Contents

G000269245

Part I: The Major Championships
(1997 and Past Results)

Part II: 1997 Season

Room 119 wants a break from golf at Forest of Arden.

What could be more relaxing for Colin Montgomerie than a golf break? If playing golf is your profession, quite a lot actually.

At the Marriott Forest of Arden Hotel & Country Club, as well as two superb golf courses, you'll find a whole range of leisure facilities. If you're looking for a golf break, or even a break from golf, there are 23 Marriott Hotels throughout the UK, 7 of which are hotel & country clubs offering golf breaks for players at any level. For reservations call 0800 221 222 or for our best ever value Golf Breaks brochure call 0800 444 878.

ITV
Teletext
p387

When you're comfortable you can do anything.

HOTELS · RESORTS · SUITES

ABERDEEN, BIRMINGHAM, BRADFORD, BRISTOL, CARDIFF, CHEPSTOW, CHESHUNT, CHICHESTER, DERBY, EDINBURGH, GLASGOW, HEATHROW, LEEDS, MAIDSTONE, MANCHESTER (1998), NEWCASTLE, PORTSMOUTH, PRESTON, SOUTHAMPTON (1998), SWANSEA, SWINDON, WARE.

Part VI: The Government of the Game

Part VII: Golf History

De Vere Hotels.
The king of the fairways.

When it comes to golfing resorts that are truly superb, just why do De Vere's rule all the rest?

Is it because our hotels offer some of the best golf resorts found in the United Kingdom?

Maybe it's because our challenging championship courses are matched by excellent off course facilities, making our golfing hospitality totally memorable.

Perhaps it's because our impeccable service and mouth-watering menus are as impressive as all our other golfing facilities on offer.

Whatever the reason, when it comes to golf holidays, we've clearly no handicaps.

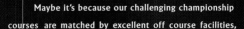

De Vere Hotels

Hotels of character, run with pride.

STOKE POGES

Stoke Poges Golf Club, Park Road, Stoke Poges, Buckinghamshire SL2 4PG
Telephone: 01753 717170 Facsimile: 01753 717181

Stoke Poges was established in 1908 and is considered by many to be the finest parkland course in the British Isles.

The course was designed by Harry Shapland Colt, a genius of the twentieth century, who went on to design many of the greatest courses in the world, including the Eden Course at St. Andrews.

The original parkland was designed in 1750 by "Capability" Brown and in 1792 by Humphry Repton. At the centre of the course is Stoke Park, the Grade I listed Clubhouse which was built for the Penn Family, the founders of Pennsylvania.

The Club is 8 miles from Heathrow Airport and only 30 minutes from central London.

Work has recently been completed on a further 9 holes, making Stoke Poges, from August 1998 a 27 hole course which has restored Colt's original design. The Club has recently installed a £500,000 irrigation system for all fairways, greens, tees, approaches and the driving range.

Stoke Poges Golf Club welcomes Societies and private visitors to use the excellent golf and conference facilities. Corporate golf days and special events can also be arranged.

Overnight accommodation is also available in 21 luxurious bedrooms on the first and second floors of the Mansion with some of the finest parkland views in the British Isles.

"You'll be hard-pressed to find a better Clubhouse in all of Britain; indeed, you'll be hard-pressed to find a more pleasant place to play in all of Britain."

GOLF MONTHLY - MAY 1996

The Captain of the Royal and Ancient Golf Club of St Andrews

Dr Alexander (Sandy) MacKechnie Mathewson drove himself in as captain of the Royal and Ancient Golf Club of St Andrews at the Club's Autumn meeting last September and holds the post for 12 months.

Born in 1923 and a member of the Royal and Ancient Golf Club since 1977, Dr Mathewson is also a member of Royal Troon and a past captain of Elie Golf House Club.

Following a school education at Irvine Royal Academy, Dr Mathewson took a degree in medicine at Glasgow University. During his army service he was a captain in the Royal Army Medical Corps and after his discharge served as general practitioner in Wishaw, Lanarkshire, for 40 years. For ten of those years he was a member of the Lanarkshire Health Board. In 1989 he was appointed Deputy Lord Lieutenant for the County of Lanark.

At the Royal and Ancient Golf Club of St Andrews he has been chairman of the Club committee and an *ex-officio* chairman of the General committee. His other interests include dogs, gardening and especially curling. He has twice been president of the Cambusnethan Curling Club.

He and his wife Dorothy have three sons, all of whom followed their father into healthcare, two being dentists in Gloucestershire and Edinburgh, and the third a doctor and R&A member at St Andrews.

During his term of office, Dr Mathewson will campaign to make the game of golf more athletic and the time to play a round shorter. He has suggested that club committees should conduct etiquette tests for new golfers to ensure they are fit to be allowed on the course.

Firm in the belief that slow play in amateur golf is influenced by the measured style of the professionals, Dr Mathewson is advocating in his year as captain for a return to what he calls 'old golfing family values', involving sound etiquette, good manners and brisk play.

'With the increasing popularity of the game, many people are taking it up without any prior knowledge or influence and no help or guidance is given,' says Dr Mathewson, who plays off 9.

Foreword

Renton Laidlaw

In a year when, for the first time in history, three players in their 20s won major titles, two events attracted extra-special attention – the phenomenal Tiger Woods scored a runaway 12-shot victory in the Masters at Augusta, living up to his potential as the most talented player to hit golf in the past 20 years, and Europe's golfers surprised everyone but themselves and their captain Severiano Ballesteros by beating the all-powerful (on paper) Americans in the Ryder Cup by Johnnie Walker.

What happened at Valderrama in September 1997 was another indication that impressive stroke-play form, which the Americans undoubtedly had, just does not guarantee match-play supremacy against a group

Renton Laidlaw

of golfers playing from the heart. Tom Kite, the American captain, could hardly have been more disappointed but his speech at the end, as the rain lashed down on the victorious Europeans, was typically generous.

The Power of the Tiger

So were the comments of his fellow players about the outstanding performance by Tiger Woods at Augusta, where Jack Nicklaus has predicted that Woods might win more Masters' Green Jackets than he and Arnold Palmer together. After having stumbled to the turn on the first day in 40, Woods played the back nine in 30 and his virtuoso performance enabled him to shoot 22-under-par for his last 63 holes and set a record-winning aggregate of 18-under-par 270, beating the previous best by one. That week Tiger Woods underlined that all the hype surrounding his turning professional less than a year earlier and the millions of contract dollars flung at him had not been misplaced.

Yet in other majors on tighter courses less well-suited to his impressive long game, Woods, who averaged 294.8 yards per drive on Tour last year, was less successful. He ran up three double bogeys at the US Open; a quadruple bogey and a triple bogey at the Open, where he also shot a third round 64; and four double bogeys at the US PGA Championship. Give him par at these holes and he would have been second twice, and fourth in the third Championship. His emergence helped US Tour Commissioner Tim Finchem sign a new deal with television which guarantees purses of $4 million for some events from 1999.

The majors are the events that annually attract most worldwide attention and all four in 1997 created global headlines. Following Woods' blistering performance at Augusta, the equally impressive giant of a man Ernie Els got the better of Montgomerie, Lehman and Maggert to take the US Open for a second time. In 1994 Els had needed a play-off to shake off Montgomerie and Loren Roberts at Oakmont, but in 1997 he won over 72 holes, clinching his triumph at the par 4 17th, the hardest hole on the course, by hitting a 5-iron to 15 feet – a classic winning shot.

Yet Els and some of his big-name colleagues, including Greg Norman, did not play well when the focus of attention turned to Royal Troon and the Open. Few journalists wrote in their previews about the chances of Justin Leonard at the Open, but the young American remained cool and putted brilliantly to edge out Sweden's US-based Jesper Parnevik and Northern Ireland's Darren Clarke to take the title. 'Being able to make the putts when I knew I needed to make them was so important,' said Leonard.

Victory for Love

Then, in August, Davis Love III, 34, finally shook off that 'best golfer around never to have won a major' tag when he clinched the US PGA Championship at Winged Foot, taking the title in the rain and against the romantic background of a

rainbow. This was perhaps the most poignant major victory of the year, not only because Love had waited so long for success in one of the events that matter in golf, but also because his late father had been a highly-respected club professional prior to his untimely death in an air crash just as Love III was beginning his career. His win left Montgomerie and the left-hander Phil Mickelson as the two golfers in that unenviable 'still-to-win-a-big-one' category. If both were to win majors in 1998, it would be more than justified. Montgomerie, in particular, is ready. He has twice lost play-offs – at the US Open to Els in 1994, and to Steve Elkington at the US PGA Championship at Riviera in 1995 – and has been second and third in two other US Opens. He has knocked on the door often enough. His time has come. At least in 1997 he won for the first time in America, when taking the individual prize in the World Cup of Golf at Kiawah Island, an event in which the Irish pair Padraig Harrington and Paul McGinley emulated the performance of Harry Bradshaw and Christy O'Connor in Mexico in 1958.

Woods, who missed only one half-way cut all year, ended the season as top money earner in the United States, with over $2 million, while the Swede Annika Sorenstam was having another great year on the LPGA Tour, winning six times and crashing through the $1 million barrier in season's earnings after a great battle for the No 1 spot with Australian Karrie Webb, winner of the Weetabix British Open at Sunningdale, and American Kelly Robbins.

Nicholas wins in US and Britain

The Swede, who has won 14 times in two years, may have achieved her goal for the year by setting a new record earnings total, but somewhat surprisingly she missed the half-way cut at her biggest event of the year, the US Open, where, for a time, it looked as if 'old-timer' (if she will excuse the phrase) Nancy Lopez might finally win her own national crown after having been three-times runner-up. In the end the title went to Alison Nicholas, a 5ft 3ins dynamo, who became a member of that unique club of players who have won both the British and US Championships. Later in the season, Miss Nicholas, requiring to finish with three birdies in the final stroke-play event on the European Tour – the Air France Madame Open at New Golf de Deauville – in order to finish second and clinch the end of the year No 1 spot on the American Express Women's Tour for the first time, did just that! All in all, European women did well internationally, with Lisa Hackney taking rookie honours in America.

In America, Steve Elkington won the Players' Championship, which aspires, as yet in vain, to be treated like a major. David Duval won three events in a row at the end of the season, including the Tour Championship, to move from 32nd to 2nd in quick time. Vijay Singh stretched his run without missing a cut to 47 events. John Daly, who walked off during the US Open, continued to battle bravely and successfully against alcoholism with the help of millionaire clubmaker Eli Callaway. Fuzzy Zoeller had cause to regret some glib remarks he made about Tiger Woods at the Masters, which cost him contracts with K-Mart and Dunlop worth an estimated $2 million a year. And Corey Pavin, Steve Stricker and 1996 US PGA champion Mark Brooks all tumbled down the rankings with dramatic form losses.

Yet it was 52-year-old Senior Tour player Hale Irwin, the former three-times US Open champion, who was the biggest prize-money earner in America in 1997 – a season which saw Lee Trevino and Jack Nicklaus fail to win. Irwin beat Woods' earnings of $2,066,833 by making $2,343,364, with the help of a record-equalling nine wins. Even then he only managed to beat Dr Gil Morgan, a six-time winner, by less than $200,000. Irwin averaged 68.92 during the year, compared to Tiger's 69.10, the third lowest average score ever on the main Tour. Montgomerie's average, by the way, was 69.37 in Europe.

The Europeans

Having missed out again on winning a major, Colin Montgomerie created history by winning the Volvo Ranking, the European money list, for a fifth year in a row, this time from Bernhard Langer who, in an injury-free season, had returned to form with four wins, including the Linde German Masters, where he became the latest golfer in Europe to shoot a 60. Since joining the Tour 10 years ago, Montgomerie has made over £6 million and for the past five years has been a remarkable 635-under-par – a measure of his much admired consistency.

Ian Woosnam won the Volvo PGA Championship, Per-Ulrik Johansson won twice and European golf's newest star, Lee Westwood, left it late to win in Europe. He had won earlier in the season in Malaysia, but he waited until the final week of the year in Europe to take the Volvo Masters over 54 holes at rain-lashed Montecastillo. The most heart-warming performance of the season was provided by José Maria Olazabal, the Spaniard whose career we (and he) thought might be over. After 18 months of inactivity because of arthritis in his feet, Olazabal came back strongly, helped in his recovery by Hans-Wilhelm Muller-Wohlfahrt from Munich who specialises in alternative medicine. Having been unable to walk, Olazabal responded to treatment, returned tentatively to action in Dubai, did well enough to finish 12th, and within a month had won the Turespaña Masters Open de Canarias. This, and other fine performances during the summer, helped him make the Ryder Cup side after having missed the 1995 match at Oak Hill.

CENTENARY CLUBS
1998

WE WOULD LIKE TO EXTEND OUR WARMEST WISHES TO THE FOLLOWING CLUBS IN THEIR CENTENARY YEAR.

Maxstoke Park Golf Club
Castle Lane, Coleshill,
Birmingham B46 1TJ.
Tel/Fax: 01675 466743

Maxstoke Park Golf Club was founded in 1898 and moved to its current location in 1946. It is set in the grounds of the 14th Century Maxstoke Castle which features scenically around much of the course. Set in rural countryside yet adjacent to all of the Midlands motorways, it has an air of tranquility in a splendid parkland scenario. A tree lined course it features several interesting water holes and whilst it is no sinecure it presents a pleasant days golf in glorious conditions.

The course is recognised as a county venue for inter-county competitions, and its members are reknowned for their friendliness and conviviality.

Boat of Garten Golf & Tennis Club
Boat of Garten,
Inverness-shire PH24 3BQ
Tel: 01479 831282

Designed by one of the grand-masters of golf course architecture, James Baird. "The Boat" is not only a demanding test of sporting skill but also a magnificent scenic setting for the game. The surrounding Highland grandeur can inspire high achievement or, in the more common event of disappointing performance, afford the comfort and consolation of communing with nature in a uniquely attractive setting.

Barnard Castle Golf Club
Harmire Road, Barnard Castle,
Co Durham DL12 8QN.
Tel: 01833 638355

Parkland course set in the valley of Teesdale with views of the Pennines. Situated north boundary of Barnard Castle on B6278.
700 Membership Hon Secretary: W C Raine Professional: Darren Pearce 18 holes Length 6,406 yards SSS 71

Records: Am 65 C Hamilton (1996) Pro 66 D Curry (1995) Visitors unrestricted - Golfing Societies welcome Fees: Weekdays £18-26 Weekends & Bank Holidays £25-32

CENTENARY CLUBS
1998

Broadstone *(Dorset)*
Golf Club
**Wentworth Drive,
Broadstone, Dorset BH18 8DQ.**

Tel/Fax: 01202 692595

The course was developed by Lord Wimborne and officially opened when the Rt Hon A J Balfour, MP, Prime Minister partnered by J H Taylor, Open Champion played against the Rt Hon John Penn, MP and James Braid, also an Open Champion.

The Broadstone (Dorset) Golf Club presents a demanding yet fair test of golf set in 250 acres of outstanding heathland, within which are many rare heathers and rare species of wildlife. The fairways range freely and separately through heather, gorse and woods of mature oaks, silver birch, pine and rhododendrons. Several holes offer magnificent views of up to 30 miles across some of the finest countryside in the south of England.

The Club has hosted the British Ladies Open Championship and Home Internationals, the English Seniors Open, the English Ladies Championships. In 1998 the Club looks forward to hosting the following events - the National Blind Golfers Championship, the English Ladies Strokeplay Championship and the English Golf Union Over 35's Strokeplay Championship. The Club has a well appointed clubhouse and a popular professional's shop.

Ashford Manor
Golf Club
**Fordbridge Road,
Ashford,**

Middlesex TW15 3RT

**Tel: 01784 257687
Fax: 01784 420355**

Ashford Manor Golf Club was formed in 1898 and has even earlier roots in the long-since defunct Staines club which played on nearby Shortwood Common, part of the Staines Moor lands.

The present clubhouse, now much changed, was originally the mansion house for the Ashford Manor Estate and parts of it have stood for some 300 years.

Despite urban development of the beautiful little Ashford village which existed when the club was formed, descriptions of the course written earlier this century remain valid today: "There is little wonder that this club is so popular, for in winter it is one of the driest courses around London, and in summer is a thing of beauty....It is so shut in by a screen of trees, so delightfully split up and diversified by woods of oak and elm, fir and cassia, so besprinkled with other foliage, as to take the townsman clean out of himself at his very first acquaintance with it."

On the Senior Tour in Europe nobody came close to matching the consistency and impressive form of Jersey-based Tommy Horton, who won six times and was second on three more occasions in 1997. Few operate the broomstick putter more effectively than former Ryder Cup player Horton.

'New breed' benefits the Ryder Cup

If the majors were dominated by the younger set – the 'new breed' as they were often called – it was the youngsters who caught the eye, too, in the Ryder Cup, with Lee Westwood, who was to win three times in the latter part of the year in Spain, Japan and Australia, proving a perfect partner for Nick Faldo. Ignacio Garrido, following his father Antonio on Cup duty, and Thomas Bjorn also played their parts in an heroic team effort at Valderrama under the enthusiastic captaincy of Severiano Ballesteros.

The match last year provided the usual quota of thrills with the result, as is normally the case these days, in doubt until the last game on the final day, after a tremendous singles fightback by the Americans, who had trailed by five points going into the last 12-game series. Although Fred Couples thrashed Ian Woosnam, ending that game at the 11th – the largest singles win in Cup history – Thomas Bjorn fought back from four down against Open champion Justin Leonard to get a vital half-point, Per-Ulrik Johansson beat Davis Love, leaving the US PGA champion winless in the match, and Costantino Rocca, who had clinched his place by shooting a career-low 62 when winning the Canon European Masters at Crans-sur-Sierre, always had the edge on Woods, whose form in the latter half of the season – he did not win after July – was indicative of his feeling some strain from being the permanent focus of attention everywhere he played. It is something he will have to get used to!

With Mickelson, Maggert and O'Meara winning, Janzen finishing par, birdie, birdie to edge out the gallant Olazabal and Lehman too strong on the last day for a tiring Garrido, who had played his part brilliantly earlier, it was left to the experienced Langer, Montgomerie and Faldo to produce the one-and-a-half points Europe needed for victory. On all three days the standard of golf had been remarkably high and this was underlined dramatically in the game featuring Faldo and Jim Furyk. When Faldo, two down, all but holed his second shot at the 14th, Furyk chipped in for a half. Then, when the three-times Masters and Open champion was inches away from an ace at the 15th, Furyk holed a bunker shot for a half, going on to win by 3 and 2. Langer had won to ensure Europe kept the Cup, but victory for the home side was dependent on the broad-shouldered Montgomerie getting at least a half with Scott Hoch in the last game on the course.

All square with one to play, Montgomerie hit a 3-wood 280 yards into the middle of the fairway at the last. Hoch finished in the trees and the result was decided. Europe had won for the fourth time in seven matches.

The Walker Cup match between Great Britain and Ireland and the Americans ended in a stroll round Quaker Ridge for a home side avenging their defeat at Royal Porthcawl two years earlier but there had been a spirited performance by reformed alcoholic Barclay Howard, who won the silver medal at the Open in refreshing style. Later in the year, however, illness forced him to cut back on his golf.

The Amateur Championship title went to Scotland's Craig Watson, who rallied in the afternoon round of the 36-hole final to beat the South African Trevor Immelman at Royal St George's.

The year marked the announcement of the new World Golf Championships series promoted by the five major Tours – the US Tour, PGA European Tour, South African, Japanese and Australasian Tours – but the year was notable for sadder reasons too.

Golf's losses

The legendary Ben Hogan, arguably the finest striker of a golf ball who had become something of a recluse at Shady Oaks in Texas, died and so too did two former US Ryder Cup captains, Jay Hebert and Dave Marr, who had made such a success of his second career as a golf commentator, first for ABC and, latterly, for NBC and the BBC. In later life Hogan, one of golf's fiercest competitors, liked his privacy but Dave Marr, who knew Hogan well, summed up a man, whose contribution to golf was so immense, this way: 'He laughed a lot away from the course but on it he was always dedicated. He was as close to perfection as any human being can be at hitting a golf ball.'

Golf writing also lost the hugely respected Dick Taylor in America after a battle with cancer, and here in Britain the literary world was saddened at the sudden and untimely death after returning from the Masters of Michael Williams, long-time golf correspondent for the *Daily Telegraph* and well-loved editor of the *Golfer's Handbook*.

Late in the year, at the age of 96, women's golf lost the incomparable Joyce Wethered (Lady Heathcoat-Amory) who won four British Women's titles and the English Women's Championship five years in a row. No less a personality than Bobby Jones once described the young Joyce as the best golfer, male or female, he had ever seen – praise indeed and, from all accounts, not misplaced.

So to 1998. More of the same from Woods and Sorenstam, a first major for Montgomerie? Who knows, but this could turn out to be Ernie Els' greatest.

Six Golfers of the Year

Renton Laidlaw

Annika Sorenstam

Just when you thought that Annika Sorenstam could hardly do better than she did in 1996, the 27-year-old from Stockholm set even higher standards in 1997, winning six times on the LPGA Tour, coming second five times and third on a further three occasions. She won two other events around the world but her end-of-year winnings in America alone totalled $1,236,789 – over $230,000 more than Australian Karrie Webb had amassed when No 1 the previous year. Indeed, such was her rivalry with Webb throughout the season that it was not until the final event – the LPGA Tour Championship – that the European star clinched both the money title and Player of the Year awards, with victory at the third hole of a play-off against Pat Hurst

© Phil Sheldon

Annika Sorenstam

and Lorie Kane, after Webb had finished tied fourth.

'I think I am living a dream and I never want to wake up,' said Sorenstam at the end of her fabulous year. 'I was Player of the Year in 1995, but this time winning that award is more special because it was my goal for the season and I felt more in control.'

Annika, who started to play golf at the age of 12, did not quite sweep the boards. Rival Webb landed the Vare Trophy, which goes to the player with the lowest scoring average. In her 25 US Tour events, Miss Webb averaged 70.00, the lowest in the award's 45-year history, to Miss Sorenstam's 70.47. Both had improved their averages over the previous year. 'It would have been great to have won the Vare Trophy again, but Karrie had a great year herself and I think I need to share some things,' said Annika

The Australian was equally complimentary. 'You know you have to play your best to beat Annika, because she will not make mistakes.' With both in contention for titles throughout the year, Kelly Robbins, third placed on the money list, was frozen out. 'I'd be No 1 if it weren't for those "kids",' she joked, 'but, seriously, they are great assets for the Tour. I just try to keep up with them.'

Colin Montgomerie

For Colin Montgomerie it was another triumphant season tinged, nevertheless, with disappointment. Another year went by without his winning a major title, although he battled all the way in the US Open at Congressional with longtime rival Ernie Els, underrated Jeff Maggert and former Open champion Tom Lehman before Els won the event for a second time.

This year he will be rearranging his schedule around the four majors to improve his chances of making the breakthrough the game's most consistent player so richly deserves, but, even if his personal battle continues on that front, he has swept all aside in Europe over the past five years. In 1997 he clinched the No 1 spot for a record-breaking fifth time, beating Peter

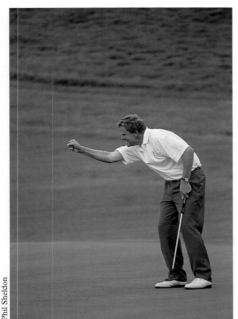

Colin Montgomerie in the Ryder Cup at Valderrama. He and Darren Clarke went on to beat Fred Couples and Davis Love III

later judged the Canon Shot of the Year in Europe. The 34-year-old Scot ended his season on a high note by winning the million dollar first prize in the Andersen Consulting World Championship, but what delighted European Tour officials just as much was his announcement that he would remain a European Tour member in 1998 and would not be moving to America. Why should he?!

Hale Irwin

If Colin Montgomerie and Bernhard Langer battled for No 1 spot in Europe, and Annika Sorenstam and Karrie Webb did the same on the LPGA Tour, the US Seniors circuit was not to be denied a remarkable duel for top honours. Hale Irwin, three times US Open champion, and Dr Gil Morgan were outstanding throughout the year, with Irwin emerging as No 1, helped by nine wins, which matched Peter Thomson's 1985 record. Irwin, winner of 20 events on the main Tour and 13 more since turning Senior two years ago, has banked more than $11 million during his career, but almost half of that has come since 1996. It is hard not to feel sorry for Morgan, who won six times during the US Senior Tour's 17th season, made $2,160,562

Oosterhuis' previous record of four successive No 1s in the early 70s. For the past five years in Europe, Montgomerie has been collectively 635 under par, and at the end of his 10th year as a professional he has become the Tour's top all-time earner, with £6,177,012, just under £120,000 more than Bernhard Langer, whose four wins last season were just not good enough to help him topple Monty from top spot. In his 10-year European career Montgomerie has had 50 top 10 finishes in 244 starts and is a remarkable 787 under par.

Finishing No 1 again and helping Europe win the Ryder Cup by Johnnie Walker were goals Montgomerie did achieve last year with his nail-biting last day performance at Valderrama outstanding. All square with one to play and requiring at least a half point from his game against Scott Hoch in the deciding singles to give Europe the overall victory team captain Seve Ballesteros had demanded, Montgomerie did what Hoch could not do. He hit his tee shot with a 3-wood 280 yards high over the trees, landing it in the ideal spot on the fairway. Hoch went in the trees. Montgomerie played his subsequent soft wedge to perfection and the Cup was won. 'That was the best tee shot I have ever struck in my life,' said Montgomerie and it was

Hale Irwin

and had to play second fiddle to a colleague who played phenomenal golf. Out of 182 rounds, Irwin shot 102 rounds in the 60s, was 466 under par for the season and had a stroke average of 68.92, second only to the record 68.89 by Lee Trevino when he won seven times in 1990.

Irwin's winnings of $2,343,364, greater incidentally than Tiger Woods' top earnings on the main Tour, were achieved with the help of a new patient approach. In 1996 he had tried to make things happen. In 1997 he just let things happen, which resulted in 18 top 10 finishes in his 23 starts. For the record, Morgan had 10 top 10 finishes in 25 starts.

Irwin's shot of the year may well have been the 3-wood he hit 245 yards to 30 feet on the final hole of the Vantage Championship for the birdie that gave him a win and pushed his earnings through the $2 million mark, but although he played two extra events in the hope of beating Thomson's nine-win record, he could only finish tied ninth and second respectively in those.

'The combination of wins is reflective of what I set out to do. I tried to keep my goals specific each week and not get caught up in the countdown,' said Irwin. 'I'm proud of the year – it would be silly not to say that – but I have never been one who is completely satisfied because that is the only way you keep going forward.'

© Phil Sheldon

Tiger Woods rewrote the record book at Augusta

Tiger Woods

If Tiger Woods is to be remembered for one performance above all others in what promises to be a long and remarkable career, it will be tough for him to improve on what he did at the Masters in April 1997. That week he became the first non-white to win a major and these are just some of the records the then 21-year-old broke that week amid the tall pines at Augusta.

His 270 winning total was a record and that 18-under-par score has been matched only once before in the 366 majors played since 1860. That was when Nick Faldo shot 18 under to win the 1990 Open. Woods' 12-stroke winning margin was the biggest in any major since the 1862 Open. His nine-stroke lead going into the final round was a record. At 21 years 3 months and 15 days he was the youngest Masters winner and the second youngest major winner behind young Tom Morris, who won the 1868 Open at age 17! Tiger was only the second golfer this century to win a major title at his first attempt as a professional although, of course, he had played in the Masters before as US Amateur Champion, a title he held for a record three years.

When he turned professional following the third of those victories in 1996, he quickly won twice in eight starts and he continued to play well in the first half of 1997. The Mercedes Championship, the Honda Classic in Thailand, the Masters, the Byron Nelson Classic and the prestigious Western Open were won by Woods, but there were no successes after that and his performance in the Ryder Cup by Johnnie Walker, in which he managed to win only one-and-a-half points, was disappointing.

Still, Woods has more than lived up to the hype that accompanied him when he turned professional. The American Associated Press worked out just how much Tiger Woods was worth to the game and came up with a staggering $650 million of 'new money'. Ticket sales at events in which he participated were up 35%. 60% more people watched US Tour golf on television because of the Tiger factor and Nike, who signed him up on what was considered a ludicrously high $40 million deal, saw its investment flourish when sales rocketed by 60%. Tom Watson summed up the Woods' influence best when he commented: 'He is a boy among men and right now he is teaching the men how to play!'

By the end of the year, Woods had earned $2,066,833 from his 21 appearances on the US Tour to finish No 1, but with a 69.10 score had been pipped by Nick Price for the low-scoring average of the season and had been out-driven

on average by only one man, John Daly, and even then by less than eight yards.

Tiger Woods, the youngest man ever to make a million on Tour (and in just nine weeks at that), rewrote much of the Tour record book and there is no reason why he should not go on rewriting it in 1998. At the end of the year, Woods was voted American Male Athlete of the Year and the story of his winning at Augusta was by a long way the American sports story of the year.

Alison Nicholas

Only two British names appear on the US Women's Open trophy – Laura Davies and her regular Solheim Cup partner Alison Nicholas who broke Nancy Lopez' heart by winning the Championship in superb style last year. Miss Lopez, enjoying a revival of fortunes, had been runner-up in the Championship three times previously, but while some might have expected she would prove the tougher on the last day, British golf's 35-year-old dynamo had other ideas. Nicholas won and Nancy Lopez had come second in her national Championship for a heartbreaking fourth time. 'I had tears in my eyes

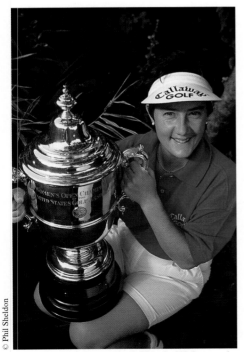

Alison Nicholas at home 1997, holding the US Open trophy

© Phil Sheldon

when Alison holed that final two-footer because I knew I no longer had a chance to win,' said Lopez. 'It was pretty tough to see.'

Ironically, years ago as she battled to sort out her game, it had been Lopez' instruction book Nicholas had turned to as a struggling 22-year-old amateur, and it had been Lopez seven years ago who had persuaded the homesick English girl to give the US Tour another go before calling it quits because she was not winning. 'I saw then that Alison was a fighter,' said Lopez and how cruelly true that was to prove at Pumpkin Ridge.

Lopez shot four rounds in the 60s – the first player ever to do so in the US Women's Open – for a 72-hole total of 275, but Nicholas finished one shot better, producing a record 10-under-par aggregate that beat by one shot the previous best set by Pat Bradley in 1981. It was tight at the end because Nicholas had been four ahead with nine to play but her European friends were never concerned about her ability to hold on. 'When Al gets in front she never backs off,' said fellow Solheim Cupper Trish Johnson. 'She's the best front-runner in the business.' Sensitive as always to the situation, Nicholas said: 'I understand that the crowd wanted Nancy to win, but they supported me just as much. Nancy is a great champion and it was a privilege to play with her. Believe me, I know how Nancy feels.'

Miss Nicholas' win gave her membership of an exclusive club of players who have won the British and US Women's Open titles. Betsy King, Laura Davies, Jane Geddes and Patty Sheehan are the only others to have achieved that fame. Nicholas' British win came in 1987 but the greatest triumph of all for the 1997 European No 1 was the 18th of her career – the victory at North Plains in Oregon that put her name on a trophy that also includes the names of Babe Zaharias, Patty Berg, Mickey Wright and Catherine Lacoste.

Justin Leonard

If few people gave much thought to Justin Leonard as a potential winner of the Open Championship at Royal Troon in 1997 it was hardly surprising. Although he had been showing more than useful form on the US Tour, winning the Kemper Open the week before the US Open Championship, his form in the British event had been nothing to write home about. In three appearances his best place finish had been 58th. This hardly augured well for his chances of taking on and beating such as Ernie Els, the reigning US Open champion, Colin Montgomerie, the European No 1 on the course over which he had learned to play, Nick Faldo and Tiger Woods. If Leonard arrived at Royal

Troon virtually unknown, however, everyone knew him by the end of the week when the 25-year-old continued the 1997 trend of players under 30 winning the majors. His final round 65 was a model of coolly controlled consistency that gave him a three-shot lead at the end over the two Europeans who shared second place – Northern Ireland's talented Darren Clarke and the extrovert Swede Jesper Parnevik, based these days on the US Tour.

Leonard went round in 69 on a blustery first day when some of the bigger stars' chances of winning were shattered; followed up with a 66; handed in a third round 72; and then putted superbly for that closing 65 and a winning 12-under-par total of 272. Woods, despite a third round 64, finished in a share of 24th place, with, among others, defending champion Tom Lehman and Montgomerie. That was 12 behind the winner. Els finished joint 10th, ten shots behind, and Greg Norman and Nick Faldo, winners of five Opens between them, had a Championship about which they had little to be satisfied. Norman finished on 287 – 15 back, and Faldo just managed to finish joint 51st.

Although both Parnevik, runner-up three years earlier to Nick Price at Turnberry, and especially Clarke believed it was going to be their week, neither played the disciplined golf in the last round that Leonard produced to win what he hopes will be the first of several majors. Five off the pace at the start on Sunday, he caught up by the 16th. His birdies at two of the last three holes saw him home comfortably enough before a knowledgable Open crowd, as always appreciative of quality play whatever the nationality of the golfer producing it.

Tom Kite, the American Ryder Cup team captain, keen to have Leonard in his side for Valderrama, had urged the young man to tie his place up with a good performance at Troon. Although Kite had left for the airport before Leonard had won, he headed back to the course on hearing the news of his success to welcome him to the side – a gesture the modest Leonard appreciated.

In previous years Leonard had had to pre-qualify for the Championship. In 1997 he was exempt for the first time and is now exempt through to 2037! Having switched two months earlier to metal woods, giving him an extra 20

Justin Leonard, the latest American to conquer Royal Troon in the Open.

© Phil Sheldon

yards in length off the tee, Leonard had more cause in the last round to thank the putter that had not worked well for him on the third day. He saved par from 18 feet at the 15th, holed from 12 feet for a birdie at the 16th to tie the lead, then rolled in a 30 footer at the 17th to move in front and put the pressure on his European rivals.

Leonard ended the year having made $1,587,531 on the US Tour for fifth spot behind Tiger Woods, David Duval, Davis Love III and Jim Furyk, but all in front of him on that list envied the fact that it was his name and not theirs that went on golf's famous claret jug. At Royal Troon international golf had witnessed the arrival on the major victory scene of a young man who has plenty of years left in which to add to his triumphs.

Walker Cup Regained by US Team 'on a Mission'

Mark Garrod   Golf Correspondent, Press Association

The Great Britain and Ireland team for the 1997 Walker Cup match at Quaker Ridge in New York doubtless subscribe to the view that sometimes it is better to travel in hope than to arrive.

In fact there was good reason for optimism in the Great Britain and Ireland camp as the team prepared for the defence of the trophy. Having beaten an American side containing Tiger Woods at Royal Porthcawl in 1995, they now faced one lacking him. In Gary Wolstenholme, Graham Rankin and Barclay Howard, the holders had three players with winning cup experience, and in Howard they had the man who less than a month before had featured on the leaderboard at the Open Championship at Royal Troon and had been the only amateur to survive the halfway cut there.

The side also included Hampshire's Justin Rose, becoming at 17 years 10 days the youngest player to appear in the match. They liked the course, they had put more work into their preparations than ever before and they fancied their chances.

It took just the opening hole of the opening foursomes, however, to place a different complexion on matters. Scotland's Steven Young hooked into the trees and the attempted recovery of his partner Howard caught a branch and shot across the fairway. Then Rose's first drive was sliced out of bounds. Partner Michael Brooks, unexpectedly finding himself hitting off the first tee, followed Young's line and Rose's next shot, the pair's fourth, struck a tree and shot across the adjoining 18th fairway.

In the third game, Wolstenholme safely found the fairway, but opponent Jason Gore out-hit him by almost 100 yards, with a drive measured at 314 yards. The omens were not good. America took a 4–0 lead, being an approximate one under par for the morning to the visitors' 24 over par. 'The occasion must have just got to them,' said captain Clive Brown.

By the end of the first day, the United States were ahead by 8½–3½, which represented something of a recovery from Brown's men, but still left a mountain to climb. And that became Everest when only Wolstenholme and Rose prevented another whitewash in the second series of foursomes. Now all Downing Gray's side

Justin Rose in the Walker Cup at Quaker Ridge

© Phil Sheldon

required to reclaim the cup was one point from the eight concluding singles, but there was never any likelihood of them settling for just that. The final score was 18–6, the second biggest winning margin in the competition's history and one which took the overall tally to 31 wins for the United States, four for Great Britain and Ireland and one tie.

The American who secured the winning point was John Harris, the 45-year-old insurance worker from Minnesota, whose record in three matches is now the most impressive of anyone through the years. The great Bobby Jones had nine victories and one defeat, but Harris's six and five defeat of 1996 Scottish champion Brooks took him to 10 wins and one loss.

It was not lost on Harris that the three American survivors of the previous match –

himself, Jerry Courville Jr and Buddy Marucci – were unbeaten this time. 'None of us had forgotten about the closing ceremony in 1995,' he said. 'It was the most humbling experience I've ever had in sport. We had to just stand there and take it. That feeling lasted for two years and we came here with a mission.'

Barclay Howard

The inability of Howard to influence the outcome was to be explained a few weeks later when the fatigue the 44-year-old had experienced at Quaker Ridge became infinitely worse and he was diagnosed as suffering from leukaemia. Treatment began immediately and the popular Scot has now had a bone marrow transplant with his sister. The entire golfing fraternity wishes him well. As the first Scot to collect the Open silver medal as leading amateur since Charlie Green in 1962, the recovering alcoholic had endeared himself to many and he earned more friends during the US Amateur Championship at Cog Hill near Chicago. After making it through to the matchplay stages, Howard disqualified himself for unwittingly having played the final hole with a different type of ball. 'Say I was walking up to win at the weekend. How could I live with myself?' he said. 'Yes, I've had my share of problems, but after 44 years you're going to start cheating? No, I could never do that.'

Howard had been a quarter-finalist in the Amateur Championship at Royal St George's, but his involvment did not end there. He stayed on to caddie for his international colleague Craig Watson, whom he had persuaded to make the long journey south. And Watson, a late convert to a broomhandle putter, duly became Scotland's third winner in six years – following Stephen Dundas in 1992 and Gordon Sherry in 1995 – with a three and two victory in the final over highly-promising South African teenager Trevor Immelman, at 17 trying to become the youngest-ever winner of the trophy.

The shock news of Howard's illness came in the week of the home internationals at Burnham and Berrow, where Scotland were unable to prevent England achieving a record fifth consecutive title. Ireland very nearly did, though. After successes over Wales and the Scots, the two sides met and it looked all over when England, led by Walker Cup pair Rose and Wolstenholme, took all five morning foursomes. But back came the Irish to lead in nine of the ten singles before Wolstenholme won the last three holes to halve

with Ken Kearney; Philip Rowe and Michael Reynard gained halves as well; and then Matt Blackey beat Adrian Morrow. The match was tied, but England kept the trophy by virtue of their 28½ points over the three days to Ireland's 26½.

In the European Team Championships at Portmarnock, however, England managed only 10th place. Ireland won the qualifying stage by a massive 15 strokes, Keith Nolan's opening 70 in horrendous conditions ranking as one of the rounds of the year, but the final was between Spain and Scotland and the Spanish became the first continental winners since Sweden in 1961. They also triumphed in the European Boys' Championship, and 17-year-old Sergio Garcia was the outstanding winner of the British Boys' Championship at Saunton. The plus-five handicapper, who the week before was 20 under par in capturing an event in France by 19 strokes, beat England's Richard Jones six and five in the 18-hole final.

On the same links, Garcia also finished third behind Welshman David Park in the English Stroke-Play Championship, the Brabazon Trophy. Both Park and Australian runner-up Geoff Ogilvy equalled the amateur course record with closing 65s, giving Park victory by four strokes with a 13-under-par total of 271 that was six shots inside the previous tournament record. His reward later was a Walker Cup debut. As you would expect, other team members tasted success during the year. Wolstenholme won the Berkshire Trophy, Rankin the Lytham Trophy and Rose, while still only 16, the St Andrews Links Trophy. Garcia had a chance of adding the European individual title in Switzerland, but finished joint second, three behind Belgian Didier de Voogt.

Matt Kuchar

Following the three-year reign of Tiger Woods as US Amateur Champion, a different home had to be found for the trophy and it turned out to be that of 19-year-old Matt Kuchar. Playing in the event for the first time, the Georgia Tech student provided a real Cinderella story by beating Randy Leen six and five in the semi-finals and then Leen's Walker Cup teammate Joel Kribel two and one in the final. 'If I had bet a buck on me at the beginning of the week, I would have won a ton of money,' said Kuchar, revealing that the thought of succeeding Woods had made him so nervous he had been physically sick before the final.

Glory Win Gives Alison the Transatlantic Double

Lewine Mair   Golf Correspondent, *The Daily Telegraph*

Alison Nicholas's glorious win in the US Women's Open did much to stop the pessimism which surrounded an anxious year for women's professional golf in Europe. The Yorkshire golfer won the biggest title of them all from no less a celebrity than Nancy Lopez. What is more, her victory was among the first on the distaff side of the modern game to receive due recognition in the golfing world as a whole. To cite just one example, she was honoured by the Association of Golf Writers of Europe, who gave her their annual trophy ahead of the Ryder Cup team which won at Valderrama.

Another US success to write home about was that of Lisa Hackney from Staffordshire who won the LPGA's Rookie of the Year award from a cosmopolitan crop of highly rated new professionals. All told, she had seven top ten finishes to sign off from the 1997 season as high as eighth on the Ping World leaderboard. Only Laura Davies from among the British contingent finished above her.

On the British amateur scene, there were grand individual performances from Alison Rose, who won both the Scottish and the British championships, and from Kim Rostron, who started the season by winning the combination of Scottish Open Stroke-Play Championship and English Match-Play. Suzanne Fanagan was a thoroughly worthy winner of the Irish Championship, while Eleanor Pilgrim won the Welsh in a year when there was a more obvious supply of strength in depth in the Principality than has been the case in years.

On the team front, however, our amateurs lost out to Sweden in the European Team Championship and to the Continent of Europe in the Vagliano Trophy – twin results to remind us that the four home countries are falling behind their Continental counterparts in some respects.

In Sweden and France, as has been noted many times over the last few years, girls benefit from playing their golf alongside boys from the moment they pick up a club. All the junior competitions are mixed, with the same applying to senior events, in which the men and women play alongside each other even in monthly medals. It is all in marked contrast to what happens in Britain, where a young girl coming into the game will probably play 90% of her club golf

Alison Nicholas

with women who are ten, twenty, thirty, forty or even fifty years older than she is.

No one would deny that she can learn a lot from these members of the ladies' section, many of whom are wonderfully canny golfers. Yet how much better it would be for her golfing welfare, not to mention her social welfare and her general enthusiasm for the game, if she were able to develop her golfing skills in mixed company.

In mid-season, Mhairi McKay and Janice Moodie, both of whom played in the Scottish women's side which lost to the Swedes in the final of the European Team Championship, left their American universities and turned professional with a view to carrying on playing in the States. Moodie earned her American player's card but McKay failed. McKay then tried for

her European tour card and succeeded but, like many other young women professionals on this side of the Atlantic, she was left to wonder whether there would be enough tournaments in Europe in 1998 to constitute a professional tour.

There were 21 tournaments down in the WPGET's handbook for 1997 but only 15 were played. If that were not bad enough, American Express, umbrella sponsors who had poured between three and four million pounds into the European women's professional scene over a three-year spell, announced last October that they would not be renewing their contract.

European Tour loses sponsor

At the time, they said that it had most to do with a 'decentralisation' policy in which the various European countries would henceforth be going their own way in terms of what they supported. John de Trafford, the Senior Vice-President of American Express, said that the decision had been reached 'with much reluctance because we have benefited in many ways from the sponsorship and our relationship with the WPGET players and officials.'

That all sounded fair enough, but it was not too long before John Petersen, who had served as the American Express presence on the women's tour, admitted that there was more besides. He said, for a start, that his company had been concerned at the women's seeming inability to hang on to quality sponsors. They had been impressed when Marks & Spencer and Wilkinson Sword came on board, but more than a little concerned when they departed the scene so soon.

Petersen added that the patchy promotion of the tournaments had not impressed. He picked out Mark McCormack's International Management Group and McDonald's as two bodies who had promoted tournaments to great effect, but spoke of other organisers whose events made just about as much impact as a club medal.

The last tournament of 1997 was a case in point. Although Alison Nicholas, the reigning US Open Champion, had hurried all the way back from Japan to try to sew up the No 1 spot on the European Order of Merit, there were more posters and publicity given that week in Deauville for the weekly horse sale than for the

golf. What a waste – especially as Miss Nicholas made her hectic dash around the world worthwhile by closing with three birdies to earn a big enough cheque to clinch that top spot.

With the season over, the hunt, headed by the selfless Miss Nicholas, was on for a replacement for Terry Coates, who had indicated several months earlier that he would be leaving early in 1998 as the Tour's Commissioner and Executive Director. Eighty people applied for the job before it was announced that John Mort, a fully qualified accountant who had arrived at the WPGET via Coopers and Lybrand, had been appointed Managing Director and asked to take care of the everyday running of the Association.

New WPGET MD takes over

The women sensed straightaway that their affairs were in good hands, for Mort's knowledge extended way beyond the Tour's facts and figures, having worked as a tournament director for a couple of years. There was a collective sigh of relief when Mort was able to reveal there would be at least nine events on the schedule and possibly as many as 11, and that did not include the Solheim Cup match and the now annual fixture against the European Seniors at the end of the year. At the time of writing the full schedule was still not available.

What is disappointing is that there is just one event in the first half of the year – the Evian Masters in June. There is the prospect however of seven tournaments in eight weeks across July and August – a run which might just lure those American-based European golfers back across the Atlantic for a longer visit. They should not need too much encouragement on that score, of course, because the European Solheim Cup side is due to be announced during the Compaq Open in Sweden towards the end of August and they will want to collect points.

Were the Europeans to win the Solheim Cup at Muirfield Village it would obviously help Managing Director Mort's task of putting the WPGET back on track. He has already gone a long way to turning things around.

Yet 1997 will be remembered more positively for what Alison Nicholas achieved on both sides of the Atlantic. It was her year.

Quotes of 1997

The Open Championship

'To me the Open is the biggest because, for a foreign player growing up in Australia, this is the one we all looked at the most: it's just one of my favourites.'   *Steve Elkington*

'The US Open is very important but I think the Open Championship, the British Open, is THE golf championship.'   *Mark O'Meara*

'It was tremendous to see my name there. I was up and down like a yo-yo towards the end but I'm joint fifth and thrilled.'   *Padraig Harrington looking at the huge leaderboard at the end*

'Nothing seemed to drop for me. Nothing went my way.'   *Ernie Els, the US Open champion*

'My game was about ten per cent off and that makes a big difference at the Open.'   *Nick Faldo who finished joint 50th*

'It was nice to walk down the 18th again and get an ovation but I wish I had been ten shots better.'   *Mark Calcavecchia, the 1989 champion*

'If I want to be considered the best player in the world I have to beat them. That is all I am trying to do.'   *Lee Westwood*

'When I played in my first Open in 1975, there were just a handful of people to choose from who really had a chance of winning a major. Nowadays there are a lot more with a realistic chance of winning one.'   *Former Open champion Nick Price*

'Coming in here and having seen Tiger Woods and Ernie Els do so well at Augusta and Congressional maybe I realised it is okay to win a tournament like this at the age I am.'   *Open champion Justin Leonard*

'Everyone has been so gracious and sincerely warm this week. I walked into a restaurant last night and everyone started clapping. You don't get that in the United States.'   *Tom Lehman, the defendng champion at Royal Troon*

'The crowds here are very respectful. They don't cheer just because you put spin on the ball like they do in the States.'   *Lee Janzen on the fans at Royal Troon*

'The fans in Britain are very knowledgable. They don't cheer for shots that you just get airborne.'   *Tiger Woods*

'Hopefully I will not have to qualify for the Open ever again, but if I do, I will.'   *Winner Justin Leonard who is exempt now until 2037*

'I still get a big thrill for this game. To do a 71 on a course like this was really something.'   *62-year-old Gary Player who will play his last Open at St Andrews in 2000*

'Today the pressure was too much. I was struggling with my game. I tried to get charged up every time I holed a putt but it was still too much of a struggle. This defeat will take longer to come to terms with than losing by a shot to Nick Price in 1994. I was thrilled to do what I did that year. This time I was confident and losing hurts more.'   *Jesper Parnevik, joint runner-up*

'Obviously I am disappointed but I do not feel I lost it. I shot level par at the weekend not a 75 or something. I had an opportunity to win and didn't but it is more experience for me.'   *Darren Clarke, who tied with Jesper Parnevik for second place*

'Everybody has been congratulating me. It means a lot to me and I hope it will inspire a lot of amateurs out there.'   *Barclay Howard, who won the silver medal as leading amateur*

US Open

'You know he is going to play well. He is such a good player under pressure that I knew that if I beat Colin (Montgomerie) I'd have a good chance of winning and that is the way it turned out.'   *Ernie Els after winning the title*

'It's a US Open. I can't smile.'   *Brad Faxon to a fan who wanted to take his picture*

'I'm not really into that history stuff.' *Ernie Els after being told that he was the first foreign golfer since Alex Smith in 1906 and 1910 to win the US Open twice and at 27 had become the youngest player to win a pair of US Opens since Jack Nicklaus won his second in 1967*

'This major business is getting me down but if I knock on the door enough, as I seem to be doing, the door will open one day. I just have to be patient.' *Colin Montgomerie after finishing runner-up to Ernie Els*

'Any time you save par out of the rough in the US Open you feel like you have escaped from jail.' *Tom Lehman about the USGA venues*

'A beaten body.' *Hale Irwin when asked what he had taken away from Congressional after shooting 13 over par*

'I've always gone into a tournament thinking I could win. This is the only tournament I have gone into hoping to finish second.' *Jack Nicklaus talking about the fact that his son Gary was playing in his first US Open*

'The people were terrific today. They could not have been nicer. Every shot I hit and every place I walked they were cheering. It was really nice. I think they thought I was playing my last round today. I'm playing some of the best golf in 10 years and I finished 13 over!' *Jack Nicklaus playing in his 41st US Open at age 57*

'Driving the ball straight is something Europeans do not do quite as well as the Americans and that is one of the reasons we have not done well in the US Open.' *Ian Woosnam who missed the halfway cut at Congressional*

US Masters

'There is no chance humanly possible that Tiger is going to lose this tournament. No way.' *Colin Montgomerie after having played with Woods on the third day*

'Even if he had average length he would be a great player.' *Lee Janzen about Tiger Woods*

'Tiger has got every shot in his bag and he does it with precision.' *Jerry Pate*

'One financial analyst said we overpaid Tiger Woods. I wonder what he is thinking now.' *Phil Knight of Nike who paid Woods an endorsement fee of $40 million when he turned professional*

'He is out there playing another game on a golf course he is going to own for a long time.' *Jack Nicklaus talking about Tiger Woods*

'To have "Fluff" (caddie Mike Cowan) with me there meant a lot. He knows my game and he has been here a lot. Some of the reads we had on the greens were tricky but I kept patience as my main thought.' *Tiger Woods*

'I'm now going off to get a picture of Mr Nicklaus and get him to sign it.' *Lee Westwood after shooting a closing 70 to finish in the top 25. Playing partner Nicklaus shot 78*

'As soon as you drive through the gate you are up. The hardest thing is to try to come down.' *Frank Nobilo on his arrival at Augusta*

'I don't know why they are hanging about out there. I won MY golf tournament.' *Tom Kite, who finished second, 12 shots behind Tiger Woods, as he waited for reporters to attend his press conference*

The USPGA Championship

'A lot of people said I had to get tougher or stronger or meaner but others said I should smile more and wave to the fans. Well, which did they want me to do?' *Winner Davis Love about his conflicting emotions on course*

'Every day I play golf I think about my dad. I know he would be extremely proud that I won not only a major but the PGA Championship. Who would have thought that a son of a PGA member would win the PGA Championship at Winged Foot – a very special place.' *Davis Love III*

'Realistically it is almost impossible to win all four majors in the same year.' *Tiger Woods admitting his goal of winning a Grand Slam after his victory at Augusta was unrealistic. Woods finished 17 shots behind winner Love*

'It was only guts and determination that got me to four over. I putted miserably all week. It's another empty year for majors but I have other goals, like winning the Ryder Cup, and the European money list is not lost yet.' *Colin Montgomerie*

'There are six hard holes, six extra hard holes and six impossible holes.' *Mark Brooks, the 1996 US PGA champion, about Winged Foot*

'I'm always scared about what is going to happen next so I don't get too excited.' *John Daly after an opening 66. He shot 73 next day and finally finished joint 29th*

'It was pretty awesome. Everyone is interested in what John is going to do. He has just unlimited talent. It is just a question of whether he can get his life together to take advantage of it.' *Tom Kite on John Daly after Daly shot an opening 66*

'I've played Winged Foot over 70 times and cannot remember it playing this tough.' *Bruce Zabriski, the Winged Foot club professional after an opening 76*

'I always though it was nice that people thought I should be in a category of players who should win a major. It is nice to get out of that category but there are some great players who should have won ahead of me.' *Davis Love III after winning*

'He knew his dad was with him. When it was all over he hugged me and I said: "Dad knows" and he said "Yes, I am sure he does."' *Penta Love, Davis Love's mother, after her son had won*

'My brother has given up an awful lot to help me with my career. We have been through good times and bad but I could not have done the job without him.' *Davis Love about his brother Mark who gave up the chance of being a club professional to caddie for Davis*

'Realistically it is almost impossible to win all four majors in the same year.' *Tiger Woods admitting his goal of winning a Grand Slam after his victory at Augusta was unrealistic. Woods finished 17 shots behind winner Love*

'I catch fish in water that is more shallow than the rough is here.' *Phil Blackmore, who tied for sixth on 281*

The 1997 Ryder Cup by Johnnie Walker

'My hat is off to the European guys. They played tough. I am still convinced we had the best 12 players in the world. I don't personally see how they could beat us.' *Tom Lehman*

'I really put out some strong teams and I thought we were going to have a great morning but the Europeans played much better on the back nine and severely out-putted us.' *Tom Kite on the fact that the US side lost the second series of four-balls 3–0 with one game halved*

'I should have been forceful in my request to the guys to come down early to play Valderrama. We still played better from tee to green but the Europeans read the putts better.' *Tom Kite who had asked his team members to visit Valderrama ahead of the game*

'With Seve you kind of get the feeling that if you ran a geiger counter over him the reading would go off the scale.' *Fred Couples about Ballesteros*

'It is mind-boggling. Our fellows had the higher rankings. We had a captain we loved and respected. We got all the pairings we wanted and we still lost. There is no rhyme nor reason to it.' *Brad Faxon*

'He was never in the way. It was always a plus to have him around. He showed me how to play a few chips, helped me with some club selections and guided me in the right direction.' *Lee Westwood about Seve Ballesteros*

'I'm sure somebody finally told Seve to leave me alone.' *Colin Montgomerie about the European captain*

'I would really like to thank the fans. The support out on the course was unbelievable.' *Colin Montgomerie*

'It has been an honour to captain this great team but now I would like to recover my game and play in the 1999 match.' *Seve Ballesteros announcing he would not want to captain the side in Boston in 1999*

'This time last year I could not walk. I am just so proud to be here. It has been brilliant. I shall never forget it.' *José Maria Olazabal, who played in all five series and made two-and-a-half points*

'I don't feel much like staying. All I can say is I am sorry for everything that has happened and I am going home now.' *Miguel Angel Martin who figured in the pre-match official team photograph as an honorary team member after having been removed from the side because of injury*

'This is an intelligent player's golf course and a great course for match-play.' *Jim Furyk*

'I gave it my all and it just was not good enough.' *Tiger Woods after losing his singles game to Costantino Rocca*

'I feel I aged five years on the back nine.' *Justin Leonard after his halved game with Thomas Bjorn. Leonard had been four up after four*

'We had our hands on the clubs but Seve was the one who played the shots.' *Ignacio Garrido on his captain*

'I was prepared for this moment. If you are mentally prepared and you control yourself you don't cry.' *Seve Ballesteros who insisted that when it seemed he was crying at the end it was only rain dripping down his face*

R&A Venues and Dates for Championships in 1998–2001

	1998	1999	2000	2001
The Amateur Championship	1–6 June Muirfield/ Gullane No 1	31 May–5 June R. County Down/ Kilkeel	5–10 June R. Liverpool/ Wallasey	4–9 June Prestwick/ Kilmarnock Barassie
The Open Championship	16–19 July R. Birkdale	15–18 July Carnoustie	20–23 July St Andrews	19–22 July R. Lytham & St Annes
(Final Qualifying)	12–13 July Hesketh Hillside Southport & Ainsdale West Lancashire	11–12 July Downfield Monifieth Montrose Panmure	16–17 July Ladybank Leven Links Lundin Scotscraig	15–16 July Fairhaven Hillside Southport & Ainsdale St Anne's Old Links
The Seniors' Open Amateur Championship	29–31 July Western Gailes & Glasgow Gailes	4–6 August Frilford Heath Red and Green	9–11 August Gullane Nos 1 & 2	8–10 August Royal Portrush Dunluce and Valley
The Boys' Home Internationals	5–7 August Jubilee Course, St Andrews	4–6 August Conwy	9–11 August Portmarnock	8–10 August Moortown
The Boys' Amateur Ch'p	10–14 August Ladybank	9–13 August R. St David's	14–18 August Hillside	13–17 August Ganton
British Mid-Amateur Ch'p	12–16 August Ganton	11–15 August Walton Heath	16–20 August Royal Troon	15–19 August Seaton Carew
The Walker Cup		11–12 September Nairn		11–12 August Ocean Forest, Sea Island, Georgia
The St Andrews Trophy	28–29 August Villa d'Este, Italy		1–2 September Turnberry	
The Jacques Leglise Trophy	28–29 August Villa d'Este, Italy	27–28 August TBA	1–2 September Turnberry	31 Aug–1 Sept TBA
The Eisenhower Trophy	19–22 November Santiago, Chile		TBA Berlin, Germany	

Future Venues and Dates for the US Major Championships

	The Masters	The US Open	US PGA Championship
1998	Augusta National, Augusta, GA	Olympic Club, San Francisco, CA	Sahalee CC, Redmond, Seattle, Washington
1999	Augusta National, Augusta, GA	Pinehurst No. 2, Pinehurst, NC	Medinah, Chicago
2000	Augusta National, Augusta, GA	Pebble Beach, Monterey CA	Valhalla, Louisville, Kentucky

The US Masters begins on the Thursday following the first Sunday in April each year.

The US Open Championship commences on the Thursday following the second Sunday in June each year.

The USPGA Championship normally commences on the second Thursday in August each year.

Venues and Dates for the 1998 Season

PGA European Tour

January
3–10   MacGregor Week, San Roque, Spain
22–25 Johnnie Walker Classic, Blue Canyon CC, Phuket, Thailand
29–1   Heineken Classic, The Vines, Perth

February
5–8   South African Open, Durban CC
12–15 Alfred Dunhill SA PGA, Houghton GC, Johannesburg
26–1   Dubai Desert Classic, Emirates GC

March
5–8   Qatar Masters, Doha GC
12–15 Moroccan Open, Golf Royal d'Agadir
19–22 Portuguese Open, Aroeira, Lisbon

April
16–19 Cannes Open, Royal Mougins, France
23–26 Peugeot Open de España, El Prat, Barcelona
30–3   Italian Open, Castelconturbia, Milan

May
7–10   Turespaña Masters Open Baleares, Santa Ponsa, Mallorca
14–17 Benson & Hedges International Open, The Oxfordshire GC
22–25 Volvo PGA Chp, Wentworth Club
29–1   Deutsche Bank – SAP Open TPC of Europe, Gut Kaden, Hamburg

June
4–7   National Car Rental English Open, Marriott Hanbury Manor
11–14 Compaq European Grand Prix, Slaley Hall, Northumberland
18–21 Madeira Island Open, Santo da Serra
25–28 Peugeot Open de France, Le Golf National, Paris

July
2–5   Murphy's Irish Open, Druids Glen, Dublin
8–11   The Standard Life Loch Lomond, Loch Lomond, Glasgow
16–19 127th Open Championship, Royal Birkdale

July *continued*
23–26 TNT Dutch Open, Hilversumsche
30–2   Volvo Scandinavian Masters, European Tour Club, Stockholm

August
6–9   German Open, venue to be announced
20–23 Smurfit European Open, The K Club, Dublin
27–30 BMW International Open, Golfclub München Nord-Eichenried

September
3–6   Canon European Masters, Crans-sur-Sierre, Switzerland
10–13 One 2 One British Masters, Marriott Forest of Arden, Warwickshire
15–17 Pre-Qualifying 1, Five Lakes GC, Chart Hills GC, Manchester GC, The Wynard Club, Woodbury Park GC
17–20 Trophée Lancôme, Saint-Nom-La-Bretèche, Paris, France
24–27 Linde German Masters, GC Gut Lärchenhof, Cologne

October
1–4   Belgacom Open, Royal Zoute, Belgium
8–11   *Alfred Dunhill Cup, St Andrews
15–18 *World Match-Play Championship, Wentworth Club
15–18 Open Novotel Perrier, Golf du Médoc, Bordeaux, France
22–25 Oki Pro-Am
27–29 Pre-Qualifying II, Pals GC, Emporda GC, Perelada GC, Panoramica GC, St Cyprien GC
29–1   Volvo Masters, Montecastillo, Spain

November
5–8   *Subaru Sarazen World Open, Chateau Elan, Atlanta
19–22 *World Cup of Golf, Gulf Harbour, Auckland, NZ
18–23 European Tour Qualifying School Finals, The San Roque Club, Real Club de Golfe, Sotogrande

* *Special event*

United States PGA Tour

January

3–4   Andersen Consulting World Championship of Golf, Grayhawk GC, Scottsdale, AZ

8–11   Mercedes Chp, La Costa Resort, Carlsbad, CA

14–18   Bob Hope Chrysler Classic, Palm Springs, CA

22–25   Phoenix Open, TPC of Scottsdale, AZ

29–1   AT&T Pebble Beach National Pro-Am, Pebble Beach, CA

February

5–8   Buick Invitational, Torrey Pines Golf Course, La Jolla, CA

12–15   United Airlines Hawaiian Open, Waialae CC, Honolulu, HA

19–22   Tucson Chrysler Classic, Tucson, AZ National Golf resort, Tucson, AZ

26–1   Nissan Open, Riviera CC, Pacific Palisades, CA

March

5–8   Doral-Ryder Open, Doral Resort, Miami, FL

12–15   Honda Classic, TPC at Heron Bay, Coral Springs, FL

19–22   Bay Hill Invitational, Bay Hill, Orlando, FL

26–29   The Players Championship, TPC at Sawgrass, Ponte Vedra Beach, FL

April

2–5   Freeport-McDermott Classic, English Turn G&CC, New Orleans, LA

9–12   The Masters, Augusta, GA

16–19   MCI Classic, Harbour Town, Hilton Head Island, SC

23–26   Great Greensboro Chrysler Classic, Forest Oaks, Greensboro, NC

30–3   Shell Houston Open, TPC at The Woodlands, TX

May

7–10   Bell South Classic, TPC at Sugarloaf, Duluth, GA

14–17   GTE Byron Nelson Classic, TPC at Las Colinas, Irving, TX

21–24   MasterCard Colonial, Colonial CC, Fort Worth, TX

28–31   Memorial Tournament, Muirfield Village GC, Dublin, OH

June

4–7   Kemper Open, TPC at Avenel, Potomac, MD

11–14   Buick Classic, Westchester CC, Rye, NY

18–21   US Open, Olympic Club, San Francisco, CA

25–28   Motorola Western Open, Cog Hill G&CC, Lemont, IL

July

2–5   Canon Greater Hartford Open, TPC at River Highlands, Cromwell, CT

9–12   Quad City Classic, Oakwood CC, Coal Valley, IL

16–19   Deposit Guaranty Golf Classic, Annandale GC, Madison, MS

23–26   CVS Charity Classic, Pleasant Valley CC, Sutton, MA

30–2   FedEx St Jude Classic, TPC at Southwind, Memphis, TN

August

6–9   Buick Open, Warwick Hills G&CC, Grand Blanc, MI

13–16   PGA Chp, Sahalee CC, Redmond, Washington

20–23   Sprint International, Castle Pines GC, Castle Rock, CO

27–30   NEC World Series of Golf, Firestone CC, Akron, OH

27–30   Greater Vancouver Open, Northview G&CC, Surrey, BC

September

3–6   Great Milwaukee Open, Brown Deer Park Golf Course, Milwaukee, WI

10–13   Bell Canadian Open, Glen Abbey, Oakville, Ontario, Canada

17–20   BC Open, En-Joie GC, Endicott, NY

24–27   Westin Texas Open, LaCantera GC, San Antonio, TX

October

1–4   Buick Challenge, Callaway Gardens Resort, Pine Mountain, GA

8–11   Michelob Chp at Kingsmill, Kingsmill GC, Williamsburg, VA

14–18   Las Vegas Invitational, TPC at Summerlin, Las Vegas, NV

22–25   Walt Disney World/Oldsmobile Classic, Lake Buena Vista, FL

29–1   The Tour Championship, East Lake, Atlanta, GA

November

5–8   Subaru Sarazen World Open Championship, The Legends at Chateau Elan, Braselton, GA

12–15   Franklin Templeton Shark Shootout, Sherwood CC, Thousand Oaks, CA

19–22   World Cup of Golf, Gulf Harbour GC, Auckland, New Zealand

December

3–6   JC Penney Classic, Westin Innisbrook Resort, Palm Harbour, FL

11–13   President's Cup, Royal Melbourne, Australia

19–20   Wendy's Three-Tour Challenge, Lake Las Vegas Resort, Henderson, NV

PGA European Seniors Tour

May

1–3 El Bosque Seniors Open, El Bosque GC, Spain

8–10 Beko Classic, Gloria Golf Resort, Turkey

15–17 AIB Irish Seniors Open, Woodbrook GC, Ireland

29–31 Philips PFA Golf Classic, Marriott Meon Valley Hotel & CC, England

June

5–7 Jersey Seniors Open, La Moye GC, Jersey

12–14 De Vere Hotels Seniors Classic, Belton Woods GC, England

19–21 Ryder Seniors Classic, Welcombe Hotel, England

25–27 Swedish Seniors, Fagelbro GC, Sweden

July

2–4 Lawrence Batley Seniors, Huddersfield GC, England

8–10 Divonne Seniors Open, Divonne GC, France

24–26 Credit Suisse Private Banking Senior Open, Bad Ragaz GC, Switzerland

31–2 Wentworth Senior Masters, Edinburgh Course, Wentworth GC, England

August

6–9 Senior British Open, Royal Portrush GC, Northern Ireland

28–31 The Belfry PGA Seniors Championship, PGA National, England

September

3–6 Golden Charter PGA Scottish Seniors Open Championship, Marriott Dalmahoy Hotel & CC, Scotland

18–20 Efteling European Trophy, Efteling Golf Park, Holland

25–27 Motor Seniors Classic, Marriott Goodwood Park Hotel & CC, England

October

9–11 Italian Seniors Open - Gianni Cigna Memorial, Marco Simone GC, Italy

15–17 Is Molas Senior Open, Is Molas GC, Sardinia

23–25 Tournament of Champions, Buckinghamshire GC, England

28–31 Seniors Tour Qualifying School, Hardelot GC, France

November

13–15 Praia D'el Rey European Cup, Praia D'el Rey GC, Portugal

US Senior PGA Tour

January

16–18 MasterCard Championship, Hualalai GC, Kailua-Kona, HA

24–25 Sr Skins Game, Mauna Lani Resort, Kohala Coast, HA

30–1 Royal Caribbean Classic, Crandon Park GC, Key Biscayne, FL

February

6–8 LG Championship, Bay Colony GC, Naples, FL

13–15 GTE Classic, TPC of Tampa Bay, Lutz, FL

20–22 American Express Invitational, TPC at Prestancia, Sarasota, FL

March

9–10 Senior Slam, Cabo del Sol GC, Los Cabos, MX

13–15 Toshiba Sr Classic, Newport Beach, CA

20–22 Liberty Mutual Legends of Golf, GC of Amelia Island, FL

27–29 Southwestern Bell Dominion, Dominion CC, San Antonio, TX

April

2–5 The Tradition, Desert Mountain, Scottsdale, AZ

16–19 PGA Seniors' Championship, PGA National GC, Palm Beach Gardens, FL

24–26 Las Vegas Sr Classic, TPC at The Canyons, Las Vegas, NV

May

1–3 Bruno's Memorial Classic, Greystone GC, Birmingham, AL

8–10 The Home Depot Invitational, TPC at Piper Glen, Charlotte, NC

15–17 Saint Luke's Classic, Loch Lloyd CC, Belton, MO

22–24 Bell Atlantic Classic, Hartefield National, Avondale, PA

29–31 Pittsburgh Sr Classic, Quicksilver GC, Midway, PA

June

5–7 Nationwide Championship, GC of Georgia, Alpharetta, GA

12–14 BellSouth Sr Classic at Opryland, Springhouse GC, Nashville, TN

18–21 AT&T Canada Sr Open, Glencoe G&CC, Calgary, Alberta

26–28 Cadillac NFL Golf Classic, Upper Montclair CC, Clifton, NJ

July

3–5 State Farm Classic, Hobbit's Glen GC, Columbia, MD

9–12 Ford Seniors Players Championship, TPC of Michigan, Dearborn, MI

17–19 Ameritech Sr Open, Kemper Lakes, Long Grove, IL

23–26 US Senior Open, Riviera CC, Pacific Palisades, CA

31–2 Franklin Quest Championship, Park Meadows CC, Park City, UT

August

7–9 Burnet Sr Classic, Bunker Hills GC, Coon Rapids, MN

14–16 First of America Classic, Egypt Valley CC, Grand Rapids, MI

21–23 Northville Long Island Classic, Meadow Brook C, Jericho, NY

28–30 BankBoston Classic, Nashawtuc CC, Concord, MA

September

4–6 Emerald Coast Classic, The Moors GC, Milton, FL

11–13 Comfort Classic, Brickyard Crossing, Indianapolis, IN

18–20 Kroger Sr Classic, The Golf Center at Kings Island, Mason, OH

25–27 Boone Valley Classic, Boone Valley GC, Augusta, MO

October

2–4 Vantage Championship, Tanglewood Park, Clemmons, NC

9–11 The Transamerica, Silverado CC, Napa, CA

16–18 Raley's Gold Rush Classic, Serrano CC, El Dorado Hills, CA

23–25 EMC^2 Kaanapali Classic, Kaanapali GC, Lahaina, HA

30–1 Pacific Bell Sr Classic, Wilshire CC, Los Angeles, CA

November

5–8 Energizer Sr Tour Championship, The Dunes, Myrtle Beach, SC

December

19–20 Lexus Challenge, La Quinta Resort, CA

19–20 Wendy's Three Tour Challenge, Lake Las Vegas Resort, Henderson, NV

Japanese Tour

March

12–15 Token Corporation Cup, Kedoin GC, Kagoshima
19–22 Dydo-Drinco Shizuoka Open, Shizuoka
26–29 Justsystem KSB Open, Ayutaki CC, Kagawa

April

2–5 Descente Classic Munsingwear Cup, Taiheiyo Club, Chiba
16–19 Tsuruya Open, Sports Shinko CC, Hyogo
23–26 Asian Tour Kirin Open, Ibaragi
30–3 The Crowns, Nagoya GC, Aichi

May

7–10 Fujisankei Classic, Kawana Hotel GC, Shizuoka
14–17 PGA Ch'p, Grandage GC, Nara
21–24 Ube Kosan Open, Ube CC, Yamaguchi
28–31 Mitsubishi Galant, Tosa CC, Kochi

June

4–7 JCB Classic Sendai, Omotezao Kokusai GC, Miyagi
11–14 Sapporo Tokyu Open, Sapporokokusai GC, Hokkaido
18–21 Yomiuri Open, Yomiuri GC, Hyogo
25–28 Mizuno Open, Setonaikai GC, Okayama

July

2–5 PGA Philanthropy, Shiromizu GC, Gunma
9–12 Yonex Open Hiroshima, Hiroshima CC, Hiroshima
23–26 Aiful Cup, Aomori CC, Aomori
30–2 NST Niigata Open, Forest GC, Niigata

August

6–9 Sanko Grand Summer Championship, Sanko 72 CC, Gunma
27–30 Hisamitsu-KBC Augusta, Keya GC, Fukuoka

September

3–6 PGA Matchplay Championship, Nidom Classic C, Hokkaido
10–13 Suntory Open, Narashino CC, Chiba
17–20 ANA Open, Sapporo GC, Hokkaido
24–27 Gene Sarazen Junior Classic, Rope C, Tochigi

October

1–4 Japan Open, Oarai GC, Ibaragi
8–11 Tokai Classic, Miyoshi CC, Aichi
15–18 Nikkei Cup Torakichi Nakamura Memorial, Fuji C, Ibaragi
22–25 Bridgestone Open, Sodegaura CC, Chiba
29–1 Philip Morris Championship, ABC GC, Hyogo

November

5–8 Acom International, Seve Ballesteros GC, Fukushima
12–15 Sumitomo Visa Taiheiyo Masters, Taiheiyo Club, Shizuoka
19–22 Dunlop Phoenix, Phoenix CC, Miyazaki
26–29 Casio World Open, Ibusuki GC, Kagoshima

December

3–6 Golf Nippon Series, Tokyo Yomiuri CC, Tokyo
10–13 Daikyo Open, Daikyo CC, Okinawa

Omega Asian Tour

January
9–10   Pre-Qualifying School, Tanjong Puteri Golf Resort, Johor Bahru, Malaysia
14–17   Qualifying School, Tanjong Puteri Golf Resort, Johor Bahru, Malaysia

March
5–8   London Myanmar Open, Bagan Golf Club, Myanmar
12–15   Classic Indian Open, Royal Calcutta Golf Club, India

April
2–5   Orient Masters, Orient G&CC, Xiamen, China
16–19   Volvo China Open, Shanghai Sun Island International Golf Club, China
30–3   Macau Open, Macau G&CC, Macau

May
14–17   Guam Open, Leo Palace Resort, Manenggon Hills, Guam
21–24   Fila Open, venue to be confirmed, Korea

July
9–12   British Open Qualifying, UK

August
6–9   Sabah Masters, Shan Shui G&CC, Malaysia
13–16   Volvo Masters of Malaysia, Kelab Golf Sultan Abdul Aziz Shah, Malaysia

August *continued*
20–23   Ericsson Singapore Open, Safra Resort & CC, Singapore
27–30   Philip Morris Asia Cup, Woo Jung Hills Country Club, Korea

September
24–27   Ta Shee Open, Ta Shee G&CC, Taiwan

October
1–4   Kuala Lumpur Open, Saujauna G&CC, Malaysia
8–11   Singapore PGA Championship, Raffles Country Club, Singapore
15–18   Asia Pacific Masters, Bintan Lagoon Golf & Beach Resort, Indonesia
22–25   ABN-AMRO Pakistan Masters, Karachi Golf Club, Pakistan
29–1   Hero Honda Masters, Delhi GC, India

November
5–8   Centennial Cup, Riviera G&CC, Philippines
12–15   Thailand Open, Thailand
19–22   Tugu Pratama PGA Chp, Damai Indah G&CC, Indonesia

December
3–6   Omega PGA Championship, Clearwater Bay G&CC, Hong Kong
9–12   Volvo Asian Match-Play Chp, Taiwan

Women's European Pro Tour

(Provisional)

June
3–6   Evian Masters, Royal Golf Club, Evian, Evian-les-Bains, France

July
23–26   Chrysler Open, TBA, Sweden

August
6–9   McDonald's WPGA Chp of Europe, The Gleneagles Hotel, Perthshire
13–16   Weetabix Women's British Open, Royal Lytham and St Annes
20–23   Compaq Open, TBA, Sweden

September
14–20   Solheim Cup, Muirfield Village GC, Dublin, Ohio, USA

Additional events were to be announced later

United States LPGA Tour

January
16–18   Healthsouth Inaugural, Grand Cypress Resort, North Course, Orlando, FL
21–24   The Office Depot, Ibis G&CC, West Palm Beach, FL

February
13–15   Los Angeles Women's Chp, Oakmont CC, Glendale, CA
19–21   Cup Noodles Hawaiian Ladies' Open, Kapolei GC, Kapolei, Oahu, HA
26–1   Australian Ladies' Masters, Royal Pines Resort, Ashmore, Goldcoast, Queensland, Australia

March
12–15   Welch's/Circle K Championship, Randolph North Golf Course, Tucson, AZ
19–22   Standard Register PING, Moon Valley CC, Phoenix, AZ
26–29   Nabisco Dinah Shore, Mission Hills CC, Rancho Mirage, CA

April
2–5   Longs Drugs Challenge, Twelve Bridges GC, Lincoln, CA
16–19   City of Hope LPGA Classic, Wachesaw Plantation, Murrells Inlet, SC
24–26   Chick-fil-A Charity Chp, Eagles Landing CC, Stockbridge, GA
30–3   Mercury Titleholders' Chp, LPGA International, Daytona Beach, FL

May
8–10   Sara Lee Classic, Hermitage GC, Old Hickory, TN
14–17   McDonald's LPGA Championship, DuPont CC, Wilmington, DE
21–24   LPGA Corning Classic, Corning CC, Corning, NY
23–24   JC Penney LPGA Skins Game, Stonebriar CC, Frisco, TX
28–31   Wegmans Rochester International, Locust Hill CC, Pittsford, NY

June
4–7   Michelob Light Classic, Forest Hills CC, St Louis, MS
11–14   Oldsmobile Classic, Walnut Hills CC, East Lansing, MI
18–21   Friendly's Classic, Crestview CC, Agawam, Mass
26–28   ShopRite LPGA Classic, Marriott Seaview Resort, Atlantic City, NJ

July
2–5   US Women's Open, Blackwolf Run Golf Resort, Kohler, WI
9–12   Jamie Farr Kroger Classic, Highland Meadows GC, Sylvania, OH
16–19   JAL Big Apple Classic, Wykagyl CC, New Rochelle, NY
24–26   Giant Eagle LPGA Classic, Avalon Lakes, Warren, OH
30–2   du Maurier Classic, Essex G&CC, Windsor, Ontario, Canada

August
7–9   Star Bank LPGA Classic, Country Club of the North, Beavercreek, OH
13–16   Weetabix Women's British Open, Royal Lytham and St Annes GC, Blackpool, Lancashire, UK
20–23   Minnesota LPGA Classic, Rush Creek GC, Maple Grove, MN
28–30   State Farm Rail Classic, The Rail GC, Springfield, IL

September
4–6   Safeway LPGA Golf Chp, Columbia Edgewater CC, Portland, OR
10–13   SAFECO Classic, Meridian Valley CC, Kent, Washington
18–20   Solheim Cup, Muirfield Village GC, Dublin, Ohio
24–27   CoreStates Betsy King Classic, Berkleigh CC, Kutztown, PA
28–29   Gillette Tour Challenge Chp, Bermuda

October
8–11   Robert Trent Jones Golf Trail LPGA Tournament of Champions, Grand National, Opelika/Auburn, AL
15–18   Samsung World Championship of Women's Golf, site TBA
30–1   Nichirei International, Tsukuba CC, Ibaraki, Japan

November
6–8   Japan Classic, Sohbu CC, Chiba, Japan
19–22   ITT LPGA Tour Championship, Desert Inn GC, Las Vegas, NV

December
3–6   JC Penney Classic, Westin Innisbrook Resort, Tarpon Springs, FL
19–20   Wendy's Three-Tour Challenge, SouthShore GC at Lake Las Vegas, Henderson, NV

Men's and Boys' Amateur Tournaments

March
24–27 Sunningdale Foursomes, Sunningdale

April
4–5 Scottish Champion of Champions, Leven Links
6–11 Scottish Boys' Championship, Murcar
10–14 West of Ireland Open Amateur Championship, Enniscrone
11–12 Duncan Putter, Southerndown
15–16 Peter McEvoy Trophy, Copt Heath
25–26 Trubshaw Trophy, Tenby and Ashburnham

May
2–3 Lytham Trophy, Royal Lytham and St Annes
2–3 Berkshire Trophy, Berkshire
9–10 Irish Amateur Open Championship, Royal Dublin
9–10 West of Scotland Championship, Dullatur
15–17 Brabazon Trophy, Formby
16–17 Welsh Open Mid–Amateur Championship (Over-25s), Pennard
23–24 St Andrews Links Trophy, St Andrews Old and New
27–28 Lagonda Trophy, Gog Magog
30–1 East of Ireland Amateur Open Championship, Co Louth

June
1–6 British Amateur Championship, Muirfield and Gullane No 1
3–5 English Open Seniors' Championship, Saunton
4–5 Irish Seniors' Amateur Open Championship, Thurles
4–6 International European Mid-Amateur Championship, Roma
6–7 Tennant Cup, Glasgow Gailes and Killermont
7 Welsh Boys' Strokeplay Championship, Tredegar Park
10–11 Welsh Seniors' Championship, Aberdovey
13–14 Scottish Open Amateur Strokeplay Championship, Moray & Elgin
13–17 Irish Amateur Close Championship, The Island
19–21 Welsh Open Strokeplay, Southerndown

June *continued*
18–21 Claremont Scottish Mid-Amateur Championship, Blairgowie
25–27 European Seniors' Championship, Ascona, Switzerland
27–28 East of Scotland Open Amateur Strokeplay, Lundin
30–1 Scottish Seniors' Open Amateur Strokeplay, Ladybank

July
2–3 English Boys' Under-16 Open Amateur Strokeplay, Radcliffe-on-Trent
8–12 European Boys' Team Championship, Gullane
13–17 North of Ireland Amateur Open Championship, Royal Portrush
21–23 Carris Trophy, Whittington Heath
21–24 Welsh Boys' Championship, North Wales GC
25–29 South of Ireland Open Amateur Championship, Lahinch
27–1 English Amateur Championship, Woodhall Spa
27–1 Scottish Amateur Championship, Prestwick
29–31 British Seniors' Championship, Western Gailes and Glasgow Gailes
27–1 Welsh Amateur Championship, Prestatyn

August
5–7 Boys' Home Internationals, St Andrews (Jubilee Course)
10–14 Boys' Championship, Ladybank
12–16 British Mid-Amateur Championship, Over-25s), Ganton
20–23 International European Amateur Championship, TBA, France
22–23 North of Scotland Open Strokeplay, Elgin
28–2g St Andrews Trophy, Villa d'Este, Italy
31–2 English Boys' County Finals, Delamere Forest

September
9–11 Home Internationals, Royal Porthcawl
12 *Golf Illustrated* Gold Vase, Walton Heath
25–27 English County Finals, Stoneham

November
19–22 Eisenhower Trophy, Santiago, Chile.

Women's and Girls' Amateur

April
25–26   Helen Holm Scottish Strokeplay, Portland and Royal Troon

May
17–19   Welsh Ladies' Close Championship, Ashburnbam
19–23   Irish Ladies' Close Championship, Clandeboye
19–23   Scottish Ladies' Close Amateur Championship, North Berwick
30–31   St Rule Trophy, St Andrews

June
9–13   Ladies' British Open Amateur Championship, Little Aston
27–29   Welsh Ladies' Strokeplay, Rolls of Monmouth

July
21–24   Irish Girls' Close Championship, Galway
21–24   Scottish Girls' Close Championship, Kilmarnock Barassi
25–26   Irish Open Strokeplay Championship, Waterford Castle
26–30   Welsh Girls' Championship, Old Padeswood

August
1–2   Curtis Cup, Minikahda Club, Minnesota
4–8   British Girls' Open Amateur Championship, Holyhead
11–13   Girls' Home Internationals, Mullingar
19–21   British Ladies' Open Amateur Strokeplay, Stirling
24–28   Burhill Family Foursomes, Burhill
31–1   Scottish Senior Ladies' Close Amateur Strokeplay, Blairgowie

September
9–11   Home Internationals, Burnham and Berrow
16–17   Welsh Senior Ladies' Championship, Padeswood and Buckley
24   Irish Senior Ladies' Close Championship, Athlone
29–1   Senior Ladies' British Amateur, Powfoot

November
12–15   Espirito Santo Trophy, Santiago, Chile

TAKE THE FAMILY FOR A WALK
ROUND THE WOODS.

Five hundred years of golfing history, and a great day
out are waiting to be discovered at the
British Golf Museum—with the
latest Philips CD-i and touch-
screen displays as your guide.
Find out the secrets of the royal,
the ancient, and the modern game and its
players. Then finish the round at our gift shop.

The British Golf Museum,
Bruce Embankment, St Andrews, Fife KY16 9AB. Telephone: 01334 478880.

PART I

The Major Championships

(1997 and Past Results)

The Open Championship

126th Open Championship *at Royal Troon* (Par 71)

Prize money: £1,586,300. Entries: 2,133. Regional qualifying courses: Beau Desert, Burnham & Berrow, Carlisle, Copt Heath, Coxmoor, Glenbervie, Hankley Common, Moortown, North Hants, Romford, South Herts, Sundridge Park, Wilmslow. Final qualifying courses: Irvine Bogside, Glasgow Gailes, Kilmarnock Barassie, Western Gailes. 156 players took part, 70 (including 1 amateur) qualified for final 36 holes.

Pos	Name	Score	Prize Money £
1	Justin Leonard (US)	69-66-72-65—272	250000
2	Darren Clarke (N. Ire)	67-66-71-71—275	150000
	Jesper Parnevik (Swe)	70-66-66-73—275	150000
4	Jim Furyk (US)	67-72-70-70—279	90000
5	Stephen Ames (T&T)	74-69-66-71—280	62500
	Padraig Harrington (Ire)	75-69-69-67—280	62500
7	Fred Couples (US)	69-68-70-74—281	40666
	Eduardo Romero (Arg)	74-68-67-72—281	40666
	Peter O'Malley (Aus)	73-70-68-70—281	40666
10	Retief Goosen (SA)	75-69-70-68—282	24300
	Lee Westwood (Eng)	73-70-67-72—282	24300
	Tom Watson (US)	71-70-70-71—282	24300
	Mark Calcavecchia (US)	74-67-72-69—282	24300
	Robert Allenby (Aus)	76-68-66-72—282	24300
	Shigeki Maruyama (Jpn)	74-69-70-69—282	24300
	Tom Kite (US)	72-67-74-69—282	24300
	Davis Love III (US)	70-71-74-67—282	24300
	Ernie Els (SA)	75-69-69-69—282	24300
	Frank Nobilo (NZ)	74-72-68-68—282	24300
20	José Maria Olazábal (Sp)	75-68-73-67—283	14500
	Mark James (Eng)	76-67-70-70—283	14500
	Brad Faxon (US)	77-67-72-67—283	14500
	Stuart Appleby (Aus)	72-72-68-71—283	14500
24	Peter Lonard (Aus)	72-70-69-73—284	10362
	Colin Montgomerie (Sco)	76-69-69-70—284	10362
	Ian Woosnam (Wal)	71-73-69-71—284	10362
	David A Russell (Eng)	75-72-68-69—284	10362
	Tiger Woods (US)	72-74-64-74—284	10362
	Tom Lehman (US)	74-72-72-66—284	10362
	Jay Haas (US)	71-70-73-70—284	10362
	Phil Mickelson (US)	76-68-69-71—284	10362
32	Mark McNulty (Zim)	78-67-72-68—285	8750
33	Jonathan Lomas (Eng)	72-71-69-74—286	8283
	David Duval (US)	73-69-73-71—286	8283
	Rodger Davis (Aus)	73-73-70-70—286	8283
36	Andrew Magee (US)	70-75-72-70—287	7950
	Greg Norman (Aus)	69-73-76-69—287	7950
38	Raymond Russell (Sco)	72-72-74-70—288	7550
	Mark O'Meara (US)	73-73-74-68—288	7550
	John Kernohan (US)	76-70-74-68—288	7550

Pos	Name	Score	Prize Money £
	Mike Bradley (US)	72-73-73-70—288	7550
	Bernhard Langer (Ger)	72-74-69-73—288	7550
	Vijay Singh (Fij)	77-69-70-72—288	7550
44	José Coceres (Arg)	76-70-71-72—289	7050
	David Tapping (Eng)	71-66-78-74—289	7050
	Curtis Strange (US)	71-71-70-77—289	7050
	Jerry Kelly (US)	76-68-72-73—289	7050
48	Steve Jones (US)	76-71-68-75—290	6700
	Jim Payne (Eng)	74-74-71-71—290	6700
	Richard Boxall (Eng)	75-71-72-72—290	6700
51	Angel Cabrera (Arg)	70-70-76-75—291	6156
	Jeff Maggert (US)	76-69-71-75—291	6156
	Wayne Riley (Aus)	74-71-75-71—291	6156
	Peter Senior (Aus)	76-70-73-72—291	6156
	Corey Pavin (US)	78-69-76-68—291	6156
	Peter Mitchell (Eng)	75-69-76-71—291	6156
	Nick Faldo (Eng)	71-73-75-72—291	6156
	Greg Turner (NZ)	76-71-72-72—291	6156
59	Payne Stewart (US)	73-74-71-74—292	5800
60	Jack Nicklaus (US)	73-74-71-75—293	5750
	Barclay Howard (Sco)(Am)	70-74-76-73—293	
61	Tom Purtzer (US)	72-71-73-78—294	5625
	Jamie Spence (Eng)	78-69-72-75—294	5625
	Steve Stricker (US)	72-73-74-75—294	5625
	Peter Teravainen (US)	74-72-73-75—294	5625
65	Paul McGinley (Ire)	76-71-77-71—295	5450
	Per-Ulrik Johansson (Swe)	72-75-73-75—295	5450
	Gary Clark (Eng)	74-72-72-77—295	5450
68	Tommy Tolles (US)	77-68-75-76—296	5350
69	Billy Andrade (US)	72-72-78-76—298	5300

36-hole cut: 147, five over par. The following players missed the cut:

70	D Howell	75-73—148	95T	N Price	78-72—150	121	TM Miller	82-72—154
	W Westner	75-73—148		G Day	78-72—150	126	M Roe	79-76—155
	A Coltart	76-72—148		S Dunlap	77-73—150		A Sandywell	80-75—155
	D Robertson	76-72—148	101	P Blackmar	76-75—151		P Hinton	78-77—155
	S Ballesteros	77-71—148		J Cook	76-75—151		D Hart	78-77—155
	P Curry	79-69—148		B Tway	78-73—151		R Green	80-75—155
	R Karlsson	76-72—148		V Phillips	80-71—151		K Eriksson	85-70—155
	G Orr	76-72—148		T Gogele	76-75—151	132	P Stankowski	80-76—156
	M Wiebe	73-75—148		I Garrido	79-72—151		S Mori	80-76—156
	M Long	78-70—148		MA Martin	79-72—151		K Duke	80-76—156
	S Elkington	76-72—148		J Steenkamer	78-73—151		G Murphy	84-72—156
	P Hedblom	76-72—148	109	S Torrance	78-74—152	136	P Azinger	79-78—157
	G Brand Jr	76-72—148		R Claydon	79-73—152		Y Taylor (Am)	81-76—157
	C Mason	78-70—148		W Bladon	78-74—152	137	B McGovern	84-74—158
	P Fulke	73-75—148		MA Jimenez	82-70—152		D Frost	81-77—158
85	B Watts	75-74—149		K Jong Duck	77-75—152		M Mamat	83-75—158
	T Björn	76-73—149		L Batchelor	77-75—152	140	R Jacquelin	81-78—159
	P Broadhurst	75-74—149		C Clark	79-73—152		S Young (Am)	79-80—159
	L Roberts	76-73—149	116	S Lyle	78-75—153	141	S Bottomley	79-81—160
	L Janzen	78-71—149		J Van de Velde	77-76—153	142	A Cejka	81-80—161
	C Parry	79-70—149		A Crerar	76-77—153	143	G Ghei	81-81—162
	C Stadler	78-71—149		M Bradley	77-76—153	144	N Sato	85-78—163
	G Player	78-71—149		G Dodd	78-75—153	145	D Edlund	87-77—164
	R Damron	76-73—149		S Webster (Am)	75-78—153		J Miller (Am)	80-84—164
	P Baker	79-70—149		D Olsson (Am)	80-73—153	146	J Ozaki	76-withdrew
	C Watson (Am)	73-76—149	121	H Miyase	79-75—154		I Baker-Finch	92-withdrew
95	S McCarron	73-77—150		R McFarlane	80-74—154		C Perry	80-withdrew
	C Rocca	75-75—150		J Remesy	79-75—154		Y Kaneko	84-withdrew
	M Brooks	80-70—150		P Haugsrud	79-75—154			

1996 at Royal Lytham & St Annes

Prize money: £1,400,000. Entries: 1,918. Regional qualifying courses: Beau Desert, Burnham & Berrow, Carlisle, Copt Heath, Coxmoor, Glenbervie, Hankley Common, Moortown, North Hants, Romford, South Herts, Sundridge Park, Wilmslow. Final qualifying courses: Fairhaven, Formby, St Anne's Old Links, Southport & Ainsdale. Qualified for final 36 holes: 77 (including 1 amateur).

Pos	Name	Score	Prize £	Pos	Name	Score	Prize £
1	T Lehman (US)	67-67-64-73—271	200000	18T	R Mediate (US)	69-70-69-72—280	15500
2	M McCumber (US)	67-69-71-66—273	125000	22	M James (Eng)	70-68-75-68—281	11875
	E Els (RSA)	68-67-71-67—273	125000		J Haas (US)	70-72-71-68—281	11875
4	N Faldo (Eng)	68-68-68-70—274	75000		T Woods (US) (Am)	75-66-70-70—281	
5	J Maggert (US)	69-70-72-65—276	50000		C Mason (Eng)	68-70-70-73—281	11875
	M Brooks (US)	67-70-68-71—276	50000		S Stricker (US)	71-70-66-74—281	11875
7	P Hedblom (Swe)	70-65-75-67—277	35000	27	B Crenshaw (US)	73-68-71-70—282	9525
	G Norman (Aus)	71-68-71-67—277	35000		T Kite (US)	77-66-69-70—282	9525
	G Turner (NZ)	72-69-68-68—277	35000		P Broadhurst (Eng)	65-72-74-71—282	9525
	F Couples (US)	67-70-69-71—277	35000		C Pavin (US)	70-66-74-72—282	9525
11	A Cejka (Ger)	73-67-71-67—278	27000		P Mitchell (Eng)	71-68-71-72—282	9525
	D Clarke (N. Ire)	70-68-69-71—278	27000		F Nobilo (NZ)	70-72-68-72—282	9525
	V Singh (Fij)	69-67-69-73—278	27000	33	E Romero (Arg)	70-71-75-67—283	7843
14	M McNulty (Zim)	69-71-70-69—279	20250		T Tolles (US)	73-70-71-69—283	7843
	D Duval (US)	76-67-66-70—279	20250		S Simpson (US)	71-69-73-70—283	7843
	P McGinley (Ire)	69-65-74-71—279	20250		E Darcy (Ire)	73-69-71-70—283	7843
	S Maruyama (Jpn)	68-70-69-72—279	20250		D Gilford (Eng)	71-67-71-74—283	7843
18	M Welch (Eng)	71-68-73-68—280	15500		M O'Meara (US)	67-69-72-75—283	7843
	P Harrington (Ire)	68-68-72-71—280	15500		H Tanaka (Jpn)	67-71-70-75—283	7843
	L Roberts (US)	67-69-72-72—280	15500		B Faxon (US)	67-73-68-75—283	7843

Other Totals: M Calcavecchia (US), P Mickelson (US), K Eriksson (Swe), D Frost (RSA) 284; C Stadler (US), B Mayfair (US), P Jacobsen (US), T Hamilton (Can), B Hughes (Aus), P Stewart (US), R Boxall (Eng), J Nicklaus (US), N Price (Zim), J Furyk (US), J Parnevik (Swe) 285; J Payne (Eng), S Lyle (Sco), R Allenby (Aus), S Ames (T&T) 286; M Jonzon (Swe), DA Weibring (US), J Sluman (US), B Barnes (Sco) 287; C Suneson (Eng), C Rocca (Ita), G Law (Sco) 288; DA Russell (Eng), B Ogle (Aus), J Daly (US) 289; H Clark (Eng) 290; B Charles (NZ) 291; D Hospital (Sp), R Todd (Can), C Strange (US), R Chapman (Eng) 292; R Goosen (RSA) 293; A Langenaeken (Bel) 298.

1995 at St Andrews

Prize money: £1,250,000. Entries: 1,836. Regional qualifying courses: Beau Desert, Blackwell, Glenbervie, Hankley Common, Lanark, Moortown, North Hants, Romford, South Herts, Sundridge, Wilmslow. Final qualifying courses: Ladybank, Leven Links, Lundin, Scotscraig. Qualified for final 36 holes: 103 (including 4 amateurs).

Pos	Name	Score	Prize £	Pos	Name	Score	Prize £
1	J Daly (US)*	67-71-73-71—282	125000	20T	D Duval (US)	71-75-70-72—288	13500
2	C Rocca (It)	69-70-70-73—282	100000		A Coltart (Sco)	70-74-71-73—288	13500
3	S Bottomley (Eng)	70-72-72-69—283	65666		B Lane (Eng)	72-73-68-75—288	13500
	M Brooks (US)	70-69-73-71—283	65666	24	L Janzen (US)	73-73-71-72—289	10316
	M Campbell (NZ)	71-71-65-76—283	65666		S Webster (Eng) (Am)	70-72-74-73—289	
6	V Singh (Fij)	68-72-73-71—284	40500		B Langer (Ger)	72-71-73-73—289	10316
	S Elkington (Aus)	72-69-69-74—284	40500		J Parnevik (Swe)	75-71-70-73—289	10316
8	M James (Eng)	72-75-68-70—285	33333		M Calcavecchia (US)	71-72-72-74—289	10316
	B Estes (US)	72-70-71-72—285	33333		B Glasson (US)	68-74-72-75—289	10316
	C Pavin (US)	69-70-72-74—285	33333		K Tomori (Jpn)	70-68-73-78—289	10316
11	P Stewart (US)	72-68-75-71—286	26000	31	R Drummond (Sco)	74-68-77-71—290	8122
	B Ogle (Aus)	73-69-71-73—286	26000		JM Olazabal (Spa)	72-72-74-72—290	8122
	S Torrance (Sco)	71-70-71-74—286	26000		D Frost (RSA)	72-72-74-72—290	8122
	E Els (RSA)	71-68-72-75—286	26000		H Sasaki (Jpn)	74-71-72-73—290	8122
15	G Norman (Aus)	71-74-72-70—287	18200		J Huston (US)	71-74-72-73—290	8122
	R Allenby (Aus)	71-74-71-71—287	18200		P Jacobsen (US)	71-76-70-73—290	8122
	B Crenshaw (US)	67-72-76-72—287	18200		D Clarke (N. Ire)	69-77-70-74—290	8122
	P-U Johansson (Swe)	69-78-68-72—287	18200		D Feherty (N. Ire)	68-75-71-76—290	8122
	B Faxon (US)	71-67-75-74—287	18200		T Watson (US)	67-76-70-77—290	8122
20	P Mitchell (Eng)	73-74-71-70—288	13500				

Other Totals: S Ballesteros (Spa), W Bennett (Eng), P Mickelson (US), M McNulty (Zim), N Faldo (Eng), B Watts (US), G Sherry (Sco) (Am), J Cook (US), N Price (Zim) 291; I Woosnam (Wal), A Forsbrand (Swe), M O'Meara (US), T Nakajima (Jpn), B Claar (US), K Green (US) 292; J Gallagher (US), P O'Malley (Aus), R Claydon (Eng) 293; P Senior (Aus), P Broadhurst (Eng), D Cooper (Eng), E Herrera (Col), T Kite (US), P Lawrie (Sco), M Gates (Eng), R Floyd (US), J Leonard (US), D Gilford (Eng) 294; P Baker (Eng), J Maggert (US), J Lomas (Eng), F Nobilo (NZ), G Player (RSA), O Karlsson (Swe), M Hallberg (Swe), S Hoch (US), G Hallberg (US), J Rivero (Spa), T Woods (US) (Am) 295.

1994 at Turnberry

Prize money: £1,100,000. Entries 1,701. Regional qualifying courses: Blackwell, Glenbervie, Hankley Common, Lanark, Moortown, North Hants, Orsett, Sherwood Forest, South Herts, Sundridge Park, Wilmslow. Final qualifying courses: Glasgow Gailes, Irvine Bogside, Kilmarnock Barassie, Western Gailes. Qualified for final 36 holes: 81 (including 1 amateur). Non-qualifiers after 36 holes with scores of 143 (or more): 75 (71 professionals, 4 amateurs)

Pos	Name	Score	Prize £	Pos	Name	Score	Prize £
1	N Price (Zim)	69-66-67-66—268	110000	20	M Brooks (US)	74-64-71-68—277	12500
2	J Parnevik (Swe)	68-66-68-67—269	88000		V Singh (Fij)	70-68-69-70—277	12500
3	F Zoeller (US)	71-66-64-70—271	74000		G Turner (NZ)	65-71-70-71—277	12500
4	A Forsbrand (Swe)	72-71-66-64—273	50666		P Senior (Aus)	68-71-67-71—277	12500
	M James (GB)	72-67-66-68—273	50666	24	B Estes (US)	72-68-72-66—278	7972
	D Feherty (GB)	68-69-66-70—273	50666		T Price (Aus)	74-65-71-68—278	7972
7	B Faxon (US)	69-65-67-73—274	36000		P Lawrie (GB)	71-69-70-68—278	7972
8	N Faldo (GB)	75-66-70-64—275	30000		J Maggert (US)	69-74-67-68—278	7972
	T Kite (US)	71-69-66-69—275	30000		T Lehman (US)	70-69-70-69—278	7972
	C Montgomerie (GB)	72-69-65-69—275	30000		E Els (RSA)	69-69-69-71—278	7972
11	R Claydon (GB)	72-71-68-65—276	19333		M Springer (US)	72-67-68-71—278	7972
	M McNulty (Zim)	71-70-68-67—276	19333		L Roberts (US)	68-69-69-72—278	7972
	F Nobilo (NZ)	69-67-72-68—276	19333		P Jacobsen (US)	69-70-67-72—278	7972
	J Lomas (GB)	66-70-72-68—276	19333		C Stadler (US)	71-69-66-72—278	7972
	M Calcavecchia (US)	71-67-70-68—276	19333		A Coltart (GB)	71-69-66-72—278	7972
	G Norman (Aus)	71-67-69-69—276	19333	35	M Davis (GB)	75-68-69-67—279	6700
	L Mize (US)	73-69-64-70—276	19333		L Janzen (US)	74-69-69-67—279	6700
	T Watson (US)	68-65-69-74—276	19333		G Evans (GB)	69-69-73-68—279	6700
	R Rafferty (GB)	71-66-65-74—276	19333				

Other Totals: D Gilford (GB), D Hospital (Sp), JM Olazabal (Sp), S Ballesteros (Sp), B Marchbank (GB), D Clarke (GB) 280; J Van De Velde (Fr), D Love III (US), M Ozaki (Jpn) 280; J Gallagher Jnr (US), D Edwards (US), G Kraft (US), H Twitty (US) 281; D Frost (SA), M Lanner (Swe), K Tomori (Jpn), T Watanabe (Jpn) 282; P Baker (GB), J Cook (US), T Nakajima (Jpn), B Watts (US), R McFarlane (GB) 283; G Brand Jr (GB), H Meshiai (Jpn), B Langer (Ger), C O'Connor Jnr (Ire), P-U Johansson (Swe), R Allenby (Aus), W Grady (Aus) 284; S Elkington (Aus), M Roe (GB), L Clements (US), C Mason (GB), R Alvarez (Arg) 285; W Bennett (GB) (Am), W Riley (Aus) 286; S Lyle (GB) 287; C Ronald (GB), C Gillies (GB) 288; B Crenshaw (US) , C Parry (Aus), J Haeggman (Swe) 289; N Henning (RSA) 291; J Daly (US) 292.

1993 at Royal St George's

Prize money: £1,017,000. Entries 1,827. Regional qualifying courses: Beau Desert, Blackwell, Coxmoor, Hankley Park, Lanark, Langley Park, North Hants, Orsett, Sherwood Forest, South Herts, Sundridge Park, Wilmslow. Final qualifying courses: Littlestone, North Foreland, Prince's and Royal Cinque Ports. Qualified for final 36 holes: 78 (77 professionals, 1 amateur). Non-qualifiers after 36 holes: 78 (73 professionals, 5 amateurs) with scores of 144 and above.

Pos	Name	Score	Prize £	Pos	Name	Score	Prize £
1	G Norman (Aus)	66-68-69-64—267	100000	14T	T Kite (US)	72-70-68-68—278	15214
2	N Faldo (GB)	69-63-70-67—269	80000	21	H Clark (GB)	67-72-70-70—279	10000
3	B Langer (Ger)	67-66-70-67—270	67000		J Parnevik (Swe)	68-74-68-69—279	10000
4	C Pavin (US)	68-66-68-70—272	50500		P Baker (GB)	70-67-74-68—279	10000
	P Senior (Aus)	66-69-70-67—272	50500	24	R Davis (Aus)	68-71-71-70—280	8400
6	N Price (Zim)	68-70-67-69—274	33166		D Frost (SA)	69-73-70-68—280	8400
	E Els (SA)	68-69-69-68—274	33166		M Roe (GB)	70-71-73-66—280	8400
	P Lawrie (GB)	72-68-69-65—274	33166	27	L Mize (US)	67-69-74-71—281	7225
9	W Grady (Aus)	74-68-64-69—275	25500		S Ballesteros (Spa)	68-73-69-71—281	7225
	F Couples (US)	68-66-72-69—275	25500		M James (GB)	70-70-70-71—281	7225
	S Simpson (US)	68-70-71-66—275	25500		D Smyth (Ire)	67-74-70-70—281	7225
12	P Stewart (US)	71-72-70-63—276	21500		Y Mizumaki (Jpn)	69-69-73-70—281	7225
13	B Lane (GB)	70-68-71-68—277	20500		M Mackenzie (GB)	72-71-71-67—281	7225
14	J Daly (US)	71-66-70-71—278	15214		I Pyman (GB) (Am)	68-72-70-71—281	
	F Zoeller (US)	66-70-71-71—278	15214	34	H Twitty (US)	71-71-67-73—282	6180
	G Morgan (US)	70-68-70-70—278	15214		R Floyd (US)	70-72-67-73—282	6180
	J Rivero (Sp)	68-73-67-70—278	15214		W Westner (SA)	67-73-72-70—282	6180
	M McNulty (Zim)	67-71-71-69—278	15214		P Broadhurst (GB)	71-69-74-68—282	6180
	M Calcavecchia (US)	66-73-71-68—278	15214		J Van de Velde (Fr)	75-67-73-67—282	6180

Other Totals: D Clarke (GB), C O'Connor Jr (Ire), A Sorensen (Den), D Waldorf (US), P Moloney (Aus), G Turner (NZ), C Mason (GB), A Magee (US), R Mediate (US) 283; L Janzen (US), S Elkington (Aus), J Huston (US) 284; J Sewell (GB), M Pinero (Spa), F Nobilo (NZ), S Torrance (GB), MA Jimenez (Spa), I Woosnam (GB), S Ames (T&T), I Garbutt (GB) 285; C Parry (Aus), T Lehman (US), V Singh (Fij), P Azinger (US) 286; J Spence (GB), O Karlsson (Swe), R Drummond (GB) 287; T Pernice (US), W Guy (GB), J Cook (GB), M Sunesson (Swe) 288; I Baker-Finch (Aus), T Purtzer (US), M Miller (GB) 289; M Harwood (Aus), P Mitchell (GB), P Fowler (Aus), D Forsman (US) 290; M Krantz (Swe) 292; R Willison (GB) 293.

1992 at Muirfield

Prize money: £950,000. Entries 1,666. Regional qualifying courses: Beau Desert, Blackwell, Coxmoor, Glenbervie, Lanark, North Hants, Orsett, Sherwood Forest, South Herts, Sundridge Park, Wilmslow. Final qualifying courses: Dunbar, Gullane, Luffness New, North Berwick. Qualified for final 36 holes: 75 (74 professionals, 1 amateur). Non-qualifiers after 36 holes: 81 (77 professionals, 4 amateurs) with scores of 143 and above.

Pos	Name	Score	Prize £	Pos	Name	Score	Prize £
1	N Faldo (GB)	66-64-69-73—272	95000	19T	I Baker-Finch (Aus)	71-71-72-68—282	11066
2	J Cook (US)	66-67-70-70—273	75000		T Kite (US)	70-69-71-72—282	11066
3	JM Olazabal (Spa)	70-67-69-68—274	64000	22	P Mitchell (GB)	69-71-72-71—283	8950
4	S Pate (US)	64-70-69-73—276	53000		P Lawrie (GB)	70-72-68-73—283	8950
5	D Hammond (US)	70-65-70-74—279	30071		T Purtzer (US)	68-69-75-71—283	8950
	A Magee (US)	67-72-70-70—279	30071	25	B Andrade (US)	69-71-70-74—284	7700
	E Els (SA)	66-69-70-74—279	30071		D Waldorf (US)	69-70-73-72—284	7700
	I Woosnam (GB)	65-73-70-71—279	30071		P Senior (Aus)	70-69-70-75—284	7700
	G Brand Jr (GB)	65-68-72-74—279	30071	28	M Calcavecchia (US)	69-71-73-72—285	6658
	M Mackenzie (Chile)	71-67-70-71—279	30071		M McNulty (Zim)	71-70-70-74—285	6658
	R Karlsson (Swe)	70-68-70-71—279	30071		J Mudd (US)	71-69-74-71—285	6658
12	J Spence (GB)	71-68-70-71—280	17383		C Parry (Aus)	67-71-76-71—285	6658
	C Beck (US)	71-68-67-74—280	17383		R Cochran (US)	71-68-72-74—285	6658
	R Floyd (US)	64-71-73-72—280	17383		M Lanner (Swe)	72-68-71-74—285	6658
	A Lyle (GB)	68-70-70-72—280	17383	34	A Forsbrand (Swe)	70-72-70-74—286	5760
	M O'Meara (US)	71-68-72-69—280	17383		C Pavin (US)	69-74-73-70—286	5760
	L Rinker (US)	69-68-70-73—280	17383		P Stewart (US)	70-73-71-72—286	5760
18	G Norman (Aus)	71-72-70-68—281	13200		S Elkington (Aus)	68-70-75-73—286	5760
19	H Irwin (US)	70-73-67-72—282	11066		T Johnstone (Zim)	72-71-74-69—286	5760

Other Totals: DW Basson (SA), L Janzen (US), L Trevino (US), S Richardson (GB), W Grady (Aus), R Rafferty (Ire) 287; M Harwood (Aus), L Wadkins (US), J Coceres (Arg), R Mediate (US), C Mann (Aus), B Marchbank (GB) 288; R Mackay (Aus), V Singh (Fij), N Price (Zim), B Lane (GB) 289; C Rocca (Ita), D Feherty (Ire), M Brooks (US), O Vincent III (US) 290; P Azinger (US), B Langer (Ger), W Riley (Aus), W Guy (GB), M Clayton (Aus) 291; C Stadler (US), R Chapman (GB), D Mijovic (Can), H Buhrmann (SA) 292; P-U Johansson (Swe), P O'Malley (Aus), A Sherbourne (GB), J Robson (GB), D Lee (GB) 293; F Funk (US) 294; P Mayo (GB) 295; J Daly (US) 298.

1991 at R Birkdale

Prize money: £900,000. Entries 1,496. Regional Qualifying Courses: Beau Desert, Blackwell, Deer Park, Hankley Common, Langley Park, Ormskirk, Orsett, Sherwood Forest, South Herts. Final Qualifying Courses: Hesketh, Hillside, Southport & Ainsdale, West Lancashire. Qualified for final 36 holes: 113 (111 professionals, 2 amateurs). Non-qualifiers after 36 holes: 43 (37 professionals, 6 amateurs) with scores of 149 and above.

Pos	Name	Score	Prize £	Pos	Name	Score	Prize £
1	I Baker-Finch (Aus)	71-71-64-66—272	90000	17T	C Beck (US)	67-78-70-66—281	10055
2	M Harwood (Aus)	68-70-69-67—274	70000		I Woosnam (GB)	70-72-69-70—281	10055
3	M O'Meara (US)	71-68-67-69—275	55000		P Broadhurst (GB)	71-73-68-69—281	10055
	F Couples (US)	72-69-70-64—275	55000		M Mouland (GB)	68-74-68-71—281	10055
5	J Mudd (US)	72-70-72-63—277	34166		A Sherborne (GB)	73-70-68-70—281	10055
	E Darcy (Ire)	73-68-66-70—277	34166		P Senior (Aus)	74-67-71-69—281	10055
	B Tway (US)	75-66-70-66—277	34166	26	C Montgomerie (GB)	71-69-71-71—282	6750
8	C Parry (Aus)	71-70-69-68—278	27500		M Reid (US)	68-71-70-73—282	6750
9	G Norman (Aus)	74-68-71-66—279	22833		W Grady (Aus)	69-70-73-70—282	6750
	B Langer (Ger)	71-71-70-67—279	22833		T Watson (US)	69-72-72-69—282	6750
	S Ballesteros (Spa)	66-73-69-71—279	22833		E Romero (Arg)	70-73-68-71—282	6750
12	M Sunesson (Swe)	72-73-68-67—280	17100		M James (GB)	72-68-70-72—282	6750
	D Williams (GB)	74-71-68-67—280	17100	32	G Hallberg (US)	68-70-73-72—283	5633
	V Singh (Fij)	71-69-69-71—280	17100		P Stewart (US)	72-72-71-68—283	5633
	R Davis (Aus)	70-71-73-66—280	17100		S Richardson (GB)	74-70-72-67—283	5633
	R Chapman (GB)	74-66-71-69—280	17100		G Brand Jr (GB)	71-72-69-71—283	5633
17	L Trevino (US)	71-72-71-67—281	10055		M Miller (GB)	73-74-67-69—283	5633
	B Lane (GB)	68-72-71-70—281	10055		C O'Connor Jr (Ire)	72-71-71-69—283	5633
	N Faldo (GB)	68-75-70-68—281	10055				

Other Totals: C Strange (US), A Forsbrand (Swe), P O'Malley (Aus), N Henke (US), M Poxon (GB), J Payne (GB) (Am) 284; G Marsh (Aus), R Gamez (US), T Kite (US), S Elkington (Aus), F Allem (SA), S Torrance (GB), C Rocca (Ita), D Love III (US), D Smyth (Ire), J Spence (GB), J Nicklaus (US), N Price (Zim), D Hammond (US) 285; G Levenson (SA), A Magee (US), H Irwin (US), S Simpson (US), T Simpson (US), J Rivero (Spa), G Player (SA) 286; MA Martin (Spa), JD Blake (US), M McLean (GB), A Oldcorn (GB), M McNulty (Zim), S Jones (US), S Pate (US), G Morgan (US), D Clarke (Ire) 287.

1990 at St Andrews

Prize money: £825,000. Entries 1,707. Regional Qualifying Courses: Blackwell, Deer Park, Hankley Common, Langley Park, Ormskirk, Orsett, Sherwood Forest, South Herts. Final Qualifying Courses: Ladybank, Leven Links, Lundin, Panmure, Scotscraig. Qualified for final 36 holes: 72 (all professionals). Non-qualifiers after 36 holes: 84 (80 professionals and 4 amateurs) with scores of 144 and above.

Pos	Name	Score	Prize £		Pos	Name	Score	Prize £
1	N Faldo (GB)	67-65-67-71—270	85000		16T	P Jacobsen (US)	68-70-70-73—281	11150
2	M McNulty (Zim)	74-68-68-65—275	60000			F Nobilo (NZ)	72-67-68-74—281	11150
	P Stewart (US)	68-68-68-71—275	60000		22	E Darcy (Ire)	71-71-72-68—282	7933
4	I Woosnam (GB)	68-69-70-69—276	40000			C Parry (Aus)	68-68-69-77—282	7933
	J Mudd (US)	72-66-72-66—276	40000			J Spence (GB)	72-65-73-72—282	7933
6	I Baker-Finch (Aus)	68-72-64-73—277	28500		25	N Price (Zim)	70-67-71-75—283	6383
	G Norman (Aus)	66-66-76-69—277	28500			F Couples (US)	71-70-70-72—283	6383
8	S Pate (US)	70-68-72-69—279	22000			C O'Connor Jr (Ire)	68-72-71-72—283	6383
	C Pavin (US)	71-69-68-71—279	22000			L Trevino (US)	69-70-73-71—283	6383
	D Hammond (US)	70-71-68-70—279	22000			J Rivero (Spa)	70-70-70-73—283	6383
	D Graham (Aus)	72-71-70-66—279	22000			J Sluman (US)	72-70-70-71—283	6383
12	V Singh (Fij)	70-69-72-69—280	16375		31	B Norton (US)	71-72-68-73—284	5125
	T Simpson (US)	70-69-69-72—280	16375			L Mize (US)	71-72-70-71—284	5125
	R Gamez (US)	70-72-67-71—280	16375			R Rafferty (N. Ire)	70-71-73-70—284	5125
	P Broadhurst (GB)	74-69-63-74—280	16375			B Crenshaw (US)	74-69-68-73—284	5125
16	M Roe (GB)	71-70-72-68—281	11150			M McCumber (US)	69-74-69-72—284	5125
	S Jones (US)	72-67-72-70—281	11150			M James (GB)	73-69-70-72—284	5125
	A Lyle (GB)	72-70-67-72—281	11150			V Fernandez (Arg)	72-67-69-76—284	5125
	JM Olazabal (Spa)	71-67-71-72—281	11150			G Powers (US)	74-69-69-72—284	5125

Other Totals: D Cooper (GB), N Ozaki (Jpn), D Pooley (US), M Hulbert (US), M Reid (US), A North (US), S Simpson (US), R Floyd (US), S Torrance (GB) 285; M O'Meara (US), C Montgomerie (GB), B Langer (Ger), P Fowler (Aus), P Azinger (US) 286; H Irwin (US), E Romero (Arg), J Bland (SA), M Allen (US) 287; D Ray (GB), A Sorensen (Den), B McCallister (US), J Rutledge (Can), D Mijovic (US), M Clayton (Aus) 288; M Poxon (GB), P Baker (GB), J Nicklaus (US), R Chapman (GB), D Canipe (US) 289; J Berendt (Arg), D Feherty (GB) 290; A Saavedra (Arg) 291; M Mackenzie (GB) 292; JM Canizares (Spa) 296.

1989 at R Troon

Prize money: £750,000. Entries 1,481. Regional Qualifying Courses: Glenbervie, Hankley Common, Langley Park, Lindrick, Little Aston, Ormskirk, Porters Park, South Herts. Final Qualifying Courses: Glasgow Gailes, Irvine (Bogside), Kilmarnock (Barassie), Western Gailes. Qualified for final 36 holes: 80 (78 professionals, 2 amateurs). Non-qualifiers after 36 holes: 76 (68 professionals, 8 amateurs) with scores of 147 and above.

Pos	Name	Score	Prize £		Pos	Name	Score	Prize £
1	M Calcavecchia (US)	71-68-68-68—275	80000		19T	D Cooper (GB)	69-70-76-68—283	8575
2	W Grady (Aus)	68-67-69-71—275	55000			T Kite (US)	70-74-67-72—283	8575
	G Norman (Aus)	69-70-72-64—275	55000			D Pooley (US)	73-70-69-71—283	8575
	(Calcavecchia won 4-hole play-off)				23	V Singh (Fij)	71-73-69-71—284	6733
4	T Watson (US)	69-68-68-72—277	40000			D Love III (US)	72-70-73-69—284	6733
5	J Mudd (US)	73-67-68-70—278	30000			JM Olazabal (Spa)	68-72-69-75—284	6733
6	F Couples (US)	68-71-68-72—279	26000		26	S Bennett (GB)	75-69-68-73—285	5800
	D Feherty (GB)	71-67-69-72—279	26000			L Wadkins (US)	72-70-69-74—285	5800
8	E Romero (Arg)	68-70-75-67—280	21000			C Beck (US)	75-69-68-73—285	5800
	P Azinger (US)	68-73-67-72—280	21000			S Simpson (US)	73-66-72-74—285	5800
	P Stewart (US)	72-65-69-74—280	21000		30	J Hawkes (SA)	75-67-69-75—286	4711
11	N Faldo (GB)	71-71-70-69—281	17000			G Koch (US)	72-71-74-69—286	4711
	M McNulty (Zim)	75-70-70-66—281	17000			J Nicklaus (US)	74-71-71-70—286	4711
13	P Walton (Ire)	69-74-69-70—282	13000			P Jacobsen (US)	71-74-71-70—286	4711
	H Clark (GB)	72-68-72-70—282	13000			B Marchbank (GB)	69-74-73-70—286	4711
	S Pate(US)	69-70-70-73—282	13000			M Martin (Spa)	68-73-72-73—286	4711
	R Chapman (GB)	76-68-67-71—282	13000			I Baker-Finch (Aus)	72-69-70-75—286	4711
	M James (GB)	69-70-71-72—282	13000			M Ozaki (Jpn)	71-73-70-72—286	4711
	C Stadler (US)	73-69-69-71—282	13000			M Davis (GB)	77-68-67-74—286	4711
19	L Mize (US)	71-74-66-72—283	8575					

Other Totals: M Harwood (Aus), T Armour III (US), J Woodland (Aus) 287; M O'Meara (US), L Trevino (US), R Floyd (US), J Rivero (Spa) 288; M McCumber (US), A Lyle (GB), N Ozaki (Jpn) 289; J Miller (US), I Woosnam (GB), C O'Connor Jr (Ire) 290; B Ogle (Aus), M Roe (GB), T Ozaki (Jpn), M Allen (US), T Johnstone (Zim), E Dussart (Fra), R Boxall (GB), G Sauers (US), B Crenshaw (US) 291; C Strange (US), D Graham (Aus), K Green (US), P Hoad (GB), B Tway (US), R Rafferty (Ire), M Reid (US), W Stephens (GB) 292; L Carbonetti (Arg), A Stephen (GB), R Claydon (GB) (Am) 293; C Gillies (GB) 294; B Faxon (US), P Teravainen (US) 295; E Aubrey (US) 296; M Sludds (Ire) 297; S Ballesteros (Spa), R Karlsson (Swe) (Am) 299; G Levenson (SA) 301; B Langer (Ger) 309.

1988 at R Lytham & St Annes

Prize money: £700,000. Entries 1,393. Regional Qualifying Courses: Beau Desert, Camberley Heath, Glenbervie, Hankley Common, Langley Park, Lindrick, Little Aston, Ormskirk, Porters Park. Final Qualifying Courses: Blackpool North Shore, Fairhaven, Lytham Green Drive, St Annes Old Links. Qualified for final 36 holes: 71 (70 professionals, 1 amateur). Non-qualifiers after 36 holes: 83 (76 professionals, 7 amateurs) with scores of 149 and above.

Pos	Name	Score	Prize £	Pos	Name	Score	Prize £
1	S Ballesteros (Spa)	67-71-70-65—273	80000	20	T Kite (US)	75-71-73-68—287	7000
2	N Price (Zim)	70-67-69-69—275	60000		R Davis (Aus)	76-71-72-68—287	7000
3	N Faldo (GB)	71-69-68-71—279	47000		G Brand Jr (GB)	72-76-68-71—287	7000
4	F Couples (US)	73-69-71-68—281	33500		B Tway (US)	71-71-72-73—287	7000
	G Koch (US)	71-72-70-68—281	33500		R Charles (NZ)	71-74-69-73—287	7000
6	P Senior (Aus)	70-73-70-69—282	27000	25	J Nicklaus (US)	75-70-75-68—288	5500
7	I Aoki (Jpn)	72-71-73-67—283	21000		I Woosnam (GB)	76-71-72-69—288	5500
	P Stewart (US)	73-75-68-67—283	21000	27	M O'Meara (US)	75-69-75-70—289	5200
	D Frost (SA)	71-75-69-68—283	21000	28	H Clark (GB)	71-72-75-72—290	4600
	A Lyle (GB)	73-69-67-74—283	21000		M McNulty (Zim)	73-73-72-72—290	4600
11	D Russell (GB)	71-74-69-70—284	16500		T Watson (US)	74-72-72-72—290	4600
	B Faxon (US)	69-74-70-71—284	16500		C Beck (US)	72-71-74-73—290	4600
13	C Strange (US)	79-69-69-68—285	14000		T Armour III (US)	73-72-72-73—290	4600
	E Romero (Arg)	72-71-69-73—285	14000		J Benepe III (US)	75-72-70-73—290	4600
	L Nelson (US)	73-71-68-73—285	14000	34	W Riley (Aus)	72-71-72-76—291	4150
16	J Rivero (Spa)	75-69-70-72—286	10500		L Wadkins (US)	73-71-71-76—291	4150
	B Crenshaw (US)	73-73-68-72—286	10500	36	G Brand (GB)	73-74-72-73—292	3950
	A Bean (US)	71-70-71-74—286	10500		JM Olazabal (Spa)	73-71-73-75—292	3950
	D Pooley (US)	70-73-69-74—286	10500				

Other Totals: J Haas (US), N Ratcliffe (GB), B Marchbank (GB), R Rafferty (Ire), G March (Aus), C Pavin (US), D Russell (GB), W Grady (Aus), K Brown (GB) 293; P Kent (GB), S Torrance (GB), P Azinger (US), A North (US), M McCumber (US) 294; P Fowler (Aus), F Zoeller (US), P Walton (GB), H Green (US), J Miller (US) 295; M Smith (GB), C Mason (GB), P Broadhurst (GB) (Am) 296; C Stadler (US), G Player (SA) 297; M James (GB), S Bishop (GB), A Sherborne (GB) 298; M Pinero (Spa) 299; P Carman 301; G Bruckner, C-H Hsieh 302; B Langer (Ger) 303; G Stafford 305; P Mitchell 308.

The Belt

Year	Winner	Score	Venue	Entrants
1860	W Park, Musselburgh	174	Prestwick	8
1861	T Morris, Sr, Prestwick	163	Prestwick	12
1862	T Morris, Sr, Prestwick	163	Prestwick	6
1863	W Park, Musselburgh	168	Prestwick	14
1864	T Morris, Sr, Prestwick	167	Prestwick	6
1865	A Strath, St Andrews	162	Prestwick	10
1866	W Park, Musselburgh	169	Prestwick	12
1867	T Morris, Sr, St Andrews	170	Prestwick	10
1868	T Morris, Jr, St Andrews	157	Prestwick	10
1869	T Morris, Jr, St Andrews	154	Prestwick	8
1870	T Morris, Jr, St Andrews	149	Prestwick	17

Having been won thrice in succession by young Tom Morris, the Belt became his property. The Championship was held in abeyance for one year. From 1872 the present cup was offered for yearly competition.

The Cup

Year	Winner	Score	Venue	Entrants
1872	T Morris, Jr, St Andrews	166	Prestwick	8
1873	T Kidd, St Andrews	179	St Andrews	26
1874	M Park, Musselburgh	159	Musselburgh	32
1875	W Park, Musselburgh	166	Prestwick	18
1876	B Martin, St Andrews	176	St Andrews	34
	(D Strath tied but refused to play off)			
1877	J Anderson, St Andrews	160	Musselburgh	24
1878	J Anderson, St Andrews	157	Prestwick	26
1879	J Anderson, St Andrews	169	St Andrews	46
1880	B Ferguson, Musselburgh	162	Musselburgh	30
1881	B Ferguson, Musselburgh	170	Prestwick	22

Year	Winner	Score	Venue	Entrants
1882	B Ferguson, Musselburgh	171	St Andrews	40
1883	W Fernie, Dumfries	159	Musselburgh	41

After a tie with B Ferguson, Musselburgh

Year	Winner	Score	Venue	Entrants
1884	J Simpson, Carnoustie	160	Prestwick	30
1885	B Martin, St Andrews	171	St Andrews	51
1886	D Brown, Musselburgh	157	Musselburgh	46
1887	W Park, Jr, Musselburgh	161	Prestwick	36
1888	J Burns, Warwick	171	St Andrews	53
1889	W Park, Jr, Musselburgh	155	Musselburgh	42

After a tie with A Kirkaldy

Year	Winner	Score	Venue	Entrants
1890	J Ball, Royal Liverpool (Am)	164	Prestwick	40
1891	H Kirkaldy, St Andrews	166	St Andrews	82

After 1891 the competition was extended to 72 holes and for the first time entry money was imposed

Year	Winner	Score	Venue	Entrants
1892	H Hilton, Royal Liverpool (Am)	305	Muirfield	66
1893	W Auchterlonie, St Andrews	322	Prestwick	72
1894	J Taylor, Winchester	326	Sandwich, R St George's	94
1895	J Taylor, Winchester	322	St Andrews	73
1896	H Vardon, Ganton	316	Muirfield	64

After a tie with J Taylor. Play-off scores for 36 holes: H Vardon 157; Taylor 161

Year	Winner	Score	Venue	Entrants
1897	H Hilton, Royal Liverpool (Am)	314	Hoylake, R Liverpool	86
1898	H Vardon, Ganton	307	Prestwick	78
1899	H Vardon, Ganton	310	Sandwich, R St George's	98
1900	J Taylor, Mid-Surrey	309	St Andrews	81
1901	J Braid, Romford	309	Muirfield	101
1902	A Herd, Huddersfield	307	Hoylake, R Liverpool	112
1903	H Vardon, Totteridge	300	Prestwick	127
1904	J White, Sunningdale	296	Sandwich, R St George's	144
1905	J Braid, Walton Heath	318	St Andrews	152
1906	J Braid, Walton Heath	300	Muirfield	183
1907	A Massy, La Boulie	312	Hoylake, R Liverpool	193

Year	Winner	Score	Venue	Qual	Ents
1908	J Braid, Walton Heath	291	Prestwick	180	
1909	J Taylor, Mid-Surrey	295	Deal, R Cinque Ports	204	
1910	J Braid, Walton Heath	299	St Andrews	210	
1911	H Vardon, Totteridge	303	Sandwich, R St George's	226	

After a tie with A Massy. The tie was over 36 holes, but Massy picked up at the 35th hole before holing out. He had taken 148 for 34 holes, and when Vardon holed out at the 35th hole his score was 143.

Year	Winner	Score	Venue	Qual	Ents
1912	E Ray, Oxhey	295	Muirfield	215	
1913	J Taylor, Mid-Surrey	304	Hoylake, R Liverpool	269	
1914	H Vardon, Totteridge	306	Prestwick	194	
1915–19	*No Championship owing to the Great War*				
1920	G Duncan, Hanger Hill	303	Deal, R Cinque Ports	81	190
1921	J Hutchison, Glenview, Chicago	296	St Andrews	85	158

After a tie with R Wethered (Am). Royal and Ancient-Play-off scores: Hutchison 150; Wethered 159.

Year	Winner	Score	Venue	Qual	Ents
1922	W Hagen, Detroit, USA	300	Sandwich, R St George's	80	225
1923	A Havers, Coombe Hill	295	Troon	88	222
1924	W Hagen, Detroit, USA	301	Hoylake, R Liverpool	86	277
1925	J Barnes, USA	300	Prestwick	83	200
1926	R Jones, USA (Am)	291	R Lytham and St Annes	117	293
1927	R Jones, USA (Am)	285	St Andrews	108	207
1928	W Hagen, USA	292	Sandwich, R St George's	113	271
1929	W Hagen, USA	292	Muirfield	109	242
1930	R Jones, USA (Am)	291	Hoylake, R Liverpool	112	296
1931	T Armour, USA	296	Carnoustie	109	215
1932	G Sarazen, USA	283	Sandwich, Prince's	110	224
1933	D Shute, USA	292	St Andrews	117	287

After a tie with C Wood, USA-Play-off scores: Shute 149; Wood 154.

Year	Winner	Score	Venue	Qual	Ents
1934	T Cotton, Waterloo, Belgium	283	Sandwich, R St George's	101	312
1935	A Perry, Leatherhead	283	Muirfield	109	264
1936	A Padgham, Sundridge Park	287	Hoylake, R Liverpool	107	286
1937	T Cotton, Ashridge	290	Carnoustie	141	258
1938	R Whitcombe, Parkstone	295	Sandwich, R St George's	120	268
1939	R Burton, Sale	290	St Andrews	129	254
1940–45	*No Championship owing to Second World War*				
1946	S Snead, USA	290	St Andrews	100	225
1947	F Daly, Balmoral	293	Hoylake, R Liverpool	100	263
1948	T Cotton, Royal Mid-Surrey	284	Muirfield	97	272
1949	A Locke, South Africa	283	Sandwich, R St George's	96	224

After a tie with H Bradshaw, Kilcroney-Play-off scores: Locke 135; Bradshaw 147.

continued

Open Championship *continued*

Year	Winner	Score	Venue	Qual	Ents
1950	A Locke, South Africa	279	Troon	93	262
1951	M Faulkner, GB	285	R Portrush	98	180
1952	A Locke, South Africa	287	R Lytham and St Annes	96	275
1953	B Hogan, USA	282	Carnoustie	91	196
1954	P Thomson, Australia	283	Birkdale	97	349
1955	P Thomson, Australia	281	St Andrews	94	301
1956	P Thomson, Australia	286	Hoylake, R Liverpool	96	360
1957	A Locke, South Africa	279	St Andrews	96	282
1958	P Thomson, Australia	278	R Lytham and St Annes	96	362

After a tie with D Thomas, Sudbury. Play-off scores: Thomson 139; Thomas 143.

Year	Winner	Score	Venue	Qual	Ents
1959	G Player, South Africa	284	Muirfield	90	285
1960	K Nagle, Australia	278	St Andrews	74	410
1961	A Palmer, USA	284	Birkdale	101	364
1962	A Palmer, USA	276	Troon	119	379
1963	R Charles, New Zealand	277	R Lytham and St Annes	119	261

After a tie with P Rodgers, USA. Play-off scores: Charles 140; Rodgers 148

Year	Winner	Score	Venue	Qual	Ents
1964	T Lema, USA	279	St Andrews	119	327
1965	P Thomson, Australia	285	R Birkdale	130	372
1966	J Nicklaus, USA	282	Muirfield	130	310
1967	R De Vicenzo, Argentina	278	Hoylake, R Liverpool	130	326
1968	G Player, South Africa	289	Carnoustie	130	309
1969	A Jacklin, GB	280	R Lytham and St Annes	129	424
1970	J Nicklaus USA	283	St Andrews	134	468

After a tie with Doug Sanders, USA. Play-off scores: Nicklaus 72; Sanders 73.

Year	Winner	Score	Venue	Qual	Ents
1971	L Trevino, USA	278	R Birkdale	150	528
1972	L Trevino, USA	278	Muirfield	150	570
1973	T Weiskopf, USA	276	Troon	150	569
1974	G Player, South Africa	282	R Lytham and St Annes	150	679
1975	T Watson, USA	279	Carnoustie	150	629

After a tie with J Newton, Australia. Play-off scores: Watson 71; Newton 72.

Year	Winner	Score	Venue	Qual	Ents
1976	J Miller, USA	279	R Birkdale	150	719
1977	T Watson, USA	268	Turnberry	150	730
1978	J Nicklaus, USA	281	St Andrews	150	788
1979	S Ballesteros, Spain	283	R Lytham and St Annes	150	885
1980	T Watson, USA	271	Muirfield	151	994
1981	B Rogers, USA	276	Sandwich, R St George's	153	971
1982	T Watson, USA	284	R Troon	176	1,121
1983	T Watson, USA	275	R Birkdale	151	1,107
1984	S Ballesteros, Spain	276	St Andrews		1,413
1985	A Lyle, GB	282	Sandwich, R St George's	149	1,361
1986	G Norman, Australia	280	Turnberry	152	1,347
1987	N Faldo, GB	279	Muirfield	153	1,407
1988	S Ballesteros, Spain	273	R Lytham and St Annes	153	1,393
1989	M Calcavecchia, USA	275	R Troon	156	1,481

After a tie with W Grady, Australia, and G Norman, Australia, Calcavecchia won a 4-hole play-off.

Year	Winner	Score	Venue	Qual	Ents
1990	N Faldo, GB	270	St Andrews	152	1,707
1991	I Baker-Finch, Australia	272	R Birkdale	156	1,496
1992	N Faldo, GB	272	Muirfield	156	1,666
1993	G Norman, Australia	267	Sandwich, R St George's	156	1,827
1994	N Price, Zimbabwe	268	Turnberry	156	1,701
1995	J Daly, USA	282	St Andrews	159	1,836

After a tie with C Rocca, Italy, Daly won a 4-hole play-off.

Year	Winner	Score	Venue	Qual	Ents
1996	T Lehman, USA	271	R Lytham & St Annes	156	1,918
1997	J Leonard, USA	272	R Troon	156	2,133

The US Open Championship

97th US Open   *at Congressional CC, Bethesda, Maryland*

36-hole cut: 147, 7 over par; 84 players qualified. Prize money: $2,600,000.

Pos	Name	Score	Prize Money $
1	Ernie Els (SA)	71-67-69-69—276	465000
2	Colin Montgomerie (Sco)	65-76-67-69—277	275000
3	Tom Lehman (US)	67-70-68-73—278	172828
4	Jeff Maggert (US)	73-66-68-74—281	120454
5	Bob Tway (US)	71-71-70-70—282	79875
	Olin Browne (US)	71-71-69-71—282	79875
	Jim Furyk (US)	74-68-69-71—282	79875
	Jay Haas (US)	73-69-68-72—282	79875
	Tommy Tolles (US)	74-67-69-72—282	79875
10	Scott McCarron (US)	73-71-69-70—283	56949
	Scott Hoch (US)	71-68-72-72—283	56949
	David Ogrin (US)	70-69-71-73—283	56949
13	Loren Roberts (US)	72-69-72-71—284	47348
	Stewart Cink (US)	71-67-74-72—284	47348
	Billy Andrade (US)	75-67-69-73—284	47348
16	Bradley Hughes (Aus)	75-70-71-69—285	40086
	José Maria Olazabal (Sp)	71-71-72-71—285	40086
	Davis Love III (US)	75-70-69-71—285	40086
19	Nick Price (Zim)	71-74-71-70—286	31915
	Lee Westwood (Eng)	71-71-73-71—286	31915
	Tiger Woods (US)	74-67-73-72—286	31915
	Paul Stankowski (US)	75-70-68-73—286	31915
	Hal Sutton (US)	66-73-73-74—286	31915
24	Len Mattiace (US)	71-75-73-68—287	24173
	Edward Fryatt (US)	72-73-73-69—287	24173
	Scott Dunlap (US)	75-66-75-71—287	24173
	Steve Elkington (Aus)	75-68-72-72—287	24173
28	Paul Goydos (US)	73-72-74-69—288	17443
	Paul Azinger (US)	72-72-74-70—288	17443
	Payne Stewart (US)	71-73-73-71—288	17443
	Mark McNulty (Zim)	67-73-75-73—288	17443
	Hideki Kase (US)	68-73-73-74—288	17443
	Fuzzy Zoeller (US)	72-73-69-74—288	17443
	Kelly Gibson (US)	72-69-72-75—288	17443
	Jeff Sluman (US)	69-72-72-75—288	17443
36	Justin Leonard (US)	69-72-78-70—289	13483
	Grant Waite (US)	72-74-72-71—289	13483
	Steve Stricker (US)	66-76-75-72—289	13483
	Mark O'Meara (US)	73-73-71-72—289	13483
	Stuart Appleby (Aus)	71-75-70-73—289	13483
	Frank Nobilo (NZ)	71-74-70-74—289	13483
	John Cook (US)	72-71-71-75—289	13483
43	Darren Clarke (N. Ire)	73-74-73-70—290	10491
	Phil Mickelson (US)	75-68-73-74—290	10491

Pos	Name	Score	Prize Money $
43T	Fred Funk (US)	73-70-72-75—290	10491
	Chris Perry (US)	70-73-71-76—290	10491
	Craig Parry (Aus)	70-74-69-77—290	10491
48	Jesper Parnevik (Swe)	72-75-73-71—291	8496
	David Duval (US)	74-73-70-74—291	8496
	Nick Faldo (Eng)	72-74-69-76—291	8496
51	David White (US)	70-72-73-77—292	7786
52	Lee Janzen (US)	72-73-75-73—293	7138
	Jack Nicklaus (US)	73-71-75-74—293	7138
	Hale Irwin (US)	70-73-76-74—293	7138
	Fred Couples (US)	75-72-72-74—293	7138
	Peter Teravainen (US)	71-73-74-75—293	7138
	Paul Broadhurst (Eng)	77-69-72-75—293	7138
58	Larry Mize (US)	70-74-76-74—294	6530
	Clarence Rose (US)	72-71-73-78—294	6530
60	Chris Smith (US)	77-69-74-75—295	6270
	Duffy Waldorf (US)	73-73-73-76—295	6270
	Rodney Butcher (US)	73-74-70-78—295	6270
	Steve Jones (US)	72-75-69-79—295	6270
64	Tom Watson (US)	72-74-72-78—296	6120
65	Dave Schreyer (US)	68-73-82-74—297	6000
	Ben Crenshaw (US)	73-74-76-74—297	6000
	Brad Faxon (US)	72-74-76-75—297	6000
68	Tom Kite (US)	75-69-82-72—298	5742
	Mike Hulbert (US)	73-73-77-75—298	5742
	Greg Kraft (US)	77-69-76-76—298	5742
	John Morse (US)	71-74-76-77—298	5742
	Stephen Ames (T&T)	73-73-75-77—298	5742
	Thomas Bjorn (Den)	71-75-73-79—298	5742
74	Jimmy Green (US)	75-72-79-73—299	5550
75	Randy Wylie (US)	71-76-77-76—300	5467
	Andrew Coltart (Sco)	74-71-76-79—300	5467
77	Dick Mast (US)	73-69-83-76—301	5275
	Greg Towne (US)	71-73-83-74—301	5275
	Vijay Singh (Fij)	71-76-77-77—301	5275
	Perry Parker (US)	75-71-77-78—301	5275
	Donnie Hammond (US)	75-71-76-79—301	5275
82	Jacob Ferenz (US)	72-75-80-76—303	5110
83	Marco Dawson (US)	75-71-80-78—304	5055
84	Slade Adams (US)	71-74-78-83—306	5000

The following players missed the half-way cut; each professional received $1000.

85	R Black	76-72—148	93T	K Perry	76-73—149
	M Clark	77-71—148		M Reid	72-77—149
	J Kribel (Am)	70-78—148		L Silveira	77-72—149
	B Langer	73-75—148		S Simpson	76-73—149
	P McGinley	75-73—148		M Swartz	77-72—149
	C Pavin	74-74—148		C Wollmann (Am)	75-74—149
	L Rinker	73-75—148	108	R Allenby	75-75—150
	L Rinker	76-72—148		K Altenhof	78-72—150
93	J Estes	74-75—149		S McRoy	73-77—150
	E Brito	74-75—149		G Nicklaus	73-77—150
	M Brooks	71-78—149		B Porter	74-76—150
	M Calcavecchia	73-76—149		C Strange	79-71—150
	PJ Cowan	73-76—149		I Woosnam	76-74—150
	K Green	75-74—149		D Zinkon	76-74—150
	J Mazza	73-76—149	116	M Bradley	77-74—151
	S Murphy	75-74—149		A Aquilar	77-74—151
	L Nelson	74-75—149		P Harrington	75-76—151

116T	R Cochran	73-78—151
	D Forsman	77-74—151
	M Gogel	80-71—151
	T Noe (Am)	75-76—151
	K Schall	74-77—151
	M Sposa	77-74—151
	D Trixler	74-77—151
	M Wiebb	71-80—151
127	JD Blake	79-73—152
	M Brisky	70-82—152
	S Hart	74-78—152
	K Jones	78-74—152
	J McGovern	72-80—152
	J Ozaki	79-73—152
	J Pillar	76-76—152
	G Robison	78-74—152
135	R Cramer	72-81—153
	B Gilder	80-73—153
	F Lickliter	71-82—153

135T	P Mitchell	75-78—153
139	R Hunter	76-78—154
	J Semeisberger (Am)	78-76—154
	D Stockton	76-78—154
	G Norman	75-79—154
143	R Bradley	77-78—155
	B Wayment	78-77—155
145	R Gunn	80-76—156
146	Ed Humenik	79-78—157
	B Kearney (Am)	76-81—157
148	B Tennyson	79-80—159
	T Tryba	80-79—159
	M Schiene	81-78—159
151	R Russell	79-81—160
	M Martin	87-73—160
153	A Morse	87-77—164
154	G Sweatt	78-89—167
	J Daly	77-withdrew
	D Toms	78-withdrew

1996 US Open   *at Oakland Hills, Birmingham, Michigan*

Prize money: $2,400,000.

Pos	Name	Score	Prize $		Pos	Name	Score	Prize $
1	S Jones (US)	74-66-69-69—278	425000		7	S Hoch (US)	73-71-71-67—282	66294
2	D Lehman III (US)	71-69-70-69—279	204801			V Singh (Fiji)	71-72-70-69—282	66294
	T Lehman (US)	71-72-65-71—279	204801			K Green (US)	73-67-72-70—282	66294
4	J Morse (US)	68-74-68-70—280	111235		10	L Janzen (US)	68-75-71-69—283	52591
5	E Els (RSA)	72-67-72-70—281	84964			G Norman (Aus)	73-66-74-70—283	52591
	J Furyk (US)	72-69-70-70—281	84964			C Montgomerie (GB)	70-72-69-72—283	52591

1995 US Open *at Shinnecock Hills, New York*

Prize money: $2,000,000

Pos	Name	Score	Prize $		Pos	Name	Score	Prize $
1	C Pavin (US)	72-69-71-68—280	350000		4T	J Haas (US)	70-73-72-69—284	66633
2	G Norman (Aus)	68-67-74-73—282	207000			D Love III (US)	72-68-73-71—284	66633
3	T Lehman (US)	70-72-67-74—283	131974			P Mickelson (US)	68-70-72-74—284	66633
4	N Lancaster (US)	70-72-77-65—284	66633		10	F Nobilo (NZ)	72-72-70-71—285	44184
	J Maggert (US)	69-72-77-66—284	66633			V Singh (Fiji)	70-71-72-72—285	44184
	B Glasson (US)	69-70-76-69—284	66633			B Tway (US)	69-69-72-75—285	44184

1994 US Open *at Oakmont, Pennsylvania*

Prize money: $1,700,000

Pos	Name	Score	Prize $		Pos	Name	Score	Prize $
1	E Els (SA)	69-71-66-73—279	320000		6	C Dennis (US)	71-71-70-71—283	49485
2	L Roberts (US)	76-69-64-70—279	141828			G Norman (Aus)	71-71-69-72—283	49485
	C Montgomerie (GB)	71-65-73-70—279	141828			T Watson (US)	68-73-68-74—283	49485
(18-hole play-off scores: Els 74, Roberts 74, Montgomerie					9	D Waldorf (US)	74-68-73-69—284	37179
78. Els beat Roberts at 2nd hole of sudden death play-off.)						J Maggert (US)	71-68-75-70—284	37179
4	C Strange (US)	70-70-70-70—280	75728			J Sluman (US)	72-69-72-71—284	37179
5	J Cook (US)	73-65-73-71—282	61318			F Nobilo (NZ)	69-71-68-76—284	37179

1993 US Open *at Baltusrol, Springfield, NJ*

Prize money: $1,600,000

Pos	Name	Score	Prize $	Pos	Name	Score	Prize $
1	L Janzen (US)	67-67-69-69—272	290000	5T	T Watson (US)	70-66-73-69—278	48730
2	P Stewart (US)	70-66-68-70—274	145000	7	E Els (SA)	71-73-68-67—279	35481
3	C Parry (Aus)	66-74-69-68—277	78556		R Floyd (US)	68-73-70-68—279	35481
	P Azinger (US)	71-68-69-69—277	78556		N Henke (US)	72-71-67-69—279	35481
5	S Hoch (US)	66-72-72-68—278	48730		F Funk (US)	70-72-67-70—279	35481

1992 US Open *at Pebble Beach, Monterey, California*

Prize money: $1,500,000

Pos	Name	Score	Prize $	Pos	Name	Score	Prize $
1	T Kite (US)	71-72-70-72—285	275000	6T	JD Blake (US)	70-74-75-73—292	32315
2	J Sluman (US)	73-74-69-71—287	137500		B Gilder (US)	73-70-75-74—292	32315
3	C Montgomerie (GB)	70-71-77-70—288	84245		B Andrade (US)	72-74-72-74—292	32315
4	N Faldo (GB)	70-76-68-77—291	54924		M Hulbert (US)	74-73-70-75—292	32315
	N Price (Zim)	71-72-77-71—291	54924		T Lehman (US)	69-74-72-77—292	32315
6	I Woosnam (GB)	72-72-69-79—292	32315		J Sindelar (US)	74-72-68-78—292	32315

United States Open Championship

Year	Winner	Runner-up	Venue	By
1894	W Dunn	W Campbell	St Andrews, NY	2 holes

After 1894 decided by stroke play

Year	Winner	Venue	Score	Year	Winner	Venue	Score
1895	HJ Rawlins	Newport	173	1927	T Armour	Oakmont	301
1896	J Foulis	Southampton	152	*(After a tie with H Cooper. Play-off: Armour 76; Cooper 79)*			
1897	J Lloyd	Wheaton, Ill	162	1928	J Farrell	Olympia Fields	294
1898	F Herd	Shinnecock Hills	328	*(After a tie with R Jones, Jr. Play-off: Farrell 143; Jones 144)*			
72 holes played from 1898				1929	R Jones, Jr (Am)	Winged Foot, NY	294
1899	W Smith	Baltimore	315	*(After a tie with A Espinosa. Play-off: Jones 141; Espinosa 164)*			
1900	H Vardon (GB)	Wheaton, Ill	313	1930	R Jones, Jr (Am)	Interlachen	287
1901	W Anderson	Myopia, Mass	315	1931	B Burke	Inverness	292
1902	L Auchterlonie	Garden City	305	*(After a tie with G von Elm. Play-off: Burke 149-148; von*			
1903	W Anderson	Baltusrol	307	*Elm 149-149)*			
1904	W Anderson	Glenview	304	1932	G Sarazen	Fresh Meadow	286
1905	W Anderson	Myopia, Mass	335	1933	J Goodman (Am)	North Shore	287
1906	A Smith	Onwentsia	291	1934	O Dutra	Merion	293
1907	A Ross	Chestnut Hill, Pa	302	1935	S Parks	Oakmont	299
1908	F McLeod	Myopia, Mass	322	1936	T Manero	Springfield	282
1909	G Sargent	Englewood, NJ	290	1937	R Guldahl	Oakland Hills	281
1910	A Smith	Philadelphia	289	1938	R Guldahl	Cherry Hills	284
(After a tie with J McDermott and M Smith)				1939	B Nelson	Philadelphia	284
1911	J McDermott	Wheaton, Ill	307	*(After a tie with C Wood and D Shute)*			
1912	J McDermott	Buffalo, NY	294	1940	W Lawson Little	Canterbury, Ohio	287
1913	F Ouimet (Am)	Brookline, Mass	304	*(After a tie with G Sarazen. Tie scores: Little 70; Sarazen 73)*			
(After a tie with H Vardon and E Ray)				1941	Craig Wood	Fort Worth, Texas	284
1914	W Hagen	Midlothian	297	1942–45	*No Championship*		
1915	J Travers (Am)	Baltusrol	290	1946	L Mangrum	Canterbury	284
1916	C Evans (Am)	Minneapolis	286	*(After a tie with B Nelson and V Ghezzie)*			
1917-18	*No Championship*			1947	L Worsham	St Louis	282
1919	W Hagen	Braeburn	301	*(After a tie with S Snead. Replay scores: Worsham 69;*			
1920	E Ray (GB)	Inverness	295	*Snead 70)*			
1921	J Barnes	Washington	289	1948	B Hogan*	Los Angeles	276
1922	G Sarazen	Glencoe	288	1949	Dr C Middlecoff	Medinah, Ill	286
1923	R Jones, Jr (Am)	Inwood, LI	295	1950	B Hogan	Merion, Pa	287
(After a tie with R Cruikshank. Play-off: Jones 76;				*(After a tie with L Mangrum and G Fazio. Replay scores:*			
Cruikshank 78)				*Hogan 69; Mangrum 73; Fazio 75)*			
1924	C Walker	Oakland Hills	297	1951	B Hogan	Oakland Hills, Mich	287
1925	W MacFarlane	Worcester	291	1952	J Boros	Dallas, Texas	281
1926	R Jones, Jr (Am)	Scioto	293	1953	B Hogan	Oakmont	283

* Winner after play-off

Year	Winner	Venue	Score
1954	E Furgol	Baltusrol	284
1955	J Fleck	San Francisco	287
(After a tie with B Hogan. Replay scores: Fleck 69; Hogan 72)			
1956	Dr C Middlecoff	Rochester	281
1957	D Mayer	Inverness	282
(After a tie with Dr C Middlecoff. Tie scores: Mayer 72;			
Middlecoff 79)			
1958	T Bolt	Tulsa, Okla	283
1959	W Casper	Winged Foot, NY	282
1960	A Palmer	Denver, Col	280
1961	G Littler	Birmingham, Mich	281
1962	J Nicklaus	Oakmont	283
(After a tie with A Palmer: Nicklaus 71; Palmer 74)			
1963	J Boros	Brookline, Mass	293
(After a tie. Play-off: J Boros 70; J Cupit 7; A Palmer 76)			
1964	K Venturi	Washington	278
1965	G Player (SA)	St Louis, Mo	282
(After a tie with K Nagle (Aus). Replay scores: Player 71;			
Nagle 74)			
1966	W Casper	San Francisco	278
(After a tie with A Palmer. Replay scores: Casper 69; Palmer 73)			
1967	J Nicklaus	Baltusrol	275
1968	L Trevino	Rochester	275
1969	O Moody	Houston, Texas	281
1970	A Jacklin (GB)	Hazeltine, Minn	281
1971	L Trevino	Merion, Pa	280
(After a tie with J Nicklaus. Play-off: Trevino 68; Nicklaus 71)			
1972	J Nicklaus	Pebble Beach	290
1973	J Miller	Oakmont, Pa	279

Year	Winner	Venue	Score
1974	H Irwin	Winged Foot, NY	287
1975	L Graham	Medinah, Ill	287
(After a tie with Mahaffey. Play-off: Graham 71; Mahaffey 73)			
1976	J Pate	Atlanta, Georgia	277
1977	H Green	Southern Hills, Tulsa	278
1978	A North	Cherry Hills	285
1979	H Irwin	Inverness, Ohio	284
1980	J Nicklaus	Baltusrol	272
1981	D Graham (Aus)	Merion, Pa	273
1982	T Watson	Pebble Beach	282
1983	L Nelson	Oakmont, Pa	280
1984	F Zoeller	Winged Foot	276
(After a tie with G Norman. Play-off: Zoeller 67; Norman 75)			
1985	A North	Oakland Hills, Mich	279
1986	R Floyd	Shinnecock Hills, NY	279
1987	S Simpson	Olympic, San Francisco	277
1988	C Strange	Brookline, Mass.	278
(After a tie with N Faldo (GB). Play-off Strange 71, Faldo 75)			
1989	C Strange	Rochester, NY	278
1990	H Irwin	Medinah	280
(After a tie with M Donald, at 1st extra hole after 18-hole			
play-off tie)			
1991	P Stewart	Hazeltine, Minn	282
1992	T Kite	Pebble Beach	285
1993	L Janzen	Baltusrol	272
1994	E Els	Oakmont, Pa	279
1995	C Pavin	Shinnecock Hills, NY	280
1996	S Jones	Oakland Hills, Mich	278
1997	E Els	Congressional, Bethesda	276

The US Masters

61st US Masters *at Augusta National GC, Georgia*
Prize money: $2,732,310

Pos	Name	Score	Prize Money $
1	Tiger Woods (US)	70-66-65-69—270	486000
2	Tom Kite (US)	77-69-66-70—282	291600
3	Tommy Tolles (US)	72-72-72-67—283	183600
4	Tom Watson (US)	75-68-69-72—284	129600
5	Costantino Rocca (Ita)	71-69-70-75—285	102600
	Paul Stankowski (US)	68-74-69-74—285	102600
7	Fred Couples (US)	72-69-73-72—286	78570
	Bernhard Langer (Ger)	72-72-74-68—286	78570
	Justin Leonard (US)	76-69-71-70—286	78570
	Davis Love III (US)	72-71-72-71—286	78570
	Jeff Sluman (US)	74-67-72-73—286	78570
12	Steve Elkington (Aus)	76-72-72-67—287	52920
	Per-Ulrik Johansson (Swe)	72-73-73-69—287	52920
	Tom Lehman (US)	73-76-69-69—287	52920
	José Maria Olazabal (Sp)	71-70-74-72—287	52920
	Willie Wood (US)	72-76-71-68—287	52920
17	Mark Calcavecchia (US)	74-73-72-69—288	39150
	Ernie Els (SA)	73-70-71-74—288	39150
	Fred Funk (US)	73-74-69-72—288	39150
	Vijay Singh (Fij)	75-74-69-70—288	39150
21	Stuart Appleby (Aus)	72-76-70-71—289	30240
	John Huston (US)	67-77-75-70—289	30240
	Jesper Parnevik (Swe)	73-72-71-73—289	30240
24	Nick Price (Zim)	71-71-75-74—291	24840
	Lee Westwood (Eng)	77-71-73-70—291	24840
26	Lee Janzen (US)	72-73-74-73—292	21195
	Craig Stadler (US)	77-72-71-72—292	21195
28	Paul Azinger (US)	69-73-77-74—293	19575
	Jim Furyk (US)	74-75-72-72—293	19575
30	Scott McCarron (US)	77-71-72-74—294	17145
	Larry Mize (US)	79-69-74-72—294	17145
	Colin Montgomerie (Sco)	72-67-74-81—294	17145
	Mark O'Meara (US)	75-74-70-75—294	17145
34	Sandy Lyle (Sco)	73-73-74-75—295	14918
	Fuzzy Zoeller (US)	75-73-69-78—295	14918
36	Duffy Waldorf (US)	74-75-72-75—296	13905
37	David Frost (SA)	74-71-73-79—297	13230
38	Scott Hoch (US)	79-68-73-78—298	12690
39	Jack Nicklaus (US)	77-70-74-78—299	11610
	Sam Torrance (Sco)	75-73-73-78—299	11610
	Ian Woosnam (Wal)	77-68-75-79—299	11610
42	Masashi Ozaki (Jpn)	74-74-74-78—300	10530
43	Cory Pavin (US)	75-74-78-74—301	9720
	Clarence Rose (US)	73-75-79-74—301	9720
45	Ben Crenshaw (US)	75-73-74-80—302	8910
46	Frank Nobilo (NZ)	76-72-74-81—303	8370

The following players missed the cut. Each professional earned $5000.

47	D Berganio Jr	72-78—150	53T	DA Weibring	78-73—151	74T	T Hogarth (Am)	80-78—
	J Cook	77-73—150	62	S Cink	75-78—153	158		
	D Duval	78-72—150		E Fiori	78-75—153	76	R Allenby	82-77—159
	D Forsman	74-76—150		J Maggert	77-76—153		M Brooks	77-82—159
	P Mickelson	76-74—150		M McNulty	81-72—153	78	B Casper Jr	83-77—160
	J Morse	77-73—150	66	T Aaron	77-77—154		C Coody	83-77—160
53	W Bladon (Am)	79-72—151		R Floyd	79-75—154		S Jones	82-78—160
	B Faxon	77-74—151		Y Keneko	77-77—154	81	K Green	87-74—161
	D Hart	74-77—151	69	S Ballesteros	81-74—155	82	L Roberts	85-77—162
	G Norman	77-74—151	70	M Bradley	79-77—156	83	G Brewer Jr	84-79—163
	D Ogrin	77-74—151		N Faldo	75-81—156		J Miller (Am)	82-81—163
	K Perry	73-78—151		S Stricker	77-79—156	85	A Palmer	89-87—176
	G Player	76-75—151		S Scott (Am)	78-79—157	86	D Ford	85-94—179
	B Tway	78-73—151	74	G Boros	79-79—158			

1996 US Masters

Prize money: $2,500,000

Pos	Name	Score	Prize $	Pos	Name	Score	Prize $
1	N Faldo (GB)	69-67-73-67—276	450000	7	D Love III (US)	72-71-74-68—285	77933
2	G Norman (Aus)	63-69-71-78—281	270000		J Maggert (US)	71-73-72-69—285	77933
3	P Mickelson (US)	65-73-72-72—282	170000		C Pavin (US)	75-66-73-71—285	77933
4	F Nobilo (NZ)	71-71-72-69—283	120000	10	S McCarron (US)	70-70-72-74—286	65000
5	S Hoch (US)	67-73-73-71—284	95000		D Frost (RSA)	70-68-74-74—286	65000
	D Waldorf (US)	72-71-69-72—284	95000				

1995 US Masters

Prize money: $2,132,000

Pos	Name	Score	Prize $	Pos	Name	Score	Prize $
1	B Crenshaw (US)	70-67-69-68—274	396000	7	S Hoch (US)	69-67-71-73—280	70950
2	D Love III (US)	69-69-71-66—275	237600		P Mickelson (US)	66-71-70-73—280	70950
3	J Haas (US)	71-64-72-70—277	127600	9	C Strange (US)	72-71-65-73—281	63800
	G Norman (Aus)	73-68-68-68—277	127600	10	F Couples (US)	71-69-67-75—282	57200
5	S Elkington (Aus)	73-67-67-72—279	83600		B Henninger (US)	70-68-68-76—282	57200
	D Frost (RSA)	66-71-71-71—279	83600				

1994 US Masters

Prize money: $1,960,000

Pos	Name	Score	Prize $	Pos	Name	Score	Prize $
1	JM Olazabal (Sp)	74-67-69-69—279	360000	5T	L Roberts (US)	75-68-72-70—285	73000
2	T Lehman (US)	70-70-69-72—281	216000	8	E Els (SA)	74-67-74-71—286	60000
3	L Mize (US)	68-71-72-71—282	136000		C Pavin (US)	71-72-73-70—286	60000
4	T Kite (US)	69-72-71-71—283	96000	10	I Baker-Finch (Aus)	71-71-71-74—287	50000
5	J Haas (US)	72-72-72-69—285	73000		R Floyd (US)	70-74-71-72—287	50000
	J McGovern (US)	72-70-71-72—285	73000		J Huston (US)	72-72-74-69—287	50000

1993 US Masters

Prize money: $1,705,700

Pos	Name	Score	Prize $	Pos	Name	Score	Prize $
1	B Langer (Ger)	68-70-69-70—277	306000	3T	L Wadkins (US)	69-72-71-71—283	81600
2	C Beck (US)	72-67-72-70—281	183600	7	JM Olazabal (Spa)	70-72-74-68—284	54850
3	T Lehman (US)	67-75-73-68—283	81600		D Forsman (US)	69-69-73-73—284	54850
	J Daly (US)	70-71-73-69—283	81600	9	P Stewart (US)	74-70-72-69—285	47600
	S Elkington (Aus)	71-70-71-71—283	81600		B Faxon (US)	71-70-72-72—285	47600

1992 US Masters

Prize money: $1,500,000

Pos	Name	Score	Prize $	Pos	Name	Score	Prize $
1	F Couples (US)	69-67-69-70—275	270000	6T	N Henke (US)	70-71-70-70—281	43829
2	R Floyd (US)	69-68-69-71—277	162000		I Baker-Finch (Aus)	70-69-68-74—281	43829
3	C Pavin (US)	72-71-68-67—278	102000		N Price (Zim)	70-71-67-73—281	43829
4	J Sluman (US)	65-74-70-71—280	66000		G Norman (Aus)	70-70-73-68—281	43829
	M O'Meara (US)	74-67-69-70—280	66000		L Mize (US)	73-69-71-68—281	43829
6	S Pate (US)	73-71-70-67—281	43829		T Schulz (US)	68-69-72-72—281	43829

US Masters

at Augusta National Golf Course, Augusta, Georgia

Players are of American nationality unless otherwise stated.

Year	Winner	Score	Year	Winner	Score
1934	H Smith	284	1968	R Goalby	277
1935	G Sarazen	282	1969	G Archer	281
1936	H Smith	285	1970	W Casper*	279
1937	B Nelson	283	1971	C Coody	279
1938	H Picard	285	1972	J Nicklaus	286
1939	R Guldahl	279	1973	T Aaron	283
1940	J Demaret	280	1974	G Player (SA)	278
1941	C Wood	280	1975	J Nicklaus	276
1942	B Nelson*	280	1976	R Floyd	271
1946	H Keiser	282	1977	T Watson	276
1947	J Demaret	281	1978	G Player (SA)	277
1948	C Harmon	279	1979	F Zoeller*	280
1949	S Snead	283	1980	S Ballesteros (Sp)	275
1950	J Demaret	282	1981	T Watson	280
1951	B Hogan	280	1982	C Stadler*	284
1952	S Snead*	286	1983	S Ballesteros (Sp)	280
1953	B Hogan	274	1984	B Crenshaw	277
1954	S Snead	289	1985	B Langer (Ger)	282
1955	C Middlecoff	279	1986	J Nicklaus	279
1956	J Burke	289	1987	L Mize*	285
1957	D Ford	283	1988	A Lyle (GB)	281
1958	A Palmer	284	1989	N Faldo (GB)*	283
1959	A Wall	284	1990	N Faldo (GB)*	278
1960	A Palmer	282	1991	I Woosnam (GB)	277
1961	G Player (SA)	280	1992	F Couples	275
1962	A Palmer*	280	1993	B Langer (Ger)	277
1963	J Nicklaus	286	1994	JM Olazabal (Sp)	279
1964	A Palmer	276	1995	B Crenshaw	274
1965	J Nicklaus	271	1996	N Faldo (GB)	276
1966	J Nicklaus	288	1997	T Woods	270
1967	G Brewer	280			

---

* *Winner after play-off*

US PGA Championship

79th US PGA Championship *at Winged Foot CC, New York*
36-hole cut: 146; 71 players qualified. Prize money: $2,600,000

Pos	Name	Score	Prize Money $
1	Davis Love III (US)	66-71-66-66—269	470000
2	Justin Leonard (US)	68-70-65-71—274	280000
3	Jeff Maggert (US)	69-69-73-65—276	175000
4	Lee Janzen (US)	69-67-74-69—279	125000
5	Tom Kite (US)	68-71-71-70—280	105000
6	Phil Blackmar (US)	70-68-74-69—281	85000
	Jim Furyk (US)	69-72-72-68—281	85000
	Scott Hoch (US)	71-72-68-70—281	85000
9	Tom Byrum (US)	69-73-70-70—282	70000
10	Tom Lehman (US)	69-72-72-70—283	60000
	Scott McCarron (US)	74-71-67-71—283	60000
	Joey Sindelar (US)	72-71-71-69—283	60000
13	David Duval (US)	70-70-71-73—284	35100
	Tim Herron (US)	72-73-68-71—284	35100
	Colin Montgomerie (Sco)	74-71-67-72—284	35100
	Greg Norman (Aus)	68-71-74-71—284	35100
	Nick Price (Zim)	72-70-72-70—284	35100
	Vijay Singh (Fij)	73-66-76-69—284	35100
	Tommy Tolles (US)	75-70-73-66—284	35100
	Kirk Triplett (US)	73-70-71-70—284	35100
	Bob Tway (US)	68-75-72-69—284	35100
	Mark O'Meara (US)	69-73-75-67—284	35100
23	Mark Calcavecchia (US)	71-74-73-67—285	22500
	Bernhard Langer (Ger)	73-71-72-69—285	22500
	Doug Martin (US)	69-75-74-67—285	22500
	Shigeki Maruyama (Jpn)	68-70-74-73—285	22500
	Kenny Perry (US)	73-68-73-71—285	22500
	John Cook (US)	71-71-74-69—285	22500
29	Paul Azinger (US)	68-73-71-74—286	13625
	Ronnie Black (US)	76-69-71-70—286	13625
	Fred Couples (US)	71-67-73-75—286	13625
	John Daly (US)	66-73-77-70—286	13625
	Paul Goydos (US)	70-72-71-73—286	13625
	Hale Irwin (US)	73-70-71-72—286	13625
	Phil Mickelson (US)	69-69-73-75—286	13625
	Frank Nobilo (NZ)	72-73-67-74—286	13625
	Don Pooley (US)	72-74-70-70—286	13625
	Payne Stewart (US)	70-70-72-74—286	13625
	Lee Westwood (Eng)	74-68-71-73—286	13625
	Tiger Woods (US)	70-70-71-75—286	13625
41	Ignacio Garrido (Sp)	70-71-75-71—287	8375
	Steve Jones (US)	69-73-75-70—287	8375
	David Ogrin (US)	74-72-71-70—287	8375
	Eduardo Romero (Arg)	71-72-72-72—287	8375
45	Thomas Bjorn (Den)	72-68-77-71—288	7375
	Steve Elkington (Aus)	72-72-70-74—288	7375

Pos	Name	Score	Prize Money $
45T	Jesper Parnevik (Swe)	76-70-71-71—288	7375
	Sam Torrance (Sco)	74-72-70-72—288	7375
49	Robert Allenby (Aus)	67-77-74-71—289	6375
	Brian Henninger (US)	74-68-75-72—289	6375
	Chris Perry (US)	68-71-73-77—289	6375
	Loren Roberts (US)	76-70-74-69—289	6375
53	Olin Browne (US)	70-73-74-73—290	5280
	Ernie Els (SA)	70-76-74-70—290	5280
	Billy Mayfair (US)	75-68-75-72—290	5280
	Taylor Smith (US)	71-71-74-74—290	5280
	Craig Stadler (US)	72-72-74-72—290	5280
58	Steve Lowery (US)	72-69-79-71—291	4700
	Larry Mize (US)	71-73-73-74—291	4700
	Lanny Wadkins (US)	72-72-77-70—291	4700
61	Stuart Appleby (Aus)	75-70-69-78—292	4333
	Jay Haas (US)	71-69-73-79—292	4333
	Russ Cochran (US)	72-73-72-75—292	4333
	Fred Funk (US)	71-74-77-70—292	4333
	Retief Goosen (SA)	72-70-74-76—292	4333
	Lee Rinker (US)	70-71-75-76—292	4333
67	Peter Jacobsen (US)	74-72-75-72—293	4100
	Per-Ulrik Johansson (Swe)	73-69-73-78—293	4100
	Paul Stankowski (US)	68-71-77-77—293	4100
70	Carlos Franco (Para)	69-74-76-75—294	4000
71	Michael Bradley (US)	73-69-80-73—295	3875
	Yoshinori Kaneko (Jpn)	72-73-76-74—295	3875
	Larry Nelson (US)	76-70-76-73—295	3875
	Costantino Rocca (Ita)	69-69-79-78—295	3875
75	Andrew Magee (US)	71-70-80-75—296	3750
76	Pete Jordan (US)	76-70-75-76—297	3675
	Kevin Sutherland (US)	73-73-73-78—297	3675

The following players missed the half-way cut:

78	B Andrade	72-75—147	103	R Gamez	74-76—150	122T	F Dobbs	80-73—153
	B Boyd	71-76—147		K Gibson	76-74—150	129	P Lonard	75-79—154
	J Carter	73-74—147		D Hart	74-76—150		B Makoski	79-75—154
	R Fehr	72-75—147		M Hulbert	75-75—150		M Standly	76-78—154
	D Frost	76-71—147		J Nicklaus	74-76—150	132	J Lee	74-81—155
	L Mattiace	72-75—147		N Ozaki	75-75—150		P Oakley	78-77—155
84	BR Brown	76-72—148		T Watson	71-79—150		B Watts	78-77—155
	R Damron	76-72—148		J Stone	75-75—150	135	S Kelly	76-80—156
	G Day	76-72—148	111	JD Blake	73-78—151		H Sutton	78-78—156
	P Harrington	77-71—148		B Chamblee	77-74—151		R Wilkin	78-78—156
	J Lankford	72-76—148		S Cink	76-75—151	138	B Crenshaw	77-80—157
	C Parry	74-74—148		B Faxon	73-78—151		J Kelly	81-76—157
	R Philo Jr	72-76—148		C Rose	74-77—151		J White	82-75—157
	S Stricker	73-75—148		J Sluman	74-77—151	141	W Grady	79-79—158
	D Toms	73-75—148		B Sowards	74-77—151		J Mason	78-80—158
	F Zoeller	73-75—148	118	M Burke Jr	77-75—152	143	J Hickson	76-84—160
94	G Boros	81-68—149		E Fiori	76-76—152	144	D Kestner	79-83—162
	M Brisky	75-74—149		JM Olazabal	79-73—152	145	M Fuller	79-84—163
	P Broadhurst	74-75—149		D Waldorf	74-78—152	146	J Paesani	79-85—164
	M Brooks	70-79—149	122	D Clarke	74-79—153	147	B Taylor	82-83—165
	B Ford	74-75—149		N Faldo	75-78—153		M Wiebe	77-77-w'drew
	J Mazza	71-78—149		S Schneiter	75-78—153		J Mahaffey	78-78-w'drew
	J Overton	77-72—149		C Strange	76-77—153		F Minoza	80-80-w'drew
	C Toulson	75-74—149		C Tucker	78-75—153			
	I Woosnam	77-72—149		B Zabriski	76-77—153			

1996 US PGA *at Valhalla, Louisville, Kentucky*

Prize money: $2,400,000

Pos	Name	Score	Prize $	Pos	Name	Score	Prize $
1	M Brooks (US)*	68-70-69-70—277	430000	8	L Janzen (US)	68-71-71-70—280	57500
2	K Perry (US)	66-72-71-68—277	260000		P-U Johansson (Swe)	73-72-66-69—280	57500
3	S Elkington (Aus)	67-74-67-70—278	140000		P Mickelson (US)	67-67-74-72—280	57500
	T Tolles (US)	69-71-71-67—278	140000		L Mize (US)	71-70-69-70—280	57500
5	J Leonard (US)	71-66-72-70—279	86666		F Nobilo (NZ)	69-72-71-68—280	57500
	J Parnevik (Swe)	73-67-69-70—279	86666		N Price (Zim)	68-71-69-72—280	57500
	V Singh (Fij)	69-69-69-72—279	86666				

1995 US PGA *at Riviera, Los Angeles*

Prize money: $2,000,000

Pos	Name	Score	Prize $	Pos	Name	Score	Prize $
1	S Elkington (Aus)*	68-67-68-64—267	360000	6T	M O'Meara (US)	64-67-69-73—273	68500
2	C Montgomerie (GB)	68-67-67-65—267	216000	8	J Haas (US)	69-71-64-70—274	50000
3	E Els (SA)	66-65-66-72—269	116000		J Leonard (US)	68-66-70-70—274	50000
	J Maggert (US)	66-69-65-69—269	116000		S Lowery (US)	69-68-68-69—274	50000
5	B Faxon (US)	70-67-71-63—271	80000		J Sluman (US)	69-67-68-70—274	50000
6	B Estes (US)	69-68-68-68—273	68500		C Stadler (US)	71-66-66-71—274	50000

1994 US PGA *at Southern Hills, Tulsa, Oklahoma*

Prize money: $1,750,000

Pos	Name	Score	Prize $	Pos	Name	Score	Prize $
1	N Price (Zim)	67-65-70-67—269	310000	7T	JM Olazabal (Spa)	72-66-70-70—278	57500
2	C Pavin (US)	70-67-69-69—275	160000	9	I Woosnam (GB)	68-72-73-66—279	41000
3	P Mickelson (US)	68-71-67-70—276	110000		T Kite (US)	72-68-69-70—279	41000
4	N Faldo (GB)	73-67-71-66—277	76666		T Watson (US)	69-72-67-71—279	41000
	G Norman (Aus)	71-69-67-70—277	76666		L Roberts (US)	69-72-67-71—279	41000
	J Cook (US)	71-67-69-70—277	76666		B Crenshaw (US)	70-67-70-72—279	41000
7	S Elkington (Aus)	73-70-66-69—278	57500				

1993 US PGA *at Inverness, Toledo, Ohio*

Prize money: $1,700,000

Pos	Name	Score	Prize $	Pos	Name	Score	Prize $
1	P Azinger (US)*	69-66-69-68—272	300000	6T	P Mickelson (US)	67-71-69-70—277	47812
2	G Norman (Aus)	68-68-67-69—272	155000		J Cook (US)	72-66-68-71—277	47812
3	N Faldo (GB)	68-68-69-68—273	105000		S Simpson (US)	64-70-71-72—277	47812
4	V Singh (Fij)	68-63-73-70—274	90000		D Hart (US)	66-68-71-72—277	47812
5	T Watson (US)	69-65-70-72—276	75000		B Estes (US)	69-66-69-73—277	47812
6	S Hoch (US)	74-68-68-67—277	47812		H Irwin (US)	68-69-67-73—277	47812
	N Henke (US)	72-70-67-68—277	47812				

1992 US PGA *at Bellerive, St Louis, Missouri*

Prize money: $1,400,000

Pos	Name	Score	Prize $	Pos	Name	Score	Prize $
1	N Price (Zim)	70-70-68-70—278	280000	7	R Cochran (US)	69-69-76-69—283	52500
2	N Faldo (GB)	68-70-76-67—281	101250		D Forsman (US)	70-73-70-70—283	52500
	J Gallagher Jr (US)	72-66-72-71—281	101250	9	D Waldorf (US)	74-73-68-69—284	40000
	J Cook (US)	71-72-67-71—281	101250		A Forsbrand (Swe)	73-71-70-70—284	40000
	G Sauers (US)	67-69-70-75—281	101250		B Claar (US)	68-73-73-70—284	40000
6	J Maggert (US)	71-72-65-74—282	60000				

* *Winner after play-off*

United States PGA Championship

Year	Winner	Runner-up	Venue	By
1916	J Barnes	J Hutchison	Siwanoy	1 hole
1919	J Barnes	F McLeod	Engineers' Club	6 and 5
1920	J Hutchison	D Edgar	Flossmoor	1 hole
1921	W Hagen	J Barnes	Inwood Club	3 and 2
1922	G Sarazen	E French	Oakmont	4 and 3
1923	G Sarazen	W Hagen	Pelham	38th hole
1924	W Hagen	J Barnes	French Lick	2 holes
1925	W Hagen	W Mehlhorn	Olympic Fields	6 and 4
1926	W Hagen	L Diegel	Salisbury	4 and 3
1927	W Hagen	J Turnesa	Dallas, Texas	1 hole
1928	L Diegel	A Espinosa	Five Farms	6 and 5
1929	L Diegel	J Farrell	Hill Crest	6 and 4
1930	T Armour	G Sarazen	Fresh Meadow	1 hole
1931	T Creavy	D Shute	Wannamoisett	2 and 1
1932	O Dutra	F Walsh	St Paul, Minnesota	4 and 3
1933	G Sarazen	W Goggin	Milwaukee	5 and 4
1934	P Runyan	C Wood	Buffalo	38th hole
1935	J Revolta	T Armour	Oklahoma	5 and 4
1936	D Shute	J Thomson	Pinehurst	3 and 2
1937	D Shute	H McSpaden	Pittsburgh	37th hole
1938	P Runyan	S Snead	Shawnee	8 and 7
1939	H Picard	B Nelson	Pomonok	37th hole
1940	B Nelson	S Snead	Hershey, Pa	1 hole
1941	V Ghezzie	B Nelson	Denver, Colo	38th hole
1942	S Snead	J Turnesa	Atlantic City	2 and 1
1943	*No Championship*			
1944	B Hamilton	B Nelson	Spokane, Wash	1 hole
1945	B Nelson	S Byrd	Dayton, Ohio	4 and 3
1946	B Hogan	E Oliver	Portland	6 and 4
1947	J Ferrier	C Harbert	Detroit	2 and 1
1948	B Hogan	M Turnesa	Norwood Hills	7 and 6
1949	S Snead	J Palmer	Richmond, Va	3 and 2
1950	C Harper	H Williams	Scioto, Ohio	4 and 3
1951	S Snead	W Burkemo	Oakmont, Pa	7 and 6
1952	J Turnesa	C Harbert	Big Spring, Louisville	1 hole
1953	W Burkemo	F Lorza	Birmingham, Michigan	2 and 1
1954	C Harbert	W Burkemo	St Paul, Minnesota	4 and 3
1955	D Ford	C Middlecoff	Detroit	4 and 3
1956	J Burke	T Kroll	Boston	3 and 2
1957	L Hebert	D Finsterwald	Miami Valley, Dayton	3 and 1

Changed to stroke play

Year	Winner	Venue	Score	Year	Winner	Venue	Score
1958	D Finsterwald	Llanerch, PA	276	1978	J Mahaffey*	Oakmont, PA	276
1959	B Rosburg	Minneapolis, MN	277	1979	D Graham*	Oakland Hills, MI	272
1960	J Hebert	Firestone, Akron, OH	281	1980	J Nicklaus	Oak Hill, NY	274
1961	J Barber*	Olympia Fields, IL	277	1981	L Nelson	Atlanta, GA	273
1962	G Player	Aronimink, PA	278	1982	R Floyd	Southern Hills, OK	272
1963	J Nicklaus	Dallas, TX	279	1983	H Sutton	Pacific Palisades, CA	274
1964	B Nichols	Columbus, OH	271	1984	L Trevino	Shoal Creek, AL	273
1965	D Marr	Laurel Valley, PA	280	1985	H Green	Cherry Hills, Denver, CO	278
1966	A Geiberger	Firestone, Akron, OH	280	1986	R Tway	Inverness, Toledo, OH	276
1967	D January*	Columbine, CO	281	1987	L Nelson*	PGA National, FL	287
1968	J Boros	Pecan Valley, TX	281	1988	J Sluman	Oaktree, OK	272
1969	R Floyd	Dayton, OH	276	1989	P Stewart	Kemper Lakes, IL	276
1970	D Stockton	Southern Hills, OK	279	1990	W Grady	Shoal Creek, AL	282
1971	J Nicklaus	PGA National, FL	281	1991	J Daly	Crooked Stick, IN	276
1972	G Player	Oakland Hills, MI	281	1992	N Price	Bellerive, MS	278
1973	J Nicklaus	Canterbury, OH	277	1993	P Azinger*	Inverness, Toledo, OH	272
1974	L Trevino	Tanglewood, NC	276	1994	N Price	Southern Hills, OK	269
1975	J Nicklaus	Firestone, Akron, OH	276	1995	S Elkington*	Riviera, LA	267
1976	D Stockton	Congressional, MD	281	1996	M Brooks*	Valhalla, Kentucky	277
1977	L Wadkins*	Pebble Beach, CA	287	1997	D Love III	Winged Foot, NY	269

* Winner after play-off

Ladies' Major Championships

Weetabix Ladies' British Open Championship

Year	Winner	Club/Country	Venue	Score	
1976	J Lee Smith	Gosforth Park	Fulford	299	
1977	V Saunders	Tyrrells Wood	Lindrick	306	
1978	J Melville	Furness	Foxhills	310	
1979	A Sheard	South Africa	Southport and Ainsdale	301	
1980	D Massey	USA	Wentworth (East)	294	
1981	D Massey	USA	Northumberland	295	
1982	Figueras-Dotti	Spain	R Birkdale	296	
1983	*Not played*				
1984	A Okamoto	Japan	Woburn	289	
1985	B King	USA	Moor Park	300	
1986	L Davies	GB	R Birkdale	283	
1987	A Nicholas	GB	St Mellion	296	
1988T	C Dibnah*	Australia	Lindrick	296	
	S Little	South Africa			
1989	J Geddes	USA	Ferndown	274	
1990	H Alfredsson	Sweden	Woburn	288	
1991	P Grice-Whittaker	GB	Woburn	284	
1992	P Sheehan	USA	Woburn	207	*(Reduced to 54 holes by rain)*
1993	K Lunn	Australia	Woburn	275	
1994	L Neumann	Sweden	Woburn	280	
1995	K Webb	Australia	Woburn	278	
1996	E Klein	USA	Woburn	277	
1997	K Webb	Australia	Sunningdale	269	

United States Ladies' Open Championship

Year	Winner	Venue	By
1946	P Berg	Spokane	5 and 4

Changed to stroke play

Year	Winner	Venue	Score	
1947	B Jamieson	Greensboro	300	
1948	B Zaharias	Atlantic City	300	
1949	L Suggs	Maryland	291	
1950	B Zaharias	Wichita	291	
1951	B Rawls	Atlanta	294	
1952	L Suggs	Bala, Philadelphia	284	
1953	B Rawls	Rochester, NY	302	*(after a tie with J Pung)*
1954	B Zaharias	Peabody, Mass	291	
1955	F Crocker	Wichita	299	
1956	K Cornelius	Duluth	302	*(after a tie with B McIntire)*
1957	B Rawls	Mamaroneck	299	
1958	M Wright	Bloomfield Hills, Mich	290	
1959	M Wright	Pittsburgh, Pa	287	
1960	B Rawls	Worchester, Mass	292	
1961	M Wright	Springfield, NJ	293	
1962	M Lindstrom	Myrtle Beach	301	
1963	M Mills	Kenwood	289	
1964	M Wright	San Diego	290	*(after a tie with R Jessen, Seattle)*
1965	C Mann	Northfield, NJ	290	*continued*

* *Winner after play-off*

United States Ladies' Open Championship *continued*

Year	Winner	Venue	Score
1966	S Spuzich	Hazeltine National GC, MN	297
1967	C Lacoste (Fr)	Hot Springs, VA	294
1968	S Berning	Moselem Springs, PA	289
1969	D Caponi	Scenic-Hills	294
1970	D Caponi	Muskogee, OK	287
1971	J Gunderson-Carner	Erie, PA	288
1972	S Berning	Mamaroneck, NY	299
1973	S Berning	Rochester, NY	290
1974	S Haynie	La Grange, IL	295
1975	S Palmer	Northfield, NJ	295
1976	J Carner	Springfield, PA	292 *(after a tie with S Palmer)*
1977	H Stacy	Hazeltine, MN	292
1978	H Stacy	Indianapolis	299
1979	J Britz	Brooklawn, CN	284
1980	A Alcott	Richland, TN	280
1981	P Bradley	La Grange, Illinois	279
1982	J Alex	Del Paso, Sacramento, CA	283
1983	J Stephenson (Aus)	Broken Arrow, OK	290
1984	H Stacy	Salem, Mass	290
1985	K Baker	Baltusrol, NJ	280
1986	J Geddes	NCR	287
1987	L Davies (GB)	Plainfield	285
(After a tie with J Carner and A Akamoto (Jpn))			
1988	L Neumann (Swe)	Baltimore	277
1989	B King	Indianwood, MI	278
1990	B King	Atlanta Athletic Club, GA	284
1991	M Mallon	Colonial, TX	283
1992	P Sheehan	Oakmont, PA	280 *(after a tie with J Inkster)*
1993	L Merton	Crooked Stick	280
1994	P Sheehan	Indianwood, MI	277
1995	A Sorenstam (Swe)	The Broadmore, Col	278
1996	A Sorenstam (Swe)	Pine Needles Lodge, NC	272
1997	A Nicholas (GB)	Pumpkin Ridge, OR	274

McDonald's LPGA Championship

(Formerly: LPGA Championship 1955–87; Mazda LPGA 1988–93)

Year	Winner	Venue	Score
1955	B Hanson	Orchard Ridge	4 & 3
1956	M Hagg	Forest Lake	291 *(after a tie with P Berg)*
1957	L Suggs	Churchill Valley	285
1958	M Wright	Churchill CC	288
1959	B Rawls	Churchill CC	288
1960	M Wright	French Lick	292
1961	M Wright	Stardust	287
1962	J Kimball	Stardust	282
1963	M Wright	Stardust	294
1964	M Mills	Stardust	278
1965	S Haynie	Stardust	279
1966	G Ehret	Stardust	282
1967	K Whitworth	Pleasant Valley	284
1968	S Post	Pleasant Valley	294 *(after a tie with K Whitworth)*
1969	B Rawls	Concord	293
1970	S Englehorn	Pleasant Valley	285 *(after a tie with K Whitworth)*
1971	K Whitworth	Pleasant Valley	288
1972	K Ahern	Pleasant Valley	293
1973	M Mills	Pleasant Valley	288
1974	S Haynie	Pleasant Valley	288
1875	K Whitworth	Pine Ridge	288
1976	B Burfeindt	Pine Ridge	287
1977	C Higuchi (Jpn)	Bay Tree	279
1978	N Lopez	Kings Island	275
1979	D Caponi	Kings Island	279
1980	S Little (SA)	Kings Island	285

Year	Winner	Venue	Score
1981	D Caponi	Kings Island	280
1982	J Stephenson (Aus)	Kings Island	279
1983	P Sheehan	Kings Island	279
1984	P Sheehan	Kings Island	272
1985	N Lopez	Kings Island	273
1986	P Bradley	Kings Island	277
1987	J Geddes	Kings Island	275
1988	S Turner	Kings Island	281
1989	N Lopez	Kings Island	274
1990	B Daniel	Bethesda	280
1991	M Mallon	Bethesda	274
1992	B King	Bethesda	267
1993	P Sheehan	Bethesda	275
1994	L Davies (GB)	Wilmington, Delaware	275
1995	K Robbins	Wilmington, Delaware	274
1996	L Davies (GB)	Wilmington, Delaware	213 *(Reduced to 54 holes due to bad weather)*
1997	C Johnson	Wilmington, Delaware	281

Nabisco Dinah Shore

(Designated major championship 1983)

Year	Winner	Venue	Score
1983	A Alcott	Mission Hills	282
1984	J Inkster	Mission Hills	280 *(after a tie with P Bradley)*
1985	A Miller	Mission Hills	278
1986	P Bradley	Mission Hills	280
1987	B King	Mission Hills	283 *(after a tie with P Sheehan)*
1988	A Alcott	Mission Hills	274
1989	J Inkster	Mission Hills	279
1990	B King	Mission Hills	283
1991	A Alcott	Mission Hills	273
1992	D Mochrie	Mission Hills	279 *(after a tie with J Inkster)*
1993	H Alfredsson (Swe)	Mission Hills	284
1994	D Andrews	Mission Hills	276
1995	N Bowen	Mission Hills	285
1996	P Sheehan	Mission Hills	281
1997	B King	Mission Hills	273

Du Maurier Classic

(Designated major championship 1979)

Year	Winner	Venue	Score
1979	A Alcott	Richelieu Valley	285
1980	P Bradley	St George's	277
1981	J Stephenson (Aus)	Summerlea	278
1982	S Haynie	St George's	280
1983	H Stacy	Beaconsfield	277
1984	J Inkster	St. George's	279
1985	P Bradley	Montreal	278
1986	P Bradley	Board of Trade	276 *(after a tie with A Okamoto)*
1987	J Rosenthal	Islesmere	272
1988	S Little (SA)	Vancouver	279
1989	T Green	Beaconsfield	279
1990	C Johnston	Westmount	276
1991	N Scranton	Vancouver	279
1992	S Steinhauer	St Charles	277
1993	B Burton	London Hunt	277 *(after a tie with B King)*
1994	M Nause	Ottawa Hunt	279
1995	J Lidback	Beaconsfield, Quebec	280
1996	L Davies	Edmonton, Alberta	277
1997	C Walker	Oakville, Ontario	278

Major Championship League Tables

Major Championship Leaders – Men

	US Open	British Open	PGA	Masters	US Amateur	British Amateur	Total Titles
Jack Nicklaus	4	3	5	6	2	0	20
Bobby Jones	4	3	0	0	5	1	13
Walter Hagen	2	4	5	0	0	0	11
John Ball	0	1	0	0	0	8	9
Ben Hogan	4	1	2	2	0	0	9
Gary Player	1	3	2	3	0	0	9
Arnold Palmer	1	2	0	4	1	0	8
Tom Watson	1	5	0	2	0	0	8
Harold Hilton	0	2	0	0	1	4	7
Gene Sarazen	2	1	3	1	0	0	7
Sam Snead	0	1	3	3	0	0	7
Harry Vardon	1	6	0	0	0	0	7
Lee Trevino	2	2	2	0	0	0	6
Nick Faldo	0	3	0	3	0	0	6

Major Championship Leaders – Women

	US Open	LPGA	Du Maurier*	Nabisco Dinah Shore†	US Amateur	British Amateur	Total Titles
Mickey Wright	4	4	0	0	0	0	8
JoAnne Carner	2	0	0	0	5	0	7
Pat Bradley	1	1	3	1	0	0	6
Betsy Rawls	4	2	0	0	0	0	6
Betsy King	2	1	0	3	0	0	6
Glenna Collett Vare	0	0	0	0	6	0	6
Juli Inkster	0	0	1	2	3	0	6
Louise Suggs	2	1	0	0	1	1	5
Babe Zaharias	3	0	0	0	1	1	5
Amy Alcott	1	0	1	3	0	0	5
Laura Davies	1	2	1	0	0	0	4

* Designated a major championship in 1979
† Designated a major championship in 1983

PART II
1997 Season
(Compiled by Roderick Williams)

World Rankings for Men's Professional Golf, 1997

Pos	Name	Country	Points	Pos	Name	Country	Points
1	Greg Norman	Aus	11.49	50T	Michael Bradley	USA	2.96
2	Tiger Woods	USA	10.76	52	David Frost	SA	2.93
3	Nick Price	Zim	9.93	53	Costantino Rocca	It	2.92
4	Ernie Els	SA	9.89	54	Eduardo Romero	Arg	2.84
5	Davis Love III	USA	9.09	55	Stewart Cink	USA	2.79
6	Phil Mickelson	USA	8.73	56	Jeff Sluman	USA	2.78
7	Colin Montgomerie	Sco	8.58	57	Jay Haas	USA	2.72
8	'Jumbo' Ozaki	Jpn	8.05	58	Duffy Waldorf	USA	2.65
9	Tom Lehman	USA	8.02	59	Carlos Franco	Par	2.58
10	Mark O'Meara	USA	7.98	60T	Retief Goosen	SA	2.56
11	Justin Leonard	USA	7.00		David Ogrin	USA	2.56
12	David Duval	USA	6.87	62	Mark Brooks	USA	2.54
13	Scott Hoch	USA	6.85	63	Billy Andrade	USA	2.48
14	Brad Faxon	USA	6.66	64	Kenny Perry	USA	2.41
15	Vijay Singh	Fij	6.54	65	Peter Lonard	Aus	2.38
16	Steve Elkington	Aus	6.49	66T	Brandt Jobe	USA	2.36
17	Nick Faldo	Eng	6.44		Kirk Triplett	USA	2.36
18	Jesper Parnevik	Swe	5.70	68	Fred Funk	USA	2.30
19T	Tom Watson	USA	5.47	69T	Frankie Minoza	Phi	2.23
	Fred Couples	USA	5.47		Tim Herron	USA	2.23
21	Bernhard Langer	Ger	5.39	71T	'Jet' Ozaki	Jpn	2.22
22	Jim Furyk	USA	5.34		Andrew Magee	USA	2.22
23	Lee Westwood	Eng	5.26	73	Thomas Bjorn	Den	2.18
24	Steve Jones	USA	5.21	74T	Phil Blackmar	USA	2.15
25	Ian Woosnam	Wal	5.06		Paul Goydos	USA	2.15
26	Frank Nobilo	NZ	4.92	76	Corey Pavin	USA	2.13
27	Loren Roberts	USA	4.88	77	Greg Turner	NZ	2.04
28	Mark Calcavecchia	USA	4.42	78	Padraig Harrington	Ire	2.03
29	Jeff Maggert	USA	4.38	79	Dudley Hart	USA	2.02
30	Mark McNulty	Zim	4.22	80	Robert Karlsson	Swe	2.00
31	Paul Stankowski	USA	4.09	81T	Ignacio Garrido	Sp	1.94
32	Tommy Tolles	USA	3.96		Stephen Ames	T&T	1.94
33	Shigeki Maruyama	Jpn	3.89	83T	Miguel A Martin	Sp	1.87
34	Lee Janzen	USA	3.79		Peter O'Malley	Aus	1.87
35	John Cook	USA	3.70	85T	Andrew Coltart	Sco	1.84
36	Darren Clarke	N. Ire	3.65		Rick Fehr	USA	1.84
37	Brian Watts	USA	3.64	87	Dan Forsman	USA	1.82
38	Tom Kite	USA	3.59	88	Rocco Mediate	USA	1.80
39	Craig Stadler	USA	3.51	89	Tom Byrum	USA	1.78
40	Craig Parry	Aus	3.49	90	Mark James	Eng	1.77
41	Bill Glasson	USA	3.47	91	Eduardo Herrera	Col	1.72
42	José Maria Olazabal	Sp	3.40	92T	Yoshinori Kaneko	Jpn	1.70
43	Steve Stricker	USA	3.30		Larry Nelson	USA	1.70
44T	Scott McCarron	USA	3.29	94	Steve Lowery	USA	1.67
	Stuart Appleby	Aus	3.29	95	Peter Senior	Aus	1.66
46	Joe Ozaki	Jpn	3.22	96T	Hal Sutton	USA	1.64
47	Payne Stewart	USA	3.15		Jay Don Blake	USA	1.64
48	Per-Ulrik Johansson	Swe	3.13	98	Larry Mize	USA	1.63
49	Bob Tway	USA	2.98	99	Raymond Russell	Sco	1.62
50	Robert Allenby	Aus	2.96	100	Russ Cochran	USA	1.61

PGA European Tour, 1997

Volvo Ranking

Pos	Name	Prize Money £	Pos	Name	Prize Money £
1	Colin MONTGOMERIE (Sco)	798947	51	Daniel CHOPRA (Swe)	120241
2	Bernhard LANGER (Ger)	692398	52	Paul LAWRIE (Sco)	117919
3	Lee WESTWOOD (Eng)	588718	53	Brian DAVIS (Eng)	117575
4	Darren CLARKE (N. Ire)	537409	54	Clinton WHITELAW (SA)	116434
5	Ian WOOSNAM (Wal)	503562	55	Robert ALLENBY (Aus)	116251
6	Ignacio GARRIDO (Sp)	411479	56	Sam TORRANCE (Sco)	115433
7	Retief GOOSEN (SA)	394597	57	Mark ROE (Eng)	114542
8	Padraig HARRINGTON (Ire)	388982	58	Thomas GÖGELE (Ger)	113807
9	José Maria OLAZABAL (Sp)	385648	59	Alex CEJKA (Ger)	111263
10	Robert KARLSSON (Swe)	364542	60	Ronan RAFFERTY (N. Ire)	110314
11	Per-Ulrik JOHANSSON (Swe)	354580	61	Carl WATTS (Eng)	109910
12	Costantino ROCCA (It)	315077	62	Mark MOULAND (Wal)	104767
13	Eduardo ROMERO (Arg)	290469	63	Steve WEBSTER (Eng)	104373
14	Mark JAMES (Eng)	271510	64	Philip WALTON (Ire)	102624
15	Thomas BJORN (Den)	264938	65	Richard BOXALL (Eng)	102007
16	Raymond RUSSELL (Sco)	250633	66	Iain PYMAN (Eng)	98881
17	Patrik SJÖLAND (Swe)	245274	67	Van PHILLIPS (Eng)	98109
18	Greg TURNER (NZ)	239869	68	Carl SUNESON (Sp)	97950
19	Joakim HAEGGMAN (Swe)	228479	69	Wayne RILEY (Aus)	97913
20	Russell CLAYDON (Eng)	225005	70	Jon ROBSON (Eng)	97569
21	Paul McGINLEY (Ire)	220278	71	Gary ORR (Scot)	96667
22	Peter O'MALLEY (Aus)	208339	72	Peter HEDBLOM (Swe)	94718
23	Sven STRÜVER (Ger)	207006	73	Stuart CAGE (Eng)	91482
24	Peter BAKER (Eng)	200819	74	Mark McNULTY (Zim)	91318
25	Paul BROADHURST (Eng)	198426	75	Santiago LUNA (Sp)	90702
26	Ross McFARLANE (Eng)	187340	76	Mats HALLBERG (Swe)	88317
27	Miguel Angel MARTIN (Sp)	187289	77	Jean VAN DE VELDE (Fr)	87829
28	Jarmo SANDELIN (Swe)	184981	78	Fabrice TARNAUD (Fr)	86639
29	José COCERES (Arg)	184332	79	Jonathan LOMAS (Eng)	84184
30	Stephen AMES (T&T)	183190	80	Katsuyoshi TOMORI (Jpn)	83460
31	David GILFORD (Eng)	182619	81	Marc FARRY (Fr)	81545
32	Roger CHAPMAN (Eng)	182354	82	Stephen ALLAN (Aus)	80564
33	David CARTER (Eng)	177820	83	Barry LANE (Eng)	78046
34	Richard GREEN (Aus)	170116	84	Fredrik JACOBSON (Swe)	77697
35	Jamie SPENCE (Eng)	160986	85	Ian GARBUTT (Eng)	73421
36	Niclas FASTH (Swe)	159370	86	Andrew OLDCORN (Sco)	72041
37	Miguel Angel JIMÉNEZ (Sp)	158413	87	Klas ERIKSSON (Swe)	70898
38	Angel CABRERA (Arg)	155429	88	Martin GATES (Eng)	70535
39	Phillip PRICE (Wal)	151602	89	Jay TOWNSEND (USA)	69123
40	Peter MITCHELL (Eng)	148329	90	Domingo HOSPITAL (Sp)	68242
41	Dennis EDLUND (Swe)	147234	91	Silvio GRAPPASONNI (It)	68185
42	Scott HENDERSON (Sco)	147000	92	Dean ROBERTSON (Sco)	67789
43	Michael LONG (NZ)	144314	93	Roger WESSELS (SA)	66865
44	Anders FORSBRAND (Swe)	141727	94	Paul EALES (Eng)	66577
45	Michael JONZON (Swe)	140078	95	José RIVERO (Sp)	65983
46	Andrew COLTART (Sco)	140042	96	Per HAUGSRUD (Nor)	63405
47	David HOWELL (Eng)	137703	97	Raymond BURNS (N. Ire)	62432
48	Peter LONARD (Aus)	134067	98	Tony JOHNSTONE (Zim)	61690
49	Gordon BRAND Jr (Sco)	133541	99	Gary EVANS (Eng)	61555
50	Wayne WESTNER (SA)	129452	100	Eamonn DARCY (Ire)	61551

Tour Results *(in chronological order)*

Johnnie Walker Classic
at Hope Island, Queensland, Australia

1	Ernie Els	70-68-71-69—278	£116660
2	Michael Long	68-68-71-72—279	60795
	Peter Lonard	69-69-69-72—279	60795

Heineken Classic
at The Vines Resort, Perth, Australia

1	Miguel Angel Martin	70-67-65-71—273	£107546
2	Fred Couples	68-70-69-67—274	60943
3	Frank Nobilo	66-69-70-70—275	30969
	Jean Van de Velde	69-69-69-68—275	30969
	Marc Farry	72-66-69-68—275	30969

South African Open
at Glendower, Johannesburg, South Africa

1	Vijay Singh	69-66-66-69—270	£71476
2	Nick Price	72-66-65-68—271	52023
3	Ernie Els	66-72-67-70—275	24066
	Mark McNulty	69-69-68-69—275	24066
	Fulton Allem	66-71-71-67—275	24066

Dimension Data Pro-Am
at Gary Player CC, Sun City, South Africa

1	Nick Price	67-66-66-69—268	£63384
2	David Frost	69-65-71-71—276	46155
3	Thomas Bjorn	67-67-71-72—277	27765

Alfred Dunhill South African PGA Championship
at Houghton GC, Johannesburg, South Africa

1	Nick Price*	67-66-70-66—269	£47319
2	David Frost	69-63-66-71—269	34457
3	Nico Van Rensburg	68-68-66-68—270	20728

Dubai Desert Classic
at Emirates GC, Dubai, United Arab Emirates

1	Richard Green*	70-68-66-68—272	£116660
2	Ian Woosnam	69-67-67-69—272	60795
	Greg Norman	71-68-67-66—272	60795

* *Winner after play-off*

Moroccan Open
at Royal Golf Links, Agadir, Morocco

1	Clinton Whitelaw	68-71-69-69—277	£58330
2	Darren Cole	72-74-69-64—279	26096
	Wayne Riley	72-72-67-68—279	26096
	Roger Chapman	74-68-70-67—279	26096

Portuguese Open
at Aroeira CC, Lisbon, Portugal

1	Michael Jonzon	67-65-68-69—269	£58330
2	Ignacio Garrido	69-71-67-65—272	38880
3	Paul Broadhurst	68-67-67-73—275	21910

Turespaña Masters Open de Canarias
at Maspalomas, San Fernando, Canary Islands

1	José Maria Olazabal	70-67-68-67—272	£61964
2	Lee Westwood	72-63-68-71—274	41302
3	Paul Broadhurst	69-72-67-68—276	20932
	Eduardo Romero	70-70-67-69—276	20932

Madeira Island Open
at Santo da Serra GC, Machico, Madeira

1	Peter Mitchell	70-63-71—204	£50000
2	Fredrik Jacobson	68-73-64—205	33330
3	Andrew Coltart	66-72-68—206	18780

Europe 1 Cannes Open
at Royal Mougins, Cannes, France

1	Stuart Cage	68-67-69-66—270	£50000
2	Paul Broadhurst	68-70-69-68—275	26055
	David Carter	68-74-71-62—275	26055

Peugeot Open de España
at Golf La Moraleja II, Madrid, Spain

1	Mark James*	67-68-73-69—277	£84843
2	Greg Norman	69-70-68-70—277	56506
3	Jarmo Sandelin	72-71-69-66—278	28677
	Eduardo Romero	68-70-71-69—278	28677

Conte of Florence Italian Open
at Gardagolf CC, Brescia, Italy

1	Bernhard Langer	71-69-69-64—273	£77897
2	José Maria Olazabal	68-71-67-68—274	51924
3	Darren Clarke	70-69-71-67—277	29259

* Winner after play-off

Benson and Hedges International Open
at The Oxfordshire GC, Thame, England

1	Bernhard Langer	70-66-71-69—276	£116660
2	Ian Woosnam	70-68-70-70—278	77770
3	Lee Westwood	69-69-70-72—280	43820

Alamo English Open
at Marriott Hanbury Manor, Ware, England

1	Per-Ulrik Johansson	70-68-64-67—269	£108330
2	Dennis Edlund	68-65-69-69—271	72210
3	Jay Townsend	72-63-70-67—272	36595
	Steve Webster	68-66-70-68—272	36595

Volvo PGA Championship
at Wentworth, Surrey

Par 72, 6957 yards. Prize money: £1,122,918

1	Ian Woosnam (Wal)	67-68-70-70—275	£183340
2	Darren Clarke (N.Ire)	66-74-66-71—277	82023
	Nick Faldo (Eng)	70-67-70-70—277	82023
	Ernie Els (SA)	69-71-67-70—277	82023
5	Colin Montgomerie (Sco)	69-69-76-64—278	46640
6	David Gilford (Eng)	67-70-72-70—279	35750
	Angel Cabrera (Arg)	73-67-70-69—279	35750
8	Dennis Edlund (Swe)	70-72-68-70—280	27500
9	Lee Westwood (Eng)	70-72-70-69—281	24530
10	Barry Lane (Eng)	69-72-69-72—282	22000
11	Eamonn Darcy (Ire)	66-75-76-67—284	18930
	Eduardo Romero (Arg)	71-70-70-73—284	18930
	Frank Nobilo (NZ)	68-71-77-68—284	18930
14	Philip Walton (Ire)	69-72-70-74—285	15510
	Raymond Burns (N.Ire)	72-71-72-70—285	15510
	Carl Mason (Eng)	73-71-69-72—285	15510
	David Carter (Eng)	68-74-70-73—285	15510
	Stephen Ames (T&T)	70-69-70-76—285	15510
19	Peter Hedblom (Swe)	73-71-75-67—286	12388
	José Maria Olazabal (Sp)	72-71-73-70—286	12388
	Miguel Angel Martin (Sp)	70-75-67-74—286	12388
	Thomas Bjorn (Den)	68-74-75-69—286	12388
	Iain Pyman (Eng)	71-73-73-69—286	12388
	Ronan Rafferty (N.Ire)	74-72-72-68—286	12388
	Jon Robson (Eng)	71-71-71-73—286	12388
	Paul Curry (Eng)	71-74-71-70—286	12388
27	Mark Davis (Eng)	70-73-73-71—287	10230
	José Coceres (Arg)	74-72-72-69—287	10230
	André Bossert (Swi)	73-70-75-69—287	10230
	Peter O'Malley (Aus)	73-71-72-71—287	10230
	Carl Suneson (Sp)	73-72-69-73—287	10230

Deutsche Bank Open – TPC of Europe
at Gut Kaden, Hamburg, Germany

1	Ross McFarlane	70-73-68-71—282	£125000
2	Gordon Brand Jr	72-72-67-72—283	65130
	Anders Forsbrand	73-68-69-73—283	65130

Compaq European Grand Prix
at Slaley Hall, Northumberland, England

1	Colin Montgomerie	69-68-68-65—270	£108330
2	Retief Goosen	69-69-68-69—275	72210
3	Lee Westwood	70-70-66-70—276	40690

Volvo German Open
at Schloss Nippenburg, Stuttgart, Germany

1	Ignacio Garrido	65-67-67-72—271	£116660
2	Russell Claydon	68-69-72-66—275	77770
3	Mark James	68-67-69-72—276	43820

Peugeot Open de France
at National GC, Paris, France

1	Retief Goosen	64-67-70-70—271	£100000
2	Jamie Spence	68-71-67-68—274	66660
3	Raymond Russell	75-68-66-66—275	28490
	Darren Clarke	70-69-67-69—275	28490
	Van Phillips	70-68-71-66—275	28490
	Martin Gates	68-67-69-71—275	28490

Murphy's Irish Open
at Druids Glen, Dublin, Ireland

1	Colin Montgomerie	68-70-69-62—269	£113636
2	Lee Westwood	65-69-70-72—276	75745
3	Nick Faldo	69-73-68-68—278	42672

Gulfstream World Invitational
at Loch Lomond, Glasgow, Scotland

1	Tom Lehman	65-66-67-67—265	£133330
2	Ernie Els	70-69-65-66—270	88880
3	Retief Goosen	71-70-69-62—272	50070

Sun Dutch Open
at Hilversumsche GC, Hilversum, Netherlands

1	Sven Struver	67-64-69-66—266	£116660
2	Russell Claydon	67-68-65-69—269	77770
3	Roger Chapman	65-71-68-67—271	39410
	Angel Cabrera	71-66-67-67—271	39410

Volvo Scandinavian Masters
at Barsebäck, Malmo, Sweden

1	Joakim Haeggman	67-69-65-69—270	£125000
2	Ignacio Garrido	67-69-71-67—274	83320
3	Mats Hallberg	72-68-67-68—275	42220
	Peter Baker	70-66-69-70—275	42220

Chemapol Czech Open
at Karlstein, Prague, Czech Republic

1	Bernhard Langer	70-67-64-63—264	£133330
2	Niclas Fasth	70-65-67-66—268	69475
	Ignacio Garrido	66-65-66-71—268	69475

Smurfit European Open
at The K Club, Dublin, Ireland

1	Per-Ulrik Johansson	68-64-66-69—267	£141660
2	Peter Baker	70-67-68-68—273	94440
3	Raymond Russell	72-69-67-66—274	47885
	José Maria Olazabal	69-73-67-65—274	47885

BMW International Open
at Golfclub München Nord-Eichenried, Munich, Germany

1	Robert Karlsson*	67-67-64-66—264	£125000
2	Carl Watts	64-68-67-65—264	83320
3	Colin Montgomerie	65-67-67-66—265	£46940

Canon European Masters
at Crans-sur-Sierre, Switzerland

1	Costantino Rocca	72-64-68-62—266	£133330
2	Robert Karlsson	68-66-69-64—267	69475
	Scott Henderson	62-66-73-66—267	69475

Trophée Lancôme
at Saint Nom-la-Bretèche, Paris, France

1	Mark O'Meara	69-67-66-69—271	£116660
2	Jarmo Sandelin	70-70-65-67—272	77770
3	Greg Norman	67-66-68-72—273	39410
	Peter O'Malley	65-68-68-72—273	39410

One 2 One British Masters
at Marriott Forest of Arden, Coventry, England

1	Greg Turner	68-71-66-70—275	£125000
2	Colin Montgomerie	72-74-67-63—276	83320
3	Mark Roe	65-74-70-70—279	46940

Linde German Masters
at Berliner G&CC, Motzener See, Berlin, Germany

1	Bernhard Langer	68-69-60-70—267	£125000
2	Colin Montgomerie	71-68-66-68—273	83320
3	Thomas Bjorn	71-68-66-69—274	46940

* *Winner after play-off*

Toyota World Match Play Championship
at Wentworth Club (West Course), Virginia Water, Surrey

Total prize fund: £650,000

First Round
Ian Woosnam beat Jesper Parnevik 4 and 3
Frank Nobilo beat Phil Mickelson at 38th hole
Brad Faxon beat Darren Clarke 2 and 1
Vijay Singh beat Tsukasa Watanabe 4 and 3
(Each loser received £30000)

Quarter-Finals
Ernie Els beat Ian Woosnam 7 and 6
Nick Price beat Frank Nobilo 6 and 5
Brad Faxon beat Colin Montgomerie 2 and 1
Vijay Singh beat Steve Elkington 5 and 4
(Each loser received £40000)

Semi-Finals
Vijay Singh beat Brad Faxon 4 and 3
Ernie Els beat Nick Price at 37th hole

Play-off for 3rd and 4th places
Brad Faxon beat Nick Price 5 and 4
(Faxon received £60000, Price received £50000)

Final
Vijay Singh beat Ernie Els 1 up
(Singh received £170000, Els received £90000)

Open Novotel Perrier
at Golf du Médoc, Bordeaux, France

1	A Forsbrand and M Jonzon★	65-74-64-140—343	£35000 each
2	S Luna and J Rivero	64-71-69-139—343	25000 each
3	M Roe and M Farry	66-73-68-141—348	13000 each
	S Ballesteros and JM Olazabal	67-73-67-141—348	13000 each
	P Hedblom and P Sjöland	66-70-68-144—348	13000 each

Oki Pro-Am
at Golf La Moraleja I & II, Madrid, Spain

1	Paul McGinley	66-67-64-69—266	£75000
2	Iain Pyman	68-69-69-64—270	50000
3	Greg Turner	69-68-67-69—273	28170

Volvo Masters
at Montecastillo, Spain

1	Lee Westwood	65-67-68—200	£166000
2	Padraig Harrington	66-70-67—203	110000
3	José Maria Olazabal	66-67-71—204	63000
4	Robert Karlsson	68-67-70—205	50600
5	Peter O'Malley	68-69-69—206	35966
	Patrik Sjöland	64-68-74—206	35966
	Mark McNulty	64-69-73—206	35966
8	Colin Montgomerie	65-71-71—207	25000
9	Eduardo Romero	71-69-68—208	19833
	Ian Woosnam	67-69-72—208	19833
	Costantino Rocca	69-65-74—208	19833

★ *Winners after play-off*

Tour Statistics, 1997

Stroke Averages

Pos	Name	Avg	Pos	Name	Avg
1	Colin Montgomerie (Sco)	69.37	16	Michael Long (NZ)	70.90
2	José Maria Olazabal (Sp)	69.70	17	José Coceres (Arg)	70.92
3	Bernhard Langer (Ger)	69.88	18	David Carter (Eng)	70.98
4	Eduardo Romero (Arg)	70.03	19	Joakim Haeggman (Swe)	70.99
5	Patrik Sjöland (Swe)	70.07	20	Mark McNulty (Zim)	71.00
6	Ian Woosnam (Wal)	70.21		Peter O'Malley (Aus)	71.00
7	Darren Clarke (N.Ire)	70.22	22	Roger Chapman (Eng)	71.04
8	Lee Westwood (Eng)	70.29		Clinton Whitelaw (SA)	71.04
9	Retief Goosen (SA)	70.47		Paul McGinley (Ire)	71.04
10	Per-Ulrik Johansson (Swe)	70.59	25	Stephen Ames (T&T)	71.07
11	Thomas Bjorn (Den)	70.61		Miguel Angel Jiménez (Sp)	71.07
12	Padraig Harrington (Ire)	70.63		Jon Robson (Eng)	71.07
13	Costantino Rocca (It)	70.69	28	Ignacio Garrido (Sp)	71.08
14	Robert Karlsson (Swe)	70.78		Greg Turner (NZ)	71.08
15	Mark James (Eng)	70.84	30	Wayne Westner (SA)	71.14

PGA European Tour Qualifying School

at Guadalmina and Sotogrande, Spain

The following 43 players won tour cards for 1998:

Pos	Name	Nationality	Score	Par
1	Chris VAN DER VELDE	Neth	72-68-71-69—280	−8
2	Fredrik HENGE	Swe	68-75-66-71—280	−8
3	Robert-Jan DERKSEN	Hol	76-66-67-71—280	−8
4	Philip GOLDING	Eng	71-68-70-71—280	−8
5	Michael CAMPBELL	NZ	69-72-67-74—282	−6
6	David THOMSON	Sco	71-70-74-68—283	−5
7	Ola ELIASSON	Swe	73-68-73-69—283	−5
8	Greg OWEN	Eng	70-76-67-70—283	−5
9	Andre STOLZ	Aus	72-67-70-74—283	−5
10	Stephen BENNETT	Eng	75-68-70-71—284	−4
11	Jeev SINGH	Ind	67-74-71-72—284	−4
12	Andrew SANDYWELL	Eng	70-70-71-73—284	−4
13	John HAWKSWORTH	Eng	73-72-70-70—285	−3
14	Andrew CLAPP	Eng	73-71-71-70—285	−3
15	Maarten LAFEBER	Hol	73-68-74-70—285	−3
16	Francis HOWLEY	Ire	71-72-71-71—285	−3
17	Henrik NYSTROM	Swe	71-75-66-73—285	−3
18	Jeff REMESY	Fr	72-72-68-73—285	−3
19	Andrew BEAL	Eng	69-71-70-75—285	−3
20	Steve ALKER	NZ	76-69-72-69—286	−2
21	Gary NICKLAUS	USA	69-73-75-69—286	−2
22	Maurico MOLINA	Arg	69-77-69-71—286	−2
23	Mark DAVIS	Eng	69-70-75-72—286	−2
24	David HIGGINS	Ire	71-72-70-73—286	−2
25	Joakim RASK	Swe	72-68-71-75—286	−2
26	Pedro LINHART	Sp	73-67-71-75—286	−2
27	Johan RYSTROM	Swe	75-74-68-70—287	−1
28	Mark BOOTH	Eng	74-73-71-69—287	−1
29	Tom GILLIS	USA	74-74-70-69—287	−1

Pos	Name	Nationality	Score	Par
30	Greig HUTCHEON	Sco	75-72-70-70—287	−1
31	Cameron CLARK	N. Ire	74-71-72-70—287	−1
32	John BICKERTON	Eng	75-68-74-70—287	−1
33	Richard COUGHLAN	Ire	71-73-71-72—287	−1
34	Robert LEE	Eng	74-71-68-74—287	−1
35	Ged FUREY	Eng	72-68-72-75—287	−1
36	Darren COLE	Aus	67-72-73-75—287	−1
37	Francisco CEA	Sp	70-78-70-70—288	0
38	Olivier EDMOND	Fr	76-71-70-71—288	0
39	Bobby COLLINS	USA	72-75-71-70—288	0
40	Ivo GINER	Sp	73-73-69-73—288	0
41	Anthony WALL	Eng	71-71-73-73—288	0
42	Mathew GOGGIN	Aus	70-72-72-74—288	0
43	Mårten OLANDER	Swe	71-71-70-76—288	0

PGA European Challenge Tour Order of Merit, 1997

Pos	Name	Prize Money £
1	Michele Reale (It)	51679
2	Kalle Brink (Swe)	36112
3	Greg Chalmers (Aus)	35267
4	Raphaël Jacquelin (Fr)	34537
5	Anssi Kankkonen (Fin)	32128
6	Nicolas Joakimides (Fr)	31497
7	David Lynn (Eng)	31341
8	Steen Tinning (Den)	29522
9	Knud Storgaard (Den)	29426
10	Craig Hainline (USA)	29368
11	Stephen Leaney (Aus)	28613
12	Heinz P Thül (Ger)	27417
13	Nicolas Vanhootegem (Bel)	26936
14	Soren Kjeldsen (Den)	26581
15	Bradley Dredge (Wal)	26415
16	Mikael Lundberg (Swe)	26200
17	José Carriles (Sp)	26198
18	Francisco Cea (Sp)	25072
19	Henrik Nystrom (Swe)	24769
20	Erol Simsek (Ger)	24700
21	Jorge Berendt (Arg)	24683
22	Fredrik Henge (Swe)	23586
23	Roger Winchester (Eng)	23077
24	Thomas Nielsen (Nor)	22587
25	Olivier Edmond (Fr)	22370
26	Warren Bennett (Eng)	22260
27	Antoine Lebouc (Fr)	21418
28	Marc Pendaries (Fr)	20820
29	David A Russell (Eng)	20183
30	Per Nyman (Swe)	19888
31	Greg Owen (Eng)	19798
32	Andrew Collison (Eng)	19236
33	Mark Litton (Wal)	18596
34	Kevin Carissimi (USA)	18290
35	Mathew Goggin (Aus)	18262
36	Ivo Giner (Sp)	17746
37	Jesus Maria Arruti (Sp)	17103
38	Robert Jan Derksen (Neth)	16754
39	Mikael Piltz (Fin)	16307
40	Magnus Persson (Swe)	15664

PGA European Challenge Tour, 1997

Tournament	Venue	Winner
16th Open de Côte d'Ivoire	Ivory Coast	Knud Storgaard (Den)
Lonrho Kenya Open	Kenya	Jorge Berendt (Arg)
Is Molas Challenge	Italy	Andrew Collison (Eng)
Campeonato de España	Spain	Ignacio Garrido (Sp)
La Pavoniere Superal Challenge	Italy	Andrew Collison (Eng)
Alianca UAP Challenge	Portugal	Anssi Kankkonen (Fin)
Canarias Challenge	Spain	Michele Reale (It)
2nd Modena Classic	Italy	Jesus Maria Arruti (Sp)

Matchmaker Austrian Open	Austria	Erol Simsek (Ger)
Himmerland Open	Denmark	Mikael Lundberg (Swe)
KB Golf Challenge	Czech Republic	Alex Cejka (Ger)
Siab Open	Sweden	Joakim Rask (Swe)
Husqvarna Open (C)	Sweden	Mikael Lundberg (Swe)
Czech Republic (C)	Czech Republic	Ondrej Trupl (Cze)
Championnat de France Pro (C)	France	Raphaël Jacquelin (Fr)
Lancia Golf Pokal (C)	Germany	Erol Simsek (Ger)
Nedcar National Open (C)	Netherlands	Brian Gee (Eng)
Italian Native Open (C)	Italy	Massimo Florioli (It)
STG Coopers & Lybrand ASPG Championship (C)	Switzerland	Juan Ciola (Swi)
Team Erhverv Danish Open	Denmark	David Lynn (Eng)
Memorial Olivier Barras#	Switzerland	Raphaël Jacquelin (Fr)
Audi Quattro Trophy	Germany	David A Russell (Eng)
Open dei Tessali	Italy	Ivo Giner (Sp)
Open des Volcans	France	Mark Litton (Wal)
Neuchatel Open•	Switzerland	Erol Simsek (Ger)
Volvo Finnish Open	Finland	Soren Kjeldsen (Den)
Rolex Trophy Pro-Am#	Switzerland	Anssi Kankkonen (Fin)
Interlaken Open	*Cancelled due to rain*	
BTC Slovenian Open	Slovenia	Kalle Brink (Swe)
Klassis Turkish Open	Turkey	Bradley Dredge (Wal)
Challenge Tour Championship	England	Greg Chalmers (Aus)
Norwegian PGA Championship (C)	Norway	Morten Hagen (Nor)
Terracottem Omnium of Belgium (C)	Belgium	Didier de Vooght[†] (Bel)
Esbjerg Danish Closed (C)	Denmark	Knud Storgaard (Den)
Finnish PGA Championship	Finland	Mikael Piltz (Fin)
Netcom Norwegian Open	Norway	Dimitri Bieri (Swi)
Steelcover Dutch Challenge	Netherlands	Raphaël Jacquelin (Fr)
Toyota PGA Championship	Denmark	Fredrik Henge (Swe)
Sovereign Russian Open	Russia	Michele Reale (It)
Ohrlings Swedish Matchplay	Sweden	Gregory Garbero (USA)
Perrier European Pro-Am	Belgium	Craig Hainline (USA)
Eulen Open Galea	Spain	Warren Bennett (Eng)
BPGT Challenge	England	Olivier Edmond (Fr)
Polish Open	*Cancelled*	
Telia InfoMedia Grand Prix	Sweden	Fredrik Henge (Swe)
San Paolo Vita Open	Italy	Mathew Goggin (Aus)
Portuguese Challenge	*Cancelled*	
Estoril Challenge	Portugal	José Carriles (Sp)
Estoril Grand Final	Portugal	Nicolas Jaokimides (Fr)

\#   *Invitational event*
(C) *Closed national event*
†   *Amateur*

Professional Men's Internationals, 1997

32nd Ryder Cup *at Valderrama, Spain*

Europe   **USA**

Day One

Fourball

JM Olazabal and C Rocca (1 hole)	1	D Love III and P Mickelson	0
N Faldo and L Westwood	0	F Couples and B Faxon (1 hole)	1
J Parnevik and P-U Johansson (1 hole)	1	T Lehman and J Furyk	0
C Montgomery and B Langer	0	T Woods and M O'Meara (3 and 2)	1
	2		**2**

Foursomes

C Rocca and JM Olazabal	0	S Hoch and L Janzen (1 hole)	1
B Langer and C Montgomerie (5 and 3)	1	M O'Meara and T Woods	0
N Faldo and L Westwood (3 and 2)	1	J Leonard and J Maggert	0
J Parnevik and I Garrido	¹/₂	T Lehman and P Mickelson	¹/₂
	2¹/₂		**1¹/₂**

Day Two

Fourball

C Montgomerie and D Clarke (1 hole)	1	F Couples and D Love III	0
I Woosnam and T Bjorn (2 and 1)	1	J Leonard and B Faxon	0
N Faldo and L Westwood (2 and 1)	1	T Woods and M O'Meara	0
JM Olazabal and I Garrido	¹/₂	P Mickelson and T Lehman	¹/₂
	3¹/₂		**¹/₂**

Foursomes

C Montgomerie and B Langer (1 hole)	1	L Janzen and J Furyk	0
N Faldo and L Westwood	0	S Hoch and J Maggert (2 and 1)	1
J Parnevik and I Garrido	¹/₂	J Leonard and T Woods	¹/₂
JM Olazabal and C Rocca (5 and 4)	1	D Love III and F Couples	0
	2¹/₂		**1¹/₂**

Day Three

Singles

I Woosnam	0	F Couples (8 and 7)	1
P-U Johansson (3 and 2)	1	D Love III	0
C Rocca (4 and 2)	1	T Woods	0
T Bjorn	¹/₂	J Leonard	¹/₂
D Clarke	0	P Mickelson (2 and 1)	1
J Parnevik	0	M O'Meara (5 and 4)	1
JM Olazabal	0	L Janzen (1 hole)	1
B Langer (2 and 1)	1	B Faxon	0
L Westwood	0	J Maggert (3 and 2)	1
C Montgomerie	¹/₂	S Hoch	¹/₂
N Faldo	0	J Furyk (3 and 2)	1
I Garrido	0	T Lehman (7 and 6)	1
	4		**8**

Result: Europe 14¹/₂, USA 13¹/₂

Alfred Dunhill Cup *at The Old Course, St Andrews*

Day One

Group 1
England beat Japan 3–0
USA beat Argentina 2–1

Group 2
Sweden beat Chinese Taipei 3–0
Australia lost to France 1–2

Group 3
South Africa beat Ireland 2–1
Scotland beat Germany 2–1

Group 4
Zimbabwe beat Korea 2–1
New Zealand beat Spain 2–1

Day Two

Group 1
USA beat Japan 3–0
England lost to Argentina 1–2

Group 2
Sweden beat France 3–0
Australia beat Chinese Taipei 2–1

Group 3
Scotland beat Ireland 2–1
South Africa beat Germany 3–0

Group 4
New Zealand beat Korea 3–0
Zimbabwe beat Spain 2–1

Day Three

Group 1
USA beat England 3–0
Argentina beat Japan 2–0

Group 2
Australia lost to Sweden 1–2
France beat Chinese Taipei 3–0

Group 3
Ireland beat Germany 2–1
South Africa beat Scotland 2–0

Group 4
Korea lost to Spain 1–2
Zimbabwe lost to New Zealand 0–3

Semi-Finals

Sweden beat USA 2–1
  J Parnevik (69) lost to M O'Meara (68)
  J Haeggman (68) beat J Leonard (72)
  P-U Johansson (71) beat B Faxon (74)

South Africa beat New Zealand 2–1
  R Goosen (67) beat M Long (72)
  D Frost (72) beat S Alker (76)
  E Els (70) lost to F Nobilo (66)

Final

South Africa beat Sweden 2–1
  R Goosen (70) beat J Parnevik (74)
  D Frost (74) lost to P-U Johansson (71)
  E Els (69) beat J Haeggman (72)

	Prize Money £				Prize Money £		
	Team	Player	Total		Team	Player	Total
Group 1				**Group 4**			
USA (1)				New Zealand (7)			
Argentina	45000	15000		Zimbabwe (2)	45000	15000	
England (8)	25500	8500		Spain	25500	8500	
Japan	19500	6500	90000	Korea	19500	6500	90000
Group 2				**Losing Semi-Finalists**			
Sweden (5)				USA (1)	95000	31666	
France	45000	15000		New Zealand	95000	31666	190000
Australia (4)	25500	8500		**Runners-up**			
Chinese Taipei	19500	6500	90000	Sweden (5)	150000	50000	150000
Group 3							
South Africa (3)				**Winners**			
Scotland (6)	45000	15000		South Africa (3)	300000	100000	300000
Ireland	25500	8500					
Germany	19500	6500	90000	**Total**			1000000

The 43rd World Cup of Golf
at Kiawah Island, South Carolina, USA

1	IRELAND (545)		
	Padraig Harrington	71-67-68-67—273	
	Paul McGinley	66-70-68-68—272	$200000 each
2	SCOTLAND (550)		
	Raymond Russell	66-72-74-72—284	
	Colin Montgomerie	68-66-66-66—266	$100000 each
3	USA (551)		
	Davis Love III	65-69-74-65—273	
	Justin Leonard	72-69-67-70—278	$62500 each
4T	WALES (554)		
	Ian Woosnam	74-72-69-64—279	
	Philip Price	72-68-69-66—275	$45000 each
	GERMANY (554)		
	Sven Strüver	70-75-67-74—286	
	Alex Cejka	63-68-65-72—268	$45000 each
6	SPAIN (555)		
	Ignacio Garrido	67-67-69-67—270	
	Miguel Angel Martin	68-74-71-72—285	$30000 each
7	ENGLAND (559)		
	Paul Broadhurst	68-74-68-72—282	
	Mark James	68-73-70-66—277	$22500 each
8	ZIMBABWE (561)		
	Tony Johnstone	73-67-72-68—280	
	Mark McNulty	68-74-71-68—281	$16000 each
9T	SOUTH AFRICA (562)		
	Ernie Els	73-68-69-69—279	
	Wayne Westner	68-71-72-72—283	$13000 each
	NEW ZEALAND (562)		
	Michael Long	69-75-67-75—286	
	Grant Waite	70-70-69-67—276	$13000 each

Individual Results

1	Colin Montgomerie (Sco)	68-66-66-66—266	$10000
2	Alex Cejka (Ger)	63-68-65-72—268	50000
3	Ignacio Garrido (Sp)	67-67-69-67—270	25000
4	Paul McGinley (Ire)	66-70-68-68—272	15000
5	Padraig Harrington (Ire)	71-67-68-67—273	10000

Miscellaneous Professional Tournaments

Andersen Consulting World Championship of Golf
at Grayhawk GC, Scottsdale, Arizona

32 of the world's top players, based on the Sony Ranking, play in four regions. The Championship is the first in professional golf to have the support and sanctioning of the five major tours – the PGA Tour of Australasia, FNB Tour of Southern Africa, Japan PGA, the PGA European Tour and the US PGA Tour.

Regional Finals

International	E Els beat S Elkington 1 hole
Japan	H Meshiai beat K Hosokawa 1 hole
USA	D Love III beat P Mickelson at 20th hole
Europe	C Montgomerie beat C Rocca 5 and 4

World Semi-Final
D Love III beat H Meshiai 1 hole
C Montgomerie beat E Els 3 and 2

Final
C Montgomerie beat D Love III 2 up

Prize money: C Montgomerie $1 million, D Love III $500000, E Els $350000, H Meshiai $300000

British Assistants' Championship (Reebok PGA Assistants' Championship)
at De Vere, Blackpool (Herons Reach)

1	P Sefton	66-72-65-70—273	£4000
2	C Benians	69-63-73-69—274	2600
	N Ludwell	71-67-68-68—274	2600

East Region PGA Championship
at Nazeing

1	N Brown*	142
2	R Mann	142
3	B Mitchell	142

Club Professional Championship
at Northop

1	B Rimmer	70-68-64-66—268	£9250
2	P Wesselingh	67-70-72-67—276	6275
3	S Bennett	75-65-70-67—277	4650

* *Winner after play-off*

Hassan II Trophy
at Golf de Dar-es-Salaam, Rabat, Morocco

1	C Montgomerie	73-68-67-69—277	$100000
2	H Nystrom	68-71-71-70—280	40000
	D Howell	67-73-72-68—280	40000

Irish Club Professional Championship
at Mount Wolseley

1	N Manchip	68-73—141	£2000
2	S Hamill	72-70—142	1350
3	L Walker	72-71—143	900

Midland Professional Championship
at PGA National GC, The Belfry, Sutton Coldfield

1	J Higgins	68-69—137	
2	P Baker	69-70—139	
	P Wesselingh	71-68—139	

Million Dollar Challenge
at Sun City, Bophuthatswana, South Africa

1	N Price	71-68-68-68—275	$1000000
2	D Love III	68-67-74-67—276	225000
	E Els	69-70-70-67—276	225000

North Region PGA Championship
at Mottram Hall, Cheshire

1	G Furey	66-66-71—203	£3000
2	D Brunton	68-67-69—204	2000
3	P Carman	74-66-68—208	970
	C Tyson	72-68-68—208	970
	P Scott	74-69-65—208	970

PGA Senior Club Professional Championship
at Coventry

1	T Horton	203	£4750
2	C Defoy	212	3500
3	S Adwick	213	2350
	A Brooks	213	2350

Subaru Sarazen World Open Championship
at The Legends at Chateau Elan, Atlanta Georgia

1	M Calcavecchia	62-67-71-71—271	$360000
2	L Westwood	71-65-70-68—274	216000
3	M McNulty	74-66-70-69—279	100500
	V Singh	69-69-70-71—279	100500

Scottish Assistants' Championship
at Balbirnie Park, Markinch

1	M Hastie	70-70-69-66—275	£650
2	N Scott-Smith	73-66-67-75—281	420
3	C Lee	75-72-66-68—281	420

Scottish PGA Matchplay Championship
at Turnberry Hotel

Semi-Finals
C Gillies beat J Greaves 2 holes
D Thomson beat G Law 3 and 2

Final
D Thomson beat C Gillies 2 holes

Scottish Professional Championship
at Downfield, Dundee

1	G Law	70-68-73-73—284	£5000
2	A Webster	71-71-70-72—284	3300
3	F Mann	73-68-71-73—285	1690
	A Crerar	70-70-75-70—285	1690

Smurfit Irish Professional Championship
at Fota Island GC

1	P McGinley	70-66-75-74—285	£16000
2	S Hamill	71-68-73-74—286	7416
	J McHenry	71-75-71-69—286	7416
	D Higgins	72-70-75-69—286	7416

Southern Professional Championship
at Mill Ride, Ascot

1	P Sherman	72-66—138
2	P Creamer	70-68—138
3	G Hughes	68-72—140
	P Hughes	73-67—140

South West PGA Championship
at Manor House, Moretonhampstead

1	M Stanford (Tracy Park)	66-65—131 (-7)	£800
2	L Thompson (Knighton Heath)	63-70—133 (-5)	650
	M Thompson (Ferndown)	68-65—133 (-5)	650

Sunderland of Scotland Masters
at Cawder GC, Bishopbriggs

1	L Vennet	69-70-66-66—271	£3600
2	C Gillies	70-68-68-67—273	2600
3	A Crerar	66-67-70-71—274	1735

Sunningdale Foursomes
at Sunningdale, Berkshire

Semi-Finals
J Robinson and D Jones beat W Riley and G Smith 1 hole
Mrs J Hall and Miss H Wadsworth beat J Kemp and M Wilcox 6 and 5

Final
Mrs J Hall and Miss H Wadsworth beat J Robinson and D Jones 4 and 3

Welsh Professional Championship
at Vale of Glamorgan

1	M Ellis	71-68—139	£5500
2	M Mouland	73-67—140	3000
3	M Peet	73-68—141	2500

West of England PGA Championship
at St Mellion, Cornwall

1	L Thompson*	69-66-73—208	£1100
2	S Little	74-64-70—208	1100
	K Spurgeon	71-68-69—208	1100

West Region PGA Championship
at Woodbury Park

1	M Thompson	70-72-69—211	£2000
2	R Arnold	71-71-71—213	1350
	I Harrison	68-70-75—213	1350

Wadworth 6X Western Open
at Bowood, Wiltshire

1	J Higgins	71-72-71-70—284	£3500
2	J Taylor	74-72-70-72—288	2500
3	N Job	72-71-73-73—289	1250
	G Milne	73-76-69-71—289	1250
	M Stanford	75-72-69-73—289	1250

* Winner after play-off

PGA European Seniors' Tour, 1997

Final Order of Merit

Pos	Name	Prize Money £	Pos	Name	Prize Money £
1	Tommy HORTON (Eng)	158427	26	Hugh INGGS (SA)	22844
2	Noel RATCLIFFE (Aus)	86060	27	Tienie BRITZ (SA)	22533
3	Antonio GARRIDO (Sp)	62671	28	John GARNER (Eng)	22516
4	Brian WAITES (Eng)	61978	29	Bill HARDWICK (Can)	22418
5	Jim RHODES (Eng)	55839	30	JR DELICH (USA)	21396
6	Malcolm GREGSON (Eng)	50526	31	Harry FLATMAN (Eng)	21021
7	José Maria CANIZARES (Sp)	48955	32	Bob MENNE (USA)	20448
8	David CREAMER (Eng)	45631	33	Craig DEFOY (Wal)	20426
9	Maurice BEMBRIDGE (Eng)	42841	34	Steve WILD (Eng)	20289
10	Ian RICHARDSON (Eng)	41468	35	John FOURIE (SA)	19157
11	Renato CAMPAGNOLI (It)	39764	36	Snell LANCASTER (USA)	18928
12	Neil COLES (Eng)	37990	37	Terry GALE (Aus)	18843
13	David JONES (N. Ire)	36733	38	Lloyd MONROE (USA)	18297
14	DeRay SIMON (USA)	36251	39	Jan BJORNSSON (Swe)	16008
15	Walter HALL (USA)	33295	40	Vincent TSHABALALA (SA)	15482
16	David HUISH (Sco)	31629	41	José Maria ROCA (Sp)	15271
17	Bobby VERWEY (SA)	31548	42	Randall VINES (Aus)	13398
18	Paul LEONARD (N. Ire)	28957	43	Joe CARR (USA)	12918
19	Norman WOOD (Sco)	28886	44	Doug DALZIEL (USA)	12499
20	Eddie POLLAND (N. Ire)	26811	45	Agim BARDHA (USA)	12488
21	Alberto CROCE (It)	26259	46	Chick EVANS (USA)	12310
22	Brian HUGGETT (Wal)	26190	47	Gordon PARKHILL (N. Ire)	11280
23	TR JONES (USA)	25476	48	John MORGAN (Eng)	10800
24	Liam HIGGINS (Ire)	23574	49	Hugh JACKSON (N. Ire)	10495
25	Guy HUNT (Eng)	23152	50	Peter TOWNSEND (Eng)	10302

Tour Results *(in chronological order)*

Beko/Öger Turkish Seniors' Open
at National GC, Antalya, Turkey

1	Tommy Horton	69-70-69—208	£25503
2	Maurice Bembridge	69-72-69—210	16956
3	Joe Carr	68-74-69—211	9508

AIB Irish Seniors' Classic
at St Margarets GC, Dublin

1	Tommy Horton	71-69-68—208	£12100
2	Noel Ratcliffe	66-72-72—210	7900
3	Malcolm Gregson	71-72-69—212	4600

Philips PFA Golf Classic
at Marriott St Pierre Hotel & CC, Wales

1	DeRay Simon	69-69-74—212	£12500
2	Tommy Horton	69-72-77—218	8300
3	Jim Rhodes	69-74-76—219	3640
	Malcolm Gregson	71-72-76—219	3640
	Antonio Garrido	72-73-74—219	3640
	Tienie Britz	76-70-73—219	3640
	Brian Huggett	72-74-73—219	3640

Jersey Seniors' Open
at La Moye, Jersey

1	Tommy Horton	69-67-68—204	£15000
2	Craig Defoy	71-70-69—210	10000
3	José Maria Canizares	71-70-72—213	5070
	Paul Leonard	69-70-74—213	5070

De Vere Hotels Seniors' Classic
at Belton Woods, Lincs

1	TR Jones	68-73-71—212	£13350
2	Tommy Horton	71-70-72—213	8900
3	Arnold O'Connor	70-72-72—214	4143
	David Creamer	71-70-73—214	4143
	Noel Ratcliffe	69-71-74—214	4143

Ryder Collingtree Seniors' Classic
at Collingtree Park, Northampton

1	Neil Coles	68-71-69—208	£15000
2	Antonio Garrido	72-75-68—215	7845
	Brian Waites	69-72-74—215	7845

Manadans Affarer Seniors'
at Fågelbro, Sweden

1	Noel Ratcliffe	69-67-68—204	£12000
2	Stephen Wild	67-68-76—211	7850
3	Norman Wood	68-72-72—212	4600

Lawrence Batley Seniors'
at Huddersfield, Yorkshire

1	Antonio Garrido	70-68-68—206	£13000
2	Renato Campagnoli	70-68-69—207	8440
3	Malcolm Gregson	68-72-68—208	4043
	Bill Hardwick	70-71-67—208	4043
	Brian Waites	71-65-72—208	4043

Senior German Open
at Owingen-Überlingen, Germany

1	Noel Ratcliffe	66-69-69—204	£16660
2	David Creamer	72-69-65—206	11100
3	David Jones	67-69-71—207	6260

Senior British Open
at Royal Portrush, Northern Ireland

1	Gary Player*	68-70-72-68—278	£58330
2	John Bland	66-72-70-70—278	38850
3	Noel Ratcliffe	70-65-75-69—279	19705
	Jim Rhodes	69-71-71-68—279	19705

Shell Wentworth Senior Masters
at Wentworth Club

1	Gary Player	69-68-70—207	£20830
2	David Creamer	69-68-71—208	10845
	José Maria Canizares	72-68-68—208	10845

Credit Suisse Private Banking Seniors' Open
at Bad Ragaz, Switzerland

1	Brian Waites	63-69-71—203	£16660
2	Malcolm Gregson	68-69-66—203	11100
3	Noel Ratcliffe	64-70-70—204	5630
	Hugh Inggs	64-69-71—204	5630

The Belfry PGA Seniors' Championship
at The Belfry, North Warwickshire

1	Walter Hall	69-69-69-70—277	£25000
2	Tommy Horton	68-71-73-68—280	16640
3	Antonio Garrido	68-70-69-75—282	8365
	José Maria Canizares	68-74-72-68—282	8365

Motor City Senior Classic
at Marriott Goodwood Park Hotel & CC

1	Ian Richardson	70-67-71—208	£12500
2	Eddie Polland	66-70-73—209	6497
	DeRay Simon	67-73-69—209	6497

Scottish Seniors' Open
at Newmachar, Aberdeen

1	Tommy Horton	70-62—132	£16660
2	JR Delich	72-69—141	11100
3	Michael Murphy	69-74—143	5166
	José Maria Roca	73-70—143	5166
	Jim Rhodes	73-70—143	5166

Clubhaus Seniors' Classic
at Benton Hall, Essex

1	Tommy Horton	68-71-64—203	£12450
2	David Jones	69-68-68—205	8250
3	Malcolm Gregson	68-71-68—207	4650

* *Winner after play-off*

Senior Tournament of Champions
at Buckinghamshire GC, Denham

1	Tommy Horton	69-67-68—204	£20000
2	José Maria Canizares	68-66-73—207	13300
3	Alberto Croce	76-69-67—212	6750
	David Huish	70-70-72—212	6750

US PGA Tour, 1997

Money List

Pos	Name	Prize Money $	Pos	Name	Prize Money $
1	Tiger Woods	2066833	51	Duffy Waldorf	458074
2	David Duval	1885308	52	Kevin Sutherland	455860
3	Davis Love III	1635953	53	Robert Damron	455604
4	Jim Furyk	1619480	54	Hal Sutton	453928
5	Justin Leonard	1587531	55	Fred Couples	448385
6	Scott Hoch	1393788	56	Dan Forsman	443034
7	Greg Norman	1345856	57	Jay Haas	437895
8	Steve Elkington	1320411	58	Nick Faldo	431326
9	Ernie Els	1243008	59	Lee Rinker	415442
10	Brad Faxon	1233505	60	Dudley Hart	410188
11	Phil Mickelson	1225390	61	Paul Goydos	396241
12	Jesper Parnevik	1217587	62	Brent Geiberger	395472
13	Mark O'Meara	1124560	63	Craig Parry	387603
14	Mark Calcavecchia	1117365	64	Doug Martin	383593
15	Loren Roberts	1089140	65	Jay Don Blake	378484
16	Vijay Singh	1059236	66	Brad Fabel	375122
17	Nick Price	1053845	67	Mike Brisky	367112
18	Stuart Appleby	1003356	68	Grant Waite	362320
19	Tom Lehman	960584	69	Bob Estes	340057
20	Steve Jones	959108	70	Brandel Chamblee	334664
21	Paul Stankowski	929405	71	Brian Henninger	329864
22	Bill Glasson	926405	72	Rick Fehr	327204
23	Frank Nobilo	891315	73	Mike Reid	325551
24	Lee Janzen	877832	74	Skip Kendall	320800
25	Scott McCarron	852459	75	Mike Standly	318939
26	Jeff Maggert	835884	76	Mike Hulbert	317247
27	Tommy Tolles	825793	77	Len Mattiace	315656
28	John Cook	815903	78	Don Pooley	312660
29	Stewart Cink	809580	79	Billy Mayfair	304083
30	Andrew Magee	752007	80	Ted Tryba	303399
31	Billy Andrade	665602	81	Brad Bryant	295365
32	Phil Blackmar	642400	82	Peter Jacobsen	294931
33	Tim Herron	640997	83	David Edwards	292096
34	Jeff Sluman	634203	84	David Sutherland	288663
35	Tom Kite	631252	85	Mark Wiebe	285139
36	David Ogrin	593683	86	Robert Gamez	283434
37	Colin Montgomerie	578991	87	Darren Clarke	282816
38	Fred Funk	544419	88	Jim Carter	279834
39	Kirk Triplett	541023	89	Gabriel Hjerstedt	279624
40	Payne Stewart	538289	90	Kenny Perry	270081
41	Craig Stadler	525304	91	Billy Ray Brown	268709
42	Tom Byrum	525161	92	Kelly Gibson	267230
43	Bob Tway	507523	93	Paul Azinger	262045
44	Steve Lowery	480467	94	Olin Browne	261810
45	Tom Watson	479146	95	Steve Pate	261436
46	Russ Cochran	470929	96	Phil Tataurangi	256930
47	Michael Bradley	465887	97	Clarence Rose	256481
48	Chris Perry	460984	98	Glen Day	248323
49	David Toms	460355	99	Larry Mize	246773
50	David Frost	458700	100	Joe Durant	240936

Tour Results *(in chronological order)*

Mercedes Championship
at La Costa, Carlsbad, California

1	Tiger Woods*	70-67-65—202	$216000
2	Tom Lehman	66-67-69—202	129600
3	Guy Boros	69-68-70—207	81600

(Weather curtailed tournament)

Bob Hope Chrysler Classic
at Indian Wells, California

1	John Cook	66-69-67-62-63—327	$270000
2	Mark Calcavecchia	64-67-66-64-67—328	162000
3	Jesper Parnevik	66-70-68-66-62—332	102000

Phoenix Open
at Scottsdale, Arizona

1	Steve Jones	62-64-65-67—258	$270000
2	Jesper Parnevik	66-66-70-67—269	162000
3	Nick Price	64-72-65-69—270	102000

AT&T Pebble Beach National Pro-Am
at Pebble Beach, California

1	Mark O'Meara	67-67-67-67—268	$342000
2	David Duval	65-71-62-71—269	167200
	Tiger Woods	70-72-63-64—269	167200

Buick Invitational
at Torrey Pines, La Jolla, California

1	Mark O'Meara	67-66-71-71—275	$270000
2	David Ogrin	67-71-70-69—277	78107
	Duffy Waldorf	70-66-72-69—277	78107
	Donnie Hammond	73-67-68-69—277	78107
	Lee Janzen	71-65-71-70—277	78107
	Jesper Parnevik	70-66-69-72—277	78107
	Craig Stadler	67-68-70-72—277	78107
	Mike Hulbert	68-69-67-73—277	78107

United Airlines Hawaiian Open
at Waialae, Honolulu

1	Paul Stankowski*	71-66-64-70—271	$216000
2	Jim Furyk	70-67-66-68—271	105600
	Mike Reid	62-72-66-71—271	105600

---

* *Winner after play-off*

Tucson Chrysler Classic
at Tucson National, Tucson, Arizona

1	Jeff Sluman	75-68-65-67—275	$234000
2	Steve Jones	66-68-72-70—276	140400
3	Brad Bryant	68-69-67-73—277	75400
	Paul Stankowski	72-65-69-71—277	75400

Nissan Open
at Riviera, Pacific Palisades, California

1	Nick Faldo	66-70-68-68—272	$252000
2	Craig Stadler	71-66-68-70—275	151200
3	Scott Hoch	65-71-71-69—276	95200

Doral-Ryder Open
at Doral, Miami, Florida

1	Steve Elkington	70-66-70-69—275	$324000
2	Larry Nelson	72-66-69-70—277	158400
	Nick Price	68-67-70-72—277	158400

Honda Classic
at TPC at Heron Bay, Coral Springs, Florida

1	Stuart Appleby	68-68-67-71—274	$270000
2	Payne Stewart	68-68-68-71—275	132000
	Michael Bradley	69-65-73-68—275	132000

Bay Hill Invitational
at Bay Hill, Orlando, Florida

1	Phil Mickelson	72-65-70-65—272	$270000
2	Stuart Appleby	73-63-70-69—275	162000
3	Mark O'Meara	72-66-68-70—276	78000
	Payne Stewart	69-70-70-67—276	78000
	Omar Uresti	69-67-69-71—276	78000

The Players' Championship
at TPC at Sawgrass, Ponte Vedra Beach, Florida

1	Steve Elkington	66-69-68-69—272	$630000
2	Scott Hoch	69-71-65-74—279	378000
3	Loren Roberts	70-74-67-69—280	238000
4	Brad Faxon	70-69-72-70—281	168000

Freeport-McDermott Classic
at English Turn, New Orleans, Louisiana

1	Brad Faxon	68-69-66-69—272	$270000
2	Bill Glasson	71-72-66-66—275	132000
	Jesper Parnevik	72-69-68-66—275	132000

MCI Classic
at Harbour Town, Hilton Head, South Carolina

1	Nick Price	65-69-69-66—269	$270000
2	Brad Faxon	66-69-70-70—275	132000
	Jesper Parnevik	72-71-66-66—275	132000

Greater Greensboro Chrysler Classic
at Forest Oaks, Greensboro, North Carolina

1	Frank Nobilo*	69-69-69-67—274	$342000
2	Brad Faxon	67-70-65-72—274	205200
3	Kirk Triplett	67-69-69-70—275	129200

Shell Houston Open
at TPC at The Woodlands, Houston, Texas

1	Phil Blackmar*	68-71-67-70—276	$288000
2	Kevin Sutherland	68-72-66-70—276	172800
3	Steve Elkington	69-74-70-65—278	108800

BellSouth Classic
at TPC at Sugarloaf, Duluth, Georgia

1	Scott McCarron	70-69-66-69—274	$270000
2	David Duval	66-66-73-72—277	112000
	Brian Henninger	70-71-68-68—277	112000
	Lee Janzen	69-70-70-68—277	112000

GTE Byron Nelson Classic
at TPC at Las Colinas, Cottonwood Valley, Irving, Texas

1	Tiger Woods	64-64-67-68—263	$324000
2	Lee Rinker	65-63-69-68—265	194400
	Dan Forsman	67-64-66-70—267	104400
	Tom Watson	65-66-69-72—267	104400

Mastercard Colonial
at Colonial, Fort Worth, Texas

1	David Frost	66-63-69-67—265	$288000
2	Brad Faxon	63-66-70-68—267	140800
	David Ogrin	66-67-62-67—267	140800

Memorial Tournament
at Muirfield Village, Dublin, Ohio

1	Vijay Singh	70-65-67—202	$342000
2	Jim Furyk	71-66-67—204	167200
	Greg Norman	71-69-64—204	167200

(Weather curtailed tournament)

---

* Winner after play-off

Kemper Open
at TPC at Avenel, Potomac, Maryland

1	Justin Leonard	69-69-69-67—274	$270000
2	Mark Wiebe	69-67-66-73—275	162000
3	Nick Faldo	73-65-68-71—277	72000
	Greg Norman	66-71-73-67—277	72000
	Nick Price	66-72-72-67—277	72000
	Mike Springer	68-70-67-72—277	72000

Buick Classic
at Westchester, Harrison, New York

1	Ernie Els	64-68-67-69—268	$270000
2	Jeff Maggert	67-69-66-68—270	162000
3	Robert Damron	71-66-68-69—274	87000
	Jim Furyk	67-68-69-70—274	87000

Fedex St Jude Classic
at TPC at Southwind, Memphis, Tennessee

1	Greg Norman	68-65-69-66—268	$270000
2	Dudley Hart	69-68-66-66—269	162000
3	Robert Damron	65-66-69-70—270	87000
	Craig Parry	69-69-66-66—270	87000

Motorola Western Open
at Cog Hill, Lemont, Illinois

1	Tiger Woods	67-72-68-68—275	$360000
2	Frank Nobilo	71-70-67-70—278	216000
3	Justin Leonard	71-64-72-72—279	104000
	Steve Lowery	70-72-66-71—279	104000
	Jeff Sluman	69-69-74-67—279	104000

Quad City Classic
at Oakwood, Coal Valley, Illinois

1	David Toms	67-66-67-65—265	$243000
2	Brandel Chamblee	71-65-65-67—268	100800
	Robert Gamez	67-65-69-67—268	100800
	Jimmy Johnston	70-67-69-62—268	100800

Deposit Guaranty Golf Classic
at Annandale, Madison, Mississippi

1	Billy Ray Brown	69-66-69-67—271	$180000
2	Mike Standly	69-67-70-66—272	108000
3	Mike Brisky	64-74-67-68—273	68000

Canon Greater Hartford Open
at TPC at River Highlands, Cromwell, Connecticut

1	Stewart Cink	69-67-65-66—267	$270000
2	Tom Byrum	66-68-65-69—268	112000
	Brandel Chamblee	68-65-69-66—268	112000
	Jeff Maggert	67-66-64-71—268	112000

Sprint International
at Castle Pines, Castle Rock, Colorado

Event used modified Stableford System

1	Phil Mickelson	14-13-12-9—48 pts	$306000
2	Stuart Appleby	9-10-13-9—41	183600
3	Skip Kendall	10-12-12-4—38	115600

Buick Open
at Warwick Hills, Grand Blanc, Michigan

1	Vijay Singh	67-73-67-66—273	$270000
2	Tom Byrum	72-68-70-67—277	83375
	Russ Cochran	68-69-73-67—277	83375
	Ernie Els	68-63-72-74—277	83375
	Brad Fabel	69-67-70-71—277	83375
	Joe Ozaki	67-71-70-69—277	83375
	Curtis Strange	72-66-68-71—277	83375

NEC World Series of Golf
at Firestone, Akron, Ohio

1	Greg Norman	68-68-70-67—273	$396000
2	Phil Mickelson	67-72-66-72—277	237600
3	John Cook	68-69-67-74—278	114400
	Fred Funk	70-69-71-68—278	114400
	Tiger Woods	67-72-69-70—278	114400

Greater Vancouver Open
at Northview, Surrey, British Columbia, Canada

1	Mark Calcavecchia	68-66-65-66—265	$270000
2	Andrew Magee	65-71-65-65—266	162000
3	Bob Estes	66-67-69-65—267	102000

Greater Milwaukee Open
at Brown Deer Park, Milwaukee, Wisconsin

1	Scott Hoch	70-66-66-66—268	$234000
2	Loren Roberts	67-69-67-66—269	114400
	David Sutherland	70-65-65-69—269	114400

Bell Canadian Open
at Royal Montreal, Ile Bizard, Quebec

1	Steve Jones	71-68-67-69—275	$270000
2	Greg Norman	66-72-69-69—276	162000
3	Phil Tataurangi	69-67-72-69—277	102000

CVS Charity Classic
at Pleasant Valley, Sutton, Massachusetts

1	Loren Roberts	67-67-68-64—266	$216000
2	Bill Glasson	66-67-67-67—267	129600
3	Peter Jacobsen	68-65-70-65—268	81600

LaCantera Texas Open
at LaCantera, San Antonio, Texas

1	Tim Herron	71-67-64-69—271	$252000
2	Rick Fehr	70-67-66-70—273	123200
	Brent Geiberger	67-72-69-65—273	123200

BC Open
at En-Joie, Endicott, New York

1	Gabriel Hjerstedt	70-69-66-70—275	$234000
2	Chris Perry	69-69-69-69—276	97066
	Lee Rinker	70-68-72-66—276	97066
	Andrew Magee	67-70-69-70—276	97066

Buick Challenge
at Callaway Gardens, Pine Mountain, Georgia

1	Davis Love III	67-65-67-68—267	$216000
2	Stewart Cink	70-64-67-70—271	129600
3	Steve Lowery	69-71-72-60—272	69600
	Hal Sutton	67-65-74-66—272	69600

Michelob Championship
at Kingsmill, Williamsburg, Virginia

1	David Duval*	67-66-71-67—271	$279000
2	Duffy Waldorf	63-69-69-70—271	136400
	Grant Waite	69-67-68-67—271	136400

Walt Disney World/Oldsmobile Classic
at Lake Buena Vista, Florida

1	David Duval*	65-70-65-70—270	$270000
2	Dan Forsman	67-69-65-69—270	162000
3	Len Mattiace	67-66-65-74—272	87000
	Ted Tryba	67-68-68-69—272	87000

Las Vegas Invitational
at TPC at Summerlin, Las Vegas, Nevada

1	Bill Glasson	63-65-75-71-66—340	$324000
2	David Edwards	68-66-69-72-66—341	158400
	Billy Mayfair	65-63-73-73-67—341	158400

Tour Championship
at Champions GC, Houston, Texas

1	David Duval	66-69-70-68—273	$720000
2	Jim Furyk	66-68-73-67—274	432000
3	Davis Love III	68-68-69-70—275	276000

★ *Winner after play-off*

Official Tour Statistics, 1997

Driving Distance
(Average yards per drive)

		Yds
1	John Daly	302.0
2	Tiger Woods	294.8
3	Bill Glasson	287.5
4	Davis Love III	285.8
5	Phil Mickelson	284.1
	Chip Sullivan	284.1
7	Scott McCarron	283.8
8	Fred Couples	283.5

Total Driving
(Distance and accuracy)

1	Joe Durant
2	Hal Sutton
3	Grant Waite
4	Kenny Perry
5	Tom Byrum
6	Bill Glasson
7	Tom Lehman
8	Rocco Mediate

Greens in Regulation
(Percentage in par or better)

		%
1	Tom Lehman	72.7
2	John Cook	71.1
3	Hal Sutton	70.9
4	Bill Glasson	70.3
	Tiger Woods	70.3
6	Mark Calcavecchia	70.1
	Bob Tway	70.1
	Fuzzy Zoeller	70.1

Driving Accuracy
(Percentage in fairway)

		%
1	Allen Doyle	80.0
2	Fred Funk	79.8
3	Larry Mize	79.5
4	Nick Price	79.3
5	Jim Furyk	79.2
6	Nick Faldo	78.7
7	David Edwards	78.2
8	Loren Roberts	77.7

Putting Leaders
(Average number per green reached in regulation)

		Avg
1	Don Pooley	1.718
2	Lee Janzen	1.726
3	Loren Roberts	1.734
4	Brad Faxon	1.736
5	Mark O'Meara	1.742
6	Jim Furyk	1.743
7	Mike Brisky	1.745
8	Phil Blackmar	1.747

Sand Saves
(Percentage from greenside bunkers)

		%
1	Bob Estes	70.3
2	Ronnie Black	66.3
3	Frank Nobilo	64.6
4	Jay Haas	64.5
5	Stuart Appleby	64.2
6	Kevin Sutherland	63.8
	John Morse	63.8
8	Willie Wood	62.6

All-Around
(Best overall performance in all categoreies)

1	Bill Glasson
2	Tom Byrum
3	Greg Norman
4	Tom Lehman
5	Mark Calcavecchia
6	Scott Hoch
7	Tiger Woods
8	Jay Haas

US Senior PGA Tour, 1997

Money List

Pos	Name	Prize Money $	Pos	Name	Prize Money $
1	Hale Irwin	2343364	26	Hubert Green	556402
2	Gil Morgan	2160562	27	Jim Colbert	556000
3	Isao Aoki	1410499	28	Bob Duval	555601
4	Jay Sigel	1294838	29	Bud Allin	535064
5	David Graham	1173579	30	Frank Conner	528346
6	John Bland	1169707	31	Jimmy Powell	518576
7	Graham Marsh	1128578	32	Bob Dickson	480521
8	Hugh Baiocchi	906565	33	JC Snead	476149
9	Larry Gilbert	902816	34	Gibby Gilbert	440533
10	Dave Stockton	854611	35	Kermit Zarley	429442
11	Bob Eastwood	838908	36	Dana Quigley	427774
12	John Jacobs	802942	37	George Archer	407605
13	Dave Eichelberger	794322	38	Dewitt Weaver	395232
14	Bruce Summerhays	776804	39	Bruce Crampton	390287
15	Lee Trevino	733912	40	Leonard Thompson	384806
16	Jack Kiefer	732735	41	Mike McCullough	373282
17	Vicente Fernandez	689915	42	Chi Chi Rodriguez	372359
18	Walter Morgan	687676	43	Dale Douglass	366803
19	Bob Murphy	685611	44	Brian Barnes	354886
20	Mike Hill	678640	45	John D Morgan	349302
21	Bob Charles	623467	46	John Schroeder	345233
22	Jim Dent	590646	47	Simon Hobday	327085
23	Ray Floyd	584755	48	Terry Dill	325522
24	Tom Wargo	567419	49	Larry Nelson	312457
25	Jerry McGee	562794	50	Bobby Stroble	311970

Tour Results *(in chronological order)*

Mastercard Challenge
at Hualalai Resort, Kailua-Kona, Hawaii

1	Hale Irwin	73-68-68—209	$186000
2	Gil Morgan	72-69-70—211	110000
3	Bob Charles	74-69-69—214	90000

Royal Caribbean Classic
at Crandon Park, Key Biscayne, Florida

1	Gibby Gilbert	70-66-66—202	$127500
2	David Graham	71-67-68—206	74800
3	Isao Aoki	71-67-69—207	56100
	John Schroeder	71-69-67—207	56100

LG Championship
at Bay Colony, Naples, Florida

1	Hale Irwin	70-66-65—201	$150000
2	Bob Murphy	68-69-65—202	88000

GTE Classic
at TPC of Tampa Bay, Lutz, Florida

1	David Graham	71-68-65—204	$135000
2	Bob Dickson	69-71-67—207	79200
3	Ray Floyd	72-66-70—208	54000
	Hubert Green	69-73-66—208	54000
	Bruce Summerhays	73-68-67—208	54000

American Express Invitational
at TPC at Prestancia, Sarasota, Florida

1	Bud Allin	68-68-69—205	$180000
2	Jim Colbert	68-71-67—206	105600
3	Bruce Summerhays	71-70-67—208	72000
	Jim Albus	69-70-69—208	72000
	Mike Hill	73-66-69—208	72000

Toshiba Senior Classic
at Newport Beach, California

1	Bob Murphy*	65-70-72—207	$150000
2	Jay Sigel	69-68-70—207	88000
3	Isao Aoki	68-71-69—208	60000
	Gil Morgan	69-69-70—208	60000
	Bob Charles	68-68-72—208	60000

Liberty Mutual Legends of Golf
at PGA West, La Quinta, California

1	J Bland and G Marsh	63-64-65—192	$200000
2	H Green and G Morgan	65-63-67—195	100000
3	T Wargo and C Peete	67-64-65—196	58333
	T Jacklin and D Graham	67-64-65—196	58333
	G Gilbert and JC Snead	65-63-68—196	58333

Southwestern Bell Dominion
at Dominion, San Antonio, Texas

1	David Graham	68-69-69—206	120000
2	John Jacobs	67-71-69—207	70400
3	John Bland	70-71-67—208	52800
	Ray Floyd	73-66-69—208	52800

The Tradition
at Desert Mountain, Scottsdale, Arizona

1	Gil Morgan	66-66-67-67—266	$180000
2	Isao Aoki	66-68-70-68—272	105600
3	John Jacobs	66-68-70-70—274	86400

* *Winner after play-off*

PGA Seniors Championship
at PGA National, Palm Beach Gardens, Florida

1	Hale Irwin	69-65-72-68—274	$216000
2	Jack Nicklaus	71-72-73-70—286	105000
	Dale Douglass	70-76-71-69—286	105000

Las Vegas Senior Classic
at TPC at The Canyons, Las Vegas, Nevada

1	Hale Irwin	70-65-72—207	$150000
2	Isao Aoki	66-71-71—208	89000
3	Jim Colbert	72-66-73—211	66900
	John Jacobs	70-67-74—211	66900

Bruno's Memorial Classic
at Greystone, Birmingham, Alabama

1	Jay Sigel	68-67-70—205	$172500
2	Gil Morgan	67-72-69—208	101200
3	Isao Aoki	69-71-70—210	82800

Home Depot Invitational
at TPC at Piper Glen, Charlotte, North Carolina

1	Jim Dent*	68-70-70—208	$135000
2	Larry Gilbert	68-70-70—208	72000
	Lee Trevino	70-71-67—208	72000

Cadillac NFL Classic
at Upper Montclair, Clifton, New Jersey

1	Bruce Crampton*	76-67-67—210	$142500
2	Hugh Baiocchi	71-70-69—210	83600
3	Dave Stockton	74-67-71—212	68400

Bell Atlantic Classic
at Chester Valley, Malvern, Pennsylvania

1	Bob Eastwood	66-69—135	$150000
2	John Bland	67-69—136	80000
	Bob E Smith	69-67—136	80000

(Weather curtailed tournament)

Ameritech Senior Open
at Kemper Lakes, Long Grove, Illinois

1	Gil Morgan	67-69-74—210	$180000
2	Hale Irwin	71-66-74—211	105600
3	Bob Eastwood	70-71-71—212	86400

★ Winner after play-off

BellSouth Classic
at Springhouse, Nashville, Tennessee

1	Gil Morgan	69-66-67—202	$195000
2	John Bland	69-67-68—204	114400
3	Larry Gilbert	70-68-68—206	93600

Du Maurier Champions
at St George's, Etobicoke, Ontario, Canada

1	Jack Kiefer	65-67-69-68—269	$165000
2	Jim Colbert	65-65-70-71—271	96800
3	Graham Marsh	65-66-70-72—273	79200

Nationwide Championship
at GC of Georgia, Alpharetta, Georgia

1	Graham Marsh	67-68-70—205	$195000
2	Hale Irwin	68-69-69—206	114400
3	David Graham	68-72-69—209	93600

US Senior Open
at Olympia Fields, Illinois

1	Graham Marsh	72-67-67-74—280	$232500
2	John Bland	69-70-69-73—281	137500
3	Gil Morgan	69-74-71-68—282	73320
	Tom Wargo	69-70-73-70—282	73320

Kroger Senior Classic
at Kings Island, Mason, Ohio

1	Jay Sigel	66-63-66—195	$150000
2	Isao Aoki	68-67-67—202	88000
3	Larry Gilbert	68-66-70—204	60000
	John Jacobs	68-71-65—204	60000
	David Ojala	65-68-71—204	60000

Ford Players Championship
at TPC of Michigan, Dearborn, Michigan

1	Larry Gilbert	67-68-72-67—274	$270000
2	Isao Aoki	70-68-71-68—277	120600
	Bob Dickson	72-66-69-70—277	120600
	Jack Kiefer	72-70-67-68—277	120600
	Dave Stockton	68-70-69-70—277	120600

Burnet Senior Classic
at Bunker Hills, Coon Rapids, Minnesota

1	Hale Irwin	65-68-66—199	$202500
2	Lee Trevino	66-68-67—201	118800
3	Larry Gilbert	65-71-68—204	97200

Franklin Quest Championship
at Park Meadows, Park City, Utah

1	Dave Stockton	69-64-68—201	$150000
2	Kermit Zarley	67-69-67—203	88000
3	Hugh Baiocchi	67-71-66—204	66000
	Larry Ziegler	70-70-64—204	66000

Bank Boston Classic
at Nashawtuc, Concord, Massachussetts

1	Hale Irwin	69-67-67—203	$150000
2	Jerry McGee	68-70-67—205	80000
	Bob Wynn	71-68-66—205	80000

Northville Long Island Classic
at Meadow Brook, Jericho, New York

1	Dana Quigley*	67-67-70—204	$150000
2	Jay Sigel	68-70-66—204	88000
3	José Maria Canizares	64-70-71—205	60000
	Ray Floyd	70-69-66—205	60000
	Hubert Green	65-70-70—205	60000

First of America Classic
at Egypt Valley, Ada, Michigan

1	Gil Morgan	69-67-71—207	$150000
2	Bob Duval	68-70-70—208	88000
3	John D Morgan	68-73-69—210	72000

Saint Luke's Classic
at Loch Lloyd, Belton, Missouri

1	Bruce Summerhays*	63-71-65—199	$150000
2	Hugh Baiocchi	63-65-71—199	88000
3	Dave Stockton	68-68-64—200	72000

Pittsburgh Senior Classic
at Midway, Pennsylvania

1	Hugh Baiocchi*	70-70-66—206	$165000
2	Bob Duval	68-68-70—206	96800
3	Walter Morgan	69-72-66—207	79200

Bank One Classic
at Kearney Hill Links, Lexington, Kentucky

1	Vicente Fernandez	67-69-67—203	$120000
2	Isao Aoki	72-65-67—204	70400
3	Walter H Hall	66-71-68—205	52800
	Buddy Whitten	72-67-66—205	52800

* *Winner after play-off*

Boone Valley Classic
at Boone Valley, Augusta, Missouri

1	Hale Irwin	70-65-65—200	$195000
2	Gil Morgan	70-67-65—202	114400
3	John Bland	69-68-68—205	93600

Comfort Classic
at Brickyard Crossing, Indianopolis, Indiana

1	David Graham	67-68-65—200	$157500
2	Bud Allin	70-65-66—201	84000
	Larry Nelson	69-65-67—201	84000

Emerald Coast Classic
at The Moors, Milton, Florida

1	Isao Aoki*	71-60-65—196	$165000
2	Gil Morgan	64-68-64—196	96800
3	Bob Duval	66-66-68—200	60500
	Simon Hobday	67-63-70—200	60500
	Hale Irwin	65-66-69—200	60500
	Jay Sigel	69-66-65—200	60500

Vantage Championship
at Tanglewood Park, Clemmons, North Carolina

1	Hale Irwin	64-62-69—195	$225000
2	Dave Eichelberger	66-68-62—196	132000
3	Larry Nelson	66-65-69—200	108000

The Transamerica
at Silverado, Napa, California

1	Dave Eichelberger	67-68-70—205	$120000
2	Frank Conner	72-70-67—209	53600
	Terry Dill	68-70-71—209	53600
	John Jacobs	67-70-72—209	53600
	DeWitt Weaver	69-67-73—209	53600

Hyatt Maui Kaanapali Classic
at Kaanapali, Hawaii

1	Hale Irwin	67-63-70—200	$127500
2	Mike Hill	70-64-69—203	68000
	Bruce Summerhays	64-65-74—203	68000

Raley's Gold Rush
at Serrano, El Dorado Hills, California

1	Bob Eastwood	67-69-68—204	$135000
2	Rick Acton	73-65-68—206	79200
3	Jim Dent	69-69-70—208	59400
	John Jacobs	71-70-67—208	59400

Ralph's Senior Classic
at Wilshire, Los Angeles, California

1	Gil Morgan	67-66-65—198	$150000
2	George Archer	67-68-64—199	88000
3	Jimmy Powell	68-67-68—203	72000

Energizer Senior Tour Championship
at The Dunes, Myrtle Beach, South Carolina

1	Gil Morgan	69-66-66-71—272	$328000
2	Hale Irwin	68-67-68-71—274	187000
3	Isao Aoki	70-69-73-67—279	154000

Official Tour Statistics, 1997

Driving Distance
(Average yards per drive)

		Yds
1	John Jacobs	290.7
2	Terry Dill	286.6
3	Jay Sigel	285.3
4	Gil Morgan	281.8
5	Bob Duval	278.6
6	David Graham	278.4
7	Ray Floyd	278.3
8	Dan Wood	276.3
9	DeWitt Weaver	275.4

Greens in Regulation
(Percentage in par or better)

		%
1	Hale Irwin	76.2
2	Gil Morgan	74.1
3	Jay Sigel	73.3
4	Hugh Baiocchi	72.2
5	John Bland	72.0
6	David Graham	70.0
7	Brian Barnes	69.5
8	Isao Aoki	69.4
9	Bob Charles	69.1
	Vicente Fernandez	69.1

Putting Leaders
(Average number per green reached in regulation)

		Avg
1	Hale Irwin	1.734
2	Gil Morgan	1.746
3	Graham Marsh	1.756
4	Dave Stockton	1.762
5	Isao Aoki	1.763
6	Frank Conner	1.764
7	Ray Floyd	1.768
8	Lee Trevino	1.772

Driving Accuracy
(Percentage in fairway)

		%
1	John Bland	81.0
2	Calvin Peete	78.9
3	Bob Murphy	76.9
	Bob E Smith	76.9
	David Oakley	76.9
6	Hubert Green	76.7
7	Hale Irwin	76.5
8	Chi Chi Rodriguez	75.6
9	Walter Zembriski	75.0
10	David Ojala	74.9

Sand Saves
(Percentage from greenside bunkers)

		%
1	Isao Aoki	64.7
2	John Schroeder	61.7
3	Jerry McGee	59.1
4	Bob Eastwood	59.0
5	Homero Blancas	58.8
6	Don January	56.8
7	Jimmy Powell	56.5
8	John Bland	56.1
9	Simon Hobday	55.5
10	Bob Duval	55.2

Scoring Average

		Avg
1	Hale Irwin	68.92
2	Gil Morgan	69.29
3	Isao Aoki	70.03
4	Jay Sigel	70.37
5	John Bland	70.39
6	David Graham	70.40
7	Graham Marsh	70.47
8	Hugh Baiocchi	70.66
9	Larry Gilbert	70.71
10	Dave Stockton	70.78

Omega Asian Tour, 1997

Tour Results

Tournament	Winner	Score	Prize Money US$
Qualifying School, Malaysia	Jim Rutledge (Can)	277 (−11)	—
Asian Honda Classic, Thailand	Tiger Woods (US)	268 (−20)	48450
Vietnam Open	Andrew Bonhomme (Aus)	273 (−15)	32300
London Myanmar Open	Boonchu Ruangkit (Thai)	273 (−15)	32300
DFS Galleria Guam Open	Gerry Norquist (US)	210 (−6)	40372
Satelindo Indonesian Open	Craig Parry (Aus)	280 (−8)	44412
Volvo China Open	Cheng Jun (PRC)	280 (−8)	72000
Sabah Masters, Malaysia	Des Terblanche (SA)	281 (−7)	32300
SingTel Ericsson Singapore Open	Zaw Moe (Malay)	277 (−11)	80750
Philip Morris Asia Cup, Korea	Park No-Soek (Kor)	279 (−9)	80750
Asia Pacific Ericsson, Indonesia	Darren Cole (Aus)	275 (−13)	80750
Mild Seven KL Open, Malaysia	Charlie Wi (Kor)	277 (−11)	48450
Yokohama Singapore PGA	Prayad Marksaeng (Thai)	277 (−11)	32300
ABN-AMRO Pakistan	Thammanoon Sriroj (Thai)	274 (−14)	32300
Dubai Creek Open	Adrian Percey (Aus)	272 (−16)	40375
Hero Honda Masters, India	Ted Purdy (US)	277 (−11)	32300
Ta Shee Open Championship Taiwan	Wang Ter-chang (Tai)	282 (−6)	40375
Volvo Masters, Malaysia	Christian Pena (US)	276 (−12)	32300
Lexus International, Thailand	Prayad Marksaeng (Thai)	270 (−18)	32300
Tugu Pratama PGA Chp, Indonesia	Clay Devers (US)	276 (−12)	48450
Andersen Consulting Hong Kong Open	Frank Nobilo (NZ)	267 (−17)	58345
Omega PGA Chp, Hong Kong	Rodrigo Cuello (Phi)	270 (−10)	80750
Volvo Asian Matchplay	Des Terblanche (SA)	2 up	40375

Final Order of Merit

Pos	Name	Prize Money $	Events played	Pos	Name	Prize Money $	Events played
1	Mike Cunning (USA)	170619	17	11	Rodrigo Cuello (Phi)	97260	9
2	Prayad Marksaeng (Thai)	123806	16	12	Adrian Percey (Aus)	97238	14
3	Lu Wen-teh (Tai)	114716	12	13	Thammanoon Sriroj (Thai)	89068	15
4	Ted Purdy (USA)	111574	14	14	Cheng Jun (PRC)	86773	9
5	Jeev Milkha Singh (Ind)	110841	14	15	Fran Quinn (USA)	84828	8
6	Gerry Norquist (USA)	110436	14	16	Kang Wook-soon (Kor)	82594	11
7	Jim Rutledge (Can)	105898	12	17	Charlie Wi (Kor)	81711	13
8	Des Terblanche (SA)	100972	9	18	Mo Joong-kyung (Kor)	80210	18
9	Craig Kamps (SA)	100508	20	19	Boonchu Ruangkit (Thai)	80053	12
10	Clay Devers (USA)	98600	13	20	Chang Tse-peng (Tai)	77945	19

Australasian Tour, 1997

Tour Results

Australian Masters
at Huntingdale GC, Melbourne

1	B Hughes	63-72-66-67—268	Aus$142102
2	M Goggin	66-68-68-71—273	80527
3	R Gibson	69-67-71-68—275	45592
	F Nobilo	70-68-70-67—275	45592

Australian Open
at Metropolitan GC, Melbourne

1	L Westwood*	68-66-68-72—274	Aus$189470
2	G Norman	68-67-66-73—274	107370
3	C Parry	70-70-70-65—275	71050

New Zealand Open
at Auckland GC, Auckland

1	G Turner	69-69-71-69—278	NZ$94730
2	J-L Guepy	76-67-75-67—285	38158
	A Coltart	71-70-75-69—285	38158
	L Parsons	72-65-73-75—285	38158

Other Tournaments

Tournament	Winner	Score	Prize Money US$
Asia Pacific Masters	Darren Cole	72-64-68-71—275	86750
Australian PGA Championship	Andrew Coltart	72-71-66-76—285	94735
Tournament Players Championship	Greg Chalmers	71-70-67-68—276	142102
Coolum Classic	Craig Parry	70-68-71-67—276	52100
Victorian Open	Bradley King	68-65-67-72—272	37890
Johnnie Walker Classic	Tiger Woods	72-71-71-65—279	133330
Heineken Classic	Thomas Bjørn	70-68-68-74—280	£108935
Greg Norman International	Greg Norman	68-73-64-67—272	189470
Canon Challenge	Peter O'Malley	63-73-64-71—271	94736
ANZ Tour Championship	Matthew Goggin	66-68-71-73—278	94736

---

* *Winner after play-off*

Final Order of Merit

Pos	Player	Prize Money $
1	Andrew Coltart	316107
2	Peter O'Malley	264533
3	Greg Chalmers	263926
4	Matthew Goggin	220417
5	Robert Allenby	213234
6	Peter Lonard	210433
7	Stuart Appleby	178612
8	Bradley Hughes	170525
9	Craig Parry	161881
10	Bradley King	145814
11	Darren Cole	136263
12	Stephen Leaney	129311
13	Lucas Parsons	116482
14	Shane Tait	109321
15	Scott Laycock	106838
16	Paul Gow	103219
17	Paul Devenport	101622
18	Jean-Louis Guepy	100242
19	Jeev Singh	96390
20	Nicholas O'Hern	87073
21	Kenny Druce	86199
22	Stephen Allan	85293
23	Michael Long	84420
24	Peter Senior	81463
25	Rick Gibson	72450

Japan Tour, 1997

Tour Results

Tournament	Winner	Score	Total prize fund ¥
Token Corporation Cup	Masashi Ozaki	269 (–19)	100,000,000
Dydo Drinco Shizuoka Open	Hisayuki Sasaki	274 (–14)	100,000,000
JustSystem KSB Open	Kenchiro Fukabori	276 (–12)	70,000,000
Descente Classic Munsingwear Cup	Peter Teravainen	270 (–14)	100,000,000
Tsuruya Open	Mitsuo Harada	279 (–9)	100,000,000
Asian Tour Kirin Open	Jong-Duck Kim	278 (–10)	100,000,000
The Crowns	Masashi Ozaki	267 (–13)	120,000,000
Fuji–Sankei Classic	Kenichi Kuboya	279 (–5)	120,000,000
Japan PGA Championship	Shigeki Maruyama	272 (–16)	100,000,000
Ube-Kosan Open	Shigenori Mori	267 (–17)	100,000,000
Mitsubishi Galant	Masashi Ozaki	278 (–10)	120,000,000
JCB Classic Sendai	Nobuhito Sato	267 (–17)	100,000,000
Sapporo Tokyu Open	Hirofumi Miyase	275 (–13)	100,000,000
Yomiuri Open	Shigeki Maruyama	267 (–17)	100,000,000
Mizuno Open	Brian Watts	278 (–10)	100,000,000
PGA Philanthropy Tournament	Naomichi Ozaki	267 (–17)	100,000,000
Yonex Open Hiroshima	Naomichi Ozaki	276 (–12)	80,000,000
Nikkei Cup	Chang-Ting Yeh	272 (–16)	100,000,000
NST Niigata Open	Kazuhiko Hosokawa	277 (–11)	60,000,000
Sanko Grand Summer Championship	Shoichi Kuwabara	271 (–17)	100,000,000
Acom International (PGA Ch'p)	Kazuo Kanayama	41 pts	100,000,000
Hisamitsu-KBC Augusta	Masashi Ozaki	266 (–22)	100,000,000
PGA Matchplay Ch'p Promis Cup	Shigeki Maruyama		80,000,000
Suntory Open	Hiroyuki Fujita	274 (–14)	100,000,000
Ana Open	Shinichi Yokota	273 (–15)	100,000,000
Gene Sarazen Junior Classic	Eduardo Herrera	276 (–12)	110,000,000
Japan Open	Craig Parry	286 (+2)	120,000,000
Tokai Classic	Brandt Jobe	278 (–10)	110,000,000
Golf Digest Tournament	Brandt Jobe	267 (–17)	100,000,000
Bridgestone Open	Masashi Ozaki	273 (–15)	120,000,000
Philip Morris Championship	Brian Watts	280 (–8)	200,000,000
Sumitomo Visa Taiheiyo Masters	Lee Westwood	272 (–16)	150,000,000
Dunlop Phoenix	Tom Watson	275 (–9)	200,000,000
Casio World Open	Mitsutaka Kusakabe	278 (–10)	150,000,000
Golf Nippon Series	Shigeki Maruyama	268 (–16)	100,000,000
Daikyo Open	Kenichi Kuboya	263 (–21)	120,000,000

Final Order of Merit

Pos	Player	Prize Money ¥
1	Masashi Ozaki	170,847,633
2	Shigeki Naruyama	152,774,420
3	Brian Watts	111,153,198
4	Naomichi Ozaki	96,994,361
5	Tateo Ozaki	77,555,311
6	Brandt Jobe	69,759,886
7	Shoichi Kuwabara	60,883,113
8	Carlos Franco	56,321,628
9	Hirofumi Miyase	55,784,409
10	Frankie Minoza	54,192,571
11	Toru Suzuki	51,444,184
12	Kenchiro Fukabori	51,427,473
13	Eduardo Herrera	51,050,800
14	Kenichi Kuboya	50,740,771
15	Hajine Meshiai	44,547,120
16	Eiji Misoguchi	44,409,460
17	Tsukasa Watanabe	44,362,747
18	Hiroyuki Fujita	43,935,360
19	Mitsutaka Kusakabe	43,303,400
20	Shigemasa Higaki	42,539,160
21	Craig Parry	42,340,000
22	Mitsuo Harada	42,020,640
23	Peter Teravainen	39,921,168
24	Shinichi Yokota	39,038,496
25	Kakame Yokoo	38,027,502

South African PGA Tour, 1996/7

Tour Results

South African Open Championship
at Glendower, Johannesburg

1	Vijay Singh	69-66-66-69—270	R529300
2	Nick Price	72-66-65-68—271	385250
3	Ernie Els	66-72-67-70—275	178220
	Mark McNulty	69-69-68-69—275	178220
	Fulton Allem	66-71-71-67—275	178220

Other tournaments

Tournament	Winner	Score	Prize Money Rand
Zimbabwe Open	M McNulty	72-61-68-69—270	63200
San Lameer South African Masters	M McNulty	71-68-70-67—276	118500
Nashua Wild Coast Sun Challenge	M McNulty	66-68-70-66—270	118500
FNB Players Championship	W Schutte	69-71-69-65—274	118500
Dimension Data	N Price	67-66-66-69—268	458109
Alfred Dunhill PGA Championship	N Price	67-66-70-66—269	342827
Hollard Royal Swazi Sun Open	W Druian	70-64-65-70—269	79000

Final Order of Merit

Pos	Player	Prize Money Rand	Pos	Player	Prize Money Rand
1	Nick Price (Zim)	1223026	11	Chris Williams (SA)	157554
2	Mark McNulty (Zim)	619426	12	Marco Gortana (SA)	156339
3	Retief Goosen (SA)	301303	13	Clinton Whitelaw (SA)	151741
4	Nico van Rensburg (SA)	269289	14	Trevor Dodds (Nam)	144946
5	Wayne Westner (SA)	255810	15	Chris Davison (SA)	132402
6	Justin Hobday (SA)	219321	16	James Kingston (SA)	129639
7	Desvonde Botes (SA)	205982	17	Wayne Bradley (SA)	125855
8	Warren Schutte (SA)	194437	18	Bobby Lincoln (SA)	120673
9	Ronnie McCann (US)	180676	19	Ashley Roestoff (SA)	116088
10	Warrick Druian (SA)	174034	20	Adilson da Silva (Bra)	115440

South American PGA Tour, 1997

Tour Results

Tournament	Winner	Score	Prize Money $
World Nature Games	R Gonzalez	65-69-70-70—274	36000
Ecuador Open	G Rojas	71-67-70-69—277	18000
Peru Open	P Jonas	69-68-65-67—269	21600
Litoral Open	A Saavadra	66-69-65-66—266	21600
Argentine Masters	B Langer	73-69-68-67—277	30600
Los Leones Chile Open	G Rojas	69-67-67-69—272	16200
Prince of Wales Open	R Gonzalez	67-68-68-66—269	28000
Argentina Open	J Furyk	67-70-68-70—275	70000

Final Order of Merit

Pos	Player	Prize Money$
1	Ricardo Gonzalez (Arg)	97504
	Jim Furyk (USA)	70000
2	Gustavo Rojas (Arg)	43986
3	Tim Hegna (USA)	38578
4	Mathias Gronberg (Swe)	34021
	Angel Cabrera (Arg)	31625
	Bernhard Langer (Ger)	30600
	Cris Dimarco (USA)	29666
5	Danny Mijovic (Can)	26161
6	Ruben Alvarez (Arg)	24671
	Philip Jonas (Can)	23700
7	Raul Fretes (Par)	23228
8	Angel Franco (Par)	22982
9	Armando Saavadra (Arg)	22800
	Jorge Berendt (Arg)	22520
10	José Cantero	22232

NB Players without a position did not play in enough tournaments to gain official ranking.

1997 Ping Leaderboard World Ranking for Women's Professional Golf

Pos	Name	Nationality	Points
1	Annika Sorenstam	Swe	476.50
2	Karrie Webb	Aus	459.39
3	Laura Davies	Eng	337.68
4	Kelly Robbins	USA	330.84
5	Liselotte Neumann	Swe	224.00
6	Chris Johnson	USA	211.83
7	Michelle McGann	USA	177.48
8	Lisa Hackney	Eng	169.08
9	Dottie Pepper	USA	168.03
10	Juli Inkster	USA	167.99
11	Helen Alfredsson	Swe	166.61
12	Alison Nicholas	Eng	165.83
13	Tammie Green	USA	161.41
14	Nancy Lopez	USA	159.98
15	Jane Geddes	USA	155.47
16	Akiko Fukushima	Jpn	154.08
17	Marie Laure de Lorenzi	Fr	150.43
18	Trish Johnson	Eng	139.26
19	Rosie Jones	USA	132.23
20	Meg Mallon	USA	129.00
21	Donna Andrews	USA	123.73
22	Hiromi Kobayashi	Jpn	122.85
23	Betsy King	USA	117.83
24	Brandie Burton	USA	115.91
25	Pat Hurst	USA	114.50
26	Lorie Kane	USA	113.16
27	Barb Mucha	USA	105.47
28	Emilee Klein	USA	102.96
29	Terry-Jo Myers	USA	94.58
30	Tina Barrett	USA	94.45
31	Kris Tschetter	USA	90.45
32	Patty Sheehan	USA	89.27
33	Joanne Morley	Eng	89.02
34	Kaori Higo	Jpn	86.19
35	Kaori Harada	Jpn	85.89
36	Marnie McGuire	NZ	84.95
37	Deb Richard	USA	82.08
38	Karen Lunn	Aus	79.10
39	Colleen Walker	USA	78.92
40	Mayumi Murai	Jpn	77.63
41	Kathryn Marshall	Sco	76.64
42	Patricia Meunier Lebouc	Fr	76.41
43	Amy Fruhwirth	USA	75.00
44	Ikuyo Shiotani	Jpn	74.97
4	Kim Saiki	USA	74.25
46	Cindy Figg-Currier	USA	73.60
47	Penny Hammel	USA	71.50
48	Aki Takamura	Jpn	71.00
49	Shani Waugh	Aus	70.25
50	Michele Redman	USA	69.43

American Express Women's Professional Golf European Tour, 1997

Final Order of Merit

Pos	Name	Prize Money £	Pos	Name	Prize Money £
1	Alison Nicholas (Eng)	94589	51	Nadene Gole (Aus)	10751
2	Helen Alfredsson (Swe)	92927	52	Nicola Moult (Eng)	10545
3	Marie Laure de Lorenzi (Fr)	89523	53	Kirsty Taylor (Eng)	10523
4	Laura Davies (Eng)	77424	54	Johanna Head (Eng)	10510
5	Karen Lunn (Aus)	65142	55	Myra Murray (Sco)	10460
6	Patricia Meunier Lebouc (Fr)	52999	56	Samantha Head (Eng)	10214
7	Joanne Morley (Eng)	48217	57	Vibeke Stensrud (Nor)	10017
8	Anne-Marie Knight (Aus)	47135	58	Deni Booker (Aus)	9535
9	Trish Johnson (Eng)	45742	59	Sarah Carbon (GB)	9487
10	Maria Hjorth (Swe)	39536	60	Estefania Knuth (USA)	8947
11	Joanne Mills (Aus)	37037	61	Petra Rigby-Jinglov (Swe)	8813
12	Laurette Maritz (SA)	36280	62	Iben Tinning (Den)	8573
13	Lynnette Brooky (NZ)	35662	63	Mette Hageman (Neth)	8234
14	Lora Fairclough (Eng)	35606	64	Xonia Wunsch-Ruiz (Sp)	7963
15	Helen Wadsworth (Wal)	32799	65	Caryn Louw (SA)	7867
16	Loraine Lambert (Eng)	32727	66	Anna Radford (GB)	7392
17	Shani Waugh (Aus)	32645	67	Mia Lojdahl (Swe)	7328
18	Natascha Fink (Austria)	28294	68	Tracey Craik (Eng)	7278
19	Karina Orum (Den)	27421	69	Marlene Hedblom (Swe)	7260
20	Pernilla Sterner (Swe)	26502	70	Katharina Poppmeier (Ger)	7227
21	Mandy Sutton (Eng)	24025	71	Sara Forster (Eng)	7213
22	Asa Gottmo (Swe)	23915	72	Caroline Hall (Eng)	6998
23	Sally Prosser (Eng)	23870	73	Helene Koch (Swe)	6848
24	Susan Farron (NZ)	22583	74	Sandrine Mendiburu (Fr)	6470
25	Laura Navarro (Sp)	21945	75	Kristel Mourgue d'Algue (Fr)	6276
26	Valerie van Ryckegham (Bel)	20542	76	Nicola Murray (Eng)	6126
27	Wendy Dicks (Eng)	20350	77	Lara Tadiotto (Bel)	5441
28	Dale Reid (Sco)	20205	78	Marie-Josée Rouleau (Fr)	5410
29	Karen Pearce (Eng)	19542	79	Janet Soulsby (Eng)	5302
30	Anna Berg (Swe)	19333	80	Nicole Lowien (Aus)	5055
31	Corinne Dibnah (Aus)	19163	81	Claire Duffy (Eng)	4529
32	Jane Leary (Aus)	18898	82	Maureen Madill (Ire)	4395
33	Fiona Pike (Aus)	18642	83	Marina Arruti (Sp)	4318
34	Federica Dassu (It)	18616	84	Marie-Therese Pistolet-Boselli (Fr)	4284
35	Tina Fischer (Ger)	18437	85	Isabella Maconi (It)	4235
36	Anna-Carin Jonasson (Swe)	18023	86	Regine Lautens (Swi)	4221
37	Raquel Carriedo (Sp)	17798	87	Susan Elliott (Eng)	3950
38	Diane Barnard (Eng)	17075	88	Julie Castanier	3707
39	Julie Forbes (Eng)	16274	89	Susan Moon (US)	3368
40	Martina Koch (Swe)	15882	90	Karolina Anderson (Swe)	3301
41	Gillian Stewart (Sco)	15818	91	Lotte Greve (Den)	3257
42	Valerie Michaud (Fr)	15350	92	Mary Grace Estuesta (Phil)	3218
43	Barbara Pestana (SA)	14482	93	Charlotta Eliasson Wharton (Swe)	2815
44	Stephanie Dallongeville (Fr)	13716	94	Lisa Jensen (US)	2777
45	Sophie Gustafson (Swe)	13522	95	Katharina Larsson (Swe)	2702
46	Amaia Arruti (Sp)	13312	96	Emma-Jane Smith (Eng)	2614
47	Sara Melin (Swe)	12892	97	Lisa Educate (Eng)	2515
48	Catherine Schmitt (Ger)	12651	98	Sofie Eriksson (Swe)	2400
49	Patricia Gonzalez (Col)	12084	99	Sara Eklund (Swe)	2391
50	Debbie Dowling (Eng)	11587	100	Marika Preti (It)	2332

Tour Results *(in chronological order)*

Weetabix Women's British Open
at Sunningdale (Old), Sunningdale, Ascot

Pos	Name	Score	Prize Money £
1	K Webb	65-70-63-71—269	82500
2	R Jones	70-70-66-71—277	52000
3	A Sorenstam	72-70-69-67—278	36750
4	B Burton	73-69-71-67—280	27000
5	L Hackney	74-69-67-71—281	20000
	C Matthew	70-70-70-71—281	20000
7	W Doolan	74-70-68-70—282	14000
	T Barrett	70-72-70-70—282	14000
9	C Johnson	71-71-73-68—283	11500
10	C Sorenstam	71-70-72-71—284	10100
	B King	71-72-68-73—284	10100
12	J Lidback	71-74-70-70—285	7414
	M Hirase	76-65-74-70—285	7414
	L Neumann	68-75-71-71—285	7414
	J Inkster	69-71-73-72—285	7414
	B Mucha	72-67-73-73—285	7414
	H Dobson	73-69-69-74—285	7414
	K Marshall	70-68-73-74—285	7414
19	C Hj Koch	76-71-71-68—286	5837
	L Lambert	70-73-73-70—286	5837
	C Dibnah	72-71-70-73—286	5837
	A Dibos	71-72-70-73—286	5837
23	L Davies	74-73-69-71—287	5300
	R Hetherington	75-70-71-71—287	5300
	K Tschetter	73-70-72-72—287	5300
26	E Klein	69-74-70-75—288	5000
27	S Farron	72-75-75-67—289	4475
	B Whitehead	71-74-77-67—289	4475
	J Morley	75-69-76-69—289	4475
	L Brooky	72-73-72-72—289	4475
	H Alfredsson	69-76-72-72—289	4475
	J Moodie	74-71-71-73—289	4475
33	K Lunn	74-71-75-70—290	3875
	P Hurst	76-72-70-72—290	3875
	S Cavalleri (Am)	70-73-73-74—290	
36	S Maynor	72-74-74-71—291	3650
37	S Strudwick	72-74-74-72—292	3350
	D Richard	71-72-75-74—292	3350
	G Graham	73-73-71-75—292	3350
40	M Estill	74-74-76-69—293	3000
	S Steinhauer	72-76-73-72—293	3000
	K Parker-Gregory	75-73-70-75—293	3000
43	P Meunier Lebouc	76-72-78-68—294	2600
	A Gottmo	75-70-76-73—294	2600
	S Prosser	72-72-77-73—294	2600
	A Fruhwirth	75-69-76-74—294	2600
	S Waugh	73-72-73-76—294	2600
48	M Spencer-Devlin	71-74-80-70—295	2210
	H Kobayashi	75-73-74-73—295	2210
	F Dassu	76-69-77-73—295	2210
51	T Green	74-72-79-71—296	1990
	A Yamaoka	73-73-74-76—296	1990
	T Johnson	68-70-82-76—296	1990
	E Esterl (Am)	75-70-76-75—296	
55	S Croce	76-72-75-74—297	1745

Pos	Name	Score	Prize Money £
55T	C Pierce	73-75-75-74—297	1745
	J Lee	78-69-73-77—297	1745
	W Dicks	73-74-73-77—297	1745
59	M Koch	73-75-77-73—298	1428
	K Taylor	73-74-77-74—298	1428
	H Wadsworth	77-69-77-75—298	1428
	L Fairclough	73-72-78-75—298	1428
	L Kane	70-75-77-76—298	1428
	M Murray	74-74-71-79—298	1428
65	C Figg-Currier	75-72-75-77—299	1250
66	N Moult	74-70-83-74—301	1156
	D Barnard	74-74-78-75—301	1156
	S Gustafson	76-71-73-81—301	1156
69	S Dallongeville	71-77-76-78—302	1090

36-hole cut: 148, four over par. The following players missed the cut:

70	D Andrews	78-71—149	95	B Pestana	78-74—152		C Louw	74-81—155
	HF Tseng	76-73—149		K Harada	78-74—152	122	J Mills	86-70—156
	WS Ko	76-73—149		A Berg	78-74—152		M McGeorge	82-74—156
	A Nicholas	75-74—149		D Eggeling	77-75—152		N Gole	80-76—156
	I Shiotani	72-77—149		K Pearce	77-75—152		N Lopez	77-79—156
	V Michaud	71-78—149		C Nilsmark	77-75—152	126	J Forbes	81-76—157
76	K Golden	77-73—150		N Lowien	74-78—152		A Rogers	79-78—157
	A Read	76-74—150	102	K Poppmeier	79-74—153		G Stewart	78-79—157
	P Bradley	75-75—150		P Sterner	78-75—153		S Mendiburu	74-83—157
	M Lojdahl	75-75—150		C Schmitt	77-76—153	130	S Head	77-81—158
	AM Knight	75-75—150		A Arruti	74-79—153	131	L Navarro	82-77—159
	T Poulton	74-76—150		V Stensrud	72-81—153		L Tadiotto	78-81—159
	K Mourgue		107	P Wright	80-74—154		N Fink	76-83—159
	d'Algue	74-76—150		M Hageman	79-75—154	134	K Weiss	84-76—160
	T Loveys	74-76—150		B Hackett (Am)	79-75—154		D Reid	81-79—160
	A Alcott	70-80—150		N Bowen	77-77—154	136	L Percival	83-79—162
85	A Benz	79-72—151		D Booker	77-77—154		S Sanderson (Am)	79-83—162
	C Duffy	79-72—151		ML de Lorenzi	74-80—154	138	F Pike	85-80—165
	M Sutton	78-73—151	113	M McKay	82-73—155			
	A Rose (Am)	76-75—151		K Orum	81-74—155		C Shreyer	DQC
	S Redman	75-76—151		C Larsson	81-74—155		E Knuth	WDC
	S Melin	75-76—151		C Hall	80-75—155		M Lunn	WDC
	L Maritz	73-78—151		X Wunsch Ruiz	79-76—155		L Lindley	WDC
	M Hjorth	73-78—151		N Murray	79-76—155		M Hedblom	WDC
	AC Jonasson	71-80—151		J Leary	78-77—155		P Grice-Whittaker	WD
	F Muraguchi	70-81—151		J Arnold	78-77—155			

Estoril Ladies' Open
at Clube de Golf do Estoril, Estoril, Portugal

1	M Sutton	63-68-71—202	£13500
2	K Orum	66-66-71—203	9135
	S Waugh	68-73-66—207	6300

Amex Tour Players Classic
at The Tytherington Club, Macclesfield, UK

1	K Lunn	74-67-71-71—283	£15000
2	P Meunier Lebouc	75-69-66-74—284	8575
	T Fischer	69-69-73-73—284	8575

Ford–Stimorol Danish Open
at Vejle, Denmark

1	L Davies	68-70-69—207	£13500
2	M Hjorth	73-73-64—210	9135
3	ML de Lorenzi	72-69-72—213	5580
	K Lunn	73-71-69—213	5580

Deesse Ladies' Swiss Open
at Lausanne, Swizerland

1	ML de Lorenzi★	72-68-70-70—280	£13500
2	T Johnson	68-73-70-69—280	9135
3	K Lunn	66-71-73-72—282	6300

Evian Masters
at Royal Evian, Evian-Les-Bains, France

1	H Kobayashi★	69-67-69-69—274	£63750
2	A Nicholas	68-68-68-70—274	43031
3	ML de Lorenzi	73-69-71-67—280	29750

Guardian Irish Open
at Castleknock, Dublin

1	P Lebouc	74-70-69-71—284	£16500
2	L Navarro	73-73-70-69—285	11165
3	A Nicholas	73-74-70-69—286	7700

Ladies' German Open
at Marriott Treudelberg GC, Hamburg, Germany

1	J Mills★	71-71-70-71—283	£15000
2	L Brooky	68-74-70-71—283	10150
3	J Morley	72-68-70-74—284	7000

McDonald's WPGA Championship of Europe
at Gleneagles, Stirling, Scotland

1	H Alfredsson	74-65-67-70—276	£45000
2	C Sorenstam	74-68-70-68—280	25725
	K Marshall	70-69-71-70—280	25725

Compaq Open
at Stockholm, Sweden

1	A Sorenstam	67-67-73-70—277	£45000
2	C Nilsmark	71-72-69-71—283	30450
3	N Lopez	66-71-74-74—285	21000

French Ladies' Open
at Paris International, Paris, France

1	K Lunn	72-70-69-70—281	£15000
2	L Maritz	72-70-70-73—285	10150
3	T Johnson	74-69-72-71—286	7000

★ *Winner after play-off*

Hennessy Cup
at Golf und Land-club, Cologne, Germany

1	L Davies	75-71-68-74—288	£45000
2	AM Knight	74-74-69-72—289	30400
3	A Nicholas	74-70-72-74—290	16616
	H Alfredsson	72-71-75-72—290	16616
	L Hackney	71-75-72-72—290	16616

Sicilian Open
at Il Picciolo, Sicily

1	V Van Ryckeghem★	72-65-75-76—288	£15000
2	P Gonzalez	70-71-68-69—288	10150
3	ML de Lorenzi	71-73-74-71—289	6200
	K Orum	73-74-71-71—289	6200

Air France Madame Open
at Deauville, France

1	L Lambert	71-73-69—213	£9000
2	A Nicholas	73-69-73—215	6090
3	S Waugh	67-77-72—216	3720
	V Michaud	70-72-74—216	3720

PGA European Tour Qualifying School

at Aroeira, Portugal

The following 41 players won tour cards for 1998:

Pos	Name	Score	Pos	Name	Score
1	L Philo	71-70-72-76—289	22	R Sakkarainen	80-74-74-77—305
2	L Kreutz	73-70-72-75—290	23	I Maconi	72-77-76-80—305
3	AB Sancher Torreblanca	74-71-74-72—291	24	M Burstrom	76-75-73-81—305
4	M McKay	74-75-72-72—293	25	J van Hagen	79-77-75-75—306
5	L West	72-71-76-74—293	26	T Lipp	76-76-74-80—306
6	S Cavalleri	75-73-70-76—294	27	M De Boer	76-73-75-82—306
7	MT Pistolet-Boselli	76-73-75-72—296	28	A Pascalie	83-74-76-74—307
8	L Educate	73-75-74-74—296	29	J Crowe	78-74-79-76—307
9	A Rogers	76-73-72-77—298	30	H Hopkins	74-76-81-76—307
10	T Poulton	76-69-75-78—298	31	K Thomas	79-75-75-78—307
11	A Munt	74-71-75-79—299	32	L Greve	77-75-77-78—307
12	M Madill	75-75-76-74—300	33	S Dickens	77-79-72-79—307
13	S Moon	78-72-75-75—300	34	S Gallagher	76-75-75-81—307
14	L Dermott	76-71-75-78—300	35	W Wisbon	76-76-73-82—307
15	R Lautens	78-76-75-73—302	36	T Coll	81-76-77-74—308
16	E Esterl	73-75-79-75—302	37	N Karlsson	75-78-79-76—308
17	S Eklund	74-76-74-78—302	38	M Wright	78-80-72-78—308
18	A Barbe	80-73-77-73—303	39	E Aron	80-76-75-78—309
19	J Oliver	76-75-77-75—303	40	L Hed	81-74-76-78—309
20	C Duffy	76-74-74-79—303	41	E Fields	76-73-76-84—309
21	K Espinasse	76-76-81-72—305			

★ *Winner after play-off*

US Ladies' PGA Tour, 1997

Money Winners

Pos	Name	Prize Money $	Pos	Name	Prize Money $
1	Annika Sorenstam	1076789	39	Nanci Bowen	199163
2	Karrie Webb	947356	40	Penny Hammel	195135
3	Kelly Robbins	870657	41	Wendy Doolan	194506
4	Chris Johnson	703167	42	Alicia Dibos	190991
5	Tammie Green	580813	43	Karen Weiss	189812
6	Juli Inkster	532988	44	Helen Alfredsson	189441
7	Liselotte Neumann	483577	45	Leta Lindley	188828
8	Laura Davies	472119	46	Nancy Harvey	187339
9	Betsy King	461680	47	Dawn Coe-Jones	183903
10	Nancy Lopez	437886	48	Patty Sheehan	179453
11	Michelle McGann	412556	49	Dana Dormann	176655
12	Rosie Jones	371847	50	Wendy Ward	175264
13	Donna Andrews	368567	51	Danielle Ammaccapane	148352
14	Colleen Walker	365719	52	Susie Redman	143688
15	Lisa Hackney	351272	53	Rachel Hetherington	138019
16	Lorie Kane	350964	54	Mayumi Hirase	130547
17	Jane Geddes	323372	55	Helen Dobson	129482
18	Alison Nicholas	320602	56	Kim Williams	129063
19	Tina Barrett	308370	57	Pat Bradley	127376
20	Cindy Figg-Currier	306815	58	Dale Eggeling	126888
21	Terry-Jo Myers	305063	59	Jenny Lidback	125505
22	Barb Mucha	300295	60	Charlotta Sorenstam	118195
23	Brandie Burton	290922	61	Jan Stephenson	116793
24	Michele Redman	285879	62	Vickie Odegard	111553
25	Dottie Pepper	281200	63	Joan Pitcock	110294
26	Kris Tschetter	276609	64	Kristal Parker	110230
27	Sherri Steinhauer	258350	65	Cathy Johnston-Forbes	104951
28	Deb Richard	254275	66	Trish Johnson	104574
29	Pat Hurst	250299	67	Laurel Kean	101533
30	Hiromi Kobayashi	247550	68	Marianne Morris	98272
31	Meg Mallon	239337	69	Jane Crafter	96885
32	Gail Graham	223040	70	Caroline Pierce	92480
33	Catriona Matthew	221276	71	Stefania Croce	92286
34	Cindy Schreyer	212371	72	Becky Iverson	90862
35	Kim Saiki	210858	73	Kris Monaghan	89282
36	Emilee Klein	208865	74	Barb Whitehead	85292
37	Amy Fruwirth	200419	75	Laurie Brower	84406
38	Kathryn Marshall	199187			

Tour Results *(in chronological order)*

Chrysler-Plymouth Tournament of Champions
at Weston Hills, Fort Lauderdale, Florida

1	Annika Sorenstam	72-66-68-66—272	$115000
2	Karrie Webb	69-68-69-70—276	72000
3	Barb Mucha	72-66-69-70—277	52500

HealthSouth Inaugural
Lake Buena Vista, Florida

1	Michelle McGann*	66-72-69—207	$90000
2	Karrie Webb	68-70-69—207	55855
3	Beth Daniel	69-72-70—211	40759

Diet Dr Pepper National Pro-Am
at Ibis G&CC, West Palm Beach, Florida

1	Kelly Robbins*	66-69-69-67—271	$75000
2	Emilee Klein	71-67-70-63—271	46546
3	Chris Johnson	68-73-67-67—275	33966

Los Angeles Women's Championship
at Oakmont, Glendale, California

1	Terry-Jo Myers	74-66-66—206	$97500
2	Annika Sorenstam	66-69-73—208	60510
3	Alicia Dibos	71-73-67—211	29698
	Kelly Robbins	73-69-69—211	29698
	Catrin Nilsmark	73-69-69—211	29698
	Donna Andrews	68-73-70—211	29698
	Ellie Gibson	69-69-73—211	29698

Cup Noodles Hawaiian Ladies' Open
at Kapolei, Oahu, Hawaii

1	Annika Sorenstam	67-66-73—206	$97500
2	Meg Mallon	69-68-70—207	60510
3	Betsy King	67-72-69—208	44156

Alpine Australian Ladies' Masters
at Royal Pines, Gold Coast, Australia

1	Gail Graham	66-68-71-68—273	$97500
2	Karrie Webb	69-66-66-73—274	61666
3	Laura Davies	69-72-68-66—275	45000

Welch's–Circle K Championship
at Randolph Park, Tucson, Arizona

1	Donna Andrews	68-67-70-68—273	$75000
2	Tina Barrett	68-70-67-69—274	46546
3	Dale Eggeling	68-71-67-69—275	30192
	Annika Sorenstam	67-68-69-71—275	30192

* *Winner after play-off*

Standard Register Ping
at Moon Valley, Phoenix, Arizona

1	Laura Davies*	70-69-70-68—277	$127500
2	Kelly Robbins	67-68-73-69—277	79129
3	Laurie Brower	69-72-70-70—281	51327
	Barb Mucha	65-70-73-73—281	51327

Nabisco Dinah Shore
at Mission Hills, Rancho Mirage, California

1	Betsy King	71-67-67-71—276	$135000
2	Kris Tschetter	66-76-66-70—278	83783
3	Kelly Robbins	70-67-68-74—279	54346
	Amy Fruhwirth	69-70-68-72—279	54346

Longs Drugs Challenge
at Twelve Bridges, Lincoln, California

1	Annika Sorenstam*	73-68-71-73—285	$75000
2	Pamela Kometani	71-77-67-70—285	46546
3	Jan Stephenson	74-70-70-72—286	30192
	Juli Inkster	72-68-73-73—286	30192

Susan G Komen International
at Wachesaw East, Murrells Inlet, South Carolina

1	Karrie Webb	72-72-66-66—276	$75000
2	Lorie Kane	72-70-67-69—278	35463
	Cathy Johnston-Forbes	69-73-66-70—278	35463
	Nanci Bowen	65-73-70-70—278	35463

Chick-Fil-A Charity Championship
at Eagle's Landing, Stockbridge, Georgia

1	Nancy Lopez	71-66—137	$82500
2	Tina Barrett	70-69—139	39208
	Deb Richard	69-70—139	39208
	Karrie Webb	69-70—139	39208
(Weather curtailed tournament)			

Sprint Titleholders Championship
at LPGA International, Daytona Beach, Florida

1	Tammie Green	66-67-69-72—274	$180000
2	Annika Sorenstam	71-69-70-66—276	111711
3	Cindy Schreyer	69-71-70-67—277	65416
	Kelly Robbins	72-67-69-69—277	65416
	Karrie Webb	68-71-69-69—277	65416

Sara Lee Classic
at Hermitage GC, Old Hickory, Tennessee

1	Terry-Jo Myers*	70-67-70—207	$101250
2	Laurel Kean	69-72-66—207	54345
	Nancy Harvey	67-72-68—207	54345

* *Winner after play-off*

McDonald's LPGA Championship
at Du Pont, Wilmington, Delaware

1	Chris Johnson*	68-73-69-71—281	$180000
2	Leta Lindley	72-69-69-71—281	111711
3	Annika Sorenstam	70-73-72-67—282	81519

Corning Classic
at Corning, New York

1	Rosie Jones*	72-69-71-65—277	$97500
2	Tammie Green	71-70-67-69—277	60510
3	Helen Dobson	73-70-68-67—278	44156

Michelob Light Classic
at Forest Hills, St Louis, Missouri

1	Annika Sorenstam	70-69-66-72—277	$90000
2	Hiromi Kobayashi	69-68-69-74—280	55855
3	Karrie Webb	70-71-71-72—284	40759

Oldsmobile Classic
at Walnut Hills, East Lansing, Michigan

1	Pat Hurst	68-70-71-70—279	$90000
2	Juli Inkster	69-70-71-70—280	55855
3	Kim Saiki	73-68-71-69—281	36230
	Susie Redman	70-70-70-71—281	36230

Edina Realty Classic
at Rush Creek, Maple Grove, Minnesota

1	Danielle Ammaccapane	70-70-68—208	$90000
2	Hiromi Kobayashi	69-70-70—209	38494
	Jane Geddes	70-67-72—209	38494
	Catriona Matthew	69-68-72—209	38494
	Mayumi Hirase	69-68-72—209	38494

Rochester International
at Locust Hill, Pittsford, New York

1	Penny Hammel	71-70-70-68—279	$90000
2	Tammie Green	71-71-70-68—280	43589
	Dottie Pepper	69-69-71-71—280	43589
	Nanci Bowen	68-67-74-71—280	43589

Shoprite LPGA Classic
at Greater Bay Resort, Somers Point, New Jersey

1	Michelle McGann	72-65-64—201	$135000
2	Annika Sorenstam	65-68-71—204	85384
3	Juli Inkster	71-69-66—206	62307

Winner after play-off

Jamie Farr Kroger Classic
at Highland Meadows, Toledo, Ohio

1	Kelly Robbins	67-64-67-67—265	$105000
2	Tammie Green	67-69-70-67—273	65165
3	Nancy Lopez	68-66-71-69—274	47553

52nd US Women's Open
at Pumpkin Ridge, Cornelius, Oregon

1	Alison Nicholas	70-66-67-71—274	$232500
2	Nancy Lopez	69-68-69-69—275	137500
3	Kelly Robbins	68-69-74-66—277	86708
4	Karrie Webb	73-72-65-68—278	60432
5	Stefania Croce	72-69-71-67—279	46159
	Lisa Hackney	71-70-67-71—279	46159

JAL Big Apple Classic
at Wykagyl, New Rochelle, New York

1	Michele Redman	64-67-71-70—272	$112500
2	Annika Sorenstam	71-68-67-69—275	69819
3	Meg Mallon	71-70-67-68—276	50949

Giant Eagle Classic
at Avalon Lakes, Warren, Ohio

1	Tammie Green*	64-71-68—203	$90000
2	Laura Davies	67-66-70—203	55855
3	Cindy Figg-Currier	67-69-70—206	40759

Du Maurier Classic
at Glen Abbey, Oakville, Ontario, Canada

1	Colleen Walker	68-72-73-65—278	$180000
2	Liselotte Neumann	71-67-73-69—280	111711
3	Betsy King	71-69-72-69—281	72461

Friendly's Classic
at Crestview, Agawam. Massachusetts

1	Deb Richard	72-70-68-67—277	$82500
2	Chris Johnson	68-72-70-68—278	51201
3	Brandie Burton	73-70-69-68—280	37363

Star Bank Classic
at CC of the North, Beavercreek, Ohio

1	Colleen Walker	67-69-67—203	$82500
2	Terry-Jo Myers	72-67-66—205	51201
3	Laura Davies	71-68-67—206	27330
	Tammie Green	68-70-68—206	27330
	Kim Williams	69-67-70—206	27330
	Dottie Pepper	68-66-72—206	27330

* *Winner after play-off*

State Farm Rail Classic
at Rail GC, Springfield, Illinois

1	Cindy Figg-Currier*	69-63-68—200	$90000
2	Kris Tschetter	68-68-64—200	48307
	Lorie Kane	67-68-65—200	48307

Safeway Championship
at Columbia Edgewater, Portland, Oregon

1	Chris Johnson	70-70-66—206	$82500
2	Kim Saiki	69-72-66—207	44282
	Lisa Hackney	68-69-70—207	44282

Safeco Classic
at Meridian Valley, Kent, Washington

1	Karrie Webb	67-67-71-67—272	$82500
2	Annika Sorenstam	67-71-66-69—273	51201
3	Patty Sheehan	69-68-65-75—277	37363

Welch's Championship
at Blue Hill CC, Canton, Massachusetts

1	Liselotte Neumann	67-70-69-70—276	$82500
2	Nancy Harvey	67-68-71-73—279	51201
3	Karrie Webb	69-70-71-72—282	37363

Fieldcrest Cannon Classic
at Peninsula, Charlotte, North Carolina

1	Wendy Ward	66-65-64-70—265	$82500
2	Jane Geddes	69-66-67-65—267	44282
	Rosie Jones	67-69-65-66—267	44282

CoreStates Betsy King Classic
at Berkleigh, Kutztown, Pennsylvania

1	Annika Sorenstam	70-67-68-69—274	$90000
2	Kelly Robbins	72-69-65-70—276	55855
3	Wendy Doolan	70-72-69-66—277	29814
	Juli Inkster	70-72-68-67—277	29814
	Betsy King	70-68-67-72—277	29814
	Catriona Matthew	67-70-70-70—277	29814

World Championship of Women's Golf
at Lakeside CC, Seoul, South Korea

1	Juli Inkster*	67-74-72-67—280	$131000
2	Kelly Robbins	69-74-68-69—280	62500
	Helen Alfredsson	70-71-66-73—280	62500

---

* Winner after play-off

Toray Japan Queens Cup
at Seta GC, Shiga, Japan

1	Liselotte Neumann	68-70-67—205	$112500
2	Lorie Kane	70-69-67—206	69819
3	Lisa Hackney	69-71-67—207	45288
	Chris Johnson	67-72-68—207	45288

Japan Ladies' PGA Tour, 1997

Tour Results

Tournament	Winner	Total Prize Fund ¥
Daikin Orchid Ladies' Tournament	Woo-Soon Ko	60,000,000
Saishunkan Ladies'	Chiyako Yamazaki	60,000,000
Yellow Hat Tokyo Ladies'	Susuko Maeda	50,000,000
Kensyoen Ladies' Dogo	Kaori Harada	50,000,000
Mitsukoshi Cup	Akemi Yamaoka	60,000,000
Nasuogawa Open	Woo-Soon Ko	50,000,000
Katockichi Queen's	Jae-Sook Won	50,000,000
Gunze Cup World Ladies'	Tseng-Hsiu Feng	60,000,000
Yakult Ladies	Tomiko Ikebuchi	60,000,000
Chukyo TV Bridgestone Ladies'	Aki Takamura	50,000,000
Toto Motors Ladies'	Yoko Inoue	50,000,000
Mitsubishi Denki Ladies'	Akiko Fukushima	50,000,000
Suntory Ladies' Open	Ikuyo Shiotani	50,000,000
Dunlop Twin Lakes	Ok-Hee Ku	50,000,000
Japan Women's Open	Ayako Okamoto	70,000,000
Tohoto Ladies'	Suzuko Maeda	50,000,000
Toyo Suisan Ladies' Hokkaido	Kaori Higo	50,000,000
Resort Trust Open	Fumiko Muraguchi	50,000,000
Golf 5 Ladies'	Akiko Fukushima	50,000,000
Mizuno Ladies'	Aiko Takasu	60,000,000
NEC Karuizawa 72	Yuka Irie	60,000,000
New Caterpillar Mitsubishi Ladies'	Takayo Bandoh	60,000,000
Goyo Kensetsu Ladies'	Michiko Hattori	60,000,000
Fujisankei Classic	Aki Takamura	60,000,000
Japan LPGA Ch'ship	Akiko Fukushima	70,000,000
Yukizirusi Tokai Classic	Akiko Fukushima	60,000,000
Miyagi TV Cup	Michiko Hattori	50,000,000
Kosaido Cup	Akiko Fukushima	60,000,000
TaKaRa World Invitational	Liselotte Neumann	80,000,000
Fujitsu Ladies'	Aiko Takasu	60,000,000
Kibun Classic	Annika Sorenstam	70,000,000
Torey Japan Queen's Cup	Liselotte Neumann	82,500,000
Itoen Ladies	Helen Alfredsson	60,000,000
Daioseishi Elleair Open	Ok-Hee Ku	65,000,000
JLPGA Meiji Nyugyo Cup	Akiko Fukushima	60,000,000

Final Order of Merit

Pos	Name	Prize Money ¥
1	Akiko Fukushima	99,594,094
2	Ok-Hee Ku	59,141,950
3	Ikuyo Shiotani	52,585,450
4	Natsuko Noro	42,667,039
5	Aki Takamura	42,182,388
6	Woo-Soon Ko	41,911,472
7	Kaori Higo	41,603,137
8	Akemi Yamaoka	38,834,551
9	Fumiko Muraguchi	37,551,510
10	Suzuko Maeda	35,944,708
11	Marnie McGuire	35,644,527
12	Michiko Hattori	33,508,485
13	Aiko Takasu	33,182,250
14	Kaori Harada	31,477,811
15	Mayumi Murai	31,225,171

Men's Amateur Tournaments

The 102nd Amateur Championship
at Royal St Georges and Royal Cinque Ports

369 players from 19 countries played in 36-hole qualifying competition.
84 qualified on 156 or better for matchplay stage.

First Round

C Nickens beat F Stolear 3 and 2
S Wakefield beat G Homewood 4 and 3
S Philipson beat S Webster at 19th
S Martin beat C Duke 4 and 3
S Davis beat J Hepworth 2 and 1
P Fenton beat P Neels at 20th
M Allen beat J Lupton 2 holes
S Sheehan beat K Aitala 2 and 1
I Goroneskoul beat N Zitny at 19th
R Quiros beat J Carter 4 and 3
J Morgan beat C Bausek 2 and 1
M Wilcox beat A Wainwright at 21st
R Duck beat C Rodgers 2 and 1
B Mason beat M Houghton 4 and 3
J Herbert beat J Little 3 and 2
G Birch Jr beat C Percy 2 holes
E Aubert beat I Lyner at 19th
D Gleeson beat M Eliasson 1 hole
D Griffiths beat N Parkinson at 19th
M King beat M Haeraas 4 and 3

Second Round

M Carver beat JC Aguero 2 and 1
R Price beat I Reay 5 and 3
J Clive beat P Streeter 4 and 3
J Torines beat M Loftus 3 and 2
D Patrick beat A Forsyth 3 and 2
C Watson beat J Donaldson 5 and 4
M Blackey beat P Lawrie 5 and 3
G Fox beat D Harris 2 and 1
B Howard beat P Purhonen 2 and 1
J Thalamy beat S McCarthy 3 and 2
P Hansson beat C Elliot 2 and 1
D Park beat L Kelly 6 and 5
C Nickens beat M Pilkington 2 and 1
C Edwards beat S Wakefield 3 and 2
S Philipson beat G Rankin at 20th
M Brooks beat S Martin 1 hole
R Hislop beat S Davis 1 hole
T Immelman beat P Fenton 2 and 1
M Allen beat C Smith 3 and 2

S Sheehan beat J Fanagan at 20th
S Little beat I Goroneskoul 1 hole
P Hedges beat R Quiros 7 and 6
JM Lara beat J Morgan 4 and 3
J Rose beat M Wilcox 2 and 1
R Duck beat M Orveland 2 holes
B Mason beat P Stuart 4 and 2
B Payne beat J Herbert 1 hole
J Backstrom beat G Birch Jr 3 and 2
E Aubert beat D Olsson 4 and 3
D Gleeson beat N Kraay 4 and 3
D Griffiths beat J Bunch 2 and 1
M King beat P Nelson 1 hole

Third Round

Price beat Carver 5 and 3
Clive beat Torines 3 and 2
Watson beat Patrick 1 hole
Fox beat Blackey 1 hole
Howard beat Thalamy at 19th
Park beat Hansson 3 and 2
Edwards beat Nickens 2 and 1
Brooks beat Philipson 3 and 1
Immelman beat Hislop 4 and 3
Sheehan beat Allen 2 and 1
Little beat Hedges 4 and 3
Rose beat Lara 6 and 5
Mason beat Duck 3 and 2
Payne beat Backstrom 3 and 2
Gleeson beat Aubert 1 hole
Griffiths beat King 1 hole

Fourth Round

Clive beat Price 3 and 2
Watson beat Fox 2 and 1
Howard beat Park 3 and 2
Edwards beat Brooks 1 hole
Immelman beat Sheehan 3 and 2
Little beat Rose 7 and 5
Mason beat Payne 6 and 5
Griffiths beat Gleeson 5 and 4

continued

The 102nd Amateur Championship *continued*

Quarter Finals
Watson beat Clive at 19th
Edwards beat Howard 2 holes
Immelman beat Little 4 and 3
Griffiths beat Mason 1 hole

Semi-Finals
Watson beat Edwards 1 hole
Immelman beat Griffiths 1 hole

Final (36 holes)
Watson beat Immelman 3 and 2

US Amateur Championship
at Cog Hill, Lemont, Illinois

Semi-finals
M Kuchar beat R Leen 6 and 5
J Kribel beat B Elder 3 and 1

Final
M Kuchar beat J Kribel 2 and 1

Walker Cup
at Quaker Ridge, New York, USA

Great Britain & Ireland		USA	
Day One			
Foursomes			
B Howard and S Young	0	B Elder and J Kribel (4 and 3)	1
J Rose and M Brooks	0	J Courville and B Marucci (5 and 4)	1
G Wolstenholme and K Nolan	0	J Gore and J Harris (6 and 4)	1
R Coughlan and D Park	0	R Leen and C Wollmann (1 hole)	1
	0		4
Singles			
S Young (5 and 4)	1	D Delcher	0
C Watson (1 hole)	1	S Scott	0
B Howard	0	B Elder (5 and 4)	1
J Rose (1 hole)	1	J Kribel	0
K Nolan	0	R Leen (3 and 2)	1
G Rankin	0	J Gore (3 and 2)	1
R Coughlan	1/2	C Wollmann	1/2
G Wolstenholme	0	J Harris (1 hole)	1
	3 1/2		4 1/2
Day Two			
Foursomes			
S Young and C Watson	0	J Harris and B Elder (3 and 2)	1
B Howard and G Rankin	0	J Courville and B Marucci (5 and 4)	1
R Coughlan and D Park	0	D Delcher and S Scott (1 hole)	1
G Wolstenholme and J Rose (2 and 1)	1	R Leen and C Wollmann	0
	1		3

continued

Great Britain & Ireland		**USA**	
Day Two			
Singles			
S Young (2 and 1)	1	J Kribel	0
C Watson	1/2	J Gore	1/2
J Rose	0	J Courville (3 and 2)	1
K Nolan	0	B Elder (2 and 1)	1
M Brooks	0	J Harris (6 and 5)	1
D Park	0	B Marucci (4 and 3)	1
G Wolstenholme	0	D Delcher (2 and 1)	1
R Coughlan	0	S Scott (2 and 1)	1
	1¹/₂		6¹/₂

Result: USA 18, Great Britain and Ireland 6

European Amateur Championship
at Geneva, Switzerland

1	D de Vooght (Bel)	71-69-69-69—278
2	S Garcia (Sp)	72-70-71-68—281
	R Duck (Eng)	70-72-71-68—281
	L Donald (Eng)	72-67-70-72—281

European Team Championship
at Portmarnock

Quarter Finals

Scotland beat Iceland	5¹/₂–1¹/₂
Ireland beat Holland	6–1
Sweden beat Denmark	5–2
Spain beat Germany	4¹/₂–2¹/₂

Semi-Finals

Spain beat Ireland	4¹/₂–2¹/₂
Scotland beat Sweden	4¹/₂–2¹/₂

Final

Spain beat Scotland	4¹/₂–2¹/₂

European Club Cup
at Parco de Medici, Rome

1	Racing Club, France	417
2	Royal Mid-Surrey, England	431
3	Aalborg, Denmark	432

Other Scores

7	Blairgowrie, Scotland	446
8	County Sligo, Ireland	447
9	Wrexham, Wales	451

Leading Individual Scores

R Gillot (Fr)	67-71-65—203
T Haveman (Den)	71-68-72—211
K Ekjford (Nor)	75-69-70—214
C Ravetto (Fr)	75-68-71—214
C Rodgers (Eng)	76-71-68—215

Men's Home Internationals
at Burnham & Berrow

England beat Wales	$10^1/2$–$4^1/2$
Ireland beat Scotland	$10^1/2$–$4^1/2$
England beat Scotland	$10^1/2$–$4^1/2$
Ireland beat Wales	$8^1/2$–$6^1/2$
England halved with Ireland	$7^1/2$–$7^1/2$
Scotland beat Wales	9–6

Result: England 3, Ireland 2, Scotland 1, Wales 0

British Seniors' Open Amateur Championship
at Sherwood Forest

1	G Bradley (US)	69-74-73—216
2	R Coogan	73-72-73—218
3	R Smethurst	77-74-70—221

British Mid-Amateur Championship
at Prestwick

Quarter Finals
L McLaughlin beat G Crawford 1 hole
S Philipson beat F Illouz 3 and 1
G Thomson beat R Booth 1 hole
W Bryson beat R Darlington 2 and 1

Semi-Finals
S Philipson beat L McLaughlin at 20th
G Thomson beat W Bryson at 19th

Final
S Philipson beat G Thomson at 19th

England *v* Spain
at La Manga, Spain

England		**Spain**	
Day One			
Foursomes			
G Wolstenholme and J Rose (1 hole)	1	S Garcia and A Saura	0
M Reynard and K Wallbank (3 and 1)	1	JM Lara and M Bedia	0
S Webster and M Blackey (3 and 2)	1	A Salto and JC Aquero	0
L Donald and R Wiggins (5 and 4)	1	R Quiros and R Vera	0
	4		0
Singles			
G Wolstenholme	$1/2$	S Garcia	$1/2$
J Rose (1 hole)	1	JM Lara	0
M Carver (5 and 4)	1	A Pons	0
M Reynard	0	A Salto (2 and 1)	1
L Donald	$1/2$	R Quiros	$1/2$
R Wiggins (3 and 2)	1	JC Aquero	0
M Blackey	$1/2$	A Saura	$1/2$
S Webster (3 and 1)	1	R Vera	0
	$5^1/2$		$2^1/2$

continued

England

Spain

Day Two

Foursomes

G Wolstenholme and J Rose (2 and 1)	1	A Pons and R Vera	0
M Carver and R Wiggins	0	A Salto and R Quiros (3 and 2)	1
K Wallbank and M Reynard	0	S Garcia and JM Lara (1 hole)	1
S Webster and M Blackey (5 and 4)	1	JC Aquero and A Saura	0
	2		**2**

Singles

J Rose	$1/2$	A Salto	$1/2$
M Carver (2 holes)	1	R Quiros	0
L Donald	$1/2$	S Garcia	$1/2$
K Wallbank	0	JM Lara (3 and 2)	1
R Wiggins (2 and 1)	1	A Saura	0
M Blackey (2 and 1)	1	R Vera	0
S Webster (1 hole)	1	JC Aquero	0
G Wolstenholme	0	M Bedia (2 and 1)	1
	5		**3**

Result: England $16^{1}/_{2}$, Spain $7^{1}/_{2}$

English Amateur Championship
at Royal Liverpool

Quarter Finals
M Blackey beat S Dyson 1 hole
A Wainwright beat S Webster 3 and 1
K Ferrie beat M Reynard 5 and 4
P Rowe beat R Finch 1 hole

Semi-Finals
A Wainwright beat M Blackey 3 and 2
P Rowe beat K Ferrie 2 and 1

Final
A Wainwright beat P Rowe 2 and 1

Irish Amateur Championship
at Fota Island

Semi-Finals
P Lawrie beat P Gribben 5 and 4
K Kearney beat S Quinlivan 6 and 5

Final
K Kearney beat P Lawrie 5 and 4

Scottish Amateur Championship
at Carnoustie

Semi-Finals
C Hislop beat S Twynholm 3 and 1
S Cairns beat D Paton 4 and 3

Final
C Hislop beat S Cairns 5 and 3

Welsh Amateur Championship
at Pyle & Kenfig

Semi-Finals
JR Donaldson beat A Smith 3 and 2
M Pilkington beat C Rees 3 and 2

Final (36 holes)
JR Donaldson beat M Pilkington 5 and 4

English Open Amateur Stroke Play Championship (for the Brabazon Trophy)
at Saunton

1	D Park	69-70-67-65—271
2	G Ogilvy	74-66-70-65—275
3	S Garcia	68-73-68-67—276

Irish Open Stroke Play Championship
at Fota Island, Cork

1	K Nolan	68-69-70-72—279
2	R Coughlan	69-72-69-75—285
3	N Fox	68-72-71-74—285

Scottish Stroke Play Championship
at Monifieth and Panmure

1	DB Howard	68-66-63-74-271
2	G Ogilvy	74-69-67-69—279
3	R Wiggins	67-71-70-71—279

Welsh Open Stroke Play Championship
at Conwy

1	G Wolstenholme	71-71-72-72—286
2	Y Taylor	69-75-73-70—287
3	R Price	71-76-73-70—290

All-Ireland Inter-County Championship
at Doneghal

Semi-Finals

Wicklow beat Roscommon	3–2
Cork beat Londonderry	3½–1½

Final

Cork beat Wicklow	4–1

Aberconwy Trophy
at Conwy/Llandudno (Maesdu), Gwynedd

1	I Campbell	71-72-78-77—298
2	G Marsden	69-80-74-77—300
3	C Davies	72-74-81-74—301
	N Van Hagen	76-71-76-78—301

The Antlers
at Royal Mid-Surrey

1	S Kay and R Peacock	73-70—143
2	L Baker and P Davies	71-77—148
3	MH Dixon and D Bill	76-73—149

Berkhamsted Trophy
at Berkhamsted, Hertfordshire

1	P Streeter	73-70—143
2	L Donald	72-72—144
	J Rose	74-70—144

The Berkshire Trophy
at The Berkshire GC

1	G Wolstenholme	67-69-70-69—275
2	H Stenson	72-71-69-64—276
3	N Richardson	70-67-73-71—281
	J Doherty	68-72-70-71—281

Burhill Family Foursomes
at Burhill, Surrey

Final
Mrs J Clink and T Clink beat Mrs L Scchiari and S Scchiari 7 and 6

Cameron Corbett Vase
at Haggs Castle, Glasgow

1	C Watson	67-66-67-68—268
2	G Rankin	66-68-69-67—270
3	M Loftus	69-65-68-70—272

Central England Open Men's Foursomes
at Woodhall Spa

Semi-Finals
R Pauley and D Lever beat J Peck and G Bassi 2 and 1
G Shaw and C Radford beat P Birkin and S Cox 2 and 1

Final
G Shaw and C Radford beat R Pauley and D Lever 7 and 5

Craigmillar Park Open
at Craigmillar Park, Edinburgh

1	C Hislop	67-68-66-67—268
2	G Rankin	69-66-65-68—268
3	A Farmer	66-69-71-67—273
	SC Smith	78-68-66-69—273

Duncan Putter
at Southerndown, Bridgend, Glamorgan

1	M Pilkington	66-71-70-76—283
2	M Sanders	69-72-73-70—284
3	J Donaldson	70-75-70-70—285
	J Morgan	69-73-72-71—285

East of Ireland Amateur Open Championship
at Co Louth

1	S Quinlivan	74-74-78-77—303
2	G McGimpsey	76-76-77-76—305
3	E Power	74-78-78-76—306

East of Scotland Open Amateur Stroke Play Championship
at Lundin Links

1	S Meiklejohn	287
2	C Hislop	289
	S Whiteford	289

English Champion Club Championship
at Sandiway

1	Royal Mid-Surrey	281
	(C Rogers, R Rea, M Booker)	
2	Hinkley	284
	(J Cayless, J Herbert, J Powell))	
3	Ashford Manor	285
	(P Brown, G Homewood, S Samphire)	

English County Finals
at Ferndown, Dorset

Day One

Leicestershire and Rutland	3	Sussex	6
Yorkshire	8	Cornwall	1

Day Two

Leicestershire and Rutland	3½	Cornwall	5½
Sussex	2½	Yorkshire	6½

Day Three

Sussex	7	Cornwall	2
Leicestershire and Rutland	3	Yorkshire	9

Result
1 Yorkshire, 2 Sussex, 3 Cornwall, 4 Leicestershire & Rutland

English County Champions Tournament
at Woodhall Spa

1	J Herbert (Leics)	74-71—145
2	T Whitehouse (Warwicks)	75-71—146
3	C Duke (Herts)	76-71—147

English Open Mid-Amateur Championship for the Logan Trophy
at Stockport

1	C Banks	69-70-72—211
2	P Williams	72-71-71—214
3	M Kingsley	71-72-72—215

English Seniors' Championship
at West Hill & Woking

1	D Lane	68-73-74—215
2	H Hopkinson	73-67-76—216
3	D Harrison	74-71-73—218

Fathers and Sons Foursomes
at West Hill, Surrey

Semi-Finals
DR and M Baxter beat M and R Taggert at 19th
TWG and R Betts beat GL and G Bradbury at 19th

Final
DR and M Baxter beat TWG and R Betts 1 up

Frame Trophy
at Worplesdon, Surrey

1	B Turner*	75-71-80—226
2	M Johnson	72-78-76—226
3	JBL Webster	77-78-75—227
	ML Kirby	74-77-76—227

Golf Illustrated Gold Vase
at Walton Heath

1	M James	68-64—142
2	C Rogers	73-73—146
3	R Binney	74-73—147

Hampshire Hog
at North Hants

1	G Wolstenholme*	68-67—135
2	J Rose	67-68—135
3	B Mason	65-72—137

Halford Hewitt Cup
at Royal Cinque Ports, Deal, Kent

| Oundle beat Harrow | 3–2 |

* *Winner after play-off*

Irish Seniors Amateur Open Championship
at Oughterard GC

1	B Wilson	79-73—152
2	E Condren	77-77—154
3	A Thornquist	71-83—154

John Cross Bowl
at Worplesdon

1	CA Banks	70-66—136
2	NJ Pimm	71-71—142
	R Fenwick	71-71—142
	IR Attoe	70-72—142

King George V Coronation Cup
at Porters Park, Hertfordshire

1	J Knight	64-72—136
2	J Rose	71-67—138
	M Blackey	71-67—138
	M James	70-68—138

Lagonda Trophy
at Gog Magog, Cambridge

1	L Donald	72-67-69-71—279
2	G Wolstenholme	72-71-66-72—281
3	C Rodgers	72-73-68-69—282
	J Miller	71-70-71-70—282
	M Searle	70-69-69-74—282
	R Duck	71-68-72-71—282

Leven Gold Medal
at Leven Links, Fife

1	S Carmichael*	69-68-71-70—278
2	A Thomson	66-73-69-70—278
3	S MacKenzie	73-74-66-66—279

London Amateur Foursomes
at Walton Heath

Semi-Finals
South Beds beat Grimsdyke 3 and 2
West Herts beat Walton Heath 3 and 2

Final
West Herts beat South Beds 2 and 1

Lytham Trophy
at Royal Lytham & St Annes

1	G Rankin	71-70-67-71—279
2	L Kelly	71-70-71-76—288
3	B Howard	72-70-74-73—289

* *Winner after play-off*

Midland Open Amateur Championship
at Little Aston and Sutton Coldfield

1	P Streeter	72-69-72-76—289
2	S Wakefield	75-73-73-69—290
3	R Duck	73-76-69-73—291

North of Ireland Championship
at Royal Portrush

Semi-Finals
G McGimpsey beat A McCormick 5 and 4
M Sinclair beat D Dunne 4 and 3

Final
M Sinclair beat G McGimpsey 2 and 1

North of Scotland Open Championship
at Moray

| 1 | G Crawford | 72-66-71-72—281 |

Oxford *v* Cambridge Varsity Match
at Royal St Georges

Foursomes:	Oxford beat Cambridge	3^1/2–1^1/2
Singles:	Oxford beat Cambridge	7^1/2–2^1/2
Result:	Oxford beat Cambridge	11–4

Oxford and Cambridge Society
The President's Putter
at Rye

Semi-Finals
CR Rotheroe beat AL Woolnough 2 and 1
SD Ellis beat JM Warman 5 and 4

Final
CR Rotheroe beat SD Ellis 3 and 2

Prince of Wales Challenge
at Royal Cinque Ports, Deal

| 1 | J Carter | 78-76—154 |

St Andrews Links Trophy
at St Andrews

1	J Rose*	67-72-73-72—284
2	M Orveland	74-71-67-72—284
3	G Rankin	65-75-71-74—285

* *Winner after play-off*

St David's Gold Cross
at Royal St David's, Harlech

1	M Pilkington*	295
2	R Leonard	295

Scottish Champion of Champions
at Leven Links, Fife

1	G Rankin	274

Scottish Mid-Amateur Championship
at Cawder

Semi-Finals
H McDonald beat P Haggerty 5 and 3
C Carson beat C Barrowman 1 hole

Final
H McDonald beat C Carson 3 and 2

Scottish Seniors Championship
at Killermont, Glasgow

1	C Green	137
2	C Mackenzie	144

Selborne Salver
at Blackmoor

1	R Binney	66-72—138
2	M Blackey	70-69—139
3	J Rose	72-68—140

South of Ireland Championship
at Lahinch

Semi-Finals
A McCormick beat A Meharg 4 and 3
P Collier beat J Kavanagh 2 holes

Final
P Collier beat A McCormick 1 hole

Tennant Cup
at Glasgow Gailes

1	C Hislop	280
2	A Forsyth	289
3	L Kelly	292

* *Winner after play-off*

Tillman Trophy
at The London Club, Kent

1	M Searle	69-73-70-72—284
2	J Crampton	71-74-73-69—287
3	P Streeter	73-75-73-71—292
	C Rodgers	70-75-74-73—292

Trubshaw Cup
at Ashburnham and Tenby, Dyfed

1	M Pilkington	76-70-68-73—287

Welsh Inter-Counties Championship
at Borth and Ynyslas, Dyfed

1	Glamorgan
2	Gwent
3	Anglesey
	Brecon & Radnor

Welsh Mid-Amateur Championship
at Southerndown

1	S Merrill	76-74-75—225
2	C Platt	73-74-82—229
3	CA Bevan	77-77-77—231

Welsh Seniors Championship
at Aberdovey, Gwynedd

1	I Hughes	75-73—148
2	J Povall	76-75—151
3	DE Hart	79-76—155

Welsh Amateur Team Championship
at Cardigan

Semi-Finals

Wrexham beat Newport	4½–½
Cardiff beat North Wales	4–1

Final

Wrexham beat Cardiff	3–2

Welsh Champion of Champions
at Cradoc, Brecon

1	M Pilkington	146
2	M Griffiths	148

West of England Stroke Play Championship
at Saunton, Devon

1	M Reynard	74-67-69-70—280

West of Ireland Championship
at Rosses Point, Co Sligo

Semi-Finals
B Omelia beat P Gribben 3 and 2
J Fanagan beat A McCormick 1 hole

Final
J Fanagan beat B Omelia 3 and 2

West of Scotland Open Championship
at Erskine

1	C Hislop	69-69-70-73—281
2	RA Clark	73-73-69-71—286
3	E Moir	73-76-75-66—290
	G Lowson	75-70-72-73—290

Worplesdon Scratch Mixed Foursomes
at Worplesdon

Miss K Burton and G Wolstenholme beat K and C Quinn 6 and 5

Women's Amateur Tournaments

Vagliano Trohy –
Continent of Europe *v* Great Britain and Ireland
at Halmstad, Sweden

Europe		Great Britain and Ireland	

Day One

Foursomes

M Hedberg and U Jidflo	0	A Rose and K Rostron (5 and 4)	1
S Cavalleri and G Sergas	1/2	J Moodie and M McKay	1/2
AB Sanchez and M Prieto (2 and 1)	1	B Morgan and R Hudson	0
M Alsuguren and K Icher	1/2	E Ratcliffe and ER Power	1/2
	2		2

Singles

AB Sanchez (1 hole)	1	A Rose	0
J Lindbergh (5 and 4)	1	K Rostron	0
S Cavalleri (1 hole)	1	K Stupples	0
K Icher	0	J Moodie (2 and 1)	1
M Prieto (2 and 1)	1	M McKay	0
M Hedberg	1/2	B Morgan	1/2
G Sergas (4 and 3)	1	ER Power	0
M Alsuguren	0	E Ratcliffe (2 up)	1
	5 1/2		2 1/2

Day Two

Foursomes

S Cavalleri and G Sergas	0	A Rose and K Rostron (3 and 1)	1
M Hedberg and J Lindbergh (3 and 2)	1	J Moodie and M McKay	0
M Alsuguren and K Icher (3 and 1)	1	B Morgan and R Hudson	0
AB Sanchez and M Prieto	0	E Ratcliffe and K Stupples (3 and 1)	1
	2		2

Singles

J Lindbergh (2 and 1)	1	A Rose	0
S Cavalleri	0	J Moodie (3 and 2)	1
K Icher (4 and 3)	1	K Rostron	0
M Hedberg	0	K Stupples (3 and 2)	1
G Sergas	0	M McKay (1 hole)	1
M Prieto	1/2	B Morgan	1/2
M Alsuguren (5 and 3)	1	ER Power	0
AB Sanchez (1 hole)	1	E Ratcliffe	0
	4 1/2		3 1/2

Result: Continent of Europe 14; Great Britain and Ireland 10

British Women's Amateur Championship
at Cruden Bay

Quarter Finals
M Alsuguren beat S Cavalleri 2 holes
M McKay beat E Pilgrim 1 hole
R Morgan beat M Juul 2 and 1
A Rose beat M Zelsmann 3 and 2

Semi-Finals
M McKay beat M Alsuguren 2 and 1
A Rose beat R Morgan 2 and 1

Final
A Rose beat M McKay 4 and 3

British Women's Open Stroke Play Championship
at Silloth on Solway

1	KM Juul	293

British Senior Women's Open Amateur Championship
at Frilford Heath

1	T Wiesner	231

English Women's Amateur Championship
at Saunton

Final
K Rostron beat K Burton 4 and 2

English Women's Stroke Play Championship
at Hankley Common

1	L Tupholme	71-73-76-73—293
2	E Duggleby	71-76-76-77—300
	K Knowles	76-75-71-78—300

English Women's Seniors Stroke Play Championship
at Formby Ladies

1	A Thompson	78-74—152
2	P Meadows	74-81—155

English Women's Senior Match Play Championship
at South Winchester

Semi-Finals
C Means beat S Miller 3 and 2
G Palmer beat R Watters 2 up

Final
G Palmer beat C Means

English Women's County Championship Finals
at Ormskirk

| 1 | Surrey |
| 2 | Lancashire |

English Women's Intermediate Championship
at Abbotsley

Semi-Finals
K Smith beat K Stupples 1 up
L McGown beat L Tupholme 6 and 5

Final
K Smith beat L McGowan 2 and 1

European Women's Open Amateur Championship
at Formby

1	S Cavalleri	75-70-76-76—297
2	L Kreutz	72-76-76-77—301
3	E Ratcliffe	74-83-70-77—304
	AB Sanchez	77-75-73-79—304
	M Icher	75-74-79-76—304

Women's Home Internationals
at Lahinch

Ireland beat Wales	$6^1/2$–$2^1/2$
England beat Scotland	$6^1/2$–$2^1/2$
England beat Ireland	6–3
Scotland beat Wales	$5^1/2$–$3^1/2$
England beat Wales	5–4
Ireland beat Scotland	7–2

Final placings: 1 England, 2 Ireland, 3 Scotland, 4 Wales

Irish Women's Closed Championship
at Enniscrone

Semi-Finals
S Fanagan beat A Coffey 2 and 1
ER Power beat A O'Sullivan 2 and 1

Final
S Fanagan beat ER Power 4 and 3

Irish Women's Open Stroke Play Championship
at Waterford Castle

| 1 | Y Cassidy | 217 |
| 2 | P Gorman | 218 |

Irish Women's Senior Championship
at Athlone

1	M O'Donnell	85
2	B Ringrose	88
	V Wallis	88

Scottish Women's Closed Championship
at West Kilbride

Semi-Finals
A Rose beat S Wood 3 and 2
H Monaghan beat C Hargan 4 and 3

Final
A Rose beat H Monaghan 3 and 2

US Women's Amateur Championship
at Brae Burn, West Newton, Massachusetts

Semi-Finals
S Cavalleri beat A Baxter 2 and 1
R Burke beat M Graff 3 and 2

Final
S Cavalleri beat R Burke 5 and 4

Welsh Women's Championship
at Northop

Final
E Pilgrim beat L Davis 4 and 2

Welsh Women's Open Stroke Play Championship
at Whitchurch

1	K Edwards	216
2	M Zelsmann	221
3	K Stupples	222

Welsh Women's Senior Championship
at Fairwood Park, Swansea

1	C Thomas	160
2	J White	168

Astor Salvor
at The Berkshire

1	J Lamb	142
2	D Rushworth	143
	S Gallagher	143

The Bridget Jackson Bowl
at Handsworth, Birmingham

1	K Macintosh	69-73—142
2	R Bailey	72-71—143

Hampshire Rose
at North Hants

1	S Sanderson	142
2	K Smith	144

Helen Holm Trophy
at Royal Troon, Ayrshire

1	K Rostron*	72-71-76—219
2	F Brown	71-72-76—219
3	L Nicholson	73-72-75—220

London Women's Foursomes
at Highgate

Semi-Finals
The Berkshire beat Harpenden at 19th
Chelmsford beat Burnham Beeches 2 and 1
Final
The Berkshire beat Chelmsford 2 and 1

Midland Women's Championship
at Wollaton Park

Final
R Bailey beat T Williamson 5 and 4

Mothers and Daughters Foursomes
at Royal Mid-Surrey

1	Mrs S Lines and Miss K Lines	121

Northern Women's Championship
at Brampton, Cumbria

Semi-Finals
S Garbutt beat K McKenna 1 hole
G Nutter beat P Simpson 3 and 2

Final
G Nutter beat S Garbutt 2 and 1

* Winner after play-off

Northern Women's Counties Championship
at Wallasey

1	Lancashire
2	Yorkshire
3	Cheshire
4	Durham
5	Northumberland
6	Cumbria

Northern Women's Foursomes
at West Lancashire

Final
L Tupholme and E Duggleby beat B Scholes and.S Warrington 1 hole

St Rule Trophy
at St Andrews

1	K Rostron	217
2	J Moodie	218

Scottish Women's County Championship
at Hilton Park

1	Dunbartonshire & Argyll
2	Fife

South-East Women's Championship
at Ashridge

Final
L Evans beat H Emms 3 and 2

Juniors and Youths

Boys and Youths

Boys' Amateur Championship   *at Saunton*

Quarter Finals
S Garcia beat C Nilsson 3 and 2
N Burrows beat S Robinson 2 and 1
M Ilonen beat M Hoey at 19th
R Jones beat R Sundgren 2 and 1

Semi-Finals
S Garcia beat N Burrows 4 and 3
R Jones beat M Ilonen 2 and 1

Final
S Garcia beat R Jones 6 and 5

Boys' Home Internationals
at Royal North Devon

Wales beat England	8–7
Ireland beat Scotland	10$^{1}/_{2}$–4$^{1}/_{2}$
Wales beat Scotland	8$^{1}/_{2}$–6$^{1}/_{2}$
Ireland beat England	9$^{1}/_{2}$–5$^{1}/_{2}$
Ireland beat Wales	10–5
Scotland beat England	8–7

Result: 1 Ireland, 2 Wales, 3 Scotland, 4 England

Wales *v* Ireland Youths' International *at Royal St Davids*

Ireland		Wales	
Foursomes			
N Howley and C McMonagle	$^{1}/_{2}$	M Palmer and K Sullivan	$^{1}/_{2}$
R Leonard and A Murray	0	M Pilkington and I Campbell (5 and 4)	1
J Foster and P Martin (5 and 3)	1	H James and M Griffiths	0
	1$^{1}/_{2}$		1$^{1}/_{2}$
Singles			
JC McMonagle (2 and 1)	1	M Pilkington	0
N Howley	0	M Palmer (3 and 2)	1
R Leonard (6 and 5)	1	H James	0
J Foster	0	K Sullivan (5 and 4)	1
A Murray	0	M Griffiths (3 and 1)	1
P Martin	0	I Campbell (4 and 3)	1
	2		4

Result: Wales 5$^{1}/_{2}$, Ireland 3$^{1}/_{2}$

Great Britain and Ireland *v* Continent of Europe Boys for the Jacques Leglise Trophy
at Aberdeen

Great Britain & Ireland		Continent of Europe	
Day One			
Foursomes			
J Rose and P Rowe (4 and 3)	1	S Reale and M Secci	0
I Campbell and M Campbell	0	S Garcia and A Hultman (3 and 2)	1
G Gordon and L Rhind	0	M Jorgensen and M Ilonen (2 and 1)	1
D Jones and N Matthews	0	R Vera and R Quiros (2 and 1)	1
	1		3
Singles			
J Rose (3 and 2)	1	L Saura	0
P Rowe (3 and 2)	1	S Reale	0
I Campbell	0	S Garcia (5 and 4)	1
L Rhind (4 and 3)	1	M Secci	0
R Jones	0	A Hultman (3 and 2)	1
G Gordon	0	M Ilonen (1 hole)	1
N Matthews	0	R Vera (1 hole)	1
D Jones	0	R Quiros (3 and 2)	1
	3		5
Day Two			
Foursomes			
J Rose and P Rowe	1/2	S Garcia and A Hultman	1/2
M Campbell and N Matthews	1/2	R Vera and R Quiros	1/2
R Jones and I Campbell	0	M Jorgensen and M Ilonen (5 and 4)	1
D Jones and L Rhind	0	M Secci and A Saura (3 and 2)	1
	1		3
Singles			
J Rose	1/2	S Garcia	1/2
P Rowe (1hole)	1	R Quiros	0
D Jones (1 hole)	1	A Hultman	0
G Gordon	0	M Ilonen (2 and 1)	1
M Campbell (1 hole)	1	R Vera	0
I Campbell (4 and 3)	1	S Reale	0
N Matthews (2 and 1)	1	L Saura	0
L Rhind (2 and 1)	1	M Jorgensen	0
	6 1/2		1 1/2

Result: Great Britain & Ireland 11 1/2, Continent of Europe 12 1/2

European Boys' Team Championship
at Bled G&CC, Slovenia

Semi-Finals

England beat Sweden	4–3
Spain beat Scotland	7–0

Final

Spain beat England	4 1/2–2 1/2

English Boys' Stroke Play Championship for the Carris Trophy
at Moor Park, Hertfordshire

1	D Griffiths	72-70-70-71—283
2	C Mayson	72-71-73-69—285
3	P Rowe	70-73-71-72—286

English Boys' Under-16 Championship for the McGregor Trophy
at Radcliffe-on-Trent, Notts

1	R Paolillo	71-73-71-70—285
2	S Godfrey	66-71-75-75—287
3	S Fromant	70-74-72-72—288

English Boys' County Finals
at Sandwell Park

Warwickshire beat Cheshire	7–2
Cornwall halved with Essex	4½–4½
Essex beat Warwickshire	5–4
Cornwall beat Cheshire	5½–3½
Warwickshire beat Cornwall	5–4
Essex beat Cheshire	7–2

Result:

1	Essex
2	Warwickshire
3	Cornwall
4	Cheshire

Irish Boys' Championship
at Galway

1	M Hoey*	77-70-70—217
2	D Jones	73-72-72—217

Irish Youths' Championship
at Malone

1	N Howley	71-72-70-71—284
2	A Murray	75-70-71-69—285
	D Jones	70-73-69-73—285

Scottish Boys' Championship
at Dunbar

Semi-Finals
M Donaldson beat G Gordon 1 hole
L Rhind beat M Anderson 4 and 3

Final
M Donaldson beat L Rhind 1 hole

* Winner after play-off

Scottish Boys' Stroke Play Championship
at Downfield, Dundee

1	L Rhind	69-73-75-70—287
2	M Donaldson	72-74-75-74—295
3	B Hume	75-77-75-73—300

Scottish Boys' Under-16 Stroke Play Championship
at Glenbervie

1	D Inglis	70-69—139
2	M Lawrie	70-73—143
3	J Rae	75-72—147

Scottish Youths' Open Stroke Play Championship
at Cawder

1	S Young	269
2	K Baraka	278
3	M Loftus	279

Welsh Boys' Championship
at Glamorgan

Semi-Finals
I Campbell beat A Smith 4 and 3
A Lee beat D Morteo 3 and 2

Final
A Lee beat I Campbell 4 and 3

Welsh Boys' Under-15 Championship
at Vale of Llangollan

1	RW Johnson	75-75—150
2	GJ Reynolds	72-80—152
3	RJ Nardozzo	75-78—153

Welsh Open Youths' Championship
at Cradoc

1	N Matthews	71-72-73-79—295
2	I Campbell	73-73-75-77—298
3	HL James	74-75-70-80—299

Peter McEvoy Trophy
at Copt Heath

1	P Rowe	68-71-79-72—290
2	J Lupton	73-72-74-72—291
3	O Wilson	77-69-74-73—293

Doug Sanders World Junior Championship
at Newmachar, Aberdeen

1	A Scott (Aust)	71-70-70-70—281
2	M Secci (It)	73-72-74-70—289
3	A Baddeley (Aus)	74-73-72-72—291

World Junior Team Championship
at Hamamura Onsen G&CC, Tottori, Japan

1	USA	864
2	Japan	880
3	England	885

Girls

British Girls' Open Championship
at West Kilbride

Final
C Laurens beat M Nagl 2 and 1

Girls' Home International Championship for the Stroyan Cup
at Forfar

England beat Ireland	8–1
Scotland halved with Wales	4¹/₂–4¹/₂
Scotland beat Ireland	7–2
England beat Wales	6¹/₂–2¹/₂
Wales beat Ireland	6¹/₂–2¹/₂
England beat Scotland	5¹/₂–3¹/₂

Final placings
1 England, 2 Scotland, 3 Wales, 4 Ireland

English Girls' Championship
at Kingsdown

Semi-Finals
C Ritson beat K Fisher 2 and 1
S McKevitt beat S Garbutt 1 up

Final
S McKevitt beat C Ritson 3 and 2

Irish Girls' Championship
at Lay/Bettystown

Semi-Finals
C Coughlan beat A Burke 1 hole
J Gannon beat P Murphy 4 and 2

Final
J Gannon beat C Coughlan 3 and 2

Scottish Girls' Championship
at Dunfermline

Semi-Finals
V Laing beat P McKay 4 and 3
A Walker beat S Laing 1 hole

Final
V Laing beat A Walker 5 and 4

Welsh Girls' Championship
at Perhos

Semi-Finals
R Brewerton beat K Evans 2 and 1
K Stark beat K Hollyman 2 and 1

Final
R Brewerton beat K Stark at 19th hole

Golf Foundation Tournament Winners

Team Championship for Schools 1997

International Final at Loch Lomond

1st France

Lycee Bellevue, Toulouse

Raphael Pellicioli	77-76—153
Thomas Liarte	71-72—143
Cedric Francisco	82-73—155
	451

2nd Australia

Kooralbyn International School, Queensland

Adam Scott	71-79—150
Gavin Flint	74-77—151
Peter Briant	80-77—157
	458

3rd Ireland

Summerhill College, Sligo

Eoin Moriarty	75-75—150
Sean McTernan	73-74—147
Martin McTernan	81-86—167
	464

4th South Africa

Pretoria Boys High School, Pretoria

Patrick Simunic	79-78—157
Robert Scherman	82-74—156
Kelso Hannay	82-77—159
	472

5th England

Queen Elizabeth's Grammar, Blackburn

Nicholas Dougherty	75-73—148
Paul Clarkson	86-81—167
Jonathan Ashton	83-76—159
	474

6th Scotland

Dollar Academy, Dollar

Peter Whiteford	70-74—144
Andrew Paton	84-83—167
Scott Stewart	82-85—167
	478

7th Wales

Yale College, Wrexham

Graeme Hill	86-83—169
Michael Jones	75-73—148
Richard Parsons	82-80—162
	479

8th New Zealand

Timaru Boys' High School, Timaru

Craig Palmer	79-79—158
Simon Attridge	80-77—157
Gareth Andrews	82-88—170
	485

9th Sweden

Polhemsskolan, Lund

Anna Jonsson*	84-82—166
Martin Svensson	76-82—158
Magnus Andren	85-77—162
	486

10th India

Modern School, Delhi

Saurabh Bahuguna	82-78—160
Bikram Singh	79-83—162
Shiv Kapur	81-84—165
	487

11th Germany

Liebfrauenschule Köln, Köln

Norman Wingen	87-92—179
Klaus Frohlich	82-92—174
Robert Frohlich	90-84—174
	527

12th Netherlands

Rynlands Lyceum, Wassenaar

Nick Davis	89-w/d—w/d
Alex van Tienhoven	102-93—195
Alexander Wijnen	94-87—181
	w/d

PGA European Tour Trophy

Thomas Liarte, France	71-72—143

* Girl

Golf Foundation/Weetabix Age Group Championships
at Patshull Park, Shropshire

Boys

Under 16
Marcus Stam (Royal Liverpool)	71-73—144
Rob Perrett (Clevedon)	72-74—146
Peter Wheatcroft (Worksop)	75-75—150
Yasin Ali (Ealing)	73-78—151
Scott Davey (Yelverton)	75-77—152
James Wright (Caldy)	79-74—153

Under 14
Stuart Robinson (Thames Ditton)	78-74—152
John Maxwell (Muckhart)	81-80—161
Daniel Smith (Kenwick Park)	84-79—163
Sam Wright (Oakmere Park)	84-79—163
Daniel Morris (Prenton)	87-77—164
David Lane (Canons Brook)	79-85—164

Under 15
Gary Lockerbie (Keswick)	75-72—147
Owen Stewart (Tulliallan)	79-74—153
Andrew Haydon (Sonning)	76-77—153
Christian Smith (Coxmoor)	80-76—156
Stephen Lewton (Woburn)	78-79—157
Scott Wilson (Phoenix)	74-83—157

Under 13
James Turner (Newmarket Links)	77-81—158
Lee Shepherd (Cleckheaton)	78-81—159
Bobby Wallace (Canmore)	83-80—163
James Ruth (Tavistock)	82-83—165
Jack Budgen (E. Sussex National)	83-83—166
Adam Stott (Reddish Vale)	84-83—167

Girls

Under 17
Vikki Laing (Musselburgh)	77-76—153
Caroline Cole (Monmouthshire)	79-77—156
Kamilla Lawton (Prestbury)	76-80—156
Lucy Powell (Royal North Devon)	79-78—157
Michele Fossett (Broome Manor)	90-78—168
Stephanie Brodie (Davenport)	84-85—169

Under 15
Louise Kenney (Pitreavie)	77-75—152
Laura Archer (Telford)	79-85—164
Heather McRae (Callander)	87-90—177
Laura Eastwood (Hurdwick)	87-94—181
Sophie Walker (Kenwick Park)	89-92—181
Danielle Roseberry (Durham City)	87-94—181

Under 16
Rachel Bell (Northcliffe)	83-81—164
Martina Gillen (Beaverstown)	85-80—165
Nichola Craig (Lanark)	84-85—169
Claudine Beaver (R. Lytham & St Annes)	81-89—170
Rebecca Edmunds (Enville)	88-84—172
Rachel Freshwater (Silverstone)	92-84—176

Duke of York Trophy winners
Marcus Stam (Royal Liverpool) 140; Louise Kenney (Pitreavie) 152

Golf Foundation Team Championship for Schools for the R&A Trophy

Year	Winner	Country	Venue
1987	Klippans Gymnasieskola	Sweden	Foxhills
1988	Klippans Gymnasieskola	Sweden	Sunningdale
1989	Marks Gymnasium	Sweden	St Andrews
1990	Lycée Bellevue	France	St Andrews
1991	Lycée Bellevue	France	Sunningdale
1992	Lycée Bellevue	France	St Andrews
1993	Lycée Bellevue	France	Gleneagles
1994	Lycée Bellevue	France	St Andrews
1995	Kelvin Grove High School	Australia	Sunningdale
1996	Welkom Gymnasium	South Africa	Blairgowrie
1997	Lycée Bellevue	France	Loch Lomond

Golf Foundation Award Winners

Year	Winner	Club
1982	Lindsey Anderson	Tain
1983	Nigel Osborne Clarke	Shirehampton
1984	Wayne Henry	Redbourn
1985	David Grantham	Hull
1986	Matthew Stanford	Saltford
1987	Jane Marchant	Whittington Barracks
1988	*Boys:* Ian Garbutt	Wheatley
	Girls: Lisa Dermott	St Melyd
1989	*Boys:* Lee Westwood	Worksop
	Girls: Lynn McCool	Strabane
1990	*Boys:* Keith Law	Forfar
	Girls: Mhairi McKay	Turnberry
1991	*Boys:* Gary Harris	Broome Manor
	Girls: Nicola Buxton	Woodsome Hall
1992	*Boys:* Shaun Devenney	Strabane
	Girls: Mhairi McKay	Turnberry
1993	*Boys:* Craig Williams	Greigiau
	Girls: Georgina Simpson	Cleckheaton & Dist
1994	*Boys:* Denny Lucas	Worksop
	Girls: Rebecca Hudson	Wheatley
1995	*Boys:* Justin Rose	North Hants
	Girls: Rebecca Hudson	Wheatley
1996	*Boys:* Mark Pilkington	Nefyn & District GC and Pwllheli
	Girls: Fame More	Chesterfield GC and Lindrick GC
1997	*Boys:* Nicholas Dougherty	Shaw Hill, Lancs
	Girls: Rebecca Brewerton	Abergele & Pensarn

Awards

Association of Golf Writers' Trophy

Awarded to the man or woman who, in the opinion
of golf writers, has done most for golf during the year

1951 Max Faulkner	1974 Peter Oosterhuis
1952 Miss Elizabeth Price	1975 Golf Foundation
1953 Joe Carr	1976 Great Britain & Ireland Eisenhower Trophy Team
1954 Mrs Roy Smith (Miss Frances Stephens)	1977 Christy O'Connor
1955 Ladies' Golf Union's Touring Team	1978 Peter McEvoy
1956 John Beharrell	1979 Severiano Ballesteros
1957 Dai Rees	1980 Sandy Lyle
1958 Harry Bradshaw	1981 Bernhard Langer
1959 Eric Brown	1982 Gordon Brand Jr
1960 Sir Stuart Goodwin (sponsor of international golf)	1983 Nick Faldo
1961 Commdr Charles Roe (ex-hon secretary, PGA)	1984 Severiano Ballesteros
1962 Mrs Marley Spearman, British Ladies' Champion 1961–1962	1985 European Ryder Cup Team
1963 Michael Lunt, Amateur Champion, 1963	1986 Great Britain and Ireland Curtis Cup Team
1964 Great Britain & Ireland Eisenhower Trophy Team	1987 European Ryder Cup Team
1965 Gerald Micklem, golf administrator, President, English Golf Union	1988 Sandy Lyle
	1989 Great Britain & Ireland Walker Cup Team
1966 Ronnie Shade	1990 Nick Faldo
1967 John Panton	1991 Severiano Ballesteros
1968 Michael Bonallack	1992 European Solheim Cup Team
1969 Tony Jacklin	1993 Bernhard Langer
1970 Tony Jacklin	1994 Laura Davies
1971 Great Britain & Ireland Walker Cup Team	1995 European Ryder Cup Team
1972 Miss Michelle Walker	1996 Colin Montgomerie
1973 Peter Oosterhuis	1997 Alison Nicholas

Harry Vardon Trophy

Awarded to the PGA member heading the Order of Merit at the end of the season

1937	Charles Whitcombe	1961	Christy O'Connor	1980	Sandy Lyle
1938	Henry Cotton	1962	Christy O'Connor	1981	Bernhard Langer
1939	Roger Whitcombe	1963	Neil Coles	1982	Greg Norman
1940–45	*In abeyance*	1964	Peter Alliss	1983	Nick Faldo
1946	Bobby Locke	1965	Bernard Hunt	1984	Bernhard Langer
1947	Norman Von Nida	1966	Peter Alliss	1985	Sandy Lyle
1948	Charlie Ward	1967	Malcolm Gregson	1986	Severiano Ballesteros
1949	Charlie Ward	1968	Brian Huggett	1987	Ian Woosnam
1950	Bobby Locke	1969	Bernard Gallacher	1988	Severiano Ballesteros
1951	John Panton	1970	Neil Coles	1989	Ronan Rafferty
1952	Harry Weetman	1971	Peter Oosterhuis	1990	Ian Woosnam
1953	Flory van Donck	1972	Peter Oosterhuis	1991	Severiano Ballesteros
1954	Bobby Locke	1973	Peter Oosterhuis	1992	Nick Faldo
1955	Dai Rees	1974	Peter Oosterhuis	1993	Colin Montgomerie
1956	Harry Weetman	1975	Dale Hayes	1994	Colin Montgomerie
1957	Eric Brown	1976	Severiano Ballesteros	1995	Colin Montgomerie
1958	Bernard Hunt	1977	Severiano Ballesteros	1996	Colin Montgomerie
1959	Dai Rees	1978	Severiano Ballesteros	1997	Colin Montgomerie
1960	Bernard Hunt	1979	Sandy Lyle		

Rookie of the Year

1960	Tommy Goodwin	1980	Paul Hoad
1961	Alex Caygill	1981	Jeremy Bennett
1962	*No Award*	1982	Gordon Brand Jr
1963	Tony Jacklin	1983	Grant Turner
1964	*No Award*	1984	Philip Parkin
1966	Robin Liddle	1985	Paul Thomas
1967	*No Award*	1986	José Maria Olazabal
1968	Bernard Gallacher	1987	Peter Baker
1969	Peter Oosterhuis	1988	Colin Montgomerie
1970	Stuart Brown	1989	Paul Broadhurst
1971	David Llewellyn	1990	Russell Claydon
1972	Sam Torrance	1991	Per-Ulrik Johansson
1973	Philip Elson	1992	Jim Payne
1974	Carl Mason	1993	Gary Orr
1975	*No Award*	1994	Jonathan Lomas
1976	Mark James	1995	Jarmo Sandelin
1977	Nick Faldo	1996	Thomas Bjorn
1978	Sandy Lyle	1997	Scott Henderson
1979	Mike Miller		

Daily Telegraph Woman Golfer of the Year *(Formerly The Avia Award)*

1982	Jane Connachan	1992	GB&I Curtis Cup
1983	Jill Thornhill		Team, Captain Liz
1984	Gillian Stewart		Boatman
	and Claire Waite	1993	Catriona Lambert
1985	Belle Robertson		and Julie Hall
1986	GB&I Curtis Cup	1994	GB&I Curtis Cup
	Team		Team, Captain Liz
1987	Linda Bayman		Boatman
1988	GB&I Curtis Cup	1995	Julie Hall
	Team	1996	GB&I Curtis Cup
1989	Helen Dobson		Team
1990	Angela Uzielli	1997	Alison Rose
1991	Joanne Morley		

Bobby Jones Award

Awarded by USGA for distinguished sportsmanship in golf

1955	Francis Ouimet	1978	Bob Hope and
1956	Bill Campbell		Bing Crosby
1957	Babe Zaharias	1979	Tom Kite
1958	Margaret Curtis	1980	Charles Yates
1959	Findlay Douglas	1981	Mrs JoAnne Carner
1960	Charles Evans Jr	1982	Billy Joe Patton
1961	Joe Carr	1983	Mrs Maureen Garrett
1962	Horton-Smith	1984	Jay Sigel
1963	Patty Berg	1985	Fuzzy Zoeller
1964	Charles Coe	1986	Jess W Sweetser
1965	Mrs Edwin Vare	1987	Tom Watson
1966	Gary Player	1988	Isaac B Grainger
1967	Richard Tufts	1989	Chi-Chi Rodriquez
1968	Robert Dickson	1990	Peggy Kirk Bell
1969	Gerald Micklem	1991	Ben Grenshaw
1970	Roberto De Vicenzo	1992	Gene Sarazen
1971	Arnold Palmer	1993	PJ Boatwright Jr
1972	Michael Bonallack	1994	Lewis Oehmig
1973	Gene Littler	1995	Herbert Warren
1974	Byron Nelson		Wind
1975	Jack Nicklaus	1996	Betsy Rawls
1976	Ben Hogan	1997	Fred Brand
1977	Joseph C Dey		

The US Vardon Trophy

The award is made to the member of the US PGA who completes 60 rounds or more, with the lowest scoring average over the calendar year.

1948	Ben Hogan	1973	Bruce Crampton
1949	Sam Snead	1974	Lee Trevino
1950	Sam Snead	1975	Bruce Crampton
1951	Lloyd Mangrum	1976	Don January
1952	Jack Burke	1977	Tom Watson
1953	Lloyd Mangrum	1978	Tom Watson
1954	Ed Harrison	1979	Tom Watson
1955	Sam Snead	1980	Lee Trevino
1956	Cary Middlecoff	1981	Tom Kite
1957	Dow Finsterwald	1982	Tom Kite
1958	Bob Rosburg	1983	Ray Floyd
1959	Art Wall	1984	Calvin Peete
1960	Billy Casper	1985	Don Pooley
1961	Arnold Palmer	1986	Scott Hoch
1962	Arnold Palmer	1987	Dan Pohl
1963	Billy Casper	1988	Chip Beck
1964	Arnold Palmer	1989	Greg Norman
1965	Billy Casper	1990	Greg Norman
1966	Billy Casper	1991	Fred Couples
1967	Arnold Palmer	1992	Fred Couples
1968	Billy Casper	1993	Nick Price
1969	Dave Hill	1994	Greg Norman
1970	Lee Trevino	1995	Steve Elkington
1971	Lee Trevino	1996	Tom Lehman
1972	Lee Trevino	1997	Nick Price

US PGA Player of the Year Award

1948	Ben Hogan	1973	Jack Nicklaus
1949	Sam Snead	1974	Johnny Miller
1950	Ben Hogan	1975	Jack Nicklaus
1951	Ben Hogan	1976	Jack Nicklaus
1952	Julius Boros	1977	Tom Watson
1953	Ben Hogan	1978	Tom Watson
1954	Ed Furgol	1979	Tom Watson
1955	Doug Ford	1980	Tom Watson
1956	Jack Burke	1981	Bill Rogers
1957	Dick Mayer	1982	Tom Watson
1958	Dow Finsterwald	1983	Hal Sutton
1959	Art Wall	1984	Tom Watson
1960	Arnold Palmer	1985	Lanny Wadkins
1961	Jerry Barner	1986	Bob Tway
1962	Arnold Palmer	1987	Paul Azinger
1963	Julius Boros	1988	Curtis Strange
1964	Ken Venturi	1989	Tom Kite
1965	Dave Marr	1990	Nick Faldo
1966	Billy Casper	1991	Corey Pavin
1967	Jack Nicklaus	1992	Fred Couples
1968	*not awarded*	1993	Nick Price
1969	Orville Moody	1994	Nick Price
1970	Billy Casper	1995	Greg Norman
1971	Lee Trevino	1996	Tom Lehman
1972	Jack Nicklaus	1997	Tiger Woods

Arnold Palmer

Awarded to the US PGA Tour leading money-winner

1981	Tom Kite	1990	Greg Norman
1982	Craig Stadler	1991	Corey Pavin
1983	Hal Sutton	1992	Fred Couples
1984	Tom Watson	1993	Nick Price
1985	Curtis Strange	1994	Nick Price
1986	Greg Norman	1995	Greg Norman
1987	Paul Azinger	1996	Tom Lehman
1988	Curtis Strange	1997	Tiger Woods
1989	Tom Kite		

US PGA Tour Player of the Year

1990	Wayne Levi	1994	Nick Price
1991	Fred Couples	1995	Greg Norman
1992	Fred Couples	1996	Tom Lehman
1993	Nick Price	1997	Tiger Woods

US LPGA Rolex Player of the Year

1980	Beth Daniel	1989	Betsy King
1981	JoAnne Carner	1990	Beth Daniel
1982	JoAnne Carner	1991	Pat Bradley
1983	Patty Sheehan	1992	Dottie Mochrie
1984	Betsy King	1993	Betsy King
1985	Nancy Lopez	1994	Beth Daniel
1986	Pat Bradley	1995	Annika Sorenstam
1987	Ayako Okamoto	1996	Laura Davies
1988	Nancy Lopez	1997	Annika Sorenstam

US LPGA Vare Trophy

		Scoring average
1980	Amy Alcott	71.51
1981	JoAnne Carner	71.75
1982	JoAnne Carner	71.49
1983	JoAnne Carner	71.41
1984	Patty Sheehan	71.40
1985	Nancy Lopez	70.73
1986	Pat Bradley	71.10
1987	Betsy King	71.14
1988	Colleen Walker	71.26
1989	Beth Daniel	70.38
1990	Beth Daniel	70.54
1991	Pat Bradley	70.66
1992	Dottie Mochrie	70.80
1993	Nancy Lopez	70.83
1994	Beth Daniel	70.90
1995	Annika Sorenstam	71.00
1996	Annika Sorenstam	70.47
1997	Karrie Webb	70.01

US LPGA Gatorade Rookie of the Year

1980	Myra Van Hoose
1981	Patty Sheehan
1982	Patti Rizzo
1983	Stephanie Farwig
1984	Juli Inkster
1985	Penny Hammel
1986	Jody Rosenthal
1987	Tammie Green
1988	Liselotte Neumann (Swi)
1989	Pamela Wright (GB)
1990	Hiromi Kobayashi (Jap)
1991	Brandie Burton
1992	Helen Alfredsson (Swe)
1993	Suzanne Strudwick (GB)
1994	Annika Sorenstam (Swe)
1995	Pat Hurst
1996	Karrie Webb (Aus)
1997	Lisa Hackney

Vivien Saunders Trophy

Awarded to the Women Professional Golfers' European Tour winner of the stroke play averages

		Scoring average
1991	Alison Nicholas	71.71
1992	Laura Davies	70.35
1993	Laura Davies	71.63
1994	Liselotte Neumann	69.56
1995	Annika Sorenstam	69.75
1996	Marie Laure de Lorenzi	71.39
1997	Marie Laure de Lorenzi	72.20

Joyce Wethered Trophy

Awarded to the outstanding amateur under the age of 25

1994	Janice Moodie
1995	Rebecca Hudson
1996	Mhairi McKay
1997	Rebecca Hudson

PART III

Past Tournament Results

British and Irish National Championships

Amateur Championship

Year	Winner	Runner-up	Venue	By	Ent
1885	A MacFie	H Hutchinson	Hoylake, R Liverpool	7 and 6	44
1886	H Hutchinson	H Lamb	St Andrews	7 and 6	42
1887	H Hutchinson	J Ball	Hoylake, R Liverpool	1 hole	33
1888	J Ball	J Laidlay	Prestwick	5 and 4	38
1889	J Laidlay	L Melville	St Andrews	2 and 1	40
1890	J Ball	J Laidlay	Hoylake, R Liverpool	4 and 3	44
1891	J Laidlay	H Hilton	St Andrews	20th hole	50
1892	J Ball	H Hilton	Sandwich, R St George's	3 and 1	45
1893	P Anderson	J Laidlay	Prestwick	1 hole	44
1894	J Ball	S Fergusson	Hoylake, R Liverpool	1 hole	64
1895	L Melville	J Ball	St Andrews	19th hole	68
1896*	F Tait	H Hilton	Sandwich, R St George's	8 and 7	64

36 holes played on and after this date

Year	Winner	Runner-up	Venue	By	Ent
1897	A Allan	J Robb	Muirfield	4 and 2	74
1898	F Tait	S Fergusson	Hoylake, R Liverpool	7 and 5	77
1899	J Ball	F Tait	Prestwick	37th hole	101
1900	H Hilton	J Robb	Sandwich, R St George's	8 and 7	68
1901	H Hilton	J Low	St Andrews	1 hole	116
1902	C Hutchings	S Fry	Hoylake, R Liverpool	1 hole	114
1903	R Maxwell	H Hutchinson	Muirfield	7 and 5	142
1904	W Travis (USA)	E Blackwell	Sandwich, R St George's	4 and 3	104
1905	A Barry	Hon O Scott	Prestwick	3 and 2	148
1906	J Robb	C Lingen	Hoylake, R Liverpool	4 and 3	166
1907	J Ball	C Palmer	St Andrews	6 and 4	200
1908	E Lassen	H Taylor	Sandwich, R St George's	7 and 6	197
1909	R Maxwell	Capt C Hutchison	Muirfield	1 hole	170
1910	J Ball	C Aylmer	Hoylake, R Liverpool	10 and 9	160
1911	H Hilton	E Lassen	Prestwick	4 and 3	146
1912	J Ball	A Mitchell	Westward Ho!, R North Devon	38th hole	134
1913	H Hilton	R Harris	St Andrews	6 and 5	198
1914	J Jenkins	C Hezlet	Sandwich, R St George's	3 and 2	232
1915–19	*No Championship owing to the Great War*				
1920	C Tolley	R Gardner (USA)	Muirfield	37th hole	165
1921	W Hunter	A Graham	Hoylake, R Liverpool	12 and 11	223
1922	E Holderness	J Caven	Prestwick	1 hole	252
1923	R Wethered	R Harris	Deal, R Cinque Ports	7 and 6	209
1924	E Holderness	E Storey	St Andrews	3 and 2	201
1925	R Harris	K Fradgley	Westward Ho!, R North Devon	13 and 12	151
1926	J Sweetser (USA)	A Simpson	Muirfield	6 and 5	216
1927	Dr W Tweddell	D Landale	Hoylake, R Liverpool	7 and 6	197
1928	T Perkins	R Wethered	Prestwick	6 and 4	220
1929	C Tolley	J Smith	Sandwich, R St George's	4 and 3	253
1930	R Jones (USA)	R Wethered	St Andrews	7 and 6	271
1931	E Smith	J De Forest	Westward Ho!, R North Devon	1 hole	171
1932	J De Forest	E Fiddian	Muirfield	3 and 1	235
1933	Hon M Scott	T Bourn	Hoylake, R Liverpool	4 and 3	269
1934	W Lawson Little (USA)	J Wallace	Prestwick	14 and 13	225
1935	W Lawson Little (USA)	Dr W Tweddell	R Lytham and St Annes	1 hole	232
1936	H Thomson	J Ferrier (Aus)	St Andrews	2 holes	283
1937	R Sweeney, Jr (USA)	L Munn	Sandwich, R St George's	3 and 2	223
1938	C Yates (USA)	R Ewing	Troon	3 and 2	241
1939	A Kyle	A Duncan	Hoylake, R Liverpool	2 and 1	167
1940–45	*Suspended during Second World War*				
1946	J Bruen	R Sweeny (USA)	Birkdale	4 and 3	263
1947	W Turnesa (USA)	R Chapman (USA)	Carnoustie	3 and 2	200

Year	Winner	Runner-up	Venue	By	Ent
1948	F Stranahan (USA)	C Stowe	Sandwich, R St George's	5 and 4	168
1949	S McCready	W Turnesa (USA)	Portmarnock	2 and 1	204
1950	F Stranahan (USA)	R Chapman (USA)	St Andrews	8 and 6	324
1951	R Chapman (USA)	C Coe (USA)	R Porthcawl	5 and 4	192
1952	E Ward (USA)	F Stranahan (USA)	Prestwick	6 and 5	286
1953	J Carr	E Harvie Ward (USA)	Hoylake, R Liverpool	2 holes	279
1954	D Bachli (Aus)	W Campbell (USA)	Muirfield	2 and 1	286
1955	J Conrad (USA)	A Slater	R Lytham and St Annes	3 and 2	240
1956	J Beharrell	L Taylor	Troon	5 and 4	200
1957	R Reid Jack	H Ridgley (USA)	Formby	2 and 1	200
In 1956 and 1957 the Quarter Finals, Semi-Finals and Final were played over 36 holes					
1958	J Carr	A Thirlwell	St Andrews	3 and 2	488
In 1958, Semi-Finals and Final only were played over 36 holes					
1959	D Beman (USA)	W Hyndman (USA)	Sandwich, R St George's	3 and 2	362
1960	J Carr	R Cochran (USA)	R Portrush	8 and 7	183
1961	M Bonallack	J Walker	Turnberry	6 and 4	250
1962	R Davies (USA)	J Povall	Hoylake, R Liverpool	1 hole	256
1963	M Lunt	J Blackwell	St Andrews	2 and 1	256
1964	G Clark	M Lunt	Ganton	39th hole	220
1965	M Bonallack	C Clark	R Porthcawl	2 and 1	176
1966	R Cole (SA)	R Shade	Carnoustie (18 holes)	3 and 2	206
1967	R Dickson (USA)	R Cerrudo (USA)	Formby	2 and 1	
1968	M Bonallack	J Carr	Troon	7 and 6	249
1969	M Bonallack	W Hyndman (USA)	Hoylake, R Liverpool	3 and 2	245
1970	M Bonallack	W Hyndman (USA)	Newcastle, R Co Down	8 and 7	256
1971	S Melnyk (USA)	J Simons (USA)	Carnoustie	3 and 2	256
1972	T Homer	A Thirlwell	Sandwich, R St George's	4 and 3	253
1973	R Siderowf (USA)	P Moody	R Porthcawl	5 and 3	222
1974	T Homer	J Gabrielsen (USA)	Muirfield	2 holes	330
1975	M Giles (USA)	M James	Hoylake, R Liverpool	8 and 7	206
1976	R Siderowf (USA)	J Davies	St Andrews	37th hole	289
1977	P McEvoy	H Campbell	Ganton	5 and 4	235
1978	P McEvoy	P McKellar	R Troon	4 and 3	353
1979	J Sigel (USA)	S Hoch (USA)	Hillside	3 and 2	285
1980	D Evans	D Suddards (SA)	R Porthcawl	4 and 3	265
1981	P Ploujoux (Fra)	J Hirsch (USA)	St Andrews	4 and 2	256
1982	M Thompson	A Stubbs	Deal, R Cinque Ports	4 and 3	245
1983	A Parkin	J Holtgrieve (USA)	Turnberry	5 and 4	288
1984	JM Olazabal (Spa)	C Montgomerie	Formby	5 and 4	291
1985	G McGimpsey	G Homewood	R Dornoch	8 and 7	457
1986	D Curry	G Birtwell	R Lytham and St Annes	11 and 9	427
1987	P Mayo	P McEvoy	Prestwick	3 and 1	373
1988	C Hardin (Swe)	B Fouchee (SA)	R Porthcawl	1 hole	391
1989	S Dodd	C Cassells	R Birkdale	5 and 3	378
1990	R Muntz (Neth)	A Macara	Muirfield	7 and 6	510
1991	G Wolstenholme	B May (USA)	Ganton	8 and 6	345
1992	S Dundas	B Dredge	Carnoustie	7 and 6	364
1993	I Pyman	P Page	R Portrush	37th hole	279
1994	L James	G Sherry	Nairn	2 and 1	288
1995	G Sherry	M Reynard	Hoylake, R Liverpool	7 and 6	288
1996	W Bladon	R Beames	Turnberry	1 hole	288
1997	C Watson	T Immelman	R St Georges, R Cinque Ports	3 and 2	369

Senior Open Amateur Championship

Year	Winner	Venue	Score	
1969	R Pattinson	Formby	154	
1970	K Bamber	Prestwick	150	
1971	GH Pickard	Deal, R Cinque Ports; Sandwich, R St George's	150	
1972	TC Hartley	St Andrews	147	
1973	JT Jones	Longniddry	142	
1974	MA Ivor-Jones	Moortown	149	
1975	HJ Roberts	Turnberry	138	
1976	WM Crichton	Berkshire	149	
1977	Dr TE Donaldson	Panmure	228	
1978	RJ White	Formby	225	
1979	RJ White	Harlech, R St David's	226	
1980	JM Cannon	Prestwick St Nicholas	218	
1981	T Branton	Hoylake, R Liverpool	227	*continued*

Senior Open Amateur Championship *continued*

Year	Winner	Venue	Score
1982	RL Glading	Blairgowrie	218
1983	AJ Swann (USA)	Walton Heath	222
1984	JC Owens (USA)	Western Gailes	222
1985	D Morey (USA)	Hesketh	223
1986	AN Sturrock	Panmure	229
1987	B Soyars (USA)	Deal, R Cinque Ports	226
1988	CW Green	Barnton, Edinburgh	221
1989	CW Green	Moortown and Alwoodley	226
1990	CW Green	The Berkshire	207
1991	CW Green	Prestwick	219
1992	C Hartland	Purdis Heath	221
1993	CW Green	R Aberdeen and Murcar	150
1994	CW Green	Formby, Southport & Ainsdale	223
1995	G Steel	Hankley Common	218
1996	J Hirsch	Blairgowrie	210
1997	G Bradley (USA)	Sherwood Forest	216

Ladies' British Open Amateur Championship

Year	Winner	Runner-up	Venue	By
1893	Lady Margaret Scott	Miss I Pearson	St Annes	7 and 5
1894	Lady Margaret Scott	Miss I Pearson	Littlestone	3 and 2
1895	Lady Margaret Scott	Miss E Lythgoe	Portrush	5 and 4
1896	Miss Pascoe	Miss L Thomson	Hoylake, R Liverpool	3 and 2
1897	Miss EC Orr	Miss Orr	Gullane	4 and 2
1898	Miss L Thomson	Miss EC Neville	Yarmouth	7 and 5
1899	Miss M Hezlet	Miss Magill	Newcastle Co Down	2 and 1
1900	Miss Adair	Miss Neville	Westward Ho!, R North Devon	6 and 5
1901	Miss Graham	Miss Adair	Aberdovey	3 and 1
1902	Miss M Hezlet	Miss E Neville	Deal	19th hole
1903	Miss Adair	Miss F Walker-Leigh	Portrush	4 and 3
1904	Miss L Dod	Miss M Hezlet	Troon	1 hole
1905	Miss B Thompson	Miss ME Stuart	Cromer	3 and 2
1906	Mrs Kennon	Miss B Thompson	Burnham	4 and 3
1907	Miss M Hezlet	Miss F Hezlet	Newcastle Co Down	2 and 1
1908	Miss M Titterton	Miss D Campbell	St Andrews	19th hole
1909	Miss D Campbell	Miss F Hezlet	Birkdale	4 and 3
1910	Miss Grant Suttie	Miss L Moore	Westward Ho!, R North Devon	6 and 4
1911	Miss D Campbell	Miss V Hezlet	Portrush	3 and 2
1912	Miss G Ravenscroft	Miss S Temple	Turnberry	3 and 2

(Final played over 36 holes after 1912)

1913	Miss M Dodd	Miss Chubb	St Annes	8 and 6
1914	Miss C Leitch	Miss G Ravenscroft	Hunstanton	2 and 1
1915–18	*No Championship owing to the Great War*			
1919	*Should have been played at Burnham in October, but abandoned owing to Railway Strike*			
1920	Miss C Leitch	Miss M Griffiths	Newcastle Co Down	7 and 6
1921	Miss C Leitch	Miss J Wethered	Turnberry	4 and 3
1922	Miss J Wethered	Miss C Leitch	Prince's, Sandwich, R St George's	9 and 7
1923	Miss D Chambers	Miss A Macbeth	Burnham, Somerset	2 holes
1924	Miss J Wethered	Mrs Cautley	Portrush	7 and 6
1925	Miss J Wethered	Miss C Leitch	Troon	37th hole
1926	Miss C Leitch	Mrs Garon	Harlech	8 and 7
1927	Miss Thion de la Chaume (Fr)	Miss Pearson	Newcastle Co Down	5 and 4
1928	Miss N Le Blan (Fr)	Miss S Marshall	Hunstanton	3 and 2
1929	Miss J Wethered	Miss G Collett (USA)	St Andrews	3 and 1
1930	Miss D Fishwick	Miss G Collett (USA)	Formby	4 and 3
1931	Miss E Wilson	Miss W Morgan	Portmarnock	7 and 6
1932	Miss E Wilson	Miss CPR Montgomery	Saunton	7 and 6
1933	Miss E Wilson	Miss D Plumpton	Gleneagles	5 and 4
1934	Mrs AM Holm	Miss P Barton	Porthcawl	6 and 5
1935	Miss W Morgan	Miss P Barton	Newcastle Co Down	3 and 2
1936	Miss P Barton	Miss B Newell	Southport and Ainsdale	5 and 3
1937	Miss J Anderson	Miss D Park	Turnberry	6 and 4
1938	Mrs AM Holm	Miss E Corlett	Burnham	4 and 3
1939	Miss P Barton	Miss T Marks	Portrush	2 and 1
1940–45	*No Championship owing to Second World War*			
1946	GW Hetherington	P Garvey	Hunstanton	1 hole
1947	B Zaharias (USA)	J Gordon	Gullane	5 and 4

Year	Winner	Runner-up	Venue	By
1948	L Suggs (USA)	J Donald	Lytham St Annes	1 hole
1949	F Stephens	V Reddan	Harlech	5 and 4
1950	Vicomtesse de Saint Sauveur (Fr)	J Valentine	Newcastle Co Down	3 and 2
1951	PJ MacCann	F Stephens	Broadstone	4 and 3
1952	M Paterson	F Stephens	Troon	39th hole
1953	M Stewart (Can)	P Garvey	Porthcawl	7 and 6
1954	F Stephens	E Price	Ganton	4 and 3
1955	J Valentine	B Romack (USA)	Portrush	7 and 6
1956	M Smith (USA)	M Janssen (USA)	Sunningdale	8 and 7
1957	P Garvey	J Valentine	Gleneagles	4 and 3
1958	J Valentine	E Price	Hunstanton	1 hole
1959	E Price	B McCorkindale	Ascot	37th hole
1960	B McIntyre (USA)	P Garvey	Harlech	4 and 2
1961	M Spearman	DJ Robb	Carnoustie	7 and 6
1962	M Spearman	A Bonallack	Birkdale	1 hole
1963	B Varangot (Fr)	P Garvey	Newcastle Co Down	3 and 1
1964	C Sorenson (USA)	BAB Jackson	Sandwich, Prince's, R St George's	37th hole
1965	B Varangot (Fr)	IC Robertson	St Andrews	4 and 3
1966	E Chadwick	V Saunders	Ganton	3 and 2
1967	E Chadwick	M Everard	Harlech	1 hole
1968	B Varangot (Fr)	C Rubin (Fr)	Walton Heath	20th hole
1969	C Lacoste (Fr)	A Irvin	Portrush	1 hole
1970	D Oxley	IC Robertson	Gullane	1 hole
1971	M Walker	B Huke	Alwoodley	3 and 1
1972	M Walker	C Rubin (Fr)	Hunstanton	2 holes
1973	A Irvin	M Walker	Carnoustie	3 and 2
1974	C Semple (USA)	A Bonallack	Porthcawl	2 and 1
1975	N Syms (USA)	S Cadden	St Andrews	3 and 2
1976	C Panton	A Sheard	Silloth	1 hole
1977	A Uzielli	V Marvin	Hillside	6 and 5
1978	E Kennedy (Aus)	J Greenhalgh	Notts	1 hole
1979	M Madill	J Lock (Aus)	Nairn	2 and 1
1980	A Quast (USA)	L Wollin (Swe)	Woodhall Spa	3 and 1
1981	IC Robertson	W Aitken	Conway	20th hole
1982	K Douglas	G Stewart	Walton Heath	4 and 2
1983	J Thornhill	R Lautens (Switz)	Silloth	4 and 2
1984	J Rosenthal (USA)	J Brown	Royal Troon	4 and 3
1985	L Beman (Ire)	C Waite	Ganton	1 hole
1986	McGuire (NZ)	L Briars (Aus)	West Sussex	2 and 1
1987	J Collingham	S Shapcott	Harlech	19th hole
1988	J Furby	J Wade	Deal	4 and 3
1989	H Dobson	E Farquharson	Hoylake, R Liverpool	6 and 5
1990	J Hall	H Wadsworth	Dunbar	3 and 2
1991	V Michaud (Fr)	W Doolan (Aus)	Pannal	3 and 2
1992	P Pedersen (Den)	J Morley	Saunton	1 hole
1993	C Lambert	K Speak	R Lytham	3 and 2
1994	E Duggleby	C Mourgue d'Algue	Newport	3 and 1
1995	J Hall	K Mourgue d'Algue	R Portrush	3 and 2
1996	K Kuehne (USA)	B Morgan	R Liverpool	5 and 3
1997	A Rose	M McKay	Cruden Bay	4 and 3

Ladies' British Open Amateur Stroke Play Championship

Year	Winner	Venue	Score	
1969	A Irvin	Gosforth Park	295	
1970	M Everard	Birkdale	313	
1971	IC Robertson	Ayr Belleisle	302	
1972	IC Robertson	Silloth	296	
1973	A Stant	Purdis Heath	298	
1974	J Greenhalgh	Seaton Carew	302	
1975	J Greenhalgh	Gosforth Park	298	
1976*	J Lee Smith	Fulford	299	
1977*	M Everard	Lindrick	306	
1978*	J Melville	Foxhills	310	
1979	M McKenna	Moseley	305	
1980	M Mahill	Brancepeth Castle	304	
1981	J Soulsby	Norwich	300	*continued*

* Played concurrently with Ladies' British Open Championship

Ladies' British Open Amateur
Stroke Play Championship *continued*

Year	Winner	Venue	Score
1982	J Connachan	Downfield	294
1983	A Nicholas	Moortown	292
1984	C Waite	Caernarvonshire	295
1985	IC Robertson	Formby	300
1986	C Hourihane	Blairgowrie	291
1987	L Bayman	Ipswich	297
1988	K Mitchell	Porthcawl	317
1989	H Dobson	Southerness	298
1990	V Thomas	Strathaven	287
1991	J Morley	Long Ashton	297
1992	J Hockley	Frilford Heath	287
1993	J Hall	Gullane	290
1994	K Speak	Woodhall Spa	297
1995	MJ Pons (Sp)	Princes	289
1996	C Kuld (Den)	Conwy (Caernarvonshire)	289
1997	KM Juul (Den)	Silloth-on-Solway	293

Senior Ladies' British Open Amateur
Stroke Play Championship

Year	Winner	Venue	Score
1981	BM King	Formby	159
1982	P Riddiford	Ilkley	161
1983	M Birtwistle	Troon Portland	167
1984	O Semelaigne	Woodbridge	152
1985	Dr G Costello	Prestatyn	158
1986	P Riddiford	Longniddry	154
1987	O Semelaigne	Copt Heath	152
1988	C Bailey	Littlestone	156
1989	C Bailey	Wrexham	149
1990	A Uzielli	Harrogate	153
1991	A Uzielli	Ladybank	154
1992	A Uzielli	Stratford-upon-Avon	148
1993	J Thornhill	Ashburnham	151
1994	D Williams	Nottingham	154
1995	A Uzielli	Blairgowrie	152
1996	V Hassett	Pyle & Kenfig	236
1997	T Wiesner (USA)	Frilford Heath	231

English Amateur Championship

Year	Winner	Runner-up	Venue	By
1925	TF Ellison	S Robinson	Hoylake, R Liverpool	1 hole
1926	TF Ellison	Sq Ldr CH Hayward	Walton Heath	6 and 4
1927	TP Perkins	JB Beddard	Little Aston	2 and 1
1928	JA Stout	TP Perkins	R Lytham and St Annes	3 and 2
1929	W Sutton	EB Tipping	Northumberland	3 and 2
1930	TA Bourn	CE Hardman	Burhham	3 and 2
1931	LG Crawley	W Sutton	Hunstanton	1 hole
1932	EW Fiddian	AS Bradshaw	Sandwich, R St George's	1 hole
1933	J Woollam	TA Bourn	Ganton	4 and 3
1934	S Lunt	LG Crawley	Formby	37th hole
1935	J Woollam	EW Fiddian	Hollinwell	2 and 1
1936	HG Bentley	JDA Langley	Deal	5 and 4
1937	JJ Pennink	LG Crawley	Saunton	6 and 5
1938	JJ Pennink	SE Banks	Moortown	2 and 1
1939	AL Bentley	W Sutton	R Birkdale	5 and 4
1946	IR Patey	K Thom	Mid-Surrey	5 and 4
1947	GH Micklem	C Stow	Ganton	1 hole
1948	AGB Helm	HJR Roberts	Little Aston	2 and 1
1949	RJ White	C Stowe	Formby	5 and 4
1950	JDA Langley	IR Patey	Deal	1 hole

Year	Winner	Runner-up	Venue	By
1951	GP Roberts	H Bennett	Hunstanton	39th hole
1952	E Millward	TJ Shorrock	Burnham and Berrow	2 holes
1953	GH Micklem	RJ White	R Birkdale	2 and 1
1954	A Thirlwell	HG Bentley	Sandwich, R St George's	2 and 1
1955	A Thirlwell	M Burgess	Ganton	7 and 6
1956	GB Wolstenholme	H Bennett	R Lytham and St Annes	1 hole
1957	A Walker	G Whitehead	Hoylake, R Liverpool	4 and 3
1958	DN Sewell	DA Procter	Walton Heath	8 and 7
1959	GB Wolstenholme	MF Bonallack	Formby	1 hole
1960	DN Sewell	MJ Christmas	Hunstanton	41st hole
1961	I Caldwell	GJ Clark	Wentworth	37th hole
1962	MF Bonallack	MSR Lunt	Moortown	2 and 1
1963	MF Bonallack	A Thirlwell	Burnham and Berrow	4 and 3
1964	Dr D Marsh	R Foster	Hollinwell	1 hole
1965	MF Bonallack	CA Clark	Berkshire	3 and 2
1966	MSR Lunt	DJ Millensted	R Lytham and St Annes	3 and 2
1967	MF Bonallack	GE Hyde	Woodhall Spa	4 and 2
1968	MF Bonallack	PD Kelley	Ganton	12 and 11
1969	JH Cook	P Dawson	Sandwich, R St George's	6 and 4
1970	Dr D Marsh	SG Birtwell	R Birkdale	6 and 4
1971	W Humphreys	JC Davies	Burnham and Berrow	9 and 8
1972	H Ashby	R Revell	Northumberland	5 and 4
1973	H Ashby	SC Mason	Formby	5 and 4
1974	M James	JA Watts	Woodhall Spa	6 and 5
1975	N Faldo	D Eccleston	R Lytham and St Annes	6 and 4
1976	P Deeble	JC Davies	Ganton	3 and 1
1977	TR Shingler	J Mayell	Walton Heath	4 and 3
1978	P Downes	P Hoad	R Birkdale	1 hole
1979	R Chapman	A Carman	Sandwich, R St George's	6 and 5
1980	P Deeble	P McEvoy	Moortown	4 and 3
1981	D Blakeman	A Stubbs	Burnham and Berrow	3 and 1
1982	A Oldcorn	I Bradshaw	Hoylake, R Liverpool	4 and 3
1983	G Laurence	A Brewer	Wentworth	7 and 6
1984	D Gilford	M Gerrard	Woodhall Spa	4 and 3
1985	R Winchester	P Robinson	Little Aston	1 hole
1986	J Langmead	B White	Hillside	2 and 1
1987	K Weeks	R Eggo	Frilford Heath	37th hole
1988	R Claydon	D Curry	R Birkdale	38th hole
1989	S Richardson	R Eggo	Sandwich, R St George's	2 and 1
1990	I Garbutt	G Evans	Woodhall Spa	8 and 7
1991	R Willison	M Pullan	Formby	10 and 8
1992	S Cage	R Hutt	Deal	3 and 2
1993	D Fisher	R Bland	Saunton	3 and 1
1994	M Foster	A Johnson	Moortown	8 and 7
1995	M Foster	S Jarman	Hunstanton	6 and 5
1996	S Webster	D Lucas	Hollinwell	6 and 4
1997	A Wainwright	P Rowe	Hoylake, R Liverpool	2 and 1

English Open Amateur Stroke Play Championship for the Brabazon Trophy

Year	Winner	Venue	Score	
1957	D Sewell	Moortown	287	
1958	AH Perowne	Birkdale	289	
1959	D Sewell	Hollinwell	300	
1960	GB Wolstenholme	Ganton	286	
1961	RDBM Shade	Hoylake, R Liverpool	284	
1962	A Slater	Woodhall Spa	209	
1963	RDBM Shade	R Birkdale	306	
1964	MF Bonallack	Deal, R Cinque Ports	290	
1965 T	CA Clark/DJ Millensted/MJ Burgess	Formby	289	
1966	PM Townsend	Hunstanton	282	
1967	RDBM Shade	Saunton	299	
1968	MF Bonallack	Walton Heath	210	
1969 T	R Foster/MF Bonallack	Moortown	290	
1970	R Foster	Little Aston	287	
1971	MF Bonallack	Hillside	294	
1972	PH Moody	Hoylake, R Liverpool	296	
1973	R Revell	Hunstanton	294	*continued*

English Open Amateur Stroke Play Championship *continued*

Year	Winner	Venue	Score	
1974	N Sundelson	Moortown	291	
1975	A Lyle	Hollinwell	298	
1976	P Hedges	Saunton	294	
1977	A Lyle	Hoylake, R Liverpool	293	
1978	G Brand, Jr	Woodhall Spa	289	
1979	D Long	Little Aston	291	
1980 T	R Rafferty/P McEvoy	Hunstanton	293	
1981	P Way	Hillside	292	
1982	P Downes	Woburn	299	
1983	C Banks	Hollinwell	294	
1984	M Davis	Deal, R Cinque Ports	286	
1985 T	R Roper/P Baker	Seaton Carew	296	
1986	R Kaplan	Sunningdale	286	
1987	JG Robinson	Ganton	287	
1988	R Eggo	Saunton	289	
1989 T	C Rivett/RN Roderick	Hoylake, R Liverpool	293	
1990 T	O Edmond/G Evans	Burnham and Berrow	287	
1991	G Evans/M Pullan	Hunstanton	284	
1992	I Garrido	Notts	280	
1993	D Fisher	Stoneham	277	
1994	G Harris	Little Aston	280	
1995T	M Foster/CS Edwards	Hillside	283	
1996	P Fenton	R St Georges	297	
1997	D Park	Saunton	271	

English Seniors Championship

Year	Winner	Venue	Score	
1981	CR Spalding	Copt Heath	152	
1982	JL Whitworth	Lindrick	152	
1983	B Cawthray	Ross-on-Wye	154	
1984	RL Glading	Thetford	150	
1985	JR Marriott	Bristol and Clifton	153	
1986	R Hiatt	Northants County	153	
1987	I Caldwell	North Hants, Fleet	72	*(Curtailed due to storm)*
1988	G Edwards	Bromborough	222	
1989	G Clark	West Sussex	212	
1990	N Paul	Enville and Bridgnorth	217	
1991	W Williams	Gerrards Cross and Denham	217	
1992	B Cawthray	Fulford	223	
1993	G Edwards	John O'Gaunt	221	
1994T	G Steel/F Jones	Parkstone & Broadstone	72	*(Bad weather)*
1995	H Hopkinson	Copt Heath	226	
1996T	G Edwards/B Berney	West Lancs	224	
1997	D Lane	West Hill & Woking	215	

English Open Mid-Amateur Championship for the Logan Trophy

Year	Winner	Venue	Score
1988	P McEvoy	Little Aston	284
1989	A Mew	Moortown	290
1990	A Mew	Wentworth	214
1991	I Richardson	West Lancashire	223
1992	A Mew	King's Lynn	222
1993	R Godley	Southport & Ainsdale	210
1994T	I Richardson/A McLure	Trentham	217
1995	C Banks	Seacroft	222
1996	C Banks	Pannal, Harrogate	222
1997	C Banks	Stockport	211

English Club Champions

Year	Winner	Venue
1989	Ealing	Southport and Ainsdale
1990	Ealing	Goring and Streatley
1991	Trentham	Porters Park
1992	Bristol & Clifton	South Staffs
1993	Worksop	Rotherham
1994	Sandmoor	Coxmoor
1995	Sandmoor	Ipswich
1996	Hartlepool	Frilford Heath
1997	Royal Mid-Surrey	Sandiway

English County Championship (Men)

Year	Winner	Year	Winner	Year	Winner
1928	Warwickshire	1956	Staffordshire	1978	Kent
1929	Lancashire	1957	Surrey	1979	Gloucestershire
1930	Lancashire	1958	Surrey	1980	Surrey
1931	Yorkshire	1959	Northumberland	1981	Surrey
1932	Surrey	1961	Lancashire	1982	Yorkshire
1933	Yorkshire	1962	Northumberland	1983	Berks, Bucks, Oxon
1934	Worcestershire	1963	Yorkshire	1984	Yorkshire
1935	Worcestershire	1964	Northumberland	1985 T	Devon/Hertfordshire
1936	Surrey	1965	Northumberland	1986	Hertfordshire
1937	Lancashire	1966	Surrey	1987	Yorkshire
1938	Staffordshire	1967	Lancashire	1988	Warwickshire
1939	Worcestershire	1968	Surrey	1989	Middlesex
1947	Staffordshire	1969	Berks, Bucks, Oxon	1990	Warwickshire
1848	Staffordshire	1970	Gloucestershire	1991	Middlesex
1949	Lancashire	1971	Staffordshire	1992	Dorset
1950	*Not played*	1972	Berks, Bucks, Oxon	1993	Yorkshire
1951	Lancashire	1973	Yorkshire	1994	Middlesex
1952	Yorkshire	1974	Lincolnshire	1995	Lancashire
1953	Yorkshire	1975	Staffordshire	1996	Hampshire
1954	Cheshire	1976	Warwickshire	1997	Yorkshire
1955	Yorkshire	1977	Warwickshire		

English Ladies' Amateur Championship

Year	Winner	Runner-up	Venue	By
1960	M Nichol	A Bonallack	Burnham	3 and 1
1961	R Porter	P Reece	Littlestone	2 holes
1962	J Roberts	A Bonallack	Woodhall Spa	3 and 1
1963	A Bonallack	E Chadwick	Liphook	7 and 6
1964	M Spearman	M Everard	R Lytham and St Annes	6 and 5
1965	R Porter	C Cheetham	Whittington Barracks	6 and 5
1966	J Greenhalgh	JC Holmes	Hayling Island	3 and 1
1967	A Irwin	A Pickard	Alwoodley	3 and 2
1968	S Barber	D Oxley	Hunstanton	5 and 4
1969	B Dixon	M Wenyon	Burnham and Berrow	6 and 4
1970	D Oxley	S Barber	Rye	3 and 2
1971	D Oxley	S Barber	Hoylake	5 and 4
1972	M Everard	A Bonallack	Woodhall Spa	2 and 1
1973	M Walker	C Le Feuvre	Broadstone	6 and 5
1974	A Irvin	J Thornhill	Sunningdale	1 hole
1975	B Huke	L Harrold	R Birkdale	2 and 1
1976	L Harrold	A Uzielli	Hollinwell	3 and 2
1977	V Marvin	M Everard	Burnham and Berrow	1 hole
1978	V Marvin	R Porter	West Sussex	2 and 1
1979	J Greenhalgh	S Hedges	Hoylake	2 and 1
1980	B New	J Walker	Aldeburgh	3 and 2
1981	D Christison	S Cohen	Cotswold Hills	2 holes
1982	J Walter	C Nelson	Brancepeth Castle	4 and 3
1983	L Bayman	C Mackintosh	Hayling Island	4 and 3
1984	C Waite	L Bayman	Hunstanton	3 and 2
1985	P Johnson	L Bayman	Ferndown	1 hole

continued

English Ladies' Amateur Championship *continued*

Year	Winner	Runner-up	Venue	By
1986	J Thornhill	S Shapcott	Sandwich, Princes	3 and 1
1987	J Furby	M King	Alwoodley	4 and 3
1988	J Wade	S Shapcott	Little Aston	19th hole
1989	H Dobson	S Morgan	Burnham and Berrow	4 and 3
1990	A Uzielli	L Fletcher	Rye	2 and 1
1991	N Buxton	K Stupples	Sheringham	2 holes
1992	C Hall	J Hockley	St Annes Old Links	1 hole
1993	N Buxton	S Burnell	St Enodoc	2 and 1
1994	J Hall	S Sharpe	The Berkshire	1 hole
1995	J Hall	E Ratcliffe	Ipswich	2 and 1
1996	J Hockley	L Educate	Silloth	4 and 3
1997	K Rostron	K Burton	Saunton	4 and 2

English Ladies' Stroke Play Championship

Year	Winner	Venue	Score
1984	P Grice	Moor Park	300
1985	P Johnson	Northants County	301
1986	S Shapcott	Broadstone	301
1987	J Wade	Northumberland	296
1988	S Prosser	Wentworth	297
1989	S Robinson	Notts	302
1990	K Tebbet	Saunton	299
1991	J Morley	Ganton	301
1992	J Morley	Littlestone	289
1993	J Hall	King's Norton	298
1994	F Brown	Ferndown	289
1995	L Walton	Hallamshire	289
1996	S Gallagher	Little Aston	290
1997	L Tupholme	Hankley Common	293

English Ladies' Under-23 Championship

Year	Winner	Venue	Score
1978	S Bamford	Caldy	228
1979	B Cooper	Coxmoor	223
1980	B Cooper	Porters Park	226
1981	J Soulsby	Willesley Park	220
1982	M Gallagher	High Post	221
1983	P Grice	Hallamshire	219
1984	P Johnson	Moor Park	300
1985	P Johnson	Northants County	301
1986	S Shapcott	Broadstone	301
1987	J Wade	Northumberland	296
1988	J Wade	Wentworth	299
1989	A Shapcott	Notts Ladies	302
1990	K Tebbet	Saunton	299
1991	J Hockley	Saunton	303
1992	N Buxton	Littlestone	292
1993	R Millington	King's Norton	302
1994	F Brown	Ferndown	289
1995	E Fields	Hallamshire	297
1996	R Hudson	Little Aston	299
1997	R Bailey	Hankley Common	306

English Ladies' Seniors Championship

Year	Winner	Venue	Score
1988	A Thompson	Wentworth	158
1989	C Bailey	Notts Ladies	163
1990	A Thompson	Fairhaven	162
1991	C Bailey	Burnham and Berrow	155
1992	A Thompson	Pleasington	154

Year	Winner	Venue	Score
1993	A Uzielli	Hunstanton	150
1994	S Bassindale	Littlestone	163
1995	V Morgan	Tandridge	151
1996	A Uzielli	Royal North Devon	153
1997	A Thompson	Formby Ladies	152

English Ladies' Intermediate Championship

Year	Winner	Venue	Score
1982	J Rhodes	Headingley	19th hole
1983	L Davies	Worksop	2 and 1
1984	P Grice	Whittington Barracks	3 and 2
1985	S Lowe	Caldy	2 and 1
1986	S Moorcroft	Hexham	6 and 5
1987	J Wade	Sheringham	2 and 1
1988	S Morgan	Enville, Staffs	20th hole
1989	L Fairclough	Warrington	4 and 3
1990	L Fletcher	Whitley Bay	7 and 6
1991	J Morley	West Lancashire	6 and 5
1992	K Speak	South Staffs	3 and 1
1993	K Speak	Seascale	2 and 1
1994	J Oliver	Beaconsfield	2 up
1995	K Smith	Clitheroe	5 and 4
1996	R Bailey	Sandiway	3 and 2
1997	K Smith	Abbotsley	2 and 1

England and Wales (Ladies') County Championship

Year	Winner	Year	Winner	Year	Winner
1908	Lancashire	1948	Yorkshire	1974	Surrey
1909	Surrey	1949	Surrey	1975	Glamorgan
1910	Cheshire	1950	Yorkshire	1976	Staffordshire
1911	Cheshire	1951	Lancashire	1977	Essex
1912	Cheshire	1952	Lancashire	1978	Glamorgan
1913	Surrey	1953	Surrey	1979	Essex
1920	Middlesex	1954	Warwickshire	1980	Lancashire
1921	Surrey	1955	Surrey	1981	Glamorgan
1922	Surrey	1956	Kent	1982	Surrey
1923	Surrey	1957	Middlesex	1983	Surrey
1924	Surrey	1958	Lancashire	1984	Surrey/Yorkshire
1925	Surrey	1959	Middlesex	1985	Surrey
1926	Surrey	1960	Lancashire	1986	Glamorgan
1927	Yorkshire	1961	Middlesex	1987	Lancashire
1928	Cheshire	1962	Staffordshire	1988	Surrey
1929	Yorkshire	1963	Warwickshire	1989	Cheshire
1930	Surrey	1964	Lancashire	1990	Cheshire
1931	Middlesex	1965	Staffordshire	1991	Glamorgan
1932	Cheshire	1966	Lancashire	1992	Hampshire
1933	Yorkshire	1967	Lancashire	1993	Lancashire
1934	Surrey	1968	Surrey	1994	Staffordshire
1935	Essex	1969	Lancashire	1995	Hampshire
1936	Surrey	1970	Yorkshire	1996	Cheshire
1937	Surrey	1971	Kent	1997	Surrey
1938	Lancashire	1972	Kent		
1947	Surrey	1973	Northumberland		

Irish Amateur Championship

Year	Winner	Runner-up	Venue	By
1960	M Edwards	N Fogarty	Portstewart	6 and 5
1961	D Sheahan	J Brown	Rosses Point	5 and 4
1962	M Edwards	J Harrington	Baltray	42nd hole
1963	JB Carr	EC O'Brien	Killarney	2 and 1
1964	JB Carr	A McDade	Co Down	6 and 5

Irish Amateur Championship *continued*

Year	Winner	Runner-up	Venue	By
1965	JB Carr	T Craddock	Rosses Point	3 and 2
1966	D Sheahan	J Faith	Dollymount	3 and 2
1967	JB Carr	PD Flaherty	Lahinch	1 hole
1968	M O'Brien	F McCarroll	Portrush	2 and 1
1969	V Nevin	J O'Leary	Co Sligo	1 hole
1970	D Sheahan	M Bloom	Grange	2 holes
1971	P Kane	M O'Brien	Ballybunion	3 and 2
1972	K Stevenson	B Hoey	Co Down	2 and 1
1973	RKM Pollin	RM Staunton	Rosses Point	1 hole
1974	R Kane	M Gannon	Portmarnock	5 and 4
1975	MD O'Brien	JA Bryan	Cork	5 and 4
1976	D Brannigan	D O'Sullivan	Portrush	2 holes
1977	M Gannon	A Hayes	Westport	19th hole
1978	M Morris	T Cleary	Carlow	1 hole
1979	J Harrington	MA Gannon	Ballybunion	2 and 1
1980	R Rafferty	MJ Bannon	Co Down	8 and 7
1981	D Brannigan	E McMenamin	Co Sligo	19th hole
1982	P Walton	B Smyth	Woodbrook	7 and 6
1983	T Corridan	E Power	Killarney	2 holes
1984	CB Hoey	L McNamara	Malone	20th hole
1985	D O'Sullivan	D Branigan	Westport	1 hole
1986	J McHenry	P Rayfus	Dublin	4 and 3
1987	E Power	JP Fitzgerald	Tranmore	2 holes
1988	G McGimpsey	D Mulholland	Portrush	2 and 1
1989	P McGinley	N Goulding	Rosses Point	3 and 2
1990	D Clarke	P Harrington	Baltray	3 and 2
1991	G McNeill	N Goulding	Ballybunion	3 and 1
1992	G Murphy	JP Fitzgerald	Portstewart	2 and 1
1993	E Power	D Higgins	Enniscrone	3 and 2
1994	D Higgins	P Harrington	Portmarnock	20th hole
1995	P Harrington	D Coughlan	Lahinch	3 and 2
1996	P Lawrie	G McGimpsey	Royal Co Down	3 and 2
1997	K Kearney	P Lawrie	Fota Island	5 and 4

Irish Seniors' Open Amateur Championship

Year	Winner	Venue	Score
1980	GN Fogarty	Galway	144
1981	GN Fogarty	Bundoran	149
1982	J Murray	Douglas	141
1983	F Sharpe	Courtown	153
1984	J Boston	Connemara	147
1985	J Boston	Newcastle	155
1986	J Coey	Waterford	141
1987	J Murray	Castleroy	150
1988	WB Buckley	Westport	154
1989	B McCrea	Royal Belfast	150
1990	C Hartland	Cork	149
1991	C Hartland	Mullingar	147
1992	C Hartland	Athlone	145
1993	P Breen	Bangor	147
1994	B Buckley	Tramore	151
1995	B Hoey	Dundalk	151
1996	E Condren	Oughterard	148
1997	B Wilson	Knock, Belfast	152

Irish Ladies' Amateur Championship

Year	Winner	Runner-up	Venue	By
1960	P Garvey	PG McGann	Cork	5 and 3
1961	K McCann	A Sweeney	Newcastle	5 and 3
1962	P Garvey	M Earner	Baltray	7 and 6
1963	P Garvey	E Barnett	Killarney	9 and 7
1964	Z Fallon	P O'Sullivan	Portrush	37th hole

Year	Winner	Runner-up	Venue	By
1965	E Purcell	P O'Sullivan	Mullingar	3 and 2
1966	E Bradshaw	P O'Sullivan	Rosslare	3 and 2
1967	G Brandom	P O'Sullivan	Castlerock	3 and 2
1968	E Bradshaw	M McKenna	Lahinch	3 and 2
1969	M McKenna	C Hickey	Ballybunion	3 and 2
1970	P Garvey	M Earner	Portrush	2 and 1
1971	E Bradshaw	M Mooney	Baltray	3 and 1
1972	M McKenna	I Butler	Killarney	5 and 4
1973	M Mooney	M McKenna	Bundoran	2 and 1
1974	M McKenna	V Singleton	Lahinch	3 and 2
1975	M Gorry	E Bradshaw	Tramore	1 hole
1976	C Nesbitt	M McKenna	Rosses Point	20th hole
1977	M McKenna	R Hegarty	Ballybunion	2 holes
1978	M Gorry	I Butler	Grange	4 and 3
1979	M McKenna	C Nesbitt	Donegal	6 and 5
1980	C Nesbitt	C Hourihane	Lahinch	1 hole
1981	M McKenna	M Kenny	Laytown & Bettystown	1 hole
1982	M McKenna	M Madill	Portrush	2 and 1
1983	C Hourihane	V Hassett	Cork	6 and 4
1984	C Hourihane	M Madill	Rosses Point	19th hole
1985	C Hourihane	M McKenna	Waterville	4 and 3
1986	T O'Reilly	E Higgins	Castlerock	4 and 3
1987	C Hourihane	C Hickey	Lahinch	5 and 4
1988	L Bolton	E Higgins	Tramore	2 and 1
1989	M McKenna	C Wickham	West Port	19th hole
1990	ER McDaid	L Callan	The Island	2 and 1
1991	C Hourihane	E McDaid	Ballybunion	1 hole
1992	ER Power	C Hourihane	Co. Louth	1 hole
1993	E Higgins	A Rogers	R Belfast	2 and 1
1994	L Webb	H Kavanagh	Rosses Point	20th hole
1995	ER Power	S O'Brien-Kenney	Cork	1 hole
1996	B Hackett	L Behan	Tullamore	3 and 2
1997	S Fanagan	ER Power	Enniscrone	4 and 3

Scottish Amateur Championship

Year	Winner	Runner-up	Venue	By
1922	J Wilson	E Blackwell	St Andrews	19th hole
1923	TM Burrell	Dr A McCallum	Troon	1 hole
1924	WW Mackenzie	W Tulloch	Aberdeen	3 and 2
1925	JT Dobson	W Mackenzie	Muirfield	3 and 2
1926	WJ Guild	SO Shepherd	Leven	2 and 1
1927	A Jamieson, Jr	Rev D Rutherford	Gailes	22nd hole
1928	WW Mackenzie	W Dodds	Muirfield	5 and 3
1929	JT Bookless	J Dawson	Aberdeen	5 and 4
1930	K Greig	T Wallace	Carnoustie	9 and 8
1931	J Wilson	A Jamieson, Jr	Prestwick	2 and 1
1932	J McLean	K Greig	Dunbar	5 and 4
1933	J McLean	KC Forbes	Aberdeen	6 and 4
1934	J McLean	W Campbell	Western Gailes	3 and 1
1935	H Thomson	J McLean	St Andrews	2 and 1
1936	ED Hamilton	R Neill	Carnoustie	1 hole
1937	H McInally	K Patrick	Barassie	6 and 5
1938	ED Hamilton	R Rutherford	Muirfield	4 and 2
1939	H McInally	H Thomson	Prestwick	6 and 5
1946	EC Brown	R Rutherford	Carnoustie	3 and 2
1947	H McInally	J Pressley	Glasgow Gailes	10 and 8
1948	AS Flockhart	G Taylor	Balgownie, Aberdeen	7 and 6
1949	R Wright	H McInally	Muirfield	1 hole
1950	WC Gibson	D Blair	Prestwick	2 and 1
1951	JM Dykes	J Wilson	St Andrews	4 and 2
1952	FG Dewar	J Wilson	Carnoustie	4 and 3
1953	DA Blair	J McKay	Western Gailes	3 and 1
1954	JW Draper	W Gray	Nairn	4 and 3
1955	RR Jack	AC Miller	Muirfield	2 and 1
1956	Dr FWG Deighton	A MacGregor	Troon	8 and 7
1957	JS Montgomerie	J Burnside	Balgownie	2 and 1
1958	WD Smith	I Harris	Prestwick	6 and 5
1959	Dr FWG Deighton	R Murray	St Andrews	6 and 5
1960	JR Young	S Saddler	Carnoustie	5 and 3

continued

Scottish Amateur Championship *continued*

Year	Winner	Runner-up	Venue	By
1961	J Walker	ST Murray	Western Gailes	4 and 3
1962	SWT Murray	R Shade	Muirfield	2 and 1
1963	RDBM Shade	N Henderson	Troon	4 and 3
1964	RDBM Shade	J McBeath	Nairn	8 and 7
1965	RDBM Shade	G Cosh	St Andrews	4 and 2
1966	RDBM Shade	C Strachan	Western Gailes	9 and 8
1967	RDBM Shade	A Murphy	Carnoustie	5 and 4
1968	GB Cosh	R Renfrew	Muirfield	4 and 3
1969	JM Cannon	A Hall	Troon	6 and 4
1970	CW Green	H Stewart	Balgownie, Aberdeen	1 hole
1971	S Stephen	C Green	St Andrews	3 and 2
1972	HB Stuart	A Pirie	Prestwick	3 and 1
1973	IC Hutcheon	A Brodie	Carnoustie	3 and 2
1974	GH Murray	A Pirie	Western Gailes	2 and 1
1975	D Greig	G Murray	Montrose	7 and 6
1976	GH Murray	H Stuart	St Andrews	6 and 5
1977	A Brodie	P McKellar	Troon	1 hole
1978	IA Carslaw	J Cuddihy	Downfield	7 and 6
1979	K Macintosh	P McKellar	Prestwick	5 and 4
1980	D Jamieson	C Green	Balgownie, Aberdeen	2 and 1 *(18 holes)*
1981	C Dalgleish	A Thomson	Western Gailes	7 and 6
1982	CW Green	G McGregor	Carnoustie	1 hole
1983	CW Green	J Huggan	Gullane	1 hole
1984	A Moir	K Buchan	Renfrew	3 and 3
1985	D Carrick	D James	Southerness	4 and 2
1986	C Brooks	A Thomson	Monifieth	3 and 2
1987	C Montgomerie	A Watt	Nairn	9 and 8
1988	J Milligan	A Colthart	Barassie	1 hole
1989	A Thomson	A Tait	Moray	1 hole
1990	C Everett	M Thomson	Gullane	7 and 5
1991	G Lowson	L Salariya	Downfield	4 and 3
1992	S Gallacher	D Kirkpatrick	Glasgow Gailes	37th hole
1993	D Robertson	R Russell	R Dornoch	2 holes
1994	H McKibben	A Reid	Renfrew	39th hole
1995	S Mackenzie	H McKibben	Southerness	8 and 7
1996	M Brooks	A Turnbull	Dunbar	7 and 6
1997	C Hislop	S Cairns	Carnoustie	5 and 3

Scottish Open Amateur Stroke Play Championship

Year	Winner	Venue	Score
1967	BJ Gallacher	Muirfield and Gullane	291
1968	RDBM Shade	Prestwick and Prestwick St Nicholas	282
1969	JS Macdonald	Carnoustie and Monifieth	288
1970	D Hayes	Glasgow Gailes and Barassie	275
1971	IC Hutcheon	Leven and Lundin Links	277
1972	BN Nicholas	Dalmahoy and Ratho Park	290
1973 T	DM Robertson/GJ Clark	Dunbar and North Berwick	284
1974	IC Hutcheon	Blairgowrie and Alyth	283
1975	CW Green	Nairn and Nairn Dunbar	295
1976	S Martin	Monifieth and Carnoustie	299
1977	PJ McKellar	Muirfield and Gullane	299
1978	AR Taylor	Keir and Cawder	281
1979	IC Hutcheon	Lansdowne and Rosemount	286
1980	G Brand Jr	Musselburgh and R Musselburgh	207 *(54 holes)*
1981	F Walton	Erskine and Renfrew	287
1982	C Macgregor	Downfield and Camperdown	287
1983	C Murray	Irvine	291
1984	CW Green	Blairgowrie	287
1985	C Montgomerie	Dunbar	274
1986	KH Walker	Carnoustie	289
1987	D Carrick	Lundin Links	282
1988	S Easingwood	Cathkin Braes	277
1989	F Illouz	Blairgowrie	281
1990	G Hay	R Aberdeen	133 *(36 holes)*
1991	A Coltart	Renfrew	291
1992	D Robertson	Mortonhall	281

Year	Winner	Venue	Score
1993	A Reid	St Andrews	289
1994	D Downie	Letham Grange	288
1995	S Gallacher	Paisley	284
1996	A Forsyth	Cardross	279
1997	DB Howard	Monifieth and Panmure	271

Scottish Open Amateur Seniors' Championship

Year	Winner	Venue	Score
1978 T	JM Cannon/GR Carmichael	Glasgow Killermont	149
1979	A Sinclair	Glasgow Killermont	143
1980	JM Cannon	Royal Burgess	149
1981 T	IR Harris/Dr J Hastings/AN Sturrock	Glasgow Killermont	146
1982 T	JM Cannon/J Niven	Royal Burgess	143
1983	WD Smith	Glasgow Killermont	145
1984	A Sinclair	Royal Burgess	148
1985	AN Sturrock	Glasgow Killermont	143
1986	RL Glading	Royal Burgess	153
1987	I Hornsby	Glasgow Killermont	145
1988	J Hayes	Royal Burgess	143
1989	AS Mayer	Glasgow Killermont	
1990	G Hartland	Royal Burgess	146
1991	CW Green	Glasgow Killermont	140
1992	G Clark	Royal Burgess	148
1993	J Maclean	Glasgow Killermont	141
1994	DM Laurie	Ladybank	149
1995	CW Green	Glasgow	141
1996	CW Green	Western Gailes	146
1997	CW Green	Glasgow Killermont	137

Scottish Ladies' Amateur Championship

Year	Winner	Runner-up	Venue	By
1960	JS Robertson	DT Sommerville	Turnberry	2 and 1
1961	JS Wright (née Robertson)	AM Lurie	St Andrews	1 hole
1962	JB Lawrence	C Draper	R Dornoch	5 and 4
1963	JB Lawrence	IC Robertson	Troon	2 and 1
1964	JB Lawrence	SM Reid	Gullane	5 and 3
1965	IC Robertson	JB Lawrence	Nairn	5 and 4
1966	IC Robertson	M Fowler	Machrihanish	2 and 1
1967	J Hastings	A Laing	North Berwick	5 and 3
1968	J Smith	J Rennie	Carnoustie	10 and 9
1969	JH Anderson	K Lackie	West Kilbride	5 and 4
1970	A Laing	IC Robertson	Dunbar	1 hole
1971	IC Robertson	A Ferguson	R Dornoch	3 and 2
1972	IC Robertson	CJ Lugton	Machrihanish	5 and 3
1973	I Wright	Dr AJ Wilson	St Andrews	2 holes
1974	Dr AJ Wilson	K Lackie	Nairn	22nd hole
1975	LA Hope	JW Smith	Elie	1 hole
1976	S Needham	T Walker	Machrihanish	3 and 2
1977	CJ Lugton	M Thomson	R Dornoch	1 hole
1978	IC Robertson	JW Smith	Prestwick	2 holes
1979	G Stewart	LA Hope	Gullane	2 and 1
1980	IC Robertson	F Anderson	Carnoustie	1 hole
1981	A Gemmill	W Aitken	Stranraer	2 and 1
1982	J Connachan	P Wright	R Troon	19th hole
1983	G Stewart	F Anderson	North Berwick	3 and 1
1984	G Stewart	A Gemmill	R Dornoch	3 and 2
1985	A Gemmill	D Thomson	Barassie	2 and 1
1986	IC Robertson	L Hope	St Andrews	3 and 2
1987	F Anderson	C Middleton	Nairn	4 and 3
1988	S Lawson	F Anderson	Southerness	3 and 1
1989	J Huggon	L Anderson	Lossiemouth	5 and 4
1990	E Farquharson	S Huggan	Machrihanish	3 and 2
1991	C Lambert	F Anderson	Carnoustie	3 and 2
1992	J Moody	E Farquharson	R Aberdeen	2 and 1

continued

Scottish Ladies' Amateur Championship *continued*

Year	Winner	Runner-up	Venue	By
1993	C Lambert	M McKay	Prestwick St Nicholas	5 and 4
1994	C Matthew	V Melvin	Gullane	1 hole
1995	H Monaghan	S McMaster	Portpatrick	21st hole
1996	A Laing	A Rose	R Dornoch	1 hole
1997	A Rose	H Monaghan	W Kilbride	3 and 2

Welsh Amateur Championship

Year	Winner	Runner-up	Venue	By
1934	SB Roberts	GS Noon	Prestatyn	4 and 3
1935	R Chapman	GS Noon	Tenby	1 hole
1936	RM de Lloyd	G Wallis	Aberdovey	1 hole
1937	DH Lewis	R Glossop	Porthcawl	2 holes
1938	AA Duncan	SB Roberts	Rhyl	2 and 1
1946	JV Moody	A Marshman	Porthcawl	9 and 8
1947	SB Roberts	G Breen Turner	Harlech	8 and 7
1948	AA Duncan	SB Roberts	Porthcawl	2 and 1
1949	AD Evans	MA Jones	Aberdovey	2 and 1
1950	JL Morgan	DJ Bonnell	Southerndown	9 and 7
1951	JL Morgan	WI Tucker	Harlech	3 and 2
1952	AA Duncan	JL Morgan	Ashburnham	4 and 3
1953	SB Roberts	D Pearson	Prestatyn	5 and 3
1954	AA Duncan	K Thomas	Tenby	6 and 5
1955	TJ Davies	P Dunn	Harlech	38th hole
1956	A Lockley	WI Tucker	Southerndown	2 and 1
1957	ES Mills	H Griffiths	Harlech	2 and 1
1958	HC Squirrell	AD Lake	Conway	4 and 3
1959	HC Squirrell	N Rees	Porthcawl	8 and 7
1960	HC Squirrell	P Richards	Aberdovey	2 and 1
1961	AD Evans	J Toye	Ashburnham	3 and 2
1962	J Povall	HC Squirrell	Harlech	3 and 2
1963	WI Tucker	J Toye	Southerndown	4 and 3
1964	HC Squirrell	WI Tucker	Harlech	1 hole
1965	HC Squirrell	G Clay	Porthcawl	6 and 4
1966	WI Tucker	EN Davies	Aberdovey	6 and 5
1967	JK Povall	WI Tucker	Asburnham	3 and 2
1968	J Buckley	J Povall	Conway	8 and 7
1969	JL Toye	EN Davies	Porthcawl	1 hole
1970	EN Davies	J Povall	Harlech	1 hole
1971	CT Brown	HC Squirrell	Southerndown	6 and 5
1972	EN Davies	JL Toye	Prestatyn	40th hole
1973	D McLean	T Holder	Ashburnham	6 and 4
1974	S Cox	EN Davies	Caernarvonshire	3 and 2
1975	JL Toye	WI Tucker	Porthcawl	5 and 4
1976	MPD Adams	WI Tucker	Harlech	6 and 5
1977	D Stevens	JKD Povall	Southerndown	3 and 2
1978	D McLean	A Ingram	Caernarvonshire	11 and 10
1979	TJ Melia	MS Roper	Ashburnham	5 and 4
1980	DL Stevens	G Clement	Prestatyn	10 and 9
1981	S Jones	C Davies	Porthcawl	5 and 3
1982	D Wood	C Davies	Harlech	8 and 7
1983	JR Jones	AP Parkin	Southerndown	2 holes
1984	JR Jones	A Llyr	Prestatyn	1 hole
1985	ED Jones	MA Macara	Ashburnham	2 and 1
1986	C Rees	B Knight	Conwy	1 hole
1987	PM Mayo	DK Wood	Porthcawl	2 holes
1988	K Jones	RN Roderick	Harlech	40th hole
1989	S Dodd	K Jones	Tenby	2 and 1
1990	A Barnett	A Jones	Prestatyn	1 hole
1991	S Pardoe	S Jones	Ashburnham	7 and 5
1992	H Roberts	R Johnson	Pyle & Kenfig	3 and 2
1993	B Dredge	M Ellis	Southerndown	3 and 1
1994	C Evans	M Smith	Royal Porthcawl	5 and 4
1995	G Houston	C Evans	R St David's	3 and 2
1996	Y Taylor	DH Park	Ashburnham	3 and 2
1997	JR Donaldson	M Pilkington	Pyle & Kenfig	5 and 4

Welsh Amateur Stroke Play Championship

Year	Winner	Venue	Score
1967	EN Davies	Harlech	295
1968	JA Buckley	Harlech	294
1969	DL Stevens	Tenby	288
1970	JK Povall	Newport	292
1971 T	EN Davies	Harlech	296
	JL Toye		
1972	JR Jones	Pyle & Kenfig	299
1973	JR Jones	Llandudno (Maesdu)	300
1974	JL Toye	Tenby	307
1975	D McLean	Wrexham	288
1976	WI Tucker	Newport	282
1977	JA Buckley	Prestatyn	302
1978	HJ Evans	Pyle & Kenfig	300
1979	D McLean	Holyhead	289
1980	TJ Melia	Tenby	291
1981	D Evans	Wrexham	270
1982	JR Jones	Cradoc	287
1983	G Davies	Aberdovey	287
1984	RN Roderick	Newport	292
1985	MA Macara	Harlech	291
1986	M Calvert	Pyle & Kenfig	299
1987	MA Macara	Llandudno (Maesdu)	290
1988	RN Roderick	Tenby	283
1989	SC Dodd	Conwy	304

Open event since 1990

Year	Winner	Venue	Score
1990	G Houston	Pyle & Kenfig	288
1991	A Jones	R Porthcawl	290
1992	AJ Barnett	R St David's	278
1993	M Macara	Maesdu	280
1994	N Van Hootegem	St Pierre	290
1995	M Peet	Prestatyn	282
1996	M Blackey	Tenby	276
1997	G Wolstenholme	Conwy	286

Welsh Seniors' Amateur Championship

Year	Winner	Venue	Score
1975	A Marshman	Aberdovey	77 *(18 holes)*
1976	AD Evans	Aberdovey	156
1977	AE Lockley	Aberdovey	154
1978	AE Lockley	Aberdovey	75 *(18 holes)*
1979	CR Morgan	Aberdovey	158
1980	ES Mills	Aberdovey	152
1981	T Branton	Aberdovey	153
1982	WI Tucker	Aberdovey	147
1983	WS Gronow	Aberdovey	153
1984	WI Tucker	Aberdovey	150
1985	NA Lycett	Aberdovey	149
1986	E Mills	Aberdovey	154
1987	WS Gronow	Aberdovey	146
1988	NA Lycett	Aberdovey	150
1989	WI Tucker	Aberdovey	160
1990	I Hughes	Aberdovey	159
1991	RO Ward	Aberdovey	155
1992	I Hughes	Aberdovey	150
1993	G Perks	Aberdovey	149
1994T	G Perks/I Hughes/A Prytherch	Aberdovey	157
1995	I Hughes	Aberdovey	147
1996	G Isaac	Aberdovey	152
1997	I Hughes	Aberdovey	148

Welsh Ladies' Amateur Championship

Year	Winner	Runner-up	Venue	By
1960	M Barron	E Brown	Tenby	8 and 6
1961	M Oliver	N Sneddon	Aberdovey	5 and 4
1962	M Oliver	P Roberts	Radyr	4 and 2
1963	P Roberts	N Sneddon	Harlech	7 and 5
1964	M Oliver	M Wright	Southerndown	1 hole
1965	M Wright	E Brown	Prestatyn	3 and 2
1966	A Hughes	P Roberts	Ashburnham	5 and 4
1967	M Wright	C Phipps	Harlech	21st hole
1968	S Hales	M Wright	Porthcawl	3 and 2
1969	P Roberts	A Hughes	Caernarvonshire	3 and 2
1970	A Briggs	J Morris	Newport	19th hole
1971	A Briggs	EN Davies	Harlech	2 and 1
1972	A Hughes	J Rogers	Tenby	3 and 2
1973	A Briggs	J John	Holyhead	3 and 2
1974	A Briggs	Dr H Lyall	Ashburnham	3 and 2
1975	A Johnson (*née* Hughes)	K Rawlings	Prestatyn	1 hole
1976	T Perkins	A Johnson	Porthcawl	4 and 2
1977	T Perkins	P Whitley	Aberdovey	5 and 4
1978	P Light	A Briggs	Newport	2 and 1
1979	V Rawlings	A Briggs	Caernarvonshire	2 holes
1980	M Rawlings	A Briggs	Tenby	2 and 1
1981	M Rawlings	A Briggs	Harlech	5 and 3
1982	V Thomas (*née* Rawlings)	M Rawlings	Ashburnham	7 and 6
1983	V Thomas	T Thomas (*née* Perkins)	Llandudno	1 hole
1984	S Roberts	K Davies	Newport	5 and 4
1985	V Thomas	S Jump	Prestatyn	1 hole
1986	V Thomas	L Isherwood	Porthcawl	7 and 6
1987	V Thomas	S Roberts	Aberdovey	3 and 1
1988	S Roberts	F Connor	Tenby	4 and 2
1989	H Lawson	V Thomas	Conwy	2 and 1
1990	S Roberts	H Wadsworth	Ashburnham	3 and 2
1991	V Thomas	H Lawson	R St David's	4 and 3
1992	J Foster	S Boyes	Newport	4 and 3
1993	A Donne	V Thomas	Abergele & Pensarn	19th hole
1994	V Thomas	L Dermott	Royal Porthcawl	19th hole
1995	L Dermott	K Stark	Aberdovey	19th hole
1996	L Dermott	V Thomas	Tenby	4 and 3
1997	E Pilgrim	L Davis	Northop	4 and 2

Welsh Ladies' Open Amateur Stroke Play Championship

Year	Winner	Venue	Score
1981	V Thomas	Aberdovey	224
1982	V Thomas	Aberdovey	225
1983	J Thornhill	Aberdovey	239
1984	L Davies	Aberdovey	230
1985	C Swallow	Aberdovey	219
1986	H Wadsworth	Aberdovey	223
1987	S Shapcott	Newport	225
1988	S Shapcott	Newport	218
1989	V Thomas	Newport	220
1990	L Hackney	Newport	218
1991	M Sutton	R Porthcawl	224
1992	C Lambert	R Porthcawl	218
1993	J Hall	Newport	221
1994	A Rose	Newport	217
1995	F Brown	Newport	221
1996	E Duggleby	Whitchurch	223
1997	K Edwards	Whitchurch	216

Welsh Ladies' Senior Championship

Year	Winner	Venue	Score
1990	E Higgs	Vale of Llangollen	171
1991	H Lyall	Pyle and Kenfig	160
1992	P Morgan	Cardigan	83
1993	P Morgan	Pwllheli	157
1994	C Thomas	Llandudno	163
1995	C Thomas	Tredegar Park	157
1996	C Thomas	Vale of Llangollen	157
1997	C Thomas	Fairwood Park	160

Overseas National Championships

(Excluding PGA European Tour Events)

Argentine Open Championship

Year	Winner	Year	Winner
1988	M Fernandez	1993	M Calcavecchia
1989	E Romero	1994	M O'Meara
1990	V Fernandez	1995	M Calcavecchia
1991	JD Blake	1996	P Martinez
1992	C Stadler	1997	J Furyk

Australian Open Championship

Year	Winner	Score
1978	J Nicklaus	284
1979	J Newton	288
1980	G Norman	284
1981	W Rogers	282
1982	B Shearer	287
1983	P Fowler	285
1984	T Watson	281
1985	G Norman	212 *(54 holes only – rain)*
1986	R Davis	278
1987	G Norman	273
1988	M Calcavecchia	269
1989	P Senior	271
1990	J Morse	283
1991	W Riley	285
1992	S Elkington	280
1993	B Faxon	275
1994	R Allenby	280
1995	G Norman	278
1996	G Norman	280
1997	L Westwood	274

Australian PGA Championship

Year	Winner	Year	Winner
1988	W Grady	1993	I Baker-Finch
1989	P Senior	1994	A Coltart
1990	B Ogle	1995	*Not played*
1991	W Grady	1996	P Tataurangi
1992	C Parry	1997	A Coltart

Australian Ladies' Open Championship

Year	Winner
1995	L Neumann
1996	C Matthew
1997	J Crafter

Australian Amateur Championship

Year	Winner	Year	Winner
1988	S Bouvier	1993	GJ Chalmers
1989	S Conran	1994	W Bennett
1990	C Gray	1995	M Coggin
1991	L Parsons	1996	D Gleeson
1992	M Campbell	1997	K Felton

Australian Ladies' Amateur Championship

Year	Winner	Year	Winner
1988	C Bourtayre	1993	A-M Knight
1989	J Higgins	1994	T McKinnon
1990	J Shearwood	1995	J Hall (GB)
1991	L Briers	1996	D Linnertson
1992	J Leary	1997	M Ellis

Austrian Amateur Open Championship

Year	Winner	Year	Winner
1988	L Peterson	1993	N Zitny
1989	U Zilg	1994	J-J Wolff
1990	A Peterskovsky	1995	J Gruere
1991	D Vanbegin	1996	T Biermann
1992	H-C Winkler	1997	C Bausek

Austrian Ladies' Open Championship

Year	Winner	Year	Winner
1988	H-F Tseng	1993	N Fink
1989	K Poppmeier	1994	F Descampe
1990	A Rast	1995	A Heuser
1991	L Navarro	1996	E Poburski
1992	K Poppmeier	1997	T Schneeberger

Canadian Open Championship

Year	Winner	Year	Winner
1978	B Lietzke	1988	K Green
1979	L Trevino	1989	S Jones
1980	B Gilder	1990	W Levi
1981	P Oosterhuis	1991	N Price
1982	B Lietzke	1992	G Norman
1983	J Cook	1993	D Frost
1984	G Norman	1994	N Price
1985	C Strange	1995	M O'Meara
1986	B Murphy	1996	D Hart
1987	C Strange	1997	S Jones

Canadian Amateur Championship

Year	Winner	Year	Winner
1988	D Roxburgh	1993	G Simpson
1989	P Major	1994	W Sye
1990	W Sye	1995	G Willis
1991	J Kraemer	1996	R McMillan
1992	D Ritchie	1997	D Goehring

Canadian Ladies' Open Amateur Championship

Year	Winner	Year	Winner
1988	M Hattori	1993	MA Lapointe
1989	C Damphouse	1994	A Robertson
1990	S Lebrun	1995	T Lipp
1991	A Moore	1996	MA Lapointe
1992	MJ Rouleau	1997	AJ Eathorne

Côte d'Ivoire Open Championship

Year	Winner	Year	Winner
1991	D Llewellyn	1995	*Not played*
1992	M Bescanceny	1996	M Florioli
1993	*Not played*	1997	K Storegaard
1994	W Bradley		

Czechoslovak Open Amateur Championship

Year	Winner	Year	Winner
1988	M Brtek	1993	R Pientka
1989	A Krag	1994	F Mansson
1990	J Janda	1995	R Chudoba
1991	J Kunšta	1996	M Ettl
1992	R Chudoba	1997	U Paulsen

Czechoslovak Ladies' Open Amateur Championship

Year	Winner	Year	Winner
1988	A Hudcová	1993	H Dvorská
1989	A Kugelmüller	1994	L Křenková
1990	A Kugelmüller	1995	G Teissingova
1991	L Křenková	1996	G Teissingova
1992	L Křenková	1997	G Teissingova

Danish Amateur Stroke Play Championship

Year	Winner	Year	Winner
1988	B Tinning	1993	N Roerbaek-Peterson
1989	R Budde	1994	AR Hansen
1990	T Bjørn	1995	N Roerbaek-Peterson
1991	T Svendsen	1996	C Moelholm
1992	AR Hansen	1997	S Hansen

Danish Ladies' Stroke Play Championship

Year	Winner	Year	Winner
1988	J Kragh	1993	A Östberg
1989	M Brandt Anderson	1994	C Faaborg
1990	P Carlson	1995	I Tinning
1991	I Tinning	1996	C Kuld
1992	I Tinning	1997	KM Juul

French Amateur Championship

Year	Winner	Year	Winner
1988	P Barquez	1993	M Dieu
1989	C Cevaer	1994	L Pargade
1990	O Edmond	1995	R Eyraud
1991	F Cupillard	1996	S Fabrice
1992	N Joakimides	1997	G Havret

French Ladies' Open Championship

Year	Winner	Year	Winner
1988	ML de Lorenzi	1993	*Not played*
1989	S Strudwick	1994	J Forbes
1990	*Not played*	1995	L Kreutz
1991	S Strudwick	1996	L Rolner
1992	*Not played*	1997	K Lunn

French Ladies' Amateur Championship

Year	Winner	Year	Winner
1988	C Marty	1993	S Louapre-Pfeiffer
1989	C Bourtayre	1994	C Mourgue d'Algue
1990	C Bourson	1995	A Vincent
1991	V Michaud	1996	C Morgue d'Algue
1992	P Mennier	1997	M Monnet

German PGA Championship

Year	Winner	Year	Winner
1988	T Giedeon	1993	W Linnenfelser
1989	T Giedeon	1994	S Yates
1990	S Strüver	1995	D O'Flynn
1991	T Giedeon	1996	E Simsek
1992	M Pyatt	1997	E Simsek

German Ladies' Open Championship *(1993 – Hennessy Cup)*

Year	Winner	Year	Winner
1988	L Neumann	1993	L Neumann
1989	A Nicholas	1994	L Neumann
1990	A Okamoto	1995	A Sorenstam
1991	F Descampe	1996	H Alfredsson
1992	*Not played*	1997	L Davies

German Ladies' PGA Close Championship

Year	Winner	Year	Winner
1988	D Franz	1993	S Lehmeier
1989	D Franz	1994	F Fehlauer
1990	D Franz	1995	F Fehlauer
1991	S Lehmeier	1996	M Koch
1992	S Lehmeier	1997	F Fehlauer

German Open Amateur Championship

Year	Winner	Year	Winner
1989	J Steenkamer	1994	JE Schapmann
1991	JE Schapmann	1995	M Brier
1992	M Zerman	1996	G Ogilvy
1993	JE Schapmann	1997	H Forster

German Ladies' Open Amateur Championship

Year	Winner	Year	Winner
1989	M Fischer	1994	AC Jonasson
1991	E Knuth	1995	C Schmitt
1992	A Heuser	1996	M Neggers
1993	M Koch	1997	M Eberl

German Close Amateur Championship

Year	Winner	Year	Winner
1988	U Zilg	1993	T Himmel
1989	HG Reiter	1994	JE Schapmann
1990	M vom Hagen	1995	B Schlichting
1991	T Himmel	1996	F Lubenau
1992	T Himmel	1997	T Schuster

German Ladies' Close Amateur Championship

Year	Winner	Year	Winner
1988	C von Grundherr	1993	N Stillig
1989	M Fischer	1994	L Gehlen
1990	L Gehlen	1995	Dr P Peter
1991	A Heuser	1996	AJ Heuser
1992	M Fischer	1997	B Echterling

Hong Kong Open Championship

Year	Winner	Year	Winner
1988	H Chin-sheng	1993	B Watts
1989	B Claar	1994	D Frost
1990	K Green	1995	G Webb
1991	B Langer	1996	G Webb
1992	T Watson	1997	F Nobilo

India Open Championship

Year	Winner	Year	Winner
1988	L Chien-Soon	1993	A Sher
1989	R Bouchard	1994	E Aubrey
1990	A Debusk	1995	J Rutledge
1991	A Sher	1996	H Shirakata
1992	S Ginn	1997	E Fryatt

Italian Professional Championship

Year	Winner	Year	Winner
1988	A Canessa	1993	G Cali
1989	C Rocca	1994	G Cali
1990	M Mannelli	1995	E Bolognesi
1991	A Canessa	1996	L Gallardo
1992	M Reale	1997	M Florioli

Italian Open Amateur Championship

Year	Winner	Year	Winner
1988	E Giraud	1993	J Kjaerbye
1989	R Victor	1994	D Dupin
1990	M Tadini	1995	R Paolillo
1991	D Borrego	1996	H Stenson
1992	*Not played*	1997	R Quiros

Italian Close Amateur Championship

Year	Winner	Year	Winner
1988	M de Rossi	1993	F Crotti
1989	G Ferrero	1994	N Bisazza
1990	M Aragnetti	1995	A Napoleoni
1991	M Santi	1996	A Napoleoni
1992	F Pustetto	1997	A Napoleoni

Italian Ladies' Open Championship

Year	Winner	Year	Winner
1988	L Davies	1993	F Stensrud
1989	X Wunsch-Ruiz	1994	K Speak
1990	F Descampe	1995	D Booker
1991	C Dibnah	1996	L Davies
1992	L Davies	1997	C Sjöblom

Japan Open Championship

Year	Winner	Year	Winner
1988	M Ozaki	1993	S Okuda
1989	M Ozaki	1994	M Ozaki
1990	T Nakajima	1995	T Izwa
1991	T Nakajima	1996	P Teravainen
1992	M Ozaki	1997	C Parry

Japan Professional Championship

Year	Winner	Year	Winner
1988	T Ozaki	1993	M Ozaki
1989	M Ozaki	1994	H Goda
1990	H Kase	1995	H Sasaki
1991	O Masashi	1996	M Ozaki
1992	M Kuramoto	1997	S Maruyama

Japan Amateur Championship

Year	Winner	Year	Winner
1988	R Kawagishi	1993	K Yonekura
1989	K Oie	1994	S Sugimoto
1990	Y Kuramoto	1995	S Sugimoto
1991	K Miyamoto	1996	H Hoshino
1992	K Yonekura	1997	H Chia-Yuh

Kenya Open Championship

Year	Winner	Year	Winner
1988	C Platts	1993	C Maltman
1989	D Jones	1994	P Carman
1990	C O'Connor Jr	1995	J Lee
1991	J Robinson	1996	M Miller
1992	A Bossert	1997	J Berendt

Korea Open Championship

Year	Winner	Year	Winner
1988	Kwak Yu Hyun	1993	Y Kun Han
1989	Chul Sang Cho	1994	M Cunning
1990	L Kang-Sun	1995	B Jobe
1991	Choi Sang Ho	1996	Choi Kyung-Ju
1992	T Hamilton	1997	K Jong-Duck

Malaysian Open Championship

Year	Winner	Year	Winner
1988	T Tyner	1993	G Norquist
1989	J Maggert	1994	J Haeggman
1990	G Day	1995	C Devers
1991	R Gibson	1996	S Flesch
1992	V Singh	1997	L Westwood

Malaysian Women's Open Championship

Year	Winner	Year	Winner
1988	B New	1993	S Prosser
1989	N Terazawa	1994	J-S Won
1990	C Nishida	1995	C Dibnah
1991	C Nishida	1996	C Dibnah
1992	C Nishida	1997	P Rigby-Jinglov

Mauritius Open Championship

Year	Winner
1994	M McLean
1995	M Santi
1996	P Golding
1997	G Sherry

Mexican Open Championship

Year	Winner
1993	T Sieckmann
1994	C Perry
1995	J Cook
1996	S Cink
1997	F Nobilo

New Zealand Open Championship

Year	Winner	Year	Winner
1988	I Stanley	1993	P Fowler
1989	G Turner	1994	C Jones
1990	Not played	1995	L Parsons
1991	R Davis	1996	M Long
1992	G Waite	1997	G Turner

New Zealand Amateur Championship

Year	Winner	Year	Winner
1988	B Hughes	1993	P Tataurangi
1989	L Peterson	1994	P Fitzgibbon
1990	M Long	1995	S Bittle
1991	L Parsons	1996	D Somervaille
1992	R Lee	1997	C Johns

New Zealand Ladies' Amateur Championship

Year	Winner	Year	Winner
1988	E Cavill	1993	L Brooky
1989	W Sook	1994	JA Atkin
1990	L Brooky	1995	G Scott
1991	A Stott	1996	L Aldridge
1992	L Lambert	1997	J Oliver

Nigerian Open Championship

Year	Winner	Year	Winner
1988	V Singh	1993	G Manson
1989	V Singh	1994	E Korblah
1990	W Stephens	1995	L Lasisi
1991	J Lebbie	1996	*Not played*
1992	J Lebbie	1997	*Not played*

Nordic Amateur Championship *(Team event since 1993; previously Scandinavian Amateur Open)*

Year	Winner	Year	Winner
1988	H Simonsen	1993	Sweden
1989	P-U Johansson	1994	*Not played*
1990	P Magnebrandt	1995	Sweden
1991	M Olander	1996	*Not played*
1992	P Sterner	1997	Sweden

Nordic Ladies' Amateur Championship *(Previously Scandinavian Ladies's Amateur Open. Became a team event in 1993)*

Year	Winner	Year	Winner
1988	M Binau	1993	Sweden
1989	K Orum	1994	*Not played*
1990	A Dönnestad	1995	Denmark
1991	K Larsson	1996	*Not played*
1992	C Norvang	1997	Sweden

Portuguese Open Amateur Championship

Year	Winner	Year	Winner
1988	C Waesberg	1993	A Townhill
1989	S Bjorn	1994	M Backhausen
1990	R Oliveira	1995	G D'Hollander
1991	*Not played*	1996	M Lehtinen
1992	K Ekjord	1997	

Portuguese Close Amateur Championship

Year	Winner	Year	Winner
1988	R Oliveira	1993	J Carvalhosa
1989	A Castelo	1994	J Correia
1990	J Granja	1995	M Coelho
1991	J Carvalhosa	1996	S Corte-Real
1992	A Castelo	1997	S Castro Ferreira

Portuguese Ladies' Open Amateur Championship

Year	Winner	Year	Winner
1988	H Andersson	1993	M Arruti
1989	S Clauset	1994	S Dallongeville
1990	S Navarro	1995	ML de Lorenzi
1991	T Abecassis	1996	F Rossary
1992	L Navarro	1997	A Belen Sanchez

Singapore Open Championship

Year	Winner	Year	Winner
1988	G Bruckner	1993	P Maloney
1989	C-S Lu	1994	KH Han
1990	A Fernando	1995	S Conran
1991	J Kay	1996	J Kernohan
1992	B Israelson	1997	Z Moe

South African Open Championship

Year	Winner	Year	Winner
1988	W Westner	1993	C Whitelaw
1989	F Wadsworth	1994	T Johnstone
1990	T Dodds	1995	R Goosen
1991	W Westner	1996	E Els
1992	E Els	1997	V Singh

South African Masters

Year	Winner	Year	Winner
1988	J Bland	1993	T Johnstone
1989	H Baiocchi	1994	C Davison
1990	H Baiocchi	1995	S Dunlap
1991	F Allem	1996	W Westner
1992	E Els	1997	M McNulty

South African PGA Championship

Year	Winner	Year	Winner
1988	D Feherty	1993	M McNulty
1989	A Johnstone	1994	D Frost
1990	F Allem	1995	E Els
1991	R Wessels	1996	S Struver
1992	E Els	1997	N Price

South African Amateur Championship

Year	Winner	Year	Winner
1988	N Clarke	1993	L Chitengwa
1989	C Rivett	1994	B Vaughn
1990	R Goosen	1995	W Abery
1991	D Botes	1996	T Moore
1992	B Davison	1997	

South African Amateur Stroke Play Championship

Year	Winner	Year	Winner
1988	N Clarke	1993	D Kinnear
1989	E Els	1994	N Homann
1990	P Pascoe	1995	M Murles
1991	N Henning	1996	T Moore
1992	J Nelson	1997	

South African Ladies' Championship

Year	Winner	Year	Winner
1988	G Tebbutt	1993	M Adamson
1989	L Rose	1994	S Marais
1990	G Tebbutt	1995	G Tebbutt
1991	B Lunsford	1996	P Hall
1992	M Adamson	1997	

Spanish Open Amateur Championship

Year	Winner	Year	Winner
1988	S Atako	1993	F Stolear
1989	E Giraud	1994	J Healey
1990	D Clarke	1995	B Muir
1991	TJ Muñoz	1996	JM Lara
1992	M Stanford	1997	M Lafeber

Spanish Amateur Close Championship

Year	Winner	Year	Winner
1988	T Muñoz	1993	JA Vizcaya
1989	T Muñoz	1994	F Valera
1990	G de la Riva	1995	F Cisa
1991	D Borrego	1996	R Gonzalez
1992	A Prat	1997	S Garcia

Spanish Ladies' Open Amateur Championship

Year	Winner	Year	Winner
1988	I Calogero	1993	C Lambert
1989	I Calogero	1994	AC Jonasson
1990	D Bourson	1995	M Jorth
1991	C Quintarelli	1996	J Hall
1992	J Hall	1997	K Icher

Spanish Ladies' Amateur Close Championship

Year	Winner	Year	Winner
1988	S Navarro	1993	E Knuth
1989	S Navarro	1994	M Arruti
1990	E Valera	1995	I Elguezabal
1991	A Arruti	1996	P Martin
1992	E Knuth	1997	M Prieto

Swedish Professional Championship

Year	Winner	Year	Winner
1988	V Singh	1993	N Fasth
1989	L Hederström	1994	A Mednick
1990	A Mednick	1995	D Edlund
1991	J Ryström	1996	M Anglert
1992	S Bottomley	1997	M Krantz

Swedish Open International Stroke Play Championship

Year	Winner	Year	Winner
1988	P Haugsrud	1993	D Chopra
1989	A Gillner	1994	E Carlberg
1990	J Parnevik	1995	D Edlund
1991	J Sewell	1996	K Väinölä
1992	J Haeggman	1997	J Rask

Swedish Open Championship
(Close 1984–9)

Year	Winner	Year	Winner
1988	M Krantz	1993	P Haugsrud
1989	M Grankvist	1994	P Nyman
1990	E O'Connell	1995	P Thorn
1991	M Gronberg	1996	A Mednick
1992	J Cantero	1997	R Sjöberg

Swedish Ladies' Open Stroke Play Championship

Year	Winner	Year	Winner
1988	H Alfredsson	1993	D Reid
1989	S Norberg	1994	P Rigby
1990	M Bjurö	1995	M Löjdahl
1991	A Sörenstam	1996	P Rigby-Jinglov
1992	C Sörenstam	1997	M Tveit

Swedish Ladies' Open Championship *(Close before 1989)*

Year	Winner	Year	Winner
1988	H Alfredsson	1993	M Hjorth
1989	P Nilsson	1994	L Neumann
1990	J Allmark	1995	M Löjdahl
1991	L Ericsson	1996	A Berg
1992	C Hjalmarsson	1997	C Nilsmark

Swiss Open Amateur Championship

Year	Winner	Year	Winner
1988	A Bossert	1993	N Zitny
1989	M Frank	1994	M Brier
1990	M Santi	1995	A Langenaeken
1991	J Wade	1996	F Luca
1992	T Gottstein	1997	M Lafeber

Swiss Close Amateur Championship

Year	Winner	Year	Winner
1988	A Bossert	1993	J Ciola
1989	M Frank	1994	M Chatelain
1990	T Gottstein	1995	M Velan
1991	M Frank	1996	N Sulzer
1992	J Ciola	1997	M Chatelain

Swiss Ladies' Open Amateur Championship

Year	Winner	Year	Winner
1988	M Koch	1993	N Fink
1989	V Pamard	1994	A Nistri
1990	M Hagemann	1995	M Alsuguren
1991	M Hagemann	1996	M Alsuguren
1992	M Alsuguren	1997	A Gasser

Swiss Ladies' Close Amateur Championship

Year	Winner	Year	Winner
1988	E Orley	1993	L Schaufelberger
1989	C Vannini	1994	S Storjohann
1990	C Vannini	1995	B Albisetti
1991	S Ducrey	1996	S Lee
1992	S Ducrey	1997	S Lee

Thailand Open

Year	Winner
1997	C Chernock

United States Amateur Championship

Year	Winner	Runner-up	Venue	By
1946	SE Bishop	S Quick	Baltusrol	37th hole
1947	RH Riegel	J Dawson	Pebble Beach	2 and 1
1948	WP Turnesa	R Billows	Memphis, TN	2 and 1
1949	C Coe	R King	Rochester, NY	11 and 10
1950	S Urzetta	FR Stranahan	Minneapolis	39th hole
1951	WJ Maxwell	J Cagliardi	Saucon Valley, PA	4 and 3
1952	J Westland	A Mengert	Seattle	3 and 2
1953	G Littler	D Morey	Oklahoma City	1 hole
1954	A Palmer	R Sweeney	Detroit, MI	1 hole
1955	E Harvie Ward	W Hyndman	Richmond, VA	9 and 8
1956	E Harvie Ward	C Kocsis	Lake Forest, IL	5 and 4
1957	H Robbins	Dr F Taylor	Brookline	5 and 4
1958	C Coe	T Aaron	San Francisco	5 and 4
1959	J Nicklaus	C Coe	Broadmoor	1 hole
1960	DR Beman	R Gardner	St Louis, MO	6 and 4
1961	J Nicklaus	D Wysong	Pebble Beach	8 and 6
1962	LE Harris, Jr	D Gray	Pinehurst	1 hole

Year	Winner	Runner-up	Venue	By
1963	DR Beman	D Sikes	Des Moines	2 and 1
1964	W Campbell	E Tutweiler	Canterbury, OH	1 hole

Changed to stroke play

Year	Winner	Runner-up	Venue	By
1965	R Murphy		Tulsa, OK	291
1966	G Cowan		Ardmore, PA	285
1967	R Dickson		Colorado	285
1968	B Fleisher		Columbus	284
1969	S Melnyk		Oakmont	286
1970	L Wadkins		Portland	280
1971	G Cowan		Wilmington	280
1972	M Giles		Charlotte, NC	285

Reverted to match play

Year	Winner	Runner-up	Venue	By
1973	C Stadler	D Strawn	Inverness, OH	6 and 5
1974	J Pate	J Grace	Ridgewood, NJ	2 and 1
1975	F Ridley	K Fergus	Richmond, VA	2 holes
1976	B Sander	P Moore	Bel-Air	8 and 6
1977	J Fought	D Fischesser	Aronimonk, Pa	9 and 8
1978	J Cook	S Hoch	Plainfield, NJ	5 and 4
1979	M O'Meara	J Cook	Canterbury, OH	8 and 7
1980	H Sutton	B Lewis	North Carolina	9 and 8
1981	N Crosby	B Lyndley	San Francisco	37th hole
1982	J Sigel	D Tolley	The Country Club, Brookline	8 and 7
1983	J Sigel	C Perry	North Shore, Chicago	8 and 7
1984	S Verplank	S Randolph	Oak Tree, OK	4 and 3
1985	S Randolph	P Persons	Montclair, NJ	1 hole
1986	S Alexander	C Kite	Shoal Creek	5 and 3
1987	W Mayfair	E Rebmann	Jupiter Hills, FL	4 and 3
1988	E Meeks	D Yates	Hot Springs, VA	7 and 6
1989	C Patton	D Green	Merion, PA	3 and 1
1990	P Mickelson	M Zerman	Cherry Hills, CO	5 and 4
1991	M Voges	M Zerman	Honours Course, TN	7 and 6
1992	J Leonard	T Scherrer	Muirfield Village, OH	8 and 7
1993	J Harris	D Ellis	Champions, Houston	5 and 3
1994	T Woods	T Kuehne	Sawgrass	2 holes
1995	T Woods	G Marucci	Newport, Long Island, NY	2 holes
1996	T Woods	S Scott	Pumpkin Ridge, OR	38th hole
1997	M Kuchar	J Kribel	Cog Hill, Lemont, IL	2 and 1

United States Ladies' Amateur Championship

Year	Winner	Runner-up	Venue	By
1960	J Gunderson	J Ashley	Tulsa, Okla	6 and 5
1961	A Quast	P Preuss	Tacoma	14 and 13
1962	J Gunderson	A Baker	Rochester, NY	9 and 8
1963	A Quast	P Conley	Williamstown	2 and 1
1964	B McIntyre	J Gunderson	Prairie Dunes, Kansas	3 and 2
1965	J Ashley	A Quast	Denver	5 and 4
1966	J Carner (*née* Gunderson)	JD Streit	Pittsburgh	41st hole
1967	L Dill	J Ashley	Annandale, Pasadena	5 and 4
1968	J Carner	A Quast	Birmingham, Mich	5 and 4
1969	C Lacoste (Fra)	S Hamlin	Las Colinas, Texas	3 and 2
1970	M Wilkinson	C Hill	Darien, Conn	3 and 2
1971	L Baugh	B Barry	Atlanta	1 hole
1972	M Budke	C Hill	St Louis, Mo	5 and 4
1973	C Semple	A Quast	Montclair, NJ	1 hole
1974	C Hill	C Semple	Broadmoor, Seattle	5 and 4
1975	B Daniel	D Horton	Brae Burn, Mass	3 and 2
1976	D Horton	M Bretton	Del Paso, California	2 and 1
1977	B Daniel	C Sherk	Cincinnati	3 and 1
1978	C Sherk	J Oliver	Sunnybrook, Pa	4 and 3
1979	C Hill	P Sheehan	Memphis	7 and 6
1980	J Inkster	P Rizzo	Prairie Dunes, Kansas	2 holes
1981	J Inkster	L Coggan (Aus)	Portland, Oregon	1 hole
1982	J Inkster	C Hanton	Colorado Springs	4 and 3
1983	J Pacillo	S Quinlan	Canoe Brook, NJ	2 and 1
1984	D Richard	K Williams	Broadmoor, Seattle	37th hole
1985	M Hattori (Jpn)	C Stacy	Pittsburgh, PA	5 and 4
1986	K Cockerill	K McCarthy	Pasatiempo, California	9 and 7 *continued*

United States Ladies' Amateur Championship *continued*

Year	Winner	Runner-up	Venue	By
1987	K Cockerill	T Kerdyk	Barrington, RI	3 and 2
1988	P Sinn	K Noble	Minikahde, MN	6 and 5
1989	V Goetze	B Burton	Pinehurst, NC	4 and 3
1990	P Hurst	S Davis	Canoe Brook, NJ	37th hole
1991	A Fruhwirth	H Voorhees	Prairie Dunes	5 and 4
1992	V Goetze	A Sörenstam	Kemper Lakes	1 hole
1993	J McGill	S Ingram	San Diego	1 hole
1994	W Ward	J McGill	Hot Springs, VA	2 and 1
1995	K Kuehne	A-M Knight	Brookline	4 and 2
1996	K Kuehne	M Baena	Lincoln, Nebraska	2 and 1
1997	S Cavalleri	R Burke	Brae Burn, MA	5 and 4

Zambian Open Championship

Year	Winner	Year	Winner
1988	D Llewellyn	1993	P Harrison
1989	C Maltman	1994	*Not played*
1990	GJ Brand	1995	*Not played*
1991	DR Jones	1996	D Botes
1992	J Robinson	1997	*Not played*

Zimbabwe Open Championship

Year	Winner	Year	Winner
1991	K Waters	1995	N Price
1992	M McNulty	1996	N Price
1993	*Not played*	1997	M McNulty
1994	C Williams		

PGA European Tour

Johnnie Walker Asian Classic

Year	Winner	Score	Year	Winner	Score
1992	I Palmer	268	1996	I Woosnam	272
1993	N Faldo	269	1997	E Els	278
1994	G Norman	277			
1995	F Couples	277			

Austrian Open

Year	Winner	Score	Year	Winner	Score
1990	B Langer	271	1994	M Davis	270
1991	B Davis	269	1995	A Cejka	267
1992	P Mitchell	271	1996	P McGinley	269
1993	R Rafferty	274	1997	E Simsek	266

Belgian Open

Year	Winner	Score	Year	Winner	Score
1988	JM Olazabal	269	1993	D Clarke	270
1989	GJ Brand	273	1994	N Faldo	279
1990	O Sellberg	272	1995	Not played	
1991	P-U Johansson	276	1996	Not played	
1992	MA Jimenez	274	1997	Not played	

Benson and Hedges International Open

Year	Winner	Score	Year	Winner	Score
1988	P Baker	271	1993	P Broadhurst	276
1989	G Brand, Jr	272	1994	S Ballesteros	281
1990	JM Olazabal	279	1995	P O'Malley	280
1991	B Langer	286	1996	S Ames	283
1992	P Senior	287	1997	B Langer	276

BMW International Open

Year	Winner	Score	Year	Winner	Score
1989	D Feherty	269	1994	M McNulty	274
1990	P Azinger	277	1995	F Nobilo	272
1991	A Lyle	268	1996	M Farry	132
1992	P Azinger	266	1997	R Karlsson	264
1993	P Fowler	267			

British Masters

Year	Winner	Club/Country	Venue	Score
1982	G Norman	Australia	St Pierre	267
1983	I Woosnam	Wales	St Pierre	269
1984	*Not played*			
1985	L Trevino	USA	Woburn	278
1986	S Ballesteros	Spain	Woburn	275
1987	M McNulty	Zimbabwe	Woburn	274
1988	A Lyle	Scotland	Woburn	273
1989	N Faldo	England	Woburn	267
1990	M James	England	Woburn	270
1991	S Ballesteros	Spain	Woburn	275
1992	C O'Connor Jr	Ireland	Woburn	270
1993	P Baker	England	Woburn	266
1994	I Woosnam	Wales	Woburn	271
1995	S Torrance	Scotland	Collingtree	270
1996	R Allenby	Australia	Collingtree	284
1997	G Turner	New Zealand	Forest of Arden	275

Cannes Open

Year	Winner	Score	Year	Winner	Score	
1988	M McNulty	279	1993	R Davis	271	
1989	P Broadhurst	207 *(54 holes)*	1994	I Woosnam	271	
1990	M McNulty	280	1995	A Bossert	132	*Curtailed by weather*
1991	D Feherty	275	1996	R Russell	272	
1992	A Forsbrand	273	1997	S Cage	270	

Open Catalonia

Year	Winner	Score	Year	Winner	Score
1991	JM Olazabal	271	1995	P Walton	281
1992	J Rivero	280	1996	P Lawrie	135
1993	S Torrance	201 *(54 holes)*	1997	*Not played*	
1994	J Coceres	275			

Czech Open

Year	Winner	Score	Year	Winner	Score
1994	P-U Johansson	237	1997	B Langer	264
1995	P Teravainen	268			
1996	J Lomas	272			

Dubai Desert Classic

Year	Winner	Score	Year	Winner	Score
1989	M James	277	1994	E Els	268
1990	E Darcy	276	1995	F Couples	268
1991	*Not played*		1996	C Montgomerie	270
1992	S Ballesteros	272	1997	R Green	272
1993	W Westner	274			

Dutch Open

Year	Winner	Score	Year	Winner	Score
1988	M Mouland	274	1993	C Montgomerie	281
1989	JM Olazabal	277	1994	MA Jimenez	270
1990	S McAllister	274	1995	S Hoch	269
1991	P Stewart	267	1996	M McNulty	266
1992	B Langer	277	1997	S Strüver	266

English Open

Year	Winner	Venue	Score	Year	Winner	Venue	Score
1988	H Clark	R Birkdale	279	1993	I Woosnam	Forest of Arden	269
1989	M James	The Belfry	279	1994	C Montgomerie	Forest of Arden	274
1990	M James	The Belfry	284	1995	P Walton	Forest of Arden	274
1991	D Gilford	The Belfry	278	1996	R Allenby	Forest of Arden	278
1992	V Fernandez	The Belfry	283	1997	P-U Johansson	Hanbury Manor	269

European Masters – Swiss Open

Year	Winner	Score	Year	Winner	Score
1988	C Moody	268	1993	B Lane	270
1989	S Ballesteros	266	1994	E Romero	266
1990	R Rafferty	267	1995	M Gronberg	270
1991	J Hawkes	268	1996	C Montgomerie	260
1992	J Spence	271	1997	C Rocca	266

European Open

Year	Winner	Venue	Score	Year	Winner	Venue	Score
1980	T Kite	Walton Heath	284	1989	A Murray	Walton Heath	277
1981	G Marsh	Liverpool	275	1990	P Senior	Sunningdale	267
1982	M Pinero	Sunningdale	266	1991	M Harwood	Walton Heath	277
1983	I Aoki	Sunningdale	274	1992	N Faldo	Sunningdale	262
1984	G Brand Jr	Sunningdale	270	1993	G Brand Jr	East Sussex National	275
1985	B Langer	Sunningdale	269	1994	D Gilford	East Sussex National	275
1986	G Norman	Sunningdale	269	1995	B Langer	K Club, Co Kildare	280
1987	P Way	Walton Heath	279	1996	P-U Johansson	K Club, Co Kildare	277
1988	I Woosnam	Sunningdale	260	1997	P-U Johansson	K Club, Co Kildare	267

French Open

Year	Winner	Score	Year	Winner	Score
1988	N Faldo	274	1993	C Rocca	273
1989	N Faldo	273	1994	M Roe	274
1990	P Walton	275	1995	P Broadhurst	274
1991	E Romero	281	1996	R Allenby	272
1992	MA Martin	276	1997	R Goosen	271

German Masters

Year	Winner	Score	Year	Winner	Score
1988	JM Olazabal	279	1993	S Richardson	271
1989	B Langer	276	1994	S Ballesteros	270
1990	S Torrance	272	1995	A Forsbrand	264
1991	B Langer	275	1996	D Clarke	264
1992	B Lane	272	1997	B Langer	267

German Open

Year	Winner	Score	Year	Winner	Score
1988	S Ballesteros	263	1993	B Langer	269
1989	C Parry	266	1994	C Montgomerie	269
1990	M McNulty	270	1995	C Montgomerie	268
1991	M McNulty	273	1996	I Woosnam	193
1992	V Singh	262	1997	I Garrido	271

Honda Open

Year	Winner	Score	Year	Winner	Score
1992	B Langer	273	1995	*Not played*	
1993	S Torrance	278	1996	*Not played*	
1994	R Allenby	276	1997	*Not played*	

Irish Open

Year	Winner	Venue	Score	Year	Winner	Venue	Score
1988	I Woosnam	Portmarnock	278	1993	N Faldo	Mount Juliet	276
1989	I Woosnam	Portmarnock	278	1994	B Langer	Mount Juliet	275
1990	JM Olazabal	Portmarnock	282	1995	S Torrance	Mount Juliet	277
1991	N Faldo	Killarney	283	1996	C Montgomerie	Druids Glen	279
1992	N Faldo	Killarney	274	1997	C Montgomerie	Druid's Glen	269

Italian Open

Year	Winner	Score	Year	Winner	Score
1988	G Norman	270	1993	G Turner	267
1989	R Rafferty	273	1994	E Romero	272
1990	R Boxall	267	1995	S Torrance	269
1991	C Parry	279	1996	J Payne	275
1992	A Lyle	270	1997	B Langer	273

Jersey Open

Year	Winner	Score	Year	Winner	Score
1988	D Smyth	273	1993	I Palmer	268
1989	C O'Connor Jr	281	1994	P Curry	266
1990	*Not played*		1995	A Oldcorn	273
1991	S Torrance	279	1996	*Not played*	
1992	D Silva	277	1997	*Not played*	

Lyon Open

Year	Winner	Score	Year	Winner	Score
1992	DJ Russell	267	1995	*Not played*	
1993	C Rocca	267	1996	*Not played*	
1994	S Ames	282	1997	*Not played*	

Madeira Island Open

Year	Winner	Score
1993	M James	281
1994	M Lanner	206 *(curtailed)*
1995	S Luna	272
1996	J Sandelin	279
1997	P Mitchell	204 *(54 holes)*

Madrid Open

Year	Winner	Score	Year	Winner	Score
1988	D Cooper	275	1993	D Smyth	272
1989	S Ballesteros	272	1994	*Not played*	
1990	B Langer	270	1995	*Not played*	
1991	A Sherborne	272	1996	*Not played*	
1992	D Feherty	272	1997	*Not played*	

Moroccan Open

Year	Winner	Score	Year	Winner	Score
1992	D Gilford	287	1995	M James	275
1993	D Gilford	279	1996	P Hedblom	281
1994	A Forsbrand	276	1997	C Whitelaw	277

Portuguese Open

Year	Winner	Score	Year	Winner	Score
1988	M Harwood	280	1993	D Gilford	275
1989	C Montgomerie	264	1994	P Price	278
1990	M McLean	274	1995	A Hunter	277
1991	S Richardson	283	1996	W Riley	271
1992	R Rafferty	273	1997	M Jonzon	269

Scandinavian Masters

Year	Winner	Score	Year	Winner	Score
1991	C Montgomerie	270	1995	J Parnevik	270
1992	N Faldo	277	1996	L Westwood	281
1993	P Baker	278	1997	J Haeggman	270
1994	V Singh	268			

Scottish Open

Year	Winner	Venue	Score	Year	Winner	Venue	Score
1988	B Lane	Gleneagles	271	1993	J Parnevik	Gleneagles	271
1989	M Allen	Gleneagles	272	1994	C Mason	Gleneagles	265
1990	I Woosnam	Gleneagles	269	1995	W Riley	Carnoustie	276
1991	C Parry	Gleneagles	268	1996	I Woosnam	Carnoustie	289
1992	P O'Malley	Gleneagles	262	1997	*Not played*		

South African PGA

Year	Winner	Score	Year	Winner	Score
1992	E Els	271	1995	E Els	271
1993	*Not played*		1996	S Struver	202
1994	D Frost	259	1997	N Price	269

Spanish Open

Year	Winner	Score	Year	Winner	Score
1988	M James	262	1993	J Haeggman	275
1989	B Langer	281	1994	C Montgomerie	277
1990	R Davis	277	1995	S Ballesteros	274
1991	E Romero	275	1996	P Harrington	272
1992	A Sherborne	271	1997	M James	277

TPC of Europe

Year	Winner	Score
1995	B Langer	270
1996	F Nobilo	270
1997	R McFarlane	282

Trophée Lancôme

Year	Winner	Score	Year	Winner	Score
1988	S Ballesteros	269	1993	I Woosnam	267
1989	E Romero	266	1994	V Singh	263
1990	JM Olazabal	269	1995	C Montgomerie	269
1991	F Nobilo	267	1996	J Parnevik	268
1992	M Roe	267	1997	M O'Meara	271

Turespaña Open de Andalucia

Year	Winner	Score	Year	Winner	Score
1992	V Singh	277	1995	A Cejka	278
1993	A Oldcorn	285	1996	Not played	
1994	C Mason	278	1997	Not played	

Turespaña Open de Baleares

Year	Winner	Score	Year	Winner	Score
1988	S Ballesteros	272	1993	J Payne	277
1989	O Sellberg	279	1994	B Lane	269
1990	S Ballesteros	269	1995	G Turner	274
1991	G Levenson	282	1996	Not played	
1992	S Ballesteros	277	1997	Not played	

Turespaña Open de Canarias

Year	Winner	Score
1993	M James	275
1994	D Gilford	278
1995	J Sandelin	282
1996	Not played	
1997	JM Olazabal	272

Turespaña Open de Mediterranea

Year	Winner	Score	Year	Winner	Score
1990	I Woosnam	210 *(54 holes)*	1994	JM Olazabal	276
1991	I Woosnam	279	1995	R Karlsson	276
1992	JM Olazabal	276	1996	D Borrego	271
1993	F Nobilo	279	1997	Not played	

Volvo PGA Championship

(Until 1966 restricted to UK and Irish Pros. In 1967 and 1968 PGA 'open' and 'closed' were contested. From 1969 the Championship has been open.)

Year	Winner	Venue	Score	Year	Winner	Venue	Score
1955	K Bousfield	Pannal	277	1965	P Alliss	Sandwich, Prince's	286
1956	C Ward	Maesdu	282	1966	G Wostenholme	Saunton	278
1957	P Alliss	Maesdu	286	1967	M Gregson	Hunstanton	275
1958	H Bradshaw	Llandudno	287	1968	D Talbot	Dunbar	276
1959	D Rees	Ashburnham	283	1969	B Gallacher	Ashburnham	291
1960	A Stickley	Coventry *(63 holes)*	247	1970–71	Not played		
1961	B Bamford	R Mid-Surrey	266	1972	A Jacklin	Wentworth	279
1962	P Alliss	Little Aston	287	1973	P Oosterhuis	Wentworth	280
1963	P Butler	R Birkdale	306	1974	M Bembridge	Wentworth	278
1964	A Grubb	Western Gailes	287	1975	A Palmer	Sandwich, R St George's	285

Year	Winner	Venue	Score	Year	Winner	Venue	Score
1976	NC Coles	Sandwich, R St George's	280	1987	B Langer	Wentworth	270
1977	M Pinero	Sandwich, R St George's	283	1988	I Woosnam	Wentworth	274
1978	N Faldo	R Birkdale	278	1989	N Faldo	Wentworth	272
1979	V Fernandez	St Andrews	288	1990	M Harwood	Wentworth	271
1980	N Faldo	Sandwich, R St George's	283	1991	S Ballesteros	Wentworth	271
1981	N Faldo	Ganton	274	1992	T Johnstone	Wentworth	272
1982	A Jacklin	Hillside	284	1993	B Langer	Wentworth	274
1983	S Ballesteros	Sandwich, R St George's	278	1994	JM Olazabal	Wentworth	271
1984*	H Clark	Wentworth	204	1995	B Langer	Wentworth	279
1985	P Way	Wentworth	282	1996	C Rocca	Wentworth	274
1986	R Davis	Wentworth	281	1997	I Woosnam	Wentworth	275

Volvo Masters

Year	Winner	Score	Year	Winner	Score
1988	N Faldo	284	1993	C Montgomerie	274
1989	R Rafferty	282	1994	B Langer	276
1990	M Harwood	286	1995	A Cejka	282
1991	R Davis	280	1996	M McNulty	276
1992	A Lyle	287	1997*	L Westwood	200

World Match Play

Year	Winner	Runner-up	By	Year	Winner	Runner-up	By
1964	A Palmer	N Coles	2 and 1	1981	S Ballesteros	B Crenshaw	1 hole
1965	G Player	P Thomson	3 and 2	1982	S Ballesteros	A Lyle	37th hole
1966	G Player	J Nicklaus	6 and 4	1983	G Norman	N Faldo	3 and 2
1967	A Palmer	P Thomson	1 hole	1984	S Ballesteros	B Langer	2 and 1
1968	G Player	R Charles	1 hole	1985	S Ballesteros	B Langer	6 and 5
1969	R Charles	G Littler	37th hole	1986	G Norman	A Lyle	2 and 1
1970	J Nicklaus	L Trevino	2 and 1	1987	I Woosnam	A Lyle	1 hole
1971	G Player	J Nicklaus	5 and 4	1988	A Lyle	N Faldo	2 and 1
1972	T Weiskopf	L Trevino	4 and 3	1989	N Faldo	I Woosnam	1 hole
1973	G Player	G Marsh	40th hole	1990	I Woosnam	M McNulty	4 and 2
1974	H Irwin	G Player	3 and 1	1991	S Ballesteros	N Price	3 and 2
1975	H Irwin	A Geiberger	4 and 2	1992	N Faldo	J Sluman	8 and 7
1976	D Graham	H Irwin	38th hole	1993	C Pavin	N Faldo	1 hole
1977	G Marsh	R Floyd	5 and 3	1994	E Els	C Montgomerie	4 and 2
1978	I Aoki	S Owen	3 and 2	1995	E Els	S Elkington	2 and 1
1979	W Rogers	I Aoki	1 hole	1996	E Els	V Singh	3 and 2
1980	G Norman	A Lyle	1 hole	1997	V Singh	E Els	1 hole

Seniors

Senior British Open Championship

Year	Winner	Score	Year	Winner	Score
1988	G Player	272	1993	B Charles	291
1989	R Charles	269	1994	T Wargo	280
1990	G Player	280	1995	B Barnes	281
1991	B Verwey	285	1996	B Barnes	277
1992	J Fourie	282	1997	G Player	278

3 rounds only due to bad weather

Other Men's Professional Tournaments

PGA Seniors Championship

(Sponsored by Forte since 1983)

Year	Winner	Venue	Score	
1970	M Faulkner	Longniddry	288	
1971	K Nagle	Elie	269	
1972	K Bousfield	Longniddry	291	
1973	K Nagle	Elie	270	
1974	E Lester	Lundin	282	
1975	K Nagle	Longniddry	268	
1976	C O'Connor	Cambridgeshire Hotel	284	
1977	C O'Connor	Cambridgeshire Hotel	288	
1978	P Skerritt	Cambridgeshire Hotel	288	
1979	C O'Connor	Cambridgeshire Hotel	280	
1980	P Skerritt	Gleneagles Hotel	286	
1981	C O'Connor	North Berwick	287	
1982	C O'Connor	Longniddry	285	
1983	C O'Connor	Burnham and Berrow	277	
1984	E Jones	Stratford-upon-Avon	280	
1985	N Coles	Pannal, Harrogate	284	
1986	N Coles	Mere, Cheshire	276	
1987	N Coles	Turnberry	279	
1988	P Thomson	North Berwick	287	
1989	N Coles	West Hill	277	
1990	B Waites	Brough	269	
1991	B Waites	Wollaton Park	277	
1992	T Horton	R Dublin	290	
1993	B Huggett	Sunningdale	204	*(54 holes)*
1994	J Morgan	Sunningdale	203	
1995	J Morgan	Sunningdale	204	
1996	T Gale	The Belfry	284	
1997	W Hall	The Belfry	277	

Club Professionals' Championship

Year	Winner	Venue	Score
1973	DN Sewell	Calcot Park	276
1974	WB Murray	Calcot Park	275
1975	DN Sewell	Calcot Park	276
1976	WJ Ferguson	Moortown	283
1977	D Huish	Notts	284
1978	D Jones	Pannal	281
1979	D Jones	Pannal	278
1980	D Jagger	Turnberry	286
1981	M Steadman	Woburn	289
1982	D Durnian	Hill Valley	285
1983	J Farmer	Heaton Park	270
1984	D Durnian	Bolton Old Links	278
1985	R Mann	The Belfry	291
1986	D Huish	R Birkdale	278
1987	R Weir	Sandiway	273
1988	R Weir	Harlech	269
1989	B Barnes	Sandwich, Prince's	280
1990	A Webster	Carnoustie	292
1991	W McGill	King's Lynn	285

Year	Winner	Venue	Score
1992	J Hoskison	St Pierre	275
1993	C Hall	Coventry	274
1994	D Jones	North Berwick	278
1995	P Carman	West Hill	269
1996	B Longmuir	Co Louth	280
1997	B Rimmer	Northop	268

Assistants' Scottish Championship

Year	Winner	Venue	Score
1980	F Mann	Dunbar	294
1981	M Brown	West Kilbride	290
1982	R Collinson	West Kilbride	294
1983	A Webster	Stirling	285
1984	C Elliott	Stirling	285
1985	C Elliott	Falkirk Tryst	284
1986	P Helsby	Erskine	295
1987	C Innes	Hilton Park	284
1988	G Collinson	Turnberry	289
1989	C Brooks	Windyhill	282
1990	P Lawrie	Cruden Bay	279
1991	G Hume	Kilmarnock Barassie	299
1992	E McIntosh	Turnberry Hotel	266
1993	J Wither	Alloa	280
1994	S Henderson	Newmacher	283
1995	A Tait	Newmacher	276
1996	S Thompson	Newmacher	278
1997	M Hastie	Balbirnie Park	275

PGA Assistants' Championship

Year	Winner	Venue	Score
1984	G Weir	Coombe Hill	286
1985	G Coles	Coombe Hill	284
1986	J Brennand	Sand Moor	280
1987	J Hawksworth	Coombe Hill	282
1988	J Oates	Coventry	284
1989	C Brooks	Hillside	291
1990	A Ashton	Hillside	213 *(54 holes)*
1991	S Wood	Wentworth	288
1992	P Mayo	E Sussex National	285
1993	C Everett	Oaklands	280
1994	M Plummer	Burnham & Berrow	278
1995	I Sparkes	The Warwickshire	285
1996	S Purves	Moor Allerton	281
1997	P Sefton	De Vere, Blackpool	273

Irish National PGA Championship

Year	Winner	Venue	Score	
1960	C O'Connor	Warrenpoint	271	
1961	C O'Connor	Lahinch	280	
1962	C O'Connor	Bangor	264	
1963	C O'Connor	Little Island	271	
1964	E Jones	Knock	279	
1965	C O'Connor	Mullingar	283	
1966	C O'Connor	Warrenpoint	269	
1967	H Boyle	Tullamore (3 rounds)	214	
1968	C Greene	Knock	282	
1969	J Martin	Dundalk	268	
1970	H Jackson	Massareene	283	
1971	C O'Connor	Galway	278	
1972	J Kinsella	Bundoran	289	
1973	J Kinsella	Limerick	284	
1974	E Polland	Portstewart	277	
1975	C O'Connor	Carlow	275	*continued*

Irish National PGA Championship *continued*

Year	Winner	Venue	Score	
1976	P McGuirk	Waterville	291	
1977	P Skerritt	Woodbrook	281	
1978	C O'Connor	Dollymount	286	
1979	D Smyth	Dollymount	215	*(54 holes)*
1980	D Feherty	Dollymount	283	
1981	D Jones	Woodbrook	283	
1982	D Feherty	Woodbrook	287	
1983	L Higgins	Woodbrook	275	
1984	M Sludds	Skerries	277	
1985	D Smyth	Co Louth	204	*(54 holes due to bad weather)*
1986	D Smyth	Waterville	282	
1987	P Walton	Co Louth	144	*(36 holes due to bad weather)*
1988	E Darcy	Castle, Dublin	269	
1989	P Walton	Castle, Dublin	266	
1990	D Smyth	Woodbrook	271	
1991	P Walton	Woodbrook	277	
1992	E Darcy	K Club	285	
1993	M Sludds	K Club	285	
1994	D Clarke	Galway Bay	285	
1995	P Walton	Belvoir Park	273	
1996	D Smyth	Slieve Russell GC	281	
1997	P McGinley	Fota Island	285	

Scottish Professional Championship

Year	Winner	Venue	Score	
1960	EC Brown	West Kilbride	278	
1961	RT Walker	Forres	271	
1962	EC Brown	Dunbar	283	
1963	WM Miller	Crieff	284	
1964	RT Walker	Machrihanish	277	
1965	EC Brown	Forfar	271	
1966 T	EC Brown/J Panton	Cruden Bay	137	*(36 holes)*
1967	H Bannerman	Montrose	279	
1968	EC Brown	Monktonhall	286	
1969	G Cunningham	Machrihanish	284	
1970	RDBM Shade	Montrose	276	
1971	NJ Gallacher	Lundin Links	282	
1972	H Bannerman	Strathaven	268	
1973	BJ Gallacher	Kings Links, Aberdeen	276	
1974	BJ Gallacher	Drumpellier	276	
1975	D Huish	Duddingston	279	
1976	J Chillas	Haggs Castle	286	
1977	BJ Gallacher	Barnton	282	
1978	S Torrance	Strathaven	269	
1979	AWB Lyle	Glasgow Gailes	274	
1980	S Torrance	East Kilbride	273	
1981	B Barnes	Dalmahoy	275	
1982	B Barnes	Dalmahoy	286	
1983	B Gallacher	Dalmahoy	276	
1984	I Young	Dalmahoy	276	
1985	S Torrance	Dalmahoy	277	
1986	R Drummond	Glenbervie	270	
1987	R Drummond	Glenbervie	268	
1988	S Stephen	Haggs Castle	283	
1989	R Drummond	Monktonhall	274	
1990	R Drummond	Deer Park	278	
1991	S Torrance	Erskine	274	
1992	P Lawrie	Cardross	273	
1993	S Torrance	Dalmahoy	269	
1994	A Coltart	Dalmahoy	281	
1995	C Gillies	Dalmahoy	278	
1996	B Marchbank	Dalmahoy	276	
1997	G Law	Downfield	284	

Welsh Professional Championship

Year	Winner	Venue	Score
1960	RH Kemp, Jr	Llandudno	288
1961	S Mouland	Southerndown	286
1962	S Mouland	Porthcawl	302
1963	H Gould	Wrexham	291
1964	B Bielby	Tenby	297
1965	S Mouland	Penarth	281
1966	S Mouland	Conway	281
1967	S Mouland	Pyle and Kenfig	219 *(54 holes, fog)*
1968	RJ Davies	Southerndown	292
1969	S Mouland	Llandudno	277
1970	W Evans	Tredegar Park	289
1971	J Buckley	St Pierre	291
1972	J Buckley	Porthcawl	298
1973	A Griffiths	Newport	289
1974	M Hughes	Cardiff	284
1975	C DeFoy	Whitchurch	285
1976	S Cox	Radyr	284
1977	C DeFoy	Glamorganshire	135
1978	BCC Huggett	Whitchurch	145
1979 *Cancelled*			
1980	A Griffiths	Cardiff	139
1981	C DeFoy	Cardiff	139
1982	C DeFoy	Cardiff	137
1983	S Cox	Cardiff	136
1984	K Jones	Cardiff	135
1985	D Llewellyn	Whitchurch	132
1986	P Parkin	Whitchurch	142
1987	A Dodman	Cardiff	132
1988	I Woosnam	Cardiff	137
1989	K Jones	Royal Porthcawl	140
1990	P Mayo	Fairwood Park	136
1991	P Mayo	Fairwood Park	138
1992	C Evans	Asburnham	142
1993	P Price	Caerphilly	138
1994	M Plummer	Northop	133
1995	S Dodd	Northop	139
1996	M Stanford	Northop	137
1997	M Ellis	Vale of Glamorgan	139

Million Dollar Challenge

at Gary Player CC, Sun City, Bophuthatswana

Year	Winner	Score
1982 (Jan)	J Miller	277
1982 (Dec)	R Floyd	280
1983	S Ballesteros	274
1984	S Ballesteros	279
1985	B Langer	278
1986	M McNulty	282
1987	I Woosnam	274
1988	F Allem	278
1989	D Frost	276
1990	D Frost	284
1991	B Langer	272
1992	D Frost	276
1993	N Price	264
1994	N Faldo	272
1995	C Pavin	276
1996	C Montgomerie	274
1997	N Price	275

Men's Professional Internationals

Great Britain & Ireland (Europe from 1979) *v* USA

Year		Great Britain & Ireland		USA		Venue
1921	Foursomes	4	$10^1/_2$	1	$4^1/_2$	Gleneagles
(June 6)	Singles	$6^1/_2$		$3^1/_2$		
1926	Foursomes	5	$13^1/_2$	0	$1^1/_2$	Wentworth
(June 4–5)	Singles	$8^1/_2$		$1^1/_2$		

The Ryder Cup

Instituted 1927

Year		Great Britain & Ireland		USA		Venue
1927	Foursomes	1	$2^1/_2$	3	$9^1/_2$	Worcester, Mass
(June 3–4)	Singles	$1^1/_2$		$6^1/_2$		
1929	Foursomes	$1^1/_2$	7	$2^1/_2$	5	Moortown
(May 26–27)	Singles	$5^1/_2$		$2^1/_2$		
1931	Foursomes	1	3	3	9	Columbus, Ohio
(June 26–27)	Singles	2		6		
1933	Foursomes	$2^1/_2$	$6^1/_2$	$1^1/_2$	$5^1/_2$	Southport and Ainsdale
(June 26–27)	Singles	4		4		
1935	Foursomes	1	3	3	9	Ridgewood, NJ
(Sept 28–29)	Singles	2		6		
1937	Foursomes	$1^1/_2$	4	$2^1/_2$	8	Southport and Ainsdale
(June 29–30)	Singles	$2^1/_2$		$5^1/_2$		
1947	Foursomes	0	1	4	11	Portland, Oregon
(Nov 1–2)	Singles	1		7		
1949	Foursomes	3	5	1	7	Ganton
(Sept 16–17)	Singles	2		6		
1951	Foursomes	1	$2^1/_2$	3	$9^1/_2$	Pinehurst, N Carolina
(Nov 2 and 4)	Singles	$1^1/_2$		$6^1/_2$		
1953	Foursomes	1	$5^1/_2$	3	$6^1/_2$	Wentworth
(Oct 2–3)	Singles	$4^1/_2$		$3^1/_2$		
1955	Foursomes	1	4	3	8	Palm Springs, California
(Nov 5–6)	Singles	3		5		
1957	Foursomes	1	$7^1/_2$	3	$4^1/_2$	Lindrick
(Oct 4–5)	Singles	$6^1/_2$		$1^1/_2$		
1959	Foursomes	$1^1/_2$	$3^1/_2$	$2^1/_2$	$8^1/_2$	Eldorado, California
(Nov 6–7)	Singles	2		6		
1961	Foursomes	2	$9^1/_2$	6	$14^1/_2$	R Lytham and St Annes
(Oct 13–14)	Singles	$7^1/_2$		$8^1/_2$		
1963	Foursomes	2		6		Atlanta, Georgia
(Oct 11–13)	Fourball	2	9	6	23	
	Singles	5		11		
1965	Foursomes	4		4		R Birkdale
(Oct 7–9)	Fourball	3	$12^1/_2$	5	$19^1/_2$	
	Singles	$5^1/_2$		$10^1/_2$		

Year		Great Britain & Ireland		USA		Venue
1967	Foursomes	2½		5½		
(Oct 20–22)	Fourball	½	8½	7½	23½	Houston, Texas
	Singles	5½		10½		
1969	Foursomes	4½		3½		
(Oct 18–20)	Fourball	3½	16	4½	16	R Birkdale
	Singles	8		8		
1971	Foursomes	4½		3½		
(Sept 16–18)	Fourball	1½	13½	6½	18½	St Louis, Missouri
	Singles	7½		8½		
1973	Foursomes	4½		3½		
(Sept 20–22)	Fourball	3½	13	4½	19	Muirfield
	Singles	5		11		
1975	Foursomes	1		7		
(Sept 19–21)	Fourball	2½	11	5½	21	Laurel Valley, Pennsylvania
	Singles	7½		8½		
1977	Foursomes	1½		3½		
(Sept 15–17)	Fourball	1	7½	4	12½	R Lytham and St Annes
	Singles	5		5		

From 1979 players from the Continent of Europe became available for selection in addition to those from Great Britain and Ireland

Year		Europe		USA		Venue
1979	Foursomes	4½		3½		
(Sept 14–16)	Fourball	3	11	5	17	Greenbrier, WVa
	Singles	3½		8½		
1981	Foursomes	2		6		
(Sept 18–20)	Fourball	3½	9½	4½	18½	Walton Heath
	Singles	4		8		
1983	Foursomes	4		4		
(Oct 14–16)	Fourball	4	13½	4	14½	PGA National, Florida
	Singles	5½		6½		
1985	Foursomes	4		4		
(Sept 13–15)	Fourball	5	16½	3	11½	The Belfry
	Singles	7½		4½		
1987	Foursomes	4½		3½		
(Sept 13–15)	Fourball	6	15	2	13	Muirfield Village, Ohio
	Singles	4½		7½		

continued

The Ryder Cup *continued*

At The Belfry, Sutton Coldfield, on 22nd, 23rd and 24th September, 1989

Europe	Matches	USA	Matches

First Day

Foursomes

Europe	Matches	USA	Matches
N Faldo and I Woosnam (halved)	1/2	T Kite and C Strange (halved)	1/2
H Clark and M James	0	L Wadkins and P Stewart (1 hole)	1
S Ballesteros and JM Olazabal (halved)	1/2	T Watson and C Beck (halved)	1/2
B Langer and R Rafferty	0	M Calcavecchia and K Green (2 and 1)	1
	1		3

Fourball

Europe	Matches	USA	Matches
S Torrance and G Brand Jr (1 hole)	1	C Strange and P Azinger	0
H Clark and M James (3 and 2)	1	F Couples and L Wadkins	0
N Faldo and I Woosnam (2 holes)	1	M Calcavecchia and M McCumber	0
S Ballesteros and JM Olazabal (6 and 5)	1	T Watson and M O'Meara	0
	4		0

Second Day

Foursomes

Europe	Matches	USA	Matches
I Woosnam and N Faldo (3 and 2)	1	L Wadkins and P Stewart	0
G Brand Jr and S Torrance	0	C Beck and P Azinger (4 and 3)	1
C O'Connor Jr and R Rafferty	0	M Calcavecchia and K Green (3 and 2)	1
S Ballesteros and JM Olazabal (1 hole)	1	T Kite and C Strange	0
	2		2

Fourball

Europe	Matches	USA	Matches
N Faldo and I Woosnam	0	C Beck and P Azinger (2 and 1)	1
B Langer and JM Canizares	0	T Kite and M McCumber (2 and 1)	1
H Clark and M James (1 hole)	1	P Stewart and C Strange	0
S Ballesteros and JM Olazabal (4 and 2)	1	M Calcavecchia and K Green	0
	2		2

Third Day

Singles

Europe	Matches	USA	Matches
S Ballesteros	0	P Azinger (1 hole)	1
B Langer	0	C Beck (3 and 2)	1
JM Olazabal (1 hole)	1	P Stewart	0
R Rafferty (1 hole)	1	M Calcavecchia	0
H Clark	0	T Kite (8 and 7)	1
M James (3 and 2)	1	M O'Meara	0
C O'Connor Jr (1 hole)	1	F Couples	0
JM Canizares (1 hole)	1	K Green	0
G Brand Jr	0	M McCumber (1 hole)	1
S Torrance	0	T Watson (3 and 2)	1
N Faldo	0	L Wadkins (1 hole)	1
I Woosnam	0	C Strange (2 holes)	1
	5		7

Match Aggregate: Europe 14; USA 14.   Non-playing Captains: A Jacklin, Europe; R Floyd, USA.

At Kiawah Island, South Carolina, on 27th, 28th and 29th September, 1991

Europe	Matches	USA	Matches

First Day

Foursomes

S Ballesteros and JM Olazabal (2 and 1)	1	P Azinger and C Beck	0
B Langer and M James	0	R Floyd and F Couples (2 and 1)	1
D Gilford and C Montgomerie	0	L Wadkins and H Irwin (4 and 2)	1
N Faldo and I Woosnam	0	P Stewart and M Calcavecchia (1 hole)	1
	1		3

Fourball

S Torrance and D Feherty	$^1/_2$	L Wadkins and M O'Meara	$^1/_2$
S Ballesteros and JM Olazabal (2 and 1)	1	P Azinger and C Beck	0
S Richardson and M James (5 and 4)	1	C Pavin and M Calcavecchia	0
N Faldo and I Woosnam	0	R Floyd and F Couples (5 and 3)	1
	$2^1/_2$		$1^1/_2$

Second Day

Foursomes

S Torrance and D Feherty	0	H Irwin and L Wadkins (4 and 2)	1
M James and S Richardson	0	M Calcavecchia and P Stewart (1 hole)	1
N Faldo and D Gilford	0	P Azinger and M O'Meara (7 and 6)	1
S Ballesteros and JM Olazabal (3 and 2)	1	F Couples and R Floyd	0
	1		3

Fourball

I Woosnam and P Broadhurst (2 and 1)	1	P Azinger and H Irwin	0
B Langer and C Montgomerie (2 and 1)	1	S Pate and C Pavin	0
M James and S Richardson (3 and 1)	1	L Wadkins and W Levi	0
S Ballesteros and JM Olazabal	$^1/_2$	F Couples and P Stewart	$^1/_2$
	$3^1/_2$		$^1/_2$

Third Day

Singles

N Faldo (2 holes)	1	R Floyd	0
D Feherty (2 and 1)	1	P Stewart	0
C Montgomerie	$^1/_2$	M Calcavecchia	$^1/_2$
JM Olazabal	0	P Azinger (2 holes)	1
S Richardson	0	C Pavin (2 and 1)	1
S Ballesteros (3 and 2)	1	W Levi	0
I Woosnam	0	C Beck (3 and 1)	1
P Broadhurst (3 and 1)	1	M O'Meara	0
S Torrance	0	F Couples (3 and 2)	1
M James	0	L Wadkins (3 and 2)	1
B Langer	$^1/_2$	H Irwin	$^1/_2$
D Gilford (withdrawn at start of day)	$^1/_2$	S Pate (withdrawn at start of day)	$^1/_2$
	$5^1/_2$		$6^1/_2$

Match Aggregate: USA $14^1/_2$; Europe $13^1/_2$.   Non-playing Captains: D Stockton, USA; B Gallacher, Europe.

The Ryder Cup *continued*

At The Belfry, Sutton Coldfield, on 24th, 25th and 26th September, 1993

Europe	Matches	USA	Matches

First Day

Foursomes

Europe	Matches	USA	Matches
S Torrance and M James	0	L Wadkins and C Pavin (4 and 3)	1
I Woosnam and B Langer (7 and 5)	1	P Azinger and P Stewart	0
S Ballesteros and JM Olazabal	0	T Kite and D Love III (2 and 1)	1
N Faldo and C Montgomerie (4 and 3)	1	R Floyd and F Couples	0
	2		2

Fourball

Europe	Matches	USA	Matches
I Woosnam and P Baker (1 hole)	1	J Gallagher Jr and L Janzen	0
B Lane and B Langer	0	L Wadkins and C Pavin (4 and 2)	1
N Faldo and C Montgomerie	1/2	P Azinger and F Couples	1/2
S Ballesteros and JM Olazabal (4 and 3)	1	T Kite and D Love III	0
	2 1/2		1 1/2

Second Day

Foursomes

Europe	Matches	USA	Matches
N Faldo and C Montgomerie (3 and 2)	1	L Wadkins and C Pavin	0
B Langer and I Woosnam (2 and 1)	1	F Couples and P Azinger	0
P Baker and B Lane	0	R Floyd and P Stewart (3 and 2)	1
S Ballesteros and JM Olazabal (2 and 1)	1	T Kite and D Love III	0
	3		1

Fourball

Europe	Matches	USA	Matches
N Faldo and C Montgomerie	0	C Beck and J Cook (2 holes)	1
M James and C Rocca	0	C Pavin and J Gallagher Jr (5 and 4)	1
I Woosnam and P Baker (6 and 5)	1	F Couples and P Azinger	0
JM Olazabal and J Haeggman	0	R Floyd and P Stewart (2 and 1)	1
	1		3

Third Day

Singles

Europe	Matches	USA	Matches
I Woosnam	1/2	F Couples	1/2
B Lane	0	C Beck (1 hole)	1
C Montgomerie (1 hole)	1	L Janzen	0
P Baker (2 holes)	1	C Pavin	0
J Haeggman (1 hole)	1	J Cook	0
S Torrance *(withdrawn at start of day)*	1/2	L Wadkins *(withdrawn at start of day)*	1/2
M James	0	P Stewart (3 and 2)	1
C Rocca	0	D Love III (1 hole)	1
S Ballesteros	0	J Gallagher Jr (3 and 2)	1
JM Olazabal	0	R Floyd (2 holes)	1
B Langer	0	T Kite (5 and 3)	1
N Faldo	1/2	P Azinger	1/2
	4 1/2		7 1/2

Match Aggregate: Europe 13; USA 15.   Non-playing Captains: B Gallacher, Europe; T Watson, USA.

At Oak Hill, Rochester, New York, on 22nd, 23rd and 24th September, 1995

USA	Matches	Europe	Matches

First Day

Foursomes

C Pavin and T Lehman (1 hole)	1	N Faldo and C Montgomerie	0
J Haas and F Couples	0	S Torrance and C Rocca (3 and 2)	1
D Love III and J Maggert (4 and 3)	1	H Clark and M James	0
B Crenshaw and C Strange	0	B Langer and P-U Johansson (1 hole)	1
	2		**2**

Fourball

B Faxon and P Jacobsen	0	D Gilford and S Ballesteros (4 and 3)	1
J Maggert and L Roberts (6 and 5)	1	S Torrance and C Rocca	0
F Couples and D Love III (3 and 2)	1	N Faldo and C Montgomerie	0
C Pavin and P Mickelson (6 and 4)	1	B Langer and P-U Johansson	0
	3		**1**

Second Day

Foursomes

J Haas and C Strange	0	N Faldo and C Montgomerie (4 and 2)	1
D Love III and J Maggert	0	S Torrance and C Rocca (6 and 5)	1
L Roberts and P Jacobsen (1 hole)	1	I Woosnam and P Walton	0
C Pavin and L Roberts	0	B Langer and D Gilford (4 and 3)	1
	1		**3**

Fourball

B Faxon and F Couples (4 and 2)	1	S Torrance and C Montgomerie	0
D Love III and B Crenshaw	0	I Woosnam and C Rocca (3 and 2)	1
J Haas and P Mickelson (3 and 2)	1	S Ballesteros and D Gilford	0
C Pavin and L Roberts (1 hole)	1	N Faldo and B Langer	0
	3		**1**

Third Day

Singles

T Lehman (4 and 3)	1	S Ballesteros	0
P Jacobsen	0	H Clark (1 hole)	1
J Maggert	0	M James (4 and 3)	1
F Couples	1/2	I Woosnam	1/2
D Love III (3 and 2)	1	C Rocca	0
B Faxon	0	D Gilford (1 hole)	1
B Crenshaw	0	C Montgomerie (3 and 1)	1
C Strange	0	N Faldo (1 hole)	1
L Roberts	0	S Torrance (2 and 1)	1
C Pavin (3 and 2)	1	B Langer	0
J Haas	0	P Walton (1 hole)	1
P Mickelson (2 and 1)	1	P-U Johansson	0
	4 1/2		**7 1/2**

Match Aggregate: USA 13 1/2, Europe 14 1/2
Non-playing captains: L Wadkins, USA; B Gallacher, Europe

Ryder Cup *continued*

32nd – at Valderrama, Spain on 26th, 27th and 28th September, 1997

Europe	Matches	USA	Matches

First Day

Fourball

JM Olazabal and C Rocca (1 hole)	1	D Love III and P Mickelson	0
N Faldo and L Westwood	0	F Couples and B Faxon (1 hole)	1
J Parnevik and P-U Johansson (1 hole)	1	T Lehman and J Furyk	0
C Montgomerie and B Langer	0	T Woods and M O'Meara (3 and 2)	1
	2		2

Foursomes

C Rocca and JM Olazabal	0	S Hoch and L Janzen (1 hole)	1
B Langer and C Montgomerie (5 and 3)	1	M O'Meara and T Woods	0
N Faldo and L Westwood (3 and 2)	1	J Leonard and J Maggert	0
J Parnevik and I Garrido	1/2	T Lehman and P Mickelson	1/2
	2 1/2		1 1/2

Second Day

Fourball

C Montgomerie and D Clarke (1 hole)	1	F Couples and D Love III	0
I Woosnam and T Bjorn (2 and 1)	1	J Leonard and B Faxon	0
N Faldo and L Westwood (2 and 1)	1	T Woods and M O'Meara	0
JM Olazabal and I Garrido	1/2	P Mickelson and T Lehman	1/2
	3 1/2		1/2

Foursomes

C Montgomerie and B Langer (1 hole)	1	L Janzen and J Furyk	0
N Faldo and L Westwood	0	S Hoch and J Maggert (2 and 1)	1
J Parnevik and I Garrido	1/2	J Leonard and T Woods	1/2
JM Olazabal and C Rocca (5 and 4)	1	D Love III and F Couples	0
	2 1/2		1 1/2

Third Day

Singles

I Woosnam	0	F Couples (8 and 7)	1
P-U Johansson (3 and 2)	1	D Love III	0
C Rocca (4 and 2)	1	T Woods	0
T Bjorn	1/2	J Leonard	1/2
D Clarke	0	P Mickelson (2 and 1)	1
J Parnevik	0	M O'Meara (5 and 4)	1
JM Olazabal	0	L Janzen (1 hole)	1
B Langer (2 and 1)	1	B Faxon	0
L Westwood	0	J Maggert (3 and 2)	1
C Montgomerie	1/2	S Hoch	1/2
N Faldo	0	J Furyk (3 and 2)	1
I Garrido	0	T Lehman (7 and 6)	1
	4		8

Result: Europe 14 1/2, USA 13 1/2
Non-playing captains: S Ballesteros, Europe; T Kite, USA

Ryder Cup – INDIVIDUAL RECORDS

Matches were contested as Great Britain v USA from 1927–71; as Great Britain and Ireland from 1973–7; and as Europe v USA from 1979. Bold type indicates captain; in brackets – did not play.

Europe

Name	Year	Played	Won	Lost	Halved
Jimmy Adams	*1939-47-49-51-53	7	2	5	0
Percy Alliss	1929-33-35-37	6	3	2	1
Peter Alliss	1953-57-59-61-63-65-67-69	30	10	15	5
Laurie Ayton	1949	0	0	0	0
Peter Baker	1993	4	3	1	0
Severiano Ballesteros (Sp)	1979-83-85-87-89-91-93-95-(97)	37	20	12	5
Harry Bannerman	1971	5	2	2	1
Brian Barnes	1969-71-73-75-77-79	25	10	14	1
Maurice Bembridge	1969-71-73-75	16	5	8	3
Thomas Björn (Den)	1997	2	1	0	1
Aubrey Boomer	1927-29	4	2	2	0
Ken Bousfield	1949-51-55-57-59-61	10	5	5	0
Hugh Boyle	1967	3	0	3	0
Harry Bradshaw	1953-55-57	5	2	2	1
Gordon J Brand	1983	1	0	1	0
Gordon Brand Jr	1987-89	7	2	4	1
Paul Broadhurst	1991	2	2	0	0
Eric Brown	1953-55-57-59-(69)-(71)	8	4	4	0
Ken Brown	1977-79-83-85-87	13	4	9	0
Stewart Burns	1929	0	0	0	0
Dick Burton	1935-37-*39-49	5	2	3	0
Jack Busson	1935	2	0	2	0
Peter Butler	1965-69-71-73	14	3	9	2
José Maria Canizares (Sp)	1981-83-85-89	11	5	4	2
Alex Caygill	1969	1	0	0	1
Clive Clark	1973	1	0	1	0
Howard Clark	1977-81-85-87-89-95	15	7	7	1
Darren Clarke	1997	2	1	1	0
Neil Coles	1961-63-65-67-69-71-73-77	40	12	21	7
Archie Compston	1927-29-31	6	1	4	1
Henry Cotton	1929-37-*39-47-(53)	6	2	4	0
Bill Cox	1935-37	3	0	2	1
Allan Dailey	1933	0	0	0	0
Fred Daly	1947-49-51-53	8	3	4	1
Eamonn Darcy	1975-77-81-87	11	1	8	2
William Davies	1931-33	4	2	2	0
Peter Dawson	1977	3	1	2	0
Norman Drew	1959	1	0	0	1
George Duncan	1927-**29**-31	5	2	3	0
Syd Easterbrook	1931-33	3	2	1	0
Nick Faldo	1977-79-81-83-85-87-89-91-93-95-97	46	23	19	4
John Fallon	1955-(**63**)	1	1	0	0
Max Faulkner	1947-49-51-53-57	8	1	7	0
David Feherty	1991	3	1	1	1
George Gadd	1927	0	0	0	0
Bernard Gallacher	1969-71-73-75-77-79-81-83-(**91**)-(**93**)-(**95**)	31	13	13	5
John Garner	1971-73	1	0	1	0
Antonio Garrido (Sp)	1979	5	1	4	0
Ignacio Garrido (Sp)	1997	4	0	1	3
David Gilford	1991-95	6	3	3	0
Eric Green	1947	0	0	0	0
Malcolm Gregson	1967	4	0	4	0
Joakim Haeggman (Swe)	1993	2	1	1	0
Tom Haliburton	1961-63	6	0	6	0
Jack Hargreaves	1951	0	0	0	0
Arthur Havers	1927-31-33	6	3	3	0
Jimmy Hitchcock	1965	3	0	3	0
Bert Hodson	1931	1	0	1	0
Reg Horne	1947	0	0	0	0
Tommy Horton	1975-77	8	1	6	1
Brian Huggett	1963-67-69-71-73-75-(**77**)	25	9	10	6
Bernard Hunt	1953-57-59-61-63-65-67-69-(**73**)-(**75**)	28	6	16	6
Geoffrey Hunt	1963	3	0	3	0
Guy Hunt	1975	3	0	2	1
Tony Jacklin	1967-69-71-73-75-77-79-(**83**)-(**85**)-(**87**)-(**89**)	35	13	14	8

continued

* Great Britain named eight members of their 1939 side, but the match was not played because of the Second World War.

Ryder Cup – INDIVIDUAL RECORDS *continued*

Name	Year	Played	Won	Lost	Halved
John Jacobs	1955-(79)-(81)	2	2	0	0
Mark James	1977-79-81-89-91-93-95	24	8	15	1
Edward Jarman	1935	1	0	1	0
Per-Ulrik Johansson (Swe)	1995-97	5	3	2	0
Herbert Jolly	1927	2	0	2	0
Michael King	1979	1	0	1	0
Sam King	1937-*39-47-49	5	1	3	1
Arthur Lacey	1933-37-(51)	3	0	3	0
Barry Lane	1993	3	0	3	0
Bernhard Langer (Ger)	1981-83-85-87-89-91-93-95-97	38	18	15	5
Arthur Lees	1947-49-51-55	8	4	4	0
Sandy Lyle	1979-81-83-85-87	18	7	9	2
Jimmy Martin	1965	1	0	1	0
Peter Mills	1957-59	1	1	0	0
Abe Mitchell	1929-31-33	6	4	2	0
Ralph Moffitt	1961	1	0	1	0
Colin Montgomerie	1991-93-95-97	18	9	6	3
Christy O'Connor, Jr	1975-89	4	1	3	0
Christy O'Connor, Sr	1955-57-59-61-63-65-67-69-71-73	36	11	21	4
José Maria Olazabal (Sp)	1987-89-91-93-97	25	14	8	3
John O'Leary	1975	4	0	4	0
Peter Oosterhuis	1971-73-75-77-79-81	28	14	11	3
Alf Padgham	1933-35-37-*39	6	0	6	0
John Panton	1951-53-61	5	0	5	0
Jesper Parnevik (Swe)	1997	4	1	1	2
Alf Perry	1933-35-37	4	0	3	1
Manuel Pinero (Sp)	1981-85	9	6	3	0
Lionel Platts	1965	5	1	2	2
Eddie Polland	1973	2	0	2	0
Ronan Rafferty	1989	3	1	2	0
Ted Ray	1927	2	0	2	0
Dai Rees	1937-*39-47-49-51-53-55-57-59-61-(67)	18	7	10	1
Steven Richardson	1991	4	2	2	0
José Rivero (Sp)	1985-87	5	2	3	0
Fred Robson	1927-29-31	6	2	4	0
Costantino Rocca (It)	1993-95-97	11	6	5	0
Syd Scott	1955	2	0	2	0
Des Smyth	1979-81	7	2	5	0
Dave Thomas	1959-63-65-67	18	3	10	5
Sam Torrance	1981-83-85-87-89-91-93-95	27	7	15	5
Peter Townsend	1969-71	11	3	8	0
Brian Waites	1983	4	1	3	0
Philip Walton	1995	2	1	1	0
Charlie Ward	1947-49-51	6	1	5	0
Paul Way	1983-85	9	6	2	1
Harry Weetman	1951-53-55-57-59-61-63-(65)	15	2	11	2
Lee Westwood	1997	5	2	3	0
Charles Whitcombe	1927-29-31-33-35-37-*39-(49)	9	3	2	4
Ernest Whitcombe	1929-31-35	6	1	4	1
Reg Whitcombe	1935-*39	1	0	1	0
George Will	1963-65-67	15	2	11	2
Norman Wood	1975	3	1	2	0
Ian Woosnam	1983-85-87-89-91-93-95-97	31	14	12	5

United States of America

Name	Year	Played	Won	Lost	Halved
Tommy Aaron	1969-73	6	1	4	1
Skip Alexander	1949-51	2	1	1	0
Paul Azinger	1989-91-93	14	5	7	2
Jerry Barber	1955-61	5	1	4	0
Miller Barber	1969-71	7	1	4	2
Herman Barron	1947	1	1	0	0
Andy Bean	1979-87	6	4	2	0
Frank Beard	1969-71	8	2	3	3
Chip Beck	1989-91-93	9	6	2	1
Homero Blancas	1973	4	2	1	1
Tommy Bolt	1955-57	4	3	1	0
Julius Boros	1959-63-65-67	16	9	3	4
Gay Brewer	1967-73	9	5	3	1

* Great Britain named eight members of their 1939 side, but the match was not played because of the Second World War.

Name	Year	Played	Won	Lost	Halved
Billy Burke	1931-33	3	3	0	0
Jack Burke	1951-53-55-57-59-(73)	8	7	1	0
Walter Burkemo	1953	1	0	1	0
Mark Calcavecchia	1987-89-91	11	5	5	1
Billy Casper	1961-63-65-67-69-71-73-75-(79)	37	20	10	7
Bill Collins	1961	3	1	2	0
Charles Coody	1971	3	0	2	1
John Cook	1993	2	1	1	0
Fred Couples	1989-91-93-95-97	20	7	9	4
Wilfred Cox	1931	2	2	0	0
Ben Crenshaw	1981-83-87-95	12	3	8	1
Jimmy Demaret	**1941-47-49-51	6	6	0	0
Gardner Dickinson	1967-71	10	9	1	0
Leo Diegel	1927-29-31-33	6	3	3	0
Dale Douglass	1969	2	0	2	0
Dave Douglas	1953	2	1	0	1
Ed Dudley	1929-33-37	4	3	1	0
Olin Dutra	1933-35	4	1	3	0
Lee Elder	1979	4	1	3	0
Al Espinosa	1927-29-31	4	2	1	1
Johnny Farrell	1927-29-31	6	3	2	1
Brad Faxon	1995-97	6	2	4	0
Dow Finsterwald	1957-59-61-63-(77)	13	9	3	1
Ray Floyd	1969-75-77-81-83-85-(89)-91-93	31	12	16	3
Doug Ford	1955-57-59-61	9	4	4	1
Ed Furgol	1957	1	0	1	0
Marty Furgol	1955	1	0	1	0
Jim Furyk	1997	3	1	2	0
Jim Gallagher Jr	1993	3	2	1	0
Al Geiberger	1967-75	9	5	1	3
Vic Ghezzi	*1939-**41	0	0	0	0
Bob Gilder	1983	4	2	2	0
Bob Goalby	1963	5	3	1	1
Johnny Golden	1927-29	3	3	0	0
Lou Graham	1973-75-77	9	5	3	1
Hubert Green	1977-79-85	7	4	3	0
Ken Green	1989	4	2	2	0
Ralph Guldahl	1937-*39	2	2	0	0
Fred Haas, Jr	1953	1	0	1	0
Jay Haas	1983-95	8	3	4	1
Walter Hagen	**1927-29-31-33-35-(37)**	9	7	1	1
Bob Hamilton	1949	2	0	2	0
Chick Harbert	1949-55	2	2	0	0
Chandler Harper	1955	1	0	1	0
Dutch (EJ) Harrison	1947-49-51	3	2	1	0
Fred Hawkins	1957	2	1	1	0
Mark Hayes	1979	3	1	2	0
Clayton Heafner	1949-51	4	3	0	1
Jay Hebert	1959-61-(71)	4	2	1	1
Lionel Hebert	1957	1	0	1	0
Dave Hill	1969-73-77	9	6	3	0
Jimmy Hines	*1939	0	0	0	0
Scott Hoch	1997	3	2	0	1
Ben Hogan	**1941-47-(49)-51-(67)	3	3	0	0
Hale Irwin	1975-77-79-81-91	20	13	5	2
Tommy Jacobs	1965	4	3	1	0
Peter Jacobsen	1985-95	6	2	4	0
Don January	1965-77	7	2	3	2
Lee Janzen	1993-97	5	2	3	0
Herman Keiser	1947	1	0	1	0
Tom Kite	1979-81-83-85-87-89-93-(97)	28	15	9	4
Ted Kroll	1953-55-57	4	3	1	0
Ky Laffoon	1935	1	0	1	0
Tom Lehman	1995-97	7	3	2	2
Tony Lema	1963-65	11	8	1	2
Justin Leonard	1997	4	0	2	2
Wayne Levi	1991	2	0	2	0
Bruce Lietzke	1981	3	0	2	1
Gene Littler	1961-63-65-67-69-71-75	27	14	5	8
Davis Love III	1993-95-97	13	5	8	0
Jeff Maggert	1995-97	7	4	3	0
John Mahaffey	1979	3	1	2	0

continued

US teams were selected in 1939 (*) and 1941 (**), but the matches were not played because of the Second World War.

Ryder Cup – INDIVIDUAL RECORDS *continued*

Name	Year	Played	Won	Lost	Halved
Mark McCumber	1989	3	2	1	0
Jerry McGee	1977	2	1	1	0
Harold McSpaden	*1939-**41	0	0	0	0
Tony Manero	1937	2	1	1	0
Lloyd Mangrum	**1941-47-49-51-53	8	6	2	0
Dave Marr	1965-(**81**)	6	4	2	0
Billy Maxwell	1963	4	4	0	0
Dick Mayer	1957	2	1	0	1
Bill Mehlhorn	1927	2	1	1	0
Dick Metz	*1939	0	0	0	0
Phil Mickelson	1995-97	7	4	1	2
Cary Middlecoff	1953-55-59	6	2	3	1
Johnny Miller	1975-81	6	2	2	2
Larry Mize	1987	4	1	1	2
Gil Morgan	1979-83	6	1	2	3
Bob Murphy	1975	4	2	1	1
Byron Nelson	1937-*39-**41-47-(**65**)	4	3	1	0
Larry Nelson	1979-81-87	13	9	3	1
Bobby Nichols	1967	5	4	0	1
Jack Nicklaus	1969-71-73-75-77-81-(**83**)-(**87**)	28	17	8	3
Andy North	1985	3	0	3	0
Ed Oliver	1947-51-53	5	3	2	0
Mark O'Meara	1985-89-91-97	12	4	7	1
Arnold Palmer	1961-**63**-65-67-71-73-(**75**)	32	22	8	2
Johnny Palmer	1949	2	0	2	0
Sam Parks	1935	1	0	0	1
Jerry Pate	1981	4	2	2	0
Steve Pate	1991	1	0	1	0
Corey Pavin	1991-93-95	8	5	3	0
Calvin Peete	1983-85	7	4	2	1
Henry Picard	1935-37-*39	4	3	1	0
Dan Pohl	1987	3	1	2	0
Johnny Pott	1963-65-67	7	5	2	0
Dave Ragan	1963	4	2	1	1
Henry Ransom	1951	1	0	1	0
Johnny Revolta	1935-37	3	2	1	0
Loren Roberts	1995	4	3	1	0
Chi Chi Rodriguez	1973	2	0	1	1
Bill Rogers	1981	4	1	2	1
Bob Rosburg	1959	2	2	0	0
Mason Rudolph	1971	3	1	1	1
Paul Runyan	1933-35-*39	4	2	2	0
Doug Sanders	1967	5	2	3	0
Gene Sarazen	1927-29-31-33-35-37-**41	12	7	2	3
Densmore Shute	1931-33-37	6	2	2	2
Dan Sikes	1969	3	2	1	0
Scott Simpson	1987	2	1	1	0
Horton Smith	1929-31-33-35-37-*39-**41	4	3	0	1
JC Snead	1971-73-75	11	9	2	0
Sam Snead	1937-*39-**41-47-49-**51**-53-55-**59**-(**69**)	13	10	2	1
Ed Sneed	1977	2	1	0	1
Mike Souchak	1959-61	6	5	1	0
Craig Stadler	1983-85	8	4	2	2
Payne Stewart	1987-89-91-93	16	7	8	1
Ken Still	1969	3	1	2	0
Dave Stockton	1971-77-(**91**)	5	3	1	1
Curtis Strange	1983-85-87-89-95	20	6	12	2
Hal Sutton	1985-87	9	3	3	3
Lee Trevino	1969-71-73-75-79-81-(**85**)	30	17	7	6
Jim Turnesa	1953	1	1	0	0
Joe Turnesa	1927-29	4	1	2	1
Ken Venturi	1965	4	1	3	0
Lanny Wadkins	1977-79-83-85-87-89-91-93-(**95**)	33	20	11	2
Art Wall, Jnr	1957-59-61	6	4	2	0
Al Watrous	1927-29	3	2	1	0
Tom Watson	1977-81-83-89-(**93**)	15	10	4	1
Tom Weiskopf	1973-75	10	7	2	1
Craig Wood	1931-33-35-**41	4	1	3	0
Tiger Woods	1997	5	1	3	1
Lew Worsham	1947	2	2	0	0
Fuzzy Zoeller	1979-83-85	10	1	8	1

US teams were selected in 1939 (*) and 1941 (**), but the matches were not played because of the Second World War.

Alfred Dunhill Cup   *(Instituted 1985)*
at St Andrews

Year	Winner	Runner-up	Year	Winner	Runner-up
1986	Australia	Japan	1992	England	Scotland
1987	England	Scotland	1993	USA	England
1988	Ireland	Australia	1994	Canada	USA
1989	USA	Japan	1995	Scotland	Zimbabwe
1990	Ireland	England	1996	America	New Zealand
1991	Sweden	South Africa	1997	South Africa	Sweden

PGA Cup   *(Instituted 1973)*

Year	Winner	Venue	Result
1973	USA	Pinehurst, USA	13–3
1974	USA	Pinehurst, USA	$11^1/_2$–$4^1/_2$
1975	USA	Hillside	$9^1/_2$–$6^1/_2$
1976	USA	Moortown	$9^1/_2$–$6^1/_2$
1977	Halved	Miss Hills, USA	$8^1/_2$–$8^1/_2$
1978	GB & I	St Mellion	$10^1/_2$–$6^1/_2$
1979	GB & I	Castletown	$12^1/_2$–$4^1/_2$
1980	USA	Oak Tree	15–6
1981	Halved	Turnberry, Isle	$10^1/_2$–$10^1/_2$
1982	USA	Knoxville, Tennessee	13–7
1983	GB & I	Muirfield	$14^1/_2$–$6^1/_2$
1984	GB & I	Turnberry	$12^1/_2$–$8^1/_2$

Played alternate years from 1984

Year	Winner	Venue	Result
1986	USA	Knollwood	16–9
1988	USA	The Belfry	$15^1/_2$–$10^1/_2$
1990	USA	Kiawah Island, S Carolina	19–7
1992	USA	K Club, Ireland	15–11
1994	USA	Palm Beach, Florida	15–11
1996	Halved	Gleneagles	13–13

President's Cup   *(Instituted 1994)*

Year	Winner	Venue	Result
1994	USA	Lake Manassas, Virginia	20–12
1996	USA	Lake Manassas, Virginia	$16^1/_2$–$15^1/_2$

World Cup of Golf   *(Called Canada Cup until 1966)*

Year	Winner	Runners-up	Venue	Score
1953	Argentina	Canada	Montreal	287
	(A Cerda and R De Vincenzo)	(S Leonard and B Kerr)		
	(Individual: A Cerda, Argentina, 140)			
1954	Australia	Argentina	Laval-Sur-Lac	556
	(P Thomson and K Nagle)	(A Cerda and R De Vincenzo)		
1955	United States	Australia	Washington	560
	(C Harbert and E Furgol)	(P Thomson and K Nagle)		
	(Individual: E Furgol, USA, after a play-off with P Thomson and F van Donck, 279)			
1956	United States	South Africa	Wentworth	567
	(B Hogan and S Snead)	(A Locke and G Player)		
	(Individual: B Hogan, USA, 277)			
1957	Japan	United States	Tokyo	557
	(T Nakamura and K Ono)	(S Snead and J Demaret)		
	(Individual: T Nakamura, Japan, 274)			
1958	Ireland	Spain	Mexico City	579
	(H Bradshaw and C O'Connor)	(A Miguel and S Miguel)		
	(Individual: A Miguel, Spain, after a play-off with H Bradshaw, 286)			
1959	Australia	United States	Melbourne	563
	(P Thomson and K Nagle)	(S Snead and C Middlecoff)		
	(Individual: S Leonard, Canada, 275, after a tie with P Thomson, Australia)			

continued

World Cup of Golf *continued*

Year	Winner	Runners-up	Venue	Score
1960	United States (S Snead and A Palmer) (Individual: F van Donck, Belgium, 279)	England (H Weetman and B Hunt)	Portmarnock	565
1961	United States (S Snead and J Demaret) (Individual: S Snead, USA, 272)	Australia (P Thomson and K Nagle)	Puerto Rico	560
1962	United States (S Snead and A Palmer) (Individual: R De Vicenzo, Argentina, 276)	Argentina (F de Luca and R De Vicenzo)	Buenos Aires	557
1963	United States (A Palmer and J Nicklaus) (Individual: J Nicklaus, USA, 237 [63 holes])	Spain (S Miguel and R Sota)	St Nom-La-Breteche	482
1964	United States (A Palmer and J Nicklaus) (Individual: J Nicklaus, USA, 276)	Argentina (R De Vicenzo and L Ruiz)	Maui, Hawaii	554
1965	South Africa (G Player and H Henning) (Individual: G Player, South Africa, 281)	Spain (A Miguel and R Sota)	Madrid	571
1966	United States (J Nicklaus and A Palmer) (Individual: G Knudson, Canada, and H Sugimoto, Japan, each 272; Knudson won play-off)	South Africa (G Player and H Henning)	Tokyo	548
1967	United States (J Nicklaus and A Palmer) (Individual: A Palmer, USA, 276)	New Zealand (R Charles and W Godfrey)	Mexico City	557
1968	Canada (A Balding and G Knudson) (Individual: A Balding, Canada, 274)	United States (J Boros and L Trevino)	Olgiata, Rome	569
1969	United States (O Moody and L Trevino) (Individual: L Trevino, USA, 275)	Japan (T Kono and H Yasuda)	Singapore	552
1970	Australia (B Devlin and D Graham) (Individual: R De Vicenzo, Argentina, 269)	Argentina (R De Vicenzo and V Fernandez)	Buenos Aires	545
1971	United States (J Nicklaus and L Trevino) (Individual: J Nicklaus, USA, 271)	South Africa (H Henning and G Player)	Palm Beach, Florida	555
1972	Taiwan (H Min-Nan and LL Huan) (Individual: H Min-Nan, Taiwan, 217 [3 rounds only])	Japan (T Kono and T Murakami)	Melbourne	438
1973	United States (J Nicklaus and J Miller) (Individual: J Miller, USA, 277)	South Africa (G Player and H Baiocchi)	Marbella, Spain	558
1974	South Africa (R Cole and D Hayes) (Individual: R Cole, South Africa, 271)	Japan (I Aoki and M Ozaki)	Caracas	554
1975	United States (J Miller and L Graham) (Individual: J Miller, USA, 275)	Taiwan (H Min-Nan and KC Hsiung)	Bangkok	554
1976	Spain (S Ballesteros and M Pinero) (Individual: EP Acosta, Mexico, 282)	United States (J Pate and D Stockton)	Palm Springs	574
1977	Spain (S Ballesteros and A Garrido) (Individual: G Player, South Africa, 289)	Philippines (R Lavares and B Arda)	Manilla, Philippines	591
1978	United States (J Mahaffey and A North) (Individual: J Mahaffey, USA, 281)	Australia (G Norman and W Grady)	Hawaii	564
1979	United States (J Mahaffey and H Irwin) (Individual: H Irwin, USA, 285)	Scotland (A Lyle and K Brown)	Glyfada, Greece	575
1980	Canada (D Halldorson and J Nelford) (Individual: A Lyle, Scotland, 282)	Scotland (A Lyle and S Martin)	Bogota	572
1981	*Not played*			
1982	Spain (M Pinero and JM Canizares) (Individual: M Pinero, Spain, 281)	United States (B Gilder and B Clampett)	Acapulco	563
1983	United States (R Caldwell and J Cook) (Individual: D Barr, Canada, 276)	Canada (D Barr and J Anderson)	Pondok Inah, Jakarta	565

Year	Winner	Runners-up	Venue	Score
1984	Spain	Scotland	Olgiata, Rome	414
	(JM Canizares and J Rivero)	(S Torrance and G Brand, Jr)		
	(Individual: JM Canizares, Spain, 205. Played over 54 holes due to storm)			
1985	Canada	England	La Quinta, Calif.	559
	(D Halidorson and D Barr)	(H Clark and P Way)		
	(Individual: H Clark, England, 272)			
1986	*Not played*			
1987	Wales (won play-off)	Scotland	Kapalua, Hawaii	574
	(I Woosnam and D Llewelyn)	(S Torrance and A Lyle)		
	(Individual: I Woosnam, Wales, 274)			
1988	United States	Japan	Royal Melbourne, Australia	560
	(B Crenshaw and M McCumber)	(T Ozaki and M Ozaki)		
	(Individual: B Crenshaw, USA, 275)			
1989	Australia	Spain	Las Brisas, Spain	
	(P Fowler and W Grady)	(JM Olazabal and JM Canizares)		
	(Individual: P Fowler. Played over 36 holes due to storms.)			
1990	Germany	England (M James andR Boxall) ⎫ tie	Grand Cypress Resort, Orlando, Florida	556
	(B Langer and T Giedeon)	Ireland (R Rafferty and D Feherty) ⎭		
	(Individual: P Stewart, USA, 271)			
1991	Sweden	Wales	La Querce, Rome	563
	(A Forsbrand and P-U Johansson)	(I Woosnam and P Price)		
	(Individual: I Woosnam, Wales, 273)			
1992	USA	Sweden	La Moraleja II, Madrid, Spain	548
	(F Couples and D Love III)	(A Forsbrand and P-U Johansson)		
	(Individual: B Ogle, Australia, 270 after a tie with I Woosnam, Wales)			
1993	USA	Zimbabwe	Lake Nona, Orlando, FL	556
	(F Couples and D Love III)	(N Price and M McNulty)		
	(Individual: B Langer, Germany, 272)			
1994	USA	Zimbabwe	Dorado Beach, Puerto Rico	536
	(F Couples and D Love III)	(M McNulty and T Johnstone)		
	(Individual: F Couples, USA, 265)			
1995	USA	Australia	Mission Hills, Shenzhen, China	543
	(F Couples and D Love III)	(B Ogle and R Allenby)		
	(Individual: D Love III, USA, 267)			
1996	South Africa	USA	Erinvale, Cape Town South Africa	547
	(E Els and W Westner)	(T Lehman and S Jones)		
	(Individual: E Els, S. Africa, 272)			
1997	Ireland	Scotland	Kiawah Island, SC	545
	(P Harrington and P McGinley)	(C Montgomerie and R Russell)		
	(Individual: C Montgomerie, Scotland, 266)			

Men's Amateur Tournaments

Berkhamsted Trophy

Year	Winner	Score	Year	Winner	Score	Year	Winner	Score
1970	R Hunter	145	1979	JC Davies	147	1989	J Payne	142
1971	A Millar	144	1980	R Knott	143	1990	J Barnes	144
1971	A Millar	144	1981	P Dennett	146	1991	G Homewood	141
1972	C Cieslewicz	148	1982	DG Lane	148	1992	P Page	141
1973	SC Mason	141	1983	J Hawksworth	146	1993	S Burnell	143
1974	P Fisher	144	1984	R Willison	139	1994	M Treleaven	140
1975	P Deeble	147	1985	F George	144	1995	J Crampton	142
1976	J Davies	144	1986	P McEvoy	144	1996	L Donald	139
1977	A Lyle	144	1987	F George	141	1997	P Streeter	143
1978	JC Davies	146	1988	J Cowgill	146			

Berkshire Trophy

Year	Winner	Score	Year	Winner	Score	Year	Winner	Score
1970	MF Bonallack	274	1979	D Williams	274	1989	J Metcalfe	
1971 T	MF Bonallack	277	1980	P Downes	280	1990	J O'Shea	271
	J Davies		1981	D Blakeman	280	1991	J Bickerton	280
1972	DP Davidson	280	1982	S Keppler	278	1992	V Phillips	274
1973	P Hedges	278	1983	S Hamer	288	1993	V Phillips	271
1974	J Downie	280	1984	JL Plaxton	276	1994T	J Knight	274
1975	N Faldo	281	1985	P McEvoy	279		A Marshall	
1976	P Hedges	284	1986	R Muscroft	280	1995	G Harris	275
1977	A Lyle	279	1987	J Robinson	275	1996	G Wolstenholme	274
1978	P Hedges	281	1988	R Claydon	276	1997	G Wolstenholme	275

Duncan Putter

Year	Winner	Score	Year	Winner	Score
1988	S Dodd	290	1993	M Thomson	289
1989	RN Roderick	280	1994	G Wolstenholme	226
1990	R Willison	311	1995	B Dredge	293
1991	R Willison	267	1996	G Wolstenholme	291
1992	R Dinsdale	213	1997	M Pilkington	283

Frame Trophy *at Worplesdon*

Year	Winner	Score	Year	Winner	Score
1988	DW Frame	229	1993	D Frame	216
1989	JRW Walkinshaw	219	1994	D Lane	222
1990	WJ Williams	224	1995	M Christmas	223
1991	DB Sheahan	223	1996	D Lane	217
1992	D Frame	223	1997	B Turner	226

Golf Illustrated Gold Vase

Year	Winner	Year	Winner	Year	Winner
1948	RD Chapman	1965	C Clark	1982	I Carslaw
1949	RJ White	1966	PM Townsend	1983	S Keppler
1950	AW Whyte	1967 T	RA Durrant/	1984	JV Marks
1951	JB Carr		MF Bonallack	1985	M Davis
1952	JDA Langley	1968	MF Bonallack	1986	R Eggo
1953	JDA Langley	1969 T	MF Bonallack/J Hayes	1987	D Lane
1954	H Ridgeley	1970	D Harrison	1988	M Turner
1955	Major DA Blair	1971	MF Bonallack/H Ashby	1989	G Wolstenholme
1956	Major DA Blair	1972 T	DP Davidson/R Hunter	1990	A Rogers
1957	G Wolstenholme	1973	J Davies	1991	R Scott
1958	M Lunt	1974	P Hedges	1992	P Page
1959	A Bussell	1975	MF Bonallack	1993T	C Challen/V Phillips
1960	D Sewell	1976	A Brodie	1994	S Burnell
1961 T	DJ Harrison/	1977	J Davies	1995	A Wall
	MF Bonallack	1978	P Thomas	1996	*Not played*
1962	BHG Chapman	1979	KJ Miller	1997	M James
1963	RH Mummery	1980	G Brand, Jr		
1964	D Moffat	1981	P Garner		

Grafton Morrish Trophy *Public Schools Old Boys' Golf Association*

Year	Winner	Year	Winner	Year	Winner
1963	Tonbridge	1975	Oundle	1987	Harrow
1964	Tonbridge	1976	Charterhouse	1988	Robert Gordon's
1965	Charterhouse	1977	Haileybury	1989	Tonbridge
1966	Charterhouse	1978	Charterhouse	1990	Clifton
1967	Charterhouse	1979	Harrow	1991	Repton
1968	Wellington	1980	Charterhouse	1992	Charterhouse
1969	Sedbergh	1981	Charterhouse	1993	Malvern
1970	Sedbergh	1982	Marlborough	1994	George Heriot's
1971	Dulwich	1983	Wellington	1995	Repton
1972	Sedbergh	1984	Sedbergh	1996	Coventry
1973	Pangbourne	1985	Warwick	1997	George Heriot's
1974	Millfield	1986	Tonbridge		

Halford-Hewitt Challenge Cup *Public Schools Old Boys' Tournament*

Year	Winner	Year	Winner	Year	Winner
1947	Harrow	1964	Fettes	1981	Watsons
1948	Winchester	1965	Rugby	1982	Charterhouse
1949	Charterhouse	1966	Charterhouse	1983	Charterhouse
1950	Rugby	1967	Eton	1984	Charterhouse
1951	Rugby	1968	Eton	1985	Harrow
1952	Harrow	1969	Eton	1986	Repton
1953	Harrow	1970	Merchiston	1987	Merchiston
1954	Rugby	1971	Charterhouse	1988	Stowe
1955	Eton	1972	Marlborough	1989	Eton
1956	Eton	1973	Rossall	1990	Tonbridge
1957	Watsons	1974	Charterhouse	1991	Shrewsbury
1958	Harrow	1975	Harrow	1992	Tonbridge
1959	Wellington	1976	Merchiston	1993	Shrewsbury
1960	Rossall	1977	Watsons	1994	Tonbridge
1961	Rossall	1978	Harrow	1995	Harrow
1962	Oundle	1979	Stowe	1996	Radley
1963	Repton	1980	Shrewsbury	1997	Oundle

Hampshire Hog *at North Hants*

Year	Winner	Year	Winner
1988	S Richardson	1993	D Hamilton
1989	P McEvoy	1994	B Ingleby
1990	J Metcalfe	1995	J Rose
1991	M Welch	1996	R Tate
1992	S Graham	1997	G Wolstenholme

The Lagonda Trophy

Year	Winner	Year	Winner
1988	R Claydon	1993	L James
1989	T Spence	1994	S Webster
1990	L Parsons	1995	P Nelson
1991	J Cook	1996	S Collingwood
1992	L Westwood	1997	L Donald

Leven Amateur Championship Gold Medal

Year	Winner	Year	Winner
1988	CE Everett	1993	L Westwood
1989	AJ Coltart	1994	B Howard
1990	C Everett	1995	S Mackenzie
1991	A Graham Lowson	1996	M Eliasson
1992	D Robertson	1997	S Carmichael

The Lytham Trophy *at Royal Lytham and St Annes*

Year	Winner	Score	Year	Winner	Score	Year	Winner	Score
1965T	MF Bonallack	295	1974	CW Green	291	1988	P Broadhurst	296
	CA Clark		1975	G Macgregor	299	1989	N Williamson	286
1966	PM Townsend	290	1976	MJ Kelley	292	1990	G Evans	291
1967	R Foster	296	1977	P Deeble	296	1991	G Evans	284
1968	R Foster	286	1978	B Marchbank	288	1992	S Cage	294
1969T	T Craddock	290	1979	P McEvoy	279	1993	T McLure	292
	SG Birtwell		1980	IC Hutcheon	293	1994	W Bennett	285
1970T	JC Farmer	296	1981	R Chapman	221	1995	S Gallacher	281
	CW Green		1982	MF Sludds	306	1996	M Carver	284
	GC Marks		1983	S McAllister	299	1997	G Rankin	279
1971	W Humphreys	292	1984	J Hawksworth	289			
1972	MF Bonallack	281	1985	L Macnamara	144			
1973 T	MG King	292	1986	S McKenna	297			
	SG Birtwell		1987	D Wood	293			

Oxford *v* Cambridge

Year	Winner	Venue	Year	Winner	Venue
1946	Cambridge	R Lytham &St Annes	1972	Cambridge	Formby
1947	Oxford	Rye	1973	Oxford	Saunton
1948	Oxford	Sandwich, R St George's	1974	Cambridge	Ganton
1949	Cambridge	Hoylake	1975	Cambridge	Hoylake
1950	Oxford	R Lytham & St Annes	1976	Cambridge	Woodhall Spa
1951	Cambridge	Rye	1977	Cambridge	Porthcawl
1952	Cambridge	Rye	1978	Oxford	Rye
1953	Cambridge	Rye	1979	Oxford	Harlech
1954	Cambridge	Rye	1980	Oxford	Hoylake
1955	Cambridge	Rye	1981	Cambridge	Formby
1956	Oxford	Formby	1982	Cambridge	Hunstanton
1957	Oxford	Sandwich, R St George's	1983	Cambridge	Sandwich, R St George's
1958	Cambridge	Rye	1984	Cambridge	Sunningdale
1959	Cambridge	Burnham & Berrow	1985	Oxford	Rye
1960	Cambridge	R Lytham & St Annes	1986	Oxford	Ganton
1961	Oxford	Sandwich, R St George's	1987	Cambridge	Formby
1962	Halved	Hunstanton	1988	Cambridge	Royal Porthcawl
1963	Cambridge	R Birkdale	1989	Cambridge	Rye
1964	Oxford	Rye	1990	Cambridge	Muirfield
1965	Cambridge	Sandwich, R St George's	1991	Cambridge	Sandwich, R St George's
1966	Cambridge	Hunstanton	1992	Oxford	R Cinque Ports
1967	Cambridge	Rye	1993	Oxford	R Liverpool
1968	Cambridge	Porthcawl	1994	Oxford	Rye
1969	Cambridge	Formby	1995	Oxford	R Lytham & St Annes
1970	Halved	Sandwich, R St George's	1996	Oxford	R West Norfolk
1971	Oxford	Rye	1997	Oxford	R St Georges

Oxford and Cambridge Golfing Society's President's Putter

Year	Winner	Year	Winner	Year	Winner
1947	LG Crawley	1964	DMA Steel	1983	ER Dexter
1948	Major AA Duncan	1965	WI Uzielli	1984	A Edmond
1949	PB Lucas	1966	MF Attenborough	1985	ER Dexter
1950	DHR Martin	1969	P Moody	1986	J Caplan
1951	LG Crawley	1970	DMA Steel	1987	CD Meacher
1952	LG Crawley	1971	GT Duncan	1988	G Woollett
1953	GH Micklem	1972	P Moody	1967	JR Midgley
1954	G Huddy	1973	AD Swanston	1989	M Froggatt
1955	G Huddy	1974	R Biggs	1968	AWJ Holmes
1956	GT Duncan	1975	CJ Weight	1990	G Woollett
1957	AE Shepperson	1976	MJ Reece	1991	B Ingleby
1958	Lt-Col AA Duncan	1977	AWJ Holmes	1992	M Cox
1959	ID Wheater	1978	MJ Reece	1993	C Weight
1960	JME Anderson	1979	*Cancelled due to snow*	1994	S Seman
1961	ID Wheater	1980	S Melville	1995	A Woolnough
1962	MF Attenborough	1981	AWJ Holmes	1996	C Rotheroe
1963	JG Blackwell	1982	DMA Steel	1997	C Rotheroe

HRH Prince of Wales Challenge Cup *at Deal*

Year	Winner	Score	Year	Winner	Score
1988	MP Palmer	144	1993	ML Welch	143
1989 T	T Lloyd/NA Farrell	146	1994	I Hardy	149
1990 T	G Homewood/BS Ingleby	145	1995	L Ferris	152
1991	S Pardoe	152	1996	J Maddock	142
1992	L Westwood	160	1997	J Carter	154

Rosebery Challenge Cup *at Ashridge*

Year	Winner	Year	Winner
1988	N Leconte	1993	M Hooper
1989	C Slattery	1994	P Wilkins
1990	C Tingey	1995	P Wilkins
1991	M Thompson	1996	J Kemp
1992	R Harris	1997	L Watcham

St Andrews Links Trophy *at St Andrews*

Year	Winner	Year	Winner
1990	S Bouvier	1994	B Howard
1991	R Willison	1995	G Rankin
1992	C Watson	1996	B Howard
1993	G Hay	1997	J Rose

St David's Gold Cross *at Royal St David's, Harlech*

Year	Winner	Year	Winner
1988	MW Calvert	1993	B Dredge
1989	AJ Barnett	1994	C Evans
1990	M Macara	1995	M Skinner
1991	RJ Dinsdale	1996	L Harpin
1992	B Dredge	1997	M Pilkington

Grand Challenge Cup *at Royal St George's, Sandwich*

Year	Winner	Year	Winner
1988	T Ryan	1993	P Sefton
1989	S Green	1994	M Welch
1990	P Sullivan	1995	J Harris
1991	D Fisher	1996	M Brooks
1992	L Westwood	1997	*Not played*

Selborne Salver *at Blackmoor GC, Hampshire*

Year	Winner	Year	Winner
1988	N Holman	1993	M Welch
1989	M Stanford	1994	W Bennett
1990	J Metcalfe	1995	S Drummond
1991	J Payne	1996	J Knight
1992	M Treleaven	1997	R Binney

Sunningdale Foursomes

Year	Winners
1970	R Barrell and Miss A Willard beat R Hunter and Miss M Everard, 2 and 1
1971	A Bird and H Flatman beat J Putt and Miss K Phillips, 3 and 2
1972	JC Davies and MG King beat JK Tullis and AJ Howard, 6 and 5
1973	JA Putt and Miss M Everard beat H Clark and SC Mason, 6 and 5
1974	PJ Butler and C Clark beat HK Clark and DN Brunyard, 1 hole
1975	*Cancelled due to snow*
1976	C Clark and M Hughesdon beat BJ Hunt and IM Stungo, 2 and 1
1977	GN Hunt and D Matthew beat D Huish and G Logan, 3 and 2
1978	GA Caygill and Miss J Greenhalgh beat A Stickley and Mrs C Caldwell, 5 and 4
1979	G Will and R Chapman beat NC Coles and D McClelland, 3 and 2
1980	NC Coles and D McClelland beat SC Mason and J O'Leary, 2 and 1
1981	A Lyddon and G Brand beat MG King and MH Dixon, 1 hole
1982	Miss MA McKenna and Miss M Madill beat Miss C Langford and Miss M Walker, 1 hole
1983	J Davies and M Devetta beat M Hughesdon and Mrs L Bayman, 4 and 3
1984	Miss M McKenna and Miss M Madill beat Miss M Walker and Miss C Langford
1985	J O'Leary and S Torrance beat B Gallacher and P Garner at 25th
1986	R Rafferty and R Chapman beat Mrs M Garner and Miss M McKenna, 1 hole
1987	I Mosey and W Humphries beat Miss G Stewart and D Huish, 3 and 2
1988	C Mason and A Chandler beat Miss M McKenna and Mrs J Garner, 5 and 3
1989	A Hare and R Claydon beat Miss V Thomas and Miss J Wade, 4 and 3
1990	Miss D Reid and Miss C Dibnah beat Miss T Craik and P Hughes, 7 and 6
1991	J Robinson and W Henry beat B Critchley and R Hunter, 4 and 3
1992	R Boxall and D Cooper beat P Sherman and P Page, 3 and 2
1993	A Beal and L James beat L Warwick and D Wood, 2 and 1
1994	S Webster and A Wall beat D Howell and G Harris, 2 holes
1995	D Cooper and R Boxall beat I Mackenzie and M Mackenzie, 2 and 1
1996	L Donald and M O'Connor beat Miss G Stewart and Miss J Forbes, 2 and 1
1997	Mrs J Hall and Miss H Wadsworth beat J Robinson and D Jones, 4 and 3

Tennant Cup

This trophy was presented by Sir Charles Tennant to the Glasgow Club in 1880. It is the oldest open amateur stroke play competition in the world. It has been a 72-hole competition since 1986.

Year	Winner	Year	Winner	Year	Winner
1970	CW Green	1980	Allan Brodie	1990	C Everett
1971	Andrew Brodie	1981	G MacDonald	1991	C Everett
1972	Allan Brodie	1982	LS Mann	1992	D Robertson
1973	PJ Smith	1983	C Dalgleish	1993	D Robertson
1974	D McCart	1984	E Wilson	1994	G Rankin
1975	CW Green	1985	CJ Brooks	1995	S Gallacher
1976	IC Hutcheon	1986	PG Irvan	1996	G Rankin
1977	S Martin	1987	J Rasmussen	1997	C Hislop
1978	IA Carslaw	1988	C Dalgleish		
1979	G Hay	1989	DG Carrick		

The Tillman Trophy *at Royal St George's, Sandwich*

Year	Winner	Year	Winner
1988	E Els	1993	C Nowicki
1989	J Cook	1994	*Not played*
1990	M Wiggett	1995	P Stuart
1991	A Tillman	1996	S Wakefield
1992	D Probert	1997	M Searle

West of England Open Amateur Championship
at Burnham & Berrow

Year	Winner	Year	Winner
1988	N Holman	1993	D Haines
1989	N Holman	1994	A Emery
1990	I West	1995	A March
1991	S Amor	1996	M Carver
1992	K Baker	1997	M Reynard

West of England Open Amateur Stroke Play Championship

Year	Winner	Year	Winner
1988	M Evans	1993	P Trew
1989	AD Hare	1994	C Nowicki
1990	I West	1995	C Clark
1991	S Amor	1996	R Wiggins
1992	M Stanford	1997	M Reynard

West of Scotland Open Amateur Championship

Year	Winner	Year	Winner
1988	S Savage	1993	B Howard
1989	AJ Elliott	1994	J Hodgson
1990	ST Knowles	1995	G Rankin
1991	A Coltart	1996	C Hislop
1992	S Henderson	1997	C Hislop

Worplesdon Mixed Foursomes

Year	Winners
1980	L Bayman and I Boyd beat L Davies and R Hurst, 1 hole
1981	J Nicholsen and MN Stern beat S Birley and RL Glading, 2 and 1
1982	B New and K Dobson beat S Cohen and J Tarbuck, 2 and 1
1983	B New and K Dobson beat N McCormack and N Briggs at 19th
1984	L Bayman and MC Hughesdon beat N McCormack and N Briggs, 5 and 4
1985	H Kaye and D Longmuir beat J Collingham and GS Melville, 5 and 3
1986	P Johnson and RN Roderick beat C Duffy and L Hawkins, 2 and 1
1987	J Nicholsen and B White beat T Craik and P Hughes, 4 and 3
1988	Mme A Larrezac and JJ Caplan beat S Bennett and BK Turner, 4 and 3
1989	J Kershaw and M Kershaw beat H Kaye and D Longmuir, 2 and 1
1990	S Keogh and A Rogers beat J Rhodes and C Banks, 3 and 1
1991	J Rhodes and C Banks beat S Ledger and J Brant, 1 hole
1992	D Henson and B Turner beat S Lambert and J Tarbuck, 4 and 2
1993	A Macdonald and S Skeldon beat Mr and Mrs KM Quinn, 3 and 2
1994	Mr and Mrs K Quinn beat C Titcombe and C Rotheroe, 3 and 2
1995	Mrs C Caldwell and P Carr beat Mrs C Bushell and G Wolstenholme at 20th
1996	Miss L Walters and M Naylor beat Miss K Burton and C Rotheroe at 20th
1997	Miss K Burton and G Wolstenholme beat K and C Quinn, 6 and 5

Men's Amateur International Tournaments and Matches

United States v Great Britain & Ireland
Unofficial

Year		Great Britain		USA		Venue
1921	Foursomes	0	3	4	9	
(May 21)	Singles	3		5		Hoylake

The Walker Cup
Instituted 1922

Year		Great Britain & Ireland		USA		Venue
1922	Foursomes	1	4	3	8	Long Island, NY
(August 29)	Singles	3		5		
1923	Foursomes	3	5$^{1}/_{2}$	1	6$^{1}/_{2}$	St Andrews
(May 18–19)	Singles	2$^{1}/_{2}$		5$^{1}/_{2}$		
1924	Foursomes	1	3	3	9	Garden City, NY
(Sept 12–13)	Singles	2		6		
1926	Foursomes	1	5$^{1}/_{2}$	3	6$^{1}/_{2}$	St Andrews
(June 2–3)	Singles	4$^{1}/_{2}$		3$^{1}/_{2}$		
1928	Foursomes	0	1	4	11	Chicago
(Aug 30–31)	Singles	1		7		
1930	Foursomes	1	2	3	10	Sandwich
(May 15–16)	Singles	1		7		
1932	Foursomes	0	2$^{1}/_{2}$	4	9$^{1}/_{2}$	Brookline, Massachusetts
(Sept 1–2)	Singles	2$^{1}/_{2}$		5$^{1}/_{2}$		
1934	Foursomes	1	2$^{1}/_{2}$	3	9$^{1}/_{2}$	St Andrews
(May 11–12)	Singles	1$^{1}/_{2}$		6$^{1}/_{2}$		
1936	Foursomes	1	1$^{1}/_{2}$	3	10$^{1}/_{2}$	Pine Valley, NJ
(Sept 2–3)	Singles	0$^{1}/_{2}$		7$^{1}/_{2}$		
1938	Foursomes	2$^{1}/_{2}$	7$^{1}/_{2}$	1$^{1}/_{2}$	4$^{1}/_{2}$	St Andrews
(June 3–4)	Singles	5		3		
1947	Foursomes	2	4	2	8	St Andrews
(May 16–17)	Singles	2		6		
1949	Foursomes	1	2	3	10	Winged Foot, NY
(Aug 19–20)	Singles	1		7		
1951	Foursomes	1	4$^{1}/_{2}$	3	7$^{1}/_{2}$	Royal Birkdale
(May 11–12)	Singles	3$^{1}/_{2}$		4$^{1}/_{2}$		
1953	Foursomes	1	3	3	9	Kittansett, Massachusetts
(Sept 4–5)	Singles	2		6		
1955	Foursomes	0	2	4	10	St Andrews
(May 20–21)	Singles	2		6		
1957	Foursomes	1$^{1}/_{2}$	3$^{1}/_{2}$	2$^{1}/_{2}$	8$^{1}/_{2}$	Minikahda
(Sept 1–2)	Singles	2		6		
1959	Foursomes	0	3	4	9	Muirfield
(May 15–16)	Singles	3		5		
1961	Foursomes	0	1	4	11	Seattle, Washington
(Sept 1–2)	Singles	1		7		

From 1963 Foursomes and Singles matches were played on both days, each match over 18 holes.

Year		Great Britain & Ireland		USA		Venue
1963	Foursomes	1	8	6	12	Turnberry
(May 24–25)	Singles	7		6		
1965	Foursomes	4	11	3	11	Baltimore, Maryland
(Sept 3–4)	Singles	7		8		
1967	Foursomes	3	7	4	13	Sandwich
(May 15–20)	Singles	4		9		
1969	Foursomes	3	8	3	10	Milwaukee, Wisconsin
(Aug 22–23)	Singles	5		7		
1971	Foursomes	5½	13	2½	11	St Andrews
(May 26–27)	Singles	7½		8½		
1973	Foursomes	1	10	7	14	Brookline, Massachusetts
(Aug 24–25)	Singles	9		7		
1975	Foursomes	3	8½	5	15½	St Andrews
(May 28–29)	Singles	5½		10½		
1977	Foursomes	3	8	5	16	Shinnecock Hills, NY
(Aug 26–27)	Singles	5		11		
1979	Foursomes	4	8½	4	15½	Muirfield
(May 30–31)	Singles	4½		11½		
1981	Foursomes	4	9	4	15	Cypress Point
(Aug 28–29)	Singles	5		11		
1983	Foursomes	4½	10½	3½	13½	Hoylake
(May 25–26)	Singles	6		10		
1985	Foursomes	3	11	5	13	Pine Valley, NJ
(Aug 21–22)	Singles	8		8		
1987	Foursomes	1	7½	7	16½	Sunningdale
(May 27–28)	Singles	6½		9½		

At Peachtree, Atlanta, 16th and 17th August, 1989

Great Britain and Ireland   **USA**

First Day

Foursomes

R Claydon and D Prosser	0	R Gamez and D Martin (3 and 2)	1
S Dodd and G McGimpsey	½	D Yates and P Mickelson	½
P McEvoy and E O'Connell (6 and 5)	1	G Lesher and J Sigel	0
J Milligan and A Hare (2 and 1)	1	D Eger and K Johnson	0
	2½		**1½**

Singles

J Milligan	0	R Gamez (7 and 6)	1
R Claydon (5 and 4)	1	D Martin	0
S Dodd	½	E Meeks	½
E O'Connell (5 and 4)	1	R Howe	0
P McEvoy (2 and 1)	1	D Yates	0
G McGimpsey	0	P Mickelson (4 and 2)	1
C Cassells (1 hole)	1	G Lesher	0
RN Roderick	½	J Sigel	½
	5		**3**

First day's aggregate: Great Britain and Ireland 7½; USA 4½

Second Day

Foursomes

P McEvoy and E O'Connell	½	R Gamez and D Martin	½
R Claydon and C Cassells (3 and 2)	1	J Sigel and G Lesher	0
J Milligan and A Hare (2 and 1)	1	D Eger and K Johnson	0
G McGimpsey and S Dodd (2 and 1)	1	P Mickelson and D Yates	0
	3½		**3½**

continued

The Walker Cup *continued*

Singles

S Dodd	0	R Gamez (1 hole)	1
A Hare	$^1/_2$	D Martin	$^1/_2$
R Claydon	0	G Lesher (3 and 2)	1
P McEvoy	0	D Yates (4 and 3)	1
E O'Connell	$^1/_2$	P Mickelson	$^1/_2$
RN Roderick	0	D Eger (4 and 2)	1
C Cassells	0	GK Johnson (4 and 2)	1
J Milligan	$^1/_2$	J Sigel	$^1/_2$
	$1^1/_2$		$6^1/_2$

Second day's aggregate: Great Britain and Ireland 5; USA 7

Grand match aggregate: Great Britain and Ireland $12^1/_2$; USA $11^1/_2$

At Portmarnock, Dublin, 5th and 6th September, 1991

Great Britain and Ireland   **USA**

First Day

Foursomes

J Milligan and G Hay	0	P Mickelson and B May (5 and 3)	1
J Payne and G Evans	0	D Duval and M Sposa (1 hole)	1
G McGimpsey and R Willison	0	M Voges and D Eger (1hole)	1
P McGinley and P Harrington	0	J Sigel and A Doyle (2 and 1)	1
	0		4

Singles

A Coltart	0	P Mickelson (4 and 3)	1
J Payne (2 and 1)	1	F Langham	0
G Evans (2 and 1)	1	D Duval	0
R Willison	0	B May (2 and 1)	1
G McGimpsey (1 hole)	1	M Sposa	0
P McGinley	0	A Doyle (6 and 4)	1
G Hay (1 hole)	1	T Scherrer	0
L White	0	J Sigel (4 and 3)	1
	4		4

First day's aggregate: Great Britain and Ireland 4; USA 8

Second Day

Foursomes

J Milligan and G McGimpsey (2 and 1)	1	M Voges and D Eger	0
J Payne and R Willison	0	D Duval and M Sposa (1 hole)	1
G Evans and A Coltart (4 and 3)	1	F Langham and T Scherrer	0
L White and P McGinley (1 hole)	1	P Mickelson and B May	0
	3		1

Singles

J Milligan	0	P Mickelson (1 hole)	1
J Payne (3 and 1)	1	A Doyle	0
G Evans	0	F Langham (4 and 2)	1
A Coltart (1 hole)	1	J Sigel	0
R Willison (3 and 2)	1	T Scherrer	0
P Harrington	0	D Eger (3 and 2)	1
G McGimpsey	0	B May (4 and 3)	1
G Hay	0	M Voges (3 and 1)	1
	3		5

Second day's aggregate: Great Britain and Ireland 6; USA 6

Grand match aggregate: Great Britain and Ireland 10; USA 14

At Interlachen, Edina, Minnesota, on 18th and 19th August, 1993

Great Britain and Ireland   **USA**

First Day

Singles

I Pyman	0	A Doyle (1 hole)	1
M Stanford (3 and 2)	1	D Berganio	0
D Robertson (3 and 2)	1	J Sigel	0
S Cage	1/2	K Mitchum	1/2
P Harrington	0	T Herron (1 hole)	1
P Page	0	D Yates (2 and 1)	1
R Russell	0	T Demsey (2 and 1)	1
R Burns	0	J Leonard (4 and 3)	1
V Phillips (2 and 1)	1	B Gay	0
B Dredge	0	J Harris (4 and 3)	1
	3¹/₂		6¹/₂

First day's aggregate: Great Britain and Ireland 3$^{1}/_{2}$; USA 6$^{1}/_{2}$

Second Day

Foursomes

I Pyman and S Cage	0	A Doyle and J Leonard (4 and 3)	1
M Stanford and P Harrington	0	D Berganio and T Demsey (3 and 2)	1
B Dredge and V Phillips	0	J Sigel and K Mitchum (3 and 2)	1
R Russsell and D Robertson	0	J Harris and T Herron (1 hole)	1
	0		4

Singles

D Robertson	0	A Doyle (4 and 3)	1
I Pyman	0	J Harris (3 and 2)	1
S Cage	0	D Yates (2 and 1)	1
P Harrington	1/2	B Gay	1/2
P Page	0	J Sigel (5 and 4)	1
V Phillips	0	T Herron (3 and 2)	1
R Russell	0	K Mitchum (4 and 2)	1
R Burns (1 hole)	1	D Berganio	0
B Dredge	0	T Demsey (3 and 2)	1
M Stanford	0	J Leonard (5 and 4)	1
	1¹/₂		8¹/₂

Second day's aggregate: Great Britain and Ireland1$^{1}/_{2}$; USA 12$^{1}/_{2}$

Grand match aggregate: Great Britain and Ireland 5; USA 19

At Royal Porthcawl, Wales, on 9th and 10th September, 1995

Great Britain and Ireland   **USA**

First Day

Foursomes

G Sherry and S Gallacher	0	J Harris and T Woods (4 and 3)	1
M Foster and D Howell	1/2	A Bratton and C Riley	1/2
G Rankin and B Howard	0	N Begay and T Jackson (4 and 3)	1
P Harrington and J Fanagan (5 and 3)	1	K Cox and T Kuehne	0
	1¹/₂		2¹/₂

Singles

G Sherry (3 and 2)	1	N Begay	0
L James	0	K Cox (1 hole)	1
M Foster (4 and 3)	1	B Marucci	0
S Gallacher (4 and 3)	1	T Jackson	0
P Harrington (2 holes)	1	J Courville	0
B Howard	1/2	A Bratton	1/2
G Rankin	0	J Harris (1 hole)	1
G Wolstenholme (1 hole)	1	T Woods	0
	5¹/₂		2¹/₂

First day's aggregate: Great Britain and Ireland 7; USA 5

continued

The Walker Cup *continued*

Second Day

Foursomes

G Sherry and S Gallacher	0	A Bratton and C Riley (4 and 2)	1
D Howell and M Foster (3 and 2)	1	K Cox and T Kuehne	0
G Wolstenholme and L James	0	B Marucci and J Courville (6 and 5)	1
P Harrington and J Fanagan (2 and 1)	1	J Harris and T Woods	0
	2		2

Singles

G Sherry (2 holes)	1	C Riley	0
D Howell (2 and 1)	1	N Begay	0
S Gallacher (3 and 2)	1	T Kuehne	0
J Fanagan (3 and 2)	1	J Courville	0
B Howard	$1/2$	T Jackson	$1/2$
M Foster	$1/2$	B Marucci	$1/2$
P Harrington	0	J Harris (3 and 2)	1
G Wolstenholme	0	T Woods (4 and 3)	1
	5		3

Second day's aggregate: Great Britain and Ireland 7; USA 5

Grand match aggregate: Great Britain and Ireland 14; USA 10

At Quaker Ridge, New York, on 9th and 10th August, 1997

Great Britain and Ireland		**USA**	

First Day

Foursomes

B Howard and S Young	0	B Elder and J Kribel (4 and 3)	1
J Rose and M Brooks	0	J Courville and B Marucci (5 and 4)	1
G Wolstenholme and K Nolan	0	J Gore and J Harris (6 and 4)	1
R Coughlan and D Park	0	R Leen and C Wollmann (1 hole)	1
	0		4

Singles

S Young (5 and 4)	1	D Delcher	0
C Watson (1 hole)	1	S Scott	0
B Howard	0	B Elder (5 and 4)	1
J Rose (1 hole)	1	J Kribel	0
K Nolan	0	R Leen (3 and 2)	1
G Rankin	0	J Gore (3 and 2)	1
R Coughlan	$1/2$	C Wollmann	$1/2$
G Wolstenholme	0	J Harris (1 hole)	1
	$3^1/2$		$4^1/2$

Day Two

Foursomes

S Young and C Watson	0	J Harris and B Elder (3 and 2)	1
B Howard and G Rankin	0	J Courville and B Marucci (5 and 4)	1
R Coughlan and D Park	0	D Delcher and S Scott (1 hole)	1
G Wolstenholme and J Rose (2 and 1)	1	R Leen and C Wollmann	0
	1		3

Singles

S Young (2 and 1)	1	J Kribel	0
C Watson	$1/2$	J Gore	$1/2$
J Rose	0	J Courville (3 and 2)	1
K Nolan	0	B Elder (2 and 1)	1
M Brooks	0	J Harris (6 and 5)	1
D Park	0	B Marucci (4 and 3)	1
G Wolstenholme	0	D Delcher (2 and 1)	1
R Coughlan	0	S Scott (2 and 1)	1
	$1^1/2$		$6^1/2$

Grand match aggregate: USA 18; Great Britain and Ireland 6

Walker Cup – INDIVIDUAL RECORDS
Great Britain and Ireland

Notes: Bold type indicates captain; in brackets, did not play.
       *Players who have also played in the Ryder Cup.

Name		Year	Played	Won	Lost	Halved
MF Attenborough	Eng	1967	2	0	2	0
CC Aylmer	Eng	1922	2	1	1	0
*P Baker	Eng	1985	3	2	1	0
JB Beck	Eng	1928-(38)-(47)	1	0	1	0
PJ Benka	Eng	1969	4	2	1	1
HG Bentley	Eng	1934-36-38	4	0	2	2
DA Blair	Scot	1955-61	4	1	3	0
C Bloice	Scot	1985	3	0	2	1
MF Bonallack	Eng	1957-59-61-63-65-67-**69-71-73**	25	8	14	3
*G Brand	Scot	1979	3	0	3	0
OC Bristowe	Eng	(1923)-24	1	0	1	0
A Brodie	Scot	1977-79	8	5	2	1
A Brooks	Scot	1969	3	2	0	1
M Brooks	Scot	1997	2	0	2	0
C Brown	Wales	**1995**-(97)	0	0	0	0
Hon WGE Brownlow	Eng	1926	2	0	2	0
J Bruen	Ire	1938-49-51	5	0	4	1
JA Buckley	Wales	1979	1	0	1	0
J Burke	Ire	1932	2	0	1	1
R Burns	Ire	1993	2	1	1	0
AF Bussell	Scot	1957	2	1	1	0
S Cage	Eng	1993	3	0	2	1
I Caldwell	Eng	1951-55	4	1	2	1
W Campbell	Scot	1930	2	0	2	0
JB Carr	Ire	1947-49-51-53-55-57-59-61-63-(65)-67	20	5	14	1
RJ Carr	Ire	1971	4	3	0	1
DG Carrick	Scot	1983-87	5	0	5	0
IA Carslaw	Scot	1979	3	1	1	1
C Cassells	Eng	1989	3	2	1	0
JR Cater	Scot	1955	1	0	1	0
J Caven	Scot	1922	2	0	2	0
BHG Chapman	Eng	1961	1	0	1	0
R Chapman	Eng	1981	4	3	1	0
MJ Christmas	Eng	1961-63	3	1	2	0
*CA Clark	Eng	1965	4	2	0	2
GJ Clark	Eng	1965	1	0	1	0
*HK Clark	Eng	1973	3	1	1	1
R Claydon	Eng	1989	4	2	2	0
A Coltart	Scot	1991	3	2	1	0
GB Cosh	Scot	1965	4	3	1	0
R Coughlan	Ire	1997	4	0	3	1
T Craddock	Ire	1967-69	6	2	3	1
LG Crawley	Eng	1932-34-38-47	6	3	3	0
B Critchley	Eng	1969	4	1	1	2
D Curry	Eng	1987	4	1	3	0
CR Dalgleish	Scot	1981	3	1	2	0
B Darwin	Eng	1922	2	1	1	0
JC Davies	Eng	1973-75-77-79	13	3	8	2
P Deeble	Eng	1977-81	5	1	4	0
FWG Deighton	Scot	(1951)-57	2	0	2	0
SC Dodd	Wales	1989	4	1	1	2
B Dredge	Wales	1993	3	0	3	0
*NV Drew	Ire	1953	1	0	1	0
AA Duncan	Wales	(1953)	0	0	0	0
JM Dykes	Scot	1936	2	0	1	1
R Eggo	Eng	1987	2	0	2	0
D Evans	Wales	1981	3	1	1	1
G Evans	Eng	1991	4	2	2	0
RC Ewing	Ire	1936-38-47-49-51-55	10	1	7	2
GRD Eyles	Eng	1975	4	2	2	0
J Fanagan	Ire	1995	3	3	0	0
EW Fiddian	Eng	1932-34	4	0	4	0
J de Forest	Eng	1932	1	0	1	0
M Foster	Eng	1995	4	2	0	2
R Foster	Eng	1965-67-69-71-73-(**79**)-(**81**)	17	2	13	2

continued

Walker Cup – INDIVIDUAL RECORDS *continued*

Name		Year	Played	Won	Lost	Halved
DW Frame	Eng	1961	1	0	1	0
S Gallacher	Scot	1995	4	2	2	0
*D Gilford	Eng	1985	1	0	1	0
P Girvan	Scot	1987	3	0	3	0
G Godwin	Eng	1979-81	7	2	4	1
CW Green	Scot	1963-69-71-73-75-(83)-(85)	17	4	10	3
RH Hardman	Eng	1928	1	0	1	0
A Hare	Eng	1989	3	2	2	0
P Harrington	Ire	1991-93-95	9	3	5	1
R Harris	Scot	(1922)-23-26	4	1	3	0
RW Hartley	Eng	1930-32	4	0	4	0
WL Hartley	Eng	1932	2	0	2	0
J Hawksworth	Eng	1985	4	2	1	1
G Hay	Scot	1991	3	1	2	0
P Hedges	Eng	1973-75	5	0	2	3
CO Hezlet	Ire	1924-26-28	6	0	5	1
GA Hill	Eng	1936-(55)	2	0	1	1
Sir EWE Holderness	Eng	1923-26-30	6	2	4	0
TWB Homer	Eng	1973	3	0	3	0
CVL Hooman	Eng	1922-23	3	†1	2	†0
WL Hope	Scot	1923-24-28	5	1	4	0
DB Howard	Scot	1995-97	6	0	4	2
D Howell	Eng	1995	3	2	0	1
G Huddy	Eng	1961	1	0	1	0
W Humphreys	Eng	1971	3	2	1	0
IC Hutcheon	Scot	1975-77-79-81	15	5	8	2
RR Jack	Scot	1957-59	4	2	2	0
L James	Eng	1995	2	0	2	0
*M James	Eng	1975	4	3	1	0
A Jamieson, Jr	Scot	1926	2	1	1	0
MJ Kelley	Eng	1977-79	7	3	3	1
SD Keppler	Eng	1983	4	0	3	1
*MG King	Eng	1969-73	7	1	5	1
AT Kyle	Scot	1938-47-51	5	2	3	0
DH Kyle	Scot	1924	1	0	1	0
JA Lang	Scot	(1930)	0	0	0	0
JDA Langley	Eng	1936-51-53	6	0	5	1
CD Lawrie	Scot	(1961)-(63)	0	0	0	0
ME Lewis	Eng	1983	1	0	1	0
PB Lucas	Eng	(1936)-47-(49)	2	1	1	0
MSR Lunt	Eng	1959-61-63-65	11	2	8	1
*AWB Lyle	Scot	1977	3	0	3	0
AR McCallum	Scot	1928	1	0	1	0
SM McCready	Ire	1949-51	3	0	3	0
JS Macdonald	Scot	1971	3	1	1	1
P McEvoy	Eng	1977-79-81-85-89	18	5	11	2
G McGimpsey	Ire	1985-89-91	11	4	5	2
P McGinley	Ire	1991	3	1	2	0
G Macgregor	Scot	1971-75-83-85-87	14	5	8	1
RC MacGregor	Scot	1953	2	0	2	0
J McHenry	Ire	1987	4	2	2	0
P McKellar	Scot	1977	1	0	1	0
WW Mackenzie	Scot	1922-23	3	1	2	0
SL McKinlay	Scot	1934	2	0	2	0
J McLean	Scot	1934-36	4	1	3	0
EA McRuvie	Scot	1932-34	4	1	2	1
JFD Madeley	Ire	1963	2	0	1	1
LS Mann	Scot	1983	4	2	1	1
B Marchbank	Scot	1979	4	2	2	0
GC Marks	Eng	1969-71-(87)-(89)	6	2	4	0
DM Marsh	Eng	(1959)-71-(73)-(75)	3	2	1	0
GNC Martin	Ire	1928	1	0	1	0
S Martin	Scot	1977	4	2	2	0
P Mayo	Wales	1985-87	4	0	3	1
GH Micklem	Eng	1947-49-53-55-(57)-(59)	6	1	5	0
DJ Millensted	Eng	1967	2	1	1	0
JW Milligan	Scot	1989-91	7	3	3	1
EB Millward	Eng	(1949)-55	2	0	2	0
WTG Milne	Scot	1973	4	2	2	0
*CS Montgomerie	Scot	1985-87	8	2	5	1
JL Morgan	Wales	1951-53-55	6	2	4	0

† CVL Hooman and J Sweetser in 1922 were all square after 36 holes; instructions to the contrary not being readily available, they played on and Hooman won at the 37th. On all other occasions halved matches have counted as such.

Name		Year	Played	Won	Lost	Halved
P Mulcare	Ire	1975	3	2	1	0
GH Murray	Scot	1977	2	1	1	0
SWT Murray	Scot	1963	4	2	2	0
WA Murray	Scot	1923-24-(26)	4	1	3	0
K Nolan	Ire	1997	3	0	3	0
E O'Connell	Ire	1989	4	2	0	2
A Oldcorn	Eng	1983	4	4	0	0
*PA Oosterhuis	Eng	1967	4	1	2	1
R Oppenheimer	Eng	**(1951)**	0	0	0	0
P Page	Eng	1993	2	0	2	0
D Park	Wales	1997	3	0	3	0
P Parkin	Wales	1983	3	2	1	0
J Payne	Eng	1991	4	2	2	0
JJF Pennink	Eng	1938	2	1	1	0
TP Perkins	Eng	1928	2	0	2	0
AH Perowne	Eng	1949-53-59	4	0	4	0
GB Peters	Scot	1936-38	4	2	1	1
V Phillips	Eng	1993	3	1	2	0
AD Pierse	Ire	1983	3	0	2	1
AK Pirie	Scot	1967	3	0	2	1
MA Poxon	Eng	1975	2	0	2	0
D Prosser	Eng	1989	1	0	1	2
I Pyman	Eng	1993	3	0	3	0
*R Rafferty	Ire	1981	4	2	2	0
G Rankin	Scot	1995-97	4	0	4	0
D Robertson	Scot	1993	3	1	2	0
J Robinson	Eng	1987	4	2	2	0
RN Roderick	Wales	1989	2	0	1	1
J Rose	Eng	1997	4	2	2	0
R Russell	Scot	1993	3	0	3	0
AC Saddler	Scot	1963-65-67-(77)	10	3	5	2
Hon M Scott	Eng	1924-**34**	4	2	2	0
R Scott, Jr	Scot	1924	1	1	0	0
PF Scrutton	Eng	1955-57	3	0	3	0
DN Sewell	Eng	1957-59	4	1	3	0
RDBM Shade	Scot	1961-63-65-67	14	6	6	2
G Shaw	Scot	1987	4	1	2	1
DB Sheahan	Ire	1963	4	2	2	0
AE Shepperson	Eng	1957-59	3	1	1	1
G Sherry	Scot	1995	4	2	2	0
AF Simpson	Scot	(1926)	0	0	0	0
JN Smith	Scot	1930	2	0	2	0
WD Smith	Scot	1959	1	0	1	0
M Stanford	Eng	1993	3	1	2	0
AR Stephen	Scot	1985	4	2	1	1
EF Storey	Eng	1924-26-28	6	1	5	0
JA Stout	Eng	1930-32	4	0	3	1
C Stowe	Eng	1938-47	4	2	2	0
HB Stuart	Scot	1971-73-75	10	4	6	0
A Thirlwell	Eng	1957	1	0	1	0
KG Thom	Eng	1949	2	0	2	0
MS Thompson	Eng	1983	3	1	2	0
H Thomson	Scot	1936-38	4	2	2	0
CJH Tolley	Eng	1922-23-**24**-26-30-34	12	4	8	0
TA Torrance	Scot	1924-28-30-**32**-34	9	3	5	1
WB Torrance	Scot	1922	2	0	2	0
*PM Townsend	Eng	1965	4	3	1	0
LP Tupling	Eng	1969	2	1	1	0
W Tweddell	Eng	**1928**-(36)	2	0	2	0
J Walker	Scot	1961	2	0	2	0
*P Walton	Ire	1981-83	8	6	2	0
C Watson	Scot	1997	3	1	1	1
*P Way	Eng	1981	4	2	2	0
RH Wethered	Eng	1922-23-26-**30**-34	9	5	3	1
L White	Eng	1991	2	1	1	0
RJ White	Eng	1947-49-51-53-55	10	6	3	1
R Willison	Eng	1991	4	1	3	0
J Wilson	Scot	1923	2	2	0	0
JC Wilson	Scot	1947-53	4	0	4	0
GB Wolstenholme	Eng	1957-59	4	1	2	1
GP Wolstenholme	Eng	1995-97	7	2	5	0
S Young	Scot	1997	4	2	2	0

continued

Walker Cup – INDIVIDUAL RECORDS *continued*
United States of America

Name	Year	Played	Won	Lost	Halved
*TD Aaron	1959	2	1	1	0
B Alexander	1987	3	2	1	0
DC Allen	1965-67	6	0	4	2
B Andrade	1987	4	2	2	0
ES Andrews	1961	1	1	0	0
D Ballenger	1973	1	1	0	0
R Baxter, jr	1957	2	2	0	0
N Begay III	1995	3	1	2	0
DR Beman	1959-61-63-65	11	7	2	2
D Berganio	1993	3	1	2	0
RE Billows	1938-49	4	2	2	0
SE Bishop	1947-49	3	2	1	0
AS Blum	1957	1	0	1	0
J Bohmann	1969	3	1	2	0
M Brannan	1977	3	1	2	0
A Bratton	1995	3	1	0	2
GF Burns	1975	3	2	1	0
C Burroughs	1985	3	1	2	0
AE Campbell	1936	2	2	0	0
JE Campbell	1957	1	0	1	0
WC Campbell	1951-53-(55)-57-65-67-71-75	18	11	4	3
RJ Cerrudo	1967	4	1	1	2
RD Chapman	1947-51-53	5	3	2	0
D Cherry	1953-55-61	5	5	0	0
D Clarke	1979	3	2	0	1
RE Cochran	1961	1	1	0	0
CR Coe	1949-51-53-(57)-59-61-63	13	7	4	2
R Commans	1981	3	1	1	1
JW Conrad	1955	2	1	1	0
J Courville Jr	1995-97	6	4	2	0
K Cox	1995	3	1	2	0
N Crosby	1983	2	1	1	0
BH Cudd	1955	2	2	0	0
RD Davies	1963	2	0	2	0
JW Dawson	1949	2	2	0	0
D Delcher	1997	3	2	1	0
T Demsey	1993	3	3	0	0
RB Dickson	1967	3	3	0	0
A Doyle	1991-93	6	5	1	0
GT Dunlap Jr	1932-34-36	5	3	1	1
D Duval	1991	3	2	1	0
D Edwards	1973	4	4	0	0
HC Egan	1934	1	1	0	0
D Eger	1991	3	2	1	0
HC Eger	1989	3	1	2	0
D Eichelberger	1965	3	1	2	0
B Elder	1997	4	4	0	0
J Ellis	1973	3	2	1	0
W Emery	1936	2	1	0	1
C Evans Jr	1922-24-28	5	3	2	0
J Farquhar	1971	3	1	2	0
*B Faxon	1983	4	3	1	0
R Fehr	1983	4	2	1	1
JW Fischer	1934-36-38-(65)	4	3	0	1
D Fischesser	1979	3	1	2	0
MA Fleckman	1967	2	0	2	0
B Fleisher	1969	4	0	2	2
J Fought	1977	4	4	0	0
WC Fownes Jr	**1922-24**	3	1	2	0
F Fuhrer	1981	3	2	1	0
JR Gabrielsen	1977-(**81**)-(**91**)	3	1	2	0
R Gamez	1989	4	3	0	1
RA Gardner	1922-**23**-24-**26**	8	6	2	0
RW Gardner	1961-63	5	4	0	1
B Gay	1993	2	0	1	1
M Giles	1969-71-73-75	15	8	2	5
HL Givan	1936	1	0	0	1
JG Goodman	1934-36-38	6	4	2	0
J Gore	1997	3	2	0	1

Name	Year	Played	Won	Lost	Halved
M Gove	1979	3	2	1	0
J Grace	1975	3	2	1	0
JA Grant	1967	2	2	0	0
AD Gray Jr	1963-65-67-(95)-(97)	12	5	6	1
JP Guilford	1922-24-26	6	4	2	0
W Gunn	1926-28	4	4	0	0
*F Haas Jr	1938	2	0	2	0
*J Haas	1975	3	3	0	0
J Haas	1985	3	1	2	0
G Hallberg	1977	3	1	2	0
GS Hamer Jr	(1947)	0	0	0	0
J Harris	1993-95-97	11	10	1	0
LE Harris Jr	1963	4	3	1	0
V Heafner	1977	3	3	0	0
SD Herron	1923	2	0	2	0
T Herron	1993	3	3	0	0
*S Hoch	1979	4	4	0	0
W Hoffer	1983	2	1	1	0
J Holtgrieve	1979-81-83	10	6	4	0
JM Hopkins	1965	3	0	2	1
R Howe	1989	1	0	1	0
W Howell	1932	1	1	0	0
W Hyndman	1957-59-61-69-71	9	6	1	2
J Inman	1969	2	2	0	0
JG Jackson	1953-55	3	3	0	0
T Jackson	1995	3	1	1	1
K Johnson	1989	3	1	2	0
HR Johnston	1923-24-28-30	6	5	1	0
RT Jones Jr	1922-24-26-**28-30**	10	9	1	0
AF Kammer	1947	2	1	1	0
M Killian	1973	3	1	2	0
C Kite	1987	3	2	1	0
*TO Kite	1971	4	2	1	1
RE Knepper	(1922)	0	0	0	0
RW Knowles	1951	1	1	0	0
G Koch	1973-75	7	4	1	2
CR Kocsis	1938-49-57	5	2	2	1
J Kribel	1997	3	1	2	0
T Kuehne	1995	3	0	3	0
F Langham	1991	3	1	2	0
R Leen	1997	3	2	1	0
*J Leonard	1993	3	3	0	0
G Lesher	1989	4	1	3	0
B Lewis Jr	1981-83-85-87	14	10	4	0
JW Lewis	1967	4	3	1	0
WL Little Jr	1934	2	2	0	0
*GA Littler	1953	2	2	0	0
B Loeffler	1987	3	2	1	0
*D Love	1985	3	2	0	1
MJ McCarthy Jr	(1928)-32	1	1	0	0
BN McCormick	1949	1	1	0	0
JB McHale	1949-51	3	2	0	1
RR Mackenzie	1926-28-30	6	5	1	0
MR Marston	1922-23-24-34	8	5	3	0
D Martin	1989	4	1	1	2
B Marucci	1995-97	6	4	1	1
L Mattiace	1987	3	2	1	0
R May	1991	4	3	1	0
B Mayfair	1987	3	3	0	0
E Meeks	1989	1	0	0	1
SN Melnyk	1969-71	7	3	3	1
*P Mickelson	1989-91	8	4	2	2
AL Miller	1969-71	8	4	3	1
L Miller	1977	4	4	0	0
K Mitchum	1993	3	2	0	1
DK Moe	1930-32	3	3	0	0
B Montgomery	1987	2	2	0	0
G Moody	1979	3	1	2	0
GT Moreland	1932-34	4	4	0	0
D Morey	1955-65	4	1	3	0
J Mudd	1981	3	3	0	0
*RJ Murphy	1967	4	1	2	1

continued

Walker Cup – INDIVIDUAL RECORDS *continued*

Name	Year	Played	Won	Lost	Halved
JF Neville	1923	1	0	1	0
*JW Nicklaus	1959-61	4	4	0	0
LW Oehmig	(1977)	0	0	0	0
FD Ouimet	1922-23-24-26-30-**32-34**-(**36**)-(**38**)-(**47**)-(**49**)	16	9	5	2
HD Paddock Jr	1951	1	0	0	1
*J Pate	1975	4	0	4	0
WJ Patton	1955-57-59-63-65-(**69**)	14	11	3	0
*C Pavin	1981	3	2	0	1
M Peck	1979	3	1	1	1
M Pfeil	1973	4	2	1	1
M Podolak	1985	2	1	0	1
SL Quick	1947	2	1	1	0
S Randolph	1985	4	2	1	1
J Rassett	1981	3	3	0	0
F Ridley	1977-(**87**)-(**89**)	3	2	1	0
RH Riegel	1947-49	4	4	0	0
C Riley	1995	3	1	1	1
H Robbins Jr	1957	2	0	1	1
*W Rogers	1973	2	1	1	0
GV Rotan	1923	2	1	1	0
*EM Rudolph	1957	2	1	0	1
B Sander	1977	3	0	3	0
T Scherrer	1991	3	0	3	0
S Scott	1997	3	2	1	0
CH Seaver	1932	2	2	0	0
RL Siderowf	1969-73-75-77-(**79**)	14	4	8	2
J Sigel	1977-79-81-**83**-85-87-89-91-93	33	18	10	5
RH Sikes	1963	3	1	2	0
JB Simons	1971	2	0	2	0
*S Simpson	1977	3	3	0	0
CB Smith	1961-63	2	0	1	1
R Smith	1936-38	4	2	2	0
R Sonnier	1985	3	0	2	1
J Sorensen	1987	3	1	1	1
M Sposa	1991	3	2	1	0
*C Stadler	1975	3	3	0	0
FR Stranahan	1947-49-51	6	3	2	1
*C Strange	1975	4	3	0	1
*H Sutton	1979-81	7	2	4	1
JW Sweetser	1922-23-24-26-28-32-(**67**)-(73)	12	7	†4	†1
FM Taylor	1957-59-61	4	4	0	0
D Tentis	1983	2	0	1	1
RS Tufts	(**1963**)	0	0	0	0
WP Turnesa	1947-49-**51**	6	3	3	0
B Tuten	1983	2	1	1	0
EM Tutweiler	1965-67	6	5	1	0
ER Updegraff	1963-65-69-(**75**)	7	3	3	1
S Urzetta	1951-53	4	4	0	0
K Venturi	1953	2	2	0	0
S Verplank	1985	4	3	0	1
M Voges	1991	3	2	1	0
GJ Voigt	1930-32-36	5	2	2	1
G Von Elm	1926-28-30	6	4	1	1
D von Tacky	1981	3	1	2	0
*JL Wadkins	1969-71	7	3	4	0
D Waldorf	1985	3	1	2	0
EH Ward	1953-55-59	6	6	0	0
MH Ward	1938-47	4	2	2	0
M West	1973-79	6	2	3	1
J Westland	1932-34-53-(**61**)	5	3	0	2
HW Wettlaufer	1959	2	2	0	0
E White	1936	2	2	0	0
OF Willing	1923-24-30	4	4	0	0
JM Winters Jr	(**1971**)	0	0	0	0
C Wollman	1997	3	1	1	1
W Wood	1983	4	1	2	1
*T Woods	1995	4	2	2	0
FJ Wright	1923	1	1	0	0
CR Yates	1936-38-(**53**)	4	3	0	1
D Yates	1989-93	6	3	2	1
RL Yost	1955	2	2	0	0

† CVL Hooman and J Sweetser in 1922 were all square after 36 holes; instructions to the contrary not being readily available, they played on and Hooman won at the 37th. On all other occasions halved matches have counted as such.

Eisenhower Trophy (World Amateur Team Championship)

Year	Winners	Runners-up	Venue	Score
1958	Australia	United States	St Andrews	918
(After a tie, Australia won the play-off by two strokes: Australia 222, United States 224)				
1960	United States	Australia	Ardmore, USA	834
1962	United States	Canada	Kawana, Japan	854
1964	Great Britain & Ireland	Canada	Olgiata, Rome	895
1966	Australia	United States	Mexico City	877
1968	United States	Great Britain & Ireland	Melbourne	868
1970	United States	New Zealand	Madrid	857
1972	United States	Australia	Buenos Aires	865
1974	United States	Japan	Dominican Rep.	888
1976	Great Britain & Ireland	Japan	Penina, Portugal	892
1978	United States	Canada	Fiji	873
1980	United States	South Africa	Pinehurst, USA	848
1982	United States	Sweden	Lausanne	859
1984	Japan	United States	Hong Kong	870
1986	Canada	United States	Caracas, Venezuela	860
1988	Great Britain & Ireland	United States	Ullva, Sweden	882
1990	Sweden	New Zealand	Christchurch, New Zealand	879
1992	New Zealand	United States	Capilano, Canada	823
1994	United States	Great Britain & Ireland	Paris, France	838
1996	Australia	Sweden	Manila, Philippines	838

European Amateur Team Championship

Year	Winner	Second	Venue
1959	Sweden		
1961	Sweden	England	Brussels, Belgium
1963	England	Sweden	Falsterbo, Sweden
1965	Ireland	Scotland	St George's, England
1967	Ireland	France	Turin, Italy
1969	England	W Germany	Hamburg, W Germany
1971	England	Scotland	Lausanne, Switzerland
1973	England	Scotland	Penina, Portugal
1975	Scotland	Italy	Killarney, Ireland
1977	Scotland	Sweden	The Haagsche, Holland
1979	England	Wales	Esbjerg, Denmark
1981	England	Scotland	St Andrews, Scotland
1983	Ireland	Spain	Chantilly, France
1985	Scotland	Sweden	Halmstad, Sweden
1987	Ireland	England	Murhof, Austria
1989	England	Scotland	Royal Porthcawl
1991	England	Italy	Puerta de Hierro
1993	Wales	England	Marianske Lasne, Czech Republic
1995	Scotland	England	Royal Antwerp, Belgium
1997	Spain	Scotland	Portmarnock

Home Internationals

Year	Winner	Year	Winner	Year	Winner
1932	Scotland	1956	Scotland	1973	England
1933	Scotland	1957	England	1974	England
1934	Scotland	1958	England	1975	Scotland
1935T	England/Ireland/Scotland	1959T	England/Ireland/Scotland	1976	Scotland
1936	Scotland	1960	England	1977	England
1937	Scotland	1961	Scotland	1978	England
1938	England	1962T	England/Ireland/Scotland	1979	No Internationals held
1939–46 No Internationals held		1963T	England/Ireland/Scotland	1980	England
1947	England	1964	England	1981	Scotland
1948	England	1965	England	1982	Scotland
1949	England	1966	England	1983	Ireland
1950	Ireland	1967	Scotland	1984	England
1951T	Ireland and Scotland	1968	England	1985	England
1952	Scotland	1969	England	1986	Scotland
1953	Scotland	1970	Scotland	1987	Ireland
1954	England	1971	Scotland	1988	England
1955	Ireland	1972T	Scotland/England	1989	England *continued*

Home Internationals *continued*

1990 *at Conwy*

England beat Wales	10 matches to 5
Ireland beat Scotland	9 matches to 6
Scotland beat England	$9^1/_2$ matches to $5^1/_2$
Ireland beat Wales	11 matches to 4
Wales beat Scotland	8 matches to 7
Ireland beat England	8 matches to 7

Winners: Ireland

1991 *at Rosses Point*

Ireland halved with Wales	$7^1/_2$ matches each
Scotland beat England	$9^1/_2$ matches to $5^1/_2$
Ireland beat England	11 matches to 4
Wales beat Scotland	8 matches to 7
England beat Wales	9 matches to 6
Ireland beat Scotland	10 matches to 5

Winners: Ireland

1992 *at Prestwick*

Ireland halved with England	$7^1/_2$ matches each
Scotland beat Wales	8 matches to 7
Ireland beat Wales	11 matches to 4
England beat Scotland	$11^1/_2$ matches to $3^1/_2$
England beat Wales	$8^1/_2$ matches to $6^1/_2$
Ireland beat Scotland	$12^1/_2$ matches to $2^1/_2$

Winners: England and Ireland tied

1993 *at Hoylake*

England beat Scotland	8 matches to 7
Wales beat Ireland	$8^1/_2$ matches to $6^1/_2$
England beat Ireland	$9^1/_2$ matches to $5^1/_2$
Wales halved with Scotland	$7^1/_2$ matches each
Ireland beat Scotland	$8^1/_2$ matches to $6^1/_2$
England halved with Wales	$7^1/_2$ matches each

Winners: England

1994 *at Ashburnham, Dyfed*

England beat Scotland	$9^1/_2$ matches to $5^1/_2$
Ireland beat Wales	$10^1/_2$ matches to $4^1/_2$
England beat Wales	10 matches to 5
Ireland beat Scotland	11 matches to 4
Scotland beat Wales	8 matches to 7
England beat Ireland	9 matches to 6

Winners: England

1995 *at Royal Portrush, Co Antrim, N. Ireland*

Ireland beat Scotland	$8^1/_2$ matches to $6^1/_2$
Wales beat England	$8^1/_2$ matches to $6^1/_2$
Scotland beat Wales	11 matches to 4
England beat Ireland	9 matches to 6
Ireland beat Wales	10 matches to 5
England beat Scotland	$9^1/_2$ matches to $5^1/_2$

Winners: England beat Ireland on countback
25 wins to $24^1/_2$

1996 *at Moray, Scotland*

England beat Wales	9 matches to 6
Ireland beat Scotland	$8^1/_2$ matches to $6^1/_2$
England halved with Scotland	$7^1/_2$ matches each
Ireland beat Wales	$9^1/_2$ matches to $5^1/_2$
England beat Ireland	10 matches to 5
Scotland beat Wales	9 matches to 6

Winners: England

1997 *at Burnham & Berrow*

England beat Wales	$10^1/_2$ matches to $4^1/_2$
Ireland beat Scotland	$10^1/_2$ matches to $4^1/_2$
England beat Scotland	$10^1/_2$ matches to $4^1/_2$
Ireland beat Wales	$8^1/_2$ matches to $6^1/_2$
England halved with Ireland	$7^1/_2$ matches to $7^1/_2$
Scotland beat Wales	9 matches to 6

Winners: England

St Andrews Trophy (Great Britain and Ireland *v* Continent of Europe) *Match instituted 1956, trophy presented 1962*

Year	Winner	Venue	Result
1956	Great Britain & Ireland	Wentworth	$12^1/_2$–$2^1/_2$
1958	Great Britain & Ireland	St Cloud, France	10–5
1960	Great Britain & Ireland	Walton Heath	13–5
1962	Great Britain & Ireland	Halmstead, Sweden	18–12
1964	Great Britain & Ireland	Muirfield	23–7
1966	Great Britain & Ireland	Bilbao, Spain	$19^1/_2$–$10^1/_2$
1968	Great Britain & Ireland	Portmarnock	20–10
1970	Great Britain & Ireland	La Zoute, Belgium	$17^1/_2$–$12^1/_2$
1972	Great Britain & Ireland	Berkshire	$19^1/_2$–$10^1/_2$
1974	Continent of Europe	Punta Ala, Italy	16–14
1976	Great Britain & Ireland	St Andrews	$18^1/_2$–$11^1/_2$
1978	Great Britain & Ireland	Bremen, Germany	$20^1/_2$–$9^1/_2$
1980	Great Britain & Ireland	Sandwich, R St George's	$19^1/_2$–$10^1/_2$
1982	Continent of Europe	Rosendaelsche, Netherlands	14–10
1984	Great Britain & Ireland	Taunton, Devon	13–11
1986	Great Britain & Ireland	Halmstead, Sweden	$14^1/_2$–$9^1/_2$
1988	Great Britain & Ireland	St Andrews	$15^1/_2$–$8^1/_2$
1990	Great Britain & Ireland	El Saler, Spain	13–11
1992	Great Britain & Ireland	R Cinque Ports	14–10
1994	Great Britain & Ireland	Chantilly, France	14–10
1996	Great Britain & Ireland	Woodhall Spa	16–8

Women's Professional Internationals

Solheim Cup
At Lake Nona GC, Florida, 16th, 17th and 18th November, 1990

Europe		USA	
Foursomes			
	Matches		**Matches**
L Davies and A Nicholas (2 and 1)	1	P Bradley and N Lopez	0
P Wright and L Neumann	0	C Gerring and D Mochrie (6 and 5)	1
D Reid and H Alfredsson	0	P Sheehan and R Jones (6 and 5)	1
T Johnson and ML de Lorenzi	0	B Daniel and B King (5 and 4)	1
	1		3
Four-balls			
T Johnson and ML de Lorenzi	0	P Sheehan and R Jones (2 and 1)	1
D Reid and H Alfredsson	0	P Bradley and N Lopez (2 and 1)	1
L Davies and A Nicholas	0	B King and B Daniel (4 and 3)	1
L Neumann and P Wright (4 and 2)	1	C Gerring and D Mochrie	0
	1		3
Singles			
H Alfredsson	0	C Gerring (4 and 3)	1
L Davies (3 and 2)	1	R Jones	0
A Nicholas	0	N Lopez (6 and 4)	1
P Wright	$^{1}/_{2}$	B King	$^{1}/_{2}$
L Neumann	0	B Daniel (7 and 6)	1
D Reid (2 and 1)	1	P Sheehan	0
ML de Lorenzi	0	D Mochrie (4 and 2)	1
T Johnson	0	P Bradley (8 and 7)	1
	$2^{1}/_{2}$		$5^{1}/_{2}$

Result: USA $11^{1}/_{2}$; Europe $4^{1}/_{2}$

At Dalmahoy on 2nd, 3rd and 4th October, 1992

Europe		USA	
First Day – Foursomes			
	Matches		**Matches**
L Davies and A Nicholas (1hole)	1	B King and B Daniel	0
L Neumann and H Alfredsson (2 and 1)	1	P Bradley and D Mochrie	0
F Descampe and T Johnson	0	A Ammaccapane and M Mallon (1hole)	1
D Reid and P Wright	$^{1}/_{2}$	P Sheehan and J Inkster	$^{1}/_{2}$
	$2^{1}/_{2}$		$1^{1}/_{2}$
Second Day – Fourball			
L Davies and A Nicholas (1 hole)	1	P Sheehan and J Inkster	0
T Johnson and F Descampe	$^{1}/_{2}$	B Burton and D Richard	$^{1}/_{2}$
P Wright and D Reid	0	M Mallon and B King (1 hole)	1
H Alfredsson and L Neumann	$^{1}/_{2}$	P Bradley and D Mochrie	$^{1}/_{2}$
	2		2

continued

Solheim Cup *continued*

Third Day – Singles

L Davies (4 and 2)	1	B Burton	0
H Alfredsson (4 and 3)	1	D Ammaccapane	0
T Johnson (2 and 1)	1	P Sheehan	0
A Nicholas	0	J Inkster (3 and 2)	1
F Descampe	0	B Daniel (2 and 1)	1
P Wright (4 and 3)	1	P Bradley	0
C Nilsmark (3 and 2)	1	M Mallon	0
K Douglas	0	D Richard (7 and 6)	1
L Neumann (2 and 1)	1	B King	0
D Reid (3 and 2)	1	D Mochrie	0
	7		3

Match aggregate: Europe 11$^1/_2$, United States 6$^1/_2$

At the Greenbrier, West Virginia, 21st, 22nd and 23rd October, 1994

USA   **Europe**

First Day – Foursomes

B Burton and D Mochrie (3 and 2)	1	H Alfredsson and L Neumann	0
B Daniel and M Mallon	0	C Nilsmark and A Sorenstam (1 hole)	1
T Green and K Robbins	0	L Fairclough and D Reid (2 and 1)	1
D Andrews and B King	0	L Davies and A Nicholas (2 holes)	1
P Sheehan and S Steinhauer (2 holes)	1	T Johnson and P Wright	0
	2		3

Second Day – Fourball

B Burton and D Mochrie (2 and 1)	1	L Davies and A Nicholas	0
B Daniel and M Mallon (6 and 5)	1	C Nilsmark and A Sorenstam	0
T Green and K Robbins	0	L Fairclough and D Reid (4 and 3)	1
D Andrews and B King (3 and 2)	1	T Johnson and P Wright	0
P Sheehan and S Steinhauer	0	H Alfredsson and L Neumann (1 hole)	1
	3		2

Third Day – Singles

B King	0	H Alfredsson (2 and 1)	1
D Mochrie (6 and 5)	1	C Nilsmark	0
B Daniel (1 hole)	1	T Johnson	0
K Robbins (4 and 2)	1	L Fairclough	0
M Mallon (1 hole)	1	P Wright	0
P Sheehan	0	A Nicholas (3 and 2)	1
B Burton (1 hole)	1	L Davies	0
T Green (3 and 2)	1	A Sorenstam	0
S Steinhauer (2 holes)	1	D Reid	0
D Andrews (3 and 2)	1	L Neumann	0
	8		2

Match aggregate: United States 13, Europe 7

At St Pierre, Chepstow, 20th–22nd September, 1996

Europe   **USA**

First Day – Foursomes

A Sorenstam and C Nilsmark	$^1/_2$	K Robbins and M McGann	$^1/_2$
L Davies and A Nicholas	0	P Sheehan and R Jones (1 hole)	1
ML de Lorenzi and D Reid	0	B Daniel and V Skinner (1 hole)	1
H Alfredsson and L Neumann	0	D Pepper and B Burton (2 and 1)	1
	$^1/_2$		3$^1/_2$

Fourball

L Davies and T Johnson (6 and 5)	1	K Robbins and P Bradley	0
A Sorenstam and K Marshall (1 hole)	1	V Skinner and J Geddes	0
L Neumann and C Nilsmark	0	D Pepper and B King (1 hole)	1
H Alfredsson and A Nicholas	$^1/_2$	M Mallon and B Daniel	$^1/_2$
	2$^1/_2$		1$^1/_2$

At St Pierre, Chepstow, 20th–22nd September, 1996

Europe		USA	
Second Day – Foursomes			
L Davies and T Johnson (4 and 3)	1	P Sheehan and R Jones	0
A Sorenstam and C Nilsmark (1 hole)	1	D Pepper and B Burton	0
L Neumann and K Marshall	$^1/_2$	M Mallon and J Geddes	$^1/_2$
ML de Lorenzi amd H Alfredsson (4 and 3)	1	K Robbins and M McGann	0
	$3^1/_2$		$^1/_2$
Fourball			
L Davies and L Hackney (6 and 5)	1	B Daniel and V Skinner	0
A Sorenstam and T Johnson	$^1/_2$	M McGann and M Mallon	$^1/_2$
ML de Lorenzi and J Morley	0	K Robbins and B King (2 and 1)	1
C Nilsmark and L Neumann (2 and 1)	1	P Sheehan and J Geddes	0
	$2^1/_2$		$1^1/_2$

Third Day – Singles			
A Sorenstam (2 and 1)	1	P Bradley	0
K Marshall	0	V Skinner (2 and 1)	1
L Davies	0	M McGann (3 and 2)	1
L Neumann	$^1/_2$	B Daniel	$^1/_2$
L Hackney	0	B Burton (1 hole)	1
T Johnson	0	D Pepper (3 and 2)	1
A Nicholas	$^1/_2$	K Robbins	$^1/_2$
ML de Lorenzi	0	B King (6 and 4)	1
J Morley	0	R Jones (5 and 4)	1
D Reid	0	J Geddes (2 holes)	1
C Nilsmark	0	P Sheehan (2 and 1)	1
H Alfredsson	0	M Mallon (4 and 2)	1
	2		10

Match aggregate: USA 17, Europe 11

INDIVIDUAL RECORDS

Brackets indicate non-playing captain

Europe

Name		Year	Played	Won	Lost	Halved
Helen Alfredsson	Swe	1990-92-94-96	13	5	6	2
Laura Davies	Eng	1990-92-94-96	14	9	5	0
Florence Descampe	Bel	1992	3	0	2	1
Kitrina Douglas	Eng	1992	1	0	1	0
Lora Fairclough	Eng	1994	3	2	1	0
Lisa Hackney	Eng	1996	2	1	1	0
Trish Johnson	Eng	1990-92-94-96	13	3	8	2
Marie-Laure de Lorenzi	Fra	1990-96	7	1	6	0
Kathryn Marshall	Sco	1996	3	1	1	1
Joanne Morley	Eng	1996	2	0	2	0
Liselotte Neumann	Swe	1990-92-94-96	14	5	6	3
Alison Nicholas	Eng	1990-92-94-96	12	5	5	2
Catrin Nilsmark	Swe	1992-94-96	9	4	4	1
Dale Reid	Sco	1990-92-94-96	11	4	6	1
Annika Sorenstam	Swe	1994-96	8	4	2	2
Mickey Walker	Eng	(1990)-(92)-(94)-(96)	0	0	0	0
Pam Wright	Sco	1990-92-94	6	1	4	1

United States

Name	Year	Played	Won	Lost	Halved
Danielle Ammacapane	1992	2	1	1	0
Donna Andrews	1994	3	2	1	0
Pat Bradley	1990-92-96	8	2	5	1
Brandie Burton	1992-94-96	8	5	2	1
JoAnne Carner	(1994)	0	0	0	0
Beth Daniel	1990-92-94-96	12	7	3	2

continued

Solheim Cup *continued*

Name	Year	Played	Won	Lost	Halved
Jane Geddes	1996	4	1	2	1
Cathy Gerring	1990	3	2	1	0
Tammie Green	1994	3	1	2	0
Juli Inkster	1992	3	1	1	1
Rosie Jones	1990-96	6	4	2	0
Betsy King	1990-92-94-96	12	7	4	1
Nancy Lopez	1990	3	2	1	0
Michelle McGann	1996	4	1	1	2
Meg Mallon	1992-94-96	10	5	2	3
Alice Miller	(1992)*	0	0	0	0
Dottie Pepper	1990-92-94-96	13	8	4	1
Judy Rankin	1996	0	0	0	0
Deb Richard	1992	2	1	0	1
Kelly Robbins	1994-96	8	2	4	2
Patty Sheehan	1990-92-94-96	13	5	7	1
Val Skinner	1996	4	2	2	0
Sherri Steinhauer	1994	3	2	1	0
Kathy Whitworth	(1990)-(92)*	0	0	0	0

* Kathy Whitworth had to return home because of a bereavement; Alice Miller took over the captaincy.

Women's Amateur Tournaments

Astor Salver *at The Berkshire*

Year	Winner	Year	Winner
1988	J Thornhill	1993	S Lambert
1989	S Sutton	1994	S Lambert
1990T	J Hall/J Morley	1995	J Oliver
1991	EJ Smith	1996	S Gallagher
1992	L Walton	1997	J Lamb

Hampshire Rose *at North Hants*

Year	Winner	Year	Winner
1988	J Thornhill	1993	C Hourihane
1989	A MacDonald	1994T	K Shepherd/K Egford
1990	S Keogh	1995	J Oliver
1991	K Egford	1996	K Stupples
1992	A Uzielli	1997	S Sanderson

Helen Holm Trophy

Year	Winner	Year	Winner
1988	E Farquharson	1993	J Hall
1989	S Robinson	1994	K Tebbet
1990	C Lambert	1995	M Hjorth
1991	J Hall	1996	J Hockley
1992	M McKay	1997	K Rostron

London Ladies' Foursomes

Year	Winner	Year	Winner
1988	Harpenden	1993	Knebworth
1989	Walton Heath	1994	Knebworth
1990	Stoke Poges	1995	The Berkshire
1991	Stoke Poges	1996	The Berkshire
1992	Chelmsford	1997	The Berkshire

Women's Amateur International Tournaments and Matches

Great Britain & Ireland *v* USA (Ladies) Curtis Cup

Year		Great Britain & Ireland		USA		Venue
1932	Foursomes	0	3½	3	5½	Wentworth
	Singles	3½		2½		
1934	Foursomes	1½	2½	1½	6½	Chevy Chase
	Singles	1		5		
1936	Foursomes	1½	4½	1½	4½	Gleneagles
	Singles	3		3		
1938	Foursomes	2½	3½	½	5½	Essex County Club
	Singles	1		5		
1948	Foursomes	1	2½	2	6½	Birkdale
	Singles	1½		4½		
1950	Foursomes	1	1½	2	7½	Buffalo
	Singles	½		5½		
1952	Foursomes	2	5	1	4	Muirfield
	Singles	3		3		
1954	Foursomes	0	3	3	6	Merion
	Singles	3		3		
1956	Foursomes	1	5	2	4	Sandwich, Prince's
	Singles	4		2		
1958	Foursomes	2	4½	1	4½	Brae Burn GC
	Singles	2½		3½		
1960	Foursomes	1	2½	2	6½	Lindrick
	Singles	1½		4½		
1962	Foursomes	0	1	3	8	Colorado Springs
	Singles	1		5		
1964	Foursomes	3½	7½	2½	10½	Porthcawl
	Singles	4		8		
1966	Foursomes	1½	5	4½	13	Hot Springs
	Singles	3½		8½		
1968	Foursomes	2½	7½	3½	10½	Newcastle, Co Down
	Singles	5		7		
1970	Foursomes	2½	6½	3½	11½	Brae Burn, USA
	Singles	4		8		
1972	Foursomes	3½	8	2½	10	Western Gailes
	Singles	4½		7½		
1974	Foursomes	2½	5	3½	13	San Francisco, California
	Singles	2½		9½		
1976	Foursomes	2	6½	4	11½	R Lytham and St Annes
	Singles	4½		7½		
1978	Foursomes	2½	6	3½	12	Apawamis, NY
	Singles	3½		8½		
1980	Foursomes	1	5	5	13	St Pierre
	Singles	4		8		
1982	Foursomes	1½	3½	4½	14½	Denver, Colorado
	Singles	2		10		
1984	Foursomes	3	8½	3	9½	Muirfield
	Singles	5½		6½		
1986	Foursomes	5½	13	½	5	Prairie Dunes, Kansas
	Singles	7½		4½		

At Royal St George's on 10th and 11th June, 1988

Great Britain and Ireland		USA	
***First Day* – Foursomes**			
L Bayman and J Wade (2 and 1)	1	T Kerdyk and K Scrivner	0
S Shapcott and K Davies (5 and 4)	1	C Scholefield and C Thompson	0
J Thornhill and V Thomas	¹/₂	L Shannon and C Keggi	¹/₂
	2¹/₂		¹/₂
Singles			
L Bayman	¹/₂	T Kerdyk	1/2
J Wade (2 holes)	1	C Scholefield	0
S Shapcott	0	C Thompson (1 hole)	1
K Davies	0	P Sinn (4 and 3)	1
S Lawson (1 hole)	1	P Cornett	0
J Thornhill (3 and 2)	1	L Shannon	0
	3¹/₂		2¹/₂
***Second Day* – Foursomes**			
L Bayman and J Wade	0	T Kerdyk and K Scrivner (1 hole)	1
S Shapcott and K Davies (2 holes)	1	L Shannon and C Keggi	0
J Thornhill and V Thomas (6 and 5)	1	C Scholefield and C Thompson	0
	2		1
Singles			
J Wade	0	T Kerdyk (2 and 1)	1
S Shapcott (3 and 2)	1	C Keggi	0
S Lawson	0	K Scrivner (4 and 3)	1
V Thomas (5 and 3)	1	P Cornett	0
L Bayman (1 hole)	1	P Sinn	0
J Thornhill	0	C Thompson (3 and 2)	1
	3		3

Aggregate: Great Britain and Ireland 11, United States 7

At Somerset Hills, New Jersey, on 28th and 29th July, 1990

Great Britain and Ireland		USA	
***First Day* – Foursomes**			
H Dobson and C Lambert	0	V Goetze and A Sander (4 and 3)	1
J Hall and K Imrie (2 and 1)	1	K Noble and M Platt	0
E Farquharson and H Wadsworth	0	C Semple-Thompson and R Weiss (3 and 1)	1
	1		2
Singles			
J Hall (2 and 1)	1	V Goetze	0
K Imrie	0	K Peterson (3 and 2)	1
E Farquharson	0	B Burton (3 and 1)	1
L Fletcher	0	R Weiss (4 and 3)	1
C Lambert	0	K Noble (1 hole)	1
V Thomas (1 hole)	1	C Semple-Thompson	0
	2		4
***Second Day* – Foursomes**			
J Hall and K Imrie	0	V Goetze and A Sander (4 and 3)	1
C Lambert and H Dobson (1 hole)	1	K Noble and M Platt	0
E Farquharson and H Wadsworth	0	K Peterson and B Burton (5 and 4)	1
	1		2
Singles			
H Dobson	0	V Goetze (4 and 3)	1
C Lambert	0	B Burton (4 and 3)	1
K Imrie	0	K Peterson (1 hole)	1
J Hall	0	K Noble (2 holes)	1
E Farquharson	0	R Weiss (2 and 1)	1
V Thomas	0	C Semple-Thompson (3 and 1)	1
	0		6

Aggregate: United States 14, Great Britain and Ireland 4

continued

Curtis Cup *continued*
At Royal Liverpool, Hoylake, on 5th and 6th June, 1992

Great Britain and Ireland		USA	
First Day – Foursomes			
J Hall and C Hall	$^1/_2$	A Fruhwirth and V Goetze	$^1/_2$
V Thomas and C Lambert (2 and 1)	1	L Shannon and S Lebrun Ingram	0
J Morley and C Hourihane (2 and 1)	1	T Hanson and C Semple Thompson	0
	$2^1/_2$		$^1/_2$
Singles			
J Morley	$^1/_2$	A Fruhwirth	$^1/_2$
J Hall	0	V Goetze (3 and 2)	1
E Farquharson (2 and 1)	1	R Weiss	0
N Buxton	0	M Lang (2 holes)	1
C Lambert (3 and 2)	1	C Semple Thompson	0
C Hall (6 and 5)	1	L Shannon	0
	$3^1/_2$		$2^1/_2$
Second Day – Foursomes			
J Hall and C Hall	$^1/_2$	A Fruhwirth and V Goetze	$^1/_2$
C Hourihane and J Morley	$^1/_2$	M Lang and R Weiss	$^1/_2$
C Lambert and V Thomas	0	T Hanson and C Semple Thompson (3 and 2)	1
	1		2
Singles			
J Morley (2 and 1)	1	A Fruhwirth	0
C Lambert (6 and 5)	1	T Hanson	0
E Farquharson	0	S Lebrun Ingram (2 and 1)	1
V Thomas	0	L Shannon (2 and 1)	1
C Hourihane	0	M Lang (2 and 1)	1
C Hall (1 hole)	1	V Goetze	0
	3		3

Result: Great Britain and Ireland 10, United States 8

At The Honors Course, Ooltewah, Chattanooga, Tennessee, on 30th–31st July 1994

Great Britain and Ireland		USA	
First Day – Singles			
J Hall	$^1/_2$	J McGill	$^1/_2$
J Moodie	0	E Klein (3 and 2)	1
L Walton (1 hole)	1	W Ward	0
M McKinlay	0	C Semple Thompson (2 and 1)	1
M McKay	0	E Port (2 and 1)	1
C Matthew (1 hole)	1	S Sparks	0
	$2^1/_2$		$3^1/_2$
Foursomes			
C Matthew and J Moodie	$^1/_2$	J McGill and S Lebrun Ingram	$^1/_2$
M McKay and K Speak	0	C Semple Thompson and E Klein (7 and 5)	1
J Hall and L Walton (6 and 5)	1	W Kaupp and E Port	0
	$1^1/_2$		$1^1/_2$
Second Day – Foursomes			
J Hall and L Walton (2 and 1)	1	J McGill and S Lebrun Ingram	0
M McKinlay and ER Power	0	C Semple Thompson and E Klein (4 and 2)	1
C Matthew and J Moodie (3 and 2)	1	W Ward and S Sparks	0
	2		1
Singles			
J Hall	0	J McGill (4 and 3)	1
C Matthew (2 and 1)	1	E Klein	0
M McKay	0	E Port (7 and 5)	1
M McKinlay (3 and 2)	1	W Kaupp	0
L Walton	0	W Ward (4 and 3)	1
J Moodie (2 holes)	1	C Semple Thompson	0
	3		3

Result: Great Britain and Ireland 9, United States 9

At Killarney, Ireland, on 21st–22nd June, 1996

Great Britain and Ireland		USA	

First Day – Foursomes

J Hall and L Educate	0	E Port and K Kuehne (2 and 1)	1
A Rose and L Dermott (3 and 1)	1	M Jemsek and B Corrie-Kuehn	0
J Moodie and M McKay	1/2	C Kerr and C Semple Thompson	1/2
	1 1/2		1 1/2

Singles

J Hall	0	S Lebrun Ingram (4 and 2)	1
K Stuples (3 and 2)	1	K Booth	0
A Rose (5 and 4)	1	B Corrie-Kuehn	0
E Ratcliff	1/2	M Jemsek	1/2
M McKay (1 hole)	1	C Kerr	0
J Moodie (3 and 1)	1	C Semple Thompson	0
	4 1/2		1 1/2

Second Day – Foursomes

J Moodie and M McKay (3 and 2)	1	K Booth and S Lebrun Ingram	0
A Rose and L Dermott (2 and 1)	1	M Jemsek and B Corrie-Kuehn	0
J Hall and L Educate	0	E Port and K Kuehne (1 hole)	1
	2		1

Singles

J Hall	0	C Kerr (1 hole)	1
E Ratcliffe (3 and 1)	1	S Lebrun Ingram	0
K Stuples	0	K Booth (3 and 2)	1
A Rose (6 and 5)	1	E Port	0
M McKay	1/2	C Semple Thompson	1/2
J Moodie (2 and 1)	1	K Kuehne	0
	3 1/2		2 1/2

Result: Great Britain and Ireland 11 1/2, United States of America 6 1/2

INDIVIDUAL RECORDS

Great Britain and Ireland

Bold print: captain; bold print in brackets: non-playing captain
Maiden name in parentheses, former surname in square brackets

Name		Year	Played	Won	Lost	Halved
Jean Anderson (Donald)	Scot	1948	6	3	3	0
Diane Bailey [Frearson] (Robb)	Eng	1962-72-(**84**)-(**86**)-(**88**)	5	2	2	1
Sally Barber (Bonallack)	Eng	1962	1	0	1	0
Pam Barton	Eng	1934-36	4	0	3	1
Linda Bayman	Eng	1988	4	2	1	1
Baba Beck (Pym)	Ire	(**1954**)	0	0	0	0
Charlotte Beddows [Watson] (Stevenson)	Scot	1932	1	0	1	0
Lilian Behan	Ire	1986	4	3	1	0
Veronica Beharrell (Anstey)	Eng	1956	1	0	1	0
Pam Benka (Tredinnick)	Eng	1966-68	4	0	3	1
Jeanne Bisgood	Eng	1950-52-54-(**70**)	4	1	3	0
Elizabeth Boatman (Collis)	Eng	(**1992**)-(**94**)	0	0	0	0
Zara Bolton (Davis)	Eng	1948-(**56**)-(**66**)-(**68**)	2	0	2	0
Angela Bonallack (Ward)	Eng	1956-58-60-62-64-66	15	6	8	1
Ita Butler (Burke)	Ire	1966-(**96**)	3	2	1	0
Nicola Buxton	Eng	1992	1	0	1	0
Lady Katherine Cairns	Eng	(**1952**)	0	0	0	0
Carole Caldwell (Redford)	Eng	1978-80	5	0	3	2
Doris Chambers	Eng	(**1934**)-(**36**)-(**48**)	0	0	0	0
Carol Comboy (Grott)	Eng	(**1978**)-(**80**)	0	0	0	0
Jane Connachan	Scot	1980-82	5	0	5	0
Elsie Corlett	Eng	1932-38-(**64**)	3	1	2	0
Diana Critchley (Fishwick)	Eng	1932-34-(**50**)	3	1	2	0

continued

Curtis Cup *continued*

Name		Year	Played	Won	Lost	Halved
Karen Davies	Wales	1986-88	7	4	1	2
Laura Davies	Eng	1984	2	1	1	0
Lisa Dermott	Wal	1996	2	2	0	0
Helen Dobson	Eng	1990	3	1	2	0
Kitrina Douglas	Eng	1982	4	0	3	1
Marjorie Draper [Peel] (Thomas)	Scot	1954	1	0	1	0
Lisa Educate (Walton)	Eng	1994-96	6	3	3	0
Mary Everard	Eng	1970-72-74-78	15	6	7	2
Elaine Farquharson	Scot	1990-92	6	1	5	0
Daisy Ferguson	Ire	(1958)	0	0	0	0
Marjory Ferguson (Fowler)	Scot	1966	1	0	1	0
Elizabeth Price Fisher (Price)	Eng	1950-52-54-56-58-60	12	7	4	1
Linzi Fletcher	Eng	1990	1	0	1	0
Maureen Garner (Madill)	Ire	1980	4	0	3	1
Marjorie Ross Garon	Eng	1936	2	1	0	1
Maureen Garrett (Ruttle)	Eng	1948-(60)	2	0	2	0
Philomena Garvey	Ire	1948-50-52-54-56-60	11	2	8	1
Carol Gibbs (Le Feuvre)	Eng	1974	3	0	3	0
Jacqueline Gordon	Eng	1948	2	1	1	0
Molly Gourlay	Eng	1932-34	4	0	2	2
Julia Greenhalgh	Eng	1964-70-74-76-78	17	6	7	4
Penny Grice-Whittaker (Grice)	Eng	1984	4	2	1	1
Caroline Hall	Eng	1992	4	2	0	2
Julie Hall (Wade)	Eng	1988-90-92-94-96	19	6	10	3
Marley Harris [Spearman] (Baker)	Eng	1960-62-64	6	2	2	2
Dorothea Hastings (Sommerville)	Scot	1958	0	0	0	0
Lady Heathcoat-Amory (Joyce Wethered)	Eng	**1932**	2	1	1	0
Dinah Henson (Oxley)	Eng	1968-70-72-76	11	3	6	2
Helen Holm (Gray)	Scot	1936-38-48	5	3	2	0
Claire Hourihane	Ire	1984-86-88-90-92	8	3	3	2
Ann Howard (Phillips)	Eng	1956-68	2	0	2	0
Beverley Huke	Eng	1972	2	0	2	0
Kathryn Imrie	Scot	1990	4	1	3	0
Ann Irvin	Eng	1962-68-70-76	12	4	7	1
Bridget Jackson	Eng	1958-64-68	8	1	6	1
Patricia Johnson	Eng	1986	4	4	0	0
Susan Langridge (Armitage)	Eng	1964-66	6	0	5	1
Joan Lawrence	Scot	1964	2	0	2	0
Shirley Lawson	Scot	1988	2	1	1	0
Wilma Leburn (Aitken)	Scot	1982	2	0	2	0
Jenny Lee Smith	Eng	1974-76	3	0	3	0
Kathryn Lumb (Phillips)	Eng	1970-72	2	1	1	0
Mhairi McKay	Scot	1994-96	7	2	3	2
Mary McKenna	Ire	1970-72-74-76-78-80-82-84-86	30	10	16	4
Myra McKinlay	Scot	1994	3	1	2	0
Suzanne McMahon (Cadden)	Scot	1976	4	0	4	0
Sheila Maher (Vaughan)	Eng	1962-64	4	1	2	1
Vanessa Marvin	Eng	1978	3	1	2	0
Catriona Matthew (Lambert)	Scot	1990-92-94	12	7	4	1
Moira Milton (Paterson)	Scot	1952	2	1	1	0
Janice Moodie	Scot	1994-96	8	5	1	2
Wanda Morgan	Eng	1932-34-36	6	0	5	1
Joanne Morley	Eng	1992	4	2	0	2
Beverley New	Eng	1984	4	1	3	0
Maire O'Donnell	Ire	(1982)	0	0	0	0
Margaret Pickard (Nichol)	Eng	1968-70	5	2	3	0
Diana Plumpton	Eng	1934	2	1	1	0
Elizabeth Pook (Chadwick)	Eng	1966	4	1	3	0
Doris Porter (Park)	Scot	1932	1	0	1	0
Eileen Rose Power (McDaid)	Ire	1994	1	0	1	0
Elaine Ratcliffe	Eng	1996	2	1	0	1
Clarrie Reddan (Tiernan)	Ire	1938-48	3	2	1	0
Joan Rennie (Hastings)	Scot	1966	2	0	1	1
Maureen Richmond (Walker)	Scot	1974	4	2	2	0
Jean Roberts	Eng	1962	1	0	1	0
Belle Robertson (McCorkindale)	Scot	1960-66-68-70-72-(74)-(76)-82-86	24	5	12	7
Claire Robinson (Nesbitt)	Ire	1980	3	0	1	2
Alison Rose	Scot	1996	4	4	0	0
Vivien Saunders	Eng	1968	4	1	2	1
Susan Shapcott	Eng	1988	4	3	1	0

Name		Year	Played	Won	Lost	Halved
Linda Simpson (Moore)	Eng	1980	3	1	1	1
Ruth Slark (Porter)	Eng	1960-62-64	7	3	3	1
Anne Smith [Stant] (Willard)	Eng	1976	1	0	1	0
Frances Smith (Stephens)	Eng	1950-52-54-56-58-60-(62)-(72)	11	7	3	1
Janet Soulsby	Eng	1982	4	1	2	1
Kirsty Speak	Eng	1994	1	0	1	0
Gillian Stewart	Scot	1980-82	4	1	3	0
Karen Stupples	Eng	1996	2	1	1	0
Tegwen Thomas (Perkins)	Wales	1974-76-78-80	14	4	8	2
Vicki Thomas (Rawlings)	Wales	1982-84-86-88-90-92	13	6	5	2
Muriel Thomson	Scot	1978	3	2	1	0
Jill Thornhill	Eng	1984-86-88	12	6	2	4
Angela Uzielli (Carrick)	Eng	1978	1	0	1	0
Jessie Valentine (Anderson)	Scot	1936-38-50-52-54-56-58	13	4	9	0
Helen Wadsworth	Wales	1990	2	0	2	0
Claire Waite	Eng	1984	4	2	2	0
Mickey Walker	Eng	1972	4	3	0	1
Pat Walker	Ire	1934-36-38	6	2	3	1
Verona Wallace-Williamson	Scot	(1938)	0	0	0	0
Nan Wardlaw (Baird)	Scot	1938	1	0	1	0
Enid Wilson	Eng	1932	2	1	1	0
Janette Wright (Robertson)	Scot	1954-56-58-60	8	3	5	0
Phyllis Wylie (Wade)	Eng	1938	1	0	0	1

United States of America

Name	Year	Played	Won	Lost	Halved
Roberta Albers	1968	2	1	0	1
Danielle Ammaccapane	1986	3	0	3	0
Kathy Baker	1982	4	3	0	1
Barbara Barrow	1976	2	1	0	1
Beth Barry	1972-74	5	3	1	1
Larua Baugh	1972	4	2	1	1
Judy Bell	1960-62-(86)-(88)	2	1	1	0
Peggy Kirk Bell (Kirk)	1950	2	1	1	0
Amy Benz	1982	3	2	1	0
Patty Berg	1936-38	4	1	2	1
Barbara Fay Boddie (White)	1964-66	8	7	0	1
Jane Booth (Bastanchury)	1970-72-74	12	9	3	0
Kellee Booth	1996	3	1	2	0
Mary Budke	1974	3	2	1	0
Brandie Burton	1990	3	3	0	0
JoAnne Carner (Gunderson)	1958-60-62-64	10	6	3	1
Lori Castillo	1980	3	2	1	0
Leona Cheney (Pressler)	1932-34-36	6	5	1	0
Sis Choate	(1974)	0	0	0	0
Peggy Conley	1964-68	6	3	1	2
Mary Ann Cook (Downey)	1956	2	1	1	0
Patricia Cornett	1978-88	4	1	2	1
Brenda Corrie-Kuehn	1996	3	0	3	0
Jean Crawford (Ashley)	1962-66-68-(72)	8	6	2	0
Clifford Ann Creed	1962	2	2	0	0
Grace Cronin (Lenczyk)	1948-50	3	2	1	0
Carolyn Cudone	1956-(70)	1	1	0	0
Beth Daniel	1976-78	8	7	1	0
Virginia Dennehy	(1958)	0	0	0	0
Mary Lou Dill	1968	3	1	1	1
Alice Dye	1970	2	1	0	1
Heather Farr	1984	3	2	1	0
Jane Fassinger	1970	1	0	1	0
Mary Lena Faulk	1954	2	1	1	0
Carol Sorensen Flenniken (Sorensen)	1964-66	8	6	1	1
Edith Flippin (Quier)	(1954)-(56)	0	0	0	0
Amy Fruhwirth	1992	4	0	1	3
Kim Gardner	1986	3	1	1	1
Charlotte Glutting	1934-36-38	5	3	1	1
Vicki Goetze	1990-92	8	4	2	2
Brenda Goldsmith	1978-80	4	2	2	0
Aniela Goldthwaite	1934-(52)	1	0	1	0
Joanne Goodwin	1960	2	1	1	0

continued

Curtis Cup *continued*

Name	Year	Played	Won	Lost	Halved
Mary Hafeman	1980	2	1	0	1
Shelley Hamkin	1968-70	8	3	3	2
Penny Hammel	1984	3	1	1	1
Nancy Hammer (Hager)	1970	2	1	1	0
Cathy Hanlon	1982	3	2	1	0
Beverley Hanson	1950	2	2	0	0
Tracy Hanson	1992	3	1	2	0
Patricia Harbottle (Lesser)	1954-56	3	2	1	0
Helen Hawes	(1964)	0	0	0	0
Kathryn Hemphill	1938	1	0	0	1
Helen Hicks	1932	2	1	1	0
Carolyn Hill	1978	2	0	0	2
Cindy Hill	1970-74-76-78	14	5	6	3
Opel Hill	1932-34-36	6	2	3	1
Marion Hollins	(1932)	0	0	0	0
Dana Howe	1984	3	1	1	1
Juli Inkster	1982	4	4	0	0
Maria Jemsek	1996	3	0	2	1
Ann Casey Johnstone	1958-60-62	4	3	1	0
Mae Murray Jones (Murray)	1952	1	0	1	0
Wendy Kaupp	1994	2	0	2	0
Caroline Keggi	1988	3	0	2	1
Tracy Kerdyk	1988	4	2	1	1
Cristie Kerr	1996	3	1	1	1
Kandi Kessler	1986	3	1	1	1
Dorothy Kielty	1948-50	4	4	0	0
Dorothy Kirby	1948-50-52-54	7	4	3	0
Martha Kirouac (Wilkinson)	1970-72	8	5	3	0
Emilee Klein	1994	4	3	1	0
Nancy Knight (Lopez)	1976	2	2	0	0
Kelli Kuehne	1996	3	2	1	0
Martha Lang	1992-(96)	3	2	0	1
Bonnie Lauer	1974	4	2	2	0
Sarah Le Brun Ingram	1992-94-96	7	2	4	1
Marjorie Lindsay	1952	2	1	1	0
Patricia Lucey (O'Sullivan)	1952	1	0	1	0
Mari McDougall	1982	2	2	0	0
Jill McGill	1994	4	1	1	2
Barbara McIntire	1958-60-62-64-66-72-(76)	16	6	6	4
Lucile Mann (Robinson)	1934	1	0	1	0
Debbie Massey	1974-76	5	5	0	0
Marion Miley	1938	2	1	0	1
Dottie Mochrie (Pepper)	1986	3	0	2	1
Evelyn Monsted	(1968)	0	0	0	0
Terri Moody	1980	2	1	0	1
Karen Noble	1990	4	2	2	0
Judith Oliver	1978-80-82-(92)	8	5	1	2
Maureen Orcutt	1932-34-36-38	8	5	3	0
Joanne Pacillo	1984	3	1	1	1
Estelle Page (Lawson)	1938-48	4	3	1	0
Katie Peterson	1990	3	3	0	0
Margaret Platt	1990	2	0	2	0
Frances Pond (Stebbins)	(1938)	0	0	0	0
Ellen Port	1994-96	6	4	2	0
Dorothy Germain Porter	1950-(66)	2	1	0	1
Phyllis Preuss	1962-64-66-68-70-(84)	15	10	4	1
Betty Probasco	(1982)	0	0	0	0
Mildred Prunaret	(1960)	0	0	0	0
Polly Riley	1948-50-52-54-56-58-(62)	10	5	5	0
Barbara Romack	1954-56-58	5	3	2	0
Jody Rosenthal	1984	3	2	0	1
Anne Sander [Welts] [Decker] (Quast)	1958-60-62-66-68-74-84-90	22	11	7	4
Cindy Scholefield	1988	3	0	3	0
Cindy Schreyer	1986	3	1	2	0
Kathleen McCarthy Scrivner (McCarthy)	1986-88	6	2	3	1
Carol Semple Thompson	1974-76-80-82-90-92-94-96	27	13	10	4
Leslie Shannon	1986-88-90-92	9	1	6	2
Patty Sheehan	1980	4	4	0	0
Pearl Sinn	1988	2	1	1	0
Grace De Moss Smith (De Moss)	1952-54	3	1	2	0
Lancy Smith	1972-78-80-82-84-(94)	16	7	5	4

Name	Year	Played	Won	Lost	Halved
Margaret Smith	1956	2	2	0	0
Stephanie Sparks	1994	2	0	2	0
Hollis Stacy	1972	2	0	1	1
Claire Stancik (Doran)	1952-54	4	4	0	0
Judy Street (Eller)	1960	2	2	0	0
Louise Suggs	1948	2	0	1	1
Nancy Roth Syms (Roth)	1964-66-76-(80)	9	3	5	1
Noreen Uihlein	1978	3	1	1	1
Virginia Van Wie	1932-34	4	3	0	1
Glenna Collett Vare (Collett)	1932-(34)-36-38-48-(50)	7	4	2	1
Wendy Ward	1994	3	1	2	0
Jane Weiss (Nelson)	1956	1	0	1	0
Robin Weiss	1990-92	5	3	1	1
Donna White (Horton)	1976	2	2	0	0
Mary Anne Widman	1984	3	2	1	0
Kimberley Williams	1986	3	0	3	0
Helen Sigel Wilson (Sigel)	1950-66-(78)	2	0	2	0
Joyce Ziske	1954	1	0	1	0

Commonwealth Tournament (Ladies')

Year	Winner	Venue
1959	Great Britain	St Andrews
1963	Great Britain	Royal Melbourne, Australia
1967	Great Britain	Ancaster, Ontario, Canada
1971	Great Britain	Hamilton, New Zealand
1975	Great Britain	Ganton, England
1979	Canada	Lake Karrinup, Perth, Australia
1983	Australia	Glendale, Edmonton, Canada
1987	Canada	Christchurch, New Zealand
1991	Great Britain	Northumberland, England
1995	Australia	Royal Sydney, Australia

European Ladies' Amateur Team Championship

Year	Winner	Second	Venue
1967	England	France	Penina, Portugal
1969	France	England	Tylosand, Sweden
1971	England	France	Ganton, England
1973	England	France	Brussels, Belgium
1975	France	Spain	Paris, France
1977	England	Spain	Sotogrande, Spain
1979	Ireland	Germany	Hermitage, Ireland
1981	Sweden	France	Troia, Portugal
1983	Ireland	England	Waterloo, Belgium
1985	England	Italy	Stavanger, Norway
1987	Sweden	Wales	Turnberry, Scotland
1989	France	England	Pals, Spain
1991	England	Sweden	Wentworth, England
1993	England	Spain	Royal Haagshe
1995	Spain	Scotland	Milan, Italy
1997	Sweden	Scotland	Nordcenter, Finland

Vagliano Trophy – Great Britain & Ireland *v* Europe

Played for biennially between teams of women amateur golfers representing the British Isles and Europe. (From 1947 to 1957 was between the British Isles and France.)

Year	Winner	Result	Venue
1959	Great Britain & Ireland	12–3	Wentworth
1961	Great Britain & Ireland	8–7	Villa d'Este
1963	Great Britain & Ireland	20–10	Muirfield
1965	Continent of Europe	17–13	Cologne
1967	Continent of Europe	15$\frac{1}{2}$–14$\frac{1}{2}$	R Lytham and St Annes

continued

Vagliano Trophy *continued*

Year	Winner	Result	Venue
1969	Continent of Europe	16–14	Chantilly
1971	Great Britain & Ireland	17½–12½	Worplesdon
1973	Great Britain & Ireland	20–10	Eindhoven
1975	Great Britain & Ireland	13½–10½	Muirfield
1977	Great Britain & Ireland	15½–8½	Malmo
1979	Halved	12–12	R Porthcawl
1981	Continent of Europe	14–10	P de Hierro
1983	Great Britain & Ireland	14–10	Woodhall Spa
1985	Great Britain & Ireland	14–10	Hamburg
1987	Great Britain & Ireland	15–9	The Berkshire
1989	Great Britain & Ireland	14½–9½	Venice
1991	Great Britain & Ireland	13½–10½	Nairn
1993	Great Britain & Ireland	13½–10½	Morfontaine
1995	Continent of Europe	14–10	Ganton
1997	Continent of Europe	14–10	Halmstad

Women's World Amateur Team Championship (Espirito Santo Trophy)

Year	Winners	Runners-up	Venue	Score
1964	France	United States	St Germain	588
1966	United States	Canada	Mexico	580
1968	United States	Australia	Melbourne	616
1970	United States	France	Madrid	598
1972	United States	France	Buenos Aires	583
1974	United States	GB & I, South Africa	Dominican Republic	620
1976	United States	France	Vilamoura, Portugal	605
1978	Australia	Canada	Fiji	596
1980	United States	Australia	Pinehurst, USA	588
1982	United States	New Zealand	Geneva, Switzerland	579
1984	United States	France	Hong Kong	585
1986	Spain	France	Caracas, Venezuela	580
1988	United States	Sweden	Drottningholm, Sweden	587
1990	United States	New Zealand	Christchurch, New Zealand	585
1992	Spain	GB & I	Vancouver, Canada	588
1994	United States	Korea	Paris, France	569
1996	Korea	Italy	Manila, Philippines	438

Women's Home Internationals

Year	Winner	Venue	Year	Winner	Venue
1948	England	R Lytham and St Annes	1971	England	Longniddry
1949	Scotland	Harlech	1972	England	R Lytham and St Annes
1950	Scotland	Newcastle Co Down	1973	England	Harlech
1951	Scotland	Broadstone	1974T	England/Scotland/ Ireland	Sandwich, Princes
1952	Scotland	Troon			
1953	England	Porthcawl	1975	England	Newport
1954	England/Scotland	GantonScotland	1976	England	Troon
1955T	England	Western Gailes	1977	England	Cork
1956	Scotland	Sunningdale	1978	England	Moortown
1957	Scotland	Troon	1979T	Scotland/Ireland	Harlech
1958	England	Hunstanton	1980	Ireland	Cruden Bay
1959	England	Hoylake	1981	Scotland	Portmarnock
1960	England	Gullane	1982	England	Burnham and Barrow
1961	Scotland	Portmarnock	1983	*Matches abandoned due to weather*	
1962	Scotland	Porthcawl	1984	England	Gullane
1963	England	Formby	1985	England	Waterville
1964	England	Troon	1986	Ireland	Whittington Barracks
1965	England	Portrush	1987	England	Ashburnham
1966	England	Woodhall Spa	1988	Scotland	Barassie
1967	England	Sunningdale	1989	England	Westport
1968	England	Porthcawl	1990	Scotland	Hunstanton
1969T	England/Scotland	Western Gailes	1991	Scotland	Aberdovey
1970	England	Killarney			

1992 *at Hamilton, Lanarkshire*

Ireland beat Wales $5^1/_2$ matches to $2^1/_2$
England halved with Scotland 4 matches each
Scotland beat Wales   6 matches to 3
England beat Ireland   8 matches to 1
Scotland beat Ireland   6 matches to 3
England beat Wales $7^1/_2$ matches to $1^1/_2$

Result: England $2^1/_2$; Scotland $2^1/_2$; Ireland 1; Wales 0

1993 *at Hermitage, Dublin*

England beat Wales   7 matches to 2
Scotland beat Ireland   5 matches to 4
England beat Ireland $5^1/_2$ matches to $3^1/_2$
Scotland beat Wales   7 matches to 2
England beat Scotland $5^1/_2$ matches to $3^1/_2$
Ireland beat Wales   7 matches to 2

Result: England 3; Scotland 2; Ireland 1; Wales 0

1994 *at Huddersfield, Yorkshire*

England beat Ireland $6^1/_2$ matches to $2^1/_2$
Scotland beat Wales $8^1/_2$ matches to $^1/_2$
England beat Wales   8 matches to 1
Scotland halved with Ireland $4^1/_2$ matches to $4^1/_2$
England beat Scotland   6 matches to 3
Ireland beat Wales $5^1/_2$ matches to $3^1/_2$

Result: England 3; Scotland $1^1/_2$; Ireland $1^1/_2$; Wales 0

1995 *at Wrexham, Clwyd*

England beat Scotland   6 matches to 3
Ireland halved with Wales $4^1/_2$ matches to $4^1/_2$
Ireland beat Scotland   5 matches to 4
Wales beat England   5 matches to 4
England beat Ireland   9 matches to 0
Scotland beat Wales   5 matches to 4

Result: England 2; Wales $1^1/_2$; Ireland $1^1/_2$; Scotland 1

1996 *at Longniddry*

Scotland beat Ireland $5^1/_2$ matches to $3^1/_2$
England beat Wales   6 matches to 3
Scotland beat Wales   5 matches to 4
England beat Ireland   6 matches to 3
England beat Scotland   5 matches to 4
Ireland beat Wales $5^1/_2$ matches to $3^1/_2$

Result: England 3; Scotland 2; Ireland 1; Wales 0

1997 *at Lahinch, Ireland*

Ireland beat Wales $6^1/_2$ matches to $2^1/_2$
England beat Scotland $6^1/_2$ matches to $2^1/_2$
England beat Ireland   6 matches to 3
Scotland beat Wales $5^1/_2$ matches to $3^1/_2$
England beat Wales   5 matches to 4
Ireland beat Scotland   7 matches to 2

Result: England 3; Ireland 2; Scotland 1; Wales 0

Juniors and Youths

Boys' Amateur Championship

Year	Winner	Runner-up	Venue	By	
1921	ADD Mathieson	GH Lintott	Ascot	37th hole	
1922	HS Mitchell	W Greenfield	Ascot	4 and 2	
1923	ADD Mathieson	HS Mitchell	Dunbar	3 and 2	
1924	RW Peattie	P Manuevrier	Coombe Hill	2 holes	
1925	RW Peattie	A McNair	Barnton	4 and 3	
1926	EA McRuvie	CW Timmis	Coombe Hill	1 hole	
1927	EW Fiddian	K Forbes	Barnton	4 and 2	
1928	S Scheftel	A Dobbie	Formby	6 and 5	
1929	J Lindsay	J Scott-Riddell	Barnton	6 and 4	
1930	J Lindsay	J Todd	Fulwell	9 and 8	
1931	H Thomson	F McGloin	Killermont	5 and 4	
1932	IS MacDonald	LA Hardie	R Lytham and St Annes	2 and 1	
1933	PB Lucas	W McLachlan	Carnoustie	3 and 2	
1934	RS Burles	FB Allpass	Moortown	12 and 10	
1935	JDA Langley	R Norris	Balgownie, Aberdeen	6 and 5	
1936	J Bruen	W Innes	Birkdale	11 and 9	
1937	IM Roberts	J Stewart	Bruntsfield	8 and 7	
1938	W Smeaton	T Snowball	Moor Park	3 and 2	
1939	SB Williamson	KG Thom	Carnoustie	4 and 2	
1940-45	*Suspended during War*				
1946	AFD MacGregor	DF Dunstan	Bruntsfield	7 and 5	
1947	J Armour	I Caldwell	Hoylake	5 and 4	
1948	JD Pritchett	DH Reid	Barasssie	37th hole	
1949	H MacAnespie	NV Drew	St Andrews	3 and 2	
1950	J Glover	I Young	R Lytham and St Annes	2 and 1	
1951	N Dunn	MSR Lunt	Prestwick	6 and 5	
1952	M Bonallack	AE Shepperson	Formby	37th hole	
1953	AE Shepperson	AT Booth	Dunbar	6 and 4	
1954	AF Bussell	K Warren	Hoylake	38th hole	
1955	SC Wilson	BJK Aitken	Barassie	39th hole	
1956	JF Ferguson	CW Cole	Sunningdale	2 and 1	
1957	D Ball	J Wilson	Carnoustie	2 and 1	
1958	R Braddon	IM Stungo	Moortown	4 and 3	
1959	AR Murphy	EM Shamash	Pollok	3 and 1	
1960	P Cros	PO Green	Olton	5 and 3	
1961	FS Morris	C Clark	Dalmahoy	3 and 2	
1962	PM Townsend	DC Penman	R Mid-Surrey	1 hole	
1963	AHC Soutar	DI Rigby	Prestwick	2 and 1	
1964	PM Townsend	RD Gray	Formby	9 and 8	
1965	GR Milne	DK Midgley	Gullane	4 and 2	
1966	A Phillips	A Muller	Moortown	12 and 11	
1967	LP Tupling	SC Evans	Western Gailes	4 and 2	
1968	SC Evans	K Dabson	St Annes Old Links	3 and 2	
1969	M Foster	M Gray	Dunbar	37th hole	
1970	ID Gradwell	JE Murray	Hillside	1 hole	
1971	H Clark	G Harvey	Barassie	6 and 5	
1972	G Harvey	R Newsome	Moortown	7 and 5	
1973	DM Robertson	S Betti	Blairgowrie	5 and 3	
1974	TR Shannon	A Lyle	Hoylake	10 and 9	
1975	B Marchbank	A Lyle	Bruntsfield	1 hole	
1976	M Mouland	G Hargreaves	Sunningdale	6 and 5	
1977	I Ford	CR Dalgleish	Downfield	1 hole	
1978	S Keppler	M Stokes	Seaton Carew	3 and 2	
1979	R Rafferty	D Ray	Barassie	6 and 5	
1980	D Muscroft	A Llyr	Formby	7 and 6	*continued*

Boys' Amateur Championship *continued*

Year	Winner	Runner-up	Venue	By
1981	J Lopez	R Weedon	Gullane	4 and 3
1982	M Grieve	G Hickman	Burnham and Barrow	37th hole
1983	JM Olazabal	M Pendaries	Glenbervie	6 and 5
1984	L Vannett	A Mednick	Royal Porthcawl	2 and 1
1985	J Cook	W Henry	Barnton	5 and 4
1986	L Walker	G King	Seaton Carew	5 and 4
1987	C O'Carrol	P Olsson	Barassie	3 and 1
1988	S Pardoe	D Haines	Formby	3 and 2
1989	C Watts	C Fraser	Nairn	5 and 3
1990	M Welch	M Ellis	Hunstanton	3 and 1
1991	F Valera	R Walton	Montrose	4 and 3
1992	L Westerberg	T Biermann	R Mid-Surrey	3 and 2
1993	D Howell	V Gustavsson	Glenbervie	3 and 1
1994	C Smith	C Rodgers	Little Aston	2 and 1
1995	S Young	S Walker	Dunbar	7 and 6
1996	K Ferrie	M Pilkington	Littlestone	2 and 1
1997	S Garcia	R Jones	Saunton	6 and 5

Boys' Internationals

England v Scotland

Year	Winner	Result	Venue	Year	Winner	Result	Venue
1946	England	$8^1/_2$–$3^1/_2$	Bruntsfield	1972	England	$13^1/_2$–$1^1/_2$	Moortown
1947	England	7–5	Hoylake	1973	England	9–6	Blairgowrie
1948	England	9–3	Barassie	1974	England	11–4	Liverpool
1949	Scotland	8–4	St Andrews	1975	England	$9^1/_2$–$5^1/_2$	Bruntsfield
1950	Scotland	$8^1/_2$–$3^1/_2$	R Lytham and St Annes	1976	Scotland	8–7	Sunningdale
1951	England	7–5	Prestwick	1977	England	8–7	Downfield
1952	England	$6^1/_2$–$5^1/_2$	Formby	1978	Scotland	$8^1/_2$–$6^1/_2$	Seaton Carew
1953	Scotland	7–5	Dunbar	1979	England	11–4	Barassie
1954	England	$6^1/_2$–$5^1/_2$	Hoylake	1980	England	9–6	Formby
1955	Scotland	9–3	Barassie	1981	Halved	$7^1/_2$–$7^1/_2$	Gullane
1956	England	$7^1/_2$–$4^1/_2$	Sunningdale	1982	England	8–7	Burnham & Berrow
1957	Scotland	$7^1/_2$–$4^1/_2$	Carnoustie	1983	England	8–7	Glenbervie
1958	England	7–5	Moortown	1984	England	$9^1/_2$–$5^1/_2$	Porthcawl
1959	England	$8^1/_2$–$3^1/_2$	Pollok	1985	England	10–5	Barnton
1960	England	10–2	Olton	1986	Scotland	$8^1/_2$–$6^1/_2$	Seaton Carew
1961	Scotland	7–5	Dalmahoy	1987	Scotland	8–7	Barassie
1962	England	$6^1/_2$–$5^1/_2$	R Mid-Surrey	1988	England	11–4	Formby
1963	Scotland	9–3	Prestwick	1989	England	8–7	Nairn
1964	England	9–3	Formby	1990	Scotland	$10^1/_2$–$4^1/_2$	Hunstanton
1965	England	10–5	Gullane	1991	England	10–5	Montrose
1966	England	12–3	Moortown	1992	Scotland	10–5	R Mid-Surrey
1967	Scotland	8–7	Western Gailes	1993	England	8–7	Glenbervie
1968	England	10–5	St Annes Old Links	1994	England	10–5	Little Aston
1969	England	12–3	Dunbar	1995	Scotland	8–7	Dunbar
1970	England	12–3	Hillside	1996	England	8–7	Littlestone
1971	Halved	$7^1/_2$–$7^1/_2$	Barassie	1997	Scotland	8–7	R North Devon

Wales v Ireland

Year	Winner	Result	Venue	Year	Winner	Result	Venue
1972	Ireland	5–4	Moortown	1985	Ireland	$11^1/_2$–$3^1/_2$	Barnton
1973	Ireland	$5^1/_2$–$3^1/_2$	Blairgowrie	1986	Ireland	$8^1/_2$–$6^1/_2$	Seaton Carew
1974	Wales	5–4	Hoylake	1987	Wales	$10^1/_2$–$4^1/_2$	Barassie
1975	Wales	$6^1/_2$–$2^1/_2$	Bruntsfield	1988	Wales	8–7	Formby
1976	Wales	$71/2$–$1^1/_2$	Sunningdale	1989	Wales	$10^1/_2$–$4^1/_2$	Nairn
1977	Ireland	$61/2$–$51/2$	Downfield	1990	Ireland	$8^1/_2$–$6^1/_2$	Hunstanton
1978	Wales	8–4	Seaton Carew	1991	Wales	10–5	Montrose
1979	Ireland	$9^1/_2$–$2^1/_2$	Barassie	1992	Wales	9–6	R Mid-Surrey
1980	Wales	$6^1/_2$–$5^1/_2$	Formby	1993	Ireland	11–4	Glenbervie
1981	Ireland	8–4	Gullane	1994	Ireland	$8^1/_2$–$6^1/_2$	Little Aston
1982	Wales	9–3	Burnham & Berrow	1995	Wales	8–2	Dunbar
1983	Ireland	7–5	Glenbervie	1996	Ireland	$9^1/_2$–$5^1/_2$	Littlestone
1984	Wales	$6^1/_2$–$5^1/_2$	Porthcawl	1997	Ireland	10–5	R North Devon

R & A Trophy

This trophy is played between England, Scotland, Wales and Ireland and was introduced in 1985.

Year	Winner	Venue
1985 T	England/Ireland	Barnton
1986	Ireland	Seaton Carew
1987	Scotland	Barassie
1988	England	Formby
1989	England	Nairn
1990	Scotland	Hunstanton
1991	England	Montrose
1992 T	Wales/Scotland	R Mid-Surrey
1993	England	Glenbervie
1994	England	Little Aston
1995	Scotland	Dunbar
1996	England	Littlestone
1997	Ireland	R North DEvon

British Youths' Open Amateur Championship

Year	Winner	Club/Country	Venue	Score
1954	JS More	Swanston, Edinburgh	Erskine	287
1955	B Stockdale	Royal Lytham St Annes	Pannal	297
1956	AF Bussell	Coxmoor	Barnton	287
1957	G Will	St Andrews	Pannal	290
1958	RH Kemp	Glamorganshire	Dumfries and County	281
1959	RA Jowle	Moseley	Pannal	286
1960	GA Caygill	Sunningdale	Pannal	279
1961	JS Martin	Kilbirnie Place	Bruntsfield	284
1962	GA Caygill	Sunningdale	Pannal	287
1963	AJ Low	St Andrews University	Pollok	283
1964	BW Barnes	Burnham and Berrow	Pannal	290
1965	PM Townsend	Porters Park	Cosforth Park	281
1966	PA Oosterhuis	Dulwich and Sydenham	Dalmahoy	219 *(54 holes)*
1967	PJ Benka	Addington	Copt Heath	278
1968	PJ Benka	Addington	Ayr Belleisle	281
1969	JH Cook	Calcot Park	Lindrick	289
1970	B Dassu	Italy	Barnton	276
1971	P Elson	Coventry	Northamptonshire	277
1972	AH Chandler	Regent Park	Glasgow Gailes	281
1973	SC Mason	Goring and Streatley	Southport and Ainsdale	284
1974	DM Robertson	Dunbar	Downfield	284
1975	N Faldo	Welwyn Garden City	Pannal	278
1976	ME Lewis	Henbury	Gullane	277
1977	A Lyle	Hawkstone Park	Moor Park	285
1978	B Marchbank	Auchterarder	East Renfrewshire	278
1979	G Brand Jr	Knowle	Woodhall Spa	291
1980	G Hay	Hilton Park	Troon	303
1981	T Antevik	Sweden	West Lancashire	290
1982	AP Parkin	Newtown	St Andrews New	280
1983	P Mayo	Newport	Sunningdale	290
1984	R Morris	Padeswick and Buckley	Blairgowrie	281
1985	JM Olazabal	Spain	Ganton	281
1986	D Gilford	GB	Carnoustie	283
1987 T	J Cook*	GB	Hollinwell	283
	O Nordberg	Sweden		
1988 T	C Cassells	Murcar	Royal Aberdeen	275
	C Cevaer*	France		
1989 T	M Smith*	Brokenhurst Manor	Ashburnham	285
	A Coltart	Thornhill		
1990	M Gronberg	Sweden	Southerness	275
1991	J Payne	Sandilands	Woodhall Spa	287
1992	W Bennett	Ruislip	Northumberland	282
1993	L Westwood	Worksop	Glasgow Gailes	278
1994	F Jacobson	Sweden	Royal St David's	277
1995	*Not played*			
1996	*Not played*			
1997	*Not played*			

★ *Winner after play-off*

Youths' Internationals England v Scotland

Year	Winner	Result	Venue	Year	Winner	Result	Venue
1955	England	13–5	Pannal	1977	Scotland	9½–5½	Moor Park
1956	Scotland	+17 holes	Burgess	1978	Scotland	8½–6½	East Renfrewshire
1957	Not played			1979	Halved	7½–7½	Woodhall Spa
1958	England	+4 holes	Dumfries & County	1980	Scotland	9–6	Troon
1959	Scotland	12–6	Pannal	1981	Scotland	8–7	West Lancs
1960	Scotland	11½–6½	Pannal	1982	Halved	7½–7½	St Andrews New
1961	England	11½–6½	Bruntsfield	1983	Scotland	8½–6½	Sunningdale
1962	England	9½–8½	Pannal	1984	Scotland	9–6	Blairgowrie
1963	Scotland	9–6	Pollok	1985	Halved	7½–7½	Ganton
1964	Scotland	9–6	Pannal	1986	Scotland	8–7	Carnoustie
1965	Scotland	10½–3½	Northumberland	1987	England	9½–5½	Hollinwell
1966	England	9½–5½	Dalmahoy	1988	England	10–5	R. Aberdeen
1967	Halved	7½–7½	Copt Heath	1989	England	9–6	Ashburnham
1968	Scotland	8½–6½	Ayr Belleisle	1990	England	9–6	Southerness
1969	England	8½–6½	Lindrick	1991T	England	7½–7½	Woodhall Spa
1970	Scotland	8½–6½	Barnton		Scotland		
1971	England	11–4	Northampton County	1992	Scotland	10–5	Northumberland
1972	England	11–4	Glasgow Gailes	1993	England	8–7	Glasgow Gailes
1973	England	10–5	Southport & Ainsdale	1994	Scotland	9½–5½	Royal St David's
1974	England	9–6	Downfield	1995	Not played		
1975	Scotland	11–4	Pannal	1996	Not played		
1976	England	8½–6½	Gullane	1997	Not played		

Great Britain & Ireland v Continent of Europe, Youths (EGA Trophy)

Year	Winner	Result	Venue	Year	Winner	Result	Venue
1967	GB&I	8–7	Copt Heath	1983	GB&I	11–13	Punta Ala, Italy
1968	GB&I	11–4	Ayr Belleisle	1984	Halved	6–6	Blairgowrie
1969	GB&I	13½–1½	Lindrick	1985	GB&I	8–4	Ganton
1970	GB&I	10½–4½	Barnton	1986	GB&I	13½–10½	Bilbao, Spain
1971	GB&I	10–5	Northampton County	1987	Europe	7–5	Hollinwell
1972	GB&I	11½–3½	Glasgow Gailes	1988	GB&I	13½–10½	Copenhagen
1973	GB&I	10–5	Southport & Ainsdale	1989	GB&I	8½–3½	Ashburnham
1974	GB&I	10–5	Downfield	1990	GB&I	14½–9½	Oporto, Portugal
1975	GB&I	9–6	Pannal	1991	GB&I	14½–9½	Dalmahoy
1976	GB&I	17–13	Chantilly	1992	Europe	14–10	Bremen, Germany
1977	GB&I	11½–3½	Moor Park	1993	GB&I	16–8	Royal Troon
1978	GB&I	12½–2½	East Renfrewshire	1994	GB&I	18–6	Golf de Pan, Holland
1979	GB&I	12–3	Woodhall Spa	1995	Not played		
1980	Europe	13–11	Lunds Akademiska	1996	Not played		
1981*	GB&I	7½–4½	West Lancs	1997	Not played		
1982	GB&I	7½–4½	St Andrews New				

English Boys' Amateur Open Stroke Play Championship (Formerly Carris Trophy)

Year	Winner	Score	Year	Winner	Score	Year	Winner	Score
1935	R Upex	75	1960	PM Baxter	150	1979	P Hammond	288
1936	JDA Langley	152	1961	DJ Miller	143	1980	MP McLean	290
1937	RJ White	149	1962	FS Morris	145	1981	D Gilford	290
1938	IP Garrow	147	1963	EJ Threlfall	147	1982	M Jarvis	298
1939	CW Warren	149	1964	PM Townsend	148	1983	P Baker	288
1946	AH Perowne	158	1965	G McKay	145	1984	J Coe	283
1947	I Caldwell	159	1966	A Black	151	1985	P Baker	286
1948	I Caldwell	152	1967	RF Brown	147	1986	G Evans	292
1949	PB Hine	148	1968	P Dawson	149	1987	D Bathgate	289
1950	J Glover	144	1969	ID Gradwell	150	1988	P Page	284
1951	I Young	154	1970	MF Foster	146	1989	I Garbutt	285
1952	N Thygesen	150	1971	RJ Evans	146	1990	M Welch	276
1953	N Johnson	148	1972	L Donovan	143	1991	I Pyman	284
1954	K Warren	149	1973	S Hadfield	148	1992	M Foster	286
1955	ID Wheater	151	1974	KJ Brown	304	1993	J Harris	285
1956	G Maisey	141	1975	A Lyle	270	1994	R Duck	280
1957	G Maisey	145	1976	H Stott	285	1995	J Rose	266
1958	J Hamilton	149	1977	R Mugglestone	293	1996	G Storm	281
1959	RT Walker	152	1978	J Plaxton	144	1997	D Griffiths	283

* Singles curtailed owing to weather

Peter McEvoy Trophy *at Copt Heath*

Year	Winner	Year	Winner
1988	P Sefton	1993	S Webster
1989	D Bathgate	1994	J Harris
1990	P Sherman	1995	C Duke
1991	L Westwood	1996	M Pilkington
1992	B Davis	1997	P Rowe

Scottish Boys' Championship

Year	Winner	Runner–up	Venue	By
1960	L Carver	S Wilson	North Berwick	6 and 5
1961	K Thomson	G Wilson	North Berwick	10 and 8
1962	HF Urquhart	S MacDonald	North Berwick	3 and 2
1963	FS Morris	I Clark	North Berwick	9 and 8
1964	WR Lockie	MD Cleghorn	North Berwick	1 hole
1965	RL Penman	J Wood	North Berwick	9 and 8
1966	J McTear	DG Greig	North Berwick	4 and 3
1967	DG Greig	I Cannon	North Berwick	2 and 1
1968	RD Weir	M Grubb	North Berwick	6 and 4
1969	RP Fyfe	IP Doig	North Berwick	4 and 2
1970	S Stephen	M Henry	North Berwick	38th hole
1971	JE Murray	AA Mackay	North Berwick	4 and 3
1972	DM Robertson	G Cairns	North Berwick	9 and 8
1973	R Watson	H Alexander	North Berwick	8 and 7
1974	DM Robertson	J Cuddihy	North Berwick	6 and 5
1975	A Brown	J Cuddihy	North Berwick	6 and 4
1976	B Marchbank	J Cuddihy	Dunbar	2 and 1
1977	JS Taylor	GJ Webster	Dunbar	3 and 2
1978	J Huggan	KW Stables	Dunbar	2 and 1
1979	DR Weir	S Morrison	West Kilbride	5 and 3
1980	R Gregan	AJ Currie	Dunbar	2 and 1
1981	C Stewart	G Mellon	Dunbar	3 and 2
1982	A Smith	J White	Dunbar	39th hole
1983	C Gillies	C Innes	Dunbar	38th hole
1984	K Buchan	L Vannet	Dunbar	2 and 1
1985	AD McQueen	FJ McCulloch	Dunbar	1 hole
1986	AG Tait	EA McIntosh	Dunbar	6 and 5
1987	AJ Coltart	SJ Bannerman	Dunbar	37th hole
1988	CA Fraser	F Clark	Dunbar	9 and 8
1989	M King	D Brolls	Dunbar	8 and 7
1990	B Collier	D Keeney	West Kilbride	2 and 1
1991	C Hislop	R Thorton	West Kilbride	11 and 9
1992	A Reid	A Forsyth	West Kilbride	2 and 1
1993	S Young	A Campbell	West Kilbride	4 and 2
1994	S Young	E Little	Dunbar	2 and 1
1995	S Young	M Donaldson	R Aberdeen	7 and 6
1996	S Whiteford	I McLaughlin	West Kilbride	3 and 2
1997	M Donaldson	L Rhind	Dunbar	1 hole

Scottish Boys' Open Stroke Play Championship

Year	Winner	Venue	Score
1970	D Chillas	Carnoustie	298
1971	JE Murray	Lanark	274
1972	S Martin	Montrose	280
1973	S Martin	Barnton	284
1974	PW Gallacher	Lundin Links	290
1975	A Webster	Kilmarnock Barassie	286
1976	A Webster	Forfar	292
1977T	J Huggan/L Mann	Renfrew	303
1978	R Fraser	Arbroath	283
1979	L Mann	Stirling	289
1980	ASK Glen	Forfar	288
1981	J Gullen	Bellshill	296
1982	D Purdie	Monifieth	296
1983	L Vannet	Barassie	286
1984	K Walker	Carnoustie	280

Year	Winner	Venue	Score
1985	G Matthew	Baberton	297
1986	G Cassells	Edzell	294
1987	C Ronald	Lanark	287
1988	M Urquhart	Dumfries and County	280
1989	C Fraser	Stirling	282
1990	N Archibald	Monifieth	292
1991	S Gallacher	Crieff	280
1992	S Gallacher	Monifieth	288
1993	J Bunch	Powfoot	292
1994	S Young	Drumpellier	288
1995	C Lee	Arbroath	284
1996	M Brown	Dullatur	286
1997	L Rhind	Downfield	287

Welsh Boys' Championship

Year	Winner	Runner–up	Venue	By
1960	C Gilford	JL Toye	Llandrindod Wells	5 and 4
1961	AR Porter	JL Toye	Llandrindod Wells	3 and 2
1962	RC Waddilove	W Wadrup	Harlech	20th hole
1963	G Matthews	R Witchell	Penarth	6 and 5
1964	D Lloyd	M Walters	Conway	2 and 1
1965	G Matthews	DG Lloyd	Wenvoe Castle	7 and 6
1966	J Buckley	DP Owen	Holyhead	4 and 2
1967	J Buckley	DL Stevens	Glamorganshire	2 and 1
1968	J Buckley	C Brown	Maesdu	1 hole
1969	K Dabson	P Light	Glamorganshire	5 and 3
1970	P Tadman	A Morgan	Conway	2 and 1
1971	R Jenkins	TJ Melia	Ashburnham	3 and 2
1972	MG Chugg	RM Jones	Wrexham	3 and 2
1973	R Tate	N Duncan	Penarth	2 and 1
1974	D Williams	S Lewis	Llandudno	5 and 4
1975	G Davies	PG Garrett	Glamorganshire	20th hole
1976	JM Morrow	MG Mouland	Caernarvonshire	1 hole
1977	JM Morrow	MG Mouland	Glamorganshire	2 and 1
1978	JM Morrow	A Laking	Harlech	2 and 1
1979	P Mayo	M Hayward	Penarth	24th hole
1980	A Llyr	DK Wood	Llandudno (Maesdu)	2 and 1
1981	M Evans	P Webborn	Pontypool	5 and 4
1982	CM Rees	KH Williams	Prestatyn	2 holes
1983	MA Macara	RN Roderick	Radyr	1 hole
1984	GA Macara	D Bagg	Llandudno	1 hole
1985	B Macfarlane	R Herbert	Cardiff	1 hole
1986	C O'Carroll	GA Macara	Rhuddlan	1 hole
1987	SJ Edwards	A Herbert	Abergavenny	19th hole
1988	C Platt	P Murphy	Holyhead	2 and 1
1989	R Johnson	RL Evans	Southerndown	2 holes
1990	M Ellis	C Sheppard	Llandudno (Maesdu)	3 and 2
1991	B Dredge	A Cooper	Tenby	2 and 1
1992	Y Taylor	J Pugh	Wrexham	1 hole
1993	R Davies	S Raybould	Pyle and Kenfig	3 and 2
1994	R Peet	K Sullivan	Abergele & Pensarn	7 and 6
1995	M Palmer	O Pughe	Newport	4 and 3
1996	A Smith	M Griffiths	Borth & Ynyslas	at 19th hole
1997	A Lee	I Campbell	Glamorganshire	4 and 3

European Boys' Team Championship

Year	Winner	Venue
1980	Spain	El Prat Golf Club, Barcelona
1981	England	Olgiata Golf Club, Rome
1982	Italy	Frankfurt Golf Club, West Germany
1983	Sweden	Helsinki Golf Club, Finland
1984	Scotland	Royal St George's Golf Club, England
1985	England	Troia Golf Club, Portugal
1986	England	Turin Golf Club, Italy
1987	Scotland	Chantilly Golf Club, France
1988	France	Renfrew Golf Club, Scotland
1989	England	Lyckoma, Sweden

continued

European Boys' Team Championship *continued*

Year	Winner	Venue
1990	Spain	Reykjavik, Iceland
1991	Sweden	Oslo, Norway
1992	Scotland	Conwy, Wales
1993	Sweden	Ascona, Switzerland
1994	England	Vilamoura, Portugal
1995	England	Woodhall Spa
1996	Spain	Gut Murstatten, Austria
1997	Spain	Bled G&CC, Slovenia

Great Britain and Ireland *v* Continent of Europe, Boys (Jacques Leglise Trophy)

Year	Winner	Result	Venue	Year	Winner	Result	Venue
1958	GB&I	$11^1/_2$–$^1/_2$	Moortown	1983	GB&I	$6^1/_2$–$5^1/_2$	Glenbervie
1959	GB&I	7–2	Pollok	1984	GB&I	$6^1/_2$–$5^1/_2$	Porthcawl
1960	GB&I	8–7	Olton	1985	GB&I	$7^1/_2$–$4^1/_2$	Barnton
1961	GB&I	11–4	Dalmahoy	1986	Europe	$8^1/_2$–$3^1/_2$	Seaton Carew
1962	GB&I	11–4	Mid-Surrey	1987	GB&I	$7^1/_2$–$4^1/_2$	Barassie
1963	GB&I	12–3	Prestwick	1988	GB&I	$5^1/_2$–$2^1/_2$	Formby
1964	GB&I	12–1	Formby	1989	GB&I	$7^1/_2$–$4^1/_2$	Nairn
1965	GB&I	12–1	Gullane	1990	GB&I	10–2	Hunstanton
1966	GB&I	10–2	Moortown	1991	GB&I	$6^1/_2$–$5^1/_2$	Montrose
1967–76	*Not played*			1992	GB&I	8–7	Royal Mid–Surrey
1977	Europe	7–6	Downfield	1993	GB&I	8–7	Glenbervie
1978	Europe	7–6	Seaton Carew	1994	GB&I	$12^1/_2$–$2^1/_2$	Little Aston
1979	GB&I	$9^1/_2$–$2^1/_2$	Barassie	1995	GB&I	9–6	Dunbar
1980	GB&I	7–5	Formby	1996	Europe	13–11	Woodhall Spa
1981	GB&I	8–4	Gullane	1997	Europe	$12^1/_2$–$11^1/_2$	Aberdeen
1982	GB&I	11–1	Burnham & Berrow				

Girls' British Open Amateur Championship

Year	Winner	Runner–up	Venue	By
1960	S Clarke	AL Irvin	Barassie	2 and 1
1961	D Robb	J Roberts	Beaconsfield	3 and 2
1962	S McLaren-Smith	A Murphy	Foxton Hall	2 and 1
1963	D Oxley	B Whitehead	Gullane	2 and 1
1964	P Tredinnick	K Cumming	Camberley Heath	2 and 1
1965	A Willard	A Ward	Formby	3 and 2
1966	J Hutton	D Oxley	Troon Portland	20th hole
1967	P Burrows	J Hutton	Liphook	2 and 1
1968	C Wallace	C Reybroeck	Leven	4 and 3
1969	J de Witt Puyt	C Reybroeck	Ilkley	2 and 1
1970	C Le Feuvre	Michelle Walker	North Wales	2 and 1
1971	J Mark	Maureen Walker	North Berwick	4 and 3
1972	Maureen Walker	S Cadden	Norwich	2 and 1
1973	AM Palli	N Jeanson	Northamptonshire	2 and 1
1974	R Barry	T Perkins	Dunbar	1 hole
1975	S Cadden	L Isherwood	Henbury	4 and 3
1976	G Stewart	S Rowlands	Pyle and Kenfig	5 and 4
1977	W Aitken	S Bamford	Formby Ladies	2 and 1
1978	M L de Lorenzi	D Glenn	Largs	2 and 1
1979	S Lapaire	P Smilie	Edgbaston	19th hole
1980	J Connachan	L Bolton	Wrexham	2 holes
1981	J Connachan	P Grice	Woodbridge	20th hole
1982	C Waite	M Mackie	Edzell	6 and 5
1983	E Orley	A Walters	Leeds	7 and 6
1984	C Swallow	E Farquharson	Maesdu	1 hole
1985	S Shapcott	E Farquharson	Hesketh	3 and 1
1986	S Croce	S Bennett	West Kilbride	5 and 4
1987	H Dobson	S Croce	Barnham Broom	19th hole
1988	A Macdonald	J Posener	Pyle and Kenfig	3 and 2
1989	M McKinlay	S Eriksson	Carlisle	19th hole
1990	S Cavalleri	E Valera	Penrith	5 and 4
1991	M Hjorth	J Moodie	Whitchurch	3 and 2

Year	Winner	Runner–up	Venue	By
1992	M McKay	L Navarro	Northamptonshire	2 holes
1993	M McKay	A Vincent	Helensburgh	4 and 3
1994	A Vincent	R Hudson	Gog Magog	1 up
1995	A Lemoine	J Krantz	Northop Park	3 and 2
1996	M Monnet	C Laurens	Formby	4 and 3
1997	C Laurens	M Nagl	West Kilbride	2 and 1

English Girls' Championship

Year	Winner	Runner–up	Venue	By
1964	S Ward	P Tredinnick	Wollaton Park	2 and 1
1965	D Oxley	A Payne	Edgbaston	2 holes
1966	B Whitehead	D Oxley	Woodbridge	1 hole
1967	A Willard	G Holloway	Burhill	1 hole
1968	K Phillips	C le Feuvre	Harrogate	6 and 5
1969	C le Feuvre	K Phillips	Hawkstone Park	2 and 1
1970	C le Feuvre	M Walker	High Post	2 and 1
1971	C Eckersley	J Stevens	Liphook	4 and 3
1972	C Barker	R Kelly	Trentham	4 and 3
1973	S Parker	S Thurston	Lincoln	19th hole
1974	C Langford	L Harrold	Knowle	2 and 1
1975	M Burton	R Barry	Formby	6 and 5
1976	H Latham	D Park	Moseley	3 and 2
1977	S Bamford	S Jolly	Chelmsford	21st hole
1978	P Smillie	J Smith	Willesley Park	3 and 2
1979	L Moore	P Barry	Cirencester	1 hole
1980	P Smillie	J Soulsby	Kedleston Park	3 and 2
1981	J Soulsby	C Waite	Worksop	7 and 5
1982	C Waite	P Grice	Wilmslow	3 and 2
1983	P Grice	K Mitchell	West Surrey	2 and 1
1984	C Swallow	S Duhig	Bath	3 and 1
1985	L Fairclough	K Mitchell	Coventry	6 and 5
1986	S Shapcott	N Way	Huddersfield	7 and 6
1987	S Shapcott	S Morgan	Sandy Lodge	1 hole
1988	H Dobson	S Shapcott	Long Ashton	1 hole
1989	H Dobson	A MacDonald	Edgbaston	3 and 1
1990	C Hall	J Hockley	Bolton Old Links	20th hole
1991	N Buxton	C Hall	Knole Park	2 and 1
1992	F Brown	L Nicholson	Finham Park	2 and 1
1993	G Simpson	L Wixon	Cotswold Hills	7 and 5
1994	K Hamilton	S Forster	Whitley Bay	3 and 2
1995	R Hudson	G Nutter	Porters Park	2 and 1
1996	R Hudson	D Rushworth	Bedford	8 and 6
1997	S McKevitt	C Ritson	Kingsdown	3 and 2

Irish Girls' Championship

Year	Winner	Runner–up	Venue	By
1961	M Coburn	C McAuley	Portrush	6 and 5
1962	P Boyd	P Atkinson	Elm Park	4 and 3
1963	P Atkinson	C Scarlett	Donaghadee	8 and 7
1964	C Scarlett	A Maher	Milltown	6 and 5
1965	V Singleton	P McKenzie	Ballycastle	7 and 6
1966	M McConnell	D Hulme	Dun Laoghaire	3 and 2
1967	M McConnell	C Wallace	Portrush	6 and 5
1968	C Wallace	A McCoy	Louth	3 and 1
1969	EA McGregor	M Sheenan	Knock	6 and 5
1970	EA McGregor	J Mark	Greystones	3 and 2
1971	J Mark	C Nesbitt	Belfast	3 and 2
1972	P Smyth	M Governey	Elm Park	1 hole
1973	M Governey	R Hegarty	Mullingar	3 and 1
1974	R Hegarty	M Irvine	Castletroy	2 holes
1975	M Irvine	P Wickham	Carlow	2 and 1
1976	P Wickham	R Hegarty	Castle	5 and 3
1977	A Ferguson	R Walsh	Birr	3 and 2
1978	C Wickham	B Gleeson	Killarney	1 hole
1979	L Bolton	B Gleeson	Milltown	3 and 2
1980	B Gleeson	L Bolton	Kilkenny	5 and 3
1981	B Gleeson	E Lynn	Donegal	1 hole

continued

Irish Girls' Championship *continued*

Year	Winner	Runner–up	Venue	By
1982	D Langan	S Lynn	Headfort	5 and 4
1983	E McDaid	S Lynn	Ennis	20th hole
1984	S Sheehan	L Tormey	Thurles	6 and 4
1985	S Sheehan	D Hanna	Laytown/Bettystown	5 and 4
1986	D Mahon	T Eakin	Mallow	4 and 3
1987	V Greevy	B Ryan	Galway	8 and 7
1988	L McCool	P Gorman	Courtown	3 and 2
1989	A Rogers	R MacGuigan	Athlone	2 and 1
1990	G Doran	L McCool	Royal Portrush	3 and 1
1991	A Rogers	D Powell	Mallow	2 and 1
1992	M McGreevy	N Gorman	Kilkenny	2 and 1
1993	M McGreevy	E Dowdall	Strandhill	2 and 1
1994	A O'Leary	D Doyle	Mullingar	23rd hole
1995	P Murphy	G Hegarty	Douglas	5 and 4
1996	P Murphy	C Smyth	Warren Point	2 holes
1997	J Gannon	C Coughlan	Lay/Bettystown	3 and 2

Scottish Ladies' Junior Open Stroke Play Championship

Year	Winner	Venue	Year	Winner	Venue
1960	J Greenhalgh	Ranfurly Castle	1979	A Gemmill	Troon, Portland
1961	D Robb	Whitecraigs	1980	J Connachan	Kirkcaldy
1962	S Armitage	Dalmahoy	1981	K Douglas	Downfield
1963	A Irvin	Dumfries	1982	J Rhodes	Dumfries & Galloway
1964	M Nuttall	Dalmahoy	1983	S Lawson	Largs
1965	I Wylie	Carnoustie	1984	S Lawson	Dunbar
1966	J Smith	Douglas Park	1985	K Imrie	Ballater
1967	J Bourassa	Dunbar	1986	K Imrie	Dumfries and County
1968	K Phillips	Dumfries	1987	K Imrie	Douglas Park
1969	K Phillips	Prestonfield	1988	C Lambert	Baberton
1970	B Huke	Leven	1989	C Lambert	Dunblane New
1971	B Huke	Dalmahoy	1990	J Moodie	Royal Troon
1972	L Hope	Troon, Portland	1991	C Macdonald	Alyth
1973	G Cadden	Edzell	1992	L McCool	North Berwick
1974	S Lambie	Stranraer	1993	J Moodie	Dumfries and County
1975	S Cadden	Lanark	1994	C Agnew	Dumfries and County
1976	S Cadden	Prestonfield	1995	R Hakkarainen (Fin)	Lanark
1977	S Cadden	Edzell	1996	L Moffat	Auchterarder
1978	J Connachan	Peebles	1997	L Nicholson	Stranraer

Scottish Girls' Close Championship

Year	Winner	Runner–up	Venue	By
1960	J Hastings	A Lurie	Kilmacolm	6 and 4
1961	I Wylie	W Clark	Murrayfield	3 and 1
1962	I Wylie	U Burnet	West Kilbride	3 and 1
1963	M Norval	S MacDonald	Carnoustie	6 and 4
1964	JW Smith	C Workman	West Kilbride	2 and 1
1965	JW Smith	I Walker	Leven	7 and 5
1966	J Hutton	F Jamieson	Arbroath	2 holes
1967	J Hutton	K Lackie	West Kilbride	4 and 2
1968	M Dewar	J Crawford	Dalmahoy	2 holes
1969	C Panton	A Coutts	Edzell	23rd hole
1970	M Walker	L Bennett	Largs	3 and 2
1971	M Walker	S Kennedy	Edzell	1 hole
1972	G Cadden	C Panton	Stirling	3 and 2
1973	M Walker	M Thomson	Cowal, Dunoon	1 hole
1974	S Cadden	D Reid	Arbroath	3 and 1
1975	W Aitken	S Cadden	Leven	1 hole
1976	S Cadden	D Mitchell	Dumfries and County	4 and 2
1977	W Aitken	G Wilson	West Kilbride	2 holes
1978	J Connachan	D Mitchell	Stirling	7 and 5
1979	J Connachan	G Wilson	Dunbar	3 and 1
1980	J Connachan	P Wright	Dumfries and County	21st hole
1981	D Thomson	P Wright	Barassie	2 and 1
1982	S Lawson	D Thomson	Montrose	1 hole

Year	Winner	Runner–up	Venue	By
1983	K Imrie	D Martin	Leven	2 and 1
1984	T Craik	D Jackson	Peebles	3 and 2
1985	E Farquharson	E Moffat	West Kilbride	2 holes
1986	C Lambert	F McKay	Nairn	4 and 3
1987	S Little	L Moretti	Stirling	3 and 2
1988	J Jenkins	F McKay	Dumfries and County	4 and 3
1989	J Moodie	V Melvin	Kilmacolm	19th hole
1990	M McKay	J Moodie	Duff House Royal	3 and 2
1991	J Moodie	M McKay	Leven Links	5 and 4
1992	M McKay	L Nicholson	Powfoot	2 and 1
1993	C Agnew	H Stirling	Baberton	19th hole
1994	C Nicholson	L Moffat	Deeside	3 and 1
1995	L Moffat	F Lockhart	Paisley	2 and 1
1996	V Laing	C Hunter	Peebles	5 and 4
1997	V Laing	A Walker	Dunfermline	5 and 4

Welsh Girls' Championship

Year	Winner	Runner–up	Venue	By
1960	A Hughes	D Wilson	Llandrindod Wells	6 and 4
1961	J Morris	S Kelly	North Wales	3 and 2
1962	J Morris	P Morgan	Southerndown	4 and 3
1963	A Hughes	A Brown	Conway	8 and 7
1964	A Hughes	M Leigh	Holyhead	5 and 3
1965	A Hughes	A Reardon-Hughes	Swansea Bay	19th hole
1966	S Hales	J Rogers	Prestatyn	1 hole
1967	E Wilkie	L Humphreys	Pyle and Kenfig	1 hole
1968	L Morris	J Rogers	Portmadoc	1 hole
1969	L Morris	L Humphreys	Wenvoe Castle	5 and 3
1970	T Perkins	P Light	Rhuddlan	2 and 1
1971	P Light	P Whitley	Glamorganshire	4 and 3
1972	P Whitley	P Light	Llandudno (Maesdu)	2 and 1
1973	V Rawlings	T Perkins	Whitchurch	19th hole
1974	L Isherwood	S Rowlands	Wrexham	4 and 3
1975	L Isherwood	S Rowlands	Swansea Bay	1 hole
1976	K Rawlings	C Parry	Rhuddlan	5 and 4
1977	S Rowlands	D Taylor	Clyne	7 and 5
1978	S Rowlands	G Rees	Abergele	3 and 2
1979	M Rawlings	J Richards	St Mellons	19th hole
1980	K Davies	M Rawlings	Vale of Llangollen	19th hole
1981	M Rawlings	F Connor	Radyr	4 and 3
1982	K Davies	K Beckett	Wrexham	6 and 5
1983	N Wesley	J Foster	Whitchurch	4 and 2
1984	J Foster	J Evans	Pwllheli	6 and 5
1985	J Foster	S Caley	Langland Bay	6 and 5
1986	J Foster	L Dermott	Holyhead	3 and 2
1987	J Lloyd	S Bibbs	Cardiff	2 and 1
1988	L Dermott	A Perriam	Builth Wells	2 holes
1989	L Dermott	N Stroud	Carmarthen	4 and 2
1990	L Dermott	N Stroud	Padeswood and Buckley	6 and 4
1991	S Boyes	R Morgan	Clyne	3 and 1
1992	B Jones	S Musto	Rhuddlan	2 and 1
1993	K Stark	S Tudor-Jones	Radyr	3 and 2
1994	K Stark	J Evans	Wrexham	4 and 3
1995	E Pilgrim	L Davis	Borth and Ynyslas	2 holes
1996	K Stark	S Bourne	Monmouth	4 and 3
1997	R Brewerton	K Stark	Perhos	19th hole

European Lady Juniors' Team Championship

Year	Winner	Second	Venue
1990	Sweden	England	Shannon, Ireland
1992	Spain	Sweden	St Nom–la–Breteche, France
1994	Sweden	France	Gutenhof, Vienna, Austria
1996	France	Spain	Nairn, Scotland

Girls' Home Internationals: Stroyan Cup

Year	Winner	Venue		Year	Winner	Venue
1966	Scotland	Troon (Portland)		1982	England	Edzell
1967	England	Liphook		1983	England	Alwoodley
1968	England	Leven		1984	Scotland	Llandudno (Maesdu)
1969	England	Ilkley		1985	England	Hesketh GC
1970	England	North Wales		1986	England	West Kilbride
1971	England	North Berwick		1987	England	Barnham Broom
1972	Scotland	Royal Norwich		1988	England	Pyle and Kenfig
1973	Scotland	Northamptonshire County		1989	England	Carlisle
1974	England	Dunbar		1990	England	Penrith
1975	England	Henbury		1991	England	Whitchurch
1976	Scotland	Pyle and Kenfig		1992	Scotland	Moseley
1977	England	Formby Ladies		1993	Scotland	Helensburgh
1978	England	Largs		1994	Scotland	Gog Magog
1979	England	Edgbaston		1995	England	Northop
1980	England	Wrexham		1996	England	Formby
1981	England	Woodbridge		1997	England	Forfar

Irish Youths' Open Amateur Championship

Year	Winner	Venue	Score		Year	Winner	Venue	Score
1980	J McHenry	Clandeboye	296		1989	A Mathers	Athlone	280
1981	J McHenry	Westport	303		1990	D Errity	Dundalk	293
1982	K O'Donnell	Mullingar	286		1991	R Coughlan	Lahinch	288
1983	P Murphy	Cork	287		1992	K Nolan	Clandeboye	275
1984	JC Morris	Bangor	292		1993	CD Hislop	Co Sligo	279
1985	J McHenry	Co Sligo	287		1994	B O'Melia	Tullamore	272
1986	JC Morris	Carlow	280		1995	S Young	Ballybunion	286
1987	C Everett	Killarney	300		1996	S Young	Royal Portrush	291
1988	P McGinley	Malone	283		1997	N Howley	Galway	284

Scottish Youths' Open Amateur Stroke Play Championship

Year	Winner	Venue	Score		Year	Winner	Venue	Score
1979	A Oldcorn	Dalmahoy	217		1989	J Mackenzie	Longniddry	281
1980	G Brand, Jr	Monifieth & Ashludie	281		1990	S Bannerman	Portpatrick & Stranraer	213
1981	S Campbell	Cawder and Keir	279		1991	D Robertson	Hilton Park	273
1982	LS Mann	Leven and Scoonie	270		1992	R Russell	Nairn	296
1983	A Moir	Mortonhall	284		1993	CD Hislop	West Kilbride	284
1984	B Shields	Eastwood, Renfrew	280		1994	S Gallacher	Crieff	275
1985	H Kemp	East Kilbride	282		1995	E Little	Irvine, Ayr	280
1986	A Mednick	Cawder	282		1996	E Little	Stranraer & Portpatrick	280
1987	K Walker	Bogside	291		1997	S Young	Cawder	269
1988	P McGinley	Ladybank & Glenrothes	281					

Ulster Youths' Open Amateur Championship

Year	Winner		Year	Winner
1988	G McAllister		1993	P Collins
1989	G Moore		1994	A McCormick
1990	N Crawford		1995	P Collins
1991	P Russell		1996	R Elliott
1992	C Feenan		1997	J McKinstry

Golf Foundation Age Group Championships

Boys

Year	Under 16	Under 15	Under 14
1987	I Garbutt (Wheatley)	L Westwood (Worksop)	N Heron (Ashridge)
1988	L Westwood (Worksop)	B Collier (Callander)	S Pigott (West Malling)
1989	K Harrison (Cottesmore)	C Lane (Kingsthorpe)	G Harris (Broome Manor)
1990	C Lane (Kingsthorpe)	G Harris (Broome Manor)	P Collier (Limerick)
1991	G Harris (Broome Manor)	C Richardson (Burghley Park)	J Bajcer (Church Stretton)
1992	C Leach (Gillingham)	S Walker (Walmley)	D Kirton (Worksop)
1993	K Godfrey (St Enodoc)	S Young (Seascale)	J Rose (North Hants)
1994	A Smith (Rhondda)	T Hilton (Lewes)	A Smith (Enville)
1995	G Legg (Enmore Park)	S Robinson (Seaton Carew)	D Inglis (Glencorse)
1996	S Fromant (Orsett)	D Skinns (Canwick Park)	C Smith (Cotgrave Place)
1997	M Stam (Royal Liverpool)	G Lockerbie (Keswick)	S Robinson (Thames Ditton)

Year	Under 13
1987	M Neil (Stirling)
1988	P Drew (Worthing)
1989	A Cooper (Taymouth Castle)
1990	S Walker (Boldmere)
1991	N Rossin (John O'Gaunt)
1992	D Main (Moray)
1993	S Godfrey (St Enodoc)
1994	D Tarbotton (Hull)
1995	D Porter (Wellow)
1996	J Maxwell (Muckhart)
1997	J Turner (Newmarket Links)

Girls

Year	Under 17	Under 16	Under 15
1987		L Walton (Calcot Park)	N Buxton (Woodsome Hall)
1988		V Melvin (Clydebank & District)	J Williamson (Hadley Wood)
1989		S Boyes (Wenvoe Castle)	N Gorman (Balmoral)
1990		T Poulton (Boyce Hill)	V Hanks (Broome Manor)
1991		G Simpson (Cleckheaton & District)	D Doyle (Lahinch)
1992		H Stirling (Bridge of Allan)	G Nutter (Prestwich)
1993		K Wrigglesworth (Hornsea)	R Hudson (Wheatley)
1994		L Meredith (Wentworth)	L Moffat (W. Kilbride)
1995	R Hudson (Wheatley)	L Moffat (W. Kilbride	V Laing (Musselburgh)
1996	K Fisher (Leyland)	F More (Lindrick)	L Archer (Lilleshall Hall)
1997	V Laing (Musselburgh)	R Bell (Northcliff)	L Kenney (Pitreavie)

Year	Under 14	Under 13
1987	L Tupholme (Northcliffe)	M McKay (Turnberry)
1988	M McKay (Turnberry)	
1989	V Hanks (Broome Manor)	
1990	K Wrigglesworth (Hornsea)	
1991	E Wilcock (Sherwood Forest)	
1992	R Hudson (Wheatley)	
1993	L Walters (Ormonde Fields)	
1994	V Laing (Musselburgh)	

County and District Championships

Aberdeenshire Ladies' Championship

Year	Winner	Year	Winner
1988	L Urquhart	1993	G Penny
1989	J Forbes	1994	C Hunter
1990	E Farquharson	1995	J Matthews
1991	C Middleton	1996	S Wood
1992	R MacLennan	1997	K Moggach

Anglesey Amateur Championship

Year	Winner	Year	Winner
1988	EO Jones	1993	M Perdue
1989	M Robinson	1994	J Campbell
1990	D McLean	1995	D McLean
1991	J Campbell	1996	A Williams
1992	D McLean	1997	M Perdue

Angus Amateur Championship

Year	Winner	Year	Winner
1988	D Downie	1993	G Dough
1989	T Peebles	1994	J Rae
1990	D Leith	1995	G Hay
1991	W Taylor	1996	J Rae
1992	D Downie	1997	P Cunningham

Angus Ladies' Championship

Year	Winner	Year	Winner
1988	C Hay	1993	M Summers
1989	C Hope	1994	M Summers
1990	K Sutherland	1995	K Sutherland
1991	M Summers	1996	S Simpson
1992	M Summers	1997	S Raitt

Argyll and Bute Amateur Championship

Year	Winner	Year	Winner
1988	G Bolton	1993	G Tyre-Cole
1989	G Tyre	1994	G Bolton
1990	G Reynolds	1995	G Tyre
1991	G Bolton	1996	L Kelly
1992	G Bolton	1997	S Campbell

Ayrshire Amateur Championship

Year	Winner	Year	Winner
1988	G Blair	1993	G Sherry
1989	D Hawthorn	1994	G Lawrie
1990	R Crawford	1995	A Gourlay
1991	JA Thomson	1996	G Lawrie
1992	G Lawrie	1997	G Fox

Ayrshire Ladies' Championship

Year	Winner	Year	Winner
1988	M Wilson	1993	M Wilson
1989	A Gemmill	1994	A Gemmill
1990	C Gibson	1995	R Kennedy
1991	A Gemmill	1996	A Gemmill
1992	C Gibson	1997	A Gemmill

Bedfordshire Amateur Championship

Year	Winner	Year	Winner
1988	P Wharton	1993	C Beard
1989	C Staroscik	1994	J Kemp
1990	D Charlton	1995	I Tottingham
1991	M Wharton	1996	M Wharton
1992	L Watcham	1997	K Kemp

Bedfordshire Ladies' Championship

Year	Winner	Year	Winner
1988	S Cormack	1993	S Cormack
1989	T Gale	1994	T Gale
1990	C Cummings	1995	A Bradley
1991	E James	1996	C Hoskin
1992	S Cormack	1997	J Faris

Berks, Bucks and Oxfordshire Amateur Championship

Year	Winner	Year	Winner
1988	F George	1993	R Walton
1989	H Bareham	1994	D Fisher
1990	S Barwick	1995	D Lane
1991	VL Phillips	1996	J Carlsen
1992	VL Phillips	1997	L Donald

Berkshire Ladies' Championship

Year	Winner	Year	Winner
1988	T Smith	1993	A Uzielli
1989	L Walton	1994	J Guntrip
1990	A Uzielli	1995	A Uzielli
1991	A Uzielli	1996	S Sanderson
1992	J Guntrip	1997	L Meredith

Border Counties Ladies' Championship

Year	Winner	Year	Winner
1988	A Hunter	1993	D Turnbull
1989	A Fleming	1994	W Wells
1990	J Anderson	1995	A Fleming
1991	J Anderson	1996	K Inkpen
1992	J Anderson	1997	J Anderson

Border Golfers' Association Amateur Championship

Year	Winner	Year	Winner
1988	W Renwick	1993	D Valentine
1989	A Turnbull	1994	M Thomson
1990	M Thomson	1995	M Thomson
1991	A Turnbull	1996	D Ballantyne
1992	M Thomson	1997	W Simpson

Bucks Ladies' Championship

Year	Winner	Year	Winner
1988	C Hourihane	1993	C Watson
1989	C Hourihane	1994	P Williamson
1990	C Watson	1995	C Dowling
1991	C Watson	1996	C Watson
1992	C Watson	1997	C Watson

Caernarfonshire and District Amateur Championship

Year	Winner	Year	Winner
1988	D McLean	1993	E Jones
1989	W Jones	1994	D McLean
1990	D McLean	1995	S Pritchard
1991	J Dabecki	1996	A Williams
1992	D McLean	1997	*Not played*

Caernarfonshire Amateur Championship Cup

Year	Winner	Year	Winner
1989	M Sheppard	1994	J Dabecki
1990	I Jones	1995	J Dabecki
1991	R Williams	1996	M Pilkington
1992	MA Macara	1997	*Not played*
1993	L Harpin		

Caernarfonshire and Anglesey Ladies' Championship

Year	Winner	Year	Winner
1988	S Turner	1993	A Lewis
1989	S Roberts	1994	C Thomas
1990	S Roberts	1995	L Davies
1991	*Not played*	1996	L Davies
1992	S Turner	1997	F Vaughan Thomas

Cambridgeshire Amateur Championship

Year	Winner	Year	Winner
1988	R Claydon	1993	LG Yearn
1989	B Jackson	1994	A Emery
1990	G Stevenson	1995	S Jarvis
1991	M Seaton	1996	P Rains
1992	LG Yearn	1997	O Cousins

Cambridgeshire and Hunts Ladies' Championship

Year	Winner	Year	Winner
1988	S Meadows	1993	T Eakin
1989	J Hatcher	1994	T Eakin
1990	J Walter	1995	P Parker
1991	J Walter	1996	J Walter
1992	T Eakin	1997	J Walter

Channel Islands Amateur Championship

Year	Winner	Year	Winner
1988	DA Rowlinson	1993	B Eggo
1989	TA Gray	1994	C Chevalier
1990	TA Gray	1995	C Chevalier
1991	R Eggo	1996	R Eggo
1992	C Chevalier	1997	R Williamson

Channel Islands Ladies' Championship

Year	Winner	Year	Winner
1988	L Cummins	1993	L Cummins
1989	L Cummins	1994	L Cummins
1990	L Cummins	1995	M Chamberlayne
1991	L Cummins	1996	J Deeley
1992	V Bougourd	1997	J Deeley

Cheshire Amateur Championship

Year	Winner	Year	Winner
1988	P Bailey	1993	J Hodgson
1989	P Bailey	1994	J Hodgson
1990	J Berry	1995	C Smethurst
1991	D Bathgate	1996	D Vaughan
1992	A Hill	1997	N Pabari

Cheshire Ladies' Championship

Year	Winner	Year	Winner
1988	J Morley	1993	J Morley
1989	J Morley	1994	F Brown
1990	J Morley	1995	E Ratcliffe
1991	F Brown	1996	L Dermott
1992	J Morley	1997	E Ratcliffe

Clackmannanshire Amateur Championship

Year	Winner	Year	Winner
1989	J Gullen	1994	P McLeod
1990	P MacLeod	1995	I Ross
1991	AJ Watson	1996	R Stewart
1992	G Kennedy	1997	G Bowie
1993	S Horne		

Cornwall Amateur Championship

Year	Winner	Year	Winner
1988	P Clayton	1993	C Phillips
1989	C Phillips	1994	R Binney
1990	M Edmunds	1995	M Lock
1991	I Veale	1996	I Veale
1992	P Clayton	1997	P Darlington

Cornwall Ladies' Championship

Year	Winner	Year	Winner
1988	S Currie	1993	J Ryder
1989	S Currie	1994	E Fields
1990	S Currie	1995	L Simpson
1991	S Currie	1996	L Simpson
1992	G Fields	1997	L Simpson

County Champions' Tournament (England)

(Formerly President's Bowl)

Year	Winner
1962 T	G Edwards, Cheshire
	A Thirwell, Northumberland
1963 T	M Burgess, Sussex/R Foster, Yorks
1964	M Attenborough, Kent
1965	M Lees, Lincs
1966	R Stephenson, Middx
1967	P Benka, Surrey
1968	G Hyde, Sussex
1969	A Holmes, Herts
1970	M King, Berks, Bucks and Oxon
1971	M Lee, Yorks
1972	P Berry, Glos
1973	A Chandler, Lancs
1974 T	G Hyde, Sussex/A Lyle, Shrops & Hereford
1975	N Faldo, Herts
1976	R Brown, Devon
1977	M Walls, Cumbria
1978	I Simpson, Notts
1979	N Burch, Essex
1980	D Lane, Berks, Bucks and Oxon
1981	M Kelly, Yorks
1982	P Deeble, Northumberland
1983	N Chesses, Warwickshire
1984 T	N Briggs, Herts/P McEvoy, Warwickshire
1985	P Robinson, Herts
1986	A Gelsthorpe, Yorks
1987 T	F George, Berks, Bucks & Oxon
	D Fay, Surrey
1988	R Claydon, Cambridge
1989	R Willison, Middlesex
1990 T	P Streeter, Lincs/R Sloman, Kent
1991	T Allen, Warwickshire
1992	L Westwood, Notts
1993	R Walker, Durham
1994	G Wolstenholme, Glos
1995	S Webster, Warwickshire
1996	J Herbert, Leics/G Wolstenholme, Glos
1997	J Herbert, Leicestershire & Rutland

Cumbria Amateur Championship *(Formerly Cumberland and Westmorland Amateur Championship)*

Year	Winner	Year	Winner
1988	G Waters	1993	R Secular
1989	G Winter	1994	B Story
1990	G Winter	1995	N Mitchell
1991	G Winter	1996	R Secular
1992	A Greenbank	1997	G Watson

Cumbria Ladies' Championship

Year	Winner	Year	Winner
1988	D Thomson	1993	J Currie
1989	S Tuck	1994	J Currie
1990	S Tuck	1995	J Viles
1991	J Currie	1996	R Bruce
1992	J Currie	1997	J Blaydes

Denbighshire and Flintshire Ladies' Championship

Year	Winner	Year	Winner
1988	S Thomas	1993	S Lovatt
1989	S Thomas	1994	A Donne
1990	L Dermott	1995	S Lovatt
1991	B Jones	1996	B Jones
1992	B Jones	1997	R Brewerton

Derbyshire Amateur Championship

Year	Winner	Year	Winner
1988	N Wylde	1993	G Shaw
1989	P Eastwood	1994	J Feeney
1990	R Fletcher	1995	G Shaw
1991	J Feeney	1996	J Feeney
1992	J Feeney	1997	AS Humpston

Derbyshire Ladies' Championship

Year	Winner	Year	Winner
1988	A Howe	1993	L Holmes
1989	D Andrews	1994	L Walters
1990	D Andrews	1995	L Holmes
1991	L Holmes	1996	L Shaw
1992	L Holmes	1997	L Walters

Derbyshire Open Championship

Year	Winner	Year	Winner
1988	G Shaw	1993	J Feeney (Am)
1989	D Clark (Am)	1994	D Thompson
1990	M Deeley	1995	J Feeney (Am)
1991	J Feeney (Am)	1996	DJ Russell
1992	J Feeney (Am)	1997	

Derbyshire Professional Championship

Year	Winner	Year	Winner
1988	M McLean	1993	K Cross
1989	N Hallam	1994	D Stafford
1990	M Deeley	1995	A Carnall
1991	W Bird	1996	C Cross
1992	J Proctor	1997	A Carnall

Devon Amateur Championship

Year	Winner	Year	Winner
1988	J Langmead	1993	R Goodey
1989	R Barrow	1994	M Crossfield
1990	G Milne	1995	A Capping
1991	A Richards	1996	D Eva
1992	D Lewis	1997	G Ruth

Devon Ladies' Championship

Year	Winner	Year	Winner
1988	J Hurley	1993	K Tebbet
1989	S Germain	1994	K Tebbet
1990	V Holloway	1995	J Roberts
1991	K Tebbet	1996	R Cirin
1992	K Tebbet	1997	J Roberts

Devon Open Championship

Year	Winner	Year	Winner
1988	D Sheppard	1994	I Higgins
1989	D Sheppard	1995	B Austin
1990	G Tomkinson	1996	J Langmead
1991	R Troake	1997	J Langmead
1992	R Troake		
1993T	D Sheppard		
	T McSherry		

Dorset Amateur Championship

Year	Winner	Year	Winner
1988	A Lawrence	1993	A Lawrence
1989	A Lawrence	1994	M Davies
1990	P McMullen	1995	M Davies
1991	A Lawrence	1996	A Lawrence
1992	L James	1997	J Baldwin

Dorset Ladies' Championship

Year	Winner	Year	Winner
1988	H Delew	1993	S Sanderson
1989	T Loveys	1994	W Russell
1990	T Loveys	1995	A Monk
1991	H Davidson	1996	C Brown
1992	S Lowe	1997	A Monk

Dumfriesshire Ladies' Championship

Year	Winner	Year	Winner
1988	D Douglas	1993	G Adamson
1989	D Douglas	1994	F Watson
1990	L Armstrong	1995	D Douglas
1991	M Morrison	1996	C Adamson
1992	D Douglas	1997	L Wells

Durham Ladies' Championship

Year	Winner	Year	Winner
1988	L Chesterton	1993	L Keers
1989	L Still	1994	P Dobson
1990	B Mansfield	1995	K Lee
1991	P Dobson	1996	A Dobson
1992	L Still	1997	K Lee

Dunbartonshire Amateur Championship

Year	Winner	Year	Winner
1988	J Laird	1993	F Jardine
1989	D Shaw	1994	D Carrick
1990	J Kinloch	1995	T McKeown
1991	T McKeown	1996	K MacNair
1992	D Shaw	1997	S Carmichael

East Anglian Ladies' Championship

Year	Winner	Year	Winner
1988	R Farrow	1993	T Eakin
1989	L Still	1994	T Eakin
1990	J Sheldrick	1995	S Little
1991	J Walter	1996	C O'Grady
1992	T Eakin	1997	T Williamson

Dunbartonshire Amateur Match Play Championship

Year	Winner	Year	Winner
1988	R Blair	1993	F Jardine
1989	C Stewart	1994	F Hutchison
1990	D Shaw	1995	F Jardine
1991	F Jardine	1996	A Leitch
1992	R Blair	1997	S McLeitch

East Anglian Open Championship

Year	Winner	Year	Winner
1988	P Kent	1993	A George
1989	R Mitchell	1994	R Mann
1990	N Wichelow	1995	N Brown
1991	M Mackenzie	1996	N Brown
1992	L Fickling	1997	I Poulter

Dunbartonshire and Argyll Ladies' Championship

Year	Winner	Year	Winner
1988	V McAlister	1993	M McKinlay
1989	M McKinlay	1994	V Melvin
1990	M McKinlay	1995	A Laing
1991	M McKinlay	1996	V Melvin
1992	J Moodie	1997	K Burns

East Lothian Ladies' Championship

Year	Winner	Year	Winner
1988	C Lugton	1993	S McMester
1989	C Lugton	1994	C Matthew
1990	C Lambert	1995	H Monaghan
1991	S Spiewak	1996	H Monaghan
1992	C Lambert	1997	S McMaster

Durham Amateur Championship

Year	Winner	Year	Winner
1988	J Ellwood	1993	R Walker
1989	G Bell	1994	J Kennedy
1990	R Walker	1995	A McLure
1991	C Kilgour	1996	S Ord
1992	A McLure	1997	J Dryden

East of Ireland Open Amateur Championship

Year	Winner	Year	Winner
1988	G McGimpsey	1993	R Burns
1989	D Clarke	1994	G McGimpsey
1990	D O'Sullivan	1995	D Brannigan
1991	P Hogan	1996	N Fox
1992	R Burns	1997	S Quinlivan

Eastern Division Ladies' Championship (Scotland)

Year	Winner	Year	Winner
1988	J Ford	1993	A Rose
1989	H Rose	1994	J Ford
1990	A Hendry	1995	L Nicholson
1991	C Lambert	1996	H Monaghan
1992	J Ford	1997	S Grant

East of Scotland Open Amateur Stroke Play

Year	Winner	Year	Winner
1988	C Everett	1993	S Meiklejohn
1989	K Hird	1994	A Reid
1990	G Lawrie	1995	G Davidson
1991	R Clark	1996	C Hislop
1992	ST Knowles	1997	S Meiklejohn

Essex Amateur Championship

Year	Winner	Year	Winner
1988	R Scott	1993	R Coles
1989	V Cox	1994	R Coles
1990	Null and void	1995	D Salisbury
1991	D Lee	1996	G Clark
1992	D Lee	1997	B Taylor

Essex Ladies' Championship

Year	Winner	Year	Winner
1988	W Dicks	1993	T Poulton
1989	A MacDonald	1994	T Wilson
1990	S Bennett	1995	G Scase
1991	M King	1996	G Scase
1992	F Edmond	1997	S Barber

Essex Open Championship

Year	Winner	Year	Winner
1988	H Flatman	1993	A Blackburn
1989	H Flatman	1994	D Jones
1990	G Burrows	1995	J Robson
1991	R Joyce	1996	S Khan
1992	C Platts	1997	V Cox

Essex Professional Championship

Year	Winner	Year	Winner
1988	K Ashdown	1993	T Wheals
1989	C Williams	1994	V Cox
1990	C Cox	1995	M Stokes
1991	S Cipa	1996	P Joiner
1992	P Barham	1997	M Stokes

Fife Amateur Championship

Year	Winner	Year	Winner
1988	A Mathers	1993	DA Paton
1989	D Spriddle	1994	C MacDougall
1990	D Spriddle	1995	D Paton
1991	GD McNab	1996	B Erskine
1992	N Urquhart	1997	S Meiklejohn

Fife County Ladies' Championship

Year	Winner	Year	Winner
1988	J Lawrence	1993	K Milne
1989	J Ford	1994	L Bennett
1990	J Lawrence	1995	K Milne
1991	C McDonald	1996	E Moffat
1992	A Watson	1997	J Hall

Galloway Ladies' Championship

Year	Winner	Year	Winner
1988	M Wright	1993	H Nesbit
1989	F Rennie	1994	C Meldrum
1990	F Rennie	1995	T Dodds
1991	M Wright	1996	A Cairns
1992	C Meldrum	1997	S McMurtrie

Glamorgan Amateur Championship

Year	Winner	Year	Winner
1988	I Booth	1993	M Stimson
1989	B Knight	1994	N Edwards
1990	P Bloomfield	1995	S Roberts
1991	R Maliphant	1996	N Edwards
1992	CM Rees	1997	Y Taylor

Glamorgan County Ladies' Championship

Year	Winner	Year	Winner
1988	V Thomas	1993	V Thomas
1989	V Thomas	1994	V Thomas
1990	A Perriam	1995	J Thomas
1991	V Thomas	1996	V Thomas
1992	J Foster	1997	V Thomas

Glasgow Match Play Championship

Year	Winner	Year	Winner
1988	J Finnigan	1993	M Pairman
1989	L McLaughlin	1994	C Kelly
1990	C Barrowman	1995	C Kelly
1991	C Barrowman	1996	M Loftus
1992	C Barrowman	1997	G Lamond

Glasgow Stroke Play Championship

Year	Winner	Year	Winner
1988	D Martin	1993	CE Watson
1989	G Shaw	1994	G Crawford
1990	H Kemp	1995	D Lamond
1991	C Barrowman	1996	A Forsyth
1992	G Crawford	1997	J Finnigan

Gloucestershire Amateur Championship

Year	Winner	Year	Winner
1988	J Webber	1993	G Wolstenholme
1989	R Broad	1994	G Wolstenholme
1990	D Hares	1995	T Smith
1991	J Webber	1996	G Wolstenholme
1992	G Wolstenholme	1997	M Unwin

Gloucestershire Ladies' Championship

Year	Winner	Year	Winner
1988	S Elliott	1993	C Hamilton
1989	S Elliott	1994	K Hamilton
1990	M Mayes	1995	N Sutton
1991	C Hall	1996	J Clingan
1992	C Hall	1997	C Lipscombe

Gwent Amateur Championship

(Formerly Monmouthshire Amateur Championship)

Year	Winner	Year	Winner
1988	A Williams	1993	A Harray
1989	P Glyn	1994	B Dredge
1990	M Hayward	1995	C Dinsdale
1991	E Foster	1996	M Hayward
1992	CN Evans	1997	R Price

Hampshire, Isle of Wight and Channel Islands Amateur Championship

Year	Winner	Year	Winner
1988	S Richardson	1993	M Blackey
1989	M Smith	1994	R Bland
1990	M Wiggett	1995	M Le Mesurier
1991	AD Mew	1996	M Blackey
1992	C Chevalier	1997	S Stanley

Hampshire, Isle of Wight and Channel Islands Open Championship

Year	Winner	Year	Winner
1988	K Bowden	1993	R Bland
1989	J Coles	1994	R Bland
1990	R Watkins	1995	R Bland
1991	R Adams	1996	G Hughes
1992	I Benson	1997	M Blackey

Hampshire Ladies' Championship

Year	Winner	Year	Winner
1988	C Stirling	1993	K Egford
1989	S Pickles	1994	K Egford
1990	A MacDonald	1995	H Wheeler
1991	H Wheeler	1996	C Stirling
1992	A MacDonald	1997	H Wheeler

Hampshire Professional Match Play Championship

Year	Winner	Year	Winner
1988	K Bowden	1993	K Saunders
1989	I Young	1994	M Wheeler
1990	K Bowden	1995	M Wheeler
1991	S Ward	1996	J Le Roux
1992	J Hay	1997	D Harris

Hampshire PGA Championship

Year	Winner	Year	Winner
1988	G Stubbington	1993	R Edwards
1989	J Coles	1994	G Hughes
1990	S Watson	1995	I Benson
1991	J Hay	1996	R Bland
1992	I Benson	1997	J Lovell

Herts Amateur Championship

Year	Winner	Year	Winner
1988	J Ambridge	1993	S Burnell
1989	S Hankin	1994	G Maly
1990	N Leconte	1995	H Steel
1991	M Peake	1996	S Little
1992	S Burnell	1997	C Duke

Herts Ladies' Championship

Year	Winner	Year	Winner
1988	T Jeary	1993	C Hawkes
1989	H Kaye	1994	J Oliver
1990	S Alison	1995	J Oliver
1991	A Magee	1996	K Evans
1992	S Alison	1997	K Evans

Herts Professional Championship

Year	Winner	Year	Winner
1988	N Brown	1994T	N Brown
1989	N Lawrence		D Tapping
1990	N Brown	1995	N Brown
1991	L Jones	1996	R Hurd
1992	P Cherry	1997	P Winston
1993	L Jones		

Isle of Wight Ladies' Championship

Year	Winner	Year	Winner
1988	M Butler	1993	M Ankers
1989	M Ankers	1994	J Hurd
1990	M Ankers	1995	J Hurd
1991	M Ankers	1996	M Ankers
1992	G Fahy	1997	

Kent Amateur Championship

Year	Winner	Year	Winner
1988	W Hodkin	1993	G Brown
1989	S Green	1994	B Barham
1990	R Sloman	1995	T Milford
1991	P Oliver	1996	B Barham
1992	P Sherman	1997	D Ottoway

Kent Ladies' Championship

Year	Winner	Year	Winner
1988	C Caldwell	1993	M Sutton
1989	S Sutton	1994	M Sutton
1990	H Wadsworth	1995	C Caldwell
1991	H Wadsworth	1996	K Stupples
1992	C Caldwell	1997	S Butchers

Kent Open Championship

Year	Winner	Year	Winner
1988	J Bennett	1993	N Haynes
1989	R Cameron	1994	T Berry
1990	S Barr	1995	T Milford
1991	S Wood	1996	S Green
1992	S Barr	1997	S Page

Kent Professional Championship

Year	Winner	Year	Winner
1988	R Cameron	1993	R Cameron
1989	P Lyons	1994	M Lawrence
1990	R Cameron	1995	T Poole
1991	R Cameron	1996	A Butterfield
1992	M Lawrence	1997	P Lyons

Lanarkshire Amateur Championship

Year	Winner	Year	Winner
1988	G Jones	1993	D Brown
1989	J Taylor	1994	W Bryson
1990	G Shanks	1995	K Nisbet
1991	D Blair	1996	K Ralston
1992	W Bryson	1997	W Bryson

Lanarkshire Ladies' County Championship

Year	Winner	Year	Winner
1988	F McKay (*née* Needham)	1993	M Hughes
1989	K Dallas	1994	J Gardner
1990	A Hendry	1995	R Rankin
1991	A Hendry	1996	A Prentice
1992	F McKay	1997	L Lloyd

Lancashire Amateur Championship

Year	Winner	Year	Winner
1988	M Kingsley	1993	G Helsby
1989	R Bardsley	1994	K Wallbank
1990	T Foster	1995	G Boardman
1991	GS Lacy	1996	G Boardman
1992	R Hutt	1997	D Johnson

Lancashire Ladies' Championship

Year	Winner	Year	Winner
1988	L Fairclough	1993	K Rostron
1989	C Blackshaw	1994	G Nutter
1990	L Fairclough	1995	G Nutter
1991	A Baines	1996	A Murray
1992	J Collingham	1997	G Nutter

Lancashire Open Championship

Year	Winner	Year	Winner
1988	P Wesselingh	1993	L Edwards
1989	M Jones	1994	A Lancaster
1990	P Allan	1995	G Furey
1991	G Furey	1996	G Furey
1992	S Townend	1997	G Furey

Leicestershire and Rutland Amateur Championship

Year	Winner	Year	Winner
1988	A Martinez	1993	P Frith
1989	J Cayless	1994	I Lyner
1990	D Gibson	1995	P Frith
1991	D Gibson	1996	J Herbert
1992	D Gibson	1997	J Herbert

Leicestershire and Rutland Ladies' Championship

Year	Winner	Year	Winner
1988	A Walters	1993	M Page
1989	M Page	1994	M Page
1990	R Reed	1995	C Gay
1991	A Jenno	1996	H Lowe
1992	H Summ	1997	J Morris

Leicestershire and Rutland Open Championship

Year	Winner	Year	Winner
1988	D Gibson	1993	P Frith
1989	R Adams	1994	J Herbert
1990	R Larratt	1995	I Lyner
1991	CM Harries	1996	D Gibson
1992	*Not played*	1997	N Bland

Lincolnshire Amateur Championship

Year	Winner	Year	Winner
1988	P Streeter	1993	J Crampton
1989	J Payne	1994	J Crampton
1990	P Streeter	1995	J Crampton
1991	J Payne	1996	P Streeter
1992	P Streeter	1997	P Streeter

Lincolnshire Ladies' Championship

Year	Winner	Year	Winner
1988	H Dobson	1993	R Broughton
1989	H Dobson	1994	S Brook
1990	A Johns	1995	A Thompson
1991	A Thompson	1996	M Willerton
1992	R Jones	1997	A Thompson

Lincolnshire Open Championship

Year	Winner	Year	Winner
1988	J Heib	1993	S Bennett
1989	A Hare	1994	S Brewer
1990	A Butler (Am)	1995	S Cox
1991	J Payne (Am)	1996	S Bennett
1992	P Streeter (Am)	1997	M Ling

Lothians Amateur Championship

Year	Winner	Year	Winner
1988	B Shields	1993	S Smith
1989	K Hastings	1994	S Smith
1990	S Middleton	1995	S Smith
1991	C MacPhail	1996	N Shillinglaw
1992	C MacPhail	1997	K Nicholson

Manx Amateur Championship

Year	Winner	Year	Winner
1988	G Kelly	1993	G Wilson
1989	G Ashe	1994	R Sayle
1990	M Pugh	1995	G Wilson
1991	GK Gelling	1996	G Wilson
1992	G Wilson	1997	P McMullan

Middlesex Amateur Championship

Year	Winner	Year	Winner
1988	A Rogers	1993	GA Homewood
1989	R Willison	1994	W Bennett
1990	A Rogers	1995	G Clark
1991	J O'Shea	1996	S Kay
1992	WJ Bennett	1997	C Austin

Middlesex Ladies' Championship

Year	Winner	Year	Winner
1988	S Keogh	1993	L Housman
1989	S Keogh	1994	M Henderson
1990	S Keogh	1995	J Sadler
1991	J Dannhauser	1996	P Ramchand
1992	J Sadler	1997	J Barnett

Middlesex Open Championship

Year	Winner	Year	Winner
1988	L Fickling	1993	GA Homewood
1989	L Fickling	1994	N Wichelow
1990	R Willison (Am)	1995	N Wichelow
1991	R Willison (Am)	1996	C Austin (Am)
1992	GA Homewood	1997	L Fickling

Midland Close Championship

Year	Winner	Year	Winner
1988	A Hare	1993	M Roberts
1989	J Cook	1994	M Foster
1990	J Bickerton	1995	C Banks
1991	P Streeter	1996	I Lyner
1992	I Richardson	1997	M Keeling

Midland Open Amateur Championship

Year	Winner	Year	Winner
1988	R Winchester	1993	N Williamson
1989	J Cook	1994	D Howell
1990	J Bickerton	1995	G Harris
1991	P Sefton	1996	M Carver
1992	M McGuire	1997	P Streeter

Midland Masters

Year	Winner	Year	Winner
1988	B Waites	1993	*Not played*
1989	C Haycock	1994	C Hall
1990	J King	1995	J Higgins
1991	S Rose	1996	*Not played*
1992	C Hall	1997	*Not played*

Midland Ladies' Championship

Year	Winner	Year	Winner
1988	S Roberts	1993	R Bolas
1989	R Bolas	1994	J Morris
1990	J Hockley	1995	K Edwards
1991	R Millington	1996	S Gallagher
1992	R Bolas	1997	R Bailey

Midland Professional Match Play Championship

Year	Winner	Year	Winner
1988	J Higgins	1993	C Clark
1989	K Hayward	1994	N Turley
1990	G Farr	1995	D Eddiford
1991	B Waites	1996	S Bennett
1992	J Higgins	1997	J Higgins

Midland Professional Stroke Play Championship

Year	Winner	Year	Winner
1988	G Farr	1993	P Baker
1989	J Higgins	1994	P Baker
1990	G Stafford	1995	S Rose
1991	K Dickens	1996	DJ Russell
1992	J Higgins	1997	J Higgins

Midland Boys' Amateur Championship

Year	Winner	Year	Winner
1988	AJ Salt	1994	R Duck
1989	M Wilson	1995	C Richardson
1990	ML Welch	1996T	S Walker
1991	S Drummond		K Cliffe
1992	S Drummond	1997	K Hale
1993	S Webster		

Midland Senior Championship

Year	Winner	Year	Winner
1988	TE Kelsall	1994	G Pope
1989	RG Hiatt	1995	T Squires
1990	A Harrison	1996	JC Thomas
1991	DS Kirkland	1997T	EW Hammond
1992	A Guest		C Moir
1993	J Humphries		MA Smith

Midlothian Ladies' Championship

Year	Winner	Year	Winner
1988	M Stavert	1993	E Bruce
1989	E Bruce	1994	E Bruce
1990	E Jack	1995	P Silver
1991	E Bruce	1996	M Quigley
1992	K Marshall	1997	P Silver

Mid-Wales Ladies' Championship

Year	Winner	Year	Winner
1988	S James	1993	A Owen
1989	S Wilson	1994	G Gibb
1990	P Morgan	1995	J James
1991	T Gittens	1996	L Davies
1992	P Morgan	1997	K Humphries

Monmouthshire Ladies' Championship

Year	Winner	Year	Winner
1988	H Armstrong	1993	S Musto
1989	B Chambers	1994	E Pilgrim
1990	W Wood	1995	E Pilgrim
1991	W Wood	1996	C Waite
1992	R Morgan	1997	S O'Sullivan

Norfolk Amateur Championship

Year	Winner	Year	Winner
1988	N Williamson	1993	DA Edwards
1989	N Williamson	1994	J Durrant
1990	P Little	1995	I Ellis
1991	CJ Lamb	1996	P Little
1992	A Marshall	1997	G Price

Norfolk Ladies' Championship

Year	Winner	Year	Winner
1988	L Elliott	1993	T Williamson
1989	T Keeley	1994	J Wilkerson
1990	T Ireland	1995	J Wilkerson
1991	T Williamson	1996	C Grady
1992	T Williamson	1997	T Williamson

Norfolk Open Championship

Year	Winner	Year	Winner
1988	M Few	1993	A Collison
1989	M Few	1994	J Hill
1990	A Brydon	1995	M Barrett
1991	I Hardy	1996	M Barrett
1992	C Green	1997	N Lythgoe

Norfolk Professional Championship

Year	Winner	Year	Winner
1988	M Few	1993	A Collison
1989	M Few	1994	A Collison
1990	M Few	1995	P Briggs
1991	A Collison	1996	P Bower
1992	A Collison	1997	T Varney

Northamptonshire Amateur Championship

Year	Winner	Year	Winner
1988	D Ellson	1993	S McIlwain
1989	N Goodman	1994	A Print
1990	A Print	1995	A Lord
1991	S McDonald	1996	I Dallas
1992	AJ Wilson	1997	P Langrish-Smith

Northamptonshire Ladies' Championship

Year	Winner	Year	Winner
1988	A Duck	1993	S Sharpe
1989	C Gibbs	1994	S Sharpe
1990	C Gibbs	1995	S Sharpe
1991	C Gibbs	1996	S Carter
1992	G Gibbs	1997	S Carter

Northern Region PGA Championship

Year	Winner	Year	Winner
1988	K Waters	1993	C Smiley
1989	S Bottomley	1994	P Wesselingh
1990	J Morgan	1995	G Furey
1991	H Selby-Green	1996	S Townend
1992	P Cowen	1997	G Furey

Northern Counties (Scotland) Ladies' Championship

Year	Winner	Year	Winner
1988	I McIntosh	1993	S Alexander
1989	E Fiskin	1994	L Roxburgh
1990	F McKay	1995	F McKay
1991	M Vass	1996	F McLennan
1992	I Shannon	1997	E Vass

North of Ireland Open Amateur Championship

Year	Winner	Year	Winner
1988	N Anderson	1993	G McGimpsey
1989	N Anderson	1994	N Ludwell
1990	D Clarke	1995	F Nolan
1991	G McGimpsey	1996	M McGinley
1992	G McGimpsey	1997	M Sinclair

Northern Open Championship

Year	Winner	Year	Winner
1988	D Huish	1993	K Stables
1989	C Brooks	1994	K Stables
1990	C Brooks	1995	J Higgins
1991	C Cassells	1996	S Henderson
1992	P Smith	1997	D Thomson

Northern Ladies' Championship

Year	Winner	Year	Winner
1988	K Tebbet	1993	A Brighouse
1989	L Fletcher	1994	G Nutter
1990	L Fairclough	1995	K Rostron
1991	C White	1996	K Rostron
1992	G Simpson	1997	G Nutter

Northumberland Amateur Championship

Year	Winner	Year	Winner
1988	J Metcalfe	1993	P Taylor
1989	J Metcalfe	1994	S Twynholm
1990	K Fairbairn	1995	M Hall
1991	K Fairbairn	1996	K Cademy-Taylor
1992	S Philipson	1997	D Clark

Northumberland Ladies' Championship

Year	Winner	Year	Winner
1988	D Glenn	1993	H Wilson
1989	D Glenn	1994	D Glenn
1990	L Fletcher	1995	H Wilson
1991	C Hall	1996	C Hall
1992	C Hall	1997	C Hall

Northern Division Ladies' Championship (Scotland)

Year	Winner	Year	Winner
1988	K Imrie	1993	S Alexander
1989	S Wood	1994	J Matthews
1990	K Imrie	1995	J Harrison
1991	C Middleton	1996	J Harrison
1992	S Alexander	1997	C Hunter

North of Scotland Open Amateur Stroke Play Championship

Year	Winner	Year	Winner
1988	K Hird	1993	D Downie
1989	G Hickman	1994	E Forbes
1990	S McIntosh	1995	R Beames
1991	S Henderson	1996	S McIntosh
1992	K Buchan	1997	

Nottinghamshire Amateur Championship

Year	Winner	Year	Winner
1988	C Banks	1993	L Westwood
1989	P Shaw	1994	D Lucas
1990	L White	1995	H Hopkinson
1991	L White	1996	D McJannet
1992	L Westwood	1997	O Wilson

Nottinghamshire Ladies' Championship

Year	Winner	Year	Winner
1988	A Ferguson	1993	L Rayner
1989	A Peters	1994	G Palmer
1990	L Broughton	1995	G Palmer
1991	L Broughton	1996	L Wright
1992	S Bishop	1997	J Collingham

Nottinghamshire Open Championship

Year	Winner	Year	Winner
1988	C Banks (Am)	1993	J King
1989	P Hinton	1994	J King
1990	C Hall	1995	J King
1991	C Jepson	1996	D McJannet
1992	J King	1997	R Ellis

Oxfordshire Ladies' Championship

Year	Winner	Year	Winner
1988	T Craik	1993	N Sparks
1989	L King	1994	L King
1990	N Sparks	1995	L King
1991	L King	1996	L King
1992	L King	1997	L King

Perth and Kinross Amateur Stroke Play Championship

Year	Winner	Year	Winner
1988	E Lindsay	1993	T McLevy
1989	A Campbell	1994	E Lindsay
1990	G Smith	1995	S Herd
1991	D Robertson	1996	M Rose
1992	B Grieve	1997	N Macdonald

Perth and Kinross Ladies' Championship

Year	Winner	Year	Winner
1988	V Pringle	1993	E Wilson
1989	A Sharp	1994	C Dunbar
1990	S Mailer	1995	F Farquharson
1991	I Shannon	1996	E Wilson
1992	S Mailer	1997	N Harding

Renfrewshire Amateur Championship

Year	Winner	Year	Winner
1988	E Grey	1993	R Clark
1989	R Clark	1994	M Carmichael
1990	R Clark	1995	R Adam
1991	R Clark	1996	S Nicol
1992	G Urquhart	1997	D Owens

Renfrewshire County Ladies' Championship

Year	Winner	Year	Winner
1988	S Lawson	1993	K Fitzgerald
1989	D Jackson	1994	C Agnew
1990	D Jackson	1995	D Jackson
1991	D Jackson	1996	D Jackson
1992	D Jackson	1997	L Robertson

Scottish Area Team Championship

Year	Winner	Year	Winner
1988	Lothians	1993	Lothians
1989	Lanarkshire	1994	Lothians
1990	North East	1995	North
1991	Glasgow	1996	Renfrewshire
1992	North East	1997	Lothians

Scottish Champion of Champions

Year	Winner	Year	Winner
1970	A Horne	1984	S Stephen
1971	D Black	1985	I Brotherston
1972	R Strachan	1986	I Hutcheon
1973	*Not held*	1987	G Shaw
1974	M Niven	1988	I Hutcheon
1975	A Brodie	1989	J Milligan
1976	A Brodie	1990	J Milligan
1977	V Reid	1991	G Hay
1978	D Greig	1992	D Robertson
1979	B Marchbank	1993	R Russell
1980	I Hutcheon	1994	G Sherry
1981	I Hutcheon	1995	S Gallacher
1982	G Macgregor	1996	M Brooks
1983	D Carrick	1997	G Rankin

Scottish Foursomes Tournament – *Glasgow Evening Times* Trophy

Year	Winner	Year	Winner
1988	Irvine Ravenspark	1993	Baberton
1989	Cochrane Leith	1994	Standard Life
1990	Dunblane New	1995	Ratho Park
1991	Irvine Ravenspark	1996	Cardross
1992	Cochrane Castle	1997	Cardross

Scottish Ladies' County Championship

Year	Winner	Year	Winner
1988	Lanarkshire	1993	Gullane
1989	Lanarkshire	1994	East Lothian
1990	East Lothian	1995	Fife
1991	East Lothian	1996	East Lothian
1992	Dunbartonshire & Argyll	1997	Dunbartonshire & Argyll

Scottish Ladies' Foursomes

Year	Winner	Year	Winner
1988	Gullane	1993	North Berwick
1989	Gullane	1994	Turnberry
1990	Gullane	1995	Gullane
1991	West of Scotland Girls' Golf Assoc.	1996	Hilton Park
1992	Haggs Castle	1997	Stirling

Shropshire and Herefordshire Amateur Championship

Year	Winner	Year	Winner
1988	S Thomas	1993	M Welch
1989	M Welch	1994	M Welch
1990	M Welch	1995	D Park
1991	M Welch	1996	D Harris
1992	M Welch	1997	K Preece

Shropshire Ladies' Championship

Year	Winner	Year	Winner
1988	A Jackson	1993	A Johnson
1989	C Gauge	1994	A Johnson
1990	J Marvell	1995	B Smith
1991	A Johnson	1996	B Smith
1992	A Johnson	1997	S Heath

Somerset Amateur Championship

Year	Winner	Year	Winner
1988	C Edwards	1993	C Edwards
1989	C Edwards	1994	C Edwards
1990	C Edwards	1995	B Whittock
1991	C Edwards	1996	D Dixon
1992	C Edwards	1997	R Swords

Somerset Ladies' Championship

Year	Winner	Year	Winner
1988	C Whiting	1993	R Murr
1989	K Nicholls	1994	S Burnell
1990	K Nicholls	1995	L Wixon
1991	S Whiting	1996	L Wixon
1992	C Whiting	1997	L Wixon

South-Eastern Ladies' Championship

Year	Winner	Year	Winner
1988	C Stirling	1993	K Smith
1989	A MacDonald	1994	K Egford
1990	A MacDonald	1995	K Smith
1991	K Egford	1996	J Oliver
1992	A MacDonald	1997	L Evans

South Professional Championship

Year	Winner	Year	Winner
1988	P Harrison	1993	G Smith
1989	W Grant	1994	R Edwards
1990	Not played	1995	P Sefton
1991	J Hoskison	1996	P Hughes
1992	J Hoskison	1997	P Sherman

Southern Assistants Championship

Year	Winner	Year	Winner
1988	J Sewell	1993	R Edwards
1989	J Sewell	1994	M Wheeler
1990	Not played	1995	P Lyons
1991	G Orr	1996	D Parris
1992	G Orr	1997	A Lovelace

Southern Assistants Match Play Championship

Year	Winner	Year	Winner
1988	Not played	1993	N Gorman
1989	Not played	1994	M Groombridge
1990	G Orr	1995	M Groombridge
1991	I Roper	1996	A Butterfield
1992	G McQuitty	1997	B Hodkin

South of Ireland Open Amateur Championship

Year	Winner	Year	Winner
1988	MA Gannon	1993	P Sheehan
1989	S Keenan	1994	D Higgins
1990	D Clarke	1995	J Fanagan
1991	P McGinley	1996	A Morrow
1992	L MacNamara	1997	P Collier

South of Scotland Championship

Year	Winner	Year	Winner
1988	A Coltart	1993	D Wallis
1989	V Reid	1994	I Reid
1990	B Kerr	1995	B Scott
1991	J Power	1996	E Little
1992	J Wright	1997	I Brotherston

Southern Division Ladies' Championship (Scotland)

Year	Winner	Year	Winner
1988	S Simpson	1993	C Meldrum
1989	F Rennie	1994	D Douglas
1990	F Rennie	1995	J Anderson
1991	J Anderson	1996	D Douglas
1992	D Douglas	1997	J Anderson

South of Scotland Ladies' Championship

Year	Winner	Year	Winner
1988	M Wright	1993	D Douglas
1989	M Wright	1994	F Rennie
1990	M Wright	1995	C Meldrum
1991	F Rennie	1996	S McMurtrie
1992	M Wilson	1997	J Anderson

South-Western Ladies' Championship

Year	Winner	Year	Winner
1988	V Thomas	1993	E Fields
1989	C Hall	1994	R Morgan
1990	V Thomas	1995	E Fields
1991	V Thomas	1996	B Morgan
1992	C Hall	1997	E Pilgrim

South-Western Counties Amateur Championship

Year	Winner	Year	Winner
1988	J Langmead	1993	B Sandry
1989	K Jones	1994	A Lawrence
1990	S Amor	1995	S McCarthy
1991	P McMullen	1996	D Marsh
1992	S Edgley	1997	S McCarthy

Staffordshire Amateur Championship

Year	Winner	Year	Winner
1988	P Sweetsur	1993	C Poxon
1989	C Poxon	1994	R Mayfield
1990	P Sweetsur	1995	T Ryder
1991	M McGuire	1996	R Parkes
1992	M McGuire	1997	SD Wakefield

Staffordshire Ladies' Championship

Year	Winner	Year	Winner
1988	D Boyd	1993	R Bolas
1989	R Bolas	1994	S Gallagher
1990	R Bolas	1995	K Edwards
1991	R Bolas	1996	S Gallagher
1992	P Hale	1997	K Edwards

Staffordshire Open Championship

Year	Winner	Year	Winner
1988	J Rhodes	1993	M McGuire
1989	M Passmore	1994	D Scott
1990	J Rhodes	1995	I Proverbs
1991	M McGuire	1996	B Rimmer
1992	J Rhodes	1997	A Roger

Staffordshire and Shropshire Stroke Play Championship

Year	Winner	Year	Winner
1988	J Annable	1993	J Rhodes
1989	J Higgins	1994	J Rhodes
1990	G Farr	1995	B Stevens
1991	M Knight	1996	J Higgins
1992	S Russell	1997	R Fisher

Stirlingshire Amateur Championship

Year	Winner	Year	Winner
1988	H Anderson	1993	D Smith
1989	S Russell	1994	K McArthur
1990	K Goodwin	1995	K Brunton
1991	K Goodwin	1996	G McDonald
1992	H Anderson	1997	

Stirling and Clackmannan County Ladies' Championship

Year	Winner	Year	Winner
1988	J Harrison	1993	H Stirling
1989	J Abernethy	1994	H Stirling
1990	A Rose	1995	S Grant
1991	A Rose	1996	H Hume
1992	A Rose	1997	S Grant

Suffolk Amateur Championship

Year	Winner	Year	Winner
1988	J Whitby	1993	J Maddock
1989	M Turner	1994	J Maddock
1990	J Booth	1995	D Quinney
1991	N Meadows	1996	J Keely
1992	P Buckle	1997	J Maddock

Suffolk Ladies' Championship

Year	Winner	Year	Winner
1988	S Dawson	1993	J Hall
1989	J Hall	1994	J Hockley
1990	J Hall	1995	J Hall
1991	J Hall	1996	J Hockley
1992	J Hall	1997	L Wright

Suffolk Open Championship

Year	Winner	Year	Winner
1988	J Maddock	1993	R Mann
1989	M Elsworthy	1994	L Patterson
1990	S Crosby (Am)	1995	R Mann
1991	R Mann	1996	S McPherson
1992	R Mann	1997	P Wilby

Suffolk Professional Championship

Year	Winner	Year	Winner
1988	S Whymark	1994	L Patterson
1989	S Whymark	1995	R Mann
1990	R Mann	1996	T Cooper
1991	K Golding	1997T	A Lucas
1992	R Mann		C Jenkins
1993	K Golding		

Surrey Amateur Championship

Year	Winner	Year	Winner
1988	A Carter	1993	A Raitt
1989	T Lloyd	1994	M Ellis
1990	J Good	1995	A Wall
1991	A Tillman	1996	M Palmer
1992	A Wall	1997	T Paterson

Surrey Ladies' Championship

Year	Winner	Year	Winner
1988	C Bailey	1993	S Lambert
1989	J Thornhill	1994	S Lambert
1990	W Wooldridge	1995	J Thornhill
1991	J Thornhill	1996	L McGowan
1992	J Thornhill	1997	J Thornhill

Sussex Amateur Championship

Year	Winner	Year	Winner
1988	D Alderson	1993	M Galway
1989	P Hurring	1994	P Clevely
1990	D Arnold	1995	M Allen
1991	R Lowles	1996	M Harris
1992	M Galway	1997	M Harris

Sussex Ladies' Championship

Year	Winner	Year	Winner
1988	M Cornelius	1993	C Titcomb
1989	M Cornelius	1994	J Head
1990	M Cornelius	1995	Z Steel
1991	K Mitchell	1996	C Court
1992	J Head	1997	C Court

Sussex Open Championship

Year	Winner	Year	Winner
1988	S Rolley	1993	N Burke
1989	M Groombridge (Am)	1994	K Hinton
		1995	J Blamires
1990	Not played	1996	K Macdonald
1991	J Pinsent	1997	K Macdonald
1992	P Harrison		

Ulster Professional Championship

Year	Winner	Year	Winner
1988	J Heggarty	1993	D Jones
1989	D Feherty	1994	P Russell
1990	J Heggarty	1995	R Burns
1991	D Carson	1996	J Heggarty
1992	D Clarke	1997	D Mooney

Warwickshire Ladies' Championship

Year	Winner	Year	Winner
1988	S Morgan	1993	S Morgan
1989	S Morgan	1994	S Westhall
1990	S Morgan	1995	S Westhall
1991	S Morgan	1996	C Dowling
1992	N Moutt	1997	C Dowling

Warwickshire Amateur Championship

Year	Winner	Year	Winner
1988	A Allen	1993	G Marston
1989	J Cook	1994	N Connolly
1990	J Cook	1995	S Webster
1991	A Allen	1996	A Carey
1992	G Lord	1997	T Whitehouse

Warwickshire Professional Stroke Play Championship

Year	Winner	Year	Winner
1988	C Wicketts	1993	G Marston
1989	T Rouse	1994	S Webster (Am)
1990	N McEwan	1995	J Cook
1991	M Jennings	1996	S Edwards
1992	A Allen	1997	C Phillips

Warwickshire Open Championship

Year	Winner	Year	Winner
1988	A Allen (Am)	1993	A Bownes
1989	A Allen (Am)	1994	D White
1990	M Biddle (Am)	1995	C Dowling
1991	A Allen (Am)	1996	P Chalkley
1992	P Chalkley	1997	D Barton

Warwickshire Professional Matchplay Championship

Year	Winner	Year	Winner
1988	C Wicketts	1993	A Bands
1989	T Rouse	1994	C Wicketts
1990	N McEwan	1995	J Cook
1991	D Quinn	1996	C Phillips
1992	C Harrison	1997	L Bashford

Welsh Team Championship

Year	Winner	Year	Winner
1988	Ashburnham	1993	Morriston
1989	Cardiff	1994	Monmouthshire
1990	Whitchurch	1995	Ashburnham
1991	Wrexham	1996	Pyle & Kenfig
1992	Llanwern	1997	Wrexham

Welsh Ladies' Team Championship

Year	Winner	Year	Winner
1988	Pennard	1992	Whitchurch
1989	Llandudno (Maesdu)	1993	Pennard
		1994	St Pierre
1990	Llandudno (Maesdu)	1995	R. St Davids
		1996	R. St Davids
1991	Wenvoe Castle	1997	St Pierre

West of Ireland Open Amateur Championship

Year	Winner	Year	Winner
1988	G McGimpsey	1993	G McGimpsey
1989	P McInerney	1994	P Harrington
1990	N Goulding	1995	E Brady
1991	N Goulding	1996	G McGimpsey
1992	K Kearney	1997	J Flanagan

West of Scotland Close Amateur Championship

Year	Winner	Year	Winner
1988	G King	1993	R Weir
1989	G Lawrie	1994	A Forsyth
1990	B Smith	1995	D Howard
1991	W Bryson	1996	A Forsyth
1992	D Robertson	1997	*Not played*

West of Scotland Open Amateur Championship

Year	Winner	Year	Winner
1988	S Savage	1993	B Howard
1989	A Elliot	1994	J Hodgson
1990	S Knowles	1995	G Rankin
1991	A Coltart	1996	C Hislop
1992	S Henderson	1997	C Hislop

Western Division Ladies' Championship (Scotland)

Year	Winner	Year	Winner
1988	S Lawson	1993	J Moodie
1989	K Dallas	1994	V Melvin
1990	S Spiewak	1995	A Hendry
1991	J Moodie	1996	K Fitzgerald
1992	M McKinlay	1997	C Malcolm

West Region PGA Championship

(Previously West of England Professional Championship)

Year	Winner	Year	Winner
1988	M Thomas	1993	P Mayo
1989	G Laing	1994	S Little
1990	P Price	1995	M Thompson
1991	S Dodd	1996	M McEwan
1992	M Thomas	1997	M Thompson

Wigtownshire Championship

Year	Winner	Year	Winner
1988	K Hardie	1993	K Hardie
1989	D Taylor	1994	K Hardie
1990	R Burns	1995	R O'Keefe
1991	G Sharp	1996	E Little
1992	R O'Keefe	1997	R Shaw

Wiltshire Amateur Championship

Year	Winner	Year	Winner
1988	G Clough	1993	RE Searle
1989	A Burch	1994	R Searle
1990	N Williams	1995	N Mumford
1991	R White	1996	A Mutch
1992	D Howell	1997	P Bicknell

Wiltshire Ladies' Championship

Year	Winner	Year	Winner
1988	S Sutton	1993	V Hanks
1989	J Lawrence	1994	S Sutton
1990	M Johnston	1995	J Lamb
1991	S Sutton	1996	J Lamb
1992	S Sutton	1997	J Lamb

Wiltshire Professional Championship

(Now known as the 'Hills' Wiltshire Pro Champ)

Year	Winner	Year	Winner
1988	R Emery	1993T	G Emerson
1989	G Emerson		D Ray
1990	G Clough	1994	S Robertson
1991	A Beal	1995	G Laing
1992	G Emerson	1996	B Sandry
		1997	M Smith

Worcestershire Amateur Championship

Year	Winner	Year	Winner
1988	D Prosser	1993	M Reynard
1989	S Braithwaite	1994	R Sadler
1990	D Eddiford	1995	M Reynard
1991	J Bickerton	1996	M Reynard
1992	M Reynard	1997	S Braithwaite

Worcestershire Ladies' Championship

Year	Winner	Year	Winner
1988	J Blaymire	1993	L Jones
1989	L Waring	1994	N Lawrenson
1990	J Deeley	1995	S Tufnall
1991	L Jones	1996	N Lawrenson
1992	L Montgomery	1997	N Lawrenson

Worcestershire Open Championship

Year	Winner	Year	Winner
1988	D Eddiford	1993	P Scarrett
1989	K Hayward	1994	S Edwards
1990	J Bickerton	1995	C Clark
1991	MC Reynard	1996	D Clee
1992	A Robinson	1997	P Scarrett

Worcestershire Professional Stroke Play Championship

Year	Winner	Year	Winner
1988	C Haycock	1993	F Clark
1989	K Hayward	1994	C Clark
1990	K Hayward	1995	I Clark
1991	L Bashford	1996	F Clark
1992	R Cameron	1997	I Clark

Yorkshire Amateur Championship

Year	Winner	Year	Winner
1988	S Field	1993	J Healey
1989	G Harland	1994	P Wood
1990	P Wood	1995	J Ellis
1991	ML Pullan	1996	R Jones
1992	ID Pyman	1997	R Jones

Yorkshire Amateur Stroke Play Championship

Year	Winner	Year	Winner
1988	C Rawson	1994	N Ludwell
1989	S East	1995T	N Gibson
1990	L Walker		J Hepworth
1991	D Delaney	1996	N Emmerson
1992	J Docker	1997	A Wright
1993	J Roberts		

Yorkshire Ladies' Championship

Year	Winner	Year	Winner
1988	J Furby	1993	N Buxton
1989	K Firth	1994	N Buxton
1990	N Buxton	1995	R Hudson
1991	N Buxton	1996	J Aldersley
1992	N Buxton	1997	R Hudson

Yorkshire Professional Championship

Year	Winner	Year	Winner
1988	M Higginbottom	1993	A Nicholson
1989	D Stirling	1994	L Turner
1990	D Stirling	1995	R Golding
1991	S Elliott	1996	N Ludwell
1992	L Turner	1997	S Robinson

PART IV

Who's Who in Golf

Compiled by Alan Elliott

British Isles Players

Abbreviations used

Cls Club membership
Maj The Open, US Open, USPGA, US Masters (men) Ladies British Open, US Women's Open, USLPGA (ladies)
Chp Amateur Championship or Ladies British Open Amateur (or, within text, any championship)
Nat The player's national championship
Trn Tournament(s)
Oth Other national championship or tournament
Reg Regional tournaments
Int International team appearances
Eur European Tour or general European tournament(s)
US Tournament(s) in United States or Canada
RoW Tournament(s) in the rest of the world
Sen Senior
Jun Junior
Mis Miscellaneous information
r/u runner up
s/f semi-finalist
tied A lost play-off after first place tie
Eur(L) T Ch European (Ladies) Amateur Team Championship

Captaincy is indicated by the year printed in bold type; years in bold type within brackets indicate non-playing captain.

Aitken, Wilma *See* **Leburn**

Alliss, Peter
Born Berlin on 28th February, 1931. Turned Professional 1946
PROFESSIONAL
Eur Spanish Open 1956-58. Italian Open, Portuguese Open 1958.
Trn Daks 1954; Dunlop 1955; PGA Close 1957; Dunlop 1959; Sprite 1960 (shared). PGA Close 1962; Daks 1963 (shared); Swallow-Penfold, Esso Golden 1964; PGA Close, Jeyes 1965; Martini (shared), Rediffusion 1966; Agfa-Gevaert 1967; Piccadilly 1969; Sunningdale Foursomes 1958-61; Wentworth Pro-Am Foursomes 1959
Oth British Assistants 1952
RoW Brazilian Open 1961
Reg West of England Open Professional 1956-58-62-66
Int Ryder Cup 1953-57-59-61-63-65-67-69; UKvEurope 1954-55-56; England in World Cup

1954-55-57-58-59-61-62-64-66-67; Home International **1967**
Mis Vardon Trophy 1964-66; PGA Captain 1962-87; Author, TV commentator. Golf course architect.
AMATEUR
Jun Int England Boys 1946

Anderson, Fiona
Born Perth on 24th August, 1954
Cls Blairgowrie
Nat Scottish Ladies Amateur 1987. r/u 1980-83-88
Reg North of Scotland Ladies 1977. Scottish Universities Champion 1975
Int Vagliano Trophy 1987. Scotland (Home Int) 1977-79-80-81-83-84-86-87-88-89-90-91-92; Eur(L) T Ch 1979-83-87-91

Anderson, Jessie *See* **Valentine**

Anstey, Veronica *See* **Beharrell**

Attenborough, Michael F

Born Britford, nr Salisbury in October, 1939

Cls	Chislehurst, Royal St George's, Royal & Ancient
Oth	Scandinavian Amateur 1965
Trn	Hampshire Hog 1960. President's Putter 1962-66. County Champion of Champions 1964. Duncan Putter 1966. Prince of Wales Challenge Cup 1969
Reg	Kent Amateur 1963-64-65
Int	Walker Cup 1967. GBvEurope 1966-68. England (Home Int) 1964-66-67-68; Eur T Ch 1967
Mis	Captain of Royal & Ancient 1989/90

Bailey, Diane, MBE [Frearson], (*née* Robb)

Born Wolverhampton on 31st August, 1943

Cls	Enville (Hon), Reigate Heath, Betchworth Park
Chp	British Ladies Amateur r/u 1961
Trn	Worplesdon Mixed Foursomes 1971. Avia Foursomes 1972
Reg	Staffordshire Ladies 1961. Lincolnshire Ladies 1966-67. Midland Ladies 1966
Int	Curtis Cup 1962-72-(**84**)-(**86**)-(**88**). Vagliano Trophy 1961-(**83**)-(**85**). Espirito Santo 1968. England (Home Int) 1961-62-71. Commonwealth Team Ch (**1983**).
Mis	Surrey Ladies County Captain 1981-2
Jun	British Girls 1961. Scottish Girls Open Stroke Play 1959-61
Int	England Girls 1957-61

Baker, Peter

Born Shifnal on 7th October, 1967. Turned Professional 1986

PROFESSIONAL

Eur	Benson & Hedges International 1988; Dunhill British Masters, Scandinavian Masters 1993
Oth	UAP U25 European Open 1990; Midland Professional Chp 1993-94; Tournoi Perrier de Paris 1994
Int	Ryder Cup 1993; England in Dunhill Cup 1993 (r/u)
Mis	Rookie of the Year 1987

AMATEUR

Nat	English Open Amateur Stroke Play 1985 (shared)
Reg	Shropshire & Herefordshire Amateur 1983-84-85
Trn	Tillman Trophy 1985
Int	Walker Cup 1985; GBIvEurope 1986; England (Home Int) 1985
Jun	Carris Trophy 1983-85

Bannerman, Harry

Born Aberdeen on 5th March, 1942. Turned Professional 1965

PROFESSIONAL

Oth	Scottish Professional 1967-72. Northern Scottish Open 1967-69-72. East of Scotland PGA Match Play 1969. Scottish Coca Cola 1976
Int	Ryder Cup 1971. Scotland in World Cup 1967-72; in Double Diamond 1972-74
Mis	Frank Moran Trophy 1972

AMATEUR

Reg	North of Scotland Stroke Play 1962; North-East Scotland Stroke Play 1963-64-65
Jun Int	Scottish Boys 1959

Barber, Sally (*née* Bonallack)

Born Chigwell, Essex on 9th April, 1938. Turned Professional 1979. Reinstated Amateur 1982

AMATEUR

Cls	Thorpe Hall, Thorndon Park, Hunstanton (Hon), Killarney (Hon)
Nat	English Ladies Amateur 1968; r/u 1970-71
Oth	German Ladies 1958
Trn	Astor Salver 1972; Avia Foursomes 1976
Reg	Essex Ladies 1958-59-60-61-62-63-66-67-70-71; London Foursomes 1984
Int	Curtis Cup 1962; Vagliano Trophy 1961-69; England (Home Int) 1960-61-62-63-68-70-72-77-(**78**) Eur(L) T Ch 1969-71. CW (**1995**)

Barnes, Brian

Born Addington, Surrey on 3rd June, 1945. Turned Professional 1964

PROFESSIONAL

Eur	Agfacolor 1969; Martini International 1972; Dutch Open 1974; French Open 1975; Sun Alliance PGA Match Play 1976; Spanish Open, Greater Manchester Open 1978; Italian Open, Portuguese Open 1979; Tournament Players Chp 1981
Oth	Scottish Professional 1981-82; Coca Cola Young Professionals 1969; East of Scotland Professional 1975; Northern Scottish Open 1978; PGA Club Professional Chp 1989
RoW	Flame Lily (Rhodesia) 1967; Australian Masters 1970; Zambian Open 1979-81; Kenya Open 1981
Sen	Senior British Open 1995-96
Int	Ryder Cup 1969-71-73-75-77-79; Hennessy–Cognac Cup 1974-76-78-80; v South Africa; Scotland in World Cup 1974-75-76-77; in Double Diamond 1972-73-74-75-76-77; in PGA Cup 1990

AMATEUR

Reg	Somerset Amateur 1964; South Western Counties Amateur 1964
Jun	British Youths 1964
Int	English Youths 1964

Bayman, Linda (*née* Denison-Pender)

Born 10th June, 1948

Nat	English Ladies Amateur 1983; Ladies British Amateur Stroke Play 1987
Trn	Avia Foursomes 1969-71-73-79-80; Worplesdon Mixed Foursomes 1980-84; Astor Salver 1983-84; Critchley Salver 1984
Reg	Kent Ladies 1968-72-73-78
Int	Curtis Cup 1988; Vagliano Trophy 1971-73-85-87; Espirito Santo 1988; England (Home Int) 1971-72-73-83-84-85-87-88-95; Eur(L) T Ch 1983-85-87-(**97**)
Jun	Kent Girls 1966
Mis	Avia Woman Golfer of the Year 1987; Doris Chambers Trophy 1987-88-89; Angus Trophy 1987-89

Behan, Lillian

Born Co Kildare on 12th January, 1965. Turned Professional 1986

AMATEUR

Chp	Ladies British Open Amateur 1985
Trn	The Curragh Scratch Cup 1986

Int   Curtis Cup 1986; Vagliano Trophy 1985;
Ireland (Home Int) 1984-85-86; Eur(L) T Ch
1985

Beharrell, John Charles
Born Solihull, Warwickshire on 2nd May, 1938

Cls   Royal & Ancient, Edgbaston, Aldeburgh.
Hon member of Little Aston, Blackwell,
Handsworth
Chp   Amateur Champion 1956
Trn   Antlers Royal Mid-Surrey 1960.
Reg   Central England Mixed Foursomes 1956-57-75
Int   GB*v*Europe 1956; *v*Professionals 1956. England
(Home Int) 1956
Jun Int English Boy 1955

Beharrell, Veronica *(née Anstey)*
Born Birmingham on 14th January, 1935

Cls   Edgbaston (Hon), Little Aston
Oth   Australian Ladies, New Zealand Ladies 1955;
Victoria Ladies Open 1955
Reg   Warwickshire Ladies 1955-56-57-58-60-71-72-
75; Central England Mixed Foursomes 1957-75
Int   Curtis Cup 1956. England (Home Int) 1955-56-
58-(61)
Jun Int English Girls 1953

Benka, Peter
Born London on 18th September, 1946

Cls   Addington, West Sussex
Nat   Scottish Open Amateur Stroke Play r/u 1969
Oth   Dutch Amateur 1972
Trn   County Champion of Champions 1967;
Sunningdale Foursomes 1969; St George's
Challenge Cup 1969. Mullingar Trophy 1970;
St George's Hill Trophy 1971-75; John Cross
Bowl 1994
Reg   Surrey Amateur 1967-68
Int   Walker Cup 1969; GBI*v*Europe 1970; England
(Home Int) 1967-68-69-70; Eur T Ch 1969
Jun   British Youths 1967-68
Int   Boys 1964; Youths 1966-67-68

Bennett, Warren
*Born Ruislip on 20th August, 1971. Turned
Professional 1994*

Maj   Open: leading amateur 1994
PROFESSIONAL
Oth   Dutch Challenge Open 1995; Challenge Eulen
Open Galea 1997
AMATEUR
Nat   English Open Amateur Stroke Play (Brabazon)
r/u 1994
Oth   Australian Centennial Amateur 1994;
International Team Chp Sydney
Trn   St Andrews Links Trophy r/u 1994. Selborne
Salver; Lytham Trophy 1994.
Reg   Middlesex Chp 1994
Int   GBI *v* Europe 1994; Eisenhower Trophy 1994;
England (Home Int) 1992-93-94; *v* France
1994
Jun Int English Youths 1991-92; British Youths 1992

Bentley, Arnold Lewis
Born Southport on 11th June, 1911

Cls   Royal & Ancient, Hesketh (Hon), Royal Birkdale
Nat   English Amateur 1939
Int   England (Home Int) 1936-37; *v*France 1937-39
Mis   Played for British Seniors 1969
Jun Int Boys 1928

Bisgood, Jeanne, CBE
Born Richmond, Surrey on 11th August, 1923

Cls   Parkstone (Hon)
Nat   English Ladies 1951-53-57
Oth   Swedish Ladies 1952; Italian Ladies, German
Ladies 1953; Portuguese Ladies 1954;
Norwegian Ladies 1955.
Trn   Astor Salver 1951-52-53; Roehampton Gold
Cup 1951-52-53. Daily Graphic Cup 1945-51
Reg   South Eastern Ladies 1950-52; Surrey Ladies
1951-53-69
Int   Curtis Cup 1950-52-54-(70); England (Home
Int) 1949-50-51-52-53-54-56-58

Bladon, Warren
Born Coventry on 4th May, 1966

Cls   Kenilworth
Chp   Amateur Champion 1996
Trn   Guinness Open 1984, 1993
Reg   Warwickshire Champion 1985
Int   GBI *v* Europe 1996; England (Home Int) 1996

Boatman, Elizabeth *(née Collis)*
Born 7th April, 1944

Nat   English Ladies s/f 1974
Reg   Essex Ladies 1964-65-69-80-83
Int   England (Home Int) 1974-80-(**84**)-(**85**)-(**90**)-
(**91**); Eur(L) T Ch (**1985**)-(**87**)-(**91**); (GBI)
Commonwealth Trn (1987)-(**91**); Vagliano
Trophy (**1987**); Curtis Cup (**1992**)-(**94**)
Mis   Chairman ELGA 1989

Bonallack, Michael Francis, OBE
Born Chigwell on 31st December, 1934

Cls   Thorpe Hall, Pine Valley, Elie.
Maj   Leading Amateur in Open 1968-71
Chp   Amateur Champion 1961-65-68-69-70; s/f 1958-
72-77
Nat   English Amateur 1962-63-65-67-68; r/u 1959;
English Open Amateur Stroke Play 1964-68-69
(tied)-71; r/u 1959-66-67
Trn   Berkshire Trophy 1957-61-65-68-70-71
(shared); Hampshire Hog 1957-79; Worplesdon
Mixed Foursomes 1958; Sunningdale
Foursomes 1959; Golf Illustrated Golf Vase
1961 (shared)-67 (shared)-68-69 (shared)-71-
75; Scrutton Jug 1961-64-66-68-70-71; Lytham
Trophy 1965 (shared)-72; Antlers Royal Mid-
Surrey 1964; St George's Challenge Cup 1965-
68-81; Prince of Wales Challenge Cup 1967
Reg   Essex Amateur 1954-57-59-60-61-63-64-68-69-
70-72; Essex Open 1969; East Anglian Open
1973
Int   Walker Cup 1957-59-61-63-65-67-**69-71**-73; GB
Commonwealth Team 1959-63-**67-71**-(75);
Eisenhower Trophy 1960-62-64-66-**68**

(individual winner, shared)-**70-72**; *v*Professionals 1957-58-59-60; v Europe 1958-60-62-64-66-68-70-72. England (Home Int) 1957 to 72-74 (**1962** to **67**); Eur T Ch 1959-61-63-65-67-69-71

Jun British Boys 1952
Mis AGW Trophy 1968; Bobby Jones Award 1972; PGA Chairman 1976 to 1981; Chairman Golf Foundation 1977; President English Golf Union 1982. Best equal individual score Eisenhower Trophy 1968. Chairman Royal & Ancient Selection Committee 1975 to 1979. Donald Ross Award 1991. Gerald Micklem Award 1991. Ambassador of Golf Award 1995. Secretary to Royal & Ancient since 1983

Bonallack, Angela (*née* Ward)
Born Birchington on 7th April, 1937
Cls Prince's, Thorpe Hall, St Rule
Chp Ladies British Open Amateur r/u 1962-74
Nat English Ladies 1958-63, r/u 1960-62-72. British Ladies r/u 1962-74
Oth Swedish Ladies, German Ladies 1955; Scandinavian Ladies 1956; Portuguese Ladies 1957
Trn Astor Salver 1957-58-60-61-66; Worplesdon Mixed Foursomes 1958; Kayser-Bondor Foursomes 1958 (shared); Astor Prince's 1968; Avia Foursomes 1976; Roehampton Gold Cup 1980.
Reg Essex Ladies 1968-69-73-74-76-77-78-82; South East Ladies 1957-65; Kent Ladies' 1955-56-58
Int Curtis Cup 1956-58-60-62-64-66. Vagliano Trophy 1959-61-63. England (Home Int) 1956 to 1964; 1966-72
Jun British Girls 1955
Mis Leading amateur Colgate European Ladies' Open 1975-76

Bousfield, Kenneth
Born Marston Moor on 2nd October, 1919. Turned Professional 1938
Eur German Open 1955-59. Swiss Open, Belgian Open 1958; Portuguese Open 1960-61
Trn News Chronicle 1951; PGA Match Play 1955. PGA Close 1955; Yorkshire Evening News 1956 (shared); Dunlop 1957. Sprite 1959. Irish Hospitals 1960 (shared); Swallow-Penfold 1961. Maritime Foursomes (with G Low) 1957; Lord Derby Trn (Formby) 1959; Ryder Cup Re-Union Foursomes (A Caygill) 1964.
Oth Gleneagles Pro-Am 1964. Surrey Open 1951, 1975; Surrey Match Play 1967
Reg Southern England Professional 1951-57-74. Pringle Seniors 1972
Int Ryder Cup 1949-51-55-57-59-61; England in World Cup 1956-57

Brand, Gordon J
Born Cambridge on 6th August, 1955. Turned Professional 1976
PROFESSIONAL
Maj Open r/u 1986
Eur Volvo Belgian Open 1989
RoW Ivory Coast Open 1981; Nigerian Open 1983; Nigerian Open, Ivory Coast Open 1986; Zimbabwe Open 1987; Ivory Coast Open 1988; Zambian Open 1990

Int Ryder Cup 1983; Nissan Cup 1986; England in World Cup 1983; Dunhill Cup 1986-87 (winners)
Mis Tooting Bec Cup 1981-86; Braid-Taylor Memorial Medal 1986; Headed Safari Tour Order of Merit 1983, 1986, 1987
AMATEUR
Int GBI*v*Europe 1976; England (Home Int) 1976

Brand, Gordon Jr
Born Burntisland, Fife on 19th August, 1958. Turned Professional 1981
Cls Hon member of Woodhall Spa, Knowle
PROFESSIONAL
Eur Coral Classic, Bob Hope British Classic 1982; Celtic International, Panasonic European Open 1984; KLM Dutch Open, Scandinavian Enterprise Open 1987; Benson & Hedges International 1989; GA European Open 1993
RoW South Australian Open 1988
Oth PGA Qualifying School winner 1981
Int Ryder Cup 1987-89; Nissan Cup 1985; Kirin Cup 1988; Four Tours World Chp 1989; Scotland in World Cup 1984-85-88-89-90-92-94; in Dunhill Cup 1985-86-87 (r/u)-88-89-91-92(r/u)-93-94-97.
Mis Rookie of the Year 1982; AGW Trophy 1982
AMATEUR
Nat English Open Amateur Stroke Play 1978; Scottish Open Amateur Stroke Play 1980
Oth Swedish Open Amateur Stroke Play 1979; Portuguese Amateur 1981
Trn Golf Illustrated Gold Vase 1980; Sunningdale Foursomes 1981
Reg Gloucestershire Amateur 1977; South-Western Counties Amateur 1977-78
Int Walker Cup 1979; Eisenhower Trophy 1978-80; GB*v*Europe 1978-80; Scotland (Home Int) 1978-80; *v*England 1979; *v*Italy 1979; *v*France 1980-81; *v*Belgium 1980; Eur T Ch 1979
Jun British Youths 1979; Scottish Youths 1980
Int Youths 1977-78-79

Briggs, Audrey (*née* Brown)
Born Kent on 31st January, 1945
Cls Royal Liverpool
Nat Welsh Ladies 1970-71-73-74, r/u 1978-79-80-81
Reg Sussex Ladies 1969. Cheshire Ladies 1971-73-76-80-81. North of England Ladies 1976
Int Vagliano Trophy 1971-73. Wales (Home Int) 1969 to 84, Eur(L) T Ch 1969-71-73-75-77-79-81-83; Fiat Trophy 1978-79-80

Broadhurst, Paul
Born Staffordshire on 14th August, 1965. Turned Professional 1988
Maj Leading amateur in Open 1988
PROFESSIONAL
Eur Crédit Lyonnais Cannes Open 1989; Motorola Classic 1990; European Pro-Celebrity 1991; B&H International Open 1993; Open de France 1995
Int Ryder Cup 1991. England in Dunhill Cup 1991; World Cup 1995-97. Four Tours World Chp 1991
Mis Rookie of the Year 1989; Tooting Bec Cup 1990
AMATEUR
Trn Lytham Trophy 1988
Int (GBI)*v*Europe 1988. England (Home Int) 1986-87

Brodie, Allan

Born Glasgow on 25th September, 1947

Cls Balmore (Hon), Glasgow
Chp Amateur s/f 1976
Nat Scottish Amateur 1977; r/u 1973. Scottish Open Amateur Stroke Play r/u 1970
Trn Tennant Cup 1972-80; Golf Illustrated Gold Vase 1976
Reg West of Scotland Open Amateur 1974; Dunbartonshire Amateur Stroke Play 1975-76
Int Walker Cup 1977-79; Eisenhower Trophy 1978; GBI vEurope 1974-76-78-80; Scotland (Home Int) 1970-72-73-74-75-76-77-78-80; Eur T Ch 1973-77-79; vBelgium, Spain 1977; vFrance 1978; vEngland, Italy 1979
Jun Int Youths 1966-67

Brown, Audrey *See* Briggs

Brown, Kenneth

Born Harpenden, Herts on 9th January, 1957. Turned Professional 1974

Eur Carrolls Irish Open 1978; KLM Dutch Open 1983; Glasgow Classic 1984; Four Stars Pro-Celebrity 1985
US Southern Open 1987
RoW Kenya Open 1983
Oth Hertfordshire Open 1975
Int Ryder Cup 1977-79-83-85-87; Hennessy-Cognac Cup 1978-84; Kirin Cup 1987. Scotland: Double Diamond 1977; World Cup 1977-78-79-83
Mis Tooting Bec Cup 1980
Jun Carris Trophy 1974
Int Boys 1974

Burke, Ita *See* Butler

Bussell, Alan Francis

Born Glasgow on 25th February, 1937

Cls Whitecraigs (Hon), Coxmoor (Hon), Chevin
Chp Amateur s/f 1957
Trn Antlers Royal Mid-Surrey 1956. Golf Illustrated Gold Vase 1959
Reg Nottinghamshire Amateur 1959-60-62-63-64-68-69. Nottinghamshire Open 1960-62. Nottinghamshire Match Play 1960-62. Renfrewshire Amateur 1955
Int Walker Cup 1957. GBvEurope 1956-62; v Professionals 1956-57-59. Scotland (Home Int) 1956-57-58-61; vScandinavia 1956-60
Jun British Boys 1954. Boy International 1954. British Youths 1956. Youth International 1954-55-56

Butler, Ita *(née Burke)*

Born Nenagh, Co Tipperary

Cls Hon member of Elm Park, Killarney, Woodbrook, Nenagh
Nat Irish Ladies r/u 1972-78
Reg Leinster Ladies three times. Munster and Midland Ladies twice
Int Curtis Cup 1966-**96**. World Team Championship 1966-(**94**). Vagliano Trophy 1965-(91)-(93). Ireland (World Cup) 1964; (Home Int) 1962-63-64-65-66-68-71-72-73-76-77-78-79; Eur T Ch 1967; Fiat Trophy 1978

Butler, Peter J

Born Birmingham on 25th March, 1932. Turned Professional 1948

Cls French Open 1968. Colombian Open 1975
Trn Swallow-Penfold 1959. Yorkshire Evening News 1962; PGA Close 1963. Bowmaker 1963-67. Cox Moore 1964. PGA Match Play r/u 1964-75. Martini 1965. Piccadilly 1965-67. Penfold, Wills 1968. RTV 1969. Classic International 1971. Sumrie 1974 Evian International 1963. Grand Bahama Invitation Open 1971-72
Reg Midland Open 1956-58-60-65-69. Midland Professional 1961.
Sen Lawrence Batley Seniors 1993
Oth Gleneagles Pro-Am 1963. Sunningdale Foursomes 1974
Int Ryder Cup 1965-69-71-73. England in World Cup. 1969-70-73. England in Double Diamond 1971-72-76. GBIvEurope 1976. PGA Cup 1978-79-81-82-84
Mis Equal lowest round in British events of 61. Second in Order of Merit 1968. PGA Captain 1972

Buxton, Nicola

Born 9th March, 1973

Cls Woodsome Hall
Nat English Ladies 1991-93; English Ladies Stroke Play r/u 1992; English U-23 and U-21 Stroke Play 1992
Oth Portuguese Women's Open r/u 1994
Trn Critchley Salver 1991
Reg Yorkshire Ladies 1989-90-91
Int Curtis Cup 1992; Vagliano Trophy 1991-93; England (Home Int) 1991-92-93; Eur(L) T Ch 1991
Jun English Girls 1991

Cadden, Suzanne *See* McMahon

Cage, Stuart

Born 16th July, 1973. Turned Professional 1993

PROFESSIONAL
Eur Europe 1 Cannes Open 1997
Oth Open Divonne 1994
AMATEUR
Nat English Amateur 1992
Trn Lytham Trophy 1992
Int (GBI) Walker Cup 1993. England (Home Int) 1993
Jun Int (England) Boys 1991; Youths 1992

Caldwell, Ian

Born Streatham on 17th May, 1930

Cls Royal & Ancient, Sunningdale, Walton Heath
Nat English Amateur 1961
Trn Prince of Wales Challenge Cup 1950-51-52. Boyd Quaich 1954.
Reg Surrey Amateur 1961
Int Walker Cup 1951-55. GB Commonwealth Team 1954. GBIvEurope 1955. England (Home Int) 1950-51-52-53-54-55-56-57-61
Jun Carris Trophy 1947-48

Caldwell, Carole (née Redford)
Born Kingston, Surrey on 23rd April, 1949

Cls Canterbury (Hon)
Trn Newmark-Avia International 1973. Roehampton Gold Cup 1973-75-78; Hampshire Rose 1973, 1984; Avia Foursomes 1974; Critchley Salver 1974; Canadian Ladies Foursomes 1978; London Foursomes 1984
Oth Portuguese Ladies 1980
Reg South Eastern Ladies 1973-78. Kent Ladies 1970-75-77-86. Berkshire Ladies 1982
Int Curtis Cup 1978-80; Vagliano Trophy 1973; England (Home Int) 1973-78-79-80
Mis Playing captain of LGU U-23 team to tour Canada 1973. Lost at 27th hole in first round of American Ladies Amateur 1978

Carr, Joseph B
Born Dublin on 18th February, 1922

Cls Sutton (Hon)
Maj Leading Amateur in Open 1956-58
Chp Amateur Champion 1953-58-60, r/u 1968 s/f 1952-54.
Nat Irish Amateur 1954-57-63-64-65-67, r/u 1951-59. Irish Open Amateur 1946-50-54-56, r/u 1947-48-51; US Amateur s/f 1961
Trn Golf Illustrated Gold Vase 1951. Gleneagles Saxone 1955. Berkshire Trophy 1959. Formby Hare 1962. Mullingar Trophy 1963. Antlers Royal Mid-Surrey 1970
Reg South of Ireland Open Amateur 1948-66-69. East of Ireland Open Amateur 1941-43-45-46-48-56-57-58-60-61-64-69. West of Ireland Open Amateur 1946-47-48-51-53-54-56-58-60-61-62-66
Int Walker Cup 1947-49-51-53-55-57-59-61-**63**-(**65**)-67. GBIvEurope 1954-56-**64**-66-68. Eisenhower Trophy 1958-60-(**64**)-(**66**). Ireland (Home Int) 1947 to 1969 Eur T Ch 1965-67-69
Mis AGW Trophy 1953. Bobby Jones Award 1961. Walter Hagen Award 1967. Captain of Royal & Ancient 1991/92

Carrick, David
Born Glasgow on 28th January, 1957

Nat Scottish Amateur 1985. Scottish Open Amateur Stroke Play 1987
Trn Scottish Champion of Champions 1983. Glasgow Amateur 1980-81
Reg Dunbartonshire Amateur 1979-80-82-83
Int Walker Cup 1983-87. GBI v Europe 1986. Scotland (Home Int) 1981 to 1989; vItaly 1988; vFrance 1989; Eur T Ch 1989; vWest Germany 1987
Mis Braid Panton Trophy 1987

Chadwick, Elizabeth See Pook

Chapman, Roger
Born in Nakuru, Kenya on 1st May, 1959. Turned Professional 1981

PROFESSIONAL
RoW Zimbabwe Open 1988
Trn Sunningdale Open Foursomes 1986

Mis Tooting Bec Cup 1991(shared)
AMATEUR
Nat English Amateur 1979
Trn Duncan Putter (shared), Lytham Trophy 1981; Sunningdale Open Foursomes 1979
Int Walker Cup 1981; GBIvEurope 1980; England (Home Int) 1980-81; Eur T Ch 1981

Christmas, Martin J
Born 1939

Cls West Sussex, Addington
Chp Amateur s/f 1961-64-65
Nat English Amateur r/u 1960. English Open Amateur Stroke Play r/u 1960
Trn Gleneagles Pro-Am 1961. Wentworth Pro-Am Foursomes 1962
Oth Belgian Open Amateur 1976
Reg Sussex Amateur 1962
Int Walker Cup 1961-63. Eisenhower Trophy 1962. GBvEurope 1960-62-64. England (Home Int) 1960-61-62-63-64

Clark, Clive Anthony
Born Winchester, Hants on 27th June, 1945. Turned Professional 1965

PROFESSIONAL
Maj Open (tied) 3rd 1967 (leading British player)
Trn Danish Open 1966; Bowmaker Agfa-Gevaert 1968; John Player Trophy 1970; Sumrie 1974
Int Ryder Cup 1973
AMATEUR
Chp Amateur r/u 1965
Nat English Amateur r/u 1965. English Open Amateur Stroke Play 1965 (tied)
Trn Lytham Trophy 1965 (tied). *Golf Illustrated* Gold Vase, Scrutton Jug 1965
Oth Sunningdale Foursomes 1974-76
Int Walker Cup 1965. GBIvEurope 1964. England (Home Int) 1964-65
Mis Braid-Taylor Memorial Medal 1967; TV commentator. Golf course architect

Clark, Howard K
Born Leeds on 26th August, 1954. Turned Professional October 1973

PROFESSIONAL
Eur Portuguese Open, Madrid Open 1978; Cepsa Madrid Open, Whyte & Mackay PGA Chp 1984; Jersey Open, Glasgow Open 1985; Cepsa Madrid Open, Peugeot Spanish Open 1986; Moroccan Open, PLM Open 1987; English Open 1988
Oth U-25 TPD 1976
Int Ryder Cup 1977-81-85-87-89-95; Nissan Cup 1985-86; Hennessy-Cognac Cup 1978-84; England in World Cup 1978-84-85 (individual winner)-87; Dunhill Cup 1985-86-87 (winners)-89-90(r/u)-94-95
AMATEUR
Chp Amateur s/f 1973
Reg Yorkshire Amateur 1973
Int Walker Cup 1973; England (Home Int) 1973
Jun British Boys 1971
Int Boys 1969-71; Youths 1971-72-73

Clarke, Darren

Born Dungannon on 14th August, 1968. Turned Professional 1990

PROFESSIONAL
Maj Open r/u 1997
Eur Alfred Dunhill Open 1993; Linde German Masters 1996
Int Ireland in World Cup 1994-95-96; Dunhill Cup 1994-95-96
AMATEUR
Nat Irish Amateur 1990; Spanish Open Amateur 1990
Int Ireland (Home Int) 1987-89; (GBI) v Europe 1990

Claydon, Russell

Born on 19th November, 1965. Turned Professional 1989

Maj Leading amateur in Open 1989
PROFESSIONAL
Int England: Dunhill Cup 1997
Mis Rookie of the Year 1990
AMATEUR
Nat English Amateur 1988
RoW Australian Masters r/u 1989
Trn St George's Challenge Cup 1986; Berkshire Trophy, County Champion of Champions 1988; St Andrews Links Trophy 1989; Sunningdale Open Foursomes 1989
Reg Cambridge Amateur 1987-88
Oth UAP U-25 European Open r/u 1988
Int Walker Cup 1989; England (Home Int) 1988 Eur T Ch 1989

Coles, Neil, MBE

Born London on 26th September, 1934. Turned Professional 1950

Maj Open 3rd 1961; r/u 1973; leading British player 1975 (7th)
Eur German Open 1971. Spanish Open 1973
Trn Ballantine 1961. Senior Service 1962. Daks 1963 (tied)-64-70-71 (tied). Martini 1963 (tied). Engadine Open 1963. Bowmaker 1964-70. PGA Match Play 1964-65-73, r/u 1966-72-78. Carrolls 1965-71. Pringle, Dunlop Masters 1966. Sumrie 1970-73. Shell BP Italy, Walworth Aloyco Italy 1970; Penfold 1971. Sunbeam 1972. Wills 1974. Penfold PGA 1976. Tournament Players' Championship 1977. Sanyo Open 1982
Oth British Assistants 1956. Sunningdale Foursomes 1962-67-80. Wentworth Pro-Am Foursomes 1963-70. Southern England Professionals 1970
Int Ryder Cup 1961-63-65-67-69-71-73-77. England in World Cup 1963-68. England in Double Diamond 1971-73-75-76-77. Hennessy-Cognac Cup 1974-76-78-80
Sen Seniors British Open 1987. PGA Seniors Chp 1985-86-87-89. Geneva Seniors Open 1991. Collingtree Homes Senior Classic 1992. Gary Player Seniors Classic 1993. Collingtree Seniors 1995. Ryder Collingtree Classic 1997
Mis Harry Vardon Trophy 1963-70. Second in Order of Merit 1987. Chairman PGA European Tour. Golf course architect.

Collingham, Janet *(née* Melville)

Born Barrow-in-Furness on 16th March, 1958

Cls Notts Ladies
Chp Ladies British Open Amateur 1987
Nat Ladies British Open Amateur Stroke Play 1978
Trn Worplesdon Mixed Foursomes 1979. Northern Foursomes 1977-78. Mary McCalley Trophy 1980
Reg Highland Open 1978. Midland Ladies 1986. Lancashire Champion 1983-86
Int Vagliano Trophy 1979-87. England (Home Int) 1978-79-81-84-86-87-92; Eur(L) T Ch 1979. Girls International 1976-(81)
Mis Varsity Athlete in golf at Florida International University 1980-81; Duncan Salver 1978

Collis, Elizabeth *See* **Boatman**

Coltart, Andrew John

Born Dumfries on 12th May, 1970. Turned Professional 1991

Cls Thornhill
PROFESSIONAL
RoW Australian PGA 1994-97
Oth Scottish Professional 1994
Int Scotland: Dunhill Cup 1994-95(winners)-96, World Cup 1994-95-96
AMATEUR
Nat Scottish Amateur r/u 1988; Scottish Open Amateur Stroke Play 1991
Trn Leven Gold Medal 1989
Reg West of Scotland 1991
Int Walker Cup 1991. Eisenhower Trophy 1990; GBI v Europe 1990. Scotland (Home Int) 1988-89-90; Eur T Ch 1989-91; Nixdorf Nations Cup 1990; v Sweden, Italy 1990
Oth Leone de San Marco 1990
Jun British Youths r/u 1989-90; Scottish Boys 1987

Cosh, Gordon B

Born Glasgow on 26th March, 1939

Cls Troon, Royal Aberdeen, Bruntsfield Links. Hon member of Cowglen, Killarney
Nat Scottish Amateur 1968, r/u 1965. Scottish Open Amateur Stroke Play r/u 1968
Trn Newlands Trophy 1980
Reg West of Scotland Amateur 1961-64-65-66. Glasgow County Match Play 1965-66. Glasgow Amateur 1969. Glasgow County Stroke Play 1972-74
Int Walker Cup 1965. Eisenhower Trophy 1966-68. GB Commonwealth Team 1967. GBIvEurope 1966-68. Scotland (Home Int) 1964-65-66-67-68-69; Eur T Ch 1965-**69**
Jun Int Youths 1959-60

Craddock, Tom

Born Malahide on 16th December, 1931

Cls Malahide, Donabate, Sutton, The Island Malahide, Malone, Woodbrook, Mullingar, Carlow, Howth, Tara, Killarney
Nat Irish Amateur 1959, r/u 1965. Irish Open Amateur 1958
Trn Lytham Trophy 1969
Reg East of Ireland Open Amateur 1959-65-66

Int	Walker Cup 1967-69. Ireland (Home Int) 1955-56-57-58-59-60-65-66-67-69; Eur T Ch 1967-71

Critchley, Bruce

Born 9th December, 1942

Cls	Sunningdale, Killarney (Hon)
Chp	Amateur s/f 1970
Trn	Worplesdon Mixed Foursomes 1961. Sunningdale Foursomes 1964. Hampshire Hog 1969. Antlers Royal Mid-Surrey 1974
Reg	Surrey Amateur 1969
Int	Walker Cup 1969. GBIvEurope 1970. England (Home Int) 1962-69-70; Eur T Ch 1969
Mis	TV commentator. Co-founder annual match between former Ryder Cup v Walker Cup Players

Curry, David H

Born 6th July, 1963. Turned Professional 1988

Chp	Amateur Champion 1986
Trn	Selborne Salver 1984
Int	(GBI) Walker Cup 1987, Eisenhower Trophy 1986, vEurope 1986-88. England (Home Int) 1984-86-87, vFrance 1988

Dalgleish, Colin R

Born Glasgow on 24th September, 1960

Cls	Helensburgh (Hon), Millstone Mills (Hon)
Nat	Scottish Amateur 1981
Trn	Tennant Cup 1983-88
RoW	East of India Amateur 1981. Indian Amateur r/u 1981. Lake Macquarie International Stroke-Play Champion (Australia) 1983
Oth	Scottish Universities Champion 1983
Int	Walker Cup 1981. Scotland (Home Int) 1981-82-83; vFrance 1982; Eur T Ch 1981-83. GBvEurope 1982. EuropevSouth America 1982. Scottish Captain 1994-95-96
Jun	International Junior Masters 1977. Belgian Junior Championship 1980. British Boys r/u 1977. British Youths r/u 1979-82. Boy International 1976-77-78. Youth International 1979-80-81-82

Darcy, Eamonn

Born Delgany on 7th August, 1952. Turned Professional 1969

Eur	Spanish Open 1983; Belgian Open 1987; Desert Classic 1990
Trn	Sumrie 1976-78. Greater Manchester Open 1977
RoW	Air New Zealand Open 1980. Cock o' the North Open 1981. Kenya Open 1982. Mufulira Open 1984. West Lakes Classic (Aus) 1981
Oth	Irish Dunlop 1976. Cacharel World Under-25 1976. Irish Match Play 1981
Int	Ryder Cup 1975-77-81-87. Ireland in Double Diamond 1975-76-77. Ireland in World Cup 1976-77-83-84-85-87-91. GBIvEurope 1976; vSouth Africa 1976. Hennessy-Cognac Cup 1976-84. Dunhill Cup 1987-88 (winners)-91
Mis	Second in Order of Merit 1976; Tooting Bec Cup 1980(shared)-1991(shared); Braid Taylor Memorial Medal 1991

Davies, John C

Born London on 14th February, 1948

Cls	Mid-Surrey, Sunningdale, Royal Cinque Ports, Killarney
Chp	Amateur r/u 1976.
Nat	English Amateur r/u 1971-76. English Open Amateur Stroke Play r/u 1977
Trn	Berkshire Trophy 1969-71 (tied). Royal St George's Challenge Cup 1972-73-74-75-76-77. Sunningdale Foursomes 1968-72. Antlers Royal Mid-Surrey 1969-75-77. Golf Illustrated Gold Vase 1973-77. Prince of Wales Cup 1975. Berkhamsted Trophy 1976-78-79
Oth	Second equal in South African Open Amateur Stroke Play 1974
Reg	Surrey Amateur 1971-72-77
Int	Walker Cup 1973-75-77-79. Eisenhower Trophy 1974-76 (winners). GBIvEurope 1972-74-76-78; England (Home Int) 1969-70-71-72-73-74-78; Eur T Ch 1973-75-77
Mis	Member of European Team to tour South Africa 1974

Davies, Karen L

Born 19th June, 1965. Turned Professional 1988

PROFESSIONAL

Int	Sunrise Cup 1992

AMATEUR

Oth	Florida State Tournament 1985. South-Eastern USA Championship 1985
Int	Curtis Cup 1986-88. Wales (Home Int) 1981-82-83 (Eur L U-22) 1981-82-83-84-85-86; Eur(L) T Ch 1987, Commonwealth Team 1987
Jun	Welsh Girls 1980-82

Davies, Laura, MBE

Born Coventry on 5th October, 1963. Turned Professional 1985

Maj	Ladies British Open 1986; r/u 1987. US Women's Open 1987; McDonald's LPGA 1994-96

PROFESSIONAL

Eur	Belgian Ladies Open 1985; McEwan's Wirral Classic, Greater Manchester Tournament, Ladies Spanish Open 1986; Italian Open 1987; Italian Open, Ford Ladies Classic, Biarritz Ladies Open 1988; Laing Charity Ladies Classic 1989; AGF Biarritz Ladies Open 1990; Valextra Classic 1991; European Ladies Open, Ladies English Open, BMW Ladies Italian Open 1992; Ladies English Open 1993; Ladies Irish Open, Ladies Scottish Open 1994; Evian Masters, Irish Holidays Open, Welsh Open, English Open 1995; Evian Masters, English Open, Open de Sicilia 1996; Danish Open, Hennessy Cup 1997
US	Tucson Open, Toledo Classic 1988; Lady Keystone Open 1989; Inamori Classic 1991; McDonald's Chp 1993; Standard Register Ping, Sara Lee Classic 1994; Standard Register Ping, Chick-fil-A Charity Chp 1995; Standard Register Ping, du Maurier Classic, Star Bank LPGA Classic 1996; Standard Register Ping 1997
RoW	Itoki Classic (Jpn) 1989-95; Australian Ladies' Masters 1993-94, Thailand Open 1993-94; Itoen Ladies (Jpn) 1994-95
Int	Solheim Cup 1990-92-94; Sunrise Cup 1992; (for LPGA) Nichirei International 1993

Mis Rookie of the Year 1985. Order of Merit winner 1985-86-92-96. Hon. Member of WPGET 1993. Top of LPGA Money List 1994. Ping No. 1 1994. AGW Trophy 1994. American Golf Writers LPGA Player of the Year 1994-96. Rolex Player of the Year 1996. Vivien Saunders Trophy 1992-93

AMATEUR
Nat Welsh Open Stroke Play 1984
Oth English Intermediate 1983
Trn London Foursomes 1981
Reg South-Eastern Champion 1983-84
Int Curtis Cup 1984; Vilmorin Cup 1984; England (Home Int) 1983-84
Jun Surrey Girls 1982

Deeble, Peter George

Born Alnwick on 27th February, 1954

Cls Alnmouth, Alnwick, Hon member of Ponteland, Hexham, Rothbury, Washington, Tynedale
Nat English Amateur 1976-80
Trn Antlers Royal Mid-Surrey 1976. Lytham Trophy 1977. Berkhamsted Trophy 1975. County Champion of Champions 1982
Reg Northumberland Amateur 1975-82-83. Northumberland Stroke Play 1973-75-77-78-79. Northumberland and Durham Open 1976
Int Walker Cup 1977-81. GBI *v*Europe 1978. Europe v South America 1980. GB in Colombian International 1978. England (Home Int) 1975-76-77-78-80-81-83; Eur T Ch 1979-81; *v*Scotland 1979; *v*France 1982. England in Fiat Trophy 1980
Jun Int Boys 1970-71. Youths 1973-75-76

Deighton, Dr FWG

Born Glasgow on 21st May, 1927

Cls Royal & Ancient, Western Gailes, Elie, Glasgow, Hilton Park (Hon), North Hants
Nat Scottish Amateur 1956-59
Trn Edward Trophy 1954. Gleneagles Silver Tassie 1956. Tennant Cup 1958-60-64
Oth Boyd Quaich 1947 (tied). Royal & Ancient Silver Cross 1953-60-63-70-73. Royal Medal 1956-59-61-63-66-73. Glennie Medal 1956-58-59-60-66-70-73
Reg West of Scotland Amateur 1959. Dunbartonshire Amateur 1949-50-53-54. Glasgow Amateur 1951-55
Int Walker Cup 1951-57. GB Commonwealth Team 1954-59. GBI*v*Professionals 1956-57. Scotland (Home Int) 1950-52-53-56-58-59-60; *v*South Africa 1954; v New Zealand 1954; *v*Scandinavia 1956
Mis Member of British Touring Team to South Africa 1952

Dobson, Helen

Born Skegness on 25th February, 1971. Turned Professional 1990

PROFESSIONAL
Eur BMW European Masters 1993
US LPGA: State Farm Rail Classic 1993
Int Union Cup 1994
AMATEUR
Chp Ladies British Open Amateur 1989

Nat Ladies British Open Amateur Stroke Play 1989; English Ladies 1989
Trn Wentworth Scratch Trophy, Bridget Jackson Bowl 1989
Oth World Fourball (with Elaine Farquharson) 1989
Int Curtis Cup 1990; Vagliano Trophy 1989; England (Home Int) 1987-88-89; Eur(L) T Ch 1989
Jun British Girls 1987; English Girls 1988-89
Jun Int English Girls 1988
Mis Duncan Salver 1989. Avia Woman Golfer of the Year 1989.

Dodd, Stephen

Born Cardiff on 15th July, 1966. Turned Professional 1990

PROFESSIONAL
Eur Memorial Olivier Barras 1991; Bank of Austria Open 1992
Reg West Region PGA 1991. Welsh PGA 1995
AMATEUR
Chp Amateur Champion 1989
Nat Welsh Amateur 1989
Trn Silver Dragon, WI Tucker Trophy 1987; Duncan Putter, Carad Trophy, Cardiff Feathers, Golden Lamp 1988
Int Walker Cup 1989; Wales (Home Int) 1985-87-88-89, Eur T Ch 1987

Douglas, Kitrina

Born Bristol on 6th September, 1960. Turned Professional 1984

Maj Ladies British Open 3rd 1990
PROFESSIONAL
Eur Ford Classic, Swedish Ladies Open, Rookie of the Year 1984; Mitsubishi Colt Cars, Jersey Open 1986; Hennessy-Cognac Ladies Cup 1987; St Moritz Ladies Classic, Godiva European Masters 1989; English Open 1991; BMW European Masters 1992
Int Solheim Cup 1992
Mis Rookie of the Year 1984
AMATEUR
Chp British Ladies 1982
Oth Portuguese Champion 1983
Trn Critchley Salver 1983
Reg Gloucestershire Champion 1980-81-82-83-84
Int Curtis Cup 1982. Vagliano Trophy 1983. England (Home Int) 1981-82. Eur(L) T Ch 1983
Jun Scottish Girls Stroke-Play 1981

Dowling, Claire (*née* Hourihane)

Born 18th February, 1958

Cls Woodbrook
Nat Irish Ladies 1983-84-85-87-91; r/u 1980. British Ladies Stroke Play 1986; r/u 1990
Trn South Atlantic (USA) 1983; Hampshire Rose 1986; Critchley Salver 1990
Reg South Ireland Cup 1977; Leinster Ladies 1980
Int Curtis Cup 1984-86-88-90-92; Vagliano Trophy 1981-83-85-87-89-91; Espirito Santo 1986-90; Ireland (Home Int) 1979 to 1992, **1996**; Eur(L) T Ch 1981-83-85-87-89-**97**

Dowling, Deborah
Born Wimbledon on 26th July, 1962. Turned Professional 1981
PROFESSIONAL
Eur Jersey Open, Woodhall Hills Trn 1983; Portuguese Ladies Open 1985; Eastleigh Classic, Laing Ladies Classic 1986; Bloor Homes Eastleigh Classic 1989
RoW Singapore Open 1996
Int Union Cup 1994
AMATEUR
Reg Surrey Champion 1980
Int England (Home Int) 1981 Eur(L) T Ch 1981

Dredge, Bradley
Born Gwent, Wales on 6th July, 1973. Turned Professional 1995
PROFESSIONAL
Oth Klassis Turkish Open 1997
AMATEUR
Chp Amateur r/u 1992
Nat European Amateur r/u 1992
Trn St David's Gold Cross 1992; Welsh Trn of Champions 1994; Duncan Putter, Trubshaw Cup 1995
Int Walker Cup 1993; (GB) Eisenhower Trophy 1992, v Europe 1994; Wales (Home Int) 1992-93-94-95; Eur T Ch 1995
Jun Welsh Boys 1991

Drew, Norman Vico
Born Belfast on 25th May, 1932. Turned Professional 1958
PROFESSIONAL
Trn Yorkshire Evening News, Irish Dunlop 1959
Oth Irish Professional 1959; Ulster Professional 1966-72
Int Ryder Cup 1959; Ireland in World Cup 1960-61
AMATEUR
Nat Irish Open Amateur 1952-53
Reg North of Ireland Open Amateur 1950-52; East of Ireland Open Amateur 1952
Int Walker Cup 1953; Ireland (Home Int) 1952-53

Dundas, Stephen
Born Glasgow on 20th December, 1973
Cls Haggs Castle
Chp Amateur Champion 1992
Nat Scottish Amateur s/f 1992
Int Scotland (Home Int) 1992-93
Jun Glasgow Boys Stroke Play, Match Play 1988-89; West of Scotland Boys 1988
Jun Int Scotland Boys 1989

Educate, Lisa (*née* Walton)
Born 17th June, 1972
Cls Calcot Park
Nat English Women's Stroke Play U-18 Award 1989; Welsh Ladies' Stroke Play U-21 1991
Trn Todd Bowl 1990; Sunningdale Gold Vase 1989; Pleasington Putter 1991; Ping Lady Sun Dial Collegiate Trn 1991

Int Curtis Cup 1994-96; Espirito Santo 1994; Vagliano Trophy 1993-95; CW 1995; England (Home Int) 1991-94-95; Eur L T Ch 1993-95
Jun Int English Girls 1988-89-90

Evans, Albert David
Born Newton, Brecon, Wales on 28th August, 1911
Cls Royal & Ancient, Royal Porthcawl. Hon member of Brecon, Ross-on-Wye, Hereford, Worcestershire, Builth Wells, Pennard, Monmouth, Killarney
Chp Welsh Amateur 1949-61
Reg Herefordshire Amateur 1938-46-49-51-53-54-55-59-60-61-62. Breconshire Amateur 1929-31-32-33-34-37
Int Wales (Home Int) 1931-32-33-34-35-38-39-47-48-49-50-51-52-53-54-55-56-**60-61-62-63-64-65**; v Australia 1954
Mis Walker Cup Selector 1964-75

Evans, Duncan
Born Crewe on 23rd January, 1959
Cls Hon member of Leek, Conway, Holyhead, Royal Porthcawl, Westwood
Chp Amateur Champion 1980
Nat Welsh Amateur Stroke Play Championship 1981, r/u 1980
Reg Staffordshire Amateur 1979. Aberconwy Trophy 1981
Int Walker Cup 1981. GBIvEurope, EuropevSouth America 1980. Wales (Home Int) 1978-80; vIreland 1979; in Fiat Trophy 1980. Eur T Ch 1981
Jun Int Youths 1980

Evans, Gary
Born Rustington on 22nd February, 1969. Turned Professional 1991
Cls Worthing
Nat English Amateur r/u 1990; English Open Amateur Stroke Play 1990-91
Trn Lytham Trophy 1990-91; St Andrews Trophy r/u 1991
Int Walker Cup 1991; Eisenhower Trophy 1990; England (Home Int) 1990; Eur T Ch 1991
Jun Int British Youths 1989; English Youths 1989; English Boys 1986

Everard, Mrs D Mary
Born Sheffield on 8th October, 1942
Cls Hallamshire (Hon), Woodhall Spa (Hon), Kilton Forest (Hon), Lindrick
Maj Ladies British Open r/u 1977
Chp Ladies British Open Amateur r/u 1967
Nat Ladies British Open Amateur Stroke Play 1970-77, r/u 1971-73; English Ladies 1972, r/u 1964-77
Trn Astor Salver 1967-68-78. Hovis Ladies 1967. Roehampton Gold Cup 1970. Sunningdale Foursomes 1973. Hoylake Mixed Foursomes 1965-67-71-76. Avia Foursomes 1978
Reg North of England Ladies 1972. Yorkshire Ladies 1964-67-72-73-77

Int   Curtis Cup 1970-72-74-78. Vagliano Trophy
1967-69-71-73. GB Commonwealth Team
1971. World Team Championship 1968-72-78,
England (Home Int) 1964-67-70-72-73-77-78;
Eur(L) T Ch 1967-71-73-77
Mis   Member of British team to tour Australia 1973.
Captain English team to tour Kenya 1973

Faldo, Nicholas Alexander, MBE
Born Welwyn Garden City on 18th July, 1957.
Turned Professional 1976
PROFESSIONAL
Maj   Open Champion 1987-90-92, r/u 1993; 3rd 1988;
US Open r/u 1988 (tied) 3rd 1990; US Masters
1989-90-96; US PGA r/u 1992; 3rd 1993
Eur   Colgate PGA 1978; Sun Alliance PGA 1980;
Sun Alliance 1981; Haig Whisky TPC 1982;
French Open, Martini Int'l, Lawrence Batley
Int'l, Car Care Plan Int'l, Ebel Swiss Open
European Masters 1983; Car Care Plan Int'l
1984; Peugeot Spanish Open 1987; Peugeot
French Open, Volvo Masters 1988; Volvo PGA,
Dunhill British Masters, Peugeot French Open,
Suntory World Match Play 1989; Carrolls Irish
Open 1991; Carrolls Irish Open, Scandinavian
Masters, GA European Open, Toyota World
Match Play 1992; Johnnie Walker Classic,
Carrolls Irish Open 1993; Alfred Dunhill Open
1994
US   Heritage Classic 1984; Doral–Ryder Open 1995;
Nissan Open 1997
RoW   ICL Int'l 1979; Johnnie Walker Asian Classic
1990; Johnnie Walker World Chp 1992; Million
Dollar Challenge 1994
Oth   Skol Lager 1977
Int   Ryder Cup 1977-79-81-83-85-87-89-91-93-95-
97; Nissan Cup 1986; Kirin Cup 1987-88;
Hennessy-Cognac Cup 1978-80-82-84; England
in World Cup 1977-91; in Double Diamond
1977; in Dunhill Cup 1985-86-87 (winners)-88-
91-93(r/u); Four Tours Chp 1990
Mis   Rookie of the Year 1977; Harry Vardon Trophy
1983-92; AGW Trophy 1983-90; Braid-Taylor
Memorial Medal 1983-84-87-88-90;
BBC Sports Personality of the Year 1989;
US PGA Player of the Year 1990; Tooting Bec
Cup 1992. World Golf Hall of Fame 1997
AMATEUR
Nat   English Amateur 1975
Trn   Berkshire Trophy, Scrutton Jug, County
Champion of Champions 1975
Reg   Hertfordshire Amateur 1975
Oth   South African GU Special Stroke Chp 1975
Int   GB Commonwealth Trn 1975; England (Home
Int) 1975
Jun   British Youths 1975
Int   Boys 1974; Youths 1975

Farquharson-Black, Elaine
Born Aberdeen on 21st March, 1968. Turned
Professional 1992. Reinstated Amateur
Cls   Deeside
PROFESSIONAL
Int   Union Cup 1994
AMATEUR
Chp   Ladies British Open Amateur r/u 1989
Nat   Scottish Ladies 1990

Oth   World Fourball (with Helen Dobson) 1989
Trn   Helen Holm Trophy 1987
Reg   Aberdeenshire Ladies 1983-86-87
Int   Curtis Cup 1990-92; Vagliano Trophy 1989-91;
Commonwealth Trn 1991; Scotland (Home Int)
1987-88-89-90-91-97; Eur(L) T Ch 1989-91
Jun   British Girls r/u 1984-85; Scottish Girls 1985
Int   Scottish Girls 1982-84-85; Eur Jun(L) T Ch
1986-88

Faulkner, Max
Born Bexhill, Sussex on 29th July, 1916. Turned
Professional June 1933
Maj   Open Champion 1951
Eur   Spanish Open 1952-53-57. Portuguese Open
1968
Trn   Dunlop Southport 1946. Dunlop 1949-52.
Penfold Foursomes 1949. Lotus 1949. Dunlop
Masters 1951. PGA Match Play 1953. Irish
Hospitals 1959
Reg   West of England Open Professional 1947.
Southern England Professional 1964.
Oth   Sunningdale Open Foursomes 1964; Pringle
Seniors 1968-70
Int   Ryder Cup 1947-49-51-53-57; PGA Cup 1975

Feherty, David
Born in Bangor, NI on 13th August, 1958. Turned
Professional 1976
Eur   Italian Open, Bells Scottish Open 1986; BMW
International Open 1989; Cannes Open 1991;
Iberia Madrid Open 1992
RoW   ICL International 1984; Lexington PGA 1988;
Bells Cup (SA) 1992
Int   Ryder Cup 1991. Ireland: Dunhill Cup 1986-90
(winners) -91-93; World Cup 1990; Four Tours
World Chp 1990-91
Mis   Braid-Taylor Memorial Medal 1989

Ferguson, Marjory (*née* Fowler)
Born North Berwick on 15th May, 1937
Cls   North Berwick, Gullane, Killarney (Hon)
Nat   Scottish Ladies r/u 1966-71
Oth   Portuguese Ladies 1960
Reg   East of Scotland Ladies 1959-60-62-75. East
Lothian Ladies 1957-58-59-60-61-62-63-64-66-
67-69-74-81
Int   Curtis Cup 1966. Vagliano Trophy 1965. Scotland
(Home Int) 1959-62-63-64-65-66-67-69-70;
Eur(L) T Ch 1965-67-71

Le Feuvre, Carol *See* Gibbs
Fiddian, Eric Westwood
Born Stourbridge on 28th March, 1910
Cls   Stourbridge, Handsworth, Lindrick
Chp   Amateur r/u 1932
Nat   English Amateur 1932, r/u 1935. Irish Open
Amateur r/u 1933
Reg   Worcestershire Amateur 1928-30-50. Midland
Counties 1931
Int   Walker Cup 1932-34. England (Home Int)
1929-30-31-32-33-34-35
Jun   Boys 1927

Int English Boys 1926-27
Mis Had two holes-in-one in the Final of 1933 Irish
Open Amateur

Fletcher, Linzi

Born on 21st January, 1968
Cls Alnmouth
Nat English Ladies r/u 1990; English Womens
Intermediate 1990
Trn Critchley Salver 1989; Wentworth Scratch
Trophy 1990
Int Curtis Cup 1990; GB Commonwealth Trn
1991; England (Home Int) 1989-90; Eur(L) T
Ch 1991

Forster, Dorothy *See* Humphreys

Foster, Mark B

*Born Worksop on 1st August, 1975. Turned
Professional 1996*
Cls Worksop; Hunstanton (Hon)
Nat English Amateur 1994-95; English Open
Amateur Stroke Play 1995
Reg Midland Counties Champion 1994
Int Walker Cup 1995; England (Home Int) 1994-
95; v Spain 1995; Eur T Ch 1995
Jun Carris Trophy 1992; European Youths 1994
Jun Int English Boys 1991-92-93 (captain); British Boys
1992; British Youths 1994
Mis McEvoy Trophy r/u 1993

Foster, Rodney

Born Shipley, Yorkshire on 13th October, 1941
Cls Royal & Ancient, Hon member of Bradford,
Halifax, Leeds, West Bowling, Ilkley, East
Bierley
Chp Amateur s/f 1962-65
Nat English Amateur r/u 1964. English Open
Amateur Stroke Play 1969 (tied)-70, r/u 1965
Trn Berkshire Trophy 1964. Lytham Trophy 1967-
68. County Champion of Champions 1963 (tied)
Reg Yorkshire Amateur 1963-64-65-67-70
Int Walker Cup 1965-67-69-71-73-(**79**).
GBI v Europe 1964-66-68-70-(**80**). Eisenhower
Trophy 1964-70-(**80**). GB Commonwealth
Team 1967-71. England (Home Int) 1963-64-
66-67-68-69-70-71-72-(**76**)-(**77**)-(78); Eur T Ch
1963-65-67-69-71-73-(77)
Jun Int Boys 1958. Youths 1959

Fowler, Marjory *See* Ferguson

Frearson, Diane *See* Bailey

Gallacher, Bernard, OBE

*Born Bathgate on 9th February, 1949. Turned
Professional 1967*
PROFESSIONAL
Eur Spanish Open 1977; French Open 1979
Trn Schweppes, Wills 1969; Martini International
1971; Carrolls International, Dunlop Masters
1974; Dunlop Masters 1975; Tournament

Players Chp 1980; Greater Manchester Open
1981; Martini International; Jersey Open 1982;
Jersey Open 1984
Oth Scottish Professional 1971-73-74-77; Coca-Cola
Young Professionals 1973
RoW Zambia Eagle Open, Zambia Cock o' the North
1969; Mufulira Open 1970
Int Ryder Cup 1969-71-73-75-77-79-81-83-(**91**)-
(**93**)-(**95**); Hennessy-Cognac Cup 1974-78-82-
84; Scotland in World Cup 1969-71-74-82-83;
in Double Diamond 1971-72-73-74-75-76-77;
vSouth Africa 1976
Mis Rookie of the Year 1968; Harry Vardon Trophy
1969 (then youngest winner); Scottish
Sportsman of the Year 1969; Frank Moran
Trophy 1973
AMATEUR
Nat Scottish Open Amateur Stroke Play 1967
Int Scotland (Home Int) 1967
Jun Int Boys 1965-66

Gallacher, Stephen

Born Dechmont on 1 November, 1974
Cls Bathgate
Chp Amateur: leading qualifier 1994
Nat Scottish Amateur 1992; European Individual
Amateur 1994; Scottish Amateur Stroke Play
1995
Reg Lothians Stroke Play 1992
Trn Scottish Champion of Champions, Tennant
Cup, Lytham Trophy 1995
Int Walker Cup 1995; World Cup 1994; Scotland
(Home Int) 1992-93-94-95; v Italy, v Spain
1994; v Sweden, v France 1995; Eur T Ch
1993-95; Eisenhower Trophy 1994
Jun Scottish Boys Chp 1991-92; Scottish Youths
Chp 1994
Jun Int Scottish Boys 1991-92; British Boys 1992;
Scottish Youths 1992-93-94; British Youths
1994

Garrett, Maureen *(née* Ruttle)

Born 22nd August, 1922
Oth French Ladies 1964
Int Curtis Cup **1960**. England (Home Int). **1960**.
Vagliano Trophy **1961**
Mis LGU President 1982-85. Bobby Jones Award
1983

Garvey, Philomena K

*Born Drogheda, Co Louth on 26th April, 1927.
Turned Professional 1964, subsequently reinstated
Amateur*
Cls Co Down, Co Louth, Portrush, Milltown
Chp British Ladies 1957, r/u 1946-53-60-63
Nat Irish Ladies 1946-47-48-50-51-53-54-55-57-58-
59-60-62-63-70
Trn Worplesdon Mixed Foursomes 1955
Reg Munster Ladies 1951
Int Curtis Cup 1948-50-52-54-56-60. GBI v France
1949-51-53-55; vBelgium 1951-53. Vagliano
Trophy 1959-63. Ireland (Home Int) 1947-48-
49-50-51-52-53-54-55-56-59-60-61-62-63-69;
vAustralia 1950
Mis Quarter-finalist US Ladies 1950

Gibbs, Carol (*née* Le Feuvre)
Born Jersey on 18th October, 1951

Cls	Jersey, Lee-on-the-Solent
Nat	English Ladies r/u 1973
Oth	Dutch Ladies 1972
Trn	Avia Foursomes 1974
Reg	Jersey Ladies 1966-67-68. Hampshire Ladies 1970-71-72-73-74-76. South-Eastern Ladies 1974
Int	Curtis Cup 1974. Vagliano Trophy 1973. England (Home Int) 1971-72-73-74; Eur(L) T Ch 1973
Jun	English Girls 1969-70. British Girls 1970
Int	English Girls 1968-69-70
Mis	Member of LGU Team to tour Australia 1973, and Under-25 team to tour Canada 1973

Gilford, David
Born 14th September, 1965. Turned Professional 1986

PROFESSIONAL

Eur	Johnnie Walker International 1990; English Open 1991; Moroccan Open 1992-93; Portuguese Open 1993; Open de Tenerife, European Open 1994
RoW	Tobago International 1992
Oth	Silvermere Satellite Trophy 1987
Int	Ryder Cup 1991-95. (England) Dunhill Cup 1992(winners). World Cup 1992-93

AMATEUR

Nat	English Amateur 1984
Trn	Lagonda Trophy 1986
Int	Walker Cup 1985. GBIvEurope 1986. England (Home Int) 1983-84-85; Eisenhower Trophy 1984.
Jun	British Youths 1986. Carris Trophy 1981

Glover, John
Born Belfast on 3rd March, 1933

Cls	Killarney (Hon), New Club, St Andrews
Trn	Formby Hare 1963
Oth	British Universities 1954-55
Reg	Lancashire Amateur 1970
Int	Ireland (Home Int) 1951-52-53-55-59-60-62-70
Jun	Boy Champion 1950. Carris Trophy 1950
Mis	Secretary Royal & Ancient Rules of Golf Committee until December 1995

Green, Charles Wilson, OBE
Born Dumbarton on 2nd August, 1932

Cls	Dumbarton, Cardross, Helensburgh
Maj	Leading amateur in Open 1962
Nat	Scottish Amateur 1970-82-83, r/u 1971-80. Scottish Open Amateur Stroke Play 1975, 1984, r/u 1967-83. British Seniors 1988-89-90-91, r/u 1992-96. Scottish Seniors 1991-95-96
Trn	Lytham Trophy 1970 (tied)-74. Eden Tournament 1959. Tennant Cup 1968-70-75. Edward Trophy 1968-73-74-75
Reg	West of Scotland Amateur 1962-70-79. Dunbartonshire Amateur 1960-67-68-73-77. Dunbartonshire Match Play 1965-67-69-71-74. Glasgow Amateur 1979
Int	Walker Cup 1963-69-71-73-75-(83)-(85); GBI v Scandinavia 1962; vEurope 1962-66-68-70-72-

74-76. Eisenhower Trophy 1970-72-84-86. GB Commonwealth Team 1971. Scotland (Home Int) 1961to 1965; 1967 to 1978; **1980**; vAustralia 1964, Eur T Ch 1965-67-69-71-73-75-77-**79**-81-83; vBelgium 1973-75-77-78; vSpain 1977; vItaly 1979; vEngland 1979

Mis	Frank Moran Trophy 1974. British Selector 1980. Scottish Sports Photographer Award 1983

Greenhalgh, Julia *See* Merrill

Gregson, Malcolm Edward
Born Leicester on 15th August, 1943. Turned Professional 1961

Trn	Schweppes 1967. RTV 1967. Daks 1967-68. Martini 1967 (tied). Sumrie 1972
RoW	Zambia Cock o' the North 1974. Gambian Open 1981
Oth	Pannal Foursomes 1964. British Assistants 1964
Int	Ryder Cup 1967. England in World Cup 1967. GBI v France 1966. Sumrie 1972 England in Double Diamond 1975. (Sen) European Cup 1997
Mis	Harry Vardon Trophy 1967
Am	Boy International 1959-60

Grice-Whittaker, Penny
Born Sheffield on 11th September, 1964. Turned Professional 1985

PROFESSIONAL

Maj	Women's British Open 1991
Eur	Belgian Open 1986; Longines Classic 1991

AMATEUR

Nat	English Intermediate Champion 1984; English Stroke Play 1984; English Ladies U-23 Chp 1983
Reg	Yorkshire Champion 1981-82-83. Northern Foursomes 1984
Int	Curtis Cup 1984. England (Home Int) 1983-84. Eur(L) T Ch 1983. Vilmorin Trophy 1984. Espirito Santo 1984
Jun	English Girls 1983

Hackney, Lisa
Born Stoke-on-Trent on 24th September, 1967. Turned Professional 1991

PROFESSIONAL

Eur	Welsh Open 1996
RoW	Indonesian Open 1995
Int	Solheim Cup 1996; (for LPGA) Nichirei International 1997
Mis	Gatorade Rookie of the Year 1997; Kosaido Asian Order of Merit 1995

AMATEUR

Int	England (Home Int) 1990

Hall, Caroline
Born on 4th November, 1973. Turned Professional 1992

PROFESSIONAL

Eur	Ladies Danish Open 1995
Int	Union Cup 1994

AMATEUR

Chp	Ladies British Open Amateur s/f 1991

Nat	English Ladies Under-18 Stroke Play 1991; English Ladies 1992
Trn	Frilford Heath Scratch Cup 1990; Cotswold Hills Gold Vase 1990-91
Reg	Gloucestershire Ladies 1991
Int	Curtis Cup 1992; Vagliano Trophy 1991; England (Home Int) 1991-92; Eur(L) T Ch 1991
Jun	English Girls 1990, r/u 1991

Hall, Julie (née Wade)

Born Ipswich on 10th March, 1967

Cls	Ladybank, Felixstowe Ferry
Chp	Ladies British Open Amateur 1990-95
Nat	English Ladies Intermediate 1987; English Ladies Stroke Play 1987-93; English Ladies 1988-94-95; British Ladies Amateur Stroke Play 1988(r/u)-93; Welsh Women's Open Stroke Play 1993
Oth	World Fourball Chp (with Helen Wadsworth) 1987; Australian Women's Amateur 1995; Spanish Ladies Open Amateur 1992-96
Reg	Suffolk Chp 7 times; Suffolk Stroke Play 10 times. Fife Chp 1997
Trn	Critchley Salver 1988; Astor Salver 1990; Helen Holm Trophy 1991-93; Wentworth Scratch Cup 1993; Hermitage Scratch Cup 1994; Sunningdale Foursomes (with Helen Wadsworth) 1997
Int	Curtis Cup 1988-90-92-94-96; England (Home Int) 1987 to 1995, Eur(L) T Ch 1987-89-91-93-95; GBI Espirito Santo 1988-90-94, Vagliano Trophy 1989-91-93-95; Commonwealth Trn 1991-95
Mis	Winner of the Doris Chambers Trophy, the Angus Trophy and *The Daily Telegraph* Woman Golfer of the Year Trophy 1993 (shared). *The Daily Telegraph* Woman Golfer of the Year 1995. Secretary of the LGU 1996.

Harrington, Padraig

Born Dublin on 31st August, 1971. Turned Professional 1995

PROFESSIONAL

Eur	Open de España 1996
Int	Ireland in Dunhill Cup 1996-97; World Cup 1996-97 (winners)

AMATEUR

Nat	Irish Open Amateur 1995; Irish Close Amateur r/u 1990-94-95
Oth	Sherry Cup 1991
Int	Walker Cup 1991-93-95. Ireland (Home Int) 1990-91-92-95; Eur T Ch 1991-95. GBI v Europe 1992-94
Jun Int	GBI Youths 1990-91; Boys 1988-89; Ireland Youths 1990-91; Boys 1987-88-89

Harris, Marley [Spearman]

Born on 11th January, 1928

Cls	Sudbury
Chp	British Ladies 1961-62
Nat	English Ladies 1964
Trn	Spalding Ladies 1956; Worplesdon Mixed Foursomes r/u 1956-64; Kayser-Bondor Foursomes 1958 (tied); London Ladies Foursomes 1960; Astor Salver 1964-65; Astor

Princes' Trophy 1964-65; Sunningdale Foursomes, Casa Pupo Foursomes, Roehampton Gold Cup, Hovis Ladies 1965

RoW	New Zealand Ladies Stroke Play 1963
Reg	Middlesex Ladies 1955-56-57-58-59-61-64-65. South-East Ladies 1956-58-61
Int	Curtis Cup 1960-62-64. Vagliano Trophy 1959-61. GB Commonwealth Trn 1959-63. England (Home Int) 1955 to 65
Mis	AGW Trophy 1962. Non-playing captain English Team European Team Championship 1971

Hay, Garry

Born Perth on 27th August, 1959

Cls	Hilton Park, Downfield
Nat	Scottish Amateur Stroke Play 1990, r/u 1980
Trn	Tennant Cup 1979. Scottish Champion of Champions 1991; St Andrews Links Trophy 1993
Int	Walker Cup 1991. Scotland (Home Int) 1980-88-90-91-92; v England 1979; v Belgium 1980; v France 1980-82-89-91-93; v Italy 1988-92-94; v Sweden 1992; v Spain 1994. GBI v Europe 1980
Jun	British Youths 1980

Hedges, Peter J

Born 30th March, 1947

Cls	Langley Park (Hon), Royal Cinque Ports, Addington, Wildernesse, Royal & Ancient
Nat	English Open Amateur Stroke Play 1976
Trn	Royal St George's Challenge Cup 1970. Prince of Wales Challenge Cup 1972-73-74-77. Berkshire Trophy 1973-76-78. Golf Illustrated Gold Vase 1974. Scrutton Jug 1976
Reg	Kent Amateur 1968-71-79. Kent Open 1970-74
Int	Walker Cup 1973-75. GBIvEurope 1974-76 Eisenhower Trophy 1974. England (Home Int) 1970-73-74-75-76-77-78-82; Eur T Ch 1973-75-77
Jun	Youth International 1968
Mis	Member of European Team to tour South Africa 1974

Henson, Dinah (née Oxley)

Born Dorking on 17th October, 1948

Cls	Hon member of West Byfleet, Killarney, Fairfield, USA
Chp	British Ladies 1970.
Nat	English Ladies 1970-71, r/u 1968. British Ladies Stroke Play r/u 1969
Trn	Wills Ladies 1969-70-71. Worplesdon Mixed Foursomes 1968-77. Newmark International 1975 (tied)-77
Reg	Surrey Ladies 1967-70-71-76
Int	Curtis Cup 1968-70-72-76. Vagliano Trophy 1967-69-71. Espirito Santo 1970. GB Commonwealth Trn 1967-71. England (Home Int) 1967-68-69-70-75-76-77-78; Eur(L) T Ch 1971-77
Jun	British Girls 1963. English Girls 1965. French Girls 1969. Girl International 1964-65-66
Mis	Daks Woman Golfer of the Year 1970. Leading Amateur Colgate European Ladies Open 1974

Hetherington, Jean (née McClure) See Holmes

Holmes, Jean [Hetherington] (née McClure)

Born Wanstead, Essex on 17th August, 1923

Cls Wanstead, Hunstanton, Thorndon Park
Chp British Ladies 1946, r/u 1958.
Nat English Ladies r/u 1966
Reg Nottinghamshire Ladies 1949-50-51. Essex Ladies 1956-57
Int England (Home Int) 1957-66-(67)

Homer, Trevor Walter Brian

Born Bloxwich on 8th September, 1943. Turned Professional July 1974. Reinstated as Amateur in 1978

Chp Amateur Champion 1972-74
Trn Leicestershire Fox 1972. Harlech Gold Cross 1970
Int Walker Cup 1973. Eisenhower Trophy 1972. GBI vEurope 1972. England (Home Int) 1972-73; Eur T Ch 1973

Horton, Tommy

Born St Helens, on 16th June, 1941. Turned Professional 1957

Trn RTV 1968. PGA Match Play 1970. Gallaher Ulster 1971. Piccadilly 1972. Penfold 1974. Uniroyal International 1976. Dunlop Masters 1978
RoW South African Open 1970. Nigerian Open 1973. Zambian Open 1977. Tobago Open 1975. Gambian Open 1975
Sen Forte PGA Senior Chp 1992; Shell Scottish Seniors, Collingtree Seniors, Zurich Lexus Trophy 1993; Irish Senior Masters, St Pierre Seniors Classic 1994; De Vere Hotels Seniors Classic, Seniors Club Pro Chp 1995; Castle Royal European Seniors Classic, Stella Seniors Open, Northern Electric Seniors, The Players Chp 1996; Turkish Seniors Open, Irish Seniors Open, Jersey Seniors Open, Scottish Seniors Open, Clubhaus Seniors Classic, Senior Trn of Champions 1997
Int Ryder Cup 1975-77. GBIvFrance 1966. England in World Cup 1976. England in Double Diamond 1971-74-75-76-77. GBIvEurope 1974-76. (Sen) European Cup 1997 (Captain)
Mis Second in Order of Merit 1967. PGA Captain 1978; Braid-Taylor Memorial Medal 1976-77; Seniors Order of Merit winner (John Jacobs Trophy) 1993-96-97

Hourihane, Claire *See* Dowling

Howard, D Barclay

Born Johnstone on 27th January, 1953

Cls Cochrane Castle
Maj Leading Amateur in Open Chp 1997
Nat Scottish Amateur sf 1971, 1994; Scottish Stroke-play 1997, r/u 1979; European Amateur r/u 1996
Trn St Andrews Links Trophy 1994-96; Leven Gold Medal 1994; Cameron Corbett Vase 1975-84-95
Reg West of Scotland Strokeplay 1980-93; Glasgow Open 1996
Int Walker Cup 1995-97; Eisenhower Trophy 1996; GBI v Europe 1980-94-96; Scotland (Home Int) 1980-81-82-83-93-94-95-96; v Belgium 1980;

v France 1980-81-83-95-97; v Italy 1984-94; v Sweden 1995-97; Eur T Ch 1981-95-97; v Spain 1996
Jun Scottish Boys 1969-70; Scottish Youths 1971-72-73-74; British Youths 1971-72-73-74
Mis Scottish Order of Merit winner 1994-96.

Huggan, Shirley Margaret (née Lawson)

Born Glasgow on 16th September, 1964

Cls Eastwood, Rock Ridge, USA
Nat Scottish Ladies Amateur 1988-89 r/u 1990; Taunton Trophy 1987
Reg West of Scotland Ladies 1986-88; Renfrewshire Ladies 1985-86-87-88
Int Curtis Cup 1988; Scotland (Home Int) 1985-86-87-88-89; Eur(L) T Ch 1985-87-89; GBI Vagliano Trophy 1989
Jun Scottish Girls 1982; Scottish Girls Stroke Play 1983-84; r/u 1982-85
Int Girls 1980-81-82

Huggett, Brian George Charles, MBE

Born Porthcawl on 18th November, 1936. Turned Professional 1951

Maj Open r/u 1965. 3rd 1962
Eur Dutch Open 1962. German Open 1963. Portuguese Open 1974
Trn Cox-Moore 1963. Smart-Weston 1965. Sumrie 1968-72. PGA Close 1967. Martini 1967 (tied)-68. Shell Winter Tournament 1967-68. PGA Match Play 1968, r/u 1977. Daks 1969-71 (tied). Bowmaker 1969 (tied). Carrolls 1970. Dunlop Masters 1970. British Airways-Avis 1978
RoW Singapore International 1962. Algarve Open 1970
Sen Anvil Seniors Classic, Northern Electric Seniors 1992; Northern Electric Seniors, Forte PGA Seniors 1993; Spanish Seniors Open 1994; Windsor Senior Masters, Scottish Seniors Open 1995
Oth Sunningdale Foursomes 1957. British Assistants 1958. Gleneagles Pro-Am 1961-65. Turnberry Pro-Am 1968. Welsh Professional 1978
Reg East Anglian Open 1962-67
Int Ryder Cup 1963-67-69-71-73-75-(77). Wales in World Cup 1963-64-65-68-69-70-71-76-79. Wales in Double Diamond 1971-72-73-74-75-76-77. GBIvEurope 1974-78
Mis Vardon Trophy 1968

Huke, Beverly Joan Mary

Born Great Yarmouth on 10th May, 1951. Turned Professional 1978

Cls Cotswold Hills (Hon), Windmill Hill (Hon), Leighton Buzzard, Panmure Barry
Chp British Ladies r/u 1971
Nat English Ladies 1975
Eur Carlsberg (Ballater) 1979. Carlsberg (Rosemount) 1980. NABS Pro-Am 1st Pro Individual 1981. Brickendon Grange and Stourbridge Pro-Am 1983; Lark Valley Classic 1983 (shared); White Horse Whisky Challenge Trophy 1983. Trusthouse Forte Classic 1985. German Ladies Open 1984. Wester Volkswagen Classic 1986
Trn Roehampton Gold Cup 1971. Renfrew Rose Bowl 1976-77-78. Helen Holm Trophy 1977

Reg	Gloucestershire Ladies 1972. Angus Ladies 1976
Int	Curtis Cup 1972. Vagliano Trophy 1971-75. England (Home Int) 1971-72-75-76-77; Eur(L) T Ch 1975-77
Jun	Scottish Girls Open Stroke Play 1970-71. Girl International 1966-67-68
Mis	Chairman WPGET 1988

Humphreys, Dorothy (*née* Forster)
Lisburn, Co Antrim on 7th May, 1927

Cls	Troon Ladies; Balmoral (Hon), Clandeboye (Hon)
Nat	Irish Ladies 1952, r/u 1951
Reg	Leinster Ladies 1951; Ulster Ladies 1952-53-57
Int	GB Commonwealth Team 1953; GB *v* France, Belgium 1953. Ireland (Home Int) 1950-51-52-53-55-56-57

Hunt, Bernard John, MBE
Born Atherstone on 2nd February, 1930. Turned Professional 1946

Maj	Open 3rd 1960; leading British player (4th) 1964
Eur	Belgian Open 1957; German Open 1961; French Open 1967
Trn	Spalding, Goodwin Foursomes, Gleneagles-Saxone 1953; Goodwin Foursomes 1954; Irish Hospitals 1956; Bowmaker 1958 (shared); Martini, Daks 1961; Carrolls, Swallow-Penfold, Smart-Weston, Gevacolour, Dunlop Masters 1963; Rediffusion 1964; Dunlop Masters, Gallaher Ulster 1965; Piccadilly 1966; Gallaher Ulster 1967; Penfold, Sumrie, Agfacolor 1970; Wills 1971; Sumrie 1973
Reg	Southern England Professional 1959-60-62-67; West of England Open Professional 1960-61
Oth	British Assistants 1953; Algarve Open, BP Italy 1969
RoW	Egyptian Open 1956; Brazilian Open 1962
Int	Ryder Cup 1953-57-59-61-63-65-67-69-(73)-(75); England in World Cup 1958-59-60-62-63-64-68; in Double Diamond 1971-72-73
Mis	Harry Vardon Trophy 1958-60-65. PGA Captain 1966

Hutcheon, Ian C
Born Monifieth, Angus on 22nd February, 1942

Cls	Monifieth (Hon), Grange and Dundee (Hon)
Nat	Scottish Amateur 1973. Scottish Open Amateur Stroke Play 1971-74-79
Trn	Tennant Cup 1976; Lytham Trophy 1980; Scottish Champion of Champions 1980-81-86-88; Leven Gold Medal 1981-82
Oth	North of Spain Stroke Play 1972
Reg	Scottish Central District Amateur 1972. Angus Match Play 1965-70-72. Angus Stroke Play 1968-71-72-74. North of Scotland District Amateur Stroke Play 1975-76-82
Int	GBI *v*Europe 1974-76. Eisenhower Trophy 1974-76 (winners and joint winning individual)-80. Scotland (Home Int) 1971-72-73-74-75-76-77-78-80; Eur T Ch 1973-75-77-79-81; *v*Spain 1972-77; *v*Belgium 1973-75-77-78-80; *v*France 1978-80-81; *v*Italy 1979; in First Trophy 1979. GBI in Dominican International 1973. Walker Cup 1975-77-79-81. GBI in Colombian International 1975. GB Commonwealth Trn 1975
Mis	Frank Moran Trophy 1976

Imrie, Kathryn *See* **Marshall**

Irvin, Ann Lesley
Born 11th April, 1943

Cls	Lytham (Hon), Lytham Green Drive (Hon)
Chp	British Ladies 1973, r/u 1969
Nat	English Ladies 1967-74. British Ladies Stroke Play 1969
Trn	Roehampton Gold Cup 1967-68-69-72-76. Hovis Ladies 1966-68-70. Avia Foursomes 1968
Reg	Northern Ladies 1963-64. Lancashire Ladies 1965-67-69-71-72-74. Northern Foursomes Championship 1973
Int	Curtis Cup 1962-68-70-76. Vagliano Trophy 1961-63-65-67-69-71-73-75. GB Commonwealth Trn 1967-75. England (Home Int) 1962-63-65-67-68-69-70-71-72-73-75; Eur(L) T Ch 1965-67-69-71-73-75
Jun	French Girls 1963
Int	Girls 1960-61; British Girls 1961
Mis	Daks Woman Golfer of the Year 1968-69. Captain of British Team to tour Australia 1973. Lancashire 1981. County Captain 1979. England Junior Captain. 1981-82. International Selector 1981-82. England Selector 1981-82. County Selector and Junior Organiser

Jack, Robert Reid
Born Cumbernauld on 17th January, 1924

Cls	Dullatur
Maj	Leading Amateur in Open 1959
Chp	Amateur Champion 1957
Nat	Scottish Amateur 1955
Trn	Edward Trophy 1959. Tennant Cup 1961
Oth	Royal & Ancient Royal Medal 1965-67. Silver Cross 1956-66. Glennie Medal 1965
Reg	Glasgow Amateur 1953-54-58. Dunbartonshire Match Play 1949
Int	Walker Cup 1957-59. Eisenhower Trophy 1958. GB Commonwealth Trn 1959. GBI*v*Europe 1956. Scotland (Home Int) 1950-51-54-55-56-57-58-59-61; *v*Scandinavia 1956-58

Jacklin, Tony, CBE
Born Scunthorpe on 7th July, 1944. Turned Professional 1962

PROFESSIONAL

Maj	Open 1969, 3rd 1971-72; US Open 1970
Eur	Blaxnit 1966; Pringle, Dunlop Masters 1967; Wills, Lancôme Trophy 1970; Benson & Hedges Festival 1971; Viyella PGA Close 1972; Dunlop Masters, Italian Open 1973; Scandinavian Enterprise Open 1974; Kerrygold International Classic 1976; German Open 1979; Jersey Open 1981; Sun Alliance PGA 1982
Oth	British Assistants 1964; English Professional 1977
US	Greater Jacksonville Open 1968-72
RoW	Kimberley 1966 (shared); Forest Products, New Zealand, New Zealand PGA 1967; Dunlop International Australia 1972; Los Lagartos Open 1973-74; Venezuelan Open 1979
Sen	US Tour: First of America Classic 1994; Franklin Quest 1995
Int	Ryder Cup 1967-69-71-73-75-77-79-(83)-(85)-(87)-(89); Hennessy-Cognac 1976; England in

World Cup 1966-70-71-72; in Double Diamond 1972-73-74-76-77
Mis   Rookie of the Year 1963; Hon Life President PGA; first British player since Harry Vardon to hold Open and US Open simultaneously; Braid-Taylor Memorial Medal 1969-70-71-72
AMATEUR
Reg   Lincolnshire Open 1961

Jackson, Barbara Amy Bridget
Born Birmingham on 10th July, 1936
Cls   Royal St David's, Edgbaston. Hon member of Handsworth, Hunstanton, Killarney
Chp   British Ladies r/u 1964.
Nat   English Ladies 1956, r/u 1958
Trn   Fairway and Hazard Foursomes 1954. Kayser Bondor Foursomes 1962. Avia Foursomes 1967. Worplesdon Mixed Foursomes 1960. Astor Prince's 1963
Oth   German Ladies 1956. Canadian Ladies 1967
Reg   Midland Ladies 1954-56-57-58-59-60-69. Staffordshire Ladies 1954-56-57-58-59-63-64-67-69-76
Int   Curtis Cup 1958-64-68. Vagliano Trophy 1959-63-65-67-(73)-(75). GB Commonwealth Team 1959-67. Espirito Santo 1964. England (Home Int) 1955-56-57-58-59-63-64-65-66-(73)-(74); Eur(L) T Ch (**1975**),*v*France 1964-66
Jun   British Girls 1954
Mis   LGU International Selector 1983. English and GBI Selector 1983 to 1988. Chairman of English Ladies Association 1970-71

Jacobs, John Robert Maurice
Born Lindrick, Yorkshire on 14th March, 1925. Turned Professional 1947
Eur   Dutch Open 1957
RoW   South African Match Play 1957
Int   Ryder Cup 1955-(**79**)-(**81**). GBI*v*Continent 1954-55-58
Mis   Former PGA Tournament Director-General. TV commentator. Coach to many international teams

James, Lee
Born Poole on 27th January, 1973. Turned Professional 1995
PROFESSIONAL
Oth   Challenge First Modena Classic Open 1996
AMATEUR
Chp   Amateur Champion 1994
Nat   European Amateur r/u 1994
Int   Walker Cup 1995; GBI *v* Europe 1994; World Cup 1994; England (Home Int) 1993-94-95; *v* France 1994; *v* Spain 1995; Eur T Ch 1995

James, Mark H
Born Manchester on 28th October, 1953. Turned Professional 1975
PROFESSIONAL
Maj   Open 3rd 1981
Eur   Sun Alliance Match Play 1978; Welsh Classic,

Carroll's Irish Open 1979; Carroll's Irish Open, Italian Open 1980; Tunisian Open 1983; GSI Open 1985; Benson & Hedges International 1986; Peugeot Spanish Open 1988; Karl Litten Desert Classic, AGF Open, NM English Open 1989; Dunhill British Masters, English Open 1990; Madeira Island Open, Open de Canarias 1993; Moroccan Open 1995; Open de España 1997
RoW   Lusaka Open 1977; Sao Paulo Open 1981; South African TPC 1988
Int   Ryder Cup 1977-79-81-89-91-93-95; Hennessy-Cognac 1976-78-80-82 (individual winner)-84; World Cup 1978-79-82-84-87-88-90-93-97; Dunhill Cup 1988-89-90(r/u)-93(r/u)-95-97; Kirin Cup 1988; Four Tours World Chp 1989-90
Mis   Tooting Bec Cup 1976; Braid-Taylor Memorial Medal 1976-79-81; Rookie of the Year 1976
AMATEUR
Chp   Amateur r/u 1975
Nat   English Amateur 1974
Trn   Leicestershire Fox 1974
Int   Walker Cup 1975; England (Home Int) 1974-75; Eur T Ch 1975
Jun Int   (England) Boys 1971; Youths 1974-75

Johnson, Patricia (Trish)
Born Bristol on 17th January, 1966. Turned Professional 1987
PROFESSIONAL
Eur   McEwan's Wirral Classic, Bloor Homes Eastleigh Classic, Woolmark Match Play 1987; Hennessy Cup, Bloor Homes Eastleigh Classic, European Open, Longines Classic 1990; Spanish Classic 1992; European Open, French Open 1996
US   LPGA Qualifying School 1987; Las Vegas LPGA, Atlanta Women's Chp 1993; Fieldcrest Cannon Classic 1996
Int   Solheim Cup 1990-92-94-96; Sunrise Cup 1992 (individual winner); European Cup 1997; (for LPGA) Nichirei International 1993
Mis   Rookie of the Year 1987. Woolmark Order of Merit leader 1990
AMATEUR
Nat   English Ladies 1985. English Ladies Stroke Play 1985
Trn   Roehampton Gold Cup 1986
Reg   South-Western Ladies 1984
Int   Curtis Cup 1986; Espirito Santo 1986; Vagliano Trophy 1985; England (Home Int) 1984-85-86; Eur (L) T Ch 1985
Jun   Devon Girls 1982

Jones, John Roger
Born Old Colwyn, Denbighshire on 14th June, 1944
Cls   Langland Bay (Hon)
Nat   Welsh Amateur Stroke Play 1972-73-82, r/u 1983. Welsh Amateur 1983
Trn   Harlech Gold Cross 1976
Reg   Denbighshire Amateur 1969-71. Caernarfonshire and Anglesey Amateur 1970 (tied)-72-74-75. Glamorgan Amateur 1977-79. North Wales Amateur 1976. Carmarthenshire Amateur 1979-80. Landsdowne Trophy (Channel League) Stroke Play 1979-80-83

Int Wales (Home Int) 1970-72-73-77-78-80-81-82-83; Eur T Ch 1973-79-81-83; vDenmark 1976-80; vIreland 1979; vSwitzerland 1980; vSpain 1980; in Asian Team Championship 1979

Kelley, Michael John
Born Scarborough on 6th February, 1945
Cls Ganton, Hon member of Scarborough North Cliff, Bridlington, Bradford
Trn Lytham Trophy 1976. Antlers Royal Mid-Surrey 1972
Reg Yorkshire Amateur 1969-74-81. Yorkshire Open 1969-75. Champion of Champions 1981
Int Walker Cup 1977-79. Eisenhower Trophy 1976 (winners). GBI vEurope 1976-78-82; GBI in Colombian International 1978. England (Home Int) 1974-75-76-77-78-80-81-82-88; Eur T Ch 1977-79; vFrance 1982
Jun Int Boys 1962. Youths 1965-66

King, Michael
Born London on 15th February, 1950. Turned Professional 1974
PROFESSIONAL
Eur Tournament Players Chp 1979
Int Ryder Cup 1979; England in World Cup 1979
AMATEUR
Trn St George's Hill Trophy 1970; County Champion of Champions 1970; Sunningdale Foursomes 1972; Lytham Trophy 1973 (shared)
Reg Berks, Bucks & Oxon Amateur 1968-69-70-73-74; Berks, Bucks & Oxon Open 1968-73
Int Walker Cup 1969-73; GB Commonwealth Trn 1971; vEurope 1972; England (Home Int) 1971-72-73; Eur T Ch 1971-73

King, Samuel Leonard
Born Sevenoaks, Kent on 27th March, 1911
Maj Open 3rd 1939
Trn *Daily Mail* 1937. *Yorkshire Evening News* 1944-49
Oth British Assistants 1933. Dunlop-Southern 1936-37. Sunningdale Foursomes 1948. Teachers Senior 1961-62
Int Ryder Cup 1937-47-49. England 1934-36-37-38

Lambert, Catriona *See* **Matthew**

Lane, Barry
Born Hayes, Middlesex on 21st June, 1960. Turned Professional 1976
Eur Equity & Law Challenge 1987; Scottish Open 1988; Mercedes German Masters 1992; European Masters 1993; Open de Baleares 1994
RoW Jamaica Open 1983
Oth Andersen Consulting World Chp 1995
Int Ryder Cup 1993; (England) Dunhill Cup 1988-94-95-96; World Cup 1988-94

Lawrence, Joan B
Born Kinghorn, Fife on 20th April, 1930
Cls Honorary member of Dunfermline, Aberdour, Killarney
Chp Scottish Ladies 1962-63-64, r/u 1965. Scottish Veteran Ladies Champion 1982

Reg East of Scotland Ladies 1971-72. Fife Ladies fifteen times winner 1953-90
Int Curtis Cup 1964. World Team Champion 1964. GB Commonwealth Trn **1971**. Vagliano Trophy 1963-65. Scotland (Home Int) 1959 to 70-(77); Eur(L) T Ch 1965-67-**69**-71-(77)
Jun Girl International 1949
Mis LGU International Selector 1973-74-75-76-80-81-82-83. Treasurer Scottish Ladies Golfing Association from 1980. Chairman LGU Executive 1989

Leburn, Wilma (*née* Aitken)
Born 24th January, 1959
Trn Helen Holm Trophy 1978-80-82. Avia Foursomes 1982
Reg West of Scotland 1978-80-81. Renfrewshire Champion 1978-79-80-81-82
Int Curtis Cup 1982. Vagliano Trophy 1981-83. Scotland (Home Int) 1978-79-80-81-82-83. Vilmorin Cup 1979. Eur(L) T Ch 1979-81-83
Jun Scottish Girls 1975-77. West of Scotland Girls 1977. British Girls 1977
Int Scottish Girls 1975-77-78

Lee-Smith, Jenny
Born Newcastle-upon-Tyne on 2nd December, 1948. Turned Professional 1977
Maj Ladies British Open 1976 (as amateur)
PROFESSIONAL
Eur Carlsberg 1979; Carlsberg, Robert Windsor Trn, Volvo Swedish International, Manchester Evening News Classic 1980; Sports Space Trn, McEwan's Lager Welsh Classic, Lambert & Butler Match Play 1981; Ford Classic 1982; British Olivetti 1984
Mis Order of Merit winner 1981-82
AMATEUR
Nat Ladies British Open Amateur Stroke Play 1976
Trn Wills Match Play 1974; Newmark 1976; Hoylake Mixed Foursomes 1969
Reg Northumberland Ladies 1972-73-74
Int Curtis Cup 1974-76; Espirito Santo 1976; GB Commonwealth Trn 1975; Colombian International 1975; England (Home Int) 1973-74-75-76; Eur(L) T Ch 1975
Mis Daks Woman Golfer of the Year 1976

Lucas, Percy Belgrave, CBE, DSO, DFC
Born Sandwich Bay, Kent on 2nd September, 1915
Cls Sandy Lodge, Walton Heath, Prince's, Royal West Norfolk
Trs Berkshire Trophy 1947-49. St George's Challenge Cup 1947. Prince of Wales Challenge Cup 1947. President's Putter 1949
Reg Herts Amateur 1946-47
Int Walker Cup 1936-47-(**49**). GBI vProfessionals 1935. England (Home Int) 1936-48-**49**; vFrance 1936-47
Jun British Boys 1933.
Int Boys 1930-31-32-33
Mis President Golf Foundation 1963–66; President National Golf Clubs Advisory Association 1963–69; President Association of Golf Club Secretaries 1968–74; Member UK Sports Council 1971–83; author

Lumb, Kathryn (née Phillips)

Born Bradford on 24th February, 1952

Cls	Hon member of Bradford, West Bowling, Killarney, Filton
Reg	Central England Mixed Foursomes 1966-70. Yorkshire Ladies 1968-69
Int	Curtis Cup 1970-72. Vagliano Trophy 1969-71. England (Home Int) 1968-69-70-71; Eur(L) T Ch 1969
Jun	English Girls 1968. Scottish Girls Open Stroke Play 1968-69. French Girls 1970
Int	Girls 1967-68-69

Lunt, Michael Stanley Randle

Born Birmingham on 20th May, 1935

Cls	Royal & Ancient, Walton Heath, St Enodoc, Hon. mem. of Blackwell, Royal St David's, Moseley, Edgbaston, Stourbridge, Willesley Park, Kibworth, Handsworth, King's Norton, Dudley
Chp	Amateur Champion 1963, r/u 1964
Nat	English Amateur 1966, r/u 1962. English Open Amateur Stroke Play r/u 1961
Trn	Golf Illustrated Gold Vase 1958, Harlech Gold Cross 1959-61-64-65-66-67. Leicestershire Fox 1966
Reg	Midland Counties Amateur 1960-62
Int	Walker Cup 1959-61-62-65. Eisenhower Trophy 1964 GB Commonwealth Team 1963. England (Home Int) 1956-57-58-59-60-62-63-64-66-(72)-(73)-(74)-(75). Eur T Ch (1973)-(75)
Jun	Boy International 1949-50-51-52
Mis	AGW Trophy 1963. President Midland Counties Golf Association 1978 to 1980

Lyle, Alexander Walter Barr (Sandy), MBE

Born Shrewsbury on 9th February, 1958. Turned Professional 1977

PROFESSIONAL

Maj	Open Champion 1985. US Masters 1988
Eur	Jersey Open, Scandinavian Enterprise Open, European Open 1979; Coral Classic 1980; French Open, Lawrence Batley International 1981; Lawrence Batley International 1982; Madrid Open 1983; Italian Open, Lancôme Trophy 1984; Benson & Hedges International 1985; German Masters 1987; Dunhill British Masters, Suntory World Match Play 1988; BMW International Open 1991; Italian Open, Volvo Masters 1992
US	Greater Greensboro Open 1986; Tournament Players Championship 1987; Phoenix Open, Greater Greensboro Open 1988
Oth	PGA Qualifying School winner 1977; Scottish Professional Chp 1979
RoW	Nigerian Open 1978; Casio World Open, Kapalua International (Hawaii) 1984
Int	Ryder Cup 1979-81-83-85-87; Nissan Cup 1985-86, Kirin Cup 1987-88; Hennessy-Cognac Cup 1980-84; Scotland in World Cup 1979-80 (Individual Winner) -87(r/u); Dunhill Cup 1985-86-87 (r/u)-88-89-90-92(r/u)
Mis	Rookie of the Year 1978; Harry Vardon Trophy 1979-80-85; AGW Trophy 1980-88; Tooting

Bec Cup 1982-88; Braid-Taylor Memorial Medal 1985; Frank Moran Trophy 1985

AMATEUR

Nat	English Open Amateur Stroke Play 1975-77
Trn	County Champion of Champions 1974; Hampshire Hog, Berkshire Trophy, Scrutton Jug, Berkhamsted Trophy 1977
Reg	Midland Amateur, Shropshire & Herefordshire Amateur 1974; Midland Open 1975; Shropshire & Herefordshire Amateur 1976
Int	Walker Cup 1977; GB Commonwealth Trn 1975; GBIvEurope 1976; England (Home Int) 1975-76-77, Eur T Ch 1977
Jun	Carris Trophy 1975; British Youths 1977; r/u British Boys 1974-75
Int	Boys 1972-73-74-75
Mis	In 1975 represented England in Boy, Youth and Full Internationals

McCann, Catherine (née Smye)

Born Clonmel, Co Tipperary in 1922

Cls	Tullamore
Chp	British Ladies 1951
Nat	Irish Ladies 1949-61, r/u 1947-52-57-60
Reg	Munster Ladies 1958, Irish Midland Ladies 1952-57-58
Int	Curtis Cup 1952. Ireland (Home Int) 1947-48-49-50-51-52-53-54-56-57-58-60-61-62; vNew Zealand 1953; vCanada 1953

McClure, Jean   *See* Holmes

McCorkindale, Isabella   *See* Robertson

McEvoy, Peter

Born London on 22nd March, 1953

Cls	Copt Heath (Hon), R&A
Maj	Open leading amateur 1978-79
Chp	Amateur Champion 1977-78, r/u 1987
Nat	English Open Amateur Stroke Play 1980 (tied), r/u 1978. English Amateur r/u 1980
Trn	Duncan Putter 1978-80-87; Scrutton Jug 1978-80-85; Lytham Trophy 1978; Selborne Salver 1979-80; Leicestershire Fox 1976; Lagonda Trophy 1980; Berkshire Trophy 1985; County Champion of Champions 1984 (shared); Berkhamsted Trophy 1986; Hampshire Hog 1989
Oth	British Universities Stroke Play 1973
Reg	Warwickshire Match Play 1973-75-81; Warwickshire Amateur 1974-76-77-80-84; Warwickshire Open 1973-74; West of England Open Amateur Stroke Play 1977-80-84; Midland Open Amateur Stroke Play 1978; Midland Scratch Cup (Ireland) 1982-83-84-88
Int	Walker Cup 1977-79-81-85-89; Eisenhower Trophy 1978-80-84-86-88 (winners) (leading individual); GBI v Europe 1978-80-82-84-86-88; England (Home Int) 1976-77-78-80-81-82-83-84-85-86-87-88-89-91; v Scotland 1979; Eur T Ch 1977-79-81-83-85-87-89; in Fiat Trophy 1980; vFrance 1982-84-86-88-90; v Spain 1985-87-89. England Captain 1995
Jun	Youth International 1974
Mis	Only British amateur to complete 72 holes in US Masters (1978); AGW Trophy 1978; most capped England player

McGimpsey, Garth M
Born 17th July, 1955

Cls Bangor, Royal Portrush, Royal Co Down
Chp Amateur Champion 1985, s/f 1989
Nat Irish Amateur 1985-88
Reg North of Ireland 1978-84-91-92, West of Ireland 1984-88-96, East of Ireland 1988-94, r/u 1979-80
Int Walker Cup 1985-89-91. GBIvEurope 1984-86-88-92. Eisenhower Trophy 1984-86-88 (winners). Ireland (Home Int) 1978; 1980 to 1997. Eur T Ch 1981-89-91-95-97
Mis Irish long-driving champion 1977; UK long-driving champion 1979

McGinley, Paul
Born Dublin on 16th December, 1966. Turned Professional 1991

PROFESSIONAL
Eur Höhe Brücke Open 1996; Oki Pro-Am 1997
Oth UAP U-25 European Open 1991
Int (Ireland) Dunhill Cup 1993-96-97; World Cup 1993-97 (winners)
AMATEUR
Nat Irish Amateur 1989
Reg South of Ireland 1991
Oth Long Beach Open 1990
Int Walker Cup 1991; Ireland (Home Int) 1989-90
Jun Irish Youths, Scottish Youths 1988

Macgregor, George
Born Edinburgh on 19th August, 1944

Cls Glencorse, Killarney (Hon), West Linton (Hon)
Nat Scottish Open Amateur Stroke Play 1982 r/u 1975-79-80
Trn Lytham Trophy 1975. Leven Gold Medal 1987
Reg Lothians Amateur 1968. South-East Scotland Amateur 1972-75-79-80-81. East of Scotland Open Amateur 1979-82
Int Walker Cup 1971-75-83-85-87-(**91**). Eisenhower Trophy 1982. GBIvEurope 1970-74-84. GB Commonwealth Trn 1971-75. Scotland (Home Int) 1969-70-71-72-73-74-75-76-80-81-82-83-84-85-86-87; Eur T Ch 1971-73-75-81-83-85-87; v Belgium 1973-75-80; v England 1979; v France 1981-82; Scotland v Sweden 1983
Jun Int Youths 1964-65-66
Mis Leading Amateur Wills PGA Open 1970-71

McKay, Mhairi
Born Glasgow on 18th April, 1975. Turned Professional 1997

AMATEUR
Nat British Ladies Stroke Play U-23 (Duncan Salver), U-21 (Dinwiddy Trophy) 1993; Scottish Ladies 1993(r/u); Scottish U-21 Stroke Play 1991(r/u)-92-93
Trn Mackie Bowl 1991-93; Helen Holm Trophy 1992; Riccarton Rosebowl 1993-96
Int Curtis Cup 1994-96; Espirito Santo 1996; Vagliano Trophy 1993-95-97; Commonwealth Trn 1995; Scotland (Home Int) 1991-92-93-94-96; Eur (L) T Ch 1993-95

Jun British Girls 1992-93; Scottish Girls 1990-91(r/u)-92; Belgian Junior 1992
Jun Int Scottish Girls 1989-90-91-92-93; Jun Eur 1990-92-94-96
Mis *Daily Telegraph* Junior Golfer of the Year 1991. Golf scholarship to Stanford University. Angus Trophy 1996. Joyce Wethered Trophy 1996

McKenna, Mary A
Born Dublin on 29th April, 1949

Cls Donabate
Nat British Ladies Open Amateur Stroke Play 1979, r/u 1976. Irish Ladies 1969-72-74-77-79-81-82-89, r/u 1968-73-76. Irish Women's Close Ch 1981
Trn Dorothy Grey Stroke Play 1970-71-73. Players No 6 Cup 1971-72-74. Avia Foursomes 1977-84-86. Hermitage Scratch Cup 1975-79
Reg South of Ireland Scratch Cup 1973-74-76-79
Int Curtis Cup 1970-72-74-76-78-80-82-84-86. Vagliano Trophy 1969-71-73-75-77-79-81-85-87-(**95**). Espirito Santo 1970-74-76-**86**; Ireland (Home Int) 1968 to 1991; Eur(L) T Ch 1969-71-73-75-77-79-81-83-85-87; in Fiat Trophy 1979
Mis S/f US Women's Western 1972, Broadmoor Trn 1972 and US Women's Amateur 1980. Captain of LGU Touring Team to South Africa 1974. Leading Amateur Colgate European LPGA 1977 (tied)-79. Daks Woman Golfer of the Year 1979. Smyth Salver 1984. Taunton Trophy 1976

McLean, David
Born Holyhead on 30th January, 1947

Cls Holyhead, Baron Hill, Killarney
Nat Welsh Amateur 1973-78. Welsh Amateur Stroke Play 1975-79
Trn Duncan Putter 1982
Reg North Wales Amateur 1971-75-77-81. Caernarfonshire Amateur 1966-68-69-70 (tied)-77-79-81-82. Anglesey Amateur 1965-67-68-69-70-72-73-74-76-78-79-80-81-82
Int Wales (Home Int) 1968-69-70-71-72-73-74-75-76-77-78-80-81-82-83-85-86-88; Eur T Ch 1975-77-79-81-83; vFrance 1975-76; vDenmark 1976-80-82; vIreland 1979; vSpain 1980; vAustria 1982; v Switzerland 1980-82; in Fiat Trophy 1978-79; in Asian Team Championship 1979

McMahon, Suzanne (*née* Cadden)
Born Old Kilpatrick, Dunbartonshire on 8th October, 1957

Cls Troon
Chp British Ladies r/u 1975. British Ladies Stroke Play r/u 1975
Nat Scottish Ladies Foursomes 1972
Reg Dunbartonshire Ladies 1976-77-79
Int Curtis Cup 1976. Vagliano Trophy 1975. Scotland (Home Int) 1974-75-76-77-79; Eur(L) T Ch 1975
Jun Scottish Girls 1974-76. Scottish Girls Open Stroke Play 1976-77. British Girls 1975. Girl International 1972-73-74-75-76. World Junior Championship 1973
Mis Daks Woman Golfer of the Year 1975

Madill, Maureen

Born Coleraine, Co Derry on 1st February, 1958.
Turned Professional 1986

Chp	Ladies British Amateur 1979
Nat	Ladies British Open Amateur Stroke Play 1980. Irish Foursomes 1980
Maj	Avia Foursomes 1980-85.
Reg	North-West Scratch Cup 1978. Ulster Ladies 1980
Int	Curtis Cup 1980. Espirito Santo 1980; Vagliano Trophy 1979-81-85. GB Commonwealth Trn 1979. Ireland (Home Int) 1978-79-80-81-82-83; Eur(L) T Ch 1979-81-83
Jun Int	Girls 1972-73-74-75-76

Marks, Geoffrey C

Born Hanley, Stoke-on-Trent, in November, 1938

Cls	Hon member of Trentham, Trentham Park, Greenway Hall, Killarney, Walsall, Newcastle, Trevose, Stone. Royal & Ancient
Chp	Amateur s/f 1968-75
Nat	English Open Amateur Stroke Play r/u 1973-75
Trn	Scrutton Jug 1967. Prince of Wales Challenge Cup 1968. Leicestershire Fox 1968. Lytham Trophy 1970 (tied). Harlech Gold Cup 1974. Homer Salver 1977
Reg	Midland Amateur 1967. Staffordshire Amateur1959-60-63-66-67-68-69-73
Int	Walker Cup 1969-71-**87**. Eisenhower Trophy 1970. GBI*v*Europe 1968-70. England (Home Int) 1963-67-68-69-70-71-74-75-(**80**)-(**81**)-(**82**)-(**83**); Eur T Ch 1967-69-71-75. GB Commonwealth Trn 1975. GBI in Colombian International 1975
Jun Int	Boys 1955-56. Youths 1957-58-59-60
Mis	England Selector 1980-81-82-83 (chairman); R&A Selection Committee (chairman) 1989-93. President English Golf Union 1995

Marsh, Dr David Max

Born Southport on 29th April, 1934

Cls	Royal & Ancient, Hon member of Southport & Ainsdale, Ormskirk, West Lancashire, Worlington & Newmarket, Hillside, Clitheroe, Whalley
Nat	English Amateur 1964-70
Trn	Antlers Royal Mid-Surrey 1964-66. Formby Hare 1968. Boyd Quaich 1957
Int	Walker Cup 1959-71-(**73**)-(**75**); GBI*v*Europe 1958-(**72**)-(**74**). GBI*v*Professionals 1959. England (Home Int) 1956-57-58-59-60-64-65-66-**68**-**69**-**70**-71-72; Eur T Ch 1971
Jun Int	Boys 1951
Mis	EGU Selector 1974. British Selector 1975. Chairman R & A Selection Committee 1979-83. President EGU 1987. Captain of R & A 1990/91

Marshall, Kathryn (*née* Imrie)

Born Southend on 8th June, 1967. Turned
Professional 1990

Maj	Ladies British Open 3rd1993; leading amateur 1988 (Smyth Salver)
PROFESSIONAL	
US	Toledo Classic 1995
Int	Solheim Cup 1996; European Cup 1997

AMATEUR

Trn	St Rule Trophy 1985; Riccarton Rosebowl 1985; Roehampton Gold Cup 1990
Reg	Highland Open 1985; North of Scotland Ladies Amateur 1988-90; Northern Counties Ladies Open Stroke Play 1986-87-88-89; Angus Ladies 1982-83-84-85
Int	Curtis Cup 1990; Vagliano Trophy 1989; Scotland (Home Int) 1984-88-89; Eur(L) T Ch 1987-89
Mis	Taunton Trophy 1986; winner of two NCAA events whilst at University of Arizona (1985-89); Doris Chambers Trophy, Angus Trophy 1990
Jun	Scottish Girls Open Stroke Play 1985-86-87

Marvin, Vanessa Price

Born Cosford on 30th December, 1954. Turned
Professional 1978

PROFESSIONAL

Eur	Carlsberg Trn 1979

AMATEUR

Chp	British Ladies Amateur r/u 1977
Nat	English Ladies Amateur 1977-78.
Trn	Hampshire Rose 1975-78 (tied). Roehampton Gold Cup 1976. Newmark-Avia 1978
Reg	Yorkshire Ladies 1975-78. North of England Ladies 1975
Int	Curtis Cup 1978. Vagliano Trophy 1977. England (Home Int) 1977-78; Eur(L) T Ch 1977; in Fiat Trophy 1978
Mis	Leading amateur Colgate European LPGA 1977. Daks Woman Golfer of the Year 1978

Matthew, Catriona (*née* Lambert)

Born on 25th August, 1969. Turned Professional 1994

PROFESSIONAL

RoW	Australian Ladies Open 1996

AMATEUR

Chp	British Ladies 1993
Nat	Scottish Ladies 1991-93-94. Welsh Women's Open Stroke Play 1992
Trn	Roehampton Gold Cup 1989; Helen Holm Trophy 1990; British Universities Women's Chp 1990; St Rule Trophy, Ness Trophy 1993; Astor Salver 1994
Int	Curtis Cup 1990-92-94; Espirito Santo 1992; Vagliano Trophy 1989-91-93; Commonwealth Trn 1991; Scotland (Home Int) 1989-90-91-92-93; Eur(L) T Ch 1989-91
Jun	Scottish Girls 1986; Scottish Girls Open Stroke Play 1988-89, r/u 1987

Matthews, Tegwen [Thomas] (*née* Perkins)

Born Cardiff on 2nd October, 1955

Cls	Wenvoe Castle, Porthcawl, Pennard
Nat	Welsh Ladies Amateur 1976-77. Welsh Ladies Open Amateur Stroke Play 1980. British Ladies Amateur Stroke Play r/u 1974
Trn	Wills Match Play 1973. Avia Foursomes 1977; Worplesdon Mixed Foursomes 1973-78
Reg	South-Western Ladies 1973-74-76. Glamorganshire Ladies 1972-74-75-77-78-80-81-83
Int	Curtis Cup 1974-76-78-80. Vagliano Trophy 1973-75-77-79. Espirito Santo 1974. GB Commonwealth Trn 1975-79. GBI: Colombian Int. 1977-79. Wales (Home Int) 1972 to 84; Eur(L) T Ch 1975-77-79-81-83; in Fiat Trophy 1978

Jun	Welsh Girls 1970.
Int	Girls 1970-71-72-73
Mis	Dinwiddy Trophy 1973-74. 1974: in LGU Team touring SA; first Welsh player in Curtis Cup team; Taunton Trophy. 1976: first Welsh woman player to win all matches in Home Ints; Daks Woman Golfer of the Year (joint). Duncan Salver 1974-76

Mayo, Paul M
Born Newport, Gwent on 6th January, 1963. Turned Professional 1988
PROFESSIONAL

Nat	Welsh PGA 1990-91
Int	Wales Dunhill Cup 1993

AMATEUR

Maj	Leading Amateur in Open 1987
Chp	Amateur Champion 1987
Nat	Welsh Amateur 1987
Reg	Gwent Amateur 1982
Int	Walker Cup 1985-87; GBIvEurope 1986; Wales (Home Int) 1982-87
Jun	British Youths 1983; Welsh Boys 1979

Merrill, Julia (*née* Greenhalgh)
Born Bolton on 6th January, 1941

Cls	Pleasington (Hon), Killarney, Ganton, Hermitage
Chp	Ladies British Open Amateur r/u 1978
Nat	British Ladies Stroke Play 1974-75. Runner-up British English Ladies 1966-79. Welsh Ladies Open Amateur Stroke Play 1977
Trn	Astor Salver 1969-79. Hermitage Cup, Hampshire Rose 1977. Sunningdale Foursomes 1978
Oth	New Zealand Ladies 1963
Reg	Lancashire Ladies 1961-62-66-68-73-75-76-77-78; Northern Ladies 1961-62
Int	Curtis Cup 1964-70-74-76-78. Vagliano Trophy 1961-65-75-77. GB Commonwealth Trn 1963-75. Espirito Santo **1970-74**-78. England (Home Int) 1960-61-63-66-69-70-71-76-77-78; Eur(L) T Ch 1971-75-77-79
Jun	Scottish Girls Open Stroke Play 1960. Girl International 1957-58-59
Mis	Leading Amateur (4th) in Australian Wills Ladies Open Stroke Play 1974. Daks Woman Golfer of the Year 1974. Taunton Trophy 1975-77. Doris Chambers Trophy 1977

Milligan, James W
Born Irvine on 15th June, 1963

Cls	Kilmarnock (Barassie)
Nat	Scottish Amateur 1988
Trn	Scottish Champion of Champions 1989-90
Int	Walker Cup 1989-91; Scotland (Home Int) 1986-87-88-89-90-91-92; vWest Germany 1987; vItaly 1988-90; vSweden 1990-92; Eur T Ch 1989-91; GBIvEurope 1988-90-92; Eisenhower Trophy 1988 (winners)-90
Jun	Scottish Youths 1984

Milton, Moira (*née* Paterson)
Born 18th December, 1923

Cls	Turnhouse, Gullane (Hon), Lenzie, Maccauvlei
Chp	British Ladies 1952
Nat	Scottish Ladies r/u 1951

Reg	Dunbartonshire Ladies 1949. Midlothian Ladies 1962
Int	Curtis Cup 1952. GBIvFrance 1949-50; vBelgium 1950; Scotland (Home Int) 1949-50-51-52; vAustralia 1951; vSouth Africa 1951; Eur(L) T Ch (**1973**)
Mis	Member of LGU Team to South Africa 1951

Montgomerie, Colin S
Born Glasgow on 23rd June, 1963. Turned Professional 1987
PROFESSIONAL

Maj	US Open r/u 1994-97, 3rd 1992; USPGA r/u 1995 (tied)
Eur	Portuguese Open 1989; Scandinavian Masters 1991; Dutch Open, Volvo Masters 1993; Open de España, English Open, German Open 1994; German Open, Trophée Lancôme 1995; Dubai Desert Classic, Irish Open, European Masters 1996; Andersen Consulting Eur Chp, Compaq Eur Grand Prix, Murphy's Irish Open 1997
RoW	Nedbank Million Dollar Challenge 1996; King Hussein II Trophy, Andersen Consulting World Cup 1997
Int	Ryder Cup 1991-93-95-97; Scotland in Dunhill Cup 1988-91-92(r/u)-93-94-95(winners)-96-97; in World Cup 1988-91-92-93-97 (r/u, individual winner); Four Tours World Chp 1991
Mis	Rookie of the Year 1988; Harry Vardon Trophy 1993-94-95-96-97; Johnnie Walker Golfer of the Year 1995-96-97; AGW Trophy 1996

AMATEUR

Chp	Amateur r/u 1984
Nat	Scottish Open Amateur Stroke Play 1985; Scottish Amateur 1987
Int	Walker Cup 1985-87; Eisenhower Trophy 1984-86; GBIvEurope 1986; Scotland (Home Int) 1984-85-86 Eur T Ch 1985; vSweden 1984-86; vFrance 1985

Montgomerie, John Speir
Born Cambuslang on 7th August, 1913

Cls	Royal & Ancient, Cambuslang, Kilmarnock (Barassie), Pollok
Nat	Scottish Amateur 1957
Reg	Lanarkshire Amateur 1951-54
Int	Scotland (Home Int) 1957-(**62**)-(**63**); vScandinavia 1958
Mis	Non-playing captain Scottish Team Eur T Ch 1965. Walker Cup Selector 1957 to 1965. President Scottish Golf Union 1965-66

Moodie, Janice
Born 31st May, 1973. Turned Professional 1997
AMATEUR

Nat	British Ladies Stroke Play r/u 1991; winner U-23 (Duncan Salver) and U-21 (Dinwiddy Trophy) 1990-91; Scottish Ladies 1992; Scottish U-21 Stroke Play 1990-93
Trn	Munross Trophy, Mary McCallay Trophy; Inverness Stroke Play 1993
Reg	West of Scotland Ladies 1991
Int	Curtis Cup 1994-96; Vagliano Trophy 1993-95-97; Espirito Santo 1996; Commonwealth Trn 1995; Scotland (Home Int) 1990-91-92; Eur (L) T Ch 1991-93-95-97

Jun Scottish Girls 1989-90(r/u)-91; British Girls s/f 1989-91

Jun Int Scottish Girls 1989-90 (r/u)-91; Eur Jun(L) T Ch 1990-92

Mis Doris Chambers Trophy, Angus Trophy 1993; Wilson PGA Junior Chp 1990. Currently a golf scholar at San José State University. Joyce Wethered Trophy 1994

Morley, Joanne
Born 30th December, 1966. Turned Professional 1994

Cls Sale
Maj Leading Amateur in Women's British Open (Smyth Salver) 1989-93
PROFESSIONAL
Eur Ladies German Open 1996; European Cup 1997
Int Solheim Cup 1996; Union Cup 1994
AMATEUR
Nat Ladies British Amateur r/u 1992; Ladies British Amateur Stroke Play 1991; English Ladies Close Amateur Stroke Play 1991-92, r/u 1990; English Intermediate 1991
Trn St Rule Trophy 1987; Wentworth Scratch Cup 1988(tied); Avia Foursomes (with L Fairclough) 1989; Astor Salver 1990
Int Curtis Cup 1992; Vagliano Trophy 1991-93; Espirito Santo 1992; England (Home Int) 1990-91-92-93; Eur(L) T Ch 1991
Mis Taunton Trophy 1991; Daily Telegraph Woman Golfer of the Year 1991

Murray, Gordon H
Born Paisley on 19th December, 1936

Cls Fereneze (Hon)
Nat Scottish Amateur 1974-76, r/u 1975; Scottish Stroke Play 1983
Reg West of Scotland Amateur 1971-73-76-78
Int Walker Cup 1977. GBIvEurope 1978. Scotland (Home Int) 1973-74-75-76-77-78-83 Eur T Ch 1975-77; vSpain 1974-77; vBelgium 1975-77

Nesbitt, Claire *See* Robinson

New, Beverley Jayne
Born Bristol on 30th July, 1960. Turned Professional 1984

PROFESSIONAL
Eur Broadway Group Wirral Classic 1988
RoW Thailand Ladies Open 1987; Malaysian Ladies Open 1988
AMATEUR
Nat English Ladies 1980; Welsh Ladies Stroke Play r/u 1979
Trn Hampshire Rose 1980; WPGA United Friendly Insurance Trn, Worplesdon Mixed Foursomes 1982; Roehampton Gold Cup, Worplesdon Mixed Foursomes, Martin Bowl 1983
Reg Somerset Ladies 1979-80-81-82-83; Bristol & District Open 1983
Int Curtis Cup 1984; Vagliano Trophy 1983; England (Home Int) 1980-81-82-83; Eur(L) T Ch 1981-83; Fiat Trophy 1980
Mis Doris Chambers Trophy 1983

Nichol, Margaret *See* Pickard

Nicholas, Alison
Born Gibraltar on 6th March, 1962. Turned Professional 1984

PROFESSIONAL
Maj Ladies British Open 1987, 3rd 1988; US Women's Open 1997
Eur Laing Charity Classic 1987; Variety Club Classic, British Olivetti, Guernsey Open 1988; Lufthansa German Open, Gislaved Open 1989; Variety Club Classic 1990; Open de Paris 1992; Scottish Open 1995; Guardian Irish Holidays Open 1996
US Corning Classic, Ping-Cellular One Chp 1995
RoW Malaysian Open, Western Open (Aus) 1992
Int Solheim Cup 1990-92-94-96; (for LPGA) Nichirei International 1995-97; European Cup 1997
Mis Vivien Saunders Trophy 1991. Order of Merit winner 1997
AMATEUR
Nat Ladies British Open Amateur Stroke Play 1983
Reg Yorkshire Ladies 1984; Northern Foursomes 1983
Jun North of England Girls 1982-83
Mis Taunton Trophy 1983; Duncan Salver 1983

O'Connor, Christy
Born Galway on 21st December, 1924

Maj Open r/u 1965, 3rd 1958-61
Trn Swallow-Penfold 1955. Dunlop Masters 1956-59. Spalding 1956 (tied). PGA Match Play 1957. Daks 1959. Ballantine 1960. Irish Hospitals 1960-62. Carling-Caledonian 1961. Martini 1963 (tied)-64. Jeyes 1964. Carrolls 1964-66-67-72. Senior Service 1965; Gallaher Ulster 1966-68-69. Alcan International 1968 (tied). Bowmaker 1970. John Player Classic 1970
Oth Ulster Professional 1953-54. Irish Professional 1958-60-61-62-63-65-66-71-75-77. Irish Dunlop 1962-65-66-67. Gleneagles Pro-Am 1962. Southern Ireland Professional 1969-76. Sean Connery Pro-Am 1970
Sen PGA Seniors 1976-77-79-81-82-83. World Seniors 1976-77
Int Ryder Cup 1955-57-59-61-63-65-67-69-71-73. GBI vCommonwealth 1956. Ireland in World Cup 1956-57-58 (winners) -59-60-61-62-63-64-66-67-68-69-71-75. Ireland in Double Diamond 1971-72-73-74-75-76-77
Mis Harry Vardon Trophy 1961-62. Second in order of Merit 1964 (equal)-65-66-69-70. AGW Trophy 1977

O'Connor, Christy, Jr
Born Galway on 19th August, 1948. Turned Professional 1965

Maj Open 3rd 1985
Eur Martini 1975 (tied). Carrolls Irish Open 1975. Sumrie 1976-78. Jersey European Airways Open 1989. Dunhill British Masters 1992
Oth Irish Dunlop 1974. Carrolls Irish Match Play 1975-77
RoW Zambian Open 1974. Kenya Open 1990
Int Ryder Cup 1975-89. Ireland in Double Diamond 1972-74-76-77. Ireland in World Cup 1974-75-78-85-89-92. Hennessy-Cognac 1974-84. GBI vSouth Africa 1976. Dunhill Cup 1985-89-92
Mis Braid Taylor Memorial Medal 1976-83. Tooting Bec Cup 1985

O'Leary, John E

Born Dublin on 19th August, 1949. Turned Professional 1970

PROFESSIONAL

Trn   Sumrie 1975. Greater Manchester Open 1976. Carrolls Irish Open 1982; Irish Dunlop 1972

RoW   Holiday Inns (Swaziland) 1975

Int   Ryder Cup 1975; Ireland in World Cup 1972-80-82; Ireland in Double Diamond 1972-73-74-75-76-77; GBI v Europe 1976-78-82

AMATEUR

Reg   South of Ireland Amateur 1970.

Int   Ireland (Home Int) 1969-70; Eur T Ch 1969

Jun Int Youths 1970

Oosterhuis, Peter A

Born London on 3rd May, 1948. Turned Professional November 1968

PROFESSIONAL

Maj   Open r/u 1974-82; leading British player 1975 (7th), 1978 (6th) US Masters 3rd 1973

Eur   Agfacolor, Sunbeam Pro-Am, Piccadilly 1971; Penfold 1972; French Open, Piccadilly, Viyella PGA 1973; French Open, Italian Open 1974

US   Canadian Open 1981

RoW   General Motors South Africa 1970; Transvaal Open, Schoeman Park, Rhodesian Dunlop Masters 1971; Glen Anil Classic 1972; Rothman's Match Play South Africa, Maracaibo Open 1973; El Paraiso Open 1974

Oth   Sunningdale Foursomes 1969; Coca-Cola Young Professionals 1970-72

Reg   Southern England Professional 1971

Int   Ryder Cup 1971-73-75-77-79-81; Hennessy-Cognac 1974; England in World Cup 1971-73, in Double Diamond 1973-74

Mis   Rookie of the Year 1969; Harry Vardon Trophy 1971-72-73-74; AGW Trophy 1973-74

AMATEUR

Trn   Berkshire Trophy 1966

Int   Walker Cup 1967; Eisenhower Trophy 1968; England (Home Int) 1966-67-68

Jun   British Youths 1966

Int   Boys 1964-65; Youths 1966-67-68

O'Sullivan, Dr William M

Born Killarney on 13th March, 1911

Cls   Waterville, Killarney (Hon), Dooks (Hon), Tralee (Hon), Muskerry (Hon), Cork (Hon), Ballybunion (Hon)

Chp   Irish Open Amateur 1949, r/u 1936-53. Irish Amateur r/u 1940

Int   Ireland (Home Int) 1934-35-36-37-38-47-48-49-50-51-53-54. President Golfing Union of Ireland 1959-60

Oxley, Dinah *See* Henson

Panton-Lewis, Catherine Rita

Born Bridge of Allan, Stirlingshire on 14th June, 1955. Turned Professional 1978

Cls   Glenbervie (Hon), Pitlochry (Hon), Silloth (Hon), South Herts

PROFESSIONAL

Eur   Carlsberg Tournament 1979. State Express Ladies

Ch'p 1979. Elizabeth Ann Classic 1980. European Ladies Champion 1981. Moben Kitchens Classic 1982. Qualified for USLPGA Tour, January 1983. Smirnoff Irish Classic, UBM Northern Classic 1983, Dunham Forest Pro-Am 1983. McEwans Wirral Caldy Classic 1985. Delsjö Open 1985. Portuguese Open 1986-87. Scottish Open 1988

Int   Union Cup 1994

Mis   Order of Merit winner 1979

AMATEUR

Chp   Ladies British Open Amateur 1976

Reg   East of Scotland Ladies 1976

Int   Espirito Santo 1976. Vagliano Trophy 1977. Scotland (Home Int) 1972-73-76-77-78; Eur(L) T Ch 1973-77

Jun   Scottish Girls 1969. Girl Int 1969-70-71-72-73

Mis   Scottish Sportswoman of the Year 1976. Member of LGU under-25 team to tour Canada 1973

Panton, John, MBE

Born Pitlochry, Perthshire on 9th October, 1916. Turned Professional 1935

Maj   Leading British player in 1956 Open (5th)

Trn   Silver King 1950. Daks 1951. North-British-Harrogate 1952. Goodwin Foursomes 1952. Yorkshire Evening News 1954. PGA Match Play 1956, r/u 1968

Eur   Woodlawn Invitation Open (Germany) 1958-59-60

Oth   West of Scotland Professional 1947-48-52-54-55-61-63. Scottish Professional 1948-49-50-51-54-55-59-66 (tied). Northern Open 1948-51-52-56-59-60-62. West of Scotland PGA Match Play 1954-55-56-64. Goodwin Foursomes 1952. Gleneagles-Saxone 1956

Sen   Pringle Seniors 1967-69. World Seniors 1967

Int   Ryder Cup 1951-53-61. Scotland in World Cup 1955-56-57-58-59-60-62-63-64-65-66-68

Mis   Harry Vardon Trophy 1951. AGW Trophy 1967. Hon Professional to Royal & Ancient from 1988

Parkin, Philip

Born Doncaster on 12th December, 1961. Turned Professional 1984

PROFESSIONAL

Reg   Welsh PGA 1986

Int   Wales in World Cup 1984-89; Dunhill Cup 1985-86-87-89-90-91; Hennessy-Cognac Cup 1984

Mis   Rookie of the Year 1984. Commentator for Sky TV

AMATEUR

Chp   Amateur Champion 1983

Int   Walker Cup 1983. Wales (Home Int) 1980-81-82.

Jun   British Youths 1982

Paterson, Moira *See* Milton

Payne, Jim

Born Louth, Lincolnshire on 17th April, 1970. Turned Professional 1991

PROFESSIONAL

Maj   Leading Amateur in Open 1991

Eur   Open de Baleares 1993; Italian Open 1996

Int   World Cup 1996

AMATEUR

Trn	Berkhamsted Trophy 1989; Selborne Salver 1991
Oth	Greek Amateur 1989, European Amateur 1991
Reg	West of England Stroke Play 1990
Int	Walker Cup 1991; England (Home Int) 1989-90; Eur T Ch 1991; GBI v Europe 1990
Jun	British Youths 1991
Int	English Youths 1989-90-91
Mis	PGA European Rookie of the Year 1992

Perkins, Tegwen *See* Matthews

Perowne, Arthur Herbert
Born Norwich on 21st February, 1930

Cls	Royal Norwich, Hunstanton, West Norfolk
Chp	English Open Amateur Stroke Play 1958
Oth	Swedish Amateur 1974
Trn	Berkshire Trophy 1958 (tied)
Reg	East Anglia Open 1952. Norfolk Amateur 1948-51-52-53-54-55-56-57-58-60-61. Norfolk Open 1964
Int	Walker Cup 1949-53-59. Eisenhower Trophy 1958. GBI v Denmark 1955; *v* Professionals 1956-58. England (Home Int) 1947-48-49-50-51-53-54-55-57; *v* France 1950-54-56-59; *v* Sweden 1947; *v* Denmark 1947
Jun	Carris Trophy 1946
Int	Boys 1946

Phillips, Kathryn *See* Lumb

Pickard, Margaret (*née* Nichol)
Born 25th April, 1938

Cls	Alnmouth (Hon)
Nat	English Ladies 1960, r/u 1957-67
Reg	Northern Ladies 1957-58. Northumberland Ladies 1956-57-58-61-62-64-65-66-67-69-70-71-76-77-82
Int	Curtis Cup 1968-70. Vagliano Trophy 1959-61-67. England (Home Int) 1957-58-59-60-61-67-69-(**83**). Eur(L) T Ch (**1983**)

Pirie, Alex Kemp
Born Aberdeen on 21st June, 1942

Cls	Hazelhead (Hon), Cruden Bay
Nat	Scottish Amateur r/u 1972-74
Trn	Eden Tournament 1963.
Reg	Northern Scottish Open 1970. West of Scotland Open Amateur 1972. East of Scotland Open Amateur Stroke Play 1975. North East Scotland Match Play 1964-66-67-68-71-73. Aberdeenshire Stroke Play 1966-68
Int	Walker Cup 1967. GBI*v*Europe 1970. Scotland (Home Int) 1966-67-68-69-70-71-72-73-74-75; Eur T Ch 1967-69; *v*Belgium 1973-75; *v* Spain 1974

Pook, Elizabeth (*née* Chadwick)
Born Inverness on 4th April, 1943

Cls	Bramall Park (Hon), Anglesey (Rhosneigr)
Chp	British Ladies 1966-67.
Nat	English Ladies r/u 1963. Italian Ladies r/u 1967

Reg	Central England Mixed Foursomes 1962-63-64 North of England Ladies 1965-66-67. Cheshire Ladies 1963-64-65-66-67
Trn	Avia Foursomes (with C Lacoste) r/u 1967
Int	Curtis Cup 1966. GB Commonwealth 1967. GBI*v*Europe 1963-65-67. England (Home Int) 1963-65-66-67; Eur(L) T Ch 1967; *v*France 1965
Jun	Girl International 1961

Porter, Ruth *See* Slark

Price Fisher, Elizabeth
Born London on 17th January, 1923. Turned Professional 1968, reinstated as Amateur 1971

Cls	Hankley Common, Farnham, Berkshire
Chp	British Ladies 1959, r/u 1954-58
Nat	English Ladies r/u 1947-54-55
Oth	Danish Ladies 1952. Portuguese Ladies 1964
Trn	Spalding Ladies 1955-59. Astor Salver 1955-56-59. Fairway and Hazard Foursomes 1954-60. Kayser Bondor Foursomes 1958 (tied). Roehampton Gold Cup 1960. Central England Mixed Foursomes 1971-76-82
Reg	South Eastern Ladies 1955-59-60-69. Surrey Ladies 1954-55-56-57-58-59-60
Int	Curtis Cup 1950-52-54-56-58-60. Vagliano Trophy 1959. GBI*v*Canada 1950-54-58; *v*France 1953-55-57; *v*Belgium 1953-55-57. GB Commonwealth Team 1955-59. England (Home Int) 1948-51-52-53-54-55-56-57-58-59-60
Mis	AGW Trophy 1952

Pyman, Iain
Born Whitby on 3rd March, 1973

Cls	Sand Moor
Maj	Open Chp 1993; leading amateur 1993
Chp	Amateur Champion 1993
Trn	Formby Hare 1992
Oth	Top amateur in NSW Open (Aus)
Reg	Yorkshire champion 1992
Int	GBI Walker Cup 1993; England (Home Int) 1993
Jun	Carris Trophy 1991; Yorkshire Youths 1993
Jun Int	GBI Boys 1991; England Boys 1991

Rafferty, Ronan
Born Newry on 13th January, 1964. Turned Professional 1981

PROFESSIONAL

Eur	Equity & Law Challenge 1988; Lancia Italian Open, Scandinavian Enterprise Open, Volvo Masters 1989; PLM Open, Swiss Open 1990; Portuguese Open 1992; Austrian Open 1993
RoW	Venezuelan Open 1982; South Australian Open, New Zealand Open 1987; Australian Match Play 1988; Coca-Cola Classic (Aus) 1990; Daikyo Palm Meadow (Aus) 1992
Int	Ryder Cup 1989; Kirin Cup 1988; Four Tours World Chp 1989-90-91; GBI*v*Australia 1988; Hennessy-Cognac 1984; Ireland in World Cup 1983-84-87-88-91-92-93; Dunhill Cup 1986-87-88(winners)-89-90(winners)-91-92-93-95
Mis	Harry Vardon Trophy 1989

AMATEUR
Nat Irish Amateur 1980; English Amateur Open
      Stroke Play 1980(tied)
Int Walker Cup 1981; Eisenhower Trophy 1980;
      GBI*v*Europe 1980; Ireland (Home Int) 1980;
      *v*Wales 1979; *v*France, Germany, Sweden 1980;
      Fiat Trophy 1980; Eur T Ch 1981
Jun British Boys 1979; Irish Youths 1979; Ulster
      Youths 1979
Int Boys 1978-79; Youths 1979-80

Rawlings, Vicki *See* **Thomas**

Redford, Carole *See* **Caldwell**

Reid, Dale
Born Ladybank, Fife on 20th March, 1959. Turned
Professional 1979
PROFESSIONAL
Eur Carlsberg (Coventry) 1980. Carlsberg
      (Gleneagles), Moben Kitchens 1981. Guernsey
      Open 1982. United Friendly, International
      Classic 1983. Caldy Classic 1983. UBM Classic,
      JS Bloor Classic 1984. Ulster Volkswagen
      Classic, Brend Hotels International 1985. British
      Olivetti 1986. Volmac Open, European Open,
      Bowring Scottish Open, Volkswagen Classic
      1987. European Open, Toshiba Players Chp
      1988. Haninge Open 1990. Ford Ladies Classic,
      Eastleigh Classic 1991
Oth Sunningdale Foursomes (with C. Dibnah) 1990
Int Solheim Cup 1990-92-94-96; Sunrise Cup 1992;
      Union Cup 1994
Mis Order of Merit winner 1984-87; first Honorary
      Member of WPGET 1991
AMATEUR
Int Scotland (Home Int) 1978
Jun Fife Girls 1973-75
Jun Int Scottish Girls International 1974-75-76-77

Richardson, Steven
Born Windsor on 24th July, 1966. Turned
Professional 1989
PROFESSIONAL
Eur Girona Open, Portuguese Open 1991; German
      Masters 1993
Int Ryder Cup 1991; England in Dunhill Cup 1991-
      92(winners); World Cup 1991-92; Four Tours
      World Chp 1991
AMATEUR
Nat English Amateur 1989
Int England (Home Int) 1986-87-88

Robb, Diane *See* **Bailey**

Robertson, Dean
Born Sarnia, Canada on 11th July, 1970. Turned
Professional 1993
Cls Cochrane Castle
PROFESSIONAL
Trn HIS Assistants 1994
AMATEUR
Nat Scottish Amateur Stroke Play 1993, r/u 1993

Trn Scottish Champion of Champions 1992;
      Tennant Cup 1992-93; Leven Gold Medal 1992
Int GBI Walker Cup 1993; *v*Europe 1992;
      Eisenhower Trophy 1992; Scotland (Home Int)
      1991-92-93; v Sweden 1992, v Italy 1992
Mis Scottish Golfer of the Year 1992

Robertson, Isabella (Belle), MBE
Born Southend, Argyll, on 11th April, 1936
Cls Dunaverty (Hon)
Maj Ladies British Open: leading amateur (Smyth
      Salver); r/u 1980-81
Chp Ladies British Open Amateur 1981, r/u 1959-
      65-70
Nat Ladies British Open Amateur Stroke Play 1971-
      72-85; Scottish Ladies 1965-66-71-72-78-80; r/u
      1959-63-70
Oth New Zealand Ladies Match Play 1971
Trn Sunningdale Foursomes 1960; Avia Foursomes
      1972-81-84-86; Helen Holm Trophy 1973-79-
      86; Players No 6 Cup 1973-76; Roehampton
      Gold Cup 1978 (tied)-79-81-82
Reg West of Scotland Ladies 1957-64-66-69;
      Dunbartonshire Ladies 1958 to 1963, 1965-66-
      68-69-78
Sen US Women's Amateur Seniors r/u 1991
Int Curtis Cup 1960-66-68-70-72-(74)-(76)-82-86;
      Vagliano Trophy 1959-63-65-69-71-81; Espirito
      Santo 1964-66-68-72-80-82; GB
      Commonwealth Trn 1971-(75); Scotland (Home
      Int) 1958 to 1966, 69-72-73-78-80-81-82
      Eur(L) T Ch 1965-67-69-71-73-81-83; Fiat
      Trophy 1978-80
Mis Daks Woman Golfer of the Year 1971-81; Frank
      Moran Trophy 1971; leading qualifier US Ladies
      Amateur 1978; Scottish Sportswoman of the
      Year 1968-71-78-81; Avia Woman Golfer of the
      Year 1985

Robertson, Janette *See* **Wright**

Roe, Mark
Born Sheffield on 20th February, 1963. Turned
Professional 1981
Eur Catalan Open 1989; Trophée Lancôme 1992;
      Open de France 1994
Int England in World Cup 1989-94-95; Dunhill
      Cup 1994

Rose, Alison
Born Stirling on 18th June, 1968
Cls Stirling
Chp Ladies' British Open Amateur 1997
Nat Welsh Open Amateur Stroke Play 1994; Scottish
      Ladies r/u 1996
Reg East of Scotland Ladies 1988-90-93;
      Stirlingshire Ladies 1990-91-92
Trn St Rule Trophy 1991; Mary McCallay Trophy
      1995
Int Curtis Cup 1996; Vagliano Trophy 1995-97;
      Commonwealth Trn 1995. Scotland (Home Int)
      1990 to 1997; Eur(L) T Ch 1991-93-95-97
Jun Int Jun Eur(L) T Ch 1988
Mis Order of Merit winner 1994-96. Taunton Trophy
      1996

Russell, Raymond

Born Edinburgh on 26th July, 1972. Turned Professional 1993

PROFESSIONAL

Eur Cannes Open 1996
Int Scotland in Dunhill Cup 1996-97; World Cup 1997 (r/u)

AMATEUR

Int Walker Cup 1993; Scotland (Home Int) 1992-93; Eur T Ch 1993
Jun Scottish Youths 1992

Saddler, AC

Born Forfar, Angus on 11th August, 1935

Cls Forfar, Carnoustie
Nat Scottish Amateur r/u 1960
Trn Berkshire Trophy 1962
Int Walker Cup 1963-65-67-(77) Eisenhower Trophy 1962-(76) (winners)-78. GB Commonwealth Trn 1959-63-67; vEurope 1960-62-66-(76)-(78); vProfessionals 1959-61. Scotland (Home Int) 1959-60-61-62-63-65-(74)-(75)-(76)-(77); Eur T Ch (1975)-(77)

Saunders, Vivien Inez

Born Sutton on 24th November, 1946. Turned Professional 1969

PROFESSIONAL

Maj Ladies British Open 1977
Trn Avia Foursomes 1978; Keighley Trophy 1981; British Car Auctions 1980
US 1969 First European to qualify for LPGA tour
RoW Schweppes-Tarax Open (Australia), Chrysler Open (Australia) 1973
Mis Founder WPGA & Chairman 1978-79

AMATEUR

Chp Ladies British Open Amateur r/u 1966
Trn Avia Foursomes 1967
Int Curtis Cup 1968; Vagliano Trophy 1967; GB Commonwealth Team 1967; England (Home Int) 1967-68 Eur(L) T Ch 1967; vFrance 1966-67
Jun Int Girls 1964-65-66-67

Sewell, Douglas

Born Woking on 19th November, 1929. Turned Professional 1960

PROFESSIONAL

Trn Martini International 1970 (shared); Wentworth Pro-Am Foursomes 1968
Reg West of England Open Professional 1968-70
Int PGA Cup 1973-74-75

AMATEUR

Nat English Amateur 1958-60; English Open Amateur Stroke-Play 1957-59
Trn Scrutton Jug 1959; Golf Illustrated Gold Vase 1960; Sunningdale Foursomes 1959
Reg Surrey Amateur 1954-56-58
Int Walker Cup 1957-59; Eisenhower Trophy 1960; GB Commonwealth Trn 1959; England (Home Int) 1956-57-58-59-60

Sheahan, Dr David B

Born Southsea, England on 25th February, 1940

Cls Grange
Nat Irish Amateur 1961-66-70

Shepperson, AE

Born Sutton-in-Ashfield on 8th April, 1936

Cls Coxmoor (Hon), Notts
Nat English Open Amateur Stroke Play r/u 1958-62
Trn President's Putter 1957
Reg Nottinghamshire Amateur 1955-58-61-65. Nottinghamshire Open 1955-58
Int Walker Cup 1957-59. England (Home Int) 1956-57-58-59-60-62
Jun British Boys 1953

Sherry, Gordon

Born Kilmarnock on 8th April, 1974

Cls Kilmarnock Barassie
Chp Amateur Champion 1995; r/u 1994
Nat Scottish Amateur sf 1994; European Amateur r/u 1994
Trn St Andrews Links r/u 1995; Edward Trophy 1993-94; Scottish Champion of Champions 1994; Boyd Quaich 1993
Reg Ayrshire Matchplay 1992; Ayrshire Strokeplay 1993; Scotland South-East District 1994
Oth Scottish Universities Champion 1993; European Club Cup Champion 1994
Int Walker Cup 1995; Eisenhower Trophy 1994; GBI v Europe 1994; Scotland (Home Int) 1993-94-95; v France 1993-95; v Spain 1994; v Sweden 1995; Eur T Ch 1995
Jun Int European Youths, Scottish Youths 1994; European Boys (Champions) 1992; Scottish Boys (Champions) 1992
Mis Scottish Amateur Golfer of the Year 1995

Sinclair, Alexander, OBE

Born West Kilbride, Ayrshire on 6th July, 1920

Cls Royal & Ancient, Honorary member of West Kilbride, Drumpellier, Bothwell Castle, Royal Troon
Trn Newlands Trophy 1950
Oth Royal & Ancient Silver Cross 1972. Royal Medal 1977. Scottish Open Amateur Seniors 1979
Reg West of Scotland Amateur 1950. Lanarkshire Amateur 1952-59-61. Glasgow Amateur 1961
Int Scotland (Home Int) 1950-(66)-(67). Eur T Ch (1967)
Mis Chairman R & A Selection Committee from 1969 to 1975. Leading Amateur (joint second) in Northern Open 1948. President Scottish Golf Union 1976-78. Frank Moran Trophy 1978. Chairman R & A Amateur Status Committee 1979-81. President European Golf Association 1981-82-83. Captain of R&A 1988/89. President of Golf Foundation from 1990

Slark, Ruth (*née* Porter)

Born Chesterfield on 6th May, 1939

Cls Long Ashton (Hon), Bath, Burnham and Berrow, Reigate Heath, Walton Heath

---

Trn Jeyes Professional 1962 (as an Amateur); Frame Trophy 1991
Oth Boyd Quaich 1962
Int Walker Cup 1963. GBIvEurope 1962-64. Ireland (Home Int) 1961-62-63-64-65-66-67-70; Eur T Ch 1965-67 (winners both times)

Nat	English Ladies 1959-61-65, r/u 1978
Oth	Australian Ladies r/u 1963
Trn	Astor Prince's 1961. Fairway and Hazard Foursomes 1958. Roehampton Gold Cup 1963. Astor Salver 1962-63. Hovis Ladies 1966 (tied). Avia Foursomes 1968
Reg	South Western Ladies 1956-57-60-61-62-64-65-66-67-69-72-77-79. Gloucestershire Ladies 1957-59-61-62-63-64-66-67-69-73-74-75-76-77
Int	Curtis Cup 1960-62-64. Vagliano Trophy 1959-61-65. GB Commonwealth Team 1963. Espirito Santo 1964-66. England (Home Int) 1959-60-61-62-64-65-66-68-75-78; Eur(L) T Ch 1965
Jun	British Girls 1956. Scottish Girls Open Stroke Play 1958. Girls International 1955-56-57
Mis	Taunton Trophy 1978

Smith, William Dickson
Born Glasgow on 2nd February, 1918

Cls	Prestwick (Hon), Royal & Ancient, Royal Troon, Selkirk (Hon), Southerness, Gullane
Maj	Leading amateur (5th) in Open 1957
Nat	Scottish Amateur 1958. Scottish Senior Open Amateur 1983
Oth	Indian Open Amateur 1945. Portuguese Open Amateur 1967-70.
Trn	Worplesdon Mixed Foursomes 1957. Royal & Ancient Royal Medal 1971
Reg	Border Amateur 1949-51-57-63. Dumfriesshire Amateur 1956
Int	Walker Cup 1959. GBI v Europe 1958. Scotland (Home Int) 1957-58-59-60-63-(83); vScandinavia 1958-60

Smye, Catherine *See* McCann

Smyth, Des
Born Drogheda on 12th February, 1953. Turned Professional 1973

PROFESSIONAL

Trn	PGA Match Play 1979. Newcastle Brown 900, Greater Manchester Open 1980. Coral Classic 1981. Sanyo Open 1983. Jersey Open 1988. Madrid Open 1993
Oth	Irish PGA 1979-90. Carrolls Irish Match Play, Irish Dunlop 1980. Irish Masters 1994.
Int	Ryder Cup 1979-81. Ireland in World Cup 1979-80-82-83-88-89. Hennessy-Cognac Cup 1980-82-84. Dunhill Cup 1985-86-87-88 (winners)

AMATEUR

Int	Ireland (Home Int) 1972-73; Eur T Ch 1973

Speak, Kirsty
Born on 18th June, 1971

Cls	Clitheroe
Chp	British Ladies r/u 1993
Nat	English Intermediate 1990(r/u)-92-93; British Ladies Stroke Play 1994
Trn	Pleasington Putter 1990; Bridget Jackson Bowl 1994; Wentworth Scratch 1994
Oth	World Student Chp 1992
Int	Curtis Cup 1994; Vagliano Trophy 1993; Espirito Santo 1994; England (Home Int) 1993-94; Eur(L) T Ch 1993

Spearman, Marley *See* Harris

Squirrell, Hew Crawford
Born Cardiff on 15th August, 1932

Cls	Hon member of Cardiff, Moseley, Killarney
Nat	Welsh Amateur 1958-59-60-64-65, r/u 1962-71
Trn	Antlers Royal Mid-Surrey 1959-61. Hampshire Hog 1961. Berkhamsted Trophy 1960-63. Boyd Quaich 1955
Reg	Glamorgan Amateur 1959-65. Herts Amateur 1963-73
Int	Wales (Home Int) 1955-56-57-58-59-60-61-62-63-64-65-66-67-68-**69-70-71**-73-74-75; Eur T Ch 1965-67-69-71-75; vFrance 1975
Mis	Deputy-Director Golf Foundation

Stephen, Alexander R (Sandy)
Born St Andrews on 8th January, 1954. Turned Professional 1985

Cls	Lundin (Hon), Muckhart (Hon), Broomieknowe

PROFESSIONAL

Trn	Scottish Professional Chp 1988

AMATEUR

Nat	Scottish Amateur 1971
Trn	Scottish Champion of Champions 1984. Leven Gold Medal 1984
Reg	North of Scotland Open Amateur 1972-77. Fife Amateur 1973. Lothians Amateur 1978; East of Scotland Open Amateur 1974-77-83-84. West of Scotland Open Amateur 1975
Int	Walker Cup 1985. GBIvEurope 1972. Scotland (Home Int) 1971-72-73-74-75-76-77-84-85; Eur T Ch 1975-85; vSpain 1974; vBelgium 1975-77-78
Jun	Scottish Boys 1970.
Int	Boys 1970-71. Youths 1972-73-74-75
Mis	Finished third in World Boys International Trophy (USA) 1970

Stewart, Gillian
Born Inverness on 21st October, 1958. Turned Professional 1985

Cls	Inverness (Hon), Nairn

PROFESSIONAL

Eur	IBM European Open 1984 (as amateur). Ford Ladies Classic 1985-87
Int	Union Cup 1994

AMATEUR

Nat	Scottish Ladies 1979-83-84. Ladies British Open Amateur r/u 1982
Trn	Helen Holm Trophy 1981-84
Reg	Northern Counties Ladies 1976-78-82. North of Scotland Ladies 1975-78-80-82-83
Int	Curtis Cup 1980-82. GB Commonwealth Team 1979-83. Vagliano Trophy 1979-81-83. Espirito Santo 1982-84. Scotland (Home Int) 1979-80-81-82-83-84; Eur(L) T Ch 1979-81-83
Jun	British Girls 1976. Scottish U-19 Stroke Play Champion 1975
Int	Girls 1975-76-77
Mis	Member of Scottish team which won the 1980 European Junior Team Championship. Avia Woman Golfer of the Year 1984

Stuart, Hugh Bannerman

Born Forres on 27th June, 1942

Cls Forres (Hon), Murcar (Hon)
Chp Amateur s/f 1974
Nat Scottish Amateur 1972, r/u 1970-76
Reg North of Scotland Amateur 1967-74. Moray Amateur 1960. Nairnshire Amateur 1966
Int Walker Cup 1971-73-75; GB Commonwealth Trn 1971; Eisenhower Trophy 1972; GBI v Europe 1968-72-74. Scotland (Home Int) 1967-68-70-71-72-73-74-76; Eur T Ch 1969-71-73-75; vBelgium 1973-75
Jun Scottish Boys 1959
Int Boys 1959
Mis Won all his matches in 1971 Walker Cup. In European Team touring South Africa 1974

Thirlwell, Alan

Born 8th August, 1928

Cls Gosforth, Formby
Chp Amateur r/u 1958-72
Nat English Amateur 1954-55, r/u 1963. English Open Amateur Stroke Play r/u 1964
Trn County Champion of Champions 1962. Wentworth Pro-Am Foursomes 1960-61-68
Reg Northumberland Amateur 1952-55-62-64. Northumberland and Durham Open 1960
Int Walker Cup 1957. GB Commonwealth Trn 1954-63. GBIvEurope 1956-58; vDenmark 1955; v Professionals 1963. England (Home Int) 1951-52-54-55-56-57-58-59-63-64; vFrance 1954-56-59
Mis Canadian Amateur s/f 1957. EGU Selector 1974 to 1977. Secretary CONGU

Thomas, David C

Born Newcastle-upon-Tyne on 16th August, 1934. Turned Professional 1949

Maj Open r/u 1958 (tied), r/u 1966
Eur Belgian Open 1955. Dutch Open 1958. French Open 1959
Trn Esso Golden 1961 (tied)-62-66. PGA Matchplay, Olgiata Trophy (Rome) 1963. Silentnight 1965 (tied). Penfold-Swallow, Jeyes 1966. Penfold 1968 (tied). Graham Textiles 1969. Pains-Wessex 1969
RoW Caltex (NZ) 1958-59
Oth British Assistants 1955. Wentworth Pro-Am Foursomes 1960-61
Int Ryder Cup 1959-63-65-67. Wales in World Cup 1957-58-59-60-61-62-63-66-67-69-70. Wales in Double Diamond 1972-73
Mis Won qualifying competition for US Open 1964

Thomas, Vicki (*née* Rawlings)

Born Northampton on 27th October, 1954

Cls Pennard
Maj Leading Amateur in Women's British Open (Smyth Salver) 1986
Nat Welsh Ladies Amateur 1979-82-83-85-86-87-91-94; British Ladies Amateur Stroke Play 1990, r/u 1979. Welsh Ladies Open Stroke Play 1981-82-89, r/u 1980

Trn Roehampton Gold Cup 1983-85. Cotswold Gold Vase 1983. Keithley Trophy 1983. Sunningdale Foursomes 1989. Welsh Trn of Champions 1991-94
Reg Glamorganshire Ladies 1970-71-79; Women's South-West Chp 1991
Oth Women's Greek Amateur Stroke Play 1991
Int Curtis Cup 1982-84-86-88-90-92; GB Commonwealth Trn 1979-83-87-91; Vagliano Trophy 1979-83-85-87-89-91; Espirito Santo 1990; Wales (Home Int) 1971 to 1997; Eur(L) T Ch 1973-75-77-79-81-83-87-91
Jun Welsh Girls 1973
Int Girls 1969-70-71-72-73
Mis Taunton Trophy 1979

Thomson, Muriel

Born Aberdeen on 12th December, 1954. Turned Professional 1979

PROFESSIONAL
Eur Carlsberg, Viscount Double Glazing, Barnham Broom 1980; Elizabeth Ann Classic 1981; Guernsey Open, Sands International 1984; Laing Classic 1985; Irish Open, Ford Classic 1986
Mis Order of Merit winner 1980-83; Frank Moran Trophy 1981
AMATEUR
Nat Scottish Ladies r/u 1977
Trn Helen Holm Trophy 1975-76; Canadian Ladies Foursomes 1978
Reg North of Scotland Ladies 1973-74; Aberdeenshire Ladies 1977
Int Curtis Cup 1978; Vagliano Trophy 1977; Espirito Santo 1978; GBI in Colombian International 1979; Scotland (Home Int) 1974-75-76-77-78; Eur(L) T Ch 1975-77

Thornhill, Jill

Born 18th August, 1942

Cls Walton Heath, Silloth-on-Solway
Chp Ladies British Open Amateur 1983
Nat English Ladies 1986, r/u 1974. Ladies British Open Amateur Stroke Play r/u 1987
Trn Avia Foursomes 1970-83. Astor Salver 1972-75. Newmark International 1974. Worplesdon Mixed Foursomes 1975. Hampshire Rose 1982-87
Eur Belgian Ladies 1967
Reg South Eastern Ladies 1964-64-85. Surrey Ladies 1962-64-65-73-74-77-78-81-82-83-84
Int Curtis Cup 1984-86-88-(90). Vagliano Trophy 1965-83-85-87-(90). England (Home Int) 1964-65-74-82-83-84-85-86 -87-88. Commonwealth Trn 1983; Eur(L) T Ch 1983
Sen British Ladies Seniors 1993, r/u 1994
Mis Doris Chambers Trophy 1986. Avia Woman Golfer of the Year 1983

Torrance, Sam

Born Largs, Ayrshire on 24th August, 1953. Turned Professional 1970

PROFESSIONAL
Eur Piccadilly Medal, Martini International 1976; Carrolls Irish Open 1981; Spanish Open, Portuguese Open 1982; Scandinavian Enterprise and Portuguese Opens 1983; Tunisian and Sanyo

Opens, Benson & Hedges International 1984; Monte Carlo Open 1985; Lancia Italian Open 1987; German Masters 1990; Jersey Open 1991; Kronenbourg, Catalan and Honda Opens 1993; Italian and Irish Opens, British Masters 1995

Oth U-25 Match Play 1972; Scottish Uniroyal 1975; Scottish Professional 1978-80-91-93

RoW Zambian Open 1975; Colombian Open 1979; Australian PGA 1980

Int Ryder Cup 1981-83-85-87-89-91-93-95; Hennessy-Cognac Cup 1976-80-82-84; Nissan Cup 1985; Four Tours World Chp 1991; Scotland in World Cup 1976-78-82-84-85-87-89-90-91-93-95; Double Diamond 1973-76-77; Dunhill Cup 1985-86-87-89-90-91-93-95(winners)

Mis Rookie of the Year 1972; Tooting Bec Cup 1984

AMATEUR

Jun Int Scottish Boys 1970

Townsend, Peter Michael Paul

Born Cambridge on 16th September, 1946. Turned Professional 1966

PROFESSIONAL

Eur Dutch Open 1967; Swiss Open, Carrolls Irish Match Play 1971; Carrolls Irish Match Play 1976; Irish Dunlop 1977

Oth PGA Close, Coca-Cola Young Professionals 1968

US Chesterfield 1968

RoW Western Australia Open 1968; Caracas Open 1969; Walworth Aloyco 1971; Los Lagaratos Open 1972; ICL International (SA) 1975; Moroccan Grand Prix, Los Lagaratos, Caribbean and Zambian Opens 1978; Laurent Perrier 1981

Int Ryder Cup 1969-71; Hennessy-Cognac 1974; England in World Cup 1969-74; in Double Diamond 1971-72-74

Mis Captain PGA 1984

AMATEUR

Nat English Open Amateur Stroke Play 1966

Trn Duncan Putter 1965; Mullingar Trophy 1965-66; Lytham Trophy 1966; *Golf Illustrated* Golf Vase 1966; Prince of Wales Challenge Cup 1966; St George's Challenge Cup 1966; Berkhamsted Trophy 1966

Reg Herts Amateur 1964

Int Walker Cup 1965; Eisenhower Trophy 1966; GBIvEurope 1966; England (Home Int) 1965-66

Jun British Boys 1962-64; British Youths 1965

Int Boys 1961-62-63-64; Youths 1965

Tucker, William Iestyn

Born Nantyglo, Monmouth on 9th December, 1926

Cls Monmouthshire, Brecon, Killarney, Morlais Castle, Tredegar and Rhymney, Pontynewydd, Llantrisant, Radyr, Whitehall

Nat Welsh Amateur 1933-36, r/u 1951-56-64-67-75-76. Welsh Amateur Stroke Play 1976

Trn Duncan Putter 1960-61 (tied)-63-69-76

Reg Monmouthshire Amateur 1949, 1952 to 63, 1967-69-74. Gwent Amateur 1976

Int Wales (Home Int) 1949 to 72, 1974-75; Eur T Ch 1965-67-69-75; vAustralia 1953; vFrance 1975. Captain Welsh Team 1966-67-68

Uzielli, Angela *(née Carrick)*

Born Swanton Morley, Norfolk on 1st February, 1940

Cls Berkshire (Hon),

Chp British Ladies Open Amateur 1977.

Nat English Ladies 1990, r/u 1976

Trn Astor Salver 1971-73 (tied)-77-81. Roehampton Gold Cup 1977. Avia Foursomes 1982. Hampshire Rose 1985

Reg Berkshire Ladies 1976-77-78-79-80-81-83

Int Curtis Cup 1978. Vagliano Trophy 1977. England (Home Int) 1976-77-78-90; Eur(L) T Ch 1977

Sen British Ladies Seniors 1990-91-92-95, r/u 1993-96

Mis Daks Woman Golfer of the Year 1977; *Daily Telegraph* Woman Golfer of the Year 1990

Valentine, Jessie, MBE *(née Anderson)*

Born Perth on 18th March, 1915. Turned Professional 1960

Cls Honorary member of Craigie Hill, St Rule, Hunstanton, Blairgowrie, Murrayshall

Chp British Ladies 1937-55-58, r/u 1950-57

Nat Scottish Ladies 1938-39-51-53-55-56, r/u 1934-54

Oth New Zealand Ladies 1935. French Ladies 1936

Trn Spalding Ladies 1957. Kayser Bondor Foursomes 1959-61. Worplesdon Mixed Foursomes 1963-64-65

Reg East of Scotland Ladies 1936-38-39-50

Int Curtis Cup 1936-38-50-52-54-56-58. GBI v France 1935-36-38-39-47-49-51-55; vBelgium 1949-51-54-55; vCanada 1938-50. GB Commonwealth Trn 1953-55-(59). Scotland (Home Int) 1934-35-36-37-38-39-47-49-50-51-52-53-54-55-56-57-58

Jun British Girls 1933

Mis Canadian Ladies s/f 1938. Member of LGU Team to Australia and New Zealand 1935. Frank Moran Trophy 1967

Vaughan, Sheila *See* **Maher**

Wade, Julie *See* **Hall**

Wadsworth, Helen Elizabeth

Born on the Gower, Swansea on 7th April, 1964. Turned Professional 1991

PROFESSIONAL

Eur BMW European Masters 1994

Int Sunrise Cup 1992

Mis Rookie of the Year 1991

AMATEUR

Chp British Ladies Open Amateur r/u 1990 s/f 1988

Nat Welsh Ladies Open Amateur Stroke Play 1986. Welsh Ladies r/u 1990

Oth World Fourball Chp with Julie Hall 1987

Trn Astor Salver, Wentworth Scratch Trophy 1985; Sunningdale Foursomes (with Julie Hall) 1997

Reg Kent Ladies 1990

Int Curtis Cup 1990. Wales (Home Int) 1987-88-89-90; Eur(L) T Ch 1985-87-89

Jun South-East Girls 1981

Int Wales (Jun Eur T Ch) 1983

Mis Leading amateur, Ladies European Open 1990. Taunton Trophy 1990

Waites, Brian J

Born Bolton on 1st March, 1940. Turned Professional 1957

Eur Tournament Players' Championship 1978. Car Care Plan International 1982
RoW Kenya Open 1980. Mufulira Open (Zambia) 1980-82. Cock o' the North (Zambia) Open 1985
Oth National ProAm Chp 1979
Reg Midland Open 1971-76-81. Midland Professional Stroke Play 1972-77-78-79. Midland Professional Match Play 1972-73-74.
Sen PGA Seniors 1990-91; D-Day Sen Open 1994; Northern Electric Seniors 1995; Crédit Suisse Seniors Open 1997
Int Ryder Cup 1983; PGA Cup 1973-75-76-77-78-90; GBI vEurope 1980; Hennessy-Cognac Cup 1984; England in World Cup 1980-82-83; (Sen) European Cup 1997

Walker, Carole Michelle (Mickey), OBE

Born Alwoodley, nr Leeds on 17th December, 1952. Turned Professional 1973

PROFESSIONAL
Maj Ladies British Open r/u 1979
Eur Carlsberg 1979; Lambert & Butler Match Play 1980; Carlsberg 1981; Sands International 1983; Baume-Mercier Classic, Lorne Stewart Match Play 1984
Oth Sunningdale Foursomes 1982
Int Solheim Cup (1990)-(92)-(94)-(96)
AMATEUR
Chp Ladies British Open Amateur 1971-72; r/u 1973
Nat Ladies British Open Amateur Stroke Play r/u 1972; English Ladies 1973
Oth Portuguese Ladies Amateur, US Trans-Mississippi 1972; Spanish Ladies Amateur 1973
Trn Hovis Ladies 1972
Int Curtis Cup 1972; GB Commonwealth Trn 1971; Espirito Santo 1972; Vagliano Trophy 1971; England (Home Int) 1970-72 Eur(L) T Ch 1971-73
Jun French Girls U-22 Open 1971
Int English Girls 1969-70-71
Mis AGW Trophy 1972; Daks Women Golfer of the Year 1972; Duncan Salver 1972

Walton, Lisa *See* **Educate**

Walton, Philip

Born Dublin on 28th March, 1962. Turned Professional 1983

PROFESSIONAL
Eur French Open 1990, Open Catalonia, English Open 1995
Trn Irish Professional 1989-91
Int Ryder Cup 1995; Ireland in World Cup 1995; Dunhill Cup 1989-90 (winners)-92-94-95
AMATEUR
Nat Scottish Open Amateur Stroke Play 1981. Irish Amateur 1982
Int Walker Cup 1981-83; Eisenhower Trophy 1982. Ireland (Home Int) 1980-81; Eur T Ch 1981

Ward, Angela *See* **Bonallack**

Ward, Charles Harold

Born Birmingham on 16th September, 1911

Maj Open 3rd 1948-51, leading British player (4th) 1946
Trn Daily Mail Victory 1945. Silver King (tied), Yorkshire Evening News 1948. Spalding, North British-Harrogate, Dunlop Masters 1949. Daily Mail 1950. Dunlop, Lotus 1951. PGA Close 1956
Oth West of England Open Professional 1937. Daily Telegraph Pro-Am 1947-48. Midland Professional 1933-34-50-53-55-63. Midland Open 1949-51-52-54-57
Int Ryder Cup 1947-49-51
Mis Vardon Trophy 1948-49

Watson, Craig

Born Glasgow on 1st August 1966

Cls East Renfrewshire
Chp Amateur Champion 1997
Nat Scottish Amateur s/f 1996; Scottish Mid-Amateur 1994
Trn St Andrews Links Trophy 1992; Cameron-Corbett Vase 1996-97
Int Walker Cup 1997; Scotland (Home Int) 1991-92-94-95-96-97; Eur T Ch 1997

Way, Paul

Born Kingsbury, Middlesex on 12th March, 1963. Turned Professional 1981

PROFESSIONAL
Eur KLM Dutch Open 1982. Whyte & McKay PGA 1985. European Open 1987
RoW South African Charity Classic 1985
Int Ryder Cup 1983-85. England in World Cup 1985. Dunhill Cup 1985
AMATEUR
Nat English Open Amateur Stroke Play 1981
Int Walker Cup 1981. England (Home Int) 1981; Eur T Ch 1981

Westwood, Lee

Born Worksop on 24th April, 1973. Turned Professional 1993

PROFESSIONAL
Eur Scandinavian Masters, Volvo Masters 1997
RoW Taiheiyo Masters 1996-97; Malaysian Open, Australian Open 1997
Int Ryder Cup 1997; England in Dunhill Cup 1996-97
AMATEUR
Trn Peter McEvoy Trophy 1991; Lagonda Trophy 1992; Leven Gold Medal 1993
Int England (Home Int) 1993
Jun British Youths 1993

White, Ronald James

Born Wallasey on 9th April, 1921

Cls Hon member of Royal Birkdale, Woolton, Buxton and High Peak, Killarney
Nat English Amateur 1949 r/u, 1953. English Open Amateur Stroke Play 1950-51
Trn Golf Illustrated Gold Vase 1949. Daily Telegraph Pro-Am 1947-49

Sen British Seniors Open Amateur 1978-79
Reg Lancashire Amateur 1948
Int Walker Cup 1947-49-51-53-55. England (Home Int) 1947-48-49-53; France 1947-48
Jun Carris Trophy 1937
Int Boys 1936-37-38

Whitlock, Susan *See* Hedges

Willison, Ricky Brian
Born Ruislip on 30th July, 1959. Turned Professional 1991
PROFESSIONAL
Oth Stockley Park Challenge 1994; Tunisian Open Challenge 1995
AMATEUR
Nat English Amateur 1991, s/f 1988
Trn St George's Challenge Cup 1983; Berkhamsted Trophy 1984; Duncan Putter 1990-91; St Andrews Links Trophy 1991
Reg English Champion of Champions 1989
Oth Lake McQuarie Open (Aus), Greek Amateur Stroke Play 1990
Int Walker Cup 1991; England (Home Int) 1988-89-90; Eur T Ch 1989-91. GBI v Europe 1990; Eisenhower Trophy 1990
Mis Scrutton Jug 1991

Wilson, Enid
Born Stonebroom, nr Alfreton, Derbyshire on 15th March, 1910
Cls Hon member of Notts, Sherwood Forest, Chesterfield, Bramley, Sandy Lodge, Knole Park, North Hants, Crowborough
Chp British Ladies 1931-32-33.
Nat English Ladies 1928-30, r/u 1927; US Ladies Amateur s/f 1931-33
Trn Roehampton Gold Cup 1930
Reg Midland Ladies 1926-28-29-30. Derbyshire Ladies 1925-26. Cheshire Ladies 1933
Int Curtis Cup 1932. England (Home Int) 1928-29-30
Jun British Girls 1925

Wolstenholme, Gary Peter
Born Egham, Surrey on 21st August, 1960
Cls Bristol & Clifton, The Leicestershire, Scarborough North Cliff, County Sligo, Kilworth Springs
Chp Amateur Champion 1991
Nat British Mid-Amateur 1995, 1996
Oth Chinese Amateur 1993, Emirates Amateur 1995, Finnish Amateur 1996
Trn Berkshire Trophy 1996; Duncan Putter 1994-96; Gloucestershire County Champion 1992-93-94-96; Leicestershire Matchplay Champion 1984-85-86-88; Leicestershire Silver Fox 1984-85-89; Leicestershire Spring Tournament 1986, *Golf Illustrated* Gold Vase 1989; Ealing Open 1990; Bristol Open 1990-93; City & County Strokeplay 1994-95; Ross Scratch Trophy 1993; Long Ashton Vase 1990-92-93; Failand Cup 1989-90-91-93; John Cheatle Open Scratch Foursomes 1987-88-89-90

Reg English Counties Champion of Champions 1994-96; West of England Strokeplay 1987; Midland Open (Amateur) 1986; Midland Closed Strokeplay 1986; West Midland Amateur 1987
Int Walker Cup 1995-97; Eisenhower Trophy 1996. GBI v Europe 1992-94-96; England (Home Int) 1988 to 1997; v France 1988-90-92-94; v Spain 1989-91-93-95; Eur T Ch 1995-97
Mis Cameron Trophy 1984-86-89; Duchess Salver 1990-92-93; Scrutton Jug 1996; Leading Amateur B&H Int 1993

Woosnam, Ian, MBE
Born Oswestry on 2nd March, 1958. Turned Professional 1976
PROFESSIONAL
Maj Open 3rd 1986; US Open r/u 1989; US Masters 1991
Eur Swiss Open 1982; Silk Cut Masters 1983; Scandinavian Enterprise Open 1984; Lawrence Batley TPC 1986; Jersey Open, Cepsa Madrid Open, Bell's Scottish Open, Lancôme Trophy, Suntory World Match Play 1987; Volvo PGA, Carrolls Irish Open, Panasonic European Open 1988; Carrolls Irish Open 1989; Mediterranean Open, Monte Carlo Open, Bell's Scottish Open, Suntory World Match Play, Epson Grand Prix 1990; Mediterranean Open, Monte Carlo Open 1991; Monte Carlo Open 1992; English Open, Lancôme Trophy 1993; Cannes Open, Dunhill British Masters 1994; Johnnie Walker Classic, Heineken Classic, Scottish Open, German Open 1996; Volvo PGA Chp 1997
US USF&G Classic, Grand Slam of Golf 1991
Oth *News of the World* U-23 Match Play 1979; Cacharel U-25 Chp 1982
RoW Zambian Open 1985; Kenya Open 1986; Hong Kong Open 1987; Heineken Classic (ANZ) 1996
Reg Welsh PGA 1988
Int Ryder Cup 1983-85-87-89-91-93-95-97; Nissan Cup 1985-86; Kirin Cup 1987; Four Tours World Chp 1989-90; GBIvAustralia 1988; Hennessy-Cognac Cup 1982-84; Wales in World Cup 1980-82-83-84-85-87 (winners; also individual winner)-90-91 (r/u; individual winner)-92-93-96-97; in Dunhill Cup 1985-86-87-88-89-90-91-93-95
Mis Harry Vardon Trophy 1987-90
AMATEUR
Reg Shropshire & Herefordshire Amateur 1975

Wright, Janette *(née* Robertson)
Born Glasgow on 7th January, 1935
Cls Honorary member of Lenzie, Troon, Cruden Bay, Aboyne, St Rule
Nat Scottish Ladies 1959-60-61-73, r/u 1958
Trn Kayser Bondor Foursomes 1958 (tied)-61. Worplesdon Mixed Foursomes 1959
Reg North of Scotland Ladies 1970. Lanarkshire Ladies 1954-55-56-57-58-59. West of Scotland Ladies 1956-58-59
Int Curtis Cup 1954-56-58-60. Vagliano Trophy 1959-61. GBI v France 1957; v Belgium 1957; v Canada 1954. GB Commonwealth Team 1959. Scotland (Home Int) 1952-53-54-55-56-

57-58-59-60-61-63-65-66-67-73-(**78**)-(**79**)-(**80**).
Eur(L) T Ch 1965-73-(**79**)
Jun   British Girls 1950.
Int   Girls 1950-51-52-53

Wright, Pamela
*Born Aboyne on 26th June, 1964. Turned Professional
1988*
PROFESSIONAL
Int   Europe Solheim Cup 1990-92-94; Scotland
Sunrise Cup 1992

Mis   Gatorade Rookie of the Year 1989
AMATEUR
Nat   British U-18 Stroke Play 1981; British Ladies
Stroke Play r/u 1981; Scottish Ladies Junior
Stroke Play r/u 1980; Scottish Ladies r/u 1982;
Scottish Ladies Stroke Play 1985
Reg   North of Scotland Ladies 1984
Int   GBI Vagliano 1981; Scotland (Home Int) 1981
to 1984; Eur(L) T Ch 1987
Jun   Scottish Girls r/u 1980-81
Mis   All-American 1987-88; Collegiate Player of the
Year 1988

Overseas Players

See page 286 for list of abbreviations

Aaron, Tommy
Born Gainesville, Georgia, USA on 22nd February, 1937. Turned Professional 1961
PROFESSIONAL
Maj US Masters 1973; USPGA r/u 1972
Eur Lancôme Trophy 1972
US Canadian Open 1969; Georgia-Pacific Atlanta Golf Classic 1970
Sen Kaanapali Classic 1992
Int Ryder Cup 1969-73
AMATEUR
Nat US Amateur r/u 1958
Int Walker Cup 1959

Alcott, Amy
Born Kansas City, Missouri, USA on 22nd February, 1956. Turned Professional 1975
PROFESSIONAL
Maj US Women's Open 1980, 3rd 1984-91; USLPGA r/u 1988
US 29 LPGA wins 1975 to 1992
Mis Gatorade Rookie of the Year 1975; Vare Trophy, *Golf Magazine* Player of the Year 1980; Founders Cup 1986
AMATEUR
Jun USGA Girls 1973

Alfredsson, Helen
Born Göteborg on 9th April, 1965. Turned Professional 1989
Maj Ladies British Open 1990, r/u 1991; US Women's Open, 3rd 1993
PROFESSIONAL
Eur Hennessy Ladies Cup, Trophée Coconut Skol, Benson & Hedges Trophy (with A Forsbrand 1991; Hennessy Ladies Cup 1992; Evian Masters 1994; Hennessy Ladies Cup 1996; McDonald's WPGA Chp of Europe 1997
US Nabisco Dinah Shore 1993
RoW Queensland Women's Open, Ellair Open (Japan) 1991; Itoki Classic 1992; Itoen Ladies 1997
Int Solheim Cup 1990-92-94-96; Sunrise Cup 1990 (winners)-92(winners); (for LPGA) Nichirei International 1993-95
Mis Rookie of the Year 1989; Gatorade Rookie of the Year 1992
AMATEUR
Nat Swedish Ladies 1986-87-88; Swedish Ladies Open Stroke Play 1988

Int Sweden (Eur(L) T Ch) 1983-85-87 (winners) Espirito Santo 1988(r/u)

Allenby, Robert
Born Melbourne on 12th July, 1971. Turned Professional 1992
PROFESSIONAL
Eur Honda Open 1994; English Open, Open de France, British Masters 1996
RoW Johnnie Walker Classic 1992; Players Chp (ANZ) 1993; Australian Open 1994; Heineken Classic (ANZ) 1995
Oth Perak Masters (Malaysia) 1992
Int President's Cup 1996; World Cup r/u 1995; Dunhill Cup 1997
AMATEUR
Reg Victorian Amateur 1990

Aoki, Isao
Born Abiko, Chiba, Japan on 31st August, 1942. Turned Professional 1964
Eur World Match Play Chp 1978. European Open 1983
US Hawaiian Open 1983
RoW Japan PGA 1973-81-86; Japan Open 1983-87; Dunlop Jap International 1987; Tokai Classic, Casio World Open, Coca Cola Classic (Aust) 1989; Mitsubishi Gallant 1990-92; Casio World Open 1992
Sen US Tour Nationwide Chp 1992; Bank One Senior Classic, Brickyard Crossing Chp 1994; American Express Grand Slam, Bank of Boston Senior Golf Classic 1995; BellSouth Classic, Kroger Senior Classic 1996; Emerald Coast Classic 1997
Int Japan v US 1982-83-84. Dunhill Cup 1985. Nissan Cup 1985. Kirin Cup 1987-88

Azinger, Paul William
Born Holyoke, Massachusetts, USA on 6th January, 1960. Turned Professional 1981
Maj Open r/u 1987; US Open 3rd 1993; USPGA 1993, r/u 1988
Eur BMW International Open 1990-92
US 1987-three; 1988-one; 1989-one; 1990-one; 1991-one; 1992-one (Tour Chp); 1993-two (Memorial Trn, New England Classic)
Int Ryder Cup 1989-91-93. World Cup 1989
Mis USPGA Player of the Year 1987

Baiocchi, Hugh

Born Johannesburg, South Africa on 17th August, 1946. Turned Professional 1971

PROFESSIONAL

Eur	Swiss Open 1973; Dutch Open 1975; Scandinavian Enterprise Open 1976; PGA Match Play 1977; Swiss Open 1979; State Express Classic 1983
RoW	South African Open 1978; South African PGA 1980; Western Province Open, SA International Classic 1973; Transvaal Open 1974-76; Rhodesian Dunlop Masters, Swaziland Holiday Inns, 1976; Zimbabwe Open, Vaal Reefs Open 1980; Twee Jongegezellen Masters 1989
Sen	Pittsburgh Sen Classic 1997
Int	South Africa in World Cup 1973-77-79; Hennessy-Cognac Cup 1982
Mis	Captain SA PGA 1978-79

AMATEUR

Nat	South African Amateur 1970
Oth	Brazilian Amateur 1968

Baker, Kathy

Born Albany, New York, USA on 20th March, 1961. Turned Professional 1983.

PROFESSIONAL

Maj	US Women's Open 1985

AMATEUR

Int	Curtis Cup 1982; Espirito Santo 1982 (winners)

Baker-Finch, Ian

Born Nambour, Queensland, Australia on 24th October, 1960. Turned Professional 1979

Maj	Open Champion 1991
Eur	Scandinavian Open 1985
US	Colonial National Invitation 1989
RoW	New Zealand Open 1983; Australian Match Play 1987; Australian Masters 1988; Western Australian Open, NSW Open, Queensland PGA 1984; Victoria Open 1985; *Golf Digest* 1987; Pocarisweat Open 1988; Vines Classic 1992; Australian PGA 1993
Int	Nissan Cup 1986; Kirin Cup 1987-88; Four Tours World Chp 1990(winners)-91; Dunhill Cup 1992

Ballesteros, Severiano

Born Pedreña, Spain on 9th April, 1957. Turned Professional 1974

Maj	Open Champion 1979-84-88; r/u 1976. US Open 3rd 1987. US Masters 1980-83 r/u 1985-87; 3rd 1982
Eur	Dutch Open, Lancôme Trophy 1976; French Open, Uniroyal International, Swiss Open 1977; Martini International, German Open, Scandinavian Enterprise Open, Swiss Open 1978; English Classic 1979; Madrid Open, Martini International, Dutch Open 1980; Scandinavian Enterprise Open, Spanish Open, Suntory World Match Play 1981; Madrid Open, French Open, Suntory World Match Play 1982; Sun Alliance PGA, Irish Open, Lancôme Trophy 1983. Suntory World Match Play 1984; Irish Open, French Open, Sanyo Open, Spanish Open, Suntory World Match Play 1985; British Masters, Irish Open, Monte Carlo Open, French Open, Dutch Open,

Lancôme Trophy (tied) 1986; Suze Open 1987; Open de Baleares, Scandinavian Enterprise Open, German Open, Lancôme Trophy 1988. Cepsa Madrid Open; Epson Grand Prix; Ebel European Masters-Swiss Open 1989; Open de Baleares 1990. Volvo PGA, Dunhill British Masters, Toyota World Match Play 1991; Dubai Desert Classic, Open de Baleares 1992; Benson & Hedges International Open, German Masters 1994; Tournoi Perrier de Paris, Open de España 1995

US	Greater Greensboro Open 1978; Westchester Classic 1983-88; USF&G Classic 1985
RoW	Japanese Open, Dunlop Phoenix , Otago Classic 1977; Japanese Open, Kenya Open 1978; Dunlop Phoenix, Australian PGA 1981; Visa Taiheiyo Masters 1988; Chunichi Crowns 1991
Int	Ryder Cup 1979-83-85-87-89-91-93-95-(97); Hennessy-Cognac Cup 1976-78; Spain in World Cup 1975-76(winners)-77(winners)-91; Dunhill Cup 1985-86-88
Mis	Harry Vardon Trophy 1976-77-78-86-88-91; AGW Trophy 1979-84-91; Ritz Club Golfer of the Year 1988-91; World Golf Hall of Fame 1997

Barber, Miller

Born Shreveport, Louisiana, USA on 31st March, 1931. Turned Professional 1958

US	11 wins 1964 to 1978
Sen	US Seniors PGA 1981. US Seniors Open 1982-84-85.US Sen Tour 24 wins 1981-89
Int	Ryder Cup 1969-71

Beck, Chip

Born Fayetteville, North Carolina, USA on 12th September, 1956. Turned Professional 1978

Maj	US Open r/u 1986-89; US Masters r/u 1993
US	Los Angeles Open, USF & G Classic 1988; Buick Open 1990; Freeport Classic 1992
Int	Ryder Cup 1989-91-93; Dunhill Cup 1988
Mis	Vardon Trophy 1988

Beman, Deane R

Born Washington, DC, USA on 22nd April, 1938. Turned Professional 1987

Maj	US Open r/u 1969, leading amateur 1962

PROFESSIONAL

US	Texas Open 1969; Greater Milwaukee Open; Quad Cities Open 1972; Shrine-Robinson Classic 1973
Mis	Commissioner of US PGA Tour since 1974; Herb Graffis Award 1987

AMATEUR

Chp	Amateur Champion 1960
Nat	US Amateur 1960-63, r/u 1966
Reg	Eastern Amateur 1960-61-63-64
Int	Walker Cup 1959-61-63-65; Eisenhower Trophy 1960(winners)-62(winners)-64-66(r/u)

Berg, Patty

Born Minneapolis, USA on 13th February, 1918. Turned Professional 1940 (Founder member of LPGA)

PROFESSIONAL

Maj	US Women's Open 1946, r/u 1957
US	57 LPGA wins 1941-62 Western Open 1941-48-51-55-57-58; Titleholders Chp 1948-53-55-57)

Mis Leading money winner 1954-55-57; Bobby Jones Award 1963; Ben Hogan Award 1975; first President of USLPGA; LPGA Hall of Fame 1951; World Golf Hall of Fame 1974; Founder's Cup 1981; Old Tom Morris Award 1986

AMATEUR

Nat US Ladies Amateur 1938

Reg Western Amateur 1938

Trn 29 amateur wins 1934-40

Int Curtis Cup 1936-38

Bevione, Isa *See* Goldschmid

Bjorn, Thomas
Born Silkeborg, Denmark on 18th February, 1971. Turned Professional 1993

PROFESSIONAL

Eur Loch Lomond Invitational 1996

Oth Challenge Himmerland Open, Interlaken Open, Esbjerg Danish Closed, Coca-Cola Open 1995

Int Ryder Cup 1997; World Cup 1996-97

Mis Rookie of the Year 1996. First Dane to play in Ryder Cup

AMATEUR

Nat Danish Amateur 1990-91

Bradley, Pat
Born Westford, Massachusetts, USA on 24th March, 1951. Turned Professional 1974

Maj US Women's Open 1981, r/u 1991, 3rd 1989; USLPGA 1986 r/u 1991, 3rd 1984-85-94

US 32 LPGA wins 1976 to 1996

RoW Colgate Far East Open 1975; JC Penney Classic 1978-89

Int Solheim Cup 1990-92-96

Mis Rolex Player of the Year 1986-91; Vare Trophy 1986-91; Mazda-LPGA Series 1983-86; *Golf Magazine* Player of the Year 1986; Ben Hogan, Powell Award 1991; LPGA Hall of Fame 1991

Brooks, Mark
Born Fort Worth, Texas, USA on 25th March, 1961. Turned Professional 1983

Maj Open 3rd 1995; USPGA 1996

US Greater Hartford Open 1988; Greater Greensboro Open, Greater Milwaukee Open 1991; Kemper Open 1994; Bob Hope Chrysler Classic, Shell Houston Open 1996

Int President's Cup 1996

Burke, Jack, Jr
Born Fort Worth, Texas, USA in January, 1923. Turned Professional 1940

Maj USPGA 1956; US Masters 1956, r/u 1952

US 15 wins 1950 to 1963

Int Ryder Cup 1951-53-55-57-59-(**73**)

Mis USPGA Player of the Year 1956

Calcavecchia, Mark
Born Laurel, Nebraska, USA on 12th June, 1960. Turned Professional 1981

Maj Open Champion 1989; US Masters r/u 1988

US WSW Golf Classic 1986 Honda Classic 1987, Bank of Boston Classic 1988; Phoenix Open,

Nissan Los Angeles Open 1989; Phoenix Open 1992; BellSouth Classic 1995; Greater Vancouver Open 1997

RoW Australian Open 1988; Argentine Open 1993

Oth Subaru Sarazen World Open 1997

Int Ryder Cup 1987-89-91; Dunhill Cup 1989 (winners)-90; Kirin Cup 1987; Four Tours World Chp 1990

Campbell, William Cammack
Born West Virginia, USA on 5th May, 1923

Chp Amateur r/u 1954

Nat US Amateur 1964

Oth Canadian Amateur r/u 1952-54-65; Mexican Amateur 1956

Reg North & South Amateur 1950-53-57-67. Tam O'Shanter World Amateur 1948-49. Ontario Amateur 1967

Sen USGA Seniors 1979-80. US Seniors Open r/u 1980

Int Walker Cup 1951-53-55-57-65-67-71-75. Eisenhower Trophy 1964-(**68**)

Mis Bobby Jones Award 1956. President USGA 1983. Captain R&A 1987/88. Old Tom Morris Award 1991; World Golf Hall of Fame 1990

Canizares, José Maria
Born Madrid on 18th February, 1947. Turned Professional 1967

Eur Lancia D'Oro 1972; Avis Jersey Open; Bob Hope British Classic 1980; Italian Open 1981; Bob Hope British Classic 1983; Benson & Hedges Trophy (with Tania Abitbol) 1990; Roma Masters 1992

RoW Kenya Open 1984

Int Ryder Cup 1981-83-85-89; Hennessy-Cognac Cup 1974-76-78-80-82-84; Spain in World Cup 1974-80-82(winners)-83-84(winners; individual winner)-85-87-89; Dunhill Cup 1985-87-89-90; Double Diamond 1974; (Sen) European Cup 1997

Caponi, Donna
Born Detroit, Michigan, USA on 29th January, 1945. Turned Professional 1965

Maj US Women's Open 1969-70. USLPGA 1979-81

Eur Colgate European Open 1975

US 24 LPGA wins 1969 to 1981

Mis *LA Times* Woman Golfer of the Year 1970; Mickey Wright Award 1980-81

Carner, JoAnne *(née* Gunderson)
Born Kirkland, Washington, USA on 4th April, 1939. Turned Professional 1970

PROFESSIONAL

Maj US Women's Open 1971-76, r/u 1975-78-82-83-87 (tied); USLPGA r/u 1974-82

US 42 LPGA wins 1970 to 85

RoW Australian Ladies Open 1975

Int Solheim Cup (**1994**)

Mis Rolex Player of the Year 1974-81-82; Vare Trophy 1974-75-81-82-83; Gatorade Rookie of the Year 1970; *Golf Magazine* Player of the Year 1974-81-82; LPGA Hall of Fame 1982; World Golf Hall of Fame 1985; Bobby Jones Award 1981; Mickey Wright Award 1974-82

AMATEUR

Nat	US Ladies Amateur 1957-60-62-66-68, r/u 1956-64
Trn	LPGA Burdine's Invitational 1969 (as amateur)
Reg	Western Ladies Open Amateur 1959
Int	Curtis Cup 1958-60-62-64
Jun	US Girls 1956

Casper, Billy

Born in San Diego, California, USA on 24th June, 1931. Turned Professional 1954

Maj	US Open 1959-66; USPGA r/u 1958-65-71; US Masters 1970, r/u 1969
Eur	Lancôme Trophy 1974; Italian Open 1975
Oth	Alcan Golfer of the Year 1969; Lancia D'Oro 1974
US	51 wins 1956 to 1975; Canadian Open 1967
RoW	Brazilian Open 1959-60; Moroccan Grand Prix 1973-75; Mexican Open 1977
Sen	US: 9 wins 1982-89. US Senior Open 1983
Int	Ryder Cup 1961-63-65-67-69-71-73-75-(79)
Mis	Vardon Trophy 1960-63-65-66-68; leading money winner 1966-68. USPGA Player of the Year 1966-70; Byron Nelson Award 1966-68-70. World Golf Hall of Fame 1978; USPGA Hall of Fame 1982

Cavalleri, Silvia

Born Milan, Italy on 10th October, 1972. Turned Professional 1997

Cls	Milan
Chp	US Ladies Amateur 1997
Nat	European Ladies Chp 1996-97; World Chp (Individual) 1996
Jun	Italian National Junior Chp 1985-87-90-92-93; Italian Girls 1987-89-90; British Girls 1990
Int	Italy Eur(L)T Ch 1997

Cejka, Alexander

Born Marienbad on 2nd December, 1970. Turned Professional 1989

Eur	Open Andalucia, Hohe Brucke Open, Volvo Masters 1995
Oth	Czech Open 1990-92; Audi Quattro Open 1991-93; KB Golf Challenge 1997
Int	Germany in Dunhill Cup 1994-95-97; World Cup 1996-97

Charles, Robert J (Bob)

Born Carterton, New Zealand on 14th March, 1936. Turned Profesional 1960

PROFESSIONAL

Maj	Open Champion 1963, r/u 1968-69; US Open 3rd 1964-70; USPGA r/u 1968
Eur	Bowmaker 1961; Engadine Open, Swiss Open, Daks 1962; Piccadilly World Match Play 1969, r/u 1968; John Player Classic, Dunlop Masters 1972; Scandinavian Enterprise Open 1973; Swiss Open 1974
US	4 wins 1963 to 1974; Canadian Open 1968
RoW	New Zealand Open 1954 (as amateur)-66-70-73, r/u 1974; New Zealand Professional 1961-79-80; 17 other trn wins in New Zealand 1961-78; South African Open 1973

Sen	Volvo Seniors British Open 1989-93; US Sen Tour 22 wins 1986-94; Japan Sen 3 wins
Int	New Zealand in World Cup 1962 to 1968, 1971-72; Dunhill Cup 1985-86
Mis	First New Zealander and first left-handed player to win the Open

AMATEUR

Int	Eisenhower Trophy 1960

Coe, Charles R

Born Oklahoma City, USA on 26th October, 1923

Maj	US Masters r/u 1961
Chp	Amateur r/u 1951
Nat	US Amateur 1949-58; r/u 1959
Reg	Western Amateur 1950
Int	Walker Cup 1949-51-53-(57)-59-61-63. Eisenhower Trophy 1960
Mis	Bobby Jones Award 1964

Cole, Robert

Born Springs, South Africa on 11th May, 1948. Turned Professional 1966

PROFESSIONAL

Maj	Open 3rd 1975
US	Buick Open 1977
RoW	South African Open 1974-80; Dunlop Masters (SA) 1969; Natal Open 1969-70-72; Cape Classic 1970; Transvaal Open 1972; Rhodesian Masters 1972; Vavasseur (SA) 1974
Int	South Africa in World Cup 1969-74 (winners; individual winner)-76

AMATEUR

Chp	Amateur 1966
Nat	English Open Amateur Stroke Play r/u 1966
Trn	*Golf Illustrated* Gold Vase 1966 (shared)
Int	Eisenhower Trophy 1966

Cook, John

Born Toledo, Ohio, USA on 2nd October, 1957. Turned Professional 1979

PROFESSIONAL

Maj	Open r/u 1992; USPGA r/u 1992
US	Bing Crosby National ProAm 1981; Canadian Open 1983; The International 1987; Bob Hope Chrysler Classic, Hawaiian Open, Las Vegas Invitational 1992; St Jude Open, CVS Charity Classic 1996; Bob Hope Chrysler Classic 1997
RoW	Sao Paulo–Brazilian Open 1982; Mexican Open 1995
Int	Ryder Cup 1993; World Cup 1983

AMATEUR

Nat	US Amateur 1978
Int	US World Cup 1979
Jun	World Juniors 1974
Mis	All-American 1977-78-79

Couples, Fred

Born Seattle, Washington, USA on 3rd October, 1959. Turned Professional 1980

Maj	Open 3rd 1991; US Open leading amateur 1978, 3rd 1991; US Masters 1992; USPGA r/u 1990, 3rd 1982
Eur	Dubai Desert Classic, Johnnie Walker Classic 1995

US 13 wins 1983-96 (The Players Chp 1996)
RoW Tournoi Perrier de Paris, Johnnie Walker World Chp 1991-95
Int Ryder Cup 1989-91-93-95-97; Four Tours World Chp 1990(individual winner)-91; Dunhill Cup 1991-92-93(winners)-94(r/u); World Cup 1992(winners)-93(winners)-94(winners; individual winner)-95(winners); President's Cup 1994-96
Mis Vardon Trophy 1991-92; USPGA Player of the Year 1991-92; Arnold Palmer Award 1992

Crenshaw, Ben

Born Austin, Texas, USA on 11th January, 1952. Turned Professional 1973
PROFESSIONAL
Maj Open r/u 1978-79, 3rd 1980; US Open leading amateur 1970, 3rd 1975; USPGA r/u 1979; US Masters 1984-95, r/u 1976-83, 3rd 1989-91
Eur Carrolls Irish Open 1976
US 19 wins 1973 to 1996
RoW Australian Open r/u 1978; Mexican Open 1982
Oth Grand Slam of Golf 1995
Int Ryder Cup 1981-83-87-95; US in World Cup 1972-87-88(winners; individual winner); Kirin Cup 1988
Mis Rookie of the Year 1974; Byron Nelson Award 1976; William Richardson Award 1989; Bobby Jones Award 1991; US Ryder Cup Captain-elect 1999
AMATEUR
Trn NCAA Chp 1971-72(shared)-73
Int Eisenhower Trophy 1972(winners)

Daly, John

Born Sacramento, California, USA on 28th April, 1966. Turned Professional 1984
Maj Open Champion 1995; US Masters 3rd 1993; USPGA 1991
PROFESSIONAL
US BC Open 1992; BellSouth Classic 1994
Oth Ben Hogan Utah Classic 1990; Missouri Open 1987
Int Dunhill Cup 1993(winners)
Mis USPGA Rookie of the Year 1991
AMATEUR
Reg Missouri and Arkansas State Amateur 1983-84

Daniel, Beth

Born Charleston, South Carolina, USA on 14th October, 1956. Turned Professional October, 1978
Maj USLPGA 1990, r/u 1984
PROFESSIONAL
US 32 LPGA wins 1979 to 1995 (Ping Welch's Chp 1995)
RoW World Ladies Championship (Japan) 1979
Oth JC Penney Classic (with D Love III) 1994-95
Int Solheim Cup 1990-92-94-96; Nichirei Int 1995
Mis USLPGA Rookie of the Year 1979; USLPGA leading money winner 1980; Rolex Player of the Year 1980-90-94; Vare Trophy 1989-90-94; Order of Merit winner 1990; Mickey Wright Award 1990-94
AMATEUR
Nat US Ladies Amateur 1975-77
Int Curtis Cup 1976-78

Davies, Richard

Born USA on 29th October, 1930
Maj US Open leading amateur 1963
Chp Amateur Champion 1962
Int Walker Cup 1963

Davis, Rodger

Born Sydney, New South Wales, Australia on 18th May, 1951. Turned Professional 1974
Maj Open r/u 1987
Eur State Express Classic 1981; Whyte & Mackay PGA 1986; Wang Four Stars 1988; Spanish Open, Wang Four Stars 1990; Volvo Masters 1991; Cannes Open 1993
RoW Australian Open 1986; New Zealand Open 1986-91; South Australia Open 1978; Victoria Open 1979; New South Wales Open 1989; Palm Meadows Cup 1990; Sanctuary Cove Classic 1991-92
Int World Cup 1985-87-91-93; Dunhill Cup 1986 (winners)-87-88-90-92; Nissan Cup 1986; Kirin Cup 1987-88, Four Tours World Chp 1990 (winners)-91

Decker, Anne *See* Sander

Descampe, Florence

Born Belgium on 1st June, 1969. Turned Professional 1988
PROFESSIONAL
Eur Danish Ladies Open 1988; Valextra Classic, Italian Open, Woolmark Ladies Match Play 1990; Ladies German Open 1991; Ladies Austrian Open 1994
US McCall's LPGA Classic 1992
Int Solheim Cup 1992
AMATEUR
Nat European Amateur 1988; Belgian Ladies Match Play 1987
Jun Belgian Junior Champion 1987

Dibnah, Corinne

Born Brisbane, Australia on 29th July, 1962. Turned Professional 1984
Maj Women's British Open 1988, r/u 1992
PROFESSIONAL
Eur 12 WPGET wins 1986-92 (Ladies Italian Open 1994)
RoW Indonesian Open, Malaysian JAL Open 1996
Oth Sunningdale Foursomes (with Dale Reid) 1990
Int Sunrise Cup 1992
Mis Woolmark Order of Merit winner 1991
AMATEUR
Nat Australian Ladies 1981. New Zealand Ladies 1983
Int Commonwealth Tournament 1983 (winners)

Dickson, Robert B

Born McAlester, Oklahoma, USA on 25th January, 1944. Turned Professional 1968
PROFESSIONAL
US 2 wins 1968-73
AMATEUR
Chp Amateur Champion 1967
Nat US Amateur 1967

Int Walker Cup 1967
Mis One of only four to win British and US Amateur titles in the same year. Bobby Jones Award 1968.

Duval, David
Born Jacksonville, Fl, USA on 9th November, 1971. Turned Professional 1993
PROFESSIONAL
US Michelob Chp, Walt Disney Classic, The Tour Chp 1997
Oth Nike Wichita Open, Nike Tour Chp 1993
Int President's Cup 1996
AMATEUR
Int Walker Cup 1991

Elkington, Steve
Born Inverell, Australia on 8th December, 1962. Turned Professional 1985
PROFESSIONAL
Maj US Masters 3rd 1993; USPGA 1995; 3rd 1996
US Greater Greensboro Open 1990; Trn Players Chp 1991; Infiniti Trn of Champions 1992; Buick Southern Open 1994; Mercedes Chp 1995; Doral-Ryder Open 1997
RoW Australian Open 1992
Int President's Cup 1994-96; Dunhill Cup 1994-95-96-97; World Cup 1994
Mis Vardon Trophy 1995
AMATEUR
Nat Australia-New Zealand Amateur 1980; Australian Amateur 1981
Jun Doug Sanders Jun World Chp 1981
Mis All-American 1984-85

Els, Ernie
Born Johannesburg on 17th October, 1969. Turned Professional 1989
PROFESSIONAL
Maj Open r/u 1996; US Open 1994-97; USPGA 3rd 1995
Eur Dubai Desert Classic, Toyota World Match Play Chp 1994-95-96; Lexington PGA 1995; Johnnie Walker Classic 1997
US Sarazen World Open 1994; Byron Nelson Classic 1995; Buick Classic 1996-97; Andersen Consulting Int Chp 1997
RoW SA Open, SA Masters (Jpn), SAPGA, Swazi Sun Classic, Goodyear Classic, SA Trn Players Chp 1992; Dunlop Phoenix 1993; Johnnie Walker World Chp 1994; SA Bells Cup, SA PGA 1995
Int SA in Dunhill Cup 1992-93-94-95-96-97 (winners); World Cup 1992-93-96 (winners) (individual winner)-97; Alfred Dunhill Challenge 1995; President's Cup 1996
Mis USPGA Rookie of the Year 1994
AMATEUR
Nat SA Amateur 1986; SA Amateur Strokeplay 1989
Trn Tillman Trophy 1988

Faxon, Brad
Born Oceanport, NJ, USA on 1st August, 1961. Turned Professional 1983
PROFESSIONAL
US Provident Classic 1986; Buick Open 1991; New England Classic, The Invitational 1992;

Freeport-McDermott Classic 1997
RoW Australian Open 1993
Oth Fred Meyer Challenge (with G Norman) 1995-96
Int Ryder Cup 1995-97
AMATEUR
Int Walker Cup 1983

Fernandez, Vicente
Born Corrientes, Argentina on 5th May, 1946. Turned Professional 1964
Eur Dutch Open 1970; Benson & Hedges 1975; Colgate PGA 1979; Tenerife Open 1990; English Open 1992
RoW Argentine Open 1968-69-81-90; Maracaibo Open 1972; Brazil Open 1977-83-84
Sen US Burnet Seniors Classic 1996; Bank One Classic 1997
Int World Cup 1970-72-78-84-85. Dunhill Cup 1986-88-89

Finsterwald, Dow
Born Athens, Ohio, USA on 6th September, 1929. Turned Professional 1951
Maj US Open 3rd 1960; USPGA 1958; r/u 1957; US Masters r/u 1962 (tied), 3rd, 1960
US 11 wins 1955 to 1963; Canadian Open 1956
Int Ryder Cup 1957-59-61-63-(77)
Mis Vardon Trophy 1957; USPGA Player of the Year 1958

Floyd, Ray
Born Fort Bragg, North Carolina, USA on 4th September, 1942. Turned Professional 1961
Maj Open r/u 1978; 3rd 1981; US Open 1986; US Masters 1976, r/u 1985-90-92; USPGA 1969-82, r/u 1976
US 22 wins 1963 to 1994
RoW Brazilian Open 1978; Daiwa KBC Augusta Open (Japan) 1991
Sen US Tour 16 wins 1992-96 (Senior Tour Chp 1992-94); USPGA Seniors Chp 1995; Senior Players Chp 1996
Int Ryder Cup 1969-75-77-83-(**89**)-91-93. Dunhill Cup 1985-86. Nissan Cup 1985
Mis Rookie of the Year 1963. Vardon Trophy 1983. World Golf Hall of Fame 1989.

Ford, Doug
Born West Haven, Connecticut, USA on 6th August, 1922. Turned Professional 1949
Maj US Masters 1957; r/u 1958. USPGA 1955
US 15 wins 1955 to 1962; Canadian Open 1959-63
Sen 1987-one
Int Ryder Cup 1955-57-59-61
Mis USPGA Player of the Year 1955

Forsbrand, Anders
Born Filipstad, Sweden on 1st April, 1961. Turned Professional 1981
PROFESSIONAL
Eur Ebel European Masters–Swiss Open 1987; Open di Firenze, Benson & Hedges Trophy (with H Alfredsson) 1991; Open di Firenze, Cannes

Open, Equity & Law Challenge 1992; Moroccan Open 1994; German Masters 1995
Oth Swedish PGA 1982; Open Novotel Perrier (with M Jonzon) 1997
Int Hennessy-Cognac Cup 1984; Kirin Cup 1984; World Cup 1984-85-88-91(winners)-92-93; Dunhill Cup 1985-86-87-88-91(winners)-92-94

Frost, David
Born Cape Town, South Africa on 11th September, 1959
Eur Cannes Open 1984
RoW South African Open 1986; Million Dollar Challenge 1989-90-92; Dunlop Phoenix Open 1992; Lexington PGA, Hong Kong Open 1994
US 1988-two; 1989-one; 1990-one; 1992-one; 1993-two; 1994-one; 1997-one (MasterCard Colonial)
Int South Africa in Dunhill Cup 1991(r/u)-92-94-95-97 (winners); President's Cup 1994-96; Alfred Dunhill Challenge 1995

Furyk, Jim
Born West Chester, PA, USA on 12th May, 1970. Turned Professional 1992
US Las Vegas Invitational 1995; Hawaiian Open 1996
Oth Nike Mississippi Gulf Coast Classic 1993
Int Ryder Cup 1997

Garrido, Ignacio
Born Madrid, Spain on 27th March, 1972. Turned Professional 1993
PROFESSIONAL
Eur Volvo German Open 1997
RoW Hassan II Trophy 1996
Oth Challenge AGF (Fr), Spanish PGA 1993; Cepsa APG 1996
Int Ryder Cup 1997; Spain in Dunhill Cup 1997; World Cup 1996-97
Mis His father played in first European Ryder Cup in 1979
AMATEUR
Nat English Open Amateur Strokeplay (Brabazon) 1992

Geddes, Jane
Born Huntingdon, New York, USA on 5th February, 1960. Turned Professional 1983
Maj Ladies British Open 1989; US Women's Open 1986; USLPGA 1987
US Boston Five Classic 1986; Women's Kemper Open, GNA Glendale Federal Classic, Toledo Classic, Boston Five Classic 1987; Jamaica Classic, Atlantic City Classic 1991; Oldsmobile Classic 1993; Chicago Challenge 1994
RoW Australian Women's Masters 1990-92
Int Solheim Cup 1996; Sunrise Cup 1992; Nichirei Int 1993-95-96-97

Giles, Marvin
Maj US Open leading amateur 1973
Chp Amateur Champion 1975
Nat US Amateur Champion 1972, r/u 1967-68-69
Int Walker Cup 1969-71-73-75. Eisenhower Trophy (winners) 1968-70-72

Goldschmid, Isa *(née* Bevione)
Born Italy
Nat Italian Ladies' Close 1947-51-53-54-55-56-57-58-59-60-61-62-63-64-65-66-67-69-71-73-74. Italian Ladies' Open 1952-57-58-60-61-63-64-67-68-69
Oth Spanish Ladies 1952. French Ladies 1975
Trn Kayser Bondor 1963
Int Vagliano Trophy 1959-61-63-65-67-69-71-73-(77) Eur v United States 1968. Italy in Espirito Santo 1964-66-68-70-72

Grady, Wayne
Born Brisbane, Queensland, Australia on 26th July, 1957. Turned Professional 1978
Maj Open r/u 1989 (tied); USPGA 1990
Eur German Open 1984
US Westchester Classic 1989
RoW Australia PGA 1991; West Lakes Classic (Aus) 1978
Int Australia in World Cup 1978-83-89 (winners); Nissan Cup 1985; Four Tours Chp 1990 (winners); Dunhill Cup 1989-90-91; Alfred Dunhill Challenge 1995

Graham, David
Born Windsor, Tasmania on 23rd May, 1946. Turned Professional 1962
Maj Open 3rd 1985; US Open 1981; USPGA 1979
Eur French Open 1970; Piccadilly World Match Play 1976; Lancôme Trophy 1982
US 6 wins 1972-83
RoW Australian Open 1977, r/u 1972; Australian Wills Masters 1975; Thailand Open, Victoria Open, Tasmanian Open, Yomiuri Open 1970; Caracas Open, Japanese Airlines 1971; Chunichi Crowns (Japan) 1976; West Lakes Classic (Aust), New Zealand Open 1979; Queensland Open 1987
Sen Southwestern Bell Dominion, GTE Classic, Comfort Classic 1997
Int President's Cup 1994

Graham, Lou
Born Nashville, Tennessee, USA on 7th January, 1938. Turned Professional 1962
Maj US Open 1975; r/u 1977
US 1967-one. 1972-one. 1979-three.
Int Ryder Cup 1973-75-77. World Cup 1975(winners)

Green, Hubert
Born Birmingham, Alabama, USA on 18th December, 1946. Turned Professional 1970
Maj US Open 1977. US Masters r/u 1978. US PGA 1985
Eur Carrolls Irish Open 1977
US 16 wins 1971 to 1984
RoW Dunlop Phoenix (Japan) 1975
Int Ryder Cup 1977-79-85. USA in World Cup 1977
Mis Rookie of the Year 1971

Guadagnino, Kathy *See* Baker

Gunderson, JoAnne *See* Carner

Haas, Jay

Born St Louis, MO, USA on 2nd December, 1953.
Turned Professional 1976

PROFESSIONAL
Maj	US Masters 3rd 1995
US	9 wins 1978 to 1993
RoW	Mexican Open 1991
Int	Ryder Cup 1983-95; President's Cup 1994

AMATEUR
Int	Walker Cup 1975

Haeggman, Joakim

Born Kalmar, Sweden on 28th August, 1969. Turned Professional 1989

Eur	Peugeot Open d'España 1993
RoW	Malaysian Open 1994
Oth	Wermland Open 1990; St Compaq Open 1992
Int	Ryder Cup1993; Sweden in Dunhill Cup 1993-94-97 (r/u); World Cup 1993-94-97
Mis	First Swede to play for Europe in Ryder Cup

Harper, Chandler

Born Portsmouth, Virginia, USA on 10th March, 1914. Turned Professional 1934

Maj	USPGA 1950
US	Won over 20 tournaments. Ten times Virginia Open Champion.
Sen	National Seniors 1965 World Senior Professional, USPGA Seniors 1968.
Int	Ryder Cup 1955
Mis	Elected to USPGA Hall of Fame 1969. In 1941 scored round of 58 (29-29) on 6100 yards, Portsmouth, Virginia

Harris, John

Born Edina, Minnesota, USA in 1952

Chp	US Amateur 1993; qf 1995
Int	Walker Cup 1993-95-97; Eisenhower Trophy 1994

Harwood, Mike

Born Sydney, NSW, Australia on 8th January, 1959 Turned Professional 1979

Maj	Open r/u 1991
Eur	Portuguese Open 1988; PLM Open 1989; Volvo PGA, Volvo Masters 1990; European Open 1991
RoW	Australian PGA 1986; Fijian Open, Pacific Harbour Open 1984; South Australian Open 1990.
Int	Australia in World Cup1984; Dunhill Cup 1991; Four Tours World Chp 1991

Hayes, Dale

Born Pretoria, South Africa on 1st July, 1952. Turned Professional 1970

PROFESSIONAL
Eur	Spanish Open 1971; Swiss Open 1975; Italian Open, French Open 1978; Spanish Open 1979
Oth	Coca-Cola Young Professionals 1974; PGA U-25 1975
RoW	South African Open 1976, leading amateur 1969; South African PGA 1974-75-76; 12 wins in Southern Africa 1970-76; Brazilian Open 1970; Bogota Open 1979

Int	South Africa in World Cup 1974(winners)-76
Mis	Accles & Pollock Award 1973; Harry Vardon Trophy 1975

AMATEUR
Nat	South African Amateur Stroke Play 1969-70
Oth	English Open Amateur Stroke Play r/u 1969; German Amateur 1969; Scottish Open Amateur Stroke Play 1970
Trn	*Golf Illustrated* Gold Vase 1969 (shared)
Int	Eisenhower Trophy 1970(r/u individual)
Jun	World Junior Chp 1969

Haynie, Sandra

Born Fort Worth, Texas, USA on 4th June 1943.
Turned Professional 1961

Maj	US Open 1965-74, r/u 1963-70-82; USLPGA 1974, r/u 1975-83
US	42 LPGA wins 1962-82
Mis	Rolex Player of the Year 1970; LPGA Hall of Fame 1977

Henning, Harold

Born Johannesburg, South Africa on 3rd October, 1934. Turned Professional 1953

Maj	Open 3rd 1960-70.
Trn	Daks 1958 (tied). Yorkshire Evening News 1958 (tied). Spalding 1959 (tied). Sprite 1960. Pringle 1964
Nat	South African Open 1957-62. South African PGA 1965-66-67-72
Eur	Italian Open 1957. Swiss Open 1960-64. Danish Open 1960-64-65. German Open 1965.
RoW	Malaysian Open 1966
US	2 wins 1966-70
Sen	US Liberty Mutual Legends 1993
Oth	Transvaal Open 1957. Natal Open 1957. Western Province Open 1957-59. Cock o' the North 1959. Engadine Open 1966. South African International Classic 1972. ICL International (SA) 1980
Int	South Africa in World Cup 1957-58-59-61-65 (winners)-66-67-69-70-71

Hjorth, Maria

Born Sweden on 15th October, 1973. Turned Professional 1996

PROFESSIONAL
Int	European Cup 1997

AMATEUR
Oth	Finnish Ladies, Norwegian Ladies 1990; Spanish Open 1995; Eur Women's Individual Chp 1995; Sherry Cup 1995
Trn	St Rule Trophy, Helen Holm Trophy 1995; R&A Bursars' Trn 1995
Int	Vagliano Trophy 1995; Sweden in Espirito Santo 1994; Eur(L) T Ch 1995
Mis	Swedish Order of Merit 1991. Golf bursary at University of Stirling

Hoch, Scott

Born Raleigh, NC, USA on 24th November, 1955.
Turned Professional 1979

PROFESSIONAL
Maj	US Masters r/u 1989; US PGA 3rd 1987
Eur	Dutch Open 1995

US 8 wins 1980 to 1997 (Greater Milwaukee Open 1997)
RoW Pacific Masters, Casio World Open 1982-86; Korean Open 1990-91
Oth Andersen Consulting US Chp 1996
Int Ryder Cup 1997; President's Cup 1994-96
Mis Vardon Trophy 1986
AMATEUR
Int Walker Cup 1979; Eisenhower Trophy 1978

Hyndman, William III
Born 25th December, 1915

Chp Amateur r/u 1959-69-70
Nat US Amateur r/u 1955
Sen US Seniors 1973
Int Walker Cup 1957-59-61-71. Eisenhower Trophy 1958-60

Inkster, Juli
Born Santa Cruz, California, USA on 24th June, 1960. Turned Professional 1983
PROFESSIONAL
Maj US Women's Open r/u 1992; USLPGA 3rd 1986
US 15 wins 1983 to 1992 (JAL Big Apple Classic, 1992)
Int Solheim Cup 1992
Mis Gatorade Rookie of the Year 1984
AMATEUR
Nat US Ladies Amateur 1980-81-82
Int Curtis Cup 1982; World Cup 1980-82

Irwin, Hale
Born Joplin, Montana, USA on 3rd June, 1945. Turned Professional 1968
Maj Open r/u 1983; US Open 1974-79-90, 3rd 1975
Eur Piccadilly World Match Play 1974-75
US 20 wins 1971 to 1994 (MCI Heritage Classic 1994)
RoW Australian PGA 1978. South African PGA 1978. Bridgestone 1981
Sen US Ameritech Senior Open, Vantage Chp 1995; American Express Invitational, USPGA Seniors Chp 1996; MasterCard Chp, LG Chp, USPGA Seniors Chp, Las Vegas Sen Classic, Burnet Sen Classic, Bank Boston Classic, Boone Valley Classic, Vantage Chp 1997
Int Ryder Cup 1975-77-79-81-91. USA in World Cup 1974-79 (winners and individual winner); President's Cup 1994
Mis World Golf Hall of Fame 1992

Jacobsen, Peter
Born Portland, Oregon, USA on 4th March, 1954. Turned Professional 1976
PROFESSIONAL
US Buick-Goodwrench Open 1980; Greater Hartford Open, Colonial National Invitation 1984; Bob Hope Chrysler Classic 1990; AT&T Pebble Beach Pro-Am, Buick Invitational of California 1995
RoW Western Australia Open 1979
Oth Oregon Open, North California Open 1976
Int Ryder Cup 1985-95
AMATEUR
Mis All-American 1974-76

January, Don
Born Plainview, Texas, USA on 20th November, 1929. Turned Professional 1955
Maj USPGA 1967; r/u 1961-76
US 11 wins 1956 to 1976
Sen US Sen Tour 22 wins 1980-87
Int Ryder Cup 1965-67

Janzen, Lee
Born Austin, MN, USA on 28th August, 1964. Turned Professional 1986
Maj US Open 1993
US Northern Telecom Open 1992; Phoenix Open 1993; Buick Classic 1994; The Players Chp, Kemper Open, The Sprint International 1995
Int Ryder Cup 1993-97; Dunhill Cup 1995
Mis All-American 1985-86

Johansson, Per-Ulrik
Born Uppsala, Sweden on 6th December, 1966. Turned Professional 1990
PROFESSIONAL
Eur Renault Belgian Open 1991; Czech Open 1994; European Open 1996; English Open, European Open 1997
Int Ryder Cup 1995-97; Sweden in World Cup 1991(winners); Dunhill Cup 1991(winners)-92-95-97 (r/u)
Mis Sir Henry Cotton Rookie of the Year 1991
AMATEUR
Trn Leven Gold Medal 1986
Mis Arizona State University Team 1990

Jones, Steve
Born Artesia, New Mexico, USA on 27th December, 1958. Turned Professional 1981
Maj US Open 1996
US AT&T Pebble Beach National Pro-Am 1988; MONY Trn of Champions, Bob Hope Chrysler Classic, Canadian Open 1989; Phoenix Open, Bell Canadian Open 1997
Int World Cup 1996 (r/u)
Mis Bike accident in 1991 caused him to miss 3 years

King, Betsy
Born Reading, Pennsylvania, USA on 13th August, 1955. Turned Professional 1977
Maj British Open 1985, r/u 1984; US Open 1989-90, 3rd 1986; USLPGA 1992, r/u 1987
US 31 LPGA wins 1984 to 1997 (Nabisco Dinah Shore 1997)
Int Solheim Cup 1990-92-94-96
Mis *Golf Magazine* Player of the Year 1984-89; Founder's Cup 1989; Rolex Player of the Year 1984-89-93; Vare Trophy 1987; LPGA Hall of Fame 1995

Kite, Tom
Born Austin, Texas, USA on 9th December, 1949. Turned Professional 1972
PROFESSIONAL
Maj Open r/u 1978; US Open 1992; US Masters r/u 1983-86-97, 3rd 1977

US	19 wins 1976 to 1993 (Bob Hope Classic, Los Angeles Open 1993)
RoW	Auckland Classic (NZ) 1974
Oth	Oki Pro-Am 1996
Int	Ryder Cup 1979-81-83-85-87-89-93-(**97**); Kirin Cup 1987(individual winner); Dunhill Cup 1989 (winners)-90-92-94(r/u); World Cup 1984-85
Mis	Rookie of the Year 1973; Vardon Trophy 1981-82; Arnold Palmer Award 1981-89; Bobby Jones Award 1979; Golf Writers Player of the Year 1981; USPGA Player of the Year 1989.

AMATEUR

Chp	Amateur s/f 1971
Nat	US Amateur r/u 1970
Trn	NCAA Chp 1972(shared)
Int	Walker Cup 1971; Eisenhower Trophy 1970 (winners)

Klein, Emilee

Born Santa Monica, California, USA on 11th June, 1974. Turned Professional 1994

PROFESSIONAL

Maj	Weetabix Women's British Open 1996, LPGA Ping Welch's Chp 1996

AMATEUR

Reg	Californian Women's Amateur 1989-92
Oth	NCAA Chp 1994
Jun	US Girls 1991
Int	Curtis Cup 1994

Knight, Nancy *See* **Lopez**

Kuehne, Kelli

Born Texas, USA in 1978

Maj	Ladies British Amateur 1996; US Women's Amateur 1995-96
Jun	US Girls 1994
Int	Curtis Cup 1996; Espirito Santo 1996

Lacoste, Catherine *See* **Prado**

Langer, Bernhard

Born Anhausen, Germany on 27th August, 1957. Turned Professional 1972

Maj	Open r/u 1981-84, 3rd 1985-86-93; US Masters 1985-93
Eur	Dunlop Masters 1980; German Open, Bob Hope Classic 1981; German Open 1982; Italian Open, Glasgow Golf Classic, St Mellion TPC 1983; French, Dutch, Irish and Spanish Opens 1984; German and European Opens 1985; Lancôme Trophy(shared), German Open 1986; Whyte & Mackay PGA, Irish Open 1987; Epson Grand Prix 1988; Peugeot Spanish Open, German Masters 1989; Cepsa Madrid and Austrian Opens 1990; B&H International Open, German Masters 1991; Dutch and Honda Opens 1992; Volvo PGA, German Open 1993; Murphy's Irish Open, Volvo Masters 1994; Volvo PGA Chp, Deutsche Bank Open – TPC of Europe, European Open 1995; Italian Open, B&H International Open, Czech Open, German Masters 1997
Oth	German Close Professional, Cacherel U-25 Chp 1979; Belgian Classic 1987
US	Sea Pines Heritage Classic 1985

RoW	Colombian Open 1980; Johnnie Walker Trn, Casio World Open 1983; Australian Masters 1985; Hong Kong Open, Million Dollar Challenge 1991; Hong Kong Alfred Dunhill Masters 1996; Argentine Masters 1997
Int	Ryder Cup 1981-83-85-87-89-91-93-95-97; Hennessy-Cognac Cup 1976-78-80-**82**; Germany in World Cup 1976-77-78-79-80-90 (winners)-91-92-93 (individual winner)-94-96; Four Tours World Chp 1989-90; Nissan Cup 1985-86; Kirin Cup 1987; Dunhill Cup 1992-94
Mis	Harry Vardon Trophy 1981-84; AGW Trophy 1981-93. Ritz Club Trophy 1985; PGAET Golfer of the Year 1993

Lehman, Tom

Born Austin, Minnesota, USA on 7th March, 1959. Turned Professional 1982

Maj	Open Champion 1996; US Open r/u 1996, 3rd 1997; US Masters 3rd 1993, r/u 1994
Eur	Loch Lomond World Invitational 1997
US	Memorial Trn 1994; Colonial 1995; The Tour Chp 1996
RoW	Casio World Open 1993
Oth	Grand Slam of Golf 1996
Int	Ryder Cup 1995-97; President's Cup 1994; World Cup 1996 (r/u)
Mis	Ben Hogan Player of the Year 1991; Vardon Trophy 1996

Leonard, Justin

Born Dallas, TX, USA on 15th June, 1972. Turned Professional 1994

PROFESSIONAL

Maj	Open Champion 1997; USPGA r/u 1997
US	Buick Open 1996; Kemper Open 1997
Int	Ryder Cup 1997; President's Cup 1996; USA in World Cup 1997

AMATEUR

Nat	US Amateur 1992
Int	Walker Cup 1993; Eisenhower Trophy 1992

Littler, Gene

Born San Diego, California, USA on 21st July, 1930. Turned Professional 1954

PROFESSIONAL

Maj	US Open 1961, r/u 1954; USPGA r/u 1977; US Masters r/u 1970(tied)
US	26 wins 1955 to 1977; Canadian Open 1965
RoW	Taiheiyo Pacific Masters 1974-75; Australian Masters 1980; Yellow Pages (SA) 1977
Sen	1987-two
Int	Ryder Cup 1961-63-65-67-69-71-75
Mis	Byron Nelson Award 1959; Bobby Jones Award, Ben Hogan Award 1973; USPGA Hall of Fame 1982; World Golf Hall of Fame 1990

AMATEUR

Nat	US Amateur 1953
Int	Walker Cup 1953

Lopez, Nancy

Born Torrance, California, USA on 6th January, 1957. Turned Professional July, 1977

Maj	US Women's Open r/u 1975 (leading amateur)-77-89-97; US LPGA 1978-85-89

PROFESSIONAL
Eur Colgate European 1978-79
US 48 LPGA wins 1978 to 1997 (Chick-Fil-A Charity Chp 1997)
RoW Colgate Far East 1978
Int Solheim Cup 1990
Mis Rolex Player of the Year 1978-79-85-88; Vare Trophy 1978-79-85; Mazda-LPGA Series 1985; Gatorade Rookie of the Year 1978; Powell Award 1987; *Golf Magazine* Player of the Year 1978-79-85; LPGA Hall of Fame 1987; World Golf Hall of Fame 1989
AMATEUR
Oth Mexican Ladies Amateur 1975
Int Curtis Cup 1976; Espirito Santo 1976 (winners)
Jun US Girls 1972-74

de Lorenzi, Marie-Laure

Born Biarritz, France on 21st January, 1961. Turned Professional 1986
PROFESSIONAL
Maj Women's British Open (3rd) 1989-92
Eur BMW Ladies German Open, Belgian Ladies Godiva Open 1987; French Open, Volmac Open, Hennessy Ladies Cup, Gothenburg Ladies Open, Laing Charity Classic, Woolmark Match Play Chp, Qualitair Ladies Spanish Open, Benson & Hedges Trophy (with M McNulty) 1988; Ford Ladies Classic, Hennessy Ladies Cup, BMW Ladies Classic 1989; Ford Ladies Classic 1990; Var Open de France Féminin 1993; Spanish Open 1994; Ladies Open Costa Azul, Staatsloterij Dutch Open, French Ladies Open 1995; Swiss Open 1997
Int Solheim Cup 1990-96; Sunrise Cup 1992; European Cup 1997 (captain)
Mis Woolmark Order of Merit winner 1988-89. Vivien Saunders Trophy 1996
AMATEUR
Nat French Close Chp 1983
Oth Spanish Ladies 1978-80-83; South African Ladies', South African Ladies' Stroke Play 1981
Int France Eur(L) T Ch 1977-83; Vagliano Trophy 1983
Jun French Girls 1976; British Girls 1978
Mis Doris Chambers Trophy 1982-85; Angus Trophy 1980

Love III, Davis

Born Charlotte, NC, USA on 13th April, 1964. Turned Professional 1985
PROFESSIONAL
Maj US Open r/u 1996; USPGA 1997
US Heritage Classic 1987-91-92; The International 1990; Trn Players Chp, Greater Greensboro Open, Kapalua International 1992; Infiniti Trn of Champions, Las Vegas Invitational 1993; Freeport McMoran Classic 1995; Buick Invitational 1996; Andersen Consulting US, Buick Challenge, Lincoln-Mercury Kapalua International 1997
Oth JC Penney Classic (with B Daniel) 1994-95
Int (US) Ryder Cup 1993-95-97; Dunhill Cup 1992-93; World Cup 1992(winners)-93(winners)-94(winners)-95(winners; individual winner)-97; President's Cup 1994
AMATEUR
Int Walker Cup 1985

Lunn, Karen

Born Sydney, Australia on 21st March, 1966. Turned Professional 1985
PROFESSIONAL
Maj Ladies British Open 1993
Eur Borlange Ladies Open 1986; European Masters 1988-90; Slovenian Open 1992; AmEx Tour Players Classic, French Open 1997
RoW Thailand Ladies Open 1988; Daikyo Challenge 1990
Int European Cup 1997
Mis Spalding Order of Merit winner 1993
AMATEUR
Reg Queensland Ladies Amateur, Victoria Ladies Match Play, South Australian Ladies Stroke Play 1984
Jun NSW Junior, Australian Schoolgirls 1982; Queensland Junior 1984
Int NSW Juniors 1981-85

McIntire, Barbara

Maj US Women's Open r/u 1956
Chp Ladies British Amateur 1960
Nat US Ladies Amateur 1959-64
Int Curtis Cup 1958-60-62-64-66-72

McNulty, Mark

Born Zimbabwe on 25th October, 1953. Turned Professional 1977
Maj Open r/u 1990
Eur Greater Manchester Open 1979; German Open 1980; Portuguese Open 1986; German Open, 4 Stars Pro-Celebrity, Dunhill Masters 1987; Cannes Open, Benson & Hedges Trophy (with Marie-Laure de Lorenzi) 1988; Torres Monte Carlo Open 1989; Cannes Open, German Open 1990-91, BMW Int'l Open 1994; Dimension Data Pro-Am, Dutch Open, Volvo Masters 1996
RoW SA Open 1987, SA Masters 1982-86-97; 25 wins 1980 to 1997; Malay Open 1980; Zimbabwe Open 1992-96
Int (Zimbabwe) Dunhill Cup 1993-94-95-96-97; World Cup 1993(r/u)-94(r/u)-95-96-97; President's Cup 1994-96; Alfred Dunhill Challenge 1995

Maggert, Jeff

Born Columbia, MO, USA on 20th February, 1964. Turned Professional 1986
Maj USPGA 3rd 1995-97
US Walt Disney World Classic 1993
RoW Malaysian Open 1989; Vines Classic (ANZ) 1990
Oth Nike Knoxville Open, Buffalo Open 1990
Int Ryder Cup 1995-97; President's Cup 1994

Mallon, Meg

Born Natick, Maryland, USA on 14th April, 1963. Turned Professional 1986.
Maj US Women's Open 1991; US LPGA 1991
PROFESSIONAL
US Oldsmobile Classic, Trophée-Urban World Chp 1991; Ping Welch's Chp, Sara Lee Classic 1993; Hawaiian Ladies Open, Sara Lee Classic 1996
RoW Daikyo World Chp 1991

Int   Solheim Cup 1992-94-96; Sunrise Cup 1992;
Nichirei International 1995
AMATEUR
Oth   Michigan Ladies Amateur 1983

Marsh, Graham, MBE
Born Kalgoorlie, Western Australia on 14th January, 1944. Turned Professional 1968

Eur   Swiss Open 1970; German Open 1972;
Sunbeam Electric 1973; Benson & Hedges International 1976; Colgate World Match Play, Lancôme Trophy 1977; Dutch Open, Dunlop Masters 1979; Benson & Hedges International 1980; European Open 1981; Dutch Open 1985
US   1977-one
RoW   Watties Open (NZ) 1970; Indian Open, Spalding Masters (NZ) 1971; Indian Open, Thailand Open 1973; Malaysian Open 1974; Malaysian Open 1975; Western Australian Open 1976; 17 wins in Japan 1972-81; Sapporo-Tokyu Open (Jpn) 1989; Tokai Classic 1990
Sen   US: Bruno's Memorial Classic 1995; Paine Webber Invitational 1996; Nationwide Chp, US Sen Open 1997
Int   Dunhill Cup 1985(winners); Nissan Cup 1986; Kirin Cup 1987; Four Tours World Chp 1991
Mis   USPGA Rookie of the Year 1977; Australian Sportsman of the Year 1977

Massey, Debbie
Born Grosse Pointe, Michigan, USA on 5th November, 1950. Turned Professional 1977.

Maj   Ladies British Open 1980-81; US Women's Open leading amateur 1974; USLPGA 3rd 1983
PROFESSIONAL
US   Mizuno Japan Classic 1977; Wheeling Classic 1979; Mazda Japan Classic 1990
Mis   Gatorade Rookie of the Year 1977
AMATEUR
Oth   Canadian Ladies Amateur 1974-75-76
Reg   Western Amateur 1972-75; Eastern Amateur 1975
Int   Curtis Cup 1974-76; Espirito Santo 1976
Mis   Doris Chambers Trophy, Angus Trophy 1976

Mayfair, Billy
Born Phoenix, Arizona, USA on 6th August, 1966. Turned Professional 1988

PROFESSIONAL
US   Greater Milwaukee Open 1993; Motorola Western Open, The Tour Chp 1995
Int   Four Tours World Chp 1991
AMATEUR
Nat   US Amateur 1987
Oth   US Public Links 1986; Arizona Stroke Play Chp 1985-87
Int   Walker Cup 1987

Melnyk, Steve
Born Brunswick, Georgia, USA on 26th February, 1947. Turned Professional 1971

AMATEUR
Maj   Leading amateur Open and US Masters 1970
Chp   Amateur Champion 1971
Nat   US Amateur 1969
Reg   Western Amateur 1969. Eastern Amateur 1970

Int   Walker Cup 1969-71
Mis   US Amateur Golfer of the Year 1969

Mickelson, Phil
Born Arizona, USA. Turned Professional 1991

Maj   Leading amateur in US Open 1991, US Masters 3rd 1996; USPGA 3rd 1994
PROFESSIONAL
US   Tucson Open 1991 (as amateur); Buick Invitational of California, The International 1993; Mercedes Chp 1994; Northern Telecom Open 1995; Nortel Open, Phoenix Open, Byron Nelson Classic, NEC World Series 1996; Bay Hill Invitational, Sprint International 1997; Mercedes Chp 1998
Int   Ryder Cup 1995-97; President's Cup 1994-96; Dunhill Cup 1996 (winners)-97
AMATEUR
Nat   US Amateur 1990
Oth   NCAA Chp 1989-90-92
Int   Walker Cup 1989-91
Mis   Plays left-handed

Middlecoff, Cary
Born Halls, Tennessee, USA on 6th January, 1921. Turned Professional 1947

Maj   US Open 1949-56, r/u 1957; USPGA r/u 1955; US Masters 1955, r/u 1948
US   37 wins 194 to 19-61
Int   Ryder Cup 1953-55-59; World Cup 1959
Mis   Byron Nelson Award 1955; Vardon Trophy 1956; USPGA Hall of Fame 1974; World Golf Hall of Fame 1986

Miller, Johnny Lawrence
Born San Francisco, USA on 29th April, 1947. Turned Professional 1969

Maj   Open Champion 1976, r/u 1973, 3rd 1975; US Open 1973, leading amateur 1966; US Masters r/u 1971-75
Eur   Lancôme Trophy 1973-79
US   24 wins 1971 to 1994 (AT&T Pebble Beach 1994)
RoW   Dunlop Phoenix International (Jpn) 1974. Otago Classic (NZ) 1972
Int   Ryder Cup 1975-81; World Cup 1973 (winners; individual winner)-75 (winners; individual winner)-80; v Japan 1983
Mis   USPGA Player of the Year 1974. US leading money winner 1974

Mize, Larry Hogan
Born Augusta, Georgia, USA on 23rd September, 1958. Turned Professional 1980

Maj   US Masters 1987; 3rd 1994
US   Memphis Classic 1983; Northern Telecom Open, Buick Open 1993
RoW   Casio World Open (Jpn) 1988; Dunlop Phoenix Open 1989-90; Johnnie Walker World Chp 1993
Int   Ryder Cup 1987

Muntz, Rolf
Born Voorschoten, Netherlands on 26th March, 1969. Turned Professional 1993

PROFESSIONAL
Oth   Nedcar Open, Neuchatel Open 1994; Nedcar National Open, Challenge Changeurs 1995

AMATEUR

Chp Amateur Champion 1990

Nat Dutch Open Amateur 1989

Trn Lancôme Trophy 1988-89

Int Europe v GBI 1990-92; Dutch National Team 1989-90

Jun Dutch Junior Match Play, Dutch Junior Stroke Play 1989; Dutch International Junior Open 1989

Int Dutch Boys 1986-87

Nagle, Kelvin DG

Born North Sydney, Australia on 21st December, 1920. Turned Professional 1946

Maj Open Champion 1960, r/u 1962; US Open r/u 1965 (tied)

Eur Irish Hospitals, Dunlop, French Open 1961. Bowmaker 1962-65. Esso Golden 1963-67

US Canadian Open 1964

RoW Australian Open 1959. Australian Professional 1949-54-58-59-65-68. New Zealand Professional 1957-58-60-70-73-74-75. New Zealand Open 1957-58-62-64-67-68-69. In New Zealand BP 1968; Caltex 1969, Garden City, 1969, Otago Charity Classic 1970-76. Stars Travel 1970. In Australia: West End 1968-72-74, New South Wales Open 1968. Victoria Open 1969, NBN Newcastle 1970, New South Wales Professional 1971, South Coast Open 1975, Western Australia PGA 1977

Sen World Seniors 1971-75; British Seniors 1971-73-75(winners)

Int Australia in World Cup 1954(winners) 55-58-59-(winners)-60-61-62-65-66

Mis Honorary Member of Royal & Ancient.

Nakajima, Tsuneyuki

Born Kiryu City, Gumma, Japan on 20th October, 1954. Turned Professional 1975

Maj USPGA 3rd 1988

RoW Japan Amateur 1973. Japan Open 1985-86-90-91. Japan PGA 1983-84-86-92; 23 wins 1984 to 1995 (Fuji Sankei Classic 1995)

Int Dunhill Cup 1986. Nissan Cup 1986(individual winner). Kirin Cup 1987-88. World Cup 1996

Nelson, Byron

Born Fort Worth, Texas, USA on 4th February, 1912. Turned Professional 1932

Maj US Open 1939; r/u 1946; USPGA 1940-45, r/u 1939-41-44; US Masters 1937-42, r/u 1941-47

Eur French Open 1955

US 54 wins 1935-one 1936-one 1937-two 1938-two 1939-three 1940-two 1941-three 1942-three 1944-six 1945-fifteen 1946-five

Int Ryder Cup 1937-47

Mis Vardon Trophy 1939; leading money winner 1944-45; USPGA Hall of Fame 1953; World Golf Hall of Fame 1974; Bobby Jones Award 1974; 11 consecutive tour wins March-August 1945, and 18 for the year.

Nelson, Larry Gene

Born Fort Payne, Alabama, USA on 10th September, 1947. Turned Professional 1971

Maj US Open 1983, 3rd 1991; USPGA 1981-87

US 4 wins 1979 to 1988

RoW Suntory Open (Japan) 1989; Dunlop Phoenix Open (Japan) 1991

Int Ryder Cup 1979-81-87

Neumann, Liselotte

Born Finspang, Sweden on 20th May, 1966. Turned Professional 1985

PROFESSIONAL

Maj Weetabix Women's British Open 1994; US Women's Open 1988, 3rd 1995; USLPGA r/u 1986-92, 3rd 1994

Eur 10 wins 1985 to 1995 (Trygg Hansa Open 1995)

US Mazda Japan Classic 1991; Minnesota LPGA Classic, GHP Heartland Classic 1994; Chrysler Plymouth Trn of Champions, Ping Welch's Chp, Edina Realty LPGA Classic 1996; Welch's Chp, Toray Japan Queens Cup 1997

RoW Singapore Open 1987; Takara Invitational (Jpn) 1993

Int Solheim Cup 1990-92-94-96; Sunrise Cup 1992(winners) (individual winner); (for LPGA) Nichirei International 1995-96-97

Mis Gatorade Rookie of the Year 1988. Vivien Saunders Trophy 1994

AMATEUR

Nat Swedish Ladies Open 1982-83; Swedish Ladies Match Play 1983

Int Sweden (Eur(L) T Ch) 1983. Espirito Santo 1982-84; Vagliano Trophy 1983

Newton, Jack

Born Sydney, Australia on 30th January, 1950. Turned Professional 1969

Maj Open r/u 1975 (tied); US Masters r/u 1980

Nat Australian Open 1979

Eur Benson & Hedges Festival, Dutch Open 1972; Benson & Hedges PGA Match Play 1974; Sumrie 1975

US 1978-one

RoW City of Auckland Classic (NZ) 1972. Amoco Forbes (Aust) 1972. Nigerian Open 1974. Cock o' the North (Zambia) 1976. Mufulira Open 1976. New South Wales Open 1976-79

Mis Seriously injured on tarmac by aeroplane propeller accident 1983

Nicklaus, Jack William

Born Columbus, Ohio, USA on 21st January, 1940. Turned Professional 1961

Maj Open Champion 1966-70-78, r/u 1964-67-72-76-79, 3rd 1963-74-75; US Open 1962-67-72-80, r/u 1960 (leading am)-68-71(tied)-82, leading am (4th) 1961; USPGA 1963-71-73-75-80, r/u 1964-65-74-83, 3rd 1967-77; US Masters 1963-65-66-72-75-86, r/u 1964-71-77-81, 3rd 1973-76

PROFESSIONAL

Eur Piccadilly World Match Play 1970, r/u 1966-71

US 71 wins 1962-84; World Series 1962-63-67-70-76

RoW Australian Open 1964-68-71-75-76-78; Dunlop International (Aust) 1971; Indonesian Open 1994

Sen US Sen Tour 10 wins 1990-96 (US Senior Open, USPGA Seniors 1991; US Seniors Open 1993)

Int   Ryder Cup 1969-71-73-75-77-81-(83)-(87);
World Cup 1963(winners; individual winner)-
64(winners; individual winner)-65-66(winners)-
67(winners)-71(winners; individual winner)-
73(winners)

Mis   Rookie of the Year 1962; USPGA Player of the
Year 1967-72-73-75-76; leading money winner
1964-65-67-71-72-73-75-76; Byron Nelson
Award 1964-65-67-72-73; Bobby Jones Award
1975; Walter Hagen Award 1980; World Golf
Hall of Fame 1974; US Sportsman of the Year
1978; Card Walker Award 1983; Honorary
Member of Royal & Ancient

AMATEUR

Nat   US Amateur 1959-61

Trn   NCAA Chp 1961

Int   Walker Cup 1959-61; Eisenhower Trophy
1960(winners; individual winner)

Nobilo, Frank

Born Auckland, New Zealand on 14th May, 1960.
Turned Professional 1979

PROFESSIONAL

Eur   PLM Open 1988; Lancôme Trophy 1991; Open
Mediterrania 1993; BMW International Open
1995; Deutsche Bank TPC of Europe 1996

US   Greater Greensboro Classic 1997

RoW   New South Wales PGA 1982; New Zealand
PGA 1985-87; Indonesian Open 1994; Hong
Kong Open 1997

Oth   New Zealand U-25 Stroke Play 1979; Sarazen
World Open 1995-96

Int   New Zealand in World Cup 1982-87-88-90-93-
94-95; Dunhill Cup 1985-86-87-89-90-92-94-
95-96-97; President's Cup 1994-96; Alfred
Dunhill Challenge 1995

Mis   Rookie of the Year 1981

AMATEUR

Nat   New Zealand Amateur 1978

Norman, Greg

Born Mt Isa, Queensland, Australia on 10th
February, 1955. Turned Professional 1976

Maj   Open Champion 1986-93, r/u 1989(tied); US
Open r/u 1984(tied), r/u 1995; USPGA
1986(r/u)-93(tied); US Masters r/u 1986-
1987(tied)-96, 3rd 1989-95

Eur   Martini 1977; Martini 1979; Scandinavian Enter-
prise Open, French Open, Suntory World Match
Play 1980; Martini, Dunlop Masters 1981; Dunlop
Masters, Benson & Hedges Int'l, State Express
Classic 1982; Suntory World Match Play 1983;
European Open, Suntory World Match Play 1986;
Italian Open 1988; Johnnie Walker Classic 1994

US   Kemper Open, Canadian Open 1984;
Panasonic-Las Vegas Invitational, Kemper Open
1986; MCI Heritage Classic 1988; The
International, Greater Milwaukee Open 1989;
Doral Ryder Open 1990; Canadian Open 1992;
Doral Ryder Open 1993; The Players Chp 1994;
Memorial Trn, Greater Hartford Open, NEC
World Series 1995; Doral Ryder Open 1996;
FedEx St Jude Classic, NEC World Series 1997

RoW   Australian Open 1980-85-95-96; Australian
Masters 1984-87-89-90; Australian PGA 1984-
85; Australian TPC 1988-89; West Lakes Classic
(Aus) 1976; South Seas Classic (Fiji), NSW

Open 1978; Hong Kong Open 1979; NSW
Open, Hong Kong Open 1983; Victoria Open
1984; NSW, Queensland, South Australian and
Western Australian Opens 1986; ESP Open,
Palm Meadows Cup 1988; Chunichi Crowns
1989; Taiheiyo Masters 1993; Ford Open 1996

Oth   Andersen Consulting World Chp 1996

Int   Australia in World Cup 1976-78; Dunhill Cup
1985(winners)-1986(winners)-87-88-89-90-92-
94-95-96; Nissan Cup 1985-86, Kirin Cup
1987; test match v GBI 1988; Alfred Dunhill
Challenge 1995; President's Cup 1996

Mis   Harry Vardon Trophy 1982; Arnold Palmer
Award 1986-90; Mary Bea Porter Award 1988;
Vardon Trophy 1989-90-94; Sony Ranking No 1
1995-96-97

North, Andy

Born Thorp, Wisconsin, USA on 9th March, 1950.
Turned Professional 1972

Maj   US Open 1978-85

US   1 win 1977

Int   US in World Cup 1978

Mis   ESPN commentator

Okamoto, Ayako

Born Hiroshima, Japan on 2nd April, 1951. Turned
Professional 1976

Maj   Ladies British Open 1984; US Women's Open
r/u 1987 (tied), 3rd 1986; USLPGA r/u 1989-91,
3rd 1986-87-88

Eur   German Open 1990

US   17 wins 1982 to 1992

RoW   Japan Women's Open, Itoen Ladies (Jpn) 1993

Int   Nichirei International 1996

Mis   Rolex Player of the Year 1987; Mazda-LPGA
Series 1984-87

Olazabal, José Maria

Born Fuenterrabia, Spain on 5th February, 1966.
Turned Professional 1985

Maj   Open 3rd 1992; US Masters 1994, 1991(r/u)

PROFESSIONAL

Eur   Ebel European Masters -Swiss Open, Sanyo
Open 1986; Volvo Belgian Open, German
Masters 1988; Tenerife Open, KLM Dutch
Open 1989; Benson & Hedges International,
Carrolls Irish Open, Lancôme Trophy 1990;
Catalonia Open, Epson Grand Prix 1991; Open
de Tenerife, Open Mediterrania 1992;
Turespaña Open Mediterrania, Volvo PGA Chp
1994; Tournoi Perrier de Paris 1995; Turespaña
Masters 1997

US   NEC World Series 1990-94; Wild Coast Skins
Game 1990; The International 1991

RoW   Japanese Masters 1989

Int   Ryder Cup 1987-89-91-93-97; Kirin Cup 1987;
Spain in Dunhill Cup 1986-87-88-89-92; Four
Tours World Chp 1989; World Cup 1989.

Mis   PGA Qualifying School winner 1985

AMATEUR

Chp   Amateur Champion 1984

Nat   Spanish Open Amateur 1983

Oth   Italian Open Amateur 1983

Jun   British Boys 1983; Belgian International Youths
Chp 1984; British Youths 1985

O'Meara, Mark
Born Goldsboro, North Carolina, USA on 13th January, 1957. Turned Professional 1980
PROFESSIONAL
Maj Open 3rd 1985-91; US Open 3rd 1988
Eur Lawrence Batley International 1987; Trophée Lancôme 1997
US Greater Milwaukee Open 1984; Bing Crosby Pro-Am, Hawaiian Open 1985; AT&T Pebble Beach National Pro-Am 1989-90; Texas Open 1990; Walt Disney World Classic 1991; AT&T Pebble Beach National Pro-Am 1992; Canadian Open, Honda Classic 1995; Mercedes Chp, Greater Greensboro Open 1996; AT&T Pebble Beach National Pro-Am, Buick Invitational 1997
RoW Kapalua International, Fuji Sankei Classic (Jap) 1985; Australian Masters 1986
Int Ryder Cup 1985-89-91-97; Nissan Cup 1985; Dunhill Cup 1985-86-87-96 (winners)-97; US v Japan 1984; President's Cup 1996
Mis Rookie of the Year 1981
AMATEUR
Nat US Amateur 1979
Oth Mexican Amateur 1979

Ozaki, Masashi 'Jumbo'
Born Kaiman Town, Tokushima, Japan on 24th January, 1947. Turned Professional 1980
RoW Japan Open 1974-88-89-94; Japan PGA 1971-74-89-91-93; Japan Match Play 1989; Japan Tour 78 wins 1984 to 1997
Oth Dunlop International Open (Asa) 1992
Int Nissan Cup 1986; Kirin Cup 1987; Four Tours World Chp 1989; President's Cup 1996

Palmer, Arnold
Born Latrobe, Pennsylvania, USA on 10th September, 1929. Turned Professional 1954
PROFESSIONAL
Maj Open Champion 1961-62, r/u 1960; US Open 1960, r/u 1962-63(tied)-66(tied)-67, 3rd 1972; USPGA r/u 1964-68-70; US Masters 1958-60-62-64, r/u 1961-65, 3rd 1959
Eur Piccadilly World Match Play 1964-67; Lancôme Trophy 1971; Penfold PGA, Spanish Open 1975
US 61 wins 1956-four 1957-four 1958-two 1959-three 1960-six 1961-five 1962-six 1963-seven 1964-one 1965-one 1966-four 1967-four 1968-two 1969-two 1970-one 1971-four 1973-one. Canadian Open 1955; Canadian PGA 1980
RoW Australian Open 1966
Int Ryder Cup 1961-63-65-67-71-73-(75); World Cup 1960-62-63-64-66-67 (winners each year; individual winner 1967); President's Cup 1996
Mis USPGA Player of the Year 1960-62; Vardon Trophy 1961-62-64-67; leading money winner 1958-60-62-63; Byron Nelson Award 1957-60-61-62-63; World Golf Hall of Fame 1974; USPGA Hall of Fame 1980; Bobby Jones Award 1971; William Richardson Award 1970; Walter Hagen Award 1981; Old Tom Morris Award 1983; Honorary Member of Royal & Ancient
AMATEUR
Nat US Amateur 1954

Parnevik, Jesper
Born Danderyd, Stockholm on 7th March, 1965. Turned Professional 1986
PROFESSIONAL
Maj Open r/u 1994-97
Eur Bell's Scottish Open 1993; Volvo Scandinavian Masters 1995; Trophée Lancôme 1996
US Phoenix Open 1998
Oth Ramlosa Trophy, Odense Open, Open Passing Shot 1988; SI/Compaq Open 1990
Int Ryder Cup 1997; Sweden in Dunhill Cup 1993-94-95-97 (r/u); World Cup 1994
AMATEUR
Int Sweden in World Cup 1984-86

Parry, Craig
Born Sunshine, Victoria, Australia on 12th January, 1966. Turned Professional 1985
Maj US Open 3rd 1993
Eur Wang Four Stars National Pro-Celebrity, German Open 1989; Italian Open, Scottish Open 1991
US Canadian TPC 1987
RoW Australian Masters, Australian PGA 1992; NSW Open, South Australian PGA 1987; Bridgestone Open 1989; NSW Open 1992; Australian Masters 1994; Greg Norman Holden Classic 1995; Australian Masters 1996; Japan Open 1997; Schweppes Coolum Classic 1997
Int Kirin Cup 1988; Four Tours World Chp 1990(winners)-91; Dunhill Cup 1991-93; President's Cup 1994-96

Pate, Jerry
Born Macon, Georgia, USA on 16th September, 1953. Turned Professional 1975
PROFESSIONAL
Maj US Open 1976; r/u 1979; USPGA 1978; US Masters 3rd 1982
US 4 wins 1977 to 1982; Canadian Open 1976
RoW Taiheiyo Pacific Masters 1976; Brazilian Open 1980
Int Ryder Cup 1981; USA in World Cup 1976
Mis Rookie of the Year 1976
AMATEUR
Nat US Amateur 1974
Int Walker Cup 1975

Pavin, Corey
Born Oxnard, California, USA on 16th November, 1959. Turned Professional 1981
PROFESSIONAL
Maj US Open 1995; US Masters 3rd 1992; USPGA r/u 1994
Eur German Open 1983; Toyota World Match Play 1993
US 13 wins 1984 to 1996 (MasterCard Colonial 1996)
RoW SA PGA 1983; Tokai Classic (Jpn) 1994; Volvo Asian Masters 1995; Nedbank Million Dollar Challenge 1995
Int Ryder Cup 1991-93-95; Nissan Cup 1985; President's Cup 1994-96
Mis USPGA Player of the Year 1991; Arnold Palmer Award 1991
AMATEUR
Int Walker Cup 1981

Pepper, Dottie
Born Saratoga Springs, NY on 17th August, 1965.
Turned Professional 1987
PROFESSIONAL
US   Oldsmobile LPGA Classic 1989; Crestar Classic
     1990; Nabisco Dinah Shore, Sega Women's Chp,
     Welch's Classic, Sun Times Challenge 1992;
     World Chp of Women's Golf 1993;
     Chrysler–Plymouth Trn of Champions 1994;
     Ping Welch's Chp; McCall's LPGA Classic 1995;
     Rochester International, Shoprite LPGA Classic,
     Friendly's Classic, Safeway LPGA Chp 1996
RoW Tokyo Ladies Open (Jpn) 1989
Oth JC Penney Classic, Wendy's Three-Tour
     Challenge 1992
Int Solheim Cup 1990-92-94-96
Mis Rolex Player of the Year 1992; Vare Trophy 1992
AMATEUR
Reg New York State Champion 1981

Pinero, Manuel
*Born Badajoz, Spain on 1st September, 1952. Turned
Professional 1968*
Eur Madrid Open 1974; Swiss Open 1976; Penfold
     PGA 1977; English Classic 1980; Madrid Open,
     Swiss Open 1981; European Open 1982; Cepsa
     Madrid Open, Italian Open 1985
Oth Spanish Professional 1972-73
Int Ryder Cup 1981-85; Hennessy-Cognac Cup
     1974-76-78-80-82; Spain in World Cup 1974-
     76(winners)-78-79-80-82(winners; individual
     winner)-83-85-88; Dunhill Cup 1985

Player, Gary
*Born Johannesburg, South Africa on 1st November,
1935. Turned Professional 1953*
Maj Open Champion 1959-68-74, 3rd 1967; US Open
     1965, r/u 1958-79; USPGA 1962-72, r/u 1969; US
     Masters 1961-74-78, r/u 1962(tied)-65, 3rd 1970
Eur Dunlop 1956; Piccadilly World Match Play
     1965-66-68-71-73; Ibergolf European Chp
     1974; Lancôme Trophy 1975
US   21 wins 1958-78; World Series 1965-68-72
RoW South African Open 1956-60-65-66-67-68-69-
     72-75-76-77-79-81; South African PGA 1968-
     79-81; South African Masters 1959-60-64-67-
     71-72-73-74-76-76(2)-79; Australian Open
     1958-62-63-65-69-70-74; Australian PGA 1957;
     Brazilian Open 1972-74; Chile Open 1980; Ivory
     Coast Open 1980; Transvaal Open 1959-60-62-
     66; Natal Open 1958-60-66-68; Western
     Province Open 1968-71-72; General Motors
     (SA) 1971-75-76; Rothmans Match Play (SA)
     1973; Int'l Classic (SA) 1974; ICL Int'l (SA)
     1977; Johannesburg Int'l, Sun City Classic 1979;
     Wills Masters (Aust) 1968; Dunlop Int'l (Aus)
     1970; Japan Airlines Open 1972
Sen USPGA Senior Open 1987-88; Senior TPC
     1987; Volvo Seniors British Open 1988-90-97;
     US Sen Tour 18 wins 1985 to 1995 (Bank One
     Classic 1995); Irish Sen Masters 1993; Shell
     Wentworth Senior Masters 1997
Int South Africa in World Cup 1956-57-58-59-60-
     62-63-64-65(winners; individual winner) -66-67-
     68-71-72-73-77(individual winner); Dunhill Cup
     1991 (r/u)

Mis US leading money winner 1961; Bobby Jones
     Award 1966; World Golf Hall of Fame 1974;
     William Richardson Award 1976; SA PGA
     captain 1977, president 1978; Honorary member
     of the R&A

Ploujoux, Philippe
*Born La Bouille, Seine Maritime, France on 20th
February, 1955*
Chp Amateur Champion 1981
Nat French Amateur Close Match Play 1977
Oth International Moroccan Stroke Play 1977
Int Continental Team (St Andrews Trophy-5 times
     (including winners 1982) Continental Youth
     Team-4 times. Represented France more than 50
     times
Jun French Youths Match Play 1972-73-74-75-76.
     French Boys 1969-70

Prado, Catherine *(née Lacoste)*
Born Paris on 27th June, 1945
Maj US Women's Open 1967
Chp Ladies British Open Amateur 1969
Nat French Ladies Open Amateur 1967-69-70-72.
     French Ladies Close Amateur 1968-69
Oth US Ladies' Amateur 1969; Spanish Ladies
     Amateur 1969-72-76
Reg Western Ladies Amateur 1968
Trn Astor Princes' 1966; Worplesdon Foursomes
     1967; Hovis 1969
Int Espirito Santo 1964 (winners; individual
     winner)-68 (individual winner)
Mis Doris Chambers Trophy 1967-69; First amateur,
     first non-American and youngest player at that
     time to win the US Women's Open

Price, Nick
*Born Durban, South Africa on 28th January, 1957.
Turned Professional 1977*
Maj Open Champion 1994, r/u 1982-1988; US PGA
     1992-94
Eur Swiss Open 1980; Lancôme Trophy 1985;
     Dimension Data Pro-Am, South African PGA
     1997
US   World Series 1983; Byron Nelson Classic,
     Canadian Open 1991; Texas Open 1992; Players
     Chp, Greater Hartford Open, Sprint Western
     Open, St Jude Classic 1993; Honda Classic,
     SouthWestern Bell Colonial, Motorola Western
     Open, Canadian Open 1994; MCI Classic 1997
RoW South African Masters 1980; Vaal Reefs Open
     (SA) 1982; ICL International (SA) 1985-93;
     South Australian Open 1989; Hassan II Trophy
     (Morocco) 1995; Zimbabwe Open, Nedbank
     Million Dollar Challenge 1997
Int Zimbabwe in Dunhill Cup 1993-94-95-96-97;
     World Cup 1993 (r/u); President's Cup 1994-
     96; Alfred Dunhill Challenge 1995
Mis Arnold Palmer Award and USPGA Player of the
     Year 1993-94; Vardon Trophy 1993-97 Sony
     Ranking No. 1 1994

Quast, Anne *See Sander*

Rawls, Betsy

Born Spartanburg, South Carolina, USA on 4th May, 1928. Turned Professional 1951

Maj US Women's Open 1951-53-57-60, r/u 50(as amateur)-61; USLPGA 1959-69
US 55 LPGA wins 1951 to 1972 (incl Western Open 1952-59)
Mis Vare Trophy 1959; LPGA Hall of Fame 1960; World Golf Hall of Fame 1987; Patty Berg Award 1980; Bobby Jones Award 1996

Rivero, José

Born Spain on 20th September, 1955. Turned Professional 1973

Eur Lawrence Batley International 1984. French Open 1987. Monte Carlo Open 1988. Open de Catalonia 1992
Int Ryder Cup 1985-87. World Cup 1984 (winners)-87-88-90-91-93-94. Dunhill Cup 1986-87-88-90-91-92-94 Kirin Cup 1988

Roberts, Loren

Born San Luis Obispo, California, USA on 24th June, 1955. Turned Professional 1975

Maj US Open r/u 1994
US Nestle Invitational 1994-95; MCI Classic, Greater Milwaukee Open 1996; CVS Charity Classic 1997
Int President's Cup 1994; Ryder Cup 1995

Rocca, Costantino

Born Bergamo, Italy on 4th December, 1956. Turned Professional 1981

Maj Open r/u (tied) 1995
Eur Open du Grand Lyon, Peugeot Open de France 1993; Volvo PGA 1996; Canon European Masters 1997
Oth Rolex ProAm (Swi) 1988
Int Ryder Cup 1993-95-97; Italy in World Cup 1993-94-95
Mis First Italian to play for Europe in the Ryder Cup

Rogers, William Charles (Bill)

Born Waco, Texas, USA on 10th September, 1951. Turned Professional 1974

PROFESSIONAL
Maj Open Champion 1981; US Open r/u 1981, 3rd 1982
Eur Suntory World Match Play 1979
US 1978-one, 1981-three, 1983-one
Oth Pacific Masters 1977
RoW Suntory Open (Jap) 1980; NSW Open, Australian Open, Suntory Open (Jap) 1981
Int Ryder Cup 1981
Mis USPGA Player of the Year 1981
AMATEUR
Int Walker Cup 1973

Romero, Eduardo

Born Cordoba, Argentina on 12th July, 1954. Turned Professional 1982

Eur Lancôme Trophy 1989; Volvo Open di Firenze 1990; Spanish Open, French Open 1991; Italian Open, European Masters 1994

RoW Argentine Open 1989; Argentine PGA 1983-86; Chile Open 1984-86
Int Argentina in Dunhill Cup 1988-89-90-95-97; World Cup 1983-84-87-88-91-93-94-95

Rosenthal, Jody

Born Minneapolis, Minnesota, USA on 18th October, 1962. Turned Professional 1985

PROFESSIONAL
US United Virginia Bank Classic, du Maurier Classic 1987
Mis Gatorade Rookie of the Year 1986
AMATEUR
Chp Ladies British Open Amateur 1984
Int Curtis Cup 1984; Espirito Santo 1984(winners)

St Sauveur, Vicomtesse de *See* Segard

Sander, Anne [Welts] [Decker] (*née* Quast)

Chp Ladies British Open Amateur 1980.
Nat US Ladies Amateur 1958-61-63, r/u 1965-68-73
Int Curtis Cup 1958-60-62-66-68-74-84-90; Espirito Santo 1966(winners)-68(winners)
Mis Doris Chambers Trophy 1973-74; Angus Trophy 1974

Sarazen, Gene

Born Harrison, New York, USA on 27th February, 1902. Turned Professional 1920

Maj Open Champion 1932, r/u 1928, 3rd 1931-33; US Open 1922-32, r/u 1934-40; USPGA 1922-23-33, r/u 1930; US Masters 1935
Eur North of England Professional 1923
US 1922-one 1925-one 1927-two 1928-two 1930-two 1935-one 1936-one 1937-two 1938-one 1939-one 1941-one; USPGA Seniors 1954-58
RoW Australian Open 1936
Int Ryder Cup 1927-29-31-33-35-37
Mis PGA Hall of Fame 1940; World Golf Hall of Fame 1974; William Richardson Award 1966; Old Tom Morris Award 1988; Bobby Jones Award 1992; one of the few to win the Open and the US Open in the same year; Honorary Member of the Royal & Ancient

Segard, Mme Patrick [De St Sauveur]

(*née* Lally Vagliano)

Chp British Ladies 1950.
Trn Worplesdon Foursomes 1962. Avia Foursomes 1966. Kayser-Bondor Foursomes 1960
Nat French Ladies' Open 1948-50-51-52. French Ladies' Close 1939-46-49-50-51-54
Oth Swiss Ladies 1949-65. Luxembourg Ladies 1949. Italian Ladies 1949-51. Spanish Ladies 1951
Int France 1937-38-39-47-48-49-50-51-52-53-54-55-56-57-58-59-60-61-62-63-64-65-70. Vagliano Trophy 1959-61-63-65-(75)
Jun British Girls 1937
Mis Chairman of The Women's Committee of World Amateur Golf Council 1964 to 1972

Semple Thompson, Carol
Chp British Ladies 1974.
Nat US Ladies' Amateur 1973
Trn Newmark International 1975 (tied), r/u 1974
Int Curtis Cup 1974-77-80-82-90-94. World Team
Championship 1974(winners)-80 (winners)

Senior, Peter
*Born Singapore on 31st July, 1959. Turned
Professional 1978*
Eur PLM Open 1986; Monte Carlo Open 1987;
Panasonic European Open 1990; Benson &
Hedges International Open 1992
RoW New South Wales PGA, Rich River Classic,
(South Australian Open) 1979; Queensland
Open, New South Wales PGA 1984;
Queensland PGA 1987; Australian Open,
Australian PGA 1989; Johnnie Walker Classic
1989-91; Australian Masters 1991; Bridgestone
Open (Jpn) 1992; Vines Classic, Chunichi
Crowns (Jpn) 1993; Canon Challenge 1994;
Dunlop Open (Jpn), Australian Masters 1995;
Holden Classic, Canon Challenge 1996-97
Int Australia in Dunhill Cup 1987. Kirin Cup 1987;
World Cup 1988-90. Four Tours World Chp
1990 (winners); President's Cup 1994-96

Sheehan, Patty
*Born Middlebury, Vermont, USA on 27th October,
1956. Turned Professional 1980*
PROFESSIONAL
Maj Women's British Open 1992-94; US Women's
Open 1992-94, r/u 1983-88-90; USLPGA 1983-
84-93, r/u 1982
US 33 LPGA wins 1981 to 1996 (Nabisco Dinah
Shore 1996)
Int Solheim Cup 1990-92-94-96
Mis Gatorade Rookie of the Year 1981; Rolex Player
of the Year 1983; Vare Trophy 1984; Founders
Cup 1985; LPGA Hall of Fame 1993
AMATEUR
Nat US Ladies' Amateur r/u 1979
Int Curtis Cup 1980

Siderowf, Dick
Maj US Open leading amateur 1968
Chp Amateur Champion 1973-76
Oth Canadian Amateur 1971
Int Walker Cup 1969-73-75-77-(**79**). Eisenhower
Trophy 1968-76

Sigel, Jay
*Born Narberth, PA, USA on 13th November, 1943.
Turned Professional 1993*
PROFESSIONAL
Sen US Tour GTE West Classic 1994; Bruno's
Memorial Classic, Kroger Senior Classic 1997
AMATEUR
Maj US Open leading amateur 1984; US Masters
leading amateur 1981-82-88
Chp Amateur Champion 1979
Nat US Amateur 1982-83
Int Walker Cup 1977-79-81-**83**-85-87-89-91-93
Mis Most wins (18) in Walker Cup matches; Bobby
Jones Award 1984

Simpson, Scott William
*Born San Diego, California, USA on 17th September,
1955. Turned Professional 1977*
PROFESSIONAL
Maj US Open 1987, r/u 1991 (tied)
US 1980-one. 1984-one. 1987-one (Greater Greens-
boro Open); Bell South Atlanta Classic 1989
RoW 1984-two wins (Chunichi Crowns, Dunlop
Phoenix)
Int Ryder Cup 1987. Kirin Cup 1987
AMATEUR
Trn NCAA Chp 1976-77

Singh, Vijay
*Born Lautoka, Fiji on 22nd February, 1963. Turned
Professional 1982*
Eur Volvo Open 1989; El Bosque Open 1990; Open
de Andalucia, German Open 1992; Scandinavian
Masters, Trophée Lancôme 1994; South African
Open, Toyota World Match Play Chp 1997
US Buick Classic 1993; Phoenix Open, Buick
Classic 1995; Memorial Trn, Buick Open 1997
RoW Malay PGA 1984; Nigerian Open, Swedish PGA
1988; Zimbabwe Open, Nigerian Open, Ivory
Coast Open 1989; Hassan Trophy (Morocco)
1991; Malaysian Open 1992; Bell's Cup (SA)
1993; President's Cup 1994
Int Alfred Dunhill Challenge 1995; President's Cup
1996
Mis USPGA Rookie of the Year 1993

Snead, Samuel Jackson
*Born Hot Springs, Virginia, USA on 27th May,
1912. Turned Professional 1934*
Maj Open Champion 1946; US Open r/u 1937-47-
49-53; USPGA 1942-49-51, r/u 1938-40, 3rd
1974; US Masters 1949-52-54, r/u 1939-57
US 84 wins 1936 to 1965; Canadian Open 1938-40-
41
Sen USPGA Seniors 1964-65-67-70-72-73 World
Senior Professional 1964-65-70-72-73
Int Ryder Cup 1937-47-49-**51**-53-55-59-(**69**); USA
in World Cup 1954-56-57-58-59-60-61-62;
(winners 56-60-61-62; individual winner 1961)
Mis US leading money winner 1938-49-50. USPGA
Player of the Year 1949. Oldest professional to
win a Tour event in 1965. Unofficially credited
with 164 victories (including 84 official USPGA
tournaments) in his long career of which full
details are not available. Finished second equal
in a 1974 USPGA tournament aged 61 and third
equal in the 1974 USPGA Chp aged 62. 24
holes-in-one

Somerville, Charles Ross
Born London, Ontario, Canada on 4th May, 1903
Nat Canadian Amateur 1926-28-30-31-35-37; r/u
1924-25-34-38
Oth US Amateur 1932
Reg Ontario Amateur 1927-28-29-37. Manitoba
Amateur 1926. Canadian Seniors 1960-61
(tied)-65-66 (tied)
Mis President Royal Canadian Golf Association 1957

Sorenstam, Annika

Born Stockholm, Sweden on 9th October, 1970.
Turned Professional 1992

PROFESSIONAL

Maj British Women's Open r/u 1994; 3rd 1995; US Women's Open 1995-96

Eur OVB Damen Open, Hennessy Cup 1995; Trygg-Hansa Open 1996; Compaq Open 1997

US LPGA GHP Heartland Classic, World Chp of Women's Golf 1995; Betsy King Classic, World Chp of Women's Golf 1996; Trn of Champions, Hawaiian Ladies Open, Long's Drugs Challenge, Michelob Light Classic, Betsy King Classic, ITT Tour Chp 1997

RoW Holden Australian Open 1994

Int Solheim Cup 1994-96

Mis Rookie of the Year 1993; LPGA Rookie of the Year 1994; Rolex Player of the Year 1995-97; Vare Trophy 1995-96; Leading Money Winner Vivien Saunders Trophy 1995; Mickey Wright Award 1995-97

AMATEUR

Nat US Women's Amateur r/u 1992

Int Espirito Santo 1992 (individual winner); Swedish Ladies 1987 to 1992; NCAA All-American 1991-92

Stacy, Hollis

Born Savannah, Georgia, USA on 16th March, 1954. Turned Professional 1974

PROFESSIONAL

Maj US Women's Open 1977-78-84; r/u 1980

US 14 wins 1977 to 1985

AMATEUR

Int Curtis Cup 1972

Jun US Girls 1969-70-71

Stadler, Craig

Born San Diego, California, USA on 2nd June, 1953. Turned Professional 1975

PROFESSIONAL

Maj US Masters 1982, 3rd 1988

Eur Scandinavian Enterprise Open 1990

US 12 wins 1980-96 (Nissan Open 1996)

RoW Argentine Open 1992

Int Ryder Cup 1983-85

Mis Arnold Palmer Award 1982

AMATEUR

Nat US Amateur 1973

Int Walker Cup 1975

Stephenson, Jan

Born Sydney, NSW, Australia on 22nd December, 1951. Turned Professional 1973

Chp US Women's Open 1983. LPGA 1982

Nat Australian Ladies Open 1973-77

US 13 wins 1976 to 1986; 1987-two

Int Sunrise Cup 1992

Mis Gatorade Rookie of the Year 1974

Stewart, Payne

Born Springfield, Missouri, USA on 30th January, 1957. Turned Professional 1979

Maj Open r/u 1985-90; US Open 1991, r/u 1993; USPGA 1989

Eur Dutch Open 1991

US 9 wins 1982–95 (Shell Houston Open 1995)

RoW Indian Open, Indonesian Open 1981; Tweed Head Classic (Aust) 1982; Jun Classic (Jap) 1985

Int Ryder Cup 1987-89-91-93; Nissan Cup 1986; Kirin Cup 1988; Four Tours World Chp 1990; World Cup 1990 (individual winner); Dunhill Cup 1993 (winners)

Stockton, Dave

Born San Bernardino, California, USA on 2nd November, 1941. Turned Professional 1964

Maj US Open r/u 1978. USPGA 1970-76. US Masters r/u 1974.

US 1967-two wins; 1968-two; 1971-one; 1973-one; 1974-three; 1967 to 1974-nine

Sen 14 wins 1991 to 1997; US Senior Players Chp 1992; US Seniors Open 1996

Int Ryder Cup 1971-77-(**91**). World Cup 1970-76

Stranahan, Frank R

Born Toledo, Ohio, USA on 5th August, 1922. Turned Professional 1954

PROFESSIONAL

Maj Open r/u 1947-53, leading amateur 1947-49-50-51-53

US 1955-one, 1958-one

AMATEUR

Chp Amateur 1948-50, r/u 1952

Nat US Amateur r/u 1950

Oth Mexican Amateur 1946-48-51; Canadian Amateur 1947-48

Reg North & South Amateur 1946-49-52; Western Amateur 1946-49-51-53; Tam o' Shanter All-American Amateur 1948-49-50-51-52-53; Tam o' Shanter World Amateur 1950-51-52-53-54

Int Walker Cup 1947-49-51

Strange, Curtis

Born Norfolk, Virginia, USA on 20th January, 1955. Turned Professional 1976

PROFESSIONAL

Maj US Open 1988-89, 3rd 1984; USPGA r/u 1989; US Masters r/u 1985

Oth Canadian Open 1985-87

US 14 wins 1979 to 1988

RoW Palm Meadows Cup (Aus) 1989

Int Ryder Cup 1983-85-87-89-95. Dunhill Cup 1985-87-88-89 (winners)-90-91-94(r/u). Nissan Cup 1985. Kirin Cup 1987-88

Mis Arnold Palmer Award 1985-87. USPGA Player of the Year 1988

AMATEUR

Int Walker Cup 1975; Eisenhower Trophy 1974

Streit, Marlene Stewart

Born Cereal, Alberta, Canada on 9th March, 1934

Chp Ladies British Amateur 1953

Nat Canadian Ladies Open 1951-54-55-56-58-59-63-68-72-73. Canadian Ladies Close 1951 to 1957, 1963-68

Oth US Ladies Amateur 1956; r/u 1966. Australian Ladies 1963

Reg Ontario Provincial 1951-56-57-58. US North and South Ladies 1956

Int   Canadian Commonwealth Team 1959-63-**79**
Mis   Canadian Athlete of the Year 1951-53-56.
          Canadian Woman Athlete of the Year 1951-53-
          56-60-63

Stricker, Steve
*Born Edgerton, Wisconsin, USA on 23rd February,
1967. Turned Professional 1990*
US   Kemper Open, Motorola Western Open 1996
Oth   Victoria Open (Canada) 1990; Canadian PGA
          1993
Int   Dunhill Cup 1996 (winners)

Suggs, Louise
*Born Atlanta, Georgia, USA on 7th September, 1923.
Turned Professional 1948*
PROFESSIONAL
Maj   US Women's Open 1949-52, r/u 1951-55-58-
          59-63; USLPGA 1957, r/u 1955-60-61-63
US   50 LPGA wins 1949 to 1962 (incl Titleholders
          Chp 1946(as amateur)-54-56-59; Western Open
          1946-47(both as amateur)-49-53
Mis   Leading money winner 1953-60; Vare Trophy
          1957; LPGA Hall of Fame 1951; World Golf
          Hall of Fame 1979. Founder Member of
          LPGA
AMATEUR
Chp   British Ladies 1948
Nat   US Ladies Amateur 1947
Int   Curtis Cup 1948

Sutton, Hal
*Born Shreveport, Louisiana, USA on 28th April,
1958. Turned Professional 1981*
Maj   USPGA 1983
US   8 wins 1982–95 (BC Open 1995)
Int   Ryder Cup 1985-87; Nissan Cup 1986; v Japan
          1983
Mis   Arnold Palmer Award 1983; Golf Writers Player of
          the Year 1983; USPGA Player of the Year 1983
AMATEUR
Nat   US Amateur 1980
Int   Walker Cup 1979-81

Thomson, Peter W, CBE
*Born Melbourne, Australia on 23rd August, 1929.
Turned Professional 1949*
Maj   Open Champion 1954-55-56-58-65, r/u 1952-
          53-57, 3rd 1969
Eur   PGA Match Play 1954; *Yorkshire Evening News*
          1957; Dunlop, Daks(shared) 1958; Italian Open,
          Spanish Open 1959; German Open, *Yorkshire
          Evening News*, Bowmaker, Daks 1960; PGA
          Match Play, *Yorkshire Evening News*, Esso
          Golden(shared), Dunlop Masters 1961; Martini
          International, Piccadilly 1962; Daks 1965; PGA
          Match Play 1966; Alcan International, PGA
          Match Play, Esso Golden(tied) 1967; Dunlop
          Masters 1968; Martini International
          1970(shared); Wills 1972
US   1956-one, 1957-one
RoW   Australian Open 1951-67-72, r/u 1950, leading
          amateur 1948; Australian Professional 1967;
          New Zealand Open 1950-51-53-55-59-60-61-
          65-71; New Zealand Professional 1953; Hong

Kong Open 1960-65-67; India Open 1963-76;
Philippines Open 1964; New Zealand Caltex
1967; Victorian Open 1973
Sen   PGA Seniors Chp 1988
Int   Australia in World Cup 1953-54(winners)-55-
          56-67-59(winners)-60-61-62-65-69; President's
          Cup (**1996**)
Mis   World Golf Hall of Fame 1988. Honorary
          Member of Royal & Ancient

Trevino, Lee
*Born Dallas, Texas, USA on 1st December, 1939.
Turned Professional 1961*
Maj   Open Champion 1971-72, r/u 1980, 3rd 1970;
          US Open 1968-71; USPGA 1974-84, r/u 1985
Eur   Benson & Hedges International, Lancôme
          Trophy 1978; Lancôme Trophy 1980; Dunhill
          British Masters 1985
US   27 wins: 1968-one, 1969-one, 1970-two, 1971-
          three, 1972-three, 1973-two, 1974-one, 1975-
          one, 1976-one, 1978-one, 1980-three, 1981-one;
          World Series 1974; Canadian Open 1971-77-79;
          Canadian PGA 1979-83
RoW   Chrysler Classic (Aust) 1973; Mexican Open
          1975; Moroccan Grand Prix 1977
Sen   US Sen Tour 27 wins 1990 to 1996; USPGA
          Senior Open 1990; USPGA Seniors Chp 1992-
          94; Fuji Electric Grand Slam (Jpn) 1993
Int   Ryder Cup 1969-71-73-75-79-81-(**85**); World
          Cup 1968-69(winners; individual winner) -70-
          71(winners) -74
Mis   Rookie of the Year 1967; leading money winner
          1970; USPGA Player of the Year 1971; Vardon
          Trophy 1970-71-72-74-80; Byron Nelson Award
          1971; Ben Hogan Award 1981; World Golf Hall
          of Fame 1981; William Richardson Award 1985

Vagliano, Lally   *See* **Segard**

Varangot, Brigitte
Born Biarritz, France on 1st May, 1940
Chp   Ladies British Open Amateur 1963-65-68
Nat   French Ladies Open Amateur 1961-62-64-65-
          66-73, r/u 1960-63-67-70; French Ladies Close
          Amateur 1959-61-63-70
Oth   Italian Ladies 1970
Trn   Kayser-Bondor Foursomes; Casa Pupo
          Foursomes 1965; Avia Foursomes 1966-73
Int   France in Vagliano Trophy 1959-61-63-65-69-71;
          Espirito Santo 1964(winners)-66-68-70-72-74

De Vicenzo, Roberto
*Born Buenos Aires, Argentina on 14th April, 1923.
Turned Professional 1938*
Maj   Open Champion 1967, r/u 1950, 3rd 1948-49-
          56-60-64-69; US Masters r/u 1968
Eur   Belgian Open, Dutch Open, French Open 1950;
          French Open 1960; French Open, German
          Open 1964; Spanish Open 1966
US   1951-two 1953-one 1957-two 1966-one
RoW   Argentine Open 1944-49-51-52-58-65-67-70-
          74; Argentine Professional 1944-45-47-48-49-
          51-52; Chile Open 1946; Colombia Open 1947;
          Uruguay Open 1949; Mexican Open 1951;
          Panama Open 1952; Mexican Open 1953;

Jamaican Open 1956; Brazilian Open, Jamaican Open 1957; Brazilian Open 1960-63-64; Bogota Open 1969; Panama Open, Brazilian Open, Caracas Open 1973; Panama Open 1974

Sen	USPGA Seniors 1974; World Senior Professional 1974; Legends of Golf 1979; US Senior Open 1980
Int	Argentina in World Cup 1953(winners) -54-55-62(individual winner) -63-64-65-66-68-69-70 (individual winner) -71-72-73-74; Mexico in World Cup 1956-59-60-61
Mis	Bobby Jones Award 1970; William Richardson Award 1971; Walter Hagen Award 1979; USPGA Hall of Fame 1979; World Golf Hall of Fame 1989; Honorary Member of the R&A.

Wadkins, Lanny

Born Richmond, Virginia, USA on 5th December, 1949. Turned Professional 1971

PROFESSIONAL

Maj	US Open r/u 1986; USPGA 1977, r/u 1982-84-87, 3rd 1973; US Masters 3rd 1990-91-93
US	20 wins 1972 to 1991; World Series 1977, r/u 1990; Greater Hartford Open 1992
RoW	Victoria PGA (Aust) 1978
Int	Ryder Cup 1977-79-83-85-87-89-91-93-(**95**); World Cup 1977-84-85; v Japan 1982-83; Nissan Cup 1985; Kirin Cup 1987; Four Tours World Chp 1991
Mis	USPGA Player of the Year 1985; Rookie of the Year 1972

AMATEUR

Nat	US Amateur 1970
Reg	Western Amateur 1970; Southern Amateur 1968-70; Eastern Amateur 1969
Int	Walker Cup 1969-71; Eisenhower Trophy 1970(winners)

Ward, Harvie

Born Tarboro, North Carolina, USA in 1926. Turned Professional 1973

Chp	Amateur Champion 1952; r/u 1953
Nat	US Amateur 1955-56
Oth	Canadian Amateur 1964
Trn	NCAA Chp 1949
Reg	North and South Amateur 1948
Int	Walker Cup 1953-55-59

Watson, Tom

Born Kansas City, Missouri, USA on 4th September, 1949. Turned Professional 1971

Maj	Open Champion 1975-77-80-82-83, r/u 1984; US Open 1982, r/u 1983-87, 3rd 1980; USPGA r/u 1978; US Masters 1977-81, r/u 1978-79-84, 3rd 1991
US	32 wins: 1974-one, 1975-one, 1977-three, 1978-five, 1979-five, 1980-five, 1981-four, 1982-two, 1984-three, 1987-one, 1996-one (Memorial Trn). World Series 1975-80
RoW	Phoenix Open (Jpn) 1980; Hong Kong Open 1992; Dunlop Phoenix (Jpn) 1997
Int	Ryder Cup 1977-81-83-89-(93); v Japan 1982-84
Mis	Vardon Trophy 1977-78-79; leading money winner 1977-78-79-80-84; USPGA Player of the Year 1977-78-79-80-82-84; Bobby Jones Award

1986; World Golf Hall of Fame 1988; William Richardson Award 1991; Old Tom Morris Award 1991

Webb, Karrie

Born Ayr, Old Australia on 21st December, 1974. Turned Professional 1994

PROFESSIONAL

Maj	British Women's Open 1995-97
US	HealthSouth Inaugural, Sprint Titleholders Chp, Safeco Classic 1996; Komen International, Safeco Classic 1997
Int	Nichirei International 1996
Mis	Rookie of the Year 1995; Gatorade Rookie of the Year 1996; Mickey Wright Award 1996; Vare Trophy 1997

AMATEUR

Nat	Australian Stroke Play 1994
Oth	Queensland, New South Wales and Victoria Stroke Play 1994

Weiskopf, Tom

Born Massillon, Ohio, USA on 9th November, 1942. Turned Professional 1964

Maj	Open Champion 1973; US Open r/u 1976; 3rd 1973-77; USPGA 3rd 1975; US Masters r/u 1969-72-74-75
Eur	Piccadilly World Match Play 1972
US	1968-two, 1971-two, 1972-one, 1973-three, 1975-one, 1977-one, 1978-one, 1982-one; World Series 1973; Canadian Open 1973-75
RoW	South African PGA 1973; Argentine Open 1979
Sen	US Tour Franklin Quest Chp 1994; US Seniors Open 1995; SBC Dominion Seniors, Pittsburgh Senior Classic 1996
Int	Ryder Cup 1973-75; USA in World Cup 1972

Welts, Anne *See* **Sander**

Whitworth, Kathy

Born Monahans, Texas, USA on 27th September, 1939. Turned Professional 1959

Maj	US Open r/u 1971; USLPGA 1967-71-75, r/u 1968-70
US	88 LPGA wins 1962-85 (incl Titleholder's Chp 1965-66; Western Open 1967)
Int	Solheim Cup (**1990**)-(**92**)
Mis	Rolex Player of the Year 1966-67-68-69-71-72-73. Vare Trophy 1965-66-67-69-70-71-72. William Richardson Award 1986; Woman Athlete of the Year 1965-66; LPGA Hall of Fame; World Golf Hall of Fame 1982; Powell Award 1986; Patty Berg Award 1987

Woods, Eldrick 'Tiger'

Born Cypress, CA, USA on 30th December, 1975. Turned Professional 1996

PROFESSIONAL

Maj	US Masters 1997
Eur	Johnnie Walker Classic 1998
US	Las Vegas Invitational, Walt Disney World/ Oldsmobile Classic 1996; Mercedes Chp, Byron Nelson Classic, Motorola Western Open 1997

Int   Ryder Cup 1997
Mis   Rolex Player of the Year 1996; USPGA Player of the Year 1997
AMATEUR
Nat   US amateur 1994-95-96
Reg   Western amateur, Pacific North West amateur 1994
Int   Walker Cup 1995; Eisenhower Trophy 1994
Jun   USGA Junior National Chp 1991-92-93
Jun Int Rolex Junior All American 1990-91-92-93
Mis   Nine holes in 48 at age 3; won Junior World Trns in 1984-85-88-89; Golf Digest Player of the Year 1991-92; Golf World Player of the Year 1993. Entered Stanford University 1994

Wright, Mary Kathryn (Mickey)

Born San Diego, California, USA on 14th February, 1935. Turned Professional 1954

Maj   US Open 1958-59-61-64, r/u 1968, leading amateur 1954; USLPGA 1958-60-61-63, r/u 1964-66
US   82 LPGA wins 1956-73 (inc. Titleholders Chp 1961-62; Western Open 1962-63-66; 13 wins in 1963)

Mis   Leading money winner 1961-62-63-64; Vare Trophy 1960-61-62-63-64; LPGA Hall of Fame 1964; World Golf Hall of Fame 1976; Woman Athlete of the Year 1963-64

Yates, Charles Richard

Born Atlanta, Georgia, USA on 9th September, 1913

Maj   US Masters leading amateur 1934-39-40
Chp   Amateur Champion 1938
Reg   Western Amateur 1935.
Int   Walker Cup 1936-38-(53)
Mis   Bobby Jones Award 1980

Zoeller, Frank Urban (Fuzzy)

Born New Albany, Indiana, USA on 11th November, 1951. Turned Professional 1973

Maj   US Open 1984, 3rd 1994; USPGA r/u 1981; US Masters 1979
US   1979-two, 1983-two, 1985-one, 1986-three
Int   Ryder Cup 1979-83-85
Mis   Bobby Jones Award 1985. Ben Hogan Award 1986

British Isles International Players, Professional Men

Since 1979 the 'Great Britain and Ireland' team format for the Ryder Cup match against the United States has been widened to include professionals from the Continent of Europe

Adams, J
(Scotland): v England 1932-33-34-35-36-37-38; v Wales 1937-38; v Ireland 1937-38. (GBI): Ryder Cup 1947-49-51-53

Affleck, P
(Wales): Dunhill Cup 1995-96

Ainslie, T
(Scotland): v Ireland 1936

Alliss, Percy
(England): v Scotland 1932-33-34-35-36-37; v Ireland 1932-38; v Wales 1938. (GBI): v France 1929; Ryder Cup 1929-31-33-35-37

Alliss, Peter
(England): Canada Cup 1954-55-57-58-59-61-62-64-66; World Cup 1967. (GBI): Ryder Cup 1953-57-59-61-63-65-67-69

Anderson, Joe
(Scotland): v Ireland 1932

Anderson, W
(Scotland): v Ireland 1936; v England 1937; v Wales 1937

Ayton, LB
(Scotland): v England 1910-12-13-33-34

Ayton, JB, jr
(Scotland): v England 1937. (GBI): Ryder Cup 1949

Baker, P
(England): Dunhill Cup 1993 (r/u). (Eur): Ryder Cup 1993

Ballantine, J
(Scotland): v England 1932-36

Ballingall, J
(Scotland): v England 1938; Ireland 1938; v Wales 1938

Bamford, BJ
(England): Canada Cup 1961

Bannerman, H
(Scotland): World Cup 1967-72. (GBI): Ryder Cup 1971

Barber, T
(England): v Ireland 1932-33

Barnes, BW
(Scotland): World Cup 1974-75-76-77. (GBI): Ryder Cup 1969-71-73-75-77-79; v Europe 1974-76-78-80; v South Africa 1976

Batley, JB
(England): v Scotland 1912

Beck, AG
(England): v Wales 1938; v Ireland 1938

Bembridge, M
(England): World Cup 1974-75. (GBI): Ryder Cup 1969-71-73-75; v South Africa 1976. (Sen) European Cup 1997

Boomer, A
(England): (GBI): v America 1926; Ryder Cup 1927-29

Bousfield, K
(England): Canada Cup 1956-57. (GBI): Ryder Cup 1949-51-55-57-59-61

Boxall, R
(England): Dunhill Cup 1990; World Cup 1990

Boyle, HF
(Ireland): World Cup 1967. (GBI): Ryder Cup 1967

Bradshaw, H
(Ireland): Canada Cup 1954-55-56-57-58-59; v Scotland 1937-38; v Wales 1937; v England 1938. (GBI): Ryder Cup 1953-55-57

Braid, J
(Scotland): v England 1903-04-05-06-07-09-10-12. (GBI): v America 1921

Branch, WJ
(England): v Scotland 1936

Brand, G, jr
(Scotland): World Cup 1984-85-88-89-90-92-94; Dunhill Cup 1985-86-87-88-89-91-92-93-94-97; (Eur): Nissan Cup 1985; Kirin Cup 1988; Four Tours World Chp 1989; (GBI): Ryder Cup 1987-89; v Australia 1988

Brand, GJ
(England): World Cup 1983; Dunhill Cup 1986-87 (winners). (GBI): Ryder Cup 1983; (Eur) Nissan Cup 1986

Broadhurst, P
(England): Dunhill Cup 1991; World Cup 1997. (Eur) Ryder Cup 1991; Four Tours World Chp 1991-95

Brown, EC
(Scotland): Canada Cup 1954-55-56-57-58-59-60-61-62-65-66; World Cup 1987-68. (GBI): Ryder Cup 1953-55-57-59

Brown, K
(Scotland): World Cup 1977-78-79-83. (GBI): Ryder Cup 1977-79-83-85-87; v Europe 1978; (Eur) Kirin Cup 1987

Burns, S
(Scotland): v England 1932. (GBI): Ryder Cup 1929

Burton, J
(England): v Ireland 1933

Burton, R
(England): v Scotland 1935-36-37-38; v Ireland 1938; v Wales 1938. (GBI): Ryder Cup 1935-37-49

Busson, JH
(England): v Scotland 1938

Busson, JJ
(England): *v* Scotland 1934-35-36-37. (GBI): Ryder Cup 1935

Butler, PJ
(England): World Cup 1969-70-73. (GBI): Ryder Cup 1965-69-71-73; *v* Europe 1976

Callum, WS
(Scotland): *v* Ireland 1935

Campbell, J
(Scotland): *v* Ireland 1936

Carrol, LJ
(Ireland): *v* Scotland 1937-38; *v* Wales 1937; *v* England 1938

Cassidy, D
(Ireland): *v* Scotland 1936-37; *v* Wales 1937

Cassidy, J
(Ireland): *v* England 1933; *v* Scotland 1934-35

Cawsey, GH
(England): *v* Scotland 1906-07

Caygill, GA
(England): (GBI): Ryder Cup 1969

Clark, C
(England): (GBI): Ryder Cup 1973

Clark, HK
(England): World Cup 1978-84-85-87; Dunhill Cup 1985-86-87 (winners)-89-90(r/u)-94-95. (GBI): Ryder Cup 1977-81-85-87-89-95; *v* Australia 1988; *v* Europe 1978-84. (Eur): Nissan Cup 1985

Clarke, D
(Ireland): Dunhill Cup 1994-95-96-97; World Cup 1994-95-96. (GBI): Ryder Cup 1997

Claydon, R
(England): Dunhill Cup 1997

Coles, NC
(England): Canada Cup 1963; World Cup 1968. (GBI): Ryder Cup 1961-63-65-67-69-71-73-77; *v* Europe 1974-76-78-80

Collinge, T
(England): *v* Scotland 1937

Collins, JF
(England): *v* Scotland 1903-04

Coltart, A
(Scotland): Dunhill Cup 1994-95 (winners)-96; World Cup 1994-95-96

Coltart, F
(Scotland): *v* England 1909

Compston, A
(England): *v* Scotland 1932-35; *v* Ireland 1932. (GBI): *v* America 1926, Ryder Cup 1927-29-31; *v* France 1929

Cotton, TH
(England): (GBI): Ryder Cup 1929-37-47; *v* France 1929

Cox, S
(Wales): World Cup 1975

Cox, WJ
(England): *v* Scotland 1935-36-37. (GBI): Ryder Cup 1935-37

Curtis, D
(England): *v* Scotland 1934-38; *v* Ireland 1938; *v* Wales 1938

Dabson, K
(Wales): World Cup 1972

Dailey, A
(Scotland): *v* England 1932-33-34-35-36-38; *v* Ireland 1938; *v* Wales 1938. (GBI): Ryder Cup 1933

Daly, F
(Ireland): *v* Scotland 1936-37-38; *v* England 1938; *v* Wales 1937; Canada Cup 1954-55. (GBI): Ryder Cup 1947-49-51-53

Darcy, E
(Ireland): World Cup 1976-77-83-84-85-87; Dunhill Cup 1987-88(winners) -91. (GBI): Ryder Cup 1975-77-81-87; *v* Europe 1976-84; *v* South Africa 1976

Davies, R
(Wales): World Cup 1968

Davies, WH
(England): *v* Scotland 1932-33; *v* Ireland 1932-33. (GBI): Ryder Cup 1931-33

Davis, W
(Scotland): *v* Ireland 1933-34-35-36-37-38; *v* England 1937-38; *v* Wales 1937-38

Dawson, P
(England): World Cup 1977. (GBI): Ryder Cup 1977

De Foy, CB
(Wales): World Cup 1971-73-74-75-76-77-78

Denny, CS
(England): *v* Scotland 1936

Dobson, T
(Scotland): *v* England 1932-33-34-35-36-37; *v* Ireland 1932-33-34-35-36-37-38; *v* Wales 1937-38

Don, W
(Scotland): *v* Ireland 1935-36

Donaldson, J
(Scotland): *v* England 1932-35-38; *v* Ireland 1937; *v* Wales 1937

Dornan, R
(Scotland): *v* Ireland 1932

Drew, NV
(Ireland): Canada Cup 1960-61. (GBI): Ryder Cup 1959

Duncan, G
(Scotland): *v* England 1906-07-09-10-12-13-32-34-35-36-37. (GBI): *v* America 1921-26, Ryder Cup 1927-29-31

Durnian, D
(England): World Cup 1989; Dunhill Cup 1989

Durward, JG
(Scotland): *v* Ireland 1934; *v* England 1937

Easterbrook, S
(England): *v* Scotland 1932-33-34-35-38; *v* Ireland 1933. (GBI): Ryder Cup 1931-33

Edgar, J
(Ireland): *v* Scotland 1938

Fairweather, S
(Ireland): *v* England 1932; *v* Scotland 1933. (Scotland): *v* England 1933-35-36; *v* Ireland 1938; *v* Wales 1938

Faldo, NA
(England): World Cup 1977-91; Dunhill Cup 1985-86-87 (winners) -88-91-93 (r/u). (GBI): Ryder Cup 1977-79-81-83-85-87-89-91-93-95-97; *v* Europe 1978-80-82-84; *v* Rest of World 1982. (Eur) Nissan Cup 1986. Kirin Cup 1987; Four Tours World Chp 1990

Fallon, J
(Scotland): *v* England 1936-37-38; *v* Ireland 1937-38; *v* Wales 1937-38. (GBI): Ryder Cup 1955

Faulkner, M
(England): (GBI): Ryder Cup 1947-49-51-53-57

Feherty, D
(Ireland): World Cup 1990; Dunhill Cup 1985-86-90(winners) -91-93; (Eur): Ryder Cup 1991; Four Tours World Chp 1990-91

Fenton, WB
(Scotland): *v* England 1932; *v* Ireland 1932-33

Fernie, TR
(Scotland): *v* England 1910-12-13-33

Foster, M
(England): World Cup 1976.
(GBI): *v* Europe 1976

Gadd, B
(England): *v* Scotland 1933-35-38;
v Ireland 1933-38; *v* Wales 1938

Gadd, G
(England): (GBI): *v* America 1926,
Ryder Cup 1927

Gallacher, BJ
(Scotland): World Cup 1969-71-74-82-83. (GBI): Ryder Cup 1969-71-73-75-77-79-81-83-91 (Captain) -93(Captain)-95(Captain); *v* Europe 1974-78-82-84; *v* South Africa 1976; *v* Rest of World 1982

Garner, JR
(England): (GBI): Ryder Cup 1971-73

Gaudin, PJ
(England): *v* Scotland 1905-06-07-09-12-13

Gilford, D
(England): World Cup 1992-93;
Dunhill Cup 1992(winners);
(Eur): Ryder Cup 1991-95

Good, G
(Scotland): *v* England 1934-36

Gould, H
(Wales): Canada Cup 1954-55

Gow, A
(Scotland): *v* England 1912

Grabham, C
(Wales): *v* England 1938;
v Scotland 1938

Grant, T
(Scotland): *v* England 1913

Gray, E
(England): *v* Scotland 1904-05-07

Green, E
(England): (GBI): Ryder Cup 1947

Green, T
(England): *v* Scotland 1935.
(Wales): *v* Scotland 1937-38;
v Ireland 1937; *v* England 1938

Greene, C
(Ireland): Canada Cup 1965

Gregson, M
(England): World Cup 1967.
(GBI): Ryder Cup 1967. (Sen)
European Cup 1997

Haliburton, TB
(Scotland): *v* Ireland 1935-36-38;
v England 1938; *v* Wales 1938;
Canada Cup 1954. (GBI): Ryder
Cup 1961-63

Hamill, J
(Ireland): *v* Scotland 1933-34-35;
v England 1932-33

Hargreaves, J
(England): (GBI): Ryder Cup 1951

Harrington, P
(Ireland): Dunhill Cup 1996-97;
World Cup 1996-97 (winners)

Hastings, W
(Scotland): England 1937-38;
v Wales 1937-38; *v* Ireland 1937-38

Havers, AG
(England): *v* Scotland 1932-33-34;
v Ireland 1932-33. (GBI): *v*
America 1921-26, Ryder Cup 1927-31-33; *v* France 1929

Healing, SF
(Wales): *v* Scotland 1938

Hepburn, J
(Scotland): *v* England 1903-05-06-07-09-10-12-13

Herd, A
(Scotland): *v* England 1903-04-05-06-09-10-12-13-32

Hill, EF
(Wales): *v* Scotland 1937-38;
v Ireland 1937; *v* England 1938

Hitchcock, J
(England): (GBI): Ryder Cup 1965

Hodson, B
(England): *v* Ireland 1933. (Wales):
v Scotland 1937-38;*v* Ireland 1937;
v England 1938. (GBI): Ryder Cup
1931

Holley, W
(Ireland): *v* Scotland 1933-34-35-36-38; *v* England 1932-33-38

Horne, R
(England): (GBI): Ryder Cup 1947

Horton, T
(England): World Cup 1976. (GBI):
v Europe 1974-76; Ryder Cup 1975-77. (Sen) European Cup 1997

Houston, D
(Scotland): *v* Ireland 1934

Huggett, BGC
(Wales): Canada Cup 1963-64-65;
World Cup 1968-69-70-71-76-79.
(GBI): Ryder Cup 1963-67-69-71-73-75; *v* Europe 1974-78

Huish, D
(Scotland): World Cup 1973

Hunt, BJ
(England): Canada Cup 1958-59-60-62-63-64; World Cup 1968.
(GBI): Ryder Cup 1953-57-59-61-63-65-67-69

Hunt, GL
(England): World Cup 1972-75.
(GBI): *v* Europe 1974; Ryder Cup
1975

Hunt, Geoffrey M
(England): (GBI): Ryder Cup 1963

Hunter, W
(Scotland): *v* England 1906-07-09-10

Hutton, GC
(Scotland): *v* Ireland 1936-37;
v England 1937-38; *v* Wales 1937

Ingram, D
(Scotland): World Cup 1973

Jacklin, A
(England): Canada Cup 1966;
World Cup 1970-71-72.
(GBI): Ryder Cup 1967-69-71-73-75-77-79-83(captain) -85(captain)
-87(captain) -89(captain); *v* Europe
1976-82; *v* Rest of World 1982

Jackson, H
(Ireland): World Cup 1970-71

Jacobs, JRM
(England): (GBI): Ryder Cup 1955

Jagger, D
(England): (GBI): *v* Europe 1976

James, G
(Wales): *v* Scotland 1937; *v* Ireland
1937

James, MH
(England): World Cup 1978-79-82-84-87-88-93-97; Dunhill Cup
1988-89-90(r/u)-93(r/u)-95-97.
(GBI): Ryder Cup 1977-79-81-89-91-93-95;
v Europe 1978-80-82; *v* Rest of
World 1982; *v* Australia 1988;
(Eur): Kirin Cup 1988; Four Tours
World Chp 1989-90

Jarman, EW
(England): *v* Scotland 1935. (GBI):
Ryder Cup 1935

Job, N
(England): (GBI): *v* Europe 1980

Jolly, HC
(England): (GBI): *v* America 1926,
Ryder Cup 1927; *v* France 1929

Jones, DC
(Wales): v Scotland 1937-38;
v Ireland 1937; v England 1938

Jones, E
(Ireland): Canada Cup 1965

Jones, R
(England): v Scotland 1903-04-05-
06-07-09-10-12-13

Jones, T
(Wales): v Scotland 1936; v Ireland
1937; v England 1938

Kenyon, EWH
(England): v Scotland 1932;
v Ireland 1932

King, M
(England): World Cup 1979.
(GBI): Ryder Cup 1979

King, SL
(England): v Scotland 1934-36-37-
38; v Wales 1938; v Ireland 1938.
(GBI): Ryder Cup 1937-47-49

Kinsella, J
(Ireland): World Cup 1968-69-72-
73

Kinsella, W
(Ireland): v Scotland 1937-38;
v England 1938

Knight, G
(Scotland): v England 1937

Lacey, AJ
(England): v Scotland 1932-33-34-
36-37-38; v Ireland 1932-33-38;
v Wales 1938. (GBI): Ryder Cup
1933-37

Laidlaw, W
(Scotland): v England 1935-36-38;
v Ireland 1937; v Wales 1937

Lane, B
(England): World Cup 1988-94;
Dunhill Cup 1988-94-95-96.
(Eur): Ryder Cup 1993

Lawrie, P
(Scotland): World Cup 1996

Lees, A
(England): v Scotland 1938;
v Wales 1938; v Ireland 1938.
(GBI): Ryder Cup 1947-49-51-55

Llewellyn, D
(Wales): World Cup 1974-85-87
(winners)-88; Dunhill Cup 1985-
88. (GBI): v Europe 1984

Lloyd, F
(Wales): v Scotland 1937-38;
v Ireland 1937; v England 1938

Lockhart, G
(Scotland): v Ireland 1934-35

Lomas, J
(England): Dunhill Cup 1996

Lyle, AWB
(Scotland): World Cup 1979-80-87;
Dunhill Cup 1985-86-87-88-89-90-
92. (GBI): Ryder Cup 1979-81-83-
85-87; v Europe 1980-82-84; v
Rest of World 1982; v Australia
1988. (Eur): Nissan Cup 1985-86;
Kirin Cup 1987.

McCartney, J
(Ireland): v Scotland 1932-33-34-
35-36-37-38; v England 1932-33-
38; v Wales 1937

McCulloch, D
(Scotland): v England 1932-33-34-
35-36-37; v Ireland 1932-33-34-35

McDermott, M
(Ireland): v England 1932;
v Scotland 1932

McDowall, J
(Scotland): v England 1932-33-34-
35-36; v Ireland 1933-34-35-36

McEwan, P
(Scotland): v England 1907

McGinley, P
(Ireland): Dunhill Cup 1993-94-96-
97, World Cup 1993-94-97(winners)

McIntosh, G
(Scotland): v England 1938;
v Ireland 1938; v Wales 1938

McKenna, J
(Ireland): v Scotland 1936-37-38;
v Wales 1937-38; v England 1938

McKenna, R
(Ireland): v Scotland 1933-35;
v England 1933

McMillan, J
(Scotland): v England 1933-34-35;
v Ireland 1933-34

McMinn, W
(Scotland): v England 1932-33-34

McNeill, H
(Ireland): v England 1932

Mahon, PJ
(Ireland): v Scotland 1932-33-34-
35-36-37-38; v Wales 1937-38;
v England 1932-33-38

Martin, J
(Ireland): Canada Cup 1962-63-64-
66; World Cup 1970.
(GBI): Ryder Cup 1965

Martin, S
(Scotland): World Cup 1980

Mason, SC
(England): World Cup 1980.
(GBI): v Europe 1980

Mayo, CH
(England): v Scotland 1907-09-10-
12-13

Mayo, P
(Wales): Dunhill Cup 1993

Mills, RP
(England): (GBI): Ryder Cup 1957

Mitchell, A
(England): v Scotland 1932-33-34.
(GBI): v America 1921-26, Ryder
Cup 1929-31-33

Mitchell, P
(England): World Cup 1996

Moffitt, R
(England): (GBI): Ryder Cup 1961

Montgomerie, C
(Scotland): World Cup 1988-91-92-
93-97(individual winner); Dunhill
Cup 1988-91-92-93-94-95(winners)-
96-97. (Eur): Ryder Cup 1991-93-
95-97; Four Tours World Chp 1991

Mouland, M
(Wales): World Cup 1988-89-90-92-
93-95-96; Dunhill Cup 1986-87-88-
89-93-95-96. (Eur): Kirin Cup 1988.

Mouland, S
(Wales): Canada Cup 1965-66;
World Cup 1967

O'Brien, W
(Ireland): v Scotland 1934-36-37;
v Wales 1937

Ockenden, J
(England): (GBI): v America 1921

O'Connor, C
(Ireland): Canada Cup 1956-57-58-
59-60-61-62-63-64-66;
World Cup 1967-68-69-71-73.
(GBI): Ryder Cup 1955-57-59-61-
63-65-67-69-71-73

O'Connor, C, jr
(Ireland): World Cup 1974-75-78-
85-89-92; Dunhill Cup 1985-89-
92. (GBI): Ryder Cup 1975-89;
v Europe 1974-84; v South Africa
1976

O'Connor, P
(Ireland): v Scotland 1932-33-34-
35-36; v England 1932-33

Oke, WG
(England): v Scotland 1932

O'Leary, JE
(Ireland): World Cup 1972-80-82.
(GBI): Ryder Cup 1975;
v Europe 1976-78-82; v Rest of
World 1982

O'Neill, J
(Ireland): v England 1933

O'Neill, M
(Ireland): v Scotland 1933-34;
v England 1933

Oosterhuis, PA
(England): World Cup 1971.
(GBI): Ryder Cup 1971-73-75-77-
79-81; v Europe 1974

Padgham, AH
(England): v Scotland 1932-33-34-
35-36-37-38; v Ireland 1932-33-38;
v Wales 1938. (GBI): Ryder Cup
1933-35-37

Panton, J
(Scotland): Canada Cup 1955-56-
57-58-59-60-61-62-63-64-65-66;
World Cup 1968. (GBI): Ryder
Cup 1951-53-61

Park, J
(Scotland): v England 1909

Parkin, P
(Wales): World Cup 1984-89;
Dunhill Cup 1985-86-87-89-90-91.
(GBI): v Europe 1984

Patterson, E
(Ireland): v Scotland 1933-34-35-
36; v England 1933; v Wales 1937

Payne, J
(England): World Cup 1996

Perry, A
(England); v Ireland 1932;
v Scotland 1933-36-38. (GBI):
Ryder Cup 1933-35-37

Pickett, C
(Wales): v Scotland 1937-38;
v Ireland 1937; v England 1938

Platts, L
(Wales): (GBI): Ryder Cup 1965

Polland, E
(Ireland): World Cup 1973-74-76-77-
78-79. (GBI): Ryder Cup 1973;
v Europe 1974-76-78-80; v South
Ryder Cup 1976

Pope, CW
(Ireland): v England 1932;
v Scotland 1932

Price, P
(Wales): Dunhill Cup 1991-96;
World Cup 1994-95-97

Rafferty, R
(Ireland): World Cup 1983-84-87-
88-90-91-92-93; Dunhill Cup 1986-
87-88(winners)-89-90(winners)-91-
92-93-95. (GBI): v Europe 1984; v
Australia 1988. (Eur): Ryder Cup
1989; Kirin Cup 1988; Four Tours
World Chp 1989-90-91

Rainford, P
(England): v Scotland 1903-07

Ray, E
(England): v Scotland 1903-04-05-
06-07-09-10-12-13.
(GBI): v America 1921-26, Ryder
Cup 1927

Rees, DJ
(Wales): v Scotland 1937-38;
v Ireland 1937; England 1938;
Canada Cup 1954-56-57-58-59-60-
61-62-64. (GBI): Ryder Cup 1937-
47-49-51-53-55-57-59-61

Reid, W
(England): v Scotland 1906-07

Renouf, TG
(England): v Scotland 1903-04-05-
10-13

Richardson, S
(England): Dunhill Cup 1991-
92(winners); World Cup 1992.
(Eur): Ryder Cup 1991; Four
Tours World Chp 1991

Ritchie, WL
(Scotland): v England 1913

Robertson, F
(Scotland): v Ireland 1933;
v England 1938

Robertson, P
(Scotland): v England 1932;
v Ireland 1932-34

Robson, F
(England): v Scotland 1909-10.
(GBI): v America 1926, Ryder Cup
1927-29-31

Roe, M
(England): World Cup 1989-94-95;
Dunhill Cup 1994

Rowe, AJ
(England): v Scotland 1903-06-07

Russell, R
(Scotland): Dunhill Cup 1996-97;
World Cup 1997

Sayers, B, jr
(Scotland): v England 1906-07-09

Scott, SS
(England): (GBI): Ryder Cup 1955

Seymour, M
(England): v Scotland 1932-33;
v Ireland 1932-33. (Scotland): v
Ireland 1932

Shade, RDBM
(Scotland): World Cup 1970-71-72

Sherlock, JG
(England): v Scotland 1903-04-05-
06-07-09-10-12-13.
(GBI): v America 1921

Simpson, A
(Scotland): v England 1904

Smalldon, D
(Wales): Canada Cup 1955-56

Smith, CR
(Scotland): v England 1903-04-07-
09-13

Smith, GE
(Scotland): v Ireland 1932

Smyth, D
(Ireland): World Cup 1979-80-82-
83-88-89; Dunhill Cup 1985-86-
87-88 (winners). (GBI): Ryder Cup
1979-81; v Europe 1980-82-84;
v Rest of World 1982

Snell, D
(England): Canada Cup 1965

Spark, W
(Scotland): v Ireland 1933-35-37;
v England 1935; v Wales 1937

Spence, J
(England): Dunhill Cup 1992
(winners)

Stevenson, P
(Ireland): v Scotland 1933-34-35-
36-38; v England 1933-38

Sutton, M
(England): Canada Cup 1955

Taylor, JH
(England): v Scotland 1903-04-05-
06-07-09-10-12-13
(GBI): v America 1921

Taylor, JJ
(England): v Scotland 1937

Taylor, Josh
(England): v Scotland 1913.
(GBI): v America 1921

Thomas, DC
(Wales): Canada Cup 1957-58-59-
60-61-62-63-66; World Cup 1967-
69-70. (GBI): Ryder Cup 1959-63-
65-67

Thompson, R
(Scotland): v England 1903-04-05-
06-07-09-10-12

Tingey, A
(England): v Scotland 1903-05

Torrance, S
(Scotland): World Cup 1976-78-82-84-85-87-89-90-93-95; Dunhill Cup 1985-86-87-89-90-91-93-95 (winners). (GBI): v Europe 1976-78-80-82-84; Ryder Cup 1981-83-85-87-89-91-93-95; v Rest of World 1982. (Eur): Nissan Cup 1985; Four Tours World Chp 1991

Townsend, P
(England): World Cup 1969-74. (GBI): Ryder Cup 1969-71; v Europe 1974

Twine, WT
(England): v Ireland 1932

Vardon, H
(England): (GBI): v America 1921

Vaughan, DI
(Wales): World Cup 1972-73-77-78-79-80

Waites, BJ
(England): World Cup 1980-82-83. (GBI): v Europe 1980-82-84; v Rest of World 1982; Ryder Cup 1983. (Sen) European Cup 1997

Walker, RT
(Scotland): Canada Cup 1964

Wallace, L
(Ireland): v England 1932; v Scotland 1932

Walton P
(Ireland): Dunhill Cup 1989-90 (winners)-92-94-95; World Cup 1995. (Eur): Ryder Cup 1995

Ward, CH
(England): v Ireland 1932. (GBI): Ryder Cup 1947-49-51

Watt, T
(Scotland): v England 1907

Watt, W
(Scotland): v England 1912-13

Way, P
(England): Dunhill Cup 1985; World Cup 1985. (GBI): Ryder Cup 1983-85

Weetman, H
(England): Canada Cup 1954-56-60. (GBI): Ryder Cup 1951-53-55-57-59-61-63

Westwood, L
(England): Dunhill Cup 1996-97. (GBI): Ryder Cup 1997

Whitcombe, CA
(England): v Scotland 1932-33-34-35-36-37-38; v Ireland 1933. (GBI): Ryder Cup 1927-29-31-33-35-37; v France 1929

Whitcombe, EE
(England): v Scotland 1938; v Wales 1938; v Ireland 1938

Whitcombe, ER
(England): v Scotland 1932; v Ireland 1933. (GBI): v America 1926, Ryder Cup 1929-31-35; v France 1929

Whitcombe, RA
(England): v Scotland 1933-34-35-36-37-38. (GBI): Ryder Cup 1935

White, J
(Scotland): v England 1903-04-05-06-07-09-12-13

Wilcock, P
(England): World Cup 1973

Will, G
(Scotland): Canada Cup 1963; World Cup 1969-70. (GBI): Ryder Cup 1963-65-67

Williams, K
(Wales): v Scotland 1937-38; v Ireland 1937; v England 1938

Williamson, T
(England): v Scotland 1904-05-06-07-09-10-12-13

Wilson, RG
(England): v Scotland 1913

Wilson, T
(Scotland): v England 1933-34; v Ireland 1932-33-34

Wolstenholme, GB
(England): Canada Cup 1965

Wood, N
(Scotland): World Cup 1975. (GBI): Ryder Cup 1975

Woosnam, I
(Wales): World Cup 1980-82-83-84-85-87 (winners)-90-91-92-93-94-96-97; Dunhill Cup 1985-86-87-88-89-90-91-93-95. (GBI): v Europe 1982-84; v Rest of World 1982; Ryder Cup 1983-85-87-89-91-93-95-97; v Australia 1988. (Eur): Nissan Cup 1985-86. Kirin Cup 1987; Four Tours World Chp 1989-90

British Isles International Players, Amateur Men

Abbreviations:

CW   Commonwealth Tournament (Team from UK)
Eur T Ch   played in European Team Championship for home country
Home Int   played in Home International matches

Adams, MPD
(Wales): Home Int 1969-70-71-72-75-76-77; Eur T Ch 1971

Aitken, AR
(Scotland): v England 1906-07-08

Alexander, DW
(Scotland): Home Int 1958;
v Scandinavia 1958

Allison, A
(Ireland): v England 1928;
v Scotland 1929

Anderson, N
(Ireland): Home Int 1985-86-87-88-89-90-93. Eur T Ch 1989.
(GBI): v Europe 1988

Anderson, RB
(Scotland): v Scandinavia 1960-62;
Home Int 1962-63

Andrew, R
(Scotland): v England 1905-06-07-08-09-10

Armour, A
(Scotland): v England 1922

Armour, TD
(GBI): v America 1921

Ashby, H
(England): Home Int 1972-73-74.
(GBI): Dominican Int 1973.
(GBI): v Europe 1974

Atkinson, HN
(Wales): v Ireland 1913

Attenborough, M
(England): Home Int 1964-66-67-68; Eur T Ch 1967. (GBI): Walker Cup 1967; v Europe 1966-68

Aylmer, CC
(England): v Scotland 1911-22-23-24. (GBI): v America 1921, Walker Cup 1922

Babington, A
(Ireland): v Wales 1913

Baker, P
(England): Home Int 1985. (GBI):
Walker Cup 1985; v Europe 1986

Baker, RN
(Ireland): Home Int 1975

Ball, J
(England): v Scotland 1902-03-04-05-06-07-08-09-10-11-12

Bamford, JL
(Ireland): Home Int 1954-56

Banks, C
(England): Home Int 1983

Banks, SE
(England): Home Int 1934-38

Bannerman, SJ
(Scotland): Home Int 1988;
v Sweden 1990

Bardsley, R
(England): Home Int 1987;
v France 1988

Barker, HH
(England): v Scotland 1907

Barnett, A
(Wales): Home Int 1989-90-91;
Eur T Chp 1991

Barrie, GC
(Scotland): Home Int 1981-83;
v Sweden 1983

Barry, AG
(England): v Scotland 1906-07

Bathgate, D
(England): Home Int 1990

Bayliss, RP
(England): v Ireland 1929; Home
Int 1933-34

Bayne, PWGA
(Wales): Home Int 1949

Beames, R
(Scotland): Home Int 1995-96;
v Spain 1996; v France, Sweden 1997; (GBI) v Europe 1996

Beamish, CH
(Ireland): Home Int 1950-51-53-56

Beck, JB
(England): v Scotland 1926-30;
Home Int 1933.
(GBI): Walker Cup 1928-38
(Captain) -47 (Captain)

Beddard, JB
(England): v Wales/Ireland 1925;
v Ireland 1929; v Scotland 1927-28-29

Beharrell, JC
(England): Home Int 1956

Bell, HE
(Ireland): v Wales 1930; Home Int 1932

Bell, RK
(England): Home Int 1947

Benka, PJ
(England): Home Int 1967-68-69-70: Eur T Ch 1969. (GBI): Walker Cup 1969; v Europe 1970

Bennett, H
(England): Home Int 1948-49-51

Bennett, S
(England): v Scotland 1979

Bennett, W
(England): Home Int 1992-93-94;
v France 1994. (GBI) v Europe 1994; Eisenhower Trophy 1994

Bentley, AL
(England): Home Int 1936-37;
v France 1937-39

Bentley, HG
(England): *v* Ireland 1931;
v Scotland 1931. Home Int 1932-
33-34-35-36-37-38-47; *v* France
1934-35-36-37-39-54. (GBI):
Walker Cup 1934-36-38

Berry, P
(England): Home Int 1972.
(GBI): *v* Europe 1972

Bevan, RJ
(Wales): Home Int 1964-65-66-67-
73-74

Beveridge, HW
(Scotland): *v* England 1908

Birnie, J
(Scotland): *v* Ireland 1927

Birtwell, SG
(England): Home Int 1968-70-73

Black, D
(Scotland): Home Int 1966-67

Black, FC
(Scotland): Home Int 1962-64-65-
66-68; *v* Scandinavia 1962; Eur T
Ch 1965-67. (GBI): *v* Europe 1966

Black, GT
(Scotland): Home Int 1952-53;
v South Africa 1954

Black, JL
(Wales): Home Int 1932-33-34-35-36

Black, WC
(Scotland): Home Int 1964-65

Blackey, M
(England): *v* France 1994-96;
v Spain 1995; Home Int 1995-96-
97; Eur T Ch 1997

Blackwell, EBH
(Scotland): *v* England 1902-04-05-
06-07-09-10-12-23-24-25

Bladon, W
(England): Home Int 1996;
(GBI) *v* Europe 1996

Blair, DA
(Scotland): Home Int 1948-49-51-
52-53-55-56-57; *v* Scandinavia
1956-58-62. (GBI): Walker Cup
1955-61; CW 1954

Blakeman, D
(England): Home Int 1981;
v France 1982

Bland, R
(England): Home Int 1994-95;
v Spain 1995

Bloice, C
(Scotland): Home Int 1985-86;
v France 1985; Eur T Ch 1985;
v Italy 1986; *v* Sweden 1986.
(GBI): Walker Cup 1985

Bloxham, JA
(England): Home Int 1966

Blyth, AD
(Scotland): *v* England 1904

Bonallack, MF
(England): Home Int 1957-58-59-
60-61-62-63-64-65-66-67-68-69-70-
71-72-73-74; Eur T Ch 1969-71.
(GBI): Walker Cup 1957-59-61-63-
65-67-69 (Captain) -71 (Captain) -
73; *v* Europe 1958-62-64-66-68-70-
72; CW 1959-63-67-71; Eisenhower
Trophy 1960-62-64-66-68-70-72

Bonnell, DJ
(Wales): Home Int 1949-50-51

Bookless, JT
(Scotland): *v* England 1930-31;
v Ireland 1930; *v* Wales 1931

Bottomley, S
(England): Home Int 1986

Bourn, TA
(England): *v* Ireland 1928;
v Scotland 1930; Home Int 1933-
34; *v* France 1934.
(GBI): *v* Australia 1934

Bowen, J
(Ireland): Home Int 1961

Bowman, TH
(England): Home Int 1932

Boxall, R
(England): Home Int 1980-81-82;
v France 1982

Boyd, HA
(Ireland): *v* Wales 1913-23

Bradshaw, AS
(England): Home Int 1932

Bradshaw, EI
(England): *v* Scotland 1979; Eur T
Ch 1979

Brady, E
(Ireland): Home Int 1995

Braid, HM
(Scotland): *v* England 1922-23

Bramston, JAT
(England): *v* Scotland 1902

Brand, GJ
(England): Home Int 1976.
(GBI) *v* Europe 1976

Brand Jr, G
(Scotland): Home Int 1978-80;
v England 1979; Eur T Ch 1979;
v Italy 1979; *v* Belgium 1980;
v France 1980-81. (GBI): Walker

Cup 1979; *v* Europe 1978-80;
Eisenhower Trophy 1978-80

Branigan, D
(Ireland): Home Int 1975-76-77-80-
81-82-86; Eur T Ch 1977-81; *v* West
Germany, France, Sweden 1976

Bretherton, CF
(England): *v* Scotland 1922-23-24-
25; *v* Wales/Ireland 1925

Briscoe, A
(Ireland): *v* England 1928-29-30-
31; *v* Scotland 1929-30-31; *v* Wales
1929-30-31; Home Int 1932-33-38

Bristowe, OC
(GBI): Walker Cup 1923-24

Broad, RD
(Wales): *v* Ireland 1979; Home Int
1980-81-82-84; Eur T Ch 1981

Broadhurst, P
(England): Home Int 1986-87;
v France 1988. (GBI) *v* Europe
1988

Brock, J
(Scotland) *v* Ireland 1929; Home
Int 1932

Brodie, Allan
(Scotland): Home Int 1970-72-73-
74-75-76-77-78-80; Eur T Ch
1973-77-79; *v* England 1979; *v* Italy
1979; *v* Belgium 1977; *v* Spain
1977; *v* France 1978. (GBI): Walker
Cup 1977-79; *v* Europe 1974-76-
78-80; Eisenhower Trophy 1978

Brodie, Andrew
(Scotland): Home Int 1968-69;
v Spain 1974

Bromley-Davenport, E
(England): Home Int 1938-51

Brooks, A
(Scotland): Home Int 1968-69;
Eur T Ch 1969. (GBI): Walker Cup
1969

Brooks, CJ
(Scotland): Home Int 1984-85;
v Sweden 1984-86; *v* Italy 1986.
(GBI): *v* Europe 1986

Brooks, M
(Scotland): *v* Austria 1994; Home
Int 1995-96; *v* Spain 1996;
v France, Sweden 1997; Eur T Ch
1997. (GBI) Walker Cup 1997;
v Europe 1996; Eisenhower Trophy
1996

Brotherston, IR
(Scotland): Home Int 1984-85;
v France 1985; Eur T Ch 1985

Brough, S
(England): Home Int 1952-55-59-
60; *v* France 1952-60. (GBI): *v*
Europe 1960

Brown, CT
(Wales): Home Int 1970-71-72-73-74-75-77-78-80-88 (captain); Eur T Ch 1973; v Denmark 1977-80; v Ireland 1979; v Switzerland, Spain 1980; (GBI) v Walker Cup 1995 (Captain); v Europe 1996 (Captain)

Brown, D
(Wales): v Ireland 1923-30-31; v England 1925; v Scotland 1931

Brown, JC
(Ireland): Home Int 1933-34-35-36-37-38-48-52-53

Brownlow, Hon WGE
(GBI): Walker Cup 1926

Bruen, J
(Ireland): Home Int 1937-38-49-50. (GBI): Walker Cup 1938-49-51

Bryson, WS
(Scotland): Home Int 1991-92-93; v Sweden 1992; v Italy 1992; v France 1993; v Spain 1994

Bucher, AMM
(Scotland): Home Int 1954-55-56; v Scandinavia 1956

Buckley, JA
(Wales): Home Int 1967-68-69-76-77-78; Eur T Ch 1967-69; v Denmark 1976-77. (GBI): Walker Cup 1979

Burch, N
(England): Home Int 1974

Burgess, MJ
(England): Home Int 1963-64-67; Eur T Ch 1967

Burke, J
(Ireland): v England 1929-30-31; v Wales 1929-30-31; v Scotland 1930-31; Home Int 1932-33-34-35-36-37-38-47-48-49. (GBI): Walker Cup 1932

Burns, M
(Ireland): Home Int 1973-75-83

Burns, R
(Ireland): Home Int 1991-92. (GBI): Walker Cup 1993; v Europe 1992; Eisenhower Trophy 1992

Burnside, J
(Scotland): Home Int 1956-57

Burrell, TM
(Scotland): v England 1924

Bussell, AF
(Scotland): Home Int 1956-57-58-61; v Scandinavia 1956-60. (GBI): Walker Cup 1957; v Europe 1956-62

Butterworth, JR
(England): v France 1954

Cage, S
(England): Home Int 1992. (GBI): Walker Cup 1993

Cairnes, HM
(Ireland): v Wales 1913-25; v England 1904; v Scotland 1904-27

Cairns, S
(Scotland): Home Int 1997

Caldwell, I
(England): Home Int 1950-51-52-53-54-55-56-57-58-59-61; v France 1950. (GBI): Walker Cup 1951-55

Calvert, M
(Wales): Home Int 1983-84-86-87-89-91

Cameron, D
(Scotland): Home Int 1938-51

Campbell, A
(Wales): Home Int 1996-97

Campbell, Bart, Sir Guy C
(Scotland): v England 1909-10-11

Campbell, HM
(Scotland): Home Int 1962-64-68; v Scandinavia 1962; v Australia 1964; Eur T Ch 1965-79 (Captain). (GBI): v Europe 1964

Campbell, JGS
(Scotland): Home Int 1947-48

Campbell, W
(Scotland): v Ireland 1927-28-29-30-31; v England 1928-29-30-31; v Wales 1931; Home Int 1933-34-35-36. (GBI): Walker Cup 1930

Cannon, JHS
(England): v Ireland/Wales 1925

Cannon, JM
(Scotland): Home Int 1969; v Spain 1974

Carman, A
(England): v Scotland 1979; Home Int 1980

Carr, FC
(England): v Scotland 1911

Carr, JB
(Ireland): Home Int 1947 to 1969; Eur T Ch 1965-67-69. (GBI): Walker Cup 1947-49-51-53-55-57-59-61-63-65 (Captain) -67 (Captain); v Europe 1954-56-64-66-68; Eisenhower Trophy 1958-60

Carr, JJ
(Ireland): Home Int 1981-82-83

Carr, JP
(Wales): v Ireland 1913

Carr, JR
(Ireland): v Wales 1930-31; v England 1931; Home Int 1933

Carr, R
(Ireland): Home Int 1970-71; Eur T Ch 1971; (GBI): Walker Cup 1971

Carrgill, PM
(England): Home Int 1978

Carrick, DG
(Scotland): Home Int 1981 to 1989; v West Germany 1987; v Italy 1984-86-88; v France 1987-89; v Sweden 1983-84-86; Eur T Ch 1987-89 (Captain)-91 (Captain). (GBI): Walker Cup 1983-87; v Europe 1986

Carroll, CA
(Ireland): v Wales 1924

Carroll, JP
(Ireland): Home Int 1948-49-50-51-62

Carroll, W
(Ireland): v Wales 1913-23-24-25; v England 1925; v Scotland 1929; Home Int 1932

Carslaw, IA
(Scotland): Home Int 1976-77-78-80-81; Eur T Ch 1977-79; v England 1979; v Italy 1979; v Spain 1977; v Belgium 1978; v France 1978-83. (GBI): Walker Cup 1979; v Europe 1978

Carver, M
(England): Home Int 1996; Eur T Ch 1997

Carvill, J
(Ireland): Home Int 1989; Eur T Ch 1989. (GBI): v Europe 1990

Cashell, BG
(Ireland): Home Int 1978; v France, West Germany, Sweden 1978

Cassells, C
(England): Home Int 1989

Castle, H
(England): v Scotland 1903-04

Cater, JR
(Scotland): Home Int 1952-53-54-55-56; v South Africa 1954; v Scandinavia 1956. (GBI): Walker Cup 1955

Caul, P
(Ireland): Home Int 1968-69-71-72-73-74-75

Caven, J
(Scotland): v England 1926. (GBI): Walker Cup 1922

Chapman, BHG
(England): Home Int 1961-62.
(GBI): Walker Cup 1961;
v Europe 1962

Chapman, JA
(Wales): v Ireland 1923-29-30-31;
v Scotland 1931; v England 1925

Chapman, R
(Wales): v Ireland 1929; Home Int
1932-34-35-36

Chapman, R
(England): v Scotland 1979; Home
Int 1980-81; Eur T Ch 1981.
(GBI): Walker Cup 1981; v Europe
1980

Charles, WB
(Wales): v Ireland 1924

Chillas, D
(Scotland): Home Int 1971

Christmas, MJ
(England): Home Int 1960-61-62-
63-64. (GBI): Walker Cup 1961-
63; v Europe 1962-64; Eisenhower
Trophy 1962

Clark, CA
(England): Home Int 1964. (GBI):
Walker Cup 1965; v Europe 1964

Clark, G
(England): Home Int 1995

Clark, GJ
(England): Home Int 1961-64-66-
67-68-71. (GBI): Walker Cup
1965; v Europe 1964-66.

Clark, HK
(England): Home Int 1973.
(GBI): Walker Cup 1973

Clark, MD
(Wales): v Ireland 1947

Clarke, D
(Ireland): Home Int 1987-89;
(GBI): v Europe 1990

Clay, G
(Wales): Home Int 1962

Claydon, R
(England): Home Int 1988; Eur T
Ch 1989; (GBI): Walker Cup 1989

Cleary, T
(Ireland): Home Int 1976-77-78-
82-83-84-85-86; v Wales 1979;
v France, West Germany, Sweden
1976

Clement, G
(Wales): v Ireland 1979

Cochran, JS
(Scotland): Home Int 1966

Collier, B
(Scotland): Home Int 1994;
v Austria 1994

Colt, HS
(England): v Scotland 1908

Coltart, A
(Scotland): Home Int 1988-89-90;
Eur T Ch 1989-91; v Sweden 1990;
v Italy 1990; Nixdorf Nations Cup
1990; v France 1991. (GBI):
Walker Cup 1991; v Europe 1990;
Eisenhower Trophy 1990

Cook, J
(England): Home Int 1989-90

Cook, JH
(England): Home Int 1969

Corcoran, DK
(Ireland): Home Int 1972-73; Eur
T Ch 1973

Corridan, T
(Ireland): Home Int 1983-84-91-92

Cosh, GB
(Scotland): Home Int 1964-65-66-
67-68-69; Eur T Ch 1965-69
(Captain). (GBI): Walker Cup 1965;
v Europe 1966-68; CW 1967;
Eisenhower Trophy 1966-68

Coughlan, R
(Ireland): Home Int 1991-94. (GBI):
Walker Cup 1997; Eur T Ch 1997

Coulter, JG
(Wales): Home Int 1951-52

Coutts, FJ
(Scotland): Home Int 1980-81-82;
Eur T Ch 1981-83; v France 1981-
82-83

Cox, S
(Wales): Home Int 1970-71-72-73-
74; Eur T Ch 1971-73

Crabbe, JL
(Ireland): v Wales 1925; v Scotland
1927-28

Craddock, T
(Ireland): Home Int 1955-56-57-
58-59-60-67-68-69-70; Eur T Ch
1971. (GBI): Walker Cup 1967-69

Craigan, RM
(Ireland): Home Int 1963-64

Crawford, DR
(Scotland): Home Int 1990-91; Eur
T Ch 1991; v France 1991

Crawley, LG
(England): v Ireland 1931;
v Scotland 1931; Home Int 1932-
33-34-36-37-38-47-48-49-54-55;
v France 1936-37-38-49.
(GBI): Walker Cup 1932-34-38-47

Critchley, B
(England): Home Int 1962-69-70;
Eur T Ch 1969. (GBI): Walker Cup
1969; v Europe 1970

Crosbie, GF
(Ireland): Home Int 1953-55-56-
57-88 (captain)

Crowley, M
(Ireland): v England 1928-29-30-31;
v Wales l929-31; v Scotland 1929-
30-31; Home Int 1932

Cuddihy, J
(Scotland): Home Int 1977-78

Curry, DH
(England): Home Int 1984-86-87;
v France 1988. (GBI): Walker Cup
1987; v Europe 1986-88;
Eisenhower Trophy 1986

Dalgleish, CR
(Scotland): Home Int 1981-82-83-
89-95(Captain); Eur T Ch 1982;
Eur T Ch 1981-83-93(Captain)-
95(Captain); Nixdorf Nations Cup
1989. (GBI): Walker Cup 1981;
v Europe 1982

Darwin, B
(England): v Scotland 1902-04-05-
08-09-10-23-24. (GBI): Walker
Cup 1922

Davies, EN
(Wales): Home Int 1959-60-61-62-
63-64-65-66-67-68-69-70-71-72-
73-74; Eur T Ch 1969-71-73

Davies, FE
(Ireland): v Wales 1923

Davies, G
(Wales): v Denmark 1977; Home
Int 1981-82-83

Davies, HE
(Wales): Home Int 1933-34-36

Davies, JC
(England) Home Int 1969-71-72-73-
74-78; Eur T Ch 1973-75-77.(GBI):
Walker Cup 1973-75-77-79;
v Europe 1972-74-76-78; Eisenhower
Trophy 1974-76 (winners)

Davies, M
(England): Home Int 1984-85

Davies, TJ
(Wales): Home Int 1954-55-56-57-
58-58-60

Davison, C
(England): Home Int 1989

Dawson, JE
(Scotland): v Ireland 1927-29-30-
31; v England 1930-31; v Wales
1931; Home Int 1932-33-34-34-37

Dawson, M
(Scotland): Home Int 1963-65-66

Dawson, P
(England): Home Int 1969

De Bendern, Count J (John
de Forest)
(England): v Scotland, Ireland
1931. (GBI): Walker Cup 1932

Deboys, A
(Scotland): Home Int 1956-59-60;
v Scandinavia 1960

Deeble, P
(England): Home Int 1975-76-77-
78-80-81-83-84; v France 1982;
v Scotland 1979; Eur T Ch 1979-
81. (GBI): Walker Cup 1977-81;
v Europe 1978; Colombian Int
1978

Deighton, FWG
(Scotland): Home Int 1950-52-53-
56-58-59-60; v South Africa 1954;
v New Zealand 1954; v Scandinavia
1956. (GBI): Walker Cup 1951-57;
CW 1954-59

Denholm, RB
(Scotland): v Ireland 1927-29-31;
v Wales 1931; v England 1931;
Home Int 1932-33-34

Dewar, FG
(Scotland): Home Int 1952-53-55;
v South Africa 1954; Eur T Ch
1971 (Captain)-73 (Captain)

Dick, CE
(Scotland): v England 1902-03-04-
05-09-12

Dickson, HM
(Scotland): v Ireland 1929-31

Dickson, JR
(Ireland): Eur T Ch 1977; Home
Int 1980

Dinsdale, R
(Wales): Home Int 1991-92-93

Disley, A
(Wales): Home Int 1976-77-78;
v Denmark 1977; v Ireland 1979

Dodd, SC
(Wales):Home Int 1985-87-88-89.
(GBI): Walker Cup 1989

Donald, L
(England): Home Int 1996-97;
v France 1996

Donaldson, J
(Wales): Home Int 1996-97; Eur T
Ch 1997

Donellan, B
(Ireland): Home Int 1952

Dowie, A
(Scotland): Home Int 1949

Downes, P
(England): Home Int 1976-77-78-
80-81-82; Eur T Ch 1977-79-81.
(GBI): v Europe 1980

Downie, D
(Scotland): Home Int 1993-94;
v Italy 1994; v Spain 1994;
v Sweden 1995; v France 1995

Downie, JJ
(England): Home Int 1974

Draper, JW
(Scotland): Home Int 1954

Dredge, B
(Wales): Home Int 1992-93-94-95;
Eur T Ch 1995. (GBI): Walker Cup
1993; Eisenhower Trophy 1992; v
Europe 1994

Drew, NV
(Ireland): Home Int 1952-53.
(GBI): Walker Cup 1953

Drummond, S
(England): Home Int 1995

Duck, R
(England): Home Int 1997

Duffy, I
(Wales): Home Int 1975

Duncan, AA
(Wales): Home Int 1933-34-36-38-
47-48-49-50-51-52-53-54-55-56-57-
58-59. (GBI): Walker Cup (Captain)
1953

Duncan, GT
(Wales): Home Int 1952-53-54-55-
56-57-58

Duncan, J, jr
(Wales): v Ireland 1913

Duncan, J
(Ireland): Home Int 1959-60-61

Dundas, S
(Scotland): Home Int 1992-93

Dunn, NW
(England): v Ireland 1928

Dunn, P
(Wales): Home Int 1957-58-59-60-
61-62-63-65-66

Dunne, D
(Ireland): Home Int 1997

Dunne, E
(Ireland): Home Int 1973-74-76-
77; v Wales 1979; Eur T Ch 1975

Durrant, RA
(England): Home Int 1967; Eur T
Ch 1967

Dykes, JM
(Scotland): Home Int 1934-35-36-
48-49-51. (GBI): Walker Cup 1936

Easingwood, SR
(Scotland): Home Int 1986-87-88-
90; v Italy 1988-90; v France 1987-
89; Eur T Ch 1989

Eaves, CH
(Wales): Home Int 1935-36-38-47-
48-49

Edwards, B
(Ireland): Home Int 1961-62-64-
65-66-67-68-69-73

Edwards, CS
(England): Home Int 1991-92-93-
94-95-97; v France 1992-94-96;
v Spain 1993-95; Eur T Ch 1995

Edwards, M
(Ireland): Home Int 1956-57-58-
60-61-62

Edwards, N
(Wales): Home Int 1995-96-97; Eur
T Ch 1997

Edwards, S
(Wales): Home Int 1992

Edwards, TH
(Wales): Home Int 1947

Egan, TW
(Ireland): Home Int 1952-53-59-
60-62-67-68; Eur T Ch 1967-69

Eggo, R
(England): Home Int 1986-87-88-
89-90; v France 1988.
(GBI): Walker Cup 1987; v Europe
1988

Elliot, A
(Scotland): Home Int 1989;
v France 1989; Eur T Ch 1989

Elliot, C
(Scotland): Home Int 1982;
v France 1983

Elliot, IA
(Ireland): Home Int 1975-77-78;
Eur T Ch 1975, v France, West
Germany, Sweden 1978

Ellis, HC
(England): v Scotland 1902-12

Ellis, M
(Wales): Home Int 1992-93-94-95-
96; (GBI): v Europe 1996

Ellison, TF
(England): v Scotland 1922-25-26-
27

Emerson, T
(Wales): Home Int 1932

Emery, G
(Wales): *v* Ireland 1925; Home Int
1933-36-38

Errity, D
(Ireland): Home Int 1990

Evans, AD
(Wales): *v* Scotland 1931-35;
v Ireland 1931; Home Int 1932-33-
34-35-38-47-49-50-51-52-53-54-
55-56-61

Evans, C
(Wales): Home Int 1990-91-92-93-
94-95; Eur T Ch 1995

Evans, Duncan
(Wales): Home Int 1978-80-81;
v Ireland 1979; Eur T Ch 1981.
(GBI) Walker Cup 1981; *v* Europe
1980

Evans, G
(England): Home Int 1961

Evans, G
(England): Home Int 1990; Eur T
Ch 1991. (GBI) Walker Cup 1991;
Eisenhower Trophy 1990

Evans, HJ
(Wales): Home Int 1976-77-78-80-
81-84-85-87-88; *v* France 1976;
v Denmark 1977-80; *v* Ireland
1979; Eur T Ch 1979-81;
v Switzerland, Spain 1980

Evans, M Gear
(Wales): *v* Ireland 1930-31;
v Scotland 1931

Everett, C
(Scotland): Home Int 1988-89-90;
v Italy 1988-90; *v* France 1988-89-
91; Eur T Ch 1989-91; Nixdorf
Nations Cup 1989-90; *v* Sweden
1990

Ewing, RC
(Ireland): Home Int 1934-35-36-
37-38-47-48-49-50-51-53-54-55-
56-57-58. (GBI): Walker Cup
1936-38-47-49-51-55

Eyles, GR
(England): Home Int 1974-75; Eur
T Ch 1975. (GBI): Walker Cup
1975; *v* Europe 1974; Eisenhower
Trophy 1974

Fairbairn, KA
(England): Home Int 1988

Fairchild, CEL
(Wales): *v* Ireland 1923; *v* England
1925

Fairchild, LJ
(Wales): *v* Ireland 1924

Fairlie, WE
(Scotland): *v* England 1912

Faldo, N
(England): Home Int 1975. (GBI):
CW 1975

Fanagan, J
(Ireland): Home Int 1989 to 1997;
Eur T Ch 1995-97. (GBI): Walker
Cup 1995; *v* Europe 1992-96

Farmer, A
(Scotland): Home Int 1997

Farmer, JC
(Scotland): Home Int 1970

Fenton, P
(England): Home Int 1996

Ferguson, M
(Ireland): Home Int 1952

Ferguson, WJ
(Ireland): Home Int 1952-54-55-
58-59-61

Fergusson, S Mure
(Scotland): *v* England 1902-03-04

Ffrench, WF
(Ireland): *v* Scotland 1929; Home
Int 1932

Fiddian, EW
(England): *v* Scotland 1929-30-31;
v Ireland 1929-30-31; Home Int
1932-33-34-35; *v* France 1934.
(GBI): Walker Cup 1932-34

Fisher, D
(England): Home Int 1993-94;
v France 1994. (GBI): *v* Europe
1994

Fitzgibbon, JF
(Ireland): Home Int 1955-56-57

Fitzsimmons, J
(Ireland): Home Int 1938-47-48

Flaherty, JA
(Ireland): Home Int 1934-35-36-37

Flaherty, PD
(Ireland): Home Int 1967; Eur T
Ch 1967-69

Fleming, J
(Scotland): Home Int 1987

Fleury, RA
(Ireland): Home Int 1974

Flockhart, AS
(Scotland): Home Int 1948-49

Fogarty, GN
(Ireland): Home Int 1956-58-63-
64-67

Fogg, HN
(England): Home Int 1933

Forbes, E
(Scotland): Home Int 1996; *v* Italy
1996; *v* France, Sweden 1997

Forsyth, A
(Scotland): Home Int 1996;
v Italy 1996; *v* France, Sweden
1997; Eur T Ch 1997

Foster, M
(England): Home Int 1994-95;
v Spain 1995; Eur T Ch 1995.
(GBI): Walker Cup 1995

Foster, MF
(England): Home Int 1973

Foster, R
(England): Home Int 1963-64-66-
67-68-69-70-71-72; Eur T Ch
1967-69-71-73. (GBI): Walker Cup
1965-67-69-71-73-79 (Captain) -
81 (Captain); *v* Europe 1964-66-
68-70; CW 1967-71; Eisenhower
Trophy 1964-70-80(Captain)

Fowler, WH
(England): *v* Scotland 1903-04-05

Fox, G
(Scotland): Home Int 1997

Fox, N
(Ireland): Home Int 1996-97; Eur
T Ch 1997

Fox, SJ
(England): Home Int 1956-57-58

Frame, DW
(England): Home Int 1958-59-60-
61-62-63. (GBI): Walker Cup 1961

Francis, F
(England): Home Int 1936; *v* France
1935-36

Frazier, K
(England): Home Int 1938

Froggatt, P
(Ireland): Home Int 1957

Fry, SH
(England): *v* Scotland 1902-03-04-
05-06-07-09

Gairdner, JR
(Scotland): *v* England 1902

Gallacher, BJ
(Scotland): Home Int 1967

Gallacher, S
(Scotland): Home Int 1992-93-94-
95; *v* Italy 1994; *v* Spain 1994;
v Sweden 1995; *v* France 1995; Eur
T Ch 1993-95. (GBI): Walker Cup
1995; Eisenhower Trophy 1994

Galloway, RF
(Scotland): Home Int 1957-58-59;
v Scandinavia 1958

Gannon, MA
(Ireland): Home Int 1973-74-77-
78-80-81-83-84-87-88-89-90;
v France, West Germany, Sweden
1978-80; Eur T Ch 1979-81-89.
(GBI): v Europe 1974-78

Garbutt, I
(England): Home Int 1990-91-92;
Eur T Ch 1991; v France 1992.
(GBI): v Europe 1992

Garner, PF
(England): Home Int 1977-78-80;
v Scotland 1979

Garnet, LG
(England): v France 1934.
(GBI): v Australia 1934

Garson, R
(Scotland): v Ireland 1927-28-29

Gent, J
(England): v Ireland 1930; Home
Int 1938

Gibb, C
(Scotland): v England 1927;
v Ireland 1928

Gibson, WC
(Scotland): Home Int 1950-51

Gilford, CF
(Wales): Home Int 1963-64-65-66-
67

Gilford, D
(England): Home Int 1983-84-85.
(GBI): Walker Cup 1985; v Europe
1986; Eisenhower Trophy 1984

Gill, WJ
(Ireland): v Wales 1931; Home Int
1932-33-34-35-36-37

Gillies, HD
(England): v Scotland 1908-25-26-27

Girvan, P
(Scotland): Home Int 1986; West
Germany 1987; Eur T Ch 1987.
(GBI): Walker Cup 1987

Glossop, R
(Wales): Home Int 1935-37-38-47

Glover, J
(Ireland): Home Int 1951-52-53-
55-59-60-70

Godwin, G
(England): Home Int 1976-77-78-
80-81; v Scotland 1979;
v France 1982; Eur T Ch 1979-81.
(GBI): Walker Cup 1979-81

Goulding, N
(Ireland): Home Int 1988-89-90-
91-92; Eur T Ch 1991

Graham, AJ
(Scotland): v England 1925

Graham, J
(Scotland): v England 1902-03-04-
05-06-07-08-09-10-11

Graham, JSS
(Ireland): Home Int 1938-50-51

Gray, CD
(England): Home Int 1932

Green, CW
(Scotland): Home Int 1961 to
1978; Eur T Ch 1965-67-69-71-73-
75-77-79-81 (Captain)-83 (Captain);
v Scandinavia 1962; v Australia
1964; v Belgium 1973-75-77-78;
v Spain 1977; v Italy 1979; v
England 1979. (GBI): Walker Cup
1963-69-71-73-75-83 (Captain) -
85 (Captain); v Europe 1962-66-
68-70-72-74-76; CW 1971;
Eisenhower Trophy 1970-72-84
(Captain)-86 (Captain)

Green, HB
(England): v Scotland 1979

Green, PO
(England): Home Int 1961-62-63.
(GBI): CW 1963

Greene, R
(Ireland): Home Int 1933

Greig, DG
(Scotland): Home Int 1972-73-75.
(GBI): CW 1975

Greig, K
(Scotland): Home Int 1933

Gribben, P
(Ireland): Home Int 1997

Griffiths, HGB
(Wales): v Ireland 1923-24-25

Griffiths, HS
(Wales): v England 1958

Griffiths, JA
(Wales): Home Int 1933

Guerin, M
(Ireland): Home Int 1961-62-63

Guild, WJ
(Scotland): v England 1925-27-28;
v Ireland 1927-28

Hales, JP
(Wales): v Scotland 1963

Hall, A
(Wales): Home Int 1994

Hall, AH
(Scotland): Home Int 1962-66-69

Hall, D
(Wales): Home Int 1932-37

Hall, K
(Wales): Home Int 1955-59

Hambro, AV
(England): v Scotland 1905-08-09-
10-22

Hamilton, CJ
(Wales): v Ireland 1913

Hamilton, ED
(Scotland): Home Int 1936-37-38

Hamer, S
(England): Home Int 1983-84

Hanway, M
(Ireland): Home Int 1971-74

Hardman, RH
(England): v Scotland 1927-28.
(GBI): Walker Cup 1928

Hare, A
(England): Home Int 1988; Eur T
Ch 1989. (GBI) Walker Cup 1989

Hare, WCD
(Scotland): Home Int 1953; v New
Zealand 1954

Harpin, L
(Wales): Home Int 1996

Harrhy, A
(Wales): Home Int 1988-89-95

Harrington, J
(Ireland): Home Int 1960-61-74-75-
76; Eur T Ch 1975; v Wales 1979

Harrington, P
(Ireland): Home Int 1990-91-92-
93-94-95; Eur T Ch 1991-95.
(GBI): Walker Cup 1991-93-95;
v Europe 1992-94

Harris, D
(Wales): Home Int 1997

Harris, G
(England): Home Int 1994; v Spain
1995; Eur T Ch 1995

Harris, IR
(Scotland): Home Int 1955-56-58-59

Harris, R
(Scotland): v England 1905-08-10-
11-12-22-23-24-25-26-27-28
(GBI): Walker Cup 1922 (Captain)
-23 (Captain) -26 (Captain)

Harrison, JW
(Wales): Home Int 1937-50

Hartley, RW
(England): v Scotland 1926-27-28-
29-30-31; v Ireland 1928-29-30-31;
Home Int 1933-34-35. (GBI):
Walker Cup 1930-32

Hartley, WL
(England): v Ireland/Wales 1925;
v Scotland 1927-31;v Ireland 1928-
31; Home Int 1932-33; v France
1935.(GBI): Walker Cup 1932

Hassall, JE
(England): v Scotland 1923;
v Ireland/Wales 1925

Hastings, JL
(Scotland): Home Int 1957-58;
v Scandinavia 1958

Hawksworth, J
(England): Home Int 1984-85.
(GBI): Walker Cup 1985

Hay, G
(Scotland): v England 1979; Home
Int 1980-88-90-91-92; v Belgium
1980; v France 1980-82-89-91-93;
v Italy 1988-92-94; v Sweden 1992;
v Spain 1994; Eur T Ch 1991-93.
(GBI): v Europe 1980; Walker Cup
1991

Hay, J
(Scotland): Home Int 1972

Hayes, JA
(Ireland): Home Int 1977

Hayward, CH
(England): v Scotland 1925;
v Ireland 1928

Healy, TM
(Ireland): v Scotland 1931;
v England 1931

Heather, D
(Ireland): Home Int 1976; v France,
West Germany, Sweden 1976

Hedges, PJ
(England): Home Int 1970-73-74-
75-76-77-78-82-83; Eur T Ch
1973-75-77. (GBI): Walker Cup
1973-75; v Europe 1974-76;
Eisenhower Trophy 1996

Hegarty, J
(Ireland): Home Int 1975

Hegarty, TD
(Ireland): Home Int 1957

Helm, AGB
(England): Home Int 1948

Henderson, J
(Ireland): v Wales 1923

Henderson, N
(Scotland): Home Int 1963-64

Henriques, GLQ
(England): v Ireland 1930

Henry, W
(England): Home Int 1987;
v France 1988

Herlihy, B
(Ireland): Home Int 1950

Herne, KTC
(Wales): v Ireland 1913

Heverin, AJ
(Ireland): Home Int 1978; v France,
West Germany, Sweden 1978

Hezlet, CO
(Ireland): v Wales 1923-25-27-29-
31; v Scotland 1927-28-29-30-31;
v England 1929-30-31. (GBI):
Walker Cup 1924-26-28; v South
Africa 1927

Higgins, D
(Ireland): Home Int 1993-94

Higgins, L
(Ireland): Home Int 1968-70-71

Hill, GA
(England): Home Int 1936-37.
(GBI): Walker Cup 1936-55 (Captain)

Hilton, HH
(England): v Scotland 1902-03-04-
05-06-07-09-10-11-12

Hird, K
(Scotland): Home Int 1987-88-89;
Nixdorf Nations Cup 1989; v Italy
1990

Hislop, C
(Scotland): Home Int 1994-96;
v Austria 1994; v Italy 1996

Hoad, PGJ
(England): Home Int 1978;
v Scotland 1979

Hodgson, C
(England): v Scotland 1924

Hodgson, J
(England): Home Int 1994

Hoey, TBC
(Ireland): Home Int 1970-71-72-
73-77-84; Eur T Ch 1971-77

Hogan, P
(Ireland): Home Int 1985-86-87-
88; Eur T Ch 1991

Holderness, Sir EWE
(England): v Scotland 1922-23-24-
25-26-28. (GBI): v America 1921,
Walker Cup 1923-26-30

Holmes, AW
(England): Home Int 1962

Homer, TWB
(England): Home Int 1972-73; Eur
T Ch 1973. (GBI): Walker Cup
1973; v Europe 1972; Eisenhower
Trophy 1972

Homewood, G
(England): Home Int 1985-91;
Eur T Ch 1991

Hooman, CVL
(England): v Scotland 1910-22.
(GBI): Walker Cup 1922-23

Hope, WL
(Scotland): v England 1923-25-26-
27-28-29. (GBI): Walker Cup
1923-24-28

Horne, A
(Scotland): Home Int 1971

Horne, S
(Scotland): Home Int 1997

Hosie, JR
(Scotland): Home Int 1936

Houston, G
(Wales): Home Int 1990-91-92-93-
94-95; Eur T Ch 1991-95

Howard, DB
(Scotland): v England 1979; Home
Int 1980-81-82-83-93-94-95-96;
v Belgium 1980; v France 1980-81-
83-95-97; v Italy 1984-94; v Spain
1994-96; v Sweden 1995-97. Eur T
Ch 1981-95-97; (GBI): Walker Cup
1995-97; v Europe 1980-94-96;
Eisenhower Trophy 1996

Howell, D
(England): Home Int 1994-95;
v Spain 1995; Eur T Ch 1995.
(GBI) Walker Cup 1995

Howell, HR
(Wales): v Ireland 1923-24-25-29-
30-31; v England 1925; v Scotland
1931; Home Int 1932-34-35-36-37-
38-47

Howell, H Logan
(Wales): v Ireland 1925

Huddy, G
(England): Home Int 1960-61-62.
(GBI): Walker Cup 1961

Huggan, J
(Scotland): Home Int 1981-82-83-
84; v France 1982-83; v Sweden
1983; v Italy 1984; Eur T Ch 1981

Hughes, I
(Wales): Home Int 1954-55-56

Hulme, WJ
(Ireland): Home Int 1955-56-57

Humphrey, JG
(Wales): v Ireland 1925

Humphreys, AR
(Ireland): v England 1957

Humphreys, DI
(Wales): Home Int 1972

Humphreys, W
(England): Home Int 1970-71; Eur
T Ch 1971. (GBI): Walker Cup
1971; v Europe 1970

Hunter, NM
(Scotland): *v* England 1903-12

Hunter, R
(Scotland): Home Int 1996

Hunter, WI
(Scotland): *v* England 1922

Hutcheon, I
(Scotland): Home Int 1971-72-73-74-75-76-77-78-80; *v* Belgium 1973-75-77-78-80; *v* Spain 1977; *v* France 1978-80-81; *v* Italy 1979; *v* Sweden 1983; Eur T Ch 1973-75-77-79-81. (GBI): Walker Cup 1975-77-79-81; *v* Europe 1974-76; Eisenhower Trophy 1974-76 (winners)-80; CW 1975; Dominican Int 1973; Colombian Int 1975

Hutchings, C
(England): *v* Scotland 1902

Hutchinson, HG
(England): *v* Scotland 1902-03-04-06-07-09

Hutchison, CK
(Scotland): *v* England 1904-05-06-07-08-09-10-11-12

Hutt, R
(England): Home Int 1991-92-93

Hutton, R
(Ireland): Home Int 1991

Hyde, GE
(England): Home Int 1967-68

Illingworth, G
(England): *v* Scotland 1929; *v* France 1937

Inglis, MJ
(England): Home Int 1977

Isitt, GH
(Wales): *v* Ireland 1923

Jack, RR
(Scotland): Home Int 1950-51-54-55-56-57-58-59-61; *v* New Zealand 1954; *v* Scandinavia 1956-58. (GBI): Walker Cup 1957-59; *v* Europe 1956; Eisenhower Trophy 1958; CW 1959

Jack, WS
(Scotland): Home Int 1955

Jacob, NE
(Wales): Home Int 1932-33-34-35-36

James, D
(Scotland): Home Int 1985

James, L
(England): Home Int 1993-94-95; *v* France 1994; *v* Spain 1995; Eur T Ch 1995. (GBI): Walker Cup 1995; *v* Europe 1994; Eisenhower Trophy 1994

James, M
(England): Home Int 1974-75; Eur T Ch 1975. (GBI): Walker Cup 1975

James, RD
(England): Home Int 1974-75

Jameson, JF
(Ireland): *v* Wales 1913-24

Jamieson, A, jr
(Scotland): *v* England 1927-28-31; *v* Ireland 1928-31; *v* Wales 1931; Home Int 1932-33-36-37. (GBI): Walker Cup 1926

Jamieson, D
(Scotland): Home Int 1980

Jenkins, JLC
(Scotland): *v* England 1908-12-22-24-26-28; *v* Ireland 1928. (GBI): *v* America 1921

Jermine, JG
(Wales): Home Int 1972-73-74-75-76-82; Eur T Ch 1975-77; *v* France 1975

Jobson, RH
(England): *v* Ireland 1928

Johnson, R
(Wales): Home Int 1990-92-93-94; Eur T Ch 1991. (GBI) *v* Europe 1994

Johnson, TWG
(Ireland): *v* England 1929

Johnstone, JW
(Scotland): Home Int 1970-71

Jones, A
(Wales): Home Int 1989-90; Eur T Ch 1991

Jones, DK
(Wales): Home Int 1973

Jones, EO
(Wales): Home Int 1983-85-86

Jones, JG Parry
(Wales): Home Int 1959-60

Jones, JL
(Wales): Home Int 1933-34-36

Jones, JR
(Wales): Home Int 1970-72-73-77-78-80-81-82-83-84-85; Eur T Ch 1973-79-81; *v* Denmark 1976-80; *v* Ireland 1979; *v* Switzerland, Spain 1980; *v* Ireland 1979

Jones, JW
(England): Home Int 1948-49-50-51-52-54-55

Jones, KG
(Wales): Home Int 1988

Jones, MA
(Wales): Home Int 1947-48-49-50-51-53-54-57

Jones, Malcolm F
(Wales): Home Int 1933

Jones, SP
(Wales): Home Int 1981-82-83-84-85-86-88-89-91-93

Kane, RM
(Ireland): Home Int 1967-68-71-72-74-78; Eur T Ch 1971-79; *v* Wales 1979. (GBI): *v* Europe 1974

Kearney, K
(Ireland): Home Int 1988-89-90-92-94-95-97

Keenan, S
(Ireland): Home Int 1989

Kelleher, WA
(Ireland): Home Int 1962

Kelley, MJ
(England): Home Int 1974-75-76-77-78-80-81-82-88(Captain); *v* France 1982; Eur T Ch 1977-79. (GBI): Walker Cup 1977-79; *v* Europe 1976-78; Eisenhower Trophy 1976 (winners); Colombian Int 1978

Kelley, PD
(England): Home Int 1965-66-68

Kelly, L
(Scotland): Home Int 1997

Kelly, NS
(Ireland): Home Int 1966

Keppler, SD
(England): Home Int 1982-83; *v* France 1982. (GBI): Walker Cup 1983

Kilduff, AJ
(Ireland): *v* Scotland 1928

Killey, GC
(Scotland): *v* Ireland 1928

King, M
(England): Home Int 1969-70-71-72-73; Eur T Ch 1971-73 (GBI): Walker Cup 1969-73; *v* Europe 1970-72; CW 1971

Kirkpatrick, D
(Scotland): Home Int 1992; *v* France 1993; Eur T Ch 1993

Kissock, B
(Ireland): Home Int 1961-62-74-76; v France, West Germany, Sweden 1978

Kitchin, JE
(England): v France 1949

Knight, B
(Wales): Home Int 1986

Knight, J
(England): v France 1996

Knipe, RG
(Wales): Home Int 1953-54-55-56

Knowles, ST
(Scotland): Home Int 1990-91-92; v France 1991

Knowles, WR
(Wales): v England 1948

Kyle, AT
(Scotland): Home Int 1938-47-49-50-51-52-53.
(GBI): Walker Cup 1938-47-51; v South Africa 1952

Kyle, DH
(Scotland): v England 1924-30.
(GBI): Walker Cup 1924

Kyle, EP
(Scotland): v England 1925

Laidlay, JE
(Scotland): v England 1902-03-04-05-06-07-08-09-10-11

Lake, AD
(Wales): Home Int 1958

Lang, JA
(Scotland): v England 1929-31; v Ireland 1929-30-31; v Wales 1931. (GBI): Walker Cup 1930

Langley, JDA
(England): Home Int 1950-51-52-53; v France 1950. (GBI): Walker Cup 1936-51-53

Langmead, J
(England): Home Int 1986

Lassen, EA
(England): v Scotland 1909-10-11-12

Last, CN
(Wales): Home Int 1975

Laurence, C
(England): Home Int 1983-84-85

Lawrie, CD
(Scotland): Home Int 1949-50-55-56-57-58; v Sweden 1950; v Scandinavia 1956-58. (GBI): Walker Cup 1961 (Captain) -63 (Captain); v South Africa 1952; v Europe 1960

(Captain)-62 (Captain); Eisenhower Trophy 1960 (Captain)-62 (Captain)

Lawrie, GA
(Scotland): Home Int 1990-91; Eur T Ch 1991

Lawrie P
(Ireland): Home Int 1996; Eur T Ch 1997

Layton, EN
(England): v Scotland 1922-23-26; v Ireland/Wales 1925

Lee, IGF
(Scotland): Home Int 1958-59-60-61-62; v Scandinavia 1960

Lee, JN
(Wales): Home Int 1988-89; Eur T Ch 1991

Lee, M
(England): Home Int 1950

Lee, MG
(England): Home Int 1965

Lehane, N
(Ireland): Home Int 1976; v France, West Germany, Sweden 1976

Lewis, DH
(Wales): Home Int 1935-36-37-38

Lewis, DR
(Wales): v Ireland 1925-29-30-31; v Scotland 1931; Home Int 1932-34

Lewis, ME
(England): Home Int 1980-81-82; v France 1982. (GBI): Walker Cup 1983

Lewis, R Cofe
(Wales): v Ireland 1925

Leyden, PJ
(Ireland): Home Int 1953-55-56-57-59

Lincoln, AC
(England): v Scotland 1907

Lindsay, J
(Scotland): Home Int 1933-34-35-36

Little, E
(Scotland): v Italy 1996

Lloyd, HM
(Wales): v Ireland 1913

Lloyd, RM de
(Wales): v Scotland 1931; v Ireland 1931; Home Int 1932-33-34-35-36-37-38-47-48

Llyr, A
(Wales): Home Int 1984-85

Lockhart, G
(Scotland): v England 1911-12

Lockley, AE
(Wales): Home Int 1956-57-58-62

Logan, GW
(England): Home Int 1973

Long, D
(Ireland): Home Int 1973-74-80-81-82-83-84; v Wales 1979; Eur T Ch 1979

Low, AJ
(Scotland): Home Int 1964-65; Eur T Ch 1965; v Australia 1964

Low, JL
(Scotland): v England 1904

Lowdon, CJ
(Scotland): v Ireland 1927

Lowe, A
(Ireland): v Wales 1924; v England 1925-28; v Scotland 1927-28

Lowson, AG
(Scotland): Home Int 1989-90-91-97; v Sweden 1990-92; v Italy 1992

Lucas, D
(England): Home Int 1996

Lucas, PB
(England): Home Int 1936-48-49; v France 1936. (GBI): Walker Cup 1936-47-49 (Captain)

Ludwell, N
(England): Home Int 1991; v France 1992

Lunt, MSR
(England): Home Int 1956-57-58-59-60-62-63-64-66. (GBI): Walker Cup 1959-61-63-65; v Europe 1964; CW 1963; Eisenhower Trophy 1964

Lunt, S
(England): Home Int 1932-33-34-35; v France 1934-35-39

Lygate, M
(Scotland): Home Int 1970-75-88 (Captain); Eur T Ch 1971-85 (Captain)-87 (Captain)

Lyle, AWB
(England): Home Int 1975-76-77; Eur T Ch 1977. (GBI): Walker Cup 1977; CW 1975; v Europe 1976

Lynn, D
(England): Home Int 1995

Lyon, JS
(England): Home Int 1937-38

Lyons, P
(Ireland): Home Int 1986

McAllister, SD
(Scotland): Home Int 1983;
v Sweden 1983; Eur T Ch 1983

Macara, MA
(Wales): Home Int 1983-84-85-87-
89-90-91-92-93

McArthur, W
(Scotland): Home Int 1952-54;
v South Africa 1954

McBeath, J
(Scotland): Home Int 1964

McBride, D
(Scotland): Home Int 1932

McCallum, AR
(Scotland): v England 1929. (GBI):
Walker Cup 1928

McCarrol, F
(Ireland): Home Int 1968-69

McCart, DM
(Scotland): Home Int 1977-78;
v Belgium 1978; v France 1978

McCarthy, L
(Ireland): Home Int 1953-54-55-56

McConnell, FP
(Ireland): v Wales 1929-30-31;
v England 1929-30-31;v Scotland
1930-31; Home Int 1934

McConnell, RM
(Ireland): v Wales 1924-25-29-30-
31; v England 1925-28-29-30-31;
v Scotland 1927-28-29-31; Home
Int 1934-35-36-37

McConnell, WG
(Ireland): v England 1925

McCormack, JD
(Ireland): v Wales 1913-24;
v England 1928, Home Int 1932-
33-34-35-36-37

McCormick, A
(Ireland): Home Int 1997

McCrea, WE
(Ireland): Home Int 1965-66-67;
Eur T Ch 1965

McCready, SM
(Ireland): Home Int 1947-49-50-
52-54. (GBI): Walker Cup 1949-51

McDaid, B
(Ireland): v Wales 1979

MacDonald, GK
(Scotland): Home Int 1978-81-82; v
England 1979; v France 1981-82-83

McDonald, H
(Scotland): Home Int 1970

Macdonald, JS
(Scotland): Home Int 1969-70-71-
72; v Belgium 1973; Eur T Ch
1971. (GBI): Walker Cup 1971;
v Europe 1970

McEvoy, P
(England): Home Int 1976-77-78-
80-81-83-84-85-86-87-88-89-91,
Captain 1994 to 1997; v Scotland
1979; v France 1982-88-92; Eur T
Ch 1977-79-81-89; (GBI): Walker
Cup 1977-79-81-85-89; v Europe
1978-80-86-88; Eisenhower Trophy
1978-80-84-86-88 (winners)

Macfarlane, CB
(Scotland): v England 1912

McGimpsey, G
(Ireland): Home Int 1978 and 1980
to 1997; v Wales 1979; Eur T Ch
1981-89-91-95-97. (GBI): Walker
Cup 1985-89-91; v Europe 1986-
88-90-92; Eisenhower Trophy
1984-86-88 (winners)

McGinley, M
(Ireland): Home Int 1996

McGinley, P
(Ireland): Home Int 1989-90; Eur T
Ch 1991. (GBI): Walker Cup 1991

Macgregor, A
(Scotland): v Scandinavia 1956

Macgregor, G
(Scotland): Home Int 1969 to 1976,
1980 to 1987; v Belgium 1973-75-
80; v England 1979; v Sweden 1983-
84-86; v Italy 1984-86; v France
1981-82-85-87; Eur T Ch 1971-73-
75-81-83-85-87. (GBI): Walker Cup
1971-75-83-85-87-91 (Captain)-93
(Captain); v Europe 1970-74-84;
CW 1971-75; Eisenhower Trophy
1982

MacGregor, RC
(Scotland): Home Int 1951-52-53-
54; v New Zealand 1954. (GBI):
Walker Cup 1953

McGuire, M
(England): Home Int 1992

McHenry, J
(Ireland): Home Int 1985-86.
(GBI): Walker Cup 1987

McInally, H
(Scotland): Home Int 1937-47-48

McInally, RH
(Ireland): Home Int 1949-51

McIntosh, EA
(Scotland): Home Int 1989

Macintosh, KW
(Scotland): v England 1979; Home

Int 1980; v France 1980; v Belgium
1980. (GBI): v Europe 1980

McKay, G
(Scotland): Home Int 1969

McKay, JR
(Scotland): Home Int 1950-51-52-
54; v New Zealand 1954

McKellar, PJ
(Scotland): Home Int 1976-77-78;
v Belgium 1978; v France 1978;
v England 1979. (GBI): Walker
Cup 1977; v Europe 1978

Mackenzie, F
(Scotland): v England 1902-03

MacKenzie, S
(Scotland): Home Int 1990-93-94-
95-96-97; v Italy 1994; v Spain
1994-96; v France, Sweden 1997

Mackenzie, WW
(Scotland): v England 1923-26-27-
29; v Ireland 1930. (GBI): Walker
Cup 1922-23

Mackeown, HN
(Ireland): Home Int 1973; Eur T
Ch 1973

McKibbin, H
(Scotland): Home Int 1994-95;
v Sweden 1995; v France 1995; Eur
T Ch 1995; v Spain 1996

Mackie, GW
(Scotland): Home Int 1948-50

McKinlay, SL
(Scotland): v England 1929-30-31;
v Ireland 1930; v Wales 1931;
Home Int 1932-33-35-37-47.
(GBI): Walker Cup 1934

McKinna, RA
(Scotland): Home Int 1938

McKinnon, A
(Scotland): Home Int 1947-52

McLean, D
(Wales): Home Int 1968-69-70-71-
72-73-74-75-76-77-78-80-81-82-
83-85-86-88-90; Eur T Ch 1975-
77-79-81; v France 1975-76;
v Denmark 1976-80; v Ireland
1979; v Switzerland, Spain 1980

McLean, J
(Scotland): Home Int 1932-33-34-
35-36. (GBI): Walker Cup 1934-
36; v Australia 1934

McLeod, AE
(Scotland): Home Int 1937-38

McLeod, WS
(Scotland): Home Int 1935-37-38-
47-48-49-50-51; v Sweden 1950

McMenamin, E
(Ireland): Home Int 1981

McMullan, C
(Ireland): Home Int 1933-34-35

McNair, AA
(Scotland): v Ireland 1929

MacNamara, L
(Ireland): Home Int 1977-83-84-85-86-87-88-89-90-91-92;
Eur T Ch 1977-91

McNeill, G
(Ireland): Home Int 1991-93

McRuvie, EA
(Scotland): v England 1929-30-31;
v Ireland 1930-31; v Wales 1931;
Home Int 1932-33-34-35-36. (GBI):
Walker Cup 1932-34

McTear, J
(Scotland): Home Int 1971

Madeley, JFD
(Ireland): Home Int 1959-60-61-62-63-64. (GBI): Walker Cup 1963;
v Europe 1962

Mahon, RJ
(Ireland): Home Int 1938-52-54-55

Maliphant, FR
(Wales): Home Int 1932

Malone, B
(Ireland): Home Int 1959-64-69-71-75; Eur T Ch 1971-75

Manford, GC
(Scotland): v England 1922-23

Manley, N
(Ireland): v Wales 1924; v England
1928; v Scotland 1927-28

Mann, LS
(Scotland): Home Int 1982-83;
v Sweden 1983; Eur T Ch 1983.
(GBI): Walker Cup 1983

Marchbank, B
(Scotland): Home Int 1978; v Italy
1979; Eur T Ch 1979. (GBI):
Walker Cup 1979; v Europe 1976-78; Eisenhower Trophy 1978

Marks, GC
(England): Home Int 1963-67-68-69-70-71-74-75-82; Eur T Ch 1967-69-71-75; v France 1982 (Captain).
(GBI): Walker Cup 1969-71-87
(Captain)-89 (Captain); v Europe
1968-70; Eisenhower Trophy 1970;
CW 1975; Colombian Int 1975.

Marren, JM
(Ireland): v Wales 1925

Marsden, G
(Wales): Home Int 1994

Marsh, DM
(England): Home Int 1956-57-58-59-60-64-66-68-69-70-71-72; Eur
T Ch 1971. (GBI): Walker Cup
1959-71-73 (Captain) -75
(Captain); v Europe 1958

Marshman, A
(Wales): Home Int 1952

Marston, CC
(Wales): v Ireland 1929-30-31;
v Scotland 1931

Martin, DHR
(England): Home Int 1938;
v France 1934-49

Martin, GNC
(Ireland): v Wales 1923-29;
v Scotland 1928-29-30; v England
1929-30. (GBI): Walker Cup 1928

Martin, S
(Scotland): Home Int 1975-76-77;
Eur T Ch 1977; v Belgium 1977;
v Spain 1977. (GBI): Walker Cup
1977; v Europe 1976; Eisenhower
Trophy 1976 (winners)

Mason, SC
(England): Home Int 1973

Mathias-Thomas, FEL
(Wales): v Ireland 1924-25

Matthews, RL
(Wales): Home Int 1935-37

Maxwell, R
(Scotland): v England 1902-03-04-05-06-07-09-10

Mayo, PM
(Wales): Home Int 1982-87.
(GBI): Walker Cup 1985-87

Meharg, W
(Ireland): Home Int 1957

Melia, TJ
(Wales): Home Int 1976-77-78-80-81-82; v Ireland 1979; Eur T Ch
1977-79; v Denmark 1976-80;
v Switzerland, Spain 1980

Mellin, GL
(England): v Scotland 1922

Melville, LM Balfour
(Scotland): v England 1902-03

Melville, TE
(Scotland): Home Int 1974

Menzies, A
(Scotland): v England 1925

Metcalfe, J
(England): Home Int 1989.
(GBI) v Europe 1990

Micklem, GH
(England): Home Int 1947-48-49-50-51-52-53-54-55. (GBI): Walker
Cup 1947-49-53-55-57 (Captain)-59 (Captain); Eisenhower Trophy
1958 (Captain)

Mill, JW
(Scotland): Home Int 1953-54

Millensted, DJ
(England): Home Int 1966; Eur T
Ch 1967. (GBI): Walker Cup 1967;
CW 1967

Miller, AC
(Scotland): Home Int 1954-55

Miller, MJ
(Scotland): Home Int 1974-75-77-78; v Belgium 1978; v France 1978

Milligan, JW
(Scotland): Home Int 1986-87-88-89-90-91-92; v West Germany 1987;
v Italy 1988-90-92; v France 1987-89-91; Eur T Ch 1987-89-91;
Nixdorf Nations Cup 1989; v
Sweden 1986-90-92. (GBI): Walker
Cup 1989-91; Eisenhower Trophy
1988(winners)-90; v Europe 1988-92

Mills, ES
(Wales): Home Int 1957

Millward, EB
(England): Home Int 1950-52-53-54-55. (GBI): Walker Cup 1949-55

Milne, WTG
(Scotland): Home Int 1972-73;
Eur T Ch 1973; v Belgium 1973.
(GBI): Walker Cup 1973

Mitchell, A
(England): v Scotland 1910-11-12

Mitchell, CS
(England): Home Int 1975-76-78

Mitchell, FH
(England): v Scotland 1906-07-08

Mitchell, JWH
(Wales): Home Int 1964-65-66

Moffat, DM
(England): Home Int 1961-63-67;
v France 1959-60

Moir, A
(Scotland): Home Int 1983-84;
v Sweden 1984; v Italy 1984;
v France 1985; Eur T Ch 1985.
(GBI): v Europe 1984

Montgomerie, CS
(Scotland): Home Int 1984-85-86;
v West Germany 1987; v Sweden
1984-86; v Italy 1984; v France
1985; Eur T Ch 1985-87. (GBI):
Walker Cup 1985-87; v Europe
1986; Eisenhower Trophy 1984-86

Montgomerie, JS
(Scotland): Home Int 1957;
v Scandinavia 1958; Eur T Ch 1965
(Captain)

Montmorency, RH de
(England): v Scotland 1908;
v Wales/Ireland 1925; v South
Africa 1927. (GBI): v America 1921

Moody, JV
(Wales): Home Int 1947-48-49-51-
56-58-59-60-61

Moody, PH
(England): Home Int 1971-72.
(GBI): v Europe 1972

Moore, GJ
(Ireland): v England 1928; v Wales
1929

Morgan, JL
(Wales): 1948-49-50-51-52-53-54-
55-56-57-58-59-60-61-62-64-68.
(GBI): Walker Cup 1951-53-55

Morris, FS
(Scotland): Home Int 1963

Morris, JC
(Ireland): Home Int 1993-94-95-
96-97; Eur T Ch 1995

Morris, MF
(Ireland): Home Int 1978-80-82-83-
84; v Wales 1979; Eur T Ch 1979;
v France, W. Germany, Sweden
1980

Morris, R
(Wales): Home Int 1983-86-87

Morris, TS
(Wales): v Ireland 1924-29-30

Morrison, JH
(Scotland): v Scandinavia 1960

Morrison, JSF
(England): v Ireland 1930

Morrow, AJC
(Ireland): Home Int 1975-83-92-
93-96-97

Morrow, JM
(Wales): v Ireland 1979; Home
Int 1980-81; Eur T Ch 1979-81;
v Denmark 1980, v Switzerland
1980, v Spain 1980

Mosey, IJ
(England): Home Int 1971

Moss, AV
(Wales): Home Int 1965-66-68

Mouland, MG
(Wales): Home Int 1978-81;
v Ireland 1979; Eur T Ch 1979

Moxon, GA
(Wales): v Ireland 1929-30

Mulcare, P
(Ireland): Home Int 1968-69-70-
71-72-74-78-80; v France, West
Germany, Sweden 1978-80; Eur T
Ch 1975-79. (GBI): Walker Cup
1975; v Europe 1972

Mulholland, D
(Ireland): Home Int 1988

Munn, E
(Ireland): v Wales 1913-23-24;
v Scotland 1927

Munn, L
(Ireland): v Wales 1913-23-24;
Home Int 1936-37

Munro, RAG
(Scotland): Home Int 1960

Murdoch, D
(Scotland): Home Int 1964

Murphy, AR
(Scotland): Home Int 1961-67

Murphy, G
(Ireland): Home Int 1992-93-94-
95; Eur T Ch 1995

Murphy, P
(Ireland): Home Int 1985-86

Murray, GH
(Scotland): Home Int 1973-74-75-
76-77-78-83; v Spain 1974-77;
v Belgium 1975-77; Eur T Ch
1975-77. (GBI): Walker Cup 1977;
v Europe 1978

Murray, P
(Ireland): Home Int 1995-96

Murray, SWT
(Scotland): Home Int 1959-60-61-
62-63; v Scandinavia 1960. (GBI):
Walker Cup 1963; v Europe 1958-62

Murray, WA
(Scotland): v England 1923-24-25-
26-27. (GBI): Walker Cup 1923-24

Murray, WB
(Scotland): Home Int 1967-68-69;
Eur T Ch 1969

Muscroft, R
(England): Home Int 1986

Nash A
(England): Home Int 1988-89

Neech, DG
(England): Home Int 1961

Neill, JH
(Ireland): Home Int 1938-47-48-49

Neill, R
(Scotland): Home Int 1936

Nelson, P
(England): v France 1996

Nestor, JM
(Ireland): Home Int 1962-63-64

Nevin, V
(Ireland): Home Int 1960-63-65-
67-69-72; Eur T Ch 1967-69-73

Newey, AS
(England): Home Int 1932

Newman, JE
(Wales): Home Int 1932

Newton, H
(Wales): v Ireland 1929

Nicholson, J
(Ireland): Home Int 1932

Nolan, K
(Ireland): Home Int 1992-93-94-
95-96; Eur T Ch 1995-97. (GBI):
Walker Cup 1997; v Europe 1996;
Eisenhower Trophy 1996

Noon, GS
(Wales): Home Int 1935-36-37

Noon, J
(Scotland): Home Int 1987

O'Boyle, P
(Ireland): Eur T Ch 1977

O'Brien, MD
(Ireland): Home Int 1968-69-70-
71-72-75-76-77; Eur T Ch 1971;
v France, West Germany, Sweden
1976

O'Carroll, C
(Wales): Home Int 1989-90-91-92-
93; Eur T Ch 1991

O'Connell, A
(Ireland): Home Int 1967-70-71

O'Connell, E
(Ireland): Home Int 1985; Eur T
Ch 1989. (GBI): Walker Cup 1989;
v Europe 1988; Eisenhower Trophy
1988 (winners)

O'Leary, JE
(Ireland): Home Int 1969-70; Eur
T Ch 1969

O'Neill, JJ
(Ireland): Home Int 1968

O'Rourke, P
(Ireland): Home Int 1980-81-82-
84-85

O'Sullivan, DF
(Ireland): Home Int 1976-85-86-
87-91; Eur T Ch 1977

O'Sullivan, WM
(Ireland): Home Int 1934-35-36-37-38-47-48-49-50-51-53-54

Oldcorn, A
(England): Home Int 1982-83.
(GBI): Walker Cup 1983;
Eisenhower Trophy 1982

Omelia, B
(Ireland): Home Int 1994-95-96-97

Oosterhuis, PA
(England): Home Int 1966-67-68.
(GBI): Walker Cup 1967; v Europe 1968; Eisenhower Trophy 1968

Oppenheimer, RH
(England): v Ireland 1928-29-30;
v Scotland 1930. (GBI): Walker Cup 1957 (Captain)

Osgood, TH
(Scotland): v England 1925

Owen, JB
(Wales): Home Int 1971

Owens, GF
(Wales): Home Int 1960-61

Ownes, GH
(Ireland): Home Int 1935-37-38-47

Page, P
(England): Home Int 1993.
(GBI): Walker Cup 1993

Palferman, H
(Wales): Home Int 1950-53

Palmer, DJ
(England): Home Int 1962-63

Pardoe, S
(Wales): Home Int 1991

Parfitt, RWM
(Wales): v Ireland 1924

Park, D
(Wales): Home Int 1994-95-96-97;
Eur T Ch 1995-97. (GBI) Walker Cup 1997

Parkin, AP
(Wales): Home Int 1980-81-82.
(GBI): Walker Cup 1983

Parry, JR
(Wales): Home Int 1966-75-76-77;
v France 1976

Patey, IR
(England): Home Int 1952;
v France 1948-49-50

Paton, DA
(Scotland): Home Int 1991

Patrick, D
(Scotland): Home Int 1997

Patrick, KG
(Scotland): Home Int 1937

Patterson, AH
(Ireland): v Wales 1913

Pattinson, R
(England): Home Int 1949

Payne, J
(England): Home Int 1950-51

Payne, J
(England): Home Int 1989-90; Eur T Ch 1991. (GBI): Walker Cup 1991; v Europe 1990

Pearson, AG
(GBI): v South Africa 1927

Pearson, MJ
(England): Home Int 1951-52

Pease, JWB (*later* Lord Wardington)
(England): v Scotland 1903-04-05-06

Peet, M
(Wales): Home Int 1995-96

Pennink, JJF
(England): Home Int 1937-38-47;
v France 1937-38-39. (GBI):
Walker Cup 1938

Perkins, TP
(England): v Scotland 1927-28-29.
(GBI): Walker Cup 1928

Perowne, AH
(England): Home Int 1947-48-49-50-51-53-54-55-57. (GBI): Walker Cup 1949-53-59; Eisenhower Trophy 1958

Peters, GB
(Scotland): Home Int 1934-35-36-37-38. (GBI): Walker Cup 1936-38

Peters, JL
(Wales): Home Int 1987-88-89

Philipson, S
(England): Home Int 1997

Phillips, LA
(Wales): v Ireland 1913

Phillips, V
(GBI): Walker Cup 1993

Pierse, AD
(Ireland): Home Int 1976-77-78-80-81-82-83-84-85-87-88; v Wales 1979; v France, West Germany, Sweden 1980; Eur T Ch 1981.
(GBI): Walker Cup 1983; v Europe 1980; Eisenhower Trophy 1982

Pilkington, M
(Wales): Home Int 1997; Eur T Ch 1997

Pinch, AG
(Wales): Home Int 1969

Pirie, AK
(Scotland): Home Int 1966 to 1975;
Eur T Ch 1967-69; v Belgium 1973-75; v Spain 1974.
(GBI): Walker Cup 1967; v Europe 1970

Plaxton, J
(England): Home Int 1983-84

Pollin, RKM
(Ireland): Home Int 1971; Eur T Ch 1973

Pollock, VA
(England): v Scotland 1908

Povall, J
(Wales): Home Int 1960-61-62-63-65-66-67-68-69-70-71-72-73-74-75-76-77; Eur T Ch 1967-69-71-73-75-77; v France 1975-76; v Denmark 1976. (GBI): v Europe 1962

Powell, WA
(England): v Scotland 1923-24;
v Wales/Ireland 1925

Power, E
(Ireland): Home Int 1987-88-93-94-95-97

Power, M
(Ireland): Home Int 1947-48-49-50-51-52-54

Poxon, MA
(England): Home Int 1975-76;
Eur T Ch 1975. (GBI): Walker Cup 1975

Pressdee, RNG
(Wales): Home Int 1958-59-60-61-62

Pressley, J
(Scotland): Home Int 1947-48-49

Price, JP
(Wales): Home Int 1986-87-88

Price, R
(Wales): Home Int 1994-96-97

Prosser, D
(England): Eur T Ch 1989

Pugh, O
(Wales): Home Int 1997

Pugh, RS
(Wales): v Ireland 1923-24-29

Pullan, M
(England): Home Int 1991-92

Purcell, J
(Ireland): Home Int 1973

Pyman, I
(England): Home Int 1993.
(GBI): Walker Cup 1993

Raeside, A
(Scotland): v Ireland 1929

Rafferty, R
(Ireland): v Wales 1979; Home Int 1980-81; v France, West Germany, Sweden 1980; Eur T Ch 1981. (GBI): Walker Cup 1981; v Europe 1980; Eisenhower Trophy 1980

Rainey, WHE
(Ireland): Home Int 1962

Rankin, G
(Scotland): Home Int 1994-95-97; v Sweden 1995-97; v France 1995-97; Eur T Ch 1995-97; v Spain 1996. (GBI): Walker Cup 1995-97

Rawlinson, D
(England): Home Int 1949-50-52-53

Ray, D
(England): Home Int 1982; v France 1982

Rayfus, P
(Ireland): Home Int 1986-87-88

Reade, HE
(Ireland): v Wales 1913

Reddan, B
(Ireland): Home Int 1987

Rees, CN
(Wales): Home Int 1986-88-89-91-92-94-95-96-97

Rees, DA
(Wales): Home Int 1961-62-63-64

Reid, A
(Scotland): Home Int 1993-94-95; Eur T Ch 1993-95; v Spain 1994; v Italy 1994; v France 1995

Renfrew, RL
(Scotland): Home Int 1964

Renwick, G, jr
(Wales): v Ireland 1923

Revell, RP
(England): Home Int 1972-73; Eur T Ch 1973

Reynard, M
(England): Home Int 1996-97; v France 1996

Ricardo, W
(Wales); v Ireland 1930-31; v Scotland 1931

Rice, JH
(Ireland): Home Int 1947-52

Rice-Jones, L
(Wales): v Ireland 1924

Richards, PM
(Wales): Home Int 1960-61-62-63-71

Richardson, S
(England): Home Int 1986-87-88

Risdon, PWL
(England): Home Int 1935-36

Robb, J, jr
(Scotland): v England 1902-03-05-06-07

Robb, WM
(Scotland): Home Int 1935

Roberts, AT
(Scotland): v Ireland 1931

Roberts, GP
(England): Home Int 1951-53; v France 1949

Roberts, GW
(Scotland): Home Int 1937-38

Roberts, H
(Wales): Home Int 1992-93

Roberts, HJ
(England): Home Int 1947-48-53

Roberts, J
(Wales): Home Int 1937

Roberts, SB
(Wales): Home Int 1932-33-34-35-37-38-47-48-49-50-51-52-53-54

Roberts, WJ
(Wales): Home Int 1948-49-50-51-52-53-54

Robertson, A
(England): Home Int 1986-87; v France 1988

Robertson, CW
(Ireland): v Wales 1930; v Scotland 1930

Robertson, D
(Scotland): Home Int 1991-92-93; v Sweden 1992; v Italy 1992; v France 1993; Eur T Ch 1993. (GBI): Walker Cup 1993; v Europe 1992; Eisenhower Trophy 1992

Robertson, DM
(Scotland): Home Int 1973-74; v Spain 1974

Robertson-Durham, JA
(Scotland): v England 1911

Robinson, J
(England): v Ireland 1928

Robinson, J
(England): Home Int 1986. (GBI): Walker Cup 1987

Robinson, S
(England): v Scotland 1925; v Ireland 1928-29-30

Roderick, RN
(Wales): Home Int 1983-84-85-86-87-88. (GBI) v Europe 1988. (GBI): Walker Cup 1989

Rogers, A
(England): Home Int 1991; v France 1992

Rolfe, B
(Wales): Home Int 1963-65

Roobottom, EL
(Wales): Home Int 1967

Roper, HS
(England): v Ireland 1931; v Scotland 1931

Roper, MS
(Wales): v Ireland 1979

Roper, R
(England): Home Int 1984-85-86-87

Rose, J
(England): Home Int 1997; Eur T Ch 1997. (GBI) Walker Cup 1997

Rothwell, J
(England): Home Int 1947-48

Rowe, P
(England): Home Int 1997

Russell, R
(Scotland): Home Int 1992-93; v France 1993; Eur T Ch 1993. (GBI): Walker Cup 1993

Rutherford, DS
(Scotland): v Ireland 1929

Rutherford, R
(Scotland): Home Int 1938-47

Saddler, AC
(Scotland): Home Int 1959-60-61-62-63-64-66; v Scandinavia 1962; Eur T Ch 1965-67-(75)-(77). (GBI): Walker Cup 1963-65-67-77 (Captain); v Europe 1960-62-64-66; CW 1959-63-67; Eisenhower Trophy 1962-76(Captain/winners)

Sandywell, A
(England): Home Int 1990; Eur T Ch 1991

Scannel, BJ
(Ireland): Home Int 1947-48-49-50-51-53-54

Scott, KB
(England): Home Int 1937-38; v France 1938

Scott, Hon M
(England): v Scotland 1911-12-23-24-25-26. (GBI): Walker Cup 1924-34 (Captain); v Australia 1934

Scott, Hon O
(England): v Scotland 1902-05-06

Scott, R, jr
(Scotland): *v* England 1924-28.
(GBI): Walker Cup 1924

Scott, WGF
(Scotland): *v* Ireland 1927

Scratton, EWHB
(England): *v* Scotland 1912

Scroggie: FH
(Scotland): *v* England 1910

Scrutton, PF
(England): Home Int 1950-55.
(GBI): Walker Cup 1955-57

Sewell, D
(England): Home Int 1956-57-58-59-60. (GBI): Walker Cup 1957-59;
CW 1959; Eisenhower Trophy 1960

Shade, RDBM
(Scotland): Home Int 1957, 1960
to 1968; *v* Scandinavia 1960-62;
Eur T Ch 1965-67. (GBI): Walker
Cup 1961-63-65-67; *v* Europe
1962-64-66-68; Eisenhower Trophy
1962-64-66-68; CW 1963-67;
v Australia 1964

Shaw, G
(Scotland): Home Int 1984-86-87-88-90; *v* West Germany 1987;
v Sweden 1984; *v* France 1987;
Eur T Ch 1987. (GBI): Walker Cup
1987

Sheals, HS
(Ireland): *v* Wales 1929; *v* England
1929-30-31; *v* Scotland 1930;
Home Int 1932-33

Sheahan, D
(Ireland): Home Int 1961-62-63-64-65-66-67-70. (GBI): Walker
Cup 1963; *v* Europe 1962-64-67

Sheppard, M
(Wales): Home Int 1990

Shepperson, AE
(England): Home Int 1956-57-58-59-60-62. (GBI): Walker Cup 1957-59

Sherborne, A
(England): Home Int 1982-83-84

Sherry, G
(Scotland): Home Int 1993-94-95;
v France 1993-95; *v* Spain 1994;
v Sweden 1995; Eur T Ch 1995.
(GBI): Walker Cup 1995; *v* Europe
1994; Eisenhower Trophy 1994

Shields, B
(Scotland):Home Int 1986

Shingler, TR
(England): Home Int 1977

Shorrock, TJ
(England): *v* France 1952

Simcox, R
(Ireland): *v* Wales 1930-31;
v Scotland 1930-31; *v* England
1931; Home Int 1932-33-34-35-36-38

Simpson, AF
(Scotland): *v* Ireland 1928;
v England 1927

Simpson, JG
(Scotland): *v* England 1906-07-08-09-11-12-22-24-26.
(GBI): *v* America 1921

Sinclair, A
(Scotland): Home Int 1950; Eur T
Ch 1967 (Captain)

Slark, WA
(England): Home Int 1957

Slater, A
(England): Home Int 1955-62

Slattery, B
(Ireland): Home Int 1947-48

Sludds, MF
(Ireland): Home Int 1982

Smith, Eric M
(England): *v* Ireland 1931;
v Scotland 1931

Smith, Everard
(England): *v* Scotland 1908-09-10-12

Smith, GF
(England): *v* Scotland 1902-03

Smith, JN
(Scotland): *v* Ireland 1928-30-31;
v England 1929-30-31; *v* Wales
1931; Home Int 1932-33-34.
(GBI): Walker Cup 1930

Smith, JR
(England): Home Int 1932

Smith, LOM
(England): Home Int 1963

Smith, M
(Wales): Home Int 1993-94-95-96-97; Eur T Ch 1995-97

Smith, S
(Scotland): *v* Austria 1994

Smith, VH
(Wales): *v* Ireland 1924-25

Smith, W
(England): Home Int 1972.
(GBI): *v* Europe 1972

Smith, WD
(Scotland): Home Int 1957-58-59-60-63; *v* Scandinavia 1958-60.
(GBI): Walker Cup 1959; *v* Europe
1958

Smyth, D
(Ireland): Home Int 1972-73;
Eur T Ch 1973

Smyth, DW
(Ireland): *v* Wales 1923-30;
v England 1930; *v* Scotland 1931;
Home Int 1933

Smyth, HB
(Ireland): Home Int 1974-75-76-78; Eur T Ch 1975-79; *v* France,
West Germany, Sweden 1976.
(GBI): *v* Europe 1976

Smyth, V
(Ireland): Home Int 1981-82

Snowdon, J
(England): Home Int 1934

Soulby, DEB
(Ireland): *v* Wales 1929-30;
v England 1929-30; *v* Scotland
1929-30

Spiller, EF
(Ireland): *v* Wales 1924; *v* England
1928; *v* Scotland 1928-29

Spring, G
(Ireland): Home Int 1996

Squirrell, HC
(Wales): Home Int 1955 to 1971,
1973 to 1975; Eur T Ch 1967-69-71-75; *v* France 1975

Stanford, M
(England): Home Int 1991-92-93;
v France 1992. (GBI): Walker Cup
1993; *v* Europe 1992; Eisenhower
Trophy 1992

Staunton, R
(Ireland): Home Int 1964-65-72;
Eur T Ch 1973

Steel, DMA
(England): Home Int 1970

Stephen, AR
(Scotland): Home Int 1971-72-73-74-75-76-77-84-85; Eur T Ch
1975-85; *v* France 1985; *v* Spain
1974; *v* Belgium 1975-77-78.
(GBI): Walker Cup 1985; *v* Europe
1972

Stevens, DI
(Wales): Home Int 1968-69-70-74-75-76-77-78-80-82; Eur T Ch 1969-77; *v* France 1976; *v* Denmark 1977

Stevens, LB
(England): *v* Scotland 1912

Stevenson, A
(Scotland): Home Int 1949

Stevenson, JB
(Scotland): *v* Ireland 1931; Home
Int 1932-38-47-49-50-51

Stevenson, JF
(Ireland): *v* Wales 1923-24;
v England 1925

Stevenson, K
(Ireland): Home Int 1972

Stockdale, B
(England): Home Int 1964-65

Stoker, K
(Wales): *v* Ireland 1923-24

Stokoe, GC
(Wales): *v* England 1925; *v* Ireland
1929-30

Storey, EF
(England): *v* Scotland 1924-25-26-
27-28-30; Home Int 1936; *v* France
1936. (GBI): Walker Cup 1924-26-28

Stott, HAN
(England): Home Int 1976-77

Stout, JA
(England): *v* Scotland 1928-29-30-
31; *v* Ireland 1929-31. (GBI):
Walker Cup 1930-32

Stowe, C
(England): Home Int 1935-36-37-
38-47-49-54; *v* France 1938-39-49.
(GBI): Walker Cup 1938-47

Strachan, CJL
(Scotland): Home Int 1965-66-67;
Eur T Ch 1967

Straker, R
(England): Home Int 1932

Streeter, P
(England): Home Int 1992;
v France 1994-96

Stuart, HB
(Scotland): Home Int 1967-68-69-
70-71-72-73-74-76; Eur T Ch
1969-71-73-75; *v* Belgium 1973-
75; (GBI): Walker Cup 1971-73-
75; *v* Europe 1968-72-74; CW
1971; Eisenhower Trophy 1972

Stuart, JE
(Scotland): Home Int 1959

Stubbs, AK
(England): Home Int 1982

Suneson, C
(England): Home Int 1988; Eur T
Ch 1989

Sutherland, DMG
(England): Home Int 1947

Sutton, W
(England): *v* Scotland 1929-31; *v*
Ireland 1929-30-31

Symonds, A
(Wales): *v* Ireland 1925

Taggart, J
(Ireland): Home Int 1953

Tait, AG
(Scotland): Home Int 1987-88-89;
Nixdorf Nations Cup 1989

Tate, JK
(England): Home Int 1954-55-56

Taylor, GN
(Scotland): Home Int 1948

Taylor, HE
(England): *v* Scotland 1911

Taylor, JS
(Scotland): *v* England 1979; Home
Int 1980; *v* Belgium 1980;
v France 1980

Taylor, LG
(Scotland): Home Int 1955-56

Taylor, TPD
(Wales): Home Int 1963

Taylor, Y
(Wales): Home Int 1995-96-97; Eur
T Ch 1995-97

Thirlwell, A
(England): Home Int 1951-52-54-
55-56-57-58-63-64. (GBI): Walker
Cup 1957; *v* Europe 1956-58-64;
CW 1953-64

Thirsk, TJ
(England): *v* Ireland 1929; Home
Int 1933-34-35-36-37-38;
v France 1935-36-37-38-39

Thom, KG
(England): Home Int 1947-48-49-
53. (GBI): Walker Cup 1949

Thomas, I
(England): Home Int 1933

Thomas, KR
(Wales): Home Int 1951-52

Thompson, ASG
(England): Home Int 1935-37

Thompson, MS
(England): Home Int 1982. (GBI):
Walker Cup 1983

Thomson, AP
(Scotland): Home Int 1970; Eur T
Ch 1971

Thomson, G
(Scotland): Home Int 1996

Thomson, H
(Scotland): Home Int 1934-35-36-
37-38. (GBI): Walker Cup 1936-38

Thomson, JA
(Scotland): Home Int 1981-82-83-
84-85-86-87-88-89-91-92; Eur T
Ch 1983; *v* West Germany 1987;

v Italy 1984-86-88-90; *v* Sweden
1990

Thorburn, K
(Scotland): *v* England 1928;
v Ireland 1927

Timbey, JC
(Ireland): *v* Scotland 1928-31;
v Wales 1931

Timmis, CW
(England): *v* Ireland 1930; Home
Int. 1936-37

Tipping, EB
(England): *v* Ireland 1930

Tipple, ER
(England): *v* Ireland 1928-29;
Home Int 1932

Tolley, CJH
(England): *v* Scotland 1922-23-24-
25-26-27-28-29-30; Home Int
1936-37-38; *v* Ireland/Wales 1925;
v France 1938. (GBI): *v* America
1921, Walker Cup 1922-23-24
(Captain) -26-30-34; *v* South Africa
1927

Tooth, EA
(Wales): *v* Ireland 1913

Torrance, TA
(Scotland): *v* England 1922-23-25-
26-28-29-30; Home Int 1933.
(GBI): Walker Cup 1924-28-30-32
(Captain) -34

Torrance, WB
(Scotland): *v* England 1922-23-24-
26-27-28-30; *v* Ireland 1928-29-30.
(GBI): Walker Cup 1922

Townsend, PM
(England): Home Int 1965-66.
(GBI): Walker Cup 1965; *v* Europe
1966; Eisenhower Trophy 1966

Toye, JL
(Wales): Home Int 1963-64-65-66-
67-69-70-71-72-73-74-76-78; Eur T
Ch 1971-73-75-77; *v* France 1975

Tredinnick, SV
(England): Home Int 1950

Tucker, WI
(Wales): Home Int 1949 to 1972,
1974-75; Eur T Ch 1967-69-75;
v France 1975

Tulloch, W
(Scotland): *v* England 1927-29-30-
31; *v* Ireland 1930-31; *v* Wales
1931; Home Int 1932

Tupling, LP
(England): Home Int 1969; Eur T
Ch 1969. (GBI): Walker Cup 1969

Turnbull, A
(Scotland): Home Int 1995-96-97;
v France 1995; *v* Spain 1996

Turnbull, CH
(Wales): *v* Ireland 1913-25

Turner, A
(England): Home Int 1952

Turner, GB
(Wales): Home Int 1947-48-49-50-51-52-55-56

Tweddell, W
(England): *v* Scotland 1928-29-30; Home Int 1935.(GBI): Walker Cup 1928 (Captain) -36 (Captain)

Twynholm, S
(Scotland): Home Int 1990. Nixdorf Nations Cup 1990

Urquhart, M
(Scotland): Home Int 1993; *v* Italy 1996

Vannet, L
(Scotland): Home Int 1984

Waddell, G
(Ireland): *v* Wales 1925

Wainwright, A
(England): Home Int 1997

Walker, J
(Scotland): Home Int 1954-55-57-58-60-61-62-63; *v* Scandinavia 1958-62. (GBI): Walker Cup 1961; *v* Europe 1958-60

Walker, KH
(Scotland): Home Int 1985-86

Walker, MS
(England): *v* Ireland/Wales 1925

Walker, RS
(Scotland): Home Int 1935-36

Wallbank, K
(England): Home Int 1996-97; *v* France 1996

Wallis, G
(Wales): Home Int 1934-36-37-38

Walls, MPD
(England): Home Int 1980-81-85

Walters, EM
(Wales): Home Int 1967-68-69; Eur T Ch 1969

Walton, AR
(England): Home Int 1934-35

Walton, P
(Ireland): *v* Wales 1979: Home Int 1980-81; *v* France, Germany, Sweden 1980; Eur T Ch 1981. (GBI): Walker Cup 1981-83; Eisenhower Trophy 1982

Warren, KT
(England): Home Int 1962

Watson, CR
(Scotland): Home Int 1991-92-94-95-96-97; *v* Sweden 1992-97; *v* Italy 1992; *v* Austria 1994; *v* Spain 1996; *v* France 1997; Eur T Ch 1997. (GBI) Walker Cup 1997

Watt, AW
(Scotland): Home Int 1987

Watts, C
(England): Home Int 1991-92; *v* France 1992

Way, P
(England): Home Int 1981; Eur T Ch 1981. (GBI): Walker Cup 1981.

Webster, AJ
(Scotland): Home Int 1978

Webster, F
(Ireland): Home Int 1949

Webster, S
(England): Home Int 1995-96; Eur T Ch 1997

Weeks, K
(England): Home Int 1987-88; *v* France 1988

Welch, L
(Ireland): Home Int 1936

Welch, M
(England): Home Int 1993-94; *v* France 1994

Wemyss, DS
(Scotland): Home Int 1937

Werner, LE
(Ireland): *v* Wales 1925

West, CH
(Ireland): *v* England 1928; Home Int 1932

Westwood, L
(England): Home Int 1993

Wethered, RH
(England): *v* Scotland 1922-23-24-25-26-27-28-29-30. (GBI): *v* America 1921, Walker Cup 1922-23-26-30 (Captain) -34

White, L
(England): Home Int 1990; Eur T Ch 1991. (GBI): Walker Cup 1991

White, RJ
(England): Home Int 1947-48-49-53-54. (GBI): Walker Cup 1947-49-51-53-55

Whyte, AW
(Scotland): Home Int 1934

Wiggett, M
(England): Home Int 1990

Wiggins, R
(England): Home Int 1996; Eur T Ch 1997. (GBI): *v* Europe 1996

Wight, R
(Scotland): *v* Sweden 1950

Wilkie, DF
(Scotland): Home Int 1962-63-65-67-68

Wilkie, G
(Scotland): *v* England 1911

Wilkie, GT
(Wales): Home Int 1938

Wilkinson, S
(Wales): Home Int 1990-91

Willcox, FS
(Wales): *v* Scotland 1931; *v* Ireland 1931

Williams, DF
(England): *v* Scotland 1979

Williams KH
(Wales): Home Int 1983-84-85-86-87

Williams, PG
(Wales): *v* Ireland 1925

Williamson, SB
(Scotland): Home Int 1947-48-49-51-52

Willison, R
(England): Home Int 1988-89-90; Eur T Ch 1989-91. (GBI): Walker Cup 1991; *v* Europe 1990. Eisenhower Trophy 1990

Wills, M
(Wales): Home Int 1990

Wilson, E
(Scotland): Home Int 1985

Wilson, J
(Scotland): *v* England 1922-23-24-26; *v* Ireland 1932. (GBI): Walker Cup 1923

Wilson, JC
(Scotland): Home Int 1947-48-49-51-52-53; *v* Sweden 1950; *v* New Zealand 1954. (GBI): Walker Cup 1947-53; *v* South Africa 1954; CW 1954

Wilson, P
(Scotland): Home Int 1976; Belgium 1977

Winchester, R
(England): Home Int 1985-87-89

Winfield, HB
(Wales): *v* Ireland 1913

Winter, G
(England): Home Int 1991

Wise, WS
(England): Home Int 1947

Wolstenholme, GB
(England): Home Int 1953-55-56-57-58-59-60 (GBI): Walker Cup 1957-59; Eisenhower Trophy 1958-60; CW 1959

Wolstenholme, GP
(England): Home Int 1988 to 1997; v France 1988-92-94; v Spain 1989-91-95; Eur T Ch 1995-97. (GBI): Walker Cup 1995-97; v Europe 1992-94; Eisenhower Trophy 1996

Wood, DK
(Wales): Home Int 1982-83-84-85-86-87

Woollam, J
(England): Home Int 1933-34-35; v France 1935

Woolley, FA
(England): v Scotland 1910-11-12

Woosnam, I
(Wales): v France 1976

Worthington, JS
(England): v Scotland 1905

Wright, I
(Scotland): Home Int 1958-59-60-61; v Scandinavia 1960-62

Yeo, J
(England): Home 1971

Young, D
(Ireland): Home Int 1969-70-77

Young, ID
(Scotland): Home Int 1981-82; v France 1982. (GBI): v Europe 1982

Young, JR
(Scotland): Home Int 1960-61-65; v Scandinavia 1960. (GB): v Europe 1960

Young, S
(Scotland): Home Int 1996; v Italy 1996; Eur T Ch 1997. (GBI) Walker Cup 1997

Zacharias, JP
(England): Home Int 1935

Zoete, HW de
(England): v Scotland 1903-04-06-07

British Isles International Players, Amateur Women

Abbreviations

CW — Commonwealth Tournament (Team from UK)
Eur L T Ch — played in European Ladies Amateur Team Championship
Home Int — played in Home International matches
Previous surnames are shown in brackets.

Agnew, C
(Scotland): Home Int 1995

Aitken, E (Young)
(Scotland): Home Int 1954

Alexander, M
(Ireland): Home Int 1920-21-22-30

Allen, F
(England): Home Int 1952

Allington Hughes, Miss
(Wales): Home Int 1908-09-10-12-14-22-25

Anderson, E
(Scotland): Home Int 1910-11-12-21-25

Anderson, F
(Scotland): Home Int 1977-79-80-81-83-84-86-87-88-89-90-91-92; Eur L T Ch 1979-83-87-91. (GBI): Vagliano Trophy 1987

Anderson, H
(Scotland): Home Int 1964-65-68-69-70-71; Eur L T Ch 1969. (GBI): Vagliano Trophy 1969

Anderson, J (Donald)
(Scotland): Home Int 1947-48-49-50-51-52-53. (GBI): Curtis Cup 1948-50-52

Anderson, L.
(Scotland): Home Int 1986-87-88-89; Eur L T Ch 1987-89

Anderson, VH
(Scotland): Home Int 1907

Arbuthnot, M
(Ireland): Home Int 1921

Archer, A (Rampton)
(England): Home Int 1968 (Captain)

Armstrong, M
(Ireland): Home Int 1906

Ashcombe, Lady
(Wales): Home Int 1950-51-52-53-54

Aubertin, Mrs
(Wales): Home Int 1908-09-10

Bailey, D [Frearson] (Robb)
(England): Home Int 1961-62-71; Eur L T Ch 1968-93 (Captain). (GBI): Curtis Cup 1962-72-84 (Captain)-86 (Captain)-88(Captain); Vagliano Trophy 1961-83(Captain)-85 (Captain); CW 1983

Baker, J
(Wales): Home Int 1990

Bald, J
(Scotland): Home Int 1968-69-71; Eur L T Ch 1969

Barber, S (Bonallack)
(England): Home Int 1960-61-62-68-70-72-77-78 (Captain); Eur L T Ch 1969-71. (GBI): Curtis Cup 1962; Vagliano Trophy 1961-63-69; CW 1995(Captain); Espirito Santo 1996 (Captain)

Barclay, C (Brisbane)
(Scotland): Home Int 1953-61-68

Bargh Etherington, B (Whitehead)
(England): Home Int 1974

Barlow, Mrs
(Ireland): Home Int 1921

Barron, M
(Wales): Home Int 1929-30-31-34-35-36-37-38-39-47-48-49-50-51-52-53-54-55-56-57-58-60-61-62-63

Barry, L
(England): Home Int 1911-12-13-14

Barry, P
(England): Home Int 1982

Barton, P
(England): Home Int 1935-36-37-38-39. (GBI): Curtis Cup 1934-36

Bastin, G
(England): Home Int 1920-21-22-23-24-25

Bayliss, Mrs
(Wales): Home Int 1921

Bayman, L (Denison Pender)
(England): Home Int 1971-72-73-83-84-85-87-88-95(Captain)-96(Captain); Eur L T Ch 1985-87-89-97(Captain). (GBI) Curtis Cup 1988; Vagliano Trophy 1971-85-87; Espirito Santo 1988

Baynes, Mrs CE
(Scotland): Home Int 1921-22

Beck, B (Pim)
(Ireland): Home Int 1930-31-32-33-34-36-37-47-48-49-50-51-52-53-54-55-56-58-59-61

Beckett, J
(Ireland): Home Int 1962-66-67-68: Eur L T Ch 1967

Beddows, C [Watson] (Stevenson)
(Scotland): Home Int 1913-14-21-22-23-27-29-30-31-32-33-34-35-36-37-39-47-48-49-50-51. (GBI): Curtis Cup 1932

Behan, L
(Ireland): Home Int 1984-85-86-96. (GBI): Curtis Cup 1986; Vagliano Trophy 1985

Beharrell, V (Anstey)
(England): Home Int 1955-56-57-61 (Captain). (GBI): Curtis Cup 1956

Benka, P (Tredinnick)
(England): Home Int 1967.
(GBI): Curtis Cup 1966-68;
Vagliano Trophy 1967

Bennett, L
(Scotland): Home Int 1977-80-81

Benton, MH
(Scotland): Home Int 1914

Biggs, A (Whittaker)
(England): (GBI): Vagliano Trophy
1959

Birmingham, M
(Ireland): Home Int 1967(Captain)

Bisgood, J
(England) Home Int 1949-50-51-
52-53-54-56-58. (GBI): Curtis Cup
1950-52-54-70(Captain)

Blair, N (Menzies)
(Scotland): Home Int 1955

Blake, Miss
(Ireland): Home Int 1931-32-34-
35-36

Blaymire, J
(England): Home Int 1971-88-
89(Captain)

Bloodworth, D (Lewis)
(Wales): Home Int 1954-55-56-57-60

Boatman, EA (Collis)
(England): Home Int 1974-80-84
(Captain)-85 (Captain)-90
(Captain)-91 (Captain); Eur L T
Ch 1985 (Captain)-87 (Captain).
(GBI): Curtis Cup 1992 (Captain)-
94 (Captain); CW 1987 (Captain)-
91 (Captain)

Bolas, R
(England): Home Int 1992

Bolton, Z (Bonner Davis)
(England): Home Int 1939-48-49-
50-51-55-(Captain)-56. (GBI):
Curtis Cup 1948-56(Captain)-
66(Captain)-68(Captain)-94
(Captain); CW 1967

Bonallack, A (Ward)
(England): Home Int 1956-57-58-
59-60-61-62-63-64-65 (Captain)-
66-72. (GBI): Curtis Cup 1956-58-
60-62-64-66; Vagliano Trophy
1959-61-63

Bostock, M
(England): Home Int 1954
(Captain)

Bourn, Mrs
(England): Home Int 1909-12

Bowhill, M (Robertson-
Durham)
(Scotland): Home Int 1936-37-38

Boyd, J
(Ireland): Home Int 1912-13-14

Boyes, S
(Wales): Home Int 1992

Bradley, K (Rawlings)
(Wales): Home Int 1975-76-77-78-
79-82-83

Bradshaw, E
(Ireland): Home Int 1964-66-67-
68-69-70-71-74-75-80
(Captain)-81(Captain); Eur L T Ch
1969-71-75. (GBI): Vagliano
Trophy 1969-71

Brandom, G
(Ireland): Home Int 1965-66-67-
68; Eur L T Ch 1967.
(GBI): Vagliano Trophy 1967

Brearley, M
(Wales): Home Int 1937-38

Brennan, R (Hegarty)
(Ireland): Home Int 1974-75-76-
77-78-79-81

Brewerton, R
(Wales): Home Int 1997

Brice, Mrs
(Ireland): Home Int 1948

Bridges, Mrs
(Wales): Home Int 1933-38-39

Briggs, A (Brown)
(Wales): Home Int 1969-70-71-72-
73-74-75-76-77-78-79-80-81
(Captain) -82 (Captain)-83
(Captain) -84-93 (Captain); Eur L
T Ch 1971-75. (GBI): Vagliano
Trophy 1971-75

Brinton, Mrs
(Ireland): Home Int 1922

Bromley-Davenport, I
(Rieben)
(Wales): Home Int 1932-33-34-35-
36-48-50-51-52-53-54-55-56

Brook, D
(Wales): Home Int 1913

Brooks, E
(Ireland): Home Int 1953-54-56

Broun, JG
(Scotland): Home Int 1905-06-07-
21

Brown, B
(Ireland): Home Int 1960

Brown, E (Jones)
(Wales): Home Int 1947-48-49-50-
52-53-57-58-59-60-61-62-63-64-
65-66-68-69-70

Brown, F
(England): Home Int 1994-96-97;
Eur L T Ch 1997

Brown, Mrs FW (Gilroy)
(Scotland): Home Int 1905-06-07-
08-09-10-11-13-21

Brown, J
(Wales): Home Int 1960-61-62-64-
65; Eur L T Ch 1965-69

Brown, J
(England): Home Int 1984

Brown, TWL
(Scotland): Home Int 1924-25

Brown, Mrs
(Wales): Home Int 1924-25-27

Brownlow, Miss
(Ireland): Home Int 1923

Bryan-Smith, S
(Wales): Home Int 1947-48-49-50-
51-52-56

Burnell, S
(England): Home Int 1993; Eur L
T Ch 1993

Burrell, Mrs
(Wales): Home Int 1939

Burton, H (Mitchell)
(Scotland): Home Int 1931-55-56-
59(Captain). (GBI): Vagliano
Trophy 1961

Burton, M
(England): Eur L T Ch 1997

Burton, M
(England): Home Int 1975-76

Butler, I (Burke)
(Ireland): Home Int 1962-63-64-
65-66-68-70-71-72-73-76-77-78-
79-86(Captain)-87(Captain); Eur L
T Ch 1967. (GBI): Curtis Cup
1966-96(Captain); Vagliano Trophy
1965; Espirito Santo 1964-66

Buxton, N
(England): Home Int 1991-92-93;
Eur LT Ch 1991-93.
(GBI): Curtis Cup 1992; Vagliano
Trophy 1991-93

Byrne, A (Sweeney)
(Ireland): Home Int 1959-60-61-
62-63-90(Captain)-91(Captain)

Cadden, G
(Scotland): Home Int 1974-75-
95(Captain)-96(Captain); Eur L T
Ch 1997(Captain). (GBI) Vagliano
Trophy 1997 (Captain)

Cairns, Lady Katherine
(England): Home Int 1947-48-50-
51-52-53-54. (GBI): Curtis Cup
1952(Captain)

Caldwell, C (Redford)
(England): Home Int 1973-78-79-
80. (GBI): Curtis Cup 1978-80;
Vagliano Trophy 1973

Callen, L
(Ireland): Home Int 1990

Campbell, J (Burnett)
(Scotland): Home Int 1960

Cann, M (Nuttall)
(England): Home Int 1966

Carrick, P (Bullard)
(England): Home Int 1939-47

Caryl, M
(Wales): Home Int 1929

Casement, M (Harrison)
(Ireland): Home Int 1909-10-11-
12-13-14

Cassidy, Y
(Ireland): Home Int 1994-95

Cautley, B (Hawtrey)
(England): Home Int 1912-13-14-
22-23-24-25-27

Chambers, D
(England): Home Int 1906-07-09-
10-11-12-20-24-25. (GBI): Curtis
Cup 1934 (Captain)-36 (Captain)-
38 (Captain)

Christison, D
(England): Home Int 1981

Chugg, P (Light)
(Wales): Home Int 1973-74-75-76-
77-78-86-87-88-96; Eur L T Ch
1975-87

Clark, G (Atkinson)
(England): Home Int 1955

Clarke, Mrs ML
(England): Home Int 1933-35

Clarke, P
(England): Home Int 1981

Clarke, Mrs
(Ireland): Home Int 1922

Clarkson, H (Reynolds)
(Wales): Home Int 1935-38-39

Clay, E
(Wales): Home Int 1912

Clement, V
(England): Home Int 1932-34-35

Close, M (Wenyon)
(England): Home Int 1968-69; Eur
L T Ch 1969. (GBI): Vagliano
Trophy 1969

Coats, Mrs G
(Scotland): Home Int 1931-32-33-34

Cochrane, K
(Scotland): Home Int 1924-25-28-
29-30

Coffey, A
(Ireland): Home Int 1995-96-97;
Eur L T Ch 1997

Collett, P
(England): Home Int 1910

Collingham, J (Melville)
(England): Home Int 1978-79-81-
84-86-87-92; Eur L T Ch 1989.
(GBI): Vagliano Trophy 1979-87;
CW 1987

Colquhoun, H
(Ireland): Home Int 1959-60-61-63

Comboy, C (Grott)
(England): Home Int 1975 (Captain)
-76 (Captain). (GBI): Curtis Cup
1978 (Captain)-80 (Captain);
Vagliano Trophy 1977 (Captain)-
1979 (Captain); Espirito Santo 1978
(Captain); CW 1979

Connachan, J
(Scotland): Home Int 1979-80-81-
82-83. (GBI): Curtis Cup 1980-82;
Vagliano Trophy 1981-83; Espirito
Santo 1980-82; CW 1983

Coote, Miss
(Ireland): Home Int 1925-28-29

Copley, K (Lackie)
(Scotland): Home Int 1974-75

Corlett, E
(England): Home Int 1927-29-30-
31-32-33-35-36-37-38-39.(GBI):
Curtis Cup 1932-38-64 (Captain)

Costello, G
(Ireland): Home Int 1973-
84(Captain)-85(Captain)

Cotton, S (German)
(England): Home Int 1967-68; Eur
L T Ch 1967. (GBI): Vagliano
Trophy 1967

Couper, M
(Scotland): Home Int 1929-34-35-
36-37-39-56

Cowley, Lady
(Wales): Home Int 1907-09

Cox, Margaret
(Wales): Home Int 1924-25

Cox, Nell
(Wales): Home Int 1954

Craik, T
(Scotland): Home Int 1988

Cramsie, F (Hezlet)
(Ireland): Home Int 1905-06-07-
08-09-10-13-20-24

Crawford, I (Wylie)
(Scotland): Home Int 1970-71-72

Cresswell, K (Stuart)
(Scotland): Home Int 1909-10-11-
12-14

Critchley, D (Fishwick)
(England): Home Int 1930-31-32-
33-35-36-47. (GBI): Curtis Cup
1932-34-50 (Captain)

Croft, A
(England): Home Int 1927

Cross, M
(Wales): Home Int 1922

Cruickshank, DM (Jenkins)
(Scotland): Home Int 1910-11-12

Crummack, Miss
(England): Home Int 1909

Cuming, Mrs
(Ireland): Home Int 1910

Cunninghame, S
(Wales): Home Int 1922-25-29-31

Cuthell, R (Adair)
(Ireland): Home Int 1908

Dampney, S
(Wales): Home Int 1924-25-27-28-
29-30

David, Mrs
(Wales): Home Int 1908

Davidson, B (Inglis)
(Scotland): Home Int 1928

Davies, K
(Wales): Home Int 1981-82-83;
Eur L T Ch 1987. (GBI): Curtis
Cup 1986-88; Vagliano Trophy
1987; CW 1987

Davies, L
(England): Home Int 1983-84.
(GBI): Curtis Cup 1984;
CW 1987

Davies, P (Griffiths)
(Wales): Home Int 1965-66-67-68-
70-71-73; Eur L T Ch 1971

Davis, L
(Wales): Home Int 1997; Eur L T
Ch 1997

Deacon, Mrs
(Wales): Home Int 1912-14

Denny, A (Barrett)
(England): Home Int 1951

Dering, Mrs
(Ireland): Home Int 1923

Dermott, L
(Wales): Home Int 1987-88-89-91-92-93-94-95-96; Eur L T Ch 1991-93. (GBI): Curtis Cup 1996

Dickson, M
(Ireland): Home Int 1909

Dobson, H
(England): Home Int 1987-88-89; Eur L T Ch 1989. (GBI): Curtis Cup 1990; Vagliano Trophy 1989

Dod, L
(England): Home Int 1905

Donne, A
(Wales): Home Int 1993-94; Eur L T Ch 1993

Douglas, K
(England): Home Int 1981-82-83. (GBI): Curtis Cup 1982; Vagliano Trophy 1983

Dowdall, E
(Ireland): Home Int 1997

Dowling, C (Hourihane)
(Ireland): Home Int 1979 to 1992; Eur L T Ch 1981-83-85-87-89-97(Captain). (GBI):Curtis Cup 1984-86-88-90-92; Vagliano Trophy 1981-83-85-87-89-91; Espirito Santo 1986-90

Dowling, D
(England): Home Int 1979

Draper, M [Peel] (Thomas)
(Scotland): Home Int 1929-34-38-49-50-51-52-53-54(Captain)-55 (Captain)-56-57-58-61 (Captain)-62. (GBI): Curtis Cup 1954; Vagliano Trophy 1963 (Captain)

Duggleby, E
(England): Home Int 1994-95-96; Eur L T Ch 1995. (GBI): Vagliano Trophy 1995

Duncan, B
(Wales): Home Int 1907-08-09-10-12

Duncan, M
(Wales): Home Int 1922-23-28-34

Duncan, MJ (Wood)
(Scotland): Home Int 1925-27-28-39

Durlacher, Mrs
(Ireland): Home Int 1905-06-07-08-09-10-14

Durrant, B [Green] (Lowe)
(England): Home Int 1954

Dwyer, Mrs
(Ireland): 1928

Eakin, P (James)
(Ireland): Home Int 1967

Eakin, T
(Ireland): Home Int 1990-91-92-93-94; Eur L T Ch 1993

Earner, M
(Ireland): Home Int 1960-61-62-63-70

Edmond, F (Macdonald)
(England): Home Int 1991; Eur LT Ch 1991. (GBI): Vagliano Trophy 1991

Educate, L (Walton)
(England): Home Int 1991-94-95; Eur L T Ch 1993-95. (GBI): Curtis Cup 1994-96; Vagliano Trophy 1993-95; CW 1995

Edwards, E
(Wales): Home Int 1949-50

Edwards, J
(Wales): Home Int 1932-33-34-36-37

Edwards, J (Morris)
(Wales): Home Int 1962-63-66-67-68-69-70-77(Captain)-78(Captain)-79 (Captain); Eur L T Ch 1967-69-93(Captain)

Egford, K
(England): Home Int 1992-94

Ellis, E
(Ireland): Home Int 1932-35-37-38

Ellis Griffiths (Mrs)
(Wales): Home Int 1907-08-09-12-13

Emery, MJ
(Wales): Home Int 1928-29-30-31-32-33-34-35-36-37-38-47

Evans, H
(England): Home Int 1908

Evans, N
(Wales): Home Int 1908-09-10-13

Evans, N
(Wales): Home Int 1996-97; Eur L T Ch 1997

Everard, M
(England): Home Int 1964-67-69-70-72-73-77-78; Eur L T Ch 1967-71-77. (GBI): Curtis Cup 1970-72-74-78; Vagliano Trophy 1967-69-71-73; Espirito Santo 1968-72-78; CW 1971

Fairclough, L
(England): Home Int 1988-89-90; Eur L T Ch 1989. (GBI): Vagliano Trophy 1989

Falconer, V (Lamb)
(Scotland): Home Int 1932-36-37-47-48-49-50-51-52-53-54-55-56

Fanagan, S
(Ireland): Home Int 1995-96-97; Eur L T Ch 1997

Farie-Anderson, J
(Scotland): Home Int 1924

Farquharson-Black, E
(Scotland): Home Int 1987-88-89-90-91-97; Eur L T Ch 1989-91. (GBI): Curtis Cup 1990-92; Vagliano Trophy 1989-91; CW 1991

Ferguson, A
(Ireland): Home Int 1989

Ferguson, D
(Ireland): Home Int 1927-28-29-30-31-32-34-35-36-37-38-61 (Captain). (GBI): Curtis Cup 1958(Captain)

Ferguson, M (Fowler)
(Scotland): Home Int 1959-62-63-64-65-66-67-69-70-85; Eur L T Ch 1965-67-71. (GBI): Curtis Cup 1966; Vagliano Trophy 1965

Ferguson R (Ogden)
(England): Home Int 1957

Fields, E
(England): Home Int 1995-96

Fitzgibbon, M
(Ireland): Home Int 1920-21-29-30-31-32-33

FitzPatrick, O (Heskin)
(Ireland): Home Int 1967

Fletcher, L
(England): Home Int 1989-90; Eur LT Ch 1991. (GBI): Curtis Cup 1990; CW 1991

Fletcher, P (Sherlock)
(Ireland): Home Int 1932-34-35-36-38-39-54-55-66 (Captain)

Forbes, J
(Scotland): Home Int 1985-86-87-88-89; Eur L T Ch 1987-89

Ford, J
(Scotland): Home Int 1993-94-95

Foster, C
(England): Home Int 1905-06-09

Fowler, J
(England): Home Int 1928

Franklin Thomas, E
(Wales): Home Int 1909

Freeguard, C
(Wales): Home Int 1927

Furby, J
(England): Home Int 1987-88; Eur L T Ch 1987

Fyshe, M
(England): Home Int 1938

Gallagher, S
(Scotland): Home Int 1983-84

Gardiner, A
(Ireland): Home Int 1927-29

Garfield Evans, PR
(Whittaker)
(Wales): Home Int 1948-49-50-51-
52-53-54-55(Captain)-56(Captain)
-57 (Captain)-58(Captain)

Garon, MR
(England): Home Int 1927-28-32-
33-34-36-37-38. (GBI): Curtis Cup
1936

Garrett, M (Ruttle)
(England): Home Int 1947-48-50-
53-59(Captain)-60(Captain)-
63(Captain). (GBI): Curtis Cup
1948-60(Captain); Vagliano Trophy
1959

Garvey, P
(Ireland): Home Int 1947-48-49-
50-51-52-53-54(Captain)-56-57
(Captain) -58(Captain)-59(Captain)
-60(Captain)-61-62-63-68-69.
(GBI): Curtis Cup 1948-50-52-54-
56-60; Vagliano Trophy 1959-63

Gaynor, Z (Fallon)
(Ireland): Home Int 1952-53-54-
55-56-57-58-59-60-61-62-63-64-
65-68-69-70-72 (Captain). (GBI):
Espirito Santo 1964

Gear Evans, A
(Wales): Home Int 1932-33-34

Gee, Hon. J (Hives)
(England): Home Int 1950-51-52

Gemmill, A
(Scotland): Home Int 1981-82-84-
85-86-87-88-89-91-97(Captain)

Gethin Griffith, S
(Wales): Home Int 1914-22-23-24-
28-29-30-31-35

Gibb, M (Titterton)
(England): Home Int 1906-07-08-
10-12

Gibbs, C (Le Feuvre)
(England): Home Int 1971-72-73-
74. (GBI): Curtis Cup 1974;
Vagliano Trophy 1973

Gibbs, S
(Wales): Home Int 1933-34-39

Gildea, Miss
(Ireland): Home Int 1936-37-38-39

Glendinning, D
(Ireland): Home Int 1937-54

Glennie, H
(Scotland): Home Int 1959

Glover, A
(Scotland): Home Int 1905-06-08-
09-12

Gold, N
(England): Home Int 1929-31-32

Gordon, J
369(England): Home Int 1947-48-
49-52-53. (GBI): Curtis Cup 1948

Gorman, S
(Ireland): Home Int 1976-79-80-
81-82-92(Captain)-93(Captain);
Eur L T Ch 1993(Captain)

Gorry, Mary
(Ireland): Home Int 1971-72-73-
74-75-76-77-78-79-80-88-89
(Captain); Eur L T Ch 1971-75.
(GBI): Vagliano Trophy 1977

Gotto, Mrs C
(Ireland): Home Int 1923

Gotto, Mrs L
(Ireland): Home Int 1920

Gourlay, M
(England): Home Int 1923-24-27-
28-29-30-32-33-34-38-57(Captain).
(GBI): Curtis Cup 1932-34

Gow, J
(Scotland): Home Int 1923-24-27-
28

Graham, MA
(Scotland): Home Int 1905-06

Graham, N
(Ireland): Home Int 1908-09-10-12

Granger Harrison, Mrs
(Scotland): Home Int 1922

Grant-Suttie, E
(Scotland): Home Int 1908-10-11-
14-22-23

Grant-Suttie, R
(Scotland): Home Int 1914

Green, B (Pockett)
(England): Home Int 1939

Grice-Whittaker, P (Grice)
(England): Home Int 1983-84.
(GBI): Curtis Cup 1984; Espirito
Santo 1984

Griffith, W
(Wales): Home Int 1981

Griffiths, M
(England): Home Int 1920-21

Greenlees, E
(Scotland): Home Int 1924

Greenlees, Y
(Scotland): Home Int 1928-30-31-
33-34-35-38

Guadella, E (Leitch)
(England): Home Int 1908-10-20-
21-22-27-28-29-30-33

Gubbins, Miss
(Ireland): Home Int 1905

Hackett, B
(Ireland): Home Int 1993-94-96

Hackney, L
(England): Home Int 1990

Haig, J (Mathias Thomas)
(Wales): Home Int 1938-39

Hall, C
(England): Home Int 1991-92; Eur
LT Ch 1991. (GBI): Curtis Cup
1992; Vagliano Trophy 1991

Hall, CM
(England): Home Int 1985

Hall, J (Wade)
(England): Home Int 1987 to 1995;
Eur L T Ch 1987-89-91-93-95.
(GBI): Curtis Cup 1988-90-92-94-
96; Espirito Santo 1988-90-94;
Vagliano Trophy 1989-91-93-95;
CW 1991-95

Hall, Mrs
(Ireland): Home Int 1927-30

Hamilton, S (McKinven)
(Scotland): Home Int 1965

Hambro, W (Martin Smith)
(England): Home Int 1914

Hamilton, J
(England): Home Int 1937-38-39

Hammond, T
(England): Home Int 1985

Hampson, M
(England): Home Int 1954

Hanna, D
(Ireland): Home Int 1987-88

Harrington, D
(Ireland): Home Int 1923

Harris, M [Spearman]
(England): Home Int 1955-56-57-
58-59-60-61-62-63-64-65; Eur L T
Ch 1965-71. (GBI): Curtis Cup
1960-62-64; Vagliano Trophy
1959-61-65; Espirito Santo 1964

Harrold, L
(England): Home Int 1974-75-76

Hartill, D
(England): Home Int 1923

Hartley, E
(England): Home Int 1964(Captain)

Hartley, R
(Wales): Home Int 1958-59-62

Hastings, D (Sommerville)
(Scotland): Home Int 1955-56-57-58-59-60-61-62-63. (GBI): Curtis Cup 1958; Vagliano Trophy 1963

Hay, J (Pelham Burn)
(Scotland): Home Int 1959

Hayter, J (Yuille)
(England): Home Int 1956

Hazlett, VP
(Ireland): Home Int 1956(Captain)

Healy, B (Gleeson)
(Ireland): Home Int 1980-82

Heathcoat-Amory, Lady
(Joyce Wethered)
(England): Home Int 1921-22-23-24-25-29. (GBI): Curtis Cup 1932(Captain)

Hedges, S (Whitlock)
(England): Home Int 1979. (GBI): Vagliano Trophy 1979; CW 1979

Hedley Hill, Miss
(Wales): Home Int 1922

Hegarty, G
(Ireland): Home Int 1955-56-64(Captain)

Helme, E
(England): Home Int 1911-12-13-20

Heming Johnson, G
(England): Home Int 1909-11-13

Henson, D (Oxley)
(England): Home Int 1967-68-69-70-75-76-77-78; Eur L T Ch 1971-77. (GBI): Curtis Cup 1968-70-72-76; Vagliano Trophy 1967-69-71; Espirito Santo 1970; CW 1967-71

Heskin, A
(Ireland): Home Int 1968-69-70-72-75-77-82(Captain)-83(Captain)

Hetherington, Mrs (Gittens)
(England): Home Int 1909

Hewett, G
(Ireland): Home Int 1923-24

Hezlet, Mrs
(Ireland): Home Int 1910

Hickey, C
(Ireland): Home Int 1969-75 (Captain)-76(Captain)

Higgins, E
(Ireland): Home Int 1981 to 1988, 1991 to 1996; Eur L T Ch 1987-93

Hill, J
(England): Home Int 1986

Hill, Mrs
(Wales): Home Int 1924

Hockley, J
(England): Home Int 1991-92-93-96. (GBI): Espirito Santo 1992; Vagliano Trophy 1993

Hodge, S (Shapcott)
(England): Home Int 1986-88; Eur L T Ch 1987. (GBI): Curtis Cup 1988; Vagliano Trophy 1987; CW 1987; Espirito Santo 1988

Hodgson, M
(England): Home Int 1939

Holland, I (Hurst)
(Ireland): Home Int 1958

Holm, H (Gray)
(Scotland): Home Int 1932-33-34-35-36-37-38-47-48-50-51-55-57. (GBI): Curtis Cup 1936-38-48

Holmes, A
(England): Home Int 1931

Holmes, J [Hetherington] (McClure)
(England): Home Int 1957-66-67(Captain)

Hooman, EM [Gavin]
(England): Home Int 1910-11

Hope, LA
(Scotland): Home Int 1975-76-80-84-85-86-87-88(Captain)-89 (Captain)-90 (Captain)

Hort, K
(Wales): Home Int 1929

Howard, A (Phillips)
(England): Home Int 1953-54-55-56-57-58-79(Captain)-80(Captain). (GBI): Curtis Cup 1956-58

Hudson, R
(England): Home Int 1996-97; Eur L T Ch 1997. (GBI): Vagliano Trophy 1997

Huggan, S (Lawson)
(Scotland): Home Int 1985-86-87-88-89; Eur L T Ch 1985-87-89. (GBI): Curtis Cup 1988, Vagliano Trophy 1989

Hughes, J
(Wales): Home Int 1967-71-88-89(Captain); Eur L T Ch 1971

Hughes, Miss
(Wales): Home Int 1907

Huke, B
(England): Home Int 1971-72-75-76-77. (GBI): Curtis Cup 1972; Vagliano Trophy 1975

Hulton, V (Hezlet)
(Ireland): Home Int 1905-07-09-10-11-12-20-21

Humphreys, A (Coulman)
(Wales): Home Int 1969-70-71

Humphreys, D (Forster)
(Ireland): Home Int 1951-52-53-55-57

Hunter, D (Tucker)
(England): Home Int 1905

Hurd, D [Howe] (Campbell)
(Scotland): Home Int 1905-06-08-09-11-28-30

Hurst, Mrs
(Wales): Home Int 1921-22-23-25-27-28

Hyland, B
(Ireland): Home Int 1964-65-66

Inghram, E (Lever)
(Wales): Home Int 1947-48-49-50-51-52-53-54-55-56-57-58-64-65

Irvin, A
(England): Home Int 1962-63-65-67-68-69-70-71-72-73-75; Eur L T Ch 1965-67-69-71. (GBI): Curtis Cup 1962-68-70-76; Vagliano Trophy 1961-63-65-67-69-71-73-75; Espirito Santo 1982(Captain); CW 1967-75

Irvine, Miss
(Wales): Home Int 1930

Isaac, Mrs
(Wales): Home Int 1924

Isherwood, L
(Wales): Home Int 1972-76-77-78-80-86-88-89-90-91

Jack, E (Philip)
(Scotland): Home Int 1962-63-64-81(Captain)-82(Captain)

Jackson, B
(Ireland): Home Int 1937-38-39-50

Jackson, B
(England): Home Int 1955-56-57-58-59-63-64-65-66-73(Captain)-74(Captain). (GBI): Curtis Cup 1958-64-68; Vagliano Trophy 1959-63-65-67-73(Captain)-75(Captain); Espirito Santo 1964; CW 1959-67

Jackson, D
(Scotland): Home Int 1990

Jackson, Mrs H
(Ireland): Home Int 1921

Jackson, J
(Ireland): Home Int 1912-13-14-
20-21-22-23-24-25-27-28-29-30

Jackson, Mrs L
(Ireland): Home Int 1910-12-14-
20-22-25

Jameson, S (Tobin)
(Ireland): Home Int 1913-14-20-
24-25-27

Jenkin, B
(Wales): Home Int 1959

Jenkins, J (Owen)
(Wales): Home Int 1953-56

John, J
(Wales): Home Int 1974

Johns, A
(England): Home Int 1987-88-89

Johnson, A (Hughes)
(Wales): Home Int 1964, 1966 to
1976, 1978-79-85-95(Captain);
Eur L T Ch 1965-67-69-71

Johnson, J (Roberts)
(Wales): Home Int 1955

Johnson, M
(England): Home Int 1934-35

Johnson, PM
(England): Home Int 1984-85-86;
Eur L T Ch 1985. (GBI): Curtis
Cup 1986; Vagliano Trophy 1985;
Espirito Santo 1986

Johnson, R
(Wales): Home Int 1955

Jones, A (Gwyther)
(Wales): Home Int 1959

Jones, B
(Wales): Home Int 1994-95-96; Eur
L T Ch 1993

Jones, K
(Wales): Home Int 1959(Captain)-
1960(Captain)-61(Captain)

Jones, M (De Lloyd)
(Wales): Home Int 1951

Jones, Mrs
(Wales): Home Int 1932-35

Justice, M
(Wales): Home Int 1931-32

Kavanagh, H
(Ireland): Home Int 1993-94-95-
97; Eur L T Ch 1997. (GBI):
Vagliano Trophy 1995

Kaye, H (Williamson)
(England): Home Int 1986
(Captain) -87(Captain)

Keenan, D
(Ireland): Home Int 1989

Keiller, G [Style]
(England): Home Int 1948-49-52

Kelway Bamber, Mrs
(Scotland): Home Int 1923-27-33

Kennedy, D (Fowler)
(England): Home Int 1923-24-25-
27-28-29

Kennion, Mrs (Kenyon Stow)
(England) Home Int 1910

Kerr, J
(Scotland): Home Int 1947-48-49-54

Kidd, Mrs
(Ireland): Home Int 1934-37

King Mrs
(Ireland): Home Int 1923-25-27-29

Kinloch, Miss
(Scotland): Home Int 1913-14

Kirkwood, Mrs
(Ireland): Home Int 1955

Knight, Mrs
(Scotland): Home Int 1922

Kyle, B [Rhodes] (Norris)
(England): Home Int 1937-38-39-
48-49

Kyle, E
(Scotland): Home Int 1909-10

Laing, A
(Scotland): Home Int 1966-67-70-
71-73(Captain)-74(Captain); Eur L
T Ch 1967. (GBI): Vagliano
Trophy 1967

Laing, A
(Scotland): Home Int 1995-96-97;
Eur L T Ch 1997

Laing, V
(Scotland): Home Int 1997

Lambert, S (Cohen)
(England): Home Int 1979-80-93-
94-95; Eur L T Ch 1995.
(GBI): Vagliano Trophy 1979-95

Lambie, S
(Scotland): Home Int 1976

Laming Evans, Mrs
(Wales): Home Int 1922-23

Langford, Mrs
(Wales): Home Int 1937

Langridge, S (Armitage)
(England): Home Int 1963-64-65-
66; Eur L T Ch 1965. (GBI): Curtis
Cup 1964-66; Vagliano Trophy
1963-65

Large, P (Davies)
(England): Home Int 1951-52-
81(Captain)-82(Captain)

Larkin, C (McAuley)
(Ireland): Home Int 1966-67-68-
69-70-71-72; Eur L T Ch 1971

Latchford, B
(Ireland): Home Int 1931-33

Latham Hall, E (Chubb)
(England): Home Int 1928

Lauder, G
(Ireland): Home Int 1911

Lauder, R
(Ireland): Home Int 1911

Lawrence, JB
(Scotland): Home Int 1959-60-61-
62-63-64-65-66-67-68-69-70-
77(Captain); Eur L T Ch 1965-67-
69-71. (GBI): Curtis Cup 1964;
Vagliano Trophy 1963-65; Espirito
Santo 1964; CW 1971

Lawson, H
(Wales): Home Int 1989-90-91-92-
97; Eur L T Ch 1991-93-97

Lebrun, W (Aitken)
(Scotland): Home Int 1978-79-80-
81-82-83-85. (GBI): Curtis Cup
1982; Vagliano Trophy 1981-83

Leaver, B
(Wales): Home Int 1912-14-21

Lee Smith, J
(England): Home Int 1973-74-75-
76. (GBI): Curtis Cup 1974-76;
Espirito Santo 1976; CW 1975

Leete, Mrs IG
(Scotland): Home Int 1933

Leitch, C
(England): Home Int 1910-11-12-
13-14-20-21-22-24-25-27-28

Leitch, M
(England): Home Int 1912-14

Little, S
(Scotland): Home Int 1993

Llewellyn, Miss
(Wales): Home Int 1912-13-14-21-
22-23

Lloyd, J
(Wales): Home Int 1988

Lloyd, P
(Wales): Home Int 1935-36

Lloyd Davies, VH
(Wales): Home Int 1913

Lloyd Roberts, V
(Wales): Home Int 1907-08-10

Lloyd Williams, Miss
(Wales): Home Int 1909-10-12-14

Lobbett, P
(England): Home Int 1922-24-27-29-30

Lovatt, S
(Wales): Home Int 1994-95

Lowry, Mrs
(Ireland): Home Int 1947

Luckin, B (Cooper)
(England): Home Int 1980

Lugton, C
(Scotland): Home Int 1968-72-73-75(Captain)-76(Captain)-77-78-80

Lumb, K (Phillips)
(England): Home Int 1968-69-70-71; Eur L T Ch 1969. (GBI):
Curtis Cup 1972; Vagliano Trophy 1969-71

Lyons, T (Ross Steen)
(England): Home Int 1959.
(GBI): Vagliano Trophy 1959

MacAndrew, F
(Scotland): Home Int 1913-14

Macbeth, M (Dodd)
(England): Home Int 1913-14-20-21-22-23-24-25

MacCann, K
(Ireland): Home Int 1984-85-86

MacCann, K (Smye)
(Ireland): Home Int 1947-48-49-50-51-52-53-54-56-57-58-60-61-62-64-65(Captain)

McCarthy, A
(Ireland): Home Int 1951-52

McCarthy, D
(Ireland): Home Int 1988-90-91-95; Eur L T Ch 1993

McCool, L
(Ireland): Home Int 1993

McCulloch, J
(Scotland): Home Int 1921-22-23-24-27-29-30-31-32-33-35-60(Captain)

McDaid, E (O'Grady)
(Ireland): Home Int 1959

Macdonald, F
(England): Home Int 1990

Macdonald, K
(Scotland): Home Int 1928-29

MacGeach, C
(Ireland): Home Int 1938-39-48-49-50

McGreevy, M
(Ireland): Home Int 1996-97; Eur L T Ch 1997

McGreevy, V
(Ireland): Home Int 1987-90-92

McIntosh, B (Dixon)
(England): Home Int 1969-70;
Eur L T Ch 1969. (GBI): Vagliano Trophy 1969

MacIntosh, I
(Scotland): Home Int 1991(Captain)-92(Captain)-93(Captain); Eur L T Ch 1993(Captain)

McIntyre, J
(England): Home Int 1949-54

McKay, F
(Scotland): Home Int 1992-93-94; Eur L T Ch 1993

McKay, M
(Scotland): Home Int 1991-93-94-96; Eur L T Ch 1993-95.
(GBI): Curtis Cup 1994-96;
Vagliano Trophy 1993-95-97;
CW 1995; Espirito Santo 1996

MacKean, Mrs
(Wales): Home Int 1938-39-47

McKenna, M
(Ireland): Home Int 1968 to 1991-93; Eur L T Ch 1969-71-75-87.
(GBI): Curtis Cup 1970-72-74-76-78-80-82-84-86; Vagliano Trophy 1969-71-73-75-77-79-81-85-87-95(Captain); Espirito Santo 1970-74-76-86(Captain)-90(Captain)

Mackenzie, A
(Scotland): Home Int 1921

McKinlay, M
(Scotland): Home Int 1990-92-93; Eur L T Ch 1993. (GBI): Curtis Cup 1994

McLarty, E
(Scotland): Home Int 1966
(Captain) -67(Captain)-68(Captain)

McMahon, S (Cadden)
(Scotland): Home Int 1974-75-76-77-79. (GBI): Curtis Cup 1976;
Vagliano Trophy 1975

McMaster, S
(Scotland): Home Int 1994-95-96-97; Eur L T Ch 1995-97

McNair, W
(England): Home Int 1921

McNeil, K
(Scotland): Home Int 1969(Captain)-70(Captain)

McNeile, CL
(Ireland): Home Int 1906

McQuillan, Y
(Ireland): Home Int 1985-86

MacTier, Mrs
(Wales): Home Int 1927

Madeley, M (Coburn)
(Ireland): Home Int 1964-69; Eur L T Ch 1969

Madill, M
(Ireland): Home Int 1978-79-80-81-82-83-84-85. (GBI): Curtis Cup 1980; Vagliano Trophy 1979-81-85; Espirito Santo 1980; CW 1979

Madill, Mrs
(Ireland): Home Int 1920-24-25-27-28-29-33

Magee, A-M
(Wales): Home Int 1991-92-93-94

Magill, J
(Ireland): Home Int 1907-11-13

Maher, S (Vaughan)
(England): Home Int 1960-61-62-63-64. (GBI): Curtis Cup 1962-64;
Vagliano Trophy 1961; CW 1963

Mahon, D
(Ireland): Home Int 1989-90

Main, M (Farquhar)
(Scotland): Home Int 1950-51

Maitland, M
(Scotland): Home Int 1905-06-08-12-13

Mallam, Mrs S
(Ireland): Home Int 1922-23

Marks, Mrs T
(Ireland): Home Int 1950

Marks, Mrs
(Ireland): Home Int 1930-31-33-35

Marley, MV
(Wales): Home Int 1921-22-23-30-37

Marr, H (Cameron)
(Scotland): Home Int 1927-28-29-30-31

Marshall, K (Imrie)
(Scotland): Home Int 1984-85-89.
Eur L T Ch 1987-89 (GBI): Curtis Cup 1990; Vagliano Trophy 1989

Martin, P [Whitworth Jones] (Low)
(Wales): Home Int 1948-50-56-59-60-61

Marvin, V
(England): Home Int 1977-78;
Eur L T Ch 1977. (GBI): Curtis
Cup 1978; Vagliano Trophy 1977

Mason, Mrs
(Wales): Home Int 1923

Mather, H
(Scotland): Home Int 1905-09-12-
13-14

Matthew, C (Lambert)
(Scotland): Home Int 1989-90-91-
92-93; Eur L T Ch 1989-91-93.
(GBI): Curtis Cup 1990-92-94;
Vagliano Trophy 1989-91-93;
Espirito Santo 1992; CW 1991

Matthews, T [Thomas]
(Perkins)
(Wales): Home Int 1972-73-74-75-
76-77-78-79-80-81-82-83-84;
Eur L T Ch 1975.
(GBI): Curtis Cup 1974-76-78-80;
Vagliano Trophy 1973-75-77-79;
Espirito Santo 1974; CW 1975-79

Mellis, Mrs
(Scotland): Home Int 1924-27

Melvin, V
(Scotland): Home Int 1994-96

Menton, D
(Ireland): Home Int 1949

Menzies, M
(Scotland): Home Int 1962(Captain)

Merrill, J (Greenhalgh)
(England): Home Int 1960-61-63-
66-69-70-71-75-76-77-78; Eur L T
Ch 1971-77. (GBI): Curtis Cup
1964-70-74-76-78; Vagliano Trophy
1961-65-75-77; Espirito Santo
1970-74(Captain)-78; CW 1963

Millar, D
(Ireland): Home Int 1928

Milligan, J (Mark)
(Ireland): Home Int 1971-72-73

Mills, I
(Wales): Home Int 1935-36-37-39-
47-48

Milton, M (Paterson)
(Scotland): Home Int 1948-49-50-
51-52. (GBI): Curtis Cup 1952

Mitchell, J
(Ireland): Home Int 1930

Moffat, L
(Scotland): Home Int 1996

Monaghan, H
(Scotland): Home Int 1995-96-97;
Eur L T Ch 1997

Moodie, J
(Scotland): Home Int 1990-91-92;
Eur L T Ch 1991-93-95-97. (GBI):
Curtis Cup 1994-96; Vagliano
Trophy 1993-95-97; Espirito Santo
1996; CW 1995

Mooney, M
(Ireland): Home Int 1972-73; Eur
L T Ch 1971. (GBI): Vagliano
Trophy 1973

Moorcroft, S
(England): Home Int 1985-86; Eur
L T Ch 1985-87

Moore, S
(Ireland): Home Int 1937-38-39-
47-48-49-68(Captain)

Moran, V (Singleton)
(Ireland): Home Int 1970-71-73-
74-75; Eur L T Ch 1971-75

Morant, E
(England): Home Int 1906-10

Morgan, R
(Wales): Home Int 1996-97; Eur L
T Ch 1997. (GBI): Vagliano
Trophy 1997

Morgan, S
(England): Home Int 1989; Eur L
T Ch 1989

Morgan, W
(England): Home Int 1931-32-33-
34-35-36-37. (GBI): Curtis Cup
32-34-36

Morgan, Miss
(Wales): Home Int 1912-13-14

Moriarty, M (Irvine)
(Ireland): Home Int 1979

Morley, J
(England): Home Int 1990-91-92-
93; Eur L T Ch 1991-93. (GBI):
Curtis Cup 1992; Vagliano Trophy
1991-93; Espirito Santo 1992

Morris, L (Moore)
(England): Home Int 1912-13

Morris, Mrs de B
(Ireland): Home Int 1933

Morrison, G (Cheetham)
(England): Home Int 1965-
69(Captain). (GBI): Vagliano
Trophy 1965

Morrison, G (Cradock-
Hartopp)
(England): Home Int 1936

Mountford, S
(Wales): Home Int 1989-90-91-92;
Eur L T Ch 1991

Murray, Rachel
(Ireland): Home Int 1952

Murray, S (Jolly)
(England): Home Int 1976

Musgrove, Mrs
(Wales): Home Int 1923-24

Myles, M
(Scotland): Home Int 1955-57-59-
60-67

Neill-Fraser, M
(Scotland): Home Int 1905-06-07-
08-09-10-11-12-13-14

Nes, K (Garnham)
(England): Home Int 1931-32-33-
36-37-38-39

Nevile, E
(England): Home Int 1905-06-08-
10

New, B
(England): Home Int 1980-81-82-
83. (GBI): Curtis Cup 1984;
Vagliano Trophy 1983

Newell, B
(England): Home Int 1936

Newman, L
(Wales): Home Int 1927-31

Newton, B (Brown)
(England): Home Int 1930-33-34-
35-36-37

Nicholls, M
(Wales): Home Int 1962(Captain)

Nicholson, J (Hutton)
(Scotland): Home Int 1969-70;
Eur L T Ch 1971. (GBI): CW 1971

Nicholson, L
(Scotland): Home Int 1994-95-96-
97; Eur L T Ch 1995-97

Nicholson, Mrs WH
(Scotland): Home Int 1910-13

Nimmo, H
(Scotland): Home Int 1936-38-39

Norris, J (Smith)
(Scotland): Home Int 1966-67-68-
69-70-71-72-75-76-77-78-79-
83(Captain)-84(Captain)-
84(Captain); Eur L T Ch 1971.
(GBI): Vagliano Trophy 1977

Norwell, I (Watt)
(Scotland): Home Int 1954

Nutting, P (Jameson)
(Ireland): Home Int 1927-28

O'Brien, A
(Ireland): Home Int 1969

O'Brien Kenney, S
(Ireland): Home Int 1977-78-83-84-85-86

O'Donnell, M
(Ireland): Home Int 1974-77 (Captain) -78(Captain)-79 (Captain); Eur L T Ch 1980 (Captain). (GBI): Curtis Cup 1982; Vagliano Trophy 1981 (Captain)

O'Donohoe, A
(Ireland): Home Int 1948-49-50-51-53-73(Captain)-74 (Captain)

O'Hare, S
(Ireland): Home Int 1921-22

O'Reilly, T (Moran)
(Ireland): Home Int 1977-78-86-88-95(Captain); Eur L T Ch 1987

O'Sullivan, A
(Ireland): Home Int 1982-83-84-92-94-95-96; Eur L T Ch 1993-97

O'Sullivan, P
(Ireland): Home Int 1950-51-52-53-54-55-56-57-58-59-60-63-64-65-66-67-69 (Captain)-70(Captain)-71(Captain); Eur L T Ch 1971(Captain)

Oliver, J
(England): Home Int 1995

Oliver, M (Jones)
(Wales): Home Int 1955-60-61-62-63-64-65-66. (GBI): Espirito Santo 1964

Ormsby, Miss
(Ireland): Home Int 1909-10-11

Orr, P (Boyd)
(Ireland): Home Int 1971

Orr, Mrs
(Wales): Home Int 1924

Owen, E
(Wales): Home Int 1947

Panton-Lewis, C (Panton)
(Scotland): Home Int 1972-73-76-77-78. (GBI): Vagliano Trophy 1977; Espirito Santo 1976

Park, Mrs
(Scotland): Home Int 1952

Parker, S
(England): Home Int 1973

Patey, Mrs
(Scotland): Home Int 1922-23

Pearson, D
(England): Home Int 1928-29-30-31-32-34

Percy, G (Mitchell)
(Scotland): Home Int 1927-28-30-31

Perriam, A
(Wales): Home Int 1988-90-91-92; Eur L T Ch 1991

Phelips, M
(Wales): Home Int 1913-14-21

Phillips, ME
(England): Home Int 1905

Phillips, Mrs
(Wales): Home Int 1921

Pickard, M (Nichol)
(England): Home Int 1958-59-60-61-67-69-83(Captain). (GBI): Curtis Cup 1968-70; Vagliano Trophy 1959-61-67

Pilgrim, E
(Wales): Home Int 1995-97; Eur L T Ch 1997

Pim, Mrs
(Ireland): Home Int 1908

Pook, E (Chadwick)
(England): Home Int 1963-65-66-67; Eur L T Ch 1967.(GBI): Curtis Cup 1966; Vagliano Trophy 1963-67; CW 1967

Porter, D (Park)
(Scotland): Home Int 1922-25-27-29-30-31-32-33-34-35-37-38-47-48. (GBI): Curtis Cup 1932

Porter, M (Lazenby)
(England): Home Int 1931-32

Powell, M
(Wales): Home Int 1908-09-10-12

Power, ER (McDaid)
(Ireland): Home Int 1987 to 1997; Eur L T Ch 1987-93-97. (GBI): Curtis Cup 1994; Vagliano Trophy 1995-97

Price, M (Greaves)
(England): Home Int 1956(Captain)

Price Fisher, E (Price)
(England): Home Int 1948-51-52-53-54-55-56-57-58-59-60. (GBI): Curtis Cup 1950-52-54-56-58-60; Vagliano Trophy 1959; CW 1959

Proctor, Mrs
(Wales): Home Int 1907

Provis, I (Kyle)
(Scotland): Home Int 1910-11

Purcell, E
(Ireland): Home Int 1965-66-67-72-73

Purvis-Russell-Montgomery, C
(Scotland): Home Int 1921-22-23-25-28-29-30-31-32-33-34-35-36-37-38-39-47-48-49-50-52

Pyman, B
(Wales): Home Int 1925-28-29-30-32-33-34-35-36-37-38

Rabbidge, R
(England): Home Int 1931

Ratcliffe, E
(England): Home Int 1995-96-97; Eur L T Ch 1995-97. (GBI): Espirito Santo 1996; Vagliano Trophy 1997

Rawlings, M
(Wales): Home Int 1979-80-81-83-84-85-86-87. (GBI): Vagliano Trophy 1981

Rawlinson, T (Walker)
(Scotland): Home Int 1970-71-73-76. (GBI): Vagliano Trophy 1973

Read, P
(England): Home Int 1922

Reddan, C (Tiernan)
(Ireland): Home Int 1935-36-38-39-47-48-49. (GBI): Curtis Cup 1938-48

Reddan, MV
(Ireland): Home Int 1955

Reece, P (Millington)
(England): Home Int 1966(Captain)

Rees, G
(Wales): Home Int 1981

Rees, MB
(Wales): Home Int 1927-31

Reid, A (Lurie)
(Scotland) Home Int 1960-61-62-63-64-66. (GBI): Vagliano Trophy 1961

Reid, A (Kyle)
(Scotland): Home Int 1923-24-25

Reid, D
(Scotland): Home Int 1978-79

Remer, H
(England): Home Int 1909

Rennie, J (Hastings)
(Scotland): Home Int 1961-65-66-67-71-72; Eur L T Ch 1967. (GBI): Curtis Cup 1966; Vagliano Trophy 1961-67

Rhys, J
(Wales): Home Int 1979

Rice, J
(Ireland): Home Int 1924-27-29

Richards, D
(Wales): Home Int 1994-95-96

Richards, J
(Wales): Home Int 1980-82-83-85

Richards, S
(Wales): Home Int 1967

Richardson, Mrs
(England): Home Int 1907-09

Richmond, M (Walker)
(Scotland): Home Int 1972-73-74-75-77-78. (GBI): Curtis Cup 1974;
Vagliano Trophy 1975

Rieben, Mrs
(Wales): Home Int 1927-28-29-30-31-32-33

Rigby, F (Macbeth)
(Scotland): Home Int 1912-13

Ritchie, C (Park)
(Scotland): Home Int 1939-47-48-51-52-53-64(Captain)

Roberts, B
(Wales): Home Int 1984(Captain)-85(Captain)-86(Captain)

Roberts, E (Pentony)
(Ireland): Home Int 1932-33-34-35-36-39

Roberts, E (Barnett)
(Ireland): Home Int 1961-62-63-64-65; Eur L T Ch 1964

Roberts, G
(Wales): Home Int 1949-52-53-54

Roberts, M (Brown)
(Scotland): Home Int 1965(Captain). (GBI): Espirito Santo 1964

Roberts, P
(Wales): Home Int 1950-51-53-55-56-57-58-59-60-61-62-63-64 (Captain) -65 (Captain)-66 (Captain) -67 (Captain)-68-69-70; Eur L T Ch 1965-67-69. (GBI): Espirito Santo 1964

Roberts, S
(Wales): Home Int 1983-84-85-86-87-88-89-90; Eur L T Ch 1983-87

Robertson, B (McCorkindale)
(Scotland): Home Int 1958-59-60-61-62-63-64-65-66-69-72-73-78-80-81-82-84 -85-86; Eur L T Ch 1965-67(Captain)-69-71(Captain). (GBI): Curtis Cup 1960-66-68-70-72-74(Captain)-76(Captain)-82-86; Vagliano Trophy 1959-63-69-71-

81-85; CW 1971-75(Captain); Espirito Santo 1964-66-68(Captain)-72-80-82

Robertson, D
(Scotland): Home Int 1907

Robertson, E
(Scotland): Home Int 1924

Robertson, G
(Scotland): Home Int 1907-08-09

Robinson, C (Nesbitt)
(Ireland): Home Int 1974-75-76-77-78-79-80-81. (GBI): Curtis Cup 1980; Vagliano Trophy 1979

Robinson, R (Bayly)
(Ireland): Home Int 1947-56-57

Robinson, S
(England): Home Int 1989

Roche, Mrs
(Ireland): Home Int 1922

Rogers, A
(Ireland): Home Int 1992-93; Eur L T Ch 1993

Rogers, J
(Wales): Home Int 1972

Rose, A
(Scotland): Home Int 1990 to 1997; Eur L T Ch 1991-93-95-97. (GBI): Curtis Cup 1996; Vagliano Trophy 1995-97; CW 1995

Roskrow, M
(England): Home Int 1948-50

Ross, M (Hezlet)
(Ireland): Home Int 1905-06-07-08-11-12

Rostron, K
(England): Home Int 1996-97; Eur L T Ch 1997. (GBI): Vagliano Trophy 1997

Roxburgh, L
(Scotland): Home Int 1993-94-95

Roy, S (Needham)
(Scotland): Home Int 1969-71-72-73-74-75-76-83. (GBI): Vagliano Trophy 1973-75

Rudgard, G
(England): Home Int 1931-32-50-51-52

Rusack, J
(Scotland): Home Int 1908

Sabine, D (Plumpton)
(England): Home Int 1934-35. (GBI): Curtis Cup 1934

Saunders, V
(England): Home Int 1967-68; Eur L T Ch 1967. (GBI): Curtis Cup 1968; Vagliano Trophy 1967; CW 1967

Scott Chard, Mrs
(Wales) Home Int 1928-30

Seddon, N
(Wales): Home Int 1962-63-74 (Captain)-75(Captain)-76 (Captain)

Selkirk, H
(Wales): Home Int 1925-28

Shapcott, A
(England): Home Int 1989

Shaw, P
(Wales): Home Int 1913

Sheldon, A
(Wales): Home Int 1981

Sheppard, E (Pears)
(England): Home Int 1947

Simpson, L (Moore)
(England): Home Int 1979-80

Singleton, B (Henderson)
(Scotland): Home Int 1939-52-53-54-55-56-57-58-60-61-62-63-64-65

Slade, Lady
(Ireland): Home Int 1906

Slark, R (Porter)
(England): Home Int 1959-60-61-62-64-65-66-68-78; Eur L T Ch 1965; Espirito Santo 1964. (GBI): Curtis Cup 1960-62-64; Vagliano Trophy 1959-61-65; Espirito Santo 1966(Captain); CW 1963

Slocombe, E (Davies)
(Wales): Home Int 1974-75

Smalley, Mrs A
(Wales): Home Int 1924-25-31-32-33-34

Smillie, P
(England): Home Int 1985-86

Smith, A [Stant] (Willard)
(England): Home Int 1974-75-76. (GBI): Curtis Cup 1976; Vagliano Trophy 1975; CW 1959-63

Smith, E
(England): Home Int 1991

Smith, F (Stephens)
(England): Home Int 1947-48-49-50-51-52-53-54-55-59-62 (Captain)-71(Captain) -72 (Captain). (GBI): Curtis Cup 1950-52-54-56-58-60-62(non-playing Captain)-72(non-playing Captain); Vagliano Trophy 1959-71; CW 1959-63

Smith, K
(England): Home Int 1997

Smith, Mrs L
(Ireland): Home Int 1913-14-21-22-23-25

Smythe, M
(Ireland): Home Int 1947-48-49-50-51-52-53-54-55-56-58-59-62(Captain)

Sowter, Mrs
(Wales): Home Int 1923

Speak, K
(England): Home Int 1993-94; Eur L T Ch 1993. (GBI): Curtis Cup 1994; Vagliano Trophy 1993; Espirito Santo 1994

Speir, M
(Scotland): Home Int 1957-64-68-71(Captain)-72(Captain)

Stark, K
(Wales): Home Int 1995-96

Starrett, L (Malone)
(Ireland): Home Int 1975-76-77-78-80

Stavert, M
(Scotland): Home Int 1979

Steel, Mrs DC
(Scotland): Home Int 1925

Steel, E
(England): Home Int 1905-06-07-08-11

Stewart, G
(Scotland): Home Int 1979-80-81-82-83-84; Eur L T Ch 1982-84. (GBI): Curtis Cup 1980-82; Vagliano Trophy 1979-81-83; CW 1979-83

Stewart, L (Scraggie)
(Scotland): Home Int 1921-22-23

Stocker, J
(England): Home Int 1922-23

Stockton, Mrs
(Wales): Home Int 1949

Storry, Mrs
(Wales): Home Int 1910-14

Stroud, N
(Wales): Home Int 1989

Stuart, M
(Ireland): Home Int 1905-07-08

Stuart-French, Miss
(Ireland): Home Int 1922

Stupples, K
(England): Home Int 1995-96-97; Eur L T Ch 1995-97. (GBI): Curtis Cup 1996; Vagliano Trophy 1997

Sugden, J (Machin)
(England): Home Int 1953-54-55

Summers, M (Mackie)
(Scotland): Home Int 1986

Sumpter, Mrs
(England): Home Int 1907-08-12-14-24

Sutherland Pilch, R (Barton)
(England): Home Int 1947-49-50-58(Captain)

Swallow, C
(England): Home Int 1985; Eur L T Ch 1985

Sweeney, L
(Ireland): Home Int 1991

Tamworth, Mrs
(England): Home Int 1908

Taylor, I
(Ireland): Home Int 1930

Teacher, F
(Scotland): Home Int 1908-09-11-12-13

Tebbet, K
(England): Home Int 1990-94

Temple, S
(England): Home Int 1913-14

Temple Dobell, G (Ravenscroft)
(England): Home Int 1911-12-13-14-20-21-25-30

Thomas, C (Phipps)
(Wales): Home Int 1959-63-64-65-66-67-68-69-70-71-72-73-76-77-80

Thomas, I
(Wales): Home Int 1910

Thomas, J (Foster)
(Wales): Home Int 1984-85-86-87-92-93-95; Eur L T Ch 1987-89-91-93

Thomas, O
(Wales): Home Int 1921

Thomas, S (Rowlands)
(Wales): Home Int 1977-82-84-85

Thomas, V (Rawlings)
(Wales): Home Int 1971 to 1997; Eur L T Ch 1973-75-77-79-81-83-87-91-97. (GBI): Curtis Cup 1982-84-86-88-90; Vagliano Trophy 1979-83 -85-87-89-91; CW 1979-83-87-91. Espirito Santo 1990

Thompson, M
(Wales): Home Int 1937-38-39

Thompson, M (Wallis)
(England): Home Int 1948-49

Thompson, M
(Scotland): Home Int 1949

Thomson, D
(Scotland): Home Int 1982-83-85-87

Thomson, M
(Scotland): Home Int 1907

Thomson, M
(Scotland): Home Int 1974-75-76-77-78; Eur L T Ch 1978. (GBI): Curtis Cup 1978; Vagliano Trophy 1977

Thornhill, J (Woodside)
(England): Home Int 1965-74-82-83-84-85-86-87-88; Eur L T Ch 1965-85-87. (GBI): Curtis Cup 1984-86-88; Vagliano Trophy 1965-83-85-87-89(Captain); CW 1983-87

Thornhill, Miss
(Ireland): Home Int 1924-25

Thornton, Mrs
(Ireland): Home Int 1924

Todd, Mrs
(Ireland): Home Int 1931-32-34-35-36

Thomlinson, J [Evans] (Roberts)
(England): Home Int 1962-64. (GBI): Curtis Cup 1962; Vagliano Trophy 1963

Treharne, A [Mills]
(Wales): Home Int 1952-61

Turner, B
(England): Home Int 1908

Turner, S (Jump)
(Wales): Home Int 1982-84-85-86-91-93

Tynte, V
(Ireland): Home Int 1905-06-08-09-11-12-13-14

Uzielli, A (Carrick)
(England): Home Int 1976-77-78-90-92(Captain)-93(Captain); Eur L T Ch 1977. (GBI): Curtis Cup 1978; Vagliano Trophy 1977

Valentine, J (Anderson)
(Scotland): Home Int 1934-35-36-37-38-39-47-49-50-51-52-53-54-55-56 (Captain)-57-58. (GBI): Curtis Cup 1938-48-50-52-54-56-58; CW 1959

Valentine, P (Whitley)
(Wales): Home Int 1973-74-75-77-78-79-80-90 (Captain)

Veitch, F
(Scotland): Home Int 1912

Wadsworth, H
(Wales): Home Int 1987-88-89-90;
Eur L T Ch 1987-90. (GBI): Curtis
Cup 1990

Waite, C
(England): Home Int 1981-82-83-
84, Eur L T Ch 1985. (GBI): Curtis
Cup 1984; Vagliano Trophy 1983;
Espirito Santo 1984; CW 1983

Wakelin, H
(Wales): Home Int 1955

Walker, B (Thompson)
(England): Home Int 1905-06-07-
08-09-11

Walker, M
(England): Home Int 1970-72;
Eur L T Ch 1971. (GBI): Curtis
Cup 1972; Vagliano Trophy 1971;
CW 1971

Walker, P
(Ireland): Home Int 1928-29-30-
31-32-33-34-35-36-37-38-39-48.
(GBI): Curtis Cup 1934-36-38

Walker-Leigh, F
(Ireland): Home Int 1907-08-09-
11-12-13-14

Wallace-Williamson, V
(Scotland): Home Int 1932.
(GBI): Curtis Cup 1938 (Captain)

Walsh, R
(Ireland): Home Int 1987

Walter, J
(England): Home Int 1974-79-80-
82-86

Wardlaw, N (Baird)
(Scotland): Home Int 1932-35-36-
37-38-39-47-48. (GBI): Curtis Cup
1938

Watson, C (Nelson)
(England): Home Int 1982

Webb, L (Bolton)
(Ireland): Home Int 1981-82-88-
89-91-92-94

Webster, S (Hales)
(Wales): Home Int 1968-69-72-
91(Captain)

Wesley, N
(Wales): Home Int 1986

Westall, S (Maudsley)
(England): Home Int 1973

Weston, R
(Wales): Home Int 1927

Whieldon, Miss
(Wales): Home Int 1908

Wickham, C
(Ireland): Home Int 1983-89

Wickham, P
(Ireland): Home Int 1976-83-87;
Eur L T Ch 1987

Williams, M
(Wales): Home Int 1936

Williamson, C (Barker)
(England): Home Int 1979-80-81

Willock-Pollen, G
(England): Home Int 1907

Wilson, A
(Scotland): Home Int 1973-74-85
(Captain)

Wilson, E
(England): Home Int 1928-29-30.
(GBI): Curtis Cup 1932

Wilson, Mrs
(Ireland): Home Int 1931

Wilson Jones, D
(Wales): Home Int 1952

Winn, J
(England): Home Int 1920-21-23-
25

Wooldridge, W (Shaw)
(Scotland): Home Int 1982

Wragg, M
(England): Home Int 1929

Wright, J (Robertson)
(Scotland): Home Int 1952-53-
54-55-56-57-58-59-60-61-63-65-
67-73-78 (Captain)-79(Captain)-
80(Captain)-86(Captain); Eur L T
Ch 1965. (GBI): Curtis Cup 1954-
56-58-60; Vagliano Trophy 1959-
61-63; CW 1959

Wright, M
(Scotland): Home Int 1990-91-92;
Eur L T Ch 1991

Wright, N (Cook)
(Wales): Home Int 1938-47-48-49-
51-52-53-54-57-58-59-60-62-63-
64-66-67-68-71 (Captain)-
72(Captain)-73(Captain); Eur L T
Ch 1965-71 (Captain). (GBI):
Espirito Santo 1964

Wright, P
(Scotland): Home Int 1981-82-83-
84; Eur L T Ch 1987.
(GBI): Vagliano Trophy 1981

Wylie, P (Wade)
(England): Home Int 1934-35-
36-37-38-47. (GBI): Curtis Cup
1938

Association of Golf Writers

(L) = Life member
(H) = Honorary member

Adamson, Tony

Aitken, Michael

(L) Baker, John E

Ballantine, John

Birtill, David
Manchester Evening News

Bisher, Firman
Atlanta Journal

Blackstock, Dixon

Blighton, Bill

Blomqvist, Jan
Golf Digest Sverige

Bolze, Gerd A

Booth, Alan

Bowden, Ken

Britten, Mike

(H) Butler, Frank

Callander, Colin
Golf Monthly

Campbell, Malcolm

Carter, Jane
Women and Golf

Chapman, Jeremy
The Sporting Life

Clark, Bill
Sunday Mirror, Belfast

Clough, Frank

Corrigan, Peter

Creighton, Brian
Reuters

Crockett, Scott

Dabell, Norman

Davies, Bob
*Wolverhampton Express
and Star*

Davies, David
The Guardian

Davies, Patricia

Dempster, Martin

Donald, Peter

Ebbinge, Jan B

(L) Edwards, Leslie

Elliott, Bill

Ellison, Stanley

Farquharson, Colin

Farrell, Andrew
The Independent

Fenton, John

Ferrier, Bob

Figar, Jose
Adesport, Madrid

Frederick, Adrian

Garrod, Mark
Press Association

Gilleece, Dermot
The Irish Times

Glover, Tim
Daily Express

Godsiff, Peter

Goodner, Ross

Green, Bob

Green, Robert

Grimsley, Will

Hamilton, David

Harding, Colin
Hampshire Golf

Hardy, Martin

Haslam, Peter
Golf World

Hedley, Alan
The Journal, Newcastle-
upon-Tyne

Hennessy, John

Hermann, Philippe
Tribune de Geneva

Herron, Allan
The People

Higgs, Peter
Mail on Sunday

Hopkins, John
The Times

Howard, Jock
Golf World

(L) Huggins, Percy

Ingham, John

Jacobs, Raymond

Jansen, Anders
Svensk Golf

Jenkins, Dan

Kahn, Elizabeth

Kelly, Jeff
Andalucia Golf

Lafaurie, André-Jean

Laidlaw, Renton
Golfer's Handbook

Lawrenson, Derek
Sunday Telegraph

Leitao, Jaoá Morais
Pluripress

(L) Lincoln, Stanley

MacCullum, Scott

McDonnell, Michael
Daily Mail

Mackie, Keith

Macniven, Ian

MacVicar, Jock
Daily Express

Magowan, Jack
Belfast Telegraph

Mair, Norman

Mair, Lewine
Daily Telegraph

Maitland, Bobby

Mancinelli, Piero
Parliamo di Golf, Milan

Masters, Peter
Golf World

Mearing, Paddy

Moody, John

Mossop, James

Mulqueen, Charles
Cork Examiner

Nicol, Alister

Oakley, John

Ortega, Jesús Ruiz
Golf, Madrid

Ostermann, Ted

Pargeter, John

Pastor, Nuria
La Vanguardia, Barcelona

Pinner, John

(H) Place, Tom

(H) Platts, Mitchell

Plumridge, Chris

Potter, Bryan

Price Fisher, Elizabeth

Ramsey, Tom
News International,
Australia

Redmond, John

Reece, John K

Reid, Philip
Irish Times

Riach, Ian

Richardson, Gordon

Robertson, Bill
Today's Golfer

Robertson, Jack

Rodrigo, Robert
(Bob Rodney)

Roseforte, Tim

Ross, John

Ruddy, Pat
Golfers Companion

(L) Ryde, Peter

St John, Lauren
Sunday Times

(L) Scatchard, Charles

Scott, Graham

Seitz, Nick

Severino, Dick
Golf Features Service,
San Diego

Simmons, Richard

Simpson, Gordon
Daily Record

Skelton, Ronald

Smart, Chris
Mid-Glamorgan Press
Agency

Smith, Colm
Irish Independent

Somers, Robert

Spander, Art

Spink, Alex

(L) Steel, Donald

Stenson, Tony
Daily Mirror

Stobbs, John

Tait, Alistair
Golf Monthly

(H) Thornberry, Henry W

Trillo Amores, Isabel

(H) Ullyett, Roy

Van Esbeck, Edmund

Ward, Barry E

Webb, Mel

Whitbread, John S
Surrey Herald

White, Gordon S

Wilson, Mark

Wind, Herbert Warren

Wood, Ian

Wright, Ben

Zachrisson, Goran

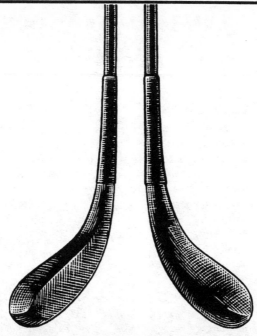

TAKE THE FAMILY FOR A WALK
ROUND THE WOODS.

Five hundred years of golfing history, and a great day

out are waiting to be discovered at the

British Golf Museum—with the

latest Philips CD-i and touch-

screen displays as your guide.

Find out the secrets of the royal,

the ancient, and the modern game and its

players. Then finish the round at our gift shop.

British Golf Museum
St Andrews

WINNER OF
7
SEVEN MAJOR AWARDS

The British Golf Museum,
Bruce Embankment, St Andrews, Fife KY16 9AB. Telephone: 01334 478880.

Buyer's Guide to Good Golfing and Golf Course Maintenance

This compact but informative guide to manufacturers and organisations offering services to golf clubs and individual golfers includes a wide number of categories, from services to personal accessories and golfing equipment to golf course maintenance.

AFTER-DINNER SPEAKERS
ANTIQUES
ARBORICULTURE LANDSCAPING/ CONSTRUCTION
ARCHITECTS, CONSTRUCTORS & CONSULTANTS
AUDIOS/VIDEOS
AWARDS, PRIZES & TROPHIES
BADGES & TIES
BAG/MEMBERSHIP TAGS
BAGS/GOLF ACCESSORIES
BALL MANUFACTURERS/SUPPLIERS
BOOKSELLERS & PUBLISHERS
BULK CONSTRUCTION MATERIAL SUPPLIES
BUSINESS CONSULTANTS
CARTOONS & CARICATURES
CARTS, TROLLEYS & BUGGIES
CELEBRITIES & AFTER-DINNER SPEAKERS
CHARITY ORGANISATIONS
CLOTHING/GOLFWEAR
CLUB MANAGEMENT CONSULTANTS
CLUB MANUFACTURERS
CLUBHOUSE FURNISHINGS & FLOOR COVERINGS
COMPUTER SYSTEMS
CORPORATE GIFTS & EVENTS
COURSE MEASUREMENT
COURSE UPGRADING/MAINTENANCE
DISTRIBUTORS & WHOLESALERS
DRIVING RANGE & PRACTICE EQUIPMENT
EDUCATION/TEACHING AIDS
ELECTRONIC POINT-OF-SALE
GIFTS & NOVELTIES
GOLF BAG STANDS/STORAGE
GOLF CLUB REPAIRS
GOLF COURSE DISTANCE GUIDES
GOLF COURSE FURNISHINGS
GOLF DEVELOPMENT, MAINTENANCE & MANAGEMENT
GOLF GRIPS & SHAFTS

GOLF HOLIDAYS/ TOUR OPERATORS HOME & OVERSEAS
GOLFING AIDS/PRACTICE EQUIPMENT
GOVERNING BODIES
GREEN KEEPING & DRIVING RANGE VEHICLES
HONOURS BOARDS
INSURANCE
IRRIGATION EQUIPMENT/DESIGN & INSTALLATION
JEWELLERY
LOCKER MANUFACTURERS
MAIL ORDER
PERSONAL ACCESSORIES
PERSONALISED PRODUCTS
PICTURES & PRINTS
PRACTICE NETTING/CAGES
PRECEPT GOLF BALLS
PROMOTION/PUBLICITY
PROPERTY CONSULTANTS
PUTTER MANUFACTURERS
RANGE BALL MANUFACTURERS
REMOTE CONTROLLED TROLLEYS
SCORECARDS & SCOREPLANNERS
SHOE ACCESSORIES
SIGNS & MARKERS
SIMULATORS/ANALYSERS
SPIKE-PROOF CARPETS
STOCK CONTROL MANAGEMENT
TEE SIGNS
THERMAL WEAR
TOWELS
TUITION
UMBRELLAS
ULTRASONIC CLUB CLEANERS
WATER STORAGE/TANKS
WEATHERWEAR
WET-WEATHER SCORECARD HOLDERS
WINTER/ALL-WEATHER TEE MATS

AFTER-DINNER SPEAKERS

Now You're Talking
After Dinner Speaker Agency
Stone Cottage, Main Street, Ireby,
Kirkby Lonsdale, Lancashire LA6 2JQ.
Tel (01524) 242221
*website: http://www.users.globalnet.co.uk/
ndave*

We have over 350 speakers, comedians and
celebrities for everything from corporate events,
company golf days and Captain's dinners to
conferences, seminars and motivational events.
We book nationwide. Fairest prices guaranteed.
Please ring Dave Dutton now.

ANTIQUES

Antique Golf
10 Glasgow Road, Paisley PA1 3QG.
Tel/Fax 0141-889 1860
e-mail: Robert@dmcsoft.com
website: www.dmcsoft.com/antiquegolf

The most extensive range of antique golf clubs
and memorabilia in the world, all clubs drawn
from the period 1840 to 1920. We supply
individual collectors, golf clubs, and the
corporate marketplace. For a preview ask for
our catalogue or view our website.

Schotten Trophies
- Manfred Schotten Antiques
109 High Street, Burford,
Oxfordshire OX18 4RH.
Tel (01993) 822302 Fax (01993) 822055
website: http://www.schotten.com

Exquisite hand crafted trophies in traditional
style, designed, manufactured and hand
finished in our own workshop by craftsmen
using solid woods, brass and bronze. Also
available are golf antiques, clubs, novelty items,
desk sets etc, and golf club furnishings. (See
advertisement page 403 for further details.)

ARBORICULTURE LANDSCAPING/ CONSTRUCTION

Practicality Brown Ltd
Iver Stud, Iver, Buckinghamshire SL0 9LA.
Tel (01753) 652022 Fax (01753) 653007

Practicality Brown Limited provides a range of
arboricultural services - tree moving (up to
70cm girth), tree supplying and planting, and a
total no-burn site clearance package backed by
forest residue chippers capable of handling stem
sizes up to 25cm diameter. *Pathform*™
hardwood chip is supplied for golf course paths
nationwide.

ARCHITECTS, CONSTRUCTORS & CONSULTANTS

ADAS
Gleadthorpe Grange,
Meden Vale, Mansfield,
Nottinghamshire NG20 9PD.
Tel (01623) 846742 Fax (01623) 847424

The *Whole in One* for new and existing courses.
Combining the science, knowledge and skills
from nearly 60 years involvement with
countryside development, our comprehensive
UK service provides feasibility studies;
landscape, ecology, planning and design;
project and aftercare management.

M J Abbott Ltd
Bratch Lane,
Dinton, Salisbury,
Wiltshire SP3 5EB.
Tel (01722) 716361 Fax (01722) 716828

M J Abbott Limited offer a range of specialist
services to the golf and leisure industry.
Recognised as one of Britain's leading
companies offering Rain Bird irrigation systems.
Land drainage, golf course construction and
maintenance are all undertaken by experienced
employees utilising the company's own specially
adapted machinery. (See advertisement page 16
for further details.)

British Institute
of Golf Course Architects
Merrist Wood House,
Worplesdon,
Guildford, Surrey GU3 3PE.
Tel (01483) 884036 Fax (01483) 884037

Professional Institute of qualified golf course
architects officially recognised by the Royal &
Ancient and English Golf Union.

Christy O'Connor Jnr, Ltd
Weir House,
Kilcolgan,
Galway, Ireland.
Tel +353 91 796475 Fax +353 91 796476

Golf course architect and course re-modelling.
Built 20 golf courses in Ireland and Europe.
Ryder Cup and World Cup player.

C J Collins Construction Ltd
**Bridge Farm House, Cuckfield Road,
Burgess Hill, West Sussex RH15 8RE.**
Tel (01444) 242993 Fax (01444) 247318

The UK's foremost constructor of golf courses and the English Golf Union's appointed contractors. Nationally respected for complete new courses and highly acclaimed for remodelling and upgrading works with existing clubs. Member of BAGCC. Driving range consultancy and construction.

Dave Thomas Ltd
**Philip House, 6 Stamford Road, Bowden,
Altrincham, Cheshire WA14 2JU.**
Tel 0161-929 8600 Fax 0161-929 5060

Golf course design consultants. The design of golf courses and the re-modelling of existing golf courses.

David Hemstock Associates
**Golf Course Architects & Consultants
Suite 4a, Northmill, Bridgefoot,
Belper, Derbyshire DE56 1YD.**
*Tel (01773) 827115 Fax (01773) 821284
e-mail: David_Hemstock@golf-design.
demon.co.uk
website: www.golf-design.demon.co.uk*

40 projects since 1991, from championship-quality new to total re-modelling of existing; Europe to China. Design and documentation, project and maintenance management, clubhouse design, through the qualified and experienced team of David Hemstock, BSc IEng., Les Watts, B.Arch., and Geoff Porter, NDH.

Fox Contracting (Owmby) Ltd
**Caenby Hall, Caenby Corner,
Market Rasen LN8 2BU.**
Tel (01673) 878444 Fax (01673) 878644

Fox Contracting (Owmby) Limited - The contracting division of the Fox group of companies was founded early 1991. Since its formation the company has successfully completed many new developments together with completing upgrading and redevelopment works on existing courses.

Golf Landscapes Ltd
**Ashwells Road, Bentley, Brentwood,
Essex CM15 9SR.**
Tel (01277) 373720 Fax (01277) 374834

The country's leading specialists in golf course construction, drainage and contract maintenance, working throughout Europe with leading international golf course architects. (See advertisement page 387 for further details.)

Greens of Scotland
**Cruickshank Building,
Craibstone Estate,
Bucksburn, Aberdeen AB21 9TR.**
Tel (01224) 711106 Fax (01224) 714591

An international golf course consultancy providing specialist skills for feasibility studies, planning, course design, buildings design, course construction, project management and turf agronomy. Our project range covers alterations, renovations, driving ranges and new courses.

J Hamilton Stutt
**Golf Course Architect
12 Bingham Avenue,
Poole,
Dorset BH14 8NE.**
Tel (01202) 708406

Founder member of the British Institute of Golf Course Architects. One of Europe's most experienced golf course architects. Personal attention throughout to each new project.

John Greasley Ltd
**Ashfield House,
1154 Melton Road,
Syston, Leicester LE7 2HB.**
Tel 0116-269 6766 Fax 0116-269 6866

John Greasley established his company in 1984 and has specialised in the construction of new courses, along with alterations, improvements and refurbishment on existing ones. Works have been completed on some of the countries oldest and most prestigious courses.

Jonathan C Gaunt
**Golf Course Architect
44 Stanmore Road,
London E11 3BU.**
*Tel 0181-532 9181 Fax 0181-532 9553
e-mail: jonathangaunt@compuserve.com
website: http://www.integrity.co.uk/golf/
gaunt*

Since 1990 Jonathan has had over 17 new courses built and is currently advising over 20 existing courses throughout the British Isles and in Portugal, Turkey and Denmark. Preferring a 'hands-on' approach, all design work and construction supervision is undertaken by him personally. Member of the BIGCA.

Land Unit Construction Ltd

Hanslope, Milton Keynes,
Buckinghamshire MK19 7BX.
Tel (01908) 510414 Fax (01908) 511056

We have the knowledge and experience gained over 20 years in golf course construction and constantly work with many of the country's leading golf course architects to provide clients with unparalleled quality of service.

Neil Coles & Associates

International Golf Course Architecture
19 Broadwater Road, Burwood Park,
Walton on Thames, Surrey KT12 5DB.
Tel (01932) 226895 Fax (01932) 222685

Designers of high quality golf courses throughout the UK and Europe, constructed to a fixed budget. Minor alterations to existing courses also undertaken, with over 20 years' experience. Member of the BIGCA.

P S D Agronomy Ltd

42 Garstang Road, Preston,
Lancashire PR1 1NA.
Tel (01772) 884450 Fax (01772) 884445

A specialist team of golf course agronomists working throughout the UK and Europe. Whether building a new course, extending an existing one or just making the best of what you have - we have the technical expertise to help.

Peter Alliss Golf Course Design

10 St Georges Yard, Farnham,
Surrey GU9 7AW.
Tel (01252) 717711 Fax (01252) 717722
e-mail: roy@allissgolf.demon.co.uk

Peter Alliss has been designing golf courses for over 30 years. All designs are supervised by him. The company offers a service from initial route plan, planning submission, construction drawings and specification to final plans. (See advertisement page 403 for further details.)

Robert J Browne

Laytown and Bettystown Golf Club
Bettystown, Co Meath, Ireland.
Tel +353 41 28793 Fax +353 41 28506

Ireland's leading professional golf course architect. Consultation on all aspects of golf course architecture, maps, specifications, management. Modern ideas showing flare and ingenuity. Numerous successful developments completed and acclaimed. New layouts and renovations. Member of the PGAA. (See advertisement page 387 for further details.)

Roger Jones Golf Associates

Allman House, Tralee Road, Killarney,
Co Kerry, Ireland.
Tel/Fax +353 64 35581

Golf architecture, construction supervision and development consultancy, including agronomy and hydrology in conjunction with PSD, for new developments and existing courses, large or small, in Ireland, UK, Europe and Middle East.

Ryder Golf Services

50 Gally Hill Road, Church Crookham,
Hampshire GU13 0QF.
Tel (01252) 617542 Fax (01252) 812082

Specialist consultancy providing advanced CAD services to architects, contractors, developers and clubs for: Feasibility studies; planning applications; course design and re-design; construction cost planning; environmental impact analysis; contract drawings; bills of quantities, 3D visualisations.

Swan Golf Designs Ltd

Telfords Barn, Willingale, Ongar,
Essex CM5 0QF.
Tel (01277) 896229 Fax (01277) 896300

Professional golf course architects with traditional values, offering initial appraisals, conceptual designs, detailed design work and construction management. Specialising in improvements of existing golf courses, extensions, re-design of greens and tees etc, including restorations of classic old courses.

Total Golf Design & Construction

Tall Pines Golf Club, Cooks Bridle Path,
Downside Backwell, Bristol BS19 3DS.
Tel/Fax (01275) 474869

Over 20 years' experience of golf course design and construction in the UK and Europe. Course upgrading work undertaken on a fixed price basis. Full member of the Professional Golfers' Architects Association.

Whitnell Contracts Ltd

Woodlands, Ellis Road, Boxted,
Colchester CO4 5RN.
Tel (01206) 272834 Fax (01206) 272104

Golf course construction, refurbishment and alterations undertaken by the professionals. A hands-on management team combined with an experienced work force utilising a modern fleet of in-house machinery and equipment, working throughout UK and Europe.

Golf Books & Videos

PO Box 444,
10 Theatre Square, Swindon,
Wiltshire SN1 1QX.
Tel (01793) 523170 Fax (01793) 432070
Freephone (orders only): 0500 007077

We supply new and recently published golf
books and videos. Free list available on request.
Fast, efficient, worldwide mail order service.

Birkdale Promotions

97 Old Watford Road,
Bricket Wood,
Nr St Albans, Hertfordshire AL2 3UN.
Tel (01923) 671225 Fax (01923) 662522

An exclusive range of bronze figurines,
silverplated golf trophies, crystal, shields,
antique replica plaques - all suitable for clubs,
societies and corporate events. Our in-house
engraving enables each to be personalised to
your specification and delivery can be made to
any address worldwide. Please call for our free
colour brochure and price list. (See
advertisement page 393 for further details.)

Chorley & Saunders Golf Art

Chequers End,
Chequers Lane,
Preston Village,
Hitchin, Hertfordshire SG4 7TY.
Tel/Fax (01462) 440277

Richard Chorley, England's premier golf artist.
Private Commissions. Original oil paintings,
drawings and limited edition prints. Prints
signed by the artist, numbered and embossed.
Collection of classic courses and golfing greats.
Ideal corporate and captain's prizes gifts.

The Cricketer Ltd

Beech Hanger,
Ashurst,
Nr Tunbridge Wells, Kent TN3 9TE.
Tel (01892) 740697 Fax (01892) 740588

The Sports Gifts catalogue has a unique
collection of gifts and trophies for golfing
fanatics to suit every occasion. Items include
brass golf bag paperweights, golf club wall
plaques, golf ball clocks, bookends and frames
and a golf charm bracelet and amusing golf
mugs. Ring for free catalogue.

Derek Burridge (Wholesale) Ltd

Awards House,
Unit 15, The Metro Centre,
Springfield Road, Hayes,
Middlesex UB4 0LE.
Tel 0181-569 0123 Fax 0181-569 0111

The country's leading suppliers of golf prizes.
We offer a vast range of silverplate, crystal,
china, clocks, leather goods and sporting
trophies, all at trade prices. Glass and
silverplate in-house engraving service. Next day
delivery throughout the UK. Call for brochure.
(See advertisement page 21 for further details).

Galloway Crystal

New Abbey Road,
Beeswing,
by Dumfries DG2 8ED.
Tel/Fax (01387) 760643
e-mail: mcc@gallowayglass.demon.co.uk
website: www.dmcsoft.com/scotplay

Specialist plain and cut crystal suppliers and
engravers. Many innovative golfing gift ideas
through our Muirfield collection and our St
Andrews collection. Personalisation our
speciality. Ask for our catalogue along with club
and reseller price lists.

Golf Classics Ltd

Tom Stewart Lane,
St Andrews KY16 8YB.
Tel (01334) 479191 Fax (01334) 479360

Traditional hand made wood putters,
completely useable. The finest possible
presentation item for a discerning golfer.
Individual or company names can be
incorporated. And now - new from Golf
Classics - the unique *Swilcan Bridge* replicate
putter.

Grandison Golf Gallery

25 Hyndland Road,
Glasgow G12 9UZ.
Tel/Fax 0141-339 9438

Finest quality limited edition prints of the
world's premier golfing venues by award-
winning artist William Grandison. Gifts and
prizes of distinction for the discerning golfer.
Free catalogue available.

Heritage Golf International Ltd

No 2 Tower Estate,
Warpsgrove Lane,
Chalgrove, Oxfordshire OX44 7XZ.
Tel (0410) 760739 Fax (01938) 561478

Produce hand crafted models of individual golf holes either commissioned by the club involved or a replica of a world famous golf hole. Individually produced and hand painted to exacting standards, mounted on a plinth with a bronze name plate, they make perfect gifts and prizes for the golfer that has everything.

In the Picture

28-29 Weybourne Road Industrial Estate,
Sheringham,
Norfolk NR26 8HF.
Tel (01263) 822265 Fax (01263) 822097

In the Picture - The Golf Collection is the world's leading publisher of historic golf imagery. Over 200 images have been produced. Series include both Open and limited editions. Hall of Fame collection; hand coloureds; Open champions; Humour on the Links; Ladies on the Links. Greetings and postcards. For prizes, presentations, club or office decor.

Schotten Trophies
- Manfred Schotten Antiques

109 High Street, Burford,
Oxfordshire OX18 4RH.
Tel (01993) 822302 Fax (01993) 822055
website: http;//www.schotten.com

 Exquisite hand crafted trophies in traditional style, designed, manufactured and hand finished in our own workshop by craftsmen using solid woods, brass and bronze. Also available are golf antiques, clubs, novelty items, desk sets etc, and golf club furnishings. (See advertisement page 403 for further details.)

Solent Souvenirs Ltd

Hamble Bank,
40 Newtown Road,
Warsash,
Southampton, Hampshire SO31 9FZ.
Tel (01489) 577985 Fax (01489) 577886

Britain's premier supplier of specialised golf jewellery and quality gifts. Many items designed and manufactured exclusively for us and unobtainable elsewhere. Replace that traditional trophy with an elegant prize which will be both useful and cherished. Most items delivered overnight.

Elizabeth Parker

The Charles Parker Building,
Midland Road,
Higham Ferrers,
Northamptonshire NN10 8DN.
Tel (01933) 418099 Fax (01933) 358058
e-mail: liziparker@compserve.com

Gold and silver wire hand embroidered blazer badges and silk or polyester ties all produced to your own club logo. Also suppliers of ties, badges, cuff links, key rings and blazer buttons. Quotations and artwork supplied by return.

Bryants of Leeds

Speedwell Street,
Meanwood Road,
Leeds, West Yorkshire LS6 2TD.
Tel 0113-243 0744 Fax 0113-242 6330
e-mail: sales@bryants.co.uk
website: www.bryants.co.uk

Bryants of Leeds is the leading supplier of personalised golf merchandise. Golf club membership bag tags are available in four different shapes as well as a variety of colours. Also available are annual membership labels, membership cards as well as course cards and car window stickers.

H M T Plastics Ltd

PO Box 195,
Haywards Heath,
West Sussex RH16 1FQ.
Tel/Fax (01444) 416088

Bag tags supplied in nine colours either round, pear shaped maxi or sunrise to accommodate club logo, from a choice of six print colours. Adhesive year sticker available in choice of nine colours and sold separately. (See advertisement page 387 for further details.)

Rogue Golf Company Ltd

The Downs Farm,
Reigate Road,
Ewell, Surrey KT17 3BY.
Tel 0181-786 8896 Fax 0181-394 1895

Manufacture and supply of innovative golf equipment including metalwoods, irons, bags and accessories. The range incorporates a fresh, youthful image combined with high quality products sourced predominently from USA.

BAGS/GOLF ACCESSORIES

Bulldog Trading Ltd
Unit 8, Waterloo Avenue,
Chelmsley Wood Industrial Estate,
Solihull North B37 6QQ.
Tel/Fax 0121-779 7575

Manufacturer of on-course golf bags, golf
accessories and personalised products for golf
clubs and corporate days.

Glenscot Golf Ltd
Osborne Court, Thelwall New Road,
Warrington, Cheshire WA4 2LS.
Tel (01925) 861740 Fax (01925) 861750
e-mail: Glenscotgo@aol.com

Glenscot Golf are manufacturers and
distributors of the Seal brand of component golf
equipment. All of which is made to measure up
to your exact specifications. This is completed
by a full range of quality golf bags.

Hymax Products (UK) Ltd
Unit 19 Team Valley Business Centre,
Earlsway Team Valley,
Gateshead NE11 0RQ.
Tel 0191-491 1138 Fax 0191-487 1911
e-mail: hymaxuk@cabeinet.co.uk
website: www.hymax.co.uk

Manufacture of golf accessories and corporate
gift packs. Unique and innovative British made
goods. *Gifts that the golfer uses.*

Prosimmon Golf (UK) Ltd
21 Monkspath Business Park,
Highlands Road, Shirley,
Solihull, West Midlands B90 4NZ.
Tel 0121-744 9551 Fax 0121-744 9541

Manufacturers of Premium golf clubs, bags and
rainwear including the *Icon* range of golf clubs
featuring the revolutionary *Torsionally Tuned*
graphite and steel shafts. Designers of unique
Matchplay custom programme.

Sun Mountain Sports
c/o Golf Products Ltd
The Downs Farm, Reigate Road,
Ewell, Surrey KT17 3BY.
Tel 0181-786 8896 Fax 0181-394 1895

Distribution of a superb range of American
made golf bags including innovative,
lightweight stand and carry bags as well as new
trolley bag offerings. One of the world's leading
suppliers of golf bags and related products.

Wilson Sporting Goods Co Ltd
1 Tanners Yard, London Road,
Bagshot, Surrey GU19 5HD.
Tel (01294) 316300 Fax (01294) 316255

Wilson manufactures and supplies a full range
for the golfer. Two New *Superstar* products
include - the Fatshaft iron - a widebody shaft
construction giving greater stability through
impact, resulting in increased distance and
accuracy. Available in steel, graphite, left-hand
and ladies, with two head designs. The Staff
Titanium golf ball features a Titanium core
giving better direct transfer of energy resulting
in greater distance and accuracy. A new
magnesium surlyn cover offers the ultimate in
breakthrough feel. It is available as the *Spin,*
Distance and *Balata.*

BALL MANUFACTURERS/ SUPPLIERS

Professional Golf Company SDN BHD
4 Jalan Tandang, Petaling Jaya,
Malaysia 46050.
Tel +603 7918833 Fax +603 7925414

Manufacturing and marketing of *Thommo* golf
balls endorsed by Peter Thomson, five time
British Open champion. New - The *Thommo*
titanium series for extra distance, spin and
superb feel. Specialised in corporate logo balls
and undertakes contract manufacturing and
driving range balls.

Second Chance Ltd
Second Chance House, Clifton Road,
Blackpool, Lancashire FY4 4QA.
Tel (01253) 767244 Fax (01253) 792656
e-mail: second.chance@blackpool.net
website: http://www.blackpool.net/golfnet

We supply four grades of *American Lake Balls*
and a range of Balata balls. Our new 6, 12, 24
and 36 allow packing by brand, ie. 12 Titleist or
12 Strata. We also sell range balls.
(See advertisement page 11 for details.)

Wilson Sporting Goods Co Ltd
1 Tanners Yard, London Road,
Bagshot, Surrey GU19 5HD.
Tel (01294) 316300 Fax (01294) 316255

Wilson manufactures and supplies a full range
for the golfer. Two New *Superstar* products
include - the Fatshaft iron - a widebody shaft
construction giving greater stability through
impact, resulting in increased distance and

Continued over

accuracy. Available in steel, graphite, left-hand and ladies, with two head designs. The Staff Titanium golf ball features a Titanium core giving better direct transfer of energy resulting in greater distance and accuracy. A new magnesium surlyn cover offers the ultimate in breakthrough feel. It is available as the *Spin, Distance* and *Balata.*

BOOKSELLERS & PUBLISHERS

Golf Books & Videos
PO Box 444,
10 Theatre Square,
Swindon, Wiltshire SN1 1QX.
Tel (01793) 523170 Fax (01793) 432070
Freephone (orders only): 0500 007077

We supply new and recently published golf books and videos. Free list available on request. Fast, efficient, worldwide mail order service.

Philip Woodrow
50 Kniveton Park,
Ilkeston,
Derbyshire DE7 5FD.
Tel/Fax 0115-930 6771

Golf books for fun and profit. Catalogue of secondhand out-of-print and collectable titles, from the very recent to the very old. Categorised according to content, eg. history, biography, ladies' golf, courses and architecture, instruction and reference etc.

Rhod McEwan Golf Books
Glengarden,
Ballater,
Aberdeenshire AB35 5UB.
Tel (013397) 55429 Fax (013397) 55995

Rare and out of print golf books. Catalogue available on request. Publisher of golf titles. We are always looking to purchase golf books in any quantity. (See advertisement page 387 for further details.)

Steve Schofield Golf Books
29 Nichols Way,
Wetherby,
West Yorkshire LS22 6AD.
Tel/Fax (01937) 581276
e-mail: steve@golfbooks.u-net.com

Classic golf books for sale, new, old and antiquarian. Books on golf history, architecture, biography, club and ball collecting and instruction. Free catalogue on request.

BULK CONSTRUCTION MATERIAL SUPPLIES

Banks Amenity Products Ltd
2 Angel Court, Dairy Yard, High Street,
Market Harborough,
Leicestershire LE16 7NL.
Tel (01858) 464346 Fax (01858) 434734

Manufacturers and distributors of bulk materials for golf course construction and maintenance. Our extensive range includes rootzones, top dressings, divot mixes, screened fensoil and loams, fairway dressings and bunker sands.

BUSINESS CONSULTANTS

Greenscape Golf Management (GSGM)
13A Flemings Lane, Killarney,
Co Kerry, Ireland.
Tel/Fax +353 64 35581

GSGM specialises in the operational management of golf facilities on behalf of owners, investors and developers as well as management consultancy to owner-operated facilities, their financial advisers or financiers. GSGM also specialises in corporate golf event management.

CARTOONS & CARICATURES

Norman Hood Cartoons
98B Main Street, Alrewas,
Burton-on-Trent, Staffordshire DE13 7AE.
Tel (01283) 790993 Fax (01283) 791593

Superb cartoons and caricatures for those golfing occasions and personalities. Norman Hood specialises in the sports industry, especially golf. Individuals and groups. Remember those special times with a unique, humorous hand drawn cartoon. Perfect for amusing club or company greetings cards. Write or telephone for information.

CARTS, TROLLEYS & BUGGIES

A La Carts
Beechwood, Bakeham Lane,
Englefield Green TW20 9TU.
Tel/Fax (01784) 472982

Manufacturers and distributors of single and two-seat golf buggies. Also special-purpose vehicles. New and reconditioned.

Chip 'N' Chub (Melex) Ltd
3 Drayton Avenue,
Ealing,
London W13 0LE.
Tel 0181-997 4885 Fax 0181-997 4825
e-mail: ChipnChubLtd@BTinternet.com

Sales of new and used Melex golf and utility cars to include full after-sales service UK wide, with full stocks of all spares. Demo and loan vehicles available and all finance packages subject to status. (See advertisement page 21 for further details.)

Club Car UK Plc
Dunmore Court,
Wootton Road,
Abingdon, Oxfordshire OX13 6BH.
Tel (01235) 537575 Fax (01235) 537576

New sole UK distributor of Club-Car offering a range of 2-8-seater golf cars (electric/petrol engine), in a variety of colours and optional extras. Available on outright purchase or contract hire to suit your requirements.

Fraser Products Ltd
Turn Street,
Syston, Leicester LE7 1HP.
Tel 0116-269 3609 Fax 0116-269 3596

Manufacturers of two models of the Fraser *Foldaway* powered trolley. One which has been purposely designed for hire by the professionals - and one for personal use. Producers of the *Fraser Fairway* pull trolleys.

Middlemore Ltd
Valley Road Works,
Sedgley, Dudley,
West Midlands DY3 1TS.
Tel (01902) 673360 Fax (01902) 880783

Manufacturers of *Electra Caddie Classic* and *Compact* one piece foldaway powered trolleys, also introducing factory the new 4-wheel single seater *Rydeon 2000* buggy that you load in the boot of your car!

Yamaha Motor (UK) Ltd
Sopwith Drive,
Brooklands, Weybridge, Surrey KT13 0UZ.
Tel (01932) 358000 Fax (01932) 358030

Suppliers of petrol and electric golf cars for clubs and individuals. Fleet contracts with optional purchase and lease schemes, full maintenance and service support. On and off-course utility vehicles, multi-passenger cars and beverage units.

CELEBRITIES & AFTER-DINNER SPEAKERS

Now You're Talking After Dinner Speaker Agency
Stone Cottage,
Main Street, Ireby,
Kirkby Lonsdale, Lancashire LA6 2JQ.
Tel (01524) 242221
website: http://www.users.globalnet.co.uk/ndave

We have over 350 speakers, comedians and celebrities for everything from corporate events, company golf days and Captain's dinners to conferences, seminars and motivational events. We book nationwide. Fairest prices guaranteed. Please ring Dave Dutton now.

CHARITY ORGANISATIONS

Sun Longest Day Challenge - The Marathon of Golf
PO Box 42,
Lymington,
Hampshire SO41 9UH.
Tel/Fax (01590) 675535

The *Challenge* offers golfers of every ability the chance to put something back into the community and have fun doing so. The object is to play 72 holes on or about the *Longest Day of the Year - June 21,* and by your efforts raise money to help your favoured charity. For details call our Helpline 01590 688887. (See advertisement page 12 for further details.)

CLOTHING/GOLFWEAR

Cape Crest Rainwear
Unit 12, Fenlake Industrial Estate,
Fenlake Road,
Bedfordshire MK42 0HB.
Tel (01234) 211707 Fax (01234) 269948
website: www.capecrest.co.uk
info@capecrest.co.uk

Cape Crest Rainwear has a large range of clothing for inclement weather. We have two ranges of suits for men and for ladies with soft microfibre outer and two year guaranteed waterproof breathable linings. We also have waterproof tops, quilted tops, windtops and waterproof lined sweaters. All are competitively priced.

Normandy Sports & Clothing
20 St Edmunds,
Berkhamsted,
Hertfordshire HP4 2HT.
Tel (01442) 865372 Fax (01442) 874480

European distributor of the world's leading personalised golf accessories company - Golf Design USA. Also supplier of personalised clothing, headwear etc. Embroidery or print. No minimum order and speedy delivery. Full colour brochures available. Telephone Bob James.

Sunderland of Scotland Ltd
PO Box 14,
Glasgow G2 1ER.
Tel 0141-552 3261 Fax 0141-552 8518

Sunderland of Scotland manufacture high quality golf rainwear in Scotland. All rainsuits are tour tested and guaranteed waterproof and breathable, a variety of fabrics including Goretex being used. Sunderlands also manufacture the famous Sunderland Original Weatherbeater and Classic Windproof Pullover. Official supplier to PGA, PGAE, LPGA and St Andrews Links Trust.

CLUB MANAGEMENT CONSULTANTS

Greenscape
Golf Management (GSGM)
13A Flemings Lane,
Killarney,
Co Kerry, Ireland.
Tel/Fax +353 64 35581

GSGM specialises in the operational management of golf facilities on behalf of owners, investors and developers as well as management consultancy to owner-operated facilities, their financial advisers or financiers. GSGM also specialises in corporate golf event management.

CLUB MANUFACTURERS

Alan Morgan Golf Club Specialist
7a Kingswood Close,
Holbrooks,
Coventry CV6 4AZ.
Tel (01203) 668100 Fax (01203) 681851

Since 1981 we have offered a high quality specialised repair service including frequency matching, Loft 'n' Lie, O.E.M. assembly and hand crafted clubs. We are a member of the Professional Clubmakers Society.

Aldila UK
12 Heather Road, Binley Woods,
Coventry CV3 2DE.
Tel/Fax (01203) 545651

World's leading manufacturer of graphite golf shafts, including the Clubmaker series, Classic series, Speciality series, Valve series and G Loomis shafts.

Bronty Golf Co Ltd
81A Bradford Road, Stanningley,
Pudsey, West Yorkshire LS28 6AT.
Tel 0113-257 7266 Fax 0113-257 0771

Manufacturers of high quality British made custom golf clubs, putters and specialist clubs. Authentic replicas and hickory shafted putters etc.

Callaway Golf UK Ltd
Units C63 & C64 Barwell Business Park,
Leatherhead Road, Chessington,
Surrey KT9 2NY.
Tel 0181-391 0111 Fax 0181-391 9399

Manufacturer of golf clubs and accessories. Rainwear. Callaway Golf are now the UK distributor for Odyssey Golf.

Cleveland Golf UK
Unit 1, The Griffin Centre, Staines Road,
Feltham, Middlesex TW14 0HS.
Tel 0181-893 2218 Fax 0181-893 2323

Cleveland Golf, pioneers in golf club technology offer a range of VAS (Vibration Absorbing System) woods, irons and putters. With patents on both the VAS system and inset hosel, Cleveland boast the most advanced and stable clubs available. Cleveland also manufactures a range of speciality wedges used by most of the top tour players around the world.

Glenscot Golf Ltd
Osborne Court, Thelwall New Road,
Warrington, Cheshire WA4 2LS.
Tel (01925) 861740 Fax (01925) 861750
e-mail: Glenscotgo@aol.com

Glenscot Golf are manufacturers and distributors of the Seal brand of component golf equipment. All of which is made to measure up to your exact specifications. This is completed by a full range of quality golf bags.

Prosimmon Golf (UK) Ltd
21 Monkspath Business Park,
Highlands Road, Shirley, Solihull,
West Midlands B90 4NZ.
Tel 0121-744 9551 Fax 0121-744 9541

Manufacturers of Premium golf clubs, bags and rainwear including the *Icon* range of golf clubs featuring the revolutionary *Torsionally Tuned* graphite and steel shafts. Designers of unique *Matchplay* custom programme.

Rogue Golf Company Ltd
The Downs Farm, Reigate Road,
Ewell, Surrey KT17 3BY.
Tel 0181-786 8896 Fax 0181-394 1895

Manufacture and supply of innovative golf equipment including metalwoods, irons, bags and accessories. The range incorporates a fresh, youthful image combined with high quality products sourced predominently from USA.

True Temper UK/Europe
c/o Tucker Fasteners,
Walsall Road, Birmingham B42 1BP.
Tel 0121-331 2276 Fax 0121-331 2286

Golf shaft manufacturer both steel and graphite. Dynamic Gold used by the world's leading players and achieving the Grand Slam, all four majors. In 1997 Sensicore the revolutionary vibration damping system new to the market.

Wilson Sporting Goods Co Ltd
1 Tanners Yard, London Road,
Bagshot, Surrey GU19 5HD.
Tel (01294) 316300 Fax (01294) 316255

Wilson manufactures and supplies a full range for the golfer. Two New *Superstar* products include - the Fatshaft iron - a widebody shaft construction giving greater stability through impact, resulting in increased distance and accuracy. Available in steel, graphite, left-hand and ladies, with two head designs. The Staff Titanium golf ball features a Titanium core giving better direct transfer of energy resulting in greater distance and accuracy. A new magnesium surlyn cover offers the ultimate in breakthrough feel. It is available as the *Spin*, *Distance* and *Balata*.

Yonex UK Ltd
74 Wood Lane, White City,
London W12 7RH.
Tel 0181-742 9777 Fax 0181-742 9612

Importer and distributor of Yonex golf, tennis and badminton products in the United Kingdom. Professionals like Scott Hoch and Phil Mickelson use Yonex golf products, and 80% of badminton professionals use Yonex rackets.

CLUBHOUSE FURNISHINGS & FLOOR COVERINGS

Club Class Cabinets
10-11 Charfleets Close,
Canvey Island,
Essex SS8 0PW.
Tel (01268) 681045 Fax (01268) 681286

Club Class Cabinetwork offer a bespoke design and build service in cabinet making, dedicated to the golfing fraternity. Products range from simple hard-wearing storage lockers to sophisticated, polished cabinets in exotic hardwoods and veneers.

Firth Carpets Ltd
Clifton Mills,
Brighouse,
West Yorkshire HD6 4EJ.
Tel (01484) 713371 Fax (01484) 711128

Comprehensive ranges of carpets for clubhouse, pro shops etc including from stock or custom design in spike-proof qualities. Free advice on all aspects of carpet and installation available.

Frank Dineley
T/A Merseyside Carpets
Heald House,
Heald Street,
Liverpool L19 2JG.
Tel/Fax 0151-722 6217

Suppliers and fitters of contract carpets and vinyls etc. Spike resistant carpet and special logo carpets for clubhouses and golfing hotels.

Old Golf by John Preston
7-9 The Lane,
West Mersea,
Colchester, Essex CO5 8NU.
Tel/Fax (01206) 382181

Furniture and personal accessories with a golfing theme. The Old Golf collection creates a comfortable ambiance for clubhouse, hotel or home, from refurbishment to new clubhouse projects. The exclusive range of personal accessories offers a wide choice of quality golf-themed gifts for all occasions. (See advertisements pages 11 & 16 for further details.)

Schotten Trophies
- Manfred Schotten Antiques
109 High Street, Burford,
Oxfordshire OX18 4RH.
Tel (01993) 822302 Fax (01993) 822055
website: http://www.schotten.com

Exquisite hand crafted trophies in traditional style, designed, manufactured and hand finished in our own workshop by craftsmen using solid woods, brass and bronze. Also available are golf antiques, clubs, novelty items, desk sets etc, and golf club furnishings. (See advertisement page 403 for further details.)

Stackit
1 Stokesay Fore, Telford,
Shropshire IF7 4QA.
Tel (01952) 277772 Fax (01952) 277797

Producers of *Golf Organisers* for hotel bedroom, clubhouse and personal use. Also *Golf Bag Stands* for driving ranges and *External Furniture* for driving range and golf course use - from our stock or to your specification.

CORPORATE GIFTS & EVENTS

Hymax Products (UK) Ltd
Unit 19 Team Valley Business Centre,
Earlsway Team Valley,
Gateshead NE11 0RQ.
Tel 0191-491 1138 Fax 0191-487 1911
e-mail: hymaxuk@cabeinet.co.uk
website: www.hymax.co.uk

Manufacture of golf accessories and corporate gift packs. Unique and innovative British made goods. *Gifts that the golfer uses.*

On Course Leisure Management
Hiam Business Centre, New Road,
Maulden, Bedfordshire MK45 2BG.
Tel/Fax (01525) 840606

On Course Leisure Management arrange tailor-made golf holidays for individuals, families or groups: and comprehensive corporate golf packages throughout the UK and worldwide.

COMPUTER SYSTEMS

Euro Systems Projects (ESP)
Europa House,
8 Kimpton Link Business Park,
Kimpton Road, Sutton, Surrey SM3 9PF.
Tel 0181-641 7216 Fax 0181-641 3179

ESP is universally recognised as the UK's

market leader for integrated point-of-sale and management systems. GOLFMASTER has been specifically designed for both the golf professional and the golf club, and encompasses all aspects encountered when running a successful and profitable golf operation.

Pro Shop Keeper Ltd
140 Portway, Stratford, London E15 3QW.
Tel (01727) 835155 Fax (01727) 837881

Pro Shop Keeper is a low cost fully integrated till and stock control system. It can use almost any existing pc. Please contact Carl or Tony on 01727 835155.

COURSE UPGRADING/ MAINTENANCE

ADAS
Gleadthorpe Grange, Meden Vale,
Mansfield, Nottinghamshire NG20 9PD.
Tel (01623) 846742 Fax (01623) 847424

The *Whole in One* for new and existing courses. Combining the science, knowledge and skills from nearly 60 years involvement with countryside development, our comprehensive UK service provides feasibility studies; landscape, ecology, planning and design; project and aftercare management.

M J Abbott Ltd
Bratch Lane, Dinton, Salisbury,
Wiltshire SP3 5EB.
Tel (01722) 716361 Fax (01722) 716828

M J Abbott Limited offer a range of specialist services to the golf and leisure industry. Recognised as one of Britain's leading companies offering Rain Bird irrigation systems. Land drainage, golf course construction and maintenance are all undertaken by experienced employees utilising the company's own specially adapted machinery. (See advertisement page 16 for further details.)

Banks Amenity Products Ltd
2 Angel Court, Dairy Yard, High Street,
Market Harborough,
Leicestershire LE16 7NL.
Tel (01858) 464346 Fax (01858) 434734

Manufacturers and distributors of bulk materials for golf course construction and maintenance. Our extensive range includes rootzones, top dressings, divot mixes, screened fensoil and loams, fairway dressings and bunker sands.

Christy O'Connor Jnr, Ltd
Weir House, Kilcolgan, Galway, Ireland.
Tel +353 91 796475 Fax +353 91 796476

Golf course architect and course re-modelling. Built 20 golf courses in Ireland and Europe. Ryder Cup and World Cup player.

J Clubb Ltd
Church Hill, Wilmington, Dartford, Kent DA2 7DZ.
Tel (01322) 225431 Fax (01322) 289932

Producers and distributors of washed sand for bunkers and root zone mixes.

Dave Thomas Ltd
Philip House, 6 Stamford Road, Bowden, Altrincham, Cheshire WA14 2JU.
Tel 0161-929 8600 Fax 0161-929 5060

Golf course design consultants. The design of golf courses and the re-modelling of existing golf courses.

David Hemstock Associates
Golf Course Architects & Consultants
Suite 4a, Northmill, Bridgefoot, Belper, Derbyshire DE56 1YD.
Tel (01773) 827115 Fax (01773) 821284
e-mail: David_Hemstock@golf-design.dem on/co.uk
website: www.golf-design.demon.co.uk

40 projects since 1991, from championship-quality new to total re-modelling of existing; Europe to China. Design and documentation, project and maintenance management, clubhouse design, through the qualified and experienced team of David Hemstock, BSc IEng., Les Watts, B.Arch., and Geoff Porter, NDH.

European Golf Machinery
Street Garage, Bucklesham, Ipswich, Suffolk IP10 0DN.
Tel (01473) 659815 Fax (01473) 659045

Manufacturers of driving range equipment including golf ball collectors, dispensers, ball washers and elevators. Kawasaki ATV and Mule Distributors. Exclusive diesel engined Mule utility vehicle. (See advertisement page 393 for further details.)

Fox Contracting (Owmby) Ltd
Caenby Hall, Caenby Corner, Market Rasen LN8 2BU.
Tel (01673) 878444 Fax (01673) 878644

Fox Contracting (Owmby) Limited - The contracting division of the Fox group of companies was founded early 1991. Since its formation the company has successfully completed many new developments together with completing upgrading and redevelopment works on existing courses.

Golf Landscapes Ltd
Ashwells Road, Bentley, Brentwood, Essex CM15 9SR.
Tel (01277) 373720 Fax (01277) 374834

The country's leading specialists in golf course construction, drainage and contract maintenance, working throughout Europe with leading international golf course architects. (See advertisement page 387 for further details.)

Greens of Scotland
Cruickshank Building, Craibstone Estate, Bucksburn, Aberdeen AB21 9TR.
Tel (01224) 711106 Fax (01224) 714591

An international golf course consultancy providing specialist skills for feasibility studies, planning, course design, buildings design, course construction, project management and turf agronomy. Our project range covers alterations, renovations, driving ranges and new courses.

John Greasley Ltd
Ashfield House, 1154 Melton Road, Syston, Leicester LE7 2HB.
Tel 0116-269 6766 Fax 0116-269 6866

John Greasley established his company in 1984 and has specialised in the construction of new courses, along with alterations, improvements and refurbishment on existing ones. Works have been completed on some of the countries oldest and most prestigeous courses.

Jonathan C Gaunt
Golf Course Architect
44 Stanmore Road, London E11 3BU.
Tel 0181-532 9181 Fax 0181-532 9553
e-mail: jonathangaunt@compuserve.com
website: http://www.integrity.co.uk/golf/ gaunt

Since 1990 Jonathan has had over 17 new courses built and is currently advising over 20 existing courses throughout the British Isles and in Portugal, Turkey and Denmark. Preferring a 'hands-on' approach, all design work and construction supervision is undertaken by him personally. Member of the BIGCA.

Land Unit Construction Ltd
Hanslope, Milton Keynes,
Buckinghamshire MK19 7BX.
Tel (01908) 510414 Fax (01908) 511056

We have the knowledge and experience gained over 20 years in golf course construction and constantly work with many of the country's leading golf course architects to provide clients with unparalleled quality of service.

Neil Coles & Associates
International Golf Course Architecture
19 Broadwater Road, Burwood Park,
Walton on Thames, Surrey KT12 5DB.
Tel (01932) 226895 Fax (01932) 222685

Designers of high quality golf courses throughout the UK and Europe, constructed to a fixed budget. Minor alterations to existing courses also undertaken, with over 20 years' experience. Member of the BIGCA.

P S D Agronomy Ltd
42 Garstang Road, Preston,
Lancashire PR1 1NA.
Tel (01772) 884450 Fax (01772) 884445

A specialist team of golf course agronomists working throughout the UK and Europe. Whether building a new course, extending an existing one or just making the best of what you have - we have the technical expertise to help.

Peter Alliss Golf Course Design
10 St Georges Yard, Farnham,
Surrey GU9 7AW.
Tel (01252) 717711 Fax (01252) 717722
e-mail: roy@allissgolf.demon.co.uk

Peter Alliss has been designing golf courses for over 30 years. All designs are supervised by him. The company offers a service from initial route plan, planning submission, construction drawings and specification to final plans. (See advertisement page 403 for further details.)

Practicality Brown Ltd
Iver Stud, Iver, Buckinghamshire SL0 9LA.
Tel (01753) 652022 Fax (01753) 653007

Practicality Brown Limited provides a range of arboricultural services - tree moving (up to 70cm girth), tree supplying and planting, and a total no-burn site clearance package backed by forest residue chippers capable of handling stem sizes up to 25cm diameter. *Pathform*™ hardwood chip is supplied for golf course paths nationwide.

Robert J Browne
Laytown and Bettystown Golf Club
Bettystown,
Co Meath, Ireland.
Tel +353 41 28793 Fax +353 41 28506

Ireland's leading professional golf course architect. Consultation on all aspects of golf course architecture, maps, specifications, management. Modern ideas showing flare and ingenuity. Numerous successful developments completed and acclaimed. New layouts and renovations. Member of the PGAA. (See advertisement page 387 for further details.)

Roger Jones Golf Associates
Allman House,
Tralee Road, Killarney,
Co Kerry, Ireland.
Tel/Fax +353 64 35581

Golf architecture, construction supervision and development consultancy, including agronomy and hydrology in conjunction with PSD, for new developments and existing courses, large or small, in Ireland, UK, Europe and Middle East.

Ryder Golf Services
50 Gally Hill Road,
Church Crookham,
Hampshire GU13 0QF.
Tel (01252) 617542 Fax (01252) 812082

Specialist consultancy providing advanced CAD services to architects, contractors, developers and clubs for: Feasibility studies; planning applications; course design and re-design; construction cost planning; environmental impact analysis; contract drawings; bills of quantities, 3D visualisations.

Swan Golf Designs Ltd
Telfords Barn,
Willingale,
Ongar, Essex CM5 0QF.
Tel (01277) 896229 Fax (01277) 896300

Professional golf course architects with traditional values, offering initial appraisals, conceptual designs, detailed design work and construction management. Specialising in improvements of existing golf courses, extensions, re-design of greens and tees etc, including restorations of classic old courses.

Toro Commercial Products
Lely (UK) Ltd
Station Road, St Neots, Huntingdon,
Cambridgeshire PE19 1QH.
Tel (01480) 476971 Fax (01480) 216167

Toro offer an extensive range of professional turf maintenance equipment which includes: greens mowers, fairway mowers, triplex mowers, rotary mowers, aeration and utility vehicles. Toro manufacture to an exceptionally high quality and give unrivalled quality of cut.

Total Golf Design & Construction
Tall Pines Golf Club, Cooks Bridle Path,
Downside Backwell, Bristol BS19 3DS.
Tel/Fax (01275) 474869

Over 20 years' experience of golf course design and construction in the UK and Europe. Course upgrading work undertaken on a fixed price basis. Full member of the Professional Golfers' Architects Association.

Whitnell Contracts Ltd
Woodlands, Ellis Road, Boxted,
Colchester CO4 5RN.
Tel (01206) 272834 Fax (01206) 272104

Golf course construction, refurbishment and alterations undertaken by the professionals. A hands-on management team combined with an experienced work force utilising a modern fleet of in-house machinery and equipment, working throughout UK and Europe.

COURSE MEASUREMENT

Eagle Promotions Ltd
Eagle House, 1 Clearway Court,
139-141 Croydon Road, Caterham,
Surrey CR3 6PF.
Tel (01883) 344244 Fax (01883) 341777

Eagle Promotions offer a comprehensive range of products from certified course measurement and tee signs through to scorecards, yardage books, green fee tickets, members' tags, event and leader boards, honours boards, clubhouse and general course signage. For further information please contact Philip McInley on 01883 344244.

Strokesport
Abbey Mill Business Centre,
Paisley PA1 1TJ.
Tel 0141-848 1199 Fax 0141-887 1642

Measurement and survey to professional standard. Certification accepted by National Golf unions. Leading specialists in course measurement. We are also publishers of STROKESAVER Distance Guides which are recognised as the most accurate and useful golf course management aids worldwide. STROKESAVER provides professionals and clubs with a constant profit centre. (See advertisement page 16 for further details.)

Vickers Sports Optics
Unit 9, 35 Revenge Road,
Lordswood, Kent ME5 8DW.
Tel (01634) 201284 Fax (01634) 201286

Bushnells Yardage *Pro*™ 400 instantaneously measures distances up to 400 yards with incredible accuracy (±1 yard). Know whether - you can reach the green in one - clear the water or bunker - it's safe to hit or how far I have driven/hit the ball.

DISTRIBUTORS & WHOLESALERS

Aldila UK
12 Heather Road, Binley Woods,
Coventry CV3 2DE.
Tel/Fax (01203) 545651

Aldila Golf equipment distributors: Diamond Golf Ltd, 4/5 Rudford Industrial Estate, Ford Road, Arundel BN18 0BS Tel (01903) 726999 Fax (01903) 726998; Golfsmith (Europe) Ltd, Leewood Business Park, Upton Road, Huntingdon PE17 5XQ Tel (01480) 891909 Fax (01480) 891836; Gratex Golf, Golf House, Broad Lane, Bradford, West Yorkshire. Tel (01274) 664289 Fax (01274) 656040.

Cleveland Golf UK
Unit 1, The Griffin Centre, Staines Road,
Feltham, Middlesex TW14 0HS.
Tel 0181-893 2218 Fax 0181-893 2323

Cleveland Golf, pioneers in golf club technology offer a range of VAS (Vibration Absorbing System) woods, irons and putters. With patents on both the VAS system and inset hosel, Cleveland boast the most advanced and stable clubs available. Cleveland also manufactures a range of speciality wedges used by most of the top tour players around the world.

J Clubb Ltd
Church Hill,
Wilmington,
Dartford, Kent DA2 7DZ.
Tel (01322) 225431 Fax (01322) 289932

Producers and distributors of washed sand for bunkers and root zone mixes.

Dimensions in Sport
Airport House,
Purley Way,
Croydon, Surrey CR0 0XZ.
Tel 0181-680 2017 Fax 0181-681 5171

Dimensions in Sport are the European distributors for the complete range of Precept golf balls. These high performance products are endorsed by, amongst others, Nick Faldo and Mick Price. There is also a logo ball service.

Eaton Ltd - Golf Pride Grips
Units 1 & 2 Stirling Centre,
Northfields Industrial Estate,
Market Deeping,
Nr Peterborough PE6 8LB.
Tel (01778) 341555

Manufacturers of golf grips for over 45 years, they have been the leader in golf grip technology and the leader in rubber and cord grip sales for both professional and amateur players alike.

Fraser Products Ltd
Turn Street,
Syston, Leicester LE7 1HP.
Tel 0116-269 3609 Fax 0116-269 3596

Manufacturers of two models of the *Fraser Foldaway* powered trolley. One which has been purposely designed for hire by the professionals - and one for personal use. Producers of the *Fraser Fairway* pull trolleys.

Old Golf by John Preston
7-9 The Lane,
West Mersea,
Colchester, Essex C05 8NU.
Tel/Fax (01206) 382181

Furniture and personal accessories with a golfing theme. The Old Golf collection creates a comfortable ambiance for clubhouse, hotel or home, from refurbishment to new clubhouse projects. The exclusive range of personal accessories offers a wide choice of quality golf-themed gifts for all occasions. (See advertisements pages 11 & 16 for further details.)

Sun Mountain Sports
c/o Golf Products Ltd
The Downs Farm,
Reigate Road,
Ewell, Surrey KT17 3BY.
Tel 0181-786 8896 Fax 0181-394 1895

Distribution of a superb range of American made golf bags including innovative, lightweight stand and carry bags as well as new trolley bag offerings. One of the world's leading suppliers of golf bags and related products.

Yonex UK Ltd
74 Wood Lane,
White City,
London W12 7RH.
Tel 0181-742 9777 Fax 0181-742 9612

Importer and distributor of Yonex golf, tennis and badminton products in the United Kingdom. Professionals like Scott Hoch and Phil Mickelson use Yonex golf products, and 80% of badminton professionals use Yonex rackets.

DRIVING RANGE & PRACTICE EQUIPMENT

Easy Picker Europe Ltd
Badcock House, Unit 11a,
Dolphin Park, Castle Road,
Eurolink Industrial Centre,
Sittingbourne, Kent ME10 3RL.
Tel (01795) 427333 Fax (01795) 425222

Manufacturers of golf driving range equipment including Epic ball dispensers, ball pickers, ball washers, conveyor and ancillary products. Easy Picker Europe are the UK sole distributor for Astroturf range mats and golf surfaces, together with winter tees, walkways and putting surfaces.

European Golf Machinery
Street Garage,
Bucklesham,
Ipswich, Suffolk IP10 0DN.
Tel (01473) 659815 Fax (01473) 659045

Manufacturers of driving range equipment including golf ball collectors, dispensers, ball washers and elevators. Kawasaki ATV and Mule Distributors. Exclusive diesel engined Mule utility vehicle. (See advertisement page 393 for further details.)

Golftek (UK) Ltd
Curtis Road,
Dorking,
Surrey RH4 1XD.
Tel (01306) 741888 Fax (01306) 877888

Distributor of the world's best golf swing, club fitting analyser and three dimensional golf simulator, as on TV. Distributor of the best DIGITISED VIDEO system available. Sports coach as well as video teaching systems. Europe's largest manufacturer of golf mats, portarange nets and cage nets.

Heritage Fairway Ltd
1 St Johns Road,
Hove,
East Sussex BN3 2FB.
Tel (01273) 220116 Fax (01273) 747517

UK manufacturers of golf range equipment including manual and electronic ball dispensers. Academy ball washers and washing systems, ball conveyors and ball collectors. Also suppliers of ancillary equipment: Range mats, winter tee mats, range balls, baskets, target nets and range markers. (See advertisement page 21 for further details.)

H Pattisson & Co Ltd
Pattisson House,
Addison Road,
Chesham,
Buckinghamshire HP5 2BD.
Tel (01494) 794646 Fax (01494) 794747

At Pattissons we are continually improving our products and services so that you, the customer, always receives the best. We have over a 100 years of servicing the golf industry and believe that there is no reason to go anywhere else for your golf course furnishings. With our direct van sales service and our network of UK and European distributors, including our NEW Pattisson offices in Spain, we can offer a comprehensive service to all our customers.

Range Servant UK Ltd
Hempstead Road,
Hunton Bridge,
Watford, Hertfordshire WD1 3NJ.
Tel/Fax (01923) 263777

Manufacture and market golf range and practice ground equipment. Golf ball dispensers, golf ball washers, golf ball collectors, play mats for ranges and practice grounds - winter tee mats a speciality, range balls and baskets.

Tildenet Ltd
Hartcliffe Way, Bristol BS3 5RJ.
Tel 0117-966 9684 Fax 0117-923 1251

Supply and installation of the ultimate netting based solutions for the world of golf. Including perimeter safety netting, practice nets to cater for professionals, warm-up tees, advanced players and beginners. Anti-ball plugging netting, target nets, target greens anti-dazzle netting. And for the greenkeeper - grass growth acceleration technology and bunker membrane.

EDUCATION/TEACHING AIDS

Chartex Products International Ltd
20 Grasmere, Liden, Swindon,
Wiltshire SN3 6LE.
Tel (01793) 530880 Fax (01793) 491035

Golf Fitness Programmes - *Keeping Fit for Better Golf* is a new, unique programme of exercises designed to help improve stamina, suppleness and strength for enhanced control and greater distance. The 36-page book, plus the warm-up stretching booklet is supplemented with two thera-band rubber tubes for progressive strength training. Endorsed by the PGA of Europe.

Golf Projects Ltd
The Lodge,
East Sussex National Golf Club,
Uckfield, East Sussex TN22 5ES.
Tel (01825) 880250 Fax (01825) 880251

Distributors of hi-tech golf teaching and entertainment systems including the Astar digital video teaching system and Deadsolid simulators and analysers.

ELECTRONIC POINT-OF-SALE

Euro Systems Projects (ESP)
Europa House,
8 Kimpton Link Business Park,
Kimpton Road, Sutton, Surrey SM3 9PF.
Tel 0181-641 7216 Fax 0181-641 3179

ESP is universally recognised as the UK's market leader for integrated point-of-sale and management systems. GOLFMASTER has been specifically designed for both the golf professional and the golf club, and encompasses all aspects encountered when running a successful and profitable golf operation.

Antique Golf

10 Glasgow Road,
Paisley PA1 3QG.
Tel 0141-889 1860 Fax 0141-889 1860
e-mail: Robert@dmcsoft.com
website: www.dmcsoft.com/antiquegolf

The most extensive range of antique golf clubs and memorabilia in the world, all clubs drawn from the period 1840 to 1920. We supply individual collectors, golf clubs, and the corporate marketplace. For a preview ask for our catalogue or view our website.

Birkdale Promotions

97 Old Watford Road,
Bricket Wood,
Nr St Albans, Hertfordshire AL2 3UN.
Tel (01923) 671225 Fax (01923) 662522

An exclusive range of bronze figurines, silverplated golf trophies, crystal, shields, antique replica plaques - all suitable for clubs, societies and corporate events. Our in-house engraving enables each to be personalised to your specification and delivery can be made to any address worldwide. Please call for our free colour brochure and price list. (See advertisement page 393 for further details.)

The Cricketer Ltd

Beech Hanger,
Ashurst,
Nr Tunbridge Wells, Kent TN3 9TE.
Tel (01892) 740697 Fax (01892) 740588

The Sports Gifts catalogue has a unique collection of gifts and trophies for golfing fanatics to suit every occasion. Items include brass golf bag paperweights, golf club wall plaques, golf ball clocks, bookends and frames and a golf charm bracelet and amusing golf mugs. Ring for free catalogue.

Heritage Golf International Ltd

No 2 Tower Estate,
Warpsgrove Lane,
Chalgrove, Oxfordshire OX44 7XZ.
Tel (0410) 760739 Fax (01938) 561478

Produce hand crafted models of individual golf holes either commissioned by the club involved or a replica of a world famous golf hole. Individually produced and hand painted to exacting standards, mounted on a plinth with a bronze name plate, they make perfect gifts and prizes for the golfer that has everything.

Old Golf by John Preston

7-9 The Lane, West Mersea,
Colchester, Essex CO5 8NU.
Tel/Fax (01206) 382181

Furniture and personal accessories with a golfing theme. The Old Golf collection creates a comfortable ambiance for clubhouse, hotel or home, from refurbishment to new clubhouse projects. The exclusive range of personal accessories offers a wide choice of quality golf-themed gifts for all occasions. (See advertisements pages 11 & 16 for further details.)

Schotten Trophies - Manfred Schotten Antiques

109 High Street, Burford,
Oxfordshire OX18 4RH.
Tel (01993) 822302 Fax (01993) 822055
website: http://www.schotten.com

Exquisite hand crafted trophies in traditional style, designed, manufactured and hand finished in our own workshop by craftsmen using solid woods, brass and bronze. Also available are golf antiques, clubs, novelty items, desk sets etc, and golf club furnishings. (See advertisement page 403 for further details.)

Tee-Time

MAP House, The Tanneries, East Street,
Titchfield, Hampshire PO14 4AR.
Tel (01705) 412526 Fax (01705) 413589

Unique and *monsoon-proof*, the Tee-Time scorecard wallet lets you write down your score without exposing your scorecard to the rain...and hand in a dry, legible card to the committee. Come rain, come shine, a genuine and valued accessory for daily use.

Stackit

1 Stokesay Fore, Telford,
Shropshire IF7 4QA.
Tel (01952) 277772 Fax (01952) 277797

Producers of *Golf Organisers* for hotel bedroom, clubhouse and personal use. Also *Golf Bag Stands* for driving ranges and *External Furniture* for driving range and golf course use - from our stock or to your specification.

GOLF CLUB REPAIRS

Alan Morgan Golf Club Specialist
7a Kingswood Close, Holbrooks,
Coventry CV6 4AZ.
Tel (01203) 668100 Fax (01203) 681851

Since 1981 we have offered a high quality specialised repair service including frequency matching, Loft 'n' Lie, O.E.M. assembly and hand crafted clubs. We are a member of the Professional Clubmakers Society.

GOLF COURSE DISTANCE GUIDES

Strokesport
Abbey Mill Business Centre,
Paisley PA1 1TJ.
Tel 0141-848 1199 Fax 0141-887 1642

We are publishers of STROKESAVER Distance Guides which are recognised as the most accurate and useful golf course management aids worldwide. STROKESAVER provides professionals and clubs with a constant profit centre. Course Measurement - Measurement and survey to professional standard. Certification accepted by National Golf unions. Leading specialists in course measurement. (See advertisement page 16 for further details.)

Vickers Sports Optics
Unit 9, 35 Revenge Road, Lordswood,
Kent ME5 8DW.
Tel (01634) 201284 Fax (01634) 201286

Bushnells Yardage *Pro*™ *400* instantaneously measures distances up to 400 yards with incredible accuracy (±1 yard). Know whether - you can reach the green in one - clear the water or bunker - it's safe to hit or how far I have driven or hit the ball.

GOLF COURSE FURNISHINGS

H Pattisson & Co Ltd
Pattisson House, Addison Road,
Chesham, Buckinghamshire HP5 2BD.
Tel (01494) 794646 Fax (01494) 794747

At Pattissons we are continually improving our products and services so that you, the customer, always receives the best. We have over a 100 years of servicing the golf industry and believe that there is no reason to go anywhere else for your golf course furnishings. With our direct van sales service and our network of UK and European distributors, including our NEW

Pattisson offices in Spain, we can offer a comprehensive service to all our customers.

GOLF GRIPS & SHAFTS

Eaton Ltd - Golf Pride Grips
Units 1 & 2 Stirling Centre,
Northfields Industrial Estate,
Market Deeping,
Nr Peterborough PE6 8LB.
Tel (01778) 341555

Manufacturers of golf grips for over 45 years, they have been the leader in golf grip technology and the leader in rubber and cord grip sales for both professional and amateur players alike.

True Temper UK/Europe
c/o Tucker Fasteners,
Walsall Road,
Birmingham B42 1BP.
Tel 0121-331 2276 Fax 0121-331 2286

Golf shaft manufacturer both steel and graphite. Dynamic Gold used by the world's leading players and achieving the Grand Slam, all four majors. In 1997 Sensicore the revolutionary vibration damping system new to the market.

GOLF HOLIDAYS/TOUR OPERATORS - HOME & OVERSEAS

3D Golf plc
61 New Road,
Ayr KA8 8HH.
Tel (01292) 263331 Fax (01292) 286424
website: www.3dgolf.co.uk

UK's largest golf holiday company. For over 20 years we have given the British golfer *The best Golf Holiday Deals in the Business* to Spain, Portugal, France and Corfu. Phone for a brochure or video.

Edenside House
Edenside,
St Andrews KY15 9SQ
Tel (01334) 838108 Fax (01334) 835493
e-mail: 106076.2226@compuserve.com

Golf tours of Scotland and Ireland arranged through this AA 4Q selected guesthouse. St Andrews two and a half miles (five minutes by car). 9 double/twin en suite rooms, some ground floor, all with colour TV and beverage tray. Extensive breakfast menu, exclusively non-smoking. Ample parking

Eire Golf

Fossa, Killarney,
Co Kerry, Ireland.
Tel +353 64 31638 Fax +353 64 31736

As specialists in Irish golf holidays, we offer you complete fully inclusive packages to all Ireland. Golfers and non-golfers the itineraries are full and comprehensive without compromise. *The personal company looking after you.*

Golf Par Excellence

Conplan House,
Nork Way,
Banstead, Surrey SM7 1NU.
Tel (01737) 211818 Fax (01737) 211820

Holidays for the discerning golfer. Carefully selected French chateaux, hotels and quiet country houses, close to the pick of the excellent golf courses. Ferry/tunnel bookings and reserved tee-times. Competition week/ends and society days throughout the year.

J D Golf Tours

18 Tullyglass Hill,
Shannon, Co Clare, Ireland.
Tel +353 61 364000 Fax +353 61 361360

We will arrange personalised tours covering the whole of Britain and Ireland, pre-booking accommodation, green fees, ground transport, ferry or flight. Contact us for brochure and further information. Freephone 0800 626 324.

On Course Leisure Management

Hiam Business Centre,
New Road, Maulden,
Bedfordshire MK45 2BG.
Tel/Fax (01525) 840606

On Course Leisure Management arrange tailor-made golf holidays for individuals, families or groups: and comprehensive corporate golf packages throughout the UK and worldwide.

The Scottish National Sports Centre - Inverclyde

Burnside Road, Largs,
Ayrshire KA30 8RW.
Tel (01475) 674666

Residential tuition courses for all abilities using the purpose- built SGU golf facility. Top PGA teaching professionals. Driving bays, video playback swing analysis, training bunkers and variety of types of green.

GOLFING AIDS/PRACTICE EQUIPMENT

Pan European (Golf) 1973 (PEP)

Old Mill Works, High Street, Maldon,
Essex CM9 5EH.
Tel/Fax (01621) 851700

Products include a wide range of practice nets and mats for beginners through to professionals. We also make a commercial range of nets and mats for clubs, stores and leisure centres. Worldwide export sales our speciality.

Smart Golf UK

PO Box 220, Southport,
Merseyside PR8 26H.
Tel (01704) 575575 Fax (01704) 575566

Suppliers of the most realistic and accurate indoor golf simulators in the world, together with swing analysis systems. Smart Golf is the acknowledged expert in the creation of profitable installations and has a proven track record.

GOVERNING BODIES

English Golf Union

The National Golf Centre, The Broadway,
Woodhall Spa, Lincolnshire LN10 6PU.
Tel (01526) 354500 Fax (01526) 354020

The governing body for mens' amateur golf in England on behalf of its members, promotes the game and offers to them the facilities of the National Golf Centre. A major new initiative is the scheme enabling casual golfers access to an EGU handicap. (See advertisement page 12 for further details.)

GREEN KEEPING & DRIVING RANGE VEHICLES

Club Car UK Plc

Dunmore Court, Wootton Road,
Abingdon, Oxfordshire OX13 6BH.
Tel (01235) 537575 Fax (01235) 537576

New sole UK distributor of Carryall. The right tools for the job that is the whole idea behind our transport and utility vehicles. They are the most durable, dependable vehicles on the course. Outright purchase, contract hire or lease purchase terms available.

Toro Commercial Products

Lely (UK) Ltd
Station Road, St Neots, Huntingdon,
Cambridgeshire PE19 1QH.
Tel (01480) 476971 Fax (01480) 216167

Toro offer an extensive range of professional turf maintenance equipment which includes: green mowers, fairway mowers, triplex mowers, rotary mowers, aeration and utility vehicles. Toro manufacture to an exceptionally high quality and give unrivalled quality of cut.

HONOURS BOARDS

Eagle Promotions Ltd

Eagle House, 1 Clearway Court,
139-141 Croydon Road, Caterham,
Surrey CR3 6PF.
Tel (01883) 344244 Fax (01883) 341777

Eagle Promotions offer a comprehensive range of products from certified course measurement and tee signs through to scorecards, yardage books, green fee tickets, members' tags, event and leader boards, honours boards, clubhouse and general course signage. For further information please contact Philip McInley on 01883 344244.

Kronologic Honours Board System

2 Dromonby Lane, Kirkby,
Cleveland TS9 5LD.
Tel/Fax (01642) 711055

25 year exclusively hand made - singles and doubles - honour boards complete with moulded gold inlay frame surround, including engraved title plates. Winners' names in gold relief lettering as standard. Outstanding visual impact with innovative, in-house, low cost easy annual updating facility. (See advertisement page 21 for further details.)

INSURANCE

Golfplan

International Golf Insurance
Redcliffe House, Whitehouse Street,
Bristol BS3 4AU.
Tel 0117-963 6198 Fax 0117-923 1058
e-mail: golfplan@dial.pipex.com
website: http://www.golfplan.co.uk

Golfplan, endorsed by the PGA, is Europe's largest specialist golf insurance provider. A Golfplan policy covers individual golfers against personal liability; accidental damage to third party property; golf equipment; personal effects; equipment hire charges; tournament entry fees; membership fees; personal accident; Hole-in-One; free legal advice. Contact your professional or call Golfplan quoting Ref: GHB2

IRRIGATION EQUIPMENT/DESIGN & INSTALLATION

M J Abbott Ltd

Bratch Lane,
Dinton, Salisbury,
Wiltshire SP3 5EB.
Tel (01722) 716361 Fax (01722) 716828

M J Abbott Limited offer a range of specialist services to the golf and leisure industry. Recognised as one of Britain's leading companies offering Rain Bird irrigation systems. Land drainage, golf course construction and maintenance are all undertaken by experienced employees utilising the company's own specially adapted machinery. (See advertisement page 16 for further details.)

British Overhead Irrigation Ltd

Upper Halliford Green,
Shepperton,
Middlesex TW17 8SB.
Tel (01932) 788301 Fax (01932) 780437

Established 75 years, British Overhead Irrigation provide a complete professional, independent golf course irrigation engineering service - design, installation, upgrading and maintenance. Also manufacture *Wizard* fairway self-travelling sprinklers and sectional covers for circular butyl-lined water storage tanks.

I S S Aquaturf Systems Ltd

Unit 6, The Bourne Centre,
Salisbury Business Park,
Southampton Road,
Salisbury,
Wiltshire SP1 2NY.
Tel (01722) 412510 Fax (01722) 413025

ISS Aquaturf Systems Limited are master dealers for *Hunter Industries* operating throughout southern England in the design, supply and installation of automatic pop-up irrigation systems for golf courses. The company has been in business for nearly 20 years and specialises in providing quality systems at competitive prices.

Landline Ltd
1 Bluebridge Industrial Estate,
Halstead, Essex CO9 2EX.
Tel (01787) 476699 Fax (01787) 472507

Supply and install impermeable waterproof
liners to water features, irrigation reservoirs and
ponds. A technical advisory service is available
for all aspects of liner installation. We offer
customers a professional and complete service,
backed by almost 20 years of practical
experience of a specialised industry.

Ocmis Irrigation (UK) Ltd
Head Office: Higher Burrow,
Kingsbury, Martock, Somerset TA12 6BU.
Tel (01460) 241939 Fax (01460) 242198

Scotland: Broadmeadow, Harburn,
West Calder, West Lothian EH55 8RT
Tel 0131-220 2102

Ocmis Irrigation offer the complete irrigation
service including the design, supply and
installation of Rain Bird, Buckner and Hunter
irrigation systems. Complete after-sales service
and full maintenance and service contracts for
all types and makes of irrigation systems.

Watermation
Sprinklers & Controls Ltd
Tongham Road, Aldershot,
Hampshire GU12 4AA.
Tel (01252) 336838

Manufacturer, design, installation and
maintenance of quality golf course irrigation
equipment including computer controllers and
full range of heavy duty impact and gear drive
sprinklers. Installations on hundreds of golf
courses in the UK and worldwide.

York & Martin
39 Salisbury Street, Fordingbridge,
Hampshire SP6 1AB.
Tel (01425) 652087 Fax (01425) 652476

Independent irrigation consultants providing
objective advice on all irrigation related matters
including water souring, existing system
evaluation, system designs and specifications
project supervision etc. Operating throughout
the UK and mainland Europe.

*IF YOUR ORGANISATION
IS NOT LISTED HERE CALL
(01494) 782376*

Solent Souvenirs Ltd
Hamble Bank, 40 Newtown Road, Warsash,
Southampton, Hampshire SO31 9FZ.
Tel (01489) 577985 Fax (01489) 577886

Britain's premier supplier of specialised golf
jewellery and quality gifts. Many items designed
and manufactured exclusively for us and
unobtainable elsewhere. Replace that traditional
trophy with an elegant prize which will be both
useful and cherished. Most items delivered
overnight.

Club Class Cabinets
10-11 Charfleets Close,
Canvey Island, Essex SS8 0PW.
Tel (01268) 681045 Fax (01268) 681286

Club Class Cabinetwork offer a bespoke design
and build service in cabinet making, dedicated
to the golfing fraternity. Products range from
simple hard-wearing storage lockers to
sophisticated, polished cabinets in exotic
hardwoods and veneers.

Birkdale Promotions
97 Old Watford Road, Bricket Wood,
Nr St Albans, Hertfordshire AL2 3UN.
Tel (01923) 671225 Fax (01923) 662522

An exclusive range of bronze figurines,
silverplated golf trophies, crystal, shields,
antique replica plaques - all suitable for clubs,
societies and corporate events. Our in-house
engraving enables each to be personalised to
your specification and delivery can be made to
any address worldwide. Please call for our free
colour brochure and price list. (See
advertisement page 393 for further details.)

Derek Burridge (Wholesale) Ltd
Awards House, Unit 15, The Metro Centre,
Springfield Road, Hayes,
Middlesex UB4 0LE.
Tel 0181-569 0123 Fax 0181-569 0111

The country's leading suppliers of golf prizes.
We offer a vast range of silverplate, crystal,
china, clocks, leather goods and sporting
trophies, all at trade prices. Glass and silverplate in-house engraving service. Next day
delivery throughout the UK. Call for brochure.
(See advertisement page 21)

Golf Books & Videos
PO Box 444,
10 Theatre Square, Swindon,
Wiltshire SN1 1QX.
Tel (01793) 523170 Fax (01793) 432070
Freephone (orders only): 0500 007077

We supply new and recently published golf
books and videos. Free list available on request.
Fast, efficient, worldwide mail order service.

Philip Woodrow
50 Kniveton Park, Ilkeston,
Derbyshire DE7 5FD.
Tel/Fax 0115-930 6771

Golf books for fun and profit. Catalogue of
secondhand out-of-print and collectable titles,
from the very recent to the very old.
Categorised according to content, eg. history,
biography, ladies' golf, courses and
architecture, instruction and reference etc.

Solent Souvenirs Ltd
Hamble Bank, 40 Newtown Road, Warsash,
Southampton, Hampshire SO31 9FZ.
Tel (01489) 577985 Fax (01489) 577886

Britain's premier supplier of specialised golf
jewellery and quality gifts. Many items designed
and manufactured exclusively for us and
unobtainable elsewhere. Replace that traditional
trophy with an elegant prize which will be both
useful and cherished. Most items delivered
overnight.

Steve Schofield Golf Books
29 Nichols Way, Wetherby,
West Yorkshire LS22 6AD.
Tel/Fax (01937) 581276
e-mail: steve@golfbooks.u-net.com

Classic golf books for sale, new, old and
antiquarian. Books on golf history, architecture,
biography, club and ball collecting and
instruction. Free catalogue on request.

PERSONAL ACCESSORIES

Cleveland Golf UK
Unit 1, The Griffin Centre, Staines Road,
Feltham, Middlesex TW14 0HS.
Tel 0181-893 2218 Fax 0181-893 2323

Cleveland Golf, pioneers in golf club
technology offer a range of VAS (Vibration
Absorbing System) woods, irons and putters.
With patents on both the VAS system and inset
hosel, Cleveland boast the most advanced and
stable clubs available. Cleveland also

manufactures a range of speciality wedges used
by most of the top tour players around the
world.

Old Golf by John Preston
7-9 The Lane,
West Mersea,
Colchester, Essex CO5 8NU.
Tel/Fax (01206) 382181

Furniture and personal accessories with a
golfing theme. The Old Golf collection creates a
comfortable ambiance for clubhouse, hotel or
home, from refurbishment to new clubhouse
projects. The exclusive range of personal
accessories offers a wide choice of quality golf-
themed gifts for all occasions. (See advertisements pages 11 & 16 for further details.)

N S Pyramid Ltd
Unit 5, Ashburton Industrial Estate,
Ross-on-Wye,
Herefordshire HR9 7BW.
Tel (01989) 767676 Fax (01989) 766450

Actual manufacturers of British made top
quality golf accessories and personalised on-
course merchandise for golf days, societies and
tournaments. Support British Industry.

Rogue Golf Company Ltd
The Downs Farm,
Reigate Road,
Ewell, Surrey KT17 3BY.
Tel 0181-786 8896 Fax 0181-394 1895

Manufacture and supply of innovative golf
equipment including metalwoods, irons, bags
and accessories. The range incorporates a fresh,
youthful image combined with high quality
products sourced predominently from USA.

Softspikes® UK
Distributed by:
The Grass Roots Company Ltd
5 Cheltenham Close,
West Tytherington,
Macclesfield, Cheshire SK10 2WD.
Tel (01625) 422136 Fax (01625) 422137
e-mail: sales@softspikes.co.uk

The world's No 1 plastic alternative to metal
spikes. We offer a complete programme to golf
courses wishing to ban the use of metal spikes
and a network of agents servicing retail outlets
nationwide.

Brollies Limited
45 Allerton Road, Woolton Village,
Liverpool L25 7AL.
Tel 0151-421 0250 Fax 0151-421 0091

Brollies Limited carry a comprehensive range in best quality British made Hoyland and Fox Frame umbrellas. Also available seat sticks, twinbrellas, garden parasols, imported double ribbed golf umbrellas and golf ball retrievers. All printed or unprinted.

Bryants of Leeds
Speedwell Street, Meanwood Road,
Leeds, West Yorkshire LS6 2TD.
Tel 0113-243 0744 Fax 0113-242 6330
e-mail: sales@bryants.co.uk
website: www.bryants.co.uk

Bryants of Leeds are the leading supplier of personalised golf merchandise. Golf club membership bag tags are available in four different shapes as well as a variety of colours. Also available are annual membership labels, membership cards as well as course cards and car window stickers.

Bulldog Trading Ltd
Unit 8, Waterloo Avenue,
Chelmsley Wood Industrial Estate,
Solihull North B37 6QQ.
Tel/Fax 0121-779 7575

Manufacturer of on-course golf bags, golf accessories and personalised products for golf clubs and corporate days.

Derek Burridge (Wholesale) Ltd
Awards House, Unit 15, The Metro Centre,
Springfield Road, Hayes,
Middlesex UB4 0LE.
Tel 0181-569 0123 Fax 0181-569 0111

The country's leading suppliers of golf prizes. We offer a vast range of silverplate, crystal, china, clocks, leather goods and sporting trophies, all at trade prices. Glass and silverplate in-house engraving service. Next day delivery throughout the UK. Call for brochure. (See advertisement page 21 for further details.)

Elizabeth Parker
The Charles Parker Building,
Midland Road, Higham Ferrers,
Northamptonshire NN10 8DN.
Tel (01933) 418099 Fax (01933) 358058
e-mail: liziparker@compuserve.com

Gold and silver wire hand embroidered blazer badges and silk or polyester ties all produced to your own club logo. Also suppliers of ties, badges, cuff links, key rings and blazer buttons. Quotations and artwork supplied by return.

Galloway Crystal
New Abbey Road,
Beeswing,
by Dumfries DG2 8ED.
Tel/Fax (01387) 760643
e-mail: mcc@gallowayglass.demon.co.uk
website: www.dmcsoft.com/scotplay

Specialist plain and cut crystal suppliers and engravers. Many innovative golfing gift ideas through our Muirfield collection and our St Andrews collection. Personalisation our speciality. Ask for our catalogue along with club and reseller price lists.

H M T Plastics Ltd
PO Box 195,
Haywards Heath,
West Sussex RH16 1FQ.
Tel/Fax (01444) 416088

Bag tags supplied in nine colours either round, pear shaped maxi or sunrise to accommodate club logo, from a choice of six print colours. Adhesive year stickers available in choice of nine colours and sold separately. (See advertisement page 387 for further details.)

The Highland Connection
38 Watt Road,
Glasgow G52 4RW.
Tel 0141-882 8340 Fax 0141-882 7090

The Highland Connection supply the golf professionals at the best known golf clubs throughout the UK with their own distinctive woven golf towels made in Glasgow, Scotland. Embroidered towels in various quantities also available.

Normandy Sports & Clothing
20 St Edmunds,
Berkhamsted,
Hertfordshire HP4 2HT.
Tel (01442) 865372 Fax (01442) 874480

European distributor of the world's leading personalised golf accessories company - Golf Design USA. Also supplier of personalised clothing, headwear etc. Embroidery or print. No minimum order and speedy delivery. Full colour brochures available. Telephone Bob James.

PICTURES & PRINTS

Chorley & Saunders Golf Art
**Chequers End, Chequers Lane,
Preston Village,
Hitchin, Hertfordshire SG4 7TY.**
Tel/Fax (01462) 440277

Richard Chorley, England's premier golf artist. Private Commissions. Original oil paintings, drawings and limited edition prints. Prints signed by the artist, numbered and embossed. Collection of classic courses and golfing greats. Ideal corporate and captain's prizes gifts.

Grandison Golf Gallery
25 Hyndland Road, Glasgow G12 9UZ.
Tel/Fax 0141-339 9438

Finest quality limited edition prints of the world's premier golfing venues by award-winning artist William Grandison. Gifts and prizes of distinction for the discerning golfer. Free catalogue available.

In the Picture
**28-29 Weybourne Road Industrial Estate,
Sheringham, Norfolk NR26 8HF.**
Tel (01263) 822265 Fax (01263) 822097

In the Picture - The Golf Collection is the world's leading publisher of historic golf imagery. Over 200 images have been produced. Series include both Open and limited editions. Hall of Fame collection; hand coloureds; Open champions; Humour on the Links; Ladies on the Links. Greetings and postcards. For prizes, presentations, club or office decor.

PRACTICE NETTING/CAGES

Golftek (UK) Ltd
Curtis Road, Dorking, Surrey RH4 1XD.
Tel (01306) 741888 Fax (01306) 877888

Distributor of the world's best golf swing, club fitting analyser and three dimensional golf simulator, as on TV. Distributor of the best DIGITISED VIDEO system available. Sports coach as well as video teaching systems. Europe's largest manufacturer of golf mats, portarange nets and cage nets.

Links Leisure
**Unit 22, Civic Industrial Park,
Whitchurch, Shropshire SY13 ITT.**
Tel (01948) 663002 Fax (01948) 666381

Manufactured from heavy duty box sections finished in green plastic coating, the net measuring 3.5m x 3.5m can be supplied in singles or multiples and comes complete with heavy duty baffle net.

Pan European (Golf) 1973 (PEP)
**Old Mill Works,
High Street,
Maldon, Essex CM9 5EH.**
Tel/Fax (01621) 851700

Products include a wide range of practice nets and mats for beginners through to professionals. We also make a commercial range of nets and mats for clubs, stores and leisure centres. Worldwide export sales our speciality.

Tildenet Ltd
**Hartcliffe Way,
Bristol BS3 5RJ.**
Tel 0117-966 9684 Fax 0117-923 1251

Supply and installation of the ultimate netting based solutions for the world of golf. Including perimeter safety netting, practice nets to cater for professionals, warm-up tees, advanced players and beginners. Anti-ball plugging netting, target nets, target greens anti-dazzle netting. And for the greenkeeper - grass growth acceleration technology and bunker membrane.

PRECEPT GOLF BALLS

Dimensions in Sport
**Airport House,
Purley Way,
Croydon, Surrey CR0 0XZ.**
Tel 0181-680 2017 Fax 0181-681 5171

Dimensions in Sport are the European distributors for the complete range of Precept golf balls. These high performance products are endorsed by, amongst others, Nick Faldo and Mick Price. There is also a logo ball service.

PROMOTION/PUBLICITY

Bryants of Leeds
**Speedwell Street,
Meanwood Road,
Leeds, West Yorkshire LS6 2TD.**
*Tel 0113-243 0744 Fax 0113-242 6330
e-mail: sales@bryants.co.uk
website: www.bryants.co.uk*

Bryants of Leeds are the leading supplier of personalised golf merchandise. Before you organise your next promotion or corporate golf day call for a free copy of our colour brochure to help make your event a success.

The Highland Connection
38 Watt Road,
Glasgow G52 4RW.
Tel 0141-882 8340 Fax 0141-882 7090

The Highland Connection supply the golf professionals at the best known golf clubs throughout the UK with their own distinctive woven golf towels made in Glasgow, Scotland. Embroidered towels in various quantities also available.

Norman Hood Cartoons
98B Main Street,
Alrewas,
Burton-on-Trent, Staffordshire DE13 7AE.
Tel (01283) 790993 Fax (01283) 791593

Superb cartoons and caricatures for those golfing occasions and personalities. Norman Hood specialises in the sports industry, especially golf. Individuals and groups. Remember those special times with a unique, humorous hand drawn cartoon. Perfect for amusing club or company greetings cards. Write or telephone for information.

N S Pyramid Ltd
Unit 5, Ashburton Industrial Estate,
Ross-on-Wye, Herefordshire HR9 7BW.
Tel (01989) 767676 Fax (01989) 766450

Actual manufacturers of British made top quality golf accessories and personalised on-course merchandise for golf days, societies and tournaments. Support British Industry.

PROPERTY CONSULTANTS

Edward Symmons Hotel & Leisure
11-14 Grafton Street, London W1X 3LA.
Tel 0171-344 4554 Fax 0171-344 4555

Consultant surveyors providing specialist property advice to the golf and leisure industry. Established track record in sales, valuations, acquisitions, development appraisals, rating and feasibility studies throughout the UK and Europe. (See advertisement page 393 for further details.)

PUTTER MANUFACTURERS

Bronty Golf Co Ltd
81A Bradford Road, Stanningley, Pudsey,
West Yorkshire LS28 6AT.
Tel 0113-257 7266 Fax 0113-257 0771

Manufacturers of high quality British made custom golf clubs, putters and specialist clubs. Authentic replicas and hickory shafted putters etc.

Callaway Golf UK Ltd
Units C63 & C64 Barwell Business Park,
Leatherhead Road,
Chessington,
Surrey KT9 2NY.
Tel 0181-391 0111 Fax 0181-391 9399

Manufacturer of golf clubs and accessories. Rainwear. Callaway Golf is now the UK distributor for Odyssey Golf.

Golf Classics Ltd
Tom Stewart Lane,
St Andrews KY16 8YB.
Tel (01334) 479191 Fax (01334) 479360

Traditional hand made wood putters, completely useable. The finest possible presentation item for a discerning golfer. Individual or company names can be incorporated. And now - new from Golf Classics - the unique *Swilcan Bridge* replicate putter.

RANGE BALL MANUFACTURERS

Heritage Fairway Ltd
1 St Johns Road,
Hove,
East Sussex BN3 2FB.
Tel (01273) 220116 Fax (01273) 747517

UK manufacturers of golf range equipment including manual and electronic ball dispensers. Academy ball washers and washing systems, ball conveyors and ball collectors. Also suppliers of ancillary equipment: Range mats, winter tee mats, range balls, baskets, target nets and range markers. (See advertisement page 21 for further details.)

Professional Golf Company SDN BHD
4 Jalan Tandang,
Petaling Jaya,
Malaysia 46050.
Tel +603 7918833 Fax +603 7925414

Manufacturing and marketing of *Thommo* golf balls endorsed by Peter Thomson, five time British Open champion. New - The *Thommo* titanium series for extra distance, spin and superb feel. Specialised in corporate logo balls and undertakes contract manufacturing and driving range balls.

REMOTE CONTROLLED TROLLEYS

Middlemore Ltd
Valley Road Works, Sedgley, Dudley, West Midlands DY3 1TS.
Tel (01902) 673360 Fax (01902) 880783

Distributors of the world's foremost remote controlled powered golf trolley - the *Lectronic Kaddy Phoenix*. There is no other all aluminium remote controlled unit loaded with features this model has to offer. Test drive one today.

SCORECARDS & SCOREPLANNERS

Eagle Promotions Ltd
Eagle House, 1 Clearway Court, 139-141 Croydon Road, Caterham, Surrey CR3 6PF.
Tel (01883) 344244 Fax (01883) 341777

Eagle Promotions offer a comprehensive range of products from certified course measurement and tee signs through to scorecards, yardage books, green fee tickets, members' tags, event and leader boards, honours boards, clubhouse and general course signage. For further information please contact Philip McInley on 01883 344244.

SHOE ACCESSORIES

Softspikes® UK
Distributed by:
The Grass Roots Company Ltd
5 Cheltenham Close, West Tytherington, Macclesfield, Cheshire SK10 2WD.
Tel (01625) 422136 Fax (01625) 422137
e-mail: sales@softspikes.co.uk

The world's No 1 plastic alternative to metal spikes. We offer a complete programme to golf courses wishing to ban the use of metal spikes and a network of agents servicing retail outlets nationwide.

SIGNS & MARKERS

Alpha Signs
23 Henham Road, Debden Green, Saffron Walden, Essex CB11 3NA.
Tel (01279) 850555

Specialising in the manufacture of high quality golf signs. Our comprehensive range includes tee-signs, directional and interior signage in many materials. All signs custom designed to

suit the individual course. Ask for our 1998 brochure.

Links Leisure
Unit 22, Civic Industrial Park, Whitchurch, Shropshire SY13 ITT.
Tel (01948) 663002 Fax (01948) 666381

Cast from strong durable GRC the Pro-Tee golf signs come in three sizes and are designed to suit the individual course. They can be painted to six standard colours and supplied with a variety of stands.

SIMULATORS/ANALYSERS

Golf Projects Ltd
The Lodge,
East Sussex National Golf Club,
Uckfield, East Sussex TN22 5ES.
Tel (01825) 880250 Fax (01825) 880251

Distributors of hi-tech golf teaching and entertainment systems including the Astar digital video teaching system and Deadsolid simulators and analysers.

Golftek (UK) Ltd
Curtis Road, Dorking, Surrey RH4 1XD.
Tel (01306) 741888 Fax (01306) 877888

Distributor of the world's best golf swing, club fitting analyser and three dimensional golf simulator, as on TV. Distributor of the best *digitised video* system available. Sports coach as well as video teaching systems. Europe's largest manufacturer of golf mats, portarange nets and cage nets.

Smart Golf UK
PO Box 220, Southport, Merseyside PR8 26H.
Tel (01704) 575575 Fax (01704) 575566

Suppliers of the most realistic and accurate indoor golf simulators in the world, together with swing analysis systems. Smart Golf is the acknowledged expert in the creation of profitable installations and has a proven track record.

SPIKE-PROOF CARPETS

Firth Carpets Ltd
Clifton Mills, Brighouse,
West Yorkshire HD6 4EJ.
Tel (01484) 713371 Fax (01484) 711128

Comprehensive ranges of carpets for clubhouse,
pro shops etc including from stock or custom
design in spike-proof qualities. Free advice on
all aspects of carpet and installation available.

Frank Dineley
T/A Merseyside Carpets
Heald House, Heald Street,
Liverpool L19 2JG.
Tel/Fax 0151-722 6217

Suppliers and fitters of contract carpets and
vinyls etc. Spike resistant carpet and special
logo carpets for clubhouses and golfing hotels.

STOCK CONTROL MANAGEMENT

Pro Shop Keeper Ltd
140 Portway, Stratford, London E15 3QW.
Tel (01727) 835155 Fax (01727) 837881

Pro Shop Keeper is a low cost fully integrated
till and stock control system. It can use almost
any existing pc. Please contact Carl or Tony on
01727 835155.

TEE SIGNS

Alpha Signs
23 Henham Road, Debden Green,
Saffron Walden, Essex CB11 3NA.
Tel (01279) 850555

Specialising in the manufacture of high quality
golf signs. Our comprehensive range includes
tee-signs, directional and interior signage in
many materials. All signs custom designed to
suit the individual course. Ask for our 1998
brochure.

THERMAL WEAR

Mycoal Warm Packs Ltd
Unit 1, Imperial Park, Empress Road,
Southampton SO14 0JW.
Tel (01703) 211068 Fax (01703) 231398

Suppliers and manufacturers of the ever
popular handwarmers and thermo-mittens. All
enquiries welcomed. Nothing too small or too
large.

TOWELS

The Highland Connection
38 Watt Road,
Glasgow G52 4RW.
Tel 0141-882 8340 Fax 0141-882 7090

The Highland Connection supply the golf
professionals at the best known golf clubs
throughout the UK with their own distinctive
woven golf towels made in Glasgow, Scotland.
Embroidered towels in various quantities also
available.

TUITION

Beaufort Golf Course
Churchtown,
Beaufort, Killarney,
Co Kerry, Ireland.
Tel +353 64 44440 Fax +353 64 44752

A traditional Kerry welcome awaits you at the
Friendliest Course in Kerry. Challenging 18-hole
par 71 championship course, buggies and
caddies for hire, excellent golf shop, bar food
and snacks. Tuition can be arranged with our
golf professional. Societies and groups
welcome. (See advertisement page 28 for
further details.)

Cannington Golf Course
Cannington College,
Cannington,
Bridgwater, Somerset TA5 2LS.
Tel (01278) 655050 Fax (01278) 655055

Designed by Martin Hawtree of Oxford and
built to highest international specifications in
1992 by Brian D Pierson Ltd under the
consultancy of top agronomists Jim Arthur and
Gordon Child. Together they have produced
arguably the best 9-hole golf course in the west
of England. With its 'Links-Like' appearance, in
high summer the subtle contours make for a
testing round of golf for the scratch golfer, yet
are receptive for the beginner with its wide open
spaces, at 2,929 yards par 34 . Beating par will
take skill and courage.

Rodway Hill Golf Course
Newent Road, Highnam,
Gloucestershire GL2 8DN.
Tel (01452) 384222 Fax (01989) 766450

An 18-hole pay and play par 68 course two
miles south west of Gloucester, with panoramic
views of the Cotswolds. It has a well stocked
shop, practice and teaching facilities. Hire kit
available. Societies welcome.

The Scottish National Sports Centre - Inverclyde
Burnside Road, Largs,
Ayrshire KA30 8RW.
Tel (01475) 674666

Residential tuition courses for all abilities using the purpose- built SGU golf facility. Top PGA teaching professionals. Driving bays, video playback swing analysis, training bunkers and variety of types of green.

UMBRELLAS

Brollies Limited
45 Allerton Road,
Woolton Village,
Liverpool L25 7AL.
Tel 0151-421 0250 Fax 0151-421 0091

Brollies Limited carry a comprehensive range in best quality British made Hoyland and Fox Frame umbrellas. Also available seat sticks, twinbrellas, garden parasols, imported double ribbed golf umbrellas and golf ball retrievers. All printed or unprinted.

ULTRASONIC CLUB CLEANERS

K M E
Spa Court, Spa Lane,
Harrogate,
North Yorkshire HG2 7JF.
Tel (01423) 888853 Fax (01423) 887001

The ultrasonic club cleaner - Full set of clubs cleaned in two minutes (grips and clubheads). Restores tackiness to your grips. Cleans grooves on the clubface. Simple and safe to use. Token operated. Three years warranty (UK only). Provides an excellent service whilst generating extra revenue. Endorsed and recommended by Bill Ferguson.

WATER STORAGE/TANKS

British Overhead Irrigation Ltd
Upper Halliford Green,
Shepperton, Middlesex TW17 8SB.
Tel (01932) 788301 Fax (01932) 780437

Established 75 years, British Overhead Irrigation provide a complete professional, independent golf course irrigation engineering service - design, installation, upgrading and maintenance. Also manufacture *Wizard* fairway self-travelling sprinklers and sectional covers for circular butyl-lined water storage tanks.

I S S Aquaturf Systems Ltd
Unit 6, The Bourne Centre,
Salisbury Business Park,
Southampton Road,
Salisbury, Wiltshire SP1 2NY.
Tel (01722) 412510 Fax (01722) 413025

ISS Aquaturf Systems Limited are master dealers for *Hunter Industries* operating throughout southern England in the design, supply and installation of automatic pop-up irrigation systems for golf courses. The company has been in business for nearly 20 years and specialises in providing quality systems at competitive prices.

Landline Ltd
1 Bluebridge Industrial Estate,
Halstead,
Essex CO9 2EX.
Tel (01787) 476699 Fax (01787) 472507

Supply and install impermeable waterproof liners to water features, irrigation reservoirs and ponds. A technical advisory service is available for all aspects of liner installation. We offer customers a professional and complete service, backed by almost 20 years of practical experience of a specialised industry.

WEATHERWEAR

Cape Crest Rainwear
Unit 12, Fenlake Industrial Estate,
Fenlake Road,
Bedfordshire MK42 0HB.
Tel (01234) 211707 Fax (01234) 269948
website: www.capecrest.co.uk
info@capecrest.co.uk

Cape Crest Rainwear has a large range of clothing for inclement weather. We have two ranges of suits for men and for ladies with soft microfibre outer and two year guaranteed waterproof breathable linings. We also have waterproof tops, quilted tops, windtops and waterproof lined sweaters. All are competitively priced.

Mycoal Warm Packs Ltd
Unit 1, Imperial Park,
Empress Road, Southampton SO14 0JW.
Tel (01703) 211068 Fax (01703) 231398

Suppliers and manufacturers of the ever popular handwarmers and thermo-mittens. All enquiries welcomed. Nothing too small or too large.

Sunderland of Scotland Ltd
PO Box 14,
Glasgow G2 1ER.
Tel 0141-552 3261 Fax 0141-552 8518

Sunderland of Scotland manufacture high quality golf rainwear in Scotland. All rainsuits are tour tested and guaranteed waterproof and breathable, a variety of fabrics including Goretex being used. Sunderlands also manufacture the famous Sunderland Original Weatherbeater and Classic Windproof Pullover. Official supplier to PGA, PGAE, LPGA and St Andrews Links Trust.

WET-WEATHER SCORECARD HOLDERS

Tee-Time
MAP House,
The Tanneries, East Street,
Titchfield, Hampshire PO14 4AR.
Tel (01705) 412526 Fax (01705) 413589

Unique and *monsoon-proof*, the Tee-Time scorecard wallet lets you write down your score without exposing your scorecard to the rain...and hand in a dry, legible card to the committee. Come rain, come shine, a genuine and valued accessory for daily use.

WINTER/ALL-WEATHER TEE MATS

Easy Picker Europe Ltd
Badcock House, Unit 11a, Dolphin Park,
Castle Road, Eurolink Industrial Centre,
Sittingbourne, Kent ME10 3RL.
Tel (01795) 427333 Fax (01795) 425222

Manufacturers of golf driving range equipment including Epic ball dispensers, ball pickers, ball washers, conveyor and ancillary products. Easy Picker Europe are the UK sole distributor for Astroturf range mats and golf surfaces, together with winter tees, walkways and putting surfaces.

Heritage Fairway Ltd
1 St Johns Road, Hove,
East Sussex BN3 2FB.
Tel (01273) 220116 Fax (01273) 747517

UK manufacturers of golf range equipment including manual and electronic ball dispensers. Academy ball washers and washing systems, ball conveyors and ball collectors. Also suppliers of ancillary equipment: Range mats, winter tee mats, range balls, baskets, target nets and range markers. (See advertisement page 21 for further details.)

Links Leisure
Unit 22, Civic Industrial Park,
Whitchurch, Shropshire SY13 ITT.
Tel (01948) 663002 Fax (01948) 666381

The Pro-Tee all-weather golf mat gives the golfer a flat, solid surface on which to stand. Couple this with the unique tee peg retention slot and the Pro-Tee gives the ideal substitute for the natural grass surface. The Pro-Tee is supplied in three sizes, 1.5m x 1.0m, 2.0m x 1.0m and 1.5m x 1.5m, the first two having three replaceable grass sections.

Range Servant UK Ltd
Hempstead Road, Hunton Bridge,
Watford, Hertfordshire WD1 3NJ.
Tel/Fax (01923) 263777

Manufacture and market golf range and practice ground equipment. Golf ball dispensers, golf ball washers, golf ball collectors, play mats for ranges and practice grounds - winter tee mats a speciality, range balls and baskets.

LATE ENTRY

GOLF DEVELOPMENT, MAINTENANCE & MANAGEMENT

Barrelfield Golf Ltd
302 Ewell Road
Surbiton, Surrey KT6 7AQ
Tel 0181-390 6566 Fax 0181-390 8830

Barrelfield Golf Limited has an unrivalled track record in the development, marketing, management and maintenance of profitable golf clubs in Britain. Other services include feasability studies and arranging finance. For further information contact Melvin Thomas, Tel: 0181-390 6566.

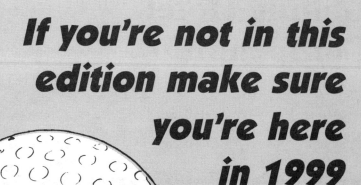
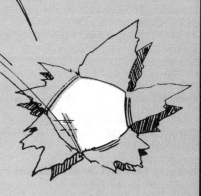

Golfing Hotel Compendium

The Golfing Hotel Compendium is a comprehensive source of information for golfers wishing to find the most comfortable place to stay at or close to some of the finest courses in the country. This section has been compiled from the premier hotels, guest houses and self-catering facilities in the British Isles which include golf among their many attractions.

If readers wish especially to recommend an establishment which is not listed in this section of the Royal & Ancient Golfer's Handbook the editors will be happy to be advised.

ENGLAND

South West

Alverton Manor Country House Hotel
Truro, Cornwall TR1 1XQ.
Tel (01872) 276633 Fax (01872) 2222989

AA/RAC 3-Star; Award-Winning 2-AA Rosettes Restaurant; Johansen's Guide; West Country Tourist Board 4-Crown Highly Commended; *Best Loved Hotels of the World*. Cornwall's premier house hotel in the cathedral city of Truro. A former convent dating from c1700. Quietly set in six acres of terraced grounds and centrally situated for all Cornish golf courses.

Bel Alp House Country Hotel
Haytor, Nr Bovey Tracey, South Devon TQ13 9XX.
Tel (01364) 661217 Fax (01364) 661292

Small, elegant country house in a most spectacular setting providing a remarkable standard of food, comfort and hospitality. Close to many excellent South Devon golf courses plus perfect peace and quiet.

Berry Head Hotel
Berry Head Road, Brixham, Devon TQ5 9AJ.
Tel (01803) 853225 Fax (01803) 882084

AA 3-Star; ETB 4-Crown Commended. In an area of outstanding natural beauty the Berry Head Hotel is surrounded by six acres of secluded grounds and yet only a short walk from the fishing port of Brixham. All bedrooms en suite with full facilities. Private functions and seminars catered for. Walking, sailing and angling all available locally. Golf can be arranged at Churston Golf Club only three miles away. Indoor heated swimming pool.

Boscundle Manor
Tregrehan, St Austell, Cornwall PL25 3RL.
Tel (01726) 813557 Fax (01726) 814997

A small attractive and beautifully furnished country house hotel with luxury accommodation and extensive facilities including practice golf area, games room, and both indoor and outdoor swimming pools. Local fresh food and outstanding wine list.

Burnham & Berrow Golf Club

The Dormy,
St Cristopher's Way,
Burnham-on-Sea, Somerset TA8 2PE.
Tel (01278) 785760

18-hole championship links golf course and 9-hole course. Dormy accommodation available. (See advertisement page 22 for further details.)

Cape Cornwall Golf & Country Club

St Just, Penzance,
Cornwall TR19 7NL.
Tel/Fax (01736) 788611

FIRST and LAST 18-hole coastal course in England, par 69 SSS68. En suite and self-catering accommodation inclusive of golf, gym, swimming, spa, sauna. April to September B&B £37 per person Thursday/Sunday; £30 per person Monday to Wednesday. Green fee £20 weekday and weekends.

The Centurion Hotel & Fosseway Golf & Country Club

Charlton Lane,
Midsomer Norton,
Bath, Somerset BA3 4BD.
Tel (01761) 417711 Fax (01761) 418357

AA/RAC 3-Star hotel with 44 luxurious rooms, just ten miles from Bath, family run with excellent cuisine. Private gardens, family-sized indoor pool, squash courts, indoor and outdoor bowling greens, 9-hole golf course, four bars - all waiting to welcome you.

China Fleet Country Club

Saltash, Cornwall PL12 6LJ.
Tel (01752) 848668 Fax (01752) 848456

Situated in 180 acres of Cornish countryside, 40 self-catering 4- and 6-berth apartments, 18-hole par 72 golf, 28-bay driving range, pool, health suite, gymnasium, racket sports, bars, restaurant and coffee shop. (See advertisement page 32 for further details.)

Commodore Hotel

Beach Road, Sand Bay,
Kewstoke,
Weston-Super-Mare, Somerset BS22 9UZ.
Tel (01934) 415778 Fax (01934) 636483

AA/RAC 3-Star. Peaceful and stylish haven dedicated to fine food and service. Reduced green fees at both Weston and Worlebury clubs Special break/party rates. AA/RAC awards for cuisine and service.

Dormy Hotel

New Road, Ferndown, Dorset BH22 8ES.
Tel (01202) 872121 Fax (01202) 895388

Adjacent to Ferndown Golf Course and in reach of seventeen top quality local golf courses. Our superb leisure facilities make an excellent addition to the golf packages that we offer throughout the year. (Part of the De Vere Hotels Group - see advertisement page 7 for further details.)

The Duke of Cornwall Hotel

Millbay Road, Plymouth, Devon PL1 3LG.
Tel (01752) 266256 Fax (01752) 600062

3-Star Victorian style city centre hotel. 70 en suite bedrooms with every modern comfort. Awarded an AA Rosette for food and service. Conference and banqueting facilities for up to 300 delegates. Friendly and professional staff. Easily accessible from all routes.

The Holland Inn Hotel

Hatt, Saltash, Cornwall PL12 6PJ.
Tel (01752) 844044 Fax (01752) 849701

30 en suite spacious chalets, Sky TV, ample car parking adjacent to the rooms. Situated one mile from the St Mellion Golf Club and two miles from the China Fleet Club. Rates £25 single £35 double.

The Jarvis Gloucester Hotel & Country Club

Robinswood Hill, Matson Lane,
Gloucester GL4 6EA.
Tel (01452) 525653

Extensive leisure facilities including indoor swimming pool, sauna, gymnasium, solarium. Squash courts, tennis courts, snooker, pool. Championship dry ski slopes. Full 18-hole and 9-hole par 3 courses.

Penscot Hotel & Maypole Restaurant

The Square, Shipham, Nr Cheddar,
North Somerset BS25 1TW.
Tel (01934) 842659 Fax (01934) 842576

A lovely old world hotel, c1450. Cosy and peaceful with a homely friendly atmosphere. A delightful place to unwind. Two attractive lounges with well stocked bar, TV and log fires. 16 well appointed bedrooms, 13 en suite, all with complimentary beverage making facilities. Restaurant offers freshly prepared home cooking, varied menu, vegetarians catered for. Excellent wine list. Ideal location for

continued over

golfing breaks. Eight courses within ten miles. Drying facilities, on-site parking. Special rates for societies. (See advertisement page 419 for further details.)

Penventon Hotel
Redruth,
Cornwall TR15 1TE.
Tel (01209) 214141 Fax (01209) 219164

AA/RAC 3-Star Rosette. Large country house hotel, parkland setting, central for six courses. Superior restaurant, resident pianists, three bars, nightclub, indoor pool complex, sauna, jacuzzi, robes provided, masseuse, hairdresser. Special bargain rates all year. Colour brochures. A Cornish welcome awaits you. Open all year.

Pines Hotel
Burlington Road, Swanage,
Dorset BH19 1LT.
Tel (01929) 425211

50-bedroom family run 3-Star hotel. All bedrooms have private bathroom, telephone and colour TV. One and a half miles from Isle of Purbeck Golf Club. Within easy reach of all Dorset courses.

Polurrian Hotel
Mullion,
Lizard Peninsula,
Helston, Cornwall TR12 7EN.
Tel (01326) 240421 Fax (01326) 240083

AA 3-Star; ETB 4-Crown Highly Commended. Every comfort and warmest of welcomes awaits you at the Polurrian Hotel. Set in an enchanting position overlooking its own private cove, this is the ideal location for walking or just relaxing. Superb leisure facilities including gym, sauna, solarium, tennis, indoor and outdoor pools, play areas and registered crèche. Golf can be arranged at Mullion Golf Club just two miles away.

Riversford Hotel
Limers Lane,
Bideford,
Devon EX39 2RG.
Tel (01237) 474239 Fax (01237) 421661

Peace and tranquility in gardens beside the river Torridge. A relaxing retreat after a day on the fairways of North Devon. Excellent food, a flexible lounge bar and comfortable en suite bedrooms. Concessionary golf at North Devon only five minutes from hotel.

The Slipway Hotel
The Harbour Front, Port Isaac,
Cornwall PL29 3RH.
Tel/Fax (01208) 880264

Set in the heart of this beautiful old fishing village the Slipway is the ideal base for a Cornish holiday and is situated within easy striking distance of sailing facilities at Rock and several excellent golf courses including the championship course of St Enodoc.

Stakis Puckrup Hall Hotel & Golf Club
Puckrup, Tewkesbury,
Gloucestershire GL20 6EL.
Tel (01684) 296200 Fax (01684) 850788

If golf is your chosen sport, Stakis Puckrup Hall is an excellent choice. Established trees, lakes and parkland play host to a challenging and beautifully tended par 70 championship course, situated between the Cotswold and Malvern hills. (See advertisement page 419 for further details.)

Tewkesbury Park Hotel Country Club Resort
Lincoln Green Lane, Tewkesbury,
Gloucestershire GL20 7DN.
Tel (01684) 295405 Fax (01684) 292386

This 78-bedroom hotel with modern facilities is surrounded by its own 18-hole golf course. It also offers heated indoor pool, sauna, jacuzzi, solarium, health and beauty salon, squash and floodlit tennis courts, steam room and fitness centre. (See advertisement page 421 for further details.)

Trevose Golf & Country Club
Constantine Bay, Padstow,
North Cornwall PL28 8JB.
Tel (01841) 520208 Fax (01841) 521057
e-mail: @trevose-gc.co.uk
website: http://www.trevose-gc.co.uk

Trevose offers not only great golf (championship 18-hole course, a 9-hole full length (3,100 yards) par 35 plus a 9-hole short course) but also a first class clubhouse and restaurant, three hard all-weather tennis courts, a heated outdoor swimming pool in the summer, a games room for the kids and a boutique. Accommodation is available in bungalows, chalets, luxury flats and dormy suites. send for our detailed, full colour brochure.

Welbeck Manor
& Sparkwell Golf Course
Blacklands, Sparkwell, Plymouth,
Devon PL7 5DF.
Tel/Fax (01752) 837219

A testing 9-hole, pay as you play course and
also a par 3 course, set in 60 acres of parkland.
Facilities include a well equipped golf shop,
excellent hotel accommodation, restaurant and
bar. Open to the public. Golf societies welcome.

Woodbury Park Golf Club
Woodbury Castle, Exeter, Devon EX5 1JJ.
Tel (01395) 233382 Fax (01395) 233384

Five luxury lodges situated with 27 holes of a
championship standard golf course. The lodges
are an ideal venue for a short golf break. The
Nigel Mansell owned resort also has extensive
leisure facilities.

Yeoldon House Hotel
Durrant Lane, Northam, Bideford,
Devon EX39 2RL.
Tel (01237) 474400 Fax (01237) 476618

Play the oldest course in England: Royal North
Devon. We take pride in our excellent cuisine
and fine wines. Our rooms are comfortable and
perfect to rest those well golfed bones. Societies
and parties of any number welcome. ETB 4-
Crown Highly Commended. £40-£50 Single,
£70-£90 Double.

South East

Ashdown Forest Golf Hotel
Chapel Lane, Forest Row,
East Sussex RH18 5BB.
Tel (01342) 824866 Fax (01342) 824869
e-mail: reservations@ashgolf.demon.co.uk
website: http://www.ashgolf.demon.co.uk

Newly refurbished hotel with 19 en suite
bedrooms, large function room, conference
facilities, restaurant and two bars. Hotel
operates the Royal Ashdown Forest Golf Club
West Course. Several other courses
incorporated in residential golf breaks. (See
advertisement page 421 for further details.)

The Bell Hotel
The Quay, Sandwich, Kent CT13 9EF.
Tel (01304) 613388 Fax (01304) 615308

The perfect base when playing Royal St
Georges, Prince's, and Royal Cinque Ports - all
within ten minutes drive. Relax in traditional

comfort in historic surroundings. Individually
designed rooms with en suite throughout.
Special inclusive golf breaks with the *Prince's
Golf Club*. (See advertisement page 423 for
further details.)

Botley Park Hotel
Golf & Country Club
Winchester Road, Boorley Green, Botley,
Hampshire SO3 2UA.
Tel (01489) 780888 Fax (01489) 789242

Set in 176 acres of rolling Hampshire
countryside, this 4-Star hotel has 100 en suite
bedrooms, superb restaurant, extensive leisure
facilities and its own picturesque and
challenging 18-hole par 70 golf course and
driving range. (See advertisement page 421 for
further details).

Burlington Hotel
Bellevue Road, Ventnor,
Isle of Wight PO38 1DB.
Tel (01983) 852113 Fax (01983) 853862

A charming, detached Victorian hotel with
panoramic sea views. Licensed. Car park.
Centrally heated. All en suite bedrooms with
colour TV, tea/coffee-making facilities and
telephone. Near to all the Island's golf courses -
reduced green fees. Special 4-night ferry
inclusive packages B&B and evening meal from
£155 per person including VAT.AA/RAC 3-
Star; ETB 4-Crown Highly Commended.

Cottesmore
Golf & Country Club
Buchan Hill, Pease Pottage, Crawley,
West Sussex RH11 9AT.
Tel (01293) 528256 Fax (01293) 522819

12 en suite bedrooms overlooking peaceful
undulating Sussex countryside. Guests can
enjoy two full 18-hole mature golf courses,
tennis, squash, indoor pool, spa bath, steam
room, sauna and gymnasium. Ten minutes from
Gatwick, one mile from the Pease Pottage exit
(J11) off the M23.

Dale Hill Hotel
Ticehurst, Wadhurst,
East Sussex TN5 7DQ.
Tel (01580) 200112

Highly commended luxurious hotel situated in
an area of outstanding national beauty, with
elegant health club and highly acclaimed 18-
hole golf course. New Ian Woosnam
championship course opened September, 1997.

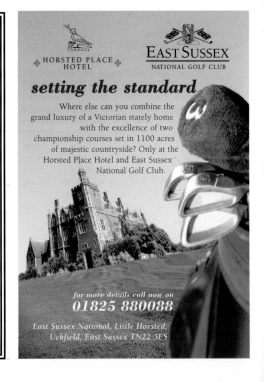

Donnington Grove Country Club Golf Hotel & Conference Centre

Grove Road,
Donnington,
Newbury, Berkshire RG14 2LA.
Tel (01635) 581000 Fax (01635) 552259

18-hole parkland/moorland championship course designed by Dave Thomas. The clubhouse and hotel are located within a beautifully renovated 18th-century gothic mansion. This will provide an ideal setting for your society, company golf day or conference stay.

The Dormy House - Seaford

Seaford Golf Club,
East Blatchington,
Seaford, East Sussex BN25 2JD.
Tel (01323) 892442

The Dormy House provides comfortable accommodation for eighteen guests in 9 twin-bedded en suit bedrooms on the first floor of the clubhouse, and 2 single rooms in our bungalow annexe. For latest brochure ring 01323 892442.

Five Lakes Hotel Golf & Country Club

Colchester Road,
Tolleshunt Knights,
Maldon, Essex CM9 8HX.
Tel (01621) 868888 Fax (01621) 869696

Luxury country club nestling in 320 acres of Essex countryside, close to the Roman town of Colchester and 'Constable Country'. Extensive facilities include a 4-Star hotel, two 18-hole golf courses - the Lakes course a PGA European Tour qualifying course designed by Neil Coles, indoor and outdoor tennis, squash, indoor pool, jacuzzi, steam, sauna, gymnasium, health spa, aerobics studio, snooker and crèche. Golf packages and leisure breaks available on request.

The Flackley Ash Hotel

Peasmarsh,
Rye,
East Sussex TN31 6YH.
Tel (01797) 230651 Fax (01797) 230510

3-Star Georgian country house hotel set in beautiful grounds with croquet lawn. Indoor swimming pool, whirlpool spa, saunas, mini-gym and 'beautique'. Extensive wine list, a friendly welcome and an AA Rosette for our food.

Gatton Manor Hotel Golf & Country Club Ltd

Ockley,
Nr Dorking, Surrey RH5 5PQ.
Tel (01306) 627555

Set amidst its own 18-hole golf course in 200 acres of parklands and lakes, situated between London and the south coast, in the heart of the Surrey countryside. Superb all en suite accommodation overlooking the golf course and grounds. À la carte restaurants, large lounge bar, conference suites, gym and health club.

Hanbury Manor

Ware,
Hertfordshire SG12 0SD.
Tel (01920) 487722 Fax (01920) 487692

5-Star country resort, yet only 25 miles north of central London. Championship golf course (1997 ALAMO English Open), state of the art health spa, three award-winning restaurants and 96 deluxe bedrooms. Ten conference rooms. (See advertisement page 4 for further details.)

Horsted Place Sporting Estate

Little Horsted,
Uckfield,
East Sussex TN22 5TS.
Tel (01825) 750581 Fax (01825) 750459
Club Tel: (01825) 880088/Fax: 880066
Combine Victorian elegance and luxury at Horsted Place Hotel with exceptional golf on one of the two spectacular courses at East Sussex National Golf Club. If you require golf tuition there is a superb golf academy which has its own three hole course. Experience for yourself challenging golf and exceptional accommodation in beautiful surroundings. (See advertisement page 421 for further details.)

Lansdowne Hotel

King Edward's Parade,
Eastbourne,
East Sussex BN21 4EE.
Tel (01323) 725174 Fax (01323) 739721

RAC/AA 3-Star. Play 36 holes a day on choice of seven courses; we book your tee-off time. Two nights with green fees, light lunch at club and use of our drying room. 1 April to 31 May, £140; 1 June to 30 September, £150; 1 October to 31 December, £135; 1 January to 28 February, £135; 1 to 31 March, £138. Extra days pro rata. (See advertisement page 425 for further details.)

Manor of Groves
Golf & Country Club
High Wych, Sawbridgeworth,
Hertfordshire CM21 0LA.
Tel (01279) 722333 Fax (01279) 726972

This superb 18-hole golf course set around its own Georgian manor house offers the ideal setting for that break away. Along with its special rated packages, and golf school, the clubhouse facilities include superb cuisine, bar, and a function room suitable for all occasions.

Marriott Goodwood Park
Hotel & Country Club
Goodwood, Nr Chichester,
West Sussex PO18 0QB.
Tel (01243) 775537 Fax (01243) 520120

Country club hotel set in the 12,000 acre Goodwood Estate with a testing 18-hole golf course and superb leisure facilities including golf range, practice area, putting green and fully equipped sports shop. (See advertisement page 4 for further details.)

Marriott Meon Valley
Hotel & Country Club
Sandy Lane, Shedfield, Nr Southampton,
Hampshire SO32 2HQ.
Tel (01329) 833455 Fax (01329) 834411

Set in 225 acres of Hampshire parkland, the Marriott Meon Valley Hotel offers a challenging 18-hole golf course and an equally testing 9-hole course. The hotel also offers extensive leisure and conference facilities. (See advertisement page 4 for further details.)

Marriott Tudor Park
Hotel & Country Club
Ashford Road, Bearsted, Maidstone,
Kent ME14 4NQ.
Tel (01622) 734334 Fax (01622) 735360

Situated in the Garden of England, Tudor Park is set in a 220 acre former deer park. Its superb golf course is designed by Donald Steel. The hotel also offers excellent accommodation, leisure and conference facilities. (See advertisement page 4 for further details.)

Sondes Lodge
14 Sondes Road, Deal, Kent CT14 7BW.
Tel (01304) 368741

AA 4-Q Selected; ETB Commended. Victorian 3-bedroom guesthouse. Full en suite available. Fifteen minutes from the famous Royal St

George's and Prince's golf clubs. Ten minutes from Deal's Royal Cinque Ports course. Visa accepted. Contact Jayne or Tony Hulme.

South Lodge Hotel
Lower Beeding, Nr Horsham,
West Sussex RH13 6PS.
Tel (01403) 891711 Fax (01403) 891766

South Lodge Hotel is a Victorian country house set in 93 acres of wooded parkland. Each of our 39 rooms is individually designed. Enjoy golf at our *two 18-hole championship courses* at Mannings Heath, tennis, croquet, petanque, putting or snooker. (See advertisement page 423 for further details.)

The Springs Hotel
Wallingford Road, North Stoke,
Wallingford, Oxon OX10 6BE.
Tel (01491) 836687 Fax (01491) 836877

Situated twix Oxford and Henley this Tudor-style country house offers, 30 en suite luxurious rooms, AA-2 Rosette restaurant, outdoor swimming pool and an 18-hole par 72 golf course. Your comfort and well-being are our priority.

Stocks Hotel Golf & Country Club
Stocks Road, Aldbury, Nr Tring,
Hertfordshire HP23 5RX.
Tel (01442) 851341 Fax (01442) 851253

A championship 18-hole all-weather golf course, PGA Game Improvement Centre. Chipping and putting greens, practice fairway. Full stocked professional shop. 18 bedrooms, two restaurants, riding stables, full leisure facilities, conference rooms.

Witney Four Pillars Hotel
Ducklington Lane, Witney,
Oxfordshire OX8 7TJ.
Tel (01993) 779777 Fax (01993) 703467

Golf can be pre-booked by our Witney hotel on two courses, one is a new lakes course, 18-hole 6,700 yards par 71. The other is ten miles away also an 18-hole 6,700 yards 72 par.

East Anglia

Abbotsley Golf Hotel
Eynesbury Hardwicke, St Neots,
Cambridgeshire PE19 4XN.
Tel (01480) 474000 Fax (01480) 471018

Friendly country house hotel set amidst two 18-
continued over

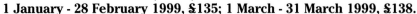 

hole courses. *Golf Monthly* "The Abbotsley course - the design is a revelation. The presentation superb." Award-winning gardens; relaxed atmosphere. Home of Vivien Saunders golf schools.

Barnham Broom Hotel
Golf, Conference & Leisure Centre
Honingham Road, Barnham Broom,
Norwich, Norfolk NR9 4DD.
Tel (01603) 759393 Fax (01603) 758224

EETB 4-Crown; AA Rosette. East Anglia's finest conference and leisure centre lies in 250 acres of countryside. 53 fully equipped bedrooms include family rooms, served by Flints restaurant and sports snack bar. Four squash courts, snooker, heated indoor swimming pool and spa jets, tennis and 36-hole golf. *Golfing Getaways* from £120. (See advertisement page 425 for further details.)

Beaumaris Hotel
15 South Street, Sheringham,
Norfolk NR26 8LL.
Tel (01263) 822370 Fax (01263) 821421

Established and run by the same family for fifty years with a reputation for personal service and excellent English cuisine. 22 en suite bedrooms. AA 2-Star Ashley Courtenay Recommended; EATB 4-Crown Commended. Three minutes' walk Sheringham's exhilarating cliff top golf course.

Cambridgeshire Moat House Hotel
Bar Hill,
Cambridge CB3 8EU.
Tel (01954) 780098 Fax (01954) 780010

18-hole championship golf course set in 134 acres of parkland. Golf professional David Vernon. Newly built clubhouse and golf shop. 99 en suite bedrooms. Extensive leisure facilities. Five miles north of Cambridge on A14. Visitors welcome.

The Golf Club - Thorpeness
Thorpeness, Nr Aldeburgh,
Suffolk IP16 4NH.
Tel (01728) 452176 Fax (01728) 453868

One of East Anglia's finest and most challenging 18-hole courses. Handicap certificate required, advisable to book in advance. Accommodation, bars, restaurant, golf shop, tennis courts and course set adjacent to picturesque coastal village on Suffolk Heritage coast. (See advertisement page 423 for further details.)

Oaklands Hotel
89 Yarmouth Road,
Thorpe St Andrew,
Norwich NR7 OHH.
Tel (01603) 434471 Fax (01603) 700318

RAC 3-Star hotel set in its own grounds overlooking the Yare Valley river. It is situated within easy reach of several local golf clubs, and is renowned for its excellent food, wine and service.

Wentworth Hotel
Wentworth Road,
Aldeburgh,
Suffolk IP15 5BD.
Tel (01728) 452312 Fax (01728) 454343

Country house hotel with sea views. 38 bedrooms all with colour TV, radio and tea-maker. Two comfortable lounges, cosy bar, log fires and antique furniture. Our restaurant specialises in local, fresh produce and seafood.

White Horse Hotel
Station Road,
Leiston, Suffolk IP16 4HD.
Tel (01728) 830694 Fax (01728) 833105

Close to three excellent courses in the heart of Suffolk Heritage coast. Friendly bars, excellent food, 12 rooms, 11 en suite, all with TV and telephone. Bargain weekend breaks all year.

Northamptonshire

Farthingstone Hotel & Golf Course
Farthingstone,
Towcester,
Northamptonshire NN12 8HA.
Tel (01327) 361291 Fax (01327) 361645

Set in glorious wooded countryside, just 90 minutes outside London. Farthingstone Hotel offers 16 superb en suite rooms, a challenging 18-hole golf course, squash court, full size snooker tables, and a carvery restaurant. Highly competitive tariffs.

The Queen Eleanor Hotel
London Road,
Wootton,
Northampton NN4 0JN.
Tel (01604) 762468 Fax (01604) 706191

Built in the 1880s located within one mile of the M1. Whether it is for a business meeting, a wedding or function or an overnight stay - a warm welcome awaits you.

East Midlands

Belton Woods Hotel

Belton,
Nr Grantham,
Lincolnshire NG32 2LN.
Tel (01476) 593200 Fax (01476) 574547

A magnificent hotel, golf and leisure resort set in 475 acres of glorious countryside. Two challenging 18-hole championship golf courses, 9-hole course, driving range, putting green and extensive leisure facilities. 136 bedrooms. (Part of the De Vere Hotels Group - see advertisement page 7 for further details.)

Dower House Hotel

Manor Estate,
Woodhall Spa,
Lincolnshire LN10 6PY.
Tel (01526) 352588 Fax (01526) 354045

Situated within the Manor Estate the Dower House overlooks the new Woodhall 18-hole golf course. The hotel is renowned for food and wine. 3-Crown Commended. Golfing parties' tariff available.

Eagle Lodge Hotel

The Breadway,
Woodhall Spa,
Lincolnshire LN10 6SP.
Tel (01526) 353231 Fax (01526) 352797

A privately owned hotel only one and a half miles from championship golf course. Good food, good atmosphere and friendly staff will make your stay an enjoyable one. Good golf courses close by. DB&B £36 per person, B&B £28 per person.

The Grange & Links Hotel

Sea Lane, Sandilands, Sutton-on-Sea,
Lincolnshire LN12 2RA.
Tel (01507) 441334 Fax (01507) 443033

3-Star 30-bedroom hotel with own 18-hole links course. Two tennis courts, snooker and ballroom. Award-winning hotel renowned for superb cuisine, friendliness, comfort and service.

Marriott Breadsall Priory Hotel & Country Club

Moor Road, Morley, Nr Derby,
Derbyshire DE7 6DL.
Tel (01332) 832235 Fax (01332) 833509

Based on a 13th-century mansion set in 400 acres of stunning parkland, Breadsall Priory offers two superb golf courses, excellent accommodation and comprehensive leisure and conference facilities. (See advertisement page 4 for further details.)

Petwood Hotel

Woodhall Spa, Lincolnshire LN10 6QF.
Tel (01526) 352411 Fax (01526) 353473

Built at the turn of the century, this traditional country house is set in a 30 acre estate, close to Woodhall Spa's championship golf course. 47 en suite bedrooms. Snooker, croquet and putting. Popular restaurant specialising in local produce.

The Toft House Hotel & Golf Course

Toft, Nr Bourne, Lincolnshire PE10 0JT.
Tel (01778) 590614 Fax (01778) 590264

The hotel is a family run, 22-bedroom converted farmhouse with its own 18-hole par 72 golf course covering 107 acres of undulating land with picturesque views of the lake and surrounding countryside.

West Midlands

The Belfry

Wishaw, North Warwickshire B76 9PR.
Tel (01675) 470033 Fax (01675) 470256

The Belfry, venue for three Ryder Cup matches and a unique fourth returning in 2001, is one of Europe's foremost business, golf and leisure resorts. Top class facilities includes 324 4-Star bedrooms, five restaurants, eight bars and Bel Air nightclub. Leisure facilities include gym, indoor pool, sauna, snooker and beautician to name but a few. Three golf courses including the Brabazon, PGA National and Derby courses. Floodlit driving range and putting green, largest on-course golf leisure and lifestyle shop in Europe which opened in May 1997. (Part of the De Vere Hotels Group - see advertisement page 427 for further details.)

The Chequers Inn

Fladbury, Nr Pershore,
Worcestershire WR10 2PZ.
Tel (01386) 860276 Fax (01386) 861286

A 14th-century inn containing cosy beamed restaurant and bar with magnificent open fire. Situated between Evesham and Pershore on the edge of the Cotswolds. Golf breaks include four days golf at different courses and three nights dinner, bed and breakfast.

Coleshill Hotel
152 High Street, Coleshill,
Warwicks B46 3BG.
Tel (01675) 465527 Fax (01675) 464013

Five miles from the Belfry, five miles from the Forest of Arden, the Coleshill hotel is the ideal venue for golfing parties. 23 very well appointed rooms, character bar, delightful relaxing restaurant - and we know golfers! Special prices for golfers *plus the Coleshill Hotel Challenge Trophy!*

Hawkstone Park Hotel
Weston-under-Redcastle, Shrewsbury,
Shropshire SY4 5UY.
Tel (01939) 200611 Fax (01939) 200311

The recently refurbished Hawkstone Park Hotel and Golf Centre has two contrasting 18-hole golf courses; the Hawkstone, famous for its mature picturesque parkland setting, and the redeveloped Windmill offering undulating landscape and strategic water features.

Ingon Manor Golf & Country Club
Ingon Lane, Snitterfield,
Nr Stratford-upon-Avon,
Warwickshire CV37 0QE.
Tel (01789) 731857 Fax (01789) 731657

Located two miles from Stratford, close to the A46. Par 72, 18-hole golf course, 6,554 yards white tees, 6,091 yards yellow tees. Driving range and practice area. All day bar and catering. Accommodation available.

Marriott Forest of Arden Hotel & Country Club
Maxstoke Lane, Meriden,
Warwickshire CV7 7HR.
Tel (01676) 522335 Fax (01676) 523711

Set in 10,000 acres of Warwickshire countryside, the Forest of Arden, host to the One-2-One British Masters, offers some of Britain's best golfing alongside first class accommodation, leisure and conference facilities. (See advertisement page 4 for further details.)

Nailcote Hall Hotel
Nailcote Lane, Berkswell,
Warwickshire CV7 7DE.
Tel (01203) 466174 Fax (01203) 470720

Delightful and challenging championship 9-hole par 3 course designed to test any golfer's short game. Set in the grounds of this 17th-century black and white Jacobean country house hotel, used by Cromwell in the English Civil War.

Patshull Park Hotel Golf & Country Club
Pattingham, Shropshire WV6 7HR.
Tel (01902) 700100 Fax (01902) 700874

Parkland, lakeside 18-hole championship John Jacobs' designed course in grounds of the Earl of Dartmouth estate. Corporate, society and residential packages. 49 en suite bedrooms, swimming pool, leisure centre, gymnasium, fishing. Restaurant and Bunkers coffee shop.

The Redfern Hotel
Cleobury Mortimer,
Shropshire DY14 8AA.
Tel (01299) 270395 Fax (01299) 271011

Family run 2-Star; 4-Crown Commended hotel with AA Rosette and RAC Merit award for food. Fifteen golf courses within a short drive. Reasonable inclusive prices with unlimited golf available.

Telford Golf & Country Club
Great Hay,
Sutton Hill, Telford,
Shropshire TF7 4DT.
Tel (01952) 429977 Fax (01952) 586602

Overlooking the Ironbridge Gorge, the hotel offers its own 18-hole championship course. Floodlit driving range and practice areas. The extensive leisure facilities include squash courts, swimming pool, gymnasium, snooker, whirlpool, sauna and steam rooms. There is a resident masseur. (See advertisement page 429 for further details.)

Welcombe Hotel & Golf Course
Warwick Road, Stratford-upon-Avon,
Warwickshire CV37 0NR.
Tel (01789) 295252 Fax (01789) 414666

A 4-Star Jacobean-style mansion set within its own 6,217 yards private golf course. A newly created clubhouse and pro shop within the hotel's 157 acres enhance the parkland course.

Whitefields Hotel Golf & Country Club
Coventry Road, Thurlaston, Nr Rugby,
Warwickshire CV23 9JR.
Tel (01788) 521800 Fax (01788) 521695

18-hole course 6,223 yards. Driving range, putting green 18. 33 en suite rooms. Four conference rooms. Bars and à la carte restaurant. Societies welcome seven days. Call the secretary on 01788 815555. Reservations 01788 521800.

Yorkshire & Humberside

Aldwark Manor Golf Hotel

Aldwark, Alne, York, Yorkshire YO6 2NF.
(Hotel) Tel (01347) 838146
(Golf) Tel (01347) 838353
Fax (01347) 838867

This fully restored Victorian manor offers its guests all modern facilities with superb food, wine and country location to complement the 18-hole par 71 parkland course, which holds many surprises for our visitors. Open all year round to non-residents. Twelve miles from York and Harrogate on the river Ure. (See advertisement page 429 for further details.)

Alfreda Guest House

Heslington Lane, Fulford, York YO1 4HN.
Tel (01904) 631698

Family run Edwardian residence in large grounds. Parking, security lighting/camera. En suite rooms, colour TV, radio, direct dial telephones, tea/coffee-making facilities, double glazing. Gas central heating. Five minutes' walk Fulford golf. Contact Elizabeth - 01904 631698.

Cave Castle Golf Hotel

South Cave, Brough,
East Yorkshire HU15 2EU.
Tel (01430) 421286 Fax (01430) 421118

Superb manor house in 160 acres of parkland situated at foot of the Wolds. Five minutes from M62 motorway link and fifteen minutes from Hull. 25 en suite bedrooms with restaurant, function and conference facilities. Own 18-hole golf course 6,524 yards SSS 71. Golf breaks, societies and non-members welcome.

Central Hotel

1-3 The Crescent, Scarborough,
Yorkshire YO11 2PW.
Tel (01723) 365766 Fax (01723) 360448

Refurbished, elegant Georgian hotel in town centre. Own car park. 30 fully equipped en suite rooms. Public bar. Food served from 12 noon to midnight every day. Pool table. Lift to all floors. Five golf courses within 20 mile radius.

The Dormy - Harrogate Golf Club

Forest Lane Head, Harrogate,
North Yorkshire HG2 7TF.
Tel (01423) 862999

A long established 18-hole golf course set amongst mature trees formerly part of the Forest of Knaresborough. Visitors are assured of a warm reception in the extensively refurbished clubhouse and restaurant. Dormy accommodation available. (See advertisement page 25 for further details.)

The Harewood Arms Hotel

Harrogate Road,
Harewood,
Nr Leeds, West Yorkshire LS17 9LH.
Tel 0113-288 6566 Fax 0113-288 6064

Ideally located for businessmen and tourists. Seven miles from the commercial centre of Leeds and seven miles from the spa town of Harrogate. The hotel is conveniently situated for discovering the charm of the Yorkshire Dales, with an abundance of things to see and do. (See advertisement page 429 for further details.)

The Hobbit Hotel

Hob Lane, Norland,
Sowerby Bridge,
West Yorkshire HX6 3QL.
Tel (01422) 832202 Fax (01422) 835381

Inn-style hotel with panoramic views. All bedrooms en suite. Choose from restaurant or bar bistro for reputable food at affordable prices. Good selection of ales. Activities include golf within 500 yards, Murder Mystery, day at the races, horseriding, 2.00 am entertainments licence.

Oulton Hall Hotel

Rothwell Lane, Oulton, Leeds LS26 8HN.
Tel 0113-282 1000

This elegant 5-Star Yorkshire hotel complete with 19th-century style formal gardens, is situated adjacent to the Oulton Park Golf Club where guests have the choice of either 18- or 9-hole courses set in spectacular White Rose countryside. Facilities also include a 22-bay driving range. (Part of the De Vere Hotels Group - see advertisement page 7 for further details.)

Rudding Park Hotel

Follifoot, Harrogate,
North Yorkshire HG3 1JH.
Tel (01423) 871350 Fax: (01423) 872286

Rudding Park, situated two and half miles south of Harrogate, is the ideal venue for the discerning golfer. It offers a contemporary 4-Star AA/RAC hotel as well as an 18-hole, par 72 parkland golf course. (See advertisement page 427 for further details.)

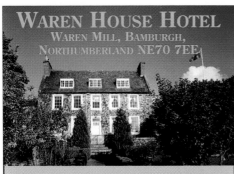

Sea Brink Hotel

3 The Beach,
Filey,
North Yorkshire YO14 9LA.
Tel (01723) 513257 Fax (01723) 514139

STB 3-Crown Commended; AA/RAC 2-Star. Traditional seafront hotel overlooking beautiful Filey Bay. 9 en suite rooms, many with sea views. Centrally heated, colour TV, telephone/clock radio and hospitality tray. Licensed restaurant and coffee shop. Five golf courses nearby including Ganton.

North West

Alvaston Hall Hotel

Middlewich Road,
Nantwich,
Cheshire CW5 6PD.
Tel (01270) 624341 Fax (01270) 623395

Established hotel in picturesque setting close to Nantwich. Newly developed clubhouse and challenging 9-hole course with water and hill features. Golf professional on-site with well equipped shop. Members of the Cheshire and English Golf Union. Teaching Centre for PGA.

Carden Park Hotel Golf Resort & Spa

Nr Chester,
Cheshire CH3 9DQ.
Tel (01829) 731000 Fax (01829) 731032

Set in 750-acres of beautiful Cheshire countryside near Chester. A true golf resort with two 18-hole golf courses - the mature Cheshire course and the new Nicklaus course, the 9-hole par 3 Azalea course and Europe's first Jack Nicklaus Residential Golf School. The superb AA/RAC 4-Star hotel also has an extensive spa and there are many other leisure facilities on the estate. For further information and a brochure call Liz Mole on 01829 731000. (See advertisement page 431 for further details.)

Clifton Arms Hotel

West Beach,
Lytham, Lancashire FY8 5QJ.
Tel (01253) 739898 Fax (01253) 730657

The Clifton Arms Hotel is set in the picturesque town of Lytham. Overlooking Lytham Green and seafront it is ideally situated for all local golf courses, including Royal Lytham, Fairhaven, Greendrive and Old Links.

De Vere Hotel Blackpool

East Park Drive,
Blackpool,
Lancashire FY3 8LL.
Tel (01253) 838866

De Vere Hotel Blackpool adds a touch of 4-Star elegance to one of Europe's most popular tourist destinations. Extensive facilities include: 164 bedrooms, first class restaurant, three bars, six conference rooms, indoor swimming pool, 18-bay floodlit driving range and an 18-hole championship golf course designed by Peter Alliss and Clive Clark. The course regularly hosts corporate golf and society days and was the recent venue for both the PGA Northern Championship and Reebok PGA and Lancashire Open. (Part of the De Vere Hotels Group - see advertisement page 7 for further details.)

The Dormy House

Royal Lytham & St Anne's Golf Club,
Links Gate,
Lytham St Anne's,
Lancashire FY8 3LQ.
Tel (01253) 724206 Fax (01253) 780946

Ideal for small parties wishing to play the championship course. Accommodation for men only. Apply to the assistant secretary. (See advertisement page 22 for further details.)

Forte Posthouse - Lancaster

Waterside Park,
Caton Road, Lancaster,
Lancashire LA1 3RA.
Tel (01524) 65999 Fax (01524) 841265

Modern, friendly hotel situated on the banks of the river Lune. Conveniently located for discovering the beauty of the Lake District. Facilities include leisure club, to relax and unwind, and informal restaurant. Six 18-hole courses within 25 miles.

The George Hotel

Devonshire Street,
Penrith,
Cumbria CA11 7SU.
Tel (01768) 862696 Fax (01768) 868223

Privately owned hotel. All rooms with private facilities, TV, direct dial telephone, hospitality tray, radio and baby listening system. Private car park. Double or twin room from £58.00. Single room from £42.75 inclusive of VAT and full English breakfast.

The Imperial Hotel - Blackpool
North Promenade, Blackpool,
Lancashire FY7 2HB.
Tel (01253) 623971 Fax (01255) 751784

Overlooking the sea on North Promenade, the Imperial's fine Victorian building still retains the glory of its past, whilst offering the facilities you would associate with a world class hotel. (See advertisement page 431 for further details.)

Jarvis Alma Lodge
149 Buxton Road, Stockport,
Greater Manchester 5KZ 6EL.
Tel 0161-483 4431

Located on the southern edge of Stockport, within easy access to M63, M56, M6 and M62. 52 bedrooms with one suite, all rooms have radio, colour TV, direct dial telephone, hair-dryer, tea/coffee-making facilities etc. Extensive car park. Seven miles from Manchester airport.

Llyndir Hall Hotel
Llyndir Lane, Rossett,
Nr Chester LL12 0AY.
Tel (01244) 571648 Fax (01244) 571258

Set in peaceful countryside six miles from the historic city of Chester. AA 3-Star hotel with leisure facilities. 38 bedrooms all en suite with satellite TV. Excellent restaurant. Located close to many superb golf courses. (See advertisement page 431 for further details.)

Metropole Hotel
3 Portland Street, Southport,
Merseyside PR8 1LL.
Tel (01704) 536836 Fax (01704) 549041

RAC/AA 2-Star hotel. Centrally situated and close to Royal Birkdale and other championship courses. Fully licensed - late bar facilities for residents. Full size snooker table. Reduced rates for golfers. Golfing proprietors will assist with tee reservations.

Mottram Hall Hotel
Wilmslow Road, Mottram St Andrew,
Prestbury, Cheshire SK10 4QT.
Tel (01625) 828135

Mottram Hall is an elegant 18th-century Georgian building, set in secluded parkland with delightful ornamental gardens and lake. The 4-Star hotel has 132 luxury bedrooms, conference facilities for up to 275 guests, a luxurious leisure club, and a superb 18-hole championship golf course designed by international golf architect Dave Thomas. Leisure facilities include spacious swimming pool, spa, saunas and steam rooms, fully equipped gym - even a full sized soccer pitch utilised by European football champions, Germany, who stayed here in 1996. (Part of the De Vere Hotels Group - see advertisement page 7 for further details.)

The Prince of Wales Hotel
Lord Street, Southport,
Merseyside PR8 1JS.
Tel (01704) 536688 Fax (01704) 543932

Since 1876 the Prince of Wales Hotel has been the premier hotel in Southport - the Golfers' Paradise. Used as the base for the Ryder Cup and British Open over the years, the hotel provides quality 4-Star accommodation. 103 rooms, two restaurants and bars. We are able to arrange tee-times at any of the twelve courses in the area including Royal Birkdale. The hotel, located centrally in Southport, offers free car parking. (See advertisement page 429 for further details.)

The Royal Clifton Hotel
The Promenade, Southport,
Merseyside PR8 1RB.
Tel (01704) 533771 Fax (01704) 500657

Southport's premier 3-Star Best Western hotel is just five minutes from Royal Birkdale and a plethora of championship courses are nearby. Relax in our superb health club and wine and dine in our award-winning restaurant. Special golfing breaks available.

Seapark Apartments
51 Alexandra Road, Southport,
Merseyside PR9 9HD.
Tel (01704) 500444 Fax (01704) 531703

The Open Championship Royal Birkdale 1998 Seapark is situated within walking distance of the town centre and three miles from the course. The accommodation at Seapark ranges from studio to 5-bedroomed apartments. Every luxury apartment is self contained, has fully fitted kitchens, TV, video and is also serviced daily.

St David's Park Hotel
St David's Park, Ewloe, Nr Chester,
Flintshire CH5 3YB.
Tel (01244) 520800 Fax (01244) 520930

AA 4-Star hotel with extensive leisure facilities, including gym and swimming pool. 145 bedrooms and suites, excellent restaurant.
continued over

Northop Country Park Golf Club only five minutes away, and Carden Park Golf Resort 20 minutes. Special golf packages available. (See advertisement page 431 for further details.)

Tufton Arms Hotel
Market Square,
Appleby-in-Westmorland,
Cumbria CA16 6XA.
Tel (017683) 51593 Fax (017683) 52761

Family owned 16th-century coaching inn, offering renowned AA Rosette and RAC Merit awarded cuisine, and warm hospitality. Ideal exploring base for lakes and dales, with nearby Appleby's 18-hole challenging moorland course.

The Waterford Hotel
37 Leicester Street,
Southport,
Merseyside PR9 0EX.
Tel/Fax (01705) 530559

Close to many golf courses including Royal Birkdale. Ideally located for exploring Southport's shops, restaurants and bars. Well appointed en suite bedrooms, most with lake views. Residents' bar and restaurant. Car parking. Drying facilities.

Isle of Man

Castletown Golf Links Hotel
Derbyhaven, Castletown,
Isle of Man IM9 1UA.
Tel (01624) 822201 Fax (01624) 625535

Situated on our own peninsula, our championship golf course of 6,700 yards, with all holes having sea views, is a real test of links golf. The hotel facilities are of a luxurious 3-Star standard.

North East

Linden Hall Golf Club
Longhorsley, Morpeth,
Northumberland NE65 8XF.
Tel (01670) 788050 Fax (01670) 788544

Linden Hall Golf Club is located within the grounds of Linden Hall Hotel, a 4-Star, 5-Crown Georgian manor country house hotel. The 18-hole, 6,809 yard, SSS 73 golf course is set within mature woodland, rolling parkland with established burns and lakes amidst a stunning backdrop of the Cheviot hills and Northumbrian coastline.

Ramside Hall Hotel & Golf Club
Carrville, Durham DH1 1TD.
Tel 0191-386 5282 Fax 0191-386 0399

Set in 220 acres on the outsksirts of the cathedral city of Durham and surrounded by a stimulating 27-hole golf course. 3-Star; 4-Crown High Commended. 80 luxury bedrooms, restaurant, grill room and carvery. Conference and banqueting facilities. Superb floodlit driving range and practice areas. (See advertisement page 433 for further details.)

Waren House Hotel
Waren Mill, Bamburgh,
Northumberland NE70 7EE.
Tel (01668) 214581 Fax (01668) 214484

Traditional country house hotel in six acres wooded grounds and gardens on edge of Budle Bay just two miles from Bamburgh. Superb accommodation, excellent Northumbrian cuisine and over 250 reasonably priced wines to choose from. Children over 14 welcome. (See advertisement page 433 for further details.)

White Swan Hotel
Bondgate Within, Alnwick,
Northumberland NE66 1TD.
Tel (01665) 602109 Fax (01665) 504100

AA 3-Star 17th-century coaching inn. Over ten courses within 25 miles. Packages arranged, tee-times booked. Spectacular coastline. Also racing breaks.

SCOTLAND

Scottish Borders

Castle Hotel - Coldstream
11 High Street, Coldstream,
Berwickshire TD12 4AP.
Tel/Fax (01890) 882830

Small family run hotel offering en suite accommodation 400 metres from Hirsel Golf Club, Kelso club eight miles, Berwick club fourteen miles. Public bar open all day. B&B £25 per person.

Kelvin House Hotel
53 Main Street, Glenluce,
Wigtownshire DG8 0PP.
Tel/Fax (01581) 300303

Family run 3-Crown en suite hotel. Renowned

continued over

for food, wine and real ales. The hotel is a member of *Taste of Burns*. Five golf courses nearby with concessionary rates at all five of them.

The Marine Hotel
Cromwell Road, North Berwick,
East Lothian EH39 4LZ.
Tel (01620) 892406 Fax (01620) 894480

Superb 80-bedroom sporting hotel overlooking the North Berwick West Links with fabulous sea and golfing views. Home-from-home for many of the world's top golfers and famed for friendly service and traditional value for money holidays. For non-golfers there is swimming, tennis and snooker. Families, individuals and golfing parties enjoy the relaxed atmosphere of this all-year-round holiday hotel. Special seasonal leisure breaks and holiday rates. (See advertisement page 435 for further details.)

Sunlaws House Hotel
& Roxburghe Golf Course
Kelso, Roxburghshire TD5 8JZ.
Tel (01573) 450331 Fax (01573) 450611

22-bedroom hotel owned by the Duke and Duchess of Roxburghe. Luxury accommodation, superb cuisine. The 18-hole championship standard Roxburghe golf course, designed by Dave Thomas, surrounds the hotel.

Tweeddale Arms Hotel
High Street, Gifford,
East Lothian EH41 4QU.
Tel (01620) 810240 Fax (01620) 810488

Situated in the conservation village of Gifford eighteen miles from Edinburgh. We have eighteen of the finest golf courses to cater for everyone, from novice to champion, all within easy reach of the hotel. In addition to the excellent amenities and outstanding personal service the hotel offers warmth and hospitality in the true Scottish tradition.

South

Auchen Castle Hotel
Beattock, Moffat,
Dumfries-shire DG10 9SH.
Tel (01683) 300407 Fax (01683) 300667

This beautiful mansion, just off the A74, is convenient to Moffat, Lockerbie, Dumfries and Powfoot golf courses. The excellent restaurant, elegant rooms, private trout loch and gardens, all make for an ideal golfing break.

Cally Palace Hotel
Gatehouse of Fleet DG7 2DL.
Tel (01557) 814341 Fax (01557) 814522

This award-winning 4-Star country mansion has its own exclusive par 70, 18-hole golf course sculpted perfectly into the surrounding 150 acres of mature parkland. Other facilities include fishing loch and leisure complex.

Clonyard House Hotel
Colvend,
Dalbeattie, Kirkshire DG5 4QW.
Tel (01556) 630372 Fax (01556) 630422

Family run country hotel in quiet grounds. Excellent restaurant, also informal meals in our lively bar. Ground floor rooms with facilities including direct dial telephone. Five golf courses within a ten mile radius, including Southerness. Double room £32.50 per person. Special rates for golfing parties.

Powfoot Golf Hotel
Links Avenue,
Powfoot, Annan,
Dumfrieshire DG12 5PN.
Tel (01461) 700254 Fax (01461) 700288

Privately owned 18-bedroom hotel adjacent to and overlooking golf course and Solway Firth. Several other excellent golf courses in area. All bedrooms en suite complete with colour TV, direct dial telephone and hostess tray. Excellent wine list and our menus include local produce like Solway salmon, prime Galloway steaks, duck and venison. Golf packages available. Telephone for details.

Central & East

Ardchoille Farmhouse
Dunshalt,
Nr Auchtermuchty,
Fife KY14 7EY.
Tel/Fax (01337) 828414

First class accommodation in the midst of golfing country. Ladybank three miles, St Andrews within easy reach. Superb food and comfort. Golf parties of six - 3 twin bedrooms; en suite facilities, colour TV and tea/coffee-making facilities. DB&B reasonable rates. Safe parking. 5-Q AA Premier Selected; RAC Highly Acclaimed; Taste of Scotland; STB 3-Crown Highly Commended. Holder of REHIS diploma in advanced food hygiene. Welcome host.

Location:
Two miles from Tenby. Off the A4139 Tenby-Pembroke coast road.

Penally ABBEY

Country House Hotel

PENALLY, Nr TENBY, PEMBROKESHIRE.
Tel: 01834 843033   Fax: 01834 844714

THE HOTEL FOR ALL SEASONS

Set in five acres, Penally Abbey, one of Pembroke's loveliest country houses, enjoys spectacular sea views across the golf course and Carmarthen Bay. Exquisitely furnished bedrooms, all en-suite, centrally heated, colour TV, telephone, hairdryer and tea/coffee-making facilities.
Mouth watering dishes of fresh seasonal delicacies are served in our candlelit restaurant, complemented by excellent wines from our cellar.

SILVERWOOD GOLF HOTEL & Country Club

SILVERWOOD GOLF CENTRE ON SITE

18 Hole Parkland Course
9 Hole Par 3 Course
Driving Range Floodlit

WEEKEND GOLF PACKAGES
(Thursday to Sunday inclusive)

1 Day Special 1 Bed & Breakfast 1 Evening Meal Plus 1 Day's Golf £40 per person sharing.

3 Day Special 3 Bed & Breakfast 3 Evening Meals Plus 3 Days' Golf £110 per person sharing.

KILN ROAD, LURGAN,
CO ARMAGH BT66 6NF

Tel: (01762) 327722
Fax: (01762) 325290
R of I: (08 01762) 327722

Where nothing is taken for granted ...Except Perfection

During your stay at the Limerick Inn Hotel, we want you to forget everything and relax, and with 32 golf courses in the Shannonside region, we feel sure that our hotel will be above par - and the golf well below!

Here you'll find the amenities of a modern hotel combined with the comforts of an ideal home,

- 153 luxury ensuite bedrooms
- Extensive Health & Leisure Centre, with superb sports facilities and Hair & Beauty Salon
- Top class restaurant serving the finest in Irish and French Cuisine

That's why we take as much of the worry from you as possible, leaving you to enjoy yourself at the acclaimed Limerick Inn Hotel.

For further information, contact us on +353-61-326666

LIMERICK INN HOTEL

Seriously Interested in You

Situated 12 miles from Shannon International Airport and 3 miles from Limerick City on the main Limerick/Ennis N7 Road.
ENNIS ROAD, LIMERICK. TEL. +353-61-326666 FAX +353-61-326281 e-mail: limerick-inn@limerick-inn.ie http://www.commerce.ie/cl/limerick-inn

Auchterarder House
Auchterarder, Perthshire PH3 1DZ.
Tel (01764) 663646 Fax (01764) 662939

40 golf courses within a 20 mile radius of Auchterarder. We can organise hunting, fishing, riding, off-road driving, sight-seeing castles, lochs, mountains, distilleries, guided walks and biking. Gourmet dining in exclusive country house setting. (Member of the Wren's Hotel Group - see advertisement page 439 for further details.)

Balbirnie House Hotel
Balbirnie Park, Markinch,
by Glenrothes, Fife KY7 6NE.
Tel (01592) 610066 Fax (01592) 610529

Balbirnie is an elegant 18th-century mansion in a 416 acre park. AA 4-Red Star; 5-Crown Deluxe STB with 30 rooms/suites. Ideally located for Ladybank, St Andrews, Carnoustie. Balbirnie Park Golf Course within the Park.

Balgeddie House Hotel
Balgeddie Way, Glenrothes North,
Fife KY6 3ET.
Tel (01592) 742511 Fax (01592) 621702
e-mail: balgeddie@easynet.co.uk

AA/RAC 3-Star; STB 4-Crown. Beautifully situated in immaculate gardens in the heart of some of the country's finest golf courses. All bedrooms have private bathroom, satellite TV, telephone, radio, tea-making facilities. Elegant cocktail bar/restaurant - table d'hôte/à la carte menus. Golf packages arranged. (See advertisement page 25 for further details.)

The Barnton Thistle Hotel
Queensferry Road, Edinburgh EH4 6AS.
Tel 0131-339 1144

Situated four miles from the centre of Edinburgh. Within walking distance of the Royal Burgess Golfing Society and a short distance from Lothian's numerous golf courses. 50 bedrooms all en suite. Restaurant and three bars.

Caledonian Hotel
81 High Street, Leven, Fife KY8 4NG.
Tel (01333) 424101 Fax (01333) 421241

The Caledonian Hotel is centrally located within Fife. Leven itself has two excellent golf courses, one of which is used for many national and international qualifying events. A 4-Crown STB hotel.

Crusoe Hotel
2 Main Street, Lower Largo, Fife KY8 6BT.
Tel (01333) 320759 Fax (01333) 320865

Crusoe Hotel is situated at the water's edge and has 12 en suite bedrooms and a suite. À la carte and table d'hôte meals served in the Castaway restaurant, seafood and flambé dishes a speciality. Discount given for groups of eight plus.

Dalmunzie House Hotel
Spittal O'Glenshee, Blairgowrie,
Perthshire PH10 7QG.
Tel (01250) 885224 Fax (01250) 885225

Set in the Highlands with our own 9-hole course. This friendly country house offers an ideal base for a golfing holiday with excellent local courses at Blairgowrie, Pitlochry, Alyth and many more. AA Rosette for food. (See advertisement page 435 for further details.)

Drumoig Golf Club & Hotel
Drumoig, Leuchars, St Andrews,
Fife KY16 0BE.
Tel (01382) 541800 Fax (01382) 542211

Superb new golf hotel only ten minutes from St Andrews. 24 fully equipped en suite lodge bedrooms, well stocked bar, lounge and à la carte restaurant. Own 18-hole tournament standard golf course. Ideally located for touring Fife, Tayside and Perthshire.

Edenside House
Edenside, St Andrews KY16 9SQ.
Tel (01334) 838108 Fax (01334) 838493
e-mail: 106076.2226@compuserve.com

AA 4-Q selected guest house in superb waterfront location. St Andrews only two and a half miles (five minutes by car). 9 double/twin en suite rooms, some ground floor, all with colour TV and beverage tray etc. Extensive breakfast menu, exclusively non-smoking, ample parking. *Also Golf Tours of Scotland/Ireland* by associated tour company.

Gleddoch House
Langbank, Renfrewshire PA14 6YE.
Tel (01475) 540711 Fax (01475) 540201

Country house hotel overlooking the river Clyde within easy reach of Glasgow and airport. Own golf course (par 72, 6,300 yards). Pro shop, clubhouse with own restaurant, bar, squash, horseriding, clay pigeon shooting and off-road driving. Golf Societies welcome.

The Glynhill Leisure Hotel
169 Paisley Road, Nr Glasgow Airport, Renfrew PA4 8XB.
Tel 0141-886 5555 Fax 0141-885 2838

AA/RAC 3-Star; STB 4-Crown Commended. Ideally located, convenient for central Scotland's many golf courses and clubs. 125 comfortable en suite bedrooms. Two excellent restaurants (dinner dances every Friday and Saturday), and a superb leisure club for relaxation and enjoyment.

Goldenstones Hotel
Queens Road, Dunbar, East Lothian EH42 1LG.
Tel (01368) 862356 Fax (01368) 865644

STB 3-Crown. We can arrange tee-times for you at some of the finest Scottish golf courses, including Muirfield, Dunbar and North Berwick. There are nineteen superb courses all within half an hour of the hotel.

Golf Hotel
34 Dirleton Avenue, North Berwick, East Lothian EH39 4BH.
Tel/Fax (01620) 892202

Family run hotel ideal for golfers wishing to play any of East Lothian's sixteen courses. Starting times arranged. Lounge bar, TV lounge, rooms with private bathroom and colour TV.

Green Craigs
Aberlady, East Lothian EH32 0PY.
Tel (01875) 870301 Fax (01875) 870440

The white house set on the bay overlooking Edinburgh is the Green Craigs restaurant, bistro and hotel. All 6 rooms en suite, colour TV, tea/coffee-making facilities, with toiletries, mineral water and fresh fruit as added extras. Exceptionally good food and wines. Nineteen golf courses within the county with Muirfield only five minutes away. Courtesy bus and limo service for diners.

Hazelbank Hotel
28 The Scores, St Andrews, Fife KY16 9AS.
Tel (01334) 72466

Situated 400 yards from R&A clubhouse overlooking St Andrews Bay this family run hotel offers quality accommodation (STB 3-Crown Commended) at affordable prices. All rooms en suite. Rates 1998 £25 - £48 per person B&B, double/twin.

Inchview Hotel
69 Kinghorn Road, Burntisland, Fife KY3 9EB.
Tel (01592) 872239 Fax (01592) 874866

4-Crown STB Commended; AA 2-Star family run hotel with comfortable accommodation overlooking the Forth Estuary. Excellent cuisine in the restaurant and real ales in the lounge bar. A convenient base for some of the best golf courses. 25 minutes from Edinburgh

The Inn at Lathones
By Largoward, St Andrews, Fife KY9 1JE.
Tel (01334) 840494 Fax (01334) 840694

This charming old coaching inn is set in one of the most beautiful areas of Scotland, just five miles from the famous university town of St Andrews on the A915 towards Kirkcaldy. In 1997 the inn was purchased and returned to its former glory as a traditional coaching inn, with open log fire, friendly ghosts, great food and ales, whilst still offering modern day comforts, and the friendliest of people to look after your every need. Seventeen golf courses within nine miles of the inn.

Kinloch House Hotel
By Blairgowrie, Perthshire PH10 6SG.
Tel (01250) 884237

Kinloch House offers an almost unique proposition for golfers. 35 courses within an hour's drive, planning of rounds and booking of tee-times, sportsman's room with every facility and the best of Scottish hospitality. In-house health and fitness centre. AA 3-Red Star; 3-Rosettes.

Lairds Hotel
13 Philip Street, Carnoustie, Tayside DD7 6EB.
Tel (01241) 852182

You are warmly invited to Lairds 18th-century family run hotel where we specialise in golf packages. Rooms are en suite with beverage making facilities, satellite TV and full restaurant facilities. Five minutes from golf courses.

Letham Grange
Colliston, by Arbroath DD11 4RL.
Tel (01241) 890373 Fax (01241) 890725

42-bedrooms, Victorian mansion, with 36-holes of superb golf. First class facilities set in the heartland of golf. Company/society golf outings/ breaks welcome. (See advertisement page 437 for further details.)

445

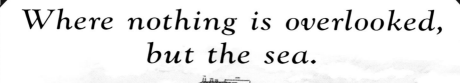

The Links Hotel - Montrose
Mid Links, Montrose DD10 8RL.
Tel (01674) 671000 Fax (01674) 672698

Use the hotel as a base to enjoy the pleasures of Angus, sandy beaches, golf courses, Glen Esk, House of Dun, Montrose Basin Nature Reserve, local museum distillery, and Glamis Castle. (See advertisement page 435 for further details.)

Loch Monzievaird Chalets
Ochtertyre, Crieff, Perthshire P47 4JR.
Tel (01764) 652586 Fax (01764) 652555

The beautiful grounds at Loch Monzievaird, are hidden away one mile from Crieff. Our Norwegian and Danish chalets are laid out amongst ancient oak, beech and scots pine. 20 golf courses within half an hour's drive!

The Mallard
East Links Road, Gullane,
East Lothian EH31 2AF.
Tel (01620) 843288 Fax (01620) 843200

4-Crown Commended. Situated overlooking Gullane's famous golf course. Special golfing breaks available all year round. We offer hospitality with informality to the golfer and non-golfer.

Marriott Dalmahoy Hotel & Country Club
Kirknewton, Nr Edinburgh,
Midlothian EH27 8EB.
Tel 0131-333 1845 Fax 0131-335 3203

Set in over 1,000 acres of Scottish woodland and almost in the shadow of the Pentland Hills, Dalmahoy offers something special for every golfer. A regular European tour venue, only seven miles from Edinburgh. Two outstanding courses - East Championship Course and the West Course. 4-Star hotel with 115 bedrooms and excellent conference facilities. Swimming pool, jet pool, sauna/steam room, resistance and CV gymnasium, tennis courts, golf and leisure shop, Long Weekend restaurant, health and beauty salon and club bar. Floodlit driving range with tuition, video facilities and short game area. (See advertisement page 4 for further details.)

Navitie Guest House
Nr Loch Leven, Lochgelly, Fife KY5 8LR.
Tel (01592) 860295 Fax (01592) 869769

10-bedroom house set in four acres. Quiet location, private parking. All rooms en suite, centrally heated, tea/coffee making facilities, TV in all rooms. Sauna. Guests' lounge with log fire. Over 100 golf courses from a two to 30 minutes' drive! STB 3-Crown Commended

Old Course Hotel - St Andrews Golf Resort & Spa
St Andrews,
Fife KY16 9SP.
Tel (01334) 474371 Fax (01334) 477668

This luxury 125-bedroom hotel overlooks the 17th Road Hole of the Old Course and is a five minute walk to the beach and town. Facilities include health spa with swimming pool, whirlpool, fitness room and full range of massage and beauty treatments. The hotel now has its own championship golf course, the Duke's Course. Open to non-residents, with residents enjoying guaranteed tee-times and reduced green fees.

The Old Manse Guest House
136 Main Street,
Newmills, By Culross,
Fife KY12 8SX.
Tel (01383) 880150

STB Commended. Overlooking the Forth, ample parking. Edinburgh and St Andrews within easy reach. 6 bedrooms, 3 with en suite, all with TV, tea/coffee facilities. Will assist with itinerary. Rooms £16 - £22 B&B.

The Park Hotel - Dundee
Coupar Angus Road,
Dundee DD2 3HY.
Tel (01382) 610691 Fax (01382) 612633

Small hotel with 12 bedrooms, personally run with excellent standards at budget prices. Restaurant and function facilities. (See advertisement page 435 for further details.)

The Park Hotel - Montrose
John Street,
Montrose, Angus DD10 8RJ.
Tel (01674) 673415 Fax (01674) 677091

Family owned 3-Star 59-bedroom hotel, quietly situated yet close to town centre. Golf, tennis and all sports and leisure facilities. Recently refurbished brasserie bar and restaurant offering quality, variety and exceptional value for money. Superb golf packages tailor-made to your requirements, including Montrose Medal, Carnoustie, Letham Grange and Edzell. (See advertisement page 437 for further details.)

Rescobie Hotel
Leslie, Glenrothes, Fife KY6 2BQ.
Tel (01592) 742143 Fax (01592) 620231
e-mail: Rescobie@easynet.co.uk
AA/RAC 2-Star; STB 4-Crown. A small country house hotel with 10 fully equipped bedrooms and an AA Rosette for its excellent food. Positioned centrally between Carnoustie, Dalmahoy, Gleneagles and St Andrews. Over 100 golf courses are within easy driving range. (See advertisement page 433 for further details.)

Richmond Park Hotel
26 Linlithgow Road, Bowness,
Central Region EH51 0DN.
Tel (01506) 823213 Fax (01506) 822717
A warm welcome assured at the 4-Crown Commended Richmond Park. Recently extended to offer 46 luxury bedrooms. À la carte restaurant and lounge-diner. Overlooking river Forth. Minutes from many of Central Scotland's finest courses.

Rusacks Hotel Golf Club
Pilmour Links, St Andrews, Fife KY16 9JQ.
Tel (01334) 474321 Fax (01334) 477896
Golf Club Tel/Fax (01334) 479176
Rusacks Hotel, overlooking the first and last fairways of the Old Course, provides outstanding facilities for golfers. The Rusacks Golf Club, situated within the hotel, offers guests a full golf booking service, lockers, sauna, solarium, club bar and golf shop. Voted one of the *Top Ten Golf Hotels in the World.* STB 5-Crown.

The Scores Hotel
St Andrews, Fife, KY16 9BB.
Tel (01334) 472451 Fax (01334) 473947
Overlooking St Andrews Bay and the Royal & Ancient clubhouse, this famous 3-Star hotel is only yards from the 1st tee of the Old Course and a short stroll from the historic town centre. 30 en suite rooms, noted restaurant, parking.

St Andrews Golf Hotel
St Andrews, Fife KY16 9AS.
Tel (01334) 472611 Fax (01334) 472188
AA 3-Star and Rossette; STB 4-Crown Deluxe. Most comfortable, traditional Scottish hotel (all bedrooms en suite). Fine restaurant. Extensive cellar. On the seafront 220 yards from the 'Old Course'. Let us arrange your golf in Scotland. (See advertisement page 437 for further details.)

Highlands, Islands & North

Aberdeen Airport Thistle Hotel
Argyll Road, Aberdeen AB2 0DU.
Tel (01224) 725252 Fax (01224) 723745
Just off the main A96 to Inverness - The Gateway to Grampian Highlands - 20 golf courses in Aberdeen to choose from. Up to 50% discount at weekends. Please quote R & A Golfer's Handbook.

Alton Burn Hotel
Alton Burn Road, Nairn IV12 5ND.
Tel (01667) 452051 Fax (01667) 456697
Superb family run hotel overlooking Nairn golf course, with many courses a short drive away. All 25 bedrooms have private facilities, tea-maker and TV. Special rates for golfing parties. We can arrange tee-times etc for you. *Walker Cup venue 1999.*

Castle Hotel - Huntly
Huntly, Aberdeenshire AB54 4SH.
(01466) 792696
In our own grounds above Huntly golf course this family run hotel offers peace and tranquility for the individual or groups. Ideally situated for numerous courses in the north east, all within easy 'driving' range.

Corrour House Hotel
Inverdruie, Aviemore PH22 1QH.
Tel (01479) 810220 Fax (01479) 811500
A lovely country house hotel with charm and character, set in four acres of garden and woodland with spectacular views of the Cairngorm mountains. Where golfing guests return year after year to enjoy superb comfort, food and wines. Set in the heart of Strathspey, half a mile from Aviemore with six delightful courses nearby. Recommended by leading hotel guides. STB 3-Crown Commended; Taste of Scotland.

Craigellachie Hotel
Craigellachie, Speyside,
Banffshire AB38 9SR.
Tel (01340) 881204 Fax (01340) 881253
Ideally located for enjoying the best of golf in Scotland with many golf courses within one hour's drive including links, parkland, championship moorland. The Craigellachie is fully refurbished providing true Highland hospitality. Call for brochure today. STB 4-Crown Deluxe.

Culloden House
Milton of Culloden, Inverness IV1 2NZ.
Tel (01463) 790461 Fax (01463) 792181

Easy to access and a short drive to Royal Dornoch, Nairn and four local golf courses. This STB 5-Crown Deluxe Georgian country house sits in 40 acres of tranquil parkland only minutes from Dalcross airport and Inverness.

Dornoch Castle
Dornoch, Sutherland IV25 3SD.
Tel (01862) 810216 Fax (01862) 810981

Formerly a bishop's palace, the hotel has 17 bedrooms. The panelled cocktail bar, elegant lounge and Bishop's Room restaurant overlook historic Dornoch Cathedral. AA, RAC, STB 4-Crown Commended.

Dunraven Lodge
Golf Road, Strathpeffer IV14 9AS.
Tel/Fax (01997) 421210

Kim and Judy offer relaxed and informal atmosphere, home from home, Honesty bar, full size snooker table and sauna room. Balcony bedrooms all en suite with beautiful views. 150 metres from golf course. Stalking and fishing can be arranged.

Fairwinds Hotel
Carr-Bridge, Inverness-shire PH23 3AA.
Tel/Fax (01479) 841240

Former Victorian manse set in seven acres of ground that has been converted to an STB 4-Star hotel. Personal service with good food and wines. Village golf course plus five courses within easy reach.

Kingsmills Hotel
Culcabock Road, Inverness IV2 3LP.
Tel (01463) 237166 Fax (01463) 718480

Overlooking Inverness golf club and centrally located for Royal Dornoch and the Nairn golf clubs, this 4-Star luxurious Swallow hotel offers purpose-built GOLF VILLAS and extensive leisure facilities with a 3-hole pitch and putt course.

Machrie Hotel
& Golf Links Course
Port Ellen, Isle of Islay, Argyll PA42 7AN.
Tel (01496) 310310 Fax (01496) 302404

Play a hidden gem of a course. Traditional 18-hole championship links course situated on the doorstep of the Machrie Hotel. Superior and standard accommodation, excellent food and friendly service. Self-catering and golf packages also available.

Ramleh Hotel
& Fingal's Restaurant
2 Academy Street, Nairn,
Inverness-shire IV12 4RJ.
Tel (01667) 453551 Fax (01667) 456577

1994 Les Routiers British Restaurant of the Year. George and Carol Woodhouse offer a warm welcome to their 10-bedroomed hotel and renowned restaurant. Close to both of Nairn's championship courses, many more within 30 miles. Beautiful beaches, whisky and castle trails.

The Royal Hotel - Fortrose
Fortrose, Ross-shire IV10 8SU.
Tel (01381) 620236

Friendly Highland hotel 20 minutes from Inverness. 15 well appointed bedrooms, large lounge, two bars, dining room serving a wide menu including traditional Scottish home cooking. 12 golf courses including Nairn and Royal Dornoch within three quarters of an hour's drive.

The Royal Hotel - Tain
High Street, Tain, Ross-shire IV19 1AB.
Tel (01862) 892013 Fax (01862) 893450

The Royal Hotel is a 120 year old Victorian hotel situated in the heart of the finest golfing territory in the Highlands. Enjoy cuisine prepared by our award-winning French chef, whilst benefiting from our very competitive rates.

West

Barons Craig Hotel
Rockliffe, By Dalbeattie,
Kirkcudbrightshire DG5 4QF.
Tel (01556) 630225

STB 4-Crown Commended; RAC 3-Star. This imposing granite structured hotel dated 1880 is situated in nine acres of wooded area with lush lawns and gardens overlooking the Solway and Rough Firth. 22 bedrooms all with private bathrooms and showers. Well appointed lounges and restaurant. Excellent 18-hole golf courses within easy reach. List available on request.

Carlton Toby Hotel
187 Ayr Road, Prestwick,
Ayrshire KA9 1TP.
Tel (01292) 476811 Fax (01292) 673712

Recently refurbished, the Carlton Toby Hotel is set in its own grounds. Ideally located for Ayr, Prestwick and Troon centres. Two minutes' walk from Centrum Ice Arena. All rooms are en suite, have tea/coffee-making facilities, Sky TV, hairdryer and telephone.

County Hotel - Ayr
Wellington Square, Ayr KA7 1EY.
Tel (01292) 263368 Fax (01292) 282781

Superb golf in the south west coast of Scotland, and a friendly family run hotel offering full facilities including residents' bar with a choice of 30 malt whiskies. Bar snacks to fine dining available. Pay and Stay Golf - ask for group rates. (See advertisement page 439 for further details.)

Dunduff House
Dunduff Farm, Dunure, Ayr KA7 4LH.
Tel (01292) 500225 Fax (01292) 500222

Situated on the edge of Dunure overlooking Arran and Firth of Clyde. Golf courses include Royal Troon, Turnberry and many more interesting courses. All rooms have TV, radio, tea-making facilities, wash hand basin. Two double rooms have en suite facilities. STB Highly Commended 2-Crown; AA Selected 4-Q. Self-catering cottage available sleeps four.

Hospitality Inn
46 Annick Road, Irvine KA11 4LD.
Freephone 0800 731 9323
Fax (01294) 277287

Located on the beautiful Ayrshire coast this modern 4-Star hotel, with its own private 9-hole golf course and spectacular indoor lagoon, makes this the ideal base for the golfing enthusiast to relax. Individual fully inclusive golf packages available.

Malin Court Hotel & Restaurant
Turnberry, Ayrshire KA26 9PB.
Tel (01655) 331457 Fax (01655) 331072

Situated in the heart of Burns' country on the beautiful Ayrshire coast, overlooking Turnberry's famous golf course. There are 17 well appointed bedrooms. The best of modern Scottish food is served, complemented by an extensive wine list. Golf can be arranged locally on twelve courses.

Manor Park Hotel
Monkton,
By Prestwick Airport,
Ayrshire KA9 2RJ.
Tel/Fax (01292) 479365

The hotel, built in the early 1990s, is situated in a rural location, surrounded by scenic countryside. It offers 12 individually furnished, spacious rooms. Conservatory/restaurant with quality cuisine and Courtyard function suite. Golf enthusiasts may take advantage of some of Scotland's most famous golf courses situated just a few minutes' drive from the hotel.

Parson's Lodge
15 Main Street,
Patna, Ayrshire KA6 7LN.
Tel (01292) 531306

Situated eight miles south east of Ayr on the A713. All rooms have colour TV with private facilities. Bistro restaurant, licensed. Ideally situated for golfing in Ayrshire. STB 3-Crown Commended. Small parties only - maximum of six.

South Beach Hotel
South Beach,
Troon, Ayrshire KA10 6EG.
Tel (01292) 312033 Fax (01292) 318438

3-Star 4-Crown Commended privately run hotel facing the sea. Golfers' paradise, fifteen courses within easy reach. Royal Troon being most famous. 30 bedrooms all en suite. Golf can be arranged. Friendly atmosphere.

Turnberry Hotel Golf Courses & Spa
Ayrshire KA26 9LT.
Tel (01655) 331000 Fax (01655) 331706

One of the world's finest luxury hotel, golf and spa resorts. Edwardian country house overlooking its own Ailsa and Arran championship courses. The Ailsa is ranked 16th in the world and was the venue for the 1994 Open Championship.

West End Hotel
West Bay, Dunoon PA23 7HU.
Tel (01369) 702907 Fax (01369) 706266
website: wwwdesign.co.uk/westend.
Teletext page 254.

Family run, fully licensed hotel. Single and twin rooms available. Very attractive rates for golfing parties. Five minutes from the superb Cowal championship course.

WALES

Welsh Borders

Belmont Lodge & Golf Course
Belmont, Hereford HR2 9SA.
Tel (01432) 352666 Fax (01432) 358090

18-hole golf course running along the beautiful Wye Valley with a 30-bedroomed hotel on-site. Other facilities include bar, restaurant, fishing, bowling, tennis and snooker. Only a mile and a half from Hereford city centre.

Cadmore Lodge Hotel
St Michaels,
Tenbury Wells,
Worcestershire WR15 8TQ.
Tel/Fax (01584) 810044

A warm welcome awaits at Cadmore Lodge Hotel. Excellent cuisine from chefs with imagination and flair. 9-hole golf course par 68 SSS 65 (18 holes). Two fishing lakes for trout and course fishing. Indoor swimming pool, with spa, steam room and cardio-vascular equipment. (See advertisement page 439 for further details.)

Pen-y-Dyffryn Country Hotel
Rhydycroesau,
Nr Oswestry,
Shropshire SY10 7JD.
Tel/Fax (01691) 653700

Quietly situated former Georgian rectory in spectacular hill-country right on Shropshire/ Wales border. AA Rosette food award. All rooms have TV and en suite facilities. Exclusive 2-for-1 green fees at Oswestry Mile End and Chirk courses. Six courses within 20 minutes. DB&B from £45 per person per night.

The Talbot Hotel
West Street, Leominster,
Herefordshire HR6 8EP.
Tel (01568) 616347 Fax (01568) 614880

A privately owned town centre hotel, parts of which date from the 15th-century, is to be found in the small, ancient market town of Leominster. Good food and friendly staff with comfortable surroundings help to make your golfing break enjoyable. Courses of preference and tee-off times arranged for your society/party at nearby recommended courses of Leominster, Herefordshire, Kington, Upper Sapey, Ludlow and Belmont. Two days golf plus DB&B £140 inclusive

North

Bedford Hotel
The Promenade, Craig-y-Don,
Llandudno LL30 1BN.
Tel (01492) 879661 Fax (01492) 860185

Ideally situated on the promenade with easy access to six golf courses, two of which are championship standards. Within the hotel is Gigolo Italian restaurant renowned for its style and cuisine, open late in the evenings.

Holyhead Golf Club
Lon Garreg Fawr, Trearddur Bay,
Anglesey LL65 2YG.
Tel/Fax (01407) 763279

Comfortable twin-bedded accommodation is available at the Holyhead Golf Club, with all meals provided in the club restaurant. Enjoy excellent golf on heathland course with spectacular view to Snowdonia. Reservations ring 01407 763279.

Imperial Hotel - Llandudno
The Promenade, Llandudno,
Gwynedd LL30 1AP.
Tel (01492) 877466 Fax (01492) 878043

100-bedroomed hotel with extensive leisure facilities including 45' indoor swimming pool. Ideally situated for all North Wales' golf courses. Award-winning restaurant and private dining room for up to 30 available.

The Links Hotel - Conwy
Conwy Road, Llandudno, Conwy,
Gwynedd LL30 1PN.
Tel (01492) 879180

A small, family run hotel/public house, situated near the premier courses in the area. The hotel is close to the town's amenities and its own huge car park.

Pen-y-Dyffryn Country Hotel
See Welsh Borders

Royal Sportsman
131 High Street, Porthmadog,
Gwynedd LL49 9HA.
Tel (01766) 512015 Fax (01766) 512490

Delightful hotel in centre of Porthmadog. All rooms en suite with usual facilities, excellent cuisine, private garage for residents. Golf package inclusive of green fees and half board, tee-times arranged. Five courses within 30 minutes of hotel. (See advertisement page 439 for further details.)

South & South West

Carlton Hotel & Restaurant
654-656 Mumbles Road, Mumbles,
Nr Swansea SA3 4EA.
Tel/Fax (01792) 360450

Very friendly 3-Crown hotel near five golf courses. Perfect for parties of golfers. Private bar. All rooms, mostly en suite, have TV, telephone and tea/coffee-making facilities. Restaurant available (table d'hôte). In the heart of Mumbles with panoramic views.

The Court Hotel
Lamphey, Pembroke,
Pembrokeshire SA71 5NT.
Tel (01646) 672273 Fax (01646) 672480

One of Wales' leading country hotels. Deluxe bedrooms, superb leisure centre, swimming pool, jacuzzi, gym, sauna and floodlit tennis. Special arrangements with Tenby, South Pembrokeshire, Trefloyne and Haverfordwest golf clubs. Excellent food and wine - local produce. A Best Western Hotel.

The Dormy
Royal Porthcawl Golf Club,
Rest Bay, Porthcawl,
Mid Glamorgan CF36 3UW.
Tel (01656) 782251 Fax (01656) 771687

Luxury dormy accommodation for parties of up to twelve persons. Apply to the secretary. (See advertisement page 26 for further details.)

Fairways Hotel
The Seafront, Porthcawl,
Mid-Glamorgan CF36 3LS.
Tel (01656) 782085 & 783544
Fax (01656) 785351

Bedrooms en suite with telephone and TV. Residents lounge. Seaview. Restaurant lunches and dinner. Full à la carte and table d'hôte. Sunday lunches. Wedding receptions and parties. Lounge and restaurant bars. Bar meals. Near six golf courses.

Marriott St Pierre Hotel & Country Club
St Pierre Park, Chepstow NP6 6YA.
Tel (01291) 625261 Fax (01291) 629975

St Pierre has recently undergone a multi-million pound refurbishment. Set in 400 acres of exceptional parkland, the hotel offers two superb golf courses, including the Old Course, host to the 1996 Solheim Cup. Extensive leisure and conference facilities. (See advertisement page 4 for further details.)

Penally Abbey
Penally, Nr Tenby, South Pembrokeshire,
Dyfed SA70 7PY.
Tel (01834) 843033 Fax (01834) 844714

We overlook Tenby's 18-hole championship course and are 30 minutes from three other courses. 12 rooms en suite. (See advertisement page 441 for further details.)

Porthcawl Hotel
John Street, Porthcawl,
Mid-Glamorgan CF36 3AP.
Tel (01656) 782257 & 783810
Fax (01656) 772040

All bedrooms en suite with telephone and television. Lounge and wine bar. Daily bar meals and Sunday lunches. Wedding receptions and parties. Outside catering. *Streets* nightclub. Health and fitness centre. Near six golf courses and shopping centre.

CHANNEL ISLANDS

La Grande Mare Hotel Golf Club
La Grande Mare, Vazon, Castel, Guernsey.
Tel (01481) 56576 & 53544
Fax (01481) 55194

Beautifully appointed luxury hotel with 18-hole golf course playing off 14 greens. Professional shop and tuition on-site. First class, well priced restaurant. 2-AA Rosettes. Beachside location. Golfing breaks catered for.

Les Arches Hotel
Archirondel, Gorey, St Martin,
Jersey JE3 6DR.
Tel (01534) 853839 Fax (01534) 856660

3-Star hotel overlooking France. Private access to beach. All rooms en suite with TV. One and a half miles from Royal Jersey Golf Club. Swimming pool, garden, tennis court, golf net, sauna, mini-gym and bars. Restaurant. Bed and breakfast rates from £29. Special discount for golfers.

The Moorings Hotel & Restaurant
Gorey Pier, Gorey, Jersey JE3 6EW.
Tel (01534) 853633 Fax (01534) 857618

3-Star intimate and luxurious 17-bedroom hotel overlooking the quaint Gorey harbour and the sandy bay of Grouville. Half a mile from the Royal Jersey Golf Club. Renowned for its

continued over

superb food, seafood a speciality. Open all year. Special rates for golfers at any time.

The St Pierre Park Hotel
Rohais, St Peter Port, Guernsey GYI 1FD.
Tel (01481) 728282 Fax (01481) 712041

This 4-Star hotel offers extensive leisure facilities including a 9-hole par 3 golf course, designed by Tony Jacklin. Three tennis courts and a health suite with heated indoor swimming pool, spa bath, saunas, steam rooms, solaria and exercise room.

NORTHERN IRELAND

Beach House Hotel
61 Beach Road, Portballintrae, Co Antrim BT57 8RT.
Tel (012657) 31214 Fax (012657) 31664

With spectacular views of Scotland and Donegal, our seafront hotel is close to Old Bushmills Distillery and the Giant's Causeway. Central to six links courses including Royal Portrush, and is renowned for good food, accommodation and family hospitality.

Glassdrumman Lodge
85 Mill Road, Annalong, Co Down BT34 4RH.
Tel (013967) 68451 Fax (013967) 67041

Nestling in the Mourne mountains is this 10-bedroomed country house where comfort and hospitality go hand in hand. The dining room is well acclaimed for serving good local produce grown mainly on the farm and gardens.

Radisson Roe Park Hotel & Golf Resort
Roe Park, Limauady, Co Londonderry BT49 9LB.
Tel (015047) 22222 Fax (015047) 22313

Northern Ireland's premier golf and leisure resort featuring 64 luxurious bedrooms, O'Cahan's bar, Coach House brasserie, Courtyard restaurant, Fairways leisure club and the Eden health and beauty salon. 18-hole championship parkland course, driving range, putting green and golf shop.

The Silverwood Hotel
Kiln Road, Lurgan, Craigavon BT66 6NF.
Tel (01762) 327722 Fax (01762) 325290

The hotel lies within a complex of an 18-hole golf course, putting courses, driving range, gym

and a certified ski slope. Also available - game and coarse fishing, sailing, winter skiing, windsurfing, bird and wildlife reserve and parascending. (See advertisement page 441 for further details.)

EIRE

Aberdeen Lodge Hotel
53-55 Park Avenue, off Ailsbury Road, Ballsbridge, Dublin 4, Ireland.
Tel +353 1 2838155 Fax +353 1 2837877

In the embassy district of Dublin City, this award-winning 4-Star hotel is a luxurious combination of Edwardian grace, fine foods and modern comfort, all that one expects of a private hotel - including suites with jacuzzi and executive facilities. Landscaped gardens and guests' car park. Ideal base for your tailor-made golfing itinerary at Druid's Glen, Portmarnock, St Margaret's and many major championship courses. (A member of the Green Book of Ireland - see advertisement page 447 for further details.)

Aghadoe Heights Hotel
Killarney, Co Kerry, Ireland.
Tel +353 64 31766 Fax +353 64 31345.

Stunning panoramic views, comfort, good food and personal service are the keynotes of this luxury 5-Star hotel, with its rooftop restaurant and superb indoor leisure facilities. Perfectly located for playing Ireland's premier golf courses including Killarney, Tralee, Ballybunion and Waterville.

The Alexander Hotel at Merrion Square
Dublin 2, Ireland.
Tel +353 1 6073700 Fax +353 1 6615663

Contemporary style deluxe hotel ideally located in Dublin City centre and within 20 minutes of numerous golf courses, including Royal Dublin, Portmarnock and St Margarets. Tee-times arranged on request.

Ballyroe Hotel
Ballyheigue Road, Tralee, Co Kerry, Ireland.
Tel +353 66 26796 Fax +353 66 25066

Kerry is an idyllic setting for a hotel and a golf course, therefore the Ballyroe hotel is perfectly situated. Some of Ireland's premier golf courses including Tralee, Killarney, Ballybunion and Waterville are within striking distance.

Spectacular views, well appointed accommodation, friendly service and fine cuisine are the keynotes of this delightful property. Beautiful sandy beaches, scenic tours and many historic buildings can also be enjoyed from this ideally located hotel. (A member of the Green Book of Ireland - see advertisement page 447 for further details.)

The Davenport Hotel at Merrion Square
Dublin 2, Ireland.
Tel +353 1 607 3500 Fax +353 1 661 5663

Traditional style deluxe hotel and Global Partner of Inter-Continental Hotels. Located in Dublin City centre and within 20 minutes of all major golf courses. Tee-times arranged on request. Private valet car parking.

Deer Park Hotel & Golf Courses
Howth, Co Dublin, Ireland.
Tel +353 1 832 2624 Fax +353 1 839 2405

78-bedroom 3-Star hotel with four parkland courses. Ireland's largest golf complex. Just nine miles from Dublin City and airport. Great value all-inclusive golf weekend rates available. (See advertisement page 443 for further details.)

Dromoland Castle
Newmarket-on-Fergus, Co Clare, Ireland.
Tel +353 61 368144 Fax +353 61 363355

Dromoland Castle is a magnificent renaissance castle on 375 acres of parkland. It offers the highest accommodation standards, and award-winning restaurant. Activities include golf, clay pigeon shooting, horseriding and fishing, we also have a fully equipped health centre. The castle is located eight miles from Shannon International airport in County Clare.

Ferrycarrig Hotel
Ferrycarrig Bridge, Wexford, Ireland.
Tel +353 53 20999 Fax +353 53 20982

The hotel boasts one of the most inspiring locations of any hotel in Ireland with fabulous views over river Slaney Estuary. Facilities include 90 bedrooms and suites. AA 2-Rosette waterfront restaurants, fabulous health and fitness club, 20 metre pool. *Part owners of St Helen's Bay Golf Club.*

Finnstown Country House Hotel & Golf Course
Newcastle Road, Lucan, Co Dublin, Ireland.
Tel +353 1 62 80644 Fax +353 1 62 81088

Finnstown Country House Hotel is located eight miles west of Dublin City. Its excellent facilities include a 9-hole golf course, leisure centre with pool, and a superb restaurant. At Finnstown the perfect golfing break awaits you. (Ref. 37)

Fitzpatrick Bunratty
Bunratty, Co Clare, Ireland.
Tel +353 61 361177 Fax +353 61 471252

In the picturesque village of Bunratty, beside medieval castle and Folk Park. Four miles from Shannon airport. Play Lahinch, Dromoland, Shannon and Woodstock from here. Truffles restaurant, lively bar, popular with locals. Airport and golf transfers on request.

Fitzpatrick Castle Dublin
Killiney, Co Dublin, Ireland.
Tel +353 1 284 0700 Fax +353 1 285 0207

4-Star hotel, set in magnificent gardens, overlooking Dublin Bay. PJ's restaurant, cocktail bar and extensive leisure centre. Easy drive to Blainroe, Charlesland, and exciting new Druid's Glen golf courses. Courtesy coach transfers to airport and golf on request.

Fitzpatrick Cork
Tivoli, Cork, Ireland.
Tel +353 21 507533 Fax +353 21 507641

Five minutes by car from city centre. Accessible to Little Island, Harbour Point, Fota and Lee Valley courses. Excellent fitness centre with 9-hole golf course. PJ's restaurant, two bars. Entertainment on Fridays and Saturdays. Jazz brunch on Sundays. Airport and golf transfers on request.

Galway Bay Golf & Country Club Hotel
Renville, Oranmore, Co Galway, Ireland.
Tel +353 91 790500 Fax +353 91 790510

Galway Bay Golf and Country Club Hotel and Golfing Village enjoys the tranquility of the Renville Peninsula and yet is only eight miles from vibrant Galway City. The hotel, with 92 standard and deluxe en suite rooms, provides a magnificent setting for visitors coming to this special part of the west of Ireland. The guest rooms offer panoramic views of the golf course, Renville Park and Galway Bay as it stretches out to the Atlantic Ocean. Activities include fishing, golfing, scenic walks and horseriding. (See advertisement page 443 for further details.)

The Glendalough Hotel
Glendalough,
Co Wickford, Ireland.
Tel +353 404 45135 Fax +353 404 45142

Situated in Ireland's *Garden of Golf* with spectacular golf in a beautiful setting. The Glendalough Hotel offers distinctive Irish hospitality in a world famous location. Courses include Druid's Glen, the European Club and Woodenbridge.

Granville Hotel
The Quay,
Waterford, Ireland.
Tel +353 51 855111 Fax +353 51 870307

RAC 4-Star Waterford's most prestigious city centre hotel. It has been elegantly refurbished, retaining its olde worlde character. This family run hotel has two award-winning restaurants also friendly bar. Ten golf courses within 20 minutes. Golf packages arranged on request.

Halpins Hotel
& Vittles Restaurant
Erin Street,
Kilkee, Co Clare, Ireland.
Tel +353 65 56032 Fax +353 65 56317

The highly acclaimed 3-Star Halpins Hotel and award-winning Vittles restaurant are a combination of old world charm, fine food, vintage wines and modern comforts, overlooking old Victorian Kilkee. Close to Shannon airport, Kilimer car ferry and cliffs of Moher. Kilkee is surely a golfer's haven within one hour's drive of eleven championship courses including Lahinch and Ballybunion. Contact us to plan your west coast golfing break. (A member of the Green Book of Ireland - see advertisement page 447 for further details.)

Hotel Europe
Killarney,
Co Kerry, Ireland.
Tel +353 64 31900 Fax +353 64 32118

Overlooking the famous lakes of Killarney, adjacent to Killeen, Mahony's Point golf courses, the Hotel Europe is within easy reach of Beaufort, Dunloe, Killorglin, Ross, Dooks, Ballybunion, Tralee and Waterville. Other facilities include 25 metres swimming pool, sauna, gymnasium, free horseriding with our own string of Haflinger horses, free indoor tennis courts and billiards. Fishing and boating on the lakes of Killarney.

Hunter's Hotel
Rathnew, Co Wicklow, Ireland.
Tel +353 404 40106 Fax +353 404 40338

270 year old coaching inn run by the same family for the past 170 years. Ideal centre for golf holidays. Sixteen 18-hole courses within half an hour, nearest three minutes' drive away.

International (Best Western) Hotel
Killarney, Co Kerry, Ireland.
Tel +353 64 31816 Fax +353 64 31837

From our modernised town centre hotel we will arrange your golf at Killarney (two championship courses), Ballybunion, Waterville, Tralee etc. Family run hotel close to good shopping and restaurants. We know what golfers require.

Jennings Hotel
& Rose Garden Restaurant
Old Westport Road, Castlebar,
Co Mayo, Ireland.
Tel/Fax +353 94 23111

Jennings hotel, is located in an area convenient to some of the best golf courses on the west coast of Ireland, including Castlebar, Westport, Enniscrone and Rosses Point. The golf enthusiast will find this hotel an ideal place to stay with excellent cuisine, facilities and service. Magnificent scenery, tranquil, sandy beaches and a wide range of cultural attractions can also be experienced form this centrally located hotel. (A member of the Green Book of Ireland -see advertisement page 447 for further details.)

Jordans Townhouse & Restaurant
Newry Street, Carlingford,
Co Louth, Ireland.
Tel +353 42 73223 Fax +353 42 73827

Jordans Townhouse, listed in *The 100 Best Places to Stay and Dine* and also Egon Ronay 6 Commendation holder, is equidistant from Royal County Down in Northern Ireland and County Louth Golf Club and also has five other 18-hole courses within 20 minutes.

Kathleen's Country House
Tralee Road (N22), Killarney,
Co Kerry, Ireland.
Tel +353 64 32810 Fax +353 64 32340

Kathleen's is a charming private hotel, 5-Q AA registered; 4-Star ITB; 1993 award-winning *'RAC Guesthouse of the Year'*. 17 delightful bedrooms furnished in antique pine with private bathroom, orthopaedic beds, telephone, TV/

radio, tea/coffee-making facilities, hairdryer. Ideal golfing base for Killarney, Tralee, Waterville, Dooks and Ballybunion. (See advertisement page 445 for further details.)

The Kildare Hotel & Country Club
At Straffan,
Co Kildare, Ireland.
Tel +353 601 7300 Fax +353 601 7399
e-mail: hotel@kclub.ie

Located 30 minutes from Dublin. Arnold Palmer designed 18-hole championship golf course, clubhouse, practice area and driving range. Resident golf professional Ernie Jones. Home to *The Smurfit European Open* since September 1995 until the year 2000. Hotel AA 5-Red Stars. Fishing, health club and sports centre with indoor and outdoor tennis. (See advertisement page 443 for details.)

Killarney Heights Hotel
Cork Road,
Killarney,
Co Kerry, Ireland.
Tel +353 64 31158 Fax +353 64 35198

This family owned 71-bedroom hotel, opened 1996, is located only a few miles from Killarney, Tralee, Ballybunion and Waterville golf clubs. Other major visitor attractions are Ring of Kerry, Killarney's lakes and mountains and panoramic scenery.

Limerick Inn Hotel
Ennis Road,
Limerick, Ireland.
Tel +353 61 326666 Fax +353 61 326281

The Limerick Inn is located in the heart of Ireland's lovely Shannonside. All 153 bedrooms have private bathroom, direct dial telephone, radio and TV. The hotel has a modern health and leisure centre and full conference facilities. (See advertisement page 441 for further details.)

Marine Links Hotel
Ballybunion,
Co Kerry, Ireland.
Tel +353 68 27139 Fax +353 68 27666

The Marine Links is just one mile from Ballybunion Golf Club. All our en suite bedrooms have multi-channel TV, telephone and tea/coffee-making facilities. Our seafood restaurant is renowned. Concession green fees. RAC Restaurant and Hospitality Award winners 1995/96/1997.

The Mont Clare Hotel
Merrion Square,
Dublin 2, Ireland.
Tel +353 1 6073800 Fax +353 1 6615663

Traditional Dublin hotel centrally located at Merrion Square and within 20 minutes of numerous golf courses, including Royal Dublin and Portmarnock. Tee-times arranged on request. Complimentary valet car parking.

Mount Falcon Castle
Ballina,
Co Mayo, Ireland.
Tel +353 96 70811 Fax +353 96 71517

Mount Falcon Castle offers tranquility and the quiet comfort of log fires and superb cuisine in a country house atmosphere. Within easy reach of three magnificent courses all situated in areas of outstanding natural beauty in the wild and wonderful west of Ireland.

Mount Juliet
Thomastown,
Co Kilkenny, Ireland.
Tel +353 56 24455 Fax +353 56 24766

Deluxe accommodation in the elegant Mount Juliet House or the informal Hunters Yard. Ireland's premier sporting estate offers guests on-site fishing, horseriding, tennis, stylish leisure centre, David Leadbetter Golf Academy. Home of the Irish Open, 1993, 1994 and 1995.

Parknasilla Great Southern Hotel
Parknasilla,
Sneen, Co Kerry, Ireland.
Tel +353 64 45122 Fax +353 64 45323

The Parknasilla celebrated its centenary in 1995. This 4-Star 84-bedroom hotel has just completely rebuilt its 9-hole golf course, making it one of the most scenic in Ireland. Wide range of leisure activities available.

Portmarnock Hotel & Golf Links
Strand Road,
Portmarnock,
Co Dublin, Ireland.
Tel +353 1 846 0611 Fax +353 1 846 2442

This prestigious new development is located 15 minutes from Dublin airport and 25 minutes from the city centre. The hotel's 18-hole golf links was designed by Bernard Langer and is the only PGA European Tour course in Ireland. (See advertisement page 445 for further details.)

Powerscourt Golf Club
Enniskerry,
Co Wicklow, Ireland.
Tel +353 1 204 6033 Fax +353 1 276 1303

Studio apartment accommodation is available on the estate. Each apartment is beautifully furnished and has a fully equipped kitchen, a twin bedded room and en suite bathroom. Enjoy the tranquillity and privacy in this thousand acre estate within strolling distance of the golf course and clubhouse where full restaurant and bar facilities are conveniently located. (See advertisement page 32 for further details.)

Ross Lake House Hotel
Rosscahill, Oughterard,
Co Galway, Ireland.
Tel +353 91 550109 & 550154
Fax +353 91 550184

Located fourteen miles from Galway City, and three miles from the picturesque golfing and fishing village of Oughterard. An ideal base for golfing in the west of Ireland. Great golf, quality food and a homely atmosphere awaits you. (See advertisement page 447 for further details.)

The Slieve Russell Hotel Golf & Country Club
Ballyconnell, Co Cavan, Ireland.
Tel +353 49 26444 Fax +353 49 26474

Located only two hours' drive from both Dublin and Belfast, the Slieve Russell is a complete resort with its 5-Star leisure facilities, championship 18-hole golf course. 151 superbly appointed bedrooms and a selection of restaurants and bars. Conference and banqueting suites - The *Perfect* location for business or pleasure.

Springfort Hall
Mallow, Co Cork, Ireland.
Tel +353 22 21278 Fax +353 22 21557

Springfort Hall, offers an excellent choice of exceptional golf courses - Mallow, Doneraile, Lee Valley, Muskerry, Little Island, Fota Island Harbour Point, and many more, are all within easy reach. This 18th-century Georgian manor house is the ideal base for exploring the delights of Cork and Kerry. Situated in beautiful private grounds, Springfort Hall offers exceptional standards of quality, service and cuisine. (A member of the Green Book of Ireland - see advertisement page 447 for further details.)

St Helen's Bay Golf & Country Club
St Helens, Kilrane, Rosslare Harbour,
Co Wexford, Ireland.
Tel +353 53 33234 Fax +353 53 33803

Luxury on-site accommodation together with tennis courts, leisure room and sauna. Full bar/catering facilities available in the clubhouse. Superbly located championship 18-hole golf course, which has blended the best of parkland characteristics with a finish that is true links and plenty of difficulty. Situated only five minutes from Rosslare ferryport. Green fee and society friendly, playable all year round.

Tinakilly Country House & Restaurant
Rathnew, Wicklow, Co Wicklow, Ireland.
Tel +353 404 69274 Fax +353 404 67806

4-Star ITB; RAC Blue Ribbon; AA Red Star and a Small Luxury Hotel of the World. Renowned for splendid fresh food in elegant Victorian surroundings, Tinakilly is situated in seven acres of gardens and has 40 bedrooms, mostly junior suites, with sea views. 29 miles from Dublin, eight miles from Druid's Glen, home of the 1996/97/1998 Irish Open, and locally, European Club, Blainroe, Woodenbridge, Wicklow and Delgany. Special golf brochure available. Don't miss Powerscourt Gardens, Glendalough, Wicklow mountains and Ballykissangel!

LATE ENTRY

SCOTLAND Central & East

Templar Lodge Hotel
(Formerly the Queen's Hotel)
Gullane
East Lothian EH31 2AS
Tel 01620 842275 Fax 01620 842970

The hotel has been recently refurbished to a high standard and is within easy access of all East Lothian golf courses - Gullane No.1 said to be the oldest in the country including Muirfield, host to the Open.

Mention the Royal & Ancient
Golfer's Handbook when you
make your enquiries

Golf Club Facilities

This section, included for the first time in 1992, lists clubs which can offer hotel accommodation, and hotels which have their own golf facilties. They are able to provide for society or corporate days, and in some instances offer an extensive range of other sports and leisure activities. A sub-section also includes driving ranges, practice grounds and leisure complexes

Abbotsley Golf Hotel
Eynesbury Hardwicke,
St Neots,
Cambridgeshire PE19 4XN.
Tel (01480) 474000 Fax (01480) 471018

Friendly country house hotel set amidst two 18-hole courses. *Golf Monthly* "The Abbotsley course - the design is a revelation. The presentation superb." Award-winning gardens; relaxed atmosphere. Home of Vivien Saunders golf schools.

Aldwark Manor Golf Hotel
Aldwark,
Alne, York,
West Yorkshire YO6 2NF.
Tel (Hotel) (01347) 838146
(Golf) (01347) 838353
Fax (01347) 838867

Aldwark Manor extends a warm welcome to everyone. Situated in the Vale of York is a 6,171 yard par 71 golf course, laid out in easy walking parkland with the river Ure meandering beside a number of fairways. The ideal venue for your society or company golf day. (See advertisement page 429 for further details.)

Alvaston Hall Hotel
Middlewich Road, Nantwich,
Cheshire CW5 6PD.
Tel (01270) 624341 Fax (01270) 623395

Established hotel in picturesque setting close to Nantwich. Newly developed clubhouse and challenging 9-hole course with water and hill features. Golf professional on-site with well equipped shop. Members of the Cheshire and English Golf Union. Teaching Centre for PGA.

Ashdown Forest Golf Hotel
Chapel Lane,
Forest Row,
East Sussex RH18 5BB.
Tel (01342) 824866 Fax (01342) 824869
e-mail:reservatins@ashgolf.demon.co.uk
website: http://www.ashgolf.demon.co.uk

Newly refurbished hotel with 19 en suite bedrooms, large function room, conference facilities, restaurant and two bars. Hotel operates the Royal Ashdown Forest Golf Club West Course, 18-holes, 5,606 yards SSS 67. Several other courses incorporated in residential golf breaks. (See advertisement page 421 for further details.)

Ayr - Scotland
For information on accommodation available in South Ayrshire whilst playing at one or more of the many courses in the *Heart of Scotland's Golf Country* as detailed on page 30.
Contact the Ayrshire and Arran Tourist Board on 01292 288688.
(See advertisement page 30 for further details.)

Ballater Golf Club
Victoria Road,
Ballater AB35 5QX.
Tel (013397) 55567 Fax (013397) 55057

The most scenic golf course in Scotland, slightly undulating, medium length course situated in the heart of Royal Deeside. A delightful golfing experience which is enjoyed by golfers of all calibre. Situated 42 miles west of Aberdeen with Balmoral Castle a mere eight miles up river.
(See advertisement page 25 for further details.)

Barnham Broom Hotel

Golf, Conference & Leisure Centre
Honingham Road, Barnham Broom,
Norwich, Norfolk NR9 4DD.
Tel (01603) 759393 Fax (01603) 758224

EETB 4-Crown; AA Rosette. East Anglia's finest conference and leisure centre lies in 250 acres of countryside. 53 fully equipped bedrooms include family rooms, served by Flints restaurant and sports snack bar. Four squash courts, snooker, heated indoor swimming pool and spa jets, tennis and 36-hole golf. *Golfing Getaways* from £120. (See advertisement page 425 for further details.)

Beaufort Golf Course

Churchtown, Beaufort, Killarney,
Co Kerry, Ireland.
Tel +353 64 44440 Fax +353 64 44752

A traditional Kerry welcome awaits you at *the Friendliest Course in Kerry*. Challenging 18-hole par 71 championship course, buggies and caddies for hire, excellent golf shop, bar food and snacks. Tuition can be arranged with our golf professional. Societies and groups welcome. (See advertisement page 28 for further details.)

The Belfry

Wishaw, North Warwickshire B76 9PR.
Tel (01675) 470033 Fax (01675) 470256

The Belfry, venue for three Ryder Cup matches and a unique fourth returning in 2001, is one of Europe's foremost business, golf and leisure resorts. Top class facilities includes 324 4-Star bedrooms, five restaurants, eight bars and Bel Air nightclub. Leisure facilities include gym, indoor pool, sauna, snooker and beautician to name but a few. Three golf courses including the Brabazon, PGA National and Derby courses. Floodlit driving range and putting green, largest on-course golf leisure and lifestyle shop in Europe which opened in May 1997. (Part of the De Vere Hotels group - see advertisement page 427 for further details.)

Belleisle Golf Course

Belleisle Park, Ayr.
c/o South Ayrshire Council, Burns House,
Burns Statue Square, Ayr KA7 1UT.
Tel (01292) 616269/616270

18-holes, length of course 6,431 yards SSS 72. For advance reservations telephone (01292) 441258. Practice area, caddy cars, catering and bar facilities are available. Visitors welcome all week. Professional David Gemmell (01292)

441314. (See advertisement page 30 for further details.)

Belmont Lodge & Golf Course

Belmont, Hereford HR2 9SA.
Tel (01432) 352666 Fax (01432) 358090

18-hole golf course running along the beautiful Wye Valley with a 30-bedroomed hotel on-site. Other facilities include bar, restaurant, fishing, bowling, tennis and snooker. Only a mile and a half from Hereford city centre.

Belton Woods Hotel

Belton, Nr Grantham,
Lincolnshire NG32 2LN.
Tel (01476) 593200 Fax (01476) 574547

A magnificent hotel, golf and leisure resort set in 475 acres of glorious countryside. Two challenging 18-hole championship golf courses, 9-hole course, driving range, putting green and extensive leisure facilities. 136 bedrooms. (Part of the De Vere Hotels Group - see advertisement page 7 for further details.)

Borth and Ynyslas Golf Club

Borth, Ceredigion SY24 5JS.
Tel/Fax (01970) 871202

18 holes links course adjoining Borth beach. Humps and hollows provide great variation, although the topography and springy turf make for easy walking. Professional's shop, practice area, modern clubhouse with bar and catering.

Botley Park Hotel
Golf & Country Club

Winchester Road, Boorley Green, Botley,
Hampshire SO3 2UA.
Tel (01489) 780888 Fax (01489) 789242

Set in 176 acres of rolling Hampshire countryside, this 4-Star hotel has 100 en suite bedrooms, superb restaurant, extensive leisure facilities and its own picturesque and challenging 18-hole par 70 golf course and driving range. (See advertisement page 421 for further details).

The Burgess Hill Golf Academy

Cuckfield Road, Burgess Hill,
West Sussex RH15 8RE.
Tel (01444) 258585

New 24-bay, undercover, floodlit driving range and practice facilities. Superb new 9-hole par 3 golf course. Open seven days a week, 7am to 10pm. PGA professionals for lessons and pro shop for all your golfing requirements.

Burnham & Berrow Golf Club
St Cristopher's Way, Burnham-on-Sea,
Somerset TA8 2PE.
Tel (01278) 785760

18-hole championship links golf course and 9-
hole course. Dormy accommodation available.
(See advertisement page 22 for further details.)

Bushey Hall Golf Club
Bushey Hall Drive,
Bushey,
Hertfordshire WD2 2EP.
Tel (01923) 222253 Fax (01923) 229759
Pro Shop Tel (01923) 225802

 Established 1890 Bushey Hall Golf Club has
one of the oldest and best established courses in
Hertfordshire. Facilities include a fully
equipped pro shop, practice net, clubhouse
restaurant and bar. Open for membership. Pay
as you play operated. (See advertisement page
25 for further details.)

Cadmore Lodge Hotel
St Michaels,
Tenbury Wells,
Worcestershire WR15 8TQ.
Tel/Fax (01584) 810044

A warm welcome awaits at Cadmore Lodge
Hotel. Excellent cuisine from chefs with
imagination and flair. 9-hole golf course par 68
SSS 65 (18 holes). Two fishing lakes for trout
and course fishing. Indoor swimming pool, with
spa, steam room and cardio-vascular
equipment. (See advertisement page 439 for
further details.)

Cally Palace Hotel
Gatehouse of Fleet DG7 2DL.
Tel (01557) 814341 Fax (01557) 814522

This award-winning 4-Star country mansion
has its own exclusive par 70, 18-hole golf
course sculpted perfectly into the surrounding
150 acres of mature parkland. Other facilities
include fishing loch and leisure complex.

Cambridgeshire Moat House Hotel
Bar Hill,
Cambridge CB3 8EU.
Tel (01954) 780098 Fax (01954) 780010

18-hole championship golf course set in 134
acres of parkland. Golf professional David
Vernon. Newly built clubhouse and golf shop.
99 en suite bedrooms. Extensive leisure
facilities. Five miles north of Cambridge on
A14. Visitors welcome.

Cannington Golf Course
Cannington College, Cannington,
Bridgwater, Somerset TA5 2LS.
Tel/Fax (01278) 655050

Designed by Martin Hawtree of Oxford and
built to highest international specifications in
1992 by Brian D Pierson Ltd under the
consultancy of top agronomists Jim Arthur and
Gordon Child. Together they have produced
arguably the best 9-hole golf course in the west
of England. With its 'Links-Like' appearance, in
high summer the subtle contours make for a
testing round of golf for the scratch golfer, yet
are receptive for the beginner with its wide open
spaces, at 2,929 yards par 34. Beating par will
take skill and courage.

Cape Cornwall Golf & Country Club
St Just, Penzance, Cornwall TR19 7NL.
Tel/Fax (01736) 788611

FIRST and LAST 18-hole coastal course in
England, par 69 SSS 68. En suite and self-
catering accommodation inclusive of golf, gym,
swimming, spa, sauna. April to September B&B
£37 per person Thursday/Sunday; £30 per
person Monday to Wednesday. Green fee £20
weekday and weekends.

Carden Park Hotel Golf Resort & Spa
Nr Chester, Cheshire CH3 9DQ.
Tel (01829) 731000 Fax (01829) 731032

Set in 750-acres of beautiful Cheshire
countryside near Chester. A true golf resort
with two 18-hole golf courses - the mature
Cheshire course and the new Nicklaus course,
the 9-hole par 3 Azalea course and Europe's
first Jack Nicklaus Residential Golf School. The
superb AA/RAC 4-Star hotel also has an
extensive spa and there are many other leisure
facilities on the estate. For further information
and a brochure call Liz Mole on 01829 731000.
(See advertisement page 431 for further
details.)

Castletown Golf Links Hotel
Derbyhaven, Castletown,
Isle of Man IM9 1UA.
Tel (01624) 822201 Fax (01624) 625535

Situated on our own peninsula, our
championship golf course of 6,700 yards, with
all holes having sea views, is a real test of links
golf. The hotel facilities are of a luxurious 3-
Star standard.

Cave Castle Golf Hotel
South Cave, Brough,
East Yorkshire HU15 2EU.
Tel (01430) 421286 Fax (01430) 421118

Superb manor house in 160 acres of parkland situated at foot of the Wolds. Five minutes from M62 motorway link and fifteen minutes from Hull. 25 en suite bedrooms with restaurant, function and conference facilities. Own 18-hole golf course 6,524 yards SSS 71. Golf breaks, societies and non-members welcome.

The Centurion Hotel & Fosseway Golf & Country Club
Charlton Lane,
Midsomer Norton,
Bath, Somerset BA3 4BD.
Tel (01761) 417711 Fax (01761) 418357

AA/RAC 3-Star hotel with 44 luxurious rooms, just ten miles from Bath, family run with excellent cuisine. Private gardens, family-sized indoor pool, squash courts, indoor and outdoor bowling greens, 9-hole golf course, four bars - all waiting to welcome you.

China Fleet Country Club
Saltash, Cornwall PL12 6LJ.
Tel (01752) 848668 Fax (01752) 848456

Situated in 180 acres of Cornish countryside, 40 self-catering 4- and 6-berth apartments, 18-hole par 72 golf, 28-bay driving range, pool, health suite, gymnasium, racket sports, bars, restaurant and coffee shop. (See advertisement page 32 for further details.)

Cottesmore Golf & Country Club
Buchan Hill, Pease Pottage, Crawley,
West Sussex RH11 9AT.
Tel (01293) 528256 Fax (01293) 522819

12 en suite bedrooms overlooking peaceful undulating Sussex countryside. Guests can enjoy two full 18-hole mature golf courses, tennis, squash, indoor pool, spa bath, steam room, sauna and gymnasium. Ten minutes from Gatwick, one mile from the Pease Pottage exit (J11) off the M23.

Courtown Golf Club
Kiltennel, Gorey,
Co Wexford, Ireland.
Tel +353 55 25166 Fax +353 55 25553

The quality of this excellent course is matched by its luxurious clubhouse, bar and catering facilities. (See advertisement page 28 for further details.)

Dale Hill Hotel
Ticehurst, Wadhurst,
East Sussex TN5 7DQ.
Tel (01580) 200112

Highly commended luxurious hotel situated in an area of outstanding national beauty, with elegant health club and highly acclaimed 18-hole golf course. New Ian Woosnam championship course opened September, 1997.

Dalmilling Golf Course
Westwood Avenue, Ayr.
c/o South Ayrshire Council,
Burns House,
Burns Statue Square, Ayr KA7 1UT.
Tel (01292) 616269/616270

18-holes, length of course 5,724 yards SSS 68. For advance reservations telephone (01292) 263893. Practice area, caddy cars, catering and bar facilities available. Visitors welcome all week. Professional Philip Cheyney (01292) 263893. (See advertisement page 30 for further details.)

Darley Golf Course
Harling Drive, Troon KA10 6NF.
c/o South Ayrshire Council, Burns House,
Burns Statue Square, Ayr KA7 1UT.
Tel (01292) 616269/616270

18-holes, length of course 6,501 yards SSS 72. For advance reservations telephone (01292) 312464. Practice area, caddy cars, catering and bar facilities are available. Visitors are welcome all week. Professional Gordon McKinley (01292) 315566. (See advertisement page 30 for further details.)

De Vere Hotel Blackpool
East Park Drive,
Blackpool,
Lancashire FY3 8LL.
Tel (01253) 838866

De Vere Hotel Blackpool adds a touch of 4-Star elegance to one of Europe's most popular tourist destinations. Extensive facilities include: 164 bedrooms, first class restaurant, three bars, six conference rooms, indoor swimming pool, 18-bay floodlit driving range and an 18-hole championship golf course designed by Peter Alliss and Clive Clark. The course regularly hosts corporate golf and society days and was the recent venue for both the PGA Northern Championship and Reebok PGA and Lancashire Open. (Part of the De Vere Hotels Group - see advertisement page 7 for further details.)

Deer Park Hotel & Golf Courses
Howth, Co Dublin, Ireland.
Tel +353 1 832 2624 Fax +353 1 839 2405

78-bedroom 3-Star hotel with four parkland courses. Ireland's largest golf complex. Just nine miles from Dublin City and airport. Great value all-inclusive golf weekend rates available. (See advertisement page 443 for further details.)

Donnington Grove Country Club Golf Hotel & Conference Centre
Grove Road, Donnington, Newbury, Berkshire RG14 2LA.
Tel (01635) 581000 Fax (01635) 552259

18-hole parkland/moorland championship course designed by Dave Thomas. The clubhouse and hotel are located within a beautifully renovated 18th-century gothic mansion. This will provide an ideal setting for your society, company golf day or conference stay.

Dromoland Castle
Newmarket-on-Fergus, Co Clare, Ireland.
Tel +353 61 368144 Fax +353 61 363355

Dromoland Castle is a magnificent renaissance castle on 375 acres of parkland. It offers the highest accommodation standards, and award-winning restaurant. Activities include golf, clay pigeon shooting, horseriding and fishing, we also have a fully equipped health centre. The castle is located eight miles from Shannon International airport in County Clare.

Drumoig Golf Club & Hotel
Drumoig, Leuchars, St Andrews, Fife KY16 0BE.
Tel (01382) 541800 Fax (01382) 542211

Superb new golf hotel only ten minutes from St Andrews. 24 fully equipped en suite lodge bedrooms, well stocked bar, lounge and à la carte restaurant. Own 18-hole tournament standard golf course. Ideally located for touring Fife, Tayside and Perthshire.

Farthingstone Hotel & Golf Course
Farthingstone, Towcester, Northamptonshire NN12 8HA.
Tel (01327) 361291 Fax (01327) 361645

Set in glorious wooded countryside, just 90 minutes outside London. Farthingstone Hotel offers 16 superb en suite rooms, a challenging 18-hole golf course, squash court, full size snooker tables, and a carvery restaurant. Highly competitive tariffs.

Finnstown Country House Hotel & Golf Course
Newcastle Road, Lucan, Co Dublin, Ireland.
Tel +353 1 62 80644 Fax +353 1 62 81088

Finnstown Country House Hotel is located eight miles west of Dublin City. Its excellent facilities include a 9-hole golf course, leisure centre with pool, and a superb restaurant. At Finnstown the perfect golfing break awaits you. (Ref. 37)

Five Lakes Hotel Golf & Country Club
Colchester Road, Tolleshunt Knights, Maldon, Essex CM9 8HX.
Tel (01621) 868888 Fax (01621) 869696

Luxury country club nestling in 320 acres of Essex countryside, close to the Roman town of Colchester and 'Constable Country'. Extensive facilities include a 4-Star hotel, two 18-hole golf courses - the Lakes course a PGA European Tour qualifying course designed by Neil Coles, indoor and outdoor tennis, squash, indoor pool, jacuzzi, steam, sauna, gymnasium, health spa, aerobics studio, snooker and crèche. Golf packeges and leisure breaks available on request.

Fullarton Golf Course
Harling Drive, Troon KA10 6NF.
c/o South Ayrshire Council, Burns House, Burns Statue Square, Ayr KA7 1UT.
Tel (01292) 616269/616270

18-holes, length of course 4,919 yards SSS 63. For advance reservations telephone (01292) 312464. Practice area, caddy cars, catering and bar facilities are available. Visitors are welcome all week. Professional Gordon McKinley (01292) 315566. (See advertisement page 30 for further details.)

Gainsborough Golf Club
Thonock, Gainsborough, Lincolnshire DN21 1PZ.
Tel (01427) 613088 Fax (01427) 810172

The Karsten Lakes championship course, designed by Neil Coles, MBE, is part of a 36-hole complex set amongst undulating Lincolnshire parkland. The two courses are complemented with a 4-Star clubhouse offering restaurant and conference facilities. Society and corporate golf parties welcome.

Galway Bay
Golf & Country Club Hotel
Renville, Oranmore,
Co Galway, Ireland.
Tel +353 91 790500 Fax +353 91 790510

Galway Bay Golf and Country Club Hotel and
Golfing Village enjoys the tranquility of the
Renville Peninsula and yet is only eight miles
from vibrant Galway City. The hotel, with 92
standard and deluxe en suite rooms, provides a
magnificent setting for visitors coming to this
special part of the west of Ireland. The guest
rooms offer panoramic views of the golf course,
Renville Park and Galway Bay as it stretches
out to the Atlantic Ocean. Activities include
fishing, golfing, scenic walks and horseriding.
(See advertisement page 443 for further
details.)

Gatton Manor Hotel
Golf & Country Club Ltd
Ockley, Nr Dorking,
Surrey RH5 5PQ.
Tel (01306) 627555

Set amidst its own 18-hole golf course in 200
acres of parklands and lakes, situated between
London and the south coast, in the heart of the
Surrey countryside. Superb all en suite
accommodation overlooking the golf course and
grounds. À la carte restaurants, large lounge
bar, conference suites, gym and health club.

Girvan Golf Course
Golf Course Road, Girvan.
c/o South Ayrshire Council,
Burns House, Burns Statue Square,
Ayr KA7 1UT.
Tel (01292) 616269/616270

18-holes, length of course 5,095 yards SSS 64.
For advance reservations telephone (01465)
714346. Practice area, trolleys available for
hire, catering and bar facilities available.
Visitors welcome all week. (See advertisement
page 30 for further details.)

Gleddoch House
Langbank,
Renfrewshire PA14 6YE.
Tel (01475) 540711 Fax (01475) 540201

Country house hotel overlooking the river
Clyde within easy reach of Glasgow and airport.
Own golf course (par 72, 6,300 yards). Pro
shop, clubhouse with own restaurant, bar,
squash, horseriding, clay pigeon shooting and
off-road driving. Golf Societies welcome.

Gosforth Park
Golfing Complex Ltd
(Parklands Golf Course)
High Gosforth Park,
Newcastle-upon-Tyne NE3 5HQ.
Tel 0191-236 4480

The complex has an 18-hole golf course, 45-bay
two tier floodlit driving range, 9-hole pitch and
putt course and putting green. Also pro shop,
bar and restaurant. Open to non-members.

The Grange & Links Hotel
Sea Lane, Sandilands,
Sutton-on-Sea,
Lincolnshire LN12 2RA.
Tel (01507) 441334 Fax (01507) 443033

3-Star 30-bedroom hotel with own 18-hole
links course. Two tennis courts, snooker and
ballroom. Award-winning hotel renowned for
superb cuisine, friendliness, comfort and
service.

Hanbury Manor
Ware,
Hertfordshire SG12 0SD.
Tel (01920) 487722 Fax (01920) 487692

5-Star country resort, yet only 25 miles north of
central London. Championship golf course
(1997 ALAMO English Open), state of the art
health spa, three award-winning restaurants and
96 deluxe bedrooms. Ten conference rooms.
(See advertisement page 4 for further details.)

Harrogate Golf Club
Forest Lane Head, Harrogate,
North Yorkshire HG2 7TF.
Tel (01423) 862999

A long established 18-hole golf course set
amongst mature trees formerly part of the
Forest of Knaresborough. Visitors are assured
of a warm reception in the extensively
refurbished clubhouse and restaurant. Dormy
accommodation available. (See advertisement
page 25 for further details.)

Hawkstone Park Hotel
Weston-under-Redcastle, Shrewsbury,
Shropshire SY4 5UY.
Tel (01939) 200611 Fax (01939) 200311

The recently refurbished Hawkstone Park Hotel
and Golf Centre has two contrasting 18-hole
golf courses; the Hawkstone, famous for its
mature picturesque parkland setting, and the
redeveloped Windmill offering undulating
landscape and strategic water features.

Hertfordshire Golf & Country Club

Broxbournebury Mansion,
White Stubbs Lane, Broxbourne,
Hertfordshire EN10 7PY.
Tel (01992) 466666 Fax (01992) 470326

Set in spectacular countryside enjoy excellent golf on our Nicklaus 18-hole course, 30-bay floodlit driving range and golf academy. Voted Top Ten Best New Courses in the UK by Golf World. 80-seater brasserie-style restaurant and clubhouse with spike bar and conference rooms for 12 to 150. Societies welcome - handicap required. (See advertisement page 22 for further details.)

Hollywood Lakes Golf Club

Ballyboughal, Co Dublin, Ireland.
Tel +353 1 843 3406/7 Fax +353 1 843 3002

Parkland course featuring water hazards and lakes at 5 holes and also the longest par 5 in Ireland at 630 yards (14th hole). (See advertisement page 30 for details.)

Holyhead Golf Club

Lon Garreg Fawr, Treaddur Bay,
Anglesey LL65 2YG.
Tel/Fax (01407) 763279

Excellent golf on heathland course with spectacular view to Snowdonia. Golf accommodation is available in twin-bedded rooms. All meals provided in club restaurant. Reservations ring 01407 763279.

Horam Park Golf Club

Chiddingly Road, Horam,
East Sussex TN21 0JJ.
Tel (01435) 813477 Fax (01435) 813677

9-hole golf course 18 tee positions, pitch 'n' putt course, 16-bay driving range open 8am to 10pm seven days. Extensive pro shop, bar, restaurant, PGA qualified teaching professionals. Societies and visitors welcome. Specialises in corporate days.

Horsted Place Sporting Estate

Little Horsted, Uckfield,
East Sussex TN22 5TS.
(Hotel) Tel (01825) 750581
Fax (01825) 750459
(Club) Tel (01825) 880088
Fax (01825) 880066

Combine Victorian elegance and luxury at Horsted Place Hotel with exceptional golf on one of the two spectacular courses at East Sussex National Golf Club. If you require golf tuition there is a superb golf academy which has its own three hole course. Experience for yourself challenging golf and exceptional accommodation in beautiful surroundings. (See advertisement page 421 for further details.)

Hospitality Inn

46 Annick Road,
Irvine KA11 4LD.
Freephone 0800 731 9323
Fax(01294) 277287

Located on the beautiful Ayrshire coast this modern 4-Star hotel, with its own private 9-hole golf course and spectacular indoor lagoon, makes this the ideal base for the golfing enthusiast to relax. Individual fully inclusive golf packages available.

Ingon Manor Golf & Country Club

Ingon Lane,
Snitterfield,
Nr Stratford upon Avon,
Warwickshire CV37 0QE.
Tel (01789) 731857 Fax (01789) 731657

Located two miles from Stratford, close to the A46. Par 72, 18-hole golf course, 6,554 yards white tees, 6,091 yards yellow tees. Driving range and practice area. All day bar and catering. Accommodation available.

The Jarvis Gloucester Hotel & Country Club

Robinswood Hill,
Matson Lane,
Gloucester GL4 6EA.
Tel (01452) 525653

Extensive leisure facilities including indoor swimming pool, sauna, gymnasium, solarium. Squash courts, tennis courts, snooker, pool. Championship dry ski slopes. Full 18-hole and 9-hole par 3 courses.

The K Club

At Straffan,
Co Kildare, Ireland.
Tel +353 1 601 7200 Fax +353 1 601 7299

Located 30 minutes from Dublin. Arnold Palmer designed 18-hole championship golf course, clubhouse, practice area and driving range. Resident golf professional Ernie Jones. Home to The Smurfit European Open since September 1995 until the year 2000. Hotel AA 5-Red Stars. Fishing, health club and sports centre with indoor and outdoor tennis. (See advertisement page 443 for further details.)

La Grande Mare Hotel Golf Club
La Grande Mare,
Vazon, Castel, Guernsey.
Tel (01481) 56576&53544 Fax(01481) 55194

Beautifully appointed luxury hotel with 18-hole golf course playing off 14 greens. Professional shop and tuition on-site. First class, well priced restaurant. 2-AA Rosettes. Beachside location. Golfing breaks catered for.

Laytown & Bettystown Golf Club
Bettystown, Co Meath, Ireland.
Tel +353 41 27170 Fax +353·41 28506

A traditional links, 18-holes par 70. Exceptional greens 12 months. Half hour north of Dublin airport. Hospitality assured, all services. Ryder Cup men Des Smyth and Philip Walton have won the Captain's Prize. (Regular tournament venue.)

Letham Grange
Colliston, by Arbroath DD11 4RL.
Tel (01241) 890373 Fax (01241) 890725

42-bedrooms, Victorian mansion, with 36-holes of superb golf. First class facilities set in the heartland of golf. Company/society golf outings/breaks welcome. (See advertisement page 437 for further details.)

Linden Hall Golf Club
Longhorsley, Morpeth,
Northumberland NE65 8XF.
Tel (01670) 788050 Fax (01670) 788544

Linden Hall Golf Club is located within the grounds of Linden Hall Hotel, a 4-Star, 5-Crown Georgian manor country house hotel. The 18-hole, 6,809 yard, SSS 73 golf course is set within mature woodland, rolling parkland with established burns and lakes amidst a stunning backdrop of the Cheviot hills and Northumbrian coastline.

Lochgreen Golf Course
Harling Drive, Troon KA10 6NF.
c/o South Ayrshire Council,
Burns House, Burns Statue Square,
Ayr KA7 1UT.
Tel (01292) 616269/616270

18-holes, length of course 6,822 yards SSS 73. For advance reservations telephone (01292) 312464. Practice area, caddy cars and catering facilities are available. Visitors are welcome all week. Professional Gordon McKinley (01292) 315566. (See advertisement page 30 for further details.)

Machrie Hotel & Golf Links Course
Port Ellen,
Isle of Islay, Argyll PA42 7AN.
Tel (01496) 310310 Fax (01496) 302404

Play a hidden gem of a course. Traditional 18-hole championship links course situated on the doorstep of the Machrie Hotel. Superior and standard accommodation, excellent food and friendly service. Self-catering and golf packages also available.

Mannings Heath Golf Club
Fullers, Hammerpond Road,
Mannings Heath,
Horsham,
West Sussex RH13 6PH.
Tel (01403) 210228 Fax (01403) 270974

Mannings Heath Golf Club was founded in 1905. With *two 18-hole championship courses* providing a challenging test to the discerning golfer. 'Fullers', the family mansion has been tastefully restored to provide first class clubhouse facilities for all our clients. Overnight accommodation available at South Lodge Hotel nearby. (See advertisement page 423 for further details.)

Manor of Groves Golf & Country Club
High Wych,
Sawbridgeworth,
Hertfordshire CM21 0LA.
Tel (01279) 722333 Fax (01279) 726972

This superb 18-hole golf course set around its own Georgian manor house offers the ideal setting for that break away. Along with its special rated packages, and golf school, the clubhouse facilities include superb cuisine, bar, and a function room suitable for all occasions.

Marriott Breadsall Priory Hotel & Country Club
Moor Road,
Morley,
Nr Derby, Derbyshire DE7 6DL.
Tel (01332) 832235 Fax (01332) 833509

Based on a 13th-century mansion set in 400 acres of stunning parkland, Breadsall Priory offers two superb golf courses, excellent accommodation and comprehensive leisure and conference facilities. (See advertisement page 4 for further details.)

Marriott Dalmahoy
Hotel & Country Club
Kirknewton, Nr Edinburgh,
Midlothian EH27 8EB.
Tel 0131-333 1845 Fax 0131-335 3203

Set in over 1,000 acres of Scottish woodland
and almost in the shadow of the Pentland Hills,
Dalmahoy offers something special for every
golfer. A regular European tour venue, only
seven miles from Edinburgh. Two outstanding
courses - East Championship Course and the
West Course. 4-Star hotel with 115 bedrooms
and excellent conference facilities. Swimming
pool, jet pool, sauna/steam room, resistance and
CV gymnasium, tennis courts, golf and leisure
shop, Long Weekend restaurant, health and
beauty salon and club bar. Floodlit driving
range with tuition, video facilities and short
game area. (See advertisement page 4 for
further details.)

Marriott Forest of Arden
Hotel & Country Club
Maxstoke Lane, Meriden,
Warwickshire CV7 7HR.
Tel (01676) 522335 Fax (01676) 523711

Set in 10,000 acres of Warwickshire
countryside, the Forest of Arden, host to the
One-2-One British Masters, offers some of
Britain's best golfing alongside first class
accommodation, leisure and conference
facilities. (See advertisement page 4 for further
details.)

Marriott Goodwood Park
Hotel & Country Club
Goodwood, Nr Chichester,
West Sussex PO18 0QB.
Tel (01243) 775537 Fax (01243) 520120

Country club hotel set in the 12,000 acre
Goodwood Estate with a testing 18-hole golf
course and superb leisure facilities including
golf range, practice area, putting green and fully
equipped sports shop. (See advertisement page
4 for further details.)

Marriott Meon Valley
Hotel & Country Club
Sandy Lane, Shedfield, Nr Southampton,
Hampshire SO32 2HQ.
Tel (01329) 833455 Fax (01329) 834411

Set in 225 acres of Hampshire parkland, the
Marriott Meon Valley Hotel offers a challenging
18-hole golf course and an equally testing 9-
hole course. The hotel also offers extensive

leisure and conference facilities. (See
advertisement page 4 for further details.)

Marriott St Pierre
Hotel & Country Club
St Pierre Park, Chepstow NP6 6YA.
Tel (01291) 625261 Fax (01291) 629975

St Pierre has recently undergone a multi-million
pound refurbishment. Set in 400 acres of
exceptional parkland, the hotel offers two
superb golf courses, including the Old Course,
host to the 1996 Solheim Cup. Extensive
leisure and conference facilities. (See
advertisement page 4 for further details.)

Marriott Tudor Park
Hotel & Country Club
Ashford Road, Bearsted, Maidstone,
Kent ME14 4NQ.
Tel (01622) 734334 Fax (01622) 735360

Situated in the Garden of England, Tudor Park
is set in a 220 acre former deer park. Its superb
golf course is designed by Donald Steel. The
hotel also offers excellent accommodation,
leisure and conference facilities. (See
advertisement page 4 for further details.)

Maybole Golf Course
Memorial Park, Maybole.
c/o South Ayrshire Council, Burns House,
Burns Statue Square, Ayr KA7 1UT.
Tel (01292) 616269/616270

9-holes, length of course 2,635 yards SSS 33.
For advance reservations telephone (01292)
263893. Trolleys available for hire. Visitors
welcome all week. (See advertisement page 30
for further details.)

Mentmore Golf & Country Club
Mentmore, Nr Leighton Buzzard,
Bedfordshire LU7 0UA.
Tel (01296) 662020 Fax (01296) 662592

Two 18-hole championship golf courses.
Rothschild Course par 72, 6,763 yards.
Rosebery Course par 72, 6,777 yards. Practice
range. Restaurant, swimming pool, sauna,
jacuzzi and steam room.

Mersey Valley Golf Club (1995)
Warrington Road, Bold Heath,
Widnes, Cheshire WA8 3XL.
Tel/Fax 0151-424 6060

Conference facilities, corporate golf days and
memberships, societies and visitors welcome.
Buggy hire. We specialise in corporate golf days

- easy walking course. 20 minutes from Liverpool and Manchester, two miles junction 7, M62. Superb bar and catering facilities.

Mottram Hall Hotel
Wilmslow Road, Mottram St Andrew, Prestbury, Cheshire SK10 4QT.
Tel (01625) 828135

Mottram Hall is an elegant 18th-century Georgian building, set in secluded parkland with delightful ornamental gardens and lake. The 4-Star hotel has 132 luxury bedrooms, conference facilities for up to 275 guests, a luxurious leisure club, and a superb 18-hole championship golf course designed by international golf architect Dave Thomas. Leisure facilities include spacious swimming pool, spa, saunas and steam rooms, fully equipped gym - even a full sized soccer pitch utilised by European football champions, Germany, who stayed here in 1996. (Part of the De Vere Hotels Group - see advertisement page 7 for further details.)

Mount Juliet
Thomastown, Co Kilkenny, Ireland.
Tel +353 56 24455 Fax +353 56 24766

Deluxe accommodation in the elegant Mount Juliet House or the informal Hunters Yard. Ireland's premier sporting estate offers guests on-site fishing, horseriding, tennis, stylish leisure centre, David Leadbetter Golf Academy. Home of the Irish Open, 1993, 1994 and 1995.

Nailcote Hall Hotel
Nailcote Lane, Berkswell, Warwickshire CV7 7DE.
Tel (01203) 466174 Fax (01203) 470720

Delightful and challenging championship 9-hole par 3 course designed to test any golfers short game. Set in the grounds of this 17th-century black and white Jacobean country house hotel, used by Cromwell in the English Civil War.

Newbury Racecourse Golf Club
The Racecourse, Newbury, Berkshire RG14 7NZ.
Tel (01635) 551464 Fax (01635) 528354

A heathland/links 6,500 yards 18-hole golf course with 20-bay floodlit driving range. Memberships are available and golfers can play on a pay and play basis. Fully stocked pro shop and excellent clubhouse which can cater for society bookings. (See advertisement page 22 for further details.)

Northop Country Park Golf Club
Northop, Flintshire CH7 6WA.
Tel (01352) 840440 Fax (01352) 840445

John Jacob's designed par 72, 18-hole championship course in 247 acres of mature parkland. Driving range, pratice greens and pro shop plus two all-weather tennis courts, gym and sauna. Award-winning restaurant. Overnight accommodation available at nearby St David's Park Hotel five minutes away. (See advertisement page 431 for further details.)

Old Course Hotel - St Andrews Golf Resort & Spa
St Andrews, Fife KY16 9SP.
Tel (01334) 474371 Fax (01334) 477668

This luxury 125-bedroom hotel overlooks the 17th Road Hole of the Old Course and is a five minute walk to the beach and town. Facilities include health spa with swimming pool, whirlpool, fitness room and full range of massage and beauty treatments. The hotel now has its own championship golf course, the Duke's Course. Open to non-residents, with residents enjoying guaranteed tee-times and reduced green fees.

Oulton Hall Hotel
Rothwell Lane, Oulton, Leeds LS26 8HN.
Tel 0113-282 1000

This elegant 5-Star Yorkshire hotel complete with 19th-century style formal gardens, is situated adjacent to the Oulton Park Golf Club where guests have the choice of either 18- or 9-hole courses set in spectacular White Rose countryside. Facilities also include a 22-bay driving range. (Part of the De Vere Hotels Group - see advertisement page 7 for further details.)

Parknasilla Great Southern Hotel
Parknasilla, Sneen, Co Kerry, Ireland.
Tel +353 64 45122 Fax +353 64 45323

The Parknasilla celebrated its Centenary in 1995. This 4-Star 84-bedroom hotel has just completely rebuilt its 9-hole golf course, making it one of the most scenic in Ireland. Wide range of leisure activities available.

Patshull Park Hotel Golf & Country Club
Pattingham, Shropshire WV6 7HR.
Tel (01902) 700100 Fax (01902) 700874

Parkland, lakeside 18-hole championship John Jacobs' designed course in grounds of the Earl of Dartmouth estate. Corporate, society and residential packages. 49 en suite bedrooms, swimming pool, leisure centre, gymnasium, fishing. Restaurant and Bunkers coffee shop.

Penrith Golf Club
Salkeld Road, Penrith,
Cumbria CA11 8SG.
Tel (01768) 891919

The club, which is 108 years old, is easily accessible from junction 41 on the M6 motorway and lies half a mile east of Penrith, enjoying panoramic views to the Lakeland hills. Visitors are very welcome to play this excellent course. (See advertisement page 30 for further details.)

Peterhead Golf Club
Craigewan Links, Riverside Drive,
Peterhead AB42 1LT.
Tel (01779) 472149 & 480725

One of the oldest clubs in the world. Beautiful links which are neither flat or too hilly, a joy to play. Recommended for the serious low handicapper and the normal club golfer who wants the challenge of a lifetime. (See advertisement page 28 for further details.)

Portmarnock Hotel & Golf Links
Strand Road, Portmarnock, Co Dublin, Ireland.
Tel +353 1 846 0611 Fax +353 1 846 2442

This prestigious new development is located 15 minutes from Dublin airport and 25 minutes from the city centre. The hotel's 18-hole golf links was designed by Bernard Langer and is the only PGA European Tour course in Ireland. (See advertisement page 445 for further details.)

Powerscourt Golf Club
Enniskerry, Co Wicklow, Ireland.
Tel +353 1 204 6033 Fax +353 1 276 1303

An Inspiring Course in a Spectacular Location. Powerscourt is a free draining course with links characteristics. Built to championship standard, with top quality tees and exceptional tiered greens, it is set in some of Ireland's most beautiful parkland. Studio apartment accommodation is available on the estate, within strolling distance of the clubhouse. (See advertisement page 32 for further details.)

Radisson Roe Park Hotel & Golf Resort
Roe Park, Limauady,
Co Londonderry, N. Ireland BT49 9LB.
Tel (015047) 22222 Fax (015047) 22313

Northern Ireland's premier golf and leisure resort featuring 64 luxurious bedrooms, O'Cahan's bar, Coach House brasserie, Courtyard restaurant, Fairways leisure club and the Eden health and beauty salon. 18-hole championship parkland course, driving range, putting green and golf shop.

Ramside Hall Hotel & Golf Club
Carrville, Durham DH1 1TD.
Tel 0191-386 5282 Fax 0191-386 0399

Set in 220 acres on the outsksirts of the cathedral city of Durham and surrounded by a stimulating 27-hole golf course. 3-Star; 4-Crown High Commended. 80 luxury bedrooms, restaurant, grill room and carvery. Conference and banqueting facilities. Superb floodlit driving range and practice areas. (See advertisement page 433 for further details.)

Rodway Hill Golf Course
Newent Road, Highnam,
Gloucestershire GL2 8DN.
Tel (01452) 384222 Fax (01989) 766450

An 18-hole pay and play par 68 course two miles south west of Gloucester, with panoramic views of the Cotswolds. It has a well stocked shop, practice and teaching facilities. Hire kit available. Societies welcome.

Royal Lytham & St Anne's Golf Club
Links Gate, Lytham St Anne's FY8 3LQ.
Tel (01253) 724206 Fax (01253) 780946

Ideal for small parties wishing to play the championship course. Accommodation for men only. Apply to the assistant secretary. (See advertisement page 22 for further details.)

Royal Porthcawl Golf Club
Rest Bay, Porthcawl,
Mid Glamorgan CF36 3UW.
Tel (01656) 782251 Fax (01656) 771687

Luxury dormy accommodation for parties of up to twelve persons. Apply to the secretary. (See advertisement page 26 for further details.)

Rudding Park Golf

**Rudding Park, Harrogate,
North Yorkshire HG3 1DJ.**
Tel (01423) 872100 Fax: (01423) 873011

Superb floodlit driving range and golf academy.
Complete the golf experience on our 18-hole,
par 72 parkland course. Corporate and society
bookings welcome. (See advertisement page
427 for further details.)

Rusacks Hotel Golf Club

Pilmour Links, St Andrews, Fife KY16 9JQ.
*Tel (01334) 474321 Fax (01334) 477896
Golf Club Tel/Fax (01334) 479176*

Rusacks Hotel, overlooking the first and last
fairways of the Old Course, provides outstanding facilities for golfers. The Rusacks Golf
Club, situated within the hotel, offers guests a
full golf booking service, lockers, sauna, solarium, club bar and golf shop. Voted one of the
Top Ten Golf Hotels in the World. STB 5-Crown.

Sand Moor Golf Club

Alwoodley Lane, Leeds LS17 7DJ.
Tel 0113-268 5180

A golfing paradise created out of a barren moor,
with magnificent views of the surrounding
countryside. The course is an excellent
challenge of golf. Refurbishment of the
clubhouse during 1997 have improved still
further the quality of facilities available. (See
advertisement page 26 for further details.)

Seafield Golf Course

**Belleisle Park, Ayr.
c/o South Ayrshire Council, Burns House,
Burns Statue Square, Ayr KA7 1UT.**
Tel (01292) 616269/616270

18-holes, length of course 5,498 yards SSS 66.
For advance reservations telephone (01292)
441258. Practice area, caddy cars, catering and
bar facilities available. Visitors welcome all
week. Professional David Gemmell (01292)
441314. (See advertisement page 30.)

Seaford Golf Club

**East Blatchington, Seaford,
East Sussex BN25 2JD.**
Tel (01323) 892442

The Dormy House provides comfortable
accommodation for eighteen guests in 9 twin-
bedded en suite bedrooms on the first floor of
the clubhouse, and 2 single rooms in our
bungalow annexe. For latest brochure ring
01323 892442.

Sedlescombe Golf Club

**Kent Street, Sedlescombe,
East Sussex TN33 0SD.**
Tel (01424) 870898 Fax (01424) 870855

9-hole golf course, alternative second 9-holes,
pitch and putt course. 24-bay floodlit driving
range. Bar and restaurant. All facilities open to
the public. Societies and corporate days
welcome.

The Silverwood Hotel

Kiln Road, Lurgan, Craigavon BT66 6NF.
Tel (01762) 327722 Fax (01762) 325290

The hotel lies within a complex of an 18-hole
golf course, putting courses, driving range, gym
and a certified ski slope. Also available - game
and coarse fishing, sailing, winter skiing,
windsurfing, bird and wildlife reserve and
parascending. (See advertisement page 441 for
further details.)

The Slieve Russell Hotel Golf & Country Club

Ballyconnell, Co Cavan, Ireland.
Tel +353 49 26444 Fax +353 49 26474

Located only two hours' drive from both
Dublin and Belfast, the Slieve Russell is a
complete resort with its 5-Star leisure facilities,
championship 18-hole golf course. 151 superbly
appointed bedrooms and a selection of
restaurants and bars. Conference and
banqueting suites - 'The *Perfect*' location for
business or pleasure.

The Springs Hotel

**Wallingford Road, North Stoke,
Wallingford, Oxon OX10 6BE.**
Tel (01491) 836687 Fax (01491) 836877

Situated twix Oxford and Henley this Tudor-
style country house offers, 30 en suite luxurious
rooms, AA-2 Rosette restaurant, outdoor swimming pool and an 18-hole par 72 golf course.
Your comfort and well-being are our priority.

St Helen's Bay Golf & Country Club

**St Helens, Kilrane, Rosslare Harbour,
Co Wexford, Ireland.**
Tel +353 53 33234 Fax +353 53 33803

Superbly located championship 18-hole golf
course, which has blended the best of parkland
characteristics with a finish that is true links and
plenty of difficulty. Luxury on-site
accommodation together with tennis courts,

continued over

leisure room and sauna. Full bar and catering facilities available in the clubhouse. Situated only five minutes from Rosslare ferryport. Green fee and society-friendly, playable all year round.

The St Pierre Park Hotel
Rohais, St Peter Port,
Guernsey GYl 1FD.
Tel (01481) 728282 Fax (01481) 712041

This 4-Star hotel offers extensive leisure facilities including a 9-hole par 3 golf course, designed by Tony Jacklin. Three tennis courts and a health suite with heated indoor swimming pool, spa bath, saunas, steam rooms, solaria and exercise room.

Stakis Puckrup Hall Hotel & Golf Club
Puckrup,
Tewkesbury,
Gloucestershire GL20 6EL.
Tel (01684) 296200 Fax (01684) 850788

If golf is your chosen sport, Stakis Puckrup Hall is an excellent choice. Established trees, lakes and parkland play host to a challenging and beautifully tended par 70 championship course, situated between the Cotswold and Malvern hills. (See advertisement page 419 for further details.)

Stocks Hotel Golf & Country Club
Stocks Road,
Aldbury, Nr Tring,
Hertfordshire HP23 5RX.
Tel (01442) 851341 Fax (01442) 851253

A championship 18-hole all-weather golf course, PGA Game Improvement Centre. Chipping and putting greens, practice fairway. Full stocked professional shop. 18 bedrooms, two restaurants, riding stables, full leisure facilities, conference rooms.

Stoke Poges Golf Club
Park Road,
Stoke Poges,
Buckinghamshire SL2 4PG.
Tel (01753) 717170 Fax (01753) 717181

Golf Club of the Year 1996. The ultimate venue for both corporate and social entertaining (six conference rooms, three restaurants and 21 bedrooms). Providing outstanding service and cuisine in unique surroundings close to London and Heathrow. (See advertisement page 8 for further details.)

Sunlaws House Hotel & Roxburghe Golf Course
Kelso, Roxburghshire TD5 8JZ.
Tel (01573) 450331 Fax (01573) 450611

22-bedroom hotel owned by the Duke and Duchess of Roxburghe. Luxury accommodation, superb cuisine. The 18-hole championship standard Roxburghe golf course, designed by Dave Thomas, surrounds the hotel.

Sweetwoods Park Golf Club
Cowden, Edenbridge, Kent TN8 7JN.
Tel (01342) 850729 Fax (01342) 850866

Situated two miles west of Edenbridge off juntion 6 of the M25. Simply the best value in golf around. Excellent 18-holes 6,512 yards par 72 course and floodlit driving range. (See advertisement page 26 for details.)

Telford Golf & Country Club
Great Hay, Sutton Hill, Telford,
Shropshire TF7 4DT.
Tel (01952) 429977 Fax (01952) 586602

Overlooking the Ironbridge Gorge, the hotel offers its own 18-hole championship course. Floodlit driving range and practice areas. The extensive leisure facilities include squash courts, swimming pool, gymnasium, snooker, whirlpool, sauna and steam rooms. There is a resident masseur. (See advertisement page 429.)

Tewkesbury Park Hotel Country Club Resort
Lincoln Green Lane, Tewkesbury,
Gloucestershire GL20 7DN.
Tel (01684) 295405 Fax (01684) 292386

This 78-bedroom hotel with modern facilities is surrounded by its own 18-hole golf course and offers a heated indoor pool, sauna, jacuzzi, solarium, health and beauty salon, squash and floodlit tennis courts, steam room and fitness centre. (See advertisement page 421.)

The Golf Club - Thorpeness
Thorpeness, Nr Aldeburgh,
Suffolk IP16 4NH.
Tel (01728) 452176 Fax (01728) 453868

One of East Anglia's finest and most challenging 18-hole courses. Handicap certificate required, advisable to book in advance. Accommodation, bars, restaurant, golf shop, tennis courts and course set adjacent to picturesque coastal village on Suffolk Heritage coast. (See advertisement page 423 for further details.)

The Toft House
Hotel & Golf Course
Toft, Nr Bourne, Lincolnshire PE10 0JT.
Tel (01778) 590614 Fax (01778) 590264

The hotel is a family run, 22-bedroom converted farmhouse with its own 18-hole par 72 golf course covering 107 acres of undulating land with picturesque views of the lake and surrounding countryside.

Trevose Golf & Country Club
Constantine Bay, Padstow,
North Cornwall PL28 8JB.
Tel (01841) 520208 Fax (01841) 521057
e-mail: @trevose-gc.co.uk
website: http://www.trevose-gc.co.uk

Trevose offers not only great golf (championship 18-hole course, a 9-hole full length (3,100 yards) par 35 plus a 9-hole short course) but also a first class clubhouse and restaurant, three hard all-weather tennis courts, a heated outdoor swimming pool in the summer, a games room for the kids and a boutique. Accommodation is available in bungalows, chalets, luxury flats and dormy suites. send for our detailed, full colour brochure

Turnberry Hotel
Golf Courses & Spa
Ayrshire KA26 9LT.
Tel (01655) 331000 Fax (01655) 331706

One of the world's finest luxury hotel, golf and spa resorts. Edwardian country house overlooking its own Ailsa and Arran championship courses. The Ailsa is ranked 16th in the world and was the venue for the 1994 Open Championship.

Welbeck Manor & Sparkwell
Golf Course
Blacklands, Sparkwell, Plymouth,
Devon PL7 5DF.
Tel/Fax (01752) 837219

A testing 9-hole, pay as you play course and also a par 3 course, set in 60 acres of parkland. Facilities include a well equipped golf shop, excellent hotel accommodation, restaurant and bar. Open to the public. Golf societies welcome.

Welcombe Hotel & Golf Course
Warwick Road, Stratford-upon-Avon,
Warwickshire CV37 0NR.
Tel (01789) 295252 Fax (01789) 414666

A 4-Star Jacobean-style mansion set within its own 6,217 yards private golf course. A newly created clubhouse and pro shop within the hotel's 157 acres enhance the parkland course.

Whitefields Hotel
Golf & Country Club
Coventry Road, Thurlaston, Nr Rugby,
Warwickshire CV23 9JR.
Tel (01788) 521800 Fax (01788) 521695

18-hole course 6,223 yards. Driving range, putting green 18. 33 en suite rooms. Four conference rooms, bars and à la carte restaurant. Societies welcome seven days. Call the secretary on 01788 815555. Reservations 01788 521800.

Woodbury Park Golf Club
Woodbury Castle, Exeter, Devon EX5 1JJ.
Tel (01395) 233382 Fax (01395) 233384

Five luxury lodges situated with 27 holes of a championship standard golf course. The lodges are an ideal venue for a short golf break. The Nigel Mansell owned resort also has extensive leisure facilities.

DRIVING RANGES
& PRACTICE GROUNDS

The Burgess Hill Golf Academy
Cuckfield Road, Burgess Hill,
West Sussex RH15 8RE.
Tel (01444) 258585

New 24-bay, undercover, floodlit driving range and comprehensive practice facilities. Superb new 9-hole par 3 golf course. Open seven days a week, 7am to 10pm. PGA professionals for lessons and pro shop for all your golfing requirements.

Carden Park Hotel
Golf Resort & Spa
Nr Chester, Cheshire CH3 9DQ.
Tel (01829) 731000 Fax (01829) 731032

Set in 750-acres of beautiful Cheshire countryside near Chester. A true golf resort with two 18-hole golf courses - the mature Cheshire course and the new Nicklaus course, the 9-hole par 3 Azalea course and Europe's first Jack Nicklaus Residential Golf School. The superb AA/RAC 4-Star hotel also has an extensive spa and there are many other leisure facilities on the estate. For further information and a brochure call Liz Mole on 01829 731000. (See advertisement page 432.)

Gosforth Park
Golfing Complex Ltd
**(Parklands Golf Course
High Gosforth Park,
Newcastle-upon-Tyne NE3 5HQ.**
Tel 0191-236 4480

The complex has an 18-hole golf course, 45-bay
two tier floodlit driving range, 9-hole pitch and
putt course and putting green. Also pro shop,
bar and restaurant. Open to non-members.

The Hertfordshire
Golf & Country Club
**Broxbournebury Mansion,
White Stubbs Lane,
Broxbourne, Hertfordshire EN10 7PY.**
Tel (01992) 466666 Fax (01992) 470326

Set in spectacular countryside enjoy excellent
golf on our Nicklaus 18-hole course, 30-bay
floodlit driving range and golf academy. Voted
Top Ten Best New Courses in the UK by Golf
World. 80-seater brasserie-style restaurant and
clubhouse with spike bar and conference rooms
for 12 to 150. Societies welcome - handicap
required. (See advertisement page 22 for further
details.)

Horam Park Golf Club
**Chiddingly Road,
Horam,
East Sussex TN21 0JJ.**
Tel (01435) 813477 Fax (01435) 813677

9-hole golf course 18 tee positions, pitch 'n'
putt course, 16-bay driving range open 8am to
10pm seven days. Extensive pro shop, bar,
restaurant, PGA qualified teaching
professionals. Societies and visitors welcome.
Specialises in corporate days.

The K Club
**At Straffan,
Co Kildare, Ireland.**
Tel +353 1 601 7200 Fax +353 1 601 7299

Located 30 minutes from Dublin. Arnold
Palmer designed 18-hole championship golf
course, clubhouse, practice area and driving
range. Resident golf professional Ernie Jones.
Home to The Smurfit European Open since
September 1995 until the year 2000. Hotel AA
5-Red Stars. Fishing, health club and sports
centre with indoor and outdoor tennis. (See
advertisement page 443 for further details.)

Rudding Park Golf
**Rudding Park, Harrogate,
North Yorkshire HG3 1DJ.**
Tel (01423) 872100 Fax: (01423) 873011

Superb floodlit driving range and golf academy.
Complete the golf experience on our 18-hole,
par 72 parkland course. Corporate and society
bookings welcome. (See advertisement page
427 for further details.)

Sedlescombe Golf Club
**Kent Street, Sedlescombe,
East Sussex TN33 0SD.**
Tel (01424) 870898 Fax (01424) 870855

9-hole golf course, alternative second 9-holes,
pitch and putt course. 24-bay floodlit driving
range. Bar and restaurant. All facilities open to
the public. Societies and corporate days
welcome.

Telford Golf & Country Club
**Great Hay, Sutton Hill, Telford,
Shropshire TF7 4DT.**
Tel (01952) 429977 Fax (01952) 586602

Overlooking the Ironbridge Gorge, the hotel
offers its own 18-hole championship course.
Floodlit driving range and practice areas. The
extensive leisure facilities include squash courts,
swimming pool, gymnasium, snooker,
whirlpool, sauna and steam rooms. There is a
resident masseur. (See advertisement page 429
for further details.)

Ideal locations for society days, special functions and group golfing weekends

Index of Advertisers

Continued over

PART V

Clubs and Courses in the British Isles and Europe

Compiled by Jan Bennett

1998 Centenary Clubs

The following clubs celebrate their centenaries in 1998:

England

Ashford Manor
Barnard Castle
Broadstone
Church Stretton
Congleton
Ealing
Hessle
Hornsea
Market Harborough
Maxstoke Park
Northumberland
Sickleholme
Tolladine
West Bowling
Wigan
Willingdon
Wimbledon Park
Worcester G&CC

Scotland

Boat-of-Garten
Burntisland Golf House Club
Canmore
Gairloch
Leslie
The St Rule Club

Ireland

County Meath
Youghal

Golf Clubs and Courses in the British Isles

How to use this section

1. Geographical divisions

In England, Ireland and Wales clubs are listed in alphabetical order within counties. Listing is generally under geographical county, and sometimes under the county of affiliation.

In Scotland, counties are generally grouped under recognised administrative regions.

European clubs are listed in alphabetical order by country, and grouped under regional headings. In some areas, only 18-hole courses are included.

All clubs and courses are listed in the general index at the back of the book.

2. Club details

After the name of the club is the date of foundation (where available).

Courses are private unless otherwise stated. Many public courses have members' clubs which play over them; information on these clubs can be obtained from the course concerned.

The address is the postal address of each club or course. If the postal county is different from the one under which the club or course is listed, it will be shown in the address.

Tel: club telephone number general use.

Mem: total number of playing members. The number of lady members (L) and juniors (J) are sometimes shown separately.

Sec/Pro: telephone numbers for Secretaries and Professionals are shown if different from the club telephone number.

Holes: course length refers to medal tee yardages whenever possible.

Recs: Professional, Amateur and Ladies' Course Records.

V'tors: playing opportunities and restrictions for unaccompanied visitors.

Fees: green fees are quoted for visitors if they are permitted to play unaccompanied by a member. The basic cost per round or per day (D) is shown first, then, in brackets, the cost of a weekend and/or Bank Holiday round. Weekly (W) and monthly (M) are sometimes shown. *Green fees quoted are the most up to date supplied by each club.*

Loc: general location of course.

Mis: other facilities/useful information.

Arch: course architect/designer.

3. Abbreviations

WD Weekdays.
WE Weekends.
BH Bank Holidays.
U Unrestricted.
M With a member, ie casual visitors are not allowed. Only visitors playing with a member are permitted on the days stated.
H Handicap cerificate required.
I Introduction, ie visitors are permitted on the days stated if they have a letter of introduction from their own club or their own club's membership card.
XL No ladies allowed on the days stated.
NA No visitors allowed.
SOC Recognised Golfing Societies welcome if previous arrangements made with secretary.
CR Course Rating (Europe)

The following information is as up to date as possible at the time of going to press. For the accuracy of this information we are indebted to the club secretaries who supply the details, but we are always pleased to be notified of any inaccuracies.

Great Britain and Ireland County Index

List of new entries in 1998

England

Cambridgeshire
Cambridge
Malton

Channel Islands
Les Ormes

Cheshire
Antrobus
Styal

Cornwall
Trethorne

Derbyshire
Brailsford

Devon
Portmore Golf Park
Teign Valley

Durham
The Wynyard

Essex
Elsenham Golf Centre

Gloucestershire
Kendleshire

Hampshire
The Hampshire
Park

Lancashire
Mossock Hall

Leicestershire
Six Hills

Lincolnshire
Forest Pines
Waltham Windmill

Merseyside
Houghwood

Norfolk
Caldecott Hall

Northamptonshire
Kingfisher CC
Stoke Albany

Northumberland
Linden Hall

Oxfordshire
Kirtlington
The Springs

Sussex (West)
Rustington

Yorkshire (East)
Allerthorpe Park
Kilnwick Percy

Yorkshire (South)
Robin Hood
Rother Valley

Yorkshire (West)
Crow Nest Park
Fardew
The Manor

Scotland

Aberdeenshire
Longside
Meldrum House

Fife
Charleton

Midlothian
Melville Golf Centre

Inverness
Castle Heather

Perth & Kinross
Whitemoss

Stirlingshire
Balfron

West Coast
Isle of Harris

Ireland

Co Antrim
Down Royal
Gracehill
Greenacres

Co Carlow
Mount Wolseley

Co Cork
Fernhill

Co Down
Ardminnan
Blackwood
Rockmount
Temple

Co Dublin
Citywest
Swords

Co Galway
Bearna

Co Kerry
Ballyheigue Castle
Kerries
Ross

Co Limerick
Abbeyfeale

Co Louth
Towneley Hall

Co Roscommon
Strokestown

Co Tyrone
Auchnacloy

Co Wexford
Tara Glen

Co Wicklow
Djouce Mountain
Druid's Glen
Powerscourt
Rathsallagh
Roundwood

Wales

Carmarthenshire
Derllys

Denbighshire
Moss Valley
Pen-y-Cae
Plassey

Flintshire
Kinsale

Isle of Anglesey
Storws Wen

Monmouthshire
Wernddu Golf
  Centre

South Glamorgan
Cottrell Park

West Glamorgan
Lakeside

Stop Press

Stoke Albany (1997)
Ashley Road, Stoke Albany, Market Harborough
LE16 8PL, Northamptonshire
Tel   (01858) 535208
Fax   (01858) 535505
Mem 400
Sec   R Want
Pro   A Clifford
Holes 18 L 6132 yds Par 71 SSS 69
V'tors U SOC
Loc   Between Market Harborough and Corby (A427)
Arch Hawtree

England

Bedfordshire

Aspley Guise & Woburn Sands (1914)
West Hill, Aspley Guise, Milton Keynes MK17 8DX

Tel	**(01908) 582264**
Mem	560
Sec	B Hunt (01908) 583596
Pro	D Marsden (01908) 582974
Holes	18 L 6135 yds SSS 70
Recs	Am–67 M Wharton
	Pro–68 P Webster
V'tors	WD–H WE/BH–MH
	SOC–Wed & Fri
Fees	£23 D–£29
Loc	2 miles W of M1 Junction 13
Arch	Herd/Sandow

Aylesbury Vale (1991)
Wing, Leighton Buzzard LU7 0UJ

Tel	**(01525) 240196**
Fax	(01525) 240848
Mem	600
Sec	C Wright (Sec/Mgr)
Pro	D Marsden (01525) 240197
Holes	18 L 6612 yds Par 72 SSS 72
Recs	Am–69 C Beesley (1997)
	Pro–69 D Armor (1993)
V'tors	WD–U WE–U phone first
	SOC–WD
Fees	£10 (£21)
Loc	3 miles W of Leighton
	Buzzard on Wing-Stewkley
	road
Mis	Driving range
Arch	Sq Ldr Don Wright

Beadlow Manor Hotel G&CC (1973)
Beadlow, Shefford SG17 5PH

Tel	**(01525) 860800**
Fax	(01525) 861345
Mem	700
Sec	R Tommey (01525) 843398
Pro	P Hetherington (01525)
	861292
Holes	18 L 6238 yds SSS 71
	18 L 6042 yds SSS 70
Recs	Am–71 C Skinner
	Pro–66 L Fickling
V'tors	U H SOC
Fees	On application
Loc	2 miles W of Shefford on A507
Mis	Driving range

Bedford & County (1912)
Green Lane, Clapham, Bedford MK41 6ET

Tel	**(01234) 352617**
Fax	(01234) 357195
Mem	600
Sec	E Bullock (Mgr)
Pro	E Bullock (01234) 359189
Holes	18 L 6399 yds SSS 70

Recs	Am–66 C Allen (1980),
	SD Folbigg (1990),
	D West (1996)
	Pro–66 M King (1978)
	Ladies–69 R Hudson (1996)
V'tors	WD–U H WE–M SOC
Fees	WD–£27.50
Loc	2 miles NW of Bedford on A6

Bedfordshire (1891)
Bromham Rd, Biddenham, Bedford MK40 4AF

Tel	**(01234) 261669**
Fax	(01234) 261669
Mem	600
Sec	CD Carrington (Gen Mgr)
Pro	P Saunders (01234) 353653
Holes	18 L 6305 yds SSS 70
Recs	Am–63 JC Kemp
	Pro–65 K Warren
V'tors	WD–U phone first WE–M
	before noon SOC–WD
Fees	On application
Loc	2 miles NW of Bedford (A428)

Chalgrave Manor
Dunstable Road, Chalgrave, Toddington LU5 6JN

Tel	**(01525) 876556**
Fax	(01525) 876556
Mem	450
Sec	S Rumball
Pro	M Brewer (01525) 876554
Holes	18 L 6382 yds Par 72 SSS 70
Recs	Am–69 M Parrett (1995)
	Pro–69 M Brewer (1994)
V'tors	U SOC–WD
Fees	£10 (£15)
Loc	2 miles W of M1 Junction 12
	on A5120
Mis	Practice range
Arch	Mike Palmer

Colmworth (1992)
New Road, Colmworth MK44 2NV

Tel	**(01234) 378181**
Fax	(01234) 376235
Mem	350
Sec	P Watmough
	(01234) 266636
Pro	S Bryden (01234) 378822
Holes	18 L 6420 yds Par 70 SSS 71
V'tors	U SOC
Fees	£10 (£15)
Loc	6 miles N of Bedford,
	off Kimbolton road
Arch	John Glasgow

Colworth (1985)
Unilever Research, Sharnbrook, Bedford MK44 1LQ

Tel	**(01234) 222076**
Mem	405
Sec	S Pound
Holes	9 L 2626 yds Par 68 SSS 66
Recs	Am–69 W Young (1997)

V'tors	M
Fees	D–£6
Loc	Sharnbrook, 10 miles N of
	Bedford, off A6

Dunstable Downs (1907)
Whipsnade Road, Dunstable LU6 2NB

Tel	**(01582) 604472**
Fax	(01582) 478700
Mem	640
Sec	JP Pyne
Pro	M Weldon (01582) 662806
Holes	18 L 6255 yds SSS 70
Recs	Am–64 J Todd (1989)
	Pro–64 K Golding (1992)
V'tors	WD–H WE–M SOC–WD exc
	Wed
Fees	£18 D–£28
Loc	2 miles SW of Dunstable on
	B4541. M1 Junction 11
Arch	James Braid

Griffin (1985)
Chaul End Road, Caddington LU1 4AX

Tel	**(01582) 415573**
Mem	450
Sec	Mrs J Johnson
Holes	18 L 6161 yds Par 71 SSS 69
Recs	Am–63 M Ecart (1993)
V'tors	WD–U WE/BH–phone first
	SOC
Fees	D–£10 (£15)
Loc	3 miles W of Luton on A505
	between Dunstable and
	Caddington. M1 Junction 11

Henlow (1985)
Henlow Camp, Henlow SG16 6DN

Tel	**(01462) 851515 Ext 7083**
Fax	(01462) 851515 Ext 7687
Mem	250
Sec	CJ Harwood (01462) 851515
	(Ext 7769)
Pro	Beverley Huke (01908) 310247
Holes	9 L 5618 yds SSS 67
Recs	Am–68 R Shimwell (1995)
V'tors	M
Fees	D–£5
Loc	3 miles SE of Shefford on
	A600

John O'Gaunt (1948)
Sutton Park, Sandy, Biggleswade SG19 2LY

Tel	**(01767) 260360**
Fax	(01767) 261381
Mem	1450
Sec	To be appointed
Pro	P Round (01767) 260094
Holes	John O'Gaunt 18 L 6513 yds
	SSS 71
	Carthagena 18 L 5869 yds
	SSS 69
Recs	Am–64 N Wharton
	Pro–67 SC Evans

V'tors H–phone first SOC–WD
Fees £45 (£50)
Loc 3 miles NE of Biggleswade
on B1040
Arch Hawtree

Leighton Buzzard

(1925)
*Plantation Road, Leighton Buzzard
LU7 7JF*
Tel (01525) 373811/373812
Mem 650
Sec J Burchell (01525) 373811
Pro L Scarbrow (01525) 372143
Holes 18 L 6101 yds SSS 70
Recs Am–66 S Wells (1993)
Pro–66 N Brown (1997)
V'tors WD exc Tues–U H
WE/BH–MH
Fees £20 D–£27
Loc Heath and Reach, 1 mile N of
Leighton Buzzard. M1
Junction 12

Millbrook (1980)

Ampthill MK45 2JB
Tel (01525) 840252
Fax (01525) 406249
Mem 520
Sec M Williamson (Mgr)
Pro D Armor (01525) 402269
Holes 18 L 6530 yds SSS 71
V'tors WD–U exc Thurs WE–NA
before 2pm
Fees £15 (£25)
Loc 4 miles from M1 Junctions 12
or 13 on A507
Arch W Sutherland

Mount Pleasant (1992)

Pay and play
*Station Road, Lower Stondon, Henlow
SG16 6JL*
Tel (01462) 850999
Fax (01462) 850257
Mem 300
Sec D Simkins (Prop)
Pro M Roberts
Holes 9 L 6003 yds Par 70 SSS 69
V'tors U SOC–WD
Fees 9 holes–£6 (£8);
18 holes–£10.50 (£14.50)
Loc 4 miles N of Hitchin, off A600
Arch Derek Young

Mowsbury (1975)

Public
Kimbolton Road, Bedford MK41 8DQ
Tel (01234) 216374/771041
Mem 611
Sec LW Allan
Pro M Summers
Holes 18 L 6514 yds SSS 71
Recs Am–64
Pro–66
V'tors U
Fees £5 (£8)
Loc 2 miles N of Bedford on B660
Mis Driving range
Arch Hawtree

Pavenham Park (1994)

Pavenham, Bedford MK43 7PE
Tel (01234) 822202
Fax (01234) 826602
Mem 700
Sec M Rizzi
Pro ZL Thompson
Holes 18 L 6353 yds SSS 71
V'tors WD–U WE–M SOC–WD
Fees £15
Loc 4 miles NW of Bedford on A6
Arch Zac Thompson

South Beds (1892)

Warden Hill Road, Luton LU2 7AA
Tel (01582) 575201
Fax (01582) 495381
Mem 850
Sec (01582) 591500
Pro E Cogle (01582) 591209
Holes Galley 18 L 6332 yds SSS 71
Warden 9 L 4954 yds SSS 64
Recs Am–64 I Tottingham (1993)
V'tors Galley WD–U (Ladies
Day–Tues) WE/BH–H exc
comp days–NA SOC
Warden–U
Fees Galley £19 D–£29 (£26
D–£38); Warden £7 (£10)
Loc 3 miles N of Luton, E of A6

Stockwood Park (1973)

Public
*Stockwood Park, London Rd, Luton
LU1 4LX*
Tel (01582) 413704
Fax (01582) 481001
Mem 900
Sec Mrs B McMillan
Pro G McCarthy
Holes 18 L 6049 yds SSS 69
Recs Am–67 D Smith (1993)
Pro–66 T Minshall
V'tors U
Fees £7.50 (£9.90)
Loc 1 mile S of Luton on A6. M1
Junction 10
Mis Driving range

Tilsworth (1972)

Public
*Dunstable Rd, Tilsworth, Dunstable
LU7 9PU*
Tel (01525) 2107210722
Fax (01525) 210465
Mem 370
Pro N Webb (Mgr)
Holes 18 L 5303 yds Par 69 SSS 66
Recs Am–68 J Howells
Pro–65 N Webb
V'tors U SOC
Fees £8 (£10)
Loc 2 miles N of Dunstable (A5)
Mis Driving range

Wyboston Lakes (1978)

Public
Wyboston Lakes, Wyboston MK44 3AL
Tel (01480) 223004
Fax (01480) 216652

Mem 300
Sec B Chinn (Mgr)
Pro P Ashwell (01480) 223004
Holes 18 L 5721 yds SSS 69
Recs Am–69
Pro–64 P Ashwell
V'tors WD–U WE–booking SOC
Fees £10 (£14)
Loc S of St Neots, off A1 and
St Neots by-pass
Mis Driving range
Arch Neil Ockden

Berkshire

Bearwood (1986)

*Mole Road, Sindlesham, Wokingham
RG11 5DB*
Tel (01734) 761330
Fax (01734) 772687
Mem 550
Sec BFC Tustin (Mgr) (01734)
760060
Pro (01734) 760156
Holes 9 L 5614 yds SSS 68
Recs Am–68 J Carpenter (1995)
Pro–66 JB Tustin (1995)
V'tors WD–H before 4pm –M after
4pm WE/BH–M
Fees 18 holes–£15; 9 holes–£8
Loc 1 mile SW of Winnersh, on
B3030. M4 Junction 10
Mis Driving range

Bearwood Lakes (1996)

Bearwood Road, Sindlesham RG41 4SJ
Tel (0118) 979 7900
Fax (0118) 979 2911
Mem 750
Sec S Evans (Gen Mgr)
Pro E Inglis (0118) 978 3030
Holes 18 L 6800 yds Par 72 SSS 72
V'tors M H
Fees £25 (£30)
Loc 1 mile S of M4 Junction 10,
between Wokingham and
Sindlesham
Arch Martin Hawtree

The Berkshire (1928)

Swinley Road, Ascot SL5 8AY
Tel (01344) 621495
Mem 935
Sec Maj PD Clarke
(01344) 621496
Pro P Anderson (01344) 622351
Holes Red 18 L 6369 yds SSS 71
Blue 18 L 6260 yds SSS 71
V'tors WD–I WE/BH–M
Fees On application
Loc 3 miles from Ascot on A332
Arch Herbert Fowler

Bird Hills (1985)

Public
*Drift Road, Hawthorn Hill,
Maidenhead SL6 3ST*
Tel (01628) 771030/75588/26035
Fax (01628) 31023

Sec	A Kibblewhite
Pro	S Kelly, C Cowie
Holes	18 L 6212 yds SSS 69
	Pro–65 S Kelly (1988)
V'tors	U SOC–WD
Fees	On application
Loc	4 miles S of Maidenhead on A330
Mis	Floodlit driving range

Blue Mountain Golf Centre (1993)

Pay and play
Wood Lane, Binfield RG42 4EX

Tel	(01344) 300220
Fax	(01344) 360960
Mem	1200
Pro	N Dainton
Holes	18 L 6097 yds SSS 70
Recs	Am–69 C Challen (1993)
	Pro–63 P Simpson
V'tors	U SOC
Fees	£14 (£18)
Loc	1 mile W of Bracknell on B3408. M4 Junction 10
Mis	Driving range. Golf Academy

Calcot Park (1930)

Bath Road, Calcot, Reading RG31 7RN

Tel	(0118) 942 7124
Fax	(0118) 945 3373
Mem	750
Sec	T Harris
Pro	IJ Campbell
	(0118) 942 7797
Holes	18 L 6283 yds SSS 70
Recs	Am–65 R Walton (1994)
	Pro–63 C Defoy (1983)
	Ladies–69 L Walton (1992)
V'tors	WD–I H WE/BH–M SOC
Fees	On application
Loc	3 miles W of Reading on A4. M4 Junction 12
Arch	HS Colt

Castle Royle (1994)

Knowl Hill, Reading RG10 9XA

Tel	(01628) 829252
Sec	B Lee, G Payne (Props)
Pro	P Stanwick
Holes	18 L 6700 yds Par 72
V'tors	M
Loc	2 miles W of Maidenhead (A4). M4 Junction 8/9
Arch	Neil Coles

Datchet (1890)

Buccleuch Road, Datchet SL3 9BP

Tel	(01753) 543887
Mem	210 50(L) 25(J)
Sec	J Knight (01753) 541872
Pro	J Goodman (01753) 542755
Holes	9 L 5978 yds SSS 69
Recs	Am–66 S McKee (1996)
	Pro–63 N Wood (1979)
V'tors	WD–U before 3pm –M after 3pm WE–M SOC
Fees	£16 D–£24
Loc	Slough, Windsor 2 miles

Donnington Grove CC

Donnington, Newbury RG13 2LA

Tel	(01635) 581000
Fax	(01635) 552259
Mem	250
Sec	E Tanaka (Mgr)
Pro	G Williams
Holes	18 L 7050 yds Par 72 SSS 74
V'tors	U SOC–WD/BH
Fees	£20 D–£30 (£30 D–£45)
Loc	NW of Newbury, off old Oxford road (B4494) or A4. M4 Junction 13
Arch	Dave Thomas

Donnington Valley (1985)

Old Oxford Road, Donnington, Newbury RG14 3AG

Tel	(01635) 32488
Mem	500
Sec	LC Storey
Pro	N Mitchell
Holes	18 L 4029 yds SSS 60
V'tors	U
Fees	On application
Loc	N of Newbury, off Old Oxford road

Downshire (1973)

Public
Easthampstead Park, Wokingham RG11 3DH

Tel	(01344) 302030
Fax	(01344) 301020
Sec	DM Coles
Pro	W Humphreys
Holes	18 L 6382 yds SSS 70
Recs	Am–67 T Smith
	Pro–66 M King
V'tors	U SOC
Fees	Summer–£12.50 (£15.50)
	Winter–£11 (£12.50)
Loc	Off Nine Mile Ride
Mis	Driving range. Pitch & putt

East Berkshire (1903)

Ravenswood Ave, Crowthorne RG45 6BD

Tel	(01344) 772041
Fax	(01344) 777378
Mem	700
Sec	JF Stocker
Pro	A Roe (01344) 774112
Holes	18 L 6345 yds SSS 70
Recs	Am–64 J Brant (1992)
V'tors	WD–H WE/BH–M SOC
Fees	£35
Loc	Nr Crowthorne Station
Arch	P Paxton

Goring & Streatley (1895)

Rectory Road, Streatley-on-Thames RG8 9QA

Tel	(01491) 872688
Fax	(01491) 875224
Mem	740 115(L) 50(J)
Sec	J Menzies (01491) 873229
Pro	R Mason (01491) 873715
Holes	18 L 6320 yds SSS 70
Recs	Am–65 DG Lane
	Pro–62 P Simpson
V'tors	WD–U WE/BH–M SOC–WD

Fees	£22 D–£30 (£25 D–£40)
Loc	10 miles NW of Reading on A417
Arch	Tom Dunne

Hennerton (1992)

Crazies Hill Road, Wargrave RG10 8LT

Tel	(01734) 401000/404778
Fax	(01734) 401042
Mem	500
Sec	PJ Hearn
Pro	W Farrow (01734) 404778
Holes	9 L 2730 yds SSS 34
Recs	Am–66 C Pilbrow (1994)
V'tors	WD–U WE–pm only SOC
Fees	18 holes–£12 (£18)
	9 holes–£9 (£14)
Loc	Between Maidenhead and Reading (A4/A321)
Mis	Driving range
Arch	Dion Beard

Hurst (1979)

Public
Sandford Lane, Hurst, Wokingham RG10 0SQ

Tel	(01734) 344355
Sec	AG Poncia (Hon)
Pro	P Watson
Holes	9 L 3015 yds SSS 70
Fees	On application
Loc	Reading 5 miles. Wokingham 3 miles

Maidenhead (1896)

Shoppenhangers Road, Maidenhead SL6 2PZ

Tel	(01628) 624693
Mem	600
Sec	JSW Scott
Pro	S Geary (01628) 624067
Holes	18 L 6360 yds SSS 70
Recs	Am–S Maynard (1992)
	Pro–64 AN Walker,
	G Wolstenholme
V'tors	WD–H Fri–M after noon WE–M
Fees	D–£35
Loc	Off A308, nr Maidenhead Station

Mapledurham (1992)

Mapledurham, Reading RG4 7UD

Tel	(01734) 463353
Fax	(01734) 463363
Mem	650
Sec	N Wootten
Pro	D Burton
Holes	18 L 5625 yds SSS 69
V'tors	U
Fees	£14 (£17)
Loc	4 miles NW of Reading, off A4074
Arch	MRM Sandow

Mill Ride (1990)

Mill Ride, Ascot SL5 8LT

Tel	(01344) 886777
Fax	(01344) 886820
Mem	300

Sec G Irvine (Gen Mgr)
Pro M Palmer
Holes 18 L 6752 yds SSS 72
Recs Am–68 G Weeks (1992)
       Pro–64 G Hughesdon
V'tors H SOC
Fees On application
Loc 2 miles W of Ascot
Arch Donald Steel

Newbury & Crookham
(1873)
Bury's Bank Road, Greenham
Common, Newbury RG19 8BZ
Tel (01635) 40035
Fax (01635) 40045
Mem 626
Sec Mrs JR Hearsey
Pro DW Harris (01635) 31201
Holes 18 L 5940 yds SSS 68
Recs Am–63 G Woodham (1996)
       Pro–65 J Lovell (1996)
V'tors WD–U H WE–M (recognised
        club members)
Fees £20
Loc 2 miles SE of Newbury

Newbury Racecourse
(1994)
The Racecourse, Newbury RG14 7NZ
Tel (01635) 551464
Fax (01635) 528354
Mem 300
Sec R Pridham (Mgr)
       (01635) 40015
Pro N Mitchell (01635) 551464
Holes 18 L 6311 yds Par 70 SSS 70
Recs Am–69 E Richardson (1996)
V'tors U SOC
Fees £12 (£16)
Loc 4 miles S of M4 Junction 13
       on A34
Mis Driving range

Reading (1910)
17 Kidmore End Road, Emmer Green,
Reading RG4 8SG
Tel (01734) 472169
Mem 725
Sec T Jackson (01734) 472909
Pro AR Wild (01734) 476115
Holes 18 L 6212 yds SSS 70
Recs Am–66 B Smith
       Pro–64 TP Morrison
V'tors Mon–Thurs–UH
        Fri/WE/BH–M
        SOC–Tues–Thurs
Fees £30
Loc 2 miles N of Reading, off
       Peppard Road (B481)

Royal Ascot (1887)
Winkfield Road, Ascot SL5 7LJ
Tel (01344) 25175
Fax (01344) 872330
Mem 600
Sec NCW Barker
Pro A White (01344) 24656
Holes 18 L 5716 yds SSS 68

Recs Am–65 M Milne,
       G Woodman
       Pro–67 B Lane
V'tors M SOC
Fees On application
Loc On Ascot Heath, inside Ascot
       racecourse. Windsor 4 miles
Arch JH Taylor

The Royal Household
(1901)
Buckingham Palace, London
SW1A 1AA
Tel (0171) 930 4832
Fax (0171) 839 5950
Mem 200
Sec A Barrett
Holes 9 L 4560 yds SSS 62
V'tors Strictly by invitation
Loc Home Park, Windsor Castle
Arch Muir Ferguson

Sand Martins (1993)
Finchampstead Road, Wokingham
RG11 3RQ
Tel (0118) 979 2711
Fax (0118) 977 0282
Mem 790
Sec Sue Grindell (Mgr)
Pro AJ Hall (0118) 977 0265
Holes 18 L 6204 yds Par 70
       SSS 70
Recs Am–69 L Gauthier (1997)
       Pro–64 I Mosey (1997)
V'tors WD–U WE–NA SOC
Fees £22
Loc 1 mile S of Wokingham.
       M4 Junction 10
Mis Driving range
Arch ET Fox

Sonning (1914)
Duffield Road, Sonning, Reading
RG4 6GJ
Tel (0118) 969 3332
Fax (0118) 944 8409
Mem 700
Sec PF Williams
Pro RT McDougall
       (0118) 969 2910
Holes 18 L 6366 yds SSS 70
Recs Am–65 J Lush
       Pro–65 B Lane
V'tors WD–H WE–M
Fees On application
Loc 1¹/₂ miles E of A329(M).
       S of A4, nr Sonning

Sulham Valley (1992)
Pincents Lane, Calcot, Reading
RG3 5UQ
Tel (01734) 305959
Fax (01734) 305002
Mem 700
Sec To be appointed
Pro Tina Tetley
Holes 18 L 6121 yds Par 71
V'tors U SOC
Fees £20 (£25)
Loc M4 Junction 12, 1 mile

Swinley Forest (1909)
Coronation Road, Ascot
SL9 5LE
Tel (01344) 20197
Fax (01344) 874733
Mem 310
Sec IL Pearce
       (01344) 874979
Pro RC Parker
       (01344) 874811
Holes 18 L 5952 yds SSS 69
Recs Am–65 IL Pearce
       Pro–62 R Chapman
V'tors M
Fees £65
Loc S of Ascot
Arch HS Colt

Temple (1909)
Henley Road, Hurley, Maidenhead
SL6 5LH
Tel (01628) 824795
Fax (01628) 828119
Mem 450
Sec Lt Col JCF Hunt
       (01628) 824795
Pro J Whiteley
       (01628) 824254
Holes 18 L 6206 yds SSS 70
Recs Am–63 S Hodsdon
V'tors WD–H WE/BH–M SOC
Fees £25 (£30)
Loc Between Maidenhead and
       Henley on A4130. M4
       Junction 8/9. M40 Junction 4
Arch Willie Park Jr

West Berkshire (1975)
Chaddleworth, Newbury
RG16 0HS
Tel (01488) 638574
Mem 500
Sec Mrs CM Clayton
Pro P Simpson
       (01488) 638851
Holes 18 L 7059 yds SSS 74
Recs Am–71 D Murphy (1993)
       Pro–65 W Grant (1994)
       Ladies–75 D Edwards (1995)
V'tors WD–U WE–M SOC–WD
Fees £16 D–£24
Loc Off A338 to Wantage. M4
       Junction 14

Winter Hill (1976)
Grange Lane, Cookham SL6 9RP
Tel (01628) 527613
Fax (01628) 527613
Mem 800
Sec JE Hoskings
Pro R Frost (01628) 527610
Holes 18 L 6408 yds SSS 71
Recs Am–63 J Ackland-Snow
       (1996)
V'tors WD–U WE–M SOC
Fees £25
Loc Maidenhead 3 miles
Arch Charles Lawrie

Buckinghamshire

Abbey Hill (1975)

Monks Way, Two Mile Ash, Milton Keynes MK8 8AA

Tel	**(01908) 563845**
Mem	500
Sec	Mrs L Bentley
Pro	G Woodham
Holes	18 L 6193 yds SSS 69
	Par 3 course
Recs	Am–67 T Mernagh
	Pro–67 S Roche
V'tors	U
Fees	On application
Loc	2 miles S of Stony Stratford
Mis	Driving range

Aylesbury Golf Centre (1992)

Public

Hulcott Lane, Bierton HP22 5GA

Tel	**(01296) 393644**
Sec	K Partington (Mgr)
Pro	M Kierstenson
Holes	9 L 5488 yds SSS 68
V'tors	U
Fees	£9 (£10)
Loc	1 mile N of Aylesbury on A418
Mis	Driving range. Extension to 18 holes in 1998
Arch	TS Benwell

Beaconsfield (1914)

Seer Green, Beaconsfield HP9 2UR

Tel	**(01494) 676545**
Fax	**(01494) 681148**
Mem	862
Sec	RE Thomas
Pro	M Brothers
	(01494) 676616
Holes	18 L 6487 yds Par 72 SSS 71
Recs	Am–66 D Haines
	Pro–63 E Murray
V'tors	WD–H WE–NA
Fees	£30
Loc	2 miles E of Beaconsfield. M40 Junction 2
Mis	Driving range
Arch	HS Colt

Buckingham (1914)

Tingewick Road, Buckingham MK18 4AE

Tel	**(01280) 813282 (Clubhouse)**
Fax	**(01280) 821812**
Mem	680
Sec	T Gates (Gen Mgr)
	(01280) 815566
Pro	T Gates (01280) 815210
Holes	18 L 6082 yds SSS 69
Recs	Am–67 S Impey (1993)
	Pro–67 S Watson (1990)
V'tors	WD–U WE–M SOC–Tues & Thurs
Fees	£28
Loc	2 miles SW of Buckingham on A421

Buckinghamshire (1992)

Denham Court, Denham Court Drive, Denham UB9 5BG

Tel	**(01895) 835777**
Fax	**(01895) 835210**
Mem	650
Sec	KN Munt (Mgr)
Pro	J O'Leary
Holes	18 L 6880 yds SSS 72
Recs	Am–70 P Kilgour
	Pro–70 G Lee
V'tors	I or M SOC–WD exc Fri
Fees	£35.25 (£47)
Loc	Off A40(M). M25 Junction 16b/M40 Junction 1
Mis	Driving range (Members)
Arch	John Jacobs

Burnham Beeches (1891)

Green Lane, Burnham, Slough SL1 8EG

Tel	**(01628) 661150**
Fax	**(01628) 668968**
Mem	670
Sec	AJ Buckner (Mgr) (01628) 661448
Pro	R Bolton (01628) 661661
Holes	18 L 6449 yds SSS 71
Recs	Am–66 LC Donald
	Pro–64 H Flatman
V'tors	WD–I WE/BH–M H
Fees	£28 D–£42
Loc	4 miles W of Slough

Chalfont Park (1994)

Three Households, Chalfont St Giles HP8 4LW

Tel	**(01494) 876293**
Mem	720
Sec	G Harvey (Golf Dir)
Pro	M Griffiths
Holes	18 L 5300 yds SSS 68
V'tors	U SOC–WD
Fees	£18
Loc	3 miles N of M40 Junction 2
Arch	Jonathan Gaunt

Chartridge Park (1989)

Chartridge, Chesham HP5 2TF

Tel	**(01494) 791772**
Fax	**(01494) 786462**
Mem	700
Sec	Mr & Mrs P Gibbins
Pro	P Gibbins
Holes	18 L 5516 yds SSS 66
Recs	Am–64 S Richards (1997)
	Pro–67 P Gibbins (1995)
V'tors	U SOC
Fees	£20 (£25)
Loc	2 miles NW of Chesham. 9 miles W of M25 Junction 18
Arch	John Jacobs

Chesham & Ley Hill (1900)

Ley Hill, Chesham HP5 1UZ

Tel	**(01494) 784541**
Fax	**(01494) 785506**
Mem	422
Sec	B Durand
Holes	9 L 5240 yds SSS 66
Recs	Am–62 GA Knowes
	Pro–65 M Lovegrove
V'tors	Mon & Thurs–U Wed–U after noon Fri–U before 4pm –M after 4pm Tues–M after 3pm WE/BH–M SOC–Thurs only
Fees	On application
Loc	Chesham 2 miles
Mis	Course closed Sun after 2pm from 1st Apr–30th Sept

Chiltern Forest

Aston Hill, Halton, Aylesbury HP22 5NQ

Tel	**(01296) 631267**
Fax	**(01296) 631267**
Mem	600
Sec	S Thornton (01296) 631267
Pro	C Skeet (01296) 631817
Holes	18 L 5765 yds SSS 70
Recs	Am–68 R Conway-Lye (1992)
	Pro–64 I Mosey,
	M Booth (1997)
V'tors	WD–U WE–M SOC
Fees	D–£23
Loc	5 miles SE of Aylesbury, off A4011

Denham (1910)

Tilehouse Lane, Denham UB9 5DE

Tel	**(01895) 832022**
Fax	**(01895) 835340**
Mem	800
Sec	M Miller
Pro	S Campbell (01895) 832801
Holes	18 L 6439 yds SSS 71
Recs	Am–66 DMA Steel
	Pro–68 J Sheridan
V'tors	Mon–Thurs–I H Fri–Sun/BH–M
Fees	£35 D–£50
Loc	2 miles NW of Uxbridge
Arch	HS Colt

Ellesborough (1906)

Butlers Cross, Aylesbury HP17 0TZ

Tel	**(01296) 622114**
Fax	**(01296) 622114**
Mem	700
Sec	PMJ York (Gen Mgr)
Pro	M Squire (01296) 623126
Holes	18 L 6283 yds SSS 71
Recs	Am–64 C Roake
	Pro–66 T Ashton
V'tors	WE/BH–M WD–I or H SOC–Wed & Thurs only
Fees	On application
Loc	1 mile W of Wendover

Farnham Park (1974)

Public

Park Road, Stoke Poges, Slough SL2 4PJ

Tel	**(01753) 643332**
Mem	600
Sec	Mrs M Brooker
	(01753) 647065
Pro	P Warner
Holes	18 L 6172 yds SSS 71
Recs	Am–66 P Robshaw
	Pro–68 T Bowers

V'tors U
Fees £9 (£12)
Loc 2 miles N of Slough
Arch Hawtree

Flackwell Heath (1905)

Treadaway Road, Flackwell Heath,
High Wycombe HP10 9PE
Tel (01628) 520027
Fax (01628) 530040
Mem 750
Sec Pamela Morgan
(01628) 520929
Pro P Watson (01628) 523017
Holes 18 L 6207 yds SSS 70
Recs Am–63 PJ Collett
Pro–64 M Booth
V'tors WD–H WE–M SOC–Wed &
Thurs
Fees £30
Loc Between High Wycombe and
Beaconsfield, off A40. M40
Junction 3/4

Gerrards Cross (1934)

Chalfont Park, Gerrards Cross
SL9 0QA
Tel (01753) 883263
Fax (01753) 883593
Mem 825
Sec Inger Perkins
Pro M Barr (01753) 885300
Holes 18 L 6212 yds SSS 70
Recs Am–64 R Gill (1997)
Pro–63 AP Barr
V'tors WD–H WE/BH–M SOC
Fees £32 D–£44
Loc 1 mile from Station, off A413

Harewood Downs (1908)

Cokes Lane, Chalfont St Giles
HP8 4TA
Tel (01494) 762308
Fax (01494) 766869
Mem 700
Sec Wg Cdr MR Cannon
(01494) 762184
Pro GC Morris (01494) 764102
Holes 18 L 5958 yds SSS 69
Recs Am–65 AL Parsons
Pro–65 JM Hume
V'tors WD–H WE/BH–H XL before
noon SOC
Fees £27 (£33)
Loc 2 miles E of Amersham, off
A413

Harleyford (1996)

Harleyford Estate, Henley Road,
Marlow SL7 2SP
Tel (01628) 402300
Fax (01628) 478434
Mem 750
Sec R Eades (Mgr)
(01628) 402338
Pro A Barr (01628) 402300
Holes 18 L 6604 yds Par 72 SSS 72
V'tors U H
Fees £40 (£60)
Loc 1 mile W of Marlow
Arch Donald Steel

Hazlemere G&CC

(1982)
Penn Road, Hazlemere, High Wycombe
HP15 7LR
Tel (01494) 714722
Fax (01494) 713914
Mem 850
Sec DE Hudson
Pro SR Morvell
(01494) 718298
Holes 18 L 5855 yds SSS 68
Recs Am–65 N Bennett (1995)
Pro–62 M Booth (1994)
V'tors WD–U WE–booking req
SOC–WD
Fees £25 (£40)
Loc 3 miles NE of High Wycombe
on B474
Arch Terry Murray

Iver (1983)

Hollow Hill Lane, Iver SL0 0JJ
Tel (01753) 655615
Mem 500
Sec G Noble
Pro K Teschner
Holes 9 L 6248 yds SSS 72
Recs Am–68 D Sargood (1990)
V'tors U SOC
Fees 18 holes–£10 (£13.50)
9 holes–£5.50 (£7)
Loc ½ mile from Langley station,
off Langley Park Road. M4
Junction 5, 2 miles

Ivinghoe (1967)

Wellcroft, Ivinghoe, Leighton Buzzard
LU7 9EF
Tel (01296) 668696
Fax (01296) 662755
Mem 250
Sec Mrs SE Garrad
(0296) 662478
Pro PW Garrad
(01296) 668696
Holes 9 L 4508 yds SSS 62
Recs Am–61 J Dillon (1984)
Pro–57 M Flitney (1994)
V'tors WD–U WE–U after 8am
SOC
Fees 18 holes–£7 (£8); 9 holes–£5
Loc 3 miles N of Tring. M1
Junction 11, 5 miles
Arch R Garrad

Lambourne (1992)

Dropmore Road, Burnham SL1 8NF
Tel (01628) 666755
Fax (01628) 663301
Mem 600
Sec W Sheffield
Pro D Hart (Golf Dir) (01628)
662936
Holes 18 L 6771 yds SSS 73
Recs Am–70 C Challen
V'tors H or I
Fees £30 (£40)
Loc 1 mile N of Burnham. M40
Junction 2. M4 Junction 7
Arch Donald Steel

Little Chalfont (1981)

Lodge Lane, Little Chalfont, Amersham
Tel (01494) 764877
Fax (01494) 762860
Mem 400
Sec JM Dunne
Pro B Woodhouse (01494)
762942
Holes 9 L 5852 yds SSS 68
Recs Am–76 D Brown
Pro–65 S Parker
V'tors U SOC
Fees On application
Loc Chalfont & Latimer Station
½ mile
Arch JM Dunne

Mentmore G&CC

(1992)
Mentmore, Leighton Buzzard
LU7 0UA
Tel (01296) 662020
Fax (01296) 662592
Mem 1100
Sec M Fallows (Man Dir)
Pro P Elson
Holes Rothschild 18 L 6777 yds
SSS 72
Rosebery 18 L 6850 yds
SSS 73
V'tors WD–H WE/BH–H by
appointment SOC
Fees £30 D–£45
Loc 4 miles S of Leighton Buzzard
Mis Driving range
Arch Bob Sandow

Princes Risborough

(1990)
Lee Road, Saunderton Lee, Princes
Risborough HP27 9NX
Tel (01844) 346989 (Clubhouse)
Fax (01844) 274938
Mem 400
Sec JF Tubb (Man Dir)
Pro (01844) 274567
Holes 9 L 5017 yds SSS 66 Par 68
Recs Am–68 J Forrest (1994)
Pro–62 M Booth (1994)
V'tors U SOC
Fees £14 (£18)
Loc 7 miles NW of High
Wycombe on A4010
Arch Guy Hunt

Richings Park G&CC

(1996)
North Park, Iver SL0 9DL
Tel (01753) 655352
Fax (01753) 655409
Mem 650
Sec S Hodsdon (Mgr)
(01753) 655370
Pro M Heys (01753) 655352
Holes 18 L 6094 yds Par 70 SSS 69
V'tors WD–U WE–M
Fees £17
Loc Nr M4 Junction 5
Mis Driving range
Arch Alan Higgins

Silverstone (1992)

Pay and play
*Silverstone Road, Stowe, Buckingham
MK18 5LH*

Tel	**(01280) 850005**
Fax	(01280) 850080
Mem	670
Sec	D Mears, J Faulkner (Props)
Pro	R Holt
Holes	18 L 6164 yds SSS 70
V'tors	U–booking advisable SOC–WD
Fees	£8 (£12)
Loc	Opposite Silverstone Race Circuit, N of Buckingham
Mis	Driving range
Arch	David Snell

Stoke Poges (1908)

Park Road, Stoke Poges SL2 4PG

Tel	**(01753) 717170**
Fax	(01753) 717181
Mem	600
Sec	RC Pickering
Pro	T Morrison
Holes	18 L 6670 yds SSS 71
Recs	Am–65 BA Price, V Phillips, D Fisher Pro–65 J Hudson
V'tors	U
Fees	£45 D–£65 W–£100
Loc	2 miles N of Slough
Arch	HS Colt

Stowe (1974)

Stowe, Buckingham MK18 5EH

Mem	300
Sec	Mrs CM Shaw (01280) 813650
Holes	9 L 4573 yds SSS 63
V'tors	WD/WE 8am–1pm & after 7pm–M; School holidays–M SOC
Fees	On application
Loc	M1 Junction 16. 4 miles NW of Buckingham

Thorney Park (1992)

Thorney Mill Lane, Iver SL0 9AL

Tel	**(01895) 422095**
Fax	(01895) 431307
Mem	200
Sec	L Grundon
Pro	A Killing
Holes	9 L 3000 yds SSS 34
Recs	Am–S Walker
V'tors	U SOC
Fees	9 holes–£7 (£9) 18 holes–£10 (£13)
Loc	3 miles N of M4 Junction 5 (B470)
Mis	Practice range
Arch	S Adby

Three Locks (1992)

*Great Brickhill, Milton Keynes
MK17 9BH*

Tel	**(01525) 270470**
Fax	(01525) 270470
Mem	300
Sec	P Critchley

Holes	18 L 6025 yds Par 70 SSS 68
Recs	Am–67 G Tarbox (1995)
V'tors	U SOC exc Sun
Fees	£12.50 (£14.50)
Loc	N of Leighton Buzzard on A4146. M1 Junction 14
Arch	MRM Sandow

Wavendon Golf Centre (1990)

*Lower End Road, Wavendon, Milton
Keynes MK17 8DA*

Tel	**(01908) 281811**
Fax	(01908) 281257
Mem	250
Sec	J Droke
Pro	G Iron
Holes	18 L 5460 yds Par 67 SSS 66 9 hole Par 3 course
V'tors	U SOC
Fees	£10 (£14)
Loc	2 miles W of M1 Junction 13
Mis	Floodlit driving range

Weston Turville (1974)

*New Road, Weston Turville, Aylesbury
HP22 5QT*

Tel	**(01296) 424084**
Fax	(01296) 395376
Mem	600
Sec	BJ Hill
Pro	C George (01296) 425949
Holes	18 L 6100 yds SSS 69
Recs	Am–71 S Allder
V'tors	U
Fees	£15 (£20)
Loc	1 1/2 miles SE of Aylesbury

Wexham Park (1979)

Pay and play
*Wexham Street, Wexham, Slough
SL3 6ND*

Tel	**(01753) 663271**
Fax	(01753) 663210
Mem	850
Sec	B Foyster
Pro	D Morgan (01753) 663425
Holes	18 L 5323 yds SSS 66 Green 9 L 2283 yds SSS 32 Red 9 L 2851 yds SSS 34
V'tors	U SOC–WD/Sat & Sun pm
Fees	18 hole–£10 (£13.50) 9 hole–£5.50 (£7)
Loc	2 miles N of Slough
Mis	Driving range
Arch	David Morgan

Whiteleaf (1904)

*Whiteleaf, Princes Risborough
HP27 0LY*

Tel	**(01844) 343097/274058**
Mem	300
Sec	Mrs F Ward
Pro	KS Ward (01844) 345472
Holes	9 L 5391 yds SSS 66
Recs	Am–66 GE Oates Pro–63 MM Caines
V'tors	WD–U WE–M SOC
Fees	£18
Loc	Princes Risborough 2 miles

Windmill Hill (1972)

Public
*Tattenhoe Lane, Bletchley, Milton
Keynes MK3 7RB*

Tel	**(01908) 648149 (Clubhouse)**
Fax	(01908) 271478
Mem	450
Sec	Mrs PM Long
Pro	C Clingan (01908) 378623
Holes	18 L 6773 yds SSS 72
Recs	Am–69 RJ Long Pro–66 C Defoy
V'tors	U SOC
Fees	£8.50 (£11.85)
Loc	4 miles from M1 Junction 14, on A421
Mis	Floodlit driving range
Arch	Henry Cotton

Woburn (1976)

*Bow Brickhill, Milton Keynes
MK17 9LJ*

Tel	**(01908) 370756**
Fax	(01908) 378436
Sec	A Hay (Man Dir) Glenna Beasley (Sec)
Pro	L Blacklock (01908) 647987
Holes	Duke's 18 L 6961 yds SSS 74 Duchess 18 L 6651 yds SSS 72
Recs	Duke's Pro–63 P Baker, I Woosnam Ladies Pro–64 J Geddes Duchess Ladies Pro–67 S Waugh
V'tors	WD–H (by arrangement) WE–M
Fees	By arrangement
Loc	1/2 mile E of A5. 4 miles W of M1 Junction 13
Arch	Charles Lawrie (Duke's)

Wycombe Heights (1991)

Public
*Rayners Avenue, Loudwater, High
Wycombe HP10 9SW*

Tel	**(01494) 816686**
Fax	(01494) 816728
Mem	1200
Sec	P Talbot (01494) 813185
Pro	A Bishop (01494) 812862
Holes	18 L 6300 yds Par 70 SSS 72 18 hole Par 3 course
V'tors	U SOC
Fees	£11 (£14.95)
Loc	1/2 mile from M40 Junction 3, on A40 to Wycombe
Mis	Driving range
Arch	John Jacobs

Cambridgeshire

Abbotsley (1986)

*Eynesbury Hardwicke, St Neots
PE19 4XN*

Tel	**(01480) 210033/474000**
Fax	(01480) 471018
Mem	550
Sec	Heather Inman
Pro	Vivien Saunders
Holes	18 L 6311 yds SSS 72

Recs Am–70 H Watts (1997)
Pro–69 S Whymark (1984)
V'tors WD/BH–U WE–M before
2.30pm –U after 2.30pm SOC
Fees £25 (£30)
Loc 2 miles SE of St Neots on
B1046. M11 Junction 13
(A428)

Abbotsley Cromwell

Pay and play
*Eynesbury Hardwicke, St Neots
PE19 4XN*
Tel (01480) 215153
Fax (01480) 403280
Mem 250
Sec Heather Inman
Pro G Dixon
Holes 18 L 6087 yds SSS 69
V'tors U SOC
Fees £12 (£15)
Loc 2 miles SE of St Neots on
B1046. M11 Junction 13
(A428)
Mis Floodlit driving range

Bourn (1991)

*Toft Road, Bourn, Cambridge
CB3 7TT*
Tel (01954) 718057
Fax (01954) 718908
Pro C Watson (01954) 718958
Holes 18 L 6417 yds SSS 71
Recs Am–68 A Stubbs (1996)
Pro–67 P Dimmock
V'tors U SOC–WD
Fees On application
Loc 8 miles W of Cambridge, off
B1046. M11 Junction 12

Brampton Park (1991)

*Buckden Road, Brampton, Huntingdon
PE18 8NF*
Tel (01480) 434700
Fax (01480) 411145
Mem 650
Sec MN Staveley (Gen Mgr)
Pro A Currie (01480) 434705
Holes 18 L 6300 yds SSS 72
Recs Am–70 R Beadles (1997)
Pro–67 N Brown (1992)
Ladies–67 P Parker (1995)
V'tors U
Fees £20 D–£30 (D–£40)
Loc 3 miles W of Huntingdon, off
A1/A604
Arch Simon Gidman

Cambridge

*Station Road, Longstanton, Cambridge
CB4 5DR*
Tel (01954) 789388
Mem 200
Sec K Green
Pro G Huggett
Holes 18 L 6736 yds Par 72 SSS 74
V'tors U SOC
Fees £9 (£11)
Loc 12 miles NW of Cambridge,
off A14 (B1050)
Mis Floodlit driving range

Cambridge Meridian

*Comberton Road, Toft, Cambridge
CB3 7RY*
Tel (01223) 264700
Fax (01223) 264701
Mem 610
Sec J Allen (Sec/Mgr)
Pro M Clemons
(01223) 264702
Holes 18 L 6651 yds Par 73
SSS 72
Recs Am–72 G Hopkinson (1994)
V'tors U SOC
Fees £18 (£20)
Loc 3 miles SW of Cambridge on
B1046. M11 Junction 12
Arch Alliss/Clark

Cambridgeshire Moat House (1974)

Bar Hill, Cambridge CB3 8EU
Tel (01954) 780555
Fax (01954) 780010
Mem 550
Sec D Hefferland
Pro D Vernon
(01954) 780098
Holes 18 L 6734 yds SSS 72
Recs Am–68 P Way
Pro–68 P Townsend
V'tors U SOC
Fees £15 D–£25 (£30)
Loc 5 miles NW of Cambridge
on A14

Elton Furze (1993)

*Bullock Road, Haddon, Peterborough
PE7 3TT*
Tel (01832) 280189
Fax (01832) 280299
Mem 440
Sec Angela Hyde
Pro F Kiddie (01832) 280614
Holes 18 L 6289 yds SSS 70
Recs Am–67 E Couduit (1996)
Pro–69 F Kiddie (1994)
V'tors WD–phone in advance SOC
Fees On application
Loc 4 miles W of Peterborough on
old A605
Mis Driving range
Arch Roger Fitton

Ely City (1961)

Cambridge Road, Ely CB7 4HX
Tel (01353) 662751
Fax (01353) 668636
Mem 950
Sec MS Hoare (Mgr)
Pro A George (01353) 663317
(Touring Pro H Baiocchi)
Holes 18 L 6627 yds SSS 72
Recs Am–66 L Yearn
Pro–66 L Trevino
Ladies Am–71 K Miller
Ladies Pro–68 B Lunsford
V'tors WD–H WE–H
SOC–Tues–Fri
Fees £26 (£32)
Loc 12 miles N of Cambridge
Arch Henry Cotton

Girton (1936)

Dodford Lane, Girton CB3 0QE
Tel (01223) 276169
Fax (01223) 277150
Mem 800
Sec Mrs MA Cornwell
Pro S Thomson (01223) 276991
Holes 18 L 6085 yds SSS 69
Recs Am–67 C Sherriff (1993)
V'tors WD–U WE/BH–M SOC
Fees £18 D–£20
Loc 3 miles N of Cambridge
(A604)

The Gog Magog (1901)

Shelford Bottom, Cambridge CB2 4AB
Tel (01223) 247626
Fax (01223) 414990
Mem 1200
Sec I Skellern
Pro I Bamborough (01223)
246058
Holes Old 18 L 6398 yds SSS 70
Wandlebury 18 L 6754 yds
SSS 73
Recs Am–64 RW Guy, MT Seaton,
DWG Woods, L James,
R Claydon, M Landrum,
T Milford, J Cook
Pro–60 J Boast
Ladies–69 J Hockley
V'tors WD–I or H WE/BH–M
SOC–WD exc Wed
Fees Old–£30 D–£37.50
Loc 2 miles S of Cambridge on
A1307 (A604)
Arch Hawtree

Hemingford Abbots (1991)

*New Farm Lodge, Cambridge Road,
Hemingford Abbots PE18 9HQ*
Tel (01480) 495000
Fax (01480) 496149
Mem 410
Sec BJ Smith
Pro B Mylward (01480) 492939
Holes 9 L 5468 yds SSS 68
V'tors WD–U WE–M before 1pm
–U after 1pm
Fees On application
Loc 2 miles S of Huntingdon on
A604
Mis Floodlit driving range

Heydon Grange G & CC (1994)

Heydon, Royston SG8 7NS
Tel (01763) 208988
Fax (01763) 208926
Mem 200
Sec AJ Swatton
Pro S Bonham
Holes 18 L 6512 yds SSS 71
9 L 3249 yds SSS 71
V'tors U SOC
Fees £15 (£20)
Loc 4 miles E of Royston on A505.
M11 Junction 10
Arch Walker/Young

Lakeside Lodge (1992)

Fen Road, Pidley, Huntingdon
PE17 3DD

Tel	**(01487) 740540**
Fax	(01487) 740852
Mem	350
Sec	Mrs J Hopkins
Pro	A Headley (01487) 741541
Holes	18 L 6821 yds SSS 73
	9 hole Par 3 course
V'tors	U SOC
Fees	£9 (£15)
Loc	4 miles N of St Ives on B1040
Mis	Driving range
Arch	A Headley

Malton (1993)

Pay and play
Malton Lane, Meldreth, Royston
SG8 6PE

Tel	**(01763) 262200**
Fax	(01763) 262209
Mem	450
Sec	A Boyce (01638) 751222
Pro	G Dixon (01763) 262200
Holes	18 L 6708 yds Par 72 SSS 72
V'tors	U SOC–exc WE–NA before 11am
Fees	£10 (£12)
Loc	8 miles SW of Cambridge, off A10. 5 miles SW of M11 Junction 11
Mis	Driving range
Arch	Bruce Critchley

March (1922)

Frogs Abbey, Grange Rd, March
PE15 0YH

Tel	**(01354) 652364**
Mem	400
Sec	Lt Cdr LE Taylor RN
Pro	J Hadland
Holes	9 L 6210 yds SSS 70
Recs	Am–67 JW Kisby, J Greenall
V'tors	H SOC–WD
Fees	£15
Loc	18 miles E of Peterborough on A141

Old Nene G&CC (1992)

Muchwood Lane, Bodsey, Ramsey
PE17 1XQ

Tel	**(01487) 813519**
Mem	200
Sec	PB Cade
Pro	S Mills (01487) 710122
Holes	9 L 5675 yds SSS 68
Recs	Am–R Dale (1995)
V'tors	U SOC
Fees	18 holes–£10 (£13) 9 holes–£7 (£9)
Loc	1 mile N of Ramsey, towards Ramsey Mereside
Mis	Driving range
Arch	Richard Edrich

Orton Meadows (1987)

Public
Ham Lane, Peterborough PE2 0UU

Tel	**(01733) 237478**
Mem	626

Sec	Mrs S Ramsay (01733) 234769
Pro	N Grant, J Mitchell
Holes	18 L 5800 yds SSS 68
Recs	Am–69 J Wood (1997)
	Pro–69 J Mitchell (1996)
V'tors	U–phone Pro
Fees	£9.50 (£12)
Loc	2 miles SW of Peterborough on old A605
Mis	12 hole pitch & putt
Arch	D & R Fitton

Peterborough Milton (1937)

Milton Ferry, Peterborough PE6 7AG

Tel	**(01733) 380204**
Fax	(01733) 380489
Mem	800
Sec	Mrs D Adams (01733) 380489
Pro	M Gallagher (01733) 380793
Holes	18 L 6462 yds SSS 72
Recs	Am–66 M Peacock (1995)
	Pro–62 S Bennett (1996)
V'tors	WD–U WE–M SOC
Fees	£20 (£25)
Loc	4 miles W of Peterborough on A47
Arch	James Braid

Ramsey (1964)

4 Abbey Terrace, Ramsey, Huntingdon
PE17 1DD

Tel	**(01487) 812600**
Fax	(01487) 815746
Mem	750
Sec	RAR Hill
Pro	S Scott (01487) 813022
Holes	18 L 6163 yds Par 71 SSS 70
Recs	Am–65 S Train (1996)
	Pro–66 R Robertson (1994)
V'tors	WD–H WE/BH–M SOC
Fees	£25
Loc	12 miles SE of Peterborough
Arch	J Hamilton Stutt

St Ives (1923)

St Ives, Huntingdon PE17 4RS

Tel	**(01480) 64459**
Fax	(01480) 468392
Mem	385
Sec	BE Dunn (01480) 468392
Pro	D Glasby (01480) 466067
Holes	9 L 6100 yds SSS 69
Recs	Am–67 Fl-Lt CJB Murdoch
	Pro–61 P Alliss
V'tors	WD–U H WE–M
Fees	£20
Loc	5 miles E of Huntingdon

St Neot's (1890)

Crosshall Road, St Neot's PE19 4AE

Tel	**(01480) 472363**
Fax	(01480) 472363
Mem	600
Sec	AR Peck (Mgr) (01480) 472363
Pro	G Bithrey (01480) 476513
Holes	18 L 6074 yds SSS 69
Recs	Am–65 O Cousins
	Pro–65 M Gallacher, H Flatman

V'tors	WD–H WE–M
Fees	On application
Loc	By A1/B1048 Junction

Thorney Golf Centre (1991)

Public
English Drove, Thorney, Peterborough
PE6 0TJ

Tel	**(01733) 270570**
Fax	(01733) 270842
Sec	Jane Hind
Pro	M Templeman
Holes	Fen 18 L 6104 yds SSS 69
	Lakes 18 L 6402 yds SSS 71
	9 hole Par 3 course
Recs	Fen Am–71 M Perkins (1992)
	Pro–66 M Templeman (1993)
	Lakes Am–66 I Whittingham (1997)
	Pro–69 J Darroch (1996)
V'tors	Lakes WD–U SOC WE–M
Fees	Fen £6 (£8); Lakes £10 (£16)
Loc	8 miles E of Peterborough, off A47
Mis	Floodlit driving range
Arch	A Dow

Thorpe Wood (1975)

Public
Nene Parkway, Peterborough PE3 6SE

Tel	**(01733) 267701**
Fax	(01733) 332774
Sec	R Palmer
Pro	D Fitton, R Fitton
Holes	18 L 7086 yds SSS 74
Recs	Am–71 J Frankum (1992)
	Pro–71 R Fitton (1986)
	Ladies–72 S Sharpe (1992)
V'tors	U–booking required SOC–WD
Fees	£9.50 (£12)
Loc	3 miles W of Peterborough, on A47
Arch	Alliss/Thomas

Channel Islands

Alderney

Route des Carrieres, Alderney GY9 3YD

Tel	**(01481) 822835**
Fax	(01481) 823609
Mem	320
Sec	HCA Armstrong (01481) 822057
Pro	None
Holes	9 L 5006 yds Par 64 SSS 65
Recs	Am–65 M Hugman
V'tors	U SOC
Fees	£12.50 (£17.50)
Loc	1 mile E of St Anne

La Grande Mare (1994)

Vazon Bay, Castel, Guernsey

Tel	**(01481) 55313**
Fax	(01481) 55194
Mem	650
Sec	J Vermeulen (01481) 53544
Pro	M Groves (01481) 53432

Holes 18 L 5112 yds SSS 66
Recs Am–63 I Thomas (1997)
V'tors U–booking necessary SOC
Fees D–£25 (£28)
Loc Vazon Bay, W coast of Guernsey
Arch Hawtree

Les Mielles G&CC (1994)

Public
St Ouens Bay, Jersey
Tel (01534) 482787
Fax (01534) 485414
Mem 1500
Sec J Le Brun (Golf Dir)
Holes 18 L 5654 yds Par 70
V'tors H or Green Card
Fees £18 (£20)
Loc Five Mile Road, St Ouens Bay
Mis Driving range
Arch Le Brun/Whitehead

La Moye (1902)

La Moye, St Brelade, Jersey JE3 8GQ
Tel (01534) 43401,
(01534) 47166 (Bookings)
Fax (01534) 47289
Mem 1350
Sec CHM Greetham
Pro M Deeley (01534) 43130
Holes 18 L 6664 yds SSS 72
Recs Am–68 T Gray (1996)
Pro–62 G Brand Jr
V'tors I H SOC–9.30–11am and 2.30–4pm WE–after 2.30pm
Fees £40 D–£60 (£45) W–£180
Loc 2 miles from Jersey Airport
Mis Driving range
Arch James Braid

Les Ormes (1996)

Pay and play
Mont à la Brune, St Brelade, Jersey JE3 8FL
Tel (01534) 499077/44464
Fax (01534) 499122
Mem 600
Sec G Stubbs (01534) 44464
Pro A Chamberlain (01534) 499077
Holes 9 L 5018 yds Par 66 SSS 65
V'tors U SOC
Fees 9 holes–£11 (£13); 18 holes–£16 (£20)
Loc Mont à la Brune, nr Airport
Mis Driving range

Royal Guernsey (1890)

L'Ancresse, Guernsey
Tel (01481) 47022
Fax (01481) 43960
Mem 1520
Sec M de Laune (Club Mgr)
R Eggo (Golf Mgr)
Pro N Wood (01481) 45070
Holes 18 L 6206 yds SSS 70
Recs Am–64 R Eggo (1986)
Pro–64 P Cunningham
V'tors WD–H WE–M
Fees £34
Loc 3 miles N of St Peter Port
Mis Driving range

Royal Jersey (1878)

Grouville, Jersey JE3 9BD
Tel (01534) 854416
Fax (01534) 854684
Mem 1300
Sec RC Leader
Pro T Horton (01534) 852234
Holes 18 L 6059 yds SSS 70
Recs Am–64 R Harrop (1989)
Pro–64 P Le Chevalier (1988)
V'tors WD–H after 10am WE/BH–H after 2.30pm
Fees £40 (£40)
Loc 4 miles E of St Helier

St Clements (1925)

Public
St Clements, Jersey JE2 6QN
Tel (01534) 821938
Pro R Marks
Holes 9 L 3972 yds SSS 61
Recs Am–61 T Gray, B McCarthy
V'tors U exc Sun am–NA
Fees On application
Loc 1 mile E of St Helier

St Pierre Park

Rohais, St Peter Port, Guernsey GY1 1FD
Tel (01481) 727039
Mem 290
Pro R Corbet (Mgr)
Holes 9 hole Par 3 course
V'tors U SOC
Fees 18 holes–£15 (£17)
Loc 1 mile W of St Peter Port
Mis Driving range
Arch Tony Jacklin

Cheshire

Alder Root (1993)

Alder Root Lane, Winwick, Warrington WA2 8RZ
Tel (01925) 291919
Fax (01925) 291919
Mem 450
Sec Mrs K Young
Pro T Yarwood (01925) 291932
Holes 10 L 5820 yds Par 69 SSS 68
Recs Am–67 I Dallimore (1996)
V'tors WD–U SOC
Fees £16 (£18)
Loc 4 miles N of Warrington (A49). M6 Junction 22. M62 Junction 9
Arch Millington/Lander

Alderley Edge (1907)

Brook Lane, Alderley Edge SK9 7RU
Tel (01625) 585583
Mem 212 90(L) 40(J) 40(5)
Sec JBD Page
Pro P Bowring (01625) 584493
Holes 9 L 5823 yds SSS 68
Recs Am–62 RF Brindle (1993)
Pro–63 MJ Slater (1994)
V'tors M or H SOC
Fees £18 (£22)
Loc 12 miles S of Manchester

Altrincham Municipal (1893)

Public
Stockport Road, Timperley, Altrincham WA15 7LP
Tel (0161) 928 0761
Mem 276
Sec RA Berrisford
Pro S Partington
Holes 18 L 6204 yds Par 71 SSS 69
Recs Am–67
Pro–67
V'tors U
Fees £6 (£8.40)
Loc 1 mile W of Altrincham (A560)
Mis Driving range

Alvaston Hall (1992)

Middlewich Road, Nantwich CW5 6PD
Tel (01270) 624341
Mem 296
Sec MJ Conroy
Pro K Valentine
Holes 9 L 3612 yds Par 64 SSS 59
Recs Am–64 MJ Conroy (1995)
V'tors U
Fees £9 (£9)
Loc 11 miles W of M6 Junction 18 on A530
Mis Driving range
Arch K Valentine

Antrobus

Foggs Lane, Antrobus, Northwich CW9 6JQ
Tel (01925) 730890
Fax (01925) 730100
Mem 550
Sec Miss C Axford
Pro P Farrance (01925) 730900
Holes 18 L 6220 yds Par 72 SSS 72
V'tors H SOC
Fees £18 (£20)
Loc Nr M56 Junction 10, on A559 to Northwich
Mis Driving range
Arch M Slater

Ashton-on-Mersey (1897)

Church Lane, Sale M33 5QQ
Tel (0161) 973 3220
Mem 180 70(L) 40(J)
Sec DE McMahon (0161) 976 4390
Pro MJ Williams (0161) 962 3727
Holes 9 L 3073 yds SSS 69
Recs Am–66 P Bolton (1997)
Pro–67 R Williamson, D Cooper, MJ Williams
V'tors WD–U H exc Tues–NA before 3pm WE–M
Fees £18
Loc 5 miles W of Manchester. M63 Junction 7, 1½ miles

Astbury (1922)

Peel Lane, Astbury, Congleton CW12 4RE
Tel (01260) 272772 (Clubhouse)
Mem 700
Sec C Radley (01260) 279139

Pro A Salt (01260) 298663
Holes 18 L 6296 yds SSS 70
Recs Am–61 IA Jones (1996)
Pro–69 I Mosey (1979)
V'tors WD–H or M WE–M
SOC–Thurs only
Fees £25 SOC–£20
Loc 1 mile S of Congleton, off A34

Birchwood (1979)

Kelvin Close, Birchwood, Warrington WA3 7PB
Tel (01925) 818819
Fax (01925) 822403
Mem 745
Sec A Harper
Pro P McEwan (01925) 816574
Holes 18 L 6727 yds Par 71 SSS 73
Recs Am–67 A Stokes
Pro–65 P Affleck
V'tors U SOC–Mon/Wed/Thurs
Fees £18 D–£26 (£34)
Loc M62 Junction 11, 2 miles.
Signs to 'Science Park North'
Arch TJA Macauley

Bramall Park (1894)

20 Manor Road, Bramhall, Stockport SK7 3LY
Tel (0161) 485 3119 (Clubhouse)
Fax (0161) 485 7101
Mem 715
Sec IR McNeill (0161) 485 7101
Pro M Proffit (0161) 485 2205
Holes 18 L 6214 yds SSS 70
Recs Am–65 SM Hughes (1993)
Pro–63 D Cooper (1984)
V'tors I
Fees £25 (£35)
Loc 8 miles S of Manchester
(A5102)

Bramhall (1905)

Ladythorn Road, Bramhall, Stockport SK7 2EY
Tel (0161) 439 4057
Fax (0161) 439 0264
Mem 300 155(L) 85(J)
Sec BJ Cluley (Hon)
(0161) 439 6092
Pro R Green (0161) 439 1171
Holes 18 L 6300 yds SSS 70
Recs Am–63 G Bradley (1994)
Pro–66 I Higby (1987)
V'tors U exc Thurs SOC–Wed
Fees £24 D–£28 (£31 D–£38)
Loc S of Stockport, off A5102

Carden Park (1993)

Carden, Broxton, Chester CH3 9DQ
Tel (01829) 731600
Fax (01829) 731636
Mem 234
Sec D Nutter, D Llewelyn
Pro D Williams (01829) 731500
Holes Cheshire 18 L 6564 yds
SSS 73; Nicklaus 18L 7010
yds Par 72; 9 hole Par 3 course
Recs Am–74 J Clorley (1995)
Pro–67 S Edwards (1996)
V'tors H SOC
Fees £30 (£30)

Loc 10 miles S of Chester on A534
Mis Golf School. Driving range
Arch Alan Higgins

Cheadle (1885)

Shiers Drive, Cheadle Road, Cheadle SK8 1HW
Tel (0161) 428 2160
Mem 350
Sec RS Lee (0161) 491 4452
Pro S Booth (0161) 428 9878
Holes 9 L 5006 yds SSS 65
Recs Am–63 PS Griffiths (1991)
V'tors H or I exc Tues & Sat–NA
SOC
Fees £18 (£22.50)
Loc 1 mile S of Cheadle. M63
Junction 11, 2 miles

Chester (1901)

Curzon Park, Chester CH4 8AR
Tel (01244) 675130
Fax (01244) 676667
Mem 840
Sec VFC Wood (01244) 677760
Pro G Parton (01244) 671185
Holes 18 L 6508 yds SSS 71
Recs Am–66 R Howell
Pro–66 D Screeton
V'tors U H SOC
Fees £23 (£28)
Loc Chester 1 mile

Congleton (1898)

Biddulph Road, Congleton CW12 3LZ
Tel (01260) 273540
Mem 440
Sec R Walsh
Pro JA Colclough (01260) 271083
Holes 12 L 5103 yds Par 68 SSS 65
Recs Am–60 M Griffiths (1989)
Pro–59 N Coles (1968)
V'tors U H SOC
Fees £14 (£20)
Loc 1¹/₂ miles E of Congleton on
A527

Crewe (1911)

Fields Road, Haslington, Crewe CW1 5TB
Tel (01270) 584227 (Steward)
Fax (01270) 584099
Mem 628
Sec Ms PM Stratton
(01270) 584099
Pro M Booker (01270) 585032
Holes 18 L 6424 yds SSS 71
Recs Am–65 CR Smethurst (1995)
Pro–65 M Brunton (1994)
V'tors WD–U WE/BH–M SOC
Fees £27 After 1pm–£22
Loc 2 miles NE of Crewe Station,
off A534. 5 miles W of M6
Junction 17

Davenport (1913)

Worth Hall, Middlewood Road, Poynton, Stockport SK12 1TS
Tel (01625) 876951
Fax (01625) 876951
Mem 650
Sec DW Scott

Pro W Harris (01625) 877319
Holes 18 L 6027 yds SSS 69
Recs Am–64 R Lauder
Pro–67 B Evans
V'tors U exc Sat–NA SOC–Tues &
Thurs
Fees £25 (£30)
Loc 5 miles S of Stockport

Delamere Forest (1910)

Station Road, Delamere, Northwich CW8 2JE
Tel (01606) 883264
Fax (01606) 883800
Mem 400
Sec TG Owen (01606) 883800
Pro EB Jones (01606) 883307
Holes 18 L 6328 yds SSS 70
Recs Am–65 J Brown
Pro–63 M Bembridge
V'tors WD–U WE–2 ball only SOC
Fees £30 D–£40 (£35)
Loc 10 miles E of Chester, off
B5152
Arch Herbert Fowler

Disley (1889)

Stanley Hall Lane, Disley, Stockport SK12 2JX
Tel (01663) 762071
Mem 500
Sec D English
Pro AG Esplin (01663) 762884
Holes 18 L 6015 yds SSS 69
Recs Am–67 P Leadbetter
Pro–63 B Charles
V'tors WD–U exc Thurs WE/BH–M
Fees £25 (£30)
Loc 6 miles S of Stockport on A6

Dukinfield (1913)

Yew Tree Lane, Dukinfield SK16 5DB
Tel (0161) 338 2340
Mem 300 80(L) 65(J)
Sec L Holmes (0161) 366 0542
Pro J Lowe
Holes 18 L 5203 yds SSS 66
Recs Am–7 C Kenworthy
V'tors WD–U exc Wed pm WE–M
SOC
Fees £16.50
Loc 6 miles E of Manchester

Dunham Forest G&CC (1961)

Oldfield Lane, Altrincham WA14 4TY
Tel (0161) 928 2605
Fax (0161) 929 8975
Mem 600
Sec Mrs S Klaus
Pro I Wrigley (0161) 928 2727
Holes 18 L 6636 yds SSS 72
V'tors WD–U WE/BH–M SOC exc
12–1pm
Fees £35 (£40)
Loc 1 mile SW of Altrincham

Eaton (1965)

Guy Lane, Waverton, Chester CH3 7PH
Tel (01244) 335885
Fax (01244) 335782

Mem 550
Sec GC Parry
Pro N Dunroe (01244) 335826
Holes 18 L 6562 yds SSS 71
Recs Am–69 M Picton (1994)
V'tors H SOC–WD
Fees On application
Loc 3 miles SE of Chester, off A41
Arch Donald Steel

Ellesmere Port (1971)
Public
Chester Road, Childer Thornton, South Wirral L66 1QF
Tel (0151) 339 7689
Mem 350
Sec P Walker
Pro D Yates
Holes 18 L 6432 yds SSS 71
Recs Am–66 A Waterhouse
Pro–67 B Evans, A Caygill
V'tors WD–U WE–arrange with Pro
SOC–WD
Fees £5.60 (£6.50)
Loc 9 miles N of Chester on A41

Frodsham (1990)
Simons Lane, Frodsham WA6 6HE
Tel (01928) 732159
Fax (01928) 734070
Mem 550
Sec EI Roylance
Pro G Tonge (01928) 739442
Holes 18 L 6298 yds SSS 70
V'tors WD/BH–U WE–M
SOC–WD
Fees £25 (£30)
Loc 9 miles NE of Chester (A56).
M56 Junction 12, 3 miles
Arch John Day

Gatley (1911)
Waterfall Farm, Styal Road, Heald Green, Cheadle SK8 3TW
Tel (0161) 437 2091
Mem 400
Sec P Hannam
Pro AJ Ayre (0161) 436 2830
Holes 9 L 5934 yds SSS 68
Recs Am–67 M Hoyland
Pro–63 C Timperley
V'tors WD exc Tues–arrange with
Sec WE/Tues–NA
Fees £20
Loc 7 miles S of Manchester.
Manchester Airport 2 miles

Hale (1903)
Rappax Road, Hale WA15 0NU
Tel (0161) 980 4225
Mem 300
Sec JW Hughes
Pro M Grantham
(0161) 904 0835
Holes 9 L 5780 yds SSS 68
Recs Am–66 PF Veitch
Pro–65 D Durnian
V'tors WD–U exc Thurs–NA before
5pm WE/BH–M SOC
Fees D–£20
Loc 2 miles SE of Altrincham

Hazel Grove (1912)
Hazel Grove, Stockport SK7 6LU
Tel (0161) 483 3217
Mem 550
Sec HAG Carlisle (0161) 483 3978
Pro ME Hill (0161) 483 7272
Holes 18 L 6310 yds SSS 71
Recs Am–65 D Parkin
Pro–67 M Slater
V'tors U
Fees £22.50 (£27.50)
Loc 3 miles S of Stockport (A6)

Heaton Moor (1892)
Mauldeth Road, Heaton Mersey, Stockport SK4 3NX
Tel (0161) 432 2134
Mem 550
Sec JR Smith (0161) 442 8054
Pro SJ Marsh (0161) 432 0846
Holes 18 L 5968 yds SSS 69
Recs Am–66 D Howarth
Pro–66 D Cooper
V'tors U SOC
Fees £23 (£31)
Loc 2 miles from M63 Junction 12,
off A5145

Helsby (1901)
Tower's Lane, Helsby, Warrington WA6 0JB
Tel (01928) 722021
Mem 600
Sec D Leigh
Pro M Jones (01928) 725457
Holes 18 L 6229 yds SSS 70
Recs Am–69 D Stallard
Pro–68 I Wright
V'tors H WE–NA SOC–Tues &
Thurs
Fees £22
Loc 1 mile SE of M56 Junction 14,
off Primrose Lane
Arch James Braid

Heyrose (1990)
Budworth Road, Tabley, Knutsford WA16 0HY
Tel (01565) 733664/733623
Fax (01565) 733664
Mem 700
Sec C Stewart (01565) 733664
Pro M Redrup (01565) 734267
Holes 18 L 6515 yds SSS 71
Pro–68
V'tors U SOC
Fees £19 (£24)
Loc 3 miles W of Knutsford, off
Pickmere Lane. M6 Junction 19

Houldsworth (1910)
Houldsworth Park, Houldsworth Street, Reddish, Stockport SK5 6BN
Tel (0161) 442 9611
Fax (0161) 442 1712
Mem 625
Sec SW Zielinski (0161) 442 1712
Pro D Naylor (0161) 442 1714
Holes 18 L 6209 yds Par 71 SSS 70
Recs Am–67 R Arnold
Pro–63 D Vaughan

V'tors U SOC
Fees £20 (£25)
Loc 4 miles S of Manchester

Knights Grange (1983)
Public
Grange Lane, Winsford CW7 2PT
Tel (01606) 552780
Sec Mrs P Littler (Mgr)
Pro G Moore (01606) 75476
Holes 9 L 5720 yds SSS 68
V'tors U SOC
Fees 18 holes–£3.50 (£5.10)
9 holes–£2.70 (£3.95)
Loc Knights Grange Sports
Complex

Knutsford (1891)
Mereheath Lane, Knutsford WA16 6HS
Tel (01565) 633355
Mem 250
Sec JM Long
Pro A Gillies
Holes 9 L 6288 yds SSS 70
Recs Am–65 B Stockdale
Pro–65 D Cooper
V'tors H exc Wed–NA SOC
Fees £18 (£25)
Loc Knutsford ½ mile

Leigh (1906)
Kenyon Hall, Culcheth, Warrington WA3 4BG
Tel (01925) 763130
Fax (01925) 765097
Mem 700
Sec PF Saunders (01925) 762943
Pro A Baguley (01925) 762013
Holes 18 L 5892 yds SSS 68
Recs Am–63 WN Denton (1997)
Pro–65 A Baguley (1997)
V'tors U H SOC
Fees £26 (£33)
Loc 5 miles NE of Warrington
Arch James Braid

Lymm (1907)
Whitbarrow Road, Lymm WA13 9AN
Tel (01925) 752177
Fax (01925) 755020
Mem 400 100(L) 75(J) 50(5)
Sec A Spencer (01925) 755020
Pro S McCarthy (01925) 755054
Holes 18 L 6304 yds SSS 70
Recs Am–68 CN Brown (1987)
Pro–69 S Lyle (1987)
V'tors WD–H WE–M SOC–Wed
Fees £20 (£28)
Loc 5 miles SE of Warrington. M6
Junction 20

Macclesfield (1889)
The Hollins, Macclesfield SK11 7EA
Tel (01625) 423227
Fax (01625) 260061
Mem 600
Sec A Gronert (01625) 615845
Pro T Taylor (01625) 616952
Holes 18 L 5769 yds SSS 68
Recs Am–66 J Donaldson

V'tors WD/BH–H WE–M SOC–WD
Fees £20 (£25)
Loc SE edge of Macclesfield
Arch Hawtree

Malkins Bank (1980)

Public
Malkins Bank, Sandbach
Tel (01270) 765931
Pro D Wheeler
Holes 18 L 6071 yds SSS 69
Recs Am–65 J Parry (1994)
V'tors U SOC
Fees £6.70 (£7.70) (1996)
Loc 2 miles S of Sandbach via A534/A533. M6 Junction 17

Marple (1892)

Barnsfold Road, Hawk Green, Marple, Stockport SK6 7EL
Tel (0161) 427 2311
Fax (0161) 427 1125
Mem 435 100(L) 60(J)
Sec MR Baguley (0161) 427 1125
Pro D Myers (0161) 427 1195
Holes 18 L 5552 yds SSS 67
Recs Am–66 T Christie (1984)
Pro–64 I Spencer (1995)
V'tors WD–U exc Thurs–NA WE/BH–M SOC
Fees £20 (£30)
Loc 2 miles from High Lane North, off A6

Mellor & Townscliffe (1894)

Tarden, Gibb Lane, Mellor, Stockport SK6 5NA
Tel (0161) 427 2208
Mem 700
Sec G Lee
Pro G Broadley (0161) 427 5759
Holes 18 L 5925 yds SSS 69
Recs Am–68 GD Williams (1988), MG Senior, AJH Ellis (1992) Pro–64 MJ Slater (1977)
V'tors WD–U WE–M SOC
Fees £20 (£27.50)
Loc 7 miles SE of Stockport, off A626

Mere G&CC (1934)

Chester Road, Mere, Knutsford WA16 6LJ
Tel (01565) 830155
Fax (01565) 830713
Mem 375 200(L) 40(J)
Sec WG Squires, Karen Bucksey
Pro P Eyre (01565) 830219
Holes 18 L 6817 yds SSS 73
Recs Am–65 S Andrew (1996) Pro–64 D Clarke (1995)
V'tors WE/BH–M Wed & Fri–M Mon/Tues/Thurs–H SOC
Fees D–£60
Loc 1 mile E of M6 Junction 19. 2 miles W of M56 Junction 7
Mis Driving range–members and green fees only
Arch James Braid

Mersey Valley (1995)

Warrington Road, Bold Heath, Widnes WA8 3XL
Tel (0151) 424 6060
Fax (0151) 424 6060
Mem 550
Sec A Rigby
Pro A Stevenson
Holes 18 L 6300 yds SSS 70
V'tors U
Fees £15 (£20)
Loc M62 Junction 7, 2 miles
Arch RMR Bush

Mottram Hall Hotel (1991)

Wilmslow Road, Mottram St Andrew, Prestbury SK10 4QT
Tel (01625) 828135
Fax (01625) 829284
Mem 500
Sec D Goodwin
Pro T Rastall
Holes 18 L 7006 yds SSS 74 Pro–66 J Matthews (1991)
V'tors U H
Fees £39 (£44)
Loc 4 miles SE of Wilmslow
Arch Dave Thomas

New Mills (1907)

Shaw Marsh, New Mills, Stockport SK12 4QE
Tel (01663) 743485
Mem 350
Sec R Tuson (01663) 747205
Pro S James (01663) 746161
Holes 9 L 5633 yds SSS 67
Recs Am–66 N Coverley Pro–64 E Litchfield
V'tors WD–U WE–M SOC
Fees On application
Loc 8 miles SE of Stockport

Portal G&CC (1992)

Cobblers Cross Lane, Tarporley CW6 0DJ
Tel (01829) 733933
Fax (01829) 733928
Mem 250
Sec D Wills (Golf Dir)
Pro M Slater
Holes 18 L 7037 yds SSS 73 Pro–67 D Clare, D Wills, D Cooper
V'tors U H SOC
Fees £40
Loc 11 miles SE of Chester on A51. M6 Junctions 16 or 19
Mis Driving range
Arch Donald Steel

Portal Premier (1990)

Forest Road, Tarporley CW6 0JA
Tel (01829) 733884
Fax (01829) 733666
Mem 550
Sec K Brain (Golf Dir)
Pro Miss J Statham (01829) 733703

Holes 18 L 6508 yds SSS 71
Recs Am–67 P Mayoh Pro–69 B Rimmer
V'tors U SOC–WD
Fees £30 (£35)
Loc 1 mile N of Tarporley on A49 Warrington road
Mis Driving range
Arch Tim Rouse

Poulton Park (1980)

Dig Lane, Cinnamon Brow
Tel (01925) 812034/822802
Fax (01925) 822802
Mem 360
Sec K Berry
Pro D Newing (01925) 825220
Holes 9 L 4978 metres SSS 66
Recs Am–64 I Quirk
V'tors WD–NA 5–6pm WE–NA 12–2pm
Fees £18 (£19)
Loc Off Crab Lane, Fearnhead

Prestbury (1920)

Macclesfield Road, Prestbury, Macclesfield SK10 4BJ
Tel (01625) 829388
Fax (01625) 828241
Mem 725
Sec Dianne Bradley (01625) 828241
Pro N Summerfield (01625) 828242
Holes 18 L 6359 yds SSS 71
Recs Am–64 P Bolton Pro–67 D Brunton
V'tors WD–I WE–M SOC–Thurs
Fees £38
Loc 2 miles NW of Macclesfield

Pryors Hayes (1993)

Willington Road, Oscroft, Tarvin CH3 8NL
Tel (01829) 741250
Fax (01829) 741250
Mem 600
Sec T Berrisford
Pro N Rothe (01829) 740140
Holes 18 L 6074 yds Par 69 SSS 69
Recs Am–69 D Amitage (1997)
V'tors U SOC
Fees £15 (£20)
Loc 5 miles E of Chester
Arch Day

Queens Park (1985)

Public
Queens Park Drive, Crewe CW2 7SB
Tel (01270) 666724
Mem 250
Sec KF Lear (01270) 628352
Pro R Johnson
Holes 9 L 4920 yds SSS 64
Recs Am–67 A Jennings (1994)
V'tors WD–U WE–U after 12 noon SOC
Fees £4.60 (£6.10)
Loc 2 miles from Crewe, off Victoria Avenue

Reasecheath (1987)

Reasecheath College, Reasecheath,
Nantwich CW5 6DF

Tel	**(01270) 625131**
Fax	(01270) 625665
Mem	350
Sec	GM Oakes (Hon)
Holes	9 L 3726 yds SSS 58
V'tors	M SOC–WD
Fees	£5
Loc	2 miles NW of Nantwich on College campus
Arch	D Mortram

Reddish Vale (1912)

Southcliffe Road, Reddish, Stockport
SK5 7EE

Tel	**(0161) 480 2359**
Fax	(0161) 477 8242
Mem	600
Sec	RG Dean
Pro	RA Brown (0161) 480 3824
Holes	18 L 6086 yds SSS 69
Recs	Am–64 KR Gorton, D Young Pro–67 R Williamson, P Cheetham, D Fletcher
V'tors	WD–U exc 12.30–1.30pm–M WE–M SOC–WD
Fees	£22
Loc	1 mile NNE of Stockport
Arch	Dr A Mackenzie

Ringway (1909)

Hale Mount, Hale Barns, Altrincham
WA15 8SW

Tel	**(0161) 904 9609**
Mem	345 165(L) 41(J)
Sec	D Wright (0161) 980 2630
Pro	N Ryan (0161) 980 8432
Holes	18 L 6494 yds SSS 71
Recs	Am–67 RE Preston Pro–66 M Hollingworth
V'tors	Tues–NA before 3pm Fri–M Sun–NA before 11am SOC
Fees	£28 (£34)
Loc	8 miles S of Manchester, off M56 Junction 6 (A538)

Romiley (1897)

Goosehouse Green, Romiley, Stockport
SK6 4LJ

Tel	**(0161) 430 2392**
Mem	700
Sec	P Trafford
Pro	G Butler (0161) 430 7122
Holes	18 L 6454 yds Par 70 SSS 71
Recs	Am–67 CC Harrison Pro–67 D Roberts
V'tors	U SOC
Fees	£24 (£33)
Loc	Station ¾ mile (B6104)

Runcorn (1909)

Clifton Road, Runcorn WA7 4SU

Tel	**(01928) 572093 (Members)**
Fax	(01928) 574214
Mem	375 80(L) 80(J)
Sec	WB Reading (01928) 574214
Pro	S Dooley (01928) 564791
Holes	18 L 6035 yds SSS 69
Recs	Am–58 L Kopanski (1995)
V'tors	WD–U H exc comp days WE–M SOC
Fees	£18
Loc	Runcorn (A557). M56 Junction 12

St Michaels Jubilee (1977)

Public
Dundalk Road, Widnes WA8 8BS

Tel	**(0151) 424 6230**
Mem	200
Sec	KB Stevenson
Pro	R Bilton (01295) 65241
Holes	18 L 5612 yds SSS 67
Recs	Am–67 I O'Connor (1989)
V'tors	U
Fees	On application

Sale (1913)

Sale Lodge, Golf Road, Sale M33 2XU

Tel	**(0161) 973 3404**
Fax	(0161) 962 4217
Mem	600
Sec	JH Prow (Gen Mgr) (0161) 973 1638
Pro	M Stewart (0161) 973 1730
Holes	18 L 6351 yds SSS 70
Recs	Am–61 C Wetton Pro–65 D Brunton
V'tors	U SOC–WD
Fees	£28 (£33)
Loc	N boundary of Sale. M63 Junction 8

Sandbach (1895)

Middlewich Road, Sandbach
CW11 1FH

Tel	**(01270) 762117**
Mem	240 115(L) 50(J)
Sec	AF Pearson
Holes	9 L 5598 yds SSS 67
Recs	Am–63 DN Hughes
V'tors	WD–U WE/BH–M
Fees	D–£16
Loc	1 mile W of Sandbach (A533). M6 Junction 17

Sandiway (1921)

Chester Road, Sandiway CW8 2DJ

Tel	**(01606) 882606**
Fax	(01606) 888548
Mem	730
Sec	MC Gilyeat (01606) 883247
Pro	W Laird (01606) 883180
Holes	18 L 6435 yds SSS 72
Recs	Am–67 G Stewart Pro–65 D Huish
V'tors	H SOC
Fees	£35 (£40)
Loc	15 miles E of Chester on A556
Arch	Ted Ray

Shrigley Hall (1989)

Shrigley Park, Pott Shrigley,
Macclesfield SK10 5SB

Tel	**(01625) 575757**
Fax	(01625) 573323
Mem	400

Sec	G Hay
Pro	GA Ogden (01625) 575626
Holes	18 L 6281 yds SSS 71
Recs	Am–69 J Murphy (1995) Pro–67 D Durnian (1995)
V'tors	H SOC
Fees	£25 (£30)
Loc	5 miles NE of Macclesfield, off A523. M6 Junction 18
Arch	Donald Steel

Stamford (1901)

Oakfield House, Huddersfield Road,
Stalybridge SK15 3PY

Tel	**(01457) 832126**
Mem	500
Sec	BD Matthews
Pro	B Badger (01457) 834829
Holes	18 L 5701 yds SSS 68
Recs	Am–68 A Derry
V'tors	WD–U WE comp days–after 2.30pm SOC–WD
Fees	On application
Loc	NE boundary of Stalybridge on B6175

Stockport (1906)

Offerton Road, Offerton, Stockport
SK2 5HL

Tel	**(0161) 427 2001 (Members)**
Fax	(0161) 449 8293
Mem	510
Sec	WR Bosanko (0161) 427 8369
Pro	M Peel (0161) 427 2421
Holes	18 L 6326 yds SSS 71
Recs	Am–67 JR Whittaker, S Fraser-Thompson, SM Hughes, P Pearse Pro–66 E Lester Ladies–68 RA Hughes
V'tors	SOC–WD
Fees	£35 (£45)
Loc	4 miles SE of Stockport on A627

Styal (1994)

Station Road, Styal SK9 4JN

Tel	**(01625) 531359**
Fax	(01625) 530063
Mem	650
Sec	W Higham (01625) 530063
Pro	G Traynor (01625) 530063
Holes	18 L 6301 yds Par 71 SSS 70
V'tors	U SOC
Fees	£12 (£16)
Loc	2 miles from M56 Junction 5
Mis	Floodlit driving range
Arch	T Holmes

The Tytherington Club (1986)

Macclesfield SK10 2JP

Tel	**(01625) 434562**
Fax	(01625) 430882
Mem	800
Sec	To be appointed
Pro	J Foss
Holes	18 L 6737 yds SSS 73
Recs	Am–68 J Hodgson Pro–71 P Affleck, L Turner Ladies Pro–63 L Davies

V'tors U H SOC–WD
Fees £28 D–£35 (£34 D–£45)
Loc N of Macclesfield (A523)
Mis Driving range
Arch Thomas/Dawson

Upton-by-Chester (1934)

Upton Lane, Chester CH2 1EE
Tel (01244) 381183
Fax (01244) 376955
Mem 750
Sec JB Durban
Pro PA Gardner (01244) 381333
Holes 18 L 5850 yds SSS 68
Recs Am–62 J Davies
Pro–66 A Perry
V'tors U SOC–WD
Fees £20 (£25)
Loc Off Liverpool road, near
'Frog' PH

Vicars Cross (1939)

*Tarvin Road, Great Barrow, Chester
CH3 7HN*
Tel (01244) 335174
Mem 800
Sec Mrs K Hunt
Pro JA Forsythe (01244) 335595
Holes 18 L 6243 yds SSS 70
V'tors U SOC–Tues & Thurs
Fees £22 (£22)
Loc 3 miles E of Chester on A51
Arch E Parr

Walton Hall (1972)

Public
*Warrington Road, Higher Walton,
Warrington WA4 5LU*
Tel (01925) 266775
Mem 350
Sec I England
Pro J Jackson (01925) 263061
Holes 18 L 6843 yds Par 72 SSS 73
Recs Am–70 R Davies (1988)
V'tors U SOC
Fees £6.50 (£8)
Loc 2 miles S of Warrington. M56
Junctions 10/11
Arch Dave Thomas

Warrington (1903)

Hill Warren, Appleton WA4 5HR
Tel (01925) 261620
Fax (01925) 265933
Mem 875
Sec NF Morrall (01925) 261775
Pro R Mackay (01925) 265431
Holes 18 L 6305 yds SSS 70
Recs Am–66 JR Bennett
Pro–65 EG Lester
V'tors U SOC–Wed
Fees On application
Loc 3 miles S of Warrington

Werneth Low (1912)

*Werneth Low Road, Gee Cross, Hyde
SK14 3AF*
Tel (0161) 368 2503
Mem 315 60(L) 40(J)
Sec R Clapham (0161) 366 0837
Pro T Bacchus

Holes 11 L 6113 yds Par 70 SSS 69
Recs Am–67 S Madden
Pro–57 D Cooper
V'tors U exc Sun–NA Sat/BH–M
SOC
Fees £15
Loc 2 miles SE of Hyde, nr Gee
Cross. M67 Junction 4
Arch Peter Campbell

Widnes (1924)

Highfield Road, Widnes WA8 7DT
Tel (0151) 424 2440
Fax (0151) 495 2849
Mem 600
Sec MM Cresswell
(0151) 424 2995
Pro J O'Brien (0151) 420 7467
Holes 18 L 5729 yds SSS 68
Recs Am–64 F Whitfield (1990)
Pro–64 A Murray (1976)
V'tors WD–U WE–H NA on comp
days SOC–Thurs
Fees £20 (£30)
Loc Station ½ mile

Wilmslow (1889)

*Great Warford, Mobberley, Knutsford
WA16 7AY*
Tel (01565) 872148
Fax (01565) 872172
Mem 780
Sec Mrs MI Padfield
Pro J Nowicki (01565) 873620
Holes 18 L 6607 yds SSS 72
Recs Am–66 C Nowicki (1995)
Pro–62 C Corrigan (1994)
V'tors U H exc Wed–NA before 3pm
Fees £30 (£40)
Loc 3 miles W of Alderley Edge

Cornwall

Bowood (1992)

*Valley Truckle, Lanteglos, Camelford
PL32 9RT*
Tel (01840) 213017
Mem 300
Sec T Japes
Pro B Patterson
Holes 18 L 6692 yds SSS 72
V'tors H (phone first) SOC
Fees £23 (£25)
Loc 2 miles SW of Camelford, off
A39, on to B3266
Mis Driving range

Bude & North Cornwall (1891)

Burn View, Bude EX23 8DA
Tel (01288) 352006
Fax (01288) 356855
Mem 500 220(L) 60(J)
Sec PK Brown
Pro J Yeo
Holes 18 L 6057 yds SSS 70
Recs Am–65 S Rickard
Pro–67 B Austin
Ladies–73 S Currie

V'tors WD–H 9.30–12.30pm,
2–5pm and after 6.30pm
WE–restricted SOC
Fees £20 D–£28 (£25)
Loc Bude town centre

Budock Vean Hotel (1922)

Falmouth TR11 5LG
Tel (01326) 250288
Fax (01326) 250892
Mem 250
Sec E Duncan
Pro A Ramsden (Golf Mgr)
Holes 9 L 5153 yds SSS 65
Recs Am–61 RJ Sadler
Pro–64 D Short
V'tors H
Fees D–£14 (D–£18)
Loc Falmouth 5 miles

Cape Cornwall G&CC (1990)

St Just, Penzance TR19 7NL
Tel (01736) 788611
Fax (01736) 788611
Mem 450
Sec M Waters
Pro S Richards (01736) 788867
Holes 18 L 5650 yds SSS 68
V'tors WD/Sat–U Sun–NA before
noon SOC
Fees £20 (£20)
Loc 1 mile W of St Just. 8 miles W
of Penzance, off A3071
Arch R Hamilton

Carlyon Bay (1926)

Carlyon Bay, St Austell PL25 3RD
Tel (01726) 814250
Fax (01726) 814250
Mem 500
Sec Y Lister, P Clemo
Pro M Rowe (01726) 814228
Holes 18 L 6650 yds SSS 71
Recs Am–68 A Nash
Pro–65 N Coles
V'tors U–book with Pro
Fees £29
Loc 2 miles E of St Austell
Arch J Hamilton Stutt

China Fleet CC (1991)

Saltash PL12 6LJ
Tel (01752) 848668
Fax (01752) 848456
Mem 600
Sec DW O'Sullivan
Pro RA Moore
Holes 18 L 6551 yds SSS 72
Recs Am–69 I Ashenden (1993)
V'tors H–by arrangement SOC
Fees On application
Loc 1 mile from Tamar Bridge,
off A38
Mis Floodlit driving range
Arch Martin Hawtree

Culrose

Royal Naval Air Station, Culdrose
Tel (01326) 574121 Ext 2413
Mem 173

Sec D Wearne (Mgr)
(01326) 572977
Holes 18 L 6432 yds Par 72 SSS 71
Recs Am–74 P McDonald
V'tors M–play restricted to WE and
evenings
Fees D–£5 (D–£5)
Loc 1 mile S of Helston on A3083

Falmouth (1894)

Swanpool Road, Falmouth TR11 5BQ
Tel **(01326) 311262/314296**
Fax (01326) 317783
Mem 500
Sec R Wooldridge
Pro B Patterson (Golf Dir)
Holes 18 L 6061 yds Par 72 SSS 70
V'tors U H SOC
Fees £20 D–£26
Loc ¼ mile W of Swanpool Beach
Mis Driving range

Isles of Scilly (1904)

St Mary's, Isles of Scilly TR21 0NF
Tel **(01720) 422692**
Fax (01720) 422049
Mem 130
Sec S Watt
Holes 9 L 6001 yds SSS 69
Recs Am–70 M Twynham
Pro–66 G Ryall, P Evans
V'tors WD–U Sun–M
Fees £16
Loc Hughtown 1½ miles
Arch Horace Hutchinson

Killiow Golf Park (1987)

Killiow, Kea, Truro TR3 6AG
Tel **(01872) 270246**
Fax (01872) 240915
Mem 545
Sec D Pratt, J Penrose (Prop)
Holes 18 L 3946 yds Par 62
V'tors WD–U WE–NA before
10.30am
Fees £10
Loc 2½ miles S of Truro, off A39
Mis Driving range

Lanhydrock (1991)

Lostwithiel Road, Bodmin PL30 5AQ
Tel **(01208) 73600**
Fax (01208) 77325
Mem 400
Sec G Bond (Gen Mgr)
Pro J Broadway
Holes 18 L 6169 yds Par 71 SSS 68
Recs Am–66 R Binney (1996)
Pro–65 A Nash (1996)
V'tors U SOC
Fees On application
Loc 1 mile S of Bodmin, off B3268
Mis Driving range
Arch J Hamilton Stutt

Launceston (1927)

St Stephen, Launceston PL15 8HF
Tel **(01566) 773442**
Fax (01566) 777506
Mem 900

Sec BJ Grant
Pro J Tozer
Holes 18 L 6407 yds SSS 71
Recs Am–67 C Phillips (1987)
Pro–64 S Little (1989)
V'tors WD–U H WE–NA SOC
Fees D–£24
Loc 1 mile N of Launceston, off
Bude road
Arch J Hamilton Stutt

Looe (1933)

Bin Down, Looe PL13 1PX
Tel **(01503) 240239**
Fax (01503) 240864
Mem 600
Sec G Bond (Gen Mgr)
Pro A MacDonald
Holes 18 L 5940 yds SSS 68
Recs Am–64 I Veale (1993)
V'tors U SOC
Fees On application
Loc 3 miles E of Looe
Arch Harry Vardon

Lostwithiel G&CC (1990)

Lower Polscoe, Lostwithiel PL22 0HQ
Tel **(01208) 873550**
Fax (01208) 873479
Mem 350
Sec D Higman
Pro T Nash (01208) 873822
Holes 18 L 5984 yds Par 72
Pro–70 M Hammond (1990)
V'tors WD–H WE–restricted SOC
Fees £20 (£23)
Loc ½ mile E of Lostwithiel, off
A390
Mis Driving range
Arch Stuart Wood

Merlin (1991)

Mawgan Porth, Newquay TR8 4AD
Tel **(01841) 540222**
Sec Mrs M Oliver
Holes 18 L 5227 yds SSS 67
V'tors U SOC
Fees 18 holes–£10; 9 holes–£7
Loc 2 miles N of Newquay
Mis Driving range
Arch Ross Oliver

Mullion (1895)

Cury, Helston TR12 7BP
Tel **(01326) 240685**
Mem 700
Sec G Fitter
Pro P Blundell (01326) 241176
Holes 18 L 6037 yds SSS 70
V'tors H (restricted comp days and
open days) SOC–WD
Fees £20 W–£70
Loc 6 miles S of Helston
Arch W Sich

Newquay (1890)

Tower Road, Newquay TR7 1LT
Tel **(01637) 872091**
Fax (01637) 874066
Mem 600

Sec G Binney (01637) 874354
Pro A Cullen (01637) 874830
Holes 18 L 6140 yds SSS 69
Recs Am–63 P Clayton (1989).
I Veale (1995)
Pro–63 D Haines (1994)
V'tors WD/Sat–H Sun–H SOC
Fees £21 (£21) W–£80
Loc Newquay town centre
Arch HS Colt

Perranporth (1927)

Budnic Hill, Perranporth TR6 0AB
Tel **(01872) 572454**
Mem 600
Sec PDR Barnes (01872) 573701
Pro DC Mitchell (01872) 572317
Holes 18 L 6286 yds SSS 72
Recs Am–62 P Trew (1993)
Pro–68
V'tors WD–U WE–H SOC
Fees D–£20 (D–£25)
Loc ½ mile NW of Perranporth
Arch James Braid

Praa Sands (1971)

Praa Sands, Penzance TR20 9TQ
Tel **(01736) 763445**
Fax (01736) 763399
Mem 300
Sec D & K Phillips (Props)
Holes 9 L 4122 yds Par 62 SSS 60
Recs Am–59 P Lorys (1981)
V'tors U exc Sun am
Fees £14.50 D–£20
Loc 7 miles E of Penzance on
A394 Penzance-Helston road
Arch RA Hamilton

St Austell (1912)

Tregongeeves, St Austell PL26 7DS
Tel **(01726) 74756**
Mem 780
Sec SH Davey
Pro M Rowe (01726) 68621
Holes 18 L 5981 yds SSS 69
Recs Am–67 AC Nash
Pro–64 AC Nash (1993)
V'tors SOC exc comp days
Fees On application
Loc 1½ miles W of St Austell

St Enodoc (1890)

Rock, Wadebridge PL27 6LD
Tel **(01208) 863216**
Fax (01208) 862976
Mem 1360
Sec Col L Guy OBE
Pro NJ Williams (01208) 862402
Holes Church 18 L 6207 yds SSS 70
Holywell 18 L 4165 yds
SSS 61
Recs Am–65 K Jones
Pro–67 Dai Rees
V'tors Church H–max 24 SOC
Holywell–U
Fees Church £35 (£40)
Holywell £15 (£15)
Loc 6 miles NW of Wadebridge
Arch James Braid

St Kew (1993)
Pay and play
St Kew Highway, Wadebridge, Bodmin PL30 3EF

Tel	(01208) 841500
Fax	(01208) 841500
Mem	250
Sec	MC Cole
Pro	N Rogers
Holes	9 L 4543 yds SSS 62
V'tors	U SOC
Fees	9 holes–£8.50; 18 holes–£13
Loc	2½ miles N of Wadebridge on A39
Mis	Covered driving range
Arch	David Derry

St Mellion Hotel G&CC
(1976)
St Mellion, Saltash PL12 6SD

Tel	(01579) 351351
Fax	(01579) 350537
Mem	800
Sec	R Brewer (Golf Dir)
Pro	A Milton, D Moon
Holes	Old 18 L 5782 yds SSS 68
	Nicklaus 18 L 6651 yds SSS 72
Recs	Nicklaus Am–70 C Eichstedt
	Nicklaus Pro–63 C Mason
V'tors	SOC
Fees	On application
Loc	Tamar Bridge, 5 miles NW of Saltash
Mis	Driving range for members and visitors
Arch	Hamilton Stutt/Nicklaus

Tehidy Park (1922)
Camborne TR14 0HH

Tel	(01209) 842208
Fax	(01209) 843680
Mem	1000
Sec	R Parker
Pro	J Dumbreck (01209) 842914
Holes	18 L 6241 yds SSS 71
Recs	Am–67 N Rogers (1989)
	Pro–68 J Langmead (1990)
V'tors	H
Fees	£22 (£27)
Loc	3 miles N of Camborne

Tregenna Castle Hotel
(1982)
St Ives TR26 2DE

Tel	(01736) 795254 Ext 121
Mem	297
Sec	J Goodman
Holes	18 L 3549 yds SSS 57
Recs	Am–62 G Thomas (1989)
	Pro–54 L Knapp (1986)
V'tors	U SOC
Fees	On application
Loc	St Ives 1 mile, off A3074

Treloy (1991)
Treloy, Newquay TR7 4JN

Tel	(01637) 878554
Mem	145
Sec	J Reid
Holes	9 L 2143 yds SSS 31
V'tors	U SOC
Fees	18 holes–£11.50; 9 holes–£7.50
Loc	2 miles E of Newquay on A3059
Arch	MRM Sandow

Trethorne
Kennards House, Launceston PL15 8QE

Tel	(01566) 86324
Fax	(01566) 86903
Mem	600
Sec	M Davey
Pro	C Kaminski
Holes	18 holes Par 71
V'tors	U
Fees	£16 (£17)
Loc	2 miles SW of Launceston (A30)
Mis	Driving range
Arch	Frank Frayn

Trevose (1924)
Constantine Bay, Padstow PL28 8JB

Tel	(01841) 520208
Fax	(01841) 521057
Mem	960
Sec	P Gammon (Prop)
	PW O'Shea (Sec/Mgr)
Pro	G Alliss (01841) 520261
Holes	18 L 6608 yds SSS 72
	9 L 3031 yds SSS 35
	9 L 1367 yds SSS 29
Recs	Am–67 C Phillips
	Pro–66 N Burch
V'tors	H SOC
Fees	On application
Loc	4 miles W of Padstow
Mis	3 & 4 ball times restricted (phone first)
Arch	HS Colt

Truro (1937)
Treliske, Truro TR1 3LG

Tel	(01872) 272640
Fax	(01872) 278684
Mem	900
Sec	HWD Leicester (Sec/Mgr)
	(01872) 278684
Pro	NK Bicknell (01872) 276595
Holes	18 L 5347 yds SSS 66
Recs	Am–61 AJ Ring
	Pro–60 Nash
V'tors	U H SOC
Fees	£18 (£22)
Loc	2 miles W of Truro on A390
Arch	Colt/Alison/Morrison

West Cornwall (1889)
Lelant, St Ives TR26 3DZ

Tel	(01736) 753401
Mem	825
Sec	MC Lack
Pro	P Atherton (01736) 753177
Holes	18 L 5884 yds SSS 69
Recs	Am–63 P Rowe
	Pro–64 G Emerson
V'tors	H
Fees	£20 (£25)
Loc	2 miles E of St Ives

Whitsand Bay Hotel
(1909)
Portwrinkle, Torpoint PL11 3BU

Tel	(01503) 230470 (Clubhouse)
Fax	(01503) 230329
Mem	400
Sec	GG Dyer (01503) 230164
Pro	S Poole (01503) 230778
Holes	18 L 5885 yds SSS 68
Recs	Am–62 GG Dyer (1981)
	Pro–62 M Faulkner (1948)
V'tors	U SOC
Fees	£15 (£17.50)
Loc	6 miles W of Plymouth
Arch	Willie Fernie

Cumbria

Alston Moor (1906)
The Hermitage, Alston CA9 3DB

Tel	(01434) 381675
Mem	170
Sec	H Robinson (01434) 381354
Holes	10 L 5380 yds SSS 66
Recs	Am–S Embleton (1995)
V'tors	U SOC
Fees	D–£8 (D–£10)
Loc	2 miles S of Alston on B6277

Appleby (1903)
Brackenber Moor, Appleby CA16 6LP

Tel	(017683) 51432
Mem	834
Sec	D Metcalfe (Hon)
Holes	18 L 5901 yds SSS 68
Recs	Am–63 K Bush
	Pro–69 SS Scott
V'tors	U
Fees	£14 (£18)
Loc	2 miles SE of Appleby. ½ mile N of A66
Arch	Willie Fernie

Barrow (1921)
Rakesmoor Lane, Hawcoat, Barrow-in-Furness LA14 4QB

Tel	(01229) 825444
Mem	506 110(L) 80(J)
Sec	J Slater (Hon)
Pro	J McLeod (01229) 832121
Holes	18 L 6209 yds SSS 70
Recs	Am–66 NL Brooks,
	P McNulty (1994)
	Ladies–68 J McCall (1984)
V'tors	U H Ladies Day–Fri SOC
Fees	£15 W–£60
Loc	2 miles E of Barrow, off A590

Brampton (Talkin Tarn)
(1907)
Brampton CA8 1HN

Tel	(016977) 2255
Mem	775
Sec	IJ Meldrum (01228) 23155
Pro	S Harrison (016977) 2000
Holes	18 L 6407 yds Par 72 SSS 71
Recs	Am–66 R Secular (1993),
	R Richardson (1995)
	Ladies–71 L Fletcher (1989)

V'tors U
Fees D–£20 (D–£23)
Loc B6413, 1 mile SE of Brampton
Arch James Braid

Brayton Park (1986)
Pay and play
*Lakeside Inn, Brayton Park, Aspatria
CA5 3TD*
Tel (016973) 20840
Mem 110
Sec D MacLaren
Holes 9 L 2521 yds SSS 65
V'tors U
Fees 9 holes–£5 (£6)
18 holes–£7 (£8)
Loc 1 mile N of Aspatria. 10 miles
N of Cockermouth
Mis Driving range

Carlisle (1908)
Aglionby, Carlisle CA4 8AG
Tel (01228) 513303/513029
Fax (01228) 513303
Mem 735
Sec C Ward (Mgr)
Pro JS More (01228) 513241
Holes 18 L 6278 yds SSS 70
Recs Am–63 C Hislop (1995)
Pro–63 M Archer (1993)
V'tors WD–U exc Tues–NA Sat–NA
Sun–restricted
SOC–Mon/Wed/Fri
Fees £22 D–£33 (£30 D–£40)
Loc ¼ mile E of M6 Junction 43,
on A69
Arch Mackenzie Ross

Carus Green (1996)
Pay and play
Burneside Road, Kendal LA9 6EB
Tel (01539) 721097
Fax (01539) 721097
Mem 250
Sec G Corrie
Pro None
Holes 18 L 5642 yds Par 70 SSS 68
V'tors U SOC
Fees £9 (£9)
Loc 1 mile N of Kendal on
Burneside Road

Casterton
*Sedbergh Road, Casterton, Carnforth
LA6 2LA*
Tel (015242) 71592
Mem 300
Sec J & E Makinson (Props)
Pro R Williamson
Holes 9 L 3015 yds Par 35
Recs Am–63 A Burton (1995)
V'tors U SOC
Fees £9 (£12)
Loc 1 mile NE of Kirkby Lonsdale
on A683. M6 Junction 36,
6 miles
Arch Will Adamson

Cockermouth (1896)
Embleton, Cockermouth CA13 9SG
Tel (017687) 76223/76941
Fax (017687) 76941

Mem 539
Sec RD Pollard (01900) 822650
Holes 18 L 5496 yds SSS 67
Recs Am–62 DL Bragg
V'tors WD–U before 3.30pm exc
Wed Sun–NA before 11am
and 2–3.15pm SOC
Fees £15 (£20)
Loc 4 miles E of Cockermouth
Arch James Braid

Dalston Hall (1990)
Dalston Hall, Dalston, Carlisle CA5 7JX
Tel (01228) 710165
Mem 270
Sec Jane Simpson
Holes 9 L 2700 yds SSS 67
V'tors U
Fees 9 holes–£5 (£6.50)
18 holes–£9 (£12)
Loc 5 miles SW of Carlisle on
B5299. 6 miles W of M6
Junction 42

The Dunnerholme (1905)
*Duddon Road, Askam-in-Furness
LA16 7AW*
Tel (01229) 462675
Mem 440
Sec Mrs ME Tyson
(01229) 581400
Holes 10 L 6162 yds SSS 70
Recs Am–68 H Bayliff
Pro–70 JB Ball
V'tors U
Fees £12 (£15)
Loc 6 miles N of Barrow on A595

Eden (1992)
Crosby-on-Eden, Carlisle CA6 4RA
Tel (01228) 573003
Fax (01228) 818435
Mem 550
Pro S Harrison (01228) 573003
Holes 18 L 6368 yds SSS 72
Recs Am–64 C Hislop (1997)
V'tors U SOC
Fees £15 (£20)
Loc 5 miles NE of Carlisle, off
A689. M6 Junction 44
Mis Driving range

Furness (1872)
*Walney Island, Barrow-in-Furness
LA14 3LN*
Tel (01229) 471232
Mem 700
Sec WT French
Holes 18 L 6363 yds SSS 71
Recs Am–65 M Day (1996)
Pro–65 A Chandler,
GJ Brand (1984)
V'tors H SOC
Fees £17 (£17)

Grange Fell (1952)
*Fell Road, Grange-over-Sands
LA11 6HB*
Tel (015395) 32536
Mem 300

Sec JB Asplin
(015395) 32021
Holes 9 L 4826 metres SSS 66
Recs Am–65 D Airey (1996)
Pro–66 F Robinson
V'tors U
Fees £12 (£17)
Loc W of Grange-over-Sands,
towards Cartmel

Grange-over-Sands
(1919)
*Meathop Road, Grange-over-Sands
LA11 6QX*
Tel (015395) 33180
Fax (015395) 33754
Mem 430 160(L) 30(J)
Sec JR Green (015395) 33754
Pro S Sumner-Roberts
(015395) 35937
Holes 18 L 5938 yds SSS 69
Recs Am–67 DA Shepherd
Pro–67 G Cuthbert
V'tors H SOC
Fees £18 D–£24 (£24 D–£28)
Loc E of Grange, off B5277

Kendal (1891)
The Heights, Kendal LA9 4PQ
Tel (01539) 724079 (Clubhouse),
(01539) 723499 (Bookings)
Mem 731
Sec D Leake, R Maunder (Mgr)
(01539) 733708
Pro D Turner (01539) 723499
Holes 18 L 5515 yds SSS 67
Recs Am–60 P Millar
Pro–62 D Stirling
V'tors U H SOC
Fees £16 (£20)
Loc 1 mile NW of Kendal

Keswick (1978)
Threlkeld Hall, Keswick CA12 4SX
Tel (017687) 79324, (017687)
79010 (Bookings)
Mem 900
Sec JV Simpson
Pro C Hamilton
(017687) 79010
Holes 18 L 6225 yds SSS 72
Recs Am–68 G Watson (1997)
Pro–69 I Clark (1984)
V'tors U H–book with Pro SOC
Fees D–£17 (£22)
Loc 4 miles E of Keswick (A66)
Arch E Brown

Kirkby Lonsdale
*Scaleber Lane, Barbon, Carnforth
LA6 2LJ*
Mem 600 50(J)
Sec G Hall (015242) 76365
Pro C Barrett (015242) 76366
Holes 18 L 6482 yds SSS 71
V'tors U SOC
Fees £18 (£22)
Loc 3 miles N of Kirkby Lonsdale,
off A683
Arch W Squires

Maryport (1905)

Bankend, Maryport CA15 6PA
Tel   (01900) 812605
Mem   380
Sec   A Carlton (01900) 822680
Holes 18 L 6088 yds SSS 70
Recs Am–70 D Roberts (1989)
V'tors U SOC
Fees D–£15 (£20)
Loc   1 mile N of Maryport, off B5300

Penrith (1890)

Salkeld Road, Penrith CA11 8SG
Tel   (01768) 891919/865429
Mem   750
Sec   D Noble (01768) 891919
Pro   G Key (01768) 891919
Holes 18 L 6026 yds SSS 69
Recs Am–63 JD Dockar
         Pro–61 J Metcalfe
V'tors WD–H WE/BH–H
         10.06–11.30am & after 3pm
Fees £20 D–£25 (£25 D–£30)
Loc   ½ mile E of Penrith

St Bees (1931)

Rhoda Grove, Rheda, Frizington CA26 3TE
Tel   (01946) 812105/824300
         (Clubhouse)
Mem   375
Sec   JB Campbell
Holes 9 L 5122 yds SSS 65
Recs Am–62 D Cooper
V'tors U
Fees £10 (£12)
Loc   4 miles S of Whitehaven

Seascale (1893)

Seascale CA20 1QL
Tel   (019467) 28202/28800
Fax   (019467) 28202
Mem   650
Sec   C Taylor (019467) 28202
Pro   J Graham
Holes 18 L 6416 yds Par 71 SSS 71
Recs Am–66 J Graham (1995),
         S Young (1996)
         Pro–65 MF Studds (1992)
V'tors U SOC
Fees £20 D–£25 (£25 D–£30)
Loc   15 miles S of Whitehaven
Arch Campbell/Lowe

Sedbergh (1896)

Catholes-Abbot Holme, Sedbergh LA10 5SS
Tel   (015396) 21551
Fax   (015396) 20993
Mem   350
Sec   AD Lord (015396) 20993
Pro   J Garner
Holes 9 L 5588 yds Par 70 SSS 68
Recs Am–66 A Pickering (1996)
         Pro–66 P Walker (1995)
V'tors U–phone in advance SOC H
Fees £14 D–£20 (£18 D–£25)
Loc   1 mile S of Sedbergh on Dent road. M6 Junction 37, 5 miles
Arch WG Squires

Silecroft (1903)

Silecroft, Millom LA18 4AG
Tel   (01229) 774250
Mem   320
Sec   DLA MacLardie
         (01229) 774342
Holes 9 L 5877 yds SSS 68
Recs Am–66 A Leece (1996)
         Ladies–71 J Currie (1995)
V'tors WD–U WE/BH–restricted SOC
Fees £10 (£15)
Loc   3 miles W of Millom

Silloth-on-Solway (1892)

Silloth, Carlisle CA5 4BL
Tel   (016973) 31304
Fax   (016973) 31782
Mem   800
Sec   JG Proudlock
Pro   C Weatherhead (016973) 32404
Holes 18 L 6614 yds SSS 73
Recs Am–65 J Longcake
V'tors U H–booking advisable SOC
Fees D–£25
Loc   22 miles W of Carlisle (B5302). M6 Junction 43
Arch Willie Park Jr

Silverdale (1906)

Red Bridge Lane, Silverdale, Carnforth LA5 0SP
Tel   (01524) 701300
Mem   500
Sec   PJ Watts (01524) 702074
Holes 12 L 5417 yds SSS 67
V'tors U exc Sun (Summer)–M
Fees £15 (£18)
Loc   3 miles NW of Carnforth, by Silverdale Station

Stony Holme (1974)

Public
St Aidan's Road, Carlisle CA7 1LS
Tel   (01228) 34856
Sec   DJ Daley (01228) 75641
Pro   S Ling
Holes 18 L 5775 yds Par 69 SSS 68
Recs Am–64
V'tors U SOC
Fees On application
Loc   1 mile E of Carlisle, off A69. M6 Junction 43
Arch Frank Pennink

Ulverston (1895)

Bardsea Park, Ulverston LA12 9QJ
Tel   (01229) 582824
Mem   745
Sec   P Wedgwood
Pro   MR Smith (01229) 582806
Holes 18 L 6201 yds SSS 70
Recs Am–64 AJ Edwards (1997)
         Pro–64 P Carman, G Furey (1995)
V'tors H or I SOC
Fees Summer–£25 D–£30 (£30 D–£35); Winter–£14 D–£18 (£18 D–£22)

Loc   1½ miles SW of Ulverston on A5087
Arch Herd/Colt

Windermere (1891)

Cleabarrow, Windermere LA23 3NB
Tel   (015394) 43123
Fax   (015394) 43123
Mem   700
Sec   KR Moffat
Pro   WSM Rooke (015394) 43550
Holes 18 L 5006 yds SSS 65
Recs Am–58 P Chapman (1988)
         Pro–58 D Cooper (1990)
         Ladies–68 J Blaydes (1995)
V'tors H SOC
Fees £23 (£28)
Loc   1½ miles E of Bowness
Arch George Lowe

Workington (1893)

Branthwaite Road, Workington CA14 4SS
Tel   (01900) 603460/67818
Mem   600 110(L) 85(J)
Sec   MWStG Addison
Pro   A Drabble
Holes 18 L 6252 yds SSS 70
Recs Am–65 A Drabble
V'tors H SOC
Fees £15 (£18)
Loc   2 miles SE of Workington
Arch James Braid

Derbyshire

Alfreton (1892)

Oakerthorpe, Alfreton DE55 7DH
Tel   (01773) 832070
Mem   300
Sec   E Brown
Pro   J Mellor (01773) 831901
Holes 11 L 5373 yds SSS 65
Recs Am–60 R Surgey (1995)
         Pro–65 J Smith
V'tors WD–U H before 4.30pm –M after 4.30pm WE–M SOC H
Fees £14 (£18)
Loc   W of Alfreton (A38). M1 Junction 28

Allestree Park (1949)

Public
Allestree Hall, Allestree, Derby
Tel   (01332) 550616
Sec   G Rawson (01332) 552971
Pro   A Carnell
Holes 18 L 5749 yds SSS 68
Recs Am–66 A Oates
V'tors WD–U WE–booking req SOC
Fees On application
Loc   2 miles N of Derby on A6

Ashbourne (1886)

Clifton, Ashbourne DE6 4BN
Tel   (01335) 342078
Mem   400
Sec   RG Lowe (01335) 343457

Holes 9 L 5359 yds SSS 66
V'tors U SOC
Fees £14 (£18)
Loc 2 miles W of Ashbourne on A515
Arch Frank Pennink

Bakewell (1899)

Station Road, Bakewell DE4 1GB
Tel (01629) 812307
Mem 205 67(L) 25(J)
Sec F Parker
Pro None
Holes 9 L 5840 yds SSS 68
Recs Am–63 W Hudson
V'tors WD–U WE/BH–by arrangement SOC
Fees £15 (£20)
Loc 1/2 mile NE of Bakewell and A6

Blue Circle (1985)

Cement Works, Hope S33 2RP
Tel (01433) 622315
Mem 154
Sec DS Smith
Holes 9 L 5350 yds SSS 66
Recs Am–69 B Harper
V'tors M
Loc Hope Valley

Bondhay (1991)

Bondhay Lane, Whitwell, Worksop S80 3EH
Tel (01909) 723608
Fax (01909) 720226
Sec H Hardisty
Pro M Bell
Holes 18 L 6785 yds Par 72
9 hole course
V'tors U SOC
Fees £20 (£25)
Loc 2 miles E of M1 Junction 30, off A619
Mis Driving range
Arch Donald Steel

Brailsford

Pools Head Lane, Brailsford DE6 3BU
Tel (01335) 360096
Mem 46
Sec D Garrett
Pro WD McCarthy, RG Brown
Holes 9 L 3148 yds Par 36 SSS 35
V'tors U SOC
Fees £7.50 (£10)
Loc On A52 between Derby and Ashbourne
Mis Driving range

Breadsall Priory Hotel G&CC (1976)

Moor Road, Morley, Derby DE7 6DL
Tel (01332) 832235
Fax (01332) 833509
Mem 900
Sec G Moran (Gen Mgr)
Pro A Smith (01332) 834425
Holes 18 L 6201 yds SSS 70
18 L 6028 yds SSS 69

Recs Am–66 A Thomas
Pro–66 M Glynn, DJ Russell
V'tors WD–U SOC–WD only
Fees £35–£45
Loc Morley, 5 miles N of Derby (A61)

Burton-on-Trent (1894)

43 Ashby Road East, Burton-on-Trent DE15 0PS
Tel (01283) 568708 (Clubhouse)
Fax (01283) 544551
Mem 600
Sec D Hartley (01283) 544551
Pro G Stafford (01283) 562240
Holes 18 L 6579 yds SSS 71
Recs Am–67 DI Clarke, M Grundy
Pro–65 C Hall (1994)
V'tors I H WD–NA before 9am or 1–2pm SOC
Fees £27 (£30)
Loc 3 miles E of Burton on A50
Arch HS Colt

Buxton & High Peak (1887)

Townend, Buxton SK17 7EN
Tel (01298) 23453
Fax (01298) 26263
Mem 450
Sec JW Critchlow
Pro G Brown (01298) 23112
Holes 18 L 5954 yds SSS 69
Recs Am–66 P Anderson, P Norton
Pro–63 N Hallam
V'tors U
Fees £20 (£25)
Loc NE boundary of Buxton (A6)

Carsington Water (1994)

Pay and play
Carsington, Wirksworth
Tel (01629) 85650
Mem 300
Sec GWR Coleman (Mgr) (01403) 784864
Pro To be appointed
Holes 9 L 6000yds SSS
V'tors U SOC
Fees On application
Loc 8 miles NE of Ashbourne, off B5035
Arch John Ludlow

Cavendish (1925)

Gadley Lane, Buxton SK17 6XD
Tel (01298) 23494
Fax (01298) 79708
Mem 600
Sec JD Rushton
Pro P Hunstone (01298) 25052
Holes 18 L 5833 yds SSS 68
Recs Am–64 I Menzies (1992)
Pro–63 I Buckley (1988)
V'tors U H SOC–by prior arrangement with Pro
Fees £25 (£35)
Loc 3/4 mile W of Buxton Station. St John's Road (A53)
Arch Dr A Mackenzie

Chapel-en-le-Frith (1905)

The Cockyard, Manchester Road, Chapel-en-le-Frith SK23 9UH
Tel (01298) 812118
Fax (01298) 813943
Mem 569
Sec J Hilton (01298) 813943
Pro DJ Cullen (01298) 812118
Holes 18 L 6054 yds SSS 69
Recs Am–67 D Buckle (1996)
Pro–67 J Line (1996)
V'tors U
Fees £20 (£30)
Loc 13 miles SE of Stockport, off A6 (B5470)

Chesterfield (1897)

Walton, Chesterfield S42 7LA
Tel (01246) 279256
Fax (01246) 276622
Mem 590
Sec DA Peacock
Pro M McLean (01246) 276297
Holes 18 L 6247 yds SSS 70
Recs Am–65 I Wyatt
Pro–66 K Nagle, B Hutchison
V'tors WD–U H WE–M SOC
Fees £25–£34
Loc 2 miles SW of Chesterfield on A263

Chesterfield Municipal (1934)

Public
Murray House, Crow Lane, Chesterfield S41 0EQ
Tel (01246) 273887, (01246) 239500 (Bookings)
Sec J Hearnshaw
Pro C Weatherhead (01246) 203960
Holes 18 L 6013 yds SSS 69
9 hole course
Recs Pro–71 K Moss
V'tors U
Fees On application
Loc 1/4 mile past Chesterfield station
Mis Pitch & putt

Chevin (1894)

Duffield, Derby DE56 4EE
Tel (01332) 841864
Fax (01332) 841864
Mem 500 100(L) 80(J) 70(5D)
Sec JA Milner
Pro W Bird (01332) 841112
Holes 18 L 6057 yds SSS 69
Recs Am–64 P Gration (1997)
Pro–64 A Hare (1991)
V'tors WD–U WE–M SOC–WD
Fees £27
Loc 5 miles N of Derby on A6

Derby Sinfin (1923)

Public
Wilmore Road, Sinfin, Derby DE24 9HD
Tel (01332) 766323
Sec P Davidson
Pro J Siddons (01332) 766462

Holes 18 L 6163 yds SSS 69
Recs Am–67 DT James, KS Taylor
Pro–68 C Henderson
V'tors U SOC
Fees On application
Loc 1 mile S of Derby, off A52

Erewash Valley (1905)

Stanton-by-Dale, Ilkeston DE7 4QR
Tel (0115) 932 3258
Fax (0115) 932 2984
Mem 575
Sec JA Beckett (0115) 932 2984
Pro MJ Ronan (0115) 932 4667
Holes 18 L 6492 yds SSS 71
Recs Am–67 R Claydon (1988),
A Dalton (1993)
Pro–68 MJ Ronan (1981)
V'tors WE/BH–NA before noon
SOC–WD
Fees £22 D–£27 (D–£27)
Loc 10 miles E of Derby, off A52.
M1 Junction 25, 3 miles

Glossop & District (1894)

Sheffield Road, Glossop SK13 7PU
Tel (01457) 865247 (Clubhouse)
Mem 250
Sec DM Pridham
Pro D Marsh (01457) 853117
Holes 11 L 5800 yds SSS 68
Recs Am–64 MA Boothroyd
Pro–68 S Sewgolum
V'tors U SOC
Fees £15 (£20)
Loc 1 mile E of Glossop, off A57

Grassmoor Golf Centre

Pay and play
*North Wingfield Road, Grassmoor,
Chesterfield S42 5EA*
Tel (01246) 856044
Fax (01246) 853933
Mem 500
Sec A Clark
Pro P Goldthorpe
Holes 18 L 5721 yds Par 69
Recs Am–70 D Hill, C Bryan
Pro–64 P Goldthorpe
V'tors U SOC
Fees £7.50 (£10)
Loc 2 miles S of Chesterfield on
B6038. M1 Junction 29,
3 miles
Mis Floodlit driving range
Arch Hawtree

Horsley Lodge (1992)

Smalley Mill Road, Horsley DE21 5BL
Tel (01332) 780838
Fax (01332) 781118
Mem 580
Sec G Johnson
Pro P Kent (01332) 780839
Holes 18 L 6400 yds SSS 71
Recs Am–70 S Hughes (1995)
V'tors U H
Fees £18 (£18)
Loc 4 miles NE of Derby. M1
Junction 28
Mis Driving range
Arch GM White

Ilkeston (1929)

Public
*Peewit West End Drive, Ilkeston
DE7 5GH*
Tel (0115) 930 4550
Mem 100
Sec M Ogden (0115) 944 2304
Pro None
Holes 9 L 4116 yds Par 62 SSS 60
Recs Am–62 (1996)
V'tors U SOC–WD
Fees On application
Loc ½ mile E of Ilkeston

Kedleston Park (1947)

Kedleston, Quarndon, Derby DE22 5JD
Tel (01332) 840035
Fax (01332) 842329
Mem 797
Sec K Wilson
Pro DJ Russell (01332) 841685
Holes 18 L 6585 yds SSS 71
Recs Am–64 JP Feeney
Pro–65 K Waters
V'tors WD–H
Fees £27 (£35)
Loc 4 miles N of Derby. National
Trust signs to Kedleston Hall
Arch James Braid

Matlock (1907)

*Chesterfield Road, Matlock Moor,
Matlock DE4 5LZ*
Tel (01629) 582191
Mem 496 78(L) 55(J)
Sec AJ Box
Pro M Whithorn (01629) 584934
Holes 18 L 5804 yds SSS 68
Recs Am–64 N Furniss
Pro–65 W Bird
V'tors WD–U exc
12.30–1.30pm–NA
WE/BH–M SOC–WD
Fees D–£25
Loc 1½ miles NE of Matlock
(A632)

Maywood (1990)

Rushy Lane, Risley, Derby DE7 3ST
Tel (0115) 939 2306
Mem 500
Sec P Moon (Prop)
Pro (0115) 949 0043
Holes 18 L 6424 yds SSS 71
Recs Am–74 M Thomson (1995)
V'tors WD–U before 4pm WE–NA
SOC
Fees £15 (£20)
Loc Between Nottingham and
Derby. M1 Junction 25

Mickleover (1923)

Uttoxeter Road, Mickleover DE3 5AD
Tel (01332) 513339 (Clubhouse)
Mem 760
Sec D Rodgers (01332) 512092
Pro T Coxon (01332) 518662
Holes 18 L 5708 yds SSS 68
Recs Am–62 D Bartlett
Pro–63 A Skingle

V'tors U SOC–Tues & Thurs
Fees £20 (£25)
Loc 3 miles W of Derby on
A516/B5020

Ormonde Fields (1906)

*Nottingham Road, Codnor, Ripley
DE5 9RG*
Tel (01773) 742987
Mem 660
Sec K Constable
Pro P Buttifant
Holes 18 L 6011 yds SSS 69
V'tors U SOC
Fees On application
Loc A610 Ripley to Nottingham
road. M1 Junction 26, 5 miles

Pastures (1969)

*Pastures Hospital, Mickleover
DE3 5DQ*
Tel (01332) 521074
Mem 320
Sec S McWilliams
Holes 9 L 5095 yds SSS 65
Recs Am–62 C Whyatt (1989)
V'tors M SOC–WD
Loc 4 miles W of Derby
Arch JF Pennink

Shirland (1977)

Lower Delves, Shirland DE5 6AU
Tel (01773) 834935
Mem 350
Sec G Brassington
(01246) 852816
Pro NB Hallam (01773) 834935
Holes 18 L 6072 yds SSS 70
Recs Am–67 R Skingle (1990)
Pro–71 NB Hallam (1987)
V'tors WD–U WE–U after 3pm SOC
Fees £20 (£25) (1995)
Loc 1 mile N of Alfreton, off A61
by Shirland Church

Sickleholme (1898)

Bamford, Sheffield S33 0BH
Tel (01433) 651306
Mem 250 100(L) 72(J)
Sec PH Taylor (Mgr)
Pro PH Taylor
Holes 18 L 6064 yds SSS 69
Recs Am–63 IL Fletcher,
DRM Kinsey
Pro–65 AP Highfield
V'tors U exc Wed am
Fees £26 (£32)
Loc W of Sheffield, between
Hathersage and Hope (A625)

Stanedge (1934)

*Walton Hay Farm, Chesterfield
S45 0LW*
Tel (01246) 566156
Mem 300
Sec W Tyzack (01246) 276568
Holes 9 L 4867 yds SSS 64
Recs Am–64 W Steel Jr (1982),
J Weston-Taylor (1991)
Pro–65 A Skingle (1987)

V'tors WD–U before 2pm –M after
2pm Sat–M Sun–NA before
4pm –M after 4pm
Fees £15
Loc 5 miles SW of Chesterfield, off
B5057
Mis Course extension open 1998

Devon

Ashbury (1991)

Fowley Cross, Okehampton EX20 4NL
Tel **(01837) 55453**
Fax (01837) 55468
Mem 50
Sec DJ Fensom
Pro R Cade
Holes 18 L 5536 yds SSS 67
18 L 5623 yds SSS 67
18 hole Par 3 course
V'tors U
Fees £12 (£15)
Loc 4 miles W of Okehampton, off
A3079
Arch DJ Fensom

Axe Cliff (1894)

*Squires Lane, Axmouth, Seaton
EX12 4AB*
Tel **(01297) 24371**
Mem 400
Sec Mrs H Kenworthy
Pro M Dack
Holes 18 L 6040 yds SSS 70
Recs Am–64 P Raven
V'tors U H SOC
Fees £19 (£21)
Loc Nr Yacht Club at Axmouth
Bridge

Bigbury (1923)

Bigbury, Kingsbridge TQ7 4BB
Tel **(01548) 810207**
Mem 850
Sec BJ Perry (01548) 810557
Pro S Lloyd (01548) 810412
Holes 18 L 6076 yds SSS 69
Recs Am–65 CS Yeoman
Pro–65 R Tuddenham,
S Little
V'tors I H SOC
Fees D–£20 (£24)
Loc 15 miles SE of Plymouth

Chulmleigh (1976)

Leigh Road, Chulmleigh EX18 7BL
Tel **(01769) 580519**
Fax (01769) 580519
Mem 100
Sec HM Meadows
Holes Summer 18 L 1450 yds SSS 54
Winter 9 L 2372 yds SSS 56
Recs Am–51 P Andrews (1995)
Pro–48 M Blackwell (1992)
V'tors U
Fees £6.50 D–£12
Loc 1 mile N of A377 at
Chulmleigh
Arch John Goodban

Churston (1890)

Churston, Brixham TQ5 0LA
Tel **(01803) 842218**
Fax (01803) 845738
Mem 750
Sec KP Loosemore
(01803) 842751
Pro N Holman (01803) 843442
Holes 18 L 6201 yds SSS 70
Recs Am–64 RHP Knott (1989)
Pro–64 J Langmead (1995)
Ladies–70 S Guthrie (1995)
V'tors H exc Tues am–NA
Fees £22 (£27)
Loc 5 miles S of Torquay
Arch HS Colt

Dainton Park (1993)

*Totnes Road, Ipplepen, Newton Abbot
TQ12 5TN*
Tel **(01803) 813812**
Mem 500
Sec D Wood
Pro M Tyson
Holes 18 L 6210 yds SSS 70
Recs Am–70 A Davies (1995)
V'tors U SOC
Fees £14.50 (£17)
Loc 2 miles S of Newton Abbot on
A381
Mis Driving range
Arch Adrian Stiff

Dartmouth G&CC (1992)

Blackawton, Totnes TQ9 7DE
Tel **(01803) 712686**
Fax (01803) 712628
Mem 800
Sec S Butterfield
Pro J Fullard (01803) 712650
Holes Ch'ship 18 L 7191 yds SSS 74
Club 9 L 2583 yds SSS 33
V'tors WD–U phone first WE–H
SOC
Fees Ch'ship £25 (£35) Club £10
Loc 4 miles NE of Dartmouth on
A3122
Mis Driving range
Arch Jeremy Pern

Dinnaton (1989)

Ivybridge PL21 9HU
Tel **(01752) 892512/892452**
Fax (01752) 698334
Mem 300
Sec B Rimes
Pro D Ridyard (01752) 691288
Holes 9 L 4100 yds SSS 59
9 hole course Par 64
Recs Am–66 P Tuckwell (1996)
V'tors U SOC
Fees D–£10 (D–£12.50)
Loc 12 miles SE of Plymouth, off
A38/B3213
Arch Pink/Cotton

Downes Crediton (1976)

Hookway, Crediton EX17 3PT
Tel **(01363) 773991**
Fax (01363) 775060
Mem 720

Sec Mrs G Mullins, PT Lee
(01363) 773025
Pro H Finch (01363) 774464
Holes 18 L 5958 yds SSS 69
V'tors H SOC
Fees £18 D–£25 (£22)
Loc 2 miles S of Crediton, off
A377

East Devon (1902)

*North View Road, Budleigh Salterton
EX9 6DQ*
Tel **(01395) 442018**
Mem 850
Sec (01395) 443370
Pro T Underwood (01395)
445195
Holes 18 L 6214 yds SSS 70
Recs Am–65 R Winchester (1987),
R Martin (1992)
Pro–64 G Ryall (1990)
V'tors H SOC–Thurs only
Fees £27 (£35)
Loc 12 miles SE of Exeter

Elfordleigh Hotel G&CC
(1932)

*Colebrook, Plympton, Plymouth
PL7 5EB*
Tel **(01752) 336428**
Fax (01752) 344581
Mem 400
Sec Mrs P Parfitt (01752) 348425
Holes 9 L 5664 yds SSS 67
Recs Am–65 A Moon (1992)
V'tors H–phone first
Fees £15 (£20)
Loc 4 miles E of Plymouth

Exeter G&CC (1895)

Countess Wear, Exeter EX2 7AE
Tel **(01392) 874139**
Fax (01392) 874139
Mem 850
Sec KJ Ham (Golf Mgr)
Pro M Rowett (01392) 875028
Holes 18 L 6000 yds SSS 69
Recs Am–63 G Milne (1988),
D Turnbull (1995)
Pro–62 I Sparks (1990)
V'tors WD–U WE–H SOC–Thurs
Fees D–£25 (D–£25)
Loc 4 miles SE of Exeter
Arch James Braid

Fingle Glen (1992)

Tedburn St Mary, Exeter EX6 6AF
Tel **(01647) 61817**
Fax (01647) 61135
Mem 450
Sec P Miliffe
Pro S Gould
Holes 9 L 2466 yds SSS 63
Recs Am–65 J Breading (1994)
Pro–63 R Troake (1992)
V'tors U SOC
Fees 18 holes–£10 (£14)
9 holes–£7 (£8)
Loc 5 miles W of Exeter on A30
Mis Driving range

Hartland Forest G&CC
(1991)
East Yagland, Wolsery, Bideford
EX39 5RA
Tel   (01237) 431442
Fax   (01237) 431734
Mem 130
Sec   S Barker
Pro   S Barker
Holes 18 L 6015 yds Par 71 SSS 69
V'tors U SOC
Fees On application
Loc   6 miles S of Clovelly, off A39
Arch John Hepplewhite

Hele Park Golf Centre
Pay and play
Ashburton Road, Newton Abbot
TQ12 6JN
Tel   (01626) 336060
Fax   (01626) 332661
Mem 270
Sec   W Stanbury (01626) 336060
Pro   J Langmead
Holes 9 L 2584 yds SSS 65
Recs Am–64 J Beare (1996)
V'tors U
Fees £8.50 (£11.50)
Loc   W of Newton Abbot on A383
Mis   Driving range
Arch M Craig

Holsworthy (1937)
Kilatree, Holsworthy EX22 6LP
Tel   (01409) 253177
Fax   (01409) 253177
Mem 650
Sec   B Megson
Pro   S Chapman (01409) 254771
Holes 18 L 6062 yds SSS 69
Recs Am–64 G Webb (1995)
          Pro–67 G Ryall, R Troake
          (1987)
V'tors WD–U Sun–U after 2.30pm
Fees £15 (£20)
Loc   1 mile W of Holsworthy.
          7 miles E of Bude

Honiton (1896)
Middlehills, Honiton EX14 8TR
Tel   (01404) 44422
Fax   (01404) 42943
Mem 800
Sec   JL Carter
Pro   A Cave (01404) 42943
Holes 18 L 5902 yds SSS 68
Recs Am–67 A March (1992),
          K Harper (1996)
          Pro–66 B Dredge,
          J Langmead (1996)
          Ladies–74 J Easterbrook (1995)
V'tors U (recognised club member)
          SOC
Fees On application
Loc   2 miles S of Honiton

Hurdwick (1990)
Tavistock Hamlets, Tavistock PL19 8PZ
Tel   (01822) 612746
Mem 175

Sec   Maj RW Cullen (Mgr)
Holes 18 L 5217 yds Par 68
V'tors U SOC
Fees £14 (£14)
Loc   1 mile N of Tavistock, on
          Brentor Church road
Arch Hawtree/Bartlett

Ilfracombe (1892)
Hele Bay, Ilfracombe EX34 9RT
Tel   (01271) 862176
Fax   (01271) 867731
Mem 648
Sec   BSR Warren
Pro   D Hoare (01271) 863328
Holes 18 L 5893 yds SSS 69
Recs Am–66 PA Boot (1993),
          P Redmore (1996)
V'tors H SOC WD–NA 12–2pm
          WE/BH–U after 10am –NA
          12–2pm
Fees £19 (£20) 5D–£75
Loc   2 miles E of Ilfracombe,
          towards Combe Martin
Arch TK Weir

Libbaton (1990)
High Bickington, Umberleigh EX37 9BS
Tel   (01769) 560269
Mem 475
Sec   JH Brough
Pro   JN Phillips (01769) 560167
Holes 18 L 6494 yds SSS 72
Recs Am–67 S Herniman (1995)
V'tors U SOC
Fees £15 (£18)
Loc   1 mile S of High Bickington
          on B3217. M5 Junction 27
Mis   Floodlit driving range

Manor House Hotel
(1929)
Moretonhampstead TQ13 8RE
Tel   (01647) 440998
Fax   (01647) 440961
Mem 250
Sec   R Lewis
Pro   R Lewis
Holes 18 L 6016 yds SSS 69
Recs Am–68 G Milne (1989)
          Pro–65 G Emerson (1985)
V'tors U H SOC
Fees £22.50 (£28)
Loc   15 miles SW of Exeter on
          B3212. M5 Junction 31
Mis   Driving range
Arch JF Abercromby

Mortehoe & Woolacombe
(1992)
Easewell, Mortehoe, Ilfracombe
Tel   (01271) 870225
Mem 225
Sec   M Wilkinson (01271) 870745
Holes 9 L 4852 yds SSS 63
Recs Am–66 D Huxtable (1997)
V'tors U
Fees 9 holes–£6; 18 holes–£10
Loc   E of Mortehoe village
Arch David Hoare

Newton Abbot (1930)
Newton Abbot TQ12 6QQ
Tel   (01626) 52460
Fax   (01626) 330210
Mem 886
Sec   R Smith
Pro   M Craig (01626) 62078
Holes 18 L 5862 yds SSS 68
Recs Am–63 M Pym (1989)
          Pro–67 B Barnes (1977)
V'tors H SOC–Thurs
Fees D–£22
Loc   Stover, 3 miles N of Newton
          Abbot on A382
Arch James Braid

Okehampton (1913)
Okehampton EX20 1EF
Tel   (01837) 52113
Fax   (01837) 52734
Mem 500
Sec   CS Hicks
Pro   S Jefferies (01837) 53541
Holes 18 L 5243 yds SSS 67
Recs Am–65 D File Jr (1997)
          Pro–H Finch
V'tors H SOC
Fees On application
Loc   S boundary of Okehampton
Arch JH Taylor

Padbrook Park (1992)
Pay and play
Cullompton EX15 1RU
Tel   (01884) 38286
Fax   (01804) 34359
Mem 450
Sec   R Chard (Mgr)
Pro   S Adwick (01884) 820805
Holes 9 L 6108 yds SSS 70
V'tors U SOC–WD
Fees 18 holes–£10 (£16)
          9 holes–£7 (£8)
Loc   10 miles E of Exeter. M5
          Junction 28, 1 mile
Arch Bob Sandow

Portmore Golf Park (1997)
Pay and play
Landkey Road, Barnstaple EX32 9LB
Tel   (01271) 378378
Fax   (01271) 378378
Mem 60
Sec   C Webber
Pro   S Gould, G Ross
Holes 9 L 3176 yds Par 54
V'tors U
Fees 9 holes–£7 (£8)
          18 holes–£10 (£12)
Loc   1 mile E of Barnstaple, off
          A361
Mis   Floodlit driving range
Arch Hawtree

Royal North Devon (1864)
Golf Links Road, Westward Ho!
EX39 1HD
Tel   (01237) 473824 (Clubhouse)
Fax   (01237) 423456
Mem 1000

Sec (01237) 473817
Pro I Higgins (01237) 477598
Holes 18 L 6653 yds SSS 72
Recs Am–66 D Boughey,
S McCarthy (1995)
Pro–66 P Dawson,
KDG Nagle, MF Foster
Ladies–69 P Johnson
V'tors U H
Fees £28 D–£34 (£30 D–£36)
Loc 2 miles N of Bideford (A39)
Arch Tom Morris

Saunton (1897)

Saunton, Braunton EX33 1LG
Tel (01271) 812436
Fax (01271) 814241
Mem 1250
Sec TC Reynolds
Pro AT Mackenzie (01271) 812013
Holes East 18 L 6729 yds SSS 73
West 18 L 6403 yds SSS 71
Recs East Am–65 M Treleaven
(1993)
Pro–66 J Taylor
West Am–68 PH Watts (1991)
Pro–67 JP Langmead (1996)
V'tors U H SOC
Fees £30 D–£45 (£40 D–£55)
Loc 6 miles W of Barnstaple
Arch Fowler/Pennink

Sidmouth (1889)

Cotmaton Road, Sidmouth EX10 8SX
Tel (01395) 513023
Fax (01395) 514661
Mem 850
Sec IM Smith (01395) 513451
Pro H Barrell (01395) 516407
Holes 18 L 5068 yds SSS 65
Recs Am–59 N Winchester
Pro–62 J Robinson
V'tors U SOC
Fees £20 (£20)
Loc ½ mile W of Sidmouth. 12
miles SE of M5 Junction 30
Arch JH Taylor

Sparkwell (1993)

Pay and play
Sparkwell, Plymouth PL7 5DF
Tel (01752) 837219
Fax (01752) 837219
Mem 108
Sec G Axworthy
Pro None
Holes 9 L 5772 yds SSS 68
V'tors U SOC
Fees 18 holes–£10 (£12)
9 holes–£6 (£7)
Loc 8 miles NE of Plymouth. A38
Plympton Junction
Mis 9 hole pitch & putt
Arch J Gabb

Staddon Heights (1904)

Plymstock, Plymouth PL9 9SP
Tel (01752) 402475
Fax (01752) 401998
Mem 740
Sec K Bravant
Pro I Marshall (01752) 492630

Holes 18 L 5845 yds SSS 70
Recs Am–66 G Box
Pro–67 G Milne
V'tors WE–H SOC–WD
Fees D–£17.50 (D–£22.50)
Loc SE Plymouth, via Plymstock

Tavistock (1890)

Down Road, Tavistock PL19 9AQ
Tel (01822) 612049
Fax (01822) 612344
Mem 700
Sec R Vandenbergh
(01822) 612344
Pro D Rehaag (01822) 612316
Holes 18 L 6250 yds SSS 70
Recs Am–66 MG Symons (1981)
Pro–69 S Chadwick,
N Bicknell
Ladies–72 D Gosling (1989),
E Fields (1991)
V'tors U SOC–WD
Fees £18 (£23)
Loc Whitchurch Down

Teign Valley (1995)

Christow, Exeter EX6 7PA
Tel (01647) 253026
Fax (01647) 253026
Mem 300
Sec Sue Pearman
Pro R Stephenson (01647) 253127
Holes 18 L 5913 yds Par 70 SSS 68
V'tors U SOC
Fees £12 (£16)
Loc SW of Exeter, via A38
(B3193)
Arch Peter Nicholson

Teignmouth (1924)

Exeter Road, Teignmouth TQ14 9NY
Tel (01626) 773614
Fax (01626) 777070
Mem 900
Sec D Holloway (01626) 777070
Pro P Ward (01626) 772894
Holes 18 L 6227 yds SSS 70
Recs Am–65 JH Laidler (1980)
Pro–66 P Millhouse (1987)
V'tors WD–H (recognised club
member) WE–by appointment
SOC–WD
Fees £22 (£25)
Loc 2 miles N of Teignmouth on
B3192
Arch Dr A Mackenzie

Thurlestone (1897)

Thurlestone, Kingsbridge TQ7 3NZ
Tel (01548) 560405
Fax (01548) 560405
Mem 770
Sec R Marston
Pro P Laugher (01548) 560715
Holes 18 L 6340 yds Par 71 SSS 70
Recs Am–65 D Eva (1995)
Pro–67 PJ Yeo (1975)
V'tors I or H
Fees £26 W–£100
Loc 5 miles W of Kingsbridge, off
A379
Arch HS Colt

Tiverton (1932)

Post Hill, Tiverton EX16 4NE
Tel (01884) 252114 (Clubhouse)
Fax (01884) 252187
Mem 600 130(L) 45(J)
Sec MJ Lowry (Sec/Mgr)
(01884) 252187
Pro D Sheppard (01884) 254836
Holes 18 L 6236 yds SSS 71
Recs Am–65 SC Waddington (1977)
Pro–67 D Sheppard (1997)
Ladies–70 C Trew (1977)
V'tors H
Fees On application
Loc 5 miles W of M5 Junction 27.
1½ miles E of Tiverton on
B3391
Arch Braid/Cotton

Torquay (1910)

*Petitor Road, St Marychurch, Torquay
TQ1 4QF*
Tel (01803) 327471
Fax (01803) 316116
Mem 800
Sec BG Long (01803) 314591
Pro M Ruth (01803) 329113
Holes 18 L 6198 yds Par 69 SSS 70
Recs Am–63 AD Stubbs (1996)
Pro–65 G Emerson (1992)
V'tors H SOC
Fees £20 (£25)
Loc 2 miles N of Torquay

Torrington (1895)

Weare Trees, Torrington EX38 7EZ
Tel (01805) 622229
Mem 440
Sec GSC Green (Hon)
Holes 9 L 4419 yds Par 64 SSS 62
Recs Am–58 DL George
V'tors U exc Sun am–NA SOC
Fees £10 (£12)
Loc 1 mile W of Torrington on
Weare Gifford road

Warren (1892)

Dawlish Warren EX7 0NF
Tel (01626) 862255
Fax (01626) 888005
Mem 600
Sec D Daniell
Pro AJ Naldrett (01626) 864002
Holes 18 L 5968 yds SSS 69
Recs Am–65 J Langmead (1987)
V'tors H SOC–Mon/Wed/Fri
Fees £21 (£24)
Loc 1½ miles E of Dawlish

Waterbridge (1992)

Pay and play
Down St Mary, Crediton EX17 5LG
Tel (01363) 85111
Sec CA Petherick
Pro D Ridyard
Holes 9 L 1955 yds Par 32
V'tors U
Fees 18 holes–£9 (£12)
9 holes–£5 (£6.50)
Loc 1 mile N of Copplestone on
A337
Arch David Taylor

Woodbury Park (1992)

Woodbury Castle, Woodbury EX5 1JJ

Tel	(01395) 233382
Fax	(01395) 233384
Mem	540
Sec	PJ Flavin
Pro	A Richards
Holes	18 L 6707 yds SSS 72
	9 L 4582 yds SSS 62
Recs	Am–68 P Sweeney
	Pro–67 G Norman (1995),
	F Nobilo (1996)
V'tors	U
Fees	18 hole–£35; 9 hole–£9
Loc	10 miles E of Exeter on A3052.
	M5 Junction 30, 6 miles
Mis	Driving range
Arch	J Hamilton Stutt

Wrangaton (1895)

Golf Links Road, Wrangaton, South Brent TQ10 9HJ

Tel	(01364) 73229
Fax	(01364) 73229
Mem	790
Sec	G Williams
Pro	A Whitehead (01364) 72161
Holes	18 L 6083 yds SSS 69
Recs	Am–66 D Marsh (1996)
V'tors	H SOC
Fees	£17 (£23)
Loc	Dartmoor, 3 miles E of Ivybridge
Arch	Donald Steel

Yelverton (1904)

Golf Links Road, Yelverton PL20 6BN

Tel	(01822) 852824
Fax	(01822) 852824
Mem	600
Sec	HS Fleming (01822) 852824
Pro	T McSherry (01822) 853593
Holes	18 L 6351 yds Par 71 SSS 72
Recs	Am–68 S Davey (1997)
	Pro–69 J Langmead (1997)
V'tors	H SOC
Fees	D–£30 (£40)
Loc	6 miles N of Plymouth on A386
Arch	Herbert Fowler

Dorset

The Ashley Wood (1896)

Wimborne Road, Blandford Forum DT11 9HN

Tel	(01258) 452253
Fax	(01258) 450590
Mem	670
Sec	P Lillford
Pro	S Taylor
Holes	18 L 6276 yds Par 70 SSS 70
Recs	Am–66 S Sanger (1996)
	Pro–67 S Taylor (1996)
V'tors	U
Fees	Phone in advance
Loc	1½ miles SE of Blandford on B3082
Arch	Patrick Tallack

Bournemouth & Meyrick Park (1890)

Pay and play

Central Drive, Meyrick Park, Bournemouth BH2 6LH

Tel	(01202) 290307,
	(01202) 290862 (Bookings)
Mem	400
Pro	L Thompson
Holes	18 L 5637 yds Par 69
Recs	Am–65
	Pro–62 D Ray (1994)
V'tors	U
Fees	£11 (£12)
Loc	½ mile behind Town Hall, Bournemouth
Arch	Dunn(1894)/Colt(1925)

Bridport & West Dorset (1891)

East Cliff, West Bay, Bridport DT6 4EP

Tel	(01308) 422597
Fax	(01308) 421095
Mem	700
Sec	PJ Ridler (01308) 421095
Pro	D Parsons (01308) 421491
Holes	18 L 6028 yds SSS 69
Recs	Am–61 M Rees (1990)
	Pro–66 S Bishop (1980),
	R Crockford (1983)
V'tors	WD/Sat–U after 9.30am
	Sun–U after 1pm SOC
Fees	£22 After 2pm–£16
Loc	2 miles S of Bridport at West Bay
Mis	9 hole pitch & putt course (Summer)

Broadstone (1898)

Wentworth Drive, Broadstone BH18 8DQ

Tel	(01202) 692595
Fax	(01202) 692595
Mem	650
Sec	C Robinson
Pro	N Tokely (01202) 692835
Holes	18 L 6315 yds SSS 70
Recs	Am–66 JH Nash (1988),
	LS James (1992),
	LG Orchard (1997)
	Pro–66 R Davies (1992),
	J Langmead (1994)
V'tors	WD–H after 9.30am
	WE/BH–restricted SOC–WD
Fees	£28 D–£37
Loc	4 miles N of Poole, off A349
Arch	Dunn(1898)/Colt(1925)

The Bulbury Club (1989)

Bulbury Lane, Lytchett Matravers, Poole BH16 6EP

Tel	(01929) 459574
Fax	(01929) 459000
Mem	400
Sec	IG Brooks
Pro	N Gravelle
Holes	18 L 6313 yds Par 72 SSS 70
Recs	Pro–63 D Read (1991)
V'tors	U SOC–WD
Fees	£20
Loc	3 miles NW of Poole, off A35

Came Down (1896)

Came Down, Dorchester DT2 8NR

Tel	(01305) 812531
Fax	(01305) 813494
Mem	700
Sec	DE Matthews (Mgr) (01305) 813494
Pro	D Holmes (01305) 812670
Holes	18 L 6244 yds SSS 71
Recs	Am–66 A Louden (1993)
	Pro–63 S Robertson (1997)
V'tors	H Sun am–NA SOC
Fees	£22 (£27.50)
Loc	2 miles S of Dorchester
Arch	Taylor/Colt

Canford School

Canford School, Wimborne BH21 3AD

Tel	(01202) 841254
Fax	(01202) 881009
Mem	420
Sec	C Jervis BEd
Holes	9 L 5918 yds SSS 68
Recs	Am–69 J Lovett (1996)
V'tors	M SOC
Fees	£8
Loc	2 miles SE of Wimborne, off A341
Arch	P Boult

Chedington Court (1991)

South Perrott, Beaminster DT8 3HU

Tel	(01935) 891413
Fax	(01935) 891217
Mem	360
Sec	D Astill (Man Dir)
Holes	18 L 5950 yds SSS 69
V'tors	U SOC
Fees	£16 (£20)
Loc	4 miles SE of Crewkerne on A356
Arch	Chapman/Hemstock/Steel

Christchurch (1977)

Barrack Road, Iford, Christchurch BH23 2BA

Tel	(01202) 473817
Mem	300
Sec	J Lucas
Pro	PL Troth
Holes	9 L 4330 yds SSS 61
Recs	Am–63 P Holbert
V'tors	U
Fees	£5.40 (£6.10)
Loc	Bournemouth/Christchurch boundary
Mis	Driving range

Crane Valley (1992)

The Clubhouse, Verwood BH31 7LE

Tel	(01202) 814088
Fax	(01202) 813407
Mem	600
Sec	A Blackwell (Gen Mgr)
Pro	P Cannings
Holes	18 L 6421 yds SSS 71
	9 L 2030 yds SSS 60
Recs	Am–70 A Ross (1996)
	Pro–66 G Ryall (1996)
V'tors	H SOC 9 hole–U

Fees 18 hole–£20 (£30);
9 hole–£5.50 (£6.50)
Loc Nr Ringwood, off B3081
Verwood-Cranborne road
Mis Floodlit driving range
Arch Donald Steel

Dorset Heights (1990)

*Belchalwell, Blandford Forum
DT11 0EG*

Tel (01258) 861386
Fax (01258) 860900
Mem 350
Sec Mrs J Burton,
RBM Moore (Dir)
Pro A Stuart
Holes 18 L 6500 yds SSS 71
V'tors U SOC
Fees £12 (£15)
Loc Between Okeford Fitzpaine
and Ibberton

Dudsbury (1992)

*Christchurch Road, Ferndown
BH22 8ST*

Tel (01202) 593499
Fax (01202) 594555
Sec GH Legg
Pro R Tuddenham (01202) 594488
Holes 18 L 6765 yds Par 71 SSS 73
Recs Am–68 C Jessup (1997)
Pro–64 R Dinsdale (1995)
V'tors U
Fees On application
Loc 3 miles N of Bournemouth
(B3073)
Mis Driving range. Academy
course
Arch Donald Steel

East Dorset (1978)

Bere Regis, Wareham BH20 7NT

Tel (01929) 472244
Fax (01929) 471294
Mem 620
Sec BR Lee (Gen Mgr)
Pro D Honan
Holes Lakeland 18 L 7027 yds
SSS 75; Woodland 18 L 4887
yds SSS 64
Recs Am–71 L James (1992)
V'tors Lakeland–H SOC
Woodland–U
Fees Lakeland–£27 (£32)
Woodland–£18 (£20)
Loc 5 miles S of Bere Regis, off
Wool road
Mis Driving range
Arch Martin Hawtree

Ferndown (1923)

*119 Golf Links Road, Ferndown
BH22 8BU*

Tel (01202) 874602
Fax (01202) 873926
Mem 700
Sec E Robertson (Mgr) (01202)
874602
Pro IAB Parker (01202) 873825
Holes 18 L 6452 yds SSS 71
9 L 5604 yds SSS 68

Recs Old Am–65 JP Baldwin
Pro–68 DN Sewell
President's Am–65 SW Findlay
Pro–68 DN Sewell
V'tors WD–I H after 9.30am
SOC–Tues & Fri
Fees Old £40 (£45)
President's £15 (£20)
Loc 6 miles N of Bournemouth
Arch Harold Hilton

Ferndown Forest (1993)

Forest Links Road, Ferndown BH22 9QE

Tel (01202) 876096
Fax (01202) 894095
Mem 360
Sec K Fergus
Pro R Grafham
Holes 18 L 4610 yds Par 67
V'tors U
Fees £12 (£15)
Loc 5 miles N of Bournemouth.
N of Ferndown Bypass
Mis Floodlit driving range
Arch Hunt/Grafham

Halstock (1988)

Pay and play
Common Lane, Halstock BA22 9SF

Tel (01935) 891689
Fax (01935) 891839
Mem 200
Sec LR Church (Mgr)
Holes 18 L 4351 yds Par 65 SSS 61
Recs Am–61 R Glover (1997)
V'tors U SOC
Fees £10 (£12)
Loc 6 miles S of Yeovil, off A37
Mis Driving range

Highcliffe Castle (1913)

*107 Lymington Road, Highcliffe-on-
Sea, Christchurch BH23 4LA*

Tel (01425) 272953
Mem 350 100(L) 50(J)
Sec BE Savery
(01425) 272210
Holes 18 L 4776 yds Par 64 SSS 63
Recs Am–58 S Jenkins (1986)
Pro–59 M Butcher (1988)
V'tors H SOC
Fees £20 (£30)
Loc 8 miles E of Bournemouth

Isle of Purbeck (1892)

Studland BH19 3AB

Tel (01929) 450361
Fax (01929) 450501
Mem 500
Sec Mrs J Robinson (MD)
Pro I Brake (01929) 450354
Holes 18 L 6283 yds SSS 71
9 L 2022 yds SSS 30
Recs Am–67 N Holman
Pro–72 K Sparkes
V'tors U SOC
Fees £25 D–£32.50 (£30
D–£37.50)
Loc 3 miles N of Swanage on
B3351. Ferry from Sandbanks
to Studland
Arch HS Colt

Knighton Heath (1976)

*Francis Avenue, West Howe,
Bournemouth BH11 8NX*

Tel (01202) 572633
Fax (01202) 590774
Mem 700
Sec R Bestwick
Pro Miss J Miles
(01202) 578275
Holes 18 L 6084 yds SSS 69
Recs Am–64 H McCann (1990),
N Tanswell (1991)
Pro–64 A Beal (1990)
Ladies–69 J Brown (1990)
V'tors WD–H after 9.30am
WE–M
Fees On application
Loc 3 miles N of Poole, at
junction of A348/A3049

Lyme Regis (1893)

Timber Hill, Lyme Regis DT7 3HQ

Tel (01297) 442963,
(01297) 442043 (Steward)
Mem 750
Sec RSF McWhinney
(01297) 442963
Pro A Black (01297) 443822
Holes 18 L 6283 yds SSS 70
Recs Am–67 MR Searle,
D Gee (1996)
Pro–68 D Honan
V'tors H WD–U after 9.30am
(2.30pm Thurs) Sun–U after
noon SOC
Fees £20 After 2pm–£17
Loc Between Lyme Regis and
Charmouth, off A3502/A35

Lyons Gate (1991)

*Lyons Gate Farm, Lyons Gate,
Dorchester DT2 7AZ*

Tel (01300) 345239
Mem 125
Sec TH Wood
Pro T Lovegrove
Holes 9 L 2100 yds SSS 60
V'tors U SOC
Fees 18 holes–£7.50
9 holes–£4.50
Loc Middle Marsh, 12 miles N of
Dorchester (A352)
Arch Ken Abel

Moors Valley (1989)

Public
Horton Road, Ringwood BH24 2ET

Tel (01425) 480448
Fax (01425) 480799
Mem 310
Sec D Meharg
Pro M Torrens (01425) 479776
Holes 18 L 6270 yds SSS 70
Recs Am–74 P Cutmore
Ladies–67 A Dean
V'tors U
Fees On application
Loc 4 miles SW of Ringwood,
off A31
Mis Driving range
Arch Martin Hawtree

Parkstone (1910)

Links Road, Parkstone, Poole BH14 9QS
Tel   **(01202) 707138**
Fax   (01202) 706027
Mem   500 160(L) 50(J)
Sec   AS Kinnear
Pro   M Thomas (01202) 708092
Holes 18 L 6250 yds SSS 70
Recs   Am–65 DSL Cook,
       RA Latham, T Spence
       Pro–63 P Alliss
V'tors H WD–NA before 9.30am
       and 12.30–2.10pm
       WE–NA before 9.45am and
       12.30–2.30pm
Fees   £30 D–£40 (£40 D–£50)
Loc   3 miles W of Bournemouth,
       off A35
Arch   W Park Jr/Braid

Queens Park (1905)

Public
*Queens Park West Drive, Queens Park,
Bournemouth BH8 9BY*
Tel   **(01202) 302611/396198**
       (Bookings)
Mem   520
Sec   MJ Poole (01202) 302611
Pro   R Hill (01202) 396817
Holes 18 L 6305 yds SSS 70
Recs   Am–69 M Butcher
       Pro–66 A Caygill, H Boyle
V'tors U SOC
Fees   £10 (£12)
Loc   2 miles NE of Bournemouth
Mis   Closed Sun pm

Riversmeet Par Three

*Stony Lane South, Christchurch
BH23 1HW*
Tel   **(01202) 477987**
Fax   (01202) 470853
Mem   250
Sec   N Williams
Holes 18 L 1650 yds Par 54
V'tors U
Fees   On application
Loc   2 miles W of Bournemouth

Sherborne (1894)

Clatcombe, Sherborne DT9 4RN
Tel   **(01935) 812475**
Fax   (01935) 814218
Sec   Mrs JMC Guy (01935)
       814431
Pro   S Wright (01935) 812274
Holes 18 L 5882 yds Par 70 SSS 68
Recs   Am–62 AW Lawrence (1997)
       Pro–64 K Spurgeon, R Davis
       (1997)
V'tors H
Fees   £25 (£30)
Loc   1 mile N of Sherborne,
       off B3145

Solent Meads Par Three

Public
*Rolls Drive, Hengistbury Head,
Bournemouth*
Tel   **(01202) 420795**
Holes 18 L 2325 yds Par 54
V'tors U

Fees   On application
Loc   Hengistbury Head, S of
       Christchurch
Mis   Driving range

Sturminster Marshall
(1992)

Pay and play
*Moor Lane, Sturminster Marshall
BH21 4AH*
Tel   **(01258) 858444**
Fax   (01258) 858262
Mem   490
Sec   DR Holdsworth
Pro   G Howell
Holes 9 L 4882 yds SSS 64
Recs   Am–68
V'tors U SOC
Fees   18 holes–£10; 9 holes–£7
Loc   8 miles N of Poole on A350
Arch   John Sharkey

Wareham (1908)

Sandford Road, Wareham BH20 4DH
Tel   **(01929) 554147**
Fax   (01929) 554147
Mem   550
Sec   Maj JL Holloway
Holes 18 L 5603 yds SSS 67
Recs   Am–66 K Knott (1993)
V'tors WD–H 9.30am–5pm SOC
       WE–M
Fees   £15
Loc   Nr railway station, on A351
Arch   C Whitcombe

Weymouth (1909)

Links Road, Weymouth DT4 0PF
Tel   **(01305) 773981**
Fax   (01305) 788029
Mem   750
Sec   BR Chatham
Pro   D Lochrie (01305) 773997
Holes 18 L 5976 yds SSS 69
Recs   Am–63 MJ Watson (1987)
       Pro–60 G Emerson (1993)
       Ladies–72 T Loveys (1988)
V'tors H SOC–WD
Fees   £20 (£25)
Loc   1 mile from town centre
       (A354), off Manor roundabout
Arch   Braid/Hamilton Stutt

Durham

Barnard Castle (1898)

*Harmire Road, Barnard Castle
DL12 8QN*
Tel   **(01833) 638355**
Mem   700
Sec   GA Stoddart
Pro   D Pearce
Holes 18 L 6406 yds SSS 71
Recs   Am–68 C Hamilton (1995)
       Pro–66 D Curry (1995)
V'tors U SOC
Fees   £16 D–£24 (£24 D–£30)
Loc   N boundary of Barnard Castle
       on B6278

Beamish Park (1950)

Beamish, Stanley DH9 0RH
Tel   **(0191) 370 1382**
Fax   (0191) 370 2937
Mem   520
Sec   B Bradley
Pro   C Cole (0191) 370 1984
Holes 18 L 6205 yds SSS 70
Recs   Am–64 D Vest
V'tors WD/Sat–U before 4pm
       Sun–NA SOC
Fees   £16 (£24)
Loc   Beamish, nr Stanley
Arch   Henry Cotton

Billingham (1967)

Sandy Lane, Billingham TS22 5NA
Tel   **(01642) 554494/533816**
Fax   (01642) 533816
Mem   850
Sec   EI Douglas (01642) 533816
Pro   M Ure (01642) 557060
Holes 18 L 6430 yds SSS 71
Recs   Am–66 S Twynholm (1993)
       Pro–63 M Maith (1993)
V'tors WD–H after 9am WE/BH–H
       after 10am SOC
Fees   D–£20 (£33)
Loc   W boundary of Billingham by
       A19, E of bypass
Arch   Frank Pennink

Bishop Auckland (1894)

*High Plains, Durham Road, Bishop
Auckland DL14 8DL*
Tel   **(01388) 602198**
Mem   860
Sec   G Thatcher (01388) 663648
Pro   D Skiffington (01388) 661618
Holes 18 L 6420 yds SSS 71
Recs   Am–64 G Border (1994)
       Pro–65 P Harrison
V'tors H (closed Good Friday and
       Christmas Day)
Fees   £20 D–£24 (£26)
Loc   ½ mile NE of Bishop Auckland
Arch   James Kay

Blackwell Grange (1930)

*Briar Close, Blackwell, Darlington
DL3 8QX*
Tel   **(01325) 464464**
Mem   650
Sec   F Hewitson (Hon)
       (01325) 464458
Pro   R Givens (01325) 462088
Holes 18 L 5621 yds SSS 67
Recs   Am–63 GE Johnson
       Pro–63 M Gregson
V'tors U exc Wed 11am–2.30pm–NA
       Sat–booking req
       Sun–restricted SOC
Fees   £16 D–£22 (£20)
Loc   1 mile S of Darlington on A66
Arch   Frank Pennink

Brancepeth Castle (1924)

Brancepeth Village, Durham DH7 8EA
Tel   **(0191) 378 0075**
Fax   (0191) 378 3835
Mem   768 118(L) 74(J)

Sec K Stewart
Pro D Howdon (0191) 378 0183
Holes 18 L 6415 yds SSS 71
Recs Am–64 G Boardman (1992)
Pro–64 B Rumney (1990)
V'tors SOC–WD WE–NA
Fees £24 (£30)
Loc 5 miles W of Durham on A690
Arch HS Colt

Castle Eden & Peterlee
(1927)
Castle Eden, Hartlepool TS27 4SS
Tel (01429) 836220
Mem 650
Sec D Livingston (01429) 836510
Pro G Laidlaw (01429) 836689
Holes 18 L 6262 yds SSS 70
Recs Am–66 G Border (1987)
Pro–66 P Harrison (1995)
V'tors U
Fees £20
Loc 2 miles S of Peterlee
Arch Henry Cotton

Chester-Le-Street (1908)
Lumley Park, Chester-Le-Street DH3 4NS
Tel (0191) 388 3218
Fax (0191) 388 1220
Mem 435 130(L) 90(J)
Sec J Dodds
Pro D Fletcher (0191) 389 0157
Holes 18 L 6437 yds SSS 71
Recs Am–67 J Goss
V'tors WD–H after 9.30am –NA 12–1pm WE–NA before 10.30am or 12–2pm
Fees £20 (£25)
Loc E of Chester-Le-Street
Arch JH Taylor

Consett & District (1911)
Elmfield Road, Consett DH8 5NN
Tel (01207) 502186
Fax (01207) 505060
Mem 650
Sec B Bromley (01207) 521190
Pro C Dilley (01207) 580210
Holes 18 L 6023 yds SSS 69
Recs Am–63 J Kennedy (1996)
V'tors WD–U SOC–exc Sat
Fees £17 (£25)
Loc 14 miles N of Durham on A691
Arch Harry Vardon

Crook (1919)
Low Job's Hill, Crook DL15 9AA
Tel (01388) 762429/767926
Mem 450
Sec R Hoggarth
Pro None
Holes 18 L 6102 yds SSS 70
Recs Am–68 D Hanlon
Pro–64 K Fairbairn
V'tors U SOC
Fees £14 (£23)
Loc ½ mile E of Crook (A689)

Darlington (1908)
Haughton Grange, Darlington DL1 3JD
Tel (01325) 355324
Fax (01325) 488126
Mem 780
Sec To be appointed
Pro (01325) 484198
Holes 18 L 6270 yds SSS 70
Recs Am–67 J Howson
V'tors WD–U from 10am–12 & 2–4pm WE–M
Fees D–£23
Loc Off Salters Lane, NE of Darlington

Dinsdale Spa (1910)
Middleton St George, Darlington DL2 1DW
Tel (01325) 332222
Fax (01325) 332222
Mem 875
Sec DW Corcoran (01325) 332297
Pro C Imlah (01325) 332515
Holes 18 L 6090 yds Par 71 SSS 69
Recs Am–65 MJ Howe (1995)
Pro–65 M Joseph (1995)
V'tors WD–U exc Tues–NA WE–M
Fees D–£20
Loc 5 miles SE of Darlington

Durham City (1887)
Littleburn, Langley Moor, Durham DH7 8HL
Tel (0191) 378 0069
Mem 750
Sec LTI Wilson (0191) 386 0200
Pro S Corbally (0191) 378 0029
Holes 18 L 6326 yds SSS 70
V'tors WD–U SOC
Fees £22 (£30)
Loc 1½ miles W of Durham, off A690
Arch CC Stanton

Eaglescliffe (1914)
Yarm Road, Eaglescliffe, Stockton-on-Tees TS16 0DQ
Tel (01642) 780098
Mem 835
Sec AH Painter (01642) 780238
Pro P Bradley (01642) 790122
Holes 18 L 6275 yds SSS 70
Recs Am–63 CM Hoggart (1993)
Pro–65 N Gilkes (1993)
V'tors U SOC
Fees £24 (£30)
Loc 3 miles S of Stockton-on-Tees on A135

Hartlepool (1906)
Hart Warren, Hartlepool TS24 9QF
Tel (01429) 274398
Fax (01429) 274129
Mem 700
Sec WE Storrow (01429) 870282
Pro ME Cole (01429) 267473
Holes 18 L 6255 yds SSS 70
Recs Am–62 G Storm (1997)
Pro–65 J Harrison, D Curry

V'tors WD–U SOC
Fees £20 (£30)
Loc N boundary of Hartlepool

Hobson Municipal (1978)
Public
Hobson, Burnopfield, Newcastle-upon-Tyne
Tel (01207) 271605
Sec RJ Handrick
Pro J Ord
Holes 18 L 6403 yds SSS 71
V'tors U SOC
Fees £9 (£12)
Loc Between Gateshead and Consett on A692

Knotty Hill Golf Centre
(1992)
Pay and play
Sedgefield, Stockton-on-Tees TS21 2BB
Tel (01740) 620320
Fax (01740) 622227
Sec D Craggs (Mgr)
Holes 18 L 6517 yds Par 72 SSS 71 9 hole course
V'tors U SOC
Fees £12 (£12)
Loc 1 mile N of Sedgefield on A177. A1(M) Junction 60, 2 miles
Mis Floodlit driving range
Arch Chris Stanton

Mount Oswald (1924)
South Road, Durham City DH1 3TQ
Tel (0191) 386 7527
Fax (0191) 386 0975
Mem 120
Sec SE Reeve
Holes 18 L 6009 yds SSS 69
Recs Am–64 J Mee (1986)
Pro–66 J Mathews (1984)
V'tors U SOC
Fees £11 D–£18 (£13 D–£21)
Loc SW of Durham on A177

Norton (1989)
Pay and play
Junction Road, Norton, Stockton-on-Tees TS20 1SU
Tel (01642) 676385
Fax (01642) 608467
Pro T Miles
Holes 18 L 5870 yds SSS 71
V'tors U SOC
Fees £8 (£9)
Loc 1 mile E of A177 on B1274
Arch Tim Harper

Oakleaf Golf Complex
(1993)
Pay and play
School Aycliffe Lane, Newton Aycliffe DL5 6QZ
Tel (01325) 310820
Fax (01325) 300873
Sec A Bailey (Mgr) (01325) 300700

Pro   C Burgess
Holes   18 L 5334 yds SSS 66
V'tors   WD–U WE–booking req
Fees   £6 (£7)
Loc   1 mile W of Aycliffe on A6072, from A68
Mis   Floodlit driving range

Ramside (1995)

Ramside Hall Hotel, Carrville, Durham DH1 1TD
Tel   (0191) 386 9514
Fax   (0191) 386 9519
Mem   300
Sec   TI Flowers
Holes   27 holes:
6217-6851 yds SSS 70-73
V'tors   U H SOC
Fees   £25 (£30)
Loc   2 miles NE of Durham on A690. A1(M) Junction 62
Mis   Driving range. Golf Academy
Arch   J Gaunt

Roseberry Grange (1986)

Public
Grange Villa, Chester-Le-Street DH2 3NF
Tel   (0191) 370 0670
Mem   500
Sec   R McDermott (Hon)
Pro   A Hartley (0191) 370 0670
Holes   18 L 5892 yds SSS 68
Recs   Am–66 D Brolls (1989), D Matthews (1994)
Pro–65 B Rumney (1988)
V'tors   U SOC
Fees   £10 (£10)
Loc   3 miles W of Chester-Le-Street on A693
Mis   Driving range

Ryhope (1992)

Public
Leechmere Way, Hollycarrside, Ryhope, Sunderland SR2 0DH
Tel   (0191) 523 7333
Fax   (0191) 521 3811
Mem   300
Sec   A Brown
Pro   None
Holes   18 L 4601 yds SSS 65
Recs   Am–67 JA Nelson, A Hall
V'tors   U
Fees   £6 (£6)
Loc   2 miles SW of Sunderland, off A1018
Arch   Jonathan Gaunt

Seaham (1911)

Shrewsbury Street, Dawdon, Seaham SR7 7RD
Tel   (0191) 581 2354
Mem   550
Sec   V Smith (0191) 581 1268
Pro   T Jenkins (0191) 513 0837
Holes   18 L 5972 yds SSS 69
Recs   Am–63 C Walton (1993)
V'tors   U SOC
Fees   On application
Loc   Dawdon, 2 miles NE of A19

Seaton Carew (1874)

Tees Road, Hartlepool TS25 1DE
Tel   (01429) 266249/261040
Mem   650
Sec   PR Wilson (01429) 261473
Pro   W Hector
Holes   Old 18 L 6613 yds SSS 72
Brabazon 18 L 6855 yds SSS 73
Recs   Old Am–66 MJ Kelley, B Popple
Pro–66 N Bell
Brabazon Am–66 ID Garbutt
V'tors   U SOC
Fees   £27 (£38)
Loc   Hartlepool 2 miles
Arch   Dr A Mackenzie

South Moor (1923)

The Middles, Craghead, Stanley DH9 6AG
Tel   (01207) 232848/283525
Fax   (01207) 284616
Mem   650
Sec   B Davison (0191) 388 4523
Pro   S Cowell (01207) 283525
Holes   18 L 6445 yds Par 72 SSS 71
Recs   Am–66 G Wearmouth (1991)
Pro–67 LP Tupling (1980)
Ladies–70 PA Dobson (1987)
V'tors   WD–H WE/BH–M
SOC–WD/Sat
Fees   £14 (£25)
Loc   8 miles NW of Durham
Arch   Dr A Mackenzie

Stressholme (1976)

Public
Snipe Lane, Darlington DL2 2SA
Tel   (01325) 461002
Fax   (01325) 351826
Sec   R Taylor
Pro   M Watkins, D Patterson
Holes   18 L 6511 yds SSS 71
Recs   Am–69 S Aitken
Pro–64 N Coles
V'tors   U
Fees   On application
Loc   2 miles S of Darlington on A66
Mis   Floodlit driving range

Woodham G & CC (1983)

Burnhill Way, Newton Aycliffe DH5 4PM
Tel   (01325) 320574
Mem   610
Sec   JD Jenkinson
Pro   E Wilson
Holes   18 L 6770 yds SSS 72
Recs   Am–68 L McCavanagh
Pro–67 M Ure
V'tors   WD–U WE/BH–booking SOC
Fees   On application
Loc   1 mile N of Newton Aycliffe
Arch   J Hamilton Stutt

The Wynyard

Wellington Drive, Wynyard Park, Billingham TS22 5QJ
Tel   (01740) 644399
Fax   (01740) 644592

Sec   Lynne Lowther (Mgr)
Pro   A Oliphant
Holes   18 holes Par 72 SSS 73
Recs   Am–66 N Emmerson (1997)
Pro–63 O Edmond (1997)
V'tors   M SOC–H
Fees   On application
Loc   5 miles E of Sedgefield, between A1 and A19
Mis   Floodlit driving range
Arch   Hawtree

Essex

Abridge G&CC (1964)

Epping Lane, Stapleford Tawney RM4 1ST
Tel   (01708) 688396
Fax   (01708) 688550
Mem   650
Sec   G Winckless (01708) 688396
Pro   M Herbert (01708) 688333
Holes   18 L 6703 yds SSS 72
Recs   Am–67 R Curtis
Pro–68 D Feherty
V'tors   WD–H WE/BH–NA
Fees   £30
Loc   Theydon Bois/Epping Stations 3 miles
Arch   Henry Cotton

Ballards Gore G&CC (1980)

Gore Road, Canewdon, Rochford SS4 2DA
Tel   (01702) 258917
Mem   600
Sec   NG Patient
Pro   A Curry (01702) 258924
Holes   18 L 7062 yds SSS 74
V'tors   WD–U WE–M after 12.30pm (summer) 11.30am (winter) SOC
Fees   £16 D–£22
Loc   1½ miles NE of Rochford

Basildon (1967)

Public
Clayhill Lane, Sparrow's Hearne, Basildon SS16 5JP
Tel   (01268) 533297
Fax   (01268) 533849
Mem   320
Sec   AM Burch
Pro   W Paterson (01268) 533532
Holes   18 L 6236 yds Par 72 SSS 70
Recs   Am–70 S Rooney (1997)
Pro–67 J Fryatt (1996)
V'tors   U SOC
Fees   £9 (£15)
Loc   1 mile S of Basildon, off A176 at Kingswood roundabout

Belfairs (1926)

Public
Eastwood Road North, Leigh-on-Sea SS9 4LR
Tel   (01702) 525345 (Starter)
Pro   M Foreman (01702) 520202

Holes 18 L 5802 yds SSS 68
V'tors WD–U exc Thurs am.
Booking necessary
Fees £11 (£16)
Loc Between A127 and A13

Belhus Park (1972)

Pay and play
Belhus Park, South Ockendon
RM15 4QR
Tel (01708) 854260
Mem 280
Sec DA Faust
Pro G Lunn
Holes 18 L 5188 yds SSS 68
Recs Am–67 M Jennings, J Bearman
Pro–63 R Joyce
V'tors U
Fees £8 (£11.50)
Loc 1 mile N of A13/M25
Dartford Tunnel
Mis Floodlit driving range

Bentley G&CC (1972)

Ongar Road, Brentwood CM15 9SS
Tel (01277) 373179
Fax (01277) 375097
Mem 550
Sec JA Vivers
Pro N Garrett (01277) 372933
Holes 18 L 6709 yds SSS 72
Recs Am–71 J Moody (1987)
Pro–69 S Cipa (1988),
B Smith (1988)
V'tors WD–UH WE–M after noon
BH–after 11am SOC–WD
Fees £21 D–£28
Loc 18 miles E of London. M25
Junction 28, 3 miles

Benton Hall (1993)

Wickham Hill, Witham CM8 3LH
Tel (01376) 502454
Fax (01376) 521050
Mem 400
Sec PS Holmes (Mgr)
Pro J Hudson
Holes 18 L 6520 yds SSS 71
9 hole Par 3 course
V'tors U SOC–WD
Fees £16 (£20)
Loc Witham, 8 miles NE of
Chelmsford, off A12
Mis Driving range
Arch Walker/Cox

Birch Grove (1970)

Layer Road, Colchester CO2 0HS
Tel (01206) 734276
Mem 250
Sec Mrs M Marston
Holes 9 L 4108 yds SSS 60
Recs Am–58 A Green (1993)
V'tors U exc Sun–U after 1pm SOC
Fees D–£10
Loc 3 miles S of Colchester on
B1026

Boyce Hill (1921)

Vicarage Hill, Benfleet SS7 1PD
Tel (01268) 793625
Fax (01268) 750497

Mem 600
Sec RM Burden
Pro G Burroughs (01268) 752565
Holes 18 L 5956 yds SSS 68
Recs Am–64 N Perrin
Pro–61 G Burroughs
V'tors WD–UH WE/BH–MH
SOC–Thurs only
Fees D–£25
Loc 4 miles W of Southend
Arch James Braid

Braintree (1891)

Kings Lane, Stisted, Braintree CM7 8DA
Tel (01376) 346079
Fax (01376) 331216
Mem 700
Sec MND Robinson
Pro T Parcell (01376) 343465
Holes 18 L 6161 yds SSS 69
Recs Am–65 M Hawes, M Davis
Pro–65 P Golding
V'tors WD–U exc Fri–H Sat/BH–H
Sun–NA SOC
Fees £25 (£40)
Loc 1 mile E of Braintree, off
A120 towards Stisted
Arch Hawtree

Braxted Park (1953)

Braxted Park, Witham CM8 3EN
Tel (01376) 572372
Fax (01621) 892840
Mem 83
Sec M Woollett
Pro M Woollett
Holes 9 L 2940 yds Par 70 SSS 68
V'tors WD–U SOC–WD
Fees 18 holes–£12; 9 holes–£9
Loc 1½ miles off A12,
nr Kelvedon
Arch Sir Allen Clark

Bunsay Downs (1982)

Public
Little Baddow Road, Woodham Walter,
Maldon CM9 6RW
Tel (01245) 412648/412369
Sec MFL Durham
Pro Mickey Walker
(01245) 414662
Holes 9 L 2913 yds SSS 68
9 hole Par 3 course
V'tors WD–U WE/BH–book in
advance SOC–WD
Fees On application
Loc 7 miles E of Chelmsford,
off A414
Mis Indoor driving range

Burnham-on-Crouch
(1923)

Ferry Road, Creeksea, Burnham-on-
Crouch CM0 8PQ
Tel (01621) 782282/785508
Fax (01621) 782282
Mem 600
Sec LR Posner
Pro K Smith, S Caroy
(01621) 786280
Holes 18 L 6056 yds SSS 69

Recs Am–66 D Clarke (1966)
Pro–64 FJ Winser
V'tors WD–H WE/BH–M
Fees £22
Loc 1½ miles W of Burnham
Arch D Swan

The Burstead (1995)

Tye Common Road, Little Bursted,
Billericay CM12 9SS
Tel (01277) 631171
Fax (01277) 632766
Mem 900
Sec L Mence
Pro K Bridges
Holes 18 L 6150 yds SSS 69
V'tors WD–U H
Fees £18
Loc 2 miles S of Billericay, off
A176
Arch Patrick Tallack

Canons Brook (1962)

Elizabeth Way, Harlow CM19 5BE
Tel (01279) 421482
Fax (01279) 626393
Mem 800
Sec Dr J Stewart
Pro A McGinn (01279) 418357
Holes 18 L 6763 yds SSS 73
Recs Am–68 H Cornick
Pro–65 G Burroughs
V'tors WD–U WE/BH–M
Fees £20 D–£27
Loc 25 miles N of London
Arch Henry Cotton

Castle Point (1988)

Public
Waterside Farm, Somnes Avenue,
Canvey Island SS8 9FG
Tel (01268) 510830
Mem 300
Sec DT Pitt (01268) 750275
Pro P Joiner (01268) 510830
Holes 18 L 6153 yds SSS 69
Recs Am–67 C Ledger (1997)
V'tors U SOC
Fees £8 (£12)
Loc On A130 to Canvey Island,
off A13 Eastbound
Mis Driving range
Arch Golf Landscapes

Channels (1974)

Belsteads Farm Lane, Little Waltham,
Chelmsford CM3 3PT
Tel (01245) 440005
Fax (01245) 442032
Mem 650
Sec AM Squire
Pro IB Sinclair
(01245) 441056
Holes 18 L 6272 yds SSS 71
18 L 4779 yds Par 67 SSS 63
V'tors WD–U WE–M SOC
Fees £24 D–£35
Loc 3 miles NE of Chelmsford on
A130
Mis Pitch & putt course. Driving
range

Chelmsford (1893)

Widford, Chelmsford CM2 9AP

Tel	(01245) 250555
Fax	(01245) 256483
Mem	650
Sec	A Johnson (01245) 256483
Pro	GD Bailey (01245) 257079
Holes	18 L 5981 yds SSS 69
Recs	Am–66 B Hilsdon
	Pro–65 C Platts
V'tors	WD–H WE/BH–M SOC
Fees	£27 D–£36
Loc	Off A1016 at Widford r'bout
Arch	HS Colt

Chigwell (1925)

High Road, Chigwell IG7 5BH

Tel	(0181) 500 2059
Fax	(0181) 501 3410
Mem	700
Sec	RH Danzey
Pro	R Beard (0181) 500 2384
Holes	18 L 6279 yds SSS 70
Recs	Am–66 AM Ronald,
	JM Bint (1991)
	Pro–66 H Flatman
V'tors	WD–H WE/BH–M
Fees	£28 D–£37
Loc	13 miles NE of London (A113)

Clacton (1892)

West Road, Clacton-on-Sea CO15 1AJ

Tel	(01255) 424331
Fax	(01255) 424602
Mem	650
Sec	H Lucas (01255) 421919
Pro	SJ Levermore (01255) 426304
Holes	18 L 6532 yds SSS 71
Recs	Am–68 D Lee, A Wenn,
	D Robertson
	Pro–65 R Wheeler
V'tors	H WE/BH–H after 11am SOC
Fees	£20 (£30)
Loc	On sea front

Colchester (1909)

Braiswick, Colchester CO4 5AU

Tel	(01206) 852946
Fax	(01206) 852698
Mem	330 90(L) 70(J)
Sec	Mrs J Boorman (01206) 853396
Pro	M Angel (01206) 853920
Holes	18 L 6319 yds SS 70
Recs	Am–63 B Booth
	Pro–68 A Parcell
V'tors	WD–H WE/BH–NA SOC
Fees	£18 D–£22 (£30)
Loc	¼ mile NW of Colchester North Station, towards West Berholt on B1508
Arch	James Braid

Colne Valley (1991)

Station Road, Earls Colne CO6 2LT

Tel	(01787) 224233/224343
Fax	(01787) 224126
Mem	500
Sec	J Martin (Mgr) (01787) 224343
Pro	S Clark (01787) 224233

Holes	18 L 6301 yds SSS 70
	Pro–68 M Deal (1995)
V'tors	WD–U WE/BH–after 10.30am SOC–WD
Fees	£16 (£21)
Loc	12 miles W of Colchester (A604)
Arch	Howard Swann

Crondon Park (1994)

Stock Road, Stock CM4 9DP

Tel	(01277) 841115
Fax	(01277) 841356
Mem	875
Sec	J Lancaster
Pro	M Herbert
Holes	18 L 6585 yds SSS 71 9 hole course
V'tors	WD–U WE–M SOC–WD
Fees	£17 (£25)
Loc	5 miles S of Chelmsford on B1007. M25 Junction 28
Mis	Driving range
Arch	Martin Gillett

Epping Forest G&CC (1994)

Woolston Manor, Abridge Road, Chigwell IG7 6BX

Tel	(0181) 500 2549
Fax	(0181) 501 5452
Sec	T Peck (Sec/Mgr)
Pro	C Stephenson
Holes	18 L 6408 yds SSS 71
Recs	Am–67 D Williams (1996) Pro–66 I Ellis
V'tors	H SOC–WD
Fees	£20 (£30)
Loc	1 mile from M11 Junction 5
Mis	Floodlit driving range
Arch	Neil Coles

Elsenham Golf Centre (1997)

Hall Road, Elsenham, Bishop's Stortford CM22 6DH

Tel	(01279) 812865
Fax	(01279) 816970
Sec	O McKenna (Prop)
Pro	O McKenna
Holes	9 L 5854 yds Par 70
V'tors	U
Fees	9 holes–£9 (£12) 18 holes–£14 (£16)
Loc	Off M11, by Stansted Airport
Mis	Driving range.

Essex G&CC (1990)

Earls Colne, Colchester CO6 2NS

Tel	(01787) 224466
Fax	(01787) 224410
Mem	600
Sec	DJ Clark
Pro	D Peck
Holes	18 L 6879 yds Par 73 9 L 2771 yds Par 34
Recs	Am–69 (1995) Pro–68 P Joiner (1996)
V'tors	U SOC–WD
Fees	£16 (£20)

Loc	2 miles N of A120 at Coggeshall on B1024
Mis	Floodlit driving range.
Arch	Reg Plumbridge

The Essex Golf Complex (1993)

Pay and play

Garon Park, Eastern Avenue, Southend-on-Sea SS9 4PT

Tel	(01702) 601701
Fax	(01702) 601033
Mem	700
Sec	Mrs J Jacom
Pro	G Jacom
Holes	18 L 6237 yds SSS 70 9 hole Par 3 course
Recs	Am–67 A Gregory (1995), J Tann (1996)
V'tors	U SOC
Fees	£13 (£17)
Loc	E side of Southend-on-Sea. M25 Junction 29
Mis	Floodlit driving range
Arch	Walker/Cox

Fairlop Waters (1987)

Public

Forest Road, Barkingside, Ilford IG6 3JA

Tel	(0181) 500 9911
Mem	135
Sec	L Quinn
Pro	B Preston (0181) 501 1881
Holes	18 L 6288 yds SSS 72 9 hole Par 3 course
V'tors	U
Fees	£7.50 (£11)
Loc	2 miles from S end of M11, by Fairlop underground station
Mis	Driving range

Five Lakes Hotel G&CC (1974)

Colchester Road, Tolleshunt Knights, Maldon CM9 8HX

Tel	(01621) 868888
Fax	(01621) 869696
Mem	600
Pro	G Carter
Holes	Links 18 L 6250 yds SSS 70 Lakes 18 L 6765 yds SSS 72
Recs	Links Am–68 D Wilks (1991) Pro–68 K Ashdown (1988) Pro–63 E Dussart (1992)
V'tors	U BH–U after 1pm SOC
Fees	Links £18 (£25) Lakes £25 (£33)
Loc	8 miles S of Colchester, off B1026
Mis	Driving range
Arch	Neil Coles

Forrester Park (1975)

Beckingham Road, Great Totham, Maldon CM9 8EA

Tel	(01621) 891406
Fax	(01621) 891406
Mem	900
Sec	T Forrester-Muir
Pro	G Pike (01621) 893456
Holes	18 L 6073 yds SSS 69

Recs Am–68 K Chamberlain (1997)
V'tors WD–U WE–NA before noon
SOC–WD
Fees £17 (£17)
Loc 3 miles NE of Maldon on
B1022
Arch Everett/Forrester-Muir

Frinton (1895)

*1 The Esplanade, Frinton-on-Sea
CO13 9EP*
Tel (01255) 674618
Fax (01255) 674618
Mem 900
Sec Lt Col RW Attrill
Pro P Taggart (01255) 671618
Holes 18 L 6259 yds SSS 70
9 L 2508 yds SSS 33
Recs Am–67 IA Quick
Pro–64 A Raitt
V'tors 18 hole–H WE/BH–NA before
11.30am SOC
Fees 18 hole–D–£22; 9 hole–£7.50
Loc 18 miles E of Colchester
Arch W Park Jr/HS Colt

Gosfield Lake (1986)

*The Manor House, Gosfield, Halstead
CO9 1SE*
Tel (01787) 474747
Fax (01787) 476044
Mem 630
Sec JA O'Shea (Sec/Mgr)
Pro R Wheeler (01787) 474488
Holes Lakes 18 L 6756 yds SSS 72
Meadows 9 L 4180 yds Par 66
Recs Lakes Am–68 S Bearman
(1993)
V'tors Lakes WD–H WE(pm)–H by
arrangement SOC.
Meadows–U
Fees Lakes D–£25
Meadows D–£10
Loc 7 miles N of Braintree
(A1017)
Arch Sir H Cotton/Swann

Hainault Forest (1912)

Public
Romford Road, Chigwell Row IG7 4QW
Tel (0181) 500 2470 (Caddy
Master), (0181) 500 2097
(Clubhouse)
Mem 630
Sec WA Fowles (0181) 500 0385
Pro CS Hope (0181) 500 2131
Holes No 1 18 L 5754 yds SSS 67
No 2 18 L 6600 yds SSS 71
Recs No 1 Am–65 TG Patmore
Pro–65 AE Frost
No 2 Am–68 S Middleton
Pro–68 AE Frost
V'tors U
Fees On application
Loc Hog Hill, Redbridge

Hanover G&CC (1991)

Hullbridge Road, Rayleigh SS6 9QS
Tel (01702) 232377
Fax (01702) 231811
Mem 700

Sec T Harrold
Pro A Blackburn
Holes Georgian 18 L 6669 yds
SSS 72; Regency 18 L 3700
yds SSS 58
Recs Am –74 A Wheeler,
T Brown (1996)
Pro–69 A Blackburn (1996)
V'tors Georgian WD–H WE–M
SOC; Regency U SOC
Fees Georgian £25 D–£35
Regency £11.75 (£14.10)
Loc 3 miles NW of Southend
Arch Reg Plumbridge

Hartswood (1967)

Public
*King George's Playing Fields,
Brentwood CM14 5AE*
Tel (01277) 214830 (Bookings)
Fax (01277) 218850
Mem 400
Sec M Freeman (01227) 218850
Pro S Cole (01277) 218714
Holes 18 L 6192 yds SSS 70
Recs Am–70 A Cornell
Pro–64 M Sharman
V'tors WD–U after 1pm SOC
Fees On application
Loc E of Brentwood on A128

Harwich & Dovercourt
(1906)

*Station Road, Parkeston, Harwich
CO12 4NZ*
Tel (01255) 503616
Mem 400
Sec JA Eldridge
Holes 9 L 2950 yds SSS 69
V'tors WD–U SOC
Fees On application
Loc A120 to roundabout to
Harwich Port, course entrance
20 yds on LHS

Ilford (1907)

Wanstead Park Road, Ilford IG1 3TR
Tel (0181) 554 2930
Fax (0181) 554 0822
Mem 618
Sec PH Newson
Pro S Dowsett (0181) 554 0094
Holes 18 L 5251 yds SSS 66
Recs Am–60 P Happe (1990)
Pro–64 B Huggett, A Campbell
V'tors WD–U WE–phone Pro
Fees £13.50 (£16)
Loc S end of M11, off A406

Langdon Hills (1991)

*Lower Dunton Road, Bulphan
RM14 3TY*
Tel (01268) 548444/544300
Fax (01268) 490084
Mem 700
Sec B Hardie
Pro T Moncur, P Wernham
Holes 27 holes:
Langdon 9 L 3132 yds Par 35
Bulphan 9 L 3372 yds Par 37
Horndon 9 L 3054 yds Par 36

Recs Am–67 S McAnally
V'tors U SOC
Fees £11 (£12)
Loc SW of Basildon between A127
and A13. M25 Junction 29,
8 miles
Mis Floodlit driving range
Arch MRM Sandow

Loughton (1981)

Public
*Clays Lane, Debden Green, Loughton
IG10 2RZ*
Tel (0181) 502 2923
Mem 190
Sec A Day
Pro S Layton
Holes 9 L 4735 yds SSS 62
V'tors U–booking required SOC
Fees 18 holes–£8 (£10)
9 holes–£5 (£6)
Loc M25 Junction 26

Maldon (1891)

*Beeleigh Langford, Maldon
CM9 6LL*
Tel (01621) 853212
Mem 450
Sec GR Bezant
Holes 9 L 6253 yds SSS 70
Recs Am–71 R Byford
Pro–67 S Levermore
V'tors WD–U H WE–M SOC
Fees £15 D–£20
Loc 3 miles NW of Maldon on
B1019

Maylands (1936)

Harold Park, Romford RM3 0AZ
Tel (017083) 42055
Fax (017083) 73080
Mem 600
Sec (017083) 73080
Pro JS Hopkin
(017083) 46466
Holes 18 L 6351 yds SSS 70
Recs Am–65 I Moore (1995)
Pro–67 H Flatman
V'tors WD–I WE/BH–M SOC
Fees £20 (£30)
Loc 2 miles E of Romford on A12.
M25 Junction 28, 1 mile
Arch HS Colt

Nazeing (1992)

Middle Street, Nazeing EN9 2LW
Tel (01992) 893798/893915
Fax (01992) 893882
Mem 350
Sec J Speller (01992) 893915
Pro R Green (01992) 893798
Holes 18 L 6598 yds SSS 71
Recs Am–68 M Hales (1994)
Pro–65 P Barham (1995)
V'tors WD–H WE/BH–H after 11am
SOC
Fees £20 (£28)
Loc 3 miles SW of Harlow. M11
Junction 7
Mis Open air driving range
Arch Martin Gillett

North Weald (1996)

Rayley Lane, North Weald, Epping CM16 6AR
Tel (01992) 522118
Fax (01992) 522881
Mem 500
Sec JF Saunders
Pro M Janes (01992) 524725
Holes 18 L 6311 yds Par 71 SSS 70
V'tors WD–H WE–NA SOC–WD
Fees £17.50
Loc 1½ miles E of M11 Junction 7 on A414
Arch David Williams

Orsett (1899)

Brentwood Road, Orsett RM16 3DS
Tel (01375) 891352
Fax (01375) 892471
Mem 800
Sec KR Wilcox
Pro P Joiner (01375) 891797
Holes 18 L 6614 yds SSS 72
Recs Am–68 A Pollock, I Quick Pro–68 K Lunt
V'tors WD–H SOC–Mon–Wed only
Fees £32.50
Loc 4 miles NE of Grays on A128. M25 Junction 30/31
Arch James Braid

Regiment Way Golf Centre (1995)

Pay and play
Back Lane, Little Waltham, Chelmsford CM3 3PR
Tel (01245) 361100
Sec R Pamphilon
Pro D Marsh
Holes 9 L 4760 yds Par 65 SSS 64
V'tors U
Fees 9 holes–£8; 18 holes–£12
Loc 3 miles NE of Chelmsford (A130)
Mis Floodlit driving range

Risebridge (1972)

Pay and play
Risebridge Chase, Lower Bedfords Road, Romford RM1 4DG
Tel (01708) 741429
Mem 275
Sec J Alexander
Pro P Jennings
Holes 18 L 6280 yds SSS 70 9 hole Par 3 course
Recs Am–67 B Reeve (1979), D Girdlestone (1985)
V'tors U
Fees £8.45 (£10.50)
Loc 2 miles from M25 Junction 28, off A12
Arch F Hawtree

Rochford Hundred (1893)

Rochford Hall, Hall Road, Rochford SS4 1NW
Tel (01702) 544302
Fax (01702) 541343
Mem 340 150(L) 60(J)
Sec AH Bondfield

Pro GS Hill
Holes 18 L 6256 yds SSS 70
Recs Am–65 DK Wood Pro–65 C Tucker
V'tors WD–U H WE–M
Fees On application
Loc 4 miles N of Southend-on-Sea
Arch James Braid

Romford (1894)

Heath Drive, Gidea Park, Romford RM2 5QB
Tel (01708) 740007 (Members)
Fax (01708) 752157
Mem 680
Sec Mrs H Robinson (01708) 740986
Pro H Flatman (01708) 749393
Holes 18 L 6395 yds SSS 70
Recs Am–66 D Girdlestone Pro–65 W McColl Ladies–72 M Knights
V'tors WD–I WE–NA SOC
Fees £25 D–£35
Loc 1 mile E of Romford. 3 miles W of M25 Junction 29
Arch HS Colt

Royal Epping Forest (1888)

Public
Forest Approach, Station Road, Chingford, London E4 7AZ
Tel (0181) 529 6407
Fax (0181) 559 4664
Mem 300 50(L) 25(J)
Sec Mrs P Runciman (0181) 529 2195
Pro R Gowers (0181) 529 5708
Holes 18 L 6220 yds SSS 70
Recs Am–68 A Johns Pro–65 R Gowers
V'tors U–booking necessary SOC
Fees £9.80 (£13.40)
Loc Nr Chingford station
Mis Red coats or trousers compulsory

Saffron Walden (1919)

Windmill Hill, Saffron Walden CB10 1BX
Tel (01799) 522689
Fax (01799) 522786
Mem 950
Sec DH Smith (Mgr) (01799) 522786
Pro P Davis (01799) 527728
Holes 18 L 6606 yds SSS 72
Recs Am–65 J Dickinson (1997) Pro–63 L Fickling (1991)
V'tors WD–U H WE/BH–M SOC
Fees £30
Loc Saffron Walden, on B184

St Cleres

St Cleres Hall, Stanford-le-Hope SS17 0LX
Tel (01375) 673007
Mem 500
Sec D Wood
Pro D Wood (01375) 361565
Holes 18 holes Par 72 SSS 71
V'tors U H SOC

Fees £15 (£20)
Loc 10 miles E of M25 Junction 30/31 (A13)
Arch Adrian Stiff

Stapleford Abbotts (1989)

Horseman's Side, Tysea Hill, Stapleford Abbotts RM4 1JU
Tel (01708) 381108
Fax (01708) 386345
Mem 800
Pro D Eagle (01708 381278)
Holes Abbotts 18 L 6487 yds SSS 71 Priors 18 L 5965 yds SSS 69 Friars 9 L 1140 yds
Recs Am–70 P Daykin (1994) Pro–66 D Eagle (1994)
V'tors WD–U H WE–M SOC
Fees £10–£40
Loc 3 miles N of Romford. M25 Junction 28
Mis Tee reservations (01708) 370040/(01277) 373344
Arch Howard Swann

Stock Brook Manor (1992)

Queen's Park Avenue, Stock, Billericay CM12 0SP
Tel (01277) 653616
Fax (01277) 633063
Mem 750
Sec K Roe (Dir)
Pro K Merry
Holes 18 L 6728 yds SSS 72 9 L 2977 yds SSS 69
Recs Am–69 D Wilson (1995) Pro–66 K Merry (1995)
V'tors H–booking necessary
Fees £25 (£30)
Loc 5 miles S of Chelmsford on B1007
Mis Driving range. Par 3 course
Arch Martin Gillett

Stonyhill

Brentwood Road, Herongate CM13 3LW
Tel (01277) 811895
Fax (01277) 811304
Mem 600
Sec S Cipa (Golf Dir)
Pro M Stokes
Holes 18 L 6536 yds Par 73 SSS 71 9 L 3400 yds Par 36
V'tors U SOC–WD/WE pm
Fees £16 (£20)
Loc 4 miles E of M25 Junction 29
Mis Driving range
Arch Reg Plumbridge

Theydon Bois (1897)

Theydon Bois, Epping CM16 4EH
Tel (01992) 813054
Fax (01992) 813054
Mem 600
Sec RS Blower
Pro RJ Hall (01992) 812460
Holes 18 L 5480 yds SSS 68
Recs Am–63 B Taylor (1997) Pro–64 R Joyce (1989)
V'tors Thurs am–restricted H SOC WE–M
Fees £23 After 2pm–£20

Loc 1 mile S of Epping. M25
Junction 26
Arch James Braid

Thorndon Park (1920)

Ingrave, Brentwood CM13 3RH

Tel **(01277) 810345**
Fax (01277) 810645
Mem 450 140(L) 60(J)
Sec JE Leggitt
Pro BV White (01277) 810736
Holes 18 L 6492 yds SSS 71
Recs Am–66 MES Davis
Pro–65 BJ Hunt, B Waites
V'tors WD–I WE/BH–M
Fees £35 D–£50
Loc 2 miles SE of Brentwood on
A128
Arch HS Colt

Thorpe Hall (1907)

*Thorpe Hall Avenue, Thorpe Bay
SS1 3AT*

Tel **(01702) 582205**
Fax (01702) 582205
Mem 1000
Sec RM O'Hara
Pro WJ McColl (01702) 588195
Holes 18 L 6286 yds SSS 71
Recs Am–64 S Feltham (1995)
Pro–66 C Laurence (1993)
V'tors WD–H
Fees On application
Loc E of Southend-on-Sea

Three Rivers (1973)

*Stow Road, Purleigh, Chelmsford
CM3 6RR*

Tel **(01621) 828631**
Fax (01621) 828060
Mem 700
Sec P Davidson (Gen Mgr)
Pro To be appointed
Holes 18 L 6609 yds Par 73 SSS 71
18 L 4637 yds Par 65
V'tors WD–U WE/BH–U after
10.30am SOC
Fees £19 (£22)
Loc Cold Norton, 5 miles S of
Maldon
Mis Driving range
Arch Hawtree

Toot Hill (1991)

School Road, Toot Hill, Ongar CM5 9PU

Tel **(01277) 365747**
Mem 400
Sec Mrs Cameron
Pro M Bishop
Holes 18 L 6013 yds SSS 70
V'tors H SOC–WD
Fees £25
Loc 2 miles W of Ongar
Mis Practice range
Arch Martin Gillett

Top Meadow (1986)

Fen Lane, North Ockendon RM14 3PR

Tel **(01708) 852239 (Clubhouse)**
Sec G Bourton
Pro P King (01708) 859545

Holes 18 L 5500 yds SSS 69
9 L 1633 yds Par 30
V'tors WD–U WE–NA SOC
Fees £12
Loc N Ockendon, off B186
Mis Driving range

Towerlands (1985)

Panfield Road, Braintree CM7 5BJ

Tel **(01376) 326802**
Fax (01376) 552487
Mem 325
Sec R Crane
Pro (01376) 347951
Holes 9 L 5559 yds Par 68
V'tors WD–U WE–U after 12.30pm
SOC
Fees 18 holes–£10 (£12); 9 holes–£8
Loc 1 mile NW of Braintree
(B1053)
Mis Practice range

Upminster (1928)

114 Hall Lane, Upminster RM14 1AU

Tel **(01708) 222788**
Fax (01708) 222788
Mem 1000
Sec JA Dobson
Pro N Carr (01708) 220000
Holes 18 L 6076 yds SSS 69
Recs Am–66 A Emery, N Leonard
V'tors WD–U H exc Tues am Ladies
Day WE/BH–NA SOC
Fees £25 D–£30
Loc Station ¾ mile

Wanstead (1893)

Wanstead, London E11 2LW

Tel **(0181) 989 0604**
Fax (0181) 532 9138
Mem 650
Sec K Jones (0181) 989 3938
Pro D Hawkins (0181) 989 9876
Holes 18 L 6262 yds SSS 69
Recs Am–62 P Sullivan
Pro–64 N Coles, P Brown
V'tors WD–H WE/BH–M
Fees D–£25
Loc Off A12, nr Wanstead station
Arch James Braid

Warley Park (1975)

*Magpie Lane, Little Warley, Brentwood
CM13 3DX*

Tel **(01277) 224891**
Fax (01277) 200679
Mem 800
Sec K Regan
Pro J Groat (01277) 200441
Holes 27 hole course
Recs Am–65 M Cox (1996)
V'tors WD–H
Fees £25
Loc 2 miles S of Brentwood. M25
Junction 29
Arch Reg Plumbridge

Warren (1932)

Woodham Walter, Maldon CM9 6RW

Tel **(01245) 223258/223198**
Fax (01245) 223989
Mem 800

Sec MFL Durham
(01245) 223258
Pro Mickey Walker OBE
(01245) 224662
Holes 18 L 6211 yds SSS 69
Recs Am–65 M Robarts (1990)
Pro–66 H Flatman
V'tors WD–H WE–M SOC
Fees £25 D–£30
Loc 7 miles E of Chelmsford, off
A414
Mis Golf Academy (01245) 223198

Weald Park (1994)

*Coxtie Green Road, South Weald,
Brentwood CM14 5RJ*

Tel **(01277) 375101**
Mem 600
Sec June Mackison
Pro P Barham, F Sunderland
(01277) 375484
Holes 18 L 6612 yds SSS 72
Recs Am–68 D Mackison (1995),
R Gold, A Gibson (1996)
Pro–65 P Barham (1994)
V'tors WD–telephone booking
required WE–H NA before
noon
Fees £25 (£30)
Loc 3 miles from M25 Junction 28
(A1023)
Arch Reg Plumbridge

West Essex (1900)

*Bury Road, Sewardstonebury,
Chingford, London E4 7QL*

Tel **(0181) 529 7558**
Fax (0181) 524 7870
Mem 654
Sec D Wilson
Pro R Joyce (0181) 529 4367
Holes 18 L 6289 yds SSS 70
Recs Am–64 G Stowe (1996)
Pro–63 G Burroughs
V'tors WD–U H WE/BH–M H
SOC–Mon/Wed/Fri
Fees £25 D–£30
Loc 2 miles N of Chingford BR
station. M25 Junction 26
Mis Driving range
Arch James Braid

Woodford (1890)

*2, Sunset Avenue, Woodford Green
IG8 0ST*

Tel **(0181) 504 0553/4254**
Fax (0181) 504 3330
Mem 430
Sec GJ Cousins (0181) 504 3330
Pro A Johns (0181) 504 4254
Holes 9 L 5867 yds SSS 68
Recs Am–69 M Everitt, R Piper,
P Blaxill, MG Smith
Pro–66 C Platts, L Jones
V'tors WD–U exc Tues am–NA
Sat–M Sun–NA before noon
SOC
Fees £10–£15
Loc 11 miles NE of London
Mis Major item of red clothing to
be worn on course
Arch Tom Dunn

Gloucestershire

Brickhampton Court
Cheltenham Road, Churchdown
GL2 9QF

Tel	**(01452) 859444**
Fax	(01452) 859333
Sec	R East (Gen Mgr)
Pro	D Finch (Golf Dir)
Holes	Spa 18 L 6387 yds Par 71
	SSS 70
	Glevum 9 L 1859 yds Par 31
V'tors	U SOC
Fees	£16 D–£25 (£22.50 D–£30)
Loc	Between Cheltenham and
	Gloucester. M5 Junction 11,
	3 miles
Mis	Floodlit driving range
Arch	Simon Gidman

Bristol & Clifton (1891)
Beggar Bush Lane, Failand, Clifton,
Bristol BS8 3TH

Tel	**(01275) 393474/393117**
Fax	(01275) 394611
Mem	800
Sec	RC Bennett (01275) 393474
Pro	P Mawson (01275) 393031
Holes	18 L 6316 yds SSS 70
Recs	Am–65 G Wolstenholme
	Pro–64 P Oosterhuis
V'tors	WD–UH WE/BH–MH
Fees	On request
Loc	2 miles W of suspension bridge.
	4 miles S of M5 Junction 19

Broadway (1895)
Willersey Hill, Broadway, Worcs
WR12 7LG

Tel	**(01386) 858997**
Fax	(01386) 858643
Mem	500 160(L) 70(J)
Sec	B Carnie (Sec/Mgr)
	(01386) 853683
Pro	M Freeman (01386) 853275
Holes	18 L 6216 yds SSS 70
Recs	Am–65 M Dove
	Pro–66 D Steele, R Adams
V'tors	H exc Sat–M SOC
Fees	£27 (£33)
Loc	1½ miles E of Broadway (A44)
Arch	James Braid

Canons Court (1982)
Bradley Green, Wotton-under-Edge
GL12 7PN

Tel	**(01453) 843128**
Fax	(01453) 844151
Mem	300
Sec	AR Webb (Gen Mgr)
Holes	9 L 5323 yds SSS 68
V'tors	U
Fees	£8 (£10)
Loc	3 miles E of M5 Junction 14,
	off B4058

Chipping Sodbury
Chipping Sodbury, Bristol BS17 6PU

Tel	**(01454) 312024 (Members),**
	(01454) 315822 Catering
Fax	(01454) 319042

Mem	750
Sec	D Bird (01454) 319042
Pro	M Watts (01454) 314087
Holes	New 18 L 6912 yds SSS 73
	Old 9 L 6194 yds SSS 69
Recs	New Am–66 D Wood (1988)
	Pro–65 B Austin (1993)
V'tors	WD–U WE–pm only Sat/
	Sun am–XL SOC
Fees	New £20 (£25) Old £4 (£5)
Loc	12 miles NE of Bristol. M4
	Junction 18, 5 miles. M5
	Junction 14, 9 miles.
Arch	Fred Hawtree

Cirencester (1893)
Cheltenham Road, Bagendon,
Cirencester GL7 7BH

Tel	**(01285) 653939**
Fax	(01285) 650665
Mem	800
Sec	IA Gray (01285) 652465
Pro	P Garratt (01285) 656124
Holes	18 L 6020 yds Par 70 SSS 69
V'tors	H SOC–WD
Fees	£20 (£25)
Loc	1½ miles N of Cirencester on
	A435
Arch	James Braid

Cleeve Hill (1976)
Pay and play
Cleeve Hill, Cheltenham GL52 3PW

Tel	**(01242) 672025**
Sec	S Gilman (Mgr)
Pro	(01242) 672592
Holes	18 L 6444 yds SSS 71
V'tors	U exc Sat 11–3pm/Sun am–NA
	SOC
Fees	£8 (£10)
Loc	3 miles N of Cheltenham on
	A46 to Winchcombe
Mis	Tee booking 7 days in advance

Cotswold Edge (1980)
Upper Rushmire, Wotton-under-Edge
GL12 7PT

Tel	**(01453) 844167**
Fax	(01453) 845120
Mem	800
Sec	NJ Newman
Pro	DJ Gosling (01453) 844398
Holes	18 L 5816 yds SSS 69
Recs	Am–68 J Lathom-Sharp (1989)
	Pro–66 J Loughnane (1994)
	Ladies–70 M Mayes (1995)
V'tors	WD–U WE–M SOC
Fees	£15
Loc	2 miles NE of Wotton-under-
	Edge on B4058 Tetbury road.
	M5 Junction 14

Cotswold Hills (1902)
Ullenwood, Cheltenham GL53 9QT

Tel	**(01242) 573210**
Fax	(01242) 515264
Mem	800
Sec	A O'Reilly (01242) 515264
Pro	N Boland (01242) 515263
Holes	18 L 6716 yds SSS 72
Recs	Am–67 G Wolstenholme (1992)
	Pro–67 J Loughnane,
	S Little (1992)

V'tors	I (recognised club members)
	SOC
Fees	£24 (£30)
Loc	3 miles S of Cheltenham
Arch	MD Little

Filton (1909)
Golf Course Lane, Bristol BS34 7QS

Tel	**(0117) 969 2021**
Fax	(0117) 931 4359
Mem	800
Sec	M Burns (0117) 969 4169
Pro	JCN Lumb (0117) 969 4158
Holes	18 L 6312 yds SSS 70
Recs	Am–66 J Kitchen
	Pro–68 RH Evans
V'tors	WD–U WE/BH–M SOC–WD
Fees	£20 D–£25
Loc	4 miles N of Bristol
Arch	Hawtree

Forest Hills (1992)
Mile End Road, Coleford GL16 7BY

Tel	**(01594) 810620**
Mem	500
Sec	AR Walker (01594) 810620
Pro	None
Holes	18 L 5724 yds SSS 68
Recs	Am–P Gibson (1995)
V'tors	U SOC
Fees	£13 (£15)
Loc	1 mile W of Coleford
	(B4028)
Arch	Adrian Stiff

Forest of Dean (1973)
Lords Hill, Coleford GL16 8BD

Tel	**(01594) 832583**
Fax	(01594) 832584
Mem	500
Sec	Mrs J Sandells
Pro	J Hansel (01594) 833689
Holes	18 L 5682 yds SSS 67
V'tors	U SOC
Fees	£16 (£18)
Loc	½ mile SE of Coleford on
	Parkend road. M50, 10 miles
Arch	John Day

Gloucester Hotel (1976)
Matson Lane, Gloucester GL4 9EA

Tel	**(01452) 525653**
Mem	750
Sec	P Darnell
Pro	P Darnell (01452) 411311
Holes	18 L 6127 yds SSS 69
	9 L 1980 yds SSS 27
Recs	Am–68 J Wallace
	Pro–65 P Darnell
V'tors	U
Fees	£19 (£25)
Loc	2 miles S of Gloucester, off
	Painswick road. M5 Junction 11
Mis	Driving range

Henbury (1891)
Westbury-on-Trym, Bristol BS10 7QB

Tel	**(0117) 950 0660**
Fax	(0117) 959 1928
Mem	760
Sec	RH White (0117) 950 0044

Pro N Riley (0117) 950 2121
Holes 18 L 6039 yds SSS 70
Recs Am–62 G Wolstenholme
Pro–67 B Sandry
V'tors WD–H WE–M SOC–Tues &
Fri
Fees £21
Loc 3 miles N of Bristol, off
A4018. M5 Junction 17

Kendleshire

*Henfield Road, Coalpit Heath, Bristol
BS17 2TG*
Tel (0117) 956 7007
Fax (0117) 957 3433
Mem 750
Sec P Murphy
Pro P Barrington
(0117) 956 7000
Holes 18 L 6500 yds Par 70 SSS 71
Recs Am–73
Pro–66 D Ray
V'tors H SOC
Fees £18 (£24)
Loc 1 mile NE of Bristol.
M32 Junction 1
Mis Driving range
Arch Adrian Stiff

Knowle (1905)

*Fairway, West Town Lane, Brislington,
Bristol BS4 5DF*
Tel (0117) 977 6341
Fax (0117) 972 0615
Mem 700
Sec Mrs JD King
(0117) 977 0660
Pro GM Brand (0117) 977 9193
Holes 18 L 6016 yds SSS 69
Recs Am–61 MR Jeffery (1994)
Pro–64 S Brown
V'tors WD exc Thurs–H WE/BH–H
SOC–Thurs
Fees £22 D–£27 (£27 D–£32)
Loc Brislington Hill, 3 miles S of
Bristol, off A4
Arch JH Taylor

Lilley Brook (1922)

*Cirencester Road, Charlton Kings,
Cheltenham GL53 8EG*
Tel (01242) 526785
Fax (01242) 256880
Mem 700
Sec K Skeen
Pro F Hadden (01242) 525201
Holes 18 L 6226 yds SSS 70
Recs Am–64 B Mitten (1987)
Pro–61 S Little (1996)
V'tors WD–H or I (recognised club
members) WE–M SOC–WD
Fees £25 D–£30 (£30 D–£35)
Loc 3 miles SE of Cheltenham on
A435

Long Ashton (1893)

*Clarken Coombe, Long Ashton, Bristol
BS41 9DW*
Tel (01275) 392229
Fax (01275) 394395
Mem 750
Sec BJG Manning
(01275) 392316

Pro DP Scanlan
(01275) 392265
Holes 18 L 6077 yds SSS 70
Recs Am–66 G Wolstenholme
Pro–66 K Aitken, A Sherborne,
A Oldcorn, D Sheppard
V'tors WD–U H WE/BH–I H
SOC–Wed
Fees £26 (£35)
Loc 3 miles S of Bristol on B3128
Arch JH Taylor

Lydney (1909)

Lakeside Avenue, Lydney GL15 5QA
Tel (01594) 842614
Mem 300
Sec DA Barnard
(01594) 843940
Holes 9 L 5382 yds SSS 66
Recs Am–63 MA Barnard (1988)
Pro–68 F Goulding
V'tors WD–U WE/BH–M SOC
Fees £12 W–£35
Loc 20 miles SW of Gloucester,
off A48

Mangotsfield (1975)

*Carsons Road, Mangotsfield, Bristol
BS17 3LW*
Tel (0117) 956 5501
Mem 600
Sec C Main
Pro C Trewin
Holes 18 L 5337 yds SSS 66
Recs Am–63 N Pillinger (1990)
Ladies–77 P Chapman (1988)
V'tors U
Fees On application
Loc 6 miles NE of Bristol

Minchinhampton (1889)

Minchinhampton, Stroud GL6 9BE
Tel (01453) 832642 (Old),
(01453) 833840 (New)
Fax (01453) 833860
Mem 1860
Sec DT Calvert (01453) 833866
Pro C Steele (01453) 833860
Holes Old 18 L 6019 yds SSS 69
Avening 18 L 6279 yds SSS 70
Cherington 18 L 6320 yds
SSS 70
Recs Old Am–67 PH Fisher, L Scott
Pro–67 RA Brown
Avening Am–67 R Broad
Pro–66 K Spurgeon
Cherington Am–66 S Rose
V'tors H SOC
Fees Old–£10 (£13)
New–£25 (£30)
Loc Old–3 miles E of Stroud.
New–5 miles E of Stroud
Arch Old: R Wilson.
Avening: F Hawtree.
Cherington: M Hawtree

Naunton Downs (1993)

Naunton, Cheltenham GL54 3AE
Tel (01451) 850090
Fax (01451) 850091
Mem 900
Sec ND Powell (Golf Dir)

Pro ND Powell (01451) 850092
Holes 18 L 6078 yds Par 71 SSS 69
Recs Am–73 D Devine
V'tors U–by arrangement
Fees £19.95
Loc 5 miles SW of Stow-on-the-
Wold, off B4068
Arch Jacob Pott

Painswick (1891)

Painswick, Stroud GL6 6TL
Tel (01452) 812180
Mem 430
Sec AR Green
Pro None
Holes 18 L 4780 yds SSS 65
Recs Am–61 B Hill
V'tors WD/Sat–U Sun–M SOC
Fees £10 Sat–£15
Loc ½ mile N of Painswick on A46
Arch David Brown

Rodway (1991)

Pay and play
Highnam GL2 8DN
Tel (01452) 384222
Fax (01989) 766450
Mem 350
Sec S Williams
Pro T Grubb
Holes 18 L 5860 yds SSS 68
Recs Am–72
V'tors U SOC
Fees 18 holes–£8 (£10)
9 holes–£5 (£6)
Loc 2 miles W of Gloucester
(B4215)
Arch J Gabb

Sherdons Golf Centre
(1993)

Pay and play
Manor Farm, Tredington, Tewkesbury
Tel (01684) 274782
Fax (01684) 275358
Mem 300
Sec R Chatham
Pro P Clark
Holes 9 L 2654 yds Par 34 SSS 66
V'tors U
Fees 18 holes–£9 (£12);
9 holes–£5.50 (£7.50)
Loc 2 miles S of Tewkesbury,
off A38
Mis Driving range

Shirehampton Park
(1907)

*Park Hill, Shirehampton, Bristol
BS11 0UL*
Tel (0117) 982 3059
Fax (0117) 982 2083
Mem 600
Sec GW Rees (0117) 982 2083
Pro B Ellis (0117) 982 2488
Holes 18 L 5430 yds SSS 67
Recs Am–63 PM Fisher (1995)
V'tors WD–H WE–M SOC–Thurs
Fees £18 (£25)
Loc 2 miles E of M5 Junction 18,
on B4054

Stakis Puckrup Hall Hotel (1992)

Puckrup, Tewkesbury GL20 6EL

Tel	**(01684) 296200**
Fax	(01684) 850788
Mem	420
Sec	C Sandyford-Sykes
Pro	K Pickett
Holes	18 L 6189 yds SSS 70
Recs	Am–68 K Booth
V'tors	WD–H SOC WE–residents
Fees	£22.50 (£25)
Loc	2 miles N of Tewkesbury on A38. M50 Junction 1. M5 Junction 8
Arch	S Gidman

Stinchcombe Hill (1889)

Stinchcombe Hill, Dursley GL11 6AQ

Tel	**(01453) 542015**
Mem	550
Sec	S Johnson
Pro	P Bushell (01453) 543878
Holes	18 L 5734 yds SSS 68
Recs	Am–63 TP Smith (1992) Pro–64 I Bolt (1984)
V'tors	U–phone Pro SOC
Fees	£20 (£25)
Loc	1 mile W of Dursley
Arch	A Hoare

Tewkesbury Park Hotel (1976)

Lincoln Green Lane, Tewkesbury GL20 7DN

Tel	**(01684) 295405**
Fax	(01684) 292386
Mem	710
Sec	RS Nichol (01684) 299452
Pro	R Taylor (01684) 294892
Holes	18 L 6533 yds SSS 72 6 hole Par 3 course
Recs	Am–67 A Soutar (1995) Pro–68 D Ray (1996)
V'tors	WD–U H SOC–WD WE–residential SOC only
Fees	£25 (£30)
Loc	½ mile S of Tewkesbury on A38. M5 Junction 9, 2 miles

Thornbury Golf Centre (1992)

Bristol Road, Thornbury

Tel	**(01454) 281144**
Fax	(01454) 281177
Mem	400
Sec	I Gibson
Pro	S Hubbard
Holes	18 L 6154 yds SSS 69 Par 71 18 L 2195 yds Par 54
Recs	Am–70 A Gilbert (1996) Pro–68 G Orr (1994)
V'tors	U SOC–WD
Fees	£13.50 (£15)
Loc	10 miles N of Bristol, off A38
Mis	Driving range
Arch	Hawtree

Tracy Park (1976)

Tracy Park, Bath Road, Wick, Bristol BS15 5RN

Tel	**(0117) 937 2251**
Fax	(0117) 937 4288
Mem	950
Sec	S Taylor
Pro	R Berry (0117) 937 3521
Holes	27 holes: Avon L 6423 yds SSS 71 Bristol L 6430 yds SSS 71 Cotswold L 6189 yds SSS 69
Recs	Am–65 S Pugh Pro–64 P Pring
V'tors	WD/WE–phone first SOC
Fees	£22 (£30)
Loc	3 miles NW of Bath, off A420. M4 Junction 18

Westonbirt (1971)

Westonbirt, Tetbury GL8 8QG

Tel	**(01666) 880242**
Mem	200
Sec	Bursar, Westonbirt School
Holes	9 L 4504 yds SSS 61
Recs	Am–62 S Dunlop
V'tors	U SOC–WD
Fees	On application
Loc	3 miles S of Tetbury, off A433

Woodlands G&CC (1989)

Pay and play

Woodlands Lane, Almondsbury, Bristol BS12 4JZ

Tel	**(01454) 619319**
Fax	(01454) 619397
Sec	J Seymour
Holes	18 L 6100 yds SSS 70
V'tors	U SOC
Fees	£12 (£15)
Loc	Nr M5 Junction 16
Arch	Cliff Chapman

Woodspring G&CC (1994)

Yanley Lane, Long Ashton, Bristol BS18 9LR

Tel	**(01275) 394378**
Fax	(01275) 394473
Sec	M Pierce (Gen Mgr)
Pro	N Beer
Holes	27 holes: 6209-6587 yds Par 71-71 SSS 70-71
V'tors	W–H SOC
Fees	£25 (£28.50)
Loc	2 miles S of Bristol on A38.
Mis	Floodlit driving range
Arch	Allis/Clark

Hampshire

Alresford (1890)

Cheriton Road, Alresford SO24 0PN

Tel	**(01962) 733746**
Fax	(01962) 736040
Mem	720
Sec	P Kingston
Pro	M Scott (01962) 733998
Holes	18 L 5905 yds Par 69 SSS 68
Recs	Am–67 G Richardson (1994) Pro–64 J Barnes (1996)

V'tors	U H WE–after noon SOC
Fees	£20 D–£32 (£37)
Loc	1 mile S of Alresford on B3046
Arch	Scott Webb Young

Alton (1908)

Old Odiham Road, Alton GU34 4BU

Tel	**(01420) 82042**
Mem	370
Sec	P Brown
Pro	P Brown (01420) 86518
Holes	9 L 5744 yds SSS 68
Recs	Am–64 R Lamport (1993) Pro–62 R Edwards (1993)
V'tors	WD–U WE–H or M SOC–WD
Fees	18 holes–£12 D–£16 9 holes–£7.50
Loc	2 miles N of Alton. 6 miles S of Odiham, off B3349
Arch	James Braid

Ampfield Par Three (1963)

Winchester Road, Ampfield, Romsey SO51 9BQ

Tel	**(01794) 368480**
Mem	500
Sec	Mrs S Baker
Pro	R Benfield (01794) 368750
Holes	18 L 2478 yds SSS 53
Recs	Am–49 R Bailey Pro–49 A Timms
V'tors	WD–U WE/BH–H (phone first) SOC
Fees	£9 (£15.50)
Loc	5 miles E of Romsey on A31
Arch	Henry Cotton

Andover (1907)

51 Winchester Road, Andover SP10 2EF

Tel	**(01264) 323980**
Mem	460 70(L) 30(J)
Sec	Mrs L Brearley (01264) 358040
Pro	D Lawrence (01264) 324151
Holes	9 L 6096 yds SSS 69
Recs	Am–65 V Rusher (1993) Pro–64 I Young (1991)
V'tors	U H SOC–Mon–Wed
Fees	£10 (£22)
Loc	½ mile S of Andover on A3057
Arch	JH Taylor

Army (1883)

Laffans Road, Aldershot GU11 2HF

Tel	**(01252) 336776**
Fax	(01252) 337562
Mem	700
Sec	Maj (Retd) JWG Douglass (01252) 337272
Pro	G Cowley (01252) 336722
Holes	18 L 6579 yds SSS 71
Recs	Am–67 M Rollason Pro–67 I Benson
V'tors	WD–H–contact Sec/Mgr SOC
Fees	Special rates for Forces
Loc	Between Aldershot and Farnborough

Barton-on-Sea (1897)

Milford Road, New Milton
BH25 5PP

Tel	**(01425) 615308**
Fax	(01425) 621457
Mem	560 115(L) 50(J)
Sec	N Hallam-Jones
Pro	P Coombs (01425) 611210
Holes	27 holes:
	L 6289-6505 yds Par 72
Recs	Am–68 L Mitchelmore (1996)
	Pro–65 J Le Roux (1997)
V'tors	H NA before 9am SOC–WD
	exc Tues
Fees	D–£27.50 (D–£30)
Loc	1 mile from New Milton, off
	B3058. M27 Junction 1
Arch	J Hamilton Stutt

Basingstoke (1928)

Kempshott Park, Basingstoke
RG23 7LL

Tel	**(01256) 465990**
Fax	(01256) 331793
Mem	700
Sec	WA Jefford
Pro	I Hayes (01256) 51332
Holes	18 L 6350 yds SSS 70
Recs	Am–66 C Humphrey (1996)
	Pro–63 G Hughes (1996)
V'tors	WD–H WE–M SOC–Wed &
	Thurs
Fees	£20 D–£30
Loc	3 miles W of Basingstoke on
	A30. M3 Junction 7
Arch	James Braid

Bishopswood (1978)

Bishopswood Lane, Tadley, Basingstoke
RG26 6AT

Tel	**(01734) 815213/820312**
Fax	(01734) 815213
Mem	500
Sec	MW Phillips (Mgr)
	(01734) 812200
Pro	S Ward
Holes	9 L 6474 yds SSS 71
Recs	Am–69 C Wilkins (1987)
	Pro–66 P Bryden (1992)
V'tors	WD–U WE–M
Fees	£14
Loc	6 miles N of Basingstoke, off
	A340
Mis	Floodlit driving range
Arch	Blake/Phillips

Blackmoor (1913)

Whitehill, Bordon GU35 9EH

Tel	**(01420) 472775/475461**
Fax	(01420) 487666
Mem	680 100(L) 70(J)
Sec	Miss Christina Hayllar
Pro	S Clay (01420) 472345
Holes	18 L 6213 yds SSS 70
Recs	Am–66 NE Holman (1988)
	Pro–64 R Dickman (1990)
V'tors	H WE–NA
Fees	£30 L–£40
Loc	½ mile W of Whitehill on
	A325
Arch	HS Colt

Blacknest (1993)

Frith End, Binsted GU34 4QL

Tel	**(01420) 22888**
Fax	(01420) 22001
Mem	600
Sec	GD Lawson
Pro	I Benson
Holes	18 L 5858 yds SSS 69
	9 hole Par 3 course
V'tors	U SOC
Fees	£14 (£16) (1997)
Loc	7 miles SW of Farnham, off
	A325
Mis	Driving range

Botley Park Hotel G&CC (1989)

Winchester Road, Boorley Green, Botley
SO3 2UA

Tel	**(01489) 780888 Ext 444**
Fax	(01489) 789242
Mem	700
Sec	Miss M Johnstone
Pro	T Barter (01489) 789771
Holes	18 L 6341 yds SSS 70
Recs	Am–67 D Lawrence (1996)
	Pro–G Stubbington (1995)
V'tors	H SOC
Fees	£30
Loc	6 miles E of Southampton
	on B3354. M27 Junction 7.
	8 miles SE of M3
Mis	Driving range
Arch	Potterton/Murray

Bramshaw (1880)

Brook, Lyndhurst SO43 7HE

Tel	**(01703) 813433**
Fax	(01703) 813958
Mem	1400
Sec	RD Tingey
Pro	C Bonner (01703) 813434
Holes	Forest 18 L 5774 yds SSS 68
	Manor 18 L 6517 yds SSS 71
Recs	Forest Am–67 G Hill
	Pro–65 R Tuddenham
	Manor Am–66 M LeMesurier
	Pro–66 G Stubbington
V'tors	WD–U H WE–M
Fees	Forest £20 Manor £25
Loc	10 miles SW of Southampton.
	M27 Junction 1, 1 mile

Brokenhurst Manor (1919)

Sway Road, Brockenhurst SO42 7SG

Tel	**(01590) 623332**
Fax	(01590) 624140
Mem	800
Sec	PE Clifford
Pro	J Lovell (01590) 623092
Holes	18 L 6222 yds SSS 70
Recs	Am–63 R Bland, J Rose
	Pro–64 N Tokely
V'tors	WD–H after 9.30am
	NA–Tues–Ladies' Day SOC
Fees	£30 D–£40 (D–£45)
Loc	1 mile SW of Brockenhurst on
	B3055
Arch	HS Colt

Burley (1905)

Burley, Ringwood BH24 4BB

Tel	**(01425) 402431**
Fax	(01425) 402431
Mem	520
Sec	GJ Stride
Holes	9 L 6149 yds Par 71 SSS 69
Recs	Am–68 AS Elliott (1991),
	M Geisler, P Brine
	(1997)
V'tors	H
Fees	£14 (£16) W–£42
Loc	4 miles SE of Ringwood

Cams Hall Estate (1993)

Portchester Road, Fareham PO16 8UP

Tel	**(01329) 827222**
Fax	(01329) 827111
Mem	950
Sec	D Renton (Sec/Mgr)
Pro	J Neve (01329) 837732
Holes	27 L 6244-6477 yds SSS 71-72
Recs	Am–69 J Oxford (1994)
V'tors	U SOC
Fees	£19 (£25)
Loc	8 miles W of Portsmouth.
	M27 Junction 11
Arch	Alliss/Clarke

Chilworth Golf Centre (1989)

Main Road, Chilworth, Southampton
SO16 7JP

Tel	**(01703) 740544**
Fax	(01703) 733166
Sec	Mrs E Garner
Pro	M Butcher, J Barnes
Holes	18 L 5740 yds SSS 69
Recs	Pro–65 J Barnes (1997)
V'tors	U
Fees	£12 (£15)
Loc	Between Romsey and
	Southampton on A27
Mis	Floodlit driving range

Corhampton (1891)

Corhampton, Southampton SO32 3LP

Tel	**(01489) 877279**
Fax	(01489) 877680
Mem	750
Sec	RE Jones
Pro	I Roper (01489) 877638
Holes	18 L 6444 yds SSS 70
Recs	Am–66 R Edwards (1988),
	A Clotworthy (1992)
	Pro–64 MD Jarvis (1991),
	G Stubbington (1992)
V'tors	WD–U H WE/BH–M
	SOC–Mons & Thurs
Fees	£21 D–£31
Loc	9 miles S of Winchester

Dibden Golf Centre (1974)

Public

Main Road, Dibden, Southampton
SO45 5TB

Tel	**(01703) 845596**
Fax	(01703) 845596
Mem	700
Sec	Mrs J Lock (Hon)

Pro	A Bridge (01703) 845596
Holes	18 L 5986 yds SSS 69
	9 hole course
Recs	Am–63 R Bland (1992)
	Pro–63 I Young (1988)
V'tors	U
Fees	£10 D–£18 (£12)
Loc	10 miles W of Southampton,
	off A326 at Dibden
	roundabout
Mis	Floodlit driving range

Dummer (1993)

Dummer, Basingstoke RG25 2AR

Tel	(01256) 397888
Fax	(01256) 397889
Mem	750
Sec	K Dandridge
Pro	G Stubbington
Holes	18 L 6513 yds SSS 71
Recs	Am–68 R Aldred
	Pro–67 K Saunders, R Adams
V'tors	WD–U
Fees	£25
Loc	7 miles SW of Basingstoke.
	M3 Junction 7
Arch	Alliss/Clark

Dunwood Manor (1969)

Danes Road, Awbridge, Romsey SO5 10GF

Tel	(01794) 340549
Fax	(01794) 341215
Mem	700
Sec	JR Basford
Pro	H Teschner
	(01794) 340663
Holes	18 L 5755 yds SSS 69
Recs	Am–69 D Harris
	Pro–61 G Stubbington
V'tors	WE/BH–restricted SOC–WD
Fees	£20 (£30)
Loc	Romsey 4 miles, off A27

Fleetlands (1961)

Fareham Road, Gosport PO13 0AW

Tel	(01705) 544492
Mem	120
Sec	A Eade (01705) 544384
Holes	9 L 4852 yds SSS 64
Recs	Am–67 M Squibb,
	D Edmunds
	Pro–68 K Jackson
V'tors	M at all times
Loc	2 miles S of Fareham on A32
	Gosport road. M27
	Junction 12

Fleming Park (1973)

Public

Fleming Park, Magpie Lane, Eastleigh SO5 3LH

Tel	(01703) 612797
Sec	ABG Davis
Pro	C Strickett
Holes	18 L 4436 yds SSS 62
Recs	Am–62 D Cox (1989)
	Pro–61 J Hay
V'tors	U SOC–WD
Fees	On application
Loc	6 miles N of Southampton

Furzeley (1993)

Pay and play

Furzeley Road, Denmead PO7 6TX

Tel	(01705) 231180
Fax	(01705) 231180
Pro	D Brown
Holes	18 L 4363 yds SSS 62
V'tors	U SOC
Fees	£9.80 (£11.50)
Loc	2 miles NW of Waterlooville

Gosport & Stokes Bay (1885)

Fort Road, Haslar, Gosport PO12 2AT

Tel	(01705) 581625
Fax	(01705) 527941
Mem	450
Sec	AP Chubb (01705) 527941
Holes	9 L 5668 yds SSS 69
Recs	Am–69 M Stubley (1986)
	Pro–65 P Dawson (1985)
V'tors	U exc Sun–NA
Fees	£15 (£20)
Loc	S boundary of Gosport

Great Salterns (1914)

Public

Portsmouth Golf Centre, Burrfields Road, Portsmouth PO3 5HH

Tel	(01705) 664549
Fax	(01705) 650525
Pro	T Healy
Holes	18 L 5970 yds SSS 68
V'tors	U SOC
Fees	£11
Loc	1 mile off M27 on A2030
Mis	Driving range

The Hampshire

Winchester Road, Goodworth Clatford, Andover SP11 7TB

Tel	(01264) 357555
Fax	(01264) 356606
Mem	735
Sec	A Timms (Gen Mgr)
Pro	P Smith, J Slade
Holes	18 L 6376 yds Par
	9 hole Par 3 course
Recs	Am–69 A Lewis
	Pro–65 G Stubbington
V'tors	U SOC
Fees	£14 (£25)
Loc	1 mile SW of Andover
	(A3057)
Mis	Covered driving range
Arch	T Fiducia

Hartley Wintney (1891)

London Road, Hartley Wintney, Basingstoke RG27 8PT

Tel	(01252) 842214
Mem	410
Sec	BD Powell (01252) 844211
Pro	M Smith (01252) 843779
Holes	9 L 6096 yds SSS 69
Recs	Am–70 M Wild
	Pro–63 R Lewington
V'tors	Wed–Ladies Day
	WE/BH–restricted SOC–Tues
	& Thurs

Fees	£17 (£20)
Loc	A30 between Camberley and
	Basingstoke

Hayling (1883)

Links Lane, Hayling Island PO11 0BX

Tel	(01705) 463712/463777
Fax	(01705) 464446
Mem	800
Sec	CJ Cavill (01705) 464446
Pro	R Gadd (01705) 464491
Holes	18 L 6521 yds SSS 71
Recs	Am–65 EJ Tambling (1993)
	Pro–66 F Gilbride (1971)
V'tors	H WE/BH–after 10am
	SOC–Tues & Wed
Fees	£26 (£35)
Loc	5 miles S of Havant on A3023
Arch	Taylor(1905)/Simpson(1933)

Hockley (1915)

Twyford, Winchester SO21 1PL

Tel	(01962) 713165
Fax	(01962) 713612
Mem	750
Sec	ID Morgan (Mgr)
Pro	T Lane (01962) 713678
Holes	18 L 6296 yds SSS 70
Recs	Am–66
	Pro–64
V'tors	U H SOC
Fees	On application
Loc	2 miles S of Winchester on
	B3335
Mis	Driving range
Arch	James Braid

Leckford (1929)

Leckford, Stockbridge SO20 6JS

Tel	(01264) 810320
Mem	400
Sec	J Wood
Holes	Old 9 L 3251 yds SSS 71
	New 9 L 2281 yds SSS 62
V'tors	M
Loc	5 miles W of Andover

Lee-on-the-Solent (1905)

Brune Lane, Lee-on-the-Solent PO13 9PB

Tel	(01705) 550207
Fax	(01705) 554233
Mem	715
Sec	P Clash (Mgr)
	(01705) 551170
Pro	J Richardson (01705) 551181
Holes	18 L 5959 yds SSS 69
Recs	Am–66 S Richardson
	Pro–63 R Edwards (1993)
V'tors	WD–U H WE–M H
	SOC–Thurs
Fees	D–£25 (£30)
Loc	3 miles S of Fareham. M27
	Junction 11

Liphook (1922)

Liphook GU30 7EH

Tel	(01428) 723271/723785
Fax	(01428) 724853
Mem	700

Sec	Maj JB Morgan MBE
	(01428) 723785
Pro	I Large
Holes	18 L 6167 yds SSS 70
Recs	Am–66 M Blackey, R Eggo
	Pro–66 TR Pinner
V'tors	I H (max 24) Sun–NA before
	1pm SOC
Fees	£29 D–£37 (£37 D–£47)
Loc	1 mile S of Liphook on B2070
	(old A3)
Arch	ACG Groome

Marriott Meon Valley Hotel (1977)

Sandy Lane, Shedfield, Southampton SO32 2HQ

Tel	(01329) 833455
Fax	(01329) 834411
Mem	850
Sec	S Coney (Gen Mgr)
	GF McMenemy (Golf Dir)
Pro	J Stirling
Holes	18 L 6519 yds SSS 71
	9 L 2885 yds SSS 68
Recs	Am–66 R Tate (1996)
	Pro–67 J Garner (1987)
V'tors	H SOC
Fees	18 hole: £30 (£40)
	9 hole: £15
Loc	2 miles NW of Wickham.
	N off A334
Arch	J Hamilton Stutt

New Forest (1888)

Southampton Road, Lyndhurst SO43 7BU

Tel	(01703) 282752
Mem	750
Sec	Mrs L Dyer,
	R Macdonald (Prop)
Holes	18 L 5742 yds SSS 68
Recs	Am–64 A Hindmarch (1993)
V'tors	U exc Sun am SOC–WD
Fees	£12 (£14)
Loc	8 miles W of Southampton
	on A35

North Hants (1904)

Minley Road, Fleet GU13 8RE

Tel	(01252) 616443
Fax	(01252) 811627
Mem	550
Sec	IR Goodliffe
Pro	S Porter (01252) 616655
Holes	18 L 6257 yds Par 69 SSS 70
Recs	Am–65 JP Rose (1995),
	B Mason (1997)
	Pro–65 LR Booth,
	GM Hughes (1994)
	Ladies–65 A MacDonald,
	C Caldwell (1990)
V'tors	WD–H by prior arrangement
	WE/BH–MH SOC–Tues &
	Wed
Fees	On application
Loc	3 miles W of Farnborough on
	B3013. M3 Junction 4A
Arch	James Braid

Old Thorns (1982)

Pay and play

Longmoor Road, Griggs Green, Liphook GU30 7PE

Tel	(01428) 724555
Fax	(01428) 725036
Sec	GM Jones (Gen Mgr)
Pro	P Loxley
Holes	18 L 6533 yds SSS 71
	Pro–69 I Aoki (1982)
V'tors	U SOC
Fees	£35 (£45)
Loc	Griggs Green exit off A3
Mis	Driving range
Arch	Cdr John Harris

Otterbourne Golf Centre (1995)

Poles Lane, Otterbourne, Winchester SO21 1DZ

Tel	(01962) 775225
Fax	(01962) 775225
Sec	Mrs E Garner
Holes	9 L 1939 yds
V'tors	U
Fees	£4 (£5)
Loc	On A31 between Otterbourne
	and Hursley

Park (1995)

Pay and play

Avington, Winchester SO21 1DA

Tel	(01962) 779945 (Clubhouse)
Fax	(01962) 779955
Mem	300
Sec	R Stent (Prop) (01962) 779955
Pro	None
Holes	9 L 1949 yds Par 61 SSS 59
V'tors	U SOC
Fees	9 holes–£6 (£9)
	18 holes–£9 (£13.50)
Loc	4 miles E of Winchester.
	M3 Junction 9

Paultons Golf Centre (1993)

Pay and play

Old Salisbury Road, Ower, Romsey SO51 6AN

Tel	(01703) 813992
Fax	(01703) 813993
Sec	R Park (Golf Dir)
Pro	J Cave (01703) 814626
Holes	18 L 6238 yds SSS 71
	9 hole Academy course
V'tors	U SOC
Fees	18 holes–£15 (£20)
	9 holes–£5
Loc	Nr M27 Junction 2, at Ower
Mis	Driving range

Petersfield (1892)

Tankerdale Lane, Liss GU33 7QY

Tel	(01730) 895165
Fax	(01730) 894713
Mem	730
Sec	RR Hine
Pro	G Hughes (01730) 895216
Holes	18 L 6400 yds Par 72 SSS 71
	9 L 3010 yds SSS 68

Recs	Am–67 J Britton
	Pro–65 G Hughes
V'tors	WD–U WE/BH–NA before
	noon SOC–Mon/Wed/Fri
Fees	18 hole: £25 (£30)
	9 hole: £10 (£12)
Loc	Off A3, between Liss and
	Midhurst

Portsmouth (1926)

Public

Crookhorn Lane, Widley, Waterlooville PO7 5QL

Tel	(01705) 372210
Fax	(01705) 200766
Mem	650
Sec	D Houlihan (01705) 201827
Pro	J Banting (01705) 372210
Holes	18 L 6139 yds SSS 70
V'tors	U SOC–arrange with Pro
Fees	£8.80–£11.50
Loc	1 mile N of Portsmouth, on
	B2177

Romsey (1900)

Nursling, Southampton SO16 0XW

Tel	(01703) 732218
Fax	(01703) 741036
Mem	825
Sec	P Hargraves (01703) 734637
Pro	M Desmond (01703) 736673
Holes	18 L 5752 yds SSS 68
Recs	Am–65 J Archer (1990)
	Pro–64 J Slade (1985)
V'tors	WD–H WE/BH–M H
Fees	£21 D–£26
Loc	2 miles SE of Romsey on
	A3057. M27/M271 Junction 3

Rowlands Castle (1902)

Links Lane, Rowlands Castle PO9 6AE

Tel	(01705) 412216
Mem	800 150(L) 50(J)
Sec	KD Fisher (01705) 412784
Pro	P Klepacz (01705) 412785
Holes	18 L 6618 yds Par 72 SSS 72
Recs	Am–69 S Martin (1995)
	Pro–66 M Gregson (1974)
	Ladies–73 A Wheble (1994)
V'tors	WD–U H exc Wed
	am–restricted WE–phone first
	Sat–M SOC–Tues & Thurs
Fees	£25 (£30)
Loc	9 miles S of Petersfield, off
	A3(M). 3 miles N of Havant

Royal Winchester (1888)

Sarum Road, Winchester SO22 5QE

Tel	(01962) 852462
Fax	(01962) 865048
Mem	750
Sec	D Thomson (Mgr)
Pro	S Hunter (01962) 862473
Holes	18 L 6204 yds SSS 70
Recs	Am–65 P Arnold
	Pro–67 B Lane, D Feherty,
	K Bowden, I Roper
V'tors	WD–U H WE/BH–M
	SOC–Mon/Tues/Wed
Fees	On application
Loc	W of Winchester.
	M3 Junction 11

Sandford Springs (1988)

Wolverton, Tadley RG26 5RT
Tel   (01635) 297881
Fax   (01635) 298065
Mem   700
Sec   G Tipple
Pro   K Brake, G Edmunds (01635)
          297883
Holes 27 L 6100 yds SSS 70
V'tors WD–prior booking WE–M
          SOC–WD
Fees   £23 D–£29
Loc   8 miles NW of Basingstoke on
          A339
Arch   Hawtree

South Winchester

Pitt, Winchester SO22 5QW
Tel   (01962) 877800
Fax   (01962) 877900
Mem   675
Sec   S Wright (Gen Mgr)
Pro   R Adams (01962) 840469
Holes 18 L 7086 yds SSS 74
V'tors M
Loc   S side of Winchester on
          Romsey road
Mis   Driving range
Arch   Thomas/Alliss

Southampton Municipal
(1935)

Public
Golf Course Road, Bassett,
Southampton
Tel   (01703) 768407
Pro   J Cave
Holes 18 L 6218 yds SSS 70
          9 L 2391 yds SSS 33
Recs   Am–64 P Dedman
          Pro–62 SW Murray
V'tors U
Fees   On application
Loc   2 miles N of Southampton

Southwick Park (1977)

Pinsley Drive, Southwick PO17 6EL
Tel   (01705) 380131
Mem   650 80(L)
Sec   NW Price
Pro   J Green (01705) 380442
Holes 18 L 5972 yds SSS 69
Recs   Am–67 R Edwards, R Berry
          Pro–64 G Hughes
V'tors WD–U before 11am only
          SOC–Tues
Fees   On application. Service
          Personnel reduced rate
Loc   5 miles N of Portsmouth, off
          B2177

Southwood (1977)

Public
Ively Road, Farnborough GU14 0LJ
Tel   (01252) 548700
Sec   R Hammond
Pro   R Hammond
Holes 18 L 5738 yds SSS 68
Recs   Am–66 R Colborne (1996)
          Pro–61 R Edwards

V'tors U
Fees   £12 (£14.50)
Loc   1 mile W of Farnborough,
          off A325
Arch   M Hawtree

Stoneham (1908)

Monks Wood Close, Bassett,
Southampton SO16 3TT
Tel   (01703) 768151
Fax   (01703) 766320
Mem   800
Sec   RGM Bennett
          (01703) 769272
Pro   J Young (01703) 768397
Holes 18 L 6310 yds SSS 70
Recs   Am–63 M Blackey
          Pro–63 J Martin
V'tors U SOC–Mon/Thurs/Fri
Fees   £29 D–£36 (£40)
Loc   2 miles N of Southampton
          on A27
Arch   Willie Park

Test Valley (1992)

Micheldever Road, Overton, Basingstoke
RG25 3DS
Tel   (01256) 771737
Mem   550
Sec   RV Gardiner (Mgr)
          (01256) 770916
Pro   A Briggs (01256) 771737
Holes 18 L 6883 yds SSS 73
Recs   Pro–66 D Wyborn (1995)
V'tors U SOC
Fees   £14 (£20)
Loc   2 miles S of Overton on
          Micheldever road. M3
          Junction 8
Arch   Wright/Darcy

Tournerbury Golf Centre
(1993)

Pay and play
Tournerbury Road, Hayling Island
PO11 9DL
Tel   (01705) 462266
Pro   R Brown
Holes 9 L 2956 yds SSS 35
V'tors U SOC
Fees   9 holes–£6.80 (£7.80)
Loc   E coast of Hayling Island.
          3 miles S of Havant
Mis   Driving range

Tylney Park (1973)

Rotherwick, Basingstoke RG27 9AY
Tel   (01256) 762079
Fax   (01256) 763079
Mem   700
Sec   MR Alcock
Pro   C de Bruin (Mgr)
Holes 18 L 6108 yds SSS 69
Recs   Am–65 J Shaw
          Pro–68 S Watson (1988)
V'tors WD–U WE–M or H SOC
Fees   On application
Loc   2 miles NW of Hook.
          M3 Junction 5

Waterlooville (1907)

Cherry Tree Ave, Cowplain,
Waterlooville PO8 8AP
Tel   (01705) 263388
Fax   (01705) 347513
Mem   800
Sec   D Nairne
Pro   J Hay (01705) 256911
Holes 18 L 6602 yds SSS 72
Recs   Am–M Blackey (1997)
          Pro–64 P Hughes (1996)
          Ladies–71 K Smith (1992)
V'tors WD/WE–M H (Sun am–XL)
          SOC
Fees   £25 D–£30
Loc   10 miles N of Portsmouth
          on A3
Arch   Henry Cotton

Wellow (1991)

Ryedown Lane, East Wellow, Romsey
SO51 6BD
Tel   (01794) 322872
Mem   500
Sec   Mrs C Gurd
Pro   N Bratley (01794) 323833
Holes 27 L 6000 yds SSS 69
Recs   Am–68 A Hemington (1994)
          Pro–69 M Mills (1994)
V'tors U SOC–WD
Fees   £16 (£19)
Loc   2 miles W of Romsey. M27
          Junction 2, via A36
Arch   W Wiltshire

Weybrook Park (1971)

Rooksdown Lane, Basingstoke
RG24 9NT
Tel   (01256) 320347
Fax   (01256) 812973
Mem   600
Sec   GE Carpenter
Pro   A Dillon (01256) 333232
Holes 18 L 6468 yds SSS 71
V'tors WD–U WE–contact Mgr
          SOC
Fees   £15 (£20)
Loc   1¹/₂ miles N of Basingstoke

Wickham Park

Titchfield Lane, Wickham, Fareham
PO17 5PJ
Tel   (01329) 833342
Fax   (01329) 834798
Sec   T Hill (Mgr)
Pro   T Hill
Holes 18 L 6022 yds Par 70 SSS 69
Recs   Am–71 J Houghton (1996)
V'tors U SOC
Fees   £9.50 (£12.50)
Loc   2 miles N of Fareham
Arch   Jon Payn

Worldham Park (1993)

Pay and play
Cakers Lane, Worldham, Alton
GU34 3AG
Tel   (01420) 543151
Fax   (01420) 84124
Mem   500
Sec   R Buss (Hon)

Holes	18 L 5836 yds SSS 68
V'tors	WD–U WE–U after 11am
	SOC–WD
Fees	£10 (£12)
Loc	1/2 mile E of Alton on B3004
	to Bordon
Mis	Driving range
Arch	Troth/Widborne

Hereford & Worcester

Abbey Park G&CC (1985)

Dagnell End Road, Redditch B98 7BD

Tel	(01527) 63918
Fax	(01527) 65872
Mem	1200
Sec	ME Bradley
Pro	RK Cameron (01527) 68006
Holes	18 L 6411 yds SSS 71
V'tors	WD–U SOC
Fees	£10 (£12.50)
Loc	B4101, off A441 Birmingham
	road
Mis	Driving range
Arch	Donald Steel

Bank House Hotel G&CC

(1992)

Bransford, Worcester WR6 5JD

Tel	(01886) 833551
Fax	(01886) 832461
Mem	350
Sec	PAD Holmes
Pro	C George
Holes	18 L 6204 yds SSS 71
Recs	Am–64 T Duffy (1997)
	Pro–65 G George (1997)
V'tors	U SOC
Fees	£15 (£25)
Loc	3 miles SW of Worcester
	on A4103 Hereford road.
	M5 Junction 7
Mis	Driving range
Arch	Bob Sandow

Belmont Lodge (1983)

Belmont, Hereford HR2 9SA

Tel	(01432) 352666
Fax	(01432) 358090
Mem	500
Sec	T Thomas
Pro	M Welsh (01432) 352717
Holes	18 L 6511 yds SSS 71
Recs	Am–71 N Dulson
	Pro–66 S Edwards
V'tors	U SOC
Fees	On application
Loc	11/2 miles S of Hereford
	on A465
Arch	B Sandow

Blackwell (1893)

Blackwell, Bromsgrove, Worcestershire B60 1PY

Tel	(0121) 445 1994
Fax	(0121) 445 4911
Mem	300 100(L) 20(J)

Sec	JT Mead
Pro	N Blake (0121) 445 3113
Holes	18 L 6230 yds SSS 71
Recs	Am–65 M Reynard (1994)
	Pro–63 W Stephens (1994)
V'tors	WD–U H WE/BH–M
Fees	£50
Loc	3 miles E of Bromsgrove. M42
	Junction 1 (South)

Brandhall (1946)

Public

Heron Road, Oldbury, Warley B68 8AQ

Tel	(0121) 552 7475
Mem	355
Sec	DJ Hart (0121) 559 9193
Pro	C Yates (0121) 552 2195
Holes	18 L 5813 yds SSS 68
Recs	Am–63 A Salter
V'tors	U exc first 2 hrs Sat/Sun
Fees	£6.60 (£8.50)
Loc	6 miles NW of Birmingham.
	M5 Junction 2, 11/2 miles

Bromsgrove Golf Centre

(1992)

Pay and play

Stratford Road, Bromsgrove B60 1LD

Tel	(01527) 575886
Mem	900
Sec	D Went
Pro	G Long, M Davies (01527)
	575886
Holes	18 L 5869 yds SSS 68
Recs	Pro–63 C Clark (1997)
V'tors	U SOC–WD
Fees	£12.50 (£15.50)
Loc	Junction of A38/A448. M42
	Junction 1. M5 Junction 4/5
Mis	Driving range
Arch	Hawtree

Burghill Valley (1991)

Tillington Road, Burghill, Hereford HR4 7RW

Tel	(01432) 760456
Fax	(01432) 761654
Sec	K Smith (Mgr)
Pro	N Clarke (01432) 760808
Holes	18 L 6239 yds SSS 70
V'tors	U SOC
Fees	£16 (£20)
Loc	3 miles N of Hereford,
	off A4110

Cadmore Lodge (1990)

Pay and play

Berrington Green, Tenbury Wells, Worcester WR15 8TQ

Tel	(01584) 810044
Mem	150
Sec	RV Farr
Pro	None
Holes	9 L 5129 yds Par 68 SSS 65
V'tors	U
Fees	D–£10 (D–£14)
Loc	2 miles S of Tenbury Wells on
	A4112

Churchill & Blakedown

(1926)

Churchill Lane, Blakedown, Kidderminster DY10 3NB

Tel	(01562) 700018
Mem	350
Sec	B Pendry
Pro	K Wheeler (01562) 700454
Holes	9 L 6472 yds Par 72 SSS 71
Recs	Am–67 R Bradshaw (1995)
V'tors	WD–U WE–M
Fees	£17.50
Loc	3 miles N of Kidderminster
	on A456

Cocks Moor Woods (1926)

Public

Alcester Road, South King's Heath, Birmingham BK1 6ER

Tel	(0121) 444 3584
Pro	S Ellis
Holes	18 L 5742 yds SSS 67
Recs	Am–67 A Osborne
	Pro–65 G Broadbent
V'tors	U
Fees	On application
Loc	6 miles S of Birmingham
	(A435)

Droitwich G&CC (1897)

Ford Lane, Droitwich WR9 0BQ

Tel	(01905) 770129
Fax	(01905) 797290
Mem	782
Sec	M Ashton (01905) 774344
Pro	CS Thompson
	(01905) 770207
Holes	18 L 6058 yds SSS 69
Recs	Am–62 S Braitwaite
V'tors	WD–U WE/BH–M
	SOC–Wed & Fri
Fees	£24
Loc	1 mile N of Droitwich, off
	A38. M5 Junction 5

Dudley (1893)

Turners Hill, Rowley Regis B65 9DP

Tel	(01384) 253719
Mem	320
Sec	RP Fortune (01384) 233877
Pro	P Taylor (01384) 254020
Holes	18 L 5654 yds SSS 69
Recs	Am–66 AA Davies
	Pro–63 R Livingstone
V'tors	WD–U WE–M
Fees	On application
Loc	2 miles S of Dudley

Evesham (1894)

Craycombe Links, Fladbury, Pershore WR10 2QS

Tel	(01386) 860395
Fax	(01386) 861356
Mem	340
Sec	FG Vincent (Hon)
	(01386) 552373
Pro	C Haynes (01386) 861144
Holes	9 L 6415 yds SSS 71
V'tors	WD–H WE–M NA on
	comp/match days SOC

Fees D–£15
Loc Fladbury, 4 miles W of
Evesham (A4538)

Fulford Heath (1933)

*Tanners Green Lane, Wythall,
Birmingham B47 6BH*
Tel **(01564) 822806 (Clubhouse)**
Fax (01564) 822629
Mem 700
Sec Mrs MA Tuckett
(01564) 824758
Pro D Down (01564) 822930
Holes 18 L 6216 yds SSS 70
Recs Am–66 S Leahy
Pro–66 D Prosser
V'tors WD–H WE/BH–M SOC
Fees On application
Loc 8 miles S of Birmingham

Gay Hill (1913)

Hollywood Lane, Birmingham B47 5PP
Tel **(0121) 430 6523/7077**
Fax (0121) 436 7796
Mem 700
Sec Mrs M Adderley
(0121) 430 8544
Pro A Potter (0121) 474 6001
Holes 18 L 6532 yds SSS 71
Recs Am–64 P Johnson (1993)
Pro–66 R Livingston
V'tors WD–U H WE–M SOC
Fees £28.50
Loc 7 miles S of Birmingham on
A435. M42 Junction 3, 3 miles

Habberley (1924)

*Trimpley Road, Kidderminster
DY11 5RG*
Tel **(01562) 745756**
Mem 250
Sec DB Lloyd
Holes 9 L 5440 yds SSS 67
Recs Am–62 M Dudley
V'tors WD–U WE–M SOC
Fees £10
Loc 3 miles NW of Kidderminster

Hagley (1980)

*Wassell Grove, Hagley, Stourbridge
DY9 9JW*
Tel **(01562) 883701**
Fax (01562) 887518
Mem 700
Sec GF Yardley
Pro I Clark (01562) 883852
Holes 18 L 6353 yds SSS 72
Recs Am–66 S Hull (1995)
Pro–69 I Clark (1990)
V'tors WD–U exc Wed NA before
1.30pm WE–M after 10am
SOC–WD
Fees £22 D–£28
Loc 5 miles SW of Birmingham on
A456. M5 Junction 3

Halesowen (1909)

The Leasowes, Halesowen B62 8QF
Tel **(0121) 550 1041**
Mem 600
Sec Mrs M Bateman
(0121) 501 3606

Pro J Nicholas (0121) 503 0593
Holes 18 L 5754 yds SSS 68
Recs Am–65 D Henn
Pro–66
V'tors WD–U WE–M SOC–WD exc
Wed
Fees £18 D–£25
Loc M5 Junction 3, 2 miles

Hereford Municipal (1983)

Public
Holmer Road, Hereford HR4 9UD
Tel **(01432) 278178**
Fax (01432) 266281
Sec P Brookes
Pro P Brookes (01432) 344376
Holes 9 L 3060 yds Par 70 SSS 69
V'tors U SOC
Fees 18 holes–£5.70 (£7.60)
9 holes–£3.50 (£4.75)
Loc Hereford Leisure Centre, A49
Leominster road

Herefordshire (1896)

*Raven's Causeway, Wormsley, Hereford
HR4 8LY*
Tel **(01432) 830219**
Mem 500 75(L) 85(J)
Sec RW Dando (Hon)
Pro D Hemming (01432) 830465
Holes 18 L 6069 yds SSS 69
Recs Am–63 D Park (1993)
Pro–61 B Barnes
V'tors U–phone first SOC
Fees £17 D–£22 (£20 D–£28)
Loc 6 miles NW of Hereford

Kidderminster (1909)

Russell Road, Kidderminster DY10 3HT
Tel **(01562) 822303**
Fax (01562) 862041
Mem 800
Sec M Burnand
Pro NP Underwood (01562)
740090
Holes 18 L 6405 yds SSS 71
Recs Am–66 MJ Houghton (1995)
Pro–68 F Clarke (1993)
Ladies–73 L Waring (1993)
V'tors WD–H WE–M SOC–Thurs
Fees £25 D–£35
Loc Signposted off A449
Wolverhampton–Worcester
road

Kings Norton (1892)

*Brockhill Lane, Weatheroak,
Alvechurch, Birmingham B48 7ED*
Tel **(01564) 826789**
Fax (01564) 826955
Mem 1050
Sec D Gutteridge (Mgr)
Pro K Hayward (01564) 822822
Holes 9 L 3382 yds SSS 36
9 L 3372 yds SSS 36
9 L 3290 yds SSS 36
V'tors WD–U WE–NA SOC
Fees £30 D–£35
Loc 7 miles S of Birmingham.
1 mile N of M42 Junction 3
Mis 12 hole short course
Arch Fred Hawtree

Kington (1926)

Bradnor Hill, Kington HR5 3RE
Tel **(01544) 230340**
Fax (01544) 340270
Mem 500
Sec GR Wictome (01544) 340270
Pro D Oliver (01544) 231320
Holes 18 L 5840 yds SSS 68
Recs Am–65 K Alexander
V'tors WE–NA before 10.15am:
restricted 1.30–2.45pm SOC
Fees £13 D–£16 (£16 D–£20)
Loc 1 mile N of Kington
Arch CK Hutchinson

Leominster (1967)

Ford Bridge, Leominster HR6 0LE
Tel **(01568) 612863 (Clubhouse)**
Fax (01568) 610055
Mem 550
Sec JA Ashcroft (01568) 610055
Pro A Ferriday (01568) 611402
Holes 18 L 6029 yds SSS 69
Recs Am–69 D Francis (1992)
Pro–71 F Clark (1992)
V'tors H SOC
Fees £14 D–£17 (£21)
Loc 3 miles S of Leominster on
A49 (Leominster By-pass)
Arch R Sandow

Lickey Hills (1927)

Public
*Lickey Hills, Rednal, Birmingham
B45 8RR*
Tel **(0121) 453 3159**
Sec MR Billingham
Pro MS March
Holes 18 L 6010 yds SSS 69
Recs Am–66 S Green
Pro–72 R Livingston
V'tors U
Fees On application
Loc 10 miles SW of Birmingham.
M5 Junction 4

Little Lakes (1975)

*Lye Head, Bewdley, Worcester
DY12 2UZ*
Tel **(01299) 266385**
Mem 400 50(L)
Sec T Norris (01562) 67495
Pro M Laing
Holes 9 L 6247 yds SSS 72
Recs Am–70 R Dean (1990)
Pro–70 R Lane (1986)
V'tors WD–U WE–NA SOC
Fees £12 D–£15
Loc 3 miles W of Bewdley, off A456

Moseley (1892)

*Springfield Road, Kings Heath,
Birmingham B14 7DX*
Tel **(0121) 444 2115**
Fax (0121) 441 4662
Mem 600
Sec RA Jowle (0121) 444 4957
Pro G Edge (0121) 444 2063
Holes 18 L 6300 yds SSS 70
Recs Am–64 C Norman (1992)
Pro–67 G Edge (1992)
Ladies–72 J Thorne (1976)

V'tors I H or M
Fees £37
Loc South Birmingham

North Worcestershire
(1907)
Frankley Beeches Road, Northfield, Birmingham B31 5LP
Tel (0121) 475 1047
Fax (0121) 476 8681
Mem 550
Sec D Wilson
Pro K Jones (0121) 475 5721
Holes 18 L 5907 yds SSS 69
Recs Am–64 DJ Russell
Pro–63 K Dickens (1988)
V'tors WD–U WE/BH–M
Fees £18 D–£25.50
Loc 7 miles SW of Birmingham, off A38
Arch James Braid

Ombersley (1991)
Bishopswood Road, Ombersley, Droitwich WR9 0LE
Tel (01905) 620747
Fax (01905) 620047
Mem 750
Sec G Glenister (Gen Mgr)
Pro G Glenister
Holes 18 L 6139 yds SSS 69
Recs Am–72
V'tors U
Fees £11.50 (£15.50)
Loc 6 miles N of Worcester, off A449
Mis Driving range
Arch David Morgan

Perdiswell Park
Pay and play
Bilford Road, Worcester WR3 8DX
Tel (01905) 754668
Fax (01905) 756608
Mem 150
Sec R Gardner
Holes 9 L 5870 yds SSS 68
V'tors U
Fees 9 holes–£4.40 (£5.80)
18 holes–£7.10 (£8.20)
Loc Worcester
Mis Extension to 18 holes in 1999

Pitcheroak (1973)
Public
Plymouth Road, Redditch B97 4PB
Tel (01527) 541054
Pro D Stewart
Holes 9 L 4584 yds SSS 62
V'tors U
Fees £5.75 (£6.75)
Loc Redditch

Redditch (1913)
Lower Grinsty, Green Lane, Callow Hill, Redditch B97 5PJ
Tel (01527) 543309
Fax (01527) 543079
Mem 883
Sec WH Kerr

Pro F Powell (01527) 546372
Holes 18 L 6671 yds SSS 72
Pro–68 G Mercer (1991)
V'tors WD–U SOC
Fees £27.50
Loc 3 miles SW of Redditch, off A441
Arch F Pennink

Ross-on-Wye (1903)
Two Park, Gorsley, Ross-on-Wye HR9 7UT
Tel (01989) 720267
Fax (01989) 720212
Mem 760
Sec GH Cason
Pro N Catchpole (01989) 720439
Holes 18 L 6500 yds SSS 73
Recs Am–69 D Powell (1994)
Pro–68 J Peters (1994)
Ladies–69 E Fields (1994)
V'tors U SOC–Wed–Fri (min 16 players)
Fees £35 D–£45 SOC–£28
Loc 5 miles N of Ross-on-Wye, by M50 Junction 3
Mis Parkland driving range
Arch CK Cotton

Sapey (1991)
Upper Sapey, Worcester WR6 6XT
Tel (01886) 853288
Fax (01886) 853485
Mem 500
Sec Miss L Stevenson
Pro C Knowles
Holes 18 L 5885 yds SSS 69
Recs Am–64 E Deasey (1994)
Pro–63 K Craggs (1994)
V'tors WD–U WE–NA before 10am SOC
Fees £15 D–£22 (£20 D–£25)
Loc 6 miles N of Bromyard on B4203. M5 Junction 5
Mis Driving range

South Herefordshire
(1992)
Twin Lakes, Upton Bishop, Ross-on-Wye HR9 7UA
Tel (01989) 780535
Fax (01989) 740611
Mem 250
Sec RLA Lee (Mgr)
Pro E Litchfield
Holes 18 L 6672 yds Par 71 SSS 72
9 hole Par 3 course
Recs Am–71 A Rock (1995)
V'tors U SOC
Fees £15 (£18)
Loc 3 miles NE of Ross-on-Wye. M50 Junction 4
Mis Floodlit driving range
Arch John Day

Stourbridge (1892)
Worcester Lane, Pedmore, Stourbridge DY8 2RB
Tel (01384) 393062
Mem 720
Sec Mrs MA Betts (01384) 395566

Pro M Male (01384) 393129
Holes 18 L 6231 yds SSS 70
Recs Am–65 J Fisher
Pro–63 WH Firkins
V'tors WD–U exc Wed before 4pm–M WE/BH–M
Fees £25
Loc 1 mile S of Stourbridge on Worcester road

Tolladine (1898)
The Fairway, Tolladine Road, Worcester WR4 9BA
Tel (01905) 21074 (Clubhouse)
Mem 270
Pro (01905) 726180
Holes 9 L 5174 yds SSS 67
Recs Am–65 T Sanders (1992)
Ladies–71 C George (1991)
V'tors WD–U before 4pm –M after 4pm WE/BH–M SOC
Fees On application
Loc M5 Junction 6, 1 mile

The Vale G&CC (1991)
Bishampton, Pershore WR10 2LZ
Tel (01386) 462781
Fax (01386) 462597
Mem 800
Sec D Cudmore
Pro Caroline Griffiths
(01386) 462520
Holes 18 L 7114 yds SSS 74
9 L 2918 yds SSS 68
Recs Am–72 G Downie (1996)
V'tors U–phone Pro SOC–WD
Fees On application
Loc 6 miles NW of Evesham, off B4084. M5 Junction 6, 8 miles
Mis Driving range
Arch M Sandow

Warley (1921)
Public
Lightwoods Hill, Warley B67 5EQ
Tel (0121) 429 2440
Pro D Owen
Holes 9 L 2606 yds SSS 64
Recs Am–62 M Daw
Pro–58 B Fereday
V'tors U
Fees On application
Loc 5 miles W of Birmingham, off A456

Wharton Park (1992)
Long Bank, Bewdley DY12 2QW
Tel (01299) 405222
Fax (01299) 405121
Mem 600
Sec CJ Price
Pro A Hoare (01299) 405163
Holes 18 L 6600 yds Par 73 SSS 72
Recs Am–64 J Toman (1996)
Pro–65 D Eddiford (1996)
V'tors U SOC
Fees £20 (£25)
Loc Bewdley By-pass on A456
Mis Driving range. Academy

For list of abbreviations see page 479

Worcester G&CC

(1898)

Boughton Park, Worcester WR2 4EZ

Tel	(01905) 422555
Mem	1005
Sec	JM Kennedy
Pro	C Colenso (01905) 422044
Holes	18 L 6251 yds SSS 70
Recs	Am–66 D Clee (1996)
	Pro–67 C Colenso (1995)
V'tors	WD–H WE–M SOC
Fees	£25
Loc	1 mile W of Worcester on A4103
Arch	Dr A Mackenzie (1926) C Colenso (1991)

Worcestershire (1879)

Wood Farm, Malvern Wells WR14 4PP

Tel	(01684) 573905
Fax	(01684) 575992
Mem	770
Sec	RG Blackwell (01684) 575992
Pro	R Lewis (01684) 564428
Holes	18 L 6449 yds SSS 71
Recs	Am–67 PM Guest, MC Reynard, S Braithwaite Pro–66 R Larratt
V'tors	WD–H WE–H after 10am
Fees	£28 (£33) W–£87
Loc	2 miles S of Gt Malvern, off A449/B4209

Wyre Forest Golf Centre

Pay and play

Zortech Avenue, Kidderminster DY11 7EX

Tel	(01299) 822682
Fax	(01299) 879433
Mem	363
Sec	D Lawrence
Pro	S Price
Holes	18 L 5790 yds Par 70 SSS 68
V'tors	U SOC
Fees	£9 (£12.50)
Loc	18 miles S of Birmingham on A451, between Kidderminster and Stourport
Mis	Floodlit driving range

Hertfordshire

Aldenham G&CC (1975)

Church Lane, Aldenham WD2 8AL

Tel	(01923) 853929
Fax	(01923) 858472
Mem	560
Sec	Mrs J Phillips
Pro	(01923) 857889
Holes	18 L 6500 yds SSS 71 9 L 2350 yds
Recs	Am–67 P Wharton (1987) Pro–69 B Charles (1982)
V'tors	U
Fees	£24 (£30)
Loc	3 miles E of Watford, off B462. M1 Junction 5

Aldwickbury Park (1995)

Piggottshill Lane, Wheathampstead Road, Harpenden AL5 1AB

Tel	(01582) 765112
Fax	(01582) 760113
Mem	700
Sec	A Knott
Pro	S Clark (01582) 760112
Holes	18 L 6032 yds Par 71 SSS 69 9 hole Par 3 course
V'tors	WD–U booking necessary WE–U after 1pm SOC–WD
Fees	£20 (£26)
Loc	E of Harpenden on Wheathampstead road. M1 Junction 9. A1(M) Junction 4
Arch	Gillett/Brown

Arkley (1909)

Rowley Green Road, Barnet EN5 3HL

Tel	(0181) 449 0394
Mem	350
Sec	J Hardie
Pro	M Porter (0181) 440 8473
Holes	9 L 6045 yds SSS 69
Recs	Am–67 D Wiggins Pro–63 LV Baker
V'tors	WD–U WE–M SOC–Wed–Fri
Fees	£20
Loc	NW of Barnet, off A1(M)
Arch	James Braid

Ashridge (1932)

Little Gaddesden, Berkhamsted HP4 1LY

Tel	(01442) 842244
Fax	(01442) 843770
Mem	700
Sec	MS Silver
Pro	A Ainsworth (01442) 842307
Holes	18 L 6547 yds SSS 71
Recs	Am–63 J Kemp (1996) Pro–66 JRM Jacobs
V'tors	WD only–phone Sec
Fees	On application
Loc	5 miles N of Berkhamsted on B4506
Arch	Campbell/Hutchison/ Hotchkin

Barkway Park (1992)

Nuthampstead Road, Barkway, Royston SG8 8EN

Tel	(01763) 849070
Fax	(01763) 849075
Mem	400
Sec	Mrs V Sadler
Pro	J Bates (01763) 848215
Holes	18 L 6997 yds SSS 74
V'tors	WD–U WE–U after 11.30am
Fees	£12 (£17)
Loc	5 miles SE of Royston, on B1368
Arch	Vivien Saunders

Batchwood Hall (1935)

Pay and play

Batchwood Drive, St Albans AL3 5XA

Tel	(01727) 833349
Fax	(01582) 793215
Mem	425

Sec	BR Mercer
Pro	J Thomson
Holes	18 L 6487 yds SSS 71
Recs	Am–67 D Tapping (1991) Pro–62 PP Wynne
V'tors	WD–U WE–NA before 10am
Fees	£9 (£11)
Loc	NW of St Albans on A5081. 5 miles S of M1 Junction 9
Arch	JH Taylor

Batchworth Park (1996)

London Road, Rickmansworth WD3 1JS

Tel	(01923) 711400
Fax	(01923) 710200
Mem	750
Sec	K Heathcote (Gen Mgr)
Pro	R Whitehead, K Jackson, M Arnold
Holes	18 L 6723 yds Par 72 SSS 72
V'tors	M
Fees	NA
Loc	1 mile SE of Rickmansworth on A404. M25 Junction 18
Mis	Indoor Academy
Arch	Dave Thomas

Berkhamsted (1890)

The Common, Berkhamsted HP4 2QB

Tel	(01442) 865832
Fax	(01442) 863730
Mem	450 120(L) 50(J)
Sec	CD Hextall
Pro	BJ Proudfoot (01442) 865851
Holes	18 L 6605 yds Par 73 SSS 72
Recs	Am–64 N Leconte (1986) Pro–69 S Proudfoot (1987)
V'tors	U H WE–M before 11.30am SOC–Wed & Fri
Fees	£22 (£35)
Loc	1 mile N of Berkhamsted. M25 Junction 21 (A41). M1 Junction 8
Arch	HS Colt/James Braid

Bishop's Stortford (1910)

Dunmow Road, Bishop's Stortford CM23 5HP

Tel	(01279) 654715
Fax	(01279) 655215
Mem	925
Sec	B Collins
Pro	V Duncan (01279) 651324
Holes	18 L 6404 yds SSS 71
Recs	Am–69 I Hardie (1997) Pro–66 M Stokes (1997) Ladies–71 A Smithet (1997)
V'tors	WD–U WE–M SOC–WD exc Tues
Fees	£20 D–£30
Loc	E of Bishop's Stortford on A1250. M11 Junction 8, ¼ mile
Arch	James Braid

Boxmoor (1890)

18 Box Lane, Hemel Hempstead HP3 0DJ

Tel	(01442) 242434 (Clubhouse)
Mem	290
Sec	P Lavis (01442) 66534

Pro None
Holes 9 L 4854 yds SSS 64
Recs Am–62 G Linton
V'tors U exc Sun–NA
Fees £10 Sat–£15
Loc 1 mile W of Hemel Hempstead on B4505 to Chesham

Brickendon Grange (1964)
Brickendon, Hertford SG13 8PD
Tel (01992) 511258
Fax (01992) 511411
Mem 650
Sec CT MacDonald
Pro J Hamilton (01992) 511218
Holes 18 L 6325 yds SSS 70
Recs Am–66 S Burnell (1991) Pro–67 S James, K Robson (1985)
V'tors WD–U H WE/BH–M SOC
Fees On application
Loc Bayford, 3 miles S of Hertford

Bridgedowm (1994)
St Albans Road, Barnet EN5 4RE
Tel (0181) 440 4120
Fax (0181) 440 4009
Mem 400
Pro D Beal
Holes 18 L 6626 yds Par 72 SSS 72
V'tors By appointment
Fees £13 (£15)
Loc 1 mile S of South Mimms on A1081. M25 Junction 23
Arch Howard Swann

Briggens House Hotel (1988)
Briggens Park, Stanstead Road, Stanstead Abbotts SG12 8LD
Tel (01279) 793742
Fax (01279) 793685
Mem 200
Sec J Carter
Pro S Carter
Holes 9 L 5825 yds SSS 69
V'tors U SOC
Fees £10.50 (£15)
Loc 4 miles E of Hertford, off A414

Brocket Hall (1992)
Welwyn AL8 7XG
Tel (01707) 390055
Fax (01707) 390052
Mem 350
Sec R Ransley
Pro K Wood (01707) 390063
Holes 18 L 6584 yds SSS 72
Recs Am–68 Ujlaki (1994) Pro–65 K Wood (1994)
V'tors M H
Fees £40 (£50)
Loc On B653 to Wheathampstead. A1(M) Junction 4
Arch Alliss/Clark

Brookmans Park (1930)
Brookmans Park, Hatfield AL9 7AT
Tel (01707) 652487
Fax (01707) 661851

Mem 775
Sec PA Gill
Pro I Jelley (01707) 652468
Holes 18 L 6473 yds SSS 71
Recs Am–66 P Embleton (1990) Pro–66 I Jelley (1990)
V'tors WD–UH WE/BH–M SOC
Fees £27
Loc 3 miles S of Hatfield, off A1000
Arch Hawtree/Taylor

Bushey G&CC (1980)
High Street, Bushey WD2 1BJ
Tel (0181) 950 2283
Fax (0181) 386 1181
Mem 600
Sec D Hourihan
Pro M Lovegrove (0181) 950 2215
Holes 9 L 3000 yds SSS 69 Pro–67
V'tors WD–before 6pm WE/BH–after 2pm Wed–closed SOC–WD exc Wed
Fees 18 holes–£10 (14) 9 holes–£7 (£9)
Loc 2 miles S of Watford on A4008
Mis Driving range

Bushey Hall (1890)
Pay and play
Bushey Hall Drive, Bushey WD2 2EP
Tel (01923) 222253
Fax (01923) 229759
Mem 400
Sec JK Smith
Pro K Wickham (01923) 225802
Holes 18 L 6099 yds SSS 69
Recs Am–66 M Bowen (1990), S Clement (1992) Pro–65 N Brown (1992), J Pinsent (1994)
V'tors U SOC–WD
Fees £10 (£17)
Loc 1 mile SE of Watford. M1 Junction 5

Chadwell Springs (1974)
Hertford Road, Ware SG12 9LE
Tel (01920) 463647
Mem 350
Sec M Scott (01920) 461447
Pro M Wall (01920) 462075
Holes 9 L 3021 yds SSS 69
V'tors WD–U WE–M
Fees £20
Loc Between Ware and Hertford on A119

Chesfield Downs Golf Centre (1991)
Pay and play
Jack's Hill, Graveley, Stevenage SG4 7EQ
Tel (01462) 482929
Fax (01462) 482930
Mem 550
Sec P McCullough
Pro Jane Fernley
Holes 18 L 6630 yds SSS 72 9 holes Par 3 course

V'tors U SOC
Fees 18 hole–£13.25 (£19.25) 9 hole–£2 (£3)
Loc B197, N of Stevenage. A1(M) Junctions 8 or 9
Mis Driving range
Arch Jonathan Gaunt

Cheshunt (1976)
Public
Park Lane, Cheshunt EN7 6QD
Tel (01992) 29777
Mem 480
Sec JG Duncan
Pro A Traynor (01992) 24009
Holes 18 L 6608 yds SSS 71
Recs Am–65 S Blight (1986)
V'tors U–booking required
Fees £9.50 (£12)
Loc Off A10 at Church Lane, Cheshunt. M25 Junction 25, 3 miles
Arch Hawtree

Chorleywood (1890)
Common Road, Chorleywood WD3 5LN
Tel (01923) 282009
Mem 220 55(L) 40(J)
Sec DW Kirkland
Pro RM Mandeville
Holes 9 L 2838 yds SSS 67
Recs Am–65 N Leconte (1990) Pro–61 M Squires (1990)
V'tors WD–U exc Tues am WE–U after 11.30am SOC
Fees £16 (£20)
Loc 3 miles N of Rickmansworth, off A404. M25 Junction 18

Danesbury Park (1992)
Codicote Road, Welwyn AL6 9SD
Tel (01438) 840100
Fax (01727) 846109
Mem 300
Sec D Snowdon
Pro G Aris
Holes 9 L 4150 yds SSS 60
V'tors M SOC–WD
Loc ³/4 mile from A1(M) Junction 6 on B656 Hitchin road
Arch Derek Snowdon

Dyrham Park CC (1963)
Galley Lane, Barnet EN5 4RA
Tel (0181) 440 3361
Fax (0181) 441 9836
Mem 600
Sec P Court
Pro W Large (0181) 440 3904
Holes 18 L 6422 yds SSS 71
Recs Am–67 D Zartz (1991) Pro–65 P Elson (1978)
V'tors M SOC–Wed
Loc 10 miles W of London, W off A1
Arch CK Cotton

East Herts (1899)
Hamels Park, Buntingford SG9 9NA
Tel (01920) 821923
Fax (01920) 823700

Mem 700
Sec C Wilkinson (01920) 821978
Pro SM Bryan (01920) 821922
Holes 18 L 6456 yds SSS 71
Recs Am–66 D Hamilton
          Pro–64 R Joyce
V'tors WD–H exc Wed–NA before
           1pm WE–M
Fees On application
Loc ¼ mile N of Puckeridge
         on A10

Elstree (1984)

Watling Street, Elstree WD6 3AA
Tel **(0181) 953 6115**
Fax (0181) 207 6390
Mem 600
Sec K Ellis
Pro M Warwick
Holes 18 L 6100 yds SSS 69
Recs Am–68 C Woodcock (1987)
V'tors U SOC
Fees On application
Loc A5183, 1 mile N of Elstree.
         M1 Junction 4
Mis Floodlit driving range

Forest Hills (1994)

*Newgate Street, Newgate Street Village
SG13 8EW*
Tel **(01707) 876825**
Fax (01707) 876825
Mem 170
Sec C Easton
Pro C Easton
Holes 9 L 3220 yds Par 72 SSS 71
Recs Am–72 N Brooks (1996)
V'tors WD–U WE/BH–by
           arrangement
Fees £15 (£20)
Loc 3 miles W of Cheshunt. M25
         Junction 25
Arch Mel Flannagan

Great Hadham (1993)

*Great Hadham Road, Bishop's Stortford
SG10 6JE*
Tel **(01279) 843558**
Fax (01279) 842122
Mem 700
Sec C Day
Pro K Lunt (01279) 843888
Holes 18 L 6854 yds SSS 73
Recs Am–68 D Kitteridge (1996)
V'tors WD–U WE/BH–NA before 12
           noon SOC
Fees £16 (£22)
Loc 3 miles SW of Bishops
         Stortford (B1004). M11
         Junction 8
Mis Driving range

Hadley Wood (1922)

*Beech Hill, Hadley Wood, Barnet
EN4 0JJ*
Tel **(0181) 449 4486**
Fax (0181) 364 8633
Mem 635
Sec Gen Mgr (0181) 449 4328
Pro P Jones (0181) 449 3285
Holes 18 L 6457 yds SSS 71

Recs Am–67 C Holton (1983),
          N Leconte (1989)
          Pro–67 P Elson (1980)
V'tors WD–H or I WE/BH–M SOC
Fees On application
Loc 10 miles N of London, off
         A111 between Potters Bar and
         Cockfosters. 2 miles S of M25
         Junction 24
Mis Practice range
Arch Dr A Mackenzie

Hanbury Manor (1990)

Ware SG12 0SD
Tel **(01920) 487722**
Fax (01920) 487692
Mem 600
Sec S Follett
Pro P Blaze
Holes 18 L 7016 yds SSS 74
V'tors M H
Loc 8 miles N of M25 Junction 25
         on A10
Arch Jack Nicklaus Jr

Harpenden (1894)

*Hammonds End, Harpenden
AL5 2AX*
Tel **(01582) 712580**
Fax (01582) 712725
Mem 800
Sec J Newton
Pro P Cherry (01582) 767124
Holes 18 L 6381 yds SSS 70
Recs Am–67 B Bulmer (1987),
          D Ramsay (1995)
          Pro–65 J Sewell (1994)
V'tors WD–U exc Thurs WE/BH–M
           SOC–WD exc Thurs
Fees £24 D–£34
Loc 6 miles N of St Albans on
         B487
Arch Hawtree/Taylor

Harpenden Common (1931)

East Common, Harpenden AL5 1BL
Tel **(01582) 712856**
Fax (01582) 715959
Mem 865
Sec RD Parry (01582) 715959
Pro D Fitzsimmons
         (01582) 460655
Holes 18 L 6214 yds SSS 70
Recs Am–67 T Turner (1997)
V'tors WD–U H WE–M SOC
Fees £23 (£28)
Loc 4 miles N of St Albans, on
         A1081
Arch K Brown (1995)

Hartsbourne G&CC (1946)

*Hartsbourne Avenue, Bushey Heath
WD2 1JW*
Tel **(0181) 950 1133**
Fax (0181) 950 5357
Mem 750
Sec Miss S Hobbs
Pro A Cardwell (0181) 950 2836

Holes 18 L 6305 yds SSS 70
          9 L 5432 yds SSS 66
Recs Am–66 J Bohn
          Pro–62 P Oosterhuis
V'tors NA SOC
Loc 5 miles SE of Watford,
         off A4008
Arch Hawtree/Taylor

Hatfield London CC (1976)

Pay and play
*Bedwell Park, Essendon, Hatfield
AL9 6JA*
Tel **(01707) 642624**
Fax (01707) 646187
Mem 308
Sec H Kawashima
Pro N Greer (01707) 650431
Holes 18 L 6880 yds SSS 72
V'tors U SOC
Fees £16 (£32)
Loc 5 miles E of Hatfield on B158.
         A1(M) Junction 4
Mis 9 hole pitch & putt course
Arch Fred Hawtree

The Hertfordshire (1995)

Pay and play
*Broxbournebury Mansion, White Stubbs
Lane, Broxbourne EN10 7PY*
Tel **(01992) 466666**
Fax (01992) 470326
Mem 690
Sec J Anderson (Dir)
Pro A Shearn
Holes 18 L 6400 yds Par 70 SSS 70
          Pro–64 B Davis (1996)
V'tors U H SOC
Fees £21 (£25)
Loc 8 miles N of M25 Junction 25,
         off A10
Mis Floodlit driving range
Arch Jack Nicklaus II

Kingsway Golf Centre (1991)

*Cambridge Road, Melbourn, Royston
SG8 6EY*
Tel **(01763) 262727**
Fax (01763) 263298
Mem 450
Sec Mrs J Trim
Pro Miss D Hastings, R Jessop
Holes 9 L 2500 yds Par 33
          9 hole Par 3 course
V'tors U SOC
Fees 9 holes–£5.50; 18 holes–£9.50
Loc N of Royston on A10
Mis Driving range

Knebworth (1908)

*Deards End Lane, Knebworth
SG3 6NL*
Tel **(01438) 812752 (Clubhouse)**
Fax (01438) 815216
Mem 1000
Sec M Parsons MBE
         (01438) 812752
Pro G Parker (01438) 812757

Holes 18 L 6492 yds SSS 71
Recs Am–66 J Phelps (1997)
　　　Pro–66 L Jones (1991)
V'tors WD–U H WE–M
　　　SOC–Mon/Tues/Thurs
Fees £30
Loc 1 mile S of Stevenage on B197
Arch Willie Park

Lamerwood (1996)

*Codicote Road, Wheathampstead
AL4 8RH*
Tel (01582) 833013
Fax (01582) 641831
Sec S Takabatake (Prop)
Pro S Williams
Holes 18 L 6588 yds Par 72
V'tors U
Fees £19 (£25)
Loc 5 miles W of A1(M)
　　　Junction 4 on B653
Arch Campbell Sinclair

Letchworth (1905)

Letchworth Lane, Letchworth SG6 3NQ
Tel (01462) 683203
Fax (01462) 484567
Mem 900
Sec AR Bailey
Pro SJ Mutimer (01462) 682713
Holes 18 L 6181 yds SSS 69
Recs Am–65 P Tandy
　　　Pro–66 NC Coles
V'tors WD–U WE–M
　　　SOC–Wed–Fri
Fees £24
Loc S of Letchworth, off A505.
　　　A1(M) Junction 9
Arch Harry Vardon

Little Hay Golf Complex (1977)

Pay and play
*Box Lane, Bovingdon, Hemel
Hempstead HP3 0DQ*
Tel (01442) 833798
Pro D Johnson (Golf Dir)
Holes 18 L 6610 yds SSS 72
　　　Pro–69
V'tors U SOC
Fees £8 (£12)
Loc 2 miles W of Hemel
　　　Hempstead, on B4505 to
　　　Chesham
Mis Driving range
Arch Hawtree

Manor of Groves G&CC (1991)

*High Wych, Sawbridgeworth
CM21 0LA*
Tel (01279) 722333
Fax (01279) 726972
Mem 450
Pro C Laurence
Holes 18 L 6280 yds SSS 70
V'tors U SOC
Fees On application
Loc 1 mile N of Harlow
Arch S Sharer

Mid Herts (1892)

*Gustard Wood, Wheathampstead
AL4 8RS*
Tel (01582) 832242
Fax (01582) 832242
Mem 500(M) 125(L)
Sec RJH Jourdan
Pro N Brown (01582) 832788
Holes 18 L 6060 yds SSS 69
Recs Am–68 P Mayles (1987)
　　　Pro–63 P Winston (1992)
V'tors WD–UH exc Tues & Wed pm
　　　WE/BH–M SOC
Fees On application
Loc 6 miles N of St Albans on
　　　B651

Mill Green (1994)

*Gypsy Lane, Mill Green, Welwyn
Garden City AL7 4TY*
Tel (01707) 276900
Fax (01707) 276898
Sec J Tubb (Gen Mgr)
Pro A Hall (01707) 270542
Holes 18 L 6615 yds Par 72 SSS 72
　　　Par 3 course
V'tors U SOC–WD
Fees £27.50 (£32.50)
Loc S of Welwyn Garden City, off
　　　A414. A1 Junction 4
Arch Clark/Alliss

Moor Park (1923)

Rickmansworth WD3 1QN
Tel (01923) 773146
Fax (01923) 777109
Mem 1700
Sec JA Davies
Pro L Farmer
Holes High 18 L 6713 yds SSS 72
　　　West 18 L 5823 yds SSS 68
Recs High Am–65 G Harris (1993)
　　　Pro–63 B Gallacher (1969)
　　　West Am–62 AJ Eisner (1984)
　　　Pro–63 AD Locke, A Lees,
　　　EE Whitcombe
V'tors WD–H WE/BH–M SOC
Fees On application
Loc 1 mile SE of Rickmansworth,
　　　off Batchworth roundabout
　　　(A4145). M25 Junction 18,
　　　2 miles
Arch HS Colt

Old Fold Manor (1910)

*Old Fold Lane, Hadley Green, Barnet
EN5 4QN*
Tel (0181) 440 9185
Fax (0181) 441 4863
Mem 520
Sec AW Dickens (Mgr)
Pro G Potter (0181) 440 7488
Holes 18 L 6481 yds SSS 71
Recs Am–66 A Clark
　　　Pro–68 SL King
V'tors WD–H WE–M SOC–Thurs &
　　　Fri
Fees £20 D–£27
Loc 1 mile N of Barnet on A1000

Oxhey Park

*Prestwick Road, South Oxhey, Watford
WD1 6DT*
Tel (01923) 248312
Mem 210
Sec D McFadden (Mgr)
Holes 9 L 1637 yds Par 58
V'tors U
Fees 9 holes–£6; 18 holes–£8
Loc 2 miles SW of Watford. M1
　　　Junction 5
Mis Driving range

Panshanger Golf Complex (1976)

*Old Herns Lane, Welwyn Garden City
AL7 2ED*
Tel (01707) 333312/333350
　　　(Bookings)
Holes 18 L 6167 yds SSS 70
　　　9 hole Par 3 course
Recs Am–71 S Walton (1987)
　　　Pro–70 R Green
V'tors U
Fees On application
Loc 2 miles off A1, via B1000 to
　　　Hertford

Porters Park (1899)

Shenley Hill, Radlett WD7 7AZ
Tel (01923) 854127
Fax (01923) 855475
Mem 650
Sec RMA Springall (Mgr)
Pro D Gleeson (01923) 854366
Holes 18 L 6313 yds SSS 70
Recs Am–65 CC Boal (1990)
　　　Pro–64 P Townsend
V'tors WD–H phone first WE/BH–M
　　　SOC–Wed & Thurs
Fees £29–£44
Loc E of Radlett on Shenley road

Potters Bar (1923)

Darkes Lane, Potters Bar EN6 1DE
Tel (01707) 652020
Fax (01707) 655051
Mem 550
Sec GL Pearce (Sec/Mgr)
Pro G Aris (01707) 652987
Holes 18 L 6279 yds SSS 70
Recs Am–66 RR Davis
　　　Pro–65 D McClelland
V'tors WD–H WE/BH–M
　　　SOC–Mon/Tues/Fri
Fees £20 D–£30
Loc 1 mile N of M25 Junction 24,
　　　off A1000
Arch James Braid

Redbourn (1970)

*Kinsbourne Green Lane, Redbourn, St
Albans AL3 7QA*
Tel (01582) 793493
Fax (01582) 794362
Sec R Fay
Pro M Varney
Holes 18 L 6506 yds SSS 71
　　　9 hole Par 3 course
Recs Am–67 R Kosmalski

V'tors WD–U booking necessary
WE/BH–H SOC–WD
Fees 18 hole: £17 (£22)
9 hole: £5 (£7.50)
Loc 4 miles N of St Albans, off A5.
1 mile S of M1 Junction 9
Mis Target golf range

Rickmansworth (1937)

Public
*Moor Lane, Rickmansworth
WD3 1QL*
Tel (01923) 775278
Mem 250
Sec RA Botham (01494) 763251
Pro A Dobbins (01923) 775278
Holes 18 L 4493 yds SSS 62
Recs Am–63 JC Jackson (1991)
V'tors U
Fees £9 (£13)
Loc ½ mile SE of Rickmansworth,
off Batchworth roundabout
(A4145). M25 Junction 18,
2 miles
Mis 9 hole pitch & putt course

Royston (1892)

Baldock Road, Royston SG8 5BG
Fax (01763) 242696
Mem 750
Sec DH Mear (01763) 242696
Pro M Hatcher (01763) 243476
Holes 18 L 6066 yds SSS 69
Recs Am–65 GA Hainsworth
Pro–63 B Waites
V'tors WD–U WE/BH–M SOC
Fees £20
Loc SW of Royston on A505

Sandy Lodge (1910)

*Sandy Lodge Lane, Northwood, Middx
HA6 2JD*
Tel (01923) 825429
Fax (01923) 824319
Mem 700
Sec RS Keating
Pro J Pinsent (01923) 825321
Holes 18 L 6347 yds SSS 71
Recs Am–66 DG Scammell (1992),
R Catlin (1994)
Pro–64 A Jacklin (1977)
V'tors H or M SOC
Fees On application
Loc Adjacent Moor Park Station
Arch Harry Vardon

Shendish Manor (1988)

Pay and play
*Shendish House, Apsley, Hemel
Hempstead HP3 0AA*
Tel (01442) 251806
Fax (01442) 230683
Sec M Thornberry
Holes 18 L 5660 yds Par 70 SSS 68
Recs Am–69 K Swatman (1991)
V'tors U SOC
Fees £15 (£20)
Loc S of Hemel Hempstead, off
A41. M25 Junction 20
Arch Cotton/Steel

South Herts (1899)

*Links Drive, Totteridge, London
N20 8QU*
Tel (0181) 445 0117
Fax (0181) 445 7569
Mem 850
Sec PF Wise (0181) 445 2035
Pro RY Mitchell
(0181) 445 4633
Holes 18 L 6470 yds SSS 71
9 L 1581 yds
Recs Am–67 R Neill (1964)
Pro–65 M Litton (1995)
V'tors WD–IH WE/BH–M
Fees On application
Loc Totteridge Lane
Arch Harry Vardon

Stevenage (1980)

Public
Aston Lane, Stevenage SG2 7EL
Tel (01438) 880424
Mem 420
Sec Mrs S Elwin
(01438) 880322
Pro S Brown (01438) 880424
Holes 18 L 6451 yds SSS 71
9 hole Par 3 course
Recs Am–69 T Carter (1990),
C Elwin (1992),
D Gibson (1995)
Pro–65 R Green (1989)
V'tors U
Fees £10 (£13)
Loc Off A602 to Hertford. A1(M)
Junction 7
Mis Driving range
Arch John Jacobs

Stocks Hotel G&CC

(1993)
*Stocks Road, Aldbury, Tring
HP23 5RX*
Tel (01442) 851341
Fax (01442) 851253
Mem 450
Pro PR Lane (Ext 308)
Holes 18 L 7016 yds SSS 74
V'tors H SOC
Fees £30 (£40)
Loc Aldbury, 2 miles E of Tring.
A41(T), 2 miles
Arch M Billcliffe

Verulam (1905)

London Road, St Albans AL1 1JG
Tel (01727) 853327
Fax (01727) 812201
Mem 640
Sec AR Crichton-Smith
Pro N Burch (01727) 861401
Holes 18 L 6448 yds Par 72 SSS 71
Recs Am–67 DCN Longmuir (1991)
Pro–65 R Mitchell (1986)
V'tors WD–H exc Mon–U
WE/BH–M SOC–Tues &
Thurs
Fees £25 (Mon–£13)
Loc 1 mile SE of St Albans on
A1081
Arch Braid/Steel

Welwyn Garden City

(1922)
*Mannicotts, High Oaks Road, Welwyn
Garden City AL8 7BP*
Tel (01707) 322722
Fax (01707) 393213
Mem 900
Sec GD Eastwood (Gen Mgr)
(01707) 325243
Pro R May (01707) 325525
Holes 18 L 6100 yds SSS 69
Recs Am–64 MJ Deal (1991),
D Crilley (1996)
Pro–63 N Faldo (1988)
V'tors WD–H WE/BH–NA
Fees On application
Loc 1 mile N of Hatfield. A1(M)
Junction 4 - B197 to Valley
Road
Arch Hawtree

West Herts (1890)

Cassiobury Park, Watford WD1 7SL
Tel (01923) 224264
Fax (01923) 222300
Mem 700
Sec CC Dodman
(01923) 236484
Pro CS Gough
(01923) 220352
Holes 18 L 6488 yds SSS 71
Recs Am–66 M Hooper (1995)
Pro–65 R Mann (1995)
Ladies–73 F Smith (1992)
V'tors WD–U WE/BH–M
SOC–Wed & Fri
Fees £20 (£30)
Loc Off A412, between Watford
and Rickmansworth
Arch Morris/Mackenzie

Whipsnade Park (1974)

Studham Lane, Dagnall HP4 1RH
Tel (01442) 842330
Fax (01442) 842090
Mem 600
Sec D Whalley
Pro M Lewendon
Holes 18 L 6812 yds SSS 72
Recs Am–71 A Calder
Pro–66 A Clapp
V'tors WD–U WE–M SOC–WD
Fees £23 D–£33
Loc 8 miles N of Hemel
Hempstead, off A4147

Whitehill (1990)

Dane End, Ware SG12 0JS
Tel (01920) 438495
Fax (01920) 438891
Mem 700
Sec Mr & Mrs A Smith (Props)
Pro D Ling
Holes 18 L 6636 yds SSS 72
V'tors H–booking necessary
Fees £15 (£18)
Loc 6 miles N of Ware (A10)
Mis Floodlit driving range

Isle of Man

Castletown (1892)

Fort Island, Derbyhaven IM9 1UA
Tel   (01624) 822201
Fax   (01624) 824633
Mem   400
Sec   R Griffiths (Hon)
Pro   M Crowe (01624) 822211
Holes 18 L 6716 yds SSS 72
Recs   Am–68 WR Ennett
          Pro–65 D Dunk
V'tors U SOC
Fees   £22.50 (£27.50)
Loc   1 mile E of Castletown
Arch   Mackenzie Ross

Douglas Municipal

(1927)
Public
Pulrose Park, Douglas
Tel   (01624) 661558
Pro   K Parry
Holes 18 L 5922 yds Par 69 SSS 68
Recs   Am–63
V'tors U
Fees   £6.30 (£12.50)
Loc   Douglas Pier 2 miles
Arch   Dr A Mackenzie

King Edward Bay

(1893)
Groudle Road, Onchan
Tel   (01624) 620430/673821
Fax   (01624) 676794
Mem   400
Sec   B Holt (01624) 670977
Pro   D Jones (01624) 672709
Holes 18 L 5457 yds SSS 65
Recs   Am–63
V'tors U SOC
Fees   £10 (£12)
Loc   1 mile N of Douglas
Arch   Tom Morris (1893 course)

Mount Murray G&CC

(1994)
Santon IM4 2HT
Tel   (01624) 661111
Fax   (01624) 611116
Mem   360
Sec   AD Dyson (Ext 3023)
Pro   AD Dyson (Ext 3023)
Holes 18 L 6664 yds SSS 72
Recs   Am–69 G Wilson (1996)
V'tors U H SOC
Fees   £18 (£24)
Loc   3 miles SW of Douglas
Mis   Driving range

Peel (1895)

Rheast Lane, Peel IM5 1BG
Tel   (01624) 842227
Fax   (01624) 843456
Mem   600
Sec   Mrs LA Cullen
          (01624) 843456
Pro   M Crowe
Holes 18 L 5914 yds SSS 68

Recs   Am–63 G Kelly
V'tors WD–U WE/BH–NA before
          10.30am SOC
Fees   £15 (£20)
Loc   10 miles W of Douglas via A1
Arch   James Braid

Port St Mary (1936)

Public
Kallow Road, Port St Mary
Tel   (01624) 834932
Sec   T Boyle (Hon)
Pro   M Crowe (01624) 822221
Holes 9 L 2711 yds SSS 66
Recs   Am–62 A Cain (1994)
V'tors WD–U WE–NA before
          10.30am SOC
Fees   On application
Loc   6 miles W of Castletown via A5

Ramsey (1891)

Brookfield, Ramsey
Tel   (01624) 813365/812244
Fax   (01624) 814736
Mem   812
Sec   Maj B Hodgson
          (01624) 812244
Pro   C Wilson (01624) 814736
Holes 18 L 6019 yds SSS 69
Recs   Am–65 S Boyd
          Pro–64 D Wills
V'tors WD–U after 10am WE–M
          SOC
Fees   £16 (£20)
Loc   N of Douglas via A18.
          W boundary of Ramsey
Arch   James Braid

Rowany (1895)

Port Erin
Tel   (01624) 834108
Fax   (01624) 834108
Mem   600
Sec   AJ Laine (Mgr) (01624)
          834072
Holes 18 L 5881 yds SSS 69
Recs   Am–65 G Wilson
V'tors U SOC
Fees   On application
Loc   6 miles W of Castletown
          via A5

Isle of Wight

Cowes (1908)

Crossfield Avenue, Cowes PO31 8HN
Tel   (01983) 280135 (Clubhouse)
Mem   300
Sec   D Weaver
          (01983) 292303
Holes 9 L 5934 yds SSS 68
Recs   Am–66 M Leek, R Greenham
V'tors H Thurs–NA before 3pm
          (Ladies Day) Fri–NA after
          5pm Sun am–NA
Fees   £15 (£18)
Loc   Nr Cowes High School
Arch   J Hamilton Stutt

Freshwater Bay (1894)

Afton Down, Freshwater PO40 9TZ
Tel   (01983) 752955
Fax   (01983) 752955
Mem   500
Sec   G Smith MBE
Holes 18 L 5725 yds SSS 68
Recs   Am–62 JE Veal (1997)
          Pro–66 T Underwood (1981)
V'tors H SOC
Fees   £20 (£24)
Loc   400 yds off Military Road

Newport (1896)

*St George's Down, Shide, Newport
PO30 3BA*
Tel   (01983) 525076
Mem   350
Sec   MJ Cunningham
Holes 9 L 5674 yds SSS 68
Recs   Am–65 J Burton (1987)
V'tors WD–U exc Wed–NA
          12–2.30pm Sat–NA before
          3.30pm Sun–NA before noon
          SOC
Fees   £15 (£17.50)
Loc   1 mile SE of Newport
Arch   Guy Hunt

Osborne (1903)

*Osborne House Estate, East Cowes
PO32 6JX*
Tel   (01983) 295421
Mem   260 90(L)
Sec   RS Jones
Holes 9 L 6372 yds SSS 70
V'tors WD–U exc Ladies Day (Tues)
          9am–1pm–NA WE–NA
          before noon SOC
Fees   £16 (£19) 5D–£60
Loc   S of East Cowes in grounds of
          Osborne House

Ryde (1921)

Binstead Road, Ryde PO33 3NF
Tel   (01983) 614809
Fax   (01983) 567418
Mem   450
Sec   ARJ Goodall
Pro   None
Holes 9 L 5287 yds SSS 66
Recs   Am–65 J Thorp
V'tors WD–U exc Wed pm Sun–NA
          before noon
Fees   £15 (£20)
Loc   On main Ryde/Newport road

Shanklin & Sandown

(1900)
Fairway Lake, Sandown PO36 9PR
Tel   (01983) 403217
Fax   (01983) 403217
Mem   650
Sec   AJ Messing
Pro   P Hammond (01983) 404424
Holes 18 L 6063 yds SSS 69
Recs   Am–65 D McToldridge,
          K Brochocki
          Pro–65 R Wynn
V'tors WD–U WE–NA before
          12 noon

For list of abbreviations see page 479

Fees £22 (£25) 3D–£55
Loc Off Sandown-Shanklin road at the Fairway in Lake
Arch Cowper/James Braid

Ventnor (1892)

Steephill Down Road, Ventnor
Tel (01983) 853326
Mem 250
Sec KM Tomes
Holes 12 L 5767 yds Par 70 SSS 68
Recs Am–73 IH Guy
V'tors WD–U exc Ladies Day–Fri Sun–NA before 1pm SOC
Fees On application
Loc NW boundary of Ventnor

Kent

Aquarius (1913)

Marmora Rd, Honor Oak, London SE22 0RY
Tel (0181) 693 1626
Mem 400
Sec S Ridgeway
Pro F Private
Holes 9 L 5246 yds SSS 66
Recs Am–62 R Hare
Pro–63 F Private
V'tors M

Ashford (1903)

Sandyhurst Lane, Ashford TN25 4NT
Tel (01233) 620180
Fax (01233) 622655
Mem 650
Sec AH Story (01233) 622655
Pro H Sherman (01233) 629644
Holes 18 L 6263 yds SSS 70
Recs Am–69 R Young
Pro–64 P Sherman
V'tors WD–H WE/BH–H SOC
Fees £20 (£42)
Loc Ashford 1½ miles (A20)
Arch Cotton

Austin Lodge (1991)

Eynsford, Swanley DA4 0HU
Tel (01322) 863000
Fax (01322) 862406
Mem 600
Sec S Bevan
Pro N Willis
Holes 18 L 6600 yds Par 73 SSS 71
Pro–66 N Willis (1995)
V'tors WD–U WE–NA before noon SOC
Fees £15 (£21)
Loc Off A225, nr Eynsford Station. M25 Junction 3, 3 miles
Mis Driving range for members and guests
Arch Peter Bevan

Barnehurst (1903)

Public
Mayplace Road East, Bexley Heath DA7 6JU
Tel (01322) 523746
Fax (01322) 554612
Mem 300
Sec B Davies (01322) 552952
Pro P Tallack (01322) 552952
Holes 9 L 5448 yds SSS 69
Pro–63 S Barr
V'tors U SOC
Fees £5.70 (£9.20)
Loc Between Crayford and Bexleyheath
Arch James Braid

Bearsted (1895)

Ware Street, Bearsted, Maidstone ME14 4PQ
Tel (01622) 738389
Fax (01622) 738198
Mem 780
Sec Mrs LM Siems (01622) 738198
Pro T Simpson (01622) 738024
Holes 18 L 6253 yds SSS 70
Recs Am–66 M Sur (1995)
Pro–67 T Spence (1995)
V'tors WD–I H WE–H M (recognised GC members) SOC
Fees £27 D–£36
Loc 2½ miles E of Maidstone

Beckenham Place Park (1907)

Public
Beckenham Hill Road, Beckenham BR3 2BP
Tel (0181) 650 2292
Fax (0181) 663 1201
Pro H Davies-Thomas
Holes 18 L 5722 yds SSS 68
Recs Am–62 S Champion
Pro–65 T Cotton
V'tors U
Fees £7.60 (£12.40) WE–booking fee
Loc Off A21 on A222

Bexleyheath (1907)

Mount Road, Bexleyheath BR8 7RJ
Tel (0181) 303 6951
Mem 350
Sec SE Squires
Holes 9 L 5239 yds SSS 66
Recs Am–65 D Fillary
V'tors WD–H before 4pm
Fees £20
Loc Station 1 mile

Birchwood Park Golf Centre (1990)

Birchwood Road, Wilmington, Dartford DA2 7HJ
Tel (01322) 660554
Fax (01322) 667283
Mem 450
Sec Julie Smith (Mgr) (01322) 662038
Pro S Cranfield (01322) 660554

Holes 18 L 6364 yds Par 71 SSS 70
9 hole course
Recs Am–63 L Venus (1994)
V'tors U SOC
Fees £14 (£18)
Loc 2 miles S of A2/A2018 Junction
Mis Driving range. Indoor teaching centre
Arch Howard Swann

Boughton (1993)

Pay and play
Brickfield Lane, Boughton, Faversham ME13 9AJ
Tel (01227) 752277
Fax (01227) 752361
Mem 300
Sec S Hall
Pro T Poole
Holes 18 L 6452 yds SSS 71
Recs Am–70 G Houston
Pro–70 T Berry, C Evans
V'tors U SOC–WD
Fees £16 (£22)
Loc NE of Boughton, nr M2/A2 interchange. 6 miles W of Canterbury
Mis Driving range
Arch Philip Sparks

Broke Hill (1993)

Sevenoaks Road, Halstead TN14 7HR
Tel (01959) 533225
Fax (01959) 532880
Sec T Collingwood
Pro C West (01959) 533810
Holes 18 L 6454 yds Par 72 SSS 71
Recs Am–70 S Lloyd (1996)
Pro–69 B Cameron (1997)
V'tors WD–U before 5pm WE–NA
Fees £30
Loc 4 miles S of Bromley on A21. M25 Junction 4
Arch David Williams

Bromley (1948)

Public
Magpie Hall Lane, Bromley BR2 8JF
Tel (0181) 462 7014
Pro A Hodgson
Holes 9 L 5538 yds SSS 66
Recs Am–66 HE Harding, KW Miles
V'tors U
Fees On application
Loc Off Bromley Common (A21)

Broome Park (1981)

Broome Park Estate, Barham, Canterbury CT4 6QX
Tel (01227) 831701
Fax (01227) 831973
Mem 600
Sec RC Cheeseworth (Ext 263)
Pro T Britz (01227) 831126
Holes 18 L 6610 yds SSS 72
Recs Am–66 A Roberts (1995)
Pro–66 B Impett (1984)
V'tors H WE–NA before noon SOC–WD
Fees £26 (£32)

Loc M2/A2-A260 Folkestone road, 1½ miles on RH side
Mis Driving range
Arch Donald Steel

Canterbury (1927)

Scotland Hills, Littlebourne Road, Canterbury CT1 1TW
Tel (01227) 453532
Fax (01227) 784277
Mem 650
Sec J Lucas
Pro P Everard (01227) 462865
Holes 18 L 6249 yds SSS 70
Recs Am–65 SP Blake
Pro–64 K Redford
V'tors WD–U H WE–NA before 3pm SOC–Tues & Thurs
Fees £27 D–£36 (£36)
Loc 1 mile E of Canterbury on A257
Arch HS Colt

Chart Hills (1993)

Weeks Lane, Biddenden TN27 8JX
Tel (01580) 292222
Fax (01580) 292233
Mem 315
Sec R Hyder (Gen Mgr)
Pro W Easdale (01580) 292148
Holes 18 L 7086 yds SSS 74
V'tors H
Fees £65 (incl lunch)
Loc 12 miles W of Ashford (A262)
Mis Golf Academy
Arch Nick Faldo

Chelsfield Lakes Golf Centre (1992)

Pay and play
Court Road, Orpington BR6 9BX
Tel (01689) 896266
Fax (01689) 824577
Mem 650
Sec S Creed (Man Dir)
Pro N Lee, D Clark
Holes 18 L 6077 yds Par 71 SSS 69
9 hole Par 3 course
V'tors U–booking required SOC
Fees £14 (£17)
Loc 1 mile from M25 Junction 4 (A224)
Mis Target golf range
Arch MRM Sandow

Cherry Lodge (1969)

Jail Lane, Biggin Hill, Westerham TN16 3AX
Tel (01959) 572250
Fax (01959) 540672
Mem 650
Sec CF Smith
Pro N Child (01959) 572989
Holes 18 L 6652 yds SSS 73
Recs Am–70 K Williams (1996)
Pro–69 S Barr (1992)
V'tors WD–U WE–M
Fees £18 D–£25
Loc 3 miles N of Westerham, off A233
Mis Driving range
Arch John Day

Chestfield (1925)

103 Chestfield Road, Whitstable CT5 3LU
Tel (01227) 794411
Mem 692
Sec MA Sutcliffe
Pro J Brotherton (01227) 793563
Holes 18 L 6181 yds SSS 70
Recs Am–64 G Pini
Pro–66 M Campos
V'tors WD–H
Fees On application
Loc 1 mile S of A299 and Chestfield Station

Chislehurst (1894)

Camden Place, Chislehurst BR7 5HJ
Tel (0181) 467 3055
Fax (0181) 295 0874
Mem 740
Sec NE Pearson (0181) 467 2782
Pro M Lawrence (0181) 467 6798
Holes 18 L 5128 yds SSS 65
Recs Am–61 J Murray (1993)
Pro–61 W Hodkin
V'tors WD–H WE–M SOC
Fees D–£25
Loc M25 Junction 3/A20/A222

Cobtree Manor Park (1984)

Public
Chatham Road, Boxley, Maidstone ME14 3AZ
Tel (01622) 753276
Sec A Ferras
Holes 18 L 5716 yds SSS 68
Recs Am–67 M White (1991)
V'tors WD–U WE/BH–(book 1 wk in advance) SOC–WD
Fees £8.50 (£13.25)
Loc 3 miles N of Maidstone on A229
Arch F Hawtree

Corinthian (1987)

Gay Dawn Farm, Fawkham, Dartford DA3 8LZ
Tel (01474) 707559
Mem 400
Sec R Fletton
Pro C McKillop
Holes 9 L 6323 yds Par 72 SSS 70
Recs Am–72 A Walker, G Hesketh (1995)
V'tors WD–U H WE/BH–NA before 1pm SOC
Fees D–£15
Loc 4 miles S of Dartford Tunnel. E of Brands Hatch along Fawkham Valley road

Cray Valley (1972)

Pay and play
Sandy Lane, St Paul's Cray, Orpington BR5 3HY
Tel (01689) 837909
Fax (01689) 891428
Mem 600
Sec J Scappatura (01689) 839677

Pro G Sheriff (01689) 837909
Holes 18 L 5624 yds SSS 67
9 L 2100 yds SSS 60
V'tors U
Fees £13 (£19)
Loc Off A20 Ruxley roundabout at Sidcup

Darenth Valley (1973)

Pay and play
Station Road, Shoreham, Sevenoaks TN14 7SA
Tel (01959) 522944 (Clubhouse)
Fax (01959) 525089
Sec JR Cooper (Mgr)
Pro S Fotheringham (01959) 522922
Holes 18 L 6327 yds Par 72 SSS 71
Recs Am–69 W Leo
Pro–65 S Wood
V'tors U–booking required SOC
Fees £13 (£18)
Loc 3 miles N of Sevenoaks, off A225

Dartford (1897)

Dartford Heath, Dartford DA1 2TN
Tel (01322) 223616
Mem 600
Sec Mrs MM Gronow
Pro G Cooke (01322) 226409
Holes 18 L 5914 yds Par 69 SSS 69
Recs Am–65 N Buttery (1992)
Pro–65 N Burke (1988)
V'tors WD–I WE–M H
Fees £28
Loc Dartford 2 miles

Deangate Ridge (1972)

Public
Duxcourt Road, Hoo, Rochester ME3 8RZ
Tel (01634) 250537
Mem 800
Sec JH Orr
Pro R Fox (01634) 251180
Holes 18 L 6300 yds SSS 70
Recs Am–67 L Brookwell (1994)
Pro–65 N Allen (1990)
V'tors U SOC
Fees £9.95 (£12.30)
Loc 7 miles NE of Rochester on A228. M2, 5 miles

Edenbridge G&CC (1973)

Crouch House Road, Edenbridge TN8 5LQ
Tel (01732) 867381
Fax (01732) 867029
Mem 1000
Sec Mrs N Taylor
Pro (01732) 865202
Holes 18 L 6604 yds SSS 72
18 L 5671 yds SSS 67
9 hole course
Recs Am–66 ACI Cox
V'tors WD/WE–booking necessary
Fees £16.50 (£22)
Loc 2 miles W of Edenbridge. M25 Junction 6
Mis Floodlit driving range. 9 hole pitch & putt course

Eltham Warren (1890)

Bexley Road, Eltham, London SE9 2PE

Tel	**(0181) 850 1166**
Mem	400
Sec	DJ Clare (0181) 850 4477
Pro	G Brett (0181) 859 7909
Holes	9 L 5840 yds SSS 68
Recs	Am–66 G Janes, D Holmes, RB Hills
	Pro–67 T Spence
V'tors	WD–I WE/BH–M SOC–Thurs only
Fees	D–£25
Loc	½ mile from Eltham station on A210

Etchinghill (1995)

Pay and play
Canterbury Road, Etchinghill CT18 8FA

Tel	**(01303) 863863**
Fax	(01303) 863210
Sec	D Stodart (Mgr)
Pro	C Hodgson (01303) 863966
Holes	18 L 6121 yds Par 70 SSS 69 9 hole Par 3 course
V'tors	U
Fees	£15 (£20)
Loc	1 mile N of M20 Junction 12 on B2065
Mis	Driving range
Arch	John Sturdy

Executive GC Cranbrook (1969)

Golford Road, Cranbrook TN17 4AL

Tel	**(01580) 712833**
Fax	(01580) 714274
Mem	500
Sec	C Cooper
Pro	A Gillard
Holes	18 L 6295 yds SSS 70
Recs	Am–67 S Coulter
	Pro–70 S Barr
V'tors	WD–U WE/BH–restricted SOC
Fees	£23 (£30) (1997)
Loc	15 miles S of Maidstone. M25 Junction 5-A21/A262
Mis	Driving range
Arch	Cdr J Harris

Faversham (1910)

Belmont Park, Faversham ME13 0HB

Tel	**(01795) 890251**
Fax	(01795) 890760
Mem	800
Sec	FW Prescott (Mgr) (01795) 890561
Pro	S Rokes (01795) 890275
Holes	18 L 6021 yds SSS 69
Recs	Am–65 R Chapman
	Pro–63 T Spence
V'tors	WD–I or H WE–M SOC
Fees	£25
Loc	Faversham and M2, 2 miles

Gillingham (1908)

Woodlands Road, Gillingham ME27 2AP

Tel	**(01634) 850999**
Fax	(01634) 574749
Mem	450 100(L) 50(J)

Sec	LP O'Grady (01634) 853017
Pro	B Impett (01634) 855862
Holes	18 L 5509 yds SSS 67
Recs	Am–65 T Williamson
	Pro–64 P Clark
V'tors	WD–I H WE/BH–M
Fees	£18 D–£25
Loc	A2/M2, 2 miles
Arch	Braid/Steel

Hawkhurst (1968)

High Street, Hawkhurst TN18 4JS

Tel	**(01580) 752396**
Fax	(01580) 754074
Mem	450
Sec	A Shipley
Pro	T Collins (01580) 753600
Holes	9 L 5709 yds SSS 68
Recs	Am–66 R Gerrard
	Pro–68 R Cameron
V'tors	WD–U WE–M SOC
Fees	18 holes–£10 (£12); 9 holes–£9
Loc	14 miles S of Tunbridge Wells on A268

Herne Bay (1895)

Eddington, Herne Bay CT6 7PG

Tel	**(01227) 374097**
Mem	480
Sec	B Warren (01227) 373964
Pro	S Dordoy (01227) 374727
Holes	18 L 5567 yds SSS 68
Recs	Am–60 SJ Wood
	Pro–65 C Clark
V'tors	WD–U WE/BH–H after noon SOC–WD
Fees	£18 D–£25 (£25)
Loc	A299 Thanet road

Hever (1993)

Hever TN8 7NG

Tel	**(01732) 700771**
Fax	(01732) 700771
Mem	700
Sec	A Chase
Pro	R Tinworth
Holes	18 L 7002 yds SSS 75
V'tors	H SOC
Fees	£29–(£45) (£45–£59)
Loc	2 miles E of Edenbridge
Arch	Peter Nicholson

High Elms (1969)

Public
High Elms Road, Downe, Orpington BR6 7SZ

Tel	**(01689) 858175**
Sec	Mrs P O'Keeffe (Hon)
Pro	P Remy
Holes	18 L 6210 yds SSS 70
Recs	Am–68 I Farman
V'tors	U
Fees	On application
Loc	Off A21 via Shire Lane

Hythe Imperial (1950)

Prince's Parade, Hythe CT21 6AE

Tel	**(01303) 267441**
Fax	(01303) 267554
Mem	445

Sec	N Jones (01303) 267554
Pro	G Ritchie (01303) 267441
Holes	9 L 5560 yds SSS 67
Recs	Am–63 PI Kaye
	Pro–63 G Ritchie
V'tors	H SOC
Fees	£20
Loc	On coast, 4 miles W of Folkestone

Kings Hill (1996)

Kings Hill, West Malling ME19 4AF

Tel	**(01732) 875040/ 842121 (Bookings)**
Fax	(01732) 875019
Mem	430
Sec	P Townson (Mgr)
Pro	C Lightfoot (01732) 842121
Holes	18 L 6622 yds Par 72 SSS 72
V'tors	WD–U WE/BH–M after 2pm (11am Winter) SOC–WD
Fees	£25
Loc	3 miles from M20 Junction 4, off A228
Arch	David Williams

Knole Park (1924)

Seal Hollow Road, Sevenoaks TN15 0HJ

Tel	**(01732) 452709**
Fax	(01732) 463159
Mem	700
Sec	PF Lamb (01732) 452150
Pro	PE Gill (01732) 451740
Holes	18 L 6249 yds SSS 70
Recs	Am–64 RW Seamer
V'tors	WD–restricted WE/BH–M H SOC
Fees	£32 D–£42
Loc	½ mile from Sevenoaks centre
Arch	JF Abercromby

Lamberhurst (1890)

Church Road, Lamberhurst TN3 8DT

Tel	**(01892) 890241**
Fax	(01892) 891140
Mem	700
Sec	P Gleeson (01892) 890591
Pro	M Travers (01892) 890552
Holes	18 L 6345 yds SSS 70
Recs	Am–69 L Ferris
	Pro–65 A Lavers
V'tors	WD–U H WE–NA before noon
Fees	£22 D–£33 (£36)
Loc	5 miles SE of Tunbridge Wells, off A21

Langley Park (1910)

Barnfield Wood Road, Beckenham BR3 6SZ

Tel	**(0181) 650 2090**
Mem	650
Sec	JL Smart (0181) 658 6849
Pro	C Staff (0181) 650 1663
Holes	18 L 6488 yds SSS 71
Recs	Am–66 T Trodd
	Pro–65 P Mitchell (1987), GT Ritchie (1991)
V'tors	WD–H WE–M SOC–WD
Fees	£35
Loc	Bromley South Station 1 mile
Arch	JH Taylor

Leeds Castle (1928)

Pay and play
Leeds Castle, Hollingbourne, Maidstone ME17 1PL
Tel (01622) 880467/765400
Fax (01622) 735616
Sec Mrs A Knowlden
Pro None
Holes 9 L 2880 yds Par 33
Recs Pro–32 A Jacklin
V'tors U SOC–WD
Fees 9 holes–£9.50
Loc 10 miles E of Maidstone (A20). M20 Junction 8, 1 mile
Mis 6-day advance booking
Arch Neil Coles

Littlestone (1888)

St Andrews Road, Littlestone, New Romney TN28 8RB
Tel (01797) 362310
Fax (01797) 362740
Mem 550
Sec Col C Moorhouse (01797) 363355
Pro S Watkins (01797) 362231
Holes 18 L 6470 yds SSS 72
Recs Am–67 G Godmon (1984), S Wood (1988), A Stracey (1995)
Pro–65 P Eales, D Clark, R Green, (1993)
V'tors WD–H WE–by arrangement SOC
Fees £30 (£45)
Loc 2 miles E of New Romney. 15 miles SE of Ashford
Arch W Laidlaw Purves/Dr A Mackenzie

The London Golf Club (1993)

South Ash Manor Estate, Ash, Sevenoaks TN15 7EN
Tel (01474) 879899
Fax (01474) 879912
Mem 400
Sec J Paulin
Pro K Morgan (Tour Pro), P Way
Holes Heritage 18 L 7208 yds Par 72 SSS 74; International 18 L 7005 yds Par 72 SSS 74
Recs Heritage Am–68 S Wakefield (1996)
Pro–68 J Nicklaus (1994)
International Am–71 J Bush (1996)
Pro–66 P Mitchell (1995)
V'tors M
Fees N/A
Loc Off A20, nr Brands Hatch at West Kingsdown
Arch Nicklaus/Kirby

Lullingstone Park (1967)

Public
Parkgate Road, Chelsfield, Orpington BR6 7PX
Tel (01959) 533793
Pro M Watt
Holes 18 L 6779 yds SSS 72
9 L 2445 yds Par 33

Recs Am–71
Pro–69
V'tors U
Fees On application
Loc Off Orpington by-pass (A224) towards Well Hill. M25 Junction 4
Mis Driving range. 9 hole pitch & putt

Lydd

Pay and play
Romney Road, Lydd, Romney Marsh TN29 9LS
Tel (01797) 320808
Fax (01797) 321482
Mem 400
Sec BM Evans (Sec/Mgr)
Pro G Richie
Holes 18 L 6517 yds Par 71 SSS 71
Recs Am–68 M Cozens (1995)
V'tors U SOC
Fees £12 (£15)
Loc 15 miles SE of Ashford (B2075)
Mis Driving range
Arch M Smith

Mid Kent (1909)

Singlewell Road, Gravesend DA11 7RB
Tel (01474) 568035
Fax (01474) 564218
Mem 1050
Sec T Potter
Pro M Foreman (01474) 332810
Holes 18 L 6218 yds SSS 70
Recs Am–64 S Barker (1995)
Pro–60 K McDonald (1993)
V'tors WD–H WE–M
Fees On application
Loc SE of Gravesend, nr A2
Arch Frank Pennink

Moatlands (1993)

Watermans Lane, Brenchley, Tonbridge TN12 6ND
Tel (01892) 724400
Fax (01892) 723300
Mem 500
Sec K Wiley
Pro S Wood (01892) 724252
Holes 18 L 7060 yds Par 72 SSS 74
V'tors WD–U H WE–H NA before noon SOC–WD exc Wed
Fees £27 (£37)
Loc Between Matfield and Paddock Wood, off B2160
Mis Driving range
Arch T Saito

Nizels (1992)

Nizels Lane, Hildenborough, Tonbridge TN11 8NX
Tel (01732) 833138
Fax (01732) 833764
Mem 700
Sec A Gemmil
Pro Mrs S Hodge (01732) 838926
Holes 18 L 6408 yds SSS 71
Recs Am–67 R Edwards
V'tors WD–U SOC

Fees £25 D–£35
Loc 4 miles from M25 on B245. A21 Tonbridge North Junction
Arch Lennan/Purnell

North Foreland (1903)

Convent Road, Broadstairs, Thanet CT10 3PU
Tel (01843) 862140
Fax (01843) 862140
Mem 800
Sec BJ Preston
Pro N Hanson (01843) 604471
Holes 18 L 6430 yds SSS 71
Recs Am–66 P Walton, A Sheppard
Pro–65 M Lawrence
V'tors WD–H WE–NA am –H pm
Fees £26 (£36)
Loc B2052, 1½ miles N of Broadstairs
Mis 18 hole pitch & putt course
Arch Fowler/Simpson

Oastpark (1993)

Malling Road, Snodland ME6 5LG
Tel (01634) 242661
Fax (01634) 240744
Mem 300
Sec Anne Green (01634) 242818
Pro J Gregory (01634) 242661
Holes 18 L 6173 yds Par 69 SSS 69
Recs Am–71 D Porthouse (1993)
V'tors U SOC
Fees £8.50 (£12)
Loc 1 mile E of M20 Junction 4

Poult Wood (1974)

Public
Higham Lane, Tonbridge TN11 9QR
Tel (01732) 364039 (Bookings), (01732) 366180 (Clubhouse)
Mem 520
Sec S Taylor
Pro C Miller
Holes 18 L 5569 yds SSS 67
9 hole course
Recs Am–64 J McIlveney
V'tors U–booking required SOC–WD
Fees £8.60 (£13.20)
Loc 1 mile N of Tonbridge, off A227
Arch Hawtree

Prince's (1904)

Sandwich Bay, Sandwich CT13 9QB
Tel (01304) 611118
Fax (01304) 612000
Mem 350
Sec WM Howie(Mgr)
Pro C Evans (01304) 613797
Holes 27 hole course (3 x 9 holes):
Dunes/Himalayas/Shore
Length 6238–6947 yds
Par 71-72 SSS 70-73
Recs Himalayas/Shore
Am–67 M Goodin
Pro–69 M Mannelli
Dunes/Himalayas Am–69
S Wood

V'tors U SOC–(book with M Stone)
Fees £36 D–£42 Sat–£39 D–£47
Sun–£40 D–£52
Loc Sandwich Bay (A256)
Mis Driving range
Arch Morrison/Campbell

Redlibbets

Fawkham, Longfield, Kent DA3 8LY
Tel (01474) 872278
Sec R Fox (Golf Dir)
Pro R Taylor
Holes 18 L 6651 yds Par 72
V'tors U SOC
Fees £25
Loc M20 Junction 2, off A20
between Fawkham and Ash

The Ridge (1993)

*Chartway Street, East Sutton,
Maidstone ME17 3DL*
Tel (01622) 844382
Fax (01622) 844168
Mem 650
Sec G Sones
Pro M Rackham
(01622) 844243
Holes 18 L 6254 yds SSS 70
V'tors WD–H SOC–Tues & Thurs
WE–NA
Fees £18
Loc 3 miles E of Maidstone, off
A274. M20 Junction 8
Mis Driving range
Arch Patrick Dawson

Rochester & Cobham Park (1891)

Park Pale, by Rochester ME2 3UL
Tel (01474) 823411
Fax (01474) 824446
Mem 720
Sec Maj JW Irvine (Mgr)
Pro J Blair (01474) 823658
Holes 18 L 6596 yds SSS 71
Pro–68 P Mitchell (1997)
V'tors WD–U H WE–M before 5pm
SOC–Tues & Thurs
Fees £26
Loc 3 miles E of Gravesend exit
(A2)
Mis Driving range
Arch D Steel

Romney Warren (1993)

Pay and play
*St Andrews Road, Littlestone, New
Romney TN28 8RB*
Tel (01797) 362231
Fax (01797) 362740
Mem 250
Sec P Rolfe (Hon)
Pro S Watkins
Holes 18 L 5126 yds SSS 65
Recs Am–69 C Moorhouse
V'tors U SOC
Fees £12 (£17)
Loc 2 miles E of New Romney. 15
miles SE of Ashford
Arch Evans/Lewis

Royal Blackheath (1608)

Court Road, Eltham, London SE9 5AF
Tel (0181) 850 1795
Fax (0181) 859 0150
Mem 700
Sec Wg Cdr R Barriball RAF
(Rtd)
Pro I McGregor
(0181) 850 1763
Holes 18 L 6219 yds SSS 70
Recs Am–68 M Harris (1994)
Pro–66 M Lawrence,
B Cameron (1993)
V'tors WD–I or H WE/BH–M SOC
Fees £30
Loc 5 miles W of M25 Junction 3
Mis Golf museum
Arch James Braid

Royal Cinque Ports (1892)

Golf Road, Deal CT14 6RF
Tel (01304) 374007 (Office),
(01304) 374328 (Clubhouse)
Fax (01304) 379530
Mem 1000+
Sec CC Hammond (01304)
367856
Pro A Reynolds (01304) 374170
Holes 18 L 6482 yds SSS 71
Recs Am–65 MF Bonallack (1964)
Pro–63 GD Manson (1981)
V'tors WD–I H
Fees On application
Loc A258, N of Deal
Mis Driving range

Royal St George's (1887)

Sandwich CT13 9PB
Tel (01304) 613090
Fax (01304) 611245
Mem 675
Sec GE Watts
Pro A Brooks (01304) 615236
Holes 18 L 6565 yds Par 70 SSS 72
Recs Am–67 H Berwick (1954),
JR Harris (1995)
M Brooks (1996)
Pro–63 N Faldo, P Stewart
(1993)
V'tors WD–I H WE–M SOC–WD
Fees £60 D–£85
Loc 1 mile E of Sandwich
Arch Dr Laidlaw Purves

Ruxley Park (1975)

Pay and play
*Sandy Lane, St Paul's Cray, Orpington
BR5 3HY*
Tel (01689) 871490
Fax (01689) 891428
Mem 500
Sec J Scappatura
Pro A Langoon
Holes 18 L 6027 yds SSS 69
9 hole Par 3 course
V'tors U
Fees £11 (£18)
Loc Off A20 Ruxley roundabout at
Sidcup
Mis Floodlit driving range

St Augustines (1907)

*Cottington Road, Cliffsend, Ramsgate
CT12 5JN*
Tel (01843) 590333
Fax (01843) 590444
Mem 650 55(J)
Sec LP Dyke
Pro DB Scott (01843) 590222
Holes 18 L 5197 yds SS 65
Recs Am–64 AD Setterfield
Pro–61 P Mitchell
V'tors H SOC–WD
Fees £21.50 (£23.50)
Loc 2 miles SW of Ramsgate from
A253 or A256. Signs to St
Augustines Cross
Arch Tom Vardon

Sene Valley (1888)

Sene, Folkestone CT18 8BL
Fax (01303) 237513
Mem 650
Sec RW Leaver (01303) 268513
Pro N Watson (01303) 268514
Holes 18 L 6196 yds SSS 69
Recs Am–65 J Hamilton
Pro–67 P Moger
V'tors H SOC
Fees £20 (£30)
Loc 2 miles N of Hythe on B2065
Arch Henry Cotton

Sheerness (1906)

*Power Station Road, Sheerness
ME12 3AE*
Tel (01795) 662585
Mem 700
Sec R Pearce
Pro W Evans (01795) 666840
Holes 18 L 6460 yds SSS 71
Recs Am–66 R Whitington (1996)
V'tors WD–U SOC–Tues–Thurs
Fees £15
Loc 9 miles N of Sittingbourne.
M20, M2 or A2 to A249

Shooter's Hill (1903)

*Lowood, Eaglesfield Road, London
SE18 3DA*
Tel (0181) 854 1216
Fax (0181) 854 0469
Mem 310 60(L) 31(J)
Sec BR Adams (0181) 854 6368
Pro M Ridge (0181) 854 0073
Holes 18 L 5721 yds SSS 68
Recs Am–63 M Holland (1984)
Pro–62 M Parker (1990)
V'tors WD–I WE/BH–M SOC–Tues
& Thurs only
Fees £20 D–£25
Loc Off A207 nr Blackheath

Shortlands (1894)

*Meadow Road, Shortlands, Bromley
BR2 0PB*
Tel (0181) 460 2471
Fax (0181) 460 8828
Mem 525
Sec PW Smeeth
(0181) 460 8828
Pro J Murray (0181) 464 6182

For list of abbreviations see page 479

Holes 9 L 5261 yds SSS 66
Recs Am–59 T Coulstock (1990)
Pro–59 N Haynes (1995)
V'tors M
Loc Ravensbourne Ave, Shortlands

Sidcup (1891)

7 Hurst Road, Sidcup DA15 9AE
Tel **(0181) 300 2864**
Mem 400
Sec K Rawlins (0181) 300 2150
Pro N Willis (0181) 309 0679
Holes 9 L 5722 yds SSS 68
Recs Am–65 M Bennett
Pro–64 D Webb
V'tors WD–H WE/BH–M SOC–WD
Fees £14
Loc On A222. A2/A20, 2 miles

Sittingbourne & Milton Regis (1929)

Wormdale, Newington, Sittingbourne ME9 7PX
Tel **(01795) 842261**
Fax (01795) 844117
Mem 525 100(L) 50(J)
Sec HDG Wylie
Pro JR Hearn (01795) 842775
Holes 18 L 6291 yds SSS 70
Recs Am–63 PA Stuart (1997)
V'tors WD–H Sat–NA Sun–M
SOC–Tues & Thurs
Fees £20
Loc 1 mile N of M2 Junction 5

Sundridge Park (1901)

Garden Road, Bromley BR1 3NE
Tel **(0181) 460 1822**
Fax (0181) 289 3050
Mem 1200
Sec D Lowton (0181) 460 0278
Pro B Cameron (0181) 460 5540
Holes East 18 L 6490 yds SSS 71
West 18 L 6007 yds SSS 69
Recs East Am–66 J MacNamara
(1995)
Pro–63 R Cameron
West Am–64 R Hurd (1993)
Pro–65 R Fidler
V'tors H SOC–WD
Fees £40
Loc 1 mile N of Bromley, by
Sundridge Park Station. M25
Junctions 3/4

Tenterden (1905)

Woodchurch Road, Tenterden TN30 7DR
Tel **(01580) 763987**
Fax (01580) 763987
Mem 650
Sec JM Wilson
Pro A Scullion (01580) 762409
Holes 18 L 6050 yds Par 70 SSS 69
Recs Am–69 R Murley (1992)
Pro–65 R Cameron (1991)
V'tors WD–U WE/BH–M Sun–NA
before noon
Fees On application
Loc 1 mile E of Tenterden on
B2067

Tudor Park Hotel (1988)

Ashford Road, Bearsted, Maidstone ME14 4NQ
Tel **(01622) 734334**
Fax (01622) 735360
Mem 750
Sec J Ladbrook
Pro J Slinger (01622) 739412
Holes 18 L 6041yds SSS 69
Recs Am–64 D Jessop (1992)
Pro–65 N Haynes (1993)
V'tors H SOC
Fees £25 (£30)
Loc 3 miles E of Maidstone on
A20. M20 Junction 8
Arch Donald Steel

Tunbridge Wells (1889)

Langton Road, Tunbridge Wells TN4 8XH
Tel **(01892) 523034**
Mem 360 86(L) 45(J)
Sec RF Mealing
(01892) 536918
Pro M Barton (01892) 541386
Holes 9 L 4728 yds SSS 62
Recs Am–59 EC Chapman
Pro–59 J Humphrey
V'tors U H SOC
Fees £15 D–£20
Loc Tunbridge Wells, next to
Spa Hotel

Upchurch River Valley (1991)

Pay and play
Oak Lane, Upchurch, Sittingbourne ME9 7AY
Tel **(01634) 360626**
Fax (01634) 387784
Mem 550
Sec AJ New (01634) 260594
Pro R Cornwell (01634) 379592
Holes 18 L 6237 yds SSS 70
9 hole Par 3 course
V'tors U SOC–WD
Fees 18 hole–£10.95 (£13.95);
9 hole–£6.75 (£8.45)
Loc 3 miles NE of Rainham, off
A2. M2 Junction 4
Mis Floodlit driving range
Arch David Smart

Walmer & Kingsdown (1909)

The Leas, Kingsdown, Deal CT14 8EP
Tel **(01304) 373256**
Fax (01304) 363017
Mem 627
Sec JP Morgan
Pro M Paget (01304) 363017
Holes 18 L 6437 yds SSS 71
Recs Am–66 P Wilson (1995)
Pro–70 M Lee
V'tors WD–H WE–after noon SOC
Fees D–£28 (£30)
Loc 2½ miles S of Deal on clifftop
Arch James Braid

Weald of Kent (1992)

Pay and play
Maidstone Road, Headcorn TN27 9PT
Tel **(01622) 890866**
Fax (01622) 891793
Mem 1000
Sec D Etheridge (Mgr)
Holes 18 L 6169 yds SSS 69
V'tors U–booking 3 days in advance
SOC
Fees £14.50 (£18.50)
Loc 5 miles S of Maidstone on
A274. M20 Junction 8
Arch John Millen

West Kent (1916)

West Hill, Downe, Orpington BR6 7JJ
Tel **(01689) 851323**
Fax (01689) 858693
Mem 750
Sec PR Stevens
Pro RS Fidler (01689) 856863
Holes 18 L 6399 yds SSS 70
Recs Am–62 DC Smith (1984)
Pro–65 H Baiocchi (1985)
V'tors WD–H or I–phone to arrange
WE/BH–M
Fees On application
Loc 5 miles S of Orpington

West Malling (1974)

Addington, Maidstone ME19 5AR
Tel **(01732) 844785**
Fax (01732) 844795
Mem 900
Sec MR Ellis
Pro D Lambert
Holes Spitfire 18 L 6142 yds Par 70
Hurricane 18 L 6240 yds
Par 70
Recs Spitfire Am–67 S Pigott
Pro–67 H Baiocchi
Hurricane Am–69 S Pigott
V'tors WD–U WE–U H after noon
Fees £20 (£30)
Loc 12 miles W of Maidstone
(A20)

Westgate & Birchington (1893)

176, Canterbury Road, Westgate-on-Sea CT8 8LT
Tel **(01843) 831115/833905**
Mem 325
Sec JM Wood
Pro R Game
Holes 18 L 4926 yds SSS 64
Pro–60 J Hickman
Ladies–60 W Morgan
V'tors H or I WD–NA before 10am
WE–NA before 11am SOC
Fees £13 (£15)
Loc 1 mile W of Westgate (A28)

Whitstable & Seasalter (1910)

Collingwood Road, Whitstable CT5 1EB
Tel **(01227) 272020**
Mem 300
Sec DB Christie

Holes 9 L 5314 yds SSS 63
V'tors WD–U WE–M
Fees On application
Loc 1 mile W of Whitstable

Wildernesse (1890)

Seal, Sevenoaks TN15 0JE
Tel (01732) 761526
Mem 700
Sec RA Foster (01732) 761199
Pro CA Walker (01732) 761527
Holes 18 L 6438 yds SSS 72
Recs Am–64 AD Tillman (1991)
Pro–65 I Grant (1980)
V'tors WD–I H
SOC–Mon/Thurs/Fri
Fees £32 D–£47
Loc 2 miles E of Sevenoaks (A25).
M25 Junction 5

Woodlands Manor (1928)

*Woodlands, Tinkerpot Lane, Sevenoaks
TN15 6AB*
Tel (01959) 523805
Mem 650
Sec EF Newman (01959) 523806
Pro A Brooks (01959) 524161
Holes 18 L 6000 yds SSS 68
Recs Am–65 N Sherman
Pro–65 N Coles
V'tors WD–U WE–H NA before
noon SOC–WD
Fees On application
Loc 4 miles S of M25 Junction 3.
Off A20 between West
Kingsdown and Otford
Arch Coles/Lyons

Wrotham Heath (1906)

*Seven Mile Lane Comp, Sevenoaks
TN15 8QZ*
Tel (01732) 884800
Mem 424 75(L) 50(J)
Sec LJ Byrne
Pro H Dearden (01732) 883854
Holes 18 L 5954 yds SSS 69
V'tors WD–H WE/BH–M
SOC–Thurs & Fri
Fees £22 D–£32
Loc 8 miles W of Maidstone on
B2016. M26/A20 Junction,
1 mile
Arch Donald Steel

Lancashire

Accrington & District
(1893)

*West End, Oswaldtwistle, Accrington
BB5 4LS*
Tel (01254) 232734
Mem 350
Sec JE Pilkington (01254) 235070
Pro W Harling (01254) 231091
Holes 18 L 6044 yds SSS 69
Recs Am–64 J Rothwell
V'tors WD/WE–U SOC
Fees On application
Loc 3 miles SW of Accrington

Ashton & Lea (1913)

*Tudor Ave, Blackpool Rd, Lea,
Preston PR4 0XA*
Tel (01772) 726480
Fax (01772) 735762
Mem 850
Sec T Ashton (01772) 735282
Pro M Greenough (01772)
720374
Holes 18 L 6346 yds SSS 70
Recs Am–65 K Wallbank (1989)
Pro–66 J Hawksworth (1988),
S Townend (1992)
Ladies–72 L Fairclough (1985)
V'tors U SOC
Fees £20 (£23)
Loc 3 miles W of Preston, off A5085
Arch J Steer

Ashton-in-Makerfield
(1902)

*Garswood Park, Liverpool Road,
Ashton-in-Makerfield WN4 0YT*
Tel (01942) 727267
Mem 500
Sec JR Hay (01942) 719330
Pro P Allan (01942) 724229
Holes 18 L 6212 yds SSS 70
Recs Am–68 GS Lacy
V'tors WD–U exc Wed WE/BH–M
SOC
Fees £25
Loc 1 mile W of Ashton-in-
Makerfield on A58. M6
Junction 23/24

Ashton-under-Lyne (1913)

*Gorsey Way, Hurst, Ashton-under-Lyne
OL6 9HT*
Tel (0161) 330 1537
Fax (0161) 330 1537
Mem 600
Sec D McGee (0161) 339 5394
Pro C Boyle (0161) 308 2095
Holes 18 L 6209 yds SSS 70
Recs Am–67 S Hamer (1992)
V'tors WD–U WE/BH–M SOC
Fees £25
Loc 8 miles E of Manchester

Bacup (1912)

Maden Road, Bacup OL13 8HY
Tel (01706) 873170
Mem 395
Sec J Garvey (01706) 874485
Holes 9 L 6008 yds SSS 69
Recs Am–67 M Butcher
V'tors U
Fees On application
Loc Bankside Lane

Baxenden & District (1913)

*Top o' th' Meadow, Baxenden,
Accrington BB5 2EA*
Tel (01254) 234555
Mem 400
Sec N Turner (01706) 225423
Holes 9 L 5702 yds SSS 68
Recs Am–68 W Horvath
Pro–66 C Tobin

V'tors WD–U WE/BH–M
Fees £15
Loc 2 miles SE of Accrington

Beacon Park (1982)

Public
*Beacon Lane, Dalton, Up Holland
WN8 7RU*
Tel (01695) 627500
Mem 250
Sec T Harris
Pro R Peters (01695) 622700
Holes 18 L 5927 yds SSS 69
Recs Am–68 D Parkin,
I Donaldson
V'tors U–book 6 days in advance
SOC
Fees On application
Loc Nr Ashurst Beacon and
M58/M6 Junction 26
Mis Driving range

Blackburn (1894)

Beardwood Brow, Blackburn BB2 7AX
Tel (01254) 51122
Fax (01254) 665578
Mem 440 90(L) 60(J)
Sec PJ Irvine
Pro A Rodwell (01254) 55942
Holes 18 L 6144 yds SSS 70
Recs Am–63 JS Reed (1991)
Pro–66 M Foster
Ladies–68 CD Blackshaw
(1994)
V'tors U SOC–WD
WE/BH–restricted
Fees £24 (£28)
Loc 1 mile NW of Blackburn
(A677). M6 Junction 31

Blackpool North Shore
(1904)

Devonshire Road, Blackpool FY2 0RD
Tel (01253) 351017
Fax (01253) 591240
Mem 980
Sec MA Nuttall (01253) 352054
Pro B Ward (01253) 354640
Holes 18 L 6443 yds SSS 71
Recs Am–66 K Wallbank (1995)
Pro–63 C O'Connor
V'tors WD–U WE–restricted SOC
Fees £25 (£30)
Loc 1/2 mile E of Queens
Promenade (B5124)

Blackpool Park (1925)

Public
*North Park Drive, Blackpool
FY3 8LS*
Mem 650
Sec D Stones (01253) 397916
Pro B Purdie (01253) 391004
Holes 18 L 6192 yds SSS 69
Recs Am–67 PCooper (1983),
D O'Connell (1992)
Pro–68 D Lewis
V'tors U–No telephone booking
Fees £9 (£10.50)
Loc 2 miles E of Blackpool,
signposted off M55

Mis Tee reservations: Blackpool
Borough Council, Town Hall,
Talbot Square, Blackpool
Arch Dr A Mackenzie

Bolton (1891)

Lostock Park, Bolton BL6 4AJ
Tel **(01204) 843278**
Fax (01204) 843067
Mem 600
Sec Mrs HM Stuart
(01204) 843067
Pro R Longworth (01204) 843073
Holes 18 L 6237 yds Par 70 SSS 70
Recs Am–66 JB Hope,
DE Roocroft, G Boardman
Pro–64 J Wright
V'tors U SOC
Fees £29 D–£33 (£36 D–£40)
Loc 3 miles W of Bolton. M61
Junction 6, 2 miles

Bolton Old Links (1891)

*Chorley Old Road, Montserrat, Bolton
BL1 5SU*
Tel **(01204) 840050**
Fax (01204) 842307
Mem 600
Sec AW Turner (01204) 842307
Pro P Horridge (01204) 843089
Holes 18 L 6406 yds SSS 72
Recs Am–66 L Mooney (1981)
Pro–64 J Cheetham (1990)
V'tors U H exc comp Sats SOC
Fees £27 (£35)
Loc 3 miles NW of Bolton on
B6226
Arch Dr A Mackenzie

Bolton Open Golf

Pay and play
*Longsight Park, Longsight Lane,
Harwood BL2 4JX*
Tel **(01204) 597659/309778**
Mem 250
Pro CR Loydall (Golf Dir)
Holes 9 hole course
Recs Am–64 S Walsh
V'tors WD–U WE–booking
necessary SOC
Fees £6.50 (£8.50)
Loc 3 miles NE of Bolton (A666)
Mis Driving range.

Brackley Municipal (1977)

Public
*Bullows Road, Little Hulton, Worsley
M38 9TR*
Tel **(0161) 790 6076**
Pro S Lomax (Mgr)
Holes 9 L 3003 yds SSS 69
V'tors U
Fees On application
Loc 2 miles NW of Walkden, off A6

Breightmet (1911)

Red Bridge, Ainsworth, Bolton BL2 5PA
Tel **(01204) 527381**
Mem 200
Sec SP Griffiths

Holes 9 L 6416 yds SSS 71
Recs Am–71 M Durham (1992))
Pro–68 P Alliss (1971)
V'tors WD–H WE–NA SOC–WD
Fees £15 (£18)
Loc 3 miles E of Bolton

Brookdale (1896)

*Medlock Road, Woodhouses, Failsworth
M35 9WQ*
Tel **(0161) 681 4534**
Fax (0161) 681 4534
Mem 650
Sec W Hilton
Pro T Cupello (0161) 681 2655
Holes 18 L 5841 yds SSS 68
Recs Am–65 G Lever, J Spicer
V'tors WD–U SOC–WD
Fees £20
Loc 5 miles NE of Manchester

Burnley (1905)

Glen View, Burnley BB11 3RW
Tel **(01282) 421045**
Mem 730
Sec GJ Butterfield
(01282) 451281
Pro WP Tye
(01282) 455266
Holes 18 L 5911 yds SSS 69
Recs Am–64 GD Haworth
Pro–66 JS Steer
V'tors U SOC
Fees £20 (£25)
Loc Via Manchester Road to
Glen View Road

Bury (1890)

*Unsworth Hall, Blackford Bridge, Bury
BL9 9TJ*
Tel **(0161) 766 4897**
Fax (0161) 796 3480
Mem 750
Sec AN Burkey
Pro S Crake (0161) 766 2213
Holes 18 L 5927 yds SSS 68
Recs Am–64 PD Hilton
Pro–64 PWT Evans
V'tors H SOC
Fees £25 (£30)
Loc A56, 5 miles N of
Manchester. 3 miles N of
M62 Junction 17

Castle Hawk (1975)

*Chadwick Lane, Castleton, Rochdale
OL11 3BY*
Tel **(01706) 640841**
Fax (01706) 860587
Mem 200
Sec J Accleton
Pro M Vipond
Holes 18 L 5398 yds SSS 68
9 L 3158 yds SSS 55
Recs Am–68 S Tyrell
Pro–66 M Vipond
V'tors U SOC
Fees D–£7 (D–£9)
Loc Castleton Station 1 mile.
M62 Junction 20

Chorley (1897)

*Hall o' th' Hill, Heath Charnock,
Chorley PR6 9HX*
Tel **(01257) 480263**
Fax (01257) 480722
Mem 550
Sec AK Tyrer
Pro GP Mutch (01257) 481245
Holes 18 L 6307 yds SSS 70
Recs Am–64 WG Bromilow
Pro–65 RN Giles
V'tors WD–I or H WE–NA SOC
Fees On application
Loc 1 mile S of Chorley at junction
A6/A673
Arch JA Steer

Clitheroe (1891)

Whalley Road, Clitheroe BB7 1PP
Tel **(01200) 422618 (Clubhouse)**
Fax (01200) 422292
Mem 638
Sec G Roberts JP (01200) 422292
Pro J Twissell (01200) 424242
Holes 18 L 6326 yds SSS 71
Recs Am–66 P Dwyer
V'tors WD–U H SOC
Fees £33 (£39)
Loc 2 miles S of Clitheroe
Mis Range
Arch James Braid

Colne (1901)

*Law Farm, Skipton Old Road, Colne
BB8 7EB*
Tel **(01282) 863391**
Mem 328
Sec JT Duerden (Hon)
Pro None
Holes 9 L 5961 yds SSS 69
Recs Am–63 M Brooks
Ladies–66 M Birtwistle
V'tors U exc comp days SOC–WD
Fees £15 (£20)
Loc 1½ miles N of Colne. From
end of M65, signs to Keighley
and then Lothersdale

Crompton & Royton
(1913)

*High Barn, Royton, Oldham
OL2 6RW*
Tel **(0161) 624 2154**
Mem 620
Sec TR Jones (0161) 624 0986
Pro DA Melling
Holes 18 L 6222 yds SSS 70
Recs Am–65 JA Osbaldeston
Pro–65 D Durnian
V'tors U SOC–WD
Fees £24 (£30)
Loc 3 miles NW of Oldham

Darwen (1893)

Winter Hill, Darwen BB3 0LB
Tel **(01254) 701287**
Mem 375 70(L) 60(J)
Sec J Kenyon (01254) 704367
Pro W Lennon (01254) 776370
Holes 18 L 5863 yds SSS 68

Recs   Am–63 J Grimshaw (1994),
           A Durkin (1997); Pro–65
V'tors U exc Tues & Sat–NA
Fees   £20 (£25)
Loc   Darwen 1½ miles

Dean Wood (1922)

*Lafford Lane, Up Holland, Skelmersdale
WN8 0QZ*
Tel   **(01695) 622219**
Fax   (01695) 622245
Mem   750
Sec   A McGregor
Pro   AB Coop
Holes 18 L 6137 yds SSS 70
Recs   Am–66 J Dawber (1973),
           B Giblin (1992)
V'tors WD–U WE/BH–M SOC
Fees   £27 (£30)
Loc   4 miles W of Wigan (A577)
Arch   James Braid

Deane (1906)

*Off Junction Road, Deane, Bolton
BL3 4NS*
Tel   **(01204) 61944**
Mem   490
Sec   P Flaxman (01204) 651808
Pro   D Martindale
Holes 18 L 5652 yds SSS 67
Recs   Am–63 S Simpson
V'tors WD–U WE–restricted
           SOC–Tues/Thurs/Fri
Fees   £20 (£25)
Loc   2 miles W of Bolton. M61
           Junction 5, 1 mile

Dunscar (1908)

*Longworth Lane, Bromley Cross, Bolton
BL7 9QY*
Tel   **(01204) 598228**
Mem   600
Sec   JW Jennings (01204) 303321
Pro   G Treadgold (01204) 592992
Holes 18 L 6085 yds Par 71 SSS 69
Recs   Am–65 GJW Hastie (1995)
           Pro–66 W Slater
V'tors WD–U WE–restricted SOC
Fees   £20 (£30)
Loc   3 miles N of Bolton, off A666

Duxbury Park (1975)

Public
*Duxbury Hall Road, Duxbury Park,
Chorley PR7 4AS*
Tel   **(01257) 265380**
Fax   (01257) 241378
Sec   R Blease
Pro   D Clarke
Holes 18 L 6270 yds SSS 70
Recs   Am–69 D Arstall
           Pro–66 J Anglada
V'tors U
Fees   £6.25 (£8.50)
Loc   1½ miles S of Chorley, off
           Wigan Lane

Fairhaven (1895)

*Lytham Hall Park, Ansdell, Lytham St
Annes FY8 4JU*
Tel   **(01253) 736741**
Fax   (01253) 731461

Mem   900
Sec   H Fielding
Pro   (01253) 736976
Holes 18 L 6883 yds SSS 73
Recs   Am–65 SG Birtwell (1967)
           Pro–64 J Leonard (1996)
V'tors WD–U WE–NA before 9am
           SOC–WD
Fees   £33 (£40)
Loc   Lytham 2 miles. St Annes
           2 miles. M55 Junction 4

Fishwick Hall (1912)

*Glenluce Drive, Farringdon Park,
Preston PR1 5TD*
Tel   **(01772) 798300**
Mem   750
Sec   RR Gearing
Pro   M Hadfield (01772) 795870
Holes 18 L 6045 yds SSS 69
Recs   Am–66 C Cross
V'tors Apply to Sec SOC
Fees   £21 (£26)
Loc   1 mile E of Preston, nr
           junction of A59 and M6
           Junction 31

Fleetwood (1932)

*Golf House, Princes Way, Fleetwood
FY7 8AF*
Tel   **(01253) 873114 (Clubhouse)**
Fax   (01253) 773573
Mem   548
Sec   R Yates (01253) 773573
Pro   S McLaughlin (01253)
           873661
Holes L 18 L 6723 yds SSS 72
Recs   Am–67 D Johnson (1994)
           Pro–70 S Bennett
V'tors U H exc Tues SOC
Fees   £24 (£30)
Loc   1 mile W of Fleetwood
Arch   A Steer

Gathurst (1913)

*Miles Lane, Shevington, Wigan
WN6 8EW*
Tel   **(01257) 252861 (Clubhouse)**
Mem   675
Sec   Mrs I Fyffe (01257) 255235
Pro   D Clarke (01257) 254909
Holes 18 L 6089 yds Par 70 SSS 69
Recs   Am–65 S Ainscough
V'tors WD–U before 5pm
           WE/BH/Wed–M SOC–WD
Fees   £22
Loc   4 miles W of Wigan. 1 mile S
           of M6 Junction 27
Arch   N Pearson-ADAS

Ghyll (1907)

*Ghyll Brow, Barnoldswick, Colne
BB18 6JH*
Tel   **(01282) 842466**
Mem   310
Sec   JL Gill (01756) 798592
Holes 9 L 5708 yds SSS 68
Recs   Am–64 M Boardman (1989)
V'tors U exc Sun–NA
Fees   £14 (£18)
Loc   7 miles N of Colne, off A56

Great Harwood (1896)

*Harwood Bar, Great Harwood
BB6 7TE*
Tel   **(01254) 884391**
Mem   175 60(L) 45(J)
Sec   A Garraway
           (01254) 886802
Holes 9 L 6413 yds SSS 71
Recs   Am–68 J Aspinall
           Pro–64 AH Padgham
V'tors U SOC
Fees   £13 (£16)
Loc   5 miles NE of Blackburn

Great Lever & Farnworth (1911)

*Plodder Lane, Farnworth, Bolton
BL4 0LQ*
Tel   **(01204) 656493**
Fax   (01204) 656137
Mem   560
Sec   MJ Ivill (01204) 656137
Pro   T Howarth
Holes 18 L 5986 yds SSS 69
Recs   Am–67 D Barr (1989)
           Ladies-B Hill (1974)
V'tors H SOC–WD
Fees   £16.50 (£27)
Loc   1½ miles S of Bolton

Green Haworth (1914)

*Green Haworth, Accrington
BB5 3SL*
Tel   **(01254) 237580**
Mem   225
Sec   K Lynch
Holes 9 L 5513 yds SSS 68
Recs   Am–67 S Ormerod (1992)
V'tors WD–U exc Wed–Ladies only
           after 5pm WE/BH–M SOC
Fees   On application
Loc   Willows Lane

Greenmount (1920)

Greenmount, Bury BL8 4LH
Tel   **(01204) 883712**
Mem   220
Sec   J Robinson
Pro   J Seed
Holes 9 L 5230 yds SSS 66
Recs   Am–63 P Hambleton (1997)
V'tors WD–U exc Tues WE–M
Fees   £15
Loc   3 miles N of Bury

Haigh Hall (1972)

Public
*Haigh Hall Country Park, Haigh,
Wigan WN2 1PE*
Tel   **(01942) 833337 (Clubhouse)**
Mem   300
Sec   W Fleetwood
Pro   I Lee (01942) 831107
Holes 18 L 6423 yds SSS 71
Recs   Am–65 G Lacy (1992)
           Pro–66 K Waters (1988)
V'tors U
Fees   £5.95 (£8.50)
Loc   2 miles NW of Wigan. M6
           Junction 27. M61 Junction 6

Harwood (1926)

Springfield, Roading Brook Road,
Bolton BL2 4JD

Tel	**(01204) 522878**
Sec	D Bamber (01204) 524233
Pro	N Dance (01204) 522878
Holes	18 L 5786 yds SSS 69
Recs	Am–63 L Irvine
V'tors	WD–U WE–M SOC
Fees	£15
Loc	4 miles NE of Bolton (B6391)
Arch	J Shuttleworth

Herons Reach (1993)

Pay and play
East Park Drive, Blackpool FY3 8LL

Tel	**(01253) 838866/766156**
Fax	(01253) 798800
Mem	550
Sec	DB Smith (Mgr)
Pro	D Naughton (01253) 766156
Holes	18 L 6461 yds SSS 71
Recs	Am–68
	Pro–67
V'tors	U H SOC
Fees	£25 (£35)
Loc	M55 Junction 4. Follow signs
	to Blackpool Zoo
Mis	Floodlit driving range
Arch	Alliss/Clark

Heysham (1910)

Trumacar Park, Middleton Road,
Heysham, Morecambe LA3 3JH

Tel	**(01524) 851011**
Fax	(01524) 853030
Mem	685
Sec	FA Bland (Sec/Mgr)
Pro	R Dône (01524) 852000
Holes	18 L 6258 yds SSS 70
Recs	Am–64 M Murray (1994)
	Pro–64 P Walker (1990)
V'tors	U H SOC
Fees	£17 D–£22 (£27)
Loc	2 miles S of Morecambe.
	M6 Junction 34, 5 miles
Arch	A Herd

Hindley Hall (1905)

Hall Lane, Hindley, Wigan WN2 2SQ

Tel	**(01942) 255131/523116**
Mem	430
Sec	GW Gooch (01942) 255131
Pro	N Brazell (01942) 255991
Holes	18 L 5913 yds SSS 68
Recs	Am–64 NG Hibbs
	Pro–65
V'tors	U SOC
Fees	£20 (£27)
Loc	2 miles S of Wigan. M61
	Junction 6

Horwich (1895)

Victoria Road, Horwich BL6 5PH

Tel	**(01204) 696980**
Mem	200
Sec	C Sherborne
Holes	9 L 5404 yds SSS 67
Recs	Am–62 S Southern
V'tors	M SOC–WD
Loc	5 miles W of Bolton

Hurlston Hall (1994)

Hurlston Lane, Southport Road,
Scarisbrick L40 8JD

Tel	**(01704) 840400**
Fax	(01704) 841404
Mem	600
Sec	G Hayes (Gen Mgr)
Pro	G Bond (01704) 841120
Holes	18 L 6746 yds SSS 72
Recs	Am–71 J Fisher (1995)
	Pro–66 D Shacklady (1996)
V'tors	H SOC
Fees	£25 (£30)
Loc	2 miles NW of Ormskirk
	(A570). M58 Junction 3
Mis	Floodlit driving range
Arch	Donald Steel

Ingol (1981)

Tanterton Hall Road, Ingol, Preston
PR2 7BY

Tel	**(01772) 734556**
Mem	700
Sec	H Parker
Pro	S Laycock
Holes	18 L 5868 yds SSS 68
Recs	Am–68
	Pro–67
V'tors	U SOC–WD
Fees	£15 (£25)
Loc	1½ miles NW of Preston
	(A6). M6 Junction 32

Knott End (1911)

Wyreside, Poulton-le-Fylde FY6 0AA

Tel	**(01253) 810254 (Clubhouse)**
Fax	(01253) 810576
Mem	660
Sec	KE Butcher (01253) 810576
Pro	P Walker (01253) 811365
Holes	18 L 5789 yds SSS 68
Recs	Am–58 M Davies (1994)
	Pro–66 P Harrison (1978)
V'tors	WD–U WE/BH–by
	arrangement SOC–WD
Fees	D–£23 (£26)
Loc	Over Wyre, 12 miles NE of
	Blackpool (A588)
Arch	James Braid

Lancaster G&CC (1932)

Ashton Hall, Ashton-with-Stodday,
Lancaster LA2 0AJ

Tel	**(01524) 752090**
Fax	(01524) 752742
Mem	525 165(L) 125(J)
Sec	DDJ Palmer (01524) 751247
Pro	DE Sutcliffe (01524) 751802
Holes	18 L 6465 yds SSS 71
Recs	Am–66 S Andrew
V'tors	WD–H SOC–WD
Fees	£32
Loc	2 miles S of Lancaster (A588)
Mis	Dormy House
Arch	James Braid

Lansil (1947)

Caton Road, Lancaster LA4 3PE

Tel	**(01524) 39269**
Mem	450
Sec	J Ollerton (01995) 601451

Holes	9 L 5608 yds SSS 67
Recs	Am–68 DC Whiteway,
	SM Humpage
V'tors	WD–U Sun–U after 1pm
Fees	£12 (£12)
Loc	A683, 2 miles E of Lancaster

Leyland (1923)

Wigan Road, Leyland PR5 2UD

Tel	**(01772) 436457**
Fax	(01772) 436457
Mem	750
Sec	J Ross
Pro	C Burgess (01772) 423425
Holes	18 L 6123 yds SSS 69
Recs	Am–62 J Mann (1991)
	Pro–66 T Hastings (1993)
V'tors	WD–U WE–M SOC–WD
Fees	£25 (1994)
Loc	M6 Junction 28, ½ mile

Lobden (1888)

Whitworth, Rochdale OL12 8XJ

Tel	**(01706) 343228**
Fax	(01706) 343228
Mem	220
Sec	N Danby (01706) 643241
Holes	9 L 5697 yds SSS 68
Recs	Am–66 C Hardman (1996)
V'tors	U
Fees	£10 (£15)
Loc	4 miles N of Rochdale

Longridge (1877)

Fell Barn, Jeffrey Hill, Longridge,
Preston PR3 2TU

Tel	**(01772) 783291**
Mem	700
Sec	DC Wensley
Pro	NS James (01772) 783291
Holes	18 L 5969 yds SSS 69
Recs	Am–65 A Taylor (1997)
V'tors	U
Fees	£15 (£25)
Loc	8 miles NE of Preston,
	off B6243

Lowes Park (1914)

Hilltop, Lowes Road, Bury BL9 6SU

Tel	**(0161) 764 1231/763 9503**
Fax	(0161) 763 9503
Mem	400
Sec	J Entwistle
Holes	9 L 6009 yds Par 70 SSS 69
Recs	Am–67 M Thornton (1996)
V'tors	WD–U exc Wed–NA
	WE/BH–by arrangement
Fees	£17 (£23)
Loc	1 mile NE of Bury, off A56

Lytham Green Drive
(1922)

Ballam Road, Lytham FY8 4LE

Tel	**(01253) 734782**
Fax	(01253) 731350
Mem	700
Sec	R Kershaw (01253) 737390
Pro	A Lancaster (01253) 737379
Holes	18 L 6168 yds SSS 69
Recs	Am–64 C Rymer (1988)
	Pro–64 E Romero (1988)

V'tors WD–U H WE–NA SOC–WD
Fees £27 (£35)
Loc Lytham St Annes

Marland (1928)

Public
Springfield Park, Bolton Road, Rochdale
OL11 4RE
Tel (01706) 49801
Fax (01706) 49801
Mem 300
Sec B Wynn
Pro D Wills
Holes 18 L 5237 yds SSS 66
Recs Am–67 C Thornsby (1993)
     Pro–67 ME Hill
V'tors WD–U WE–booking
     necessary
Fees £6.70 (£8.20)
Loc W of Rochdale (A58). M62
     Junctions 19/20, 2 miles

Marsden Park (1969)

Public
Townhouse Road, Nelson BB9 8DG
Tel (01282) 67525
Sec BD Goodwin
     (01282) 450398
Holes 18 L 5806 yds Par 70 SSS 68
Recs Am–66 A Skelton (1987)
     Pro–74 T Gillett
V'tors U SOC
Fees On application
Loc Signposted Walton Lane

Morecambe (1904)

Bare, Morecambe LA4 6AJ
Tel (01524) 418050
Fax (01524) 412841
Mem 1071
Sec Mrs J Atkinson (01524)
     412841
Pro S Fletcher (01524) 415596
Holes 18 L 5770 yds SSS 68
Recs Am–64 J Swallow, DP Carney
     Pro–63 B Gallacher,
     P Oosterhuis
V'tors U H SOC
Fees On application
Loc On coast road towards
     Carnforth (A5105)

Mossock Hall (1996)

Liverpool Road, Bickerstaffe L39 0EE
Tel (01695) 424962
Fax (01695) 424961
Mem 500
Sec D Kelly (Sec/Mgr)
     (01695) 421717
Pro M Webb (01695) 424969
Holes 18 L 6375 yds Par 71 SSS 70
V'tors U SOC
Fees £20 (£30)
Loc 3 miles E of Ormskirk

Mytton Fold (1994)

Langho BB6 8AB
Tel (01254) 240662
Fax (01254) 248119
Mem 270

Sec DB Woodburn
Pro G Coope
     (01254) 240662 Ext 235
Holes 18 L 6217 yds SSS 70
V'tors U SOC
Fees £12 (£15)
Loc 6 miles N of Blackburn, off
     A59. M6 Junction 31
Arch F Hargreaves

Nelson (1902)

Kings Causeway, Brierfield, Nelson
BB9 0EU
Tel (01282) 614583
Fax (01282) 606226
Mem 550
Sec BR Thomason
Pro N Sumner
     (01282) 617000
Holes 18 L 5967 yds SSS 69
Recs Am–63 N Nuttley (1995)
     Pro–68 H Shoesmith
V'tors WD–U H exc Thurs–NA
     WE–U exc Sat before 4pm
     SOC
Fees £25 (£30)
Loc 2 miles N of Burnley

Oldham (1892)

Lees New Road, Oldham OL4 5EN
Tel (0161) 624 4986
Mem 300 45(L) 35(J)
Pro J Peel (0161) 626 8346
Holes 18 L 5045 yds SSS 65
Recs Am–66 D Maloney (1987)
     Pro–65 E Smith
V'tors U SOC–WD
Fees On application
Loc Off Oldham-Stalybridge road

Ormskirk (1899)

Cranes Lane, Lathom, Ormskirk
L40 5UJ
Tel (01695) 572112
Mem 300
Sec RDJ Lawrence (01695)
     572227
Pro J Hammond
     (01695) 572074
Holes 18 L 6358 yds SSS 70
Recs Am–63 DJ Eccleston
     Pro–67 MJ Slater
V'tors I exc Sat–NA SOC
Fees £30 Wed–£35 Sun–£35
     D–£40
Loc 2 miles E of Ormskirk

Penwortham (1908)

Blundell Lane, Penwortham, Preston
PR1 0AX
Tel (01772) 743207
Fax (01772) 744630
Mem 700
Sec J Parkinson (01772) 744630
Pro N Marshall (01772) 742345
Holes 18 L 6056 yds SSS 69
Recs Am–62 A Gillespie
     Pro–66 W Fletcher
V'tors WD–U WE–no parties
Fees £22 (£28)
Loc 1½ miles W of Preston (A59)

Pleasington (1891)

Pleasington, Blackburn BB2 5JF
Tel (01254) 202177
Fax (01254) 201028
Mem 520
Sec JF Howarth
Pro GJ Furey (01254) 201630
Holes 18 L 6445 yds SSS 71
Recs Am–65 J Covill (1992)
     Pro–65 D Stirling (1993)
V'tors H
Fees £36 (£42)
Loc 3 miles SW of Blackburn

Poulton-le-Fylde (1982)

Public
Myrtle Farm, Breck Road, Poulton,
Blackpool
Tel (01253) 892444
Mem 250
Sec G Schofield
Pro L Ware
Holes 9 L 2979 yds SSS 69
Recs Am–72 R Walker,
     L Chenery (1992)
     Pro–74 C Mawdesley
V'tors U
Fees On application
Loc 3 miles NE of Blackpool
Mis Indoor driving range

Preston (1892)

Fulwood Hall Lane, Fulwood, Preston
PR2 8DD
Tel (01772) 700436 (Clubhouse)
Fax (01772) 794234
Mem 800
Sec DJ Sanders (01772) 700011
Pro PA Wells (01772) 700022
Holes 18 L 6233 yds SSS 70
Recs Am–65 MA Holmes, J Wright
     Pro–66 JM Hulme
V'tors WD–U H WE–M SOC–WD
Fees £22 D–£27
Loc 1½ miles W of M6
     Junction 32
Arch James Braid

Regent Park (Bolton)
(1931)

Public
Links Road, Chorley New Road, Bolton
BL2 9XX
Tel (01204) 844170
Mem 260
Sec D Bunting
Pro B Longworth (01204) 842336
Holes 18 L 6221yds Par 70 SSS 69
Recs Am–62 N Jameson (1995)
     Pro–68 L Alamby
V'tors U SOC–WD
Fees £6 (£8)
Loc A673, 3 miles W of Bolton.
     M61 Junction 6

Rishton (1927)

Eachill Links, Hawthorn Drive, Rishton
BB1 4HG
Tel (01254) 884442
Fax (01254) 51946
Mem 302

Sec T Charnock (Hon)
Holes 9 L 6097 yds SSS 69
Recs Am–68 K Sheridan
Pro–68 J Matthews
V'tors WD–U WE–M
Fees £12
Loc 3 miles E of Blackburn
Arch Thomas/Alliss

Rochdale (1888)

Edenfield Road, Bagslate, Rochdale
OL11 5YR
Tel (01706) 646024 (Clubhouse)
Fax (01706) 643818
Mem 750
Sec (01706) 643818
Pro A Laverty (01706) 522104
Holes 18 L 6031 yds SSS 69
Recs Am–65 SM Lord (1992)
Pro–65 J Hammond (1989)
V'tors U
Fees £25 (£30)
Loc 3 miles from M62 Junction 20
on A680

Rossendale (1903)

Ewood Lane, Head Haslingden,
Rossendale BB4 6LH
Tel (01706) 831339
Mem 682
Sec JR Swain (01706)
831339/214968
Pro SJ Nicholls (01706) 213616
Holes 18 L 6293 yds SSS 70
Recs Am–64 AG Westwell
Pro–67 D Screeton
Ladies–72 J Ruff
V'tors WD/Sun–U Sat–M
Fees £22.50 (£27.50)
Loc 7 miles N of Bury, nr end
of M66

Royal Lytham & St Annes (1886)

Links Gate, Lytham St Annes
FY8 3LQ
Tel (01253) 724206
Fax (01253) 780946
Mem 600
Sec LB Goodwin FCA
Pro E Birchenough (01253)
720094
Holes 18 L 6685 yds SSS 73
Recs Am–66 R Foster, T Craddock
Pro–65 C O'Connor,
BGC Huggett, W Longmuir,
S Ballesteros
V'tors WD–I H
Fees £75 (incl lunch)
Loc St Annes 1 mile (A584)
Mis Dormy House

Saddleworth (1904)

Mountain Ash, Uppermill, Oldham
OL3 6LT
Tel (01457) 873653
Fax (01457) 820647
Mem 700
Sec AE Gleave
Pro ET Shard
Holes 18 L 5976 yds SSS 69

Recs Am–65 RC Hughes
Pro–69 M Melling, A Gillies
V'tors U
Fees £23 (£30)
Loc 5 miles E of Oldham
Arch Mackenzie/Leaver

St Annes Old Links (1901)

Highbury Road, Lytham St Annes
FY8 2LD
Tel (01253) 723597
Fax (01253) 781506
Mem 945
Sec PW Ray
Pro GG Hardiman (01253) 722432
Holes 18 L 6616 yds SSS 72
Recs Am–66 RD Squire, AC Nash
Pro–65 R Sailer, T Bjorn,
M Florioli, R Boxall
V'tors WD–NA before 9.30am and
12–1.30pm WE/BH–arrange
with Sec SOC
Fees £35 (£45)
Loc Between St Annes and
Blackpool, off A584
Arch Herd

Shaw Hill Hotel G&CC (1925)

Preston Road, Whittle-le-Woods,
Chorley PR6 7PP
Tel (01257) 269221
Fax (01257) 261223
Mem 500
Sec F Wharton
Pro D Clarke (01257) 279222
Holes 18 L 6405 yds SSS 71
Recs Am–66 N Hopwood (1991)
Pro–69 I Evans (1984)
V'tors WD–U H SOC
Fees £30 (£40)
Loc A6, 1¹/₂ miles N of Chorley.
M61 Junction 8. M6
Junction 28

Standish Court (1995)

Rectory Lane, Standish, Wigan
WN6 0XD
Tel (01257) 425777
Fax (01257) 425888
Mem 500
Sec PC Dawson
Pro T Kershaw
Holes 18 L 5650 yds Par 68 SSS 66
V'tors U SOC
Fees £10 (£15)
Loc M6 Junction 27, 2 miles
Arch Patrick Dawson

Stonyhurst Park (1980)

Stonyhurst, Hurst Green, Blackburn
BB6 9QB
Tel (01254) 826478
Mem 315
Sec TA Cooke (01200) 23089
Holes 9 L 5529 yds SSS 66
V'tors WD–phone first WE–M
Fees £12
Loc 5 miles SW of Clitheroe
(B6243)
Mis Green fees payable at Bayley
Arms, Hurst Green

Towneley (1932)

Public
Towneley Park, Todmorden Road,
Burnley BB11 3ED
Tel (01282) 451636
Mem 300
Sec N Clark (01282) 414455
Pro (01282) 38473
Holes 18 L 5811 yds Par 70 SSS 68
9 hole course
Recs Am–67 T Foster (1990)
Pro–65 D Whittaker (1985)
V'tors U
Fees £6 (£7)
Loc 1¹/₂ miles E of Burnley

Tunshill (1901)

Kiln Lane, Milnrow, Rochdale
Tel (01706) 342095
Mem 180
Sec D Hardman
Holes 9 L 5742 yds SSS 68
Recs Am–66 D Williams (1994)
V'tors WD–U WE–M SOC
Fees On application
Loc 2 miles E of Rochdale. M62
Junction 21

Turton (1908)

Wood End Farm, Bromley Cross, Bolton
BL7 9QH
Tel (01204) 852235
Mem 370 70(L) 21(J)
Sec JF Moorhouse (01204)
301791
Holes 18 L 5901 yds Par 69
SSS 68
V'tors WD–U exc Wed–NA
11.30–2.30pm WE/BH–M
Fees £17
Loc 3¹/₂ miles N of Bolton

Walmersley (1906)

Garrett's Close, Walmersley, Bury
BL9 6TE
Tel (0161) 764 1429
Mem 450
Sec RO Goldstein
Pro S Crake (0161) 763 9050
Holes 18 L 5341 yds SSS 67
V'tors WD–U exc Tues–NA Sat–NA
Sun–M SOC–Wed–Fri
Fees D–£20
Loc 2 miles N of Bury (A56). S of
M66 Junction 1
Arch SG Marnoch

Werneth (1909)

Green Lane, Garden Suburb, Oldham
OL8 3AZ
Tel (0161) 624 1190
Mem 400
Sec JH Barlow
Pro R Penny
Holes 18 L 5363 yds SSS 66
Recs Am–62 LA Lawton
Pro–63 S Holden
V'tors WD–U WE–M SOC
Fees £16.50
Loc 2 miles S of Oldham

Westhoughton (1929)

Long Island, Westhoughton, Bolton
BL5 2BR

Tel	(01942) 811085
Fax	(01942) 608958
Mem	230
Sec	F Donohue
Pro	J Seed
Holes	9 L 5834 yds SSS 68
Recs	Am–64 T Woodward
V'tors	WD–U WE/BH–M
Fees	D–£15
Loc	4 miles SW of Bolton on A58

Whalley (1912)

Long Leese Barn, Clerkhill, Whalley,
Blackburn BB7 9DR

Tel	(01254) 822236
Mem	475
Sec	JS Dawson (01254) 886313
Pro	H Smith
Holes	9 L 6258 yds Par 72 SSS 70
Recs	Am–70 G Blades (1996)
	Ladies–75 D Dawson (1996)
V'tors	U exc Sat (Apr–Oct)
	SOC–WD
Fees	£15 (£20)
Loc	7 miles NE of Blackburn

Whittaker (1906)

Littleborough OL5 0LH

Tel	(01706) 378310
Mem	135
Sec	GA Smith (01484) 428546
Holes	9 L 5576 yds SSS 67
Recs	Am–61 D Kernick
	Pro–65 MT Hoyle
V'tors	WD/Sat–U Sun–NA
Fees	£12 (£15)
Loc	1½ miles N of Littleborough, off A58
Arch	NP Stott

Wigan (1898)

Arley Hall, Haigh, Wigan WN1 2UH

Tel	(01257) 421360
Mem	280
Sec	E Walmsley
Holes	9 L 6058 yds SSS 69
Recs	Am–68 RM Hodson
V'tors	U exc Tues & Sat
Fees	£25 (£30)
Loc	4 miles N of Wigan, off A5106/ B5239. M6 Junction 27

Wilpshire (1890)

72 Whalley Road, Wilpshire, Blackburn
BB1 9LF

Tel	(01254) 248260
Fax	(01254) 248260
Mem	650
Sec	J Ditchfield
Pro	W Slaven (01254) 249558
Holes	18 L 5911 yds SSS 68
Recs	Am–64 H Green (1975), MJ Savage (1978), PC Livesey (1990) Pro–61 J Hawkesworth (1989)
V'tors	WD–U WE/BH–on request
Fees	£25 (£30)
Loc	3 miles NE of Blackburn, off A666

Leicestershire

Beedles Lake (1993)

Pay and play
170 Broome Lane, East Goscote
LE7 3WQ

Tel	(0116) 260 6759
Mem	336
Sec	D Lilley
Pro	SA Byrne
Holes	18 L 6573 yds Par 72 SSS 71
Recs	Am–71
V'tors	U SOC
Fees	£8 (£10)
Loc	4 miles N of Leicester on B5328, off A46
Mis	Driving range
Arch	D Tucker

Birstall (1901)

Station Road, Birstall, Leicester
LE4 3BB

Tel	(0116) 267 4450
Fax	(0116) 267 4322
Mem	430 107(L) 50(J)
Sec	Mrs SE Chilton (0116) 267 4322
Pro	D Clark (0116) 267 5245
Holes	18 L 6222 yds SSS 70
Recs	Am–63 PA Frith, DE Gibson Pro–62 RS Larratt
V'tors	Mon/Wed/Fri–I Other days–M SOC
Fees	£20 D–£25
Loc	3 miles N of Leicester (A6)

Blaby (1991)

Pay and play
Lutterworth Road, Blaby LE8 3DB

Tel	(0116) 278 4804
Pro	B Morris
Holes	9 L 2600 yds SSS 68
V'tors	U
Fees	18 holes–£6 (£8)
Loc	S of Blaby village
Mis	Driving range

Breedon Priory (1990)

Wilson, Derby DE73 1LG

Tel	(01332) 863081
Fax	(01332) 863081
Mem	850
Sec	KM Stevenson
Pro	B Hill
Holes	18 L 5338 yds Par 68 SSS 66
Recs	Am–64 S Marriott (1997) Pro–68 T Coxon (1992)
V'tors	WD–U WE–NA before 2pm phone first SOC–WD
Fees	£14 (£16)
Loc	3½ miles W of M1 Junction 23A on A453
Arch	Snell/Ashton

Charnwood Forest (1890)

Breakback Road, Woodhouse Eaves,
Loughborough LE12 8TA

Tel	(01509) 890259
Fax	(01509) 890925
Mem	330

Sec	J Clarke (01530) 835579 (H)
Holes	9 L 5960 yds SSS 69
Recs	Am–64 C Radford (1992)
V'tors	WD–H WE/BH–NA SOC–Wed–Fri
Fees	£15 (£25)
Loc	M1 Junction 23, 3 miles

Cosby (1895)

Chapel Lane, Broughton Road, Cosby,
Leicester LE9 1RG

Tel	(0116) 286 4759
Fax	(0116) 286 4484
Mem	690
Sec	GT Kirkpatrick
Pro	M Wing (0116) 284 8275
Holes	18 L 6417 yds Par 71 SSS 71
Recs	Am–67 DE Gibson Pro–69 T Westwood Ladies–74 A Genno
V'tors	WD–U H before 4pm WE/BH–M H SOC–WD–H
Fees	£22 D–£26
Loc	½ mile S of Cosby. 7 miles S of Leicester

Enderby (1986)

Public
Mill Lane, Enderby, Leicester
LE9 5NW

Tel	(0116) 284 9388
Sec	LJ Speake (0116) 284 1133
Pro	C D'Araujo
Holes	9 L 4356 yds SSS 61
V'tors	U
Fees	18 holes–£5.50 (£7.50)
Loc	Enderby 2 miles. M1 Junction 21

Glen Gorse (1933)

Glen Road, Oadby, Leicester
LE2 4RF

Tel	(0116) 271 2226/271 4159
Fax	(0116) 271 4159
Mem	360 110(L) 60(J)
Sec	M Goodson (0116) 271 4159
Pro	D Fitzpatrick (0116) 271 3748
Holes	18 L 6648 yds SSS 72
Recs	Am–69 J Powell (1996) Pro–67 G Coysh (1996) Ladies–70 M Page (1992)
V'tors	WD–U WE/BH–M SOC–WD
Fees	£24 D–£28.50
Loc	3 miles S of Leicester on A6

Greetham Valley (1992)

Greetham, Oakham LE15 7NP

Tel	(01780) 460004
Fax	(01780) 460623
Mem	800
Sec	FE Hinch
Pro	J Pengelly (01780) 460666
Holes	27 holes SSS 71 9 hole Par 3 course
Recs	Am–64 T Sweet (1997) Pro–65 J Pengelly (1997)
V'tors	U SOC–WD
Fees	£20 (£24)
Loc	5 miles NE of Oakham (B668)
Mis	Floodlit driving range

Hinckley (1983)

Leicester Road, Hinckley LE10 3DR
Tel (01455) 615124
Fax (01455) 890841
Mem 650
Pro R Jones (01455) 615014
Holes 18 L 6517 yds SSS 71
Recs Am–65 J Cayless (1996)
Pro–67 K Dickens (1987)
V'tors WD–U exc Tues Sat–NA
before 4pm Sun–M after
11am SOC
Fees £25
Loc NE of Hinckley on A4668

Humberstone Heights

(1978)
Public
Gipsy Lane, Leicester LE5 0TB
Tel (0116) 276 1905/3680
Mem 400
Sec F Lock (0116) 276 3680
Pro P Highfield (0116) 276 4674
Holes 18 L 6343 yds SSS 70
Recs Am–68 S Sansome
Pro–66 C Hall
V'tors U SOC–WD
Fees On application
Loc 3 miles E of Leicester, off A47
Mis Driving range. Pitch & putt
course
Arch Hawtree

Kibworth (1904)

*Weir Road, Kibworth Beauchamp,
Leicester LE8 0LP*
Tel (0116) 279 2301
Fax (0116) 279 2301
Mem 700
Sec PD Ind (Mgr), Mrs Y Yeomans
Pro R Larratt (0116) 279 2283
Holes 18 L 6312 yds SSS 70
Recs Am–67 EE Feasey, C Noble
(1991)
Pro–64 P Broadhurst (1991)
V'tors WD–U WE–M SOC–WD
Fees £22
Loc 9 miles SE of Leicester on A6
Mis Driving range

Kilworth Springs (1993)

*South Kilworth Road, North Kilworth,
Lutterworth LE17 6HJ*
Tel (01858) 575082
Fax (01858) 575078
Mem 514
Sec K Mattock
Pro N Melvin
Holes 18 L 6718 yds SSS 72
V'tors U SOC
Fees £17 (£21)
Loc 4 miles E of M1 Junction 20
Mis Driving range

Kirby Muxloe (1893)

*Station Road, Kirby Muxloe, Leicester
LE9 2EP*
Tel (0116) 239 3107
Fax (0116) 239 3457
Mem 425

Sec H Taylor (Sec/Mgr)
(0116) 239 3457
Pro RT Stephenson
(0116) 239 2813
Holes 18 L 6351 yds SSS 70
Recs Am–66 P Bosworth,
J Coulthurst (1994)
Pro–62 J Higgins (1993)
V'tors WD–U before 3.45pm exc
Tues–NA WE–Captain's
permission only SOC–H
Fees £22 D–£28
Loc 3 miles W of Leicester
Mis Driving range for members
and green fees only

Langton Park G&CC

(1994)
Langton Hall, Leicester LE16 7TY
Tel (01858) 545374
Fax (01858) 545358
Mem 200
Sec J Window
Holes 18 L 6724 yds SSS 72
V'tors H or I SOC
Fees On application
Loc 12 miles SE of Leicester, off
A6. 2 miles N of Market
Harborough
Arch Hawtree

Leicestershire (1890)

Evington Lane, Leicester LE5 6DJ
Tel (0116) 273 6035
Fax (0116) 273 8825
Mem 750
Sec JL Adams (0116) 273 8825
Pro JR Turnbull (0116) 273 6730
Holes 18 L 6330 yds SSS 70
Recs Am–64 IR Lyner, DJ Bush
Pro–63 H Henning, I Mosey,
S Sherratt
V'tors U H SOC
Fees £24 (£29)
Loc 2 miles E of Leicester

Leicestershire Forest

(1991)
Markfield Lane, Botcheston LE9 9FJ
Tel (01455) 824800
Mem 460
Sec M Fixter
Pro M Wing
Holes 18 L 6111 yds SSS 69
V'tors U–phone first
Fees On application
Loc 6 miles W of Leicester. M1
Junction 22, 4 miles
Mis Driving range
Arch York/Fixter

Lingdale (1967)

*Joe Moore's Lane, Woodhouse Eaves,
Loughborough LE12 8TF*
Tel (01509) 890703
Mem 609
Sec M Green
Pro P Sellears (01509) 890684
Holes 18 L 6545 yds SSS 71
Recs Am–68 R Walker (1994)
Pro–70 R Larratt (1992)

V'tors U SOC
Fees D–£20 (£23)
Loc 6 miles S of Loughborough.
M1 Junction 23, 4 miles

Longcliffe (1905)

*Snells Nook Lane, Nanpantan,
Loughborough LE11 3YA*
Tel (01509) 216321
Mem 550
Sec G Harle (01509) 239129
Pro I Bailey (01509) 231450
Holes 18 L 6611 yds SSS 72
Recs Am–68 S Critchley
Pro–67 ID Bailey
V'tors WD–H WE–M
Fees £25
Loc 3 miles SW of Loughborough.
M1 Junction 23

Luffenham Heath (1911)

Ketton, Stamford, Lincs PE9 3UU
Tel (01780) 720205
Mem 555
Sec IF Davenport
Pro I Burnett (01780) 720298
Holes 18 L 6273 yds SSS 70
Recs Am–64 M Welch
Pro–67 PJ Butler, RL Moffitt
V'tors U H SOC–WD
Fees £35 (£40)
Loc 5 miles W of Stamford on
A6121
Arch James Braid

Lutterworth (1904)

Lutterworth, Leicester LE17 5HN
Tel (01455) 552532
Fax (01455) 553586
Mem 670
Sec JD Jaynes
Pro R Tisdall (01455) 557199
Holes 18 L 6229 yds SSS 70
Recs Am–71 M Howkins
V'tors WD–U WE–M SOC
Fees £20 D–£26
Loc By M1 Junction 20

Market Harborough (1898)

*Great Oxendon Road, Market
Harborough LE16 8NF*
Tel (01858) 463684
Mem 560
Sec JR Ingleby (01858) 525688
Pro FJ Baxter (01858) 463684
Holes 18 L 6022 yds Par 70 SSS 69
Recs Am–67 K Bonser (1995)
Pro–63 FJ Baxter (1994)
V'tors WD–U WE–M SOC–WD
Fees £20 D–£25
Loc 1 mile S of Mkt Harborough
on A508
Arch Howard Swan

Melton Mowbray (1925)

*Waltham Rd, Thorpe Arnold, Melton
Mowbray LE14 4SD*
Tel (01664) 562118
Fax (01664) 562118
Mem 575

Sec Mrs EA Sallis
Pro J Hetherington
(01664) 569629
Holes 18 L 6222 yds SSS 70
V'tors U H before 3pm –M after
3pm SOC
Fees £20 (£25)
Loc 2 miles NE of Melton
Mowbray on A607

Oadby (1974)
Public
Leicester Road Racecourse, Oadby,
Leicester LE2 4AB
Tel (0116) 270 9052/270 0215
Pro S Ward (0116) 270 9052
Holes 18 L 6376 yds Par 72 SSS 70
Recs Am–65 S Davis (1988)
Pro–73 C O'Connor Jr
V'tors WD–U WE/BH–book with
Pro SOC–WD
Fees £6 (£9)
Loc 2 miles SE of Leicester (A6)

Park Hill (1994)
Park Hill, Seagrave LE12 7NG
Tel (01509) 815454
Fax (01509) 816062
Mem 300
Sec SL Hardy
Pro DC Mee (01509) 815775
Holes 18 L 7219 yds Par 73 SSS 74
V'tors U SOC
Fees £20 D–£28 (£24 D–£36)
Loc 6 miles N of Leicester on A46

RAF Cottesmore (1982)
Oakham, Leicester LE15 7BL
Tel (01572) 812241 Ext 429
Mem 219
Sec PA Cuttle
Holes 9 L 5622 yds SSS 67
Recs Am–64 P Holiday (1993)
V'tors M
Fees £5
Loc RAF Cottesmore

RAF North Luffenham
(1975)
RAF North Luffenham, Oakham
LE15 8RL
Tel (01780) 720041 Ext 7523
Mem 350 62(L) 25(J)
Sec S Nicholson
Holes 9 L 6048 yds Par 70 SSS 69
Recs Am–71 D Lilley
V'tors U SOC
Fees D–£8
Loc ½ mile from S shore of
Rutland Water

Rothley Park (1911)
Westfield Lane, Rothley, Leicester
LE7 7LH
Tel (0116) 230 2019
Sec BS Durham (0116) 230 2809
Pro A Collins (0116) 230 3023
Holes 18 L 6487 yds SSS 71
Recs Am–67 EE Feasey
Pro–68 PJ Dolan

V'tors WD–H exc Tues–NA
WE/BH–NA SOC
Fees £25 D–£30
Loc 6 miles N of Leicester,
W of A6

Rutland County (1991)
Great Casterton, Stamford PE9 4AQ
Tel (01780) 460239/460330
Fax (01780) 460437
Sec S Lowe (Golf Dir)
Pro J Darroch
Holes 18 L 6401 yds SSS 71
9 hole Par 3 course
Recs Am–68 (1997)
Pro–64 J Darroch (1993)
V'tors U H SOC
Fees £17.50 (£22.50)
Loc 3 miles N of Stamford on A1
Mis Driving range
Arch Cameron Sinclair

Scraptoft (1928)
Beeby Road, Scraptoft, Leicester LE7 9SJ
Tel (0116) 241 9000
Fax (0116) 241 8863
Mem 545
Sec D Osborn (0116) 241 8863
Pro S Wood (0116) 241 9138
Holes 18 L 6235 yds Par 70 SSS 70
Recs Am–67 L Towers
V'tors WD–U WE–M SOC–WD
Fees £20 D–£25
Loc 3 miles E of Leicester

Six Hills
Pay and play
Six Hills, Melton Mowbray LE14 3PR
Tel (01509) 881225
Mem 105
Sec Mrs J Showler
Pro M Alls
Holes 18 L 5808 yds Par 73 SSS 68
V'tors U
Fees £8 (£10)
Loc 10 miles N of leicester, off A46

Ullesthorpe Court Hotel
(1976)
Frolesworth Road, Ullesthorpe,
Lutterworth
Tel (01455) 209023
Fax (01455) 202537
Mem 600
Sec PE Woolley
Pro D Bowring (01455) 209150
Holes 18 L 6650 yds SSS 72
Recs Am–70 M Hodgson
Pro–68
V'tors U SOC–WD
Fees £13.50 D–£21.50
Loc 3 miles NW of Lutterworth,
off B577

Western Park (1920)
Public
Scudamore Road, Leicester LE3 1UQ
Tel (0116) 287 2339/287 6158
Mem 300
Sec IA Nicholson

Pro BN Whipham
(0116) 287 2339
Holes 18 L 6532 yds SSS 71
Recs Am–66 G Jones
V'tors U
Fees On application
Loc 4 miles W of Leicester. M1
Junction 21, 3 miles

Whetstone (1965)
Cambridge Road, Cosby, Leicester
LE9 5SH
Tel (0116) 286 1424
Fax (0116) 286 1424
Mem 600
Sec J Collins
Pro N Leatherland, D Raitt
Holes 18 L 5795 yds SSS 68
Recs Am–68 R Fines (1994)
Pro–64 D Raitt (1989)
V'tors U SOC
Fees £10 (£13)
Loc S boundary of Leicester
Mis Driving range
Arch E Callaway

Willesley Park (1921)
Measham Road, Ashby-de-la-Zouch
LE65 2PF
Tel (01530) 411532
Mem 600 99(L) 38(J)
Sec RE Brown (01530) 414596
Pro C Hancock (01530) 414820
Holes 18 L 6304 yds SSS 70
Recs Am–64 P Frith,
M McGuire (1993)
Pro–65 L Jones (1990)
V'tors WD–H WE/BH–H after
9.30am SOC
Fees 308 (£35)
Loc 2 miles S of Ashby on B5006.
M1 Junctions 22/23/24.
A42(M) Junction 12

Lincolnshire

Ashby Decoy (1936)
Ashby Decoy, Burringham Road,
Scunthorpe DN17 2AB
Tel (01724) 842913
Fax (01724) 271708
Mem 520 130(L) 65(J)
Sec KR Ford (01724) 866561
Pro A Miller (01724) 868972
Holes 18 L 6281 yds SSS 71
Recs Am–66 L Day (1997)
Pro–66 G Vickers (1995)
V'tors WD–H Sat–M SOC–WD exc
Tues
Fees £18 (£24)
Loc 2 miles SW of Scunthorpe

Belton Park (1890)
Belton Lane, Londonthorpe Road,
Grantham NG31 9SH
Tel (01476) 567399
Fax (01476) 592078
Mem 950
Sec T Ireland
Pro B McKee (01476) 563911

For list of abbreviations see page 479

Holes 27 holes:
Brownlow L 6412 yds SSS71
Ancaster L 6109 yds SSS 69
Belmont L 5857 yds SSS 68
Recs Am–66 AR Midgley (1991)
Pro–65 S Bennett (1984)
V'tors U H SOC–WD exc Tues
Fees £22 (£29)
Loc 2 miles N of Grantham

Belton Woods Hotel (1991)

Belton, Grantham NG32 2LN
Tel (01476) 593200
Fax (01476) 574547
Mem 350
Pro T Roberts
Holes Lakes 18 L 6805 yds SSS 73;
Woodside 18 L 6835 yds
SSS 73; 9 hole Par 3 course
Recs Pro–68 M Ingham
V'tors U SOC
Fees £27 D–£30 (£30 D–£35)
Loc 2 miles N of Grantham on
A607 towards Lincoln
Mis Driving range
Arch Cayford

Blankney (1903)

Blankney, Lincoln LN4 3AZ
Tel (01526) 320263
Fax (01526) 322521
Mem 664 138(L) 40(J)
Sec DA Priest
Pro G Bradley (01526) 320202
Holes 18 L 6419 yds SSS 71
Recs Am–69 A Bradley (1994)
Pro–69 G Bradley (1994)
V'tors U H SOC
Fees £17 (£25)
Loc 10 miles SE of Lincoln on
B1188
Mis Indoor teaching facilities
Arch Cameron Sinclair

Boston (1962)

*Cowbridge, Horncastle Road, Boston
PE22 7EL*
Tel (01205) 362306
Fax (01205) 350589
Mem 650 115L) 60(J)
Sec DE Smith (01205) 350589
Pro TR Squires (01205) 362306
Holes 18 L 6483 yds SSS 71
Recs Am–73 J Woodcock (1993)
Pro–69 C Jepson (1994)
V'tors WD–U WE/BH–H
Fees £18 (£24)
Loc 2 miles N of Boston on B1183

Boston West (1995)

Pay and play
Hubbert's Bridge, Boston PE20 3QX
Tel (01205) 290670
Fax (01205) 280650
Mem 300
Sec Helen Owen (01205) 290602
Holes 9 L 6367 yds Par 72 SSS 70
Recs Am–67 R Owens (1996)
Pro–65 A Hare (1996)
V'tors U
Fees £5.50 (£6.50)
Loc 2 miles W of Boston on B1192

Mis Floodlit driving range
Arch Michael Zara

Burghley Park (1890)

St Martin's, Stamford PE9 3JX
Tel (01780) 753789
Fax (01780) 753789
Mem 560 140(L) 100(J)
Sec PH Mulligan
Pro G Davies (01780) 762100
Holes 18 L 6236 yds SSS 70
Recs Am–64 I Richardson (1992)
Pro–70 B Thomson (1990)
V'tors WD–U or H WE/BH–M
SOC–WD
Fees £20
Loc 1 mile S of Stamford, off A1
to B1061
Arch Rev JD Day

Canwick Park (1893)

*Canwick Park, Washingborough Road,
Lincoln LN4 1EF*
Tel (01522) 542912/522166
Mem 650
Sec DJ Dixon (01522) 542912
Pro S Williamson (01522) 536870
Holes 18 L 6150 yds SSS 69
Recs Am–65 G Davies (1997)
V'tors WD–U WE–M before 3pm
SOC–WD
Fees £15 D–£19 (£19 D–£25)
Loc 1 mile SE of Lincoln
Arch Hawtree

Carholme (1906)

Carholme Road, Lincoln LN1 1SE
Tel (01522) 523725
Fax (01522) 533733
Mem 700
Sec RD Motts
Pro G Leslie (01522) 536811
Holes 18 L 6243 yds Par 71 SSS 70
Recs Am–69 RJ Taylor (1988)
Ladies–77 J Edmondson (1993)
V'tors WD–U WE–M SOC
Fees On application
Loc Lincoln 1 mile (A57)

Cleethorpes (1894)

Kings Road, Cleethorpes DN35 0PN
Tel (01472) 814060
Mem 750
Sec GB Standaloft
Pro P Davies
Holes 18 L 6360 yds SSS 70
Recs Am–69 D Burchill (1994)
V'tors WD–U exc Wed pm
Fees £20 (£25)
Loc 1 mile S of Cleethorpes

Elsham (1900)

*Barton Road, Elsham, Brigg
DN20 0LS*
Tel (01652) 688382
Mem 650
Sec BP Nazer (Mgr)
(01652) 680291
Pro S Brewer (01652) 680432
Holes 18 L 6411 yds SSS 71

Recs Am–67 DJ Bush
Pro–69 MT Hoyle
V'tors WE–M SOC–WD
Fees £24
Loc 5 miles N of Brigg. M180
Junction 5

Forest Pines (1996)

Ermine Street, Brigg DN20 0AQ
Tel (01652) 650756
Fax (01652) 650495
Mem 350
Sec D Edwards (Golf Dir)
Pro D Edwards
Holes 27 holes: 6393-6882 yds
Par 71-73 SSS 70-73
Recs Pro–69 M Ulyett
V'tors U SOC
Fees £30 D–£35
Loc M180 Junction 4, on A15 to
Scunthorpe
Mis Floodlit driving range
Arch John Morgan

Gainsborough (1894)

Thonock, Gainsborough DN21 1PZ
Tel (01427) 613088
Fax (01427) 810172
Mem 600
Sec D Bowers
Pro S Cooper
Holes 18 L 6266 yds Par 72 SSS 70
18 L 6724 yds Par 72 SSS 72
Recs Am–66
Pro–63
V'tors U
Fees £25 D–£35
Loc N of Gainsborough
Mis Floodlit driving range
Arch Neil Coles

Gedney Hill (1991)

Public
West Drove, Gedney End Hill PE12 0NT
Tel (01406) 330922
Mem 400
Sec S McGregor
Pro D Hutton
Holes 18 L 5450 yds SSS 66
Recs Am–67 N Venters
Pro–66 D Creek (1991)
V'tors U SOC–WD
Fees £6.25 (£10.50)
Loc 4 miles from A47 on B1166
Mis Driving range
Arch C Britton

Grange Park (1992)

Pay and play
*Butterwick Road, Messingham,
Scunthorpe DN17 3PP*
Tel (01724) 762945
Fax (01724) 762851
Sec I Cannon (Mgr)
Holes 13 L 4112 yds SSS 48
9 hole Par 3 course
V'tors U
Fees £5.50 (£7.50)
Loc 5 miles from Messingham.
M180 Junction 3
Mis Floodlit driving range
Arch RW Price

Grimsby (1922)

Littlecoates Road, Grimsby
DN34 4LU

Tel	**(01472) 342823 (Clubhouse)**
Fax	(01472) 342630
Mem	720 150(L) 70(J)
Sec	BJ Hoggett (01472) 342630
Pro	R Smith (01472) 356981
Holes	18 L 6098 yds Par 70 SSS 69
Recs	Am–66 M James
	Pro–66 BJ Hunt
V'tors	WD–U Sat pm/Sun am–XL
	SOC–WD
Fees	£20 D–£25 (£25)
Loc	1 mile W of Grimsby, off A46.
	1 mile from A180
Arch	HS Colt

Hirst Priory

Crowle, Scunthorpe DN17 4BU

Tel	**(01724) 711619**
Mem	400
Sec	J Hammond
Pro	E Highfield
Holes	18 L 6199 yds Par 71 SSS 69
Recs	Am–63
	Pro–67
V'tors	U SOC
Fees	£11.75 (£14.50)
Loc	3 miles N of M180 Junction 2,
	on A161 to Crowle

Holme Hall (1908)

Holme Lane, Bottesford, Scunthorpe
DN16 3RF

Tel	**(01724) 282053 (Caterer)**
Fax	(01724) 282053
Mem	470 90(L) 50(J)
Sec	G Smith (01724) 862078
Pro	R McKiernan (01724) 851816
Holes	18 L 6475 yds SSS 71
Recs	Am–65 K Spencer
	Pro–66 B Thompson
V'tors	WD–U WE–M H SOC–WD
Fees	£20 D–£22
Loc	4 miles SE of Scunthorpe.
	M180 Junction 4

Horncastle (1990)

West Ashby, Horncastle LN9 5PP

Tel	**(01507) 526800**
Mem	300
Sec	RC Chantry
Pro	EC Wright
Holes	18 L 5717 yds SSS 70
Recs	Am–71 J Page
V'tors	U SOC
Fees	£10 D–£15
Loc	1 mile N of Horncastle,
	off A158
Mis	Floodlit driving range
Arch	EC Wright

Immingham (1975)

St Andrews Lane, Off Church Lane,
Immingham DN40 2EU

Tel	**(01469) 575298**
Fax	(01469) 577636
Mem	650
Sec	P Boulton (Mgr)
Pro	N Harding (01469) 575493
Holes	18 L 6215 yds SSS 70

Recs	Am–69 C Tuck (1997)
	Pro–65 S Bennett
V'tors	WD–U WE–M Sun–NA
	before noon SOC–WD
Fees	£15 (£20)
Loc	N of St Andrew's Church,
	Immingham
Arch	Hawtree/Pennink

Kenwick Park (1992)

Kenwick Hall, Louth LN11 8NY

Tel	**(01507) 605134**
Fax	(01507) 606556
Sec	PG Shillington
Pro	E Sharp (01507) 607161
Holes	18 L 6815 yds Par 72 SSS 73
Recs	Am–72 P Spence (1996)
	Pro–67 S Bennett (1995)
V'tors	U SOC
Fees	D–£25 (£35)
Loc	1 mile SE of Louth
Mis	Teaching Academy. Driving
	range
Arch	Patrick Tallack

Kingsway (1971)

Public
Kingsway, Scunthorpe DN15 7ER

Tel	**(01724) 840945**
Sec	C Mann
Pro	C Mann
Holes	9 L 1915 yds SSS 59
V'tors	U
Fees	On application
Loc	¾ mile W of Scunthorpe,
	off A18

Kirton Holme (1992)

Pay and play
Holme Road, Kirton Holme, Boston
PE20 1SY

Tel	**(01205) 290669**
Fax	(01205) 290385
Mem	360
Sec	Mrs T Welberry (01205)
	290560
Pro	Alison Johns (01205) 369948
Holes	9 L 2884 yds SSS 68
Recs	Am–71 R Ellis (1995)
V'tors	U SOC–WD
Fees	£7.70 (£8.80)
Loc	3 miles W of Boston, off A52
Arch	DW Welberry

Lincoln (1891)

Torksey, Lincoln LN1 2EG

Tel	**(01427) 718721**
Mem	600
Sec	DB Linton
Pro	A Carter (01427) 718273
Holes	18 L 6438 yds SSS 71
Recs	Am–66 A Thain, P Taylor
	Pro–65 M James
V'tors	WD–H SOC
Fees	£22 D–£28
Loc	12 miles NW of Lincoln,
	off A156

Louth (1965)

Crowtree Lane, Louth LN11 9LJ

Tel	**(01507) 602554**
Fax	(01507) 603681

Mem	700
Sec	M Covey (Mgr),
	Mrs TL Covey (01507) 603681
Pro	AJ Blundell (01507) 604648
Holes	18 L 6424 yds SSS 71
Recs	Am–64 D Smith (1991)
	Pro–69 C Hall (1989)
V'tors	U SOC–WD
Fees	£16 D–£22 (£25 D–£30)
Loc	W side of Louth

Manor (Laceby) (1992)

Laceby Manor, Laceby, Grimsby
DN37 7EA

Tel	**(01472) 873468**
Fax	(01472) 276706
Mem	500
Sec	Mrs J Mackay, G Mackay
	(Mgr)
Holes	18 L 6354 yds SSS 70
V'tors	U SOC
Fees	D–£14 (D–£20)
Loc	5 miles W of Grimsby at
	Barton Street (A18)
Arch	Nicholson/Rushton

Market Rasen (1922)

Legsby Road, Market Rasen
LN8 3DZ

Tel	**(01673) 842319**
Mem	550
Sec	JA Brown
Pro	AM Chester
	(01673) 842416
Holes	18 L 6043 yds SSS 69
Recs	Am–66 C Osbourne (1990)
	Pro–65 S Bennett (1989)
V'tors	WD–I WE/BH–M SOC
Fees	£18 D–£25
Loc	1 mile E of Market Rasen

Millfield (1985)

Public
Laughterton, Lincoln LN1 2LB

Tel	**(01427) 718255/718473**
Mem	600
Sec	PG Guthrie
Holes	18 L 5973 yds SSS 69
	15 L 4300 yds
	9 hole Par 3 course
V'tors	U
Fees	£10
Loc	9 miles W of Lincoln
Mis	Driving range

Normanby Hall (1978)

Public
Normanby Park, Scunthorpe
DN15 9HU

Tel	**(01724) 280444 Ext 852**
	(Bookings)
Mem	800
Sec	I Green
Pro	C Mann (01724) 720226
Holes	18 L 6548 yds SSS 71
Recs	Am–68
	Pro–68 N Bundy
V'tors	U SOC–WD
Fees	£10 D–£15 (£12)
Loc	5 miles N of Scunthorpe
Arch	Hawtree

North Shore (1910)

North Shore Road, Skegness
PE25 1DN

Tel	**(01754) 763298**
Fax	(01754) 761902
Mem	450
Sec	B Howard (01754) 763298
Pro	J Cornelius
	(01754) 764822
Holes	18 L 6254 yds SSS 71
Recs	Am–71 G Hunter (1989)
V'tors	H SOC–WD
Fees	On application
Loc	1 mile N of Skegness
Arch	James Braid

RAF Waddington

Waddington, Lincoln LN5 9NB

Tel	**(01522) 720271 Ext 7958**
Mem	90
Sec	D Bennett
Holes	9 L 5519 yds SSS 69
Recs	Am–68 T Graham (1987)
V'tors	By prior arrangement
Fees	On application
Loc	4 miles S of Lincoln (A607)

Sandilands (1900)

Sandilands, Sutton-on-Sea
LN12 2RJ

Tel	**(01507) 441432**
Mem	400
Sec	D Mumby (01507) 441617
Holes	18 L 5995 yds SSS 69
Recs	Am–66 JR Payne
	Pro–63 FG Allott
V'tors	U SOC
Fees	£15 (£20)
Loc	1 mile S of Sutton-on-Sea, off A52

Seacroft (1895)

Seacroft, Skegness PE25 3AU

Tel	**(01754) 763020**
Fax	(01754) 763020
Mem	340 190(L) 90(J)
Sec	FA Williams (Sec/Mgr)
Pro	R Lawie (01754) 769624
Holes	18 L 6479 yds SSS 71
Recs	Am–67 DR Rose
	Pro–67 J Heib (1988)
V'tors	WD–U H WE–XL before 11am
Fees	£25 (£30)
Loc	S boundary of Skegness

Sleaford (1905)

Willoughby Road, South Rauceby,
Sleaford NG34 8PL

Tel	**(01529) 488273**
Mem	650
Sec	TGE Churms
Pro	J Wilson (01529) 488644
Holes	18 L 6443 yds SSS 71
Recs	Am–65 A Hare (1988)
V'tors	U H exc Sun–NA (Winter) SOC–WD
Fees	£18 (£25)
Loc	1 mile W of Sleaford on A153
Arch	Tom Williamson

South Kyme (1990)

Skinners Lane, South Kyme, Lincoln
LN4 4AT

Tel	**(01526) 861113**
Sec	A Maplethorpe
Pro	P Chamberlain
Holes	18 L 6597 yds SSS 71
Recs	Am–69 C Hill (1995)
	Pro–67 A Hare (1994)
V'tors	U SOC
Fees	£10 (£12)
Loc	2 miles from A17 on B1395
Mis	6 hole practice course
Arch	Graham Bradley

Spalding (1908)

Surfleet, Spalding PE11 4EA

Tel	**(01775) 680234**
Mem	750
Sec	BW Walker (01775) 680386
Pro	J Spencer (01775) 680474
Holes	18 L 6478 yds SSS 71
Recs	Am–62 J Crampton (1996)
	Pro–65 J Spencer
V'tors	U H SOC–Tues after 2pm & Thurs
Fees	On application
Loc	4 miles N of Spalding, off A16
Arch	Spencer/Ward/Price

Stoke Rochford (1924)

Great North Rd, Grantham NG33 5EW

Tel	**(01476) 530275**
Mem	515
Sec	JM Butler
Pro	A Dow (01476) 530218
Holes	18 L 6252 yds SSS 70
Recs	Am–65 A Hare, J Payne, M Wilson
	Pro–65 A Dow
V'tors	WD–U WE/BH–U after 10.30am
Fees	On application
Loc	6 miles S of Grantham (A1)
Arch	Maj Hotchkin (1935)

Sudbrook Moor (1991)

Public

Charity Lane, Carlton Scroop,
Grantham NG32 3AT

Tel	**(01400) 250796**
Fax	(01400) 250796
Sec	Judith Hutton
Pro	T Hutton (01400) 250796
Holes	9 L 4712 yds Par 66 SSS 61
V'tors	U–booking required
Fees	D–£5 (D–£7)
Loc	6 miles NE of Grantham (A607)
Arch	Tim Hutton

Sutton Bridge (1914)

New Road, Sutton Bridge, Spalding

Tel	**(01406) 350323 (Clubhouse)**
Mem	340
Sec	KC Buckle (01945) 870455
Holes	9 L 5820 yds SSS 68
	Pro–62 CJ Norton
V'tors	WD–H WE–NA
Fees	£17
Loc	8 miles N of Wisbech (A17)

Toft Hotel (1988)

Toft, Bourne PE10 0JT

Tel	**(01778) 590616**
Fax	(01778) 590264
Mem	500
Pro	M Jackson
Holes	18 L 6486 yds Par 72 SSS 71
V'tors	U
Fees	£12 (£17)
Loc	8 miles from Stamford on A6121
Arch	D & R Fitton

Waltham Windmill (1997)

Cheapside, Waltham, Grimsby
DN37 0HT

Tel	**(01472) 824109**
Mem	450
Sec	J Pearce (Mgr)
Pro	N Burkitt (01472) 823963
Holes	18 L 6406 yds Par 71 SSS 70
Recs	Pro–S Bennett (1997)
V'tors	WD–U SOC
Fees	£18 (£25)
Loc	2 miles S of Grimsby, off A16
Arch	Fox/Payne

Woodhall Spa (1905)

Woodhall Spa LN10 6PU

Tel	**(01526) 352511**
Fax	(01526) 352778
Mem	475
Sec	BH Fawcett
Pro	CC Elliot (01526) 353229
Holes	18 L 6921 yds SSS 73
Recs	Am–68 R Hutt, D Robertson
V'tors	H–booking essential SOC
Fees	EGU Members–£30 D–£50 Non-EGU Members–£40 D–£65
Loc	19 miles SE of Lincoln (B1191)
Arch	Col SV Hotchkin MC

Woodthorpe Hall (1986)

Woodthorpe, Alford LN13 0DD

Tel	**(01507) 450294**
Fax	(01507) 463664
Mem	400
Sec	PC Bell (01507) 463664
Holes	18 L 5140 yds Par 67 SSS 65
Recs	Am–63 BJ Day (1996)
V'tors	U SOC
Fees	D–£10
Loc	3 miles N of Alford, off B1371. 8 miles SE of Louth

London clubs

Aquarius (Kent)

Beckenham (Kent)

Bush Hill Park (Middlesex)

Chingford (Essex)

Dulwich & Sydenham Hill (Surrey)

Eltham Warren (Kent)

Finchley (Middlesex)

Hampstead (Middlesex)

Hendon (Middlesex)

Highgate (Middlesex)

London Scottish (Surrey)

Mill Hill (Middlesex)

Muswell Hill (Middlesex)

North Middlesex
(Middlesex)

Picketts Lock (Middlesex)

Richmond Park (Surrey)

Roehampton (Essex)

Royal Blackheath (Essex)

Royal Epping Forest
(Essex)

Royal Wimbledon (Surrey)

Shooter's Hill (Essex)

South Herts
(Hertfordshire)

Springfield Park (Surrey)

Trent Park (Middlesex)

Wanstead (Essex)

West Essex (Essex)

Wimbledon Common
(Surrey)

Wimbledon Park (Surrey)

Manchester (Greater)

Blackley (1907)
Victoria Avenue, Manchester M9 6HW

Tel	(0161) 643 2980
Mem	750
Sec	CB Leggott (0161) 654 7770
Pro	A Cowan (0161) 643 3912
Holes	18 L 6235 yds SSS 70
Recs	Am–65 D Royle
	Pro–66 J Nixon
V'tors	WD–U WE–M SOC–WD exc
	Thurs
Fees	£24
Loc	North Manchester

Chorlton-cum-Hardy (1903)
Barlow Hall, Barlow Hall Road, Manchester M21 7JJ

Tel	(0161) 881 3139
Fax	(0161) 881 5830
Mem	650
Sec	Mrs K Poole (0161) 881 5830
Pro	D Screeton (0161) 881 9911
Holes	18 L 5980 yds SSS 69

Recs	Am–64 P Bolton
	Pro–65 M Turner
V'tors	U H SOC–Thurs
Fees	£22 (£27)
Loc	4 miles S of Manchester
	(A5103/A5145)

Davyhulme Park (1910)
Gleneagles Road, Davyhulme, Manchester M41 8SA

Tel	(0161) 748 2856 (Clubhouse)
Mem	600
Sec	GR Swarbrick (0161) 748 2260
Pro	D Butler (0161) 748 3931
Holes	18 L 6237 yds SSS 70
Recs	Am–67 TF Sharp, B Connor,
	D Dunwoodie
	Pro–68 KG Geddes, D Rees
V'tors	WD–H exc Wed & Fri–NA
	Sat–NA Sun–M
	SOC–Mon/Tues/Thurs
Fees	£24–£30
Loc	7 miles SW of Manchester

Denton (1909)
Manchester Road, Denton, Manchester M34 2GG

Tel	(0161) 336 3218
Fax	(0161) 336 4751
Mem	670
Sec	R Wickham
Pro	M Hollingsworth
	(0161) 336 2070
Holes	18 L 6541 yds SSS 71
Recs	Am–66 R Bardsley (1993)
	Pro–68 D Cooper, S Scanlon,
	D Durnian
V'tors	WD–U WE/BH–NA before
	3pm SOC
Fees	£25 (£30)
Loc	M66 Junction 11, A57 to
	Manchester

Didsbury (1891)
Ford Lane, Northenden, Manchester M22 4NQ

Tel	(0161) 998 9278
Fax	(0161) 998 9278
Mem	760
Sec	AL Watson (Mgr)
Pro	P Barber (061) 998 2811
Holes	18 L 6273 yds SSS 70
Recs	Am–66 PR Dalby (1991)
	Pro–63 P Eales (1995),
	D Valentine (1996)
V'tors	WD–U H exc 9–10am &
	12–1.30pm–NA WE–U H
	10.30–11.30am & after 4pm
Fees	£26 (£30)
Loc	6 miles S of Manchester. M63
	Junction 9

Ellesmere (1913)
Old Clough Lane, Worsley, Manchester M28 7HZ

Tel	(0161) 790 2122
Mem	380 80(L) 75(J)
Sec	A Chapman (0161) 799 0554
Pro	T Morley (0161) 790 8591
Holes	18 L 6248 yds SSS 70
Recs	Am–67 BA Toone
	Pro–68 S Wakefield

V'tors	U exc comp days (check with
	Pro) SOC–WD
Fees	£20 (£24)
Loc	6 miles W of Manchester, nr
	junction of M62/A580

Fairfield Golf & Sailing Club (1892)
Booth Road, Audenshaw, Manchester M34 5GA

Tel	(0161) 370 1641
Mem	550
Sec	J Humphries (0161) 336 3950
Pro	SA Pownell (0161) 370 2292
Holes	18 L 5664 yds SSS 68
Recs	Am–65 PW Wrigley,
	ARS Pownell
V'tors	WD–U WE–NA before noon
	SOC–WD
Fees	£18 (£24)
Loc	5 miles E of Manchester on
	A635

Flixton (1893)
Church Road, Flixton, Urmston, Manchester M41 6EP

Tel	(0161) 748 2116
Mem	400
Sec	JG Frankland (0161) 747 0296
Pro	D Proctor (0161) 746 7160
Holes	9 L 6410 yds SSS 71
Recs	Am–66 MJ Wallwork (1995)
	Pro–65 P Reeves (1985)
V'tors	WD–U exc Wed SOC
Fees	£15
Loc	6 miles SW of Manchester on
	B5213. M63 Junction 6

Heaton Park (1912)
Public
Heaton Park, Prestwich, Manchester M25 5SW

Tel	(0161) 798 0295
Sec	V Marcroft
Pro	None
Holes	18 L 5849 yds SSS 68
Recs	Am–66 J Griffiths (1986),
	S Pilling (1988)
	Pro–65 AP Thomson, B Evans,
	I Collins, M Gray
V'tors	U SOC
Fees	On application
Loc	North Manchester, via M62
	and M66 to Middleton Road

Manchester (1882)
Hopwood Cottage, Rochdale Road, Middleton, Manchester M24 2QP

Tel	(0161) 643 2718,
	(0161) 643 0023 (Bookings)
Fax	(0161) 643 9174
Mem	700
Sec	KG Flett (0161) 643 3202
Pro	B Connor (0161) 643 2638
Holes	18 L 6450 yds SSS 72
Recs	Am–66 RE Tattersall,
	M Russell, RB Smithies
	Pro–64 D Lynn,
	M Stevenson, S Delagrange
V'tors	WD–H WE–NA SOC
Fees	D–£30 (£45)

Loc 7 miles N of Manchester.
M62 Junction 20
Mis Driving range–members and
green fees only
Arch HS Colt

North Manchester (1894)

*Rhodes House, Manchester Old Road,
Middleton, Manchester M24 4PE*

Tel (0161) 643 9033
Fax (0161) 643 7775
Mem 430 65(L) 40(J)
Sec D Parkinson
Pro C Smellie (0161) 643 7094
Holes 18 L 6542 yds SSS 72
Recs Am–66 J Cheetham
Pro–66 G Furey
V'tors U SOC
Fees £23 (£23)
Loc 5 miles N of Manchester.
M62 Junction 18
Arch A Compston

Northenden (1913)

Palatine Road, Manchester M22 4FR

Tel (0161) 998 4738
Fax (0161) 945 5592
Mem 700
Sec RN Kemp (Sec/Mgr)
Pro PA Scott
Holes 18 L 6503 yds SSS 71
Recs Am–67 JEB Waddell
Pro–64 D Durnian
V'tors U SOC
Fees £25 (£30)
Loc 5 miles S of Manchester.
M63 Junction 9

Old Manchester (1818)

Tel (0161) 766 4157
Sec PT Goodall, 9 Ashbourne
Grove, Whitefield M45 7NJ
Holes Club without a course

Pike Fold (1909)

*Cooper Lane, Victoria Avenue,
Blackley, Manchester M9 2QQ*

Tel (0161) 740 1136
Mem 300
Sec H Adams
Pro None
Holes 9 L 5789 yds SSS 68
Recs Am–66 P Bradley (1989)
Pro–66 JE Wiggett
V'tors WD–U WE/BH–M SOC
Fees D–£15
Loc 5 miles N of Manchester.
M62 Junction 18, 2 miles

Prestwich (1908)

Hilton Lane, Prestwich M25 9XB

Tel (0161) 773 2544
Mem 500
Sec WV Trees (0161) 773 4578
Pro S Wakefield (0161) 773 1404
Holes 18 L 4806 yds SSS 63
Recs Am–60 J Liwosz
V'tors WD–H WE–NA before 3pm
SOC
Fees £16 (£18)
Loc 2½ miles N of Manchester,
off A56. M63 Junction 17

Stand (1904)

*The Dales, Ashbourne Grove,
Whitefield, Manchester M45 7NL*

Tel (0161) 766 2388
Fax (0161) 796 3234
Mem 700
Sec EB Taylor (0161) 766 3197
Pro M Dance (0161) 766 2214
Holes 18 L 6411 yds SSS 71
Recs Am–67 J Seddon (1990)
Pro–67 PM Eales
V'tors U SOC–WD
Fees £25 (£30)
Loc 5 miles N of Manchester.
M62 Junction 17
Arch Alex Herd

Swinton Park (1926)

*East Lancashire Road, Swinton,
Manchester M27 5LX*

Tel (0161) 794 1785
Mem 450 120(L) 50(J)
Sec F Slater (0161) 794 0861
Pro J Wilson (0161) 793 8077
Holes 18 L 6712 yds SSS 72
Recs Am–66 J Thornley (1984)
Pro–65 D Wheeler (1992)
V'tors WD–U WE–M SOC–Tues
Fees On application
Loc On A580, 5 miles NW of
Manchester

Whitefield (1932)

*Higher Lane, Whitefield, Manchester
M45 7EZ*

Tel (0161) 766 2728
Fax (0161) 767 9502
Mem 500
Sec Miss J Peatfield
(0161) 766 2904
Pro P Reeves (0161) 766 3096
Holes 18 L 6045 yds SSS 69
18 L 5755 yds SSS 68
V'tors U SOC–WD
Fees £25 (£35)
Loc 4 miles N of Manchester.
M62 Junction 17

William Wroe (1973)

Public
*Pennybridge Lane, Flixton, Manchester
M31 3DL*

Tel (0161) 748 8680
Pro B Parkinson
Holes 18 L 4395 yds SSS 61
Recs Am–60 C Meadows,
D Dunwoodie
V'tors U–booking necessary
Fees On application
Loc 6 miles SW of Manchester, by
M63 Junction 4

Withington (1892)

*243 Palatine Road, West Didsbury,
Manchester M20 2UE*

Tel (0161) 445 3912
Mem 340 97(L) 38(J)
Sec TH Glover (0161) 445 9544
Pro RJ Ling (0161) 445 4861
Holes 18 L 6410 yds SSS 70
Recs Am–65 MC Keates (1995)
Pro–66 R Leach (1995)

V'tors WD–H exc Thurs SOC
Fees On application
Loc 6 miles S of Manchester on
B5166

Worsley (1894)

*Stableford Avenue, Monton Green,
Eccles, Manchester M30 8AP*

Tel (0161) 789 4202
Mem 625
Sec R Pizzey MBE
Pro C Cousins
Holes 18 L 6217 yds SSS 70
Recs Am–65 D Harding (1994)
V'tors I NA–9–9.45am &
12.15–1.30pm
Fees £20
Loc 5 miles W of Manchester

Merseyside

Allerton Municipal (1934)

Public
Allerton Road, Liverpool 18

Tel (0151) 428 1046
Pro B Large
Holes 18 L 5494 yds SSS 65
9 hole course
V'tors U SOC
Fees On application
Loc 5 miles S of Liverpool

Arrowe Park (1931)

Public
*Arrowe Park, Woodchurch, Birkenhead,
Wirral L49 5LW*

Tel (0151) 677 1527
Sec K Finlay
Pro C Didsbury
Holes 18 L 6377 yds SSS 70
Recs Am–66 D Ball (1995)
V'tors U
Fees £6 (£6)
Loc 3 miles S of Birkenhead on
A552. M53 Junction 3, 1 mile

Bidston (1913)

Bidston Link Road, Wallasey L44 2HR

Tel (0151) 638 3412
Mem 500
Sec JJ Gleeson
Pro S Hubbard (0151) 630 6650
Holes 18 L 6207 yds SSS 70
Recs Am–64 S Earnden (1993)
Pro–68 JM Hume
V'tors WD–U WE–M SOC
Fees On application
Loc Off Bidston Link Road

Blundells Hill

Blundells Lane, Rainhill L35 6NA

Tel (01744) 24892
Fax (01744) 28861
Mem 600
Sec A Roberts
Pro A Sproston
Holes 18 L 6347 yds Par 71
V'tors U SOC

For list of abbreviations see page 479

Fees £20 (£30)
Loc 3 miles SW of St Helens. M62 Junction 7
Arch Steve Marnoch

Bootle (1934)

Dunnings Bridge Road, Litherland L30 2PP

Tel (0151) 928 6196
Mem 400
Sec J Morgan (Hon)
Pro A Bradshaw (0151) 928 1371
Holes 18 L 6362 yds SSS 70
Recs Am–64 S Ashcroft
Pro–69 R Boobyer
V'tors U–book by phone SOC
Fees £4.80 (£6.25)
Loc 5 miles N of Liverpool (A565)
Arch Fred Stevens

Bowring (1913)

Public
Bowring Park, Roby Road, Huyton L36 4HD

Tel (0151) 489 1901
Pro D Weston
Holes 9 L 5592 yds SSS 66
Recs Am–67 G Spurrier
V'tors U
Fees On application
Loc 6 miles N of Liverpool. M62 Junction 5

Brackenwood (1933)

Public
Brackenwood Lane, Bebington, Wirral L63 2LY

Tel (0151) 608 3093
Pro C Disbury
Holes 18 L 6131 yds SSS 69
Recs Am–67 D Charlton
Pro–64 C Disbury
V'tors U SOC
Fees On application
Loc Nr M53 Junction 4

Bromborough (1904)

Raby Hall Road, Bromborough L63 0NW

Tel (0151) 334 2155
Fax (0151) 334 0303
Mem 800
Sec JT Barraclough (0151) 334 2978
Pro G Berry (0151) 334 4499
Holes 18 L 6650 yds SSS 73
Recs Am–67 J Berry, GM Edwards, GJ Bradley, P Bailey
V'tors U–contact Pro in advance
Fees £28 (£30)
Loc Mid Wirral, M53 Junction 4

Caldy (1907)

Links Hey Road, Caldy, Wirral L48 1NB

Tel (0151) 625 5660
Fax (0151) 625 7394
Mem 875
Sec TDM Bacon
Pro K Jones (0151) 625 1818
Holes 18 L 6675 yds SSS 73
Recs Am–67 JR Berry

V'tors WD–U exc before 9.30am and from 1–2pm (booking necessary) SOC
Fees On application
Loc 1½ miles S of West Kirby

Childwall (1913)

Naylor's Road, Gateacre, Liverpool L27 2YB

Tel (0151) 487 0654
Fax (0151) 487 0882
Mem 650
Sec KG Jennions (Mgr)
Pro N Parr (0151) 487 9871
Holes 18 L 6425 yds SSS 71
Recs Am–66 M Gamble
V'tors WE/BH/Tues–restricted
Fees £26 (£35)
Loc 7 miles E of Liverpool. M62 Junction 6, 2 miles
Arch James Braid

Eastham Lodge (1973)

117 Ferry Road, Eastham, Wirral L62 0AP

Tel (0151) 327 1483
Fax (0151) 327 3003
Mem 608
Sec CS Camden (0151) 327 3003
Pro R Boobyer (0151) 327 3008
Holes 18 L 5706 yds SSS 68
V'tors WD–U WE/BH–M SOC–Tues
Fees £22
Loc 6 miles S of Birkenhead, off A41. M53 Junction 5. Signs to Eastham Country Park

Formby (1884)

Golf Road, Formby, Liverpool L37 1LQ

Tel (01704) 872164
Fax (01704) 833028
Mem 600
Sec To be appointed
Pro C Harrison (01704) 873090
Holes 18 L 6993 yds SSS 74
Recs Am–66 I Pyman, MJC Hudson
Pro–65 NC Coles
V'tors WD–I H SOC
Fees £50
Loc By Freshfield Station
Arch Willie Park

Formby Ladies' (1896)

Formby, Liverpool L37 1YL

Tel (01704) 874127
Sec Mrs V Bailey (01704) 873493
Pro C Harrison (01704) 873090
Holes 18 L 5426 yds SSS 71
Recs Am–60 CD Lee
V'tors U–phone first SOC
Fees £30 (£35)
Loc Formby, off A565

Grange Park (1891)

Prescot Road, St Helens WA10 3AD

Tel (01744) 22980 (Members)
Fax (01744) 26318
Mem 730

Sec CV Hadley (01744) 26318
Pro P Roberts (01744) 28785
Holes 18 L 6480 yds SSS 71
Recs Am–65 G Boardman (1989), K Wallbank (1995)
Pro–66 R Ellis (1986)
V'tors I SOC–WD exc Tues
Fees £24 (£36)
Loc 1½ miles W of St Helens on A58

Haydock Park (1877)

Golborne Park, Newton Lane, Newton-le-Willows WA12 0HX

Tel (01925) 224389
Fax (01925) 228525
Mem 390 120(L)
Sec JV Smith (01925) 228525
Pro PE Kenwright (01925) 226944
Holes 18 L 6043 yds SSS 69
Recs Am–65 D Pilkington, P Boydell, K Sargent, P Eckersley
V'tors H or I SOC–WD exc Tues
Fees £25
Loc 1 mile E of M6 Junction 23

Hesketh (1885)

Cockle Dick's Lane, Cambridge Road, Southport PR9 9QQ

Tel (01704) 530226
Fax (01704) 539250
Mem 650
Sec MG Senior (01704) 536897
Pro J Donoghue (01704) 530050
Holes 18 L 6522 yds SSS 72
Recs Am–66 MP Thorpe
Pro–64 D Hayes
V'tors WD–U WE/BH–restricted SOC
Fees £35 D–£40 (£50)
Loc 1 mile N of Southport (A565)

Heswall (1902)

Cottage Lane, Gayton, Heswall, Wirral L60 8PB

Tel (0151) 342 1237
Fax (0151) 342 1237
Mem 902
Sec RJ Butler
Pro AE Thompson (0151) 342 7431
Holes 18 L 6492 yds SSS 72
Recs Am–62 CJ Sands (1994)
Pro–66 AE Thompson (1990)
V'tors U H BH–NA SOC–Wed & Fri
Fees £35 (£40)
Loc 8 miles NW of Chester off A540. M53 Junction 4

Hillside (1909)

Hastings Road, Hillside, Southport PR8 2LU

Tel (01704) 569902
Fax (01704) 563192
Mem 800
Sec JG Graham (01704) 567169
Pro B Seddon (01704) 568360
Holes 18 L 6850 yds SSS 74

Recs Am–67 I Garbutt, J Payne
Pro–66 M O'Grady, R Craig
V'tors By arrangement with Sec
Fees D–£40 (£50)
Loc Southport

Houghwood

Billinge Hill, Crank Road, Crank,
St Helens WA11 8RL
Tel (01744) 894444
Fax (01744) 894754
Mem 630
Sec K Pilling
Pro D Clarke (01744) 894444
Holes 18 L 6202 yds SSS 69
Recs Am–69 I Harrison (1997)
V'tors WD–U SOC–WD
Fees £14 (£17)
Loc 5 miles N of St Helens, off
A580 (B5201). M6 Junctions
24/25
Arch N Pearson

Hoylake Municipal (1933)

Public
Carr Lane, Hoylake, Wirral L47 4BQ
Tel (0151) 632 2956/4883
(Bookings)
Sec A Peacock
Pro S Hooton
Holes 18 L 6330 yds SSS 70
Recs Am–67 T Manning (1989)
Pro–64 T Bennett (1982)
V'tors WD–U WE–phone booking
1 week in advance SOC
Fees £6
Loc 4 miles W of Birkenhead
Arch James Braid

Huyton & Prescot (1905)

Hurst Park, Huyton Lane, Huyton
L36 1UA
Tel (0151) 489 1138
Fax (0151) 489 0797
Mem 700
Sec Mrs S Threlfall (0151) 489
3948
Pro M Harrison (0151) 489 2022
Holes 18 L 5839 yds SSS 68
Recs Am–67
V'tors WD–U WE–H SOC–WD
Fees On application
Loc 7 miles E of Liverpool. 1 mile
S of Prescot on B5199. M57
Junction 2

Leasowe (1891)

Leasowe Road, Moreton, Wirral
L46 3RD
Tel (0151) 677 5852
Fax (0151) 604 1424
Mem 610
Sec EJ Reeves (Mgr)
Pro AJ Ayre (0151) 678 5460
Holes 18 L 6263 yds SSS 70
Recs Am–63 J Maddocks
V'tors WD–U WE–H
Fees D–£20 (D–£25)
Loc 1 mile N of Queensway
Tunnel. M53 Junction 1
Arch John Ball Jr

Lee Park (1954)

Childwall Valley Road, Gateacre,
Liverpool L27 3YA
Tel (0151) 487 9861 (Clubhouse)
Mem 550
Sec Mrs D Barr (0151) 487 3882
Holes 18 L 6024 yds SSS 69
V'tors SOC
Fees On application
Loc 7 miles SE of Liverpool
(B5171)

Liverpool Municipal (1967)

Public
Ingoe Lane, Kirkby, Liverpool L32 4SS
Tel (0151) 546 5435
Pro D Weston
Holes 18 L 6571 yds SSS 71
Recs Am–70 J Paton (1986)
Pro–70
V'tors U WE–booking required SOC
Fees On application
Loc M57 Junction 6 to B5192

Prenton (1905)

Golf Links Road, Prenton, Birkenhead
L42 8LW
Tel (0151) 608 1461
Fax (0151) 609 1580
Mem 470 100(L) 51(J)
Sec WFW Disley (0151) 608 1053
Pro R Thompson (0151) 608
1636
Holes 18 L 6429 yds SSS 71
Recs Am–65 P Langford (1993)
V'tors U SOC–Wed & Fri
Fees £30 (£35)
Loc Outskirts of Birkenhead. M53
Junction 3

RLGC Village Play (1895)

Hoylake, Wirral L47 4AL
Mem 40
Sec CJ Peddie (0151) 625 1587
Holes Play over Royal Liverpool

Royal Birkdale (1889)

Waterloo Road, Birkdale, Southport
PR8 2LX
Tel (01704) 569913
Fax (01704) 562327
Sec NT Crewe (01704) 567920
Pro RN Bradbeer (01704) 568857
Holes 18 L 6703 yds SSS 73
Recs Am–67 G Hamerton (1995)
Pro–63 J Mudd (1991 Open)
V'tors I H SOC
Fees £55 D–£75 (£75)
Loc 1½ miles S of Southport
(A565)
Arch George Lowe

Royal Liverpool (1869)

Meols Drive, Hoylake L47 4AL
Tel (0151) 632 3101/3102
Fax (0151) 632 6737
Mem 810
Sec Gp Capt CT Moore CBE

Pro J Heggarty
(0151) 632 5868
Holes 18 L 6835 yds SSS 74
Recs Am–67 C Nowicki (1993)
Pro–64 B Waites
V'tors H SOC
Fees On application
Loc On A553 from M53
Junction 2

Sherdley Park Municipal

Public
Sherdley Park, St Helens
Tel (01744) 813149
Fax (01744) 817967
Sec B Collins (Mgr)
Pro PR Parkinson
Holes 18 L 5974 yds SSS 69
Recs Am–68 J Greenough
V'tors U SOC
Fees £7 (£8)
Loc 2 miles E of St Helens (A570).
M62 Junction 7, 2 miles
Mis Driving range

Southport & Ainsdale (1907)

Bradshaws Lane, Ainsdale, Southport
PR8 3LG
Tel (01704) 578092
Fax (01704) 570896
Mem 390 110(L) 78(J)
Sec NA Wilson (01704) 578000
Pro M Houghton (01704) 577316
Holes 18 L 6612 yds SSS 73
Recs Am–66 RAR Hutt (1991)
Pro–62 C Moody (1991)
V'tors WD–9.30am–12 & 2.30–4pm
WE/BH–M
Fees £35 D–£45 (£45)
Loc 3 miles S of Southport on
A565
Arch James Braid

Southport Municipal (1914)

Public
Park Road West, Southport PR9 0JS
Tel (01704) 535286
Pro W Fletcher
Holes 18 L 6253 yds SSS 69
Pro–67 W Fletcher (1986)
V'tors U SOC
Fees On application
Loc N end of Southport
promenade

Southport Old Links (1926)

Moss Lane, Southport PR9 7QS
Tel (01704) 28207
Mem 450
Sec BE Kenyon
Holes 9 L 6224 yds SSS 71
Recs Am–68 J Robinson
V'tors U exc WE comp days/BH–NA
SOC–WD
Fees £18 (£25)
Loc Churchtown, 3 miles NE of
Southport

Wallasey (1891)

Bayswater Road, Wallasey L45 8LA

Tel	**(0151) 639 3630**
Fax	(0151) 638 8988
Mem	350 90(L) 50(J)
Sec	Mrs LM Dolman
	(0151) 691 1024
Pro	M Adams (0151) 638 3888
Holes	18 L 6607 yds SSS 73
Recs	Am–68 P Morgan
	Pro–66 P Barber
V'tors	H SOC
Fees	On application
Loc	M53–signs to New Brighton
Arch	Tom Morris

Warren (1911)

Public

Grove Road, Wallasey, Wirral

Tel	**(0151) 639 8323 (Clubhouse)**
Pro	K Lamb (051) 639 5730
Holes	9 L 5914 yds SSS 68
Recs	Am–66 J Hayes
	Pro–66 JA MacLachlan
V'tors	U
Fees	On application
Loc	Wallasey

West Derby (1896)

Yew Tree Lane, Liverpool L12 9HQ

Tel	**(0151) 228 1540**
Fax	(0151) 259 0505
Mem	550
Sec	AP Milne (0151) 254 1034
Pro	A Witherup (0151) 220 5478
Holes	18 L 6257 yds SSS 70
Recs	Am–67 JT Paton
	Pro–67 AC Coop
V'tors	SOC–WD after 9.30am
Fees	£25 (£30)
Loc	2 miles E of Liverpool, off
	A580–West Derby Junction

West Lancashire (1873)

*Blundellsands, Crosby, Liverpool
L23 8SZ*

Tel	**(0151) 924 4115**
Fax	(0151) 931 4448
Mem	700
Sec	DD Wilson (0151) 924 1076
Pro	T Hastings (0151) 924 5662
Holes	18 L 6767 yds SSS 73
Recs	Am–68 J Payne
	Pro–66 C Mason
V'tors	H SOC–WD exc Tues
Fees	£35 D–£50 (£60)
Loc	Between Liverpool and
	Southport, off A565
Arch	CK Cotton

Wirral Ladies (1894)

*93 Bidston Road, Birkenhead, Wirral
L43 6TS*

Tel	**(0151) 652 1255**
Fax	(0151) 653 4323
Mem	450
Sec	Mrs SA Headford
Pro	A Law (0151) 652 2468
Holes	18 L 4966 yds SSS 70 (Ladies)
	18 L 5170 yds SSS 66 (Men)

Recs	Am–71 Miss H Lyall
V'tors	U H SOC
Fees	On application
Loc	Birkenhead ½ mile. M53,
	2 miles

Woolton (1901)

*Doe Park, Speke Road, Woolton,
Liverpool L25 7TZ*

Tel	**(0151) 486 1601**
Fax	(0151) 486 1664
Mem	750
Sec	SH King (0151) 486 2298
Pro	A Gibson (0151) 486 1298
Holes	18 L 5706 yds SSS 68
Recs	Am–63 J Edwards
	Pro–66 DJ Rees
V'tors	U exc comp days
Fees	£20 (£28)
Loc	SE Liverpool

Middlesex

Airlinks (1984)

Public

Southall Lane, Hounslow TW5 9PE

Tel	**(0181) 561 1418**
Fax	(0181) 813 6284
Sec	M Hutchins (Mgr)
Pro	C Woodcock
Holes	18 L 6001 yds SSS 69
Recs	Am–60 K Dempster
	Pro–70 R Critchin (1995)
V'tors	WD–U Sat am–NA
Fees	£10.75 (£13.50)
Loc	Just off M4 Junction 3
Mis	Floodlit driving range
Arch	Alliss/Taylor

Ashford Manor (1898)

*Fordbridge Road, Ashford
TW15 3RT*

Tel	**(01784) 252049**
Fax	(01784) 420355
Mem	800
Sec	DG Seward
	(01784) 257687
Pro	M Finney (01784) 255940
Holes	18 L 6352 yds SSS 70
Recs	Am–65 GA Homewood
	(1989)
	Pro–64 D Talbot
V'tors	H
Fees	£25
Loc	Ashford, off A308

Brent Valley (1938)

Public

Church Road, Hanwell, London W7

Tel	**(0181) 567 1287 (Bookings)**
Mem	195
Sec	P Bryant
Pro	P Bryant
Holes	18 L 5426 yds SSS 66
Recs	Am–62 T Greenwood (1996)
	Pro–61 R Green (1988)
V'tors	U SOC
Fees	On application

Bush Hill Park (1895)

*Bush Hill, Winchmore Hill, London
N21 2BU*

Tel	**(0181) 360 5738**
Fax	(0181) 360 5583
Mem	665
Sec	To be appointed
Pro	A Andrews (0181) 360 4103
Holes	18 L 5825 yds SSS 68
Recs	Am–63 PD Lawrence
	Pro–63 W McColl
V'tors	WD–H WE–M SOC
Fees	£24 (£32)
Loc	S of Enfield

C&L Country Club (1991)

West End Road, Northolt UB5 6RD

Tel	**(0181) 845 5662**
Holes	9 L 4440 yds SSS 62
V'tors	U SOC
Fees	£10
Loc	A40, opp Northolt Airport
Arch	Patrick Tallack

Crews Hill (1920)

*Cattlegate Road, Crews Hill, Enfield
EN2 8AZ*

Tel	**(0181) 363 0787**
Fax	(0181) 364 5641
Mem	600
Sec	EJ Hunt (0181) 363 6674
Pro	J Reynolds (0181) 366 7422
Holes	18 L 6208 yds SSS 70
Recs	Am–68 S Bishop
	Pro–65 H Flatman
V'tors	WD–I H WE/BH–M SOC
Fees	On application
Loc	2½ miles N of Enfield. M25
	Junction 24
Arch	HS Colt

Ealing (1898)

Perivale Lane, Greenford UB6 8SS

Tel	**(0181) 997 0937**
Fax	(0181) 998 0756
Mem	600
Sec	Mrs SA Taylor
Pro	I Parsons (0181) 997 3959
Holes	18 L 6216 yds SSS 70
Recs	Am–64 R Neill, C Challens
	Pro–64 R Verwey
V'tors	WD–U H WE/BH–M
Fees	On application
Loc	Marble Arch 6 miles on A40
Arch	HS Colt

Enfield (1893)

Old Park Road South, Enfield EN2 7DA

Tel	**(0181) 363 3970**
Fax	(0181) 342 0381
Mem	625
Sec	NA Challis (0181) 342 0313
Pro	L Fickling (0181) 366 4492
Holes	18 L 6154 yds SSS 70
Recs	Am–62 T Greenwood
	Pro–66 L Fickling
V'tors	WD–H WE/BH–M SOC–WD
Fees	£25 D–£30
Loc	1 mile NE of Enfield. M25
	Junction 24–A1005
Arch	James Braid

Finchley (1929)

Nether Court, Frith Lane, London NW7 1PU

Tel	**(0181) 346 2436**
Fax	(0181) 343 4205
Mem	550
Sec	WD Keene
Pro	DM Brown (0181) 346 5086
Holes	18 L 6411 yds SSS 71
Recs	Am–65 D Chatterton
	Pro–67 T Moore
V'tors	WD–U WE–pm only SOC
Fees	On application
Loc	M1 Junction 2
Arch	James Braid

Fulwell (1904)

Wellington Road, Hampton Hill TW12 1JY

Fax	(0181) 977 7732
Mem	750
Sec	PF Butcher (0181) 977 2733
Pro	N Turner (0181) 977 3844
Holes	18 L 6544 yds SSS 71
Recs	Am–65 P Wharton (1992)
	Pro–63 P Buchan (1982)
V'tors	WD–I WE–M SOC
Fees	£30 (£35)
Loc	Opposite Fulwell Station

Grim's Dyke (1910)

Oxhey Lane, Hatch End, Pinner HA5 4AL

Tel	**(0181) 428 4093**
Fax	(0181) 421 5494
Mem	575
Sec	PH Payne (0181) 428 4539
Pro	J Rule (0181) 428 7484
Holes	18 L 5600 yds SSS 67
Recs	Am–65 J Thornton (1988)
	Pro–61 G Kemble (1995)
V'tors	WD–U H WE–M SOC
Fees	£20 D–£25
Loc	2 miles NW of Harrow (A4008)
Arch	James Braid

Hampstead (1893)

Winnington Road, London N2 0TU

Tel	**(0181) 455 0203**
Fax	(0181) 731 6194
Mem	435
Sec	KF Young
Pro	PJ Brown (0181) 455 7089
Holes	9 L 5812 yds SSS 68
Recs	Am–66 RDA Smith
	Pro–65 D Stevenson
V'tors	Phone Pro first SOC
Fees	£30 (£35)
Loc	1 mile from Hampstead, nr Spaniards Inn
Arch	Tom Dunn

Harrow School (1978)

High Street, Harrow-on-the-Hill HA1 3HW

Mem	440 100(L) 10(J)
Sec	PG Dunbar (0181) 869 1253
Holes	9 L 3690 yds SSS 57
Recs	Am–58
V'tors	M
Loc	Harrow School
Arch	Donald Steel

Haste Hill (1933)

Public

The Drive, Northwood HA6 1HN

Tel	**(01923) 825224**
Fax	(01923) 826485
Mem	250
Sec	R Rodgers
Pro	A Hart
Holes	18 L 5794 yds SSS 68
Recs	Am–65 M Stanton
V'tors	U SOC
Fees	£10.85 (£15.85)
Loc	Northwood-Hillingdon

Heath Park (1975)

Stockley Road, West Drayton

Tel	**(01895) 444232**
Fax	(01895) 445122
Mem	180
Sec	J O'Loughlin (Prop)
Holes	9 L 3800 yds SSS 62
Recs	Am–65 P Moor (1994)
V'tors	U SOC
Fees	18 holes–£5.50 (£6.50)
Loc	Holiday Inn, Heathrow

Hendon (1903)

Ashley Walk, Devonshire Road, London NW7 1DG

Tel	**(0181) 346 6023**
Fax	(0181) 343 1974
Mem	560
Sec	DE Cooper
Pro	S Murray (0181) 346 8990
Holes	18 L 6266 yds SSS 70
Recs	Am–68 AL MacLeod
	Pro–66 SWT Murray
V'tors	WD–U WE/BH–bookings SOC
Fees	£25 D–£30 (£35)
Loc	M1 Junction 2, by Copthall Sports Centre
Arch	HS Colt

Highgate (1904)

Denewood Road, Highgate, London N6 4AH

Tel	**(0181) 340 1906 (Clubhouse)**
Fax	(0181) 348 9152
Mem	700
Sec	JG Wilson (0181) 340 3745
Pro	R Turner (0181) 340 5467
Holes	18 L 5964 yds SSS 69
Recs	Am–66 D Kingsman, P Bax, G Clarke, CR Lloyd
	Pro–66 I Martin (1987)
V'tors	WD–U exc Wed–NA WE/BH–M SOC
Fees	£27
Loc	Off Sheldon Avenue

Hillingdon (1892)

18 Dorset Way, Hillingdon, Uxbridge UB10 0JR

Tel	**(01895) 239810**
Fax	(01895) 233956
Mem	375

Sec	KJ Newton (01895) 233956
Pro	PCR Smith (01895) 460035
Holes	9 L 5459 yds SSS 67
Recs	Am–62 J Hall
	Pro–61 N Wichelow
V'tors	WD–U exc Thurs 12–4pm WE pm–M H SOC–WD
Fees	£15 D–£27
Loc	Off Uxbridge Road, opposite St John's Church

Horsenden Hill (1935)

Public

Woodland Rise, Greenford UB6 0RD

Tel	**(0181) 902 4555**
Pro	T Martin
Holes	9 L 3264 yds SSS 56
V'tors	U
Fees	On application
Loc	Greenford

Hounslow Heath (1979)

Public

Staines Road, Hounslow TW4 5DS

Tel	**(0181) 570 5271**
Mem	200
Sec	G Wakefield
Holes	18 L 5901 yds SSS 68
V'tors	WD–U WE–booking essential
Fees	£7.30 (£10.20)
Loc	Opposite Green Lane, Staines Road (A315)
Arch	Fraser

Lee Valley (1973)

Pay and play

Lee Valley Leisure, Picketts Lock Lane, Edmonton, London N9 0AS

Tel	**(0181) 803 3611**
Pro	RG Gerken
Holes	18 L 4902 yds SSS 64
V'tors	WD–U WE–booking advisable
Fees	£10 (£13)
Loc	1 mile N of North Circular Rd, Edmonton on Meridian Way
Mis	Floodlit driving range

London Golf Centre (1984)

Public

Ruislip Road, Northolt UB5 6QZ

Tel	**(0181) 841 6162/845 2332**
Fax	(0181) 842 2097
Sec	JP Clifford (Gen Mgr), N Sturgess
Pro	G Newall (0181) 845 3180
Holes	9 L 5838 yds SSS 69
Recs	Am–71 D Clark (1990)
	Pro–67 J Livesley (1990)
V'tors	U SOC
Fees	9 holes–£5; 18 holes–£9
Loc	Off A40, nr Polish war memorial
Mis	Driving range

Mill Hill (1925)

100 Barnet Way, Mill Hill, London NW7 3AL

Tel	**(0181) 959 2282**
Fax	(0181) 906 0731
Mem	450

Sec G Mabon (0181) 959 2339
Pro G Harvey (0181) 959 7261
Holes 18 L 6309 yds SSS 70
Recs Am–65 H Aarons
Pro–67 J Hudson
V'tors WD–U H WE/BH–U H after
11.30am SOC–Mon/Wed/Fri
Fees £22.50 (£30)
Loc ¾ mile N of Apex Corner, nr
A1/A41 junction
Arch Abercromby/Colt

Muswell Hill (1893)

*Rhodes Avenue, Wood Green, London
N22 4UT*

Tel **(0181) 888 2044**
Fax (0181) 889 9380
Mem 500
Sec JAB Connors (0181) 888 1764
Pro D Wilton (0181) 888 8046
Holes 18 L 6474 yds SSS 71
Recs Am–67 PJ Montague
Pro–65 H Weetman
V'tors WD–U WE–book with Pro
SOC
Fees £23 D–£33 (£35)
Loc 1 mile from Bounds Green
Station

North Middlesex (1928)

*The Manor House, Friern Barnet Lane,
Whetstone, London N20 0NL*

Tel **(0181) 445 1732**
Mem 600
Sec MR Tapsell (Mgr)
(0181) 445 1604
Pro ASR Roberts (0181) 445 3060
Holes 18 L 5625 yds SSS 67
Recs Am–65 M Cohen
Pro–64 S Levermore
V'tors WE/BH–restricted SOC–WD
Fees £22 (£30)
Loc 5 miles S of M25 Junction 23,
between Barnet and Finchley
Arch Willie Park Jr

Northolt (1991)

Pay and play
Huxley Close, Northolt UB5 5UL

Tel **(0181) 841 5550**
Mem 250
Sec L Gribben
Pro I Godleman
Holes 9 hole course Par 56 SSS 55
V'tors U SOC
Fees £5
Loc Nr M40 Target roundabout
Mis Driving range

Northwood (1891)

*Rickmansworth Road, Northwood
HA6 2QW*

Tel **(01923) 825329**
Fax (01923) 840150
Mem 560
Sec D Thompson (01923) 821384
Pro CJ Holdsworth (01923) 820112
Holes 18 L 6553 yds SSS 71
Recs Am–68 JC Haynes (1997)
Pro–67 J Bland (1977)
V'tors WD–H WE/BH–NA SOC

Fees £25 (£35)
Loc 3 miles SE of Rickmansworth
(A404)
Arch James Braid

Perivale Park (1932)

Public
*Stockdove Way, Argyle Road, Greenford
UB6 8EN*

Sec GC Taylor
Pro P Bryant (0181) 575 7116
Holes 9 L 5296 yds SSS 65
Recs Am–63 W McWilliams
Pro–63
V'tors U
Fees 9 holes–£4.40 (£6.50);
18 holes–£11.50
Loc 1 mile E of Greenford, off A40

Pinner Hill (1927)

*Southview Road, Pinner Hill
HA5 3YA*

Tel **(0181) 866 0963**
Fax (0181) 868 4817
Mem 770
Sec RJ Tibbs
Pro M Grieve (0181) 866 2109
Holes 18 L 6266 yds SSS 70
Recs Am–63 SR Warrin
Pro–67 TH Cotton, G Player,
T Wilkes, G Low, J Warren
V'tors WD–H exc Wed & Thurs–U
Sun/BH–M SOC
Fees £25 (£32) exc Wed &
Thurs–£12
Loc 1 mile W from Pinner Green
Arch JH Taylor

Ruislip (1936)

Public
Ickenham Road, Ruislip HA4 7DQ

Tel **(01895) 638835**
Fax (01923) 822877
Mem 450
Sec BJ Channing (01895) 636963
Pro G Lloyd
Holes 18 L 5702 yds Par 69 SSS 68
Recs Am–64 W Bennet
Pro–65 A George
V'tors U SOC
Fees £10 (£12.50–£15)
Loc W Ruislip BR/LTE Station
Mis Driving range
Arch A Herd

Stanmore (1893)

*29 Gordon Avenue, Stanmore
HA7 2RL*

Tel **(0181) 954 2599**
Mem 590
Sec AW Schooling
Pro VR Law (0181) 954 2646
Holes 18 L 5860 yds SSS 68
Recs Am–64 P Hardy (1994)
Pro–62 V Law (1984)
V'tors WD–H WE/BH–M
SOC–Wed & Thurs
Fees £25
Loc Between Stanmore and
Belmont, off Old Church
Lane

Stockley Park (1993)

Pay and play
*The Clubhouse, Stockley Park, Uxbridge
UB11 1AQ*

Tel **(0181) 813 5700**
Fax (0181) 813 5655
Sec N Munro
Pro A Knox
Holes 18 L 6548 yds SSS 71
V'tors U SOC
Fees £23 (£33)
Loc Heathrow Airport, 2 miles.
M4 Junction 4, 1 mile
Arch Robert Trent Jones Sr

Strawberry Hill (1900)

*Wellesley Road, Strawberry Hill,
Twickenham TW2 5SD*

Tel **(0181) 894 1246**
Mem 350
Sec Mrs M King (0181) 894 0165
Pro P Buchan (0181) 898 2082
Holes 9 L 2381 yds Par 64 SSS 62
Recs Am–61 RE Heryet
Pro–59 H Fullicks, R Gerken,
K Bousfield
V'tors WD–U WE–M XL
Fees £20
Loc Strawberry Hill Station
Arch JH Taylor

Sudbury (1920)

Bridgewater Road, Wembley HA0 1AL

Tel **(0181) 902 3713**
Fax (0181) 903 2966
Mem 640
Sec AJ Poole (Gen Mgr)
Pro N Jordan (0181) 902 7910
Holes 18 L 6282 yds SSS 70
Recs Am–63 T Greenwood,
L White
Pro–65 J Gill
V'tors WD–H WE–M SOC
Fees On application
Loc Junction of A4005/A4090

Sunbury (1993)

Charlton Lane, Shepperton TW17 8QA

Tel **(01932) 772898**
Fax (01932) 866120
Mem 450
Sec P Davison
Pro A Hardaway
Holes 9 L 3105 yds SSS 70
V'tors U
Fees £6.50 (£15)
Loc M3 Junction 1, 1 mile
Mis Floodlit driving range

Trent Park (1973)

Public
Bramley Road, Southgate, London N14

Tel **(0181) 366 7432**
Fax (0181) 368 3823
Pro T Sheaff
Holes 18 L 6008 yds SSS 69
Recs Am–65 M Skinner (1989)
Pro–64 V Law (1979)
V'tors WD–U SOC WE–NA before
11am

Fees £10.60 (£13.50)
Loc Nr Oakwood Tube station
Mis Driving range

Twickenham Park (1977)
Pay and play
Staines Road, Twickenham TW2 5JD
Tel (0181) 783 1698
Fax (0181) 941 9134
Pro Suzy Watt (0181) 783 1698
Holes 9 L 6014 yds SSS 69
V'tors U
Fees On application
Loc 2 miles NW of Hampton
Court, nr end of M3
Mis Floodlit driving range

Uxbridge (1947)
Public
*The Drive, Harefield Place, Uxbridge
UB10 8PA*
Tel (01895) 231169
Fax (01895) 810262
Pro P Howard (01895) 237287
Holes 18 L 5711 yds SSS 68
Recs Am–65 A Schyns (1988)
Pro–64 P Smith (1994)
V'tors U SOC
Fees £10 (£15)
Loc 2 miles N of Uxbridge. B467
off A40 towards Ruislip

West Middlesex (1891)
Greenford Road, Southall UB1 3EE
Tel (0181) 574 3450
Mem 700
Sec PJ Furness
Pro IP Harris (0181) 574 1800
Holes 18 L 6119 yds SSS 69
Recs Am–65 J Walsh
Pro–64 L Farmer
V'tors WD–U WE–NA
Fees Tues/Thurs/Fri–£15.50
(£27.50) Mon & Wed–£10
Loc Junction of Uxbridge Road
and Greenford Road
Arch James Braid

Whitewebbs (1932)
Public
*Beggars Hollow, Clay Hill, Enfield
EN2 9JN*
Tel (0181) 363 2951
Mem 200
Sec IF Forsyth
Pro P Garlick (0181) 363 4454
Holes 18 L 5863 yds SSS 68
Recs Am–61 C Smith
Pro–68 D Lewis
V'tors U
Fees £10 (£12)
Loc 1 mile N of Enfield

Wyke Green (1928)
*Syon Lane, Isleworth, Osterley
TW7 5PT*
Tel (0181) 560 8777
Fax (0181) 569 8390
Mem 700
Sec DG Seward

Pro DA Holmes (0181) 847 0685
Holes 18 L 6242 yds SSS 70
Recs Am–65 MR Johnson
Pro–64 C DeFoy
V'tors WD–U WE/BH–M SOC
Fees £25 After 3pm–£15
Loc 1/2 mile from Gillette Corner
(A4)

Norfolk

Barnham Broom Hotel
(1977)
Barnham Broom, Norwich NR9 4DD
Tel (01603) 759393
Fax (01603) 758224
Mem 600
Sec A Long (Man Dir),
P Ballingall (Golf Dir)
Pro S Beckham
Holes Valley 18 L 6470 yds SSS 71
Hill 18 L 6628 yds SSS 72
Recs Valley Am–69 A Elliot
Pro–65 J Higgins
Hill Am–71 A Marshall
V'tors I or H WE/BH–NA (exc hotel
residents) SOC
Fees £27 Residents–£19
Loc 8 miles SW of Norwich, off
A47. 4 miles NW of
Wymondham, off A11
Arch Pennink/Steel

Bawburgh (1978)
*Glen Lodge, Marlingford Road,
Bawburgh, Norwich NR9 3LU*
Tel (01603) 740404
Fax (01603) 740403
Mem 650
Sec I Ladbrooke (Golf Dir),
J Barnard
Pro C Potter (01603) 742323
Holes 18 L 6224 yds SSS 70
Recs Am–67 K Parfitt
Pro–67 T Varney, A Hemsley
V'tors U–phone first SOC
Fees £18 (£22)
Loc 2 miles W of Norwich, off A47
Norwich Southern Bypass
Mis Floodlit driving range. Golf
Academy
Arch Shaun Manser

Caldecott Hall
*Caldecott Hall, Beccles Road, Fritton,
Gt Yarmouth NR31 9EY*
Tel (01493) 488488
Fax (01493) 488561
Mem 400
Sec P Riches
Pro M Snazell
Holes 18 L 6476 yds Par 71 SSS 71
9 hole Par 3 course
V'tors H SOC
Fees £15 (£20)
Loc 5 miles SW of Gt Yarmouth
on A413
Mis Floodlit driving range. 9 hole
pitch & putt

Costessey Park (1983)
*Costessey Park, Costessey, Norwich
NR8 5AL*
Tel (01603) 746333
Fax (01603) 746185
Mem 500
Sec CL House
Pro S Cook (01603) 747085
Holes 18 L 6104 yds Par 72 SSS 69
V'tors U SOC–WD
Fees On application
Loc 3 miles W of Norwich, off A47
at Round Well PH

Dereham (1934)
Quebec Road, Dereham NR19 2DS
Tel (01362) 695900
Fax (01362) 695904
Mem 390
Sec W Sargeant
Pro R Curtis (01362) 695631
Holes 9 L 6225 yds SSS 70
Recs Am–64 AC Marshall (1995)
Pro–65 M Elsworthy (1986)
V'tors H WE–M
Fees £20
Loc Dereham 1/2 mile

Dunham (1987)
Little Dunham, King's Lynn PE32 2DF
Tel (01328) 701718
Fax (01328) 701906
Mem 250
Sec J Glencross
Pro J Laing (01485) 520076
Holes 9 L 2269 yds SSS 62
V'tors U SOC
Fees £9 (£12)
Loc 4 miles NE of Swaffham, off
A47. Signs from Necton
Arch Cecil Denny

Dunston Hall (1994)
Pay and play
*Ipswich Road, Dunston, Norwich
NR14 8PQ*
Tel (01508) 470178
Fax (01508) 471499
Mem 250
Sec J Hillis
Pro P Briggs
Holes 18 L 6200 yds Par 71 SSS 70
V'tors U
Fees £20 (£25)
Loc 5 miles S of Norwich on A140
Mis Driving range
Arch John Glasgow

Eagles (1990)
*School Road, Tilney All Saints, Kings
Lynn PE34 4RS*
Tel (01553) 827147
Fax (01553) 829777
Mem 300
Sec D Horn
Pro N Pickerell
Holes 9 L 2142 yds SSS 61
Par 3 course
V'tors U
Fees 9 holes–£5.75 (£6.75)

Loc   5 miles W of Kings Lynn
on A47
Mis   Driving range
Arch   David Horn

Eaton (1910)

Newmarket Road, Norwich NR4 6SF
Tel   **(01603) 452881**
Fax   (01603) 451686
Mem   640 135(L) 70(J)
Sec   DLP Sochon (01603) 451686
Pro   M Allen (01603) 452478
Holes   18 L 6135 yds SSS 69
Recs   Am–64 AK Nichols (1990),
M Barrett (1996)
Pro–65 M Spooner (1988)
V'tors   H WE–NA before noon SOC
Fees   £17 (£22)
Loc   S Norwich, off A11

Fakenham (1973)

The Race Course, Fakenham
Tel   **(01328) 862867**
Mem   510
Sec   G Cocker (01328) 855665
Pro   C Williams (01328) 863534
Holes   9 L 6174 yds SSS 69
Pro–65 K Golding (1991)
V'tors   WD–U WE–NA before
12 noon SOC
Fees   £14 (£18)
Loc   Fakenham racecourse

Feltwell (1976)

*Thor Ave, Wilton Road, Feltwell
IP26 4AY*
Tel   **(01842) 827644**
Mem   400
Sec   PJ Jessop
Pro   P Field
Holes   9 L 6260 yds SSS 70
Recs   Am–68 S Dupe (1994)
V'tors   U SOC–WD
Fees   £14 (£22)
Loc   1 mile S of Feltwell on B1112
Mis   Former Feltwell aerodrome

Gorleston (1906)

*Warren Road, Gorleston, Gt Yarmouth
NR31 6JT*
Tel   **(01493) 661911**
Mem   900
Sec   NP Longbottom
(01493) 661911
Pro   N Brown (01493) 662103
Holes   18 L 6400 yds SSS 71
Recs   Am–68 J Maddock (1981)
Pro–66 R Mann (1991)
V'tors   U H SOC
Fees   D–£20 (D–£25) W–£85
Loc   S of Gorleston, off A12
Arch   JH Taylor

Great Yarmouth & Caister (1882)

*Beach House, Caister-on-Sea,
Gt Yarmouth NR30 5TD*
Tel   **(01493) 720421**
Mem   700
Sec   HJ Harvey (01493) 728699
Pro   R Foster

Holes   18 L 6330 yds SSS 70
Recs   Am–65 C Green
Pro–66 E Murray
V'tors   WE–NA before noon SOC
Fees   £27 (£30)
Loc   Caister-on-Sea

Hunstanton (1891)

*Golf Course Road, Old Hunstanton
PE36 6JQ*
Tel   **(01485) 532811**
Fax   (01485) 532319
Mem   650 250(L) 60(J)
Sec   MT Whybrow
Pro   J Carter (01485) 532751
Holes   18 L 6735 yds SSS 72
Recs   Am–65 S Robertson (1989)
Pro–65 ME Gregson (1967)
V'tors   WD–H after 9.30am WE–H
after 10.30am SOC
Fees   D–£45 (£55)
Loc   1½ miles NE of Hunstanton
Mis   2-ball play only
Arch   George Fernie

King's Lynn (1923)

Castle Rising, King's Lynn PE31 6BD
Tel   **(01553) 631656**
Fax   (01553) 631036
Mem   980
Sec   GJ Higgins (01553) 631654
Pro   C Hanlon (01553) 631655
Holes   18 L 6646 yds SSS 72
Recs   Am–68 J Jones (1993)
Pro–64 P Hinton (1991)
Ladies–75 W Fryer (1985)
V'tors   WD–U H WE/BH–NA SOC
Fees   £33 (£40)
Loc   4 miles NE of King's Lynn,
off A149
Arch   Alliss/Thomas

Links Country Park Hotel

West Runton, Cromer NR27 9QH
Tel   **(01263) 838383**
Fax   (01263) 838264
Mem   300
Sec   CL Savage (Hon)
Pro   L Patterson (01263) 838215
Holes   9 L 4814 yds SSS 64
Recs   Am–64 CJ Lamb (1988)
Pro–65 R Mann,
GR Harvey (1987)
V'tors   U
Fees   £20 (£25)
Loc   3 miles W of Cromer (A149)
Arch   JH Taylor

Mattishall (1990)

South Green, Mattishall, Dereham
Tel   **(01362) 850464**
Mem   300
Sec   Miss B Todd
Holes   9 L 6218 yds SSS 70
V'tors   WD–U WE–U before noon
SOC
Fees   £8 (£10)
Loc   6 miles E of Dereham (B1063)
Mis   9 hole pitch & putt
Arch   BC Todd

Middleton Hall (1989)

Middleton, King's Lynn PE32 1RH
Tel   **(01553) 841800**
Mem   550
Sec   Ellen Bompas
Pro   P Whittle (01553) 841801
Holes   18 L 6007 yds SSS 69
Recs   Am–71 D Wooley
V'tors   U SOC
Fees   £20 (£25)
Loc   2 miles SE of King's Lynn
on A47
Mis   Driving range
Arch   D Scott

Mundesley (1901)

Links Road, Mundesley NR11 8ES
Tel   **(01263) 720279**
Fax   (01263) 720279
Mem   450
Sec   P Clarke (Sec/Mgr)
(01263) 720095
Pro   TG Symmons (01831) 455461
Holes   9 L 5377 yds SSS 66
V'tors   WD–U exc Wed 11.30–
3.30pm WE–NA before
11.30am
Fees   £17.50 (£20)
Loc   7 miles SE of Cromer

The Norfolk G&CC (1993)

*Hingham Road, Reymerston, Norwich
NR9 4QQ*
Tel   **(01362) 850297**
Fax   (01362) 850614
Mem   400
Sec   C Nunn (Gen Mgr)
Pro   Alison Sheard
(01362) 850778
Holes   18 L 6603 yds SSS 72
Recs   Am–72 J Tavener (1994)
V'tors   WD–U before 4pm –M after
4pm WE/BH–NA before noon
SOC
Fees   £16 (£20)
Loc   14 miles W of Norwich, off
B1135 Dereham to
Wymondham road
Mis   9 hole pitch & putt course

RAF Marham (1974)

RAF Marham, King's Lynn PE33 9NP
Mem   353
Sec   LS Candlish (01760) 337261
(Ext 7262)
Holes   9 L 5244 yds SSS 66
Recs   Am–71
V'tors   By prior arrangement–U exc
Sun am
Loc   11 miles SE of King's Lynn,
nr Narborough
Mis   Course situated on MOD
land, and may be closed
without prior notice

Richmond Park (1990)

Saham Road, Watton IP25 6EA
Tel   **(01953) 881803**
Fax   (01953) 881817
Mem   600

Sec	Gp Capt E Durham RAF (Rtd)
Pro	A Hemsley
Holes	18 L 6300 yds SSS 70
Recs	Am–71 D Glenn (1994)
	Pro–69 F Kiddie (1995)
V'tors	WD–U WE–H before noon
	SOC
Fees	£18 (£24)
Loc	½ mile NW of Watton
Mis	Driving range
Arch	Scott/Jessup

Royal Cromer (1888)

Overstrand Road, Cromer NR27 0JH

Tel	(01263) 512884
Fax	(01263) 512884
Mem	700
Sec	BA Howson
Pro	RJ Page (01263) 512267
Holes	18 L 6508 yds SSS 71
Recs	Am–67 T Hurrell (1993)
	Pro–69 C Williams,
	R Waugh (1991)
V'tors	H SOC–WD
Fees	£28 (£34)
Loc	1 mile E of Cromer on B1159
Arch	HS Colt/JH Taylor

Royal Norwich (1893)

Drayton High Road, Hellesdon,
Norwich NR6 5AH

Tel	(01603) 425712
Mem	700
Sec	J Meggy (01603) 429928
Pro	D Futter (01603) 408459
Holes	18 L 6603 yds SSS 72
Recs	Am–67 A Barker (1981)
	Pro–66 HJ Boyle (1971)
V'tors	WE/BH–restricted SOC
Fees	D–£30 (£36)
Loc	½ mile W of Norwich ring
	road, on Fakenham road
Arch	James Braid

Royal West Norfolk (1892)

Brancaster, King's Lynn PE31 8AX

Tel	(01485) 210223
Fax	(01485) 210087
Mem	760
Sec	Maj NA Carrington Smith
	(01485) 210087
Pro	RE Kimber (01485) 210616
Holes	18 L 6428 yds SSS 71
Recs	Am–67 AH Perowne
	Pro–66 M Elsworthy
V'tors	M No four balls allowed
	mid-July–mid-Sept WE–NA
	before 10am SOC
Fees	£39 (£49)
Loc	7 miles E of Hunstanton on
	A419
Arch	Holcombe Ingleby

Ryston Park (1932)

Ely Road, Denver, Downham Market
PE38 0HH

Tel	(01366) 382133
Mem	320
Sec	WJ Flogdell (01366) 383834
Pro	None
Holes	9 L 6310 yds SSS 70

Recs	Am–66 JP Alflatt (1975)
V'tors	WD–H WE/BH–M SOC
Fees	£15 D–£20
Loc	1 mile S of Downham Market
	on A10
Arch	James Braid

Sheringham (1891)

Sheringham NR26 8HG

Tel	(01263) 822038
Fax	(01263) 825189
Mem	700
Sec	MJ Garrett (01263) 823488
Pro	MW Jubb (01263) 822980
Holes	18 L 6464 yds SSS 71
Recs	Am–65 J Little (1995)
	Pro–66 R Mann (1991)
V'tors	WD–U H after 9.30am SOC
Fees	£32 (£37)
Loc	½ mile W of Sheringham
	(A149)
Arch	Tom Dunn

Sprowston Park (1980)

Pay and play
Wroxham Road, Sprowston, Norwich
NR9 8RP

Tel	(01603) 410657
Fax	(01603) 788884
Mem	500
Sec	G Porter
Pro	P Grice (01603) 417264
Holes	18 L 5982 yds SSS 70
Recs	Am–65 M Frary
	Pro–65 N Catchpole
V'tors	U SOC
Fees	£14 (£17)
Loc	2 miles NE of Norwich on
	A1151
Mis	Floodlit driving range

Swaffham (1922)

Cley Road, Swaffham PE37 8AE

Tel	(01760) 721611
Mem	500
Sec	R Joslin
Pro	P Field
Holes	9 L 6252 yds SSS 70
Recs	Am–68 G Head
	Pro–64 CJ Norton
V'tors	WD–U WE–M exc Sun
	am–NA
Fees	£18
Loc	1½ miles SW of Swaffham

Thetford (1912)

Brandon Road, Thetford IP24 3NE

Tel	(01842) 752258 (Clubhouse)
Fax	(01842) 766212
Mem	700
Sec	Mrs SA Redpath (01842)
	752169
Pro	G Kitley (01842) 752662
Holes	18 L 6879 yds SSS 73
Recs	Am -66 MP Williamson
	Pro–68 C Green
	Ladies–74 S Saunders
V'tors	H SOC–Wed–Fri
Fees	£32
Loc	2 miles W of Thetford
	(B1107), off A11 By-pass

Wensum Valley (1990)

Beech Avenue, Taverham, Norwich
NR8 6HP

Tel	(01603) 261012
Fax	(01603) 261664
Mem	850
Sec	Miss B Todd
Pro	T Varney
Holes	18 L 6000 yds SSS 69
	18 L 4862 yds SSS 66
Recs	Am–69 P Robson (1993)
	Pro–67 M Spooner (1990)
V'tors	WD–U H WE–NA before
	noon SOC
Fees	£15 (£18)
Loc	4 miles NW of Norwich on
	A1067
Mis	Floodlit driving range
Arch	BC Todd

Weston Park (1993)

Weston Longville, Norwich NR9 5JW

Tel	(01603) 872363
Fax	(01603) 873040
Mem	400
Sec	RR Wright (Gen Mgr),
	DF Cottier
Pro	MR Few (01603) 872998
Holes	18 L 6603 yds SSS 72
V'tors	WD–U H
Fees	£24 (£29)
Loc	7 miles NW of Norwich,
	off A1067
Arch	John Glasgow

Northamptonshire

Cold Ashby (1974)

Stanford Road, Cold Ashby,
Northampton NN6 6EP

Tel	(01604) 740548
Fax	(01604) 740548
Mem	600 40(L) 40(J)
Sec	DA Croxton (Prop)
Pro	S Rose (01604) 740099
Holes	27 L 6308 yds Par 72 SSS 70
Recs	Am–69 G Croxton (1997)
	Pro–65 J Higgins (1996)
V'tors	WD–U WE–U after 12 noon
	(if booked) SOC
Fees	£15 (£23)
Loc	11 miles N of Northampton,
	nr A5199/A14 Junction.
	7 miles E of M1 Junction 18
Arch	David Croxton

Collingtree Park (1990)

Windingbrook Lane, Northampton
NN4 0XN

Tel	(01604) 700000
Fax	(01604) 702600
Mem	900
Sec	Miss J Byrne
Pro	G Pook
Holes	18 L 6695 yds SSS 72
Recs	Am–67 S Bottomley (1993)
	Pro–66 M Persson (1994)
	Ladies Pro–69 J Hill (1994)
V'tors	H SOC

Fees £30 (£40)
Loc ½ mile E of M1 Junction 15
Mis Floodlit driving range
Arch Johnny Miller

Corby (1965)
Public
Stamford Road, Weldon, Corby
Tel (01536) 260756
Fax (01536) 260756
Pro G Brown
Holes 18 L 6677 yds SSS 72
Recs Am–75 R Beekie, M Scott,
WF Kearney
Pro–70 RH Kemp
V'tors U SOC–WD
Fees On application
Loc 4 miles E of Corby (A43)

Daventry & District (1922)
Norton Road, Daventry NN11 5LS
Tel (01327) 702829
Mem 350
Sec J Grainger (01327) 706245
Pro None
Holes 9 L 5812 yds Par 69 SSS 68
V'tors WD–U Sun–NA before 11am
SOC–phone Pro
Fees £8 (£10)
Loc 2 miles E of Daventry

Delapre (1976)
Public
Eagle Drive, Nene Valley Way,
Northampton NN4 7DU
Tel (01604) 764036/763957
Fax (01604) 706378
Mem 1000
Sec JS Corby (01604) 763957
Pro J Corby, J Cuddihy
(01604) 764036
Holes 18 L 6293 yds SSS 70
9 L 2146 yds SSS 32
2 x 9 holes Par 3 courses
Recs Am–66 M McNally
V'tors U SOC
Fees £8 (£11)
Loc 3 miles from M1 Junction 15,
on A508/A45
Mis Pitch & putt. Driving range
Arch Jacobs/Corby

Embankment (1975)
The Embankment, Wellingborough
NN8 1LD
Tel (01933) 228465
Mem 175
Sec JB Andrew, E Walden (Mgr)
Holes 9 L 3374 yds SSS 57
Recs Am–58
V'tors WD–M
Fees £4
Loc 1 mile SE of Wellingborough
Arch TH Neal

Farthingstone Hotel (1974)
Farthingstone, Towcester NN12 8HA
Tel (01327) 361291
Fax (01327) 361645
Mem 400

Sec DC Donaldson (Prop/Mgr)
Pro (01327) 361533
Holes 18 L 6248 yds SSS 71
Recs Am–63 C Lawrence (1996)
Pro–66 D Thorp (1984),
M Gallagher (1985),
K Dickens (1989)
V'tors U SOC
Fees £10 D–£15 (£15 D–£20)
SOC–from £10
Loc 4 miles W of A5 on
Farthingstone-Everdon road.
M1 Junction 16, 6 miles

Hellidon Lakes Hotel & CC (1991)
Hellidon, Daventry NN11 6LN
Tel (01327) 62550
Fax (01327) 62559
Mem 500
Sec J Nicoll
Pro G Wills (01327) 62551
Holes 18 L 6700 yds SSS 72
9 L 5582 yds SSS 67
Recs Am–70 P Hutchinson (1995)
V'tors U H SOC
Fees £15 (£20)
Loc 7 miles SW of Daventry,
via A361.
Mis Driving range
Arch David Snell

Kettering (1891)
Headlands, Kettering NN15 6XA
Tel (01536) 511104
Mem 700 100(L) 50(J)
Sec DG Buckby (01536) 511104
Pro K Theobald (01536) 81014
Holes 18 L 6087 yds SSS 69
Recs Am–65 A Draper (1992)
Pro–64 P Smith (1991)
V'tors WD–U WE/BH–M SOC
Fees £15 D–£22
Loc S boundary of Kettering
Arch Tom Morris

Kingfisher CC
Pay and play
Buckingham Road, Deanshanger,
Milton Keynes MK18 6DG
Tel (01908) 562332
Fax (01908) 260857
Mem 200
Sec Maj DM Barraclough
(01908) 560217
Pro None
Holes 9 L 5471 yds Par 70 SSS 67
V'tors U SOC
Fees £5.50 (£10.50)
Loc NW of Milton Keynes on
A422 to Buckingham
Mis Covered driving range
Arch Donald Steel

Kingsthorpe (1908)
Kingsley Road, Northampton NN2 7BU
Tel (01604) 711173
Fax (01604) 710610
Mem 600
Sec JE Harris (01604) 710610
Pro P Armstrong (01604) 719602

Holes 18 L 5918 yds SSS 69
Recs Am–63 S McDonald
Pro–64 B Larratt
V'tors WD–U WE/BH–M H
SOC–WD
Fees D–£25
Loc 2 miles N of Northampton
centre, off A508

Northampton (1893)
Harlestone, Northampton NN7 4EF
Tel (01604) 845102
Fax (01604) 820262
Mem 595 134(L) 65(J)
Sec RL Jones (01604) 845155
Pro K Dickens (01604) 845167
Holes 18 L 6615 yds Par 72 SSS 72
Recs Am–67 GH Keates (1996)
Pro–67 D Eddiford, J Higgins,
A Hare (1995)
Ladies–74 S Carter (1997)
V'tors WD–U H WE–M SOC
Fees £30
Loc 4 miles NW of Northampton,
on A428 beyond Harlestone
Arch Donald Steel

Northamptonshire County (1909)
Church Brampton, Northampton
NN6 8AZ
Tel (01604) 842170
Mem 650
Sec ME Wadley (01604) 843025
Pro T Rouse (01604) 842226
Holes 18 L 6503 yds SSS 71
Recs Am–65 R Duck (1994)
Pro–64 J Higgins (1990)
V'tors H SOC
Fees Summer–£37.50 (£37.50)
Winter–£27.50 (£27.50)
Loc 5 miles NW of Northampton,
off A50
Arch HS Colt

Oundle (1893)
Benefield Road, Oundle PE8 4EZ
Tel (01832) 273267
Fax (01832) 273267
Mem 600
Sec G Brooks (Gen Mgr)
Pro R Keys (01832) 272273
Holes 18 L 6235 yds SSS 70
Recs Am–68
Pro–67
V'tors WD–U WE–M before 10.30am
–U after 10.30am SOC
Fees £22 (£30)
Loc 1½ miles W of Oundle on A427

Overstone Park (1994)
Watermark Leisure, Billing Lane,
Northampton NN6 0AP
Tel (01604) 647666
Fax (01604) 642635
Mem 450
Sec B Willoughby
Pro B Mudge (01604) 643555
Holes 18 L 6602 yds SSS 72
V'tors M
Fees £14 (£18)

Loc   4 miles E of Northampton,
      off A45. M1 Junction 15
Mis   Driving range
Arch Donald Steel

Rushden (1919)

Kimbolton Road, Chelveston,
Wellingborough NN9 6AN

Tel   (01933) 418511
Mem   350
Sec   SP Trayhorn
Holes   10 L 6335 yds Par 71 SSS 70
Recs   Am–69
V'tors WD–U exc Wed pm
        WE/BH–M SOC
Fees   £15
Loc   On A45, 2 miles E of Higham
        Ferrers

Staverton Park (1977)

Staverton Park, Staverton, Daventry
NN11 6JT

Tel   (01327) 302000/302118
Fax   (01327) 311428
Sec   D Entwhistle (Gen Mgr),
        Mrs A Radford (Sec)
Pro   R Mudge (01327) 705506
Holes   18 L 6634 yds SSS 72
Recs   Am–67
        Pro–64
V'tors U SOC
Fees   On application
Loc   1 mile SW of Daventry, off
        A425. M1 Junctions 16/18.
        M40 Junction 11
Mis   Driving range

Wellingborough (1893)

Harrowden Hall, Great Harrowden,
Wellingborough NN9 5AD

Tel   (01933) 677234/673022
Fax   (01933) 679379
Mem   850
Sec   R Tomlin (01933) 677234
Pro   D Clifford (01933) 678752
Holes   18 L 6620 yds SSS 72
Recs   Am–69 J Campbell (1993)
        Pro–68 M Gallagher (1993)
V'tors WD–U H exc Tues WE–M
        SOC–WD exc Tues
Fees   D–£35
Loc   2 miles N of Wellingborough
        on A509
Arch   Hawtree

Whittlebury Park G&CC

(1992)

Whittlebury, Towcester NN12 8XW

Tel   (01327) 858092
Fax   (01327) 858009
Mem   450
Sec   PJ Tomlin
Pro   M Leung (01327) 858588
Holes   36 holes:
        5000-7000 yds SSS 66-72
V'tors U H SOC
Fees   £18 D–£30 (£25 D–£35)
Loc   4 miles S of Towcester
        on A413
Mis   Driving range. Indoor golf
        centre
Arch   Cameron Sinclair

Northumberland

Allendale (1906)

High Studdon, Allenheads Road,
Allendale, Hexham NE47 9DH

Mem   140 30(L) 9(J)
Sec   Ann Egdell (Hon)
        (01434) 345005
Holes   9 L 5044 yds SSS 65
V'tors U BH–NA before 2pm SOC
Fees   £10
Loc   1½ miles S of Allendale on
        B6295

Alnmouth (1869)

Foxton Hall, Alnmouth NE66 3BE

Tel   (01665) 830231
Fax   (01665) 830922
Mem   800
Sec   C Jobson
Pro   Shop (01665) 830043
Holes   18 L 6484 yds SSS 71
Recs   Am–64 IS Ferrie (1996)
V'tors Mon/Tues/Thurs–H (restricted)
        SOC
Fees   D–£27
Loc   5 miles SE of Alnwick
Mis   Dormy House
Arch   HS Colt

Alnmouth Village (1869)

Marine Road, Alnmouth NE66 2RZ

Tel   (01665) 830370
Mem   340
Sec   W Maclean (01665) 602096
Holes   9 L 6020 yds SSS 70
Recs   Am–63 D Weddell
V'tors H
Fees   £15 (£20)
Loc   Alnmouth

Alnwick (1907)

Swansfield Park, Alnwick

Tel   (01665) 602632
Mem   500
Sec   LE Stewart (01665) 602499
Holes   18 L 6250 yds SSS 70
V'tors U
Fees   D–£15 (D–£20)
Loc   Alnwick, off A1
Arch   Rochester/Rae

Arcot Hall (1909)

Dudley, Cramlington NE23 7QP

Tel   (0191) 236 2794
Fax   (0191) 217 0370
Mem   660
Sec   JM Forteath QGM
        (0191) 236 2794
Pro   GM Cant (0191) 236 2147
Holes   18 L 6389 yds SSS 70
Recs   Am–65 G Pickup (1990),
        A Leach,
        D Caldicott (1994)
        Pro–64 B Rumney (1997)
V'tors WD–H WE/BH–M SOC
Fees   D–£26 (£30) After 3pm–£21
Loc   7 miles N of Newcastle, off A1
Arch   James Braid

Bamburgh Castle (1904)

The Club House, 40 The Wynding,
Bamburgh NE69 7DE

Tel   (01668) 214378
Mem   670
Sec   TC Osborne (01668) 214321
Holes   18 L 5621 yds Par 68 SSS 67
Recs   Am–64 M Dawson (1994)
V'tors WD–U H WE/BH–M SOC
Fees   D–£25 (£30 D–£35)
Loc   5 miles E of A1, via B1341
        or B1342
Arch   George Rochester

Bedlingtonshire (1972)

Public
Acorn Bank, Bedlington

Tel   (01670) 822457
Mem   966
Sec   E Ramsay
Pro   M Webb (01670) 822087
Holes   18 L 6224 metres SSS 73
Recs   Am–68 D Gray
        Pro–64 D Curry
V'tors U
Fees   £15 (£20)
Loc   12 miles N of Newcastle
        (A1068)
Arch   Frank Pennink

Belford (1993)

South Road, Belford NE70 7HY

Tel   (01668) 213433
Fax   (01668) 213919
Mem   300
Sec   AM Gilhome
Pro   None
Holes   9 L 6304 yds SSS 70
Recs   Am–72 MB Turnbull (1995)
V'tors U SOC
Fees   On application
Loc   15 miles N of Alnwick, off A1
Mis   Driving range
Arch   Nigel Williams

Bellingham (1893)

Boggle Hole, Bellingham NE48 2DT

Tel   (01434) 220530
Fax   (01434) 220160
Mem   630
Sec   P Cordiner (01434) 220182
Holes   18 L 6077 yds Par 70 SSS 70
Recs   Am–69 S Robinson (1997)
V'tors U exc comp days SOC
Fees   £15 (£20)
Loc   15 miles N of Hexham, off
        B6320
Mis   Driving range
Arch   I Wilson

Berwick-upon-Tweed

(1890)

Gostwick Beal, Berwick-upon-Tweed
TD15 2RW

Tel   (01289) 387256
Fax   (01289) 387256
Mem   550
Sec   AE French
Pro   P Terras (01289) 387380
Holes   18 L 6449 yds SSS 71

Recs   Am–69 M Hindhaugh (1995)
        Pro–69 GJ Brand
        Ladies–72 J Lee-Smith
V'tors WD–U WE–U 10–12 and
        after 2pm SOC
Fees   £20 D–£25 (£25 D–£32)
Loc   5 miles S of Berwick, off A1
Arch   James Braid

Blyth (1905)

New Delaval, Blyth NE24 4DB
Tel   (01670) 540110
Mem   800
Sec   J Tate, L Morpeth
Pro   A Brown (01670) 356514
Holes 18 L 6498 yds SSS 71
Recs   Am–65 S Brooks (1997)
V'tors WD–U WE/BH–M SOC–WD
        before 3pm
Fees   £18 D–£20
Loc   W end of Plessey Road, Blyth

Burgham Park G&CC

(1994)
Felton, Morpeth NE65 8QP
Tel   (01670) 787898
Fax   (01670) 787164
Mem   650
Sec   J Carr
Pro   S McNally (01670) 787978
Holes 18 L 6751 yds SSS 72
Recs   Am–68 I Paxton (1997)
V'tors U SOC
Fees   On application
Loc   7 miles N of Morpeth on A1
Mis   Pitch & putt course
Arch   Andrew Mair

Close House (1968)

*Close House, Heddon-on-the-Wall,
Newcastle-upon-Tyne NE15 0HT*
Tel   (01661) 852953
Mem   1000
Sec   J Pearson
Pro   M Webb
Holes 18 L 5587 yds SSS 67
Recs   Am–61 DJ Craig
V'tors M SOC–WD
Fees   D–£18
Loc   9 miles W of Newcastle on A69
Arch   Hawtree

Dunstanburgh Castle

(1900)
Embleton NE66 3XQ
Tel   (01665) 576562
Mem   387
Sec   PFC Gilbert (Mgr)
Holes 18 L 6298 yds SSS 70
Recs   Am–69
V'tors U
Fees   £15 (£20)
Loc   7 miles NE of Alnwick
        on B1339
Arch   James Braid

Haltwhistle

*Banktop, Greenhead, Haltwhistle
NE49 9JR*
Tel   (016977) 47367 (Club)
Mem   300

Sec   WE Barnes (Hon)
Pro   J Metcalf
Holes 18 L 5474 yds SSS 67
V'tors U SOC
Fees   D–£12
Loc   3 miles W of Haltwhistle
        on A69
Arch   Andrew Mair

Hexham (1892)

Spital Park, Hexham NE46 3RZ
Tel   (01434) 602057
Fax   (01434) 601865
Mem   700
Sec   AN Harris (01434) 603072
Pro   MW Forster (01434) 604904
Holes 18 L 6272 yds SSS 70
Recs   Am–64 JP Arnott (1994)
        Pro–67 I Waugh
V'tors U
Fees   £25 (£32) W–£100
Loc   21 miles W of Newcastle (A69)

Linden Hall

Longhorsley, Morpeth NE65 8XF
Tel   (01670) 788050
Mem   250
Sec   D Curry (Sec/Mgr)
Pro   D Curry
Holes 18 L 6809 yds SSS 73
V'tors H SOC
Fees   £22.50 (£30)
Loc   8 miles NW of Morpeth, off
        A697
Mis   Driving range
Arch   Jonathan Gaunt

Magdalene Fields (1903)

Pay and play
Magdalene Fields, Berwick-upon-Tweed
Tel   (01289) 306384
Mem   400
Sec   MJ Lynch
Holes 18 L 6407 yds SSS 71
Recs   Am–65 J Patterson (1995)
V'tors U SOC
Fees   £16 (£18)
Loc   Berwick-upon-Tweed 1 mile
Arch   Park/Jefferson/Thompson

Matfen Hall (1994)

Matfen, Hexham
Tel   (01661) 886500
Fax   (01661) 886146
Mem   350
Sec   D Harrison
Pro   J Harrison
Holes 18 L 6732 yds Par 72
        9 hole Par 3 course
        Pro–67 D Curry (1995)
V'tors U
Fees   £19 (£23)
Loc   12 miles W of Newcastle,
        off B6318
Mis   Practice range
Arch   Mair/James

Morpeth (1907)

The Common, Morpeth NE61 2BT
Tel   (01670) 504942
Fax   (01670) 504918

Mem   700
Sec   KD Cazaly (01670) 504942
Pro   MR Jackson (01670) 515675
Holes 18 L 5671 metres SSS 69
Recs   Am–65 MD Hall (1995)
        Pro–68 T Horton (1976)
V'tors H SOC
Fees   £20 (£25)
Loc   1 mile S of Morpeth on A197

Newbiggin (1884)

Newbiggin-by-the-Sea NE64 6DW
Tel   (01670) 817344 (Clubhouse)
Fax   (01670) 520236
Mem   500
Sec   GW Beattie (01670) 852959
Pro   M Webb (01670) 817833
Holes 18 L 6452 yds SSS 71
Recs   Am–65 J McCallum
        Pro–68 K Saint
V'tors U after 10am exc comp
        days–NA SOC
Fees   D–£14 (D–£19)
Loc   Newbiggin, nr Church Point

Ponteland (1927)

*53 Bell Villas, Ponteland, Newcastle-
upon-Tyne NE20 9BD*
Tel   (01661) 822689
Mem   460 150(L) 100(J)
Sec   J Hillyer
Pro   A Crosby
Holes 18 L 6524 yds SSS 71
Recs   Am–65 RJ Wiggins (1997)
        Pro–63 B Rumney (1994)
V'tors WD–U WE/BH–M
Fees   £22.50
Loc   6 miles NW of Newcastle on
        A696, nr Airport

Prudhoe (1930)

*Eastwood Park, Prudhoe-on-Tyne
NE42 5DX*
Tel   (01661) 832466
Mem   450
Sec   GB Garratt
Pro   J Crawford (01661) 836188
Holes 18 L 5862 yds SSS 68
Recs   Am–63 CN Hunter
        Pro–65 A Crosby
V'tors WD–U
Fees   £20 (£25)
Loc   15 miles W of Newcastle
        (A695)

Rothbury (1891)

*Old Race Course, Rothbury, Morpeth
NE65 7TR*
Tel   (01669) 621271
Mem   369
Sec   WT Bathgate (01669) 620718
Pro   None
Holes 9 L 5681 yds SSS 67
Recs   Am–65 PA Arkle (1996)
V'tors WD–U exc Tues after 4pm &
        Wed am WE–NA SOC
Fees   D–£11 (D–£16)
Loc   15 miles N of Morpeth on
        A697. W side of Rothbury
Arch   JB Radcliffe

Seahouses (1913)

Beadnell Road, Seahouses NE68 7XT
Tel **(01665) 720794**
Mem 600
Sec JA Stevens (01665) 720809
Holes 18 L 5462 yds SSS 67
Recs Am–64 K Johnston (1993)
V'tors U SOC
Fees £16 (£20)
Loc 14 miles N of Alnwick. 9 miles
E of A1 on B1340

Slaley Hall G&CC
(1988)

Slaley, Hexham NE47 0BY
Tel **(01434) 673350**
Fax (01434) 673152
Mem 350
Sec DG Burton
Pro M Stancer
(01434) 673154
Holes 18 L 7021 yds SSS 74
Recs Am–71 J Dryden (1994),
A McBride (1995)
Pro–65 R Drummond (1996)
V'tors WD–H SOC
Fees £40 D–£65
Loc 20 miles W of Newcastle. 7
miles S of Corbridge, off A68
Mis Driving range
Arch Dave Thomas

Stocksfield (1913)

New Ridley, Stocksfield NE43 7RE
Tel **(01661) 843041**
Mem 410 100(L) 70(J)
Sec B Slade
Pro S McKenna
Holes 18 L 5978 yds SSS 70
Recs Am–66 I Rourke, S Oliver
Pro–63 S McKenna
V'tors U SOC–exc Wed & Sat
Fees £18 (£20)
Loc 2 miles S of Stocksfield.
3 miles E of A68
Arch F Pennink

Swarland Hall (1993)

*Coast View, Swarland, Morpeth
NE65 9JG*
Tel **(01670) 787940 (Clubhouse)**
Sec K Rutter (01670) 787010
Pro D Fletcher (01670) 787010
Holes 18 L 6628 yds SSS 72
V'tors U
Fees £14 (£18)
Loc 8 miles S of Alnwick, 1 mile
W of A1

Tynedale (1908)

Public
Tyne Green, Hexham
Tel **(01434) 608154**
Sec J McDiarmid
Pro Mrs C Brown
Holes 9 L 5706 yds SSS 68
Recs Am–63
V'tors U exc Sun–booking necessary
Fees £10 (£12) (1993)
Loc S side of Hexham

Warkworth (1891)

*The Links, Warkworth, Morpeth
NE65 0SW*
Tel **(01665) 711596**
Mem 400
Sec JA Gray (01665) 711556
Holes 9 L 5870 yds SSS 68
Recs Am–65 C Shell
V'tors U exc Tues & Sat SOC
Fees D–£12 (D–£20)
Loc 9 miles SE of Alnwick (A1068)
Arch Tom Morris

Wooler (1975)

*Dod Law, Doddington, Wooler
NE71 6EA*
Mem 250
Sec WH Henderson (01668)
281137
Pro None
Holes 9 L 6372 yds SSS 70
Recs Am–72 K Fairbairn, C Renton,
M Thompson (1992),
S Lowrey (1996)
V'tors U SOC
Fees D–£10 (D–£15)
Loc 3 miles N of Wooler on B6525

Nottinghamshire

Beeston Fields (1923)

Beeston, Nottingham NG9 3DD
Tel **(0115) 925 7062**
Fax (0115) 925 4280
Mem 525 222(L) 60(J)
Sec J Lewis
Pro A Wardle (0115) 922 0872
Holes 18 L 6404 yds SSS 71
Recs Am–66 P Benson (1984)
Pro–65 G Owen (1995)
V'tors U SOC
Fees £20 (£25)
Loc 4 miles W of Nottingham.
M1 Junction 25
Arch Tom Williamson

Bulwell Forest (1902)

Public
*Hucknall Road, Bulwell, Nottingham
NG6 9LQ*
Tel **(0115) 977 0576**
Fax (0115) 977 1229
Mem 400
Sec D Waddilove (Hon)
Pro L Rawlings (0115) 976 3172
Holes 18 L 5746 yds SSS 68
Recs Am–63 J Worthy
Pro–62 CD Hall
V'tors U
Fees £10
Loc 4 miles N of Nottingham.
M1 Junction 26, 3 miles

Chilwell Manor (1906)

*Meadow Lane, Chilwell, Nottingham
NG9 5AE*
Tel **(0115) 925 8958**
Fax (0115) 922 0575
Mem 700

Sec RA Westcott
Pro P Wilson (0115) 925 8993
Holes 18 L 6395 yds Par 70 SSS 70
Recs Am–67 C Gray
Pro–66 B Waites
V'tors U SOC
Fees £18 (£20)
Loc 4 miles W of Nottingham
on A6005

College Pines (1993)

*Worksop College Drive, Sparken Hill,
Worksop S80 3AP*
Tel **(01909) 501431**
Mem 550
Sec C Snell (Golf Dir)
Pro C Snell (01909) 501431
Holes 18 L 6663 yds SSS 72
Recs Am–71 W Beeston (1994)
Pro–69 B Hunt (1994)
V'tors U–phone first SOC
Fees £12 (£18)
Loc 1 mile SE of Worksop on
B6034, off Worksop Bypass
Mis Driving range
Arch David Snell

Cotgrave Place G&CC
(1991)

Stragglethorpe NG12 3HB
Tel **(0115) 933 3344/933 5500**
Mem 400
Sec CC Rathbone
Pro G Towne (0115) 933 4686
Holes 27 L 6560 yds SSS 71-72
V'tors U
Fees £14 (£17)
Loc 4 miles SE of Nottingham,
off A52
Mis Driving range
Arch Small/Glasgow

Coxmoor (1913)

*Coxmoor Road, Sutton-in-Ashfield
NG17 5LF*
Tel **(01623) 557359**
Fax (01623) 557359
Mem 650
Sec N Cockbill
Pro D Ridley (01623) 559906
Holes 18 L 6501 yds SSS 72
Recs Am–65 P Fenton
Pro–65 G Owen
V'tors H exc Ladies Day–Tues
WE–NA SOC
Fees D–£28
Loc 1½ miles S of Mansfield.
4 miles NE of M1 Junction 27
on A611

Edwalton (1982)

Public
Edwalton, Nottingham
Tel **(0115) 923 4775**
Sec Mrs DJ Parkes (Hon)
Pro J Staples
Holes 9 L 3336 yds SSS 36
9 hole Par 3 course
Recs Am–73
Pro–72
V'tors U
Fees On application

Loc 2 miles S of Nottingham
(A606)
Mis Driving range

Kilton Forest (1978)
Public
Blyth Road, Worksop S81 0TL
Tel **(01909) 472488**
Mem 364
Sec G Lawman (Hon)
(01909) 485994
Pro PW Foster (01909) 486563
Holes 18 L 6344 yds Par 72 SSS 71
Recs Am–68 B Hurt (1993)
Pro–71 B Hurt (1995)
V'tors WD–U WE–booking
necessary SOC
Fees £7.85 (£10.25)
Loc 1 mile NE of Worksop on
B6045

Leen Valley Golf Centre
(1994)
Pay and play
Wigwam Lane, Hucknall NG15 7TA
Tel **(0115) 964 2037**
Fax (0115) 964 2724
Sec BR Goodman (Gen Mgr)
Pro S Smith (01623) 422764
Holes 18 L 6233 yds Par 72 SSS 70
Recs Am–73 J Wright (1996)
V'tors U SOC–WD
Fees £8.50 (£9.50)
Loc ½ mile from Hucknall town
centre
Arch Tom Hodgetts

Mansfield Woodhouse
(1973)
Public
Mansfield Woodhouse NG19 9EU
Tel **(01623) 23521**
Sec M Stuart
Pro L Highfield Jr
Holes 9 L 2411 yds SSS 65
Recs Am–67 S Fisher
Pro–L Highfield Jr
V'tors U
Fees £3
Loc 2 miles N of Mansfield (A60)

Mapperley (1903)
*Central Avenue, Plains Road,
Mapperley, Nottingham NG3 5RH*
Tel **(0115) 955 6672**
Mem 650
Sec A Newton
Pro M Allen (0115) 955 6673
Holes 18 L 6283 yds SSS 70
Recs Am–68 P Benson (1991)
Pro–69 D Ridley (1990)
V'tors U SOC
Fees £12 D–£15
Loc 3 miles NE of Nottingham,
off B684

Newark (1901)
*Kelwick, Coddington, Newark
NG24 2QX*
Tel **(01636) 626241**
Fax (01636) 626497

Mem 600
Sec AW Morgans (01636) 626282
Pro PA Lockley (01636) 626492
Holes 18 L 6421 yds SSS 71
Recs Am–66 J Johnson
Pro–65 HA Bennett
Ladies–71 E Glasby
V'tors H SOC
Fees £22 (£27)
Loc 4 miles E of Newark on A17

Nottingham City (1910)
Public
*Lawton Drive, Bulwell, Nottingham
NG6 8BL*
Tel **(0115) 927 8021**
Fax (0115) 927 6916
Mem 460
Sec AS Otter (0115) 927 6916
Pro CR Jepson (0115) 927 2767
Holes 18 L 6218 yds SSS 70
Recs Am–65 D Weir (1994)
Pro–66 T Smart
V'tors WD–U WE–NA before noon
SOC
Fees £10 (£10)
Loc 5 miles N of Nottingham.
M1 Junction 26

Notts (1887)
*Hollinwell, Kirkby-in-Ashfield
NG17 7QR*
Tel **(01623) 752042/753225**
Fax (01623) 753655
Mem 500
Sec SFC Goldie (01623) 753225
Pro BJ Waites (01623) 753087
Holes 18 L 7030 yds Par 72 SSS 74
Recs Am–66 AR Gelsthorpe
Pro–64 J Bland
V'tors WD–H WE/BH–M
Fees On application
Loc 4 miles S of Mansfield on
A611. M1 Junction 27
Mis Driving range-green fees only
Arch Willie Park Jr

Oakmere Park (1974)
Oaks Lane, Oxton NG25 0RH
Tel **(0115) 965 3545**
Fax (0115) 965 5628
Mem 450
Sec J Wright (Dir)
Pro S Meade (0115) 965 3545
Holes 18 L 6617 yds SSS 72
9 L 3495 yds SSS 37
Recs Am–69 J Vaughan
Pro–65 J Mellor
V'tors WD–U WE/BH–arrange times
with Mgr SOC
Fees 18 hole–£16 (£20)
9 hole–£6 (£8)
Loc 8 miles NE of Nottingham on
A614
Mis Floodlit driving range
Arch F Pennink

Radcliffe-on-Trent (1909)
*Dewberry Lane, Cropwell Road,
Radcliffe-on-Trent NG12 2JH*
Tel **(0115) 933 3000**
Fax (0115) 911 6991

Mem 670
Sec L Wake
Pro R Ellis (0115) 933 2396
Holes 18 L 6381 yds Par 70 SSS 71
Recs Am–64 M Harris (1994)
Pro–66 I Ball (1995)
Ladies–73 M Harris (1983)
V'tors H SOC–Wed only
Fees £23 (£28)
Loc 6 miles E of Nottingham,
off A52
Arch Tom Williamson

Ramsdale Park Golf Centre (1992)
Pay and play
Oxton Road, Calverton NG14 6NU
Tel **(0115) 965 5600**
Fax (0115) 965 4105
Sec B Jenkinson (Mgr)
Pro R Macey
Holes 18 L 6546 yds SSS 71
18 hole Par 3 course
Recs Pro–69 G Orr (1993)
V'tors U SOC–WD
Fees £13.50
Loc 5 miles NE of Nottingham on
B6386
Mis Floodlit driving range
Arch Hawtree

Retford (1921)
Brecks Road, Ordsall, Retford DN22 7UA
Tel **(01777) 703733**
Mem 700
Sec A Harrison (01777) 860682
Pro S Betteridge
Holes 18 L 6370 yds SSS 70
Recs Am–67 PJ Grout (1993)
V'tors WD–U WE–M SOC–WD
Fees £19 D–£23
Loc 2 miles SW of Retford, off
A638 or A620. M1
Junction 30

Ruddington Grange
(1988)
*Wilford Road, Ruddington, Nottingham
NG11 6NB*
Tel **(0115) 984 6141**
Fax (0115) 940 5165
Mem 600
Sec J Smith (Mgr), AR Dessaur
Pro R Simpson (0115) 921 1951
Holes 18 L 6490 yds SSS 72
Recs Am–72 B Cifton (1995)
Pro–68 C Hall (1990)
V'tors U H BH–U exc comp days
SOC
Fees D–£15 (£22.50)
Loc 3 miles S of Nottingham

Rushcliffe (1910)
*Stocking Lane, East Leake,
Loughborough LE12 5RL*
Tel **(01509) 852959**
Mem 654
Sec DJ Barnes
Pro C Hall (01509) 852701
Holes 18 L 6090 yds SSS 69
V'tors SOC–WD

Fees D–£22
Loc 9 miles S of Nottingham. M1
Junction 24

Serlby Park (1905)
Serlby, Doncaster DN10 6BA
Tel (01777) 818268
Mem 250
Sec R Wilkinson (01302) 536336
Holes 9 L 5370 yds SSS 66
Recs Am–63 A Pugsley (1988)
Pro–65 M Bembridge (1965)
V'tors M
Loc 12 miles S of Doncaster,
between A614 and A638

Sherwood Forest (1895)
Eakring Road, Mansfield NG18 3EW
Tel (01623) 26689
Fax (01623) 26689
Mem 648
Sec K Hall
Pro K Hall (01623) 27403
Holes 18 L 6714 yds SSS 73
Recs Am–67 S Fisher
Pro–68 C Gray, G Stafford
V'tors H SOC–WD
Fees On application to Sec
Loc 2 miles E of Mansfield (A617)
Arch HS Colt/James Braid

Southwell (1993)
*Southwell Racecourse, Rolleston,
Newark NG25 0TS*
Tel (01636) 815294
Fax (01636) 812271
Mem 300
Sec C Lissaman
Pro S Meade (01636) 816501
Holes 18 L 5710 yds Par 71 SSS 68
V'tors U SOC
Fees £15
Loc 6 miles W of Newark on A617.
Course adjacent to racetrack
Arch RA Muddle

Springwater (1991)
Pay and play
*Moor Lane, Calverton, Nottingham
NG14 6FZ*
Tel (0115) 965 2129
Mem 300
Sec W Turner (0115) 965 2565
Pro P Wharmsby (0115) 965 2129
Holes 9 L 3203 yds Par 72 SSS 71
Recs Am–69 R Overton (1995)
V'tors U SOC
Fees £9 (£13)
Loc Off A6097 between Lowdham
and Oxton
Mis Extension to 18 holes Spring
1998
Arch ADAS/McEvoy

Stanton-on-the-Wolds (1906)
Stanton Lane, Keyworth NG12 5BH
Tel (0115) 937 2044
Mem 500 167(L) 100(J)
Sec HG Gray FCA
(0115) 937 2006

Pro N Hernon ((0115) 937 2390
Holes 18 L 6437 yds SSS 71
Recs Am–67 CA Banks, PJ Whitt
Pro–68 N Turley
V'tors WD–U exc comp days WE–M
SOC
Fees D–£20 SOC–£25–£30
Loc 9 miles S of Nottingham

Trent Lock Golf Centre (1991)
*Lock Lane, Sawley, Long Eaton
NG10 3DD*
Tel (0115) 946 4398
Fax (0115) 946 1183
Mem 550
Sec R Bluck
Pro M Taylor
Holes 18 hole course Par 72 SSS 70
V'tors U SOC
Fees £11
Loc S of Long Eaton. M1
Junction 25
Mis Driving range
Arch E McCausland

Wollaton Park (1927)
Wollaton Park, Nottingham NG8 1BT
Tel (0115) 978 7574
Fax (0115) 978 7574
Mem 700
Sec MT Harvey
Pro J Lower (0115) 978 4834
Holes 18 L 6445 yds SSS 71
Recs Am–65 L White
Pro–64 L White
V'tors U SOC
Fees On application
Loc 2 miles SW of Nottingham
Arch T Williamson

Worksop (1914)
Windmill Lane, Worksop S80 2SQ
Tel (01909) 472696
Mem 500
Sec PG Jordan (01909) 477731
Pro JR King (01909) 477732
Holes 18 L 6651 yds SSS 72
Recs Am–70 D Bagshaw
Pro–69 A Carter
V'tors WD–U H (phone first)
WE/BH–M SOC
Fees On application
Loc 1 mile SE of Worksop, off
A6009 via by-pass (A57). M1
Junction 30, 9 miles

Oxfordshire

Aspect Park (1988)
*Remenham Hill, Henley-on-Thames
RG9 3EH*
Tel (01491) 578306
Fax (01491) 578306
Mem 600
Sec T Winsland
Pro T Notley (01491) 577562
Holes 18 L 6559 yds Par 72 SSS 71
V'tors WD–U WE–restricted before
noon SOC

Fees £20 (£25)
Loc 1 mile E of Henley. M40
Junction 4, 8 miles
Mis Driving range. Pitch & putt
Arch T Winsland

Badgemore Park (1972)
Henley-on-Thames RG9 4NR
Tel (01491) 573667 (Clubhouse)
Fax (01491) 576899
Mem 600
Sec J Connell (Mgr) (01491)
572206
Pro J Dunn (01491) 574175
Holes 18 L 6112 yds SSS 69
Recs Am–67 SJ Mann
Pro–65 M Howell
V'tors WD–U WE–pm only
SOC–WD
Fees £15 (£25)
Loc ¾ mile W of Henley on B290

Banbury (1994)
*Aynho Road, Adderbury, Banbury
OX17 3NT*
Tel (01295) 810419
Fax (01295) 810056
Mem 100
Sec MA Reed (Prop), Sarah Jarrett
Holes 18 L 6365 yds Par 71 SSS 70
Recs Am–74 K Moggridge (1996)
Pro–72 G Wills (1994)
V'tors U SOC
Fees £8 (£10)
Loc 6 miles S of Banbury on
B4100. M40 Junction 10
or 11
Mis Undergoing reconstruction in
1998
Arch Reed/Payn

Brailes (1992)
*Sutton Lane, Lower Brailes, Banbury
OX15 5BB*
Tel (01608) 685336
Mem 430
Sec RAS Malir
Pro M Bendall (01608) 685633
Holes 18 L 6270 yds Par 71 SSS 70
Recs Am–72 I Mold (1996)
V'tors U SOC–WD
Fees £16 (£22)
Loc 3 miles E of Shipston-on-
Stour on B4035. M40
Junction 11, 10 miles
Arch BA Hull

Burford (1936)
Burford OX18 4JG
Tel (01993) 822149
Mem 680
Sec R Cane (01993) 822583
Pro N Allen (01993) 822344
Holes 18 L 6405 yds SSS 71
Recs Am–67 DE Giles
Pro–67 H Weetman
V'tors WD–H SOC
Fees On application
Loc 19 miles W of Oxford on A40

Carswell CC (1993)

Carswell, Faringdon SN7 8PU

Tel (01367) 870422
Mem 300
Sec G Lisi (Prop)
Pro G Robbins
Holes 18 L 6133 yds Par 72
Recs Am–73 I Lewis (1994)
Pro–68 S Defoy (1993),
J Nicholas, M Booth (1994)
V'tors U SOC
Fees £12 (£15)
Loc 12 miles W of Oxford on
A420
Mis Floodlit driving range

Cherwell Edge (1980)

Chacombe, Banbury OX17 2EN

Tel (01295) 711591
Fax (01295) 712404
Mem 566
Sec RA Beare
Pro J Kingston
Holes 18 L 5947 yds SSS 68
Recs Am–67 K Cole (1995)
Pro–64 M Booth (1995)
Ladies–76 J Lane (1990)
V'tors U SOC–WD
Fees £10 (£13.50)
Loc 3 miles E of Banbury on B4525
Mis Driving range

Chesterton (1973)

Chesterton, Bicester OX6 8TE

Tel (01869) 241204
Mem 550
Sec BT Carter
Pro JW Wilkshire (01869) 242023
Holes 18 L 6224 yds SSS 70
Recs Am–68 D Grant (1994)
Pro–68 B Lane (1983)
V'tors U SOC–WD
Fees £12 (£18)
Loc 2 miles SW of Bicester.
M40 Junction 9

Chipping Norton (1890)

*Southcombe, Chipping Norton
OX7 5QH*

Tel (01608) 642383
Fax (01608) 645422
Mem 900
Sec AJB Norman
Pro D Craik Jr (01608) 643356
Holes 18 L 6280 yds SSS 70
Recs Am–67 A Perrie, J Morewood,
A Jones
Pro–62 T Ashton (1996)
V'tors WD–U WE–M
Fees £20
Loc 1 mile E of Chipping Norton
on A44

Drayton Park (1992)

Pay and play
*Steventon Road, Drayton, Abingdon
OX14 2RR*

Tel (01235) 550607/528989
Fax (01235) 525731
Mem 600

Sec (01235) 528989
Pro Dinah Masey (01235) 550607
Holes 18 L 6000 yds SSS 67
9 hole Par 3 course
Recs Am–65 O Cooper (1996)
V'tors U SOC
Fees £12 (£15)
Loc 5 miles S of Oxford on A34.
M4 Junction 13
Mis Floodlit driving range
Arch Hawtree

Frilford Heath (1908)

Frilford Heath, Abingdon OX13 5NW

Tel (01865) 390864
Fax (01865) 390823
Mem 1200 210(L)
Sec JW Kleynhans
Pro DC Craik (01865) 390887
Holes Red 18 L 6768 yds SSS 73
Green 18 L 6006 yds SSS 69
Blue 18 L 6726 yds SSS 73
Recs Red Am–69 J Gallagher (1997)
Green Am–63 K Johnson
(1997)
Blue Am–67 G Storm,
G Wolstenholme (1996)
V'tors WD–I H WE/BH–M SOC
Fees £45 (£60)
Loc 3 miles W of Abingdon
A338
Arch Blue-Simon Gidman

Hadden Hill (1990)

Pay and play
Wallingford Road, Didcot OX11 9BJ

Tel (01235) 510410
Fax (01235) 510410
Mem 420 62(L)
Sec MV Morley
Pro D Halford, A Waters
Holes 18 L 6563 yds SSS 71
Recs Am–65 N Hammond (1995)
V'tors WD–U SOC–WD
Fees £12 (£15)
Loc E of Didcot on A4130
Mis Floodlit driving range
Arch MV Morley

Henley (1908)

*Harpsden, Henley-on-Thames
RG9 4HG*

Tel (01491) 575781
Fax (01491) 412179
Mem 750
Sec AM Chaundy
(01491) 575742
Pro M Howell (01491) 575710
Holes 18 L 6329 yds SSS 70
Recs Am–65 D Griffin (1989)
Pro–63 R Lee (1996)
V'tors WD–H WE–M SOC
Fees D–£30
Loc 1 mile S of Henley (A4155)
Arch James Braid

Huntercombe (1901)

Nuffield, Henley-on-Thames RG9 5SL

Tel (01491) 641207
Fax (01491) 642060
Mem 700

Sec Lt Col TJ Hutchison
Pro JB Draycott
(01491) 641241
Holes 18 L 6261 yds SSS 70
Recs Am–64 MH Dixon
Pro–63 J Morris
V'tors H–by appointment only
SOC–WD
Fees D–£38
Loc 6 miles W of Henley on
A4130
Mis Foursomes and singles only
Arch Willie Park Jr

Kirtlington (1995)

Kirtlington OX5 3JY

Tel (01869) 351133
Fax (01869) 331143
Mem 230
Sec K MacNiven (Sec/Mgr)
Pro P Hughes (01869) 351133
Holes 18 holes Par 70 SSS 69
Recs Am–69 A Dowzanskyj,
B Moggridge (1997)
V'tors U SOC
Fees £15 (£20)
Loc 1 mile from Kirtlington on
A4095. M40 Junction 9
Arch G Webster

Lyneham (1992)

*Lyneham, Chipping Norton
OX7 6QQ*

Tel (01993) 831841
Fax (01993) 831775
Mem 700
Sec CJT Howkins
Pro R Jefferies
Holes 18 L 6669 yds SSS 72
Recs Am–67 D Yates (1996)
Pro–66 P Saunders (1996)
V'tors U SOC
Fees £13 (£16)
Loc 4 miles W of Chipping
Norton, off A361
Mis Driving range
Arch D Carpenter

North Oxford (1907)

Banbury Road, Oxford OX2 8EZ

Tel (01865) 554415
Fax (01865) 515921
Mem 701
Sec GW Pullin
(01865) 554924
Pro R Harris (01865) 553977
Holes 18 L 5805 yds SSS 67
Recs Am–64 S Donaghey
Pro–62 F George
V'tors WD–U WE–M SOC–WD exc
Thurs
Fees On application
Loc 4 miles N of Oxford, off
A4260 to Kidlington

The Oxfordshire (1993)

*Rycote Lane, Milton Common, Thame
OX9 2PU*

Tel (01844) 278300
Fax (01844) 278003
Mem 650

Sec   M Kayanuma (Gen Mgr)
Pro   I Mosey
Holes 18 L 7187 yds SSS 76
Recs   Am–68 A Wall (1995)
       Pro–65 E Romero (1997)
       Ladies Am–73 E Fields
       (1995), J Oliver (1996)
       Ladies Pro–64 M-L de Lorenzi
       (1996)
V'tors M
Fees   On application
Loc   1½ miles W of Thame on
       A329. M40 Junction 7,
       2 miles
Mis   Driving range
Arch   Rees Jones

RAF Benson (1975)

Royal Air Force, Benson
Tel   (01491) 837766
Mem   200
Sec   Sgt P Hersey RAF
       (01491) 838091
Holes 9 L 4395 yds Par 63 SSS 61
Recs   Am–63 R Mills (1991)
V'tors M
Loc   3½ miles NE of Wallingford

Rye Hill

Milcombe, Banbury OX15 4RU
Tel   (01295) 721818
Fax   (01295) 720911
Pro   L Bond
Holes 18 L 6569 yds Par 71
V'tors WD–U WE–booking
       necessary
Fees   £12 (£15)
Loc   5 miles SW of Banbury, off
       A361. M40 Junction 11
Mis   Academy holes

Southfield (1875)

Hill Top Road, Oxford OX4 1PF
Tel   (01865) 242158
Fax   (01865) 242158
Mem   700
Sec   TJ Sullivan
Pro   A Rees (01865) 244258
Holes 18 L 6230 yds SSS 70
Recs   Am–66 CM Barrett,
       GL Morley
       Pro–61 A Rees
V'tors WD–U WE/BH–M H SOC
Fees   £24
Loc   2 miles E of Oxford
Arch   HS Colt

The Springs (1998)

*Wallingford Road, North Stoke,
Wallingford OX10 6BE*
Tel   (01491) 836687
Fax   (01491) 836877
Mem   550
Sec   M Herbert
Pro   M Herbert
Holes 18 L 6440 yds Par 72
V'tors By arrangement SOC–WD
Fees   £22 (£30)
Loc   2 miles SW of Wallingford on
       B4009. M40 Junction 6
Arch   Brian Huggett

Studley Wood (1996)

*The Straight Mile, Horton-cum-Studley,
Oxford OX33 1BF*
Tel   (01865) 351144
Fax   (01865) 351166
Mem   750
Sec   P Fox
Pro   T Williams (01865) 351122
Holes 18 L 6711 yds Par 73 SSS 73
Recs   Am–70 J Carlsen (1997)
       Pro–65 L Stanford (1997)
       Ladies–73 L King (1996)
V'tors U SOC
Fees   £21 (£30)
Loc   4 miles NE of Oxford. M40
       Junction 8
Mis   Driving range. Golf academy
Arch   Simon Gidman

Tadmarton Heath (1922)

Wigginton, Banbury OX15 5HL
Tel   (01608) 737278
Fax   (01608) 730548
Mem   600
Sec   RE Wackrill
Pro   T Jones (01608) 730047
Holes 18 L 5917 yds SSS 69
Recs   Am–64 I Manning
       Pro–63 G Smith
V'tors WD–H by appointment
       WE–M SOC–WD
Fees   £26 After 2pm–£18
Loc   5 miles SW of Banbury, off
       B4035
Arch   Maj CJ Hutchison

Waterstock (1994)

Pay and play
*Thame Road, Waterstock, Oxford
OX33 1HT*
Tel   (01844) 338093
Fax   (01844) 338036
Mem   500
Sec   AJ Wyatt
Pro   A Wyatt
Holes 18 L 6535 yds Par 73
Recs   Am–68 D Watson
V'tors U SOC
Fees   £12 (£16)
Loc   E of Oxford on A418. M40
       Junction 8
Mis   Floodlit driving range
Arch   Donald Steel

Witney Lakes (1994)

Pay and play
Downs Road, Witney OX8 5SY
Tel   (01993) 779000
Fax   (01993) 778866
Mem   450
Sec   Miss S John (Mgr)
Pro   JP Hunt
Holes 18 L 6460 yds SSS 71
Recs   Am–71 G Corkish (1995)
       Pro–72 S Richardson (1994)
V'tors U
Fees   £13 (£18)
Loc   2 miles W of Witney on
       B4047
Mis   Floodlit driving range
Arch   Simon Gidman

Shropshire

Arscott (1992)

*Arscott, Pontesbury, Shrewsbury
SY5 0XP*
Tel   (01743) 860114
Mem   550
Sec   B Harper (01743) 262342
Pro   G Sawyer (01743) 860881
Holes 18 L 6112 yds SSS 69
Recs   Am–72 R Edwards (1993)
V'tors WD–U WE/BH–M before
       noon SOC
Fees   £15.50 (£20.50)
Loc   5 miles SW of Shrewsbury,
       off A488
Arch   Martin Hamer

Bridgnorth (1889)

Stanley Lane, Bridgnorth WV16 4SF
Tel   (01746) 763315
Mem   690
Sec   KD Cole (01746) 764179
Pro   P Hinton (01746) 762045
Holes 18 L 6638 yds SSS 72
Recs   Am–67 C Banks (1985)
       Pro–66 P Hinton (1989)
V'tors H SOC
Fees   £20 (£30)
Loc   1 mile N of Bridgnorth

Chesterton Valley

Chesterton, Worfield, Bridgnorth
Tel   (01476) 783682
Mem   250
Sec   P Hinton
Pro   P Hinton
Holes 9 L 3392 yds Par 74 SSS 72
V'tors U–phone first
Fees   £6 (£6)
Loc   10 miles W of Wolverhampton
       on B4176

Church Stretton (1898)

Trevor Hill, Church Stretton SY6 6JH
Tel   (01694) 722281
Mem   470
Sec   R Broughton
       (01694) 722633
Pro   P Seal (01743) 873751
Holes 18 L 5020 yds SSS 65
Recs   Am–62 NJ Evans (1993)
V'tors H WE–NA before 10.30am
       SOC
Fees   £12 (£18)
Loc   ½ mile W of Church Stretton,
       off A49
Arch   James Braid

Cleobury Mortimer

(1993)
*Wyre Common, Cleobury Mortimer
DY14 8HQ*
Tel   (01299) 271112 (Clubhouse)
Fax   (01299) 271468
Mem   600
Sec   G Pain
Pro   G Farr
Holes 18 L 6363 yds Par 71 SSS 70

Recs Am–67 A Sykes (1997)
        Pro–70 T Stevens (1997)
V'tors WD–U H WE–M H SOC
Fees £16.50 (£19.50)
Loc   10 miles SW of Kidderminster
        on A4117
Mis   Driving range

Hawkstone Park (1920)

*Weston-under-Redcastle, Shrewsbury
SY4 5UY*

Tel   (01939) 200611
Fax   (01939) 200311
Mem   700
Sec   KL Brazier
Pro   P Wesselingh
Holes Hawkstone 18 L 6491 yds
        SSS 72; Windmill 18 L 6764
        yds SSS 72
        Academy 6 holes Par 3 course
Recs Am–65 M Welch
        Pro–65 A Jacklin, AWB Lyle
        Ladies–71 S Parker
V'tors U
Fees £28 D–£42 (£36 D–£50)
Loc   10 miles S of Whitchurch. 14
        miles N of Shrewsbury on A49
Mis   Driving range
Arch Braid/Huggett

Hill Valley G&CC (1975)

Terrick Road, Whitchurch SY13 4JZ

Tel   (01948) 663584
Fax   (01948) 665927
Mem   600
Sec   RB Walker
Pro   AR Minshall (01948) 663032
Holes Main 18 L 6517 yds SSS 71
        No 2 18 L 5285 yds SSS 66
Recs Am–67 M Welch
        Pro–64 M Welch, W Milne
V'tors U
Fees Main–£19 (£25) No 2–£6 (£9)
Loc   1 mile N of Whitchurch, off
        A41/A49 Bypass
Arch Alliss/Thomas

Lilleshall Hall (1937)

*Abbey Road, Lilleshall, Newport
TF10 9AS*

Tel   (01952) 603840/604776
Fax   (01952) 604776
Mem   600
Sec   FR Price (01952) 604776
Pro   NW Bramall (01952) 604104
Holes 18 L 5789 yds SSS 68
Recs Am–65 P Baker
        Pro–70 J Anderson
        Ladies–71 L Archer
V'tors WD–U WE–M SOC
Fees £20 (BH–£30)
Loc   3 miles S of Newport between
        Lilleshall and Sheriffhales.
        M54 Junction 4
Arch HS Colt

Llanymynech (1933)

Pant, Oswestry SY10 8LB

Tel   (01691) 830542
Mem   760
Sec   DR Thomas (01691) 830983

Pro   A Griffiths (01691) 830879
Holes 18 L 6114 yds Par 70 SSS 69
Recs Am–66 M Evans (1984)
        Pro–65 I Woosnam (1983)
V'tors U before 4.30pm –M after
        4.30pm SOC–WD
Fees £15 (£20)
Loc   5 miles S of Oswestry on A483

Ludlow (1889)

Bromfield, Ludlow SY8 2BT

Tel   (01584) 856285
Mem   550
Sec   CR Vane Percy
Pro   R Price (01584) 856366
Holes 18 L 6277 yds SSS 70
Recs Am–69 R Rodgers (1996)
        Pro–66 G Farr (1996)
V'tors H SOC–WD
Fees D–£18 (D–£24)
Loc   2 miles N of Ludlow (A49)

Market Drayton (1925)

Sutton, Market Drayton TF9 1LX

Tel   (01630) 652266
Fax   (01630) 652266
Mem   500
Sec   EG Davies
Pro   R Clewes
Holes 18 L 6290 yds SSS 71
Recs Am–70 S Thomas (1991)
V'tors WD–U WE–NA
Fees £20
Loc   1 mile S of Market Drayton

Meole Brace (1976)

Public

Meole Brace, Shrewsbury SY2 6QQ

Tel   (01743) 364050
Fax   (01743) 364050
Pro   I Doran
Holes 9 L 2915 yds SSS 68
Recs Am–68 J Mansell
        Pro–68 R Cockcroft
V'tors WD–U WE–book in advance
Fees On application
Loc   1 mile S of Shrewsbury.
        Junction A5/A49

Mile End (1992)

Mile End, Oswestry SY11 4JE

Tel   (01691) 670580
Fax   (01691) 670580
Sec   R Thompson
Pro   S Carpenter
        (01691) 671246
Holes 18 L 6194 yds SSS 69
Recs Am–70 S Kerr (1996)
V'tors SOC–WD
Fees £10 D–£14 (£14 D–£18)
Loc   1 mile from Oswestry, off A5
Mis   Driving range
Arch Price/Gough

Oswestry (1930)

Aston Park, Oswestry SY11 4JJ

Tel   (01691) 610221
Fax   (01691) 610535
Mem   880
Sec   A Jennings (01691) 610535

Pro   D Skelton (01691) 610448
Holes 18 L 6038 yds SSS 69
Recs Am–62 AL Strange (1978)
        Pro–62 DJ Probert (1996)
V'tors M or H SOC–WD
Fees £20 (£28)
Loc   3 miles SE of Oswestry on A5
Arch James Braid

Severn Meadows (1990)

Pay and play

Highley, Bridgnorth WV16 6HZ

Tel   (01746) 862212
Mem   190
Sec   C Harrison
Pro   None
Holes 9 L 5258 yds Par 68 SSS 67
V'tors WD–U WE–booking required
Fees £10 (£12)
Loc   8 miles S of Bridgnorth on
        B4555

Shifnal (1929)

Decker Hill, Shifnal TF11 8QL

Tel   (01952) 460467/460330
Fax   (01952) 460330
Mem   500
Sec   PW Holden (01952) 460330
Pro   J Flanaghan (01952) 460457
Holes 18 L 6422 yds SSS 71
Recs Am–65 C Watts
        Pro–64 P Baker
V'tors WD–phone first WE/BH–M
Fees On application
Loc   1 mile NE of Shifnal. M54
        Junction 4, 2 miles

Shrewsbury (1891)

Condover, Shrewsbury SY5 7BL

Tel   (01743) 872976
Fax   (01743) 874647
Mem   529 184(L) 70(J)
Sec   Mrs SM Kenny (01743)
        872977
Pro   P Seal (01743) 873751
Holes 18 L 6178 yds Par 70 SSS 69
Recs Am–60 JR Burn
V'tors H SOC
Fees £18 (£23)
Loc   4 miles S of Shrewsbury

The Shropshire (1992)

Pay and play

*Muxton Grange, Muxton, Telford
TF2 8PQ*

Tel   (01952) 677866
Fax   (01952) 677844
Mem   500
Sec   S Mackintosh
Pro   D Thorp
Holes 27 holes:
        9 L 3286 yds; 9 L 3303 yds;
        9 L 3334 yds SSS 70-72
Recs Am–70 R Wheeler (1996)
V'tors U SOC
Fees £12 (£18)
Loc   4 miles NW of Telford
        (B5060). M54 Junction 4
Mis   Floodlit driving range. Pitch &
        putt course
Arch Martin Hawtree

Telford G & C Moat House (1976)

*Great Hay, Sutton Heights, Telford
TF7 4DT*

Tel	**(01952) 429977**
Fax	(01952) 586602
Mem	500
Sec	I Lucas (Ext 286)
Pro	I Doran (01952) 586052
Holes	18 L 6761 yds SSS 72
	9 hole Par 3 course
Recs	Am–66 C Bufton (1986)
	Pro–62 D Thorpe (1983)
V'tors	H SOC
Fees	£25 (£30)
Loc	4 miles SE of Telford, off A442
Mis	Driving range
Arch	John Harris

Worfield (1991)

Worfield, Bridgnorth WV15 5HE

Tel	**(01746) 716541**
Fax	(01746) 716302
Mem	450
Sec	W Weaver (Gen Mgr)
	(01746) 716372
Pro	S Russell (01746) 716541
Holes	18 L 6801 yds SSS 73
Recs	Am–69 N Doody (1997)
	Pro–69 D Probert (1995)
V'tors	U SOC
Fees	£15 (£20)
Loc	7 miles W of Wolverhampton
	on A454
Arch	Gough/Williams

Wrekin (1905)

Wellington, Telford TF6 5BX

Tel	**(01952) 244032**
Fax	(01952) 252906
Mem	400 100(L) 90(J)
Sec	AK McCririck
Pro	K Housden (01952) 223101
Holes	18 L 5657 yds SSS 67
Recs	Am–64 S Price, AJ Ford
	(1993), A Stephenson (1994)
	Pro–67 C Holmes
V'tors	WD–U before 5pm –M after
	5pm SOC
Fees	£18 (£25)
Loc	Wellington, off B5061

Somerset

Bath (1880)

*Sham Castle, North Road, Bath
BA2 6JG*

Tel	**(01225) 425182**
Fax	(01225) 331027
Mem	730
Sec	PE Ware (01225) 463834
Pro	P Hancox (01225) 466953
Holes	18 L 6438 yds SSS 71
Recs	Am–69 R McCue (1995)
	Pro–66 M McEwan (1997)
V'tors	H SOC
Fees	£25 (£30)
Loc	1½ miles SE of Bath, off A36
Arch	HS Colt

Brean (1973)

*Coast Road, Brean, Burnham-on-Sea
TA8 2RT*

Tel	**(01278) 751595**
Fax	(01278) 751595
Mem	400
Sec	WS Martin (Hon)
Pro	S Spencer (01278) 751570
Holes	18 L 5565 yds SSS 67
Recs	Am–69 B Reeves (1963)
V'tors	WD–U H WE–pm only
	SOC–WD
Fees	On application
Loc	4 miles N of Burnham-on-Sea.
	M5 Junction 22, 6 miles

Burnham & Berrow (1890)

*St Christopher's Way, Burnham-on-Sea
TA8 2PE*

Tel	**(01278) 783137**
Fax	(01278) 795440
Mem	800
Sec	Mrs EL Sloman
	785760
Pro	M Crowther-Smith
	(01278) 784545
Holes	18 L 6606 yds SSS 73
	9 L 6332 yds SSS 72
Recs	Medal Am–66 SJ Martin
	C'ship Am–66 DG Haines
	(1993)
V'tors	I SOC
Fees	18 hole: £36 (£50);
	9 hole: £10
Loc	1 mile N of Burnham-on-Sea
	on B3140
Mis	Dormy House

Cannington (1993)

Pay and play

*Cannington College, Bridgwater
TA5 2LS*

Tel	**(01278) 655050**
Fax	(01278) 652479
Mem	200
Sec	R Macrow (Mgr)
Pro	R Macrow
Holes	9 L 2929 yds SSS 68
V'tors	U exc Wed eve–restricted
Fees	18 holes–£10 (£12);
	9 holes–£6.50 (£7.50)
Loc	4 miles NW of Bridgwater on
	A39. M5 Junction 24
Arch	Hawtree

Clevedon

Castle Road, Clevedon BS21 7AA

Tel	**(01275) 873140**
Fax	(01275) 341228
Mem	800
Sec	M Heggie (Mgr)
	(01275) 874057
Pro	M Heggie (01275) 874704
Holes	18 L 6042 yds SSS 69
Recs	Am–65 N Barker (1995),
	JE Morgan (1997)
	Pro–64 M Plummer (1995)
V'tors	WD–U H exc Wed am
	WE/BH–U H (phone first)
	SOC
Fees	£20 D–£25 (£30)

Loc	Off Holly Lane, Walton,
	Clevedon. M5 Junction 20
Arch	JH Taylor

Enmore Park (1906)

Enmore, Bridgwater TA5 2AN

Tel	**(01278) 671244 (Members)**
Fax	(01278) 671481
Mem	780
Sec	D Weston (01278) 671481
Pro	N Wixon (01278) 671519
Holes	18 L 6406 yds SSS 71
Recs	Am–66 T Lawrence (1990),
	D Dixon Jr (1994)
	Pro–64 R Davis (1994)
	Ladies–70 K Nicholls (1989),
	L Wixon (1994)
V'tors	U SOC–WD
Fees	£18 (£25)
Loc	3 miles W of Bridgwater,
	off Durleigh road.
	M5 Junctions 23/24
Arch	Hawtree

Entry Hill (1985)

Public

Entry Hill, Bath BA2 5NA

Tel	**(01225) 834248**
Sec	J Sercombe
Pro	T Tapley
Holes	9 L 4206 yds SSS 61
Recs	Am–63 I Hulley (1992),
	A Peates (1996)
V'tors	WD/WE–booking only
Fees	18 holes–£7.85 (£8.95)
	9 holes–£4.95 (£5.60)
Loc	1 mile S of Bath, off A367

Farrington (1992)

*Marsh Lane, Farrington Gurney, Bristol
BS39 6TS*

Tel	**(01761) 241274 (Clubhouse),**
	(01761) 453440
Fax	(01761) 241274
Mem	700
Sec	Mrs PM Thompson
Pro	P Thompson (01761) 241787
Holes	18 L 6693 yds Par 72 SSS 72
	9 L 3022 yds Par 54 SSS 53
Recs	Am–73 S Ponfield (1997)
	Pro–68 S Little (1997)
V'tors	U SOC–WD
Fees	18 hole–£20 (£30)
	9 hole–£8 (£10)
Loc	12 miles S of Bristol (A37)
	10 miles S of Bath (A39)
Mis	Floodlit driving range
Arch	Peter Thompson

Fosseway CC (1970)

*Charlton Lane, Midsomer Norton, Bath
BA3 4BD*

Tel	**(01761) 412214**
Fax	(01761) 418357
Mem	438
Sec	RF Jones (Mgr)
Holes	9 L 4608 yds SSS 65
Recs	Am–55 M Chedgy (1985)
V'tors	WD–U exc Wed–M after 5pm
	WE–NA before 1.30pm
Fees	£9 (£11)
Loc	10 miles SW of Bath on A367

Frome Golf Centre

Pay and play
Critchill Manor, Frome BA11 4LJ
Tel   (01373) 453410
Fax   (01373) 453410
Mem   300
Sec   Mrs S Austin
Pro   A Wright
Holes 18 hole course Par 66 SSS 64
Recs   Pro–53 A Wright
V'tors U
Fees   £10 D–£14 (£12 D–£16)
Loc   12 miles S of Bath
Mis   Driving range

Isle of Wedmore (1992)

*Lineage, Lascots Hill, Wedmore
BS28 4QT*
Tel   (01934) 712452
Fax   (01934) 713696
Mem   560
Sec   AC Edwards (01934) 713649
Pro   G Coombe (01934) 712452
Holes 18 L 6006 yds Par 70 SSS 69
Recs   Am–70 J Body (1994)
V'tors U SOC–WD
Fees   £12.50 (£18.50)
Loc   ³⁄₄ mile N of Wedmore.
         M5 Junction 22
Arch   Terry Murray

Kingweston (1983)

*(Sec) Mead Run, Compton Street,
Compton Dundon, Somerton TA11 6PP*
Tel   (01458) 43921
Mem   200
Sec   JG Willetts
Holes 9 L 4516 yds SSS 62
V'tors M exc Wed & Sat 2–5pm–NA
Fees   NA
Loc   1 mile SE of Butleigh. 2 miles
         SE of Glastonbury

Lansdown (1894)

Lansdown, Bath BA1 9BT
Tel   (01225) 422138
Fax   (01225) 339252
Mem   750
Sec   Mrs E Bacon
Pro   T Mercer (01225) 420242
Holes 18 L 6316 yds SSS 70
Recs   Am–66 VL Phillips (1992)
         Pro–64 D Ray (1995)
V'tors H SOC
Fees   £18 (£18)
Loc   2 miles NW of Bath, by
         racecourse. M4 Junction 18,
         6 miles
Arch   HS Colt

Long Sutton (1991)

Pay and play
Long Load, Langport TA10 9JU
Tel   (01458) 241017
Mem   500
Sec   GC Bennett
Pro   M Blackwell
Holes 18 L 6367 yds SSS 71
Recs   Am–70 B Parker
V'tors WD–U WE–booking required
         SOC

Fees   £14 (£17)
Loc   3 miles E of Langport
Mis   Driving range
Arch   Patrick Dawson

Mendip (1908)

Gurney Slade, Bath BA3 4UT
Tel   (01749) 840570
Fax   (01749) 841439
Mem   700
Sec   Mrs JP Howe
Pro   RF Lee (01749) 840793
Holes 18 L 6330 yds SSS 70
Recs   Am–65 M Stephens (1992)
         Pro–64 N Blenkarne (1987)
V'tors WD–U WE–H SOC–WD
Fees   £20 (£30)
Loc   3 miles N of Shepton Mallet
         (A37)
Arch   CK Cotton

Mendip Spring (1992)

Honeyhall Lane, Congresbury BS49 5JT
Tel   (01934) 853137/852322
Fax   (01934) 853021
Mem   400
Sec   I Harrison (Mgr)
Pro   J Blackburn
Holes 18 L 6334 yds SSS 70
         9 L 2392 yds SSS 68
Recs   Am–64 I Harrison
V'tors U
Fees   18 hole: £21 (£27)
         9 hole: £7 (£7.50)
Loc   Congresbury. M5 Junction 21.
Mis   Driving range
Arch   Langholt

Minehead & West Somerset (1882)

*The Warren, Warren Road, Minehead
TA24 5SJ*
Tel   (01643) 702057
Fax   (01643) 705095
Mem   604
Sec   LS Harper
Pro   I Read (01643) 704378
Holes 18 L 6228 yds SSS 71
Recs   Am–66 M Luckett
         Pro–66 BJ Hunt
V'tors U after 9.30am SOC
Fees   £22 (£25) W–£80
Loc   E end of sea front

Oake Manor (1993)

Oake, Taunton TA4 1BA
Tel   (01823) 461993
Fax   (01823) 461995
Mem   600
Sec   R Gardner (Golf Mgr)
Pro   R Gardner
Holes 18 L 6109 yds Par 70 SSS 69
Recs   Am–68 B Downs (1996)
         Pro–66 M Watson (1996)
V'tors U–phone first SOC
Fees   £15.50 (£18)
Loc   4 miles W of Taunton, off
         B3227. M5 Junctions 25/26
         onto A38
Mis   Driving range
Arch   Adrian Stiff

Orchardleigh (1996)

Frome BA11 2PH
Tel   (01373) 454200/454206
         (Bookings)
Fax   (01373) 454202
Mem   500
Sec   J Willder (Gen Mgr)
Pro   P Green
Holes 18 L 6810 yds Par 72 SSS 73
Recs   Am–71 P Chilvers (1996)
         Pro–67 N Mitchell (1996)
         Ladies–76 C Nicholson (1996)
V'tors WD/BH–U WE–U after 11am
         SOC
Fees   £20 D–£30 (£25 D–£35)
Loc   2 miles NW of Frome on
         A362. 12 miles S of Bath
Mis   Driving range
Arch   Brian Huggett

Puxton Park (1992)

Pay and play
Puxton, Weston-super-Mare BS24 6TA
Tel   (01934) 876942
Pro   C Ancsell
Holes 18 L 6600 yds Par 72
V'tors U SOC
Fees   £8 (£10)
Loc   A370, 2 miles E of M5
         Junction 21

Saltford (1904)

*Golf Club Lane, Saltford, Bristol
BS18 3AA*
Tel   (01225) 873220
Fax   (01225) 873525
Mem   650
Sec   V Radnedge (01225) 873513
Pro   D Millensted (01225) 872043
Holes 18 L 6081 yds SSS 69
Recs   Am–64 D Young
         Pro–63 S Little
V'tors U SOC–Mon & Thurs
Fees   £22 (£28)
Loc   7 miles SE of Bristol

Stockwood Vale (1991)

Public
*Stockwood Lane, Keynsham, Bristol
BS18 2ER*
Tel   (0117) 986 6505
Mem   500
Sec   M Edenborough
Pro   J Richards
Holes 18 L 6031 yds SSS 71
V'tors U SOC
Fees   £12 (£14)
Loc   1 mile SE of Bristol, off A4174
Mis   Driving range
Arch   Ramsay

Tall Pines (1991)

Public
*Cooks Bridle Path, Downside, Backwell,
Bristol BS19 3DS*
Tel   (01275) 472076
Fax   (01275) 474869
Sec   T Murray
Pro   A Murray
Holes 18 L 6100yds SSS 69
V'tors U SOC

Fees £12 (£14)
Loc 8 miles SW of Bristol
(A470/A38)
Arch Terry Murray

Taunton & Pickeridge

(1892)

Corfe, Taunton TA3 7BY
Tel **(01823) 421240**
Fax (01823) 421742
Mem 630
Sec GW Sayers (01823) 421537
Pro G Milne (01823) 421790
Holes 18 L 5927 yds SSS 68
Recs Am–63 SN Richards (1992)
Pro–61 M Plummer (1994)
V'tors H SOC
Fees On application
Loc 5 miles S of Taunton on B3170
Arch Hawtree

Taunton Vale (1991)

Creech Heathfield, Taunton TA3 5EY
Tel **(01823) 412220**
Fax (01823) 413583
Mem 670
Sec Mrs JA Thomas
Pro M Keitch (01823) 412880
Holes 18 L 6142 yds Par 70 SSS 69
9 L 2004 yds Par 64 SSS 60
Recs Am–68 M Luckett (1997)
Pro–66 J Palmer (1995)
V'tors U SOC
Fees 18 hole: £15 (£19)
9 hole: £7.50 (£9.50)
Loc 3 miles N of Taunton, off
A361. M5 Junctions 24/25
Mis Floodlit driving range
Arch John Pyne

Tickenham (1991)

*Clevedon Road, Tickenham, Bristol
BS21 6SB*
Tel **(01275) 856626**
Mem 150
Pro A Sutcliffe
Holes 9 L 2000 yds
V'tors U SOC
Fees 18 holes–£9 (£10)
Loc 2 miles E of M5 Junction 20
on B3130, nr Nailsea
Mis Floodlit driving range
Arch Andrew Sutcliffe

Vivary (1928)

Public
Vivary Park, Taunton TA1 3JW
Tel **(01823) 289274 (Clubhouse)**
Mem 500
Sec G Potter
Pro M Steadman (01823) 333875
Holes 18 L 4620 yds SSS 63
V'tors U SOC–WD
Fees £7.50
Loc Centre of Taunton
Arch Herbert Fowler

Wells (1893)

East Horrington Road, Wells BA5 3DS
Tel **(01749) 672868**
Fax (01749) 675005
Mem 750

Sec CD Alexander (Sec/Mgr)
(01749) 675005
Pro A Bishop (01749) 679059
Holes 18 L 6015 yds SSS 69
Recs Am–66 M Stevens (1993),
B Whittock (1995)
V'tors WD–U WE–H SOC–WD
Fees £18 (£22) Mon–Fri £60
Loc 1½ miles E of Wells, off
Radstock road
Mis Floodlit driving range

Weston-super-Mare

(1892)

*Uphill Road North, Weston-super-Mare
BS23 4NQ*
Tel **(01934) 626968**
Fax (01934) 626968
Mem 752
Sec J Keight (01934) 626968
Pro M La Band (01934) 633360
Holes 18 L 6251 yds SSS 70
Recs Am–64 B Porter, S Martin
Pro–66 G Ryall
V'tors H SOC
Fees £24 (£35) W–£75
Loc Weston-super-Mare
Arch T Dunn

Wheathill (1993)

Pay and play
Wheathill, Somerton TA11 7HG
Tel **(01963) 240667**
Fax (01963) 240230
Mem 200
Sec A Lyddon (Sec/Mgr)
Pro A England
Holes 18 L 5362 yds SSS 66
4 holes Par 3 course
Pro–63 J Goymer
V'tors U SOC
Fees £10 (£12)
Loc 3 miles W of Castle Cary
on B3153

Windwhistle G&CC

(1932)

Cricket St Thomas, Chard TA20 4DG
Tel **(01460) 30231**
Fax (01460) 30055
Mem 550
Sec IN Dodd
Pro D Driver
Holes 18 L 6470 yds SSS 71
Recs Am–69
V'tors U–phone first SOC
Fees On application
Loc Windwhistle, 3 miles E of
Chard on A30, opp Wildlife
Park. M5 Junction 25, 12 miles
Arch JH Taylor/L Fisher

Worlebury (1908)

*Monks Hill, Worlebury, Weston-super-
Mare BS22 9SX*
Tel **(01934) 623214**
Fax (01934) 625789
Mem 640
Sec MW Penny (01934) 625789
Pro G Marks (01934) 418473
Holes 18 L 5963 yds SSS 69

Recs Am–67 I Heppenstall,
P Simmonds (1992)
Pro–66 G Marks (1992)
V'tors H SOC–WD
Fees £20 (£30)
Loc 2 miles NE of Weston,
off A370
Arch Hawtree

Yeovil (1919)

Sherborne Road, Yeovil BA21 5BW
Tel **(01935) 475949 (Clubhouse)**
Fax (01935) 411283
Mem 685 165(L) 70(J)
Sec R Wilmott (01935) 422965
Pro G Kite (01935) 473763
Holes 18 L 6144 yds SSS 70
9 L 4876 yds SSS 65
Recs Am–64 J Pounder (1991)
Pro–65 G Laing (1987),
R Troake (1989),
S Little, G Hampshire (1991)
V'tors WD–U H WE/BH–H
(WD/WE–phone Pro) SOC
Fees 18 hole: £25 (£30)
9 hole: £15 (£18)
Loc 1 mile from Yeovil on A30 to
Sherborne
Arch Fowler/Alison

Staffordshire

Alsager G&CC (1992)

*Audley Road, Alsager, Stoke-on-Trent
ST7 2UR*
Tel **(01270) 875700**
Fax (01270) 882207
Mem 640
Sec J Olmes
Holes 18 L 6193 yds SSS 70
Recs Am–68 K Statham (1991)
V'tors WD–U before 5pm –M after
5pm WE/BH–M SOC
Fees £21
Loc 5 miles W of Crewe.
M6 Junction 16

Barlaston (1987)

Meaford Road, Stone ST15 8UX
Tel **(01782) 372867**
Fax (01782) 372867
Mem 650
Pro I Rogers (01782) 372795
Holes 18 L 5800 yds SSS 68
Recs Am–65 D Lynn (1995)
V'tors WD–U WE–NA before 10am
Fees On application
Loc ½ mile S of Barlaston.
M6 Junction 14/15

Beau Desert (1921)

Hazel Slade, Cannock WS12 5PJ
Tel **(01543) 422626/422773**
Fax (01543) 451137
Mem 500
Sec AJR Fairfield (01543) 422626
Pro B Stevens (01543) 422492
Holes 18 L 6310 yds SSS 71
Recs Am–65 N Isherwood (1995)
Pro–64 T Minshall

V'tors WD–U WE–phone in advance
BH–NA SOC
Fees £35 (£45)
Loc 4 miles NE of Cannock,
off A460

Bloxwich (1924)

Stafford Road, Bloxwich WS3 3PQ
Tel (01922) 405724
Fax (01922) 476593
Mem 595
Sec DA Frost (01922) 476593
Pro RJ Dance
Holes 18 L 6286 yds SSS 70
Recs Am–67 R Fleming
Pro–65 J Rhodes
V'tors WD–U WE–M SOC
Fees £25 (£30)
Loc N of Walsall on A34

Branston G&CC (1975)

*Burton Road, Branston, Burton-on-
Trent DE14 3DP*
Tel (01283) 512211
Fax (01283) 566984
Mem 800
Sec G Pyle (Golf Mgr)
Pro G Prince
Holes 18 L 6632 yds Par 71 SSS 72
Recs Am–70 B Wood
Pro–67 B Rimmer (1996)
V'tors WD–U WE–M before noon
SOC
Fees £25 (£35)
Loc 1/2 mile S of Burton (A38)
Mis Driving range
Arch G Hamshall

Brocton Hall (1894)

Brocton, Stafford ST17 0TH
Tel (01785) 662627
Fax (01785) 661591
Mem 500
Sec WR Lanyon (01785) 661901
Pro R Johnson (01785) 661485
Holes 18 L 6095 yds SSS 69
Recs Am–66 P Sutton
V'tors I H SOC
Fees £28 (£33)
Loc 4 miles SE of Stafford, off A34
Arch Harry Vardon

Burslem (1907)

*Wood Farm, High Lane, Stoke-on-
Trent ST6 7JT*
Tel (01782) 837006
Mem 300
Sec FL Barnes (01270) 873692
Holes 9 L 5360 yds SSS 66
Recs Am–64 M Keeling (1988)
Pro–66 T Williamson
V'tors WD–U WE–NA
Fees £16
Loc Burslem 2 miles

Calderfields (1983)

Aldridge Road, Walsall WS4 2JS
Tel (01922) 640540 (Clubhouse),
(01922) 32243 (Bookings)
Fax (01922) 38787
Mem 550

Sec JE Hampshire
Holes 18 L 6636 yds SSS 72
V'tors U SOC
Fees £10
Loc 1 mile N of Walsall (A454).
M6 Junction 10
Mis Floodlit driving range

Cannock Park (1993)

Public
Stafford Road, Cannock WS11 2AL
Tel (01543) 578850
Fax (01543) 578850
Mem 270
Sec JN Bradbury (01543) 572800
Pro D Dunk
Holes 18 L 5048 yds SSS 65
V'tors U SOC–WD
Fees £7 (£8)
Loc 1/2 mile N of Cannock on A34.
M6 Junction 11, 2 miles
Arch John Mainland

The Craythorne (1972)

*Craythorne Road, Stretton, Burton-on-
Trent DE13 0AZ*
Tel (01283) 564329
Fax (01283) 511908
Mem 500
Sec AA Wright (Man Dir)
Pro S Hadfield (01283) 533745
Holes 18 L 5255 yds Par 68 SSS 67
Recs Am–66 AA Wright (1997)
V'tors WD–U SOC
Fees £18 (£22)
Loc Stretton, 1 1/2 miles N of
Burton. A38/A5121 Junction
Mis Floodlit driving range. Pitch &
putt course

Dartmouth (1910)

Vale Street, West Bromwich B71 4DW
Tel (0121) 588 2131
Mem 350
Sec CF Wade
Pro G Dean
Holes 9 L 6060 yds SSS 70
Recs Am–66 T Cheese (1991)
Pro–70 P Lester
V'tors WD–U WE–M SOC–Tues &
Thurs
Fees D–£20
Loc 1 mile from W Bromwich,
behind Churchfields High
School. Junction M5/M6

Drayton Park (1897)

Drayton Park, Tamworth B78 3TN
Tel (01827) 251139
Fax (01827) 284035
Mem 450
Sec AO Rammell JP
Pro MW Passmore (01827)
251478
Holes 18 L 6414 yds SSS 71
Recs Am–62 M McGuire (1993)
Pro–65 DJ Russell (1987)
V'tors WD–H WE/BH–NA
SOC–Tues & Thurs
Fees R/D–£29
Loc 2 miles S of Tamworth (A4091)
Arch James Braid

Druids Heath (1974)

Stonnall Road, Aldridge WS9 8JZ
Tel (01922) 55595
Mem 577 75(L) 45(J)
Sec PJ Bradford
Pro S Elliott (01922) 59523
Holes 18 L 6659 yds Par 72 SSS 73
Recs Am–69 M Pearce
V'tors WD–U WE–M
Fees £25 (£32)
Loc 6 miles NW of Sutton
Coldfield, off A452

Enville (1935)

*Highgate Common, Enville, Stourbridge
DY7 5BN*
Tel (01384) 872074
Fax (01384) 873396
Mem 900
Sec RJ Bannister (Sec/Mgr)
(01384) 872074
Pro S Power (01384) 872585
Holes Highgate 18 L 6471 yds
SSS 72; Lodge 18 L 6275 yds
SSS 70
Recs Highgate Am–67 PJ Randle
(1991)
Pro–65 J Stafford (1991)
Lodge Am–67 C Elston
(1996)
V'tors WD–U WE/BH–M H SOC
Fees £28–£38
Loc 6 miles W of Stourbridge

Goldenhill (1983)

Public
*Mobberley Road, Goldenhill, Stoke-on-
Trent ST6 5SS*
Tel (01782) 784715
Fax (01782) 775940
Mem 600
Sec P Jones
Pro A Clingan
Holes 18 L 5957 yds SSS 68
V'tors U SOC–book with Pro
Fees £6 (£7)
Loc Between Tunstall and
Kidsgrove, off A50

Great Barr (1961)

Chapel Lane, Birmingham B43 7BA
Tel (0121) 357 1232
Mem 600
Sec Mrs JS Pembridge
(0121) 358 4376
Pro R Spragg (0121) 357 5270
Holes 18 L 6545 yds SSS 72
Recs Am–67 CM Lambert,
CD Webb
Pro–71 J Higgins
V'tors WD–U WE–I (h'cap max 18)
SOC
Fees £25
Loc 6 miles NW of Birmingham.
M6 Junction 7

Greenway Hall (1908)

Stockton Brook, Stoke-on-Trent ST9 9LJ
Tel (01782) 503158
Mem 550
Sec A Pedley

Holes 18 L 5676 yds SSS 67
Recs Am–65 A Bailey, A Dathan
V'tors WD–U SOC
Fees £14
Loc 5 miles N of Stoke, off A53

Handsworth (1895)

Sunningdale Close, Handsworth Wood,
Birmingham B20 1NP
Tel (0121) 554 3387
Mem 850
Sec PS Hodnett (Hon)
Pro L Bashford (0121) 523 3594
Holes 18 L 6267 yds SSS 70
Recs Am–65 P Johnson (1994)
Pro–71 HF Boyce
V'tors WD–U WE/BH–M SOC
Fees £30
Loc 3 miles NW of Birmingham.
M5 Junction 1. M6 Junction 7

Himley Hall (1980)

Public
Himley Hall Park, Dudley DY3 4DF
Tel (01902) 895207
Mem 300
Sec M Harris
Holes 9 L 3145 yds SSS 36
9 hole short course
Recs Am–69 K Baker
V'tors WD–U WE/BH–restricted
Fees 18 holes–£7.50 (£8)
9 holes–£5.20 (£5.50)
Loc Grounds of Himley Hall Park.
B4176, off A449
Arch A & K Baker

Ingestre Park (1977)

Ingestre, Stafford ST18 0RE
Tel (01889) 270061
Fax (01889) 270845
Mem 740
Sec CJ Radmore (Mgr) (01889)
270845
Pro D Scullion (01889) 270304
Holes 18 L 6334 yds SSS 70
Recs Am–67 D Hughes (1990)
Pro–68 D Scullion (1982)
Ladies–71 K Edwards (1996)
V'tors WD–H before 3.30pm
WE/BH–M SOC–WD exc
Wed
Fees £23 D–£28
Loc 6 miles E of Stafford, off
Tixall Road. M6 Junctions
13/14
Arch Hawtree

Izaak Walton

Cold Norton, Stone ST15 0NS
Tel (01785) 760900
Mem 375
Sec TT Tyler
Pro J Brown
Holes 18 L 6281 yds SSS 72
Recs Am–72 G Dollochin (1995)
V'tors U SOC
Fees £15 (£20)
Loc 7 miles NW of Stafford on
B2056. M6 Junction 14
Mis Driving range

Lakeside (1969)

Rugeley Power Station, Rugeley
WS15 1PR
Tel (01889) 575667
Fax (01889) 576412
Mem 550
Sec BJ Cary
Holes 18 L 5478 yds SSS 68
Recs Am–68 S Rodgers
V'tors M
Loc 2 miles SE of Rugeley
on A513

Leek (1892)

Big Birchall, Leek ST13 5RE
Tel (01538) 385889
Mem 500 100(L) 60(J)
Sec F Cutts (01538) 384779
Pro P Stubbs (01538) 384767
Holes 18 L 6240 yds SSS 70
Recs Am–61 D Evans
Pro–65 P Baker
V'tors U H before 3pm –M after
3pm SOC–Wed only
Fees £24 (£30)
Loc ½ mile S of Leek on A520

Little Aston (1908)

Streetly, Sutton Coldfield B74 3AN
Tel (0121) 353 2066
Fax (0121) 353 2942
Mem 250
Sec NH Russell (0121) 353 2942
Pro J Anderson (0121) 353 0330
Holes 18 L 6670 yds SSS 73
Recs Am–64
Pro–68
V'tors H–by prior arrangement
WE–XL
Fees On application
Loc 4 miles NW of Sutton
Coldfield, off A454
Arch Harry Vardon

Manor (Kingstone) (1991)

Leese Hill, Kingstone, Uttoxeter
ST14 8QT
Tel (01889) 563234
Mem 280
Sec A Campbell
Holes 9 hole course
V'tors U
Fees £10 (£15)
Loc 4 miles W of Uttoxeter
Mis Driving range
Arch E Anderson

Newcastle Municipal (1973)

Public
Keele Road, Newcastle-under-Lyme
ST5 5AB
Tel (01782) 627596
Sec GA Bytheway
Pro C Smith
Holes 18 L 5822 metres SSS 70
Recs Am–70 P Rowe
Pro–68 P Rowe
V'tors U
Fees £6.50 (£8.40)

Loc 2 miles W of Newcastle on
A525, opposite University.
M6 Junction 15
Mis Driving range

Newcastle-under-Lyme (1908)

Whitmore Road, Newcastle-under-Lyme
ST5 2QB
Tel (01782) 616583
Fax (01782) 617006
Mem 575
Sec KP Geddes (Sec/Mgr)
(01782) 617006
Pro P Symonds (01782) 618526
Holes 18 L 6317 yds SSS 71
Recs Am–64 MC Keates (1989)
Pro–68 A Pauly (1988)
V'tors WD–U H WE/BH–M SOC
Fees On application
Loc 2 miles SW of Newcastle-
under-Lyme on A53

Onneley (1968)

Onneley, Crewe, Cheshire CW3 5QF
Tel (01782) 750577
Mem 410
Sec P Ball (01782) 846759
Pro None
Holes 9 L 5584 yds SSS 67
Recs Am–67 D Davenport
V'tors WD–U Sat/BH–M Sun–NA
SOC–Mon/Thurs/Fri
Fees £15
Loc 8 miles W of Newcastle,
off A51
Arch A Benson

Oxley Park (1914)

Stafford Road, Bushbury,
Wolverhampton WV10 6DE
Tel (01902) 420506
Fax (01902) 712241
Mem 550
Sec Mrs K Mann (01902) 425892
Pro LA Burlison (01902) 425445
Holes 18 L 6168 yds SSS 69
Recs Am–67 CD Woolley,
MS Roberts (1995)
Pro–65 P Weaver (1987)
V'tors U SOC
Fees £25 (£25)
Loc 1 mile N of Wolverhampton,
off A449
Arch HS Colt

Parkhall (1989)

Public
Hulme Road, Weston Coyney, Stoke-on-
Trent ST3 5BH
Tel (01782) 599584
Sec N Worrall (Mgr)
(01831) 456409
Pro A Clingan
Holes 18 L 2335 yds Par 54
Recs Am–53 N Worrall (1991)
V'tors WE–booking necessary SOC
Fees On application
Loc 3 miles E of Stoke. Longton
1 mile

Patshull Park Hotel
G&CC (1980)

Pattingham, Wolverhampton WV6 7HR

Tel	**(01902) 700100/700342**
Fax	(01902) 700874
Mem	395
Sec	K Roberts
Pro	J Higgins
Holes	18 L 6412 yds SSS 71
Recs	Am–67 S Weir
	Pro–63 J Higgins
V'tors	U H SOC
Fees	£22.50 (£27.50)
Loc	7 miles W of Wolverhampton, off A41. M54 Junction 3, 5 miles
Arch	John Jacobs

Penn (1908)

Penn Common, Wolverhampton WV4 5JN

Tel	**(01902) 341142**
Mem	650
Sec	MH Jones
Pro	A Briscoe (01902) 330472
Holes	18 L 6462 yds SSS 71
Recs	Am–67 C Upton, M Weston
	Pro–70 J Rhodes, R Cameron
V'tors	WD–U WE–M SOC
Fees	£20 (Nov–Feb £15)
Loc	2 miles SW of Wolverhampton, off A449

Perton Park (1990)

Wrottesley Park Road, Perton, Wolverhampton WV6 7HL

Tel	**(01902) 380103/380073**
Fax	(01902) 326219
Mem	300
Sec	E Greenway (Mgr)
Pro	J Harrold (01902) 380073
Holes	18 L 6620 yds SSS 72
V'tors	U SOC
Fees	£10 (£15)
Loc	6 miles W of Wolverhampton, off A454
Mis	Driving range

St Thomas's Priory
(1995)

Armitage Lane, Armitage, Rugeley WS15 1ED

Tel	**(01543) 491116**
Fax	(01543) 492244
Mem	500
Sec	J Bissell
Pro	S Berry (01543) 492096
Holes	18 L 5969 yds SSS 70
Recs	Pro–67 M McGuire (1997)
V'tors	M SOC–WD
Fees	On application
Loc	1 mile SE of Rugeley on A513, opp Ash Tree Inn
Arch	Paul Mulholland

Sandwell Park (1897)

Birmingham Road, West Bromwich B71 4JJ

Tel	**(0121) 553 4637**
Fax	(0121) 525 1651
Mem	600

Sec	DA Paterson
Pro	N Wylie (0121) 553 4384
Holes	18 L 6470 yds SSS 72
Recs	Am–65 J Bromley (1997)
	Pro–67 F Clark (1994),
	I Clark (1997)
V'tors	WD–U WE–MH SOC–WD
Fees	£25–£35
Loc	West Bromwich/Birmingham boundary. By M5 Junction 1
Arch	HS Colt

Sedgley (1992)

Pay and play

Sandyfields Road, Sedgley, Dudley DY3 3DL

Tel	**(01902) 880503**
Mem	150
Sec	JA Cox
Pro	G Mercer
Holes	9 L 3150 yds SSS 71
V'tors	WD–U WE–booking advised
Fees	9 holes–£5 (£5.50)
	18 holes–£7 (£7.50)
Loc	1/2 mile from Sedgley, off A463 between Dudley and Wolverhampton
Mis	Driving range
Arch	WG Cox

Seedy Mill (1991)

Elmhurst, Lichfield WS13 3HE

Tel	**(01543) 417333**
Fax	(01543) 418098
Mem	1100
Sec	G Roberts (Gen Mgr)
Pro	R O'Hanlon
Holes	18 L 6305 yds SSS 70
	9 hole Par 3 course
V'tors	U H SOC
Fees	On application
Loc	2 miles N of Lichfield on A515
Mis	Floodlit driving range
Arch	Hawtree

South Staffordshire
(1892)

Danescourt Road, Tettenhall, Wolverhampton WV6 9BQ

Tel	**(01902) 751065**
Fax	(01902) 741753
Mem	600
Sec	JA Macklin
Pro	J Rhodes (01902) 754816
Holes	18 L 6513 yds SSS 71
Recs	Am–69 IS Guest (1996)
	Pro–67 D Gilford (1984)
	Ladies–73 A Bullock (1994)
V'tors	WD–U WE/BH–M or by arrangement SOC
Fees	£34 D–£40 (£47)
Loc	3 miles W of Wolverhampton, off A41
Arch	Harry Vardon

Stafford Castle (1907)

Newport Road, Stafford ST16 1BP

Tel	**(01785) 223821**
Mem	440
Sec	DH Fellowes
Holes	9 L 6382 yds Par 71 SSS 70

Recs	Am–68 J Campion (1992)
V'tors	WD–U WE–after 1pm
Fees	£14 (£18)
Loc	1/2 mile W of Stafford

Stone (1896)

The Fillybrooks, Stone ST15 0NB

Tel	**(01785) 813103**
Mem	314
Sec	PR Farley (01785) 284875
Holes	9 L 6299 yds Par 71 SSS 70
Recs	Am–68 A Hurst (1991)
	Ladies–75 DR Pursell (1995)
V'tors	WD–U WE/BH–M SOC–WD
Fees	£20
Loc	1/2 mile W of Stone on A34

Swindon (1976)

Bridgnorth Road, Swindon, Dudley DY3 4PU

Tel	**(01902) 897031**
Fax	(01902) 326219
Mem	500
Sec	E Greenway (Mgr)
Pro	P Lester (01902) 896191
Holes	18 L 6081 yds SSS 69
	9 hole Par 3 course
Recs	Am–68 N Bennett (1990)
V'tors	U SOC–WD
Fees	£18 (£27)
Loc	5 miles SW of Wolverhampton on B4176
Mis	Driving range

Tamworth (1978)

Public

Eagle Drive, Amington, Tamworth B77 4EG

Tel	**(01827) 53850**
Mem	500
Pro	D Scott
Holes	18 L 6695 yds SSS 72
Recs	Am–67 CJ Christison
	Pro–65 BN Jones
V'tors	U SOC–WD
Fees	On application
Loc	2 1/2 miles E of Tamworth on B5000. M42, 3 miles

Trentham (1894)

14 Barlaston Old Road, Trentham, Stoke-on-Trent ST4 8HB

Tel	**(01782) 642347**
Mem	680
Sec	RN Portas (01782) 658109
Pro	S Wilson (01782) 657309
Holes	18 L 6644 yds SSS 72
Recs	Am–63 DA Lynn (1995)
	Pro–68 D Gilford (1991)
V'tors	WD–U H WE/BH–M (or enquire Sec) SOC–WD
Fees	£25
Loc	3 miles S of Newcastle, off A34. M6 Junction 15

Trentham Park (1936)

Trentham Park, Stoke-on-Trent ST4 8AE

Tel	**(01782) 642245**
Fax	(01782) 658800

For list of abbreviations see page 479

Mem   500 100(L) 50(J)
Sec   RN Portas (01782) 658800
Pro   (01782) 642125
Holes   18 L 6403 yds SSS 71
Recs   Am–67 S Clarke
Pro–68 D Gilford, R Rafferty
V'tors   H SOC–Wed & Fri
Fees   £22.50 (£30)
Loc   4 miles S of Newcastle on
A34. M6 Junction 15, 1 mile

Uttoxeter (1970)

Wood Lane, Uttoxeter ST14 8JR
Tel   (01889) 565108
Fax   (01889) 566552
Mem   780
Sec   Mrs G Davies (01889) 566552
Pro   AD McCandless
(01889) 564884
Holes   18 L 5475 yds SSS 68
Recs   Am–64 B Belcher (1992)
V'tors   WD–U WE–by arrangement
SOC
Fees   £15 D–£22 (£17)
Loc   Uttoxeter racecourse ½ mile

Walsall (1907)

Broadway, Walsall WS1 3EY
Tel   (01922) 613512
Fax   (01922) 616460
Mem   600
Sec   E Murray (01922) 613512
Pro   R Lambert (01922) 626766
Holes   18 L 6232 yds SSS 70
Recs   Am–65 P Brown, S Wakefield
(1997)
V'tors   WD–U WE–M SOC
Fees   £33
Loc   1 mile S of Walsall, off A34.
M6 Junction 7
Arch   McKenzie

Wergs (1990)

Pay and play
Keepers Lane, Tettenhall WV6 8UA
Tel   (01902) 742225
Fax   (01902) 744748
Mem   255
Sec   Mrs G Parsons
Holes   18 L 6949 yds Par 72 SSS 73
Recs   Am–74 T Mathers (1991)
Pro–74 D Prosser (1990)
V'tors   U
Fees   D–£13.50 (D–£17)
Loc   3 miles W of Wolverhampton
on A41
Arch   CW Moseley

Westwood (1923)

Newcastle Road, Wallbridge, Leek
ST13 7AA
Tel   (01538) 398385
Fax   (01538) 382485
Mem   550
Sec   C Plant
Pro   N Hyde
Holes   18 L 6207 yds SSS 70
Recs   Am–66 M Sales
V'tors   U SOC–WD
Fees   WD–£18
Loc   W boundary of Leek on A53

Whiston Hall (1971)

Whiston, Cheadle ST10 2HZ
Tel   (01538) 266260
Fax   (01538) 383600
Mem   500
Sec   HL Wainscott (Mgr)
Holes   18 L 5742 yds SSS 69
V'tors   U SOC
Fees   £12 (£16)
Loc   8 miles NE of Stoke-on-Trent
on A52, nr Alton Towers

Whittington Heath (1886)

Tamworth Road, Lichfield WS14 9PW
Tel   (01543) 432317 (Admin),
(01543) 432212 (Steward)
Fax   (01543) 432317
Mem   670
Sec   Mrs JA Burton (Admin),
R Walsh (Comp Sec)
Pro   AR Sadler (01543) 432261
Holes   18 L 6448 yds SSS 71
V'tors   WD–H or I WE/BH + day
after–M SOC–Wed & Thurs
Fees   £24 D–£32
Loc   2½ miles E of Lichfield on
Tamworth road (A51)

Wolstanton (1904)

Dimsdale Old Hall, Hassam Parade,
Wolstanton, Newcastle ST5 9DR
Tel   (01782) 616995
Mem   625
Sec   Ms VJ Downend
(01782) 622413
Pro   S Arnold (01782) 622718
Holes   18 L 5807 yds SSS 68
Recs   Am–63 P Sweetsur
Pro–66 CH Ward
V'tors   WD–H WE–M SOC–WD
Fees   £20
Loc   1½ miles NW of Newcastle
(A34)

Suffolk

Aldeburgh (1884)

Aldeburgh IP15 5PE
Tel   (01728) 452408
Fax   (01728) 452937
Mem   879
Sec   IM Simpson (01728) 452890
Pro   K Preston (01728) 453309
Holes   18 L 6330 yds SSS 71
9 L 2114 yds SSS 64
Recs   Am–65 J Lloyd
Pro–67 JM Johnson
V'tors   H SOC
Fees   On application
Loc   6 miles E of A12 (A1094)
Arch   W Fernie/J Thompson

Beccles (1899)

The Common, Beccles NR34 9BX
Tel   (01502) 712244
Mem   200
Sec   Mrs LW Allen (01502) 712479
Holes   9 L 2696 yds SSS 67
Recs   Am–65 S Shulver

V'tors   WD–U Sun–M SOC
Fees   £11 (£13)
Loc   10 miles W of Lowestoft
(A146)

Brett Vale

Noakes Road, Raydon, Ipswich IP7 5LR
Tel   (01473) 310718
Fax   (01473) 824482
Sec   LJ Morrison
Pro   R Taylor
Holes   18 L 5847 yds Par 70
V'tors   U–booking advisable
SOC–WD
Fees   £15 (£17.50)
Loc   10 miles SW of Ipswich, off
A12 (B1070)
Mis   Golf academy

Bungay & Waveney Valley (1889)

Outney Common, Bungay NR35 1DS
Tel   (01986) 892337
Mem   673
Sec   RW Stacey
Pro   N Whyte
Holes   18 L 6063 yds SSS 69
Recs   Am–64 D Wood
Pro–64 T Spurgeon
V'tors   WD–U WE–M SOC–WD
Fees   D–£24
Loc   ½ mile W of Bungay, on
N side of A143
Arch   James Braid

Bury St Edmunds (1922)

Tut Hill, Bury St Edmunds IP28 6LG
Tel   (01284) 755979
Fax   (01284) 763288
Mem   650 180(L)
Sec   JC Sayer
Pro   M Jillings (01284) 755978
Holes   18 L 6678 yds Par 72 SSS 72
9 L 2217 yds Par 31 SSS 31
Recs   Am–69 S Goodman, A Currie,
J Maddock (1993),
C Wright (1997)
Pro–67 K Golding (1989)
V'tors   WD/BH–U WE–M SOC–WD
Fees   18 hole: £24
9 hole: £12 (£13)
Loc   2 miles W of Bury St
Edmunds on B1106, off A14
Arch   Ted Ray

Cretingham (1984)

Grove Farm, Cretingham, Woodbridge
IP13 7BA
Tel   (01728) 685275
Fax   (01728) 685037
Mem   300
Sec   C Jenkins (Prop)
Pro   C Jenkins
Holes   9 L 2260 yds Par 33
Pro–61 T Johnson (1994)
V'tors   U
Fees   18 holes–£8 (£10)
Loc   2 miles SE of Earl Soham.
11 miles N of Ipswich
Mis   Practice range. Pitch & putt
course
Arch   J Austin

Diss (1903)

Stuston Common, Diss IP22 3JB

Tel	**(01379) 642847**
Mem	700
Sec	J Bell (01379) 641025
Pro	N Taylor (01379) 644399
Holes	18 L 6238 yds SSS 70
Recs	Am–72 S Brawn (1993)
	Pro–67 R Curtis (1993)
V'tors	WD only
Fees	£20
Loc	1 mile SE of Diss, off A140

Felixstowe Ferry (1880)

Ferry Road, Felixstowe IP4 9RY

Tel	**(01394) 283060**
Mem	850
Sec	RH Owens (01394) 286834
Pro	I Macpherson (01394) 283975
Holes	18 L 6308 yds SSS 70
	9 L 2986 yds Par 35
Recs	Am–67 S Macpherson (1993)
	Pro–65 I Richardson (1979),
	L Paterson
V'tors	M H WD before 10.30am
	SOC. 9 hole course–U
Fees	£26
Loc	2 miles NE of Felixstowe,
	towards Felixstowe Ferry
Arch	Henry Cotton (1947)

Flempton (1895)

Bury St Edmunds IP28 6HQ

Tel	**(01284) 728291**
Mem	250
Sec	JF Taylor
Pro	M Jillings
Holes	9 L 6240 yds SSS 70
Recs	Am–67 Lt J Reynolds
	Pro–69 J Arbon
V'tors	WD–H WE/BH–M
Fees	£22 D–£28
Loc	4 miles NW of Bury St
	Edmunds on A1101
Arch	JH Taylor

Fynn Valley (1992)

Witnesham, Ipswich IP6 9JA

Tel	**(01473) 785267**
Fax	(01473) 785632
Mem	650
Sec	T Tyrrell
Pro	P Wilby, G Crane
	(01473) 785463
Holes	18 L 5873 yds Par 68 SSS 68
	9 hole Par 3 course
Recs	Am–68 M Millett
	Pro–64 P Curry,
	M Stokes (1995)
V'tors	U exc Sun am SOC
Fees	£15 (£18)
Loc	2 miles N of Ipswich on B1077
Mis	Driving range
Arch	Tony Tyrrell

Haverhill (1974)

Coupals Road, Haverhill CB9 7UW

Tel	**(01440) 761951**
Fax	(01440) 761951
Mem	550
Sec	Mrs J Edwards

Pro	S Mayfield (01440) 712628
Holes	18 L 5898 yds SSS 70
Recs	Am–66 A Carter (1991),
	R Cramsie (1993)
	Pro–66 C Cook
V'tors	U–phone Pro SOC–Tues &
	Thurs
Fees	£14 (£18)
Loc	1 mile E of Haverhill, off
	A604. Signs to Calford Green
Arch	Charles Lawrie

Hintlesham Hall (1991)

Hintlesham, Ipswich IP8 3NS

Tel	**(01473) 652761**
Fax	(01473) 652463
Mem	350
Sec	Tina Shannon (Mgr)
Pro	A Spink
Holes	18 L 6638 yds SSS 72
Recs	Am–67 P McEvoy (1991)
	Pro–68 A Lucas (1997)
V'tors	WD–U WE–NA before 2pm
	SOC
Fees	£27
Loc	4 miles W of Ipswich on A1071
Arch	Hawtree

Ipswich (Purdis Heath) (1895)

Purdis Heath, Bucklesham Road, Ipswich IP3 8UQ

Tel	**(01473) 727474 (Steward)**
Fax	(01473) 715236
Mem	740
Sec	To be appointed
	(01473) 728941
Pro	SJ Whymark (01473) 724017
Holes	18 L 6405 yds SSS 71
	9 L 1950 yds Par 31
Recs	Am–64 JVT Marks
	Pro–67 RA Knight
V'tors	18 hole–H SOC 9 hole–U
Fees	18 hole–£35 (£36)
	9 hole–£10
Loc	3 miles E of Ipswich
Arch	James Braid

Links (Newmarket) (1902)

Cambridge Road, Newmarket CB8 0TG

Tel	**(01638) 663000**
Fax	(01638) 661476
Mem	685
Sec	Lt Cdr DM Baird RN
Pro	J Sharkey (01638) 662395
Holes	18 L 6424 yds SSS 71
Recs	Am–66 R Wiseman
	Pro–64 N Mitchell
	Ladies–68 T Eakin
V'tors	H exc Sun–M before 11.30am
	SOC
Fees	£28 (£32)
Loc	1 mile SW of Newmarket

Newton Green (1907)

Newton Green, Sudbury CO10 0QN

Tel	**(01787) 77501**
Mem	550
Sec	K Mazdon (01787) 377217
Pro	K Lovelock (01787) 313215
Holes	18 L 5893 yds SSS 69

V'tors	WD–U WE–M before 12 –U
	after 12 SOC
Fees	£14 (£14)
Loc	4 miles S of Sudbury on A134

Rookery Park (1891)

Carlton Colville, Lowestoft NR33 8HJ

Tel	**(01502) 560380**
Fax	(01502) 560380
Mem	1000
Sec	SR Cooper
Pro	M Elsworthy (01502) 515103
Holes	18 L 6729 yds SSS 72
	9 hole Par 3 course
Recs	Am–71 G Long (1985)
	Pro–66 R Mann (1995)
V'tors	WD–U Sat/BH–after 11am
	Sun–NA SOC
Fees	£25 (£30)
Loc	3 miles W of Lowestoft (A146)

Royal Worlington & Newmarket (1893)

Golf Links Road, Worlington, Bury St Edmunds IP28 8SD

Tel	**(01638) 712216**
Fax	(01638) 717787
Mem	310
Sec	Maj GWM Hipkin
Pro	M Hawkins (01638) 715224
Holes	9 L 6210 yds SSS 70
Recs	Am–67 DJ Millensted
	Pro–66 EE Beverley
V'tors	I or H–phone first WE–NA
Fees	D–£35 After 2pm–£25
Loc	6 miles NE of Newmarket,
	off A11
Arch	Tom Dunn

Rushmere (1927)

Rushmere Heath, Ipswich IP4 5QQ

Tel	**(01473) 727109**
Fax	(01473) 725648
Mem	800
Sec	PL Coles (01473) 725648
Pro	NTJ McNeill
	(01473) 728076
Holes	18 L 6262 yds SSS 70
Recs	Am–66 F Knights (1989),
	M Turner (1990)
	Pro–67 NTJ McNeill(1984),
	S Beckham (1985)
V'tors	WD–H WE/BH–H after
	2.30pm
Fees	£20
Loc	3 miles E of Ipswich, off
	Woodbridge road (A1214)

St Helena (1990)

Bramfield Road, Halesworth IP19 9XA

Tel	**(01986) 875567**
Fax	(01986) 874565
Mem	400
Sec	Mrs RK Ward
Pro	PM Heil
Holes	18 L 6580 yds SSS 72
	9 hole course SSS 36
Recs	Am–71 N Land (1995)
	Pro–68 PM Heil (1994)
V'tors	H SOC
Fees	18 hole–£15 D–£19 (£21)
	9 hole–£7.50

Loc 1 mile S of Halesworth,
off A144
Mis Floodlit driving range
Arch JW Johnson

Seckford (1991)

Seckford Hall Road, Great Bealings,
Woodbridge IP13 6NT
Tel (01394) 388000
Fax (01394) 382818
Mem 300
Sec T Pennock (Golf Dir)
Pro J Skinner
Holes 18 L 5303 yds Par 69 SSS 66
Recs Am–63 S Jay
Pro–63 J Skinner
V'tors U–booking necessary SOC
Fees £13 (£15)
Loc SW of Woodbridge, off A12
Mis Driving range
Arch J Johnson

Southwold (1884)

The Common, Southwold IP18 6TB
Tel (01502) 723234
Mem 450
Sec MS Lumsden (01502) 723248
Pro B Allen (01502) 723790
Holes 9 L 6050 yds SSS 69
Recs Am–67 S Fitzgerald
Pro–65 R Mann
V'tors U (subject to fixtures)
Fees £18 (£22)
Loc 35 miles NE of Ipswich

Stoke-by-Nayland (1972)

Keepers Lane, Leavenheath, Colchester
CO6 4PZ
Tel (01206) 262836
Fax (01206) 263356
Mem 1400
Pro K Lovelock (01206) 262769
Holes Gainsborough 18 L 6498 yds
SSS 71; Constable 18 L 6544
yds SSS 71
Recs Gainsborough Am–68
K Browne (1997);
Pro–67 K Golding (1997)
Constable Am–66 K Browne
(1997); Pro–70 J Hudson,
H Flatman (1990)
V'tors WD–U WE/BH–H after 10am
SOC
Fees £20 (£24)
Loc Off A134 Colchester-Sudbury
road on B1068
Mis Driving range

Stowmarket (1962)

Lower Road, Onehouse, Stowmarket
IP14 3DA
Tel (01449) 736392
Fax (01449) 736826
Mem 600
Sec J Edwards-Hayes
(01449) 736473
Pro D Burl
Holes 18 L 6119 yds SSS 69
Recs Am–66 M Darling
Pro–66 H Flatman
V'tors H SOC–Thurs & Fri

Fees £23 (£29)
Loc 2½ miles SW of Stowmarket
Mis Driving range

The Suffolk G&CC (1974)

St John's Hill Plantation, The Street,
Fornham All Saints,
Bury St Edmunds IP28 6JQ
Tel (01284) 706777
Fax (01284) 706721
Mem 600
Sec DJ Clark
Pro None
Holes 18 L 6077 yds SSS 69
V'tors U SOC
Fees £10 (£12)
Loc 2 miles NW of Bury St
Edmunds, off B1106

Thorpeness Golf Hotel (1923)

Thorpeness, Leiston IP16 4NH
Tel (01728) 452176
Fax (01728) 453868
Mem 250
Sec NW Griffin
Pro (01728) 454926
Holes 18 L 6271 yds SSS 71
Recs Am–66 J Marks
Pro–67 K McDonald
V'tors U
Fees On application
Loc 2 miles N of Aldeburgh
Arch James Braid

Ufford Park Hotel (1992)

Yarmouth Road, Ufford, Woodbridge
IP12 1QW
Tel (01394) 382836
Fax (01394) 383582
Mem 300
Sec S Robertson
Pro S Robertson
Holes 18 L 6325 yds SSS 71
Recs Am–67 J Maddock
Pro–67 C Green
V'tors U SOC
Fees £14 (£18)
Loc 2 miles N of Woodbridge,
off A12
Arch P Pilgrim

Waldringfield Heath (1983)

Newbourne Road, Waldringfield,
Woodbridge IP12 4PT
Tel (01473) 736768
Fax (01473) 736436
Mem 610
Sec LJ McWade
Pro R Mann, A Lucas
(01473) 736417
Holes 18 L 6141 yds SSS 69
Recs Am–70 S Simmonds (1995)
Pro–68 A Dobson (1995)
V'tors WD–U WE/BH–M before
noon SOC–WD
Fees On application
Loc 3 miles E of Ipswich, off A12
Arch P Pilgrem

Woodbridge (1893)

Bromeswell Heath, Woodbridge
IP12 2PF
Tel (01394) 382038
Fax (01394) 382392
Mem 930
Sec Capt LA Harpum RN
Pro A Hubert (01394) 383213
Holes 18 L 6299 yds SSS 70
9 L 6308 yds SSS 70
Recs Am–64 JVT Marks (1983)
Pro–65 F Sunderland (1970)
V'tors WD–H WE/BH–M SOC
Fees 18 hole: £30; 9 hole: £15
Loc 2 miles E of Woodbridge on
A1152 towards Orford
Arch F Hawtree

Surrey

The Addington (1913)

205 Shirley Church Road, Croydon
CR0 5AB
Tel (0181) 777 1055
Sec JW Beale
Holes 18 L 6242 yds SSS 71
Recs Am–66 P Benka
Pro–68 F Robson
V'tors H SOC–WD
Fees On application
Loc E Croydon 2½ miles
Arch JF Abercromby

Addington Court (1931)

Public
Featherbed Lane, Addington, Croydon
CR0 9AA
Tel (0181) 657 0281
Fax (0181) 651 0282
Sec G Cotton
Pro G Cotton
Holes Old 18 L 5577 yds SSS 67
Falconwood 18 L 5513 yds
SSS 66
Lower 9 L 1812 yds SSS 62
Recs Am–62 S Griffiths (1994)
Pro–60 W Grant,
C DeFoy (1992)
V'tors U
Fees Old £11.50 (£12.95)
Falconwood £9.99 (£11.50)
9 hole–£6.95
Loc 3 miles E of Croydon
Mis 18 hole pitch & putt course
Arch F Hawtree Sr

Addington Palace (1923)

Addington Park, Gravel Hill, Addington
CR0 5BB
Tel (0181) 654 3061
Fax (0181) 655 3632
Mem 700
Sec LM Dennis-Smither
Pro R Williams (0181) 654 1786
Holes 18 L 6410 yds SSS 71
Recs Am–63 R Glading
Pro–65 AD Locke
V'tors WD–H WE/BH–M
Fees £30
Loc 2 miles E of Croydon Station

Banstead Downs (1890)

Burdon Lane, Belmont, Sutton
SM2 7DD

Tel	**(0181) 642 2284**
Fax	(0181) 642 5252
Mem	650
Sec	RHA Steele
Pro	R Dickman (0181) 642 6884
Holes	18 L 6194 yds SSS 69
Recs	Am–64 P Brittain (1992)
	Pro–64 M Wheeler (1995)
V'tors	WD–H WE/BH–M
	SOC–Thurs
Fees	£30. After 12 noon–£20
Loc	1 mile S of Sutton

Barrow Hills (1970)

Longcross, Chertsey KT16 0DS

Tel	**(01344) 635770**
Mem	320
Sec	RW Routley (01932) 848117
Holes	18 L 3090 yds SSS 53
Recs	Am–58 EJ Sewell (1979)
V'tors	M
Fees	On application
Loc	4 miles W of Chertsey

Betchworth Park (1911)

Reigate Road, Dorking RH4 1NZ

Tel	**(01306) 882052**
Fax	(01306) 877462
Mem	725
Sec	B Weeds
Pro	A Tocher (01306) 884334
Holes	18 L 6266 yds SSS 70
Recs	Am–64 M Osborne (1995)
	Pro–65 NC Coles
V'tors	WD–by arrangement exc Tues
	& Wed am WE–NA exc Sun
	pm
Fees	£33 (£45)
Loc	1 mile E of Dorking on A25
Arch	HS Colt

Bletchingley (1993)

Church Lane, Bletchingley RH1 4LP

Tel	**(01883) 744666**
Fax	(01883) 744284
Mem	600
Sec	CT Manktelow (Mgr)
Pro	A Dyer (01883) 744848
Holes	18 L 6504 yds Par 72 SSS 71
V'tors	WD–U WE–M SOC
Fees	£18 (£25)
Loc	1 mile S of M25 Junction 6
	on A25

Bowenhurst

Mill Lane, Crondall, Farnham
GU10 5RP

Tel	**(01252) 851695**
Fax	(01252) 851695
Mem	202
Sec	GL Corbey
Pro	C Cowie (01252) 851344
Holes	9 L 2007 yds Par 62 SSS 60
V'tors	U SOC
Fees	18 holes–£9 (£12);
	9 holes–£5 (£6.50)
Loc	2 miles SW of Farnham on
	A287. M3 Junction 5
Mis	Driving range

Bramley (1913)

Bramley, Guildford GU5 0AL

Tel	**(01483) 893042**
Fax	(01483) 894673
Mem	800
Sec	Ms M Lambert
	(01483) 892696
Pro	G Peddie (01483) 893685
Holes	18 L 5990 yds SSS 69
Recs	Am–65 J Jones (1993)
	Pro–63 P Hughes (1994)
V'tors	WD–U WE–M SOC–WD
Fees	£27 D–£33
Loc	3 miles S of Guildford
	on A281
Mis	Driving range–members and
	green fees only
Arch	Mayo/Braid

Burhill (1907)

Burwood Road, Walton-on-Thames
KT12 4BL

Tel	**(01932) 227345**
Fax	(01932) 267159
Mem	1100
Sec	G Hogg
Pro	L Johnson (01932) 221729
Holes	18 L 6224 yds SSS 70
Recs	Am–64 RJ Pollitt (1991)
	Pro–65 G Orr (1988)
V'tors	WD–H WE/BH–M
Fees	On application
Loc	Between Walton-on-Thames
	and Cobham, off Burwood
	Road
Mis	Game Improvement Centre
Arch	Willie Park

Camberley Heath (1913)

Golf Drive, Camberley GU15 1JG

Tel	**(01276) 23258**
Fax	(01276) 692505
Mem	725
Sec	J Greenwood
Pro	G Ralph (01276) 27905
Holes	18 L 6337 yds SSS 70
V'tors	WD–H WE–M SOC H
Fees	On application
Loc	1½ miles S of Camberley
	on A325
Arch	HS Colt

Central London Golf Centre (1992)

Public
Burntwood Lane, Wandsworth, London
SW17 0AT

Tel	**(0181) 871 2468**
Fax	(0181) 871 2468
Mem	320
Sec	J Robson
Pro	J Robson
Holes	9 L 4658 yds SSS 62
V'tors	WD–U WE–NA before
	12 noon SOC
Fees	£6.50 (£8.50)
Loc	Off Burntwood Lane SW17
Arch	Patrick Tallack

Chessington Golf Centre (1983)

Pay and play
Garrison Lane, Chessington
KT9 2LW

Tel	**(0181) 391 0948**
Fax	(0181) 397 2068
Mem	120
Sec	J Lafferty
Holes	9 L 1400 yds Par 54 SSS 50
Recs	Am–60 N Murphy
	Pro–54 R Hunter
V'tors	U
Fees	£4.50 (£5.40)
Loc	Off A243, opp Chessington
	South Station. M25
	Junction 9
Mis	Driving range

Chiddingfold (1994)

Petworth Road, Chiddingfold
GU8 4SL

Tel	**(01428) 685888**
Fax	(01428) 685939
Mem	400
Sec	Mrs L Pascolini (Gen Mgr)
	Mrs V Farrow (Admin)
Pro	P Creamer
Holes	18 L 5482 yds Par 70 SSS 67
Recs	Am–67 D Brown (1995)
	Pro–64 P Creamer (1995)
V'tors	U SOC
Fees	£18 (£25)
Loc	On A283 between Petworth
	and Guildford
Arch	Johnathan Gaunt

Chipstead (1906)

How Lane, Chipstead, Coulsdon
CR5 3LN

Tel	**(01737) 551053**
Fax	(01737) 555404
Mem	600
Sec	SLD Spencer-Skeen
	(01737) 555781
Pro	G Torbett (01737) 554939
Holes	18 L 5450 yds SSS 67
Recs	Am–63 B Sharples (1995)
	Pro–64 P Mitchell (1994)
V'tors	WD–U WE/BH–M
Fees	£25 After 2pm–£20
Loc	Nr Chipstead Station

Chobham (1994)

Chobham Road, Knaphill, Woking
GU21 2TZ

Tel	**(01276) 855584**
Fax	(01276) 855663
Mem	750
Sec	D Cross
Pro	R Thomas
Holes	18 L 5821 yds Par 69 SSS 68
Recs	Am–65 J Rose
	Pro–61 G Harris, R Boxall
V'tors	M H–restricted SOC
Fees	£24 (£30)
Loc	3 miles E of M3 Junction 3
	between Chobham and
	Knaphill (A3046)
Arch	Alliss/Clark

Clandon Regis (1994)

Epsom Road, West Clandon GU4 7TT
Tel (01483) 224888
Fax (01483) 211781
Mem 558
Sec N Caplin
Pro S Lloyd
Holes 18 L 6412 yds Par 72 SSS 71
Recs Am–68 A Booth (1996)
Pro–65 P Hughes (1995)
V'tors WD–U SOC–WD
Fees £26
Loc 3 miles E of Guildford on A246

Coombe Hill (1911)

Golf Club Drive, Coombe Lane West, Kingston KT2 7DF
Tel (0181) 942 2284
Fax (0181) 949 5815
Mem 553
Sec Mrs C De Foy
Pro C De Foy (0181) 949 3713
Holes 18 L 6303 yds SSS 71
Recs Am–66 C Boal
Pro–67 B Gallagher
V'tors WD–I or H WE–NA SOC
Fees D–£65
Loc 1 mile W of New Malden on A238
Arch JF Abercromby

Coombe Wood (1904)

George Road, Kingston Hill, Kingston-upon-Thames KT2 7NS
Tel (0181) 942 3828 (Clubhouse)
Fax (0181) 942 0388
Mem 640
Sec PM Urwin (0181) 942 0388
Pro D Butler (0181) 942 6764
Holes 18 L 5299 yds SSS 66
Recs Am–61 M Heath (1997)
Pro–60 D Butler (1987)
V'tors WD–U H after 9am
WE/BH–M SOC–WD
Fees On application
Loc 1 mile E of Kingston-upon-Thames, off A3 at Robin Hood roundabout or Coombe junction
Arch Williamson

Coulsdon Manor (1937)

Pay and play
Coulsdon Court Road, Coulsdon, Croydon CR5 2LL
Tel (0181) 668 0414
Fax (0181) 668 3118
Pro (0181) 660 6083
Holes 18 L 6037 yds SSS 70
Recs Am–66 K Smale
Pro–66 G Ralph
V'tors U
Fees £13 (£16)
Loc 5 miles S of Croydon on B2030. M25 Junction 7
Arch HS Colt

Croham Hurst (1911)

Croham Road, South Croydon CR2 7HJ
Tel (0181) 657 5581
Fax (0181) 657 3229
Mem 515 110(L) 50(J)

Sec R Passingham (Mgr)
Pro E Stillwell (0181) 657 7705
Holes 18 L 6286 yds SSS 70
Recs Am–64 CF Staroscik (1991)
Pro–66 B Firkins
V'tors WD–I WE/BH–M
Fees £33 (£42)
Loc 1 mile from S Croydon. M25 Junction 6-A22-B270-B269

Cuddington (1929)

Banstead Road, Banstead SM7 1RD
Tel (0181) 393 0952
Fax (0181) 786 7025
Mem 760
Sec DM Scott
Pro M Warner (0181) 393 5850
Holes 18 L 6394 yds SSS 70
Recs Am–68 S Stuart
Pro–61 J Spence
V'tors WD–I WE–M
Fees £35 (£40)
Loc Nr Banstead Station
Arch HS Colt

Dorking (1897)

Deepdene Avenue, Chart Park, Dorking RH5 4BX
Tel (01306) 886917
Fax (01306) 886917
Mem 420
Sec JB Hawkins
Pro P Napier
Holes 9 L 5163 yds SSS 65
Recs Am–61 R Mann
Pro–62 A King
V'tors WD–U WE/BH–M
SOC–WD
Fees £12
Loc 1 mile S of Dorking on A24
Arch James Braid

Drift (1976)

The Drift, East Horsley KT24 5HD
Tel (01483) 284641
Fax (01483) 284642
Mem 700
Sec C Rose
Pro J Hagen (01483) 284772
Holes 18 L 6425 yds SSS 72
Recs Am–71 B Rowan
Pro–71 J Bennett
V'tors WD–U SOC
Fees £30 After 1pm–£20
Loc 2 miles off A3 (B2039). M25 Junction 10

Duke's Dene (1996)

Slines New Road, Woldingham CR3 7HA
Tel (01883) 653501
Fax (01883) 653502
Mem 800
Sec D Sherette (Gen Mgr)
Pro P Thornley (01883) 653541
Holes 18 L 6322 yds Par 71 SSS 70
V'tors U SOC
Fees £25 (£30)
Loc 2½ miles N of M25 Junction 6
Arch Bradford Benz

Dulwich & Sydenham Hill (1894)

Grange Lane, College Road, London SE21 7LH
Tel (0181) 693 3961
Fax (0181) 693 2481
Mem 850
Sec Mrs S Alexander
Pro D Baillie (0181) 693 8491
Holes 18 L 6051 yds SSS 69
Recs Am–64 J Piner
Pro–63 LF Rowe
V'tors WD–H WE/BH–M SOC
Fees £25

Dunsfold Aerodrome (1965)

Dunsfold Aerodrome, Godalming GU8 4BS
Tel (01483) 265472
Mem 270
Sec F Tuck (01483) 265403
Pro None
Holes 9 L 6099 yds Par 70 SSS 69
Recs Am–70 R Arkwright (1991)
V'tors M
Fees £5 (£5)
Loc 10 miles S of Guildford, off A281
Arch Sharkey/Hayward

Effingham (1927)

Effingham Crossroads, Effingham KT24 5PZ
Tel (01372) 452203
Fax (01372) 459959
Mem 980
Sec RW Lamb
Pro S Hoatson (01372) 452606
Holes 18 L 6524 yds SSS 71
Recs Am–64 M Feltham (1997)
Pro–65 B Barnes (1984)
V'tors WD–H WE/BH–M
Fees £35 After 2pm–£27.50
Loc 8 miles N of Guildford on A246
Arch HS Colt

Epsom (1889)

Longdown Lane South, Epsom Downs, Epsom KT17 4JR
Tel (01372) 721666
Fax (01372) 817183
Mem 800
Sec JH Carter FCA
Pro R Goudie (01372) 741867
Holes 18 L 5701 yds SSS 68
Recs Am–68 D Barnett (1994)
Pro–62 K MacDonald (1996)
V'tors WD–U exc Tues am
WE/BH–NA before noon SOC
Fees £20
Loc ¾ mile NE of Epsom Racecourse

Farnham (1896)

The Sands, Farnham GU10 1PX
Tel (01252) 783163
Fax (01252) 781185
Mem 750

Sec Jill Brazill (01252) 782109
Pro G Cowlishaw (01252) 782198
Holes 18 L 6313 yds SSS 70
Recs Am–67 G Walmsley (1988)
Pro–66 B Cameron (1995)
V'tors WD–H WE–M SOC–Wed &
Thurs
Fees £30 D–£38
Loc 1 mile E of Farnham, off A31

Farnham Park Par Three
(1966)
Pay and play
Farnham Park, Farnham GU9 0AU
Tel (01252) 715216
Fax (01252) 718246
Mem 59
Sec P Chapman
Pro P Chapman
Holes 9 L 1163 yds Par 54
Recs Am–51 DW Bryant (1997)
Pro–56 G Wheeler (1966)
V'tors U
Fees £3.90 (£4.40)
Loc By Farnham Castle
Arch Henry Cotton

Fernfell G&CC (1985)
Barhatch Lane, Cranleigh GU6 7NG
Tel (01483) 268855
Fax (01483) 267251
Mem 600
Sec M Hale
Pro T Longmuir (01483) 277188
Holes 18 L 5648 yds SSS 67
Recs Am–66 R Edwards (1997)
Pro–64 A Lovelace (1995)
V'tors WD–U WE/BH–pm only
SOC–WD
Fees £20 (£25)
Loc 1 mile from Cranleigh,
off A281
Mis Driving range

Foxhills (1975)
Stonehill Road, Ottershaw KT16 0EL
Tel (01932) 872050
Fax (01932) 874762
Mem 975
Sec A Laking (Mgr)
Pro A Good (01932) 873961
Holes 18 L 6680 yds SSS 73
18 L 6547 yds SSS 72
9 hole course
Pro–65 P Dawson
V'tors WD–U WE–NA before noon
SOC–WD am
Fees £45 D–£65 (£55)
Loc 2 miles SW of Chertsey
on B386
Mis Driving range
Arch FW Hawtree

Gatton Manor Hotel G&CC (1969)
Standon Lane, Ockley, Dorking RH5 5PQ
Tel (01306) 627555
Fax (01306) 627713
Mem 250
Sec LC Heath

Pro R Sargent (01306) 627557
Holes 18 L 6653 yds SSS 72
Recs Am–72 J McLaren (1985)
Pro–73 R Sargent (1985)
V'tors U exc Sun before 1 pm–NA
SOC–WD
Fees £21 (£28)
Loc 1½ miles SW of Ockley,
off A29. M25 Junction 9,
S on A24
Mis Driving range
Arch Henry Cotton

Goal Farm Par Three
(1977)
Public
Gole Road, Pirbright GU24 OP2
Tel (01483) 473183/473205
Sec R & J Church (Props)
Pro K Warne
Holes 9 hole Par 3 course
Recs Am–45 P Wakefield (1991)
V'tors Sat/Thurs am–restricted
SOC–WD
Fees £7 (£7.50)
Loc 7 miles NW of Guildford

Guildford (1886)
High Path Road, Merrow, Guildford GU1 2HL
Tel (01483) 563941
Fax (01483) 453228
Mem 600
Sec BJ Green
Pro PG Hollington
(01483) 566765
Holes 18 L 6090 yds SSS 70
Recs Am–64 DG Lintott (1989)
Pro–66 H Stott (1996)
V'tors WD–U WE–M SOC–WD
Fees £25
Loc 2 miles E of Guildford
on A246

Hankley Common (1896)
Tilford, Farnham GU10 2DD
Tel (01252) 792493
Fax (01252) 795699
Mem 700
Sec JKA O'Brien
Pro P Stow (01252) 793761
Holes 18 L 6438 yds SSS 71
Recs Am–66 J Lee (1987)
Pro–62 H Stott (1988),
M Nichols (1994)
V'tors WD–U WE–discretion of Sec
Fees £40 (£50)
Loc 3 miles SE of Farnham on
Tilford road

Hazelwood Golf Centre
Pay and play
Croysdale Avenue, Green Street, Sunbury-on-Thames TW16 6QU
Tel (01932) 770932
Fax (01932) 770933
Mem 292
Sec J Reed
Pro P Erasmus
Holes 9 L 5660 yds Par 35 SSS 67
Recs Am–64 C Gough (1997)

V'tors U SOC
Fees £7 (£8.50)
Loc M3 Junction 1, 1 mile
Mis Driving range. Golf academy
Arch Jonathan Gaunt

Hindhead (1904)
Churt Road, Hindhead GU26 6HX
Tel (01428) 604614
Fax (01428) 608508
Mem 500 50(L) 60(J)
Sec Miss A McMenemy
Pro N Ogilvy (01428) 604458
Holes 18 L 6373 yds SSS 70
Recs Am–64 M Lassam
Pro–63 A Tillman
V'tors WD–U WE–by arrangement
H SOC–Wed & Thurs
Fees £36 (£44)
Loc 1½ miles N of Hindhead
on A287. M25 Junction 10,
25 miles

Hoebridge Golf Centre
(1982)
Public
Old Woking Road, Old Woking GU22 8JH
Tel (01483) 722611
Fax (01483) 740369
Mem 480
Sec P Gaylor (Mgr)
Pro TD Powell
Holes 18 L 6587 yds SSS 71
Inter 9 L 2294 yds Par 33
18 hole Par 3 course
V'tors U
Fees 18 hole: £15 (£17);
Inter: £8.50; Par 3–£7
Loc Between Old Woking and
West Byfleet on B382
Mis Floodlit driving range
Arch Jacobs/Hawtree

Home Park (1895)
Hampton Wick, Kingston-upon-Thames KT1 4AD
Tel (0181) 977 6645
Fax (0181) 977 4414
Mem 500
Sec BW O'Farrell
(0181) 977 2423
Pro L Roberts (0181) 977 2658
Holes 18 L 6610 yds SSS 71
V'tors U
Fees £15 (£25)
Loc 1 mile W of Kingston

Horton Park CC (1993)
Hook Road, Epsom KT19 8QG
Tel (0181) 393 8400 (Enquiries),
(0181) 394 2626 (Bookings)
Fax (0181) 394 1369
Mem 510
Sec P Hart (Gen Mgr)
(0181) 393 8400
Pro J Robson, G Clements
(0181) 394 2626
Holes 18 L 5197 yds SSS 66
V'tors U SOC
Fees £11 (£13)

Loc 1 mile from A3, W of Ewell.
M25 Junction 9
Mis Driving range
Arch Patrick Tallack

Hurtmore (1991)

Pay and play
Hurtmore Road, Hurtmore, Godalming
GU7 2RN
Tel (01483) 426492
Fax (01483) 426121
Mem 200
Sec E McKee
Pro Maxine Burton
Holes 18 L 5444 yds SSS 66
V'tors WD–U WE–booking advisable
SOC
Fees £10 (£14)
Loc 5 miles S of Guildford on A3.
M25 Junction 10
Arch Alliss/Clark

Kingswood (1928)

Sandy Lane, Kingswood, Tadworth
KT20 6NE
Tel (01737) 833316
Fax (01737) 833920
Mem 770
Sec S Fitzgibbon (01737) 832188
Pro J Dodds (01737) 832334
Holes 18 L 6904 yds SSS 73
Recs Am–70 P Stanford
Pro–67 R Blackie
V'tors U SOC
Fees £32 (£42)
Loc 5 miles S of Sutton on A217.
M25 Junction 8, 2 miles
Mis Driving range
Arch James Braid

Laleham (1907)

Laleham Reach, Chertsey KT16 8RP
Tel (01932) 564211
Fax (01932) 564448
Mem 600
Sec Mrs PA Kennett
Pro H Stott
Holes 18 L 6203 yds SSS 70
Recs Am–65 K Archer (1995)
Pro–65 C Defoy (1986)
V'tors WD–U 9.30–4.30pm WE–M
SOC–Mon–Wed
Fees £18–£25
Loc 2 miles S of Staines, opposite
Thorpe Park

Leatherhead (1903)

Kingston Road, Leatherhead KT22 0EE
Tel (01372) 843966
Fax (01372) 842241
Mem 600
Sec R Beswick
Pro S Norman (01372) 843956
Holes 18 L 6203 yds SSS 70
Recs Am–66 J Double (1996)
Pro–65 J Sewell (1992),
S Norman (1993)
V'tors U SOC
Fees £30 (£45)
Loc On A243 to Chessington.
M25 Junction 9

Limpsfield Chart (1889)

Westerham Road, Limpsfield RH8 0SL
Tel (01883) 723405/722106
Mem 350
Sec DS Adams
Pro None
Holes 9 L 5718 yds SSS 68
Recs Am–67 N Simmons
Pro–64 B Huggett
V'tors WD–U exc Thurs (Ladies
Day) WE–M or by
appointment SOC
Fees £18 (£20)
Loc 2 miles E of Oxted

Lingfield Park (1987)

Racecourse Road, Lingfield RH7 6PQ
Tel (01342) 834602
Fax (01342) 836077
Mem 700
Sec J Russell
Pro C Morley (01342) 832659
Holes 18 L 6500 yds SSS 72
Recs Am–70 G Sutton (1995)
Pro–69 S Defoy (1996)
V'tors WD–U WE/BH–M SOC–WD
Fees £27 (£37)
Loc Next to Lingfield racecourse.
M25 Junction 6
Mis Driving range

London Scottish (1865)

Windmill Enclosure, Wimbledon
Common, London SW19 5NQ
Tel (0181) 788 0135
Fax (0181) 789 7517
Mem 250
Sec S Barr (0181) 789 7517
Pro S Barr (0181) 789 1207
Holes 18 L 5458 yds Par 68 SSS 66
Recs Am–64 A Glickberg (1975)
Pro–62 P Sefton (1996)
V'tors WD–U WE/BH–NA SOC
Fees On application
Loc Wimbledon Common
Mis Red upper garment must be
worn
Arch Willie Dunn/Tom Dunn

Malden (1893)

Traps Lane, New Malden KT3 4RS
Tel (0181) 942 0654
Fax (0181) 336 2219
Mem 800
Sec PG Fletcher
Pro R Hunter (0181) 942 6009
Holes 18 L 6295 yds SSS 70
Recs Am–65 G Lashford
Pro–63 P Talbot
V'tors WD–U WE–restricted
SOC–Wed–Fri
Fees On application
Loc Off A3, between Wimbledon
and Kingston

Merrist Wood (1997)

Coombe Lane, Worplesdon, Guildford
GU3 3PE
Tel (01483) 884045
Fax (01483) 884047
Mem 700

Sec R Penley-Martin (Gen Mgr)
Pro A Kirk (01483) 884050
Holes 18 L 6575 yds Par 72 SSS 71
V'tors H SOC–WD
Fees £35 D–£60 (£50)
Loc 2 miles W of Guildford, off
A323
Arch David Williams

Milford

Station Lane, Milford GU8 5HS
Tel (01483) 419200
Fax (01483) 419199
Mem 750
Sec M Hatch (Mgr)
Pro N English (01483) 416291
Holes 18 L 5960 yds Par 69 SSS 68
Recs Am–65 D Jenkins
Pro–64 M Nicholls
V'tors WD–H WE–restricted SOC
Fees £19.50 (£35)
Loc 3 miles SW of Guildford,
off A3
Arch Alliss/Clark

Mitcham (1924)

Carshalton Road, Mitcham
Junction CR4 4HN
Tel (0181) 648 1508
Fax (0181) 648 4197
Mem 450
Sec WJ Dutch (0181) 648 4197
Pro JA Godfrey (0181) 640 4280
Holes 18 L 5931 yds SSS 68
Recs Am–D Wilde
V'tors WD–U WE–NA before
1.30pm SOC
Fees £13 (£13)
Loc Mitcham Junction Station

Moore Place (1926)

Public
Portsmouth Road, Esher KT10 9LN
Tel (01372) 463533
Fax (01372) 460274
Mem 160
Sec D Allen (Mgr)
Pro D Allen
Holes 9 L 4216 yds SSS 58
Recs Am–29 W Cavanagh
Pro–25 P Loxley
V'tors U
Fees £5.80 (£7.70)
Loc Centre of Esher
Arch D Allen

New Zealand (1895)

Woodham Lane, Addlestone
KT15 3QD
Tel (01932) 345049
Fax (01932) 342891
Mem 300
Sec J Manley (01932) 342891
Pro VR Elvidge (01932) 349619
Holes 18 L 6012 yds SSS 69
Recs Am–66 P Cannings
Pro–72 A Herd
V'tors By request
Fees On application
Loc Woking 3 miles. West Byfleet
1 mile. Weybridge 5 miles

North Downs (1899)
Northdown Road, Woldingham
CR3 7AA

Tel	**(01883) 653397**
Fax	(01883) 652832
Mem	650
Sec	JAL Smith (Mgr)
	(01883) 652057
Pro	M Homewood (01883)
	653004
Holes	18 L 5843 yds SSS 68
Recs	Am–66 M Smallcorn (1989),
	AL Smith (1996),
	HJ Young (1997)
	Pro–65 W Humphreys (1987)
V'tors	WD–U WE–M
	SOC–Tues/Wed/Fri
Fees	£25
Loc	3 miles E of Caterham.
	M25 Junction 6
Arch	JF Pennink

Oak Park (1984)
Heath Lane, Crondall, Farnham
GU10 5PB

Tel	**(01252) 850880**
Fax	(01252) 850851
Mem	500
Sec	Mrs R Smythe (Prop)
Pro	S Coaker (01252) 850066
Holes	Woodland 18 L 6318 yds
	SSS 70
	Village 9 L 3279 yds Par 36
Recs	Am–71 A Wheeler (1994)
	Pro–67 K Jackson (1995)
V'tors	H I SOC Village–U
Fees	Woodland £20 (£30);
	Village £10 (£12)
Loc	Off A287 Farnham-Odiham
	road. M3 Junction 5, 4 miles
Mis	Floodlit driving range
Arch	Patrick Dawson

Oaks Sports Centre (1973)
Public
Woodmansterne Road, Carshalton
SM5 4AN

Tel	**(0181) 643 8363**
Fax	(0181) 770 7303
Mem	1000
Pro	G Horley
Holes	18 L 6023 yds SSS 69
	9 hole course
Recs	Pro–66 G Horley
V'tors	U
Fees	18 hole: £12 (£14)
	9 hole: £5.65 (£6.60)
Loc	2 miles from Sutton on B278
Mis	Floodlit driving range

Pachesham Park Golf Centre (1990)
Pay and play
Oaklawn Road, Leatherhead KT22 0BT

Tel	**(01372) 843453**
Fax	(01372) 844076
Mem	420
Sec	P Taylor
Pro	P Taylor
Holes	9 L 2804 yds Par 35
Recs	Pro–67 W Grant (1997)

V'tors	U SOC
Fees	9 holes–£7.50 (£9)
Loc	NW of Leatherhead, off A244.
	M25 Junction 9
Mis	Driving range
Arch	P Taylor

Pine Ridge (1992)
Old Bisley Road, Frimley, Camberley
GU16 5NX

Tel	**(01276) 20770**
Fax	(01276) 678837
Pro	A Kelso
Holes	18 L 6458 yds SSS 71
Recs	Am–65 V Phillips (1993)
	Pro–67 C Montgomerie (1993)
V'tors	U
Fees	£16 (£20)
Loc	Off Maultway, between
	Lightwater and Frimley.
	M3 Junction 3, 2 miles
Mis	Floodlit driving range
Arch	Clive D Smith

Purley Downs (1894)
106 Purley Downs Road, Purley, South
Croydon CR2 0RB

Tel	**(0181) 657 8347**
Fax	(0181) 651 5044
Mem	700
Sec	PC Gallienne
Pro	G Wilson
	(0181) 651 0819
Holes	18 L 6230 yds SSS 70
Recs	Am–65 MD Dawton
	Pro–64 R Blackie
V'tors	WD–I WE–M
Fees	On application
Loc	3 miles S of Croydon (A235)

Puttenham (1894)
Puttenham, Guildford GU3 1AL

Tel	**(01483) 810498**
Fax	(01483) 810988
Mem	500
Sec	G Simmons
Pro	G Simmons
	(01483) 810277
Holes	18 L 6200 yds SSS 70
Recs	Am–67 L Boxall (1996)
V'tors	WD–by prior appointment
	WE/BH–M SOC–Wed &
	Thurs
Fees	On application
Loc	Midway between Guildford
	and Farnham on Hog's Back

Pyrford (1993)
Warren Lane, Pyrford GU22 8XR

Tel	**(01483) 723555**
Fax	(01483) 729777
Sec	D Renton
Pro	J Bennett (01483) 751070
Holes	18 L 6201 yds SSS 70
Recs	Am–73 A Kikkidas
	Pro–64 J Bennett
V'tors	H SOC
Fees	£35 (£50)
Loc	2 miles from A3 at Ripley
Arch	Alliss/Clark

RAC Country Club (1913)
Woodcote Park, Epsom KT18 7EW

Tel	**(01372) 276311**
Fax	(01372) 276117
Sec	K Symons
Pro	I Howieson (01372) 279514
Holes	Old 18 L 6709 yds SSS 72
	Coronation 18 L 5598 yds
	SSS 67
Recs	Old Am–68 GW Nielsen
	(1994)
	Old Pro–66 M Roe (1997)
V'tors	M SOC
Loc	Epsom Station 1 3/4 miles
Arch	Fowler/Myddleton

Redhill (1993)
Pay and play
Canada Avenue, Redhill RH1 5BF

Tel	**(01737) 770204**
Fax	(01737) 760046
Mem	90
Sec	S Furlonger
Pro	T Clingan
Holes	9 L 1903 yds Par 31 SSS 59
V'tors	U SOC
Fees	9 holes–£4.50 (£5.75)
Loc	1 1/2 miles S of Redhill on A23.
	Grounds of East Surrey
	Hospital
Mis	Floodlit driving range
Arch	Peter Casemore

Redhill & Reigate (1887)
Clarence Lodge, Pendleton Road, Redhill
RH1 6LB

Tel	**(01737) 244626/244433**
Mem	500
Sec	C Brown (01737) 240777
Pro	W Pike (01737) 244433
Holes	18 L 5238 yds SSS 66
V'tors	WD–U WE–phone first SOC
Fees	£11 (£16)
Loc	1 mile S of Redhill on A23

Reigate Heath (1895)
The Club House, Reigate Heath
RH2 8QR

Tel	**(01737) 242610**
Fax	(01737) 226793
Mem	330 80(L) 60(J)
Sec	RJ Perkins (01737) 226793
Pro	B Davies
Holes	9 L 5658 yds SSS 67
Recs	Am–65 H Maurice (1995)
	Pro–65 P Loxley (1977)
V'tors	WD–U Sun/BH–M
	SOC–Wed & Thurs
Fees	On application
Loc	W boundary of Reigate Heath

Reigate Hill
Gatton Bottom, Reigate RH2 0TU

Tel	**(01737) 645577**
Fax	(01737) 642650
Mem	650
Sec	AP Barclay
Pro	M Platts (01737) 646070
Holes	18 L 6175 yds Par 72 SSS 70

V'tors WD–U WE–M SOC
Fees £25
Loc 1 mile from M25 Junction 8, off A217
Arch David Williams

Richmond (1891)

Sudbrook Park, Richmond TW10 7AS
Tel **(0181) 940 1463**
Fax (0181) 332 7914
Mem 500
Sec RL Wilkins (0181) 940 4351
Pro N Job (0181) 940 7792
Holes 18 L 6007 yds SSS 69
Recs Am–63 A Riley, T Cowgill
Pro–63 N Price
V'tors WD–H
Fees £38
Loc Between Richmond and Kingston-upon-Thames

Richmond Park (1923)

Public
Roehampton Gate, Richmond Park, London SW15 5JR
Tel **(0181) 876 3205/1795**
Fax (0181) 878 1354
Sec AJ Gourvish
Pro D Bown
Holes Dukes 18 L 6036 yds SSS 68
Princes 18 L 5868 yds SSS 67
V'tors WD–U WE–booking necessary SOC–WD
Fees On application
Loc In Richmond Park
Mis Driving range
Arch Hawtree

Roehampton (1901)

Roehampton Lane, London SW15 5LR
Tel **(0181) 876 1621**
Fax (0181) 392 2386
Mem 1200
Sec M Yates (Chief Exec) (0181) 876 5505; JW Tucker (Mgr) (0181) 876 1621
Pro AL Scott (0181) 876 3858
Holes 18 L 6065 yds SSS 69
Recs Am–67 AL Scott
Pro–62 H Stott
V'tors WD/WE–Introduced by member
Fees On application
Loc 1 mile W of Putney, off South Circular

Roker Park (1993)

Pay and play
Holly Lane, Aldershot Road, Guildford GU3 3PB
Tel **(01483) 236677**
Mem 200
Sec C Tegg
Pro K Warn (01483) 236677
Holes 9 L 3037 yds SSS 72
V'tors U SOC
Fees £7 (£8.50)
Loc 2 miles W of Guildford on A323
Mis Driving range
Arch Alan Helling

Royal Mid-Surrey (1892)

Old Deer Park, Richmond TW9 2SB
Tel **(0181) 940 1894**
Fax (0181) 332 2957
Mem 1250
Sec MSR Lunt
Pro D Talbot (0181) 940 0459
Holes Outer 18 L 6385 yds SSS 70
Inner 18 L 5446 yds SSS 67
Recs Outer Am–62 P Cunningham
Pro–64 R Charles, B Gallacher
V'tors WD–H or M WE/BH–M SOC
Fees £55
Loc Nr Richmond roundabout, off A316
Arch JH Taylor

Royal Wimbledon (1865)

29 Camp Road, Wimbledon, London SW19 4UW
Tel **(0181) 946 2125**
Fax (0181) 944 8652
Mem 800
Sec PJT Svehlik
Pro H Boyle (0181) 946 4606
Holes 18 L 6362 yds SSS 70
Recs Am–66 JFM Connolly
Pro–71 R Burton
V'tors NA
Arch HS Colt

Rusper (1992)

Rusper Road, Newdigate RH5 5BX
Tel **(01293) 871456,**
(01293) 871871 (Bookings)
Fax (01293) 871456
Mem 270
Sec G Hems
Pro Janice Arnold (01293) 871871
Holes 9 L 6218 yds SSS 69
Recs Am–72 I Tween (1996)
Pro–67 R Dickman (1994)
V'tors U
Fees 18 holes–£11.50 (£15.50)
9 holes–£7 (£8.50)
Loc 5 miles S of Dorking, off A24
Mis Driving range
Arch AW Blunden

St George's Hill (1912)

Golf Club Road, St George's Hill, Weybridge KT13 0NL
Tel **(01932) 847758**
Fax (01932) 821564
Mem 600
Sec J Robinson
Pro AC Rattue (01932) 843523
Holes 27 L 6097-6569 yds SSS 69-71
Recs Am–65 D Swanston
Pro–64 A Raitt
V'tors WD–I H WE/BH–M SOC–Wed–Fri
Fees £50 D–£65
Loc 2 miles N of M25/A3 Junction, on B374
Arch HS Colt

Sandown Park (1970)

Public
More Lane, Esher KT10 8AN
Tel **(01372) 461234**
Sec P Barriball (Mgr)

Pro R Catley Smith
Holes 9 L 5658 yds SSS 67
9 hole Par 3 course
Recs Am–68 M Mabbott (1993)
V'tors U–closed on race days
Fees £6 (£7.50)
Loc Sandown Park Racecourse
Mis Floodlit driving range
Arch John Jacobs

Selsdon Park Hotel (1929)

Addington Road, Sanderstead, South Croydon CR2 8YA
Tel **(0181) 657 8811**
Fax (0181) 651 3401
Sec Mrs C Screene
Pro M Churchill (0181) 657 4129
Holes 18 L 6473 yds SSS 71
Recs Am–68 M Welch
Pro–64 M Job
V'tors U SOC (min 12 golfers)
Fees £20 (£30)
Loc 3 miles S of Croydon on A2022 Purley-Addington road
Mis Driving range
Arch JH Taylor

Shirley Park (1914)

194 Addiscombe Road, Croydon CR0 7LB
Tel **(0181) 654 1143**
Fax (0181) 654 6733
Mem 600
Sec A Baird
Pro P Webb (0181) 654 8767
Holes 18 L 6210 yds SSS 70
Recs Am–66 J Good
Pro–65 J Bennett
V'tors WD–U WE/BH–M SOC
Fees £30
Loc On A232, 1 mile E of East Croydon Station

Silvermere (1976)

Pay and play
Redhill Road, Cobham KT11 1EF
Tel **(01932) 867275**
Mem 900
Sec Mrs P Devereux
Pro D McClelland
Holes 18 L 6333 yds SSS 71
Pro–65 S Rolley (1986)
V'tors WD–U WE–NA before 1pm SOC
Fees £18.50 (£25)
Loc 1/2 mile from M25 Junction 10 on B366 to Byfleet
Mis Floodlit driving range

Sunningdale (1900)

Ridgemount Road, Sunningdale SL5 9RW
Tel **(01344) 621681**
Fax (01344) 624154
Mem 800
Sec S Zuill
Pro K Maxwell (01344) 620128
Holes Old 18 L 6609 yds SSS 72
New 18 L 6703 yds SSS 72

Recs Old Am–66 MC Hughesdon
Pro–62 N Faldo
New Am–62 C Challen
Pro–64 GJ Player
V'tors Mon–Thurs–I Fri/WE–M
Fees Old £100 New £75
Loc Sunningdale Station ¼ mile,
off A30
Arch Willie Park/HS Colt

Sunningdale Ladies (1902)

Cross Road, Sunningdale SL5 9RX
Tel (01344) 20507
Mem 400
Sec JF Darroch
Holes 18 L 3622 yds SSS 60
V'tors WD/WE–by appointment. No
3 or 4 balls before 11am
Fees Ladies £18 (£20)
Men £22 (£27)
Loc Sunningdale Station ¼ mile
Arch HS Colt

Surbiton (1895)

Woodstock Lane, Chessington KT9 1UG
Tel (0181) 398 3101
Fax (0181) 339 0992
Mem 750
Sec DR Crockford
Pro P Milton (0181) 398 6619
Holes 18 L 6055 yds SSS 69
Recs Am–63 N Reilly
Pro–63 C de Foy
V'tors WD–H WE/BH–M
Fees £30 D–£45
Loc 2 miles E of Esher

Sutton Green

Sutton Green, Woking GU4 7QF
Tel (01483) 747898
Sec J Buchanan
Pro T Dawson (01483) 766849
Holes 18 L 6300 yds Par 71 SSS 70
V'tors U
Fees £25 (£30)
Loc 2 miles S of Woking

Tandridge (1925)

Oxted RH8 9NQ
Tel (01883) 712273 (Clubhouse)
Fax (01883) 730537
Mem 750
Sec Lt Cdr SE Kennard RN
(01883) 712274
Pro A Farquhar (01883) 713701
Holes 18 L 6250 yds SSS 70
Recs Am–68 JC Robson
Pro–69 BGC Huggett
V'tors Mon/Wed/Thurs only–H
SOC–Mon/Wed/Thurs
Fees On application
Loc 5 miles E of Redhill, off A25.
M25 Junction 6
Arch HS Colt

Thames Ditton & Esher (1892)

Portsmouth Road, Esher KT10 9AL
Tel (0181) 398 1551
Mem 300
Sec D Kaye

Pro M Rodbard
Holes 9 L 5419 yds SSS 65
Recs Am–61 T Petitt
Pro–61 D Regan
V'tors WD–U WE–by arrangement
Fees £10 (£12)
Loc Esher

Tyrrells Wood (1924)

Tyrrells Wood, Leatherhead KT22 8QP
Tel (01372) 376025 (2 lines)
Fax (01372) 360836
Mem 744
Sec CGR Kydd
Pro M Taylor (01372) 375200
Holes 18 L 6282 yds SSS 70
Recs Am–67 P Earl (1988)
Pro–65 P Hoad (1988)
V'tors WD–I BH/Sat–NA Sun–NA
before noon SOC
Fees £34 (£44)
Loc 2 miles SE of Leatherhead,
off A24 nr Headley. M25
Junction 9, 1 mile

Walton Heath (1903)

*Deans Lane, Walton-on-the-Hill,
Tadworth KT20 7TP*
Tel (01737) 812060
Fax (01737) 814225
Mem 900
Sec N Lomas (01737) 812380
Pro K Macpherson
(01737) 812152
Holes Old 18 L 6801 yds SSS 73
New 18 L 6609 yds SSS 72
Recs Old Am–68 R Revell
Pro–65 P Townsend
New Am–67 JK Tate,
AJ Wells, RDH Hall
Pro–64 C Clark
Ch'ship Pro–64 I Woosnam
(1987), M Harwood (1991)
V'tors WD–I H WE/BH–M SOC
Fees On application
Loc 18 miles S of London on
A217/B2032. 2 miles N of
M25 Junction 8
Arch WH Fowler

The Wentworth Club (1924)

*Wentworth Drive, Virginia Water
GU25 4LS*
Tel (01344) 842201
Fax (01344) 842804
Mem 2335
Sec J Grant (Admin)
Pro D Rennie (01344) 846306
Holes West 18 L 6957 yds SSS 74
East 18 L 6176 yds SSS 70
Edinburgh 18 L 6979 yds
SSS 73
Executive 9 L 1902 yds Par 27
Recs West Am–72 P McEvoy
Pro–63 W Riley
East Am–65 G Wolstenholme
Pro–62 DN Sewell, G Will
Edinburgh Pro–67 G Orr
V'tors WD–H by prior arrangement
WE–M SOC–WD
Fees On application

Loc 21 miles SW of London at
A30/A329 junction. M25
Junction 13, 8 miles
Mis Driving range
Arch HS Colt (East/West).
Jacobs/Player (Edinburgh)

West Byfleet (1906)

*Sheerwater Road, West Byfleet
KT14 6AA*
Tel (01932) 345230
Fax (01932) 340667
Mem 550
Sec DG Lee (Gen Mgr)
(01932) 343433
Pro D Regan (01932) 346584
Holes 18 L 6211 yds SSS 70
Recs Am–66 W Calderwood
Pro–65 R Dickman,
N Gorman (1994)
V'tors WD–U WE/BH–NA SOC
Fees £30 D–£38
Loc West Byfleet ½ mile on A245.
M25 Junction 10 or 11
Arch CS Butchart

West Hill (1909)

*Bagshot Road, Brookwood
GU24 0BH*
Tel (01483) 474365/472110
Fax (01483) 474252
Mem 550
Sec MC Swatton
Pro JA Clements (01483) 473172
Holes 18 L 6368 yds SSS 70
Recs Am–65 A Carter
Pro–62 G Brown
V'tors WD–H WE–M SOC
Fees £35 D–£45
Loc 5 miles W of Woking
on A322

West Surrey (1910)

Enton Green, Godalming GU8 5AF
Tel (01483) 421275
Fax (01483) 415419
Mem 750
Sec RT Crabb
Pro A Tawse (01483) 417278
Holes 18 L 6259 yds SSS 70
Recs Am–66 SD Cook
Pro–65 G Orr
V'tors H SOC–Wed/Thurs/Fri
Fees £27 (£47)
Loc ½ mile SE of Milford Station
Arch Herbert Fowler

Wildwood (1992)

Horsham Road, Afold GU6 8JE
Tel (01403) 753255
Fax (01403) 752005
Sec A Hill
Pro N Parfrement
Holes 18 L 6650 yds SSS 72
Pro–67 H Stott (1993)
V'tors H SOC–WD
Fees D–£25 (£37.50)
Loc 10 miles S of Guildford on
A281
Mis Driving range
Arch Hawtree

Wimbledon Common
(1908)

19 Camp Road, Wimbledon Common, London SW19 4UW

Tel	(0181) 946 0294
Fax	(0181) 947 8697
Mem	250
Sec	BK Cox (0181) 946 7571
Pro	JS Jukes
Holes	18 L 5438 yds SSS 66
Recs	Am–63 MA Woodward, TP Standish
	Pro–64 JS Jukes
V'tors	WD–U WE–M Sun pm BH–NA
Fees	£15
Loc	Wimbledon Common
Mis	Pillarbox red outer garment must be worn. London Scottish play here

Wimbledon Park (1898)

Home Park Road, London SW19 7HR

Tel	(0181) 946 1002
Fax	(0181) 944 8688
Mem	650
Sec	PJ Dell (0181) 946 1250
Pro	D Wingrove (0181) 946 4053
Holes	18 L 5492 yds SSS 66
Recs	Am–60 D Braggins
	Pro–60 M Gerrard
V'tors	WD–H I WE/BH–after 3pm SOC
Fees	D–£40 (£40)
Loc	Opp All England Lawn Tennis Club

Windlemere (1978)

Pay and play

Windlesham Road, West End, Woking GU24 9QL

Tel	(01276) 858727
Fax	(01276) 678837
Sec	CD Smith
Pro	D Thomas
Holes	9 L 5346 yds SSS 66
V'tors	U
Fees	9 holes–£7.50 (£9)
Loc	A319 at Lightwater/West End
Mis	Floodlit driving range
Arch	Clive D Smith

Windlesham (1994)

Grove End, Bagshot GU19 5HY

Tel	(01276) 452220
Fax	(01276) 452290
Mem	800
Sec	AJ Walters
Pro	L Mucklow (01276) 472323
Holes	18 L 6515 yds SSS 71
Recs	Am–68 G Woodman (1996)
V'tors	H–phone first SOC–WD
Fees	£40 (£50)
Loc	½ mile N of M3 Junction 3, off A30/A322
Mis	Driving range
Arch	Tommy Horton

The Wisley (1991)

Ripley, Woking GU23 6QU

Tel	(01483) 211022
Fax	(01483) 211662
Mem	700
Sec	JR Arthur OBE
Pro	W Reid (01483) 211213
Holes	27 holes SSS 73:
	Church 9 L 3355 yds
	Garden 9 L 3385 yds
	Mill 9 L 3473 yds
Recs	Am–69 T Gottstein (1995)
V'tors	M
Loc	1 mile S of M25 Junction 10
Arch	Robert Trent Jones Jr

Woking (1893)

Pond Road, Hook Heath, Woking GU22 0JZ

Tel	(01483) 760053
Fax	(01483) 772441
Mem	500
Sec	Lt Col IJ Holmes
Pro	J Thorne (01483) 769582
Holes	18 L 6340 yds SSS 70
Recs	Am–65 PJ Benka (1968)
V'tors	WD–I H WE/BH–M
Fees	£45
Loc	W of Woking in St John's/ Hook Heath area
Arch	Tom Dunn

Woodcote Park
(1912)

Meadow Hill, Bridle Way, Coulsdon CR5 2QQ

Tel	(0181) 660 0176
Fax	(0181) 668 2788
Mem	630
Sec	TJ Fensom (0181) 668 2788
Pro	D Hudspith (0181) 668 1843
Holes	18 L 6669 yds SSS 72
Recs	Am–66 S Keppler
	Pro–66 C Bonner
V'tors	WD–U WE–M
Fees	£30 D–£40
Loc	Purley 2 miles

Worplesdon (1908)

Heath House Road, Woking GU22 0RA

Tel	(01483) 472277
Fax	(01483) 473303
Mem	580
Sec	JT Christine
Pro	JT Christine (01483) 473287
Holes	18 L 6440 yds SSS 71
Recs	Am–64 KG Jones (1988), AD Tillman (1991)
	Pro–62
	Ladies–67 W Wooldridge
V'tors	WD–H WE–M
Fees	On application
Loc	E of Woking, off A322. 6 miles S of M3 Junction 3

Sussex (East)

Ashdown Forest Golf Hotel

Chapel Lane, Forest Row RH18 5BB

Tel	(01342) 824866
Fax	(01342) 824869
Mem	150 (Anderida GS)
Sec	LR Anderson (Hotel Mgr)
Pro	M Landsborough (01342) 822247
Holes	18 L 5606 yds SSS 67
V'tors	U SOC
Fees	£16 (£21)
Loc	4 miles S of E Grinstead. 12 miles W of Tunbridge Wells
Mis	Royal Ashdown Forest West Course

Brighton & Hove (1887)

Devils Dyke Road, Brighton BN1 8YJ

Tel	(01273) 556482
Fax	(01273) 556482
Mem	373
Sec	MD Harrity
Pro	P Bonsall (01273) 540560
Holes	9 L 5710 yds SSS 68
Recs	Am–65 A Schofield (1992)
V'tors	U SOC Sun–NA before noon
Fees	£15 (£25)
Loc	4 miles N of Brighton
Arch	James Braid

Cooden Beach (1912)

Cooden Beach, Bexhill-on-Sea TN39 4TR

Tel	(01424) 842040
Fax	(01424) 842040
Mem	700
Sec	TE Hawes
Pro	J Sim (01424) 843938
Holes	18 L 6470 yds SSS 71
Recs	Am–69 CM Skinner, MP Owen
	Pro–67 D Geall
V'tors	H SOC
Fees	£29 (£35)
Loc	W boundary of Bexhill
Arch	Herbert Fowler

Crowborough Beacon
(1895)

Beacon Road, Crowborough TN6 1UJ

Tel	(01892) 661511
Fax	(01892) 667339
Mem	700
Sec	Mrs V Harwood (01892) 661511
Pro	D Newnham (01892) 653877
Holes	18 L 6256 yds SSS 70
Recs	Am–64 GCD Carter, SF Robson, I McKellow (1993), G Smith (1997)
	Pro–66 D Geal (1992)
V'tors	I H WE/BH–M
Fees	£25–£40
Loc	9 miles S of Tunbridge Wells on A26

Dale Hill Hotel (1973)

Ticehurst, Wadhurst TN5 7DQ

Tel	**(01580) 200112**
Fax	(01580) 201249
Mem	640
Sec	Jane Griffiths (Sec/Mgr)
Pro	A Good (01580) 201090
Holes	18 L 6106 yds SSS 69
	Pro–68 K MacDonald
V'tors	WD–U WE/BH–H phone first SOC
Fees	£20 (£30)
Loc	B2087, off A21 at Flimwell
Mis	Driving range. 2nd course open 1997

Dewlands Manor (1992)

Pay and play
Cottage Hill, Rotherfield TN6 3JN

Tel	**(01892) 852266**
Fax	(01892) 853015
Sec	R Page
Pro	N Godin
Holes	9 L 3186 yds Par 36
V'tors	U–phone first
Fees	9 holes–£13 (£15)
	18 holes–£24 (£28)
Loc	½ mile S of Rotherfield, off A267/B2101. 10 miles S of Tunbridge Wells. M25 Junction 5
Arch	Reg Godin

The Dyke (1906)

Devil's Dyke, Dyke Road, Brighton BN1 8YJ

Tel	**(01273) 857296**
Fax	(01273) 857078
Mem	750
Sec	TR White
Pro	(01273) 857260
Holes	18 L 6611 yds SSS 72
Recs	Am–68 S Crooks
	Pro–66 I Dryden
V'tors	U exc Sun–NA
Fees	£25 D–£35 (£35)
Loc	4 miles N of Brighton
Arch	Fred Hawtree

East Brighton (1893)

Roedean Road, Brighton BN2 5RA

Tel	**(01273) 604838**
Fax	(01273) 680277
Mem	650
Sec	DM Jackson
Pro	RS Goodway (01273) 603989
Holes	18 L 6346 yds SSS 70
Recs	Am–67 AW Schofield (1995)
	Pro–63 S King
V'tors	WD–U H after 9am WE–NA before 11am SOC
Fees	£17 D–£22 (£20 D–£30)
Loc	1½ miles E of Town Centre, overlooking Marina
Arch	James Braid

East Sussex National (1989)

Little Horsted, Uckfield TN22 5ES

Tel	**(01825) 880088**
Fax	(01825) 880066
Mem	770
Sec	P Lewin (Golf Dir)
Pro	I Naylor (01825) 880256
Holes	East 18 L 7138 yds SSS 74
	West 18 L 7154 yds SSS 74
Recs	East Am–68 M Watson (1993)
	East Pro–65 G Brand Jr (1993)
	West Pro–64 T Bjorn (1995)
V'tors	U on one course
Fees	Summer–£45 Winter–£35
Loc	2 miles S of Uckfield, on A22
Mis	Driving range. Golf academy
Arch	Bob Cupp

Eastbourne Downs (1907)

East Dean Road, Eastbourne BN20 8ES

Tel	**(01323) 720827**
Fax	(01323) 412506
Mem	650
Sec	AJ Reeves
Pro	T Marshall (01323) 732264
Holes	18 L 6601 yds SSS 72
Recs	Am–67 J Collison (1988)
	Pro–70 B Gallacher
V'tors	WD–U WE–NA before 11am
Fees	D–£20
Loc	1 mile W of Eastbourne on A259
Arch	JH Taylor

Eastbourne Golfing Park (1992)

Pay and play
Lottbridge Drove, Eastbourne BN23 6QJ

Tel	**(01323) 520400**
Fax	(01323) 520400
Mem	250
Sec	R Cruttenden
Pro	B Finch
Holes	9 L 5046 yds SSS 65
Recs	Am–64 G Murray (1994)
V'tors	U
Fees	£8 (£12)
Loc	½ mile S of Hampden Park
Mis	Floodlit driving range
Arch	David Ashton

Hastings (1973)

Public
Beauport Park, Battle Road, St Leonards-on-Sea TN38 0TA

Tel	**(01424) 852977**
Sec	Mrs H Hovenden
Pro	C Giddins (01424) 852981
Holes	18 L 6248 yds SSS 71
Recs	Am–69 V Massarella (1981)
	Pro–72 S Hall (1987)
V'tors	U–booking necessary SOC
Fees	£10.30 (£13)
Loc	3 miles N of Hastings, off A2100 Battle road
Mis	Driving range

Highwoods (1925)

Ellerslie Lane, Bexhill-on-Sea TN39 4LJ

Tel	**(01424) 212625**
Fax	(01424) 216866
Mem	800
Sec	JE Osborough
Pro	MJ Andrews (01424) 212770
Holes	18 L 6218 yds SSS 70
	Pro–68 C Clark (1976)
V'tors	WD/Sat–H Sun am–M Sun pm–H
Fees	£25 (£30)
Loc	2 miles N of Bexhill
Arch	JH Taylor

Hollingbury Park (1909)

Public
Ditchling Road, Brighton BN1 7HS

Tel	**(01273) 552010**
Fax	(01273) 552010
Mem	300
Sec	BCL Rumary
Pro	G Crompton (01273) 500086
Holes	18 L 6415 yds SSS 71
Recs	Am–67 P Plant (1997)
	Pro–65 J Spence (1989)
V'tors	U SOC
Fees	£11 D–£17 (£15)
Loc	1 mile NE of Brighton

Holtye (1893)

Holtye, Cowden, Edenbridge TN8 7ED

Tel	**(01342) 850635**
Fax	(01342) 850576
Mem	430
Sec	JP Holmes (01342) 850576
Pro	K Hinton (01342) 850957
Holes	9 L 5325 yds SSS 66
Recs	Am–65 PD Scarles, JA Couling, BD Clarke, L Bridges
	Pro–62 K Hinton
V'tors	WD–U exc Wed/Thurs am–NA WE–NA before noon SOC–Tues & Fri
Fees	D–£15 (£18)
Loc	4 miles E of E Grinstead on A264

Horam Park (1985)

Pay and play
Chiddingly Road, Horam TN21 0JJ

Tel	**(014353) 813477**
Fax	(014353) 813677
Mem	400
Sec	Mrs G Lloyd
Pro	M Jarvis
Holes	9 L 5864 yds SSS 70
	Pro–64 J Pinsent (1988)
V'tors	U exc Sat–M before 4pm SOC
Fees	18 holes–£14 D–£15 9 holes–£8.50 D–£9
Loc	½ mile S of Horam towards Chiddingley. 12 miles N of Eastbourne on A267
Mis	Floodlit driving range
Arch	Glen Johnson

Lewes (1896)

Chapel Hill, Lewes BN7 2BB

Tel	**(01273) 473245**
Mem	700
Sec	AG Redshaw (01273) 483474
Pro	P Dobson (01273) 483823
Holes	18 L 6218 yds Par 71 SSS 70
Recs	Am–65 M Hilton (1996)
	Pro–67 CA Burgess (1988)
V'tors	WD–U WE–NA before 2pm SOC

Fees £18 (£30)
Loc ½ mile from Lewes at E end of Cliffe High Street

Mid Sussex (1995)
Spatham Lane, Ditchling BN6 8XJ
Tel (01273) 846567
Fax (01273) 845767
Mem 600
Sec J Tippett-Iles (Mgr)
Pro C Connell
Holes 18 L 6450 yds Par 71 SSS 71
Pro–68 A Murray,
D Mills (1996)
V'tors WD–U WE–M SOC–WD
Fees £20
Loc 1 mile E of Ditchling
Mis Driving range
Arch David Williams

Nevill (1914)
Benhall Mill Road, Tunbridge Wells TN2 5JW
Tel (01892) 525818
Fax (01892) 517861
Mem 579 152(L) 55(J)
Sec Miss KNR Pudner
Pro P Huggett (01892) 532941
Holes 18 L 6349 yds SSS 70
Recs Am–64 J Harris (1994)
Pro–66 M Warner (1988)
V'tors WD–H WE/BH–M
Fees £33
Loc Tunbridge Wells 1 mile

Peacehaven (1895)
Brighton Road, Newhaven BN9 9UH
Tel (01273) 514049
Mem 290
Sec DM Jackson (01273) 512571
Pro G Williams (01273) 512602
Holes 9 L 5235 yds SSS 66
Recs Am–65 J Harris (1993)
V'tors WD–U WE/BH–after 11am SOC
Fees £11 (£17)
Loc 8 miles E of Brighton on A259
Arch James Braid

Piltdown (1904)
Piltdown, Uckfield TN22 3XB
Tel (01825) 722033
Fax (01825) 724192
Mem 400
Sec JC Duncan (Hon)
Pro J Amos (01825) 722389
Holes 18 L 6070 yds SSS 69
Recs Am–67 A Smith (1988)
Pro–69 S Frost, P Lovesey
V'tors I or H exc BH/Tues am/Thurs am/Sun am SOC
Fees £27.50 D–£32
Loc 1 mile W of Maresfield, off A272 towards Isfield

Royal Ashdown Forest (1888)
Chapel Lane, Forest Row, East Grinstead RH18 5LR
Tel (01342) 822018
Fax (01342) 825211

Mem 450
Sec DJ Scrivens
Pro MA Landsborough (01342) 822247
Holes Old 18 L 6477 yds SSS 71
West 18 L 5606 yds SSS 67
Recs Old Am–67 RA Darlington (1987), NJ Harrington (1996)
Pro–62 HA Padgham
V'tors On application (phone first)
Fees D–£36 (£36 D–£42)
Loc 4 miles S of E Grinstead on B2110 Hartfield road. M25 Junction 6

Royal Eastbourne (1887)
Paradise Drive, Eastbourne BN20 8BP
Tel (01323) 729738
Fax (01323) 729738
Mem 850
Sec PG White
Pro R Wooller (01323) 736986
Holes 18 L 6118 yds SSS 69
9 L 2147 yds SSS 32
Recs Am–62 J Beland (1991)
Pro–62 J Pinsent (1987)
V'tors U H SOC
Fees 18 hole: 20 (£25)
9 hole: £12
Loc ½ mile from Town Hall

Rye (1894)
Camber, Rye TN31 7QS
Tel (01797) 225241/225460
Fax (01797) 225460
Mem 979 115(L) 125(J)
Sec Lt Col CJW Gilbert
Pro MP Lee (01797) 225218
Holes 18 L 6308 yds SSS 71
9 L 6141 yds SSS 70
Recs Am–64 P Hurring (1988),
G Wolstenholme (1994),
JE Ambridge (1996)
Pro–63 G Ralph (1994)
V'tors M
Loc 3 miles E of Rye on B2075
Arch HS Colt

Seaford (1887)
East Blatchington, Seaford BN25 2JD
Tel (01323) 892442
Fax (01323) 894113
Mem 420 110(L) 37(J)
Sec RN Vandenbergh
Pro (01323) 894160
Holes 18 L 6233 yds SSS 70
Recs Am–66 EA Snow, A Flygt
Pro–67 H Weetman
V'tors WD–U after 9.30am exc Tues WE–M SOC
Fees £25 D–£35
Loc 1 mile N of Seaford (A259)
Arch JH Taylor

Seaford Head (1907)
Public
Southdown Road, Seaford BN25 4JS
Tel (01323) 890139
Sec JT Wass
Pro AJ Lowles
Holes 18 L 5812 yds SSS 68

Recs Am–65 D Hills
Pro–64 M Andrews
V'tors U
Fees £12 D–£18 (£14.50 D–£20)
Loc 8 miles W of Eastbourne.
¾ mile S of A259

Sedlescombe (1990)
Kent Street, Sedlescombe TN33 0SD
Tel (01424) 870898
Fax (01424) 870855
Mem 380
Sec Mrs A Briggs
Pro J Andrews
Holes 18 L 6218 yds Par 72
V'tors WD–H WE–M
Fees On application
Loc 5 miles N of Hastings
Mis Floodlit driving range
Arch Glen Johnson

Sweetwoods Park (1994)
Cowden, Edenbridge TN8 7JN
Tel (01342) 850729
Fax (01342) 850866
Mem 800
Sec G Myles
Pro B Wynn
Holes 18 L 6516 yds Par 72
Recs Am–66 S Randall
Pro–65 K Kelsall
V'tors U SOC–WD
Fees £18 (£27)
Loc 5 miles E of E Grinstead on A264
Mis Driving range
Arch P Strand

Waterhall (1923)
Public
Waterhall Road, Brighton BN1 8YR
Tel (01273) 508658
Mem 300
Sec MR Lee (Hon)
Pro P Charman
Holes 18 L 5775 yds SSS 68
Recs Am–66 R Vance
V'tors WD–U WE–U after 8am
Fees £10.50 (£14.50)
Loc 3 miles N of Brighton between A23 and A27. 1 mile N of A2308

Wellshurst G&CC (1992)
North Street, Hellingly BN27 4EE
Tel (01435) 813636
Fax (01435) 812444
Mem 300
Sec M Adams (Man Dir)
Pro M Round (01435) 813456
Holes 18 L 5771 yds SSS 68
V'tors U SOC
Fees £14 (£17.50)
Loc 2 miles N of Hailsham on A267
Mis Driving range

West Hove (1910)
Church Farm, Hangleton, Hove BN3 8AN
Tel (01273) 413411 (Clubhouse)
Fax (01273) 439988

Sec	K Haste (Mgr)
	(01273) 419738
Pro	D Cook (01273) 413494
Holes	18 L 6201 yds SSS 70 Par 70
	Pro–70 G McWhitty
V'tors	U–phone first SOC
Fees	On application
Loc	N of Brighton By-pass. 2nd
	junction W from A23 flyover
Mis	Practice driving range
Arch	Hawtree

Willingdon (1898)

Southdown Road, Eastbourne
BN20 9AA

Tel	(01323) 410983
Mem	550
Sec	Mrs J Packham
	(01323) 410981
Pro	JN Debenham
	(01323) 410984
Holes	18 L 6049 yds SSS 69
Recs	Am–64 DM Sewell (1986)
	Pro–62 J Sewell (1990)
V'tors	WD–U H WE–MH exc Sun
	am–NA SOC–H
Fees	D–£24 (£27)
Loc	½ mile N of Eastbourne,
	off A22
Arch	JH Taylor/Dr A Mackenzie

Sussex (West)

Avisford Park (1990)

Pay and play
Yapton Lane, Walberton, Arundel
BH18 0LS

Tel	(01243) 554611
Fax	(01243) 555580
Mem	75
Sec	J Beach
Pro	R Beach
Holes	18 L 5703 yds SSS 68
	Pro–68 R Beach (1994)
V'tors	U SOC
Fees	£14 (£15)
Loc	4 miles W of Arundel on A27

Bognor Regis (1892)

Downview Road, Felpham, Bognor
Regis PO22 8JD

Tel	(01243) 865867
Fax	(01243) 860719
Mem	650
Sec	BD Poston
	(01243) 821929
Pro	S Bassil (01243) 865209
Holes	18 L 6238 yds Par 70 SSS 70
Recs	Am–64 M Harris (1995)
	Pro–64 JR Day (1992), C
	Fogden (1997)
V'tors	WD–I or H after 9.30am
	WE/BH–M (Apr–Sept) –I H
	(Oct–Mar) SOC–WD
Fees	£25 (£30)
Loc	2 miles E of Bognor Regis,
	off A259
Arch	James Braid

Burgess Hill

Pay and play
Cuckfield Road, Burgess Hill

Tel	(01444) 258585
Fax	(01444) 247318
Sec	CJ Collins (Mgr)
Holes	9 hole Par 3 course
V'tors	U
Fees	On application
Loc	N of Burgess Hill
Mis	Floodlit driving range
Arch	Steel/Collins

Chartham Park (1993)

Felcourt, East Grinstead RH19 2JT

Tel	(01342) 870340
Fax	(01342) 870719
Sec	Denise Leech
Pro	I Dryden
Holes	18 L 6688 yds Par 72 SSS 72
V'tors	WD–U WE–U after 11am
Fees	£27 (£40)
Loc	2 miles N of East Grinstead,
	off A22
Mis	Driving range

Chichester (1990)

Hunston Village, Chichester PO20 6AX

Tel	(01243) 533833
Fax	(01243) 539922
Mem	700
Sec	A Dowling (01243) 536666
Pro	S James
Holes	Cathedral 18 L 6461 yds
	SSS 71; Tower 18 L 6175 yds
	SSS 72; 9 hole Par 3 course
Recs	Cathedral Am–69 P Duke
	Tower Pro–67 C Rota
V'tors	U SOC
Fees	Tower–£15 (£19.50)
	Cathedral–£20 (£28)
Loc	2 miles S of A27 on B2145
	to Selsey
Mis	Driving range
Arch	Phillip Sanders

Copthorne (1892)

Borers Arm Road, Copthorne
RH10 3LL

Tel	(01342) 712508
Fax	(01342) 717682
Mem	565
Sec	DJ MacInnes (01342) 712033
Pro	J Burrell (01342) 712405
Holes	18 L 6505 yds SSS 71
Recs	Am–66 D Arnold
	Pro–66 K MacDonald
V'tors	WD–U WE/BH–after 1pm
	SOC
Fees	£30 (£35)
Loc	1 mile E of M23 Junction 10,
	on A264
Arch	James Braid

Cottesmore (1975)

Buchan Hill, Pease Pottage, Crawley
RH11 9AT

Tel	(01293) 528256
Fax	(01293) 522819
Mem	1200
Sec	M Topper

Pro	A Prior (01293) 535399
Holes	Griffin 18 L 6248 yds Par 71
	SSS 70; Phoenix 18 L 5514
	yds Par 69 SSS 67
Recs	Old Am–66 S Pardoe
	Pro–67 R Tinworth
V'tors	WD–U WE–NA before 11am
	SOC–WD
Fees	Griffin–£25 (£31)
	Phoenix–£16 (£21)
Loc	4 miles S of Crawley, off M23
	Junction 11
Arch	MD Rogerson

Cowdray Park (1920)

Petworth Road, Midhurst GU29 0BB

Tel	(01730) 812088
Fax	(01730) 813599
Mem	700
Sec	JK McIver (01730) 813599
Pro	R Gough (01730) 812091
Holes	18 L 6212 yds SSS 70
Recs	Am–67 S Brown (1994)
	Pro–66 G Ralph (1989)
V'tors	WD/Sat–H NA before 9.30am
	Sun/BH–H NA before 10am
	SOC–Wed & Thurs
Fees	£20 (£25)
Loc	1 mile E of Midhurst on A272
Arch	T Simpson

Effingham Park (1980)

West Park Road, Copthorne
RH10 3EU

Tel	(01342) 716528
Fax	(01342) 716039
Mem	320
Sec	J O'Donovan (Mgr)
	(01342) 712138
Pro	M Root
Holes	9 L 1815 yds Par 30
Recs	Am–29
	Pro–26
V'tors	WD–U exc Wed & Thurs
	before 12 noon WE–U after
	11.30am
Fees	£8 D–£11.50 (£9 D–£13.50)
Loc	B2028/B2039.
	M23 Junction 10
Mis	Golf academy
Arch	Francisco Escario

Foxbridge (1993)

Foxbridge Lane, Plaistow RH14 0LB

Tel	(01403) 753303/753343
	(Bookings)
Fax	(01403) 753433
Mem	300
Sec	Miss K Harridge
Holes	9 L 3118 yds SSS 70
V'tors	M SOC
Loc	15 miles S of Guildford,
	off B2133
Arch	Paul Clark

Gatwick Manor (1975)

London Road, Lowfield Heath, Crawley
RH10 2ST

Tel	(01293) 538587
Pro	C Jenkins
Holes	9 L 1246 yds SSS 28
	Pro–24 C Jenkins (1991)

V'tors U SOC
Fees 9 holes–£3
Loc A23 to Crawley, 1 mile past Gatwick Airport
Arch Patrick Tallack

Goodwood (1892)

Goodwood, Chichester PO18 0PN
Tel (01243) 785012 (Members)
Fax (01243) 781741
Mem 900
Sec CAR Pickup (01243) 774968
Pro K MacDonald (01243) 774994
Holes 18 L 6401 yds SSS 71
Recs Am–67 C Fogden (1993) Pro–64 G Orr (1992)
V'tors WD–H after 9am WE–H after 10am SOC–Wed & Thurs
Fees £32 (£42)
Loc 3 miles NE of Chichester, on road to racecourse
Arch James Braid

Goodwood Park G&CC

(1989)
Goodwood, Chichester PO18 0QB
Tel (01243) 775987
Mem 750
Sec B Geoghegan (Sec/Mgr)
Pro A Wratting
Holes 18 L 6530 yds SSS 72
V'tors WD–H WE/BH–NA before noon H SOC
Fees £30 (£40)
Loc 4 miles N of Chichester
Arch Donald Steel

Ham Manor (1936)

West Drive, Angmering, Littlehampton BN16 4JE
Tel (01903) 783288
Fax (01903) 850886
Mem 860
Sec VJ Chaszczewski
Pro S Buckley (01903) 783732
Holes 18 L 6216 yds SSS 70
Recs Am–64 F Wieland (1987) Pro–62 TA Horton
V'tors WD/WE–H
Fees On application
Loc Between Worthing and Littlehampton
Arch HS Colt

Hassocks (1995)

Pay and play
London Road, Hassocks BN6 9NA
Tel (01273) 846990
Fax (01273) 846070
Mem 350
Sec S Boakes (Mgr) (01273) 846630
Pro C Ledger (01273) 846990
Holes 18 L 5754 yds Par 70 SSS 68
Recs Am–64 S Murray (1995) Pro–64 C Ledger (1995)
V'tors U
Fees £12.50 (£16.25)
Loc 1 mile S of Burgess Hill on A273. 7 miles N of Brighton
Arch Paul Wright

Haywards Heath (1922)

High Beech Lane, Haywards Heath RH16 1SL
Tel (01444) 414310
Fax (01444) 458319
Mem 771
Sec JE Jarman (01444) 414457
Pro M Henning (01444) 414866
Holes 18 L 6204 yds SSS 70
Recs Am–68 T Hilton Pro–66 P Sefton
V'tors WD/WE–H–restricted SOC–Wed & Thurs
Fees £26 (£36)
Loc 2 miles N of Haywards Heath, off B2112

Hill Barn (1935)

Public
Hill Barn Lane, Worthing BN14 9QE
Tel (01903) 237301
Pro AP Higgins
Holes 18 L 6224 yds SSS 70
Recs Am–66 H Francis, B Roberts Pro–63 J Kinsella
V'tors U
Fees £12.50 (£13.50)
Loc NE of A27 at Warren Road roundabout
Arch Hawtree

Horsham (1993)

Pay and play
Worthing Road, Horsham RH13 7AX
Tel (01403) 271525
Fax (01403) 274528
Mem 240
Sec J Ellwood (01403) 271525
Pro N Burke (Mgr)
Holes 9 L 2061 yds Par 33 SSS 30
Recs Am–61 J Ellwood (1995) Pro–55 J Spence (1993)
V'tors U SOC
Fees 9 holes–£6 (£7)
Loc 1 mile S of Horsham, off A24

Ifield (1927)

Rusper Road, Ifield, Crawley RH11 0LN
Tel (01293) 520222
Fax (01293) 612973
Mem 875
Sec B Gazzard
Pro J Earl (01293) 523088
Holes 18 L 6330 yds SSS 70
Recs Am–67 C Paterson Pro–65 G Cowlishaw, P Mitchell
V'tors WD–H WE–M SOC
Fees £20 D–£30
Loc W of Crawley. M23 Junction 11

Littlehampton (1889)

170 Rope Walk, Littlehampton BN17 5DL
Tel (01903) 717170
Fax (01903) 726629
Mem 650
Sec KR Palmer (Sec/Mgr)
Pro G McQuitty (01903) 716369

Holes 18 L 6244 yds SSS 70
Recs Am–66 J Jones Pro–65 D Cook
V'tors WD–U after 9.30am WE/BH–NA before noon SOC
Fees £24 (£30)
Loc W bank of River Arun, Littlehampton

Mannings Heath (1905)

Fullers, Hammerpond Road, Mannings Heath, Horsham RH13 6PG
Tel (01403) 210228
Fax (01403) 270974
Mem 730
Sec J Curtis
Pro C Tucker (01403) 210228
Holes Waterfall 18 L 6378 yds SSS 70; Kingfisher 18 L 6305 yds SSS 70
Recs Am–66 J Newsome Pro–66 R Willison
V'tors U H SOC
Fees £32 (£40)
Loc 3 miles SE of Horsham (A281). M23 Junction 11
Mis Driving range
Arch Kingfisher-David Williams

Osiers Farm (1991)

Osiers Farm, Petworth GU28 9LX
Tel (01798) 344097
Fax (01798) 342528
Mem 100
Pro R Mace (Golf Dir)
Holes 18 L 6191 yds Par 71 SSS 66
V'tors U SOC
Fees 18 holes–£10 D–£12.50; 9 holes–£7.50
Loc 1½ miles N of Petworth on A283
Arch C & T Duncton

Paxhill Park (1990)

East Mascalls Lane, Lindfield RH16 2QN
Tel (01444) 484467
Fax (01444) 482709
Mem 540
Sec JD Bowen
Pro S Dunkley
Holes 18 L 6196 yds SSS 68
Recs Am–67 E Pagden (1993)
V'tors WD–U WE–pm only
Fees £15 (£20)
Loc 1 mile N of Lindfield, off B2028. 4 miles NE of Haywards Heath
Mis Driving range
Arch Patrick Tallack

Pease Pottage (1986)

Horsham Road, Pease Pottage, Crawley RH11 9AP
Tel (01293) 521706
Mem 56
Sec A Venn
Pro M Root
Holes 9 L 3511 yds SSS 57
Recs Am–63 M Bolton Smith (1992) Pro–58 S Mantel (1992)

V'tors U
Fees £8 (£11)
Loc S of Crawley, off A23
Mis Driving range

Pyecombe (1894)

Pyecombe, Brighton BN45 7FF
Tel (01273) 845372
Fax (01273) 843338
Mem 650
Pro CR White (01273) 845398
Holes 18 L 6278 yds SSS 70
Recs Am–67 TM Greenfield
Pro–66 JA Brown
Ladies–68 A Greenfield
V'tors WD–U exc Tues after 9.15am
WE–U after 2pm
SOC–Mon/Wed/Thurs
Fees £15 (£25)
Loc 6 miles N of Brighton on A273

Rustington (1992)

Golfers Lane, Rustington BN16 4NB
Tel (01903) 850790
Fax (01903) 850982
Pro D Reffin
Holes 18 L 5735 yds Par 70 SSS 68
V'tors U SOC
Fees On application
Loc On A259 between Worthing
and Littlehampton
Mis Floodlit driving range
Arch David Williams

Selsey (1906)

Golf Links Lane, Selsey PO20 9DR
Tel (01243) 602203
Mem 400
Sec P Carter (01243) 605176
Pro P Grindley
Holes 9 L 5834 yds SSS 68
Recs Am–64 S Gill
Pro–63 C Giddins, P Hurring
V'tors U
Fees £12 (£17)
Loc 7 miles S of Chichester

Shillinglee Park (1980)

Pay and play
Chiddingfold, Godalming GU8 4TA
Tel (01428) 653237
Fax (01428) 644391
Mem 400
Sec R Mace (Prop)
Pro R Mace
Holes 9 L 2500 yds Par 32
Recs Am–65
V'tors U SOC exc Sat am
Fees £11 D–£12.50 (£13 D–£16)
9 holes–£7.50
Loc 2½ miles SE of Chiddingfold
Mis Pitch & putt course
Arch Roger Mace

Singing Hills (1992)

Pay and play
Albourne, Brighton BN6 9EB
Tel (01273) 835353
Fax (01273) 835444
Mem 400

Sec V Street
Pro W Street
Holes 27 holes SSS 69-72:
River 9 L 2826 yds
Valley 9 L 3348 yds
Lakes 9 L 3253 yds
Recs Am–67 B Anderson (1992)
Pro–66 R Frost (1993)
V'tors U SOC
Fees £18 (£26)
Loc 6 miles N of Brighton, off
B2117
Mis Driving range
Arch MRM Sandow

Slinfold Park (1993)

*Stane Street, Slinfold, Horsham
RH13 7RE*
Tel (01403) 791154
Fax (01403) 791465
Mem 600
Sec RP King
Pro G McKay
(01403) 791555
Holes 18 L 6450 yds SSS 71
9 hole course
Recs Am–68 N Darnell
V'tors U SOC
Fees £20 (£25)
Loc 3 miles W of Horsham (A29)
Mis Driving range
Arch John Fortune

Tilgate Forest (1982)

Public
*Titmus Drive, Tilgate, Crawley
RH10 5EU*
Tel (01293) 530103
Fax (01293) 523478
Mem 320
Sec T Reagan
Pro S Trussell, D McClelland
Holes 18 L 6359 yds SSS 70
9 hole Par 3 course
Recs Am–70 L Cooper (1997)
Pro–68 J Hodgkinson (1986)
V'tors U SOC–Mon–Thurs
Fees 18 hole–£12 (£16)
9 hole–£4 (£5.30)
Loc 1½ miles SE of Crawley. M23
Junction 11
Mis Driving range

West Chiltington (1988)

Pay and play
*Broadford Bridge Road, West
Chiltington RH20 2YA*
Tel (01798) 813574
Fax (01798) 812631
Mem 700
Sec D Thomson (Mgr)
Pro G Downer
(01798) 812115
Holes 18 L 5969 yds Par 70 SSS 69
9 hole Par 3 course
Recs Am–66 R Ellis (1995)
Pro–62 B Barnes (1991)
V'tors U SOC
Fees £12.50 (£15)
Loc 2 miles E of Pulborough
Mis Driving range
Arch Faulkner/Barnes

West Sussex (1930)

*Golf Club Lane, Wiggonholt,
Pulborough RH20 2EN*
Tel (01798) 872563
Fax (01798) 872033
Mem 800
Sec CP Simpson
Pro T Packham (01798) 872426
Holes 18 L 6221 yds SSS 70
Recs Am–61 G Evans
V'tors WD–I H after 9.30am exc
Fri–M SOC–Thurs
Fees On application
Loc 1½ miles E of Pulborough
on A283
Arch Campbell/Hutcheson

Worthing (1905)

Links Road, Worthing BN14 9QZ
Tel (01903) 260801
Fax (01903) 694664
Mem 1000
Sec IJ Evans
Pro S Rolley (01903) 260718
Holes Lower 18 L 6530 yds SSS 72
Upper 18 L 5243 yds SSS 66
Recs Lower Am–62 P Drew (1994)
Pro–66 P Harrison (1992)
V'tors WD–U H WE–confirm in
advance with Pro
Fees On application
Loc Central Station 1½ miles
(A27), nr A24 Junction
Arch HS Colt

Tyne & Wear

Backworth (1937)

*The Hall, Backworth, Shiremoor,
Newcastle-upon-Tyne NE27 0AH*
Tel (0191) 268 1048
Mem 400
Sec D Carruthers
Pro None
Holes 9 L 5930 yds SSS 69
Recs Am–66
V'tors Mon & Fri–U Tues–Thurs–M
after 5pm WE–after 12.30pm
exc comp Sats–after 6pm
Fees On application
Loc Off Tyne Tunnel link road,
Holystone roundabout

Birtley (1922)

Birtley Lane, Birtley DH3 2LR
Tel (0191) 410 2207
Mem 220
Sec K Thomas
Holes 9 L 5660 yds SSS 67
Recs Am–63 I McEntee
V'tors WD–U exc Fri pm–M
WE/BH–M SOC
Fees £12
Loc 3 miles from Birtley service
area on A1(M)

Boldon (1912)

Dipe Lane, East Boldon NE36 0PQ
Tel (0191) 536 4182 (Clubhouse)
Fax (0191) 537 2270

Mem 700
Sec RW Benton (0191) 536 5360
Pro Phipps Golf (0191) 536 5835
Holes 18 L 6348 yds SSS 70
Recs Am–67 GR Simpson (1987)
Pro–66 M Archer (1993)
V'tors WD–U WE/BH–NA before
3.30pm
Fees On application
Loc 8 miles SE of Newcastle

City of Newcastle (1891)

Three Mile Bridge, Gosforth, Newcastle-upon-Tyne NE3 2DR
Tel (0191) 285 1775
Fax (0191) 284 0700
Mem 400 110(L) 60(J)
Sec AJ Matthew (Mgr)
Pro AJ Matthew (0191) 285 5481
Holes 18 L 6528 yds SSS 71
Recs Am–64 S Harrison (1995)
Pro–66 AJ Brown (1996)
V'tors U
Fees £21 (£26)
Loc B1318, 3 miles N of Newcastle
Arch Harry Vardon

Garesfield (1922)

Chopwell NE17 7AP
Tel (01207) 561278/561309
Fax (01207) 561309
Mem 700
Sec EM Thirlwell
Pro D Race (01207) 563082
Holes 18 L 6196 yds SSS 70
Recs Am–68 I Turner (1991)
Pro–70 D Dunk (1978)
V'tors WD–U WE/BH–NA before
4.30pm SOC
Fees On application
Loc 7 miles SW of Newcastle,
between High Spen and
Chopwell

Gosforth (1906)

Broadway East, Gosforth, Newcastle-upon-Tyne NE3 5ER
Tel (0191) 285 6710
Mem 370 100(L) 50(J)
Sec JE Stephenson (0191) 285
3495
Pro G Garland (0191) 285 0553
Holes 18 L 6024 yds SSS 69
Recs Am–65 I Potter (1992)
V'tors WD–U WE–M before 4pm
–U after 4pm SOC
Fees £20
Loc 3 miles N of Newcastle,
off A6125

Heworth (1911)

Gingling Gate, Heworth, Gateshead NE10 8XY
Tel (0191) 469 2137
Mem 600
Sec G Holbrow (0191) 469 9832
Pro None
Holes 18 L 6404 yds SSS 71
Recs Am–65 D Moralee
Pro–69 P Highmoor
V'tors WD–U WE–NA before noon
Fees £15 (£15)
Loc SE boundary of Gateshead

Houghton-le-Spring (1908)

Copt Hill, Houghton-le-Spring DH5 8LU
Tel (0191) 584 1198
Mem 600
Sec N Wales (0191) 584 0048
Pro (0191) 584 7421
Holes 18 L 6416 yds Par 72 SSS 71
Recs Am–66 J Ellison
V'tors U SOC
Fees £20 (£27)
Loc 3 miles SW of Sunderland

Newcastle United (1892)

Ponteland Road, Cowgate, Newcastle-upon-Tyne NE5 3JW
Tel (0191) 286 4693 (Clubhouse)
Mem 500
Sec J Simpson
Pro (0191) 286 9998
Holes 18 L 6596 yds SSS 71
Recs Am–64 G Grant (1993)
V'tors WD–U WE/BH–M
Fees On application
Loc Nuns Moor, 2 miles W of city
centre

Northumberland (1898)

High Gosforth Park, Newcastle-upon-Tyne NE3 5HT
Tel (0191) 236 2498
Fax (0191) 236 2498
Mem 500
Sec SC Owram
Pro None
Holes 18 L 6629 yds SSS 72
Recs Am–67 W Bennett,
PH Coulthard
Pro–65 A Jacklin, T Horton
V'tors WD–I BH–M
Fees £35–£45
Loc 5 miles N of Newcastle
Arch HS Colt/James Braid

Parklands (1971)

High Gosforth Park, Newcastle-upon-Tyne NE3 5HQ
Tel (0191) 236 4480/4867
Mem 770
Sec B Woof
Pro B Rumney
Holes 18 L 6060 yds Par 71 SSS 69
Recs Am–66 S Johnston,
G Hewitt
Pro–65 B Rumney
V'tors U
Fees £15 (£18)
Loc 5 miles N of Newcastle
Mis 9 hole pitch & putt course.
Driving range

Ravensworth (1906)

Moss Heaps, Wrekenton, Gateshead NE9 7UU
Tel (0191) 487 6014/2843
Mem 550
Sec WR Walker (0191) 416 4794
Pro S Cowell (0191) 491 3475
Holes 18 L 5872 yds SSS 68

Recs Am–63 K Kelly
Pro–64 T Horton
V'tors U H SOC
Fees £19 (£28)
Loc 3 miles S of Newcastle
on B1296

Ryton (1891)

Doctor Stanners, Clara Vale, Ryton NE40 3TD
Tel (0191) 413 3253
Fax (0191) 413 1642
Mem 600
Sec S Dix
Holes 18 L 5499 metres SSS 69
Recs Am–69 P Brougham, S Dix,
P Highmoor
V'tors WD–U WE–M SOC
Fees £15 (£20)
Loc 7 miles W of Newcastle,
off A695

South Shields (1893)

Cleadon Hills, South Shields NE34 8EG
Tel (0191) 456 0475
Mem 700
Sec WH Loades (0191) 456 8942
Pro G Parsons (0191) 456 0110
Holes 18 L 6264 yds SSS 70
Recs Am–64 J Dryden (1993)
Pro–64 M Gregson (1978)
V'tors U SOC
Fees On application
Loc Cleadon Hills

Tynemouth (1913)

Spital Dene, Tynemouth, North Shields NE30 2ER
Tel (0191) 257 4578
Fax (0191) 259 5193
Mem 824
Sec W Storey (0191) 257 3381
Pro J McKenna (0191) 258 0728
Holes 18 L 6403 yds SSS 71
Recs Am–65 CS Hill
Pro–64 J Ord
V'tors WD–U 9.30am–5pm –NA
before 9.30am and after 5pm
WE/BH–M
Fees £20
Loc 8 miles E of Newcastle
Arch Willie Park

Tyneside (1879)

Westfield Lane, Ryton NE40 3QE
Tel (0191) 413 2177
Fax (0191) 413 2742
Mem 660
Sec RW Knighting
(0191) 413 2742
Pro M Gunn (0191) 413 1600
Holes 18 L 6042 yds SSS 69
Recs Am–65 CW Philipson,
G Lawson
Pro–65 JR Harrison
V'tors WD–U (exc 11.30–1.30pm)
WE–NA before 3pm SOC
Fees £20 (£30)
Loc 7 miles W of Newcastle. S of
river, off A695
Arch HS Colt

For list of abbreviations see page 479

Wallsend (1973)
Public
Rheydt Avenue, Bigges Main, Wallsend
NE28 8SU
Tel   **(0191) 262 1973**
Sec   D Souter
Pro   K Phillips (0191) 262 4231
Holes 18 L 6608 yds SSS 72
Recs   Am–66 A Dobson (1997)
V'tors U
Fees   £12 (£14)
Loc   Between Newcastle and
        Wallsend on coast road
Mis   Driving range
Arch   G Showball

Washington (1980)
Stone Cellar Road, Usworth, District 12,
Washington NE37 1PH
Tel   **(0191) 402 9988**
Fax   **(0191) 415 1166**
Sec   S Purdy
Pro   W Marshall (0191) 417 8346
Holes 18 L 6604 yds SSS 72
Recs   Am–68 D Godfrey (1996)
        Pro–64 P Harrison (1991)
V'tors U SOC
Fees   £19 (£27.50)
Loc   Off A1(M), on A195
Mis   Driving range. 9 hole pitch
        & putt

Wearside (1892)
Coxgreen, Sunderland SR4 9JT
Tel   **(0191) 534 2518**
Fax   **(0191) 534 2518**
Mem   650
Sec   N Hildrew
Pro   D Brolls (0191) 534 4269
Holes 18 L 6315 yds SSS 70
        Par 3 course
Recs   Am–64 R Walker
        Pro–63 J Harrison
V'tors H SOC
Fees   £25 (£32)
Loc   2 miles W of Sunderland,
        off A183, by A19

Westerhope (1941)
Whorlton Grange, Westerhope,
Newcastle-upon-Tyne NE5 1PP
Tel   **(0191) 286 9125**
Mem   778
Sec   R Pears (0191) 286 7636
Pro   N Brown (0191) 286 0594
Holes 18 L 6407 yds SSS 71
Recs   Am–64 R Roper, S Phillipson
        Pro–67 D Russell
V'tors WD–U
Fees   £16
Loc   5 miles W of Newcastle

Whickham (1911)
Hollinside Park, Fellside Road,
Whickham, Newcastle-upon-
Tyne NE16 5BA
Tel   **(0191) 488 7309 (Clubhouse)**
Fax   **(0191) 488 1576**
Mem   630
Sec   ME Pearse (0191) 488 1576
Pro   J Ord (0191) 488 8591

Holes 18 L 5878 yds Par 68 SSS 68
Recs   Am–61 AJ McLure
V'tors U
Fees   £20 (£25)
Loc   5 miles SW of Newcastle

Whitburn (1931)
Lizard Lane, South Shields NE34 7AF
Tel   **(0191) 529 2144**
Mem   550 73(L) 42(J)
Sec   Mrs V Atkinson
        (0191) 529 4944
Pro   D Stephenson (0191) 529 4210
Holes 18 L 5900 yds Par 69 SSS 68
Recs   Am–64 G Wilkinson (1997)
V'tors U SOC–WD exc Tues
Fees   £17.50 (£22.50)
Loc   2 miles N of Sunderland on
        coast
Arch   Colt/Alison/Morrison

Whitley Bay (1890)
Claremont Road, Whitley Bay
NE26 3UF
Tel   **(0191) 252 0180**
Fax   **(0191) 297 0030**
Mem   700
Sec   B Dockar
Pro   G Shipley (0191) 252 5688
Holes 18 L 6529 yds SSS 71
Recs   Am–68 PB Taylor
        Pro–66 J Fourie
V'tors WD–U WE–M
Fees   £22 D–£30
Loc   10 miles E of Newcastle

Warwickshire

Ansty (1992)
Brinklow Road, Ansty, Coventry
CV7 9JH
Tel   **(01203) 621341/621305**
Fax   **(01203) 602671**
Mem   450
Sec   R Challis
Pro   J Reay
Holes 18 L 6079 yds Par 71 SSS 69
V'tors U SOC
Fees   £9 (£13)
Loc   Between Ansty and Brinklow
        (B4029). M6 Junction 2,
        1 mile.
Mis   Driving range
Arch   D Morgan

Atherstone (1894)
The Outwoods, Coleshill Road,
Atherstone CV9 2RL
Tel   **(01827) 713110**
Mem   400 40(L) 40(J)
Sec   VA Walton (01827) 892568
Pro   To be appointed
Holes 18 L 6006 yds Par 72 SSS 70
Recs   Am–69 S Webster (1995)
V'tors WD–H WE–M SOC–WD
Fees   D–£17 BH–£20
Loc   ¼ mile from Atherstone on
        Coleshill road

The Belfry (1977)
Public
Lichfield Road, Wishaw B76 9PR
Tel   **(01675) 470301**
Fax   **(01675) 470178**
Sec   R Maxfield
Pro   P McGovern
Holes Brabazon 18 L 7177 yds
        SSS 72; Derby 18 L 6009 yds
        SSS 69; PGA National 18 L
        7072 yds SSS 72
V'tors H SOC
Fees   Brabazon–£75; Derby–£35;
        PGA National–£60
Loc   2 miles N of M42 Junction 9,
        off A446
Mis   Driving range
Arch   Brabazon and Derby: Alliss/
        Thomas. PGA National:
        Thomas

Bidford Grange (1992)
Stratford Road, Bidford-on-Avon
B50 4LY
Tel   **(01789) 490319**
Fax   **(01789) 778184**
Mem   310
Sec   M Smith (Mgr)
Pro   D Webber
Holes 18 L 7233 yds Par 72 SSS 74
Recs   Am–66 D Webber
        Pro–71 M Dove
V'tors U SOC
Fees   £12 (£15)
Loc   5 miles W of Stratford-on-
        Avon on B439
Arch   Swann/Tillman/Granger

Boldmere (1936)
Public
Monmouth Drive, Sutton Coldfield,
Birmingham BJ3 6JR
Tel   **(0121) 354 3379**
Mem   300
Sec   R Leeson
Pro   T Short
Holes 18 L 4463 yds SSS 62
Recs   Am–57 G Marston (1987)
        Pro–57 P Weaver (1987)
V'tors U
Fees   £8.50 (£9)
Loc   By Sutton Park, 1 mile W of
        Sutton Coldfield

City of Coventry
(Brandon Wood) (1977)
Public
Brandon Lane, Coventry CV8 3GQ
Tel   **(01203) 543141**
Fax   **(01203) 545108**
Mem   500
Sec   C Gledhill
Pro   C Gledhill
Holes 18 L 6610 yds SSS 72
        Pro–68 AR Sadler
V'tors U SOC
Fees   On application
Loc   6 miles SE of Coventry,
        off A45(S)
Mis   Floodlit driving range

Copt Heath (1907)

1220 Warwick Road, Knowle, Solihull
B93 9LN

Tel	(01564) 772650
Fax	(01564) 771022
Mem	700
Sec	W Lenton
Pro	BJ Barton (01564) 776155
Holes	18 L 6508 yds SSS 71
Recs	Am–67 JMH Mayell,
	PI Chalkley, G Storm
	Pro–67 D Stokes
V'tors	WD–H WE/BH–M SOC
Fees	£35
Loc	2 miles S of Solihull on A4141

Coventry (1887)

Finham Park, Coventry CV3 6PJ

Tel	(01203) 411123
Fax	(01203) 690131
Mem	750
Sec	B Fox (01203) 414152
Pro	P Weaver (01203) 411298
Holes	18 L 6613 yds SSS 72
Recs	Am–66 P Downes
	Pro–64 C Hall,
	A Webster (1993)
	Ladies Pro–62 J Arnold (1990)
V'tors	WD–H
Fees	£30
Loc	2 miles S of Coventry on A444/4113

Coventry Hearsall (1894)

Beechwood Avenue, Coventry CV5 6DF

Tel	(01203) 713470
Fax	(01203) 691534
Mem	450
Sec	Mrs ME Hudson
Pro	M Tarn (01203) 713156
Holes	18 L 5983 yds SSS 69
Recs	Am–64 W Nicolson (1992)
	Pro–66 B Morris (1987)
V'tors	WD–U WE–M
Fees	D–£24
Loc	1½ miles S of Coventry, off A45

Crocketts Manor G&CC (1994)

Birmingham Road, Henley-in-Arden
B95 5QA

Tel	(01564) 793715
Fax	(01564) 795754
Mem	600
Sec	S Edwin (Golf Mgr)
Pro	S Edwin
Holes	18 L 6933 yds SSS 73
	9 hole Par 3 course
V'tors	U–booking required SOC–H
Fees	£20 D–£25 (£25 D–£30)
Loc	N of Stratford-on-Avon on A3400. M40 Junction 16, 3 miles
Mis	Driving range. Golf Academy
Arch	N Selwyn-Smith

Edgbaston (1896)

Church Road, Edgbaston, Birmingham
B15 3TB

Tel	(0121) 454 1736
Fax	(0121) 454 2395

Mem	885
Sec	P Heath
Pro	AH Bownes
	(0121) 454 3226
Holes	18 L 6118 yds SSS 69
Recs	Am–66 J Cook (1990)
	Pro–65 J Rhodes
V'tors	H SOC
Fees	£37.50 (£50)
Loc	1½ miles S of Birmingham, off A38
Arch	HS Colt

GPT (formerly Grange GC)

Copsewood, Coventry CV3 1HS

Tel	(01203) 451465
Mem	350
Sec	E Soutar (Hon)
Holes	9 L 6002 yds SSS 69
Recs	Am–70
V'tors	WD–U before 2.30pm
	Sat–NA Sun–NA before noon
Fees	£10 Sun–£15
Loc	2½ miles E of Coventry on A428
Arch	TJ McAuley

Harborne (1893)

40 Tennal Road, Harborne,
Birmingham B32 2JE

Tel	(0121) 427 1728
Mem	600
Sec	GA Tozer
	(0121) 427 3058
Pro	A Quarterman
	(0121) 427 3512
Holes	18 L 6235 yds SSS 70
Recs	Am–65 RC Ellis
	Pro–65 E Cogle
V'tors	WD–U WE/BH–M SOC
Fees	£30 D–£35
Loc	3 miles SW of Birmingham. M5 Junction 3
Arch	HS Colt

Harborne Church Farm (1926)

Public
Vicarage Road, Harborne, Birmingham
B17 0SN

Tel	(0121) 427 1204
Fax	(0121) 428 3126
Mem	180
Sec	B Flanagan
Pro	P Johnson
Holes	9 L 4882 yds Par 66 SSS 64
Recs	Am–62 J McAllister
V'tors	U
Fees	18 holes–£8 (£8.50)
	9 holes–£5 (£5.50)
Loc	3 miles SW of Birmingham

Hatchford Brook (1969)

Public
Coventry Road, Sheldon, Birmingham
B26 3PY

Tel	(0121) 743 9821
Sec	ID Thompson (0121) 779 3780
Pro	M Hampton
Holes	18 L 6155 yds Par 69 SSS 69

Recs	Am–69 A Allen (1987),
	G Weaver (1994)
	Pro–68 P Smith (1988),
	J Kelly (1995)
V'tors	U SOC–WD
Fees	On application
Loc	City boundary close to airport. A45/M42 Junction

Hilltop (1979)

Public
Park Lane, Handsworth, Birmingham
B21 8LJ

Tel	(0121) 554 4463
Pro	K Highfield
Holes	18 L 6114 yds SSS 69
Recs	Am–66 H Ali
	Pro–65 BN Jones
V'tors	U
Fees	On application
Loc	Sandwell Valley. M5 Junction 1

Ingon Manor (1993)

Ingon Lane, Snitterfield, Stratford-on-
Avon CV37 0QE

Tel	(01789) 731857
Mem	300
Pro	M Reay
Holes	18 L 6554 yds Par 72 SSS 71
Recs	Am–74 J Webber (1993)
	Pro–74 P Broadhurst (1993)
V'tors	H SOC
Fees	£12 (£25)
Loc	3 miles N of Stratford-on-Avon, off A461. M40 Junction 15
Arch	David Hemstock

Kenilworth (1889)

Crewe Lane, Kenilworth CV8 2EA

Tel	(01926) 854296
Fax	(01926) 864453
Mem	750
Sec	JH McTavish
	(01926) 858517
Pro	S Yates (01926) 512732
Holes	18 L 6413 yds SSS 71
Recs	Am–62 WL Bladon (1995)
V'tors	U H BH–M SOC
Fees	£28 (£37)
Loc	1½ miles E of Kenilworth. 5 miles S of Coventry
Arch	Hawtree

Ladbrook Park (1908)

Poolhead Lane, Tanworth-in-Arden,
Solihull B94 5ED

Tel	(01564) 742264
Fax	(01564) 742909
Mem	700
Sec	Mrs SE Burrows (Admin)
Pro	R Mountford (01564) 742581
Holes	18 L 6427 yds SSS 71
Recs	Am–67 PJ Sant
	Pro–65 RDS Livingston
V'tors	WD–U H WE/BH–M H
Fees	On application
Loc	12 miles S of Birmingham. M42 Junction 3
Arch	HS Colt

Leamington & County
(1908)

Golf Lane, Whitnash, Leamington Spa
CV31 2QA

Tel	(01926) 425961
Fax	(01926) 425961
Mem	650
Sec	SM Cooknell
Pro	I Grant (01926) 428014
Holes	18 L 6430 yds SSS 71
Recs	Am–65 RG Hiatt
	Pro–66 D Thomas
V'tors	U SOC
Fees	£25 (£40)
Loc	1½ miles S of Leamington Spa
Arch	HS Colt

Marriott Forest of Arden Hotel (1970)

Maxstoke Lane, Meriden, Coventry
CV7 7HR

Tel	(01676) 522335
Fax	(01676) 523711
Mem	650
Pro	K Thomas (0958) 632170
Holes	Arden 18 L 6718 yds Par 72 SSS 73; Aylesford 18 L 6525 yds Par 72 SSS 71
Recs	Pro–63 C Montgomerie (1997)
V'tors	WD–U SOC–WD
Fees	Arden–£60 (£70) Aylesford–£35 (£40)
Loc	9 miles W of Coventry, off A45. M6 Junction 4
Mis	Driving range
Arch	Donald Steel

Maxstoke Park (1898)

Castle Lane, Coleshill, Birmingham
B46 2RD

Tel	(01675) 466743
Fax	(01675) 466743
Mem	600
Sec	D Haywood
Pro	N McEwan (01675) 464915
Holes	18 L 6442 yds SSS 71
Recs	Am–64 AM Allen
	Pro–65 C O'Connor Jr
V'tors	WD–U WE–M
Fees	£25
Loc	3 miles SE of Coleshill

Moor Hall (1932)

Moor Hall Drive, Four Oaks, Sutton
Coldfield B75 6LN

Tel	(0121) 308 6130
Mem	628
Sec	RV Wood
Pro	A Partridge (0121) 308 5106
Holes	18 L 6249 yds SSS 70
Recs	Am–65 J Cook
	Pro–64 J Higgins
V'tors	WD–U H exc Thurs–U after 1pm WE/BH–M
Fees	£30 D–£40
Loc	1 mile E of Sutton Coldfield

Newbold Comyn (1973)
Public

Newbold Terrace East, Leamington Spa

Tel	(01926) 421157
Mem	191

Sec	AA Pierce
Pro	D Knight
Holes	18 L 6315 yds SSS 70
Recs	Am–70 G Knight
	Pro–S Hutchinson (1987)
V'tors	WD–U WE–booking 1 week in advance SOC
Fees	£7.30 (£9.50)
Loc	Off Willes Road (B4099)

North Warwickshire
(1894)

Hampton Lane, Meriden, Coventry
CV7 7LL

Tel	(01676) 522915
Fax	(01676) 522915
Mem	450
Sec	EG Barnes (Hon)
Pro	D Ingram (01676) 522259
Holes	9 L 6362 yds SSS 70
Recs	Am–64 A Allen (1993)
V'tors	WD–U WE/BH–M SOC
Fees	£18
Loc	6 miles W of Coventry, off A45

Nuneaton (1906)

Golf Drive, Whitestone, Nuneaton

Tel	(01203) 347810
Fax	(01203) 327563
Mem	650
Sec	G Pinder
Pro	S Bainbridge (01203) 340201
Holes	18 L 6412 yds SSS 71
Recs	Am–67 P Broadhurst
	Pro–67 C Holmes
V'tors	WD–U H WE–M SOC
Fees	£25 D–£30
Loc	2 miles S of Nuneaton

Oakridge

Arley Lane, Ansley Village, Nuneaton
CV10 9PH

Tel	(01676) 541389
Fax	(01676) 542709
Mem	500
Sec	Mrs S Lovric (Admin)
Pro	I Sadler
Holes	18 L 6242 yds Par 71 SSS 70
V'tors	U SOC–WD
Fees	£15
Loc	B4112 from Nuneaton. M6 Junction 3
Arch	Algie Jayes

Olton (1893)

Mirfield Road, Solihull B91 1JH

Tel	(0121) 705 1083
Fax	(0121) 711 2010
Mem	600
Sec	JB Mawby (0121) 704 1936
Pro	MP Daubney (0121) 705 7296
Holes	18 L 6232 yds SSS 71
Recs	Am–63 J Berry
	Pro–64 I Clark
V'tors	WD–U exc Wed am WE–M
Fees	£25–£35
Loc	7 miles SE of Birmingham (A41)

Purley Chase (1980)

Pipers Lane, Ridge Lane, Nuneaton
CV10 0RB

Tel	(01203) 393118
Mem	600
Sec	Linda Jackson
Holes	18 L 6772 yds SSS 72
Recs	Am–72 P Broadhurst
	Pro–64 P Elson
V'tors	WD/BH–U WE–U after 2.30pm SOC
Fees	On application
Loc	4 miles WNW of Nuneaton on B4114 (A47) A5 Mancetter Island
Mis	Driving range

Pype Hayes (1932)
Public

Eachelhurst Road, Walmley, Sutton
Coldfield B76 8EP

Tel	(0121) 351 1014
Fax	(0121) 313 0206
Mem	320
Sec	L Brogan
Pro	JF Bayliss
Holes	18 L 5996 yds SSS 69
Recs	Am–66 A Sheard (1992)
	Pro–59 J Cawsey (1954)
V'tors	U
Fees	On application
Loc	5 miles NE of Birmingham

Robin Hood (1893)

St Bernards Road, Solihull B92 7DJ

Tel	(0121) 706 0159
Fax	(0121) 706 0806
Mem	650
Sec	B Cook (0121) 706 0061
Pro	A Harvey (0121) 706 0806
Holes	18 L 6635 yds SSS 72
Recs	Am–68 J Draper (1988), GW Barton (1993)
V'tors	WD–U WE/BH–M SOC–WD H
Fees	£29 D–£35
Loc	7 miles S of Birmingham
Arch	HS Colt

Rugby (1891)

Clifton Road, Rugby CV21 3RD

Tel	(01788) 542306
Fax	(01788) 542306
Mem	750
Sec	N Towler
Pro	A Peach (01788) 575134
Holes	18 L 5614 yds SSS 67
Recs	Am–64 J Wilson, P Godding, S Warren
	Pro–64 A Peach
V'tors	WD–U WE/BH–M SOC
Fees	On application
Loc	1 mile N of Rugby on B5414

Shirley (1956)

Stratford Road, Monkspath, Shirley,
Solihull B90 4EW

Tel	(0121) 744 6001
Fax	(0121) 745 8220
Mem	570
Sec	Mrs VA Duggan

Pro S Bottrill (0121) 745 4979
Holes 18 L 6510 yds SSS 71
Recs Am–67 N Burdekin
V'tors WD–U WE–M SOC
Fees £25 D–£35
Loc 8 miles S of Birmingham, nr M42 Junction 4

Sphinx (1948)

Sphinx Drive, Coventry CV3 1WA
Tel (01203) 451361
Mem 300
Sec GE Brownbridge (01203) 597731
Holes 9 L 4262 yds SSS 60
Recs Am–61 G Mason (1994)
V'tors Fri/WE–M after 4.30pm SOC
Fees £8 (£10)
Loc Nr Binley Road, Coventry

Stoneleigh Deer Park (1992)

The Old Deer Park, Coventry Road, Stoneleigh CV8 3DR
Tel (01203) 639991
Fax (01203) 692471
Mem 900
Sec AJ Sledger
Pro S Mouland
Holes 18 L 6083 yds SSS 71
9 hole Par 3 course
V'tors WD–U WE–NA before noon SOC–WD
Fees On application
Loc ½ mile E of Stoneleigh
Arch K Harrison

Stratford Oaks (1991)

Bearley Road, Snitterfield, Stratford-on-Avon CV37 0EZ
Tel (01789) 731982
Fax (01789) 731981
Mem 600
Sec ND Powell (Golf Dir)
Pro A Dunbar
Holes 18 L 6100 yds SSS 71
Recs Am–67 S Millington (1992)
Pro–66 D Eddiford (1992)
V'tors WD–U WE–U booking necessary
Fees £15 (£20)
Loc 4 miles NE of Stratford-on-Avon
Mis Driving range
Arch Howard Swann

Stratford-on-Avon (1894)

Tiddington Road, Stratford-on-Avon CV37 7BA
Tel (01789) 297296
Mem 770
Sec (01789) 205749
Pro D Sutherland (01789) 205677
Holes 18 L 6311 yds SSS 70
Recs Am–63 I Roberts
Pro–64 M Gallagher
V'tors U H SOC
Fees On application
Loc ½ mile E of Stratford-on-Avon on B4086

Sutton Coldfield (1889)

110 Thornhill Road, Sutton Coldfield B74 3ER
Tel (0121) 353 2014
Fax (0121) 353 5503
Mem 600
Sec RF Fletcher, Mrs T Rennie (0121) 353 9633
Pro JK Hayes (0121) 353 9633
Holes 18 L 6541 yds SSS 71
Recs Am–65 L Jacks (1986)
Pro–64 PA Elson (1978)
V'tors U H SOC
Fees £25 (£35)
Loc 9 miles N of Birmingham, off B4138

Tidbury Green (1994)

Pay and play
Tilehouse Lane, Shirley, Solihull B90 1HP
Tel (01564) 824460
Mem 300
Sec Lucy Broadhurst
Pro R Thompson
Holes 9 L 2473 yds Par 34
V'tors U SOC
Fees 18 holes–£9 (£9)
9 holes–£6 (£6)
Loc 2 miles from M42 Junction 4, nr Earlswood Lakes
Mis Driving range
Arch Derek Stevenson

Walmley (1902)

Brooks Road, Wylde Green, Sutton Coldfield B72 1HR
Tel (0121) 377 7272
Fax (0121) 377 7272
Mem 700
Sec MJ Roberts
Pro CJ Wicketts (0121) 373 7103
Holes 18 L 6537 yds SSS 72
Recs Am–67 J Phillips (1997)
Pro–66 D Prosser (1997)
V'tors WD–U WE–M SOC
Fees £30 D–£35
Loc N boundary of Birmingham

Warwick (1971)

Public
Warwick Racecourse, Warwick CV34 6HW
Tel (01926) 494316
Sec Mrs R Dunkley
Pro P Sharp (01926) 491284
Holes 9 L 2682 yds SSS 66
Recs Am–67 R Buckingham
Pro–70 P Sharp
V'tors U exc while racing in progress
Fees £4 (£5)
Loc Centre of Warwick Racecourse
Mis Driving range

The Warwickshire (1993)

Leek Wootton, Warwick CV35 7QT
Tel (01926) 409409
Fax (01926) 408409
Mem 800
Sec G Ivory

Pro J Cook
Holes 18 L 7178 yds SSS 74
18 L 7154 yds SSS 74
9 hole Par 3 course
Pro–68 P Baker (1993)
V'tors H
Fees £35 (£35)
Loc 1 mile N of Warwick, off A46. M40 Junction 15
Mis Driving range
Arch Karl Litton

Welcombe Hotel

Warwick Road, Stratford-on-Avon CV37 0NR
Tel (01789) 299012
Fax (01789) 414666
Mem 120
Sec J Moore (01789) 295252
Pro C Mason (01789) 299012
Holes 18 L 6294 yds SSS 70
Recs Am–67 R Fletcher (1997)
Pro–64 S Dodd (1997)
V'tors U H
Fees D–£40 (D–£45)
Loc 1½ miles NE of Stratford-on-Avon on A439 towards Warwick
Mis Practice range
Arch T McAuley

Whitefields Hotel (1992)

Coventry Road, Thurlaston, Rugby CV23 9JR
Tel (01788) 521800
Fax (01788) 521695
Mem 650
Sec B Coleman
Pro M Chamberlain (01788) 522393
Holes 18 L 6433 yds Par 71 SSS 70
Recs Am–69 A Stephenson
V'tors U SOC
Fees £18 (£22)
Loc 3 miles SW of Rugby at A45/M45 Junction
Mis Driving range

Widney Manor (1993)

Pay and play
Saintbury Drive, Widney Manor, Solihull B91 3SZ
Tel (0121) 711 3646
Fax (0121) 711 3691
Mem 475
Sec T Atkinson (Sec/Mgr)
Pro T Atkinson
Holes 18 L 5001 yds Par 68
V'tors U–booking 5 days in advance SOC
Fees £8.80 (£12)
Loc 3 miles from M42 Junction 4, off A34

Windmill Village (1990)

Birmingham Road, Allesley, Coventry CV5 9AL
Tel (01203) 404041
Fax (01203) 407016
Mem 500
Sec M Harrhy (Mgr)

For list of abbreviations see page 479

Pro   R Hunter (01203) 404041
Holes 18 L 5169 yds Par 70
Recs Am–68
          Pro–67 R Hunter (1996)
V'tors U SOC
Fees £9.95 (£12.95)
Loc   3 miles W of Coventry on A45
Arch Hunter/Harrhy

Wishaw (1995)

Bulls Lane, Wishaw, Sutton Coldfield B76 9AA

Tel   **(0121) 313 2110**
Sec   C Samways
Pro   R Griffin
Holes 18 L 5481 yds Par 72 SSS 67
V'tors U SOC
Fees £10 (£15)
Loc   3 miles NW of M42
          Junction 9

Wiltshire

Bowood G&CC (1992)

Derry Hill, Calne SN11 9PQ

Tel   **(01249) 822228**
Fax   (01249) 822218
Mem   400
Sec   E Schofield (Mkting Mgr)
Pro   N Blenkarne (Golf Dir)
Holes 18 L 7317 yds Par 73 SSS 74
Recs Am–69 C Edwards (1995)
          Pro–67 N Brown (1994)
V'tors U–booking required WE–M
          before noon SOC
Fees £32 D–£42
Loc   3 miles SE of Chippenham on
          A342. M4 Junction 14 (A4)
Mis   Driving range. 3 Academy
          holes
Arch David Thomas

Bradford-on-Avon (1991)

Trowbridge Road, Bradford-on-Avon

Tel   **(01225) 868268**
Pro   G Sawyer
Holes 9 L 2100 metres SSS 61
V'tors WD–U WE–pm only
Fees 9 holes–£6.50; 18 holes–£10
Loc   SE of Bradford, nr River Avon

Brinkworth (1984)

Longmans Farm, Brinkworth, Chippenham SN15 5DG

Tel   **(01666) 510277**
Mem   250
Sec   J Sheppard
Holes 18 L 5900 yds SSS 69
V'tors U SOC
Fees On application
Loc   2 miles from Brinkworth
          (B4042). 12 miles NE of
          Chippenham

Broome Manor (1976)

Public

Pipers Way, Swindon SN3 1RG

Tel   **(01793) 532403**
Fax   (01793) 433255
Mem   800

Sec   T Watt (Mgr)(01793) 495761
Pro   B Sandry (01793) 532403
Holes 18 L 6283 yds SSS 70
          9 L 2690 yds SSS 67
Recs Am–62 G Harris (1994)
          Pro–66 M Bevan (1989)
V'tors U
Fees 18 hole: £10.50; 9 hole: £6.50
Loc   Swindon 2 miles.
          M4 Junction 15
Mis   Floodlit driving range
Arch F Hawtree

Chippenham (1896)

Malmesbury Road, Chippenham SN15 5LT

Tel   **(01249) 652040**
Fax   (01249) 446681
Mem   650
Sec   D Maddison
Pro   W Creamer (01249) 655519
Holes 18 L 5540 yds SSS 67
Recs Am–64 RE Searle (1993)
          Pro–64 B Sandry
V'tors U WE–M SOC
Fees £20 (£25)
Loc   1 mile N of Chippenham,
          off A350. M4 Junction 17

Cricklade Hotel (1992)

Common Hill, Cricklade SN6 6HA

Tel   **(01793) 750751**
Fax   (01793) 751767
Mem   140
Sec   T Hooley
Pro   I Bolt
Holes 9 L 1830 yds SSS 57
V'tors WD–U SOC–WD
Fees £16 D–£25
Loc   ½ mile W of Cricklade on
          B4040. M4 Junctions 15/16
Arch Bolt/Smith

Cumberwell Park (1994)

Bradford-on-Avon BA15 2PQ

Tel   **(01225) 863322**
Fax   (01225) 868160
Mem   800
Sec   R Smith (Mgr)
Pro   J Jacobs
Holes 18 L 6807 yds SSS 73
Recs Pro–63 S Little
V'tors H SOC
Fees £18 (£25)
Loc   Between Bradford-on-Avon
          and Bath on A363. M4
          Junction 18
Arch Adrian Stiff

Erlestoke Sands (1992)

Erlestoke, Devizes SN10 5UB

Tel   **(01380) 831069**
Fax   (01380) 831069
Mem   740
Sec   M Pugsley
Pro   A Marsh (01380) 831027
Holes 18 L 6406 yds Par 73 SSS 71
Recs Am–71 P Oakey (1993)
          Pro–68 S Little (1996)
V'tors U–book with Pro SOC
Fees £16 (£25)

Loc   6 miles E of Westbury on
          B3098
Mis   Driving area. 3 Academy holes
Arch Adrian Stiff

Hamptworth G&CC (1994)

Elmtree Farmhouse, Hamptworth Road, Landford SP5 2DU

Tel   **(01794) 390155**
Fax   (01794) 390022
Sec   P Stevens
Holes 18 L 6516 yds SSS
V'tors H
Fees £25 D–£30
Loc   10 miles SE of Salisbury, off
          A36/B3079. M27 Junction 2,
          6 miles

High Post (1922)

Great Durnford, Salisbury SP4 6AT

Tel   **(01722) 782231**
Fax   (01722) 782356
Mem   590
Sec   NI Symington (01722) 782356
Pro   I Welding (01722) 782219
Holes 18 L 6305 yds Par 70 SSS 70
Recs Am–64 K Weeks, RE Searle
          Pro–65 P Alliss, N Sutton
V'tors WD–U WE/BH–H SOC
Fees £23 D–£28 (£35) SOC–£32
Loc   4 miles N of Salisbury on A345

Highworth (1990)

Swindon Road, Highworth SN6 7SJ

Tel   **(01793) 766014**
Pro   M Toombs
Holes 9 L 3220 yds SSS 70
V'tors U SOC
Fees £4.50 (£5)
Loc   5 miles N of Swindon (A361)
Mis   9 hole pitch & putt

Kingsdown (1880)

Kingsdown, Corsham SN13 8BS

Tel   **(01225) 742530**
Mem   500 105(L) 45(J)
Sec   J Prosser (01225) 743472
Pro   A Butler (01225) 742634
Holes 18 L 6445 yds SSS 71
Recs Am–66 S Hodges (1991)
          Pro–64 M Wiggett (1993)
V'tors WD–H WE–M
Fees £22
Loc   5 miles E of Bath

Manor House (1992)

Castle Combe SN14 7PL

Tel   **(01249) 782982**
Fax   (01249) 782992
Mem   400
Sec   Susan Auld (Gen Mgr)
Pro   C Smith (Golf Dir)
Holes 18 L 6340 yds SSS 71
Recs Am–73 M Hodges (1995)
V'tors U H–booking necessary SOC
Fees £35 (£45)
Loc   N of Castle Combe, off
          B4039. M4 Junction 17,
          4 miles
Mis   Driving range
Arch Alliss/Clarke

Marlborough (1888)

The Common, Marlborough SN8 1DU
Tel   **(01672) 512147**
Fax   (01672) 513164
Mem   750
Sec   JAD Sullivan
Pro   S Amor (01672) 512493
Holes 18 L 6526 yds SSS 71
Recs   Am–61 G Harris
       Pro–63 B Sandry
V'tors WD/WE–H SOC
Fees   £21 D–£32 (£40)
Loc   ½ mile N of Marlborough
       (A346)

Monkton Park Par Three

(1975)
Pay and play
Chippenham SN15 3PP
Tel   **(01249) 653928**
Fax   (01249) 653928
Mem   100
Sec   MR & BJ Dawson (Props)
Holes 9 hole Par 3 course
Recs   Am–23 J Dawson (1991)
V'tors U
Fees   18 holes–£4.75 (£5)
       9 holes–£3.25 (£3.50)
Loc   Centre of Chippenham.
       M4 Junction 17
Arch   M Dawson

North Wilts (1890)

Bishops' Cannings, Devizes SN10 2LP
Tel   **(01380) 860257**
Fax   (01380) 860877
Mem   600 96(L) 90(J)
Sec   Mrs P Stephenson
       (01380) 860627
Pro   GJ Laing (Golf Mgr)
       (01380) 860330
Holes 18 L 6333 yds SSS 70
Recs   Am–65 N Williams (1996)
       Pro–66 GJ Laing
       Ladies–72 S Firmston (1997)
V'tors U exc Xmas Day–Jan 31–M
       SOC
Fees   £19 (£25)
Loc   1 mile from A4, E of Calne

Oaksey Park (1991)

Pay and play
Oaksey, Malmesbury SN16 9SB
Tel   **(01666) 577995**
Fax   (01666) 577174
Holes 9 L 2900 yds SSS 68
V'tors U SOC
Fees   £10 (£15)
Loc   8 miles NE of Malmesbury,
       off A429
Mis   Driving range
Arch   Chapman/Warren

Ogbourne Downs (1907)

*Ogbourne St George, Marlborough
SN8 1TB*
Tel   **(01672) 841217**
Mem   700
Sec   DJ Knight (01672) 841327
Pro   C Harraway (01672) 841287

Holes 18 L 6353 yds SSS 70
Recs   Am–66 RJ Binsted,
       S Robertson
       Pro–65 I Bolt, G Wraith
V'tors WD–H WE–M SOC–WD
Fees   £20 (£30)
Loc   5 miles S of M4 Junction 15,
       on A346
Arch   JH Taylor

RMCS Shrivenham

(1953)
*RMCS Shrivenham, Swindon
SN6 8LA*
Tel   **(01793) 785725**
Mem   500
Sec   R Humphrey (Mgr)
Holes 18 L 5684 yds SSS 69
Recs   Am–65 GNH Evans
V'tors M SOC
Fees   £8 (£10)
Loc   Grounds of Royal Military
       College of Science. Entry
       must be arranged with Mgr

Salisbury & South Wilts

(1888)
Netherhampton, Salisbury SP2 8PR
Tel   **(01722) 742645**
Fax   (01722) 742645
Mem   1100
Sec   J Newcomb (Sec/Mgr)
Pro   G Emerson (01722) 742929
Holes 18 L 6528 yds SSS 71
       9 hole course Par 34
Recs   Am–65 D Hutton
       Pro–61 S Little
V'tors WD–U WE–H SOC–WD
Fees   £25 (£40)
Loc   Wilton, 3 miles SW of
       Salisbury on A3094
Arch   Taylor/Gidman

Shrivenham Park (1967)

Pay and play
*Penny Hooks, Shrivenham, Swindon
SN6 8EX*
Tel   **(01793) 783853**
Fax   (01793) 782999
Mem   400
Sec   Mrs A Briggs
Pro   J Goodson
Holes 18 L 5713 yds SSS 69
V'tors U SOC
Fees   £10.50 (£12.50 D–£16.50)
Loc   4 miles E of Swindon, off
       A420. M4 Junction 15
Arch   Glen Johnson

Thoulstone Park (1992)

Chapmanslade, Westbury BA13 4AQ
Tel   **(01373) 832825**
Fax   (01373) 832821
Sec   Mrs J Pearce
Pro   T Isaacs (01373) 832808
Holes 18 L 6300 yds Par 71 SSS 70
Recs   Am–69 S Wilson (1994)
       Pro–67 T Nash (1992)
V'tors U SOC–WD
Fees   £16 (£22.50)

Loc   12 miles S of Bath, off A36
Mis   Driving range
Arch   MRM Sandow

Tidworth Garrison

(1908)
Bulford Road, Tidworth SP9 7AF
Tel   **(01980) 842321 (Clubhouse)**
Fax   (01980) 842301
Mem   700
Sec   Lt Col DFT Tucker (Mgr)
       (01980) 842301
Pro   T Gosden (01980) 842393
Holes 18 L 6101 yds SSS 69
Recs   Am–66 C Akrill (1992)
       Pro–62 I Benson (1995)
V'tors SOC–Tues & Thurs
Fees   £20
Loc   1 mile SW of Tidworth on
       Bulford road (A338)
Arch   Donald Steel

Upavon (RAF) (1918)

Douglas Avenue, Upavon SN9 6BQ
Tel   **(01980) 630787**
Fax   (01980) 630787
Mem   550
Sec   L Mitchell
Pro   R Blake (01980) 630281
Holes 18 L 6415 yds SSS 71
Recs   Am–71 R Greenwood (1997)
V'tors WD–U WE–M before noon
       –U after noon SOC–WD
Fees   £15 (£20)
Loc   2 miles SE of Upavon on
       A342
Arch   R Blake

West Wilts (1891)

Elm Hill, Warminster BA12 0AU
Tel   **(01985) 212702**
Fax   (01985) 219809
Mem   570 70(L) 70(J)
Sec   DJ Spratt (01985) 213133
Pro   AJ Lamb (01985) 212110
Holes 18 L 5709 yds SSS 68
Recs   Am–62 CG Burton (1989)
       Pro–61 I Bolt,
       I Harrison (1997)
V'tors WD–U H WE–U H after
       noon –NA before noon
Fees   £15 D–£24 (£35)
Loc   Off A350, on Westbury road
Arch   JH Taylor

The Wiltshire (1993)

*Vastern, Wootton Bassett, Swindon
SN4 7PB*
Tel   **(01793) 849999**
Fax   (01793) 849988
Mem   600
Sec   RG Lipscombe (Gen Mgr)
Pro   A Gray
Holes 18 L 6522 yds SSS 72
Recs   Am–67
V'tors U SOC
Fees   £30 (£30)
Loc   1 mile S of Wootton Bassett.
       M4 Junction 16
Arch   Alliss/Clark

Wrag Barn G&CC
(1990)
Shrivenham Road, Highworth, Swindon
SN6 7QQ
Tel   (01793) 861327
Fax   (01793) 861325
Mem   462
Sec   Mrs S Manners
Pro   B Loughrey (01793) 766027
Holes   18 L 6600 yds SSS 71
Recs   Am–71 P Poulton (1993)
          Pro–66 G Clough (1992)
V'tors   WD–U WE–NA before noon
          SOC–WD
Fees   £22 (£27)
Loc   6 miles NE of Swindon on
          B4000. M4 Junction 15,
          8 miles
Mis   Driving range
Arch   Hawtree

Yorkshire (East)

Allerthorpe Park
Allerthorpe, York YO4 4RL
Tel   (01759) 306686
Fax   (01759) 304308
Mem   350
Sec   Linda Ridley
Pro   None
Holes   13 L 5514 yds Par 68 SSS 67
V'tors   U SOC
Fees   £14 (£14)
Loc   2 miles W of Pocklington, off
          A1079
Arch   JG Hatcliffe

Beverley & East Riding
(1889)
The Westwood, Beverley HU17 8RG
Tel   (01482) 867190
Fax   (01482) 868757
Mem   530
Sec   B Granville (01482) 868757
Pro   I Mackie (01482) 869519
Holes   18 L 5972 yds SSS 69
Recs   Am–65 N Burnley (1994)
V'tors   U SOC–WD
Fees   £12 (£16)
Loc   Beverley-Walkington road
          (B1230)

Boothferry
(1982)
Public
*Spaldington Lane, Spaldington, Goole
DN14 7NG*
Tel   (01430) 430364
Pro   N Bundy
Holes   18 L 6593 yds SSS 72
Recs   Am–70 R Giles (1988)
          Pro–70 M Ingham (1984),
          Rolley (1987)
V'tors   U SOC
Fees   On application
Loc   3 miles N of Howden on
          B1288. M62 Junction 37,
          2 miles
Arch   Donald Steel

Bridlington
(1905)
Belvedere Road, Bridlington YO15 3NA
Tel   (01262) 672092/606367
Fax   (01262) 606367
Mem   623
Sec   C Greenwood (01262) 606367
Pro   ARA Howarth (01262) 674721
Holes   18 L 6577 yds SSS 71
Recs   Am–66 R Webster (1997)
          Pro–69 J Healey (1996)
V'tors   U exc Sun–NA
Fees   £14 (£30)
Loc   1½ miles S of Bridlington, off
          A165
Arch   James Braid

The Bridlington Links
(1993)
Pay and play
*Flamborough Road, Marton,
Bridlington YO15 1DW*
Tel   (01262) 401584
Fax   (01262) 401702
Mem   300
Sec   PM Hancock (Gen Mgr)
Pro   S Raybould
Holes   18 L 6720 yds SSS 72
          9 hole course
Recs   Am–69 J Smith (1995)
V'tors   U
Fees   £12 (£15)
Loc   2 miles N of Bridlington on
          B1255
Mis   Floodlit driving range.
          3 Academy holes
Arch   Howard Swann

Brough
(1893)
Cave Road, Brough HU15 1HB
Tel   (01482) 667374
Fax   (01482) 667291
Mem   800
Sec   WG Burleigh (01482) 667291
Pro   G Townhill (01482) 667483
Holes   18 L 6183 yds SSS 69
Recs   Am–65 AG McKelvie (1997)
          Pro–64 B Thompson (1993)
V'tors   WD–U exc Wed–NA
Fees   £35
Loc   10 miles W of Hull on A63

Cave Castle Hotel
(1989)
South Cave, N Humberside HU15 2EU
Tel   (01430) 421286/422245
          (Hotel)
Fax   (01430) 421118
Sec   C Welton
Pro   J Lynch (01430) 421286
Holes   18 L 6409 yds SSS 71
V'tors   U SOC
Fees   £12.50 (£18)
Loc   10 miles W of Hull.
          Junction of A63/M62

Cherry Burton
(1993)
Pay and play
*Leconfield Road, Cherry Burton,
Beverley*
Tel   (01964) 550924
Mem   220

Sec   A Ashby (Mgr)
Pro   A Ashby
Holes   9 L 2278 yds Par 33 SSS 62
Recs   Am–62 P Killeen (1995)
V'tors   U SOC
Fees   £7 (£10)
Loc   2 miles N of Beverley, off
          Malton road
Mis   Driving range

Cottingham
*Woodhill Way, Cottingham, Hull
HU16 5RZ*
Tel   (01482) 842394
Fax   (01482) 846030
Mem   500
Sec   J Wiles (01482) 846030
Pro   CW Gray (01482) 842394
Holes   18 L 6230 yds Par 72 SSS 69
V'tors   WD–U WE/BH–M before
          11am SOC
Fees   £14 D–£20 (£20 D–£30)
Loc   3 miles N of Hull, off A164
Mis   Driving range

Driffield
(1934)
*Sunderlandwick, Driffield
YO25 9AD*
Tel   (01377) 253116 (Clubhouse),
          (01377) 240599 (Office)
Fax   (01377) 240599
Mem   634
Pro   (01377) 240448
Holes   18 L 6212 yds SSS 70
Recs   Am–67 G Drewery (1985),
          KA Gray (1994)
V'tors   H I SOC
Fees   R/D–£18 (R/D–£25)
Loc   S of Driffield on A164

Flamborough Head
(1932)
*Lighthouse Road, Flamborough,
Bridlington YO15 1AR*
Tel   (01262) 850333/850417
Fax   (01262) 850279
Mem   400
Sec   GS Thornton
          (01262) 850683
Holes   18 L 5973 yds SSS 69
Recs   Am–70 E Skaggs
V'tors   U
Fees   £16 (£19) W–£64
Loc   5 miles NE of Bridlington

Ganstead Park
(1976)
*Longdales Lane, Coniston, Hull
HU11 4LB*
Tel   (01482) 811280 (Steward)
Fax   (01482) 874754
Mem   700
Sec   G Drewery
          (01482) 874754
Pro   M Smee (01482) 811121
Holes   18 L 6801 yds SSS 73
V'tors   U H WE–NA before noon
          SOC
Fees   On application
Loc   5 miles E of Hull on A165
Arch   Peter Green

Hainsworth Park (1983)

Brandesburton, Driffield YO25 8RT

Tel   **(01964) 542362**
Fax   (01964) 542362
Mem   450
Sec   Maj R Kilpatrick (Mgr)
       BW Atkin (Prop)
Holes 18 L 6027 yds SSS 69
V'tors U SOC
Fees   £12 (£15)
Loc   6 miles NW of Beverley, off
       A165 at Brandesburton
       roundabout

Hessle (1898)

Westfield Road, Cottingham HU16 5YL

Tel   **(01482) 650171**
Fax   (01482) 652679
Mem   680
Sec   RL Dorsey
Pro   G Fieldsend (01482) 650190
Holes 18 L 6604 yds SSS 72
Recs   Am–68 PM Blanshard (1997)
       Pro–69 B Thompson (1980)
       Ladies–72 E Duggleby (1994)
V'tors WD–U exc Tues 9am–1pm
       WE–NA before 11am
Fees   £20 (£28)
Loc   3 miles SW of Cottingham
Arch   Thomas/Alliss

Hornsea (1898)

Rolston Road, Hornsea HU18 1XG

Tel   **(01964) 535488**
Fax   (01964) 534989
Mem   600
Sec   BW Kirton (01964) 532020
Pro   B Thompson (01964) 534989
Holes 18 L 6685 yds SSS 72
Recs   Am–66 A Wright (1967)
       Pro–66 G Brown (1991)
V'tors WD–U WE–restricted SOC
Fees   £19 D–£26
Loc   300 yds past Hornsea Free
       Port
Arch   Mackenzie/Braid

Hull (1921)

*The Hall, 27 Packman Lane, Kirk Ella,
Hull HU10 7JT*

Tel   **(01482) 653026**
Fax   (01482) 658919
Mem   800
Sec   R Toothill (Gen Mgr)
       (01482) 658919
Pro   D Jagger (01482) 653074
Holes 18 L 6246 yds SSS 70
Recs   Am–64 JD Dockar, R Roper
       Pro–66 D Dunk, N Hunt,
       S Smith, D Jagger
V'tors WD–U WE–NA
Fees   £25 D–£30
Loc   5 miles W of Hull

Kilnwick Percy (1995)

Kilnwick Percy, Pocklington YO4 2UF

Tel   **(01759) 303090**
Mem   350
Sec   Mrs A Clayton (Sec/Mgr)
Pro   J Townhill
Holes 18 L 6214 yds Par 70 SSS 70

V'tors U SOC
Fees   £10 (£13)
Loc   1 mile E of Pocklington,
       off B1246
Arch   John Day

Springhead Park (1930)

Public
Willerby Road, Hull HU5 5JE

Tel   **656309**
Sec   A Farr (Hon) (01482) 501126
Pro   B Herrington
Holes 18 L 6402 yds SSS 71
Recs   Am–69 AD Hill, A Wright
       Pro–65 S Rolley
V'tors U SOC–phone Sec
Fees   £6 (£7.80) (1997)
Loc   4 miles W of Hull

Sutton Park (1935)

Public
Salthouse Road, Hull HU8 9HF

Tel   **(01482) 374242**
Fax   (01482) 701428
Mem   300
Sec   L Derrett (Hon)
Pro   P Rushworth (01482) 711450
Holes 18 L 6251 yds SSS 70
Recs   Am–67 A Wright
       Pro–64 L Herrington
V'tors U SOC–exc Sun
Fees   £6.50 (£8.50)
Loc   3 miles E of Hull on A165

Withernsea (1907)

*Chestnut Avenue, Withernsea
HU19 2PG*

Tel   **(01964) 612258 (Clubhouse)**
Mem   329 40(L) 40(J)
Sec   Mrs J Jackson (01964) 612078
Pro   G Harrison (01482) 492720
Holes 9 L 6191 yds Par 72 SSS 69
Recs   Am–BJ Hayes
V'tors WD–U WE/BH–M before
       3pm SOC
Fees   £10
Loc   17 miles E of Hull on A1033.
       S side of Withernsea

Yorkshire (North)

Aldwark Manor (1978)

Aldwark, Alne, York YO6 2NF

Tel   **(01347) 838353**
Fax   (01347) 838867
Sec   GF Platt (Golf Dir)
Holes 18 L 6171 yds Par 71 SSS 70
Recs   Am–70 RW Smart (1994)
       Pro–69 N Squire (1992)
V'tors U SOC
Fees   £20 D–£25 (£25 D–£30)
Loc   5 miles SE of Boroughbridge,
       off A1. 13 miles NW of York,
       off A19

Ampleforth College (1962)

*56 High Street, Helmsley, York
YO6 5AE*

Mem   175
Sec   JE Atkinson (01439) 770678

Holes 10 L 4018 yds SSS 63
V'tors U exc WD 2–4pm SOC–WD
Fees   £8 (£12)
Loc   Driveway of Gilling Castle.
       18 miles N of York (B1363)
Mis   Green fees payable at Fairfax
       Arms, Gilling East
Arch   Rev Jerome Lambert OSB

Bedale (1894)

Leyburn Road, Bedale DL8 1EZ

Tel   **(01677) 422568**
Mem   600 60(J)
Sec   GA Shepherdson
       (01677) 422451
Pro   AD Johnson
       (01677) 422443
Holes 18 L 6565 yds SSS 71
Recs   Am–68 R Lawson (1994)
       Pro–76 N Walton (1992)
V'tors U SOC
Fees   £18 (£24)
Loc   N boundary of Bedale

Bentham (1922)

*Robin Lane, Bentham, Lancaster
LA2 7AG*

Tel   **(015242) 61018**
Mem   450
Sec   JM Philipson (015242) 62455
Holes 9 L 5760 yds SSS 69
Recs   Am–67 CJ Carter (1992)
V'tors U SOC
Fees   £14 (£20) W–£56
Loc   NE of Lancaster on B6480
       towards Settle. 13 miles E of
       M6 Junction 34

Catterick (1930)

*Leyburn Road, Catterick Garrison
DL9 3QE*

Tel   **(01748) 833401**
Fax   (01748) 833268
Mem   700
Sec   JK Mayberry (Sec/Mgr)
       (01748) 833268
Pro   A Marshall (01748) 833671
Holes 18 L 6329 yds SSS 70
Recs   Am–65 CS Carveth
       Pro–69 D Edwards
V'tors WD–U H SOC
Fees   £20 (£25)
Loc   6 miles SW of Scotch Corner,
       via A1
Arch   Arthur Day

Cleveland (1887)

Queen Street, Redcar TS10 1BT

Tel   **(01642) 483693**
Fax   (01642) 471798
Mem   800
Sec   LR Manley
       (01642) 471798
Pro   S Wynn (01642) 483462
Holes 18 L 6707 yds SSS 72
Recs   Am–66 CM Nolan (1996)
       Pro–70 B Hardcastle (1976)
V'tors WD–U after 9.30am
       WE/BH–no parties SOC
Fees   £20 (£30)
Loc   S bank of River Tees

Cocksford (1992)
Stutton, Tadcaster LS24 9NG

Tel	**(01937) 834253**
Fax	(01937) 834253
Sec	Gill Coxon
Pro	G Thompson
Holes	18 L 5570 yds Par 71 SSS 69
	9 L 2470 yds Par 33
	Pro–71 M Maith (1994)
V'tors	WD–U WE–by arrangement
	SOC
Fees	£16 D–£20 (£22 D–25)
Loc	1½ miles S of Tadcaster

Crimple Valley (1976)
Pay and play
*Hookstone Wood Road, Harrogate
HG2 8PN*

Tel	**(01423) 883485**
Fax	(01423) 881018
Mem	200
Sec	P Lumb
Pro	P Lumb
Holes	9 L 2500 yds SSS 33
V'tors	U
Fees	9 holes–£4.50 (£5);
	18 holes–£7.50 D–£10
Loc	1 mile S of Harrogate, off A61,
	by Yorkshire Showground
Arch	R Lumb

Drax (1989)
Drax, Selby YO8 8PQ

Mem	465
Sec	J Leedham (01757) 702247
Holes	9 L 5510 yds Par 68 SSS 67
Recs	Am–70 A Dick (1993)
V'tors	M
Fees	£5 (£7)
Loc	5 miles S of Selby, off A1041
Arch	JM Scott

Easingwold (1930)
*Stillington Road, Easingwold, York
YO6 3ET*

Tel	**(01347) 821486**
Fax	(01347) 822474
Mem	625
Sec	DB Stockley (01347) 822474
Pro	J Hughes (01347) 821964
Holes	18 L 6285 yds SSS 70
Recs	Am–67 JP Miller
	Pro–65 G Brown
V'tors	U
Fees	D–£25 (£30)
Loc	12 miles N of York on A19.
	S end of Easingwold
Arch	Hawtree

Filey (1897)
West Ave, Filey YO14 9BQ

Tel	**(01723) 513293**
Fax	(01723) 514952
Mem	768
Sec	MS Scutt
Pro	GM Hutchinson
	(01723) 513134
Holes	18 L 6112 yds SSS 69
Recs	Am–65 P Blanchard
	Pro–64 AS Murray

V'tors	U H SOC
Fees	£21 (£27) Summer
	£16 (£21) Winter
Loc	1 mile S of Filey centre
Arch	James Braid

Forest of Galtres (1993)
*Moorlands Road, Skelton, York
YO3 3RF*

Tel	**(01904) 766198**
Fax	(01904) 766198
Mem	450
Sec	Mrs SJ Procter
Pro	N Suckling
Holes	18 L 6312 yds Par 72 SSS 70
Recs	Am–72 S Spear (1997)
	Pro–67 N Suckling (1995)
V'tors	U SOC
Fees	£16 (£21)
Loc	Skelton, 4 miles N of York.
	1½ miles off A19
Arch	Simon Gidman

Forest Park (1991)
Stockton-on Forest, York YO3 9UW

Tel	**(01904) 400425**
Mem	650
Sec	N Crossley
	(01904) 400688
Pro	None
Holes	18 L 6660 yds Par 71 SSS 72
	9 L 3186 yds Par 70 SSS 70
Recs	Am–71
V'tors	U SOC
Fees	£16 D–£22 (D–£28)
Loc	1½ miles from E end of A64
	York By-pass
Mis	Driving range

Fulford (1906)
Heslington Lane, York YO1 5DY

Tel	**(01904) 413579**
Fax	(01904) 416918
Mem	700
Sec	R Bramley BEM MIMgt
Pro	B Hessay (01904) 412882
Holes	18 L 6775 yds SSS 72
Recs	Am–66 G Harland (1989)
	Pro–62 I Woosnam (1985)
V'tors	By arrangement with Sec
Fees	£30 D–£40 (£40)
Loc	2 miles S of York (A64)
Arch	Major C McKenzie

Ganton (1891)
*Station Road, Ganton, Scarborough
YO12 4PA*

Tel	**(01944) 710329**
Mem	600
Sec	Maj RG Woolsey
Pro	G Brown (01944) 710260
Holes	18 L 6734 yds SSS 74
Recs	Am–67 G Boardman
	Pro–65 N Coles
V'tors	By prior arrangement
Fees	On application
Loc	11 miles SW of Scarborough
	on A64
Arch	Dunn/Vardon/Braid/Colt

Harrogate (1892)
Forest Lane Head, Harrogate HG2 7TF

Tel	**(01423) 863158 (Clubhouse)**
Fax	(01423) 860073
Mem	700
Sec	G Merryweather
	(01423) 862999
Pro	P Johnson (01423) 862547
Holes	18 L 6241 yds SSS 70
Recs	Am–65 NA Fegan (1995)
	Pro–63 P Scott (1994)
	Ladies–69 R Skaife (1993)
V'tors	WD–U WE/BH–enquire first
	SOC–WD exc Tues
Fees	£28 D–£32 (£40)
Loc	2 miles E of Harrogate on
	Knaresborough road (A59)
Arch	Sandy Herd

Heworth (1911)
*Muncaster House, Muncastergate, York
YO3 9JX*

Tel	**(01904) 424618**
Mem	345 80(L) 50(J)
Sec	RJ Hunt (01904) 426156
Pro	G Roberts (01904) 422389
Holes	12 L 6141 yds SSS 69
V'tors	U
Fees	£12 (£16)
Loc	NE boundary of York (A1036)

Hunley Hall (1993)
Brotton, Saltburn TS12 2QQ

Tel	**(01287) 676216**
Fax	(01287) 678250
Mem	500
Sec	E Lillie
Pro	A Brook (01287) 677444
Holes	18 L 6918 yds Par 73 SSS 73
Recs	Am–69 JJ Jackson (1997)
V'tors	U SOC–exc Sun
Fees	£18 (£25)
Loc	15 miles SE of Middlesbrough
	on A174
Mis	Floodlit driving range
Arch	John Morgan

Kirkbymoorside (1951)
*Manor Vale, Kirkbymoorside, York
YO6 6EG*

Tel	**(01751) 431525**
Mem	650
Sec	AR Holmes
Holes	18 L 6101 yds SSS 69
Recs	Am–65 S Dunn (1995)
	Ladies–69 J Brown
V'tors	U between 9.30–12.30 and
	after 1.30pm
Fees	£18 (£25)
Loc	A170 between Helmsley and
	Pickering

Knaresborough (1920)
*Boroughbridge Road, Knaresborough
HG5 0QQ*

Tel	**(01423) 863219**
Fax	(01423) 869345
Mem	795
Sec	Gp Capt JI Barrow (Mgr)
	(01423) 862690
Pro	GJ Vickers (01423) 864865

Holes 18 L 6433 yds SSS 71
Recs Am–68 JR McVicar (1995)
Pro–69 A Miller (1994)
V'tors U SOC
Fees £22.50 (£27.50)
Loc 1½ miles N of Knaresborough on A6055
Arch Hawtree

Malton & Norton (1910)

Welham Park, Welham Road, Norton, Malton YO17 9QE
Tel (01653) 692959
Fax (01653) 697912
Mem 820
Sec WG Wade (01653) 697912
Pro SI Robinson (01653) 693882
Holes 27 holes:
Welham L 6456 yds SSS 71
Park L 6231 yds SSS 70
Derwent L 6267 yds SSS 70
V'tors WD–U WE–restricted on match days H SOC
Fees £22 (£28)
Loc 18 miles NE of York (A64)

Masham (1895)

Burnholme, Swinton Road, Masham, Ripon HG4 4HT
Tel (01765) 689379
Fax (01765) 689491
Mem 332
Sec (01765) 689491
Holes 9 L 6068 yds SSS 69
V'tors WD–U before 5pm WE–M BH–NA
Fees £15
Loc 10 miles N of Ripon, off A6108

Middlesbrough (1908)

Brass Castle Lane, Marton, Middlesbrough TS8 9EE
Tel (01642) 311515
Fax (01642) 319607
Mem 950
Sec BC Hunt
Pro DJ Jones (01642) 311766
Holes 18 L 6215 yds SSS 70
Recs Am–64 JW Lupton (1996)
Pro–65 D Padgett (1993)
V'tors U
Fees D–£28 (£34)
Loc 3 miles S of Middlesbrough

Middlesbrough Municipal (1977)

Public
Ladgate Lane, Middlesbrough TS5 7YZ
Tel (01642) 315533
Fax (01642) 300726
Mem 625
Sec J Dilworth (Hon)
Pro A Hope (01642) 300720
Holes 18 L 6333 yds SSS 70
Recs Am–67 J Wharton (1995)
Pro–67 B Gallagher (1981)
V'tors U
Fees £7.75 (£9.75)
Loc 2 miles S of Middlesbrough on A174
Mis Floodlit driving range

Oakdale (1914)

Oakdale, Harrogate HG1 2LN
Tel (01423) 567162
Fax (01423) 536030
Mem 775
Sec D Rodgers
Pro C Dell (01423) 560510
Holes 18 L 6456 yds SSS 71
Recs Am–61 M Fountain (1997)
Pro–66 P Hall (1989)
V'tors WD–U 9.30–12.30 and after 2pm SOC–WD
Fees £27 D–£40
Loc ½ mile NE of Royal Hall, Harrogate
Arch Dr A Mackenzie

Pannal (1906)

Follifoot Road, Pannal, Harrogate HG3 1ES
Tel (01423) 871641
Fax (01423) 870043
Mem 780
Sec R Braddon (01423) 872628
Pro M Burgess (01423) 872620
Holes 18 L 6618 yds SSS 72
Recs Am–62 SR Macfarlane (1984)
Pro–65 A Nicholson (1993)
V'tors WD–H 9.30–12 and after 1.30pm WE–H 11–12 and after 2.30pm SOC
Fees £37 D–£45 (£45)
Loc 2½ miles S of Harrogate, on A61

Pike Hills (1920)

Tadcaster Road, Askham Bryan, York YO2 3UW
Tel (01904) 700797
Fax (01904) 700797
Mem 750
Sec L Hargrave
Pro I Gradwell (01904) 708756
Holes 18 L 6146 yds SSS 69
Recs Am–67 C Weir (1995)
V'tors WD–U H before 4.30pm –M after 4.30pm SOC–WD
Fees £18 D–£24
Loc 3 miles SW of York on A64

Richmond (1892)

Bend Hagg, Richmond DL10 5EX
Tel (01748) 825319
Mem 600
Sec BD Aston (01748) 823231
Pro P Jackson (01748) 822457
Holes 18 L 5769 yds SSS 68
Recs Am–AP Jackson
Pro–64 J Harrison, P Harrison
V'tors U
Fees £18 (£25)
Loc 3 miles SW of Scotch Corner
Arch Frank Pennink

Ripon City (1905)

Palace Road, Ripon HG4 3HH
Tel (01765) 603640
Mem 650 100(L) 45(J)
Sec B Denbigh-White
Pro T Davis (01765) 600411

Holes 18 L 6120 yds SSS 69
Recs Am–63
V'tors U SOC
Fees £18 (£25)
Loc 1 mile N of Ripon on A6108
Arch ADAS

Romanby (1993)

Pay and play
Yafforth Road, Northallerton DL7 0PE
Tel (01609) 779988
Fax (01609) 779084
Mem 500
Sec G McDonnell (01609) 778855
Pro T Jenkins
Holes 18 L 6663 yds SSS 72
V'tors U SOC
Fees £14 (£18)
Loc 1 mile W of Northallerton on B6271
Mis Floodlit driving range
Arch Will Adamson

Rudding Park (1995)

Pay and play
Rudding Park, Harrogate HG3 1DJ
Tel (01423) 872100
Fax (01423) 873011
Sec M Mackaness (Sec/Mgr)
Pro S Hotham (01423) 873400
Holes 18 L 6871 yds SSS 72
V'tors U H SOC
Fees £18.50 (£20)
Loc 2 miles S of Harrogate (A658)
Mis Driving range. Golf Academy
Arch Hawtree

Saltburn (1894)

Hob Hill, Saltburn-by-the-Sea TS12 1NJ
Tel (01287) 622812
Mem 900
Sec D Becker
Pro M Nutter (01287) 624653
Holes 18 L 5846 yds SSS 68
Recs Am–66
Pro–62 D Rees
V'tors H SOC
Fees £19 (£24)
Loc 1 mile S of Saltburn

Scarborough North Cliff (1909)

North Cliff Avenue, Burniston Road, Scarborough YO12 6PP
Tel (01723) 360786
Fax (01723) 362134
Mem 860
Sec JR Freeman
Pro SN Deller (01723) 365920
Holes 18 L 6425 yds SSS 71
Recs Am–66 F Anderson
V'tors U exc Sun before 10am and comp days H SOC
Fees £18 D–£25 (£22 D–£28)
Loc 2 miles N of Scarborough on coast road
Arch James Braid

For list of abbreviations see page 479

Scarborough South Cliff (1903)

*Deepdale Avenue, Scarborough
YO11 2UE*

Tel	**(01723) 360522**
Fax	(01723) 374737
Mem	565
Sec	RK Oakes (01723) 374737
Pro	AR Skingle (01723) 365150
Holes	18 L 6039 yds SSS 69
Recs	Am–64 J Smith (1994)
	Pro–66 MJ Slater (1987)
V'tors	U H
Fees	£20 (£25)
Loc	1 mile S of Scarborough

Scarthingwell (1993)

Scarthingwell, Tadcaster LS24 9DG

Tel	**(01937) 557878**
Fax	(01937) 557909
Mem	400
Pro	S Footman (01937) 557864
Holes	18 L 6759 yds Par 71 SSS 72
V'tors	U SOC
Fees	£16 (£18)
Loc	4 miles S of Tadcaster
	on A162

Selby (1907)

Mill Lane, Brayton, Selby YO8 9LD

Tel	**(01757) 228622**
Mem	749
Sec	JN Proctor
Pro	A Smith (01757) 228785
Holes	18 L 6246 yds SSS 70
Recs	Am–65 L Walker, N Ludwell
	Pro–64 D Matthew
V'tors	WD–H WE–NA
	SOC–Wed–Fri
Fees	£23 D–£25
Loc	3 miles SW of Selby, off A19
	at Brayton. 5 miles N of M62
	Junction 34
Arch	JH Taylor/Hawtree

Settle (1895)

Giggleswick, Settle BD24

Tel	**(01729) 825288**
Mem	250
Sec	RG Bannier (01729) 823596
Holes	9 L 5414 yds SSS 66
Recs	Am–62 M Gray (1996)
	Pro–59 L Turner (1995)
V'tors	U exc Sun–restricted SOC
Fees	D–£10
Loc	1 mile N of Settle on A65
Arch	Tom Vardon

Skipton (1893)

Off NW Bypass, Skipton BD23 1LL

Tel	**(01756) 795657**
Fax	(01756) 796665
Mem	720
Sec	EJ Paterson
Pro	P Robinson (01756) 793257
Holes	18 L 6087 yds SSS 70
Recs	Am–66 BJ Mallinson (1995)
V'tors	U SOC
Fees	£23 (£25)
Loc	Skipton 1 mile

Tees-side (1901)

Acklam Road, Thornaby TS17 7JS

Tel	**(01642) 676249**
Fax	(01642) 676252
Mem	600
Sec	D Watson (01642) 616516
Pro	K Hall (01642) 673822
Holes	18 L 6535 yds Par 72 SSS 71
Recs	Am–66 J Miller, M Rigby
V'tors	WD–U before 4.30pm WE–U
	after 11am BH–M before
	11am SOC
Fees	D–£26 (£30)
Loc	2 miles S of Stockton on
	A1130. ½ mile from A19

Thirsk & Northallerton (1914)

Thornton-le-Street, Thirsk YO7 4AB

Tel	**(01845) 522170**
Mem	500
Sec	JS Weatherall (01845) 525115
Pro	R Garner (01845) 526216
Holes	18 L 6495 yds SSS 71
Recs	Am–68 I Richardson
	Pro–68 J Harrison
V'tors	WD/Sat–U H Sun–M SOC
Fees	£20 D–£25 Sat/BH–£25
Loc	2 miles N of Thirsk, nr A19
	and A168 roundabout
Arch	ADAS

Whitby (1892)

*Sandsend Road, Low Straggleton,
Whitby YO21 3SR*

Tel	**(01947) 602768**
Fax	(01947) 600660
Mem	900
Sec	T Graham (01947) 600660
Pro	R Wood (01947) 602719
Holes	18 L 6134 yds SSS 70
Recs	Am–67
	Pro–68
V'tors	U H SOC
Fees	£20 (£25)
Loc	2 miles N of Whitby on A174

Wilton (1952)

Wilton, Redcar TS10 4QY

Tel	**(01642) 465265**
Mem	863
Sec	JCP Elder
Pro	Pat Smillie (01642) 452730
Holes	18 L 6145 yds SSS 69
Recs	Am–64 BM Christie (1991)
	Pro–68 S Hunt
	Ladies–75 V Duncan (1984)
V'tors	WD–U after 10am Sat–NA
	Sun/BH–U after 10am
	SOC–WD exc Tues
Fees	D–£18 (D–£24)
Loc	3 miles W of Redcar on A174–
	signs to Wilton Castle

York (1890)

*Lords Moor Lane, Strensall, York
YO3 5XF*

Tel	**(01904) 491840**
Fax	(01904) 491852
Mem	380 123(L) 100(J)
Sec	RV Braddon
Pro	A Mason (01904) 490304
Holes	18 L 6312 yds SSS 70
Recs	Am–66 D Oxley (1990)
	Pro–66 P Fowler
V'tors	U–phone Sec SOC
Fees	£22 D–£28 (£36)
Loc	2 miles N of York ring road
	(A1237)
Arch	JH Taylor

Yorkshire (South)

Abbeydale (1895)

*Twentywell Lane, Dore, Sheffield
S17 4QA*

Tel	**(0114) 236 0763**
Fax	(0114) 236 0762
Mem	700
Sec	Mrs KM Johnston
Pro	N Perry (0114) 236 5633
Holes	18 L 6419 yds SSS 71
V'tors	U SOC–Tues & Fri
Fees	£35 (£40)
Loc	5 miles S of Sheffield, off A621

Austerfield Park (1974)

*Cross Lane, Austerfield, Doncaster
DN10 6RF*

Tel	**(01302) 710841**
Fax	(01302) 710841
Mem	370 45(L) 35(J)
Sec	A Bradley (01709) 518930
Pro	P Rothery (01302) 710850
Holes	18 L 6900 yds SSS 73
	9 hole Par 3 course
Recs	Am–69 D Hemsworth (1995)
	Pro–67 J Brennand (1988)
V'tors	WD–U WE–after 10am SOC
Fees	£16 (£21)
Loc	2 miles NE of Bawtry, off A614
Mis	Driving range

Barnsley (1925)

Public
*Wakefield Road, Staincross, Barnsley
S75 6JZ*

Tel	**(01226) 382856**
Sec	L Lammas
Pro	M Melling (01226) 382954
Holes	18 L 5951 yds Par 69 SSS 69
Recs	Am–64 RI Shaw (1988)
	Pro–62 M Melling (1986)
V'tors	U
Fees	£8 (£8.50)
Loc	4 miles N of Barnsley on A61

Beauchief Municipal (1925)

Public
*Beauchief, Abbey Lane, Sheffield
S8 0DB*

Tel	**(0114) 236 7274/262 0040**
Mem	450
Sec	JG Pearson (0114) 230 6720
Pro	A Highfield
Holes	18 L 5452 yds SSS 66
Recs	Am–65 PW Hickinson
	Pro–63 P Tupling
V'tors	U
Fees	£9
Loc	A621 Sheffield

Birley Wood (1974)
Public
Birley Lane, Sheffield S12 3BP
Tel   (0114) 264 7262
Mem   294
Sec   M Hollis
Pro   P Ball
Holes 18 L 5483 yds SSS 67
Recs   Am–66 S Pearson (1991)
            Pro–67 D Muscroft (1990)
V'tors U
Fees   £7 (£8)
Loc   4 miles S of Sheffield on
            A616. M1 Junction 30

Concord Park (1952)
Public
Shiregreen Lane, Sheffield S5 6AE
Tel   (0114) 257 0274/257 0053
Sec   B Shepherd
Pro   None
Holes 18 L 4321 yds SSS 62
Recs   Am–56 S Ridal (1991)
V'tors U
Fees   £5.20
Loc   M1 Junction 34, 1 mile

Crookhill Park (1974)
Public
Conisborough, Doncaster DN12 2AH
Tel   (01709) 862979
Mem   500
Sec   C Gouldin
Pro   R Swaine
Holes 18 L 5839 yds SSS 68
Recs   Am–64 A Clegg, S Clegg
            Pro–70
V'tors U
Fees   £8.75 (£9.95)
Loc   3 miles W of Doncaster (A630)

Doncaster (1894)
*Bawtry Road, Bessacarr, Doncaster
DN4 7PD*
Tel   (01302) 865632
Fax   (01302) 865994
Mem   375
Sec   RJ Perkins
Pro   G Bailey (01302) 868404
Holes 18 L 6230 yds SSS 70
Recs   Am–66 H Green
            Pro–66 H Clark
V'tors WD–U H WE/BH–NA before
            11.30am SOC–WD
Fees   £20 (£25)
Loc   4½ miles S of Doncaster
            on A638
Arch   Mackenzie/Hawtree

Doncaster Town Moor
(1895)
*Bawtry Road, Belle Vue, Doncaster
DN4 5HU*
Tel   (01302) 533778
Mem   540
Sec   J Stoddart
Pro   SC Poole (01302) 535286
Holes 18 L 6001 yds SSS 69
Recs   Am–66 P Miller (1994)
            Pro–63 D Shacklady (1995)
V'tors U exc Sun–NA before
            11.30am SOC

Fees   £14 (£16)
Loc   Inside racecourse. Clubhouse
            on A638

Dore & Totley (1913)
*Bradway Road, Bradway, Sheffield
S17 4QR*
Tel   (0114) 236 0492
Fax   (0114) 235 3436
Mem   580
Sec   JR Johnson (0114) 236 9872
Pro   G Watkinson (0114) 236 6844
Holes 18 L 6265 yds SSS 70
Recs   Am–65 NM Parkinson
            Pro–64 P Cowen
V'tors WD–U exc Wed–NA before
            1pm Sat–M Sun–NA before
            11am SOC–Tues & Thurs
Fees   £20 D–£26
Loc   5 miles SW of Sheffield,
            off A61

Grange Park (1972)
*Upper Wortley Road, Kimberworth,
Rotherham S61 2SJ*
Tel   (01709) 558884
Sec   R Charity (01709) 583400
Pro   E Clark (01709) 559497
Holes 18 L 6461 yds SSS 71
Recs   Am–65 M Hammond
            Pro–68 G Tickell
V'tors U
Fees   £9.50 (£10)
Loc   2 miles W of Rotherham on
            A629
Mis   Driving range

Hallamshire (1897)
Sandygate, Sheffield S10 4LA
Tel   (0114) 230 1007
Fax   (0114) 230 2153
Mem   600
Sec   K Sharrocks (0114) 230 2153
Pro   G Tickell (0114) 230 5222
Holes 18 L 6359 yds SSS 71
Recs   Am–66 W Bremner, P Nelson
            Pro–63 JW Wilkinson
V'tors H SOC–WD
Fees   £33 (£38)
Loc   W boundary of Sheffield

Hallowes (1892)
Dronfield, Sheffield S18 6UR
Tel   (01246) 413734
Mem   508
Sec   R Warriss
Pro   P Dunn (01246) 411196
Holes 18 L 6342 yds SSS 71
Recs   Am–66 S Priest (1989),
            MJ Nolan (1996)
            Pro–64 PL Cowen (1991)
V'tors WD–U WE–M
Fees   £20 D–£27
Loc   6 miles S of Sheffield on
            B6057

Hickleton (1909)
Hickleton, Doncaster DN5 7BE
Tel   (01709) 896081
Fax   (01709) 896081
Mem   525

Sec   I Wright
Pro   P Shepherd
            (01709) 888436
Holes 18 L 6208 yds SSS 71
Recs   Am–69 A Herbert (1995)
V'tors WD–U WE–NA before noon
            SOC
Fees   £21 (£26)
Loc   6 miles W of Doncaster
            on A635
Arch   Huggett/Coles

Hillsborough (1920)
Worrall Road, Sheffield S6 4BE
Tel   (0114) 234 3608
Fax   (0114) 234 9151
Mem   533
Sec   KA Dungey
            (0114) 234 9151
Pro   G Walker (0114) 233 2666
Holes 18 L 6035 yds SSS 70
Recs   Am–64 JE Laycock (1987),
            MI Mackenzie (1992)
            Pro–63 CW Gray (1987)
V'tors H SOC
Fees   £28 (£35)
Loc   Wadsley, Sheffield
Mis   Driving range

Lees Hall (1907)
*Hemsworth Road, Norton, Sheffield
S8 8LL*
Tel   (0114) 255 4402
Mem   550
Sec   JW Poulson (0114) 255 2900
Pro   S Mackinder
Holes 18 L 6137 yds SSS 69
Recs   Am–65 AR Gellsthorpe
            Pro–63 B Hutchinson
V'tors U SOC
Fees   £20 (£30)
Loc   3 miles S of Sheffield. E of A61

Lindrick (1891)
*Lindrick Common, Worksop, Notts
S81 8BH*
Tel   (01909) 485802
Fax   (01909) 488685
Mem   500
Sec   Lt Cdr RJM Jack RN
            (01909) 475282
Pro   PL Cowen (01909) 475820
Holes 18 L 6615 yds SSS 72
Recs   Am–65 DF Livingston
            Pro–65 G Bond, J Morgan
V'tors U H–by prior arrangement exc
            Tues SOC–WD
Fees   £45 (£45)
Loc   4 miles W of Worksop on
            A57. M1 Junction 31

Owston Park (1988)
Public
*Owston Hall, Owston, Doncaster
DN6 9JF*
Tel   (01302) 330821
Holes 9 L 6148 yds SSS 71
V'tors U
Fees   On application
Loc   5 miles N of Doncaster on A19
Arch   Michael Parker

Phoenix (1932)

*Pavilion Lane, Brinsworth, Rotherham
S60 5PA*

Tel	**(01709) 363788**
Fax	(01709) 363788
Mem	700
Sec	J Burrows (01709) 370759
Pro	M Roberts (01709) 382624
Holes	18 L 6145 yds SSS 69
Recs	Am–65
V'tors	U
Fees	D–£21
Loc	2 miles S of Rotherham. M1 Junction 34
Mis	Driving range
Arch	H Cotton

Renishaw Park (1911)

*Golf House, Mill Lane, Renishaw,
Sheffield S21 3UZ*

Tel	**(01246) 432044**
Mem	450
Sec	TJ Childs
Pro	J Oates (01246) 435484
Holes	18 L 6262 yds SSS 70
Recs	Am–64 CS Bright Pro–66 D Dunk
V'tors	H SOC
Fees	£21 D–£29.50 (£34)
Loc	7 miles SE of Sheffield. 2 miles W of M1 Junction 30

Robin Hood (1996)

*Owston Hall, Owston, Doncaster
DN6 9JF*

Tel	**(01302) 722800**
Fax	(01302) 728885
Mem	200
Sec	R Baker
Pro	To be appointed
Holes	18 L 6937 yds SSS 72
V'tors	U SOC
Fees	£10 (£12)
Loc	5 miles N of Doncaster on A19 (B1220)
Arch	Will Adamson

Rother Valley Golf Centre (1996)

*Mansfield Road, Wales Bar, Sheffield
S31 8PE*

Tel	**(0114) 247 3000**
Fax	(0114) 247 6000
Mem	600
Sec	MC Shattock (Mgr)
Pro	JK Ripley
Holes	18 L 6602 yds Par 72 SSS 72 9 hole Par 3 course
Recs	Am–71 M Armitage (1997) Pro–71 R Wragg (1997)
V'tors	U SOC
Fees	£10 (£16) Mon–£7.50
Loc	Rother Valley Country Park, 2 miles S of M1 Junction 31
Mis	Floodlit driving range
Arch	Shattock/Roe

Rotherham (1903)

Thrybergh Park, Rotherham S65 4NU

Tel	**(01709) 850466**
Fax	(01709) 855288
Mem	400

Sec	G Smalley (01709) 850812
Pro	S Thornhill (01709) 850480
Holes	18 L 6324 yds SSS 70
Recs	Am–65 ID Garbutt (1992), L Westwood (1993) Pro–66 B Hutchison
V'tors	WD–U SOC
Fees	£28 (£35)
Loc	4 miles E of Rotherham on A630

Roundwood (1976)

*Green Lane, Rawmarsh, Rotherham
S62 6LA*

Tel	**(01709) 523471**
Mem	400
Sec	AW Hawke (01709) 382123
Holes	9 L 5646 yds SSS 67
V'tors	WE–NA before 5pm on comp days SOC–WD
Fees	£12 (£15)
Loc	2 miles N of Rotherham on A633

Sandhill (1993)

Pay and play
Little Houghton, Barnsley S72 0HW

Tel	**(01226) 753444**
Mem	275
Sec	GD Bell
Holes	18 L 6250 yds SSS 70
Recs	Am–69 P Kelly (1996)
V'tors	U SOC
Fees	£8 (£11)
Loc	6 miles E of Barnsley, off A635
Mis	Driving range
Arch	John Royston

Sheffield Transport (1923)

Meadow Head, Sheffield S8 7RE

Tel	**(0114) 237 3216**
Mem	125
Sec	AE Mason
Holes	18 L 3966 yds SSS 62
Recs	Am–62 VR Hutton, E Tonks, PR Pemberton
V'tors	M
Loc	S of Sheffield on A61

Silkstone (1893)

*Field Head, Elmhirst Lane, Silkstone,
Barnsley S75 4LD*

Tel	**(01226) 790328**
Mem	600
Sec	J Goulding
Pro	K Guy (01226) 790128
Holes	18 L 6069 yds SSS 70
Recs	Am–64 D Kershaw (1995)
V'tors	WD–U SOC–WD
Fees	D–£26 SOC(12+)–£38
Loc	1 mile W of M1 Junction 37 on A628

Sitwell Park (1913)

Shrogs Wood Road, Rotherham S60 4BY

Tel	**(01709) 541046**
Fax	(01709) 703637

Mem	500
Sec	G Simmonite
Pro	N Taylor (01709) 540961
Holes	18 L 6250 yds SSS 70
Recs	Am–61 R Jones (1994)
V'tors	WD–U Sat–M Sun–NA before 11.30am SOC
Fees	£24 D–£28 (£28)
Loc	2½ miles E of Rotherham on A631. M18 Junction 1
Arch	Dr A Mackenzie

Stocksbridge & District (1924)

*30 Royd Lane, Townend, Deepcar,
Sheffield S30 5RZ*

Tel	**(0114) 288 2003**
Mem	300
Sec	S Lee (0114) 288 2408
Pro	T Brookes
Holes	18 L 5200 yds Par 65 SSS 65
Recs	Am–60 I Batty (1996) Pro–61 TJ Brookes (1996)
V'tors	U SOC
Fees	£17 (£26)
Loc	9 miles W of Sheffield (A616)

Tankersley Park (1907)

High Green, Sheffield S30 4LG

Tel	**(0114) 246 8247**
Mem	574
Sec	PA Bagshaw
Pro	I Kirk (0114) 245 5583
Holes	18 L 6212 yds Par 69 SSS 70
Recs	Am–65 D Platts Pro–69 W Atkinson
V'tors	WD–U WE–M SOC–WD
Fees	£22 D–£26 (£26)
Loc	Chapeltown, 7 miles N of Sheffield. M1 Junctions 35A/36
Arch	Hawtree

Thorne (1980)

*Kirton Lane, Thorne, Doncaster
DN8 5RJ*

Tel	**(01405) 812054**
Sec	P Kitteridge (01302) 813827
Pro	RD Highfield
Holes	18 L 5366 yds SSS 65
V'tors	U
Fees	£7.60 (£8.60)
Loc	10 miles NE of Doncaster. M18 Junction 5/6
Arch	RD Highfield

Tinsley Park (1920)

Public
*High Hazel Park, Darnell, Sheffield
S9 4PE*

Tel	**(0114) 256 0237**
Mem	560
Sec	SP Edwards
Pro	AP Highfield
Holes	18 L 6103 yds SSS 69
Recs	Am–68 SJ Thorpe Pro–66 D Snell
V'tors	U
Fees	£7.50
Loc	M1 Junction 32, 1 mile

For list of abbreviations see page 479

Wath-upon-Dearne (1904)
Abdy Rawmarsh, Rotherham S62 7SJ
Tel (01709) 872149/878609
Fax (01709) 878609
Mem 680
Sec DMC Vallance
(01709) 872048
Pro C Bassett (01709) 878677
Holes 18 L 5857 yds SSS 68
V'tors WD–U WE/BH–M SOC
Fees £21
Loc Abdy Farm, 1¹/₂ miles S of
Wath-upon-Dearne

Wheatley (1913)
Armthorpe Road, Doncaster DN2 5QB
Tel (01302) 831655
Mem 385 100(L) 50(J)
Pro S Fox (01302) 834085
Holes 18 L 6405 yds SSS 71
Recs Am–65 D Lawrence
Pro–64 I Garbutt
Ladies–63 R Hudson
V'tors U SOC
Fees £24 (£30)
Loc 3 miles NE of Doncaster

Wombwell Hillies (1989)
Public
*Wentworth View, Wombwell, Barnsley
S73 0LA*
Tel (01226) 754433
Sec S Rolbiecki (Mgr)
Holes 9 L 2095 yds SSS 60
V'tors U
Fees On application
Loc 4 miles SE of Barnsley

Wortley (1894)
*Hermit Hill Lane, Wortley, Sheffield
S35 7DP*
Tel (0114) 288 8469
Fax (0114) 288 8649
Mem 400
Sec WHM Hoyland
Pro I Kirk (0114) 288 6490
Holes 18 L 6033 yds SSS 69
Recs Am–65
Pro–64
V'tors WD–U WE–NA before 10am
SOC
Fees £25 (£30)
Loc 2 miles W of M1 Junction 36,
off A629

Yorkshire (West)

Alwoodley (1908)
*Wigton Lane, Alwoodley, Leeds
LS17 8SA*
Tel (0113) 268 1680
Fax (0113) 293 9458
Mem 450
Sec RCW Banks
Pro JR Green (0113) 268 9603
Holes 18 L 6686 yds SSS 73
Recs Am–67 SJM Peel
Pro–68 D Fitton
V'tors SOC–WD

Fees £50 (£60)
Loc 5 miles N of Leeds on A61
Arch Dr A Mackenzie

Baildon (1896)
Moorgate, Baildon, Shipley BD17 5PP
Tel (01274) 584266
Mem 500
Sec B Sugden (01274) 593023
Pro R Masters (01274) 595162
Holes 18 L 6225 yds SSS 70
Recs Am–63 I Martin
Pro–64 G Brand, D Durnian
V'tors WD–U before 5pm (restricted
Tues) WE/BH–restricted
Fees £16 (£20)
Loc 5 miles N of Bradford,
off A6038
Arch Tom Morris/James Braid

Ben Rhydding (1947)
*High Wood, Ben Rhydding, Ilkley
LS9 8SB*
Tel (01943) 608759
Mem 195 60(L) 36(J)
Sec A Leverton
Holes 9 L 4711 yds SSS 64
Recs Am–64 H Barker (1987)
Pro–64 GJ Brand (1984)
V'tors WD–U exc Wed pm & Thurs
am WE–M
Fees £10 (£15)
Loc 2 miles SE of Ilkley

Bingley St Ives (1931)
St Ives Estate, Bingley BD16 1AT
Tel (01274) 562436
Fax (01274) 511788
Sec Mrs M Welch
Pro R Firth (01274) 562506
Holes 18 L 6480 yds SSS 71
Recs Am–64 R Jones
Pro–62 N Faldo
Ladies–70 H Butterfield
V'tors WD–U before 4pm
Fees £24 D–£27
Loc 6 miles NW of Bradford,
off A650

Bracken Ghyll (1993)
*Skipton Road, Addingham, Ilkley
LS29 0SL*
Tel (01943) 830691 (Clubhouse)
Mem 400
Sec Chloe Walker (01943) 831207
Pro None
Holes 9 L 6560 yds Par 74 SSS 71
Recs Am–63 A Emptage (1995)
V'tors WD/BH–U WE–NA before
noon on comp days SOC
Fees £10 (£14)
Loc 3 miles W of Ilkley on old A65
to Addingham
Mis Indoor practice area
Arch OCM Associates

Bradford (1891)
*Hawksworth Lane, Guiseley, Leeds
LS20 8NP*
Tel (01943) 875570
Fax (01943) 875570
Mem 550

Sec T Eagle
Pro S Weldon (01943) 873719
Holes 18 L 6259 yds SSS 71
Recs Am–66 WJ Dowswell
V'tors WD–U WE–NA before noon
SOC–WD
Fees On application
Loc 8 miles N of Bradford, off
A6038. 10 miles N of Leeds
on A650

Bradford Moor (1907)
*Scarr Hall, Pollard Lane, Bradford
BD2 4RW*
Tel (01274) 771716
Mem 350
Sec CP Bedford
Pro R Hughes (01274) 771718
Holes 9 L 5854 yds SSS 68
Recs Am–65 N Bell (1997)
Pro–69 H Waller
V'tors WD–U
Fees £8–£12
Loc 2 miles N of Bradford

Bradley Park (1978)
Public
Bradley Road, Huddersfield HD2 1PZ
Tel (01484) 223772
Fax (01484) 451613
Mem 300
Sec K Blackwell
Pro PE Reilly
Holes 18 L 6202 yds SSS 70
9 hole Par 3 course
Recs Am–69 R Hall
Pro–64 P Carman
V'tors U SOC
Fees £9.50 (£11.50)
Loc 2 miles N of Huddersfield, off
A6107, M62 Junction 25
Mis Floodlit driving range

Branshaw (1912)
*Branshaw Moor, Oakworth, Keighley
BD22 7ES*
Tel (01535) 643235
Mem 525
Sec T O'Hara
Pro M Tyler (01535) 647441
Holes 18 L 5858 yds SSS 69
Recs Am–65 D Eeles (1990)
Pro–64 G Moore (1997)
V'tors WD–U SOC–WD
Fees £15 (£20)
Loc 2 miles SW of Keighley on
B6143
Arch James Braid/Dr A Mackenzie

Calverley (1984)
Woodhall Lane, Pudsey LS28 5JX
Tel (0113) 256 9244
Fax (0113) 256 9244
Mem 700
Sec WW Gardner
Pro D Johnson
Holes 18 L 5527 yds SSS 67
9 hole course
Recs Am–67 N Wendal-Jones
V'tors WD–U WE–pm only
Fees £12 (£17)
Loc 4 miles NE of Bradford

For list of abbreviations see page 479

Castle Fields (1900)

Rastrick Common, Brighouse

Mem	140
Sec	J Briggs (01484) 716217
Holes	6 L 2406 yds SSS 50
Recs	Am–54
V'tors	M
Loc	1 mile S of Brighouse

City of Wakefield (1936)

Public

Lupset Park, Horbury Road, Wakefield WF2 8QS

Tel	**(01924) 367442**
Sec	Mrs P Ambler
Pro	R Holland (01924) 360282
Holes	18 L 6319 yds SSS 70
Recs	Am–67 SJ Topp (1995)
	Pro–67 L Turner (1995)
	Ladies–71 J Oxley
V'tors	U SOC–WD
Fees	On application
Loc	A642, 2 miles W of Wakefield. 2 miles E of M1 Junction 39/40
Arch	JSF Morrison

Clayton (1906)

Thornton View Road, Clayton, Bradford BD14 6JX

Tel	**(01274) 880047**
Mem	210 35(L) 35(J)
Sec	DA Smith (01274) 572311
Holes	9 L 5515 yds SSS 67
Recs	Am–65 ND Hawkins
V'tors	WD–U Sat–U Sun–after 4pm
Fees	£10 D–£12 (£12)
Loc	3 miles W of Bradford, off A647

Cleckheaton & District (1900)

483 Bradford Road, Cleckheaton BD19 6BU

Tel	**(01274) 874118 (Clubhouse)**
Fax	(01274) 871382
Mem	572
Sec	Mrs R Newsholme (Asst Sec) (01274) 851266
Pro	M Ingham (01274) 851267
Holes	18 L 5860 yds SSS 69
Recs	Am–62 CA Bloice (1985)
	Pro–E Wilson (1989)
V'tors	U SOC
Fees	£23 (£30)
Loc	Nr M62 Junction 26–A638

Crosland Heath (1914)

Felks Stile Road, Crosland Heath, Huddersfield HD4 7AF

Tel	**(01484) 653216**
Mem	320
Sec	D Walker (01484) 653262
Pro	C Gaunt (01484) 653877
Holes	18 L 6004 yds SSS 70
Recs	Am–64 P Fenton (1997)
	Pro–65 S Dellar
V'tors	U SOC
Fees	On application
Loc	3 miles W of Huddersfield, off A62

Crow Nest Park (1994)

Pay and play

Coach Road, Hove Edge, Brighouse HD6 2LN

Tel	**(01484) 401121**
Fax	(01422) 201216
Mem	200
Sec	P Knowles (01422) 201216
Pro	B Parry (01484) 401121
Holes	9 L 6020 yds Par 70 SSS 69
V'tors	WD–U WE–U before noon
Fees	£13 (£16)
Loc	5 miles E of Halifax. M62 Junction 25
Mis	Driving range
Arch	Will Adamson

Dewsbury District (1891)

The Pinnacle, Sands Lane, Mirfield WF14 8HJ

Tel	**(01924) 492399**
Mem	650
Sec	CB Rhodes
Pro	N Hirst (01924) 496030
Holes	18 L 6360 yds SSS 71
Recs	Am–68 P Robinson (1996)
	Pro–67 P Cowen (1996)
V'tors	WD–U WE–M –U after 4pm SOC
Fees	£18 (£18)
Loc	2 miles W of Dewsbury, off A644

East Bierley (1928)

South View Road, Bierley, Bradford

Tel	**(01274) 681023**
Mem	156 47(L) 30(J)
Sec	RJ Welch (01274) 683666
Holes	9 L 4692 yds SSS 63
Recs	Am–59 R Watts
	Pro–62 B Hill
V'tors	U exc Mon–NA after 4pm Sun–NA
Fees	£10 (£12.50)
Loc	4 miles SE of Bradford

Elland (1910)

Hammerstones Leach Lane, Hullen Edge, Elland HX5 0TA

Tel	**(01422) 372505**
Mem	265
Sec	AD Blackburn (01422) 372014
Pro	N Krzywicki (01422) 374886
Holes	9 L 2763 yds SSS 66
Recs	Am–64 C Hartland
V'tors	U
Fees	£14 (£25)
Loc	Elland 1 mile. M62 Junction 24, signpost Blackley

Fardew (1993)

Pay and play

Nursery Farm, Carr Lane, East Morton, Keighley BD20 5RY

Tel	**(01274) 561229**
Fax	(01274) 561438
Mem	100
Sec	GA Richardson
Pro	L Turner
Holes	9 L 3104 yds Par 72 SSS 70

(Crow Nest Park continued)

Recs	Am–70 R Foster (1993)
	Pro–66 L Turner (1994)
V'tors	U SOC
Fees	9 holes–£7 (£8); 18 holes–£12 (£14)
Loc	10 miles E of Skipton on old A650. M606, 10 miles
Arch	Will Adamson

Ferrybridge "C" (1976)

PO Box 39, Stranglands Lane, Knottingley WF11 8SQ

Tel	**(01977) 674188**
Mem	305
Sec	TD Ellis
Holes	9 L 5211 yds SSS 66
Recs	Am–66 L Agar (1995)
V'tors	M
Fees	D–£6 (D–£7)
Loc	½ mile off A1, on B6136
Arch	NE Pugh

Fulneck (1892)

Fulneck, Pudsey LS28 8NT

Tel	**(0113) 256 5191**
Mem	290
Sec	J Brogden (0113) 257 4049
Holes	9 L 5456 yds SSS 67
Recs	Am–64 I Holdsworth
V'tors	WD–U WE/BH–M SOC
Fees	£14
Loc	5 miles W of Leeds

Garforth (1913)

Long Lane, Garforth, Leeds LS25 2DS

Tel	**(0113) 286 2021**
Fax	(0113) 286 3308
Mem	550
Sec	NC Brown (0113) 286 3308
Pro	K Findlater (0113) 286 2063
Holes	18 L 6327 yds SSS 70
Recs	Am–63 AR Gelsthorpe
V'tors	WD–U H WE/BH–M SOC
Fees	£26 D–£30
Loc	9 miles E of Leeds, between Garforth and Barwick-in-Elmet

Gotts Park (1933)

Public

Armley Ridge Road, Armley, Leeds LS12 2QX

Tel	**(0113) 234 2019**
Mem	300
Sec	M Gill (0113) 256 2994
Pro	JK Simpson
Holes	18 L 4960 yds SSS 64
V'tors	U
Fees	On application
Loc	2 miles W of Leeds

Halifax (1895)

Union Lane, Ogden, Halifax HX2 8XR

Tel	**(01422) 244171**
Fax	(01422) 241459
Mem	450
Sec	G Horrocks-Taylor
Pro	M Allison (01422) 240047
Holes	18 L 6038 yds SSS 70
Recs	Am–64 A Wainwright
	Pro–65 W Good

V'tors U WD–parties welcome SOC
Fees On application
Loc 4 miles N of Halifax on A629
Arch Alex Herd/James Braid

Halifax Bradley Hall
(1907)
Holywell Green, Halifax HX4 9AN
Tel **(01422) 374108**
Mem 608
Sec JR Burton (01484) 715797
Pro P Wood (01422) 370231
Holes 18 L 6213 yds SSS 70
Recs Am–65 AR Whitworth
V'tors U SOC
Fees £18 (£28)
Loc S of Halifax on A6112

Halifax West End (1913)
Paddock Lane, Highroad Well, Halifax HX2 0NT
Tel **(01422) 353608**
Fax (01442) 341878
Mem 340 110(L) 60(J)
Sec BR Thomas (01422) 341878
Pro D Rishworth (01422) 363293
Holes 18 L 5951 yds SSS 69
Recs Am–64 SC Ingham
Pro–64 AJ Bickerdike
V'tors U SOC
Fees £20 (£25)
Loc 2 miles NW of Halifax

Hanging Heaton (1922)
Whitecross Road, Bennett Lane, Dewsbury WF12 7DT
Tel **(01924) 461606**
Fax (01924) 430100
Mem 550
Sec SM Simpson (01924) 461729
Pro (01924) 467077
Holes 9 L 2868 yds SSS 67
Recs Am–65 J Maguire (1997)
Pro–65 M Pearson (1988)
V'tors WD–U WE–M
Fees £12
Loc Dewsbury ¾ mile (A653)

Headingley (1892)
Back Church Lane, Adel, Leeds LS16 8DW
Tel **(0113) 267 3052 (Clubhouse)**
Fax (0113) 281 7334
Mem 675
Sec JR Burns JP (Mgr)
(0113) 267 9573
Pro SA Foster (0113) 267 5100
Holes 18 L 6298 yds SSS 70
Recs Am–66 SD Mason (1995)
Pro–64 S Field (1990)
V'tors U SOC
Fees £30 D–£35 (£40)
Loc 5 miles NW of Leeds, off A660

Headley (1907)
Headley Lane, Thornton, Bradford BD13 3LX
Tel **(01274) 833481**
Fax (01274) 670398
Mem 270 35(L) 35(J)

Sec K Allan (01274) 670398
Holes 9 L 4914 yds SSS 64
Recs Am–61 A Cording (1985)
Pro–66 M Ingham (1982)
V'tors WD–U WE–M SOC
Fees On application
Loc 5 miles W of Bradford
(B6145)

Hebden Bridge (1930)
Wadsworth, Hebden Bridge HX7 8PH
Tel **(01422) 842896**
Mem 300
Sec Miss S Greenwood
(01422) 842732
Holes 9 L 5064 yds SSS 65
Recs Am–63 IS Marsland (1978),
PJ Richardson (1989),
IR Powell (1994)
Pro–63 M Ingham (1974)
V'tors WD–U
Fees £12 (£15)
Loc 1 mile N of Hebden Bridge

Horsforth (1907)
Layton Rise, Layton Road, Horsforth, Leeds LS18 5EX
Tel **(0113) 258 6819**
Mem 365 90(L) 85(J)
Sec E Northard
Pro N Bell (0113) 258 5200
Holes 18 L 6293 yds SSS 70
Recs Am–66 SG Hurd
Pro–67 HW Muscroft
V'tors U SOC
Fees D–£24 (£30)
Loc 6 miles NW of Leeds

Howley Hall (1900)
Scotchman Lane, Morley, Leeds LS27 0NX
Tel **(01924) 472432**
Fax (01924) 478417
Mem 465
Sec K Spencer (01924) 478417
Pro SA Spinks (01924) 473852
Holes 18 L 6058 yds Par 71 SSS 69
Recs Am–66 JD Roberts (1994)
V'tors U
Fees £21 D–£25 (D–£30)
Loc 4 miles SW of Leeds on
B6123

Huddersfield (1891)
Fixby Hall, Lightridge Road, Huddersfield HD2 2EP
Tel **(01484) 420110**
Fax (01484) 424623
Mem 576
Sec JM Seatter (Gen Mgr),
Mrs D Lockett (01484)
426203
Pro P Carman (01484) 426463
Holes 18 L 6432 yds SSS 71
Recs Am–64 S Hurd (1994)
Pro–64 D Padgett (1991)
V'tors U SOC–WD
Fees £33 D–£45 (£45 D–£60)
Loc 2 miles N of Huddersfield, off
A6107. M62 Junction 24

Ilkley (1890)
Myddelton, Ilkley LS29 0BE
Tel **(01943) 607277**
Fax (01943) 816130
Mem 530
Sec AK Hatfield (01943) 600214
Pro JL Hammond (01943)
607463
Holes 18 L 6260 yds SSS 70
Recs Am–65 AC Flather (1984)
Pro–66 CS Montgomerie
(1990)
V'tors U
Fees £35 (£40)
Loc NW of Ilkley, off A65

Keighley (1904)
Howden Park, Utley, Keighley BD20 6DH
Tel **(01535) 603179**
Fax (01535) 604778
Mem 600
Sec CL Hodge (01535) 604778
Pro M Bradley (01535) 665370
Holes 18 L 6141 yds SSS 70
Recs Am–64 AW Utley (1995)
Pro–65 J Holchaks
V'tors WD–U ex Tues Sat–NA
Sun/BH–NA before 2pm
Fees £22 D–£26 (£24 D–£28)
Loc 1 mile W of Keighley on A629

Leeds (1896)
Elmete Road, Roundhay, Leeds LS8 2LJ
Tel **(0113) 265 8775**
Fax (0113) 232 3369
Mem 545
Sec SJ Clarkson (0113) 265 9203
Pro S Longster (0113) 265 8786
Holes 18 L 6092 yds SSS 69
Recs Am–63 M Lawson
Pro–63 P Hall
V'tors WD–U WE–M
Fees £25 D–£32
Loc 4 miles NE of Leeds, off A58

Leeds Golf Centre (1994)
Pay and play
Wike Ridge Lane, Shadwell, Leeds LS17 9JW
Tel **(0113) 288 6000**
Fax (0113) 288 6185
Mem 500
Sec D Dourambers
Pro N Harvey
Holes 18 L 6800 yds SSS 72
12 hole Par 3 course
V'tors U SOC
Fees £12.50 (£12.50)
Loc NE of Leeds, between A58
and A61
Mis Driving range. Golf Academy
Arch Donald Steel

Lightcliffe (1907)
Knowle Top Road, Lightcliffe HX3 8SW
Tel **(01422) 202459**
Mem 170 95(L) 84(J)
Sec JA Vachell (01422) 358490

Pro R Kershaw
Holes 9 L 5368 metres SSS 68
Recs Am–66 JR Denham,
CRC Denham
V'tors U H–exc comp days Sun
am–M SOC
Fees £15 (£20)
Loc 3 miles E of Halifax (A58)

Lofthouse Hill

*Leeds Road, Lofthouse Hill, Wakefield
WF3 3LR*
Tel (01924) 823703
Fax (01924) 823703
Sec N Todd
Pro B Janes (01924) 820048
Holes 9 L 3167 yds Par 35
V'tors M SOC
Fees 18 holes–£17.50;
9 holes–£10
Loc Between Leeds and Wakefield
Mis Driving range

Longley Park (1911)

Maple Street, Huddersfield HD5 9AX
Tel (01484) 426932
Mem 400
Sec D Palliser
Pro J Ambler (01484) 422304
Holes 9 L 5269 yds Par 66 SSS 66
Recs Am–61 SA Martin (1997)
Pro–65 PW Booth
V'tors WD–U exc Thurs
WE–restricted
Fees £13.50 (£16)
Loc Huddersfield ½ mile

Low Laithes (1925)

*Park Mill Lane, Flushdyke, Ossett
WF5 9AP*
Tel (01924) 273275
Fax (01924) 266067
Mem 575
Sec KN Pinder (01924) 266067
Pro P Browning (01924) 274667
Holes 18 L 6468 yds SSS 71
Recs Am–67
Pro–68
V'tors U WE–no parties SOC–WD
Fees £19 D–£23 (£32)
Loc 2 miles W of Wakefield.
M1 Junction 40
Arch Dr A Mackenzie

The Manor

*Bradford Road, Drighlington, Bradford
BD11 1AB*
Tel (0113) 285 2644
Mem 300
Sec J Crompton (Sec/Mgr)
Pro J Crompton
Holes 18 L 6508 yds Par 72 SSS 71
Recs Am–73 J Gill (1997)
Pro–67 J Crompton (1995)
V'tors U SOC–exc Sat
Fees £15 (£15)
Loc 1 mile from M62 Junction 27,
off A650
Mis Floodlit driving range.
6 holes pitch & putt
Arch David Hemstock

Marsden (1921)

*Hemplow, Marsden, Huddersfield
HD7 6NN*
Tel (01484) 844253
Mem 200 49(L) 22(J)
Sec D Horncastle
Holes 9 L 5702 yds SSS 68
Recs Am–63 AJ Bickerdike
Pro–A Bickerdike
V'tors WD–U Sat–NA before 4pm
Sun–M SOC
Fees £10
Loc 8 miles W of Huddersfield,
off A62
Arch Dr A Mackenzie

Meltham (1908)

*Thick Hollins Hall, Meltham,
Huddersfield HD7 3DQ*
Tel (01484) 850227
Mem 450
Sec J Holdsworth (Hon)
Pro PF Davies (01484) 851521
Holes 18 L 6305 yds SSS 70
Recs Am–65 A Sheard
Pro–69 W Casper
V'tors H
Fees £20 (£25)
Loc 5 miles SW of Huddersfield
(B6107)

Mid Yorkshire (1993)

*Havercroft Lane, Darrington, Pontefract
WF8 3BP*
Tel (01977) 704522
Fax (01977) 600823
Mem 600
Sec IM Collins (Mgr)
Pro W Heywood (01977) 600844
Holes 18 L 6340 yds SSS 71
V'tors U H SOC
Fees £15 (£25)
Loc Nr A1/M62 junction
Mis Floodlit driving range
Arch Steve Marnoch

Middleton Park (1933)

Public
*Ring Road, Beeston Park, Middleton
LS10 3TN*
Tel (0113) 270 9506
Mem 310
Sec TC Foster (0113) 252 2215
Pro S Shaw
Holes 18 L 5233 yds SSS 66
Recs Am–63 S Nicholson
V'tors U
Fees On application
Loc 3 miles S of Leeds

Moor Allerton (1923)

Coal Road, Wike, Leeds LS17 9NH
Tel (0113) 266 1154
Fax (0113) 237 1124
Mem 1200
Sec J Denton (Hon)
Pro R Lane (0113) 266 5209
Holes 27 holes:
6470-6843 yds SSS 73-74
Recs Am–65 K Wallbank (1994)
Pro–65 B Waites
V'tors WD/Sat–U Sun–NA SOC

Moortown (1909)

Harrogate Road, Leeds LS17 7DB
Tel (0113) 268 6521
Fax (0113) 268 0986
Mem 580
Sec CA Moore
Pro B Hutchinson (0113) 268 3636
Holes 18 L 6826 yds SSS 74
Recs Am–69 C Turner, R Treweek
Pro–66 D McPherson
V'tors H
Fees £42 D–£50 (£47 D–£55)
Loc 5½ miles N of Leeds on A61
Arch Dr A Mackenzie

Normanton (1903)

*Snydale Road, Normanton, Wakefield
WF6 1PA*
Tel (01924) 892943
Mem 300
Sec J McElhinney
Pro M Evans (01924) 220134
Holes 9 L 5323 yds SSS 66
Recs Am–65 R Booth (1992)
Pro–65 A Wright (1991)
Ladies–69 D Evans (1992)
V'tors U exc Sun–NA
Fees On application
Loc 1 mile from M62 Junction 31.
A655 towards Wakefield

Northcliffe (1921)

*High Bank Lane, Shipley, Bradford
BD18 4LJ*
Tel (01274) 584085
Fax (01274) 596731
Mem 750
Sec HR Archer (01274) 596731
Pro M Hillas (01274) 587193
Holes 18 L 6104 yds SSS 69
Recs Am–64 J Firth (1996)
Pro–67 M James
V'tors U SOC
Fees £20 (£25)
Loc 3 miles NW of Bradford, off
A650 Keighley road
Arch James Braid

Otley (1906)

West Busk Lane, Otley LS21 3NG
Tel (01943) 461015
Fax (01943) 850387
Mem 700
Sec Mrs P Bates (01943) 465329
Pro (01943) 463403
Holes 18 L 6225 yds SSS 70
Recs Am–65 M Wood (1966)
Pro–62 GJ Brand (1988)
V'tors U exc Sat–NA SOC
Fees £24 (£30)
Loc 1 mile W of Otley, off A6038

Oulton Park (1990)

Public
Oulton, Rothwell, Leeds LS26 8EX
Tel (0113) 282 3152
Fax (0113) 282 6290

Mem 390
Sec A Booth (Mgr)
Pro S Gromett
Holes 18 L 6479 yds SSS 71
9 L 3287 yds SSS 35
Recs Am–69 A Cole (1995)
Pro–65 P Wesselingh (1995)
V'tors U SOC
Fees 18 hole–£10–20
Loc 5 miles SE of Leeds, off A642.
N of M62 Junction 30
Mis Driving range
Arch Alliss/Thomas

Outlane (1906)

*Slack Lane, Outlane, Huddersfield
HD3 3YL*
Tel (01422) 374762
Mem 500
Sec A Armstrong
Pro D Chapman
Holes 18 L 6010 yds SSS 70
Recs Am–67 NJ Nuttall
Pro–67 D Chapman
V'tors U SOC
Fees £18 (£27)
Loc 4 miles W of Huddersfield, off
A640. M62 Junction 23

Painthorpe House (1961)

*Painthorpe Lane, Crigglestone,
Wakefield WF4 3HE*
Tel (01924) 255083
Fax (01924) 252022
Mem 180
Sec H Kershaw (01924) 274527
Holes 9 L 4520 yds SSS 62
Recs Am–64 J Turner,
J Whitehouse (1986)
V'tors U exc Sun–NA
Fees £6 Sat–£10
Loc 1 mile SE of M1 Junction 39

Phoenix Park (1922)

Phoenix Park, Thornbury, Bradford 3
Tel (01274) 667573
Mem 180
Sec C Lally (01274) 668218
Pro None
Holes 9 L 4982 yds SSS 64
Recs Am–61 S Carey
V'tors WD/BH–U WE–NA
Fees On application
Loc Thornbury Roundabout
(A647)

Pontefract & District (1900)

Park Lane, Pontefract WF8 4QS
Tel (01977) 792241
Fax (01977) 792241
Mem 841
Sec WT Smith (Mgr)
(01977) 792241
Pro NJ Newman (01977) 706806
Holes 18 L 6227 yds SSS 70
Recs Am–63 DC Rooke
Pro–67 GW Townhill
V'tors I SOC–WD exc Wed
Fees £25 (£32)
Loc Pontefract 1 mile on B6134.
M62 Junction 32

Pontefract Park (1973)

Public
Park Road, Pontefract
Tel (01977) 702799
Holes 18 L 4068 yds SSS 62
V'tors U
Fees On application
Loc Between Pontefract and M62
roundabout, nr racecourse

Queensbury (1923)

*Brighouse Road, Queensbury, Bradford
BD13 1QF*
Tel (01274) 882155
Mem 230 55(L) 40(J)
Sec H Andrew
Pro G Howard (01274) 816864
Holes 9 L 5102 yds SSS 65
Recs Am–64 S Rogers,
H Wilkerson
Pro–63 P Cowan
V'tors U
Fees £10 (£20)
Loc 4 miles SW of Bradford
(A647)

Rawdon (1896)

*Buckstone Drive, Micklefield Lane,
Rawdon LS19 6BD*
Tel (0113) 250 6040
Mem 220 55(L) 50(J)
Sec RA Adams
(0113) 250 6064
Pro (0113) 250 5017
Holes 9 L 5982 yds SSS 69
Recs Am–64 A Coverdale
V'tors WD–H WE/BH–M SOC
Fees £16
Loc 6 miles NW of Leeds nr
A65/A658 junction

Riddlesden (1927)

Howden Rough, Riddlesden, Keighley
Tel (01535) 602148
Mem 400
Sec Mrs KM Brooksbank
(01535) 607646
Holes 18 L 4295 yds Par 63 SSS 61
Recs Am–60 M Mitchell (1987)
Pro–59 P Cowan (1983)
V'tors U exc Sun–NA before 2pm
Fees £10 (£15)
Loc 1 mile from Riddlesden, off
Scott Lane West. 3 miles N of
Keighley, off A650

Roundhay (1923)

Public
Park Lane, Leeds LS8 2EJ
Tel (0113) 266 2695
Mem 400
Sec RH McLachlan
Pro JA Pape (0113) 266 1686
Holes 9 L 5322 yds SSS 65
Recs Am–61 R Taylor
Pro–62 M Bembridge
V'tors U
Fees On application
Loc N of Leeds, off Moortown
Ring Road

Ryburn (1910)

Norland, Sowerby Bridge, Halifax
Tel (01422) 831355
Mem 200
Sec J Hoyle (01422) 843070
Holes 9 L 4907 yds SSS 64
Recs Am–64 DS Lumb (1987)
Pro–61 M Pearson (1987)
V'tors U
Fees £15 (£20)
Loc 3 miles S of Halifax

Sand Moor (1926)

Alwoodley Lane, Leeds LS17 7DJ
Tel (0113) 268 1685
Fax (0113) 268 5180
Mem 540
Sec BF Precious (0113) 268 5180
Pro P Tupling (0113) 268 3925
Holes 18 L 6429 yds SSS 71
Recs Am–63 SR Cage (1993)
Pro–62 S Holden (1991)
V'tors WD–H by arrangement
WE–NA
Fees £30 (£38)
Loc 5 miles N of Leeds, off A61

Scarcroft (1937)

Syke Lane, Leeds LS14 3BQ
Tel (0113) 289 2263
Mem 580
Sec TB Davey MBE
(0113) 289 2311
Pro D Tear (0113) 289 2780
Holes 18 L 6426 yds SSS 71
Recs Am–64 J Roberts (1995)
Pro–65 D Padgett (1990)
V'tors WD–U WE/BH–M or by
arrangement SOC–WD exc
Mon
Fees £26 (£40)
Loc 7 miles N of Leeds, off A58

Shipley (1896)

*Beckfoot Lane, Cottingley Bridge,
Bingley BD16 1LX*
Tel (01274) 563212
Mem 600
Sec GM Shaw (01274) 568652
Pro JR Parry (01274) 563674
Holes 18 L 6218 yds SSS 70
Recs Am–66 GM Shaw (1975),
IC Bottomley (1991),
I Pyman (1993), JP Miller,
D Mansell, D Wright (1996)
Pro–64 M Ingham (1987)
V'tors WD–U exc Tues–NA before
2pm Sat–NA before 4pm
Fees £27 (£36)
Loc 6 miles N of Bradford on
A650
Arch Colt/Alison/Mackenzie/Braid

Silsden (1913)

*Brunthwaite, Silsden, Keighley
BD20 0HN*
Tel (01535) 652998
Mem 300
Sec G Davey
Holes 14 L 4870 yds SSS 64
Recs Am–61
V'tors Sat–restricted Sun–U after 1pm

Fees On application
Loc 5 miles N of Keighley,
off A6034

South Bradford (1906)

Pearson Road, Odsal, Bradford
BD6 1BH

Tel (01274) 679195
Mem 200
Pro I Marshall (01274) 673346
Holes 9 L 6004 yds SSS 69
Recs Am–65 GM Yarnold
Pro–67 S Miguel, A Caygill
V'tors WD–U WE–M
Fees On application
Loc Bradford 2 miles, nr Odsal
Stadium

South Leeds (1914)

Gipsy Lane, Ring Road, Beeston,
Leeds LS11 5TU

Tel (0113) 270 0479
Mem 500
Sec J Neal (0113) 277 1676
Pro M Lewis (0113) 270 2598
Holes 18 L 5865 yds SSS 68
Recs Am–65 R Lister
Pro–68 J Pitts
V'tors WD–U WE–M SOC
Fees £18 (£25)
Loc 4 miles S of Leeds. 2 miles
from M62 and M1

Temple Newsam (1923)

Public
Temple Newsam Road, Halton, Leeds
LS15 0LN

Tel (0113) 264 5624
Mem 500
Sec G Gower
Pro J Pape (0113) 264 7362
Holes Lord Irwin 18 L 6448 yds
SSS 71; Lady Dorothy Wood
18 L 6029 yds SSS 70
V'tors U SOC
Fees Summer–£8 (£9.50)
Winter–£7 (£8.50)
Loc 5 miles E of Leeds, off A63

Todmorden (1894)

Rive Rocks, Cross Stone, Todmorden,
Lancs 0L14 8RD

Tel (01706) 812986
Mem 180 40(L) 30(J)
Sec PH Eastwood
Holes 9 L 5878 yds SSS 68
Recs Am–67 G Morgan, J May
Pro–68 B Hunt, 69 M Welch
V'tors WD/BH–U WE–M SOC–WD
Fees £15 (£20)
Loc 1 mile N of Todmorden,
off A646

Wakefield (1891)

28 Woodthorpe Lane, Sandal,
Wakefield WF2 6JH

Tel (01924) 255104
Mem 500
Sec JW Wood (01924) 258778
Pro IM Wright (01924) 255380
Holes 18 L 6613 yds SSS 72

Recs Am–66 S Cage (1992)
Pro–68 HW Muscroft (1982)
V'tors U SOC–Wed–Fri
Fees £22 (£30)
Loc 3 miles S of Wakefield on
A61. M1 Junction 39

Waterton Park (1995)

The Balk, Walton, Wakefield WF2 6QL

Tel (01924) 259525
Fax (01924) 256969
Mem 650
Sec M Dredge
Pro P Hall (01924) 255557
Holes 18 L 6843 yds Par 72 SSS 73
Recs Am–75 D Pitts
V'tors M
Loc 4 miles SE of Wakefield centre
Arch Simon Gidman

West Bowling (1898)

Newall Hall, Rooley Lane, Bradford
BD5 8LB

Tel (01274) 724449
Fax (01274) 393207
Mem 500
Sec MEL Lynn (01274) 393207
Pro IA Marshall (01274) 728036
Holes 18 L 5769 yds SSS 68
Recs Am–65 D Chalmers (1995)
V'tors WD–U H SOC
Fees £26 (£30)
Loc Junction of M606 and
Bradford Ring Road East

West Bradford (1900)

Chellow Grange, Haworth Road,
Bradford BD9 6NP

Tel (01274) 542767
Mem 450
Sec GA Nixon (Hon)
Pro NM Barber (01274) 542102
Holes 18 L 5723 yds SSS 68
Recs Am–63 RJ Ellis (1984)
Pro–66
V'tors U
Fees £18 (£18)
Loc 3 miles W of Bradford (B6269)

Wetherby (1910)

Linton Lane, Linton, Wetherby
LS22 4JF

Tel (01937) 580089
Fax (01937) 581915
Mem 630
Sec JR Nicholson
Pro D Padgett (01937) 583375
Holes 18 L 6235 yds SSS 70
Recs Am–63 S Dyson (1996)
Pro–63 JR Green (1997)
V'tors WE–U after 10am SOC–Mon
& Tues
Fees £25 (£36)
Loc ¾ mile W of Wetherby. A1
Wetherby roundabout

Whitwood (1987)

Public
Altofts Lane, Whitwood, Castleford
WF10 5PZ

Tel (01977) 512835
Sec S Hicks (Hon)

Pro R Holland
Holes 9 L 6176 yds SSS 69
V'tors WD–U WE–booking
necessary
Fees On application
Loc 2 miles SW of Castleford
(A655). M62 Junction 31

Willow Valley (1994)

Pay and play
Clifton, Brighouse HD6 4JB

Tel (01274) 878624
Fax (01274) 852805
Mem 200
Sec A Cobbett
Pro J Haworth
Holes 18 & 9 hole courses
V'tors U
Fees 18 hole–£20; 9 hole–£6–10
Loc SW of Leeds, M62 Junction 25
Mis Driving range
Arch Jonathan Gaunt

Woodhall Hills (1905)

Woodhall Road, Calverley, Pudsey
LS28 5UN

Tel (0113) 256 4771 (Clubhouse)
Mem 450
Sec ID Mackland (0113) 255
4594
Pro W Lockett (0113) 256 2857
Holes 18 L 6001 yds SSS 69
Recs Am–63 AJ Dufton
V'tors WD–U Sat–U after 4.30pm
Sun–U after 10.30am
Fees D–£20.50 (D–£25.50)
Loc 4 miles E of Bradford, off
A647, by Calverley Golf Club

Woodsome Hall (1922)

Woodsome Hall, Fenay Bridge,
Huddersfield HD8 0LQ

Tel (01484) 602971
Fax (01484) 608260
Mem 394 194(L) 103(J)
Sec AS Guest
Pro M Higginbottom
(01484) 602034
Holes 18 L 6080 yds SSS 69
Recs Am–65 M Broadbent
Pro–65 D Jagger
V'tors U H exc Tues–NA before
4pm SOC
Fees £27.50 (£35)
Loc 6 miles SE of Huddersfield on
A629 Penistone road

Woolley Park (1995)

Woolley, Wakefield WF4 2JS

Tel (01226) 380144 (Bookings)
Fax (01226) 390295
Mem 500
Sec D Rowbottom (Prop)
(01226) 382209
Pro JK Ripley
Holes 18 L 6471 yds Par 70 SSS 71
V'tors WD–U WE–restricted SOC
Fees £10 (£15)
Loc 5 miles S of Wakefield on
A61. M1 Junction 38, 2 miles
Arch M Shattock

Ireland

Co Antrim

Ballycastle (1890)
Cushendall Road, Ballycastle BT64 6QP
Tel (012657) 62536
Fax (012657) 69909
Mem 920
Sec HA Fraser (Hon)
Pro I McLaughlin (012657) 62506
Holes 18 L 5812 yds SSS 69
Recs Am–66 F Fleming (1962),
    J McAleese, RJ McCoy,
    E Hughes
    Pro–64 F Daly
V'tors U H SOC
Fees £18 (£25) (1997)
Loc Between Portrush and
    Cushendall (A2)

Ballyclare (1923)
*25 Springvale Road, Ballyclare
BT39 9JW*
Tel (01960) 342352 (Clubhouse)
Fax (01960) 322696
Mem 440
Sec H McConnell (01960) 322696
Holes 18 L 5840 yds SSS 71
Recs Am–69 J Foster
    Pro–69 S Hamill
V'tors WD–U WE–NA before 4pm
Fees £16 (£22)
Loc 1½ miles N of Ballyclare.
    14 miles N of Belfast

Ballymena (1902)
*128 Raceview Road, Ballymena
BT42 4HY*
Tel (01266) 861207/861487
Mem 824
Sec C McAuley (Hon)
Pro J Gallagher (01266) 861652
Holes 18 L 5245 metres SSS 67
Recs Am–62 D Cunning
V'tors WD/Sun–U SOC
Fees On application
Loc 2 miles E of Ballymena on A42

Bentra
Public
*Slaughterford Road, Whitehead
BT38 9TG*
Tel (01960) 378996
Sec N Houston (01960) 351711
Holes 9 L 3155 yds Par 37 SSS 35
V'tors U
Fees £6.75 (£10.50)
Loc 4 miles N of Carrickfergus on
    A2 Larne road

Bushfoot (1890)
*50 Bushfoot Road, Portballintrae
BT57 8RR*
Tel (012657) 31317
Mem 860
Sec J Knox Thompson (Sec/Mgr)
Holes 9 L 5876 yds SSS 67

Recs Am–63 A McIlroy (1990)
V'tors U Sat–NA after noon SOC
Fees £13 (£16)
Loc 1 mile N of Bushmills. 4 miles
    E of Portrush

Cairndhu (1928)
*192 Coast Road, Ballygally, Larne
BT40 2QC*
Tel (01574) 583248
Fax (01574) 583324
Mem 875
Sec N Moore (01574) 583324
Pro R Walker (01574) 583417
Holes 18 L 6112 yds SSS 69
Recs Am–64 B McMillen,
    R Houston
    Pro–64 D Jones, P Townsend
V'tors U exc Sat–NA
Fees £18 (£24) Mon/Wed–£15
Loc 4 miles N of Larne
Arch JSF Morrison

Carrickfergus (1926)
*35 North Road, Carrickfergus
BT38 8LP*
Tel (01960) 363713
Fax (01960) 363023
Mem 850
Sec RJ Campbell (Sec/Mgr)
Pro R Stevenson (01960) 351803
Holes 18 L 5752 yds SSS 68
Recs Am–64 R Donald
    Pro–66 T Halpin
V'tors U
Fees £14 (£20)
Loc 8 miles E of Belfast, off A2

Cushendall (1937)
21 Shore Road, Cushendall BT44 0QQ
Tel (012667) 71318
Mem 824
Sec S McLaughlin (012667)
    58366
Holes 9 L 4834 m SSS 63
Recs Am–62 A McCallin (1995)
V'tors WE–restricted SOC
Fees £10 (£15)
Loc Cushendall, 25 miles N
    of Larne

Down Royal (1990)
Dungarton Road, Maze, Lisburn
Tel (01846) 621339
Fax (01846) 621339
Mem 26
Sec J Tinnion (Mgr)
Holes 18 L 6058 m Par 72 SSS 69
V'tors U
Fees £14 (£17)

Gracehill (1995)
*141 Ballinlea Road, Stranocum,
Ballymoney BT53 8PX*
Tel (012657) 51209
Fax (012657) 51209
Mem 260

Sec M McClure (Mgr)
Pro J Gillen, Mrs M Gillen
Holes 18 L 6800 metres Par 72
V'tors U
Fees £12 (£15)
Loc 6 miles N of Ballymoney
    (B66)

Greenacres (1996)
*153 Ballyrobert Road, Ballyclare
BT39 9RT*
Tel (01960) 354111
Fax (01960) 354166
Mem 249
Sec M Brown
Pro G Mercer
Holes 18 L 6020 yds Par 71 SSS 68
V'tors U
Fees £12 Fri–£16 (£18)
Loc 3 miles from Corrs Corner
    on B56
Mis Floodlit driving range

Greenisland (1894)
*156 Upper Road, Greenisland,
Carrickfergus BT38 8RW*
Tel (01232) 862236
Mem 510
Sec J Wyness (01232) 864583
Holes 9 L 5536 metres Par 71
    SSS 69
Recs Am–65
V'tors WD–U Sat–NA before 5pm
    SOC–exc Sat
Fees £12 (£18)
Loc 9 miles NE of Belfast
Arch H Middleton

Lambeg (1986)
Bells Lane, Lambeg, Lisburn
Tel (01846) 662738
Mem 200
Sec T Burrell
Pro I Murdock
Holes 9 L 4383 metres SSS 65
Recs Am–64 A Mason (1993)
V'tors U SOC
Fees £6 (£6.50)
Loc SW of Belfast, off Lisburn road

Larne (1894)
*54 Ferris Bay Road, Islandmagee,
Larne BT40 3RT*
Tel (01960) 382228
Mem 420
Sec KJ Hedley (01960) 382127
Holes 9 L 6114 yds SSS 69
Recs Am–66 IA Nesbitt,
    BR Hobson
    Pro–68 N Drew
V'tors WD–U WE–M after 5pm
    SOC–WD/Sun
Fees £8 (£15)
Loc 6 miles N of Whitehead on
    Browns Bay road
Arch George Baillie

Lisburn (1891)

68 Eglantine Road, Lisburn BT27 5RQ
Tel   (01846) 677216
Fax   (01846) 603608
Mem   1421
Sec   GE McVeigh (Sec/Mgr)
Pro   BR Campbell (01846) 677217
Holes   18 L 6647 yds SSS 72
Recs   Am–65 P Grant (1990)
            Pro–64 D Feherty (1989)
V'tors WD–U WE–M
            SOC–Mon/Thurs/Fri
Fees   £25 (£30)
Loc   3 miles S of Lisburn on A3
Arch   Hawtree

Mallusk (1992)

Mallusk, Newtownabbey
Mem   75
Sec   J Smith
Holes   9 L 4444 metres SSS 62
V'tors U
Fees   £4.50 (£7)
Loc   4 miles NW of
            Newtownabbey (B95)

Massereene (1895)

51 Lough Road, Antrim BT41 4DQ
Tel   (01849) 429293
Fax   (01849) 487661
Mem   850
Sec   Mrs S Greene (01849) 428096
Pro   J Smyth (01849) 464074
Holes   18 L 6614 yds SSS 71
Recs   Am–66 T Coulter
V'tors U SOC
Fees   £20 (£25)
Loc   1 mile S of Antrim

Royal Portrush (1888)

Dunluce Road, Portrush BT56 8JQ
Tel   (01265) 822311
Fax   (01265) 823139
Mem   1042 256(L)
Sec   Miss W Erskine
Pro   DA Stevenson (01265) 823335
Holes   Dunluce 18 L 6772 yds
            SSS 73; Valley 18 L 6273 yds
            SSS 70; Skerries 9 hole course
Recs   Dunluce Am–67
            G McGimpsey
            Pro–66 J Hargreaves
            Valley Am–65 MJC Hoey
V'tors WD–I H exc Wed & Fri
            pm–NA Sat–NA before 3pm
            Sun–NA before 10.30am SOC
Fees   Dunluce £55 (£65)
            Valley £22 (£30)
Loc   Portrush Coastal Rd ½ mile
Arch   HS Colt

Whitehead (1904)

*McCrae's Brae, Whitehead,
Carrickfergus BT38 9NZ*
Tel   (01960) 353792
Mem   910
Sec   J Niblock, R Patrick
            (01960) 353631
Pro   C Farr (01960) 353118
Holes   18 L 6426 yds SSS 71
Recs   Am–68 A Hope

V'tors WD–U WE–M SOC–exc Sat
Fees   £12 (£18)
Loc   ½ mile from Whitehead, off
            road to Island Magee

Co Armagh

Ashfield (1990)

Freeduff, Cullyhanna
Tel   (01693) 868180
Mem   150
Sec   J Quinn (Sec/Mgr)
Pro   E Maney
Holes   18 L 6540 yds SSS 69
V'tors U
Fees   On application
Loc   6 miles S of
            Newtownhamilton (B135)
Mis   Driving range
Arch   Frank Ainsworth

County Armagh (1893)

Newry Road, Armagh BT60 1EN
Tel   (01861) 522501
Fax   (01861) 525861
Mem   900
Sec   M Grant (01861) 525861
Pro   A Rankin (01861) 525864
Holes   18 L 6184 yds SSS 69
V'tors U SOC–WD
Fees   £12 (£18)
Loc   40 miles SW of Belfast by M1

Edenmore (1992)

*Drumnabreeze Road, Macheralin,
Craigavon BT67 0RH*
Tel   (01846) 611310
Fax   (01846) 613310
Mem   332
Sec   K Logan (Sec/Mgr)
Holes   18 L 6244 yds Par 71 SSS 70
Recs   Am–71 I Moore (1997)
V'tors U SOC
Fees   £10 Fri–£12 Sat–£15
Loc   4 miles E of Lurgan (A3)
Arch   F Ainsworth

Lurgan (1893)

The Demesne, Lurgan BT67 9BN
Tel   (01762) 322087 (Clubhouse)
Fax   (01762) 325306
Mem   878
Sec   Mrs G Turkington
Pro   D Paul (01762) 321068
Holes   18 L 5836 metres SSS 70
Recs   Am–65 T Cummins (1990)
            Pro–65 B Todd
V'tors U SOC–Mon/Thurs/Fri am/
            Sun am
Fees   £15 (£20)
Loc   Nr Brownlow Castle, Lurgan
Arch   Frank Pennink

Portadown (1906)

192 Gilford Road, Portadown BT63 5LF
Tel   (01762) 355356
Mem   1004
Sec   Mrs ME Holloway

Pro   P Stevenson (01762) 334655
Holes   18 L 6119 yds SSS 70
Recs   Am–A Poole (1996)
            Pro–63
V'tors WD–U exc Tues
Fees   £16 (£20)
Loc   3 miles S of Portadown,
            towards Gilford

Silverwood (1983)

Public
Turmoyra Lane, Silverwood, Lurgan
Tel   (01762) 326606
Mem   180
Sec   V McCorry (Sec/Mgr)
Holes   18 L 6496 yds SSS 72
V'tors U
Fees   £7 (£10)
Loc   Lurgan 1 mile.
            M1 Junction 10
Mis   Floodlit driving range

Tandragee (1922)

Markethill Road, Tandragee BT62 2ER
Tel   (01762) 840727 (Clubhouse)
Fax   (01762) 840664
Mem   1210
Sec   B Carson (01762) 841272
Pro   P Stevenson (01762) 841761
Holes   18 L 5754 metres Par 71
            SSS 70
Recs   Am–62 P Topley
            Pro–65 W Sullivan (1983)
V'tors U SOC
Fees   £15 (£21)
Loc   8 miles S of Portadown
            on A27
Arch   F Hawtree

Belfast

Ballyearl Golf Centre

Public
*585 Doagh Road, Newtownabbey
BT36 5RZ*
Tel   (01232) 848287
Fax   (01232) 844896
Pro   J Robinson (01232) 840899
Holes   9 L 2362 yds Par 3 course
V'tors U
Fees   £4.50 (£5.30)
Loc   N of Mossley on B59, via A8
Mis   Floodlit driving range

Balmoral (1914)

518 Lisburn Road, Belfast BT9 6GX
Tel   (01232) 381514
Fax   (01232) 669505
Mem   1002
Sec   RC McConkey (Mgr)
Pro   G Bleakley (01232) 667747
Holes   18 L 5909 metres SSS 70
Recs   Am–66 M Wilson
            Pro–64 D Jones
V'tors U exc Sat SOC–Mon & Thurs
Fees   £20 Wed–£24 (£30)
Loc   2 miles S of Belfast by
            Kings Hall

Belvoir Park (1927)

Church Road, Newtownbreda, Belfast BT8 4AN

Tel	**(01232) 491693**
Fax	(01232) 646113
Mem	1100
Sec	KH Graham (01232) 491693
Pro	GM Kelly (01232) 646714
Holes	18 L 6501 yds SSS 71
Recs	Am–66 TS Anderson,
	JN Browne
	Pro–65 G Fairweather,
	P Walton (1995)
V'tors	U exc Sat–NA
Fees	£33 (£38)
Loc	3 miles S of Belfast centre,
	off Newcastle road
Arch	HS Colt

Cliftonville (1911)

Westland Road, Belfast BT14 6NH

Tel	**(01232) 744158/746595**
Mem	429
Sec	JM Henderson (Hon)
Holes	9 L 6242 yds SSS 70
Recs	Am–66 WRA Tennant,
	IA Nesbitt, B Doherty Jr,
	M Donnelly
	Pro–67 S Hamill
V'tors	U exc Sat
Fees	£12 (£15)
Loc	Belfast

Dunmurry (1905)

91 Dunmurry Lane, Dunmurry, Belfast BT17 9JS

Tel	**(01232) 610834**
Fax	(01232) 602540
Mem	493 127(L) 117(J)
Sec	ID McBride (Sec/Mgr)
Pro	J Dolan (01232) 621314
Holes	18 L 5832 yds SSS 68
Recs	Am–64 D Flannagan
	Pro–67 P Leonard
V'tors	Tues & Thurs–NA after 5pm
	Sat–NA before 5pm SOC
Fees	£17 (£26) SOC–£16 (£20)
Loc	Belfast 5 miles
Arch	T McAuley

Fortwilliam (1891)

Downview Avenue, Belfast B15 4EZ

Tel	**(01232) 370770**
Fax	(01232) 781891
Mem	1100
Sec	M Purdy
Pro	P Hanna (01232) 770980
Holes	18 L 5973 yds SSS 69
Recs	Am–67 A O'Neill
	Pro–65 P Leonard
V'tors	U SOC
Fees	£20 (£27)
Loc	2 miles N of Belfast on A2

Gilnahirk (1983)

Public

Manns Corner, Upper Braniel Road, Belfast

Tel	**(01232) 448477**
Mem	200
Sec	H Moore

Pro	K Gray
Holes	9 L 2699 metres SSS 68
Recs	Am–65 T McIver (1993)
V'tors	U
Fees	On application
Loc	3 miles SE of Belfast, off A23

The Knock Club (1895)

Summerfield, Dundonald, Belfast BT16 0QX

Tel	**(01232) 482249**
Fax	(01232) 483251
Mem	900
Sec	SG Managh (01232) 483251
Pro	G Fairweather (01232) 483825
Holes	18 L 6407 yds SSS 71
Recs	Am–66 DT Alderdice
	Pro–69 PR McGuirk
V'tors	U SOC–Mon & Thurs
Fees	D–£20 (£25)
Loc	4 miles E of Belfast on the
	Upper Newtownards Road
Arch	Colt/Mackenzie/Alison

Malone (1895)

240 Upper Malone Road, Dunmurry, Belfast BT17 9LB

Tel	**(01232) 612695**
Fax	(01232) 431394
Mem	759 379(L) 211(J)
Sec	JNS Agate (01232) 612758
Pro	M McGee (01232) 614917
Holes	18 L 6654 yds SSS 71
	9 L 3191 yds SSS 36
	Pro–68 E Jones
V'tors	Wed–NA after 2pm Sat–NA
	before 5pm SOC–Mon &
	Thurs
Fees	£32 (£37)
Loc	6 miles S of Belfast
Arch	J Harris/CK Cotton

Ormeau (1893)

50 Park Road, Belfast BT7 2EX

Tel	**(01232) 641069 (Members)**
Fax	(01232) 646250
Mem	280 70(L) 45(J)
Sec	R Kirk (01232) 640700
Pro	(01232) 640999
Holes	9 L 5308 yds SSS 65
Recs	Am–56 E Donaldson (1995)
V'tors	U SOC
Fees	£12 (£14.50)
Loc	2 miles S of Belfast

Shandon Park (1926)

73 Shandon Park, Belfast BT5 6NY

Tel	**(01232) 793730**
Fax	(01232) 402773
Mem	1100
Sec	MG Corsar (Mgr) (01232)
	401856
Pro	B Wilson (01232) 797859
Holes	18 L 6261 yds SSS 70
Recs	Am–64 N Anderson
	Pro–68 CP Posnett
V'tors	WD–U Sat–NA before 5pm
	SOC
Fees	£22 (£27)
Loc	3 miles E of Belfast on the
	Knock road

Co Carlow

Borris (1908)

Deerpark, Borris

Tel	**(0503) 73143**
Mem	380
Holes	9 L 6120 yds Par 70 SSS 69
Recs	Am–66 D Todd (1996)
V'tors	WD–U Sun–M SOC–WD/Sat
Fees	£12
Loc	Borris

Carlow (1899)

Deer Park, Dublin Road, Carlow

Tel	**(0503) 31695**
Fax	(0503) 40065
Mem	1300
Sec	Mrs M Meaney
Pro	A Gilbert (0503) 41745
Holes	18 L 5844 metres Par 70
	SSS 71
Recs	Am–64 J Kavanagh (1994)
	Pro–68 C O'Connor
V'tors	U SOC–WD
Fees	£22 (£27) SOC–£20 (£25)
Loc	2 miles N of Carlow. 50 miles
	S of Dublin (N7)
Arch	Tom Simpson

Mount Wolseley (1996)

Tullow

Tel	**(0503) 51674**
Fax	(0503) 52123
Mem	250
Sec	D Morrissey (Mgr)
Pro	J Bolger
Holes	18 L 6497 m Par 72 SSS 74
V'tors	U
Fees	£20 (£25)
Loc	15 miles E of Carlow (R275)

Co Cavan

Belturbet (1950)

Erne Hill, Belturbet

Tel	**(049) 22287**
Mem	175
Sec	PF Coffey (049) 22498
Pro	None
Holes	9 L 5347 yds SSS 65
Recs	Am–64 J Costello (1982)
V'tors	U SOC
Fees	£7 (£8)
Loc	1 mile E of Belturbet

Blacklion (1962)

Toam, Blacklion, via Sligo

Tel	**(072) 53024**
Mem	220
Sec	R Thompson (Hon)
Holes	9 L 5544 metres SSS 69
V'tors	U SOC
Fees	D–£8 (D–£10)
Loc	12 miles SW of Enniskillen on
	A4 to N16
Arch	Eddie Hackett

Cabra Castle (1978)

Kingscourt
Mem   130
Holes 9 L 5308 metres SSS 68
V'tors U exc Sun–NA SOC
Fees   D–£9
Loc   2 miles E of Kingscourt

County Cavan (1894)

Arnmore House, Drumelis, Cavan
Tel   (049) 31283
Mem   760
Sec   J Sheridan (049) 32045
Holes 18 L 5519 metres SSS 69
Recs   Am–66 A Cafferty
       Pro–65 J Purcell (1987)
V'tors Mon/Tues/Thurs–U
Fees   IR£10 (IR£12)
Loc   2 miles W of Cavan on
       Killeshandra road

Slieve Russell (1994)

Ballyconnell
Tel   (049) 26444
Fax   (049) 26474
Mem   350
Sec   PJ Creamer (049) 26458
Pro   L McCool (049) 26458
Holes 18 L 7053 yds Par 72 SSS 74
       9 hole Par 3 course
Recs   Am–71 K Smith
       Pro–68 P Walton
V'tors U SOC
Fees   £28 Sat–£36
Loc   15 miles N of Cavan Town
Mis   Driving range
Arch   Paddy Merrigan

Virginia (1945)

Park Hotel, Virginia
Tel   (049) 47235
Mem   307
Sec   J Greene (Hon)
Holes 9 L 4900 metres SSS 62
Recs   Am–54 PJ O'Reilly
V'tors U
Fees   £8
Loc   35 miles SE of Cavan,
       nr Lough Ramor (N3)

Co Clare

Clonlara (1993)

Clonlara
Tel   (061) 354141
Mem   91
Holes 9 L 5289 metres Par 70 SSS 69
V'tors U
Fees   £7 (£10)
Loc   8 miles NE of Limerick

Drumoland Castle (1964)

Newmarket–on–Fergus
Tel   (061) 368144/368444
Fax   (061) 363355
Mem   400
Sec   J O'Halloran (061) 368244
Pro   P Murphy
Holes 18 L 6098 yds SSS 71
Recs   Am–74 Dr C Hackett (1986)

V'tors U SOC
Fees   D–£20 (£25)
Loc   18 miles NW of Limerick.
       Shannon Airport 4 miles

East Clare (1992)

Bodyke
Tel   (061) 921322
Mem   130
Sec   A Mawhinney (Sec/Mgr)
Holes 9 L 5675 metres Par 72 SSS 70
V'tors U
Fees   £5
Loc   20 miles E of Ennis (R352)

Ennis (1907)

Drumbiggle Road, Ennis
Tel   (065) 24074
Fax   (065) 41848
Mem   860
Sec   J Normoyle
Pro   M Ward (065) 20690
Holes 18 L 5275 metres SSS 68
Recs   Am–65 L Pyne
       Pro–66 P Skerritt
V'tors U exc Sun SOC
Fees   £18 SOC–£13/£15
Loc   ¹/₂ mile NW of Ennis, off N18

Kilkee (1896)

East End, Kilkee
Tel   (065) 56048
Fax   (065) 56977
Mem   579
Sec   M Haugh
Holes 18 L 5928 metres Par 71
       SSS 71
Recs   Am–68 D Nagle, N Cotter
V'tors U SOC
Fees   £20
Loc   End of Kilkee Promenade.
       10 miles NW of Kilrush
Arch   Eddie Hackett

Kilrush (1934)

Parknamoney, Kilrush
Tel   (065) 51138
Fax   (065) 52633
Mem   338
Sec   G Kelly (065) 59005
Holes 18 L 5986 yds Par 70 SSS 69
Recs   Am–68 P King (1995)
V'tors U SOC
Fees   £16 (£18)
Loc   25 miles SW of Ennis
Arch   Arthur Spring

Lahinch (1892)

Lahinch
Tel   (065) 81003
Fax   (065) 81592
Mem   1250
Sec   A Reardon (Sec/Mgr)
Pro   R McCavery (065) 81408
Holes Old 18 L 6699 yds SSS 73
       Castle 18 L 5620 yds SSS 69
V'tors WD–U WE–NA 9–10.30am
       and 1–2pm SOC
Fees   Old–£45; Castle–£25
Loc   20 miles NW of Ennis on T69
Arch   Morris/Gibson/Mackenzie/
       Harris

Shannon (1966)

Shannon Airport
Tel   (061) 471020
Fax   (061) 471507
Mem   800
Sec   DJ Lempriere (061) 471849
Pro   A Pyke (061) 471551
Holes 18 L 6854 yds SSS 72
Recs   Am–63 J Purcell
       Pro–65 D Durnian
V'tors WD–U SOC
Fees   £20 (£25)
Loc   Shannon Airport

Spanish Point (1915)

Spanish Point, Miltown Malbay
Tel   (065) 84198
Mem   100
Sec   G O'Loughlin
Holes 9 L 3820 yds SSS 58
Recs   Am–27 D Twomey
       Pro–23 P Skerritt
V'tors U
Fees   £10
Loc   2 mile S of Miltown Malbay
       (N67). 20 miles W of Ennis

Woodstock (1993)

Shanaway Road, Ennis
Tel   (065) 29463
Fax   (065) 20304
Mem   350
Sec   AM Russell (Sec/Mgr)
Holes 18 L 5879 metres SSS 71
V'tors U
Fees   £20 (£25)
Arch   Arthur Spring

Co Cork

Bandon (1910)

Castlebernard, Bandon
Tel   (023) 41111/44544
Fax   (023) 44690
Mem   520
Sec   B O'Neill (Hon)
Pro   P O'Boyle (023) 42224
Holes 18 L 5663 metres Par 70
       SSS 69
Recs   Am–66 J Carroll
V'tors U
Fees   £12 (£15)
Loc   Bandon 1¹/₂ miles. 18 miles
       SW of Cork

Bantry Park (1975)

Donemark, Bantry, West Cork
Tel   (027) 50579
Fax   (027) 50579
Mem   420
Sec   Enda J Lonergan (Mgr)
Pro   F Condon
Holes 18 L 5914 metres Par 71
       SSS 72
Recs   Am–71 B Aylmer (1997)
       Pro–66 C O'Connor Jr
V'tors WD–U before 4.30 pm
       WE/BH–booking necessary
       SOC

Fees   £18 (£20)
Loc   1 mile N of Bantry on
Glengarriff road (N71)
Arch   E Hackett/C O'Connor, Jnr

Berehaven (1902)

Millcove, Castletownbere
Tel   (027) 70700
Mem   118
Sec   H Barry (Sec/Mgr)
(027) 70252
Holes   9 L 2605 yds SSS 66
Recs   Am–65 T Harrington (1990)
V'tors   U SOC
Fees   £10 (£10)
Loc   2 miles E of Castletownbere
on Glengarriff road

Charleville (1909)

Charleville
Tel   (063) 81257
Fax   (063) 81274
Mem   650
Sec   M Keane (Sec/Mgr)
Pro   None
Holes   18 L 6430 yds SSS 69
9 L 6750 yds SSS 72
Recs   Am–65 K Carey (1995)
Ladies–68 S Keane (1990)
V'tors   WD–U WE–book in advance
SOC
Fees   £15 (£17) SOC–£13.50 (£15)
Loc   35 miles N of Cork on
Limerick road

Cobh (1987)

Ballywilliam, Cobh
Tel   (021) 812399
Fax   (021) 812615
Mem   250
Sec   DA Kilcullen
Holes   9 L 4576 metres SSS 64
Recs   Am–63 P McGee Jr
Pro–64 C O'Connor Sr
V'tors   WD–U WE–NA
Fees   £8 (£9)
Loc   1 mile N of Cobh. 16 miles
SE of Cork
Arch   Eddie Hackett

Coosheen (1989)

Schull
Tel   (028) 28182
Mem   164
Sec   D Morgan
Holes   9 L 3362 metres Par 60 SSS 61
V'tors   U
Fees   £6 (£8)
Loc   20 miles S of Bantry

Cork (1888)

Little Island, Cork
Tel   (021) 353451/353037
Fax   (021) 353410
Mem   350 160 (L)
Sec   M Sands (021) 353451
Pro   P Hickey (021) 353421
Holes   18 L 6065 metres SSS 72
Recs   Am–66 T Cleary
Pro–66 J Hegarty

V'tors   WD–U H exc 12–2pm –M
after 4pm Thurs–(Ladies
Day)–phone in advance
WE–NA before 2.30pm H
Fees   £35 (£40)
Loc   5 miles E of Cork, off N25
Arch   Dr A Mackenzie

Doneraile (1927)

Doneraile
Tel   (022) 24137
Mem   152
Holes   9 L 5528 yds SSS 67
V'tors   U
Fees   On application
Loc   8 miles NW of Mallow

Douglas (1909)

Douglas, Cork
Tel   (021) 891086
Fax   (021) 895297
Mem   839
Sec   B Barrett (Mgr) (021) 895297
Pro   GS Nicholson (021) 362055
Holes   18 L 5664 metres SSS 69
Recs   Am–64 P Morris
Pro–64 E Darcy
V'tors   WD–U exc Tues WE–NA
before 2pm SOC–WD
Fees   IR£19 (IR£21)
Loc   Cork 3 miles

Dunmore (1967)

Dunmore House, Muckross, Clonakilty
Tel   (023) 33352
Mem   163
Sec   P Hogan (Hon)
Holes   9 L 4464 yds SSS 61
Recs   Am–65
Pro–62
V'tors   WD–U exc Wed WE–M SOC
Fees   £10
Loc   3 miles S of Clonakilty
Arch   Eddie Hackett

East Cork (1971)

Gortacrue, Midleton
Tel   (021) 631687
Fax   (021) 613695
Mem   600
Sec   M Moloney (Sec/Mgr)
Pro   D MacFarlane
Holes   18 L 5207 metres SSS 67
Recs   Am–65 G Murphy (1995)
V'tors   WD–U WE–NA before noon
BH–U
Fees   £15
Loc   2 miles N of Midleton on L35
Arch   Eddie Hackett

Fermoy (1892)

Corrin, Fermoy
Tel   (025) 32694
Fax   (025) 33072
Mem   800
Sec   S Hallihan
Pro   B Moriarty (025) 31472
Holes   18 L 5795 metres SSS 70
V'tors   U SOC
Fees   £12 (£15)
Loc   2 miles S of Fermoy, off N8

Fernhill (1994)

Carrigaline
Tel   (021) 372226
Fax   (021) 371011
Mem   60
Sec   A Thompson (Mgr)
Holes   18 L 5602 m Par 70 SSS 68
V'tors   U
Fees   £12 (£14)
Loc   10 miles SE of Cork (R609)
Arch   ML Bowes

Fota Island (1993)

Carrigtwohill, Cork
Tel   (021) 883710
Fax   (021) 883713
Mem   400
Sec   K Mulcahy (Sec/Mgr)
Pro   K Morris
Holes   18 L 6886 yds Par 72 SSS 74
Recs   Am–67 P Harrington
V'tors   U
Fees   £32 (£37)
Loc   8 miles E of Cork on N25
Mis   Driving range
Arch   O'Connor Jr/McEvoy

Frankfield (1984)

Frankfield, Douglas
Tel   (021) 361199
Mem   280
Pro   D Whyte
Holes   9 L 4621 metres SSS 65
Recs   Am–64
V'tors   U SOC
Fees   £5
Loc   S of Cork
Mis   Driving range

Glengarriff (1935)

Glengarriff
Tel   (027) 63150
Mem   170
Sec   N Deasy (Hon)
Holes   9 L 4094 metres SSS 66
V'tors   U
Fees   D–£12
Loc   1 mile E of Glengarriff (N71)

Harbour Point (1991)

Clash, Little Island
Tel   (021) 353094
Fax   (021) 354408
Mem   250
Sec   Ms N O'Connell (Sec/Mgr)
Holes   18 L 6063 yds SSS 72
V'tors   U SOC
Fees   £12.50–£22
Loc   5 miles E of Cork
Mis   Floodlit driving range
Arch   Paddy Merrigan

Kanturk (1971)

Fairy Hill, Kanturk
Tel   (029) 50534
Mem   350
Sec   J Pigott (029) 50588
Holes   18 L 6262 yds Par 72 SSS 70
Recs   Am–72 D O'Riordan,
M Archdeacon (1987),
J O'Connor (1989)

V'tors U
Fees £10
Loc 2 miles SW of Kanturk
    (R579)
Arch R Barry

Kinsale Farrangalway
(1993)
Farrangalway, Kinsale
Tel (021) 774722
Fax (021) 773114
Mem 740
Sec Deirdre O'Sullivan
Pro G Broderick (021) 773258
Holes 18 L 6609 yds SSS 72
Recs Am–70 K McCarthy
    Pro–69 G Broderick
V'tors WD–U WE–NA SOC
Fees £20 (£25)
Loc 3 miles NW of Kinsale.
    18 miles S of Cork
Arch Jack Kenneally

Kinsale Ringenane (1912)
Ringenane, Belgooly, Kinsale
Tel (021) 772197
Mem 740
Sec C McCloskey
Pro None
Holes 9 L 5332 yds SSS 68
Recs Am–63 K McCarthy
V'tors U SOC
Fees £15
Loc 2 miles E of Kinsale (R600).
    16 miles S of Cork

Lee Valley G&CC (1993)
Clashanure, Ovens, Cork
Tel (021) 331721
Fax (021) 331695
Mem 350
Sec Kathleen Curzon
Pro B McDaid
Holes 18 L 6800 yds SSS 72
Recs Am–71 D McFarlane (1993)
    Pro–68 F Couples (1993)
V'tors U SOC
Fees £22 (£25)
Loc 8 miles W of Cork (N22)
Mis Floodlit driving range
Arch C O'Connor Jr

Macroom (1924)
Lackaduve, Macroom
Tel (026) 41072
Fax (026) 41391
Mem 550
Sec L Gould
Pro None
Holes 18 L 5598 metres SSS 70
Recs Am–66 J Mills
V'tors U H SOC
Fees D–IR£13 (IR£16)
Loc Macroom Town, through
    Castle Arch. 25 miles W of
    Cork

Mahon (1980)
Cloverhill, Blackrock, Cork
Tel (021) 362480
Mem 250

Holes 18 L 4818 metres SSS 66
V'tors U
Fees £9 (£9.50)
Loc SE of Cork City

Mallow (1948)
Ballyellis, Mallow
Tel (022) 21145
Fax (022) 42501
Mem 1500
Sec V Devlin
Pro S Conway
Holes 18 L 6559 yds SSS 72
Recs Am–67 J Murphy (1995)
V'tors WD–U before 5pm SOC
Fees £18 (£22)
Loc 1 mile SE of Mallow Bridge
    on Killavullen road
Arch J Harris

Mitchelstown (1908)
Mitchelstown
Tel (025) 24072
Mem 500
Sec J Mullins
Holes 15 L 5057 metres SSS 67
Recs Am–65 A Spratt
V'tors U SOC
Fees £10 (£10)
Loc 30 miles NE of Cork
Arch David Jones

Monkstown (1908)
Parkgarriffe, Monkstown
Tel (021) 841376
Fax (021) 841376
Mem 900
Sec GA Finn
Pro B Murphy (021) 841686
Holes 18 L 5669 metres SSS 69
Recs Am–66 J Morris Jr (1988)
    Pro–67 K Morris (1992)
V'tors U H SOC
Fees £23 (£26)
Loc 7 miles SE of Cork

Muskerry (1897)
Carrigrohane
Tel (021) 385297
Fax (021) 385297
Mem 755
Sec JJ Moynihan
Pro WM Lehane (021) 381445
Holes 18 L 5786 metres SSS 71
Recs Am–64 K Bornemann
    Pro–66 J Hegerty
V'tors Restricted at certain
    times–phone first SOC
Fees £12.50 –£22 (£23)
Loc 7 miles NW of Cork. 2 miles
    W of Blarney

Old Head (1997)
Kinsale
Tel (021) 778444
Fax (021) 778022
Sec R Cawley (Mgr)
Holes 18 L 7100 yds SSS 72
V'tors U SOC
Fees £50 (£60)
Loc 7 miles S of Kinsale
Arch R Kirby/J Carr

Raffeen Creek (1989)
Ringaskiddy
Tel (021) 378430
Mem 450
Sec P Farry (Mgr)
Holes 9 L 5800 yds SSS 68
Recs Am–67 J Hornibrook (1993)
    Pro–71 C O'Connor Sr (1989)
V'tors WD–U WE–U after noon
Fees IR£10 (IR£13)
Loc 1 mile from Ringaskiddy
    Ferryport
Arch Eddie Hackett

Skibbereen (1931)
Licknavar, Skibbereen
Tel (028) 21227/22340
Mem 376
Sec Carmel O'Driscoll (Hon)
Pro None
Holes 18 L 5900 metres Par 70
    SSS 68
Recs Am–68 J Kenneally (1993)
V'tors U SOC–Sat
Fees £12 (£15)
Loc 1 mile W of Skibbereen.
    52 miles SW of Cork
Mis Driving range
Arch Eddie Hackett

Youghal (1898)
Knockaverry, Youghal
Tel (024) 92787
Fax (024) 92641
Mem 640
Sec Margaret O'Sullivan
Pro L Burns (024) 92590
Holes 18 L 5646 metres SSS 69
Recs Am–67 T Kenefick (1992)
V'tors U
Fees D–IR£14
Loc 30 miles E of Cork on N25
    from Rosslare
Arch Cdr Harris

Co Donegal

Ballybofey & Stranorlar
(1957)
Stranorlar, Ballybofey
Tel (074) 31093
Mem 450
Sec A Harkin (074) 31228
Holes 18 L 5922 yds SSS 68
Recs Am–64 E McMenamin (1992)
V'tors U SOC
Fees £12 SOC–£10
Loc Stranorlar ¼ mile
Arch PC Carr

Ballyliffin (1947)
Inishowen, Ballyliffin
Tel (077) 76119
Fax (077) 76672
Mem 828
Sec RG Fox (Gen Mgr)
    KJ O'Doherty (Hon)
Pro None

Holes Old 18 L 6611 yds SSS 72
Glashedy 18 L 6837 yds Par 72
Recs Old Pro–64 H O'Neill
Glashedy Pro–67 G Loughery
V'tors U SOC–WD
Fees Old IR£17 (IR£20)
Glashedy IR£25 (IR£30)
Loc 8 miles N of Buncrana.
15 miles N of Londonderry
Arch Glashedy–Craddock/Ruddy

Buncrana (1951)
Buncrana
Tel (077) 62279
Mem 175
Sec F McGrory (Hon)
Pro NS Doherty
Holes 9 L 4250 metres SSS 62
V'tors U
Fees £6
Loc 1 mile S of Buncrana, off R238

Bundoran (1894)
Bundoran
Tel (072) 41302
Fax (072) 42014
Mem 400
Sec J McGagh (Sec/Mgr)
Pro D Robinson
Holes 18 L 6159 yds SSS 70
Recs Am–66
Pro–66
V'tors WD–U WE–restricted SOC
Fees £16 (£18)
Loc E boundary of Bundoran.
20 miles S of Donegal
Arch H Vardon

Cruit Island (1985)
Kincasslagh, Dunglow
Tel (075) 43296
Mem 190
Pro None
Holes 9 L 5297 yds SSS 66
V'tors U SOC
Fees £7 (£9)
Loc 5 miles N of Dunglow, off R259

Donegal (1960)
Murvagh, Laghey
Tel (073) 34054
Fax (073) 34377
Mem 590
Sec J Nixon (073) 22166
J McBride (Admin)
Holes 18 L 7271 yds SSS 73
Recs Am–68 M Gannon
V'tors H SOC–exc Sun
Fees £18 (£25)
Loc 7 miles S of Donegal on N15
Arch Eddie Hackett

Dunfanaghy (1903)
Dunfanaghy, Letterkenny
Tel (074) 36335
Mem 300
Sec S Sterritt (074) 25432
Holes 18 L 5066 metres SSS 66
Recs Am–64 J Brogan
Pro–66 L Wallace
V'tors U SOC

Fees IR£11 (IR£13)
Loc 25 miles NW of Letterkenny
on N56

Greencastle (1892)
Greencastle
Tel (077) 81013
Mem 600
Sec PJ Keys (077) 81228
Holes 18 L 5211 metres SSS 67
Recs Am–67 F McCarroll (1993)
V'tors WD–U WE–restricted SOC
Fees £12 (£18)
Loc 21 miles NE of Londonderry,
nr Moville
Arch Eddie Hackett

Gweedore (1926)
Magheragallon, Derrybeg, Letterkenny
Tel (075) 31140
Mem 145
Holes 9 L 6201 yds SSS 69
V'tors U
Fees £7 (£8)
Loc 3 miles N of Gweedore,
off R257

Letterkenny (1913)
Barnhill, Letterkenny
Tel (074) 21150
Mem 490
Pro N McCole
Holes 18 L 6299 yds SSS 71
Recs Am–67 P Shiels
Pro–68 J Gallagher
V'tors U SOC
Fees £10 SOC–£6
Loc 1 mile E of Letterkenny
Arch Eddie Hackett

Narin & Portnoo (1931)
Narin, Portnoo
Tel (075) 45107
Fax (074) 25185
Mem 436
Sec E Bonner (Hon)
Pro None
Holes 18 L 5950 yds Par 69 SSS 68
Recs Am–64 B McBride (1980)
Pro–63 R Browne (1980)
V'tors WD–U H Sat–restricted
9.30–11.30am & 1–2.30pm
Sun–restricted SOC
Fees £13 (£16) SOC–£10
Loc 6 miles N of Ardara. West
Donegal

North West (1891)
Lisfannon, Fahan
Tel (077) 61027
Fax (077) 63284
Mem 520
Sec D Coyle (Hon)
Pro S McBriarty (077) 61715
Holes 18 L 6239 yds SSS 71
Recs Am–65 F Friel
Pro–64 M Doherty
V'tors U
Fees IR£15 (IR£20)
Loc 2 miles S of Buncrana.
12 miles N of Londonderry

Otway (1893)
Saltpans, Rathmullan, Letterkenny
Tel (074) 58319
Mem 97
Sec T Morrison (Hon)
Holes 9 L 4234 yds SSS 60
Recs Am–60 D Gallagher
V'tors U
Fees £7
Loc 15 miles NE of Letterkenny,
by Lough Swilly

Portsalon (1891)
Portsalon, Letterkenny
Tel (074) 59459
Mem 300
Sec C Toland (Hon)
Holes 18 L 5878 yds Par 69 SSS 68
Recs Am–66 K McLaughlin (1994)
Pro–71 J Henderson
V'tors U
Fees £10 (£12)
Loc 20 miles N of Letterkenny

Redcastle (1983)
Redcastle, Moville
Tel (077) 82073
Mem 120
Holes 9 L 6046 yds SSS 70
V'tors U
Fees £10 (£12)
Loc 15 miles NE of Londonderry,
by Lough Foyle (R238)

Rosapenna (1894)
Downings, Rosapenna
Tel (074) 55301
Fax (074) 55128
Mem 300
Sec MJ Gallagher (Hon)
Pro D Patterson
Holes 18 L 6254 yds SSS 71
Recs Am–M McGinley, D Boyce
Pro–68 F Daly
V'tors U
Fees IR£15
Loc 20 miles N of Letterkenny
Mis Golf academy
Arch Morris/Vardon/Braid

Co Down

Ardglass (1896)
Castle Place, Ardglass BT30 7TP
Tel (01396) 841219
Fax (01396) 841841
Mem 841
Sec Miss D Polly
Pro P Farrell (01396) 841022
Holes 18 L 5542 metres Par 70
SSS 69
Recs Am–65 D Baker
Pro–64 K Morris
V'tors U SOC
Fees £17 (£22)
Loc 7 miles SE of Downpatrick
on B1

Ardminnan (1995)

15 Ardminnan Road, Portaferry
BT22 1QJ

Tel	**(01247) 771321**
Fax	(01247) 771321
Mem	170
Sec	S McCrea (Mgr)
Pro	J Peden
Holes	9 L 2766 m Par 70 SSS 69
V'tors	U
Fees	£10 (£15)
Loc	10 miles E of Downpatrick via ferry. 18 miles SE of Newtownards (A20)
Arch	Frank Ainsworth

Banbridge (1913)

Huntly Road, Banbridge BT32 3UR

Tel	**(018206) 62342**
Fax	(018206) 69400
Mem	850
Sec	H Carson (Sec/Mgr) (018206) 62211
Holes	18 L 5376 metres SSS 68
Recs	Am–62 R Leonard
V'tors	U SOC
Fees	£10 (£20)
Loc	1 mile W of Banbridge

Bangor (1903)

Broadway, Bangor BT20 4RH

Tel	**(01247) 270922**
Fax	(01247) 453394
Mem	1100
Sec	DJ Ryan (Sec/Mgr)
Holes	18 L 6424 yds SSS 71
Recs	Am–64 P Barry Pro–66 C O'Connor
V'tors	WD–U exc –M 1–2pm Wed–U before 4.45pm Sat–NA SOC–Mon & Wed
Fees	£17.50 Sun–£25
Loc	1 mile S of Bangor, off Donaghadee road
Arch	James Braid

Blackwood (1995)

150 Crawfordsburn Road, Bangor
BT19 1GB

Tel	**(01247) 852706**
Fax	(01247) 853785
Mem	351
Sec	J Kennedy
Holes	2 x 18 hole courses
V'tors	U
Fees	On application
Loc	W of Bangor
Mis	Driving range

Bright Castle (1970)

14 Coniamstown Road, Bright,
Downpatrick BT30 8LU

Tel	**(01396) 841319**
Mem	54
Holes	18 L 6730 yds SSS 74
Recs	Am–70 A Ennis
V'tors	U SOC
Fees	£10 (£12)
Loc	5 miles S of Downpatrick, off Killough road (B176)

Carnalea (1927)

Station Road, Bangor BT19 1EZ

Tel	**(01247) 465004**
Fax	(01247) 273989
Mem	800
Sec	JH Crozier (01247) 270368
Pro	T Loughran (01247) 270122
Holes	18 L 5584 yds SSS 67
Recs	Am–63 A Robinson (1991)
V'tors	U SOC–WD
Fees	£13 (£17)
Loc	By Carnalea Station, Bangor

Clandeboye (1933)

Conlig, Newtownards BT23 3PN

Tel	**(01247) 271767/473706**
Fax	(01247) 473711
Mem	1291
Sec	W Donald (01247) 271767
Pro	P Gregory (01247) 271750
Holes	Dufferin 18 L 5915 metres SSS 71; Ava 18 L 5172 metres SSS 68
Recs	Am–65 S King Pro–68 J Heggarty, D Jones, D Feherty
V'tors	WD–U WE–M SOC
Fees	Dufferin–£25 Ava–£20
Loc	Conlig, off A21 Bangor–Newtownards road
Arch	Von Limburger/Alliss/Thomas

Crossgar (1993)

Derryboye Road, Crossgar

Tel	**(01396) 831523**
Holes	9 L 4139 metres Par 64 SSS 63
V'tors	U
Fees	£8 (£10)
Loc	6 miles N of Downpatrick (A7)

Donaghadee (1899)

Warren Road, Donaghadee BT21 0PQ

Tel	**(01247) 883624**
Fax	(01247) 888891
Mem	1250
Sec	K Patton
Pro	G Drew (01247) 882392
Holes	18 L 5570 metres Par 71
Recs	Am–65 J Nelson (1977), J McBurney (1994) Pro–69 E Clarke
V'tors	U exc Sat–NA SOC–Mon/Wed/Fri
Fees	£14 (£18)
Loc	6 miles S of Bangor on coast road. 18 miles E of Belfast

Downpatrick (1932)

Saul Road, Downpatrick BT30 6PA

Tel	**(01396) 612152/615947**
Fax	(01396) 617502
Mem	850
Sec	A Carson (01396) 615947
Pro	(01396) 615167
Holes	18 L 5702 metres SSS 69
Recs	Am–64 D Baker (1990)
V'tors	U SOC
Fees	£15 (£20)
Loc	25 miles SE of Belfast (A1). Downpatrick 1½ miles
Arch	Hawtree

Helen's Bay (1896)

Golf Road, Helen's Bay, Bangor
BT19 1TL

Tel	**(01247) 852601 (Clubhouse)**
Fax	(01247) 852815
Mem	480
Sec	LWL Mann (01247) 852815
Holes	9 L 5181 metres SSS 67
Recs	Am–67 PT Dorman (1996) Pro–67 L Esdale
V'tors	WD/Sun–U Tues/Thurs/Sat–restricted SOC–WD exc Tues
Fees	On application
Loc	9 miles E of Belfast, off A2

Holywood (1904)

Nuns Walk, Demesne Road, Holywood
BT18 9LE

Tel	**(01232) 422138**
Fax	(01232) 425040
Mem	800
Sec	D Jenkins (01232) 423135
Pro	M Bannon (01232) 425503
Holes	18 L 5885 yds SSS 68
Recs	Am–61 J Watts Pro–64 M Bannon
V'tors	WD–U exc 1.30–2.15pm Sat–after 5pm
Fees	£15 (£21)
Loc	5 miles E of Belfast on Bangor road

Kilkeel (1948)

Mourne Park, Ballyardle, Kilkeel
BT34 4LB

Tel	**(016937) 62296/65095**
Fax	(016937) 65095
Mem	672
Sec	SC McBride (016937) 63787
Holes	18 L 6625 yds SSS 72
Recs	Am–70 SP McVeigh (1996)
V'tors	U SOC–exc BH/Sat
Fees	£16 (£18)
Loc	3 miles W of Kilkeel on Newry road
Mis	Driving range
Arch	Eddie Hackett

Kirkistown Castle (1902)

142 Main Road, Cloughey,
Newtownards BT22 1JA

Tel	**(012477) 71233/71353**
Fax	(012477) 71699
Mem	924
Sec	G Graham (012477) 71233
Pro	J Peden (012477) 71004
Holes	18 L 5628 metres SSS 70
Recs	Am–68 Jas Brown Pro–71 RJ Polley, C O'Connor
V'tors	WD–U WE/BH–NA 1st tee 9.30–10.30am and 12–1.30pm SOC
Fees	£13 (£20)
Loc	25 miles SE of Belfast
Arch	James Braid

Mahee Island (1930)

Comber, Belfast BT23 6ET

Tel	**(01238) 541234**
Mem	500
Sec	T Reid (Hon)

Pro A McCracken
Holes 9 L 2790 yds SSS 67
Recs Am–63 W McClements (1995)
Pro–65 N Drew
V'tors U exc Sat–NA before 5pm
SOC–WD exc Mon
Fees £10 (£15)
Loc Strangford Lough, 14 miles
SE of Belfast

Mount Ober G&CC

Ballymaconaghy Road, Knockbracken, Belfast BT8 4SB
Tel (01232) 792108 (Bookings)
Fax (01232) 705862
Mem 600
Sec P Laverty (Hon)
Pro G Loughrey (01232) 401811
Holes 18 L 5312 yds SSS 68
Recs Am–66
Pro–68
V'tors WD–U Sat–NA before 3pm
Sun–NA before 10.30am SOC
Fees £11 (£14)
Loc 2 miles SW of Belfast, nr Four
Winds
Mis Floodlit driving range

Mourne (1946)

*36 Golf Links Road, Newcastle
BT33 0AN*
Tel (013967) 23218
Mem 275
Sec EJ Kane (Sec/Mgr)
N McCready (Hon)
Holes Play over Royal Co Down

Ringdufferin (1993)

*Ringdufferin Road, Toye, Killyleagh
BT30 9PH*
Tel (01396) 828812
Mem 232
Holes 18 L 4698 metres Par 68
SSS 66
V'tors U
Fees £8 (£10)
Loc 2 miles N of Killyleagh, off A22

Rockmount (1995)

*28 Drumalig Road, Carryduff, Belfast
BT8 8EQ*
Tel (01232) 812279
Fax (01232) 815851
Mem 700
Sec D Patterson (Mgr)
Holes 18 L 6373 yds Par 72 SSS 71
V'tors U
Fees £18 (£22)
Loc 8 miles S of Belfast (A24)

Royal Belfast (1881)

Holywood, Craigavad BT19 0BP
Tel (01232) 428165
Fax (01232) 421404
Mem 1200
Sec Mrs SH Morrison
Pro C Spence (01232) 428586
Holes 18 L 6184 yds SSS 70
Recs Am–69 B Purdy (1991)
Pro–65 D Clark (1992)

V'tors I Sat–NA before 4.30pm
Fees £30 (£35)
Loc E of Belfast on A2

Royal County Down (1889)

Newcastle BT33 0AN
Tel (013967) 23314
Fax (013967) 26281
Mem 450
Sec PE Rolph
Pro KJ Whitson (013967) 22419
Holes Ch'ship 18 L 7037 yds SSS 74
Annesley 18 L 4681 yds SSS 63
Recs Ch'ship Am–66 J Bruen,
JM Jamison, HB Smyth
Pro–67 A Compston, B Gadd
V'tors Contact Sec
Fees Ch'ship–£60 (£70)
Annesley–£15 (£20)
Loc 30 miles S of Belfast
Arch Tom Morris

Scrabo (1907)

*233 Scrabo Road, Newtownards
BT23 4SL*
Tel (01247) 812355
Fax (01247) 822919
Mem 958
Sec J Fraser (Sec/Mgr)
Pro A Cardwell (01247) 817848
Holes 18 L 5699 metres SSS 71
Recs Am–65 J Rea (1991)
Pro–67 N Drew (1987)
V'tors WD–U WE–after 5pm SOC
Fees £8 (£15)
Loc 2 miles W of Newtownards,
by Scrabo Tower

The Spa (1907)

Grove Road, Ballynahinch BT24 8BR
Tel (01238) 562365
Mem 895
Sec TG Magee
Holes 18 L 6003 metres SSS 72
Recs Am–67 R Wallace
V'tors U exc Wed–NA after 3pm
Sat–NA
Fees £14 (£18)
Loc 1 mile S of Ballynahinch.
15 miles S of Belfast

Temple (1994)

*60 Church Road, Boardmills, Lisburn,
Bt27 6UP*
Tel (01846) 639213
Fax (01846) 638637
Mem 300
Sec D Kinnear (Sec/Mgr)
Holes 9 L 5451 yds Par 68 SSS 66
V'tors U
Fees £10 (£14)
Loc Lisburn

Warrenpoint (1893)

*Lower Dromore Rd, Warrenpoint
BT34 3LN*
Tel (016937) 52219
Fax (016937) 52918
Mem 1066
Sec J McMahon (016937) 53695

Pro N Shaw (016937) 52371
Holes 18 L 5628 metres SSS 70
Recs Am–66 K Stevenson
Pro–69 S Hamill
V'tors U SOC
Fees £17 (£23)
Loc 5 miles S of Newry

Co Dublin

Balbriggan (1945)

Blackhall, Balbriggan
Tel (01) 841 2229
Fax (01) 841 3927
Mem 600
Sec M O'Halloran (Sec/Mgr)
Holes 18 L 5881 metres SSS 71
V'tors WD–U WE–M SOC
Fees £16 (£18)
Loc 2 miles S of Balbriggan on
N1. 18 miles N of Dublin
Arch Paramour/Stillwell

Balcarrick (1972)

Corballis, Donabate
Tel (01) 843 6228
Fax (01) 843 6957
Sec J Byrne
Holes 18 L 5167 metres SSS 71
V'tors WD–U Sat–NA before 10am
Sun–NA SOC
Fees £10 (£15)
Loc 2 miles E of Donabate.
18 miles N of Dublin

Ballinascorney (1971)

Ballinascorney, Tallaght, Dublin
Tel (01) 512516/512082
Mem 500
Holes 18 L 5464 yds SSS 67
V'tors WD–U
Fees £10 (£16)
Loc 8 miles SW of Dublin

Beaverstown (1985)

Beaverstown, Donabate
Tel (01) 843 6439
Fax (01) 843 6721
Mem 800
Sec E Smyth (Sec/Mgr)
Holes 18 L 5855 metres SSS 71
Recs Am–72 M Perry (1987)
Pro–67 T Judd (1995)
V'tors WD–U WE/BH–M SOC
Fees £14 (£22.50)
Loc 4 miles N of Dublin Airport
Arch Eddie Hackett

Beech Park (1983)

Johnstown, Rathcoole
Tel (01) 458 0522/458 0100
Fax (01) 458 8365
Mem 550
Sec J Deally (Sec/Mgr)
Pro None
Holes 18 L 5730 metres SSS 70
Recs Am–71 P Stapleton (1990)
Pro–67 B Todd (1989)

V'tors WD–U exc Tues/Wed–M
WE–M BH–NA
Fees £22
Loc Rathcoole 1 mile on Kilteel
road. SW of Dublin
Arch Eddie Hackett

Citywest (1994)

Saggart
Tel (01) 458 8566
Fax (01) 831 5779
Mem 170
Sec B Cooling (Mgr)
Holes 18 L 6441 yds Par 71 SSS 71
V'tors U
Fees £27 (£30)
Loc 10 miles SW of Dublin, off N7

Coldwinters (1994)

Newtown House, St Margaret's
Tel (01) 864 0324
Fax (01) 834 1400
Mem 375
Sec Mrs K Yates
Pro R Machin
Holes 18 L 5973 metres SSS 71
9 L 3133 metres SSS 31
V'tors U
Fees £8.50 (£12.50)
Loc NW of Dublin. Airport
2 miles
Mis Driving range. Golf Academy
Arch Martin Hawtree

Corrstown (1993)

Corrstown, Killsallaghan
Tel (01) 864 0533/4
Fax (01) 864 0537
Mem 900
Sec J Kelly
Pro P Gittens
Holes 18 L 6077 metres Par 72
SSS 71; 9 L 5584 metres
Par 70 SSS 69
V'tors Booking necessary
Fees £17 (£20)
Loc Dublin Airport 6 miles
Arch E Connaughton

Donabate (1925)

Balcarrick, Donabate
Tel (01) 843 6059/6346/6001
Fax (01) 843 5012
Mem 913
Sec B Judd (01) 843 6346
Pro H Jackson
Holes 18 L 6187 yds SSS 69
Recs Am–67 D Hanratty
Pro–65 M Murphy
V'tors WE/BH–NA
Fees £20
Loc 8 miles N of Dublin Airport
on N1

Dublin Mountain (1993)

Gortlum, Brittas
Tel (01) 458 2622
Sec D Carolan
Holes 18 L 5433 metres Par 70
SSS 69

V'tors U
Fees £6 (£8)
Loc SW of Dublin

Dun Laoghaire (1910)

Eglinton Park, Dun Laoghaire
Tel (01) 280 1055
Fax (01) 280 4868
Mem 972
Sec T Stewart (01) 280 3916
Pro O Mulhall (01) 280 1694
Holes 18 L 5478 metres SSS 69
Recs Am–66 N Mannion
Pro–65 P Skerritt
V'tors WD–U exc 12–1.30pm SOC
Fees IR£26
Loc 7 miles S of Dublin. Ferry
Port 1 mile
Arch HS Colt

Finnstown

Finnstown House Hotel, Lucan
Tel (01) 628 0644
Fax (01) 628 1088
Mem 300
Sec M Doyle (01) 836 3423
Holes 9 L 5172 yds SSS 64
Recs Am–65 C Kane (1996)
V'tors H SOC
Fees £12 (£16)
Loc 7 miles W of Dublin
Arch B Browne

Forrest Little (1972)

Forrest Little, Cloghran
Tel (01) 840 1183/840 1763
Fax (01) 840 1000
Mem 900
Sec T Greany (Sec/Mgr)
Pro T Judd
Holes 18 L 5865 metres SSS 70
Recs Am–67 T Judd (1984)
Pro–65 C O'Connor Jr (1984)
V'tors WD–U WE–NA
Fees IR£18
Loc Nr Dublin Airport
Arch F Hawtree

Hermitage (1905)

Lucan
Tel (01) 626 5396
Mem 1153
Sec Kay Russell (01) 626 8491
Pro C Carroll (01) 626 8072
Holes 18 L 6032 metres SSS 71
Recs Am–65 T Moran
Pro–65 R Davis
V'tors U SOC–WD
Fees £25 (£35)
Loc Lucan 2 miles. 8 miles W
of Dublin

Hollywood Lakes (1992)

Ballyboughal
Tel (01) 843 3406/7
Fax (01) 843 3002
Mem 350
Sec A Brogan (Sec/Mgr)
Holes 18 L 6834 yds Par 72 SSS 72
Recs Am–69 M Hogan (1993)
V'tors WD–U WE/BH–U after noon

Fees £17 (£22)
Loc 10 miles N of Dublin Airport
Arch Mel Flanagan

The Island (1890)

Corballis, Donabate
Tel (01) 843 6104
Fax (01) 843 6860
Mem 600
Sec J Finn (01) 843 6462
Pro K Kelleher (01) 843 5002
Holes 18 L 6053 metres SSS 72
Recs Am–67 T Smith (1997)
V'tors WD–U WE–NA
Fees £40
Loc 14 miles N of Dublin
Arch Hawtree

Killiney (1903)

Ballinclea Road, Killiney
Tel (01) 285 1983
Fax (01) 285 2823
Mem 520
Sec H Keegan (Sec/Mgr)
(01) 285 2823
Pro P O'Boyle (01) 285 6294
Holes 9 L 6220 yds SSS 70
Recs Am–72 N Duke
Pro–65 H Bradshaw
V'tors U
Fees D–£20
Loc 8 miles S of Dublin
Arch E Connaughton

Kilternan (1987)

Kilternan
Tel (01) 295 5559
Fax (01) 295 5670
Mem 906
Sec J Kinsella
Pro G Hendley (01) 295 2986
Holes 18 L 5413 yds SSS 67
Recs Am–69 S Foley (1991)
Pro–68 J Hegarty (1996)
V'tors U SOC
Fees £16 (£20)
Loc 12 miles S of Dublin
Arch Eddie Connaughton

Lucan (1897)

Celbridge Road, Lucan
Tel (01) 628 0246
Fax (01) 628 2929
Mem 740
Sec T O'Donnell (Sec/Mgr)
(01) 628 2106
Holes 18 L 5958 metres Par 71
SSS 71
Recs Am–68 B Dowling
V'tors WD–U WE/BH–M SOC–WD
exc Thurs
Fees £18
Loc 14 miles W of Dublin,
nr Lucan on N4
Arch Eddie Hackett

Luttrelstown Castle (1993)

Clonsilla, Dublin 15
Tel (01) 808 9988
Fax (01) 808 9989
Mem 400

Sec P Smith (Gen Mgr)
Pro G Campbell (Golf Dir)
Holes 18 L 6384 metres Par 72
SSS 73
Recs Am–67 J O'Brien (1996)
Pro–66 J Young (1994)
V'tors U SOC
Fees £40 (£45)
Loc 7 miles W of Dublin
Mis Driving range
Arch Bielenberg/Connaughton

Malahide (1892)

Beechwood, The Grange, Malahide
Tel (01) 846 1611
Fax (01) 846 1270
Mem 850
Sec T Gallagher (Sec/Mgr)
Pro D Barton
Holes 27 holes:
6257–6633 yds SSS 70–72
Recs Am–70 PA Hearne Jr
V'tors WD–U WE–by arrangement
SOC
Fees £30 (£40)
Loc 1½ miles S of Malahide.
10 miles N of Dublin,
nr Airport
Arch Eddie Hackett

Milltown (1907)

*Lower Churchtown Road, Milltown,
Dublin 14*
Tel (01) 497 6090
Fax (01) 497 6008
Mem 1432
Sec W Johnston (Sec/Mgr)
Pro J Harnett (01) 497 7072
Holes 18 L 5638 metres Par 71
SSS 69
Recs Am–67 J O'Brien
Pro–64 C Greene
V'tors WD–U exc Tues & Wed pm
Fri/WE–M BH–NA
SOC–Mon & Thurs before
3.45pm
Fees £34
Loc 4 miles S of Dublin centre
Arch Freddie Davis

Portmarnock (1894)

Portmarnock
Tel (01) 846 2968
Fax (01) 846 2601
Mem 971
Sec JJ Quigley
Pro J Purcell (01) 846 2634
Holes 27 holes:
6361–6497 metres SSS 74–75
Recs Am–68 JB Carr
Pro–64 S Lyle (1989)
V'tors I WE–XL
Fees IR£65 (IR£80)
Loc 8 miles NE of Dublin

Portmarnock Hotel (1995)

Strand Road, Portmarnock
Tel (01) 846 0611
Fax (01) 846 1077
Sec Moira Cassidy (Golf Dir)
(01) 846 1800

Holes 18 L 6260 metres Par 71
SSS 73
Recs Pro–67 D Smyth (1997)
V'tors U H
Fees £50 Residents–£30
Loc 8 miles NE of Dublin. Airport
15 mins
Arch Bernhard Langer

Rush (1943)

Rush
Tel (01) 843 7548
Mem 360
Sec BJ Clear (Sec/Mgr)
(01) 843 8177
Holes 9 L 5598 metres SSS 69
Recs Am–68 PJ Dolan
V'tors WD–U WE–M
Fees £15
Loc 16 miles N of Dublin, off R127

St Margaret's G&CC (1993)

St Margaret's, Dublin
Tel (01) 864 0400
Fax (01) 864 0289
Mem 200
Sec A McKenna (Sec/Mgr)
Holes 18 L 6900 yds SSS 73
Pro–69 C Monaghan (1993)
Ladies Pro–66 L Davies (1995)
V'tors U SOC
Fees £40 (£40)
Loc 3 miles NW of Dublin
Airport, between N1/N2
Mis Driving range
Arch Craddock/Ruddy

Skerries (1906)

Skerries
Tel (01) 849 1204 (Clubhouse)
Fax (01) 849 1591
Mem 908
Sec A Burns (01) 849 1567
Pro J Kinsella (01) 849 0925
Holes 18 L 6081 metres SSS 72
V'tors U SOC
Fees IR£20 (IR£25)
Loc 20 miles N of Dublin

Slade Valley (1970)

Lynch Park, Brittas
Tel (01) 458 2739
Fax (01) 458 2784
Mem 800
Sec P Maguire (01) 458 2183
Pro J Dignam
Holes 18 L 5337 metres SSS 68
Recs Am–65
Pro–64
V'tors WD–U am WE–M
Fees £17
Loc 8 miles W of Dublin, off N4
Arch Sullivan/O'Brien

Swords (1996)

Balheary Avenue, Swords
Tel (01) 840 9819
Mem 230
Sec O McGuiness (Mgr)
Holes 18 L 5677 m Par 71 SSS 70

V'tors U
Fees £8 (£10)
Loc 10 miles N of Dublin,
nr Airport

Westmanstown (1988)

Clonsilla, Dublin 15
Tel (01) 820 5817
Mem 950
Holes 18 L 5819 metres SSS 70
V'tors U SOC
Fees £15 (£20)
Loc 15 miles W of Dublin,
nr Lucan
Arch Eddie Hackett

Woodbrook (1921)

Dublin Road, Bray
Tel (01) 282 4799
Fax (01) 282 1950
Mem 950
Sec B O'Neill (Gen Mgr)
Pro W Kinsella
Holes 18 L 6221 metres SSS 72
Recs Am–L Macnamara
Pro–D Smyth, J McHenry
Ladies Pro–L Davies
V'tors WD–U WE–phone Sec SOC
Fees £35 (£40)
Loc 11 miles SE of Dublin on N11
Arch P McEvoy

Dublin City

Carrickmines (1900)

Golf Lane, Carrickmines, Dublin 18
Tel (01) 295 5972
Mem 500
Sec AN McEachern (Hon)
Holes 9 L 6103 yds SSS 69
Recs Am–68
Pro–68
V'tors U exc Wed/Sat–NA
Fees £20 Sun–£23 Sat–NA
Loc 6 miles S of Dublin

Castle (1913)

Woodside Drive, Rathfarnham, Dublin 14
Tel (01) 490 4207
Fax (01) 492 0264
Mem 800
Sec LF Blackburne (Sec/Mgr)
Pro D Kinsella (01) 492 0272
Holes 18 L 6270 yds SSS 68
Recs Am–67 J Pender
Pro–63 P Townsend
V'tors Mon/Thurs/Fri–U Wed–U
before 12.30pm WE/BH–M
SOC
Fees £35
Loc 5 miles S of Dublin

Clontarf (1912)

*Donnycarney House, Malahide Road,
Dublin 3*
Tel (01) 833 1892
Fax (01) 833 1933
Mem 1035
Sec N Rooney (Mgr)

Pro   J Craddock (01) 833 1877
Holes 18 L 5447 metres SSS 68
Recs   Am–66 R Murray
           Pro–64 H Bradshaw
V'tors WD–U WE–M SOC
Fees   £26
Loc   2 miles NE of Dublin city
           centre
Arch   HS Colt

Deer Park (1974)

Deer Park Hotel, Howth Castle, Howth
Tel   **(01) 8222624**
Fax   (01) 8392405
Mem   312
Sec   JP Doran (Hon) (01) 8326039
Pro   None
Holes 18 L 6781 yds Par 72 SSS 71
           18 L 6475 yds Par 72 SSS 70
           12 hole Par 3 course
Recs   Am–71 P Coldrick (1995)
V'tors U SOC
Fees   £8.90 (£11.50)
Loc   8 miles NE of Dublin
Arch   F Hawtree

Edmondstown (1944)

Rathfarnham, Dublin 16
Tel   **(01) 493 2461**
Fax   (01) 493 3152
Mem   600
Sec   S Davies (01) 493 1082
Pro   A Crofton (01) 494 1049
Holes 18 L 5663 metres Par 70
           SSS 70
Recs   Am–68 A Bernstein
V'tors WD/BH–U SOC
Fees   £25 (£30) Summer
           £20 (£25) Winter
Loc   5 miles S of Dublin
Arch   McAllister

Elm Green (1996)

Castleknock, Dublin 15
Tel   **(01) 820 0797**
Fax   (01) 820 8134
Sec   J Lambe (Hon)
Holes 18 L 5300 m Par 71 SSS 68
V'tors U
Fees   £11 (£16)
Loc   NW Dublin

Elm Park (1927)

Nutley House, Donnybrook, Dublin 4
Tel   **(01) 269 3438/269 3014**
Fax   (01) 269 4505
Mem   1750
Sec   A McCormack (01) 269 3438
Pro   S Green (01) 269 2650
Holes 18 L 5374 metres SSS 68
Recs   Am–63 PF Hogan
           Pro–63 P Townsend
V'tors U–phone Pro
Fees   £35 (£45)
Loc   3 miles S of Dublin

Foxrock (1893)

Torquay Road, Foxrock, Dublin 18
Tel   **(01) 289 5668**
Fax   (01) 289 4943

Mem   550
Sec   WM Daly (01) 289 3992
Pro   D Walker (01) 289 3414
Holes 9 L 5667 metres SSS 69
Recs   Am–68 D Campbell,
           M Sludds
           Pro–66 M Murphy
V'tors WD/BH/Sun–M Tues &
           Sat–NA
Fees   £20
Loc   5 miles S of Dublin

Grange (1911)

Whitechurch Road, Rathfarnham,
Dublin 16
Tel   **(01) 493 2832**
Fax   (01) 493 9490
Mem   1050 235(L) 210(J)
Sec   JA O'Donoghue
           (01) 493 2889
Pro   B Hamill (01) 493 2299
Holes 18 L 5517 metres SSS 69
Recs   Am–64 WB Buckley
           Pro–62 C O'Connor Jr
V'tors WD–U exc Tues/Wed
           pm–NA WE–M
Fees   £30
Loc   Rathfarnham, 5 miles from
           centre of Dublin

Hazel Grove (1988)

Mount Seskin Road, Jobstown,
Tallaght, Dublin 24
Tel   **(01) 452 0911**
Mem   400 175(L)
Sec   J Matthews
Pro   None
Holes 9 L 5300 metres SSS 67
Recs   Am–61 H Donnelly (1996)
           Ladies–61 M O'Connell (1996)
V'tors Mon/Wed/Fri–U Sun–NA
           Tues/Thurs/Sat–restricted
Fees   £9
Loc   3 miles from Tallaght, off
           Blessington road
Arch   Eddie Hackett

Howth (1916)

Carrickbrack Road, Sutton,
Dublin 13
Tel   **(01) 832 3055**
Fax   (01) 832 1793
Mem   1200
Sec   Ms A MacNeice
Pro   JF McGuirk (01) 839 3895
Holes 18 L 5618 metres SSS 69
Recs   Am–66 M Roe
           Pro–71
V'tors WD–U exc Wed WE–M
Fees   £18 Fri–£20
Loc   9 miles NE of Dublin, nr
           Sutton Cross

Kilmashogue (1994)

College Road, Whitechurch,
Dublin 16
Tel   **(088) 682360**
Fax   (01) 493 0729
Mem   355
Sec   V O'Kelly (Hon)
Pro   W Sullivan

Holes 9 L 5320 m Par 70 SSS 70
Fees   £10
Loc   Dublin

Newlands (1926)

Clondalkin, Dublin 22
Tel   **(01) 459 2903**
Fax   (01) 459 3498
Mem   1086
Sec   AT O'Neill (01) 459 3157
Pro   K O'Donnell (01) 459 3538
Holes 18 L 6184 yds SSS 69
Recs   Am–66 R Burdon, P Hanley Jr
           Pro–68 C O'Connor
V'tors WD–U am WE/BH–NA SOC
Fees   IR£30
Loc   6 miles SW of Dublin at
           Newlands Cross (N7)
Arch   James Braid

Rathfarnham (1899)

Newtown, Dublin 16
Tel   **(01) 493 1201/493 1561**
Fax   (01) 493 1561
Mem   561
Sec   DO Tipping (01) 493 1201
Pro   B O'Hara
Holes 9 L 5787 metres SSS 70
Recs   Am–69 R Hayden
V'tors U exc Tues & Sat–NA
Fees   £22.50
Loc   6 miles S of Dublin
Arch   John Jacobs

Royal Dublin (1885)

North Bull Island, Dollymount,
Dublin 3
Tel   **(01) 833 6346**
Fax   (01) 833 6504
Mem   900
Sec   JA Lambe (01) 833 1262
Pro   L Owens (01) 833 6477
           (Touring Pro C O'Connor Sr)
Holes 18 L 6922 yds SSS 73
Recs   Am–67 G O'Donovan (1984)
           Pro–63 B Langer, G Cullen
           (1985)
V'tors U H exc Wed Sat–NA before
           4pm SOC–WD
Fees   IR£50 (IR£60)
Loc   3 miles NE of Dublin, on
           coast road to Howth
Mis   Practice range. Indoor tuition
Arch   HS Colt

St Anne's (1921)

North Bull Island, Dollymount,
Dublin 5
Tel   **(01) 833 2797/6471**
Fax   (01) 833 4618
Mem   520
Sec   W Bornemann (01) 833 6471
Pro   P Skerritt
Holes 18 L 5797 metres Par 70
           SSS 70
Recs   Am–67 S Rodgers
           Pro–64 P Skerritt
V'tors WE/BH–NA SOC
Fees   £25 (£30)
Loc   Dublin 5 miles
Arch   Eddie Hackett

Stackstown (1975)

Kellystown Road, Rathfarnham, Dublin 16

Tel	**(01) 942338/941993**
Mem	1120
Sec	K Lawlor (Sec/Mgr)
Pro	M Kavanagh (01) 944561
Holes	18 L 5952 metres SSS 72
Recs	Am–70 P Harrington
V'tors	WD–U SOC
Fees	£12 (£15)
Loc	7 miles SE of Dublin

Sutton (1890)

Cush Point, Burrow Road, Sutton, Dublin 13

Tel	**(01) 323013**
Fax	(01) 321603
Mem	221 185(L) 63(J)
Sec	H O'Neill
Pro	N Lynch
Holes	9 L 5522 yds SSS 67
Recs	Am–64 M Hanway
	Pro–64 L Owens (1987)
V'tors	Tues–NA Sat–NA before 5.30pm
Fees	£15 (£20)
Loc	7 miles E of Dublin

Co Fermanagh

Castlehume

Castle Hume, Enniskillen BT93 7ED

Tel	**(01365) 327077**
Fax	(01365) 327076
Mem	150
Sec	Helen Keenan (Sec/Mgr)
Holes	18 L 6139 metres SSS 70
Recs	Am–69
V'tors	U
Fees	£12 (£18)
Loc	Enniskillen
Mis	Driving range
Arch	Tony Carroll

Enniskillen (1896)

Castlecoole, Enniskillen BT74 6HZ

Tel	**(01365) 325250**
Mem	600
Sec	R Millar
Pro	None
Holes	18 L 5574 metres SSS 70
Recs	Am–67 D Robinson (1992)
V'tors	U SOC
Fees	D–£12 (£15)
Loc	1 mile SE of Enniskillen, on Castlecoole Estate
Arch	TJ McAuley

Co Galway

Athenry (1902)

Palmerstown, Oranmore

Tel	**(091) 794466/790765**
Fax	(091) 794971
Mem	700
Sec	P Flattery (091) 753772
Pro	D Cunningham (091) 790843
Holes	18 L 6100 yds SSS 69
Recs	Am–69 S McCormack (1995)
V'tors	WD/Sat–U Sun–M SOC
Fees	£15
Loc	10 miles E of Galway on Athenry road
Arch	Eddie Hackett

Ballinasloe (1894)

Rossgloss, Ballinasloe

Tel	**(0905) 42126**
Fax	(0905) 42538
Mem	800
Sec	J Millane
Holes	18 L 5865 metres SSS 70
Recs	Am–64 M Quinn
	Pro–66 C O'Connor
	Ladies–68 M Madden
V'tors	U SOC
Fees	£14
Loc	Ballinasloe 2 miles
Arch	Eddie Hackett

Bearna (1996)

Corboley, Bearna

Tel	**(091) 592677**
Sec	K Cantrell (Hon)
Holes	18 L 5746 m Par 72 SSS 72
V'tors	U
Fees	On application

Connemara (1973)

Ballyconnelly, Clifden

Tel	**(095) 23502/23602**
Fax	(095) 23662
Mem	700
Sec	J McLaughlin (Sec/Mgr)
Pro	H O'Neill (095) 23502
Holes	18 L 6560 metres SSS 72
Recs	Am–67 D Mortimer (1996)
	Pro–68
V'tors	U H SOC
Fees	£25
Loc	8 miles SW of Clifden
Arch	Eddie Hackett

Connemara Isles

Annaghvane, Lettermore, Connemara

Tel	**(091) 572498**
Fax	(091) 572214
Mem	95
Sec	P O'Conghaile (Sec/Mgr)
Holes	9 L 5168 yds Par 70 SSS 67
Recs	Am–PO Suilleabhain (1997)
V'tors	U SOC
Fees	£10
Loc	3 miles W of Costello
Arch	Craddock/Ruddy

Galway (1895)

Blackrock, Salthill, Galway

Tel	**(091) 522033**
Fax	(091) 522033
Mem	1020
Sec	P Fahy
Pro	D Wallace (091) 523038
Holes	18 L 5828 metres SSS 70
V'tors	Restricted Tues & Sun
Fees	£18 (£23)
Loc	3 miles W of Galway City

Galway Bay G&CC (1993)

Renville, Oranmore

Tel	**(091) 790500**
Fax	(091) 790510
Mem	400
Sec	R Counihan
Pro	E O'Connor (091) 790503
Holes	18 L 6350 metres SSS 73
V'tors	U H SOC
Fees	£25–£35
Loc	10 miles E of Galway City (N18)
Mis	Driving range. Golf Academy
Arch	C O'Connor Jr

Gort (1924)

Castlequarter, Gort

Tel	**(091) 632244**
Mem	460
Sec	S Devlin (Hon) (091) 631281
Pro	None
Holes	18 L 5979 metres SSS 71
V'tors	U exc Sun am SOC
Fees	£12 (£12)
Loc	20 miles S of Galway
Arch	C O'Connor Jr

Loughrea (1924)

Graigue, Loughrea

Tel	**(091) 41049**
Mem	400
Sec	C McGuinness (Hon)
Holes	18 L 5613 yds SSS 68
Recs	Am–67 S Glynn
V'tors	U SOC
Fees	On application
Loc	1 mile N of Loughrea, off Dublin–Galway road. 20 miles E of Galway
Arch	Eddie Hackett

Mountbellew (1929)

Mountbellew, Ballinasloe

Tel	**(0905) 79259**
Mem	300
Holes	9 L 5564 yds SSS 66
Recs	Am–68 I Hayden
V'tors	U SOC
Fees	On application
Loc	50km NE of Galway on N63

Oughterard (1973)

Gortreevagh, Oughterard

Tel	**(091) 552131**
Fax	(091) 552733
Mem	850
Sec	J Waters (Hon)
Pro	M Ryan (Ext 226)
Holes	18 L 6150 yds SSS 69
Recs	Am–67 T Hargrove (1995)
V'tors	U SOC
Fees	£15
Loc	15 miles NW of Galway on N59
Arch	Harris

Portumna (1907)

Ennis Road, Portumna

Tel	**(0509) 41059**
Mem	570

Sec R Clarke (Hon)
Holes 18 L 5474 metres Par 68
SSS 67
Recs Am–68 W Carty (1995),
S Breen (1996)
Pro–63 H Bradshaw
V'tors U SOC
Fees £12
Loc 40 miles SE of Galway on
Lough Derg

Tuam (1907)

Barnacurragh, Tuam
Tel **(093) 28993**
Fax (093) 26003
Mem 700
Sec V Gaffney (Sec/Mgr)
Pro L Smyth (093) 24091
Holes 18 L 5944 metres SSS 71
Recs Am–68 D Williams (1996)
Pro–68 R Rafferty (1983)
V'tors Sun–NA SOC–WD
Fees £10
Loc 20 miles N of Galway
Arch Eddie Hackett

Co Kerry

Ardfert (1993)

Sackville, Ardfert, Tralee
Tel **(066) 34744**
Fax (066) 34744
Mem 171
Sec Sinead Maunsell
Pro N Cassidy
Holes 9 hole course
V'tors U
Fees 9 holes–£9; 18 holes–£14
Loc 60 miles NW of Tralee
(R551)
Mis Driving range
Arch James Healy

Ballybunion (1893)

Sandhill Road, Ballybunion
Tel **(068) 27146**
Fax (068) 27387
Mem 648
Sec J McKenna (Sec/Mgr)
Pro B O'Callaghan
Holes Old 18 L 6542 yds SSS 72
Cashen 18 L 6477 yds SSS 70
Recs Am–67 P Mulcare
V'tors U SOC
Fees Old–£55; New–£30;
Old+New D–£72
Loc 2 miles S of Ballybunion.
50 miles W of Limerick,
via Tarbert

Ballyheigue Castle
(1995)

Ballyheigue, Tralee
Tel **(066) 33555**
Fax (066) 33147
Mem 180
Sec JP Broderick (Mgr)
Holes 9 L 6292 m Par 72 SSS 74
V'tors U

Fees £17
Loc 15 miles NW of Tralee (R551)

Beaufort (1994)

Churchtown, Beaufort, Killarney
Tel **(064) 44440**
Fax (064) 44752
Mem 180
Sec C Kelly
Pro H Duggan
Holes 18 L 6605 yds Par 71 SSS 72
V'tors WD–H SOC
Fees £25 (£30)
Loc 7 miles W of Killarney,
off N72
Arch Dr Arthur Spring

Castlegregory

Stradbally, Castlegregory
Tel **(066) 39444**
Mem 296
Sec M Moloney (Sec/Mgr)
Holes 9 L 5340 metres SSS 68
V'tors U SOC
Fees £14 (£14)
Loc 18 miles W of Tralee
Arch Arthur Spring

Ceann Sibeal (1924)

Ballyferriter
Tel **(066) 56255/56408**
Fax (066) 56409
Mem 460
Pro D O'Connor
Holes 18 L 6690 yds SSS 71
V'tors U SOC
Fees D–£22 W–£100
Loc Dingle Peninsula,
W of Tralee
Arch Hackett/O'Connor Jr

Dooks (1889)

Glenbeigh
Tel **(066) 68205/68200**
Fax (066) 68476
Mem 585
Sec M Shanahan (Sec/Mgr)
(066) 67370
Holes 18 L 5346 metres SSS 68
Recs Am–72 MI McGillicuddy
(1992)
V'tors WD–U H before 5pm
WE/BH–phone first SOC
Fees £20 (£20)
Loc 3 miles N of Glenbeigh, on
Ring of Kerry

Kenmare (1903)

Kenmare
Tel **(064) 41291**
Fax (064) 42061
Mem 349
Sec M MacGearailt
Pro None
Holes 18 L 5441 metres SSS 69
V'tors U SOC
Fees £15 (£18)
Loc 20 miles S of Killarney on
Cork road
Arch Eddie Hackett

Kerries (1995)

Tralee
Tel **(066) 22112**
Mem 280
Sec M Barrett (Mgr)
Holes 9 L 2718 m Par 35 SSS 39
V'tors U
Fees £14

Killarney (1893)

Mahoney's Point, Killarney
Tel **(064) 31034**
Fax (064) 33065
Mem 1500
Sec T Prendergast
Pro T Coveney (064) 31615
Holes Mahoney's Point 18 L
6164 metres SSS 72
Killeen 18 L 6475 metres
SSS 73
Recs Mahoney's Point Am–68
S Coyne (1968)
Killeen Am–73 DF O'Sullivan
Pro–65 D Feherty
V'tors H SOC
Fees £38
Loc 3 miles W of Killarney (R562)
Mis Lackabane course open
May 1999
Arch Mahoney's Point: Longhurst/
Campbell; Killeen: Hackett/
O'Sullivan

Killorglin (1992)

Steelroe, Killorglin
Tel **(066) 61979**
Fax (066) 61437
Mem 230
Sec B Dodd
Pro None
Holes 18 L 6464 yds SSS 72
Recs Am–64 S Harmon (1997)
V'tors U SOC
Fees IR£14 (IR£16)
Loc 1 mile from Killorglin on
Tralee road (N70). 12 miles
W of Killarney
Arch Eddie Hackett

Parknasilla (1974)

Parknasilla, Sneem
Tel **(064) 45122**
Fax (064) 45323
Mem 110
Sec M Walsh
Holes 9 L 6044 yds Par 72 SSS 70
V'tors U
Fees £12
Loc Great Southern Hotel, 2 miles
E of Sneem on Ring of Kerry
Mis Driving range

Ross (1995)

Ross Road, Killarney
Tel **(064) 31125**
Fax (064) 31860
Mem 80
Sec M Doyle (Mgr)
Holes 9 L 5674 m Par 72 SSS 72
V'tors U
Fees £15

For list of abbreviations see page 479

Tralee (1896)

West Barrow, Ardfert
Tel (066) 36379
Fax (066) 36008
Mem 1000
Pro None
Holes 18 L 6252 metres SSS 71
Recs Am–66 G O'Sullivan (1987)
V'tors WD–U H before 4.30pm exc
Wed–restricted WE/BH–NA
exc 11–12.30–H SOC–WD
Fees £30 (£40)
Loc 8 miles NW of Tralee on
Spa/Fenit road
Arch Arnold Palmer

Waterville (1889)

Ring of Kerry, Waterville
Tel (066) 74102
Fax (066) 74482
Mem 320
Sec N Cronin
Pro L Higgins
Holes 18 L 7184 yds SSS 74
Recs Pro–65 L Higgins
V'tors U H SOC
Fees £50
Loc ¼ mile N of Waterville on
Ring of Kerry
Mis Driving range
Arch Hackett/Mulcahy

Co Kildare

Athy (1906)

Geraldine, Athy
Tel (0507) 31729
Mem 350
Holes 18 L 6308 yds SSS 70
V'tors WD–U Sat–M SOC
Fees £10 (£15)
Loc 1 mile N of Athy on Kildare
road

Bodenstown (1983)

Bodenstown, Sallins
Tel (045) 97096
Mem 650
Sec P Cunningham (Hon)
Holes Old 18 L 6132 metres SSS 71
Ladyhill 18 L 5278 metres
SSS 68
Recs Am–71 J Gray (1991)
V'tors U exc WE–NA (Old course)
Fees Old–£10; Ladyhill–£9
Loc 4 miles N of Naas on Clane
road. 18 miles W of Dublin,
off N7

Castlewarden G&CC (1989)

Straffan
Tel (01) 458 9254
Fax (01) 458 9254
Mem 550 200(L)
Sec J Ferriter (Hon)
Pro G Egan (01) 458 8219

Holes 18 L 6624 yds Par 72 SSS 71
V'tors WD–U WE–M SOC
Fees £17
Loc 13 miles W of Dublin, off N4
Arch Halpin/Browne

Cill Dara (1920)

Little Curragh, Kildare Town
Tel (045) 521433/521295
Mem 400
Sec P Flanagan (Hon)
Pro M O'Boyle
Holes 9 L 5842 metres SSS 70
Recs Am–67 T Royce, P Doyle
(1989)
V'tors WD–U before 2pm exc
Wed–NA Sat–NA after noon
Sun/BH–NA SOC
Fees £10 (£12)
Loc 1 mile W of Kildare town

Craddockstown (1983)

Craddockstown, Naas
Tel (045) 97610
Mem 580
Holes 18 L 6134 metres Par 71
SSS 72
V'tors U
Fees £12 (£15)
Loc Naas

The Curragh (1883)

Curragh
Tel (045) 441238/441714
Mem 500 160(L)
Sec Ann Culleton
(045) 441714
Pro G Burke (045) 441896
Holes 18 L 6035 metres SSS 70
Recs Am–63 I Stewart (1997)
Pro–63 L Walker (1997)
Ladies–68 L Behan (1997)
V'tors WD–check with Sec
Fees On application
Loc 3 miles S of Newbridge

Highfield (1992)

Highfield House, Carbury
Tel (0405) 31021
Fax (0405) 31021
Mem 450
Sec P Duggan (Sec/Mgr)
Pro None
Holes 18 L 5707 m SSS 69
V'tors WD–U WE–U after 10am
Fees £8 (£12)
Loc 32 miles W of Dublin on N4
Arch Alan Duggan

The K Club (1991)

Kildare Hotel & CC, Straffan
Tel (01) 601 7300
Fax (01) 601 7399
Mem 527
Sec P Crowe (Golf Dir)
Pro E Jones
Holes 18 L 7200 yds SSS 72
Recs Pro–64 C Montgomerie
(1997)
V'tors U H SOC–WD

Fees IR£120
Loc 18 miles SW of Dublin (N7)
Mis Driving range
Arch Arnold Palmer

Killeen (1986)

Killeenbeg, Kill
Tel (045) 866003
Fax (045) 875881
Mem 300
Sec P Carey
Pro None
Holes 18 L 5815 metres Par 71
SSS 70
V'tors WD–U WE–NA before 10am
Fees £13 (£15)
Loc 2 miles off N7 on Sallins road
Arch Ruddy/Craddock

Knockanally (1985)

Donadea, North Kildare
Tel (045) 869322
Fax (045) 869322
Mem 500
Sec N Lyons
Holes 18 L 6424 yds SSS 71
Recs Pro–66 K O'Donnell, D James
(1988)
V'tors U
Fees £18 (£22)
Loc 20 miles W of Dublin on
Galway road (M4)
Arch N Lyons

Leixlip (1994)

Leixlip
Tel (01) 624 4978
Fax (01) 624 6185
Mem 180
Sec J McKone
Holes 9 L 5920 yds Par 72 SSS 70
V'tors U
Fees £13 (£15)
Loc 10 miles W of Dublin on N4
Arch Eddie Hackett

Naas (1896)

Kerdiffstown, Naas
Tel (045) 874644
Fax (045) 874644
Mem 514
Sec M Conway
Holes 18 L 5660 metres SSS 70
V'tors U SOC
Fees £15 (£20)
Loc 2 miles N of Naas
Arch Arthur Spring

Woodlands (1985)

Coill Dubh, Naas
Tel (045) 860777
Mem 325
Sec J Russell
Holes 9 L 5600 metres SSS 66
V'tors U
Fees £6 (£7)
Loc Naas

For list of abbreviations see page 479

Co Kilkenny

Callan (1929)
Geraldine, Callan
Tel   **(056) 25136**
Mem   350
Sec   M Duggan (Hon)
Holes 9 L 5844 yds SSS 68
Recs   Am–70 J Madden
       Pro–71 M Kavanagh
V'tors U SOC
Fees   £8
Loc   1 mile SE of Callan. 10 miles
       SW of Kilkenny

Castlecomer (1935)
Dromgoole, Castlecomer
Tel   **(056) 41139**
Mem   425
Sec   M Doheny (Hon)
Holes 9 L 5923 metres SSS 71
Recs   Am–69 K Kenny (1994)
V'tors U
Fees   £8 (£10)
Loc   11 miles N of Kilkenny

Kilkenny (1896)
Glendine, Kilkenny
Tel   **(056) 65400**
Fax   (056) 65400
Mem   950
Sec   S O'Neill (056) 65400
Pro   N Leahy (056) 61730
Holes 18 L 6435 yds SSS 70
Recs   Am–64 G Stewart
       Pro–68 B Todd
V'tors U
Fees   £20 (£22)
Loc   1 mile N of Kilkenny

Mount Juliet (1991)
Thomastown
Tel   **(056) 24455**
Fax   (056) 24522
Sec   T Judge
Pro   M Reid
Holes 18 L 7143 yds SSS 74
Recs   Pro–65 N Faldo (1993)
V'tors U
Fees   £70 (£75)
Loc   10 miles S of Kilkenny, off
       Dublin–Waterford road.
Mis   Driving range–residents and
       green fees. Golf Academy
Arch   Jack Nicklaus

Co Laois

Abbeyleix (1895)
Rathmoyle, Abbeyleix
Tel   **(0502) 31450**
Mem   280
Sec   GP O'Hara (Hon)
Holes 9 L 5680 yds SSS 69
V'tors WD–U WE–NA SOC–WD/
       Sat
Fees   £8 (£10)

Loc   10 miles S of Portlaoise.
       60 miles SW of Dublin on
       Cork road

Heath (Portlaoise)
(1930)
The Heath, Portlaoise
Tel   **(0502) 46533**
Mem   540
Sec   P Malone (0502) 21074
Pro   E Doyle (0502) 46622
Holes 18 L 6247 yds SSS 70
Recs   Am–67 T Tyrrell (1983)
V'tors U
Fees   On application
Loc   4 miles E of Portlaoise
Mis   Floodlit driving range

Mountrath (1929)
Knockanina, Mountrath
Tel   **(0502) 32558**
Mem   400
Sec   J Mulhare (0502) 32421
Holes 18 L 6020 yds Par 71 SSS 69
Recs   Am–68 S Carter
V'tors U
Fees   £10
Loc   10 miles W of Portlaoise.
       Mountrath 2 miles

Portarlington (1909)
Garryhinch, Portarlington
Tel   **(0502) 23115**
Fax   (0502) 23044
Mem   450
Sec   M Turley (Hon)
Holes 18 L 6004 metres Par 72
       SSS 71
Recs   Am–70 M Turley (1997)
V'tors WD–U WE–restricted
Fees   £14 (£17)
Loc   Between Portarlington and
       Mountmellick on L116

Rathdowney (1931)
Coulnaboul West, Rathdowney
Tel   **(0505) 46170**
Mem   181
Sec   S Bolger (Hon)
Holes 9 L 6086 yds Par 70 SSS 69
Recs   Am–71 J O'Malley
V'tors U exc Sun–NA SOC
Fees   £6
Loc   1 mile S of Rathdowney.
       20 miles SW of Portlaoise
Arch   Eddie Hackett

Co Leitrim

Ballinamore (1941)
Creevy, Ballinamore
Tel   **(078) 44346**
Mem   86
Sec   P Duignan (Hon)
Holes 9 L 5204 yds SSS 66
Recs   Am–68 D Gannon
V'tors U SOC

Fees   D–£5
Loc   2 miles N of Ballinamore.
       20 miles NE of
       Carrick–on–Shannon

Carrick–on–Shannon
(1910)
Woodbrook, Carrick–on–Shannon
Tel   **(079) 67015**
Mem   210
Sec   A McNally (Sec/Mgr)
Holes 9 L 5584 yds SSS 68
V'tors U
Fees   IR£12
Loc   4 miles W of Carrick–on–
       Shannon on N4

Co Limerick

Abbeyfeale (1993)
Dromtrasna Collins, Abbeyfeale
Tel   **(068) 32033**
Mem   85
Sec   M O'Riordan (Mgr)
Pro   D Power
Holes 9 L 4004 yds Par 62 SSS 61
V'tors U
Fees   £6
Loc   12 miles SW of Newcastle
       West

Adare Manor (1900)
Adare
Tel   **(061) 396204**
Mem   580
Sec   TR Healy (Hon)
Holes 18 L 5396 metres SSS 69
V'tors WD–U WE–M
Fees   D–£15
Loc   10 miles SW of Limerick

Castletroy (1937)
Castletroy, Limerick
Tel   **(061) 335261**
Fax   (061) 335373
Mem   940
Sec   L Hayes (061) 335753
Pro   (061) 338283 (Shop)
Holes 18 L 5793 metres SSS 71
V'tors WD–U Sat am–U Sat
       pm/Sun–M
       SOC–Mon/Wed/Fri
Fees   £22 (£22)
Loc   2 miles N of Limerick on
       Dublin road

Killeline (1993)
Newcastle West
Tel   **(069) 61600**
Fax   (069) 62853
Mem   278
Sec   J McCoy
Holes 18 L 6700 yds Par 72
V'tors U
Fees   £12

Limerick (1891)

Ballyclough, Limerick

Tel	(061) 414083
Fax	(061) 415146
Mem	1325
Sec	D McDonogh (061) 415146
Pro	J Cassidy (061) 412492
Holes	18 L 6479 yds SSS 71
Recs	Am–68 M Morrissey (1994)
	Pro–67 P Broadhurst (1995)
V'tors	WD–U before 5pm exc Tues
	WE–M SOC–WD
Fees	£22.50
Loc	3 miles S of Limerick

Limerick County G&CC

Ballyneety

Tel	(061) 351881
Fax	(061) 351384
Mem	250
Sec	Vari McGreevy (Mgr)
Pro	P Murphy
Holes	18 L 6137 metres Par 72 SSS 74
V'tors	U SOC
Fees	£20 (£25)
Loc	5 miles S of Limerick (R512)
Mis	Driving range
Arch	Des Smyth

Newcastle West (1938)

Ardagh

Tel	(069) 76500
Fax	(069) 76511
Mem	450 112(L)
Sec	P Lyons (Sec/Mgr)
Holes	18 L 5905 metres SSS 72
Recs	Am–61 A Spring (1996)
V'tors	U exc Sun–U after 4pm SOC
Fees	£18
Loc	6 miles N of Newcastle West, off N21
Mis	Floodlit driving range
Arch	Arthur Spring

Co Londonderry

Benone Par Three

53 Benone Avenue, Benone, Limavady BT49 0LQ

Tel	(015047) 50555
Sec	CL Smith
Holes	9 L 1427 yds Par 3 course
V'tors	U
Fees	On application
Loc	12 miles N of Limavady on A2 coast road

Brown Trout (1984)

209 Agivey Road, Aghadowey, Coleraine

Tel	(01265) 868209
Fax	(01265) 868878
Mem	210
Sec	B O'Hara (Sec/Mgr)
Pro	K Revie
Holes	9 L 2800 yds SSS 68
Recs	Am–64 D Mulholland
V'tors	U SOC

Fees	£10 (£15)
Loc	8 miles S of Coleraine at junction of A54/B66
Arch	W O'Hara Sr

Castlerock (1901)

Circular Road, Castlerock BT51 4TJ

Tel	(01265) 848314
Fax	(01265) 848314
Mem	1100
Sec	RG McBride
Pro	`. Kelly
Holes	18 L 6121 metres SSS 72
	9 L 2457 metres SSS 34
Recs	Am–67 D Mulholland
V'tors	WD–U exc Fri SOC
Fees	18 hole: £25 (£35)
	9 hole: £8 (£12)
Loc	5 miles W of Coleraine on A2
Arch	Ben Sayers

City of Derry (1912)

49 Victoria Road, Londonderry BT47 2PU

Tel	(01504) 311610/46369
Mem	692
Sec	PJ Doherty
Pro	M Doherty
	(01504) 311496
Holes	Prehen 18 L 6487 yds SSS 71
	Dunhugh 9 L 4708 yds SSS 63
Recs	Am–68 D Ballentine
V'tors	WD–U before 4pm –M after 4pm WE–U H SOC
Fees	Prehen £11 (£13)
	Dunhugh £5
Loc	3 miles from E end of Craigavon Bridge towards Strabane

Foyle (1994)

Alder Road, Londonderry BT48 8DB

Tel	(01504) 352222
Fax	(01504) 353967
Mem	177
Sec	M Lapsley
Pro	K McLaughlin
Holes	18 L 6678 metres SSS 72
	9 hole course
V'tors	U
Fees	£12 (£15)
Loc	Londonderry
Mis	Driving range
Arch	Frank Ainsworth

Kilrea (1920)

Drumagarner Road, Kilrea

Tel	(01266) 821048
Mem	310
Sec	DP Clarke
Holes	9 L 4532 yds SSS 62
Recs	Am–61 R Rees (1982), T Moore (1989)
V'tors	Tues & Wed–NA after 5pm Sat–NA after 12 noon
Fees	£10 (£12.50)
Loc	Nr Kilrea on Maghera road. 15 miles S of Coleraine

Moyola Park (1976)

15 Curran Road, Castledawson, Magherafelt BT45 8DG

Tel	(01648) 468468
Fax	(01648) 468468
Mem	940
Sec	LWP Hastings (Hon)
Pro	V Teague (01648) 468830
Holes	18 L 6062 yds Par 71
Recs	Am–67 R Evans
	Pro–67 J Loughrey
V'tors	U SOC exc Sat
Fees	£16 (£25)
Loc	40 miles NW of Belfast by M2. 35 miles S of Coleraine
Arch	Don Patterson

Portstewart (1894)

117 Strand Road, Portstewart BT55 7PG

Tel	(01265) 832015
Fax	(01265) 834097
Mem	1524
Sec	M Moss BA
	(01265) 833839
Pro	A Hunter (01265) 832601
Holes	Strand 18 L 6784 yds SSS 73
	Riverside 9 L 2662 yds Par 32
	Town 18 L 4733 yds SSS 62
Recs	Strand Am–67 D Ballentine, M Kilgore (1997)
V'tors	SOC–by arrangement
Fees	Strand–£40 (£60); Riverside–£10 (£15); Town £8 (£12)
Loc	W boundary of Portstewart. N of Coleraine

Roe Park (1993)

Limavaddy BT49 9LB

Tel	(015047) 22212
Mem	300
Sec	D Brockerton
Pro	S Duffy
Holes	18 L 6318 yds Par 70 SSS 71
V'tors	U
Fees	£16 (£20)
Loc	Limavaddy

Co Longford

County Longford (1900)

Glack, Dublin Road, Longford

Tel	(043) 46310
Fax	(043) 47082
Mem	327
Sec	M Connellan
Pro	None
Holes	18 L 6008 yds SSS 69
Recs	Am–P Mitchell
V'tors	U SOC
Fees	On application
Loc	Longford ½ mile on Dublin road
Arch	Eddie Hackett

Co Louth

Ardee (1911)
Ardee
Tel   (041) 53227/56283
Fax   (041) 56137
Mem   650
Sec   K McCarthy (Sec/Mgr)
          (041) 53227
Holes 18 L 6348 yds SSS 71
Recs   Am–67 J Carroll
          Pro–70 C O'Connor
V'tors U SOC
Fees   £17 (£17)
Loc   ½ mile N of Ardee
Arch   Eddie Hackett

County Louth (1892)
Baltray, Drogheda
Tel   (041) 22327
Fax   (041) 22969
Mem   1055
Sec   M Delany (041) 22329
Pro   P McGuirk (041) 22444
Holes 18 L 6783 yds SSS 72
Recs   Am–66 R Burns
          Pro–67 P Cowen
V'tors By prior arrangement
Fees   On request
Loc   3 miles NE of Drogheda
Arch   Tom Simpson

Dundalk (1905)
Blackrock, Dundalk
Tel   (042) 21731
Fax   (042) 22022
Mem   850
Sec   J Carroll (042) 21731
Pro   J Cassidy (042) 22102
Holes 18 L 6115 metres SSS 72
V'tors U SOC
Fees   £17 (£21)
Loc   3 miles S of Dundalk

Greenore (1896)
Greenore
Tel   (042) 73212
Fax   (042) 73678
Mem   500
Sec   B Rafferty (Sec/Mgr)
Holes 18 L 6506 yds SSS 71
Recs   Am–68 E McCarten
          Pro–68 A Cardwell
V'tors WD–U before 5pm
          WE/BH–by arrangement
          SOC
Fees   £12 (£18)
Loc   15 miles E of Dundalk on
          Carlingford Lough
Arch   Eddie Hackett

Killinbeg (1991)
Killin Park, Dundalk
Tel   (042) 39303
Mem   100
Sec   D Bell (Sec/Mgr)
Pro   None
Holes 12 L 3322 yds SSS 69
V'tors U SOC

Fees   £7 (£10)
Loc   2 miles NW of Dundalk on
          Castletown road

Seapoint (1993)
Termonfeckin, Drogheda
Tel   (041) 22333
Fax   (041) 22331
Mem   300
Sec   S Kelly (Mgr)
Pro   D Carroll
Holes 18 L 5900 metres SSS 71
Recs   Am–72 D Branigan (1993)
V'tors U SOC
Fees   £22.50 (£27.50)
Loc   5 miles NE of Drogheda
          (R166)
Arch   Smyth/Branigan

Towneley Hall (1994)
Tullyallen, Drogheda
Tel   (041) 42229
Fax   (041) 31762
Mem   125
Sec   J Grennan (Hon)
Holes 9 L 5221 m Par 71 SSS 69
V'tors U
Fees   £6 (£7)
Loc   5 miles NW of Drogheda,
          off R168

Co Mayo

Achill Island (1951)
Keel, Achill
Tel   (098) 43456
Mem   100
Sec   P Lavelle (Hon)
Holes 9 L 2689 metres Par 70 SSS 67
Recs   Am–69 J Lawlor (1990)
V'tors U H SOC
Fees   On application
Loc   50 miles NW of Westport, on
          Achill Island
Arch   P Skerritt

Ashford Castle
Cong
Tel   (092) 46003
Holes 9 L 4500 yds SSS 68
V'tors U SOC
Fees   £15
Loc   25 miles N of Galway on
          Lough Corrib
Arch   Eddie Hackett

Ballina (1910)
Mossgrove, Shanaghy, Ballina
Tel   (096) 21050
Fax   (096) 21050
Mem   460
Sec   V Frawley (096) 21795
Holes 18 L 6103 yds SSS 69
Recs   Am–69 N Dee (1996)
V'tors WD–U Sun–NA before noon
          SOC–WD
Fees   £12 (£16)
Loc   1 mile E of Ballina

Ballinrobe (1895)
Castlebar Road, Ballinrobe
Tel   (092) 41448
Mem   300
Sec   P Holian (092) 41659
Holes 9 L 5790 yds SSS 68
Recs   Am–67 B Finlay
V'tors U exc Sun–NA SOC
Fees   D–£10 W–£40
Loc   2 miles NW of Ballinrobe

Ballyhaunis (1929)
Coolnaha, Ballyhaunis
Tel   (0907) 30014
Mem   300
Sec   JG Forde (Hon)
Holes 9 L 5413 metres Par 70 SSS 68
Recs   Am–69 P Charlton (1995)
V'tors U exc Thurs (Ladies Day)–M
          Sun–NA SOC–WD
Fees   £8
Loc   2 miles N of Ballyhaunis

Belmullet (1925)
Carne, Belmullet
Tel   (097) 82292/81051
Fax   (097) 81477
Mem   300
Sec   A Valkenburg (097) 82292
Holes 18 L 6119 metres SSS 72
V'tors U SOC
Fees   £17 W–£70
Loc   2 miles W of Belmullet.
          40 miles W of Ballina
Arch   Eddie Hackett

Castlebar (1910)
Rocklands, Castlebar
Tel   (094) 21649
Fax   (094) 26088
Mem   650
Holes 18 L 6229 yds SSS 70
Recs   Am–67 D Kelly
V'tors U exc Sun
Fees   £12 (£15)
Loc   1 mile S of Castlebar, on
          Galway road

Claremorris (1917)
Castlemagarrett, Claremorris
Tel   (094) 71527
Mem   270
Sec   W Feeley (Hon)
Pro   D Kearney
Holes 9 L 6454 yds SSS 69
Recs   Am–66 P Killeen
          Pro–63 C O'Connor
V'tors WD–U before noon Sat–U
          before noon SOC
Fees   £8 (£10)
Loc   2 miles S of Claremorris (N17)
Mis   Extension to 18 holes April
          1998
Arch   Tom Craddock

Mulrany (1968)
Mulrany, Westport
Tel   (098) 36262
Mem   100
Sec   D Nevin (Hon)

Holes 9 L 6255 yds Par 71 SSS 69
V'tors U
Fees D–£8
Loc 20 miles NW of Castlebar

Swinford (1922)
Brabazon Park, Swinford
Tel (094) 51378
Mem 300
Sec T Regan (094) 51502
Holes 9 L 5901 yds SSS 68
Recs Am–70 B Finlay (1991)
V'tors U SOC–exc Sun
Fees D–£10 (£15)
Loc S of Swinford, off Kiltimagh road

Westport (1908)
Carowholly, Westport
Tel (098) 28262/27070
Fax (098) 27217
Mem 700
Sec P Smyth (Mgr)
Pro A Mealia
Holes 18 L 6653 yds SSS 72
Recs Am–65 L Gibbons (1984)
V'tors U SOC
Fees £18 (£23)
Loc 2 miles W of Westport
Arch F Hawtree

Co Meath

Ashbourne (1991)
Archerstown, Ashbourne
Tel (01) 835 2005
Mem 645
Sec R Sheehan
Holes 18 L 5778 metres Par 71 SSS 70
V'tors WD–U WE–NA before 1pm SOC
Fees £17 (£17)
Loc 12 miles N of Dublin, off N2
Arch Des Smyth

The Black Bush (1987)
Thomastown, Dunshaughlin
Tel (01) 825 0021
Mem 900
Sec I Yorston
Pro None
Holes 18 L 6930 yds SSS 73
9 L 2800 yds SSS 35
V'tors WD–U WE–NA before 4pm SOC
Fees On application
Loc 1 mile E of Dunshaughlin, off N3. 20 miles NW of Dublin
Mis Driving range for members and green fees
Arch Robert J Browne

County Meath (1898)
Newtownmoynagh, Trim
Tel (046) 31463
Fax (046) 37554
Mem 500

Sec JJ Ennis (046) 31825
Pro None
Holes 18 L 6720 yds SSS 72
Recs Am–68 P Rayfus
V'tors WD–U exc Ladies day
WE–restricted SOC–exc Sun
Fees £15 (£18)
Loc 2 miles SW of Trim. 25 miles NW of Dublin
Arch Hackett/Craddock

Gormanston College (1961)
Franciscan College, Gormanston
Tel (01) 841 2203
Fax (01) 841 2874
Mem 160
Sec Br Laurence Brady
Pro B Browne
Holes 9 L 1973 metres
Recs Am–60 G Ormsby (1992)
V'tors NA
Loc 22 miles N of Dublin

Headfort (1928)
Kells
Tel (046) 40857
Fax (046) 49282
Mem 993
Sec Enda Carroll (046) 40146
Pro B McGovern (046) 40639
Holes 18 L 6007 metres SSS 71
Recs Am–67 D McGrane (1990)
Pro–64 D Smyth (1973)
V'tors U SOC exc Sun
Fees £18 (£22)
Loc 65km NW of Dublin

Kilcock (1985)
Gallow, Kilcock
Tel (01) 628 7283
Mem 230
Sec F Reid (Hon)
Holes 9 L 5364 metres SSS 68
V'tors U
Fees £7 (£9)
Loc 20 miles W of Dublin (N4)

Laytown & Bettystown (1909)
Bettystown
Tel (041) 27170/27534
Fax (041) 28506
Mem 850
Sec Stella Garvey–Hoey
Pro RJ Browne (041) 28793
Holes 18 L 6254 yds SSS 69
V'tors U SOC–WD
Fees On application
Loc 25 miles N of Dublin

Moor Park (1993)
Mooretown, Navan
Tel (046) 27661
Mem 130
Sec M Fagan
Holes 18 L 5600 metres Par 72 SSS 69
V'tors U

Fees On application
Loc Navan

Royal Tara (1923)
Bellinter, Navan
Tel (046) 25244/25508/25584
Fax (046) 25508
Mem 1000
Sec P O'Brien
Pro A Whiston
Holes 18 L 5757 yds Par 71
9 L 3184 yds Par 35
Recs Am–66 M McQuaid
V'tors U
Fees £16 (£20)
Loc 25 miles N of Dublin, off N3

Co Monaghan

Castleblayney (1985)
Muckno Park, Castleblayney
Tel (042) 49485
Mem 275
Sec A McNally (042) 46570
Holes 9 L 2678 yds SSS 66
Recs Am–70 J McCarthy (1987)
V'tors U SOC
Fees £8 (£10)
Loc Castleblayney town centre. 18 miles SE of Monaghan
Arch R Browne

Clones (1913)
Hilton Park, Clones
Tel (049) 56017
Mem 245
Sec P McGrane (042) 42333
Holes 9 L 5790 yds SSS 68
Recs Am–64 D McGuigan
V'tors WD–U Sun–NA before noon
Fees £8 (£10)
Loc Hilton Park, 2½ miles from Clones

Mannan Castle (1993)
Donaghmoyne, Carrickmacross
Tel (042) 63308
Fax (042) 63195
Mem 340
Sec R Howell (042) 62531
Holes 9 L 6008 metres Par 72 SSS 71
V'tors U
Fees £10 (£10)
Loc 4 miles N of Carrickmacross

Nuremore (1964)
Nuremore, Carrickmacross
Tel (042) 61438
Mem 220
Pro M Cassidy
Holes 18 L 6246 yds SSS 74
V'tors U
Fees On application
Loc 1 mile S of Carrickmacross on Dublin road
Arch Eddie Hackett

Rossmore (1916)

Rossmore Park, Monaghan

Tel (047) 81316
Mem 500
Sec J McKenna (Hon)
Holes 18 L 6082 yds Par 70 SSS 68
Recs Am–64 R Berry
V'tors WD–U WE/BH–U SOC
Fees £15
Loc 2 miles S of Monaghan on Cootehill road
Arch Des Smyth

Co Offaly

Birr (1893)

The Glenns, Birr

Tel (0509) 20082
Mem 750
Sec J McMenamin (Hon)
Holes 18 L 6216 yds SSS 70
Recs Am–62 P Lawrie
Pro–68 RJ Browne
V'tors U SOC–exc Sun–NA 11.30–12
Fees £12 (£14)
Loc 2 miles W of Birr
Mis Driving range

Castlebarnagh (1992)

Daingean

Tel (0506) 53384
Mem 86
Sec E Mangan
Holes 18 L 5595 metres Par 71 SSS 69
V'tors U
Fees £6 (£8)
Loc 12 miles E of Tullamore (R402)

Edenderry (1910)

Kishavanna, Edenderry

Tel (0405) 31072
Mem 750
Sec N Dempsey (0405) 31575
Holes 18 L 6121 metres Par 72 SSS 72
Recs Am–66 J Brady (1995)
V'tors WD–U exc Thurs (Ladies Day) WE–restricted SOC
Fees £12 (£14)
Loc 1 mile E of Edenderry
Arch Havers/Hackett

Tullamore (1896)

Brookfield, Tullamore

Tel (0506) 21439
Mem 993
Sec A Marsden (Hon)
Pro D McArdle (0506) 51757
Holes 18 L 6322 yds SSS 70
Recs Am–64 D White
Pro–68 H Boyle, J Martin, D Jones
V'tors WD–U exc Tues (Ladies Day) Sat–M 12.30–3pm Sun–NA SOC

Fees £12 (£15)
Loc 2½ miles S of Tullamore, off Birr road
Arch James Braid

Co Roscommon

Athlone (1892)

Hodson Bay, Athlone

Tel (0902) 92073/92235
Fax (0902) 94080
Mem 900
Sec T Corry (Hon)
Pro M Quinn
Holes 18 L 5922 metres SSS 71
V'tors U SOC
Fees D–£15 (£18)
Loc 3 miles N of Athlone on Roscommon road
Arch F Hawtree

Ballaghaderreen (1937)

Aughalustia, Ballaghaderreen

Tel (0907) 60295
Mem 150
Sec B Clancy (Hon)
Holes 9 L 5663 yds SSS 66
V'tors U SOC
Fees £6
Loc Ballaghaderreen 3 miles
Arch P Skerritt

Boyle (1911)

Knockadoobrusna, Roscommon Road, Boyle

Tel (079) 62594
Mem 287
Sec P Nangle (Hon)
(079) 63288
Holes 9 L 4957 metres SSS 65
Recs Am–65 A Wynne (1987)
V'tors U SOC
Fees £7
Loc 1½ miles S of Boyle
Arch Eddie Hackett

Castlerea (1905)

Clonallis, Castlerea

Tel (0907) 20068/20705
Mem 200
Sec J Mulligan (Hon)
Holes 9 L 5466 yds SSS 66
Recs Am–63 R de Lacy Staunton
V'tors WD/Sat–U Sun–by arrangement
Fees £8 (£10)
Loc Knock Road, Castlerea

Roscommon (1904)

Moate Park, Roscommon

Tel (0903) 26382
Mem 500
Sec B Campbell (Hon)
Holes 18 L 6290 metres Par 72 SSS 69
Recs Am–64 K Kearney (1992)
V'tors WD–U WE/BH–restricted SOC

Fees £15 SOC–£10
Loc 1 mile S of Roscommon
Arch Eddie Connaughton

Strokestown (1992)

Cloonfinlough, Strokestown

Mem 150
Holes 9 L 5230 m Par 68 SSS 67
V'tors U
Fees £5
Loc 15 miles N of Roscommon (R368)

Co Sligo

Ballymote (1940)

Ballinascarron, Ballymote

Tel (071) 83158
Mem 250
Sec EJ Stagg (Hon)
Holes 9 L 5302 metres SSS 67
Recs Am–67 P Mullen
V'tors U
Fees D–£7 (£7)
Loc 15 miles S of Sligo

County Sligo (1894)

Rosses Point

Tel (071) 77134/77186
Fax (071) 77460
Mem 1169
Sec RG Dunne
Pro L Robinson (071) 77171
Holes 18 L 6037 metres SSS 72
Recs Am–66 F Howley (1991)
Pro–67 C O'Connor Sr (1975)
V'tors U–booking required
Fees £27 (£35)
Loc 5 miles NW of Sligo
Arch Colt/Allison

Enniscrone (1931)

Ballina Road, Enniscrone

Tel (096) 36297
Fax (096) 36657
Mem 700
Sec JM Fleming (Hon)
Pro C McGoldrick (096) 36666
Holes 18 L 6620 yds SSS 72
Recs Am–69 D Basquil
Pro–71 C O'Connor Sr, J O'Leary
V'tors WD–U WE/BH–phone first SOC
Fees D–£18 (£24)
Loc S of Enniscrone. Ballina 13 km
Mis Driving range
Arch Eddie Hackett

Strandhill (1932)

Strandhill

Tel (071) 68188
Fax (071) 68811
Mem 450
Sec Sandra Corcoran
(071) 68725
Holes 18 L 6032 yds Par 69 SSS 68

V'tors WD–U WE/BH–restricted
SOC
Fees IR£15 (IR£18)
Loc 6 miles W of Sligo

Tubbercurry (1990)

Ballymote Road, Tubbercurry
Tel (071) 85849
Mem 250
Sec B Kilgannon (071) 86124
Holes 9 L 5478 metres SSS 69
V'tors U
Fees £10
Loc 20 miles S of Sligo
Arch Eddie Hackett

Co Tipperary

Ballykisteen G&CC
(1994)

Monard
Tel (052) 51439
Mem 260
Sec Josephine Ryan
Pro D Reddan
Holes 18 L 6765 yds Par 72 SSS 73
V'tors U SOC–book in advance
Fees £20
Loc 3 miles W of Tipperary town
Mis Driving range
Arch Des Smyth

Cahir Park (1968)

Kilcommon, Cahir
Tel (052) 41474
Mem 187
Sec M Fitzgerald (Hon)
Pro D Foran
Holes 9 L 5690 yds SSS 69
Recs Am–68
V'tors U SOC–WD/Sat
Fees £10
Loc 1 mile S of Cahir
Arch Eddie Hackett

Carrick–on–Suir (1939)

Garravoone, Carrick–on–Suir
Tel (051) 640047
Fax (051) 640558
Mem 500
Sec A Murphy (Sec/Mgr)
Holes 18 L 6061 metres Par 72
SSS 70
V'tors U exc Sun–NA before 11am
SOC–WD/Sat
Fees £12 (£14)
Loc 2 miles S of Carrick on
Dungarvan road
Arch Eddie Hackett

Clonmel (1911)

Lyreanearla, Mountain Road, Clonmel
Tel (052) 21138/24050
Fax (052) 24050
Mem 931
Sec A Myles–Keating
(052) 24050
Pro R Hayes (052) 24050

Holes 18 L 6330 yds SSS 70
Recs Am–63 M O'Neill
V'tors WD–U WE–SOC
Fees £18 (£20)
Loc 2 miles SW of Clonmel
Arch Eddie Hackett

County Tipperary G&CC
(1993)

Dundrum House Hotel, Dundrum, Cashel
Tel (062) 71116
Fax (062) 71366
Mem 120
Sec W Crowe (Mgr)
Holes 18 L 6682 yds SSS 73
V'tors U SOC
Fees £15 (£20)
Loc 6 miles W of Cashel
Arch Philip Walton

Nenagh (1929)

Beechwood, Nenagh
Tel (067) 31476
Fax (067) 34808
Mem 700
Sec PJ Hayes (Hon)
Pro G Morrison (067) 33242
Holes 18 L 5483 metres Par 69
SSS 68
Recs Am–64 P Lyons (1984)
V'tors U SOC
Fees £15
Loc 3 miles NE of Nenagh on old
Birr road
Arch Dr A Mackenzie/Hackett

Roscrea (1892)

Derryvale, Roscrea
Tel (0505) 21130
Mem 350
Sec K McDonnell (Hon)
Holes 18 L 5706 metres SSS 70
V'tors U
Fees £10 (£12)
Loc 2 miles E of Roscrea on
Dublin road (N7)
Arch Arthur Spring

Templemore (1970)

Manna South, Templemore
Tel (0504) 31400
Mem 240
Sec JK Moloughney (Hon)
Holes 9 L 5442 yds SSS 67
Recs Am–68
V'tors U exc Sun SOC
Fees £5 (£10)
Loc ½ mile S of Templemore

Thurles (1909)

Turtulla, Thurles
Tel (0504) 21983
Fax (0504) 24647
Mem 850
Sec A Howell
Pro S Hunt
Holes 18 L 5904 metres SSS 71
Recs Am–66 DF O'Sullivan
Pro–70 H Bradshaw

V'tors U
Fees £18
Loc 1 mile S of Thurles

Tipperary (1896)

Rathanny, Tipperary
Tel (062) 51119
Mem 460
Sec J Considine (Hon)
Holes 9 L 5805 metres SSS 70
Recs Am–69
V'tors U SOC
Fees D–£10
Loc Tipperary 1 mile

Co Tyrone

Auchnacloy (1995)

99 Tullyvar Road, Auchnacloy
Tel (01662) 557050
Mem 146
Sec E Hadden (Mgr)
Holes 9 L 5017 metres Par 70
SSS 68
V'tors U
Fees £10 (£12)
Loc 12 miles SW of Dungannon
(B35)

Dungannon (1890)

34 Springfield Lane, Mullaghmore, Dungannon BT70 1QX
Tel (018687) 22098/27338
Mem 585
Sec LRP Agnew
Pro None
Holes 18 L 5818 yds SSS 68
Recs Am–68 D Fitzpatrick (1993)
V'tors U
Fees £15 (£18)
Loc 1 mile NW of Dungannon on
Donaghmore road

Fintona (1904)

Eccleville Desmesne, Fintona
Tel (01662) 841480/840777
Fax (01662) 841480
Mem 400
Sec D Montague (Hon)
Holes 9 L 5765 metres Par 72
SSS 70
Recs Am–68 E Donnell
Pro–69 L Higgins, J Kinsilla,
L Robinson
V'tors U exc comp days SOC
Fees £12 (£15)
Loc 8 miles S of Omagh

Killymoon (1889)

200 Killymoon Road, Cookstown BT80 8TW
Tel (016487) 63762/62254
Fax (016487) 63762
Mem 950
Sec B Rouse (016487) 63762
Pro (016487) 63460
Holes 18 L 5488 metres SSS 69

Recs Am–64 A O'Neill
Pro–65 D Smyth
V'tors U H SOC
Fees £14 (£18)
Loc 1 mile S of Cookstown, off
A29

Newtownstewart (1914)

*38 Golf Course Road, Newtownstewart
BT78 4HU*
Tel **(016626) 61466**
Fax (016626) 62506
Mem 700
Sec JE Mackin (016626) 71487
Pro None
Holes 18 L 5341 metres Par 70
SSS 69
Recs Am–65 G Forbes,
I Moore (1996)
Pro–66 J Fisher (1978)
V'tors WD–U WE–NA after noon
SOC
Fees £10 (£15)
Loc 2 miles SW of
Newtownstewart on B84

Omagh (1910)

*83A Dublin Road, Omagh
BT78 1HQ*
Tel **(01662) 243160/241442**
Mem 917
Sec Mrs FEA Caldwell,
JA McElholm
Pro None
Holes 18 L 5382 metres SSS 68
Recs Am–WR Barton (1993)
Ladies–61 BM Taylor (1992)
V'tors U SOC
Fees £10 (£15)
Loc ½ mile from Omagh on A5

Strabane (1908)

Ballycolman, Strabane BT82 9PH
Tel **(01504) 382271/382007**
Fax (01504) 382007
Mem 600
Sec E Kennedy (01504) 382007
Pro None
Holes 18 L 5552 metres SSS 69
Recs Am–63 E Kennedy
Pro–69
V'tors WD–U WE–by arrangement
SOC
Fees £10 (£12)
Loc ½ mile from Strabane,
nr Fir Trees Hotel

Co Waterford

Dungarvan (1924)

Knocknagranagh, Dungarvan
Tel **(058) 43310/41605**
Fax (058) 44113
Mem 600
Sec T Whelan
Pro (058) 44707
Holes 18 L 6134 metres Par 72
SSS 73
Recs Am–66 S Norris (1994)

V'tors U SOC
Fees £15 (£20)
Loc 2 miles E of Dungarvan on
N25. 25 miles W of Waterford
Arch Maurice Fives

Dunmore East (1993)

Dunmore East
Tel **(051) 383151**
Fax (051) 383151
Mem 300
Sec M Skehan
Holes 18 L 6655 yds Par 72 SSS 70
V'tors U
Fees £10 (£14)
Loc 10 miles S of Waterford
(R684)
Arch J O'Riordan

Faithlegg (1993)

Faithlegg House, Faithlegg
Tel **(051) 82241**
Fax (051) 82664
Mem 60
Sec V McGreevy (Golf Admin)
Pro T Higgins
Holes 18 L 6057 metres SSS 72
V'tors U SOC
Fees £20
Loc 6 miles E of Waterford City
on Dunmore East road
Arch Patrick Merrigan

Gold Coast (1993)

Ballinacourty, Dungarvan
Tel **(058) 42249/44055**
Fax (058) 43378
Mem 400
Sec T Considine (058) 44055
Pro None
Holes 18 L 6171 metres Par 72
SSS 72
V'tors U SOC
Fees £15 (£18)
Loc E of Dungarvan, off R675
Arch M Fives

Lismore (1965)

Ballyin, Lismore
Tel **(058) 54026**
Mem 250
Sec P Norris
Holes 9 L 5291 metres SSS 67
V'tors WD–U before 5pm –M after
5pm WE–phone first
SOC–exc Sun
Fees £8 (£10)
Loc 1 mile N of Lismore, off N72

Tramore (1894)

Newtown Hill, Tramore
Tel **(051) 386170/381247**
Fax (051) 390961
Mem 1396
Sec J Cox (Sec/Mgr)
Pro D Kiely
Holes 18 L 6055 metres SSS 73
Recs Am–66 E Power
Pro–66 H Boyle
V'tors U

Fees £25 (£30)
Loc 7 miles S of Waterford
Arch Capt Tippett

Waterford (1912)

Newrath, Waterford
Tel **(051) 74182**
Fax (051) 53405
Mem 961
Sec J Condon (Sec/Mgr)
(051) 76748
Pro E Condon (051) 54256
Holes 18 L 5722 metres SSS 70
Recs Am–65 J Morris (1992)
V'tors U
Fees £17 (£20)
Loc 1 mile N of Waterford (N25)
Arch Willie Park/James Braid

Waterford Castle (1991)

The Island, Waterford
Tel **(051) 71633**
Fax (051) 79316
Sec D Brennan
Holes 18 L 6790 yds Par 72
V'tors H SOC
Fees £25
Loc 2 miles E of Waterford, off
R683. Island in River Suir
Arch Des Smyth

West Waterford (1993)

Dungarvan
Tel **(058) 43216/41475**
Fax (058) 44343
Mem 150
Sec AA Spratt
Pro To be appointed
Holes 18 L 6802 yds Par 72
V'tors U SOC
Fees £18 (£22)
Loc 2 miles W of Dungarvan,
off N25
Arch Eddie Hackett

Co Westmeath

Delvin Castle (1992)

Clonyn, Delvin
Tel **(044) 64315**
Mem 200
Sec A Lee
Pro D Leenaghan
Holes 18 L 5809 metres Par 70
SSS 68
V'tors U
Fees £7 (£10)
Loc 15 miles NE of Mullingar
(N52)

Glasson G & CC

Glasson, Athlone
Tel **(0902) 85120**
Fax (0902) 85444
Holes 18 L 7083 yds Par 72
V'tors U
Fees £22 (£25)
Loc 6 miles NE of Athlone (N55)
Arch C O'Connor Jr

Moate (1901)

Ballinagarby, Moate

Tel	(0902) 81271/81270
Mem	600
Sec	J Creggy (Hon)
Holes	18 L 6294 yds SSS 70
V'tors	U SOC–WD
Fees	£10 (£13)
Loc	Moate village centre
Arch	Bobby Browne

Mount Temple (1991)

Mount Temple, Moate

Tel	(0902) 81841/81545
Fax	(0902) 81957
Mem	150
Sec	M & M Dolan (Props)
Pro	None
Holes	18 L 6500 yds SSS 71
Recs	Am–K Buckley (1996)
V'tors	U H SOC
Fees	£14 (£16)
Loc	3 miles N of N6, between Athlone and Moate
Arch	Michael Dolan

Mullingar (1894)

Belvedere, Mullingar

Tel	(044) 48366/48629
Fax	(044) 41499
Mem	586
Sec	C Mulligan (Sec/Mgr)
Pro	J Burns
Holes	18 L 6370 yds SSS 71
Recs	Am–63 P Walton Pro–64
V'tors	U SOC
Fees	£16 (£23)
Loc	3 miles S of Mullingar (M52)
Arch	James Braid

Co Wexford

Courtown (1936)

Kiltennel, Gorey

Tel	(055) 25166/25432
Fax	(055) 25553
Mem	800
Sec	J Finn (Sec/Mgr)
Pro	J Coone (055) 25558
Holes	18 L 6398 yds SSS 71
Recs	Am–67 J McGill (1987) Pro–68 M Murphy (1976)
V'tors	U SOC
Fees	£12–£17 (£15–£20)
Loc	2 miles SE of Gorey
Arch	Harris

Enniscorthy (1908)

Knockmarshal, Enniscorthy

Tel	(054) 33191
Fax	(054) 33191
Mem	700
Sec	Ann Byrne
Pro	M Sludds (054) 37600
Holes	18 L 5808 metres SSS 72
Recs	Am–69 C Morris (1990)

V'tors	U exc Tues & Sun–phone first SOC
Fees	£16 (£18)
Loc	1½ miles SW of Enniscorthy on New Ross road

New Ross (1905)

Tinneranny, New Ross

Tel	(051) 421433
Fax	(051) 420098
Mem	740
Sec	Kathleen Daly (Sec/Mgr)
Holes	18 L 5751 metres SSS 70
Recs	Am–66 M O'Brien Pro–65 C O'Connor
V'tors	U exc Sun SOC
Fees	£10 (£15)
Loc	1 mile W of New Ross

Rosslare (1905)

Rosslare Strand, Rosslare

Tel	(053) 32203 (Bookings)
Fax	(053) 32203
Mem	1000
Sec	JF Hall (Mgr)
Pro	A Skerritt (053) 32238
Holes	Old 18 L 6577 yds Par 72 SSS 72; New 9 L 3153 yds Par 70 SSS 70
Recs	Am–66 A Duggan (1996)
V'tors	U SOC
Fees	18 hole–£22 (£30) 9 hole–£9–13
Loc	10 miles S of Wexford. Rosslare Ferry 6 miles
Arch	Hawtree/Taylor/O'Connor Jr

St Helen's Bay (1993)

St Helen's, Kilrane, Rosslare Harbour

Tel	(053) 33234/33669
Fax	(053) 33803
Mem	200
Sec	L Byrne
Pro	None
Holes	18 L 6091 metres SSS 72
V'tors	U SOC
Fees	£20
Loc	Nr Rosslare Ferry terminal
Arch	Philip Walton

Tara Glen (1993)

Ballymoney, Courtown

Tel	(055) 25413
Fax	(055) 25612
Holes	9 hole course
V'tors	U
Fees	On application
Loc	4 miles E of Gorey. 12 miles S of Arklow

Wexford (1960)

Mulgannon, Wexford

Tel	(053) 42238
Mem	586
Sec	P Daly (Hon)
Pro	P Roche (053) 46300
Holes	18 L 6338 yds Par 72 SSS 70
V'tors	U SOC
Fees	£14 (£15)
Loc	Wexford ½ mile

Co Wicklow

Arklow (1927)

Abbeylands, Arklow

Tel	(0402) 32492
Fax	(0402) 32971
Mem	500
Sec	B Timmons (Hon)
Pro	None
Holes	18 L 5770 yds SSS 67
Recs	Am–65 J Groomes (1994)
V'tors	WD–U Sat–U after 5pm Sun–NA SOC
Fees	£15
Loc	1 mile from Arklow
Arch	Eddie Hackett

Baltinglass (1928)

Baltinglass

Tel	(0508) 81350
Fax	(0508) 81350
Mem	399
Sec	F Doyle (Hon)
Pro	M Murphy
Holes	9 L 6070 yds SSS 69
Recs	Am–66 D Coakley Pro–70 S Hunt
V'tors	U SOC
Fees	£10 (£12)
Loc	38 miles S of Dublin (N81)

Blainroe (1978)

Blainroe

Tel	(0404) 68168
Fax	(0404) 69369
Mem	830
Sec	W O'Sullivan (Sec/Mgr)
Pro	J McDonald
Holes	18 L 6171 metres SSS 72
Recs	Am–71 L Corcoran (1996) Pro–68
V'tors	U
Fees	£25 (£35)
Loc	3 miles S of Wicklow on coast
Arch	CW Hawtree

Bray (1897)

Ravenswell Road, Bray

Tel	(01) 286 2484
Fax	(01) 286 2484
Mem	275
Sec	T Brennan (Sec/Mgr)
Pro	M Walby
Holes	9 L 5230 metres SSS 70
Recs	Am–65 K Nolan (1994)
V'tors	U before 6pm SOC–WD
Fees	£17
Loc	12 miles S of Dublin

Charlesland G&CC (1993)

Greystones

Tel	(01) 287 6764
Fax	(01) 287 3882
Sec	M Doherty (Golf Admin)
Pro	P Heeney
Holes	18 L 6739 yds Par 72
V'tors	U SOC

Fees   IR£23 (IR£28)
Loc   18 miles SE of Dublin
Arch   Eddie Hackett

Coollattin (1950)

Coollattin, Shillelagh
Tel   (055) 29125
Mem   355
Sec   R McCrea (Hon)
Holes   9 L 6203 yds SSS 70
Fees   £10 (£12)
Loc   50 miles S of Dublin in
        Wicklow Mountains

Delgany (1908)

Delgany
Tel   (01) 287 4536
Fax   (01) 287 3977
Mem   882
Sec   RJ Kelly (Sec/Mgr)
Pro   G Kavanagh (01) 287 4697
Holes   18 L 6025 yds SSS 69
Recs   Am–63 J May (1978)
        Pro–61 K Morris (1997)
V'tors U exc comp days
        SOC–Mon/Thurs/Fri
Fees   £23 (£27)
Loc   18 miles S of Dublin,
        nr Greystones, off N11
Arch   H Vardon

Djouce Mountain

(1997)
Roundwood
Tel   (01) 281 8585
Mem   130
Sec   D McGillycuddy (Mgr)
Holes   9 L 6087 metres Par 71
        SSS 69
V'tors U SOC
Fees   £10 (£12)
Loc   15 miles NW of Wicklow
        (R764)
Arch   Eddie Hackett

Druid's Glen (1995)

Newtownmountkennedy
Tel   (01) 287 3600
Fax   (01) 287 3699
Mem   100
Sec   D Flinn (Gen Mgr)
Pro   E Darcy
Holes   18 L 7026 yds Par 71 SSS 74
Recs   Pro–62 C Montgomerie
        (1997)
V'tors U SOC
Fees   £75
Loc   20 miles S of Dublin (N11)
Mis   Golf Academy
Arch   Craddock/Ruddy

The European Club

(1989)
Brittas Bay, Wicklow
Tel   (0404) 47415
Fax   (01) 280 8457
Mem   120
Sec   P Ruddy
Pro   None

Holes   18 L 6800 yds SSS 71
V'tors H SOC
Fees   £25 (£30)
Loc   30 miles S of Dublin, off N11
Arch   Pat Ruddy

Glenmalure (1993)

Greenane, Rathdrum
Tel   (0404) 46679
Fax   (0404) 46783
Mem   170
Sec   C Morris (Mgr)
Holes   18 L 5237 metres SSS 66
V'tors U SOC
Fees   IR£12 (IR£15)
Loc   2 miles SW of Rathdrum on
        Glenmalure road
Arch   Suttle/McEvoy

Greystones (1895)

Greystones
Tel   (01) 287 6624
Fax   (01) 287 3749
Mem   850
Sec   O Walsh (01) 287 4136
Pro   K Daly (01) 287 5308
Holes   18 L 5401 metres SSS 68
Recs   Am–67
        Pro–66
V'tors WD–U
Fees   £20 (£24)
Loc   Greystones, 18 miles S of
        Dublin

Kilcoole (1992)

Kilcoole
Tel   (01) 287 2066
Mem   250
Sec   P McEntaggert
Holes   9 L 5506 metres Par 70 SSS
        69
Recs   Am–71 R Mullen (1993)
V'tors WD–U WE–NA before noon
        SOC–WD
Fees   £10 (£12)
Loc   S of Kilcoole on Newcastle
        road, off N11
Arch   Brian Williams

Old Conna (1987)

Ferndale Road, Bray
Tel   (01) 282 6055
Fax   (01) 282 5611
Mem   750
Sec   D Diviney (Sec/Mgr)
Pro   P McDaid (01) 272 0022
Holes   18 L 6551 yds SSS 72
V'tors WD–U before 4pm
        WE/BH–NA SOC
Fees   £22.50
Loc   2 miles N of Bray. 12 miles
        S of Dublin
Arch   Eddie Hackett

Powerscourt (1996)

Enniskerry
Tel   (01) 276 0503
Fax   (01) 276 1303
Mem   700
Sec   M Slazenger (Mgr)

Pro   P Thompson
Holes   18 L 5858 m Par 72 SSS 72
V'tors U
Fees   £45 (£55)
Loc   Enniskerry, 5 miles W of Bray

Rathsallagh (1993)

Dunlavin
Tel   (045) 403316
Fax   (045) 403295
Mem   188
Sec   M Bermingham (Mgr)
Holes   18 L 5943 m Par 72 SSS 72
V'tors U
Fees   £30 (£40)
Loc   14 miles S of Naas (R412)

Roundwood (1995)

Newtownmountkennedy
Tel   (01) 281 8488
Fax   (01) 284 3642
Sec   M McGuirk (Hon)
Holes   18 L 6685 yds Par 72
        SSS 72
Loc   15 miles NW of Wicklow
        (R764)

Tulfarris (1987)

Blessington Lakes
Tel   (045) 864574
Fax   (045) 864423
Mem   200
Sec   A Williams (Mgr)
        (045) 401662
Pro   A Williams
Holes   9 L 2806 metres SSS 69
V'tors U SOC
Fees   £12 (£15)
Loc   30 miles S of Dublin,
        off N81
Mis   Extension to 18 holes 1998
Arch   Patrick Merrigan

Wicklow (1904)

Dunbur Road, Wicklow
Tel   (0404) 67379
Mem   450
Sec   J Kelly (Hon)
Pro   D Daly (0404) 66122
Holes   18 L 5695 metres SSS 70
V'tors SOC–WD/Sat
Fees   £18 (£20)
Loc   32 miles S of Dublin, nr
        Wicklow town
Arch   Craddock/Ruddy

Woodenbridge (1884)

Woodenbridge, Arklow
Tel   (0402) 35202
Fax   (0402) 35202
Mem   550
Sec   H Crummy
Holes   18 L 6344 yds Par 71
        SSS 71
Recs   Am–71 RJ Moran (1994)
V'tors U exc Sat & Thurs
Fees   £25 (£30)
Loc   4 miles W of Arklow. 45 miles
        S of Dublin
Arch   Patrick Merrigan

For list of abbreviations see page 479

Scotland

Angus

Arbroath (1903)

Public
Elliot, Arbroath DD11 2PE

Tel **(01241) 872069 (Clubhouse)**,
(01241) 875837 (Bookings)
Mem 650
Sec L Robb
Pro L Ewart (01241) 875837
Holes 18 L 6185 yds Par 70 SSS 69
Recs Am–67 P McKechnie,
C Lee (1995)
V'tors WD–U SOC WE–NA before
10am
Fees £15 D–£20 (£20 D–£30)
Loc 1 mile SW of Arbroath on A92
Arch James Braid

Brechin (1893)

Trinity, Brechin DD9 7PD

Tel **(01356) 622383**
Mem 650
Sec AB May (01356) 622326
Pro S Rennie (01356) 625270
Holes 18 L 6200 yds SSS 70
Recs Am–65 G Tough
V'tors U exc Wed SOC
Fees £14 D–19 (£18 D–27)
Loc 1 mile N of Brechin on B90

Caird Park (1926)

Public
*Mains Loan, Caird Park, Dundee
DD4 9BX*

Tel **(01382) 453606**
Mem 350
Sec G Martin (01382) 504064
Pro J Black (01382) 459438
Holes 18 L 6303 yds SSS 70
Yellow 9 L 1692 yds SSS 29
Red 9 L 1983 yds SSS 29
Recs Am–67 G Lochead (1995)
V'tors U SOC
Fees On application
Loc Off Kingsway by-pass, N of
Dundee

Camperdown (1960)

Public
Camperdown Park, Dundee

Tel **(01382) 623398**
Mem 330
Sec R Gordon (01382) 814445
Pro R Brown
Holes 18 L 6561 yds SSS 72
Recs Am–67 G Bell
V'tors U
Fees On application
Loc 2 miles NW of Dundee (A923)

Downfield (1932)

Turnberry Ave, Dundee DD2 3QP

Tel **(01382) 825595**
Fax (01382) 813111
Mem 750
Sec BD Liddle

Pro KS Hutton (01382) 889246
Holes 18 L 6822 yds SSS 73
Recs Am–67 P Cunningham (1997)
Pro–65 A Crerar (1995)
V'tors WD–U 9.30–noon and
2.18–3.42pm WE–limited
access after 2pm
Fees £16–31 D–£26–46 (£21–36)
Loc N of Dundee, off A923

Edzell (1895)

High St, Edzell DD9 7TF

Tel **(01356) 648235**
Fax (01356) 648094
Mem 650
Sec IG Farquhar (01356) 647283
Pro AJ Webster (01356) 648462
Holes 18 L 6348 yds SSS 71
Recs Am–62 JKA Bruce (1997)
Pro–67 I Young (1992)
V'tors WD–NA 4.45–6.15pm
WE–NA 7.30–10.30am &
12–2pm SOC
Fees £20 D–£30 (£26 D–£39)
Loc 6 miles N of Brechin
Mis Driving range
Arch Bob Simpson

Forfar (1871)

*Cunninghill, Arbroath Road, Forfar
DD8 2RL*

Tel **(01307) 462120**
Fax (01307) 468495
Mem 500 140(L) 100(J)
Sec W Baird (01307) 463773
Pro P McNiven (01307) 465683
Holes 18 L 6052 yds Par 69 SSS 70
Recs Am–61 KG Law (1995)
Pro–65 E Brown
V'tors U exc Sat SOC
Fees £17 (£22)
Loc 1½ miles E of Forfar
Arch James Braid

Kirriemuir (1908)

Northmuir, Kirriemuir DD8 4PN

Tel **(01575) 72144 (Clubhouse)**,
**(01575) 73317 (Starter/
Admin)**
Fax **(01575) 74608**
Mem 600
Sec A Caira (Mgr)
Pro A Caira (01575) 73317
Holes 18 L 5510 yds SSS 67
Recs Am–62 JL Adamson
Pro–63 D Huish
V'tors WD–U WE–NA SOC
Fees £16 D–£22
Loc NE outskirts of Kirriemuir.
17 miles N of Dundee
Arch James Braid

Letham Grange (1987)

*Letham Grange, Colliston, Arbroath
DD11 4RL*

Tel **(01241) 890377**
Fax (01241) 890414

Mem 780
Sec Miss C Grainger
Pro S Moir
Holes Old 18 L 6968 yds SSS 73
New 18 L 5528 yds SSS 68
Recs Old Am–69 D Downie (1994)
New Am–62 L McLaughlin
(1994)
Old Pro–67 J Metcalfe,
J Bickerton (1994)
V'tors WD–U exc Tues before 10am
WE–M before 10.30am &
12.30–2pm (Old) –M before
9am & 1–2pm (New) BH–U
SOC
Fees Old £24 D–£36 (£33);
New £15.50 D–£22 (£18)
Loc 4 miles NW of Arbroath
on A993
Arch Old: Steel/Smith
New: T MacAuley

Monifieth Golf Links

*Medal Starter's Box, Princes Street,
Monifieth DD5 4AW*

Tel **(01382) 532767 (Medal)**,
(01382) 532967 (Ashludie)
Fax (01382) 535553
Mem 1700
Sec HR Nicoll (01382) 535553
Pro I McLeod (01382) 532945
Holes Medal 18 L 6650 yds SSS 72
Ashludie 18 L 5123 SSS 66
Recs Am–63 JL Adamson
Pro–64 S Sewgolum
V'tors WD–U Sat–NA before 2pm
Sun–NA before 10am SOC
Fees Medal £26 D–£36 (£30)
Ashludie £15 D–£21 (£16
D–£24)
Loc 6 miles E of Dundee
Mis Abertay, Broughty,
Grange/Dundee and
Monifieth clubs play here

Montrose (1562)

Public
Traill Drive, Montrose DD10 8SW

Tel **(01674) 672932**
Fax (01674) 671800
Mem 1300
Sec Mrs M Stewart
Pro K Stables (01674) 672634
Holes Medal 18 L 6470 yds SSS 72
Broomfield 18 L 4815 yds
SSS 63
Recs Medal Am–64 G Tough
(1991)
Pro–63 P Wardell (1997)
V'tors WD–U Sat–NA before 2.30pm
Sun–NA before 10am
Fees Medal £20 (£28);
Broomfield £10 (£14)
Loc 1 mile from Montrose,
off A90
Mis Royal Montrose, Caledonia
and Mercantile clubs play here

Montrose Caledonia

(1896)

Dorward Road, Montrose DD10 8SW

Tel	(01674) 672313
Sec	P McIntosh
	(01674) 676789
Holes	Play over Montrose courses

Montrose Mercantile

East Links, Montrose DD10 8SW

Tel	(01674) 672408
Mem	980
Sec	DD Scott (01674) 675716
Holes	Play over Montrose courses

Panmure (1845)

Barry, Carnoustie DD7 7RT

Tel	(01241) 853120
Fax	(01241) 859737
Mem	500
Sec	Maj (Retd) GW Paton
	(01241) 855120
Pro	N Mackintosh
	(01241) 852460
Holes	18 L 6317 yds Par 70 SSS 71
Recs	Am–66 I Frame (1984)
	Pro–62 C Moody (1990)
V'tors	WD/Sun–U Sat–NA
Fees	£28 D–£42
Loc	2 miles W of Carnoustie,
	off A930

Royal Montrose (1810)

Dorward Road, Montrose DD10 8SW

Tel	(01674) 672376
Mem	650
Sec	JS Richardson
	(01674) 676000
Holes	Play over Montrose courses

Carnoustie Clubs

Carnoustie (1842)

3 Links Parade, Carnoustie DD7 7JE

Tel	(01241) 852480
Fax	(01241) 856459
Mem	900
Sec	DW Curtis
Holes	Play over Carnoustie courses

Carnoustie Caledonia

(1887)

Links Parade, Carnoustie DD7 7JF

Tel	(01241) 852115
Mem	640
Sec	DC Thomson
Holes	Play over Carnoustie courses

Carnoustie Ladies

(1873)

12 Links Parade, Carnoustie DD7 6AZ

Tel	(01241) 855252
Mem	106
Sec	Mrs J Clark (01241) 859457
Holes	Play over Carnoustie courses

Carnoustie Mercantile

(1896)

Links Parade, Carnoustie DD7 7JE

Mem	50
Sec	DG Ogilvie
	(01356) 647304 Police
	House, Dunlappie Road,
	Edzell DD9 7UB
Holes	Play over Carnoustie courses

Dalhousie (1868)

c/o Glencoe Hotel, Links Parade, Carnoustie DD7 7JF

Tel	(01241) 853273
Mem	150
Sec	WM Osler
Holes	Play over Carnoustie courses

Carnoustie Courses

Buddon Links (1981)

Public

Links Parade, Carnoustie DD7 7JE

Tel	(01241) 853249 (Starter),
	(01241) 853789 (Bookings)
Fax	(01241) 852720
Sec	EJC Smith
Holes	18 L 5420 yds SSS 66
V'tors	WD–U WE–U after 11am
Fees	£15
Loc	12 miles E of Dundee, by A92
	or A930

Burnside (1914)

Public

Links Parade, Carnoustie DD7 7JE

Tel	(01241) 855344 (Starter),
	(01241) 853789 (Bookings)
Fax	(01241) 852720
Sec	EJC Smith
Holes	18 L 6020 yds SSS 69
	Pro–62 A Tait
V'tors	WD–U Sat–U after 2pm
	Sun–U after 11.30am
Fees	£19
Loc	12 miles E of Dundee, by A92
	or A930

Carnoustie Championship (16th)

Public

Links Parade, Carnoustie DD7 7JE

Tel	(01241) 853249 (Starter),
	(01241) 853789 (Bookings)
Fax	(01241) 852720
Sec	EJC Smith
Holes	18 L 6941 yds SSS 75
	Pro–64 A Tait,
	C Montgomerie
V'tors	WD–H Sat–H after 2pm
	Sun–H after 11.30am
Fees	£52
Loc	12 miles E of Dundee, by A92
	or A930

Argyll & Bute

Blairmore & Strone

(1896)

High Road, Strone, Dunoon PA23 8JJ

Tel	(01369) 840676
Mem	130
Sec	JK Clark (01369) 840467
Holes	9 L 2122 yds SSS 62
Recs	Am–63 JA Kirby (1987)
V'tors	Mon–NA after 6pm Sat–NA
	12–4pm
Fees	D–£5 (D–£10) W–£30
Loc	Strone, 8 miles N of Dunoon
Arch	James Braid

Bute (1888)

Kingarth, Isle of Bute

Mem	115
Sec	I McDougall
	(01700) 504369
Holes	9 L 2497 yds SSS 64
Recs	Am–65 G McArthur (1990)
V'tors	U Sat–U after 12.30pm
Fees	D–£6
Loc	Stravanan Bay, 6 miles S of
	Rothesay, off A845

Carradale (1906)

Carradale, Campbeltown PA28 6SA

Tel	(01583) 431643
Mem	324
Sec	JR Ogilvie
Pro	None
Holes	9 L 2392 yds SSS 64
Recs	Am–62 JW Campbell (1994)
	Pro–68 R Weir (1994)
V'tors	U
Fees	D–£8
Loc	Carradale, 15 miles N of
	Campbeltown (B842)

Colonsay

Isle of Colonsay PA61 7YP

Tel	(019512) 316
Mem	100
Sec	K Byrne
Holes	18 L 4775 yds Par 72
V'tors	U
Fees	On application
Loc	W coast of Colonsay, at
	Machrins

Cowal (1891)

Ardenslate Road, Dunoon PA23 8LT

Tel	(01369) 702216
Fax	(01369) 705673
Mem	900
Sec	Mrs W Fraser
	(01369) 705673
Pro	RD Weir (01369) 702395
Holes	18 L 6063 yds SSS 70
Recs	Am–64 LW Kelly (1997)
	Pro–63 RD Weir (1991)
V'tors	WD–U WE–restricted SOC
Fees	On application
Loc	NE boundary of Dunoon
Arch	James Braid (1928)

Craignure (1895)

Scallastle, Craignure, Isle of Mull
PA64 5AP
Tel	**(01680) 812487/812416**
Fax	(01680) 300402
Mem	92
Sec	DS Howitt
Holes	9 L 5072 yds SSS 65
Recs	Am–72
V'tors	U
Fees	£10 D–£12
Loc	1 mile N of Craignure Ferry Terminal (Oban 40mins)
Mis	Course re-designed 1979

Dalmally (1986)

Old Saw Mill, Dalmally PA33 1AS
Tel	**(01838) 200373**
Mem	120
Sec	AJ Burke (01838) 200370
Pro	None
Holes	9 L 2277 yds Par 64 SSS 63
Recs	Am–64 K MacIntyre (1994)
V'tors	U
Fees	R/D–£10
Loc	1 mile W of Dalmally on A85

Dunaverty (1889)

Southend, Campbeltown PA28 6RF
Tel	**(01586) 830677**
Mem	399
Sec	DS Ure
Holes	18 L 4799 yds SSS 64
Recs	Am–58
V'tors	U
Fees	£13
Loc	10 miles S of Campbeltown

Gigha (1992)

Isle of Gigha, Kintyre PA41 7AA
Tel	**(01583) 505287**
Mem	30
Sec	M Tart
Holes	9 L 5042 yds SSS 65
V'tors	U
Fees	D–£10
Loc	Off W coast of Kintyre

Glencruitten (1905)

Glencruitten Road, Oban PA34 4PU
Tel	**(01631) 562868**
Mem	350 105(L) 115(J)
Sec	AG Brown (01631) 564604
Pro	G Clark (01631) 564115
Holes	18 L 4452 yds SSS 63
Recs	Am–55 JM Wilson Pro–60 H Bannerman, G Cunningham
V'tors	U
Fees	On application
Loc	Oban 1 mile
Arch	James Braid

Innellan (1891)

Knockamillie Road, Innellan
Tel	**(01369) 830242**
Mem	200
Sec	A Wilson (01369) 702573
Holes	9 L 4878 yds SSS 64
Recs	Am–63
V'tors	U SOC
Fees	£10 (£10)
Loc	4 miles S of Dunoon (A815)

Inveraray (1893)

c/o 2 The Maltlands, Inveraray
Tel	**(01499) 302508**
Mem	160
Sec	S Bell
Holes	9 L 5600 yds SSS 67
V'tors	U SOC
Fees	D–£8 (£10)
Loc	1 mile S of Inveraray on A83

Kyles of Bute (1907)

Tighnabruaich PA21 2EE
Tel	**(01700) 811603**
Mem	160
Sec	J Thomson
Holes	9 L 2389 yds SSS 32
Recs	Am–62 F McDonald (1996)
V'tors	U
Fees	D–£8 W–£10
Loc	26 miles W of Dunoon

Lochgilphead (1963)

Blarbuie Road, Lochgilphead PA31 8LE
Tel	**(01546) 602340**
Mem	250
Sec	N McKay (01546) 603840
Holes	9 L 4484 yds SSS 63
Recs	Am–59 R Willan Pro–62 R Weir (1991)
V'tors	U SOC
Fees	D–£10 (D–£10)
Loc	½ mile N of Lochgilphead by Hospital

Machrie Hotel (1891)

Port Ellen, Isle of Islay PA42 7AN
Tel	**(01496) 302310**
Fax	(01496) 302404
Mem	292
Sec	T Dunn
Holes	18 L 6226 yds SSS 70
Recs	Am–66 I Middleton Pro–67 M Seymour
V'tors	U SOC
Fees	£20
Loc	Machrie, 5 miles N of Port Ellen
Mis	Driving range
Arch	Willie Campbell

Machrihanish (1876)

Machrihanish, Campbeltown
PA28 6PT
Tel	**(01586) 810213**
Fax	(01586) 810221
Mem	525 135(L) 80(J)
Sec	Mrs A Anderson
Pro	K Campbell (01586) 810277
Holes	18 L 6228 yds SSS 71 9 hole course
Recs	Am–65 I McLennan Jr Pro–64 B Lockie
V'tors	U
Fees	£23 D–£32 exc Sat–£38
Loc	5 miles W of Campbeltown

Millport (1888)

Millport, Isle of Cumbrae KA28 0HB
Tel	**(01475) 530311**
Mem	288 120(L) 78(J)
Sec	JT McGill (01475) 530306
Pro	K Docherty (01475) 530305
Holes	18 L 5828 yds SSS 69
Recs	Am–64 AD Harrington (1981)
V'tors	U SOC
Fees	£14.50 D–£18.50 (£18.50 D–£24.50) W–£51 M–£134
Loc	W of Millport (Largs car ferry)
Arch	James Braid

Port Bannatyne (1912)

Bannatyne Mains Road, Port
Bannatyne, Isle of Bute PA20 0PH
Tel	**(01700) 504544**
Mem	180
Sec	IL MacLeod (01700) 502009
Holes	13 L 4730 yds SSS 67
Recs	Am–61 J Ewing Pro–64 W Watson
V'tors	U
Fees	£14 (£14)
Loc	2 miles N of Rothesay, Isle of Bute

Rothesay (1892)

Canada Hill, Rothesay PA20 9HN
Tel	**(01700) 502244**
Fax	(01700) 503554
Mem	350
Sec	A Shore
Pro	J Dougal (01700) 503554
Holes	18 L 5395 yds SSS 66
Recs	Am–62 G Reynolds (1993) Pro–72 RDBM Shade (1968)
V'tors	WD–U WE–book with Pro SOC
Fees	£15 (£24) W–£80
Loc	1 mile E of Rothesay
Mis	Practice range
Arch	Braid/Sayers

Tarbert (1910)

Kilberry Road, Tarbert PA29 6XX
Tel	**(01880) 820565**
Mem	101
Sec	P Cupples (01880) 820536
Holes	9 L 4460 yds SSS 63
Recs	Am–62 D Lamont (1990) Pro–63
V'tors	U SOC
Fees	£5 D–£8 W–£30
Loc	1 mile W of Tarbert on B8024, off A83

Tobermory (1896)

Erray Road, Tobermory, Isle of Mull
PA75 6PS
Fax	(01688) 302140
Mem	180
Sec	J Weir (01688) 302338
Holes	9 L 2492 yds SSS 64
Recs	Am–65 G Davidson (1994) Ladies 72 J Jack (1993)
V'tors	U
Fees	D–£12 W–£40

Loc Tobermory, Isle of Mull
Mis Tickets from Western Isles
Hotel
Arch David Adams

Vaul (1920)

Scarinish, Isle of Tiree PA77 6TP
Mem 100
Sec P Campbell (01879) 220334
Holes 9 L 2837 yds Par 72 SSS 68
V'tors U
Fees On application
Loc 3 miles N of Scarinish, E end
of Tiree. 40 min flight from
Glasgow

Ayrshire

Annanhill (1957)

Public
Irvine Road, Kilmarnock KA3 2RT
Tel (01563) 21512 (Starter)
Mem 350
Sec T Denham
(01563) 521644
Holes 18 L 6270 yds SSS 70
Recs Am–65 I McKenzie
Pro–65 J Farmer
V'tors WD/Sun–U Sat–NA SOC–exc
Sat
Fees £10 (£16)
Loc 1 mile W of Kilmarnock
Arch J McLean

Ardeer (1880)

*Greenhead Avenue, Stevenston
KA20 4JX*
Tel (01294) 464542/465316
Fax (01294) 465316
Mem 500
Sec P Watson (01294) 605243
Pro R Summerfield (Shop)
(01294) 601327
Holes 18 L 6409 yds SSS 72
Recs Am–67 J Shearer
Pro–68 A Brooks, I Stanley,
R Walker (1971)
V'tors U exc Sat–NA SOC–WD
Fees £12 D–£22 Sun–£20 D–£30
Loc ½ mile N of Stevenston,
off A78
Arch H Stutt

Auchenharvie (1981)

Public
*Moor Park Road, West Brewery Park,
Saltcoats KA20 3HU*
Mem 80
Sec A Breslin (01294) 469361
Pro R Rodgers (01292) 603103
Holes 9 L 5300 yds SSS 66
Recs Am–67 R Galloway, J Murphy,
P Rodgers, A Wylie
V'tors WD–U WE–U after 9.30am
Fees On application
Loc Low road between Saltcoats
and Stevenston
Mis Driving range

Ballochmyle (1937)

Ballochmyle, Mauchline KA5 6LE
Tel (01290) 550469
Fax (01290) 553150
Mem 860
Sec A Williams
Pro None
Holes 18 L 5952 yds SSS 69
Recs Am–64 G Holland (1996)
Pro–65 A Hunter (1987)
V'tors WD/WE–U BH–M SOC exc
Wed/Sat/BH
Fees On application
Loc 1 mile S of Mauchline
on B705, off A76

Beith (1896)

Bigholm Road, Beith KA15 2JQ
Tel (01505) 503166
Mem 380
Sec EJ Armstrong
Holes 18 L 5616 yds SSS 68
Recs Am–64 K Ross
V'tors U before 5pm exc Sat &
Sun pm
Fees £10 (£15)
Loc 1 mile NE of Beith. 12 miles
NE of Paisley

Belleisle (1927)

Public
Bellisle Park, Doonfoot Road, Ayr
Tel (01292) 441258
Fax (01292) 442632
Pro D Gemmell (Golf Mgr)
(01292) 441314
Holes 18 L 6477 yds SSS 72
Recs Am–63 K Gimson
Pro–64 J Farmer
Ladies–71 B Robinson
V'tors WD–U WE–H
Fees £17 D–£24
Loc S of Ayr in Belleisle Park
Arch James Braid

Brodick (1897)

Brodick, Isle of Arran
Tel (01770) 302349
Fax (01770) 302349
Mem 580
Sec HM Macrae
Pro PS McCalla
(01770) 302513
Holes 18 L 4736 yds SSS 64
Recs Am–62 A Gold
V'tors U SOC
Fees £12 D–£17 (£17 D–£25)
Loc Brodick Pier 1 mile

Brunston Castle (1992)

Dailly, Girvan KA26 9RH
Tel (01465) 811471
Fax (01465) 811545
Mem 350
Sec P McCloy (Gen Mgr)
Pro D McKenzie
Holes 18 L 6792 yds SSS 72
V'tors U–booking necessary SOC
Fees £25 D–£40
Loc 4 miles E of Girvan
Arch Donald Steel

Caprington

Public
*Ayr Road, Caprington, Kilmarnock
KA1 4UW*
Tel (01563) 21915 (Starter)
Mem 400
Sec F McCulloch
Holes 18 L 5460 yds SSS 69
9 hole course
Recs Am–63 S Fraser
Pro–66 E Brown
V'tors U
Fees On application
Loc 1 mile S of Kilmarnock
(B7038)

Corrie (1892)

Corrie, Sannox, Isle of Arran KA27 8JD
Tel (01770) 810223
Mem 200
Sec R Stevenson (01770) 810268
Holes 9 L 1948 yds SSS 61
Recs Am–57 A Gold (1966)
V'tors U exc Sat pm
Fees D–£7 W–£30
Loc 6 miles N of Brodick

Dalmilling (1961)

Public
Westwood Avenue, Ayr KA8 0QY
Tel (01292) 263893
Fax (01292) 610543
Pro P Cheyney (Golf Mgr)
Holes 18 L 5724 yds SSS 68
Recs Am–61 G McKay
V'tors U
Fees £11 D–£18
Loc NE boundary of Ayr, nr Ayr
racecourse

Doon Valley (1927)

Hillside, Patna
Tel (01292) 531607
Mem 90
Sec J Green
Pro None
Holes 9 L 5654 yds SSS 68
V'tors U
Fees £5 (£5)
Loc 8 miles SE of Ayr (A713)

Girvan (1900)

Public
Golf Course Road, Girvan KA26 9HW
Tel (01465) 714272/714346
(Starter)
Fax (01465) 714346
Holes 18 L 5095 yds SSS 64
Recs Am–61 J Cannon
Pro–61 K Stevely
V'tors U
Fees £11 D–£18
Loc N side of Girvan (A77).
22 miles S of Ayr

Glasgow GC Gailes (1892)

Gailes, Irvine KA11 5AE
Tel (01294) 311258
Fax (0141) 942 0770 (Sec)
Mem 1200

Sec DW Deas (0141) 942 2011
Pro J Steven (01294) 311561
Holes 18 L 6513 yds Par 71 SSS 72
Recs Am–65 GC Sherry, LW Kelly
Pro–64 C Gillies
V'tors WD–I WE/BH–NA before
2.30pm SOC
Fees £42 D–£52 (£47)
Loc 1 mile S of Irvine, off A78
Arch Willie Park Jr

Irvine (1887)

Bogside, Irvine KA12 8SN
Tel (01294) 78139
Mem 450
Sec A Morton (01294) 75979
Pro K Erskine (01294) 75626
Holes 18 L 6408 yds SSS 71
Recs Am–65 DA Roxburgh (1981)
Pro–66 R Weir (1987)
V'tors U SOC–WD
Fees On application
Loc 1 mile N of Irvine towards
Kilwinning

Irvine Ravenspark (1907)

Public
Kidsneuk Lane, Irvine KA12 8SR
Tel (01294) 271293
Mem 400
Sec G Robertson
Pro P Bond (01294) 276467
Holes 18 L 6429 yds SSS 71
Recs Am–65 GJ Robertson
V'tors U
Fees £4 (£14)
Loc N side of Irvine, off A737.
7 miles N of Troon

Kilbirnie Place (1922)

Largs Road, Kilbirnie KA25 7AT
Tel (01505) 683398
Mem 450
Sec JC Walker
Pro None
Holes 18 L 5411 yds SSS 67
Recs Am–64 G McLean
V'tors WD–U
Fees On application
Loc ½ mile W of Kilbirnie, S of
A760. 15 miles SW of Paisley

Kilmarnock (Barassie) (1887)

*29 Hillhouse Road, Barassie, Troon
KA10 6SY*
Tel (01292) 311077
Fax (01292) 313920
Mem 500
Sec RL Bryce (01292) 313920
Pro G Howie (01292) 311322
Holes 18 L 6484 yds SSS 73
9 L 2888 yds SSS 34
Recs Am–72 JB Morrison (1997)
V'tors WE/Wed–NA SOC–Tues &
Thurs
Fees £32.50 D–£50
Loc Opp Barassie Railway Station
Arch Theodore Moone

Lamlash (1889)

Lamlash, Isle of Arran KA27 8JU
Tel (01770) 600296 (Clubhouse),
(01770) 600196 (Starter)
Fax (01770) 600296
Mem 450
Sec J Henderson
Pro None
Holes 18 L 4640 yds SSS 64
Recs Am–61 D MacFarlane (1997)
Ladies–66 B Livingston (1992)
V'tors U SOC
Fees £10 D–£14 (£12 D–£18)
Loc 3 miles S of Brodick on A841
Arch Auchterlonie/Fernie

Largs (1891)

Irvine Road, Largs KA30 8EU
Tel (01475) 674681 (Clubhouse)
Fax (01475) 673594
Mem 800
Sec DH Macgillivray
(01475) 673594
Pro R Collinson (01475) 686192
Holes 18 L 6115 yds Par 70 SSS 71
Recs Am–64 C White (1989)
Pro–63 J Greaves (1997)
V'tors U
Fees £25 D–£35
Loc 1 mile S of Largs on A78

Lochranza (1991)

Pay and play
Lochranza, Isle of Arran KA27 8HL
Tel (0177083) 0273
Fax (0177083) 0273
Sec IM Robertson
Holes 9 L 5600 yds SSS 70
Recs Am–74 D McAllister (1993)
V'tors U SOC–May–Oct
Fees 18 holes–£8
Loc 14 miles N of Brodick
Arch IM Robertson

Loudoun Gowf (1909)

Galston KA4 8PA
Tel (01563) 820551
Mem 650
Sec TR Richmond (01563)
821993
Holes 18 L 6016 yds SSS 69
Recs Am–61 AG Todd
V'tors WD–U WE–M
Fees £17 D–£29 (1997)
Loc 5 miles E of Kilmarnock
on A71

Machrie Bay (1900)

*Machrie Bay, Brodick, Isle of Arran
KA27 8DZ*
Tel (01770) 850232
Mem 260
Sec J Milesi
Holes 9 L 2200 yds SSS 32
Recs Am–62 A Kelso
Pro–59 W Hagen
V'tors U
Fees D–£5 W–£15
Loc 9 miles W of Brodick
Arch William Fernie

Maybole (1970)

Public
Memorial Park, Maybole KA19
Holes 9 L 2635 yds SSS 65
Recs Am–64 WW McCulloch
V'tors U
Fees £7 D–£11
Loc S of Maybole, off A77. 8 miles
S of Ayr

Muirkirk (1991)

Pay and play
*c/o 1 Cairn View, Muirkirk
KA18 3QW*
Tel (01290) 661556
Fax (01290) 661556
Mem 100
Sec Mrs M Casagranda
Holes 9 L 5366 yds SSS 67
V'tors U SOC
Fees £6 (£6)
Loc 12 miles W of M74 Junction
12 on A70

New Cumnock (1901)

*Lochill, Cumnock Road, New Cumnock
KA18 4BQ*
Tel (01290) 423659
Mem 250
Sec D Scott
Holes 9 L 2588 yds SSS 65
Recs Am–62 R Hodge (1992)
V'tors U exc Sun am–NA
Fees £5 D–£8
Loc 1 mile W of New Cumnock
Arch William Fernie

Prestwick (1851)

2 Links Road, Prestwick KA9 1QG
Tel (01292) 477404
Fax (01292) 477255
Mem 580
Sec IT Bunch
Pro FC Rennie
(01292) 479483
Holes 18 L 6668 yds SSS 73
Recs Am–68 PM Mayo, P Deeble,
B Andrade (1987)
Pro–67 EC Brown,
C O'Connor
V'tors WD–I on application only
Fees On application
Loc Prestwick Airport 1 mile,
nr Railway Station

Prestwick St Cuthbert (1899)

East Road, Prestwick KA9 2SX
Tel (01292) 477101
Fax (01292) 671730
Mem 865
Sec JC Rutherford
Holes 18 L 6470 yds SSS 71
Recs Am–65 S Wallace (1996)
Ladies–67 CA Gibson (1992)
V'tors WD–U WE/BH–M
SOC–WD
Fees £20 D–£27
Loc ½ mile E of Prestwick

Prestwick St Nicholas
(1851)
*Grangemuir Road, Prestwick
KA9 1SN*
Tel   (01292) 477608
Fax   (01292) 678570
Mem   600 155(L) 68(J)
Sec   GBS Thomson
Pro   Shop (01292) 678559
Holes   18 L 5952 yds SSS 69
Recs   Am–65 G Lawrie
        Pro–63 A Johnstone
V'tors WD–U WE–NA exc Sun pm
Fees   £30 D–£45 Sun pm–£35
Loc   Prestwick
Arch   C Hunter

Routenburn (1914)
Greenock Road, Largs KA30 9AH
Tel   (01475) 673230
Mem   400
Sec   J Thomson (Mgr)
Pro   G McQueen
        (01475) 687240
Holes   18 L 5650 yds SSS 68
Recs   Am–64 B Moore
        Pro–65 S Torrance
V'tors U SOC–WD
Fees   £6.60 (£11)
Loc   N of Largs, off A78
Arch   James Braid

Royal Troon (1878)
Craigend Road, Troon KA10 6EP
Tel   (01292) 311555
Fax   (01292) 318204
Mem   800
Sec   JW Chandler
Pro   RB Anderson (01292) 313281
Holes   Old 18 L 7097 yds SSS 74;
        Portland 18 L 6289 yds
        SSS 71
Recs   Old Am–70 CW Green,
        J Harkis, R Claydon,
        DW Hawthorn
        Pro–64 G Norman (1989),
        E Woods (1997)
        Portland Am–65 GS Reynolds
        Pro–65 WG Cunningham
V'tors Booking required.
        Mon/Tues/Thurs only–H
        (max 20) WE–NA
Fees   Old + Portland D–£110
        Portland D–£70 (inc Lunch)
Loc   SE side of Troon (B749).
        Prestwick Airport 3 miles
Mis   Practice range
Arch   W Fernie

Seafield (1930)
Public
Belleisle Park, Doonfoot Road, Ayr
Tel   (01292) 441258
Fax   (01292) 442632
Pro   D Gemmell (Golf Mgr)
        (01292) 441314
Holes   18 L 5498 yds SSS 66
Recs   Am–65 R Gibson
V'tors U
Fees   £11 D–£18
Loc   S of Ayr in Belleisle Park

Shiskine (1896)
*Shiskine, Blackwaterfoot, Isle of
Arran KA27*
Tel   (01770) 860226
Mem   550 154(L) 42(J)
Sec   Mrs F Crawford (01770)
        860293 J Faulkner (01770)
        860392
Holes   12 L 2990 yds SSS 42
Recs   Am–39 J Melvin, J Brown
        Pro–36 DH McGillivray
V'tors U SOC
Fees   £10 W–£30
Loc   11 miles SW of Brodick

Skelmorlie (1891)
Skelmorlie PA17 5ES
Tel   (01475) 520152
Mem   390
Sec   Mrs A Fahey (Hon)
Holes   13 L 5056 yds SSS 65
Recs   Am–61 J McCreadie (1992)
        Pro–69 J Braid, G Duncan
V'tors U exc Sat (Apr–Oct)
Fees   D–£16 Sun–£18
Loc   Wemyss Bay Station 1½ miles
Arch   James Braid

Troon Municipal
Public
Harling Drive, Troon KA10 6NF
Tel   (01292) 312464
Fax   (01292) 312578
Pro   G McKinlay
Holes   Lochgreen 18 L 6785 yds
        SSS 73; Darley 18 L 6501 yds
        SSS 72; Fullarton 18 L
        4822 yds SSS 63
Recs   Lochgreen Am–66 R Milligan
        Pro–65 J Chillas
        Darley Am–66 M Rossi
        Pro–66 J White
        Fullarton Am–58 A McQueen
V'tors U SOC
Fees   Lochgreen £17 D–£24
        Darley £13 D–£23
        Fullarton £11 D–£18
Loc   4 miles N of Prestwick at
        Station Brae

Troon Portland (1894)
1 Crosbie Road, Troon KA10
Tel   (01292) 313488
Mem   120
Sec   J Irving
Holes   Play over Portland at Royal
        Troon

Troon St Meddans (1907)
Harling Drive, Troon KA10 6NF
Mem   200
Sec   R Lamont (01294) 552878
Holes   Play over Troon Municipal
        courses Lochgreen and Darley

Turnberry Hotel (1906)
Turnberry KA26 9LT
Tel   (01655) 331000
Fax   (01655) 331706
Sec   E Bowman (Mgr)

Pro   B Gunson
Holes   Ailsa 18 L 6976 yds SSS 72
        Arran 18 L 6014 yds SSS 69
Recs   Ailsa Am–70 GK MacDonald
        Pro–63 M Hayes, G Norman
        (1986)
        Arran Am–66 AP Parkin
        Pro–65 E McIntosh,
        C Ronald, S McGregor
V'tors On application
Fees   On application
Loc   5 miles N of Girvan on A77
Arch   Hutchison/Mackenzie Ross

West Kilbride (1893)
*Fullerton Drive, Seamill, West Kilbride
KA23 9HT*
Tel   (01294) 823911
Fax   (01294) 823911
Mem   900
Sec   H Armour
Pro   G Ross (01294) 823042
Holes   18 L 6452 yds SSS 71
Recs   Am–63 G Fox (1995)
        Pro–63 F Mann, J McCredie
        (1997)
V'tors WD–U WE–M BH–NA SOC
Fees   On application
Loc   West Kilbride
Arch   Old Tom Morris/James Braid

Western Gailes (1897)
Gailes, Irvine KA11 5AE
Tel   (01294) 311649
Fax   (01294) 312312
Mem   450
Sec   AM McBean
Holes   18 L 6639 yds SSS 73
Recs   Am–67 RA Muscroft (1986)
        Pro–65 B Gallacher (1986)
V'tors WD–H exc Thurs (booking
        necessary)
Fees   £52 D–£84
Loc   3 miles N of Troon (A78)

Whiting Bay (1895)
*Golf Course Road, Whiting Bay, Isle of
Arran KA27 8PR*
Tel   (017707) 487
Mem   290
Sec   Mrs I I'Anson
Holes   18 L 4405 yds SSS 63
Recs   Am–58 N Auld
V'tors U
Fees   On application
Loc   8 miles S of Brodick

Borders

Duns (1894)
Hardens Road, Duns TD11 3NR
Tel   (01361) 882194
Mem   520
Sec   A Campbell (01361) 882717
Pro   None
Holes   18 L 6209 yds SSS 70
Recs   Am–65 I Angus
V'tors U SOC
Fees   £12 (£12)
Loc   1 mile W of Duns, off A6105

Eyemouth (1880)

Gunsgreen House, Eyemouth TD14 5DX

Tel	(018907) 50551
Fax	(018907) 50551
Mem	310
Sec	M Hope (018907) 50432
Pro	C Maltman
Holes	9 L 4608 metres SSS 65
Recs	Am–61 J Patterson (1991)
V'tors	WD–U
Fees	D–£10
Loc	4 miles N of border, off A1
Mis	Extending to 18 holes

Galashiels (1884)

Ladhope Recreation Ground, Galashiels TD1 2NJ

Tel	(01896) 753724
Mem	366
Sec	R Gass (01896) 755307
Holes	18 L 5309 yds SSS 67
Recs	Am–61 I Frizzel
	Pro–70 J Braid
V'tors	U SOC
Fees	£10 D–£14 (£12 D–£16)
Loc	¼ mile NE of Galashiels, off A7

Hawick (1877)

Vertish Hill, Hawick

Tel	(01450) 72293
Mem	700
Sec	J Harley
Holes	18 L 5929 yds SSS 69
Recs	Am–63 AJ Ballantyne
	Pro–64 N Faldo
V'tors	H SOC
Fees	£18 D–£25
Loc	½ mile S of Hawick

The Hirsel (1948)

Kelso Road, Coldstream TD12 4NJ

Tel	(01890) 882678
Mem	700
Sec	JC Balfour (01890) 883052
Holes	18 L 6092 yds SSS 69
Recs	Am–64 M Ledgerwood (1990)
V'tors	U SOC
Fees	£15 (£20)
Loc	½ mile W of Coldstream (A697)

Innerleithen (1886)

Leithen Water, Leithen Road, Innerleithen EH44 6NL

Tel	(01896) 830951
Mem	175
Sec	S Wyse (01896) 830071
Holes	9 L 6066 yds SSS 69
Recs	Am–66 C Fraser
V'tors	U
Fees	£10 (£13)
Loc	1 mile N of Innerleithen on Heriot road
Arch	Willie Park

Jedburgh (1892)

Dunion Road, Jedburgh

Tel	(01835) 863587
Mem	300
Sec	R Strachan
Holes	9 L 5492 yds SSS 67
Recs	Am–62 E Redpath (1990)
	Pro–66 C Montgomerie (1992)
V'tors	U
Fees	£12
Loc	Jedburgh 1 mile
Arch	Willie Park

Kelso (1887)

Berrymoss Racecourse Road, Kelso

Tel	(01573) 23009
Mem	350
Sec	JP Payne (01573) 23259
Holes	18 L 6066 yds SSS 69
Recs	Am–64 JF Thomas
V'tors	U SOC
Fees	On application
Loc	1 mile N of Kelso, inside racecourse

Langholm (1892)

Langholm

Tel	(013873) 80673/81247
Mem	150
Sec	WJ Wilson
Holes	9 L 2872 yds SSS 68
Recs	Am–63 G Davidson
V'tors	U
Fees	£10 (£10)
Loc	18 miles E of Lockerbie. 21 miles N of Carlisle on A7

Lauder (1896)

Galashiels Road, Lauder

Tel	(01578) 722526
Mem	250
Sec	D Dickson
Holes	9 L 6002 yds SSS 70
Recs	Am–66 CA Lumsden
	Pro–70 W Park Jr (1905)
V'tors	U SOC
Fees	£10
Loc	½ mile W of Lauder
Arch	W Park Jr

Melrose (1880)

Dingleton, Melrose

Tel	(0189) 682 2855
Mem	310
Sec	W MacRae (01835) 822758
Holes	9 L 5579 yds SSS 68
Recs	Am–62 G Matthew (1989)
V'tors	WD–U before 4pm
Fees	£15 D–£15
Loc	S boundary of Melrose, off A68

Minto (1928)

Denholm, Hawick

Tel	(01450) 870220
Mem	600
Sec	I Todd (01835) 862611
Pro	None
Holes	18 L 5460 yds SSS 67
Recs	Am–65 C Kerr (1994)
V'tors	U SOC
Fees	£15 (£20)
Loc	Denholm, 6 miles E of Hawick

Newcastleton

Holm Hill, Newcastleton TD9 0QD

Tel	(013873) 75257
Sec	FJ Ewart
Holes	9 L 5748 yds Par 70 SSS 68
V'tors	U SOC
Fees	D–£7 (£8) W–£35
Loc	E of Newcastleton, off B6357
Arch	J Shade

Peebles (1892)

Kirkland Street, Peebles

Tel	(01721) 720197
Mem	600
Sec	H Gilmore
Holes	18 L 6160 yds SSS 69
Recs	Am–63 C Fraser
	Pro–70 RDBM Shade
V'tors	H SOC
Fees	£17 D–£23 (£23 D–£32)
Loc	23 miles S of Edinburgh, via A703
Arch	James Braid/HS Colt

St Boswells (1899)

St Boswells TD6 0DE

Tel	(01835) 823527
Mem	320
Sec	JG Phillips (01835) 823858
Holes	9 L 5250 yds SSS 66
Recs	Am–61 CI Ovens (1989)
V'tors	U SOC
Fees	£12 D–£15 (£15)
Loc	Off A68 at St Boswells Green, by River Tweed
Arch	Willie Park/Shade

Selkirk (1883)

The Hill, Selkirk TD7 4NW

Tel	(01750) 20621
Mem	363
Sec	A Wilson (01750) 20907
Holes	9 L 5560 yds SSS 67
Recs	Am–60 MD Cleghorn
V'tors	WD–U exc Mon pm SOC
Fees	D–£15 (£15)
Loc	1 mile S of Selkirk on A7
Arch	Willie Park

Torwoodlee (1895)

Galashiels TD1 2NE

Tel	(01896) 752260
Mem	400
Sec	A Wilson
Pro	R Elliott
Holes	18 L 6200 yds Par 70 SSS 69
Recs	Am–64 Pro–70
V'tors	WD–U from 9.30am–1pm and after 2pm exc Thurs–NA from 4–6pm WE–by arrangement SOC
Fees	£15 (£20)
Loc	1 mile N of Galashiels on A7
Arch	Willie Park

Clackmannanshire

Alloa (1891)
Schawpark, Sauchie, Alloa FK10 3AX
Tel   **(01259) 722745**
Mem   550 80(L) 130(J)
Sec   P Ramage
Pro   W Bennett (01259) 724476
Holes   18 L 6240 yds Par 70 SSS 71
Recs   Am–63 AJ Liddle
    Pro–66 R Weir, G Harvey
V'tors   U WE–no parties
Fees   £16 D–£25 (£20 D–£30)
Loc   Sauchie, N of Alloa on A908
Arch   James Braid

Alva
Beauclerc Street, Alva FK12 5LH
Tel   **(01259) 760431**
Mem   320
Holes   9 L 2423 yds SSS 64
Recs   Am–62 (1997)
V'tors   U
Fees   On application
Loc   Back Road, Alva, on A91
    Stirling-St Andrews road.
    Signs to Alva Glen

Braehead (1891)
Cambus, Alloa FK10 2NT
Tel   **(01259) 725766**
Mem   800
Sec   P MacMichael
Pro   P Brookes (01259) 722078
Holes   18 L 6086 yds SSS 69
Recs   Am–64 D Mackison
V'tors   U–booking necessary SOC
Fees   £16 D–£24 (£24 D–£32)
Loc   2 miles W of Alloa (A907)
Arch   Robert Tait

Dollar (1890)
Brewlands House, Dollar FK14 7EA
Tel   **(01259) 742400**
Mem   480
Sec   JC Brown
Holes   18 L 5242 yds SSS 66
Recs   Am–64 D Ross, M Davies
V'tors   U SOC
Fees   £11 D–£15 (£20)
Loc   Dollar, off A91
Arch   Ben Sayers

Tillicoultry (1899)
Alva Road, Tillicoultry FK13 6BL
Tel   **(01259) 50124**
Mem   400
Sec   R Whitehead
Holes   9 L 2528 yds SSS 66
Recs   Am–62 J Malcolm
V'tors   WD/WE–U SOC
Fees   £10 (£15)
Loc   9 miles E of Stirling

Tulliallan (1902)
Kincardine, Alloa
Tel   **(01259) 30396**
Mem   525 53(L) 100(J)
Sec   JS McDowall (01324) 485420
Pro   S Kelly (01259) 30798

Holes   18 L 5982 yds SSS 69
Recs   Am–65 A Pickles, D Johnson
    Pro–70 D Huish, S Walker,
    G Gray
V'tors   U exc comp days
Fees   On application
Loc   5 miles SE of Alloa

Dumfries & Galloway

Castle Douglas (1905)
Abercromby Road, Castle Douglas
Tel   **(01556) 502801**
Mem   510
Sec   AD Millar (01556) 502099
Holes   9 L 5400 yds SSS 66
Recs   Am–62 W Blayney,
    J Shepherd (1989)
V'tors   U
Fees   £12
Loc   Off A75/A713, NE of
    Castle Douglas

Colvend (1908)
Sandyhills, Dalbeattie DG5 4PY
Tel   **(01556) 630398**
Mem   500
Sec   JB Henderson
Holes   18 L 4700 yds SSS 66
Recs   Am–63 W Blayney (1990),
    S McKnight (1995)
Fees   £15
Loc   6 miles S of Dalbeattie
    on A710

Crichton (1884)
Bankend Road, Dumfries DG1 4TH
Tel   **(01387) 247894**
Fax   (01387) 247894
Mem   450
Sec   Mrs JD Moor (Admin),
    BC Moor
Holes   9 L 3084 yds SSS 69
Recs   Am–64 W Herd Jr
    Pro–67 D Gemmell
V'tors   WD–U before 3pm SOC
Fees   £12
Loc   1 mile from Dumfries,
    nr Hospital

Dalbeattie (1897)
Dalbeattie
Tel   **(01556) 611421**
Mem   280
Sec   T Moffat
Holes   9 L 4200 yds SSS 60
V'tors   U
Fees   On application
Loc   14 miles SW of Dumfries

Dumfries & County (1912)
Nunfield, Edinburgh Road, Dumfries DG1 1JX
Tel   **(01387) 253585**
Mem   600 100(L) 100(J)
Sec   EC Pringle
Pro   S Syme (01387) 268918

Holes   18 L 5928 yds SSS 68
Recs   Am–64 D James,
    IR Brotherston,
    W Blayney, M Townsley
    Pro–63 A Thomson, F Mann,
    J McAlister
V'tors   WD–U exc 12.30–2pm–NA
    Sat–NA Sun–NA before 10am
Fees   £22 (£25)
Loc   1 mile NE of Dumfries,
    on A701
Arch   J Braid

Dumfries & Galloway (1880)
2 Laurieston Avenue, Maxwelltown, Dumfries
Tel   **(01387) 253582**
Mem   450
Sec   J Donnachie (01387) 263848
Pro   J Fergusson (01387) 256902
Holes   18 L 5782 yds SSS 68
Recs   Am–62 A Miller
    Pro–63 K Baxter
V'tors   U
Fees   £25 (£30)
Loc   Dumfries
Arch   Willie Fernie

Gatehouse (1921)
Gatehouse of Fleet
Tel   **(01557) 814766 (Clubhouse),**
    (01644) 450260 (Bookings)
Mem   350
Sec   JS McConchie (01557) 840239
Holes   9 L 2521 yds SSS 66
Recs   Am–60 S Martin
V'tors   U
Fees   D–£10 (D–£10)
Loc   ³⁄₄mile N of Gatehouse.
    9 miles NW of Kirkcudbright

Gretna (1991)
Kirtle View, Gretna DG16 5HD
Tel   **(01461) 338464**
Sec   G & E Birnie (Props)
Holes   9 L 6430 yds SSS 71
V'tors   U SOC
Fees   £8 (£10)
Loc   1 mile W of Gretna, off A75
Mis   Driving range
Arch   Nigel Williams

Hoddom Castle (1973)
Pay and play
Hoddom Bridge, Ecclefechan DG11 1AS
Tel   **(01576) 300251**
Sec   D Laycock
Holes   9 L 2274 yds SSS 33
V'tors   U
Fees   £5 (£6)
Loc   2 miles SW of Ecclefechan
    on B725. M74 Junction 6

Kirkcudbright (1893)
Stirling Crescent, Kirkcudbright DG6 4EZ
Tel   **(01557) 330314**
Mem   500
Sec   N Russell
Holes   18 L 5739 yds SSS 69

Recs Am–65 S McLeish (1996)
Ladies–74 M Clement (1995)
V'tors U H–phone first SOC
Fees £18 D–£23 (£15 D–£20)
Loc ½ mile from Kirkcudbright
town centre

Lochmaben (1926)

Castlehill Gate, Lochmaben DG11 1NT
Tel (01387) 810552
Mem 650
Sec JM Dickie
Holes 18 L 5357 yds SSS 66
Recs Am–63 BJ Scott (1996)
V'tors WD–U before 5pm WE–U
exc comp days SOC
Fees £16 D–£20 (£20 D–£25)
Loc 4 miles W of Lockerbie
on A709. 8 miles NE of
Dumfries
Arch James Braid

Lockerbie (1889)

Corrie Road, Lockerbie DG11 2ND
Tel (01576) 203363
Fax (01576) 203363
Mem 620
Sec J Thomson
Holes 18 L 5418 yds SSS 66
Recs Am–64 P Laurie (1997)
Ladies–74 W Murray (1997)
V'tors U exc Sun–NA before 11.30am
Fees £18 Sat–£22 Sun–£18
Loc ½ mile NE of Lockerbie,
on Corrie road
Arch James Braid

Moffat (1884)

Coatshill, Moffat DG10 9SB
Tel (01683) 220020
Mem 350
Sec TA Rankin
Pro None
Holes 18 L 5263 yds SSS 67
Recs Am–60 GJ Rodaks (1979)
V'tors WD–restricted Wed after
12 noon
Fees £18.50 D–£20 (£28 D–£30)
Loc Signposted on A701 from
Beattock (A74)
Arch Ben Sayers

New Galloway (1902)

New Galloway
Tel (01644) 430455
Mem 280
Sec AR Brown
Holes 9 L 5006 yds Par 68 SSS 67
Recs Am–64 M Billington (1997)
V'tors U
Fees D–£10
Loc S of New Galloway on A762.
20 miles N of Kirkcudbright
Arch Baillie

Newton Stewart (1981)

*Kirroughtree Avenue, Minnigaff,
Newton Stewart DG8 6PF*
Tel (01671) 402172
Mem 380

Sec J Tait
Holes 18 L 5887 yds Par 69 SSS 70
Recs Am–66 R O'Keefe (1997)
V'tors U H
Fees £17 D–£20 (£20 D–£24)
Loc N of Newton Stewart, off A75

Portpatrick (1903)

*Golf Course Road, Portpatrick
DG9 8TB*
Tel (01776) 810273
Fax (01776) 810811
Mem 530
Sec JA Horberry
Holes Dunskey 18 L 5882 yds
SSS 68
Dinvin 9 L 1504 yds Par 27
Recs Am–63 EA Little (1996)
Pro–63 G Weir,
S McAllister (1997)
Ladies–71 M Wilson,
CA Malcolm
V'tors U H SOC
Fees £18 D–£27 (£21 D–£32)
W–£80; Dinvin £8 D–£12
Loc 8 miles SW of Stranraer
Arch CW Hunter

Powfoot (1903)

Cummertrees, Annan DG12 5QE
Tel (01461) 700276
Fax (01461) 700276
Mem 820
Sec BW Sutherland MBE (Mgr)
Pro G Dick (01461) 700327
Holes 18 L 6266 yds SSS 71
Recs Am–63 C Wright,
I Thomson
Pro–67 J Stevens
V'tors WD–U Sat–NA Sun–NA
before 2pm
Fees Winter £12 5D–£48
Summer D–£30 (£23) 5D–£90
Loc 4 miles W of Annan. 15 miles
SE of Dumfries, off B724
Arch James Braid

St Medan (1905)

Monreith, Newton Stewart DG8 8NJ
Tel (01988) 700358
Mem 300
Sec D O'Neill (01988) 500555
Holes 9 L 2277 yds SSS 63
Recs Am–60 J Grundy (1990)
V'tors U SOC
Fees £12
Loc 3 miles S of Port William,
off A747

Sanquhar (1894)

Blackaddie Road, Sanquhar
Tel (01659) 50577
Mem 180
Sec Mrs J Murray (01659) 58181
Holes 9 L 5630 yds SSS 68
Recs Am–66 I Brotherston (1982),
J Copeland
V'tors U SOC
Fees On application
Loc ½ mile W of Sanquhar (A76).
30 miles N of Dumfries

Southerness (1947)

Southerness, Dumfries DG2 8AZ
Tel (01387) 880677
Fax (01387) 880644
Mem 800
Sec WD Ramage
Holes 18 L 6566 yds SSS 73
Recs Am–65 M Gronberg (1990)
Pro–71 A Crerar (1995)
V'tors H–phone first SOC
Fees D–£28 (D–£40)
Loc 16 miles S of Dumfries,
off A710
Arch Mackenzie Ross

Stranraer (1906)

Creachmore, Leswalt, Stranraer DG9 0LF
Tel (01776) 870245
Fax (01776) 870445
Mem 600
Sec BC Kelly
Holes 18 L 6308 yds SSS 72
Recs Am–66 CG Findlay, J Sproule
V'tors WE–NA before 9.30am and
11.45am–1.45pm
Fees £18 (£24)
Loc 2 miles NW of Stranraer
on A718
Arch James Braid

Thornhill (1893)

Blacknest, Thornhill DG3
Tel (01848) 330546
Mem 700
Sec JFK Crichton
Holes 18 L 6011 yds SSS 70
Recs Am–63 AJ Coltart (1990)
V'tors U
Fees On application
Loc 14 miles NW of Dumfries
(A76)

Wigtown & Bladnoch (1960)

Lightlands Terrace, Wigtown DG8 9EF
Tel (01988) 403354
Mem 190
Sec Mrs J Edmunds
Holes 9 L 2731 yds SSS 67
Recs Am–62 R Shaw (1994)
V'tors U SOC
Fees £10 (£10)
Loc Between Wigtown and
Bladnoch, off A714

Wigtownshire County (1894)

*Mains of Park, Glenluce, Newton
Stewart DG8 0NN*
Tel (01581) 300420
Mem 435
Sec R McKnight
Pro None
Holes 18 L 5847 yds SSS 68
Recs Am–67 D Taylor (1995),
R Shaw (1996)
V'tors U exc Wed–NA after 6pm
Fees £17.50 D–£22 (£19.50
D–£24)
Loc 8 miles E of Stranraer on A75
Arch W Gordon Cunningham

Dunbartonshire

Balmore (1906)

Balmore, Torrance
Tel (01360) 2120240
Mem 700
Sec GP Woolard (0141) 332 0392
Holes 18 L 5735 yds SSS 67
Recs Am–63 A Brodie
V'tors M SOC
Fees On application
Loc 4 miles N of Glasgow, off A807

Bearsden (1891)

*Thorn Road, Bearsden, Glasgow
G61 4BP*
Tel (0141) 942 2351
Mem 500
Sec JR Mercer
Holes 9 L 6014 yds SSS 69
Recs Am–67 S Hardie (1991),
P Anderson (1996)
Pro–65 R Craig (1991)
V'tors M
Loc 6 miles NW of Glasgow

Cardross (1895)

*Main Road, Cardross, Dumbarton
G82 5LB*
Tel (01389) 841213 (Clubhouse)
Fax (01389) 841754
Mem 850
Sec IT Waugh (01389) 841754
Pro R Farrell (01389) 841350
Holes 18 L 6469 yds SSS 72
Recs Am–65 J King, JLS Kinloch
(1996)
Pro–65 J White (1990)
V'tors WD–U WE–M SOC
Fees £25 D–£35
Loc 4 miles W of Dumbarton
on A814
Arch Fernie (1904)/Braid(1921)

Clober (1951)

*Craigton Road, Milngavie, Glasgow
G62 7HP*
Tel (0141) 956 1685
Mem 575
Sec TS Arthur (0141) 955 0382
Pro (0141) 956 6963 (Golf Shop)
Holes 18 L 5068 yds SSS 65
Recs Am–61 PW Smith, J Graham
V'tors WD–U before 4pm WE–M
BH–NA SOC–WD
Fees £12
Loc 7 miles NW of Glasgow

Clydebank & District (1905)

Hardgate, Clydebank G81 5QY
Tel (01389) 873289
Mem 780
Sec W Manson (01389) 800098
Pro D Pirie (01389) 878686
Holes 18 L 5823 yds SSS 68
Recs Am–64 D Galbraith (1965),
C Barrowman Jr (1993)
Pro–64 KW Walker (1994)
Ladies–68 V Melvin (1994)

V'tors WD–H
Fees On application
Loc 2 miles N of Clydebank

Clydebank Municipal (1927)

Public
*Overtoun Road, Dalmuir, Clydebank
G81 3RE*
Tel (0141) 952 8698 (Starter)
Fax (0141) 952 6372
Pro R Bowman (0141) 952 6372
Holes 18 L 5349 yds SSS 66
Recs Am–63 J Semple, P Semple
Pro–63 G Weir
V'tors U exc Sat–NA 11am–2.30pm
Fees On application
Loc 8 miles W of Glasgow

Cumbernauld (1975)

Public
*Palacerigg Country Park, Cumbernauld
G67 3HU*
Tel (01236) 734969
Mem 360
Sec DSA Cooper
Holes 18 L 6412 yds SSS 71
Recs Am–67 G Wilson
Pro–66 J Farmer
V'tors U SOC–WD only
Fees £7.50
Loc 3 miles SE of Cumbernauld
Arch Henry Cotton

Dougalston (1977)

*Strathblane Road, Milngavie,
Glasgow G62*
Tel (0141) 956 5750
Fax (0141) 956 6480
Mem 440
Sec Sandra Currie (Mgr)
Pro None
Holes 18 L 6269 yds SSS 71
Recs Am–71 J Carnegie, J McLaren
(1987)
Pro–73 B Barnes
V'tors WD–U SOC
Fees £12 D–£20
Loc 7 miles N of Glasgow on A81

Douglas Park (1897)

Hillfoot, Bearsden, Glasgow G61 2TJ
Tel (0141) 942 2220
Mem 470 270(L) 120(J)
Sec DN Nicolson
Pro D Scott (0141) 942 1482
Holes 18 L 5982 yds SSS 69
Recs Am–65 DJ Ward (1996),
IC Bell (1997)
Pro–64 C Maltman (1995)
V'tors M SOC
Loc 6 miles NW of Glasgow,
nr Hillfoot Station

Dullatur (1896)

Dullatur, Glasgow G68 0AR
Tel (01236) 723230
Mem 420 60(L)
Sec W Laing (01236) 727847
Pro D Sinclair

Holes 18 L 6253 yds SSS 70
Recs Am–62 D Kane Jr (1989)
Pro–68 J Farmer
V'tors WD–U WE–M SOC
Fees £25 After 1.30pm–£15
Loc 3 miles N of Cumbernauld

Dumbarton (1888)

Broadmeadow, Dumbarton G82 2BQ
Tel (01389) 32830
Mem 500
Sec R Turnbull
Holes 18 L 5981 yds SSS 69
Recs Am–64 CW Green
V'tors WD–U WE/BH–M
Fees On application
Loc 1 mile N of Dumbarton

Hayston (1926)

*Campsie Road, Kirkintilloch, Glasgow
G66 1RN*
Tel (0141) 776 1244
Fax (0141) 775 0723
Mem 440 70(L) 60(J)
Sec JV Carmichael (0141) 775
0723
Pro S Barnett (0141) 775 0882
Holes 18 L 6042 yds SSS 70
Recs Am–62 LS Mann
Pro–64 B Moffat
V'tors WD–I before 4.30pm –M after
4.30pm WE–M
Fees £20
Loc 1 mile N of Kirkintilloch
Arch James Braid

Helensburgh (1893)

*25 East Abercromby Street, Helensburgh
G84 9JD*
Tel (01436) 674173
Fax (01436) 671170
Mem 825
Sec D Loch
Pro D Fotheringham
(01436) 675505
Holes 18 L 6058 yds SSS 69
Recs Am–64 A Scott
Pro–65 RT Drummond,
D Chillas, B Marchbank
V'tors WD–U WE–NA
Fees On application
Loc N of Helensburgh and A814.
8 miles W of Dumbarton
Arch Tom Morris

Hilton Park (1927)

*Auldmarroch Estate, Stockiemuir Road,
Milngavie G62 7HB*
Tel (0141) 956 5124/1215
Mem 1200
Sec Mrs JA Warnock
(0141) 956 4657
Pro W McCondichie
(0141) 956 5125
Holes Hilton 18 L 6054 yds SSS 70
Allander 18 L 5374 yds SSS 66
Recs Hilton Am–65 AP McDonald,
RG Fraser, B Reid
Pro–64 AF Anderson
Allander Am–66 I Weir
Pro–62 K Baxter

V'tors WD–U before 4pm
Fees On application
Loc 8 miles NW of Glasgow
on A809
Arch James Braid

Kirkintilloch (1894)
*Todhill, Campsie Road, Kirkintilloch
G66 1RN*
Tel (0141) 776 1256
Mem 420 92(L) 104(J)
Sec IM Gray (0141) 775 2387
Holes 18 L 5269 yds SSS 66
Recs Am–61 S Shaw
Pro–68 R Weir
V'tors M SOC
Fees SOC–On application
Loc 7 miles N of Glasgow

Lenzie (1889)
19 Crosshill Road, Lenzie G66 5DA
Tel (0141) 776 1535
Mem 501 125(L) 125(J)
Sec JA Chisholm (0141) 776 6020
Pro J McCallum (0141) 777 7748
Holes 18 L 5984 yds SSS 69
Recs Am–64 S Lindsay
Pro–62 S Henderson (1995)
V'tors M SOC
Fees On application
Loc 6 miles NE of Glasgow

Loch Lomond
*Rossdhu House, Luss, Alexandria
G83 8NT*
Tel (01436) 860223
Fax (01436) 860265
Sec K Williams (Gen Mgr)
Pro C Campbell
Holes 18 L 7060 yds Par 71
Recs Pro–62 R Goosen
V'tors NA
Loc 20 miles NW of Glasgow
on A82
Arch Weiskopf/Morrish

Milngavie (1895)
*Laighpark, Milngavie, Glasgow
G62 8EP*
Tel (0141) 956 1619
Mem 390
Sec Mrs AJW Ness
Holes 18 L 5818 yds SSS 68
Recs Am–64 RGB McCallum,
R Blair, AS McGarvie
V'tors M SOC
Fees On application
Loc 7 miles NW of Glasgow

Vale of Leven (1907)
*Northfield Road, Bonhill, Alexandria
G83 9ET*
Tel (01389) 752351
Mem 600
Sec J Stewart (01389) 757691
Holes 18 L 5156 yds SSS 66
Recs Am–60 G Brown (1988)
Pro–63 EC Brown (1959)
V'tors U exc Sat (Apr–Sept) SOC
(max 36 members)

Fees £16 D–£20 (£20 D–£25)
Loc Bonhill, 3 miles N of
Dumbarton, off A82

Westerwood Hotel G&CC (1989)
*St Andrews Drive, Cumbernauld
G68 0EW*
Tel (01236) 725281 (Pro)
Fax (01236) 738478
Mem 500
Pro S Killin
Holes 18 L 6735 yds SSS 73
Recs Am–67 A Forsyth
Pro–67 G Redford
V'tors U
Fees £22.50 (£27.50)
Loc 13 miles NE of Glasgow,
off A80
Mis Driving range
Arch Dave Thomas

Windyhill (1908)
Windyhill, Bearsden G61 4QQ
Tel (0141) 942 2349
Mem 650
Sec B Davidson
Pro G Collinson (0141) 942 7157
Holes 18 L 6254 yds SSS 70
Recs Am–64 K Smyth (1994)
Pro–67 G Collinson (1989)
V'tors WD–I Sun–M SOC–WD
Fees £20
Loc 8 miles NW of Glasgow
Arch James Braid

Fife

Aberdour (1896)
Seaside Place, Aberdour KY3 0TX
Tel (01383) 860688
Fax (01383) 860050
Mem 450 170(L)
Sec TH McIntyre
(01383) 860080
Pro G McCallum
(01383) 860256
Holes 18 L 5460 yds Par 67 SSS 66
Recs Am–63 S Meiklejohn (1990)
V'tors WD–book with Pro Sat–NA
SOC
Fees £17 D–£28
Loc 8 miles SE of Dunfermline,
on coast
Arch Robertson/Anderson

Anstruther (1890)
*Marsfield Shore Road, Anstruther
KY10 3DZ*
Tel (01333) 310956
Fax (01333) 312283
Mem 500
Sec J Boal
Holes 9 L 4504 yds SSS 63
Recs Am–62 G Taylor (1992)
Pro–61 I Collins (1990)
V'tors U SOC
Fees £12 (£15)
Loc 9 miles S of St Andrews

Auchterderran (1904)
Public
Woodend Road, Cardenden KY5 0NH
Tel (01592) 721579
Mem 100
Sec W Nicolson
Holes 9 L 5400 yds SSS 66
Recs Am–66 C McRae
V'tors U
Fees On application
Loc 1 mile N of Cardenden.
6 miles W of Kirkcaldy,
off A910

Balbirnie Park (1983)
*Balbirnie Park, Markinch, Glenrothes
KY7 6NR*
Tel (01592) 612095
Fax (01592) 752006
Mem 800
Sec AD Gordon
Pro DFG Scott (01592) 752006
Holes 18 L 6210 yds SSS 70
Recs Am–66 G Birnie
Pro–69 C Gillies, S Walker
V'tors WE–booking essential
Fees £24 D–£32 (£30 D–£40)
Loc 2 miles E of Glenrothes
Arch Fraser Middleton

Ballingry (1908)
Public
*Lochore Meadows Country Park,
Crosshill, Lochgelly*
Tel (01592) 860086
Mem 150
Sec W Glencross (01592) 861316
Holes 9 L 6482 yds SSS 71
Recs Am–68 S Meiklejohn (1990)
V'tors U
Fees On application
Loc 2 miles N of Lochgelly (B920)

Burntisland (1797)
*51 Craigkennochie Terrace, Burntisland
KY3 9EN*
Tel (01592) 872728
Mem 100
Sec AD McPherson
Holes Play over Dodhead Course,
Burntisland

Burntisland Golf House Club (1898)
Dodhead, Burntisland KY3 9EY
Tel (01592) 874093
Fax (01592) 874093
Mem 800
Sec WK Taylor (Mgr)
(01592) 874093
Pro J Montgomery
(01592) 872116
Holes 18 L 5965 yds SSS 70
Recs Am–65 WT Beveridge (1997)
Pro–62 D Robertson (1995)
V'tors U
Fees £15 D–£21 (£25 D–£35)
Loc 1 mile E of Burntisland
on B923
Arch Willie Park Jr/James Braid

Canmore (1898)

Venturefair, Dunfermline
Tel   **(01383) 724969**
Mem   580 90(L) 80(J)
Sec   JC Duncan
       (01383) 726098
Pro   (01383) 728416
Holes 18 L 5437 yds SSS 66
Recs   Am–61 R Wallace
V'tors WD–U WE–restricted
Fees   £12 D–£18
Loc   1 mile N of Dunfermline
       on A823

Charleton (1994)

Pay and play
Charleton, Colinsburgh KY9 1HG
Tel   **(01333) 340505**
Fax   (01333) 340583
Pro   G Finlayson
       (01333) 426649
Holes 18 L 6149 yds SSS 70
V'tors U SOC
Fees   £16 (£20)
Loc   1 mile W of Colinsburgh,
       off B492
Mis   Driving range. 9 holes pitch
       & putt
Arch   John Salveson

Cowdenbeath (1991)

Public
Seco Place, Cowdenbeath
Tel   **(01383) 511918**
Mem   400
Sec   D Ferguson
Holes 9 L 6552 yds SSS 70
Recs   Am–68
V'tors U
Fees   On application
Loc   In Cowdenbeath, signposted
       from A909

Crail Golfing Society
(1786)

*Balcomie Clubhouse, Fifeness, Crail
KY10 3XN*
Tel   **(01333) 450278**
Fax   (01333) 450416
Mem   750 200(L)
Sec   JF Horsfield (Mgr)
       (01333) 450686
Pro   G Lennie (01333) 450960
Holes 18 L 5922 yds SSS 69
V'tors U
Fees   On application
Loc   11 miles SE of St Andrews

Cupar (1855)

Hilltarvit, Cupar KY15 5JT
Tel   **(01334) 653549**
Fax   (01334) 653549
Mem   475
Sec   JM Houston (01334) 654101
Holes 9 L 5074 yds SSS 65
Recs   Am–61 TR Spence
V'tors WD–U Sat–NA
       SOC–WD/Sun
Fees   £12 (£15)
Loc   10 miles W of St Andrews

Dunfermline (1887)

*Pitfirrane, Crossford, Dunfermline
KY12 8QW*
Tel   **(01383) 723534**
Mem   520
Sec   R De Rose
Pro   S Craig (01383) 729061
Holes 18 L 6126 yds SSS 70
Recs   Am–65 RW Malcolm
       Pro–65 A Brooks
V'tors WD/Sun–U 10–12 & 2–4pm
       Sat–M SOC–WD
Fees   £20 D–£28 (£25 D–£35)
Loc   2 miles W of Dunfermline
       on A994
Arch   JR Stutt

Dunnikier Park (1963)

Public
Dunnikier Way, Kirkcaldy KY1 3LP
Tel   **(01592) 261599**
Mem   600 35(L) 75(J)
Sec   RA Waddell (01592) 200627
Pro   G Whyte (01592) 642121
Holes 18 L 6601 yds SSS 72
Recs   Am–65 S Duthie (1988)
       Pro–65 A Hunter (1988)
V'tors U SOC
Fees   £15 (£20)
Loc   N boundary of Kirkcaldy
Arch   R Stutt

Earlsferry Thistle (1875)

Melon Park, Elie KY9 1AS
Mem   60
Sec   J Fyall
Holes Play over Golf House Club
       course

Falkland (1976)

Public
The Myre, Falkland KY7 7AA
Tel   **(01337) 857404**
Mem   350
Sec   Mrs H Horsburgh
Holes 9 L 2384 metres SSS 66
Recs   Am–62 AD Morrison (1993)
V'tors U SOC
Fees   On application
Loc   5 miles N of Glenrothes
       on A912

Glenrothes (1958)

Public
*Golf Course Road, Glenrothes
KY6 2LA*
Tel   **(01592) 754561/758686**
Mem   750 35(L) 50(J)
Sec   Mrs PV Landells (01592)
       756941
Holes 18 L 6444 yds SSS 71
Recs   Am–65 C Birrell,
       NM Urquhart
       Pro–69 R Craig, B Lawson
       Ladies–70 L McKinlay (1989)
V'tors U
Fees   £12 (£16)
Loc   Glenrothes West, off A92.
       M90 Junction 3
Arch   JR Stutt

Golf House Club (1875)

Elie, Leven KY9 1AS
Tel   **(01333) 330327**
Fax   (01333) 330895
Sec   A Sneddon (01333) 330301
Pro   R Wilson (01333) 330955
Holes 18 L 6261 yds SSS 69
       9 L 2277 yds SSS 32
Recs   Am–63 AW Mathers
       Pro–62 K Nagle
V'tors July–Sept ballot. WE–no party
       bookings. WE–NA before
       3pm (May–Sept)
Fees   £32 D–£45 (£40 D–£50)
Loc   12 miles S of St Andrews

Kinghorn Ladies (1905)

*Golf Clubhouse, McDuff Crescent,
Kinghorn KY3 9RE*
Tel   **(01592) 890345**
Mem   39
Sec   Miss E Douglas
       (01592) 890512
Holes Play over Kinghorn Municipal

Kinghorn Municipal
(1887)

Public
McDuff Crescent, Kinghorn KY3 9RE
Tel   **(01592) 890345**
Fax   (01592) 55761
Sec   JP Robertson (01592) 203397
Pro   None
Holes 18 L 5629 yds SSS 67
Recs   Am–64 G Wilkinson (1991)
V'tors U SOC
Fees   £7.60 (£10)
Loc   3 miles S of Kirkcaldy (A921)
Mis   Kinghorn and Kinghorn
       Thistle Clubs play here
Arch   Tom Morris

Kirkcaldy (1904)

Balwearie Road, Kirkcaldy KY2 5LT
Tel   **(01592) 260370**
Mem   450 100(L)
Sec   AC Thomson (01592) 205240
Pro   S McKay (01592) 203258
Holes 18 L 6040 yds SSS 70
Recs   Am–66 G Ridsdale, S Swan
V'tors U exc Sat–NA
Fees   On application
Loc   S end of Kirkcaldy

Ladybank (1879)

Annsmuir, Ladybank KY15 7RA
Tel   **(01337) 830320 (Clubhouse),
       (01337) 830725 (Starter)**
Fax   **(01337) 831505**
Mem   900
Sec   IF Sproule (01337) 830814
Pro   MJ Gray (01337) 830725
Holes 18 L 6641 yds SSS 72
Recs   Am–63 P Stewart (1995)
       Pro–65 M Brookes (1995)
V'tors WD–U 9.30am–4.30pm
       M–after 4.30pm WE–NA
       10.15am–5pm
Fees   £28 (£35)
Loc   6 miles SW of Cupar

Leslie (1898)

Balsillie Laws, Leslie, Glenrothes
KY6 3EZ
Tel   (01592) 620040
Mem   300
Sec   G Lewis
Holes   9 L 4940 yds SSS 64
Recs   Am–59 R Bremer
Pro–64 J Chillas
V'tors   U
Fees   £5 (£8)
Loc   3 miles W of Glenrothes.
M90 Junction 5/7, 11 miles

Leven Golfing Society
(1820)

Links Road, Leven KY8 4HS
Tel   (01333) 426096/424229
Fax   (01333) 424229
Mem   655
Sec   RT Wright (01333) 424229
Holes   Play over Leven Links

Leven Links (1846)

The Promenade, Leven KY8 4HS
Tel   (01333) 421390 (Starter)
Fax   (01333) 428859
Mem   1200
Sec   (01333) 428859 (Links Joint
Committee)
Holes   18 L 6434 yds SSS 71
Recs   Am–62 M Eliasson,
B Williams (1996)
Pro–63 P Hoad (1984)
V'tors   WD–U before 5pm Sat–no
parties Sun–NA before
10.30am SOC
Fees   £24 (£34)
Loc   E of Leven, on promenade.
12 miles SW of St Andrews

Leven Thistle (1867)

3 Balfour Street, Leven KY8 4JF
Tel   (01333) 426397
Mem   500
Sec   J Scott (01333) 426333
Holes   Play over Leven Links

Lochgelly (1895)

Cartmore Road, Lochgelly
Tel   (01592) 780174
Mem   450
Sec   RF Stuart (01383) 512238
Pro   None
Holes   18 L 5454 yds SSS 66
Recs   Am–65 D Sinclair (1995)
V'tors   U
Fees   £12 (£17)
Loc   NW edge of Lochgelly.
5 miles W of Kirkcaldy

Lundin (1868)

Golf Road, Lundin Links KY8 6BA
Tel   (01333) 320202
Fax   (01333) 329743
Mem   800
Sec   DR Thomson
Pro   DK Webster (01333) 320051
Holes   18 L 6394 yds SSS 71

Recs   Am–64 C Hislop
Pro–63 AD Hare
V'tors   WD–U H Sat–NA before
2.30pm Sun–M H
Fees   £27 D–£36 Sat–£36
Loc   3 miles E of Leven
Arch   James Braid

Lundin Ladies (1891)

Woodielea Road, Lundin Links
KY8 6AR
Tel   (01333) 320022/320832
Mem   350
Sec   Mrs E Davidson
(01333) 320490
Holes   9 L 4730 yds SSS 67
Recs   Am–67 Miss L Bennett
V'tors   U
Fees   On application
Loc   3 miles E of Leven

Methil (1892)

Links House, Links Road, Leven
KY8 4HS
Tel   (01333) 425535
Mem   50
Sec   ATJ Traill
Holes   Play over Leven Links

Pitreavie (1922)

Queensferry Road, Dunfermline
KY11 5PR
Tel   (01383) 722591
Mem   700
Sec   RT Mitchell MBE JP
Pro   C Mitchell (01383) 723151
Holes   18 L 6031 yds SSS 69
Recs   Am–65 D Manson (1990)
Pro–64 S Kennedy
V'tors   U–phone Pro SOC (Parties –
max 36 – must be booked in
advance)
Fees   £18 D–£24 (£35)
Loc   2 miles off M90 Junction 2,
between Rosyth and
Dunfermline
Arch   Dr A Mackenzie

St Michael's (1903)

Leuchars
Tel   (01334) 839365
Fax   (01334) 838666
Mem   550
Sec   R Smith (01334) 838666
Holes   18 L 5802 yds SSS 68
Recs   Am–69 C Smith (1996)
Pro–71 J Farmer (1996)
V'tors   Sun am–NA (Mar–Oct) SOC
Fees   D–£15
Loc   5 miles N of St Andrews
on Dundee road (A919)

Saline (1912)

Kinneddar Hill, Saline KY12 9LT
Tel   (01383) 852591
Mem   400
Sec   R Hutchison (01383) 852344
Holes   9 L 5302 yds SSS 66
Recs   Am–A Brown
V'tors   U exc medal Sat
Fees   £9 (£11)
Loc   5 miles NW of Dunfermline

Scoonie (1952)

Public
North Links, Leven KY8 1DH
Tel   (01333) 27057
Sec   KD Houston
Pro   None
Holes   18 L 5600 yds SSS 66
Recs   Am–63 P Lamont
V'tors   U SOC
Fees   On application
Loc   Adjoins Leven Links

Scotscraig (1817)

Golf Road, Tayport DD6 9DZ
Tel   (01382) 552515
Fax   (01382) 553130
Mem   750
Sec   K Gourlay
Pro   SJ Campbell
Holes   18 L 6550 yds SSS 72
Recs   Am–69 D Landsburgh
Pro–69
V'tors   WD–U WE–by prior
arrangement SOC
Fees   On application
Loc   10 miles N of St Andrews

Thornton (1921)

Station Road, Thornton KY1 4DW
Tel   (01592) 771173 (Starter)
Fax   (01592) 774955
Mem   630
Sec   BSL Main (01592) 771111
Holes   18 L 6175 yds Par 70 SSS 69
Recs   Am–64 A McDonaugh
(1994), D Imrie (1996),
S Swan (1997)
V'tors   U
Fees   £15 D–£25 (£22 D–£32)
Loc   5 miles N of Kirkcaldy,
off A92

St Andrews Clubs

New Golf Club (1902)

3-6 Gibson Place, St Andrews
KY16 9JE
Tel   (01334) 473426
Fax   (01334) 477570
Mem   1550
Sec   AJ Dochard (Sec/Mgr)
Holes   Play over St Andrews Links
courses

Royal & Ancient (1754)

St Andrews KY16 9JD
Tel   (01334) 472112
Fax   (01334) 477580
Mem   1800
Sec   MF Bonallack OBE
Holes   Play over St Andrews Links

St Andrews (1843)

Links House, The Links, St Andrews
KY16 9JB
Tel   (01334) 474637
Fax   (01334) 479577
Mem   1909

Sec K Barber (Sec/Mgr) (0334) 73017
Holes Play over St Andrews Links

St Andrews Thistle (1817)

St Andrews KY16 9JB
Mem 190
Sec DL Joy (01334) 473749
Holes Play over St Andrews Links

St Regulus Ladies'

9 Pilmour Links, St Andrews KY16 9JG
Mem 186
Sec Mrs N Davidson (01382) 543183
Holes Play over St Andrews Links

The St Rule Club (1898)

12 The Links, St Andrews KY16 9JB
Tel (01334) 472988
Mem 200
Sec Mrs JA Sanderson (Golf), Mrs J Pate (Club)
Holes Play over St Andrews Links

St Andrews Courses

Balgove Course (1993)

Public
St Andrews Links Trust, St Andrews KY16 9SF
Tel (01334) 466666
Fax (01334) 477036
Sec I Forbes (Links Mgr)
Holes 9 L 1520 yds (Beginners course)
V'tors U
Fees £7 3D–£18 W–£36
Loc St Andrews Links, on A91
Mis Driving range
Arch Donald Steel

Duke's Course (1995)

Craigtoun Park, St Andrews KY16 8NS
Tel (01334) 479947
Fax (01334) 479456
Sec Heidi Orr (Golf Admin)
Pro J Kelly
Holes 18 L 7171 yds Par 72 SSS 72
V'tors U–booking required SOC
Fees £50 D–£65
Loc Craigtoun Park
Arch Peter Thompson

Eden Course (1914)

Public
St Andrews Links Trust, St Andrews KY16 9SF
Tel (01334) 466666
Fax (01334) 477036
Sec I Forbes (Links Mgr)
Holes 18 L 6112 yds SSS 70
V'tors U SOC
Fees £8–£21
Loc St Andrews Links, on A91

Mis 3D–£77 W–£154 (unlimited play over Jubilee, New, Eden, Strathtyrum and Balgove courses). Driving range
Arch HS Colt

Jubilee Course (1897)

Public
St Andrews Links Trust, St Andrews KY16 9SF
Tel (01334) 466666
Fax (01334) 477036
Sec I Forbes (Links Mgr)
Holes 18 L 6805 yds SSS 73
V'tors U SOC
Fees £11–£29
Loc St Andrews Links, on A91. Signs to West Sands
Mis 3D–£77 W–£154 (unlimited play over Jubilee, Strathtyrum, Eden & New courses). Driving range
Arch Angus/Steel

New Course (1895)

Public
St Andrews Links Trust, St Andrews KY16 9SF
Tel (01334) 466666
Fax (01334) 477036
Sec I Forbes (Links Mgr)
Holes 18 L 6604 yds SSS 72
Recs Am–67 GM Mitchell Pro–63 F Jowle
V'tors U SOC
Fees £12–£31
Loc St Andrews Links, on A91. Signs to West Sands
Mis 3D–£77 W–£154 (unlimited play over Jubilee, New, Eden, Strathtyrum and Balgove courses). Driving range
Arch Old Tom Morris

Old Course (15th Century)

Public
St Andrews Links Trust, St Andrews KY16 9SF
Tel (01334) 466666
Fax (01334) 477036
Sec I Forbes (Links Mgr)
Holes 18 L 6566 yds SSS 72
Recs Am–66 C McLachlan Pro–65 J Leonard, J Parnevik (1997) Ladies–67 M McKay (1993)
V'tors H I No Sun play
Fees £34–£72
Loc St Andrews Links, on A91. Signs to West Sands
Mis Driving range

Strathtyrum Course (1993)

Public
St Andrews Links Trust, St Andrews KY16 9SF
Tel (01334) 466666
Fax (01334) 477036
Sec I Forbes (Links Mgr)
Holes 18 L 5094 yds Par 69 SSS 64

V'tors U SOC
Fees £7–£16
Loc St Andrews Links, on A91
Mis 3D–£77 W–£154 (unlimited play over Jubilee, New, Eden, Strathtyrum and Balgove courses). Driving range
Arch Donald Steel

Glasgow

Alexandra Park (1880)

Public
Alexandra Park, Dennistoun, Glasgow G31 8SE
Tel (0141) 556 1294
Mem 250
Sec G Campbell
Holes 9 L 4562 yds Par 62
V'tors U
Fees On application
Loc ½ mile E of Glasgow, nr M8
Arch Graham McArthur

Bishopbriggs (1906)

Brackenbrae Road, Bishopbriggs, Glasgow G64 2DX
Tel (0141) 772 1810
Fax (0141) 762 2532
Mem 400 100(L) 100(J)
Sec J Quin (0141) 772 8938
Holes 18 L 6041 yds SSS 69
Recs Am–63 M Loftus (1995) Pro–63 M Miller
V'tors M or I H
Fees On application
Loc 6 miles N of Glasgow on A803
Arch James Braid

Cathcart Castle (1895)

Mearns Road, Clarkston G76 7YL
Tel (0141) 638 0082
Mem 900
Sec IG Sutherland (0141) 638 9449
Pro D Naylor (0141) 638 3436
Holes 18 L 5832 yds SSS 68
Recs Am–62 S Black (1985) Pro–64 A White (1983)
V'tors M SOC
Fees £17 D–£25
Loc 1 mile from Clarkston on B767

Cawder (1933)

Cadder Road, Bishopbriggs, Glasgow G64 3QD
Tel (0141) 772 7101
Fax (0141) 772 4463
Mem 1200
Sec GT Stoddart (0141) 772 5167
Pro K Stevely (0141) 772 7102
Holes Cawder 18 L 6295 yds SSS 71; Keir 18 L 5877 yds SSS 68
Recs Cawder Am–68 CW Green Pro–61 I Spencer Keir Am–63 G Rodaks, GH Murray
V'tors WD–U WE–NA SOC–WD

Fees £27
Loc N of Glasgow, off A803
Kirkintilloch road
Arch Braid/Steel

Cowglen (1906)

301 Barrhead Road, Glasgow G43
Tel (0141) 632 0556
Mem 450
Sec RJG Jamieson (01292)
266600
Pro J McTear (0141) 649 9401
Holes 18 L 6006 yds SSS 69
Recs Am–63 D Barclay Howard
Pro–63 S Torrance
V'tors M
Fees £20 D–£30
Loc 3 miles SW of Glasgow (B762)

Deaconsbank (1922)

Public
Rouken Glen Park, Stewarton Road,
Eastwood, Glasgow G46
Tel (0141) 638 7044
Sec C Cosh
Holes 18 L 4800 yds SSS 63
V'tors U
Fees On application
Loc 5 miles S of Glasgow,
W of A77
Mis Driving range

Glasgow (1787)

Killermont, Bearsden, Glasgow
G61 2TW
Tel (0141) 942 1713
Fax (0141) 942 0770
Mem 800
Sec DW Deas (0141) 942 2011
Pro J Steven (0141) 942 8507
Holes 18 L 5968 yds Par 70 SSS 69
Recs Am–63 JS Cochran,
C Barrowman
Pro–65 H Weetman
V'tors M
Loc 4 miles NW of Glasgow
Arch Tom Morris Sr

Haggs Castle (1910)

70 Dumbreck Road, Dumbreck,
Glasgow G41 4SN
Tel (0141) 427 0480
Fax (0141) 427 1157
Mem 970
Sec I Harvey (0141) 427 1157
Pro J McAlister (0141) 427 3355
Holes 18 L 6464 yds SSS 72
Recs Am–64 M Goggin,
I Steel (1995)
Pro–62 S Torrance (1984)
V'tors M SOC–Weds only
Fees SOC–£27 D–£38
Loc SW Glasgow (B768)

King's Park (1934)

Public
150A Croftpark Avenue, Croftfoot,
Glasgow G54
Tel (0141) 630 1597
Sec PJ King

Holes 9 L 4236 yds Par 64 SSS 60
Recs Am–27 I Simpson
V'tors U
Fees On application
Loc Croftfoot, 3½ miles S of
Glasgow

Knightswood (1929)

Public
Knightswood Park, Lincoln Avenue,
Glasgow G13
Tel (0141) 959 6358
Mem 40
Sec J Dean (0141) 954 6495
Holes 9 L 2792 yds SSS 34
V'tors U
Fees On application
Loc 4 miles NW of Glasgow,
S of A82

Lethamhill (1933)

Public
Cumbernauld Road, Glasgow
G33 1AH
Tel (0141) 770 6220
Fax (0141) 770 0520
Holes 18 L 5946 yds SSS 68
Recs Am–70 R Harker
V'tors U
Fees £5.50 (1996)
Loc 3 miles NE of Glasgow (A80)

Linn Park (1924)

Public
Simshill Road, Glasgow G44 5TA
Tel (0141) 637 5871
Holes 18 L 4592 yds SSS 65
Recs Am–62 J Cassidy (1989)
V'tors U
Fees £5.50 (1996)
Loc 4 miles S of Glasgow,
W of B766

Littlehill (1926)

Public
Auchinairn Road, Glasgow G64 1UT
Tel (0141) 772 1916
Holes 18 L 6228 yds SSS 70
Recs Am–69
V'tors U
Fees £3.25 (£3.80)
Loc 3 miles NE of Glasgow,
E of A803

Pollok (1892)

90 Barrhead Road, Glasgow
G43 1BG
Tel (0141) 632 1080
Fax (0141) 649 1398
Mem 500
Sec A Mathison Boyd
(0141) 632 4351
Pro None
Holes 18 L 6257 yds SSS 70
Recs Am–62 G Shaw
Pro–62 G Cunningham
V'tors WD–I XL WE–NA SOC–WD
Fees £30 D–£40
Loc 3 miles SW of Glasgow
(B762). M77 Junction 3

Ralston (1904)

Strathmore Avenue, Ralston, Paisley
PA1 3DT
Tel (0141) 882 1349
Mem 440 165(L) 100(J)
Sec J Pearson
Pro J Scott (0141) 810 4925
Holes 18 L 6100 yds SSS 69
Recs Am–62 A Forsyth
Pro–62 M King
V'tors M
Loc 2 miles E of Paisley (A737)

Ruchill (1928)

Public
Ruchil Park, Brassey Street, Maryhill,
Glasgow G20
Mem 60
Sec DF Campbell
(0141) 946 7676
Holes 9 L 2240 yds SSS 31
V'tors U
Fees On application
Loc 2 miles N of Glasgow,
W of A879

Sandyhills (1905)

223 Sandyhills Road, Glasgow
G32 9NA
Tel (0141) 778 1179
Mem 700
Sec P Ward
Holes 18 L 6253 yds SSS 71
Recs Am–65 J Hay
V'tors WE–M SOC
Fees £17.50
Loc 4 miles SE of Glasgow,
N of A74

Williamwood (1906)

Clarkston Road, Netherlee, Glasgow
G44 3YR
Tel (0141) 637 1783
Mem 680
Sec P Laing
Pro J McTear (0141) 637 2715
Holes 18 L 5878 yds SSS 69
Recs Am–61 H Kemp (1990)
Pro–61 BJ Gallacher (1974)
V'tors M
Loc 5 miles S of Glasgow
Arch James Braid

Lanarkshire

Airdrie (1877)

Rochsoles, Airdrie ML6 0PQ
Tel (01236) 762195
Mem 450
Sec DM Hardie
Pro G Monks
(01236) 754360
Holes 18 L 6004 yds SSS 69
Recs Am–63 G Rankin
V'tors M I WE/BH–NA SOC
Fees £15 D–£25
Loc Airdrie 1 mile
Arch James Braid

Bellshill (1905)

Community Road, Orbiston, Bellshill
ML4 2RZ

Tel	**(01698) 745124**
Mem	680
Sec	Mrs L Kennedy (Admin)
Holes	18 L 5900 yds Par 69 SSS 69
Recs	Am–67
	Pro–70 J McCallum
V'tors	WD–U Sun–NA before
	1.30pm SOC
Fees	D–£18 (£25)
Loc	30 miles W (A725) M74
	Junction 5

Biggar (1895)

Public
The Park, Broughton Road, Biggar
ML12 6AH

Tel	**(01899) 220618 (Clubhouse)**,
	(01899) 220319 (Bookings)
Mem	250
Sec	WS Turnbull (01899) 220566
Pro	None
Holes	18 L 5416 yds SSS 66
Recs	Am–61 B Kerr (1994),
	G Venerus (1995)
	Pro–63 P Lawrie (1993)
V'tors	U–booking recommended
Fees	£9 (£10)
Loc	12 miles SE of Lanark (A702)
Arch	Willie Park

Blairbeth (1910)

Burnside, Rutherglen, Glasgow
G73 4SF

Tel	**(0141) 634 3355**
Mem	450
Sec	FT Henderson (0141) 569
	7266
Holes	18 L 5518 yds SSS 68
Recs	Am–64 D Orr
	Pro–69 WG Cunningham
V'tors	SOC–WD
Fees	On application
Loc	1 mile S of Rutherglen

Bothwell Castle (1922)

Blantyre Road, Bothwell, Glasgow
G71 8PS

Tel	**(01698) 853177**
Fax	(01698) 854052
Mem	1137
Pro	JG Niven (01698) 852052
Holes	18 L 6243 yds SSS 70
Recs	Am–62 B Howard
	Pro–61 A Crerar (1994)
V'tors	WD–U 9.30–10.30am &
	2.30–3.30pm
Fees	£20 D–£28
Loc	3 miles N of Hamilton. M74
	Junction 5

Calderbraes (1891)

57 Roundknowe Road, Uddingston
G71 7TS

Tel	**(01698) 813425**
Mem	300
Sec	S McGuigan (0141) 773 2287
Holes	9 L 5046 yds Par 66 SSS 67
Recs	Am–65 D Gilchrist (1986)

V'tors	WD–U WE–M
Fees	D–£12
Loc	Start of M74

Cambuslang (1892)

30 Westburn Drive, Cambuslang
G72 7NA

Tel	**(0141) 641 3130**
Mem	200 100(L) 75(J)
Sec	RM Dunlop
Holes	9 L 6072 yds SSS 69
Recs	Am–62 S Gillespie (1996)
V'tors	M
Fees	On application
Loc	Cambuslang Station ¾ mile

Carluke (1894)

Hallcraig, Mauldslie Road, Carluke
ML8 5HG

Tel	**(01555) 771070/770574**
Mem	460 100(L)
Sec	D Black (01555) 773086
Pro	R Forrest (01555) 751053
Holes	18 L 5805 yds SSS 68
Recs	Am–63 D Brown
	Pro–64 G Cunningham,
	R Davis, W Milne
V'tors	WD–U before 4pm
	WE/BH–NA
Fees	£18 D–£25
Loc	20 miles SE of Glasgow

Carnwath (1907)

Main Street, Carnwath ML11 8JX

Tel	**(01555) 840251**
Mem	380
Sec	To be appointed
Pro	None
Holes	18 L 5955 yds SSS 69
Recs	Am–65 B Holbrook
V'tors	WD–U before 4pm Sat–NA
	Sun–restricted
Fees	WD/Sat–D–£18
	Sun/BH–D–£22
Loc	7 miles E of Lanark

Cathkin Braes (1888)

Cathkin Road, Rutherglen, Glasgow
G73 4SE

Tel	**(0141) 634 6605**
Fax	(0141) 634 6605
Mem	900
Sec	H Millar
Pro	S Bree (0141) 634 0650
Holes	18 L 6208 yds SSS 71
Recs	Am–65 L McLaughlin (1994)
	Pro–66 C Maltman (1992)
V'tors	WD–I
Fees	£25
Loc	5 miles S of Glasgow (B759)
Arch	James Braid

Coatbridge (1971)

Public
Townhead Road, Coatbridge
ML52 2HX

Tel	**(01236) 28975**
Mem	300
Sec	O Dolan (01236) 26811
Pro	G Weir (01236) 21492

Holes	18 L 6020 yds SSS 69
Recs	Am–69 A Webster (1989)
V'tors	U
Fees	On application
Loc	Townhead, E of Glasgow.
	½ mile E of M73
Mis	Driving range

Colville Park (1922)

Jerviston Estate, Motherwell ML1 4UG

Tel	**(01698) 263017**
Fax	(01698) 263017
Mem	800 64(L) 140(J)
Sec	S Connacher (01698) 265378
Pro	Golf Shop (01698) 265779
Holes	18 L 6265 yds SSS 70
Recs	Am–65 G King
	Pro–66 SD Brown
V'tors	M SOC–WD only
Fees	D–£20
Loc	1 mile NE of Motherwell
	on A723
Arch	James Braid

Crow Wood (1925)

Cumbernauld Road, Muirhead,
Glasgow G69 9JF

Tel	**(0141) 799 2011**
Mem	700
Sec	I McInnes (0141) 779 4954
Pro	B Moffat (0141) 779 1943
Holes	18 L 6261 yds Par 71 SSS 71
Recs	Am–62 D Robertson
	Pro–66 J McTear, A Oldcorn
V'tors	WD–H (prior notice required)
	SOC
Fees	£20 D–£28
Loc	5 miles NE of Glasgow, off A80
Arch	James Braid

Douglas Water (1922)

Douglas Water, Lanark ML11 9NB

Tel	**(01555) 880361**
Mem	190
Sec	R McMillan
Holes	9 L 2916 yds SSS 69
Recs	Am–63 D Peat
V'tors	U exc Sat–restricted
Fees	£5 (£8)
Loc	7 miles S of Lanark

Drumpellier (1894)

Drumpellier Ave, Coatbridge ML5 1RX

Tel	**(01236) 424139/428723**
Mem	500
Sec	W Brownlie (01236) 428723
Pro	D Ross (01236) 432971
Holes	18 L 6227 yds SSS 70
Recs	Am–63 G Rankin
	Pro–62 C Maltman
V'tors	I
Fees	£22 D–£30
Loc	8 miles E of Glasgow

East Kilbride (1900)

Chapelside Road, Nerston, East Kilbride
G74 4PF

Tel	**(01355) 220913 (Clubhouse)**
Fax	(01355) 247728
Mem	834

Sec WG Gray
Pro W Walker (01355) 222192
Holes 18 L 6419 yds SSS 71
Recs Am–65 WF Bryce
Pro–64 D Ingram
V'tors M SOC
Fees On application
Loc 8 miles S of Glasgow

Easter Moffat (1922)

Mansion House, Plains, Airdrie
ML6 8NP
Tel **(01236) 842878**
Mem 450
Sec JG Timmons (01236) 761440
Pro B Dunbar (01236) 843015
Holes 18 L 6221 yds SSS 70
Recs Am–65 B Lees (1995)
Pro–66 R Shade (1967)
V'tors WD only BH–NA
Fees On application
Loc 3 miles E of Airdrie

Hamilton (1892)

Riccarton, Ferniegair, by Hamilton
Tel **(01698) 282872**
Mem 500
Sec GM Chapman
(01698) 459537
Pro MJ Moir (01698) 282324
Holes 18 L 6255 yds SSS 71
Recs Am–62 G Hogg, B Smith
V'tors M or by arrangement with Sec
Fees On application
Loc 1½ miles S of Hamilton
Arch James Braid

Hollandbush (1954)

Public
Acre Tophead, Lesmahagow, Coalburn
Tel **(01555) 893484**
Mem 600
Sec J Hamilton
Pro I Rae (01555) 893646
Holes 18 L 6233 yds SSS 70
Recs Am–63 G Brown, R Lynch
V'tors U
Fees £7.25 (£8.50)
Loc 10 miles SW of Lanark,
off A74, between Lesmahagow
and Coalburn

Kirkhill (1910)

Greenlees Road, Cambuslang, Glasgow
G72 8YN
Tel **(0141) 641 3083 (Clubhouse)**
Mem 570
Sec To be appointed
Holes 18 L 5889 yds SSS 69
Recs Am–63 D Martin
Pro–68 R Weir
V'tors WD–by prior arrangement
WE/BH–NA SOC
Fees On application
Loc Cambuslang, SE Glasgow

Lanark (1851)

The Moor, Lanark ML11 7RX
Tel **(01555) 663219**
Fax (01555) 663219
Mem 500 130(L) 150(J)

Sec GH Cuthill
Pro A White (01555) 661456
Holes 18 L 6426 yds SSS 71
9 hole course
Recs Am–64 CV McInally
Pro–62 C Maltman
V'tors WD–U until 4pm WE–M
Fees 18 hole: £24 D–£36
9 hole: £4
Loc 30 miles S of Glasgow,
off A74
Arch Tom Morris

Langlands (1985)

Auldhouse Road, East Kilbride
G75 9DW
Tel **(013552) 48173**
Mem 236
Sec NJ Martin (0141) 644 2623
Holes 18 L 6202 yds Par 70 SSS 70
Recs Am–64 T Hunter (1996)
V'tors U
Fees £7.25 (£8.50)
Loc 2 miles SE of East Kilbride

Larkhall

Public
Burnhead Road, Larkhall
Tel **(01698) 881113**
Mem 400
Sec I Gilmour
Holes 9 L 6754 yds SSS 72
Recs Am–67 S Crolla
V'tors U exc Tues 5–8pm & Sat
7am–5pm
Fees On application
Loc SW of Larkhall on B7109.
10 miles SE of Glasgow

Leadhills (1935)

Leadhills, Biggar ML12 6XR
Tel **(01659) 74222**
Mem 100
Sec H Shaw
Holes 9 L 2031 yds SSS 62
V'tors U
Fees On application
Loc 6 miles S of Abington, off A74

Mount Ellen (1905)

Lochend Road, Gartcosh, Glasgow
G69 9EY
Tel **(01236) 872277**
Mem 480
Sec WJ Dickson
Pro G Reilly
Holes 18 L 5525 yds SSS 68
V'tors WD–U from 9am–4pm
WE–NA
Fees On application
Loc 8 miles NE of Glasgow,
W of M73

Shotts (1895)

Blairhead, Benhar Road, Shotts
ML7 5BJ
Tel **(01501) 820431**
Mem 700
Sec J McDermott
Pro S Strachan (01501) 822658

Holes 18 L 6205 yds SSS 70
Recs Am–65 AJ Ferguson
Pro–65 B Gunson
V'tors WD–U Sat–NA before
4.30pm
Fees D–£17 (D–£20)
Loc 18 miles E of Glasgow
on B7057. M8 Junction 5,
1½ miles
Arch James Braid

Strathaven (1908)

Glasgow Road, Strathaven
ML10 6NL
Tel **(01357) 520421**
Mem 950
Sec AW Wallace
Pro M McCrorie
(01357) 521812
Holes 18 L 6226 yds SSS 70
Recs Am–65 R Scott
Pro–63 D Huish
V'tors WD–I before 4pm WE–NA
Fees On request
Loc N of Strathaven, off Glasgow
road (A726)

Strathclyde Park

Public
Mote Hill, Hamilton
Tel **(01698) 429350**
Mem 180
Sec K Will
Pro W Walker (01698) 285511
Holes 9 L 6350 yds SSS 70
Recs Am–64 JJ Smith (1993)
V'tors U exc medal days (phone
booking)
Fees £2.40
Loc Hamilton
Mis Driving range

Torrance House (1969)

Public
Strathaven Road, East Kilbride,
Glasgow G75 0QZ
Tel **(013552) 48638**
Mem 650
Sec JB Asher (013552) 49720
Pro J Dunlop (013552) 33451
Holes 18 L 6415 yds SSS 71
Recs Am–67 A Pitt
Pro–66 I Collins
V'tors U
Fees On application
Loc S of East Kilbride,
off Strathaven road (A726)

Wishaw (1897)

55 Cleland Road, Wishaw ML2 7PH
Tel **(01698) 372869**
Mem 475 100(L)
Sec R Hutchison
Pro JG Campbell
(01698) 358247
Holes 18 L 5999 yds SSS 69
Recs Am–63 G Dingwall (1996)
Pro–63 A Hunter (1989)
V'tors WD after 4pm–NA Sat–NA
Fees £13 D–£21 Sun–£26
Loc N of Wishaw town centre

For list of abbreviations see page 479

Lothians

East Lothian

Aberlady (1912)

Aberlady EH32 0QD
Mem 35
Sec K Hope (01875) 7374
Holes Play over Kilspindie course

Bass Rock (1873)

6 Harperdean Cottages, Harperdean, Haddington EH41 3SQ
Mem 110
Sec SH Butterworth
(01620) 822082
Holes Play over North Berwick

Dirleton Castle (1854)

Gullane
Tel **(01620) 843496**
Mem 100
Sec RH Atkinson
Holes Play over Gullane courses

Dunbar (1856)

East Links, Dunbar EH42 1LT
Tel **(01368) 862317**
Fax (01368) 865202
Mem 998
Sec Liz Thom
Pro D Small (01368) 862086
Holes 18 L 6426 yds SSS 71
Recs Am–64 C Craig (1996)
Pro–64 R Weir (1989)
V'tors U SOC–exc Thurs
Fees D–£30 (D–£40)
Loc ¹/₂ mile E of Dunbar. 30 miles
E of Edinburgh, off A1
Arch Tom Morris

Gifford (1904)

Edinburgh Road, Gifford EH41 4JN
Tel **(01620) 810267**
Fax (01620) 810267
Mem 450
Sec P Blyth
Holes 9 L 6243 yds SSS 70
Recs Am–64 D Shearer (1996)
Ladies–67 S McEwan (1996)
V'tors Tues/Wed/Sat–NA after 4pm
Sun–NA after noon
Fees D–£10 (£10)
Loc 4 miles S of Haddington.
20 miles SE of Edinburgh
(B6355)
Arch Willie Watt

The Glen (1906)

East Links, North Berwick EH39 4LE
Tel **(01620) 892726**
Fax (01620) 895288
Mem 650
Sec DR Montgomery
Pro None
Holes 18 L 6079 yds SSS 69
Recs Am–64 A Imlah (1992)
V'tors U–booking recommended

Fees £17 D–£25 (£20 D–£30)
Loc 25 miles E of Edinburgh,
off A198
Mis Golf shop (01620) 894596
Arch Mackenzie Ross

Gullane (1882)

Gullane EH31 2BB
Tel **(01620) 843115 (Starter)**
Fax (01620) 842327
Mem 870 300(L) 60(J)
Sec AJB Taylor (01620) 842255
Pro J Hume (01620) 843111
Holes No 1 18 L 6466 yds SSS 72
No 2 18 L 6244 yds SSS 70
No 3 18 L 5252 yds SSS 66
6 hole children's course
Recs No 1 Am–65 ME Lewis
Pro–65 J Hobday (1992)
No 2 Am–64 RCH Robertson
Pro–66 H Bannerman
V'tors No 1–H Nos 2/3–U
Fees No 1 £54 D–£80 (£67)
No 2 £23 D–£35 (£29–£44)
No 3 £14 D–£21 (£18–£26)
Children's course free
Loc 18 miles E of Edinburgh
on A198
Mis Advance booking advisable

Haddington (1865)

Amisfield Park, Haddington EH41 4PT
Tel **(01620) 823627**
Fax (01620) 822727
Mem 650
Sec S Wilson
Pro J Sandilands (01620) 822727
Holes 18 L 6317 yds SSS 70
Recs Am–69 S Doctor
V'tors WD–U WE–U 10am–12 &
2–4pm
Fees £17 (£22)
Loc 17 miles E of Edinburgh
on A1. ³/₄ mile E of
Haddington

The Honourable Company of Edinburgh Golfers (1744)

Muirfield, Gullane EH31 2EG
Tel **(01620) 842123**
Fax (01620) 842977
Mem 625
Sec Gp Capt JA Prideaux
Holes 18 L 6601 yds SSS 73
(Championship 6963 yds)
Recs Am–68 P Lyons (1995)
Pro–63 R Davis (1987)
V'tors WD–Tues & Thurs I H
WE/BH–NA SOC
Fees £65 D–£85
Loc NE outskirts of Gullane,
opposite sign for Greywalls
Hotel on A198

Kilspindie (1867)

Aberlady, Longniddry EH32 0QD
Tel **(01875) 870358**
Fax (01875) 870358
Mem 460 150(L) 60(J)
Sec RM McInnes

Pro GJ Sked (01875) 870695
Holes 18 L 4957 metres SSS 66
Recs Am–62 RJ Humble (1990)
Pro–59 E McIntosh (1996)
V'tors Phone Sec in advance WD–U
after 9.15am WE–U after
11am SOC
Fees On application
Loc Aberlady

Longniddry (1921)

Links Road, Longniddry EH32 0NL
Tel **(01875) 852141**
Fax (01875) 853371
Mem 950
Sec N Robertson
Pro WJ Gray (01875) 852228
Holes 18 L 6219 yds SSS 70
Recs Am–63 C Hardin (1987)
Pro–63 P Harrison (1987)
V'tors WD–U H SOC–Mon–Thurs
after 9.18am
Fees £27 D–£38 (£35)
Loc 13 miles E of Edinburgh,
off A1
Arch HS Colt

Luffness New (1894)

Aberlady EH32 0QA
Tel **(01620) 843114**
Fax (01620) 842933
Mem 700
Sec Lt Col JG Tedford
(01620) 843336
Pro None
Holes 18 L 6122 yds SSS 70
Recs Am–63 R Winchester
Pro–62 C O'Connor
V'tors H or I XL before 10am
WE/BH–NA SOC
Fees £35 D–£50
Loc 1 mile W of Gullane (A198)
Arch Tom Morris

Musselburgh (1938)

Monktonhall, Musselburgh
Tel **(0131) 665 2005**
Mem 800
Sec G Miller, G Finlay (Admin)
Pro F Mann (0131) 665 7055
Holes 18 L 6614 yds SSS 73
Recs Am–65 JM Noon
Pro–67 EC Brown, B Devlin,
G Cunningham, A Jacklin
Ladies–69 J Connachan
V'tors U
Fees £18 (£25)
Loc 1 mile S of Musselburgh
on B6415
Arch James Braid

Musselburgh Old Course

Public
*Silver Ring Clubhouse, Millhill,
Musselburgh EH21 7RG*
Tel **(0131) 665 6981**
Mem 150
Holes 9 L 5380 yds SSS 67
Recs Am–67 P Hosie
V'tors WD/BH–U WE–U after 1pm
Fees On application
Loc 7 miles E of Edinburgh on A1

North Berwick (1832)

West Links, Beach Road, North Berwick EH39 4BB

Tel	(01620) 892135
Fax	(01620) 893274
Mem	324
Sec	AG Flood (01620) 895040
Pro	D Huish (01620) 893233
Holes	18 L 6420 yds SSS 71
Recs	Am–66 G Sherry (1994)
	Pro–64 N Job (1994)
V'tors	U H
Fees	£30 D–£45 (£45 D–£60)
	Winter–£15 (£20)
Loc	½ mile W of North Berwick (A198). 24 miles E of Edinburgh

Royal Musselburgh (1774)

Prestongrange House, Prestonpans EH32 9RP

Tel	(01875) 810276
Fax	(01875) 810276
Mem	800
Sec	TH Hardie (Sec/Mgr)
	J Hanratty (Golf Sec)
Pro	J Henderson (01875) 810139
Holes	18 L 6237 yds SSS 70
Recs	Am–64 J Hall (1995)
V'tors	U SOC
Fees	£20 D–£35 (£35)
Loc	8 miles E of Edinburgh on B1361 North Berwick road
Arch	James Braid

Tantallon (1853)

32 Westgate, North Berwick EH39 4AH

Tel	(01620) 2114
Mem	300
Sec	T Hill
Holes	Play over North Berwick West Links

Thorntree (1856)

Prestongrange House, Prestonpans EH32 9RP

Mem	100
Sec	J Hanratty
Holes	Play over Royal Musselburgh course

Whitekirk (1995)

Whitekirk, North Berwick EH39 5PR

Tel	(01620) 870300
Fax	(01620) 870330
Sec	C Patey
Pro	C Patey (Golf Dir)
Holes	18 L 6520 yds Par 71 SSS 72
V'tors	U
Fees	£18 (£25)
Loc	3 miles SE of North Berwick (A198)
Mis	Golf Academy
Arch	Cameron Sinclair

Winterfield (1935)

Public

St Margarets, North Road, Dunbar EH42 1AU

Tel	(01368) 862280
Mem	400
Sec	M O'Donnell (01368) 862564
Pro	K Phillips (01368) 863562
Holes	18 L 5053 yds SSS 65
Recs	Am–61 R Walkinshaw,
	J Huggan
	Pro–65 SWT Murray
V'tors	U
Fees	On application–phone Pro
Loc	W side of Dunbar. 28 miles E of Edinburgh

Midlothian

Baberton (1893)

50 Baberton Avenue, Juniper Green, Edinburgh EH14 5DU

Tel	(0131) 453 3361
Mem	800
Sec	EW Horberry (0131) 453 4911
Pro	K Kelly (0131) 453 3555
Holes	18 L 6123 yds SSS 70
Recs	Am–64 RW Bradly (1989),
	D Beveridge Jr,
	BJH Tait (1991)
	Pro–62 B Barnes
	Ladies–67 KS Marshall (1997)
V'tors	I SOC–WD
Fees	£18.50 D–£28.50
Loc	5 miles SW of Edinburgh (A70)
Arch	Willie Park Jr

Braid Hills (1893)

Public

Braid Hills Road, Edinburgh EH10 6JY

Tel	(0131) 447 6666 (Starter)
Holes	No 1 18 L 5239 yds SSS 68
	No 2 18 L 4832 yds SSS 63
Recs	Am–65
V'tors	U–no phone bookings. No 2 course closed Sun
Fees	£7
Loc	3 miles S of Edinburgh (A702)
Mis	No 2 course open Apr-Oct

Braids United (1897)

22 Braid Hills Approach, Edinburgh EH10 6JY

Tel	(0131) 452 9408
Mem	100
Sec	G Hind
Holes	Play over Braids 1 and 2

Broomieknowe (1906)

36 Golf Course Road, Bonnyrigg EH19 2HZ

Tel	(0131) 663 9317
Fax	(0131) 663 2152
Mem	500
Sec	JG White
Pro	M Patchett (0131) 660 2035
Holes	18 L 6200 yds Par 70

Recs	Am–65 K Hastings (1990),
	Am–64 SJ Knowles (1994)
V'tors	WD–U WE/BH–NA
Fees	£17 D–£25 (£20)
Loc	7 miles SE of Edinburgh
Arch	Braid/Hawtree

Bruntsfield Links Golfing Society (1761)

The Clubhouse, 32 Barnton Avenue, Edinburgh EH4 6JH

Tel	(0131) 336 2006
Fax	(0131) 336 5538
Mem	1130
Sec	Cdr DM Sandford (0131) 336 1479
Pro	B Mackenzie (0131) 336 4050
Holes	18 L 6407 yds SSS 71
Recs	Am–67 AW Ritchie
V'tors	SOC–apply to Sec–H
Fees	£36 D–£50 (£42 D–£55)
Loc	3 miles W of Edinburgh
Arch	Willie Park/Dr A Mackenzie

Carrick Knowe (1930)

Public

Glendevon Park, Edinburgh EH12 5VZ

Tel	(0131) 337 1096 (Starter)
Holes	18 L 6299 yds SSS 70
Recs	Am–64 R Bradley
V'tors	U–phone bookings not accepted
Fees	On application
Loc	5 miles W of Edinburgh

Craigentinny (1891)

Public

Craigentinny Avenue, Edinburgh EH7

Tel	(0131) 554 7501 (Starter),
	(0131) 661 5351 Ext 209
Holes	18 L 5418 yds SSS 66
Recs	Am–64
V'tors	U–phone bookings not accepted
Fees	£7
Loc	2½ miles E of Edinburgh

Craigmillar Park (1895)

1 Observatory Road, Edinburgh EH9 3HG

Tel	(0131) 667 2837
Mem	425 100(L) 70(J)
Sec	T Lawson (0131) 667 0047
Pro	B McGhee (0131) 667 0047
Holes	18 L 5859 yds SSS 69
Recs	Am–64 A Mail (1992)
	Ladies–66 M Pollock (1993)
V'tors	WD–I or H before 3.30pm WE/BH–NA
Fees	On application
Loc	Blackford, S of Edinburgh
Arch	James Braid

Duddingston (1895)

Duddingston Road West, Edinburgh EH15 3QD

Tel	(0131) 661 1005
Fax	(0131) 661 4301
Mem	580
Sec	JC Small (0131) 661 7688
Pro	A McLean (0131) 661 4301

Holes 18 L 6438 yds SSS 71
Recs Am–64 G Macgregor
Pro–65 S Torrance,
C Maltman
V'tors WD–U SOC–Tues & Thurs
Fees £27 Soc–£23
Loc SE Edinburgh

Glencorse (1890)

Milton Bridge, Penicuik EH26 0RD
Tel (01968) 677177
Fax (01968) 674399
Mem 700
Sec W Oliver (01968) 677189
Pro C Jones (01968) 676481
Holes 18 L 5217 yds Par 64 SSS 66
Recs Am–60 N Shillinglaw (1996)
Pro–60 C Brooks (1994)
V'tors WD–U SOC–Mon–Thurs
Fees £18 (£24)
Loc 8 miles S of Edinburgh (A701)

Kingsknowe (1908)

*326 Lanark Road, Edinburgh
EH14 2JD*
Tel (0131) 441 1144
Fax (0131) 441 2079
Mem 819
Sec R Wallace (0131) 441 1145
Pro A Marshall (0131) 441 4030
Holes 18 L 5966 yds SSS 69
Recs Am–63 JJ Little
Pro–64 WB Murray
V'tors WD–U before 4pm
WE–phone Pro
SOC–WD before 4pm
Fees On application
Loc SW Edinburgh

Liberton (1920)

*297 Gilmerton Road, Edinburgh
EH16 5UJ*
Tel (0131) 664 3009
Fax (0131) 664 0853
Mem 795
Sec P Long
Pro I Seath (0131) 664 1056
Holes 18 L 5306 yds SSS 66
Recs Am–61 RMF Jack, D Rennie
Pro–63 JL Brash
V'tors U–phone Pro SOC–WD
Fees £17
Loc 3 miles S of Edinburgh

Lothianburn (1893)

*106a Biggar Road, Edinburgh
EH10 7DU*
Tel (0131) 445 2206
Mem 600 75(L) 100(J)
Sec WFA Jardine (0131) 445 5067
Pro K Mungall (0131) 445 2288
Holes 18 L 5568 yds SSS 68
Recs Am–66 IJ Whigham (1997)
V'tors WD–U before 4.30pm –M
after 4.30pm WE–NA
SOC–H
Fees £15 D–£21 (£21 D–£26)
Loc S of Edinburgh, on A702.
Lothianburn exit from
Edinburgh by-pass
Arch James Braid (1928)

Marriott Dalmahoy Hotel & CC

Dalmahoy, Kirknewton EH27 8EB
Tel (0131) 333 4105/1845
Fax (0131) 335 3203
Sec B Anderson (Dir),
JM Bryans (Sec)
Pro S Callan
Holes East 18 L 6677 yds SSS 72
West 18 L 5185 yds SSS 66
Recs East Am–65 M Backhausen,
F Jacobsen
Pro–62 B Barnes
West Am–65 W Morton
Pro–60 S Callan
V'tors WD–U H SOC–WD
Fees East–£48 West–£32
Loc 7 miles W of Edinburgh
on A71
Mis Floodlit driving range
Arch James Braid

Melville Golf Centre (1995)

Pay and play
*South Melville, Lasswade
EH18 1AN*
Tel (0131) 654 0224
Fax (0131) 654 0814
Mem 50
Sec Mr & Mrs MacFarlane
(Props)
Pro G Carter (0131) 663 8038
Holes 9 L 4530 yds Par 66 SSS 62
V'tors U SOC
Fees £7–£12 (£9–£16)
Loc 7 miles S of Edinburgh on A7
Mis Floodlit driving range
Arch G Webster

Merchants of Edinburgh (1907)

*Craighill Gardens, Morningside,
Edinburgh EH10 5PY*
Tel (0131) 447 1219
Mem 730
Sec AM Montgomery
Pro NEM Colquhoun
(0131) 447 8709
Holes 18 L 4889 yds SSS 64
Recs Am–59 AK Helm (1995)
Ladies–66 LM Caine (1991)
V'tors WD–U before 4pm –M after
4pm WE–M SOC–WD
Fees £15
Loc SW of Edinburgh, off A701

Mortonhall (1892)

*231 Braid Road, Edinburgh
EH10 6PB*
Tel (0131) 447 2411
Fax (0131) 447 8712
Mem 500
Sec Mrs CD Morrison
(0131) 447 6974
Pro DB Horn (0131) 447 5185
Holes 18 L 6557 yds SSS 72
Recs Am–66 C Cassells
Pro–68 G Cunningham
V'tors H SOC

Fees £30 (£40)
Loc 2 miles S of Edinburgh
on A702
Arch James Braid/FW Hawtree

Murrayfield (1896)

*43 Murrayfield Road, Edinburgh
EH12 6EU*
Tel (0131) 337 1009
Fax (0131) 313 0721
Mem 775
Sec Mrs MK Hermiston
(0131) 337 3478
Pro J Fisher (0131) 337 3479
Holes 18 L 5727 yds SSS 69
Recs Am–64 DED Neave
Pro–63 WB Murray
V'tors WD–I WE–M
Fees £25 D–£30
Loc 2 miles W of Edinburgh centre

Newbattle (1896)

*Abbey Road, Eskbank, Dalkeith
EH22 3AD*
Tel (0131) 663 2123
Fax (0131) 654 1810
Mem 600
Sec HG Stanners
(0131) 663 1819
Pro D Torrance
(0131) 660 1631
Holes 18 L 6012 yds SSS 70
Recs Am–63 S Thorburn
Pro–61 A Oldcorn
V'tors WD–U before 4pm WE–M
Fees £16 D–£24
Loc 6 miles S of Edinburgh on A7
and A68
Arch HS Colt

Portobello (1853)

Public
*Stanley Street, Portobello, Edinburgh
EH15 1JJ*
Tel (0131) 669 4361 (Starter),
(0131) 661 5351 Ext 209
Mem 60
Holes 9 L 2419 yds SSS 32
Recs Am–27
V'tors U–phone bookings not
accepted
Fees On application
Loc 4 miles E of Edinburgh on A1

Prestonfield (1920)

*6 Priestfield Road North, Edinburgh
EH16 5HS*
Tel (0131) 667 9665
Mem 800
Sec AS Robertson
Pro G MacDonald
(0131) 667 8597
Holes 18 L 6212 yds SSS 70
Recs Am–66 AM Dun,
MD Tummins (1997)
V'tors Sat–NA 8–10.30am and
12–1.30pm Sun–NA before
11.30am SOC
Fees £20 D–£30 (£30 D–£40)
Loc 2 miles SE of Edinburgh,
off A68 Dalkeith road

Ratho Park (1928)

Ratho, Newbridge, Midlothian
EH28 8NX

Tel   (0131) 333 2566/1752
Fax   (0131) 333 1752
Mem   550 98(L) 65(J)
Sec   JS Yates (0131) 333 1752
Pro   A Pate (0131) 333 1406
Holes 18 L 5900 yds SSS 68
Recs   Am–61 DM Summers (1991)
        Pro–64 WG Stowe
V'tors U SOC–Tues–Thurs
Fees   £25 D–£35 (£35)
Loc   8 miles W of Edinburgh (A71)

Ravelston (1912)

24 Ravelston Dykes Road, Edinburgh
EH4 5NZ

Tel   (0131) 315 2486
Mem   610
Sec   S Houston
Holes 9 L 5332 yds SSS 65
Recs   Am–64 JW Fraser (1994)
        Pro–67 W Murray (1987)
V'tors WD–H
Fees   £15
Loc   Off Queensferry Road (A90).
        Turn S at Blackhall
Arch   James Braid

Royal Burgess Golfing Society of Edinburgh (1735)

181 Whitehouse Road, Barnton,
Edinburgh EH4 6BY

Tel   (0131) 339 2075
Fax   (0131) 339 3712
Mem   620 50(J)
Sec   JP Audis (0131) 339 2075
Pro   G Yuille (0131) 339 6474
Holes 18 L 6494 yds SSS 71
Recs   Am–66 J Yuille (1992)
        Pro–63
V'tors I SOC
Fees   On application
Loc   Queensferry Road (A90)
Arch   Tom Morris

Silverknowes (1947)

Public
Silverknowes, Parkway, Edinburgh
EH4 5ET

Tel   (0131) 336 3843 (Starter),
        (0131) 661 5351
Mem   511
Sec   DW Scobie
Holes 18 L 6202 yds SSS 70
Recs   Am–65 K Reilly (1995)
V'tors U–phone bookings not
        accepted SOC
Fees   £7.80
Loc   4 miles W of Edinburgh

Swanston (1927)

111 Swanston Road, Fairmilehead,
Edinburgh EH10 7DS

Tel   (0131) 445 2239
Mem   500
Sec   J Allan
Pro   I Taylor (0131) 445 4002

Holes 18 L 5024 yds SSS 65
Recs   Am–63 G Millar
V'tors U exc comp days–NA
        WE–NA after 1pm
Fees   £12 D–£18 (£17 D–£22)
Loc   S of Edinburgh, off Biggar
        road (A702)

Torphin Hill (1895)

Torphin Road, Edinburgh EH13 0PG

Tel   (0131) 441 1100
Mem   450
Sec   RM Brannan
Pro   J Browne
Holes 18 L 5025 yds SSS 66
Recs   Am–65 G Campbell
V'tors WD–U WE–U exc comp days
        SOC
Fees   D–£12 (D–£20)
Loc   SW boundary of Edinburgh

Turnhouse (1897)

154 Turnhouse Road, Corstorphine,
Edinburgh EH12 0AD

Tel   (0131) 339 1014
Mem   500
Sec   AB Hay (0131) 539 5937
Pro   J Murray (0131) 339 7701
Holes 18 L 6171 yds SSS 70
Recs   Am–65 E McIntosh (1990)
        Pro–64 D Huish
V'tors M or by arrangement
Fees   On application
Loc   W of Edinburgh (A9080)

West Lothian

Bathgate (1892)

Edinburgh Road, Bathgate
EH48 1BA

Tel   (01506) 652232
Fax   (01506) 636775
Mem   580
Sec   (01506) 630505
Pro   S Strachan (01506) 630553
Holes 18 L 6326 yds SSS 70
Recs   Am–64 J McLean
        Pro–58 S Torrance (1992)
V'tors U
Fees   £15 (£30)
Loc   15 miles W of Edinburgh.
        M8 Junction 4
Arch   Wm Park Sr

Deer Park CC (1978)

Knightsridge, Livingston EH54 9PG

Tel   (01506) 38843
Fax   (01506) 35608
Mem   500
Sec   I Thomson
Pro   W Yule
Holes 18 L 6636 yds SSS 72
Recs   Am–67 D Thomson (1994)
        Pro–66
V'tors U SOC
Fees   £16 D–£22 (£26 D–£32)
Loc   N of Livingston.
        M8 Junction 3

Dundas Parks (1957)

(Sec) 52 Scotstoun Park, South
Queensferry EH30 9PQ

Mem   450
Sec   Mrs J Pennie (Hon) (0131)
        331 3179
Holes 9 L 5510 metres SSS 69
Recs   Am–66 J McLaren
V'tors M I SOC
Fees   On application
Loc   Dundas Estate (Private).
        1 mile S of Queensferry
        (A8000)

Greenburn (1953)

6 Greenburn Road, Fauldhouse
EH47 9HG

Tel   (01501) 770292
Mem   500
Sec   A Stein (01501) 741967
Pro   M Leighton
        (01501) 771187
Holes 18 L 6210 yds SSS 71
Recs   Am–65 B Watson
V'tors U
Fees   On application
Loc   4 miles S of M8 Junction 4
        (East)/Junction 5 (West)

Harburn (1921)

West Calder EH55 8RS

Tel   (01506) 871256
Fax   (01506) 871131
Mem   470 80(L) 100(J)
Sec   J McLinden
        (01506) 871131
Pro   S Mills (01506) 871582
Holes 18 L 5921 yds SSS 69
Recs   Am–62 M Kirk
        Pro–64 A Alcorn
V'tors U
Fees   £16 (£21)
Loc   2 miles S of W Calder
        on B7008, via A70 or A71

Linlithgow (1913)

Braehead, Linlithgow EH49 6QF

Tel   (01506) 842585
Fax   (01506) 842585
Mem   430
Sec   TB Thomson
Pro   D Smith (01506) 844356
Holes 18 L 5729 yds SSS 68
Recs   Am–64 J Cuddihy (1975)
        Pro–65 J White (1988)
V'tors U exc Sat–NA SOC
Fees   £15 D–£23 Sun–£23 D–£30
Loc   SW of Linlithgow, off M9

Niddry Castle (1983)

Castle Road, Winchburgh
EH52 2RQ

Tel   (01506) 891097
Mem   450
Holes 9 L 5476 yds SSS 67
Recs   Am–66 J Niven
V'tors U
Fees   £12 (£17)
Loc   10 miles W of Edinburgh
        (B9080)

Polkemmet (1981)

Public
Whitburn, Bathgate EH47 0AD
Tel   **(01501) 743905**
Holes 9 L 2967 metres SSS 37
V'tors U
Fees £1.50–£3.40
        Sun–£1.80–£4.20
Loc   Between Whitburn and
        Harthill on B7066. M8
        Junctions 4/5
Mis   Driving range

Pumpherston (1895)

*Drumshoreland Road, Pumpherston
EH53 0LF*
Tel   **(01506) 432869**
Mem   326 10(L) 57(J)
Sec   AH Docharty (01506) 854652
Holes 9 L 5434 yds SSS 67
Recs Am–64 P Drake (1996)
V'tors M SOC–WD
Loc   14 miles W of Edinburgh.
        M8 Junction 3

Uphall (1895)

Houston Mains, Uphall EH52 6JT
Tel   **(01506) 856404**
Fax   (01506) 855358
Mem   500
Sec   WA Crighton
Pro   G Law (01506) 855553
Holes 18 L 5592 yds SSS 67
Recs Am–62 L Rhind (1997)
        Pro–64 CJ Brooks, A Oldcorn
        (1992)
V'tors U
Fees £14 D–£19 (£18 D–£26)
Loc   7 miles W of Edinburgh
        Airport (A8). M8 Junction 3

West Linton (1890)

West Linton EH46 7HN
Tel   **(01968) 660463**
Mem   700
Sec   G Scott (01968) 660970
Pro   I Wright (01968) 660256
Holes 18 L 6132 yds SSS 70
Recs Am–63 S Walker (1992)
        Pro–71 B Gallacher
V'tors WD–U WE–NA before 1pm
Fees £18 D–£27 (£28) W–£75
Loc   NW of Peebles on A702.
        18 miles S of Edinburgh

West Lothian (1892)

Airngath Hill, Linlithgow EH49 7RH
Tel   **(01506) 826030**
Fax   (01506) 826030
Mem   850
Sec   MJ Todd
Pro   N Robertson (01506) 825060
Holes 18 L 6406 yds SSS 71
Recs Am–64 AG O'Neill (1990)
        Pro–68 J Farmer (1980)
V'tors WD–NA after 4pm WE–by
        arrangement
Fees On application
Loc   1 mile N of Linlithgow,
        towards Bo'ness
Arch W Park Jr/Adams/Middleton

North

Caithness & Sutherland

Bonar Bridge, Ardgay
(1904)

Bonar-Bridge IV24 3EJ
Tel   **(01863) 766199**
Fax   (01863) 766738
Mem   250
Sec   F Mussard (01863) 766375
Holes 9 L 5284 yds SSS 68
Recs Am–63 M Munro (1994)
V'tors U
Fees D–£10 (£10)
Loc   ½ mile N of Bonar-Bridge on
        A836. 12 miles W of Dornoch

Brora (1891)

Golf Road, Brora KW9 6QS
Tel   **(01408) 621417**
Sec   J Fraser
Holes 18 L 6110 yds SSS 69
Recs Am–61 J Miller
        Pro–67 D Huish
V'tors U exc comp days –H for open
        comps SOC
Fees £18 D–£24
Loc   18 miles N of Dornoch (A9)
Arch James Braid

The Carnegie Club (1995)

*Skibo Castle, Clashmore, Dornoch
IV25 3RQ*
Tel   **(01862) 894600**
Fax   (01862) 894601
Mem   120
Sec   S Toon
Pro   W Milne
Holes 18 L 6671 yds Par 71 SSS 71
V'tors H–booking required
Fees £50
Loc   3 miles SW of Dornoch
Arch Donald Steel

Durness (1988)

Balnakeil, Durness IV27 4PN
Tel   **(01971) 511364**
Mem   120
Sec   Mrs L Mackay (01971) 511364
Holes 9 L 5555 yds SSS 69
Recs Am–71 M Mackay (1996),
        D McIntosh (1997)
V'tors U
Fees D–£12 W–£50
Loc   57 miles NW of Lairg
        on A838

Golspie (1889)

Ferry Road, Golspie KW10 6ST
Tel   **(01408) 633266**
Fax   (01408) 633393
Mem   420
Sec   Mrs M MacLeod
Pro   None
Holes 18 L 5890 yds SSS 68

Recs Am–65 J Miller
        Pro–65 D Huish
V'tors U SOC
Fees £18 D–£20 (£18 D–£25)
Loc   11 miles N of Dornoch

Helmsdale (1895)

Golf Road, Helmsdale KW8 6JA
Mem   92
Sec   D Bishop
Holes 9 L 3720 yds SSS 61
V'tors U
Fees £5 D–£10 W–£25
Loc   30 miles N of Dornoch (A9)

Lybster (1926)

Main Street, Lybster KW1 6BL
Mem   100
Sec   M Bowman
Holes 9 L 1896 yds SSS 61
Recs Am–59 D Nicholson (1991),
        E Larnach (1993),
        E Newman (1995)
V'tors U SOC
Fees £5
Loc   13 miles S of Wick on A99

Reay (1893)

Reay, Thurso KW14 7RE
Tel   **(01847) 811288**
Mem   332 56(L) 34(J)
Sec   Miss P Peebles
        (01847) 811537
Pro   None
Holes 18 L 5865 yds SSS 68
Recs Am–64 GA Dunnett (1990)
        Ladies–71 E Manson (1988)
V'tors U exc comp days
Fees D–£15 W–£45
Loc   11 miles W of Thurso

Royal Dornoch (1877)

Golf Road, Dornoch IV25 3LW
Tel   **(01862) 810219**
Fax   (01862) 810792
Mem   1036 249(L) 67(J)
Sec   JS Duncan (Sec/Mgr)
        (01862) 811220
Pro   WE Skinner (01862) 810902
Holes C'ship 18 L 6514 yds SSS 73
        Struie 18 L 5438 yds SSS 66
Recs Am–66 CP Christy
        Pro–65 K Stables
V'tors H
Fees On application
Loc   45 miles N of Inverness,
        off A9, N of Dornoch
Mis   Helipad by clubhouse. Airstrip
        nearby

Thurso (1893)

Newlands of Geise, Thurso KW14 7XD
Tel   **(01847) 893807**
Mem   300
Sec   Capt D Phillips
        (01847) 895433
Holes 18 L 5828 yds SSS 69
Recs Am–63 G Dunnett (1989)
V'tors U
Fees £11
Loc   2 miles SW of Thurso

Wick (1870)
Reiss, Wick KW1 5LJ
Tel   **(01955) 602726**
Mem   311
Sec   D Shearer (01955) 602935
Holes   18 L 5976 yds SSS 69
Recs   Am–63 R Taylor (1988)
        Pro–68 Dai Rees
V'tors U
Fees   On application
Loc   3 miles N of Wick on A9

Inverness

Abernethy (1893)
Nethy Bridge PH25 3EB
Tel   **(01479) 821305**
Mem   320
Sec   DA Gill (01479) 821040
Holes   9 L 2520 yds SSS 66
Recs   Am–61 I Murray
V'tors U SOC
Fees   £10 (£14)
Loc   5 miles S of Grantown (B970)

Alness (1904)
Ardross Rd, Alness
Tel   **(01349) 883877**
Mem   300
Sec   Mrs E Taylor
Holes   9 L 2436 yds SSS 63
Recs   Am–62 C MacIver (1983)
        C Taylor (1989)
V'tors U exc Mon–NA 5–7pm SOC
Fees   On application
Loc   ¼ mile N of Alness. 10 miles
        N of Dingwall

Boat-of-Garten (1898)
Boat-of-Garten PH24 3BQ
Tel   **(01479) 831282**
Fax   (01479) 831523
Mem   599
Sec   P Smyth
Holes   18 L 5866 yds SSS 69
Recs   Am–67 DF Sharp (1991)
        Pro–64 G Harvey (1993)
V'tors U–booking advisable
Fees   £21 D–£26 (£26 D–£31)
Loc   27 miles SE of Inverness (A95)
Arch   James Braid

Carrbridge (1980)
Carrbridge PH23 3AU
Tel   **(01479) 841623 (Clubhouse)**
Mem   600
Sec   Mrs AT Baird
Holes   9 L 2623 yds Par 71 SSS 68
Recs   Am–64 G Hay (1992)
V'tors U exc comp days–NA
Fees   D–£11 (D–£12) (1997)
Loc   23 miles SE of Inverness,
        off A9

Castle Heather (1996)
Castle Heather, Inverness IV1 2AA
Tel   **(01463) 713334/5**
Fax   (01463) 712695
Mem   500

Sec   GD Thompson
        (01463) 713335
Pro   M Piggot (01463) 713334
Holes   18 L 6700 yds Par 73 SSS 72
Recs   Am–69 N Hampton (1996)
V'tors U
Fees   D–£20 (D–£25)
Loc   Culduthel, SW Inverness
Mis   Floodlit driving range

Fort Augustus (1930)
Markethill, Fort Augustus PH32 4AU
Mem   110
Sec   H Fraser (01320) 6309
Holes   9 L 5454 yds SSS 68
Recs   Am–P MacDonald (1995)
V'tors U
Fees   D–£10
Loc   W end of Fort Augustus

Fort William (1974)
North Road, Fort William PH33 6SW
Tel   **(01397) 704464**
Mem   300
Sec   G Bales
Holes   18 L 5686 metres SSS 71
V'tors U
Fees   On application
Loc   3 miles N of Fort William
        (A82)
Arch   JR Stutt

Fortrose & Rosemarkie
(1888)
Ness Road East, Fortrose IV10 8SE
Tel   **(01381) 620529**
Mem   800
Sec   Mrs M Collier
Holes   18 L 5858 yds SSS 69
Recs   Am–64 G Paterson
V'tors U SOC
Fees   £16 D–£22 (£22)
Loc   Black Isle, 12 miles N of
        Inverness
Arch   James Braid

Invergordon (1893)
*King George Street, Invergordon
IV18 0BD*
Tel   **(01349) 852715**
Mem   170 30(L) 50(J)
Sec   NR Paterson (01349) 882693
Holes   18 L 6040 yds Par 69 SSS 69
V'tors U SOC
Fees   £10 (£10)
Loc   15 miles NE of Dingwall
        (A9/B817)
Arch   A Rae (1994)

Inverness (1883)
Culcabock Road, Inverness IV2 3XQ
Tel   **(01463) 239882**
Fax   (01463) 239882
Mem   1100
Sec   G Thomson
Pro   AP Thomson (01463) 231989
Holes   18 L 6226 yds SSS 70
Recs   Am–62 ND Hampton
        Pro–62 N Scott-Smith
V'tors WE/BH–restricted SOC
Fees   £25 D–£34 (£30 D–£40)
Loc   1 mile S of Inverness

Kingussie (1891)
Gynack Road, Kingussie PH21 1LR
Tel   **(01540) 661374 (Clubhouse)**
Fax   (01540) 662066
Mem   700
Sec   ND MacWilliam
        (01540) 661600
Pro   None
Holes   18 L 5555 yds SSS 68
Recs   Am–63 ND MacWilliam
        (1994)
        Pro–66 K Hutton (1991)
V'tors U
Fees   £13.50 D–£16.50 (£15.50
        D–£20.50)
Loc   ½ mile N of Kingussie, off A9
Arch   H Vardon

Muir of Ord (1875)
*Great North Road, Muir of Ord
IV6 7SX*
Tel   **(01463) 870825**
Fax   (01463) 870825
Mem   700
Sec   D Noble
Pro   G Vivers (01463) 871311
Holes   18 L 5557 yds SSS 68
Recs   Am–61 DR McIntosh (1997)
V'tors U SOC
Fees   D–£12.50 (£16.50) W–£50
Loc   15 miles N of Inverness
        (A862)
Arch   James Braid

Newtonmore (1893)
Newtonmore PH20 1AT
Tel   **(01540) 673328**
Fax   (01540) 673878
Mem   420
Sec   RJ Cheyne (01540) 673878
Pro   R Henderson (01540) 673611
Holes   18 L 6029 yds SSS 68
Recs   Am–68 TR Spence (1995)
        Pro–68 F Couttes (1993)
V'tors U SOC
Fees   D–£10 (£15)
Loc   4 miles W of Kingussie.
        46 miles S of Inverness

Spean Bridge
Spean Bridge, Fort William
Mem   65
Sec   AJ McLaren (Pres)
        (01397) 704954
Holes   9 hole course SSS 62
V'tors U
Fees   On application
Loc   9 miles N of Fort William
        on A82

Strathpeffer Spa (1888)
Strathpeffer IV14 9AS
Tel   **(01997) 421011/421219**
Fax   (01997) 421011
Mem   350 60(L) 80(J)
Sec   N Roxburgh (01997) 421396
Pro   Shop (01997) 421011
Holes   18 L 4792 yds SSS 64
Recs   Am–60 D Krzyzanowski
        Pro–66 A Herd

For list of abbreviations see page 479

V'tors U SOC
Fees £14 D–£20
Loc ¼ mile N of Strathpeffer.
5 miles W of Dingwall
Arch Willie Park

Tain (1890)

Tain
Tel (01862) 892314
Mem 500
Sec Mrs KD Ross
Pro None
Holes 18 L 6311 yds SSS 70
Recs Am–67 M Munro (1997)
V'tors U
Fees £20 D–£26 (£24 D–£30)
Loc 35 miles N of Inverness (A9).
8 miles S of Dornoch
Arch Tom Morris

Tarbat (1909)

Portmahomack, Tain IV20 1YB
Tel (01862) 87236
Fax (01349) 853715
Mem 200
Sec D Wilson
Holes 9 L 2568 yds SSS 66
Recs Am–63 D Mackay
V'tors U H SOC
Fees D–£5 (D–£6)
Loc 10 miles E of Tain
Arch J Sutherland

Torvean (1962)

Public
Glenurquhart Road, Inverness
Tel (01463) 711434 (Starter)
Fax (01463) 225651
Mem 400
Sec Mrs KM Gray
(01463) 225651
Pro None
Holes 18 L 5784 yds SSS 68
Recs Am–65 DC Walker (1994)
Pro–70 R Weir (1988)
Ladies–70 C MacLeod (1995)
V'tors U
Fees £11 (£13)
Loc SW of Inverness on A82

Moray & Nairn

Elgin (1906)

*Hardhillock, Birnie Road, Elgin
IV30 3SX*
Tel (01343) 542338
Fax (01343) 542341
Mem 854 113(L) 150(J)
Sec DF Black
Pro I Rodger (01343) 542884
Holes 18 L 6411 yds SSS 71
Recs Am–64 NS Grant (1972)
Pro–63 K Stables (1996)
V'tors WD–U after 9.30am WE–U
after 10am SOC–WD
SOC–WE by arrangement
Fees £21 D–£27 (£27 D–£35)
Loc 1 mile S of Elgin on A941

Forres (1889)

Muiryshade, Forres IV36 0RD
Tel (01309) 672949
Mem 716 130(J)
Sec Margaret Greenaway
Pro S Aird (01309) 672250
Holes 18 L 6141 yds SSS 70
Recs Am–64 S Aird Jr
V'tors U SOC
Fees £14 (£20)
Loc 1 mile SE of Forres, off B9010

Garmouth & Kingston (1932)

Garmouth, Fochabers IV32 7LU
Tel (01343) 870388
Fax (01343) 870388
Mem 400
Sec A Robertson (01343) 870231
Holes 18 L 5395 yds SSS 66
Recs Am–64 R Roy (1996)
Pro–70
V'tors U SOC
Fees £11 D–£17 (£15 D–£20)
Loc 8 miles NE of Elgin

Grantown-on-Spey (1890)

*Golf Course Road, Grantown-on-Spey
PH26 3HY*
Tel (01479) 872079
Fax (01479) 873725
Mem 700
Sec JA Matheson (01479) 873154
Pro B Mitchell (01479) 872398
Holes 18 L 5710 yds Par 70 SSS 68
Recs Am–60 G Bain (1984)
Pro–62 D Webster
V'tors WD–U WE–U after 10am
SOC
Fees D–£18 (D–£23)
Loc E side of Grantown (A95)
Arch Willie Park

Hopeman (1923)

Hopeman, Moray IV30 2YA
Tel (01343) 830578
Fax (01343) 830152
Mem 650
Sec R Johnston
Holes 18 L 5531 yds SSS 67
Recs Am–63 K Williamson (1997)
V'tors WD–U Sat–NA before
10.30am and 12.30–2pm
Sun–NA before 9.30am SOC
Fees £12 (£17)
Loc 7 miles NW of Elgin
on B9012
Arch J McKenzie

Moray (1889)

Stotfield Road, Lossiemouth IV31 6QS
Tel (01343) 812018
Fax (01343) 815102
Mem 1500
Sec B Russell
Pro A Thomson (01343) 813330
Holes Old 18 L 6643 yds SSS 73
New 18 L 6005 yds SSS 69
V'tors U H SOC
Fees On application
Loc 6 miles N of Elgin

Nairn (1887)

Seabank Road, Nairn IV12 4HB
Tel (01667) 452103
Fax (01667) 456328
Mem 938
Sec J Somerville (01667) 453208
Pro R Fyfe (01667) 452787
Holes 18 L 6722 yds SSS 74
9 hole course
Recs Am–66 S Tomisson
Pro–65 D Small
V'tors U SOC
Fees On application
Loc Nairn West Shore (A96)
Arch Old Tom
Morris/Braid/Simpson

Nairn Dunbar (1899)

Lochloy Road, Nairn IV12 5AE
Tel (01667) 452741
Fax (01667) 456897
Mem 500
Sec Mrs SJ McLennan
Pro BR Mason (01667) 453964
Holes 18 L 6712 yds SSS 73
Recs Am–69 C Duffy
Pro–63 RM Collinson
V'tors U
Fees £25 D–£33 (£30 D–£40)
Loc In Nairn

Orkney & Shetland

Orkney (1889)

*Grainbank, Kirkwall, Orkney
KW15 1RD*
Tel (01856) 872457
Fax (01856) 874165
Mem 415
Sec LF Howard (01856) 874165
Holes 18 L 5411 yds SSS 67
Recs Am–65 KD Peace
Pro–71 I Smith
V'tors U
Fees D–£10 W–£35
Loc 1 mile W of Kirkwall

Shetland (1891)

*PO Box 18, Lerwick, Shetland
ZE1 0YW*
Tel (01595) 840369
Mem 405
Sec J Campbell (Mgr)
Holes 18 L 5776 yds SSS 68
Recs Am–67 MC Boxwell (1996)
V'tors U
Fees D–£12
Loc 3 miles N of Lerwick (A907)
Arch Fraser Middleton

Stromness (1890)

Stromness, Orkney KW16 3DU
Tel (01856) 850772
Mem 250
Sec FJ Groundwater
(01856) 850622
Holes 18 L 4762 yds SSS 63
Recs Am–61 G Dunnet
Pro–66 R Macaskill

V'tors U
Fees D–£12
Loc Stromness, 16 miles W of Kirkwall on Hoy Sound

Whalsay (1976)
Skaw Taing, Whalsay, Shetland
Tel (01806) 566481/566450
Sec HA Sandison
Pro None
Holes 18 L 6009 yds Par 70 SSS 68
Recs Am–65 IG Sandison (1993)
V'tors U SOC
Fees D–£5 W–£15
Loc 5 miles N of Symbister Ferry

West Coast

Askernish (1891)
Lochboisdale, Askernish, South Uist
Tel (01878) 700301
Fax (01878) 700309
Mem 30
Sec AL Macdonald
Pro M McPhee
Holes 9 L 5114 yds SSS 67
Recs Am–66 K Robertson
V'tors U
Fees £10
Loc 5 miles NW of Lochboisdale
Arch Tom Morris Sr

Gairloch (1898)
Gairloch IV21 2BQ
Tel (01445) 712407
Mem 285
Sec A Shinkins
Holes 9 L 2281 yds SSS 64
Recs Am–63 L Chancellor (1995)
V'tors U
Fees D–£12 W–£45
Loc 60 miles W of Dingwall in Wester Ross

Isle of Harris
Scarista, Isle of Harris
Tel (01859) 520236
Mem 66
Sec A Haddow
Pro None
Holes 9 L 2442 yds Par 68 SSS 64
V'tors U
Fees £5 (£5)
Loc 13 miles S of Tarbert on W coast

Isle of Skye (1964)
Sconser, Isle of Skye IV48 8TD
Tel (01478) 650351
Mem 180
Sec M MacDonald
Holes 9 L 4798 yds Par 66 SSS 64
Recs Am–62 M Whatley
V'tors U
Fees D–£10
Loc Between Broadford and Sligachan

Lochcarron (1911)
Lochcarron, Strathcarron IV54 8YL
Mem 156
Sec G Weighill (015202) 257
Holes 9 L 3578 yds SSS 60
V'tors U exc Sat 2–5pm–NA
Fees £7.50 W–£20
Loc ½ mile E of Lochcarron in Wester Ross

Skeabost (1982)
Skeabost Bridge, Isle of Skye IV5 9NP
Tel (01470) 532202
Fax (01470) 532454
Mem 80
Sec DJ Matheson (01470) 532319 (Skeabost House Hotel)
Holes 9 L 3224 yds SSS 59
V'tors U
Fees D–£6
Loc 6 miles NW of Portree on Dunvegan road

Stornoway (1890)
Lady Lever Park, Stornoway, Isle of Lewis HS2 0XP
Tel (01851) 702240
Mem 400
Sec H Lloyd
Holes 18 L 5252 yds Par 68 SSS 67
Recs Am–62 KW Galloway
Pro–65 JC Farmer
V'tors U exc Sun–NA SOC
Fees D–£12 W–£36
Loc Off A857 in Lews Castle, Isle of Lewis

Traigh (1900)
Traigh, Arisaig PH39 4NT
Tel (01687) 450337
Mem 160
Sec W Henderson (01687) 450645
Pro None
Holes 9 L 2456 yds Par 68 SSS 65
V'tors U
Fees D–£10 (D–£12)
Loc 2 miles N of Arisaig on A830 Fort William-Mallaig road
Arch John Salveson

North East

Aberdeen Clubs

Bon Accord (1872)
19 Golf Road, Aberdeen AB2 1QB
Tel (01224) 633464
Mem 950
Sec JB Miller
Holes Play over King's Links

Caledonian (1899)
20 Golf Road, Aberdeen AB2 1QB
Tel (01224) 632443
Mem 620
Sec JA Bridgeford
Holes Play over King's Links

Aberdeen Courses

Auchmill (1975)
Bonnyview Road, West Heatheryfold, Aberdeen AB2 7FQ
Tel (01224) 715214
Mem 300
Sec W Cameron (01464) 821217
Pro None
Holes 18 L 5883 yds Par 70 SSS 68
Recs Am–65 G McInnes (1996)
V'tors U
Fees On application
Loc 3 miles NW of Aberdeen city centre
Arch Coles/Huggett

Balnagask
Public
St Fitticks Road, Aberdeen
Tel (01224) 876407
Pro I Smith
Holes 18 L 5472 metres SSS 69
V'tors U
Fees On application
Loc 1½ miles SE of Aberdeen

Deeside (1903)
Bieldside, Aberdeen AB15 9DL
Tel (01224) 869457
Mem 600
Sec AG Macdonald (01224) 869457
Pro FJ Coutts (01224) 861041
Holes 18 L 5972 yds SSS 69
9 L 3316 yds SSS 36
Recs Am–64 AK Pirie, RH Willox, DA Rennie
Pro–63 FJ Coutts (1995)
V'tors H
Fees £25 (£30)
Loc 3 miles SW of Aberdeen on A93

Hazlehead (1927)
Public
Hazlehead, Aberdeen
Tel (01224) 321830
Pro I Smith
Holes 18 L 5673 metres SSS 70
18 L 5303 metres SSS 68
9 L 2531 metres SSS 34
Recs Am–65 D Jamieson
Pro–67 P Oosterhuis
V'tors U
Fees On application
Loc 3 miles W of Aberdeen

King's Links
Public
Golf Road, Aberdeen AB2 1QB
Tel (01224) 632269
Pro B Davidson (01224) 641577
Holes 18 L 5838 metres SSS 71
V'tors U
Fees On application
Loc 1 mile E of Aberdeen
Mis Driving range. Bon Accord, Caledonian and Northern Clubs play here

Murcar (1909)

Bridge of Don, Aberdeen AB23 8BD

Tel	**(01224) 704345**
Fax	(01224) 704345
Mem	830
Sec	D Corstorphine
	(01224) 704354
Pro	G Forbes (01224) 704370
Holes	18 L 6241 yds SSS 71
	9 L 2680 yds SSS 35
Recs	Am–65 R Grant, J Savege,
	E Morrison
	Pro–65 PA Smith
V'tors	WD–H before noon WE–H
	Sat–NA before 4pm Sun–NA
	before noon
Fees	£28 D–£38 (D–£43)
Loc	5 miles N of Aberdeen, off A92.
	9 hole course at Strabathie
Arch	A Simpson

Peterculter (1989)

Oldtown, Burnside Road, Peterculter AB14 0LN

Tel	**(01224) 735245**
Fax	(01224) 735580
Mem	889
Sec	K Anderson
Pro	D Vannet (01224) 734994
Holes	18 L 5924 yds SSS 69
Recs	Am–65 P Robb (1994)
V'tors	WD–U before 4pm WE–U
	SOC–WD exc Mon
Fees	£12–£18 (£16–£21)
Loc	8 miles W of Aberdeen
	on A93

Portlethen (1983)

Badentoy Road, Portlethen, Aberdeen AB12 4YA

Tel	**(01224) 781090**
Fax	(01224) 781090
Mem	1200
Sec	BF Mole
Pro	Muriel Thomson (01224)
	782571
Holes	18 L 6735 yds SSS 72
Recs	Am–64 GJ Esson (1997)
	Pro–62 D Vannett (1966)
V'tors	WD–U WE–NA before 11am
	SOC
Fees	£14 (£21)
Loc	6 miles S of Aberdeen on A90

Royal Aberdeen (1780)

Balgownie, Bridge of Don, Aberdeen AB23 8AT

Tel	**(01224) 702571**
Fax	(01224) 826591
Mem	350 100(J)
Sec	GF Webster
Pro	R MacAskill (01224) 702221
Holes	18 L 6372 yds SSS 71
	18 L 4066 yds SSS 60
Recs	Am–64 J Fought
	Pro–63 A Garrido
V'tors	I H SOC
Fees	£37 D–£48 (£48)
Loc	2 miles N of Aberdeen,
	off A92 Ellon road
Arch	Simpson/Braid

Westhill (1977)

Westhill Heights, Westhill AB32 6RY

Tel	**(01224) 743361 (Clubhouse)**
Fax	(01224) 742567
Mem	500
Sec	AD Joss (01224) 742567
Pro	R McDonald (01224) 740159
Holes	18 L 5849 yds SSS 69
Recs	Am–64 A Reith
	Pro–65 R McDonald
V'tors	WD–U before 4.30pm & after
	7pm –M 4.30–7pm Sat–M
	Sun–U after 10am
Fees	£11 D–£16 (£15 D–£22)
Loc	6 miles W of Aberdeen,
	off A944
Arch	Charles Lawrie

Aberdeenshire

Aboyne (1883)

Formaston Park, Aboyne

Tel	**(013398) 86328**
Fax	(013398) 87078
Mem	725 180(J)
Sec	Mrs M MacLean
	(013398) 87078
Pro	I Wright (013398) 86328
Holes	18 L 5910 yds SSS 68
Recs	Am–62 G Forbes, C Forbes
	Pro–63 S Walker
V'tors	U
Fees	On application
Loc	E end of Aboyne. 30 miles W
	of Aberdeen (A93)

Alford

Montgarrie Road, Alford AB33 8AE

Tel	**(019755) 62178**
Fax	(019755) 62178
Mem	608
Sec	B Fiddes
Pro	None
Holes	18 L 5402 yds Par 69 SSS 65
V'tors	WD–U WE–restricted
	on comp days SOC
Fees	£12 (£19)
Loc	25 miles W of Aberdeen
	on A944

Auchenblae (1894)

Public

Auchenblae

Tel	**(01561) 320331 (Bookings)**
Mem	85
Sec	J McNicoll (01561) 320678
Holes	9 L 2208 yds SSS 63
Recs	Am–62 AI Robertson,
	J McNicoll
	Pro–60 A Locke
V'tors	U exc Wed & Fri 5.30–9pm
Fees	£6 Sat–£7 Sun–£8
Loc	11 miles SW of Stonehaven.
	3 miles W of Fordoun

Ballater (1892)

Victoria Road, Ballater AB35 5QX

Tel	**(013397) 55567**
Fax	(013397) 55057
Mem	670

Sec	AE Barclay
Pro	F Smith (013397) 55658
Holes	18 L 6094 yds SSS 69
Recs	Am–61 R Damron
	Pro–62 K Stables
V'tors	U
Fees	On application
Loc	42 miles W of Aberdeen
	on A93

Banchory (1905)

Kinneskie, Banchory AB31 5TA

Tel	**(01330) 822365**
Mem	800
Sec	Mrs A Smith (Admin)
Pro	D Naylor (01330) 822447
Holes	18 L 5775 yds SSS 68
Recs	Am–60 D Reith (1990)
	Pro–61 A Thomson,
	D Matthew
V'tors	WD–U
Fees	£18 (£21)
Loc	W of Banchory, off A93

Braemar (1902)

Cluniebank Road, Braemar AB35 5XX

Tel	**(013397) 41618**
Mem	300
Sec	J Pennet (01224) 704471
Holes	18 L 4916 yds SSS 64
Recs	Am–58 J Crammond (1997)
	Pro–64 L Vannett (1988)
V'tors	U SOC
Fees	£12 D–£16 (£16 D–£21)
	W–£60
Loc	Braemar ½ mile. 17 miles W
	of Ballater
Arch	J Anderson

Buckpool (1933)

Barhill Road, Buckie AB56 1DU

Tel	**(01542) 832236**
Fax	(01542) 832236
Mem	500
Sec	Mrs E Cowie
Holes	18 L 6257 yds SSS 70
Recs	Am–65 K Buchan (1991)
	Pro–64 L Vannet (1989)
	Ladies–67 L Smith (1993)
V'tors	U
Fees	£10 D–£12 (£12 D–£18)
Loc	W end of Buckpool, ½ mile
	off A98

Cruden Bay (1899)

Cruden Bay, Peterhead AB42 0NN

Tel	**(01779) 812285**
Fax	(01779) 812945
Mem	1070
Sec	Mrs R Pittendrigh
Pro	RG Stewart (01779) 812414
Holes	18 L 6395 yds SSS 72
	9 L 5106 yds SSS 65
Recs	Am–65 C Gilbert (1997)
	Pro–65 L Vannet (1996),
	B Marchbank (1997)
V'tors	WD–U WE–H exc comp days
Fees	£35 D–£50 (£45)
Loc	22 miles NE of Aberdeen
	(A90)
Mis	Driving range
Arch	Thomas Simpson

Cullen (1879)

The Links, Cullen, Buckie AB56 2UU
Tel (01542) 840685
Mem 625
Sec LIG Findlay (01542) 840174
Pro None
Holes 18 L 4610 yds Par 63 SSS 62
Recs Am–58 B Main (1979)
    Ladies–62 M Seivwright (1993)
V'tors WD–U WE–restricted Jul/Aug
    SOC
Fees £10 D–£15 (£13 D–£18)
Loc 5 miles E of Buckie, off A98
    between Aberdeen and
    Inverness
Arch Tom Morris

Duff House Royal (1910)

The Barnyards, Banff AB45 3SX
Tel (01261) 812062
Fax (01261) 812224
Mem 547 167(L) 132(J)
Sec J Maison
Pro RS Strachan (01261) 812075
Holes 18 L 6161 yds SSS 69
Recs Am–63 DC Clark
V'tors WD–U H WE–H 8.30–11am
    and 12.30–3pm
Fees £24 (£30)
Loc Moray Firth coast, between
    Buckie and Fraserburgh
Arch Dr A & Maj CA Mackenzie

Dufftown (1896)

Dufftown AB55 4BX
Tel (01340) 820325
Fax (01340) 820325
Mem 310
Sec DM Smith
Pro None
Holes 18 L 5308 yds SSS 67
Recs Am–65 G Mercer, S Hanson,
    J Hanson (1996)
    Pro–68 A Aird (1990)
V'tors U
Fees £10 D–£15
Loc 1 mile SW of Dufftown
    on Tomintoul road

Dunecht House (1925)

Dunecht, Skene AB3 7AX
Mem 400
Sec G Lyall (01224) 740922
Holes 9 L 3135 yds SSS 70
Recs Am–72 A Angus (1987)
V'tors M
Loc 12 miles W of Aberdeen
    on A944

Fraserburgh (1881)

Philorth, Fraserburgh AB4 8TL
Tel (01346) 516616
Mem 661 67(L) 112(J)
Sec AD Stewart
Holes 18 L 6278 yds SSS 70
    9 L 3400 yds
Recs Am–66 G Watt
    Pro–67 I Smith
V'tors U SOC
Fees On application
Loc 1 mile SE of Fraserburgh

Huntly (1892)

Cooper Park, Huntly AB54 4SH
Tel (01466) 792643
Mem 800
Sec EA Stott (01466) 792360
Holes 18 L 5399 yds SSS 66
Recs Am–64 S Younger
V'tors U SOC
Fees D–£13 (D–£20) W–£65
Loc N side of Huntly. 38 miles
    NW of Aberdeen, off A96

Insch

Golf Terrace, Insch AB52 6JY
Tel (01464) 820363
Sec B Leith (01464) 820144
Holes 18 L 5287 yds SSS 69
Recs Am–66 H McKenzie (1990),
    K Harper (1994)
V'tors U
Fees On application
Loc 28 miles NW of Aberdeen,
    off A96

Inverallochy

Public
Whitelink, Inverallochy, Fraserburgh AB43 8XY
Tel (01346) 582000
Mem 280
Sec I Watt (01346) 582096
Pro None
Holes 18 L 5137 yds SSS 65
Recs Am–57 SJ Young (1997)
V'tors U
Fees D–£10 (£15)
Loc 4 miles E of Fraserburgh,
    off A92

Inverurie (1923)

Blackhall Road, Inverurie AB51 5JE
Tel (01467) 620207
Fax (01467) 621051
Mem 475 110(L)
Sec J Ramage (01467) 624080
Pro (01467) 620193
Holes 18 L 5711 yds SSS 68
Recs Am–65 R Brechin
    Ladies–74 J Tough
V'tors U SOC–WD
Fees D–£18 (£24)
Loc 1 mile W of Inverurie.
    16 miles NW of Aberdeen

Keith (1963)

Fife Park, Keith AB55 5DF
Tel (01542) 882469
Mem 400
Sec DG Shepherd
    (01542) 887934 (H)
Holes 18 L 5802 yds SSS 68
Recs Am–65
    Pro–64
V'tors U
Fees £11 (£13)
Loc Fife Park, W side of Keith

Kemnay (1908)

Monymusk Road, Kemnay AB51 5RA
Tel (01467) 642225 (Clubhouse),
    (01467) 643746 (Office)
Fax (01467) 643746

Mem 820
Sec D Imrie (01467) 643047
Pro None
Holes 18 L 5903 yds SSS 69
Recs Am–69 (1995)
    Pro–72 (1996)
V'tors U
Fees £16 D–£20 (£18 D–£22)
Loc 15 miles W of Aberdeen
    (B993)

Kintore (1911)

Kintore AB51 0UR
Tel (01467) 632631
Fax (01467) 632631
Mem 700
Sec Mrs V Graham
Holes 18 L 5985 yds SSS 69
Recs Am–65 K Bennet (1994)
    Pro–63 A Crerar,
    S Henderson (1996)
    Ladies–71 R Anderson (1995)
V'tors U
Fees £10 (£15)
Loc 12 miles NW of Aberdeen
    on A96

Longside

West End, Longside, Peterhead AB42 4XJ
Tel (01779) 821558
Mem 750
Sec S Silcock (01779) 821549
Pro None
Holes 18 L 5215 yds Par 66 SSS 66
Recs Am–69 E Brocklehurst (1996)
    Ladies–71 C Thomson (1997)
V'tors U exc Sun–NA before
    10.30am SOC
Fees £10 D–£14 Sat–£12 D–£16
    Sun–£16 D–£20
Loc 5 miles W of Peterhead
    on A590

McDonald (1927)

Ellon AB41 9AW
Tel (01358) 720576
Fax (01358) 720001
Mem 650
Sec G Ironside
Pro R Urquhart (01358) 722891
Holes 18 L 5986 yds SSS 69
Recs Am–65
    Pro–63
V'tors U
Fees On application
Loc 15 miles N of Aberdeen,
    off A90

Meldrum House (1998)

Meldrum House Estate, Oldmeldrum AB51 0AE
Tel (01651) 873553
Fax (01651) 873553
Mem 400
Sec C Farquharson (Gen Mgr)
Pro To be appointed
Holes 18 L 6350 yds Par 70
V'tors M
Fees NA
Loc 18 miles N of Aberdeen,
    on A947

Newburgh-on-Ythan
(1888)
Newburgh, Ellon AB41 0FB
Tel	(01358) 789058
Fax	(01358) 789956
Mem	380 60(L) 80(J)
Sec	E Leslie (01358) 789956
Pro	None
Holes	18 L 6162 yds SSS 70
Recs	Am–68 (1997)
V'tors	U exc Tues after 3pm–NA
Fees	On application
Loc	12 miles N of Aberdeen
	(A975)

Newmachar (1989)
Swailend, Newmachar, Aberdeen AB21 7UU
Tel	(01651) 863002
Fax	(01651) 863055
Mem	800
Sec	G McIntosh
Pro	P Smith (01651) 862127
Holes	18 L 6623 yds Par 72 SSS 74
	18 L 6388 yds Par 72 SSS 71
Recs	Am–67 M Vibe-Hastrup,
	C Benedetti (1996),
	S Young (1997)
	Pro–65 A Tait (1995)
V'tors	H SOC
Fees	Hawkshill £25 (£30)
	Swailend £15 (£20)
Loc	12 miles N of Aberdeen on A947
Mis	Driving range
Arch	Dave Thomas

Oldmeldrum (1885)
Kirkbrae, Oldmeldrum AB51 0DJ
Tel	(01651) 872648/873555
Mem	800
Sec	D Petrie (01651) 872383
Pro	J Caven (01651) 873555
Holes	18 L 5988 yds Par 70 SSS 69
Recs	Am–66 DH Clarke (1996)
V'tors	WD–U before 5pm WE–phone first
Fees	£12 (£18)
Loc	17 miles N of Aberdeen on A947

Peterhead (1841)
Craigewan Links, Peterhead AB42 1LT
Tel	(01779) 472149
Mem	620 55(L)
Holes	18 L 6173 yds SSS 71
	9 L 2237 yds SSS 62
Recs	Am–64 K Buchan (1988)
	Pro–64 J Farmer (1980)
V'tors	U exc Sat–restricted
Fees	On application
Loc	1 mile N of Peterhead
Arch	Willie Park Jr/James Braid

Rosehearty
c/o Mason's Arms, Rosehearty, Fraserburgh
Tel	(01346) 571250 (Mem Sec)
Mem	220
Sec	A Downie
Holes	9 L 2197 yds SSS 62
Recs	Am–61 M Summers (1996)
V'tors	U
Fees	D–£7 (D–£10)
Loc	4 miles W of Fraserburgh (B9031)

Rothes (1990)
Blackhall, Rothes, Aberlour AB38 7AN
Tel	(01340) 831443
Mem	270
Sec	JP Tilley (01340) 831277
Pro	None
Holes	9 L 2478 yds SSS 65
V'tors	U
Fees	£8 (£10)
Loc	½ mile SW of Rothes. 10 miles S of Elgin on A941
Arch	John Souter

Royal Tarlair (1926)
Buchan Street, Macduff AB44 1TA
Tel	(01261) 832897
Mem	520
Sec	Mrs C Davidson
Holes	18 L 5866 yds SSS 68
Recs	Am–64 A Morrison
V'tors	U
Fees	£10 D–£15 (£15 D–£20)
Loc	Macduff, 4 miles E of Banff. 45 miles E of Aberdeen

Spey Bay (1907)
Spey Bay Hotel, Spey Bay, Fochabers IV32 7PJ
Tel	(01343) 820424
Mem	180
Sec	M Dann (Mgr)
Holes	18 L 6092 yds Par 70 SSS 69
Recs	Am–66 M Cameron
V'tors	U
Fees	£10 (£13)
Loc	2 miles W of Buckie, off B9104
Mis	Driving range
Arch	Ben Sayers

Stonehaven (1888)
Cowie, Stonehaven AB39 3RH
Tel	(01569) 762124
Fax	(01569) 765973
Mem	500
Sec	WA Donald
Pro	None
Holes	18 L 5128 yds Par 66 SSS 65
Recs	Am–61 RG Forbes (1987),
	FG McCarron (1995)
V'tors	Sat–NA before 3.45pm Sun–NA before 10.45am
Fees	£15 (£20)
Loc	1 mile N of Stonehaven
Arch	A Simpson

Strathlene (1877)
Buckie AB5 2DJ
Tel	(01542) 31798
Mem	300
Sec	GML Clark
Holes	18 L 5957 yds SSS 69

Recs	Am–65 AG Ross, J Geddes
V'tors	U SOC
Fees	£10 (£15) W–£40
Loc	½ mile E of Buckie
Arch	G Smith

Tarland (1908)
Tarland AB3 4YN
Tel	(013398) 81413
Mem	300
Sec	RG Reid
Holes	9 L 5812 yds SSS 68
Recs	Am–65 C Forbes (1997)
V'tors	WD–U WE–enquiry advisable SOC–WD only
Fees	£12 (£15) (1997)
Loc	5 miles NW of Aboyne. 30 miles W of Aberdeen
Arch	Tom Morris

Torphins (1896)
Torphins AB31 4JU
Tel	(013398) 82115
Mem	370
Sec	S MacGregor (013398) 82402
Holes	9 L 4738 yds SSS 64
Recs	Am–63 J Cramond
V'tors	U SOC
Fees	£10 (£12)
Loc	W of Torphins via Wester Beltie. 6 miles NW of Banchory

Turriff (1896)
Rosehall, Turriff
Tel	(01888) 562982
Fax	(01888) 568050
Mem	814
Sec	R Grieg
Pro	R Smith (01888) 563025
Holes	18 L 6145 yds SSS 69
Recs	Am–67 A Ogg (1996) Pro–66 K Hutton (1996)
V'tors	H WE–NA before 10am SOC
Fees	£16 D–£20 (£21 D–£27)
Loc	35 miles N of Aberdeen (A947)
Arch	GM Fraser

Perth & Kinross

Aberfeldy (1895)
Taybridge Road, Aberfeldy PH15 2BH
Tel	(01887) 820535
Mem	260
Sec	C Henderson (01887) 829509
Holes	18 L 5600 yds Par 68 SSS 66
Recs	Am–65 (1997)
V'tors	U
Fees	£14 D–£22 W–£55
Loc	10 miles W of Ballinluig, off A9
Arch	Souters

Alyth (1894)

Pitcrocknie, Alyth PH11 8HF

Tel	**(01828) 632268**
Fax	(01828) 633491
Mem	850
Sec	J Docherty
Pro	T Melville (01828) 632411
Holes	18 L 6205 yds SSS 70
Recs	Am–65 J Cochrane Jr
	Pro–64 I Young
V'tors	U SOC
Fees	On application
Loc	16 miles NW of Dundee (A91)
Arch	Tom Morris/James Braid

Auchterarder (1892)

Ochil Road, Auchterarder PH3 1LS

Tel	**(01764) 662804**
Fax	(01764) 662804
Mem	765
Sec	WM Campbell (01764) 664669
Pro	G Baxter (01764) 663711
Holes	18 L 5757 yds SSS 68
Recs	Am–62 M O'Brien (1997)
V'tors	U SOC
Fees	£18 D–£26 Sat–£24 D–£36 Sun–£36
Loc	1 mile SW of Auchterarder

Bishopshire (1903)

Pay and play

Kinnesswood, Kinross

Mem	200
Sec	J Proudfoot (01592) 780203
Holes	10 L 4700 metres SSS 64
Recs	Am–63 J Morris
V'tors	U
Fees	£5 (£6)
Loc	3 miles E of Kinross (A911). M90 Junction 7
Arch	W Park

Blair Atholl (1896)

Blair Atholl PH18 5TG

Tel	**(01796) 481407**
Mem	390
Sec	JA McGregor (01796) 481274
Holes	9 L 2855 yds SSS 68
Recs	Am–66
V'tors	U
Fees	£11 (£14)
Loc	35 miles N of Perth, off A9

Blairgowrie (1889)

Rosemount, Blairgowrie PH10 6LG

Tel	**(01250) 872594**
Fax	(01250) 875451
Mem	1200
Sec	JN Simpson (Managing Sec) (01250) 872622
Pro	C Dernie (01250) 873116
Holes	Rosemount 18 L 6588 yds SSS 72
	Landsdowne 18 L 6895 yds SSS 73
	Wee 9 L 4614 yds SSS 63
Recs	Rosemount Am–64 E Giraud, W Taylor, Pro–66 G Norman

	Lansdowne Am–67 C Mitchell, Pro–69 J McAlister
V'tors	Mon/Tues/Thurs–U H 8am–12 & 2–3.30pm Wed/Fri/WE–restricted
Fees	On application
Loc	1 mile S of Blairgowrie, off A93. 15 miles N of Perth
Arch	Rosemount: James Braid; Landsdowne: Thomas/Alliss; Wee: Old Tom Morris

Callander (1890)

Aveland Road, Callander FK17 8EN

Tel	**(01877) 330090**
Fax	(01877) 330062
Mem	700
Sec	DM Davidson
Pro	W Kelly (01877) 330975
Holes	18 L 5125 yds SSS 66
Recs	Am–61 B Collier
	Pro–59 D Matthew
V'tors	U SOC
Fees	On application
Loc	Off A84, E end of Callander
Arch	Tom Morris

Comrie (1891)

Comrie PH6 2LR

Tel	**(01764) 70055**
Mem	330
Sec	GC Betty (01764) 670941
Holes	9 L 2983 yds SSS 70
Recs	Am–65 A Philp
V'tors	U
Fees	£10 (£10)
Loc	7 miles W of Crieff (A85)

Craigie Hill (1909)

Cherrybank, Perth PH2 0NE

Tel	**(01738) 624377**
Fax	(01738) 620829
Mem	625
Sec	DR Allan (01738) 620829
Pro	S Harrier (01738) 622644
Holes	18 L 5386 yds SSS 67
Recs	Am–60 G Still (1988)
	Pro–63 W Murray (1986)
V'tors	U exc Sat
Fees	£15 (£25)
Loc	W boundary of Perth
Arch	Fernie/Anderson

Crieff (1891)

Perth Road, Crieff PH7 3LR

Tel	**(01764) 652909 (Bookings)**
Fax	(01764) 655096
Mem	670
Sec	JS Miller (01764) 652397
Pro	DJW Murchie
Holes	Ferntower 18 L 6402 yds SSS 71; Dornock 9 L 4772 yds SSS 63
Recs	Ferntower Am–66 Pro–66
V'tors	U H NA–12–2pm or after 5pm SOC
Fees	Ferntower £20 (£27) Dornock £12 (£15)
Loc	1 mile NE of Crieff (A85). 17 miles W of Perth

Dalmunzie (1948)

Glenshee, Blairgowrie PH10 7QG

Tel	**(01250) 885226**
Fax	(01250) 885225
Mem	52
Sec	S Winton (Mgr)
Holes	9 L 2035 yds SSS 60
V'tors	U
Fees	£6.50 D–£10
Loc	22 miles N of Blairgowrie on A93. (Dalmunzie Hotel sign)

Dunkeld & Birnam (1892)

Fungarth, Dunkeld PH8 0HU

Tel	**(01350) 727524**
Fax	(01350) 728660
Mem	432
Sec	Mrs W Sinclair (01350) 727564
Pro	None
Holes	9 L 5240 yds SSS 66
Recs	Am–65 S McKendrick (1996)
V'tors	WD–U WE–phone first
Fees	On application
Loc	Dunkeld 1 mile, off A923. 15 miles N of Perth

Dunning (1953)

Rollo Park, Dunning PH2 0QX

Tel	**(01764) 684747**
Mem	580
Sec	Mrs M Ramsay (01764) 684237
Holes	9 L 4777 yds Par 66 SSS 63
V'tors	U
Fees	£10 D–£14 (£12)
Loc	9 miles SW of Perth, off A9

Glenalmond

Trinity College, Glenalmond

Sec	The Bursar (01738) 880275
Holes	9 L 5812 yds SSS 68
Recs	Am–70 CMW Robertson Pro–72 M Dennis
V'tors	NA
Loc	10 miles NW of Perth
Arch	James Braid

The Gleneagles Hotel

Auchterarder PH3 1NF

Tel	**(01764) 663543 (Golf), (01764) 662231 (Hotel)**
Pro	G Schofield
Holes	King's 18 L 6471 yds SSS 71 Queen's 18 L 5965 yds SSS 69 Monarch 18 L 7081 SSS 74 9 hole Par 3 course
V'tors	Residents & Members only
Fees	NA
Loc	16 miles SW of Perth on A9
Mis	Driving range. Golf Academy

Green Hotel (1900)

2 The Muirs, Kinross KY13 7AS

Tel	**(01577) 863407**
Fax	(01577) 863180
Mem	450
Sec	Mrs M Smith

Holes Red 18 L 6257 yds SSS 70
Blue 18 L 6456 yds SSS 71
V'tors U
Fees £15 D–£25 (£25 D–£35)
Loc 17 miles S of Perth. M90
Junction 6/7

Kenmore (1992)

Pay and play
*Mains of Taymouth, Kenmore,
Aberfeldy PH15 2HN*

Tel (01887) 830226
Fax (01887) 830211
Mem 120
Sec R Menzies (Mgr)
Pro None
Holes 9 L 6052 yds SSS 69
Recs Am–68 S Sutherland (1997)
V'tors U SOC
Fees 9 holes–£7 (£8);
18 holes–£10 (£12)
Loc 6 miles W of Aberfeldy
on A827
Arch D Menzies & Partners

Killin (1913)

Killin FK21 8TX
Tel (01567) 820312
Mem 298
Sec J Greaves
Holes 9 L 2410 yds SSS 65
Recs Am–61 G Smith
V'tors U SOC–Apr–Oct
Fees £12 (£15)
Loc Killin, W end of Loch Tay
Arch John Duncan

King James VI (1858)

Moncreiffe Island, Perth PH2 8NR
Tel (01738) 625170,
(01738) 632460 (Starter)
Fax (01738) 445132
Mem 675
Sec Mrs H Blair (01738) 445132
Pro A Coles (01738) 632460
Holes 18 L 5664 yds SSS 69
Recs Am–63 G Clark (1976)
Pro–62 W Guy (1991)
V'tors U exc Sat Sun–by reservation
Fees £15 D–£22 Sun D–£28
Loc Island in River Tay, Perth
Arch Tom Morris

Milnathort (1910)

South Street, Milnathort KY13 2AW
Tel (01577) 864069
Mem 400
Holes 9 L 5969 yds SSS 69
Recs Am–65 D Reid (1992)
V'tors U SOC
Fees D–£10 (£15)
Loc 1 mile N of Kinross. M90
Junction 6/7

Muckhart (1908)

Muckhart, Dollar FK14 7JH
Tel (01259) 781423
Mem 550 125(L) 100(J)
Sec AB Robertson
Pro K Salmoni
Holes 18 L 6034 yds SSS 70

9 hole course
Recs Am–66 E Carnegie (1983)
V'tors U SOC
Fees 18 hole: £15 D–£22 (£22
D–£30); 9 hole: £10
Loc A91, 3 miles E of Dollar,
towards Rumbling Bridge

Murrayshall (1981)

*Murrayshall, New Scone, Perth
PH2 7PH*
Tel (01738) 551171
Fax (01738) 552595
Mem 300
Sec A Bryan (Mgr)
Pro AT Reid (01738) 552784
Holes 18 L 5877 metres SSS 72
Recs Am–67 G Redford
Pro–67 J Farmer
V'tors U SOC–WD/WE
Fees £22 D–£30 (£27 D–£45)
Loc 3 miles NE of Perth, off A94
Mis Driving range. Indoor Golf
Centre
Arch Hamilton Stutt

Muthill (1935)

Peat Road, Muthill PH5 2AD
Tel (01764) 681523
Fax (01764) 656073
Mem 450
Sec Maj (Retd) IF Nelson
(01764) 681541
Holes 9 L 2371 yds SSS 63
Recs Am–61 C MacGregor (1991)
Pro–68 RM Jamieson,
W Milne (1985)
V'tors U SOC
Fees £12 (£15)
Loc 3 miles S of Crieff on A822

North Inch

Public
*c/o Perth & Kinross Council, 5 High
Street, Perth PH1 5JS*
Tel (01738) 636481 (Starter)
Sec G Harbut (01738) 475215
Holes 18 L 4340 metres SSS 65
V'tors U SOC
Fees On application
Loc Nr Perth and A9, by River
Tay. Signs to Bell's Sports
Centre

Pitlochry (1909)

Golf Course Road, Pitlochry PH16 5QY
Tel (01796) 472792 (Bookings)
Fax (01796) 473599
Mem 498
Sec DCM McKenzie JP
(01796) 472114
Pro G Hampton
Holes 18 L 5811 yds SSS 69
Recs Am–63 CP Christy,
MM Niven
Pro–64
V'tors U SOC
Fees D–£20 (D–£25) (1996)
Loc N side of Pitlochry (A9).
28 miles NW of Perth
Arch Fernie/Hutchison

Royal Perth Golfing Society (1833)

1/2 Atholl Crescent, Perth PH1 5NG
Tel (01738) 622265
Fax (01738) 441131
Mem 250
Sec RPJ Blake (Gen Sec) (01738)
440088, AH Anderson (Golf
Sec) (01738) 637311
Holes Play over North Inch course

St Fillans (1903)

*South Lochearn Rd, St Fillans
PH26 2NJ*
Tel (01764) 685312
Mem 400
Sec KW Foster (01764) 679509
Holes 9 L 5796 yds SSS 67
V'tors U SOC
Fees On application
Loc 12 miles W of Crieff, on A85
Arch W Auchterlonie

Strathmore Golf Centre (1995)

Pay and play
*Leroch, Alyth, Blairgowrie
PH11 8NZ*
Tel (01828) 633322
Fax (01828) 633533
Mem 300
Sec P Barron (Man Dir)
Pro None
Holes 18 L 6454 yds Par 72 SSS 72
9 L 1719 yds Par 29 SSS 58
Recs Am–68 K Grant (1997)
V'tors U SOC
Fees 18 hole: £16 (£20)
9 hole: £6
Loc 5 miles E of Blairgowrie,
off A926
Mis Floodlit driving range
Arch John Salvesen

Strathtay (1909)

*Lorne Cottage, Dalguise, Dunkeld
PH8 0JX*
Tel (01350) 727797
Mem 184
Sec TD Lind
Holes 9 L 4082 yds SSS 63
Recs Am–61 AM Deboys
V'tors U exc Mon–NA after 5pm
Sun–NA 1–4pm SOC
Fees D–£10
Loc 4 miles W of Ballinluig
(A827), towards Aberfeldy

Taymouth Castle (1923)

Kenmore, Aberfeldy PH15 2NT
Tel (01887) 830228
Fax (01887) 830765
Mem 200
Sec AA MacTaggart (Golf Dir)
Pro A Marshall
Holes 18 L 6066 yds SSS 69
Recs Am–63 MM Niven
Pro–A Learmonth (1962)

V'tors U WE–booking essential
SOC
Fees £16 D–£26 (£20 D–£36)
Loc 6 miles W of Aberfeldy
(A827)
Arch James Braid

Whitemoss (1994)

Whitemoss Road, Dunning, Perth
Tel (01738) 730300
Mem 300
Sec V Westwood
Pro None
Holes 18 L 6200 yds Par 69 SSS 69
V'tors U SOC
Fees £15 (£15)
Loc Aberuthven, 10 miles SW of
Perth, off A9

Renfrewshire

Barshaw (1920)

Public
*Barshaw Park, Glasgow Road,
Paisley*
Tel (0141) 889 2908
Fax (0141) 840 2148
Mem 103
Sec W Collins (0141) 884 2533
Holes 18 L 5703 yds SSS 67
V'tors U
Fees £6.50
Loc 1 mile E of Paisley Cross,
off A737

Bonnyton (1957)

Eaglesham, Glasgow G76 0QA
Tel (01355) 302781
Fax (01355) 303151
Mem 950
Pro K McWade
(01355) 302256
Holes 18 L 6252 yds SSS 71
Recs Am–64 A Winston
Pro–68 J Wilson
V'tors I SOC–WD
Fees £27
Loc 2 miles W of Eaglesham.
6 miles S of Glasgow

Caldwell (1903)

Caldwell, Uplawmoor
Tel (01505) 850329
Fax (01505) 850604
Mem 450
Sec HIF Harper
(01505) 850366
Pro S Forbes (01505) 850616
Holes 18 L 6228 yds SSS 70
Recs Am–64 JM Sharp (1974)
Pro–63 C Innes (1987),
G Collinson (1988),
C Gillies (1989)
V'tors WD–booking before 4pm–M
after 4pm WE–M
Fees On application
Loc 5 miles SW of Barrhead
on A736 Glasgow-Irvine road

Cochrane Castle (1895)

*Scott Avenue, Craigston, Johnstone
PA5 0HF*
Tel (01505) 320146
Fax (01505) 325338
Mem 425
Sec JC Cowan
Pro JJ Boyd (01505) 328465
Holes 18 L 6226 yds Par 71 SSS 71
Recs Am–65 R Davidson
Pro–71 S Kelly
V'tors WD–U WE–M
Fees £17 D–£25
Loc ½ mile S of Beith Road,
Johnstone
Arch Charles Hunter

East Renfrewshire
(1922)

*Loganswell, Pilmuir, Newton Mearns
G77 6RT*
Tel (013555) 500256
Mem 450
Sec AL Gillespie (0141) 333 9989
Pro GD Clarke (013555) 500206
Holes 18 L 6097 yds SSS 70
Recs Am–63 D Orr (1996)
Pro–64 CR Brooks (1989)
V'tors On application
Fees £30 D–£35
Loc 2 miles SW of Newton
Mearns
Arch James Braid

Eastwood (1893)

*Muirshield, Loganswell, Newton
Mearns, Glasgow G77 6RX*
Tel (01355) 500261
Mem 900
Sec VE Jones (01355) 500280
Pro A McGinness
(01355) 500285
Holes 18 L 5864 yds SSS 69
Recs Am–61 D Orr (1996)
Pro–66 JC Farmer (1981)
V'tors M SOC
Fees £20 D–£30
Loc 9 miles SW of Glasgow
Arch Theodore Moone

Elderslie (1909)

63 Main Road, Elderslie PA5 9AZ
Tel (01505) 323956
Fax (01505) 323956
Mem 432
Sec Mrs A Anderson
Pro R Bowman (01505) 320032
Holes 18 L 6165 yds SSS 70
Recs Am–62 G Campbell (1996)
Pro–61 D Robertson (1994)
V'tors M SOC–WD
Fees £20 D–£30
Loc 2 miles SW of Paisley

Erskine (1904)

Bishopton PA7 5PH
Tel (01505) 862302
Mem 400 200(L)
Sec TA McKillop
Pro P Thomson (01505) 862108

Holes 18 L 6287 yds SSS 70
Recs Am–66 IG Riddell
Pro–63 G Collinson
V'tors WD–I WE–M
Fees £25
Loc 5 miles NW of Paisley

Fereneze (1904)

Fereneze Avenue, Barrhead G78 1HJ
Tel (0141) 881 1519
Mem 700
Sec KWM Tudhope
(0141) 248 6976
Pro (0141) 880 7058
Holes 18 L 5962 yds SSS 70
Recs Am–67 I McMillan (1995)
Pro–65 S McAllister,
A Tait (1995)
V'tors M SOC–WD
Fees D–£20
Loc 9 miles SW of Glasgow

Gleddoch (1974)

Langbank PA14 6YE
Tel (01475) 540304
Fax (01475) 540459
Mem 600
Sec DW Tierney
Pro K Campbell
(01475) 540704
Holes 18 L 6375 yds SSS 71
Recs Am–64 M O'Hare
Pro–67 J Chillas, C Gillies
V'tors WD–U WE–restricted SOC
Fees £30
Loc 16 miles W of Glasgow
(M8/A8)
Arch J Hamilton Stutt

Gourock (1896)

Cowal View, Gourock PA19 1HD
Tel (01475) 631001
Fax (01475) 631001
Mem 538 98(L) 86(J)
Sec AD Taylor
Pro G Coyle (01475) 636834
Holes 18 L 6512 yds SSS 73
Recs Am–64 N Skinner
Pro–68 R Arnott
V'tors WD–I SOC
Fees £18 (£22)
Loc 3 miles SW of Greenock,
off A770. 7 miles W of Port
Glasgow

Greenock (1890)

Forsyth Street, Greenock PA16 8RE
Tel (01475) 720793
Mem 500 111(L) 110(J)
Sec EJ Black
Pro S Russell (01475) 787236
Holes 18 L 5888 yds SSS 68
9 L 2149 yds SSS 32
Recs Am–64 MC Mazzoni,
C McLellan, M Carmichael
Pro–66 H Thomson,
J Panton, H Boyle
V'tors WD–U WE/BH–M
Fees D–£22 (£27)
Loc 1 mile SW of Greenock on A8
Arch James Braid

Kilmacolm (1891)

Porterfield Road, Kilmacolm
PA13 4PD

Tel	(01505) 872139
Fax	(01505) 874007
Mem	776
Sec	DW Tinton
Pro	D Stewart (01505) 872695
Holes	18 L 5960 yds SSS 69
Recs	Am–64 M Stevenson
	Pro–63 R Weir, J White
V'tors	WD–U WE–M
Fees	£20
Loc	10 miles W of Paisley (A761)

Lochwinnoch (1897)

Burnfoot Road, Lochwinnoch
PA12 4AN

Tel	(01505) 842153
Mem	500
Sec	Mrs E McBride
Pro	G Reilly (01505) 843029
Holes	18 L 6243 yds SSS 71
Recs	Am–58 M Beattie (1994),
	A Finlayson (1995)
	Pro–63 M Miller (1987)
V'tors	WD–U before 4.30pm
	SOC–WD
Fees	£15 D–£20
Loc	9 miles SW of Paisley

Old Ranfurly (1905)

Ranfurly Place, Bridge of Weir
PA11 3DE

Tel	(01505) 613612 (Clubhouse)
Fax	(01505) 613214
Mem	375
Sec	R Mitchell (01505) 613214
Pro	None
Holes	18 L 6089 yds SSS 69
Recs	Am–62 A Hunter (1983)
	Pro–66 C Elliot (1984)
V'tors	WD–I WE–M SOC
Fees	On application
Loc	7 miles W of Paisley, off A761

Paisley (1895)

Braehead, Paisley PA2 8TZ

Tel	(0141) 884 2292
Fax	(0141) 884 3903
Mem	805
Sec	WJ Cunningham
	(0141) 884 3903
Pro	G Stewart (0141) 884 4114
Holes	18 L 6466 yds Par 71 SSS 72
Recs	Am–66 WB Anderson,
	S Young, M Brooke
	Pro–66 S Callan,
	G Collinson, C Gillies
V'tors	WD–H SOC
Fees	£20 D–£28 (1997)
Loc	Braehead, S of Paisley

Port Glasgow (1895)

Devol Farm, Port Glasgow
PA14 5XE

Tel	(01475) 704181
Mem	375
Sec	NL Mitchell
	(01475) 706273

Holes	18 L 5712 yds SSS 68
Recs	Am–62 M Carmichael
V'tors	WD–U before 5pm –M after
	5pm WE–NA SOC
Fees	On application
Loc	1 mile S of Port Glasgow

Ranfurly Castle (1889)

Golf Road, Bridge of Weir
PA11 3HN

Tel	(01505) 612609
Fax	(07070) 710326
Mem	360 160(L) 100(J)
Sec	J Walker
Pro	T Eckford
	(01505) 614795
Holes	18 L 6284 yds SSS 71
Recs	Am–65 WMB Brown
	Pro–65 W Lockie (1989)
V'tors	WD–H WE–M SOC–Tues
Fees	£25 D–£35
Loc	7 miles W of Paisley (A761)
Arch	Kirkcaldy/Auchterlonie

Renfrew (1894)

Blythswood Estate, Inchinnan Road,
Renfrew PA4 9EG

Tel	(0141) 886 6692
Fax	(0141) 886 1808
Mem	465 110(L) 80(J)
Sec	I Murchison
Pro	D Grant
	(0141) 885 1754
Holes	18 L 6818 yds SSS 73
Recs	Am–67 R Coultart (1991)
	Pro–65 J Farmer (1991)
V'tors	M SOC
Fees	On application
Loc	3 miles N of Paisley, nr
	Airport
Arch	Cdr JD Harris

Whinhill (1911)

Beith Road, Greenock

Tel	(01475) 24694
Mem	250
Sec	R Kirkpatrick
	(01475) 633258
Pro	None
Holes	18 L 5504 yds SSS 68
Recs	Am–64 J Callaghan (1995)
V'tors	U
Fees	On application
Loc	Upper Greenock - Largs road

Whitecraigs (1905)

72 Ayr Road, Giffnock, Glasgow
G46 6SW

Tel	(0141) 639 4530
Fax	(0141) 639 4530
Mem	1150
Sec	AG Keith CA
Pro	A Forrow
	(0141) 639 2140
Holes	18 L 6013 yds SSS 69
V'tors	WD–I WE–M SOC–WD
Fees	On application
Loc	6 miles S of Glasgow (A77),
	nr Whitecraigs Station

Stirlingshire

Aberfoyle (1890)

Braeval, Aberfoyle FK8 3UY

Tel	(018772) 382493
Mem	600
Sec	RD Steele
	(018772) 382638
Holes	18 L 5218 yds SSS 66
Recs	Am–64 EJ Barnard
V'tors	WD–U WE–NA before
	11.30am
Fees	£12 D–£16 (£16 D–£24)
Loc	Braeval, 18 miles NW of
	Stirling (A81)

Balfron (1992)

Kepculloch Road, Balfron G63

Mem	400
Sec	I Rubython
	(01360) 440915
Pro	None
Holes	9 L 5372 yds Par 68 SSS 67
V'tors	WD–U before 4pm
	WE–restricted SOC
Fees	£7
Loc	18 miles NW of Glasgow,
	off A81

Bonnybridge (1924)

Larbert Road, Bonnybridge

Tel	(01324) 812822
Mem	425
Sec	C Munn
Holes	9 L 6058 yds SSS 69
Recs	Am–64 S Hunter, J Maxwell
	Pro–66 J McTear
V'tors	WD–I
Fees	On application
Loc	3 miles W of Falkirk

Bridge of Allan (1895)

Sunnylaw, Bridge of Allan

Tel	(01786) 832332
Mem	300
Sec	S Green, M Watson
Holes	9 L 4932 yds SSS 65
Recs	Am–62 ID McFarlane
V'tors	U exc Sat
Fees	£8 (£12)
Loc	4 miles N of Stirling, off A9
Arch	Tom Morris Sr

Buchanan Castle (1936)

Drymen G63 0HY

Tel	(01360) 660369
Mem	830
Sec	R Kinsella (01360) 660307
Pro	K Baxter (01360) 660330
Holes	18 L 6015 yds SSS 69
Recs	Am–64 C Dunan
	Pro–66 D Huish, W Milne
V'tors	M or by arrangement with Sec
Fees	On application
Loc	18 miles NW of Glasgow.
	25 miles W of Stirling,
	off A811
Arch	James Braid

Campsie (1897)

Crow Road, Lennoxtown, Glasgow
G65 7HX

Tel	**(01360) 310244**
Mem	650
Sec	D Barbour
Pro	M Brennan
	(01360) 310920
Holes	18 L 5517 yds SSS 68
Recs	Am–70 M Howat (1996)
V'tors	WD–U before 4.30pm
Fees	£12
Loc	N of Lennoxtown on B822 Fintry road

Dunblane New (1923)

Perth Road, Dunblane FK15 0LJ

Tel	**(01786) 823711**
Fax	(01786) 825946
Mem	600
Sec	JH Dunsmore
Pro	RM Jamieson
Holes	18 L 5957 yds SSS 69
Recs	Am–64 GK McDonald, AY Wilson, S Morrison Pro–64 RM Jamieson
V'tors	WD–Mon/Tues/Thurs/Fri am WE–M SOC
Fees	£18 (£27)
Loc	E side of Dunblane. 6 miles N of Stirling

Falkirk (1922)

Stirling Road, Camelon, Falkirk
FK2 7YP

Tel	**(01324) 611061/612219**
Fax	(01324) 639573
Mem	700
Sec	J Elliott
Holes	18 L 6282 yds SSS 70
Recs	Am–66 Pro–66
V'tors	WD–U until 4pm Sat–NA SOC–exc Sat
Fees	£15 D–£20 Sun–£30
Loc	1½ miles W of Falkirk on A9
Arch	James Braid

Falkirk Tryst (1885)

86 Burnhead Road, Larbert
FK5 4BD

Tel	**(01324) 562415**
Mem	800

Sec	RD Wallace
	(01324) 562054
Pro	S Dunsmore
	(01324) 562091
Holes	18 L 6053 yds SSS 69
Recs	Am–62 T Gilchrist Pro–65 J Chillas
V'tors	WD–U WE–M SOC–WD
Fees	£15 D–£25
Loc	3 miles NW of Falkirk

Glenbervie (1932)

Stirling Road, Larbert FK5 4SJ

Tel	**(01324) 562605**
Fax	(01324) 551054
Mem	600
Sec	Mrs M Purves
Pro	J Chillas
	(01324) 562725
Holes	18 L 6423 yds SSS 70
Recs	Am–65 J McCallum (1996) Pro–64 G Law
V'tors	WD–I WE–M SOC–Tues & Thurs
Fees	£30 D–£45
Loc	1 mile N of Larbert on A9

Grangemouth (1973)

Public
Polmonthill, Polmont FK2 0YA

Tel	**(01324) 711500**
Mem	700
Sec	I Hutton (Hon)
Pro	SJ Campbell
	(01324) 714355
Holes	18 L 6527 yds SSS 70
Recs	Am–65 LJ Blair (1996)
V'tors	U–book with Pro SOC
Fees	£5.50 D–£8.30 (£7.40 D–£10.20)
Loc	3 miles NE of Falkirk. M9 Junction 4

Kilsyth Lennox (1900)

Tak-Ma-Doon Road, Kilsyth
G65 0RS

Tel	**(01236) 823525 (Bookings)**
Mem	250
Sec	AG Stevenson
	(01236) 823213
Holes	18 L 5930 yds Par 70
Recs	Am–66 R Irvine (1986), W Erskine (1987)

Polmont (1901)

Manuel Rigg, Maddiston, Falkirk
FK2 0LS

Tel	**(01324) 711277 (Clubhouse)**
Fax	(01324) 712504
Mem	300
Sec	P Lees
	(01324) 713811
Holes	9 L 3044 yds SSS 69
Recs	Am–66 C Fowler (1996)
V'tors	U exc Sat–NA
Fees	£7 Sun–£12
Loc	4 miles SE of Falkirk on B805

Stirling (1869)

Queen's Road, Stirling FK8 3AA

Tel	**(01786) 473801**
Fax	(01786) 450748
Mem	1000
Sec	WC McArthur
	(01786) 464098
Pro	I Collins
	(01786) 471490
Holes	18 L 6409 yds SSS 71
Recs	Am–64 KJ McArthur (1997) Pro–66 G Everitt (1993)
V'tors	WD–U SOC WE–NA
Fees	On application
Loc	King's Park, Stirling
Arch	Braid/Cotton

Strathendrick (1901)

Glasgow Road, Drymen G63

Tel	**(01360) 660695**
Mem	480
Sec	J Vickers (01360) 660675
Holes	9 L 5116 yds SSS 64
Recs	Am–60 P Haggarty Pro–64 C Dernie
V'tors	WD–U SOC–WD before 5pm
Fees	£10 D–£16
Loc	25 miles W of Stirling, off A811
Arch	W Fernie

Wales

Cardiganshire

Aberystwyth (1911)
Bryn-y-Mor, Aberystwyth SY23 2HY
Tel (01970) 615104
Fax (01970) 615104
Mem 390
Sec L Evans
Pro M Newson (01970) 625301
Holes 18 L 6109 yds SSS 71
Recs Am–67 P Richards
Pro–67 P Parkin, G Emerson
V'tors U SOC
Fees £18.50 (£22.50)
Loc Aberystwyth ½ mile
Arch H Varden

Borth & Ynyslas (1885)
Borth SY24 5JS
Tel (01970) 871202
Fax (01970) 871202
Mem 550
Sec · Miss S Wilson
Pro JG Lewis (01970) 871557
Holes 18 L 6100 yds SSS 70
Recs Am–65 M Stimson (1989),
C Evans (1993)
Pro–67 JG Lewis
Ladies–73 K Stark
V'tors WD–U WE/BH–by prior
arrangement SOC
Fees £18 (£25)
Loc 8 miles N of Aberystwyth
(B4353), off A487

Cardigan (1895)
Gwbert-on-Sea, Cardigan SA43 1PR
Tel (01239) 612035/621775
Fax (01239) 621775
Mem 600
Sec JJ Jones
Pro C Parsons
Holes 18 L 6687 yds SSS 73
Recs Am–68 R Emanuel
V'tors H SOC
Fees D–£16 (£21) W–£65
Loc 3 miles N of Cardigan
Arch Hawtree

Cilgwyn (1977)
Llangybi, Lampeter SA48 8NN
Tel (01570) 45286
Mem 290
Sec N Hill
Holes 9 L 5327 yds SSS 67
Recs Am–67 EL Jones (1991)
V'tors U SOC
Fees £10 (£15) W–£60
Loc 5 miles NE of Lampeter,
off A485 at Llangybi

Penrhos G&CC (1991)
Llanrhystud, Aberystwyth SY23 5AY
Tel (01974) 202999
Fax (01974) 202100
Mem 300
Sec R Rees-Evans
Pro P Diamond
Holes 18 L 6641 yds SSS 72
9 hole Par 3 course
Recs Am–70 I Miller (1997)
V'tors U SOC
Fees £17 (£22)
Loc 9 miles S of Aberystwyth,
off A487
Mis Driving range
Arch Jim Walters

Carmarthenshire

Ashburnham (1894)
Cliffe Terrace, Burry Port SA16 0HN
Tel (01554) 832466
Fax (01554) 832466
Mem 725
Sec DK Williams (01554) 832269
Pro RA Ryder (01554) 833846
Holes 18 L 6916 yds SSS 72
Recs Am–69 Y Taylor
Pro–71 C Evans, N Roderick
V'tors H
Fees £27 D–£32 (£32 D–£42)
Loc 5 miles W of Llanelli (A484)

Carmarthen (1907)
*Blaenycoed Road, Carmarthen
SA33 6EH*
Tel (01267) 281214
Mem 700
Sec J Coe (01267) 281588
Pro P Gillis (01267) 281493
Holes 18 L 6212 yds SSS 71
Recs Am–66 N Roderick (1997)
Pro–69 B Barnes
V'tors H SOC
Fees £18 (£25)
Loc 4 miles NW of Carmarthen

Derllys (1993)
*Derllys Court, Llysonnen Road,
Carmarthen SA33 5DT*
Tel (01267) 211575/211309
Fax (01267) 211575
Mem 48
Sec R Walters
Holes 9 L 2859 yds Par 70 SSS 66
V'tors U
Fees £9 D–£12 (£10 D–£13)
Loc 4 miles W of Carmarthen,
off A40
Arch P Johnson

Glynhir (1909)
*Glynhir Road, Llandybie, Ammanford
SA18 2TF*
Tel (01269) 850472
Fax (01269) 851365
Mem 700
Sec EP Rees, DB Jones
(01269) 851365
Pro D Prior (01269) 851010
Holes 18 L 5994 yds SSS 70
Recs Am–66 R Collins
V'tors WD/Sat–H Sun–NA
SOC–WD
Fees Winter £10 (£12) 5D–£45
Summer £16 (£22) 5D–£70
Loc 3½ miles N of Ammanford
Arch Hawtree

Conwy

Abergele & Pensarn (1910)
*Tan-y-Goppa Road, Abergele
LL22 8DS*
Tel (01745) 824034
Fax (01745) 824034
Mem 1250
Sec HE Richards
Pro I Runcie (01745) 823813
Holes 18 L 6520 yds SSS 71
Recs Am–66 D Davies (1994)
Pro–65 D Vaughan (1987)
V'tors U SOC
Fees On application
Loc Abergele Castle Grounds
Arch Hawtree

Betws-y-Coed (1977)
Clubhouse, Betws-y-Coed LL24
Tel (01690) 710556
Mem 400
Sec JH Jones
Holes 9 L 4996 yds SSS 63
Recs Am–63 DWP Hughes (1990)
V'tors U SOC
Fees £15 (£20)
Loc ½ mile off A5, in Betws-y-
Coed

Conwy (Caernarvonshire) (1890)
Morfa, Conwy LL32 8ER
Tel (01492) 593400
Fax (01492) 593363
Mem 750
Sec DL Brown (01492) 592423
Pro JP Lees (01492) 593225
Holes 18 L 6936 yds SSS 74
Recs Am–69 C Platt (1996)
V'tors H WE–restricted SOC
Fees £25 (£30)
Loc ½ mile W of Conway, off A55

Kinmel Park (1989)
Pay and play
Bodelwyddan LL18 5SR
Tel (01745) 833548
Fax (01745) 833544
Sec P Stebbings
Pro P Stebbings

Holes 9 L 1550 yds Par 29
V'tors U
Fees £3 (£3.50)
Loc Off A55, between Abergele and St Asaph
Mis Driving range. Golf Academy
Arch Peter Stebbings

Llandudno (Maesdu)

(1915)

Hospital Road, Llandudno LL30 1HU

Tel (01492) 876450
Fax (01492) 871570
Mem 1109
Sec G Dean
Pro S Boulden (01492) 875195
Holes 18 L 6513 yds SSS 72
Recs Am–67 G Jones, CT Brown, M Macara
Pro–66 PJ Butler
V'tors U H–recognised GC members SOC
Fees £25 (£30)
Loc 1 mile S of Llandudno Station, nr Hospital

Llandudno (North Wales)

(1894)

72 Bryniau Road, West Shore, Llandudno LL30 2DZ

Tel (01492) 875325
Fax (01492) 875325
Mem 560
Sec F Hopley
Pro RA Bradbury (01492) 876878
Holes 18 L 6247 yds Par 71 SSS 71
Recs Am–66 L Harpin
Pro–63 WS Collins
V'tors U SOC–phone Sec
Fees £23 (£30)
Loc ³/₄ mile from Llandudno on West Shore

Llanfairfechan (1971)

Llannerch Road, Llanfairfechan LL33 0EB

Tel (01248) 680144
Mem 352
Sec MJ Charlesworth (01248) 680524
Holes 9 L 3119 yds SSS 57
Recs Am–53 MJ Charlesworth (1983)
V'tors U
Fees £5 (£10)
Loc 7 miles E of Bangor on A55

Old Colwyn (1907)

Woodland Avenue, Old Colwyn LL29 9NL

Tel (01492) 515581
Mem 250
Sec DM Fisher
Holes 9 L 5243 yds SSS 66
Recs Am–63 C Oldham, JD Jones Roberts
Pro–67 DJ Rees
V'tors WD–U WE–by arrangement SOC
Fees £10 (£15)
Loc 2 miles E of Colwyn Bay

Penmaenmawr (1910)

Conway Old Road, Penmaenmawr LL34 6RD

Tel (01492) 623330
Mem 600
Sec Mrs JE Jones
Holes 9 L 5143 yds SSS 66
Recs Am–63 S Wilkinson
V'tors U SOC
Fees £12 (£18)
Loc 4 miles W of Conway

Rhos-on-Sea (1899)

Penrhyn Bay, Llandudno LL30 3PU

Tel (01492) 549641
Mem 600
Sec JG Yates
Pro M Jones
Holes 18 L 6064 yds SSS 69
Recs Am–69 P Knowles
Pro–66 M Greenough
V'tors U
Fees On application
Loc On coast at Rhos-on-Sea. 4 miles E of LLandudno

Denbighshire

Bryn Morfydd Hotel

(1982)

Llanrhaeadr, Denbigh LL16 4NP

Tel (01745) 890280
Fax (01745) 890488
Mem 400
Sec CS Henderson (Golf Dir)
Pro IP Jones
Holes 18 L 5660 yds SSS 67
9 hole Par 3 course
V'tors U SOC
Fees £12 (£16)
Loc 2¹/₂ miles SE of Denbigh on A525
Arch Duchess-Alliss/Thomas. Dukes-Muirhead/Henderson

Chirk (1990)

Chirk, Wrexham

Tel (01691) 774407
Fax (01691) 773878
Mem 850
Sec FA Barnes
Pro JA Fullard
Holes 18 L 7045 yds Par 72 SSS 73
9 hole Par 3 course
V'tors U after 10am SOC
Fees £15 D–£22 (£22 D–£28)
Loc 8 miles S of Wrexham on A483
Mis Driving range

Denbigh (1922)

Henllan Road, Denbigh LL16 5AA

Tel (01745) 814159
Mem 550
Sec MJ McCarthy (01745) 816669
Pro M Jones (01745) 814159
Holes 18 L 5712 yds SSS 68

Recs Am–65 OJ Roberts (1995)
Pro–69 C Defoy (1986)
V'tors U SOC
Fees On application
Loc 1 mile NW of Denbigh (B5382)

Moss Valley (1990)

Pay and play
Moss Road, Wrexham LL11 4UR

Tel (01978) 720518
Mem 100
Sec C Davies
Holes 9 L 2724 yds Par 70 SSS 66
V'tors U
Fees £4 (£5)
Loc N of Wrexham, off A541

Pen-y-Cae (1993)

Ruabon Road, Pen-y-Cae, Wrexham LL14 1TW

Tel (01978) 810108
Mem 100
Sec G Williams (Mgr)
Holes 9 L 4280 yds Par 64 SSS 62
V'tors U SOC–WD
Fees 9 holes–£5 (£6)
18 holes–£7.50 (£9.50)
Loc 6 miles S of Wrexham, via A483/A539
Arch John Day

Plassey (1992)

The Plassey, Eyton, Wrexham LL13 0SP

Tel (01978) 780020
Mem 100
Sec V Cliffe, G Hughes (Prop.)
Holes 9 L 2308 yds Par 32
V'tors U SOC
Fees £8
Loc 2 miles SW of Wrexham, off A483
Mis Driving range. Pitch & putt
Arch K Williams

Prestatyn (1905)

Marine Road East, Prestatyn LL19 7HS

Tel (01745) 854320
Fax (01745) 888353
Mem 650
Sec R Woodruff (Mgr) (01745) 888353
Pro M Staton (01745) 852083
Holes 18 L 6808 yds SSS 73
Recs Am–66 RJ Edwards (1993)
V'tors H SOC
Fees £20 (£25)
Loc 1 mile E of Prestatyn
Arch S Collins

Rhuddlan (1930)

Meliden Road, Rhuddlan LL18 6LB

Tel (01745) 590217
Fax (01745) 590472
Mem 515 155(L) 80(J)
Sec D Morris
Pro A Carr (01745) 590898
Holes 18 L 6482 yds SSS 71

Recs Am–66 D McKendrick (1995)
V'tors H or I Sun–M SOC–WD
Fees £18 (£30)
Loc 2 miles N of St Asaph, off A55
Arch F Hawtree

Rhyl (1890)

Coast Road, Rhyl LL18 3RE
Tel (01745) 353171
Fax (01745) 353171
Mem 440
Sec I StC Doig
Pro T Leah
Holes 9 L 6153 yds SSS 70
Recs Am–L Williams (1994)
Pro–67 H Cotton, C Ward, N von Nida
V'tors U SOC
Fees £12 (£15)
Loc On A548 between Rhyl and Prestatyn
Arch James Braid

Ruthin-Pwllglas (1920)

Pwllglas, Ruthin
Tel (01824) 702296
Mem 360
Sec WK Roberts (01824) 703427
Holes 10 L 5362 yds SSS 66
Recs Am–66 H Roberts
V'tors U SOC
Fees £12.50 (£18)
Loc 2½ miles S of Ruthin

St Melyd (1922)

The Paddock, Meliden Road, Prestatyn LL19 9NB
Tel (01745) 854405
Mem 400
Sec PM Storey (01745) 853574
Pro R Bradbury (01745) 888858
Holes 9 L 5857 yds SSS 68
Recs Am–65 AR Grace (1990)
Pro–66 S Wilkinson
V'tors U SOC
Fees £15 (£19)
Loc S of Prestatyn on A547

Vale of Llangollen (1908)

Holyhead Road, Llangollen LL20 7PR
Tel (01978) 860613
Fax (01978) 860906
Mem 750
Sec AD Bluck (01978) 860906
Pro DI Vaughan (01978) 860040
Holes 18 L 6656 yds Par 72 SSS 73
Recs Am–67 DE Hart (1991)
Pro–68
V'tors U SOC
Fees £20 (£25)
Loc 1½ miles E of Llangollen on A5

Wrexham (1906)

Holt Road, Wrexham LL13 9SB
Tel (01978) 261033
Mem 650
Sec JR Scott (01978) 364268

Pro R Young (01978) 351476
Holes 18 L 6233 yds Par 70 SSS 70
Recs Am–64 M Ellis (1995)
Pro–66 SJ Edwards (1993)
V'tors H SOC–WD
Fees £20 (£25)
Loc 2 miles NE of Wrexham on A534
Arch James Braid

Flintshire

Caerwys (1989)

Pay and play
Caerwys, Mold CH7 5AQ
Tel (01352) 720692
Mem 200
Sec E Barlow
Pro N Lloyd
Holes 9 L 3080 yds SSS 60
Recs Am–61 T Adamson (1989)
V'tors U SOC
Fees £4.50 (£5.50)
Loc SW of Caerwys. 1½ miles S of A55 Express Way, between Holywell and St Asaph
Arch Eleanor Barlow

Flint (1966)

Cornist Park, Flint CH6 5HJ
Tel (01352) 732327, (01244) 812974
Fax (01244) 811885
Mem 390
Sec TE Owens
Holes 9 L 5953 yds SSS 69
Recs Am–65 O O'Neil, G Houston
V'tors WD–U before 5pm SOC–WD
Fees D–£10 (£10)
Loc 1 mile SW of Flint. End of M56, 8 miles

Hawarden (1911)

Groomsdale Lane, Hawarden, Deeside CH5 3EH
Tel (01244) 531447
Mem 480
Pro C Hope (01244) 520809
Holes 18 L 5842 yds SSS 68
Recs Am–64 L Hinks-Edwards
V'tors H SOC
Fees £12.50 (£15)
Loc 6 miles W of Chester, off A55

Holywell (1906)

Brynford, Holywell CH8 8LQ
Tel (01352) 710040/713937
Fax (01352) 713937
Mem 375 60(L)
Sec EK Carney (01352) 713937
Pro J Law (01352) 710040
Holes 18 L 6100 yds Par 70 SSS 70
Recs Am–69 DP Hardie (1994)
V'tors WD–U WE–SOC
Fees £15 (£20)
Loc 2 miles S of Holywell, off A5026

Kinsale

Pay and play
Llanerchymor, Holywell CH8 9DX
Tel (01745) 561080
Fax (01745) 561079
Mem 85
Sec A Backhurst (Golf Dir)
Pro A Backhurst
Holes 9 holes Par 70 SSS 70
V'tors U
Fees 9 holes–£5.70;
18 holes–£8.50
Loc 4 miles N of Holywell on A548
Mis Floodlit driving range
Arch K Smith

Mold (1909)

Pantymwyn, Mold CH7 5EH
Tel (01352) 740318/741513
Fax (01352) 741517
Mem 350 85(L) 90(J)
Sec EJ Reeves (01352) 741513
Pro M Carty (01352) 740318
Holes 18 L 5528 yds SSS 67
Recs Am–64 N Tomlinson
Pro–64 D Wills
V'tors U SOC
Fees £16 (£23)
Loc 4 miles W of Mold
Arch Hawtree

Northop Country Park (1994)

Northop, Chester CH7 6WA
Tel (01352) 840440
Fax (01352) 840445
Sec D Llewellyn
Pro M Pritchard
Holes 18 L 6735 yds Par 72
Recs Am–68
Pro–64
V'tors U–phone first
Fees £28 (£35)
Loc 3 miles S of Flint, off A55
Mis Driving range
Arch John Jacobs

Old Padeswood (1978)

Station Road, Padeswood, Mold CH7 4JL
Tel (01244) 547701 (Clubhouse)
Mem 500
Sec R Slater
Pro A Davies (01244) 547401
Holes 18 L 6728 yds SSS 72
9 hole Par 3 course
Recs Am–66 L Lockett (1991), I Rowlands (1997)
Pro–65 I Higsby
Ladies–72 S Lovat (1994)
V'tors U exc comp days SOC–WD
Fees £16 D–£25 (£20 D–£30)
Loc 2 miles from Mold on A5118

Padeswood & Buckley (1933)

The Caia, Station Lane, Padeswood, Mold CH7 4JD
Tel (01244) 550537
Fax (01244) 541600

Mem 592
Sec JG Peters
Pro D Ashton (01244) 543636
Holes 18 L 6001 yds Par 70 SSS 69
Recs Am–66 SA Delves
V'tors WD–U 9am–4pm –M after
4pm Sat–U Sun–NA
SOC–WD Ladies Day–Wed
Fees £20 (£25)
Loc 8 miles W of Chester, off
A5118. 2nd golf club on right
Arch D Williams

Gwynedd

Aberdovey (1892)
Aberdovey LL35 0RT
Tel (01654) 767210
Fax (01654) 767027
Mem 800
Sec JM Griffiths (01654) 767493
Pro J Davies (01654) 767602
Holes 18 L 6445 yds SSS 71
Recs Am–66 BT Bell (1993)
Pro–67 J Smith
V'tors NA–8–9.30am & 1–2pm
Fees On application
Loc 3 miles W of Aberdovey
(A493)

Abersoch (1907)
Golf Road, Abersoch LL53 7EY
Tel (01758) 712622
Fax (01758) 712622
Mem 700
Sec A Drosinos Jones
Pro A Drosinos Jones
Holes 18 L 5819 yds SSS 69
V'tors U H SOC
Fees £18 (£20)
Loc ½ mile S of Abersoch (A55).
7 miles S of Pwllheli
Arch Harry Vardon

Bala (1973)
Penlan, Bala LL23 7YD
Tel (01678) 520359
Fax (01678) 521361
Mem 320
Sec Dianne Davies
Pro T Davies
Holes 10 L 4962 yds SSS 64
Recs Am–63 RJ Roberts (1997)
V'tors WD–U WE–NA pm SOC
Fees £12 (£15) W–£40
Loc 1 mile SW of Bala, off A494
to Dolgellau

Bala Lake Hotel
Bala LL23 7YF
Tel (01678) 520344/520111
Fax (01678) 521193
Mem 50
Sec D Pickering
Holes 9 L 4280 yds SSS 61
V'tors U
Fees On application
Loc 1½ miles S of Bala on B4403

Caernarfon (1907)
Aberforeshore, LLanfaglan, Caernarfon LL54 5RP
Tel (01286) 673783/678359
Fax (01286) 672535
Mem 696
Sec DJ Jones
Pro A Owen (01286) 678359
Holes 18 L 5891 yds SSS 68
Recs Am–66
Pro–64
V'tors U SOC
Fees £17 (£22)
Loc 2½ miles SW of Caernarfon

Criccieth (1905)
Ednyfed Hill, Criccieth
Tel (01766) 522154
Mem 200
Sec MG Hamilton
(01766) 522697
Holes 18 L 5755 yds SSS 68
Recs Am–63 NJ Gore (1982)
Ladies–60 F Prole (1979)
V'tors U
Fees £12 Sun–£15
Loc 4 miles W of Portmadoc

Dolgellau (1911)
Pencefn Road, Dolgellau LL40 1SL
Tel (01341) 422603
Mem 300
Sec HM Edwards
Pro None
Holes 9 L 4671 yds Par 66 SSS 63
Recs Am–63 AL Williams (1991)
Pro–61 L James (1937)
V'tors U SOC
Fees £13 (£16)
Loc ½ mile N of Dolgellau

Ffestiniog (1893)
Y Cefn, Ffestiniog
Tel (01766) 762637 (Clubhouse)
Mem 138
Sec A Roberts
(01766) 831829
Holes 9 L 5032 metres Par 68 SSS 65
V'tors U
Fees On application
Loc 1 mile E of Ffestiniog on Bala
road (B4391)

Nefyn & District (1907)
Morfa Nefyn, Pwllheli LL53 6DA
Tel (01758) 720218 (Clubhouse)
Fax (01758) 720476
Mem 750
Sec JB Owens
(01758) 720966
Pro J Froom
(01758) 720102
Holes 18 L 6548 yds SSS 71
9 L 2618 yds SSS 34
Recs Am–68 M Pilkington
Pro–67 I Woosnam
V'tors U SOC
Fees £22 D–£27 (£27 D–£35)
Loc 1½ miles W of Nefyn.
20 miles W of Caernarfon

Porthmadog (1902)
Morfa Bychan, Porthmadog LL49 9UU
Tel (01766) 512037
Fax (01766) 514638
Mem 920
Sec Mrs A Richardson (Office
Mgr) (01766) 514124
Pro P Bright (01766) 513828
Holes 18 L 6330 yds Par 70 SSS 71
Recs Am–63 J Morrow
V'tors U H SOC
Fees D–£20 (D–£26)
Loc 2 miles S of Porthmadog,
towards Black Rock Sands
Arch James Braid

Pwllheli (1900)
Golf Road, Pwllheli LL53 5PS
Tel (01758) 701644
Mem 820
Sec RE Williams
Pro GD Verity (01758) 612520
Holes 18 L 6091 yds SSS 69
Recs Am–66 MG Hughes (1988)
Pro–67 D Screeton
V'tors U
Fees D–£18 (D–£25)
Loc ½ mile SW of Pwllheli
Arch James Braid

Royal St David's (1894)
Harlech LL46 2UB
Tel (01766) 780203
Fax (01766) 781110
Mem 700
Sec DL Morkill (01766) 780361
Pro J Barnett (01766) 780857
Holes 18 L 6427 yds SSS 72
Recs Am–64 C Platt (1992)
Pro–64 K Stables (1988)
V'tors U H–booking necessary SOC
Fees D–£30 (D–£35)
Loc W of Harlech on A496

St Deiniol (1905)
Penybryn, Bangor LL57 1PX
Tel (01248) 353098
Mem 500
Sec EW Jones
Holes 18 L 5048 metres SSS 67
Recs Am–61 CG Edwards (1995)
V'tors U
Fees £12 (£16)
Loc Off A5/A55 Junction, 1 mile E
of Bangor on A5122
Arch James Braid

Isle of Anglesey

Anglesey (1914)
Station Road, Rhosneigr LL64 5QX
Tel (01407) 810219
Mem 450
Sec A Jones (Sec/Mgr)
(01407) 810930
Pro M Harrison (01407) 811202
Holes 18 L 6330 yds SSS 70
Recs Am–66 M Robinson (1990)
Pro–65 B Rimmer (1994)

V'tors U H SOC
Fees £15 (£20)
Loc 8 miles SE of Holyhead,
off A4080

Baron Hill (1895)
Beaumaris LL58 8YW
Tel (01248) 810231
Mem 360
Sec A Pleming
Holes 9 L 5062 metres SSS 68
Recs Am–65 AW Jones
V'tors U exc comp days SOC–WD &
Sat (apply Sec)
Fees £12 W–£45
Loc 1 mile SW of Beaumaris

Bull Bay (1913)
Bull Bay Road, Amlwch LL68 9RY
Tel (01407) 830213
Fax (01407) 832612
Mem 850
Sec I Furlong (Sec/Mgr)
(01407) 830960
Pro J Burns (01407) 831188
Holes 18 L 6217 yds SSS 70
Recs Am–60 T Blackwell (1996)
Pro–64 A Barnett (1995)
V'tors H SOC
Fees £15 (£20)
Loc ¹/₂ mile W of Amlwch on
A5025
Arch WH Fowler

Holyhead (1912)
Trearddur Bay, Holyhead LL65 2YG
Tel (01407) 763279/762119
Fax (01407) 763279
Mem 484 225(L) 109(J)
Sec JA Williams
Pro S Elliott (01407) 762022
Holes 18 L 5540 metres SSS 70
Recs Am–67 M Owen
Pro–69 H Gould
V'tors H SOC
Fees £17.50 D–£22 (£22.50
D–£27)
Loc 2 miles S of Holyhead
Arch James Braid

Llangefni (1983)
Public
Llangefni
Tel (01248) 722193
Pro P Lovell
Holes 9 L 1467 yds Par 28
V'tors U
Fees £2.20 (£3)
Loc ¹/₂ mile S of Llangefni,
off A5111
Arch Hawtree

Storws Wen (1996)
Brynteg, Benllech LL78 8JY
Tel (01248) 852673
Fax (01248) 852673
Mem 300
Sec C Purves
Pro None
Holes 9 L 5002 yds Par 68 SSS 63

Recs Am–67 C Brown (1996)
Pro–69 P Lovell (1996)
V'tors U SOC
Fees £10 (£13)
Loc 2 miles from Benllech on
B5108
Arch K Jones

Mid Glamorgan

Aberdare (1921)
Abernant, Aberdare CF44 0RY
Tel (01685) 871188 (Clubhouse)
Fax (01685) 872797
Mem 600
Sec JG Graham
(01685) 872797
Pro AW Palmer (01685) 878735
Holes 18 L 5875 yds SSS 69
Recs Am–64 N Edwards (1997)
Pro–67 AW Palmer
V'tors I or H Sat–M SOC
Fees £14 (£18)
Loc ¹/₂ mile E of Aberdare.
12 miles NW of Pontypridd

Bargoed (1912)
Heolddu, Bargoed
Tel (01443) 830143
Mem 548
Sec WR Coleman (01443) 830608
Pro C Coombs (01443) 836411
Holes 18 L 6233 yds SSS 69
Recs Am–65 B Dredge
V'tors WD–U WE–M SOC–WD
Fees £10 (£15)
Loc NW boundary of Bargoed.
8 miles N of Caerphilly
(A469)

Bryn Meadows Golf Hotel (1973)
The Bryn, Hengoed CF8 7SM
Tel (01495) 225590/224103
Fax (01495) 228272
Mem 550
Sec B Mayo
Pro B Hunter (01495) 221905
Holes 18 L 6156 yds SSS 69
Recs Am–69 B Dredge
Pro–68 S Price
V'tors U
Fees £17.50 (£22.50)
Loc 6 miles N of Caerphilly
(A469)
Arch Mayo/Jefferies

Caerphilly (1905)
Pencapel, Mountain Road, Caerphilly CF83 1HJ
Tel (01222) 883481
Fax (01222) 863441
Mem 765
Sec (01222) 863441
Pro R Barter (01222) 869104
Holes 13 L 6039 yds SSS 71
Recs Am–65 L Absolam
Pro–68 B Huggett

V'tors WD–U H WE–M
Fees £20 W–£40
Loc 7 miles N of Cardiff, off A469
Mis Extension to 18 holes in 1998

Castell Heights (1982)
Pay and play
Blaengwynlais, Caerphilly CF8 1NG
Tel (01222) 886666 (Bookings)
Fax (01222) 869030
Mem 600
Pro S Bebb
Holes 9 L 2688 yds SSS 66
Recs Am–32 P Page (1990)
V'tors U
Fees 9 holes–£4.50 (£5.50)
Loc 4 miles from M4 Junction 32
Mis Driving range
Arch J Page

Coed-y-Mwstwr (1996)
Coychurch, Bridgend CF35 6TN
Tel (01656) 862121
Mem 260
Sec HD James (Sec/Mgr)
Holes 9 L 5834 yds Par 69 SSS 68
Recs Am–72 P Thomas,
S Chilcott (1996)
V'tors UH SOC
Fees £15
Loc 2 miles W of M4 Junction 35

Creigiau (1921)
Creigiau, Cardiff CF4 8NN
Tel (01222) 890263
Fax (01222) 890263
Mem 700
Sec To be appointed
Pro I Luntz (01222) 891909
Holes 18 L 6063 yds SSS 70
Recs Am–67 MJ Harmer (1997)
Pro–66 R Dinsdale (1996)
V'tors WD–U WE/BH–M SOC–WD
Fees £30
Loc 5 miles NW of Cardiff. M4
Junction 34

Llantrisant & Pontyclun (1927)
Lanlay Road, Talbot Green, Llantrisant CF7 8HZ
Tel (01443) 222148
Mem 500
Sec JM Williams (01443) 224601
Pro N Watson (01443) 228169
Holes 12 L 5712 yds SSS 68
Recs Am–65 TJ Lewis (1974)
Pro–65 JJ Hastings (1982)
V'tors WD–U WE/BH–M SOC–WD
Fees On application
Loc 10 miles NW of Cardiff.
2 miles N of M4 Junction 34

Maesteg (1912)
Mount Pleasant, Neath Road, Maesteg CF34 9PR
Tel (01656) 732037
Fax (01656) 734106
Mem 720
Sec RK Lewis MBE
(01656) 734106

Pro JR Black (01656) 735742
Holes 18 L 5929 yds SSS 69
Recs Am–69 R Jenkins (1991),
M Donoghue (1992),
N Hedley (1993)
Pro–64 G Ryall (1989)
V'tors WD–H SOC
Fees £17 (£20)
Loc 1 mile W of Maesteg on
B4282. M4 Junctions 36 or 40

Merthyr Tydfil (1908)

*Cilsanws Mountain, Cefn Coed,
Merthyr Tydfil CF48 2NU*
Tel (01685) 723308
Mem 200
Sec V Price
Holes 18 L 5622 yds SSS 68
Recs Am–65 N Evans
Pro–70 J Howard
V'tors U SOC–WD
Fees £12 (£16)
Loc 2 miles N of Merthyr Tydfil,
off A470 at Cefn Coed
Arch Price/Mathias

Morlais Castle (1900)

*Pant, Dowlais, Merthyr Tydfil
CF48 2UY*
Tel (01685) 722822
Mem 400
Sec N Powell
Pro P Worthing
Holes 18 L 6320 yds SSS 71
Recs Am–67 JP Davies (1993)
V'tors WD–U Sat–NA 12–4pm
Sun–NA 8am–12noon
SOC–WD
Fees £14 (£16)
Loc 3 miles N of Merthyr Tydfil,
nr Mountain Railway

Mountain Ash (1908)

*Cefnpennar, Mountain Ash
CF45 4DT*
Tel (01443) 472265
Mem 555
Sec G Matthews (01443) 479459
Pro (01443) 478770
Holes 18 L 5535 yds SSS 67
Recs Am–63 SJ Lewis
Pro–66 R Evans
V'tors WD–U H WE–M
Fees £15
Loc 9 miles NW of Pontypridd

Mountain Lakes (1988)

Blaengwynlais, Caerphilly CF8 1NG
Tel (01222) 861128
Fax (01222) 869030
Mem 480
Sec DC Rooney (Hon)
Pro S Bebb
Holes 18 L 6300 yds SSS 72
Recs Am– 68–S Deane
Pro–68 P Price (1993)
V'tors H SOC
Fees £15 (£15)
Loc 4 miles from M4 Junction 32
Mis Driving range
Arch R Sandow

Pontypridd (1905)

*Ty Gwyn Road, Pontypridd
CF37 4DJ*
Tel (01443) 402359
Fax (01443) 491622
Mem 850
Sec Vikki Hooley
(01443) 409904
Pro W Walters (01443) 491210
Holes 18 L 5725 yds SSS 68
Recs Am–66 MC Sallam,
PL Jenkins (1989)
V'tors WD–U H WE/BH–M H
SOC–WD H
Fees On application
Loc E of Pontypridd, off A470.
12 miles NW of Cardiff

Pyle & Kenfig (1922)

Waun-y-Mer, Kenfig CF33 4PU
Tel (01656) 783093/771613
Fax (01656) 772822
Mem 860
Sec RC Thomas
Pro R Evans (01656) 772446
Holes 18 L 6655 yds SSS 73
Recs Am–68 L Harpin
Pro–67 J Longmead
V'tors WD–U H WE–M SOC
Fees D–£30
Loc 2 miles NW of Porthcawl
Arch HS Colt

Rhondda (1910)

*Penrhys, Ferndale, Rhondda
CF43 3PW*
Tel (01443) 433204
Fax (01443) 441384
Mem 500
Sec G Rees (01443) 441384
Pro R Davies (01443) 441385
Holes 18 L 6428 yds SSS 71
Recs Am–69 P Derham (1988)
Pro–67 D Ray (1991)
V'tors U H SOC
Fees £20 (£25)
Loc 6 miles W of Pontypridd

Royal Porthcawl (1891)

Rest Bay, Porthcawl CF36 3UW
Tel (01656) 782251
Fax (01656) 771687
Mem 800
Sec AW Woolcott
Pro P Evans (01656) 773702
Holes 18 L 6685 yds SSS 74
Recs Am–68 S Dodds
Pro–65 B Barnes
V'tors WD–I or H WE/BH–M
SOC–H
Fees On application
Loc 22 miles W of Cardiff. M4
Junction 37

Southerndown (1905)

Ewenny, Bridgend CF32 0QP
Tel (01656) 880326
Fax (01656) 880317
Mem 700

Sec AJ Hughes
(01656) 880476
Pro DG McMonagle
Holes 18 L 6417 yds SSS 72
Recs Am–66 H Stott
Pro–64 G Hunt
V'tors U H
Fees £25 (£35)
Loc 3 miles S of Bridgend,
nr Ogmore Castle ruins

Virginia Park (1993)

Pay and play
Virginia Park, Caerphilly CF83 SW
Tel (01222) 863919
Mem 200
Sec Mrs C Lewis
Pro R Barter (01589) 877355
Holes 9 L 4661 yds Par 66 SSS 63
V'tors U SOC
Fees On application
Loc Caerphilly, 7 miles N of
Cardiff
Mis Driving range

Whitehall (1922)

*The Pavilion, Nelson, Treharris
CF46 6ST*
Tel (01443) 740245
Mem 300
Sec VE Davies
Holes 9 L 5666 yds SSS 68
Recs Am–66 M Heames (1985)
Pro–62 I Woosnam (1980)
V'tors WD–U WE–M
Fees £15
Loc 15 miles NW of Cardiff

Monmouthshire

Alice Springs (1989)

Bettws Newydd, Usk NP5 1JY
Tel (01873) 880772 (Queens),
(01873) 880708 (Kings)
Fax (01873) 880838
Mem 350
Sec KR Morgan
Pro P Williams (01873) 880914
Holes Queens 18 L 5870 yds SSS 69
Kings 18 L 6438 yds SSS 72
V'tors U SOC
Fees £15 (£18)
Loc 3 miles N of Usk on B4598
Mis Driving range
Arch Keith Morgan

Blackwood (1914)

Cwmgelli, Blackwood NP2 1EL
Tel (01495) 223152
Mem 300
Sec AD Watkins
Pro None
Holes 9 L 5304 yds SSS 66
Recs Am–64 S Erasmus
Pro–64 F Hill
V'tors WD–I SOC WE/BH–M
Fees £14
Loc ¼ mile N of Blackwood

Caerleon (1974)

Public
Broadway, Caerleon NP6 1AY
Tel   **(01633) 420342**
Mem   150
Sec   P John
Pro   A Campbell
Holes   9 L 3092 yds SSS
          Pro–66 A Campbell
V'tors U
Fees   18 holes–£5; 9 holes–£3.30
Loc   M4 Junction 25, 3 miles
Mis   Driving range
Arch   Donald Steel

Celtic Manor Hotel G&CC (1995)

Coldra Woods, Newport NP6 1JQ
Tel   **(01633) 413000**
Fax   (01633) 410284
Mem   200
Sec   M Lovett
Pro   K Williams (01633) 410268
Holes   18 L 7001 yds Par 70 SSS 74
          18 L 4094 yds Par 61 SSS 60
V'tors H SOC
Fees   On application
Loc   E of Newport on A48. M4
          Junction 24
Mis   Golf Academy. Driving range
Arch   Robert Trent Jones Sr

Dewstow (1988)

Caerwent, Newport NP6 4AH
Tel   **(01291) 430444**
Fax   (01291) 425816
Mem   650
Sec   E Tose
Pro   M Kedward
Holes   Valley 18 L 6123 yds Par 72
          SSS 70; Park 18 L 6147 yds
          SSS 69
Recs   Valley Am–73 P Collins (1994)
V'tors WD–U WE–by arrangement
          SOC
Fees   £11 (£15)
Loc   Caerwent, 5 miles W of
          Severn Bridge, off A48
Mis   Driving range

Greenmeadow (1980)

*Treherbert Road, Croesyceiliog,
Cwmbran NP44 2BZ*
Tel   **(01633) 369321**
Mem   430
Sec   PJ Richardson
Pro   C Coombs (01633) 362626
Holes   15 L 5593 yds SSS 68
Recs   Am–66 M Challinger (1989)
          Pro–66 C Jenkins (1987)
V'tors U SOC
Fees   On application
Loc   4 miles N of Newport on
          B4042. M4 Junction 26

Llanwern (1928)

*Tennyson Avenue, Llanwern, Newport
NP6 2DY*
Tel   **(01633) 412380**
Fax   (01633) 412029
Mem   776

Sec   DJ Peak (01633) 412029
Pro   S Price (01633) 413233
Holes   18 L 6115 yds SSS 69
Recs   Am–63 B Dredge (1994)
          Pro–64 S Dodd (1992)
V'tors WD–U WE–restricted I H
          SOC
Fees   WD–£20
Loc   1 mile S of M4 Junction 24

Monmouth (1896)

Leasebrook Lane, Monmouth
Tel   **(01600) 712212**
Mem   600
Sec   Mrs E Edwards
Pro   None
Holes   18 L 5698 yds SSS 69
Recs   Am–68 R Williams (1995)
          Ladies–70 D Hill (1995)
V'tors U SOC exc BH
Fees   £15 (£20)
Loc   Signposted 1 mile along A40
          Monmouth-Ross road

Monmouthshire (1892)

Llanfoist, Abergavenny NP7 9HE
Tel   **(01873) 852606**
Fax   (01873) 852606
Mem   555 107(L) 61(J)
Sec   R Bradley
Pro   (01873) 852532
Holes   18 L 5978 yds SSS 70
Recs   Am–64 B Dredge (1990)
          Pro–62 D Thomas (1962)
V'tors U H SOC
Fees   £25 (£30)
Loc   2 miles SW of Abergavenny
Arch   James Braid

The Newport (1903)

*Great Oak, Rogerstone, Newport
NP1 9FX*
Tel   **(01633) 892643/894496**
Fax   (01633) 896676
Mem   800
Sec   JV Dinsdale
          (01633) 892643
Pro   PM Mayo
          (01633) 893271
Holes   18 L 6431 yds SSS 71
Recs   Am–64 C Mayo (1993)
          Pro–62 L Bond (1994)
V'tors WD–U H exc WE–MH
Fees   £30 (£40)
Loc   3 miles W of Newport on
          B4591. M4 Junction 27,
          1 mile

Oakdale (1990)

Pay and play
Llwynon Lane, Oakdale NP2 0NF
Tel   **(01495) 220044**
Sec   M Lewis (Dir)
Pro   C Coombs
Holes   9 L 1235 yds Par 28
V'tors U SOC
Fees   On application
Loc   15 miles NW of Newport via
          A467/B4251. M4 Junction 28
Mis   Driving range
Arch   Ian Goodenough

Parc (1990)

Pay and play
*Church Lane, Coedkernew, Newport
NP1 9TU*
Tel   **(01633) 680933**
Fax   (01633) 681011
Mem   450
Sec   C Hicks (Mgr), M Cleary (Sec)
Pro   J Skuse (01633) 680955
Holes   18 L 5512 yds SSS 67
Recs   Am–68 A Skidmore
V'tors U SOC
Fees   £11 (£13)
Loc   2 miles W of Newport on A48.
          M4 Junction 28
Mis   Floodlit driving range
Arch   B Thomas

Pontnewydd (1875)

West Pontnewydd, Cwmbran NP44 1AB
Tel   **(01633) 482170**
Mem   250
Sec   HR Gabe (01633) 867185
Holes   10 L 5353 yds SSS 67
Recs   Am–62 M Hayward
V'tors WD–U WE–M SOC
Fees   £16
Loc   W outskirts of Cwmbran

Pontypool (1903)

*Lasgarn Lane, Trevethin, Pontypool
NP4 8TR*
Tel   **(01495) 763655**
Mem   607 68(L) 34(J)
Sec   PM Jones
Pro   J Howard (01495) 755544
Holes   18 L 5963 yds SSS 69
Recs   Am–64 M Hayward (1982)
          NR Davies (1985)
          Pro–64 A Sherborne,
          M Plummer (1995)
V'tors U H SOC
Fees   £20 (£24)
Loc   1 mile N of Pontypool (A4042)

The Rolls of Monmouth (1982)

The Hendre, Monmouth NP5 4HG
Tel   **(01600) 715353**
Fax   (01600) 713115
Mem   200
Sec   Mrs SJ Orton
Pro   None
Holes   18 L 6733 yds SSS 73
Recs   Am–71 D Wills
          Pro–68 M Thomas (1983)
V'tors U SOC
Fees   £32 (£37)
Loc   3½ miles W of Monmouth
          on B4233

St Pierre (1962)

St Pierre Park, Chepstow NP6 6YA
Tel   **(01291) 625261**
Fax   (01291) 629975
Mem   840
Sec   TJ Cleary
Pro   Shop (01291) 635205
Holes   18 L 6785 yds SSS 73
          18 L 5732 yds SSS 68

Recs	Old Am–69 N Van Hootegem
	Pro–64 JM Olazabal
	New Am–63 M Bearcroft
V'tors	H SOC–WD
Fees	On application
Loc	2 miles W of Chepstow (A48)
Mis	Driving range
Arch	CK Cotton

Shirenewton (1995)

Shirenewton, Chepstow NP6 6RL

Tel	**(01291) 641642**
Fax	(01291) 641831
Sec	G Morris
Holes	18 L 6820 yds Par 72 SSS 72
V'tors	U SOC
Fees	£16 (£20)
Loc	5 miles W of Chepstow, off B4235. M4 Junction 22

Tredegar & Rhymney (1921)

Tredegar, Rhymney

Tel	**(01685) 840743/843400**
Fax	(01685) 843440
Mem	204
Sec	P Kenealy
Holes	9 L 5564 yds SSS 67
Recs	Am–69 J Davies
V'tors	U
Fees	£10 (£12.50)
Loc	1½ miles W of Tredegar

Tredegar Park (1923)

Bassaleg Road, Newport NP9 3PX

Tel	**(01633) 895219**
Fax	(01633) 897152
Mem	800
Sec	RT Howell (01633) 894433
Pro	ML Morgan (01633) 894517
Holes	18 L 6097 yds SSS 70
Recs	Am–67 A Wesson
V'tors	H
Fees	D–£25 (D–£30)
Loc	W of Newport, off M4 Junction 27

Wernddu Golf Centre

Old Ross Road, Abergavenny NP7 8NG

Tel	**(01873) 856223**
Fax	(01873) 852177
Mem	520
Sec	DG Watkins
Pro	AA Ashmead
Holes	18 L 5500 yds Par 68 SSS 67
Recs	Am–64 I Chivers (1997)
V'tors	U
Fees	9 holes–£10; 18 holes–£15
Loc	1½ miles NE of Abergavenny on B4521
Mis	Floodlit driving range

West Monmouthshire (1906)

Golf Road, Pond Road, Nantyglo NP3 4QT

Tel	**(01495) 310233/311361**
Fax	(01495) 311361
Mem	600

Sec	SE Williams (01495) 310233
Holes	18 L 6118 yds SSS 69
Recs	Am–66 D Phillips (1994)
V'tors	WD/Sat–U Sun–M SOC–WD
Fees	£18
Loc	Nr Dunlop Semtex, off Brynmawr Bypass, towards Winchestown
Arch	Ben Sayers

Woodlake Park (1993)

Glascoed, Usk NP4 0TE

Tel	**(01291) 673933**
Fax	(01291) 672764
Mem	450
Sec	MJ Wood
Pro	A Pritchard (01291) 671043
Holes	18 L 6300 yds Par 71 SSS 72
Recs	Am–67 R Price (1997)
	Pro–67 M Wootton (1994)
	Ladies–73 C Cole (1997)
V'tors	H SOC
Fees	Summer–£20 (£20)
	Winter–£15 (£20)
Loc	3 miles W of Usk, nr Llandegfedd reservoir

Pembrokeshire

Haverfordwest (1904)

Arnolds Down, Haverfordwest SA61 2XQ

Tel	**(01437) 763565**
Fax	(01437) 764143
Mem	800
Sec	MA Harding (01437) 764523
Pro	A Pile (01437) 768409
Holes	18 L 6005 yds SSS 69
Recs	Am–63 R Scott (1997)
	Pro–64 AJ Pile (1995)
	Ladies–72 F Jones (1994)
V'tors	U SOC
Fees	£18 (£22)
Loc	1 mile E of Haverfordwest on A40

Milford Haven (1913)

Hubberston, Milford Haven SA72 3RX

Tel	**(01646) 692368**
Fax	(01646) 697762
Mem	380 65(L) 90(J)
Sec	WS Brown
Pro	(01646) 697762
Holes	18 L 6071 yds SSS 71
Recs	Am–66 L Rees
	Pro–68 J Taylor
V'tors	U SOC
Fees	£15 (£20)
Loc	W boundary of Milford Haven

Newport (Pembs) (1925)

Newport SA42 0NR

Tel	**(01239) 820244**
Fax	(01239) 820244
Mem	350
Sec	R Dietrich
Pro	C Parsons (01239) 615359
Holes	9 L 3089 yds SSS 68
Recs	Am–67 A Evans

V'tors	U SOC
Fees	£15
Loc	2½ miles NW of Newport, towards Newport Beach
Arch	James Braid

Priskilly Forest (1992)

Castle Morris, Haverfordwest SA62 5EH

Tel	**(01348) 840276**
Sec	P Evans
Holes	9 L 5712 yds Par 70 SSS 68
V'tors	U SOC
Fees	9 holes–£7; 18 holes–£10
Loc	2 miles off A40 at Letterston
Arch	J Walters

St Davids City (1902)

Whitesands Bay, St Davids

Tel	**(01437) 721751 (Clubhouse)**
Mem	200
Sec	CWJ Snushall
	(01437) 720312
Holes	9 L 6121 yds SSS 70
Recs	Am–67 KB Walsh (1989)
V'tors	U SOC
Fees	D–£14
Loc	2 miles W of St Davids. 15 miles NW of Haverfordwest

South Pembrokeshire (1970)

Military Road, Pembroke Dock SA72 6SE

Tel	**(01646) 621453**
Mem	350
Sec	WD Owen (01646) 621453/ 621804
Pro	None
Holes	18 L 5638 yds SSS 69
Recs	Am–65 A Jones
V'tors	U before 4.30pm SOC
Fees	On application
Loc	Pembroke Dock

Tenby (1888)

The Burrows, Tenby SA70 7NP

Tel	**(01834) 842787/842978**
Mem	800
Sec	JA Pearson (01834) 842978
Pro	M Hawkey (01834) 844447
Holes	18 L 6450 yds SSS 71
Recs	Am–65 M Peet
V'tors	H SOC
Fees	£20 (£24)
Loc	Tenby, South Beach
Arch	James Braid

Trefloyne (1996)

Trefloyne Park, Penally, Tenby SA70 7RG

Tel	**(01834) 842165**
Mem	149
Pro	S Laidler
Holes	18 L 6635 yds Par 71
V'tors	U SOC
Fees	£17.50 (£21.50)
Loc	1½ miles W of Tenby, off A4139 Pembroke road
Arch	FH Gilman

Powys

Brecon (1902)
Newton Park, Llanfaes, Brecon LD3 8PA

Tel	**(01874) 622004**
Mem	210
Sec	DHE Roderick (01874) 625547
Holes	9 L 5256 yds SSS 66
Recs	Am–61 R Dixon Pro–66 WO Moses
V'tors	U SOC
Fees	£10
Loc	1/2 mile W of Brecon on A40
Arch	James Braid

Builth Wells (1923)
Golf Club Road, Builth Wells LD2 3NF

Tel	**(01982) 553296**
Fax	(01982) 551064
Mem	425
Sec	JN Jones
Pro	R Truman
Holes	18 L 5376 yds SSS 67
Recs	Am–65
V'tors	U H SOC
Fees	£13 D–£17 (£19 D–£23)
Loc	W of Builth Wells on Llandovery road (A483)

Cradoc (1967)
Penoyre Park, Cradoc, Brecon LD3 9LP

Tel	**(01874) 623658**
Fax	(01874) 611711
Mem	750
Sec	GSW Davies
Pro	R Davies (01874) 625524
Holes	18 L 6301 yds SSS 72
Recs	Am–65 DK Wood (1982)
V'tors	U Sun–M SOC
Fees	£20 (£25)
Loc	2 miles NW of Brecon, off B4520
Arch	CK Cotton

Knighton (1913)
Little Ffrydd Wood, Knighton LD7 1EF

Tel	**(01547) 528646**
Mem	150
Sec	AW Aspley (Hon)
Holes	9 L 5320 yds Par 68 SSS 66
Recs	Am–66 M Caine, A Williams Pro–71 H Vardon
V'tors	U SOC
Fees	£8 (£10)
Loc	SW of Knighton. 20 miles NE of Llandrindod Wells
Arch	H Vardon

Llandrindod (1905)
Llandrindod Wells LD1 5NY

Tel	**(01597) 823873/822010**
Fax	(01597) 823873
Mem	420
Sec	GR Harris
Pro	None
Holes	18 L 5759 yds SSS 69

Recs	Am–65 CJ Davies (1988)
V'tors	U SOC
Fees	£12 (£20)
Loc	1 mile E of Llandrindod Wells
Arch	Harry Vardon

Machynlleth (1905)
Ffordd Drenewydd, Machynlleth SY20 8UH

Tel	**(01654) 702000**
Mem	231
Holes	9 L 5726 yds SSS 67
Recs	Am–65 Pro–65
V'tors	U Sun–NA before 11.30am SOC
Fees	£12 (£15)
Loc	1 mile E of Machynlleth, off A489

Rhosgoch (1991)
Rhosgoch, Builth Wells LD2 3JY

Tel	**(01497) 851251**
Mem	150
Sec	R Meredith
Holes	9 L 4842 yds SSS 64
V'tors	U SOC
Fees	£7 (£10)
Loc	5 miles N of Hay-on-Wye

St Giles Newtown (1895)
Pool Road, Newtown SY16 3AJ

Tel	**(01686) 625844**
Mem	350
Pro	DP Owen
Holes	9 L 6006 yds SSS 69
Recs	Am–67 F Costanzo Pro–64 AP Parkin
V'tors	U SOC
Fees	£12.50 (£15)
Loc	1 mile E of Newtown (A483). 14 miles SW of Welshpool

St Idloes (1920)
Penrhallt, Llanidloes SY18 6LG

Tel	**(01686) 412559**
Fax	(01926) 889536
Mem	292
Sec	JC Green
Pro	P Parkin
Holes	9 L 5510 yds SSS 66
Recs	Am–63 J Davies
V'tors	U H Sun–restricted SOC
Fees	£10 (£12) W–£45
Loc	1/2 mile from Llanidloes on Trefeglwys road (B4569)

Welsh Border Golf Complex (1991)
Bulthy Farm, Bulthy, Middletown SY21 8ER

Tel	**(01743) 884247**
Fax	(01939) 290502
Mem	200
Sec	P Nicholson
Pro	A Griffiths
Holes	9 L 3050 yds SSS 72 9 hole Par 3 course
V'tors	U SOC
Fees	£14

Loc	Between Shrewsbury and Welshpool on A458
Mis	Driving range
Arch	A Griffiths

Welshpool (1929)
Golfa Hill, Welshpool SY21 9AQ

Tel	**(01938) 83249**
Mem	500
Sec	DB Pritchard (01938) 552215
Pro	None
Holes	18 L 5708 yds SSS 69
Recs	Am–65 DH Ryan Pro–69 S Bowen
V'tors	U H
Fees	£10 (£20)
Loc	41/2 miles W of Welshpool, on Dolgellau road (A458)
Arch	James Braid

South Glamorgan

Brynhill (1921)
Port Road, Barry CF62 8PN

Tel	**(01446) 735061**
Mem	700
Sec	P Gershenson (01446) 720277
Pro	P Fountain (01446) 733660
Holes	18 L 5947 yds SSS 70
Recs	Am–65 C O'Carroll, N Caulfield Ladies–62 A Phillips (1990)
V'tors	WD/Sat–H Sun–NA SOC–WD
Fees	£20 Sat–£25 SOC–£17
Loc	A4050, 8 miles SW of Cardiff

Cardiff (1921)
Sherborne Avenue, Cyncoed, Cardiff CF2 6SJ

Tel	**(01222) 753067**
Fax	(01222) 752134
Mem	930
Sec	K Lloyd (01222) 753320
Pro	T Hanson (01222) 754772
Holes	18 L 6015 yds SSS 70
Recs	Am–65 SP Jones
V'tors	WD–H WE–M SOC–Thurs
Fees	£30 (£35)
Loc	3 miles N of Cardiff. 2 miles W of Pentwyn exit of A48(M). M4 Junction 29

Cottrell Park (1996)
St Nicholas, Cardiff CF5 6JY

Tel	**(01446) 781781**
Fax	(01446) 781707
Mem	900
Sec	D Marchant
Pro	M Pycroft
Holes	18 L 6606 yds Par 72 SSS 72 9 L 2807 yds Par 70 SSS 67
Recs	Am–71 S Pitt (1997) Pro–67 P Mayo (1997)
V'tors	U SOC–Mon & Tues
Fees	18 holes–£19 (£25) 9 holes–£9.50 (£12.50)

Loc 4 miles W of Cardiff on A48.
M4 Junction 33
Mis Driving range
Arch Bob Sandow

Dinas Powis (1914)

Old Highwalls, Dinas Powis CF6 4AJ
Tel (01222) 512727
Fax (01222) 512727
Mem 650
Sec JF Fraser
Pro G Bennett (01222) 513682
Holes 18 L 5486 yds SSS 67
Recs Am–65 P Davidson
Pro–67 P Fountain
V'tors H SOC
Fees D–£22 (D–£27)
Loc 3 miles SW of Cardiff
(A4055)

Glamorganshire (1890)

Lavernock Road, Penarth CF64 5UP
Tel (01222) 701185
Fax (01222) 701185
Mem 700
Sec AM Reed-Gibbs
(01222) 701185
Pro A Kerr-Smith
(01222) 707401
Holes 18 L 6181 yds SSS 70
Recs Am–65 MG Mouland (1979),
N Grimmitt (1989),
B Rigby (1997)
Pro–65 A Jacklin (1969)
V'tors WD/WE–H SOC
Fees £28 (£30)
Loc 5 miles SW of Cardiff

Llanishen (1905)

Cwm, Lisvane, Cardiff CF4 5UD
Tel (01222) 752205
Fax (01222) 755078
Mem 700
Sec PH Plumb (Sec/Mgr)
(01222) 755078
Pro RA Jones
(01222) 755076
Holes 18 L 5296 yds SSS 66
Recs Am–63 B Townley (1994)
Pro–63 JT Taylor
V'tors WD–U WE–M H SOC–Thurs
& Fri
Fees £24
Loc 5 miles N of Cardiff

Peterstone

*Peterstone, Wentloog, Cardiff
CF3 8TN*
Tel (01633) 680009
Fax (01633) 680563
Mem 700
Sec R Williams
Pro R Harries
Holes 18 L 6555 yds Par 72
SSS 72
Recs Am–67 S Vickery (1996)
V'tors U SOC–WD
Fees £15 (£19.50)
Loc 3 miles S of Castleton, off
A48. M4 Junction 28
Arch Robert Sandow

Radyr (1902)

Drysgol Road, Radyr, Cardiff CF4 8BS
Tel (01222) 842408
Fax (01222) 843914
Mem 880
Sec AM Edwards (Mgr)
Pro R Butterworth (01222) 842476
Holes 18 L 6031 yds SSS 70
Recs Am–62 C Evans
Pro–63 PW Evans, JD Grundy
V'tors WD–H WE–M
SOC–Wed/Thurs/Fri
Fees D–£32
Loc 5 miles NW of Cardiff,
off A4119

RAF St Athan (1977)

St Athan, Barry CF62 4WA
Tel (01446) 751043
Mem 450
Sec PF Woodhouse
(01446) 797186
Pro N Gillette (01446) 751043
Holes 9 L 6452 yds SSS 72
V'tors U exc Sun am–NA
Fees £10 (£15)
Loc 2 miles E of Llantwit Major.
10 miles S of Bridgend

St Andrews Major (1993)

*Coldbrook Road, Cadoxton, Barry
CF6 3BB*
Tel (01446) 722227
Holes 9 L 2931 yds
V'tors U
Fees On application
Loc Barry Docks Link road. M4
Junction 33
Arch MRM Leisure

St Mary's Hotel G&CC
(1990)

Pay and play
St Mary's Hill, Pencoed CF35 5EA
Tel (01656) 860280/861100
Fax (01656) 863400
Mem 750
Sec Kay Brazell (01656) 861100
Pro J Peters (01656) 861599
Holes 18 L 5273 yds Par 69 SSS 68
9 L 2426 yds Par 35 SSS 34
Recs Am–63 L Janes (1996)
Pro–64 R Troake
V'tors H SOC–WD
Fees 18 hole: £14 (£16)
9 hole: £4 (£5)
Loc Off M4 Junction 35
Mis Floodlit driving range

St Mellons (1937)

St Mellons, Cardiff CF3 8XS
Tel (01633) 680401
Fax (01633) 681219
Mem 500 93(L) 70(J)
Sec Mrs K Newling
(01633) 680408
Pro B Thomas (01633) 680101
Holes 18 L 6225 yds SSS 70
Recs Am–67 S Hopkins
Pro–66 E Foster

V'tors WD–U WE–M
Fees £26
Loc 4 miles E of Cardiff on A48

Vale of Glamorgan G&CC

Hensol Park, Hensol CF7 8JY
Tel (01443) 222221
Fax (01443) 222220
Mem 900
Sec Mrs G Golding
Pro P Johnson
Holes Lake 18 L 6507 yds Par 72
Hensol 9 L 3115 yds Par 36
Pro–67 G Ryall
V'tors H SOC
Fees £25 (£30)
Loc 1 mile from M 4 Junction 34
Mis Driving range. Golf
Academy
Arch Peter Johnson

Wenvoe Castle (1936)

Wenvoe, Cardiff CF5 6BE
Tel (01222) 591094
Fax (01222) 594371
Mem 540 100(L) 66(J)
Sec N Sims (01222) 594371
Pro R Day (01222) 593649
Holes 18 L 6422 yds SSS 71
Recs Am–68 N Jones (1989)
Pro–66 PW Evans (1990)
V'tors WD–H WE/BH–M SOC–WD
Fees £24
Loc 4 miles W of Cardiff, off A4050

Whitchurch (1915)

*Pantmawr Road, Whitchurch, Cardiff
CF4 6XD*
Tel (01222) 620125
Fax (01222) 529860
Mem 780
Sec JW King (01222) 620985
Pro E Clark (01222) 614660
Holes 18 L 6321 yds Par 71
SSS 71
Recs Am–63 B Dredge (1992)
Pro–62 I Woosnam (1986)
V'tors WD–U WE/BH–M H
SOC–Thurs
Fees £30 (£35)
Loc 3 miles NW of Cardiff on
A470. M4 Junction 32

West Glamorgan

Allt-y-Graban (1993)

*Allt-y-Graban Road, Pontlliw, Swansea
SA4 1DT*
Tel (01792) 885757
Mem 154
Sec Mrs M Lewis (Mgr)
Pro S Rees
Holes 9 L 2210 yds Par 66 SSS 63
V'tors U SOC
Fees 18 holes–£9 (£9)
9 holes–£6 (£6)
Loc 3 miles of M4 Junction 47,
on A48
Arch FG Thomas

Clyne (1920)

120 Owls Lodge Lane, Mayals,
Swansea SA3 5DP

Tel	**(01792) 401989**
Fax	(01792) 401078
Mem	850
Sec	KC Crawford
Pro	M Bevan (01792) 402094
Holes	18 L 6334 yds SSS 71
Recs	Am–66 C Dickens(1982)
	Pro–64 M Bevan (1990)
V'tors	WD–U before 2.30pm WE–U
	H SOC
Fees	£24 (£30)
Loc	3 miles SW of Swansea
Mis	Driving range
Arch	Colt/Harris

Earlswood (1993)

Public

Jersey Marine, Neath SA10 6JP

Tel	**(01792) 321578**
Sec	Mrs D Goatcher
	(01792) 812198
Pro	M Day
Holes	18 L 5174 yds SSS 68
V'tors	U SOC
Fees	£8
Loc	5 miles E of Swansea (B4290)

Fairwood Park (1969)

Blackhills Lane, Upper Killay, Swansea
SA2 7JN

Tel	**(01792) 203648**
Fax	(01792) 297849
Mem	650
Sec	J Beer, J Pettifer (Mgr)
Pro	G Hughes (01792) 299194
Holes	18 L 6741 yds SSS 72
Recs	Am–69 R Maliphant,
	I Roberts (1989)
	Pro–67 J Lomas (1989),
	A Griffiths,
	M Wooton (1990)
V'tors	U SOC
Fees	£25 (£30)
Loc	4 miles W of Swansea
	(A4118)
Arch	Hawtree

Glynneath (1931)

Penycraig, Pontneathvaughan,
Glynneath SA11 5UH

Tel	**(01639) 720452**
Mem	640
Sec	RM Ellis (01639) 720679
Holes	18 L 5707 yds SSS 68
Recs	Am–66 JL Davies
	Pro–66 P Mayo
V'tors	WD–U H WE–M SOC–WD
Fees	£15 (£18)
Loc	2 miles NW of Glynneath on
	B4242. 15 miles NE of
	Swansea
Arch	Cotton/Pennink/Lawrie

Inco (1965)

Clydach, Swansea

Tel	**(01792) 844216**
Mem	260

Sec	DGS Murdoch
	(01792) 843336
Holes	18 L 6064 yds SSS 69
V'tors	U
Fees	On application
Loc	N of Swansea (A4067)

Lakeside (1992)

Pay and play

Water Street, Margam, Port Talbot
SA13 2PA

Tel	**(01639) 899959**
Mem	250
Sec	G Hanbury
Pro	M Wootton
Holes	18 L 4390 yds Par 62 SSS 63
Recs	Am–65 R Clarke (1997)
	Pro–61 M Wootton (1997)
V'tors	U SOC
Fees	£9 (£9)
Loc	Nr M4 Junction 38
Mis	Driving range
Arch	M Wootton

Langland Bay (1904)

Langland, Swansea SA3 4QR

Tel	**(01792) 366023**
Fax	(01792) 361082
Mem	700
Sec	PLE Wilkins
	(01792) 361721
Pro	M Evans (01792) 366186
Holes	18 L 5830 yds SSS 69
Recs	Am–63 K Jones,
	S Dodd (1989)
	Pro–66 J Lee
V'tors	U SOC
Fees	£25 (£28)
Loc	6 miles S of Swansea
	(A4067)

Morriston (1919)

160 Clasemont Road, Morriston,
Swansea SA6 6AJ

Tel	**(01792) 771079**
Fax	(01792) 796528
Mem	425
Sec	WA Jefford (Sec/Mgr),
	R Kelly (01792) 796528
Pro	DA Rees (01792) 772335
Holes	18 L 5785 yds SSS 68
Recs	Am–61 M Gorvett (1994)
	Pro–64 DA Rees
V'tors	U H SOC–WD
Fees	£21 (£30)
Loc	4 miles N of Swansea on A48.
	M4 Junction 46, 1 mile

Neath (1934)

Cadoxton, Neath SA10 8AH

Tel	**(01639) 643615**
Mem	520
Sec	DM Hughes
	(01639) 632759
Pro	EM Bennett
	(01639) 633693
Holes	18 L 6500 yds SSS 72
Recs	Am–66 AL Cooper (1993)
	Pro–66 F Hill
V'tors	WD–U WE–M SOC

Fees	£20
Loc	2 miles NE of Neath (B4434)
Arch	James Braid

Palleg (1930)

Palleg Road, Lower Cwmtwrch,
Swansea Valley SA9 1QT

Tel	**(01639) 842193**
Mem	200
Sec	DW Moses
Holes	9 L 3209 yds SSS 72
Recs	Am–71 C Williams,
	N Turner (1990)
V'tors	WD–U WE–NA
Fees	On application
Loc	Ystalyfera 1 mile. 15 miles NE
	of Swansea (A4067)

Pennard (1896)

2 Southgate Road, Southgate, Swansea
SA3 2BT

Tel	**(01792) 233131**
Fax	(01792) 234797
Mem	775
Sec	EM Howell (01792) 233131/
	873335
Pro	MV Bennett
	(01792) 233451
Holes	18 L 6265 yds SSS 72
Recs	Am–68 D Evans
	Pro–68 A Beal (1995)
V'tors	U H SOC–WD only
Fees	£24 (£30) W–£80
Loc	8 miles W of Swansea, by
	A4067 and B4436

Pontardawe (1924)

Cefn Llan, Pontardawe, Swansea
SA8 4SH

Tel	**(01792) 863118**
Fax	(01792) 830041
Mem	610
Sec	CR Hopkin (Hon),
	Mrs M Griffiths (Admin)
Pro	G Hopkins
	(01792) 830977
Holes	18 L 6038 yds SSS 70
Recs	Am–64 B Fisher (1993)
	Pro–71 D Thomas,
	R Brook
V'tors	H SOC–WD
Fees	£20
Loc	5 miles N of M4 Junction 45,
	off A4067

Swansea Bay (1892)

Jersey Marine, Neath SA10 6JP

Tel	**(01792) 812198**
Mem	400
Sec	Mrs D Goatcher
	(01792) 814153
Pro	M Day (01792) 816159
Holes	18 L 6605 yds SSS 72
Recs	Am–71 C Smith
V'tors	U SOC
Fees	£16 (£22)
Loc	5 miles E of Swansea,
	off A483

Clubs and Courses in Continental Europe

Austria

Innsbruck & Tirol

Achensee (1934)
6213 Pertisau/Achensee
Tel   (05243) 5377
Fax   (05243) 6202
Holes 18 L 5501 m SSS 70
V'tors U H
Fees   450s (520s)
Loc   Pertisau, 50 km NE of
       Innsbruck

Innsbruck-Igls (1956)
6074 Rinn, Oberdorf 11
Tel   (05223) 8177
Fax   (05223) 8343
Holes Rinn 18 L 5935 m SSS 71
       Lans 9 L 4657 m SSS 66
V'tors H-booking necessary
Fees   460s (580s)
Loc   Rinn, 10 km E of Innsbruck.
       Lans, 8 km from Innsbruck

Kaiserwinkl GC Kössen
(1988)
6345 Kössen, Mühlau 1
Tel   (05375) 2122
Fax   (05375) 2122-13
Holes 18 L 5927 m SSS 72
V'tors H
Fees   550s (600s)
Loc   30 km N of Kitzbühel,
       nr German border
Arch   Donald Harradine

Kitzbühel (1955)
Schloss Kaps, 6370 Kitzbühel/Tirol
Tel   (05356) 3007
Fax   (05356) 73018
Holes 9 L 6085 m SSS 72
V'tors H
Fees   450s (550s)
Loc   Kitzbühel
Arch   J Morrison

Kitzbühel-Schwarzsee
(1988)
6370 Kitzbühel, Golfweg
Schwarzsee 35
Tel   (05356) 71645
Fax   (05356) 72785
Holes 18 L 6247 m SSS 72
V'tors H-booking necessary
Fees   650-750s
Loc   4 km from Kitzbühel
Arch   G Hauser

Seefeld-Wildmoos
(1968)
6100 Seefeld, Postfach 22
Tel   (05212) 3003-0
Fax   (05212) 3722-22
Holes 18 L 5967 m SSS 72
V'tors H-booking necessary
Fees   490-730s
Loc   7 km W of Seefeld. 24 km W
       of Innsbruck
Arch   Donald Harradine

Klagenfurt & South

Austria-Wörther See
9062 Moosburg, Golfstr 2
Tel   (04272) 83486, (04272)
       82302 (Golf academy)
Fax   (04272) 82055
Holes 18 L 6216 m SSS 72
Fees   550s
Loc   6 km N of Wörther See
Arch   G Hauser

Bad Kleinkirchheim-Reichenau (1984)
9546 Bad Kleinkirchheim, Postfach 9
Tel   (04275) 594
Fax   (04240) 8282-18
Holes 18 L 6084 m SSS 72
V'tors H
Fees   550s
Loc   Kleinkirchheim, 50 km NW
       of Klagenfurt, via Route 95
Arch   Donald Harradine

Kärntner (1927)
9082 Maria Wörth, Dellach 16
Tel   (04273) 2515
Fax   (04273) 2606
Holes 18 L 5744 m SSS 71
V'tors H
Fees   D-600s
Loc   Dellach, S side of Wörther
       See. 15 km W of Klagenfurt

Klopeiner See-Turnersee
(1988)
9122 St Kanzian, Grabelsdorf 94
Tel   (04239) 3800
Fax   (04239) 3800-18
Holes 18 L 6114 m SSS 72
V'tors U
Fees   600s
Loc   25 km E of Klagenfurt
Arch   Donald Harradine

Wörther See/Velden
(1988)
9231 Köstenberg, Oberdorf 70
Tel   (04274) 7045/7087
Fax   (04274) 708715
Pro   M Burrows, B Knutson,
       H Wiegele
Holes 18 L 6152 m SSS 72
V'tors H
Fees   600s
Loc   30 km W of Klagenfurt.
       12 km from Velden
Arch   Erhardt/Rossknecht

Linz & North

Amstetten-Ferschnitz
(1972)
3325 Ferschnitz, Gut Edla 18
Holes 9 L 5948 m SSS 70
V'tors U H
Fees   350s (450s)
Loc   70 km E of Linz
Arch   McIntosh

Böhmerwald GC
Ulrichsberg (1990)
4161 Ulrichsberg, Seitelschlag 50
Tel   (07288) 8200
Fax   (07288) 8422
Holes 18 L 6240 m SSS 73
       9 hole Par 3 course
V'tors U H
Fees   450s (550s)
Loc   65 km NW of Linz
Arch   Rossknecht/Erhardt

Herzog Tassilo (1991)
Blankenbergerstr 30, 4540 Bad Hall
Tel   (07258) 5480
Fax   (07258) 5480
Holes 18 L 5710 m SSS 70
V'tors U
Fees   450s (550s)
Loc   30 km SW of Linz
Arch   Peter Mayerhofer

Kremstal (1989)
Schachen 20, 4531 Kematen/Krems
Tel   (07228) 29230
Fax   (07228) 2927
Holes 18 L 5692 m Par 70
V'tors H
Fees   300s (400s)
Loc   20 km W of Linz
Arch   Peter Mayerhofer

Linz-St Florian (1960)
4490 St Florian, Tillysburg 28
Tel   (07223) 828730
Fax   (07223) 828737
Holes 18 L 6091 m Par 72 SSS 72
V'tors H
Fees   600s (780s)
Loc   St Florian, 15 km SE of Linz
Arch   Donald Harradine

Maria Theresia (1989)
Letten 5, 4680 Haag am Hausruck
Tel   (07732) 3944
Fax   (07732) 3944-9
Holes 18 L 6055 m Par 72 SSS 72
V'tors H
Fees   450s (550s)
Loc   Between Passau and Wels.
       A8 exit Haag
Arch   Angst/Stärk

Mühlviertel (1990)
4222 St Georgen, Am Luftenberg 1
Tel   (07237) 3893
Fax   (07237) 3893
Holes 18 L 6041 m SSS 72

V'tors U H
Fees   500s (600s)
Loc   15 km NE of Linz
Arch   Keith Preston

Ottenstein (1988)

3532 Niedergrünbach 60
Tel   (02826) 7476
Fax   (02826) 7476-4
Holes   18 L 6172 m SSS 72
V'tors U
Fees   450s (550s)
Loc   90 km NE of Linz.
   100 km NW of Vienna
Arch   Preston/Zinterl/Erhardt

St Oswald-Freistadt
(1988)

Promenade 22, 4271 St Oswald
Tel   (07945) 7938
Fax   (07945) 79384
Holes   9 L 5888 m Par 72
V'tors WD–UH WE–U H restricted
Fees   350s (450s)
Loc   40 km N of Linz
Arch   Mel Flannaghan

St Pölten Schloss Goldegg (1989)

3100 St Pölten Schloss Goldegg
Tel   (02741) 7360/7060
Fax   (02741) 73608
Holes   18 L 6249 m SSS 73
V'tors H or I
Fees   400s (500s)
Loc   8 km NW of St Pölten.
   60 km W of Vienna

Schloss Ernegg (1973)

3261 Steinakirchen, Schlosshotel Ernegg
Tel   (07488) 6770,
   (07488) 214 (May-Oct)
Fax   (07488) 6771/71171
Holes   18 L 5699 m SSS 70
   9 L 2076 m SSS 62
V'tors U
Fees   450s (550s)
Loc   Steinakirchen, 60 km SE of
   Linz
Arch   Tucker/Day

Traunsee-Kircham

4656 Kircham, Kampesberg 38
Tel   (07619) 2576
Fax   (07619) 2576-11
Holes   18 L 5714 m SSS 70
V'tors U
Fees   450s (550s)
Loc   10 km E of Gmunden.
   50 km SW of Linz

Waldviertel

3874 Haugschlag 160
Tel   (02865) 8441
Fax   (02865) 8441-22
Holes   18 L 6140 m SSS 72
   18 hole Par 3 course
V'tors H

Fees   490s (600s)
Loc   25 km N of Gmund.
   140 km NW of Vienna

Weitra (1989)

3970 Weitra, Hausschachen
Tel   (02856) 2058
Fax   (02856) 20584
Holes   9 L 5726 m Par 70 SSS 70
V'tors WD–U WE–H
Fees   300s (400s)
Loc   75 km NE of Linz, nr Czech
   border
Arch   M Gansdorfer

Wels (1981)

4616 Weisskirchen, Weyerbach 37
Tel   (07243) 56038
Fax   (07243) 56685
Holes   18 L 6100 m SSS 72
V'tors H
Fees   500s (600s)
Loc   5 km from Salzburg-Vienna
   highway. 8 km SE of Wels
Mis   Pitch & putt
Arch   Hauser/Hunt Hastings

Salzburg Region

Bad Gastein (1960)

5640 Bad Gastein, Golfstrasse 6
Tel   (06434) 2775
Fax   (06434) 2775-4
Holes   9 L 5986 m SSS 72
V'tors H
Fees   390s (500s)
Loc   Bad Gastein 2 km. Salzburg
   100 km
Arch   B von Limburger

Goldegg

5622 Goldegg, Postfach 6
Tel   (06415) 8585
Fax   (06415) 8585-4
Holes   18 L 5762 m Par 70
Fees   500s (550s)
Loc   60 km SW of Salzburg

Gut Altentann (1989)

Hof 54, 5302 Henndorf am Wallersee
Tel   (06214) 6026-0
Fax   (06214) 6105-81
Holes   18 L 6223 m SSS 72
V'tors H–booking necessary
Fees   750–850s
Loc   Henndorf, 16 km N of
   Salzburg
Arch   Jack Nicklaus

Gut Brandlhof G&CC
(1983)

5760 Saalfelden am Steinernen Meer, Hohlwegen 3
Tel   (06582) 2176-555
Fax   (06582) 2176-529
Holes   18 L 6218 m SSS 72
   6 hole short course

V'tors I H
Fees   550s (650s)
Loc   Saalfelden, 70 km SW of
   Salzburg towards Zell am See
Arch   Kofler

Kobernausserwald

5242 St Johann a.Walde, Strass 1
Tel   (07743) 2719
Fax   (07743) 2719
Holes   18 L 5963 m Par 71 SSS 71
V'tors U
Fees   200s (350s)
Loc   30 km E of Salzburg
Arch   Heinz Schmidbauer

Lungau/Katschberg
(1991)

5582 St Michael, Postfach 44
Tel   (06477) 7448
Fax   (06477) 7448-4
Holes   18 L 6372 m SSS 72
   9 L 2502 m Par 56
V'tors U
Fees   520s (620s)
Loc   St Michael, 120 km S of
   Salzburg
Arch   Keith Preston

Radstadt Tauerngolf
(1990)

Römerstrasse 18, 5550 Radstadt
Tel   (06452) 51110
Fax   (06452) 7336
Holes   18 L 6124 m SSS 72
   9 hole Par 3 course
V'tors U
Fees   520s (620s)
Loc   70 km NW of Salzburg

St Lorenz Mondsee
(1986)

St Lorenz 400, 5310 Mondsee
Tel   (06232) 3835-0
Fax   (06232) 3835-83
Holes   18 L 6036 m SSS 72
V'tors H
Fees   500s (650s)
Loc   Mondsee, 25 km E of
   Salzburg
Arch   Marc Miller

Salzburg Klesheim
(1955)

5071 Wals bei Salzburg, Schloss Klesheim
Tel   (0662) 850851
Holes   9 L 5700 m SSS 70
V'tors U H
Fees   450s (450s)
Loc   5 km N of Salzburg

Salzkammergut (1933)

4820 Bad Ischl, Postfach 506
Tel   (06132) 26340
Fax   (06132) 26708
Holes   18 L 5900 m SSS 71
V'tors U

Fees 500 (600s)
Loc   6 km W of Bad Ischl,
          nr Strobl. 50 km E of Salzburg

Schloss Fuschl (1964)

5322 Hof/Salzburg
Tel   **(06229) 390**
Holes 9 L 3694 m SSS 61
Fees   250–300s
Loc   Hof, 12 km E of Salzburg

Urslautal (1991)

Schinking 1, 5760 Saalfelden
Tel   **(06584) 2000**
Fax   (06584) 7475-10
Holes 18 L 6030 m SSS 71
V'tors U H
Fees   620s (690s)
Loc   80 km SW of Salzburg
Arch   Keith Preston

Zell am See-Kaprun

(1983)
5700 Zell am See-Kaprun, Golfstr 25
Tel   **(06542) 56161**
Fax   (06542) 56161-16
Holes 18 L 6218 m Par 72 SSS 72
           18 L 6056 m Par 72 SSS 72
V'tors H
Fees   650s (750s)
Loc   Zell am See, 80 km SW of
           Salzburg
Arch   Donald Harradine

Steiermark

Andritz (1993)

Andritzer Reichsstr 157, 8046 Graz
Tel   **(0316) 676820**
Fax   (0316) 676820-9
Holes 9 L 1211 m SSS 54
V'tors U
Fees   130–180s
Loc   5 km from centre of Graz
Arch   Michael Pinner

Bad Gleichenberg (1984)

Am Hoffeld 3, 8344 Bad Gleichenberg
Tel   **(03159) 3717**
Fax   (03159) 3065
Holes 9 L 5904 m Par 72 SSS 72
V'tors H
Fees   350s (450s)
Loc   60 km NW of Graz
Arch   Hauser

Dachstein Tauern

(1990)
8967 Haus/Ennstal, Oberhaus 59
Tel   **(03686) 2630**
Fax   (03686) 2630-15
Holes 18 L 5910 m SSS 71
V'tors U
Fees   525s (625s)
Loc   2 km from Schladming.
           100 km SE of Salzburg
Arch   Bernhard Langer

Ennstal-Weissenbach

G&LC (1978)

8940 Liezen, Postfach 193
Tel   **(03612) 24821**
Fax   (03612) 24821-4
Holes 18 L 5604 m SSS 70
V'tors U H
Fees   400s (450s)
Loc   3 km SW of Liezen.
           100 km SE of Salzburg
Arch   Gert Aigner

Furstenfeld (1984)

8282 Loipersdorf, Gillersdorf 50
Tel   **(03382) 8533**
Fax   (03382) 8633
Holes 18 L 6192 m SSS 72
V'tors U
Fees   475s (575s)
Loc   50 km E of Graz

Graz (1989)

8051 Graz-Thal, Windhof 137
Tel   **(0316) 572867**
Fax   (0316) 572867-4
Holes 9 L 5229 m SSS 70
V'tors U
Fees   350–500s (550s)
Loc   10 km W of Graz
Arch   Herwig Zisser

Gut Murstätten (1989)

8403 Lebring, Oedt 14
Tel   **(03182) 3555**
Fax   (03182) 3688
Holes 18 L 6398 m SSS 74
           9 L 3034 m SSS 72
V'tors H
Fees   550s (650s)
Loc   25 km S of Graz
Arch   J Dudok van Heel

Maria Lankowitz (1992)

*Puchbacher Str 109, 8591 Maria
Lankowitz*
Tel   **(03144) 6970**
Fax   (03144) 6970-4
Holes 18 L 6121 m SSS 72
V'tors U
Fees   430s (550s)
Loc   40 km W of Graz
Arch   Herwig Zisser

Murhof (1963)

8130 Frohnleiten, Adriach 53
Tel   **(03126) 3010**
Fax   (03126) 3000-29
Holes 18 L 6381 m SSS 73
V'tors U H
Fees   620s (800s)
Loc   Frohnleiten, 25 km N of Graz.
           150 km S of Vienna
Arch   B von Limburger

Reiting G&CC (1990)

8772 Traboch, Schulweg 7
Tel   **(0663) 833308/(03847) 5008**
Fax   (03847) 5682
Holes 9 L 6300 m Par 73 SSS 72

V'tors U
Fees   350s (390s)
Loc   60 km N of Graz

St Lorenzen (1990)

8642 St Lorenzen, Gassing 22
Tel   **(03864) 3961**
Fax   (03864) 3961-2
Holes 9 L 5374 m Par 70 SSS 70
V'tors U
Fees   300s (350s)
Loc   60 km N of Graz, nr
           Kapfenberg
Arch   Manfred Flasch

Schloss Frauenthal (1988)

8530 Deutschlandsberg, Ulrichsberg 7
Tel   **(03462) 5717**
Fax   (03462) 5717-5
Holes 18 L 5447 m SSS 70
V'tors U H
Fees   500s (600s)
Loc   30 km SW of Graz
Arch   Stephan Breisach

Schloss Pichlarn (1972)

8952 Irdning, Ennstal Steiermark
Tel   **(03682) 24393**
Fax   (03682) 24393
Holes 18 L 6158 m SSS 72
V'tors U
Fees   500s (650s)
Loc   2 km E of Irdning, off
           Salzburg–Graz road.
           120 km SE of Salzburg
Arch   Donald Harradine

Vienna & East

Adamstal (1994)

Gaupmannsgraben 21, 3172 Ramsal
Tel   **(02764) 3500**
Fax   (02764) 3500-15
Holes 9 L 4696–5326 m Par 70
           (18 holes from July 1998)
V'tors U
Fees   400s (550s)
Loc   65 km SW of Vienna
Arch   Jeff Howes

Bad Tatzmannsdorf

G&CC (1991)

*Am Golfplatz 2, 7431 Bad
Tatzmannsdorf*
Tel   **(03353) 8282-0**
Fax   (03353) 8282-735
Holes 18 L 6304 m SSS 73
           9 L 3660 m SSS 60
V'tors U H
Fees   18 hole:520s (650s);
           9 hole:350s (400s)
Loc   120 km SE of Vienna
Arch   Rossknecht/Erhardt

Brunn G&CC (1988)

2345 Brunn/Gebirge, Rennweg 50
Tel   **(02236) 31572/33711**
Fax   (02236) 33863

Holes 18 L 6138 m Par 70 SSS 70
V'tors H
Fees 550s (650s)
Loc 10 km S of Vienna
Arch G Hauser

Colony Club Gutenhof
(1988)
2325 Himberg, Gutenhof
Tel (02235) 87055-0
Fax (02235) 87055-14
Holes East 18 L 6335 m SSS 73
West 18 L 6397 m SSS 73
V'tors H
Fees 500s (750s)
Loc 7 km SE of Vienna
Arch Rossknecht/Erhardt

Danube Golf-Wien
(1995)
Weingartenallee 22, 1220 Wien
Tel (0222) 25072
Fax (0222) 25072-44
Holes 18 L 6130 m SSS 72
V'tors H
Fees 550s (550s)
Loc 15 km NE of Vienna
Arch Rossknecht/Erhardt

Enzesfeld (1970)
2551 Enzesfeld
Tel (02256) 81272
Fax (02256) 81272-4
Holes 18 L 6176 m SSS 72
V'tors H
Fees 500s (750s)
Loc 32 km S of Vienna. A2
Junction 29 (Leobersdorf)
Arch John Harris

Föhrenwald (1968)
2700 Wiener Neustadt, Postfach 105
Tel (02622) 29171
Fax (02622) 25334
Holes 18 L 6043 m SSS 72
V'tors H
Fees 400s (500s)
Loc 5 km S of Wiener Neustadt
on Route B54

Hainburg/Donau
(1977)
2410 Hainburg, Auf der Heide 762
Tel (02165) 62628
Fax (02165) 65331
Holes 18 L 6064 m SSS 72
V'tors H
Fees 400s (600s)
Loc 50 km E of Vienna
Arch G Hauser

Lechner 'BN' (1990)
Pichl 1, 2871 Zöbern
Tel (02642) 8451
Fax (02642) 8451
Holes 9 L 4088m Par 64 SSS 63
V'tors H

Fees 300s (400s)
Loc 90 km S of Vienna via A2
Arch Anton Reithofer

Neusiedlersee-Donnerskirchen (1988)
7082 Donnerskirchen
Tel (02683) 8171
Fax (02683) 817231
Holes 18 L 5937 m SSS 72
V'tors H
Fees 500s (500s)
Loc 45 km SE of Vienna
Arch Rossknecht-Erhardt

Schloss Ebreichsdorf
(1988)
2483 Ebreichsdorf, Schlossallee 1
Tel (02254)73888
Fax (02254) 73888-13
Holes 18 L 6246 m SSS 72
V'tors WD–H WE–on request
Fees 500s (700s)
Loc 28 km S of Vienna
Arch Keith Preston

Schloss Schönborn
2013 Schönborn
Tel (02267) 2863/2879
Fax (02267) 2879-19
Holes 27 L 6265-6474 m SSS 73
V'tors U H
Fees 500s (750s)
Loc 40 km N of Vienna

Schönfeld (1989)
A-2291 Schönfeld, Am Golfplatz 1
Tel (02213) 2063
Fax (02213) 20631
Holes 18 L 6175 m SSS 73
9 hole Par 3 course
V'tors 18 hole:WD–I WE–H
Fees 18 hole:500s (650s);
9 hole:300s (400s)
Loc 35 km E of Vienna
Arch G Hauser

Semmering (1926)
2680 Semmering
Tel (02664) 8154
Fax (02664) 2114
Holes 9 L 3786 m SSS 60
V'tors H
Fees 350s (450s)
Loc 30 km SW of Vienna
Neustadt

Wien (1901)
1020 Wien, Freudenau 65a
Tel (0222) 728 9564
(Clubhouse), 728 9667
(Caddymaster)
Fax (0222) 728 9564-20
Holes 18 L 5861 m SSS 71
V'tors WE–NA
Fees 800s
Loc 10 mins SE of Vienna

Wienerberg (1989)
1100 Wien, Gutheil Schoder 9
Tel (0222) 66123-7000
Fax (0222) 66123-7789
Holes 9 L 5710 m SSS 70
V'tors H
Fees 500s
Loc Vienna District 10
Arch G Hauser

Wienerwald (1981)
1130 Wien, Altgasse 27
Tel (0222) 877 3111 (Sec)
Holes 9 L 4652 m SSS 65
V'tors H
Fees 300s (500s)
Loc Laaben, 35 km W of Vienna
Arch Herbert Illo Holy

Vorarlberg

Bludenz-Braz (1996)
Oberradin 60, 6751 Braz bei Bludenz
Tel (05552) 33503
Fax (05552) 33503-3
Holes 13 L 5284 m Par 70
V'tors H
Fees D–380s (D–420s)
Loc 5 km E of Bludenz
Arch Maurice O'Fives

Montafon-Zelfen (1992)
6774 Tschagguns, Zelfenstrasse
Tel (05556) 77011
Fax (05556) 77011
Holes 9 L 3708 m Par 62 SSS 60
V'tors U H
Fees 300s
Loc 60 km S of Lake Constance

Belgium

Antwerp Region

Bossenstein (1989)
Moor 16, Bossenstein Kasteel, 2520 Broechem
Tel (03) 485 64 46
Fax (03) 485 78 41
Holes 18 L 6203 m SSS 72
9 hole course
V'tors H
Fees 1000fr (1500fr)
Loc 15 km E of Antwerp. 5 km
N of Lier
Arch Paul Rolin

Cleydael (1988)
Kasteel Cleydael, 2630 Aartselaar
Tel (03) 887 00 79/887 18 74
Fax (03) 887 00 15
Holes 18 L 6059 m SSS 72

V'tors H WE–NA before 2pm
Fees 1500fr (2000fr)
Loc 8 km S of Antwerp. 40 km N
of Brussels
Arch Paul Rolin

Inter-Mol (1984)

Goorstraat, 2400 Mol
Tel (014) 57 12 85/45 05 09
Fax (014) 58 42 73
Holes 9 L 1493 m Par 28
V'tors H
Fees 400fr (600fr)
Loc Mol, 60 km E of Antwerp

Kempense (1986)

Kiezelweg 78, 2400 Mol
Tel (014) 81 46 41 (Clubhouse),
(014) 81 62 34 (Caddymaster)
Fax (014) 81 62 78
Holes 18 L 5904 m SSS 72
V'tors H
Fees 1000fr (1500fr)
Loc 60 km E of Antwerp
Arch Marc de Keyser

Lille (1988)

Haarlebeek 3, 2418 Lille
Tel (014) 55 19 30
Fax (014) 55 19 31
Pro S Baeyens
Holes 9 L 4582 m SSS 65
V'tors U
Fees 600fr (800fr)
Loc Lille, 10 km SW of Turnhout,
nr E7. 25 km E of Antwerp

Rinkven G&CC (1980)

Sint Jobsteenweg 120, 2970 Schilde
Tel (03) 380 12 85
Fax (03) 384 29 33
Holes 27 hole course
V'tors H–phone before visit
Fees 1500fr (2500fr)
Loc 17 km NE of Antwerp,
off E19

Royal Antwerp (1888)

Georges Capiaulei 2, 2950 Kapellen
Tel (03) 666 84 56
Fax (03) 666 44 37
Holes 18 L 6140 m SSS 73
9 L 2264 m SSS 33
V'tors WD–H (phone first)
Fees 1500–2000fr
Loc Kapellen, 20 km N of
Antwerp
Arch Willie Park/T Simpson
(1920)

Steenhoven (1985)

Steenhoven 89, 2400 Postel-Mol
Tel (014) 37 36 61
Fax (014) 37 36 62
Holes 18 L 5950 m SSS 71
V'tors H–booking necessary
Fees 1500fr (2500fr)
Loc 30 mins W of Antwerp
Arch Pierre de Broqueville

Ternesse G&CC (1976)

Uilenbaan 15, 2160 Wommelgem
Tel (03) 355 14 30
Fax (03) 355 14 35
Holes 18 L 5876 m SSS 72
9 hole course
V'tors H–30
Fees 1500fr (2500fr)
Loc 5 km E of Antwerp on E313
Arch HJ Baker

Ardennes & South

Andenne (1988)

*Ferme du Moulin 52, Stud,
5300 Andenne*
Tel (085) 84 34 04
Fax (085) 84 34 04
Holes 9 L 2447 m SSS 66
V'tors U
Fees 500fr (700fr)
Loc Andenne, 20 km E of Namur
Arch C Bertier

Château Royal d'Ardenne

5560 Houyet Dinant
Tel (082) 66 62 28
Fax (082) 66 74 53
Holes 18 L 5363 m SSS 71
V'tors H
Fees 1000fr (1500fr)
Loc 9 km SE of Dinant on
Rochefort road

Falnuée (1987)

Rue E Pirson 55, 5032 Mazy
Tel (081) 63 30 90
Fax (081) 63 37 64
Holes 18 L 5700 m SSS 70
V'tors H
Fees 900fr (1400fr)
Loc 18 km NW of Namur. Mons-
Liège highway Junction 13
Arch J Jottrand

Five Nations CC

Ferme du Grand Scley, 5372 Méan
Tel (086) 32 32 32
Fax (086) 32 30 11
Holes 18 L 6066 m Par 72
V'tors U
Fees 1500fr (2000fr)
Loc 30 km S of Liège
Arch Gary Player

Mont Garni (1989)

*Rue du Mont Garni 3, 7331 Saint
Ghislain*
Tel (065) 62 27 19
Fax (065) 62 34 10
Holes 18 L 6353 m SSS 73
V'tors H
Fees 1000fr (1500fr)

Loc St Ghislain, 15 km W of
Mons. 65 km SW of Brussels
Arch T Macauley

Rougemont

*Chemin du Beau Vallon 45,
5170 Profondeville*
Tel (081) 41 14 18
Fax (081) 41 21 42
Holes 18 L 5645 m SSS 72
V'tors U
Fees 1000fr (1250fr)
Loc 10 km S of Namur

Royal GC du Hainaut (1933)

Rue de la Verrerie 2, 7050 Erbisoeul
Tel (065) 22 96 10 (Clubhouse),
(065) 22 94 74 (Sec)
Fax (065) 22 51 54
Holes 9 L 3117 m Par 36
9 L 2925 m Par 36
9 L 3218 m Par 36
V'tors U H (max 36)
Fees 1500fr (2000fr)
Loc 6 km NW of Mons towards
Ath on N56. Paris-Brussels
motorway Junction 23
Arch Martin Hawtree

Brussels & Brabant

Bercuit (1965)

Les Gottes 3, 1390 Grez-Doiceau
Tel (010) 84 15 01
Fax (010) 84 55 95
Holes 18 L 5986 m SSS 72
V'tors U H
Fees D–1450fr (2500fr)
Loc Grez-Doiceau, 27 km SE of
Brussels. Brussels-Namur
highway exit 8
Arch Robert Trent Jones Sr

Brabantse (1982)

Steenwagenstraat 11, 1820 Melsbroek
Tel (02) 751 82 05
Fax (02) 751 84 25
Holes 18 L 5156 m SSS 69
V'tors H
Fees 1000fr (1500fr)
Loc 10 km NE of Brussels, nr
airport
Arch Paul Rolin

La Bruyère (1988)

*Rue Jumerée 1, 1495 Sart-Dames-
Avelines*
Tel (071) 87 72 67
Fax (071) 87 72 67
Holes 18 L 5937 m SSS 71
V'tors U
Fees 900fr (1300fr)
Loc 40 km S of Brussels towards
Charleroi
Arch Theys

Château de la Bawette
(1988)
Chaussée du Chateau 5, 1300 Wavre
Tel   (010) 22 33 32
Fax   (010) 22 90 04
Holes Parc 18 L 6076 m SSS 72
       Champs 9 L 2146 m SSS 63
V'tors H–booking required
Fees   Parc–1200fr (2000fr)
       Champs–800fr (1300fr)
Loc   1 km N of Wavre. 20 km SE
       of Brussels. E411 Exit 5
Arch   Tom Macauley

Château de la Tournette
Chemin de Baudemont 23, 1400 Nivelles
Tel   (067) 21 95 25/22 02 30
Fax   (067) 21 95 17
Holes 18 L 6031 m Par 72
       18 L 6024 m Par 71
V'tors U H
Fees   1200fr (2000fr)
Loc   29 km S of Brussels (E19)
Arch   Alliss/Clark

L'Empereur (1989)
*Rue Emile François 9, 1474 Ways
(Genappe)*
Tel   (067) 77 15 71
Fax   (067) 77 18 33
Holes 18 L 6037 m SSS 72
       9 L 1600 m Par 31
V'tors U H
Fees   18 hole:1000fr (1800fr);
       9 hole:700fr (900fr)
Loc   25 km S of Brussels
Arch   Marcel Vercruyce

Hulencourt
*Bruyère d'Hulencourt 15, 1472 Vieux
Genappe*
Tel   (067) 79 40 40
Fax   (067) 79 40 48
Holes 18 L 6215 m SSS 72
       9 hole Par 3 course
V'tors H–max 28
Fees   1500fr (2500fr)
Loc   30 km S of Brussels
Arch   JM Rossi

Kampenhout
Wildersedreef 56, 1910 Kampenhout
Tel   (016) 65 12 16
Fax   (016) 65 16 80
Holes 18 L 6142 m SSS 72
V'tors U
Fees   1000fr (1500fr)
Loc   15 km NE of Brussels (E19)
Arch   R de Vooght

Keerbergen (1968)
Vlieghavelaan 50, 3140 Keerbergen
Tel   (015) 23 49 61
Fax   (015) 23 57 37
Holes 18 L 5503 m SSS 70
V'tors H
Fees   1100fr (1500fr)
Loc   30 km NE of Brussels
Arch   Frank Pennink

Louvain-la-Neuve
Dreve de Lauzelle, 1348 Ottignies
Tel   (010) 45 28 01
Fax   (010) 45 44 17
Holes 18 L 6226 m SSS 73
V'tors U
Fees   1200fr (2000fr)
Loc   20 km SE of Brussels,
       off E411
Arch   J Dudok van Heel

Overijse
Gemslaan 55, 3090 Overijse
Tel   (02) 687 50 30
Fax   (02) 687 37 68
Holes 9 L 5782 m SSS 71
V'tors H
Fees   800fr (1500fr)
Loc   10 km S of Brussels
Arch   Rossi

Pierpont (1992)
*1 Grand Pierpont, 6210 Frasnes-lez-
Gosselies*
Tel   (071) 85 17 75/85 14 19
Fax   (071) 85 15 43
Holes 18 L 6257 m Par 72
       5 hole Par 3 course
V'tors U
Fees   800fr (1800fr)
Loc   30 km S of Brussels via N5
Arch   J Dudok van Heel

Rigenée (1981)
*Rue de Châtelet 62,
1495 Villers-la-Ville*
Tel   (071) 87 77 65
Fax   (071) 87 77 83
Holes 18 L 6031 m SSS 73
V'tors H
Fees   1100fr (1700fr)
Loc   35 km S of Brussels towards
       Charleroi
Arch   Rolin/Descampe

Royal Amicale
Anderlecht (1987)
Rue Scholle 1, 1070 Bruxelles
Tel   (02) 521 16 87
Fax   (02) 521 51 56
Holes 18 L 5320 m Par 71 SSS 69
V'tors H
Fees   1000fr (1500fr)
Loc   SW Brussels

Royal Golf Club de
Belgique (1906)
*Château de Ravenstein,
3080 Tervuren*
Tel   (02) 767 58 01
Fax   (02) 767 28 41
Holes 18 L 6075 m SSS 72
       9 L 1960 m Par 32
V'tors H–max 20 (men) 24 (ladies)
       phone first
Fees   2000fr (3000fr)
Loc   Tervuren, 10 km E of Brussels
Arch   Simpson

Royal Waterloo (1923)
*Vieux Chemin de Wavre 50,
1380 Ohain*
Tel   (02) 633 18 50/633 15 97
Fax   (02) 633 28 66
Holes 18 L 6211 m SSS 72
       18 L 6224 m SSS 73
       9 L 2143 m SSS 33
V'tors WD–H
Fees   D–1750fr (D–2950fr)
Loc   22 km SE of Brussels
Arch   Hawtree/Rolin

Sept Fontaines (1987)
*1021, Chaussée d'Alsemberg,
1420 Braine l'Alleud*
Tel   (02) 353 02 46/353 03 46
Fax   (02) 354 68 75
Holes 18 L 6047 m SSS 72
       18 L 4870 m SSS 67
       9 hole short course
V'tors U H
Fees   1200fr (2100fr)
Loc   Braine, 15 km S of Brussels.
       Motorway exit 15 (Huizingen)
Arch   Rossi

Winge G&CC (1988)
*Leuvense Steenweg 206, 3390 Sint Joris
Winge*
Tel   (016) 63 40 53
Fax   (016) 63 21 40
Holes 18 L 6149 m SSS 73
V'tors H
Fees   1300–1800fr
Loc   35 km E of Brussels via
       Leuven
Arch   P Townsend

East

Avernas
*Route de Grand Hallet 19A,
4280 Hannut*
Tel   (019) 51 30 66
Fax   (019) 51 30 66
Holes 9 L 2674 m SSS 68
V'tors H
Fees   600fr (800fr)
Loc   40 km W of Liège
Arch   Hawtree/Cappart

Durbuy (1991)
*Route d'Oppagne 34, 6940 Barvaux-su-
Ourthe*
Tel   (086) 21 44 54, (086) 21 44 49
Holes 18 L 5963 m SSS 72
       9 hole Par 3 course
V'tors U
Fees   1100fr (1500fr)
Loc   45 km S of Liège
Arch   Martin Hawtree

Flanders-Nippon (1988)
Vissenbroekstraat 15, 3500 Hasselt
Tel   (011) 26 34 80
Fax   (011) 24 34 81

Holes 18 L 5922 m SSS 72
9 L 1726 m SSS 32
V'tors U
Fees 1000fr (1500fr)
Loc Hasselt, 85 km E of Brussels
Arch Rolin/Wirtz

Henri-Chapelle (1988)

Rue du Vivier 3, 4841 Henri-Chapelle
Tel (087) 88 19 91
Fax (087) 88 36 55
Holes 18 L 6040 m SSS 72
9 L 2168 m SSS 34
Par 3 course
V'tors 18 hole:WE–H
Fees 18 hole:1200–1600fr;
9 hole:900–1200fr
Loc 15 km NE of Liège. 25 km
N of Maastricht
Arch Steensels/Dudok van Heel

International Gomze (1986)

*Sur Counachamps 8, 4140 Gomze
Andoumont*
Tel (041) 360 92 07
Fax (041) 360 92 06
Holes 18 L 5918 m SSS 72
V'tors U H
Fees On application
Loc 15 km S of Liège. Spa 20 km
Arch Paul Rolin

Limburg G&CC (1966)

Golfstraat 1, 3530 Houthalen
Tel (089) 38 35 43
Fax (089) 84 12 08
Holes 18 L 6128 m SSS 72
V'tors H
Fees 1450fr (1850fr)
Loc Houthalen, 15 km N of
Hasselt
Arch Hawtree

Royal GC du Sart Tilman (1939)

Route du Condroz 541, 4031 Liège
Tel (041) 336 20 21
Fax (041) 337 20 26
Holes 18 L 6002 m SSS 72
V'tors H–booking required
Fees D–1500fr (2000fr)
Loc 10 km S of Liège on Route
620 (N35), towards Marche
Arch T Simpson

Royal Golf des Fagnes (1930)

1 Ave de l'Hippodrome, 4900 Spa
Tel (087) 77 16 13
Fax (087) 77 23 36
Holes 18 L 6010 m SSS 72
V'tors H–booking required
Fees 1300–1600fr (2200fr)
Loc 5 km N of Spa. 35 km SE of
Liège
Arch T Simpson

Spiegelven GC Genk (1988)

Wiemesmeerstraat 109, 3600 Genk
Tel (089) 35 96 16
Fax (089) 36 41 84
Holes 18 L 6198 m SSS 72
9 hole Par 3 course
V'tors H
Fees 1300fr (1800fr)
Loc Genk, 18 km E of Hasselt.
20 km N of Maastricht
Arch Ron Kirby

West & Oost Vlaanderen

Damme G&CC (1987)

Doornstraat 16, 8340 Damme-Sijsele
Tel (050) 35 35 72
Fax (050) 35 89 25
Holes 18 L 6046 m SSS 72
9 hole short course
V'tors H
Fees 1450fr (1950fr)
Loc 7 km E of Bruges. Knokke
15 km
Arch J Dudok van Heel

Oudenaarde G&CC (1975)

*Kasteel Petegem, Kortrykstraat 52,
9790 Wortegem-Petegem*
Tel (055) 33 41 61
Fax (055) 31 98 49
Holes 18 L 6172 m Par 72
9 L 2536 m Par 34
V'tors H
Fees 1200fr (1500fr)
Loc 3 km SW of Oudenaarde
Arch HJ Baker

De Palingbeek (1991)

Eekhofstraat 14, 8902 Hollebeke-Ieper
Tel (057) 20 04 36
Fax (057) 21 89 58
Holes 18 L 6165 m Par 72
V'tors H
Fees 1200fr (1500fr)
Loc 5 km SE of Ieper, nr Hollebeke
Arch HJ Baker

Royal Latem (1909)

9830 St Martens-Latem
Tel (09) 282 54 11
Fax (09) 282 90 19
Holes 18 L 5767 m SSS 70
V'tors H
Fees 1750fr (2250fr)
Loc 10 km SW of Ghent on route
N43 Ghent-Deinze

Royal Ostend (1903)

Koninklijke Baan 2, 8420 De Haan
Tel (059) 23 32 83
Fax (059) 23 37 49
Holes 18 L 5517 m SSS 70

V'tors H–36
Fees 1200–1500fr (1900–2200fr)
Loc 8 km N of Ostend towards
De Haan
Arch M Hawtree (1993/4)

Royal Zoute (1909)

Caddiespad 14, 8300 Knokke-le-Zoute
Tel (050) 60 16 17 (Clubhouse),
(050) 60 37 81 (Starter)
Fax (050) 62 30 29
Holes No 1 18 L 6172 m SSS 73
No 2 18 L 3607 m SSS 60
V'tors H No 1 course–max 20
WE–restricted
Fees 1800–2300fr (2000–3000fr)
Loc Knokke-Heist
Arch HS Colt

Waregem

Bergstraat 41, 8790 Waregem
Tel (056) 60 88 08
Fax (056) 61 29 42
Holes 18 L 6038 m SSS 72
V'tors H Sun–NA before 1pm
Fees 1000fr (1600fr)
Loc 30 km SW of Ghent (E17)
Arch Paul Rolin

Czech Republic

Karlovy Vary (1904)

*Prazska 125, PO Box 60,
360 01 Karlovy Vary*
Tel (017) 333 1001-2
Fax (017) 333 1101
Holes 18 L 6226 m SSS 72
V'tors H
Fees 1000kcs (1200kcs)
Loc 8 km from Karlovy Vary
(Road 6)
Arch Noskowski

Lísnice (1928)

252 03 Lísnice
Tel (0305) 92660
Holes 9 L 5002 m SSS 67
V'tors H
Fees 400kcs
Loc 30 km from Prague towards
Dobris

Lokomotiva-Brno (1967)

c/o Chlupova 7, 602 00 Brno
Tel (05) 744615
Fax (05) 759309
Holes 9 L 4632 m SSS 68
V'tors H
Fees 100kcs (180kcs)
Loc Svratka, 80 km NW of Brno.
100 km SE of Prague
Arch Chocholac

Mariánské Lázne (1905)

PO Box 267, 353 01 Mariánské Lázne
Tel **(0165) 4300**
Fax (0165) 625195
Holes 18 L 6195 m SSS 72
V'tors H
Fees D–1000kcs
Loc 2 km NE of Mariánské Lázne, opposite Golf Hotel

Park GC Ostrava (1968)

747 15 Silherovice
Tel **(069) 975 4144**
Fax (069) 975 4144
Holes 18 L 5838 m SSS 71
V'tors H
Fees D–600kcs
Loc 15 km N of Ostrava

Podebrady (1964)

PO Box 7, 29001 Podebrady
Tel **(0324) 3483**
Fax (0324) 3483
Holes 9 L 6240 m SSS 72
V'tors U
Fees 300kcs (400kcs)
Loc E side of Podebrady
Arch Wagner/Havelka

Praha (1926)

Na Morani 4, 128 00 Praha 2
Tel **(02) 292828/644 3828**
Fax (02) 292828
Holes 9 L 5960 m SSS 72
Fees 200kcs (400kcs)
Loc Prague-Motol, towards Plzen

Semily (1970)

Pod Cernym Mostem 476/1, 513 01 Semily 1
Tel **(0431) 622411/622412/4428**
Fax (0431) 622413
Holes 9 L 4160 m Par 64 SSS 64
V'tors WD–U WE–NA
Fees D–300kcs
Loc 2 km from Semily. 100 km NE of Prague
Arch Schovánek/Janata

Denmark
Bornholm Island

Bornholm (1972)

Plantagevej 3B, 3700 Rønne
Tel **56 95 68 54**
Fax 56 95 68 53
Holes 18 L 4819 m Par 68
9 hole Par 3 course
V'tors H
Fees 160kr
Loc 4 km E of Rønne, off Route 38 towards Aakirkeby

Nexø

Dueodde Golfbane, Strandmarksvejen 14, 3730 Nexø
Tel **56 48 89 87**
Fax 56 48 89 69
Holes 18 L 5631 m Par 70 CR 70.4
V'tors H
Fees 170kr (170kr)
Loc 12 km S of Nexø, nr Dueodde beach
Arch Frederik Dreyer

Nordbornholm-Rø (1987)

Spellingevej 3, Rø, 3760 Gudhjem
Tel **56 48 40 50**
Fax 56 48 40 52
Holes 18 L 5512 m SSS 71
V'tors WD–U WE–H
Fees D–170kr
Loc Rø, 8 km W of Gudhjem. 22 km NE of Rønne
Arch Anders Amilon

Funen

Faaborg (1989)

Dalkildegards Allee 1, 5600 Faaborg
Tel **62 61 77 43**
Fax 62 61 79 34
Holes 9 L 5710 m SSS 70
V'tors U H
Fees D–140kr
Loc 35 km S of Odense
Arch Frederik Dreyer

Lillebaelt (1990)

O.Hougvej 130, 5500 Middelfart
Tel **64 41 80 11**
Fax 64 41 14 11
Holes 18 L 5586 m Par 71 CR 69.1
V'tors H
Fees D–180kr (D–180kr)
Loc 2 km from Middelfart. 45 km W of Odense
Arch Malling Petersen

Odense (1927)

Hestehaven 200, 5220 Odense SØ
Tel **65 95 90 00**
Fax 65 95 90 88
Holes 18 L 6156 m CR 71
9 L 4154 m CR 61
V'tors U
Fees 200kr
Loc SE outskirts of Odense
Arch Jan Sederholm

Odense Eventyr (1993)

Falen 227, 5250 Odense SV
Tel **66 17 11 44**
Fax 66 17 11 37
Holes 27 L 8580 m SSS 72
V'tors H
Fees 220kr (250kr)
Loc 5 km SW of Odense
Arch Michael Møller

SCT Knuds (1954)

Slipshavnsvej 16, 5800 Nyborg
Tel **65 31 12 12**
Fax 65 30 28 04
Holes 18 L 5810 m CR 72
V'tors H
Fees 200kr D–250kr (430kr)
Loc 3 km SE of Nyborg
Arch Cotton/Dreyer

Svendborg (1970)

Tordensgaardevej 5, Sørup, 5700 Svendborg
Tel **62 22 40 77**
Fax 62 20 29 77
Holes 18 L 5535 m SSS 70
V'tors U
Fees 160kr (190kr)
Loc 4 km NW of Svendborg
Arch Frederik Dreyer

Vestfyns (1974)

Rønnemosegård, Krengerupvej 27, 5620 Glamsbjerg
Tel **64 72 21 24**
Fax 64 72 27 37
Holes 18 L 5629 m Par 71 CR 71
V'tors H
Fees 170kr (200kr)
Loc Glamsbjerg, 25 km SW of Odense

Greenland

Sondie Arctic Desert (1990)

Box 58, 3910 Kangerlussuaq, Greenland
Tel **29 91 14 13**
Fax 29 91 11 74
Holes 18 L 5521 m SSS 72
V'tors U
Fees 50kr
Loc 2 km E of Kangerlussuaq airport
Mis Sand fairways and greens
Arch Ulf Larson

Jutland

Aalborg (1908)

Jaegersprisvej 35, Restup Enge, 9000 Aalborg
Tel **98 34 14 76**
Fax 98 34 15 84
Holes 18 L 6003 m CR 72.4
V'tors H (max 36)
Fees D–250kr (250 kr)
Loc 7 km SW of Aalborg
Arch R Harris

Aarhus (1931)

Ny Moesgaardvej 50, 8270 Hojbjerg
Tel **86 27 63 22**
Fax 86 27 63 21
Holes 18 L 5725 m CR 71
V'tors H

Fees D–180kr (D–220kr)
Loc 6 km S of Aarhus, Route 451
Arch Brian Huggett

Blokhus Klit (1993)

Hunetorpvej 115, Box 230,
9490 Pandrup
Tel 98 20 95 00
Fax 98 20 95 01
Holes 18 L 5765 m CR 71
V'tors U H
Fees 200kr (250kr)
Loc 35 km NW of Aalborg
Arch Frederik Dreyer

Breinholtgård (1992)

Koksspangvej 17-19,
6710 Esbjerg V
Tel 75 11 57 00
Fax 75 11 55 12
Holes 18 L 5855 m Par 71 CR 72
V'tors U
Fees 200kr
Loc 11 km N of Esbjerg
Arch Gaunt/Trådsdahl

Brønderslev (1971)

PO Box 94, 9700 Brønderslev
Tel 98 82 32 81
Fax 98 82 45 25
Holes 18 L 5683 m CR 71
9 hole short course
V'tors H WE–booking necessary
Fees 180kr (200kr)
Loc 3 km W of Brønderslev
Arch Erik Schnack

Dejbjerg (1966)

Letagervej 1, Dejbjerg, 6900 Skjern
Tel 97 35 09 59/97 35 00 09
Holes 18 L 5275 m SSS 69
V'tors U H–max 36
Fees D–140kr (D–170kr)
Loc 6 km N of Skjern. 25 km from
W coast on Skjern-Ringkøbing
road (Route 28)
Arch Schnack/Dreyer

Ebeltoft (1966)

Strandgårdshøj 8a, 8400 Ebeltoft
Tel 86 34 47 87/86 36 10 64
Holes 18 L 5027 m Par 68 CR 67.6
V'tors U
Fees D–160kr
Loc 1 km N of Ebeltoft
Arch Frederik Dreyer

Esbjerg (1921)

Sønderhedevej 11, Marbaek,
6710 Esbjerg
Tel 75 26 92 19
Fax 75 26 94 19
Holes 18 L 6434 m CR 71
9 L 5520 m CR 70
V'tors U H
Fees 200kr
Loc 15 km N of Esbjerg
Arch Frederik Dreyer

Fanø Golf-Links (1901)

Nordby, 6720 Fanø
Tel 75 16 14 00
Fax 75 16 14 00
Holes 18 L 4450 m CR 65
V'tors U
Fees D–170kr
Loc W side of Fanø Island. Take
ferry from Esbjerg

Grenaa (1981)

Vestermarken 1, 8500 Grenaa
Tel (86) 32 79 29/30 95 99
Holes 18 L 5773 m SSS 70
V'tors U
Fees 150kr
Loc 1 km W of Grenaa. 60 km NE
of Aarhus
Arch Dreyer/Sommer

Gyttegård (1978)

Billundvej 43, 7250 Hejnsvig
Tel 75 33 56 49
Fax 75 33 68 20
Holes 18 L 5673 m SSS 70
V'tors H
Fees 150kr (200kr)
Loc 2 km NE of Hejnsvig. 10 km
S of Grindsted
Arch Amilon/Bossen

Haderslev (1971)

Simmerstedvej 151, 6100 Haderslev
Tel 74 52 83 01
Fax 74 53 36 01
Holes 18 L 5233 m CR 69
V'tors H
Fees 180kr (200kr)
Loc 2 km NW of Haderslev

Han Herreds

Starkaervej 20, 9690 Fjerritslev
Tel 98 21 26 66
Fax 98 21 26 77
Holes 18 L 5359 m CR 71
V'tors H
Fees 150kr
Loc 1 km N of Fjerritslev.
40 km W of Aalborg

Henne (1989)

Hennebysvej 30, 6854 Henne
Tel 75 25 56 10/40 81 39 88
Fax 75 25 56 61
Holes 18 L 6054 m SSS 73
9 hole Par 3 course
V'tors U
Fees D–170kr
Loc 19 km NW of Varde. 35 km
N of Esbjerg
Arch Frederik Dreyer

Herning

Golfvej 2, 7400 Herning
Tel 97 21 00 33
Fax 97 21 00 34
Holes 18 L 5571 m SSS 70
V'tors H

Fees 150kr (200kr)
Loc 2 km E of Herning on
Route 15
Arch Frederik Dreyer

Himmerland G&CC (1979)

Centervej 1, Gatten, 9640 Farsö
Tel 96 49 61 00
Fax 98 66 14 56
Holes Old 18 L 5422 m SSS 69
Par 70; New 18 L 6102 m
SSS 74 Par 73; 18 hole Par 3
course
V'tors H
Fees 170kr D–220kr (240kr
D–290kr)
Loc Gatten, 35 km NW of Hobro
towards Løgstør (Route 29)
Arch Jan Sederström

Hjarbaek Fjord (1992)

Lynderup, 8832 Skals
Tel 86 69 62 88
Fax 86 69 62 68
Holes 27 L 8595 m SSS 72
V'tors H
Fees 190kr (220kr)
Loc 17 km NW of Viborg
Arch Henrik Jacobsen

Hjorring (1985)

Vinstrupvej, PO Box 215,
9800 Hjorring
Tel 98 91 18 28
Fax 98 90 31 00
Holes 18 L 5943 m SSS 72
V'tors H WE–NA 9–11am
Fees 180kr
Loc N of Hjorring. 50 km N
of Aalborg
Arch Erik Schnack

Holmsland Klit

Klevevej 19, Søndervig,
6950 Ringkøbing
Tel 97 33 88 00
Fax 97 33 86 80
Holes 18 L 5611 m SSS 69
V'tors H
Fees 175kr
Loc 10 km W of Ringkøbing
Arch Leif Baekgaard

Holstebro (1970)

Råsted, 7570 Vemb
Tel 97 48 51 55
Holes 18 L 5853 m SSS 72
9 L 2510 m
V'tors H
Fees D–180kr (200kr)
Loc 13 km W of Holstebro
Arch Schnack/Hingebjerg

Horsens (1972)

Silkeborgvej 44, 8700 Horsens
Tel 75 61 51 51
Holes 18 L 6020 m SSS 72
6 hole short course

Fees 160kr
Loc 1 km W of Horsens towards
Silkeborg
Arch Jan Sederholm

Hvide Klit (1972)

Hvideklitvej 28, 9982 Aalbaek
Tel 98 48 90 21/48 84 26
Fax 98 48 91 12
Holes 18 L 5875 m SSS 72
V'tors H
Fees 160kr (220kr)
Loc 3 km N of Aalbaek. 24 km
N of Frederikshavn
Arch Anders Amilon

Juelsminde (1973)

Bobroholtvej 11a, 7130 Juelsminde
Tel 75 69 34 92
Fax 75 69 46 11
Holes 18 L 5680 m SSS 72
V'tors U H
Fees 170kr
Loc 20 km S of Horsens on coast.
2 km N of Juelsminde
Arch Mehlsen/Jacobsen/Møller

Kaj Lykke

Kirkebrovej 5, 6740 Bramming
Tel 75 10 22 46
Holes 18 L 5975 m Par 72
Par 3 course
V'tors H
Fees 200kr
Loc 18 km E of Esbjerg
Arch Bent Nielsen

Kalo (1992)

Aarhusvej 32, 8410 Rønde
Tel 86 37 36 00
Fax 86 37 36 46
Holes 18 L 5936 m CR 72.2
V'tors U
Fees 220kr (250kr)
Loc 20 km E of Aarhus
Arch Frederik Dreyer

Kolding (1933)

Emerholtsvej 15, 6000 Kolding
Tel 75 52 37 93
Fax 75 52 42 42
Holes 18 L 5376 m SSS 69
9 L 2065 m
V'tors U
Fees 160kr (200kr)
Loc 3 km N of Kolding
Arch Jan Sederholm

Lemvig (1986)

Søgårdevejen 6, 7620 Lemvig
Tel 97 81 09 20
Fax 97 81 09 20
Holes 18 L 5890 m CR 72
V'tors U
Fees 150kr (150kr)
Loc 2 km N of Lemvig. 35 km
NE of Holsterbro
Arch Frederik Dreyer

Løkken (1990)

*Vrenstedvej 226, PO Box 43,
9480 Løkken*
Tel 98 99 26 57/98 99 10 33
Fax 98 99 22 21
Holes 18 L 5896 m Par 72
9 L 2964 m Par 29
V'tors U
Fees D–160kr
Loc 45 km NW of Aalborg
Arch Kaj Andersen

Nordvestjysk (1971)

Nystrupvej 19, 7700 Thisted
Tel 97 97 41 41
Holes 18 L 5675 m CR 72
V'tors H
Fees 150kr (150kr)
Loc 17 km NW of Thisted
Arch Schnack/Jacobsen

Randers (1958)

Himmelbovej, Fladbro, 8900 Randers
Tel 86 42 88 69
Fax 86 40 88 69
Holes 18 L 5453 m SSS 70
9 hole Par 3 course
Fees 150kr (180kr)
Loc 5 km W of Randers towards
Silkeborg
Arch Mogens Harbo

Ribe (1979)

*Rønnehave, Snepsgårdevej 14,
Postboks 37, 6760#Ribe*
Tel 75 44 12 30
Holes 18 L 5430 m SSS 68
V'tors U
Fees 100kr (120kr)
Loc 8 km SE of Ribe on
Haderslev road
Arch Frederik Dreyer

Rold Skov

Golfvej 1, 9520 Skørping
Tel 98 39 26 99
Fax 98 39 26 52
Holes 18 L 5850 m SSS 72
V'tors U
Fees 170kr
Loc 30 km S of Aalborg
Arch Henrik Jacobsen

Royal Oak (1992)

Golfvej, Jels, 6630 Rødding
Tel 74 55 32 94
Fax 74 55 32 95
Holes 18 L 5967 m Par 72
V'tors H–booking necessary
Fees 280kr (280kr)
Loc 25 km SW of Kolding

Saeby

Vandløsvej 50, 9300 Saeby
Tel 98 46 76 77
Fax 98 46 11 24
Holes 18 L 5944 m SSS 72
V'tors U

Fees 180kr (200kr)
Loc Saeby, 12 km S of
Fredrikshavn
Arch Anders Amilon

Silkeborg (1966)

Sensommervej 15C, 8600 Silkeborg
Tel 86 85 33 99
Fax 86 85 35 22
Holes 18 L 5975 m SSS 72
V'tors U
Fees 200kr (250kr)
Loc 5 km E of Silkeborg
Arch Frederik Dreyer

Skanderborg (1991)

Hylke Møllevej 2, 8660 Skanderborg
Tel 86 53 86 88
Holes 9 L 2668 m SSS 68
6 hole Par 3 course
V'tors U
Fees 100kr (150kr)
Loc 20 km S of Aarhus by Lake
Skanderborg
Arch Frederik Dreyer

Skive (1973)

Frugtparken 15, 7800 Skive
Tel 97 52 44 09
Holes 9 L 5682 m CR 70
V'tors U
Fees 120kr
Loc 3 km NW of Skive.
32 km NW of Viborg
Arch Erik Schnack

Sønderjyllands (1968)

Uge Hedegård, 6360 Tinglev
Tel 74 68 75 25
Fax 74 68 75 05
Holes 18 L 5771 m SSS 70
V'tors H
Fees 180kr (220kr)
Loc 3 km NE of Tinglev. 15 km
S of Abenraa
Arch Erik Schnack

Varde (1991)

Gellerupvej 111b, 6800 Varde
Tel 75 22 49 44
Holes 18 L 5809 m SSS 70
V'tors H
Fees 150kr
Loc 20 km N of Esbjerg
Arch Erik Fauerholt

Vejle (1970)

Faellesletgard, Ibaekvej, 7100 Vejle
Tel 75 85 81 85
Fax 75 85 83 01
Holes 27 holes:
5677-6148 m Par 71-73
9 hole Par 3 course
V'tors H
Fees 250kr (250kr)
Loc 5 km SE of Vejle
Arch J Malling Pedersen

Viborg (1973)

Moellevej 26, Overlund, 8800 Viborg
Tel   86 67 30 10
Fax   86 67 34 15
Holes 18 L 5767 m CR 72
V'tors WD–H 48 WE–H 36
Fees   170kr (200kr)
Loc   2 km E of Viborg
Arch   Frederik Dreyer

Zealand

Asserbo (1946)

Bødkergaardsvej, 3300 Frederiksvaerk
Tel   47 72 14 90
Fax   47 72 14 26
Holes 18 L 5861 m Par 72
V'tors H
Fees   200kr (250kr)
Loc   3 km from Frederiksvaerk
       towards Liseleje
Arch   Ross/Samuelsen

Copenhagen (1898)

Dyrehaven 2, 2800 Lyngby
Tel   39 63 04 83
Fax   39 63 46 83
Holes 18 L 5761 m SSS 71
V'tors WD–U WE–NA before noon
Fees   200kr (250kr)
Loc   13 km N of Copenhagen, in
       deer park

Dragør

Kalvebodvej 100, 2791 Dragør
Tel   32 53 89 75
Fax   32 53 88 09
Holes 18 L 5864 m SSS 71
       6 hole Par 3 course
V'tors WD–U WE–U H
Fees   180kr (230kr)
Loc   15 km SE of Copenhagen
       centre, nr Airport
Arch   Henning Jensen/Kierkegaard

Frederikssund (1974)

Egelundsgården, Skovnaesvej 9,
3630 Jaegerspris
Tel   47 31 08 77
Fax   47 31 21 88
Holes 18 L 5937 m SSS 71
V'tors WD–U H WE–H 30
Fees   175kr (225kr)
Loc   3 km S of Frederikssund
       towards Skibby (Route 53)
Arch   Dreyer/Samuelsen

Furesø (1974)

Hestkøbgård, Hestkøb Vaenge 4,
3460 Birkerød
Tel   42 81 74 44
Fax   45 82 02 24
Holes 27 holes:
       5328-5641 m CR 70-71
V'tors H WD–NA before 9am
       WE–NA before 11am
Fees   200kr (280kr)
Loc   25 km N of Copenhagen
Arch   Jan Sederholm

Gilleleje (1970)

Ferlevej 52, 3250 Gilleleje
Tel   49 71 80 56
Fax   49 71 80 86
Holes 18 L 6641 yds CR 72
V'tors H–36
Fees   220–250kr
Loc   62 km N of Copenhagen
Arch   Jan Sederholm

Hedeland (1980)

Staerkendevej 232A, 2640 Hedehusene
Tel   46 13 61 88/46 13 61 69
Fax   46 13 62 78
Holes 18 L 6040 m Par 72
       9 hole Par 3 course
V'tors H
Fees   160kr (200kr)
Loc   7 km SE of Roskilde.
       20 km SW of Copenhagen
Arch   Jan Sederholm

Helsingør

GL Hellebaekvej, 3000 Helsingør
Tel   49 21 29 70
Fax   49 21 09 70
Holes 18 L 5612 m SSS 71
V'tors U
Fees   230kr (300kr)
Loc   2 km N of Helsingør

Hillerød (1966)

Nysøgårdsvej 9, Hammersholt,
3400 Hillerød
Tel   42 26 50 46/42 25 40 30 (Pro)
Fax   42 25 29 87
Holes 18 L 5453 m CR 71
V'tors H WE–NA before noon
Fees   200kr (250kr)
Loc   3 km S of Hillerød
Arch   Sederholm/Knudsen

Holbaek (1964)

Dragerupvej 50, 4300 Holbaek
Tel   59 43 45 79
Holes 18 L 5290 m Par 70
V'tors U H
Fees   160kr (200kr)
Loc   Kirsebaerholmen, 2 km E of
       Holbaek
Arch   Dreyer/Sederholm

Kalundborg (1974)

Kildekaergård, Rosnaesvej 225,
4400 Kalundborg
Tel   53 50 13 85
Holes 9 L 5064 m SSS 68
V'tors U
Fees   100kr (140kr)
Loc   Rosnaes, 8 km W of
       Kalundborg
Arch   Jan Sederholm

Køge (1970)

Gl.Hastrupvej12, 4600 Køge
Tel   53 65 10 00
Fax   53 65 13 45
Holes 18 L 6042 m SSS 71

V'tors WE–H max 30
Fees   150kr (210kr)
Loc   3 km S of Køge. Copenhagen
       38 km

Kokkedal (1971)

Kokkedal Alle 9, 2970 Horsholm
Tel   45 76 99 59
Fax   45 76 99 03
Holes 18 L 5936 m SSS 72
V'tors H–WE pm only
Fees   200kr (250kr)
Loc   Hørsholm, 30 km N of
       Copenhagen
Arch   Frank Pennink

Korsør (1964)

Tårnborgparken, Postbox 53,
4220 Korsør
Tel   53 57 18 36
Fax   53 57 18 39
Holes 18 L 5998 m CR 71
       6 hole Par 3 course
V'tors H WE–NA before 10am
Fees   150 (200kr)
Loc   1 km E of Korsør, on Korsør
       Bay

Mølleåens (1970)

Stenbaekgård, Rosenlundvej 3, 3540
Lynge
Tel   48 18 86 31/48 18 86 36 (Pro)
Fax   48 18 86 43
Holes 18 L 5494 m SSS 69
V'tors H
Fees   190kr (240kr)
Loc   32 km NW of Copenhagen
Arch   Jan Sederholm

Odsherred (1967)

4573 Højby
Tel   59 30 20 76
Holes 18 L 5710 m Par 71
V'tors H
Fees   160kr (190kr)
Loc   5 km SW of Nykøbing
Arch   Amilon/Dreyer

Roskilde (1973)

Gedevad, Kongemarken 30, 4000
Roskilde
Tel   42 37 01 80/46 32 61 00 (Pro)
Holes 18 L 5700 m SSS 71
V'tors H
Fees   160kr (210kr)
Loc   5 km W of Roskilde
Arch   Jan Sederholm

Rungsted (1937)

Vestre Stationsvej 16, 2960 Rungsted
Kyst
Tel   45 86 34 44
Fax   45 86 57 70
Holes 18 L 6058 m SSS 73
V'tors H WE–NA before 1pm
Fees   300kr
Loc   Rungsted, 24 km N of
       Copenhagen
Arch   Maj CA Mackenzie

Simon's Golf Club
(1993)
Nybovej 5, 3490 Kvistgaard
Tel   49 19 14 78
Fax   49 19 14 70
Holes 18 L 6200 m SSS 74
V'tors H–max 36
Fees   275kr (375kr)
Loc   10 km S of Helsingør.
       35 km N of Copenhagen
Arch   Martin Hawtree

Skjoldenaesholm
(1992)
4174 Jystrup
Tel   53 62 82 93
Fax   53 62 85 82
Holes 18 L 5974 m SSS 71
V'tors H–max 36
Fees   230kr (280kr)
Loc   10 km N of Ringsted.
       60 km SW of Copenhagen
Arch   Otto Bojesen

Skovlunde Herlev
(1980)
Syvendehusvej 111, 2730 Herlev
Tel   44 68 90 09
Fax   44 68 90 04
Holes 18 L 4824 m Par 68 CR 66
       9 hole Par 3 course
V'tors U
Fees   160kr (220kr)
Loc   Herlev/Ballerup, 15 km NW
       of Copenhagen
Arch   Torben Starup

Søllerød
Brillerne 9, 2840 Holte
Tel   42 80 17 84, 42 80 18 77 (Pro)
Fax   45 80 70 08
Holes 18 L 5872 m SSS 72
V'tors U
Fees   220kr (300kr)
Loc   19 km N of Copenhagen

Sorø (1979)
Suserupvej 7a, 4180 Sorø
Tel   53 64 93 95
Fax   57 84 85 58
Holes 18 L 5693 m Par 71 CR 72
V'tors H–max 48
Fees   180kr (220kr)
Loc   6 km S of Sorø. 15 km W of
       Ringsted
Arch   Jan Sederholm

Sydsjaellands (1974)
Borupgården, Mogenstrup,
4700 Naestved
Tel   53 76 15 55
Fax   53 76 15 88
Holes 18 L 5675 m SSS 70
V'tors H
Fees   160kr (200kr)
Loc   10 km SE of Naestved
       towards Praestø
Arch   Dreyer/Amilon

Vallensbaek
Golfsvinget 16-20, 2625 Vallensbaek
Tel   43 62 18 99
Fax   43 62 18 33
Holes 18 L 6119 m Par 71
       9 L 3130 m
V'tors H
Fees   180kr (240kr)
Loc   15 km W of Copenhagen
Arch   Frederik Dreyer

Finland

Central

Botnia (1988)
Pl 87, 61801 Kauhajoki
Tel   (06) 232 4663
Fax   (06) 231 3089
Holes 9 L 2969 m SSS 72
Fees   100fmk
Loc   8 km S of Kauhajoki.
       300 km NW of Helsinki
Arch   Kosti Kuronen

Etelä Pojhanmaan
(1986)
Isokoskentie 533, 60550 Nurmo
Tel   (964) 423 4545
Fax   (964) 423 4547
Holes 18 L 6210 m SSS 74
Fees   160fmk
Loc   5 km E of Seinäjoki.
       300 km NW of Helsinki

Jyväs Golf (1978)
PL 411, 40101 Jyväskylä
Tel   (941) 244008
Fax   (941) 244008
Holes 9 L 5636 m SSS 72
V'tors U
Fees   120fmk
Loc   2 km S of Jyväskylä
Arch   T Valtakari

Karelia Golf (1987)
Vaskiportintie, 80780 Kontioniemi
Tel   (013) 732411
Fax   (013) 732472
Holes 18 L 6223 m SSS 74
V'tors U H
Fees   170fmk
Loc   18 km N of Joensuu.
       460 km NE of Helsinki
Arch   Kosti Kuronen

Kokkolan (1957)
P O Box 164, 67101 Kokkola
Tel   (06) 822 1636
Fax   (06) 822 1630
Holes 18 L 5572 m SSS 71
V'tors U
Fees   140fmk

Loc   3 km S of Kokkola. 500 km
       N of Helsinki
Arch   KJ Indola

Laukaan Golf (1989)
41530 Laukaa
Tel   (941) 832801
Fax   (941) 832705
Holes 18 L 6200 m SSS 75
Fees   120fmk (150fmk)
Loc   28 km NE of Jyväskylä.
       300 km N of Helsinki

Pirilö Golf (1989)
Vanha Pirilontie, 68600 Pietarsaari,
Jakobstad
Tel   (06) 723 0262
Fax   (06) 723 0262
Holes 9 L 2815m SSS 72
V'tors WD/Sat–U before 5pm
       Sun–U after 3pm
Fees   D–90fmk
Loc   4 km E of Jakobstad.
       480 km NW of Helsinki on
       west coast

Tarina Golf Puijo (1988)
Golftie 135, 71800 Siilinjärvi
Tel   (017) 462 5299
Fax   (017) 462 5269
Holes 18 L 5779 m Par 73
V'tors U H
Fees   160fmk (180fmk)
Loc   21 km N of Kuopio
       (Route 5)
Arch   Kosti Kuronen

Vaasan (1969)
Golfkenttätie 61, 65380 Vaasa
Tel   (961) 356 9989
Fax   (961) 356 9091
Holes 18 L 5630 m Par 72 SSS 71
V'tors H or Green card
Fees   120fmk
Loc   Kraklund, 6 km SE of Vaasa
       on Route 724. 417 km NW
       of Helsinki
Arch   Björn Eriksson

Helsinki & South

Alands (1978)
P O Box 111, 22101 Mariehamn
Tel   (928) 43883
Fax   (928) 19034
Holes 27 L 5565 m SSS 71
Fees   160fmk (180fmk)
Loc   25 km N of Mariehamn,
       Aland (off SW coast of
       Finland)

Aura Golf (1958)
Ruissalo 85, 20100 Turku
Tel   (02) 258 9201
Fax   (02) 258 9121

Holes 18 L 5843 m SSS 71
V'tors H
Fees 200fmk
Loc Ruissalo Island, 9 km W of
Turku
Arch Pekka Sivula

Espoo Ringside Golf
(1990)
Niipperintie 20, 02920 Espoo
Tel (09) 841814
Fax (09) 841814
Holes 18 L 5855 m SSS 72
V'tors H
Fees 120fmk (200fmk)
Loc 20 km NW of Helsinki
Arch Kosti Kuronen

Espoon Golfseura
(1982)
P O Box 26, 02781 Espoo
Tel (90) 811212
Fax (90) 811153
Holes 18 L 5930 m SSS 73
V'tors H
Fees 130fmk
Loc Espoo, 24 km W of Helsinki
Arch Jan Sederholm

Helsingin Golfklubi
(1932)
Talin Kartano, 00350 Helsinki
Tel (90) 550235/557899
Fax (90) 565 3596
Holes 18 L 5870 m SSS 72
V'tors H–max 24 (men) 30 (ladies)
Fees 180fmk (200fmk)
Loc 7 km W of Helsinki

Hyvinkään (1989)
Golftie 63, 05880 Hyvinkää
Tel (019) 489390
Fax (019) 489392
Holes 18 L 5890 m Par 72
V'tors U H
Fees 120fmk (160fmk)
Loc 3 km N of Hyvinkää. 50 km
N of Helsinki
Arch Kosti Kuronen

Keimola Golf Oy
(1988)
Kirkantie 32, 01750 Vantaa
Tel (09) 896991
Fax (09) 896790
Holes 27 L 5870-5924 m
SSS 71-74
V'tors WD–U before 3pm –M after
3pm WE–M H
Fees 160fmk
Loc 15 km N of Helsinki
Arch Pekka Wesamaa

Kurk Golf (1985)
02550 Evitskog
Tel (09) 819 0480
Fax (09) 819 04810

Holes 18 L 5848 m Par 72
V'tors H
Fees 180fmk (200fmk)
Loc 40 km W of Helsinki
Arch Reijo Hillberg

Master Golf (1988)
Bodomintie 4, 02940 Espoo
Tel (90) 853 7002
Fax (90) 853 7027
Holes 27 L 5866-6109 m SSS 73-4
V'tors U
Fees 180fmk (220fmk)
Loc 25 km NW of Helsinki
Arch Kuronen/Persson

Meri-Teijo (1990)
*Mathildedalin Kartano, 25660
Mathildedal*
Tel (924) 363801
Fax (924) 363890
Holes 18 L 6163 m SSS 75
Fees 100fmk (150fmk)
Loc 20 km S of Salo. 70 km E of
Turku

Messilä (1988)
Messiläntie 240, 15980 Messilä
Tel (03) 753 8171
Fax (03) 753 8174
Holes 18 L 6013 m Par 73
V'tors WD–U before 3pm
Fees D–180fmk
Loc 8 km W of Lahti. 100 km N
of Helsinki
Arch Kosti Kuronen

Nevas Golf (1988)
01190 Box
Tel (90) 272 6313
Fax (90) 272 6345
Holes 18 L 5267 m SSS 71
V'tors U
Fees 110fmk (150fmk)
Loc 30 km E of Helsinki
Arch Kosti Kuronen

Nordcenter G&CC
(1988)
10410 Aminnefors
Tel (911) 238850
Fax (911) 238871
Holes 18 L 6375 m SSS 74
18 L 6069 m SSS 71
V'tors H
Fees 200fmk
Loc 80 km W of Helsinki
Arch Fream/Benz

Nurmijärven (1990)
Ratasillantie, 05100 Röykkä
Tel (90) 276 8890
Holes 27 L 6002-6214 m SSS 73-5
V'tors U
Fees 150fmk
Loc 23 km W of Klaukkala.
50 km NW of Helsinki

Pickala Golf (1986)
Pickala Village, 02580 Siuntio
Tel (90) 296 6251
Fax (90) 296 6190
Holes Seaside 18 L 5820 m SSS 72
Park 18 L 5897 m SSS 72
V'tors H
Fees 170fmk (200fmk)
Loc 42 km W of Helsinki, on
South coast
Arch Reijo Hillberg

Ruukkigolf (1986)
Brödtorp, 10420 Skuru
Tel (019) 245 4485
Fax (019) 245 4285
Holes 18 L 6165 m Par 72
V'tors U
Fees 120fmk (170fmk)
Loc 85 km W of Helsinki
Arch Lasse Heikkinen

St Laurence (1989)
Kaivurinkatu, 08200 Lohja
Tel (912) 386603
Fax (912) 386666
Holes 18 L 6247 m Par 72
9 L 3248 m Par 36
V'tors WD–U H before 3pm WE–U
H after 1pm
Fees 160fmk (200fmk)
Loc 50 km W of Helsinki
Arch Kosti Kuronen

Sarfvik (1984)
P O Box 27, 02321 Espoo
Tel (09) 297 7122
Fax (09) 297 7134
Holes 18 L 5680 m SSS 72
18 L 5399 m SSS 72
V'tors WD–U H 10am–2pm
Fees 250fmk
Loc 20 km W of Helsinki
Arch Jan Sederholm

Sea Golf Rönnäs (1989)
Rönnäs, 07750 Isnäs
Tel (915) 34434
Fax (915) 34458
Holes 18 L 6035 m SSS 74
Fees 150fmk
Loc 27 km SE of Porvoo. 80 km
E of Helsinki

Seaside Golf (1989)
Harjattulantie 84, 20960 Turku
Tel (921) 587100
Fax (921) 34458
Holes 18 L 6348 m SSS 75
Fees 150fmk
Loc 22 km S of Turku

Suur-Helsingin (1965)
Rinnekodintie 29, 02980 Espoo
Tel (90) 855 8687
Fax (90) 855 0648
Holes Lakisto 18 L 5551 m SSS 71
Luukki 18 L 5083 m SSS 70

Fees 150fmk
Loc 25 km N of Helsinki

Golf Talma (1989)
Nygårdintie, 04240 Talma
Tel (09) 239 6166
Fax (09) 239 6131
Holes 18 L 5855 m SSS 72
  9 L 2895 m SSS 36
  9 hole Par 3 course
V'tors H
Fees 135fmk (200fmk)
Loc 35 km N of Helsinki
Arch Henrik Wartiainen

Tuusula (1983)
P O Box 178, 04301 Tuusula
Tel (90) 259466
Fax (90) 254660
Holes 18 L 6363 m SSS 72
V'tors H
Fees 120–160fmk
Loc 30 km N of Helsinki,
  nr airport

Virvik Golf (1981)
Virvik, 06100 Porvoo
Tel (915) 579292
Fax (915) 579292
Holes 18 L 5855 m SSS 72
V'tors H
Fees 120fmk (140fmk)
Loc 18 km SE of Porvoo. 66 km
  E of Helsinki
Arch Reijo Louhimo

North

Green Zone Golf (1987)
Näräntie, 95400 Tornio
Tel (9698) 431711
Fax (9698) 431710
Holes 18 L 5870 m SSS 73
V'tors U
Fees 120fmk
Loc 2 km N of Tornio. 140 km N
  of Oulu, on Finnish/Swedish
  border
Arch Ake Persson

Katinkulta (1990)
88610 Vuokatti
Tel (08) 669 7488
Fax (08) 664 0710
Holes 18 L 6000 m SSS 74
V'tors H
Fees 150fmk (250fmk)
Loc 36 km E of Kajaani.
  600 km N of Helsinki
Arch Jan Sederholm

Oulu (1964)
Isokatu 99, 90120 Oulu
Tel (981) 371666/531 5222
Fax (981) 379728/531 5129
Holes 18 L 6160 m SSS 73
  9 L 2990 m SSS 73

V'tors U
Fees 130–150fmk
Loc Sanginsuu, 18 km E of Oulu
Arch Ronald Fream

Pielis Golf (1988)
Lomatie 1, 75500 Nurmes
Tel (013) 480734
Fax (013) 480743
Holes 9 L 5730 m SSS 72
V'tors U
Fees 120fmk
Loc 4 km E of Nurmes. 500 km
  N of Helsinki
Arch Kosti Kuronen

Raahentienoon Golf
(1990)
Kastellintie 44, 92320 Siikajoki
Tel (982) 241060
Holes 9 L 6190m SSS 73
Fees 100fmk
Loc 20 km N of Raahe.
  540 km NW of Helsinki

St Lake Golf (1993)
86800 Pyhäsalmi
Tel (984) 882001
Fax (984) 882001
Holes 9 L 2670 m SSS 72
Fees 100fmk
Loc Pyhäsalmi, 500 km N of
  Helsinki

South East

Hartolan Kunikkaalinen
(1992)
Kaikolantie, 19601 Hartola
Tel (03) 883 4310
Holes 9 L 2845 m SSS 71
V'tors H
Fees 120fmk
Loc 1 km S of Hartola. 80 km
  N of Lahti
Arch Kosti Kuronen

Imatran Golf (1986)
Golftie 11, 55800 Imatra
Tel (954) 473 4954
Fax (954) 473 4953
Holes 18 L 6141 m SSS 74
V'tors U
Fees 130fmk (160fmk)
Loc 6 km N of Imatra. 270 km
  E of Helsinki
Arch Kosti Kuronen

Kartano Golf (1988)
P O Box 60, 79601 Joroinen
Tel (972) 572257
Fax (972) 572263
Holes 18 L 5714 m SSS 73
V'tors U
Fees 130fmk (170fmk)

Loc 20 km S of Varkaus.
  330 km NE of Helsinki
Arch Ake Persson

Kerigolf (1990)
Hotellikylä Kerimaa,
58200 Kerimäki
Tel (015) 252496
Fax (015) 252124
Holes 18 L 6218 m Par 72 SSS 75
V'tors H
Fees 170fmk
Loc 15 km E of Savonlinna.
  350 km NE of Helsinki
Arch Ronald Fream

Koski Golf (1987)
Eerolan Golfkeskus,
45700 Kuusankoski
Tel (05) 374 7622
Fax (05) 374 7820
Holes 18 L 6375 m Par 73
V'tors H
Fees D–120fmk (D–160fmk)
Loc 3 km E of Kuusankoski.
  70 km E of Lahti
Arch Kosti Kuronen

Kymen Golf (1964)
Mussalo Golfcourse, 48310 Kotka
Tel (952) 605333
Fax (952) 605073
Holes 18 L 6004 m SSS 74
V'tors H
Fees 100fmk (120fmk)
Loc 5 km W of Kotka, Mussalo
  Island. 130 km E of Helsinki
Arch Kosti Kuronen

Lahden Golf (1959)
P O Box 67, 15141 Lahti
Tel (918) 784 1311
Fax (918) 784 1311
Holes 18 L 5823 m SSS 73
V'tors U H
Fees 130fmk
Loc 6 km NE of Lahti. 110 km
  NE of Helsinki

Mikkelin Golf (1967)
Kalervonkatu 5, 50130 Mikkeli
Tel (955) 151759
Fax (955) 151771
Holes 9 L 2845 m SSS 71
Fees 80fmk
Loc 2 km SW of Mikkeli.
  240 km NE of Helsinki
Arch E Inoranta

Porrassalmi (1989)
Annila, 50100 Mikkeli
Tel (015) 335518/335446
Fax (015) 335446
Holes 18 L 5140 m SSS 68
V'tors H
Fees 160–180fmk
Loc 5 km S of Mikkeli

Vierumäen Golfseura
(1988)
Suomen Urheiluopisto, 19120
Vierumäki
Tel (918) 124501
Fax (918) 124630
Holes 18 L 5755 m SSS 73
Fees 150fmk
Loc 25 km NE of Lahti

Viipurin Golf (1938)
Kahilanniemi, 53130 Lapeenranta
Tel (952) 16840
Holes 9 L 2708 m SSS 70
Loc 2 km E of Lappeenranta,
behind Etelä-Saimaa Hospital

South West

Aulangon (1959)
13600 Hämeenlinna
Tel (917) 74070
Holes 9 L 2450 m SSS 67
Fees 100fmk
Loc 5 km NW of Hämeenlinna.
100 km NW of Helsinki

Porin Golfkerho
(1939)
P O Box 25, 28601 Pori
Tel (02) 630 3888
Fax (02) 630 38813
Holes 18 L 6160 m SSS 74
V'tors H
Fees 150fmk
Loc 5 km NW of Pori, at
Kalafornia
Arch Reijo Louhimo

Rauman Golf (1989)
Pomppuistentie, 26510 Uotila
Tel (938) 823 0450
Fax (938) 823 0941
Holes 9 L 3095 m SSS 72
Fees 100fmk
Loc 3 km E of Rauma.
192 km NW of Helsinki

River Golf (1988)
Taivalkunta, 37120 Nokia
Tel (931) 340 0234
Fax (931) 3400 235
Holes 18 L 5810 m SSS 72
V'tors U
Fees 150fmk (170fmk)
Loc Nokia, 20 km W of Tampere
Arch Kosti Kuronen

Salo Golf (1988)
Liikuntapuisto 8, 24100 Salo
Tel (924) 317321
Holes 18 L 5824 m SSS 73
Fees 100fmk (120fmk)
Loc 110 km W of Helsinki

Skärgården (1980)
Finbyvägen 87, PO Box 110,
21601 Pargas
Tel (921) 882001
Fax (921) 882001
Holes 9 L 5740 m SSS 72
V'tors U
Fees 100fmk
Loc 25 km S of Turku
Arch Kosti Kuronen

Tammer Golf (1965)
P O Box 269, 33101 Tampere
Tel (931) 613316
Fax (931) 613130
Holes 18 L 5870 m SSS 72
Fees 150fmk
Loc Ruotula, 5 km NE of
Tampere

Tawast G&CC (1987)
Tawastintie 48, 13270 Hämeenlinna
Tel (03) 619 7502
Fax (03) 619 7503
Holes 18 L 6063 m SSS 73
V'tors H
Fees 180fmk
Loc 5 km E of Hämeenlinna
Arch Reijo Hillberg

Vammala (1991)
38100 Karkku
Tel (932) 34070
Fax (932) 34070
Holes 18 L 5701 m SSS 71
V'tors H
Fees 130fmk
Loc 11 km N of Vammala.
210 km NW of Helsinki
Arch Kosti Kuronen

Wiurila G&CC (1990)
Viurilantie 126, 24910 Halikko
Tel (924) 371400
Fax (924) 371404
Holes 18 L 6160 m SSS 74
Fees 100fmk (150fmk)
Loc 5 km W of Salo. 115 km W
of Helsinki

Yyteri Golf (1988)
P O Box 230, 28101 Pori
Tel (02) 638 0380
Fax (02) 638 0385
Holes 18 L 5738 m SSS 72
Fees 150fmk
Loc 20 km W of Pori
Arch Reijo Louhimo

France

Bordeaux &
South West

Albret (1986)
Le Pusocq, 47230 Barbaste
Tel 05 53 65 53 69
Fax 05 53 65 61 19
Holes 18 L 5911 m SSS 71
V'tors U
Fees 140fr (170fr)
Loc Barbaste, 30 km W of Agen
Arch JL Pega

Arcachon (1955)
35 Bd d'Arcachon, 33260 La Teste De
Buch
Tel 05 56 54 44 00
Fax 05 56 66 86 32
Holes 18 L 5930 m SSS 71
V'tors U H
Fees D–160–250fr
Loc 60 km SW of Bordeaux
Arch CR Blandford

Arcangues (1991)
64200 Arcangues
Tel 05 59 43 10 56
Fax 05 59 43 12 60
Holes 18 L 6142 m Par 72
V'tors U
Fees 230–300fr
Loc 3 km SE of Biarritz
Arch Ronald Fream

Ardilouse (1980)
Domaine de l'Ardilouse,
33680 Lacanau-Océan
Tel 05 56 03 25 60
Fax 05 56 26 30 57
Holes 18 L 5932 m SSS 72
V'tors H
Fees 160–190fr (240fr)
Loc 45 km W of Bordeaux
Arch John Harris

Biarritz (1888)
Ave Edith Cavell, 64200 Biarritz
Tel 05 59 03 71 80
Fax 05 59 03 26 74
Holes 18 L 5376 m SSS 68
V'tors U
Fees 220–320fr
Loc Biarritz
Arch Willie Dunn

Biscarrosse (1989)
Route d'Ispe, 40600 Biscarrosse
Tel 05 58 09 84 93
Fax 05 58 09 84 50
Holes Lake 9 L 2172 m SSS 32
Forest 9 L 3030 m SSS 36
V'tors U
Fees 160–250fr
Loc 80 km SW of Bordeaux
Arch Brizon/Veyssieres

Blue Green-Artiguelouve
(1986)

Domaine St Michel, Pau-Artiguelouve,
64230 Artiguelouve

Tel	05 59 83 09 29
Fax	05 59 83 14 05
Holes	18 L 6063 m Par 71
V'tors	U
Fees	190fr (235fr)
Loc	8 km NW of Pau, off Bayonne road
Arch	J Garaialde

Blue Green-Seignosse Golf Hotel (1989)

Avenue du Belvedère,
40510 Seignosse

Tel	05 58 41 68 30
Fax	05 58 41 68 31
Holes	18 L 6124 m Par 72
V'tors	U
Fees	200–330fr
Loc	30 km N of Biarritz, nr Airport
Arch	Robert von Hagge

Bordeaux-Cameyrac
(1972)

Cameyrac, 33450 St Sulpice

Tel	05 56 72 96 79
Fax	05 56 72 86 56
Holes	18 L 5927 m SSS 72 / 9 L 1188 m Par 28
Fees	150fr (200fr)
Loc	15 km E of Bordeaux
Arch	Jacques Quenot

Bordeaux-Lac (1977)

Avenue de Pernon,
33300 Bordeaux

Tel	05 56 50 92 72
Fax	05 56 29 01 84
Holes	18 L 6156 m SSS 72 / 18 L 6159 m SSS 72
Fees	180fr (220fr)
Loc	2 km N of Bordeaux
Arch	Jean Bourret

Bordelais (1900)

Domaine de Kater, Rue de Kater,
33200 Bordeaux-Caudéran

Tel	05 56 28 56 04
Fax	05 56 28 59 71
Holes	18 L 4833 m SSS 67
V'tors	H–restricted Tues
Fees	190fr (250fr)
Loc	3 km NW of Bordeaux

Casteljaloux (1989)

Avenue du Lac, 47700 Casteljaloux

Tel	05 53 93 51 60
Fax	05 53 93 04 10
Holes	18 L 5916 m SSS 72
V'tors	U
Fees	150–200fr (180–220fr)
Loc	60 km NW of Agen
Arch	Michel Gayon

Castelnaud (1987)

'La Menuisière', 47290 Castelnaud de
Gratecambe

Tel	05 53 01 74 64
Fax	05 53 01 78 99
Holes	18 L 6322 m SSS 73 / 9 L 2184 m SSS 27
Loc	10 km N of Villeneuve on N21. 40 km N of Agen

Chantaco (1928)

Route d'Ascain,
64500 St Jean-de-Luz

Tel	05 59 26 14 22/ 05 59 26 19 22
Fax	05 59 26 48 37
Holes	18 L 5722 m SSS 70
V'tors	U
Fees	260fr (340fr)
Loc	2 km S of St Jean-de-Luz, on Route d'Ascain
Arch	HS Colt

Château des Vigiers
(1990)

24240 Monestier

Tel	05 53 61 50 00
Fax	05 53 61 50 20
Holes	18 L 6003 m Par 72 / 6 hole Academy course
V'tors	H
Fees	195–300fr
Loc	15 km SW of Bergerac. 75 km E of Bordeaux
Arch	Donald Steel

Chiberta (1926)

Boulevard des Plages, 64600 Anglet

Tel	05 59 63 83 20
Fax	05 59 63 30 56
Holes	18 L 5650 m SSS 70
V'tors	H–booking required
Fees	240–320fr
Loc	3 km N of Biarritz. Airport 5 km
Arch	T Simpson

Croix de Mortemart
(1987)

St Felix de Reillac, 24260 Le Bugue

Tel	05 53 03 27 55
Holes	18 L 6222 m Par 72
V'tors	U
Fees	150–180fr W–720fr
Loc	30 km S of Perigueux, between La Douze and Le Bugue (D710)
Arch	Martine Lacroix

Graves et Sauternais
(1989)

St Pardon de Conques,
33210 Langon

Tel	05 56 62 25 43
Holes	18 L 5810 m SSS 71
Loc	5 km from Langon. 45 km SW of Bordeaux via A62

Gujan (1990)

Route de Souguinet, 33470 Gujan
Mestras

Tel	05 57 52 73 73
Fax	05 56 66 10 93
Holes	18 L 6225 m SSS 72 / 9 L 2635 m SSS 35
V'tors	U
Fees	18 hole–200–270fr / 9 hole–140–170fr
Loc	12 km E of Arcachon on RN 250. 40 km W of Bordeaux
Arch	Alain Prat

Hossegor (1930)

Ave du Golf BP#95, 40150 Hossegor

Tel	05 58 43 56 99
Fax	05 58 43 98 52
Holes	18 L 6001 m SSS 71
V'tors	H
Fees	230–350fr
Loc	15 km N of Bayonne, on coast
Arch	J Morrison

Makila

Route de Cambo, 64200 Bassussarry

Tel	05 59 58 42 42
Fax	05 59 58 42 48
Holes	18 L 6176 m SSS 72
V'tors	H
Fees	220–300fr
Loc	5 km SE of Biarritz. Airport 2 km
Arch	R Roquemore

Médoc

Chemin de Courmateau, Louens,
33290 Le Pian Médoc

Tel	05 56 70 11 90
Fax	05 56 70 11 99
Holes	Chateaux 18 L 6316 m SSS 73; Vignes 18 L 6220 m SSS 73
V'tors	H
Fees	230fr (300fr)
Loc	20 km NW of Bordeaux
Arch	Coore/Whitman

Moliets (1989)

Rue Mathieu Desbieys, 40660 Moliets

Tel	05 58 48 54 65
Fax	05 58 48 54 88
Holes	18 L 6172 m SSS 73 / 9 hole course
V'tors	U
Fees	250–320fr
Loc	Moliets, 30 km N of Bayonne. 40 km W of Dax
Arch	Robert Trent Jones Sr

La Nivelle (1907)

Place William Sharp,
64500 Ciboure

Tel	05 59 47 18 99/ 05 59 47 19 72
Holes	18 L 5570 m SSS 69
Fees	220–320fr (1991)
Loc	2 km S of St Jean-de-Luz

Pau (1856)
Rue de Golf, 64140 Pau-Billère
Tel   05 59 32 02 33
Fax   05 59 62 42 57
Holes   18 L 5312 m SSS 69
V'tors H
Fees   200fr (250fr)
Loc   2 km S of Pau. Bordeaux
            200 km
Arch   Willie Dunn

Périgueux (1980)
Domaine de Saltgourde,
24430 Marsac
Tel   05 53 53 02 35
Fax   05 53 09 46 29
Holes   18 L 6120 m SSS 72
Fees   D–180fr
Loc   3 km W of Périgueux, via
            Angoulême-Riberac road
Arch   Robert Berthet

Pessac (1989)
Rue de la Princesse, 33600 Pessac
Tel   05 57 26 03 33
Fax   05 56 36 52 89
Holes   18 L 5567-5935 m SSS 72
            9 L 2911 m SSS 36
            9 hole Par 3 course
V'tors U
Fees   200fr (260fr)
Loc   4 km W of Bordeaux
Arch   Olivier Brizon

Scottish Golf d'Aubertin
(1987)
64290 Aubertin
Tel   05 59 82 70 69
Holes   18 L 4806 m Par 66
V'tors U
Fees   100fr (120fr)
Loc   20 km S of Pau

Stade Montois (1993)
Pessourdat, 40090 Saint Avit
Tel   05 58 75 63 05
Fax   05 58 06 80 72
Holes   18 L 5944 m Par 71
V'tors U
Fees   180fr (180fr)
Loc   Pau 80 km. Biarritz 100 km
Arch   J Garaialde

Brittany

Ajoncs d'Or (1976)
Kergrain Lantic, 22410 Saint-Quay
Portrieux
Tel   02 96 71 90 74
Fax   02 96 71 40 83
Holes   18 L 6125 m SSS 72
V'tors U
Fees   170–190fr
Loc   17 km N of Saint-Brieuc.
            6 km W of Étables-sur-Mer

Baden
Kernic, 56870 Baden
Tel   02 97 57 18 96
Fax   02 97 57 22 05
Holes   18 L 6145 m SSS 73
V'tors U
Fees   155–240fr
Loc   12 km SW of Vannes
Arch   Yves Bureau

Boisgelin (1987)
Pléhédel, 22290 Lanvollon
Tel   02 96 22 31 24
Holes   18 hole course
V'tors U
Fees   100fr (150fr)
Loc   10 km S of Paimpol on D7.
            35 km from Saint-Brieuc

Brest-Iroise (1976)
Parc de Lann-Rohou, Saint-Urbain,
29800 Landerneau
Tel   02 98 85 16 17
Holes   18 L 5672 m Par 71
            9 L 3329 m Par 37
V'tors U H
Fees   210fr (230fr)
Loc   25 km E of Brest
Arch   M Fenn

Cicé-Blossac (1992)
Domaine de Cicé-Blossac,
35170 Bruz
Tel   02 99 52 79 79
Fax   02 99 57 93 60
Holes   18 L 6343 m SSS 72
V'tors U
Fees   150–250fr
Loc   Bruz, SW of Rennes (N177)
Arch   Macauley/Quenouille

Dinard (1887)
35800 St-Briac-sur-Mer
Tel   02 99 88 32 07
Fax   02 99 88 04 53
Holes   18 L 5137 m Par 68
Fees   190fr (220fr)
Loc   8 km W of Dinard. 15 km W
            of Saint-Malo

La Freslonnière
(1989)
Le Bois Briand, 35650 Le Rheu
Tel   02 99 14 84 09
Fax   02 99 14 94 98
Holes   18 L 5756 m SSS 72
V'tors U
Fees   200fr (250fr)
Loc   4 km SW of Rennes,
            off N24
Arch   A du Bouexic

L'Odet (1987)
Clohars-Fouesnant, 29950 Benodet
Tel   02 98 54 87 88
Fax   02 98 54 61 40
Holes   18 L 6235 m SSS 73
            9 hole Par 3 course

V'tors U H
Fees   160–255fr
Loc   6 km S of Benodet. 15 km SE
            of Quimper
Arch   Robert Berthet

Les Ormes (1988)
Château des Ormes, Epiniac,
35120 Dol-de-Bretagne
Tel   02 99 73 49 60
Fax   02 99 73 49 55
Holes   18 L 6070 m SSS 72
V'tors U
Fees   185–240fr
Loc   8 km S of Dol, off D795
Arch   A d'Ormesson

Pen Guen (1926)
22380 Saint-Cast-le-Guildo
Tel   02 96 41 91 20
Fax   02 96 41 77 62
Holes   18 L 4967m SSS 68
V'tors U
Fees   195–235fr
Loc   25 km W of Dinard. 30 km
            W of Saint-Malo

Pléneuf-Val André
Rue de la Plage des Vallées,
22370 Pléneuf-Val André
Tel   02 96 63 01 12
Fax   02 96 63 01 06
Holes   18 L 6052 m Par 72
V'tors U
Fees   160–270fr
Loc   30 km E of St Brieuc on coast.
            60 km W of St Malo
Arch   Alain Prat

Ploemeur Océan
Saint-Jude, Kerham,
56270 Ploemeur
Tel   02 97 32 81 82
Fax   02 97 32 80 90
Holes   18 L 5957 m SSS 72
V'tors U H
Fees   155–240fr
Loc   10 km from Lorient-Brest
            road, exit Ploemeur
Arch   Macauley/Quenouille

Quimper-Cornouaille
(1959)
Manoir du Mesmeur,
29940 La Forêt-Fouesnant
Tel   02 98 56 97 09
Holes   18 L 5657 m SSS 71
Fees   D–150fr
Loc   15 km SE of Quimper
Arch   F Hawtree

Rennes Saint Jacques
B P 1117, 37136 St-Jacques-de-la-
Lande
Tel   02 99 30 18 18
Fax   02 99 31 51 04
Holes   18 L 6135 m Par 72
            9 L 2100 m Par 32
            9 hole short course

V'tors U
Fees 155–240fr
Loc 5 km SW of Rennes
Arch Robert Berthet

Rhuys-Kerver (1988)

Formule Golf, Domaine de Kerver,
56730 St-Gildas-de-Rhuys
Tel 02 97 45 30 09
Fax 02 97 45 36 58
Holes 18 L 6197 m SSS 73
V'tors U
Fees 150–230fr
Loc 30 km S of Vannes
Arch Olivier Brizon

Les Rochers (1989)

Route d'Argentré du Plessis 3,
35500 Vitré
Tel 02 99 96 52 52
Fax 02 99 96 79 34
Holes 18 L 5721 m Par 72
V'tors U
Fees 160fr (160fr)
Loc Vitré, 30 km E of Rennes
Arch JC Varro

Sables-d'Or-les-Pins

(1925)
22240 Fréhel
Tel 02 96 41 42 57
Fax 02 96 41 51 44
Holes 18 L 5586 m SSS 71
V'tors U
Fees 180–220fr
Loc 6 km SW of Fréhel. 30 km
W of Dinard

St Laurent (1975)

Ploemel, 56400 Auray
Tel 02 97 56 85 18
Fax 02 97 56 89 99
Sec 6
Holes 18 L 6212 m SSS 72
9 L 2705 m SSS 35
V'tors U
Fees 155–255fr
Loc Ploemel, 16 km SW of Auray
Arch Fenn/Bureau

St Malo-Le Tronchet

(1986)
Le Tronchet, 35540 Miniac-Morvan
Tel 02 99 58 96 69
Holes 18 L 6049 m SSS 72
9 L 2684 m SSS 36
V'tors U
Fees D–220fr
Loc 23 km S of St Malo,
off RN 137
Arch Hubert Chesneau

St Samson (1965)

Route de Kérénoc, 22560 Pleumeur-
Bodou
Tel 02 96 23 87 34
Fax 02 96 23 84 59
Holes 18 L 5807 m Par 71
V'tors U

Fees 210fr (380fr)
Loc 7 km N of Lannion on
Tregastel road
Arch Hawtree

Sauzon (1987)

Les Poulins, 56360 Belle-Ile-en-Mer
Tel 02 97 31 64 65
Holes 18 L 5820 m SSS 72
V'tors U
Fees 180fr
Loc Island off S coast of Brittany,
near Quiberon
Arch Yves Bureau

Val Queven (1990)

Kerrousseau, 56530 Queven
Tel 02 97 05 17 96
Fax 02 97 05 19 18
Holes 18 L 6127 m SSS 72
V'tors U Sun–restricted
Fees 160–250fr
Loc 10 km W of Lorient
Arch Yves Bureau

Burgundy & Auvergne

Beaune-Levernois

(1990)
21200 Levernois
Tel 03 80 24 10 29
Fax 03 80 24 03 78
Holes 18 L 6116 m Par 72
9 hole short course
V'tors U
Fees 160fr (220fr)
Loc 5 km SE of Beaune
(D470/D111)
Arch Ch Piot

Chalon-sur-Saône

(1976)
Parc de Saint Nicolas, 71380 Chatenoy-
en-Bresse
Tel 03 85 93 49 65
Fax 03 85 93 56 95
Holes 18 L 5859 m SSS 71
V'tors U
Fees D–145fr
Loc 3 km SE of Chalon. 125 km N
of Lyon
Arch Michel Rio

Chambon-sur-Lignon

(1986)
Riondet, La Pierre de la Lune,
43400 Le Chambon-sur-Lignon
Tel 71 59 28 10
Fax 71 65 87 14
Holes 18 L 6110 m Par 72
V'tors U
Fees On application
Loc 60 km NW of Saint Etienne.
120 km NW of Lyon
Arch Michel Gayon

Château d'Avoise

(1992)
9 Rue de Mâcon, 71210 Montchanin
Tel 85 78 19 19
Fax 85 78 15 16
Holes 18 L 6350 m Par 72
V'tors WD–U WE–H
Fees 160fr (200fr)
Loc 25 km W of Chalon
Arch Martin Hawtree

Château de Chailly

Chailly-sur-Armançon,
21320 Pouilly-en-Auxois
Tel 80 90 30 40
Fax 80 90 30 05
Holes 18 L 6146 m SSS 72
V'tors U
Fees 200fr (300fr)
Loc 45 km SW of Dijon
Arch Sprecher/Watine

Château de la Salle

(1989)
71260 La Salle-Mâcon Nord
Tel 03 85 36 09 71
Fax 03 85 36 60 70
Holes 18 L 6024 m SSS 71
V'tors U
Fees 150fr (200fr)
Loc 12 km NW of Mâcon. Lyon
70 km
Arch Robert Berthet

Le Coiroux (1977)

19190 Aubazine
Tel 55 27 25 66
Fax 55 27 29 33
Holes 18 L 5400 m Par 70
V'tors U
Fees 170fr (190fr)
Loc 15 km E of Brive
Arch Hubert Chesneau

Dijon-Bourgogne

(1972)
Bois des Norges,
21490 Norges-la-Ville
Tel 03 80 35 71 10
Fax 03 80 35 79 27
Holes 18 L 6179 m SSS 72
V'tors U
Fees 180fr (250fr)
Loc 10 km N of Dijon towards
Langres
Arch Fenn/Radcliffe

Domaine de Roncemay

(1989)
89110 Chassy
Tel 03 86 73 69 87
Fax 03 86 73 69 46
Holes 18 L 6401 m SSS 73
V'tors WE–restricted
Fees 200fr (300fr)
Loc 15 km NW of Auxerre
Arch Jeremy Pern

For list of abbreviations see page 479

La Fredière (1988)
La Fredière, Céron, 71110 Marcigny
Tel   85 25 27 40
Fax   85 25 35 01
Holes   18 L 4529 m SSS 68
V'tors U
Fees   150–180fr
Loc   35 km NW of Roanne
Arch   Gilles Charmat

La Jonchère
Montgrenier, 23230 Gouzon
Tel   55 62 23 05
Holes   18 L 5858 m SSS 71
V'tors U
Fees   140fr (180fr)
Loc   30 km SW of Montluçon.
           100 km NE of Limoges
Arch   J-L Pega

Limoges-St Lazare
(1976)
Avenue du Golf, 87000 Limoges
Tel   55 28 30 02
Holes   18 L 6238 m SSS 73
V'tors U
Fees   90fr
Loc   2 km S of Limoges on
           RN20
Arch   Hubert Chesneau

Mâcon La Salle
*La Salle-Mâcon Nord,
71260 La Salle*
Tel   85 36 09 71
Fax   85 36 06 70
Holes   18 L 6024 m Par 71
           9 hole Par 3 course
V'tors H or green card
Fees   150fr (200fr)
Loc   15 km N of Mâcon (A6)
Arch   Robert Berthet

Le Nivernais
Le Bardonnay, 58470 Magny Cours
Tel   86 58 18 30
Fax   86 58 04 04
Holes   18 L 5670 m Par 71
Fees   130fr (180fr)
Loc   12 km S of Nevers on N7.
           50 km N of Moulins
Arch   Alain Prat

La Porcelaine
Célicroux, 87350 Panazol
Tel   05 55 31 10 69
Fax   05 55 31 10 69
Holes   18 L 6035 m SSS 72
V'tors U
Fees   150–200fr
Loc   6 km NE of Limoges
Arch   Jean Garaialde

Sporting Club de Vichy
(1907)
Allée Baugnies, 03700 Bellerive/Allier
Tel   70 32 39 11
Fax   70 32 00 54
Holes   18 L 5463 m SSS 70
V'tors H
Fees   190–250fr
Loc   In Vichy
Arch   Arnaud Massy

Val de Cher (1975)
03190 Nassigny
Tel   70 06 71 15
Holes   18 L 5450 m Par 70
V'tors U
Fees   150fr (200fr)
Loc   20 km N of Montluçon on
           N144
Arch   Bourret/Vigand

Les Volcans (1984)
La Bruyère des Moines, 63870 Orcines
Tel   73 62 15 51
Fax   73 62 26 52
Holes   18 L 6286 m SSS 73
           9 L 1377 m SSS 29
V'tors U H
Fees   200fr (250fr)
Loc   12 km W of Clermont-
           Ferrand on RN 141
Arch   Lucien Roux

Centre

Les Aisses (1992)
RN20 Sud, 45240 La Ferté St Aubin
Tel   02 38 64 80 87
Fax   02 38 64 80 85
Holes   27 L 6200 m Par 72
V'tors U
Fees   180fr (250fr)
Loc   30 km S of Orléans. 140 km
           S of Paris
Arch   Olivier Brizon

Ardrée (1988)
37360 St Antoine-du-Rocher
Tel   47 56 77 38
Fax   47 56 79 96
Holes   18 L 5758 m Par 70
V'tors U
Fees   200–260fr
Loc   10 km N of Tours
Arch   Olivier Brizon

Les Bordes (1987)
41220 Saint Laurent-Nouan
Tel   02 54 87 72 13
Fax   02 54 87 78 61
Holes   18 L 6412 m Par 72
V'tors U
Fees   350fr (550fr)
Loc   30 km SW of Orléans
Arch   Robert van Hagge

Château de Cheverny
La Rousselière, 41700 Cheverny
Tel   02 54 79 24 70
Fax   02 54 79 25 52
Holes   18 L 6276 m Par 71
V'tors H
Fees   190fr (260fr)
Loc   15 km S of Blois. 200 km SW
           of Paris, via A10
Arch   O Van der Vinckt

Château de Maintenon
(1988)
*Route de Gallardon,
8130 Maintenon*
Tel   37 27 18 09
Fax   37 27 10 12
Holes   18 L 6393 m SSS 74
           9 L 1541 m SSS 30
V'tors WD–U WE–restricted
Fees   250fr (450fr)
Loc   20 km W of Rambouillet
           (D906). 70 km SW of Paris
Arch   Michel Gayon

Château des Forges
(1991)
*Domaine des Forges,
79340 Menigoute*
Tel   49 69 91 77
Holes   18 L 6400 m Par 74
           9 L 3200 m Par 37
V'tors U
Fees   200fr (250fr)
Loc   30 km W of Poitiers
Arch   Bjorn Eriksson

Château des Sept Tours
(1989)
*Le Vivier des Landes, 37330 Courcelles
de Touraine*
Tel   47 24 69 75
Fax   47 24 23 74
Holes   18 L 6194 m Par 72
V'tors U
Fees   180fr (240fr)
Loc   35 km NW of Tours
Arch   Donald Harradine

Cognac (1987)
Saint-Brice, 16100 Cognac
Tel   45 32 18 17
Fax   45 35 10 76
Holes   18 L 6142 m SSS 72
V'tors H
Fees   200–230fr
Loc   5 km E of Cognac
Arch   Jean Garaialde

Le Connétable (1987)
*Parc Thermal,
86270 La Roche Posay*
Tel   05 49 86 25 10
Fax   05 49 19 48 40
Holes   18 L 5840 m SSS 72
V'tors U
Fees   150fr (180fr)
Loc   La Roche-Posay, 20 km E of
           Châtellerault. 40 km NE of
           Poitiers
Arch   JP Fourès

Domaine de Vaugouard

(1987)

Chemin des Bois, Fontenay-sur-Loing, 45210 Ferrières

Tel	02 38 95 81 52
Fax	02 38 95 79 78
Holes	18 L 5914 m SSS 72
V'tors	U
Fees	190fr (350fr)
Loc	10 km N of Montargis. 100 km S of Paris
Arch	Fromanger/Adam

Les Dryades

36160 Pouligny-Notre-Dame

Tel	54 30 28 00
Holes	18 L 6120 m SSS 72
V'tors	U
Fees	200fr (250fr)
Loc	10 km S of La Châtre (D940). 60 km SW of Bourges
Arch	Michel Gayon

Haut-Poitou (1987)

86130 Saint-Cyr

Tel	05 49 62 53 62
Fax	05 49 88 77 14
Holes	18 L 6590 m SSS 75
	9 L 1800 m Par 31
V'tors	U
Fees	170fr Sun–200fr
Loc	20 km N of Poitiers. 70 km S of Tours
Arch	HG Baker

Loudun (1985)

Domaine St Hilaire, 86120 Roiffe

Tel	05 49 98 78 06
Fax	05 49 98 72 57
Holes	18 L 6343 m Par 72
V'tors	U
Fees	125–135fr (165–175fr)
Loc	18 km N of Loudun. 15 km S of Saumur
Arch	Hubert Chesneau

Marcilly (1986)

Domaine de la Plaine, 45240 Marcilly-en-Villette

Tel	02 38 76 11 73
Fax	02 38 76 18 73
Holes	18 L 6324 m SSS 73
	9 hole course
V'tors	U
Fees	130fr (170fr)
Loc	20 km SE of Orléans
Arch	Olivier Brizon

Mazières (1987)

Le Petit Chêne, 79310 Mazières-en-Gâtine

Tel	49 63 20 95
Fax	49 63 33 75
Holes	18 L 6060 m SSS 72
V'tors	U
Fees	150fr (195fr)
Loc	15 km SW of Parthenay. 25 km NE of Niort
Arch	Robert Berthet

Mignaloux Beauvoir

Domaine de Beauvoir, 86550 Mignaloux Beauvoir

Tel	49 46 70 27
Fax	49 55 31 95
Holes	18 L 6032 m SSS 71
V'tors	WD–U WE–H
Fees	170–200fr
Loc	6 km SE of Poitiers (RN147)
Arch	Olivier Brizon

Oleron

La Vieille Perrotine, 17310 St Pierre d'Oleron

Tel	46 47 11 59
Fax	46 47 49 59
Holes	9 L 3000 m SSS 36
	6 hole short course
V'tors	U
Fees	D–100fr (D–140fr)
Loc	Island S of La Rochelle. A10 Junction 25 (Saintes)
Arch	Olivier Brizon

Orléans Val de Loire

Château de la Touche, 45450 Donnery

Tel	38 59 25 15/38 59 20 48
Fax	38 57 01 98
Holes	18 L 5771 m SSS 71
V'tors	U
Fees	180fr (250fr)
Loc	16 km E of Orléans
Arch	Trent Jones/Van der Vinckt

Le Perche (1987)

La Vallée des Aulnes, 28400 Souancé au Perche

Tel	02 37 29 17 33
Fax	02 37 29 12 88
Holes	18 L 6073 m Par 72
V'tors	U
Fees	180fr (280fr)
Loc	60 km SW of Chartres (D9). 130 km SW of Paris
Arch	Laurent Hechly

La Picardière

Chemin de la Picardière, 18100 Vierzon

Tel	48 75 21 43
Fax	48 71 87 61
Holes	18 L 6077 m Par 72
V'tors	U
Fees	170fr (220fr)
Loc	75 km S of Orléans, off A71
Arch	JL Pega

La Prée-La Rochelle

(1990)

La Richardière, 17137 Marsilly

Tel	46 01 24 42
Fax	46 01 25 84
Holes	18 L 6012 m SSS 72
V'tors	U
Fees	160–240fr
Loc	6 km N of La Rochelle
Arch	Olivier Brizon

Prieuré de Ganay

(1991)

41220 Saint Laurent-Nouan

Tel	02 54 87 26 24
Fax	02 54 87 72 50
Holes	27 hole course
V'tors	U
Fees	100fr (120fr)
Loc	130 km S of Paris
Arch	Jim Shirley

Royan (1977)

Maine-Gaudin, 17420 Saint-Palais

Tel	05 46 23 16 24
Fax	05 46 23 23 38
Holes	18 L 5970 m SSS 71
	6 hole short course
V'tors	U
Fees	150–240fr
Loc	Saint-Palais, 7 km W of Royan
Arch	Robert Berthet

Saintonge (1953)

Fontcouverte, 17100 Saintes

Tel	05 46 74 27 61
Fax	05 46 92 17 92
Holes	18 L 4790 m Par 68
V'tors	U
Fees	150–200fr
Loc	2 km NE of Saintes
Arch	Hervé Bertrand

Sancerrois (1989)

St Thibault, 18300 Sancerre

Tel	02 48 54 11 22
Fax	02 48 54 28 03
Holes	18 L 5820 m SSS 71
V'tors	U
Fees	120–170fr (180–220fr)
Loc	45 km NE of Bourges
Arch	Didier Fruchet

Sologne (1955)

Route de Jouy-le-Potier, 45240 La Ferté St Aubin

Tel	02 38 76 57 33
Fax	02 38 76 68 79
Holes	18 L 6400 yds SSS 72
V'tors	U
Fees	120fr (170fr)
Loc	25 km S of Orléans on RN20

Sully-sur-Loire (1965)

L'Ousseau, 45600 Viglain

Tel	38 36 52 08
Holes	18 L 6154 m SSS 72
	9 L 3155 m SSS 36
Loc	3 km SW of Sully-sur-Loire

Touraine (1971)

Château de la Touche, 37510 Ballan-Miré

Tel	02 47 53 20 28
Fax	02 47 53 31 54
Holes	18 L 5671 m SSS 71
V'tors	WE–H
Fees	D–230fr (D–300fr)
Loc	Villandry, 8 km SW of Tours
Arch	Michael Fenn

For list of abbreviations see page 479

Val de l'Indre (1989)

Villedieu-sur-Indre, 36320 Tregonce
Tel   54 26 59 44
Holes 18 L 6250 m SSS 72
Fees   140–190fr
Loc   12 km NW of Chateauroux.
       80 km SE of Tours on
       RN 143
Arch   Yves Bureau

Channel Coast & North

Abbeville (1989)

Route du Val, 80132 Grand-Laviers
Tel   03 22 24 98 58
Fax   03 22 24 49 61
Holes 18 L 6080 m Par 73
V'tors U
Fees   150fr (180fr)
Loc   3 km NW of Abbeville
Arch   Didier Fruchet

L'Ailette

02000 Laon
Tel   23 24 83 99
Fax   23 24 84 66
Holes 18 L 6127 m Par 72
       9 hole short course
V'tors WD–H WE–H restricted
Fees   185fr (240fr)
Loc   13 km S of Laon. 45 km NW
       of Reims
Arch   Michel Gayon

Amiens (1951)

Route d'Amiens, 80115 Querrieu
Tel   03 22 93 04 26
Fax   03 22 93 04 61
Holes 18 L 6114 m SSS 72
V'tors U
Fees   130–150fr (200–250fr)
Loc   7 km NE of Amiens (D929)
Arch   Ross/Pennink

Apremont (1992)

60300 Apremont
Tel   03 44 25 61 11
Fax   03 44 25 11 72
Holes 18 L 6436 m SSS 73
V'tors H
Fees   280fr (480fr)
Loc   45 km N of Paris
Arch   John Jacobs

Arras (1989)

Rue Briquet Taillandier, 62223 Anzin-St-Aubin
Tel   03 21 50 24 24
Fax   03 21 50 29 71
Holes 18 L 6150 m SSS 72
V'tors U
Fees   190fr (250fr)
Loc   50 km S of Lille. 110 km SE
       of Calais
Arch   JC Cornillot

Belle Dune

*Promenade de Marquenterre,
80790 Fort-Mahon-Plage*
Tel   22 23 45 50
Fax   22 23 93 41
Holes 18 L 5909 m Par 72 SSS 71
V'tors H or Green card
Fees   155–200fr
Loc   25 km S of Le Touquet on
       coast
Arch   JM Rossi

Blue Green-Chantilly Golf Hotel (1991)

*Route d'Apremont, 60500 Vineuil
St-Firmin*
Tel   03 44 58 47 74
Fax   03 44 58 50 28
Holes 18 L 6209 m SSS 72
V'tors U
Fees   150–290fr
Loc   40 km N of Paris (A1)
Arch   Huau/Nelson

Bois de Ruminghem (1991)

*1613 Rue St Antoine,
62370 Ruminghem*
Tel   21 85 30 33
Fax   21 36 38 38
Holes 18 L 6115 m Par 73
V'tors U
Fees   140fr (160fr)
Loc   30 km SE of Calais
Arch   Bill Baker

Bondues (1968)

*Château de la Vigne BP 54,
59587 Bondues Cedex*
Tel   03 20 23 20 62
Fax   03 20 23 24 11
Holes 18 L 6223 m SSS 73
       18 L 6000 m SSS 72
V'tors H–max 30
Fees   D–200fr (D–300fr)
Loc   10 km NE of Lille
Arch   Hawtree/Trent Jones

Brigode (1970)

*36 Avenue de Golf,
59650 Villeneuve D'Ascq*
Tel   20 91 17 86
Fax   20 05 96 36
Holes 18 L 6182 m SSS 72
V'tors WD–H (High season)
Fees   200fr (300fr)
Loc   8 km NE of Lille
Arch   HJ Baker

Champagne (1986)

02130 Villers-Agron
Tel   03 23 71 62 08
Fax   03 23 71 62 08
Holes 18 L 5760 m SSS 72
V'tors U
Fees   170fr (230fr)
Loc   25 km SW of Reims,
       via E50
Arch   JC Cornillot

Chantilly (1909)

*Allée de la Ménagerie, 6
0500 Chantilly*
Tel   03 44 57 04 43
Fax   03 44 57 26 54
Holes Vineuil 18 L 6597 m SSS 71
       Longeres 18 L 6378 m
       SSS 72
V'tors WE–NA
Fees   WD–350fr
Loc   45 km N of Paris
Arch   Tom Simpson

Château de Raray

*4 Rue Nicolas de Lancy,
60810 Raray*
Tel   03 44 54 70 61
Fax   03 44 54 74 97
Holes 18 L 6455 m Par 72
       9 L 2921 m Par 35
V'tors H
Fees   150–220fr (250–350fr)
Loc   60 km N of Paris (A1)
Arch   Patrick Leglise

Chaumont-en-Vexin (1963)

Château de Bertichère, 60240 Chaumont-en-Vexin
Tel   44 49 00 81/44 49 14 76
Holes 18 L 6195 m SSS 72
V'tors H
Fees   200fr (400fr)
Loc   65 km NW of Paris
Arch   Donald Harradine

Compiègne (1896)

Ave Royale, 60200 Compiègne
Tel   44 40 15 73
Fax   44 40 23 59
Holes 18 L 6017 m SSS 71
V'tors U H
Fees   200fr (300fr)
Loc   Compiègne, 80 km NE
       of Paris

Deauville l'Amiraute (1992)

*Departementale 278, Tourgéville,
14800 Deauville*
Tel   02 31 14 42 00
Fax   02 31 88 32 00
Holes 18 L 6055 m Par 73
V'tors U
Fees   220–250fr (330–350fr)
Loc   4 km S of Deauville
Arch   Bill Baker

Domaine du Tilleul (1984)

Landouzy-la-Ville, 02140 Vervins
Tel   03 23 98 48 00
Fax   03 23 98 46 46
Holes 18 L 5203 m SSS 71
V'tors Groups 10+ welcome
Fees   100–150fr (150–180fr)
Loc   7 km S of Hirson. 65 km N of
       Reims

Dunkerque (1991)

Fort Vallières, Coudekerque-Village,
59380 Bergues
Tel 28 61 07 43
Fax 28 60 05 93
Holes 18 L 6300 m SSS 71
Fees 160fr (200fr)
Loc 5 km E of Dunkerque
Arch Robert Berthet

Hardelot Dunes Course
(1991)

Ave du Golf, 62152 Hardelot
Tel 03 21 91 90 90
Holes 18 L 6031 m SSS 73
V'tors U
Fees 290–340fr
Loc 15 km S of Boulogne
Arch Paul Rolin

Hardelot Pins Course

Ave du Golf, 62152 Hardelot
Tel 03 21 83 73 10
Fax 03 21 83 24 33
Holes 18 L 5870 m SSS 72
V'tors U
Fees 290–340fr
Loc 15 km S of Boulogne
Arch Tom Simpson

International Club du
Lys (1929)

Rond-Point du Grand Cerf,
0260 Lamorlaye
Tel 03 44 21 26 00
Fax 03 44 21 35 52
Holes 18 L 6022 m Par 71
          18 L 4770 m Par 66
V'tors WD–H WE–H (booking
          necessary)
Fees WD–250fr
Loc 5 km S of Chantilly. 40 km
          N of Paris
Arch Tom Simpson

Masako Ohya (1990)

Château d'Humières, 60113 Monchy-
Humières
Tel 44 42 39 51
Fax 44 42 48 92
Holes 18 L 6176 m SSS 73
V'tors U
Fees 180fr (270fr)
Loc 80 km N of Paris.
          A1 Junction 11

Morfontaine (1926)

60128 Mortefontaine
Tel 44 54 68 27
Holes 18 L 6063 m SSS 72
          9 L 2550 m SSS 35
V'tors Members' guests only
Fees NA
Loc 10 km S of Senlis. N of Paris
Arch Tom Simpson

Mormal (1991)

Bois St Pierre, 59144 Preux-au-Sart
Tel 03 27 63 07 00
Fax 03 27 39 93 62
Holes 18 L 6022 m Par 72
V'tors H
Fees 170fr (220fr)
Loc 15 km E of Valenciennes,
          off RN49
Arch JC Cornillot

Nampont-St-Martin
(1978)

Maison Forte, 80120 Nampont-
St-Martin
Tel 03 22 29 92 90/
          03 22 29 89 87
Fax 03 22 29 97 54
Holes Cygnes 18 L 6048 m SSS 72
          Belvedère 18 L 5211 m SSS 70
V'tors U
Fees 130–150fr (200–240fr)
Loc 12 km S of Montreuil-sur-
          Mer. 50 km S of Boulogne
Arch Thomas Chatterton

Pelves (1991)

Chemin de l'Enfer, 62118 Pelves
Tel 21 58 95 42
Fax 21 24 00 04
Holes 18 L 5958 m SSS 72
V'tors U
Fees 130fr (150fr)
Loc 40 km S of Lille. 180 km N
          of Paris
Arch Ogama

Rebetz (1988)

Route de Noailles, 60240 Chaumont-
en-Vexin
Tel 03 44 49 15 54
Fax 03 44 49 14 26
Holes 18 L 6409 m SSS 73
V'tors H
Fees 150fr (350fr)
Loc Chaumont-en-Vexin,
          65 km NW of Paris, via D43
Arch J-P Fourès

Saint-Omer

Chemin des Bois, Acquin-Westbécourt,
62380 Lumbres
Tel 03 21 38 59 90
Fax 03 21 38 59 90
Holes 18 L 6400 m Par 72
          9 L 2015 m Par 31
V'tors U
Fees 140–250fr (190–290fr)
Loc 10 km W of Saint-Omer.
          40 km S of Calais
Arch J Dudok van Heel

Le Sart (1910)

5 Rue Jean-Jaurès, 59650 Villeneuve
D'Ascq
Tel 03 20 72 02 51
Fax 03 20 98 73 28
Holes 18 L 5721 m SSS 71
V'tors H
Fees 250fr (300fr 2D–500fr)

Loc 5 km E of Lille. Motorway
          Lille-Gand Junction 9
          (Breucq-Le Sart)
Arch Allan Macbeth

Thumeries (1935)

Bois Lenglart, 59239 Thumeries
Tel 03 20 86 58 98
Fax 03 20 86 52 66
Holes 18 L 5933 m SSS 72
V'tors U
Fees 180fr (250fr)
Loc 10 km N of Douai. 15 km S
          of Lille
Arch Boomer/Rossi

Le Touquet 'La Forêt'
(1904)

Ave du Golf BP 41,
62520 Le Touquet
Tel 03 21 06 28 00
Fax 03 21 06 28 01
Holes 18 L 5722 m SSS 71
V'tors U H
Fees 250fr (320fr)
Loc 2 km S of Le Touquet.
          30 km S of Boulogne
Arch H Hutchinson

Le Touquet 'La Mer'
(1930)

Ave du Golf BP 41,
62520 Le Touquet
Tel 03 21 06 28 00
Fax 03 21 06 28 01
Holes 18 L 6330 m SSS 74
V'tors U H
Fees 270fr (350fr)
Loc As 'La Forêt'
Arch HS Colt

Le Touquet 'Le Manoir'
(1994)

Ave du Golf BP 41,
62520 Le Touquet
Tel 03 21 06 28 00
Fax 03 21 06 28 01
Holes 9 L 2816 m Par 35
V'tors U
Fees 160fr (210fr)
Loc As "La Forêt'
Arch HJ Baker

Vert Parc (1991)

3 Route d'Ecuelles, 59480 Illies
Tel 20 29 37 87
Fax 20 29 37 87
Holes 18 L 6328 m SSS 73
V'tors U
Fees 140fr (220fr)
Loc 18 km SW of Lille
Arch Patrice Simon

Wimereux (1906)

Route d'Ambleteuse, 62930 Wimereux
Tel 03 21 32 43 20
Fax 03 21 33 62 21
Holes 18 L 6150 m Par 72

V'tors H
Fees 185–210fr (200–250fr)
Loc 6 km N of Boulogne on D940.
30 km S of Calais
Arch Campbell/Hutchinson

Corsica

Spano (1989)

Cocody Village, Commune de Lumio,
20260 Calvi
Tel 95 60 75 52
Fax 95 60 70 73
Holes 9 L 2200 m SSS 64
V'tors U
Fees 110–120fr
Loc Calvi
Arch Olivier Brizon

Spérone (1990)

Domaine de Spérone, 20169 Bonifacio
Tel 04 95 73 17 13
Fax 04 95 73 17 85
Holes 18 L 6130 m SSS 73
V'tors H–max 28
Fees 330fr W–1400fr
Loc S point of Corsica, SE of
Bonifacio. 25 km S of Airport
Arch Robert Trent Jones Sr

Ile de France

Ableiges (1989)

95450 Ableiges
Tel 01 30 27 97 00
Fax 01 30 27 97 10
Holes 18 L 6261 m Par 72
9 L 2137 m Par 33
V'tors 18 holes–U H (max 30)
Fees 18 holes–150fr (250fr)
9 holes–120fr (150fr)
Loc 40 km NW of Paris, nr Cergy
Pontoise
Arch Pern/Garaialde

Belesbat (1989)

Courdimanche-sur-Essonne,
91820 Boutigny-sur-Essonne
Tel 69 23 19 00
Fax 69 23 19 01
Holes 18 L 6047 m SSS 72
V'tors H–Booking required
Fees 200fr (400fr)
Loc 50 km S of Paris, between
Etampes and Fontainebleau
Arch Fromanger/Adam

Bellefontaine (1987)

95270 Bellefontaine
Tel 01 34 71 05 02
Fax 01 34 71 90 90
Holes 27 holes:
6098–6306 m Par 72
V'tors U
Fees 200fr (350fr)
Loc 27 km N of Paris
Arch Michel Gayon

Bondoufle (1990)

Departmentale 31, 91070 Bondoufle
Tel 60 86 41 71
Fax 60 86 41 56
Holes 18 L 6161 m SSS 73
V'tors U H
Fees 100–200fr (250–300fr)
Loc 30 km S of Paris
Arch Michel Gayon

Bussy-St-Georges (1988)

Promenade des Golfeurs, 77600 Bussy-
St-Georges
Tel 64 66 00 00
Fax 64 66 22 92
Holes 18 L 5924 m SSS 72
V'tors U
Fees 120–150fr (250–280fr)
Loc 20 km E of Paris. Motorway
A4 Junction 12
Arch Rolin/Cornillot

Cély (1990)

Le Château, Route de Saint-Germain,
77930 Cély-en-Bière
Tel 64 38 03 07
Fax 64 38 08 78
Holes 18 L 6026 m SSS 72
V'tors H
Fees 300fr (400fr)
Loc Fontainebleau 15 km
Arch Adam/Fromanger

Cergy Pontoise (1988)

2 Allee de l'Obstacle d'Eau,
95490 Vaureal
Tel 34 21 03 48
Fax 34 21 03 34
Holes 18 6100 m SSS 72
V'tors WD–U WE–U H
Fees 160fr (260fr)
Loc 30 km NW of Paris. A15
Junction 12
Arch Michel Gayon

Chevannes-Mennecy (1994)

91750 Chevannes
Tel 01 64 99 88 74
Fax 01 64 99 88 67
Holes 18 L 6307 m Par 72
V'tors U
Fees 120fr (200fr)
Loc 45 km S of Paris
Arch A d'Ormesson

Clement Ader (1990)

Domaine Château Pereire,
77220 Gretz
Tel 64 07 34 10
Fax 64 07 82 10
Holes 18 L 6350 m Par 72
V'tors U
Fees 200fr (450fr)
Loc 30 km SE of Paris
Arch M Saito

Coudray (1960)

Ave du Coudray, 91830 Le Coudray-
Montceaux
Tel 01 64 93 81 76
Fax 01 64 93 99 95
Holes 18 L 5733 m Par 71
9 L 1500 m Par 30
V'tors H
Fees 260fr (380fr)
Loc 35 km S of Paris on A6
(Junction 11)
Arch CK Cotton

Courson Monteloup (1991)

91680 Bruyères-le-Chatel
Tel 01 64 58 80 80
Fax 01 64 58 83 06
Holes 36 hole course:
6171–6520 m SSS 72-75
V'tors WD–U WE–M exc Jul/Aug
Fees 230fr (400fr)
Loc 35 km SW of Paris, off Route
D3
Arch Robert von Hagge

Crécy-la-Chapelle (1987)

Ferme de Monpichet, 77580 Crécy-la-
Chapelle
Tel 64 04 70 75
Holes 18 L 6211 m SSS 72
V'tors U
Fees 80fr (200fr)
Loc 20 km E of Paris by A4

Domont-Montmorency

Route de Montmorency,
95330 Domont
Tel 01 39 91 07 50
Fax 01 39 91 25 70
Holes 18 L 5775 m SSS 71
V'tors H
Fees 250fr (480fr)
Loc 18 km N of Paris
Arch Hawtree

Étiolles (1990)

Vieux Chemin de Paris, 91450 Étiolles
Tel 01 60 75 49 49
Fax 01 60 75 64 20
Holes 18 L 6239 m Par 74
9 L 2665 m SSS 36
V'tors U
Fees 260fr (390fr)
Loc 30 km S of Paris
Arch Michel Gayon

Fontainebleau (1909)

Route d'Orleans, 77300 Fontainebleau
Tel 64 22 22 95
Fax 64 22 63 76
Holes 18 L 6074 m SSS 72
V'tors WD–U WE–Jul/Aug only
Fees 350fr (500fr)
Loc 1 km SW of Fontainebleau.
60 km SE of Paris
Arch Simpson/M Hawtree

Fontenailles (1991)

Domaine de Bois Boudran,
77370 Fontenailles

Tel	01 64 60 51 00
Fax	01 60 67 52 12
Holes	18 L 6256 m SSS 74
	9 L 2870 m
V'tors	WD–U WE–H
Fees	180–200fr (320–450fr)
Loc	60 km SE of Paris
Arch	Michel Gayon

Forges-les-Bains (1989)

Rue du Général Leclerc, 91470 Forges-
les-Bains

Tel	01 64 91 48 18
Fax	01 64 91 40 52
Holes	18 L 6167 m SSS 72
V'tors	H or Green card
Fees	200fr (330fr)
Loc	35 km S of Paris, off A10
Arch	JM Rossi

La Forteresse (1989)

Domaine de la Forteresse, 77940
Thoury-Ferrottes

Tel	01 60 96 95 10
Fax	01 60 96 01 41
Holes	18 L 6025 m Par 72
V'tors	H or Green card
Fees	180fr (350fr)
Loc	25 km SE of Fontainebleau
Arch	Fromanger/Adam

Greenparc (1993)

Route de Villepech, 91280 St Pierre-
du-Perray

Tel	60 75 40 60
Fax	60 75 40 04
Holes	18 L 5839 m SSS 71
V'tors	U
Fees	125fr (250fr)
Loc	30 km SW of Paris
Arch	Robin Nelson

L'Isle Adam (1995)

1 Chemin des Vanneaux, 95290 L'Isle
Adam

Tel	01 34 08 11 11
Fax	01 34 08 11 19
Holes	18 L 6230 m Par 72
V'tors	U
Fees	150–250fr (250–375fr)
Loc	30 km N of Paris
Arch	Ronald Fream

Meaux-Boutigny (1985)

Rue de Barrois, 77470 Boutigny

Tel	60 25 63 98
Holes	18 L 5981 m SSS 72
	9 L 1499 m SSS 30
V'tors	U
Fees	180fr (300fr)
Loc	45 km E of Paris-Highway 4
Arch	Michel Gayon

Mont Griffon

BP 7, 95270 Luzarches

Tel	01 34 68 10 10
Fax	01 34 68 04 37
Holes	18 L 5905 m SSS 70
V'tors	U
Fees	200fr (350fr)
Loc	27 km N of Paris
Arch	Nelson/Huau/Dongradi

Ormesson (1969)

Chemin du Belvedère, 94490 Ormesson-
sur-Marne

Tel	01 45 76 20 71
Fax	01 45 94 86 85
Holes	18 L 6130 m SSS 72
V'tors	H
Fees	200fr (350fr)
Loc	21 km SE of Paris
Arch	Harris/CK Cotton

Ozoir-la-Ferrière (1926)

Château des Agneaux, 77330 Ozoir-la-
Ferrière

Tel	01 60 02 60 79
Fax	01 64 40 28 20
Holes	18 L 5840 m Par 71 SSS 70
	9 L 2700 m Par 35
V'tors	U H
Fees	18 hole:200fr (400fr);
	9 hole:130fr (200fr)
Loc	25 km SE of Paris via A4
	(Porte de Bercy)

Paris International (1991)

18 Route du Golf, 95560 Baillet-en-
France

Tel	34 69 90 00
Fax	34 69 97 15
Holes	18 L 6319 m SSS 72
V'tors	I or M
Fees	450fr (700fr)
Loc	24 km NW of Paris
Arch	Jack Nicklaus

St Aubin (1976)

Route du Golf, 91190 St Aubin

Tel	69 41 25 19
Fax	69 41 02 25
Holes	18 L 5971 m SSS 71
	9 L 1918 m SSS 31
V'tors	U
Fees	100fr (200fr)
Loc	30 km SW of Paris
Arch	Berthet/Rio

St Germain-les-Corbeil

6 Ave du Golf, 91250 St Germain-les-
Corbeil

Tel	60 75 81 54
Fax	60 75 52 89
Holes	18 L 5800 m SSS 71
Loc	30 km S of Paris

St Pierre du Perray (1974)

Melun-Sénart, St Pierre du Perray,
91100 Corbeil

Tel	60 75 17 47
Holes	18 L 6169 m SSS 72
Loc	30 km SE of Paris, off N6
Arch	Hubert Chesneau

Seraincourt (1964)

Gaillonnet-Seraincourt, 95450 Vigny

Tel	34 75 47 28
Fax	34 75 75 47
Holes	18 L 5760 m SSS 70
V'tors	WD–U WE–H
Fees	150fr (300fr)
Loc	35 km NW of Paris

Villarceaux (1971)

Château du Couvent,
95710 Chaussy

Tel	34 67 73 83
Fax	34 67 72 66
Holes	18 L 6175 m SSS 72
V'tors	H
Fees	150–180fr (200–300fr)
Loc	60 km NW of Paris
Arch	M Backer

Languedoc-Roussillon

Cap d'Agde (1989)

4 Ave des Alizés, 34300 Cap d'Agde

Tel	67 26 54 40
Fax	67 26 97 00
Holes	18 L 6160 m SSS 72
V'tors	U
Fees	195–235fr
Loc	25 km E of Béziers
Arch	Ronald Fream

Coulondres (1984)

72 Rue des Erables, 34980 Saint-Gely-
du-Fesc

Tel	04 67 84 13 75
Fax	04 67 84 06 33
Holes	18 L 6175 m SSS 73
V'tors	U
Fees	150fr (200fr)
Loc	10 km N of Montpellier
	towards Ganges
Arch	Donald Harradine

Falgos (1992)

BP 9, 66260 St Laurent-de-Cerdans

Tel	04 68 39 51 42
Fax	04 68 39 52 30
Holes	18 L 5044 m SSS 68
V'tors	U
Fees	200fr (250fr)
Loc	60 km S of Perpignan,
	nr Spanish border (D115)
Arch	H Urachaiz

For list of abbreviations see page 479

Fontcaude (1991)
Domaine de Fontcaude, 34990 Juvignac
Tel   04 67 03 34 30
Fax   04 67 03 34 51
Holes 18 L 6992 m SSS 72
           9 hole short course
V'tors U
Fees   200–250fr
Loc   6 km W of Montpellier
Arch   C Pitman

La Grande-Motte (1987)
Clubhouse du Golf, 34280 La Grande-Motte
Tel   04 67 56 05 00
Fax   04 67 29 18 84
Holes 18 L 6200 m Par 72
           18 L 4000 m Par 58
           6 hole short course
V'tors U
Fees   200fr (260fr)
Loc   18 km E of Montpellier
Arch   Robert Trent Jones

Montpellier Massane
(1988)
Domaine de Massane, 34670 Baillargues
Tel   04 67 87 87 87
Fax   04 67 87 87 90
Holes 18 L 6231 m Par 72
           9 hole Par 3 course
V'tors U
Fees   200fr (260fr)
Loc   9 km E of Montpellier. A9
           Junction 28
Arch   Ronald Fream

Nîmes Campagne
(1968)
Route de Saint Gilles, 30900 Nîmes
Tel   04 66 70 17 37
Fax   04 66 70 03 14
Holes 18 L 6135 m SSS 72
V'tors H
Fees   220fr (250fr)
Loc   7 km S of Nîmes, by Airport
Arch   Morandi/Harradine

Nîmes-Vacquerolles
(1990)
Route de Sauve, 30900 Nîmes
Tel   04 66 23 33 33
Fax   04 66 23 94 94
Holes 18 L 6300 m SSS 72
V'tors U
Fees   170fr (230fr)
Loc   W of Nîmes centre (D999)
Arch   W Baker

St Cyprien (1974)
Le Mas D'Huston, 66750 St Cyprien Plage
Tel   68 37 63 63
Fax   68 37 64 64
Holes 18 L 6480 m SSS 73
           9 L 2724 m SSS 35
V'tors U H
Fees   195fr (250fr)

Loc   15 km SE of Perpignan
Arch   Wright/Tomlinson

St Thomas (1992)
Route de Pézenas, 34500 Béziers
Tel   67 98 62 01
Fax   67 98 61 01
Holes 18 L 6130 m Par 72
V'tors U
Fees   200–250fr (240–250fr)
Loc   7 km NE of Béziers (RN 113)
Arch   Patrice Lambert

Loire Valley

Angers (1963)
Moulin de Pistrait, 49320 St Jean des Mauvrets
Tel   41 91 96 56
Holes 18 L 5460 m Par 70
Fees   170fr (220fr)
Loc   14 km SE of Angers. Right
           bank of Loire.

Anjou G&CC (1990)
Route de Cheffes, 49330 Champigné
Tel   02 41 42 01 01
Fax   02 41 42 04 37
Holes 18 L 6227 m SSS 72
           6 hole short course
V'tors U H
Fees   180fr (220fr)
Loc   23 km N of Angers
Arch   F Hawtree

Avrillé (1988)
Château de la Perrière, 49240 Avrillé
Tel   41 69 22 50
Fax   41 34 44 60
Holes 18 L 6116 m SSS 71
           9 hole Par 3 course
V'tors U
Fees   195fr (230fr)
Loc   5 km N of Angers
Arch   Robert Berthet

La Baule (1976)
44117 Saint-André-des Eaux
Tel   02 40 60 46 18
Fax   02 40 60 41 41
Holes 18 L 6055 m SSS 72
V'tors H
Fees   190–320fr
Loc   Avrillac, 3 km NE of La Baule
Arch   Alliss/Thomas/Gayon

La Bretesche (1967)
Domaine de la Bretesche, 44780 Missillac
Tel   02 51 76 86 86
Fax   02 40 88 36 28
Holes 18 L 6080 m SSS 72
V'tors U
Fees   180fr (300fr)
Loc   8 km NW of Pontchâteau,
           between Nantes and Vannes
Arch   Bill Baker

Cholet (1989)
Allée du Chêne Landry, 49300 Cholet
Tel   41 71 05 01
Fax   41 56 06 94
Holes 18 L 5792 m Par 71
V'tors WD–U WE–H
Fees   175fr (195fr)
Loc   2 km N of Cholet. 52 km SE
           of Nantes
Arch   Olivier Brizon

La Domangère
La Roche-sur-Yon, Route de la Rochelle, 85310 Nesmy
Tel   51 07 60 15
Fax   51 07 64 09
Holes 18 L 6480 m SSS 72
V'tors U
Fees   140–230fr (180–230fr)
Loc   6 km S of La Roche-sur-Yon.
           70 km S of Nantes
Arch   Michel Gayon

Epinay (1991)
Boulevard de l'Epinay, 44470 Carquefou
Tel   40 52 73 74
Fax   40 52 73 20
Holes 18 L 5790 m SSS 71
V'tors U
Fees   160fr (220fr)
Loc   NE of Nantes
Arch   M Hawtree

Fontenelles
Saint-Gilles-Croix-de-Vie, 85220 Aiguillon-sur-Vie
Tel   51 54 13 94
Fax   51 55 45 77
Holes 18 L 6185 m Par 72
V'tors U
Fees   100–220fr
Loc   6 km E of St-Gilles-Croix-de-
           Vie. 75 km SW of Nantes
Arch   Yves Bureau

Ile d'Or (1988)
BP 10, 49270 La Varenne
Tel   40 98 58 00
Fax   40 98 51 62
Holes 18 L 6292 m Par 72
           9 L 1217 m Par 27
V'tors U
Fees   140fr (220fr)
Loc   30 km NE of Nantes
Arch   Michel Gayon

Laval-Changé (1972)
Le Jariel, 53000 Changé-les-Laval
Tel   02 43 53 16 03
Fax   02 43 49 35 15
Holes 18 L 6068 m Par 72 SSS 72
           9 L 3388 m
V'tors WD–U WE–NA
Fees   180fr (220fr)
Loc   5 km N of Laval. 60 km E of
           Rennes
Arch   JP Foures

Le Mans Mulsanne
(1961)
Route de Tours, 72230 Mulsanne
Tel 43 42 00 36
Fax 43 42 21 31
Holes 18 L 5821 m SSS 71
V'tors H
Fees 200–360fr (240–400fr)
Loc Mulsanne, 12 km S of Le Mans

Nantes
44360 Vigneux de Bretagne
Tel 02 40 63 25 82
Holes 18 L 5940 m SSS 72
V'tors H
Fees 170fr (250fr)
Loc 12 km NW of Nantes
Arch Frank Pennink

Nantes Erdre (1990)
Chemin du Bout des Landes, 44300 Nantes
Tel 02 40 59 21 21
Fax 02 51 84 94 50
Holes 18 L 6003 m SSS 71
V'tors U
Fees 170fr (220fr)
Loc Nantes
Arch Yves Bureau

Les Olonnes
Gazé, 85340 Olonne-sur-Mer
Tel 51 33 16 16
Fax 51 30 10 45
Holes 18 L 6127 m Par 72
V'tors U
Fees 120–250fr
Loc 3 km N of Les Sables d'Olonne
Arch Bruno Parpoil

Pornic (1912)
49 Boulevard de l'Océan, Sainte-Marie/Mer, 44210 Pornic
Tel 40 82 06 69
Fax 40 82 80 65
Holes 18 L 6119 m SSS 72
V'tors U
Fees 105–230fr
Loc 1 km E of Pornic. 30 km S of La Baule
Arch Michel Gayon

Port Bourgenay (1990)
Avenue de la Mine, Port Bourgenay, 85440 Talmont-St-Hilaire
Tel 02 51 23 35 45
Fax 02 51 23 35 48
Holes 18 L 5800 m SSS 72
V'tors U
Fees 110–270fr
Loc 10 km SE of Sables d'Olonne. 100 km S of Nantes
Arch Pierre Thevenin

Sablé-Solesmes
Domaine de l'Outinière, Route de Pincé, 72300 Sablé-sur-Sarthe
Tel 02 43 95 28 78
Fax 02 43 92 39 05

Holes 27 holes SSS 72:
Forêt 9 L 3197 m
Rivière 9 L 2992 m
Cascade 9 L 3069 m
V'tors U
Fees 190–280fr
Loc 40 km SW of Le Mans
Arch Michel Gayon

St Jean-de-Monts (1988)
Ave des Pays de Monts, 85160 Saint Jean-de-Monts
Tel 51 58 82 73
Fax 51 59 18 32
Holes 18 L 5962 m SSS 72
V'tors U
Loc 60 km SW of Nantes on coast

Sargé (1990)
Rue du Golf, 72190 Sargé-les Le Mans
Tel 02 43 76 25 07
Fax 02 43 76 45 25
Holes 18 L 6054 m SSS 72
V'tors U
Fees 120fr (180fr)
Loc 6 km E of Le Mans
Arch Antoine d'Ormesson

Savenay (1990)
44260 Savenay
Tel 40 56 88 05
Fax 40 56 89 04
Holes 18 L 6335 m Par 73
9 L 1122 m Par 30
V'tors U
Fees 150–230fr
Loc 36 km W of Nantes. 30 km E of La Baule
Arch Michel Gayon

Normandy

Bagnoles-de-l'Orne
(1988)
Route de Domfront, 61140 Bagnoles-de-l'Orne
Tel 33 37 81 42
Holes 9 L 2400 m SSS 66
Fees 120fr (150fr)
Loc Bagnoles, 80 km S of Caen

Bellême-St-Martin
(1988)
Les Sablons, 61130 Bellême
Tel 33 73 00 07
Fax 33 73 00 17
Holes 18 L 6011 m SSS 72
V'tors U
Fees 170fr (250fr)
Loc 40 km NE of Le Mans
Arch Eric Vialatel

Beuzeval-Houlgate (1981)
Route de Gonneville, 14510 Houlgate
Tel 02 31 24 80 49
Fax 02 31 28 04 48
Holes 18 L 5558 m SSS 72

V'tors U
Fees 130–240fr
Loc 2 km S of Houlgate. 15 km SW of Deauville
Arch Alliss/Thomas

Cabourg-Le Home
(1907)
38 Av Président Réné Coty, Le Home Varaville, 14390 Cabourg
Tel 02 31 91 25 56
Fax 02 31 91 18 30
Holes 18 L 5234 m SSS 68
V'tors H
Fees 130–260fr
Loc 4 km W of Cabourg
Arch Jackson/Brizon

Caen (1990)
Le Vallon, 14112 Bieville-Beuville
Tel 31 94 72 09
Fax 31 47 45 30
Holes 18 holes SSS 72 Par 72
9 hole course
V'tors U
Fees 160fr (200fr)
Loc 5 km N of Caen (D60)
Arch F Hawtree

Champ de Bataille
Château du Champ de Bataille, 27110 Le Neubourg
Tel 32 35 03 72
Fax 32 35 83 10
Holes 18 L 6575 m SSS 72
V'tors U
Fees 220fr (330fr)
Loc 28 km NW of Evreux. 45 km SW of Rouen
Arch Nelson/Huau

Cherbourg (1973)
Domaine des Roches, 50470 La Glacerie
Tel 33 44 45 48
Holes 9 L 2791 m SSS 35
V'tors H
Fees 120fr
Loc 6 km S of Cherbourg

Clécy (1988)
Manoir de Cantelou, 14570 Clécy
Tel 02 31 69 72 72
Fax 02 31 69 70 22
Holes 18 L 5965 m Par 72
V'tors U
Fees 130–250fr
Loc 30 km S of Caen, via D562
Arch W Baker

Coutainville (1925)
Ave du Golf, 50230 Agon-Coutainville
Tel 33 47 03 31
Holes 9 L 5210 m SSS 68
V'tors H
Fees 150fr
Loc 12 km W of Coutances. 75 km S of Cherbourg

Dieppe-Pourville (1897)

51 Route de Pourville, 76200 Dieppe

Tel	35 84 25 05
Fax	35 84 97 11
Holes	18 L 5763 m SSS 70
V'tors	U
Fees	150–190fr (190–230fr)
Loc	2 km W of Dieppe towards Pourville
Arch	Willie Park

Étretat (1908)

BP No 7, Route du Havre, 76790 Étretat

Tel	35 27 04 89
Holes	18 L 5994 m SSS 72
V'tors	H
Fees	250–310fr
Loc	25 km N of Le Havre. Étretat 1 km
Arch	Chantepie/Fruchet

Fontenay-en-Cotentin (1975)

Fontenay-sur-Mer, 50310 Montebourg

Tel	33 21 44 27
Holes	9 L 2954 m Par 36
V'tors	U
Fees	110fr (140fr)
Loc	32 km SE of Cherbourg, via RN13/D42

Forêt Verte

Bosc Guerard, 76710 Montville

Tel	35 33 62 94
Holes	18 L 7000 yds SSS 72
V'tors	U
Fees	120fr (180fr)
Loc	10 km N of Rouen
Arch	Thierry Huau

Granville (1912)

Bréville, 50290 Bréhal

Tel	02 33 50 23 06
Fax	02 33 61 91 87
Holes	18 L 5854 m Par 71
	9 L 2323 m Par 33
V'tors	U
Fees	18 hole–155fr (225fr)
	9 hole–100fr (130fr)
Loc	5 km N of Granville
Arch	Colt/Allison/Hawtree

Le Havre (1933)

Hameau Saint-Supplix, 76930 Octeville-sur-Mer

Tel	35 46 36 50
Fax	35 46 32 66
Holes	18 L 5830 m SSS 70
V'tors	H
Fees	150fr (250fr)
Loc	10 km N of Le Havre

Léry Poses (1989)

BP 7, 27740 Poses

Tel	32 59 47 42
Holes	18 L 6242 m SSS 73
	9 hole Par 3 course

V'tors	U
Fees	150fr (200fr)
Loc	25 km SE of Rouen
Arch	J Baker

New Golf Deauville (1929)

14 Saint Arnoult, 14800 Deauville

Tel	02 31 14 24 24
Fax	02 31 14 24 25
Holes	18 L 5933 m SSS 71
	9 L 3033 m SSS 72
V'tors	U–booking required
Fees	250–350fr
Loc	3 km S of Deauville
Arch	Simpson/Cotton

Omaha Beach (1986)

Ferme St Sauveur, 14520 Port-en-Bessin

Tel	02 31 21 72 94
Fax	02 31 51 79 61
Holes	18 L 6229 m SSS 72
	9 L 2875 m SSS 35
V'tors	U H
Fees	150–220fr (260fr)
Loc	8 km N of Bayeux
Arch	Yves Bureau

Parc de Brotonne (1991)

Jumièges, 76480 Duclair

Tel	02 35 05 32 97
Fax	02 35 37 99 97
Holes	18 L 6040 m SSS 72
V'tors	U
Fees	100fr (160fr)
Loc	20 km W of Rouen
Arch	JP Fourès

Rouen-Mont St Aignan (1911)

Rue Francis Poulenc, 76130 Mont St Aignan

Tel	02 35 76 38 65
Fax	02 35 75 13 86
Holes	18 L 5522 m SSS 70
V'tors	H WE–H after 4pm
Fees	180fr (250fr)
Loc	4 km N of Rouen

St Gatien Deauville (1987)

14130 St Gatien-des-Bois

Tel	31 65 19 99
Fax	31 65 11 24
Holes	18 L 6272 m Par 72
	9 L 3035 m Par 36
V'tors	U
Fees	200fr (300fr)
Loc	8 km E of Deauville
Arch	Olivier Brizon

St Julien

St Julien-sur-Calonne, 14130 Pont-l'Évêque

Tel	31 64 30 30
Fax	31 64 12 43
Holes	18 L 6290 m SSS 73
	9 L 2133 m SSS 33
V'tors	U

Fees	130–160fr (190–230fr)
Loc	3 km SE of Pont l'Évêque
Arch	Prat/Baker

St Saëns (1987)

76680 St Saëns

Tel	35 34 25 24
Fax	35 34 43 33
Holes	18 L 6004 m SSS 71
V'tors	U
Fees	D–125fr (D–250fr)
Loc	30 km NE of Rouen
Arch	D Robinson

Le Vaudreuil (1962)

27100 Le Vaudreuil

Tel	32 59 02 60
Fax	32 59 43 88
Holes	18 L 6411 m SSS 73
V'tors	H
Fees	170fr (250fr)
Loc	6 km NE of Louviers. 25 km SE of Rouen
Arch	F Hawtree

North East

Ammerschwihr

BP 19, Route des Trois Épis, 68770 Ammerschwihr

Tel	89 47 17 30
Fax	89 47 17 77
Holes	18 L 5795 m Par 70
	9 hole short course
V'tors	U
Fees	200fr (250fr)
Loc	8 km W of Colmar. 70 km S of Strasbourg
Arch	Robert Berthet

Bâle G&CC (1928)

Rue de Wentzwiller, 68220 Hagenthal-le-Bas

Tel	03 89 68 50 91
Fax	03 89 68 55 66
Holes	18 L 6255 m Par 72 SSS 73
V'tors	WD–H (max 32) WE–M
Fees	320fr (360fr)
Loc	15 km SW of Basle
Arch	B von Limburger

Besançon (1968)

La Chevillotte, 25620 Mamirolle

Tel	03 81 55 73 54
Fax	03 81 55 88 64
Holes	18 L 6070 m SSS 73
V'tors	H
Fees	200fr (250fr)
Loc	12 km E of Besançon
Arch	Michael Fenn

Bitche (1988)

Rue des Prés, 57230 Bitche

Tel	87 96 15 30
Fax	87 96 08 04
Holes	18 L 6082 m SSS 72
	9 L 2293 m SSS 34

V'tors U
Fees 18 hole–170fr (250fr)
9 hole–120fr (150fr)
Loc 75 km NW of Strasbourg.
55 km SE of Saarbrücken
Arch Fromanger

Châlons-en-Champagne
(1988)
La Grande Romanie, 51460 Courtisols
Tel 07 55 24 30
Fax 26 66 66 81
Holes 18 L 6578 m SSS 76
V'tors U
Fees D–200fr (D–250fr)
Loc 6 km from A4/A26 Junction,
nr Châlons-sur-Marne. A26
Junction 28
Arch Alain Tribout

Château de Bournel
(1990)
25680 Cubry
Tel 81 86 00 10
Fax 81 86 01 06
Holes 18 L 5985 m SSS 72
Fees 180fr (270fr)
Loc 50 km NE of Besançon
Arch Robert Berthet

Combles-en-Barrois
(1948)
14 Rue Basse, 55000 Combles-en-Barrois
Tel 03 29 45 16 03
Fax 03 29 45 16 06
Holes 18 L 6100 m Par 72
V'tors U
Fees 180fr (200fr)
Loc 80 km W of Nancy, nr Bar-le-
Duc
Arch Michel Gayon

Épinal (1985)
Rue du Merle-Blanc, 88001 Épinal
Tel 29 34 65 97
Holes 18 L 5700 m SSS 70
V'tors H
Fees 100fr
Loc Épinal, 70 km S of Nancy
Arch Michel Gayon

Faulquemont-Pontpierre
(1993)
Rue du Golf, 57380 Faulquemont
Tel 87 29 21 21
Fax 87 90 76 25
Holes 18 L 6000 m SSS 72
9 hole par 3 course
V'tors U
Fees 140fr (200fr)
Loc 30 km E of Metz
Arch Flipo/Fourès

Forêt d'Orient
BP13 Rouilly-Sacey, 10220 Piney
Tel 25 46 37 78
Holes 18 L 6120 m Par 72

V'tors U
Fees 150fr (200fr)
Loc 20 km E of Troyes
Arch E Rossi

La Grange aux Ormes
La Grange aux Ormes, 57157 Marly
Tel 03 87 63 10 62
Fax 03 87 55 01 77
Holes 18 L 6200 m Par 72
9 L 2001 m Par 31
V'tors U H
Fees 200fr (230fr)
Loc 3 km S of Metz
Arch Philippe Gourdon

Kempferhof (1988)
351 Rue du Moulin, 67115 Plobsheim
Tel 88 98 72 72
Fax 88 98 74 76
Holes 18 L 6020 m SSS 72
V'tors H
Fees 330fr (450fr)
Loc 10 km S of Strasbourg
Arch Robert von Hagge

La Largue G&CC
(1988)
*Chemin du Largweg,
68580 Mooslargue*
Tel 03 89 07 67 67
Fax 03 89 25 62 83
Holes 18 L 6150 m SSS 72
V'tors WD–H WE–NA before
noon H
Fees 220fr (320fr)
Loc 25 km W of Basle
Arch Jean Garaialde

Metz-Cherisey (1963)
Château de Cherisey, 57420 Cherisey
Tel 03 87 52 70 18
Fax 03 87 52 42 44
Holes 18 L 6172 m SSS 72
V'tors H
Fees 200fr (250fr)
Loc 15 km SE of Metz
Arch Donald Harradine

Nancy-Aingeray (1962)
Aingeray, 54460 Liverdun
Tel 03 83 24 53 87
Holes 18 L 5577 m SSS 69
V'tors H
Fees 200fr (250fr)
Loc 17 km NW of Nancy
Arch Michael Fenn

Nancy-Pulnoy (1993)
10 Rue du Golf, 54425 Pulnoy
Tel 03 83 18 10 18
Fax 03 83 18 10 19
Holes 18 L 6000 m SSS 72
9 hole Par 3 course
V'tors WD–U WE–H
Fees 170fr (250fr)
Loc 10 km E of Nancy
Arch Hawtree/Flipo

Prunevelle (1930)
*Ferme des Petits-Bans,
25420 Dampierre-sur-le-Doubs*
Tel 81 98 11 77
Fax 81 90 28 65
Holes 18 L 6281 m SSS 73
Fees 200fr (250fr)
Loc 10 km S of Montbéliard, on
D126

Reims-Champagne
(1928)
*Château des Dames de France,
51390 Gueux*
Tel 03 26 05 46 10
Fax 03 26 05 46 19
Holes 18 L 6026 m SSS 72
V'tors U
Fees 200fr (250fr)
Loc 10 km W of Reims
Arch Michael Fenn

Rhin Mulhouse (1969)
Ile du Rhin, 68490 Chalampe
Tel 89 26 07 86
Fax 89 26 27 80
Holes 18 L 5991 m SSS 72
V'tors WE–M
Fees 240fr (330fr)
Loc 20 km E of Mulhouse
Arch Donald Harradine

Rougemont-le-Château
*Route de Masevaux, 90110 Rougemont-
le-Château*
Tel 03 84 23 74 74
Fax 03 84 23 03 15
Holes 18 L 6002 m SSS 72
V'tors U H
Fees 180fr (300fr)
Loc 18 km NE of Belfort.
25 km NW of Mulhouse
Arch Robert Berthet

Strasbourg (1934)
Route du Rhin, 67400 Illkirch
Tel 88 66 17 22
Fax 88 65 05 67
Holes 27 holes:
6105-6138 m SSS 72-73
V'tors WD–H (max 35)
Fees WD only–230fr
Loc 10 km S of Strasbourg
Arch Donald Harradine

Technopole de Metz
Rue Félix Savart, 57070 Metz
Tel 87 20 33 11
Fax 87 76 34 05
Holes 18 L 5774 m SSS 71
6 hole Par 3 course
V'tors H or Green card
Fees 170fr (190fr)
Loc SE of Metz centre
Arch Robert Berthet

Troyes-Cordelière (1957)

Château de la Cordelière,
10210 Chaource
Tel   25 40 18 76
Fax   25 40 13 66
Holes   18 L 6154 m SSS 72
V'tors   H
Fees   180fr (250fr)
Loc   NE of Chaource on N443.
             30 km SE of Troyes
Arch   P Hirigoyen

Val de Sorne

Vernantois, 39570 Lons-le-Saunier
Tel   84 43 04 80
Fax   84 47 31 21
Holes   18 L 6000 m SSS 72
V'tors   U
Fees   170–190fr (200–250fr)
Loc   4kms SE of Lons-le-Saunier,
             between Geneva and Lyon
Arch   Hugues Lambert

La Vitarderie (1986)

Chemin de Bourdonnerie BP#41,
51700 Dormans
Tel   26 58 25 09
Fax   26 59 33 88
Holes   18 L 5969 m SSS 72
V'tors   U
Fees   100fr (150fr)
Loc   Dormans, 20 km SW of Reims
Arch   Olivier Brizon

Vittel

BP 122, 88804 Vittel-Cedex
Tel   29 08 18 80 (1 May-31 Oct)
Holes   St Jean 18 L 6326 m SSS 72
             Peulin 18 L 6100 m SSS 72
             9 hole course
Fees   200fr Sat–250fr Sun–200fr
Loc   Vittel, 70 km S of Nancy
Arch   Allison/Morrison/Begin

La Wantzenau (1991)

C D 302, 67610 La Wantzenau
Tel   03 88 96 37 73
Fax   03 88 96 34 71
Holes   18 L 6400 m SSS 72
V'tors   H
Fees   260fr (400fr)
Loc   12 km N of Strasbourg
Arch   Pern/Garaialde

Paris Region

Béthemont-Chisan CC

12 Rue du Parc de Béthemont, 78300
Poissy
Tel   39 75 51 13
Fax   39 75 49 90
Holes   18 L 6035 m SSS 72
V'tors   U
Fees   300fr (500fr)
Loc   30 km W of Paris
Arch   Bernhard Langer

La Boulie

La Boulie, 78000 Versailles
Tel   39 50 59 41
Holes   18 L 6055 m SSS 71
             18 L 6206 m SSS 72
             9 hole course
V'tors   H WE–M
Fees   430fr
Loc   15 km SW of Paris

Disneyland Paris

(1992)
1 Allee de la Mare Houleuse,
77400 Magny-le-Hongre
Tel   60 45 68 04
Fax   60 45 68 33
Holes   18 L 6221 m Par 72
             9 L 2905 m Par 36
V'tors   U
Fees   18 hole: 120–160fr
             (200–270fr)
             9 hole: 100–120fr (120–170fr)
Loc   32 km E of Paris via A4
Arch   Ronald Fream

Feucherolles (1992)

78810 Feucherolles
Tel   01 30 54 94 94
Fax   01 30 54 92 37
Holes   18 L 6358 m Par 72
V'tors   U
Fees   300–350fr (380–490fr)
Loc   23 km W of Paris
Arch   JM Poellot

Fourqueux (1963)

Rue Saint Nom 36,
78112 Fourqueux
Tel   34 51 41 47
Fax   39 21 00 70
Holes   27 holes:
             5615-6025 m Par 73-74
V'tors   WD–U WE–M
Fees   350fr (390fr)
Loc   4 km SW of St Germain-en-
             Laye, W of Paris

Isabella (1969)

RN12, Sainte-Appoline,
78370 Plaisir
Tel   30 54 10 62
Fax   30 54 67 58
Holes   18 L 5629 m SSS 71
V'tors   WD–H WE–NA
Fees   250fr
Loc   28 km W of Paris (RN12)
Arch   Paul Rolin

Joyenval (1992)

Chemin de la Tuilerie,
78240 Chambourcy
Tel   39 22 27 50
Fax   39 79 12 90
Holes   Retz 18 L 6211 m Par 72
             Marly 18 L 6249 m Par 72
V'tors   M
Loc   25 km N of Paris, nr St
             Germain-en-Laye
Arch   Robert Trent Jones Sr

National Golf Club (1990)

2 Avenue du Golf, 78280 Guyancourt
Tel   01 30 43 36 00
Fax   01 30 43 85 58
Holes   Albatros 18 L 6515 m Par 72
             Aigle 18 L 5936 m Par 71
             Oiselet 9 L 2198 m Par 32
V'tors   H or Green card
Fees   150–240fr (225–360fr)
Loc   St Quentin-en-Yvelines, SW
             of Paris, beyond Versailles
             (D36)
Arch   Chesneau

Le Prieuré (1965)

78440 Sailly
Tel   34 76 70 12
Fax   34 76 71 62
Holes   Ouest 18 L 6274 m SSS 72
             Est 18 L 6157 m SSS 72
V'tors   WD–H
Fees   260fr
Loc   Sailly, 10 km NW of Meulan
             (D130). 45 km NW of Paris
Arch   F Hawtree

Rochefort (1964)

78730 Rochefort-en-Yvelines
Tel   30 41 31 81
Fax   30 41 94 01
Holes   18 L 5735 m SSS 71
V'tors   U
Fees   250–450fr
Loc   45 km SW of Paris
Arch   Hawtree

St Cloud (1911)

60 Rue du 19 Janvier,
Garches 92380
Tel   01 47 01 01 85
Fax   01 47 01 19 57
Holes   18 L 5975 m SSS 72
             18 L 4867 m SSS 67
V'tors   H
Fees   440fr Sat–540fr Sun–600fr
Loc   Porte Dauphine, 9 km W of
             Paris
Arch   HS Colt

St Germain (1922)

Route de Poissy, 78100 St Germain-
en-Laye
Tel   01 39 10 30 30
Fax   01 39 10 30 31
Holes   18 L 6117 m SSS 72
             9 L 2030 m SSS 33
V'tors   WD–H WE–M
Fees   400fr
Loc   20 km W of Paris
Arch   HS Colt

St Nom-La-Bretèche

(1959)
Hameau Tuilerie-Bignon,
78860 St Nom-La-Bretèche
Tel   01 30 80 04 40
Fax   01 34 62 60 44
Holes   18 L 6685 yds SSS 72
             18 L 6712 yds SSS 72

V'tors H
Fees   WD only–485fr
Loc   24 km W of Paris on A-13
Arch   F Hawtree

St Quentin-en-Yvelines

RD 912, 78190 Trappes
Tel   30 50 86 40
Holes   18 L 5900 m SSS 71
18 L 5753 m SSS 70
V'tors H
Fees   150fr (210fr)
Loc   20 km SW of Paris
Arch   Hubert Chesneau

Tremblay Golf Academy
(1991)

78490 Le Tremblay-sur-Mauldre
Tel   01 34 94 25 25
Fax   01 34 94 25 30
Holes   9 L 3100 m SSS 72
9 hole short course
V'tors H
Fees   100fr (140–180fr)
Loc   35 km W of Paris
Arch   Robert Berthet

La Vaucouleurs   (1987)

Rue de l'Eglise, 78910 Civry-la-Forêt
Tel   01 34 87 62 29
Fax   01 34 87 70 09
Holes   Rivière 18 L 6298 m Par 73
Vallons 18 L 5630 m SSS 70
V'tors H or Green card
Fees   200fr (350fr)
Loc   50 km W of Paris, between
Mantes and Houdan
Arch   Michel Gayon

Les Yvelines

Château de la Couharde,
78940 La-Queue-les-Yvelines
Tel   01 34 86 48 89
Fax   01 34 86 50 31
Holes   18 L 6344 m Par 72
9 L 2065 m Par 31
V'tors U
Fees   170fr (290fr)
Loc   Montfort-l'Amaury, 45 km
W of Paris
Arch   HJ Baker

Provence &
Côte d'Azur

Aix Marseille   (1935)

13290 Les Milles
Tel   04 42 24 40 41/
04 42 24 23 01
Fax   04 42 39 97 48
Holes   18 L 6291 m SSS 73
V'tors H
Fees   D–150–220fr (D–250fr)
Loc   7 km SW of Aix-en-Provence.
15 km N of Marseille

Barbaroux   (1989)

Route de Cabasse, 83170 Brignoles
Tel   04 94 69 63 63
Fax   04 94 59 00 93
Holes   18 L 6367 m SSS 72
V'tors U
Fees   260fr (260fr)
Loc   Brignoles, 50 km E of Aix.
40 km N of Toulon
Arch   PB Dye/PD Dye

Les Baux de Provence
(1987)

Domaine de Manville,
13520 Les Baux-de-Provence
Tel   90 54 40 20
Fax   90 54 40 93
Holes   9 L 2812 m SSS 36
V'tors U H
Fees   D–250fr 9 holes–100fr (150fr)
Loc   15 km NE of Arles. 15 km S
of Avignon. 80 km W of
Marseilles
Arch   Martin Hawtree

Beauvallon-Grimaud

Boulevard des Collines, 83120 Sainte-
Maxime
Tel   94 96 16 98
Holes   9 L 2503 m SSS 34
V'tors H
Fees   200–240fr
Loc   3 km SW of Sainte Maxime

Biot   (1930)

La Bastide du Roi, 06410 Biot
Tel   93 65 08 48
Fax   93 65 05 63
Holes   18 L 5054 m Par 70
V'tors U
Fees   200fr
Loc   Antibes 5 km. Nice 15 km

Cannes-Mandelieu
(1891)

Route de Golf, 06210 Mandelieu
Tel   93 49 55 39
Fax   93 49 92 90
Holes   18 L 5871 m SSS 71
9 L 2852 m SSS 33
V'tors U
Fees   260fr (300fr)
Loc   Mandelieu, 7 km W
of Cannes

Cannes-Mougins
(1925)

175 Route d'Antibes, 06250 Mougins
Tel   93 75 79 13
Fax   93 75 27 60
Holes   18 L 6304 m SSS 72
V'tors H
Fees   320fr (360fr)
Loc   8 km NE of Cannes (D35)
Arch   Colt/Simpson (1925).
Alliss/Thomas (1977)

Château L'Arc   (1985)

Domaine de Château L'Arc,
13710 Fuveau
Tel   42 53 28 38
Fax   42 29 08 41
Holes   18 L 6300 m SSS 71
V'tors U
Fees   250fr (290fr)
Loc   15 km SE of Aix-en-Provence
Arch   Michel Gayon

Châteaublanc

Les Plans, 84310 Morières-les-
Avignon
Tel   04 90 33 39 08
Fax   04 90 33 43 24
Holes   18 L 6141 m SSS 72
9 L 1267 m Par 28
V'tors H
Fees   170fr (210fr)
Loc   5 km SE of Avignon,
nr Airport
Arch   Thierry Sprecher

Digne-les-Bains   (1990)

St Pierre de Gaubert,
0400 Digne-les-Bains
Tel   92 30 58 00
Fax   92 30 58 39
Holes   18 L 5861 m SSS 72
V'tors U
Fees   160–200fr
Loc   100 km NE of Aix-en-
Provence
Arch   Robert Berthet

Estérel Latitudes   (1989)

Ave du Golf, 83700 St Raphaël
Tel   04 94 82 47 88
Fax   04 94 44 64 61
Holes   18 L 5921 m SSS 71
9 L 1392 m Par 29
V'tors U H
Fees   285fr
Loc   6 km N of St-Raphaël
Arch   Robert Trent Jones

Frégate   (1992)

Domaine de Frégate RD#559,
83270 St Cyr-sur-Mer
Tel   04 94 32 50 50
Fax   04 94 29 96 94
Holes   18 L 6210 m SSS 72
9 hole short course
V'tors U H
Fees   260fr (300fr)
Loc   25 km W of Toulon on coast
Arch   Ronald Fream

Gap-Bayard   (1988)

Centre d'Oxygénation, 05000 Gap
Tel   04 92 50 16 83
Fax   04 92 50 17 05
Holes   18 L 6023 m SSS 72
V'tors U
Fees   180fr (195fr)
Loc   7 km N of Gap. 80 km S of
Grenoble
Arch   Hugues Lambert

Grand Avignon (1989)

BP 121, Les Chênes Verts, 84270
Vedene
Tel   90 31 49 94
Fax   90 31 01 21
Holes 18 L 6046 m SSS 69
           9 hole short course
V'tors U
Fees   200–230fr
Loc   Vedene, 5 km NE of Avignon
Arch   G Roumeas

La Grande Bastide (1990)

Chemin des Picholines,
06740 Châteauneuf de Grasse
Tel   04 93 77 70 08
Fax   04 93 77 72 36
Holes 18 L 6105 m SSS 72
V'tors U H
Fees   270fr (300fr)
Loc   Grasse, 17 km N of Cannes
Arch   Cabell Robinson

Grasse CC (1992)

1 Route des Trois Ponts, 06130 Grasse
Tel   04 93 60 55 44
Fax   04 93 60 55 19
Holes 18 L 6021 m SSS 72
V'tors U
Fees   265fr (290fr)
Loc   18 km N of Cannes
Arch   JP Fourès

Le Lavandou

2 Ave du Cap Nègre, Cavalière,
83980 Le Lavandou
Tel   94 05 75 80
Holes 18 L 5649 m Par 72
V'tors U
Fees   250–350fr
Loc   50 km E of Toulon, between
           Hyères and St Tropez
Arch   Yves Bureau

Monte Carlo (1910)

Route du Mont-Agel, 06320 La Turbie
Tel   04 93 41 09 11
Fax   04 93 41 09 55
Holes 18 L 5679 m SSS 71
V'tors H
Fees   350fr (450fr)
Loc   Mont Agel, La Turbie,
           10 km N of Monte Carlo

Opio-Valbonne (1966)

Château de la Begude, Route de
Roquefort-les-Pins, 06650 Opio
Tel   04 93 12 00 08
Fax   04 93 12 26 00
Holes 18 L 5892 m SSS 72
V'tors H
Fees   320fr (350fr)
Loc   15 km N of Cannes
Arch   Donald Harradine

Pierrevert (1986)

La Grande Gardette, 04860 Pierrevert
Tel   04 92 72 17 19
Fax   04 92 72 59 12

Holes 18 L 6040 m SSS 72
V'tors U
Fees   200fr
Loc   5 km SW of Manosque.
           45 km NE of Aix
Arch   Artea

Pont Royal (1992)

Pont Royal, 13370 Mallemort
Tel   04 90 57 40 79
Fax   04 90 59 45 83
Holes 18 L 6248 m SSS 74
V'tors H
Fees   200–300fr
Loc   35 km SE of Avignon on N7,
           between Avignon and Aix
Arch   Severiano Ballesteros

Provence G&CC (1991)

Route de Fontaine de Vaucluse, L'Isle
sur la Sorgue, 84800 Saumane
Tel   90 20 20 65
Fax   90 20 32 01
Holes 18 L 6045 m SSS 72
           9 hole short course
V'tors U
Fees   200fr (240fr)
Loc   20 km E of Avignon
Arch   Jean Garaialde

Riviera Golf (1991)

Avenue des Amazones, 06210
Mandelieu
Tel   (04) 92 97 67 67
Fax   (04) 92 97 66 57
Holes 18 L 5736 m SSS 72
V'tors H–max 24 (men) 28 (ladies)
Fees   270fr
Loc   10 km SW of Cannes, off A8
Arch   Robert Trent Jones

Roquebrune (1989)

CD 7, 83520 Roquebrune-sur-Argens
Tel   94 82 92 91
Fax   94 82 94 74
Holes 18 L 6031 m SSS 71
V'tors H
Fees   240fr (240fr)
Loc   35 km N of Saint-Tropez.
           40 km SW of Cannes
Arch   Udo Barth

Royal Mougins (1993)

424 Avenue du Roi, 06250 Mougins
Tel   04 92 92 49 69
Fax   04 92 92 49 70
Holes 18 L 6004 m SSS 72
V'tors H or I
Fees   800fr (inc lunch)
Loc   5 km N of Cannes
Arch   Robert von Hagge

La Sainte-Baume (1988)

83860 Nans-les-Pins
Tel   04 94 78 60 12
Fax   04 94 78 63 52
Holes 18 L 6134 m SSS 72
V'tors U
Fees   190fr (250fr)

Loc   30 km S of Aix-en-Provence,
           via A8 (exit Saint Maximin)
Arch   Robert Berthet

Sainte-Maxime

Route de Débarquement,
83120 Sainte-Maxime
Tel   94 49 26 60
Fax   94 49 00 39
Holes 18 L 6155 m SSS 71
V'tors H
Fees   280fr
Loc   15 km N of Saint Tropez.
           80 km W of Nice (RN98)
Arch   Donald Harradine

St Endreol (1992)

Route de Bagnols-en-Forêt,
83920 La Motte
Tel   04 94 99 22 99
Fax   04 94 99 23 99
Holes 18 L 6219 m SSS 73
V'tors U H
Fees   280–300fr
Loc   30 km N of St Tropez.
           30 km W of Cannes
Arch   Michel Gayon

La Salette (1988)

Impasse des Vaudrans,
13011 La Valentine Marseille
Tel   04 91 27 12 16
Fax   04 91 27 21 33
Holes 18 L 5436 m SSS 69
V'tors U
Fees   190fr (250fr)
Loc   Nr centre of Marseilles
Arch   Michel Gayon

Servanes (1989)

Domaine de Servanes, 13890 Mouriès
Tel   04 90 47 59 95
Fax   04 90 47 52 58
Holes 18 L 6100m SSS 72
V'tors H
Fees   200fr (250fr)
Loc   35 km S of Avignon
Arch   Sprecher/Watine

Taulane

Domaine du Château de Taulane RN
85, 83840 La Martre
Tel   04 93 60 31 30
Fax   04 93 60 33 23
Holes 18 L 6250 m Par 72
V'tors H
Fees   200–300fr (350fr)
Loc   55 km N of Cannes on N85
           (Route Napoleon)
Arch   Gary Player

Valcros (1964)

Domaine de Valcros, 83250 La Londe-
les-Maures
Tel   04 94 66 81 02
Fax   04 94 35 03 73
Holes 18 L 5274 m SSS 68
V'tors H
Fees   230fr (280fr)
Loc   10 km W of Le Lavandou
Arch   F Hawtree

Valescure (1895)

BP 451, 83704 St-Raphaël Cedex

Tel	94 82 40 46
Fax	94 82 41 42
Holes	18 L 5067 m Par 68
V'tors	U H
Fees	250fr
Loc	5 km E of St-Raphaël
Arch	Lord Ashcombe

Vievola (1978)

06430 Tende

Tel	93 04 61 02
Fax	93 04 73 89
Holes	9 L 2004 m SSS 62
V'tors	U
Fees	120fr (150fr)
Loc	4 km from Italian border (RN 204). 40 km N of Monte Carlo
Mis	Open May-Oct

Rhône-Alps

Aix-les-Bains (1913)

Avenue du Golf, 73100 Aix-les-Bains

Tel	79 61 23 35
Fax	79 34 06 01
Holes	18 L 5597 m SSS 71
V'tors	H
Fees	200fr (300fr)
Loc	3 km S of Aix

Albon (1989)

Domaine de Senaud, Albon, 26140 St Rambert d'Albon

Tel	04 75 03 03 90
Fax	04 75 03 11 01
Holes	18 L 6108 m Par 72
	9 L 1260 m Par 29
V'tors	U
Fees	180–240fr
Loc	60 km S of Lyon, motorway exit Chanas
Arch	Antoine d'Ormesson

Annecy (1953)

Echarvines, 74290 Talloires

Tel	50 60 12 89
Fax	50 60 08 80
Holes	18 L 5017 m SSS 68
V'tors	H
Fees	200–250fr
Loc	13 km E of Annecy
Arch	Cecil Blandford

Annonay-Gourdan (1988)

Domaine de Gourdan, 07430 Saint Clair

Tel	75 67 03 84
Fax	75 67 79 50
Holes	18 L 5900 m SSS 71
V'tors	U
Fees	180fr (210fr)
Loc	35 km SE of St Etienne. 50 km SW of Lyon
Arch	Sprecher/Watine

Les Arcs

B P 18, 73706 Les Arcs Cedex

Tel	79 07 43 95
Fax	79 07 47 65
Holes	18 L 5547 m SSS 70
V'tors	H
Fees	150–200fr
Loc	90 km E of Chambery on N90

Le Beaujolais (1991)

69480 Lucenay-Anse

Tel	74 67 04 44
Fax	74 67 09 60
Holes	18 L 6137 m SSS 72
V'tors	U H
Fees	190fr (260fr)
Loc	25 km N of Lyon

Bossey G&CC (1985)

Château de Crevin, 74160 Bossey

Tel	04 50 43 95 50
Fax	04 50 95 32 57
Holes	18 L 6022 m Par 71
V'tors	WD–U WE–NA
Fees	300fr
Loc	6 km S of Geneva
Arch	Robert Trent Jones Jr

La Bresse

Domaine de Mary, 01400 Condessiat

Tel	74 51 42 09
Fax	74 51 40 09
Holes	18 L 6217 m Par 72
V'tors	WD–U WE–H
Fees	200fr (250fr)
Loc	15 km SW of Bourg-en-Bresse, via RN73
Arch	Jeremy Pern

Chamonix (1934)

BP 31, 74402 Chamonix Cedex

Tel	50 53 06 28
Fax	50 53 38 69
Holes	18 L 6087 m SSS 72
V'tors	H
Fees	200–300fr
Loc	3 km N of Chamonix (RN 506). Geneva 80 km
Arch	Robert Trent Jones Sr

Le Clou (1985)

01330 Villars-les-Dombes

Tel	74 98 19 65
Fax	74 98 15 15
Holes	18 L 5000 m SSS 67
V'tors	WD–U WE–H
Fees	D–160fr (D–200fr)
Loc	30 km NE of Lyon

La Commanderie (1964)

L'Aumusse-Crottet, 01290 Pont-de-Veyle

Tel	85 30 44 12
Fax	85 30 55 02
Holes	18 L 5560 m SSS 69
V'tors	H
Fees	150fr (200fr)
Loc	7 km E of Mâcon on RN 79

Corrençon-en-Vercors (1987)

Les Ritons, 38250 Corrençon-en-Vercors

Tel	76 95 80 42
Fax	76 95 84 63
Holes	18 L 5550 m Par 71
V'tors	U
Fees	150–200fr (180–250fr)
Loc	35 km S of Grenoble, off D531
Arch	Hugues Lambert

Divonne (1931)

01220 Divonne-les-Bains

Tel	50 40 34 11
Fax	50 40 34 25
Holes	18 L 6035 m SSS 72
V'tors	H–max 35
Fees	300fr (500fr)
Loc	Divonne 1/2 km. 18 km N of Geneva
Arch	Nakowsky

La Dombes (1986)

01390 Mionnay

Tel	78 91 84 84
Fax	78 91 02 73
Holes	18 L 6060 m SSS 71
V'tors	U
Fees	180fr (250fr)
Loc	20 km N of Lyon towards Bourg

Esery (1990)

Esery, 74930 Reignier

Tel	04 50 36 58 70
Fax	04 50 36 57 62
Holes	18 L 6350 m SSS 73
	9 L 2024 m SSS 31
V'tors	WD–H WE–NA
Fees	280fr
Loc	10 km S of Geneva
Arch	Michel Gayon

Flaine-Les-Carroz (1984)

74300 Flaine

Tel	50 90 85 44
Fax	50 90 88 21
Holes	18 L 3693 m Par 63
V'tors	U
Fees	140fr
Loc	4 km N of Flaine. 60 km SE of Geneva Airport
Arch	Robert Berthet

Giez (1991)

Lac d'Annecy, 74210 Giez

Tel	04 50 44 48 41
Fax	04 50 32 55 93
Holes	18 L 5820 m Par 72
	9 L 2250 m Par 33
V'tors	H or Green card
Fees	210–260fr
Loc	20 km SE of Annecy
Arch	Didier Fruchet

Le Gouverneur

Château du Breuil, 01390 Monthieux
Tel   72 26 40 34
Fax   72 26 41 61
Holes 18 L 6477 m Par 72
           18 L 5959 m Par 72
           9 L 2365 m Par 34
V'tors H or green card
Fees   180fr (250fr)
Loc   NE of Lyon, off A46
Arch   Fruchet/Sprecher

Grenoble-Bresson (1990)

Route de Montavie, 38320 Eybens
Tel   04 76 73 65 00
Fax   04 76 73 65 51
Holes 18 L 6343 m SSS 72
V'tors U
Fees   230fr (270fr)
Loc   10 km SE of Grenoble
Arch   Robert Trent Jones Jr

Grenoble-Charmeil

38210 St Quentin-sur-Isère
Tel   04 76 93 67 28
Fax   04 76 93 62 04
Holes 18 L 6200 m Par 73
V'tors U
Fees   185fr (250fr)
Loc   20 km NW of Grenoble,
           off A49
Arch   Perl/Garaialde

Grenoble-Uriage (1921)

Les Alberges, 38410 Uriage
Tel   04 76 89 03 47
Fax   04 76 73 65 51
Holes 9 L 2005 m SSS 32
V'tors U
Fees   130fr (160fr)
Loc   15 km E of Grenoble
Arch   Watine/Sprecher

Lyon (1921)

38280 Villette-d'Anthon
Tel   04 78 31 11 33
Fax   04 72 02 48 27
Holes 18 L 6229 m SSS 72
           18 L 6727 m SSS 74
V'tors U H
Fees   220fr (330fr)
Loc   20 km E of Lyon
Arch   Fenn/Lambert

Lyon-Chassieu

Route de Lyon, 69680 Chassieu
Tel   04 78 90 84 77
Fax   04 78 90 88 85
Holes 18 L 5941 m Par 70
V'tors H
Fees   160fr (220fr)
Loc   10 km E of Lyon
Arch   Chris Pittman

Lyon-Verger (1977)

69360 Saint-Symphorien D'Ozon
Tel   04 78 02 84 20
Fax   04 78 02 08 12
Holes 18 L 5800 m SSS 69
V'tors U

Fees   180fr (250fr)
Loc   14 km S of Lyon on A7, or
           RN7 2 km S of Feyzin

Maison Blanche G&CC (1991)

01170 Echenevex
Tel   50 42 44 42
Fax   50 42 44 43
Holes 18 L 6246 m SSS 72
           9 L 1757 m Par 31
V'tors WD–U H (max 30)
Fees   300fr (1995)
Loc   15 km from Geneva
Arch   Harradine/Dongradi

Méribel (1973)

BP 54, 73553 Méribel Cedex
Tel   79 00 52 67
Fax   79 00 38 85
Holes 18 L 5319 m SSS 70
V'tors H
Fees   150–270fr
Loc   15 km S of Moutiers. 35 km
           S of Albertville
Arch   Sprecher/Watine

Mont-d'Arbois (1964)

74120 Megève
Tel   50 21 29 79
Fax   50 93 02 63
Holes 18 L 6100 m SSS 72
V'tors WE–restricted. Booking
           required Jul/Aug
Fees   200–300fr
Loc   3 km SE of Megève
Arch   Henry Cotton

Royal Golf Club (1904)

Rive Sud du lac de Genève, 74500 Évian
Tel   04 50 75 46 66
Fax   04 50 75 65 54
Holes 18 L 6030 m SSS 72
V'tors H
Fees   D–190–310fr (D–290–380fr)
Loc   2 km W of Évian. 40 km NE
           of Geneva Airport
Arch   Cabell Robinson

St Etienne (1989)

62 Rue St Simon, 42000 St Etienne
Tel   04 77 32 14 63
Fax   04 77 33 61 23
Holes 18 L 5700 m Par 72
V'tors U
Fees   180fr (230fr)
Loc   Nr centre of St Etienne. Lyon
           60 km
Arch   Thierry Sprecher

Salvagny

*100 Rue des Granges, 69890 La Tour
de Salvagny*
Tel   78 48 83 60
Fax   78 48 00 16
Holes 18 L 6300 m SSS 73 Par 72
V'tors U
Fees   200fr (290fr)
Loc   Lyon 20 km
Arch   Drancourt

La Sorelle (1991)

*Domaine de Gravagnieux,
01320 Villette-sur-Ain*
Tel   74 35 47 27
Fax   74 35 44 51
Holes 18 L 6100 m SSS 72
V'tors U
Fees   140fr (190fr)
Loc   50 km NE of Lyon
Arch   Patrick Jacquier

Tignes (1968)

Val Claret, 73320 Tignes
Tel   79 06 37 42 (Summer)
Fax   79 06 35 64
Holes 18 L 4810 m SSS 68
V'tors H–max 35
Fees   200fr
Loc   50 km E of Moutiers, off
           D902, nr Italian border.
           70 km S of Chamonix

Valdaine (1989)

*Domaine de la Valdaine, Montboucher/
Jabron, 26740 Montelimar-Montboucher*
Tel   75 01 86 66
Fax   75 01 24 49
Holes 18 L 5631 m SSS 71
V'tors U
Fees   180fr (260fr)
Loc   4 km E of Montelimar.
           50 km S of Valence
Arch   TJ Macauley

Valence St Didier (1983)

26300 St Didier de Charpey
Tel   75 59 67 01
Fax   75 59 68 19
Holes 18 L 5807 m SSS 71
V'tors U
Fees   160fr (210fr)
Loc   12 km E of Valence
Arch   Thierry Sprecher

Toulouse &
Pyrenees

Albi Lasbordes (1989)

Château de Lasbordes, 81000 Albi
Tel   05 63 54 98 07
Fax   05 63 47 21 55
Holes 18 L 6200 m SSS 72
V'tors U
Fees   170fr (230fr)
Loc   70 km NE of Toulouse
Arch   Garaialde/Pern

Ariège (1986)

09240 La Bastide-de-Serou
Tel   61 64 56 78
Fax   61 64 57 99
Holes 18 L 6000 m SSS 71
V'tors H
Fees   120fr (170fr)
Loc   Unjat, 17 km NW of Foix
Arch   Michel Gayon

La Bigorre (1992)
Pouzac, 65200 Bagnères de Bigorre
Tel   62 91 06 20
Holes   18 L 5909 m SSS 72
V'tors U
Fees   150fr
Loc   18 km S of Tarbes. 150 km
          W of Toulouse
Arch   Olivier Brizon

Château de Terrides
(1986)
Domaine de Terrides,
82100 Labourgade
Tel   63 95 61 07
Fax   63 95 64 97
Holes   18 L 6420 m SSS 71
V'tors U
Fees   150fr (200fr)
Loc   45 km NW of Toulouse
Arch   J-P Foures

Embats
Route de Montesquiou, 32000 Auch
Tel   05 62 05 20 80/
          05 62 61 10 11
Fax   05 62 05 92 55
Holes   18 L 4751 m SSS 65
V'tors U
Fees   150fr (170fr)
Loc   4 km W of Auch. 80 km W
          of Toulouse
Arch   André Migret

Étangs de Fiac (1987)
Brazis, 81500 Fiac
Tel   05 63 70 64 70
Fax   05 63 75 32 91
Holes   18 L 5800 m SSS 71
V'tors U
Fees   150–220fr
Loc   45 km NE of Toulouse
Arch   M Hawtree

Florentin-Gaillac
(1990)
Le Bosc, Florentin,
81150 Marssac-sur-Tarn
Tel   63 55 20 50
Fax   63 53 26 41
Holes   18 L 6150 m SSS 71
V'tors U
Fees   170–210fr
Loc   10 km W of Albi. 70 km NE
          of Toulouse
Arch   Robert Berthet

Guinlet (1986)
32800 Eauze
Tel   62 09 80 84
Fax   62 09 84 50
Holes   18 L 5565 m Par 71
V'tors U
Fees   150fr (180fr)
Loc   60 km SW of Agen.
          150 km SE of Bordeaux
Arch   M Thevenin

Lannemezan
La Demi-Lune, 65300 Lannemezan
Tel   62 98 01 01
Holes   18 L 5872 m Par 70
V'tors H
Fees   150–190fr (180–210fr)
Loc   38 km SE of Tarbes
Arch   Hirigoyen/Laserre

Lourdes
Lac de Lourdes, 65100 Lourdes
Tel   62 42 02 06
Holes   18 L 5675 m SSS 72
V'tors U
Fees   160fr (180fr)
Loc   4 km W of Lourdes
Arch   Olivier Brizon

Luchon (1908)
BP 40, 31110 Bagnères de Luchon
Tel   61 79 03 27
Holes   9 L 2375 m SSS 66
V'tors H
Fees   130fr (170fr)
Loc   Luchon, 90 km SE of Tarbes.
          145 km S of Toulouse
Mis   Open Mar-Nov
Arch   Fenn/Hawtree

Mazamet-La Barouge
(1956)
81660 Pont de l'Arn
Tel   63 61 08 00/63 67 06 72
Fax   63 61 13 03
Holes   18 L 5623 m SSS 70
V'tors U
Fees   160fr (220fr)
Loc   2 km N of Mazamet. 80 km
          E of Toulouse. 80 km W of
          Béziers
Arch   Mackenzie Ross/Hawtree

Toulouse (1951)
31320 Vieille-Toulouse
Tel   05 61 73 45 48
Fax   05 62 19 04 67
Holes   18 L 5602 m SSS 69
V'tors U
Fees   180fr (250fr)
Loc   8 km S of Toulouse
Arch   Hawtree

Toulouse-La Ramée
Ferme Cousturier, 31170 Tournefeuille
Tel   05 61 07 09 09
Fax   05 61 07 15 93
Holes   18 L 5605 m SSS 69
          9 hole short course
V'tors H
Fees   120fr (150fr)
Loc   SW of Toulouse
Arch   Hawtree

Toulouse-Palmola (1974)
Route d'Albi, 31660 Buzet-sur-Tarn
Tel   05 61 84 20 50
Fax   05 61 84 48 92
Holes   18 L 6156 m SSS 73

V'tors H
Fees   210fr (300–350fr)
Loc   18 km NE of Toulouse. A68
          Junction 4
Arch   Michael Fenn

Toulouse-Seilh
Route de Grenade, 31840 Seilh
Tel   05 61 42 59 30
Fax   05 61 42 34 17
Holes   Red 18 L 6122 m SSS 72
          Yellow 18 L 4202 m SSS 64
V'tors H
Fees   150–200fr (200–250fr)
Loc   15 km N of Toulouse.
          Blagnac Airport 5 km
Mis   Pitch & putt
Arch   Jean Garaialde

Toulouse-Teoula
71 Avenue des Landes, 31830 Plaisance du Touch
Tel   05 61 91 98 80
Fax   05 61 91 49 66
Holes   18 L 5500 m Par 69
V'tors H or green card
Fees   150fr (200fr)
Loc   15 km W of Toulouse
Arch   Martin Hawtree

Les Tumulus (1987)
1 Rue du Bois, 65310 Laloubère
Tel   05 62 45 14 50
Fax   05 62 45 14 50
Holes   18 L 5050 m Par 70
V'tors U
Fees   150fr (200fr)
Loc   5 km S of Tarbes, towards
          Bagnères
Arch   Charles de Ginestet

Germany

Aachen & Saar

Aachen (1927)
Schürzelter Str 300, 52074 Aachen
Tel   (0241) 12501
Fax   (0241) 171075
Holes   18 L 6063 m Par 72
V'tors H
Fees   D–50DM (D–70DM)
Loc   Seffent, 5 km NW of Aachen
Arch   Murray/Morrison/Pennink

Eifel (1977)
Kölner Str, 54576 Hillesheim
Tel   (06593) 1241
Fax   (06593) 9421
Holes   18 L 6017 m Par 72
V'tors H–phone before play
Fees   60DM (80DM)
Loc   70 km S of Cologne
Arch   Grohs/Preismann

Haus Kambach (1989)

Kambachstrasse 9-13, 52249
Eschweiler-Kinzweiler
Tel **(02403) 37615**
Fax (02403) 21270
Holes 18 L 6178 m SSS 72
V'tors U
Fees 60DM (70DM)
Loc 20 km NE of Aachen
Arch Dieter Sziedat

Nahetal (1971)

Drei Buchen, 55583 Bad Münster am
Stein
Tel **(06708) 2145/3032**
Fax (06708) 1731
Holes 18 L 6065 m SSS 72
V'tors H
Fees 60DM (80DM)
Loc 6 km S of Bad Kreuznach.
70 km SW of Frankfurt
Arch Armin Keller

Pfalz Neustadt (1971)

Im Lochbusch, 67435 Neustadt
Tel **(06327) 97420**
Fax (06327) 974218
Holes 18 L 6180 m SSS 72
V'tors U H WE–NA before 3pm
Fees 75DM (100DM)
Loc Geinsheim, 15 km SE of
Neustadt towards Speyer

Saarbrücken (1961)

Oberlimbergerweg, 66798 Wallerfangen-
Gisingen
Tel **(06837) 91800/1584**
Fax (06837) 91801
Holes 18 L 6231 m SSS 73
V'tors H
Fees 80DM (100DM)
Loc B406 towards Wallerfangen.
8 km N of Saarlouis
Arch Donald Harradine

Websweiler Hof (1991)

Websweiler Hof, 66424 Homburg
Tel **(06841) 71111**
Fax (06841) 755555
Holes 18 L 6188 m Par 72 SSS 74
V'tors U H
Fees 60DM (80DM)
Loc 35 km E of Saarbrücken

Westpfalz Schwarzbachtal (1988)

66509 Rieschweiler
Tel **(06336) 6442**
Fax (06336) 6408
Holes 18 L 5740 m SSS 70
V'tors H
Fees 50DM (70DM)
Loc 40 km E of Saarbrücken

Woodlawn

6792 Ramstein Flugplatz
Tel **(06371) 476240**
Fax (06371) 42158
Holes 18 L 6225 yds Par 70

V'tors Military GC–visitors restricted
Fees $13 ($16)
Loc Ramstein 3 km. Kaiserlautern
10 km

Berlin & East

Berlin am Schäferberg

Am Wildgatter 47, 14109 Berlin
Tel **(030) 805 2328**
Fax (030) 805 2328
Holes 18 L 5689 m SSS 70
V'tors WE–M H–booking required
Fees $60
Loc SW Berlin. Motorway exit
Wannsee, towards Glienicker
Brücke

Berlin G&CC (1924)

Golfweg 22, 14109 Berlin,
US Forces Europe
Tel **819 6533**
Fax 805 5534
Holes 18 L 6350 yds Par 70
V'tors WD–H WE–M
Fees $40 ($50)
Loc Wannsee District (Berlin)
Arch Percy Alliss

Berlin G&CC Motzener See (1991)

Am Golfplatz 5, 15741 Motzen
Tel **(033769) 50130**
Fax (033769) 50134
Holes 18 L 6330 m SSS 73
9 L 2756 m SSS 54
V'tors H–booking required
Fees 90DM (110DM)
Loc 30 km S of Berlin
Arch Kurt Rossknecht

Berlin Wannsee (1895)

Golfweg 22, 14109 Berlin
Tel **806 7060**
Holes 18 L 6088 m SSS 72
9 L 4442 m SSS 64
V'tors WD–U H WE–M
Fees 100DM (120DM)
Loc 17 km SW of Berlin
Arch Harris Bros (1925)

Berliner GC Gatow (1990)

Kladower Damm 182-288, Flugplatz
Gatow, 14089 Berlin
Tel **(030) 365 76 60**
Fax (030) 365 76 60
Holes 9 L 5687 m SSS 70
V'tors H
Fees 40DM (50DM)
Loc 16 km from Berlin

Elbflorenz GC Dresden (1992)

Ferdinand von Schillstr 2,
01728 Possendorf
Tel **(035206) 2430**
Fax (035206) 24317

Holes 18 holes Par 73
V'tors H
Fees 65DM (75DM)
Loc Dresden 12 km
Arch Dieter Sziedat

Potsdamer Tremmen (1990)

Tremmener Landstrasse,
14641 Tremmen
Tel **(033233) 80244**
Fax (033233) 80957
Holes 18 L 5921 m Par 72
V'tors H
Fees 60DM (80DM)
Loc SW of Berlin

Semlin am See (1992)

Ferchesarerstrasse, 14715 Semlin
Tel **(03385) 5540**
Fax (03385) 554400
Holes 18 L 6348 m SSS 73
V'tors H
Fees 60DM (90DM)
Loc 80 km W of Berlin (B5/B188)
Arch Christoph Städler

Bremen & North West

Club Zur Vahr (1905)

Bgm-Spitta-Allee 34, 28329 Bremen
Tel **Bremen (0421) 204480,**
Garlstedt (04795) 417
Fax (0421) 244 9248
Holes Garlstedt 18 L 6535 m Par 74
SSS 75; Bremen 9 L 5862 m
Par 71 SSS 71
V'tors WD–H WE–M
Fees Garlstedt–70DM
Bremen–50DM
Loc Garlstedt-30 km N of
Bremen. Vahr-Bremen
Arch B von Limburger

Küsten GC Hohe Klint (1978)

Hohe Klint, 27478 Cuxhaven
Tel **(04723) 2737**
Fax (04723) 5022
Holes 18 L 6150 m SSS 72
V'tors U H
Fees 50DM (70DM)
Loc 12 km SW of Cuxhaven on
Route 6, nr Oxstedt

Münster-Wilkinghege (1963)

Steinfurterstr 448, 48159 Münster
Tel **(0251) 211201**
Fax (0251) 261518
Holes 18 L 5955 m SSS 71
V'tors WD–H WE–I
Fees 50DM (70DM)
Loc 2 km N of Münster

Oldenburgischer (1964)

Am Golfplatz 1, 26180 Rastede
Tel (04402) 7240
Fax (04402) 70417
Holes 18 L 6117 m SSS 72
V'tors WD–U WE–M
Fees 50DM (60DM)
Loc 10 km N of Oldenburg, nr Rastede
Arch Von Limburger/Schantmeyer

Osnabrück (1955)

Karmannstr 1, 49084 Osnabrück
Tel (05402) 5636
Fax (05402) 5257
Holes 18 L 5881 m Par 71
V'tors U
Fees 60DM (70DM)
Loc 13 km SE of Osnabrück

Ostfriesland (1980)

Postbox 1220, 26634 Wiesmoor
Tel (04944) 6440
Fax (04944) 6441
Holes 18 L 6256 m SSS 73
V'tors U
Fees 50DM (60DM)
Loc 25 km SW of Wilhelmshaven
Arch Frank Pennink

RAF Gütersloh

RAF Gütersloh BFPO#47
Tel (05241) 842409
Holes 9 L 5761 yds SSS 68
Loc 5 km W of Gütersloh

Senne GC Gut Welschof

Augustdorferstr 70, 33758 Schloss Holte-Stukenbrock
Tel (05207) 920936
Fax (05207) 88788
Holes 18 L 6246 m SSS 72
V'tors U H
Fees 50DM (70DM)
Loc 20 km S of Bielefeld
Arch Christoph Städler

Soltau (1982)

Hof Loh, 29614 Soltau
Tel (05191) 14077
Fax (05191) 2593
Holes 18 L 6274 m SSS 73
9 L 2340 m SSS 54
V'tors H
Fees 50DM (60DM)
Loc Tetendorf, S of Soltau

Syke (1989)

Schultenweg 1, 28857 Syke-Okel
Tel (04242) 8230
Fax (04242) 8255
Holes 18 L 6266 m Par 73
V'tors U H
Fees 50DM (60DM)
Loc 20 km S of Bremen

Tietlingen (1979)

29683 Fallingbostel
Tel (05162) 3889
Fax (05162) 7564

Holes 18 L 6193 m Par 72 SSS 73
V'tors H
Fees 50DM (60DM)
Loc 65 km N of Hanover, between Walsrode and Fallingbostel
Arch Bruns/Chadwick

Vechta-Welpe (1989)

Welpe 2, 49377 Vechta
Tel (04441) 5539/82168
Fax (04441) 852480
Holes 18 L 6105 m Par 72
V'tors H
Fees 50DM (70DM)
Loc 50 km SW of Bremen
Arch Rainer Preissmann

Verden (1988)

Holtumer Str 24, 27283 Verden
Tel (04230) 1470
Fax (04230) 1550
Holes 18 holes Par 72
V'tors U
Fees 50DM (60DM)
Loc 30 km E of Bremen, nr Walle

Westfälischer Gütersloh

Gütersloher Str 127, 33397 Rietberg
Tel (05244) 2340/10528
Fax (05244) 1388
Holes 18 L 6135 m SSS 72
V'tors U H
Fees 50DM (70DM)
Loc 8 km SE of Gütersloh, nr Neuenkirchen
Arch B von Limburger

Central

Bad Kissingen (1911)

Euerdorferstr 11, 97688 Bad Kissingen
Tel (0971) 3608
Fax (0971) 60140
Holes 18 L 5675 m SSS 70
V'tors U H
Fees 60DM (75DM)
Loc Bad Kissingen 2 km. 65 km N of Würzburg

Bad Lippspringe (1989)

Senne 1, 33173 Bad Lippspringe
Tel (05252) 53794
Fax (05252) 53811
Holes 18 L 5826 m Par 73 SSS 72
9 L 5214 m Par 68 SSS 68
V'tors H
Fees 40–50DM (50–60DM)
Loc 9 km E of Paderborn, off Route 1

Dillenburg

Auf dem Altscheid, 35687 Dillenburg
Tel (02771) 5001
Fax (02771) 5002
Holes 18 L 6115 m Par 72
V'tors U H
Fees 65DM (80DM)

Loc 30 km S of Siegen. 100 km N of Frankfurt

Frankfurter (1913)

Golfstrasse 41, 60528 Frankfurt/Main
Tel (069) 666 2318
Fax (069) 666 7018
Holes 18 L 6455 yds SSS 71
V'tors H–28 max
Fees 85DM (100DM)
Loc 6 km SW of Frankfurt, nr Airport

Hanau-Wilhelmsbad (1958)

Wilhelmsbader Allee 32, 63454 Hanau
Tel (06181) 82071
Fax (06181) 86967
Holes 18 L 6227 m Par 73
V'tors WD–H WE–M H
Fees 80DM (100DM)
Loc 4 km NW of Hanau on B8-40/AB66. Frankfurt 15 km
Arch Ernst Kothe

Heidelberg-Lobenfeld (1968)

Biddersbacherhof, 74931 Lobbach-Lobenfeld
Tel (06226) 952110
Fax (06226) 952115
Holes 18 L 5989 m SSS 72
V'tors WD–H WE–M H
Fees 60DM (80DM)
Loc 20 km E of Heidelberg
Arch Donald Harradine

Hofgut Kolnhausen (1992)

35423 Lich
Tel (06404) 91071
Fax (06404) 91072
Holes 18 L 6065m SSS 72
V'tors H–booking necessary Sun–M
Fees 80DM (100DM)
Loc 45 km N of Frankfurt
Arch Heinz Fehring

Homburger (1899)

Saalburgchaussee 2, 61350 Bad Homburg
Tel (06172) 306808
Fax (06172) 32648
Holes 10 holes Par 70 SSS 69
V'tors H
Fees 50DM (70DM)
Loc On B456 to Usingen

Idstein-Wörsdorf (1989)

Gut Henriettenthal, 65510 Idstein-Wörsdorf
Tel (06126) 9322-0
Fax (06126) 9322-22
Holes 18 L 6165 m SSS 72
V'tors WD–H WE–M
Fees 70DM (100DM)

Loc   25 km N of Wiesbaden
Arch Kurt Rossknecht

Jacobsberg (1990)
Im Tal der Loreley, 56154 Boppard
Tel   (06742) 808491
Fax   (06742) 808493
Holes 18 L 6351 m Par 72 SSS 72
V'tors U
Fees 70DM (90DM)
Loc   80 km N of Mainz
Arch Wolfgang Jersombek

Kronberg G&LC (1954)
Schloss Friedrichshof, Hainstr 25,
61476 Kronberg/Taunus
Tel   (06173) 1426
Fax   (06173) 5953
Holes 18 L 5183 m SSS 68
V'tors WD–U H WE–M H
Fees 70DM (90DM)
Loc   16 km NW of Frankfurt
Arch Ernst Kothe

Kurhessischer GC Oberaula (1987)
Postfach 31, 36278 Oberaula
Tel   (06628) 1573
Fax   (06628) 1573
Holes 18 L 6050 m SSS 72
V'tors U H
Fees D–50DM (D–70DM)
Loc   50 km S of Kassel, nr Kircheim
Arch Deutsche Golf Consult

Main-Taunus (1979)
Lange Seegewann 2,
65205 Wiesbaden
Tel   (06122) 52550/52208(Sec)
Holes 18 L 6045 m SSS 72
V'tors H
Loc   15 km NW of Frankfurt Airport

Mannheim-Viernheim (1930)
Alte Mannheimer Str 3,
68519 Viernheim
Tel   (06204) 71313 (Clubhouse),
         (06204) 78737 (Sec)
Fax   (06204) 740181
Holes 9 L 6060 m SSS 72
V'tors WD–H WE–M H (Summer)
Fees 50DM (60DM)
Loc   10 km NE of Mannheim

Mittelrheinischer Bad Ems (1938)
Denzerheide, 56130 Bad Ems
Tel   (02603) 6541
Fax   (02603) 13995
Holes 18 L 6050 m SSS 72
V'tors H
Fees 80DM (110DM)
Loc   13 km E of Koblenz, nr Bad Ems (6km)
Arch Karl Hoffmann

Neuhof
Hofgut Neuhof, 63303 Dreieich
Tel   (06102) 327927
Fax   (06102) 327012
Holes 18 L 6151 m SSS 72
V'tors WD–H WE–M
Fees 100DM
Loc   Hofgut Neuhof, S of Frankfurt, off A3
Arch Patrick Merrigan

Oberhessischer Marburg (1973)
Maximilianenhof, 35091 Cölbe-Bernsdorf
Tel   (06427) 2728/2824 (Pro)
Fax   (06427) 3090
Holes 9 L 6098 m SSS 72
V'tors I H
Fees 50DM (70DM)
Loc   8 km N of Marburg, off B3 towards Reddehausen

Paderborner Land (1983)
Wilseder Weg 25, 33102 Paderborn
Tel   (05251) 4377
Holes 18 L 5670 m SSS 68
Fees 20DM (30DM)
Loc   Salzkotten/Thule, between B-1 and B-64

Rhein Main (1977)
Steubenstrasse 9, 65189 Wiesbaden
Tel   (0611) 373014
Holes 18 L 6116 m SSS 71
V'tors M
Fees $50
Loc   Wiesbaden 6 km

Rheinblick
Weisser Weg, 65201 Wiesbaden-
Frauenstein
Tel   (0611) 420675
Fax   (0611) 941 0434
Holes 18 L 6604 yds SSS 70
V'tors Limited to Monday play only
Fees $50
Loc   2 km from Wiesbaden at Hessen

Rheintal (1971)
An der Bundesstrr 291,
68723 Oftersheim
Tel   (06202) 56390
Holes 18 L 5840 m SSS 71
Fees On application
Loc   Oftersheim, SE of Mannheim

Rhoen (1971)
Am Golfplatz, 36145 Hofbieber
Tel   (06657) 1334
Fax   (06657) 1754
Holes 18 L 5686 m SSS 70
V'tors H
Fees 50DM (70DM)
Loc   Hofbieber, 11 km E of Fulda
Arch Kurt Peters

Schloss Braunfels (1970)
Homburger Hof, 35619 Braunfels
Tel   (06442) 4530
Fax   (06442) 6683
Holes 18 L 6320 m SSS 73
V'tors WD–H (max 36) WE–H NA 10am–3pm
Fees D–70DM (90DM)
Loc   70 km N of Frankfurt

Schloss Sickendorf (1990)
Schloss Sickendorf, 36341 Lauterbach
Tel   (06641) 96130
Fax   (06641) 961335
Holes 18 L 6124 m SSS 72
V'tors H
Fees 50DM (70DM)
Loc   30 km W of Fulda. 120 km E of Frankfurt
Arch Spangemacher

Sennelager (British Army) (1963)
Bad Lippspringe BFPO#16
Tel   (05252) 53794
Fax   (05252) 53811
Holes Old 18 L 5754 m SSS 72
         New 9 L 5214 m SSS 68
V'tors U
Fees (Forces) 30DM (40DM)
         (Civilians) 50DM (60DM)
Loc   9 km E of Paderborn, off Route 1

Spessart (1972)
Golfplatz Alsberg, 63628 Bad Soden-
Salmünster
Tel   (06056) 91580
Fax   (06056) 915820
Holes 18 L 6051 m SSS 72
V'tors H
Fees 60DM (90DM) W–250DM
Loc   70 km NE of Frankfurt, via A66 towards Fulda
Arch Elliot Rowan

Stromberg-Schindeldorf (1987)
Park Village Golfanlagen, Buchenring 6,
55442 Stromberg
Tel   (06724) 93080
Fax   (06724) 930818
Holes 18 L 5161 Par 68 SSS 68
V'tors U H–booking necessary
Fees 60DM (85DM)
Loc   5 km from A61 exit Stromberg

Taunus Weilrod (1979)
Merzhauser Landstr, 61276 Weilrod-
Altweilnau
Tel   (06083) 95050
Fax   (06083) 950515
Holes 18 L 5981 m SSS 72
V'tors H
Fees 65DM (90DM)
Loc   25 km NW of Bad Homburg
Arch Donald Harradine

For list of abbreviations see page 479

Wiesbadener (1893)

Chausseehaus 17, 65199 Wiesbaden

Tel	(0611) 460238
Fax	(0611) 463251
Holes	9 L 5320 m SSS 68
V'tors	WD–H (Max36) WE–H
	(max 28)
Fees	60DM (80DM)
Loc	8 km NW of Wiesbaden,
	towards Schlangenbad
Arch	Hirsch

Wiesloch-Hohenhardter Hof G&LC (1983)

Hohenhardter Hof, 69168 Wiesloch-Baiertal

Tel	(06222) 72081
Fax	(06222) 71718
Holes	18 L 6080 m SSS 72
V'tors	WD–H WE–H
Fees	60DM (80DM)
Loc	17 km S of Heidelberg
Arch	Harradine/Weishaupt

Hamburg & North

Altenhof (1971)

Eckernförde, 24340 Altenhof

Tel	(04351) 41227,
	(04351) 45800 (Pro)
Fax	(04351) 41227
Holes	18 L 6066 m SSS 72
V'tors	H
Fees	50DM (70DM)
Loc	3 km S of Eckernförde.
	25 km NW of Kiel
Arch	Donald Harradine

Brodauer Mühle (1986)

Baumallee 14, 23730 Gut Beusloe

Tel	(04561) 8140
Fax	(04561) 8140
Holes	18 L 6113 m Par 72 SSS 72
V'tors	U H–36
Fees	50DM (80DM)
Loc	30 km N of Lübeck
Arch	Siegmann/Osterkamp

Buchholz-Nordheide

An der Rehm 25, 21244 Bucholz

Tel	(04181) 36200
Fax	(04181) 97294
Holes	18 L 6130 m SSS 72
V'tors	WD–U H WE–H I before
	10am
Fees	60DM (80DM)
Loc	30 km S of Hamburg

Buxtehude (1982)

Zum Lehmfeld 1, 21614 Buxtehude

Tel	(04161) 81333
Fax	(04161) 87268
Holes	18 L 6480 m SSS 74
V'tors	WD–H WE–H before 9.30am
	–M after 9.30am
Fees	50–60DM (60–80DM)
Loc	30 km SW of Hamburg on
	Route 73 from Harburg
Arch	Wolfgang Siegmann

Föhr (1966)

25938 Nieblum

Tel	(04681) 580455
Fax	(04681) 580456
Holes	18 L 6089 m SSS 72
V'tors	H
Fees	60DM (70DM)
Loc	3 km SW of Wyk, by Airport

Gut Grambek (1981)

Schlosstr 21, 23883 Grambek

Tel	(04542) 841474
Fax	(04542) 841476
Holes	18 L 6029 m SSS 71
V'tors	H
Fees	50DM (70DM)
Loc	30 km S of Lübeck. 50 km
	E of Hamburg

Gut Kaden (1984)

Kadenerstrasse 9, 25486 Alveslohe

Tel	(04193) 9929–0
Fax	(04193) 992919
Holes	18 L 6076 m Par 72
	9 hole course
V'tors	U H
Fees	60DM (90DM)
Loc	Alveslohe, 30 km N of
	Hamburg

Gut Waldhof (1969)

Am Waldhof, 24629 Kisdorferwohld

Tel	(04194) 99740
Fax	(04194) 1251
Holes	18 L 6044 m Par 72
V'tors	WD–H WE–M
Fees	50DM (70DM)
Loc	34 km N of Hamburg via
	Autobahn A7 to Kaltenkirchen,
	or via route B432

Hamburg (1906)

In de Bargen 59, 22587 Hamburg

Tel	(040) 812177
Fax	(040) 817315
Holes	18 L 5925 m SSS 72
V'tors	H WE–M
Fees	75DM (80DM)
Loc	Blankenese, 14 km W of
	Hamburg
Arch	Colt/Allison/Morrison

Hamburg Holm (1993)

Haverkamp 1, 25488 Holm

Tel	(04103) 91330
Fax	(04103) 913313
Holes	18 L 6170 m Par 72
V'tors	WD–U WE–M
Fees	65DM (80DM)
Loc	20 km W of Hamburg
Arch	Harradine/Rossknecht

Hamburg-Ahrensburg (1964)

Am Haidschlag 39–45, 22926 Ahrensburg

Tel	(04102) 51309
Fax	(04102) 81410
Holes	18 L 5782 m SSS 71

V'tors	WE–M only
Fees	60DM (70DM)
Loc	20 km NE of Hamburg.
	Motorway exit Ahrensburg

Hamburg-Waldorfer (1960)

Schevenbarg, 22949 Ammersbek

Tel	(040) 605 1337
Fax	(040) 605 4879
Holes	18 L 6154 m SSS 73
	18 hole pitch & putt course
V'tors	WD–U H WE–M H
Fees	70DM (85DM)
Loc	20 km N of Hamburg
Arch	B von Limburger

Hamburger GC in der Lüneburger Heide (1957)

Am Golfplatz 24, 21218 Seevetal

Tel	(04105) 2331
Fax	(04105) 52571
Holes	18 L 5903 m SSS 71
V'tors	WD–U WE–M
Fees	60DM (80DM)
Loc	25 km S of Hamburg
Arch	Morrison/Gärtner

Hoisdorf (1977)

Hof Bornbek/Hoisdorf, 22952 Lütjensee

Tel	(04107) 7831
Fax	(04107) 9934
Holes	18 L 5958 m Par 71
V'tors	WD–U WE–M only
Fees	70DM (80M)
Loc	25 km NE of Hamburg

Jersbek

Oberteicher Weg, 22941 Jersbek

Tel	(04532) 23555
Fax	(04532) 24779
Holes	18 L 5867 m SSS 71
V'tors	WD–H or I WE–M
Fees	50DM (60DM)
Loc	20 km N of Hamburg
Arch	Von Schinkel

Kieler GC Havighorst (1988)

Havighorster Weg 20, 24211 Havighorst

Tel	(04302) 965980
Fax	(04302) 965981
Holes	18 L 6242 m Par 73 SSS 73
V'tors	WD–U H WE–H
Fees	50DM (60DM)
Loc	10 km S of Kiel. 85 km N of
	Hamburg
Arch	Udo Barth

Lübeck-Travemünder (1921)

Kowitzberg 41, 23570 Lübeck-Travemünde

Tel	(04502) 74018
Fax	(04502) 72182
Holes	18 L 6071 m SSS 72

V'tors H
Fees 60DM (80DM)
Loc 18 km NE of Lübeck.
    70 km NE of Hamburg

Maritim Timmendorfer Strand (1973)

Am Golfplatz 3, 23669 Timmendorfer Strand
Tel (04503) 5152
Fax (04503) 86344
Holes North 18 L 6065 m SSS 72
    South 18 L 3755 m SSS 60
V'tors WE–booking required
Fees North D–60DM (D–90DM)
    South D–50DM (D–75DM)
Loc 15 km N of Lübeck
Arch B von Limburger

Mittelholsteinischer Aukrug (1969)

Zum Glasberg 9, 24613 Aukrug-Bargfeld
Tel (04873) 595
Fax (04873) 1698
Holes 18 L 6140 m SSS 72
V'tors WD–H WE–H booking
    necessary
Fees 45DM (60DM)
Loc 10 km W of Neumunster.
    Mitte exit on Route 430

An der Pinnau (1982)

Pinnerbergerstr 81a, 25451 Quickborn
Tel (04106) 81800
Fax (04106) 82003
Holes 18 L 6490 m SSS 74
    18 L 6115 m SSS 72
V'tors H or I
Fees 60DM (80DM)
Loc 25 km NW of Hamburg,
    nr Renzel

Am Sachsenwald (1985)

Am Riesenbett, 21521 Dassendorf
Tel (04104) 6120
Fax (04104) 6551
Holes 18 L 6118 m SSS 72
V'tors H
Fees 50DM (60DM)
Loc 20 km SE of Hamburg
Arch Deutsche Golf Consult

St Dionys (1972)

Widukindweg, 21357 St Dionys
Tel (04133) 6277
Fax (04133) 6281
Holes 18 L 6118 m SSS 72
V'tors By appointment only
Fees 60DM (80DM)
Loc 10 km N of Lüneburg

Schloss Breitenberg

25524 Breitenberg
Tel (04828) 8188
Fax (04828) 8100
Holes 18 hole course
V'tors H
Fees 60DM (70DM)
Loc 50 km N of Hamburg
Arch Gerd Osterkamp

Schloss Lüdersburg (1985)

21379 Lüdersburg bei Lüneburg
Tel (04139) 6970-0
Fax (04139) 6970 70
Holes 18/9 L 6091 m SSS 73
    9 hole Par 3 course
V'tors U H
Fees 30–60DM (80DM)
Loc 12 km E of Lüneburg.
    55 km SE of Hamburg
Arch Wolfgang Siegmann

Sylt

Am Golfplatz, 25996 Wenningstedt
Tel (04651) 45311
Fax (04651) 45692
Holes 18 L 6200 m SSS 72
V'tors H
Fees 50–100DM
Loc Sylt Island, 75 km W of
    Flensburg

Treudelberg G&CC (1990)

Lemsahler Landstr 45, 22397 Hamburg
Tel (040) 608 22500
Fax (040) 608 22444
Holes 18 L 6182 m SSS 72
    9 hole pitch & putt
V'tors U H
Fees 70DM (90DM)
Loc N of Hamburg centre
Arch Donald Steel

Uhlenhorst (1989)

24229 Uhlenhorst
Tel (04349) 539
Fax (04349) 1434
Holes 18 L 6195 m SSS 72
V'tors U
Fees 50DM (60DM)
Loc 8 km N of Kiel
Arch Donald Harradine

Auf der Wendlohe

Oldesloerstr 251, 22457 Hamburg
Tel (040) 550 5014/5
Fax (040) 550 3668
Holes 27 holes:
    5675-6050 m SSS 72
V'tors WE–M
Fees WD–60DM
Loc 15 km N of Hamburg
Arch Ernst-Dietmar Hess

Wentorf-Reinbeker (1901)

Golfstrasse 2, 21465 Wentorf
Tel (040) 729 78066
Fax (040) 729 78067
Holes 18 L 5698 m SSS 70
V'tors WD–U H WE–M
Fees 60DM (70DM)
Loc 20 km SE of Hamburg
Arch Ernst Hess

Worpswede (1974)

Giehlermühlen, 27729 Vollersode
Tel (04763) 7313
Fax (04763) 6193
Holes 18 L 6200 m SSS 72
V'tors WD–U H WE–M H
Fees 50DM (60DM)
Loc Giehlermuhlen, 20 km N of
    Bremen, off B74
Arch Siegmann

Hanover & Weserbergland

Bad Salzuflen G&LC

Schwaghof 4, 32108 Bad Salzuflen
Tel (05222) 10773
Fax (05222) 13954
Holes 18 L 6138 m Par 72
V'tors H
Fees 60DM (70DM)
Loc 3 km NE of Bad Salzuflen
Arch B von Limburger

Braunschweig (1926)

Schwartzkopffstr 10, 38126 Braunschweig
Tel (0531) 691369
Holes 18 L 5893 m SSS 71
Loc Braunschweig 5 km

Burgdorf (1970)

Waldstr 15, 31303 Burgdorf-Ehlershausen
Tel (05085) 7628
Fax (05085) 6617
Holes 18 L 6426 m SSS 74
V'tors H
Fees 50DM (70DM)
Loc Burgdorf-Ehlershausen,
    20 km NE of Hanover

Gifhorn (1982)

Wilscher Weg 56, 38503 Gifhorn
Tel (05371) 16737
Fax (05371) 51092
Holes 18 L 5972 m SSS 72
V'tors H
Fees 50DM (70DM)
Loc 30 km N of Braunschweig

Göttingen (1969)

Levershausen, 37154 Northeim
Tel (05551) 61915
Fax (05551) 61863
Holes 18 L 6050 m SSS 72
V'tors H
Fees 50DM (60DM)
Loc 20 km N of Göttingen,
    towards Northeim
Arch Dr Siegmann

Hannover (1923)

Am Blauen See, 30823 Garbsen
Tel (05137) 73235

Holes 18 L 5855 m SSS 71
Loc   15 km NW of Hanover

Herzogstadt Celle
(1985)
Beukenbusch 1, 29229 Celle
Tel   (05086) 395
Fax   (05086) 8288
Holes 18 L 5915 m SSS 71
V'tors H
Fees 50DM (60DM)
Loc   6 km NE of Celle, towards
      Lüneburg. 40 km NE of
      Hanover
Arch Wolfgang Siegmann

Isernhagen (1983)
Auf Gut Lohne, 30916 Isernhagen
Tel   (05139) 2998
Fax   (05139) 27033
Holes 18 L 6379 m SSS 73
V'tors H–(max 34)
Fees 50DM (70DM)
Loc   Gut Lohne, 12 km NE of
      Hanover

Kassel-Wilhelmshöhe
(1958)
Ehlenerstr 21, 34131 Kassel
Tel   (0561) 33509
Fax   (0561) 37729
Holes 18 L 5691 m SSS 70
V'tors U H
Fees 60DM (80DM)
Loc   Wilhelmshöhe, 5 km W of
      Kassel
Arch Donald Harradine

Lipperland zu Lage
*Ottenhauserstr 100,
32791 Lage/Lippe*
Tel   (05232) 66829
Fax   (05232) 18165
Holes 18 L 6260 m SSS 73
V'tors H
Fees 30DM (40DM)
Loc   22 km E of Bielefeld
Arch Heinz Wolters

Lippischer (1980)
*Huxollweg 21A, 32825 Blomberg-
Cappel*
Tel   (05231) 459
Fax   (05236) 8102
Holes 18 L 6110 m SSS 72
Fees 50DM (60DM)
Loc   12 km E of Detmold

Pyrmonter (1961)
Postfach 100 828, 31758 Hameln
Tel   (05281) 8196
Fax   (05281) 8196
Holes 18 L 5775 m SSS 70
V'tors H
Fees 50DM (60DM)
Loc   4 km S of Bad Pyrmont.
      20 km SW of Hameln
Arch Donald Harradine

Ravensberger Land
*Sudstrasse 96, 32130 Enger-
Pödinghausen*
Tel   (09224) 7308
Fax   (09224) 79682
Holes 18 hole course SSS 72
V'tors WD–H WE–M
Fees 30DM (40DM)
Loc   25 km NE of Bielefeld
      towards Herford
Arch Heinz Wolters

Schloss Schwöbber
(1985)
Wirtschaftshof, 31855 Aerzen
Tel   (05154) 2004
Holes 18 L 6222 m SSS 73
      18 hole short course
Loc   10 km SW of Hameln.
      60 km SW of Hanover

Sieben-Berge Rheden
(1965)
Postfach 1152, 31021 Gronau
Tel   (05182) 52336
Fax   (05182) 52336
Holes 18 L 5856 m SSS 71
V'tors U H
Fees 50DM (60DM)
Loc   35 km S of Hanover
Arch B von Limburger

Weserbergland (1982)
Weissenfelder Mühle, Polle
Tel   (05535) 8842
Fax   (05535) 1225
Holes 18 holes SSS 72
V'tors H
Fees 50DM (60DM)
Loc   35 km S of Hameln

Munich &
South Bavaria

Altötting-Burghausen
(1986)
Piesing 4, 84533 Haiming
Tel   (08678) 986903
Fax   (08678) 986905
Holes 18 L 6281 m SSS 72/73
      9 L 3730 m SSS 60
      9 L 3101 m SSS 71/2
V'tors U
Fees 60DM (80DM)
Loc   Schloss Piesing, 4 km N of
      Burghausen towards Haiming
Arch G von Mecklenberg

Augsburg (1959)
*Engelshofer Str 2, 86399 Bobingen-
Burgwalden*
Tel   (08234) 5621
Fax   (08234) 7855
Holes 18 L 5833 m SSS 71

V'tors U
Fees 60DM (80DM)
Loc   18 km SW of Augsburg

Bad Tölz (1973)
83646 Wackersberg
Tel   (08041) 9994
Fax   (08041) 2116
Holes 9 L 2886 m SSS 71
V'tors WD–H WE–M
Fees 50DM (60DM)
Loc   5 km W of Bad Tölz. 55 km S
      of Munich

Bad Wörishofen
Schlingenerstr 27, 87668 Rieden
Tel   (08346) 777
Holes 18 L 6318 m SSS 71
Loc   10 km S of Bad Wörishofen

Beuerberg (1982)
Gut Sterz, 82547 Beuerberg
Tel   (08179) 671/728
Fax   (08179) 5234
Holes 18 L 6518 m SSS 74
V'tors WD–H WE–M H
Fees 90DM (100DM)
Loc   Beuerberg, 45 km SW of
      Munich
Arch Donald Harradine

Im Chiemgau (1982)
Kötzing 1, 83339 Chieming-Hart
Tel   (08669) 7557
Fax   (08669) 78153
Holes 18 L 6200 m SSS 73
      9 hole Par 3 course
V'tors WD–H
Fees D–70DM (D–100DM)
Loc   40 km W of Salzburg
Arch J Dudok van Heel

Erding-Grünbach (1973)
Am Kellerberg, 85461 Grünbach
Tel   (08122) 6465
Fax   (08122) 49684
Holes 18 L 6109 m SSS 72
V'tors WD–H (max 35) WE–H (max
      28)
Fees 60DM (80DM)
Loc   40 km NE of Munich

Eschenried (1983)
Kurfürstenweg 10, 85232 Eschenried
Tel   (08131) 87238/79650
Fax   (08131) 567418
Holes 18 L 6088 m Par 72 SSS 73
V'tors U H
Fees 70DM (90DM)
Loc   8 km NW of Munich
Arch G von Mecklenburg

Falkenhof G&LC (1983)
PO Box 1560, 84483 Burghausen
Tel   (08678) 8996
Fax   (08677) 65146
Holes 9 L 3030 m SSS 72
Fees 30DM (60DM)

Loc   Falkenhof-Marktl, 48 km N of
Salzburg. 100 km E of Munich
Arch   Kurt Rossknecht

Feldafing (1926)

Tutzinger Str 15, 82340 Feldafing
Tel   (08157) 9334-0
Fax   (08157) 9334-99
Holes   18 L 5724 m SSS 71
V'tors   WD–H WE–M
Fees   100DM (120DM)
Loc   32 km S of Munich
Arch   B von Limburger

Garmisch-Partenkirchen
(1928)

*Postfach 1345, 82453 Garmisch-
Partenkirchen*
Tel   (08824) 8344
Fax   (08824) 325
Holes   18 L 6190 m SSS 72
Fees   65DM (85DM)
Loc   11 km N of Garmisch

Gut Rieden

Gut Rieden, 82319 Starnberg
Tel   (08151) 90770
Fax   (08151) 907711
Holes   18 L 6046 yds SSS 72
V'tors   H WE–M
Fees   80DM (100DM)
Loc   25 km S of Munich

Hohenpähl (1988)

82396 Pähl
Tel   (08808) 1330
Fax   (08808) 775
Holes   18 L 6080 m Par 71 SSS 73
18 L 5765 m Par 71 SSS 72
V'tors   WD–H WE–M H
Fees   90DM (100DM)
Loc   40 km S of Munich on B2
Arch   Kurt Rossknecht

Holledau

Weihern 3, 84104 Rudelzhausen
Tel   (08756) 96010
Fax   (08756) 815
Holes   18 L 6085 m SSS 72
9 hole course
V'tors   U H
Fees   50DM (70DM)
Loc   55 km N of Munich

Höslwang im Chiemgau
(1975)

Kronberg 3, 83129 Höslwang
Tel   (08075) 714
Fax   (08075) 8134
Holes   18 L 8500 m Par 72
V'tors   H
Fees   60DM (80DM)
Loc   80 km S of Munich
Arch   Thomas Himmel

Iffeldorf

Gut Rettenberg, 82393 Iffeldorf
Tel   (08856) 925555
Fax   (08856) 925559

Holes   18 L 5904 m SSS 71
V'tors   U
Fees   80DM (100DM)
Loc   45 km S of Munich
Arch   Hery Beer

Landshut (1989)

*Oberlippach 2,
84095 Furth-Landshut*
Tel   (08704) 8378
Fax   (08704) 8379
Holes   18 L 6251 m SSS 73
V'tors   H
Fees   70DM (90DM)
Loc   65 km E of Munich
Arch   Kurt Rossknecht

Mangfalltal G&LC

Oed 1, 83620 Feldkirchen-Westerham
Tel   (08063) 6300
Holes   18 L 5740 m SSS 72
Fees   40DM (55DM)
Loc   40 km SE of Munich

Margarethenhof am
Tegernsee (1982)

*Gut Steinberg PF#1101,
83701 Gmund am Tegernsee*
Tel   (08022) 7506-0
Fax   (08022) 74818
Holes   18 L 6056 m SSS 72
V'tors   WD–H WE–before 10am
Fees   100DM (120DM)
Loc   Tegernsee, 45 km S of
Munich
Arch   Frank Pennink

München Nord-
Eichenried (1989)

Münchnerstr 57, 85452 Eichenried
Tel   (08123) 93080
Fax   (08123) 930893
Holes   18 L 6318 m Par 73
V'tors   U
Fees   80DM (100DM)
Loc   19 km NE of Munich
Arch   Kurt Rossknecht

München West-
Odelzhausen (1988)

Gut Todtenried, 85235 Odelzhausen
Tel   (08134) 1618
Fax   (08134) 7623
Holes   18 L 6169 m Par 72 SSS 72
V'tors   I
Fees   60DM (90DM)
Loc   35 km NW of Munich

München-Riedhof

82544 Egling-Riedhof
Tel   (08171) 7065
Fax   (08171) 72452
Holes   18 L 6216 m SSS 72
V'tors   WD–U H
Loc   25 km S of München
Arch   Heinz Fehring

Münchener (1910)

Tölzerstrasse 95, 82064 Strasslach
Tel   (08170) 450
Fax   (08170) 611
Holes   Strasslach 27 L 6177 m SSS 72
Thalkirchen 9 L 2528 m
SSS 69
V'tors   WD–H WE–M
Fees   WD–100DM
Loc   Strasslach: 10 km from
Munich. Thalkirchen: Munich

Olching (1979)

Feurstrasse 89, 82140 Olching
Tel   (08142) 48290
Fax   (08142) 482914
Holes   18 L 6042 m Par 72
V'tors   H WE–NA
Fees   80DM (100DM)
Loc   15 km W of Munich
Arch   J Dudok van Heel

Pfaffing Wasserburger

*München Ost, Köckmühle,
83539 Pfaffing*
Tel   (08076) 1718
Fax   (08076) 8594
Holes   18 L 6212 m SSS 73
9 hole course
V'tors   U H
Fees   70DM (90DM)
Loc   50 km E of Münich
Arch   Kurt Rossknecht

St Eurach G&LC (1973)

Eurach 8, 82393 Iffeldorf
Tel   (08801) 1332
Fax   (08801) 2523
Holes   18 L 6509 m SSS 74
V'tors   H exc Wed & Fri pm–NA
WE–NA
Fees   100DM
Loc   40 km S of Munich
Arch   Donald Harradine

Schloss Klingenburg-
Günzburg (1978)

*Schloss Klingenburg,
89341 Jettingen-Scheppach*
Tel   (08225) 3030
Fax   (08225) 30350
Holes   18 L 6237 m SSS 72
V'tors   H
Fees   70DM (100DM)
Loc   40 km W of Augsburg.
5 km from Stuttgart-Munich
motorway, exit Burgau
Arch   Harradine/Sziedat

Schloss Maxlrain

*Freitung 14, 83104 Maxlrain-
Tuntenhausen*
Tel   (08061) 1403
Fax   (08061) 30146
Holes   18 L 6357 m Par 72 SSS 73
9 hole Par 3 course
V'tors   U H
Fees   50–90DM
Loc   40 km S of Munich
Arch   Paul Krings

Starnberg (1986)

Uneringerstr, 82319 Starnberg
Tel (08151) 12157
Fax (08151) 29115
Holes 18 L 6057 m Par 72
V'tors WD–H WE–NA
Fees 70DM
Loc 30 km S of Munich
Arch Kurt Rossknecht

Tegernseer GC Bad Wiessee (1958)

Robognerhof 1, 83707 Bad Wiessee
Tel (08022) 8769
Fax (08022) 82747
Holes 18 L 5501 m SSS 69
V'tors WD–H
Fees 90DM
Loc Tegernsee, 50 km S of Munich

Tutzing (1983)

82327 Tutzing-Deixlfurt
Tel (08158) 3600
Fax (08158) 7234
Holes 18 L 6159 m SSS 72
V'tors U H
Fees 80DM (100DM)
Loc Starnberger See, 30 km SW of Munich

Wittelsbacher GC Rohrenfeld-Neuburg (1988)

Gut Rohrenfeld, 86633 Neuburg/Donau
Tel (08431) 44118
Fax (08431) 41301
Holes 18 L 6350 m SSS 73
V'tors U H
Fees 70DM (90DM)
Loc 7 km E of Neuburg. 70 km NW of Munich
Arch J Dudok van Heel

Wörthsee (1982)

Gut Schluifeld, 82237 Wörthsee
Tel (08153) 3872
Fax (08153) 4280
Holes 18 L 6300 m SSS 73
V'tors WD–H WE–NA
Fees 80DM (100DM)
Loc Wörthsee, 20 km W of Munich
Arch Kurt Rossknecht

Nuremberg & North Bavaria

Abenberg (1988)

Am Golfplatz 19, 91183 Abenberg
Tel (09178) 98960
Fax (09178) 989698
Holes 18 holes Par 72 SSS 72
V'tors WD–H
Fees 70DM (90DM)
Loc 10 km S of Schwabach. 30 km S of Nuremberg

Bad Griesbach

Holzhäuser 8, 94086 Bad Griesbach
Tel (08532) 790-0
Fax (08532) 790-45
Holes Uttlau 18 L 6115 m SSS 72
Lederbach 18 L 5998 m
SSS 71; Brunnwies 18 L
6029 m SSS 71
V'tors I
Fees 80DM (100DM)
Loc 28 km SW of Passau
Arch Kurt Rossknecht

Bad Windsheim (1992)

Am Weinturm 2, 91438 Bad Windsheim
Tel (09841) 5027
Fax (09841) 3448
Holes 18 L 6265 m Par 73 SSS 73
V'tors U
Fees 60DM (80DM)
Loc 40 km W of Nuremberg (B470)

Bamberg (1973)

Postfach 1525, 96006 Bamberg
Tel (09547) 7212/7109
Fax (09547) 7817
Holes 18 L 6175 m SSS 72
V'tors H
Fees 60DM (80DM)
Loc Gut Leimershof, 16 km N of Bamberg
Arch Dieter Sziedat

Donau GC Passau-Rassbach (1986)

Rassbach 8, 94136 Thyrnau-Passau
Tel (08501) 91313
Fax (08501) 91314
Holes 18 L 6165 m SSS 72
V'tors U
Fees 60DM (70DM)
Loc 10 km E of Passau
Arch Götz Mecklenburg

Fränkische Schweiz (1974)

Kanndorf 8, 91316 Ebermannstadt
Tel (09194) 4827
Fax (09194) 5410
Holes 18 L 6050 m SSS 72
V'tors H
Fees 60DM (80DM)
Loc 5 km E of Ebermannstadt. 40 km N of Nuremberg

Fürth (1992)

Vacherstrasse 261, 90768 Fürth
Tel (0911) 757522
Fax (0911) 757522
Holes 18 L 6478 yds SSS 71
V'tors H
Fees 50DM (70DM)
Loc 20 km W of Nuremburg

Hof (1985)

Postfach 1324, 95012 Hof
Tel (09281) 43749
Fax (09821) 60318/709999
Holes 18 L 6040 m SSS 72
V'tors H
Fees 50DM (70DM)
Loc 2 km NE of Hof (B173)
Arch Dieter Sziedat

Ingolstadt (1977)

Spitzmühle, Gerolfingerstr, 85049 Ingolstadt
Tel (0841) 85778
Holes 18 L 5500 m SSS 69
Fees On application
Loc 3 km from Ingolstadt towards Gerolfing

Lauterhofen (1987)

Ruppertslohe 18, 92283 Lauterhofen
Tel (09186) 1574
Fax (09186) 1527
Holes 18 L 6054 m SSS 72
V'tors H
Fees 60DM (80DM)
Loc 25 km SE of Nuremberg
Arch Dillschnitter

Lichtenau-Weickershof (1980)

Weickershof 1, 91586 Lichtenau
Tel (09827) 92040
Fax (09827) 9204-44
Holes 18 L 6218 m SSS 72
V'tors WD–H (max 35) WE–M
Fees 60DM (80DM)
Loc 10 km E of Ansbach
Arch Dieter Sziedat

Oberfranken Thurnau (1965)

Postfach 1349, 95304 Kulmbach
Tel (09228) 319
Fax (09228) 7219
Holes 18 L 6152 m SSS 72
V'tors I H
Fees 70DM (90DM)
Loc Thurnau, 18 km NW of Bayreuth. 14 km SW of Kulmbach
Arch Donald Harradine

Oberpfälzer Wald G&LC (1977)

Ödengrub, 92431 Kemnath bei Fuhrn
Tel (09439) 466
Fax (09439) 1247
Holes 18 L 5799 m SSS 71
V'tors I
Fees 50DM (60DM)
Loc 10 km E of Schwarzenfeld, towards Neunburg
Arch Max Haseneder

Oberzwieselau (1990)

94227 Lindberg
Tel (01049) 9922/2367
Fax (01049) 9922/2924
Holes 18 L 6214 yds SSS 72
V'tors H–(max 36)

Fees   70DM (90DM)
Loc   170 km NE of Munich

Regensburg G&LC

(1966)

*Jagdschloss Thiergarten, 93177
Altenthann*
Tel   (09403) 505
Fax   (09403) 4391
Holes   18 L 5785 m SSS 71
V'tors U
Fees   60DM (90DM)
Loc   14 km E of Regensburg, nr
            Walhalla
Arch   Donald Harradine

Regensburg-Sinzing

Minoritenhof 1, 93161 Sinzing
Tel   (0941) 32504
Fax   (0941) 36299
Holes   18 L 5984 m SSS 72
            6 hole short course
V'tors U H
Fees   60DM (70DM)
Loc   7 km SW of Regensburg

Am Reichswald (1960)

Schiestlstr 100, 90427 Nürnberg
Tel   (0911) 305730
Fax   (0911) 301200
Holes   18 L 6345 m SSS 72
V'tors U H
Fees   70DM (100DM)
Loc   10 km N of Nuremberg

Rottaler G&CC (1972)

Am Fischgartl 2, 84332 Herbertsfelden
Tel   (08561) 5969
Fax   (08561) 2646
Holes   18 L 6105 m Par 72 SSS 72
V'tors U
Fees   60DM (70DM)
Loc   5 km W of Pfarrkirchen on
            B388. 120 km E of Munich
Arch   Donald Harradine

Sagmühle (1984)

*Golfplatz Sagmühle 1, 94086 Bad
Griesbach*
Tel   (08532) 2038
Fax   (08532) 3165
Holes   18 L 6168 m SSS 72
V'tors H
Fees   70DM (80DM)
Loc   25 km SW of Passau
Arch   Kurt Rossknecht

Schloss Fahrenbach

(1993)

95709 Tröstau
Tel   (09232) 882-256
Fax   (09232) 882-345
Holes   18 L 5858 m Par 71
V'tors U
Fees   £15 (£25)
Loc   15 km W of Marktredwitz.
            40 km E of Bayreuth
Arch   Deutsche Golf Consult

Schlossberg (1985)

Grünbach 8, 94419 Reisbach
Tel   (08734) 7035
Fax   (08734) 7795
Holes   18 L 6070 m SSS 72
V'tors U
Fees   50DM (70DM)
Loc   Sommershausen, 15 km from
            Dingolfing. 100 km NE of
            Munich, off Route 11

Schmidmühlen G&CC

(1968)

Am Theilberg, 92287 Schmidmühlen
Holes   18 L 5946 m SSS 72
Loc   35 km NW of Regensburg

Schwanhof (1994)

*Klaus Conrad Allee 1, 92706 Luhe-
Wildenau*
Tel   (09607) 92020
Fax   (09607) 920248
Holes   18 hole course SSS 72
V'tors U H
Fees   60DM (80DM)
Loc   80 km N of Regensburg
Arch   Pate/Weisshaupt

Rhineland

Ahaus

*Schmäinghook 36, 48683 Ahaus-
Alstätte*
Tel   (02567) 405
Fax   (02567) 3524
Holes   18 hole course SSS 72
            6 hole Par 3 course
V'tors U H
Fees   60DM (80DM)
Loc   60 km W of Münster
Arch   Deutsche Golf Consult

Bad Neuenahr G&LC

(1979)

*Remagener Weg, 53474 Bad Neuenahr-
Ahrweiler*
Tel   (02641) 2325
Fax   (02641) 29750
Holes   18 L 6060 m SSS 72
V'tors WD-H WE-H before 10am &
            after 4pm
Fees   70DM (90DM)
Loc   Bad Neuenahr, 40 km S
            of Bonn
Arch   Grohs/Preismann

Bergisch-Land

Siebeneickerst 386, 42111 Wuppertal
Tel   (02053) 7177
Fax   (02053) 7303
Holes   18 L 6037 m SSS 72
V'tors WD-H WE-M
Fees   80DM
Loc   Elberfeld, 8 km W of
            Wuppertal

Bochum (1982)

Im Mailand 127, 44797 Bochum
Tel   (0234) 799832
Fax   (0234) 795775
Holes   18 L 5300 m SSS 68
V'tors WD-H
Fees   60DM (80DM)
Loc   Bochum-Stiepel, 7 km S
            of Bochum

Bonn-Godesberg in
Wachtberg (1960)

*Landgrabenweg, 53343 Wachtberg-
Niederbachen*
Tel   (0228) 344003
Fax   (0228) 340820
Holes   18 L 5900 m Par 71
V'tors WD-H WE-M
Fees   70DM (90DM)
Loc   Niederbachem, 4 km from
            Bad Godesberg
Arch   M Peters

Burg Overbach (1984)

Postfach 1213, 53799 Much
Tel   (02245) 5550
Fax   (02245) 8247
Holes   18 L 6056 m SSS 72
V'tors H
Fees   60DM (80DM)
Loc   Much, 45 km E of Cologne,
            off A4
Arch   Deutsch Golf Consult

Castrop-Rauxel

*Dortmunder Str 383, 44577 Castrop-
Rauxel*
Tel   (02305) 62027
Fax   (02305) 61410
Holes   18 L 6181 m SSS 72
Fees   55DM (80DM)
Loc   10 km W of Dortmund

Dortmund (1956)

Reichmarkstr 12, 44265 Dortmund
Tel   (0231) 774133/774609
Fax   (0231) 774403
Holes   18 L 6174 m SSS 72
V'tors WE-M
Fees   60DM (80DM)
Loc   8 km S of Dortmund

Düsseldorf (1961)

Rommerljansweg 12, 40882 Ratingen
Tel   (02102) 81092
Fax   (02102) 81782
Holes   18 L 5905 m SSS 71
V'tors WD-U WE-M
Loc   11 km N of Düsseldorf

Düsseldorf Hösel

In den Höfen 32, 40883 Ratingen
Tel   (02102) 68629
Holes   18 L 6160 m SSS 72
Loc   Hösel, 15 km NE of
            Düsseldorf

Elfrather Mühle (1991)

An der Elfrather Mühle 145,
47802 Krefeld
Tel **(02151) 4969-12-14**
Fax (02151) 477459
Holes 18 L 6061 m Par 72 SSS 73
V'tors WD–H 36 WE–H 28
Fees 60–80DM (80–100DM)
Loc Krefeld 7 km. Düsseldorf
25 km
Arch Ron Kirby

Erftaue (1991)

Zur Mühlenerft 1,
41517 Grevenbroich
Tel **(02181) 280637**
Fax (02181) 280639
Holes 18 L 6039 m Par 72
V'tors WD–H WE–H after 1pm
Fees 60DM (80DM)
Loc 25 km SW of Düsseldorf
Arch Karl Grohs

Essen Haus Oefte

(1959)
Laupendahler Landstr, 45219 Essen
Tel **(02054) 83911**
Holes 18 L 6100 m SSS 72
Fees 80DM (100DM)
Loc 14 km SW of Essen

Essen-Heidhausen

(1970)
Preutenborbeckstr 36, 45239 Essen
Tel **(0201) 404111**
Holes 18 L 5937 m SSS 71
Loc 10 km S of Essen on B224,
nr Werden

Gut Heckenhof (1993)

53783 Eitorf
Tel **(02243) 83137**
Fax (02243) 83426
Holes 18 L 6214 m SSS 72
V'tors H
Fees On request
Loc 40 km SE of Cologne
Arch William Amick

Haus Bey (1992)

41334 Nettetal
Tel **(02153) 9197-0**
Fax (02153) 919750
Holes 18 L 6116 m SSS 72
V'tors WD–U H WE–M H
Fees 60DM (80DM)
Loc 40 km NW of Düsseldorf
Arch Paul Krings

Hubbelrath (1961)

Bergische Landstr 700,
40629 Düsseldorf
Tel **(02104) 72178/71848**
Fax (02104) 75685
Holes East 18 L 6208 m SSS 72
West 18 L 4325 m SSS 62
V'tors WD–U exc 12–3pm WE–M

Fees 100DM (120DM)
Loc Hubbelrath, 13 km E of
Düsseldorf, on Route B7
Arch B von Limburger

Hummelbachaue Neuss

(1987)
Norfer Kirchstrasse, 41469 Neuss
Tel **(02137) 91910**
Fax (02137) 4016
Holes 18 L 6091 m Par 73
V'tors WD–H WE–M
Fees 40–80DM (80DM)
Loc 5 km W of Düsseldorf
Arch Udo Barth

Issum-Niederrhein (1973)

Pauenweg 68, 47661 Issum 1
Tel **(02835) 3626**
Fax (02835) 4267
Holes 18 L 5728 m SSS 70
V'tors H
Fees 60DM (70DM)
Loc 10 km E of Geldern
Arch Harradine

Juliana (1979)

Frielinghausen 1, 45549 Sprockhövel
Tel **(0202) 647070/648220**
Fax (0202) 649891
Holes 18 L 6100 m SSS 71
V'tors H
Fees 50DM (80DM)
Loc 30 km E of Düsseldorf
Arch De Buer

Köln G&LC

Golfplatz 2, 51429 Bergisch Gladbach
Tel **(02204) 63114/63138**
Fax (02204) 68192
Holes 18 L 6090 m Par 72
V'tors H
Fees 80DM (100DM)
Loc 15 km E of Cologne

Krefeld (1930)

Eltweg 2, 47809 Krefeld
Tel **(02151) 570071/72**
Holes 18 L 6060 m SSS 72
V'tors WD–U H
Fees 80DM (100DM)
Loc 7 km SE of Krefeld.
Düsseldorf 16 km
Arch B von Limburger

Nordkirchen

Am Golfplatz 6, 59394 Nordkirchen
Tel **(02596) 9191**
Fax (02596) 9195
Holes 18 L 6200 m SSS 71
V'tors WD–I WE–H
Fees 60DM (70DM)
Loc 30 km S of Münster
Arch Christoph Städtler

RAF Germany (1956)

RAF Brüggen BFPO#25
Tel **(02163) 80049**
Fax (02163) 80934

Holes 18 L 6522 yds SSS 71
V'tors WD–U
Fees 35DM
Loc On B230, 1 km from Dutch/
German border. 25 km W of
Mönchengladbach

Rhein Sieg (1971)

Postfach 1216, 53759 Hennef
Tel **(02242) 6501**
Holes 18 L 6081 m Par 72
Loc Hennef, 30 km SE of Cologne

St Barbara's Royal Dortmund (1969)

Hesslingweg, 44309 Dortmund
Tel **(0231) 202551**
Fax (0231) 259183
Holes 18 L 5967 m SSS 73
V'tors H–by prior arrangement
Fees 60DM (80DM)
Loc Dortmund Brackel
Arch Brig Jones/Maj Coleman

Schloss Georghausen

(1962)
Georghausen 8, 51789 Lindlar-
Hommerich
Tel **(02207) 4938**
Fax (02207) 81230
Holes 18 L 6045 m SSS 72
V'tors H
Fees 60DM (80DM)
Loc 30 km E of Cologne

Schloss Myllendonk

(1965)
Myllendonkerstr 113,
41352 Korschenbroich 1
Tel **(02161) 641049**
Fax (02161) 648806
Holes 18 L 6120 m SSS 72
V'tors H
Fees 90DM (100DM)
Loc Korschenbroich, 5 km E of
Mönchengladbach

Schmitzhof (1975)

Arsbeckerstr 160, 41844 Wegberg
Tel **(02436) 39090**
Fax (02436) 390915
Holes 18 L 6115 m SSS 72
V'tors H
Fees 70DM (90DM)
Loc Wegberg-Merbeck, 20 km
SW of Mönchengladbach

Schwarze Heide

Gahlenerstrasse 44, 46244 Bottrop-
Kirchellen
Tel **(02045) 82488**
Fax (02045) 83077
Holes 18 L 6051 m SSS 72
V'tors I H
Fees 50DM (70DM)
Loc 55 km N of Düsseldorf
Arch Peter Drecker

Unna-Fröndenberg

(1985)

Schwarzer Weg 1,
58730 Fröndenberg

Tel   (02373) 70068
Fax   (02373) 70069
Holes 18 L 6177 m SSS 72
V'tors M H (max 34)
Fees   60DM (80DM)
Loc   25 km W of Dortmund
Arch   Karl Grohs

Vestischer GC Recklinghausen (1974)

Bockholterstr 475, 45659
Recklinghausen

Tel   (02361) 93420
Fax   (02361) 934240
Holes 18 L 6111 m SSS 72
V'tors WD–H exc Mon–NA
       WE–M
Fees   80DM (100DM)
Loc   Nr Loemühle Airport, N of
       Recklinghausen
Arch   Donald Harradine

Wasserburg Anholt

(1972)

Am Schloss 3, 46419 Isselburg Anholt

Tel   (02874) 3444
Fax   (02874) 29164
Holes 18 L 6115 m SSS 72
V'tors WD–U WE–H
Fees   50DM (80DM)
Loc   Parkhotel, Wasserburg
       Anholt. 15 km W
       of Bocholt

Westerwald (1979)

Postfach 1231, 57621 Hachenburg

Tel   (02666) 8220
Holes 18 holes SSS 72
Fees   35M (45DM)
Loc   Hachenburg, 60 km E of
       Bonn

Stuttgart & South West

Allgäuer G&LC (1984)

Hofgut Boschach, 87724 Ottobeuren

Tel   (08332) 1310
Fax   (08332) 5161
Holes 18 L 6215 m SSS 72
       6 hole short course
V'tors H
Fees   60DM (80DM)
Loc   2 km S of Ottobeuren.
       20 km N of Kempten

Bad Liebenzell

Golfplatz 9, 75378 Bad Liebenzell

Tel   (07052) 1574
Fax   (07052) 5302
Holes 18 L 6121 m Par 72 SSS 72

V'tors H–(max 33) WE–M
       10.30am–2pm
Fees   60DM (80DM)
Loc   35 km W of Stuttgart
Arch   Felix Elger

Bad Rappenau (1989)

Ehrenbergstrasse 25a, 74906 Bad
Rappenau

Tel   (07264) 3666
Fax   (07264) 3838
Holes 18 L 6103 m SSS 72
V'tors U H
Fees   60DM (80DM)
Loc   10 km NW of Heilbronn
Arch   Karl Gross

Baden Hills GC Rastatt

(1982)

Postfach 2, 76549 Hügelsheim

Tel   (07229) 5346
Fax   (07229) 5347
Holes 18 L 5906 m Par 71
V'tors H–booking necessary WD–U
       before 5pm WE–M before 3pm
Fees   D–50DM (D–70DM)
Loc   10 km W of Badeb-Baden.
       50 km N of Strasbourg

Baden-Baden (1901)

Fremersbergstr 127,
76530 Baden-Baden

Tel   (07221) 23579
Fax   (07221) 23528
Holes 18 L 4413 m Par 64
V'tors U
Fees   65DM (90DM)
Loc   3 km S of Baden-Baden
Arch   Harry Vardon

Bodensee (1986)

Lampertsweiler 51, 88138 Weissensberg

Tel   (08389) 89190
Fax   (08389) 89191
Holes 18 L 6112 m SSS 72
V'tors H
Fees   70DM (90DM)
Loc   5 km NE of Lindau/Bodensee
Arch   Robert Trent Jones Sr

Freiburg (1970)

Krüttweg 1, 79199 Kirchzarten

Tel   (07661) 9847-0
Fax   (07661) 984747
Holes 18 L 6068 m SSS 72
V'tors H
Fees   60DM (70DM)
Loc   Freiburg-Kappel/Kirchzarten
Arch   B von Limburger

Hechingen Hohenzollern

(1955)

Postfach 1124, 72379 Hechingen

Tel   (07471) 6478
Holes 18 holes SSS 72
V'tors WE–M
Fees   On application
Loc   Hechingen, 50 km S of
       Stuttgart

Heilbronn-Hohenlohe

(1964)

Hofgasse, 74639 Zweiflingen-
Friedrichsruhe

Tel   (07941) 920810
Fax   (07941) 920819
Holes 18 L 6082 m SSS 72
V'tors H
Fees   60DM (90DM)
Loc   25 km W of Heilbronn,
       nr Öhringen

Hohenstaufen (1959)

Unter den Ramsberg, 73072 Donzdorf-
Reichenbach

Tel   (07162) 27171/20050
Holes 18 L 6540 yds SSS 72
Loc   15 km E of Goppingen.
       45 km E of Stuttgart

Konstanz (1965)

Langenrain, Kargegg, 78476 Allensbach

Tel   (07533) 5124
Fax   (07533) 4897
Holes 18 L 6058 m SSS 72
V'tors WD–I WE–H max 28
Fees   70DM (90DM)
Loc   15 km NW of Konstanz,
       nr Langenrain

Lindau-Bad Schachen

(1954)

Am Schönbühl 5, 88131 Lindau

Tel   (08382) 78090
Fax   (08382) 78998
Holes 18 L 5871 m Par 71 SSS 71
Fees   80DM (100DM)
Loc   Nr Lindau, Bodensee

Markgräflerland Kandern (1984)

Feuerbacher Str 35, 79400 Kandern

Tel   (07626) 1043
Fax   (07626) 1433
Holes 18 L 6044 m Par 72 SSS 71
V'tors WD–U WE–M
Fees   60DM (80DM)
Loc   Kandern, 10 km N of
       Lörrach. 14 km NW of Basle
Arch   Grohs/Benz

Neckartal (1974)

Aldingerstr, Gebäude 975,
71638 Ludwigsburg-Pattonville

Tel   (07141) 871319
Fax   (07141) 81716
Holes 18 L 6310 m SSS 73
V'tors WD–U WE–M
Fees   70DM (75DM)
Loc   5 km NE of Stuttgart, nr
       Kornwestheim
Arch   B von Limburger

Obere Alp (1989)

Am Golfplatz 1-3, 79780 Stühlingen

Tel   (07703) 9203-0
Fax   (07703) 9203-18

Holes 18 L 6216 m SSS 72
9 L 3664 m SSS 60
V'tors H
Fees 18 hole: 60DM (90DM)
9 hole: 45DM (60DM)
Loc 40 km N of Zürich, nr Swiss
border
Arch Karl Grohs

Oberschwaben-Bad Waldsee (1968)

Hofgut Hopfenweiler,
88339 Bad Waldsee
Tel (07524) 5900
Fax (07524) 6106
Holes 18 L 6148 m SSS 72
V'tors H–(max 34)
Fees 65DM (90DM)
Loc Bad Waldsee, 60 km SW
of Ulm
Arch Donald Harradine

Oeschberghof L&GC (1976)

Golfplatz 1, 78166 Donaueschingen
Tel (0771) 84525
Fax (0771) 84540
Holes 18 L 6580 m SSS 74
9 L 4120 m SSS 62
V'tors H
Fees 80DM (120DM)
Loc Donaueschingen, 60 km E
of Freiburg
Arch Deutsche Golf Consult

Owingen-Überlingen

Alte Owinger Str, 88696 Owingen
Tel (07551) 83040
Fax (07551) 830422
Holes 18 L 6148 m SSS 72
V'tors H
Fees 60DM (90DM)
Loc 5 km N of Überlingen, nr
Lake Konstanz

Pforzheim Karlshäuser Hof

Karlshäuser Weg,
75248 Ölbronn-Dürrn
Tel (07237) 9100
Fax (07237) 5161
Holes 18 hole course SSS 72
V'tors H
Fees 60DM (80DM)
Loc 6 km N of Pforzheim.
30 km E of Karlsruhe
Arch Reinhold Weishaupt

Reutlingen-Sonnenbühl (1987)

Im Zerg, 72820 Sonnenbühl
Tel (07128) 92660
Fax (07128) 926692
Holes 18 L 6085 m SSS 72
V'tors H
Fees 60DM (80DM)
Loc 40 km S of Stuttgart

Rhein Badenweiler (1971)

79401 Badenweiler
Tel (07632) 7970
Fax (07632) 797150
Holes 18 L 6134 m SSS 72
V'tors WD–H WE–M
Fees 60DM (90DM)
Loc 16 km W of Badenweiler.
30 km SW of Freiburg
Arch Donald Harradine

Schloss Langenstein (1991)

Schloss Langenstein, 78359 Orsingen-
Nenzingen
Tel (07774) 50651
Fax (07774) 50699
Holes 18 L 6389 m SSS 73
9 hole course
V'tors WD–H WE–H (restricted)
Fees 80DM (100DM)
Loc 120 km S of Stuttgart.
75 km NE of Zürich
Arch Rod Whitman

Schloss Liebenstein (1982)

Postfach 27, 74380 Neckarwestheim
Tel (07133) 9878-0
Fax (07133) 9878-18
Holes 27 L 5890-6361 m
SSS 71-73
V'tors U
Fees 60DM (80DM)
Loc 35 km N of Stuttgart
Arch Donald Harradine

Schloss Weitenburg (1984)

Sommerhalde 11, 7
2181 Starzach-Sulzau
Tel (07472) 8061
Fax (07472) 8062
Holes 18 L 6069 m SSS 72/73
9 hole course
V'tors I
Fees 18 hole:70DM (90DM)
9 hole:30DM (40DM)
Loc 50 km SW of Stuttgart in
Neckar Valley
Arch Heinz Fehring

Sonnenalp (1976)

Hotel Sonnenalp,
87527 Ofterschwang
Tel (08321) 27276 (Sec)
Fax (08321) 272242
Holes 18 L 5938 m SSS 71
Fees 95DM
Loc 4 km W of Sonthofen
Arch Donald Harradine

Steisslingen (1991)

Kapellenstr 4a, 78256 Steisslingen-
Wiechs
Tel (07738) 7196
Fax (07738) 7196

Holes 18 L 6145 m SSS 72
V'tors U
Fees 55DM (85DM)
Loc 30 km N of Konstanz
Arch Dave Thomas

Stuttgarter Solitude (1927)

71297 Mönsheim
Tel (07044) 5852
Fax (07044) 5357
Holes 18 L 6045 m Par 72 SSS 72
V'tors WD–H max 28 WE–M phone
first
Fees 80DM (100DM)
Loc 15 km W of Stuttgart
Arch K von Limburger

Ulm/Neu-Ulm (1963)

Wochenauer Hof 2, 89186 Illerrieden
Tel (07306) 919420
Fax (07306) 919422
Holes 18 L 6076 m SSS 72
V'tors H
Fees 60DM (80DM)
Loc 15 km S of Ulm
Arch Deutsche Golf Consult

Waldegg-Wiggensbach (1988)

Hof Waldegg, 87487 Wiggensbach
Tel (08370) 93073
Fax (08370) 93074
Holes 18 L 5462 m SSS 69
V'tors H–max 36
Fees 60DM (80DM)
Loc 10 km W of Kempten,
nr Swiss/Austrian border

Greece

Afandou (1973)

Afandou, Rhodes
Tel (0241) 51255
Holes 18 L 6060 m Par 72
V'tors U
Fees 4000–4500dra
Loc Afandou, 20 km S of Rhodes
town

Corfu (1972)

PO Box 71, Ropa Valley,
49100 Corfu
Tel (0661) 94220/1
Fax (0661) 94220
Holes 18 L 6300 m SSS 72
Fees 6000–10.000dra
Loc Ermones Bay, 16 km W of
Corfu town

Glyfada (1962)

PO Box 70116, 166-10 Glyfada,
Athens
Tel   (01894) 6459
Fax   (01894) 6834
Holes 18 L 6189 m Par 72
V'tors H
Fees   11.000dra (15.000dra)
Loc   12 km S of Athens
Arch   Donald Harradine

Porto Carras G&CC
(1979)

Porto Carras, Halkidiki
Tel   (0375) 71381/71221
Holes 18 L 6086 m SSS 72
Loc   Sithonia Peninsula,
       100 km SE of Thessaloniki

Iceland

Akureyri (1935)

PO Box 317, 602 Akureyri
Tel   (462) 2974
Fax   (461) 1755
Holes 18 L 5783 m SSS 73
V'tors U H
Fees   £15
Loc   1 km from Akureyri (N coast)
Arch   Solnes/Gudmundsson

Borgarness (1973)

PO Box 112, 310 Borgarnes
Tel   (0437) 1663
Fax   (0437) 2063
Holes 9 L 5260 m SSS 71
V'tors U
Fees   1200Ikr
Loc   5 km from Borgarnes.
       100 km N of Reykjavik
       (W coast)

Éskifjardar (1976)

735 Éskifirdi
Holes 9 L 4412 m SSS 66
Fees   D–1000 Ikr
Loc   3 km W of Éskifjördur
       (E coast)

Hornafjardar

Hornafirdi
Tel   (7) 8030
Holes 9 L 3610 m SSS 63
Loc   Hofn (SE coast)

Húsavík (1967)

PO Box 23, Kötlum, 640 Húsavík
Tel   (6) 41000
Holes 9 L 2686 m SSS 70
V'tors U
Fees   1000Ikr
Loc   2 km from Húsavík (N coast)

Mis   Open June-Sept
Arch   Nils Skjöld

Isafjardar (1978)

PO Box 367, Isafjördur
Tel   (4) 3696 (Captain)
Holes 9 L 4860 m SSS 68
Fees   1000Ikr
Loc   3 km W of Isafjördur
       (NW coast)

Jökull (1973)

Vallholt 15, 355 Olafsvík
Tel   (3) 61198/61666
Holes 9 L 4530 m SSS 65
Fees   D–1000 Ikr
Loc   5 km SE of Olafsvík (W coast)

Keilir (1967)

Box 148, 222 Hafnarfjördur
Tel   (1) 565 3360
Fax   (1) 565 2560
Holes 18 L 5110 m SSS 68
V'tors U
Fees   £17 (£20)
Loc   Hafnarfjördur, 10 km S of
       Reykjavik (SW coast)

Leynir (1965)

PO Box 9, 300 Akranes
Tel   (431) 2711
Fax   (431) 3711
Holes 11 L 5445 m CR 70.3
V'tors U
Fees   1500Ikr
Loc   2 km from Akranes (SW coast)
Arch   H Thorsteinsson

Ness-Nesklúbburinn
(1964)

PO Box 66, 172 Seltjarnarnes
Tel   (561) 1930
Fax   (561) 1966
Holes 9 L 5374 m SSS 71
V'tors U
Fees   1500 Ikr
Loc   3 km W of Reykjavík

Olafsfjordur (1968)

Vesturgata 12, 625 Olafsfjordur
Tel   (6) 62364
Fax   (6) 62374
Holes 9 L 4570 m SSS 67
Fees   £8
Loc   60 km NW of Akureyri
       (N coast)
Mis   Open Jun-Oct

Reykjavíkur (1934)

Grafarholti, Box 12068,
132 Reykjavik
Tel   (1) 587 2211,
       (1) 587 2215 (Pro)
Fax   (1) 587 2212
Holes 18 L 5962 m SSS 73
V'tors U

Fees   2600 Ikr
Loc   8 km E of Reykjavík
Arch   Nils Skjold

Saudárkróks (1970)

Saudárkrókur
Tel   (5) 35075
Holes 9 L 5708 m SSS 71
Loc   2 km W of Saudárkrókur
       (N coast)

Sudurnesja (1964)

PO Box 112, 230 Keflavik
Tel   (2) 14100
Holes 18 L 5961 m SSS 73
Loc   N of Keflavik (SW coast).
       Airport 5 km

Vestmannaeyja (1938)

Vestmannaeyja Island
Tel   (481) 2363
Fax   (481) 2362
Holes 18 L 5601 m SSS 69
V'tors U
Fees   D–1500Ikr
Loc   2 km W of town centre.
       Large island off S coast.
       20 min flight from
       Reykjavík.

Italy

Como, Milan & Bergamo

Ambrosiano (1994)

Cascina Bertacca, 20080 Bubbiano-
Milan
Tel   (0290) 840820
Fax   (0290) 849365
Holes 18 L 6047 m Par 72
V'tors U
Fees   60.000L (90.000L)
Loc   25 km SW of Milan
Arch   Cornish/Silva

Barlassina CC (1956)

Via Privata Golf 42, 20030 Birago di
Camnago (MI)
Tel   (0362) 560621/2/3
Fax   (0362) 560934
Holes 18 L 6184 m SSS 72
V'tors WD–U
Fees   110.000L (155.000L)
Loc   22 km N of Milan
Arch   J Morrison

Bergamo L'Albenza
(1960)
*Via Longoni 12, 24030 Almenno San
Bartolomeo*
Tel   **(035) 640028/640707**
Fax   (035) 640028
Holes 18 L 6198 m SSS 72
          9 L 2962 m SSS 36
V'tors WD–U
Fees   70.000L (120.000L)
Loc   13 km NW of Bergamo.
          Milan 45 km
Arch   Cotton/Sutton

Brianza (1996)
*Cascina Cazzo,
20040 Usmate Velate*
Tel   **(039) 682 9089**
Fax   (039) 682 9059
Holes 18 L 5729 m Par 71 SSS 70
V'tors U
Fees   50.000L (80.000L)
Loc   24 km NE of Milan.
          Monza 6 km
Arch   Marco Croze

Carimate (1962)
Via Airoldi, 22060 Carimate
Tel   **(031) 790226**
Fax   (031) 790226
Holes 18 L 5982 m SSS 71
V'tors U H
Fees   70.000L (100.000L)
Loc   15 km S of Como. 27 km N
          of Milan
Arch   Pier Mancinelli

Castelconturbia (1984)
Via Suno, 28010 Agrate Conturbia
Tel   **(0322) 832093**
Fax   (0322) 832428
Holes Red 9 L 3330 m Par 36
          Yellow 9 L 3070 m Par 36
          Blue 9 L 3210 m Par 36
V'tors WD–H WE–M H
Fees   95.000L (150.000L)
Loc   23 km N of Novara.
          Milan 60 km
Arch   Robert Trent Jones Sr

Franciacorta (1986)
*Loc Castagnola, 25040 Nigoline di
Corte Franca, (Brescia)*
Tel   **(030) 984167**
Fax   (030) 984393
Holes 18 L 6065 m SSS 72
          9 hole Par 3 course
V'tors U
Fees   70.000L (100.000L)
Loc   Nigoline, 25 km E of Bergamo.
          Autostrada A4 exit Rovato
Arch   Dye/Croze

Lanzo Intelvi (1962)
22024 Lanzo Intelvi (CO)
Tel   **(031) 840169**
Holes 9 L 2438 m SSS 66
Loc   32 km NW of Como
Mis   Open May-Oct

Menaggio & Cadenabbia
(1907)
Via Golf 12, 22010 Grandola E Uniti
Tel   **(0344) 32103**
Fax   (0344) 30780
Holes 18 L 5455 m Par 70 SSS 69
V'tors WD–U H WE–H restricted
Fees   80.000L (110.000L)
Loc   5 km W of Menaggio.
          40 km N of Como
Arch   John Harris

Milano (1928)
20052 Parco di Monza (MI)
Tel   **(039) 303081/2/3**
Fax   (039) 304427
Holes 18 L 6414 m SSS 73
          9 L 2976 m SSS 36
V'tors WD–H WE–by appointment
Fees   96.000L (144.000L)
Loc   6 km N of Monza. 18 km
          NE of Milan
Arch   Gannon/Blandford

Molinetto CC (1982)
*SS Padana Superiore 11,
20063 Cernusco S/N (MI)*
Tel   **(02) 9210 5128/9210 5983**
Fax   (02) 9210 6635
Holes 18 L 6010 m Par 71
V'tors WD–H WE–restricted
Fees   80.000L (100.000L)
Loc   Cernusco, 10 km E of Milan

Monticello (1975)
Via Volta 4, 22070 Cassina Rizzardi
Tel   **(031) 928055**
Fax   (031) 880207
Holes 18 L 6413 m SSS 72
          18 L 6056 m SSS 72
V'tors WD–H WE–NA
Fees   80.000L (100.000L)
Loc   10 km SE of Como
Arch   Jim Fazio

La Pinetina (1971)
Via al Golf 4, 22070 Appiano Gentile
Tel   **(031) 933202**
Fax   (031) 890342
Holes 18 L 6001 m SSS 71
V'tors WD–U WE–booking
          necessary
Fees   70.000L (110.000L)
Loc   12 km SW of Como. Milan
          25 km

Le Robinie (1992)
*Via per Busto Arsizio 9, 21058 Solbiate
Olona (VA)*
Tel   **(039) 331 329260**
Fax   (039) 331 329266
Holes 18 L 6250 m Par 72 SSS 74
V'tors WD–U WE–H
Fees   80.000L (120.000L)
Loc   25 km NW of Milan.
          Malpensa Airport 6 km
Arch   Jack Nicklaus

La Rossera (1970)
Via Montebello 4, 24060 Chiuduno
Tel   **(035) 838600**
Fax   (035) 442 7047
Holes 9 L 2510 m SSS 68
V'tors U
Fees   45.000L (65.000L)
Loc   2 km from Chiuduno.
          18 km SE of Bergamo

Le Rovedine (1978)
*Via Carlo Marx, 20090 Noverasco di
Opera (MI)*
Tel   **(02) 5760 6420/5760 2730**
Fax   (02) 5760 6405
Holes 18 L 6307 m SSS 72
V'tors U
Fees   50.000L (75.000L)
Loc   4 km S of Milan

Royal Sant'Anna (1978)
22040 Annone di Brianza (CO)
Tel   **(0341) 577551**
Fax   (0341) 260143
Holes 18 L 4500 m SSS 64
Loc   15 km SE of Como. Milan
          40 km

Varese (1934)
*Via Vittorio Veneto 32,
21020 Luvinate (VA)*
Tel   **(0332) 227394/229302**
Fax   (0332) 222107
Holes 18 L 5936 m SSS 72
V'tors WD–U H
Fees   80.000L (120.000L)
Loc   5 km NW of Varese
Arch   Gannon/Blandford

Vigevano (1974)
*Via Chitola 49,
27029 Vigevano (PV)*
Tel   **(0381) 346628/346077**
Fax   (0381) 346091
Holes 18 L 5678 m SSS 72
Loc   25 km SE of Novara.
          35 km SW of Milan

Villa D'Este (1926)
Via Cantù 13, 22030 Montorfano (CO)
Tel   **(031) 200200**
Fax   (031) 200786
Holes 18 L 5787 m SSS 71
V'tors I H
Fees   80.000L (120.000L)
Loc   Montorfano, 7 km SE of
          Como
Arch   Peter Gannon

Zoate
20067 Zoate di Tribiano (MI)
Tel   **(02) 9063 2183/9063 1861**
Fax   (02) 9063 1861
Holes 18 L 6122 m Par 72
V'tors WD–U H
Fees   70.000L (100.000L)
Loc   Zoate, 17 km SE of Milan
Arch   Marmori

Elba

Acquabona (1971)

57037 Portoferraio, Isola di Elba (LI)
Tel   (0565) 940066
Fax   (0565) 933410
Holes 9 L 5144 m SSS 67
V'tors U
Fees   45.000–65.000L
Loc   5 km NW of Porto Azzurro.
           6 km NW of Porto Ferraio
Arch   Gianni Albertini

Emilia Romagna

Adriatic GC Cervia
(1985)

Via Jelenia Gora No 6,
48016 Cervia-Milano Marittima
Tel   (0544) 992786/992370
Fax   (0544) 993410
Holes 18 L 6246 m SSS 72
V'tors U H
Fees   85.000L (100.000L)
Loc   20 km SE of Ravenna
Arch   Marco Croze

Bologna (1959)

Via Sabattini 69, 40050 Monte San
Pietro (BO)
Tel   (051) 969100
Fax   (051) 672 0017
Holes 18 L 6171 m SSS 72
V'tors U
Fees   60.000L (90.000L)
Loc   20 km W of Bologna
Arch   Harris/Cotton

Croara (1976)

29010 Croara di Gazzola
Tel   (0523) 977105/977148
Fax   (0523) 977100
Holes 18 L 6065 m SSS 72
V'tors H
Fees   50.000L (70.000L)
Loc   16 km SW of Piacenza.
           84 km SE of Milan
Arch   Buratti/Croze

Matilde di Canossa

Via Casinazzo 1,
42100 San Bartolomeo
Tel   (0522) 371295
Fax   (0522) 371204
Holes 18 L 6231 m SSS 72
V'tors U
Fees   50.000L (80.000L)
Loc   50 km NW of Bologna
Arch   Marco Croze

La Rocca (1985)

Via Campi 8, 43038 Sala Baganza
(PR)
Tel   (0521) 834037
Fax   (0521) 834575
Holes 18 L 6076 m SSS 71

V'tors U
Fees   60.000L (80.000L)
Loc   8 km S of Parma
Arch   Marco Croze

La Torre (1992)

Via Limisano 10, Riolo Terme (RA)
Tel   (0546) 74035
Fax   (0546) 74076
Holes 18 L 6350 m Par 72
V'tors H
Fees   40.000L (50.000L)
Loc   30 km SW of Bologna
Arch   Alberto Croze

Gulf of Genoa

Degli Ulivi (1932)

Via Campo Golf 59, 18038 Sanremo
Tel   (0184) 557093
Fax   (0184) 557388
Holes 18 L 5203 m SSS 67
V'tors U
Fees   60.000L (95.000L)
Loc   5 km N of Sanremo
Arch   Peter Gannon

Garlenda (1965)

Via Golf 7, 17030 Garlenda
Tel   (0182) 580012
Fax   (0182) 580561
Holes 18 L 6047 m Par 72 SSS 71
V'tors WE–H
Fees   80.000L (130.000L)
Loc   15 km N of Alassio
Arch   John Harris

Marigola (1975)

Via Vallata 5, 19032 Lerici (SP)
Tel   (0187) 970193
Fax   (0187) 970193
Holes 9 L 2116 m Par 49
V'tors U
Fees   30.000L (35.000L)
Loc   6 km SE of La Spezia
Arch   Franco Marmori

Pineta di Arenzano
(1959)

Piazza del Golf 3, 16011 Arenzano
(GE)
Tel   (010) 911 1817
Fax   (010) 911 1270
Holes 9 L 5527 m SSS 70
V'tors H
Fees   60.000L (85.000L)
Loc   Arenzano Pineta, 20 km W
           of Genoa
Arch   Donald Harradine

Rapallo (1930)

Via Mameli 377, 16035 Rapallo
(GE)
Tel   (0185) 261777
Fax   (0185) 261779
Holes 18 L 5638 m Par 70

V'tors H WE–NA before noon
Fees   80.000L (Sat–120.000L)
Loc   25 km SE of Genoa. A12
           motorway exit Rapallo

Versilia (1990)

Via Sipe 100, 55045 Pietrasanta
(LU)
Tel   (0584) 88 15 74
Fax   (0584) 75 22 72
Holes 18 L 6115 m Par 72
V'tors U H
Fees   70.000L (80.000L)
Loc   30 km N of Pisa on coast,
           nr Forte dei Marmi
Arch   Marco Croze

Lake Garda & Dolomites

Asiago (1967)

Via Meltar 2, 36012 Asiago (VI)
Tel   (0424) 462721
Fax   (0424) 462721
Holes 18 L 6005 m SSS 71
V'tors U H
Fees   80.000L (100.000L)
Loc   3 km N of Asiago. 50 km N
           of Vicenza
Arch   P Harradine

Bogliaco (1912)

Via Golf 11, 25088 Toscolano
Maderno
Tel   (0365) 643006
Fax   (0365) 643006
Holes 9 L 2572 m SSS 67
V'tors H
Fees   50.000L (70.000L)
Loc   Lake Garda, 40 km NE
           of Brescia

Ca' degli Ulivi (1988)

Via Ghiandare 2, 37010 Marciaga di
Costermano (VR)
Tel   (045) 725 6463/725 6485
Fax   (045) 725 6876
Holes 18 L 6000m SSS 72
           9 hole course
Loc   Above village of Garda.
           Verona Airport 35 km

Campo Carlo Magno
(1922)

Golf Hotel, 38084 Madonna di
Campiglio (TN)
Tel   (0465) 441003
Fax   (0465) 440298
Holes 9 L 5148 m SSS 67
V'tors H
Fees   75.000–100.000L
Loc   Madonna di Campiglio 1 km.
           74 km NW of Trento
Arch   Henry Cotton

Folgaria (1987)
Loc Costa di Folgaria, 38064 Folgaria (TN)
Tel (0464) 720480
Fax (0464) 720480
Holes 9 L 2582 m SSS 70
V'tors H
Fees 60.000L (70.000L)
Loc 30 km S of Trento, off A22
Arch Marco Croze

Gardagolf CC (1985)
Via Angelo Omodeo 2, 25080 Soiano Del Lago (BS)
Tel (0365) 674707 (Sec)
Fax (0365) 674788
Holes 18 L 6505 m SSS 74
9 L 2635 m Par 35
V'tors H
Fees 85.000L (115.000L)
Loc Lake Garda, 30 km NE of Brescia
Arch Cotton/Pennink/Steel

Karersee-Carezza
Loc Carezza 171, 39056 Welschofen-Nova Levante
Tel (0471) 612200
Fax (0471) 612200
Holes 9 L 5340 m SSS 68
V'tors H
Fees 60.000L (70.000L)
Loc 30 km S of Bolzano
Arch Marco Croze

Petersberg (1987)
Unterwinkel 5, 39040 Petersberg (BZ)
Tel (0471) 615122
Fax (0471) 615229
Holes 18 L 5100 m SSS 66
V'tors U
Fees 75.000L (95.000L)
Loc 35 km SE of Bolzano, nr Nova Ponente
Arch Marco Croze

Ponte di Legno (1980)
Corso Milano 36, 25056 Ponte di Legno (BS)
Tel (0364) 900306
Fax (0364) 900555
Holes 9 L 4803 m SSS 68
V'tors U
Fees 40.000L (60.000L)
Loc 90 km W of Trento, nr San Michele
Arch Caremoli

Verona (1963)
Ca' del Sale 15, 37066 Sommacampagna
Tel (045) 510060
Fax (045) 510242
Holes 18 L 6054 m SSS 72
V'tors H WE–M
Fees 100.000L (110.000L)
Loc 7 km W of Verona
Arch John Harris

Naples & South

Napoli (1983)
Via Campiglione 11, 80072 Arco Felice (NA)
Tel (081) 526 4296
Holes 9 L 4776 m SSS 68
V'tors M
Fees 30.000L (35.000L)
Loc Pozzuoli, 10 km W of Naples

Porto d'Orra (1977)
PB 102, 88063 Catanzaro Lido
Tel (0961) 791045
Fax (0961) 791444
Holes 9 L 5686 m SSS 70
Fees 35.000L (35.000L)
Loc 9 km N of Catanzaro Lido on coast

Riva Dei Tessali (1971)
74011 Castellaneta
Tel (099) 843 9251
Fax (099) 843 9255
Holes 18 L 5960 m SSS 71
V'tors U
Fees 60.000L
Loc 34 km SW of Taranto
Arch Marco Croze

San Michele
Loc Bosco 8/9, 87022 Cetraro (CS)
Tel (0982) 91012
Fax (0982) 91430
Holes 9 L 2760 m SSS 70
V'tors U H
Fees 30.000L (35.000L)
Loc Cetraro, 50 km N of Cosenza. 250 km SE of Naples
Arch Piero Mancinelli

Rome & Centre

Castelgandolfo (1987)
Via Santo Spirito 13, 00040 Castelgandolfo
Tel (06) 931 2301/931 3084
Fax (06) 931 2244
Holes 18 L 6025 m SSS 72
V'tors U H Sun–restricted
Fees 60.000L (100.000L)
Loc 22 km SE of Rome
Arch Robert Trent Jones

Eucalyptus (1988)
Via Cogna 5, 04011 Aprilia (Roma)
Tel (06) 926252/926 8120
Fax (06) 926 8502
Holes 18 L 6310 m Par 72 SSS 73
V'tors WD–U WE–U H
Fees 40.000L (50.000L)
Loc 20 km S of Rome on Aprilia–Anzio road
Arch D'Onofrio/Mancinelli

Fioranello
CP 96, 00040 Santa Maria delle Mole (RM)
Tel (06) 713 8058
Fax (06) 713 8212
Holes 18 L 5417 m Par 70
Fees 40.000L (50.000L)
Loc Santa Maria, 17 km SE of Rome

Fiuggi (1928)
Superstrada Anticolana 1, 03015 Fiuggi (FR)
Tel (0775) 55250
Fax (0775) 506742
Holes 9 L 5697 m SSS 70
V'tors U
Loc 60 km SE of Rome

Marco Simone (1989)
Via di Marco Simone, 00012 Guidonia (RM)
Tel (0774) 366469
Fax (0774) 366476
Holes 18 L 6317 m SSS 73
18 hole course Par 64
V'tors U
Fees 80.000L (100.000L)
Loc 17 km NE of Rome
Arch Fazio/Mezzacane

Nettuno
Via della Campana 18, 00048 Nettuno (RM)
Tel (06) 981 9419
Fax (06) 981 9419
Holes 18 L 6260 m SSS 72
V'tors U H
Fees 40.000L (50.000L)
Loc 60 km S of Rome on coast
Arch Marco Croze

Olgiata (1961)
Largo Olgiata 15, 00123 Roma
Tel (06) 308 9141
Fax (06) 308 9968
Holes 18 L 6347 m SSS 73
9 L 2947 m SSS 71
V'tors U
Fees 70.000L (120.000L)
Loc 19 km NW of Rome, nr La Storta
Arch CK Cotton

Parco de' Medici (1989)
Viale Parco de' Medici 20, 00149 Roma
Tel (06) 655 3477
Fax (06) 655 3344
Holes 18 L 6318 m SSS 73
V'tors U
Fees 90.000L
Loc 15 km SW of Rome, nr Airport
Arch P Fazio

Pescara (1992)

Contrado Cerreto 58, 66010 Miglianico (CH)
Tel   **(0871) 959566**
Fax   (0871) 950363
Holes   18 L 6184 m Par 72 SSS 72
V'tors U
Fees   50.000L (70.000L)
Loc   S of Pescara (Adriatic coast)

Le Querce

San Martino, 01015 Sutri (VT)
Tel   **(0761) 68789**
Fax   (0761) 68142
Holes   18 L 6433 m SSS 72
V'tors U
Fees   50.000L (70.000L)
Loc   42 km N of Rome
Arch   Fazio/Mezzacane

Roma (1903)

*Via Appia Nuova 716A,
00178 Roma*
Tel   **(06) 780 3407**
Fax   (06) 783 46219
Holes   18 L 5825 m SSS 72
V'tors WD–H WE–M H
Fees   80.000L (110.000L)
Loc   7 km SE of Rome towards
        Ciampino

Tarquinia

*Loc Pian di Spille, Via degli Alina 271,
01016 Marina Velca/Tarquinia (VT)*
Tel   **(0766) 812109**
Holes   9 L 5442 m SSS 69
Loc   80 km N of Rome on coast

Torvaianica

Via Enna 30, 00040 Marina di Ardea
Tel   **(06) 913 3250**
Fax   (06) 913 3592
Holes   9 L 4416 m SSS 64
V'tors H
Fees   20.000L
Loc   30 km S of Rome
Arch   Leonardo Basili

Sardinia

Is Molas (1975)

CP 49, 09010 Pula
Tel   **(070) 924 1013/4**
Fax   (070) 924 1015
Holes   18 L 6383 m SSS 72
Fees   80.000L (100.000L)
Loc   Pula, 32 km S of Cagliari
Arch   Cotton/Pennink/Lurie

Pevero GC Costa Smeralda (1972)

07020 Porto Cervo
Tel   **(0789) 96072/96210/96211**
Fax   (0789) 96572
Holes   18 L 6186 m SSS 72

V'tors U
Fees   80.000–200.000L
Loc   Porto Cervo, 30 km N of
        Olbia, on Costa Smeralda
Arch   Robert Trent Jones

Turin & Piemonte

Alpino Di Stresa (1924)

Viale Golf Panorama 49, 28839 Vezzo (VB)
Tel   **(0323) 20642/20101**
Fax   (0323) 20642
Holes   9 L 5397 m Par 69 SSS 68
V'tors WE–U WE–restricted
Fees   18 holes–50.000L (70.000L)
        9 holes–35.000L (50.000L)
Loc   7 km W of Stresa. Milan
        80 km
Arch   Peter Gannon

Biella Le Betulle (1958)

Valcarozza, 13050 Magnano (VC)
Tel   **(015) 679151**
Fax   (015) 679276
Holes   18 L 6427 m SSS 72
V'tors U
Fees   90.000L (110.000L)
Loc   17 km SW of Biella
Arch   John Morrison

Cervino (1955)

11021 Cervinia-Breuil (AO)
Tel   **(0166) 949131**
Fax   (0116) 949131
Holes   9 L 4796 m SSS 66
V'tors U
Fees   50.000L–70.000L
Loc   53 km NE of Aosta
Arch   Donald Harradine

Cherasco CC (1983)

*Loc Fraschetta, Cascina Roma,
12062 Cherasco (CN)*
Tel   **(0172) 489772/488489**
Fax   (0172) 488304
Holes   18 L 5947 m Par 72 SSS 71
V'tors H
Fees   50.000L (80.000L)
Loc   Cherasco, 45 km S of Turin
Arch   Gianmarco Croze

Claviere (1923)

Strada Nazionale 45, 10050 Claviere (TO)
Tel   **(0122) 878917**
Holes   9 L 4650 m SSS 65
V'tors U
Fees   70.000L
Loc   96 km W of Turin
Arch   Luzi

Courmayeur

11013 Courmayeur (AO)
Tel   **(0165) 89103**
Holes   9 L 2650 m SSS 67
Loc   5 km NE of Courmayeur

Le Fronde (1973)

Via Sant-Agostino 68, 10051 Avigliana (TO)
Tel   **(011) 932 8053/0540**
Fax   (011) 932 0928
Holes   18 L 5976 m SSS 71
V'tors WD–U WE–H max 34
Fees   60.000L (80.000L)
Loc   Avigliana, 20 km W of Turin
Arch   John Harris

Iles Borromees

*Loc Motta Rossa, 28010 Brovello
Carpugnino (VB)*
Tel   **(0323) 929285/929192**
Fax   (0323) 929190
Holes   18 L 6445 m SSS 72
V'tors U
Fees   80.000L (100.000L)
Loc   5 km S of Stresa. 80 km NW
        of Milan
Arch   Marco Croze

Golf dei Laghi (1993)

*Via Trevisani 6, 21028 Travedona
Monate (VA)*
Tel   **(0332) 978101**
Fax   (0332) 977532
Holes   18 L 6400 m Par 72 SSS 73
V'tors H
Fees   60.000L (100.000L)
Loc   30 km SW of Varese.
        50 km NW of Milan
Arch   Piero Mancinelli

Margara (1975)

Via Tenuta Margara 5, 15043 Fubine (AL)
Tel   **(0131) 778555**
Fax   (0131) 778772
Holes   18 L 6045 m SSS 72
Loc   15 km NW of Alessandria

La Margherita

Strada Pralormo 29, Carmagnola (TO)
Tel   **(011) 979 5113**
Fax   (011) 979 5204
Holes   18 L 6339 m SSS 73
V'tors U
Fees   50.000L (80.000L)
Loc   20 km S of Turin
Arch   Croze/Ferraris

Piandisole (1964)

Via Pineta 1, 28057 Premeno (NO)
Tel   **(0323) 587100**
Holes   9 L 2830 m SSS 67
Fees   40.000L (60.000L)
Loc   Premeno, 30 km N of Stresa

I Roveri (1971)

Rotta Cerbiatta 24, 10070 Fiano (TO)
Tel (011) 923 5719/923 5667
Fax (011) 923 5668
Holes 18 L 6218 m SSS 72
9 L 3107 m SSS 36
V'tors WE–NA
Fees 80.000L (100.000L)
Loc 16 km NW of Turin. Caselle
Airport 10 km
Arch Robert Trent Jones

Santa Croce

Fraz Mellana, 12012 Bóves (CN)
Tel (0171) 387041
Fax (0171) 387512
Holes 18 L 6000 m SSS 72
V'tors U
Fees 50.000L (70.000L)
Loc 80 km S of Turin, nr Cúneo
Arch Graham Cooke

La Serra (1970)

Via Astigliano 42, 15048 Valenza (AL)
Tel (0131) 954778
Fax (0131) 928294
Holes 9 L 2820 m SSS 70
V'tors H
Fees 25.000L (40.000L)
Loc 4 km W of Valenza. 7 km
N of Alessandria
Arch Migliorini

Sestrieres (1932)

Piazza Agnelli 4, 10058 Sestrieres (TO)
Tel (0122) 755170/76243
Fax (0122) 76294
Holes 18 L 4598 m Par 67 SSS 65
V'tors U H
Fees 55.000L (80.000L)
Loc Sestrieres, 96 km W of Turin

Stupinigi (1972)

Corso Unione Sovietica 506, 10135 Torino
Tel (011) 347 2640
Fax (011) 397 8038
Holes 9 L 2175 m SSS 63
Loc Mirafiore, Turin

Torino (1924)

Via Grange 137, 10070 Fiano Torinese
Tel (011) 923 5440/923 5670
Fax (011) 923 5886
Holes 18 L 6216 m SSS 72
18 L 6214 m SSS 72
V'tors U
Fees 80.000L (100.000L)
Loc 23 km NW of Turin
Arch Morrison/Croze/Cooke

Vinovo (1986)

Via Debouche, 10048 Vinovo (TO)
Tel (011) 965 3880/2263
Fax (011) 962 3748
Holes 9 L 4278 m Par 64

V'tors U
Fees 50.000L (60.000L)
Loc 3 km SW of Turin
Arch Croce/Chiaravigcio

Tuscany & Umbria

Casentino (1985)

Loc Il Palazzo, 52014 Poppi (Arezzo)
Tel (0575) 529810
Fax (0575) 520167
Holes 9 L 5550 m Par 72 SSS 69
V'tors WD–U WE–H
Fees 40.000L (50.000L)
Loc Poppi, 50 km SE of Florence
Arch R Brami

Castelfalfi G&CC

50050 Montaione (FI)
Tel (0571) 698093/4
Fax (0571) 698098
Holes 18 L 6095 m SSS 73
V'tors H
Fees 50.000L
Loc 45 km SW of Florence
Arch Pier Mancinelli

Conero GC Sirolo (1987)

Via Betellico 6, 60020 Sirolo (AN)
Tel (071) 736 0613
Fax (071) 736 0380
Holes 18 L 6185 m Par 72
9 hole course Par 29
V'tors U
Fees 60.000L (80.000L)
Loc Sirolo, 20 km SE of Ancona.
Falconara Airport 25 km
Arch Marco Croze

Cosmopolitan G&CC

(1992)
Viale Pisorno 60, 56018 Tirrenia
Tel (050) 33633
Fax (050) 33085
Holes 18 L 6291 m SSS 73
V'tors U
Fees 60.000L
Loc 15 km SW of Pisa
Arch David Mezzacane

Firenze Ugolino

Strada Chiantigiana 3, 50015 Grassina
Tel (055) 205 1009/203 1085
Fax (055) 230 1141
Holes 18 L 5785 m SSS 70
V'tors U
Fees 50.000L (70.000L)
Loc Grassina, 9 km S of Florence

Lamborghini-Panicale

(1992)
Loc Soderi 1, 06064 Panicale (PG)
Tel (075) 837582
Fax (075) 837582

Holes 9 L 2860 m SSS 36
V'tors H
Fees 35.000L (45.000L)
Loc 30 km W of Perugia, nr Lake
Trasimeno
Arch Lamborghini Ferruccio

Montecatini (1985)

Via Dei Brogi 5, Loc Pievaccia, 51015 Monsummano Terme
Tel (0572) 62218
Fax (0572) 617435
Holes 18 L 5932 m SSS 71
V'tors WD–U H
Fees 70.000L (80.000L)
Loc 8 km SE of Montecatini
Terme. 50 km SW of
Florence (A11)
Arch Marco Croze

Le Pavoniere (1986)

Via della Fattoria 6, 50047 Prato
Tel (0574) 620855
Fax (0574) 624558
Holes 18 L 6464 m Par 72 SSS 73
V'tors U
Fees 50.000L (70.000L)
Loc Prato 10 km. 25 km W of
Florence
Arch Arnold Palmer

Perugia (1960)

06074 Santa Sabina-Ellera
Tel (075) 517 2204
Fax (075) 517 2370
Holes 18 L 5650 m SSS 71
V'tors U
Fees 60.000L (70.000L)
Loc 6 km NW of Perugia
Arch David Mezzacane

Poggio dei Medici

Via S Gavino 27, 50038 Scarperia, Firenze
Tel (055) 843 0436
Fax (055) 843 0439
Holes 18 L 6367 m Par 73
V'tors U
Fees 60.000L (75.000L)
Loc 30 km from Florence
Arch Fioravanti/Dassù

Punta Ala (1964)

Via del Golf 1, 58040 Punta Ala (GR)
Tel (0564) 922121/922719
Fax (0564) 920182
Holes 18 L 6213 m SSS 72
V'tors U
Fees 50.000–90.000L
Loc 40 km NW of Grosseto. Siena
90 km. Florence 150 km

Tirrenia (1968)

Viale San Guido, 56018 Tirrenia (PI)
Tel (050) 37518
Fax (050) 33286
Holes 9 L 3065 m SSS 72
Loc 15 km SW of Pisa on coast

Venice &
North East

Albarella
*Isola de Albarella, 45010 Rosolina
(RO)*
Tel	**(0426) 330124**
Fax	(0426) 330628
Holes	18 L 6040 m SSS 72
V'tors	H
Fees	70.000L (90.000L)
Loc	64 km S of Venice
Arch	Harris/Croze

Ca' della Nave (1986)
*Piazza Vittoria 14,
30030 Martellago*
Tel	**(041) 540 1555**
Fax	(041) 540 1926
Holes	18 L 6380 m SSS 73
	9 L 1240 m Par 28
V'tors	H
Fees	80.000L (100.000L)
Loc	Martellago, 12 km NW of
	Venice
Arch	Arnold Palmer

Cansiglio (1956)
CP 152, 31029 Vittorio Veneto
Tel	**(0438) 585398**
Fax	(0438) 585398
Holes	18 L 6007 m SSS 71
V'tors	WD–U WE–H
Fees	65.000L (85.000L)
Loc	21 km NE of Vittorio Veneto.
	80 km NE of Venice
Arch	Trent Jones/Croze

Colli Berici (1986)
*Strada Monti Comunali,
36040 Brendola (VI)*
Tel	**(0444) 601780**
Fax	(0444) 400777
Holes	18 L 5798 m SSS 71
V'tors	U
Fees	80.000L (100.000L)
Loc	Vicenza 10 km. Venice 70 km
Arch	Marco Croze

Frassanelle (1990)
35030 Frassanelle di Rovolon (PD)
Tel	**(049) 991 0722**
Fax	(049) 991 0722
Holes	18 L 6180 m SSS 72
V'tors	H
Fees	80.000L (100.000L)
Loc	20 km S of Padova, nr Via
	dei Colli
Arch	Marco Croze

Lignano
*Via Bonifica 3, 33054 Lignano
Sabbiadoro*
Tel	**(0431) 428025**
Fax	(0431) 423230
Holes	18 L 6280 m SSS 72
V'tors	H

Fees	60.000L (80.000L)
Loc	90 km E of Venice on coast
Arch	Marco Croze

La Montecchia (1989)
*Via Montecchia 12,
35030 Selvazzano (PD)*
Tel	**(049) 805 5550**
Fax	(049) 805 5737
Holes	18 L 6318 m SSS 73
	9 L 3012 m Par 36
V'tors	U H
Fees	90.000L (110.000L)
Loc	8 km W of Padova. 40 km W
	of Venice
Arch	T Macauley

Padova (1966)
35050 Valsanzibio di Galzignano
Tel	**(049) 913 0078**
Fax	(049) 913 1193
Holes	18 L 6053 m SSS 72
Loc	Valsanzibio, 20 km S of
	Padua

San Floriano-Gorizia
(1987)
*Castello di San Floriano,
34070 San Floriano del Collio (GO)*
Tel	**(0481) 884252/884234**
Fax	(0481) 884252
Holes	9 L 4200 m Par 66
V'tors	U
Fees	40.000L
Loc	6 km NW of Gorizia.
	50 km SE of Udine,
	nr Slovenian border
Arch	Pellicciari

Trieste (1954)
Via Padriciano 80, 34012 Trieste
Tel	**(040) 226159/227062**
Fax	(040) 226159
Holes	9 L 5826 m SSS 71
Loc	Padriciano, 7 km E of Trieste

Udine (1971)
*Via dei Fagi 1, Località Villaverde,
33034 Fagagna (UD)*
Tel	**(0432) 800418**
Fax	(0432) 800418
Holes	9 L 2944 m Par 72 SSS 71
V'tors	H
Fees	60.000L
Loc	15 km NW of Udine
Arch	Marco Croze

Venezia (1928)
*Via del Forte, 30011 Alberoni
(Venezia)*
Tel	**(041) 731015/731333**
Fax	(041) 731339
Holes	18 L 6199 m SSS 72
V'tors	U H
Fees	90.000L (100.000L)
Loc	Venice Lido
Arch	Cruickshank/Cotton

Villa Condulmer (1960)
*Via della Croce 3, 31021 Zerman di
Mogliano Veneto*
Tel	**(041) 457062**
Fax	(041) 457202
Holes	18 L 5995 m SSS 71
	9 hole short course
Fees	60.000L (Sun–80.000L)
Loc	Mogliano Veneto, 17 km N of
	Venice
Arch	Harris/Croze

Luxembourg

Clervaux (1990)
B P 5, 9701 Clervaux
Tel	**92 93 95**
Fax	92 94 51
Holes	18 holes SSS 72
V'tors	H
Fees	980fl (1300fl)
Loc	3 km from Clervaux, North
	Luxembourg

Gaichel
Rue de Eischen, 8469 La Gaichel
Tel	**39 71 08**
Fax	39 00 75
Holes	9 L 5170 m SSS 70
V'tors	U H
Fees	700fr (900fr)
Loc	10 km W of Mersch on
	Belgian border. Arlon 3 km

Grand-Ducal de
Luxembourg (1936)
1 Route de Trèves, 2633 Senningerberg
Tel	**34 00 90**
Fax	34 83 91
Holes	18 L 5765 m SSS 71
V'tors	H
Fees	1500fr (2000fr)
Loc	7 km N of Luxembourg
Arch	Maj Simpson

Kikuoka CC Chant Val
(1991)
Scheierhaff, 5412 Canach
Tel	**35 61 35**
Fax	35 74 50
Holes	18 L 6404 m SSS 74
V'tors	H
Fees	1400fr–2060fr (2575fr)
Loc	20 km E of Luxembourg City
Arch	Iwao Uematsu

Golf de Luxembourg
Domaine de Belenhaff, 6141 Junglinster
Tel	**78 00 68-1**
Fax	78 71 28
Holes	18 L 6179 m Par 72
V'tors	H or Green card
Fees	1650fl (1950fl)
Loc	17 km NE of Luxembourg

Malta

Royal Malta (1888)
Marsa HMR 15, Malta
Tel   (035) 23 38 51
Fax   (035) 23 18 09
Holes 18 L 5020 m SSS 68
V'tors U H exc Thurs–NA before
            11am Sat/BH–NA before
            noon
Fees   £M10
Loc   Marsa, 3 miles from Valetta

Netherlands

Amsterdam &
Noord Holland

Amsterdam Old Course
(1990)
Zwarte Laantje 4, 1099 CE Amsterdam
Tel   (020) 694 3650
Fax   (020) 663 4621
Holes 9 L 5264 m SSS 68
V'tors WE–H
Fees   75fl (90fl)
Loc   5 km SE of Amsterdam

Amsterdamse (1934)
Bauduinlaan 35, 1047 HK Amsterdam
Tel   (020) 497 7866
Fax   (020) 497 5966
Holes 18 L 6124 m CR 73.1
V'tors WD–H WE–M
Fees   65–100fl
Loc   10 km W of Amsterdam
Arch   Rolin/Jol

Haarlemmermeersche
*Spieringweg, Cruquiusdijk 122,
2141 EV Vijfhuizen*
Tel   (023) 558 3124
Fax   (023) 558 1554
Holes 9 L 6087 m SSS 72
           9 hole short course
V'tors H
Fees   50fl
Loc   Haarlemmermeer, W of
            Amsterdam
Arch   C O'Connor Jr

Kennemer G&CC (1910)
Kennemerweg 78, 2042 XT Zandvoort
Tel   (023) 571 2836/8456
Fax   (023) 571 9520
Holes 27 holes CR 71.9-72.0:
           Van Hengel 9 L 2951 m
           Pennink 9 L 2916 m
           Colt 9 L 2942 m
V'tors H WE–NA before 3pm
Fees   125fl
Loc   Zandvoort, 6 km W of Haarlem
Arch   Colt/Pennink

De Noordhollandse (1982)
Sluispolderweg 6, 1817 BM Alkmaar
Tel   (072) 515 6807
Fax   (072) 511 0510
Holes 18 L 6084 m SSS 72
V'tors H or proficiency card
Fees   50–75fl (75–100fl)
Loc   2 km N of Alkmaar
Arch   Ryks/Dudok van Heel

Olympus (1973)
*Abcouderstraatweg 46,
1105 AA Amsterdam Zuid-Oost*
Tel   (0294) 285373
Fax   (0294) 286347
Holes 18 L 5926 m SSS 71
V'tors U–phone first
Fees   55fl
Loc   SE of Amsterdam, nr A2 and
            AMC Hospital
Arch   Dudok van Heel/Jol

Purmer (1989)
*Westerweg 60, Postbus 587,
1440 AN Purmerend*
Tel   (0299) 462143
Fax   (0299) 462143
Holes 18 L 6079 m SSS 70
           9 hole course
V'tors H
Fees   55–100fl
Loc   16 km N of Amsterdam
Arch   Huxley

Spaarnwoude (1977)
Het Hoge Land 3, 1981 LT Velsen
Tel   (023) 538 2708
Fax   (023) 538 7274
Holes 18 L 5676 m SSS 70
           9 L 2981 m SSS 36
           18 hole short course
V'tors H
Fees   40fl
Loc   14 km W of Amsterdam.
            10 km NE of Haarlem
Arch   Pennink/Jol

Zaanse (1988)
Zuiderweg 68, 1456 NH Wijdewormer
Tel   (029) 947 9123
Holes 9 L 5282 m SSS 68
V'tors WD–H WE–H before noon
            and after 3pm
Fees   40fl (50fl)
Loc   15 km NE of Amsterdam
Arch   Gerard Jol

Breda &
South West

Brugse Vaart (1993)
Brugse Vaart 10, 4501 NE Oostburg
Tel   (0117) 453410
Fax   (0117) 455511
Holes 18 L 6195 m SSS 72
V'tors U
Fees   55fl (65fl)
Loc   15 km N of Bruges, nr Knokke
Arch   Devos/Bauwens

Domburgsche (1914)
Schelpweg 26, 4357 BP Domburg
Tel   (0118) 586106
Fax   (0118) 586109
Holes 9 L 5402 m SSS 69
V'tors H
Fees   55fl (65fl)
Loc   15 km NW of Middelburg

Grevelingenhout (1988)
Oudendijk 3, 4311 NA Bruinisse
Tel   (0111) 482650
Fax   (0111) 481566
Holes 18 L 5951 m CR 70.7
           9 hole Par 3 course
V'tors WD–U H WE–NA
Fees   75fl (95fl)
Loc   55 km SW of Rotterdam
Arch   Donald Harradine

Oosterhoutse (1985)
Dukaatstraat 21, 4903 RN Oosterhout
Tel   (0162) 458759
Fax   (0162) 433285
Holes 18 L 6128 m SSS 71
V'tors WD–U H WE–M
Fees   70fl (75fl)
Loc   10 km NE of Breda
Arch   J Dudok van Heel

Reymerswael (1986)
Grensweg 21, 4411 ST Rilland Bath
Tel   (0113) 551265
Fax   (0113) 551264
Holes 9 L 5986 m SSS 72
V'tors H
Fees   40fl (50fl)
Loc   20 km W of Bergen op Zoom.
            50 km W of Breda, off A58
Arch   J Dudok van Heel

Toxandria (1928)
Veenstraat 89, 5124 NC Molenschot
Tel   (0161) 411200
Fax   (0161) 411715
Holes 18 L 5974 m SSS 71
V'tors WD–I phone first
Fees   75fl (100fl)
Loc   8 km E of Breda
Arch   Morrison/Dudok van Heel

De Woeste Kop (1986)
Justaasweg 4, 4571 NB Axel
Tel   (0115) 564467/564831 (Pro)
Fax   (0115) 564467
Holes 9 L 5444 m SSS 69
V'tors U
Fees   30fl (50fl)
Loc   45 km W of Antwerp
Arch   Paneels/Bosch

Wouwse Plantage (1981)
*Zoomvlietweg 66, 4725 TD Wouwse
Plantage*
Tel   (01657) 9593
Holes 18 L 5909 m SSS 71
V'tors H WE–M
Fees   60fl (70fl)

Loc   10 km E of Bergen-op-Zoom,
nr Roosendaal
Arch   Pennink/Rolin

East Central

Breuninkhof
Bussloselaan 6, 7383 RP Bussloo
Tel   (0571) 261955
Fax   (0571) 262089
Holes   9 L 6178 m SSS 72
V'tors   H
Fees   55fl (65fl)
Loc   100 km E of Amsterdam
Arch   Eschauzier

Edese (1978)
Papendallaan 22, 6816 VD Arnhem
Tel   (026) 482 1985
Fax   (026) 482 1348
Holes   18 L 5740 m SSS 70
V'tors   H
Fees   60fl (80fl)
Loc   National Sportcentrum
Papendal. NW of Arnhem,
towards Ede
Arch   Pennink/Dudok van Heel

Hattemse G&CC (1930)
Veenwal 11, 8051 AS Hattem
Tel   (038) 444 1909
Holes   9 L 5808 yds SSS 68
V'tors   WD–H WE–M+H
Fees   40fl (50fl)
Loc   Hattem, 5 km S of Zwolle
Arch   Del Court van Krimpen

Keppelse (1926)
c/o Rozenstraat 11, 7255 XS Hengelo
Tel   (0314) 381416
Fax   (0575) 464399
Holes   9 L 5360 m SSS 68
Fees   55fl (65fl)
Loc   Laag-Keppel, 25 km E of
Arnhem
Arch   JP Eschauzier

De Koepel (1983)
Postbox 88, 7640 AB Wierden
Tel   (0546) 576150/574070
Fax   (0546) 574070
Holes   9 L 2863 m SSS 70
V'tors   WE–H
Fees   50fl (60fl)
Loc   7 km W of Almelo
Arch   F Pennink

Nunspeetse G&CC (1987)
Plesmanlaan 30, Nunspeet
Tel   (03412) 61758
Fax   (03412) 61149
Holes   27 L 6100 m SSS 71
V'tors   U
Fees   70fl (85fl)
Loc   Nunspeet, 25 km SW of
Zwolle
Arch   Paul Rolin

Rosendaelsche (1895)
Apeldoornseweg 450,
6816 SN Arnhem
Tel   (026) 442 1438
Fax   (026) 351 1196
Holes   18 L 6057 m SSS 72
V'tors   WD–H WE–NA
Fees   85fl
Loc   5 km N of Arnhem on Route
N50
Arch   Frank Pennink

Sallandsche De Hoek (1934)
PO Box 24, 7430 AA Diepenveen
Tel   (0570) 593269
Fax   (0570) 593269
Holes   18 L 5889 m SSS 71
V'tors   H
Fees   75fl (90fl)
Loc   6 km N of Deventer
Arch   Pennink/Steel

Twentsche (1926)
*Almelosestraat 17, 7495 TG Ambt
Delden*
Tel   (074) 384 1167
Fax   (074) 384 1067
Holes   18 L 6208 m SSS 72
V'tors   H
Fees   80fl (90fl)
Loc   4 km N of Delden
Arch   TJ McAuley

Veluwse (1957)
Nr 57, 7346 AC Hoog Soeren
Tel   (055) 519 1275
Fax   (055) 519 1275
Holes   9 L 6264 yds SSS 70
V'tors   WD–U WD–H
Fees   60fl (70fl)
Loc   5 km W of Apeldoorn

Eindhoven & South East

De Berendonck (1985)
Weg Door de Berendonck 40,
6603 LP Wijchen
Tel   (024) 642 0039
Fax   (024) 641 1254
Holes   18 L 5671 m Par 71 SSS 70
V'tors   WE–restricted
Fees   55fl (65fl)
Loc   5 km SW of Nijmegen
Arch   J Dudok van Heel

Best G&CC
Golflaan 1, 5683 RZ Best
Tel   (04993) 91443
Fax   (04993) 93221
Holes   18 L 6079 m SSS 71
V'tors   U
Fees   60fl (80fl)
Loc   Best, 5 km NW of Eindhoven
Arch   J Dudok van Heel

Crossmoor G&CC (1986)
Laurabosweg 8, 6006 VR Weert
Tel   (0495) 518438
Fax   (0495) 518709
Holes   18 L 6052 m SSS 72
9 hole Par 3 course
V'tors   H
Fees   60fl (80fl)
Loc   Weert/Altweertheide,
30 km SE of Eindhoven
Arch   J Dudok van Heel

De Dommel (1928)
*Zegenwerp 12, 5271 NC
St Michielsgestel*
Tel   (07355) 12316
Fax   (07355) 19168
Holes   18 L 5607 m SSS 69
V'tors   WD–H WE–NA
Fees   75fl (90fl)
Loc   10 km S of Hertogenbosch
Arch   Colt/Steel

Eindhovensche (1930)
*Eindhovenseweg 300, 5553 VB
Valkenswaard*
Tel   (040) 201 4816
Fax   (040) 204 4038
Holes   18 L 5918 m SSS 71
V'tors   H
Fees   70fl (100fl)
Loc   8 km S of Eindhoven
Arch   HS Colt

Geysteren G&CC (1974)
Het Spekt 2, 5862 AZ Geysteren
Tel   (0478) 531809/532592
Fax   (0478) 532963
Holes   18 L 6090 m SSS 72
V'tors   WD–H WE–M
Fees   80fl (100fl)
Loc   Off N271, nr Wanssum.
25 km N of Venlo
Arch   Pennink/Steel

Haviksoord (1976)
*Maarheezerweg Nrd 11,
5595 XG Leende (NB)*
Tel   (040) 206 1818
Fax   (040) 206 2761
Holes   9 L 5880 m SSS 71
V'tors   H
Fees   40fl (50fl)
Loc   10 km S of Eindhoven

Het Rijk van Nijmegen (1985)
Postweg 17, 6561 KJ Groesbeek
Tel   (024) 397 6644
Fax   (024) 397 6942
Holes   18 L 6010 m SSS 71
18 L 5747 m SSS 70
V'tors   H
Fees   65fl (80fl)
Loc   5 km E of Nijmegen
Arch   Paul Rolin

De Schoot (1973)

Schootsedijk 18,
5491 TD Sint Oedenrode
Tel (04134) 73011
Fax (04134) 79256
Holes 9 L 2630 m SSS 68
V'tors U
Fees 40fl (45fl)
Loc 20 km N of Eindhoven
Arch A Rijks

Tongelreep G&CC (1984)

Charles Roelslaan 15,
5644 ZX Eindhoven
Tel (040) 252 0963
Holes 9 L 5260 m SSS 69
V'tors WD–H WE–H by
introduction only
Fees 30fl (40fl)
Loc Eindhoven
Arch J van Rooy

Limburg Province

Brunssummerheide (1985)

Rimburgerweg 50, Brunssum
Tel (045) 270968
Fax (045) 273939
Holes 27 L 5933 m SSS 71
9 hole Par 3 course
V'tors U H
Fees 60fl (75fl)
Loc 25 km NE of Maastricht

Hoenshuis G&CC (1987)

Hoensweg 17,
6367 GN Voerendaal
Tel (045) 753300/754488
Fax (045) 750900
Holes 18 L 6074 m SSS 72
V'tors WE–NA 10am–2pm
Fees 60fl (90fl)
Loc Limburg, 10 km NE of
Maastricht
Arch Paul Rolin

De Zuid Limburgse G&CC (1956)

Dalbissenweg 22,
6281 NC Mechelen
Tel (043) 455 1397 (Clubhouse),
(043) 455 1254 (Sec)
Fax (043) 455 1576
Holes 18 L 5924 m SSS 71
V'tors WD–U WE–H
Fees 60fl (90fl)
Loc Mechelen, 25 km SE of
Maastricht
Arch Hawtree/Snelder/Rolin

North

Gelpenberg (1970)

Gebbeveenweg 1, 7854 TD Aalden
Tel (0591) 371784/371929
Fax (0591) 372422
Holes 18 L 6031 m Par 71
V'tors H
Fees 60fl (70fl)
Loc 16 km W of Emmen
Arch Pennink/Steel

Holthuizen (1985)

Oosteinde 7a, 9301 ZP Roden
Tel (050) 501 5103
Holes 9 L 6079 m SSS 72
V'tors H
Fees 70fl (80fl)
Loc 10 km S of Groningen
Arch A Rijks

Lauswolt G&CC (1964)

Van Harinxmaweg 8A, PO Box 36,
9244 ZN Beetsterzwaag
Tel (0512) 382594/383590
Fax (0512) 383739
Holes 18 L 6008 m CR 70.4
V'tors H
Fees 100fl (125fl)
Loc Beetsterzwaag, 5 km S of
Drachten
Arch Pennink/Steel

Noord Nederlandse G&CC (1950)

Pollselaan 5, 9756 CJ Glimmen
Tel (050) 406 2004
Fax (050) 406 1922
Holes 18 L 4891 m SSS 70
V'tors H
Fees 60fl (90fl)
Loc 12 km S of Groningen,
off A28

De Semslanden (1989)

Nieuwe Dijk 1, 9514 BX
Gasselternijveen
Tel (0599) 565353/564661
Fax (0599) 564661
Holes 9 L 6078 m CR 132
V'tors H
Fees 40fl (50fl)
Loc 20 km W of Assen
Arch Eschauzier/Thate

Vegilinbosschen

Legemeersterweg 18,
8527 DS Legemeer
Tel (0513) 499466
Fax (0513) 499777
Holes 18 L 5765 m SSS 71
V'tors H
Fees 60fl (80fl)
Loc 100 km N of Amsterdam
Arch Allen Rijks

Rotterdam & The Hague

Broekpolder (1981)

Watersportweg 100, 3138 HD
Vlaardingen
Tel (010) 249 5566,
(010) 249 5555/249 5577
Fax (010) 249 5579
Holes 18 L 6048 m SSS 72
V'tors H
Fees 75–100fl (100–125fl)
Loc 15 km W of Rotterdam,
off A20
Arch Frank Pennink

Capelle a/d Ijssel (1977)

Gravenweg 311, 2905 LB Capelle a/d
Ijssel
Tel (010) 442 2485
Fax (010) 442 2485
Holes 18 L 5214 m SSS 68
V'tors WD–U WE–M
Fees 65fl (75fl)
Loc 5 km S of Rotterdam
Arch Donald Harradine

Cromstrijen (1989)

Veerweg 26, 3281 LX Numansdorp
Tel (0186) 654455
Fax (0186) 654681
Holes 18 L 6168 m Par 72
9 L 3710 m Par 62
V'tors WD–U H WE–M H
Fees 80fl (95fl)
Loc 30 km S of Rotterdam (A29)
Arch Tom McAuley

De Hooge Bergsche (1989)

Rottebandreef 40, 2661 JK
Bergschenhoek
Tel (010) 522 0052/522 0703
Fax (010) 521 9350
Holes 18 L 5370 m SSS 68
V'tors U
Fees 50fl (65fl)
Loc Bergschenhoek, 2 km NE of
Rotterdam
Arch Gerard Jol

Kleiburg (1974)

Postbus 137, 3230 AC Brielle
Tel (0181) 413330
Fax (0181) 419691
Holes 18 L 5652 m SSS 69
V'tors U
Fees 50–65fl
Loc 25 km W of Rotterdam
Arch Pennink/Jol

Koninklijke Haagsche G&CC (1893)

Groot Haesebroekeseweg 22,
2243 EC Wassenaar
Tel (070) 517 9607
Fax (070) 514 0171
Holes 18 L 5674 m SSS 71

V'tors WD–H (max 26) WE–M
Fees   150fl
Loc   6 km N of The Hague
Arch   Allison/Colt

Kralingen (1933)
Kralingseweg 200,
3062 CG Rotterdam
Tel   **(010) 452 2283**
Holes 9 L 5277 yds SSS 66
V'tors H
Fees   35fl (45fl)
Loc   5 km from centre of
       Rotterdam
Arch   Copijn/Cotton

De Merwelanden (1985)
Golfbaan Crayestein, Baanhoekweg 50,
3313 LP Dordrecht
Tel   **(078) 621 1221**
Fax   (078) 616 1036
Holes 18 L 5722 m Par 71
V'tors U
Fees   50fl (70fl)
Loc   20 km SE of Rotterdam
Arch   H & C Kuijsters

Noordwijkse (1915)
Randweg 25, PO Box 70,
2200 AB Noordwijk
Tel   **(0252) 373761**
Fax   (0252) 370044
Holes 18 L 5879 m CR 71.8
V'tors WD–H before noon and after
       3pm
Fees   110fl
Loc   5 km N of Noordwyk.
       15 km NW of Leiden
Arch   Frank Pennink

Rijswijkse (1987)
Delftweg 58, 2289 AL Rijswijk
Tel   **(070) 319 2424**
Fax   (070) 399 5040
Holes 18 L 6159 m Par 72
       CR 70.2
V'tors U H
Fees   70fl (90fl)
Loc   5 km SE of The Hague
Arch   Donald Steel

Rozenstein (1984)
Hoge Klei 1, 2242 XZ Wassenaar
Tel   **(070) 511 7846**
Fax   (070) 511 9302
Holes 18 L 5820 m SSS 70
V'tors H
Fees   60fl (90fl)
Loc   14 km NE of The Hague
Arch   Dudok van Heel/Jol

Zeegersloot (1984)
Kromme Aarweg 5, PO Box 190,
2400 AD Alphen a/d Rijn
Tel   **(0172) 474567**
Fax   (0172) 494660
Holes 18 L 5793 m SSS 70
       9 hole Par 3 course
V'tors U H

Fees   18 hole–50fl (70fl);
       9–hole:25fl (35fl)
Loc   Alphen, 15 km N of Gouda.
       20 km S of Amsterdam
Arch   Gerard Jol

Utrecht & Hilversum

Almeerderhout (1986)
Watersnipweg 19-21,
1341 AA Almere
Tel   **(036) 538 4444**
Fax   (036) 538 4435
Holes 27 L 6004–6046 m
       CR 71.9–72.2
       9 hole Par 3 course
V'tors WD–U WE–M (Max
       h'cap 28)
Fees   55fl (65fl)
Loc   30 km N of Hilversum
Arch   Dudok van Heel/Ryks

Anderstein
Woudenbergseweg 13a, 3953 ME
Maarsbergen
Tel   **(0343) 431330**
Fax   (0343) 432062
Holes 18 L 6015 m SSS 71
V'tors WD–U WE–M only
Fees   70–100fl
Loc   20 km E of Utrecht
Arch   Jol/Dudok van Heel

De Batouwe (1990)
Oost Kanaalweg 1, 4011 LA Zoelen
Tel   **(03446) 24370**
Fax   (03446) 13096
Holes 18 L 5717 m Par 72 SSS 70
       9 hole Par 3 course
V'tors U H–booking necessary
Fees   60fl (80fl)
Loc   Tiel, 25 km SE of Utrecht
Arch   Alan Rijks

Flevoland
Bosweg 98, 8231 DZ Lelystad
Tel   **(03200) 30077**
Holes 9 L 5888 m SSS 71
V'tors WD–U H WE–M+H
Fees   D–45fl (D–55fl)
Loc   Island of Flevoland. 1 km
       NW of Lelystad. 45 km N
       of Hilversum
Arch   JS Eschauzier

De Haar (1974)
PO Box 104, Parkweg 5, 3450 AC
Vleuten
Tel   **(030) 677 2860**
Fax   (030) 677 3903
Holes 9 L 6650 yds SSS 71
V'tors WD–H WE–NA
Fees   100fl (150fl)
Loc   10 km NW of Utrecht
Arch   F Pennink

Hilversumsche (1910)
Soestdijkerstraatweg 172, 1213 XJ
Hilversum
Tel   **(035) 685 7060**
Fax   (035) 685 3813
Holes 18 L 6098 m Par 72
V'tors Phone booking necessary
Fees   75fl (100fl)
Loc   3 km E of Hilversum, nr Baarn
Arch   Burrows/Colt

De Hoge Kleij (1985)
Appelweg 4, 3832 RK Leusden
Tel   **(033) 461 6944**
Fax   (033) 465 2921
Holes 18 L 6046 m SSS 72
V'tors H
Fees   65fl (95fl)
Loc   1 km SE of Amersfoort
       20 km NE of Utrecht via A28
Arch   Donald Steel

Nieuwegeinse (1985)
Postbus 486, 3437 AL Nieuwegein
Tel   **(030) 604 2192/0769**
Fax   (030) 604 2192
Holes 9 L 4630 m Par 68 SSS 65
V'tors WD–U WE–NA before 4pm
Fees   45fl
Loc   7 km S of Utrecht
Arch   Paul Rolin

Utrechtse 'De Pan' (1894)
Amersfoortseweg 1, 3735 LJ Bosch en
Duin
Tel   **(030) 695 6427**
Fax   (030) 696 3769
Holes 18 L 5707 m Par 72 SSS 70
V'tors WD–H (phone first) WE–NA
Fees   90fl
Loc   10 km E of Utrecht, off A28
Arch   HS Colt

Zeewolde
Golflaan 1, 3896 LL Zeewolde
Tel   **(036) 522 2103**
Fax   (036) 522 4100
Holes 27 holes Par 72
V'tors WE–H
Fees   50fl (75fl)
Loc   20 km N of Hilversum.
       60 km NE of Amsterdam

Norway

Arendal og Omegn (1986)
Nes Verk, 4900 Tvedestrand
Tel   37 16 03 60
Fax   37 16 02 11
Holes 18 L 5528 m Par 72
V'tors U
Fees   200kr (250kr)
Loc   Nes Verk, 20 km E of Arendal
       (E18). 95 km NE of
       Kristiansand

Baerum

P O Box 31, 1355 Baerum
Tel 67 56 30 85
Fax 67 56 03 87
Holes 18 L 5300 m SSS 71
9 hole short course
V'tors WD–U H WE–M H between
11am–4pm. Booking advisable
Fees 200kr (250kr)
Loc 10 km W of Oslo. 10 km N
of Sandvika

Bergen (1937)

PO Box 470, 5001 Bergen
Tel 05 18 20 77
Holes 9 L 4461 m SSS 66
Fees D–150kr
Loc 8 km N of Bergen

Borre

Semb Hovedgaard, 3186 Horten
Tel 33 07 32 40
Fax 33 07 32 41
Holes 18 L 6120 m SSS 73
V'tors H
Fees 200kr (250kr)
Loc Horten, 50 km S of Drammen.
100 km SW of Oslo
Arch T Nordström

Borregaard (1927)

PO Box 348, 1701 Sarpsborg
Tel 69 12 15 00
Fax 69 15 74 11
Holes 9 L 4500 m SSS 65
V'tors H
Fees 120kr
Loc Opsund, 1 km N of Sarpsborg

Drøbak

Belsjøveien 50, 1440 Drøbak
Tel 64 93 16 80
Fax 64 93 39 80
Holes 18 L 5188 m SSS 71
V'tors H
Fees 200kr (250kr)
Loc 40 km SE of Oslo
Arch Hauser

Elverum (1980)

PO Box 71, 2401 Elverum
Tel 62 41 35 88
Fax 62 41 55 13
Holes 18 L 5845 m Par 72
V'tors H
Fees 200kr (220kr)
Loc Starmoen Fritidspark,
10 km E of Elverum. 35 km E
of Hamar. 150 km N of Oslo

Grenland (1976)

Luksefjellvn 578, 3721 Skien
Tel 35 59 07 03
Fax 35 59 06 10
Holes 18 L 5777 m Par 72
V'tors U
Fees 200kr
Loc 6 km from Skien
Arch Jan Sederholm

Groruddalen (1988)

Postboks 4 Vestli, 0911 Oslo
Tel 22 21 67 18
Holes 9 L 2520 m SSS 54
V'tors U–before 2pm
Fees 100kr (150kr)
Loc 15 km N of Oslo
Arch Leif Nilsson

Hemsedal (1994)

3560 Hemsedal
Tel 32 06 23 77
Fax 32 06 01 92
Holes 9 L 4816 m Par 68
V'tors U H
Fees 150kr (190kr)
Loc 40 km N of Gol. 380 km
NW of Oslo
Arch Leif Nilsson

Kjekstad (1976)

PO Box 201, 3440 Røyken
Tel 31 28 58 50/31 28 53 53
Fax 31 28 91 55
Holes 18 L 5100 m SSS 67
V'tors H
Fees 200kr
Loc 12 km SE of Drammen on
Route 282. 40 km SW of Oslo
Arch Jan Sederholm

Kristiansand (1973)

PO Box 6090, Søm, 4602 Kristiansand
Tel 38 04 35 85
Fax 38 04 34 15
Holes 9 L 2485 m SSS 70
V'tors U
Fees D–150kr
Loc 8 km E of Kristiansand (E18)

Larvik (1989)

Fritzøe Gård, 3267 Larvik
Tel 33 18 33 11
Fax 33 18 76 44
Holes 18 L 6147 m Par 72
V'tors H
Fees 200kr (250kr)
Loc 3 km S of Larvik on R301
to Stavern
Arch Jan Sederholm

Narvik (1992)

PO Box 85, 8523 Elvegard
Tel 76 95 12 01
Fax 76 95 03 33
Holes 18 L 5890 m Par 72
V'tors U H
Fees 250kr
Loc 30 km S of Narvik
Arch Jan Sederholm

Nes (1988)

Rommen Golfpark, 2160 Vormsund
Tel 63 90 29 29
Fax 63 90 21 60
Holes 18 L 6081 m Par 72
V'tors H or Green card
Fees 200kr (250kr)
Loc 50 km NE of Oslo, via E6/RV2
Arch Hauser

Onsoy

Postboks 458, 1601 Fredrikstad
Tel 69 33 35 90/69 33 35 55
Fax 69 33 35 24
Holes 18 L 5600 m SSS 72
V'tors U
Fees 200–250kr
Loc 10 km W of Fredrikstad.
Oslo 80 km
Arch Andersen/Mejstedt

Oppdal (1987)

PO Box 19, 7340 Oppdal
Holes 9 L 2621 m Par 68
V'tors U
Fees 150kr
Loc 120 km S of Trondheim
Arch Jan Sederholm

Oppegård (1985)

P O Box 137, 1412 Sofiemyr
Tel 66 99 18 75
Fax 66 99 18 95
Holes 18 L 5280 m Par 71
V'tors U H
Fees 200kr (250kr)
Loc 22 km S of Oslo

Oslo (1924)

Bogstad, 0757 Oslo
Tel 22 51 05 60
Fax 22 51 05 61
Holes 18 L 6719 yds SSS 72
V'tors H–Max 20 (men) 28 (ladies)
WD–restricted before 2pm
WE–restricted after 2pm
Fees 275kr (325kr)
Loc 8 km NW of Oslo. Signs to
'Bogstad Camping'.

Østmarka (1989)

Postboks 63, 1914 Ytre Enebakk
Tel 64 92 41 11
Fax 64 92 47 55
Holes 18 L 5640 m
V'tors H
Fees 200kr (250kr)
Loc 35 km E of Oslo

Oustoen CC (1965)

PO Box 100, 1330 Oslo Lufthavn
Tel 67 53 52 95/22 56 33 54
Fax 67 53 95 44
Holes 18 L 5400m SSS 72
V'tors M
Fees 350kr
Loc Small island in Oslofjord,
10 km W of Oslo

Skjeberg (1986)

PO Box 3014, Kurland, 1701 Sarpsborg
Tel 69 16 63 10
Holes 18 L 5500 m SSS 72
V'tors U
Fees 130kr (150kr)
Loc Hevingen, 2 km N of
Sarpsborg
Arch Jan Sederholm

Sorknes

Sorknes Gaard, 2450 Rena
Tel   62 44 18 70
Fax   62 44 00 27
Holes 18 L 6150 m SSS 72
V'tors U
Fees   200kr (230kr)
Loc   170 km N of Oslo
Arch   Juul Soegaard

Stavanger (1956)

Longebakke 45, 4042 Hafrsfjord
Tel   51 55 54 31
Fax   51 55 73 11
Holes 18 L 5751 m Par 71
V'tors H
Fees   250kr
Loc   6 km SW of Stavanger
Arch   F Smith

Trondheim (1950)

PO Box 169, 7001 Trondheim
Tel   73 53 18 85/92 01 74 47
Fax   73 52 75 05
Holes 9 L 5632 m SSS 72
V'tors H or Green Card
Fees   150kr
Loc   Trondheim 3 km

Vestfold (1958)

PO Box 64, 3173 Vear
Tel   33 36 56 55 (Sec)
Fax   33 36 60 25
Holes 18 L 5851 m SSS 73
V'tors H
Fees   200kr
Loc   Tønsberg 8 km
Arch   F Smith

Portugal

Algarve

Alto Golf (1991)

P O Box 1, Alvor, 8500 Portimão
Tel   (082) 416913/401045-7
Fax   (082) 401046
Holes 18 L 6125 m SSS 73
V'tors H
Fees   8750esc
Loc   2 km W of Portimão
Arch   Cotton/Dobereiner

Carvoeiro (1991)

Vale Currais, Praia do Carvoeiro,
Apartado 24, 8401#Lagoa#Codex
Tel   (082) 342168
Fax   (082) 342189
Holes Quinta do Gramacho 18 L
           5919 m Par 72 SSS 71;
           Vale de Pinta 18 L 5861 m
           Par 71 SSS 71

V'tors U
Fees   8500esc
Loc   10 km E of Portimao.
           60 km W of Faro, nr Lagoa
Arch   Ronald Fream

Palmares (1975)

Meia Praia, 8600 Lagos
Tel   (082) 762953
Fax   (082) 762534
Holes 18 L 5961 m SSS 72
V'tors U
Fees   7000esc
Loc   Meia Praia, 5 km E of Lagos
Arch   Frank Pennink

Parque da Floresta

(1987)
Vale do Poço, Budens, 8650 Vila do
Bispo
Tel   (082) 695333
Fax   (082) 695157
Holes 18 L 5787 m SSS 72
V'tors U
Fees   7900esc
Loc   16 km W of Lagos, nr Salema
Arch   Pepe Gancedo

Penina (1966)

PO Box 146, Penina, 8502 Portimão
Tel   (082) 415415
Fax   (082) 415000
Holes Championship 18 L 6343 m
           SSS 73; Resort 9 L 3987 m
           SSS 71; Academy 9 L 1851 m
           Par 30
V'tors H
Fees   Championship–10.500esc
           Resort–6000esc
           Academy–5000esc
Loc   5 km W of Portimão. 12 km E
           of Lagos
Arch   Henry Cotton

Pine Cliffs G&CC

(1991)
Sheraton Algarve Hotel, Praia da
Falesia, 8200 Albufeira
Tel   (089) 500100/501999
Fax   (089) 501950
Holes 9 L 2324 m SSS 67
V'tors U H
Fees   9 holes–5500esc
Loc   7 km W of Vilamoura
Arch   Martin Hawtree

Pinheiros Altos (1992)

Quinta do Lago, 8135 Almancil
Tel   (089) 394340
Fax   (089) 394392
Holes 18 L 6236 m Par 72
V'tors U–phone first
Fees   13.000esc
Loc   Quinta do Lago, 15 km W
           of Faro
Arch   Ronald Fream

Quinta do Lago (1974)

Quinta Do Lago, 8135 Almancil
Tel   (089) 390700/9
Fax   (089) 394013
Holes Quinta do Lago 18 L 6488 m
           SSS 72; Ria Formosa 18 L
           6205 m SSS 72
V'tors H–by prior arrangement
Fees   13.000esc
Loc   15 km W of Faro. Airport
           20 km
Arch   Mitchell/Lee

Salgados

Apartado 2266, Vale do Rabelho,
8200 Albufeira
Tel   (089) 591111
Fax   (089) 591112
Holes 18 L 6000 m Par 72
V'tors U
Fees   On application
Loc   W of Albufeira
Arch   P de Vasconcelos

San Lorenzo (1988)

Quinta do Lago, 8135 Almancil
Tel   (089) 396522
Fax   (089) 396908
Holes 18 L 6238 m SSS 73
V'tors H–restricted
Fees   18.000esc
Loc   16 km W of Faro
Arch   Joseph Lee

Vale de Milho (1990)

Apt 273, Praia do Carvoeiro, 8400 Lagoa
Tel   (082) 358502
Fax   (082) 358497
Holes 9 L 1845 m Par 27
V'tors U
Fees   18 holes–4000esc
           9 holes–2950esc
Loc   Jorge de Lagos Village.
           Carvoeiro 2 km
Arch   Dave Thomas

Vale do Lobo (1968)

8137 Vale Do Lobo
Tel   (089) 393939
Fax   (089) 394742
Holes Ocean 18 L 5493 m Par 71
           Royal 18 L 6175 m Par 72
V'tors H
Fees   15.000esc
Loc   19 km W of Faro. Airport
           19 km
Arch   Cotton/Roquemore

Vila Sol (1991)

Alto do Semino, Vilamoura,
8125 Quarteira
Tel   (089) 302144/5/6
Fax   (089) 302147
Holes 18 L 6189 m SSS 72
V'tors U H
Fees   11.000 esc
Loc   5 km E of Vilamoura. Faro
           Airport 10 km
Arch   Donald Steel

Vilamoura Laguna
(1990)
Vilamoura, 8125 Quarteira
Tel (089) 380724
Fax (089) 380726
Holes Norte 9 L 2935 m; Este 9 L
2953 m; Sul 9 L 3180 m
V'tors H–max 28(M) 36(L)
Fees 18 holes–10.000esc
Loc As Vilamoura Old
Arch Joseph Lee

Vilamoura Old (1969)
Vilamoura, 8125 Quarteira
Tel (089) 322650
Fax (089) 322658
Holes 18 L 5988 m Par 73 SSS 72
V'tors H–max 24(M) 28(L) Soft
spikes only
Fees 18.000esc
Loc Quarteira, 25 km W of Faro
Arch Frank Pennink

Vilamoura Pinhal (1976)
Vilamoura, 8125 Quarteira
Tel (089) 321562
Fax (089) 321411
Holes 18 L 6300 m Par 72 SSS 71
V'tors H–max 28(M) 36(L)
Fees 11.000esc
Loc As Vilamoura Old
Arch Pennink/Trent Jones

Azores

Batalha (1995)
*Rua do Bom Jesus, Aflitos, 9545 Fenais
da Luz (Açores)*
Tel (096) 498559/498560
Fax (096) 498284
Holes 18 L 6419 m SSS 72
V'tors U
Fees D–6000esc
Loc Sao Miguel Island. Ponta
Delgada 10 km
Arch Cameron/Powell

Furnas (1939)
*Rua do Bom Jesus, Aflitos, 9545 Fenais
da Luz (Açores)*
Tel (096) 498559/498560
Fax (096) 498284
Holes 18 L 6229 m SSS 72
V'tors U
Fees D–6000esc
Loc São Miguel Island. Furnas
Villa 5 km
Arch Mackenzie Ross

Terceira Island (1954)
C P 15, 9760 Praia da Victória
Fax (095) 92445
Holes 18 L 5695 m SSS 70
V'tors U H
Fees US$ 30
Loc 13 km NE of Angra do
Heroismo

Lisbon &
Central Portugal

Aroeira (1972)
*Herdade da Aroeira, Fonte da Telha,
2825 Monte da Caparica*
Tel (01) 297 1345
Fax (01) 297 1283
Holes 18 L 6040 m SSS 72
V'tors U H
Fees 6000esc (10.000esc)
Loc 20 km S of Lisbon, off Setúbal/
Costa da Caparica road
Arch Frank Pennink

Estoril (1945)
Avenida República, 2765 Estoril
Tel (01) 468 0176/468 1376
Fax (01) 468 2796
Holes 18 L 5210 m SSS 68
9 L 2350 m SSS 65
V'tors WD–U WE–M
Fees 8250esc (11.0000esc)
Loc N of Estoril on Sintra road.
30 km W of Lisbon
Arch Mackenzie Ross

Estoril-Sol Golf
Academy (1976)
Quinta do Outeira, Linhó, 2710 Sintra
Tel (01) 923 2461
Fax (01) 923 2461
Holes 9 L 4228 m Par 62
V'tors U
Fees 3900esc
Loc 7 km N of Estoril. Lisbon
35 km
Arch Harris/Fream

Lisbon Sports Club (1922)
Casal da Carregueira-Belas, 2475 Belas
Tel (01) 431 0077
Fax (01) 431 2482
Holes 18 L 5278 m SSS 69
V'tors U
Fees D–7000esc (9000esc)
Loc Belas, 20 km NW of Lisbon
Arch Hawtree

Montado
Algeruz, 2950 Palmela
Tel (065) 706775
Fax (065) 706648
Holes 18 L 6060 m SSS 72
V'tors U
Fees 5000P
Loc 5 km E of Setúbal. 40 km S
of Lisbon
Arch Duarte Sotomayor

Penha Longa (1992)
Lagoa Azul, Linhó, 2710 Sintra
Tel (01) 924 9011
Fax (01) 924 9024
Holes Atlantic 18 L 6290 m Par 72
Monastery 9 L 2588 m Par 35
V'tors U H
Fees Atlantic 12.000esc (17.000esc)
Monastery 4500esc (6500esc)

Loc 8 km N of Estoril. 17 km
W of Lisbon
Arch Robert Trent Jones Jr

Quinta da Beloura
Estrada de Albarraque, 2710 Sintra
Tel (01) 924 0021
Fax (01) 924 0061
Holes 18 L 5878 m Par 72
V'tors U
Fees On application
Loc Between Estoril and Sintra,
off N9
Arch R Roquemore

Quinta da Marinha (1984)
Quinta da Marinha, 2750 Cascais
Tel (01) 486 9881
Fax (01) 486 9032
Holes 18 L 6014 m SSS 71
V'tors U
Fees 7900esc (9500esc)
Loc 2 km W of Cascais. 32 km
W of Lisbon
Arch Robert Trent Jones

Quinta do Peru
Quinta do Conde, 2830 Quinta do Conde
Tel (01) 213 4320/22
Fax (01) 213 4321
Holes 18 L 6308 m Par 72
V'tors U
Fees On application
Loc E of Lisbon on EN10
Arch R Roquemore

Tróia Golf
Torralta, Tróia, 2900 Setúbal
Tel (065) 44112
Fax (065) 44315
Holes 18 L 6338 m SSS 74
V'tors U
Fees 4500esc (5500esc)
Loc S of Setúbal on Tróia
peninsula. 50 km S of Lisbon
Arch Robert Trent Jones

Vimeiro
*Praia do Porto Novo, Vimeiro,
2560 Torres Vedras*
Tel (061) 984157
Fax (061) 984621
Holes 9 L 4781 m SSS 67
V'tors U
Fees D–1500esc. Hotel guests free
Loc Vimeiro, 20 km N of Torres
Vedras. 65 km N of Lisbon
Arch Frank Pennink

Madeira

Madeira (1991)
Sto Antonio da Serra, 9200 Machico
Tel (091) 552345/552356
Fax (091) 552367
Holes 18 L 6040 m Par 72
9 hole course
V'tors U
Fees 8000esc

Loc 25 km E of Funchal.
Airport 3 km
Arch Robert Trent Jones

Palheiro (1993)

Sitio do Balancal, Sao Gonçalo,
9050 Funchal
Tel (091) 792116
Fax (091) 792456
Holes 18 L 6022 m SSS 71
V'tors May–Sept–U Oct–April–H
Fees D–£40
Loc 5 km from Funchal, off
Airport road to Camacha
Arch Cabell Robinson

North

Estela (1989)

Rio Alto, Estela, 4490 Póvoa de Varzim
Tel (052) 612400
Fax (052) 612701
Holes 18 L 6188 m SSS 73
V'tors H
Fees 7500esc
Loc 7 km N of Póvoa de Varzim.
40 km N of Oporto (Route 13)
Arch Duarte Sottomayor

Golden Eagle

Quinta do Brincal, Arrouquelas,
2040 Rio Maior
Tel (043) 98383
Fax (043) 98167
Holes 18 L 6203 m Par 72
V'tors U
Fees On application
Loc N of Lisbon, off IC2 towards
Leiria
Arch R Roquemore

Miramar (1962)

Av Sacadura Cabral, Miramar,
4405 Valadares
Tel (02) 762 2067
Fax (02) 762 7859
Holes 9 L 2573 m SSS 67
V'tors H WE–NA after 10am
Fees 7500esc (9000esc)
Loc 8 km S of Oporto

Oporto (1890)

Sisto-Paramos, 4500 Espinho
Tel (02) 722008
Fax (02) 726895
Holes 18 L 5780 m SSS 70
V'tors H WE–restricted
Fees 10.000esc
Loc Espinho, 15 km S of Oporto

Vidago

Pavilhão do Golfe, 5425 Vidago
Tel (076) 97356
Fax (076) 996622
Holes 9 L 2256m SSS 64
Loc 50 km N of Vila Real.
130 km NE of Oporto
Arch Mackenzie Ross

Slovenia

CC Golf Bled (1937)

Cesta Svobode 13, 4260 Bled
Tel (064) 718 230
Fax (064) 718 225
Holes 18 L 6320 m SSS 73
9 L 6168 m SSS 72
V'tors H 24
Fees £24 (£27)
Loc 3 km W of Bled. 50 km NW
of Ljubljana, nr Austro-Italian
border
Arch Donald Harradine

Castle Mokrice (1992)

Terme Catez, Topliska Cesta 35,
68250 Brezice
Tel (0608) 57000/1
Fax (0608) 57007
Holes 18 holes SSS 70
V'tors H
Fees 44DEM (48DEM)
Loc 30 km N of Zagreb
Arch Donald Harradine

Lipica (1989)

Lipica 5, 66210 Sezana
Tel (067) 31580
Fax (067) 72818
Holes 9 L 6240 m SSS 71
V'tors U
Fees £12 (£18)
Loc 11 km NE of Trieste.
85 km SW of Ljubljana
Arch Donald Harradine

Spain

Alicante & Murcía

Bonalba (1996)

Muchamiel, Alicante
Holes 18L 6190 m Par 72
V'tors U
Fees 4500P (5000P)
Loc 10 km N of Alicante.
A7 Junction 67
Arch Ramón Espinosa

Don Cayo (1974)

Conde de Altea 49, Altea (Alicante)
Tel (96) 584 80 46
Fax (96) 584 11 88
Holes 9 L 6156 m SSS 72
V'tors U H
Fees D–3800P
Loc 4 km N of Altea, nr Callosa
Arch Barber/Sanz

Ifach (1974)

Crta Moraira-Calpe Km 3, Apdo 28,
03720 Benisa (Alicante)
Tel (96) 649 71 14
Fax (96) 649 71 14
Holes 9 L 3408 m SSS 59
V'tors U
Fees D–3300P
Loc 9 km N of Calpe, towards
Moraira
Arch Javier Arana

Jávea (1981)

Apartado 148, 03730 Jávea, (Alicante)
Tel (96) 579 25 84
Fax (96) 646 05 54
Holes 9 L 6070 m SSS 72
V'tors H
Fees D–4500P
Loc Lluca, Jávea. 90 km NE of
Alicante
Arch Francisco Moreno

La Manga (1971)

30385 Los Belones, Cartagena
Tel (968) 13 72 34
Fax (968) 15 72 72
Holes North 18 L 5780 m SSS 70
South 18 L 6259 m SSS 73
Princesa 18 L 5971 m SSS 72
V'tors U
Fees D–5250P
Loc 30 km NE of Cartagena, nr
Murcia airport
Arch RD Putman

La Marquesa (1989)

Ciudad Quesada II, 03170 Rojales,
(Alicante)
Tel (96) 671 42 58
Fax (96) 671 42 67
Holes 18 L 5840 m Par 72 SSS 70
V'tors U
Fees D–4200P
Loc Rojales, 40 km S of Alicante
Arch Justo Quesada

Las Ramblas (1991)

Crta Alicante-Cartagena Km50,
03189 Urb Villamartin, Orihuela
(Alicante)
Tel (96) 532 20 11
Fax (96) 676 51 58
Holes 18 L 5770 m SSS 71
V'tors U H
Fees 4000P
Loc 9 km S of Torrevieja
Arch José Gancedo

Real Campoamor (1989)

Crta Cartagena-Alicante Km48, Apdo
17, 03189 Orihuela-Costa (Alicante)
Tel (96) 532 13 66
Fax (96) 532 24 54
Holes 18 L 6203 m Par 72 SSS 73
V'tors U H
Fees 5000P
Loc Torrevieja 9 km (N332)
Arch C Gracia Caselles

La Sella (1991)

Ctra La Jara-Jesús Pobre, 03749 Jesús Pobre (Alicante)

Tel	(96) 645 42 52/645 41 10
Fax	(96) 645 42 01
Holes	18 L 6028 m SSS 71
V'tors	U H
Fees	5000–6000P
Loc	Denia 5 km
Arch	Juan de la Cuadra

Villamartin (1972)

Crta Alicante-Cartagena Km50, 03189 Urb Villamartin, Orihuela (Alicante)

Tel	(96) 676 51 27/676 51 60
Fax	(96) 676 51 58
Holes	18 L 6132 m SSS 72
V'tors	U H
Fees	5000P
Loc	8 km S of Torrevieja
Arch	Paul Putman

Almería

Almerimar (1976)

Urb Almerimar, 04700 El Ejido

Tel	(950) 48 02 34
Fax	(950) 49 72 33
Holes	18 L 6111 m SSS 72
V'tors	U
Fees	4500P W–20.000P
Loc	35 km W of Almería
Arch	Gary Player

Cortijo Grande (1976)

Apdo 2, Cortijo Grande, 04630 Turre

Tel	(951) 47 91 76
Holes	9 holes course SSS 36
Loc	20 km W of Turre. 85 km N of Almería, nr Mojácar

Playa Serena (1979)

Urb Playa Serena, 04740 Roquetas de Mar

Tel	(950) 33 30 55
Fax	(950) 33 30 55
Holes	18 L 6301 m SSS 72
V'tors	H
Fees	3500P
Loc	20 km S of Almería
Arch	Gallardo/Alliss

Balearic Islands

Canyamel

Urb Canyamel, Crta de Cuevas, 07580 Capdepera, Mallorca

Tel	(971) 56 44 57
Fax	(971) 56 53 80
Holes	18 L 6115 m SSS 72
V'tors	H
Fees	7500P
Loc	70 km NE of Palma, nr Cala Ratjada
Arch	José Gancedo

Capdepera (1989)

Apdo 6, 07580 Capdepera, Mallorca

Tel	(971) 56 58 75/56 58 57
Fax	(971) 56 58 74
Holes	18 L 6284 m SSS 72
V'tors	U H
Fees	7500P
Loc	71 km E of Palma, between Artá and Capdepera
Arch	Maples/Pape

Club Son Parc (1977)

Apdo 634, Mahón, Menorca

Tel	(971) 37 98 14
Fax	(971) 36 88 06
Holes	9 L 2791 m SSS 69
V'tors	U H
Fees	D–5000P
Loc	Mercadel, 18 km N of Mahón
Arch	JF Martínez

Ibiza (1990)

Apdo 1270, 07840 Santa Eulalia

Tel	(971) 19 61 18
Fax	(971) 19 60 51
Holes	18 L 6083 m SSS 72
	9 L 5867 m SSS 70
V'tors	H
Fees	6000P
Loc	7 km N of Ibiza town
Arch	Thomas/Rivero

Pollensa (1986)

Ctra Palma-Pollensa Km 49, 07460 Pollensa, Mallorca-Baleares

Tel	(971) 53 32 16
Fax	(971) 53 32 65
Holes	9 L 5304 m Par 70 SSS 70
V'tors	U
Fees	6900P
Loc	Pollensa, 45 km N of Palma
Arch	José Gancedo

Poniente (1978)

Costa de Calvia, Mallorca

Tel	(971) 13 01 48
Fax	(971) 13 01 76
Holes	18 L 6430 m SSS 72
V'tors	U
Fees	8200P
Loc	12 km SW of Palma towards Cala Figuera
Arch	John Harris

Pula Golf (1995)

Predio de Pul, 07550 Capdepera, Mallorca

Tel	(971) 81 70 34
Fax	(971) 81 70 35
Holes	18 L 6003 m Par 71
V'tors	U H
Fees	8500P
Loc	70 km NE of Palma
Arch	Francisco López

Real Menorca (1976)

Apartado 97, 07780 Mahón, Menorca

Tel	(971) 36 39 00
Holes	9 L 5724 m SSS 72
Loc	7 km N of Mahón
Arch	John Harris

Royal Bendinat (1986)

C. Campoamor, 07015 Calviá, Mallorca

Tel	(971) 40 52 00
Fax	(971) 70 07 86
Holes	18 L 5768 m SSS 71
V'tors	U H
Fees	7000P
Loc	7 km W of Palma
Arch	Martin Hawtree

Santa Ponsa (1976)

Santa Ponsa, 07180 Calvia (Mallorca)

Tel	(971) 69 02 11/69 08 00
Fax	(971) 69 33 64
Holes	No 1 18 L 6520 m SSS 74
	No 2 18 L 6053 m SSS 73
V'tors	No 1–U H No 2–NA
Fees	6900P
Loc	18 km W of Palma
Arch	Folco Nardi

Son Servera (1967)

Costa de Los Pinos, 07759 Son Servera, Mallorca

Tel	(971) 84 00 96
Fax	(971) 84 01 60
Holes	9 L 5956 m SSS 72
V'tors	H
Fees	D–7000P
Loc	Son Servera, 64 km E of Palma
Arch	John Harris

Son Vida (1964)

Urb Son Vida, 07013 Palma de Mallorca

Tel	(971) 79 12 10
Fax	(971) 79 11 27
Holes	18 L 5740 m SSS 71
V'tors	U H
Fees	8100P
Loc	3 km NW of Palma
Arch	FW Hawtree

Vall d'Or (1986)

Apdo 23, 07660 Cala D'Or, Mallorca

Tel	(971) 83 70 68/83 70 01
Fax	(971) 83 72 99
Holes	18 L 5799 m SSS 71
V'tors	H
Fees	7800P
Loc	60 km E of Palma, between Cala d'Or and Porto Colóm
Arch	Benz/Bendly

Barcelona &
Cataluña

Aro-Mas Nou (1990)
Apdo 429, 17250 Playa de Aro
Tel **(972) 82 69 00**
Fax (972) 82 69 06
Holes 18 L 6218 m Par 72
9 holes Par 3 course
V'tors U H
Fees 5500P (8000P)
Loc 35 km SE of Gerona on coast.
A7 exit 9
Arch Ramón Espinosa

Bonmont Terres Noves
(1990)
*Urb Terres Noves, 43330 Montroig
(Tarragona)*
Tel **(977) 81 81 40**
Fax (977) 81 81 46
Holes 18 L 6371 m SSS 72
V'tors U H
Fees 5000P (7000P)
Loc S of Tarragona. 130 km S of
Barcelona
Arch Robert Trent Jones Jr

Can Bosch (1984)
*Trav de les Corts 322,
08029 Barcelona*
Tel **(93) 405 04 22/866 25 71**
Fax (93) 419 9659
Holes 9 L 3027 m SSS 71
V'tors U H
Fees 3000P (6000P)
Loc 35 km NE of Barcelona
Arch Ramon Espinosa

Costa Brava (1962)
*La Masia, 17246 Sta Cristina d'Aro
(Gerona)*
Tel **(972) 83 71 50**
Fax (972) 83 72 72
Holes 18 L 5573 m SSS 70
V'tors H
Fees 5500–7500P
Loc Playa de Aro 5 km. 30 km
SE of Gerona
Arch J Hamilton Stutt

Costa Dorada (1983)
Apartado 600, 43080 Tarragona
Tel **(977) 65 33 61**
Holes 18 L 6223 m SSS 73
Loc Tarragona
Arch José Gancedo

Empordà (1990)
*Crta Torroella de Montgri,
17257 Gualta (Gerona)*
Tel **(972) 76 04 50/76 01 36**
Fax (972) 75 71 00
Holes 27 L 5855-6112 m SSS 70-71
V'tors U H
Fees 5500P (8500P)

Girona (1992)
*Urb Golf Girona, 17481 Sant Julià de
Ramis, (Girona)*
Tel **(972) 17 16 41**
Fax (972) 17 16 82
Holes 18 L 6100 m Par 72 SSS 72
V'tors H–booking required
Fees 4500P (6000P)
Loc Sant Julià de Ramis,
4 km from Gerona
Arch Hawtree

Llavaneras (1945)
*Camino del Golf, 08392 San Andres de
Llavaneras, (Barcelona)*
Tel **(93) 792 60 50**
Fax (93) 795 25 58
Holes 18 L 4644 m SSS 66
V'tors U H
Fees 6000P (12.000P)
Loc 4 km N of Mataró. 34 km N
of Barcelona (A19)
Arch Hawtree/Espinosa

Masia Bach (1990)
*Ctra Martorell-Capellades,
08781 Sant Esteve Sesrovires*
Tel **(93) 772 6310**
Fax (93) 772 6356
Holes 18 L 6039 m SSS 72
9 L 3780 m SSS 60
V'tors H
Fees 5750P (17.250P)
Loc 30 km NW of Barcelona
Arch JM Olazábal

Osona Montanya (1988)
*Masia L'Estanyol, 08553 El Brull
(Barcelona)*
Tel **(93) 884 01 70**
Fax (93) 884 04 07
Holes 18 L 6036 m Par 72
V'tors U H
Loc 60 km NE of Barcelona
Arch Dave Thomas

Pals
*Ctra de la Platja de Pals,
17526 Gerona*
Tel **(972) 63 60 06**
Fax (972) 63 70 09
Holes 18 L 6222 m SSS 72
Fees D–4500–8500P
Loc 40 km E of Gerona.
135 km NE of Barcelona
Arch FW Hawtree

Peralada (1993)
La Garriga, 17491 Peralada, Girona
Tel **(972) 53 82 87**
Fax (972) 53 82 36
Holes 18 L 6128 m SSS 72
V'tors H
Fees 6000P (7500P)

Loc 35 km E of Gerona, nr Pals.
130 km N of Barcelona
Arch Robert von Hagge

Loc Costa Brava, on French
border. 40 km S of Perpignan
Airport, nr Llançà
Arch Jorge Soler

Real Cerdaña (1929)
Apdo 63, Puigcerdá, (Gerona)
Tel **(972) 88 13 38**
Holes 18 L 5735 m SSS 70
Loc Cerdaña, 1 km from
Puigcerdá
Arch Javier Arana

Real Golf El Prat (1956)
*Apdo 10, 8820 El Prat de Llobregat,
(Barcelona)*
Tel **(93) 379 02 78**
Fax (93) 370 51 02
Holes 4 x 9 holes:
6070-6266 m SSS 73-74
V'tors WD–H WE–M H
Fees 9500P (19.090P)
Loc El Prat, Airport 3 km.
15 km S of Barcelona
Arch Arana/Thomas

Reus Aiguesverds (1989)
*Crta Cambrils, Mas Guardià,
43206 Reus*
Tel **(977) 75 27 25**
Fax (977) 75 19 38
Holes 18 L 6905 yds SSS 72
V'tors U
Fees 5000–6000P
Loc 10 km W of Tarragona.
100 km S of Barcelona

Sant Cugat (1914)
08190 Sant Cugat del Valles
Tel **(93) 674 39 08/674 39 58**
Holes 18 L 5209 m SSS 68
Loc 20 km NW of Barcelona

Sant Jordi
*Urb Sant Jordi d'Alfama, 4
3860 Ametlla de Mar, (Tarragona)*
Tel **(977) 49 34 57**
Fax (977) 49 32 77
Holes 9 L 5696 m SSS 70
V'tors U H
Fees 3500P
Loc 50 km S of Tarragona
Arch Lauresno Nomen

Terramar (1922)
Apdo 6, 08870 Sitges
Tel **(93) 894 05 80/894 20 43**
Fax (93) 894 70 51
Holes 18 L 5878 m Par 72 SSS 71
V'tors H
Fees 5600–8500P
Loc Sitges, 37 km S of Barcelona
Arch Hawtree/Piñero/Fazio

Torremirona (1994)
*Ctra N260 Km46, 17744 Navata
(Girona)*
Tel **(972) 55 37 37**
Fax (972) 55 37 16
Holes 18 L 5708 m Par 70

For list of abbreviations see page 479

V'tors U
Fees 5775P (6500P)
Loc   30 km from Girona,
      nr Besalú, off A7

Vallromanes (1969)

C/Afveras, 08188 Vallromanes
Tel   (93) 572 90 64
Fax   (93) 572 93 30
Holes 18 L 6038 m SSS 72
V'tors H
Fees D–5750P (11.500P)
Loc   23 km N of Barcelona
      between Alella and Granollers.
      A7 Junction 13
Arch FW Hawtree

Burgos

Lerma (1991)

Ctra Madrid-Burgos Km195,
09340 Lerma (Burgos)
Tel   (947) 17 12 14/17 12 16
Fax   (947) 17 12 16
Holes 18 L 6235 m SSS 72
V'tors H
Fees 3500P (5500P)
Loc   30 km S of Burgos, nr Villa
      Ducal de Lerma
Arch Pepe Gancedo

Canary Islands

Amarilla (1988)

Urb Amarilla Golf, San Miguel de
Abona, 38630 Santa Cruz de Tenerife
Tel   (922) 73 03 19
Fax   (922) 73 00 85
Holes 18 L 6077 m Par 72
V'tors H
Fees 6875P
Loc   6 km SW of South Airport.
      12 km from Playa de las
      Américas
Arch Donald Steel

Costa Teguise (1978)

Apdo 170, 35080 Arrecife de Lanzarote
Tel   (928) 59 05 12
Fax   (928) 59 04 90
Holes 18 L 5853 m SSS 72
V'tors U
Fees Summer–5000P
      Winter–6400P
Loc   4 km N of Arrecife
Arch John Harris

Maspalomas (1968)

Av de Africa, Maspalomas,
35100 Las Palmas de Gran Canaria
Tel   (928) 76 25 81/76 73 43
Fax   (928) 76 82 45
Holes 18 L 6216 m SSS 72
V'tors U
Fees Summer–5000P
      Winter–8000P
Loc   S coast of Gran Canaria
Arch Mackenzie Ross

Real Golf Las Palmas
(1891)

PO Box 93, Santa Brigida, 35310 Las
Palmas, Gran#Canaria
Tel   (928) 35 10 50/35 01 04
Fax   (928) 35 01 10
Holes 18 L 5690 m SSS 71
V'tors WE–NA
Fees WD–4500P
Loc   Bandama, Las Palmas 14 km
Arch Mackenzie Ross

Real Tenerife (1932)

El Peñón, Tacoronte, Tenerife
Tel   (922) 63 66 07
Fax   (922) 63 64 80
Holes 18 L 5750 m Par 71
V'tors WD–H 8am–1pm
Fees 5720P
Loc   20 km N of Santa Cruz.
      Puerto Cruz 15 km
Arch J Laynez

Golf del Sur (1987)

San Miguel de Abona, 38620 Tenerife
(Canarias)
Tel   (922) 73 81 70
Fax   (922) 78 82 72
Holes North 9 L 2913 m SSS 36
      Links 9 L 2469 m SSS 34
      South 9 L 2957 m SSS 36
V'tors H
Fees 5500–7700P
Loc   Airport 3 km. Playa de las
      Américas 12 km
Arch Pepe Gancedo

Cordoba

Pozoblanco (1984)

Jacinto Benavente 8, 14400 Pozoblanco,
(Córdoba)
Tel   (957) 10 02 39/10 00 06
Holes 9 L 3020 m SSS 62
Loc   Pozoblanco 3 km
Arch Carlos Luca

Los Villares (1976)

Avda del Generalismo 1-2, PO Box
463, 14080 Córdoba
Tel   (957) 35 02 08
Holes 18 L 5964 m SSS 73
Loc   9 km N of Córdoba, towards
      Obejo

Galicia

Aero Club de Santiago
(1976)

General Pardiñas 34, Santiago de
Compostela (La Coruña)
Tel   (981) 59 24 00
Holes 9 L 5816 m SSS 70
Loc   Santiago Airport

Aero Club de Vigo
(1951)

Reconquista 7, 36201 Vigo
Tel   (986) 48 66 45/48 75 09
Holes 9 L 5622 m SSS 60
Loc   Peinador Airport, 8 km from
      Vigo

La Coruña (1962)

Apartado 737, 15080 La Coruña
Tel   (981) 28 52 00
Holes 18 L 5782 m SSS 72
Loc   Arteijo, 7 km SW of La Coruña
Arch Antonio Lucena

La Toja (1970)

Isla de La Toja, El Grove, Pontevedra
Tel   (986) 73 01 58/73 08 18
Fax   (986) 73 31 22
Holes 9 L 5178 m SSS 72
V'tors H
Fees 6000–9000P
Loc   La Toja island. 30 km W of
      Pontevedra
Arch Ramón Espinosa

Madrid Region

Barberán (1967)

Apartado 150.239, Cuatro Vientos,
28080 Madrid
Tel   (91) 509 12 58/509 11 40
Holes 11 L 6202 m SSS 72
V'tors U
Loc   10 km SW of Madrid
Arch Ramón Espinosa

La Dehesa (1991)

Calle Real 19, 28691 Villanueva La
Canada
Tel   (91) 815 70 22/815 70 37
Fax   (91) 815 54 68
Holes 18 L 6456 m SSS 72
V'tors M+H only
Fees 2500P (8500P)
Loc   35 km NW of Madrid
Arch Manuel Piñero

Las Encinas de Boadilla
(1984)

Crta Boadilla-Pozuelo Km 1400,
Boadilla del Monte, Madrid
Tel   (91) 633 11 00
Holes 9 L 1464 m SSS 72
Loc   Pozuelo, 12 km W of Madrid
Arch Francisco Moreno

Herreria (1966)

PO Box 28200, San Lorenzo del
Escorial, (Madrid)
Tel   (91) 890 51 11
Holes 18 L 6050 m SSS 72
Loc   Escorial, 50 km W of Madrid
Arch Antonio Lucena

Lomas-Bosque (1973)

Urb El Bosque, 28670 Villaviciosa de Odón, (Madrid)
Tel **(91) 616 75 00**
Fax (91) 616 73 93
Holes 18 L 6075 m SSS 72
9 hole Par 3 course
V'tors WD–U H WE–M H
Fees 4000–12.500P
Loc 20 km SW of Madrid
Arch RD Putman

La Moraleja (1976)

La Moraleja, Alcobendas (Madrid)
Tel **(91) 650 07 00**
Holes 18 L 6016 m SSS 72
V'tors M
Loc 9 km N of Madrid on Burgos road
Arch Jack Nicklaus

Nuevo De Madrid
(1972)

Las Matas (Madrid)
Tel **(91) 630 08 20**
Holes 18 L 5647 m SSS 70
Loc 25 km NW of Madrid on La Coruña road

Puerta de Hierro
(1904)

Avda de Miraflores, 28035 Madrid
Tel **(91) 216 1745**
Fax (91) 373 8111
Holes 18 L 6347 m SSS 73
18 L 5273 m SSS 68
V'tors M only
Fees 6900P (14.950P)
Loc 4 km N of Madrid (Route VI)
Arch Harris/Simpson

RAC de España (1967)

José Abascal 10, 28003 Madrid
Tel **(91) 657 00 01**
Holes 18 L 6505 m SSS 72
9 hole Par 3 course
Loc San Sebastián de los Reyes, 28 km N of Madrid on Burgos road
Arch Javier Arana

Somosaguas (1971)

Somosaguas, 28011 Madrid
Tel **(91) 352 16 47**
Holes 9 L 6054 m SSS 72
Loc Somosaguas
Arch John Harris

Valdeláguila (1975)

Urb Valdeláguila, Villalbilla, (Madrid)
Tel **(91) 885 96 59**
Fax (91) 885 96 59
Holes 9 L 5714 m SSS 70
V'tors WD–U WE–NA
Fees 3000P
Loc 8 km S of Alcalá de Henares

Villa de Madrid CC
(1932)

Crta Castilla, 28040 Madrid
Tel **(91) 357 21 32**
Fax (91) 549 07 97
Holes 27 L 5900-6321 m SSS 73-74
V'tors U H
Fees 1950P (2900P)
Loc 4 km NW of Madrid, in the Casa del Campo
Arch Javier Arana

Málaga Region

Alhaurín (1994)

Crta 426 Km15, Alhaurín el Grande
Tel **(952) 59 59 70**
Fax (952) 59 45 86
Holes 18 L 6221 m Par 72
18 hole Par 3 course
9 hole Par 3 course
V'tors U
Fees 5000P
Loc 6 km from Mijas
Arch Severiano Ballesteros

Añoreta (1989)

Avenida del Golf, 29730 Rincón de la Victoria, (Málaga)
Tel **(952) 40 40 00**
Fax (952) 40 40 50
Holes 18 L 5976 m SSS 71
V'tors U
Fees 2500P (3000P)
Loc 12 km E of Málaga
Arch JM Canizares

La Cala (1991)

La Cala de Mijas, 29647 Mijas-Costa (Málaga)
Tel **(952) 58 91 01,**
(952) 58 91 00
Fax (952) 58 91 05
Holes North 18 L 6160 m SSS 72
South 18 L 5960 m SSS 71
6 hole Par 3 course
V'tors U H
Fees 4500–7500P
Loc 6 km from Cala de Mijas, between Fuengirola and Marbella
Arch Cabell Robinson

El Candado (1965)

Urb El Candado, El Palo, 29018 Málaga
Tel **(952) 29 93 40/1**
Holes 9 L 4676 m SSS 66
Fees 3500P
Loc El Palo, 5 km E of Málaga on Route N340
Arch Carlos Fernández

El Chaparral

Urb El Chaparral, Mijas-Costa
Tel **(952) 49 38 00**
Fax (952) 49 40 51

Holes 18 L 5700 m SSS 71
V'tors U H
Fees 4000P
Loc 5 km W of Fuengirola on N340
Arch Pepe Gancedo

Guadalhorce (1988)

Crtra de Cártama Km7, Apartado 48, 29590 Campanillas (Málaga)
Tel **(952) 17 93 78**
Fax (952) 17 93 72
Holes 18 L 6194 m SSS 72
9 hole Par 3 course
V'tors WD–H before 1pm (booking necessary) WE–M
Fees 4000–5000P
Loc 8 km W of Málaga
Arch Kosti Kuronen

Lauro (1992)

Los Caracolillos, 29130 Alaurín de la Torre, (Málaga)
Tel **(95) 241 27 67**
Fax (95) 241 47 57
Holes 18 L 5971 m SSS 71
V'tors U
Fees D–5000P
Loc 20 km SW of Málaga airport on Route C-344 towards Coín
Arch Folco Nardi

Málaga Club de Campo
(1925)

Parador de Golf, Apdo 324, 29080 Málaga
Tel **(952) 38 12 55**
Fax (952) 38 21 41
Holes 18 L 6249 m SSS 72
V'tors U
Fees 4400P
Loc Torremolinos 4 km. 12 km S of Málaga, nr Airport
Arch Tom Simpson

Mijas (1976)

Apartado 145, Fuengirola, Málaga
Tel **(952) 47 68 43**
Fax (952) 46 79 43
Holes Lagos 18 L 6548 m Par 71 SSS 74; Olivos 18 L 6009 m Par 72 SSS 72
V'tors H–booking required Oct–Apr
Fees 6200P
Loc 4 km NW of Fuengirola (Mijas Valley)
Arch Robert Trent Jones

Miraflores (1990)

Urb Riviera del Sol, 29647 Mijas-Costa
Tel **(952) 93 19 60**
Fax (952) 93 19 42
Holes 18 L 5635 m SSS 70
V'tors U
Fees 5500P
Loc 15 km E of Marbella
Arch Folco Nardi

Los Moriscos (1974)
Costa Granada, Motril (Granada)
Tel   (958) 82 55 27
Fax   (958) 25 52 51
Holes   9 L 5689 m SSS 72 Par 70
V'tors   U
Fees   2800P
Loc   8 km W of Motril, near
         Salobrena. 80 km E of Málaga
Arch   Ibergolf

La Siesta (1990)
*Sitio de Calahonda, Mijas-Costa
(Málaga)*
Tel   (952) 83 63 70
Holes   9 hole Par 3 course
Loc   20 km E of Málaga

Torrequebrada (1976)
Apdo 120, 29630 Benalmadena-Costa
Tel   (952) 44 27 42/56 11 02
Fax   (952) 56 11 29
Holes   18 L 5806 m SSS 71
V'tors   H
Fees   5000–7400P
Loc   Benalmadena, 22 km S of
         Málaga
Arch   Pepe Gancedo

Marbella & Estepona

Alcaidesa Links
*CN-340 Km124.6, 11315 La Linea
(Cádiz)*
Tel   (956) 79 10 40
Fax   (956) 79 10 41
Holes   18 L 5708 m SSS 71
V'tors   U–booking advised
Fees   8000P
Loc   15 km E of Gibraltar
Arch   Alliss/Clark

Aloha (1975)
29660 Nueva Andalucía, (Málaga)
Tel   (952) 81 08 76/81 37 50, (952)
         81 23 88 (Caddymaster)
Fax   (952) 81 23 89
Holes   18 L 6261 m SSS 72
         9 hole short course
V'tors   H–booking necessary
Fees   7500–15.000P
Loc   8 km W of Marbella, nr Puerto
         Banus
Arch   Javier Arana

Los Arqueros (1991)
*Crta de Ronda Km43, 29679 Benahavis
(Málaga)*
Tel   (952) 78 46 00
Fax   (952) 78 67 07
Holes   18 L 6130 m SSS 72
V'tors   H
Fees   4500P
Loc   5 km N of San Pedro de
         Alcántara
Arch   Severiano Ballesteros

Atalaya G&CC (1968)
Crta Benahavis 7, 29688 Málaga
Tel   (952) 88 48 01
Fax   (952) 88 57 35
Holes   18 L 5893 m Par 72
         18 L 5123 m Par 72
V'tors   U H
Fees   6000P (6000P)
Loc   12 km S of Marbella.
         60 km SW of Málaga
Arch   B von Limburger

Las Brisas (1968)
*Apdo 147, 29660 Nueva Andalucía,
(Málaga)*
Tel   (952) 81 08 75/81 30 21
Fax   (952) 81 55 18
Holes   18 L 6094 m SSS 72
V'tors   H–restricted
Fees   12.000P
Loc   8 km S of Marbella, nr Puerto
         Banus
Arch   Robert Trent Jones

La Cañada (1982)
*Ctra Guadiaro Km 1, 11311 Guadiaro
(Cádiz)*
Tel   (956) 79 41 00/79 44 11
Fax   (956) 79 42 41
Holes   9 L 2873 m SSS 72
V'tors   U
Fees   1200P
Loc   Guadiaro, 2 km from
         Sotogrande
Arch   Robert Trent Jones

La Duquesa G&CC (1987)
*Urb El Hacho, 29691 Manilva
(Málaga)*
Tel   (952) 89 04 25/89 04 26
Fax   (952) 89 00 57
Holes   18 L 6142 m SSS 72
Fees   5000P
Loc   10 km S of Estepona
Arch   Robert Trent Jones

Estepona (1989)
*Paraje Arroyo Vaquero, Apartado 274,
29680 Estepona (Málaga)*
Tel   (952) 65 14 99
Holes   18 L 6001 m SSS 71
Loc   5 km W of Estepona
Arch   Luis López

Guadalmina (1959)
*Guadalmina Alta, San Pedro de
Alcántara, 29678 Marbella (Málaga)*
Tel   (952) 88 65 22
Fax   (952) 88 34 83
Holes   North 18 L 5825 m SSS 70
         South 18 L 6075 m SSS 72
         9 hole Par 3 course
V'tors   H (max 27M/35L)
Fees   7500P
Loc   San Pedro, 12 km W of
         Marbella
Arch   Arana/Nardi

Monte Mayor (1992)
*Crta N340 Km 165, 29660 Marbella
(Málaga)*
Tel   (95) 211 30 88
Fax   (95) 211 30 87
Holes   18 L 5593 m SSS 71
V'tors   U
Fees   6000P (inc buggy)
Loc   Between San Pedro and
         Estepona, at Cancelada
Arch   Pepe Gancedo

Los Naranjos (1977)
*Apdo 64, 29660 Nueva Andalucía,
Marbella*
Tel   (952) 81 52 06/81 24 28
Fax   (952) 81 14 28
Holes   18 L 6484 m SSS 72
V'tors   U H
Fees   6800P
Loc   8 km S of Marbella, nr Puerto
         Banus
Arch   Robert Trent Jones Sr

El Paraiso (1974)
*Ctra Cádiz-Málaga Km 167, 29680
Estepona (Málaga)*
Tel   (95) 288 38 35/288 38 46
Fax   (95) 288 58 27
Holes   18 L 6116 m SSS 72
V'tors   U
Fees   D–7000P
Loc   14 km S of Marbella
Arch   Player/Kirby

La Quinta G&CC (1989)
*Urb La Quinta, 29660 Nueva
Andalucía*
Tel   (952) 78 34 62
Fax   (952) 78 34 66
Holes   27 L 5797-5945 m SSS 71-72
V'tors   U H
Fees   7900P
Loc   3 km N of San Pedro de
         Alcántara
Arch   Piñero/García-Garrido

Rio Real (1965)
*Urb Rio Real, PO Box 82,
29600 Marbella (Málaga)*
Tel   (95) 277 95 09
Fax   (95) 277 21 40
Holes   18 L 6130 m SSS 72
V'tors   U
Fees   5500P
Loc   5 km E of Marbella. Málaga
         Airport 50 km
Arch   Javier Arana

San Roque (1990)
*CN 340 Km 126, San Roque,
11360 Cádiz*
Tel   (956) 61 30 30
Fax   (956) 61 30 12/61 30 13
Holes   18 L 6440 m SSS 74
V'tors   U H
Fees   7000P
Loc   3 km W of Sotogrande.
         15 km E of Gibraltar
Arch   Dave Thomas

Santa María G&CC
Coto de los Dolores, Urb Elviria,
Crta N340 Km 192, 29600 Marbella
(Málaga)
Tel   (952) 83 03 86/83 03 88/
        83 10 36
Fax   (952) 83 08 70
Holes 9 L 5792 m SSS 71
V'tors U
Fees   4500P
Loc   10 km E of Marbella, opp
        Hotel Don Carlos
Arch   A García Garrido

Sotogrande (1964)
Paseo del Parque, Apartado 14,
Sotogrande (Cádiz)
Tel   (956) 79 50 50/79 50 51
Fax   (956) 79 50 29
Holes 18 L 6224 m SSS 74
        9 L 1299 m Par 29
Fees   8000P
Loc   30 km N of Gibraltar,
        nr Guadiaro
Arch   Robert Trent Jones

Valderrama (1985)
Apartado 1, 11310 Sotogrande
(Cádiz)
Tel   (956) 79 12 00
Fax   (956) 79 60 28
Holes 18 L 6326 m SSS 71
        9 L 1100 m SSS 27
V'tors H–12–2pm
Fees   28.000P
Loc   18 km N of Gibraltar
Arch   Robert Trent Jones Sr

North Coast

Barganiza (1982)
Apartado 277, 33080 Oviedo,
Asturias
Tel   (985) 74 24 68
Holes 18 L 5549 m SSS 70
Fees   5000P
Loc   12 km N of Oviedo on Gijon
        old road
Arch   Victor García

Castiello (1958)
Apartado de Correos 161, Gijón
Tel   (985) 36 63 13
Holes 18 L 4817 m SSS 67
V'tors WE–restricted in summer
Fees   3000P
Loc   5 km S of Gijón on Oviedo
        old road

La Cuesta
Apdo 40, 33500 Llanes
Tel   (98) 541 7084
Fax   (98) 540 1973
Holes 9 L 5456 m SSS 69
V'tors U
Fees   2500P
Loc   3 km from Llanes (N-634)

Larrabea (1989)
Crta de Landa, 01170 Legutiano,
(Alava)
Tel   (945) 46 58 44/46 58 41
Fax   (945) 46 57 25
Holes 18 L 5991 m Par 72
V'tors U
Fees   5000P (6000P)
Loc   14 km N of Vitoria,
        nr Villareal de Alava
Arch   José Gancedo

Laukariz (1976)
Laukariz-Munguía (Viscaya)
Tel   (94) 674 08 58/674 04 62
Holes 18 L 6112 m SSS 72
Loc   15 km N of Bilbao towards
        Mungía
Arch   RD Putman

La Llorea (1994)
Crta Nacional 632, Km 62, 3394
Lloreda (Gijon)
Tel   (985) 33 31 91
Fax   (985) 36 47 26
Holes 18 L 5868 m Par 72
V'tors H
Fees   5500P (6500P)
Loc   10 km E of Gijón
Arch   Roland Fabret

Real Golf Neguri (1911)
Apdo Correos 9, 48990 Algorta
Tel   (94) 469 02 00/04/08
Holes 18 L 6319 m SSS 72
        6 hole Par 3 course
Fees   6000P
Loc   La Galea, 20 km N of Bilbao
Arch   Javier Arana

Real Golf Pedreña (1928)
Apartado 233, Santander
Tel   (942) 50 00 01/50 02 66
Fax   (942) 50 04 21
Holes 18 L 5745 m SSS 70
        9 L 2740 m SSS 36
V'tors H
Fees   5600P (9000P)
Loc   20 km from Santander, on
        Bay of Santander
Arch   Colt/Ballesteros

Real San Sebastián (1910)
PO Box 6, Fuenterrabia, (Guipúzcoa)
Tel   (943) 61 68 45/61 68 46
Fax   (943) 61 14 91
Holes 18 L 6020 m SSS 71
V'tors WD–U H from 9–12 noon
        WE–NA
Fees   6000P
Loc   Jaizubia Valley, 14 km NE of
        San Sebastián
Arch   P Hirigoyen

Real Zarauz (1916)
Apartado 82, Zarauz, (Guipúzcoa)
Tel   (943) 83 01 45

Holes 9 L 5184 m SSS 68
Loc   Zarauz, 25 km W of San
        Sebastián

Pamplona

Ulzama (1965)
31779 Guerendiain (Navarra)
Tel   (948) 30 51 62
Fax   (948) 30 54 71
Holes 18 L 6246 m Par 72 SSS 73
V'tors U
Fees   On application
Loc   20 km N of Pamplona
Arch   Javier Arana

Seville & Gulf of Cadiz

Bellavista (1976)
Crta Huelva-Punta Umbria, Apdo 335,
Huelva
Tel   (955) 31 90 17
Fax   (955) 31 90 25
Holes 9 L 6270 m SSS 73
Fees   3500–5000P
Loc   Aljaraque, 6 km SW of
        Huelva, towards Punta
        Umbria

Islantilla (1993)
Urb Islantilla, Apdo 52, 21410 Isla
Cristina (Huelva)
Tel   (959) 48 60 39/48 60 49
Fax   (959) 48 61 04
Holes 27 L 5926-6142 m SSS 72-73
V'tors U H
Fees   6500P
Loc   30 km W of Huelva,
        nr Portuguese border
Arch   Canales/Recasens

Montecastillo (1993)
Carretera de Arcos, 11406 Jérez
Tel   (956) 15 12 00
Fax   (956) 15 12 09
Holes 18 L 6494 m SSS 72
V'tors H
Fees   5500P
Loc   10 km NE of Jérez. 75 km
        S of Seville
Arch   Jack Nicklaus

Novo Sancti Petri (1990)
Urb Novo Sancti Petri, Playa de la
Barrosa, 11139 Chiclana de la Frontera
Tel   (956) 49 40 05/49 44 50
Fax   (956) 49 43 50
Holes 27 L 5197-6466 m SSS 72
V'tors U H
Fees   7000P
Loc   La Barrosa, 24 km SE of
        Cádiz. Jérez Airport 50 km
Arch   Severiano Ballesteros

Pineda De Sevilla
(1939)
Apartado 1049, 41080 Sevilla
Tel **(954) 61 14 00/61 33 99**
Holes 18 L 6120 m SSS 72
Loc 3 km S of Seville on Cádiz
road
Arch R & F Medina

Real Golf Sevilla (1992)
Autovia Sevilla-Utrera, 41089
Montequinto (Sevilla)
Tel **(954) 12 43 01**
Fax (954) 12 42 29
Holes 18 L 6321 m SSS 73
V'tors U H WE–booking necessary
Fees 6000P
Loc 3 km S of Seville
Arch José María Olazabal

Sevilla Golf (1989)
Hacienda Las Minas, Ctra de Isla
Mayor, Aznalcazar (Sevilla)
Tel **(955) 75 04 14**
Holes 9 L 5910 m SSS 71
Fees 3500P (5000P)
Loc 15 km W of Seville
Arch A García Garrido

Vista Hermosa (1975)
Apartado 77, Urb Vista Hermosa,
11500 Puerto de Santa María, Cádiz
Tel **(956) 87 56 05**
Holes 9 L 5614 m SSS 70
Loc 25 km W of Cádiz

Zaudin
Crta Mairena-Tomares, 41940 Tomares
(Sevilla)
Tel **(954) 15 33 44**
Holes 18 L 6192 m Par 71 SSS 72
V'tors U
Fees On application
Loc Cornisa del Aljarafe,
3 km from Seville
Arch Gary Player

Valencia & Castellón

El Bosque (1989)
Crta Godelleta, 46370 Chiva-Valencia
Tel **(96) 180 41 42**
Fax (96) 180 40 09
Holes 18 L 6384 m SSS 74
V'tors U
Fees 5000P
Loc Nr Chiva, 24 km W of
Valencia, off Madrid road
Arch Robert Trent Jones Sr

Costa de Azahar (1960)
Ctra Grao-Benicasim, Castellón de la
Plana
Tel **(964) 22 70 64**
Holes 9 L 2724 m SSS 70

Loc 5 km NE of Castellón,
on coast
Arch Angel Pérez

Escorpión (1975)
Apartado Correos 1, Betera
(Valencia)
Tel **(96) 160 12 11**
Fax (96) 169 01 87
Holes 18 L 6345 m SSS 73
V'tors H
Fees 4000P (8000P)
Loc Betera, 20 km N of Valencia
Arch Ron Kirby

Manises (1964)
Apartado 22.029, Manises
(Valencia)
Tel **(96) 152 18 71**
Holes 9 L 6094 m Par 73
Loc 8 km W of Valencia
Arch Javier Arana

Mediterraneo CC
(1978)
Urb La Coma, Borriol, (Castellón)
Tel **(964) 32 12 27**
Fax (964) 32 13 57
Holes 18 L 6239 m SSS 73
V'tors H
Fees 3500–4500P (4500–5000P)
Loc Borriol, 4 km NW of
Castellón
Arch Ramón Espinosa

Oliva Nova (1992)
Carretera Las Marinas, 03700 Denia
Tel **(096) 285 40 00**
Holes 18 L 6445m SSS 72
V'tors U
Loc 15 km N of Denia, off A7
Arch Severiano Ballesteros

El Saler (1968)
Parador Luis Vives, 46012 El Saler
(Valencia)
Tel **(96) 161 11 86**
Fax (96) 162 70 16
Holes 18 L 6485 m SSS 75
Fees D–4500P
Loc Oliva, 18 km S of Valencia,
towards Cullera
Arch Javier Arana

Valladolid

Entrepinos (1990)
Crta Pesquerela Km1.5, 47130
Simancas, (Valladolid)
Tel **(983) 59 05 11/59 05 61**
Fax (983) 59 07 65
Holes 18 L 5208 m Par 69
V'tors U H
Fees 5000P (7000P)
Loc 15 km SW of Valladolid
Arch Manuel Piñero

Zaragoza

Aero Club de Zaragoza
(1966)
Coso 34, 50004 Zaragoza
Tel **(976) 21 43 78**
Holes 9 L 5042 m SSS 67
Loc 12 km SW of Zaragoza, by
airbase

La Penaza (1973)
Apartado 3039, Zaragoza
Tel **(976) 34 28 00/34 22 48**
Fax (976) 34 28 00
Holes 18 L 6122 m SSS 72
V'tors H
Fees D–5600P (6720P)
Loc 15 km SW of Zaragoza on
Madrid road, nr airbase
Arch FW Hawtree

Sweden

East Central

Ängsö (1979)
Björnövägen 2, 721 30 Västerås
Tel **(0171) 441012**
Fax (0171) 441049
Holes 18 hole course SSS 72
V'tors H
Fees 160kr (210kr)
Loc 15 km E of Västerås
Arch Åke Hultström

Arboga
Åkervägen 5, 732 32 Arboga
Tel **(0589) 70100**
Holes 18 L 5890 m SSS 73
V'tors U
Fees 140kr
Loc 5 km S of Arboga
Arch Sune Linde

Ärila (1951)
Nicolai, 611 92 Nyköping
Tel **(0155) 214967**
Fax (0155) 267657
Holes 18 L 5810 m Par 72
V'tors H
Fees 200kr (250kr)
Loc 5 km SE of Nyköping
Arch Sköld/Linde

Arlandastad
Norslunda Gård, 195 95 Rosersberg
Tel **(08) 590 36515**
Fax (08) 590 35518
Holes 18 L 5830 m SSS 72
9 L 1495 m SSS 29
V'tors H

Fees 250kr (320kr)
Loc 35 km N of Stockholm, nr Airport
Arch Sune Linde

Askersund (1980)

Box 3002, 696 03 Ammeberg
Tel (0583) 34442
Fax (0583) 34369
Holes 18 L 5800 m SSS 72
V'tors H
Fees 180kr
Loc 10 km SE of Askersund towards Ammeberg. 1 km on road to Kärra
Arch Ronald Fream

Burvik

Burvik, 740 12 Knutby
Tel (0174) 43060
Fax (0174) 43062
Holes 18 L 5785 m SSS 72
V'tors U
Fees On application
Loc 45 km E of Uppsala. 70 km N of Stockholm
Arch Bengt Lorichs

Edenhof (1991)

740 22 Bälinge
Tel (018) 334185
Fax (018) 334186
Holes 18 L 5898 m SSS 72
V'tors H
Fees 180kr (240kr)
Loc 17 km NW of Uppsala
Arch Sune Linde

Enköping (1970)

Box 2006, 745 02 Enköping
Tel (0171) 20830
Fax (0171) 20830
Holes 18 L 5660 m SSS 71
V'tors H
Fees 160kr (200kr)
Loc 1 km E of Enköping, off E18

Eskilstuna (1951)

Strängnäsvägen, 633 49 Eskilstuna
Tel (016) 142629
Fax (016) 148729
Holes 18 L 5610 m SSS 70
V'tors H
Fees 160kr (200kr)
Loc 2 km E of Eskilstuna. 20 km E of Örebro
Arch Douglas Brasier

Fagersta (1970)

Box 2051, 737 02 Fagersta
Tel (0223) 54060
Holes 18 L 5775 m SSS 71
Fees 100kr
Loc 7 km W of Fagersta (Route 65). 70 km N of Västerås

Frösåker (1989)

Frösåker Gård, 725 97 Västerås
Tel (021) 25401
Fax (021) 25485
Holes 18 L 5820 m SSS 72
V'tors U H
Fees 150kr (200kr)
Loc Västerås 15 km
Arch Sune Linde

Fullerö (1988)

Jotsberga, 725 91 Västerås
Tel (021) 50132
Fax (021) 50431
Holes 18 L 5707 m SSS 72
V'tors H
Fees 150kr (200kr)
Loc 6 km SW of Västerås
Arch Hultström/Sjöberg

Gripsholm (1991)

Box 133, 647 32 Mariefred
Tel (0159) 13040
Fax (0159) 13345
Holes 18 holes Par 73 course
V'tors H
Fees 180kr (250kr)
Loc 1 km from Mariefred
Arch Bengt Lorichs

Grönlund (1989)

PO Box 38, 740 10 Almunge
Tel (0174) 20670
Fax (0174) 20455
Holes 18 L 5865 m SSS 71
V'tors H
Fees 200kr (260kr)
Loc 20 km E of Uppsala. 25 km NE of Arlanda Airport
Arch Åke Persson

Gustavsvik

Box 22033, 702 02 Örebro
Tel (019) 244486
Fax (019) 246490
Holes 18 holes SSS 72
V'tors H
Fees 200kr
Loc 1 km S of Örebro
Arch Turner/Wirhed

Katrineholm (1959)

Jättorp, 641 93 Katrineholm
Tel (0150) 39270
Fax (0150) 39011
Holes 18 L 5850 m SSS 72
V'tors H
Fees 160kr (180kr)
Loc 7 km E of Katrineholm
Arch Nils Skjöld

Köping (1963)

Box 278, 731 26 Köping
Tel (0221) 81090
Fax (0221) 81277
Holes 18 L 5636 m SSS 71
V'tors U
Fees 140kr (190kr)

Loc 5 km N of Köping (Route 250)

Kumla (1987)

Box 46, 692 21 Kumla
Tel (019) 577370
Fax (019) 577373
Holes 18 L 5845 m SSS 72
V'tors U
Fees 200kr
Loc 8 km E of Kumla. 20 km SE of Örebro
Arch Jan Sederholm

Linde (1984)

Dalkarlshyttan, 711 31 Lindesberg
Tel (0581) 13960
Fax (0581) 12936
Holes 18 L 5539 m SSS 71
V'tors H
Fees 150kr (180kr)
Loc 42 km N of Örebro on R60. Lindesberg 2 km

Mosjö

Mosjö Gård, 705 94 Örebrö
Tel (019) 225780
Fax (019) 225045
Holes 18 L 6160 m SSS 74
V'tors WD–U WE–H
Fees 180kr (180kr)
Loc 10 km S of Örebrö
Arch Åke Persson

Nora (1988)

Box 108, 713 23 Nora
Tel (0587) 311660
Fax (0587) 15050
Holes 18 L 5865 m SSS 72
V'tors U
Fees 120kr (150kr)
Loc 33 km N of Örebro
Mis Open Apr-Oct

Örebro (1939)

Lanna, 719 93 Vintrosa
Tel (019) 291065
Fax (019) 291055
Holes 18 L 5870 m SSS 72
V'tors H–(max 36)
Fees 220kr
Loc 18 km W of Örebro on Route E18

Roslagen

Box 110, 761 22 Norrtälje
Tel (0176) 37194
Fax (0176) 37103
Holes 18 L 5512 m SSS 71
    9 hole course
V'tors H
Fees 150kr (200kr)
Loc 7 km N of Norrtälje

Sala (1970)

Fallet, Isätra, 733 92 Sala
Tel (0224) 53077/53055/53064
Holes 18 L 5570 m SSS 71

For list of abbreviations see page 479

Fees 100kr
Loc 8 km E of Sala towards
Uppsala, Route 67/72

Sigtunabygden (1961)
Box 89, 193 22 Sigtuna
Tel (08) 592 54012
Fax (08) 592 54167
Holes 18 L 5710 m SSS 72
Fees 210kr (270kr)
Loc Sigtuna, 50 km N of
Stockholm
Arch Nils Sköld

Södertälje (1952)
Box 91, 151 21 Södertälje
Tel (08) 550 38240
Fax (08) 550 62549
Holes 18 L 5875 m SSS 72
V'tors H WE–NA before 1pm
Fees 225kr (275kr)
Loc 4 km W of Södertälje
Arch Nils Sköld

Strängnäs (1968)
Box 21, 645 21 Strängnäs
Tel (0152) 14731
Fax (0152) 14716
Holes 18 L 5790 m SSS 72
V'tors H
Fees 150kr (200kr)
Loc 3 km S of Strängnäs
Arch Anders Amilon

Torshälla (1960)
Box 128, 64422 Torshälla
Tel (016) 358722
Fax (016) 357491
Holes 18 L 5934 m Par 72
V'tors H
Fees 160kr (180kr)
Loc 5 km N of Eskilstuna
Arch Brasier/Linde

Tortuna
Nicktuna, Tortuna, 725 96 Västerås
Tel (021) 65300
Fax (021) 65302
Holes 18 L 5750 m SSS 72
V'tors U
Fees 150kr (180kr)
Loc 10 km N of Västerås
Arch Husell/Hultström

Trosa (1972)
Box 80, 619 00 Trosa
Tel (0156) 22458
Fax (0156) 22454
Holes 18 L 5727 m SSS 72
V'tors U
Fees 180kr
Loc 5 km W of Trosa, towards
Uttervik

Upsala (1937)
Hämö Gård, Läby, 755 92 Uppsala
Tel (018) 460120
Fax (018) 461205

Holes 18 L 6176 m SSS 74
9 L 1643 m SSS 56
V'tors H
Fees 200kr (250kr)
Loc 10 km W of Uppsala
Arch Greger Paulsson

Vassunda
Smedby Gård, 741 91 Knivsta
Tel (018) 381230/381235
Fax (018) 381416
Holes 18 L 6141 m Par 72
V'tors H
Fees 220kr (250kr)
Loc 45 km N of Stockholm
Arch Sune Linde

Västerås (1931)
Bjärby, 724 81 Västerås
Tel (021) 357543
Fax (021) 357573
Holes 18 L 5380 m SSS 69
V'tors U
Fees 150kr (200kr)
Loc 2 km N of Västerås
Arch Nils Sköld

Far North

Boden (1946)
Box 107, 961 21 Boden
Tel (0921) 72051
Fax (0921) 72047
Holes 18 L 5495 m SSS 72
V'tors H
Fees 160kr
Loc 7 km S of Boden
Arch Björn Eriksson

Funäsdalsfjällen (1972)
Box 66, 840 95 Funäsdalen
Tel (0684) 21100
Fax (0684) 21100
Holes 18 L 5300 m SSS 72
V'tors U
Fees 160kr
Loc Funäsdalen, nr Norwegian
border
Arch Sköld/Linde

Gällivare-Malmberget (1973)
Box 35, 983 21 Malmberget
Tel (0970) 20782
Fax (0970) 20782
Holes 18 L 5620 m SSS 71
V'tors H
Fees 100kr
Loc 4 km N of Gällivare, towards
Malmberget
Arch Jan Sederholm

Haparanda (1989)
Mattiu 140, 953 35 Haparanda
Tel (0922) 10660
Fax (0922) 15040

Holes 18 L 6230 m SSS 73
V'tors H
Fees 160kr
Loc 125 km E of Luleå
Arch Peter Chamberlain

Härnösand (1957)
Box 52, 871 22 Härnösand
Tel (0611) 66169
Fax (0611) 66169
Holes 18 L 5410 m SSS 70
V'tors H
Fees D–180kr
Loc Vägnön, 16 km N of
Härnösand on E4, towards
Hemsö Island
Arch Nils Sköld

Kalix (1990)
Box 32, 952 21 Kalix
Tel (0923) 15945/15935
Fax (0923) 77735
Holes 18 L 5700m SSS 71
V'tors U
Fees 160kr
Loc 80 km N of Luleå
Arch Jan Sederholm

Klövsjö-Vemdalen
Box 147, 840 32 Klövsjö
Tel (0682) 23494
Holes 18 L 5732 m SSS 72
9 hole course
V'tors H or Green Card
Fees 150kr (150kr)
Loc 100 km S of Östersund
Arch Sune Linde

Luleå (1955)
Box 314, 971 09 Luleå
Tel (0920) 56300/1/2
Fax (0920) 56362
Holes 18 L 5675 m SSS 72
V'tors H
Fees 160kr
Loc Rutvik, 12 km E of Luleå
Arch Skjöld/Tideman

Östersund-Fröso (1947)
Box 40, 832 01 Frösön
Tel (063) 43001
Fax (063) 43765
Holes 18 L 6000 m SSS 73
Fees 150kr
Loc Island of Frösö

Öviks GC Puttom (1967)
Ovansjö 1970, 891 95 Arnäsvall
Tel (0660) 64091
Fax (0660) 64040
Holes 18 L 5795 m SSS 72
V'tors H
Fees 160kr
Loc 15 km N of Örnsköldsvik on
E4
Arch Nils Sköld

Piteå (1960)

Nötön, 941 90 Piteå

Tel	(0911) 14990
Fax	(0911) 14960
Holes	18 L 5325 m SSS 69
V'tors	H
Fees	150kr
Loc	2 km NE of Piteå
Arch	Jan Sederholm

Skellefteå (1967)

Box 152, 931 22 Skellefteå

Tel	(0910) 779333
Fax	(0910) 779777
Holes	27 L 6135 m SSS 72
	Par 3 course
V'tors	U H
Fees	200kr
Loc	Skellefteå 5 km
Arch	Sköld/Carlsson/Larsson

Sollefteå-Långsele (1970)

Box 213, 881 25 Sollefteå

Tel	(0620) 21477/12670
Fax	(0620) 21477/12670
Holes	18 L 5770 m SSS 72
V'tors	H
Fees	160kr (160kr)
Loc	Österforse, 15 km SW of
	Sollefteå (Route 89)
Arch	Nils Sköld

Sundsvall (1952)

Golfvägen 5, 862 00 Kvissleby

Tel	(060) 561056
Fax	(060) 561909
Holes	18 L 5885 m SSS 72
V'tors	WD–H before noon WE–H
	after 10am
Fees	180kr (200r)
Loc	Skottsund, 15 km S of
	Sundsvall

Timrå

Golfbanevägen 2, 860 32 Fagervik

Tel	(060) 570153
Fax	(060) 578136
Holes	18 L 5715 m Par 72
V'tors	H
Fees	180kr (200kr)
Loc	1 km S of Sundsvall airport
Arch	Sune Linde

Umeå (1954)

Lövön, 913 35 Holmsund

Tel	(090) 41071/41066
Fax	(090) 149120
Holes	18 L 5751 m SSS 72
	9 L 2688 m SSS 70
V'tors	U
Fees	200kr
Loc	16 km SE of Umeå
Arch	Bo Engdahl

Gothenburg

Albatross (1973)

Lillhagsvägen, 422 50 Hisings-Backa

Tel	(031) 551901/550500
Fax	(031) 555900
Holes	18 L 6020 m SSS 72
Fees	220kr (250kr)
Loc	10 km N of Gothenburg on
	Hising Island

Chalmers

PO Box 40, 438 21 Landvetter

Tel	(031) 918430
Fax	(031) 916338
Holes	18 L 5560 m SSS 71
V'tors	WD–U H before 4pm –M H
	after 4pm WE–M H before
	2pm –U H after 2pm
Fees	200kr (200kr)
Loc	20 km E of Gothenburg.
	2 km from Landvetter airport
Arch	Gyllenhammar/Henrikson

Delsjö (1962)

Kallebäck, 412 76 Göteborg

Tel	(031) 406959
Fax	(031) 407130
Holes	18 L 5703 m Par 71
V'tors	H WE–NA before 1pm
Fees	220kr (260kr)
Loc	5 km E of Gothenburg
	(Route 40)
Arch	Douglas Brasier

Forsgårdens (1982)

Gamla Forsv 1, 434 47 Kungsbacka

Tel	(0300) 13649
Fax	(0300) 71987
Holes	18 L 6110 m SSS 72
	9 L 2915 m
V'tors	WD–U WE–NA before 2pm
Fees	220kr (260kr)
Loc	1 km SE of Kungsbacka.
	20 km S of Gothenburg
Arch	Sune Linde

Göteborg (1902)

Box 2056, 436 02 Hovås

Tel	(031) 282444
Fax	(031) 685333
Holes	18 L 5935 yds SSS 70
V'tors	WD–U WE–M before 2pm
Fees	250kr (300kr)
Loc	11 km S of Gothenburg
	(Route 158)

Gullbringa (1967)

442 95 Kungälv

Tel	(0303) 227161
Fax	(0303) 227778
Holes	18 L 5775 m Par 70
	9 L 2777 m
V'tors	U
Fees	200kr
Loc	14 km W of Kungälv, towards
	Marstrand

Kungälv-Kode

Ö Knaverstad 140, 442 97 Kode

Tel	(0303) 51300
Fax	(0303) 50205
Holes	18 L 5984 m Par 72
V'tors	U
Fees	200kr
Loc	30 km N of Gothenburg
Arch	Lars Andreasson

Kungsbacka (1971)

Hamra Gård 515, 43040 Särö

Tel	(031) 936277
Fax	(031) 935085
Holes	18 L 5855 m SSS 72
	9 L 2880 m SSS 36
V'tors	WD–U WE–NA before
	2pm
Fees	220kr (260kr)
Loc	7 km N of Kungsbacka on
	Route 158
Arch	Pennink/Nordström

Lysegården (1966)

Box 532, 442 15 Kungälv

Tel	(0303) 223426
Fax	(0303) 223075
Holes	18 L 5670 m SSS 71
	9 L 5444 m SSS 70
V'tors	H
Fees	180kr
Loc	10 km N of Kungälv
Arch	Röhss/Engström

Mölndals (1979)

Box 77, 437 21 Lindome

Tel	(031) 993030
Fax	(031) 994901
Holes	18 L 5625 m SSS 73
V'tors	H WE–NA before 11am
Fees	200kr (240kr)
Loc	Lindome, 20 km S of
	Gothenburg
Arch	Ronald Fream

Öijared (1958)

PI 1082, 448 92 Floda

Tel	(0302) 30604
Fax	(0302) 35370
Holes	18 L 5875 m Par 72
	18 L 5655 m Par 71
V'tors	H WE–NA before 1pm
Fees	200kr (220kr)
Loc	35 km NE of Gothenburg
	(E20), nr Nääs
Arch	Brasier/Amilon

Partille (1986)

Box 234, 433 24 Partille

Tel	(031) 987043/987019 (Pro)
Fax	(031) 987757
Holes	18 L 5475 m SSS 71
V'tors	WD–H before 3pm WE–NA
	before 1pm
Fees	D–160kr (200kr)
Loc	Öjersjö, 10 km E of
	Gothenburg

Särö (1899)

Box 74, 430 40 Särö
Tel   (031) 936317
Fax   (031) 936572
Holes 9 holes Par 27
        9 holes Par 34
V'tors H
Fees 100kr (150kr)
Loc   10 km W of Kungsbacka.
        Gothenburg 18 km (Route 158)

Sjögärde

430 30 Frillesås
Tel   (0340) 652230
Fax   (0340) 652577
Holes 18 L 5723 m SSS 72
        6 hole short course
V'tors H
Fees 200kr (220kr)
Loc   20 km S of Kungsbacka
Arch Lars Andreasson

Stenungsund-Spekeröd
(1993)

Lundby Pl 7480, 444 93 Spekeröd
Tel   (0303) 778470
Fax   (0303) 778350
Holes 18 L 6245 m Par 72
V'tors WD–H WE–N 10–12
Fees D–220kr (D–220kr)
Loc   50 km N of Gothenburg
Arch Peter Nordwall

Stora Lundby (1983)

Torgestorp, 443 71 Grabo
Tel   (0302) 44200
Fax   (0302) 44125
Holes 18 L 6040 m Par 72
        9 hole Par 3 course
V'tors H
Fees 160kr (200kr)
Loc   25 km NE of Gothenburg
Arch Frank Pennink

Malmö &
South Coast

Barsebäck G&CC
(1969)

246 55 Löddeköpinge
Tel   (046) 776230
Fax   (046) 772630
Holes Old 18 L 5910 m Par 72
        New 18 L 6025 m Par 72
V'tors WD–H booking necessary
Fees D–320kr
Loc   35 km N of Malmö
Arch Bruce/Steel

Bokskogen (1963)

Torups Nygård, 230 40 Bara
Tel   (040) 481004
Fax   (040) 481081
Holes Old 18 L 5992 m Par 72
        New 18 L 5499 m Par 71

V'tors H WE–after 1pm Old course
Fees 200kr (260kr)
Loc   15 km SE of Malmö, off E65
Arch Amilon/Sederholm/Lorichs

Falsterbo (1909)

Fyrvägen, 239 40 Falsterbo
Tel   (040) 470078/475078
Fax   (040) 472722
Holes 18 L 6577 yds Par 71
V'tors H WE–M before noon
Fees D–220–330kr
Loc   30 km SW of Malmö
Arch Gunnar Bauer

Flommens (1935)

239 40 Falsterbo
Tel   (040) 475016
Fax   (040) 473157
Holes 18 L 5735 m SSS 72
V'tors H WE–NA before 1pm
Fees 220kr
Loc   35 km SW of Malmö

Kävlinge (1991)

Box 138, 244 22 Kävlinge
Tel   (046) 736270
Fax   (046) 736271
Holes 18 L 5800 m SSS 72
V'tors H
Fees 160kr (220kr)
Loc   12 km N of Lund
Arch Rolf Collijn

Ljunghusen (1932)

*Kinellsvag, Ljunghusen, 236 42
Höllviken*
Tel   (040) 450384
Fax   (040) 454265
Holes 3 x 9 holes:
        1-18 L 5895 m SSS 73
        10-27 L 5670 m SSS 71
        19-9 L 5455 m SSS 70
V'tors WD–U H WE–M before
        noon
Fees 220kr (260kr)
Loc   Falsterbo Peninsula.
        30 km SW of Malmö
Arch Douglas Brasier

Lunds Akademiska (1936)

Kungsmarken, 225 92 Lund
Tel   (046) 99005
Fax   (046) 99146
Holes 18 L 5780 m SSS 72
V'tors H
Fees 160kr (200kr)
Loc   5 km E of Lund
Arch Boström/Morrison

Malmö

Segesvängen, 212 27 Malmö
Tel   (040) 292535
Fax   (040) 292228
Holes 18 L 5720 m SSS 71
V'tors H
Fees 170kr (200kr)
Loc   NE of Malmö

Örestad (1986)

*Golfvägen, Habo Ljung,
234 22 Lomma*
Tel   (040) 410580
Fax   (040) 416320
Holes 18 L 6036 m Par 73
        9 L 2923 m Par 35
        18 hole Par 3 course
V'tors H
Fees 170kr (200kr)
Loc   15 km N of Malmö
Arch Åke Persson

Österlen (1945)

Lilla Vik, 272 95 Simrishamn
Tel   (0414) 24230
Fax   (0414) 24133
Holes 18 L 5855 m SSS 72
V'tors H
Fees 120–250kr
Loc   Vik, 8 km N of Simrishamn
Arch Tommy Nordström

Romeleåsen (1969)

Kvarnbrodda, 240 14 Veberöd
Tel   (046) 82012/82014
Fax   (046) 82113
Holes 18 L 5783 m SSS 72
Fees 150kr (200kr)
Loc   6 km S of Veberöd. 25 km E
        of Malmö

Söderslätts

Västra Grevie 19, 235 94 Vellinge
Tel   (040) 443039
Fax   (040) 443469
Holes 18 L 5800 m SSS 72
        9 hole Par 3 course
V'tors WD–H WE–M H before noon
Fees 160kr (200kr)
Loc   15 km SE of Malmö
Arch Sune Linde

Tegelberga (1989)

Alstad Pl 140, 231 96 Trelleborg
Tel   (040) 485690
Fax   (040) 485691
Holes 18 L 5727 m CR 75
V'tors U
Fees 120–180kr (200–220kr)
Loc   11 km N of Trelleborg.
        25 km E of Malmö
Arch Peter Chamberlain

Tomelilla

Ullstorp, 273 94 Tomelilla
Tel   (0417) 13420
Fax   (0417) 14455
Holes 18 L 6455 m Par 73 SSS 75
V'tors H
Fees 180kr (180kr)
Loc   15 km N of Ystad. 60 km
        E of Malmö
Arch Tommy Nordström

Trelleborg (1963)

Maglarp, Pl 401, 231 93 Trelleborg
Tel   (0410) 30460
Fax   (0410) 30281

Holes 18 L 5160 m Par 69
V'tors U H
Fees 180kr
Loc 5 km W of Trelleborg
Arch Brasier/Chamberlain

Vellinge (1991)

Toftadalsgård, 235 41 Vellinge
Tel (040) 443255
Fax (040) 443179
Holes 18 L 5766 m SSS 72
6 hole short course
V'tors WD–U WE–NA before noon
Fees 180kr (220kr)
Loc 16 km SE of Malmö
Arch Tommy Nordström

Ystad (1930)

Box 162, 271 24 Ystad
Tel (0411) 50350
Fax (0411) 50392
Holes 18 L 5800 m SSS 72
V'tors U
Fees 150kr
Loc 7 km E of Ystad, towards
Simrishamn
Arch Bruce/Lachmann

North

Alvkarleby

PO Box 41, 810 71 Alvkarleby
Tel (026) 72757
Holes 18 holes Par 70
V'tors U
Fees On application
Loc 25 km from Gävle (Route 76)

Avesta (1963)

Åsbo, 774 01 Avesta
Tel (0226) 55913/10866/12766
Fax (0226) 12578
Holes 18 L 5560 m SSS 71
V'tors U
Fees 170kr
Loc 3 km NE of Avesta
Arch Sune Linde

Bollnäs

Norrfly 4526, 823 91 Kilafors
Tel (0278) 50540/51310 (Shop)
Fax (0278) 51220
Holes 18 L 5870 m Par 72
V'tors H
Fees 160kr
Loc 15 km S of Bollnäs (Route 83)

Dalsjö (1989)

Box 215, 781 23 Borlänge
Tel (0243) 82800/220080
Fax (0243) 220140
Holes 18 L 5715 m Par 72
V'tors H
Fees 180kr (200kr)
Loc 5 km NE of Borlänge
Arch Jeremy Turner

Falun-Borlänge (1956)

Storgarden 10, 791 93 Falun
Tel (023) 31015
Fax (023) 31072
Holes 18 L 6085 m SSS 72
Fees 150kr
Loc Aspeboda, 8 km N of
Borlänge

Gävle (1949)

Bönavägen 23, 805 95 Gävle
Tel (026) 120333/120338
Fax (026) 516468
Holes 18 L 5735 m SSS 73
Fees 200kr (250kr)
Loc 3 km N of Gävle

Hagge (1963)

Hagge, 771 90 Ludvika
Tel (0240) 28087/28513
Fax (0240) 28515
Holes 18 L 5519 m SSS 71
V'tors H
Fees D–150kr
Loc 7 km S of Ludvika
Arch Sune Linde

Hofors (1965)

Box 117, 813 22 Hofors
Tel (0290) 85125
Fax (0290) 85101
Holes 18 L 5400 m SSS 70
V'tors U
Fees 140kr (160kr)
Loc 5 km SE of Hofors

Högbo (1962)

Daniel Tilas Väg 4,
811 92 Sandviken
Tel (026) 215015
Fax (026) 215322
Holes 18 L 5760 m Par 72
9 L 2590 m Par 35
V'tors H
Fees 160kr
Loc 6 km N of Sandviken (Route
272)
Arch Sköld/Linde

Hudiksvall (1964)

Tjuvskär, 824 01 Hudiksvall
Tel (0650) 15930
Fax (0650) 18630
Holes 18 L 5665 m SSS 72
V'tors U
Fees 160kr
Loc 4 km SE of Hudiksvall
Arch Linde/Sköld

Leksand (1977)

Box 25, 793 21 Leksand
Tel (0247) 14640
Fax (0247) 14157
Holes 18 L 5263 m SSS 70
Fees 150kr (150kr)
Loc 2 km N of Leksand

Ljusdal (1973)

Box 151, 827 23 Ljusdal
Tel (0651) 16883
Fax (0651) 16883
Holes 18 L 5920 m Par 72
V'tors U
Fees 160kr
Loc 2 km E of Ljusdal
Arch Eriksson/Skjöld

Mora (1980)

Box 264, 792 24 Mora
Tel (0250) 10182
Fax (0250) 10306
Holes 18 L 5600 m Par 72
Fees 150kr
Loc 1 km N of Mora. 40 km NW
of Rättvik
Arch Sune Linde

Rättvik (1954)

Box 29, 795 21 Rättvik
Tel (0248) 51030
Fax (0248) 12081
Holes 18 L 5350 m SSS 70
V'tors U
Fees 130–200kr
Loc 2 km N of Rättvik

Sälen (1983)

Box 20, 780 67 Sälen
Tel (0280) 20670/20671
Holes 18 L 5035 m SSS 72
V'tors U
Fees 120kr
Loc 230 km NW of Borlänge.
400 km NW of Stockholm

Säter (1984)

Box 89, 783 22 Säter
Tel (0225) 50030
Fax (0225) 51424
Holes 18 L 5781 m SSS 73
V'tors U
Fees 150kr
Loc 25 km SE of Borlänge.
180 km NW of Stockholm
Arch Sune Linde

Snöå (1990)

Snöå Bruk, 780 51 Dala-Järna
Tel (0281) 24072
Holes 18 L 5738 m SSS 72
V'tors U
Fees 150kr
Loc 80 km W of Borlänge, nr
Dala-Järna (Route 71)
Arch Åke Persson

Söderhamn (1961)

Oxtorget 1C, 826 00 Söderhamn
Tel (0270) 51300
Fax (0270) 51002
Holes 18 L 5770 m SSS 72
V'tors H
Fees 130–150kr
Loc 8 km N of Söderhamn

Sollerö (1991)
Levsnäs, 79290 Sollerön
Tel   (0250) 22236
Fax   (0250) 22854
Holes 18 L 7226 yds Par 72
V'tors H
Fees   160kr
Loc   14 km from Mora on Island
       of Sollerön in Siljan
Arch   JR Turner

Skane & South

Allerum (1992)
Pl 7592, 260 35 Ödåkra
Tel   (042) 93051
Fax   (042) 93045
Holes 18 L 6201 m SSS 73
V'tors U
Fees   130kr (200kr)
Loc   9 km NE of Helsingborg
Arch   Hans Fock

Ängelholm (1973)
Box 1117, 262 22 Ängelholm
Tel   (0431) 430260/431460
Fax   (0431) 431568
Holes 18 L 5760 m Par 72
V'tors H (max 36)
Fees   140–200kr
Loc   10 km E of Ängelholm on
       route 114
Arch   Jan Sederholm

Araslöv
Starvägen 1, 291 75 Färlöv
Tel   (044) 71600
Fax   (044) 71575
Holes 18 L 5817 m Par 71
V'tors H or Green card
Fees   150kr (200kr)
Loc   9 km NW of Kristianstad
       (Route 19)
Arch   Sune Linde

Båstad (1929)
Box 1037, 269 21 Båstad
Tel   (0431) 73136
Fax   (0431) 73331
Holes 18 L 5760 m Par 71
       18 L 6325 m Par 73
V'tors H
Fees   260kr
Loc   4 km W of Båstad (Route
       115)
Arch   Hawtree/Taylor/Nordström

Bedinge (1931)
Golfbanevägen, 231 76 Beddingestrand
Tel   (0410) 25514
Fax   (0410) 25411
Holes 18 L 5444 m SSS 70
V'tors H
Fees   D–120–200kr
Loc   Beddingestrand, 20 km E of
       Trelleborg
Arch   Åke Persson

Bjäre
Salomonhög 3086, 269 93 Båstad
Tel   (0431) 361053
Fax   (0431) 361764
Holes 18 L 5550 m SSS 71
V'tors H
Fees   D–220–250kr
Loc   2 km E of Båstad. 60 km
       N of Helsingborg
Arch   Svante Dahlgren

Bosjökloster (1974)
243 95 Höör
Tel   (0413) 25858
Fax   (0413) 25895
Holes 18 L 5890 m Par 72
V'tors H
Fees   160kr (200kr)
Loc   7 km S of Höör. 40 km
       NE of Malmö
Arch   Douglas Brasier

Carlskrona (1949)
PO Almö, 370 24 Nättraby
Tel   (0457) 35123
Fax   (0457) 35090
Holes 18 L 5485 m Par 70
V'tors U
Fees   D–200kr
Loc   18 km SW of Karlskrona
Arch   Jan Sederholm

Degeberga-Widtsköfle
Box 71, 297 21 Degeberga
Tel   (044) 355035
Fax   (044) 355035
Holes 18 L 6129 m SSS 72
       9 hole Par 3 course
V'tors U
Fees   100–170kr
Loc   20 km S of Kristianstad

Eslöv (1966)
Box 150, 241 22 Eslöv
Tel   (0413) 18610
Fax   (0413) 18610
Holes 18 L 5630 m CR 70
V'tors H
Fees   180kr (220kr)
Loc   4 km S of Eslöv (Route 113)
Arch   Thure Bruce

Hässleholm (1978)
Skyrup, 282 95 Tyringe
Tel   (0451) 53111
Fax   (0451) 53138
Holes 18 L 5830 m SSS 72
V'tors U
Fees   150kr (200kr)
Loc   15 km NW of Hässleholm
Arch   Persson/Bruce/Jensen

Helsingborg (1924)
260 40 Viken
Tel   (042) 236147
Holes 9 L 4578 m Par 68
V'tors U

Fees   120kr (140kr)
Loc   15 km NW of Helsingborg
Arch   W Hester

Karlshamn (1962)
Box 188, 374 23 Karlshamn
Tel   (0454) 50085
Fax   (0454) 50160
Holes 18 L 5861 m SSS 72
       9 holes SSS 36
V'tors H
Fees   D–200kr
Loc   Morrum, 10 km W of
       Karlshamn
Arch   Douglas Brasier

Kristianstad (1924)
Box 41, 296 21 Åhus
Tel   (044) 247656
Fax   (044) 247635
Holes 18 L 5810 m SSS 72
       9 L 2945 m SSS 36
V'tors H
Fees   D–150kr (D–200kr)
Loc   18 km SE of Kristianstad.
       Airport 20 km
Arch   Brasier/Nordström

Landskrona (1960)
Erikstorp, 261 61 Landskrona
Tel   (0418) 26010
Fax   (0418) 36868
Holes Old 18 L 5700 m SSS 71
       New 18 L 4300 m SSS 67
V'tors U
Fees   180kr (220kr)
Loc   4 km N of Landskrona,
       towards Borstahusen

Mölle (1943)
260 42 Mölle
Tel   (042) 347520
Fax   (042) 347523
Holes 18 L 5312 m Par 70
V'tors H–max 29
Fees   260kr
Loc   Mölle, 35 km NW of
       Helsingborg
Arch   Thure Bruce

Örkelljunga
Rya 472, 286 91 Örkelljunga
Tel   (0435) 53690/53640
Fax   (0435) 53670
Holes 18 L 5755 m SSS 72
V'tors H
Fees   160kr (200kr)
Loc   8 km S of Örkelljunga.
       40 km NE of Helsingborg (E4)
Arch   Hans Fock

Östra Göinge (1981)
Box 114, 289 00 Knislinge
Tel   (044) 60060
Holes 18 L 5898 m Par 72
V'tors U
Fees   140kr
Loc   20 km N of Kristianstad

Perstorp (1964)

PO Box 87, 284 00 Perstorp
Tel   (0435) 35411
Fax   (0435) 35959
Holes   18 L 5675 m SSS 71
         6 hole short course
V'tors   H
Fees   140kr (180kr)
Loc   1 km S of Perstorp. 45 km E
         of Helsingborg

Ronneby (1963)

Box 26, 372 21 Ronneby
Tel   (0457) 10315
Holes   18 L 5323 m SSS 70
Fees   160kr
Loc   3 km S of Ronneby

Rya (1934)

Rya 5500, 255 92 Helsingborg
Tel   (042) 220182
Fax   (042) 220394
Holes   18 L 5599 m SSS 71
V'tors   H
Fees   220–250kr
Loc   10 km S of Helsingborg

St Arild (1987)

Pl 1726 Fjälastorp,
260 41 Nyhamnsläge
Tel   (042) 346860
Fax   (042) 346042
Holes   18 L 5805 m SSS 72
V'tors   H
Fees   120kr (200kr)
Loc   50 km N of Helsingborg
Arch   Jan Sederholm

Skepparslov (1984)

Udarpssäteri, 291 92 Kristianstad
Tel   (044) 229508
Fax   (044) 229503
Holes   18 L 5900 m SSS 72
V'tors   U
Fees   150kr (200kr)
Loc   7 km W of Kristianstad
Arch   Rolf Collijn

Söderåsen (1966)

Box 41, 260 50 Billesholm
Tel   (042) 73337
Fax   (042) 73963
Holes   18 L 5657 m Par 71
V'tors   U
Fees   200kr
Loc   20 km E of Helsingborg
Arch   Thure Bruce

Sölvesborg

Box 63, 294 22 Sölvesborg
Tel   (0456) 70650
Fax   (0456) 70650
Holes   18 L 5900 m SSS 72
V'tors   U
Fees   120kr (160kr)
Loc   30 km E of Kristianstad
Arch   Sune Linde

Svalöv

Månstorp Pl 1365, 268 90 Svalöv
Tel   (0418) 62462
Fax   (0418) 62462
Holes   18 L 5860 m SSS 73
V'tors   U
Fees   160kr (220kr)
Loc   20 km E of Landskrona

Torekov (1924)

Box 81, 260 93 Torekov
Tel   (0431) 63355
Fax   (0431) 64916
Holes   18 L 5701 m Par 72
V'tors   Jun–Aug–H WE–M before
         noon
Fees   160–220kr
Loc   3 km N of Torekov
Arch   Nils Sköld

Trummenas

373 02 Ramdala
Tel   (0455) 60505
Holes   18 L 5600 m SSS 72
         9 hole course
V'tors   H
Fees   D–140kr W–590kr
Loc   15 km NE of Karlskrona
Arch   Ingemar Ericsson

Vasatorp (1973)

Box 13035, 250 13 Helsingborg
Tel   (042) 235058
Fax   (042) 235135
Holes   18 L 5875 m SSS 72
         9 L 2940 m
V'tors   H
Fees   250kr
Loc   8 km E of Helsingborg
Arch   Thure Bruce

Wittsjö (1962)

Ubbaltsgården, 280 22 Vittsjö
Tel   (0451) 22635
Holes   18 L 5461 m SSS 71
V'tors   U
Fees   130kr (170kr)
Loc   2 km E of Vittsjö

South East

A 6 Golfklubb

Centralvägen, 553 05 Jönköping
Tel   (036) 308130
Fax   (036) 308140
Holes   27 hole course:
         9 L 3185 m Par 38
         9 L 3115 m Par 37
         9 L 2935 m Par 36
V'tors   U H
Fees   200kr
Loc   2 km SE of Jönköping
Arch   Peter Nordwall

Älmhult (1975)

Pl 1215, 343 90 Älmhult
Tel   (0476) 14135
Fax   (0476) 16565
Holes   18 L 5407 m SSS 71
V'tors   U H
Fees   D–140kr
Loc   2 km E of Älmhult on
         Route 120
Arch   Persson/Söderberg

Åtvidaberg (1954)

Box 180, 597 24 Åtvidaberg
Tel   (0120) 35425
Fax   (0120) 13502
Holes   18 L 5856 m Par 72
V'tors   H
Fees   180kr (220kr)
Loc   30 km SE of Linköping
Arch   Douglas Brasier

Ekerum

387 92 Borgholm, Öland
Tel   (0485) 80000
Fax   (0485) 80010
Holes   18 L 6045 m CR
         9 L 2875 m CR
V'tors   U H
Fees   200–260kr
Loc   12 km S of Borgholm.
         25 km N of Öland bridge
Arch   Peter Nordwall

Eksjö (1938)

Skedhult, 575 96 Eksjö
Tel   (0381) 13525
Holes   18 L 5930 m SSS 72
V'tors   WD–U WE–H
Fees   200kr
Loc   6 km W of Eksjö on Nässjö
         road
Arch   Anders Amilon

Emmaboda (1976)

Kyrkogatan, 360 60 Vissefjärda
Tel   (0471) 20505/20540
Fax   (0471) 20440
Holes   18 L 6165 m SSS 72
V'tors   H
Fees   160kr
Loc   12 km S of Emmaboda.
         50 km N of Karlskrona

Finspång (1965)

Viberga Gård, 612 92 Finspång
Tel   (0122) 13940
Fax   (0122) 18888
Holes   18 L 5800 m SSS 72
V'tors   U
Fees   160kr (240kr)
Loc   2 km E of Finspång, Route
         51. Norrköping 25 km.
Arch   Sköld/Linde

Gotska (1986)

Box 1119, 621 22 Visby, Gotland
Tel   (0498) 215545
Fax   (0498) 215545

Holes 18 L 5202 m Par 68
    9 L 5414 m Par 72
V'tors 18 hole:H   9 hole:U
Fees 120–180kr
Loc N outskirts of Visby
Arch Jack Wenman

Gumbalde

Box 35, 620 13 Ståga, Gotland
Tel (0498) 482880
Fax (0498) 482884
Holes 18 L 5600 m SSS 71
V'tors U
Fees 160kr (180kr)
Loc 50 km SE of Visby, Gotland
    island
Arch Lars Lagergren

Hook

560 13 Hok
Tel (0393) 21420
Fax (0393) 21379
Holes 18 L 5758 m SSS 72
    18 L 5750 m SSS 73
    9 hole Par 3 course
V'tors H
Fees 220kr
Loc Hok, 30 km SE of Jönköping,
    towards Växjö
Arch Edberg/Bruce/Sederholm

Isaberg (1968)

Nissafors Bruk, 330 27 Hestra
Tel (0370) 336330
Fax (0370) 336325
Holes East 18 L 5823 m CR 72.8
    West 18 L 5568 m CR 69.4
V'tors H
Fees 220kr (250–270kr)
Loc 18 km N of Gislaved, nr
    Nissafors. 60 km S of
    Jönköping
Arch Amilon/Bruce/Persson

Jönköping (1936)

Kettilstorp, 556 27 Jönköping
Tel (036) 76567
Fax (036) 76511
Holes 18 L 6370 m SSS 70
V'tors WD–U H–phone in advance
    WE–H
Fees 200kr
Loc Kettilstorp, 3 km S of
    Jönköping
Arch Nils Sköld

Kalmar (1947)

Box 278, 391 23 Kalmar 1
Tel (0480) 472111
Fax (0480) 472314
Holes Blue 18 L 5700 m SSS 72
    Red 18 L 5634 m SSS 72
V'tors H
Fees 220kr
Loc 9 km N of Kalmar

Lagan (1966)

Box 63, 340 14 Lagan
Tel (0372) 30450/35460
Fax (0372) 35307

Holes 18 L 5600 m SSS 71
V'tors U
Fees 160kr
Loc Lagan, 10 km N of Ljungby,
    on Route E4
Arch Amilon/Persson/Magnusson

Landeryd (1987)

Bogestad Gård, 585 93 Linköping
Tel (013) 162520
Fax (013) 150493
Holes North 18 L 5675 m SSS 72
    South 18 L 5085 m SSS 68
    9 hole short course
V'tors U
Fees 220kr (240kr)
Loc 7 km SE of Linköping
Arch Nordström/Persson

Linköping (1945)

Box 10054, 580 10 Linköping
Tel (013) 120646
Fax (013) 140769
Holes 18 L 5664 m SSS 71
V'tors H
Fees 200kr (240kr)
Loc 3 km SW of Linköping
Arch Sundblom/Brasier

Mjölby (1986)

Blixberg, Miskarp, 595 92 Mjölby
Tel (0142) 12570
Fax (0142) 16553
Holes 18 L 5485 m SSS 71
V'tors H
Fees 160kr
Loc 35 km WSW of Linköping
    (E4)
Arch Åke Persson

Motala (1956)

PO Box 264, 591 23 Motala
Tel (0141) 50840 (Sec)
Holes 18 L 5905 m SSS 72
V'tors U
Fees 140kr (140kr)
Loc 3 km S of Motala via
    Route 50 or 32

Nässjö (1988)

Box 5, 571 20 Nässjö
Tel (0380) 10022
Fax (0380) 12082
Holes 18 L 5783 m Par 72
V'tors U
Fees 160kr
Loc 40 km E of Jönköping
Arch Bjorn Magnusson

Norrköping (1928)

Klinga Golfbana, 605 97 Norrköping
Tel (011) 335235/183654
Fax (011) 335014
Holes 18 L 5860 m SSS 73
V'tors U
Fees 160kr (200kr)
Loc Klinga, 9 km S of Norrköping
    on E4
Arch Nils Sköld

Oskarshamn (1972)

Box 148, 572 23 Oskarshamn
Tel (0491) 94033
Fax (0491) 94033
Holes 18 L 5545 m SSS 71
V'tors H
Fees 160kr
Loc 10 km SW of Oskarshamn,
    nr Forshult
Arch Nils Sköld

Skinnarebo

Skinnarebo, 555 93 Jönköping
Tel (036) 69075
Fax (036) 362975
Holes 18 L 5686 m SSS 71
    9 hole Par 3 course
V'tors H
Fees 180kr
Loc 14 km SW of Jönköping
Arch Björn Magnusson

Söderköping (1983)

Hylinge, 605 96 Norrköping
Tel (011) 70579
Holes 18 L 5730 m SSS 72
V'tors U
Fees 180kr
Loc Västra Husby, 9 km W of
    Söderköping
Arch Ronald Fream

Tobo (1971)

Box 101, 598 22 Vimmerby
Tel (0492) 30346
Fax (0492) 30870
Holes 18 L 5720 m SSS 73
V'tors U
Fees 160kr
Loc 10 km S of Vimmerby,
    nr Storebro. 60 km SW of
    Västervik
Arch Brasier/Jensen

Tranås (1952)

Box 430, 573 25 Tranås
Tel (0140) 311661
Fax (0140) 16161
Holes 18 L 5830 m SSS 72
V'tors U
Fees 180kr (200kr)
Loc 2 km N of Tranås

Vadstena (1957)

Hagalund 3, 592 94 Vadstena
Tel (0143) 12440
Holes 18 L 5486 m SSS 71
Fees 150kr
Loc 3 km S of Vadstena, towards
    Vaderstad

Värnamo (1962)

Box 146, 331 21 Värnamo
Tel (0370) 23123
Fax (0370) 23216
Holes 18 L 6253 m SSS 72
V'tors U
Fees 180kr
Loc 8 km E of Värnamo on
    Route 127
Arch Nils Sköld

Västervik (1959)

Box 62, 593 22 Västervik
Tel   (0490) 32420
Holes   18 L 5760 m SSS 72
Fees   150kr
Loc   1 km SE of Västervik

Växjö (1959)

Box 227, 351 05 Växjö
Tel   (0470) 21515
Fax   (0470) 21557
Holes   18 L 5860 m Par 72
V'tors H
Fees   200kr (220kr)
Loc   5 km NW of Växjö
Arch   Douglas Brasier

Vetlanda (1983)

Box 249, 574 23 Vetlanda
Tel   (0383) 18310
Fax   (0383) 19278
Holes   18 L 5552 m SSS 71
V'tors U
Fees   160kr
Loc   Östanå, 3 km W of Vetlanda.
        80 km SE of Jönköping
Arch   Jan Sederholm

Visby

Kronholmen Västergarn, 620 20
Klintehamn, Gotland
Tel   (0498) 245058
Fax   (0498) 246240
Holes   18 L 5765 m SSS 72
        9 hole course
V'tors Jun–Sept–H
Fees   200–270kr
Loc   Kronholmen, 25 km S of
        Visby, Gotland island
Arch   Nordwall/Sköld

Vreta Kloster

Box 144, 590 70 Ljungsbro
Tel   (013) 63680
Fax   (013) 66545
Holes   18 L 5666 m SSS 72
V'tors H
Fees   160kr
Loc   15 km N of Linköping
Arch   Sune Linde

South West

Alingsås (1985)

Hjälmared 4050, 441 95 Alingsås
Tel   (0322) 52421
Holes   18 L 5600 m SSS 72
V'tors U
Fees   120–150kr (200kr)
Loc   5 km SE of Alingsås towards
        Borås

Bäckavattnet (1977)

Marbäck, 305 94 Halmstad
Tel   (035) 44270
Fax   (035) 44275

Holes   18 L 5740 m SSS 72
V'tors H
Fees   180kr
Loc   13 km E of Halmstad (RD25)

Billingen (1949)

St Kulhult, 540 17 Lerdala
Tel   (0511) 80291
Fax   (0511) 80244
Holes   18 L 5470 m Par 71
V'tors H
Fees   150kr (180kr)
Loc   20 km NW of Skövde
Arch   Douglas Brasier

Borås (1933)

Östra Vik, Kråkered, 504 95 Borås
Tel   (033) 250250
Fax   (033) 250176
Holes   North 18 L 6005 m Par 72
        South 18 L 5085 m Par 69
V'tors H–booking necessary
Fees   200kr (200kr)
Loc   6 km S of Borås, on Route 41
        towards Varberg
Arch   Brasier/Persson

Ekarnas (1970)

Balders Väg 12, 467 31 Grästorp
Tel   (0514) 51450
Fax   (0514) 51450
Holes   18 L 5501 m SSS 71
V'tors H
Fees   140kr (180kr)
Loc   25 km E of Trollhättan.
        Lidköping 35 km
Arch   Jan Andersson

Falkenberg (1949)

Golfvägen, 311 72 Falkenberg
Tel   (0346) 50287
Fax   (0346) 50997
Holes   27 L 5575-5680 m SSS 72
V'tors H
Fees   140–220kr
Loc   5 km S of Falkenberg

Falköping (1965)

Box 99, 521 02 Falköping
Tel   (0515) 31270
Fax   (0515) 31389
Holes   18 L 5835 m Par 72
V'tors H
Fees   120kr (160kr)
Loc   7 km E of Falköping on Route
        46 towards Skovde
Arch   Nils Sköld

Halmstad (1930)

302 73 Halmstad
Tel   (035) 30077/30280 (Starter)
Fax   (035) 32308
Holes   18 L 6259 m CR 72.4
        18 L 5787 m CR 69.9
V'tors H WE–M before 1pm
Fees   330kr
Loc   Tylosand, 9 km W of
        Halmstad
Arch   Sundblom/Sköld/Pennink

Haverdals (1988)

Slingervägen 35, 31042 Haverdal
Tel   (035) 59530
Fax   (035) 53890
Holes   18 L 5840 m Par 72
V'tors H
Fees   220kr
Loc   11 km NW of Halmstad
Arch   Anders Amilon

Hökensås (1962)

PO Box 116, 544 00 Hjo
Tel   (0503) 16059
Fax   (0503) 16156
Holes   18 L 5540 m SSS 72
V'tors U
Fees   160kr (180kr)
Loc   8 km S of Hjo on Route 195
Arch   Sune Linde

Hulta (1972)

Box 54, 517 22 Bollebygd
Tel   (033) 288180
Fax   (033) 288227
Holes   18 L 6000 m SSS 72
V'tors H
Fees   180kr (200kr)
Loc   Bollebygd, 35 km E of
        Gothenburg
Arch   Jan Sederholm

Knistad G&CC

541 92 Skövde
Tel   (0500) 463170
Fax   (0500) 463075
Holes   18 L 5790 m SSS 72
V'tors H
Fees   200kr
Loc   10 km NE of Skövde
Arch   Jeremy Turner

Laholm (1964)

Box 101, 312 22 Laholm
Tel   (0430) 30601
Fax   (0430) 30891
Holes   18 L 5430 m SSS 70
V'tors U H
Fees   170kr (200kr)
Loc   5 miles E of Laholm on
        Route 24
Arch   Jan Sederholm

Lidköping (1967)

Box 2029, 531 02 Lidköping
Tel   (0510) 46144
Fax   (0510) 46495
Holes   18 L 5382 m CR 68.6
V'tors H
Fees   160kr
Loc   5 km E of Lidköping
Arch   Douglas Brasier

Mariestad (1975)

PO Box 299, 542 23 Mariestad
Tel   (0501) 17383
Fax   (0501) 78117

Holes 18 L 5970 m SSS 73
V'tors H
Fees 180kr
Loc 4 km W of Mariestad, at
Lake Vänern

Marks (1962)

Brättingstorpsvägen 28, 511 58 Kinna
Tel (0320) 14220
Fax (0320) 12516
Holes 18 L 5530 m SSS 69
V'tors H
Fees 140kr (180kr)
Loc Kinna, 30 km S of Borås

Onsjö (1974)

Box 6331 A, 462 42 Vänersborg
Tel (0521) 68870
Fax (0521) 68871
Holes 18 L 5730 m SSS 72
V'tors U
Fees 140kr (170kr)
Loc 3 km S of Vänersborg.
80 km N of Gothenburg

Ringenäs

Strandlida, 305 90 Halmstad
Tel (035) 59050
Fax (035) 59135
Holes 27 L 5395-5615 m CR
V'tors H
Fees D–150–200kr (D–200kr)
Loc 10 km NW of Halmstad on
coast
Arch Sune Linde

Skogaby (1988)

312 93 Laholm
Tel (0430) 60190
Holes 18 L 5555 m SSS 71
V'tors U H
Fees 120kr (160kr)
Loc 10 km E of Laholm. 30 km
SE of Halmstad
Arch J Rosengren

Töreboda (1965)

Box 18, 545 21 Töreboda
Tel (0506) 12305
Fax (0506) 12305
Holes 18 L 5355 m SSS 70
V'tors U
Fees 160kr
Loc 7 km E of Töreboda

Trollhättan (1963)

Stora Ekeskogen, 466 91 Sollebrunn
Tel (0520) 441000
Fax (0520) 441049
Holes 18 L 6200 m SSS 73
V'tors U
Fees 200kr
Loc Koberg, 20 km SE of
Trollhättan
Arch Nils Sköld

Ulricehamn (1947)

523 33 Ulricehamn
Tel (0321) 10021
Fax (0321) 16004
Holes 18 L 5509 m SSS 71
V'tors WD–H
Fees 140kr (180kr)
Loc Backasen, 2 km E of
Ulricehamn

Vara-Bjertorp

Bjertorp, 535 91 Kvänum
Tel (0512) 20260
Fax (0512) 20261
Holes 18 L 6005 m Par 73
V'tors H
Fees 140kr (180kr)
Loc 10 km N of Vara. 110 km NE
of Gothenburg (E20)
Arch Jan Sederholm

Varberg (1950)

Himle, 430 10 Tvååker
Tel (0340) 43446/37496
Fax (0340) 37440/43447
Holes East 18 L 5700 m SSS 72
West 18 L 6640 m SSS 76
V'tors H
Fees 220–280kr
Loc East:15 km E of Varberg.
West:8 km S of Varberg,
nr E6
Arch Sköld/Nordström

Vinberg (1992)

Sannagård, 311 95 Falkenberg
Tel (0346) 19020
Holes 18 L 3556 m SSS 60
V'tors U
Fees 100kr (140kr)
Loc 5 km E of Falkenberg on
coast
Arch Nilsson/Haglund

Stockholm

Ågesta (1958)

123 52 Farsta
Tel (08) 604 4538
Fax (08) 604 4397
Holes 18 L 5658 m SSS 72
9 L 3404 m SSS 62
V'tors WD–U
Fees 300kr
Loc Farsta, 15 km S of Stockholm
Arch Sköld/Sederholm

Botkyrka

Malmbro Gård, 147 91 Grödinge
Tel (08) 530 29650
Fax (08) 530 29409
Holes 18 holes SSS 73
9 hole Par 3 course
V'tors WD–U before 3pm WE–H
NA before 6pm
Fees 240kr (280kr)
Loc 30 km S of Stockholm

Bro-Bålsta (1978)

Nygårdsvägen, 197 91 Bro
Tel (08) 582 41310
Fax (08) 582 40006
Holes 18 L 6420 m Par 73
9 L 1435 m SSS 58
V'tors H (max 36)
Fees 280kr (330kr)
Loc 40 km NW of Stockholm
Arch Peter Nordwall

Djursholm (1931)

Hagbardsvägen 1, 182 63 Djursholm
Tel (08) 755 1477
Fax (08) 755 5932
Holes 18 L 5595 m SSS 71
9 L 4400 m SSS 64
V'tors WD–U H before 3pm –M
after 3pm WE–M before 3pm
–U H after 3pm
Fees 280kr
Loc 12 km N of Stockholm

Drottningholm (1958)

PO Box 183, 178 93 Drottningholm
Tel (08) 759 0085
Fax (08) 759 0851
Holes 18 L 5825 m SSS 72
V'tors WD–U H before 3pm –M
after 3pm WE–M before 3pm
–U H after 3pm
Fees 300kr
Loc 16 km W of Stockholm
Arch Sundblom/Sköld

Fågelbro G&CC

Fågelbro Säteri, 139 60 Värmdö
Tel (08) 571 40115
Fax (08) 571 40671
Holes 18 L 5445 m Par 71
V'tors WD–H WE–M
Fees 300kr (400kr)
Loc 35 km E of Stockholm
Arch Eriksson/Oredsson

Haninge (1983)

Årsta Slott, 136 91 Haninge
Tel (08) 500 32240/32270
Fax (08) 500 32340
Holes 27 L 5930 m Par 73
V'tors WD–U before 1pm –M after
1pm WE–M before 1pm –U
after 1pm
Fees 260kr (300kr)
Loc 30 km S of Stockholm towards
Nynäshamn
Arch Jan Sederholm

Ingarö (1962)

Fogelvik, 134 64 Ingarö
Tel (08) 570 28244
Fax (08) 570 28379
Holes 18 L 5515 m SSS 71
18 L 5618 m SSS 72
V'tors U H
Fees 250kr (300kr)
Loc 30 km E of Stockholm via
Route 222
Arch Sköld/Eriksson

Johannesberg G&CC
(1990)
762 95 Rimbo
Tel   (08) 512 92480
Fax   (08) 512 92390
Holes 18 L 6328 m SSS 74
       9 hole course
V'tors H
Fees   180kr (200kr)
Loc   55 km N of Stockholm
Arch   Donald Steel

Lidingö (1933)
Box 1035, 181 21 Lidingö
Tel   (08) 765 7911
Fax   (08) 765 5479
Holes 18 L 5770 m SSS 71
V'tors H
Fees   250kr
Loc   6 km NE of Stockholm

Lindö (1978)
186 92 Vallentuna
Tel   (08) 511 72260
Holes 18 L 2850 m SSS 71
Fees   200kr (250kr)
Loc   Vallentuna, 20 km N of
       Stockholm

Nynäshamn (1977)
Box 4, 148 21 Ösmo
Tel   (08) 520 27190/520 38666
Fax   (08) 520 38613
Holes 27 L 5690 m SSS 72
V'tors H–phone first
Fees   200kr (250kr)
Loc   Ösmo, 50 km S of Stockholm
Arch   Sune Linde

Österakers
Hagby 1, 184 92 Akersberga
Tel   (08) 540 85165
Fax   (08) 540 66832
Holes 18 L 5792 m SSS 72
       18 L 5780 m SSS 72
V'tors WD–H before 3pm –M after
       3pm WE–M before 2pm –H
       after 2pm
Fees   175–250kr
Loc   30 km NE of Stockholm
Arch   Jan Sederholm

Österhaninge (1992)
Box 82, 130 54 Dalarö
Tel   (08) 500 32285
Fax   (08) 501 51835
Holes 18 L 5141 m Par 69
V'tors H
Fees   150kr (200kr)
Loc   35 km S of Stockholm
Arch   B Lorichs

Parkens
Stockholm Lindö Park,
186 92 Vallentuna
Tel   (08) 511 70055 (Bookings)
Fax   (08) 511 70613
Holes 18 L 5800 m SSS 72

V'tors U H–book day before play
Fees   300kr (400kr)
Loc   30 km N of Stockholm
Arch   Persson/Bruce

PGA European Tour
(1992)
Box 133, 196 21 Kungsängen
Tel   (08) 581 65030
Fax   (08) 581 71002
Holes South 18 L 6200 m Par 70
       North 18 L 5500 m Par 70
V'tors U H
Fees   300kr (340kr)
Loc   25 km W of Stockholm via
       E18 to Brunna

Saltsjöbaden (1929)
Box 51, 133 21 Saltsjöbaden
Tel   (08) 717 0125
Fax   (08) 717 9713
Holes 18 L 5685 m SSS 72
       9 L 3640 m SSS 60
V'tors WD–U WE–M before 2pm
Fees   D–250kr
Loc   15 km E of Stockholm via
       Route 228

Sollentuna (1967)
Skillingegården, 191 77 Sollentuna
Tel   (08) 754 3625
Fax   (08) 754 1823
Holes 18 L 5895 m SSS 72
V'tors WD–H before 3pm WE–H
       after 3pm
Fees   260kr
Loc   19 km N of Stockholm.
       1 km W of E4 (Rotebro)
Arch   Nils Sköld

Stockholm (1904)
Kevingestrand 20, 182 31 Danderyd
Tel   (08) 755 0031
Fax   (08) 622 6447
Holes 18 L 5180 m SSS 69
V'tors WD–M after 3pm WE–M
       before 3pm
Fees   340kr (400kr)
Loc   7 km NE of Stockholm via
       Route E18

Täby (1968)
Skålhamra Gård, 187 70 Täby
Tel   (08) 510 23261
Fax   (08) 510 23441
Holes 18 L 5776 m SSS 73
V'tors WD–H
Fees   250–300kr
Loc   15 km N of Stockholm
Arch   Nils Sköld

Ullna (1981)
Rosenkälla, 184 92 Åkersberga
Tel   (08) 510 26075
Fax   (08) 510 26068
Holes 18 L 5825 m SSS 72
V'tors H
Fees   350kr

Loc   20 km N of Stockholm via
       Route E18
Arch   Sven Tumba

Ulriksdal
Box 8033, 171 08 Solna
Tel   (08) 857931
Holes 18 L 3900 m SSS 61
V'tors H
Fees   130kr (160kr)
Loc   8 km N of Stockholm
Arch   Alec Backhurst

Vallentuna
Box 266, 186 24 Vallentuna
Tel   (08) 511 77000/77083
Fax   (08) 511 72370
Holes 18 L 5700 m SSS 72
V'tors WD–U WE–U after 1pm
Fees   200kr (240kr)
Loc   35 km N of Stockholm
Arch   Sune Linde

Viksjö (1969)
Fjällens Gård, 175 45 Järfälla
Tel   (08) 580 31300/31310
Fax   (08) 580 31340
Holes 18 L 5930 m SSS 73
       9 L 1830 m Par 30
V'tors U
Fees   9 hole:150kr (150kr);
       18 hole:300kr (300kr)
Loc   18 km NW of Stockholm

Wäsby
Box 2017, 194 02 Upplands Väsby
Tel   (08) 510 23345/23177
Fax   (08) 510 23364
Holes 18 L 6170 m SSS 72
       9 hole course
V'tors WD–U WE–H
Fees   170kr (220kr)
Loc   20 km N of Stockholm.
       20 km S of Airport
Arch   Björn Eriksson

Wermdö G&CC (1966)
Torpa, 139 60 Värmdö
Tel   (08) 570 20849
Fax   (08) 570 20840
Holes 18 L 5577 m SSS 72
V'tors H WE–NA before 2pm
Fees   300kr (350kr)
Loc   25 km E of Stockholm via
       Route 222
Arch   Nils Sköld

West Central

Arvika
Box 197, 671 25 Arvika 1
Tel   (0570) 54133
Holes 18 L 5815 m SSS 72
V'tors U
Fees   160kr
Loc   11 km E of Arvika (Route 61)
Arch   Nils Sköld

Billerud (1961)
Valnäs, 660 40 Segmon
Tel   **(0555) 91313**
Fax   (0555) 91306
Holes 18 L 5874 m SSS 72
V'tors H
Fees   180kr
Loc   Valnäs, 15 km N of Säffle
Arch   Brasier/Sköld

Eda (1992)
Noresund, 670 40 Åmotfors
Tel   **(0571) 34101**
Fax   (0571) 34191
Holes 18 L 5575 m Par 72
V'tors U
Fees   160kr (180kr)
Loc   30 km W of Arvika
Arch   Leif Nilsson

Färgelanda
Box 23, 458 21 Färgelanda
Tel   **(0528) 20385**
Fax   (0528) 20045
Holes 18 L 6000 m SSS 71
V'tors U
Fees   160kr
Loc   23 km N of Uddevalla.
       100 km N of Gothenburg
Arch   Åke Persson

Fjällbacka (1965)
450 71 Fjällbacka
Tel   **(0525) 31150**
Fax   (0525) 32122
Holes 18 L 5850 m SSS 72
V'tors H
Fees   D–160kr
Loc   2 km N of Fjällbacka
       (Route 163)

Forsbacka (1969)
Box 136, 662 23 Åmål
Tel   **(0532) 43055**
Holes 18 L 5860 m SSS 72
V'tors U
Fees   200kr
Loc   6 km W of Åmål (Route 164)

Hammarö
Box 2080, 663 02 Hammarö
Tel   **(054) 521621**
Holes 18 L 6200 m SSS 75
Fees   160kr
Loc   11 km S of Karlstad

Karlskoga (1975)
Bricketorp 647, 691 94 Karlskoga
Tel   **(0586) 28190**
Fax   (0586) 28417
Holes 18 L 5705 m Par 72
Fees   160kr
Loc   Valåsen, 5 km E of Karlskoga
       via Route E18
Arch   Sköld/Sederholm/Engdahl

Karlstad (1957)
PO Box 294, 651 07 Karlstad
Tel   **(054) 866353**
Fax   (054) 866478
Holes 18 L 5970 m Par 72
       9 L 2875 m Par 36
V'tors H
Fees   220kr
Loc   8 km N of Karlstad (Route 63)
Arch   Sköld/Linde

Kristinehamn (1974)
Box 337, 681 26 Kristinehamn
Tel   **(0550) 82310**
Fax   (0550) 19535
Holes 18 L 5800 m SSS 72
V'tors H
Fees   200kr
Loc   3 km N of Kristinehamn
Arch   Sune Linde

Lyckorna (1967)
Box 66, 459 22 Ljungskile
Tel   **(0522) 20176**
Fax   (0522) 22304
Holes 18 L 5820 m SSS 72
V'tors H
Fees   200kr
Loc   20 km S of Uddevalla
Arch   Anders Amilon

Orust (1981)
Morlanda 9404, 474 93 Ellös
Tel   **(0304) 53170**
Fax   (0304) 53174
Holes 18 L 5770 m SSS 72
V'tors H
Fees   180kr (180kr)
Loc   Ellös, 10 km from Henön.
       80 km N of Gothenburg
Arch   Lars Andreasson

Saxå (1964)
Allegatan 17c, 682 32 Filipstad
Tel   **(0590) 24070**
Fax   (0590) 24101
Holes 18 L 5680 m SSS 73
V'tors U
Fees   160kr
Loc   15 km E of Filipstad (Route 63)

Skaftö (1963)
Röd PL 4476, 450 34 Fiskebäckskil
Tel   **(0523) 23211**
Fax   (0523) 23215
Holes 18 L 4748 m SSS 68
V'tors WD–H
Fees   100–160kr
Loc   40 km W of Uddevalla,
       through Fiskebäckskil
Arch   Sköld/Sederholm

Strömstad (1967)
Golfbanevägen, 452 90 Strömstad 1
Tel   **(0526) 61788**
Fax   (0526) 14766
Holes 18 L 5615 m SSS 71
V'tors H

Fees   180kr (200kr)
Loc   6 km N of Strömstad
Arch   Sköld/Sederholm

Sunne (1970)
Box 108, 686 23 Sunne
Tel   **(0565) 14100/14210**
Fax   (0565) 14855
Holes 18 hole course SSS 72
V'tors H
Fees   200kr
Loc   2 km S of Sunne. 60 km N of
       Karlstad on Route 45
Arch   Jan Sederholm

Torreby (1961)
Torreby Slott, 455 00 Munkedal
Tel   **(0524) 21365/21109**
Fax   (0524) 21351
Holes 18 L 5885 m SSS 72
V'tors H
Fees   D–120–180kr
Loc   Munkedal 8 km.
       Uddevalla 30 km.
Arch   Douglas Brasier

Uddeholm (1965)
Risäter 20, 683 93 Råda
Tel   **(0563) 60564**
Fax   (0563) 60017
Holes 18 L 5830 m SSS 72
V'tors U H
Fees   D–160kr
Loc   Lake Råda, 80 km N of
       Karlstad, via RD62

Switzerland

Bern

Blumisberg (1959)
3184 Wünnewil
Tel   **(026) 496 34 38**
Fax   (026) 496 35 23
Holes 18 L 6048 m SSS 73
V'tors WD–U H WE–M
Fees   80fr (80fr)
Loc   Wünnewil, 16 km SW of Bern
Arch   B von Limburger

Les Bois (1988)
Case Postale 26, 2336 Les Bois
Tel   **(032) 961 10 03**
Fax   (032) 961 10 17
Holes 9 L 3000 m Par 72
V'tors WD–U WE–M
Fees   75fr (90fr)
Loc   12 km NE of La Chaux-de-
       Fonds, on Basel road
Arch   Jeremy Pern

Neuchâtel (1928)
2072 Saint-Blaise
Tel   **(032) 753 55 50**
Fax   (032) 753 29 40

Holes 18 L 6039 m SSS 71
V'tors H
Fees 70fr (90fr)
Loc Voens/Saint-Blaise, 5 km E of
Neuchâtel. 30 km W of Bern

Wallenried (1992)

1784 Wallenried
Tel (037) 34 36 06
Fax (037) 34 36 10
Holes 18 L 6000 m SSS 72
V'tors WD–U H
Fees 70fr (90fr)
Loc 6 km W of Fribourg
Arch Ruzzo Reuss

Wylihof (1994)

4542 Luterbach
Tel (032) 682 28 28
Fax (032 682 65 17
Holes 18 L 6580 yds Par 73
V'tors WD–U H–max 30 WE–M H
Fees 90fr (90fr)
Loc 40 km N of Berne. 90 km W
of Zürich
Arch Ruzzo Reuss von Plauen

Bernese Oberland

Interlaken-Unterseen (1964)

Postfach 110, 3800 Interlaken
Tel (033) 823 60 16
Fax (033) 823 42 03
Holes 18 L 5980 m SSS 72
V'tors H
Fees 70fr (80fr)
Loc Interlaken 3 km
Arch Donald Harradine

Riederalp (1986)

3987 Riederalp
Tel (027) 927 29 32
Fax (027) 927 29 32
Holes 9 L 3066 m SSS 55
V'tors U
Fees 45fr
Loc 10 km NE of Brig
Arch Donald Harradine

Lake Geneva & South West

Bonmont (1983)

Château de Bonmont, 1275 Chéserex
Tel (022) 369 23 45
Fax (022) 369 24 17
Holes 18 L 6165 m SSS 72
V'tors WD–restricted WE–M
Fees WD–90fr
Loc 3 km from Nyon. 30 km NE
of Geneva
Arch Donald Harradine

Crans-sur-Sierre (1906)

3963 Crans-sur-Sierre-Montana
Tel (027) 41 21 68/41 27 03
Fax (027) 41 46 71/41 95 68
Holes 18 L 6260 m SSS 72
9 L 2667 m SSS 35
9 hole Par 3 course
V'tors H
Fees 18 hole–80fr W–420–500fr;
9 hole–40fr
Loc 20 km E of Sion. Geneva 2 hrs

Domaine Impérial (1987)

Villa Prangins, 1196 Gland
Tel (022) 999 06 00
Fax (022) 999 06 06
Holes 18 L 6297 m SSS 74
V'tors H–am only
Fees WD–90fr
Loc Nyon, 20 km N of Geneva
Arch Pete Dye

Geneva (1923)

70 Route de la Capite, 1223 Cologny
Tel (022) 707 48 40
Fax (022) 707 48 20
Holes 18 L 6250 m Par 72
V'tors WD–am only Tues–Fri WE–M
Fees 100fr
Loc 4 km from centre of Geneva
Arch Robert Trent Jones Sr

Lausanne (1921)

Route du Golf 3, 1000 Lausanne 25
Tel (021) 784 13 15
Fax (021) 784 13 31
Holes 18 L 6295 m SSS 74
V'tors H
Fees 80fr (100fr)
Loc 7 km N of Lausanne towards
Le Mont
Arch Narbel/Harradine/Pern

Montreux (1898)

54 Route d'Evian, 1860 Aigle
Tel (024) 466 46 16
Fax (024) 466 60 47
Holes 18 L 6143 m Par 72 SSS 73
V'tors H
Fees 70fr (90fr)
Loc Aigle, 15 km S of Montreux
Arch Donald Harradine

Sion (1995)

CP 440, Rte Vissigen 150, 1951 Sion
Tel (027) 203 79 00
Fax (027) 203 79 01
Holes 9 L 2315 m Par 66
V'tors H–booking necessary
Fees 18 holes–53fr (60fr);
9 holes–32fr (40fr)
Loc Sion, 80 km SE of Montreux
Arch JL Tronchet

Verbier (1970)

1936 Verbier
Tel (079) 412 86 48/
(027) 771 53 14
Fax (027) 771 60 93

Holes 18 L 5300 m Par 70
18 hole Par 3 course
V'tors U
Fees 25fr (50fr)
Loc Centre of Verbier
Arch Donald Harradine

Villars (1922)

C P 152, 1884 Villars
Tel (025) 35 42 14
Fax (025) 35 42 18
Holes 18 L 4093 m SSS 61
V'tors U
Fees 50fr (65fr)
Loc 7 km E of Villars towards
Les Diablerets
Arch Thierry Sprecher

Lugano & Ticino

Lugano (1923)

6983 Magliaso
Tel (091) 606 15 57/606 58 01
Fax (091) 606 65 58
Holes 18 L 5760 m SSS 71
V'tors H–(max 30)
Fees 85fr (110fr)
Loc 8 km W of Lugano towards
Ponte Tresa
Arch Harradine/Robinson

Patriziale Ascona (1928)

Via al Lido 81, 6612 Ascona
Tel (091) 791 21 32
Fax (091) 791 07 06
Holes 18 L 5948 m SSS 71
V'tors H–max 30
Fees 80fr
Loc 5 km W of Locarno
Arch CK Cotton

St Mortiz & Engadine

Arosa (1944)

Postfach 95, 7050 Arosa
Tel (081) 377 42 42
Fax (081) 377 46 77
Holes 9 L 4450 m Par 66 SSS 64
V'tors U
Fees 50fr
Loc 30 km S of Chur
Arch Donald Harradine

Bad Ragaz (1957)

Hans Albrecht Strasse, 7310 Bad Ragaz
Tel (081) 303 37 17
Fax (081) 303 37 27
Holes 18 L 5750 m SSS 71
V'tors H
Fees D–100fr
Loc 20 km N of Chur. 100 km SE
of Zürich
Arch Donald Harradine

For list of abbreviations see page 479

Davos (1929)
Postfach, 7260 Davos Dorf
Tel (081) 46 56 34
Fax (081) 46 25 55
Holes 18 L 5715 yds SSS 68
V'tors WD–U
Fees 75fr
Loc 1 km outside Davos
Arch Donald Harradine

Engadin (1893)
7503 Samedan
Tel (081) 852 52 26
Fax (081) 852 46 82
Holes 18 L 6350 m SSS 73
V'tors H
Fees 90fr
Loc Samedan, 6 km NE of
St Moritz
Arch M Verdieri

Lenzerheide Valbella (1950)
7078 Lenzerheide
Tel (081) 384 13 16
Fax (081) 384 52 22
Holes 18 L 5274 m SSS 69
V'tors H
Fees 60–80fr
Loc 20 km S of Chur towards
St Moritz
Arch Donald Harradine

Vulpera (1923)
7552 Vulpera Spa
Tel (081) 864 96 88
Fax (081) 864 96 88
Holes 9 L 1982 m SSS 62
V'tors H
Fees 50fr (60fr) W–250fr
Loc Tarasp, nr Vulpera. 60 km
NE of St Moritz
Arch Dell/Spencer

Zürich & North

Breitenloo (1964)
8309 Oberwil b. Bassersdorf
Tel (01) 836 40 80
Fax (01) 837 10 85
Holes 18 L 6125 m Par 72 SSS 72
V'tors WD–H by appointment
WE–M H
Fees 100fr
Loc 10 km NE of Zürich Airport
Arch Harradine/Pennink

Bürgenstock (1927)
6363 Bürgenstock
Tel (041) 611 05 45
Fax (041) 610 14 15
Holes 9 L 2030 m Par 35

V'tors I or H
Fees D–55fr
Loc 15 km S of Lucerne
Arch Fritz Frey

Dolder (1907)
Kurhausstrasse 66, 8032 Zürich
Tel (01) 261 50 45
Fax (01) 261 53 02
Holes 9 L 1735 m SSS 58
V'tors WD–H WE–M
Fees WD–70fr
Loc Zürich

Entfelden (1988)
Postfach 230, Muhenstrasse 52,
5036 Oberentfelden
Tel (062) 723 89 84
Fax (062) 723 84 36
Holes 9 L 3960 m SSS 60
V'tors H
Fees 50fr (70fr)
Loc 50 km W of Zürich
Arch Donald Harradine

Erlen (1988)
Schlossgut Eppishausen, Schlossstr 7,
8586 Erlen
Tel (071) 648 29 30
Fax (071) 648 29 40
Holes 18 L 5913 m SSS 72
V'tors H
Fees 80fr (110fr)
Loc 30 km NW of St Gallen.
60 km W of Zürich
Arch Deutsche Golfconsult

Hittnau-Zürich G&CC (1964)
8335 Hittnau
Tel (01) 950 24 42
Fax (01) 951 01 66
Holes 18 L 5773 m SSS 71
V'tors WD–U WE–M
Fees WD–90fr
Loc Hittnau, 30 km E of Zürich

Küssnacht (1994)
Sekretariat/Grossarni, 6403 Küssnacht
am Rigi
Tel (041) 850 70 60
Fax (041) 850 70 41
Holes 18 L 5397 m Par 68
V'tors WD–U H WE–M H
Fees 70–80fr (100fr)
Loc 20 km NE of Lucerne
Arch Peter Harradine

Lucerne (1903)
6006 Dietschiberg
Tel (041) 420 97 87
Fax (041) 420 82 48
Holes 18 L 6082 m Par 72 SSS 71-73

V'tors H
Fees 80fr (100fr)
Loc Lucerne 2 km

Ostschweizerischer (1948)
9246 Niederbüren
Tel (071) 422 18 56
Fax (071) 422 18 25
Holes 18 L 5920 m SSS 71
V'tors WD–H
Fees D–80fr (100fr)
Loc Niederbüren, 25 km NW of
St Gallen
Arch Donald Harradine

Schinznach-Bad (1929)
5116 Schinznach-Bad
Tel (056) 443 12 26
Fax (056) 443 34 83
Holes 9 L 5670 m Par 71
V'tors WD–U
Fees 70fr
Loc 6 km S of Brugg. 35 km
W of Zürich

Schönenberg (1967)
8824 Schönenberg
Tel (01) 788 16 24
Fax (01) 788 20 10
Holes 18 L 6340 m SSS 74
V'tors WD–H–by appointment
WE–M H
Fees 90fr (150fr)
Loc 20 km S of Zürich
Arch Donald Harradine

Sempachersee (1996)
6024 Hildisrieden, Lucerne
Tel (041) 462 71 71
Fax (041) 462 71 72
Holes 18 L 6130 m Par 72 SSS 72
9 L 3950 m Par 31
V'tors U H
Fees 80fr (100fr)
Loc 13 km NW of Lucerne
Arch Kurt Rossknecht

Zürich-Zumikon (1931)
8126 Zumikon
Tel (01) 918 00 50
Fax (01) 918 00 37
Holes 18 L 6360 m SSS 74
V'tors WD–by appointment
WE–M
Fees WD–100fr
Loc Zürich 10 km
Arch Donald Harradine

PART VI

Government of the Game

Introduction

The Royal & Ancient Golf Club

In Britain it is not unusual for the Governing Body of a Sport to have its origins in a private club, which later comes to be recognised as the authority through which the game is administered. The Royal & Ancient Golf Club of St Andrews is a prime example and enjoys a similar status to the Marylebone Cricket Club. With the world-wide spread of golf and cricket this century, both have emerged as the international body to which most other countries look for rulings and guidance.

The Royal & Ancient Club's records date back to 1754 when the Society of St Andrews Golfers adopted the rules which had been formulated in 1744 by the Gentlemen Golfers of Leith, later to become the Honourable Company of Edinburgh Golfers; the older club located across the Forth at Muirfield.

When in 1834 King William IV granted the St Andrews Gentlemen Golfers the right and privilege of using the title *Royal & Ancient*, the Honourable Company had temporarily lost cohesion and the R&A gradually acquired the status of the premier club. During the latter half of the Victorian age, in the 1880s and 1890s when, following the spread of the railway system, many new clubs were founded, they looked to the R&A for leadership and advice.

With the appointment of the first Rules of Golf Committee in 1897, the R&A became recognised as the Governing Authority in all countries except the United States and Mexico where the United States Golf Association controls the game. Golf federations of many countries are affiliated to the R&A. This is made clear in the *Statement of Functions* of the R&A, reproduced with the permission of the General Committee. The work of the Championship Committee is expanded in a note below, with particular reference to The Open Championship.

The success of The Open in recent years, both as a spectacle and financially, has meant that the R&A can now support fully the development of the game, while remaining the guardian of its traditions. Its encouragement of young players, especially through the Boys' Championship and the Golf Foundation, has helped produce the higher standards of play and younger champions now so apparent to all followers of the game.

Statement of Functions of the Royal & Ancient Golf Club throughout the world

With the ever continuing interest and developments in golf and the increasing complexity of the administration of the game, the Royal & Ancient Golf Club feels that a statement of its activities in this field would be of interest.

The functions for which the Club is responsible fall into three clearly defined categories. Firstly, functions of an international nature, secondly functions of a national nature, and finally the running of a Club with wide national and international Membership.

International Functions

In 1897 the Royal & Ancient became the Governing Authority on the Rules of Golf at the suggestion of the leading Golf Clubs in the United Kingdom at the time. Since then an ever increasing number of countries have sought affiliation to it, until today they number over 80, including several other Unions or Associations (eg the Ladies' Golf Union, European Golf Association, South American Golf Federation and Asia-Pacific Golf Confederation).

The Club, in its negotiations with the United States Golf Association on matters pertaining to the Rules of Golf, is not merely representing

Great Britain and Ireland, but these many countries as well.

In 1919, when it took over the running of the Open and Amateur Championships, the Royal & Ancient became responsible for the Rules of Amateur Status, and in matters pertaining thereto likewise represents these many countries.

The Royal & Ancient also supplies one of each of the two Joint Chairmen and Joint Secretaries of the World Amateur Golf Council which is responsible for the organisation of all World Amateur Team Championships.

There is a close liaison at all times with the Professional Golfers' Association and the PGA European Tour.

National Functions

Prior to the First World War, a group of Clubs had been responsible for the running of the Open and Amateur Championships. In 1919 a meeting of these Clubs confirmed that the Royal & Ancient should be the Governing Authority for the game and agreed it should assume responsibility for the two Championships.

The decision that the Royal & Ancient should be the Governing Authority was endorsed at a Meeting of the English, Scottish, Irish and Welsh Unions in 1924, at which Meeting what is now the Council of National Golf Unions was formed with the object amongst others of directing the system of Standard Scratch Scores and Handicaps.

In 1948 the Royal & Ancient took over the Boys' and in 1963 the Youths' Championship from the private interests which had previously run them; this was done at the request of the individuals concerned. In 1969 the Royal & Ancient itself inaugurated the British Seniors' Amateur Championship and in 1991 it agreed to become involved in the organisation and running of the Senior British Open Championship in conjunction with the PGA European Tour.

In 1995 it replaced The Youths' Championship with The Mid-Amateur Championship.

In addition to the organisation of five Championships, the Royal & Ancient is also responsible for the selection of Teams to represent Great Britain & Ireland in the Walker Cup, the Eisenhower Trophy, the St Andrews Trophy, and other International Tournaments. It is responsible for the organisation of such events when they are held in Great Britain and Ireland. In its World Amateur Golf Council role it takes it in turns with the USGA to organise the World Amateur Team Championships.

Club Functions

The Membership of the Club is limited to a total of 1,800, of which 1,050 may be resident in

Great Britain and Ireland and 750 elsewhere: this Overseas Membership is spread over countries throughout the world.

The Membership both at home and abroad is representative and includes many who have given and are giving great services to golf in this country and abroad to many different Unions and Associations. This permits broad and effective representation on all the Club Committees concerned with international and national functions.

Exercise of International Functions

1. Rules of Golf

(a) Committee:

The Rules of Golf Committee exists for the purpose of reviewing the Rules of Golf from time to time and of making decisions on their interpretation and publishing these decisions where necessary.

The Committee consists of twelve Members elected by the Club, of whom three retire each year and are not eligible for re-election for one year, except in the case of the Chairman and Deputy Chairman, and of up to twelve additional persons invited annually to join the Committee from Golf Authorities at home and abroad.

At present the bodies represented are:

Council of National Golf Unions
United States Golf Association
European Golf Association
Australian Golf Union
New Zealand Golf Association
Royal Canadian Golf Association
South African Golf Union
Asia-Pacific Golf Confederation
South American Golf Federation
Japan Golf Association
Ladies' Golf Union

(b) Revision of the Rules of Golf:

As the only other Governing Authority for the Rules of Golf is the USGA, the R&A works closely with this body when amendments to the Rules are under consideration for the purpose of maintaining uniformity in the Rules and their interpretation. Every four years a Conference takes place with the USGA for the purpose of discussing the proposals for changes to be made. The Rules were amended in January 1992. Although the Conference takes place quadrennially, the Rules are under constant review and investigations as to possible improvements start not long after a revision has taken place, so that ample time can be given to consult with interested parties.

Two years after a revision has taken place an important meeting is held with the USGA in the United States at the time of the Walker Cup to discuss progress and to start clearing the ground for the next Conference.

(c) Decisions:

The Rules of Golf Committee has a Decisions Sub-Committee which answers queries from Clubs and from all the Unions and Associations affiliated to the R&A. Those Decisions which seem to establish important or interesting points of interpretation are published annually jointly by the R&A and the USGA and issued world-wide. The Decisions Book can be purchased directly from the R&A.

2. Implements and Ball

The Committee consists of four Members elected by the Club, one Member of the Rules of Golf Committee and one Member of the Championship Committee, together with Consultant Members invited by the Committee to advise on technical matters. One of the elected Members retires each year but the Chairman may be re-elected immediately for the sake of continuity.

The Committee works in close co-operation with the USGA I & B Committee in interpreting the Rules and Appendices relating to the control of the form and make of golf clubs and the specifications of the golf ball to ensure that the game and established golf courses are not harmed by technical developments.

3. Rules of Amateur Status

(a) Committee:

The Committee consists of five members, of which four are elected by the Club and one provided by the Council of National Golf Unions. There are also Advisory Members to the Committee, representing the same Golfing Authorities as on the Rules of Golf Committee.

(b) Revision of Rules of Amateur Status:

A procedure, similar to that for the Rules of Golf, is adopted for revision of the Rules of Amateur Status and no policy changes are made without full consultation with all the affiliated Unions, the USGA and the PGA.

(c) Decisions:

The work of the Committee consists of (a) dealing with Applications for reinstatement to Amateur Status, (b) answering inquiries about the nature of prizes, conditions for Tournaments, etc, arising out of the increased impact of commercial sponsors on Amateur golf and the issue of guidelines and Decisions, (c) answering queries from individuals regarding their own position under the Rules and (d) controlling Scholarships and other Grants-in-aid.

Exercise of National Functions

Championship Committee

The Championship Committee is responsible for the control of the five Championships and of the International Matches and Tournaments mentioned above.

The Committee consists of eight elected Members elected by the Club, of whom two retire annually and are not eligible for re-election for one year.

For the organisation of any particular event, others may be co-opted, if required.

The work of this Committee has greatly increased in recent years, as is clearly evident from the staging of the Open Championship, for which prize money in 1998 will total £1,750,000. At the same time, more substantial reserve funds have been built up to ensure the continuance of the Open Championship as a premier world event.

The External Funds Committee makes annual donations to a number of golfing bodies, especially those concerned with the training and development of junior golf and for research on greenkeeping matters. It also make grants and loans to assist with the development of new facilities both in the UK and abroad.

Selection Committee

The Selection Committee consists of a Chairman, who is a Member of the Club, and other Members, who need not be Members of the Club, appointed by the General Committee. These other Members have for some years now been representative of each of the four Home Unions. Normally they hold their appointments for four years.

Exercise of Club Functions

The domestic affairs of the Club are run by Committees which it is not necessary to describe in this statement.

It is appropriate, however, to mention that the Club does not own a Golf Course. It is, nevertheless, much concerned with the maintenance and improvements of all four Golf Courses in St Andrews. These Courses are controlled by the St Andrews Links Trust and are run by the Links Management Committee. Three of the Trustees and four Members of the Management Committee are appointed by the Club and equal numbers are appointed by the Fife District Council. One member of the Trust is appointed by the Secretary of State for Scotland and the current MP is also a Trustee. The Club contributes an annually negotiated sum to the Trust in return for Members' playing privileges.

Finance

International Functions

After taking into account income derived from subscriptions to the Rules of Golf Decisions Service and the sale of official Rules publications, the net expenses of the Rules of Golf, Rules of Amateur Status and Rules for Implements and Ball are borne by External Activities.

National Functions

Income and expenditure of all Championships run by the R&A and the expenses of Teams representing Great Britain & Ireland are accounted for in separate divisions of one Account.

Surpluses of all income over expenditure in the External Activities Account are held in reserve to ensure the continuance of the running of the various events at a high standard.

The Royal & Ancient Golf Club as a private Members' Club does not in any way benefit from the External Activities Account.

General Committee

Responsibility for directing and co-ordinating the three functions of the R&A – as a private club, as a governing authority for golf and as the body responsible for organising and running the championships and international matches – rests with the Club's General Committee, which controls all matters of policy. The Committee consists of sixteen R&A Members, eight of whom are elected by the Club; the other eight *ex-officio* members are the Captain and Chairmen of the Finance, Implements and Ball, Membership, Club, Rules of Golf, Championship and Amateur Status Committees.

The execution of the decisions of the Club Committees and of the decisions taken by the Members at Business Meetings is in the hands of the Secretary of the R&A, who is assisted by several senior officers and the appropriate infrastructure of secretaries and clerical staff.

Contacts with Affiliated Golfing Authorities

The R&A endeavours to consult with all those Golfing Authorities concerned whenever an issue of importance arises. This covers, in particular, matters relating to Rules of Golf, Rules of Amateur Status, and the Championships.

Meetings are held when appropriate with representatives of Golfing Authorities in Great Britain & Ireland and the European Golf Association. Consultations with other Golfing Authorities abroad are regularly conducted by correspondence.

In January 1970, a Conference attended by Golfing Unions and Associations in this country and representatives of the European Golf Association was held under the auspices of the R&A to discuss all matters of mutual interest, and in particular to establish the best means of communication in the future between the Unions and Associations concerned. This was followed by a similar Conference at Chantilly, Paris in 1976.

In May 1980 the first ever International Golf Conference was held in St Andrews at which 33 countries affiliated to the R&A were represented and to which the USGA, PGA and other golfing bodies in this country sent observers. Owing to the great success of this Conference the R&A held further ones in 1985, 1989, 1993 and 1997 at which 60 countries were represented.

The R&A is represented at Meetings of the World Amateur Golf Council, the Council of National Golf Unions and on the CCPR.

October 1997 (revised)

MF Bonallack OBE
Secretary
Royal & Ancient Golf Club
of St Andrews
Fife KY16 9JD

The Championship Committee

Until 1919 the Open and Amateur Championships of Great Britain were organised by a group of leading Clubs in Scotland and England. The Club where the Championship was to be played was charged with running it for that year. In 1919, the Royal & Ancient, by then the recognised governing authority of the game, was invited to take over the responsibility for both Championships and ever since its Championship Committee has controlled both. Once the course on which a Championship is to be played has been decided, usually several years ahead, the Committee works closely with the Club concerned.

The Amateur, which is nearly as old as The Open, may have lost some of its public appeal with the growth of Professional golf and the defection of so many able young amateurs to its lucrative tour. However, the Amateur Championship is still considered the most prestigious event in the amateur game and is always played on one of the best courses.

The Championship Committee today controls several more events besides the two oldest Championships. The Boys', started privately in 1921, and the Youths', in 1954, both now come under its wing, as does the Seniors' which was inaugurated by the R&A in 1969. In addition, the biennial amateur matches against the United States and the Continent of Europe for the Walker Cup and the St Andrews Trophy respectively, are run by the Committee when played in Great Britain, as also are Boys' and Youths' Internationals against the Continent of Europe. The R&A Selection Committee chooses the team for all these amateur matches, as well as the team which competes for the Eisenhower Trophy, the World Amateur Team Championship. This was first played at St Andrews in 1958 and has since been held every two years in different parts of the world.

The remarkable development of The Open to the great occasion it is today has meant heavily increased responsibilities for the Championship Committee. TV and the media have given it an audience in millions compared with the few thousand interested in the past. The R&A's determination to match the growing interest with a new attitude and astute promotion has given the event the stature and following it now enjoys. The last 26 years have seen the winner's cheque grow from £1200 to £300,000, the total prize money from £15,000 to £1,175,000 in 1998. The financial success of The Open has provided considerable sums of money for the development of junior golf and other worthy causes connected to golf.

The R&A works closely with the Club of the course where the Championship is to be played, whose members take on many of the essential duties necessary if it is to run smoothly. These include spectator control where local Clubs take charge of a hole each, usually providing three-hour shifts of up to 16 members at a time. This can involve as many as 800 men daily. Local volunteer stewards also cover such diverse duties as course controllers, supervision of litter collection and spectator stand control. Security, courtesy transport, car park supervision and public catering, to name a few of the mass of services necessary, are provided under contract by companies expert in these fields. Close liaison with the area police authority is vital. Facilities for the Press, Television and the vast tented village, each involving several hundred people, occupy large areas and are a major limiting factor when considering possible venues for future championships.

Important for both competitors and spectators and appreciated by both is the radio network which provides up-to-the-minute scores and positions of the leading players which appear very quickly on the leader boards erected at strategic points round the course. The system developed over many years is as quick, informative and accurate as any in existence.

The Committee consists of eight Royal & Ancient members, who devote much time to their tasks. It has a full-time secretary who, together with the Secretary of the Club and some of his staff, is involved in the planning of The Open and other events throughout the year. Members of the Committee work long hours during Open week. From first light at about 5am, when the Head Greenkeeper and a nominated member of the Committee tour the course deciding the pin positions on each green for the day, to dusk when the last competitor comes in, all are occupied, mostly out on the course at selected points, in two-way radio contact with the centre, ready to give a ruling when required. In the final rounds the leading players are accompanied by a member of the committee for the whole round.

The many stands erected around the course, providing seats for sometimes 18,000 spectators, often quite close to greens, make for special problems. A loose shot which ends under a stand will probably mean the ball may be dropped without penalty in an area nearby, which has been pre-designated by the committee; this shot should be of equal difficulty as it would have been if the stand had not been there. In these cases often an official decision is required.

At the end of every round each competitor's card must be immediately checked and recorded following which, in the case of a leader, he will meet the press in the interview room.

It is the Championship Committee too which decides if any round has to be halted, postponed or cancelled due to storm and tempest. Such decisions, so difficult with so many factors, consequent on a postponement, to be considered, have been eased a little with improved weather forecasting and continuous contact with the local weather bureau.

It will be seen that the work of the Committee is never ending with the myriad tasks necessary to ensure the even flow to a Championship. The success of The Open is due to sound planning, moving with the times and the expertise of the R&A staff which is the executive arm of the Committee. The Open may be the Championship with which all are familiar; however, it must be remembered that the many other events under the R&A's control also require planning and organisation. The work for these events goes on largely unnoticed, but must not be forgotten.

Rules of Golf

As Approved by
The Royal & Ancient Golf Club
of St Andrews, Scotland
and the
United States Golf Association

28th EDITION
EFFECTIVE 1st JANUARY 1996

Contents

Relief Situations and Procedure

Other Forms of Play

Administration

Foreword
to the 1996 Edition of the Rules of Golf

The Royal & Ancient Golf Club of St Andrews and the United States Golf Association, in consultation with other golfing bodies, have carried out their customary quadrennial revision of the Rules of Golf and have agreed upon this new code to become effective from 1st January 1996.

Once again no major changes have been introduced but a number of Rules have been amended in continuance of the policy of making the Rules of Golf as clear as possible. The principal changes are summarised on page 773.

The Royal & Ancient and United States Golf Association will continue their close liaison in all matters concerning the Rules and would like to record their appreciation of the valuable assistance which they have received from other golfing bodies throughout the world.

We take this opportunity of thanking, most sincerely, our respective Committees and all those who have in many ways helped us in our endeavours.

John S Scrivener
Chairman
Rules of Golf Committee
Royal & Ancient Golf Club
of St Andrews

Trey Holland
Chairman
Rules of Golf Committee
United States Golf Association

Principal Changes introduced in the 1996 Code

DEFINITIONS

Ball in Play
Amended to include a ball substituted for the ball in play whether or not such substitution is permitted (see also Rule 15-1 and 20-4).

Ground Under Repair; Water Hazard; Lateral Water Hazard
A Committee may make a Local Rule prohibiting play from ground under repair, a water hazard or lateral water hazard if it has been defined as an environmentally-sensitive area.

RULES

Rule 6-7.   Undue Delay; Slow Play
The Committee may, in the conditions of a competition, lay down pace of play guidelines and in such a condition modify the penalty for a first offence, in stroke play, to one stroke.

Rule 6-8.   Discontinuance of Play
The Committee may provide in the conditions of competition that in potentially dangerous situations play shall be discontinued immediately following a suspension of play.

Rule 15-1.   Wrong Ball; Substituted Ball
Rule 20-4.   When Ball Dropped or Placed is in Play
If a player substitutes a ball when not permitted to do so, he loses the hole in match play or incurs a penalty of two strokes in stroke play.

Rule 25-1a.   Casual Water, Ground Under Repair and Certain Damage to Course
The Committee may make a Local Rule denying the player relief from interference with his stance.

Rule 33-2b.   New Holes
Where a single round is to be played on more than one day, the Committee may provide in the conditions of a competition that the holes and teeing grounds may be differently situated on each day of the competition.

The Rules of Golf

Section I Etiquette

Courtesy on the Course

Safety

Prior to playing a stroke or making a practice swing, the player should ensure that no one is standing close by or in a position to be hit by the club, the ball or any stones, pebbles, twigs or the like which may be moved by the stroke or swing.

Consideration for Other Players

The player who has the honour should be allowed to play before his opponent or fellow-competitor tees his ball.

No one should move, talk or stand close to or directly behind the ball or the hole when a player is addressing the ball or making a stroke.

No player should play until the players in front are out of range.

Pace of Play

In the interest of all, players should play without delay.

Players searching for a ball should signal the players behind them to pass as soon as it becomes apparent that the ball will not be easily found. They should not search for five minutes before doing so. They should not continue play until the players following them have passed and are out of range.

When the play of a hole has been completed, players should immediately leave the putting green.

If a match fails to keep its pace on the course and loses more than one clear hole on the players in front, it should invite the match following to pass.

Priority on the Course

In the absence of special rules, two-ball matches should have precedence over and be entitled to pass any three- or four-ball match, which should invite them through.

A single player has no standing and should give way to a match of any kind.

Any match playing a whole round is entitled to pass a match playing a shorter round.

Care of the Course

Holes in Bunkers

Before leaving a bunker, a player should carefully fill up and smooth over all holes and footprints made by him.

Replace Divots; Repair Ball-Marks and Damage by Spikes

Through the green, a player should ensure that any turf cut or displaced by him is replaced at once and pressed down and that any damage to the putting green made by a ball is carefully repaired. *On completion of the hole* by all players in the group, damage to the putting green caused by golf shoe spikes should be repaired.

Damage to Greens – Flagsticks, Bags, etc.

Players should ensure that, when putting down bags or the flagstick, no damage is done to the putting green and that neither they nor their caddies damage the hole by standing close to it, in handling the flagstick or in removing the ball from the hole. The flagstick should be properly replaced in the hole before the players leave the putting green. Players should not damage the putting green by leaning on their putters, particularly when removing the ball from the hole.

Golf Carts

Local notices regulating the movement of golf carts should be strictly observed.

Damage Through Practice Swings

In taking practice swings, players should avoid causing damage to the course, particularly the tees, by removing divots.

Section II Definitions

The Definitions are placed in alphabetical order and some are also repeated at the beginning of their relevant Rule. In the Rules themselves, defined terms which may be important to the application of a Rule are underlined the first time they appear.

Addressing the Ball

A player has "addressed the ball" when he has taken his stance and has also grounded his club, except that in a hazard a player has addressed the ball when he has taken his stance.

Advice

"Advice" is any counsel or suggestion which could influence a player in determining his play, the choice of a club or the method of making a stroke.

Information on the Rules or on matters of public information, such as the position of hazards or the flagstick on the putting green, is not advice.

Ball Deemed to Move
See "Move or Moved".

Ball Holed
See "Holed".

Ball Lost
See "Lost Ball".

Ball in Play
A ball is "in play" as soon as the player has made a <u>stroke</u> on the <u>teeing ground</u>. It remains in play until holed out, except when it is <u>lost, out of bounds</u> or lifted, or another ball has been substituted, whether or not such substitution is permitted; a ball so substituted becomes the ball in play.

Bunker
A "bunker" is a <u>hazard</u> consisting of a prepared area of ground, often a hollow, from which turf or soil has been removed and replaced with sand or the like. Grass-covered ground bordering or within a bunker is not part of the bunker. The margin of a bunker extends vertically downwards, but not upwards. A ball is in a bunker when it lies in or any part of it touches the bunker.

Caddie
A "caddie" is one who carries or handles a player's clubs during play and otherwise assists him in accordance with the Rules.

When one caddie is employed by more than one player, he is always deemed to be the caddie of the player whose ball is involved, and <u>equipment</u> carried by him is deemed to be that player's equipment, except when the caddie acts upon specific directions of another player, in which case he is considered to be that other player's caddie.

Casual Water
"Casual water" is any temporary accumulation of water on the <u>course</u> which is visible before or after the player takes his <u>stance</u> and is not in a <u>water</u> <u>hazard</u>. Snow and natural ice, other than frost, are either casual water or <u>loose</u> <u>impediments</u>, at the option of the player. Manufactured ice is an <u>obstruction</u>. Dew and frost are not casual water. A ball is in casual water when it lies in or any part of it touches the casual water.

Committee
The "Committee" is the committee in charge of the competition or, if the matter does not arise in a competition, the committee in charge of the <u>course</u>.

Competitor
A "competitor" is a player in a stroke competition. A "fellow-competitor" is any person with whom the competitor plays. Neither is <u>partner</u> of the other.

In stroke play foursome and four-ball competitions, where the context so admits, the word "competitor" or "fellow-competitor" includes his partner.

Course
The "course" is the whole area within which play is permitted (see Rule 33-2).

Equipment
"Equipment" is anything used, worn or carried by or for the player except any ball he has played at the hole being played and any small object, such as a coin or a tee, when used to mark the position of a ball or the extent of an area in which a ball is to be dropped. Equipment includes a golf cart, whether or not motorised. If such a cart is shared by two or more players, the cart and everything in it are deemed to be the equipment of the player whose ball is involved except that, when the cart is being moved by one of the players sharing it, the cart and everything in it are deemed to be that player's equipment.

Note: A ball played at the hole being played is equipment when it has been lifted and not put back into play.

Fellow Competitor
See "Competitor".

Flagstick
The "flagstick" is a movable straight indicator, with or without bunting or other material attached, centred in the hole to show its position. It shall be circular in cross-section.

Forecaddie
A "forecaddie" is one who is employed by the Committee to indicate to players the position of balls during play. He is an <u>outside</u> <u>agency</u>.

Ground Under Repair
"Ground under repair" is any portion of the <u>course</u> so marked by order of the Committee or so declared by its authorised representative. It includes material piled for removal and a hole made by a greenkeeper, even if not so marked. Stakes and lines defining ground under repair are in such ground. Stakes defining ground under repair are obstructions. The margin of ground under repair extends vertically downwards, but not upwards. A ball is in ground under repair when it lies in or any part of it touches the ground under repair.

Note 1: Grass cuttings and other material left on the course which have been abandoned and are not intended to be removed are not ground under repair unless so marked.

Note 2: The Committee may make a Local Rule prohibiting play from ground under repair or an environmentally-sensitive area which has been defined as ground under repair.

Hazards

A "hazard" is any <u>bunker</u> or <u>water</u> hazard.

Hole

The "hole" shall be 4¼ inches (108mm) in diameter and at least 4 inches (100mm) deep. If a lining is used, it shall be sunk at least 1 inch (25mm) below the <u>putting green</u> surface unless the nature of the soil makes it impracticable to do so; its outer diameter shall not exceed 4¼ inches (108mm).

Holed

A ball is "holed" when it is at rest within the circumference of the hole and all of it is below the level of the lip of the hole.

Honour

The side entitled to play first from the <u>teeing ground</u> is said to have the "honour".

Lateral Water Hazard

A "lateral water hazard" is a <u>water hazard</u> or that part of a water hazard so situated that it is not possible or is deemed by the Committee to be impracticable to drop a ball behind the water hazard in accordance with Rule 26-1b.

That part of a water hazard to be played as a lateral water hazard should be distinctively marked. A ball is in a lateral water hazard when it lies in or any part of it touches the lateral water hazard.

Note 1: Lateral water hazards should be defined by red stakes or lines.

Note 2: The Committee may make a Local Rule prohibiting play from an environmentally-sensitive area which has been defined as a lateral water hazard.

Line of Play

The "line of play" is the direction which the player wishes his ball to take after a stroke, plus a reasonable distance on either side of the intended direction. The line of play extends vertically upwards from the ground, but does not extend beyond the hole.

Line of Putt

The "line of putt" is the line which the player wishes his ball to take after a stroke on the <u>putting green</u>. Except with respect to Rule 16-1e, the line of putt includes a reasonable distance on either side of the intended line. The line of putt does not extend beyond the hole.

Loose Impediments

"Loose impediments" are natural objects such as stones, leaves, twigs, branches and the like, dung, worms and insects and casts or heaps made by them, provided they are not fixed or growing, are not solidly embedded and do not adhere to the ball.

Sand and loose soil are loose impediments on the <u>putting green,</u> but not elsewhere.

Snow and natural ice, other than frost, are either <u>casual water</u> or loose impediments, at the option of the player. Manufactured ice is an <u>obstruction</u>.

Dew and frost are not loose impediments.

Lost Ball

A ball is "lost" if:

a. It is not found or identified as his by the player within five minutes after the player's side or his or their caddies have begun to search for it; or

b. The player has put another ball into play under the Rules, even though he may not have searched for the original ball; or

c. The player has played any stroke with a <u>provisional ball</u> from the place where the original ball is likely to be or from a point nearer the hole than that place, whereupon the provisional ball becomes the <u>ball</u> in <u>play</u>.

Time spent in playing a <u>wrong ball</u> is not counted in the five-minute period allowed for search.

Marker

A "marker" is one who is appointed by the Committee to record a <u>competitor's</u> score in stroke play. He may be a <u>fellow-competitor</u>. He is not a <u>referee</u>.

Matches

See "Sides and Matches".

Move or Moved

A ball is deemed to have "moved" if it leaves its position and comes to rest in any other place.

Observer

An "observer" is one who is appointed by the Committee to assist a <u>referee</u> to decide questions of fact and to report to him any breach of a Rule. An observer should not attend the flagstick, stand at or mark the position of the hole, or lift the ball or mark its position.

Obstructions

An "obstruction" is anything artificial, including the artificial surfaces and sides of roads and paths and manufactured ice, except:

a. Objects defining <u>out of bounds</u>, such as walls, fences, stakes and railings;

b. Any part of an immovable artificial object which is out of bounds; and

c. Any construction declared by the Committee to be an integral part of the course.

Out of Bounds

"Out of bounds" is ground on which play is prohibited.

When out of bounds is defined by reference to stakes or a fence or as being beyond stakes or a fence, the out of bounds line is determined by the nearest inside points of the stakes or fence posts at ground level excluding angled supports.

When out of bounds is defined by a line on the ground, the line itself is out of bounds.

The out of bounds line extends vertically upwards and downwards.

A ball is out of bounds when all of it lies out of bounds.

A player may stand out of bounds to play a ball lying within bounds.

Outside Agency

An "outside agency" is any agency not part of the match or, in stroke play, not part of the competitor's side, and includes a referee, a marker, an observer and a forecaddie. Neither wind nor water is an outside agency.

Partner

A "partner" is a player associated with another player on the same side.

In a threesome, foursome, best-ball or four-ball match, where the context so admits, the word "player" includes his partner or partners.

Penalty Stroke

A "penalty stroke" is one added to the score of a player or side under certain Rules. In a threesome or foursome, penalty strokes do not affect the order of play.

Provisional Ball

A "provisional ball" is a ball played under Rule 27-2 for a ball which may be lost outside a water hazard or may be out of bounds.

Putting Green

The "putting green" is all ground of the hole being played which is specially prepared for putting or otherwise defined as such by the Committee. A ball is on the putting green when any part of it touches the putting green.

Referee

A "referee" is one who is appointed by the Committee to accompany players to decide questions of fact and apply the Rules. He shall act on any breach of a Rule which he observes or is reported to him.

A referee should not attend the flagstick, stand at or mark the position of the hole, or lift the ball or mark its position.

Rub of the Green

A "rub of the green" occurs when a ball in motion is accidentally deflected or stopped by any outside agency (see Rule 19-1).

Rule

The term "Rule" includes Local Rules made by the Committee under Rule 33-8a.

Sides and Matches

Side: A player, or two or more players who are partners.

Single: A match in which one plays against another.

Threesome: A match in which one plays against two, and each side plays one ball.

Foursome: A match in which two play against two, and each side plays one ball.

Three-ball: A match play competition in which three play against one another, each playing his own ball. Each player is playing two distinct matches.

Best ball: A match in which one plays against the better ball of two or the best ball of three players.

Four-ball: A match in which two play their better ball against the better ball of two other players.

Stance

Taking the "stance" consists in a player placing his feet in position for and preparatory to making a stroke.

Stipulated Round

The "stipulated round" consists of playing the holes of the course in their correct sequence unless otherwise authorised by the Committee. The number of holes in a stipulated round is 18 unless a smaller number is authorised by the Committee. As to extension of stipulated round in match play, see Rule 2-3.

Stroke

A "stroke" is the forward movement of the club made with the intention of fairly striking at and moving the ball, but if a player checks his downswing voluntarily before the clubhead reaches the ball he is deemed not to have made a stroke.

Teeing Ground

The "teeing ground" is the starting place for the hole to be played. It is a rectangular area two club-lengths in depth, the front and the sides of which are defined by the outside limits of two tee-markers. A ball is outside the teeing ground when all of it lies outside the teeing ground.

Through the Green

"Through the green" is the whole area of the course except

a. The teeing ground and putting green of the hole being played; and

b. All hazards on the course.

Water Hazard

A "water hazard" is any sea, lake, pond, river, ditch, surface drainage ditch or other open water course (whether or not containing water) and anything of a similar nature.

All ground or water within the margin of a

water hazard is part of the water hazard. The margin of a water hazard extends vertically upwards and downwards. Stakes and lines defining the margins of water hazards are in the hazards. Such stakes are obstructions. A ball is in a water hazard when it lies in or any part of it touches the water hazard.

Note 1: Water hazards (other than lateral water hazards) should be defined by yellow stakes or lines.

Note 2: The Committee may make a Local Rule prohibiting play from an environmentally-sensitive area which has been defined as a water hazard.

Wrong Ball

A "wrong ball" is any ball other than the player's:

    a. Ball in play,

    b. Provisional ball or

    c. Second ball played under Rule 3-3 or Rule 20-7b in stroke play.

Note: Ball in play includes a ball substituted for the ball in play whether or not such substitution is permitted.

Section III
The Rules of Play

THE GAME

Rule 1. The Game

1-1. General

The Game of Golf consists in playing a ball from the teeing ground into the hole by a stroke or successive strokes in accordance with the Rules.

1-2. Exerting Influence on Ball

No player or caddie shall take any action to influence the position or the movement of a ball except in accordance with the Rules.

    PENALTY FOR BREACH OF RULE 1-2:
      Match play – Loss of hole;
      Stroke play – Two strokes.

Note: In the case of a serious breach of Rule 1-2, the Committee may impose a penalty of disqualification.

1-3. Agreement to Waive Rules

Players shall not agree to exclude the operation of any Rule or to waive any penalty incurred.

    PENALTY FOR BREACH OF RULE 1-3:
      Match play – Disqualification of both sides;
      Stroke play – Disqualification of competitors
        concerned.

(Agreeing to play out of turn in stroke play – see Rule 10-2c.)

1-4. Points Not Covered by Rules

If any point in dispute is not covered by the Rules, the decision shall be made in accordance with equity.

Rule 2. Match Play

2-1. Winner of Hole; Reckoning of Holes

In match play the game is played by holes.

Except as otherwise provided in the Rules, a hole is won by the side which holes its ball in the fewer strokes. In a handicap match the lower net score wins the hole.

The reckoning of holes is kept by the terms: so many "holes up" or "all square", and so many "to play".

A side is "dormie" when it is as many holes up as there are holes remaining to be played.

2-2. Halved Hole

A hole is halved if each side holes out in the same number of strokes.

When a player has holed out and his opponent has been left with a stroke for the half, if the player thereafter incurs a penalty, the hole is halved.

2-3. Winner of Match

A match (which consists of a stipulated round, unless otherwise decreed by the Committee) is won by the side which is leading by a number of holes greater than the number of holes remaining to be played.

The Committee may, for the purpose of settling a tie, extend the stipulated round to as many holes as are required for a match to be won.

2-4. Concession of Next Stroke, Hole or Match

When the opponent's ball is at rest or is deemed to be at rest under Rule 16-2, the player may concede the opponent to have holed out with his next stroke and the ball may be removed by either side with a club or otherwise.

A player may concede a hole or a match at any time prior to the conclusion of the hole or the match.

Concession of a stroke, hole or match may not be declined or withdrawn.

2-5. Claims

In match play, if a doubt or dispute arises between the players and no duly authorised representative of the Committee is available within a reasonable time, the players shall continue the match without delay. Any claim, if it is to be considered by the Committee, must be made before any player in the match plays from the next teeing ground or, in the case of the last hole of the match, before all players in the match leave the putting green.

No later claim shall be considered unless it is based on facts previously unknown to the player making the claim and the player making the claim had been given wrong information (Rules 6-2a and 9) by an opponent. In any case, no later claim shall be considered after the result of the match has been officially announced, unless the Committee is satisfied that the opponent knew he was giving wrong information.

2-6. General Penalty

The penalty for a breach of a Rule in match play is loss of hole except when otherwise provided.

Rule 3. Stroke Play

3-1. Winner

The competitor who plays the stipulated round or rounds in the fewest strokes is the winner.

3-2. Failure to Hole Out

If a competitor fails to hole out at any hole and does not correct his mistake before he plays a stroke from the next teeing ground or, in the case of the last hole of the round, before he leaves the putting green, *he shall be disqualified.*

3-3. Doubt as to Procedure

a. Procedure

In stroke play only, when during play of a hole a competitor is doubtful of his rights or procedure, he may, without penalty, play a second ball. After the situation which has caused the doubt has arisen, the competitor should, before taking further action, announce to his marker or a fellow-competitor his decision to invoke this Rule and the ball with which he will score if the Rules permit.

The competitor shall report the facts to the Committee before returning his score card unless he scores the same with both balls; if he fails to do so, *he shall be disqualified.*

b. Determination of Score for Hole

If the Rules allow the procedure selected in advance by the competitor, the score with the ball selected shall be his score for the hole.

If the competitor fails to announce in advance his decision to invoke this Rule or his selection, the score with the original ball or, if the original ball is not one of the balls being played, the first ball put into play shall count if the Rules allow the procedure adopted for such ball.

Note: A second ball played under Rule 3-3 is not a provisional ball under Rule 27-2.

3-4. Refusal to Comply with a Rule

If a competitor refuses to comply with a Rule affecting the rights of another competitor, *he shall be disqualified.*

3-5. General Penalty

The penalty for a breach of a Rule in stroke play is two strokes except when otherwise provided.

CLUBS AND THE BALL

The Royal & Ancient Golf Club of St Andrews and the United States Golf Association reserve the right to change the Rules and make and change the interpretations relating to clubs, balls and other implements at any time.

Rule 4. Clubs

A player in doubt as to the conformity of a club should consult the Royal & Ancient Golf Club of St Andrews.

A manufacturer may submit to the Royal & Ancient Golf Club of St Andrews a sample of a club which is to be manufactured for a ruling as to whether the club conforms with Rule 4 and Appendix II. Such sample will become the property of the Royal & Ancient Golf Club of St Andrews for reference purposes. If a manufacturer fails to submit a sample before manufacturing and/or marketing the club, he assumes the risk of a ruling that the club does not conform with the Rules of Golf.

Where a club, or a part of a club, is required to have some specific property, this means that it must be designed and manufactured with the intention of having that property. The finished club or parts must have that property within manufacturing tolerances appropriate to the material used.

4-1. Form and Make of Clubs

A club is an implement designed to be used for striking the ball.

A putter is a club with a loft not exceeding ten degrees designed primarily for use on the putting green.

The player's clubs shall conform with the provisions of this Rule and with the specifications and interpretations set forth in Appendix II.

a. General

The club shall be composed of a shaft and a head. All parts of the club shall be fixed so that the club is one unit. The club shall not be designed to be adjustable except for weight (see also Appendix II). The club shall not be substantially different from the traditional and customary form and make, and shall have no external attachments except as otherwise permitted by the Rules.

b. Shaft

The shaft shall be straight, with the same bending and twisting properties in any direction, and shall be attached to the clubhead at the heel either directly or through a single plain neck and/or socket. A putter shaft may be attached to any point in the head.

c. Grip

The grip consists of that part of the shaft designed to be held by the player and any material added to it for the purpose of obtaining a firm hold. The grip shall be straight and plain in form, shall extend to the end of the shaft and shall not be moulded for any part of the hands.

d. Clubhead

The distance from the heel to the toe of the clubhead shall be greater than the distance from the face to the back. The clubhead shall be generally plain in shape.

The clubhead shall have only one striking face, except that a putter may have two such faces if their characteristics are the same, and they are opposite each other.

e. Club Face

The face of the club shall be hard and rigid (some exceptions may be made for putters) and, except for such markings as are permitted by Appendix II, shall be smooth and shall not have any degree of concavity.

f. Wear and Alteration

A club which conforms with Rule 4-1 when new is deemed to conform after wear through normal use. Any part of a club which has been purposely altered is regarded as new and must conform, in the altered state, with the Rules.

g. Damage

If a player's club ceases to conform with Rule 4-1 because of damage sustained in the normal course of play, the player may:
(i) use the club in its damaged state, but only for the remainder of the stipulated round during which such damage was sustained; or
(ii) without unduly delaying play, repair it.
A club which ceases to conform because of damage sustained other than in the normal course of play shall not subsequently be used during the round.

(Damage changing playing characteristics of club – see Rule 4-2.)

(Damage rendering club unfit for play – see Rule 4-4a.)

4-2. Playing Characteristics Changed

During a stipulated round, the playing characteristics of a club shall not be purposely changed by adjustment or by any other means.

If the playing characteristics of a player's club are changed during a round because of damage sustained in the normal course of play, the player may:
(i) use the club in its altered state; or
(ii) without unduly delaying play, repair it.

If the playing characteristics of a player's club are changed because of damage sustained other than in the normal course of play, the club shall not subsequently be used during the round.

Damage to a club which occurred prior to a round may be repaired during the round, provided the playing characteristics are not changed and play is not unduly delayed.

4-3. Foreign Material

Foreign material must not be applied to the club face for the purpose of influencing the movement of the ball.

PENALTY FOR BREACH OF RULE 4-1, -2 or -3: *Disqualification.*

4-4. Maximum of Fourteen Clubs

a. Selection and Replacement of Clubs

The player shall start a stipulated round with not more than fourteen clubs. He is limited to the clubs thus selected for that round except that, without unduly delaying play, he may:
(i) if he started with fewer than fourteen clubs, add any number provided his total number does not exceed fourteen; and
(ii) replace, with any club, a club which becomes unfit for play in the normal course of play.
The addition or replacement of a club or clubs may not be made by borrowing any club selected for play by any other person playing on the course.

b. Partners May Share Clubs

Partners may share clubs, provided that the total number of clubs carried by the partners so sharing does not exceed fourteen.

PENALTY FOR BREACH OF RULE 4-4a or b, REGARDLESS OF NUMBER OF EXCESS CLUBS CARRIED:

Match play – At the conclusion of the hole at which the breach is discovered, the state of the match shall be adjusted by deducting one hole for each hole at which a breach occurred. Maximum deduction per round: two holes.

Stroke play – Two strokes for each hole at which any breach occurred; maximum penalty per round: four strokes.

Bogey and par competitions – Penalties as in match play.

Stableford competitions – see Note to Rule 32-1b.

c. Excess Club Declared Out of Play

Any club carried or used in breach of this Rule shall be declared out of play by the player immediately upon discovery that a breach has occurred and thereafter shall not be used by the player during the round.

PENALTY FOR BREACH OF RULE 4-4c:
Disqualification.

Rule 5. The Ball

5-1. General

The ball the player uses shall conform to requirements specified in Appendix III on maximum weight, minimum size, spherical symmetry, initial velocity and overall distance.

Note: The Committee may require, in the conditions of a competition (Rule 33-1), that the ball the player uses must be named on the current List of Conforming Golf Balls issued by the Royal & Ancient Golf Club of St Andrews.

5-2. Foreign Material

Foreign material must not be applied to a ball for the purpose of changing its playing characteristics.

PENALTY FOR BREACH OF RULES 5-1 or
5-2: *Disqualification.*

5-3. Ball Unfit for Play

A ball is unfit for play if it is visibly cut, cracked or out of shape. A ball is not unfit for play solely because mud or other materials adhere to it, its surface is scratched or scraped or its paint is damaged or discoloured.

If a player has reason to believe his ball has become unfit for play during the play of the hole being played, he may during the play of such hole lift his ball without penalty to determine whether it is unfit.

Before lifting the ball, the player must announce his intention to his opponent in match play or his marker or a fellow-competitor in stroke play and mark the position of the ball. He may then lift and examine the ball without cleaning it and must give his opponent, marker or fellow-competitor an opportunity to examine the ball.

If he fails to comply with this procedure *he shall incur a penalty of one stroke.*

If it is determined that the ball has become unfit for play during play of the hole being played, the player may substitute another ball, placing it on the spot where the original ball lay. Otherwise, the original ball shall be replaced.

If a ball breaks into pieces as a result of a stroke, the stroke shall be cancelled and the player shall play a ball without a penalty as nearly as possible at the spot from which the original ball was played (see Rule 20-5).

*PENALTY FOR BREACH OF RULE 5-3:
Match play – Loss of hole; Stroke play – Two strokes.
*If a player incurs the general penalty for breach of Rule 5-3, no additional penalty under the Rule shall be applied.

Note: If the opponent, marker or fellow-competitor wishes to dispute a claim of unfitness, he must do so before the player plays another ball.

(Cleaning ball lifted from putting green or under any other Rule – see Rule 21.)

PLAYER'S RESPONSIBILITIES

Rule 6. The Player

Definition

A "marker" is one who is appointed by the Committee to record a <u>competitor's</u> score in stroke play. He may be a <u>fellow-competitor</u>. He is not a <u>referee</u>.

6-1. Conditions of Competition

The player is responsible for knowing the conditions under which the competition is to be played (Rule 33-1).

6-2. Handicap

a. Match Play

Before starting a match in a handicap competition, the players should determine from one another their respective handicaps. If a player begins the match having declared a higher handicap which would affect the number of strokes given or received, *he shall be disqualified;* otherwise, the player shall play off the declared handicap.

b. Stroke Play

In any round of a handicap competition, the competitor shall ensure that his handicap is recorded on his score card before it is returned to the Committee. If no handicap is recorded on his score card before it is returned, or if the recorded handicap is higher than that to which he is entitled and this affects the number of strokes received, *he shall be disqualified* from that round of the handicap competition; otherwise, the score shall stand.

Note: It is the player's responsibility to know the holes at which handicap strokes are to be given or received.

6-3. Time of Starting and Groups

a. Time of Starting

The player shall start at the time laid down by the Committee.

b. Groups

In stroke play, the competitor shall remain throughout the round in the group arranged by the Committee unless the Committee authorises or ratifies a change.

PENALTY FOR BREACH OF RULE 6-3:
Disqualification.
(Best-ball and four-ball play – see Rules 30-3a and 31-2.)

Note: The Committee may provide in the conditions of a competition (Rule 33-1) that, if the player arrives at his starting point, ready to play, within five minutes after his starting time, in the absence of circumstances which warrant waiving the penalty of disqualification as provided in Rule 33-7, the penalty for failure to start on time is *loss of the first hole in match play or two strokes at the first hole in stroke play* instead of disqualification.

6-4. Caddie

The player may have only one <u>caddie</u> at any one time, *under penalty of disqualification.*

For any breach of a Rule by his caddie, the player incurs the applicable penalty.

6-5. Ball

The responsibility for playing the proper ball rests with the player. Each player should put an identification mark on his ball.

6-6. Scoring in Stroke Play

a. Recording Scores

After each hole the <u>marker</u> should check the score with the competitor and record it. On completion of the round the marker shall sign the card and hand it to the competitor. If more than one marker records the scores, each shall sign for the part for which he is responsible.

b. Signing and Returning Card

After completion of the round, the competitor should check his score for each hole and settle any doubtful points with the Committee. He shall ensure that the marker has signed the card, countersign the card himself and return it to the Committee as soon as possible.

PENALTY FOR BREACH OF RULE 6-6b:
Disqualification.

c. Alteration of Card

No alteration may be made on a card after the competitor has returned it to the Committee.

d. Wrong Score for Hole

The competitor is responsible for the correctness of the score recorded for each hole on his card. If he returns a score for any hole lower than actually taken, *he shall be disqualified.* If he returns a score for any hole higher than actually taken, the score as returned shall stand.

Note 1: The Committee is responsible for the addition of scores and application of the handicap recorded on the card – see Rule 33-5.

Note 2: In four-ball stroke play, see also Rule 31-4 and -7a.

6-7. Undue Delay; Slow Play

The player shall play without undue delay and in accordance with any pace of play guidelines which may be laid down by the Committee.

Between completion of a hole and playing from the next teeing ground, the player shall not unduly delay play.

PENALTY FOR BREACH OF RULE 6-7:
Match play – Loss of hole;
Stroke play – Two strokes.
For subsequent offence – Disqualification.

Note 1: If the player unduly delays play between holes, he is delaying the play of the next hole and the penalty applies to that hole.

Note 2: For the purpose of preventing slow play, the Committee may, in the conditions of a competition (Rule 33-1), lay down pace of play guidelines including maximum periods of time allowed to complete a stipulated round, a hole or a stroke.

In stroke play only, the Committee may, in such a condition, modify the penalty for a breach of this Rule as follows:

First offence – One stroke;
Second offence – Two strokes.
For subsequent offence – Disqualification.

6-8. Discontinuance of Play

a. When Permitted

The player shall not discontinue play unless:
(i)   the Committee has suspended play;
(ii) he believes there is danger from lightning;
(iii) he is seeking a decision from the Committee on a doubtful or disputed point (see Rules 2-5 and 34-3); or
(iv) there is some other good reason such as sudden illness.

Bad weather is not of itself a good reason for discontinuing play.

If the player discontinues play without specific permission from the Committee, he shall report to the Committee as soon as practicable. If he does so and the Committee considers his reason satisfactory, the player incurs no penalty. Otherwise, *the player shall be disqualified.*

Exception in match play: Players discontinuing match play by agreement are not subject to disqualification unless by so doing the competition is delayed.

Note: Leaving the course does not of itself constitute discontinuance of play.

b. Procedure When Play Suspended by Committee

When play is suspended by the Committee, if the players in a match or group are between the play of two holes, they shall not resume play until the Committee has ordered a resumption of play. If they are in the process of playing a hole, they may continue provided they do so without delay. If they choose to continue, they shall discontinue either before or immediately after completing the hole, and shall not thereafter resume play until the Committee has ordered a resumption of play.

When play has been suspended by the Committee, the player shall resume play when the Committee has ordered a resumption of play.

PENALTY FOR BREACH OF RULE 6-8b:
Disqualification.

Note: The Committee may provide in the conditions of a competition (Rule 33-1) that, in potentially dangerous situations, play shall be discontinued immediately following a suspension of play by the Committee. If a player fails to discontinue play immediately, he shall be disqualified unless circumstances warrant waiving such a penalty as provided in Rule 33-7.

(Resumption of play – see Rule 33-2d.)

c. Lifting Ball When Play Discontinued

When during the play of a hole a player discontinues play under Rule 6-8a, he may lift his ball. A ball may be cleaned when so lifted. If a ball has been so lifted, the player shall, when play is resumed, place a ball on the spot from which the original ball was lifted.

PENALTY FOR BREACH OF RULE 6-8c:
Match Play – Loss of hole; Stroke play – Two strokes.

Rule 7. Practice

7-1. Before or Between Rounds

a. Match Play

On any day of a match play competition, a player may practise on the competition course before a round.

b. Stroke Play

On any day of a stroke competition or play-off, a competitor shall not practise on the competition course or test the surface of any putting green on the course before a round or play-off. When two or more rounds of a stroke competition are to be played over consecutive days, practice between those rounds on any competition course remaining to be played is prohibited.

Exception: Practice putting or chipping on or near the first teeing ground before starting a round or play-off is permitted.

PENALTY FOR BREACH OF RULE 7-1b:
Disqualification.

Note: The Committee may in the conditions of a competition (Rule 33-1) prohibit practice on the competition course on any day of a match play competition or permit practice on the competition course or part of the course (Rule 33-2c) on any day of or between rounds of a stroke competition.

7-2. During Round

A player shall not play a practice stroke either during the play of a hole or between the play of two holes except that, between the play of two holes, the player may practise putting or chipping on or near the putting green of the hole last played, any practice putting green or the teeing ground of the next hole to be played in the round, provided such practice stroke is not played from a hazard and does not unduly delay play (Rule 6-7).

Strokes played in continuing the play of a hole, the result of which has been decided, are not practice strokes.

Exception: When play has been suspended by the Committee, a player may, prior to resumption of play, practise (a) as provided in this Rule, (b) anywhere other than on the competition course and (c) as otherwise permitted by the Committee.

PENALTY FOR BREACH OF RULE 7-2:
Match play – Loss of hole; Stroke play – Two strokes.

In the event of a breach between the play of two holes, the penalty applies to the next hole.

Note 1: A practice swing is not a practice stroke and may be taken at any place, provided the player does not breach the Rules.

Note 2: The Committee may prohibit practice on or near the putting green of the hole last played.

Rule 8. Advice; Indicating Line of Play

Definitions

"Advice" is any counsel or suggestion which could influence a player in determining his play, the choice of a club or the method of making a stroke.

Information on the Rules or on matters of public information, such as the position of hazards or the flagstick on the putting green, is not advice.

The "line of play" is the direction which the player wishes his ball to take after a stroke, plus a reasonable distance on either side of the intended direction. The line of play extends vertically upwards from the ground, but does not extend beyond the hole.

8-1. Advice

During a stipulated round, a player shall not give advice to anyone in the competition except his partner. A player may ask for advice during a stipulated round from only his partner or either of their caddies.

8-2. Indicating Line of Play

a. Other Than on Putting Green

Except on the putting green, a player may have the line of play indicated to him by anyone, but no one shall be positioned by the player on or close to the line or an extension of the line beyond the hole while the <u>stroke</u> is being played. Any mark placed during the play of a hole by the player or with his knowledge to indicate the line shall be removed before the stroke is played.

Exception: Flagstick attended or held up – see Rule 17-1.

b. On the Putting Green

When the player's ball is on the <u>putting green</u>, the player, his partner or either of their caddies may, before but not during the <u>stroke</u>, point out a line for putting, but in so doing the putting green shall not be touched. No mark shall be placed anywhere to indicate a line for putting.

PENALTY FOR BREACH OF RULE: *Match play – Loss of hole; Stroke play – Two strokes.*

Note: The Committee may, in the conditions of a team competition (Rule 33-1), permit each team to appoint one person who may give <u>advice</u> (including pointing out a line for putting) to members of that team. The Committee may lay down conditions relating to the appointment and permitted conduct of such person, who must be identified to the Committee before giving advice.

Rule 9. Information as to Strokes Taken

9-1. General

The number of strokes a player has taken shall include any penalty strokes incurred.

9.2 Match Play

A player who has incurred a penalty shall inform his opponent as soon as practicable, unless he is obviously proceeding under a Rule involving a penalty and this has been observed by his opponent. If he fails so to inform his opponent he shall be deemed to have given wrong information even if he was not aware that he had incurred a penalty.

An opponent is entitled to ascertain from the player, during the play of a hole, the number of strokes he has taken and, after play of a hole, the number of strokes taken on the hole just completed.

If during the play of a hole the player gives or is deemed to give wrong information as to the number of strokes taken, he shall incur no penalty if he corrects the mistake before his opponent has played his next stroke. If the player fails so to correct the wrong information, *he shall lose the hole.*

If after play of a hole the player gives or is deemed to give wrong information as to the number of strokes taken on the hole just completed and this affects the opponent's understanding of the result of the hole, he shall incur no penalty if he corrects his mistake before any player plays

from the next <u>teeing ground</u> or, in the case of the last hole of the match, before all players leave the <u>putting green</u>. If the player fails so to correct the wrong information, *he shall lose the hole.*

9-3. Stroke Play

A competitor who has incurred a penalty should inform his marker as soon as practicable.

ORDER OF PLAY

Rule 10. Order of Play

10-1. Match Play

a. Teeing Ground

The side entitled to play first from the <u>teeing ground</u> is said to have the "honour".

The side which shall have the honour at the first teeing ground shall be determined by the order of the draw. In the absence of a draw, the honour should be decided by lot.

The side which wins a hole shall take the honour at the next teeing ground. If a hole has been halved, the side which had the honour at the previous teeing ground shall retain it.

b. Other Than on Teeing Ground

When the balls are in play, the ball farther from the hole shall be played first. If the balls are equidistant from the hole, the ball to be played first should be decided by lot.

Exception: Rule 30-3c (best-ball and four-ball match play).

c. Playing Out of Turn

If a player plays when his opponent should have played, the opponent may immediately require the player to cancel the stroke so played and, in correct order, play a ball without penalty as nearly as possible at the spot from which the original ball was last played (see Rule 20-5).

10-2. Stroke Play

a. Teeing Ground

The competitor entitled to play first from the <u>teeing ground</u> is said to have the "honour".

The competitor who shall have the honour at the first teeing ground shall be determined by the order of the draw. In the absence of a draw, the honour should be decided by lot.

The competitor with the lowest score at a hole shall take the honour at the next teeing ground. The competitor with the second lowest score shall play next and so on. If two or more competitors have the same score at a hole, they shall play from the next teeing ground in the same order as at the previous teeing ground.

b. Other Than on Teeing Ground

When the balls are in play, the ball farthest

from the hole shall be played first. If two or more balls are equidistant from the hole, the ball to be played first should be decided by lot.

Exceptions: Rules 22 (ball interfering with or assisting play) and 31-5 (four-ball stroke play).

c. Playing Out of Turn

If a competitor plays out of turn, no penalty is incurred and the ball shall be played as it lies. If, however, the Committee determines that competitors have agreed to play in an order other than that set forth in Clauses 2a and 2b of this Rule to give one of them an advantage, *they shall be disqualified.*

(Incorrect order of play in threesomes and foursomes stroke play – see Rule 29-3.)

10-3. Provisional Ball or Second Ball from Teeing Ground

If a player plays a provisional ball or a second ball from a teeing ground, he should do so after his opponent or fellow-competitor has played his first stroke. If a player plays a provisional ball or a second ball out of turn, Clauses 1c and 2c of this Rule shall apply.

10-4. Ball Moved in Measuring

If a ball is moved in measuring to determine which ball is farther from the hole, no penalty is incurred and the ball shall be replaced.

TEEING GROUND

Rule 11. Teeing Ground

Definition

The "teeing ground" is the starting place for the hole to be played. It is a rectangular area two club-lengths in depth, the front and the sides of which are defined by the outside limits of two tee-markers. A ball is outside the teeing ground when all of it lies outside the teeing ground.

11-1. Teeing

In teeing, the ball may be placed on the ground, on an irregularity of surface created by the player on the ground or on a tee, sand or other substance in order to raise it off the ground.

A player may stand outside the teeing ground to play a ball within it.

11-2. Tee-Markers

Before a player plays his first stroke with any ball from the teeing ground of the hole being played, the tee-markers are deemed to be fixed. In such circumstances, if the player moves or allows to be moved a tee-marker for the purpose of avoiding interference with his stance, the area of his intended swing or his line of play, *he shall incur the penalty for a breach of Rule 13-2.*

11-3. Ball Falling Off Tee

If a ball, when not in play, falls off a tee or is knocked off a tee by the player in addressing it, it may be re-teed without penalty, but if a stroke is made at the ball in these circumstances, whether the ball is moving or not, the stroke counts but no penalty is incurred.

11-4. Playing from Outside Teeing Ground

a. Match Play

If a player, when starting a hole, plays a ball from outside the teeing ground, the opponent may immediately require the player to cancel the stroke so played and play a ball from within the teeing ground, without penalty.

b. Stroke Play

If a competitor, when starting a hole, plays a ball from outside the teeing ground, *he shall incur a penalty of two strokes* and shall then play a ball from within the teeing ground.

If the competitor plays a stroke from the next teeing ground without first correcting his mistake or, in the case of the last hole of the round, leaves the putting green, without first declaring his intention to correct his mistake, *he shall be disqualified.*

Strokes played by a competitor from outside the teeing ground do not count in his score.

11-5. Playing from Wrong Teeing Ground

The provisions of Rule 11-4 apply.

PLAYING THE BALL

Rule 12. Searching for and Identifying Ball

Definitions

A "hazard" is any bunker or water hazard.

A "bunker" is a hazard consisting of a prepared area of ground, often a hollow, from which turf or soil has been removed and replaced with sand or the like. Grass-covered ground bordering or within a bunker is not part of the bunker. The margin of a bunker extends vertically downwards, but not upwards. A ball is in a bunker when it lies in or any part of it touches the water hazard.

A "water hazard" is any sea, lake, pond, river, ditch, surface drainage ditch or other open water course (whether or not containing water) and anything of a similar nature.

All ground or water within the margin of a water hazard is part of the water hazard. The margin of a water hazard extends vertically upwards and downwards. Stakes and lines defining the margins of water hazards are in the hazards. Such stakes are obstructions. A ball is in a water hazard when it lies in or any part of it touches the water hazard.

12-1. Searching for Ball; Seeing Ball

In searching for his ball anywhere on the course, the player may touch or bend long grass, rushes, bushes, whins, heather or the like, but only to the extent necessary to find and identify it, provided that this does not improve the lie of the ball, the area of his intended swing or his line of play.

A player is not necessarily entitled to see his ball when playing a stroke.

In a hazard, if the ball is covered by loose impediments or sand, the player may remove by probing, raking or other means as much thereof as will enable him to see a part of the ball. If an excess is removed, no penalty is incurred and the ball shall be re-covered so that only a part of the ball is visible. If the ball is moved in such removal, no penalty is incurred; the ball shall be replaced and, if necessary, re-covered. As to removal of loose impediments outside a hazard, see Rule 23.

If a ball lying in casual water, ground under repair or a hole, cast or runway made by a burrowing animal, a reptile or a bird is accidentally moved during search, no penalty is incurred; the ball shall be replaced, unless the player elects to proceed under Rule 25-1b.

If a ball is believed to be lying in water in a water hazard, the player may probe for it with a club or otherwise. If the ball is moved in so doing, no penalty is incurred; the ball shall be replaced, unless the player elects to proceed under Rule 26-1.

PENALTY FOR BREACH OF RULE 12-1:
Match play – Loss of hole; Stroke play – Two strokes.

12-2. Identifying Ball

The responsibility for playing the proper ball rests with the player. Each player should put an identification mark on his ball.

Except in a hazard, the player may, without penalty, lift a ball he believes to be his own for the purpose of identification and clean it to the extent necessary for identification. If the ball is the player's ball, he shall replace it. Before lifting the ball, the player must announce his intention to his opponent in match play or his marker or a fellow-competitor in stroke play and mark the position of the ball. He must then give his opponent, marker or fellow-competitor an opportunity to observe the lifting and replacement. If he lifts his ball without announcing his intention in advance, marking the position of the ball or giving his opponent, marker or fellow-competitor an opportunity to observe, or if he lifts his ball for identification in a hazard, or cleans it more than necessary for identification, *he shall incur a penalty of one stroke* and the ball shall be replaced.

If a player who is required to replace a ball fails to do so, *he shall incur the penalty* for a breach of Rule 20-3a, but no additional penalty under Rule 12-2 shall be applied.

Rule 13. Ball Played As It Lies; Lie, Area of Intended Swing and Line of Play; Stance

Definitions

A "hazard" is any bunker or water hazard.

A "bunker" is a hazard consisting of a prepared area of ground, often a hollow, from which turf or soil has been removed and replaced with sand or the like. Grass-covered ground bordering or within a bunker is not part of the bunker. The margin of a bunker extends vertically downwards, but not upwards. A ball is in a bunker when it lies in or any part of it touches the bunker.

A "water hazard" is any sea, lake, pond, river, ditch, surface drainage ditch or other open water course (whether or not containing water) and anything of a similar nature.

All ground or water within the margin of a water hazard is part of the water hazard. The margin of a water hazard extends vertically upwards and downwards. Stakes and lines defining the margins of water hazards are in the hazards. Such stakes are obstructions. A ball is in a water hazard when it lies in or any part of it touches the water hazard.

The "line of play" is the direction which the player wishes his ball to take after a stroke, plus a reasonable distance on either side of the intended direction. The line of play extends vertically upwards from the ground, but does not extend beyond the hole.

13-1. Ball Played As It Lies

The ball shall be played as it lies, except as otherwise provided in the Rules. (Ball at rest moved – see Rule 18.)

13-2. Improving Lie, Area of Intended Swing or Line of Play

Except as provided in the Rules, a player shall not improve or allow to be improved:

the position or lie of his ball,

the area of his intended swing,

his line of play or a reasonable extension of that line beyond the hole or

the area in which he is to drop or place a ball

by any of the following actions:

moving, bending or breaking anything growing or fixed (including immovable obstructions and objects defining out of bounds) or

removing or pressing down sand, loose soil, replaced divots, other cut turf placed in position or other irregularities of surface

except as follows:

as may occur in fairly taking his stance,

in making a stroke or the backward movement of his club for a stroke,

on the teeing ground in creating or eliminating irregularities of surface, or

on the putting green in removing sand and

loose soil as provided in Rule 16-1a or in repairing damage as provided in Rule 16-1c.

The club may be grounded only lightly and shall not be pressed on the ground.

Exception: Ball in hazard – see Rule 13-4.

13-3. Building Stance

A player is entitled to place his feet firmly in taking his stance, but he shall not build a stance.

13-4. Ball in Hazard

Except as provided in the Rules, before making a stroke at a ball which is in a hazard (whether a bunker or a water hazard), or which, having been lifted from a hazard, may be dropped or placed in the hazard, the player shall not:

a. Test the condition of the hazard or any similar hazard,

b. Touch the ground in the hazard or water in the water hazard with a club or otherwise, or

c. Touch or move a loose impediment lying in or touching the hazard.

Exceptions:

1. Provided nothing is done which constitutes testing the condition of the hazard or improves the lie of the ball, there is no penalty if the player (a) touches the ground in any hazard or water in a water hazard as a result of or to prevent falling, in removing an obstruction, in measuring or in retrieving or lifting a ball under any Rule or (b) places his clubs in a hazard.

2. The player after playing the stroke, or his caddie at any time without the authority of the player, may smooth sand or soil in the hazard, provided that, if the ball is still in the hazard, nothing is done which improves the lie of the ball or assists the player in his subsequent play of the hole.

Note: At any time, including at address or in the backward movement for the stroke, the player may touch with a club or otherwise any obstruction, any construction declared by the Committee to be an integral part of the course or any grass, bush, tree or other growing thing.

PENALTY FOR BREACH OF RULE: *Match play – Loss of hole; Stroke play – Two strokes.*
(Searching for ball – see Rule 12-1.)

Rule 14. Striking the Ball

Definition

A "stroke" is the forward movement of the club made with the intention of fairly striking at and moving the ball, but if a player checks his downswing voluntarily before the clubhead reaches the ball he is deemed not to have made a stroke.

14-1. Ball to be Fairly Struck At

The ball shall be fairly struck at with the head of the club and must not be pushed, scraped or spooned.

14-2. Assistance

In making a stroke, a player shall not accept physical assistance or protection from the elements.

PENALTY FOR BREACH OF RULE 14-1 or -2;
Match play – Loss of hole; Stroke play – Two strokes.

14-3. Artificial Devices and Unusual Equipment

A player in doubt as to whether use of an item would constitute a breach of Rule 14-3 should consult the Royal & Ancient Golf Club of St Andrews.

A manufacturer may submit to the Royal & Ancient Golf Club of St Andrews a sample of an item which is to be manufactured for a ruling as to whether its use during a stipulated round would cause a player to be in breach of Rule 14-3. Such sample will become the property of the Royal & Ancient Golf Club of St Andrews for reference purposes. If a manufacturer fails to submit a sample before manufacturing and/or marketing the club, he assumes the risk of a ruling that use of the item would be contrary to the Rules of Golf.

Except as provided in the Rules, during a stipulated round the player shall not use any artificial device or unusual equipment:

a. Which might assist him in making a stroke or in his play; or

b. For the purpose of gauging or measuring distance or conditions which might affect his play; or

c. Which might assist him in gripping the club, except that:

(i) plain gloves may be worn;

(ii) resin, powder and drying or moisturising agents may be used;

(iii) tape or gauze may be applied to the grip (provided such application does not render the grip non-conforming under Rule 4-1c); and

(iv) a towel or handkerchief may be wrapped around the grip.

PENALTY FOR BREACH OF RULE 14-3:
Disqualification.

14-4. Striking the Ball More than Once

If a player's club strikes the ball more than once in the course of a stroke, the player shall count the stroke and *add a penalty stroke*, making two strokes in all.

14-5. Playing Moving Ball

A player shall not play while his ball is moving.

Exceptions:

Ball falling off tee – Rule 11-3.

Striking the ball more than once – Rule 14-4.

Ball moving in water – Rule 14-6.

When the ball begins to move only after the player has begun the <u>stroke</u> or the backward movement of his club for the stroke, he shall incur no penalty under this Rule for playing a moving ball, but he is not exempt from any penalty incurred under the following Rules

Ball at rest moved by player – Rule 18-2a.

Ball at rest moving after address – Rule 18-2b.

Ball at rest moving after loose impediment touched – Rule 18-2c.

(Ball purposely deflected or stopped by player, partner or caddie – see Rule 1-2.)

14-6. Ball Moving in Water

When a ball is moving in water in a <u>water hazard</u>, the player may, without penalty, make a <u>stroke</u>, but he must not delay making his stroke in order to allow the wind or current to improve the position of the ball. A ball moving in water in a water hazard may be lifted if the player elects to invoke Rule 26.

PENALTY FOR BREACH OF RULE 14-5 or -6:
Match play – Loss of hole; Stroke play –
Two strokes.

Rule 15. Wrong Ball; Substituted Ball

Definition

A "wrong ball" is any ball other than the player's:

a. <u>Ball in play</u>,

b. <u>Provisional ball</u>, or

c. Second ball played under Rule 3-3 or Rule 20-7b in stroke play.

Note: Ball in play includes a ball substituted for the ball in play whether or not such substitution is permitted.

15-1. General

A player must hole out with the ball played from the <u>teeing ground</u> unless a Rule permits him to substitute another ball. If a player substitutes another ball when not so permitted, that ball is not a <u>wrong ball</u>; it becomes the ball in play and, if the error is not corrected as provided in Rule 20-6, *the player shall incur a penalty of loss of hole in match play or two strokes in stroke play.*

(Playing from wrong place – see Rule 20-7.)

15-2. Match Play

If a player plays a stroke with a <u>wrong ball</u> except in a <u>hazard</u>, *he shall lose the hole.*

If a player plays any strokes in a hazard with a wrong ball, there is no penalty. Strokes played in a hazard with a wrong ball do not count in the player's score. If the wrong ball belongs to another player, its owner shall place a ball on the spot from which the wrong ball was first played.

If the player and opponent exchange balls during the play of a hole, the first to play the wrong ball other than from a hazard shall lose the hole; when this cannot be determined, the hole shall be played out with the balls exchanged.

15-3. Stroke Play

If a competitor plays a stroke or strokes with a <u>wrong ball</u>, *he shall incur a penalty of two strokes,* unless the only stroke or strokes played with such ball were played when it was in a hazard, in which case no penalty is incurred.

The competitor must correct his mistake by playing the correct ball. If he fails to correct his mistake before he plays a stroke from the next <u>teeing ground</u> or, in the case of the last hole of the round, fails to declare his intention to correct his mistake before leaving the <u>putting green</u>, *he shall be disqualified.*

Strokes played by a competitor with a wrong ball do not count in his score.

If the wrong ball belongs to another competitor, its owner shall place a ball on the spot from which the wrong ball was first played.

(Lie of ball to be placed or replaced altered – see Rule 20-3b.)

THE PUTTING GREEN

Rule 16. The Putting Green

Definitions

The "putting green" is all ground of the hole being played which is specially prepared for putting or otherwise defined as such by the Committee. A ball is on the putting green when any part of it touches the putting green.

The "line of putt" is the line which the player wishes his ball to take after a stroke on the <u>putting green</u>. Except with respect to Rule 16-1e, the line of putt includes a reasonable distance on either side of the intended line. The line of putt does not extend beyond the hole.

A ball is "holed" when it is at rest within the circumference of the hole and all of it is below the level of the lip of the hole.

16-1. General

a. Touching Line of Putt

The <u>line of putt</u> must not be touched except:

(i)   the player may move sand and loose soil on the putting green and other <u>loose impediments</u> by picking them up or by brushing them aside with his hand or a club without pressing anything down;

(ii) in addressing the ball, the player may place the club in front of the ball without pressing anything down;

(iii) in measuring – Rule 10-4;

(iv) in lifting the ball – Rule 16-1b;

(v) in pressing down a ball-marker;

(vi) in repairing old hole plugs or ball marks on the putting green – Rule 16-1c; and

(vii) in removing movable obstructions – Rule 24-1.

(Indicating line for putting on putting green – see Rule 8-2b.)

b. Lifting Ball

A ball on the putting green may be lifted and, if desired, cleaned. A ball so lifted shall be replaced on the spot from which it was lifted.

c. Repair of Hole Plugs, Ball Marks and Other Damage

The player may repair an old hole plug or damage to the putting green caused by the impact of a ball, whether or not the player's ball lies on the putting green. If the ball is moved in the process of such repair, it shall be replaced, without penalty. Any other damage to the putting green shall not be repaired if it might assist the player in his subsequent play of the hole.

d. Testing Surface

During the play of a hole, a player shall not test the surface of the putting green by rolling a ball or roughening or scraping the surface.

e. Standing Astride or on Line of Putt

The player shall not make a stroke on the putting green from a stance astride, or with either foot touching, the line of putt or an extension of that line behind the ball.

f. Position of Caddie or Partner

While making a stroke on the putting green, the player shall not allow his caddie, his partner or his partner's caddie to position himself on or close to an extension of the line of putt behind the ball.

g. Playing Stroke While Another Ball in Motion

The player shall not play a stroke while another ball is in motion after a stroke from the putting green, except that, if a player does so, he incurs no penalty if it was his turn to play.

(Lifting ball interfering with or assisting play while another ball in motion – see Rule 22.)

PENALTY FOR BREACH OF RULE 16-1:

Match play – Loss of hole; Stroke play – Two strokes.

16-2. Ball Overhanging Hole

When any part of the ball overhangs the lip of the hole, the player is allowed enough time to reach the hole without unreasonable delay and an additional ten seconds to determine whether the ball is at rest. If by then the ball has not fallen into the hole, it is deemed to be at rest. If the ball subsequently falls into the hole, the player is deemed to have holed out with his last stroke, and *he shall add a penalty stroke to his score* for the hole; otherwise there is no penalty under this Rule.

(Undue delay – see Rule 6-7.)

Rule 17. The Flagstick

17-1. Flagstick Attended, Removed or Held Up

Before and during the stroke, the player may have the flagstick attended, removed or held up to indicate the position of the hole. This may be done only on the authority of the player before he plays his stroke.

If, prior to the stroke, the flagstick is attended, removed or held up by anyone with the player's knowledge and no objection is made, the player shall be deemed to have authorised it. If anyone attends or holds up the flagstick or stands near the hole while a stroke is being played, he shall be deemed to be attending the flagstick until the ball comes to rest.

17-2. Unauthorised Attendance

a. Match Play

In match play, an opponent or his caddie shall not, without the authority or prior knowledge of the player, attend, remove or hold up the flagstick while the player is making a stroke or his ball is in motion.

b. Stroke Play

In stroke play, if a fellow-competitor or his caddie attends, removes or holds up the flagstick without the competitor's authority or prior knowledge while the competitor is making a stroke or his ball is in motion, *the fellow-competitor shall incur the penalty* for breach of this Rule. In such circumstances, if the competitor's ball strikes the flagstick, the person attending it, or anything carried by him, the competitor incurs no penalty and the ball shall be played as it lies, except that, if the stroke was played from the putting green, the stroke shall be cancelled, the ball replaced and the stroke replayed.

PENALTY FOR BREACH OF RULE 17-1 or -2: *Match play – Loss of hole; Stroke play – Two strokes.*

17-3. Ball Striking Flagstick or Attendant

The player's ball shall not strike:

a. The flagstick when attended, removed or held up by the player, his partner or either of their caddies, or by another person with the player's authority or prior knowledge; or

b. The player's caddie, his partner or his partner's caddie when attending the flagstick, or another person attending the flagstick with the player's authority or prior knowledge, or anything carried by any such person; or

c. The flagstick in the hole, unattended, when the ball has been played from the putting green.

PENALTY FOR BREACH OF RULE 17-3;
Match play – Loss of hole; Stroke play – Two strokes, and the ball shall be played as it lies.

17-4. Ball Resting Against Flagstick

If the ball rests against the flagstick when it is in the hole, the player or another person authorised by him may move or remove the flagstick and if the ball falls into the hole, the player shall be deemed to have holed out with his last stroke; otherwise the ball, if moved, shall be placed on the lip of the hole, without penalty.

BALL MOVED, DEFLECTED OR STOPPED

Rule 18. Ball At Rest Moved

Definitions

A ball is deemed to have "moved" if it leaves its position and comes to rest in any other place.

An "outside agency" is any agency not part of the match or, in stroke play, not part of the competitor's side, and includes a referee, a marker, an observer and a forecaddie. Neither wind nor water is an outside agency.

"Equipment" is anything used, worn or carried by or for the player except any ball he has played at the hole being played and any small object, such as a coin or a tee, when used to mark the position of a ball or the extent of an area in which a ball is to be dropped. Equipment includes a golf cart, whether or not motorised. If such a cart is shared by two or more players, the cart and everything in it are deemed to be the equipment of the player whose ball is involved except that, when the cart is being moved by one of the players sharing it, the cart and everything in it are deemed to be that player's equipment.

Note: A ball played at the hole being played is equipment when it has been lifted and not put back into play.

A player has "addressed the ball" when he has taken his stance and has also grounded his club, except that in a hazard a player has addressed the ball when he has taken his stance.

Taking the "stance" consists in a player placing his feet in position for and preparatory to making a stroke.

18-1. By Outside Agency

If a ball at rest is moved by an outside agency, the player shall incur no penalty and the ball shall

be replaced before the player plays another stroke.

(Player's ball at rest moved by another ball – see Rule 18-5.)

18-2. By Player, Partner, Caddie or Equipment

a. General

When a player's ball is in play, if:

(i)   the player, his partner or either of their caddies lifts or moves it, touches it purposely (except with a club in the act of addressing it) or causes it to move except as permitted by a Rule, or

(ii) equipment of the player or his partner causes the ball to move,

the player shall incur a penalty stroke. The ball shall be replaced unless the movement of the ball occurs after the player has begun his swing and he does not discontinue his swing.

Under the Rules no penalty is incurred if a player accidentally causes his ball to move in the following circumstances:

> In measuring to determine which ball farther from hole – Rule 10-4

> In searching for covered ball in hazard or for ball in casual water, ground under repair, etc. – Rule 12-1

> In the process of repairing hole plug or ball mark – Rule 16-1c
> In the process of removing loose impediment on putting green – Rule 18-2c

> In the process of lifting ball under a Rule – Rule 20-1

> In the process of placing or replacing ball under a Rule – Rule 20-3a

> In removal of movable obstruction – Rule 24-1.

b. Ball Moving After Address

If a player's ball in play moves after he has addressed it (other than as a result of a stroke), the player shall be deemed to have moved the ball and *shall incur a penalty stroke.* The player shall replace the ball unless the movement of the ball occurs after he has begun his swing and he does not discontinue his swing.

c. Ball Moving After Loose Impediment Touched

Through the green, if the ball moves after any loose impediment lying within a club-length of it has been touched by the player, his partner or either of their caddies and before the player has addressed it, the player shall be deemed to have moved the ball and *shall incur a penalty stroke.* The player shall replace the ball unless the movement of the ball occurs after he has begun his swing and he does not discontinue his swing.

On the putting green, if the ball or the ball-marker <u>moves</u> in the process of removing any <u>loose impediment</u>, the ball or the ball-marker shall be replaced. There is no penalty provided the movement of the ball or the ball-marker is directly attributable to the removal of the loose impediment. Otherwise, *the player shall incur a penalty stroke* under Rule 18-2a or 20-1.

18-3. By Opponent, Caddie or Equipment in Match Play

a. During Search

If, during search for a player's ball, the ball is moved by an opponent, his caddie or his <u>equipment</u>, no penalty is incurred and the player shall replace the ball.

b. Other Than During Search

If, other than during search for a ball, the ball is touched or moved by an opponent, his caddie or his <u>equipment</u>, except as otherwise provided in the Rules, *the opponent shall incur a penalty stroke.* The player shall replace the ball.

(Ball moved in measuring to determine which ball farther from the hole – see Rule 10-4.)

(Playing a wrong ball – see Rule 15-2.)

18-4. By Fellow-Competitor, Caddie or Equipment in Stroke Play

If a competitor's ball is moved by a fellow-competitor, his caddie or his <u>equipment</u>, no penalty is incurred. The competitor shall replace his ball.

(Playing a wrong ball – see Rule 15-3.)

18-5. By Another Ball

If a ball in play and at rest is moved by another ball in motion after a stroke, the moved ball shall be replaced.

*PENALTY FOR BREACH OF RULE:

Match play – Loss of hole. Stroke play –
Two strokes.

*If a player who is required to replace a ball fails to do so, he shall incur the general penalty for breach of Rule 18 but no additional penalty under Rule 18 shall be applied.

Note 1: If a ball to be replaced under this Rule is not immediately recoverable, another ball may be substituted.

Note 2: If it is impossible to determine the spot on which a ball is to be placed, see Rule 20-3c.

Rule 19. Ball in Motion Deflected or Stopped

Definitions

An "outside agency" is any agency not part of the match or, in stroke play, not part of the competitor's side, and includes a referee, a marker, an observer and a forecaddie. Neither wind nor water is an outside agency.

"Equipment" is anything used, worn or carried by or for the player except any ball he has played at the hole being played and any small object, such as a coin or a tee, when used to mark the position of a ball or the extent of an area in which a ball is to be dropped. Equipment includes a golf cart, whether or not motorised. If such a cart is shared by two or more players, the cart and everything in it are deemed to be the equipment of the player whose ball is involved except that, when the cart is being moved by one of the players sharing it, the cart and everything in it are deemed to be that player's equipment.

Note: A ball played at the hole being played is equipment when it has been lifted and not put back into play.

19-1. By Outside Agency

If a ball in motion is accidentally deflected or stopped by any <u>outside</u> <u>agency</u>, it is a <u>rub</u> <u>of the green</u>, no penalty is incurred and the ball shall be played as it lies except:

a. If a ball in motion after a <u>stroke</u> other than on the <u>putting green</u> comes to rest in or on any moving or animate outside agency, the player shall, <u>through</u> <u>the green</u> or in a <u>hazard</u>, drop the ball, or on the putting green place the ball, as near as possible to the spot where the outside agency was when the ball came to rest in or on it, and

b. If a ball in motion after a stroke on the putting green is deflected or stopped by, or comes to rest in or on any moving or animate outside agency except a worm or an insect, the stroke shall be cancelled, the ball replaced and the stroke re-played.

If the ball is not immediately recoverable, another ball may be substituted.

(Player's ball deflected or stopped by another ball – see Rule 19-5.)

Note: If the referee or the Committee determines that a player's ball has been purposely deflected or stopped by an <u>outside</u> <u>agency</u>, Rule 1-4 applies to the player. If the outside agency is a fellow-competitor or his caddie, Rule 1-2 applies to the fellow-competitor.

19-2. By Player, Partner, Caddie or Equipment

a. Match Play

If a player's ball is accidentally deflected or stopped by himself, his partner or either of their caddies or <u>equipment</u>, *he shall lose the hole.*

b. Stroke Play

If a competitor's ball is accidentally deflected or stopped by himself, his partner or either of their caddies or <u>equipment</u>, *the competitor shall incur a penalty of two strokes.* The ball shall be played as it lies, except when it comes to rest in or on the competitor's, his partner's or either of their caddies' clothes or equipment, in which case the competitor shall, <u>through</u> <u>the</u> <u>green</u> or in a <u>hazard</u>, drop the ball, or on the <u>putting green</u> place the ball, as near as possible to where the article was when the ball came to rest in or on it.

Exception: Dropped Ball – see Rule 20-2a.

(Ball purposely deflected or stopped by player, partner or caddie – see Rule 1-2.)

19-3. By Opponent, Caddie or Equipment in Match Play

If a player's ball is accidentally deflected or stopped by an opponent, his caddie or his <u>equipment</u>, no penalty is incurred. The player may play the ball as it lies or, before another <u>stroke</u> is played by either side, cancel the stroke and play a ball without penalty as nearly as possible at the spot from which the original ball was last played (see Rule 20-5).

If the ball has come to rest in or on the opponent's or his caddie's clothes or equipment, the player may <u>through</u> <u>the</u> <u>green</u> or in a <u>hazard</u> drop the ball, or on the putting green place the ball, as near as possible to where the article was when the ball came to rest in or on it.

Exception: Ball striking person attending flagstick – see Rule 17-3b.

(Ball purposely deflected or stopped by opponent or caddie – see Rule 1-2.)

19-4. By Fellow-Competitor, Caddie or Equipment in Stroke Play

See Rule 19-1 regarding ball deflected by outside agency.

19-5. By Another Ball

a. At Rest

If a player's ball in motion after a stroke is deflected or stopped by a ball in play and at rest, the player shall play his ball as it lies.

In match play no penalty is incurred. In stroke play, there is no penalty unless both balls lay on the putting green prior to the stroke, in which case *the player incurs a penalty of two strokes.*

b. In Motion

If a player's ball in motion after a stroke is deflected or stopped by another ball in motion after a stroke, the player shall play his ball as it lies. There is no penalty unless the player was in breach of Rule 16-1g, in which case *he shall incur the penalty for breach of that Rule.*

Exception: If the player's ball is in motion after a stroke on the putting green and the other ball in motion is an outside agency – see Rule 19-1b.

PENALTY FOR BREACH OF RULE:
Match play – Loss of hole;
Stroke play – Two strokes.

RELIEF SITUATIONS AND PROCEDURE

Rule 20. Lifting, Dropping and Placing: Playing from Wrong Place

20-1 Lifting

A ball to be lifted under the Rules may be lifted by the player, his partner or another person authorised by the player. In any such case, the player shall be responsible for any breach of the Rules.

The position of the ball shall be marked before it is lifted under a Rule which requires it to be replaced. If it is not marked, the player *shall incur a penalty of one stroke* and the ball shall be replaced. If it is not replaced, *the player shall incur the general penalty* for breach of this Rule but no additional penalty under Rule 20-1 shall be applied.

If a ball or ball-marker is accidentally moved in the process of lifting the ball under a Rule or marking its position, the ball or the ball-marker shall be replaced. There is no penalty provided the movement of the ball or the ball-marker is directly attributable to the specific act of marking the position of, or lifting the ball. Otherwise *the player shall incur a penalty stroke* under this Rule or Rule 18-2a.

Exception: If a player incurs a penalty for failing to act in accordance with Rule 5-3 or 12-2 no additional penalty under Rule 20-1 shall be applied.

Note: The position of a ball to be lifted should be marked by placing a ball-marker, a small coin or other similar object immediately behind the ball. If the ball-marker interferes with the play, <u>stance</u> or <u>stroke</u> of another player, it should be placed one or more clubhead-lengths to one side.

20-2. Dropping and Re-dropping

a. By Whom and How

A ball to be dropped under the Rules shall be dropped by the player himself. He shall stand erect, hold the ball at shoulder height and arm's length and drop it. If a ball is dropped by any other person or in any other manner and the error is not corrected as provided in Rule 20-6, *the player shall incur a penalty stroke.*

If the ball touches the player, his partner, either of their caddies or their equipment before or after it strikes a part of the course, the ball shall be re-dropped, without penalty. There is no limit to the number of times a ball shall be re-dropped in such circumstances.

(Taking action to influence position or movement of ball – see Rule 1-2.)

b. Where to Drop

When a ball is to be dropped as near as possible to a specific spot, it shall be dropped not nearer the hole than the specific spot which, if it is not precisely known to the player, shall be estimated.

A ball when dropped must first strike a part of

the course where the applicable Rule requires it to be dropped. If it is not so dropped, Rules 20-6 and -7 apply.

c. When to Re-drop

A dropped ball shall be re-dropped without penalty if it:

(i) rolls into a <u>hazard</u>;
(ii) rolls out of a hazard;
(iii) rolls onto a <u>putting green</u>;
(iv) rolls <u>out of bounds</u>;
(v) rolls to a position where there is interference by the condition from which relief was taken under Rule 24-2 (immovable obstruction) or Rule 25-1 (abnormal ground conditions), or rolls back into the pitch-mark from which it was lifted under Rule 25-2 (embedded ball);
(vi) rolls and comes to rest more than two club-lengths from where it first struck a part of the course; or
(vii) rolls and comes to rest nearer the hole than its original position or estimated position (see Rule 20-2b) unless otherwise permitted by the Rules.
(viii) rolls and comes to rest nearer the hole than the point where the original ball last crossed the margin of the area of the hazard (Rule 25-1c(i) and (ii)) or the margin of the water hazard (Rule 26-1b) or lateral water hazard (Rule 26-1c).

If the ball when re-dropped rolls into any position listed above, it shall be placed as near as possible to the spot where it first struck a part of the course when re-dropped.

If a ball to be re-dropped or placed under this Rule is not immediately recoverable, another ball may be substituted.

20-3. Placing and Replacing

a. By Whom and Where

A ball to be placed under the Rules shall be placed by the player or his partner. If a ball is to be replaced, the player, his partner or the person who lifted or moved it shall place it on the spot from which it was lifted or moved. In any such case, the player shall be responsible for any breach of the Rules.

If a ball or ball-marker is accidentally moved in the process of placing or replacing the ball, the ball or the ball-marker shall be replaced. There is no penalty provided the movement of the ball or the ball-marker is directly attributable to the specific act of placing or replacing the ball or removing the ball-marker. Otherwise, *the player shall incur a penalty stroke* under Rule 18-2a or 20-1.

b. Lie of Ball to Be Placed or Replaced Altered

If the original lie of a ball to be placed or replaced has been altered:

(i) except in a <u>hazard</u>, the ball shall be placed in the nearest lie most similar to the original lie which is not more than one club-length from the original lie, not nearer the hole and not in a hazard;
(ii) in a <u>water</u> hazard, the ball shall be placed in accordance with Clause (i) above, except that the ball must be placed in the water hazard;
(iii) in a <u>bunker</u>, the original lie shall be recreated as nearly as possible and the ball shall be placed in that lie.

c. Spot Not Determinable

If it is impossible to determine the spot where the ball is to be placed or replaced:

(i) <u>through the green</u>, the ball shall be dropped as near as possible to the place where it lay but not in a <u>hazard</u> or on a <u>putting green</u>;
(ii) in a hazard, the ball shall be dropped in the hazard as near as possible to the place where it lay;
(iii) on the <u>putting green</u>, the ball shall be placed as near as possible to the place where it lay but not in a hazard.

d. Ball Fails to Come to Rest on Spot

If a ball when placed fails to come to rest on the spot on which it was placed, it shall be replaced without penalty. If it still fails to come to rest on that spot:

(i) except in a <u>hazard</u>, it shall be placed at the nearest spot not nearer the hole or in a hazard where it can be placed at rest;
(ii) in a hazard, it shall be placed in the hazard at the nearest spot not nearer the hole where it can be placed at rest.

If a ball when placed comes to rest on the spot on which it is placed, and it subsequently moves, there is no penalty and the ball shall be played as it lies, unless the provisions of any other Rule apply.

PENALTY FOR BREACH OF RULE 20-1, -2 or -3: *Match play – Loss of hole; Stroke play – Two strokes.*

20-4. When Ball Dropped or Placed is in Play

If the player's <u>ball in play</u> has been lifted, it is again in play when dropped or placed.

A substituted ball becomes the ball in play when it has been dropped or placed.

(Ball incorrectly substituted – see Rule 15-1.)

(Lifting ball incorrectly substituted, dropped or placed – see Rule 20-6.)

20-5. Playing Next Stroke from Where Previous Stroke Played

When, under the Rules, a player elects or is required to play his next <u>stroke</u> from where a previous stroke was played, he shall proceed as follows: if the stroke is to be played from the <u>teeing ground</u>, the ball to be played shall be played from anywhere within the teeing ground and may be teed; if the stroke is to be played from <u>through the green</u> or a <u>hazard</u>, it shall be dropped; if the stroke is to be played on the <u>putting green</u>, it shall be placed.

PENALTY FOR BREACH OF RULE 20-5:
Match play – Loss of hole; Stroke play – Two strokes.

20-6. Lifting Ball Incorrectly Substituted, Dropped or Placed

A ball incorrectly substituted, dropped or placed in a wrong place or otherwise not in accordance with the Rules but not played may be lifted, without penalty, and the player shall then proceed correctly.

20-7. Playing from Wrong Place

For a ball played from outside the teeing ground or from a wrong teeing ground – see Rule 11-4 and -5.

a. Match Play

If a player plays a stroke with a ball which has been dropped or placed in a wrong place, *he shall lose the hole.*

b. Stroke Play

If a competitor plays a stroke with his <u>ball in play</u> (i) which has been dropped or placed in a wrong place or (ii) which has been moved and not replaced in a case where the Rules require replacement, *he shall,* provided a serious breach has not occurred, *incur the penalty prescribed by the applicable Rule* and play out the hole with the ball.

If, after playing from a wrong place, a competitor becomes aware of that fact and believes that a serious breach may be involved, he may, provided he has not played a stroke from the next teeing ground or, in the case of the last hole of the round, left the putting green, declare that he will play out the hole with a second ball dropped or placed in accordance with the Rules. The competitor shall report the facts to the Committee before returning his score card; if he fails to do so, *he shall be disqualified.* The Committee shall determine whether a serious breach of the Rule occurred. If so, the score with the second ball shall count and *the competitor shall add two penalty strokes to his score with that ball.*

If a serious breach has occurred and the competitor has failed to correct it as prescribed above, *he shall be disqualified.*

Note: If a competitor plays a second ball, penalty strokes incurred by playing the ball ruled not to count and strokes subsequently taken with that ball shall be disregarded.

Rule 21. Cleaning Ball

A ball on the putting green may be cleaned when lifted under Rule 16-1b. Elsewhere, a ball may be cleaned when lifted except when it has been lifted:

a. To determine if it is unfit for play (Rule 5-3);

b. For identification (Rule 12-2), in which case it may be cleaned only to the extent necessary for identification; or

c. Because it is interfering with or assisting play (Rule 22).

If a player cleans his ball during play of a hole except as provided in this Rule, *he shall incur a penalty of one stroke* and the ball, if lifted, shall be replaced.

If a player who is required to replace a ball fails to do so, *he shall incur the penalty* for breach of Rule 20-3a, but no additional penalty under Rule 21 shall be applied.

Exception: If a player incurs a penalty for failing to act in accordance with Rule 5-3, 12-2 or 22, no additional penalty under Rule 21 shall be applied.

Rule 22. Ball Interfering with or Assisting Play

Any player may:

a. Lift his ball if he considers that the ball might assist any other player or

b. Have any other ball lifted if he considers that the ball might interfere with his play or assist the play of any other player,

but this may not be done while another ball is in motion. In stroke play, a player required to lift his ball may play first rather than lift. A ball lifted under this Rule shall be replaced.

PENALTY FOR BREACH OF RULE:
Match play – Loss of hole;
Stroke play – Two strokes.

Note: Except on the putting green, the ball may not be cleaned when lifted under this Rule – see Rule 21.

Rule 23. Loose Impediments

Definition

"Loose impediments" are natural objects such as stones, leaves, twigs, branches and the like, dung, worms and insects and casts or heaps made by them, provided they are not fixed or growing, are not solidly embedded and do not adhere to the ball.

Sand and loose soil are loose impediments on the <u>putting green</u> but not elsewhere.

Snow and natural ice, other than frost, are either <u>casual water</u> or loose impediments, at the option of the player. Manufactured ice is an obstruction.

Dew and frost are not loose impediments.

23-1. Relief

Except when both the loose impediment and the ball lie in or touch the same hazard, any loose impediment may be removed without penalty. If the ball moves, see Rule 18-2c.

When a player's ball is in motion, a loose impediment which might influence the movement of the ball shall not be removed.

> PENALTY FOR BREACH OF RULE:
> *Match play – Loss of hole;*
> *Stroke play – Two strokes.*

(Searching for ball in hazard – see Rule 12-1.)
(Touching line of putt – see Rule 16-1a.)

Rule 24. Obstructions

Definition

An "obstruction" is anything artificial, including the artificial surfaces and sides of roads and paths and manufactured ice, except:

a. Objects defining out of bounds, such as walls, fences, stakes and railings;

b. Any part of an immovable artificial object which is out of bounds; and

c. Any construction declared by the Committee to be an integral part of the course.

24-1. Movable Obstruction

A player may obtain relief from a movable obstruction as follows:

a. If the ball does not lie in or on the obstruction, the obstruction may be removed. If the ball moves, it shall be replaced, and there is no penalty provided that the movement of the ball is directly attributable to the removal of obstruction. Otherwise, Rule 18-2a applies.

b. If the ball lies in or on the obstruction, the ball may be lifted, without penalty, and the obstruction removed. The ball shall through the green or in a hazard be dropped, or on the putting green be placed, as near as possible to the spot directly under the place where the ball lay in or on the obstruction, but not nearer the hole.

The ball may be cleaned when lifted under Rule 24-1.

When a ball is in motion, an obstruction which might influence the movement of the ball, other than an attended flagstick or equipment of the players, shall not be removed.

Note: If a ball to be dropped or placed under this Rule is not immediately recoverable, another ball may be substituted.

24-2. Immovable Obstruction

a. Interference

Interference by an immovable obstruction

occurs when a ball lies in or on the obstruction, or so close to the obstruction that the obstruction interferes with the player's stance or the area of his intended swing. If the player's ball lies on the putting green, interference also occurs if an immovable obstruction on the putting green intervenes on his line of putt. Otherwise, intervention on the line of play is not, of itself, interference under this Rule.

b. Relief

Except when the ball is in a water hazard or a lateral water hazard, a player may obtain relief from interference by an immovable obstruction, without penalty, as follows:

(i) **Through the Green:** If the ball lies through the green, the point on the course nearest to where the ball lies shall be determined (without crossing over, through or under the obstruction) which (a) is not nearer the hole, (b) avoids interference (as defined) and (c) is not a hazard or on a putting green. The player shall lift the ball and drop it within one club-length of the point thus determined on a part of the course which fulfils (a), (b) and (c) above.

Note: The prohibition against crossing over, through or under the obstruction does not apply to the artificial surfaces and sides of roads and paths or when the ball lies in or on the obstruction.

(ii) **In a Bunker:** If the ball is in a bunker, the player shall lift and drop the ball in accordance with Clause (i) above, except that the ball must be dropped in the bunker.

(iii) **On the Putting Green:** If the ball lies on the putting green, the player shall lift the ball and place it in the nearest position to where it lay which affords relief from interference, but not nearer the hole nor in a hazard.

The ball may be cleaned when lifted under Rule 24-2b.

(Ball rolling to a position where there is interference by the condition from which relief was taken – see Rule 20-2c(v).)

Exception: A player may not obtain relief under Rule 24-2b if (a) it is clearly unreasonable for him to play a stroke because of interference by anything other than an immovable obstruction or (b) interference by an immovable obstruction would occur only through use of an unnecessarily abnormal stance, swing or direction of play.

Note 1: If a ball is in a water hazard (including a lateral water hazard), the player is not entitled to relief without penalty from interference by an immovable obstruction. The player shall play the ball as it lies or proceed under Rule 26-1.

Note 2: If a ball to be dropped or placed under this Rule is not immediately recoverable, another ball may be substituted.

c. Ball Lost

Except in a water hazard or a lateral water hazard, if there is reasonable evidence that a ball is lost in an immovable obstruction, the player may, without penalty, substitute another ball and follow the procedure prescribed in Rule 24-2b. For the purpose of applying this Rule, the ball shall be deemed to lie at the spot where it entered the obstruction. If the ball is lost in an underground drain pipe or culvert the entrance to which is in a hazard, a ball must be dropped in that hazard or the player may proceed under Rule 26-1, if applicable.

PENALTY FOR BREACH OF RULE:
Match play – Loss of hole;
Stroke play – Two strokes.

Rule 25. Abnormal Ground Conditions and Wrong Putting Green

Definitions

"Casual water" is any temporary accumulation of water on the course which is visible before or after the player takes his stance and is not in a water hazard. Snow and natural ice, other than frost, are casual water or loose impediments, at the option of the player. Manufactured ice is an obstruction. Dew and frost are not casual water. A ball is in casual water when it lies in or any part of it touches the casual water.

"Ground under repair" is any portion of the course so marked by order of the Committee or so declared by its authorised representative. It includes material piled for removal and a hole made by a greenkeeper, even if not so marked. Stakes and lines defining ground under repair are in such ground. Stakes defining ground under repair are obstructions. The margin of ground under repair extends vertically downwards, but not upwards. A ball is in ground under repair when it lies in or any part of it touches the ground under repair.

Note 1: Grass cuttings and other material left on the course which have been abandoned and are not intended to be removed are not ground under repair unless so marked.

Note 2: The Committee may make a Local Rule prohibiting play from ground under repair or an environmentally-sensitive area which has been defined as ground under repair.

25-1. Casual Water, Ground Under Repair and Certain Damage to Course

a. Interference

Interference by casual water, ground under repair or a hole, cast or runway made by a burrowing animal, a reptile or a bird occurs when a ball lies in or touches any of these conditions or when such a condition on the course interferes

with the player's stance or the area of his intended swing.

If the player's ball lies on the putting green, interference also occurs if such condition on the putting green intervenes on his line of putt.

If interference exists, the player may either play the ball as it lies (unless prohibited by Local Rule) or take relief as provided in Clause b.

Note: The Committee may make a Local Rule denying the player relief from interference with his stance by all or any of the conditions covered by this Rule.

b. Relief

If the player elects to take relief, he shall proceed as follows:

(i) **Through the Green:** If the ball lies through the green, the point on the course nearest to where the ball lies shall be determined which (a) is not nearer the hole, (b) avoids interference by the condition, and (c) is not in a hazard or on a putting green. The player shall lift the ball and drop it without penalty within one club-length of the point thus determined on a part of the course which fulfils (a), (b) and (c) above.

(ii) **In a Hazard:** If the ball is in a hazard, the player shall lift and drop the ball either:
(a) Without penalty, in the hazard, as near as possible to the spot where the ball lay, but not nearer the hole, on a part of the course which affords maximum available relief from the condition; or
(b) *Under penalty of one stroke,* outside the hazard, keeping the point where the ball lay directly between the hole and the spot on which the ball is dropped, with no limit to how far behind the hazard the ball may be dropped.

Exception: If a ball is in a water hazard (including a lateral water hazard), the player is not entitled to relief without penalty from a hole, cast or runway made by a burrowing animal, a reptile or a bird. The player shall play the ball as it lies or proceed under Rule 26-1.

(iii) **On the Putting Green:** If the ball lies on the putting green, the player shall lift the ball and place it without penalty in the nearest position to where it lay which affords maximum available relief from the condition, but not nearer the hole nor in a hazard.

The ball may be cleaned when lifted under Rule 25-1b.

(Ball rolling to a position where there is interference by the condition from which relief is taken – see Rule 20-2c(v).)

Exception: A player may not obtain relief under Rule 25-1b if (a) it is clearly unreasonable for him to play a stroke because of interference by anything other than a condition covered by Rule 25-1a or (b) interference by such a condition would occur only through use of an unnecessarily abnormal stance, swing or direction of play.

Note: If a ball to be dropped or placed under this Rule is not immediately recoverable, another ball may be substituted.

c. Ball Lost Under Condition Covered by Rule 25-1

It is a question of fact whether a ball lost after having been struck toward a condition covered by Rule 25-1 is lost under such condition. In order to treat the ball as lost under such condition, there must be reasonable evidence to that effect. In the absence of such evidence, the ball must be treated as a lost ball and Rule 27 applies.

(i) **Outside a Hazard:** If a ball is lost outside a hazard under a condition covered by Rule 25-1, the player may take relief as follows: the point on the course nearest to where the ball last crossed the margin of the area shall be determined which (a) is not nearer the hole than where the ball last crossed the margin, (b) avoids interference by the condition and (c) is not in a hazard or on a putting green. He shall drop a ball without penalty within one club-length of the point thus determined on a part of the course which fulfils (a), (b) and (c) above.

(ii) **In a Hazard:** If a ball is lost in a hazard under a condition covered by Rule 25-1, the player may drop a ball either:
(a) Without penalty, in the hazard, as near as possible to the point at which the original ball last crossed the margin of the area, but not nearer the hole, on a part of the course, which affords maximum available relief from the condition; or
(b) *Under penalty of one stroke,* outside the hazard, keeping the point at which the original ball last crossed the margin of the hazard directly between the hole and the spot on which the ball is dropped, with no limit to how far behind the hazard the ball may be dropped.

Exception: If a ball is in a water hazard (including a lateral water hazard), the player is not entitled to relief without penalty for a ball lost in a hole, cast or runway made by a burrowing animal, a reptile or a bird. The player shall proceed under Rule 26-1.

25-2. Embedded Ball

A ball embedded in its own pitch-mark in the ground in any closely mown area through the green may be lifted, cleaned and dropped, without penalty, as near as possible to the spot where it lay but not nearer the hole. The ball when dropped must first strike a part of the course

through the green. "Closely mown area" means any area of the course, including paths through the rough, cut to fairway height or less.

25-3. Wrong Putting Green

A player must not play a ball which lies on a putting green other than that of the hole being played. The ball must be lifted and the player must proceed as follows: the point on the course nearest to where the ball lies shall be determined which (a) is not nearer the hole and (b) is not in a hazard or on a putting green. The player shall lift the ball and drop it without penalty within one club-length of the point thus determined on a part of the course which fulfils (a) and (b) above. The ball may be cleaned when so lifted.

Note: Unless otherwise prescribed by the Committee, the term "a putting green other than that of the hole being played" includes a practice putting green or pitching green on the course.

PENALTY FOR BREACH OF RULE: *Match play – Loss of hole; Stroke play – Two strokes.*

Rule 26. Water Hazards (Including Lateral Water Hazards)

Definitions

A "water hazard" is any sea, lake, pond, river, ditch, surface drainage ditch or other open water course (whether or not containing water) and anything of a similar nature.

All ground or water within the margin of a water hazard is part of the water hazard. The margin of a water hazard extends vertically upwards and downwards. Stakes and lines defining the margins of water hazards are in the hazards. Such stakes are obstructions. A ball is in a water hazard when it lies in or any part of it touches the water hazard.

Note 1: Water hazards (other than lateral water hazards) should be defined by yellow stakes or lines.

Note 2: The Committee may make a Local Rule prohibiting play from an environmentally-sensitive area which has been defined as a water hazard.

A "lateral water hazard" is a water hazard or that part of a water hazard so situated that it is not possible or is deemed by the Committee to be impracticable to drop a ball behind the water hazard in accordance with Rule 26-1b.

That part of a water hazard to be played as a lateral water hazard should be distinctively marked. A ball is in a lateral water hazard when it lies in or any part of it touches the lateral water hazard.

Note 1: Lateral water hazards should be defined by red stakes or lines.

Note 2: The Committee may make a Local Rule prohibiting play from an environmentally-sensitive area which has been defined as a water hazard.

26-1. Ball in Water Hazard

It is a question of fact whether a ball lost after having been struck toward a <u>water hazard</u> is lost inside or outside the hazard. In order to treat the ball as lost in the hazard, there must be reasonable evidence that the ball lodged in it. In the absence of such evidence, the ball must be treated as a lost ball and Rule 27 applies.

If a ball is in or is lost in a water hazard (whether the ball lies in water or not), the player may *under penalty of one stroke:*

a. Play a ball as nearly as possible at the spot from which the original ball was last played (see Rule 20-5); or

b. Drop a ball behind the water hazard, keeping the point at which the original ball last crossed the margin of the water hazard directly between the hole and the spot on which the ball is dropped, with no limit to how far behind the water hazard the ball may be dropped; or

c. *As additional options available only if the ball last crossed the margin of a lateral water hazard,* drop a ball outside the water hazard within two club-lengths of and not nearer the hole than (i) the point where the original ball last crossed the margin of the water hazard or (ii) a point on the opposite margin of the water hazard equidistant from the hole.

The ball may be cleaned when lifted under this Rule.

(Ball moving in water in a water hazard – see Rule 14-6.)

26-2. Ball Played Within Water Hazard

a. Ball Comes to Rest in the Hazard

If a ball played from within a water hazard comes to rest in the same hazard after the stroke, the player may:

(i) proceed under Rule 26-1; or

(ii) *under penalty of one stroke,* play a ball as nearly as possible at the spot from which the last stroke from outside the hazard was played (see Rule 20-5).

If the player proceeds under Rule 26-1a, he may elect not to play the dropped ball. If he so elects, he may:

(a) proceed under Rule 26-1b, *adding the additional penalty of one stroke* prescribed by that Rule; or

(b) proceed under Rule 26-1c, if applicable, *adding the additional penalty of one stroke* prescribed by that Rule; or

(c) *add an additional penalty of one stroke* and play a ball as nearly as possible at the spot from which the last stroke from outside the hazard was played (see Rule 20-5).

b. Ball Lost or Unplayable Outside Hazard or Out of Bounds

If a ball played from within a water hazard is lost or declared unplayable outside the hazard or is out of bounds, the player, after taking *a penalty of one stroke* under Rule 27-1 or 28a, may:

(i)   play a ball as nearly as possible at the spot in the hazard from which the original ball was last played (see Rule 20-5); or

(ii) proceed under Rule 26-1b, or if applicable Rule 26-1c, *adding the additional penalty of one stroke* prescribed by the Rule and using as the reference point the point where the original ball last crossed the margin of the hazard before it came to rest in the hazard; or

(iii) *add an additional penalty of one stroke* and play a ball as nearly as possible at the spot from which the last stroke from outside the hazard was played (see Rule 20-5).

Note 1: When proceeding under Rule 26-2b, the player is not required to drop a ball under Rule 27-1 or 28a. If he does drop a ball, he is not required to play it. He may alternatively proceed under clause (ii) or (iii).

Note 2: If a ball played from within a water hazard is declared unplayable outside the hazard, nothing in Rule 26-2b precludes the player from proceeding under Rule 28b or c.

PENALTY FOR BREACH OF RULE:
Match play – Loss of hole;
Stroke play – Two strokes.

Rule 27. Ball Lost or Out of Bounds; Provisional Ball

If the original ball is lost in an immovable obstruction (Rule 24-2) or under a condition covered by Rule 25-1 (Casual water, ground under repair and certain damage to the course), the player may proceed under the applicable Rule. If the original ball is lost in a water hazard, the player shall proceed under Rule 26.

Such Rules may not be used unless there is reasonable evidence that the ball is lost in an immovable obstruction, under a condition covered by Rule 25-1 or in a water hazard.

Definitions

A ball is "lost" if:

a. It is not found or identified as his by the player within five minutes after the player's side or his or their caddies have begun to search for it; or

b. The player has put another ball into play under the Rules, even though he may not have searched for the original ball; or

c. The player has played any stroke with a <u>provisional ball</u> from the place where the original ball is likely to be or from a point nearer the hole than that place, whereupon the provisional ball becomes the <u>ball in play</u>.

Time spent in playing a <u>wrong ball</u> is not counted in the five-minute period allowed for search.

"Out of bounds" is ground on which play is prohibited.

When out of bounds is defined by reference to stakes or a fence, or as being beyond stakes or a fence, the out of bounds line is determined by the nearest inside points of the stakes or fence posts at ground level excluding angled supports.

When out of bounds is defined by a line on the ground, the line itself is out of bounds.

The out of bounds line extends vertically upwards and downwards.

A ball is out of bounds when all of it lies out of bounds.

A player may stand out of bounds to play a ball lying within bounds.

A "provisional ball" is a ball played under Rule 27-2 for a ball which may be lost outside a water hazard or may be out of bounds.

27-1. Ball Lost or Out of Bounds

If a ball is lost outside a water hazard or is out of bounds, the player shall play a ball, *under penalty of one stroke*, as nearly as possible at the spot from which the original ball was last played (see Rule 20-5).

PENALTY FOR BREACH OF RULE 27-1:
Match play – Loss of hole;
Stroke play – Two strokes.

27-2. Provisional Ball

a. Procedure

If a ball may be lost outside a water hazard or may be out of bounds, to save time the player may play another ball provisionally as nearly as possible at the spot from which the original ball was played (see Rule 20-5). The player shall inform his opponent in match play or his marker or a fellow-competitor in stroke play that he intends to play a provisional ball, and he shall play it before he or his partner goes forward to search for the original ball. If he fails to do so and plays another ball, such ball is not a provisional ball and becomes the ball in play *under penalty of stroke and distance* (Rule 27-1); the original ball is deemed to be lost.

b. When Provisional Ball Becomes Ball in Play

The player may play a provisional ball until he reaches the place where the original ball is likely to be. If he plays a stroke with the provisional ball from the place where the original ball is likely to be or from a point nearer the hole than that place, the original ball is deemed to be lost and the provisional ball becomes the ball in play *under penalty of stroke and distance* (Rule 27-1).

If the original ball is lost outside a water hazard or is out of bounds, the provisional ball becomes the ball in play, *under penalty of stroke and distance* (Rule 27-1).

c. When Provisional Ball to Be Abandoned

If the original ball is neither lost outside a water hazard nor out of bounds, the player shall abandon the provisional ball and continue play with the original ball. If he fails to do so, any further strokes played with the provisional ball shall constitute playing a wrong ball and the provisions of Rule 15 shall apply.

Note: If the original ball is in a water hazard, the player shall play the ball as it lies or proceed under Rule 26. If it is lost in a water hazard or unplayable, the player shall proceed under Rule 26 or 28, whichever is applicable.

Rule 28. Ball Unplayable

The player may declare his ball unplayable at any place on the course except when the ball is in a water hazard. The player is the sole judge as to whether his ball is unplayable.

If the player deems his ball to be unplayable, he shall, *under penalty of one stroke*:

a. Play a ball as nearly as possible at the spot from which the original ball was last played (see Rule 20-5); or

b. Drop a ball within two club-lengths of the spot where the ball lay, but not nearer the hole; or

c. Drop a ball behind the point where the ball lay, keeping that point directly between the hole and the spot on which the ball is dropped, with no limit to how far behind that point the ball may be dropped.

If the unplayable ball is in a bunker the player may proceed under Clause a, b or c. If he elects to proceed under Clause b or c, a ball must be dropped in the bunker.

The ball may be cleaned when lifted under this Rule.

PENALTY FOR BREACH OF RULE:
Match play – Loss of hole;
Stroke play – Two strokes.

OTHER FORMS OF PLAY

Rule 29. Threesomes and Foursomes

Definitions

Threesome: A match in which one plays against two, and each side plays one ball.

Foursome: A match in which two play against two, and each side plays one ball.

29-1. General

In a threesome or a foursome, during any stipulated round the partners shall play alternately from the teeing grounds and alternately during the play of each hole. Penalty strokes do not affect the order of play.

29-2. Match Play

If a player plays when his partner should have played, *his side shall lose the hole.*

29-3. Stroke Play

If the partners play a stroke or strokes in incorrect order, such stroke or strokes shall be cancelled and *the side shall incur a penalty of two strokes.* The side shall correct the error by playing a ball in correct order as nearly as possible at the spot from which it first played in incorrect order (see Rule 20-5). If the side plays a stroke from the next <u>teeing</u> <u>ground</u> without first correcting the error or, in the case of the last hole of the round, leaves the <u>putting</u> <u>green</u> without declaring its intention to correct the error, *the side shall be disqualified.*

Rule 30. Three-Ball, Best-Ball and Four-Ball Match Play

Definitions

Three-Ball: A match play competition in which three play against one another, each playing his own ball. Each player is playing two distinct matches.

Best-Ball: A match in which one plays against the better ball of two or the best ball of three players.

Four-Ball: A match in which two play their better ball against the better ball of two other players.

30-1. Rules of Golf Apply

The Rules of Golf, so far as they are not at variance with the following special Rules, shall apply to three-ball, best-ball and four-ball matches.

30-2. Three-Ball Match Play

a. Ball at Rest Moved by an Opponent

Except as otherwise provided in the Rules, if the player's ball is touched or moved by an opponent, his <u>caddie</u> or <u>equipment</u> other than during search, Rule 18-3b applies. *That opponent shall incur a penalty stroke in his match with the player,* but not in his match with the other opponent.

b. Ball Deflected or Stopped by an Opponent Accidentally

If a player's ball is accidentally deflected or stopped by an opponent, his <u>caddie</u> or <u>equipment</u>, no penalty shall be incurred. In his match with that opponent the player may play the ball as it lies or, before another stroke is played by either side, he may cancel the stroke and play a ball without penalty as nearly as possible at the spot from which the original ball was last played (see Rule 20-5). In his match with the other opponent, the ball shall be played as it lies.

Exception: Ball striking person attending flagstick – see Rule 17-3b.

(Ball purposely deflected or stopped by opponent – see Rule 1-2.)

30-3. Best-Ball and Four-Ball Match Play

a. Representation of Side

A side may be represented by one partner for all or any part of a match; all partners need not be present. An absent partner may join a match between holes, but not during play of a hole.

b. Maximum of Fourteen Clubs

The side shall be penalised for a breach of Rule 4-4 by any partner.

c. Order of Play

Balls belonging to the same side may be played in the order the side considers best.

d. Wrong Ball

If a player plays a stroke with a <u>wrong</u> <u>ball</u> except in a <u>hazard</u>, *he shall be disqualified for that hole,* but his partner incurs no penalty even if the wrong ball belongs to him. If the wrong ball belongs to another player, its owner shall place a ball on the spot from which the wrong ball was first played.

e. Disqualification of Side

(i)   *A side shall be disqualified* for a breach of any of the following by any partner:

Rule 1-3 –	Agreement to Waive Rules.
Rule 4-1, -2 or -3 –	Clubs.
Rule 5-1 or -2 –	The Ball
Rule 6-2a –	Handicap (playing off higher handicap).
Rule 6-4 –	Caddie.
Rule 6-7 –	Undue Delay; Slow Play (repeated offence)
Rule 14-3 –	Artificial Devices and Unusual Equipment.

(ii) *A side shall be disqualified* for a breach of any of the following by all partners:

Rule 6-3 –	Time of Starting and Groups.
Rule 6-8 –	Discontinuance of Play.

f. Effect of Other Penalties

If a player's breach of a Rule assists his partner's play or adversely affects an opponent's play, *the partner incurs the applicable penalty in addition to any penalty incurred by the player.*

In all other cases where a player incurs a penalty for breach of a Rule, the penalty shall not apply to his partner. Where the penalty is stated to be loss of hole, the effect shall be to disqualify the player for that hole.

g. Another Form of Match Played Concurrently

In a best-ball or four-ball match when another form of match is played concurrently, the above special Rules shall apply.

Rule 31. Four-Ball Stroke Play

In four-ball stroke play two competitors play as partners, each playing his own ball. The lower score of the partners is the score for the hole. If one partner fails to complete the play of a hole, there is no penalty.

31-1. Rules of Golf Apply
The Rules of Golf, so far as they are not at variance with the following special Rules, shall apply to four-ball stroke play.

31-2. Representation of Side
A side may be represented by either partner for all or any part of a stipulated round; both partners need not be present. An absent competitor may join his partner between holes, but not during play of a hole.

31-3. Maximum of Fourteen Clubs
The side shall be penalised for a breach of Rule 4-4 by either partner.

31-4. Scoring
The marker is required to record for each hole only the gross score of whichever partner's score is to count. The gross scores to count must be individually identifiable; otherwise *the side shall be disqualified.* Only one of the partners need be responsible for complying with Rule 6-6b.
(Wrong score – see Rule 31-7a.)

31-5. Order of Play
Balls belonging to the same side may be played in the order the side considers best.

31-6. Wrong Ball
If a competitor plays a stroke or strokes with a wrong ball except in a hazard, *he shall add two penalty strokes to his score for the hole* and shall then play the correct ball. His partner incurs no penalty even if the wrong ball belongs to him.

If the wrong ball belongs to another competitor, its owner shall place a ball on the spot from which the wrong ball was first played.

31-7. Disqualification Penalties

a. Breach by One Partner
A side shall be disqualified from the competition for a breach of any of the following by either partner:

Rule 1-3 –	Agreement to Waive Rules.
Rule 3-4 –	Refusal to Comply with Rule.
Rule 4-1, -2 or -3	Clubs.
Rule 5-1 or -2 –	The Ball.
Rule 6-2b –	Handicap (playing off higher handicap; failure to record handicap).
Rule 6-4 –	Caddie.
Rule 6-6b –	Signing and Returning Card.
Rule 6-6d –	Wrong Score for Hole, i.e. when the recorded score of the partner whose score is to count is lower

than actually taken. If the recorded score of the partner whose score is to count is higher than actually taken, it must stand as returned.

Rule 6-7 –	Undue Delay; Slow Play (repeated offence).
Rule 7-1 –	Practice Before or Between Rounds.
Rule 14-3 –	Artificial Devices and Unusual Equipment.
Rule 31-4 –	Gross Scores to count Not Individually Identifiable.

b. Breach by Both Partners
A side shall be disqualified:
(i)   for a breach by both partners of Rule 6-3 (Time of Starting and Groups) or Rule 6-8 (Discontinuance of Play), or
(ii) if, at the same hole, each partner is in breach of a Rule the penalty for which is disqualification from the competition or for a hole.

c. For the Hole Only
In all other cases where a breach of a Rule would entail disqualification, *the competitor shall be disqualified only for the hole at which the breach occurred.*

31-8. Effect of Other Penalties
If a competitor's breach of a Rule assists his partner's play, *the partner incurs the applicable penalty in addition to any penalty incurred by the competitor.*

In all other cases where a competitor incurs a penalty for breach of a Rule, the penalty shall not apply to his partner.

Rule 32. Bogey, Par and Stableford Competitions

32-1. Conditions
Bogey, par and Stableford competitions are forms of stroke competition in which play is against a fixed score at each hole. The Rules for stroke play, so far as they are not at variance with the following special Rules, apply.

a. Bogey and Par Competitions
The reckoning for bogey and par competitions is made as in match play. Any hole for which a competitor makes no return shall be regarded as a loss. The winner is the competitor who is most successful in the aggregate of holes.

The marker is responsible for marking only the gross number of strokes for each hole where the competitor makes a net score equal to or less than the fixed score.

Note: Maximum of 14 Clubs – Penalties as in match play – see Rule 4-4.

b. Stableford Competitions

The reckoning in Stableford competitions is made by points awarded in relation to a fixed score at each hole as follows:

Hole Played in	Points
More than one over fixed score or no score returned	0
One over fixed score	1
Fixed score	2
One under fixed score	3
Two under fixed score	4
Three under fixed score	5
Four under fixed score	6

The winner is the competitor who scores the highest number of points.

The marker shall be responsible for marking only the gross number of strokes at each hole where the competitor's net score earns one or more points.

Note: Maximum of 14 Clubs (Rule 4-4) – Penalties applied as follows: From total points scored for the round, deduction of two points for each hole at which any breach occurred; maximum deduction per round: four points.

32-2. Disqualification Penalties

a. From the Competition

A competitor shall be disqualified from the competition for a breach of any of the following:

Rule 1-3 –	Agreement to Waive Rules.
Rule 3-4 –	Refusal to Comply with Rule.
Rule 4-1, -2 or -3 –	Clubs.
Rule 5-1 or -2 –	The Ball.
Rule 6-2b –	Handicap (playing off higher handicap; failure to record handicap).
Rule 6-3 –	Time of Starting and Groups.
Rule 6-4 –	Caddie.
Rule 6-6b –	Signing and Returning Card.
Rule 6-6d –	Wrong Score for Hole, except that no penalty shall be incurred when a breach of this Rule does not affect the result of the hole.
Rule 6-7 –	Undue Delay; Slow Play (repeated offence).
Rule 6-8 –	Discontinuance of Play.
Rule 7-1 –	Practice Before or Between Rounds.
Rule 14-3 –	Artificial Devices and Unusual Equipment.

b. For a Hole

In all other cases where a breach of a Rule would entail disqualification, *the competitor shall be disqualified only for the hole at which the breach occurred.*

ADMINISTRATION

Rule 33. The Committee

33-1. Conditions; Waiving Rule

The Committee shall lay down the conditions under which a competition is to be played.

The Committee has no power to waive a Rule of Golf.

Certain special rules governing stroke play are so substantially different from those governing match play that combining the two forms of play is not practicable and is not permitted. The results of matches played and the scores returned in these circumstances shall not be accepted.

In stroke play the Committee may limit a referee's duties.

33-2. The Course

a. Defining Bounds and Margins

The Committee shall define accurately:
(i)   the <u>course</u> and <u>out</u> of <u>bounds,</u>
(ii) the margins of <u>water</u> <u>hazards</u> and <u>lateral water</u> <u>hazards,</u>
(iii) <u>ground</u> <u>under</u> <u>repair,</u> and
(iv) <u>obstructions</u> and integral parts of the course.

b. New Holes

New holes should be made on the day on which a stroke competition begins and at such other times as the Committee considers necessary, provided all competitors in a single round play with each hole cut in the same position.

Exception: When it is impossible for a damaged hole to be repaired so that it conforms with the Definition, the Committee may make a new hole in a nearby similar position.

Note: Where a single round is to be played on more than one day, the Committee may provide in the conditions of a competition that the holes and teeing grounds may be differently situated on each day of the competition, provided that, on any one day, all competitors play with each hole and each teeing ground in the same position.

c. Practice Ground

Where there is no practice ground available outside the area of a competition <u>course,</u> the Committee should lay down the area on which players may practise on any day of a competition, if it is practicable to do so. On any day of a stroke competition, the Committee should not normally permit practice on or to a <u>putting green</u> or from a <u>hazard</u> of the competition course.

d. Course Unplayable

If the Committee or its authorised representative considers that for any reason the course is not in a playable condition or that there are circumstances which render the proper playing of the game impossible, it may, in match play or stroke play, order a temporary suspension of play or, in stroke play, declare play null and void and cancel all scores for the round in question. When play has been temporarily suspended, it shall be resumed from where it was discontinued, even though resumption occurs on a subsequent day. When a round is cancelled, all penalties incurred in that round are cancelled.

(Procedure in discontinuing play – see Rule 6-8.)

33-3. Times of Starting and Groups

The Committee shall lay down the times of starting and, in stroke play, arrange the groups in which competitors shall play.

When a match play competition is played over an extended period, the Committee shall lay down the limit of time within which each round shall be completed. When players are allowed to arrange the date of their match within these limits, the Committee should announce that the match must be played at a stated time on the last day of the period unless the players agree to a prior date.

33-4. Handicap Stroke Table

The Committee shall publish a table indicating the order of holes at which handicap strokes are to be given or received.

33-5. Score Card

In stroke play, the Committee shall issue for each competitor a score card containing the date and the competitor's name, or in foursome, or four-ball stroke play, the competitors' names.

In stroke play, the Committee is responsible for the addition of scores and application of the handicap recorded on the card.

In four-ball stroke play, the Committee is responsible for recording the better-ball score for each hole and in the process applying the handicaps recorded on the card, and adding the better-ball scores.

In bogey, par and Stableford competitions, the Committee is responsible for applying the handicap recorded on the card and determining the result of each hole and the overall result or points total.

33-6. Decision of Ties

The Committee shall announce the manner, day and time for the decision of a halved match or of a tie, whether played on level terms or under handicap.

A halved match shall not be decided by stroke play. A tie in stroke play shall not be decided by a match.

33-7. Disqualification Penalty; Committee Discretion

A penalty of disqualification may in exceptional individual cases be waived, modified or imposed if the Committee considers such action

warranted. Any penalty less than disqualification shall not be waived or modified.

33-8. Local Rules

a. Policy

The Committee may make and publish Local Rules for abnormal conditions if they are consistent with the policy of the Governing Authority for the country concerned as set forth in Appendix I to these Rules.

b. Waiving Penalty

A penalty imposed by a Rule of Golf shall not be waived by a Local Rule.

Rule 34. Disputes and Decisions

34-1. Claims and Penalties

a. Match Play

In match play if a claim is lodged with the Committee under Rule 2-5, a decision should be given as soon as possible so that the state of the match may, if necessary, be adjusted.

If a claim is not made within the time limit provided by Rule 2-5, it shall not be considered unless it is based on facts previously unknown to the player making the claim and the player making the claim had been given wrong information (Rules 6-2a and 9) by an opponent. In any case, no later claim shall be considered after the result of the match has been officially announced, unless the Committee is satisfied that the opponent knew he was giving wrong information.

There is no time limit on applying the disqualification penalty for a breach of Rule 1-3.

b. Stroke Play

Except as provided below, in stroke play, no penalty shall be rescinded, modified or imposed after the competition has closed. A competition is deemed to have closed when the result has been officially announced or, in stroke play qualifying followed by match play, when the player has teed off in his first match.

Exceptions: A penalty of disqualification shall be imposed after the competition has closed if a competitor:

(i) was in breach of Rule 1-3 (Agreement to Waive Rules); or

(ii) returned a score card on which he had recorded a handicap which, before the competition closed, he knew was higher than that to which he was entitled, and this affected the number of strokes received (Rule 6-2b); or

(iii) returned a score for any hole lower than actually taken (Rule 6-6d) for any reason other than failure to include a penalty which, before the competition closed, he did not know he had incurred; or

(iv) knew, before the competition closed, that he had been in breach of any other Rule for which the prescribed penalty is disqualification.

34-2. Referee's Decision

If a referee has been appointed by the Committee, his decision shall be final.

34-3. Committee's Decision

In the absence of a referee, any dispute or doubtful point on the Rules shall be referred to the Committee, whose decision shall be final.

If the Committee cannot come to a decision, it shall refer the dispute or doubtful point to the Rules of Golf Committee of the Royal & Ancient Golf Club of St Andrews, whose decision shall be final.

If the dispute or doubtful point has not been referred to the Rules of Golf Committee, the player or players have the right to refer an agreed statement through the Secretary of the Club to the Rules of Golf Committee for an opinion as to the correctness of the decision given. The reply will be sent to the Secretary of the Club or Clubs concerned.

If play is conducted other than in accordance with the Rules of Golf, the Rules of Golf Committee will not give a decision on any question.

APPENDIX I

LOCAL RULES (RULE 33-8) AND CONDITIONS OF THE COMPETITION (RULE 33-1)

Part A Local Rules

Rule 33-8 provides, "The Committee may make and publish Local Rules for abnormal conditions if they are consistent with the policy of the Governing Authority for the country concerned as set forth in Appendix I to these Rules. A penalty imposed by a Rule of Golf shall not be waived by a Local Rule."

Such abnormal conditions may include those listed below. Otherwise, detailed information regarding acceptable and prohibited Local Rules is provided in "Decisions on the Rules of Golf" under Rule 33-8.

If local conditions interfere with the proper playing of the game and it is considered necessary to modify a Rule of Golf, the approval of the Governing Authority must be obtained.

1. Obstructions

a. General

Clarifying the status of objects which may be obstructions (Rule 24).

Declaring any construction to be an integral part of the course and, accordingly, not an obstruction, e.g. built-up sides of teeing grounds, putting greens and bunkers (Rules 24 and 33-2a).

b. Stones in Bunkers

Allowing the removal of stones in bunkers by declaring them to be "movable obstructions" (Rule 24).

c. Roads and Paths

(i) Declaring artificial surfaces and sides of roads and paths to be integral parts of the course, or

(ii) Providing relief of the type afforded under Rule 24-2b from roads and paths not having artificial surfaces and sides if they could unfairly affect play.

d. Fixed Sprinkler Heads

Providing relief from intervention by fixed sprinkler heads within two club-lengths of the putting green when the ball lies within two club-lengths of the sprinkler head.

e. Protection of Young Trees

Providing relief for the protection of young trees.

f. Temporary Obstructions

Specimen Local Rules for temporary obstructions (e.g. grandstands, television cables and equipment, etc) for application in Tournament Play are available from the Royal & Ancient Golf Club of St Andrews.

2. Areas of the Course Requiring Preservation

Assisting preservation of the course by defining areas, including turf nurseries, young plantations and other parts of the course under cultivation, as "ground under repair" from which play is prohibited.

3. Unusual Damage to the Course or Accumulation of Leaves (or the like)

Declaring such areas to be "ground under repair" (Rule 25). The Committee may, by Local Rule, deny relief from interference with a player's stance by such areas – see Note to Rule 25-1a.

Note: For relief from aeration holes see Specimen Local Rule 8 in part B of this Appendix.

4. Extreme Wetness, Mud, Poor Conditions and Protection of Course

(a.) Lifting an Embedded Ball, Cleaning

Where the ground is unusually soft, the Committee may, by temporary Local Rule, allow the lifting of a ball which is embedded in its own pitch-mark in the ground in an area "through the green" which is not "closely mown" (Rule 25-2) if it is satisfied that the proper playing of the game would otherwise be prevented. The Local Rule shall be for that day only or for a short period, and if practicable shall be confined to specified areas. The Committee shall withdraw the Local Rule as soon as conditions warrant and should not print it on the score card.

In similarly adverse conditions, the Committee may, by temporary Local Rule, permit the cleaning of a ball "through the green".

(b.) "Preferred Lies" and "Winter Rules"

Adverse conditions, including the poor condition of the course or the existence of mud, are sometimes so general, particularly during winter months, that the Committee may decide to grant relief by Local Rule either to protect the course or to promote fair and pleasant play. Such Local Rule shall be withdrawn as soon as conditions warrant.

5. Environmentally-Sensitive Areas

When the Committee is required to prohibit play from environmentally-sensitive areas which are on or adjoin the course, it should make a Local Rule clarifying the procedure.

An environmentally-sensitive area is an area so declared by an appropriate authority, entry into and/or play from which is prohibited for environmental reasons. Such an area may be defined as ground under repair, a water hazard, a lateral water hazard or out of bounds at the discretion of the Committee provided that, in the case of an environmentally-sensitive area which has been defined as a water hazard or a lateral water hazard, the area is, by Definition, a water hazard.

Note: The Committee may not declare an area to be environmentally-sensitive.

A specimen Local Rule is detailed in "Decisions on the Rules of Golf".

Other matters which the Committee could cover by Local Rule include:

6. Water Hazards

a. Lateral Water Hazards

Clarifying the status of sections of water hazards which may be lateral water hazards (Rule 26).

b. Provisional Ball

Permitting play of a provisional ball for a ball which may be in a water hazard of such character that it would be impracticable to determine whether the ball is in the hazard or to do so would unduly delay play. In such a case, if a provisional ball is played and the original ball is in a water hazard, the player may play the original ball as it lies or continue the provisional ball in play, but he may not proceed under Rule 26-1.

7. Defining Bounds and Margins

Specifying means used to define out of bounds, hazards, water hazards, lateral water hazards and ground under repair.

8. Dropping Zones

Establishing special areas in which balls may or shall be dropped when it is not feasible or practicable to proceed exactly in conformity with Rule 24-2b (Immovable Obstruction), Rule 25-1b or Rule 25-1c (Ground Under Repair), Rule 25-3 (Wrong Putting Green), Rule 26-1 (Water Hazards and Lateral Water Hazards) or Rule 28 (Ball Unplayable).

9. Priority on the Course

The Committee may make regulations governing Priority on the Course (see Etiquette).

Part B   Specimen Local Rules

Within the policy set out in Part A of this Appendix, the Committee may adopt a Specimen Local Rule by referring, on a score card or notice board, to the examples given below. However, Specimen Local Rules 5, 6 or 7 should not be printed or referred to on a score card as they are all of limited duration.

1. Fixed Sprinkler Heads

All fixed sprinkler heads are immovable obstructions and relief from interference by them may be obtained under Rule 24-2. In addition, if such an obstruction on or within two club-lengths of the putting green of the hole being played intervenes on the line of play between the ball and the hole, the player may obtain relief, without penalty, as follows:

If the ball lies off the putting green but not in a hazard and is within two club-lengths of the intervening obstruction, it may be lifted, cleaned and dropped at the nearest point to where the ball lay which (a) is not nearer the hole, (b) avoids such intervention and (c) is not in a hazard or on a putting green.

PENALTY FOR BREACH OF LOCAL RULE:
Match play – Loss of hole; Stroke play – Two strokes.

2. Stones in Bunkers

Stones in bunkers are movable obstructions (Rule 24-1 applies).

3. Protection of Young Trees

Protection of young trees identified by _____.
If such a tree interferes with a player's stance or the area of his intended swing, the ball must be lifted, without penalty, and dropped in accordance with the procedure prescribed in Rule 24-2b(i) (Immovable Obstruction). The ball may be cleaned when so lifted.

PENALTY FOR BREACH OF LOCAL RULE:
Match play – Loss of hole; Stroke play – Two strokes.

4. Ground Under Repair: Play Prohibited

If a player's ball lies in an area of "ground under repair" from which play is prohibited, or if such an area of "ground under repair" interferes with the player's stance or the area of his intended swing the player must take relief under Rule 25-1.
PENALTY FOR BREACH OF LOCAL RULE:
Match play – Loss of hole; Stroke play – Two strokes.

5. Lifting an Embedded Ball

(Specify the area if practicable) . . . through the green, a ball embedded in its own pitch-mark in ground other than sand may be lifted, cleaned and dropped, without penalty, as near as possible to the spot where it lay but not nearer the hole.
PENALTY FOR BREACH OF LOCAL RULE:
Match play – Loss of hole; Stroke play – Two strokes.

6. Cleaning Ball

(Specify the area if practicable) . . . through the green a ball may be lifted, cleaned and replaced without penalty.
Note: The position of the ball shall be marked before it is lifted under this Local Rule – see Rule 20-1.

7. "Preferred Lies" and "Winter Rules"

A ball lying on any "closely mown area" through the green may, without penalty, be moved or may be lifted, cleaned and placed within six inches of where it originally lay, but not nearer the hole. After the ball has been so moved or placed, it is in play.
PENALTY FOR BREACH OF LOCAL RULE:
Match play – Loss of hole; Stroke play – Two strokes.

8. Aeration Holes

If a ball comes to rest in an aeration hole, the player may, without penalty, lift the ball and clean it. Through the green, the player shall drop the ball as near as possible to where it lay, but not nearer the hole. On the putting green, the player shall place the ball at the nearest spot not nearer the hole which avoids such situation.
PENALTY FOR BREACH OF LOCAL RULE:
Match play – Loss of hole; Stroke play – Two strokes.

Part C Conditions of the Competition

Rule 33-1 provides, "The Committee shall lay down the conditions under which a competition is to be played". Such conditions should include many matters such as method of entry, eligibility, number of rounds to be played, settling ties, etc. which is not appropriate to deal with in the Rules of Golf or this Appendix. Detailed information regarding such conditions is provided in "Decisions on the Rules of Golf" under Rule 33-1.

However, there are seven matters which might be covered in the Conditions of Competition to which the Committee's attention is specifically drawn by way of a Note to the appropriate Rule. These are:

1. Specification of the Ball (Note to Rule 5-1)

a. List of Conforming Golf Balls

Arising from the regulations for ball-testing under Rule 5-1, a List of Conforming Golf Balls will be issued from time to time.

It is recommended that the List should be applied to all National and County (or equivalent) Championships and to all top class events when restricted to low handicap players. In order to apply the List to a particular competition the Committee must lay this down in the Conditions of the Competition This should be referred to in the Entry Form, and also a notice should be displayed on the Club notice board and at the 1st Tee along the following lines:

.... (Name of Event) ....

.... (Date and Club) ....

The Ball (Note to Rule 5-1)

The ball the player uses shall be named on the current List of Conforming Golf Balls issued by the Royal & Ancient Golf Club of St. Andrews.

A penalty statement will be required and must be either:

(a) "PENALTY FOR BREACH OF
    CONDITION: *Disqualification*"
        or
b) "PENALTY FOR BREACH OF
    CONDITION:
    *Match play – Loss of each hole
    at which a breach occurred.*
    *Stroke play – Two strokes for each hole
    at which a breach occurred.*"

If option (b) is adopted this only applies to use of a ball which, whilst not on the List of Conforming Golf Balls, does conform to the specifications set forth in Rule 5 and Appendix III. The penalty for use of a ball which does not so conform is disqualification.

b. One Ball Condition

If it is desired to prohibit changing brands and types of golf balls during a stipulated round, the following condition is recommended:
"Limitation on Balls Used During Round: (Note to Rule 5-1)"

(i) "One Ball" Condition

During a stipulated round, the ball the player uses must be of the same brand and type as detailed by a single entry on the current List of Conforming Golf Balls.

PENALTY FOR BREACH OF CONDITION:
Match play – At the conclusion of the hole at which the breach is discovered, the state of the match

shall be adjusted by deducting one hole for each hole at which a breach occurred; maximum deduction per round: Two holes.
Stroke play – Two strokes for each hole at which any breach occurred; maximum penalty per round: Four strokes.

(ii) **Procedure When Breach Discovered**
When a player discovers that he has used a ball in breach of this condition, he shall abandon that ball before playing from the next teeing ground and complete the round using a proper ball; otherwise, the player shall be disqualified. If discovery is made during play of a hole and the player elects to substitute a proper ball before completing that hole, the player shall place a proper ball on the spot where the ball used in breach of the condition lay.

Note: In Club events it is recommended that no such condition be applied.

2. Time of Starting (Note to Rule 6-3a)
If the Committee wishes to act in accordance with the Note, the following wording is recommended:
"If the player arrives at his starting point, ready to play, within five minutes after his starting time, in the absence of circumstances which warrant waiving the penalty of disqualification as provided in Rule 33-7, the penalty for failure to start on time is loss of the first hole to be played in match play or two strokes in stroke play. Penalty for lateness beyond five minutes is disqualification."

3. Pace of Play
The Committee may lay down pace of play guidelines, to help prevent slow play, in accordance with Note 2 to Rule 6-7.

4. Suspension of Play Due to a Dangerous Situation (Note to Rule 6-8b)
If the Committee wishes to act in accordance with the Note, the following wording is recommended:
"When play is suspended by the Committee for a dangerous situation (e.g. lightning, tornado, etc.) if the players in a match or group are between the play of two holes, they shall not resume play until the Committee has ordered a resumption of play. If they are in the process of playing a hole, they shall discontinue play immediately and shall not thereafter resume play until the Committee has ordered a resumption of play.
The signal for suspending play due to a dangerous situation will be:

PENALTY FOR BREACH OF CONDITION:
Disqualification

5. Practice
The Committee may make regulations governing practice in accordance with the Note to Rule

7-1. Exception (c) to Rule 7-2, Note 2 to Rule 7 and Rule 33-2c.

6. Advice in Team Competitions
If the Committee wishes to act in accordance with the Note, the following wording is recommended:
"In accordance with the Note to Rule 8 of the Rules of Golf each team may appoint one person (in addition to the persons from whom advice may be asked under that Rule) who may give advice to members of that team. Such person *[if it is desired to insert any restriction on who may be nominated insert such restriction here]* shall be identified to the Committee before giving advice."

7. New Holes
The Committee may provide, in accordance with the Note to Rule 33-2b, that the holes and teeing grounds for a single round competition, being held on more than one day, may be differently situated on each day.

APPENDICES II AND III

Any design in a club or ball which is not covered by Rules 4 and 5 and Appendices II and III, or which might significantly change the nature of the game, will be ruled on by the Royal & Ancient Golf Club of St Andrews and the United States Golf Association.

Appendix II

Design of Clubs

Clubs must not be substantially different from the traditional and customary form and make. Rule 4-1 prescribes general regulations for their design. The following paragraphs, which provide some specifications and clarify how Rule 4-1 is interpreted, should be read in conjunction with that Rule.
Where a club, or part of a club, is required to have some specific property, this means that it must be designed and manufactured with the intention of having that property. The finished club or part must have that property within manufacturing tolerances appropriate to the material used.

4-1a. General
Adjustability – Exception for Putters. Clubs other than putters shall not be designed to be adjustable except for weight.
Some other forms of adjustability are permitted in the design of a putter provided that:
(i) the adjustment cannot be readily made;

(ii)   all adjustable parts are firmly fixed and there is no reasonable likelihood of them working loose during a round; and

(iii)   all configurations of adjustment conform with the Rules.

The disqualification penalty for purposely changing the playing characteristics of a club during a <u>stipulated round</u> (Rule 4-2) applies to all clubs including a putter.

Note: It is recommended that all putters with adjustable parts be submitted to the Royal & Ancient Golf Club of St Andrews for a ruling.

4-1b. Shaft

Straightness. The shaft shall be straight from the top of the grip to a point not more than 5 inches (127 mm) above the sole, measured from the point where the shaft ceases to be straight along the axis of the bent part of the shaft and the neck and/or socket. (See Fig. I.)

Length. The overall length of the club shall be at least 18 inches (457 mm) measured from the top of the grip along the axis of the shaft or a straight line extension of it to the sole of the club.

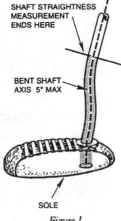

Figure I

Alignment. When the club is in its normal address position the shaft shall be so aligned that:

(i)   the projection of the straight part of the shaft on to the vertical plane through the toe and heel shall diverge from the vertical by at least 10 degrees. (See Fig. II.)

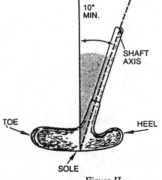

Figure II

Figure III

(ii)   the projection of the straight part of the shaft on to the vertical plane along the intended line of play shall not diverge from the vertical by more than 20 degrees. (See Fig. III.)

Except for putters, all of the heel portion of the club shall lie within 0.625 inches (16 mm) of the plane containing the axis of the straight part of the shaft and the intended (horizontal) line of play. (See Fig. IV.)

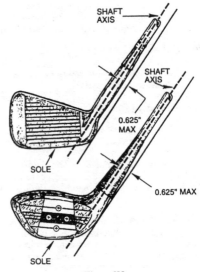

Figure IV

Bending and Twisting Properties. At any point along its length, the shaft shall:

(i)   bend in such a way that the deflection is the same regardless of how the shaft is rotated about its longitudinal axis; and

(ii)   twist the same amount in both directions.

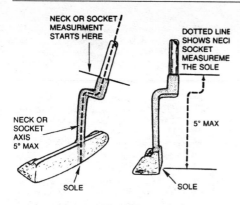

Figure V

Attachment to Clubhead. The shaft shall be attached to the clubhead at the heel either directly or through a neck and/or socket. The length from the top of the neck and/or socket to the sole of the club shall not exceed 5 inches (127 mm), measured along the axis of, and following any bend in, the neck and/or socket. (See Fig. V.)

Exception for Putters: The shaft or neck or socket of a putter may be fixed at any point in the head.

4-1c. Grip (See Fig. VI).
(i) For clubs other than putters, the grip must be circular in cross-section, except that a continuous, straight, slightly raised rib may be incorporated along the full length of the grip, and a slightly indented spiral is permitted on a wrapped grip or a replica of one.

(ii) A putter grip may have a non-circular cross-section, provided the cross-section has no concavity, is symmetrical and remains generally similar throughout the length of the grip.
(iii) The grip may be tapered but must not have any bulge or waist. Its cross-sectional dimension measured in any direction must not exceed 1.75 inches (45 mm).
(iv) For clubs other than putters the axis of the grip must coincide with the axis of the shaft.
(v) A putter may have more than one grip, provided each is circular in cross-section and the axis of each coincides with the axis of the shaft.

4-1d. Clubhead
Dimensions. The dimensions of a clubhead are measured, with the clubhead in its normal address position, on horizontal lines between vertical projections of the outermost points of (i) the heel and the toe and (ii) the face and the back. (See Fig. VII, dimension A.) If the outermost point of the heel is not clearly defined, it is deemed to be 0.625 inches (16mm) above the horizontal plane on which the club is resting in its normal address position. (See Fig. VII, dimension B.)

Plain in Shape. The clubhead shall be generally plain in shape. All parts shall be rigid, structural in nature and functional.

It is not practicable to define plain in shape precisely and comprehensively but features which are deemed to be in breach of this requirement and are therefore not permitted include:

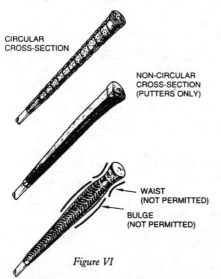

Figure VI

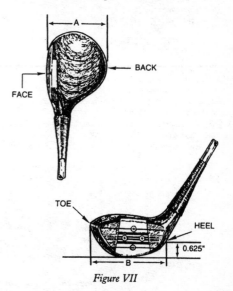

Figure VII

(a)   holes through the head,

(b)   transparent material added for other than decorative or structural purposes,

(c)   appendages to the main body of the head such as knobs, plates, rods or fins,

for the purpose of meeting dimensional specifications, for aiming or for any other purpose.

Exceptions may be made for putters.

Any furrows in or runners on the sole shall not extend into the face.

4-1e. Club Face

General. The material and construction of the face shall not have the effect at impact of a spring, or impart significantly more spin to the ball than a standard steel face, or have any other effect which would unduly influence the movement of the ball.

"Impact Area" Roughness and Material. Except for markings specified in the following paragraphs, the surface roughness within the area where impact is intended (the "impact area") must not exceed that of decorative sandblasting, or of fine milling.

The impact area must be of a single material. Exceptions may be made for wooden clubs. (See Fig. VIII, illustrative impact area.)

Figure VIII

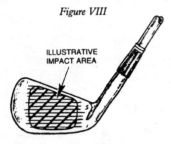

ILLUSTRATIVE
IMPACT AREA

"Impact Area" Markings. Markings in the impact area must not have sharp edges or raised lips as determined by a finger rest. Grooves or punch marks in the impact area must meet the following specifications:

(i) **Grooves.** A series of straight grooves with diverging sides and a symmetrical cross-section may be used. (See Fig. IX.) The width

and cross-section must be consistent across the face of the club and along the length of the grooves. Any rounding of groove edges shall be in the form of a radius which does not exceed 0.020 inch (0.5mm). The width of the grooves shall not exceed 0.035 inch (0.9mm), using the 30 degree method of measurement on file with the Royal & Ancient Golf Club of St Andrews. The distance between edges of adjacent grooves must not be less than three times the width of a groove, and not less than 0.075 inch (1.9mm). The depth of a groove must not exceed 0.020 inch (0.5mm).

(ii) **Punch Marks.** Punch marks may be used. The area of any such mark must not exceed 0.0044 square inch (2.8 sq mm). A mark must not be closer to an adjacent mark than 0.168 inch (4.3mm) measured from centre to centre. The depth of a punch mark must not exceed 0.040 inch (1.0mm). If punch marks are used in combination with grooves, a punch mark must not be closer to a groove than 0.168 inch (4.3mm), measured from centre to centre.

Decorative Markings. The centre of the impact area may be indicated by a design within the boundary of a square whose sides are 0.375 inch (9.5mm) in length. Such a design must not unduly influence the movement of the ball. Decorative markings are permitted outside the impact area.

Non-metallic Club Face Markings. The above specifications apply to clubs on which the impact area of the face is of metal or a material of similar hardness. They do not apply to clubs with faces made of other materials and whose loft angle is 24 degrees or less, but markings which could unduly influence the movement of the ball are prohibited. Clubs with this type of face and a loft angle exceeding 24 degrees may have grooves of maximum width 0.040 inch (1.0mm) and maximum depth of 1½ times the groove width, but must otherwise conform to the markings specifications above.

Putter Face Markings. The specifications above with regard to club face markings and surface roughness do not apply to putters.

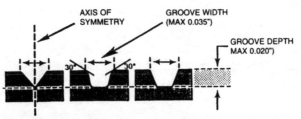

AXIS OF
SYMMETRY

GROOVE WIDTH
(MAX 0.035")

GROOVE DEPTH
MAX 0.020"

30°   30°

Figure IX: Examples of permissable cross-sections

Appendix III

The Ball

a. Weight
The weight of the ball shall not be greater than 1.620 ounces avoirdupois (45.93gm).

b. Size
The diameter of the ball shall not be less than 1.680 inches (42.67mm). This specification will be satisfied if, under its own weight, a ball falls through a 1.680 inches diameter ring gauge in fewer than 25 out of 100 randomly selected positions, the test being carried out at a temperature of 23±1°C.

c. Spherical Symmetry
The ball must not be designed, manufactured or intentionally modified to have properties which differ from those of a spherically symmetrical ball.

d. Initial Velocity
The velocity of the ball shall not be greater than 250 feet (76.2m) per second when measured on apparatus approved by the Royal & Ancient Golf Club of St. Andrews. A maximum tolerance of 2% will be allowed. The temperature of the ball when tested shall be 23±1°C.

e. Overall Distance Standard
A brand of golf ball, when tested on apparatus approved by the Royal & Ancient Golf Club of St. Andrews under the conditions set forth in the Overall Distance Standard for golf balls on file with the Royal & Ancient Golf Club of St. Andrews, shall not cover an average distance in carry and roll exceeding 280 yards (256 metres) plus a tolerance of 6%.

Note: The 6% tolerance will be reduced to a minimum of 4% as test techniques are improved

HANDICAPS

The Rules of Golf do not legislate for the allocation and adjustment of handicaps or their playing differentials. Such matters are within the jurisdiction and control of the National Union concerned and queries should be diurected accordingly.

Rules of Amateur Status

As approved by the Royal & Ancient Golf Club of St. Andrews
(Effective from 1st January 1996)

Definition of an Amateur Golfer
An Amateur Golfer is one who plays the game as a non-remunerative or non-profit-making sport.

The Governing Body
The Governing Body of golf for the Rules of Amateur Status in any country is the National Union of the country concerned except in Great Britain and Ireland where the Governing Body is the Royal & Ancient Golf Club of St. Andrews.

Any person who considers that any action he is proposing to take might endanger his Amateur Status should submit particulars to the appropriate Committee of the Governing Body for consideration.

RULE 1

Forfeiture of Amateur Status at any age

The following are examples of acts which are contrary to the Definition of an Amateur Golfer and cause forfeiture of Amateur Status:

1. Professionalism.
a. Receiving payment or compensation for serving as a Professional golfer or a teaching or playing assistant to a Professional golfer.

b. Taking any action for the purpose of becoming a Professional golfer except applying unsuccessfully for the position of a teaching or playing assistant to a Professional golfer.

Note 1. Such actions include filing application to a final or sole qualifying school or competition conducted to qualify persons to play as Professionals in tournaments; receiving services from or entering into an agreement, written or oral, with a sponsor or Professional agent; agreement to accept payment or compensation for allowing one's name or likeness as a skilled golfer to be used for any commercial purpose; and holding or retaining membership in any organisation of Professional golfers.

Note 2. Receiving payment or compensation as a shop assistant is not itself a breach of the Rules, provided duties do not include playing or giving instruction.

2. Playing for Prize Money.
Playing for prize money or its equivalent in a match, tournament or exhibition.

3. Instruction.
Receiving payment or compensation for giving instruction in playing golf, either orally, in writing, by pictures or by other demonstrations, to either individuals or groups.

Exceptions:
1. Golf instruction may be given by an employee of an educational institution or system to students of the institution or system and by camp counsellors to those in their charge, provided that the total time devoted to golf instruction during a

year comprises less than 50 per cent of the time spent during the year in the performance of all duties as such employee or counsellor.

2. Payment or compensation may be accepted for instruction in writing, provided one's ability or reputation as a golfer was not a major factor in one's employment or in the commission or sale of one's work.

4. Prizes and Testimonials.

(a) Acceptance of a prize or prize voucher of retail value exceeding as follows:

	In Europe	*Elsewhere*
For an event of more than 2 rounds	£300 } or the equivalent	{ $500 US
For an event of 2 rounds or less	£200 } or the equivalent	{ $350 US

or such lesser figure, if any, as may be decided by the Governing Body of golf in any country, or

(b) Acceptance of a testimonial in Europe of retail value exceeding £300 or the equivalent, elsewhere of retail value exceeding $500 US or the equivalent, or such lesser figure as may be decided by the Governing Body of golf in any country, or

(c) For a junior golfer, of such age as may be determined by the Governing Body of golf in any country, taking part in an event limited exclusively to juniors, acceptance of a prize or prize voucher in Europe of retail value exceeding £100 or the equivalent; elsewhere of retail value exceeding $200 US or the equivalent, or such lesser figure, if any, as may be decided by the Governing Body of golf in any country, or

(d) Conversion of a prize or prize voucher into money, or

(e) Accepting a gratuity in connection with a golfing event.

Exceptions:

1. Prizes of only symbolic value, provided that their symbolic nature is distinguished by distinctive permanent marking.

2. More than one testimonial award may be accepted from different donors even though their total retail value exceeds £300 or $500 US, provided they are not presented so as to evade such value limit for a single award.

Note 1: Events covered. The limits referred to in Clauses (a) or (c) above apply to total prize or prize vouchers received by any one person for any event or series of events in any one tournament or exhibition, including hole-in-one or other events in which golf skill is a factor.

Note 2: 'Retail value' is the price at which merchandise is available to anyone at a retail source, and the onus of proving the value of a particular prize rests with the donor.

Note 3: Purpose of prize vouchers. A prize voucher may be issued and redeemed only by the Committee in charge of a competition for the purchase of goods from a Professional's shop or other retail source, which may be specified by the Committee. It may not be used for such items as travel or hotel expenses, a bar bill, or a Club subscription.

Note 4: Maximum Value of Prizes in any event for individuals. It is recommended that the total value of scratch or each division of handicap prizes should not exceed twice the maximum retail value of prize permitted in Rule 1-4(a) and (c) in an 18-hole competition, three times in a 36-hole competition, four times in a 54-hole competition and five times in a 72-hole competition.

Note 5: Testimonial Awards. Such awards relate to notable performances or contributions to golf as distinguished from tournament prizes.

5. Lending Name or Likeness.

Because of golf skill or golf reputation receiving or contracting to receive payment, compensation or personal benefit, directly or indirectly, for allowing one's name or likeness to be used in any way for the advertisement or sale of anything, whether or not used in or appertaining to golf except as a golf author or broadcaster as permitted by Rule 1-7.

Note: A player may accept equipment from anyone dealing in such equipment provided no advertising is involved.

6. Personal Appearance.

Because of golf skill or golf reputation, receiving payment or compensation, directly or indirectly, for a personal appearance.

Exception: Actual expenses in connection with personal appearances may be paid or reimbursed provided no golf competition or exhibition is involved.

7. Broadcasting or Writing.

Because of golf skill or golf reputation, receiving payment or compensation, directly or indirectly, for broadcasting concerning golf, a golf event or golf events, writing golf articles or books, or allowing one's name to be advertised or published as the author of golf articles or books of which one is not actually the author.

Exceptions:

1. Broadcasting or writing as part of one's primary occupation or career, provided instruction in playing golf is not included (Rule 1-3).

2. Part-time broadcasting or writing, provided (a) the player is actually the author of the com-

mentary, articles or books, (b) instruction in playing golf is not included and (c) the payment or compensation does not have the purpose or effect, directly or indirectly, of financing participation in a golf competition or golf competitions.

8. Expenses.

Accepting expenses, in money or otherwise, from any source to engage in a golf competition or exhibition.

Exceptions:
A player may receive expenses, not exceeding the actual expenses incurred, as follows:

1. From a member of the family or legal guardian; *or*

2. As a player in a golf competition or exhibition limited exclusively to players who have not reached their 18th birthday prior to the year of the event; *or*

3. As a representative of his Country, County, Club or similar body in team competitions or team training camps at home or abroad, or as a representative of his Country taking part in a National Championship abroad immediately preceding or following directly upon an international team competition, where such expenses are paid by the body he represents, or by the body controlling golf in the territory he is visiting; *or*

4. As an individual nominated by a National or County Union or a Club to engage in an event at home or abroad provided that:
   (a) The player nominated has not reached such age as may be determined by the Governing Body of Golf in the country from which the nomination is made.
   (b) The expenses shall be paid only by the National Union or County Union responsible in the area from which the nomination is made or, subject to the approval of the nominating body, by the body controlling golf in the territory he is visiting. The expenses shall be limited to a *specified number of* competitive days in any one calendar year *as may be determined by the Governing Body of Golf in the country from which the nomination is made.* The expenses are deemed to include reasonable travelling time and practice days in connection with the competitive days.
   (c) Where the event is to take place abroad, the approval of the National Union of the country in which the event is to be staged and, if the nominating body is not the National Union of the country from which the nomination is made, the approval of the National Union shall first be obtained by the nominating body.
   (d) Where the event is to take place at home, and where the nomination is made by a County Union or Club, the approval of the National Union or the County Union in

the area in which the event is to be staged shall first be obtained.

(Note: The Term 'County Union' covers any Province, State or equivalent Union or Association); *or*

5. As a player invited for reasons unrelated to golf skill, e.g. celebrities, business associates, etc. to take part in golfing events; *or*

6. As a player in an exhibition in aid of a recognised Charity provided the exhibition is not run in connection with another golfing event; *or*

7. As a player in a handicap individual or handicap team sponsored golfing event where expenses are paid by the sponsor on behalf of the player to take part in the event provided the event has been approved as follows:
   (a) where the event is to take place at home the approval of the Governing Body (see Definition) shall first be obtained in advance by the sponsor, and
   (b) where the event is to take place both at home and abroad the approval of the two or more Governing Bodies shall first be obtained in advance by the sponsor. The application for this approval should be sent to the Governing Body of golf in the country where the competition commences.
   (c) where the event is to take place abroad the approval of two or more Governing Bodies shall first be obtained by the sponsor. The application for this approval should be sent to the Governing Body of golf in the country whose players shall be taking part in the event abroad

(Note 1: Business Expenses. It is permissible to play in a golf competition while on a business trip with expenses paid provided that the golf part of the expenses is borne personally and is not charged to business. Further, the business involved must be actual and substantial, and not merely a subterfuge for legitimising expenses when the primary purpose is a golf competition.)

(Note 2: Private Transport. Acceptance of private transport furnished or arranged for by a tournament sponsor, directly or indirectly, as an inducement for a player to engage in a golf competition or exhibition shall be considered accepting expenses under Rule 1-8.)

9. Scholarships.

Because of golf skill or golf reputation, accepting the benefits of a scholarship or grant-in-aid other than ones whose terms and conditions have been approved by the Amateur Status Committee of the Royal & Ancient Golf Club of St. Andrews.

10. Membership.

Because of golf skill accepting membership in a Golf Club without full payment for the class of membership for the purpose of playing for that Club.

11. Conduct Detrimental to Golf.

Any conduct, including activities in connection with golf gambling, which is considered detrimental to the best interests of the game.

Rule 2

Procedure for Enforcement and Reinstatement

1. Decision on a Breach.

Whenever information of a possible breach of the Definition of an Amateur Golfer by a player claiming to be an Amateur shall come to the attention of the appropriate Committee of the Governing Body, the Committee, after such investigation as it may deem desirable, shall decide whether a breach has occurred. Each case shall be considered on its merits. The decision of the committee shall be final.

2. Enforcement.

Upon a decision that a player has acted contrary to the Definition of an Amateur Golfer, the Committee may declare the Amateur Status of the player forfeited or require the player to refrain or desist from specified actions as a condition of retaining his Amateur Status.

The Committee shall use its best endeavours to ensure that the player is notified and may notify any interested Golf Association of any action taken under this paragraph.

3. Reinstatement.

The Committee shall have sole power to reinstate a player to Amateur Status or to deny reinstatement. Each application for reinstatement shall be decided on its merits. In considering an application for reinstatement, the Committee shall normally be guided by the following principles:

a. Awaiting Reinstatement.

The professional holds an advantage over the Amateur by reason of having devoted himself to the game as his profession; other persons infringing the Rules of Amateur Status also obtain advantages not available to the Amateur. They do not necessarily lose such advantage merely by deciding to cease infringing the Rules. Therefore, an applicant for reinstatement to Amateur Status shall undergo a period awaiting reinstatement as prescribed by the Committee.

The period awaiting reinstatement shall start from the date of the player's last breach of the Definition of an Amateur Golfer unless the Committee decides that it shall start from the date when the player's last breach became known to the Committee.

b. Period Awaiting Reinstatement.

The period awaiting reinstatement shall normally be related to the period the player was in breach. However, no applicant shall normally be eligible for reinstatement until he has conducted himself in accordance with the Definition of an Amateur Golfer for a period of at least two consecutive years. The Committee, however, reserves the right to extend or to shorten such a period. A longer period will normally be required of applicants who have been in breach for more than five years. Players of national prominence who have been in breach for more than five years shall not normally be eligible for reinstatement.

c. One Reinstatement.

A player shall not normally be reinstated more than once.

d. Status While Awaiting Reinstatement.

During the period awaiting reinstatement an applicant for reinstatement shall conform with the Definition of an Amateur Golfer.

He shall not be eligible to enter competitions as an Amateur. He may, however, enter competitions, and win a prize, solely among members of a Club of which he is a member, subject to the approval of the Club; but he may not represent such Club against other Clubs.

Forms of Application for Countries under the Jurisdiction of the Royal & Ancient Golf Club

(a) Each application for reinstatement shall be submitted on the approved form to the County Union where the applicant wishes to play as an Amateur. Such Union shall, after making all necessary enquiries, forward it through the National Union (and in the case of lady applicants, the Ladies' Golf Union) and the appropriate Professional Golfers' Association, with comments endorsed thereon, to the Governing Body of golf in that country. Forms of application for reinstatement may be obtained from the Royal & Ancient Golf Club or from the National or County Unions. The application shall include such information as the Royal & Ancient Golf Club may require from time to time and it shall be signed and certified by the applicant.

(b) Any application made in countries under the jurisdiction of the Royal & Ancient Golf Club of St. Andrews which the Governing Body of golf in that country considers to be doubtful or not to be covered by the above regulations may be submitted to the Royal & Ancient Golf Club of St. Andrews whose decision shall be final.

R. & A. POLICY ON GAMBLING

The Definition of an Amateur Golfer provides that an Amateur golfer is one who plays the game as a non-remunerative or non-profit-making sport. When gambling motives are introduced evils can arise which threaten the integrity both of the game and of the individual players.

The R&A does not object to participation in wagering among individual golfers or teams of golfers when participation in the wagering is limited to the players, the players may only wager on themselves or their teams, the sole source of all money won by players is advanced by the players and the primary purpose is the playing of the game for enjoyment.

The distinction between playing for prize money and gambling is essential to the validity of the Rules of Amateur Status. The following constitute golf wagering and not playing for prize money:

1. Participation in wagering among individual golfers.

2. Participation in wagering among teams.

Organised Amateur events open to the general golfing public and designed and promoted to create cash prizes are not approved by the R&A. Golfers participating in such events without irrevocably waiving their right to cash prizes are deemed by the R&A to be playing for prize money.

The R&A is opposed to and urges Unions and Clubs and all other sponsors of golf competitions to prohibit types of gambling such as: Calcuttas, auction sweepstakes and any other forms of gambling organised for general participation or permitting participants to bet on someone other than themselves or their teams.

Attention is drawn to Rule 1-11 relating to conduct detrimental to the game, under which players can forfeit their Amateur Status. It is the Club which, by permitting competitions where excessive gambling is involved, or illegal prizes are offered, bears the responsibility for which the individual is penalised and Unions have the power to invoke severe sanctions against a Club or individual for consistently ignoring this policy.

The Standard Scratch Score and Handicapping Scheme

Implemented 1983. Revised 1st January 1997

This scheme does not apply to ladies' clubs under the jurisdiction of the Ladies' Golf Union.

Published and administered by the Council of National Golf Unions and adopted by the Unions affiliated to the European Golf Association

Foreword

The Standard Scratch Score and Handicapping Scheme was prepared by the British Golf Unions' Joint Advisory Council in 1925 at the request of the Royal and Ancient Golf Club of St. Andrews and has been in operation throughout Great Britain and Ireland since the 1st March 1926.

The Scheme incorporated in this booklet, known as the Standard Scratch Score and Handicapping Scheme 1983, introduced a new concept in handicapping based on the system presently in use by the Australian Golf Union and which takes account of all scores returned by players under Medal Play conditions.

No change has been made in the present method of fixing the Standard Scratch Scores of courses but, on the principle that uniformity and equity in handicapping can be more effectively achieved if there is uniformity and equity in the fixing of Standard Scratch Scores, the Council of National Golf Unions has examined the Course Rating System of the United States Golf Association and has agreed that the Scratch Rating calculated by that procedure may be progressively adopted by National Unions as the Standard Scratch Score pursuant to clause 1.

A supplementary scheme is being prepared incorporating the United States Golf Association Slope Course Rating System for Unions wishing to adopt 'slope' adjusted handicaps.

Amended editions of this Scheme were published on 1st January 1986, 1st January 1989 and 1st January 1993. Further amendments since made are incorporated in this revised edition of the Scheme.

The principal changes are:

(1) Clause 1.(3) Assessment of Standard Scratch Score.

(2) Clause 11.(2) Requirement of Clubs to properly apply the Scheme.

(3) Clause 11.(7) Retention of Handicap Record Sheets by Clubs.

(4) Clause 11 Note. Procedure for dealing with complaints regarding a Club's application of the Scheme.

(5) Clause 15.(3) Amendment to procedure to obtain a Handicap.

(6) Clause 17.(3) & 17.(4) Further amendments to procedures in dealing with Suspension of Handicaps.

(7) Clause 19.(1) & 19.(2)(a) Restrictions in alteration of Handicaps to minimum of one whole stroke.

(8) Clause 19.(8) Introduction, at the discretion of Unions, of Stableford Adjustment.

(9) Clause 19. Note 2. Annual Review of Handicaps of all Members.

(10) Appendix A. New Handicap Record Sheet.

(11) Appendix G. Notes 1 to 5. Additional and revised notes relating to Handicap Allowances.

(12) Appendix H. Revised requirements relating to Computer Software.

(13) Appendix I. Recommendations for Stroke Index Allocation.

(14) Appendix J. Stableford Points Alternative (clause 19.(8)).

(15) Appendix K. Decisions. Amendments to Decisions 7 and 8, and additional Decisions 9 to 14.

PART ONE Definitions

Definition

A. UNION.
B. AREA AUTHORITY.
C. AFFILIATED CLUB.
D. HOME CLUB.
E. MEMBER.
F. HANDICAPPING AUTHORITY.
G. HANDICAP COMMITTEE.
H. HANDICAPS.
I. CATEGORIES OF HANDICAP.
J. MEASURED COURSE.
K. DISTANCE POINT.
L. MEDAL TEE.
M. MEDAL PLAY CONDITIONS.
N. QUALIFYING COMPETITION.
O. QUALIFYING SCORE.
P. AGGREGATE FOURBALL COMPETITION.
Q. STANDARD SCRATCH SCORE.
R. COMPETITION SCRATCH SCORE.
S. NETT DIFFERENTIAL.
T. BUFFER ZONE.

PART TWO The Golf Course and the Standard Scratch Score

PART THREE Handicapping

Definitions

Throughout the Scheme whenever a word or expression is used which is defined within the following definitions the word or expression is printed in capital letters.

A – Union

A UNION is any national organisation in control of amateur golf in any country.

B – Area Authority

An AREA AUTHORITY is any authority appointed by a UNION to act on behalf of that UNION for the purposes of the Scheme within a specified area.

C – Affiliated Club

An AFFILIATED CLUB is a club affiliated to a UNION or AREA AUTHORITY which pays to the UNION and AREA AUTHORITY a specified annual per capita fee in respect of each eligible MEMBER.

D – Home Club

A player's HOME CLUB is an AFFILIATED CLUB of which the player is a MEMBER. If the player is a MEMBER of more than one AFFILIATED CLUB he shall nominate one as his HOME CLUB.

E – Member

A MEMBER is an amateur golfer who is eligible to compete in all QUALIFYING COMPETITIONS arranged by an AFFILIATED CLUB subject only to exclusion by virtue of one or more of the following:

(a) Restrictions imposed relating solely to the handicap of the players who may compete; or

(b) Restrictions imposed relating solely to the age of the players who may compete; or

(c) Such other restrictions as may be permitted by the UNION provided that any restrictions so permitted shall stipulate a minimum number of QUALIFYING COMPETITIONS in a calendar year in which the MEMBER shall have a reasonable opportunity to compete.

Note: Under this definition a MEMBER need not necessarily be a member as defined by the constitution or rules of his AFFILIATED CLUB or CLUBS.

F – Handicapping Authority

The HANDICAPPING AUTHORITY for a player is his HOME CLUB subject to the overall jurisdiction of the UNION.

G – Handicap Committee

The HANDICAP COMMITTEE is the body appointed by an AFFILIATED CLUB to administer the Scheme within the CLUB.

H – Handicaps

(1) EXACT HANDICAP – a player's EXACT HANDICAP is his handicap calculated in accordance with the provisions of the Scheme to one decimal place.

(2) PLAYING HANDICAP – a player's PLAYING HANDICAP is his EXACT HANDICAP calculated to the nearest whole number (0.5 is rounded upwards).

I – Categories of Handicap

Handicaps are divided into the following CATEGORIES:

CATEGORY 1: Handicaps of 5 or less.
CATEGORY 2: Handicaps of 6 to 12 inclusive.
CATEGORY 3: Handicaps of 13 to 20 inclusive.
CATEGORY 4: Handicaps of 21 to 28 inclusive.

J – Measured Course

Any course played over by an AFFILIATED CLUB the measured length of which has been certified in accordance with the requirements of clause 2.

K – Distance Point

The DISTANCE POINT is the position of a permanent marker indicating the point from which the length of a hole is measured.

L – Medal Tee

A MEDAL TEE is a rectangular area the front of which shall not be more than 10 yards (9 metres) in front of the relevant DISTANCE POINT and the rear of which shall not be less than 2 yards (2 metres) behind the DISTANCE POINT.

Note: Special rules apply when the length of a MEASURED COURSE has been temporarily reduced – see clause 7.

M – Medal Play Conditions

MEDAL PLAY CONDITIONS prevail during stroke, par and Stableford competitions played with full handicap allowance over 18 holes under the Rules of Golf from MEDAL TEES. MEDAL PLAY CONDITIONS shall not prevail when the length of the course played varies by more than 100 yards (91 metres) from the length of the MEASURED COURSE.

Note: Special rules apply when the length of a MEASURED COURSE has been temporarily reduced – see clause 7.

N – Qualifying Competition

A QUALIFYING COMPETITION is any competition in which MEDAL PLAY CONDITIONS prevail and for which a COMPETITION SCRATCH SCORE is calculated subject to restrictions and limitations contained in the Scheme or imposed by UNIONS.

O – Qualifying Score

A QUALIFYING SCORE is any score including a "no return" returned in a QUALIFYING COMPETITION.

P – Aggregate Fourball Competition

An AGGREGATE FOURBALL COMPETITION is a QUALIFYING COMPETITION in which the completed scores at each hole of a team of not more than two amateur players are aggregated.

Q – Standard Scratch Score

The STANDARD SCRATCH SCORE is the score allotted to an 18 hole golf course after the application of clause 1.

R – Competition Scratch Score

The COMPETITION SCRATCH SCORE is the score determined by clause 20.

S – Nett Differential

The NETT DIFFERENTIAL is the difference (+ or –) between the nett score returned by a player in a QUALIFYING COMPETITION and the COMPETITION SCRATCH SCORE.

T – Buffer Zone

A score is within a player's BUFFER ZONE when a NETT DIFFERENTIAL is within the following bands for his HANDICAP CATEGORY.

CATEGORY 1	0 to +1
CATEGORY 2	0 to +2
CATEGORY 3	0 to +3
CATEGORY 4	0 to +4

Note: When a player's score is within his BUFFER ZONE his EXACT HANDICAP remains unchanged.

PART TWO

The Golf Course and the Standard Scratch Score

1. The Standard Scratch Score

1.(1) The STANDARD SCRATCH SCORE is the score which a scratch player is expected to return in ideal conditions over a MEASURED COURSE. In the case of a nine-hole course it represents two rounds.

1.(2) The allocation of STANDARD SCRATCH SCORES shall be the responsibility of the UNION.

1.(3) Unions shall direct that the Standard Scratch Score of courses under their jurisdiction shall be assessed in accordance with either:

    (a) Course Rating System of the United States Golf Association;

    (b) the procedure hereafter contained.

1.(4) In assessing the STANDARD SCRATCH SCORE

Table of Provisional Standard Scratch Scores

Standard length of Course	Lengths included in Standard Length		Provisional Standard Scratch Score
Yards	Yards	Metres	
7100	7001-7200	6402-6584	74
6900	6801-7000	6219-6401	73
6700	6601-6800	6036-6218	72
6500	6401-6600	5853-6035	71
6300	6201-6400	5670-5852	70
6100	5951-6200	5442-5669	69
5800	5701-5950	5213-5441	68
5500	5451-5700	4984-5212	67
5300	5201-5450	4756-4983	66
5100	5001-5200	4573-4755	65
4900	4801-5000	4390-4572	64
4700	4601-4800	4207-4389	63
4500	4401-4600	4024-4206	62
4300	4201-4400	3841-4023	61
4100	4001-4200	3659-3840	60

1 yard = 0.91440 metres
1 metre = 1.09361 yards

of a course, officials will take as the starting point the Provisional Standard Scratch Score from the Table. They will then consider the following points:

    (a) The terrain and general layout of the course.

    (b) Normal ground conditions – Is run average, above average or below average?

    (c) Sizes of greens and whether watered or unwatered.

    (d) Hazards – Are greens well guarded or open?

    (e) Width of fairways, the effect of trees and nature of rough.

    (f) Nearness of "out of bounds" to fairways and greens.

    (g) Average weather conditions throughout the playing year. Is the course exposed and subject to high winds for most of the year? Is it sheltered from the full effects of adverse weather?

    (h) The distance by which the length of the course varies from the standard length shown in column one of the Table.

1.(5) Having considered all these points, officials will fix the STANDARD SCRATCH SCORE of the course by:

    (a) Confirming the Provisional Standard Scratch Score as the STANDARD SCRATCH SCORE.

    (b) Adding a stroke or strokes to the Provisional Standard Scratch Score.

    (c) Deducting a stroke or strokes from the Provisional Standard Scratch Score.

1.(6) With effect from 1st January 1993 no course of less than 3,000 yards shall be allocated a STANDARD SCRATCH SCORE. At the discretion of a UNION courses between 3,000 and 4,000 yards may be allocated such STANDARD SCRATCH SCORE as the UNION shall determine.

2. Course Measurement

Measurement shall be by plan or projection along the horizontal plane from the DISTANCE POINT on the MEDAL TEE to the centre of the green of each hole.

In the case of a dog-leg hole, measurement shall be along the centre line of the fairway to the axis and then to the centre of the green. Measurement shall be carried out by a qualified surveyor, or someone competent and experienced in the handling of surveying instruments, who shall grant a certificate showing details of the length of each hole and the total playing length of the course. Subsequent alterations to the length of the course will require a certificate only for the altered hole or holes which shall be measured in the manner prescribed above.

3. Alterations to Courses

When alterations have been carried out to a course increasing or decreasing its length, the club shall submit a "Form of Application" through its AREA AUTHORITY to the UNION. In the case of a new course, a "Form of Application" shall be submitted by the club through its AREA AUTHORITY to the UNION who will fix the STANDARD SCRATCH SCORE. The UNION is responsible for all STANDARD SCRATCH SCORES in the country over which it has jurisdiction.

4. Tees

All clubs with the requisite facilities should have back and forward MEDAL TEES with a yardage measurement from each tee and a separate STANDARD SCRATCH SCORE as measured from back and forward MEDAL TEES permanently marked.

Wherever possible when courses are being remeasured the DISTANCE POINT on each MEDAL TEE should be so positioned that the tee markers when placed adjacent to the DISTANCE POINT provide a teeing area which satisfies the following recommendation of the Royal & Ancient Golf Club of St Andrews:

"Committees should bear in mind the definition of 'Teeing Ground' (Rules of Golf) which states: 'It is a rectangular area two club-lengths in depth'. The Tee Markers should be placed in such a position that the player has the benefit of the full depth to which the definition entitles him."

To facilitate the use of the correct tees the Royal & Ancient Golf Club of St Andrews recommends that tee boxes or other objects in use to mark the teeing ground shall be painted as follows:

Ladies' Standard MEDAL TEES	Red
Men's Forward MEDAL TEES	Yellow
Men's Back MEDAL TEES	White

When a National Championship is being played over a course the tee markers may be coloured Blue.

5. Par

The STANDARD SCRATCH SCORE must not be allocated amongst the individual holes, but should be printed as a total on the card. The par figure for each hole should be printed alongside each hole on the card. Par for each hole shall be fixed by the club in relation to the length and playing difficulty of each hole and shall be fixed within the following ranges:

	Yards	Metres
Par 3	0–250	0–229
Par 4	220–500	201–457
Par 5	440+	402+

e.g. if a hole is 460 yards (421 metres) it may be allotted par 4 or 5 depending upon its average playing difficulty.

The total of the Par figures for each hole of a course will not necessarily coincide with the STANDARD SCRATCH SCORE of that course. Par figures should be used for Stableford, Par, and similar competitions.

6. Preferred Lies

When preferred lies are in operation the following points shall be taken into consideration: MEDAL PLAY CONDITIONS will apply notwithstanding the application of a Local Rule for preferred lies as a result of adverse conditions during the period from 1st October to 30th April. Preferred lies may be used during that period but are not mandatory upon clubs during any part thereof. The Local Rule may apply to specified holes only. Outside that period MEDAL PLAY CONDITIONS will not apply if preferred lies are in operation unless the consent of the UNION or AREA AUTHORITY has been first obtained.

It is emphasised that preferred lies shall apply only when a Local Rule has been made and published in accordance with Appendix 1 of the Rules of Golf as follows:

"A ball lying on any 'closely mown area' through the green may, without penalty, be moved or may be lifted, cleaned and placed within six inches of where it originally lay, but not nearer the hole. After the ball has been so moved or placed, it is in play."

Penalty for breach of Local Rule: Match Play –
Loss of hole; Stroke play – Two strokes.
Note: "closely mown area" means any area of the
course, including paths through the rough, cut to
fairway height or less. (Rule 25-2).

7. Permitted Adjustment to a Measured Course

Whilst each AFFILIATED CLUB must endeavour to
maintain the length of its MEASURED COURSE at all
times MEDAL PLAY CONDITIONS nevertheless prevail when the length of a course has been reduced
in the following circumstances:

(a) When, to allow movement of the playing
position on the MEDAL TEE or the use of a
temporary green or tee, the length of the
course being played has been reduced by
not more than 100 yards (91 metres) from
the length of the MEASURED COURSE.

(b) When, to allow work to proceed on course
alterations or for reasons other than weather conditions, it is necessary to reduce the
playing length of the MEASURED COURSE by
between 100 and 300 yards (91 and 274
metres). In these circumstances, the club
shall reduce the STANDARD SCRATCH SCORE
of the MEASURED COURSE temporarily by 1
stroke and report to the UNION, or to such
other body nominated by the UNION, the
reduction in the STANDARD SCRATCH
SCORE, and the reason for it. The club
must also notify the UNION or other body
when the course has been restored to its
measured length and the official STANDARD
SCRATCH SCORE reinstated.

PART THREE
Handicapping

8. Introduction

8.(1) The Council of National Golf Unions
Standard Scratch Score and Handicapping Scheme
has been revised to achieve a uniformity and
equity in handicapping throughout Great Britain
and Ireland and other countries adopting the
Scheme. The nature of the game of golf, with its
varying playing conditions, makes handicapping a
relatively inexact operation. Nevertheless, if the
same principles are sensibly and universally
applied by HANDICAP COMMITTEES, a high degree
of uniformity in handicapping can be achieved. It
is therefore of paramount importance that all parties to the Scheme fulfil their obligations to it and
these are set out below.

8.(2) Handicapping within the Scheme is delegated to AFFILIATED CLUBS subject to the overall
jurisdiction of the UNION.

9. Rights and Obligations of the Union

The UNION:

9.(1) Shall have overall jurisdiction for the
administration of the Scheme.

9.(2) May delegate any part of that jurisdiction to
an AREA AUTHORITY.

9.(3) Shall ratify all PLAYING HANDICAPS reduced
to below scratch on the first occasion in any calendar year, immediately after the reduction.

9.(4) Shall have the right to obtain information
upon handicaps from AFFILIATED CLUBS at any
time.

9.(5) Shall establish within the UNION conditions,
restrictions and limitations to be imposed in
respect of competitions deemed to be QUALIFY-
ING COMPETITIONS.

9.(6) Shall settle any dispute referred to it. Its
decision shall be final.

9.(7) May at its discretion authorise HOME CLUBS
to increase the handicaps of players in any of the
CATEGORIES 2, 3, and 4 pursuant to clause 19.
When such authority has been given the requirements of clause 19.(2) and (3) that the increase
shall be effected by the UNION or AREA AUTHORITY
shall not apply. Notwithstanding the foregoing,
the UNION may, if it considers that handicaps
have been unjustifiably increased by a HOME
CLUB, require that club to comply with all of the
provisions of clause 19.

9.(8) May at its discretion direct that scores
returned by a player in CATEGORIES 3 and/or 4 at
a club which is not his HOME CLUB or alternatively
at a club of which he is not a MEMBER shall be disregarded for handicap increase pursuant to clause
16.(3).

9.(9) Establish a procedure to adjudicate upon
the suspension of handicaps pursuant to clause
17(1) and appoint a committee to perform duties
referred to in that clause.

9.(10) May at its discretion require a player to
return to his HOME CLUB information regarding
scores in non qualifying competitions as provided
by clause 13.(10).

9.(11) May at its discretion restrict increases of
EXACT HANDICAPS to 2.0 strokes in a calendar
year as provided by clause 16.(10)(b).

9.(12) May at its discretion authorise HOME
CLUBS to apply clause 19.(8).

10. Rights and Obligations of the Area Authority

The AREA AUTHORITY shall:

10.(1) Administer the responsibilities delegated
to it by the UNION.

10.(2) Have the right to obtain information upon
handicaps from AFFILIATED CLUBS at any time.

10.(3) Appoint a committee to perform the duties
referred to in clause 17(1).

11. Rights and Obligations of the Affiliated Club

The AFFILIATED CLUB shall:

11.(1) Act as the HANDICAPPING AUTHORITY for all members for whom it is the HOME CLUB subject to the overall jurisdiction of the UNION.

11.(2) Ensure that the Scheme is properly applied in the club. Failure by a club to comply with this requirement justifies – a UNION withdrawing the club's right to act as a HANDICAPPING AUTHORITY or imposing such conditions as the UNION consider appropriate.

11.(3) Ensure that with effect from 1st April 1997 any computer software used for the calculation of handicaps shall satisfy the requirements set out in Appendix H.

11.(4) Ensure that all handicaps are calculated in accordance with the Scheme.

11.(5) Appoint a HANDICAP COMMITTEE of which the majority shall be MEMBERS to perform the obligations set out in clause 12 below.

11.(6) Appoint a committee of which the majority shall be MEMBERS to perform the duties referred to in clause 17(1).

11.(7) Retain handicap records in respect of all present and past MEMBERS for not less than the current and previous calendar year.

Note: It is the HOME CLUB's responsibility to ensure that handicaps are maintained in accordance with the rules laid down by the Scheme. Any complaint regarding the application of the Scheme shall be made to the UNION, or AREA AUTHORITY if so delegated, which may at its discretion, carry out such investigation as it shall consider appropriate. If following such an investigation, it is found that a HOME CLUB is in breach of its responsibilities, the HOME CLUB shall be directed by the UNION or AREA AUTHORITY to review all handicaps and shall within 3 months from that direction report to the UNION or AREA AUTHORITY the manner in which matters have been rectified. Failure to resolve the matter satisfactorily would justify the UNION disaffiliating the HOME CLUB, or declaring that handicaps at that club are no longer C.O.N.G.U. Handicaps.

12. Rights and Obligations of the Handicap Committee

The HANDICAP COMMITTEE shall:

12.(1) Maintain a list in which the names of competitors must be entered prior to competing in a QUALIFYING COMPETITION at the club.

12.(2) Ensure, so far as possible, that all cards taken out in QUALIFYING COMPETITIONS are returned to the committee including incomplete cards.

12.(3) At the conclusion of each round of a QUALIFYING COMPETITION calculate the COMPETITION SCRATCH SCORE as required by clause 20.

12.(4) Post on the club's notice board all changes of MEMBERS' PLAYING HANDICAPS immediately they are made.

12.(5) Ensure that a record of MEMBERS' current PLAYING HANDICAPS is available in a prominent position in the club house.

12.(6) When the club is a player's HOME CLUB:

(a) Maintain on his behalf a handicap record sheet which shall include all the information shown in Appendix A.

(b) Ensure his scores are recorded immediately after completion of each QUALIFYING COMPETITION at the HOME CLUB or the reporting of a QUALIFYING SCORE returned elsewhere, and that all EXACT HANDICAPS are calculated in relation to scores recorded in chronological order.

(c) Keep his EXACT HANDICAP up to date at all times.

(d) Notify the UNION and AREA AUTHORITY immediately the committee reduces a MEMBER'S PLAYING HANDICAP to below scratch on the first occasion in any calendar year and obtain ratification from the UNION or, if so delegated, from the AREA AUTHORITY.
Note: The reduction is effective before ratification.

(e) Unless some other body has been appointed by the HOME CLUB for this purpose, exercise the power to suspend handicaps contained in clause 17.

(f) When a MEMBER changes his HOME CLUB send to the new HOME CLUB a copy of the player's current handicap record sheet.

(g) Specify the conditions which apply when a player wishes to obtain a handicap under the provisions of clause 15.

(h) Exercise the powers to adjust players' handicaps contained in clause 19.

(i) As required by clause 19.(5) advise players of changes made to their handicaps under the provisions of clause 19.

13. Rights and Obligations of the Player

The player shall:

13.(1) Have one handicap only which shall be allotted and adjusted by his HOME CLUB. That handicap shall apply elsewhere including other clubs of which the player is a MEMBER.

13.(2) If he is a MEMBER of more than one AFFILIATED CLUB select one as his HOME CLUB and notify that club and the others of his choice.

13.(3) Not change his HOME CLUB except by giving advance notice of the change which can take effect only at the end of a calendar year unless he has ceased to be a member of his HOME CLUB or both clubs agree to the change taking place at an earlier date.

13.(4) Report to his HOME CLUB the names of all other AFFILIATED CLUBS of which he is, becomes, or ceases to be, a MEMBER and report to all other AFFILIATED CLUBS of which he is a MEMBER:

   (a) The name of his HOME CLUB and any changes of his HOME CLUB and

   (b) Alterations to his PLAYING HANDICAP made by his HOME CLUB.

13.(5) Ensure that before competing in a QUALIFYING COMPETITION his entry has been inserted in the competition entry list.

13.(6) Ensure that all competition cards in QUALIFYING COMPETITIONS, whether or not complete, are returned to the organising committee.

13.(7) Subject to the provisions of clause 9.(8) report to his HOME CLUB immediately all QUALIFYING SCORES (including no returns) returned away from his HOME CLUB advising the HOME CLUB of the date of the QUALIFYING COMPETITION, the venue and the COMPETITION SCRATCH SCORE together with the following:

   (a) After a stroke play QUALIFYING COMPETITION the gross score returned and such further information as shall be required by the HOME CLUB.

   (b) After a Stableford QUALIFYING COMPETITION the par of the course and the number of points scored.

   (c) After a par QUALIFYING COMPETITION the par of the course and the score versus par.

Note 1: Players are reminded that failure to report scores returned away from their HOME CLUBS (including no returns) when so required by the scheme is likely to lead to the suspension of offending players' handicaps under the provisions of clause 17.

Note 2: In the event of a QUALIFYING COMPETITION being declared abandoned or scores returned being deemed by clause 20 not to be QUALIFYING SCORES the player is required to report the above information only if he has returned a NETT DIFFERENTIAL of less than zero.

13.(8) Prior to playing in any competition at a club other than his HOME CLUB ensure that any appropriate reductions to his PLAYING HANDICAP have been made or alternatively comply with the obligations set out in clause 16.(11).

13.(9) Enter his current PLAYING HANDICAP on all cards returned in a QUALIFYING COMPETITION even though the event may not be a handicap competition.

13.(10) Provide to his HOME CLUB such information regarding scores in non-qualifying competitions if so directed by a UNION.

14. Qualifying Scores

14.(1) The only scores to be recorded on a player's handicap record sheet are:

   (a) QUALIFYING SCORES as defined.

   (b) NETT DIFFERENTIALS of less than zero returned in any abandoned round of a QUALIFYING COMPETITION or in any

round of a QUALIFYING COMPETITION when that round has been deemed under the provisions of clause 20 not to be a QUALIFYING SCORE.

   (c) Correct scores in a QUALIFYING COMPETITION which are disqualified for any reason.

   (d) Scores returned in a QUALIFYING COMPETITION played over 18 holes on a course reduced in length under the provisions of clause 7.

   (e) Scores returned in a QUALIFYING COMPETITION played over a MEASURED COURSE when Local Rules are in operation for preferred lies (as permitted by clause 6) or for any other purpose provided the rules are authorised by Appendix 1 of the Rules of Golf or associated guidance notes or have been approved by the Rules of Golf Committee of the Royal & Ancient Golf Club of St Andrews.

   (f) The individual scores and no returns returned by players in AGGREGATE FOUR-BALL COMPETITIONS.

Note 1: The competition must be a QUALIFYING COMPETITION.

Note 2: QUALIFYING SCORES returned in Stableford and par competitions shall be converted into NETT DIFFERENTIALS by using the tables in Appendix C.

14.(2) The following returns shall not be accepted as QUALIFYING SCORES in any circumstances:

   (a) Scores returned in any better ball four-ball competition.

   (b) Scores returned in competitions over less than 18 holes.

   (c) Scores returned in any competition which is not played in accordance with the Rules of Golf and authorised Local Rules. e.g. A competition which limits the number of clubs permitted to less than 14.

   (d) Scores returned in an extended competition in which the player has the option of selecting the day or days on which he shall compete and/or how many returns he shall make except the following competitions in which only one return is permitted:

     (i) A competition over no more than two days which need not be consecutive, or

     (ii) A competition extended over three or more days solely to accommodate the number of players entered.

   (e) Subject to clause 14.(1)(b) scores returned in any round of a QUALIFYING COMPETITION deemed under the provisions of clause 20 not to be QUALIFYING SCORES.

   (f) Any competition other than an AGGREGATE FOURBALL COMPETITION in which competitors play in partnership with another competitor.

(g) Stableford and par competitions played with less than full handicap allowance.

(h) Scores returned in events run by organisations which are not HANDICAPPING AUTHORITIES unless such events have been previously approved by a UNION as a QUALIFYING COMPETITION.

15. Allotment of Handicaps

15.(1) The maximum handicap is 28. (Maximum EXACT HANDICAP 28.0.)

15.(2) A handicap can be allotted only to a MEMBER of an AFFILIATED CLUB.

15.(3) To obtain a handicap a player shall submit such number of cards as his HOME CLUB requires, but not less than three, at his HOME CLUB (preferably over a MEASURED COURSE) each of which shall be signed by a responsible person acceptable to the HANDICAP COMMITTEE. Any score of more than 2 over par at any hole shall be amended to 2 over par. After these adjustments have been made an EXACT HANDICAP shall be allotted equivalent to the number of strokes by which the best of the submitted rounds differs from the STANDARD SCRATCH SCORE. The HANDICAP COMMITTEE may allot a player an initial whole number EXACT HANDICAP less than the best score if it has reason to consider that a lower handicap is more appropriate to the player's ability. In exceptional circumstances a higher handicap may be allotted than that indicated by the best score.

When a player fails to return cards justifying an EXACT HANDICAP of 28.0 he may, at the discretion of the HANDICAP COMMITTEE, be given an EXACT HANDICAP of 28.0. The player's PLAYING HANDICAP shall equal the EXACT HANDICAP allotted. AFFILIATED CLUBS may at their absolute discretion refuse to allot a handicap until a specified standard has been attained.

15.(4) A player without a handicap shall not be allotted a CATEGORY 1 HANDICAP without the written authority of the UNION, or AREA AUTHORITY if so delegated.

16. Alteration of Handicaps

16.(1) Definition I divides handicaps into the following four CATEGORIES:

CATEGORY 1: Handicaps of 5 or less.
CATEGORY 2: Handicaps of 6 to 12 inclusive.
CATEGORY 3: Handicaps of 13 to 20 inclusive.
CATEGORY 4: Handicaps of 21 to 28 inclusive.

16.(2) If a player returns a NETT DIFFERENTIAL within his BUFFER ZONE his EXACT HANDICAP is not changed.

16.(3) Subject to the provisions of clauses 9.(8), 20.(3) and 20.(4), if a player returns a score with a NETT DIFFERENTIAL above his BUFFER ZONE or records a "no return" his EXACT HANDICAP is increased by 0.1.

16.(4) If a player returns a NETT DIFFERENTIAL of less than zero his EXACT HANDICAP is reduced by an amount *per stroke that the* NETT DIFFERENTIAL *is below zero*, the amount per stroke being determined by his HANDICAP CATEGORY.

16.(5) The recording of scores shall be kept by NETT DIFFERENTIAL i.e. the difference (+ or −) between the player's nett score and the COMPETITION SCRATCH SCORE. The date, NETT DIFFERENTIAL, EXACT HANDICAP and PLAYING HANDICAP must be recorded on the player's handicap record sheet together with the supplementary information shown in Appendix A.

16.(6) EXACT HANDICAPS shall be adjusted as follows, with reference to the handicap adjustment table, Appendix B.

| CATEGORY | PLAYING HANDICAP | If NETT DIFFERENTIAL is: | |
		Above BUFFER ZONE. Add *only*	Below CSS. Subtract for *each* Stroke below
1	Up to 5	0.1	0.1
2	6 to 12	0.1	0.2
3	13 to 20	0.1	0.3
4	21 to 28	0.1	0.4

For example: If a player on 11.2 returns a score with a NETT DIFFERENTIAL of 4 his EXACT HANDICAP becomes 11.3. If he then returns a score with a NETT DIFFERENTIAL of −7 his EXACT HANDICAP is reduced by 7 times 0.2 = 1.4, i.e. to an EXACT HANDICAP of 9.9 and his PLAYING HANDICAP is 10 which is immediately his new handicap.

16.(7) When a player's handicap is to be reduced so that it goes from a higher CATEGORY to a lower CATEGORY, it shall be reduced at the rate appropriate to the higher CATEGORY only so far as brings his PLAYING HANDICAP into the lower CATEGORY and the balance of the reduction shall be at the rate appropriate to the lower CATEGORY.

For example: If a player on 21.2 returns a score with a NETT DIFFERENTIAL of −6, i.e. 6 strokes below his PLAYING HANDICAP of 21, his handicap is reduced as follows:

21.2−(2 times 0.4) (i.e. −0.8)=20.4
20.4−(4 times 0.3) (i.e. −1.2)=19.2

16.(8) A player whose EXACT HANDICAP contains 0.5 or over shall be given the next higher handicap, e.g. 12.5 exact would be 13 PLAYING HANDICAP. This applies when handicaps are to be increased or reduced.

Note: EXACT HANDICAP −0.5 rounded upwards is PLAYING HANDICAP scratch and not plus one.

16.(9) Reductions of PLAYING HANDICAPS shall be made on the day the score becomes known to the HOME CLUB.

16.(10)
(a) Increases of PLAYING HANDICAPS shall be made at the end of each calendar month

or at such shorter intervals as the HOME CLUB may decide.

(b) A UNION may at its discretion restrict an increase of EXACT HANDICAPS to 2.0 strokes in a calendar year except increases granted under clause 19.

16.(11) If, for any reason, a player is unable to report to his HOME CLUB a QUALIFYING SCORE or SCORES which may have a NETT DIFFERENTIAL of less than zero or has been unable to ascertain, after reporting such scores, whether or not his PLAYING HANDICAP has been reduced, he shall then, before competing in a further competition at a club other than his HOME CLUB, either:

(a) For that competition only, make such reduction to his PLAYING HANDICAP as shall be appropriate under the Scheme by applying the COMPETITION SCRATCH SCORE if known, otherwise the STANDARD SCRATCH SCORE to his gross score, or

(b) Report to the committee organising the competition any relevant score returned which after deduction of his PLAYING HANDICAP is two above the STANDARD SCRATCH SCORE or less. The committee may, for that competition only, reduce the player's PLAYING HANDICAP.

Note: Increases to PLAYING HANDICAPS may not be made under the provisions of this sub clause.

16.(12) The procedure for the restoration of handicaps which have been lost is contained in clause 18.

17. Suspension, Lapsing and Loss of Handicaps

17.(1) Subject to the provisions of Clause 17(2) the UNION, AREA AUTHORITY or a player's HOME CLUB shall suspend the handicap of any player who in its opinion has:

(a) Constantly or blatantly failed to comply with the obligations and responsibilities imposed by this Scheme, or

(b) Conducted himself in a manner prejudicial to the interests of his UNION, AREA AUTHORITY or HOME CLUB or to the game of Golf.

The player must be notified of the period of suspension and of any other conditions imposed. No player's handicap shall be suspended without first affording him the opportunity of appearing before the committee or other body.

17.(2) Subject to any directions to the contrary issued by a UNION no proceedings pursuant to Clause 17(1) shall be considered by an AREA AUTHORITY or HOME CLUB without the written authority of the UNION. Following the receipt of a request for such an authority, UNIONS shall direct whether the UNION, the AREA AUTHORITY or HOME CLUB shall hear and determine the issue. Subject to any directions made by a UNION no authority is required in respect of proceedings brought against a MEMBER by his HOME CLUB in respect of an alleged offence committed at that club.

17.(3) Any player who requests his HOME CLUB to confirm or certify his handicap for competition entry purposes shall be deemed to have had adequate opportunity of reporting to his HOME CLUB any relevant away scores on or prior to the date and time at which the confirmation or certificate of handicap is requested. If it is established to the satisfaction of the player's HOME CLUB after due investigation that a player has so failed to report away scores his handicap may be suspended for such period as the HOME CLUB shall consider appropriate. Whilst his handicap is suspended a player shall not be eligible to compete in or enter any golf event which requires a C.O.N.G.U. handicap as a condition of entry. Following a written request from a player whose handicap has been suspended accompanied by full details of all relevant omitted scores, his HOME CLUB may re-instate his handicap appropriately adjusted. HOME CLUBS do not require the authority of the UNION or AREA AUTHORITY to proceed under this sub clause.

17.(4) UNIONS shall direct the appeal procedure to be made available to a player should he be dissatisfied with a determination under the foregoing sub clauses.

17.(5) If a player is suspended from membership of his HOME CLUB his handicap shall lapse automatically until his membership is reinstated.

17.(6) A player's handicap is lost immediately he ceases to be a MEMBER of any AFFILIATED CLUB or loses his amateur status.

17.(7) Whilst a player's handicap is suspended, lapsed or has been lost he shall not enter or compete in any competition which requires a competitor to be the holder of a C.O.N.G.U. handicap as designated by this scheme for either entering or competing in the competition.

17.(8) The suspension of a player's handicap shall apply at all AFFILIATED CLUBS of which the player is or becomes a MEMBER during the period of suspension.

18. Restoration of Handicaps

18.(1) If the handicap of a player is to be reinstated within 6 months of the date on which his handicap was lost, or suspended or lapsed upon his suspension from membership of his HOME CLUB it shall be reinstated at the same handicap the player last held. In all other cases the player shall be allotted a new handicap after he has complied with the requirements of Clause 15.

18.(2) When allotting a new handicap to a player the HANDICAP COMMITTEE shall give due consideration to the handicap he last held and a CATEGORY 1 HANDICAP shall not be allotted without the written approval of the UNION or AREA AUTHORITY if so delegated.

19. Powers of the Handicap Committee Relating to General Play

19.(1) Whenever the HANDICAP COMMITTEE of a player's HOME CLUB considers that a player's EXACT HANDICAP is too high and does not reflect his current playing ability the HANDICAP COMMITTEE must, subject to the provisions of clause 19.(3), reduce his EXACT HANDICAP by not less than one whole stroke to the figure it considers appropriate. Fractional reductions in excess of one stroke are permitted.

19.(2)(a) Whenever the HANDICAP COMMITTEE of a player's HOME CLUB considers that a player's EXACT HANDICAP is too low and does not reflect his current playing ability the HANDICAP COMMITTEE must, subject to the provisions of clause 19.(3), recommend to the UNION, or AREA AUTHORITY if so delegated, that his EXACT HANDICAP should be increased by not less than one whole stroke to the figure it considers appropriate. Fractional increases in excess of one stroke are permitted.

(b) In the event of a UNION delegating to HOME CLUBS the unconditional authority to increase the handicaps of players in any of the CATEGORIES 2, 3 and 4 HOME CLUBS need not submit to the UNION or AREA AUTHORITY proposals in respect of any changes of handicaps of players in the nominated CATEGORIES.

19.(3) When the HANDICAP COMMITTEE has decided

(a) That the EXACT HANDICAP of a CATEGORY 1 player shall be reduced, or

(b) That the EXACT HANDICAP of a CATEGORY 2 player shall be reduced into CATEGORY 1, or

(c) That the EXACT HANDICAP of any player shall be increased (Subject to the provision of clause 9(7))

Then the HANDICAP COMMITTEE must refer the matter to the UNION, or AREA AUTHORITY if so delegated, with its recommended adjustment. The UNION or AREA AUTHORITY shall then authorise the recommended variation, reject the recommendation or refer the matter back to the HANDICAP COMMITTEE for further consideration. The UNION or AREA AUTHORITY shall be supplied with all the information upon which the recommendation is based and with any further information required.

19.(4) When deciding whether to effect or recommend an adjustment of handicap the HANDICAP COMMITTEE of the player's HOME CLUB shall consider all available information regarding the player's golfing ability.

It shall consider in particular:

(a) The frequency of QUALIFYING SCORES recently returned by the player to and below his PLAYING HANDICAP.

(b) The player's achievements in match play, four-ball better-ball competitions and other non-qualifying events.

(c) QUALIFYING SCORES returned by the player in stroke play competitions which are adversely affected by one or more particularly bad holes. It may prove helpful to take into account the number of points the player would have scored if these QUALIFYING SCORES had been in Stableford competitions played with full handicap allowance.

19.(5) The HANDICAP COMMITTEE shall advise a player of any change of handicap under this clause and the change will become effective when the player becomes aware of the adjustment.

19.(6) The HANDICAP COMMITTEE or other body organising a competition at a club which is not the player's HOME CLUB may, if it considers that his handicap is too high because of scores reported pursuant to sub clause 16.(11)(b) or for any other reason, reduce that handicap. Any reduction made under this clause shall apply only to the competition for which it is made.

19.(7) Subject to clause 19.(8) an AFFILIATED CLUB may not apply a formula by which handicaps shall be adjusted under this clause. Any handicap so adjusted shall not be a C.O.N.G.U. handicap designated under this scheme.

19.(8) UNIONS may direct Clubs within their jurisdiction that scores returned in stroke play QUALIFYING COMPETITIONS, whether or not all 18 holes have been completed, may be adjusted to the NETT DIFFERENTIAL which would have applied if the competition had been a Stableford QUALIFYING COMPETITION. No points shall be recorded on a hole where there is no score. This adjustment is for handicap purposes only, and notwithstanding the provisions of sub clause 19.(1), reductions of less than 1 stroke may be made under this sub clause. This sub clause does not apply to Category 1 handicaps and no EXACT HANDICAP can be reduced to less than 5.5.

APPENDIX J sets out a short alternative procedure and supplementary recommendations for calculating Stableford Point Score reductions authorised by this sub clause.

19.(9) Decisions made by a HANDICAP COMMITTEE, UNION or AREA AUTHORITY under this clause shall be final.

Note 1: In the interests of equitable handicapping it is essential that all HANDICAP COMMITTEES keep the handicaps of the MEMBERS for whom they act as the HOME CLUB under review and that adjustments of handicaps are considered as soon as it comes to the committee's notice that a player's handicap may no longer correctly reflect his current general golfing ability.

Note 2: Prior to the 1st March each year the HANDICAP COMMITTEE shall undertake a review of the handicaps of all MEMBERS for whom the Club

APPENDIX A

Handicap Record Sheet

Player:

Home Club: **Other Clubs:**

Handicap increases (clause 16.10(a)) made: Immediately

1	2 Date of score entry	3 Date of event	4 Round	5 Venue	6 Event	7 Gross Score	8 Clause 19.8 Adjst	9 Adjst Gross Score	10 CSS	11 Gross Dif	12 Net Dif	13 H'cap Adjst	14 Revised Exact H'cap	15 Revised Playing H'cap
		01-May-95		Handicap brought forward									21.0	21
1	06-May-95	06-May-95		Home Club	Medal	98	−1	97	72	25	4	0.0	21.0	21
2	07-May-95	07-May-95		Home Club	Medal	96		96	70	26	5	0.1	21.1	21
3	20-May-95	20-May-95		XXX Club	Medal	NR		NR	73	NR		0.1	21.2	21
4	21-May-95	21-May-95		Home Club	Medal	85		85	70	15	−6	−2.00	19.2	19
5	04-Jun-95	04-Jun-95		Home Club	Medal	90		90	70	20	1	0.0	19.2	19
6	05-Jun-95	05-Jun-95		Home Club	Stableford	n/a		n/a	70	23	4	0.1	19.3	19
7	25-Jun-95	25-Jun-95		Home Club	Medal	97	−1	96	70	26	7	0.1	19.4	19
8	26-Jun-95	26-Jun-95		Home Club	Medal	92		92	71	21	2	0.0	19.4	19
9	08-Jul-95	08-Jul-95	1	Home Club	Par	n/a		n/a	70	26	7	0.1	19.5	20
10	08-Jul-95	08-Jul-95	2	Home Club	Par	n/a		n/a	70	26	6	0.1	17.8 ~~19.6~~	18 ~~20~~
11	29-Jul-95	29-Jul-95		Home Club	Medal	100	−2	98	70	28	10 ~~8~~	0.1	17.9 ~~19.7~~	18 ~~20~~
12	30-Jul-95	30-Jul-95		Home Club	Medal	94		94	70	24	6 ~~4~~	0.1	18.0 ~~19.8~~	18 ~~20~~
13	06-Aug-95	06-Aug-95		Home Club	Medal	92		92	70	22	4 ~~2~~	0.1 ~~0.0~~	18.1 ~~19.8~~	18 ~~20~~
14	07-Aug-95	09-Jul-95		YYY Club	Medal	87		87	73	14	−6	Late	18.1	18
15	20-Aug-95	20-Aug-95		Home Club	Stableford	n/a		n/a	70	16	−2	−0.6	17.5	18
16	20-Aug-95			Clause 19 reduction								−1.5	16.0	16
17	21-Aug-95	21-Aug-95		Home Club	Stableford	n/a		n/a	69	18	2	0.0	16.0	16
18														

For notes to Appendix A, see opposite page

is the HOME CLUB and make such handicap adjustment as may be appropriate under the provisions of this clause.

Note 3: The HANDICAP COMMITTEE should consider dealing more severely with a player whose general standard of play is known to be improving than it should with a player who it is believed has returned scores below his general ability but whose general playing ability is not considered to be improving.

20. Competition Scratch Score

20.(1) At the conclusion of each round of a QUALIFYING COMPETITION the COMPETITION SCRATCH SCORE shall be calculated by following the procedure set out in Appendix D and applying the relevant Table in either Appendix E or F.

20.(2) In the event of one round of a QUALIFYING COMPETITION extending over more than one day the COMPETITION SCRATCH SCORE shall be calculated for each day.

20.(3) The relevant Table dictates any adjustment to be made to the STANDARD SCRATCH SCORE to provide the COMPETITION SCRATCH SCORE or to direct that the scores returned shall not count as QUALIFYING SCORES (indicated by "N/C" in the Table column heading). When the COMPETITION SCRATCH SCORE has been established all NETT DIFFERENTIALS shall be calculated in relation thereto and handicap adjustments made and entered in the player's Handicap Record Sheets. (See Definition T – BUFFER ZONE.)

20.(4) If the Table indicates that the scores returned shall not count as QUALIFYING SCORES then the COMPETITION SCRATCH SCORE shall be deemed to be three strokes more than the STANDARD SCRATCH SCORE. All players who after the application of the COMPETITION SCRATCH SCORE to their scores have returned a NETT DIFFERENTIAL of less than zero shall have their EXACT HANDICAPS reduced to the extent dictated by the NETT DIFFERENTIAL so calculated. A NETT DIFFERENTIAL of zero or above shall not result in a handicap increase.

20.(5) If a QUALIFYING COMPETITION is abandoned for any reason the COMPETITION SCRATCH SCORE shall be regarded as equal to the STANDARD SCRATCH SCORE and players returning NETT DIFFERENTIALS of less than zero shall have their EXACT HANDICAPS reduced to the extent dictated by the NETT DIFFERENTIAL. A NETT DIFFERENTIAL of zero or above shall not result in a handicap increase.

Note: UNIONS, AREA AUTHORITIES and any organisations so authorised by a UNION shall establish the COMPETITION SCRATCH SCORES for events they organise.

20.(6) Where a player is a MEMBER of two or more AFFILIATED CLUBS and competes in a QUALIFYING COMPETITION organised by two or more of those clubs and played over the same course and the score in one round is used in all the competitions then the COMPETITION SCRATCH SCORE applicable shall be that applied by his HOME CLUB or if none of the clubs is his HOME CLUB the highest COMPETITION SCRATCH SCORE shall be applied.

Notes to Appendix A

1. The provisions of clause 19.(8) have been applied to the scores shown above. Manual entries in respect of stroke play scores which are reduced by Stableford point calculation are made as follows:

    (a) the reduced NETT DIFFERENTIAL is entered in column 12.

    (b) A score equal to the reduced NETT DIFFERENTIAL plus the PLAYING HANDICAP from which the player competed is entered in column 11.

    (c) The number of strokes by which the NETT DIFFERENTIAL has been reduced is entered in column 8 and the reduced gross score entered in column 9.

2. On 4th June the player returned his card without a score recorded on one of the holes. The Stableford point calculation provided a point total which gave a NETT DIFFERENTIAL of one stroke over CSS. Despite the "No Return" the player's score is in his BUFFER ZONE and his EXACT HANDICAP remains unchanged.

3. If clause 19.(8) does not apply at the Club no entries are made in columns 8 and 9.

4. Appendix J sets out a short alternative procedure and supplementary recommendations for calculating Stableford point score reductions authorised by clause 19.(8).

5. When away scores are reported to a HOME CLUB after a later QUALIFYING COMPETITION has been entered in the Player's Record Sheet the player's EXACT HANDICAP shall be recalculated immediately to provide the EEXACT HANDICAP that would have applied if the scores had been entered in chronological order.

6. It will be noted in the above Table that the player failed to report an away score on 9th July until the 7th August. The omission resulted in the player playing in three competitions at his Home Club from a handicap of 20 instead of 18. Disqualification under Rule of Golf 6-2b is not permitted in these circumstances even if the player had been successful in winning one of the QUALIFYING COMPETITIONS. In the absence of a satisfactory explanation the HOME CLUB should consider suspending the player's handicap under clause 17.(1)

APPENDIX B
Table of Handicap Adjustments

Nett Differentials	−1	−2	−3	−4	−5	−6	−7	−8	−9	−10	−11	−12	Over Buffer Zone
Exact Handicaps Up to 5.4	−0.1	−0.2	−0.3	−0.4	−0.5	−0.6	−0.7	−0.8	−0.9	−1.0	−1.1	−1.2	+0.1
5.5–5.6	−0.2	−0.3	−0.4	−0.5	−0.6	−0.7	−0.8	−0.9	−1.0	−1.1	−1.2	−1.3	+0.1
5.7–5.8	−0.2	−0.4	−0.5	−0.6	−0.7	−0.8	−0.9	−1.0	−1.1	−1.2	−1.3	−1.4	+0.1
5.9–6.0	−0.2	−0.4	−0.6	−0.7	−0.8	−0.9	−1.0	−1.1	−1.2	−1.3	−1.4	−1.5	+0.1
6.1–6.2	−0.2	−0.4	−0.6	−0.8	−0.9	−1.0	−1.1	−1.2	−1.3	−1.4	−1.5	−1.6	+0.1
6.3–6.4	−0.2	−0.4	−0.6	−0.8	−1.0	−1.1	−1.2	−1.3	−1.4	−1.5	−1.6	−1.7	+0.1
6.5–6.6	−0.2	−0.4	−0.6	−0.8	−1.0	−1.2	−1.3	−1.4	−1.5	−1.6	−1.7	−1.8	+0.1
6.7–6.8	−0.2	−0.4	−0.6	−0.8	−1.0	−1.2	−1.4	−1.5	−1.6	−1.7	−1.8	−1.9	+0.1
6.9–7.0	−0.2	−0.4	−0.6	−0.8	−1.0	−1.2	−1.4	−1.6	−1.7	−1.8	−1.9	−2.0	+0.1
7.1–7.2	−0.2	−0.4	−0.6	−0.8	−1.0	−1.2	−1.4	−1.6	−1.8	−1.9	−2.0	−2.1	+0.1
7.3–7.4	−0.2	−0.4	−0.6	−0.8	−1.0	−1.2	−1.4	−1.6	−1.8	−2.0	−2.1	−2.2	+0.1
7.5–7.6	−0.2	−0.4	−0.6	−0.8	−1.0	−1.2	−1.4	−1.6	−1.8	−2.0	−2.2	−2.3	+0.1
7.7–12.4	−0.2	−0.4	−0.6	−0.8	−1.0	−1.2	−1.4	−1.6	−1.8	−2.0	−2.2	−2.4	+0.1
12.5–12.7	−0.3	−0.5	−0.7	−0.9	−1.1	−1.3	−1.5	−1.7	−1.9	−2.1	−2.3	−2.5	+0.1
12.8–13.0	−0.3	−0.6	−0.8	−1.0	−1.2	−1.4	−1.6	−1.8	−2.0	−2.2	−2.4	−2.6	+0.1
13.1–13.3	−0.3	−0.6	−0.9	−1.1	−1.3	−1.5	−1.7	−1.9	−2.1	−2.3	−2.5	−2.7	+0.1
13.4–13.6	−0.3	−0.6	−0.9	−1.2	−1.4	−1.6	−1.8	−2.0	−2.2	−2.4	−2.6	−2.8	+0.1
13.7–13.9	−0.3	−0.6	−0.9	−1.2	−1.5	−1.7	−1.9	−2.1	−2.3	−2.5	−2.7	−2.9	+0.1
14.0–14.2	−0.3	−0.6	−0.9	−1.2	−1.5	−1.8	−2.0	−2.2	−2.4	−2.6	−2.8	−3.0	+0.1
14.3–14.5	−0.3	−0.6	−0.9	−1.2	−1.5	−1.8	−2.1	−2.3	−2.5	−2.7	−2.9	−3.1	+0.1
14.6–14.8	−0.3	−0.6	−0.9	−1.2	−1.5	−1.8	−2.1	−2.4	−2.6	−2.8	−3.0	−3.2	+0.1
14.9–15.1	−0.3	−0.6	−0.9	−1.2	−1.5	−1.8	−2.1	−2.4	−2.7	−2.9	−3.1	−3.3	+0.1
15.2–15.4	−0.3	−0.6	−0.9	−1.2	−1.5	−1.8	−2.1	−2.4	−2.7	−3.0	−3.2	−3.4	+0.1
15.5–15.7	−0.3	−0.6	−0.9	−1.2	−1.5	−1.8	−2.1	−2.4	−2.7	−3.0	−3.3	−3.5	+0.1
15.8–20.4	−0.3	−0.6	−0.9	−1.2	−1.5	−1.8	−2.1	−2.4	−2.7	−3.0	−3.3	−3.6	+0.1
20.5–20.8	−0.4	−0.7	−1.0	−1.3	−1.6	−1.9	−2.2	−2.5	−2.8	−3.1	−3.4	−3.7	+0.1
20.9–21.2	−0.4	−0.8	−1.1	−1.4	−1.7	−2.0	−2.3	−2.6	−2.9	−3.2	−3.5	−3.8	+0.1
21.3–21.6	−0.4	−0.8	−1.2	−1.5	−1.8	−2.1	−2.4	−2.7	−3.0	−3.3	−3.6	−3.9	+0.1
21.7–22.0	−0.4	−0.8	−1.2	−1.6	−1.9	−2.2	−2.5	−2.8	−3.1	−3.4	−3.7	−4.0	+0.1
22.1–22.4	−0.4	−0.8	−1.2	−1.6	−2.0	−2.3	−2.6	−2.9	−3.2	−3.5	−3.8	−4.1	+0.1
22.5–22.8	−0.4	−0.8	−1.2	−1.6	−2.0	−2.4	−2.7	−3.0	−3.3	−3.6	−3.9	−4.2	+0.1
22.9–23.2	−0.4	−0.8	−1.2	−1.6	−2.0	−2.4	−2.8	−3.1	−3.4	−3.7	−4.0	−4.3	+0.1
23.3–23.6	−0.4	−0.8	−1.2	−1.6	−2.0	−2.4	−2.8	−3.2	−3.5	−3.8	−4.1	−4.4	+0.1
23.7–24.0	−0.4	−0.8	−1.2	−1.6	−2.0	−2.4	−2.8	−3.2	−3.6	−3.9	−4.2	−4.5	+0.1
24.1–24.4	−0.4	−0.8	−1.2	−1.6	−2.0	−2.4	−2.8	−3.2	−3.6	−4.0	−4.3	−4.6	+0.1
24.5–24.8	−0.4	−0.8	−1.2	−1.6	−2.0	−2.4	−2.8	−3.2	−3.6	−4.0	−4.4	−4.7	+0.1
24.9–28.0	−0.4	−0.8	−1.2	−1.6	−2.0	−2.4	−2.8	−3.2	−3.6	−4.0	−4.4	−4.8	+0.1

Appendix C

Table for converting Par and Stableford scores to nett differentials
(Note – the Table is based on full handicap allowance)

Score versus PAR	7 down	6 down	5 down	4 down	3 down	2 down	1 down	All Square	1 up	2 up	3 up	4 up	5 up	6 up	7 up
STABLEFORD points scored	29	30	31	32	33	34	35	36	37	38	39	40	41	42	43
Par 7 less than CSS	0	−1	−2	−3	−4	−5	−6	−7	−8	−9	−10	−11	−12	−13	−14
Par 6 less than CSS	+1	0	−1	−2	−3	−4	−5	−6	−7	−8	−9	−10	−11	−12	−13
Par 5 less than CSS	+2	+1	0	−1	−2	−3	−4	−5	−6	−7	−8	−9	−10	−11	−12
Par 4 less than CSS	+3	+2	+1	0	−1	−2	−3	−4	−5	−6	−7	−8	−9	−10	−11
Par 3 less than CSS	+4	+3	+2	+1	0	−1	−2	−3	−4	−5	−6	−7	−8	−9	−10
Par 2 less than CSS	+5	+4	+3	+2	+1	0	−1	−2	−3	−4	−5	−6	−7	−8	−9
Par 1 less than CSS	+6	+5	+4	+3	+2	+1	0	−1	−2	−3	−4	−5	−6	−7	−8
Par equal to CSS	+7	+6	+5	+4	+3	+2	+1	0	−1	−2	−3	−4	−5	−6	−7
Par 1 more than CSS	+8	+7	+6	+5	+4	+3	+2	+1	0	−1	−2	−3	−4	−5	−6
Par 2 more than CSS	+9	+8	+7	+6	+5	+4	+3	+2	+1	0	−1	−2	−3	−4	−5
Par 3 more than CSS	+10	+9	+8	+7	+6	+5	+4	+3	+2	+1	0	−1	−2	−3	−4
Par 4 more than CSS	+11	+10	+9	+8	+7	+6	+5	+4	+3	+2	+1	0	−1	−2	−3
Par 5 more than CSS	+12	+11	+10	+9	+8	+7	+6	+5	+4	+3	+2	+1	0	−1	−2
Par 6 more than CSS	+13	+12	+11	+10	+9	+8	+7	+6	+5	+4	+3	+2	+1	0	−1

Example:– (a) 3 up on a Par 72 course with a CSS of 70. Par is 2 more than CSS so Nett Differential = −1.
(b) 37 Stableford points on a course with Par 68 & CSS 69. Par is 1 less than CSS so Nett Differential = −2.

APPENDIX D

Standard Scratch Score and Handicapping Scheme

The Competition Scratch Score

Number of Competitors Including No Returns		PERCENTAGES		ROUNDED %
Category 1	A	A x 100 / D	F	I
Category 2	B	B x 100 / D	G	J
Category 3	C	100 minus boxes I & J		K
Total	D	Total:		100
Number of Nett Scores in Categories 1, 2 & 3 at 2 over SSS and better	E	E x 100 / D	H	L

Procedure

1. Enter in Boxes A, B and C the number of competitors, including no returns, from each of the Categories 1, 2 & 3.
2. Enter the total number of competitors in Categories 1, 2 and 3, including no returns, in Box D.
3. Enter in Box E the number of competitors in Categories 1, 2 and 3 who have returned nett scores two over SSS and better before any application of clause 19.8. For Par and 'Stableford competitions use the converted equivalent.
   Note: To establish the converted equivalent of a score Two over SSS calculate as follows:
   (a) Stableford Competitions = Par less SSS plus 36 less 2.
   (b) Par Competitions = Par less SSS less 2.
4. In Boxes F, G and H enter the percentages of the adjacent boxes in relation to Box D as indicated.
5. Round the number in Box F to the nearest 10% and enter the result in Box I. (5% upwards).
6. Round the number in Box G to the nearest 10% and enter the result in Box J. (5% upwards).
   Note: Occasionally the rounding of Boxes F and G will produce a total of Boxes I and J in excess of 100. When this occurs round the number in Box G downwards and insert the amended number in Box J.
7. Enter in Box K the total of Boxes I and J deducted from 100. (The percentage in Box K may not coincide with the rounded percentage Box C would give if calculated).
8. Round the number in Box H to the nearest whole number (0.5 upwards) and enter the result in Box L.
9. Select the relevant Table – Table A when the total number of competitors in Categories 1, 2 & 3 exceeds 30, otherwise Table B. Select the row which contains the percentage shown in Boxes I, J and K.
10. In the row selected find the column which includes the number in Box L. The SSS adjustment is shown in the heading of that column and that number is added to or deducted from the SSS to provide the COMPETITION SCRATCH SCORE (CSS). For each QUALIFYING COMPETITION the CSS replaces the SSS for all handicapping purposes. The BUFFER ZONES are applied to the CSS and not the SSS.
11. The heading N/C at the top of a column in the Tables indicates that scores returned shall not result in handicap increases. Reductions of handicap will be made on the basis that the CSS is three strokes higher than the SSS.
12. When a competition has been abandoned for any reason reductions of handicaps shall be on the basis that the CSS is equal to the SSS but no handicaps shall be increased.
13. In the event of all the competitors in a QUALIFYING COMPETITION holding handicaps in CATEGORY 4 the OMPETITION SCRATCH SCORE shall be the STANDARD SCRATCH SCORE.
14. HANDICAP COMMITTEES are reminded that they no longer have a discretion to determine that a QUALIFYING COMPETITION shall or shall not be "non counting".

APPENDIX E

Table A   More than 30 competitors in categories 1, 2 & 3

Categories			Adjustments to SSS to determine the CSS					
1	2	3	N/C	+3	+2	+1	0	−1
0%	0%	100%	0-4	5-7	8-10	11-15	16-30	31+
0%	10%	90%	0-4	5-7	8-11	12-15	16-32	33+
0%	20%	80%	0-5	6-7	8-11	12-16	17-34	35+
0%	30%	70%	0-5	6-8	9-12	13-17	18-36	37+
0%	40%	60%	0-5	6-8	9-12	13-18	19-38	39+
0%	50%	50%	0-5	6-8	9-13	14-19	20-40	41+
0%	60%	40%	0-5	6-9	10-14	15-20	21-41	42+
0%	70%	30%	0-5	6-9	10-14	15-21	22-43	44+
0%	80%	20%	0-5	6-9	10-15	16-22	23-45	46+
0%	90%	10%	0-6	7-10	11-15	16-23	24-47	48+
0%	100%	0%	0-6	7-10	11-16	17-24	25-49	50+
10%	0%	90%	0-5	6-8	9-12	13-17	18-34	35+
10%	10%	80%	0-5	6-8	9-12	13-18	19-36	37+
10%	20%	70%	0-5	6-8	9-13	14-18	19-38	39+
10%	30%	60%	0-5	6-9	10-13	14-19	20-39	40+
10%	40%	50%	0-5	6-9	10-14	15-20	21-41	42+
10%	50%	40%	0-5	6-9	10-14	15-21	22-43	44+
10%	60%	30%	0-6	7-9	10-15	16-22	23-45	46+
10%	70%	20%	0-6	7-10	11-16	17-23	24-47	48+
10%	80%	10%	0-6	7-10	11-16	17-24	25-49	50+
10%	90%	0%	0-6	7-10	11-17	8-25	26-51	52+
20%	0%	80%	0-5	6-8	9-13	14-19	20-38	39+
20%	10%	70%	0-5	6-9	10-14	15-20	21-39	40+
20%	20%	60%	0-5	6-9	10-14	15-21	22-41	42+
20%	30%	50%	0-6	7-9	10-15	16-22	23-43	44+
20%	40%	40%	0-6	7-10	11-15	16-22	23-45	46+
20%	50%	30%	0-6	7-10	11-16	17-23	24-47	48+
20%	60%	20%	0-6	7-10	11-16	17-24	25-49	50+
20%	70%	10%	0-6	7-11	12-17	18-25	26-51	52+
20%	80%	0%	0-6	7-11	12-18	19-26	27-53	54+
30%	0%	70%	0-6	7-9	10-14	15-21	22-41	42+
30%	10%	60%	0-6	7-10	11-15	16-22	23-43	44+
30%	20%	50%	0-6	7-10	11-16	17-23	24-45	46+
I	J	K	VALUES OF L (Percentages)					

Categories			Adjustments to SSS to determine the CSS					
1	2	3	N/C	+3	+2	+1	0	−1
30%	30%	40%	0-6	7-10	11-16	17-24	25-47	48+
30%	40%	30%	0-6	7-11	12-17	18-25	26-49	50+
30%	50%	20%	0-6	7-11	12-17	18-26	27-51	52+
30%	60%	10%	0-6	7-11	12-18	19-26	27-53	54+
30%	70%	0%	0-7	8-11	12-18	19-27	28-55	56+
40%	0%	60%	0-6	7-10	11-16	17-23	24-45	46+
40%	10%	50%	0-6	7-10	11-16	17-24	25-47	48+
40%	20%	40%	0-6	7-11	12-17	18-25	26-49	50+
40%	30%	30%	0-6	7-11	12-18	19-26	27-51	52+
40%	40%	20%	0-7	8-11	12-18	19-27	28-53	54+
40%	50%	10%	0-7	8-12	13-19	20-28	29-55	56+
40%	60%	0%	0-7	8-12	13-19	20-29	30-57	58+
50%	0%	50%	0-6	7-11	12-17	18-25	26-49	50+
50%	10%	40%	0-7	8-11	12-18	19-26	27-51	52+
50%	20%	30%	0-7	8-12	13-18	19-27	28-53	54+
50%	30%	20%	0-7	8-12	13-19	20-28	29-55	56+
50%	40%	10%	0-7	8-12	13-20	21-29	30-57	58+
50%	50%	0%	0-7	8-13	14-20	21-30	31-59	60+
60%	0%	40%	0-7	8-12	13-19	20-27	28-53	54+
60%	10%	30%	0-7	8-12	13-19	20-28	29-55	56+
60%	20%	20%	0-7	8-12	13-20	21-29	30-57	58+
60%	30%	10%	0-7	8-13	14-20	21-30	31-59	60+
60%	40%	0%	0-7	8-13	14-21	22-31	32-61	62+
70%	0%	30%	0-7	8-13	14-20	21-30	31-57	58+
70%	10%	20%	0-7	8-13	14-21	22-31	32-59	60+
70%	20%	10%	0-8	9-13	14-21	22-31	32-60	61+
70%	30%	0%	0-8	9-14	15-22	23-32	33-62	63+
80%	0%	20%	0-8	9-13	14-22	23-32	33-60	61+
80%	10%	10%	0-8	9-14	15-22	23-33	34-62	63+
80%	20%	0%	0-8	9-14	15-23	24-34	35-64	65+
90%	0%	10%	0-8	9-14	15-23	24-34	35-64	65+
90%	10%	0%	0-8	9-15	16-24	25-35	36-66	67+
100%	0%	0%	0-9	10-15	16-24	25-36	37-68	69+
I	J	K	VALUES OF L (Percentages)					

Table B Less than 31 competitors in categories 1, 2 & 3

1	2	3	N/C	+3	+2	+1	0	−1
0%	0%	100%	0-3	4-5	6-8	9-12	13-30	31+
0%	10%	90%	0-3	4-6	7-9	10-13	14-32	33+
0%	20%	80%	0-3	4-6	7-9	10-14	15-34	35+
0%	30%	70%	0-4	5-6	7-10	11-14	15-36	37+
0%	40%	60%	0-4	5-6	7-10	11-15	16-38	39+
0%	50%	50%	0-4	5-7	8-10	11-16	17-40	41+
0%	60%	40%	0-4	5-7	8-11	12-17	18-41	42+
0%	70%	30%	0-4	5-7	8-11	12-17	18-43	44+
0%	80%	20%	0-4	5-7	8-12	13-18	19-45	46+
0%	90%	10%	0-4	5-7	8-12	13-19	20-47	48+
0%	100%	0%	0-4	5-8	9-13	14-19	20-49	50+
10%	0%	90%	0-4	5-6	7-9	10-14	15-34	35+
10%	10%	80%	0-4	5-6	7-10	11-15	16-36	37+
10%	20%	70%	0-4	5-6	7-10	11-15	16-38	39+
10%	30%	60%	0-4	5-7	8-11	12-16	17-39	40+
10%	40%	50%	0-4	5-7	8-11	12-17	18-41	42+
10%	50%	40%	0-4	5-7	8-12	13-18	19-43	44+
10%	60%	30%	0-4	5-7	8-12	13-18	19-45	46+
10%	70%	20%	0-4	5-8	9-12	13-19	20-47	48+
10%	80%	10%	0-4	5-8	9-13	14-20	21-49	50+
10%	90%	0%	0-4	5-8	9-13	14-20	21-51	52+
20%	0%	80%	0-4	5-7	8-11	12-16	17-38	39+
20%	10%	70%	0-4	5-7	8-11	12-16	17-39	40+
20%	20%	60%	0-4	5-7	8-11	12-17	18-41	42+
20%	30%	50%	0-4	5-7	8-12	13-18	19-43	44+
20%	40%	40%	0-4	5-7	8-12	13-19	20-45	46+
20%	50%	30%	0-4	5-8	9-13	14-19	20-47	48+
20%	60%	20%	0-4	5-8	9-13	14-20	21-49	50+
20%	70%	10%	0-4	5-8	9-13	14-21	22-51	52+
20%	80%	0%	0-5	6-8	9-14	15-22	23-53	54+
30%	0%	70%	0-4	5-7	8-12	13-18	19-41	42+
30%	10%	60%	0-4	5-7	8-12	13-18	19-43	44+
30%	20%	50%	0-4	5-8	9-12	13-19	20-45	46+
I	**J**	**K**	**VALUES OF L (Percentages)**					

1	2	3	N/C	+3	+2	+1	0	−1
30%	30%	40%	0-4	5-8	9-13	14-20	21-47	48+
30%	40%	30%	0-4	5-8	9-13	14-20	21-49	50+
30%	50%	20%	0-5	6-8	9-14	15-21	22-51	52+
30%	60%	10%	0-5	6-9	10-14	15-22	23-53	54+
30%	70%	0%	0-5	6-9	10-15	16-23	24-55	56+
40%	0%	60%	0-4	5-8	9-13	14-19	20-45	46+
40%	10%	50%	0-4	5-8	9-13	14-20	21-47	48+
40%	20%	40%	0-5	6-8	9-14	15-21	22-49	50+
40%	30%	30%	0-5	6-8	9-14	15-21	22-51	52+
40%	40%	20%	0-5	6-9	10-14	15-22	23-53	54+
40%	50%	10%	0-5	6-9	10-15	16-23	24-55	56+
40%	60%	0%	0-5	6-9	10-15	16-24	24-57	58+
50%	0%	50%	0-5	6-8	9-14	15-21	22-49	50+
50%	10%	40%	0-5	6-9	10-14	15-22	23-51	52+
50%	20%	30%	0-5	6-9	10-15	16-22	23-53	54+
50%	30%	20%	0-5	6-9	10-15	16-23	24-55	56+
50%	40%	10%	0-5	6-9	10-16	17-24	25-57	58+
50%	50%	0%	0-5	6-10	11-16	17-25	26-59	60+
60%	0%	40%	0-5	6-9	10-15	16-23	24-53	54+
60%	10%	30%	0-5	6-9	10-15	16-24	25-55	56+
60%	20%	20%	0-5	6-9	10-16	17-24	25-57	58+
60%	30%	10%	0-5	6-10	11-16	17-25	26-59	60+
60%	40%	0%	0-5	6-10	11-17	18-26	27-61	62+
70%	0%	30%	0-5	6-10	11-16	17-25	26-57	58+
70%	10%	20%	0-5	6-10	11-16	17-25	26-59	60+
70%	20%	10%	0-5	6-10	11-17	18-26	27-60	61+
70%	30%	0%	0-5	6-10	11-17	18-27	28-62	63+
80%	0%	20%	0-5	6-10	11-17	18-26	27-60	61+
80%	10%	10%	0-6	7-10	11-18	19-27	28-62	63+
80%	20%	0%	0-6	7-11	12-18	19-28	29-64	65+
90%	0%	10%	0-6	7-11	12-18	19-28	29-64	65+
90%	10%	0%	0-6	7-11	12-19	20-29	30-66	67+
100%	0%	0%	0-6	7-11	12-19	20-30	31-68	69+
I	**J**	**K**	**VALUES OF L (Percentages)**					

Handicap Allowances

as recommended by Council of National Golf Unions

The Council of National Golf Unions recommends that the following handicap allowances shall apply in the following forms of play. The reference to handicaps in all cases refers to PLAYING HANDICAPS.

Match Play

Singles	The full difference between the HANDICAPS of the two players.
Foursomes	¹/₂ of the full difference between the aggregate HANDICAP of either side.
Four-ball (better ball)	Back marker to concede strokes to the other three players based on ³/₄ of the difference between the full handicap.

Strokes to be taken according to the Stroke Table.

Bogey or Par Competitions

Singles	Full handicap
Foursomes	¹/₂ of the aggregate HANDICAP of the partners.
Four-ball (better ball)	Each partner receives ³/₄ of full handicap.

Strokes to be taken according to the Stroke Table.

Stroke Play

Singles	Full handicap
Foursomes	¹/₂ of aggregate HANDICAPS of the partners.
Four-ball (better ball)	Each partner receives ³/₄ of the full handicap and strokes to be taken according to the Stroke Table.

Stableford Competitions

Singles	Full handicap
Foursomes	¹/₂ of aggregate HANDICAPS of the partners.
Four-ball (better ball)	Each partner receives ³/₄ of full handicap.

Strokes to be taken according to the Stroke Table and not added to the points scored.

Note 1: A UNION may at its discretion make the above recommendations mandatory.

Note 2: Half Strokes. Half strokes or over to be counted as one; smaller fractions to be disregarded except in Foursomes Stroke Play when half strokes are counted as such.

Note 3: Handicap allowances in a handicap competition must be laid down by the Committee in the Conditions of the Competition (Rules of Golf 33-1).

Note 4: In handicap competitions over 36 holes strokes should be given or taken on a basis of 2 18

hole rounds in accordance with the 18 hole Stroke Table unless the Committee introduce a special Stroke Table.

Note 5: Sudden death play-off. When extra holes are played in handicap competitions, strokes should be taken in accordance with the Stroke Table.

Computer Software relating to the Standard Scratch and Handicapping Scheme

1. With effect from 1st April 1997 any software used by Affiliated Clubs shall provide a printed record for submission, when required, to Area Authorities or National Unions which shall contain not less information than that required in the Handicap Record Sheet shown in Appendix A and the notes thereto.

2. All entries must be displayed and handicap adjustments made in chronological order.

3. The software shall not include any guidance or option contrary to the requirements of the Scheme, e.g.:

   (a) Stroke Index Allocation.

   (b) Any formula for clause 19 adjustments other than as provided in clause 19.(8).

   (c) Provision enabling Clubs to obtain reductions of handicap without handicap increases other than when so required by clauses 20.(4) and 20.(5).

Stroke Index Allocation

Rule of Golf 33-4 requires Committees to "publish a table indicating the order of holes at which handicap strokes are to be given or received". To provide consistency at Clubs it is recommended that the allocation is so made as follows:

   (a) Of paramount importance is the even spread of the strokes to be received at all handicap differences over the 18 holes.

   (b) This is best achieved by allocating the odd numbered strokes to the more difficult of the two nines, usually the longest nine, and the even numbers to the other nine.

   (c) The first and second stroke index holes should be placed close to the centre of each nine and the first six strokes should not be allocated to adjacent holes. The 7th to the 10th indexes should be allocated so that a player receiving 10 strokes does not receive three strokes on consecutive holes.

(d) None of the first eight strokes should be allocated to the 1st or the last hole, and at clubs where competitive matches may be started at the 10th hole, at the 9th or 10th holes. This avoids a player receiving an undue advantage on the 19th hole should a match continue to sudden death. Unless there are compelling reasons to the contrary, stroke indexes 9, 10, 11 and 12 should be allocated to holes 1, 9, 10 and 18 in such order as shall be appropriate.

(e) Subject to satisfying the foregoing recommendations, when selecting each stroke index in turn holes of varying length should be selected. Index 1 could be a par 5, index 2 a long par 4, index 3 a shorter par 4 and index 4 a par 3. There is no recommended order for this selection, the objective being to select in index sequence holes of varying playing difficulty. Such a selection provides more equal opportunity for all handicaps in match play and Stableford and Par competitions than an order based upon hole length or difficulty to obtain par.

Note 1: Par is not an indicator of hole difficulty. Long par 3 and 4 holes are often selected for low index allocation in preference to par 5 holes on the basis that it is easier to score par on a par 5 hole than 4 on a long par 4. Long par 3 and 4 holes are difficult pars for low handicap players but often relatively easy bogeys for players with slightly higher handicaps. Difficulty in relation to par should not be taken into account when selecting stroke indexes.

Note 2: When allocating a stroke index it should be noted that in the majority of social matches there are small handicap differences thereby making the even distribution of the lower indexes of great importance.

The above recommendations supplement those made by the Royal and Ancient Golf Club of St Andrews contained in "Guidance Notes for Club Committees".

APPENDIX J

Stableford Points Alternative (Clause 19.(8))

1. The purpose of applying a Stableford Point calculation under clause 19.(8) handicap reductions is to reduce the impact of extremely bad scores on a hole in stroke play QUALIFYING COMPETITIONS which are not truly representative of a player's golf ability.
2. If a player applies the course stroke index relevant to his handicap and scores a nett par on each

hole in a Stableford QUALIFYING COMPETITION he will have a medal score equal to the par of the course. If the par is less than the SSS he will have recorded a nett medal score below his handicap by the difference between par and SSS. If par is more than SSS the reverse applies. It is by applying this principle that point scores in a Stableford QUALIFYING COMPETITION are converted into NETT DIFFERENTIALS.

3. Any hole in a Stableford QUALIFYING COMPETITION upon which a player records no score and accordingly is not awarded any points indicates that the player would, if the hole had been completed, have scored not less than a nett double bogey. A nett double bogey on a par 3 hole = 5 strokes, on a par 4 hole = 6 strokes and on a par 5 hole = 7 strokes. E.g. on a par 4 hole a player who obtains no Stableford points would, if he had completed the hole, have taken 6 or more strokes if the index did not provide a stroke on that hole or 7 strokes or more if he had received a stroke.

4. By applying these principles it is possible to convert a stroke play medal score into the NETT DIFFERENTIAL which would have applied if the same scores had been recorded in a Stableford event *without calculating the points on each hole.* Further it is not necessary to make an adjustment when the par and SSS are not the same. It is also possible to calculate a NETT DIFFERENTIAL in a stroke play event when one or more holes have not been completed.

These adjustments are achieved as follows:

(a) All holes completed. The player's NETT DIFFERENTIAL is reduced by the number of strokes he has scored on any hole in excess of nett double bogey. Other than for plus handicap players only scores of 6 or more can be reduced on par 3 holes, 7 or more on par 4s and 8 or more on par 5s. An examination of the scores on the par 3 holes will usually identify no adjustment on those holes and thereafter only scores of 7 or more require examination (8 or more if the player's handicap is greater than 18). This process will usually show that no scores are to be reduced. If a reduction is appropriate that reduction is entered in column 8 of the Handicap Record Sheet and other numbers appropriately adjusted.

(b) Holes with no score recorded. The assessment is made as in (a) above by reducing all scores to nett double bogey. A score of nett double bogey is entered at holes where no score is recorded. The scores are totalled and the player's handicap applied. Scores are then entered in the Handicap Record Sheet commencing at column 9.

5. By applying the process of "nett double bogey" it has been found that it takes less than one fifth of the time to achieve the same result as

•

calculating the number of Stableford points. Further it is not unreasonable to ask competitors to mark all holes on their cards which are to be considered for Stableford adjustment.

6. Clubs are reminded that Stableford adjustment is optional under clause 19.(8) If no adjustment is made then no entry will be made in column 8.

7. Clubs are reminded that Stableford adjustments under clause 19.(8) are made for handicap purposes only. Clause 19.(8) does not apply to CATEGORY 1 handicaps and no EXACT HANDICAP can be reduced to less that 5.5.

APPENDIX K
Decisions

1. Scores in Extended Competitions

If from a series of any number of scores special prizes are awarded for the best eclectic score or the best nett or gross aggregate of a prescribed number of scores, the individual scores in the series will be QUALIFYING COMPETITIONS provided each score is returned under MEDAL PLAY CONDITIONS in a QUALIFYING COMPETITION, as defined in the Scheme, and not returned solely for the purpose of the eclectic, nett or gross aggregate awards.

2. Qualifying Scores

(a) If a club with a large number of QUALIFYING COMPETITIONS in the calendar year wishes to deprive certain of the competitions of their status as QUALIFYING COMPETITIONS it may do so provided competitors are so advised before play commences.

(b) It would be outside the spirit of the Handicapping Scheme to declare that all Club Medal Competitions during a specified period would not be regarded as QUALIFYING COMPETITIONS, although played under full MEDAL PLAY CONDITIONS.

(c) In both (a) and (b) above it would be more appropriate to play unofficial MEDAL COMPETITIONS under conditions which would not give them the status of QUALIFYING COMPETITIONS.

Note: A declaration that a competition is not a QUALIFYING COMPETITION disqualifies all scores returned in that competition for handicapping purposes. Thus a player returning a score below his handicap will not have his EXACT HANDICAP reduced nor will a score above a player's BUFFER ZONE increase his EXACT HANDICAP. Clause 19(4)(b) does however allow scores in non

qualifying competitions to be one of a number of considerations when deciding to effect or recommend a handicap adjustment.

(d) A competition will not lose the status of QUALIFYING COMPETITION when played under conditions when, because of work proceeding or ground conditions in the area, pegging-up has been made obligatory by the club on a restricted area of the course, provided the playing of QUALIFYING COMPETITIONS under such conditions has the prior approval of the UNION or AREA AUTHORITY.

3. Upwards adjustment of Handicaps

(a) Clubs may elect to adjust PLAYING HANDICAPS upwards at the end of each calendar month or at shorter intervals.

(b) There could be slight differences in EXACT HANDICAPS produced by each method when comparison is made at the end of a calendar month.

(c) The procedure for recording NETT DIFFERENTIALS set out in the Scheme should be adhered to whatever method is used.

(d) There is no objection to clubs electing to adjust PLAYING HANDICAPS upwards at the end of each calendar month, or at more frequent intervals, taking steps to adjust and record EXACT and PLAYING HANDICAPS so that at the end of each month they correspond with those derived by adjusting handicaps after the playing of each QUALIFYING COMPETITION.

4. Limitation of Handicaps

Clubs have inquired whether they may impose a limit of handicap to some of their competitions e.g. insist that a 24 handicap player competes from a handicap of 18. This is permitted by Rule of Golf 33-1. However, when recording the players' scores for handicapping purposes, adjustments must be made to ensure that the NETT DIFFERENTIAL is recorded from his current PLAYING HANDICAP i.e. in the example quoted 24 instead of 18.

This is comparatively simple for MEDAL COMPETITION, but is impractical for Stableford and Par competitions as it is unlikely for example that a player would record a score at a hole where a stroke allowance of one from an 18 handicap gave him no points, whereas from a handicap of 24 with a stroke allowance of two at that particular hole he might have registered one point.

5. Incomplete Cards and No Returns

(a) All cards must be returned, whether complete or not.

(b) It is expected that every player who enters for an 18-hole QUALIFYING COMPETITION intends to complete the round.

(c) Since an Incomplete Card and a No Return have the effect of increasing a player's handicap, the club would be justified in refusing to accept a card or record a 'N.R.' when the player has walked in after playing only a few holes.

(d) Cards should not be issued to players when there is obviously insufficient light for them to complete the round.

(e) Sympathetic consideration should be given to players who have had to discontinue play for any cause considered to be reasonable by the organising committee.

(f) Clauses 17 and 19 of the Scheme give clubs the discretion to deal with players who persistently submit Incomplete Cards or make No Returns if they consider they are attempting to 'build a handicap'.

6. Reduction of Handicaps during a Competition

Where the conditions of a competition do not provide otherwise the handicap of a player applying at the beginning of a competition shall apply throughout that competition.

This provision shall apply to a competition in which supplementary prizes are awarded for the best scores returned in an individual round or in combinations of individual rounds of the competition. The provisions shall not apply in circumstances where the winner is the player returning the lowest aggregate score in two or more separate competitions.

Where a player's handicap has been reduced during the course of a competition in which the original handicap continues to apply the player shall play from his reduced handicap in all other competitions commencing after the handicap reduction.

7. Overseas Scores

Scores returned in tournaments organised by the European Golf Association are QUALIFYING SCORES for handicapping purposes and must be returned to the HOME CLUB pursuant to clause 13.(7) provided COMPETITION SCRATCH SCORES have been calculated. Other scores returned in overseas tournaments may be returned and used, if considered appropriate, under the terms of clause 19.

8. Clause 19

Except under sub clause 19.(8), reductions pursuant to clause 19 can be made only when the HANDICAP COMMITTEE has reason to believe that

the handicap of a player may be too high. The Committee must consider all available information regarding the player's ability. In these circumstances a low score in a single event is not sufficient evidence alone to justify a clause 19 reduction.

If the handicap of any player is reduced other than to the extent required by clause 16 or by the correct application of clause 19, the player's handicap will not be a C.O.N.G.U. handicap and must not be used in any competition for which a C.O.N.G.U. handicap is required.

9. Plus Handicaps

When calculating the number of strokes a plus handicap player should give the course when other than full allowance is to be applied, the rounding of fractions of a stroke shall be carried out in the usual way by rounding 0.5 of a stroke upwards. However as a handicap of "plus" is mathematically a minus handicap (below zero), three quarters of a handicap of +2 equals −1.5 which rounds upwards to -1 stroke. That stroke should be conceded to the course at the hole allocated stroke index 18.

10. CSS Calculations – Club runs two separate competitions on same day

When two or more separate competitions are held by a club on the same day in which all competitors play only one round a single CSS shall be calculated by reference to the scores of the Category 1, 2 and 3 competitors in all of the competitions. If any of the competitions are over more than one round on the same day then two CSS calculations shall be made for those competitions, one for each round, and the scores in those competitions shall be excluded from the calculation of the CSS for the competition or competitions over one round.

11. Tee Areas

To ensure that when tee markers are placed adjacent to the distance point a player may tee his ball and play his stroke from within the area permitted by the Rules of Golf it is proposed that, with effect from 1st January 2001, all distance points shall be positioned on tees so that they are not less than 4 yards in front of the rear of the tee. In the intervening period Clubs are asked to reposition distance points immediately prior to reprinting score cards. Adjustments to the SSS of the course will be made initially only when the course is re-rated. At any re-rating the assessment shall be related to the revised hole measurements.

12. Disqualified Scores

Clause 14.(1)(c) of the Scheme provides that a player's handicap record shall include "Correct

Scores in a QUALIFYING COMPETITION which are disqualified for any reason".

The following are examples when, following disqualification, correct scores can be identified:

(a) Rule 3-4 – Player refuses to comply with the Rules affecting the rights of another competitor.

(b) Rule 6-2 (b) – Handicap entered on a card which is too high. If a handicap has been entered which is too low the correct handicap should be substituted for handicapping purposes.

(c) Rule 6-3 – Player failing to start at the correct time.

(d) Rule 6-6 – Card not signed by the player or his marker.

(e) Rule 6-6 (b) – Player unduly delays the return of his card.

(f) Rule 6-6 (d) – Score entered on a hole which is too low. If a score has been entered on a hole which is too high the correct score should be substituted for handicap purposes.

(g) Rule 6-7 – Player unduly delaying play.

(h) Rule 6-8 – Player discontinues play.

The following are situations where a score shall not be regarded as a correct score when the player has been disqualified:

(i) Rule 1-3 – Agreeing to waive the Rules.

(j) Rule 4-1, 4-2 & 4-3 – Using illegal clubs.

(k) Rule 6-4 – Employing more than one caddie at the same time.

(l) Rule 7-1 – Practising on the course prior to play.

(m) Rule 14-3 – Using an artificial device.

(n) Rule 15-3 – Playing a wrong ball not corrected.

(o) Rule 20-7 – Playing a ball from a wrong place.

To accept a disqualified score as a "correct score" the committee must verify the score in such manner as it shall deem appropriate. When a disqualified score has been so accepted as a QUALIFYING SCORE before the last card has been returned to the Committee, the corrected score shall be included in the calculation of the CSS. Otherwise for CSS purposes the card shall be regarded as a "no return". All penalty strokes shall be included in the score for handicap purposes.

13. Clause 19 applied at a time when the player has not returned relevant away scores

When a HOME CLUB has made a handicap adjustment pursuant to clause 19 and the player subsequently reports scores from away QUALIFYING COMPETITIONS held prior to the date of the adjustment those scores shall not be used to further adjust the player's handicap unless the effect of one or more of the scores would have been to reduce the player's exact handicap and the overall reduction would have been to less than the clause 19 adjusted exact handicap. The Club may, at its discretion, reconsider the clause 19 adjustment in the light of the further information.

14. Starting other than from the 1st Tee including 'Shotgun Starts'

Competitions in which competitors are authorised by the Committee to commence play elsewhere than from the 1st tee will be QUALIFYING COMPETITIONS for handicap purposes provided all other requirements of the Scheme are satisfied.

Stationery

Enquiries regarding storage binders and handicap record sheets suitable for use in connection with the Standard Scratch Score and Handicapping Scheme 1983 to be directed to Hon. Secretary of the Council of National Golf Unions: A. Thirlwell, 19 Birch Green, Formby, Liverpool L37 1NG. Telephone/fax 01704 831800

Forms of application for:

An alteration to the Basic Standard Scratch Score.

An addition for course value to the Provisional Standard Scratch Score.

The above forms may be obtained from the Secretaries of:

(a) County Golf Unions or District Committees.

(b) Area Authorities.

(c) National Golf Unions.

(d) Council of National Golf Unions.

Draws for Match Play Competitions

Cold Draw

When the number of entries is not a whole power of 2, i.e. 4, 8, 16, 32, 64 etc, a number of first round byes are necessary. Subtract the number of entries from the nearest of these numbers above the number of entries to give the number of byes. *Example:* (a) 28 entries – subtracting from 32 gives 4 first round byes; (b) 33 entries – subtracting from 64 gives 31 first round byes.

All names (or numbers representing names) are put in a hat and the requisite number of byes drawn out singly and placed in pairs in the second round of the draw, alternately at the top and bottom, i.e. the first two names go at the top of the draw, the next two at the bottom and so on until all the byes have been drawn. If there is an odd number of byes, the last drawn is bracketed to play against the winner of either the first or last first round match. Having drawn all the byes, the remaining names are then drawn and placed in pairs in the first round in the order drawn in the middle of the draw.

Automatic Draw

When a stroke play qualifying round(s) is used to determine the qualifiers for the ensuing match play, the automatic draw is used, based on the qualifying position of each qualifier, i.e. the leading qualifier is number 1 in the draw, the second qualifier is number 2 and so on.

The following table gives the automatic draw for up to 64 qualifiers. Use the first column for 64 qualifiers, the second column for 32 qualifiers, and so on.

64	32	16	8	4	2	1
1/64	1	1				
33/32	32		1			
17/48	17	16				
49/16	16			1		
9/56	9	9				
41/24	24		8			
25/40	25	8				
57/8	8				1	
5/60	5	5				
37/28	28		5			
21/44	21	12				
53/12	12			4		
13/52	13	13				
45/20	20		4			
29/36	29	4				
61/4	4					1
3/62	3	3				
35/30	30		3			
19/46	19	14				
51/14	14			3		
11/54	11	11				
43/22	22		6			
27/38	27	6				
59/6	6				2	
7/58	7	7				
39/26	26		7			
23/42	23	10				
55/10	10			2		
15/50	15	15				
47/18	18		2			
31/34	31	2				
63/2	2					

The Ladies' Golf Union Handicapping System

Effective from 1 February 1998

FIRST EDITION

Incorporating:

Ladies Golf Union Scratch Score System
Ladies Golf Union Handicapping System
Ladies' Golf Union Medal Competitions

The Scores, St Andrews, Fife KY16 9AT
Telephone 01334 475811
Fax 01334 472818

Index

Medal Competitions

The Ladies Golf Union Scratch Score System

1. Introduction

1.1 The basis of the Ladies' Golf Union handicapping system is that all scores used to calculate a player's abiliy must be returned on courses that have been assessed in accordance with the Ladies' Golf Union Scratch Score System and have been allocated a Scratch Score

1.2 Overseas affiliated Unions and Clubs shall be permitted to make such adjustments to these regulations as may be deemed by their Executive Committee to be necessary on account of climatic or other conditions peculiar to the territory administered by them, so long as these adjustments do not depart from the fundamental principles of the LGU Scratch Score System or contravene the Rules of Golf as laid down by the Royal and Ancient Golf Club of St. Andrews. The LGU must be informed as and when such adjustments are made

2. Definitions

2.1 Club Committee: The committee responsible for the course including, where appropriate, the Committee of the Ladies' Section where the management of the club and its course is entirely in the hands of the Committee of the Ladies' Section

2.2 Committee: The committee of the Ladies' Section of an Affiliated Club

2.3 Course Group: The Course Group is determined by the average amount of run in normal spring and autumn conditions of wind and weather

2.4 Course Rating: The Course Rating is the sum of the Ratings of the 18 individual holes

2.5 Course Value: Course Value is the basis for addition to or deduction from Course Rating on account of the presence or absence of playing difficulties

2.6 LGU Tees: Tees indicated by some permanent mark on the tee from which the measured length of the hole is taken on which the LGU Scratch Score is based. LGU teeing ground is an area indicated by RED tee markers and within ten yards in any direction of the LGU permanent mark. "LGU Tees" includes tees from which a special Scratch Score has been assessed

2.7 Scratch Player: For assessment purposes a Scratch Player is a theoretical golfer who consistently averages a carry of at least 180 yards (165 metres) from the tee, and whose second shot on a par-5 hole carries at least 170 yards (155 metres)

2.8 Scratch Score: The LGU Scratch Score of a course is the score expected from a Scratch Player in normal spring and autumn conditions of wind and weather

> 2.8.1 The Scratch Score is allotted for 18 holes
>> 2.8.1.1 in the case of a 9 hole course, for 9 holes played twice
>> 2.8.1.2 where a course has fewer than 18 but more than 9, certain specified holes played twice to make the number of holes up to 18

2.9 Scratch Score Assessor: A person or her deputy appointed by the National Organisation responsible for allocating and revising as necessary Scratch Scores in accordance with these regulations

3. Application for Scratch Score

3.1 An application for a Scratch Score for a course must be completed on an official application form and returned to the National Organisation

3.2 A Scratch Score is allocated by a Scratch Score Assessor

4. Measurement of Courses

4.1 The measurement of each course is the responsibility of the Club Committee

> 4.1.1 Measurement should be carried out by a qualified surveyor or someone competent and experienced in the handling of surveying instruments, who should
> 4.1.2 grant a certificate showing details of
>> 4.1.2.1 the method of measurement (i.e. laser, theodolite, etc.)
>> 4.1.2.2 the length of each hole and
>> 4.1.2.3 the total playing length of the course
> 4.1.3 Subsequent alterations to the length of the course will require a certificate only for the altered hole or holes, measured in the manner prescribed above

4.2 Each hole should be

> 4.2.1 measured by plan or projection
> 4.2.2 along the horizontal plane
> 4.2.3 from the LGU tee to the centre of the green

4.3 Dog-leg holes should be measured

> 4.3.1 along the centre line of the fairway to the axis and
> 4.3.2 from the axis to the centre of the green

5. Calculation of Scratch Score

5.1 The Scratch Score is compiled from the sum of the Ratings of individual holes using Rating Table in Appendix S1 with adjustments for

> 5.1.1 the amount of run assessed from Table of Course Groups in Appendix S2 and
> 5.1.2 course difficulties assessed from Course Value

5.2 Course value is assessed on the following:

> 5.2.1 lay-out of the course
> 5.2.2 side hazards (trees, gorse, ditches, etc.)
> 5.2.3 whether greens are well guarded or open
> 5.2.4 narrowness or width of fairways
> 5.2.5 nature of rough
> 5.2.6 whether the course is flat or hilly, giving rise to awkward stances
> 5.2.7 whether the course is exposed to the elements e.g. seaside courses

5.3 Course value is expressed as a number ranging from -1 to $+2$

Examples

Course Rating	71.4	Course Rating	71.6
Group 2	+ 1.0	Group 4	-1.0
Course Value	nil	Course Value	1.0
	72.4		71.6
Scratch Score: 72		**Scratch Score:** 72	

6. Alterations to Course

6.1 Permanent Alterations

Where any permanent alteration is to be made to the course resulting in an alteration of the length of a hole by more than 10 yards or material alteration to the configuration of the ground the Scratch Score Assessor must be notified so that the Scratch Score may be revised

6.2 Temporary Alterations

Where any temporary alteration is made to the course resulting in an alteration of the length of a hole by more than 10 yards or material alteration to the configuration of the ground the Scratch Score Assessor must be notified. If necessary, a Temporary Scratch Score will be confirmed for the duration of the alterations

A Scratch Score which has been revised owing to alteration of the course comes into force from the day on which the altered course is in play. A Scratch Score which has been revised for any other reason comes into force on the first day of the month following the date when notification of the alteration to the Scratch Score is received

7. Adverse Conditions

7.1 Where the Club Committee has made a Local Rule that tee pegs must be used on any closely mown area or through the green:

    7.1.1 a deduction from the Scratch Score of two strokes must be made where more than 9 holes are affected

    7.1.2 a deduction from the Scratch Score of one stroke must be made where 3 to 9 holes are affected

    7.1.3 a deduction from the Scratch Score of one stroke will be at the discretion of the Scratch Score Assessor where fewer than 3 holes are affected

In all the above instances the Scratch Score Assessor MUST be notified

7.2 Where, for the preservation of a putting green, a temporary hole is off but adjacent to the green counting scores may be returned for handicap provided

    7.2.1 the length of the hole is altered by no more than 10 yards or

    7.2.2 where the hole is altered by more than 10 yards the Scratch Score Assessor has been notified

7.3 Where more than two temporary greens are in use scores are non-counting for handicap

7.4 Where, due to annually abnormal specific conditions, such as flooding or the like, temporary alterations are in operation regularly and are ALWAYS THE SAME, a Temporary Scratch Score may be granted by application to the Scratch Score Assessor

This Temporary Scratch Score may operate for a maximum of ONE year only but may be renewed on application to the Scratch Score Assessor

8. Par

The Scratch Score is given for the course as a whole. A PAR may be allocated by the Committee for each hole with the following as a suggested guide, based on a Scratch Player

	Yards	Metres
PAR 3	up to 220	up to 200
PAR 4	200 to 430	182 to 391
PAR 5	over 409	over 372

The total of the PAR figures for each hole of a course will not necessarily coincide with the Scratch Score of that course. The Par figure is used in Stableford and Par competitions

APPENDIX S1

Rating Table

Yards	Rating	Metres
up to 100	2.7	up to 91
101 to 112	2.8	92 to 102
113 to 124	2.9	103 to 113
125 to 140	3.0	114 to 128
141 to 160	3.1	129 to 146
161 to 180	3.2	147 to 165
181 to 200	3.3	166 to 183
201 to 218	3.4	184 to 199
219 to 236	3.5	200 to 216
237 to 254	3.6	217 to 232
255 to 272	3.7	233 to 249
273 to 290	3.8	250 to 265
291 to 308	3.9	266 to 282
309 to 326	4.0	283 to 298
327 to 344	4.1	299 to 314
345 to 362	4.2	315 to 331
363 to 380	4.3	332 to 347
381 to 398	4.4	348 to 364
399 to 416	4.5	365 to 380
417 to 432	4.6	381 to 395
433 to 448	4.7	396 to 410
449 to 464	4.8	411 to 424
465 to 480	4.9	425 to 439
481 to 496	5.0	440 to 453
497 to 512	5.1	454 to 468
513 to 528	5.2	469 to 483
529 to 544	5.3	484 to 497
545 to 560	5.4	498 to 512
561 & over	5.5	513 & over

APPENDIX S2

The Course Rating is based on Group 3 (average run on tee shot 11–20 yards or 10–18 metres), and in the case of courses assessed in other Groups (after practical tests on the course in normal spring and autumn conditions of wind and weather) should be adjusted according to the following

Table of Course Groups				
When the carry from the tee is 180 yards (165 metres) and				
Group		*Yards*	*Metres*	*Adjustment*
1	the average amount of run is	nil to 5	nil to 4	+2
2	the average amount of run is	6 to 10	5 to 9	+1
3	the average amount of run is	11 to 20	10 to 18	nil
4	the average amount of run is	21 to 30	19 to 27	−1
5	the average amount of run is	31 to 40	28 to 36	−2
6	the average amount of run is	41 & over	37 & over	−3

The Ladies Golf Union Handicapping System

Introduction

1.1 The Ladies' Golf Union System of Handicapping seeks to achieve uniformity and equity of handicapping. The basis of the system is that it shall reflect a player's current form and shall be calculated according to an LGU Scratch Score and the player's handicap shall be the same in every Affiliated Club

1.2 Overseas Unions and Clubs. Overseas affiliated Unions and Clubs shall be permitted to make such adjustments to these regulations as may be deemed by their Executive Committee to be necessary on account of climatic or other conditions peculiar to the territory administered by them, so long as these adjustments do not depart from the fundamental principles of the LGU System of Handicapping as stated in the paragraph above or contravene the Rules of Golf as laid down by the Royal and Ancient Golf Club of St. Andrews. The LGU must be informed as and when such adjustments are made

2. Definitions

2.1 Affiliated Club: A golf club affiliated to the Ladies' Golf Union

2.2 Affiliated Organisation: A golfing organisation, which must have a Committee of annually elected officers, including a Secretary, conversant with the LGU System of Handicapping, who may organise Qualifying Competitions for Playing Members who must be affiliated to the Ladies' Golf Union

2.3 Buffer Zone: The nett differential range within which an Exact Handicap remains unchanged

2.4 Categories
 Category 1: Handicaps of 5 or less
 Category 2: Handicaps of 6 to 12 inclusive
 Category 3: Handicaps of 13 to 20 inclusive
 Category 4: Handicaps of 21 to 28 inclusive
 Category 5: Handicaps of 29 to 40 inclusive
 Category 6: Handicaps of 41 to 45 inclusive

2.5 Committee: The committee of the Ladies' Section of an Affiliated Club

2.6 Club Committee: The committee responsible for the course including, where appropriate, the Committee of the Ladies' Section where the management of the club and its course is entirely in the hands of the Committee of the Ladies' Section

2.7 Completed Gross Score: The total gross score for eighteen holes

2.8 Differential: The difference between the Completed Gross Score and the LGU Scratch Score of the course on which it is returned

2.9 Exact Handicap: A player's handicap calculated in accordance with these Regulations to one decimal place with a maximum of 45.0

2.10 Extra Day Score (EDS): A Completed Gross Score which is returned other than in a Qualifying Competition. A maximum of ten Extra Day Scores may be taken out in any one LGU year by a player in Category 2, 3, 4, 5 or 6. The scores must be returned on courses of Affiliated Clubs of which she is a Playing Member and used for handicap purposes

2.11 Gross Differential: The sum of the Nett Differential and the player's Playing Handicap

2.12 Handicap Adviser: A person or her deputy appointed by a National Organisation to assist Handicap Secretaries in dealing with problems and exceptional cases

2.13 Handicap Committee: At each Affiliated Club a committee of a minimum of three members, one of whom shall be the Handicap Secretary, responsible for the review of handicaps on the basis of general play

2.14 Handicap Score: A Completed Gross Score returned

2.14.1 by a Playing Member to attain or re-attain an LGU handicap

2.14.2 by an Individual Member

2.15 Handicap Secretary: A person appointed at a player's Home Club to maintain handicap records

2.16 Home Club: The Affiliated Club which a player, who is a Playing Member of more than one Affiliated Club, has nominated for the maintenance of her handicap records

2.17 Individual Member:

2.17.1 of the Ladies' Golf Union:– a player who is temporarily resident overseas for a period of not less than one year

2.17.2 of a National Organisation:– a player who is on a waiting list to become an annual Playing Member of an Affiliated Club

2.18 Lapsed Handicap: A player's handicap will be considered to have lapsed if she is no longer a Playing Member of an Affiliated Club of the Ladies' Golf Union or an Individual Member

2.19 LGU Scratch Score: The score allocated to a course by the Ladies' Golf Union in accordance with the LGU Scratch Score System and which must be clearly marked on all cards returned for handicap purposes

2.20 LGU Tees: Tees indicated by some permanent mark on the tee from which the measured length of the hole is taken on which the LGU Scratch Score is based. LGU teeing ground is an area indicated by RED tee markers and within ten yards in any direction of the LGU permanent mark. "LGU Tees" includes tees from which a special Scratch Score has been assessed

2.21 LGU Year:

2.21.1 For Affiliated Clubs in Great Britain and Ireland – the period commencing on 1 February in one year and ending on 31 January in the following year

2.21.2 For overseas Affiliated Unions or Clubs – the period whose fixed dates are as authorised by the Ladies' Golf Union

2.22 Marker: A marker is an amateur member of a recognised golf club or an Individual Member who holds or has held a handicap from a handicap authority recognised by the Ladies' Golf Union

2.23 National Organisations:

2.23.1 The English Ladies' Golf Association (ELGA)

2.23.2 The Irish Ladies' Golf Union (ILGU)

2.23.3 The Scottish Ladies' Golfing Association (SLGA)

2.23.4 The Welsh Ladies' Golf Union (WLGU)

2.23.5 For overseas Affiliated Clubs – the Ladies' Golf Union (LGU)

2.24 Nett Differential: The difference between the player's Nett Score and the LGU Scratch Score of the course on which it is returned, or the result of applying the "LGU Table for converting Par and Stableford Scores to Nett Differentials" contained in Appendix H1

2.25 Nett Score: A player's Completed Gross score adjusted by her Playing Handicap

2.26 No Return: The situation which arises when a player competes in a Qualifying Competition, or takes out an EDS, and the player fails to complete or return the score card

2.27 Open Qualifying Competition: A Qualifying Competition open to Playing Members of Affiliated Clubs and Individual Members

2.28 Playing Handicap: A player's handicap calculated in accordance with these Regulations and expressed as a whole number

2.29 Playing Member: A member of an Affiliated Club who is eligible to play in Qualifying Competitions organised by that Club

2.30 Qualifying Competition: A Stroke Play, Par or Stableford competition

2.30.1 run by an Affiliated Club or Organisation on a course with an LGU Scratch Score of not less than 60

2.30.2 played by an individual player over eighteen holes

2.30.3 held on a specified day or days approved by the Club Committee

2.30.4 where play is in twos, threes or fours at the discretion of the Committee

2.31 Qualifying Competition Score: A player's score or a "No Return" returned in a Qualifying Competition

2.32 Recognised Golf Club: Any golf club affiliated to its national organisation including overseas clubs

3. Eligibility to Hold an LGU Handicap

3.1 An LGU handicap may be obtained and held by an amateur lady golfer who is:

3.1.1 an annual Playing Member, including a five-day, country, junior or life member (whether honorary or paying) of an Affiliated Club

3.1.2 an Individual Member or

3.1.3 a temporary Playing Member of an Affiliated Club provided that a membership is to last for a period of not less than twelve months

4. Scores for LGU Handicapping

4.1 General
To be acceptable for the purposes of handicap a score must be:

4.1.1 returned in accordance with the Rules of Golf as approved by the Royal and Ancient Golf Club of St. Andrews and with the Local Rules and Bye-laws of the club which must not contravene any Rule of Golf of the Royal and Ancient Golf Club of St. Andrews or any Regulation of the Ladies' Golf Union

4.1.2 returned on the course of an Affiliated Club with an LGU Scratch Score of not less than 60 and with play from the LGU Tees

4.1.3 marked by an eligible Marker

4.1.4 that of the first round of the day on any one course, except in the case of a Qualifying Competition consisting of 36 holes played on one day when both scores shall count

4.2 Qualifying Competition Scores
The following scores are Qualifying Competition Scores for handicap purposes:

4.2.1 a Qualifying Competition Score returned on a course of an Affiliated Club

4.2.2 a Qualifying Competition Score unacceptable for any reason which does not affect the gross score at each hole

4.2.3 any score returned in a Stableford or Par Qualifying Competition from which a player has been disqualified under the Rules of Golf, Rule 6-2b, in which case

the score shall be adjusted according to the player's correct Playing Handicap

4.2.4 any score returned in a Stableford or Par Qualifying Competition played in conjunction with a Stroke Play competition in which case the score returned in the Stroke Play competition MUST be used for handicap purposes. An incomplete score returned in this situation is a "No Return"

4.3 Extra Day Scores
A maximum of ten Extra Day Scores may be returned by a player in Category 2, 3, 4, 5 or 6 during an LGU year and will count for handicap purposes as follows:

4.3.1 an Extra Day Score returned on a course of an Affiliated Club at which the player is a Playing Member, showing the current LGU Scratch Score and the date the round was played

4.3.2 an Extra Day Score unacceptable for any reason which does not affect the gross score at each hole

A player may not reduce her Exact Handicap below 5.5 on an Extra Day Score

4.4 Cards for Reduction only
Subject to Regulation 4.1, the following scores shall count for handicap purposes only if they result in a reduction in a player's Exact Handicap:

4.4.1 a score returned in a Qualifying Competition which is subsequently declared "null and void"

4.4.2 a score returned in a Qualifying Competition when less than the required number of players return scores within or below their Buffer Zone in accordance with the Qualifying Competition Table in Appendix H5

4.4.3 a Handicap Score returned by an Individual Member who holds an LGU handicap

4.5 Overseas Cards
A score returned in competition at a Recognised Golf Club under a handicap authority other than the Ladies' Golf Union shall count for handicap purposes only if it results in a Nett Differential below the player's Buffer Zone and is countersigned by an official of that club. The score card must be lodged with the Handicap Secretary of the player's Home Club

4.6 Non-counting Scores
The following scores shall NOT count for handicap

4.6.1 a score above a player's Buffer Zone returned in a Qualifying Competition when less than the required number of players have returned scores within or below their Buffer Zone in accordance with the Qualifying Competition Table in Appendix H5

4.6.2   a score returned in a best-ball or better-ball competition (see Rules of Golf, Rule 31)

4 6.3   a score returned in a Pro-Am / Am-Am team event when any team members play in the same group

4 6.4   a score returned in a competition played over less than eighteen holes

4.6.5   a score returned when a Nett Differential is calculated using **other than the player's full handicap allowance**

4.6.6   a score returned when more than two temporary greens are in use

4.6.7   a score returned in a competition which limits the number of clubs to less than 14

5. Attaining and Re-attaining an LGU Handicap

5.1 A Playing Member who has never held a handicap may attain an LGU handicap:

5.1.1   by returning a minimum of three Handicap Scores in accordance with Regulation 4.1

5.1.2   where the Marker may only mark the score of one player in a round

5.1.3   when the Exact Handicap will be the Differential of the best score returned, maximum 45.0

5.2 A Playing Member of an Affiliated Club, whose LGU handicap lapsed when her previous playing membership ceased, may re-attain an LGU handicap

5.2.1   if lapsed for less than six months - equal to her previous Exact Handicap

5.2.2   if lapsed for more than six months - by returning three Handicap Scores in accordance with Regulation 4.1
5.2.2.1 if the best Differential is the same as, or lower than, the player's last Exact Handicap then an Exact Handicap equal to that Differential will be awarded
5.2.2.2 if the best Differential is higher than the player's last Exact Handicap, her Exact Handicap will be equal to her last Exact Handicap until an adjustment has been authorised in accordance with Regulation 7

5.3 A Playing Member who holds or has held a handicap from a handicap authority other than the Ladies' Golf Union and recognised by the Ladies' Golf Union may attain an LGU handicap as follows:

5.3.1   where she holds a handicap she will be awarded an Exact Handicap equal to her current handicap

5.3.2   where her handicap has lapsed she will

be awarded an Exact Handicap in accordance with Regulation 5.2.1 or 5.2.2

The player will be expected to provide certified details of her previous handicap

5.4 A Playing Member who is a former professional golfer and who has been, or is being, reinstated as an amateur golfer, and who wishes to attain an LGU handicap must apply to the Secretary of the Ladies' Golf Union

5.4.1   The application must be accompanied by SIX scores fulfilling the conditions of Regulation 4.1 together with details of any LGU handicap held during the previous three years

5.4.2   The scores must have been completed within the twelve months immediately prior to the date of application for handicap. This twelve month period may include all or part of the time when a player awaits reinstatement

5.4.3   The Ladies' Golf Union will allot the player an Exact Handicap and thereafter her handicap will be administered and calculated in accordance with the Ladies' Golf Union Regulations

5.5 A Handicap Score must bear:

5.5.1   the name of the player

5.5.2   the date on which the score was marked

5.5.3   the signature of an eligible Marker

5.5.4   the signature of the player

5.5.5   the LGU Scratch Score of the course played

5.6 A Handicap Score returned to attain or re-attain a handicap is not an Extra Day Score

6. Calculation of Handicaps

For calculations, Nett Differentials derived from a player's Playing Handicap must be applied **in chronological order**

6.1 Calculation of Exact Handicap

A player's Exact Handicap will be reviewed every time she competes in a Qualifying Competition or (excepting Category 1 players) marks one of her ten Extra Day Scores

6.1.1   If a player returns a score with a Nett Differential within her Buffer Zone her Exact Handicap remains unchanged

6.1.2   If a player returns a score with a Nett Differential above her Buffer Zone or a "No Return" her Exact Handicap shall be increased by 0.1 provided the required number of players in a Qualifying Competition have returned scores within or below their Buffer Zone in accordance with the Qualifying Competition Table in Appendix H5

6.1.3   If a player returns a score with a Nett Differential below her Buffer Zone her Exact Handicap shall be reduced by an amount per stroke determined by her handicap category and calculated by using the "Table of Buffer Zones" shown below

For examples of handicap calculations see Appendix H2

6.2 Reducing to a Lower Category

6.2.1   The Exact Handicap shall be reduced at the rate appropriate to the higher category only so far as it brings her Playing Handicap into the lower category. The balance of the reduction shall be at the lower rate

6.2.2   When a player's Exact Handicap is to be reduced to a lower category the new handicap must be calculated using the "Table of LGU Handicap Adjustments" contained in Appendix H3

6.2.3   A player may not reduce her Exact Handicap into Category 1 with an Extra Day Score. An Extra Day Score that would reduce her handicap into Category 1 shall only reduce her Exact Handicap to 5.5

For examples of handicap reductions to lower categories see Appendix H4

6.3 Calculation of Playing Handicap

A player's Playing Handicap is her Exact Handicap rounded to the nearest WHOLE number (0.5 is rounded upwards).

For examples of rounding Exact Handicaps to Playing Handicaps see Appendix H4

6.4 Alterations to Handicaps

6.4.1   Exact Handicap
An alteration to an Exact Handicap is made when a Qualifying Competition or Extra Day Score is recorded on a Playing Member's LGU Handicap Register Form at her Home Club

6.4.2   Playing Handicap
6.4.2.1 Immediate Reduction of Playing Handicap
When a player returns a score with a Nett Differential below her Buffer Zone her Handicap Secretary must refer to the Table of Immediate Reductions of Playing Handicap in Appendix H6. Any resulting reduction in her Playing Handicap becomes operative immediately the player has been informed of the alteration by her Handicap Secretary, EXCEPT

6.4.2.1.1 in a 36, 54 or 72 hole competition played on the same day or on consecutive days
6.4.2.1.2 for the purposes of a play-off in the event of a tie in a competition resolved in this way

6.4.2.2 Monthly Alterations
An alteration to a Playing Handicap is effective from the 8th day of each month, based on the player's Exact Handicap at the end of the previous month calculated on all scores returned during the previous month and applied in chronological order EXCEPT

6.4.2.2.1 in a 36, 54 or 72 hole competition played on consecutive days spanning the 7th or 8th days of a month
6.4.2.2.2 for the purposes of a play-off in the event of a tie in a competition resolved in this way

Where an Immediate Reduction of Playing Handicap has been made during the first seven days of a month, such reduction must be repeated after the revised Playing Handicap has been calculated from the rounded Exact Handicap at the end of the Previous

TABLE OF BUFFER ZONES

CATEGORY	HANDICAP	Nett Differential within Buffer Zone	Nett Differential above Buffer Zone	Nett Differential below Buffer Zone
		NO CHANGE	INCREASE EXACT HANDICAP	DECREASE EXACT HANDICAP PER STROKE
1	5 or less	0 to +1	0.1	0.1
2	6 to 12	0 to +2	0.1	0.2
3	13 to 20	0 to +3	0.1	0.3
4	21 to 28	0 to +4	0.1	0.4
5	29 to 40	0 to +5	0.1	0.5
6	41 to 45	0 to +10	0.1	1.0

month. The amended Playing Handicap is effective from the 8th day of the month

6.4.3 Alteration under General Play

An alteration to a player's Exact Handicap under general play in accordance with Regulation 7 will result in her Playing Handicap being altered to her rounded Exact Handicap. The alterations become operative immediately the player has been informed by her Handicap Secretary

7. General Play

7.1 Each club shall form a Handicap Committee for the purpose of considering a player's ability under this Regulation

7.2 If the Handicap Committee considers that a player's handicap does not reflect her current playing ability, APPLICATION for adjustment may be made by the Handicap Committee of a player's Home Club by submitting the relevant information detailed in Appendix H7 to the National Organisation who may form a Committee for the purpose of applying this regulation subject to the following conditions:

7.2.1   If it is considered that a player's Exact Handicap is too high the Exact Handicap may be reduced by the National Organisation to a figure that reflects more closely her current playing ability. Factors to be taken into account include performance in match play, foursomes, mixed and team events and particularly if the player, for whatever reason, does not return cards for handicap either in Qualifying Competitions or as Extra Day Scores

7.2.2   If it is considered that a player's Exact Handicap is too low then the Exact Handicap may be increased by the National Organisation to a figure considered appropriate to reflect more closely her current playing ability. Factors to be taken into account include age, infirmity, illness or such change in circumstance as prevents the player from regularly returning scores acceptable for handicap

7.3 If a player considers her handicap does not reflect her current playing ability she may apply to her Handicap Committee for a revision under general play.

7.4 Exact Handicaps cannot be decreased below 5.5 or increased above 40.4 on general play

The adjusted handicap will become operative immediately the player has been informed of the alteration by her Handicap Secretary

8. Player's Responsibilities

8.1 Correct Handicap

Each player is responsible AT ALL TIMES for playing off her correct handicap (Rules of Golf, Rule 6-2) and should be able to produce an up-to-date LGU Handicap Certificate when required to do so. In case of doubt or disagreement between a player and her Handicap Secretary or Handicap Adviser as to the player's correct Playing Handicap she should play off the lower alternative until an official decision can be obtained from her Handicap Secretary, Handicap Adviser or National Organisation

8.2 Intention of Playing

It is expected that every player who registers to play in an 18-hole Qualifying Competition or indicates that she is to mark an Extra Day Score intends to complete the round

A player must indicate her intention to return a card as follows:

8.2.1   before competing in a Qualifying Competition she must register in accordance with the conditions of the competition

8.2.2   before marking an Extra Day Score she must

8.2.2.1 sign and date the Extra Day Book and

8.2.2.2 enter her name and the date on her score card

8.3 Return of Score Cards

A player must return all cards, including "No Returns", from Qualifying Competitions and Extra Day Scores

8.4 Reporting Scores

A player must report to her Handicap Secretary immediately all scores returned with a Nett Differential below her Buffer Zone.

If the player is unable to report a score with a Nett Differential below her Buffer Zone to her Handicap Secretary before playing in a further competition she must report the score to the organising committee, who shall refer to the Table of Immediate Reductions of Playing Handicap in Appendix H6 and reduce her Playing Handicap, if applicable, for that competition

8.5 Membership of more than one Club

8.5.1   A player who is a Playing Member of more than one Affiliated Club must decide which club she wishes to be her Home Club and notify the Handicap Secretary of each club of her decision and of her other playing memberships

8.5.2   A player who is a Playing Member of more than one Affiliated Club must inform the Handicap Secretary of any change to her Playing Handicap before she competes at an Affiliated Club of which she is a Playing Member other than her Home Club

8.5.3 A player who changes her Home Club must ask the Handicap Secretary of her former Home Club for a copy of her LGU Handicap Register Form and forward it, together with her LGU Handicap Certificate, to the Handicap Secretary of her new Home Club

8.5.4 An annual Playing Member of a club affiliated to the Ladies' Golf Union who also has membership of a club under the jurisdiction of a handicap authority other than the Ladies' Golf Union **must** return to her Handicap Secretary all competition scores which might **reduce** her LGU handicap, countersigned by an official of that club

9. Responsibilities of the Committee of an Affiliated Club

9.1 Compliance with the Regulations

It is the responsibility of the Committee of an Affiliated Club to ensure compliance with the Regulations of the Ladies' Golf Union governing the following:

9.1.1 the application of the LGU Scratch Score System

9.1.2 the indication of LGU Tees

9.1.3 the appointment of a Handicap Secretary

9.1.4 the appointment of a Handicap Committee

9.2 Registering Intention to Play

The Committee of an Affiliated Club must provide a list or book where a player must register her intention

9.2.1 to compete in a Qualifying Competition or

9.2.2 to mark an Extra Day Score

9.3 Status of Qualifying Competition Scores

The Committee of an Affiliated Club is responsible for applying the Qualifying Competition Table in Appendix H5 to determine whether a score returned in a Qualifying Competition above a player's Buffer Zone will result in an increase in her Exact Handicap

9.4 Handicap Secretary

It is recommended that the Handicap Secretary should be, at the very least, an *ex officio* member of the Committee. The Handicap Secretary must

9.4.1 register all scores acceptable for handicap purposes and all "No Returns"

9.4.2 retain all score cards until the end of the current LGU year

9.4.3 at a Playing Member's Home Club
9.4.3.1 calculate and record her Exact and Playing Handicaps
9.4.3.2 provide her with an up-to-date LGU Handicap Certificate when requested

9.4.4 at a club other than a Playing Member's Home Club
9.4.4.1 notify the Handicap Secretary of her Home Club of all scores acceptable for handicap purposes and "No Returns" returned at that Affiliated Club by submitting the prescribed LGU Handicap Exchange Sheet at the end of each calendar month

Handicap Advisers, or their Deputies, appointed by the National Organisations will assist Handicap Secretaries in dealing with problems and exceptional cases, referring as necessary to the National Organisation

9.5 Handicap Records

Each Affiliated Club must maintain the following records of all scores acceptable for handicap and ensure that the records are available in the clubhouse for reference by members

9.5.1 manual records
9.5.1.1 a list of Playing Handicaps
9.5.1.2 LGU Handicap Register Forms or

9.5.2 computerised records
9.5.2.1 a list of Playing Handicaps
9.5.2.2 LGU Handicap Register Forms printed at least monthly for players who have returned scores during the previous month

LGU Handicap Register Forms should be retained by the club for the immediate past TWO years for reference. LGU Handicap Register Forms for all Playing Members must be returned to the National Organisation should the club cease to be affiliated

9.6 Handicap Certificates

The Handicap Secretary of a Playing Member's Home Club is responsible for issuing an LGU Handicap Certificate on application.

9.6.1 The LGU Handicap Certificate must show:
9.6.1.1 the name of the player
9.6.1.2 the name of the player's Home Club
9.6.1.3 the player's Playing Handicap
9.6.1.4 the player's Handicap Category

9.6.2 All LGU Handicap Certificates should be checked periodically

9.6.3 A Handicap Secretary is empowered to recall the LGU Handicap Certificate of any player where she believes that the certified handicap is no longer correctly recorded

9.6.4 Should a player cease to be a member of any Affiliated Club of the Ladies' Golf Union, or of a National Organisation, her LGU Handicap Certificate is invalid and must be recalled by the Handicap Secretary of the club or the appropriate authority

9.7 Members new to an Affiliated Club

9.7.1 From Another Affiliated Club

9.7.1.1 When a new Playing Member who holds or has held an LGU handicap joins an Affiliated Club which is to be her Home Club she must be asked for her LGU Handicap Certificate and LGU Handicap Register Form. If her LGU handicap has lapsed she must re-attain an LGU handicap in accordance with the regulations

9.7.1.2 When a new Playing Member who holds or has held an LGU handicap joins an Affiliated Club which is not to be her Home Club, she must be asked to provide details of her Playing or Lapsed Handicap, with relevant dates on which it was based, and the name of her Home Club. Her Playing Handicap, if any, must be recorded immediately by the Handicap Secretary of her new club.

9.7.2 From a non-Affiliated Club

When a new Playing Member who holds or has held a handicap from a handicap authority other than the Ladies' Golf Union joins an Affiliated Club which will be her Home Club the player must provide details of her Exact or Lapsed Handicap with relevant dates on which it was based and must attain an LGU handicap in accordance with the regulations. Her Exact Handicap, if any, must be recorded immediately by the Handicap Secretary of her new club

9.8 Visiting Players

It is the responsibility of the committee organising an Open Qualifying Competition to comply with Regulation 11

9.9 Handicap Stationery

Supplies of Handicap Stationery are obtainable on application by the Handicap Secretary to her National Organisation

10. Responsibilities of the National Organisations

10.1 The National Organisations shall appoint Scratch Score Assessors who will be responsible for allotting, and revising as necessary, the LGU Scratch Scores of all courses of Affiliated Clubs in accordance with the LGU Scratch Score System

10.2 The National Organisations shall appoint Handicap Advisers and Deputies. Handicap Advisers and their Deputies will assist Handicap Secretaries in dealing with problems and exceptional cases, referring as necessary to their National Organisation

10.3 The National Organisations shall be responsible for applying the regulations on general play and may form a sub-committee for this purpose

10.4 The National Organisations shall deal with queries on the LGU Regulations or the Rules of Golf submitted by Committees, Handicap Secretaries or members of Affiliated Clubs, in accordance with the procedures laid down in regulation 12

10.5 The National Organisations shall supply handicap stationery on application by the Handicap Secretary of an Affiliated Club, including

10.5.1 LGU Handicap Certificates

10.5.2 LGU Handicap Exchange Sheets

10.5.3 LGU Handicap Register Forms

11. Responsibilities of those running Open Qualifying Competitions

The organiser responsible for running an Open Qualifying Competition must:

11.1 apply the Qualifying Competition Table in Appendix H5 to determine whether a score returned above a player's Buffer Zone will result in an increase in her Exact Handicap

11.2 return a complete list of results to the Home Club of each competitor specifying:

11.2.1 date of the competition

11.2.2 venue of the competition

11.2.3 LGU Scratch Score and Par of course played

11.2.4 result of application of Qualifying Competition Table

11.2.5 for each competitor:

11.2.5.1 name

11.2.5.2 Home Club

11.2.5.3 Playing Handicap

11.2.5.4 Gross and Nett Score or Stableford points or Par result or NR

11.2.5.5 indication if player's score is within or below Buffer Zone

11.3 retain all score cards and details of "No Returns" until the end of the current LGU year

12. Queries

Queries on LGU Regulations must be, and on the Rules of Golf may be, submitted in accordance with the following procedures:

12.1 SECRETARIES and COMMITTEES of Affiliated Clubs should submit queries to their Handicap Adviser and National Organisation in that order. Handicap queries from members should be referred to the club Handicap Secretary, the Handicap Adviser and the National Organisation in that order

12.2 MEMBERS of AFFILIATED CLUBS may submit queries to their National Organisation only if their statements are signed as read on behalf of the Committee. If there is any difference of opinion the Committee or opposing party should submit their own statement in writing

12.3 OVERSEAS UNIONS and CLUBS. In the case of clubs affiliated to the Ladies' Golf Union outside Great Britain and Ireland or directly affiliated to the LGU, queries should be submitted to the LGU. Statements should be signed as read on behalf of such Union or club Committee

Correspondence of this nature sent to the LGU and the National Organisations is filed for reference and cannot be returned.

Appendix H1
Table for Converting Par and Stableford Scores to Nett Differentials

(Note – the Table is based on full handicap allowance)

Scores versus PAR	15 down	14 down	13 down	12 down	11 down	10 down	9 down	8 down	7 down	6 down	5 down	4 down	3 down	2 down	1 down	All Square	1 up	2 up	3 up	4 up	5 up	6 up	7 up	8 up
STABLEFORD Points scored	21	22	23	24	25	26	27	28	29	30	31	32	33	34	35	36	37	38	39	40	41	42	43	44
Par 5 less than SS	+10	+9	+8	+7	+6	+5	+4	+3	+2	+1	0	-1	-2	-3	-4	-5	-6	-7	-8	-9	-10	-11	-12	-13
Par 4 less than SS	+11	+10	+9	+8	+7	+6	+5	+4	+3	+2	+1	0	-1	-2	-3	-4	-5	-6	-7	-8	-9	-10	-11	-12
Par 3 less than SS	+12	+11	+10	+9	+8	+7	+6	+5	+4	+3	+2	+1	0	-1	-2	-3	-4	-5	-6	-7	-8	-9	-10	-11
Par 2 less than SS	+13	+12	+11	+10	+9	+8	+7	+6	+5	+4	+3	+2	+1	0	-1	-2	-3	-4	-5	-6	-7	-8	-9	-10
Par 1 less than SS	+14	+13	+12	+11	+10	+9	+8	+7	+6	+5	+4	+3	+2	+1	0	-1	-2	-3	-4	-5	-6	-7	-8	-9
Par Equal to SS	+15	+14	+13	+12	+11	+10	+9	+8	+7	+6	+5	+4	+3	+2	+1	0	-1	-2	-3	-4	-5	-6	-7	-8
Par 1 more than SS	+16	+15	+14	+13	+12	+11	+10	+9	+8	+7	+6	+5	+4	+3	+2	+1	0	-1	-2	-3	-4	-5	-6	-7
Par 2 more than SS	+17	+16	+15	+14	+13	+12	+11	+10	+9	+8	+7	+6	+5	+4	+3	+2	+1	0	-1	-2	-3	-4	-5	-6
Par 3 more than SS	+18	+17	+16	+15	+14	+13	+12	+11	+10	+9	+8	+7	+6	+5	+4	+3	+2	+1	0	-1	-2	-3	-4	-5
Par 4 more than SS	+19	+18	+17	+16	+15	+14	+13	+12	+11	+10	+9	+8	+7	+6	+5	+4	+3	+2	+1	0	-1	-2	-3	-4
Par 5 more than SS	+20	+19	+18	+17	+16	+15	+14	+13	+12	+11	+10	+9	+8	+7	+6	+5	+4	+3	+2	+1	0	-1	-2	-3

Use **Table of LGU Handicap Adjustments** in Appendix H3 to establish any INCREASE or DECREASE in EXACT HANDICAP

Examples:

(a) 3 up on a Par 74 course with an SS of 72. Par is 2 more than SS, Nett Differential = – 1. Exact Handicap reduction depends upon Category

(b) 39 Stableford points on a course with Par 71 and SS 72. Par is 1 less than SS, Nett Differential = – 4. Exact Handicap reduction depends upon Category

(c) 3 down or 33 Stableford points on a course with Par and SS of 72. Nett differential is +3 and is within Buffer Zone of Categories 3, 4, 5 and 6. Exact Handicaps in Categories 1 and 2 will be increased by 0.1

APPENDIX H2

Examples of Handicap Calculations

For the purpose of illustration assume the course being played in the following examples has an LGU Scratch Score of 72

(1) Category 1 – Playing Handicap 5 or less
   (a) If a player returns a nett score of 74 or more her Exact Handicap will be increased by 0.1
   (b) If a player returns a nett score of 72 or 73 her Exact Handicap will remain unchanged
   (c) If a player returns a nett score of 71 her Exact Handicap will be reduced by 0.1

(2) Category 2 – Playing Handicap 6 to 12
   (a) If a player returns a nett score of 75 or more her Exact Handicap will be increased by 0.1
   (b) If a player returns a nett score of 72, 73, or 74 her Exact Handicap will remain unchanged
   (c) If a player returns a nett score of 71 her Exact Handicap will be reduced by 0.2

(3) Category 3 – Playing Handicap 13 to 20
   (a) If a player returns a nett score of 76 or more her Exact Handicap will be increased by 0.1
   (b) If a player returns a nett score of 72, 73, 74 or 75 her Exact Handicap will remain unchanged
   (c) If a player returns a nett score of 71 her Exact Handicap will be reduced by 0.3

(4) Category 4 – Playing Handicap 21 to 28
   (a) If a player returns a nett score of 77 or more her Exact Handicap will be increased by 0.1
   (b) If a player returns a nett score of 72, 73, 74, 75 or 76 her Exact Handicap will remain unchanged
   (c) If a player returns a nett score of 71 her Exact Handicap will be reduced by 0.4

(5) Category 5 – Playing Handicap 29 to 40
   (a) If a player returns a nett score of 78 or more her Exact Handicap will be increased by 0.1
   (b) If a player returns a nett score of 72, 73, 74, 75, 76 or 77 her Exact Handicap will remain unchanged
   (c) If a player returns a nett score of 71 her Exact Handicap will be reduced by 0.5

(6) Category 6 – Playing Handicap 41 to 45
   (a) If a player returns a nett score of 83 or more her Exact Handicap will be increased by 0.1, maximum Exact Handicap 45.0
   (b) If a player returns a nett score of 72, 73, 74, 75, 76, 77, 78, 79, 80, 81, 82 her Exact Handicap will remain unchanged
   (c) If a player returns a nett score of 71 her Exact Handicap will be reduced by 1.0

APPENDIX H3

Table of LGU Handicap Adjustments

	Nett Differential	−1	−2	−3	−4	−5	−6	−7	−8	−9	−10	−11	−12	Above Buffer Zone
	Exact Handicaps:													
Category 1	Up to 5.4	−0.1	−0.2	−0.3	−0.4	−0.5	−0.6	−0.7	−0.8	−0.9	−1.0	−1.1	−1.2	+0.1
Category 2	5.5– 5.6	−0.2	−0.3	−0.4	−0.5	−0.6	−0.7	−0.8	−0.9	−1.0	−1.1	−1.2	−1.3	+0.1
	5.7– 5.8	−0.2	−0.4	−0.5	−0.6	−0.7	−0.8	−0.9	−1.0	−1.1	−1.2	−1.3	−1.4	+0.1
	5.9– 6.0	−0.2	−0.4	−0.6	−0.7	−0.8	−0.9	−1.0	−1.1	−1.2	−1.3	−1.4	−1.5	+0.1
	6.1– 6.2	−0.2	−0.4	−0.6	−0.8	−0.9	−1.0	−1.1	−1.2	−1.3	−1.4	−1.5	−1.6	+0.1
	6.3– 6.4	−0.2	−0.4	−0.6	−0.8	−1.0	−1.1	−1.2	−1.3	−1.4	−1.5	−1.6	−1.7	+0.1
	6.5– 6.6	−0.2	−0.4	−0.6	−0.8	−1.0	−1.2	−1.3	−1.4	−1.5	−1.6	−1.7	−1.8	+0.1
	6.7– 6.8	−0.2	−0.4	−0.6	−0.8	−1.0	−1.2	−1.4	−1.5	−1.6	−1.7	−1.8	−1.9	+0.1
	6.9– 7.0	−0.2	−0.4	−0.6	−0.8	−1.0	−1.2	−1.4	−1.6	−1.7	−1.8	−1.9	−2.0	+0.1
	7.1– 7.2	−0.2	−0.4	−0.6	−0.8	−1.0	−1.2	−1.4	−1.6	−1.8	−1.9	−2.0	−2.1	+0.1
	7.3– 7.4	−0.2	−0.4	−0.6	−0.8	−1.0	−1.2	−1.4	−1.6	−1.8	−2.0	−2.1	−2.2	+0.1
	7.5– 7.6	−0.2	−0.4	−0.6	−0.8	−1.0	−1.2	−1.4	−1.6	−1.8	−2.0	−2.2	−2.3	+0.1
	7.7–12.4	−0.2	−0.4	−0.6	−0.8	−1.0	−1.2	−1.4	−1.6	−1.8	−2.0	−2.2	−2.4	+0.1
Category 3	12.5–12.7	−0.3	−0.5	−0.7	−0.9	−1.1	−1.3	−1.5	−1.7	−1.9	−2.1	−2.3	−2.5	+0.1
	12.8–13.0	−0.3	−0.6	−0.8	−1.0	−1.2	−1.4	−1.6	−1.8	−2.0	−2.2	−2.4	−2.6	+0.1
	13.1–13.3	−0.3	−0.6	−0.9	−1.1	−1.3	−1.5	−1.7	−1.9	−2.1	−2.3	−2.5	−2.7	+0.1
	13.4–13.6	−0.3	−0.6	−0.9	−1.2	−1.4	−1.6	−1.8	−2.0	−2.2	−2.4	−2.6	−2.8	+0.1
	13.7–13.9	−0.3	−0.6	−0.9	−1.2	−1.5	−1.7	−1.9	−2.1	−2.3	−2.5	−2.7	−2.9	+0.1
	14.0–14.2	−0.3	−0.6	−0.9	−1.2	−1.5	−1.8	−2.0	−2.2	−2.4	−2.6	−2.8	−3.0	+0.1
	14.3–14.5	−0.3	−0.6	−0.9	−1.2	−1.5	−1.8	−2.1	−2.3	−2.5	−2.7	−2.9	−3.1	+0.1
	14.6–14.8	−0.3	−0.6	−0.9	−1.2	−1.5	−1.8	−2.1	−2.4	−2.6	−2.8	−3.0	−3.2	+0.1
	14.9–15.1	−0.3	−0.6	−0.9	−1.2	−1.5	−1.8	−2.1	−2.4	−2.7	−2.9	−3.1	−3.3	+0.1
	15.2–15.4	−0.3	−0.6	−0.9	−1.2	−1.5	−1.8	−2.1	−2.4	−2.7	−3.0	−3.2	−3.4	+0.1
	15.5–15.7	−0.3	−0.6	−0.9	−1.2	−1.5	−1.8	−2.1	−2.4	−2.7	−3.0	−3.3	−3.5	+0.1
	15.8–20.4	−0.3	−0.6	−0.9	−1.2	−1.5	−1.8	−2.1	−2.4	−2.7	−3.0	−3.3	−3.6	+0.1
Category 4	20.5–20.8	−0.4	−0.7	−1.0	−1.3	−1.6	−1.9	−2.2	−2.5	−2.8	−3.1	−3.4	−3.7	+0.1
	20.9–21.2	−0.4	−0.8	−1.1	−1.4	−1.7	−2.0	−2.3	−2.6	−2.9	−3.2	−3.5	−3.8	+0.1
	21.3–21.6	−0.4	−0.8	−1.2	−1.5	−1.8	−2.1	−2.4	−2.7	−3.0	−3.3	−3.6	−3.9	+0.1
	21.7–22.0	−0.4	−0.8	−1.2	−1.6	−1.9	−2.2	−2.5	−2.8	−3.1	−3.4	−3.7	−4.0	+0.1
	22.1–22.4	−0.4	−0.8	−1.2	−1.6	−2.0	−2.3	−2.6	−2.9	−3.2	−3.5	−3.8	−4.1	+0.1
	22.5–22.8	−0.4	−0.8	−1.2	−1.6	−2.0	−2.4	−2.7	−3.0	−3.3	−3.6	−3.9	−4.2	+0.1
	22.9–23.2	−0.4	−0.8	−1.2	−1.6	−2.0	−2.4	−2.8	−3.1	−3.4	−3.7	−4.0	−4.3	+0.1
	23.3–23.6	−0.4	−0.8	−1.2	−1.6	−2.0	−2.4	−2.8	−3.2	−3.5	−3.8	−4.1	−4.4	+0.1
	23.7–24.0	−0.4	−0.8	−1.2	−1.6	−2.0	−2.4	−2.8	−3.2	−3.6	−3.9	−4.2	−4.5	+0.1
	24.1–24.4	−0.4	−0.8	−1.2	−1.6	−2.0	−2.4	−2.8	−3.2	−3.6	−4.0	−4.3	−4.6	+0.1
	24.5–24.8	−0.4	−0.8	−1.2	−1.6	−2.0	−2.4	−2.8	−3.2	−3.6	−4.0	−4.4	−4.7	+0.1
	24.9–28.4	−0.4	−0.8	−1.2	−1.6	−2.0	−2.4	−2.8	−3.2	−3.6	−4.0	−4.4	−4.8	+0.1
Category 5	28.5–28.9	−0.5	−0.9	−1.3	−1.7	−2.1	−2.5	−2.9	−3.3	−3.7	−4.1	−4.5	−4.9	+0.1
	29.0–29.4	−0.5	−1.0	−1.4	−1.8	−2.2	−2.6	−3.0	−3.4	−3.8	−4.2	−4.6	−5.0	+0.1
	29.5–29.9	−0.5	−1.0	−1.5	−1.9	−2.3	−2.7	−3.1	−3.5	−3.9	−4.3	−4.7	−5.1	+0.1
	30.0–30.4	−0.5	−1.0	−1.5	−2.0	−2.4	−2.8	−3.2	−3.6	−4.0	−4.4	−4.8	−5.2	+0.1
	30.5–30.9	−0.5	−1.0	−1.5	−2.0	−2.5	−2.9	−3.3	−3.7	−4.1	−4.5	−4.9	−5.3	+0.1
	31.0–31.4	−0.5	−1.0	−1.5	−2.0	−2.5	−3.0	−3.4	−3.8	−4.2	−4.6	−5.0	−5.4	+0.1
	31.5–31.9	−0.5	−1.0	−1.5	−2.0	−2.5	−3.0	−3.5	−3.9	−4.3	−4.7	−5.1	−5.5	+0.1
	32.0–32.4	−0.5	−1.0	−1.5	−2.0	−2.5	−3.0	−3.5	−4.0	−4.4	−4.8	−5.2	−5.6	+0.1
	32.5–32.9	−0.5	−1.0	−1.5	−2.0	−2.5	−3.0	−3.5	−4.0	−4.5	−4.9	−5.3	−5.7	+0.1
	33.0–33.4	−0.5	−1.0	−1.5	−2.0	−2.5	−3.0	−3.5	−4.0	−4.5	−5.0	−5.4	−5.8	+0.1
	33.5–33.9	−0.5	−1.0	−1.5	−2.0	−2.5	−3.0	−3.5	−4.0	−4.5	−5.0	−5.5	−5.9	+0.1
	34.0–40.4	−0.5	−1.0	−1.5	−2.0	−2.5	−3.0	−3.5	−4.0	−4.5	−5.0	−5.5	−6.0	+0.1
Category 6	40.5–41.4	−1.0	−1.5	−2.0	−2.5	−3.0	−3.5	−4.0	−4.5	−5.0	−5.5	−6.0	−6.5	+0.1
	41.5–42.4	−1.0	−2.0	−2.5	−3.0	−3.5	−4.0	−4.5	−5.0	−5.5	−6.0	−6.5	−7.0	+0.1
	42.5–43.4	−1.0	−2.0	−3.0	−3.5	−4.0	−4.5	−5.0	−5.5	−6.0	−6.5	−7.0	−7.5	+0.1
	43.5–44.4	−1.0	−2.0	−3.0	−4.0	−4.5	−5.0	−5.5	−6.0	−6.5	−7.0	−7.5	−8.0	+0.1
	44.5–45.0	−1.0	−2.0	−3.0	−4.0	−5.0	−5.5	−6.0	−6.5	−7.0	−7.5	−8.0	−8.5	+0.1

Examples of Handicap Reductions Resulting in Change of Category

For the purpose of illustration assume the course being played in the following examples has an LGU Scratch Score of 72

The player's Exact Handicap shall reduce at the higher rate only so far as it brings her Playing Handicap into a lower Category. The balance of the reduction shall be at the lower rate.

Example 1: Category 6 to Category 8

Exact handicap	43.7		Nett Score 65		Nett Differential −7
Reduction:	4 x 1.0 =	4.0	brings Exact Handicap to 39.7		
	3 x 0.5 =	1.5			
		5.5	NEW Exact Handicap 38.2		

Example 2: Category 5 to Category 4

Exact handicap	29.6		Nett Score 67		Nett Differential −5
Reduction:	3 x 0.5 =	1.5	brings Exact Handicap to 28.1		
	2 x 0.4 =	0.8			
		2.3	NEW Exact Handicap 27.3		

Example 3: Category 4 to Category 3

Exact handicap	21.2		Nett Score 68		Nett Differential −4
Reduction:	2 x 0.4 =	0.8	brings Exact Handicap to 20.4		
	2 x 0.3 =	0.6			
		1.4	NEW Exact Handicap 19.8		

Example 4: Category 3 to Category 2

Exact handicap	12.7		Nett Score 70		Nett Differential −2
Reduction:	1 x 0.3 =	0.3	brings Exact Handicap to 12.4		
	1 x 0.2 =	0.2			
		0.5	NEW Exact Handicap 12.2		

Example 5: Category 2 to Category 1

Exact handicap	5.6		Nett Score 69		Nett Differential −3
Reduction:	1 x 0.2 =	0.2	brings Exact Handicap to 5.4		
	2 x 0.1 =	0.2			
		0.4	NEW Exact Handicap 5.2		

Example 6

An Exact Handicap must be reduced by the correct rate relevant to the handicap category, otherwise two players with the same nett score, playing off similar handicaps but in different categories could result in the player with the higher handicap acquiring a lower Playing Handicap than a player who started the day with a lower Playing Handicap.

Player 1	Exact Handicap 12.4		Nett Score 64	Nett Differential −8	
	Reduction:	8 x 0.2 =	1.6	NEW Exact Handicap = 10.8	
Player 2	Exact Handicap 12.6		Nett Score 64	Nett Differential −8	
	Reduction:	8 x 0.3 =	2.4	NEW Exact Handicap = 10.2	INCORRECT
	Reduction:	1 x 0.3 =	0.3	brings Exact Handicap to 12.3	
		7 x 0.2 =	1.4		
			1.7	NEW Exact handicap = 10.9	CORRECT

Example 7

An Exact Handicap may not be reduced below 5.5 on an Extra Day Score

Exact Handicap 5.8	Extra Day Score		Nett Score 69	Nett Differential -3
Reduction:	2 x 0.2 =	0.4		
	1 x 0.1 =	0.1		
		0.5	NEW Exact Handicap = 5.3 INCORRECT	
			NEW Exact Handicap = 5.5 CORRECT	

Examples of rounding exact handicaps to playing handicaps

Example 8

Exact Handicap	23.5 rounded up to	Playing Handicap	24
	23.4 rounded down to		23

Example 9

Exact Handicap	0.5 rounded up to	Playing Handicap	1
	0.4 rounded down to		Scratch

Example 10

Exact Handicap	−2.5 rounded up to	Playing Handicap	+2
	−2.6 rounded down to		+3

APPENDIX H5

Qualifying Competitions

At the end of each round of a Qualifying Competition, the Organising Committee must consult the following Qualifying Competition Table to determine whether a score returned above a player's Buffer Zone will result in an increase to her Exact Handicap

Procedure:

1   Ascertain the total number of players in Categories 1–5 who have played in the round

2   Count the number of players in Categories 1–5 who have returned scores within or below their Buffer Zone

3   From the left hand column of the Qualifying Competition Table, find the range of players in Categories 1–5 who have played in the round

4   If the number of players who have returned scores within or below their Buffer Zone is less than the number shown in the corresponding right hand column of the Table the round is non-counting for handicap increases

Where a Qualifying Competition has been run on two courses, i.e. LGU Medal competition with Silver and Bronze Divisions playing on different courses, a separate assessment must be made for each course

If a Qualifying Competition is restricted solely to Category 6 players, the Exact Handicap of a player who returns a score above her Buffer Zone will be increased by 0.1, maximum Exact Handicap 45.0

Qualifying Competition Table	
Number of Players excluding Category 6	Minimum Number of Players in/below Buffer Zone
up to 14	1
15–24	2
25–34	3
35–44	4
45–54	5
55–64	6
65–74	7
75–84	8
85–94	9
95–104	10
105–114	11
115–124	12
125–134	13
135–144	14
145–154	15
155–164	16
165–174	17
175–184	18
185–194	19
195–204	20

APPENDIX H6

Immediate Reduction of Playing Handicap

When a player returns a score with a Nett Differential below her Buffer Zone her Handicap Secretary must refer to the Table of Immediate Reductions of Playing Handicap to ascertain the reduction, if any, to be made to her Playing Handicap

The reduction will become operative immediately the player has been informed of the alteration by her Handicap Secretary

If a player returns a score with a Nett Differential below her Buffer Zone and is unable to report the score to her Handicap Secretary before playing in a further competition, she must report her score to the organising committee, who shall refer to the Table of Immediate Reductions of Playing Handicap and reduce her Playing Handicap, if applicable, for that competition.

Table of Immediate Reductions of Playing Handicap													
	Nett Diff	−1	−2	−3	−4	−5	−6	−7	−8	−9	−10	−11	−12
	Playing Handicap												
Category 2	8–12								-2	-2	-2	-2	-2
Category 3	13							-2	-2	-2	-2	-2	-3
	14						-2	-2	-2	-2	-3	-3	-3
	15						-2	-2	-2	-3	-3	-3	-3
	16–20						-2	-2	-2	-3	-3	-3	-4
Category 4	21					-2	-2	-2	-3	-3	-3	-3	-4
	22				-2	-2	-2	-2	-3	-3	-3	-4	-4
	23				-2	-2	-2	-3	-3	-3	-4	-4	-4
	24				-2	-2	-2	-3	-3	-4	-4	-4	-4
	25–28				-2	-2	-2	-3	-3	-4	-4	-4	-5
Category 5	29				-2	-2	-3	-3	-3	-4	-4	-5	-5
	30				-2	-2	-3	-3	-4	-4	-4	-5	-5
	31				-2	-2	-3	-3	-4	-4	-5	-5	-5
	32–40				-2	-2	-3	-3	-4	-4	-5	-5	-6
Category 6	41	-1	-1	-2	-2	-3	-3	-4	-4	-5	-5	-6	-6
	42	-1	-2	-2	-3	-3	-4	-4	-5	-5	-6	-6	-7
	43	-1	-2	-3	-3	-4	-4	-5	-5	-6	-6	-7	-7
	44	-1	-2	-3	-4	-4	-5	-5	-6	-6	-7	-7	-8
	45	-1	-2	-3	-4	-5	-5	-6	-6	-7	-7	-8	-8
	Nett Diff	-1	-2	-3	-4	-5	-6	-7	-8	-9	-10	-11	-12

Application for Handicap Adjustment Based on General Play

An Application for adjustment of a player's Exact Handicap in accordance with general play must be made by the Handicap Committee of her Home Club and must contain the relevant scores from item 1 and information detailed in either item 2 or item 3:

1   Summary of Scores Returned by Player:

1.1 Name of player

1.2 Home Club of player

1.3 Exact Handicap of player 12 months ago

1.4 Exact Handicap of player on date of application

1.5 Qualifying Competitions

    1.5.1 number of Qualifying Competitions in which player has competed

    1.5.2 number of scores returned

    1.5.3 number of NR's

    1.5.4 number of Qualifying Competitions in which the player has competed that have resulted in the competition being declared non-counting for increases in Exact Handicaps

    1.5.5 Nett Differentials

        1.5.5.1 below Buffer Zone

        1.5.5.2 within BufferZone

        1.5.5.3 above Buffer Zone

1.6 Extra Day Scores

    1.6.1 number of Extra Day Scores marked

    1.6.2 number of NR's

    1.6.3 Nett Differentials

        1.6.3.1 below Buffer Zone

        1.6.3.2 within Buffer Zone

        1.6.3.3 above Buffer Zone

1.7 Details of best ten Gross Differentials returned during the preceding 12 months

1.8 Handicap scores returned to attain/re-attain an LGU handicap

    1.8.1 Differentials of at least three Handicap Scores

2   Application for Increase in Exact Handicap

2.1 Reason for application for increase in Exact Handicap - this may include:

    2.1.1 Alternative Day player in LGU Medal Competitions and/or other Qualifying Competitions where all or most of the competitions result in non-counting for an increase in Exact Handicap due to less than the required number of players returning scores within or below their Buffer Zone in accordance with Appendix H5 - give details

    2.1.2 Player whose previous handicap lapsed when her Playing Membership of a club ceased – give details of length of time that has elapsed since player held a handicap

    2.1.3 Age, infirmity or illness - give details

The National Organisation will assess the facts and may authorise an appropriate increase in the player's Exact Handicap within the recommendations set out below. Where a player has not held a handicap or has not returned scores for handicap for several years, the Exact Handicap will be increased with the proviso that if the player continues to return scores for handicap that do not reflect her current form her Exact Handicap may be re-assessed in six months

Exact Handicaps cannot be increased above 40.4 on general play

Recommended maximum increases:

Category 1   one or two strokes
Category 2   two or three strokes
Category 3   two or three strokes
Category 4   three or four strokes
Category 5   three or four strokes
Category 6   no increase under general play

3 Application for Decrease in Exact Handicap

    3.1 Reason for application for decrease in Exact Handicap - this may include:

    3.2 Performance in:

        3.2.1 match play competitions

        3.2.2 foursomes and four-ball competitions

        3.2.3 mixed competitions

        3.2.4 team competitions

    Details of performance in events should be supplied with the application

The National Organisation will assess the facts and may authorise an appropriate decrease in a player's Exact Handicap

Exact Handicaps cannot be decreased below 5.5 on general play

APPENDIX H8

Ladies' Golf Union Open Qualifying Competition Results

		Score in Buffer Zone:		
			Nett	Points
Date:	15 March 1998	Cat 1	75	
		Cat 2	76	
Competition:	Open Meeting - Stroke Play	Cat 3	77	
Played at Golf Club/Course:	Somewhere GC (Long Course)	Cat 4	78	
LGU Scratch Score: 74	Par: 74	Cat 5	79	

Player	Home Club	Playing Handicap	Category	Gross Score	Nett Score	Points or +/-	Score within/ below Buffer Zone
Other A N	Seaside	23	4	99	76		Y
Smith J	Seaside	26	4	106	80		
Black A	Inland	7	2	84	77		
Visitor A	Parkland	3	1	75	72		Y
Brown J	Neighbouring	14	3	79	65		Y
Newcomer A	Seaside	30	5	107	77		Y

Number of Players in Categories 1 - 5:   6
Number of Players in Categories 1 - 5 within or below Buffer Zone: 4

**LADIES' GOLF UNION
OPEN QUALIFYING COMPETITION RESULTS**

		Score in Buffer Zone:		
			Nett	Points
Date:	25 May 1998	Cat 1		37
		Cat 2		36
Competition:	Open Meeting - Stableford	Cat 3		35
Played at Golf Club/Course:	New GC	Cat 4		34
LGU Scratch Score: 72	Par: 74	Cat 5		33

Player	Home Club	Playing Handicap	Category	Gross Score	Nett Score	Points or +/-	Score within/ below Buffer Zone
Other A N	Seaside	23	4			30	
Smith J	Seaside	26	4			36	Y
Black A	Inland	7	2			40	Y
Visitor A	Parkland	3	1			36	
Brown J	Neighbouring	14	3			35	Y
Newcomer A	Seaside	30	5			32	

Number of Players in Categories 1 - 5:   6
Number of Players in Categories 1 - 5 within or below Buffer Zone: 3

LGU Handicap Register Form

APPENDIX H9

NAME   AN Other

HOME CLUB   Seaside Golf Club

OTHER CLUBS   Inland Golf Club · Holiday Golf Club

Monthly Adjustments of Playing Handicap Adjustment effective on 8th day of month based on Exact Handicap on last day of previous month

Immediate reductions – see Appendix H6

Date Played	Course	Rnd	Event	EDS per LGU year	Gross Score	H'cap	Nett Score	Points or +/-	Par	SS	Nett Diff	Gross Diff	R	Adjustment see Appendix H3	Revised Exact H'cap	Revised Playing Hcap	Cat
01 February 1998	LGU Handicap		LGU Handicap	0											21.0	21	4
12 April 1998	Seaside		Stableford			21		31	72	72	+5	26		+0.1	21.1		
14 April 1998	Seaside		LGU Medal		100	21	79			72	+7	28		+0.1	21.2		
21 April 1998	Inland		EDS	1	NR	21								+0.1	21.3		
24 April 1998	Seaside		LGU Medal		88	21	67			72	-5	16		-1.8	19.5		
24 April 1998	REDUCTION		REDUCTION													19	3
28 April 1998	Seaside		Stableford		NR	19								+0.1	19.6		
02 May 1998	Seaside		EDS	2	90	19	71			72	-1	18		-0.3	19.3		
07 May 1998	REVISION		REVISION										R		19.3	20	3
21 May 1998	Seaside		Stableford			20		27	72	72	+9	29		0.0	19.3		
27 May 1998	Holiday		Par			20		-6	69	70	+5	25		+0.1	19.4		
28 May 1998	Holiday		Trophy		94	20	74			70	+4	24		+0.1	19.5		
01 June 1998	Holiday		LGU Medal		81	20	61			70	-9	11		-2.7	16.8		
01 June 1998	REDUCTION		REDUCTION													17	3
07 June 1998	REVISION		REVISION										R			20	3
07 June 1998	REDUCTION 1/6/1998		REDUCTION 1/6/1998													17	3
17 June 1998	Neighbouring		Open Meeting		87	17	70			71	-1	16		-0.3	16.5		
24 June 1998	Woodland		Open Meeting		NR	17								+0.1	16.6		
27 June 1998	Inland	1	36 hole Trophy		91	17	74			75	-1	16		-0.3	16.3		
27 June 1998	Inland	2	36 hole Trophy		96	17	79			75	+4	21		+0.1	16.4		
07 July 1998	REVISION		REVISION										R			16	3
10 July 1998	Holiday		EDS	3	92	16	76			70	+6	22		+0.1	16.5		
12 July 1998	Seaside		Stableford			16		35	72	72	+1	17		0.0	16.5		
02 August 1998	Seaside		Par			16		+6	72	72	-6	10		-1.8	14.7		
02 August 1998	REDUCTION		REDUCTION													14	3
07 August 1998	REVISION		REVISION													17	3
07 August 1998	REDUCTION 2/8/1998		REDUCTION 2/8/1998													15	3
10 August 1998	Inland		LGU Medal		92	15	77			75	+2	17		0.0	14.7		
17 August 1998	Seaside		Stableford			15		37	72	72	-1	14		-0.3	14.4		
01 September 1998	Inland		LGU Medal		95	15	80			75	+5	20		+0.1	14.5		
07 September 1998	REVISION		REVISION													14	3

Gross Diff = Nett Diff + Handicap

R denotes Reduction Only Qualifying Competition – see Appendix H5

APPENDIX H10

Ladies' Golf Union Handicap Exchange Sheet

Scores returned at ——————— Golf Club during the month of ——————— 199

Players' HOME CLUB is ——————— Golf Club

Name of Member	Date Played	Rnd	Competition or EDS	Gross Score	H'cap	Nett Score	Points or +/–	Par	SS	Nett Diff	Gross Diff	R

Gross Diff = Nett Diff + Handicap   R denotes Reduction only Qualifying Competition

Signed: ——————————————————— Date: ———————————

Handicap Secretary

APPENDIX H11

Ladies' Golf Union Summary of Scores

Date: _____
Golf Club: _____   Home Club of the following players:

Player	Exact H'cap year ago	Exact H'cap Today	Qualifying Competitions							Extra Day Scores		Ten best Gross Differentials returned during preceding 12 months
			Played	Scores	NR's	R's	Nett Differentials			Played	NR's	Qualifying Competitions and EDS
							<BZ	=BZ	>BZ			
Other A N	20.4	22.9	30	25	5	5		7	23	4	2	23 24 25 25 25 27 28 29 31 31
Smith J	25.8	26.4	2	2					2	2		32 33 33 37
Youngster A	25.4	15.9	20	20			5	15				14 15 16 21 22 22 24 24 25 25
Weckender A	14.2	14.7	5	5		5			5	5		19 19 20 20 20 21 21 24 25 26

Notes:

Exact Handicap year ago = Exact Handicap on 01 February 1998 until new LGU Handicapping System has been in use for 1 year

R denotes Reduction only Qualifying Competition

<BZ Nett Differential below Buffer Zone =BZ Nett Differential within Buffer Zone >BZ Nett Differential above Buffer Zone

Computer Software Relating to the LGU Handicapping System

With effect from 1 February 1998, any software used by an Affiliated Club shall fulfil the following requirements:

1 At the Home Club of Playing Members

  1.1 record

    1.1.1 all Qualifying Competition Scores and Extra Day Scores (including No Returns) returned at that club

    1.1.2 all Qualifying Competition Scores and Extra Day Scores (including No Returns) returned at other clubs where a player is a Playing Member

    1.1.3 all Qualifying Competition Scores (including No Returns) returned in Open Qualifying Competitions

    1.1.4 all overseas scores that resulted in a Nett Differential below a player's Buffer Zone

    1.1.5 all Handicap Scores

  1.2 calculate Exact Handicaps in accordance with these regulations by applying scores in chronological order

  1.3 provide a facility for an Immediate Reduction of a Playing Handicap to be applied by the Handicap Secretary

  1.4 revise Playing Handicaps on the seventh day of each month in accordance with these regulations, incorporating any Immediate Reduction of Playing Handicap that has been recorded during the first seven days of the month

  1.5 print a list of up-to-date Playing Handicaps on demand

  1.6 print LGU Handicap Register Forms containing not less than the information shown in Appendix H9 at least once a month for those who have returned scores during the month

  1.7 print an LGU Summary of Scores containing not less than the information shown in Appendix H11 on demand

  1.8 provide a facility for altering an Exact and Playing Handicap following an adjustment under general play

2 At a club that is not the Home Club of Playing Members

  2.1 record all Qualifying Competition Scores and Extra Day Scores (including No Returns) and Handicap Scores returned at that club

  2.2 print an LGU Handicap Register Form when required

  2.3 print an LGU Handicap Exchange Sheet containing not less than the information shown in Appendix H10 at the end of each month when scores have been recorded

3 When requested by the Ladies' Golf Union, a software supplier, wishing to confirm compliance with the LGU Handicapping System regulations, shall provide printed records:

  3.1 LGU Handicap Register Form as shown in Appendix H9

  3.2 LGU Handicap Exchange Sheet as shown in Appendix H10 and

  3.3 LGU Summary of Scores as shown in Appendix H11

LGU Medal Competitions

1.1 Silver and Bronze Medals - General

The Ladies' Golf Union will award a Silver and Bronze Medal to each Affiliated Club for annual competition

1.1.1 Silver Division

A Silver Medal will be awarded for players with Playing Handicaps up to and including 20

1.1.2 Bronze Division

A Bronze Medal will be awarded for players with Playing Handicaps of 21 to 40 inclusive

The Handicap Secretary should apply for the Silver and Bronze Medals to the National Organisation or, in the case of overseas Affiliated Clubs to the Ladies' Golf Union, by the beginning of the LGU year

1.2 Number of LGU Medal Competitions

The Committee is responsible for running up to SIXTEEN Stroke Play competitions for the LGU Silver and Bronze Medals awarded annually to each Affiliated Club. Any, or all, of these competitions may be played in conjunction with a club Stroke Play competition, as authorised by the Committee. It is recommended that, unless climatic or other conditions make it impossible, all clubs should hold at least one LGU Medal Competition monthly

1.3 Qualifications

1.3.1 All Playing Members, **including junior members**, with a Playing Handicap of 40 or less are eligible to compete

1.3.2 A Playing Member belonging to more than one Affiliated Club may compete in LGU Medal Competitions held at each of these clubs and may even play for two medals on the same day, provided they are not played on the same course

Committees may not make a condition requiring a minimum number of scores to be returned before a member is eligible to compete

1.4 Conditions of Entry

1.4.1 Registering Intention to Compete

Before playing in an LGU Medal Competition a player must register her intention to compete by one of the following means, otherwise her score cannot be accepted

1.4.1.1 Entering, or having entered, her name in a book kept for the purpose

1.4.1.2 Entering, or having entered, her name on a prepared sheet, list or time sheet

1.4.2 Minimum number of entries

Should only one player enter the competition her score must be recorded and count for LGU Medal purposes. **If no player enters the competition the LGU Medal Competition will be deemed to have taken place unless Regulation 1.9 applies**

There shall be no compulsory draw or entry fee for players competing in LGU Medal Competitions only, but the Committee may make its own conditions regarding starting times and entry fees for any competitions played in conjunction with LGU Medal Competitions

1.5 Marking of Scores

Play may be in twos, threes or fours. Where there is a single competitor the Committee shall appoint an eligible Marker whose appointment may be authorised by the Committee retrospectively

1.6 More than one Course

Where a club has more than one course the LGU Medal Competitions need not all be played on the same course provided that all competitors in the Silver Division play the same course in any one competition and all competitors in the Bronze Division play the same course in any one competition

1.7 Alternative Day

For those clubs who have members who cannot play on the Main Medal Day, and providing the Club Committee is willing to grant the necessary permission, the Committee may arrange an Alternative Day for all or some of the LGU Medal Competitions complying with the Rules of Golf (Note to Rule 33-2b)

The Committee shall be responsible for deciding which members may play on the Alternative Day. Provision must be made for members to indicate on which day they are available in line with the following recommendations:

1.7.1 If the Club Committee limits the number of members who may compete on the Alternative Day the Committee should decide the fairest apportionment of opportunity to those wishing to play

1.7.2 The Committee may request members to indicate their preference on a prepared list or book at any time up to one week before the first day of the Competition days, whether it be the Main or the Alternative Day

1.7.3 The Committee may draw up a list of those eligible to play on the Alternative Day at the beginning of the LGU year. A

player whose name is on such a list may, at the discretion of the Committee, play on a Main Day, provided she indicates her intention to the Committee not less than one week before the first of the competition days

1.7.4 The Alternative Day should, if possible, be arranged on a date **prior** to the Main Day so that the Competition is closed at the end of the Main Day

1.7.5 If a major club competition coincides with the LGU Medal Competition it may be played on the Main Day only or the Main and Alternative Day at the discretion of the Committee

1.7.6 The aim of the Committee should be to enable as many members as possible to play in the LGU Medal Competition. To this end a restricted playing member (e.g. 5-day member) should be allowed to enter the LGU Medal Competition on whichever day her membership permits

Under no circumstances may any player compete twice in the same LGU Medal Competition

1.8 Fixing of dates

1.8.1 Main Day - the dates of the LGU Medal Competitions (minimum four and maximum sixteen) at each Affiliated Club shall be fixed by the beginning of each LGU year and posted in the clubhouse

1.8.2 Alternative Day – an Alternative Day must be arranged within seven days of the Main Day, **preferably prior to the Main Day**, in the same LGU Year and may be on any day of the week. A notice of the dates must be posted in the clubhouse at the beginning of the LGU year

1.9 Change of date

1.9.1 The date of an LGU Medal Competition may only be altered should the course be pronounced unavailable by the Club Committee or if the Committee or their authorised representative consider that for any reason the course is not in a playable condition or that there are circumstances which render the proper playing of the game impossible (Rules of Golf – Rule 33-2d)

1.9.2 The new date must be within two calendar months of the date originally fixed and within the same LGU Year and must be posted in the clubhouse. A change of date may be applied to a Main or an Alternative Day separately

1.10 Silver and Bronze Medals

The Silver and Bronze Medals will be played for annually from 1 February to 31 January. The winners will be those who return the lowest aggregate of FOUR Nett Scores in LGU Medal Competitions from 1 February to 31 January. Where more than one course or more than one LGU Scratch Score have applied the aggregate score shall be calculated as the aggregate of the Nett Differentials between the LGU Scratch Score applicable and the Nett Score returned

1.10.1 For the Silver Medal all four scores must be returned whilst the player has a Playing Handicap of 20 or under and, for the Bronze, whilst she has a Playing Handicap of 21 to 40 inclusive

1.10.2 The winning of a Silver Medal supersedes the winning of a Bronze Medal in any club in the same year

1.10.3 If two or more competitors tie, the winner shall be decided on the Nett Score of the last 9, 6, 3 or 1 hole(s) of all four cards added together. If still a tie, decision shall be by play-off over eighteen holes on current Playing Handicap. In the case of a tie where the aggregate of the Nett Differentials has had to be applied, ties shall be decided by play-off over eighteen holes on current Playing Handicap

The Handicap Secretary shall issue to the winner of the Medal in each Division a Certificate supplied by the National Organisation on which should be stated the winner's name, the name of her club and the venue and date of the LGU Medal Final at which she will be entitled to compete for the LGU Gold or Silver Medal. This information may be obtained from the LGU Poster of Events distributed to Affiliated Clubs in early January

1.11 Gold and Silver Medals

The Ladies' Golf Union will award Gold and Silver Medals for annual competition in England, Ireland, Scotland and Wales. The National Organisation shall be responsible for the organisation of the annual competitions. Winners of the Silver and Bronze Medals respectively, in their own club during the preceding LGU year are eligible to compete for the Gold and Silver Medals in their own country

1.12 LGU Pendants

An LGU Pendant will be awarded annually to the winner, in either the Silver or the Bronze Division, of the September LGU Medal Competition in each Affiliated Club. Ties shall be decided on the last 9, 6, 3 or 1 hole(s). If still a tie, decision should be by play-off over eighteen holes, on the Playing Handicap applicable on the day of the LGU Pendant competition

Where more than one course or more than one LGU Scratch Score have applied, the winner is the player with the best Nett Differential between the LGU Scratch Score of the course played and the Nett Score returned. In this instance, ties shall be decided by play-off over eighteen holes on the Playing Handicap applicable on the day of the LGU Pendant Competition. A player is eligible to win a Pendant in every Affiliated Club of which she is a Playing Member

The Handicap Secretary should apply for the Pendant to the National Organisation or, in the case of overseas Affiliated Clubs to the Ladies' Golf Union, by the beginning of the LGU year

Any club which does NOT permit a junior member with a Playing Handicap of 40 or less to compete in LGU Medal Competitions shall NOT be entitled to receive a Silver and Bronze Medal and shall NOT be entitled to receive an LGU Pendant

Governing Bodies

Home Unions

The English Golf Union

The English Golf Union was founded in 1924 and embraces 34 County Unions with over 1,550 affiliated clubs, 23 clubs overseas, and 447 Golfing Societies and Associations. Its objects are:

(1) To further the interests of Amateur Golf in England.
(2) To assist in maintaining a uniform system of handicapping.
(3) To arrange an English Championship; an English Stroke Play Championship; an English County Championship, International and other Matches and Competitions.
(4) To co-operate with the Royal & Ancient Golf Club of St Andrews and the Council of National Golf Unions.
(5) To co-operate with other National Golf Unions and Associations in such manner as may be decided.

The Scottish Golf Union

The Scottish Golf Union was founded in 1920 and embraces 661 clubs. Subject to the stipulation and declaration that the Union recognises the Royal & Ancient Golf Club of St Andrews as the Ruling Authority in the game of golf, the objects of the Union are:

(a) To foster and maintain a high standard of Amateur Golf in Scotland and to administer and organise and generally act as the governing body of amateur golf in Scotland.
(b) To institute and thereafter carry through annually a Scottish Amateur Championship, a Scottish Open Amateur Stroke Play Championship and other such competitions and matches as they consider appropriate.
(c) To administer and apply the rules of the Standard Scratch Score and Handicapping Scheme as approved by the Council of National Golf Unions from time to time.
(d) To deal with other matters of general or local interest to amateur golfers in Scotland.

The Union's organisation consists of Area Committees covering the whole of Scotland. There are 16 Areas, each having its own Association or Committee elected by the Clubs in that particular area and each Area Association or Committee elects one delegate to serve on the Executive of the Union.

Golfing Union of Ireland

The Golfing Union of Ireland, founded in 1891, embraces 275 Clubs. Its objects are:

(1) Securing the federation of the various Clubs.
(2) Arranging Amateur Championships, Inter-Provincial and Inter-Club Competitions, and International Matches.
(3) Securing a uniform standard of handicapping.
(4) Providing for advice and assistance, other than financial, to affiliated Clubs in all matters appertaining to Golf, and generally to promote the game in every way, in which this can be better done by the Union than by individual Clubs.

Its functions include the holding of the *Close* Championship for Amateur Golfers and Tournaments for Team Matches.

Its organisation consists of Provincial Councils in each of the four Provinces elected by the Clubs in the Province – each province electing a limited number of delegates to the Central Council which meets annually.

Welsh Golfing Union

The Welsh Golfing Union was founded in 1895 and is the second oldest of the four National Unions. Unlike the other Unions it is an association of Golf Clubs and Golfing Organisations. The present membership is 127. For the purpose of electing the Executive Council, Wales is divided into ten districts which between them return 22 members.

The objects of the Union are:

(a) To take any steps which may be deemed necessary to further the interests of the amateur game in Wales.
(b) To hold a Championship Meeting or Meetings each year.
(c) To encourage, financially and/or otherwise,

Inter-Club, Inter-County, and International Matches, and such other events as may be authorised by the Council.

(d) To assist in setting up and maintaining a uniform system of Handicapping.

(e) To assist in the establishment and maintenance of high standards of greenkeeping.

Note: The union recognises the Royal & Ancient Golf Club of St Andrews as the ruling authority.

The Council of National Golf Unions

At a meeting of Representatives of Golf Unions and Associations in Great Britain and Ireland, called at the special request of the Scottish Golf Union, and held in York, on 14th February, 1924, resolutions were adopted from which the Council of National Golf Unions was constituted.

The Council holds an Annual Meeting in March, and such other meetings as may be necessary. Two representatives are elected from each national Home Union – England, Scotland, Ireland and Wales – and hold office until the next Annual meeting when they are eligible for re-election.

The principal function of the Council, as laid down by the York Conference, was to formulate a system of Standard Scratch Scores and Handicapping, and to co-operate with the Royal & Ancient Championship Committee in matters coming under their jurisdiction. The responsibilities undertaken by the Council at the instance of the Royal & Ancient Golf Club or the National Unions are as follows:

1　The Standard Scratch Score and Handicapping Scheme, formulated in March, 1926, approved by the Royal & Ancient, and last revised in 1989.

2　The nomination of two members on the Board of Management of The Sports Turf Research Institute, with an experimental station at St Ives, Bingley, Yorkshire.

3　The management of the Annual Amateur International Matches between the four countries – England, Scotland, Ireland and Wales.

United States Golf Association

The USGA is the national governing body of golf. Its single most important goal is preserving the integrity and values of the game.

Formed on 22nd December, 1894, a year when two clubs proclaimed different US Amateur Champions, representatives of five clubs met at a dinner at the Calumet Club in New York City. They created a central governing body to establish uniform rules, to conduct national championships and to nurture the virtues of sportsmanship in golf.

The names of the standing committees give an idea of what the USGA does:

Rules of Golf, Championship, Amateur Status and Conduct, Implements and Ball, Handicap, Women's, Sectional Affairs, Green Section, Public Links, Women's Public Links, Junior Championship, Girls' Junior, Senior Championship, Senior Women's Championship, Bob Jones Award, Museum, Green Section Award, Finance, Public Information, Membership, Regional Association, Associates, Intercollegiate Relations, Mid-Amateur Championship, International Team Selection, Development, Turfgrass Research, Nominating.

The USGA, as the governing body of the game in the United States, makes and interprets the Rules of Golf in co-operation with the Royal & Ancient Golf Club of St Andrews, Scotland; developed and maintains the national system of handicapping; controls the standards of the ball and the implements of the game; works in turfgrass and turf management; and, generally speaking, preserves and promotes the game.

The Professional Golfers' Association

The Professional Golfers' Association was founded in 1901 to promote interest in the game of golf; to protect and advance the mutual and trade interests of its members; to arrange and hold meetings and tournaments periodically for the members; to institute and operate funds for the benefit of the members; to assist the members to obtain employment; and effect any other objects of a like nature as may be determined from time to time by the Association.

Classes of Membership

There shall be nine (9) classes of membership:

(i) **Class A** Members engaged as the nominated professional on a full-time basis at a PGA Club, PGA Course or PGA Driving Range in one of the seven Regions; and members engaged as the nominated professional on a full-time basis, at an establishment in one of the seven Regions at which the public can play and/or practise which, in the opinion of the Executive Committee does not qualify as a PGA Club, Course or Driving Range but does warrant Class A status.

Note: Class A(T) – Class A members currently engaged at an establishment which has been inspected and approved as a PGA Training Establishment and currently holds that status will be identified where appropriate by the suffix (T) after their classification.

(ii) **Class B** Members engaged by a Class A or D member to assist the nominated professional at any PGA Establishment in one of the seven Regions on a full-time basis.

(iii) **Class C** Tournament playing members (men and women).

(iv) **Class D** Members engaged as the nominated professional on a full-time basis at a PGA Establishment within the seven Regions which does not qualify as a 'Class A' establishment, or engaged on a full-time basis within the seven Regions by any other Company or any other individual designated by the Executive Committee for this purpose. (Former Class G.)

(v) **Class E** Honorary Associate Members (HAM). Those who in the opinion of the Executive Committee through their past or continuing membership justify retaining the full privileges of membership as Honorary Associate Members (HAM).

(vi) **Class F** Associate Members (AM).

(a) Those who have ceased to be eligible for other categories of membership who in the opinion of the Executive Committee through their past membership justify retaining limited privileges of membership as Associate Members; and (b) Members of the PGA European Tour or WPGET who do not qualify for Class C membership but who in the opinion of the Executive Committee justify limited privileges of membership as Associate Members.

(vii) **Class G** Honorary Life Members (HLM). Those recommended by the Board to a Special General Meeting of the Association for election as Honorary Life Members. No form of application is needed nor need reference be made to the Regional Committee concerned.

(viii) **Class H** Members who are qualified members of the Association, and ineligible for any other class of membership, engaged on a full-time basis at an establishment acceptable to the Association outside the jurisdiction of the seven Regions. (Overseas)

(ix) **Class O** Members who have not qualified at the official training centre of the Association, who are ineligible for any other class of membership, and who are current members of another PGA approved by the Association and have held such membership for not less than two years.

The Management of the Association is under the overall direction and control of a Board. The Association is divided into seven Regions each of which employs a full-time secretary and runs tournaments for the benefit of members within its Region.

The Association is responsible for arranging and obtaining sponsorship of the Ryder Cup, Club Professionals' Championship, PGA Cup matches, Seniors' Championship, PGA Assistants' Championship, Assistants' Match Play Championship and other National Championships.

Anyone who intends to become a club professional must serve a minimum of three years in registration and qualify at the PGA Training School before election as a full Member.

PGA European Tour

To be eligible to become a member of the PGA European Tour a player must possess certain minimum standards which shall be determined by the Tournament Committee. In 1976 a Qualifying School for potential new members was introduced to be held annually. The leading players are awarded cards allowing them to compete in PGA European Tour tournaments.

In 1985 the PGA European Tour became ALL EXEMPT with no more Monday pre-qualifying. Full details can be obtained from the Wentworth Headquarters.

Women Professional Golfers' European Tour

The Women Professional Golfers' European Tour (WPG European Tour) was founded in 1988 to further the development of women's professional golf throughout Europe and its membership is open to all nationalities. An amateur wishing to join the Tour must be 18 years of age, have a handicap of 1 or less and is on probation for eight rounds in tournaments, during which she must attain certain playing standards as determined by the Tournament Committee.

Government of the Amateur and Open Golf Championship

In December 1919, on the invitation of the clubs who had hitherto controlled the Amateur and Open Golf Championships, the Royal & Ancient took over the government of those events. These two championships are now controlled by a committee appointed by the Royal & Ancient Golf Club of St Andrews. The Committee is called the Royal and Ancient Golf Club Championship Committee and consists of eight members of the Club elected by the Club.

Ladies' Golf Union (LGU)

The Ladies' Golf Union was founded in 1893 with the following objects:

(1) To promote the interests of the game of Golf.

(2) To obtain a uniformity of the rules of the game by establishing a representative legislative authority.

(3) To establish a uniform system of handicapping.

(4) To act as a tribunal and court of reference on points of uncertainty.

(5) To arrange the Annual Championship Competition and obtain the funds necessary for that purpose.

After 100 years, only the language has changed, the present Constitution defining the objects as:

(1) To uphold the rules of the game, to advance and safeguard the interests of women's golf and to decide all doubtful and disputed points in connection therewith.

(2) To maintain, regulate and enforce the LGU Handicapping System.

(3) To employ the funds of The Union in such a manner as shall be deemed best for the interests of women's golf, with power to borrow or raise money to use for the same purpose.

(4) To maintain and regulate International events, Championships and Competitions held under the LGU regulations and to promote the interests of Great Britain and Ireland in Ladies International Golf.

(5) To make, maintain and publish such regulations as may be considered necessary for the above purposes.

The constituents of the LGU are:

Home Countries. The English Ladies' Golf Association (founded 1952), the Irish Ladies' Golf Union (founded 1893), the Scottish Ladies' Golfing Association (founded 1904), the Welsh Ladies' Golf Union (founded 1904), plus ladies' societies, girls' schools and ladies' clubs affiliated to these organisations. *Overseas.* Affiliated ladies' golf unions and golf clubs in the Commonwealth and any other overseas ladies' golfing organisation affiliated to the LGU.

Individual lady members of clubs within the above categories are regarded as *members of the LGU.*

The Rules of the Game and of Amateur Status, which the LGU is bound to uphold, are those published by the Royal & Ancient Golf Club of St Andrews.

In endeavouring to fulfil its responsibilities towards advancing and safeguarding women's golf, the LGU maintains contact with other golfing organisations – the Royal & Ancient Golf Club of St Andrews, the Council of National Golf Unions, the Golf Foundation, the Central Council of Physical Recreation, the Sports Council, the Women Professional Golfers' European Tour and the Women's Committee of the United States Golf Association. This contact ensures that the LGU is informed of developments and projected developments and has an opportunity

to comment upon and to influence the future of the game for women.

Either directly or through its constituent national organisations the LGU advises and is the ultimate authority on doubts or disputes which may arise in connection with the handicapping system and regulations governing competitions played under LGU conditions.

The handicapping system, together with the system for assessment of Scratch Scores, is formulated and published by the LGU. Handicap Certificates are provided by the LGU and distributed through the National Organisations and appointed club officials to every member of every affiliated club which has fulfilled the requisite conditions for obtaining an LGU handicap.

The funds of the LGU are administered by the Hon. Treasurer on the authority of the Executive Council, and the accounts are submitted annually for adoption in General Meeting.

The Women's British Open Championship, Ladies' British Amateur Championships and the Home International matches, at both senior and junior level, are organised annually by the LGU. International events involving a British or a combined British and Irish team are organised and controlled by the LGU when held in this country and the LGU acts as the co-ordinating body for the Commonwealth Tournament in whichever of the five participating countries it is held, fouryearly, by rotation. The LGU selects and trains the teams, provides the uniforms and pays all the expenses of participation, whether held in this country or overseas. The LGU also maintains and regulates certain competitions played under handicap, such as Medal Competitions, Coronation Foursomes, Challenge Bowls, Australian Spoons and the LGU Pendant Competition.

The day-to-day administration of certain of the LGU responsibilities in the home countries is undertaken by the National Organisations, such as that concerned with handicapping regulations, Scratch Scores, and the organisation of Challenge Bowls and Australian Spoons Competitions.

Membership subscriptions to the LGU are assessed on a per capita basis of the club membership. To save unnecessary expense and duplication of administrative work in the home countries LGU subscriptions are collected by the National Organisations along with their own, and transmitted in bulk to the LGU.

Policy is determined and control over all the LGU's activities is exercised by an Executive Council of eight members – two each elected by the English, Irish, Scottish and Welsh national organisations. The Chairman is elected annually by the Councillors and may hold office for one year only, during which term her place on the Council is taken by her Deputy and she has no vote other than a casting vote. The President and the Hon. Treasurer of the Union also attend and take part in Council meetings but with no vote. The Council meets five times a year.

The Annual General Meeting is held in January. The formal business includes presentation of the Report of the Executive Council for the previous year and of the Accounts for the last completed financial year, the election or re-election of President, Vice-Presidents, Hon. Treasurer and Auditors, and a report of the election of Councillors and their Deputies for the ensuing year and of the European Championship Committee representative. Voting is on the following basis: Executive Council, one each (8); members in the four home countries, one per national organisation (4) and in addition one per 100 affiliated clubs or part thereof; one per overseas Commonwealth Union with a membership of 50 or more clubs, and one per 100 individually affiliated clubs.

The Lady Golfer's Handbook is published annually by the LGU and is distributed free to all affiliated clubs and organisations and to appointed Handicap Advisers. It is also available for sale to anyone interested. It contains the regulations for handicapping and Scratch Score assessment, for British Championships and international matches (with results for the past twenty years) and for LGU competitions, and sets out the Rules of the Union. It also lists every affiliated organisation, with names and addresses of officials, and every affiliated club, with Scratch Score, county of affiliation, number of members, and other useful information.

Miscellaneous Rulings

Limitation of the Golf Ball

At the Autumn Business Meeting, 1920, of the Royal & Ancient Club the following resolution was adopted: *On and after 1st May, 1921, the weight of the ball shall not be greater than 1.62 ounces avoirdupois, and the size not less than 1.62 inches in diameter. The Rules of Golf Committee and the Executive Committee of the United States Golf Association will take whatever steps they think necessary to limit the powers of the ball with regard to distance, should any ball of greater power be introduced.* The United States Golf Association intimated, May, 1929, that they had resolved to adopt *an easier and pleasanter ball for the average golfer*, and from 1st January, 1931, to 31st December, 1932, the standards of specification of the ball in competitions under their jurisdiction was not less than 1.68 inches in diameter, and not greater than 1.55 ounces in weight. In January, 1932, another alteration was made in the specification of the ball, the weight being increased to 1.62 and the size remaining the same, viz, not less than 1.68.

The Royal Canadian Golf Association adopted the USGA specification as from 1st January, 1948. The effect of this difference between the legislation of the Royal & Ancient, the Royal Canadian Golf Association, and the USGA is that golfers competing in the United States and Canada must use a ball that is larger, but no heavier, than the ball which is legal in other parts of the world.

In May, 1951, a special committee was set up by the Royal & Ancient Golf Club and the United States Golf Association to discuss the desirability of uniformity in the Rules of Golf and the form and make of clubs and balls. The committee recommended that both sizes of ball (1.62 inches and 1.68 inches in diameter both having the same weight, 1.62 ounces) be legal in all countries. At their autumn meeting the United States Golfers' Association rejected this proposal but agreed that in international team competition in the United States, the size of the ball be not less than 1.62 inches in diameter.

The matter of a uniform ball worldwide was investigated by a special committee from the R&A and the USGA but was dropped in 1974 when the two bodies could not reach agreement.

In 1987, however, the Royal & Ancient Golf Club of St Andrews proposed and adopted an amendment which decreed that the diameter of the golf ball should be not less than 1.68 inches (42.67 mm) instead of 1.62 inches (41.15 mm). The change of rule was introduced on 1st January 1990. An official statement declared: 'With the steady and, in most countries, rapid decline in the use of the 1.62 inch ("small") ball, the R&A has been considering changing to the 1.68 inch ("large") ball for some time, but has held off from doing so mainly because of the large number of Japanese golfers still using the small ball. With the use of the small ball in Japan now dropping steadily and in most other countries now being at 10% or less, it seems an appropriate time to make this change.' A maximum initial velocity standard of not greater than 250 feet per second on special apparatus was introduced by the R&A in 1976.

The R&A issues lists of conforming golf balls annually.

Limitation of Number of Clubs

At the Business Meeting of the Royal & Ancient Golf Club, May, 1937, the Rules of Golf Committee submitted a recommendation that on and after 1st January, 1938, the preamble to the Rules of Golf shall read: *The game of golf consists of a ball being played from a teeing ground to a hole by successive strokes with clubs (not exceeding fourteen in number) and balls made in conformity with the directions laid down in the clause on 'Form and make of golf clubs and balls'.* The recommendation was not approved by the members.

In September, 1938, at the Business Meeting of

the Royal & Ancient, a similar recommendation was approved by the members, and the limitation of the number of clubs to fourteen became operative as from 1st May, 1939.

The United States Golf Association decided to limit the number of clubs to fourteen as from 1st January, 1938.

Steel-Shafted Clubs

The Royal & Ancient Golf Club authorised steel shafts in November, 1929, in the following announcement: *The Rules of Golf Committee have decided that steel shafts, as approved by the Rules of Golf Committee are declared to conform with the requirements of the clause in the Rules of Golf on the form and make of golf clubs.*

Laminated Shafts

The Rules of Golf Committee on 5th December, 1932, announced that clubs with laminated shafts built entirely of wood are permissible.

Recognised Golf Clubs

The Rules of Golf Committee, in answering a query, gave the opinion that a recognised Golf Club is one which has regularly appointed office-bearers.

The English Golf Union decided that a recognised Golf Club for the purpose of competitive golf in England is a golf club affiliated to the English Golf Union through its County Union, or where there is no County Union direct to the English Golf Union as an Associate Member.

Championship Conditions

Men

The Amateur Championship

The Championship, until 1982, was decided entirely by match play over 18 holes except for the final which was over 36 holes. Since 1983 the Championship has comprised two stroke play rounds of 18 holes each from which the leading 64 players and ties over the 36 holes qualify for the match play stages. Matches are over 18 holes except for the final which is over 36 holes.

Full particulars can be obtained from the Championship Entries Department, Royal & Ancient Golf Club, St Andrews, Fife KY16 9JD.

The Seniors' Open Amateur Championship

The Championship consists of 18 holes on each of two days, the leading 50 players and ties over the 36 holes then playing a further 18 holes the following day. Entrants must have attained the age of 55 years prior to the first day of the Championship.

Full particulars can be obtained from the Championship Entries Department, Royal & Ancient Golf Club, St Andrews, Fife KY16 9JD.

National Championships

The English, Scottish, Irish and Welsh Amateur Championships are played by holes, each match consisting of one round of 18 holes except the final which is contested over 36 holes.

Full particulars of conditions of entry and method of play can be obtained from the secretaries of the respective national Unions.

English Open Amateur Stroke Play Championship

The Championship consists of one round of 18 holes on each of two days after which the leading 40 and those tying for 40th place play a further two rounds. The remainder are eliminated.

Conditions for entry include:
Entrants must have a handicap not exceeding three.

Where the entries exceed 130, an 18-hole qualifying round is held the day before the Championship. Certain players are exempt from qualifying.

Full particulars of conditions of entry and method of play can be obtained from the Secretary, English Golf Union.

British Mid-Amateur Championship

The Championship comprises two stroke play rounds of 18 holes from which the leading 64 players over the 36 holes qualify for the match play stages. All matches including the final are over 18 holes. Entrants must have attained the age of 25 years prior to the first day of the Championship.

Full particulars can be obtained from the Championship Entries Department, Royal & Ancient Golf Club, St Andrews, Fife KY16 9JD.

Boys

Boys' Amateur Championship

The Championship is played by match play, each match including the final consisting of one round of 18 holes. Entrants must be under 18 years of age at 00.00 hours on 1st January in the year of the Championship.

Full particulars can be obtained from the Championship Entries Department, Royal & Ancient Golf Club, St Andrews, Fife KY16 9JD.

Ladies

Ladies' British Open Amateur Championship

The Championship consists of one 18-hole qualifying round on each of two days. The players returning the 64 lowest scores over 36 holes shall qualify for match play. Ties for 64th place shall be decided by hole-by-hole play-off.

Ladies' British Open Amateur Stroke Play Championship

The Championship consists of 72 holes stroke play; 18 holes are played on each of two days after which the first 32 and all ties for 32nd place qualify for a further 36 holes on the third day. Handicap limit is 4.

Ladies' British Open Championship

The Championship consists of 72 holes stroke play. 18 holes are played on each of four days, the field being reduced after the first 36 holes.

Entries accepted from lady amateurs with a handicap not exceeding scratch and from lady professionals.

Full particulars for all three Championships can be obtained from the Administrator, LGU, The Scores, St Andrews, Fife KY16 9AT.

National Championships

Conditions of entry and method of play for the English, Scottish, Welsh and Irish Ladies' Close Championships can be obtained from the Secretaries of the respective associations.

Other championships organised by the respective national associations, from whom full particulars can be obtained, include English Ladies', Intermediate, English Ladies' Stroke-Play, Scottish Girls' Open Amateur Stroke Play

(under 21) and Welsh Ladies' Open Amateur Stroke Play.

Girls

Girls' British Open Amateur Championship

The Championship consists of two 18-hole qualifying rounds, followed by match play in two flights each of sixteen players.

Conditions of entry include:

Entrants must be under 18 years of age on the 1st January in the year of the Championship.

Competitors are required to hold a certified LGU international handicap not exceeding 15, or to be members of their National Junior Team for the current year.

Full particulars can be obtained from the Administrator, LGU, The Scores, St Andrews, Fife KY16 9AT.

National Championships

The English, Scottish, Irish and Welsh Girls' Close Championships are open to all girls of relevant nationality and appropriate age which may vary from country to country. A handicap limit may be set by some countries.

Full particulars can be obtained via the secretaries of the respective associations.

International Match Conditions

Men – Amateur

Walker Cup – Great Britain and Ireland v United States of America

Deed of Gift to United States Golf Association International Challenge Trophy

Mr GH Walker of the United States presented a Cup for international competition to be known as *The United States Golf Association International Challenge Trophy*, popularly described as *The Walker Cup*.

The Cup shall be played for by teams of amateur golfers selected from Clubs under the jurisdiction of the United States Golf Association on the one side and from England, Scotland, Wales, Northern Ireland and Eire on the other.

The International Walker Cup Match shall be held every two years in the United States of America and Great Britain and Ireland alternately.

The teams shall consist of not more than ten players and a captain.

The contest consists of four foursomes and eight singles matches over 18 holes on each of two days.

St Andrews Trophy

First staged in 1956, the St Andrews Trophy is a biennial international match played between two selected teams of amateur golfers representing Great Britain and Ireland and the Continent of Europe. Each team consists of nine players and the match is played over two consecutive days with four morning foursomes followed each afternoon by eight singles. Selection of the Great Britain and Ireland team is carried out by the Selection Committee of the Royal & Ancient Golf Club. The European Golf Association select the Continent of Europe team.

Men's World Amateur Team Championship (Eisenhower Trophy)

Founded in recognition of the need for an official world amateur team championship, the first event was played at St Andrews in 1958 and the Trophy has been played for every second year in different countries around the world.

Each country enters a team of four players who play stroke play over 72 holes, the total of the three best individual scores to be counted for each round.

European Team Championship

Founded in 1959 by the European Golf Association for competition among member countries of the Association. The Championship is held biennially and played in rotation round the countries which are grouped in four geographical zones.

Each team consists of six players who play two qualifying rounds of 18 holes, the five best scores of each round constituting the team aggregate. Flights for match play are then arranged according to qualifying round rankings. For the match play, teams consist of five players, playing two foursomes in the morning and five singles in the afternoon.

A similar championship is held every year for junior teams.

From 1990, the European Golf Association began organising the International European Championships – formally known as the European Individual Amateur Championships – on an annual basis.

Home Internationals *(Raymond Trophy)*

The first official International Match recorded was in 1902 at Hoylake between England and Scotland who won 32 to 25 on a holes up basis.

In 1932 International Week was inaugurated under the auspices of the British Golf Unions' Joint Advisory Council with the full approval of the four National Golf Unions. The Council of National Golf Unions is now responsible for running the matches.

Teams of 11 players from England, Scotland, Ireland and Wales engage in matches consisting of 5 foursomes and 10 singles over 18 holes, the foursomes being in the morning and the singles in the afternoon. Each team plays every other team.

The eligibility of players to play for their country shall be their eligibility to play in the Amateur Championship of their country.

Men – Professional

Ryder Cup

This Cup was presented by Mr Samuel Ryder, St Albans, England (who died 2nd January, 1936), for competition between a team of British professionals and a team of American professionals. The trophy was first competed for in 1927. In 1929 the original conditions were varied to confine the British team to British-born professionals resident in Great Britain, and the American team to American-born professionals resident in the United States, in the year of the match. In 1977 the British team was extended to include European players. The matches are played biennially, in alternate continents, in accordance with the conditions as agreed between the respective PGAs.

World Cup *(formerly Canada Cup)*

Founded in America in 1953 as an International Team event for professional golfers with the intention of spreading international goodwill.

Each country is represented by two players, the best team score over 72 holes being the winners of the World Cup and the best individual score the International Trophy. It is played annually, but not in 1986.

Ladies

Great Britain and Ireland *v* United States (Curtis Cup)

For a trophy presented by the late Misses Margaret and Harriot Curtis of Boston, USA, for biennial competition between teams from the United States of America and Great Britain and Ireland.

The match is sponsored jointly by the United States Golf Association and the Ladies' Golf Union who may select teams of not more than 8 players.

The match consists of 3 foursomes and 6 singles of 18 holes on each of two days, the foursomes being played each morning.

Europe *v* United States (Solheim Cup)

The Solheim Cup, named after Karsten Solheim who heads the sponsoring Ping company, is the women's equivalent of the Ryder Cup. In 1990 the inaugural competition between the top women professional golfers from Europe and America took place in Florida. The matches are played biennially in alternate continents. The format is foursomes and four-ball matches on the first two days, followed by singles on the third in accordance with the conditions as agreed between the WPG European Tour and the LPGA.

Great Britain and Ireland *v* Continent of Europe (Vagliano Trophy)

For a trophy presented to the Comité des Dames de la Fédération Française de Golf and the Ladies' Golf Union by Monsieur AA Vagliano, originally for annual competition between teams of women amateur golfers from France and Great Britain and Ireland but, since 1959, by mutual agreement, for competition between teams from the Continent of Europe and Great Britain and Ireland.

The match is played biennially, alternately in Great Britain and Ireland and on the Continent of Europe, with teams of not more than 9 players plus a non-playing captain.

The match consists of 4 foursomes and 8 singles, of 18 holes on each of two days. The foursomes are played each morning.

Women's World Amateur Team Championship (Espirito Santo Trophy)

Presented by Mrs Ricardo Santo of Portugal for biennial competition between teams of not more than three women amateur golfers who represent a national association affiliated to the World Amateur Golf Council. First competed for in 1964.

The Championship consists of 72 holes stroke play, 18 holes on each of four days, the two best scores in each round constituting the team aggregate.

Commonwealth Tournament (Lady Astor Trophy)

For a trophy presented by the late Viscountess Astor CH, and the Ladies' Golf Union for competition once in every four years between teams of women amateur golfers from Commonwealth countries.

The inaugural Commonwealth Tournament was played at St Andrews in 1959 between teams from Australia, Canada, New Zealand, South Africa and Great Britain and was won by the British team. The tournament is played in rotation in the competing countries, for the present Great Britain, Australia, Canada, and New Zealand, each country being entitled to nominate 6 players including a playing or non-playing captain.

Each team plays every other team and each team match consists of 2 foursomes and 4 singles over 18 holes. The foursomes are played in the morning and the singles in the afternoon.

European Ladies' Amateur Team Championship

The Championship is held biennially between teams of amateur women golfers from the European countries. Each team consists of not more than 6 players who play two qualifying rounds, the five best scores in each round constituting the team aggregate. The match play draw is made in flights according to the position in the qualifying rounds. The match play consists of 2 foursomes and 5 singles on each of three days.

A similar championship is held in alternate years for junior ladies' teams, under 21 years of age.

Home Internationals

Teams from England, Scotland, Ireland and Wales compete annually for a trophy presented to the LGU by the late Mr TH Miller. The qualifications for a player being eligible to play for her country are the same as those laid down by each country for its Close Championship.

Each team plays each other team. The matches consist of 6 singles and 3 foursomes, each of 18 holes. Each country may nominate teams of not more than 8 players.

Boys

Home Internationals (R&A Trophy)

Teams comprising 11 players from England, Scotland, Ireland and Wales compete against one another over three days in a single round robin format. Each fixture comprises five morning foursomes followed by ten afternoon singles.

To be eligible for selection, players must be under the age of 18 at 00.00 hours on 1st January in the year of the matches.

England v Scotland; Wales v Ireland

The International Matches between England and Scotland (10 players a side) and Wales and Ireland (10 players a side) are played on the Thurs-day preceding the Boys' Championship. The following day the winners of these two matches play against each other, as do the losers. To be eligible to play in these matches a boy must qualify by age to be eligible to play in the Boys' Championship.

Great Britain and Ireland v Continent of Europe (Jacques Leglise Trophy)

The Jacques Leglise Trophy is an annual international match played between two selected teams of amateur boy golfers representing Great Britain and Ireland and the Continent of Europe. Each team consists of nine players and the match is played over two consecutive days with four morning foursomes followed each afternoon by eight singles. Selection of the Great Britain and Ireland team is carried out by the Selection Committee of the Royal & Ancient Golf Club. The European Golf Association selects the Continent of Europe team

To be eligible for selection, players must be under the age of 18 at 00.00 hours on 1st January in the year of the matches.

Girls

Home Internationals

Teams from England, Scotland, Ireland and Wales compete annually for the Stroyan Cup. The qualifications for a player for the Girls' International Matches shall be the same as those laid down by each country for its Girls' Close Championship except that a player shall be under 18 years on the 1st January in the year of the Championship.

Each team, consisting of not more than 8 players, plays each other team, a draw taking place to decide the order of play between the teams. The matches consist of 6 singles and 3 foursomes, each of 18 holes.

Golf Associations

The National Association of Public Golf Courses (Affiliated to English Golf Union)

1927 saw the foundation of the Association by the late FG Hawtree (Golf Course Architect) and the late JH Taylor (five times Open Champion). They were both farsighted enough to see the need for cohesion between *Private* golf, *Public* golf and the Local Councils. Up to the outbreak of World War II the Association struggled on, sustained by a small amount of very welcome financial support from the *News of the World*. This enabled the *unofficial* Championship to be staged.

After the War, the Association was revitalised and the Championship was recognised by the National Union, and so from a shaky start of 240 qualifiers, there are now some 3500 Public Course golfers trying to qualify, from a total estimated membership of 50,000. The success and importance of the *Public Courses Championship of England* prompted the commencement of the Championship for Ladies and then the Championship for Juniors – which share equal importance. Soon after the establishment of Individual Championships there came the introduction of various Club Team events, and these have now progressed to National Level with a vast following from Club members. Thus the Association now organises some 14 national events annually for the membership.

Some years ago it was realised that the Local Councils (Course Management Authorities) could not enjoy official recognition and membership of the County Unions or National Unions except through the Association. This has now been remedied and many CMA are full subscribing members of the Association, and many others permit the *Courtesy of the Course* for all our National and Zonal Tournaments. Advice is offered to CMA – when requested – on such matters as Course Construction, Club formation and integration, establishment of Standard Scratch Score and Par Values, and many other topics concerned with the management of the game of golf.

Some overseas organisations and Councils have already sought our advice and help in recent years, when forming their own Courses, Clubs and Associations.

The Constitutional aims have not changed over the years, and the Association is proud to have maintained these Aims through the activities provided by the National Executive of the Association. The aims are:

1. To unite the Clubs formed on Public Courses in England and Wales, and their Course Managements in the furtherance of the interests of Amateur Golf.
2. To promote Annual Public Courses Championships and such other matches, competitions and tournaments as shall be authorised by the executive of the Association.
3. To afford direct representation of Public Course Interests in the National Union.

The total organisation of the Association is wholly voluntary and honorary, from the President down through Vice-Presidents, Chairmen, Secretary, Treasurer and Zone Secretaries. It is quite fantastic for an unpaid Organisation to cover such an exacting *field* of work, but most gratifying to the National Executive who have secured the progress of recent years.

Association of Golf Club Secretaries

Membership is 1900, consisting of Secretaries and retired Secretaries of Clubs largely situated in Great Britain but also from Clubs in Europe and other parts of the world. The Association offers from its Headquarters at Weston-super-Mare advice on all aspects of managing a Golf Club including an extensive Information Library which has some 300 different items. Regular training courses are held for newly appointed and intending Secretaries. The Association's Journal *Golf Club Management* is circulated to all members monthly and regular business meetings are held within the 15 regions of the Association as well as National Conferences and Seminars.

The Association of Golf Writers

A group of 30 newspapermen attending the Walker Cup Match at St Andrews on 2 June 1938 decided there was a need for an organisation to 'protect the interests of golf writers'. Their main objective was to establish a close liaison with the governing bodies and promoters of golf.

Thus was born The Association of Golf Writers, now solidly established and rightly respected as the official negotiating body of the golfing press. The Association owes much to a membership which has included many internationally recognised names who have contributed to elevating the Association to a unique level among British sports writers' associations.

Secretary: Mark Garrod, Press Association, London House, Central Park, New Lane, Leeds LS11 5DZ.

The Sports Turf Research Institute
(Bingley, West Yorkshire)

The Institute is officially recognised as the national centre for sports and amenity turf and is the official agronomist to the Championship Committee of the R&A. It is a non-profit distributing company limited by guarantee, its affairs managed by a small Executive Committee drawn from its Members Body comprising most sports controlling bodies. Golf is represented by the nominees of the R&A, the four home Golf Unions and the Council of National Golf Unions. The British Institute of Golf Course Architects, the British & International Greenkeepers Association and the PGA European Tour are represented on its Members Body and Golf Committee.

The Institute's mission is to carry out research and promote innovation; to provide advisory and consultancy services; and to provide education and publications for subscribing clubs, sports controlling bodies and the turfgrass industry at large. Activities other than research are run from its wholly owned subsidiary company, STRI Ltd.

The British Institute of Golf Course Architects

The Institute was founded in 1970 in order to establish standards of experience, knowledge and integrity in their profession. Fellowship and Membership of the Institute demonstrates that the Golf Course Architect has designed and supervised the construction throughout of a significant number of golf courses, having completed at least six full years of practical experience. Associateship is open to those with lesser degrees of experience who have also passed the Student Education Programme and satisfied the Committee that they are responsible, ethical and competent to design and direct the construction of golf courses to the high standard required. It is further required that Fellows, Members and Associates main business activity is golf course architecture.

The British Association of Golf Course Constructors

Objects: To promote the development of the golf course construction industry, to promote the adoption of policies to ensure a high quality of workmanship and working practices, to collect and disseminate information of value regarding the construction of golf courses to other members of the association, to members of the allied industries and to the public to promote the training and education of personnel within the industry and to maintain agreed standards of golf course construction by adherence to contractual procedures and codes of practice.

British and International Golf Greenkeepers' Association

The Association was formed in 1987 resulting from an amalgamation of the British, English and Scottish Associations. The Association has an official magazine, *Greenkeeping International,* which is issued free to all members.

The objects are to promote and advance all aspects of greenkeeping; to assist and encourage the proficiency of members; to arrange an International Annual Conference, educational seminars, functions and competitions; to maintain a Benevolent Fund; to act as an employment agency; to provide a magazine; to collaborate with any body or organisation which may benefit the Association or its members or with which there may be a common interest; to carry out and perform any other duties which shall be in the general interests of the Association or its members.

National Golf Clubs' Advisory Association

The National Golf Clubs' Advisory Association was founded in 1922. The objects are to protect the interests of Golf Clubs in general and to give legal advice and direction, under the opinion of Counsel, on the administrative and legal responsibilities of Golf Clubs. In cases taken to the Courts for decisions on any points which in the opinion of the Executive Committee involve principles affecting the general interests of affiliated clubs financial assistance may sometimes be given.

European Golf Association
Association Européenne de Golf

Formed at a meeting held at Luxembourg, 20th November, 1937, membership shall be restricted to European National Amateur Golf Associations or Unions. The Association shall concern itself solely with matters of an international character.

The Association shall have as its prime objects:

(a) To encourage international development of golf and strengthen bonds of friendship between the national organisations and to encourage the formation of new ones.

(b) To co-ordinate dates of the Open and Amateur Championships of its members.

(c) To arrange when such have been decided upon, European Team Championships and Matches of international character.

(d) To decide and publish the Calendar dates of the Open and Amateur Championships and Matches.

Golf Club Stewards' Association

The Golf Club Stewards' Association was founded as early as 1912. Its members are Stewards in Golf Clubs throughout the UK and Eire. It has a National Committee and Regional Branches in the South, North-West, Midlands, East Anglia, Yorkshire, Wales and the West, North-East Scotland and Ireland. The objects of the Association are to promote the interests of members; to administer a Benevolent Fund for members in need and to arrange golf competitions and matches. It also serves as an Agency for the employment of Stewards in Golf Clubs.

Addresses of Golfing Organisations – Worldwide

National Associations

Great Britain & Ireland

Royal and Ancient Golf Club
Sec, MF Bonallack, St Andrews, Fife KY16 9JD.
Tel (01334) 472112 *Fax* (01334) 477580.

Council of National Golf Unions
Hon Sec, A Thirlwell, 19 Birch Green, Formby,
Liverpool L37 1NG. *Tel/Fax* (01704) 831800.

Ladies' Golf Union
Sec, Mrs J Hall, The Scores, St Andrews, Fife
KY16 9AT. *Tel* (01334) 475811
Fax (01334) 472818.

The Professional Golfers' Association
Sec, DKC Wright, Apollo House, The Belfry,
Sutton Coldfield, West Midlands B76 9PT.
Tel (01675) 470333 *Fax* (01675) 470674.

East Region *Sec*, S Curtis, John O'Gaunt Golf
Club, Sutton Park, Sandy, Biggleswade,
Beds SG19 2LY. *Tel* (01767) 261888
Fax (01767) 261381.

Midland Region *Sec*, A Lott, King's Norton
Golf Club, Brockhill Lane, Weatheroak,
Nr Alvechurch, Worcs B48 7ED.
Tel (01564) 824909 *Fax* (01564) 822805.

North Region *Sec*, A Salmon, No 2 Cottage,
Bolton Golf Club, Lostock Park, Chorley New
Road, Bolton, Lancs BL6 4AJ.
Tel (01204) 496137 *Fax* (01204) 847959.

South Region *Sec*, P Ward, Clandon Regis Golf
Club, Epsom Road, West Clandon, Guildford,
Surrey GU4 7TT. *Tel* (01483) 224200 *Fax*
(01483) 223224.

West Region *Sec*, R Ellis, Exeter Golf and
Country Club, Topsham Road, Countess Wear,
Exeter, Devon EX2 7AE. *Tel* (01392) 877657
Fax (01392) 876382.

Irish Region *Sec*, M McCumiskey, Dundalk Golf
Club, Blackrock, Dundalk, Co Louth, Eire.
Tel (00 353) 422 1193 *Fax* (00 353) 422 1899.

Scottish Region *Sec*, P Lloyd, Glenbervie Golf
Club, Stirling Road, Larbert FK5 4SJ.
Tel (01324) 562451 *Fax* (01324) 562190.

PGA European Tour
Exec Dir, KD Schofield CBE, PGA European
Tour, Wentworth Drive, Virginia Water, Surrey
GU25 4LX. *Tel* (01344) 842881
Fax (01344) 842929.

**Women Professional Golfers'
European Tour**
Chief Exec, T Coates, The Tytherington Club,
The Old Hall, Macclesfield, Cheshire SK10 2JP.
Tel (01625) 611444 *Fax* (01625) 610406.

Artisan Golfers' Association
Hon Sec, A Everett, 51 Rose Hill Park West,
Sutton, Surrey SM1 3LA.
Tel 0181-644 7037.

Association of Golf Club Secretaries
Sec, R Burniston, 7a Beaconsfield Road,
Weston-super-Mare, BS23 1YE.
Tel (01934) 641166 *Fax* (01934) 644254.

Association of Golf Writers
Sec, M Garrod, 106 Byng Drive, Potters Bar,
Herts EN6 1UJ. *Tel/Fax* (01707) 654112.

**British Association of Golf Course
Constructors**
Sec, JH Franks, 37 Five Mile Drive, Wolvercote,
Oxford OX2 8HT. *Tel* (01865) 516927.

British Golf Collectors Society
Sec, CH Ibbetson, PO Box 13704, North
Berwick EH39 4ZB.
Tel/Fax (01620) 895561.

The British Golf Museum
Dir, PN Lewis, Bruce Embankment, St Andrews,
Fife KY16 9AB. *Tel* (01334) 478880
Fax (01334) 473306.

**The British Institute of
Golf Course Architects**
Sec, Mrs S Rooke, Merrist Wood House,
Worplesdon, Surrey GU3 3PE.
Tel (01483) 884036 *Fax* (01483) 884037.

British & International Golf Greenkeepers Association
Exec Dir, N Thomas BA, Aldwark Manor, Aldwark, Alne, York Y06 2NF.
Tel (01347) 838581/2 *Fax* (01347) 838864.

British Left-Handed Golfers' Society
Hon Sec, AC Kirkland, 7 Ingersley Road, Bollington, Cheshire SK10 5RE.
Tel (01625) 575516.

British Turf & Landscape Irrigation Association
Sec, DG Halford, Myerscough College, Bilsborrow, Preston, Lancs PR3 0RY.
Tel (01995) 640611 *Fax* (01995) 640842.

Golf Club Stewards' Association
Sec, G Shaw, 50 The Park, St Albans, Herts AL1 4RY. *Tel* (01727) 85334.

Golf Foundation
Exec Dir, Miss L Attwood, MBE, Foundation House, Hanbury Manor, Ware, Herts SG12 0UH.
Tel (01920) 484044 *Fax* (01920) 484055.

Golf Society of Great Britain
Sec, Miss E Mountain, Hope Point, Granville Road, St Margaret's Bay, Dover, Kent CT15 6DT. *Tel* (01304) 852229.

Hole in One Golf Society
Sec, B Dickinson, PO Box 109, New Lane, Greengates, Bradford, Yorkshire BD10 9UY.
Tel (01474) 534298.

National Association of Public Golf Courses
Hon Sec, AK Witte, 35 Sinclair Grove, Golders Green, London NW11 9JH. *Tel* 0181-458 5433.

National Golf Clubs' Advisory Association
Sec, Mrs JM Brock, 2 Angel House, Portland Square, Bakewell, Derbyshire DE45 1HB
Tel (01629) 813844 *Fax* (01629) 812614.

Professional Golfers' Architects Association
Sec, NH Fletcher, Apollo House, The Belfry, Sutton Coldfield B76 9PT. *Tel* (01675) 470333
Fax (01675) 470674.

Public Schools' Old Boys' Golf Association
Jt Secs: P de Pinna, Bruins, Wythwood, Haywards Heath, West Sussex RH16 4RD.
Tel 0171-265 0071. JBM Urry, Dormers, 232 Dickens Heath Road, Shirley, Solihull, West Midlands B90 1QQ. *Tel* 0121-328 5665.

Public Schools' Golfing Society
Hon Sec, JNS Lowe, Flushing House, Church Road, Great Bookham, Surrey KT23 3JT.
Tel (01372) 458651 *Fax* (01372) 451361.

Senior Golfers' Society
Sec, Brigadier D Ross, CBE, Milland Farmhouse, Liphook, Hants GU30 7JP.

The Society of One-Armed Golfers
Hon Sec, HF Ross, 11 Campbell Place, Torrance, Glasgow G64 4HR.
Tel (01360) 622476.

Sports Turf Research Institute
Chief Exec, Dr PM Canaway, *Marketing,* Anne Wilson, St Ives Estate, Bingley, West Yorks BD16 1AU.
Tel (01274) 565131 *Fax* (01274) 561891.

Regional Associations

England

English Golf Union
Sec, PM Baxter, National Golf Centre, The Broadway, Woodhall Spa, Lincs LN10 6PU. *Tel* (01526) 354500 *Fax* (01526) 354020.
Midland Group *Sec,* RJW Baldwin, Chantry Cottage, Friar Street, Droitwich, Worcs WR9 8EQ. *Tel/Fax* (01905) 778560.
Northern Group *Hon Sec,* EG Bunting, 7 Northbrook Court, Hartlepool TS26 0DJ.
Tel (01429) 274828.
South Eastern Group *Hon Sec,* MA Hobson, 22 Wye Court, Malvern Way, Ealing, London W13 8EA. *Tel* 081-997 7466.
South Western Group *Sec,* JT Lumley, 51 Roundway Park, Devizes, Wilts SN10 2EE.
Tel (01380) 723935.

English Ladies' Golf Association
Sec, Mrs MJ Carr, Edgbaston Golf Club, Church Road, Birmingham B15 3TB.
Tel 0121-456 2088. *Fax* 0121-454 5542
Northern Division *Hon Sec,* Mrs L Young, 10 Cleehill Drive, North Shields, Tyne & Wear NE29 9EW. *Tel* 0191-257 6925.
Midlands Division *Hon Sec,* Mrs D Harris, Ivy Cottage, Lutterworth Road, Gilmorton, Lutterworth, Leics LE17 5PN. *Tel* (01455) 556093.
South-Eastern Division *Hon Sec,* Mrs R Wallis, The Bungalow, The Green, Pirbright, Woking GU24 0JE. *Tel* (01483) 476528.
South-Western Division *Hon Sec,* Mrs VJ Wilde, 19 Ferndown Close, Kingsweston, Bristol BS11 0UP. *Tel* (0117) 968 3543.

English Blind Golf Association
Sec, D Morris, 11 Riverside Avenue, Newquay, Cornwall TR7 1PL. *Tel/Fax* (01637) 875464.

English Schools' Golf Association
Hon Sec, R Snell, 20 Dykenook Close,
Whickham, Newcastle-upon-Tyne NE16 5TD.
Tel 0191-488 3538.

Bedfordshire County Golf Union
Hon Sec, C Allen, 102 Tyne Crescent, Bedford,
Beds MK41 7UW. *Tel/Fax* (01234) 216835.

Bedfordshire Ladies' County Golf Association
Hon Sec, Mrs H Molloy, Keepers Cottage,
Beadlow, Shefford, Beds SG17 5PH.
Tel (01525) 861202.

Bedfordshire & Cambridgeshire PGA
Sec, L Scarbrow, 22 Hillcrest Road, Luton
LU2 7AB. *Tel* (01582) 240197.

Berks, Bucks & Oxon PGA
Hon Sec, Mrs M Green, Wayside, Aylesbury
Road, Monks Risborough, Aylesbury, Bucks
HP27 0JS. *Tel* (01844) 343012.

Berks, Bucks & Oxon Union of Golf Clubs
Sec, R Stewart, Leyacre, Lodersfield, Lechlade,
Glos GL73DJ. *Tel/Fax* (01367) 253403.

Berkshire Ladies' County Golf Association
Hon Sec, Mrs J West, 4 Mansfield Place, Ascot,
Berks SL5 8ND. *Tel* (01344) 883682.

Buckinghamshire Ladies' County Golf Association
Hon Sec, Mrs S Munn, 'Garah', 21 Clifton Lawns,
Chesham Bois, Bucks HP6 5PT. *Tel* (01494)
433860.

Cambridgeshire Area Golf Union
Sec, RAC Blows, 2A Dukes Meadow, Stapleford,
Cambridge CB2 5BH. *Tel* (01223) 842062.

Cambs & Hunts Ladies' County Golf Association
Hon Sec, Mrs S Ramsey, 25 Leighton, Orton
Malbourne, Peterborough PE2 5QB
Tel (01733) 236502.

Channel Islands Ladies' Golf Association
Hon Sec, Mrs AGR Willis, Oakenbirch, Park
Estate, St Brelade, Jersey JE3 8EQ.
Tel (01534) 842072.

Cheshire County Ladies' Golf Association
Hon Sec, Mrs B Walker, 12 Higher Downs,
Knutsford, Cheshire WA16 8AW.
Tel (01565) 634124.

Cheshire PGA
Sec, A Salmon, No 2 Cottage, Bolton Golf Club,
Lostock Park, Chorley New Road, Bolton
BL6 4AJ. *Tel* (01204) 496137.

Cheshire Union of Golf Clubs
Hon Sec, BH Nattrass, 'Whitecliff', 6 Bryn
Seiriol, Llandudno LL30 1PD.
Tel/Fax (01492) 580518.

Cornwall Golf Union
Hon Sec, JG Rowe, 8 Lydcott Crescent,
Widegates, Looe, Cornwall PL13 1QG.
Tel/Fax (01503) 240492.

Cornwall Ladies' County Golf Association
Hon Sec, Mrs A Eddy, Penmester, Hain Walk,
St Ives, Cornwall TR26 2AF.
Tel (01736) 795392.

Cumbria Ladies' County Golf Association
Hon Sec, Mrs V Hetherington, The Patch,
Lowmoor Road, Wigton CA7 9QR.
Tel (016973) 42403.

Cumbria Union of Golf Clubs
Hon Sec, T Edmondson, Thorn Lea, Lazonby,
Penrith, Cumbria CA10 1AT. *Tel* (01768)
898231.

Derbyshire Ladies' County Golf Association
Hon Sec, Mrs J Brock, Stoney End, Gorse Ridge
Drive, Baslow, Derbyshire DE45 1SL.
Tel (01246) 583350.

Derbyshire PGA
Sec, F McCabe, Hillside, Lower Hall Close,
Holbrook, Derby DE56 0TN.
Tel (01332) 880411.

Derbyshire Union of Golf Clubs
Hon Sec, JB Kay, Tamarinda, Whitworth Road,
Darley Dale, Matlock, Derbys DE4 2HH.
Tel (01629) 734143.

Devon County Golf Union
Sec, RJ Hirst, Flat 4, 27 West Street, Tavistock,
Devon PL19 8JY. *Tel/Fax* (01822) 617750.

Devon County Ladies' Golf Association
Hon Sec, Mrs V Irish, Homefield, Aveton
Gifford, Kingsbridge, Devon TQ7 4LF.
Tel (01548) 550369.

Dorset County Golf Union
Hon Sec, Lt Col MD Hutchins, 38 Carlton
Road, Bournemouth BH1 3TG.
Tel (01202) 290821 *Fax* (01202) 311288.

Dorset Ladies' County Golf Association
Hon Sec, Mrs J Wilson, Bunkers, 19 Chiswell
Road, Canford Heath, Poole, Dorset BH17 9FB.
Tel (01202) 246332.

Durham County Golf Union
Hon Sec, GP Hope, 7 Merrion Close, Moorside,
Sunderland SR3 2QP. *Tel* 0191-528 0421
Fax 0191-522 8605.

Durham County Ladies' Golf Association
Sec, Mrs R Foy, Jolby Manor, Stapleton,
Darlington DL2 2QS. *Tel* (01325) 377500.

Essex County Amateur Golf Union
Sec, J Barbour, 181 Northumberland Avenue,
Hornchurch, Essex RM11 2HW.
Tel/Fax (01708) 543524.

Essex Ladies' County Golf Association
Hon Sec, Mrs C Davies, 26 Theydon Park Road,
Theydon Bois, Essex CM16 7LP.
Tel (01992) 813491.

Essex PGA
Sec, A Birch, 27 Curlew Crescent, Basildon,
Essex SX16 5HR. *Tel* (01268) 533849.

Gloucestershire & Somerset PGA
Sec, N Boland, Cotswold Hills GC, Ullenwood,
Cheltenham GL53 9QT. *Tel* (01242) 515263.

Gloucestershire Golf Union
Hon Sec, RF Crisp, 2 Hartley Close, Charlton
Kings, Cheltenham GL53 9DN.
Tel (01242) 514024 *Fax* (01242) 221659.

**Gloucestershire Ladies' County Golf
Association**
Hon Sec, Mrs EA Bates, 128 Claverham Road,
Claverham, Avon BS19 4LQ.
Tel (01934) 833470.

**Hampshire, Isle of Wight & Channel Islands
Golf Union**
Sec, K Maplesden, 5 Coldharbour Wood, Rake,
Liss, Hants GU33 7JJ. *Tel/Fax* (01730) 895102.

Hampshire Ladies' County Golf Association
Sec, Mrs S O'Shea, 134 Carbery Avenue,
Southbourne, Bournemouth BH6 3LH.
Tel (01202) 424651

Hampshire PGA
Sec, Mrs D Bryon, South Winchester Golf Club,
Pitt, Winchester SO22 5QV.
Tel (01962) 860928.

**Hertfordshire County Ladies' Golf
Association**
Hon Sec, Mrs A Thomson, 13 Carleton Rise,
Welwyn AL6 9RP. *Tel* (01438) 715612.

Hertfordshire Golf Union
Hon Sec, JC Harkett, 5 Willow Way, Harpenden,
Herts AL5 5JF. *Tel* (01582) 760841
Fax (01582) 462608.

Hertfordshire PGA
Hon Sec, RA Gurney, 1 Field Lane, Letchworth,
Herts SG6 3LF. *Tel* (01462) 627899.

Isle of Man Golf Union
Hon Sec, AD Horne, 27 Ballahane Close, Port
Erin, Isle of Man. *Tel* (01624) 834389.

Isle of Wight Ladies' Golf Association
Hon Sec, Mrs ED Train, 15 Rectory Drive,
Wooton, IOW PO33 4QQ. *Tel* (01983) 883169.

Kent County Golf Union
Hon Sec, JH Goby JP, St Andrew's Road,
Littlestone, New Romney, Kent TN28 8RB.
Tel (01797) 367725 *Fax* (01797) 367726.

Kent County Ladies' Golf Association
Hon Sec, Mrs S Daniel, 6 Wyvern Close,
Dartford DA1 2NA. *Tel* (01322) 271583.

Kent PGA
Joint Secs: E Impett, 20 The Grove, Barham,
Kent *Tel* (01227) 831655; R Burkin, 35 Valley
Walk, Shirley, Croydon, Surrey CR0 8SR.
Tel 0181–656 3935.

Lancashire Ladies' County Golf Association
Hon Sec, Mrs SA Hampson, Highmoor Farm,
Highmoor Lane, Wrightington, Wigan WN6 9PS.
Tel (01257) 252140.

Lancashire PGA
Sec, A Salmon, No 2 Cottage, Bolton Golf Club,
Lostock Park, Chorley New Road, Bolton
BL6 4AJ. *Tel* (01204) 496137

Lancashire Union of Golf Clubs
Sec, AV Moss, 5 Dicconson Terrace, Lytham
St Annes, Lancs FY8 5JY. *Tel* (01253) 733323
Fax (01253) 795721.

Leicestershire & Rutland Golf Union
Hon Sec, C Chamberlain, 10 Shipton Close,
The Meadows, Wigston Magna, Leicester
LE18 3WL. *Tel* (0116) 288 9862.

**Leicestershire & Rutland Ladies'
County Golf Association**
Hon Sec, Mrs AL Adams, 23 Fisher Close,
Cossington, Leicester LE7 4US.
Tel (01509) 812869.

Leicestershire PGA
Sec, D Freeman, 218 Hamilton Lane, Scraptoft,
Leics. *Tel* (0116) 241 4735.

Lincolnshire Ladies' County Association
Hon Sec, Mrs S Gee, 17 Parksgate Avenue,
Lincoln LN6 7HP. *Tel* (01522) 688778.

Lincolnshire PGA
Sec, JK Britten, Gainsborough GC, Thonock,
Gainsborough DN21 1PZ. *Tel* (01427) 612278.

Lincolnshire Union of Golf Clubs
Hon Sec, GH Moore OBE, Authorpe House,
36 Horncastle Road, Woodhall Spa LN10 6UZ.
Tel (01526) 352792.

Middlesex County Golf Union
Sec, PSV Cooke, 36 Grants Close, Mill Hill,
London NW7 1DD. *Tel* 0181-349 0414.

Middlesex Ladies' County Golf Association
Hon Sec, Ms B Popple, 9 Ashleigh Court, Avenue
Road, London N14 4EL. *Tel* 0181-886 9015.

Middlesex PGA
Sec, B Eady, 8 Woodbank Drive, Chalfont
St Giles, Bucks HP8 4RP. *Tel* (01494) 874487.

Norfolk County Golf Union
Hon Sec, RJ Trower, 12a Stanley Avenue,
Thorpe, Norwich, Norfolk NR7 0BE.
Tel/Fax (01603) 431026.

Norfolk Ladies' County Association
Hon Sec, Mrs J Foad, 28 St Leonard's Close,
Wymondham, Norfolk NR18 0JF.
Tel (01953) 602692.

Norfolk PGA
Hon Sec, DM Bray, 4 Bluebell Drive,
Sheringham, Norfolk NR26 8XE.
Tel (01263) 821905.

North East & North West PGA
Sec, R Sentance, 7 Larch Lea, Ponteland,
Newcastle-upon-Tyne NE20 9LG.
Tel (01661) 825151.

Northamptonshire Golf Union
Hon Sec, RG Halliday, 12 Edge Hill Road,
Duston, Northampton NN5 6BY.
Tel/Fax (01604) 751031.

Northamptonshire Ladies' County Golf Association
Hon Sec, Mrs J Ray, The Dairy, 12 Cotterstock
Road, Oundle PE8 5HA. *Tel* (01832) 273573.

Northamptonshire PGA
Sec, G Mobbs, Ivycroft, Back Lane, Chapel
Brampton, Northants. *Tel* (01604) 843305.

Northumberland Ladies' County Golf Association
Hon Sec, Mrs PA Smith, Clonreher, Armstrong
Cottages, Bamburgh, Northumberland
NE69 7BA. *Tel* (01668) 214216.

Northumberland Union of Golf Clubs
Hon Sec, WE Procter, 5 Oakhurst Drive, Kenton
Park, Gosforth, Newcastle-upon-Tyne NE3 4JS.
Tel 0191-274 5310 (O); 0191–285 4981 (H).

Nottinghamshire County Ladies' Golf Association
Hon Sec, Mrs BA Patrick, 18 Delville Avenue,
Keyworth, Notts, NG12 5JA.
Tel (0115) 937 3237.

Nottinghamshire PGA
Sec, RW Futer, 52 Barden Road, Mapperley,
Nottingham NG3 5QD. *Tel* (0115) 952 0956.

Nottinghamshire Union of Golf Clubs
Hon Sec, R Brown, 48 Weaverthorpe Road,
Woodthorpe, Notts NG5 4NB.
Tel/Fax (0115) 926 6560.

Oxfordshire Ladies' County Golf Association
Hon Sec, Mrs EA Sadler, 5 Manor Farm Road,
Dorchester-on-Thames OX10 7HZ.
Tel (01865) 340018.

Sheffield PGA
Sec, G Walker, Hillsborough GC, Worrall Road,
Sheffield S6 4BE. *Tel* (01742) 332666.

Shropshire & Herefordshire Union of Golf Clubs
Hon Sec, JR Davies, 23 Poplar Crescent, Bayston
Hill, Shrewsbury SY3 0QB. *Tel* (01743) 872655.

Shropshire & Hereford PGA
Sec, P Hinton, 1 Stanley Lane Cottages,
Bridgnorth, Shropshire. *Tel* (01746) 752045.

Shropshire Ladies' County Golf Association
Hon Sec, Mrs HF Davies, Brooklands, Oldwoods,
Bomere Heath, Shrewsbury SY4 3AX.
Tel (01939) 290427.

Somerset Golf Union
Hon Sec, CF Carr, 21 Greenacre, Wembdon,
Bridgwater, Somerset TA6 7RD. *Tel/Fax* (01278)
450476.

Somerset Ladies' County Golf Association
Hon Sec, Mrs D Bowerman, Ridgedown,
Blagdon Hill, Taunton TA3 7SL.
Tel (01823) 42256.

South-Western Counties Golf Association
Hon Sec/Treas, JT Lumley, Hartland, Potterne,
Devizes, Wilts SN10 5PA. *Tel* (01380) 723935.

Staffordshire Ladies' County Golf Association
Hon Sec, Mrs A Adams, 'Tanglewood',
19 Beacon Road, Walsall WS5 3LF.
Tel 0121–357 6217.

Staffordshire PGA
Sec, E Griffiths, 22 Wynn Road, Penn,
Wolverhampton. *Tel* (01902) 332180.

Staffordshire Union of Golf Clubs
Hon Sec, BA Cox, 34 Lordswood Square,
Harborne, Birmingham B17 9BS.
Tel 0121-427 4962.

Suffolk County Golf Union
Hon Sec, RA Kent, 77 Bennett Avenue, Bury St
Edmunds, Suffolk IP33 3JJ. *Tel/Fax* (01284)
705765.

Suffolk Ladies' County Golf Association
Hon Sec, Mrs S Birrell, Warren House, Great
Saxham, Bury St Edmunds IP29 5JR.
Tel (01284) 810007.

Suffolk PGA
Sec, M Jillings, Bury St Edmunds GC, Tut Hill,
Bury St Edmunds, Suffolk IP28 2LG.
Tel (01284) 755978.

Surrey County Golf Union
Hon Sec, MW Ashton, Clearglen House,
151 Frimley Road, Camberley, Surrey GU15 2PS.
Tel (01276) 677959 *Fax* (01276) 63334.

Surrey Ladies' County Golf Association
Hon Sec, Mrs D Marchant, Larchfield, Hunts
Hill, Normandy, Guildford, Surrey GU3 2AH.
Tel (01483) 810873.

Surrey PGA
Sec, P Bowles, 27 Lower Wood Road, Claygate,
Surrey KT10 0EU. *Tel* (01372) 463882.

Sussex County Golf Union
Sec, DG Pulford, 216 South Coast Road,
Peacehaven, East Sussex BN10 8JR.
Tel (01273) 589791 *Fax* (01273) 585705.

**Sussex County Ladies'
Golf Association**
Hon Sec, Mrs BJ Page, Ewerby, 7 Denmans
Close, Lindfield, West Sussex RH16 2JX.
Tel (01444) 482454.

Sussex PGA
Sec, C Pluck, 96 Cranston Avenue, Bexhill,
East Sussex TN39 3NL. *Tel* (01424) 221298.

**Warwickshire Ladies' County Golf
Association**
Hon Sec, Mrs A Parry, The Willows,
16 Rushbrook Road, Stratford-upon-Avon,
Warwicks CV37 7JW. *Tel* (01789) 204083.

Warwickshire PGA
Sec, J Tunnicliff, 80 Wychwood Ave, Knowle,
Solihull B93 9DZ. *Tel* (01675) 470809.

Warwickshire Union of Golf Clubs
Hon Sec, J Stubbings, Quaker Cottage, Wiggins
Hill Road, Wishaw, Sutton Coldfield B76 9QE.
Tel (01675) 470809.

Wiltshire County Golf Union
Hon Sec, RF Buthlay, 14 Budbury Close,
Bradford-on-Avon, Wilts. BA15 1QG.
Tel/Fax (01225) 866401.

**Wiltshire Ladies' County
Golf Association**
Hon Sec, Mrs EM Kent, 2 Colenzo Drive,
Andover, Hants SP10 1JS. *Tel* (01264) 323375.

Wiltshire PGA
Sec, L Ross, Marlborough GC, The Common,
Marlborough, Wilts. *Tel* (01672) 512493.

**Worcestershire County Ladies'
Golf Association**
Hon Sec, Mrs S Smith, 12 Russell Road,
Kidderminster DY10 3HT.
Tel (01562) 824808.

Worcestershire PGA
Sec, J Sanders, 2 Hawford House, Claines,
Worcester WR3 7SQ. *Tel* (01905) 454048.

Worcestershire Union of Golf Clubs
Hon Sec, A Boyd, The Bears Den, Upper Street,
Defford, Worcester WR8 9BG.
Tel (01386) 750657 *Fax* (01386) 750472.

**Yorkshire Ladies' County
Golf Association**
Hon Sec, Mrs M Elliott, Ingle Court, Lepton,
Huddersfield, Yorks HD8 0NN.
Tel (01484) 602011.

Yorkshire PGA
Sec, J Pape, 1 Summerhill Gardens, Leeds,
Yorks LS8 2EL. *Tel* (0113) 266 4746.

Yorkshire Union of Golf Clubs
Hon Sec, KH Dowswell, 33 George Street,
Wakefield, W Yorks WF1 1LX.
Tel (01924) 383869 *Fax* (01924) 383634.

Ireland

Golfing Union of Ireland
Gen Sec, S Smith, Glencar House, 81 Eglinton
Road, Donnybrook, Dublin 4.
Tel (00 353) 1 269 4111
Fax (00 353) 1 269 5368

Connacht Branch *Gen Sec,* S Hosty,
14 Rockbarton Green, Salthill, Galway.
Tel/Fax (00 353) 91 27072.

Leinster Branch *Sec,* P Smyth, 1 Clonskeagh
Square, Clonskeagh Road, Dublin 14.
Tel (00 353) 1 269 6977
Fax (00 353) 1 269 3602.

Munster Branch *Hon Sec,* S McMahon,
6 Town View, Mallow, Co Cork.
Tel (00 353) 22 21026 *Fax* (00 353) 22 42373

Ulster Branch *Gen Sec,* BG Edwards, 58a High
Street, Holywood, Co Down, BT18 9AE.
Tel (01232) 423708 *Fax* (01232) 426766.

Irish Ladies' Golf Union
Sec, Miss MP Turvey, 1 Clonskeagh Square,
Clonskeagh Road, Dublin 14.
Tel (00 353) 1 269 6244 *Fax* (00 353) 1 283 8670.

Eastern District *Hon Sec,* Miss E Foley,
10 Vale View Avenue, The Park, Cabinteely,
Dublin 18. *Tel* (00 353) 1 285 6853.

Midland District *Hon Sec,* Mrs N Colgan,
Cloonagoose, Borris, Kilkenny.
Tel (00 353) 503 73577

Northern District *Hon Sec,* Mrs B McCaw,
16 Merrion Avenue, Newcastle, Co. Down
BT33 0BH. *Tel* (013967) 26140.

Southern District *Hon Sec,* Mrs M Power,
36 Tracton Avenue, Montenotte, Cork.
Tel (021) 551977.

Western District *Hon Sec,* Mrs H Sweeney,
Galway Road, Roscommon.
Tel (00 353) 902 74796.

Scotland

Scottish Golf Union
Sec, Scottish National Golf Centre, Drumoig,
Leuchars, St Andrews KY16 0DW.
Tel (01382) 549500 *Fax* (01382) 549510.

Area Associations:
Angus D Speed, 7 Eastgate, Friockheim,
Arbroath DD11 4TG. (01241) 828544.

Argyll & Bute G Duncanson, 2 Mount Stewart
Road, Rothersay, Bute PA20 9DY.
Tel (01700) 502468.

Ayrshire RL Crawford, 81 Connel Crescent,
Mauchline, Ayrshire KA5 5AU.
Tel (01563) 521190 (B), (01290) 551434 (R).

Borders RG Scott, Buckholmburn, Edinburgh Road, Galashiels TD1 2EY. *Tel* (01896) 752697.

Clackmannanshire T Johnson, 75 Dewar Avenue, Kincardine FK10 4RR. *Tel* (01259) 731168 (R).

Dunbartonshire AW Jones, 107 Larkfield Road, Lenzie, Glasgow G66 3AS. *Tel* 0141-776 7430(R).

Fife BR Wright, 26 East Fergus Place, Kirkcaldy, Fife KY1 1XT. *Tel* (01592) 206605 *(office)*.

Glasgow RGJ Jamieson, 37 Eglinton Street, Beith KA21 1AZ. *Tel* (01505) 503000 *(office)*.

Lanarkshire T Logan, 41 Woodlands Drive, Coatbridge, Lanarkshire ML5 1LB. *Tel* (01236) 428799.

Lothians J Wood, 28 Stoneyhill Avenue, Musselburgh EH21 6SB. *Tel* 0131-665 4813.

North JT Jamieson, 3 Drummond Crescent, Inverness IV2 4QW. *Tel* (01463) 233624.

North-East G McIntosh, Newmachar Golf Club, Sailend, Newmachar, Aberdeen AB21 7UU. *Tel* (01651) 863002.

Perth & Kinross DY Rae, 18 Carlownie Place, Auchterarder PH3 1BT. *Tel* (01764) 662837.

Renfrewshire JI McCosh, 'Muirfield', 20 Williamson Place, Johnstone, Renfrewshire PA5 9DW. *Tel* (01505) 344613.

South JH Sommerville, Cherry Cottage, Kirkcudbright DG6 4EU. *Tel* (01557) 330445.

Stirlingshire I Hutton, 18 Turret Drive, Polmont FK2 0QW. *Tel* (01324) 712585.

Scottish Ladies' Golfing Association
Sec, Mrs LC Sommerville, Scottish National Golf Centre, Drumoig, Leuchars, Fife KY16 0BE. *Tel* (01382) 549502 *Fax* (01382) 549512.

Scottish Ladies' Golfing Association – County Golf
Hon Sec, Mrs M Clark, 13 Hillcroft Road, Banchory AB31 5TF. *Tel* (01330) 823803.

Aberdeen Ladies' County Golf Association
Hon Sec, Mrs M Robinson, 7 Carnegie Gardens, Aberdeen AB15 4AW. *Tel* (01224) 313582.

Angus Ladies' County Golf Association
Hon Sec, Mrs A Rennie, 53 Princes Street, Monifieth, Dundee DD5 4AN. *Tel* (01382) 533718.

Ayrshire Ladies' County Golf Association
Hon Sec, Mrs M Mowat, Seton Lodge, 9 Southpark Road, Ayr KA7 2TL. *Tel* (01292) 268773.

Border Counties' Ladies Golf Association
Hon Sec, Mrs M Waddell, Nether Horsburgh, Innerleithen EH44 6RE. *Tel* (01896) 830188.

Dumfriesshire Ladies' County Golf Association
Hon Sec, Miss MJ Greig, 10 Nelson Street, Dumfries DG2 9AY. *Tel* (01387) 254429.

Dunbartonshire & Argyll Ladies' County Association
Hon Sec, Mrs CM Kelly, 86 Nasmyth Avenue, Bearsden, Glasgow G61 4SQ. *Tel* 0141-942 9959.

East Lothian Ladies' County Association
Hon Sec, Mrs IG Campbell, Glenlair, Main Street, Gullane EH31 2HD. *Tel* (01620) 842534.

Fife County Ladies' Golf Association
Hon Sec, Mrs M Steele, 26 South Dewar Street, Dunfermline KY12 8AR. *Tel* (01383) 721840.

Galloway Ladies' County Golf Association
Hon Sec, Mrs EM Gemmell, Priory Croft, 3 St John Street, Whithorn DG8 8PD. *Tel* (01988) 500559.

Lanarkshire Ladies' County Golf Association
Hon Sec, Mrs M Heggie, 80 Weirwood Avenue, Garrowhill, Glasgow G69 6LM. *Tel* 0141-771 3082.

Midlothian County Ladies' Golf Association
Hon Sec, Mrs S Simpson, 85 Ravelston Dykes, Edinburgh EH12 6EZ. *Tel* 0131-337 4670.

Northern Counties' Ladies Golf Association
Hon Sec, Mrs C MacLennan, Midville, Contin IV14 9ES. *Tel* (01997) 421236.

Perth & Kinross Ladies' County Golf Association
Hon Sec, Mrs P Drysdale, Annandale, Packhill Road, Rattray, Blairgowrie PH10 7DS. *Tel* (01250) 873641.

Renfrewshire Ladies' County Golf Association
Hon Sec, Mrs M Neilson, 47 Octavia Terrace, Greenock PA16 7SR. *Tel* (01475) 724673.

Stirling & Clackmannan Ladies' Golf Association
Hon Sec, Mrs A Hunter, 22 Muirhead Road, Stenhousemuir FK5 4JA. *Tel* (01324) 554515.

Scottish Golfer's Alliance
Sec/Treas, Mrs MA Caldwell, 5 Deveron Avenue, Giffnock, Glasgow G46 6NH.

Wales

Welsh Golfing Union
Sec, R Dixon, Catsash, Newport NP6 1JQ. *Tel* (01633) 430830

Anglesey Golf Union
Hon Sec, GP Jones, 20 Gwelfor Estate, Cemaes, Anglesey LL67 0NL. *Tel* (01407) 710755.

Brecon & Radnor Golf Union
Hon Sec, DJ Davies, Garden House, Howey, Llandrindod Wells, Powys. *Tel* (01597) 824316.

Caernarvonshire & District Golfing Union
Hon Sec, RE Jones, 23 Bryn Rhos, Rhosbodrual, Caernarfon, Gwynedd LL55 2BT.
Tel (01286) 673486.

Denbighshire Golfing Union
Hon Sec, EG Howells, 10 Lon Howell, Myddleton Park, Dinbych, Clwyd CH7 3NH.

Dyfed Golfing Union
Hon Sec, J Pearson, Tenby Golf Club, The Burrows, Tenby, Dyfed SA70 9NP.
Tel (01834) 842978.

Flintshire Golfing Union
Hon Sec, H Griffith, Cornist Lodge, Cornist Park, Flint, Clwyd CH6 5HJ.
Tel (01352) 732186.

Glamorgan County Golf Union
Hon Sec, GB Hughes, 46 Gelli Fawr Road, Morriston, Swansea SA6 7PW.
Tel (01792) 773043.

Gwent Golf Union
Sec, CM Buckley, 3 Oak Court, Woodfield Park, Blackwood, Gwent NP2 0BY.
Tel (01495) 223520.

Welsh Ladies' Golf Union
Hon Sec, Mrs S Webster, Catsash, Newport NP6 1JQ. Tel/Fax (01633) 422911.

Caernarvonshire & Anglesey Ladies' County Golf Association
Hon Sec, Mrs M Bromley, Ty'r Ysgol, Borth Y Gest, Porthmadog LL49 9UF.
Tel (01766) 512573.

Denbighshire & Flintshire Ladies' County Golf Association
Sec, Mrs D Jones, Pyllan Clai, Bontuchel, Ruthin, Denbighshire LL15 2BW.
Tel (01824) 710674.

Glamorgan Ladies' County Golf Association
Sec, Mrs S Williams, 19 Trem-y-Don, Barry, South Glamorgan CF62 6QJ.
Tel (01446) 734865.

Mid Wales Ladies' County Golf Association
Sec, Miss A James, Flat 4, Penbryn Court, Lampeter, Dyfed SA48 7EU.
Tel (01570) 422463.

Monmouthshire Ladies' County Golf Association
Hon Sec, Mrs E Davidson, Jon-Len, Goldcliff, Newport NP6 2AU. Tel (01633) 274477.

Europe

European Golf Association
Place de la Croix Blanche 19, 1066 Epalinges, Lausanne, Switzerland.
Tel +41 21 784 35 32. Fax +41 21 784 35 36.

Austrian Golf Association/Austrian PGA
Sec, Mrs W Neuwirth, Haus des Sports, Prinz-Eugen-Strasse 12, 1040 Vienna.
Tel +43 1 505 3245 Fax +43 1 505 4962

Royal Belgian Golf Federation
Chausée de la Hulpe 110, 1000 Brussels.
Tel +32 2 672 23 89 Fax +32 2 672 08 97

Czech Golf Federation
Erpet Golf Centre, Strakonicka 510, 150 00 Prague 5, Czech Republic. Tel/Fax +42 2 54 45 86

Danish Golf Union
Idrattens Hus, 2605 Brondby.
Tel +45 43 26 27 00 Fax +45 43 26 27 01.

Finnish Golf Union
Radiokatu 20, SF-00240 Helsinki.
Tel +358 0 158 2244 Fax +358 0 147 145.

French Golf Federation
Sec, J Paris, 69 Avenue Victor Hugo, 75783 Paris Cedex 16. Tel +33 1 44 17 63 00
Fax +33 1 44 17 63 63.

French PGA
176 Rue Jean Jaures, 92800 Puteaux.
Tel +33 1 47 72 78 23 Fax +33 1 42 04 41 06

German Golf Association
Postfach 2106, Victoriastr 16, 65189 Wiesbaden.
Tel +49 611 990 200 Fax +49 611 990 2040.

German PGA
Hauptstrasse 6, 86356 Neusaess.
Tel +49 821 465 048.

Hellenic Golf Federation
PO Box 70003, GR 16610, Glyfada, Athens.
Tel +30 1 894 1933 Fax +30 1 894 5162.

Iceland Golf Union
Sport Center, 104 Reykjavik. Tel +354 568 6686
Fax +354 568 6086.

Italian Golf Federation
Viale Tiziano 74, 00196 Rome.
Tel +39 6 323 1825 Fax +39 6 322 0250.

Luxembourg Golf Union
C/o GC Grand-Ducal de Luxembourg, 1 Route de Trèves, 2633 Senningerberg.
Tel +352 34 00 90 Fax +352 34 83 91.

Netherlands Golf Federation
Sec, HL Heyster, PO Box 221, 3454 ZL De Meern.Tel +31 30 662 1888 Fax +31 30 662 1177.

Netherlands PGA
Sec, Mrs R Vonk, Burg. van der Borchlaan 1, 3722 GZ Bilthoven. Tel +31 30 228 7018
Fax +31 30 225 0261.

Norwegian Golf Federation
Hauger Skolevei 1, 1351 Rud. *Tel* +47 67 15 46 00
Fax +47 67 13 86 40.

Portuguese Golf Federation
Rua General Ferreira Martins 10, Miraflores,
1495 Algés. *Tel* +351 1 410 7521
Fax +351 1 410 7972.

Slovenian Golf Association
Bled G&CC, C. Svobede 13, 64260 Bled.
Tel +386 64 718230 *Fax* +386 64 718225.

Spanish Golf Association
Capitan Haya 9-5, 28020 Madrid.
Tel +34 1 555 26 82 / 555 27 57
Fax +34 1 556 32 90.

Swedish Golf Federation
Sec, B Wickberg, PO Box 84, 182 11 Danderyd.
Tel +46 8 622 1500 *Fax* +46 8 755 8439.

Swedish PGA
Sec, M Sorling, Tylosand, 302 73 Halmstad.
Tel +46 35 320 30 *Fax* +46 35 320 25.

Swiss Golf Association
Place de la Croix Blanche 19, 1066 Epalinges,
Lausanne. *Tel* +41 21 784 3531
Fax +41 21 784 3536.

Swiss PGA
Place de la Croix Blanche 19, Case Postale 14,
1066 Epalinges, Lausanne. *Tel* +41 21 784 3543
Fax +41 21 784 3536.

America: USA & Canada

Canadian Ladies' Golf Association
Golf House, Glen Abbey, 1333 Dorval Drive,
Oakville, Ontario L6J 4Z3. *Tel* +1 905 849 2542
Fax +1 905 849 0188.

Canadian PGA
13450 Dublin Line, Acton, Ontario L7J 2W7.
Tel +1 519 853 5450 *Fax* +1 519 853 5449.

Ladies Professional Golf Association
2570 West International Speedway Blvd, Suite
B, Daytona Beach, Florida 32114.
Tel +1 904 254 8800
Fax +1 904 254 4755.

National Golf Foundation
1150 South US Highway One, Jupiter, Florida
33477. *Tel* +1 407 744 6006.

PGA of America
Box 109601, 100 Avenue of the Champions,
Palm Beach Gardens, Florida 33418.
Tel +1 407 624 8400 *Fax* +1 407 624 8448.

PGA Tour
Sawgrass, Ponte Vedra, Florida 32082.
Tel +1 904 285 3700 *Fax* +1 904 285 7913.

Royal Canadian Golf Association
Golf House, Glen Abbey, 1333 Dorval Drive,
Oakville, Ontario L6J 4Z3. *Tel* +1 905 849 9700
Fax +1 905 845 7040.

United States Golf Association
Golf House, PO Box 708, Far Hills, New Jersey
07931. *Tel* +1 908 234 2300 *Fax* +1 908 234 2179.

Central America

Bahamas Golf Federation
PO Box N4568, Nassau.

Barbados Golf Association
C/o Sandy Lane Golf Club, PO Box 743,
Kingston 8.

Bermuda Golf Association
PO Box HM 433, Hamilton HM BX.
Tel +1 809 298 1367

El Salvador Golf Federation
Apartado Postal 631, San Salvador.

Jamaica Golf Association
Constant Spring GC, PO Box 743, Kingston 8.
Tel +1 809 925 2325.

Mexican Golf Association
Cincinnati, No. 40-104, Mexico 18, DF.

South America

Argentine Golf Association
Corrientes 538, Piso 11, 1043 Buenos Aires.
Tel +54 1 325 7498.

Bolivian Golf Federation
Casilla de Correo 6130, La Paz.

Brazilian Golf Federation
Rua 7 de Abril, 01044 São Paulo.

Chilean Golf Federation
Casilla 13307, Correo 21, Santiago.

Colombian Golf Union
Carrer 7A, 72-64 of Int 26 Apartado Aereo
90985, Bogotà.

Ecuador Golf Federation
Casilla 521, Guayaquil.

Paraguay Golf Association
Casilla de Correo 302, Asunción.

Peru Golf Federation
Casilla 5637, Lima.

South American Golf Federation
Casilla de Correo No. 53826, Punta Del Este,
CP 21000 – Maldonado. *Tel* +598 42 70691.

Uruguay Golf Association
Casilla 1484, Montevideo.

Venezuela Golf Federation
Local 5, Avda. Avila, La Florida, Caracas 1050.

Africa

Botswana Golf Union
PO Box 1368, Gaborone.

Ghana Golf Association
PO Box 8, Achimola.

Kenya Golf Union
PO Box 49609, Nairobi.
Tel +254 2 720074.

Kenya Ladies' Golf Union
PO Box 45615, Nairobi.

Malawi Golf Union
PO Box 1198, Blantyre.

Malawi Ladies' Golf Union
PO Box 5319, Limbe.

Namibian Golf Union
PO Box 2989, Windhoek 9000.

Nigeria Golf Union
National Sports Commission, Surulere,
PO Box 145, Lagos.

Sierra Leone Golf Federation
Freetown Golf Club, PO Box 237, Lumley Beach,
Freetown.

South African Golf Association
PO Box 391994, Bramley, South Africa 2018.
Tel +27 11 442 3723   *Fax* +27 11 442 3753.

South African Ladies' Golf Union
PO Box 135, 1930 Vereenigning, Transvaal.
Tel /Fax +27 16 231936.

South African PGA
PO Box 79432, Senderwood 2145.
Tel +27 11 485 2327
Fax +27 11 485 1799.

South African Women's PGA
PO Box 781547, Sandton 2146.
Tel +27 11 783 3213
Fax +27 11 789 1367.

Swaziland Golf Union
PO Box 1739, Mbabane.

Tanzania Golf Union
PO Box 2569, Dar-es-Salaam.
Tel +255 51 36415/6.

Tanzania Ladies' Golf Union
PO Box 286, Dar-es-Salaam.

Uganda Golf Union
Kitante Road, PO Box 2574, Kampala.

Zaire Golf Federation
BP 1648, Lubumbashi.

Zambian Golf Union
PO Box 31943, Lusaka.

Zambia Ladies' Golf Union
PO Box 90554, Luanshya.

Zimbabwe Golf Association
PO Box 3327, Harare.

Zimbabwe Ladies' Golf Union
PO Box 3814, Harare.

Asia and Far East

Asia-Pacific Golf Confederation
52, 1st Floor, Jalan Hang, Lekiu 50100,
Kuala Lumpur.

Asia Golf Tour Inc.
8,2A 8th Floor, Jaya Shopping Centre, Jalan
Semangat, 46100 Petaling Jaya, Selangor,
Malaysia. *Tel* +603 758 2784
Fax +603 758 2169.

China Golf Association
75 Lane 187, Tunhau S Road, Taipei,
Taiwan 10647.

PGA Republic of China
No 196 Pei Ling 5th Road, Taipei, Taiwan.
Tel +886 2 8220318 *Fax* +886 2 8229684.

Hong Kong Golf Association
Room 2003, Sports House, 1 Stadium Path,
Son KoPo, Causeway Bay, Hong Kong.
Tel +852 2522 8804 *Fax* +852 2845 1553.

Hong Kong PGA
110 Yu To Sang Building, 37 Queens Road,
Central, Hong Kong HX7 3751.
Tel +852 523 3171.

Indian Golf Union
Tata Centre (3rd Floor), 43 Chowringhee Road,
Calcutta 700071.

Indonesian Golf Association
C/o bank Bumi Daya,
Jln Imam Bonjol 61-PO Box 106,
Jakarta Pusat.

Japan Golf Association
606-6th Floor, Palace Building, Marunouchi,
Chiyoda-ku, Tokyo. *Tel* +81 3 3215 0003
Fax +81 3 3214 2831.

Japan Ladies PGA
7–16–3 Ginza, Chuo-ku, Tokyo 104.
Tel +81 3 3546 7801 *Fax* +81 3 3546 7805.

Japan PGA
Tel +81 3 3547 0131 *Fax* +81 3 3547 1030.

Korean Golf Association
13th Floor, Manhattan Bldg, 36-2,
Yeo-Eui-Do-Dowg, Yeong Deung Po-Ku, Seoul.
Tel +82 2 783 4748.

Malaysian Golf Association
12a Persiaran Ampang, 55000 Kuala Lumpur.
Tel +60 3 4577931 *Fax* +60 3 4565596.

Pakistan Golf Federation
PO Box No. 1295, Rawalpindi.

Philippines Golf Association
209 Administration Building, Rizal Memorial
Sports Complex, Vito Cruz, Manila.
Tel +63 2 588845 *Fax* +63 2 521 1587.

Singapore Golf Association
Thomson Road, PO Box 0172, Singapore 9157.
Tel +65 466 4892 *Fax* +65 466 4897.

Sri Lanka Golf Union
2 Gower Street, Colombo 5, Sri Lanka.

Thailand Golf Association
Railway Training Centre, Vibhavadee Rangsit
Road, Bangkok 10900. *Tel* +66 251 34988/9.

Australasia

Australian Golf Union
Golf Australia House, 153–155 Cecil Street,
South Melbourne, Victoria 3205.
Tel +61 3 9699 7944 *Fax* +61 3 9690 8510.

Women's Golf Australia
355 Moray Street, South Melbourne,
Victoria 3205. *Tel* +61 3 9690 9344
Fax +61 3 9696 2060.

Australian PGA
4/140 George Street,
Hornsby 2077 New South Wales.
Tel +61 2 476333 *Fax* +61 2 477 7625.

New Zealand Golf Association
PO Box 11842, Wellington Library,
65 Victoria Street, Wellington.
Tel +64 4 4722 967 *Fax* +64 4 4997 330.

Women's Golf New Zealand
PO Box 111-87, 65 Victoria Street, Wellington.
Tel +64 4 4726 733 *Fax* +64 4 4726 732.

New Zealand PGA
PO Box 11-934, Wellington.
Tel +64 4 4722 687 *Fax* +64 4 4712 152.

PART VII

Golf History

The Championships of Great Britain

The Open Championship

The Open Championship was initiated by Prestwick Golf Club in 1860 and was played there until 1870. The Club presented the Championship Belt which was to be held for a year by the winner and which would become the absolute property of any player who won three years in succession. The competition consisted of three rounds of the 12 holes Prestwick then had, to be played on one day. The Open did not become a four-round contest until 1892. There were few entrants in the early years and nearly all were professionals, who were sometimes also greenkeepers and clubmakers, with a few amateurs.

Young Tom Morris won the Belt outright in 1870. There was no contest the following year, but in 1872 Prestwick, the Royal and Ancient and the Honourable Company, who were still playing at Musselburgh, subscribed to provide the present trophy, which was not to be won outright. Since then only three winners would have so earned it: Jamie Anderson and Bob Ferguson during the following ten years and Peter Thomson since in 1954-56. The Championship was to be held on the courses of the three subscribing Clubs in turn. Young Tom won the first for the new cup in 1872 at St Andrews, but died tragically at the age of 24 in 1875.

The three courses continued to be used until 1892 when it was first played at Muirfield to where the Honourable Company had moved. That year was also the first in which the Championship became a 72-hole contest over two days. In 1890, at Prestwick, John Ball had become the first amateur to win. Only two others have followed his success: Harold Hilton in 1892 and 1897, and Bobby Jones in 1926, 1927 and 1930. Roger Wethered tied with Jock Hutchison at St Andrews in 1921, but lost the play-off; if he had not incurred a penalty stroke through treading on his ball in the third round, he may well have won.

The Triumvirate

The year 1894 saw the first occasion the Open was played in England at Sandwich and the first English professional to win, JH Taylor. He won again the next year and for the fifth time in 1913. Harry Vardon and James Braid were the two others of the *great triumvirate* who together won sixteen Opens between 1894 and 1914. Taylor's five wins were spread over twenty years and Vardon's six over nineteen. Braid's wins were concentrated into ten years from 1901 to 1910, all of them in Scotland. Vardon won three times at Prestwick but never at St Andrews, where Taylor and Braid both won twice. Only Taylor managed a win at Hoylake. No other player won more than once during their supremacy. The winning scores at the time were very high by today's standards, for although the courses were marginally shorter, the equipment and clothing were primitive compared with those in use now. At Sandwich Taylor's score was 326, or 38 over an average of 4s. His 304 at Hoylake in 1913 was played in appalling weather, wearing a tweed jacket, cap and boots, and using wooden shafts and leather grips. He had no protective clothing or umbrella and won by 8 strokes from Ted Ray. The last winning total over 300 was Hagen's 301 at Hoylake in 1924.

Better Standards

That improved equipment has helped combat the greater length and heavier rough of today's Championship courses is suggested by comparing the average winning scores for decades of this century.

Decade	Average winning score	Decade	Average winning score
1905–14	302	1956–65	280
1920–29	295	1966–75	280
1930–39	289	1976–85	277
1946–55	284	1986–95	273

Of the 126 Opens held so far, twenty Scots have won, twenty Americans, sixteen English, four Australians, two South Africans and one each from France, Ireland, New Zealand, Argentina, Spain and Zimbabwe. The Scots have won thirty-nine times but only twice since Braid in 1910 (Duncan in 1920 and Lyle in 1985), the USA thirty-three times, England twenty-nine, Australia nine times, South Africa seven times, Spain three times and each of the others once. Since the triumvirate's day ended, the only Englishmen to win more than once have been Sir Henry Cotton and Nick Faldo, both with three victories. The Americans have won thirty-three out of the last seventy Opens played.

It will be seen that certain nationalities tend to dominate for a decade or so; the Scots until 1893, then the English until 1914, the USA in the 1920s and until 1933 when the English had a short resuscitation. The Commonwealth were to the fore from 1949 to 1965 (Locke, Thomson, Nagle and Charles) with the Americans coming back again to win in 13 out of 18 years between 1966 and 1983. Equally dominating in their periods were Hagen and Jones in the twenties, Cotton in the thirties, Locke and Thomson the fifties, and thereafter Palmer, Nicklaus, Player, Trevino, Watson and Ballesteros.

Open Courses

Only fourteen courses have accommodated the Open. St Andrews leads with 25, followed by Prestwick, which was discarded in 1925 as unsuitable for large crowds, with 24. The second group comprises Muirfield with fourteen, Royal St George's, Sandwich twelve and Hoylake with ten. Hoylake's last Open was in 1967; that it is not used now is due not to any lack of quality of the course but to lack of space. Deal appeared in 1909 and 1920, and was due again in 1949 but the sea broke across the course, and Sandwich came in for the last time until 1981. Troon and Royal Lytham and St Annes each held an Open between the wars, Carnoustie two and Princes, Sandwich, when Sarazen won in 1932, one; this course, which was used as a tank training ground during the Second World War, has not been asked again. In 1951, Portrush, the only Irish course to stage an Open, also provided the only English winner between Cotton and Jacklin in Max Faulkner. Birkdale and Turnberry are firmly established in the rota which for many years settled at four Scottish courses – St Andrews, Muirfield, Troon and Turnberry – and three in England – Royal Lytham and St Annes, Birkdale and Royal St George's, Sandwich. In 1999, however, Carnoustie will host the championship for the first time since 1975.

Traditionally the Open is only played on links courses. While there may yet be new venues by the sea capable of being stretched and groomed to be worthy of holding an Open, the many other considerations to be weighed, such as an adequate road system to carry vast crowds and nearly as many acres as the course covers to accommodate the tented village and services, it is not easy to see where the Championship Committee will turn.

Qualifying

How does one qualify to play in an Open? Since qualifying was first introduced in 1914, there have been numerous changes. Regional qualifying was tried for a year in 1926. At one of the courses used, Sunningdale, Bobby Jones (and even he had to qualify!) played what many consider the classic round of golf: a 66, all 4s and 3s, never over par, 8 birdies, 33 putts and 33 other shots.

Until 1963 all competitors, even the holder, had to play two qualifying rounds on the Open course on the Monday and Tuesday of the Open week. The qualifiers then had one round on Wednesday, one on Thursday and the leading group of between 40 and 60 players finished with two rounds on Friday. In 1963 certain exemptions from qualifying were introduced. The two rounds on the Friday were dropped in 1966 in favour of one round each on Friday and Saturday; not until 1980 was the first round played on Thursday and the last on Sunday. As the entry continued to increase, in 1970 nearby courses were used for qualifying and in 1977 regional qualifying was reintroduced in the previous week with final qualifying on nearby courses later.

There have been surprisingly few ties involving a play-off, only thirteen in 126 Championships. The first should have been in 1876 involving David Strath and Bob Martin. However, Strath took umbrage over a complaint against him and refused to play again, Martin being declared the winner. Until 1963 ties were decided over 36 holes; the next two, between Nicklaus and Sanders at St Andrews in 1970 and Watson and Newton at Carnoustie in 1975, were played over 18. Later it was decided that in the event of a tie, the winner would be found immediately by a play-off over specified holes, followed by 'sudden death' if necessary. This happened in 1989 when Calcavecchia beat Norman and Grady over 4 holes after finishing level on 275. In 1995 there was another, John Daly beating Costantino Rocca at St Andrews.

Prize Money

In 1863 the total prize money was £10, its distribution among the fourteen entrants, six of whom were amateurs, is unknown. A year later it had risen by over 50% to £16; the winner taking £6. By 1993 the total prize fund reached £1,000,000 of which the winner received £100,000. In 1997 this had risen to £250,000. Until about 1955, the winner's and leaders' rewards were very modest; even in 1939 the cheque for the first man was £100 out of a total of £500. With some justification the prestige of winning the Open then was adjudged to be of much more value than any monetary award. The growth since the 1950s has been astonishing and is evidence that, while it is still a tremendous asset for any man to have won the Open, the authorities have recognised that it will not maintain its leading place without substantial reward.

The rapid advance of the Open to the major spectacle it has become is due to a combination of factors. Not least of these is the TV presentation of the BBC, acknowledged as the world's best in golf, the interest and enthusiasm of thousands of spectators keen to watch on the spot rather than on the box, and the Royal & Ancient's promotion of this world showpiece of golf that it has become. Behind it all has been the foresight of successive Championship Committees and, in the late 1960s and 1970s, the masterly spreading of the gospel by Keith Mackenzie, Secretary of the R&A in 1966-82, that is so ably continued by his successor, Michael Bonallack.

Laurence Viney

The Amateur Championship

Early History

Golf has always been a competitive game and club medals have been keenly contested since the nineteenth century. Many of the leading amateurs were members of several clubs and, aided by an excellent railway system, they competed against each other at such venues as St Andrews, Prestwick, Hoylake and Musselburgh. An embryonic *open amateur competition* was held in the late 1850s (the first being won by Robert Chambers, the publisher, in 1858) but there seems to have been little enthusiasm for such an event and it died around the time of the first Open Championship (1860). The best amateurs began to enter the Open from 1861. By the 1870s, there was renewed interest in organising a tournament for amateurs only but nothing happened, probably because no one club took a strong enough lead. A proposal in 1877 to the membership of the R&A that it sponsor a sort of Amateur Championship (involving club members and others nominated by members) was defeated.

It fell to the Hoylake golfers to set in motion the championship we now know as *The Amateur*. In 1884 the Secretary of Royal Liverpool, Thomas Potter, proposed that an event – open to all amateurs – should be organised. This original intention was not carried out until 1886 and so the winner of 1885 (AF Macfie) triumphed over a strong, but limited, field drawn from certain

clubs. The clubs that were responsible for the running of the championship until the R&A took over in 1920 – and who made contributions for the purchase of the trophy – were:

Royal & Ancient
Royal Burgess Golfing Society of Edinburgh
Royal Liverpool
Royal St George's
Royal Albert, Montrose
Royal North Devon
Royal Aberdeen
Royal Blackheath
Royal Wimbledon
Royal Dublin
Alnmouth
North Berwick, New Club
Panmure, Dundee
Prestwick
Bruntsfield Links Golfing Society, Edinburgh
Dalhousie
Gullane
Formby
Honourable Company of Edinburgh Golfers
Innerleven
King James VI, Perth
Kilspindie
Luffness
Tantallon
Troon
West Lancashire

The first championship was not without its teething troubles. The format which was adopted allowed both golfers to proceed to the next round if their match was halved, so the first championship had three semi-finalists – and Macfie got a bye into the final. From 1886, the usual format was adopted.

More serious than the problem of an idiosyncratic draw, however, was the question of amateur status, raised for the first time in 1886.

The committee had to decide if it should accept the entries of John Ball III and Douglas Rolland. As a 15-year-old, Ball had finished fourth in the 1878 Open at Prestwick and on the advice of Jack Morris he accepted the prize money of 10s (50p). Rolland, a stonemason, had accepted second prize in the 1884 Open. Rolland's entry to the Amateur was refused while Ball's was accepted. Ball went on to win the championship a record eight times and the Open Championship of 1890.

The Format

After such a difficult start, the format of 18-hole matches with a 36-hole final remained until 1956. This arrangement made for many closely fought matches, as shown in 1930, the year of RT Jones' Grand Slam triumph. Jones' only victory in the event came in the right year and it is worth pointing out that, in making his way to the final, he won in the fourth round at the 19th (by laying a stymie) against Cyril Tolley, the holder, and his victories in the sixth round and in the semi-final were by the narrowest of margins. In addition, the fact that the draw was not seeded sometimes meant early meetings between top golfers; for example, in 1926 the visiting American Walker Cup Team members, von Elm and Ouimet, met in the second round and von Elm went on to meet Jesse Sweetser in the third.

As a result of such events, there was some pressure for the introduction of seeding the draw but it was not until 1958 that the practice was officially adopted. In the 50s and 60s there were other changes in format in an attempt to satisfy large numbers of golfers who wished to play and to ensure a worthy winner.

The popularity of the championship has posed difficulties for the R&A. The mathematically ideal number of entrants to be fitted into a convenient format is 256. In 1950, 324 entered the championship causing golf to be played on the Old Course for 14 hours a day. In order to restrict the numbers turning up to the championship proper, an experiment in regional qualifying was held in 1958 (again a St Andrews year) and 488 players with handicaps of 5 and under played 36 holes of stroke play on 14 courses. This system was quickly replaced and in 1961 the handicap limit was lowered (to 3) and a balloting-out of higher handicaps was introduced so that 256 were left to play for the trophy. This method was followed until 1983 with the introduction of 36 holes of stroke play to find 64 players for match play, from which to find the eventual winner. The handicap limit in 1997 was 1.

There was also pressure for the introduction of 36-hole matches. As early as 1922 the R&A's championship committee canvassed the opinion of the 252 men who played that year. Nineteen of these voted in favour of 36-hole matches, seven for district qualification, fifty-two voted for a stroke play qualification followed by 18-hole matches and the others who replied wanted no change to the system. In 1956 and 1957 the last 3 rounds were played over 36 holes, in 1958 and 1959 the semi-final and final were over 36 holes and then the old format returned.

There is constant pressure on the organisers to find a format to satisfy the needs of large numbers of home and foreign players, to take into account differences in national handicapping systems, to preserve the atmosphere of the championship, to maintain match play as a central feature of top-level amateur golf and even to take into account the vagaries of the weather. The task is almost impossible.

The Winners

Any man who wins the Amateur is a considerable golfer but there are certain outstanding champions. John Ball of Royal Liverpool won the title eight times between 1888 and 1912. It is interesting to note that he never successfully defended his title. Michael Bonallack triumphed five times between 1961 and 1970, including an incredible hat-trick of victories in which he successively beat Joe Carr and Bill Hyndman twice.

Several golfers have successfully defended their title: Horace Hutchinson, Harold Hilton, Lawson Little and Peter McEvoy, while others have won twice or more – Johnny Laidlay, Freddie Tait, Bob Maxwell, Cyril Tolley, Edward Holderness, Frank Stranahan, Joe Carr and Trevor Homer.

The oldest man to win was the Hon Michael Scott, at the age of 54 in 1933. The youngest winners – John Beharrell and Bobby Cole – were both 18 years and 1 month old. Cole's victory over Ronnie Shade was achieved over 18 holes – play being affected by poor visibility. The first overseas winner was Walter Travis who won in 1904 – one consequence of his victory was the banning of the use of centre-shafted putters. The first Continental winner was the Frenchman Philippe Ploujoux, who won in 1981. A visiting Walker Cup team always made for an exciting championship and from seventeen visits to Great Britain the title crossed the Atlantic twelve times.

No doubt there have been hundreds of thrilling matches played in the Championship, but few can have been as pulsating as the 1899 final at Prestwick where Johnny Ball beat Freddie Tait at the 37th hole. The victory must have been a sweet one for Ball, since Tait, the hero of Scotland, had won the previous year over Ball's home links of Hoylake. Sadly, Tait was killed in the Boer War in 1900. *The great battle*, as Jones described his fourth round tie against Tolley in 1930, rivalled the Ball-Tait final for tense excitement, but for sheer brilliance of scoring, Michael Bonallack's first round in the 1968 final must take pride of place.

The Amateur Championship has been played for over a century and in essence it has changed remarkably little. The increasing popularity of the game at home and abroad, the lure of the professional ranks with its dependence on stroke play and the increasing commercialism of all sport notwithstanding, the Championship continues to stand for all that is great in golf.

David Christie

Famous Players of the Past

In making the difficult choice of the names to be included, effort has been made to acknowledge the outstanding players and personalities of each successive era from the early pioneers to the stars of recent times.

Alliss, Percy   (1897–1975)

Percy Alliss was one of Britain's most successful professionals between the wars. He was in the top six in the Open Championship seven times, his best finish being at Carnoustie in 1931 when he tied third, two strokes behind Tommy Armour. That same year he was also runner-up in the Canadian Open. He was a member of three Ryder Cup teams in 1933-35-37, an international honour also gained later by his son, Peter.

Much of his career was spent at Wansee club in Berlin, and it was during this time that he won the German Open in four successive years from 1926 and then again in 1933. He was Italian Open champion in 1927 and 1935 and won the British Matchplay Championship in 1933 and 1937. A most consistent performer, he was noted particularly for his long iron play.

Anderson, Jamie   (1842–1912)

Winner of three consecutive Open Championships (1877-78-79). Born at St Andrews, he was the son of *Old Daw*, a St Andrews caddie and character. Jamie began golf when 10 years old, and rapidly developed into a fine player, noted for straight hitting and good putting. Anderson's method was to play steadily and on one occasion at St Andrews he remarked that he had played 90 consecutive holes without a bad shot or one stroke made otherwise than he had intended. He was for a period professional to Ardeer Club, but returned to St Andrews to follow his vocation of playing professional.

Anderson, Willie   (1878–1910)

One of the Scottish emigrants to America, his flat swing won him the US Open in 1901, 1903, 1904 and 1905. He shares the record of four Open titles with Jones, Hogan and Nicklaus, and remains the only man to win three in a row.

Armour, Thomas D   (1896–1968)

Open Champion, 1931. US Open Champion, 1927. USPGA 1930. He had a distinguished amateur career – including the French Open Amateur and tied first place in the Canadian Open. He had the unique distinction of playing in 1921 for Britain against the US as an amateur and in 1925 as a professional for the US against Britain in the unofficial international matches that preceded the inception of the Walker Cup and Ryder Cup events. When he came to the end of his tournament career he quickly gained an outstanding reputation as a coach, and books he wrote on the technique of the game were best-sellers

Auchterlonie, William   (1872–1963)

Won the Open title at Prestwick at the age of 21 with a set of seven clubs which he had made himself and shortly afterwards founded the famous club-making firm in St Andrews. He never played with more than his seven clubs and was a great believer that a golfer had to be master of the half, three-quarter and full shots with each club. As professional to the Royal & Ancient Golf Club from 1935 to his death he saw one of his ambitions fulfilled – the Centenary Open at St Andrews in 1960.

Ball, John   (1862–1940)

One of the greatest amateur golfers of all time. His father owned the Royal Hotel, Hoylake, prior to the formation of the golf links and when there was a small racecourse on the land later formed into the Royal Liverpool Links. The links became John Ball's playground. In 1878, when fifteen years old, he competed in the Open Championship, finished fourth, eight strokes behind the winner and ahead of many famous Scottish professionals of that time. Between 1888 and 1912 he won the Amateur Championship eight times. In 1890 he was the first amateur to win the Open Championship. He played for England against Scotland continuously from 1902 to 1911, captaining the side each year. He was Amateur Champion in 1899 when war with South Africa broke out and Ball served in that campaign with the Cheshire Yeomanry and did not compete in the Championships of 1900-01-02. In the First World War he served in the Home Forces. He played in his last Amateur Championship in 1921, the year of the first American invasion, and he reached the fifth round although in his fifty-eighth year. Modest and retiring, he rarely spoke about his golf. On the morning of his last round in the Championship he remarked to a friend in the clubhouse, *If only a storm of wind and rain would sweep across the links from the Welsh hills I feel I could beat all of them once again.* But it was a week of torrid heat and he failed. He retired to his farm in North Wales, where he died in December 1940.

Barton, Miss Pamela (1917–43)

At the age of twenty-two when the Second World War broke out, Miss Pamela Barton had already achieved great fame in the golfing world. She won the Ladies' Championship, 1936-39, runner-up, 1934-35, the American Ladies' Championship, 1936 and the French Ladies' Championship, 1934. In 1936, at the age of nineteen, she held both the British and American Ladies' Championships, the first person to do so since 1909. Miss Barton played for England in the home internationals in 1935-36-37-38-39; for Great Britain *v* United

Pam Barton   Popperfoto

States in 1934-36; *v* France, 1934-36-37-38-39. She was a member of the Ladies' Golf Union teams which toured Canada and America, 1934, and Australia and New Zealand in 1935. Of a charming and cheerful disposition, Miss Barton, who became a Flight-Officer in the WAAF, was killed in a plane crash at an RAF airfield in Kent.

Boros, Julius (1920–94)

Of Hungarian extraction he is remembered for his long, lazy swing and quiet personality. He won two US Open Championships, the first in 1952 and the second 11 years later, at the age of 43, in a play-off against Arnold Palmer and Jackie Cupit. It made him the oldest winner of the title until overtaken by Hale Irwin (45) in 1990. He became the oldest US PGA champion at 48 in 1968, while his best finish in the US Masters was third in 1963 and his best in the Open Championship 15th at Muirfield in 1966.

Braid, James (1870–1950)

One of the greatest figures in golf of all times, James Braid, with Harry Vardon and JH Taylor, made up the Triumvirate which dominated British professional golf for twenty years before the First World War. He was the first person to win the Open Championship five times. This record was later equalled by Taylor and beaten by Vardon. Braid's achievements were remarkable for the short time in which they were accomplished. In ten years he won five times and was second on three occasions. His victories were in 1901, 1905, 1906, 1908, 1910. He won the Match Play Tournament four times, 1903-5-7-11, a record which was unequalled till 1950, and the French Open Championship in 1910. He played for Scotland *v* England in 1903-4-5-6-7-9-10-12 and for Great Britain against America, 1921. A joiner by trade, Braid played as an amateur in Fife and Edinburgh and in 1893 went to London and worked as a club-maker. Taylor and Vardon were well established in the golfing world before Braid turned professional in 1896 and he quickly came into prominence by finishing level with Taylor, who by that time had been Champion twice, in a challenge match. In a historic international foursomes, Braid and partner Alex Herd lost to Vardon and Taylor in a match for £400 over four courses. A tall, powerful player who lashed the ball with *divine* fury, he was famous for his imperturbability: no matter how the game was progressing he always appeared outwardly calm and it was this serenity of temperament which assisted him to his Championship victories on two occasions. A man of few words, it was once said that *Nobody could be as wise as James Braid looked.* One of the founder members of the Professional Golfers' Association, Braid did much to elevate the status of the professional golfer. Braid made a major contribution to golf architecture; Gleneagles, Rosemount, Carnoustie and Dalmahoy all bear his stamp. He was admired and respected by all who knew him, as much for his modest and kindly nature as for his prowess as a golfer. He was professional at Romford for eight years and at Walton Heath for forty-five, and was for twenty-five years an honorary member of the latter club, becoming one of its directors. He was made an honorary member of the Royal & Ancient Golf Club in the last years of his life and had the distinction of being the only honorary member of the Parliamentary Golfing Society.

Campbell, Miss Dorothy Iona (1883–1946)

Won British Ladies' Championship, 1909-11; Scottish Ladies' Championship, 1905-6-8; American Ladies' Championship, 1909-10; Canadian Ladies' Championship 1910-11-12. One of only two women golfers to win the British, American and Canadian Championships, the other being Marlene Stewart (Mrs M Stewart Streit). Played for Scotland in international matches and for British Ladies *v* American Ladies.

Compston, Archie   (1893–1962)

One of the outstanding personalities of British golf in the years between the two World Wars who fought hard to resist the developing dominance of the American invasion. He played in three Ryder Cup matches – in 1927, 1929 and 1931. In a 72-hole challenge match he beat Hagen by 18 and 17 in 1928 at Moor Park and in the Open which followed he finished third to Hagen. He tied for second place in the Open of 1925.

Cotton, Sir Henry   (1907–87)

Sir Henry Cotton bestrode the British professional golf scene as player, teacher, writer, course architect and encourager of youth from 1930 until his death in December 1987, a few days before his well-deserved knighthood was announced.

He was the only Briton to win the Open more than once in a period of 75 years, between 1914 and 1989; his three victories at Sandwich in 1934, Carnoustie in 1937 and Muirfield in 1948 were pinnacles in a dedicated, sometimes controversial, but highly successful career. All three victories contained at least one memorable round. His 65 at Sandwich (after which a golf ball was named), his last round 71 at Carnoustie in a downpour and his record 66 at Muirfield, with King George VI among the spectators, showed a style of play and of life admired by all.

No man did more to raise the status of the professional golfer. His insistence on having Hon-

Henry Cotton   Popperfoto

orary Membership of clubs to which he was attached – Waterloo Brussels, Ashridge, Royal Mid-Surrey and Temple near Maidenhead – began a practice now followed by many clubs with their professionals. As Ryder Cup player and Captain, founder-member of the Golf Foundation, and his Rookie of the Year award, he led by example. His reward, which many would say came too late, was the first knighthood given for service to golf.

His many playing successes included winning eleven Continental Opens and five finals in the *News of the World* Match Play Tournament, which at the time was second only in prestige to the Open which he won twice. He was four times selected for the Ryder Cup team, being Captain in 1937 and non-playing Captain in 1953. Captain of the PGA in 1934 and 1954, he also had many other lesser tournament wins.

During the war, in which he served in the RAF, he played exhibition matches in aid of the Red Cross and encouraged his fellow professionals to do likewise. After he retired from Championship play, he devoted his time to writing articles for the golf press and several books. He was also a great supporter of the Golf Foundation and for the development of his beloved Penina in Portugal where he spent much of his last years.

He was elected to Honorary Membership of the Royal & Ancient Club in 1968 and was aware of his coming knighthood when he died a few days before it was announced.

The Curtis Sisters:
Harriet (1878–1944)
Margaret (1880–1965)

The names of Harriet Curtis and her sister Margaret will always be remembered in golf because in 1932 they donated the Curtis Cup for biennial competition between women golfers of the United States and Great Britain and Ireland. Harriet won the US Women's Amateur championship in 1906 and played her sister Margaret in the final the following year, when Margaret won the first of her three titles. Margaret competed in the event for the last time in 1947, more than 50 years after her first appearance.

Darwin, Bernard (1876–1961)

One of the most respected and widely known personalities in the game. As a graceful and authoritative writer on golf and golfers he had no equal. He knew intimately every player and every course of note throughout the world, and his phenomenal memory, fluent pen and gentle humour established him as the top historian of the game over many years. In 1937 he was awarded the CBE for his services to literature, which included journalism, books of children's stories and other sports besides golf. He was captain of the Royal & Ancient Club in 1934-35, and played internationally for England from 1902 until 1924 and in the first Walker Cup match (1922). He had travelled to the US to report the match for *The Times* and had been called in to play and captain the side when Robert Harris fell ill. During his playing career he won many amateur titles and trophies. He was a grandson of Charles Darwin.

Demaret, Jimmy (1910–83)

One of the game's most colourful characters, stemming no doubt from the fact that he was still a nightclub singer in 1940 when he won six consecutive tournaments against very strong opposition. It culminated with the Masters which he also won in 1947 and 1950, making him the first man to collect three green jackets. It was a remarkable victory because Demaret made up seven strokes on Jim Ferrier over the last six holes, winning by two after being five behind. Demaret was a co-owner of the Champions club in Houston, where the 1967 Ryder Cup and 1969 US Open were played. His record in the Ryder Cup in the years 1947-49-51 is without parallel. He won all his six matches, two of the three foursomes being in partnership with Ben Hogan.

Duncan, George (1884–1964)

He was the last Scottish-born winner of the Open title domiciled in Britain. He won the title in 1920 and his victory was achieved after two opening rounds of 80 which left him 13 strokes behind the leader. Two years later, at Sandwich, he finished second to Hagen after one of the most exciting finishes up to that time. Hagen had finished and was already being hailed as the winner when Duncan, a very late starter, reached the 18th hole needing a 4 to tie. He failed but his round was notable as the only one under 70 in that Open and the first to break 70 in the Open since 1904. Prior to the first war, Duncan was a prominent challenger to the established Triumvirate and would probably have achieved greater fame but for the war years during which he would have been at his prime. One of the fastest players of all time, he wasted no time, especially on the greens, and his book *Golf at a Gallop* was appropriately titled.

The Dunns

The twin brothers Dunn, born at Musselburgh in 1821, were prominent in golf between 1840 and 1860. In 1849, Old Willie Dunn and Jamie Dunn played their great match against Allan Robertson and Old Tom Morris. Willie Dunn became custodian in the Blackheath Links until 1864, and he then returned to Leith, and later to North Berwick, where he died at the age of 59. Willie Dunn was celebrated for the peculiar grace of his style and, as the longest driver of his day, he was a doughty match fighter, and one of his famous games was with Allan Robertson in 1843, when he played the St Andrews champion 20 rounds, and lost by 2 rounds and 1 to play. Another famous match was in 1852, when, partnered by Sir Robert Hay, he played Allan Robertson and Old Tom. Jamie Dunn, his twin brother, was also a fine player.

Willie's son went to America, and won the first Championship of America in 1894. He was among the first to experiment with the idea of steel shafts. About 1900 he inserted thin steel rods in split cane and lancewood shafts. He invented a coneshaped paper tee, the forerunner of the wooden tee, and was a pioneer of indoor golf schools. He died in London in 1952.

Ferguson, Bob (1848–1915)

Started to caddie on Musselburgh when aged eight. In 1866, when 18, he won the first prize in the Leith Tournament, in which all the great professionals of the day took part. The late Sir Charles Tennant put up the money for young Ferguson, who, in 1868 and 1869, beat Tom Morris six times. In 1875, at Hoylake, with young Tom Morris representing Scotland in a foursome, he beat Bob Kirk, Blackheath, and John Allan,

Westward Ho!, representing England. He won the Open Championship in 1880, 1881 and 1882. In 1883 he tied with Willie Fernie, losing the 36-hole play-off by one stroke. After this Championship he became ill with typhoid, and was never able to reproduce his great form. He became the custodian of the Musselburgh links, taught the young and was widely respected in the community.

Fernie, Willie   (1851–1924)

Born in St Andrews, he went to Dumfries in 1880 as greenkeeper. In 1882 he was second to Bob Ferguson in the Open Championship and after a tie with the same player he won the Open Championship in 1883 at Musselburgh after a 36-hole play-off. He became professional to Felixstowe and Ardeer and in 1887 to Troon, and was there as professional until February, 1924. He was a very stylish player and in great demand as a teacher. He played in many important stake matches, the two biggest being against Andrew Kirkaldy over Troon, Prestwick and St Andrews which he won by 4 and 3, and against Willie Park over Musselburgh and Troon which he lost by 13 and 12. He played for Scotland against England in 1904.

Hagen, Walter   (1892–1969)

The first of the great golfers with star quality. People flocked to see him as much because he was a *character* as for his outstanding skill and many achievements. He did not want to be a millionaire, but merely to live like one, and this he did in

Walter Hagen   Popperfoto

dramatic style as when he used a hired Rolls-Royce as a changing room at the Open because professionals were not admitted to the clubhouse, and when he gave the whole of his first prize in the Open to his caddie. He also pioneered stylish dressing on the course. As a player he had great mastery of the recovery shot, nerves of steel beneath his debonair exterior and a fine putting touch. His best achievement was probably his four consecutive wins in the USPGA championship when the event was decided by matchplay over 36 holes. He won the US Open in 1914 and 1919 and the Open in 1922-24-28-29 and represented the US against Britain on seven occasions. His world tours with Kirkwood, his extrovert approach and the entertainment he provided on and off the course were the forerunners of the spectacular development of golf as a spectator sport. In spite of his being a contemporary of the immortal Bobby Jones, his personality was such that he was never overshadowed.

Herd, Alexander 'Sandy'   (1868–1944)

His life in the forefront of the game was more prolonged than his contemporaries of the Victorian era, and when he took part in his last Open at St Andrews in 1939 he was 71 and his appearances in the Championship covered a span of 54 years. A brilliant shot player, success often eluded him as he was prone to leave his putts short and to indecision. On his first appearance in the Open, at the age of 17, he possessed only four clubs and although he was frequently in contention it was not until 1902 that he won the Championship. He was the first player to win the Open using a rubber-cored ball. In 1920 at Deal and again the following year at St Andrews he was joint leader in the Open after three rounds. In 1926, aged 58, he won the PGA Match Play tournament at Royal Mid-Surrey in a 36-hole final, having played five rounds in the previous three days to reach it. Those three achievements when he was in his fifties are convincing proof of the longevity of his game. His life in golf brought him into competition with all the great Victorians – Taylor, Vardon, Kirkaldy, Braid and Park – and continued through the Jones and Hagen era up to the days of Locke, Cotton, Rees and Sarazen and others who, over 100 years after Herd's birth, were still playing Open Championship golf.

Hilton, Harold   (1869–1942)

Born at West Kirby, a few miles from Hoylake, he was one of the most scientific of golfers. He learned his game at Royal Liverpool, where he won success in boys' competitions. In 1892, the year the Open Championship was extended to 72 holes, he won, and again in 1897. He won the Amateur Championship and the Irish Open

Championship four times each, the St George's Cup twice, the American Amateur Championship once and became the first player, and the only Britisher, to hold both the US and British Amateur titles at the same time. He was small, 5 feet 7 inches, but immensely powerful in build. Hilton made a major contribution to golf literature as the first editor of *Golf Monthly*.

Hogan, Ben (1912–1997)

As one of only four golfers to date to win all four major championships – the Masters, United States Open, Open and United States PGA – Ben Hogan is assured of a place among the sport's all-time greats. He dominated the scene in America after the Second World War, playing golf of a standard few have witnessed before or since, and in 1953 came closer than anyone has ever done to achieving the Grand Slam of all four in one season. Only a clash of dates between the Open and US PGA denied him the opportunity. Yet four years earlier it had looked as if his career might be prematurely ended. Hogan and his wife were involved in a crash with a Greyhound bus in fog in Texas and there were reports that he might not survive his horrific injuries. But survive he did, and after having to learn how to walk again, he returned to action just under a year later and within weeks was a winner again

Remarkably, it had taken him almost a decade as a professional to record his first victory and he was 34 when he won the first of his nine majors, the 1946 US PGA. He was 11 under par in beating Jimmy Demaret 10 and 9 in the semi-finals, and in the final, after finding himself three down to Ed Oliver, he played the next 14 holes in eight under par and won 6 and 4. He went on to win both the US Open and US PGA in 1948 and, following his crash, added six more majors in the space of four seasons. Never fond of overseas travel, his Open Championship debut did not come until 1953, the year he won the Masters by five shots, the US Open by six and triumphed in five of the six tournaments he entered. Alien though Carnoustie must have seemed to him, he scored 73-71-70-68 to win by four strokes. It was to prove his one and only appearance in the event, but at home he continued to strive for perfection and even at the age of 54 he finished tenth in the 1967 Masters, including a round of 66 where he played the inward half in 30. His life, dramatic from the moment his father committed suicide when Ben was nine, was made into a Hollywood film entitled *Follow the Sun*, starring Glenn Ford.

Hunter, Charles (1836–1921)

A caddie and club-maker under old Tom Morris at Prestwick, he was for three years professional at the Blackheath Club, London, and succeeded old

Tom as the Prestwick Club professional in 1864. He played in the first Open Championship at Prestwick in 1860, and he was a conspicuous figure at every championship and tournament held at Prestwick, acting as starter and in charge of the house flag up till the time of his death. He did not take much part in professional competitions, preferring to attend to his club-making and his members. In fact, during one championship round, while playing a niblick shot, he received word that the Lord Ailsa wished him to come at once and pick him out a set of clubs. He put his niblick back in his bag, pocketed his ball and returned to his workshop. In 1919 he was presented with his portrait in oils by the Prestwick Club, and a replica hangs in the Club. At the Open Championship of 1914 at Prestwick, he was the recipient of a presentation from his brother professionals. As a man of fine integrity, his friendship was valued by all golfers of his time.

Hutchinson, Horace (1859–1932)

An eminent golfer from the early 80s until 1907. He was a stylish and attractive player. Won the Amateur Championship in 1886 and 1887, runner-up 1885 (the first year of the Championship), and he was in the final in 1903. He was a semi-finalist in 1896, 1901, and 1904. He represented England v Scotland 1902-3-4-6-7, and was chosen in 1905 but illness prevented him taking his place. His career in the front rank of the game extended over twenty years. He was a voluminous and pleasant writer on golf and out-door life. He was the first Englishman to captain the Royal & Ancient. In other years he was also Captain of Royal Liverpool, Royal St George's and President of Royal North Devon.

Jones, Bobby (1902–1971)

By the time he retired from competitive golf in 1930 at the age of 28, Jones had established himself as one of the greatest golfers of all time, if not the greatest. He represented America in the Walker Cup from its inauguration in 1922 until 1930 and played in the match against Great Britain in 1921. His victories included the US Open in 1923-26-29-30 (tied in 1925 and 1928 but lost the play-off; second in 1922 and 1924); US Amateur 1924-25-27-28-30 (runner-up in 1919 and 1926); Open Championship 1926-27-30; Amateur Championship 1930. In 1930, Jones reached a pinnacle which will probably never be equalled when he achieved the Grand Slam – winning in one year the Open and Amateur Championships of America and Britain.

He then retired from championship golf. His stylish swing was the subject of admiration wherever he went – full, flowing, smooth, graceful and rhythmical. Yet he was of such a nervous

Bobby Jones   Popperfoto

Kirkaldy, Andrew   (1860–1934)

A rugged type of the old school of Scottish professionals, he was the last survivor of that race. After army service in Egypt and India he was appointed professional as at Winchester. He had no liking for the steady sedate life of an English professional and after six weeks returned to his native St Andrews, where he lived the rest of his days acting as a playing professional until he was appointed professional to the Royal and Ancient Golf Club. He was a man of powerful physique. He was a beautiful golfer to watch, particularly his iron shots. In the Open Championship, 1889, he tied with Willie Park at Musselburgh, but lost on the replay. He played in many money matches and the most notable was in 1895. JH Taylor had won the Open Championship in 1894, the first English professional to do so, and prior to the Open Championship, at St Andrews in 1895, the young English champion challenged the world for £50-a-side. Kirkaldy accepted and won by a hole. Candid, outspoken, sometimes uncouth, Kirkaldy in his old age was respected by princes and peers.

Laidlay, John Ernest   (1860–1940)

Johnny Laidlay played high-quality golf for fifty years – a testimony to his technique and temperament. In all, he won more than 130 medals. At a time when golf was booming and the opposition tough, he won the Amateur Championship twice (1889, 1891) was runner-up three times and beaten semi-finalist three times. He was second in the 1893 Open Championship when his characteristically good putting failed. He played for Scotland every year from 1902 until 1911, when he was fifty-one. The longevity of his very individual swing was perhaps due to his early golfing experiences at Musselburgh where he saw Young Tom Morris, knew Willie Park well and played a lot with Bob Ferguson (including a famous round by moonlight). His contribution to the game was the overlapping grip – known erroneously as the Vardon grip. Laidlay played cricket for Scotland (vs Yorkshire – taking 6 wickets for 18 runs); he was a pioneer of wildlife photography and carved beautiful furniture.

Leitch, 'Cecil'   (1891–1977)

Although she had reached the semi-final of the British Ladies' Championship in 1908 at the age of 17 and had won the French Ladies' Championship in 1912, it was in 1914 that she really established herself as Britain's dominant woman golfer when she won the English Ladies', the French Ladies' and the British Ladies'. She retained each of these titles when they were next held after the First World War (the English in 1919 and the British and French in 1920) and

disposition that he was frequently physically sick and unable to eat during a championship.

During his championship winning years, Jones was also a keen scholar and gained first-class honours degrees in law, English literature and mechanical engineering at three different universities. He finally settled on a legal career with his own practice in Atlanta. It was there that he and his friend Clifford Roberts conceived and developed the idea of the great Augusta National course and the Masters tournament, now a fitting memorial to the *Master Golfer* himself.

In recognition of his great skill and courage, and the esteem in which he was held in Britain and at St Andrews in particular, he was made an honorary member of the Royal & Ancient in 1956 and two years later, when in St Andrews as captain of the US team in the inaugural competition for the Eisenhower Trophy, he was given the Freedom of the Burgh of St Andrews. He died on 18th December, 1971 after many years of suffering from a crippling spinal disease. As a final tribute a memorial service was held at St Andrews.

who can say how many times she might have won them in the intervening years. In all she won the French Ladies' in 1912-14-20-21-24, the English Ladies' in 1914-19, the British Ladies' in 1914-20-21-26 and the Canadian Ladies' in 1921. Her total of four victories in the British Ladies' has never been bettered and has been equalled only by her great rival Joyce Wethered, against whom in the 1920s she had many memorable matches. Miss Leitch was an outspoken person who occasionally battled with the golfing authorities. Her strong attacking play mirrored her personality. Aged 19, in 1910 she accepted the challenge from Harold Hilton, at his peak, to take on any woman golfer over 72 holes giving half a stroke (a stroke at every second hole). Miss Leitch won this famous challenge match by 2 and 1 and later also beat John Ball, eight times Amateur Champion. Right to the end of her life, Cecil Leitch took an active interest in golf, attending major events whenever possible.

Lema, Tony (1934–66)

'Champagne Tony', as he was called because of his habit of treating the golf writers after his victories, had much in common with Walter Hagen. He loved the 'high life' but behind it was steely resolve as well. A beautiful swinger of the club, he was a golfer of grace rather than power. His victory in the Open Championship of St Andrews in 1964 was remarkable because he had never played golf in Europe before. He had just won three American tournaments in quick succession but arrived late and had only 27 holes of practice. Aided by that famous local caddie, Tip Anderson, he quickly mastered these most revered of links and won by five strokes from Jack Nicklaus. A player who did nothing by halves – such as losing to Gary Player in the world matchplay championship after being seven up with 17 to play – he was killed when the private aeroplane in which he was travelling crashed on a golf course in Illinois. He was only 32.

Little, Lawson (1910–68)

As an amateur he established two records in that he won both the Amateur and American Amateur Championships in 1934 and again in 1935. In the final of the 1934 Amateur he won by the margin of 14 and 13 and for the 23 holes played he was ten under 4's. He turned professional in 1936 and won the Canadian Open in the same year and in 1940, won the US Open after a play-off.

Locke, Bobby (1917–87)

The son of Northern Irish emigrants, Artur D'Arcy Locke turned professional in 1938 after a very successful amateur career, in which he won the South

African Boys' Championship, the South African Amateur (twice) and Open Championship (twice) as well as finishing leading amateur in the Open Championships of 1936 and 1937. As a result of his visits to Britain, he developed a characteristic hook to increase his length and although never a long hitter, his deadly short game made him a formidable competitor. In his first year as a professional he won the Irish, South African and New Zealand Open Championships as well as the South African Professional title.

During the war, Locke flew Liberator bombers for nearly 2000 hours. He left the South African Air Force weighing four stones heavier and immediately resumed his winning way. Second to Snead at St Andrews in the 1946 Open, he was encouraged to visit America where he was greatly successful. He beat Snead 12–2 in a series of matches and won four tournaments in 1947, two in 1948, three in 1949 and one in 1950. Locke had bad relations with the USPGA who disliked his success and they banned him from their tournaments. Locke concentrated his efforts on Europe. He won the Open Championship four times – 1949-50-52-59 – as well as the Open Championships of Canada (1947), France (1952-53), Germany (1954), Switzerland (1954), Egypt (1954) and South Africa (six times as a professional). He also won a number of British titles including the Dunlop Masters, Spalding, the Lotus, Daks and Bowmaker Tournaments. The

Bobby Locke   Popperfoto

1957 Open Championship was the first to be shown on television and the first in which the leaders went out last. Locke won by 3 strokes and his score of 279 was the first time 280 had been beaten at St Andrews. Locke had to mark his ball on the 72nd hole and in front of the cameras replaced it on the wrong spot. The R & A decided to let his score stand as he had derived no advantage from his technical error and disqualification would have been inequitable and against the spirit of the game.

Bobby Locke will be remembered as a beautifully dressed golfer – plus fours, white shirt and tie – with a superb temperament, especially after a disastrous hole, great self discipline, the highest standards of behaviour and a wonderful short game. He was virtually in retirement when he had a serious car crash. On recovery he continued to play golf but his competitive career was at an end. He was made an honorary member of the R & A in 1976.

Longhurst, Henry   (1909–78)

After leaving Cambridge University, he acquired a job as a golf writer in which he could indulge his love of the game and be paid for it. He never ceased to be amazed at his own good fortune. His regular weekly article in the *Sunday Times* became compulsory reading for the golfing cognoscenti. From writing he became involved in radio and, later, television, through which he became world famous as a commentator.

Television was the perfect medium for his talents. His humour, easy manner, gifted observation and perception, mellow voice, calm delivery and economy of word were all perfectly suited to a slow-moving sport, and from his vast knowledge and understanding of the game, he was always able to fill in any gaps in the action with an apt story or two.

Longhurst also wrote several amusing books about different periods of his life, including a brief spell as an MP. He was awarded the CBE for his services to golf and was one of only a handful of people to be made an honorary member of the Royal & Ancient Golf Club. His own golf was good enough to have won the German Open Amateur in 1936 and to be runner-up in the French Open Amateur in 1937.

Mackenzie, Alister   (1870–1934)

A prolific designer of golf courses all over the world, Dr Alexander 'Alister' Mackenzie was a family doctor and surgeon before abandoning medicine to work full-time in golf. An early design, in conjunction with Harry S Colt, was in 1907 for Alwoodley GC, Leeds, where he was a founder member and honorary secretary until 1912. He designed and redesigned dozens of courses in Britain and did outstanding work in Australia and New Zealand. But he is best remembered for designing Cypress Point in California and, with Bobby Jones, the Augusta National in Georgia, home of the US Masters.

Massy, Arnaud   (1877–1958)

Born in Biarritz, France, he became, in 1907, the first overseas player to win the Open Championship. He won at Hoylake beating JH Taylor by two strokes. He also tied with Harry Vardon at St George's in 1911 but conceded the title at the 35th hole of the play-off.

Micklem, Gerald   (1911–88)

Gerald Micklem devoted so much of his life to the benefit of golf, both as player and administrator, that he will always be remembered for his dedication to the cause of amateurs and professionals alike. He gave his time unsparingly to the game's development, whether locally at his favourite Sunningdale, at the R&A or on the international scene. After a pre-war Oxford Blue, he was English Champion in 1947 and 1953, four times in the Walker Cup side between 1947 and 1955 and non-playing Captain in 1957 and 1959, and 12 years a Home International from 1947. He was second in the Brabazon and also won the St George's Challenge Cup, the Berkshire Trophy, the President's Putter and several R&A Members' medals.

When he ceased to play in tournaments, his administrative responsibilities were legion. Captain of many English and British teams in European and International events, he took a leading part in the development of the Open, being Chairman of the Championship Committee of the Royal & Ancient during a key period. It was in this appointment that he made his greatest contribution to the future of the game. It was his vision and enterprise which led to the spectacle that the Open is today, as the most prestigious and best organised Championship anywhere in the world. He was Captain of the Royal & Ancient Club in 1968.

To the end of his life he lent his support to most golf ventures and many were the amateurs and professionals whom he helped and who were made welcome at his home, close to Sunningdale, and who remember his generosity and advice given, based on his wide knowledge of the game.

Mitchell, Abe   (1897–1947)

The finest player who never won an Open Championship was the tribute paid by JH Taylor. He finished in the first six five times in the Open and was three times winner of the Match Play Championship. Along with Duncan and later Compston, he was one of the few British hopes against the American invasion of the twenties.

Morgan, Wanda   (1910–1995)

British Amateur champion in 1935, English champion three times (1931-36-37), also three times a member of the Curtis Cup teams of 1932-34-36, Wanda Morgan was one of the outstanding women players of the 1930s. She first made her mark in 1929 when, aged 19, she reached the semi-finals of the English Open and was promptly dubbed one of the 'Kent Kids', the other being Diana Fishwick (*née* Critchley). Wanda Morgan won the Kent Championship seven times and had the reputation of being a good wooden club player and outstanding with her iron play. She was less certain on the greens and changed both her putter and her method repeatedly. As a representative of the Dunlop sports company, her career was curtailed but she was a source of constant encouragement to the young.

The Morrises:
Old Tom   (1821–1908)
Young Tom   (1851–75)

Old Tom Morris and his son, young Tom Morris, played a prominent part in golf in the period from 1850 to 1875. The father was born at St Andrews on 16th June, 1821. At the age of eighteen, he was apprenticed to Allan Robertson in the ball-making trade. When Morris was thirty years of age, Colonel Fairlie of Coodham took him to Prestwick, and he remained there until 1865, when he returned to St Andrews and became greenkeeper to the Royal & Ancient Golf Club, a position he held until 1904.

Young Tom was born at St Andrews in 1851, and exhibited early remarkable powers as a golfer. At the age of sixteen he won the Open Professional Tournament at Montrose against the best players in the country, and he won the Championship Belt outright by scoring three successive victories in 1868-69-70. The Championship lapsed for a year, but when it was resumed in 1872, young Tom scored his fourth successive victory.

There is no doubt that young Tom was the finest golfer of his time, but the tragic death of his wife, while he was engaged playing with his father in a great golf match at North Berwick against the brothers Willie and Mungo Park, had a most depressing effect on him, and he survived his wife by only a few months. Near the finish of this match, a telegram reached North Berwick intimating that, following her confinement, young Tom's wife was dangerously ill. The telegram was held over by Provost Brodie and not handed to young Tom until the end of the match. The yacht of John Lewis, an Edinburgh golfer, was put at the service of the Morrises but before the party embarked, a second telegram brought the sad news to young Tom that his wife had died. It was a mournful party that made the voyage across the Forth to St Andrews. The brilliant young golfer never recovered from the

shock, and he died on Christmas Day of the same year, 1875, at the age of twenty-four.

There was a second son, JOF Morris, who played in professional tournaments but, although a fine golfer, he never approached the brilliant execution of his elder brother.

Old Tom competed in every Open Golf Championship up to and including 1896, the year Harry Vardon scored his first victory in the Open Championship. Old Tom died at St Andrews in 1908. He was respected throughout the golfing world for his honest, sturdy qualities. His portrait hangs in the R&A Clubhouse, and the home green at St Andrews is named in his memory. A monument, a sculpted figure of Young Tom in golfing pose, was erected by public subscription in St Andrews Cathedral Churchyard and a smaller memorial stone was placed on the grave when Old Tom died.

Ouimet, Francis   (1893–1967)

He is often described as the player who started the golf boom in the US when, as a young amateur, he tied with Harry Vardon and Ted Ray for the 1913 US Open and went on to win the play-off. In an illustrious career he won the US Amateur twice and was a member of every Walker Cup team from 1922 to 1934 and was non-playing Captain then until 1949. Ouimet was the first non-British national to be elected Captain of the R&A Golf Club in 1951. He was prominent in golf legislation and administration in America and a committee member of the USGA for many years.

The Parks

Brothers Willie and Mungo Park of Musselburgh are famous in the annals of golf for the numerous money matches they played.

Willie had the distinction of winning the very first Open Championship in 1860 and repeated his victory in 1863, 1866 and 1875. For twenty years Willie had a standing challenge in *Bell's Life*, London, to play any man in the world for £100-a-side. Willie took part in numerous matches against Tom Morris for very large stakes and in the last of these at Musselburgh in 1882, the match came to an abrupt end when Park was two up with six to play. The referee stopped play because spectators were interfering with the balls. Morris and the referee retired to Foreman's public house. Park sent a message saying if Morris did not come out and finish the match he would play the remaining holes alone and claim the stakes. This he did.

Mungo followed in his brother's footsteps by winning the Open Championship in 1874. He was for many years greenkeeper and professional at Alnmouth.

Willie's son, Willie Junior, kept up the golfing tradition of the family by winning the Open in

1887 and 1889. He designed many golf courses in Europe and America, sometimes in conjunction with property development, as at Sunningdale, and was the pioneer of the modern ideas of golf course construction. Like his forebears he took part in many private challenge matches, the one against Harry Vardon at North Berwick in 1899 being watched by the greatest crowd ever for that time and for many years afterwards. Willie Junior died in 1925 aged 61.

The third generation of this golfing family sustained a prominent golf association through Miss Doris Park (Mrs Aylmer Porter), daughter of Willie Junior, who established a distinguished record in ladies' international and championship golf.

Philp, Hugh

The master craftsman among the half-dozen club-makers located in St Andrews in the early days of the nineteenth century. He was especially skilled in making a wooden putter with a long head of pear-shaped design. He is believed to have made not many more than one hundred putters. The wooden putter was for centuries a favoured club at St Andrews for long approach putting. The creations of Hugh Philp are highly prized by golf club collectors. After his death in 1856 his business was carried on by Robert Forgan.

Picard, Henry   (1907–97)

The disappointment of finishing only fourth in the 1935 Masters after opening with rounds of 67 and 68 for a four-stroke lead was forgotten only three years later when, back in Augusta, scores of 71-72-72-70 proved good enough for a two-shot victory. The following year he added the United States PGA championship. One down with one to play against Byron Nelson, Picard made a four-foot birdie putt to force extra holes and at the 37th he holed from seven feet for another birdie while Nelson missed from five. Winner of 27 tournaments in total, ill-health affected his career thereafter, although he continued to play in the Masters until 1969. He can also be given some of the credit for Sam Snead's success, giving him a driver in 1937 which instantly solved Snead's hooking problems and turned him into the longest straight driver in the game.

Ray, Ted   (1877–1943)

Born Jersey, his early days coincided with the famous Triumvirate and it was not until 1912 that he won the Open and was runner-up the following year to Taylor. He was again runner-up in 1925 at the age of 48. In 1913 he tied for the US Open with Ouimet and Vardon, but lost the play-off. After the war he returned to America and won the US Open title in 1920 and was the last British player to hold

Dai Rees   Popperfoto

the title until Tony Jacklin, in 1970. He and Vardon were the only British players to win both the US Open and the Open until they were joined by Jacklin. Noted for his long driving and powers of recovery, he was invariably to be seen playing with a pipe clenched between his teeth.

Rees, Dai   (1913–83)

One of Britain's outstanding golfers from the 1930s to the 1960s. He played in nine Ryder Cup matches between 1937 and 1961, and was also non-playing captain in 1967. In 1957, he captained the only British team to win the Ryder Cup since 1933. He was three times a runner-up in the Open Championship and once third, and won the PGA Match Play Championship four times, and the Dunlop Masters twice, in addition to numerous other tournament successes in Britain, on the Continent of Europe and in Australasia. At the age of 60, he finished third in the Martini tournament. He was made an honorary member of the Royal & Ancient Golf Club in 1976.

Robertson, Allan   (1815–58)

According to tradition, he was never beaten in an individual stake match on level terms. A short, thick-set man, he had a beautiful, well-timed swing, and several golfers who could recall Robertson, and who saw Harry Vardon at his best, were of the opinion that there was considerable similarity in the elegance and grace of the two players. Tom Morris, senior, worked in Allan Robertson's shop, where the principal trade was making feather balls. A disagreement occurred between Robertson and Morris on the advent of the gutta ball, because Old Tom decided to play with the invention, and Allan considered the gutta might damage his trade in featheries. Allan, through agents, endeavoured to buy up all gutta balls in order to protect his industry of feather balls. Allan Robertson and Tom Morris never seem to have come together in any single match for large stakes, but it is recorded that they never lost a foursome in which they were partners.

Ryder, Samuel   (1858–1936)

Sam Ryder was a prosperous seed merchant and the Mayor of St Albans. He did not take up golf until the age of 52 but became one of the most famous names in golf as donor of the Ryder Cup, played for in biennial competition between teams of professionals from Great Britain and Ireland (now Europe) and the United States. Ryder attended an unofficial international match between British and American professionals at Wentworth in 1926 and was greatly impressed by the chivalry and camaraderie of the two sides. He declared afterwards, 'We must do this again'.The first Ryder Cup match was played the following year at Worcester, Massachusetts, and the first in Britain in 1929 at Moortown, Yorkshire.

Sayers, Bernard   (1857–1924)

Of very small stature, one of the smallest Scottish professionals, and light of build, Bernard Sayers nevertheless took a leading position in the game for over 40 years with his outstanding skill and rigid physical training. He engaged in numerous stake matches and played for Scotland against England in every match from 1903 to 1910 and in 1912 and 1913. He competed in every Open Championship from 1880 to 1923. Of a bright and sunny disposition, he contributed much to the merriment of championship and professional gatherings. He taught princes and nobles to play the game, was presented to King Edward, and received a presentation from King George, when Duke of York.

Smith, Mrs Frances (née Bunty Stephens)   (1925–78)

Dominated post-war women's golf by winning the British Ladies' Championship in 1949 and 1954 (runner-up 1951-52), the English Ladies' in 1948-54-55 (runner-up 1959) and the French

Ladies' in 1949. She represented Great Britain in the Curtis Cup on six consecutive occasions from 1950 to 1960. A pronounced pause at the top of her swing made her style most distinctive. She was awarded the OBE for her services to golf and was president of the English Ladies' Golf Association at the time of her death.

Smith, Horton   (1908–63)

Came to notice first from Joplin, Missouri, when 20 years old, and brilliantly embarked on the professional circuit in the winter of 1929 when he won all but one of the open tournaments in which he played. He was promoted to that year's Ryder Cup team and also played in 1933 and 1935. He won the first US Masters Tournament in 1934 and again in 1936 as well as more than thirty other major events. On his 21st birthday he won the French Open. He was President of the American PGA, 1952-54, and received two national distinctions: the Ben Hogan Award for overcoming illness or injury, and the Bobby Jones Award for distinguished sportsmanship in golf. The day after the Ryder Cup match which he attended in Atlanta in 1963 he collapsed and died in a Detroit hospital.

Smith, Macdonald   (1890–1949)

Born at Carnoustie, he was one of the great golfers who never won the Open Championship, in which he consistently finished in a high place, coming second in 1930 and 1932, third in 1923 and 1924, fourth in 1925 and 1934 and fifth in 1931. He went to America before he was 20. In the Open Championship at Prestwick in 1925 he entered the last round with a lead of five strokes over the field, but a wildly enthusiastic Scottish crowd of 20,000 engulfed and overwhelmed him. The sequel to these unruly scenes was the introduction of gate money the following year and Prestwick was dropped from the rota for the Open. He died in Los Angeles.

Tait, Freddie   (1870–1900)

Born at 17 Drummond Place, in Edinburgh (his father PG Tait was a Professor at Edinburgh University). He joined the R&A in 1890, and that year beat all previous St Andrews' amateur records by holing the course in 77, and in 1894 he reduced the record to 72. He was first amateur in the Open Championship in 1894, 1896 and 1899 and third in 1896 and 1897. He won the Amateur Championship in 1896 at Sandwich, beating in successive rounds GC Broadwood, Charles Hutchings, JE Laidlay, John Ball, Horace Hutchinson and HH Hilton, the strongest amateurs of the day. He repeated his victory in 1898 at Hoylake, and in 1899 he fought and lost at the 37th the historic final with John Ball at Prestwick. There is a Freddie Tait Cup given annually to the best amateur in the South African Open Championship. This cup was purchased from the surplus of the fund collected during the visit of the British amateur golfers to South Africa in 1928. He was killed in the South African War at Koodoosberg Drift, aged 30.

Taylor, John Henry   (1871–1963)

Last survivor of the famous Triumvirate – Taylor, Braid and Vardon – died at his Devonshire home in February, 1963, within a month of his 92nd birthday. Born at Northam, Devon, he had been professional at Burnham, Winchester and Royal Mid-Surrey. JH won the Open Championship five times – 1894-95-1900-09-13 – and also tied with Harry Vardon in 1896, but lost the replay. He was runner-up in 1904-05-06-14. His brilliant career included the French and German Open Championships and he was second in the US Open in 1900. Among the many honours he received were honorary membership of the R&A Golf Club in 1949. He was regarded as the pioneer of British professionalism and helped to start the Professional Golfers' Association. He did much to raise the whole status of the professional and, in the words of Bernard Darwin, *turned a feckless company into a self-respecting and respected body of men*. On his retirement in 1957 the Royal North Devon Golf Club paid him their greatest compliment by electing him President.

Tolley, Cyril   (1896–1978)

A dominant figure in amateur golf in the inter-war period. He won the first of two Amateur Championships in 1920 while still a student at Oxford and continued to win championships and represent England and Britain until 1938. Among other titles he won the Welsh Open (1921 and 1923) and remains the only amateur to have won the French Open (1924 and 1929). A powerful hitter with a delicate touch, Tolley was a crowd pleaser. He is remembered as much for a match he lost as for some of his victories. Having won the Amateur Championship in 1929, Tolley was a favourite to win at St Andrews in 1930. The draw was unseeded and he met Bobby Jones in the fourth round. A huge crowd turned out to watch a very exciting match which Jones won on the 19th with a stymie. Tolley was elected Captain of the R&A in 1948.

Travis, Walter   (1862–1925)

Born in Australia, Travis was the first overseas golfer to win the British Amateur, at Sandwich in 1904. He won the title using a centre-shafted putter, which was subsequently banned for many years. He won the US Amateur Championship in

1900, having taken up the game four years previously at the age of 35. He repeated his victory in 1901 and 1903 and was a semi-finalist five times between 1898 and 1914, winning also the stroke competition six times between 1900 and 1908. The *Old Man* as he was known is reckoned to have been one of the finest judges of distance who ever played golf. He died in New York.

Vardon, Harry   (1870–1937)

Born Grouville, Jersey, Vardon created a record by winning the Open Championship six times, his wins being in 1896, 1898, 1899, 1903, 1911 and 1914. He also won the American Open in 1900 and tied in 1913, subsequently losing the play-off. He had a serious illness in 1903 and it was said that he never quite regained his former dominance, particularly on the putting green.

That he was the foremost golfer of his time cannot be disputed and he innovated the modern upright swing and popularised the overlapping grip invented by JE Laidlay.

Had it not been for ill-health and the intervention of the First World War, his outstanding records both in the UK and America would almost certainly have been added to in later years. But in any event his profound influence on the game lives on. More than 100 years after his birth his achievements are still the standard of comparison with the latter-day giants of the game.

Harry Vardon   Popperfoto

Vare, Glenna (*née* Collett)   (1903–89)

A natural all-rounder at games, her six American Amateur championships set new standards. It was only achieved however by intense study of the mechanics of the swing and concentrated practice. She attacked the ball, with both irons and woods, with uncommon verve. Sadly, perhaps, a British Amateur title eluded her, despite being in successive finals in 1929 and 1930. In the first against Joyce Wethered at St Andrews she was three under 4s for the first 11 holes and 5-up but became victim of an outstanding counter-attack by the finest woman golfer of her time. A year later she lost again, this time unexpectedly to a little-known 19-year-old, Diana (Fishwick) Critchley, at Formby. She played in five Curtis Cup matches and was also captain, proving as popular with foe as with friend.

Walker, George   (1874–1953)

President of the United States Golf Association in 1920 and one of the instigators of the biennial Walker Cup matches between the leading amateurs of Great Britain and Ireland and the United States. He donated the trophy for the first match, played at Long Island, New York, on 29th August 1922, and won by the host country. Educated partly in England, at Stoneyhurst, Walker was an all-round sportsman and a good golfer, though not of international standard. His grandson, George Bush, became President of the United States.

Wethered, Joyce (Lady Heathcoat-Amory)   (1899–1983)

Bobby Jones once stated that Joyce Wethered was, taking into account 'the unavoidable handicap of a woman's lesser physical strength', the finest golfer he had ever seen. Her brother Roger persuaded her into competitive golf after the First World War. She was just 18 when she entered her first English Ladies' Championship in 1920, but she won it at Sherringham by beating the holder Cecil Leitch in the final aand was to remain unbeaten for the next four years, winning 33 successive matches. She also won four British Championships, equalling Leitch's record.

With her irons, her hands seldom went higher than shoulder level on either backswing or follow through and she made the game seem effortless. Jones's comment came after they played together at St Andrews. She scored 75 and he wrote: 'I had never played golf with anyone, man or woman, amateur or professional, who made me feel so utterly outclassed.' After playing in the inaugural Curtis Cup match in 1932, she forfeited her amateur status and toured America in 1935. She was reinstated as an amateur after the Second World War.

Wethered, Roger   (1899–1983)

One of the outstanding amateurs of the period between the two World Wars, Roger Wethered won the Amateur Championship in 1923 and was runner-up in 1928 and 1930. He won the President's Putter of the Oxford and Cambridge GS five times (once a tie) between 1926 and 1936, played in the Walker Cup against the United States six times between 1921 and 1934, and for England against Scotland every year from 1922 to 1930. He was captain of the Royal & Ancient in 1946. But he will probably be best remembered for the fact that he tied with Jock Hutchison, a Scot who had settled in the United States, in the 1921 Open Championship at St Andrews, despite having incurred a penalty stroke by inadvertently treading on his ball. Wethered was reluctant to stay on for the 36-hole play-off the following day because of a cricket engagement in England, but was persuaded to do so, only to be beaten by nine strokes, 150 to 159. No British amateur has come so close to winning the Open Championship since.

The Whitcombe Brothers:
Ernest   (1890–1971)
Charles   (1895–1978)
Reginald   (1898–1957)

The story of the Whitcombes is told in a limited edition publication, *The Whitcombe Brothers – A Golfing Legend*, and what a remarkable story it is. They were born in Burnham, Somerset, and won many titles between them. All three played in the 1935 Ryder Cup contest at Ridgewood, New Jersey, but only Reg, the youngest, won the Open Championship (at Sandwich in 1938). Ernest finished second to Walter Hagen in 1924 at Hoylake after leading by three strokes at one time and Charles took 76 in the final round at Muirfield in 1935 to lose by five strokes and finish third.

Wilson, Enid   (1910–96)

Between the wars of 1914–18 and then 1939–45 Enid Wilson was second only to Joyce Wethered among British women golfers. She had an outstanding record which was the result of her relish for the big occasion. Her finest years were between 1931–33 when she completed a hat-trick of victories in the British Women's Championship, all of them by wide margins. In 1931 she beat Wanda Morgan by seven and six in the final at Portmarnock. The following year at Saunton she similarly despatched Clementine Montgomery, and then in 1933 she defeated Diana Plumpton by 5 and 4 at Gleneagles. She had already won the English Championship twice, in 1928 and 1930, and, before that, the British

Girls' title in 1925. Twice, in 1931 and 1933, she was a semi-finalist in the American Championship, and played for Britain in the inaugural Curtis Cup match against the United States at Wentworth in 1932, beating Helen Hicks.

Enid Wilson had a sound, rather graceful, swing, and, though a hard worker on the practice ground, she never allowed golf to rule her life – indeed she retired from the game at a comparatively early age. Instead she turned to journalism, and for many years was the Women's Golf Correspondent of the *Daily Telegraph*, her pungent views frequently ruffling the feathers of the Ladies' Golf Union. Her book, *A Gallery of Women Golfers*, was widely acclaimed. She was a familiar figure in a long tweed skirt, which she wore in all weathers, and she compiled such a valuable collection of stamps that many of them had to be kept in the vaults of a bank. She saw out the last years of her life at her treasured Oast House at Crowborough in East Sussex.

Wood, Craig   (1901–68)

Born at Lake Placid, New York, Wood was a player of 'near misses'. Like Greg Norman many years later, Wood lost play-offs for what are known now as all the major championships even if they were not then. They were the 1933 Open Championship to Densmore Shute at St Andrews, the 1934 PGA Championship to Paul Runyan at

Buffalo, the 1935 Masters to Gene Sarazen at Augusta and the 1939 US Open to Byron Nelson at Philadelphia. However, success did finally come for Wood in 1941 when he won both the Masters and US Open. He was also a member of three American Ryder Cup teams.

Zaharias, Mrs George (Mildred Babe Didrikson) (1915–56)

In the 1932 Olympic Games she established three world records for women: 80 metres hurdles, javelin, and high jump. On giving up athletics she took up golf and won the Texas Women's Open in 1940-45-46; the Western Open, 1940-44-45-50; and the US National Women's Amateur, 1946. In 1947 she won the Ladies' Championship, the first American to do so.

In August 1947 she turned professional and went on to win the US National Women's Open, 1948-50. In winning the Tampa Open, 1951, she set up a women's world record aggregate, for the time, of 288 for 72 holes.

She was voted Woman Athlete of the year five times in 1932-45-46-47-50, and in 1949 was voted Greatest Female Athlete of the Half-Century.

The first woman to hold the post of head professional to a golf club, the *Babe* was a courageous and fighting character who left her mark in the world of sport.

Interesting Facts and Unusual Incidents

Royal Golf Clubs

● The right to the designation *Royal* is bestowed by the favour of the Sovereign or a member of the Royal House. In most cases the title is granted along with the bestowal of royal patronage on the club. The Perth Golfing Society was the first to receive the designation *Royal*. That was accorded in June 1833. King William IV bestowed the honour on the Royal & Ancient Club in 1834. The most recent Club to be so designated is the Royal Troon in 1978.

Royal and Presidential Golfers

● In the long history of the Royal and Ancient game no reigning British monarch has played in an open competition. The Duke of Windsor, when Prince of Wales in 1922, competed in the Royal & Ancient Autumn Medal at St Andrews. He also took part in competitions at Mid-Surrey, Sunningdale, Royal St George's and in the Parliamentary Handicap. He also occasionally competed in American events, sometimes partnered by a professional, and on a private visit to London in 1952 he competed in the Autumn competition of Royal St George's at Sandwich scoring 97. As Prince of Wales he had played on courses all over the world and, after his abdication, as Duke of Windsor he continued to enjoy the game for many years.

● King George VI (when Duke of York) in 1930 and the Duke of Kent in 1937 also competed in the Autumn Meeting of the Royal & Ancient, these occasions being after they had formally played themselves into the Captaincy of the Club and each returned his card in the medal round.

● King Leopold of Belgium played in the Belgian Amateur Championship at Le Zoute, the only reigning monarch ever to have played in a national championship. The Belgian King played in many competitions subsequent to his abdication. In 1949 he reached the quarter-finals of the French Amateur Championship at St Cloud, playing as Count de Rethy.

● King Baudouin of Belgium in 1958 played in the triangular match Belgium-France-Holland and won his match against a Dutch player. He also took part in the Gleneagles Hotel tournament (playing as Mr B de Rethy), partnered by Dai Rees in 1959.

● United States President George Bush accepted an invitation in 1990 to become an Honorary Member of the Royal & Ancient Golf Club of St Andrews. The honour recognised his long connection and that of his family with golf and the R&A. Both President Bush's father, Prescott Bush Sr, and his grandfather, George Herbert Walker – who donated the Walker Cup – were presidents of the United States Golf Association. Other Honorary Members of the R&A include Kel Nagle, Jack Nicklaus, Arnold Palmer, Gene Sarazen, Peter Thomson, Roberto De Vicenzo and Gary Player.

● In September 1992, the Royal & Ancient Golf Club of St Andrews announced that His Royal Highness The Duke of York had accepted the Club's invitation of Honorary Membership. The Duke of York is the third member of the Royal Family to accept membership and joins Their Royal Highnesses The Duke of Edinburgh and The Duke of Kent. In August The Duke of York visited the Club and played his first round on the Old Course, impressing the locals and caddies with his considerable skill and in particular with the length of many of his drives, said the official announcement.

First Lady Golfer

● Mary Queen of Scots, who was beheaded on 8th February, 1587, was probably the first lady golfer so mentioned by name. As evidence of her indifference to the fate of Darnley, her husband who was murdered at Kirk o' Field, Edinburgh, she was charged at her trial with having played at golf in the fields beside Seton a few days after his death.

Record Championship Victories

● In the Amateur Championship at Muirfield, 1920, Captain Carter, an Irish golfer, defeated an American entrant by 10 and 8. This is the only known instance where a player has won every hole in an Amateur Championship tie.

● In the final of the Canadian Ladies' Championship at Rivermead, Ottawa, 1921, Cecil Leitch defeated Mollie McBride by 17 and 15. Miss Leitch only lost 1 hole in the match, the ninth. She was 14 up at the end of the first round, and only 3 holes were necessary in the second round, Miss Leitch winning them all. She won 18 holes out of 21 played, lost 1, and halved 2.

● In the final of the French Ladies' Open Championship at Le Touquet in 1927, Mlle de la Chaume (St Cloud) defeated Mrs Alex Johnston (Moor Park) by 15 and 14, the largest victory in a European golf championship.

● At Prestwick in 1934, W Lawson Little, Presidio, San Francisco, defeated James Wallace, Troon Portland, by 14 and 13 in the final of the Amateur Championship, the record victory in the Amateur Championship. Wallace failed to win a single hole.

Players who have won Two or More Major Championships in the Same Year since 1916

● (The first Masters Tournament was played in 1934.)

    1922 Gene Sarazen – USPGA, US Open
    1924 Walter Hagen – USPGA, Open
    1926 Bobby Jones – US Open, Open
    1930 Bobby Jones – US Open, Open (Bobby Jones also won the US Amateur and British Amateur in this year.)
    1932 Gene Sarazen – US Open, Open
    1941 Craig Wood – Masters, US Open
    1948 Ben Hogan – USPGA, US Open
    1949 Sam Snead – USPGA, Masters
    1951 Ben Hogan – Masters, US Open
    1953 Ben Hogan – Masters, US Open, Open
    1956 Jack Burke – USPGA, Masters
    1960 Arnold Palmer – Masters, US Open
    1962 Arnold Palmer – Masters, Open
    1963 Jack Nicklaus – USPGA, Masters
    1966 Jack Nicklaus – Masters, Open
    1971 Lee Trevino – US Open, Open
    1972 Jack Nicklaus – Masters, Open
    1974 Gary Player – Masters, Open
    1975 Jack Nicklaus – USPGA, Masters
    1977 Tom Watson – Masters, Open
    1980 Jack Nicklaus – USPGA, US Open
    1982 Tom Watson – US Open, Open
    1990 Nick Faldo – Masters, Open
    1994 Nick Price – Open, US PGA

Outstanding Records in Championships, International Matches and on the Professional Circuit

● The record number of victories in the Open Championship is six, held by Harry Vardon who won in 1896-98-99-1903-11-14.

● Five-time winners of the Championship are JH Taylor in 1894-95-1900-09-13; James Braid

in 1901-05-06-08-10; Peter Thomson in 1954-55-56-58-65 and Tom Watson in 1975-77-80-82-83. Thomson's 1965 win was achieved when the Championship had become a truly international event. In 1957 he finished second behind Bobby Locke. By winning again in 1958 Thomson was prevented only by Bobby Locke from winning five consecutive Open Championships.

● Four successive victories in the Open by *Young* Tom Morris is a record so far never equalled. He won in 1868-69-70-72. (The Championship was not played in 1871.) Other four-time winners are Bobby Locke in 1949-50-52-57, Walter Hagen in 1922-24-28-29, Willie Park 1860-63-66-75, and *Old* Tom Morris 1861-62-64-67.

● Since the Championship began in 1860, players who have won three times in succession are Jamie Anderson, Bob Ferguson, and Peter Thomson.

● Robert Tyre Jones won the Open three times in 1926-27-30; the Amateur in 1930; the American Open in 1923-26-29-30; and the American Amateur in 1924-25-27-28-30. In winning the four major golf titles of the world in one year (1930) he achieved a feat unlikely ever to be equalled. Jones retired from competitive golf after winning the 1930 American Open, the last of these Championships, at the age of 28.

● Jack Nicklaus has had the most wins (six) in the US Masters Tournament, followed by Arnold Palmer with four.

● In modern times there are four championships generally regarded as standing above all others – the Open, US Open, US Masters, and USPGA. Four players have held all these titles, Gene Sarazen, Ben Hogan, Gary Player, and Jack Nicklaus, who in 1978 became the first player to have held each of them at least three times. His record in these events is – Open 1966-70-78; US Open 1962-67-72-80; US Masters 1963-65-66-72-75-86; USPGA 1963-71-73-75-80. His total of major championships is now 18.

The nearest approach to achieving the Grand Slam of the Open, US Open, US Masters and USPGA in one year was by Ben Hogan in 1953 when he won the first three and could not compete in the USPGA as it then overlapped with the Open Championship.

● In the 1996 English Amateur Championship at Hollinwell, Ian Richardson (50) and his son, Carl, of Burghley Park, Lincolnshire, both reached the semi-finals. Both lost.

● The record number of victories in the US Open is four, held by W Anderson, Bobby Jones, Ben Hogan and Jack Nicklaus.

● Bobby Jones (amateur), Gene Sarazen, Ben Hogan, Lee Trevino and Tom Watson are the only players to have won the Open and US Open Championships in the same year. Tony Jacklin won the Open in 1969 and the US Open in 1970 and for a few weeks was the holder of both.

● In winning the Amateur Championship in 1970 Michael Bonallack became the first player to win in three consecutive years.

● The English Amateur record number of victories is held by Michael Bonallack, who won the title five times.

● John Ball holds the record number of victories in the Amateur Championship, which he won eight times. Next comes Michael Bonallack (who was internationally known as *The Duke*) with five wins.

● Cecil Leitch and Joyce Wethered each won the British Ladies' title four times.

● The Scottish Amateur record was held by Ronnie Shade, who won five titles in successive years – 1963-64-65-66-67. His long reign as Champion ended when he was beaten in the fourth round of the 1968 Championship after winning 44 consecutive matches.

● Joyce Wethered established an unbeaten record by winning the English Ladies' in five successive years from 1920 to 1924 inclusive.

● In winning the Amateur Championships of Britain and America in 1934 and 1935 Lawson Little won 31 consecutive matches. Other dual winners of these championships in the same year are RT Jones (1930) and Bob Dickson (1967).

● Peter Thomson's victory in the 1971 New Zealand Open Championship was his ninth in that championship.

● In a four-week spell in 1971, Lee Trevino won in succession the US Open, the Canadian Open and the Open Championships.

● The finalists in the 1970 Amateur Championship, Michael Bonallack and Bill Hyndman, were the same as in 1969. This was the first time the same two players reached the final in successive years.

● On the US professional circuit the greatest number of consecutive victories is 11, achieved by Byron Nelson in 1945. Nelson also holds the record for most victories in one calendar year, again in 1945 when he won a total of 18 tournaments.

● Raymond Floyd, by winning the Doral Classic in March 1992, joined Sam Snead as the only winners of US Tour events in four different decades.

● Jack Nicklaus and the late Walter Hagen have had five wins each in the USPGA Championship. All Hagen's wins were in successive years and at match play; all Nicklaus's at stroke play.

● In 1953 Flori van Donck of Belgium had seven major victories in Europe, including the Open Championships of Switzerland, Italy, Holland, Germany and Belgium.

● Mrs Anne Sander won four major amateur titles each under a different name. She won the US Ladies' in 1958 as Miss Quast, in 1961 as Mrs Decker, in 1963 as Mrs Welts and the British Ladies' in 1980 as Mrs Sander.

● The highest number of appearances in the Ryder Cup matches is held by Nick Faldo who made his eleventh appearance in 1997.

● The greatest number of appearances in the Walker Cup matches is held by Irishman Joe Carr who made his tenth appearance in 1967.

● In the Curtis Cup Mary McKenna made her ninth consecutive appearance in 1986.

● Players who have represented their country in both Walker and Ryder Cup matches are, for the United States, Fred Haas, Ken Venturi, Gene Littler, Jack Nicklaus, Tommy Aaron, Mason Rudolph, Bob Murphy, Lanny Wadkins, Tom Kite, Jerry Pate, Craig Stadler, Jay Haas, Bill Rodgers, Hal Sutton, Curtis Strange, Davis Love III, Justin Leonard and Tiger Woods; and for Great Britain and Ireland, Norman Drew, Peter Townsend, Clive Clark, Peter Oosterhuis, Howard Clark, Mark James, Michael King, Paul Way, Ronan Rafferty, Sandy Lyle, David Gilford, Colin Montgomerie and Peter Baker.

Remarkable Recoveries in Match Play

● There have been two remarkable recoveries in the Walker Cup Matches. In 1930 at Sandwich, JA Stout, Great Britain, round in 68, was 4 up at the end of the first round against Donald Moe. Stout started in the second round, 3, 3, 3, and was 7 up. He was still 7 up with 13 to play. Moe, who went round in 67, won back the 7 holes to draw level at the 17th green. At the 18th or 36th of the match, Moe, after a long drive placed his iron shot within three feet of the hole and won the match by 1 hole.

● In 1936 at Pine Valley, George Voigt and Harry Girvan for America were 7 up with 11 to play against Alec Hill and Cecil Ewing. The British pair drew level at the 17th hole, or the 35th of the match, and the last hole was halved.

● In the 1965 Piccadilly Match Play Championship Gary Player beat Tony Lema after being 7 down with 17 to play.

● Bobby Cruickshank, the old Edinburgh player, had an extraordinary recovery in a 36-hole match in a USPGA Championship for he defeated Al Watrous after being 11 down with 12 to play.

● In a match at the Army GC, Aldershot, on 5th July, 1974, for the Gradoville Bowl, MC Smart was 8 down with 8 to play against Mike Cook. Smart succeeded in winning all the remaining holes and the 19th for victory.

● In the 1982 Suntory World Match Play Championship Sandy Lyle beat Nick Faldo after being 6 down with 18 to play.

Oldest Champions

Open Championship

Belt: 46 years 99 days. Tom Morris in 1867.
Cup: 44 years 93 days. Roberto De Vicenzo in 1967.

44 years 42 days. Harry Vardon in 1914.
42 years 97 days. JH Taylor in 1913.

Amateur Championship: Hon Michael Scott,
54 years, Hoylake 1933.
British Ladies Amateur: Mrs Jessie Valentine,
43 years, Hunstanton 1958.
Scottish Amateur: JM Cannon, 53 years, Troon
1969.
English Amateur: Terry Shingler, 41 years
11 months, Walton Heath 1977. Gerald
Micklem, 41 years 8 months, Royal Birkdale
1947.
US Open: Hale Irwin, 45 years, Medinah, Illi-
nois, 1990.
US Amateur: Jack Westland, 47 years, Seattle
1952. Westland was defeated in the 1931
final, 21 years previously, by Francis Ouimet
at Beverley, Chicago, Illinois.
US Masters: Jack Nicklaus, 46 years, in 1986.
USPGA: Julius Boros, 48 years, in 1968. Lee
Trevino, 43 years, in 1984.
USPGA Tour: Sam Snead, 52 years,
Greensborough Open in 1965. Julius Boros
lost play-off in Westchester Classic 1975.
Sam Snead, 61 years, equal second in Glen
Campbell Open 1974.

Youngest Champions

Open Championship

Belt: 17 years 5 months. Tom Morris, Jr in
1868.
Cup: 21 years 24 days. Willie Auchterlonie in
1893.
21 years 5 months. Tom Morris, Jr in 1872.
22 years 103 days. Severiano Ballesteros in
1979.
Amateur Championship: JC Beharrell, 18 years
1 month, Troon 1956. R Cole (S Africa) 18
years 1 month, Carnoustie 1966.
British Ladies Amateur: May Hezlett, 17 years,
Newcastle Co Down 1899. Michelle Walker,
18 years, Alwoodley 1971.
English Amateur: Nick Faldo, 18 years, Lytham
St Annes 1975. Paul Downes, 18 years,
Birkdale 1978. David Gilford, 18 years,
Woodhall Spa 1984. Ian Garbutt, 18 years,
Woodhall Spa 1990. Mark Foster, 18 years,
Moortown 1994.
English Amateur Stroke Play: Ronan Rafferty,
16 years, Hunstanton 1980.
British Ladies Open Stroke Play: Helen Dobson,
18 years, Southerness, 1989.

Disqualifications

*Disqualifications are now numerous, usually for some
irregularity over signing a scorecard or for late arrival
at the first tee. We therefore show here only incidents
in major events involving famous players or players
who were in a winning position or, alternatively, incidents which were in themselves unusual.*

● JJ McDermott, the American Open Champion
1911-12, arrived for the Open Championship at
Prestwick in 1914 to discover that he had made a
mistake of a week in the date the championship
began. The American could not play as the qualifying rounds were completed on the day he arrived.
● In the Amateur Championship at Sandwich in
1937, Brigadier-General Critchley, arriving at
Southampton from New York on the *Queen Mary*,
which had been delayed by fog, flew by specially
chartered aeroplane to Sandwich. He circled over
the clubhouse, so the officials knew he was nearly
there, but he arrived six minutes late, and his name
had been struck out. At the same championship a
player, entered from Burma, who had travelled
across the Pacific and the American Continent, and
was also on the *Queen Mary*, travelled from
Southampton by motor car and arrived four hours
after his starting time to find after journeying more
than halfway round the world he was *struck out*.
● An unprecedented disqualification was that of
A Murray in the New Zealand Open Championship, 1937. Murray, who was New Zealand
Champion in 1935, was playing with JP
Hornabrook, New Zealand Amateur Champion,
and at the 8th hole in the last round, while waiting for his partner to putt, Murray dropped a ball
on the edge of the green and made a practice putt
along the edge. Murray returned the lowest score
in the championship, but he was disqualified for
taking the practice putt.
● At the Open Championship at St Andrews in
1946, John Panton, Glenbervie, in the evening
practised putting on a green on the New Course,
which was one of the qualifying courses. He himself reported his inadvertence to the Royal &
Ancient and he was disqualified.
● At the Open Championship, Sandwich, 1949,
C Rotar, an American, qualified by four strokes
to compete in the championship but he was disqualified because he had used a putter which did
not conform to the accepted form and make of a
golf club, the socket being bent over the centre of
the club head. This is the only case where a player
has been disqualified in the Open Championship
for using an illegal club.
● In the 1957 American Women's Open Championship, Mrs Jackie Pung had the lowest score,
298 over four rounds, but lost the championship.
The card she signed for the final round read *five*
at the 4th hole instead of the correct *six*. Her total
of 72 was correct but the error, under rigid rules,
resulted in her disqualification. Betty Jameson,
who partnered Mrs Pung and also returned a
wrong score, was also disqualified.

Longest Match

● WR Chamberlain, a retired farmer, and George
New, a postmaster at Chilton Foliat, on 1st
August, 1922, met at Littlecote, the 9-hole course

of Sir Ernest Wills, and they agreed to play every Thursday afternoon over the course. This they did until New's sudden death on 13th January, 1938. An accurate record of the matches was kept giving details of each round including wind direction and playing conditions. In the elaborate system nearly two million facts were recorded. New played 814 rounds, and aggregated 86,397 strokes, of which Chamberlain took 44,008 and New 42,371. New, therefore, was 1,637 strokes up. The last round of all was halved, a suitable end to such an unusual contest.

Longest Ties

● The longest known ties in 18-hole match play rounds in major events were in an early round of the News of the World Match Play Championship at Turnberry in 1960, when WS Collins beat WJ Branch at the 31st hole and in the third round of the same tournament at Walton Heath in 1961 when Harold Henning beat Peter Alliss also at the 31st hole.
● In the 1970 Scottish Amateur Championship at Balgownie, Aberdeen, E Hammond beat J McIvor at the 29th hole in their second round tie.
● CA Palmer beat Lionel Munn at the 28th hole at Sandwich in 1908. This is the record tie of the British Amateur Championship. Munn has also been engaged in two other extended ties in the Amateur Championship. At Muirfield, in 1932, in the semi-final, he was defeated by John de Forest, the ultimate winner, at the 26th hole, and at St Andrews, in 1936, in the second round he was defeated by JL Mitchell, again at the 26th hole.

The following examples of long ties are in a different category for they occurred in competitions, either stroke play or match play, where the conditions stipulated that in the event of a tie, a further stated number of holes had to be played – in some cases 36 holes, but mostly 18. With this method a vast number of extra holes was sometimes necessary to settle ties.
● The longest known was between two American women in a tournament at Peterson (New Jersey) when 88 extra holes were required before Mrs Edwin Labaugh emerged as winner.
● In a match on the Queensland course, Australia, in October, 1933, HB Bonney and Col HCH Robertson versus BJ Canniffe and Dr Wallis Hoare required to play a further four 18-hole matches after being level at the end of the original 18 holes. In the fourth replay Hoare and Caniffe won by 3 and 2 which meant that 70 extra holes had been necessary to decide the tie.
● After finishing all square in the final of the Dudley GC's foursomes competition in 1950, FW Mannell and AG Walker played a further three 18-hole replays against T Poole and E Jones, each time finishing all square. A further 9 holes were then arranged when Mannell and

Walker won by 3 and 2 making a total of 61 extra holes to decide the tie.
● RA Whitcombe and Mark Seymour tied for first prize in the Penfold £750 Tournament at St Annes-on-Sea, in 1934. They had to play off over 36 holes and tied again. They were then required to play another 9 holes when Whitcombe won with 34 against 36. The tournament was over 72 holes. The first tie added 36 holes and the extra 9 holes made an aggregate of 117 holes to decide the winner. This is a record in first-class British golf but in no way compares with other long ties as it involved only two replays – one of 36 holes and one of 9.
● In the American Open Championship at Toledo, Ohio, in 1931, G Von Elm and Billy Burke tied for the title. Each returned aggregates of 292. On the first replay both finished in 149 for 36 holes but on the second replay Burke won with a score of 148 against 149. This is a record tie in a national open championship.
● Paul Downes was beaten by Robin Davenport at the 9th extra hole in the 4th round of the 1981 English Amateur Championship, a record marathon match for the championship.
● Severiano Ballesteros was beaten by Johnny Miller at the 9th extra hole of a sudden-death play-off at the 1982 million dollar Sun City Challenge, a record for any 72-hole professional event.
● José Maria Olazabal beat Ronan Rafferty at the 9th extra hole to win the 1989 Dutch Open on the Kennemer Golf and Country Club course.

Long Drives

It is impossible to state with any certainty what is the longest ever drive. Many long drives have never been measured and many others have most likely never been brought to our attention. Then there are several outside factors which can produce freakishly long drives, such as a strong following wind, downhill terrain or bonehard ground. Where all three of these favourable conditions prevail outstandingly long drives can be achieved. Another consideration is that a long drive made during a tournament is a different proposition from one made for length alone, either on the practice ground, a long driving competition or in a game of no consequence. All this should be borne in mind when considering the long drives shown here.
● When professional Carl Hooper hit a wayward drive on the 3rd hole (456 yards) at the Oak Hills Country Club, San Antonio, during the 1992 Texas Open, he wrote himself into the record books but out of the tournament. The ball kept bouncing and rolling on a tarmac cart path until it was stopped by a fence – 787 yards away. It took Hooper two recovery shots with a 4-iron and then an 8-iron to return to the fairway. He eventually holed out for a double bogey six and failed to survive the half-way qualifying cut.

● Tommie Campbell of Portmarnock hit a drive of 392 yards at Dun Laoghaire GC in July 1964.
● Playing in Australia, American George Bayer is reported to have driven to within chipping distance of a 589 yards hole. *It was certainly a drive of over 500 yards,* said Bayer acknowledging the strong following wind, sharp downslope where his ball landed and the bone-hard ground.
● In September, 1934, over the East Devon course, THV Haydon, Wimbledon, drove to the edge of the 9th green which was a hole of 465 yards, giving a drive of not less than 450 yards.
● EC Bliss drove 445 yards at Herne Bay in August, 1913. The drive was measured by a Government surveyor who also measured the drop in height from tee to resting place of the ball at 57 feet.

Long Carries

● At Sitwell Park, Rotherham, in 1935 the home professional, W Smithson, drove a ball which carried a dyke at 380 yards from the 2nd tee.
● George Bell, of Penrith GC, New South Wales, Australia, using a number 2 wood drove across the Nepean River, a certified carry of 309 yards in a driving contest in 1964.
● After the 1986 Irish Professional Championship at Waterville, Co. Kerry, four long-hitting professionals tried for the longest-carry record over water, across a lake in the Waterville Hotel grounds. Liam Higgins, the local professional, carried 310 yards and Paul Leonard 311, beating the previous record by 2 yards.
● In the 1972 Algarve Open at Penina, Henry Cotton vouched for a carry of 305 yards over a ditch at the 18th hole by long-hitting Spanish professional Francisco Abreu. There was virtually no wind assistance.
● At the Home International matches at Portmarnock in 1949 a driving competition was held in which all the players in all four teams competed. The actual carry was measured and the longest was 280 yards by Jimmy Bruen.
● On 6th April, 1976, Tony Jacklin hit a number of balls into Vancouver harbour, Canada, from the 495-foot high roof of a new building complex. The longest carry was measured at 389 yards.

Long Hitting

There have been numerous long hits, not on golf courses, where an outside agency has assisted the length of the shot. Such an example was a 'drive' by Liam Higgins in 1986, on the Airport runway at Baldonal, near Dublin, of 632 yards.

Longest Albatrosses

● The longest-known albatrosses (three under par) recorded at par 5 holes are:

● 647 yards-2nd hole at Guam Navy Club by Chief Petty Officer Kevin Murray of Chicago on 3rd January, 1982.
● 609 yards-15th hole at Mahaka Inn West Course, Hawaii, by John Eakin of California on 12th November, 1972.
● 602 yards-16th hole at Whiting Field Golf Course, Milton, Florida, by 27-year-old Bill Graham with a drive and a 3-wood, aided by a 25 mph tail wind.
● The longest-known albatrosses in open championships are: 580 yards-14th hole at Crans-sur-Sierre, by American Billy Casper in the 1971 Swiss Open; 558 yards-5th hole at Muirfield by American Johnny Miller in the 1972 Open Championship.
● In the 1994 German Amateur Championship at Wittelsbacher GC, Rohrenfeld, Graham Rankin, a member of the visiting Scottish national team, had a two at the 592-yard 18th.

Eagles (Multiple and Consecutive)

● Wilf Jones scored three consecutive eagles at the first three holes at Moor Hall GC when playing in a competition there on August Bank Holiday Monday 1968. He scored 3, 1, 2 at holes measuring 529 yards, 176 yards and 302 yards.
● In a round of the 1980 Jubilee Cup, a mixed foursomes match play event of Colchester GC, Mrs Nora Booth and her son Brendan scored three consecutive gross eagles of 1, 3, 2 at the 8th, 9th and 10th holes.
● Three players in a four-ball match at Kington GC, Herefordshire, on 22nd July, 1948, all had eagle 2s at the 18th hole (272 yards). They were RN Bird, R Morgan and V Timson.
● Four Americans from Wisconsin on holiday at Gleneagles in 1977 scored three eagles and a birdie at the 300-yard par-4 14th hole on the King's course. The birdie was by Dr Kim Lulloff and the eagles by Dr Gordon Meiklejohn, Richard Johnson and Jack Kubitz.
● In an open competition at Glen Innes GC, Australia on 13th November, 1977, three players in a four-ball scored eagle 3s at the 9th hole (442 metres). They were Terry Marshall, Roy McHarg and Jack Rohleder.
● David McCarthy, a member of Moortown Golf Club, Leeds, had three consecutive eagles (3,3,2) on the 4th, 5th and 6th holes during a Pro-Am competition at Lucerne, Switzerland, on 7th August, 1992.

Speed of Golf Ball and Club Head and Effect of Wind and Temperature

● In *The Search for the Perfect Swing,* a scientific study of the golf swing, a first class golfer is said to have the club head travelling at 100 mph at impact. This will cause the ball to leave the club at 135 mph. An outstandingly long hitter might manage to have the club head travelling at 130 mph which would produce a ball send-off speed of 175 mph. The resultant shot would carry 280 yards.

● According to Thomas Hardman, Wilson's director of research and development, wind will reduce or increase the flight of a golf ball by approximately 1½ yards for every mile per hour of wind. Every two degrees of temperature will make a yard difference in a ball's flight.

Most Northerly Course

● The most northerly course is the Akureyri Golf Club in Iceland which is situated 65°40' North of the equator. Not far south is the Luleö course in Sweden, at 65°35' North.

Most Southerly Course

● Golf's most southerly course is Scott Base Country Club, 13° north of the South Pole. The course is run by the New Zealand Antarctic Programme and players must be kitted in full survival gear. The most difficult aspect is finding the orange golf balls which tend to get buried in the snow. Other obstacles include penguins, seals and skuas. If the ball is stolen by a skua then a penalty of one shot is incurred; but if the ball hits a skua it counts as a birdie.

Highest Golf Courses

● The highest golf course in the world is thought to be the Tuctu GC in Peru which is 14,335 feet above sea-level. High courses are also found in Bolivia with the La Paz GC being about 13,500 feet. In the Himalayas, near the border with Tibet, a 9-hole course at 12,800 feet has been laid out by keen golfers in the Indian Army.

● The highest course in Europe is at Sestriere in the Italian Alps, 6,500 feet above sea-level.

● The highest courses in Great Britain are West Monmouthshire in Wales at 1,513 feet, Leadhills in Scotland at 1,500 feet and Church Stratton in England at 1,250 feet.

Longest Courses

● The longest course in the world is Dub's Dread GC, Piper, Kansas, USA measuring 8,101 yards (par 78).

● The longest course for the Open Championship was 7,252 yards at Carnoustie in 1968.

Longest Holes

● The longest hole in the world, as far as is known, is the 6th hole measuring 782 metres

(860 yards) at Koolan Island GC, Western Australia. The par of the hole is 7. There are several holes over 700 yards throughout the world. At Teyateyaneng, South Africa, one hole measures 619 yards.

● The longest hole for the Open Championship is 577 yards (6th hole) at Royal Troon.

Longest Tournaments

● The longest tournament held was over 144 holes in the World Open at Pinehurst, N Carolina, USA, first held in 1973. Play was over two weeks with a cut imposed at the halfway mark.

● An annual tournament is played in Germany on the longest day of the year, comprising 100 holes' medal play. The best return, in 1995, was 399 strokes.

Largest Entries

The Open – 2,133, Royal Troon, 1997.
The Amateur – 488, St Andrews, 1958.

● US Open – The US Open of 1990 received a record 6,198 entries.

● The largest entry for a PGA European Tour event was 398 for the 1978 Colgate PGA Championship. Since 1985, when the all-exempt ruling was introduced, all PGA tournaments have had 144 competitors, slightly more or less.

● In 1952, Bobby Locke, the Open Champion, played a round at Wentworth, against any golfer in Britain. Cards costing 2s. 6d. each (12½p), were taken out by 24,000 golfers. The challenge was to beat the local par by more than Locke beat the par at Wentworth; 1,641 competitors, including women, succeeded in *beating* the Champion and each received a certificate signed by him. As a result of this challenge the British Golf Foundation benefited to the extent of £3,026, the proceeds from the sale of cards. A similar tournament was held in the United States and Canada when 87,094 golfers participated; 14,667 players bettered Ben Hogan's score under handicap. The fund benefited by $80,024.

Largest Prize Money

● The Machrie Tournament of 1901 was the first tournament with a first prize of £100. It was won by JH Taylor, then Open Champion, who beat James Braid in the final.

● The richest event in the world is currently the Andersen Consulting World Championship of Golf. In 1997–98 it offered prize money of $3,650,000.

● (For prize money in the Open Championship see under Conditions and History of Open Championship.)

Holing-in-One

Odds Against

● At the Wanderers Club, Johannesburg in January, 1951, forty-nine amateurs and professionals each played three balls at a hole 146 yards long. Of the 147 balls hit, the nearest was by Koos de Beer, professional at Reading Country Club, which finished 10½ inches from the hole. Harry Bradshaw, the Irish professional who was touring with the British team in South Africa, touched the pin with his second shot, but the ball rolled on and stopped 3 feet 2 inches from the cup.

● A competition on similar lines was held in 1951 in New York when 1,409 players who had done a hole-in-one held a competition over several days at short holes on three New York golf courses. Each player was allowed a total of five shots, giving an aggregate of 7,045 shots. No player holed-in-one, and the nearest ball finished 3½ inches from the hole.

● A further illustration of the element of luck in holing-in-one is derived from an effort by Harry Gonder, an American professional, who in 1940 stood for 16 hours 25 minutes and hit 1,817 balls trying to do a 160 yard hole-in-one. He had two official witnesses and caddies to tee and retrieve the balls and count the strokes. His 1,756th shot struck the hole but stopped an inch from the hole. This was his nearest effort.

● From this and other similar information an estimate of the odds against holing-in-one at any particular hole within the range of one shot was made at somewhere between 1,500 and 2,000 to 1 by a proficient player. Subsequently, however, statistical analysis in America has come up with the following odds: a male professional or top amateur 3,708 to 1; a female professional or top amateur 4,648 to 1; an average golfer 42,952 to 1.

Hole-in-One First Recorded

● Earliest recorded hole-in-one was in 1868 at the Open Championship when Tom Morris (Young Tom) did the 8th hole 145 yards Prestwick in one stroke. This was the first of four Open Championships won successively by Young Tom.

● The first hole-in-one recorded with the 1.66 in ball was in 1972 by John G Salvesen, a member of the R&A Championship Committee. At the time this size of ball was only experimental. Salvesen used a 7-iron for his historical feat at the 11th hole on the Old Course, St Andrews.

Holing-in-One in Important Events

Since the day of the first known hole-in-one by Tom Morris Jr, at the 8th hole (145 yards) at Prestwick in the 1868 Open Championship, holes-in-one, even in

championships, have become too numerous for each to be recorded. Only where other unusual or interesting circumstances prevailed are the instances shown here.

● All hole-in-one achievements are remarkable. Many are extraordinary. Among the more amazing was that of 2-handicap Leicestershire golfer Bob Taylor, a member of the Scraptoft Club. During the final practice day for the 1974 Eastern Counties Foursomes Championship on the Hunstanton Links, he holed his tee shot with a 1-iron at the 188-yards 16th. The next day, in the first round of the competition, he repeated the feat, the only difference being that because of a change of wind he used a 6-iron. When he stepped on to the 16th tee the following day his partner jokingly offered him odds of 1,000,000 to one against holing-in-one for a third successive time. Taylor again used his 6-iron – and holed in one!

● 1878–Jamie Anderson, competing in the Open Championship at Prestwick, holed the 17th hole in one. Anderson was playing the next to last hole, and though it seemed then that he was winning easily, it turned out afterwards that if he had not taken this hole in one stroke he would very likely have lost. Anderson was just about to make his tee shot when Andy Stuart (winner of the first Irish Open Championship in 1892), who was acting as marker to Anderson, remarked he was standing outside the teeing ground, and that if he played the stroke from there he would be disqualified. Anderson picked up his ball and teed it in a proper place. Then he holed-in-one. He won the Championship by one stroke.

● On a Friday the 13th in 1990, Richard Allen holed-in-one at the 13th at the Barwon Heads Golf Club, Victoria, Australia, and then lost the hole. He was giving a handicap stroke to his opponent, brother-in-law Jason Ennels, who also holed-in-one.

● 1906–R Johnston, North Berwick, competing in the Open Championship, did the 14th hole at Muirfield in one. Johnston played with only one club throughout – an adjustable head club.

● 1959–The first hole-in-one in the US Women's Open Championship was recorded. It was by Patty Berg on the 7th hole (170 yards) at Churchill Valley CC, Pittsburgh.

● 1962–On 6th April, playing in the second round of the Schweppes Close Championship at Little Aston, H Middleton of Shandon Park, Belfast, holed his tee shot at the 159 yards 5th hole, winning a prize of £1,000. Ten minutes later, playing two matches ahead of Middleton, RA Jowle, son of the professional, Frank Jowle, holed his tee shot at the 179 yards 9th hole. As an amateur he was rewarded by the sponsors with a £30 voucher.

● 1963–By holing out in one stroke at the 18th hole (156 yards) at Moor Park on the first day of the Esso Golden round-robin tournament, HR Henning, South Africa, won the £10,000 prize offered for this feat.

● 1967–Tony Jacklin in winning the Masters tournament at St George's, Sandwich, did the 16th hole in one. His ace has an exceptional place in the records for it was seen by millions on TV, the ball in view in its flight till it went into the hole in his final round of 64.

● 1971–John Hudson, 25-year-old professional at Hendon, achieved a near miracle when he holed two consecutive holes-in-one in the Martini Tournament at Norwich. They were at the 11th and 12th holes (195 yards and 311 yards respectively) in the second round.

● 1971–In the Open Championship at Birkdale, Lionel Platts holed-in-one at the 212-yard 4th hole in the second round. This was the first instance of an Open Championship hole-in-one being recorded by television. It was incidentally Platts' seventh ace of his career.

● Nick Faldo's hole-in-one at the 14th in the 1993 Ryder Cup at The Belfry was only the second to be recorded in the history of the match. The other was by Peter Butler at Muirfield's 16th hole in 1973.

● 1973–In the 1973 Open Championship at Troon, two holes-in-one were recorded, both at the 8th hole, known as the Postage Stamp, in the first round. They were achieved by Gene Sarazen and amateur David Russell, who were by coincidence respectively the oldest and youngest competitors.

● Mrs Argea Tissies, whose husband Hermann took 15 at Royal Troon's Postage Stamp 8th hole in the 1950 Open, scored a hole-in-one at the 2nd hole at Punta Ala in the second round of the Italian Ladies' Senior Open of 1978. Exactly five years later on the same date, at the same time of day, in the same round of the same tournament at the same hole, she did it again with the same club.

● In less than two hours play in the second round of the 1989 US Open at Oak Hill Country Club, Rochester, New York, four competitors – Doug Weaver, Mark Wiebe, Jerry Pate and Nick Price – each holed the 167 yards 6th hole in one. The odds against four professionals achieving such a record in a field of 156 are reckoned at 332,000 to 1.

Holing-in-One – Longest Holes

● Bob Mitera, when a 21-year-old American student, standing 5 feet 6 inches and weighing under 12 stones, claimed the world record for the longest hole-in-one. Playing over the appropriately named Miracle Hill course at Omaha, on 7th October, 1965, Bob holed his drive at the 10th hole, 447 yards long. The ground sloped sharply downhill.

● Two longer holes-in-one have been achieved, but because they were at dog-leg holes they are not generally accepted as being the longest holes-in-one. They were 496 yards (17th hole, Teign Valley) by Shaun Lynch in July 1995 and 480 yards (5th hole, Hope CC, Arkansas) by L Bruce on 15th November, 1962.

● In March, 1961, Lou Kretlow holed his tee shot at the 427 yards 16th hole at Lake Hefner course, Oklahoma City, USA.

● The longest known hole-in-one in Great Britain was the 393-yard 7th hole at West Lancashire GC, where in 1972 the assistant professional Peter Parkinson holed his tee shot.

● Other long holes-in-one recorded in Great Britain have been 380 yards (5th hole at Tankersley Park) by David Hulley in 1961; 380 yards (12th hole at White Webbs) by Danny Dunne on 30th July, 1976; 370 yards (17th hole at Chilwell Manor, distance from the forward tee) by Ray Newton in 1977; 365 yards (10th hole at Harewood Downs) by K Saunders in 1965; 365 yards (7th hole at Catterick Garrison GC) by Leslie Bruckner on 18th July, 1980.

● The longest-recorded hole-in-one by a woman was that accomplished in September, 1949 by Marie Robie – the 393-yard hole at Furnace Brook course, Wollaston, Mass, USA.

● In April 1988, Mary Anderson, a bio-chemistry student at Trinity College, Dublin, holed-in-one at the 290-yard 6th hole at the Island GC, Co Dublin.

● In January 1985 Otto Bucher from Switzerland holed-in-one at the age of 99 on La Manga's 130-yard 12th hole.

● Six-year-old Tommy Moore aced the 145-yard fourth hole at Woodbrier, West Virginia, in 1968. He had another at the same hole before his seventh birthday.

● The youngest player ever to achieve a hole in one is now believed to be Matthew Draper, who was only five when he aced the 122-yard fourth hole at Cherwell Edge, Oxfordshire, in June 1997. He used a wood.

Holing-in-One – Greatest Number by One Person

59–Amateur Norman Manley of Long Beach, California.

50–Mancil Davis, professional at the Trophy Club, Forth Worth, Texas.

31–British professional CT le Chevalier who died in 1973.

22–British amateur, Jim Hay of Kirkintilloch GC.

10–Mrs Olga Penman, formerly of Harewood Downs GC.

At One Hole

13–Joe Lucius at 15th hole of Mohawk, Ohio.

5–Left-hander, the late Fred Francis at 7th (now 16th) hole of Cardigan GC.

Holing-in-One – Greatest Frequency

● The greatest number of holes-in-one in a calendar year is 11, by JO Boydstone of California in 1962.

● John Putt of Frilford Heath GC had six holes-in-one in 1970, followed by three in 1971.

● Douglas Porteous, of Ruchill GC, Glasgow, achieved seven holes-in-one in the space of eight months. Four of them were scored in a five-day period from 26th to 30th September, 1974, in three consecutive rounds of golf. The first two were achieved at Ruchill GC in one round, the third there two days later, and the fourth at Clydebank and District GC after another two days. The following May, Porteous had three holes-in-one, the first at Linn Park GC incredibly followed by two more in the one round at Clober GC.

● Mrs Kathleen Hetherington of West Essex has holed-in-one five times, four being at the 15th hole at West Essex. Four of her five aces were within seven months in 1966.

● Mrs Dorothy Hill of Dumfries and Galloway GC holed-in-one three times in 11 days in 1977.

● James C Reid of Brodick, aged 59 and 8 hand-icap in 1987, achieved 14 holes-in-one, all but one on Isle of Arran courses. His success was in spite of severe physical handicaps of a stiff left knee, a damaged right ankle, two discs removed from his back and a hip replacement.

Holing Successive Holes-in-One

● Successive holes-in-one are rare; successive par 4 holes-in-one may be classed as near mir-acles. NL Manley performed the most incredible feat in September, 1964, at Del Valle Country Club, Saugus, California, USA. The par 4 7th (330 yards) and 8th (290 yards) are both slightly downhill, dog-leg holes. Manley had *aces* at both, en route to a course record of 61 (par 71).

● The first recorded example in Britain of a player holing-in-one stroke at each of two succes-sive holes was achieved on 6th February, 1964, at the Walmer and Kingsdown course, Kent. The young assistant professional at that club, Roger Game (aged 17) holed out with a 4-wood at the 244-yard 7th hole, and repeated the feat at the 256-yard 8th hole, using a 5-iron.

● The first occasion of holing-in-one at consecu-tive holes in a major professional event occurred when John Hudson, 25-year-old professional at Hendon, holed-in-one at the 11th and 12th holes at Norwich during the second round of the 1971 Martini tournament. Hudson used a 4-iron at the 195-yard 11th and a driver at the 311-yard down-hill 12th hole.

● Assistant professional Tom Doty (23 years), playing in a friendly match on a course near Chicago in October, 1971, had a remarkable four-hole score which included two consecutive holes-in-one, sandwiched either side by an albatross and an eagle: 4th hole (500 yards)-2; 5th hole (360 yards dog-leg)-1; 6th hole (175 yards)-1; 7th hole (375 yards)-2. Thus he was 10 under par for four consecutive holes.

Holing-in-One Twice (or More) in the Same Round by the Same Person

What might be thought to be a very rare feat indeed – that of holing-in-one twice in the same round – has in fact happened on many occasions as the following instances show. It is, nevertheless, compared to the number of golfers in the world, still something of an outstanding achievement. The first known occasion was in 1907 when J Ireland playing in a three-ball match at Worlington holed the 5th and 18th holes in one stroke and two years later in 1909 HC Josecelyne holed the 3rd (175 yards) and the 14th (115 yards) at Acton on 24th November.

● The first mention of two holes-in-one in a round by a woman is of special note in that it was followed later by a similar feat by another lady at the same club. On 19th May, 1942, Mrs W Driver, of Balgowlah Golf Club, New South Wales, holed out in one at the 3rd and 8th holes in the same round, while on 29th July, 1948, Mrs F Burke at the same club holed out in one at the 2nd and 8th holes.

● The Rev Harold Snider, aged 75, scored his first hole-in-one on 9th June, 1976 at the 8th hole of the Ironwood course, near Phoenix. By the end of his round he had scored three holes-in-one, the other two being at the 13th (110 yards) and 14th (135 yards). Ironwood is a par-3 course, giving more opportunity for scoring holes-in-one, but, nevertheless, three holes-in-one in one round on any type of course is an outstanding achievement.

● When the Hawarden course in North Wales comprised only nine holes, Frank Mills in 1994 had two holes-in-one at the same hole in the same round. Each time, he hit a seven iron to the 134-yard third and 12th.

● The youngest player to achieve two holes-in-one in the same round is thought to be Chris-topher Anthony Jones on 14 September, 1994. At the age of 14 years and 11 months he had holes-in-one at the Sand Moor, Leeds, 137-yard 10th hole and then at the 156-yard 17th.

● The youngest woman to have performed the feat was a 17-year-old, Marjorie Merchant, play-ing at the Lomas Athletic GC, Argentina, at the 4th (170 yards) and 8th (130 yards) holes.

● Tony Hannam, left-handed, handicap 16 and age 71, followed a hole-in-one at the 142 yards 4th of the Bude and North Cornwall Golf Club course with another at the 143 yards 10th on Friday, 18th September, 1992.

Holes-in-One on the Same Day

● In July 1987, at the Skerries Club, Co Dublin, Rank Xerox sponsored two tournaments, a men's 18-hole four-ball with 134 pairs competing and a 9-hole mixed foursomes with 33. During the day each of the four par-3 holes on the course were holed-in-one, the 2nd by Noel Bollard, 5th by

Bart Reynolds, 12th by Jackie Carr and 15th by Gerry Ellis.

Two Holes-in-One at the Same Hole in the Same Game

First in World
● George Stewart and Fred Spellmeyer at the 18th hole, Forest Hills, New Jersey, USA in October 1919.

First in Great Britain
● Miss G Clutterbuck and Mrs HM Robinson at the 15th hole (120 yards), St Augustine GC, Ramsgate, on 8th May, 1925.

First in Denmark
● In a Club match in August 1987 at Himmerland, Steffan Jacobsen of Aalborg and Peter Forsberg of Himmerland halved the 15th hole in one shot, the first known occasion in Denmark.

First in Australia
● Dr & Mrs B Rankine, playing in a mixed 'Canadian foursome' event at the Osmond Club near Adelaide, South Australia in April 1987, holed-in-one in consecutive shots at the 2nd hole (162 metres), he from the men's tee with a 3-iron and his wife from the ladies' tee with a 1½ wood.

Holing-in-One – Miscellaneous Incidents

● Chemistry student Jason Bohn, aged 19, of State College, Pennsylvania, supported a charity golf event at Tuscaloosa, Alabama, in 1992 when twelve competitors were invited to try to hole-in-one at the 135-yard 2nd hole for a special prize covered by insurance. One attempt only was allowed. Bohn succeeded and was offered US$1m (paid at the rate of $5,000 a month for the next 20 years) at the cost of losing his amateur status. He took the money.
● The late Harry Vardon, who scored the greatest number of victories in the Open Championship, only once did a hole-in-one. That was in 1903 at Mundesley, Norfolk, where Vardon was convalescing from a long illness.
● Bob Hope had a hole-in-one at Palm Springs, California, at the age of 90.
● In April 1984 Joseph McCaffrey and his son, Gordon, each holed-in-one in the Spring Medal at the 164-yard 12th hole at Vale of Leven Club, Dunbartonshire.
● In a guest day at Rochford Hundred, Essex, in 1994, there were holes-in-one at all the par threes. First Paul Cairns, of Langdon Hills, holed a 4-iron at the 205-yard 15th, next Paul Francis, a member of the home club, sank a 7-iron at the 156-yard seventh and finally Jim Crabb, of Three Rivers, holed a 9-iron at the 136-yard 11th.
● In 1977, 14-year-old Gillian Field after a series of lessons holed-in-one at the 10th hole at Moor Place GC in her first round of golf.
● By holing-in-one at the 2nd hole in a match against D Graham in the 1979 Suntory World Match Play at Wentworth, Japanese professional Isao Aoki won himself a Bovis home at Gleneagles worth, inclusive of furnishings, £55,000.
● On the morning after being elected captain for 1973 of the Norwich GC, JS Murray hit his first shot as captain straight into the hole at the 169 yards first hole.
● Using the same club and ball, 11-handicap left-hander Christopher Smyth holed-in-one at the 2nd hole (170 yards) in two consecutive medal competitions at Headfort GC, Co Meath, in January, 1976.
● Playing over Rickmansworth course at Easter, 1960, Mrs AE (Paddy) Martin achieved a remarkable sequence of *aces*. On Good Friday she sank her tee shot at the third hole (125 yards). The next day, using the same ball and the same 8-iron, at the same hole, she scored another *one*. And on the Monday (same ball, same club, same hole) she again holed out from the tee.
● Alex Evans, aged eight, holed-in-one with a 4-wood at the 136-yard fourth hole at Bromborough, Merseyside, in 1994.
● In January 1985 Otto Bucher of Switzerland, aged 99, holed-in-one at the 130-yard 12th hole at the La Manga Championship South course in Spain.
● At Barton-on-Sea in February 1989 Mrs Dorothy Huntley-Flindt, aged 91, holed-in-one at the par 3 13th. The following day Mr John Chape, a fellow member in his 80s, holed the par 3 5th in one.
● In 1995 Roy Marsland of Ratho Park, Edinburgh, had three holes in one in nine days: at Prestonfield's fifth, at Ratho Park's third and at Sandilands' second.
● Michael Monk, age 82, a member of Tandridge Golf Club, Surrey, waited until 1992 to record his first hole-in-one. It continued a run of rare successes for his family. In the previous 12 months, Mr Monk's daughter, Elizabeth, 52, daughter-in-law, Celia, 48, and grandson, Jeremy, 16, had all holed in one on the same course.
● Lou Holloway, a left-hander, recorded his second hole-in-one at the Mount Derby course in New Zealand 13 years after acing the same hole while playing right-handed.
● Ryan Procop, an American schoolboy, holed-in-one at a 168-yard par 3 at Glen Eagles GC, Ohio, with a putter. He confessed that he was so disgusted with himself after a 12 on the previous hole that he just grabbed his putter and hit from the tee.
● Ernie and Shirley Marsden, of Warwick Golf Club, are believed in 1993 to have equalled the record for holes-in-one by a married couple. Each has had three, as have another English couple, Mr and Mrs BE Simmonds.

Challenge Matches

One of the first recorded professional challenge matches was in 1843 when Allan Robertson beat Willie Dunn in a 20-round match at St Andrews over 360 holes by 2 rounds and 1 to play. Thereafter until about 1905 many matches are recorded, some for up to £200 a side – a considerable sum for the time. The Morrises, the Dunns and the Parks were the main protagonists until Vardon, Braid and Taylor took over in the 1890s. Often matches were on a home-and-away basis over 72 holes or more, with many spectators; Vardon and Willie Park Jr attracted over 10,000 at North Berwick in 1899.

Between the wars Walter Hagen, Archie Compston, Henry Cotton and Bobby Locke all played several such matches. Compston surprisingly beat Hagen by 18 up and 17 to play at Moor Park in 1928; yet typically Hagen went on to win the Open the following week at Sandwich. Cotton played classic golf at Walton Heath in 1937 when he beat Densmore Shute for £500-a-side at Walton Heath by 6 and 5 over 72 holes.

Curious and Large Wagers
(See also bets recorded under Cross-Country Matches, and in Challenge Matches)

● In the Royal and Ancient Club minutes an entry on 3rd November, 1870 was made in the following terms:
Sir David Moncrieffe, Bart, of Moncrieffe, backs his life against the life of John Whyte-Melville, Esq, of Strathkinnes, for a new silver club as a present to the St Andrews Golf Club, the price of the club to be paid by the survivor and the arms of the parties to be engraved on the club, and the present bet inscribed on it. No balls to be attached to it. In testimony of which this bet is subscribed by the parties thereto.

Thirteen years later, Mr Whyte-Melville, in a feeling and appropriate speech, expressed his deep regret at the lamented death of Sir Robert Moncrieffe, one of the most distinguished and zealous supporters of the club. Whyte-Melville, while lamenting the cause that led to it, had pleasure in fulfilling the duty imposed upon him by the bet, and accordingly delivered to the captain the silver putter. Whyte-Melville in 1883 was elected captain of the club a second time; he died in his eighty-sixth year in July, 1883, before he could take office and the captaincy remained vacant for a year. His portrait hangs in the Royal & Ancient clubhouse and is one of the finest and most distinguished pictures in the smoking room.

● In 1914 Francis Ouimet, who in the previous autumn had won the American Open Championship after a triangular tie with Harry Vardon and Ted Ray, came to Great Britain with Jerome D Travers, the holder of the American amateur title, to compete in the British Amateur Championship at Sandwich. An American syndicate took a bet of £30,000 to £10,000 that one or other of the two United States champions would be the winner. It only took two rounds to decide the bet against the Americans. Ouimet was beaten by a then quite unknown player, HS Tubbs, while Travers was defeated by Charles Palmer, who was fifty-six years of age at the time.

● 1907 John Ball for a wager undertook to go round Hoylake during a dense fog in under 90, in not more than two and a quarter hours and without losing a ball. Ball played with a black ball, went round in 81, and also beat the time.

● The late Ben Sayers, for a wager, played the eighteen holes of the Burgess Society course scoring a four at every hole. Sayers was about to start against an American, when his opponent asked him what he could do the course in. *Fours* replied Sayers, meaning 72, or an average of 4s for the round. A bet was made, then the American added, *Remember a three or a five is not a four.* There were eight bogey 5s and two 3s on the Burgess course at the time Old Ben achieved his feat.

Feats of Endurance

Although golf is not a game where endurance, in the ordinary sense in which the term is employed in sport, is required, there are several instances of feats on the links which demanded great physical exertion.

● Four British golfers, Simon Gard, Nick Harley, Patrick Maxwell and his brother Alastair Maxwell, completed 14 rounds in one day at Iceland's Akureyri Golf Club, the most northern 18-hole course in the world, during June, 1991 when there was 24-hour daylight. It was claimed a record and £10,000 was raised for charity.

● In 1971 during a 24-hour period from 6 pm on 27th November until 5.15 pm on 28th November, Ian Colston completed 401 holes over the 6,061 yards Bendigo course, Victoria, Australia. Colston was a top marathon athlete but was not a golfer. However prior to his golfing marathon he took some lessons and became adept with a 6-iron, the only club he used throughout the 401 holes. The only assistance Colston had was a team of harriers to carry his 6-iron and look for his ball, and a band of motor-cyclists who provided light during the night. This is, as far as is known, the greatest number of holes played in 24 hours on foot on a full-size course.

● In 1934 Col Bill Farnham played 376 holes in 24 hours 10 minutes at the Guildford Lake Course, Guildford, Connecticut, using only a mashie and a putter.

● To raise funds for extending the Skipton GC course from 12 to 18 holes, the club professional, 24-year-old Graham Webster, played 277 holes in the hours of daylight on Monday 20th June,

1977. Playing with nothing longer than a 5-iron he averaged 81 per 18-hole round. Included in his marathon was a hole-in-one.

● Michael Moore, a 7 handicap 26-year-old member of Okehampton GC, completed on foot 15 rounds 6 holes (276 holes) there on Sunday, 25th June, 1972, in the hours of daylight. He started at 4.15 am and stopped at 9.15 pm. The distance covered was estimated at 56 miles.

● On 21st June, 1976, 5-handicapper Sandy Small played 15 rounds (270 holes) over his home course Cosby GC, length 6,128 yards, to raise money for the Society of Physically Handicapped Children. Using only a 5-iron, 9-iron and putter, Small started at 4.10 am and completed his 270th hole at 10.39 pm with the aid of car headlights. His fastest round was his first (40 minutes) and slowest his last (82 minutes). His best round of 76 was achieved in the second round.

● During the weekend of 20th-21st June, 1970, Peter Chambers of Yorkshire completed over 14 rounds of golf over the Scarborough South Cliff course. In a non-stop marathon lasting just under 24 hours, Chambers played 257 holes in 1,168 strokes, an average of 84.4 strokes per round.

● Bruce Sutherland, on the Craiglockhart Links, Edinburgh, started at 8.15 pm on 21st June, 1927, and played almost continuously until 7.30 pm on 22nd June, 1927. During the night four caddies with acetylene lamps lit the way, and lost balls were reduced to a minimum. He completed fourteen rounds. Mr Sutherland, who was a physical culture teacher, never recovered from the physical strain and died a few years later.

● Sidney Gleave, motor-cycle racer, and Ernest Smith, golf professional, Davyhulme Club, Manchester, on 12th June, 1939, played five rounds of golf in five different countries – Scotland, Ireland, Isle of Man, England and Wales. Smith had to play the five rounds under 80 in one day to win the £100 wager. They travelled by plane, and the following was their programme with time taken and Smith's score:

Start – Prestwick St Nicholas (Scotland), 3.40 am. Score 70. Time taken, 1 hour 35 minutes.

2nd Course – Bangor (Ireland), 7.15 am. Score 76. Time taken, 1 hour 30 minutes.

3rd Course – Castletown (Isle of Man), 10.15 am. Score 76. Time taken, 1 hour 40 minutes.

4th Course – Blackpool, Stanley Park (England), 1.30 pm. Score 72. Time taken, 1 hour 55 minutes.

5th Course – Hawarden (Wales), 6 pm. Score 68 (record). Time taken, 2 hours 15 minutes.

● On 19th June, 1995, Ian Botham, the former England cricketer, played four rounds of golf in Ireland, Anglesey, Scotland and England. His playing companions were Gary Price, the professional at Branston, and Tony Wright, owner of Craythorne, Burton-on-Trent, where the last 18

holes were completed. The other courses were St Margaret's, Anglesey and Dumfries & Galloway. Their first round began at 4.30 am and the last was completed at 8.30 pm.

● On Wednesday, 3rd July, 1974, ES Wilson, Whitehead, Co Antrim and Dr GW Donaldson, Newry, Co Down, played a nine-hole match in each of seven countries in the one day. The first 9 holes was at La Moye (Channel Islands) followed by Hawarden (Wales), Chester (England), Turnberry (Scotland), Castletown (Isle of Man), Dundalk (Eire) and Warrenpoint (N Ireland). They started their first round at 4.25 am and their last round at 9.25 pm. Wilson piloted his own plane throughout.

● In June 1986 to raise money for the upkeep of his medieval church, the Rector of Mark with Allerton, Somerset, the Rev Michael Pavey, played a sponsored 18 holes on 18 different courses in the Bath & Wells Diocese. With his partner, the well-known broadcaster on music, Antony Hopkins, they played the 1st at Minehead at 5.55 am and finished playing the 18th at Burnham and Berrow at 6.05 pm. They covered 240 miles in the 'round' including the distances to reach the correct tee for the 'next' hole on each course. Par for the 'round' was 70. Together the pair raised £10,500 for the church.

● To raise funds for the Marlborough Club's centenary year (1988), Laurence Ross, the Club professional, in June 1987, played 8 rounds in 12 hours. Against a par of 72, he completed the 576 holes in 3 under par, playing from back tees and walking all the way.

● As part of the 1992 Centenary Celebrations of the Royal Cinque Ports Golf Club at Deal, Kent, and to support charity, a six-handicap member, John Brazell, played all 37 royal courses in Britain and Ireland in 17 days. He won 22 matches, halved three, lost 12; hit 2,834 shots for an average score of 76.6; lost 11 balls and made 62 birdies. The aim was to raise £30,000 for Leukaemia Research and the Spastics Society.

● To raise more than £500 for the Guide Dogs for the Blind charity in the summer of 1992, Mrs Cheryle Power, a member of the Langley Park Golf Club, Beckenham, Kent, played 100 holes in a day – starting at 5 am and finishing at 8.45 pm.

● David Steele, a former European Tour player, completed 17½ rounds, 315 holes, between 6 am and 9.45 pm in 1993 at the San Roque club near Gibraltar in a total of 1,291 shots. Steele was assisted by a caddie cart and raised £15,000 for charity.

Fastest Rounds

● Dick Kimbrough, 41, completed a round on foot on 8th August, 1972, at North Platte CC, Nebraska (6,068 yards) in 30 minutes 10 seconds. He carried only a 3-iron.

● At Mowbray Course, Cape Town, November 1931, Len Richardson, who had represented South Africa in the Olympic Games, played a round which measured 6,248 yards in 31 minutes 22 seconds.

● The women's all-time record for the fastest round played on a course of at least 5,600 yards is held by Sue Ledger, 20, who completed the East Berks course in 38 minutes 8 seconds, beating the previous record by 17 minutes.

● In April, 1934, after attending a wedding in Bournemouth, Hants, Captain Gerald Moxom hurried to his club, West Hill in Surrey, to play in the captain's prize competition. With daylight fading and still dressed in his morning suit, he went round in 65 minutes and won the competition with a net 71 into the bargain.

● On 14th June, 1922, Jock Hutchison and Joe Kirkwood (Australia) played round the Old Course at St Andrews in 1 hour 20 minutes. Hutchison, out in 37, led by three holes at the ninth and won by 4 and 3.

● Fastest rounds can also take another form – the time taken for a ball to be propelled round 18 holes. The fastest known round of this type is 8 minutes 53.8 seconds on 25th August, 1979 by 42 members at Ridgemount CC Rochester, New York, a course measuring 6,161 yards. The Rules of Golf were observed but a ball was available on each tee; to be driven off the instant the ball had been holed at the preceding hole.

● The fastest round with the same ball took place in January 1992 at the Paradise Golf Club, Arizona. It took only 11 minutes 24 seconds; 91 golfers being positioned around the course ready to hit the ball as soon as it came to rest and then throwing the ball from green to tee.

Curious Scoring

● Tony Blackwell, playing off a handicap of four, broke the course record at Bull Bay, Anglesey, by four strokes when he had a gross 60 (net 56) in winning the club's town trophy in 1996. The course measured 6,217 yards.

● In the third round of the 1994 Volvo PGA Championship at Wentworth, Des Smyth, of Ireland, made birdie twos at each of the four short holes, the second, fifth, 10th and 14th. He also had a two at the second hole in the fourth round.

● RH Corbett, playing in the semi-final of the Tangye Cup at Mullion in 1916, did a score of 27. The remarkable part of Corbett's score was that it was made up of nine successive 3s, bogey being 5, 3, 4, 4, 5, 3, 4, 4, 3.

● At Little Chalfont in June 1985 Adrian Donkersley played six successive holes in 6, 5, 4, 3, 2, 1 from the 9th to the 14th holes against a par of 4, 4, 3, 4, 3, 3.

● On 2nd September, 1920, playing over Torphin, near Edinburgh, William Ingle did the first five holes in 1, 2, 3, 4, 5.

● In the summer of 1970, Keith McMillan, on holiday at Cullen, had a remarkable series of 1, 2, 3, 4, 5 at the 11th to 15th holes.

● Marc Osborne was only 14 years of age when he equalled the Betchworth Park amateur course record with a 66 in July, 1993. He was playing in the Mortimer Cup, a 36-hole medal competition, and had at the time a handicap of 6.8.

● Playing at Addington Palace, July, 1934, Ronald Jones, a member of Hendon Club, holed five consecutive holes in 5, 4, 3, 2, 1.

● Harry Dunderdale of Lincoln GC scored 5, 4, 3, 2, 1 in five consecutive holes during the first round of his club championship in 1978. The hole-in-one was the 7th, measuring 294 yards.

● At the Open Amateur Tournament of the Royal Ashdown Forest in 1936 Bobby Locke in his morning round had a score of 72, accomplishing every hole in 4.

● George Stewart of Cupar had a four at every hole over the Queen's course at Gleneagles despite forgetting to change into his golf shoes and therefore still wearing his street shoes.

● Henry Cotton told of one of the most extraordinary scoring feats ever. With some other professionals he was at Sestrieres in the thirties for the Italian Open Championship and Joe Ezar, a colourful character in those days on both sides of the Atlantic, accepted a wager from a club official – 1,000 lira for a 66 to break the course record; 2,000 for a 65; and 4,000 for a 64. *I'll do 64*, said Ezar, and proceeded to jot down the hole-by-hole score figures he would do next day for that total. With the exception of the ninth and tenth holes where his predicted score was 3, 4 and the actual score was 4, 3, he accomplished this amazing feat exactly as nominated.

● Nick Faldo scored par figures at all 18 holes in the final round of the 1987 Open Championship at Muirfield to win the title.

● During the Colts Championship at Knowle Golf Club, Bristol, Chris Newman (Cotswold Hills) scored eight consecutive 3s with birdies at four of the holes.

High Scores

● In the qualifying competition at Formby for the 1976 Open Championship, Maurice Flitcroft, a 46-year-old crane driver from Barrow-in-Furness, took 121 strokes for the first round and then withdrew saying, *I have no chance of qualifying.* Flitcroft entered as a professional but had never before played 18 holes. He had taken the game up 18 months previously but, as he was not a member of a club, had been limited to practising on a local beach. His round was made up thus: 7, 5, 6, 6, 6, 6, 12, 6, 7-61; 11, 5, 6, 8, 4, 9, 5, 7, 5-60, total 121. After his round Flitcroft said, *I've made a lot of progress in the last few months and I'm sorry I did not do better. I was trying too hard at the beginning but began to put things together at the end of the round.* R & A officials, who were not amused by the bogus professional's efforts, refunded the £30 entry money to Flitcroft's two fellow-competitors.

● Playing in the qualifying rounds of the 1965 Open Championship at Southport, an American self-styled professional entrant from Milwaukee, Walter Danecki, achieved the inglorious feat of scoring a total of 221 strokes for 36 holes, 81 over par. His first round over the Hillside course was 108, followed by a second round of 113. Walter, who afterwards admitted he felt *a little discouraged and sad*, declared that he entered because he was *after the money.*

● The highest individual scoring ever known in the rounds connected with the Open Championship occurred at Muirfield, 1935, when a Scottish professional started 7, 10, 5, 10, and took 65 to reach the 9th hole. Another 10 came at the 11th and the player decided to retire at the 12th hole. There he was in a bunker, and after playing four shots he had not regained the fairway.

● In 1883 in the Open Championship at Musselburgh, Willie Fernie, the winner, had a 10, the only time double figures appeared on the card of the Open Champion of the year. Fernie won after a tie with Bob Ferguson, and his score for the last hole in the tie was 2. He holed from just off the green to win by one stroke.

● In the first Open Championship at Prestwick in 1860 a competitor took 21, the highest score for one hole ever recorded in this event. The record is preserved in the archives of the Prestwick Golf Club, where the championship was founded.

● In the first round of the 1980 US Masters, Tom Weiskopf hit his ball into the water hazard in front of the par-3 12th hole five times and scored 13 for the hole.

● In the French Open at St Cloud, in 1968, Brian Barnes took 15 for the short 8th hole in the second round. After missing putts at which he hurriedly snatched while the ball was moving he penalised himself further by standing astride the line of a putt. The amazing result was that he actually took 12 strokes from about three feet from the hole.

● US professional Dave Hill 6-putted the fifth green at Oakmont in the 1962 US Open Championship.

● Many high scores have been made at the Road Hole at St Andrews. Davie Ayton, on one occasion, was coming in a certain winner of the Open Championship when he got on the road and took 11. In 1921, at the Open Championship, one professional took 13. In 1923, competing for the Autumn Medal of the Royal & Ancient, JB Anderson required a five and a four to win the second award, but he took 13 at the Road Hole. Anderson was close to the green in two, was twice in the

bunkers in the face of the green, and once on the road. In 1935, RH Oppenheimer tied for the Royal Medal (the first award) in the Autumn Meeting of the Royal & Ancient. On the play-off he was one stroke behind Captain Aitken when they stood on the 17th tee. Oppenheimer drove three balls out of bounds and eventually took 11 to the Road Hole.

● British professional Mark James scored 111 in the second round of the 1978 Italian Open. He played the closing holes with only his right hand due to an injury to his left hand.

● In the 1927 Shawnee Open, Tommy Armour took 23 strokes to the 17th hole. Armour had won the American Open Championship a week earlier. In an effort to play the hole in a particular way, Armour hooked ball after ball out of bounds and finished with a 21 on the card. There was some doubt about the accuracy of this figure and on reaching the clubhouse Armour stated that it should be 23. This is the highest score by a professional in a tournament.

Freak Matches

● In 1912, the late Harry Dearth, an eminent vocalist, attired in a complete suit of heavy armour, played a match at Bushey Hall. He was beaten 2 and 1.

● In 1914, at the start of the First World War, JN Farrar, a native of Hoylake, was stationed at Royston, Herts. A bet was made of 10-1 that he would not go round Royston under 100 strokes, equipped in full infantry marching order, water bottle, full field kit and haversack. Farrar went round in 94. At the camp were several golfers, including professionals, who tried the same feat but failed.

● Captain Pennington, who was killed in an air crash in 1933, took part in a match *from the air* against AJ Young, the professional at Sonning. Captain Pennington, with 80 golf balls in the locker of his machine, had to find the Sonning greens by dropping the balls as he circled over the course. The balls were covered in white cloth to ensure that they did not bounce once they struck the ground. The airman completed the course in 40 minutes, taking 29 *strokes*, while Young occupied two hours for his round of 68.

● In April 1924, at Littlehampton, Harry Rowntree, an amateur golfer, played the better ball of Edward Ray and George Duncan, receiving an allowance of 150 yards to use as he required during the round. Rowntree won by 6 and 5 and had used only 50 yards 2 feet of his handicap. At one hole Duncan had a two – Rowntree, who was 25 yards from the hole, took this distance from his handicap and won the hole in one. Ray (died 1945) afterwards declared that, conceded a handicap of one yard per round, he could win every championship in the world. And he might, when reckoning is taken of the number of times a putt just stops an inch or two or how much difference to a shot three inches will make for the lie of the ball, either in a bunker or on the fairway. Many single matches on the same system have been played. An 18 handicap player opposed to a scratch player should make a close match with an allowance of 50 yards.

● The first known instance of a golf match by telephone occurred in 1957, when the Cotswold Hills Golf Club, Cheltenham, England, won a golf tournament against the Cheltenham Golf Club, Melbourne, Australia, by six strokes. A large crowd assembled at the English club to wait for the 12,000 miles telephone call from Australia. The match had been played at the suggestion of a former member of the Cotswold Hills Club, Harry Davies, and was open to every member of the two clubs. The result of the match was decided on the aggregate of the eight best scores on each side and the English club won by 564 strokes to 570.

Golf Matches Against Other Sports

● HH Hilton and Percy Ashworth, many times racket champion, contested a driving match, the former driving a golf ball with a driver, and the latter a racket ball with a racket. Best distances: Against breeze – Golfer 182 yards; Racket player 125 yards. Down wind – Golfer 230 yards; Racket player 140 yards. Afterwards Ashworth hit a golf ball with the racket and got a greater distance than with the racket ball, but was still a long way behind the ball driven by Hilton.

● In 1913, at Wellington, Shropshire, a match between a golfer and a fisherman casting a 2½ oz weight was played. The golfer, Rupert May, took 87; the fisherman JJD Mackinlay, in difficulty because of his short casts, 102. His longest cast, 105 yards, was within 12 yards of the world record at the time, held by French angler, Decautelle. When within a rod's length of a hole he ran the weight to the rod end and dropped into the hole. Five times he broke his line, and was allowed another shot without penalty.

● In December, 1913, FMA Webster, of the London Athletic Club, and Dora Roberts, with javelins, played a match with the late Harry Vardon and Mrs Gordon Robertson, who used the regulation clubs and golf balls. The golfers conceded two-thirds in the matter of distance, and they won by 5 up and 4 to play in a contest of 18 holes. The javelin throwers had a mark of two feet square in which to *hole out* while the golfers had to get their ball into the ordinary golf hole. Mr Webster's best throw was one of 160 feet.

● Several matches have taken place between a golfer on the one side and an archer on the other. The wielder of the bow and arrow has nearly always proved the victor. In 1953 at Kirkhill Golf Course, Lanarkshire, five archers beat six golfers by two games to one. There were two special rules for the match; when an archer's arrow landed six feet from the hole or the golfer's ball three feet from the hole, they were counted as holed. When the arrows landed in bunkers or in the rough, archers lifted their arrow and added a stroke. The sixth archer in this match called off and one archer shot two arrows from each of the 18 tees.

● In 1954, at the Southbroom Club, South Africa, a match over 9 holes was played between an archer and a fisherman against two golfers. The participants were all champions of their own sphere and consisted of Vernon Adams (archer), Dennis Burd (fisherman), Jeanette Wahl (champion of Southbroom and Port Shepstone), and Ron Burd (professional at Southbroom). The conditions were that the archer had holed out when his arrows struck a small leather bag placed on the green beside the hole and in the event of his placing his approach shot within a bow's length of the pin he was deemed to have 1-putted. The fisherman, to achieve a 1-putt, had to land his sinker within a rod's length of the pin. The two golfers were ahead for brief spells, but it was the opposition who led at the deciding 9th hole where *Robin Hood* played a perfect approach for a birdie.

● An *Across England* combined match was begun on 11th October, 1965, by four golfers and two archers from Crowborough Beacon Golf Club, Sussex, accompanied by *Penny*, a white Alsatian dog, whose duty it was to find lost balls. They teed off from Carlisle Castle via Hadrian's Wall, the Pennine Way, finally holing out in the 18th hole at Newcastle United Golf Club in 612 teed shots. Casualties included 110 lost golf balls and 19 lost or broken arrows. The match took five-and-a-half days, and the distance travelled was about 60 miles. The golfers were Miss P Ward, K Meaney, K Ashdown and CA Macey; the archers were WH Hulme and T Scott. The first arrow was fired from the battlements of Carlisle Castle, a distance of nearly 300 yards, by Cumberland Champion R Willis, who also fired the second arrow right across the River Eden. R Clough, president of Newcastle United GC, holed the last two putts. The match was in aid of *Guide Dogs for the Blind* and *Friends of Crowborough Hospital.*

Cross-country Matches

● Taking 1 year, 114 days, Floyd Rood golfed his way from coast to coast across the United States. He took 114,737 shots including 3,511 penalty shots for the 3,397 mile course.

● Two Californian teenagers, Bob Aube (17) and Phil Marrone (18) went on a golfing safari in 1974 from San Francisco to Los Angeles, a trip of over 500 miles lasting 16 days. The first six days they played alongside motorways. Over 1,000 balls were used.

● In 1830, the Gold Medal winner of the Royal

& Ancient backed himself for 10 sovereigns to drive from the 1st hole at St Andrews to the toll bar at Cupar, distance nine miles, in 200 teed shots. He won easily.

● In 1848, two Edinburgh golfers played a match from Bruntsfield Links to the top of Arthur's Seat – an eminence overlooking the Scottish capital, 822 feet above sea level.

● On a winter's day in 1898, Freddie Tait backed himself to play a gutta ball in 40 teed shots from Royal St George's Clubhouse, Sandwich, to the Cinque Ports Club, Deal. He was to hole out by hitting any part of the Deal Clubhouse. The distance as the crow flies was three miles. The redoubtable Tait holed out with his 32nd shot, so effectively that the ball went through a window.

● In 1900 three members of the Hackensack (NJ) Club played a game of four-and-a-half hours over an extemporised course six miles long, which stretched from Hackensack to Paterson. Despite rain, cornfields, and wide streams, the three golfers – JW Hauleebeek, Dr ER Pfaare, and Eugene Crassons – completed the round, the first and the last named taking 305 strokes each, and Dr Pfaare 327 strokes. The players used only two clubs, the mashie and the cleek.

● On 3rd December, 1920, P Rupert Phillips and W Raymond Thomas teed up on the first tee of the Radyr Golf Club and played to the last hole at Southerndown. The distance as the crow flies was 15¹/₂ miles, but circumventing swamps, woods, and plough, they covered, approximately, 20 miles. The wager was that they would not do the hole in 1,000 strokes, but they holed out at their 608th stroke two days later. They carried large ordnance maps.

● On 12th March, 1921, A Stanley Turner, Macclesfield, played from his house to the Cat and Fiddle Inn, five miles distance, in 64 strokes. The route was broken and hilly with a rise of nearly 1,000 feet. Turner was allowed to tee up within two club lengths after each shot and the wagering was 6-4 against his doing the distance in 170 strokes.

● In 1919, a golfer drove a ball from Piccadilly Circus and, proceeding via the Strand, Fleet Street and Ludgate Hill, *holed out* at the Royal Exchange, London. The player drove off at 8 am on a Sunday, a time when the usually thronged thoroughfares were deserted.

● On 23rd April, 1939, Richard Sutton, a London stockbroker, played from Tower Bridge, London, to White's Club, St James's Street, in 142 strokes. The bet was he would not do *the course* in under 200 shots. Sutton used a putter, crossed the Thames at Southwark Bridge, and hit the ball short distances to keep out of trouble.

● Golfers produced the most original event in Ireland's three-week national festival of An Tostal, in 1953 – a cross-country competition with an advertised £1,000,000 for the man who could hole out in one. The 150 golfers drove off from the first tee at Kildare Club to hole out eventually on the 18th green, five miles away, on the nearby Curragh course, a distance of 8,800 yards. The unusual hazards to be negotiated included the main Dublin-Cork railway line and highway, the Curragh Racecourse, hoofprints left by Irish thoroughbred racehorses out exercising on the plains from nearby stables, army tank tracks and about 150 telephone lines. The Golden Ball Trophy, which is played for annually – a standard size golf ball in gold, mounted on a black marble pillar beside the silver figure of a golfer on a green marble base, designed by Captain Maurice Cogan, Army GHQ, Dublin – was for the best gross. And it went to one of the longest hitters in international golf – Amateur Champion, Irish internationalist and British Walker Cup player Joe Carr, with the remarkable score of 52.

● In 1961, as a University Charities Week stunt, four Aberdeen University students set out to golf their way up Ben Nevis (4,406 feet). About halfway up, after losing 63 balls and expending 659 strokes, the quartet conceded victory to Britain's highest mountain.

● Among several cross-country golfing exploits, one of the most arduous was faced by Iain Williamson and Tony Kent, who teed off from Cained Point on the summit of Fairfield in the Lake District. With the hole cut in the lawn of the Bishop of Carlisle's home at Rydal Park, it measured 7,200 yards and passed through the summits of Great Rigg Mann, Heron Pike and Nab Scar, descending altogether 1,900 feet. Eight balls were lost and the two golfers holed out in a combined total of 303 strokes.

Long-lived Golfers

● James Priddy, aged 80, played in the Seniors' Open at his home club, Weston-super-Mare, Avon, on 27th June, 1990, and scored a gross 70 to beat his age by 10 shots.

● The oldest golfer who ever lived is believed to have been Arthur Thompson of British Columbia, Canada. He equalled his age when 103 at Uplands GC, a course of over 6,000 yards. He died two years later.

● Nathaniel Vickers celebrated his 103rd birthday on Sunday, 9th October, 1949, and died the following day. He was the oldest member of the United States Senior Golf Association and until 1942 he competed regularly in their events and won many trophies in the various age divisions. When 100 years old, he apologised for being able to play only 9 holes a day. Vickers predicted he would live until 103 and he died a few hours after he had celebrated his birthday.

● American George Miller, who died in 1979 aged 102, played regularly when 100 years old.

● Phyllis Tidmarsh, aged 90, won a Stableford competition at Saltford Golf Club, near Bath, when she returned 42 points. Her handicap was cut from 28 to 27.

● George Swanwick, a member of Wallasey, celebrated his 90th birthday with a luncheon at the club on 1st April, 1971. He played golf several times a week, carrying his own clubs and had holed-in-one at the ages of 75 and 85. His ambition was to complete the sequence aged 95 . . . but he died in 1973 aged 92.

● The 10th Earl of Wemyss played a round on his 92nd birthday, in 1910, at Craigielaw. At the age of 87 the Earl was partnered by Harry Vardon in a match at Kilspindie, the golf course on his East Lothian estate at Gosford. After playing his ball the venerable earl mounted a pony and rode to the next shot. He died on 30th June, 1914.

● FL Callender, aged 78, in September 1932, played nine consecutive rounds in the Jubilee Vase, St Andrews. He was defeated in the ninth, the final round, by 4 and 2. Callender's handicap was 12. This is the best known achievement of a septuagenarian in golf.

● Bernard Matthews, aged 82, of Banstead Downs Club, handicap 6, holed the course in 72 gross in August 1988. A week later he holed it in 70, twelve shots below his age. He came back in 31, finishing 4, 3, 3, 2, 3, against a par of 5, 4, 3, 3, 4. Mr Matthews's eclectic score at his Club is 37, or one over 2's.

Playing in the Dark

On numerous occasions it has been necessary to hold lamps, lighted candles, or torches at holes in order that players might finish a competition. Large entries, slow play, early darkness and an eclipse of the sun have all been causes of playing in darkness.

● Since 1972, the Whitburn Golf Club at South Shields, Tyne and Wear, has held an annual Summer Solstice Competition. All competitors, who draw lots for starting tees, must begin before 4.24 and 13 seconds am, the time the sun rises over the first hole on the longest day of the year.

● At the Open Championship in Musselburgh in November 1889 many players finished when the light had so far gone that the adjacent street lamps were lit. The cards were checked by candlelight. Several players who had no chance of the championship were paid small sums to withdraw in order to permit others who had a chance to finish in daylight. This was the last championship at Musselburgh.

● At the Southern Section of the PGA tournament on 25th September, 1907, at Burnham Beeches, several players concluded the round by the aid of torch lights placed near the holes.

● In the Irish Open Championship at Portmarnock in September, 1907, a tie in the third round between WC Pickeman and A Jeffcott was postponed owing to darkness, at the 22nd hole. The next morning Pickeman won at the 24th.

● The qualifying round of the American Amateur Championship in 1910 could not be finished in one day, and several competitors had to stop their round on account of darkness, and complete it early in the morning of the following day.

● On 10th January, 1926, in the final of the President's Putter, at Rye, EF Storey and RH Wethered were all square at the 24th hole. It was 5 pm and so dark that, although a fair crowd was present, the balls could not be followed. The tie was abandoned and the Putter held jointly for the year. Each winner of the Putter affixes the ball he played; for 1926 there are two balls, respectively engraved with the names of the finalists.

● In the 1932 Walker Cup contest at Brooklyn, a total eclipse of the sun occurred.

● At Perth, on 14th September, 1932, a competition was in progress under good clear evening light, and a full bright moon. The moon rose at 7.10 and an hour later came under eclipse to the earth's surface. The light then became so bad that on the last three greens competitors holed out by the aid of the light from matches.

● At Carnoustie, 1932, in the competition for the *Craw's Nest* the large entry necessitated competitors being sent off in 3-ball matches. The late players had to be assisted by electric torches flashed on the greens.

● In February, 1950, Max Faulkner and his partner, R Dolman, in a Guildford Alliance event finished their round in complete darkness. A photographer's flash bulbs were used at the last hole to direct Faulkner's approach. Several of the other competitors also finished in darkness. At the last hole they had only the light from the clubhouse to aim at and one played his approach so boldly that he put his ball through the hall doorway and almost into the dressing room.

● On the second day of the 1969 Ryder Cup contest, the last 4-ball match ended in near total darkness on the 18th green at Royal Birkdale. With the help of the clubhouse lights the two American players, Lee Trevino and Miller Barber, along with Tony Jacklin for Britain each faced putts of around five feet to win their match. All missed and their game was halved.

The occasions mentioned above all occurred in competitions where it was not intended to play in the dark. There are, however, numerous instances where players set out to play in the dark either for bets or for novelty.

● On 29th November, 1878, RW Brown backed himself to go round the Hoylake links in 150 strokes, starting at 11 pm. The conditions of the match were that Mr Brown was only to be penalised *loss of distance* for a lost ball, and that no one was to help him to find it. He went round in 147 strokes, and won his bet by the narrow margin of three strokes.

● In 1876 David Strath backed himself to go round St Andrews under 100, in moonlight. He took 95, and did not lose a ball.

● In September 1928, at St Andrews, the first and last holes were illuminated by lanterns, and at 11 pm four members of the Royal and Ancient set out to play a foursome over the 2 holes. Electric lights, lanterns, and rockets were used to brighten the fairway, and the headlights of motor cars parked on Links Place formed a helpful battery. The 1st hole was won in four, and each side got a five at the 18th. About 1,000 spectators followed the freak match, which was played to celebrate the appointment of Angus Hambro to the captaincy of the club.

● In 1931, Rufus Stewart, professional, Kooyonga Club, South Australia, and former Australian Open Champion, played 18 holes of exhibition golf at night without losing a single ball over the Kooyonga course, and completed the round in 77.

● At Ashley Wood Golf Club, Blandford, Dorset, a night-time golf tournament was arranged annually with up to 180 golfers taking part over four nights. Over £6000 has been raised in four years for the Muscular Dystrophy Charity.

● At Pannal, 3rd July, 1937, RH Locke, playing in bright moonlight, holed his tee shot at the 15th hole, distance 220 yards, the only known case of holing-in-one under such conditions.

Fatal and Other Accidents on the Links

The history of golf is, unfortunately, marred by a great number of fatal accidents on or near the course. In the vast majority of such cases they have been caused either by careless swinging of the club or by an uncontrolled shot when the ball has struck a spectator or bystander. In addition to the fatal accidents there is an even larger number on record which have resulted in serious injury or blindness. We do not propose to list these accidents except where they have some unusual feature. We would remind all golfers of the tragic consequences which have so often been caused by momentary carelessness. The fatal accidents which follow have an unusual cause and other accidents given may have their humorous aspect.

● English tournament professional Richard Boxall was three shots off the lead in the third round of the 1991 Open Championship when he fractured his left leg driving from the 9th tee at Royal Birkdale. He was taken from the course to hospital by ambulance and was listed in the official results as 'retired' which entitled him to a consolation prize of £3000.

A month later, Russell Weir of Scotland, was competing in the European Teaching Professionals' Championship near Rotterdam when he also fractured his left leg driving from the 7th tee in the first round.

● In July, 1971, Rudolph Roy, aged 43, was killed at a Montreal course; in playing out of woods, the shaft of his club snapped, rebounded off a tree and the jagged edge plunged into his body.

● Harold Wallace, aged 75, playing at Lundin Links with two friends in 1950, was crossing the railway line which separates the fifth green and sixth tee, when a light engine knocked him down and he was killed instantly.

● In the summer of 1963, Harold Kalles, of Toronto, Canada, died six days after his throat had been cut by a golf club shaft, which broke against a tree as he was trying to play out of a bunker.

● At Jacksonville, Florida, on 18th March, 1952, two women golfers were instantly killed when hit simultaneously by the whirling propeller of a navy fighter plane. They were playing together when the plane with a dead engine coming in out of control, hit them from behind.

● In May, 1993, at Ponoka Community GC, Alberta, Canada, Richard McCulough hit a poor tee shot on the 13th hole and promptly smashed his driver angrily against a golf cart. The head of the driver and six inches of shaft flew through the air, piercing McCulough's throat and severing his carotoid artery. He died in hospital.

● Britain's first national open event for competitors aged over 80, at Moortown, Leeds in September, 1992, was marred when 81-year-old Frank Hart collapsed on the fourth tee and died. Play continued and Charles Mitchell, aged 80, won the Stableford competition with a gross score of 81 for 39 points.

● Playing in the 1993 Carlesburg-Tetley Cornish Festival at Tehidy Park, Ian Cornwell was struck on the leg by a wayward shot from a player two groups behind. Later, as he was leaving the 16th green, he was hit again, this time below the ear, by the same player, knocking him unconscious. This may be the first time that a player has been hit twice in the same round by the same player.

Lightning on the Links

There have been a considerable number of fatal and serious accidents through players and caddies having been struck by lightning on the course. The Royal & Ancient and the USGA have, since 1952, provided for discontinuance of play during lightning storms under the Rules of Golf (Rule 37, 6) and the United States Golf Association has given the following guide for personal safety during thunderstorms:

(a) Do not go out of doors or remain out during thunderstorms unless it is necessary. Stay inside of a building where it is dry, preferably away from fireplaces, stoves, and other metal objects.

(b) If there is any choice of shelter, choose in the following order:
   1. Large metal or metal-frame buildings.
   2. Dwellings or other buildings which are protected against lightning.

3. Large unprotected buildings.
4. Small unprotected buildings.

(c) If remaining out of doors is unavoidable, keep away from:
1. Small sheds and shelters if in an exposed location.
2. Isolated trees.
3. Wire fences.
4. Hilltops and wide open spaces.

(d) Seek shelter in:
1. A cave.
2. A depression in the ground.
3. A deep valley or canyon.
4. The foot of a steep or overhanging cliff.
5. Dense woods.
6. A grove of trees.

Note – Raising golf clubs or umbrellas above the head is dangerous.

● A serious incident with lightning involving well-known golfers was at the 1975 Western Open in Chicago when Lee Trevino, Jerry Heard and Bobby Nichols were all struck and had to be taken to hospital. At the same time Tony Jacklin had a club thrown 15 feet out of his hands.

● Two well-known competitors were struck by lightning in European events in 1977. They were Mark James of Britain in the Swiss Open and Severiano Ballesteros of Spain in the Scandinavian Open. Fortunately neither appeared to be badly injured.

● Two spectators were killed by lightning at the US Open and US PGA Championships in 1991.

Spectators Interfering with Balls

● Deliberate interference by spectators with balls in play during important money matches was not unknown in the old days when there was intense rivalry between the *schools* of Musselburgh, St Andrews, and North Berwick, and disputes arose in stake matches caused by the action of spectators in kicking the ball into either a favourable or an unfavourable position.

● Tom Morris, in his last match with Willie Park at Musselburgh, refused to go on because of interference by the spectators, and in the match on the same course about 40 years later, in 1895, between Willie Park Jr and JH Taylor, the barracking of the crowd and interference with play was so bad that when the Park-Vardon match came to be arranged in 1899, Vardon refused to accept Musselburgh as a venue.

● Even in modern times spectators have been known to interfere deliberately with players' balls, though it is usually by children. In the 1972 Penfold Tournament at Queen's Park, Bournemouth, Christy O'Connor Jr had his ball stolen by a young boy, but not being told of this at the time had to take the penalty for a lost ball. O'Connor finished in a tie for first place, but lost the play-off.

● In 1912 in the last round of the final of the Amateur Championship at Westward Ho! between Abe Mitchell and John Ball, the drive of the former to the short 14th hit an open umbrella held by a lady protecting herself from the heavy rain, and instead of landing on the green the ball was diverted into a bunker. Mitchell, who was leading at the time by 2 holes, lost the hole and Ball won the Championship at the 38th hole.

● In the match between the professionals of Great Britain and America at Southport in 1937 a dense crowd collected round the 15th green waiting for the Sarazen-Alliss match. The American's ball landed in the lap of a woman, who picked it up and threw it so close to the hole that Sarazen got a two against Alliss' three.

● In a memorable tie between Bobby Jones and Cyril Tolley in the 1930 Amateur Championship at St Andrews, Jones' approach to the 17th green struck spectators massed at the left end of the green and led to controversy as to whether it would otherwise have gone on to the famous road. Jones himself had deliberately played for that part of the green and had requested stewards to get the crowd back. Had the ball gone on to the road, the historic Jones Quadrilateral of the year – the Open and Amateur Championships of Britain and the United States – might not have gone into the records.

● In the 1983 Suntory World Match Play Championship at Wentworth Nick Faldo hit his second shot over the green at the 16th hole into a group of spectators. To everyone's astonishment and discomfiture the ball reappeared on the green about 30 ft from the hole, propelled there by a thoroughly misguided and anonymous spectator. The referee ruled that Faldo play the ball where it lay on the green. Faldo's opponent, Graham Marsh, understandably upset by the incident, took three putts against Faldo's two, thus losing a hole he might well otherwise have won. Faldo won the match 2 and 1, but lost in the final to Marsh's fellow Australian Greg Norman by 3 and 2.

Golf Balls Killing Animals and Fish, and Incidents with Animals

● An astounding fatality to an animal through being hit by a golf ball occurred at St Margaret's-at-Cliffe Golf Club, Kent on 13th June, 1934, when WJ Robinson, the professional, killed a cow with his tee shot to the 18th hole. The cow was standing in the fairway about 100 yards from the tee, and the ball struck her on the back of the head. She fell like a log, but staggered to her feet and walked about 50 yards before dropping again. When the players reached her she was dead.

● JW Perret, of Ystrad Mynach, playing with Chas R Halliday, of Ralston, in the qualifying rounds of the Society of One Armed Golfers' Championship over the Darley course, Troon, on 27th August, 1935, killed two gulls at successive holes with his second shots. The *deadly* shots were at the 1st and 2nd holes.

● On the first day of grouse shooting of the 1975 season (12th August), 11-year-old schoolboy Willie Fraser, of Kingussie, beat all the guns when he killed a grouse with his tee shot on the local course.

● On 10th June, 1904, while playing in the Edinburgh High Constables' Competition at Kilspindie, Captain Ferguson sent a long ball into the rough at the Target hole, and on searching for it found that it had struck and killed a young hare.

● Playing in a mixed open tournament at the Waimairi Beach Golf Club in Christchurch, New Zealand, in the summer of 1961, Mrs RT Challis found her ball in fairly long spongy grass where a placing rule applied. She picked up, placed the ball and played her stroke. A young hare leaped into the air and fell dead at her feet. She had placed the ball on the leveret without seeing it and without disturbing it.

● In 1906 in the Border Championship at Hawick, a gull and a weasel were killed by balls during the afternoon's play.

● A golfer at Newark, in May, 1907, drove his ball into the river. The ball struck a trout 2lb in weight and killed it.

● On 24th April, 1975, at Scunthorpe GC, Jim Tollan's drive at the 14th hole, called *The Mallard*, struck and killed a female mallard duck in flight. The duck was stuffed and is displayed in the Scunthorpe Clubhouse.

● A Samuel, Melbourne Club, at Sandringham, was driving with an iron club from the 17th tee, when a kitten, which had been playing in the long grass, sprang suddenly at the ball. Kitten and club arrived at the objective simultaneously, with the result that the kitten took an unexpected flight through the air, landing some 20 yards away.

● As Susan Rowlands was lining up a vital putt in the closing stages of the final of the 1978 Welsh Girls' Championship at Abergele, a tiny mouse scampered up her trouser leg. After holing the putt, the mouse ran down again. Susan, who won the final admitted that she fortunately had not known it was there.

Interference by Birds and Animals

● Crows, ravens, hawks and seagulls frequently carry off golf balls, sometimes dropping the ball actually on the green, and it is a common incident for a cow to swallow a golf ball. A plague of crows on the Liverpool course at Hoylake was addicted to golf balls – they stole 26 in one day – selecting only new balls. It was suggested that members should carry shotguns as a 15th club!

● A match was approaching a hole in a rather low-lying course, when one of the players made a crisp chip from about 30 yards from the hole. The ball trickled slowly across the green and

eventually disappeared into the hole. After a momentary pause, the ball was suddenly ejected on to the green, and out jumped a large frog.

● A large black crow named Jasper which frequented the Lithgow GC in New South Wales, Australia, stole 30 golf balls in the club's 1972 Easter Tournament.

● As Mrs Molly Whitaker was playing from a bunker at Beachwood course, Natal, South Africa, a large monkey leaped from a bush and clutched her round the neck. A caddie drove it off by clipping it with an iron club.

● In Massachusetts a goose, having been hit rather hard by a golf ball which then came to rest by the side of a water hazard, took revenge by waddling over to the ball and kicking it into the water.

● In the summer of 1963, SC King had a good drive to the 10th hole at the Guernsey Club. His partner, RW Clark, was in the rough, and King helped him to search. Returning to his ball, he found a cow eating it. Next day, at the same hole, the positions were reversed, and King was in the rough. Clark placed his woollen hat over his ball, remarking, *I'll make sure the cow doesn't eat mine.* On his return he found the cow thoroughly enjoying his hat; nothing was left but the pom-pom.

Armless, One-armed, Legless and Ambidextrous Players

● In September, 1933, at Burgess Golfing Society of Edinburgh, the first championship for one-armed golfers was held. There were 43 entries and 37 of the competitors had lost an arm in the 1914-18 war. Play was over two rounds and the championship was won by WE Thomson, Eastwood, Glasgow, with a score of 169 (82 and 87) for two rounds. The Burgess course was 6,300 yards long. Thomson drove the last green, 260 yards. The championship and an international match are played annually.

● In the Boys' Amateur Championship 1923, at Dunbar and 1949 at St Andrews, there were competitors each with one arm. The competitor in 1949, RP Reid, Cupar, Fife, who lost his arm working a machine in a butcher's shop, got through to the third round.

● There have been cases of persons with no arms playing golf. One, Thomas McAuliffe, who held the club between his right shoulder and cheek, once went round Buffalo CC, USA, in 108.

● Group Captain Bader, who lost both legs in a flying accident prior to the World War 1939-45, took part in golf competitions and reached a single-figure handicap in spite of his disability.

● In 1909, Scott of Silloth, and John Haskins of Hoylake, both one-armed golfers, played a home and away match for £20-a-side. Scott finished five up at Silloth. He was seven up and 14 to play at Hoylake but Haskins played so well that Scott eventually only won by 3 and 1. This was the first match between one-armed golfers. Haskins in 1919 was challenged by Mr Mycock, of Buxton, another one-armed player. The match was 36 holes, home and away. The first half was played over the Buxton and High Peak Links, and the latter half over the Liverpool Links, and resulted in a win for Haskins by 11 and 10. Later in the same year Haskins received another challenge to play against Alexander Smart of Aberdeen. The match was 18 holes over the Balgownie Course, and ended in favour of Haskins.

● In a match, November, 1926, between the Geduld and Sub Nigel Clubs – two golf clubs connected with the South African gold mines of the same names – each club had two players minus an arm. The natural consequence was that the quartet were matched. The players were – AWP Charteris and E Mitchell, Sub Nigel; and EP Coles and J Kirby, Geduld. This is the first record of four one-armed players in a foursome.

● At Joliet Country Club, USA, a one-armed golfer named DR Anderson drove a ball 300 yards.

● Left-handedness, but playing golf right-handed, is prevalent and for a man to throw with his left hand and play golf right-handed is considered an advantage, for Bobby Jones, Jesse Sweetser, Walter Hagen, Jim Barnes, Joe Kirkwood and more recently Johnny Miller were eminent golfers who were left-handed and ambidextrous.

● In a practice round for the Open Championship in July, 1927, at St Andrews, Len Nettlefold and Joe Kirkwood changed sets of clubs at the 9th hole. Nettlefold was a left-handed golfer and Kirkwood right-handed. They played the last nine, Kirkwood with the left-handed clubs and Nettlefold with the right-handed clubs.

● The late Harry Vardon, when he was at Ganton, got tired of giving impossible odds to his members and beating them, so he collected a set of left-handed clubs, and rating himself at scratch, conceded the handicap odds to them. He won with the same monotonous regularity.

● Ernest Jones, who was professional at the Chislehurst Club, was badly wounded in the war in France in 1916 and his right leg had to be amputated below the knee. He persevered with the game, and before the end of the year he went round the Clacton course balanced on his one leg in 72. Jones later settled in the United States where he built fame and fortune as a golf teacher.

● Major Alexander McDonald Fraser of Edinburgh had the distinction of holding two handicaps simultaneously in the same club – one when he played left-handed and the other for his right-handed play. In medal competitions he had to state before teeing up which method he would use.

● Former England test cricketer Brian Close once held a handicap of 2 playing right-handed, but after retiring from cricket in 1977 decided to apply himself as a left-handed player. His left-handed handicap at the time of his retirement was 7. Close had the distinction of once beating Ted Dexter, another distinguished test cricketer and noted golfer twice in the one day, playing right-handed in the morning and left-handed in the afternoon.

Blind and Blindfolded Golf

● Major Towse, VC, whose eyes were shot out during the South African War, 1899, was probably the first blind man to play golf. His only stipulations when playing the game were that he should be allowed to touch the ball with his hands to ascertain its position, and that his caddie could ring a small bell to indicate the position of the hole. Major Towse, who played with considerable skill, was also an expert oarsman and bridge player. He died in 1945, aged 81.

● The United States Blind Golfers' Association in 1946 promoted an Invitational Golf Tournament for the blind at Country Club, Inglewood, California. This competition is held annually and in 1953 there were 24 competitors and 11 players completed the two rounds of 36 holes. The winner was Charley Boswell who lost his eyesight leading a tank unit in Germany in 1944.

● In July, 1954, at Lambton Golf and Country Club, Toronto, the first international championship for the blind was held. It resulted in a win for Joe Lazaro, of Waltham, Mass, with a score of 220 for the two rounds. He drove the 215-yard 16th hole and just missed an ace, his ball stopping 18 inches from the hole. Charley Boswell, who won the United States Blind Golfers' Association Tournament in 1953, was second. The same Charles Boswell, of Birmingham, Alabama holed the 141-yard 14th hole at the Vestavia CC in one in October, 1970.

● Another blind person to have holed-in-one was American Ben Thomas while on holiday in South Carolina in 1978.

● Rick Sorenson undertook a bet in which, playing 18 holes blindfolded at Meadowbrook Course, Minneapolis, on 25th May, 1973, he was to pay $10 for every hole over par and receive $100 for every hole in par or better. He went round in 86 losing $70 on the deal.

● Alfred Toogood played blindfolded in a match against Tindal Atkinson at Sunningdale in 1912. Toogood was beaten 8 and 7. Previously, in 1908, I Millar, Newcastle-upon-Tyne, played a match blindfolded against AT Broughton, Birkdale, at Newcastle, County Down. Blindfold putting matches have been frequently played.

● Wing-Commander *Laddie* Lucas, DSO, DFC, MP, played over Sandy Lodge golf course in Hertfordshire on 7th August, 1954, completely blindfolded and had a score of 87.

Trick Shots

● Joe Kirkwood, Australia, specialised in public exhibitions of trick and fancy shots. He played all kinds of strokes after nominating them, and among his ordinary strokes nothing was more impressive than those hit for low flight. He played a full drive from the face of a wrist watch, and the toe of a spectator's shoe, full strokes at a suspended ball, and played for slice and pull at will, and exhibited his ambidexterity by playing left-handed strokes with right-handed clubs. Holing six balls, stymieing, a full shot at a ball catching it as it descended, and hitting 12 full shots in rapid succession, with his face turned away from the ball, were shots among his repertoire. In playing the last named Kirkwood placed the balls in a row, about six inches apart, and moved quickly along the line. Kirkwood, who was born in Australia lived for many years in America. He died in November, 1970 aged 73.

● On 2nd April, 1894, a 3-ball match was played over Musselburgh course between Messrs Grant, Bowden, and Waggot, the clubmaker, the latter teeing on the face of a watch at each tee. He finished the round in 41 the watch being undamaged in any way.

● In a match at Esher on 23rd November, 1931, George Ashdown, the professional, played his tee shot for each of the 18 holes from a rubber tee strapped to the forehead of Miss Ena Shaw.

● EA Forrest, a South African professional in a music hall turn of trick golf shots, played blindfolded shots, one being from the ball teed on the chin of his recumbent partner.

● The late Paul Hahn, an American trick specialist could hit four balls with two clubs Holding a club in each hand he hit two balls, hooking one and slicing the other with the same swing. Hahn had a repertoire of 30 trick shots. In 1955 he flew round the world, exhibiting in 14 countries and on all five continents.

Balls Colliding and Touching

● Competing in the 1980 Corfu International Championship, Sharon Peachey drove from one tee and her ball collided in mid-air with one from a competitor playing another hole. Her ball ended in a pond.

● Playing in the Cornish team championship in 1973 at West Cornwall GC Tom Scott-Brown, of West Cornwall GC, and Paddy Bradley, of Tehidy GC, saw their drives from the fourth and eighth tees collide in mid-air.

● Playing in a 4-ball match at Guernsey Club in June, 1966, all four players were near the 13th green from the tee. Two of them – DG Hare and S Machin – chipped up simultaneously; the balls collided in mid-air; Machin's ball hit the green, then the flagstick, and dropped into the hole for a birdie 2.

● In May, 1926, during the meeting of the Army Golfing Society at St Andrews, Colonel Howard and Lieutenant-Colonel Buchanan Dunlop, while playing in the foursomes against J Rodger and J Mackie, hit full iron shots for the seconds to the 16th green. Each thought he had to play his ball first, and hidden by a bunker the players struck their balls simultaneously. The balls, going towards the hole about 20 yards from the pin and five feet in the air, met with great force and dropped either side of the hole five yards apart.

● In 1972, before a luncheon celebrating the centenary year of the Ladies' Section of Royal Wimbledon GC, a 12-hole competition was held during which two competitors, Mrs L Champion and Mrs A McKendrick, driving from the eighth and ninth tees respectively, saw their balls collide in mid-air.

● In 1928, at Wentworth Falls, Australia, Dr Alcorn and EA Avery, of the Leura Club, were playing with the professional, E Barnes. The tee shots of Avery and Barnes at the 9th hole finished on opposite sides of the fairway. Unknown to each other, both players hit their seconds (chip shots) at the same time. Dr Alcorn, standing at the pin, suddenly saw two balls approaching the hole from different angles. They met in the air and then dropped into the hole.

● At Rugby, 1931, playing in a 4-ball match, H Fraser pulled his drive from the 10th tee in the direction of the ninth tee. Simultaneously a club member, driving from the ninth tee, pulled his drive. The tees were about 350 yards apart. The two balls collided in mid-air.

● Two golf balls, being played in opposite directions, collided in flight over Longniddry Golf Course on 27th June, 1953. Immediately after Stewart Elder, of Longniddry, had driven from the third tee, another ball, which had been pulled off line from the second fairway, which runs alongside the third, struck his ball about 20 feet above the ground. SJ Fleming, of Tranent, who was playing with Elder, heard a loud crack and thought Elder's ball had exploded. The balls were found undamaged about 70 yards apart.

Three and Two Balls Dislodged by One Shot

● In 1934 on the short 3rd hole (now the 13th) of Olton Course, Warwickshire, JR Horden, a scratch golfer of the club, sent his tee shot into long wet grass a few feet over the back of the green. When he played an *explosion* shot three balls dropped on to the putting green, his own and two others.

● AM Chevalier, playing at Hale, Cheshire, March, 1935, drove his ball into a grass bunker, and when he reached it there was only part of it showing. He played the shot with a niblick and to his amazement not one but three balls shot into the air. They all dropped back into the bunker and came to rest within a foot of each other. Then came another surprise. One of the *finds* was of the same manufacture and bore the same number as the ball he was playing with.

● Playing to the 9th hole, at Osborne House Club, Isle of Wight, George A Sherman lost his ball which had sunk out of sight on the sodden fairway. A few weeks later, playing from the same tee, his ball again was plugged, only the top showing. Under a local rule he lifted his ball to place it, and exactly under it lay the ball he had lost previously.

Balls in Strange Places

● Playing at the John O' Gaunt Club, Sutton, near Biggleswade (Beds), a member drove a ball which did not touch the ground until it reached London – over 40 miles away. The ball landed in a vegetable lorry which was passing the golf course and later fell out of a package of cabbages when they were unloaded at Covent Garden, London.

● In the English Open Amateur Stroke Play at Moortown in 1974, Nigel Denham, a Yorkshire County player, in the first round saw his overhit second shot to the 18th green bounce up some steps into the clubhouse. His ball went through an open door, ricocheted off a wall and came to rest in the men's bar, 20 feet from the windows. As the clubhouse was not out of bounds Denham decided to play the shot back to the green and opened a window 4 feet by 2 feet through which he pitched his ball to 12 feet from the flag. (Several weeks later the R&A declared that Denham should have been penalised two shots for opening the window. The clubhouse was an immovable obstruction and no part of it should have been moved.)

● In the Open Championship at Sandwich, 1949, Harry Bradshaw, Kilcroney, Dublin, at the 5th hole in his second round, drove into the rough and found his ball inside a beer bottle with the neck and shoulder broken off and four sharp points sticking up. Bradshaw, if he had treated the ball as in an unplayable lie might have been involved in a disqualification, so he decided to play it where it lay. With his blaster he smashed the bottle and sent the ball about 30 yards. The hole, a par 4, cost him 6.

● Kevin Sharman of Woodbridge GC hit a low, very straight drive at the club's 8th hole in 1979. After some minutes' searching, his ball was found embedded in a plastic sphere on top of the direction post.

● On the Dublin Course, 16th July, 1936, in the Irish Open Championship, AD Locke, the South African, played his tee shot at the 100-yard 12th hole, but the ball could not be found on arrival on the green. The marker removed the pin and it

was discovered that the ball had been entangled in the flag. It dropped near the edge of the hole and Locke holed the short putt for a birdie two.

● While playing a round on the Geelong Golf Club Course, Australia, Easter, 1923, Captain Charteris topped his tee shot to the short 2nd hole, which lies over a creek with deep and steep clay banks. His ball came to rest on the near slope of the creek bank. He elected to play the ball as it lay, and took his niblick. After the shot, the ball was nowhere to be seen. It was found later embedded in a mass of gluey clay stuck fast to the face of the niblick. It could not be shaken off. Charteris did what was afterwards approved by the R&A, cleaned the ball and dropped it behind without penalty.

● In October, 1929, at Blackmoor Golf Club, Bordon, Hants, a player driving from the first tee holed out his ball in the chimney of a house some 120 yards distant and some 40 yards out of bounds on the right. The owner and his wife were sitting in front of the fire when they heard a rattle in the chimney and were astonished to see a golf ball drop into the fire.

● A similar incident occurred in an inter-club match between Musselburgh and Lothianburn at Prestongrange in 1938 when a member of the former team hooked his ball at the 2nd hole and gave it up for lost. To his amazement a woman emerged from one of the houses adjacent to this part of the course and handed back the ball which she said had come down the chimney and landed on a pot which was on the fire.

● In July, 1955, J Lowrie, starter at the Eden Course, St Andrews, witnessed a freak shot. A visitor drove from the first tee just as a north-bound train was passing. He sliced the shot and the ball disappeared through an open window of a passenger compartment. Almost immediately the ball emerged again, having been thrown back on to the fairway by a man in the compartment, who waved a greeting which presumably indicated that no one was hurt.

● At Coombe Wood Golf Club a player hit a ball towards the 16th green where it landed in the vertical exhaust of a tractor which was mowing the fairway. The greenkeeper was somewhat surprised to find a temporary loss of power in the tractor. When sufficient compression had built up in the exhaust system, the ball was forced out with tremendous velocity, hit the roof of a house nearby, bounced off and landed some three feet from the pin on the green.

● When carrying out an inspection of the air conditioning system at St John's Hospital, Chelmsford, in 1993, a golf ball was found in the ventilator immediately above the operating theatre. It was probably the result of a hooked drive from the first tee at Chelmsford Golf Club, which is close by, but the ball can only have entered the duct on a rebound through a three-inch gap under a ventilator hood and then descended through a series of sharp bends to its final resting place.

● There have been many occasions when misdirected shots have finished in strange places after an unusual line of flight and bounce. At Ashford, Middlesex, John Miller, aged 69, hit his tee shot out of bounds at the 12th hole (237 yards). It struck a parked car, passed through a copse, hit more cars, jumped a canopy, flew through the clubhouse kitchen window, finishing in a cooking stock-pot, without once touching the ground. Mr Miller had previously done the hole in one on four occasions.

Balls Hit To and From Great Heights

● In 1798 two Edinburgh golfers undertook to drive a ball over the spire of St Giles' Cathedral, Edinburgh, for a wager. Mr Sceales, of Leith, and Mr Smellie, a printer, were each allowed six shots and succeeded in sending the balls well over the weather-cock, a height of more than 160 feet from the ground.

● Some years later Donald McLean, an Edinburgh lawyer, won a substantial bet by driving a ball over the Melville Monument in St Andrew Square, Edinburgh – height, 154 feet.

● Tom Morris in 1860, at the famous bridge of Ballochmyle, stood in the quarry beneath and, from a stick elevated horizontally, attempted to send golf balls over the bridge. He could raise them only to the pathway, 400 feet high, which was in itself a great feat with the gutta ball.

● Captain Ernest Carter, on 28th September, 1922, drove a ball from the roadway at the 1st tee on Harlech Links against the wall of Harlech Castle. The embattlements are 200 feet over the level of the roadway, and the point where the ball struck the embattlements was 180 yards from the point where the ball was teed. Captain Carter, who was laid odds of £100 to £1, used a baffy.

● In 1896 Freddie Tait, then a subaltern in the Black Watch, drove a ball from the Rookery, the highest building on Edinburgh Castle, in a match against a brother officer to hole out in the fountain in Princes Street Gardens 350 feet below and about 300 yards distant.

● Prior to the 1977 Lancôme Tournament in Paris, Arnold Palmer hit three balls from the second stage of the Eiffel Tower, over 300 feet above ground. The longest was measured at 403 yards. One ball was hooked and hit a bus but no serious damage was done as all traffic had been stopped for safety reasons.

● Long drives have been made from mountain peaks, across the gorge at Victoria Falls, from the Pyramids, high buildings in New York, and from many other similar places. As an illustration of such freakish *drives* a member of the New York Rangers' Hockey Team from the top of Mount Edith Cavell, 11,033 feet high, drove a ball which struck the Ghost Glacier 5,000 feet below and bounced off the rocky ledge another 1,000 feet – a total drop of 2,000 yards. Later, in June, 1968, from Pikes Peak, Colorado (14,110 feet), Arthur Lynskey hit a ball which travelled 200 yards horizontally but 2 miles vertically.

Remarkable Shots

● Remarkable shots are as numerous as the grains of sand; around every 19th hole, legends are recalled of astounding shots. One shot is commemorated by a memorial tablet at the 17th hole at the Lytham and St Annes Club. It was made by Bobby Jones in the final round of the Open Championship in 1926. He was partnered by Al Watrous, another American player. They had been running neck and neck and at the end of the third round, Watrous was just leading Jones with 215 against 217. At the 16th Jones drew level then on the 17th he drove into a sandy lie in broken ground. Watrous reached the green with his second. Jones took a mashie-iron (the equivalent to a 4-iron today) and hit a magnificent shot to the green to get his 4. This remarkable recovery unnerved Watrous, who 3-putted, and Jones, getting another 4 at the last hole against 5, won his first Open Championship with 291 against Watrous' 293. The tablet is near the spot where Jones played his second shot.

● Arnold Palmer (USA), playing in the second round of the Australian Wills Masters tournament at Melbourne, in October, 1964, hooked his second shot at the 9th hole high into the fork of a gum tree. Climbing 20 feet up the tree, Palmer, with the head of his 1-iron reversed, played a hammer stroke and knocked the ball some 30 yards forward, followed by a brilliant chip to the green and a putt.

● In the foursome during the Ryder Cup at Moortown in 1929, Joe Turnesa hooked the American side's second shot at the last hole behind the marquee adjoining the clubhouse, Johnny Farrel then pitched the ball over the marquee on to the green only feet away from the pin and Turnesa holed out for a 4.

Miscellaneous Incidents and Strange Golfing Facts

● Gary Player of South Africa was honoured by his country by having his portrait on new postage stamps which were issued on 12th December, 1976. It was the first time a specific golfer had ever been depicted on any country's postage stamps. In 1981 the US Postal Service introduced stamps featuring Bobby Jones and Babe Zaharias. They are the first golfers to be thus honoured by the United States.

● Gary Harris, aged 18, became the first player to make five consecutive appearances for England in the European Boys Team Championship at Vilamoura, Portugal, in 1994.

● In February, 1971, the first ever golf shots on the moon's surface were played by Captain Alan Shepard, commander of the Apollo 14 spacecraft. Captain Shepard hit two balls with an iron head attached to a makeshift shaft. With a one-handed swing he claimed he hit the first ball 200 yards aided by the reduced force of gravity on the moon. Subsequent findings put this distance in doubt. The second was a shank. Acknowledging the occasion the R&A sent Captain Shepard the following telegram: *Warmest congratulations to all of you on your great achievement and safe return. Please refer to Rules of Golf section on etiquette, paragraph 6, quote – before leaving a bunker a player should carefully fill up all holes made by him therein, unquote.* Shepard presented the club to the USGA Museum in 1974.

● Charles (Chick) Evans competed in every US Amateur Championship held between 1907 and 1962 by which time he was 72 years old. This amounted to 50 consecutive occasions discounting the six years of the two World Wars when the championship was not held.

● In winning the 1977 US Open at Southern Hills CC, Tulsa, Oklahoma, Hubert Green had to contend with a death threat. Coming off the 14th green in the final round, he was advised by USGA officials that a phone call had been received saying that he would be killed. Green decided that play should continue and happily he went on to win, unharmed.

● It was discovered at the 1977 USPGA Championship that the clubs with which Tom Watson had won the Open Championship and the US Masters earlier in the year were illegal, having grooves which exceeded the permitted specifications. The set he used in winning the 1975 Open Championship were then flown out to him and they too were found to be illegal. No retrospective action was taken.

● Mrs Fred Daly, wife of the former Open champion, saved the clubhouse of Balmoral GC, Belfast, from destruction when three men entered the professional's shop on 5th August, 1976, and left a bag containing a bomb outside the shop beside the clubhouse when refused money. Mrs Daly carried the bag over to a hedge some distance away where the bomb exploded 15 minutes later. The only damage was broken windows. On the same day several hours afterwards, Dungannon GC in Co Tyrone suffered extensive damage to the clubhouse from terrorist bombs. Co Down GC, proposed venue of the 1979 home international matches suffered bomb damage in May that year and through fear for the safety of team members the 1979 matches were cancelled.

● The Army Golfing Society and St Andrews on 21st April, 1934, played a match 200-a-side, the largest golf match ever played. Play was by foursomes. The Army won 58, St Andrews 31 and 11 were halved.

● Jamie Ortiz-Patino, owner of the Valderrama Golf Club at Sotogrande, Spain, paid a record £84,000 (increased to £92,400 with ten per cent buyers premium) for a late seventeenth- or early eighteenth-century rake iron offered at auction in Musselburgh in July, 1992. The iron, which had been kept in a garden shed, was bought to be exhibited in a museum being created in Valderrama.

● A Christie's golf auction during the week of the 1991 Open Championship created two world records. An American dealer bought a blacksmith-made iron club head dating from the seventeenth century for £44,000. It had been found 10 years before in a hedge near the North Berwick Golf Club in Scotland. Also, £165,000 was paid by a Japanese collector for an oil painting by Sir Francis Grant (1810–1878) of the 1823 Royal & Ancient captain, John Whyte-Melville, standing beside the Swilcan Burn at St Andrews. The same Japanese buyer successfully bid £35,200 for a rare gutty golf ball marking device from the workshops of Old Tom Morris in St Andrews, while an unused feathery golf ball by Allan Robertson fetched £11,000.

● In 1986 Alistair Risk and three colleagues on the 17th green at Brora, Sutherland, watched a cow giving birth to twin calves between the markers on the 18th tee, causing them to play their next tee shots from in front of the tee. Their application for a ruling from the R&A brought a Rules Committee reply that while technically a rule had been broken, their action was considered within the spirit of the game and there should be no penalty. The Secretary added that the Rules Committee hoped that mother and twins were doing well.

● In view of the increasing number of people crossing the road (known as Granny Clark's Wynd) which runs across the first and 18th fairways of the Old Course, St Andrews, as a right of way, the St Andrews Links committee decided in 1969 to control the flow by erecting traffic lights, with appropriate green for go, yellow for caution and red for stop. The lights are controlled from the starter's box on the first tee. Golfers on the first tee must wait until the lights turn to green before driving off and a notice has been erected at the Wynd warning pedestrians not to cross at yellow or stop.

● A traffic light for golfers was also installed in 1971 on one of Japan's most congested courses. After putting on the uphill 9th hole of the Fukuoka course in Southern Japan, players have to switch on a go-ahead signal for following golfers waiting to play their shots to the green.

● A 22-year-old professional at Brett Essex GC, Brentwood, David Moore, who was playing in the Mufulira Open in Zambia in 1976, was shot dead it is alleged by the man with whom he was staying for the duration of the tournament. It appeared his host then shot himself.

● Peggy Carrick and her daughter, Angela Uzielli, won the Mothers and Daughters Tournament at Royal Mid-Surrey in 1994 for the 21st time.

● Patricia Shepherd has won the ladies' club championship at Turriff GC Aberdeenshire 30 consecutive times from 1959 to 1988.

● Mrs Jackie Mercer won the South African Ladies' Championship in 1979, 31 years after her first victory in the event as Miss Jacqueline Smith.

● During the Royal & Ancient medal meeting on 25th September, 1907, a member of the Royal & Ancient drove a ball which struck the sharp point of a hatpin in the hat of a lady who was crossing the course. The ball was so firmly impaled that it remained in position. The lady was not hurt.

● John Cook, former English Amateur Champion, narrowly escaped death during an attempted coup against King Hassan of Morocco in July 1971. Cook had been playing in a tournament arranged by King Hassan, a keen golfer, and was at the King's birthday party in Rabat when rebels broke into the party demanding that the King give up his throne. Cook and many others present were taken hostage.

● When playing from the 9th tee at Lossiemouth golf course in June, 1971, Martin Robertson struck a Royal Navy jet aircraft which was coming in to land at the nearby airfield. The plane was not damaged.

● At a court in Inglewood, California, in 1978, Jim Brown was convicted of beating and choking an opponent during a dispute over where a ball should have been placed on the green.

● During the Northern Ireland troubles a home-made hand grenade was found in a bunker at Dungannon GC, Co Tyrone, on Sunday, 12th September, 1976.

● Tiger Woods, 18, became both the youngest and the first black golfer to win the United States Amateur Championship at Sawgrass in 1994.

● To mark the centenary of the Jersey Golf Club in 1978, the Jersey Post Office issued a set of four special stamps featuring Jersey's most famous golfer, Harry Vardon. The background of the 13p stamp was a brief biography of Vardon's career reproduced from the Golfer's Handbook.

● Forty-one-year-old John Mosley went for a round of golf at Delaware Park GC, Buffalo, New York, in July, 1972. He stepped on to the first tee and was challenged over a green fee by an official guard. A scuffle developed, a shot was fired and Mosley, a bullet in his chest, died on the way to hospital. His wife was awarded $131,250 in an action against the City of Buffalo and the guard. The guard was sentenced to 7½ years for second-degree manslaughter.

● When three competitors in a 1968 Pennsylvania pro-am event were about to drive from the 16th tee, two bandits (one with pistol) suddenly emerged

from the bushes, struck one of the players and robbed them of wristwatches and $300.

● In the 1932 Walker Cup match at Brooklyn, Leonard Crawley succeeded in denting the cup. An errant iron shot to the 18th green hit the cup, which was on display outside the clubhouse.

● Three golf officials appeared in court in Johannesburg, South Africa, accused of violating a 75-year-old Sunday Observance Law by staging the final round of the South African PGA championship on Sunday, 28th February, 1971. The championship should have been completed on the Saturday but heavy rain prevented any play.

● In the Open Championship of 1876, at St Andrews, Bob Martin and David Strath tied at 176. A protest was lodged against Strath alleging he played his approach to the 17th green and struck a spectator. The Royal & Ancient ordered the replay, but Strath refused to play off the tie until a decision had been given on the protest. No decision was given and Bob Martin was declared the Champion.

● At Rose Bay, New South Wales, on 11th July, 1931, DJ Bayly MacArthur, on stepping into a bunker, began to sink. MacArthur, who weighed 14 stone, shouted for help. He was rescued when up to the armpits. He had stepped on a patch of quicksand, aggravated by excess of moisture.

● The late Bobby Cruickshank was the victim of his own jubilation in the 1934 US Open at Merion. In the 4th round while in with a chance of winning he half-topped his second shot at the 11th hole. The ball was heading for a pond in front of the green but instead of ending up in the water it hit a rock and bounced on to the green. In his delight Cruickshank threw his club into the air only to receive a resounding blow on the head as it returned to earth.

● A dog with an infallible nose for finding lost golf balls was, in 1971, given honorary membership of the Waihi GC, Hamilton, New Zealand. The dog, called Chico, was trained to search for lost balls, to be sold back to the members, the money being put into the club funds.

● By 1980 Waddy, an 11-year-old beagle belonging to Bob Inglis, the secretary of Brokenhurst Manor GC, had found over 35,000 golf balls.

● Herbert M Hepworth, Headingley, Leeds, Lord Mayor of Leeds in 1906, scored one thousand holes in 2, a feat which took him 30 years to accomplish. It was celebrated by a dinner in 1931 at the Leeds club. The first 2 of all was scored on 12th June, 1901, at Cobble Hall Course, Leeds, and the 1,000th in 1931 at Alwoodley, Leeds. Hepworth died in November, 1942.

● Fiona MacDonald was the first female to play in the Oxford and Cambridge University match at Ganton in 1986.

● Mrs Sara Gibbon won the Farnham (Surrey) Club's Grandmother's competition 48 hours after her first grand-child was born.

● At Carnoustie in the first qualifying round for

the 1952 Scottish Amateur Championship a competitor drove three balls in succession out of bounds at the 1st hole and thereupon withdrew.

● In 1993, the Clark family from Hagley GC, Worcestershire, set a record for the county's three major professional events. The Worcestershire stroke play championship was won by Finlay Clark, the eldest son, who beat his father, Iain, and younger brother Cameron, who tied second. In the County Match Play it was the turn of Iain, who beat his son, Finlay, by 2 and 1 in the final. Cameron won the play-off for third place. Then in the Worcestershire Annual Pro-Am it was the turn of Cameron, with his brother, Finlay, second and father, Iain, third. To add to the achievements of the family, Cameron also won the Midland Professional Match Play Championship.

● During a Captain–Pro foursomes challenge match at Chelmsford in 1993, Club Professional Dennis Bailey, put the ball into a hole only once in all 18 holes – when he holed-in-one at the fourth.

Strange Local Rules

● The Duke of Windsor, who played on an extraordinary variety of the world's courses, once took advantage of a local rule at Jinja in Uganda and lifted his ball from a hippo's footprint without penalty.

● At the Glen Canyon course in Arizona a local rule provides that *If your ball lands within a club length of a rattlesnake you are allowed to move the ball.*

● Another local rule in Uganda read: *If a ball comes to rest in dangerous proximity to a crocodile, another ball may be dropped.*

● The 6th hole at Koolan Island GC, Western Australia also serves as a local air strip and a local rule reads: *Aircraft and vehicular traffic have right of way at all times.*

● A local rule at the RAF Waddington GC reads: *When teeing off from the 2nd, right of way must be given to taxiing aircraft.*

Record Scoring

The Open Championship

Most times champions

6   Harry Vardon, 1896-98-99-1903-11-14
5   James Braid, 1901-05-06-08-10; JH Taylor, 1894-95-1900-09-13; Peter Thomson, 1954-55-56-58-65; Tom Watson, 1975-77-80-82-83

Most times runner-up

7   Jack Nicklaus, 1964-67-68-72-76-77-79
6   JH Taylor, 1896-1904-05-06-07-14

Oldest winner

Old Tom Morris, 46 years 99 days, 1867
Roberto De Vicenzo, 44 years 93 days, 1967

Youngest winner

Young Tom Morris, 17 years 5 months 8 days, 1868
Willie Auchterlonie, 21 years 24 days, 1893
Severiano Ballesteros, 22 years 3 months 12 days, 1979

Youngest and oldest competitor

John Ball, 15 years 6 months, 1878
Gene Sarazen, 71 years 4 months 13 days, 1973

Widest margin of victory

13 strokes Old Tom Morris, 1862
12 strokes Young Tom Morris, 1870
8 strokes JH Taylor, 1900 and 1913; James Braid, 1908
6 strokes Harry Vardon, 1903; JH Taylor, 1909; Bobby Jones, 1927; Walter Hagen, 1929; Arnold Palmer, 1962; Johnny Miller, 1976

Lowest winning aggregates

267 Greg Norman, 66-68-69-64, Sandwich, 1993
268 Tom Watson, 68-70-65-65, Turnberry, 1977; Nick Price, 69-66-67-66, Turnberry, 1994
270 Nick Faldo, 67-65-67-71, St Andrews, 1990

Lowest aggregate by runner-up

269 (68-70-65-66), Jack Nicklaus, Turnberry, 1977; (69-63-70-67) Nick Faldo, Sandwich, 1993; (68-66-68-67) Jesper Parnevik, Turnberry, 1994

Lowest aggregate by an amateur

281 (68-72-70-71), Iain Pyman, Sandwich, 1993; (75, 66, 70, 70), Tiger Woods, R. Lytham, 1996

Lowest round

63 Mark Hayes, second round, Turnberry, 1977; Isao Aoki, third round, Muirfield, 1980; Greg Norman, second round, Turnberry, 1986; Paul Broadhurst, third round, St Andrews, 1990; Jodie Mudd, fourth round, Royal Birkdale, 1991; Nick Faldo, second round, Sandwich, 1993; Payne Stewart, fourth round, Sandwich, 1993

Lowest round by an amateur

66 Frank Stranahan, fourth round, Troon, 1950; Tiger Woods, second round, R. Lytham, 1996

Lowest first round

64 Craig Stadler, Royal Birkdale, 1983; Christy O'Connor Jr, Royal St George's, 1985; Rodger Davis, Muirfield, 1987; Steve Pate, Ray Floyd, Muirfield, 1992

Lowest second round

63 Mark Hayes, Turnberry, 1977; Greg Norman, Turnberry, 1986; Nick Faldo, Sandwich, 1993

Lowest third round

63 Isao Aoki, Muirfield, 1980; Paul Broadhurst, St Andrews, 1990

Lowest fourth round

63 Jodie Mudd, Royal Birkdale, 1991; Payne Stewart, Sandwich, 1993

Lowest first 36 holes

130 (66-64), Nick Faldo, Muirfield, 1992
132 (67-65), Henry Cotton, Sandwich, 1934; Nick Faldo (67-65) and Greg Norman (66-66), St Andrews, 1990; Nick Faldo (69-63), Sandwich, 1993

Lowest second 36 holes

130 (65-65), Tom Watson, Turnberry, 1977 (64-66) Ian Baker-Finch, R. Birkdale, 1991; (66-64) Anders Forsbrand, Turnberry, 1994

Lowest first 54 holes

198 (67-67-64) Tom Lehman, Royal Lytham, 1996

199 (67-65-67), Nick Faldo, St Andrews, 1990; (66-64-69) Nick Faldo, Muirfield, 1992

Lowest final 54 holes

199 (66-67-66) Nick Price, Turnberry, 1994

200 (70-65-65), Tom Watson, Turnberry, 1977; (63-70-67), Nick Faldo, Sandwich, 1993; (66-64-70), Fuzzy Zoeller, Turnberry, 1994 (66-70-64), Nick Faldo, Turnberry 1994

Lowest 9 holes

28 Denis Durnian, first 9, Royal Birkdale, 1983

Champions in three decades

Harry Vardon, 1986, 1903, 1911
JH Taylor, 1894, 1900, 1913
Gary Player, 1959, 1968, 1974

Biggest span between first and last victories

19 years, JH Taylor, 1894-1913
18 years, Harry Vardon, 1896-1914
15 years, Willie Park, 1860–75
15 years, Gary Player, 1959-74
14 years, Henry Cotton, 1934-48

Successive victories

4   Young Tom Morris, 1868-72 (no championship in 1871)

3   Jamie Anderson, 1877-79; Bob Ferguson, 1880-82, Peter Thomson, 1954-56

2   Old Tom Morris, 1861-62; JH Taylor, 1894-95; Harry Vardon, 1898-99; James Braid, 1905-06; Bobby Jones, 1926-27; Walter Hagen, 1928-29; Bobby Locke, 1949-50; Arnold Palmer, 1961-62; Lee Trevino, 1971-72; Tom Watson, 1982-83

Victories by amateurs

3 Bobby Jones, 1926-27-30
2 Harold Hilton, 1892-97
1 John Ball, 1890
Roger Wethered lost a play-off in 1921

Highest number of top five finishes

16 JH Taylor and Jack Nicklaus
15 Harry Vardon and James Braid

Players with four rounds under 70

Greg Norman (66-68-69-64), Sandwich, 1993;
Ernie Els (68-69-69-68), Sandwich, 1993;
Nick Price (69-66-67-66), Turnberry, 1994;
Jesper Parnevik (68-66-68-67), Turnberry, 1994

Highest number of rounds under 70

33 Jack Nicklaus and Nick Faldo
27 Tom Watson

23 Greg Norman
21 Lee Trevino
20 Severiano Ballesteros
19 Nick Price

Outright leader after every round

Willie Auchterlonie, 1893; JH Taylor, 1894 and 1900; James Braid, 1908; Ted Ray, 1912; Bobby Jones, 1927; Gene Sarazen, 1932; Henry Cotton, 1934; Tom Weiskopf, 1973

Record leads (since 1892)

After 18 holes: 4 strokes, James Braid, 1908; Bobby Jones, 1927; Henry Cotton, 1934; Christy O'Connor Jr, 1985

After 36 holes: 9 strokes, Henry Cotton, 1934

After 54 holes: 10 strokes, Henry Cotton, 1934; 7 strokes, Tony Lema, 1964; 6 strokes, James Braid, 1908; Tom Lehman, 1996; 5 strokes, Arnold Palmer, 1962, Bill Rogers, 1981, Nick Faldo, 1990

Champions with each round lower than previous one

Jack White, 1904, Sandwich, 80-75-72-69
James Braid, 1906, Muirfield, 77-76-74-73
Ben Hogan, 1953, Carnoustie, 73-71-70-68
Gary Player, 1959, Muirfield, 75-71-70-68

Champion with four rounds the same

Densmore Shute, 1933, St Andrews, 73-73-73-73 (excluding the play-off)

Biggest variation between rounds of a champion

14 strokes, Henry Cotton, 1934, second round 65, fourth round 79
11 strokes, Jack White, 1904, first round 80, fourth round 69; Greg Norman, 1986, first round 74, second round 63, third round 74

Biggest variation between two rounds

18 strokes: A Tingey Jr, 1923, first round 94, second 76
17 strokes, Jack Nicklaus, 1981, first round 83, second round 66; Ian Baker-Finch, 1986, first round 86, second round 69

Best comeback by champions

After 18 holes: Harry Vardon, 1896, 11 strokes behind the leader
After 36 holes: George Duncan, 1920, 13 strokes behind leader
After 54 holes: Jim Barnes, 1925, Justin Leonard, 1997, 5 strokes behind the leader

Best comeback by non–champions

Of non-champions, Greg Norman, 1989, seven strokes behind the leader and lost in a play-off

Best finishing round by a champion

64 Greg Norman, Sandwich, 1993
65 Tom Watson, Turnberry, 1977; Severiano Ballesteros, Royal Lytham, 1988; Justin Leonard, Royal Troon, 1997

Worst finishing round by a champion since 1920

79 Henry Cotton, Sandwich, 1934
78 Reg Whitcombe, Sandwich, 1938
77 Walter Hagen, Hoylake, 1924

Best opening round by a champion

66 Peter Thomson, Royal Lytham, 1958; Nick Faldo, Muirfield, 1992; Greg Norman, Sandwich, 1993
67 Henry Cotton, Sandwich, 1934; Tom Watson, R. Birkdale, 1983; Severiano Ballesteros, R. Lytham, 1988; Nick Faldo, St Andrews, 1990; John Daly, St Andrews, 1995, Tom Lehman, R. Lytham, 1996

Worst opening round by a champion since 1919

80 George Duncan, Deal, 1920 (he also had a second round of 80)
77 Walter Hagen, Hoylake, 1924

Biggest recovery in 18 holes by a champion

George Duncan, Deal, 1920, was 13 strokes behind the leader, Abe Mitchell, after 36 holes and level after 54

Most consecutive appearances

43 Gary Player, 1955–97

Championship since 1946 with the fewest rounds under 70

St Andrews, 1946; Hoylake, 1947; Portrush, 1951; Hoylake, 1956; Carnoustie, 1968. All had only two rounds under 70

Longest course

Carnoustie, 1968, 7,252 yd (6,631m)

Largest entries

2,133 in 1997, Royal Troon
1,919 in 1996, Royal Lytham

Courses most often used

St Andrews, 25; Prestwick, 24 (but not since 1925); Muirfield, 14; Sandwich, 12; Hoylake, 10; R. Lytham, 9; R. Birkdale, R. Troon 7; Musselburgh, 6; Carnoustie, 5; Turnberry, 3; Deal, 2; R. Portrush and Prince's, 1

Attendances

Year	Attendance	Year	Attendance
1962	37,098	1980	131,610
1963	24,585	1981	111,987
1964	35,954	1982	133,299
1965	32,927	1983	142,892
1966	40,182	1984	193,126
1967	29,880	1985	141,619
1968	51,819	1986	134,261
1969	46,001	1987	139,189
1970	82,593	1988	191,334
1971	70,076	1989	160,639
1972	84,746	1990	207,000
1973	78,810	1991	192,154
1974	92,796	1992	150,100
1975	85,258	1993	140,100
1976	92,021	1994	128,000
1977	87,615	1995	180,000
1978	125,271	1996	170,000
1979	134,501	1997	176,797

Prize money

Year	Total	First Prize £	Year	Total	First Prize £	Year	Total	First Prize £
1860	nil	nil	1955	3,750	1,000	1980	200,000	25,000
1863	10	nil	1958	4,850	1,000	1982	250,000	32,000
1864	16	6	1959	5,000	1,000	1983	300,000	40,000
1876	20	20	1960	7,000	1,250	1984	451,000	55,000
1889	22	8	1961	8,500	1,400	1985	530,000	65,000
1891	28.50	10	1963	8,500	1,500	1986	600,000	70,000
1892	110	(Am)	1965	10,000	1,750	1987	650,000	75,000
1893	100	30	1966	15,000	2,100	1988	700,000	80,000
1910	125	50	1968	20,000	3,000	1989	750,000	80,000
1920	225	75	1969	30,000	4,250	1990	815,000	85,000
1927	275	100	1970	40,000	5,250	1991	900,000	90,000
1930	400	100	1971	45,000	5,500	1992	950,000	95,000
1931	500	100	1972	50,000	5,500	1993	1,000,000	100,000
1946	1,000	150	1975	75,000	7,500	1994	1,100,000	110,000
1949	1,700	300	1977	100,000	10,000	1995	1,250,000	125,000
1953	2,450	500	1978	125,000	12,500	1996	1,400,000	200,000
1954	3,500	750	1979	155,000	15,500	1997	1,586,300	250,000

US Open

Most times champion
4   Willie Anderson, 1901-03-04-05; Bobby Jones, 1923-26-29-30; Ben Hogan, 1948-50-51-53; Jack Nicklaus, 1962-67-72-80

Most times runner-up
4   Bobby Jones, 1922-24-25-28; Sam Snead, 1937-47-49-53; Arnold Palmer, 1962-63-66-67; Jack Nicklaus, 1960 (am)-68-71-82

Oldest winner
Hale Irwin, 45 years, Medinah, 1990

Youngest winner
Johnny McDermott, 19 years, Chicago, 1911

Biggest winning margin
11 strokes   Willie Smith, Baltimore, 1899

Lowest winning aggregate
272   Jack Nicklaus, Baltusrol, 1980; Lee Janzen, Baltusrol, 1993

Lowest round
63   Johnny Miller, fourth round, Oakmont, 1973; Jack Nicklaus, first round, Baltusrol, 1980; Tom Weiskopf, first round, Baltusrol, 1980

Lowest 9 holes
29   Neal Lancaster, Shinnecock Hills, 1995, and Oakland Hills, 1996

Lowest first 36 holes
134   Jack Nicklaus, Baltusrol, 1980; Tze-chung Chen, Oakland Hills, 1985

Lowest final 36 holes
132   Larry Nelson, Oakmont, 1983

Most consecutive appearances
41   Jack Nicklaus 1957 to 1997

Successive victories
3   Willie Anderson, 1903-04-05

Players with four rounds under 70
Lee Trevino, 69-68-69-69, Oak Hill, 1968; Lee Janzen, 67-67-69-69, Baltusrol, 1993

Wire to wire winners
Walter Hagen, Midlothian, 1914; Jim Barnes, Columbia, 1921; Ben Hogan, Oakmont, 1953; Tony Jacklin, Hazeltine, 1970

Best opening round by a champion
63   Jack Nicklaus, Baltusrol, 1980

Worst opening round by a champion
91   Horace Rawlins, Newport, RI, 1895
Since World War II: 76 Ben Hogan, Oakland Hills, 1951

US Masters

Most times champion
6   Jack Nicklaus, 1963-65-66-72-75-86
4   Arnold Palmer, 1958-60-62-64

Most times runner-up
4   Ben Hogan, 1942-46-54-55; Jack Nicklaus, 1964-71-77-81

Oldest winner
Jack Nicklaus, 46 years, 1986

Youngest winner
Tiger Woods, 21 years, 3 months, 1997

Biggest winning margin
12 strokes   Tiger Woods, 1997

Lowest winning aggregate
270   Tiger Woods, 1997

Lowest aggregate by an amateur
281   Charles Coe, 1961 (joint second)

Lowest round
63   Nick Price, 1986; Greg Norman, 1996

Lowest 9 holes
29   Mark Calcavecchia, 1992

Lowest first 36 holes
131   Raymond Floyd, 1976

Lowest final 36 holes
131   Johnny Miller, 1975

Most appearances
45   Doug Ford 1952 to 1997
44   Sam Snead 1937 to 1983

Successive victories
2   Jack Nicklaus, 1965-66; Nick Faldo, 1989-90

Players with four rounds under 70
None

Wire to wire winners
Craig Wood, 1941; Arnold Palmer, 1960; Jack Nicklaus, 1972; Raymond Floyd, 1976

Best opening round by a champion
65   Raymond Floyd, 1976

Worst opening round by a champion
75   Craig Stadler, 1982

Albatrosses
There have been three albatross twos in the Masters at Augusta National: by Gene Sarazen at the 15th, 1935; by Bruce Devlin at the eighth, 1967; and by Jeff Maggert at the 13th, 1994.

US PGA Championship

Note: The PGA was a match play event from 1916 to 1957. Since 1958 it has been played as stroke play

Most times champion

5   Walter Hagen, 1921-24-25-26-27;
Jack Nicklaus 1963-71-73-75-80

Most times runner-up

4   Jack Nicklaus, 1964-65-74-83

Oldest winner

Julius Boros, 48 years 4 months 18 days, Pecan Valley, 1968

Youngest winner

Gene Sarazen, 20 years 5 months 22 days, Oakmont, 1922

Biggest winning margin

7 strokes   Jack Nicklaus, Oak Hill, 1980

Lowest aggregate

267   Steve Elkington and Colin Montgomerie, Riviera, 1995 – Montgomerie lost play-off

Lowest round

63   Bruce Crampton, Firestone, 1975; Raymond Floyd, Southern Hills, 1982; Gary Player, Shoal Creek, 1984; Vijay Singh, Inverness, 1993; Michael Bradley and Brad Faxon, Riviera, 1995

Most successive victories

4   Walter Hagen, 1924-25-26-27

Lowest 9 holes

28   Brad Faxon, Riviera, 1995

Lowest first 36 holes

131   Hal Sutton, Riviera, 1983; Vijay Singh, Inverness, 1993; Ernie Els and Mark O'Meara, Riviera, 1995

Lowest final 36 holes

132   Miller Barber, Dayton, 1969; Steve Elkington and Colin Montgomerie, Riviera, 1995

Most appearances

37   Arnold Palmer

Wire to wire winners

Bobby Nichols, Columbus, 1964; Raymond Floyd, Dayton, 1969; Jack Nicklaus, PGA National, 1971; Raymond Floyd, Southern Hills, 1982; Hal Sutton, Riviera, 1983

Best opening round by a champion

63   Raymond Floyd, Southern Hills, 1982

Worst opening round by a champion

75   John Mahaffey, Oakmont, 1978

European PGA Tour

Lowest 72-hole aggregate

258   (14 under par)   David Llewellyn (Wal), AGF Biarritz Open, 1988; (18 under par) Ian Woosnam (Wal), Monte Carlo Open, 1990.
259   (25 under par)   Mark McNulty (Zim), German Open at Frankfurt, 1987.

Lowest 9 holes

27   (9 under par) José María Canizares (Sp), Swiss Open at Crans-sur-Sierre, 1978; (7 under par) Robert Lee (Eng), Johnnie Walker Monte Carlo Open at Mont Agel, 1985; (6 under par) Robert Lee, Portuguese Open at Estoril, 1987; (9 under par) Joakim Haeggman (Swe), Alfred Dunhill Cup at St Andrews, 1997

Lowest 18 holes

60   (11 under par) Baldovino Dassu (It), Swiss Open at Crans-sur-Sierre, 1971; David Llewellyn (Wal), AGF Biarritz Open, 1988; (9 under par) Ian Woosnam (Wal), Torras Monte Carlo Open at Mont Agel, 1990; (12 under par) Jamie Spence, Canon European Masters at Crans-sur-Sierre, Switzerland, 1992; (10 under par) Paul Curry, Bell's Scottish Open at Gleneagles, 1992; (9 under par) both Darren Clarke and Johan Rystrom, Monte Carlo Open at Mont Agel, 1992; (12 under par) Bernhard Langer (Ger), Linde German Masters at Motzener See, 1997

Lowest 36 holes

124   (18 under par) Colin Montgomerie (Sco), Canon European Masters at Crans-sur-Sierre, 1996

Lowest first 36 holes

126   (12 under par) Darren Clarke (N. Ire), The European Monte Carlo Open at Mont Agel, 1992

Lowest 54 holes

192   (24 under par) Anders Forbrand (Swe), Ebel European Masters Swiss Open at Crans-sur-Sierre, 1987.

Largest winning margin

17 strokes   Bernhard Langer, Cacharel Under-25s' Championship in Nîmes, 1979.

Highest winning score

306   Peter Butler (Eng), Schweppes PGA Close Championship at Royal Birkdale, 1963.

Youngest winner

Dale Hayes, 18 years 290 days, Spanish Open, 1971

Oldest winner

Neil Coles, 48 years 14 days, Sanyo Open, 1982

US Tour

Lowest 72-hole aggregate

257 (27 under par) Mike Souchak, 60-68-64-65, Texas Open, 1955

Lowest 18 holes

59 Sam Snead, third round, Greenbrier Open (Sam Snead Festival), White Sulphur Springs, West Virginia, 1959; Al Geiberger, second round, Danny Thomas Memphis Classic, Colonial CC, 1977 (when preferred lies were in operation); (13 under par) Chip Beck on the 6,914-yards Sunrise GC course, Las Vegas, in the third round of the Las Vegas Invitational – he finished third but won a bonus prize of $500,000 and another $500,000 for charities

Lowest 9 holes

27 Mike Souchak, Texas Open, 1955; Andy North, BC Open, 1975

Lowest first 36 holes

126 Tommy Bolt, 1954; Paul Azinger, 1989. (On the US mini-tour a 36-hole score of 123 was achieved by Bob Risch in the 1978 Mesa Centennial Open.)

Lowest 54 holes

189 Chandler Harper, Texas Open (last three rounds), 1954

Largest winning margin

16 strokes J Douglas Edgar, Canadian Open Championship, 1919; Bobby Locke, Chicago Victory National Championship, 1948

Youngest winner

Johnny McDermott, 19 years 10 months, US Open, 1911

Oldest winner

Sam Snead, 52 years 10 months, Greater Greensboro Open, 1965

National opens – excluding Europe and USA

Lowest 72-hole aggregate

255 Peter Tupling, Nigerian Open, Lagos, 1981.

Lowest 36-hole aggregate

124 (18 under par) Sandy Lyle, Nigerian Open, Ikoyi GC, Lagos, 1978. (Lyle was in his first year as a professional.)

Lowest 18 holes

59 Gary Player, second round, Brazilian Open, Gavea GC (6,185 yards), Rio de Janeiro, 1974.

Professional events– excluding Europe and USA

Lowest 72-hole aggregate

260 Bob Charles, 66-62-69-63, Spalding Masters at Tauranga, New Zealand, 1969.

Lowest 18-hole aggregate

60 Billy Dunk (Australia), Merewether, NSW, 1970.

Lowest 9-hole aggregate

27 Bill Brask (US) at Tauranga in the New Zealand PGA in 1976.

Miscellaneous British

Women's world record

The Professional Golfers' Association in Britain claimed a women's world record for the score of 62 by Janice Arnold during a WPGA tournament in September 1990. Miss Arnold, a New Zealand professional, won the 36-hole event by 12 shots with a 17 under par total of 131 on a course of 5,815 yards at the Coventry Golf Club. The record first-round 62 with 31 out and back included seven birdies, one eagle 3 and holing of a five-iron shot for an albatross 2. Trish Johnson scored 62 (11 under par) in the 1996 French Open.

72-hole aggregate

Andrew Brooks recorded a 72-hole aggregate of 259 in winning the Skol (Scotland) tournament at Williamwood in 1974.

Lowest rounds

Playing on the ladies' course (4,020 yards) at Sunningdale on 26th September, 1961, Arthur Lees, the professional there, went round in 52, 10 under par. He went out in 26 (2, 3, 3, 4, 3, 3, 3, 3, 2) and came back in 26 (2, 3, 3, 3, 2, 3, 4, 3, 3).

AE Smith, the Woolacombe Bay professional, recorded a score of 55 in a game there with a club member on 1st January, 1936. The course measured 4,248 yards. Smith went out in 29 and came back in 26 finishing with a hole-in-one at the 18th hole.

Other low scores recorded in Britain are by CC Aylmer, an English International who went round Ranelagh in 56; George Duncan, Axenfels in 56; Harry Bannerman, Banchory in 56 in 1971; Ian Connelly, Welwyn Garden City in 56 in 1972; James Braid, Hedderwick near Dunbar in 57; H Hardman, Wirral in 58; Norman Quigley, Windermere in 58 in 1937; Robert Webster, Eaglescliffe in 58, in 1970. Harry Weetman scored 58 in a round at the 6,171 yards Croham Hurst on 30th January, 1956.

D Sewell had a round of 60 in an Alliance Meeting at Ferndown, Bournemouth, a full-size course. He scored 30 for each half and had a total of 26 putts. In September 1986, Jeffrey Burn, handicap 1, of Shrewsbury GC, scored 60 in a club competition, made up of 8 birdies, an eagle and 9 pars. He was 30 out and 30 home and no 5 on his card. Andrew Sherborne, as a 20-year-old amateur, went round Cirencester in 60 strokes. Dennis Gray completed a round at Broome Manor, Swindon (6,906 yards, SSS 73) in the summer of 1976 in 60 (28 out, 32 in).

Playing over Aberdour on 13th June, 1936, Hector Thomson, British Amateur champion, 1936, and Jack McLean, former Scottish Amateur champion, each did 61 in the second round of an exhibition. McLean in his first round had a 63, which gave him an aggregate 124 for 36 holes.

Steve Tredinnick in a friendly match against business tycoon Joe Hyman scored a 61 over West Sussex (6,211 yards) in 1970. It included a hole-in-one at the 12th (198 yards) and a 2 at the 17th (445 yards).

Another round of 61 on a full-size course was achieved by 18-year-old Michael Jones on his home course, Worthing GC (6,274 yards), in the first round of the President's Cup in May, 1974.

In the Second City Pro-Am tournament in 1970, at Handsworth, Simon Fogarty did the second 9 holes in 27 against the par of 36.

Miscellaneous USA

Lowest rounds

The lowest known scores recorded for 18 holes in America are 55 by EF Staugaard in 1935 over the 6,419 yards Montebello Park, California, and 55 by Homero Blancas in 1962 over the 5,002 yards Premier course in Longview, Texas. Staugaard in his round had 2 eagles, 13 birdies and 3 pars.

Equally outstanding is a round of 58 (13 under par) achieved by a 13-year-old boy, Douglas Beecher, on 6th July, 1976, at Pitman CC, New Jersey. The course measured 6,180 yards from the back tees, and the middle tees, off which Douglas played, were estimated by the club professional to reduce the yardage by under 180 yards.

In 1941 at a course in Portsmouth, Virginia, measuring 6,100 yards, Chandler Harper scored 58.

Jack Nicklaus in an exhibition match at Breakers Club, Palm Beach, California, in 1973 scored 59 over the 6,200 yards course.

Ben Hogan, practising on a 7,006-yard course at Palm Beach, Florida, went round in 61 – 11 under par.

The lowest 9-hole score in America is 25, held jointly by Bill Burke over the second half of the 6,384 yards Normandie CC, St Louis in May, 1970 at the age of 29; by Daniel Cavin, who had

seven 3s and two 2s on the par 36 Bill Brewer Course, Texas, in September, 1959; and by Douglas Beecher over the second half of Pitman CC, New Jersey, on 6th July, 1976, at the amazingly young age of 13. The back 9 holes of the Pitman course measured 3,150 yards (par 35) from the back tees, but even though Douglas played off the middle tees, the yardage was still over 3,000 yards for the 9 holes. He scored 8 birdies and 1 eagle.

Horton Smith scored 119 for two consecutive rounds in winning the Catalina Open in California in December, 1928. The course, however, measured only 4,700 yards.

Miscellaneous – excluding GB and USA

Tony Jacklin won the 1973 Los Lagartos Open with an aggregate of 261, 27 under par.

Henry Cotton in 1950 had a round of 56 at Monte Carlo (29 out, 27 in).

In a Pro-Am tournament prior to the 1973 Nigerian Open, British professional David Jagger went round in 59.

Max Banbury recorded a 9-hole score of 26 at Woodstock, Ontario, playing in a competition in 1952.

Women's

The lowest score recorded on a full-size course by a woman is 62 by Mary (Mickey) Wright of Dallas, Texas. This was achieved on the Hogan Park course (6,286 yards) at Midland, Texas, in November, 1964. It was equalled by 16-year-old Rae Rothfelder on 9th July, 1978, at Diamond Oak G&CC, Fort Worth, Texas, a course measuring 6,124 yards.

The lowest 72-hole score on the US Ladies' PGA circuit is 265 by Kelly Robbins in the 1997 Jamie Farr Kroger Classic and by Wendy Ward in the 1997 Fieldcrest Cannon Classic.

The lowest 9-hole score on the US Ladies' PGA circuit is 28, first achieved by Mary Beth Zimmerman in the 1984 Rail Charity Classic and since equalled by Pat Bradley, Muffin Spencer-Devlin, Peggy Kirsch and Renee Heiken.

The lowest score for 36 holes on the USLPGA circuit is 129 by Judy Dickinson in the 1985 S&H Classic.

The lowest 9-hole score on the WPGA circuit is 30 by Susan Moon at Valbonne in 1979.

In the Women's World Team Championship in Mexico in 1966, Mrs Belle Robertson, playing for the British team, was the only player to break 70. She scored 69 in the third round.

At Westgate-on-Sea GC (measuring 5,002 yards), Wanda Morgan scored 60 in an open tournament in 1929.

Since scores cannot properly be taken in match play no stroke records can be made in match play events. Nevertheless we record here two outstanding examples of low scoring in the finals of national championships. Mrs Catherine Lacoste de Prado is credited with a score of 62 in the first round of the 36-hole final of the 1972 French Ladies' Open Championship at Morfontaine. She went out in 29 and came back in 33 on a course measuring 5,933 yards. In the final of the English Ladies' Championship at Woodhall Spa in 1954, Frances Stephens (later Mrs Smith) did the first nine holes against Elizabeth Price (later Mrs Fisher) in 30. It included a hole-in-one at the 5th. The nine holes measured 3,280 yards.

Amateurs

National championships

The following examples of low scoring cannot be regarded as genuine stroke play records since they took place in match play. Nevertheless they are recorded here as being worthy of note.

Michael Bonallack in beating David Kelley in the final of the English championship in 1968 at Ganton did the first 18 holes in 61 with only one putt under two feet conceded. He was out in 32 and home in 29. The par of the course was 71.

Charles McFarlane, playing in the fourth round of the Amateur Championship at Sandwich in 1914 against Charles Evans did the first nine holes in 31, winning by 6 and 5.

This score of 31 at Sandwich was equalled on several occasions in later years there. Then, in 1948, Richard Chapman of America went out in 29 in the fourth round eventually beating Hamilton McInally, Scottish Champion in 1937, 1939 and 1947, by 9 and 7.

In the fourth round of the Amateur Championship at Hoylake in 1953, Harvie Ward, the holder, did the first nine holes against Frank Stranahan in 32. The total yardage for the holes was 3,474 yards and included one hole of 527 yards and five holes over 400 yards. Ward won by one hole.

Francis Ouimet in the first round of the American Amateur Championship in 1932 against George Voigt did the first nine holes in 30. Ouimet won by 6 and 5.

Open competitions

The 1970 South African Dunlop Masters Tournament was won by an amateur, John Fourie, with a score of 266, 14 under par. He led from start to finish with rounds of 65, 68, 65, 68, finally winning by six shots from Gary Player.

Jim Ferrier, Manly, won the New South Wales championship at Sydney in 1935 with 266. His rounds were: 67, 65, 70, 64, giving an aggregate 16 strokes better than that of the runner-up. At the time he did this amazing score Ferrier was 20 years old and an amateur.

Holes below par

Most holes below par

EF Staugaard in a round of 55 over the 6,419 yards Montbello Park, California, in 1935, had 2 eagles, 13 birdies and 3 pars.

American Jim Clouette scored 14 birdies in a round at Longhills GC, Arkansas, in 1974. The course measured 6,257 yards.

Jimmy Martin in his round of 63 in the Swallow-Penfold at Stoneham in 1961 had 1 eagle and 11 birdies.

In the Ricarton Rose Bowl at Hamilton, Scotland, in August, 1981, Wilma Aitken, a women's amateur internationalist, had 11 birdies in a round of 64, including 9 consecutive birdies from the 3rd to the 11th.

Mrs Donna Young scored 9 birdies and 1 eagle in one round in the 1975 Colgate European Women's Open.

Consecutive holes below par

Lionel Platts had ten consecutive birdies from the 8th to 17th holes at Blairgowrie GC during a practice round for the 1973 Sumrie Better-Ball tournament.

Roberto De Vicenzo in the Argentine Centre of the Republic Championship in April, 1974 at the Cordoba GC, Villa Allende, broke par at each of the first 9 holes. (By starting his round at the 10th hole they were in fact the second 9 holes played by Vicenzo.) He had 1 eagle (at the 7th hole) and 8 birdies. The par for the 3,602 yards half was 37, completed by Vicenzo in 27.

Nine consecutive holes under par have been recorded by Claude Harmon in a friendly match over Winged Foot GC, Mamaroneck, NY, in 1931; by Les Hardie at Eastern GC, Melbourne, in April, 1934; by Jimmy Smith at McCabe GC, Nashville, Tenn, in 1969; by 13-year-old Douglas Beecher, in 1976, at Pitman CC, New Jersey; by Rick Sigda at Greenfield CC, Mass, in 1979; and by Ian Jelley at Brookman Park in 1994.

TW Egan in winning the East of Ireland Championship in 1962 at Baltray had eight consecutive birdies (2nd to 9th) in the third round.

On the United States PGA tour, eight consecutive holes below par have been achieved by three players – Bob Goalby in the 1961 St Petersburg Open, Fuzzy Zoeller in the 1976 Quad Cities Open and Dewey Arnette in the 1987 Buick Open.

Fred Couples set a PGA European Tour record with twelve birdies in a round of 61 during the 1991 Scandinavian Masters on the 72-par Drottningholm course. This has since been equalled by Ernie Els (1994 Dubai Desert Classic) and by Russell Claydon and Fredrik Lindgren (1995 German Masters). Ian Woosnam, Tony Johnstone, Severiano Ballesteros, John Bickerton, Mark O'Meara and Raymond Russell share another record with eight successive birdies.

The United States Ladies' PGA record is seven consecutive holes below par achieved by Carol Mann in the Borden Classic at Columbus, Ohio in 1975.

Miss Wilma Aitken recorded nine successive birdies (from the 3rd to the 11th) in the 1981 Ricarton Rose Bowl.

Low scoring rarities

At Standerton GC, South Africa, in May 1937, FF Bennett, playing for Standerton against Witwatersrand University, did the second hole, 110 yards, in three 2s and a 1. Standerton is a 9-hole course, and in the match Bennett had to play four rounds.

In 1957 a fourball comprising HJ Marr, E Stevenson, C Bennett and WS May completed the 2nd hole (160 yards) in the grand total of 6 strokes. Marr and Stevenson both holed in one while Bennett and May both made 2.

The old Meadow Brook Club of Long Island, USA, had five par 3 holes and George Low in a round there in the 1950s scored 2 at each of them.

In a friendly match on a course near Chicago in 1971, assistant professional Tom Doty (23 years) had a remarkable low run over four consecutive holes: 4th (500 yards) 2; 5th (360 yards, dogleg) 1; 6th (175 yards) 1; 7th (375 yards) 2.

RW Bishop, playing in the Oxley Park, July medal competition in 1966, scored three consecutive 2s. They occurred at the 12th, 13th and 14th holes which measured 151, 500 and 136 yards respectively.

In the 1959 PGA Close Championship at Ashburnham, Bob Boobyer scored five 2s in one of the rounds.

American Art Wall scored three consecutive 2s in the first round of the US Masters in 1974. They were at the 4th, 5th and 6th holes, the par of which was 3, 4 and 3.

Nine consecutive 3s have been recorded by RH Corbett in 1916 in the semi-final of the Tangye Cup; by Dr James Stothers of Ralston GC over the 2,056 yards 9-hole course at Carradale, Argyll, during the summer of 1971; by Irish internationalist Brian Kissock in the Homebright Open at Carnalea GC, Bangor, in June, 1975; and by American club professional Ben Toski.

The most consecutive 3s in a British PGA event is seven by Eric Brown in the Dunlop at Gleneagles (Queen's Course) in 1960.

Hubert Green scored eight consecutive 3s in a round in the 1980 US Open.

The greatest number of 3s in one round in a British PGA event is 11 by Brian Barnes in the 1977 Skol Lager tournament at Gleneagles.

Fewest putts

The lowest known number of putts in one round is 14, achieved by Colin Collen-Smith in a round at Betchworth Park, Dorking, in June, 1947. He single-putted 14 greens and chipped into the hole on four occasions.

Professional Richard Stanwood in a round at Riverside GC, Pocatello, Idaho on 17th May, 1976 took 15 putts, chipping into the hole on five occasions.

Several instances of 16 putts in one round have been recorded in friendly games.

For 9 holes, the fewest putts is five by Ron Stutesman for the first 9 holes at Orchard Hills G&CC, Washington, USA in 1978.

Walter Hagen in nine consecutive holes on one occasion took only seven putts. He holed long putts on seven greens and chips at the other two holes.

In competitive stroke rounds in Britain and Ireland, the lowest known number of putts in one round is 18, in a medal round at Portpatrick Dunskey GC, Wilmslow GC professional Fred Taggart is reported to have taken 20 putts in a round of the 1934 Open Championship. Padraigh Hogan (Elm Park), when competing in the Junior Scratch Cup at Carlow in 1976, took only 20 putts in a round of 67.

The fewest putts in a British PGA event is believed to be 22 by Bill Large in a qualifying round over Moor Park High Course for the 1972 Benson and Hedges Match Play.

Overseas, outside the United States of America, the fewest putts is 19 achieved by Robert Wynn (GB) in a round in the 1973 Nigerian Open and by Mary Bohen (US) in the final round of the 1977 South Australian Open at Adelaide.

The USPGA record for fewest putts in one round is 18, achieved by Andy North (1990); Kenny Knox (1989); Mike McGee (1987) and Sam Trehan (1979). For 9 holes the record is 8 putts by Kenny Knox (1989), Jim Colbert (1987) and Sam Trehan (1979).

The fewest putts recorded for a 72-hole US PGA Tour event is 93 by Kenny Knox in the 1989 Heritage Classic at Harbour Town Golf Links.

The fewest putts recorded by a woman is 17, by Joan Joyce in the Lady Michelob tournament, Georgia, in May, 1982.

Index